**AA**

# ℋOTELS AND RESTAURANTS IN BRITAIN

## 1991

AA Hotels & Restaurants in Britain
**25TH**
**ANNIVERSARY**
· 1967-1991 ·

Produced by the Publishing Division of The Automobile
Association

All establishments in the Guide are regularly inspected by
the AA's hotel and restaurant inspectors. The gazetteer is
compiled by the AA's Hotel and Touring Services
Department and generated by the AA's Establishment
Database.

The atlas and town plans are prepared by the
Cartographic Department of The Automobile Association

© **The Automobile Association 1990**

**Cover Design.** The Paul Hampson Partnership
**Photographs of Whitechapel Manor Hotel,
Halmpstone Manor** – Tom Teegan.
**Elgin Hotel** – Douglas Corrance.
**The Grange Hotel** – Adrian Baker

**Illustrations:** Malcolm Henwood and Naomi Davis

**Head of Advertisement Sales:** Christopher Heard, tel
(0256) 20123 **Advertisement Production:** Karen
Weeks, tel (0256) 20123

**Typeset, printed and bound in Great Britain by**
William Clowes Limited, Beccles and London

**Colour produced by** J B Shears and Sons Ltd,
Basingstoke, Hampshire

© **The Automobile Association November 1990**

A CIP catalogue record for this book is available from the
British Library.

Published by The Automobile Association, Fanum House,
Basingstoke, Hampshire RG21 2EA

ISBN 0 7495 0201 0

# DISCOUNT SCHEME

Owners of the 1991 edition of the Hotel and
Restaurant Guide may claim a 10 per cent discount off
their room bill at more than 1,100 of the hotels listed in
the gazetteer. The hotels which have agreed to
participate in this scheme display the ⓔ symbol at the
end of their gazetteer entry.

In order to take advantage of the discount, guests
*must* remember to present their copy of the 1991
Hotel and Restaurant Guide at reception when
*checking in.* If you do not do so, the hotel may
legitimately refuse to give you the discount when you
check out. This is very important, because many hotel
accounts are now computerised and it may cause
difficulties and delays if the account has to be adjusted
at the last minute.

The discount only applies to the full-tariff room
rate, and does not apply if you are already benefiting
from any other form of discount or a special bargain
rate, including weekly terms that work out at less per
night than the full tariff for a single night's stay.

The discount is off the room rate and may not be
claimed for restaurant or bar meals or drinks. In the
case of a joint booking for a group of individuals, the
discount would only apply to the person who presents
the guide on checking in, *not* to the entire party.

If two persons are sharing a double room,
however, at the full tariff rate, the discount would apply
to the double room.

Please note that the discount may *only* be claimed
at the hotels which display the ⓔ symbol at the end of
their gazetteer entry, and that the bill must be settled
before you leave the hotel. The discount is not
applicable to company accounts.

# CONTENTS

# THE AA/SHELL GUIDE TO HOTELS AND RESTAURANTS

*An introduction from*
*Roy Reynolds, Managing Director, Shell UK Oil.*

Once more I am pleased to join with the Automobile Association in sponsoring the AA/Shell Guide to Hotels and Restaurants.

Both our organisations have long associations with motoring.

It seems there has always been a time when the highways and by-ways of Britain have featured AA services and that Shell service stations could be relied upon to be around nearly every corner.

But more than this. Both Shell and the AA have also been successful in promoting the variety and excellence of the British landscape, its towns and villages, its houses, its curiosities, its wildlife and its people. We like to think that by encouraging the motorist to look around him, we have also raised an appreciation of the freedom and the pleasures that motoring can bring.

It is a heritage of which we, in particular, are proud. And it goes back a long way. The first Shell guides to the regions of Britain were edited by John Betjeman and made their appearance in 1934. We have been producing them ever since.

It seems therefore the most natural thing in the world that we and the AA should find ourselves touching shoulders in the popular guide to all that is good in living and eating away from home.

For both our organisations, it continues to show our total commitment to you the motorist and your needs.

*Roy Reynolds*

# WHAT THEY DO FOR YOUR NSIDES, SHELL ADVANCED PETROL DOES FOR YOUR ENGINE.

Give your car a better diet. Use Shell Advanced petrol which contains a detergent that actually cleans the engine as you drive.

Which means smoother running and less carbon monoxide in the exhaust. Foods like wholemeal bread, muesli and prunes help keep your body healthy. Now you can do the same for your car by putting Shell petrol on the menu.

## YOU CAN TELL WHEN IT'S SHELL.

# SHELL ADVANCED DIESEL GIVES LESS SMOKE. IT'S USELESS.'

Compared to ordinary diesels, Shell Advanced gives out less smoke. Which is bad news for Indian chiefs who want to send smoke signals. But very good news for anyone stuck in a jam behind a truck or a bus.

Because if smoke comes in your direction, you don't need to go on the warpath. Just ask the driver to start using Shell Advanced Diesel.

**YOU CAN TELL WHEN IT'S SHELL.**

# PREFACE

I n this, the 25th Anniversary edition of the AA Guide to Hotels and Restaurants in Britain,we have, more than ever, placed the emphasis on quality. The Oxford dictionary defines 'quality' as 'degree of excellence'. Our aim with this guide is to portray the relative merits of different hotels, providing comprehensive information on the facilities and services available and giving a clear indication of the 'degree of excellence' that can be expected. The minimum standards we lay down fully reflect the findings of extensive market research to determine which facilities and services are considered essential for both business and leisure guests. However, the research also indicated that consumers were looking for a more subjective view of AA appointed hotels based on quality. It is recognised that all AA hotels meet the minimum standards set for the award of stars, but if there is more than one hotel in the same star classification, how would they relate to each other in terms of quality?

We began to address these questions with the introduction of the AA's percentage ratings for quality which we featured for the first time at 3, 4 and 5 star level in our 1990 Guide. During the past year we have extended this subjective view to include all AA appointed hotels. The very best hotels in each category are awarded Red Stars, the AA's ultimate accolade denoting outstanding all-round quality and signifying that the hotel is a top performer within its classification.

A major innovation in the gazetteer format this year is to show hotels in order of merit based on the percentage quality rating given. Entries within each town and under each star level are shown in descending order in accordance with our view of their relative quality.

The AA has always been associated with quality and it is no surprise to find that the Association's motto is 'Courtesy and Care'. In order to encourage high standards of hospitality and to recognise the improving standards of customer care in UK hotels we have decided to introduce an annual award for 'Courtesy and Care'. We asked our inspectors to select hotels around the country that place a high priority on making the guest feel totally welcome. They were told to look for hotel staff attitudes of politeness, kindness, consideration and a concern for the welfare of guests. We have featured the first fourteen hotels to be given the AA's 'Courtesy and Care' award in this guide. Our inspectors are confident you will not be disappointed with the attention you are given when staying at these hotels.

There is a mistaken belief that 'quality' can only be found at the higher star classifications. This is totally unfounded and, as our quality rating scores now clearly show, there are hotels of excellent quality at every star level. There are, in particular, some superb hotels operating at the one star level and to highlight this we feature our 'Top Twenty' one star hotels. These smaller hotels often represent outstanding value for money and usually offer a more personal, friendly approach to their guests. Try one of these hotels when you next have the opportunity—we feel sure you will be pleasantly surprised by the experience.

Because we set such high standards for AA appointed hotels, inevitably there are casualties. As soon as a hotel falls below acceptable minimum standards we delete it from our scheme. Such losses are normally well compensated by good hotels joining for the first time or returning after extensive refurbishment. As in previous years we have identified the most noteworthy of these in the 'Best Newcomers' feature. We are particularly pleased to find our national winner this year on the island of Anglesey. Tre-Ysgawen Hall, Llangefni is a lovely 3 Star Country House hotel that achieves a commendable 78% rating for quality.

Restaurants have not been forgotten either, and amongst our top 500 you will find a number of exciting newcomers that are well worth a visit. We are constantly on the look out for good new restaurants and we always listen to the recommendations received from the AA's 7.5 million members, who we think of as our part-time inspection force. We want to hear about the restaurants you like and so this 25th Anniversary edition of our guide includes a special competition to find the best restaurant description written by one of our readers. The prize is an all expenses paid meal for two at any of the top restaurants we feature.

A glance through this guide will reveal a wealth of detail about more than 4000 of the best hotels and restaurants in Britain. We demand 'quality' from the establishments in our schemes and we set the same high standards for ourselves. Our aim is to ensure that the AA's Guide to Hotels and Restaurants in Britain is the definitive guide to hotel quality. We feel sure you will find this 25th Anniversary edition the best to date.

**Albert Hampson**
Manager Hotel and Touring Services

*'We want to hear about the restaurants you like and so this 25th Anniversary edition of our guide includes a special competition to find the best restaurant description written by one of our readers.'*

# The new tunnel under the A283 is a giant leap forward. (But not for mankind.)

The frogs and toads of Storrington, West Sussex, have nothing to fear from the A283.

A specially-built tunnel now allows them to cross in safety.

The project was backed by the Shell Better Britain Campaign, a partnership between Shell and seven environmental organisations.

Securing the Campaign's backing is easy. You come to us with an idea: we come back with the information and advice you need to make it happen. In some cases we can even help with money.

Projects all over England, Scotland, Wales and N.Ireland are

being helped – turning wasteland into a picnic spot, recycling tin cans or creating a wildlife sanctuary – and hundreds more.

Whatever, or wherever your idea, start by sending the coupon.

Make like a toad. Leap at it.

To: SBBC. Red House, Hill Lane, Great Barr, Birmingham B43 6LZ.
Please send me information on the Shell Better Britain Campaign.

Name _____ Address _____

_____ Postcode _____

**20** *years*

1970 – 1990

SHELL BETTER BRITAIN CAMPAIGN

CAMPAIGN PARTNERS: NATURE CONSERVANCY COUNCIL, COUNTRYSIDE COMMISSION, COUNTRYSIDE COMMISSION FOR SCOTLAND,
BRITISH TRUST FOR CONSERVATION VOLUNTEERS, SCOTTISH CONSERVATION PROJECTS, CIVIC TRUST, SCOTTISH CIVIC TRUST, SHELL U.K.

For many years now the AA has been making awards to hotels and restaurants which we consider to be outstanding - red stars, rosettes and, more recently, high percentage ratings. Naturally, these awards, made for exceptionally high standards of accommodation, food and hospitality, reflect the degree of dedication, professionalism and effort on the part of the owners, management and staff. However, we felt that the time was right for us to make a new award on a more personal level and this award has, appropriately, been linked to the AA's motto-'Courtesy and Care'. There are a number of hotels which may not have attained the dizzy heights of red stars, but where courtesy to, and care of guests is at an exceptionally high level. Red star hotels will feature in the award list, but only where 'Courtesy and Care' are particularly to the forefront of an already top quality hotel.

Our first award winners are featured below and we think that from their stories and their comments you will get a good idea of why they have been chosen. We are sure that a stay at the hotels will confirm our choice or new ideas that we want to put into action.

## COURTESY and CARE AWARDS · AA

### ANGEL HOTEL, Bury St Edmunds

The Gough family have been in the hotel and catering business for 25 years, so Caroline Gough, who runs the Angel Hotel with her mother and brother, reckons the industry is in her blood.

'It's nice to be able to work together as a family and I like the teamwork involved. I could say that its banking the money we make that gives me the greatest satisfaction, but it wouldn't be true. What really gives me pleasure is seeing customers go away happy.

'We have put, and will continue to put a lot of effort into the hotel and it's very much part of the local community which is nice. We may not be the slickest or speediest outfit but we really do care for our guests'.

### BARDON LODGE, Blackheath London SE3.

Twelve years ago Margaret Quilter started working at Bardon Lodge as a chambermaid - today she's a director.

'I used to work with Barbara Nott the owner when I first left school and then bumped into her again years later just after she had started the hotel and needed help. I had small children then, so all I could do was chambermaiding. As the children got older I started to work full time on reception and today - I don't call myself anything, I'm just here. We all muck in and do everything anyway.

'Perhaps because the hotel started small and we've all worked together to build it up, it's still got a friendly, family atmosphere. I love the people contact and usually come into work and go home with a smile on my face. There are occasions when things don't turn out right - but that's life isn't it?'

### EMPIRE HOTEL, Llandudno

Elizabeth Maddocks worked as a State Registered Nurse until, as she put it, 'I married a fellow who owned a hotel'.

'To begin with I found it quite a contrast', admitted Elizabeth 'but it was still working with people, which I like. That was 28 years ago and now two out of three of our children are in the hotel business too.

'My father-in-law bought this hotel in 1946 and Leonard took it over from him - so it's a real family business and many of the staff have been here a really long time.

'Our customers tell us they like the relaxed atmosphere and the friendly staff. We get a lot of repeat business here and get to know people so well they become our friends.

'Even after all these years we daren't become complacent or take anything for granted so there are always corners of the hotel that need attention

### ENMORE HOTEL, Dunoon

Eleven years ago David and Angela Wilson lived in the yuppieland of the South - he was an engineer and she a teacher. But when Angela became pregnant they decided to try another stratum of life and bought the Enmore Hotel in Dunoon.

'We thought it would be nice to work together,' explained Angela 'and that if we tried to give people what we are looking for ourselves - ie making the hotel an extension of our home and the guests a part of our family - we might succeed.

'We get a lot of people from the South staying here. When they arrive they're all uptight, but after a couple of days at the laid-back pace of this part of Scotland, the magic starts to work and they don't give a damn. It's rewarding to see that, and to read the good comments that people write in our book.'

### GRAPEVINE HOTEL, Stow on the Wold

Hotel proprietor Sandra Elliott reckons that her marketing background has helped her to find out and provide the sort of service, standards and atmosphere that make guests happy.

'But ask any of our visitors to name our strongest point and I'm sure they'd say its our care', said Sandra who has

# *Arrival*

Vellore House, built in Greek Revival style, c.1836 by John Pinch the Younger for General Augustus Andrews. Tree-lined drive. Landscaped garden with Italianate grotto, gazebo, dovecote and exotic shrubs. Cedars, Wellingtonias and Copper Beeches pre-date the building.

Ebony 5″ x 4″ Field Camera, hand-made with leather and titanium. 150mm Schneider Symar-S. Aperture f22¹/₂. Exposure ¹/₄ second. Kodak 6105 daylight 100 ASA film. Through a combination of warming, frost and graduated neutral density filters. From a distance of 100 metres. Between 12 and 1 pm.

*Blues and golds and slumbering creams, floors a masterpiece in tiles, a cuisine that delights the eye as it tempts the palate. Service that makes you believe it is yesterday, after all. Rooms it may be hard to say goodbye to. Five stars hardly seem enough.*

devoted herself to building up the hotel over the last 12 years.

'We have a total caring community here; I don't think of it as a job. I care for my staff and know that they in turn care for the guests as well as for each other. I think the residents warm to this. In fact, when people make repeat visits, they often bring little gifts for the staff - perhaps a cake for the chef, fruit or flowers for the person who serviced their room when they were last here or even a present for Winston the parrot.

'I'm also very keen on training and on giving staff a career path. As the business expands, I like to encourage the staff to grow with it'.

## HOLBECK GHYLL COUNTRY HOUSE HOTEL, Windermere

There was never any doubt in the minds of David or Patricia Nicholson about what they would do for a living; they both knew from school age that they wanted to go into the hotel business. Both trained to that end and spent time working in hotels before taking the plunge to go it alone two years ago and buying the Holbeck Ghyll Hotel.

'We try and combine the highest standards and every creature comfort with a friendly staff and the sort of atmosphere in which guests' worries just evaporate away. We hope the repeat business and recommendations we receive mean we're getting it right'.

## KINLOCH HOUSE HOTEL, Blairgowrie

At the age of 40 years David Shentall decided he had worked in just about every part of the food business except running a hotel. So he and his wife Sarah looked all over Scotland for a hotel that had the potential for all-the-year-round business and that they could run themselves without a manager. They found Kinloch House.

'That was nine years ago,' said David. 'The place was a hell of a hole when we first came here - a white elephant with no customers. Now the hotel is all done up and it gives me great satisfaction to see what was once a place not to come to become *the* place to come to.

'For the future? Obviously we hope the business will continue to prosper

and certainly we shall continue to improve standards. And, having grown up in the grocery business, I feel that as long as we keep reasonably busy there won't be a need to massage prices'.

## MOORTOWN LODGE HOTEL, Ringwood

Jilly and Bob Burrows-Jones felt that their office jobs were too run of the mill and decided to make a change. As they'd always enjoyed catering and home entertaining, buying a restaurant seemed like a really good idea.

'We didn't think we'd be able to afford a hotel', explained Jilly, 'so when the particulars for Moortown Lodge dropped through our letterbox from the agency, we didn't bother even to look at them. But then we happened to be visiting the Ringwood area, remembered the hotel, went to look at it and decided then and there to take the plunge and buy it. And very enjoyable and challenging the experience has been too.

'We wanted guests to have the best of everything and to make them feel they were coming into a home. We seem to have been successful, because people keep coming back and often write us lovely complimentary letters.

'We've spent the last three years building up the business; now we feel its time to consolidate'.

## NEIGWL HOTEL, Abersoch

When Steven Heptonstall's father decided to give up working in the motor industry and buy a hotel instead, it was only natural that Steven, who was already working in the hotel and catering business, should join him in the venture.

'When my father worked in the motor trade, he spent many nights away suffering in awful hotels. He reckoned that what was wanted was a small hotel with high standards and a strong caring and family feel about it - so that's what we (my wife and mother work here too) have tried to create.

'We get a lot of satisfaction pleasing people and seeing them enjoy themselves and we get a real buzz when they make return visits.'For the future - well, we think we've got the perfect spot here, so we don't intend to move. We don't want to expand either, so we'll just go on improving what we have already'

## SHARROW BAY COUNTRY HOUSE HOTEL, Howtown

Fifty-one years ago Francis Coulson saw, fell in love with and bought this beautiful private mansion on Lake Ullswater intending to turn it into a hotel. Three years later Brian Sack, who was studying nearby, came to spend the summer at the hotel to gain work experience. 'And here I still am - like Topsy' said Brian.

Together they created the first country house hotel, gradually improving and extending the place to become the luxury, starred and rosetted establishment it is now.

'Although we've learned to delegate now we still work in the hotel ourselves' explained Francis.'We still enjoy cosseting, nurturing and nourishing our guests and making them feel needed, wanted and relaxed'.

'We both have a great love of people' added Brian 'and every day put on a performance for their benefit. This place is much more than bricks and mortar and, rather like a legend, we hope it will go on and on forever'.

## TIDES REACH HOTEL, Salcombe

The Edwards family - Roy, Pat and their son John, are no newcomers to the hotel business. In fact John is the fifth generation to become a hotelier in the West Country.

'I gave my son the chance to do something else', admitted Roy 'and he went to Cambridge University to study engineering. But he ditched that and insisted on coming into our business instead. I'm semi-retired now and John handles most of the day to day running of Tides Reach.

'For me the hotel business is my life', continued Roy. 'It's not just a job of work but something that goes much deeper than that. I really get pleasure from having guests to stay and from making sure that they have an enjoyable holiday.

'This is a very tranquil hotel, run on good old fashioned lines. Sometimes things go wrong and we all have a good laugh, but mostly things are OK, so I think we'll carry on on the same tack'.

## COURTESY AND CARE AWARDS

**TYLNEY HALL HOTEL,**
Rotherwick

Rita Mooney, General Manager of Tylney Hall, has been in the hotel business all her working life.

'I trained in hotel management and catering and then worked for Prestige and another consortium of hotels before coming here.

'For me it has become much more than a job - it's a part of my life. To work in this business you have to be totally dedicated, because otherwise with the long hours worked, you'd be labouring in vain.

'I like every aspect of the work - I like to pamper people and see them go home happy, I like the team I work with and I especially like this lovely establishment with its acres and acres of beautiful grounds.

'So long was spent planning this hotel and of course we're still always trying to improve it, but now our ambition is to achieve the very highest standards and hopefully the final accolades too'.

**WHITES HOTEL,** Lancaster Gate, London W2

Richard Senior, the young Duty Manager of Whites Hotel, started his working life in the Royal Marines, but he hated it so much he only lasted a fortnight.

'I had friends who worked in the hotel business and they always made it sound so enjoyable that I decided it might be the career for me. I applied to become a management trainee with the Mount Charlotte Group, was accepted and then spent a couple of years working at hotels in Newcastle and Cardiff before coming here.

'This hotel is the company's flagship, so I consider myself very lucky to be here. I know we work long hours, but I do enjoy the people contact and get a real buzz striving for the perfection that is required in a hotel like this and trying to give guests just that little bit extra.

'If I wake up one morning not wanting to go to work, then that will be the time to stop - but I've been in the business for six years now and it hasn't happened yet.'

**WOODHAYES COUNTRY HOUSE HOTEL,** Whimple

After 21 years spent running a variety of pubs and restaurants, Katherine and Frank Rendle felt they had fallen into a lucrative rut from which they needed a change. They decided to buy a hotel 'somewhere in the South' and eventually chose Woodhayes.

'That was two years ago and the Rendles, together with their son Michael who is now equally involved in the running of the hotel, feel their change of direction has definitely worked out for the best.

'We genuinely like and enjoy looking after people' said Katherine. 'We have all sorts staying here but we find all of them equally appreciative.

'Of course, we've still got a lot to learn and we need to be better organised. On the rare nights off that we have we visit other hotels and study what their proprietors do'.

# HOTELS and RESTAURANTS
## ~~ in BRITAIN ~~

On 12th April 1967 an AA press release announced their new 800 page AA book on hotels, designed to meet the steadily growing demand for information about the facilities provided by AA appointed hotels — the price? 17/6d, or 87½p as we now know it.

The 1991 guide, priced £11.95, reveals many of the changes over the past twenty-five years, and the style of entries has changed accordingly. Evidence of the hard sell is displayed with discounts advertised on the front cover, and, whatever happened to Brighton, the mecca of holiday hotels, piers and seaside holidays? Gone from the guide are the Metropole and Grand of the 1960s and now only one of the four hotels listed has even 3 stars.

**1967**

---

★ ★ ★ ★ ★ **Royal Bath** Bath Rd ☎25555
Impressive white-fronted large building. Casino, sauna baths, games room. Close to sea and town centre.
Open all year; licensed; 100 rooms, 76 with bath; open parking 10 cars; garage accommodation 20 cars, charge 5/-; morning coffee; last dinner 10.30 pm.

| B & B | Weekly | Lunch | Tea | Dinner | Wine | S |
|---|---|---|---|---|---|---|
| 50/-:100/- | 27:43½ gns | fr 21/- & alc | fr 7/6 & alc | 25/-:30/- & alc | fr 18/6 | 12½% |

French cooking; specialities: Escalope de Veau Elizabeth; Le Rognon de Veau Robert; Pêche Flambée Victoria.
Central heating; lift; night porter; swimming pool; TV; no dogs allowed; no coach parties.

---

**BOURNEMOUTH** Dorset Map **04** SZ09

See **Town Plan Section** During the currency of this guide some Bournemouth telephone numbers are liable to change.
See also **Christchurch, Longham & Poole**
★★★★★62% **Royal Bath** Bath Rd BH1 2EW (De Vere)
☎(0202)555555 Telex no 41375 FAX (0202) 554158
*Now 150 years old, this spaciously elegant hotel, attractively set in a commanding position overlooking the sea, has undergone major refurbishment to bring standards to an even higher level of excellence with a new leisure complex and exceptionally good conference facilities which make it particularly popular with the business fraternity. Lively dinner dances take place in the main restaurant on Saturday evenings, 'Oscar's' offering a more serious cuisine in a separate, well-appointed room and a smart and helpful staff providing competent service in all areas.*
131⇄2🛏 CTV in all bedrooms ✘ (ex guide dogs) S%
sB&B⇄£85-£95 dB&B⇄£125-£210 🅿
Lift ( 120🚗 (£3.50 per day) 🚒 ❄ CFA ⊠(heated) sauna solarium gymnasium beauty salon putting green croquet lawn *xmas*
♥ English & French V ✿ 🇿 S% Lunch fr£15.10&alc Dinner fr£21.10&alc Last dinner 10.30pm
Credit Cards 1 2 3 4 5 £

**1991**

---

Further west, in Bournemouth, The Royal Bath Hotel has been taken over by the de Vere hotel chain. Here are two entries of the same hotel, 1967 and 1991 style. Spot the differences; remember, 5/- is 25p, 10/- is 50p, 15/- is 75p and 20/- is £1:

To translate the symbols: all bedrooms now have private bath and w.c., 2 fourposter beds; colour television in all rooms; direct dial telephone in rooms; no dogs except guide dogs; single bedroom with bath and breakfast costs £85-£95 a night; double bedroom with bath and breakfast £125-£210 a night; off season bargains; lift; nightporter; 120 garage spaces for £3.50 a day; no coach parties; garden over ½-acre; conference facilities available; outdoor swimming pool (heated); sauna; solarium; gymnasium; beauty salon; putting green; croquet lawn; entertainment; facilities for children; Christmas Breaks; French cuisine, vegetarian food, morning coffee, afternoon tea; service included. Takes part in the discount scheme.

The simplicity of the 1967 entry makes it easy reading, but in the years since then hotels have had to adapt to the increasing complexity of modern life and the 1991 Guide's use of symbols is a means of giving as much information to the customer as possible. These days, 1990's office machines and conference facilities are part of the hotel's *raison d'être*, and health and leisure concerns are now recorded as leisure complexes, sports facilities and vegetarian food.

The AA's skilled hotels and restaurants inspectorate, ever on the alert regarding the well-being of the customer, has successfully moved with the times in identifying those establishments that combine quality of service and food with the needs and comfort of the potential customer. The AA's hotel rating system has developed in sophistication: Red Stars were introduced in 1979 to denote top quality hotels, and, more recently, hotels rated between one and five black stars have been further categorised by the more subjective percentage assessment that reflects the quality within the star ratings.

Hotel chains have appeared; the Lodge has arrived, offering good, functional, reasonably priced overnight accommodation,

and the acceptance of guide dogs and facilities for the disabled are now entered.

Twenty five years have elapsed between 1967 and the present. In that time the first man has landed on the moon (21st July 1969), the French onion men have gone, and Margaret Thatcher has come and almost gone, but other events have had perhaps more relevance to the changes in the Hotels and Restaurants Guide, the most significant being the change in currency and the surge in prices.

In 1971 — February to be exact — Britain changed to decimal currency — an event which brought a sigh of relief to visitors from abroad but which brought with it a rise in prices which for the newly converted public went almost unnoticed in what seemed like the change to Monopoly money. A jar of peanut butter went from 1/6d (7½p) to 16p by sleight of hand it seemed, yet representing an increase of over 100 per cent. And at the same time inflation started gathering momentum. In January 1970 it had been at its lowest at 5% but by August 1975 it was to peak at 26.9%. In 1976 the dollar fell to $1.75. Tourists flocked to the UK to take advantage of favourable exchange rates.

Inflation was to stay in double figures — anything between 10 and 20 per cent — until the mid-80s but meanwhile other notable changes had come about. In 1972 Britain joined the EEC but for the average person we seemed to gain no benefit from this and there was a strong lobby for us to get out of it. Not very long after this, in 1974, an amendment to the Appellation Contrôllée regulations issued by the French meant that the surplus wines from their best vineyards which had previously been bottled up and sold in England under the vineyard name was no longer allowed. In 1972 a bottle of Ch. Bel Air could be bought for £1.60, after the amendment the prices escalated and now the same label sells for around £16.00. And then of course, on April Fool's day, 1973 VAT came in at 10% to be reduced the following year to 8% where it stayed until June 1979 when it was increased to 15%. All these changes meant price increases which, coupled with the proliferation of credit cards in the 1980s and the increased spending power of the general public, meant that the prices of 1967 have now become unrecognisable to the modern consumer.

Living standards improved. In the 1967 Guide a notable item in General Information is 'central heating — some hotels which are indicated as having central heating often do not have it operating — especially in bedrooms — during cold weather which may prevail outside the normally recognised winter months.' There has, it seems, not only been a change in our living standards but also in the recognisable seasons. There is also a much greater demand for private bathrooms today. In 1967 a three star hotel only needed 10% of rooms with private bathrooms — today the majority must have them. Four and five star hotels are now expected to provide private bathrooms with all bedrooms — in 1967 the requirements were 20% and 75% respectively.

So what are the main differences between the old and the new guide? Physically, the modern Guide is slightly chunkier in appearance, the paper is whiter, mapping is clearer and more attractive and useful town plans have been included. Regarding the gazetteer, the answer has to be in the greatly increased number of facilities offered by establishments: a tribute to both the business acumen of the hotels who have kept abreast of the changes demanded over the years, and to the knowledgeable and accurate researching of the AA's inspectors.

As a spin-off of world concern for the environment and an increasing multi-racial society, restaurants offer more vegetarian and ethnic foods, though French cuisine still produces more award-winning restaurants.

The quality of the AA Guide has ensured its survival in spite of fashions changing faster and faster, fashions in causes, music, popular culture, education, attitudes, work and food. What once lasted a generation now lasts a year. All, that is, except some of the trusty stalwarts who have now embarked on their fourth decade of entry in the AA Hotels and Restaurants Guide. Let's wish them, and the Guide, another twenty-five years of success.

## COMPETITION RULES

# READERS Competition

To celebrate the 25th edition of Hotels and Restaurants in Britain, we are offering you, our readers, the chance to win a meal for two at the AA-appointed restaurant of your choice.

All you have to do is to write a minimum of 250 words about any restaurant and the meal you enjoyed there. The restaurant you write about need not be AA appointed.

The judges, who will include the AA's Chief Hotel Inspector and the Editor of the guide, will be looking for a lively and interesting style of writing, a sound knowledge of food and wine, and an appreciation of standards of service and general ambience.

Entries must be typed, double spaced, and must include the name and location of the restaurant. The entry form overleaf must be clearly and properly completed and attached firmly to your typed description.

Entries will be treated in the strictest confidence, but the AA will, of course, wish to publicise the winning entry and its author. The successful description will be reproduced in the next edition of the guide as part of a special feature at the front of the book and may be included, in whole or in part, in any press and publicity material produced by the AA.

Entries must be received by 3 April 1991 and the winner must take their prize by the end of June 1991.

23

★ ★ ★

West Cliff Gardens, Bournemouth, BH2 5HL
Telephone: (0202) 552659

# The Old Manor Hotel

*Leven Road, Lundin Links, Fife KY8 6AJ.*
*Telephone: 0333-320368*
*Fax: 0333-320911 Telex: 727606*

Situated on a hill overlooking Lundin Links golf course, an Open qualifying course with views over the Forth to the Lothians, the Old Manor Hotel has 20 rooms all with private facilities and radio, television etc.

The restaurant is renowned for the imaginative use of fresh local seafood and produce. The cocktail bar stocks over 100 malt whiskies, Bunter's Bar in the grounds offers pub grub in informal surroundings.

AA★★

A family run Hotel in a convenient but quiet location on the West Cliff, which has recently been re-decorated and refurbished to a very high standard. All the bedrooms have private bathrooms or shower rooms en-suite, colour T.V., central heating and tea making facilities. An excellent choice of traditionally cooked food is available in the Victorian styled restaurant.

----

## 25TH ANNIVERSARY READERS' COMPETITION

**PLEASE COMPLETE THIS FORM, IN BLOCK CAPITALS, AND ATTACH IT FIRMLY TO YOUR TYPED ENTRY.**

**RETURN TO:** The Editor, Hotels & Restaurants in Britain, Automobile Association, Fanum House, Basingstoke, Hampshire RG21 2EA

**ALL ENTRIES MUST BE RECEIVED BY 3RD APRIL 1991.**

NAME:........................................................ TELEPHONE: Home..........................................

ADDRESS: ................................................... Business..........................................

.................................................................. OCCUPATION .................................................

.................................................................. EMPLOYER.................................................

......................... POSTCODE .......................... ..................................................

**IN THE EVENT OF MY ENTRY BEING SUCCESSFUL, MY CHOICE OF RESTAURANT IS:**

Name........................................................

Address........................................................

**2nd CHOICE:**

Name........................................................

Address........................................................

I agree to abide by the rules of the competition, as set out overleaf:

**SIGNATURE:**......................................... **NAME:**......................................... **DATE:**..................
(block capitals)

*'The house itself is a handsome stone mansion, with spacious, elegant rooms, the large bay windows looking out over the peaceful Anglesey countryside.'*

## NATIONAL WINNER
### & REGIONAL WINNER-WALES

# TRE-YSGAWEN HALL
## LLANGEFNI, ANGELSEY

It has been our custom for some years now to make annual awards for the best of the new hotels in the guide. Each year we have been both charmed and impressed by the award winners and have been faced with a difficult choice between hotels of very high standard. This year is certainly no exception, and you will see that there are some wonderful buildings, excellent food, charming and enthusiastic owners or managers.... in fact very little of a tangible nature to choose between them. However, Tre-Ysgawen Hall in Anglesey was found to have that little something extra - the intangible element that makes a worthy national winner of our Best Newcomer Award. We wish them well, and have great pleasure in introducing them to you, along with our regional award winners.

Guests at Tre-Ysgawen may notice a beautifully carved slate panel let into the wall of the galley landing. The text is in Welsh, but the translation, 'With God Everything, without God Nothing' certainly describes the courage and sheer faith with which Mr and Mrs Craighead launched themselves into the restoration and transformation of this stately manor house. The motto is that of the house's original owners, the Pritchard-Rayner family, and had been preserved by a neighbour who was delighted to see it restored to its proper position.

Mr & Mrs Craighead have taken Tre-Ysgawen Hall as their first venture in hotel-keeping and are putting all their energy into making it a country-house hotel of real distinction and style. The house itself is a handsome stone mansion, with spacious, elegant rooms, the large bay windows looking out over the peaceful Anglesey countryside.

gourmand and an à la carte menu, from which the following are a small selection of dishes: hors d'oeuvres may include mousseline of scallops with fresh asparagus and parsely sauce, or an individual duck paté with ham, tongue and pistachio nuts. To follow this you might have a roast guinea fowl with glazed apples and a calvados cream sauce, or a rack of Welsh lamb with roasted shallots in a red wine sauce, and to finish, chocolate mousse flavoured with raspberry liqueur or floating islands with fresh strawberries and vanilla sauce, topped with caramel.

towards the Welsh mountains. They have furnished it in keeping, the downstairs rooms, including the reception hall from which a beautiful oak staircase rises to a galleried landing, in a restful colour scheme that sets the tone for a relaxing stay. The lounge is one of a suite of three rooms which can be opened up to form a splendid reception room for private parties. The other two rooms can be arranged to form a private conference suite, and there is a separate, enchanting 'Chinese Room' for small dinner parties. The dining room is an unusual horseshoe shape, very light and airy, with lovely views over the grounds. The 23 bedrooms are each decorated and furnished to an individual colour scheme, and are both roomy and elegant, with four-poster beds, comfortable furniture, sometimes including a chaise longue as well as armchairs. Some of the bathrooms are palatial, with 6ft jacuzzi baths, and all are extremely well appointed and furnished with high quality toiletries. The staff of 48 are very friendly and welcoming, mostly local, except for the Chef, General Manager and Maitre d'Hotel who are all experienced staff. Julian Peck, the General Manager, has all the natural charm and friendliness of manner that puts guests at their ease, combined with professionalism and a rare dedication to duty.

The chef Raymond Duthie was with the Royal Crescent at Bath when they were awarded a Michelin star and it is his ambition to repeat this achievement at Tre-Ysgawen, if not to better it, so the food here is superb. There are three separate dinner menus, a table d'hôte, a menu

When Mr and Mrs Craighead bought the house, it looked to be in a very good state of repair, but then they discovered extensive dry-rot. As he was formerly an engineer, accustomed to managing large-scale building projects in the Middle East, and she is a very capable business woman, they were not daunted, but set to work with an army of local builders and craftsmen to gut and then faithfully restore the interior, which they managed, by a miracle and a lot of hard work between September 1989 and March 1990. When they received their first guests at the beginning of March, Mrs. Craighead admitted that she felt there was only a façade - but a magnificent one - comprising the hall, the downstairs reception rooms and the first three bedrooms. From there they have gone from strength to strength, having completed all 23 bedrooms, added a new wing in the style of the main house and built on a most charming horseshoe - shaped dining room.

*'Guests' first experience of the delights to come is the entrance into the Great Hall, so imposing in English Baroque style that you half expect to see a National Trust guide.'*

# REGIONAL WINNER-SOUTH of ENGLAND

# HARTWELL HOUSE

## AYLESBURY, BUCKINGHAMSHIRE

To call Hartwell House a stately home hotel would not be an exaggeration. It is a magnificent building - part Jacobean and part Georgian - with a history going back almost a thousand years. A son of William the Conqueror once owned it, as did John, brother of Richard the Lionheart and King of England in 1199. Later the exiled King of France, Louis XVIII held court here and signed his accession papers in Hartwell's Library. The families who created the present building - the Hampdens and the Lees - were prominent at court in the 16th and 18th centuries and Royal connections were many.

After a period of decline, during this century, Historic House Hotels undertook complete restoration, achieving the highest standards. Furniture and paintings to suit the period of the house have been brought in, plasterwork and fireplaces reinstated and the gardens restored, along with their statuary.

Guests' first experience of the delights to come is the entrance into the Great Hall, so imposing in English Baroque style that you half expect to see a National Trust guide! The formalities of reception are found in the businesslike room to the right. The Rococo morning room, drawing room and library invite relaxation, while the panelled bar is an excellent place to begin the evening and peruse Aidan McCormack's imaginative menu, which explains the complexities of dishes otherwise simply named. How else would you guess that Roast Fillets of Brill would be ' ... roasted with baby fennel with a fennel and honey vinegar sauce and a navarin of shellfish, poached with rosemary and cream on a bed of beetroot coloured noodles'?

The gothic hall and staircase, both dramatic and curious with its Jacobean carved figures, leads to the bedrooms which vary considerably in size but are all beautifully appointed. Those on the first floor are huge and very grand indeed. Several of the second floor bedrooms open directly onto a charming roof garden - Louis' servants used it as a farmyard with caged birds and rabbits and greenstuff growing in large tubs.

There are some lovely walks around the grounds, through woods, along the lakeshore, taking in the statues of Frederick, Prince of Wales, William III and hercules, the Gibbs Pavilion, Gothic tower and obelisk and the bridge which was formerly the centre arch of Kew Bridge.

General Manager, Jonathan Thompson, Manager, Kevin Pearson and Restaurant Manager, Andy Paterson, head the team of staff here, with a definite policy of contact with guests. The result is a very welcoming hotel where guests feel thoroughly well looked after.

# GRANADA Hotels & Lodges

## Located on major motorways and trunk roads in Britain Granada Hotels and Lodges offer a high standard of accommodation at budget prices.

- All bedrooms have private bathroom, colour television, radio, wake up alarm and tea and coffee making facilities.
- Family rooms sleeping 4 available.
- Bedroom especially adapted for use by disabled people.
- At Granada Lodges meals may be taken in the adjacent Country Kitchen Restaurant.
- Granada Hotels have their own restaurant and bar.
- Ample free parking.
- Meeting rooms available at Granada Hotels and selected Granada Lodges.

### GRANADA
#### Hotels

M4/A34 Newbury (Chieveley) – Open Summer '91
M5 Exeter A38/A61 Alfreton
A500/A34 Stoke-on-Trent – Open Spring '91
A630/A6102 Sheffield

### GRANADA
#### Lodges

M1 Leicester (Markfield), Toddington, Woolley Edge
M4 Heston, Leigh Delamere M5 Frankley M62 Birch
M62/A1 Ferrybridge, M6 Southwaite M90 Kinross
M9/M80 Stirling A1 Grantham (Colsterworth)
Edinburgh (Musselburgh) A1(M) Washington, Blyth
A38 Saltash A36 Warminster M42/A5 Tamworth

## REGIONAL WINNER-WEST of ENGLAND

# WHITECHAPEL MANOR

### SOUTH MOLTON, DEVON

*'Inside, the house is wonderfully rambling, with hardly a straight line anywhere and old oak stairs which slope very slightly to one side.'*

Whitechapel Manor is one of Devon's finest and most historic manor houses, the present building dating from 1575. John and Patricia Shapland are the tenth owners since the earliest records in 1162, and have restored the building to the highest standards, obtaining Grade I listing as a result of their efforts. Inside, the house is wonderfully rambling, with hardly a straight line anywhere and old oak stairs which slope very slightly to one side. The luxurious refurbishments, while providing every comfort to guests, have done nothing to rob the manor of its character. The ten bedrooms, each named after an owner, vary in size from the grand four-poster room to the charming singles - one of which is still of sufficient size to house a 4'6" bed. Most of the double rooms have 6ft wide beds, the remainder 5ft.

The public rooms are of true manorial proportions, comfortably furnished in appropriate style and having a friendly, relaxing atmosphere. The real glory of the ground floor is the magnificent Jacobean carved screen which divides the hall from the drawing room, and the William and Mary panelling which has been carefully stripped of the layers of paint that had been applied by previous owners.

Dinner here is a real treat. Thierry Lepretre-Granet heads the team of three full-time chefs, producing unpretentious French provincial and English dishes with some particularly good sauces. A choice of around six starters may include sautéed duck foie gras with savoy cabbage and a Coteaux du Layon wine sauce, and a sea bass with fennel and olives. Main courses include such dishes as fillet of red deer with fresh pasta and a balsamic vinegar sauce, sirloin of beef with a green peppercorn sauce and steamed turbot with celeriac and celery strips with a noilly sauce. Potatoes are not always served, but you can make a special request for them. The wine list is well balanced and has around 120 items including good vintages.

Beautiful formal terraces lead down from the front of the house, which has 15 acres altogether, including some wonderful old trees.

# Put Quality into your Life

Clarion Foxhills Country Club, Ottershaw, Surrey

Quality Metropole Hotel, Llandrindod Wells, Powys

Clarion Norfolk Royale Hotel, Bournemouth, Dorset

Clarion Langdale Hotel & Country Club, Nr. Ambleside, Cumbria

Quality International Hotels, the 3rd largest hotel chain in the world with over 1300 hotels worldwide – offer many exciting destinations in Great Britain for both the business and the independent traveller.

Hotels in the city, country, lakeside, and by the sea. Experience the history and pageantry of London, honey-coloured cottages nestling in picture postcard gardens, trout-streams bubbling by the village green, the Cumbrian mountains and the valleys of Wales.

Quality International Hotels offer you a choice of accommodation from 4 star deluxe Clarion Hotels and Country Clubs, through Quality Hotels, Comfort Inns, and our new concept, Sleep Inns – 3 star comfort at 1 star prices!

Put Quality into your life. Call us now! **FREEPHONE 0800 44 44 44**

European Headquarters

## Quality International Hotels
2 Valentine Place, London SE1 8QH   Tel: 071-928 3333   Fax: 071-928 4762

**The Quality Choice**

*Inns·Hotels·Suites·Resorts*

Over 1300 hotels worldwide

## REGIONAL WINNER-MIDLANDS

# NORTON PLACE HOTEL

## BIRMINGHAM, WEST MIDLANDS

*'The beautifully landscaped complex includes Norton Place Hotel, The Lombard Room Restaurant, The Patrick Collection of Historic Cars and The Patrick Art Collection.'*

During his travels around the world, businessman Alexander Patrick collected ideas from the top hotels and restaurants he visited, brought them back and set about creating his idea of the ultimate place to stay and eat. The resulting Norton Place Hotel and separate Lombard Room Restaurant are part of a complex which also includes The Patrick Collection of historic cars, The Patrick

own library, open fireplace, trompe l'oeil and original works of art; and leading from it a comfortable conservatory.

The Lombard Room Restaurant is in a separate building just across the way, decorated in soft pinks and blues and with fresh flowers and the finest crystal and china. Restaurant Manager, Andrew Morgan, is a young man who has won international

Art Collection and a variety of conference and function rooms, all on a beautifully landscaped 11.5 acre site which was once a Victorian paper mill.

Each of the ten bedrooms in the single-storey building is different and everything is of the most exquisite quality, culminating in the Joseph Patrick Suite. This magnificent master suite comprises a bedroom with a grand four-poster bed, an original Louis XIV marble fireplace and limed oak panelling, a lavish en suite bathroom with a whirlpool bath, impulse shower and dolphin-style gold fixtures and a spacious conservatory. A second bedroom can be linked to the suite if required.

There is also a pleasant sitting room of comparable style, with its

awards for his waiting skills and who is totally dedicated to providing the ultimate in service. This, incidentally, does not end with the coffee and liqueurs - after the meal your car will be brought to the door, with the heater roaring if it's chilly and a cassette playing. No less dedication is shown by chef Paul Bingham, who trained at Stratford-upon-Avon College and gained experience at The White House Hotel in Regents Park, London and spent some time working in France before a number of posts in English country house hotels in the Prestige Group. Fanatical about fresh produce he cooks in the classical style, but with modern interpretation. The set price menus represent very good value.

'York stone and pillars
in the entrance hall
give an early
indication of the
quality of interior
design and decoration
throughout the
building.'

**REGIONAL WINNER-NORTH of ENGLAND**

# THE GRANGE HOTEL

## YORK, NORTH YORKSHIRE

new can be seen throughout the building.

Bedrooms are luxuriously decorated, and all have the brightest of bathrooms; conference facilities are available on the first floor in the Library and the adjoining drawing room is sunny and light with French windows. For this reason this room is also popular with hotel guests.

The Roman city of York renowned for its magnificent Minster, its circuit of walls, and many old streets and houses, is perhaps equally well known for its role as an important centre for rail and road communications in the north of England. In the 1990s it is a town that tourists love to come to. It is compact yet has museums, theatres, antique shops, a medieval street called the Shambles, the River Ouse.

18th-century houses in streets leading off from the centre contribute to the overall elegance and solidity of the city and the newly opened Grange Hotel fits easily into this pattern. It is housed is a classical Regency town house just seven minutes walk from the town centre. The owner, Savoy-trained Jeremy Cassel, and his General Manager, Andrew Harris, have converted this Grade II listed property into a visually appealing 29 bedroom hotel. York stone and pillars in the entrance hall give an early indication of the quality of interior design and decoration throughout the building. The flower-filled morning room with roaring log fire (not out of place even during summer) with its wood floor, turkish carpet and a number of deep comfortable sofas has a clublike atmosphere, with strong coloured wallpaper and portraits in oils hanging on each wall. A sympathetic combination of old and

The hotel's Ivy Restaurant, open to non-residents and accessible either from the hotel or from the street, promises good food: the chef is Cara Baird from the Roux brothers' Le Gavroche and offers French and traditional Country House cooking, complemented by a full wine list. Pictures of St Leger winners, on loan from the York Racecourse Museum, hang on the walls and contribute to the atmosphere of the room. For those wanting a less formal meal, the Brasserie, in the brick vaulted room converted from the old cellars, is a fashionably attractive setting for light meals such as king prawns in garlic and parsley, or the chef 's salad - ham, cheese and beef with green lentils and crispy garlic croutons.

What is also appealing about this hotel is the spontaneous attention of the staff to the needs of the customers. Andrew Harris, trained by Hilton hotels, has been instrumental in successfully setting up other hotel operations. His idea is to combine all elements of hotel management to create an agreeable atmosphere of wellbeing and attention to customers' needs with an unobtrusive professionalism. Cheerful staff, good food and attractive surroundings are the recipe for this and the hotel comes into our guidebook with the shine both of new paint and of staff enthusiasm to create a smart hotel of the 1990s.

·BEST NEW HOTEL AWARDS·

## REGIONAL WINNER-SCOTLAND

❖

# THE ELGIN HOTEL

### DUNFERMLINE, FIFE

❖

*'The hotel is set in its own garden of 2 acres and has views over the village green, the Firth of Forth and the Pentland Hills beyond.'*

❖

As you cross the Forth Road Bridge from Edinburgh you see to west and east clusters of houses along the shoreline. In the Firth of Forth ships swing at anchor, taking advantage of Edinburgh's cheaper mooring rates before going on to Rotterdam. If you had crossed the old Forth Bridge in the 1950s it would have been a different sight, with smoking chimneys, coal trucks clanking from the railway to the limekilns, and barges on their way to Grangemouth.

The now peaceful setting of the Firth of Forth is the main outlook from the Elgin Hotel. Charlestown itself, built in 1756 by the fifth Earl of Elgin as a planned industrial town with workers' cottages around the green, is now a commuter village which is looking forward to the added business impetus of the tourist trade. Work here has started to restore the limekilns and harbour and to provide a museum depicting the history of the village and locality.

Four years ago, Bob and June Edminson and their daughter Linzi bought the Elgin Hotel - purpose built by the tenth Earl of Elgin early this century - and gutted the building from top to bottom, restoring and decorating to the needs of the present day traveller and opened for business in 1989. The hotel is set in its own garden of 2 acres and has views over the village green, the Firth of Forth and the Pentland Hills beyond. Whilst their main business has until now come mainly from the business sector, Bob sees that his hotel, set in peaceful surroundings yet not 30 minutes from Edinburgh town centre, is just right for expanding into the holiday market. Charlestown is central to the Borders, The Trossachs and St Andrews as well as the Highlands to the north. Activities such as loch or river fishing, water sports and hill walking are all around, and there are numerous golf courses within an hour's drive.

Bedrooms at the Elgin Hotel are in fresh two-colour tones of a country print and all bedrooms have a view out over the Firth of Forth or over the village green. All have private bath/showers as well as colour televisions, hairdriers and direct dial telephones. Business executives are well catered for as there is one bedroom adaptable as a conference room and other conference facilities for parties of 25 or 50 people.

This is a hotel where value for money is to be found. Honest cooking at reasonable prices attracts non-residents to the two dining rooms. In the main dining room, where casts of the Elgin marbles can be seen above the fireplace, one can eat such delicacies as grilled salmon with cucumber and mint sauce or venison with a gammon sauce. In the Tavern Bar which is very popular with the locals, simpler fare is served such as steak pie or roast pork.

Bob and June with daughter Linzi, who comes in to give a hand in the evenings, provide a natural and attentive service which is appreciated by visitors and the locals alike.

# COUNTRY CLUB HOTELS. YOU'LL ENJOY THE EXPERIENCE.

We have created a unique environment at every Country Club Hotel.

Take a break from routine and re-charge your batteries in the relaxing surroundings of our hotels, all with extensive leisure facilities. Ten superb country locations, most with their own golf course, yet within minutes of the motorway system.

Things will look better after a few days away at a Country Club Hotel!

# BEST NEW RESTAURANTS

Each year we welcome to our guide a number of new restaurants and here we feature the five establishments which impressed our inspectors the most. We wish them every success for the future

## Stephen Bull, London WI.

Londoners have been quick to discover that at Stephen Bull's new restaurant, serious food need not always burn a hole in their pockets. The dishes are well prepared from good basic ingredients and our inspectors have particularly praised the sauces as flavoursome, of good consistency and correctly seasoned. Lunchtimes are busy here with a largely business clientele - serious eaters might prefer to wait until dinner.

## La Mouette, Llandudno, Gwynedd

Within a few weeks of its opening this smart, intimate restaurant on the Promenade, had become popular with the locals and is gaining a fine reputation. Gareth Bream was formally trained and has been responsible for the food operation at his family's hotel, The Merrion, spending his winters gaining experience in such fine restaurants as Le Manoir aux Quat'Saisons and L'Arlequin. Now he brings that experience, together with his own innovative talents, to this new venture. Service is professional and attentive by French waiters who have a good knowledge of the food and the extensive wine list.

## Markwicks Restaurant, Bristol, Avon

Markwicks Restaurant has certainly given a new lease of life to an attractive Bristol rendezvous, situated in converted vaults beneath the Commercial rooms. Stephen Markwick's cooking, which has a French bias, is extremely competent. Service is charming and polite and the wine list of some 100 bins has good world coverage at sensible prices.

## Epicurean Stow-on-the-Wold, Gloucestershire

'Jewel of the Cotswolds' is how our Inspector described this restaurant which is the first restaurant that Patrick McDonald has owned, though he has gained experience in the kitchens of some of Britain's finest hotels. He is an enthusiastic and energetic chef/proprietor who has brought fine cooking skills and modern British flair to an area which can provide him with the best raw ingredients. His imagination expands dishes that are quite common elsewhere, giving height to each course to create an immediate sense of the spectacular. Good professional service by French head waiter, Patrice Roger, is supplemented by Patrick's wife, Claire.

## Kinnaird, Dunkeld, Tayside

By the time this guide is published Kinnaird will be fully operational as a fine country manor hotel, but at the time of our Inspection we could only sample the restaurant. Chef-manager John Webber's inventive and reliable cooking has already placed Kinnaird among the best places to eat in Scotland. His cooking is modern in style, rich in flavour and generous in quantity. In view of the quality and quantity of the food here, a meal at Kinnaird represents excellent value for money.

# ONE ★ STAR HOTELS

*Top Twenty*

In the 1990 edition of the guide we introduced our new percentage awards for quality which enable prospective guests to compare the merits of hotels within a star classification. At that time the percentages were applied to three, four and five star hotels only. The exercise is now complete and in this edition all hotels will have a percentage score. One of the benefits, we feel, will be to bring about a greater appreciation of some of the one star hotels. They are usually run on a small scale, frequently by a resident family, and are more likely to offer a high degree of personal attention. Many are very conveniently situated in town centres and may have been there since the days of the mail coaches, carrying on a historic tradition of hospitality to travellers. As you will see from the percentage ratings, there are a number of establishments which, although not offer-

ing the facilities required for a higher star rating, have certainly concentrated their efforts on providing exceptional quality. Eight one star hotels have achieved Red Stars, the AA's highest accolade for excellence in hotels. These, of course, have always been easily identified by means of the list of Red Star Hotels in the preliminary pages of the guide and by their enhanced gazetteer entries. Until now, the best of the rest were not so easy to find - only the gazetteer description would give any indication of an outstanding hotel. In this edition all hotels with a high percentage are clearly identified, both with the percentage score itself and with a special highlighting of the gazetteer entry. We are delighted to be able to give these establishments the prominence they deserve and to celebrate this step forward we have selected our Top Twenty One Star Hotels for a special mention.

## 1. ★ HALMPSTONE MANOR,
Barnstaple, Devon.

The national winner of our Best Newcomer awards in the 1990 edition, Halmpstone Manor is a delightful combination of high standard accommodation and working farm. The natural warmth and hospitality of owners Charles and Jane Stanbury and their staff quickly put guests at their ease, and comfort is assured in the beautifully furnished bedrooms which have all the accoutrements of a first-class hotel room. The best local ingredients and the obvious natural talent of Jane Stanbury ensures excellent and interesting food.

## 2. ★ WHITE MOSS HOUSE,
Grasmere, Cumbria

Susan and Peter Dixon have created a real gem of a hotel at White Moss House and continue to charm their guests with the highest standards of accommodation, superb food and service that is discreet rather than outgoing. The dinner, for which we have awarded a well-earned rosette, is served at 8pm and is a set five-course meal which never fails to impress. An enormous amount of thought has gone into the pretty bedrooms which do not benefit from spaciousness, but are exceptionally well equipped down to the dimmer switches on the lighting. The success of this hotel is a tribute to the dedication and enthusiasm of the Dixons.

## 3. ★ LANGLEY HOUSE,
Wiveliscombe, Somerset

Peter and Anne Wilson and their staff bring a refreshing blend of professionalism and genuine friendliness to this lovely hotel. Dating from the 16th century and set in beautiful gardens beneath the Brendon Hills, it is only a mile from the well-beaten tourist track of the A361, but break your journey here and the lure of the North Devon resorts

are likely to fade somewhat. The warm welcome includes a glass of sherry on arrival and fresh flowers in your room and later you will be treated to a skilfully prepared set five-course dinner. The excellent cuisine, which has earned an AA Rosette award, concentrates on the freshest local produce.

## 4. ★ OLD VICARAGE COUNTRY HOUSE HOTEL, Witherslack,

Peace, tranquility, utter relaxation - all these things have been said about this idyllic hotel in southern lakeland. It is not just the quiet that attracts guests here, though. The comfortable bedrooms each individual in style, have all kinds of extras including orange juice, mineral water and Kendal Mint Cake. For more than ten years it has been run by two families - Jill and Roger Burrington-Brown and Irene and Stanley Reeve - whose caring and thoughtful approach has created the special ambience here. A set dinner in traditional style is prepared from fresh local ingredients and is complemented by a wine list of around 200 bins. Breakfast here is particularly memorable - a huge meal of Cumberland sausage, black pudding, home-produced eggs etc with excellent bread and rolls - just as well this is good walking country.'

## 5. ★ FACTOR'S HOUSE, Fort William, Highland

Set in the grounds of the very grand four red star Inverlochy Castle Hotel, this charming little establishment is by no means overshadowed by its neighbour. It provides a different style of accommodation, with the warmth and character of a private home coupled with the highest standards of comfort and food. Peter Hobbs and his staff provide a special kind of hospitality and it is this above all that makes the Factor's House such a pleasant place to stay. The fixed price menu, with a choice of four main dishes, is very good value and the bedrooms are well equipped.

## 6. ★ LANSDOWNE HOTEL, Leamington Spa, Warwickshire

David and Gillian Allen trained in Switzerland and gained experience in some large hotels before deciding that small was beautiful. In this elegant Regency building they have created a warm and happy atmosphere along with all the comforts associated with a Red Star hotel. Although Gillian takes an active part in running the hotel, she is most often found in the kitchen, preparing carefully selected dishes for the menus which always include seasonal produce. The wine list is David's personal choice and includes some unusual items.

## 7. ★ MINFFORDD HOTEL, Talyllyn, Gwynedd

Minffordd has been offering hospitality to travellers for some 300 years - first to drovers, later to teetotallers as a Temperence Hotel and now to those seeking the highest standards in peaceful surroundings. Over the last thirteen years the Pickles family have developed an individual style of hotel keeping here, with a definite emphasis away from modern services and towards old fashioned sociability. In the two comfortable lounges and cosy bar guests are encouraged to get to know each other. In the unusual dining room, although choice is limited, Jonathan Pickles' cooking is sure to please.

## 8. ★ EBURY COURT, London SW1

For over fifty years Mrs Topham has run this unique London hotel, setting standards of care and helpfulness which are carried through now by her family and their loyal staff. Small is certainly beautiful here, with pretty fabrics and china bringing considerable charm to the bedrooms. If it lacks modern facilities - less than a third of the bedrooms have private bathrooms and televisions must be requested in advance - it more than compensates with its delightful atmosphere, attention to detail and sheer quality. The food is good, too, and consists of simple British dishes, served in the stylish dining room.

## 9. 77% MOORTOWN LODGE HOTEL, Ringwood, Hants.

A recent visitor to Moortown Lodge said, 'As a female on my own, I usually feel uncomfortable in a hotel. Not here. From the moment I entered the hall I felt relaxed and welcome.' Jilly and Bob Burrows-Jones are the friendly owners, who are genuinely interested in the comfort and enjoyment of all their guests and provide service which is attentive without being intrusive. The hotel is nicely decorated throughout, and the bedrooms are well-equipped, well lit and with extras such as mineral water, chocolates, quality toiletries and a clothes brush. Jilly's evening meals are beautifully presented and full of flavour, and Bob's breakfasts are no less of a treat.

## 10. 77% THE MARSH, Leominster, Hereford & Worcester

The enthusiasm of Jacqueline and Martin Gilleland for their fine hotel is apparent almost before you get through the door, and their pride in The Marsh is justified. It

is a beautiful old timbered building which has been furnished and decorated to the highest standards. Mrs. Gilleland is one of those rare ladies who put the rest of us to shame - not only does she do the cooking, gardening and flower arranging, she has made all the lovely curtains, bed covers and cushions and even upholstered the suites and dining chairs! Her cooking is very accomplished and quite innovative with good use made of her own herbs from the garden. Martin Gilleland is an excellent and charming host, eager to talk and quick to put guests at their ease.

## 11. 76% HURSTONE HOTEL AND RESTAURANT, Waterrow, Somerset

Set in 65 acres on the edge of the Brendon Hills, this small, family-run hotel occupies a lovely 300-year-old farmhouse. It was largely re-built in the 1920s, but recent alterations have uncovered a large open fireplace and timbered ceiling in the sitting room. All of the bedrooms are on the first floor and have large south-facing windows overlooking the valley. There is an à la carte menu at dinner, with everything home made from fresh ingredients. Not only are herbs, vegetables, butter and cream produced on the farm, they also have their own prize-winning cheese, 'Hurstone'

## 12. 76% LOCH DUICH HOTEL, Ardelve, Highland

Rod and Geraldine Stenson and their friendly staff have built a reputation at Loch Duich Hotel of hospitality and good food and we have certainly received glowing reports of the cuisine from our Inspectors. Fresh local game and seafood are prepared with great skill and imagination to produce dishes that are just bursting with flavour. The atmosphere throughout the hotel is warm and homely and its situation is superb, with magnificent views of the Loch, the famous Eilean Donan Castle and the surrounding mountains

## 13. 76% WELL VIEW HOTEL, Moffat, Dumfries & Galloway.

When former teachers Janet and John Schuckardt decided to run a hotel in a popular tourist town, they asked themselves how their establishment could be different from their local competitors. Their answer was that the special strength would be their food. Janet is an enthusiastic chef, providing tempting and good quality meals using local beef, salmon and trout and she has arranged an adventurous programme of wine and food evenings including a German Evening and a Festival of Fish and Game. The hotel is a converted Victorian house in an enviable, peaceful location in the Annan valley and is, as our inspector described it, a delightful hotel.

## 14. 75% BURGOYNE HOTEL, Reeth, North Yorkshire

Our Inspector was feeling thoroughly miserable with a cold when she stayed at the Burgoyne, but was soon cheered by the warm welcome and the feeling of being well looked after. Pat and Steve Foster came into the hotel business after careers in the RAF and have created a truly homely atmosphere in the elegant surroundings of this Grade II listed 18th-century building. Rooms are light, airy and unpretentious with comfortable chairs and sofas and open stone fireplaces. Cooking had always been a hobby for Steve and now, as chef, he produces a different menu every night, with home-made soups, roulades, fish and meat dishes and puddings - all of excellent flavour.

## 15. 75% TREGARTHEN COUNTRY COTTAGE HOTEL, Mount Hawke, Cornwall.

At this pretty Cornish cottage, Clive and Mavis Hutton have created a pleasant atmosphere while providing a very high standard of accommodation. Coordinating fabrics have been used to good effect in the bedrooms, several of which have Queen-size beds and one even has a corner spa bath in its en suite bathroom. Although the menu is limited, the food is good and wholesome using fresh vegetables, seasonal produce and, of course, Cornish clotted cream. The dining room is well appointed and there are two comfortable lounges as well as the country-pub-style bar. All this, in lovely rural surroundings, just two miles from a selection of sandy surfing beaches.

## 16. 74% GLENVIEW INN, Culnacnoc, Skye

This friendly little country inn on the scenic north-east coast of Skye is run by Linda Thompson and her family, who offer traditional, informal hospitality to their guests. The six bedrooms are very attractive, each with television and facilities for making tea and coffee, and three have private shower rooms. Naturally, for an inn, there is a lively bar, but the high spot of a visit here is a meal in the dining room which offers Scottish country cooking at its best. The award of an AA Rosette is certainly well deserved. As well as the superb dinners, delicious buffet-style food, together with coffee is available all day.

## 17. 74% SUNNINGDALE, Hunstanton, Norfolk

The proprietors, Mr. and Mrs. Wright, are so friendly that guests here immediately feel relaxed and comfortable and really nothing is too much trouble - special diets, late arrivals, early departures etc - are all happily accommodated even though the couple do everything themselves. Small wonder that so many guests return again and again (you can see photographs of many of them in the lounge - and each picture tells a story!). The décor of each room is different and their experiments with colour and design have all been successful. Mrs. Wright also enjoys a culinary challenge and has won healthy eating awards, but she finds that most of the guests only want plain food. The compromise is to have a standard menu of traditional meals, with a daily choice of something more imaginative.

## 18. 73% THE MILL HOTEL, Mungrisdale, Cumbria.

Richard and Eleanor Quinlan have been at The Mill Hotel (not to be confused with the Mill Inn next door) for about seven years, providing a quiet resting place for walkers and holidaymakers in this heartland of lakes and fells. The hotel has all that you would expect of a 17th-century building, combined with all the benefits of modern facilities. Eleanor is an imaginative and expert cook, using unusual combinations of herbs and textures in her soups and producing such dishes as roast haunch of wild boar with rowan jelly and grapes with Sorbet of Muscat de beames de Venise. Traditional favourites and vegetarian alternatives are also available and, not surprisingly, the emphasis here is on dinner, bed and breakfast. The quality of the food, the service and, of course, the

surrounding countryside, is perhaps best reflected in the fact that fifty percent of the Quinlans' business is made up of repeat visitors.

## 19. 77% TYREE HOUSE HOTEL, Grantown-on-Spey, Highland

Housed in a fine old granite building in the town's main square, Tyree House Hotel provides excellent accommodation. This is, of course, a famous sporting area and proprietor, Mr. Nelson, has thoughtfully provided a secure gun and rod room for his visiting sportsmen. The comfortable bedrooms are decorated in restful shades and each has en suite facilities, television and complimentary tea, coffee and biscuits. There is a charming residents lounge in one of the front rooms on the first floor, overlooking the leafy square.

## 20. 73% WINDSOR LODGE HOTEL, Swansea, West Glamorgan.

When Mr R J. Rumble bought the property in 1969 its condition was so bad that it was offered for sale at site value only, for probable demolition. The transformation into today's Windsor Lodge Hotel has taken enormous effort and dedication, but has certainly been worthwhile. Throughout the original building and the new wing the décor is stylish and attractive, and the accommodation comfortable. The food is good, too, with well-prepared dishes accompanied by a comprehensive wine list - and we must mention the noteworthy self-service breakfast buffet. The Rumbles are very much involved in the day to day running of the hotel, along with their experienced staff, and have managed to create a country house atmosphere within the City centre.

# Comfortable, value for money accommodation for all the family

Throughout Britain, Travel Inn offers bright, modern comfortable accommodation. Easy to reach, situated in attractive locations with ample parking, just off the major roads and motorways.

There's a friendly restaurant and pub alongside every Travel Inn where you can enjoy a delicious breakfast, lunch and dinner or simply relax with a drink in the bar. Travel Inn provides exceptional value for money. £27.50 per room per night for single, double or family occupancy★ (family - 2 adults and two children up to the age of 16)

Throughout Britain, Travel Inn may be found at:

| | |
|---|---|
| BASILDON • Tel: 0268 522227 | HARLOW • Tel: 0279 442545 |
| BASINGSTOKE • Tel: 0256 811477 | HAYES • Tel: 081 573 7479 |
| CANNOCK • Tel: 0543 572721 | HEREFORD • Tel: 0432 274853 |
| CARDIFF • Tel: 0633 680070 | KENTON • Tel: 081 9071671 |
| CHEADLE • Tel: 061 499 1944 ★ | NORTHAMPTON • Tel: 0604 832340 |
| CHELTENHAM • Tel: 0242 233847 | NUNEATON • Tel: 0203 343584 |
| CHESSINGTON • Tel: 0372 744060 | PORT TALBOT • Tel: 0639 813017★ |
| CHRISTCHURCH • Tel: 0202 485376 | PRESTON • Tel: 0772 720476 |
| CROYDON • Tel: 081 686 2030 | SKIPTON • Tel: 0756 749666 ★ |
| CUMBERNAULD • Tel: 0236 725339 ★ | SOUTHAMPTON • Tel: 0703 732262 ★ |
| DOVER • Tel: 0304 213339 | TAUNTON • Tel: 0823 321112 |
| GLOUCESTER • Tel: 0452 23519 | TRING • Tel: 0442 824819 |
| GLOUCESTER • Tel: 0452 862521 | WIRRAL • Tel: 051 342 1982 ★ |
| HAGLEY • Tel: 0562 883120 | WROTHAM HEATH • Tel: 0732 884214 ★ |

★ Opening 1991

For more information on Travel Inn and latest openings nationwide:
## Tel: 0582 482224

*Perfectly placed for comfort, value and a warm welcome*

Price is correct at time of going to press. All rooms subject to availability.

# BRITAIN'S TOP HOTELS

The award of Red Stars to an hotel is the AA's highest accolade for excellence. The 72 hotels listed below are those which have been judged by our Inspectors to be the very best in their star classification, and therefore the best hotels in Britain.

New awards are made to Cliveden, Taplow, Alverton Manor, Truro, Hartwell House, Aylesbury, Whitechapel Manor, South Molton, Summer Lodge, Evershot, Maes y Neuedd, Talsarnau, Lewtrenchard Manor, Lewdown, and Wharton Lodge, Ross on Wye. Hunstrete House, Hunstrete and Middlethorpe Hall, York, make a welcome reappearance.

## ENGLAND
## AVON

HUNSTRETE ★★★⚜ Hunstrete House
A fine example of a country-house hotel, with elegant rooms and an impressive library. Hunstrete House is a delightful place to stay and standards under the new ownership are as high as ever.

THORNBURY ★★★⚜ Thornbury Castle
This imposing building hides a very comfortable, welcoming hotel behind its historic stone walls. Standards of hospitality are a tribute to the manager Peter Strong.

## BUCKINGHAMSHIRE

ASTON CLINTON ❀★★★ Bell Inn
Michael and Patsy Harris have created and maintain a delightful atmosphere at this lovely old coaching inn, famed for its atmosphere, food and fine wines.

AYLESBURY ★★★⚜ Hartwell House
A magnificent building, part Jacobean and part Georgian, now faithfully restored by Historic House Hotels to make an elegant hotel of rare distinction and character.

TAPLOW ★★★★★⚜ Cliveden
This splendid stately home, owned by the National Trust, offers guests a taste of its glittering past and provides the highest levels of quality and comfort.

## Channel Islands, Jersey

ST SAVIOUR ❀★★★★⚜ Longueville Manor
This is without doubt Jersey's finest hotel, elegant, luxurious and welcoming. Chef Andrew Baird ensures that the food is in style with the rest of the hotel.

## CHESHIRE

CHESTER ❀★★★★ Chester Grosvenor
A magnificent hotel, exceptionally well managed by Jonathan Slater and Jonathan Ritchie, the elegant 'Arkle' restaurant offers a memorable Gourmet menu, created by Chef Paul Reed.

## CORNWALL

LISKEARD ❀★★⚑ Well House
An idyllic setting gives Nick Wainford's hotel a uniquely welcoming air, and first impressions are admirably borne out by owner and staff alike. The cooking is a treat to look forward to.

TRURO ★★★ Alverton Manor
The Costello family have restored this Grade II listed manor to its former glory and provide every creature comfort.

## CUMBRIA

BRAMPTON ❀★★⚑ Farlam Hall
The pleasures to be savoured here are the peace and quiet of the wooded grounds, the excellent and uncomplicated cooking and the old-fashioned courtesy of staff and owners.

GRASMERE ❀★★★⚑ Michael's Nook
Fine antiques furnish this Victorian hotel which offers splendid lakeland views and excellent cooking.

GRASMERE ❀★ White Moss House
Our Inspectors continue to rate this one of the best small hotels in northern England, admirably run by Susan and Peter Dixon.

HOWTOWN ❀❀★★★⚑ Sharrow Bay Hotel
A hotel whose individual style and excellent cuisine, built up over many years by Brian Sack and Francis Coulson, has earned international fame.

WATERMILLOCK ★★⚑ Old Church Hotel
Definitely a favourite with our Inspectorate, the hotel's setting on the shores of Ullswater, is idyllic, and the atmosphere peaceful.

WINDERMERE ❀★★ Miller Howe
An international reputation has not detracted from the charm and individuality of John Tovey's famous hotel. Dinner continues to be an exciting and memorable event.

WITHERSLACK ★★⚑ Old Vicarage
This charming family-run hotel goes from strength to strength providing excellent food, really comfortable rooms and a welcoming atmosphere.

## DERBYSHIRE

BASLOW ★★★ Cavendish
Views over the Chatsworth estate refresh the eye and give this comfortable and friendly hotel a fitting setting.

## DEVON

BARNSTAPLE ★⚑ Halmpstone Manor
Winner of the AA Best Newcomer Award last year, this is an exceptionally charming hotel, whose owners Charles and Jane Stanbury, know how to pamper guests.

CHAGFORD ❀★★★⚑ Gidleigh Park
Location and grounds continue to be a major attraction at the Henderson's well established hotel, where Shaun Hill's cooking is more than praiseworthy.

LEWDOWN ❀★★⚑ Lewtrenchard Manor
A magnificent 17th-century house on the edge of Dartmoor retaining much of its original ornate decor.

NORTH HUISH ★★⚑ Brookdale House
Charles and Carol Trevor-Roper run this secluded hotel to perfection, offering an imaginative style of cooking in relaxed surroundings.

SOUTH MOLTON ❀★★⚑ Whitechapel Manor
A historic manor, restored and sympathetically converted by John and Patricia Shapland who have preserved its character throughout. The menus devised by Thierry Lepretre-Granet offer French provincial and English dishes.

## DORSET

EVERSHOT ★★ Summer Lodge
A delightful country hotel in an attractive village setting with the atmosphere of a welcoming private house.

GILLINGHAM ★★♨ Stock Hill House
Fine antiques furnish this splendid Victorian manor. Luxury abounds, and Peter Hauser's excellent cooking has strong Austrian overtones.

## EAST SUSSEX

BATTLE ★★★♨ Netherfield Place
Thirty acres of grounds surround this Georgian country house with its elegant restaurant and pleasant rooms.

UCKFIELD ★★★♨ Horsted Place
A magnificent hotel offering every luxury and, under the managership of Elizabeth Crookston, impeccable standards of service. Allan Garth's cooking is highly recommended.

## ESSEX

DEDHAM ✿★★★ Maison Talbooth
A very comfortable, quiet hotel, very much the creation of its well known proprietor Gerald Milsom. Its nearby restaurant, Le Talbooth, has an established reputation for fine cuisine.

## GLOUCESTERSHIRE

BUCKLAND ✿★★★♨ Buckland Manor
Lovely grounds and peaceful countryside surround this welcoming hotel where owners Adrienne and Barry Berman create the right mood to appreciate the cooking of chef Martin Pearn.

CHELTENHAM ✿★★★♨ Greenway Hotel
A beautiful hotel, run with the greatest efficiency and charm by Tony Elliott and his staff. Their new chef Edward Stephens is already extending the high reputation of the restaurant.

LOWER SLAUGHTER ★★★♨ Lower Slaughter Manor
The hotel enjoys a lovely village setting. Rooms are beautifully furnished and the welcome is friendly.

TETBURY ✿★★★♨ Calcot Manor
Ramon Farthing's cooking is the highlight of a stay at this attractive Cotswold hotel where the Ball family make guests feel instantly at home.

## HAMPSHIRE

NEW MILTON ✿★★★★♨ Chewton Glen
Long established as a luxury hotel whose fine leisure facilities include a golf course, owner Martin Skan continues to extend and improve the accommodation and facilities.

## HEREFORD & WORCESTER

BROADWAY ★★★★ Lygon Arms
A lovely old Coltswold inn with a fine reputation for high standards of accommodation and service that attracts guests from all over the world.

ROSS ON WYE ★★ Wharton Lodge
A delightful Georgian property, converted into an hotel of extremely high quality and a most welcome addition to the Guide. Hospitality from the Gough family is all that could be desired.

## KENT

ASHFORD ★★★★♨ Eastwell Manor
An imposing hotel set in 62 acres of grounds, Eastwell Manor, with its panelled walls, leather sofas and large stone-mantled fireplaces, is the epitome of English country-house hotels.

## LEICESTER

OAKHAM ✿★★★♨ Hambleton Hall
Owners Tim and Stefa Hart provide a warm welcome in the best tradition of country house hospitality. Chef Brian Baker's cooking is justifiably very popular.

## LONDON

SW1 ★★★★★ Berkeley
Formality of service and an air of dignity prevail in this distinguished hotel, where traditional standards are appreciated by a discerning and faithful clientele.

SW1 ★★★★ Goring Hotel
Praise from all quarters continues to be showered on this cheerful, family-run hotel. Rooms are well-planned and attractive, the menus interesting and the atmosphere welcoming.

SW1 ★ Ebury Court
This outstanding small hotel run for many years by Mrs Topham and now by her daughter and son-in-law, lays emphasis on comfort and high standards of service.

SW3 ❀★★★★ Capital
Proprietor David Levin is to be congratulated for making this modern hotel such a friendly and welcoming place. Its restaurant is highly recommended.

W1 ★★★★★ Claridges
A splendid Mayfair hotel, very much a London landmark and a haunt of the rich and famous. General Manager and Director Ron Jones inspires every department of the hotel with real enthusiasm.

W1 ❀❀★★★★★ Connaught
Luxury, discreet service and the maintenance of traditional standards have kept the Connaught in a pre-eminent position. The restaurant is superb.

W1 ★★★★ Athenaeum
With its rooms now all refurbished to suit the demands of an international clientele, this is fast becoming the most modern of West End hotels, with an extremely good restaurant.

W1 ★★★★ Browns Hotel
High standards of service, warmth of welcome, and a comfortable, club-like atmosphere distinguish this long-established Mayfair Hotel.

WC2 ❀★★★★★ Savoy
A world-famous hotel with a long and distinguished tradition of service to live up to. Its two restaurants are equally famous and deservedly popular.

## NORFOLK

GRIMSTON ❀★★★★⚜ Congham Hall
A handsome country-house hotel set in beautiful parkland and offering a comfortable stay in fine surroundings. Guests appreciate the lavish meals.

## NORTH YORKSHIRE

BILBROUGH ★★★⚜ Bilbrough Manor
A handsome country-house hotel, quiet and secluded, yet near to York. Service is professional and friendly, surroundings are luxurious.

YORK ★★★ Middlethorpe Hall
Overlooking York racecourse, this 17th-century mansion has been beautifully converted. Chef Kevin Francksen provides imaginative menus.

## OXFORDSHIRE

GREAT MILTON ❀❀❀★★★⚜ Le Manoir aux Quat' Saisons
Raymond Blanc's culinary skills are so celebrated that they scarcely need to be mentioned, and the setting of his lovely hotel leaves nothing to be desired.

## SOMERSET

DULVERTON ★★⚜ Ashwick House
The Exmoor countryside is the setting for this delightful Edwardian house where the Sherwood family create a peaceful welcoming atmosphere.

STON EASTON ★★★⚜ Ston Easton
A majestic Palladian mansion with elegant accommodation, run with supreme efficiency and no detail overlooked.

WIVELISCOMBE ❀★ Langley House
A small, exceptionally pretty hotel set in lovely countryside. Peter and Anne Wilson are friendly hosts, and the standard of cooking is excellent.

## SUFFOLK

HINTLESHAM ❀★★★⚜ Hintlesham Hall
In spite of a change of ownership, this beautiful and charming hotel retains its Red Stars – all the key staff have been retained and we are confident that standards will remain high.

## WARWICKSHIRE

LEAMINGTON SPA ❀❀★★★ Mallory Court
Luxurious accommodation and attentive service await guests arriving at this fine hotel set in 10 acres of gardens.

LEAMINGTON SPA ★ Lansdowne Hotel
Run by David and Gillian Allen this is a first class small hotel providing well above average facilities and cooking.

## WEST SUSSEX

EAST GRINSTEAD ❀★★★⚜ Gravetye Manor
Peter Herbert's distinguished country-house hotel set in extensive grounds has, for the past 30 years, remained a shining example of consistently high standards.

## WEST YORKSHIRE

WETHERBY ★★★⚜ Woodhall
A palatial Yorkshire mansion where staff are both warm and hospitable. The country-house atmosphere suits the excellent dinners provided by chef Simon Wood.

## WALES

### GWYNEDD

LLANDUDNO ★★★⚜️ Bodysgallen Hall
Delightful gardens surround this historic
17th-century house which has been well
restored to provide all modern comforts.

LLANDUDNO ✹★★ St. Tudno
'Delightful' is the only way of describing
this hotel run with such charm and flair by
Janette and Martin Bland. Hospitality, fine
cooking and stylish furnishings are its
hallmarks.

TALSARNAU ★★⚜️ Maes-y-Neuadd
A delightful and historic hotel, set in the
midst of beautiful countryside, it offers an
extremely high standard of service and
accommodation, which has earned the
award of red stars for the first time.

TAL-Y-LLYN ★ Minfford Hotel
A very hospitably run hotel, dating from
the 18th century, set amid breathtaking
mountain scenery but handy for travellers
as it is near the A487/B4405 junction.

## SCOTLAND

### CENTRAL

DUNBLANE ✹★★★⚜️ Cromlix House
A stately country house, set in a 5000 acre
estate, Cromlix House exudes an air of
tranquility, comfort and relaxation. The 5-
course dinners are notable.

### DUMFRIES & GALLOWAY

PORTPATRICK ✹★★⚜️ Knockinaam
Lodge
This secluded Victorian lodge with
gardens running down to a private beach
is memorable for the excellence of the
food and the charm of its surroundings.

### GRAMPIAN

BANCHORY ★★★⚜️ Banchory Lodge
This delightful Georgian mansion on the
River Dee, run by Dugald and Maggie
Jaffrey, is an ideal retreat for anglers and
holiday makers.

## HIGHLAND

ARISAIG ★★★⚜️ Arisaig House
A fine country house on the Road to the
Isles, Arisaig House is a haven of peace,
retaining many original 1930s features.

FORT WILLIAM ★★★★⚜️ Inverlochy
Castle
An outstanding hotel, providing every
luxury for its guests in a beautiful setting,
with immaculate standards of
housekeeping and service which have
earned Grete Hobbs many accolades.

FORT WILLIAM ★ The Factor's House
A charming small hotel, exceptionally well
run by Peter Hobbs and his friendly staff.
Cooking is very good, and the set menu
very good value.

WHITEBRIDGE ★★⚜️ Knockie Lodge
An 18th-century hunting lodge set high
above Loch Nan Lann, this hotel is the
ultimate retreat for those in search of
tranquility.

### STRATHCLYDE

ERISKA ★★★⚜️ Isle of Eriska Hotel
Its location, on an island rich in wildlife
and owned by the hotel's proprietor,
Robin Buchanan-Smith, gives this hotel a
unique advantage. All modern comforts
are incorporated within its baronial rooms.

KILCHRENAN ★★★⚜️ Ardanaiseig
Lovely gardens surround this secluded
hotel on the banks of Loch Awe. Jonathan
and Jane Brown are charming hosts,
dedicated to the wellbeing of their guests.

PORT APPIN ✹★★ Airds
A delightful small hotel overlooking Loch
Linnhe and set in magnificent scenery.
Friendly service combines with the best of
Scottish cooking to make guests feel
welcome and relaxed.

### TAYSIDE

AUCHTERARDER ★★★★★ Gleneagles
Renowned for its leisure and sports
facilities, which include two golf courses,
with a third under construction and an
equestrian centre, Gleneagles continues
to be in the top flight of luxury hotels.

# FOR THE PERFECT BREAK FROM WORK
# OR THE PERFECT WORKING BREAK

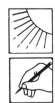

If you're looking for the perfect holiday in the South of England, Resort Hotels Carefree Breaks offer you an exciting choice of midweek, 7 day or weekend breaks (from just £19 per person per night).

At each of our comfortable 3 star hotels and coaching inns you'll enjoy a unique blend of old-fashioned courtesy and modern luxury. And you'll find our hotels are the perfect base for exploring the culture and history of the South.

Resort Hotels also offer an exceptional range of business facilities. Well-equipped conference and meeting rooms are available, and we can arrange any kind of function or banquet. Many of our hotels also now include health and leisure clubs.

Whether you're looking for the perfect place to do business or the most relaxing place to escape it, you can rely on Resort to make your stay special.

Phone Free on 0800 500 100 for details of our leisure or business programmes.

**RESORT HOTELS PLC**
2 FREDERICK TERRACE, FREDERICK PLACE,
BRIGHTON, EAST SUSSEX BN1 1AX.

## MARSTON HOTELS
• for all your •
HOTEL AND CORPORATE ENTERTAINMENT NEEDS
IN THE SOUTH EAST

| ★★★ | ★★★★ | ★★★ |
|---|---|---|
| **Bridgewood Manor Hotel** | **The Hythe Imperial** | **Stade Court Hotel** |
| Rochester, Kent | Hythe, Kent | Hythe, Kent |
| 3 star, 100 bedrooms, | 4 star, 100 bedrooms, 10 main | 3 star, 39 bedrooms, 2 main |
| 7 main Conference Rooms, | Conference Rooms, Golf | Conference Rooms plus use |
| Leisure Centre. | Course and Extensive Indoor | of Hythe Imperial Golf and |
| | and Outdoor Leisure Facilities. | Leisure Facilities. |
| Tel (0634) 201333 | Tel (0303) 267441 | Tel (0303) 268263 |
| Fax (0634) 201330 | Fax (0303) 264610 | Fax (0303) 264610 |

46

# BRITAIN'S BEST RESTAURANTS

The AA's rosette awards are given to restaurants where the cooking is of an exceptionally high standard, and where presentation of the dishes and service reach the same level of excellence. Rosette awards are a recognition of the chef's ability and are based on the subjective assessment of the AA's most experienced Inspectors.

The highest award is three rosettes, and this supreme distinction has been given to only four restaurants in the whole country; Chez Nico, owned by Nico Ladenis; Le Gavroche, owned by Albert Roux, and Le Manoir aux Quat' Saisons, owned by Raymond Blanc, retain their three rosettes and they are now joined by Pierre Koffman at Tante Claire.

L'Ortolan, owned by John Burton-Race, has been awarded two rosettes this year.

New one-rosette awards have been made to 17 restaurants:

Markwicks, *Bristol*
Chester Grosvenor, *Chester*
Le Champignon Sauvage, *Cheltenham*

Epicurean, *Stow-on-the-Wold*
Wyck Hill House Hotel, *Stow-on-the-Wold*
Normandie Hotel, *Bury*
Charingworth Manor, *Charingworth*
Plas Bodegroes, *Pwllheli*
Poppies, *Brimfield*
Keats Restaurant, *London NW3*
Stephen Bull, *London W1*
Whitechapel Manor, *South Molton*
Les Alouettes, *Claygate*
Pennyhill Park, *Bagshot*
Eslington Villa Hotel, *Gateshead*
Amberley Castle, *Amberley*
Kinnaird, *Dunkeld*

Seventeen restaurants have lost their rosettes, either because the management or chef has changed, because they have closed, or because they no longer meet the standards the AA sets for its rosette awards. Altogether only 131 restaurants (including hotel restaurants) have been awarded rosettes.

Please consult the gazetteer for full details of the establishments listed below. Some restaurants have been awarded rosettes for their dinner menu only.

## ENGLAND

### AVON

**Bristol**❀✕✕ Marwicks
**Freshford**★★★❀ Homewood Park

### BERKSHIRE

**Bray**❀❀✕✕✕✕ Waterside Restaurant
**Maidenhead**★★★★❀ Fredrick's Hotel
**Shinfield**❀❀✕✕✕ L'Ortolan

### BUCKINGHAMSHIRE

**Aston Clinton**★★★❀ Bell Inn

### CAMBRIDGESHIRE

**Ely**❀✕ The Old Fire Engine House

## CHANNEL ISLANDS

**St Saviour, Jersey**
★★★★❀ Longueville Manor Hotel

### CHESHIRE

**Chester**★★★★❀ Chester Grosvenor
**Wilmslow**★★★❀ Stanneylands Hotel

### CORNWALL

**Liskeard**★★❀ Well House Hotel
**Padstow**❀✕✕ Seafood Restaurant

### CUMBRIA

**Brampton**★★❀ Farlam Hall Hotel
**Cartmel**❀✕✕ Uplands
**Grasmere**★★★❀ Michael's Nook Hotel
★❀ White Moss House Hotel

**Howtown**❀❀★★★ Sharrow Bay Hotel
**Ulverston**❀ ✕ Bay Horse Inn
**Watermillock**★★★❀ Rampsbeck Hotel
**Windermere**★★❀ Miller Howe Hotel
❀✕ Porthole Eating House

## DEVON

**Chagford**★★★❀ Gidleigh Park Hotel
**Dartmouth**❀ ✕ ✕ Carved Angel
❀✕✕ Mansion House
**Lewdown**★★❀ Lewtrenchard Manor
**South Molton**❀★★★✌ Whitechapel Manor
**Torquay**❀✕✕ Table Restaurant

## EAST SUSSEX

**Hastings**❀✕ Roser's

## ESSEX

**Broxted**★★★❀ White Hall
**Dedham**❀✕✕ Le Talbooth

## GLOUCESTERSHIRE

**Buckland**★★★❀ Buckland Manor Hotel
**Charingworth**★★★❀ Charingworth Manor
**Cheltenham**★★★❀ Greenway Hotel
❀✕✕ Champigon Sauvage
**Cleeve Hill**❀✕✕ Redmonds at Malvern View
**Stow-on-the-Wold**❀✕✕ Epicurean
★★★❀ Wyck Hill House
**Stroud**❀✕ Oakes
**Tetbury**★★★❀ Calcot Manor Hotel
**Upper Slaughter**★★★❀ Lords of the Manor Hotel

## GT MANCHESTER

**Bury**★★★❀ Normandie Hotel

## HAMPSHIRE

**Brockenhurst**❀✕✕ Le Poussin
**Fordingbridge**❀✕ Three Lions
**Grayshott**❀✕ Woods
**New Milton**★★★★❀ Chewton Glen Hotel
**Romsey**❀✕✕ Old Manor House
**Southampton**❀✕ Golden Palace
❀✕✕ Kuti's
**Wickham**★★❀ Old House Hotel
**Winchester**★★★❀ Lainston House Hotel

## HEREFORD & WORCESTER

**Ledbury**★★❀ Hope End Hotel
**Brimfield**❀✕ Poppies

## ISLE OF WIGHT

**Seaview**★★❀ Seaview Hotel

## KENT

**Faversham**❀✕✕ Read's
**Tunbridge Wells**❀✕✕ Thackeray's House

## LANCASHIRE

**Wrightington**❀✕✕✕ High Moor

## LEICESTERSHIRE

**Oakham**★★★❀ Hambleton Hall Hotel

## LONDON

**EC2**❀✕✕✕ Le Poulbot
**NW3**❀✕✕ Keats
**SW1**❀✕ Ciboure
❀✕✕ Ken Lo's Memories of China
❀✕✕ Le Mazarin
**SW3**❀✕✕ Bibendum
★★★★❀ Capital Hotel
❀❀❀✕✕ Tante Claire
❀✕✕ Turners
**SW7**❀✕✕ Hilaire
**SW8**❀✕✕ Cavaliers
❀✕✕ L'Arlequin
**SW17**❀❀✕✕ Harveys
**W1**❀✕ Alastair Little
❀✕✕ Au Jardin des Gourmets
❀❀❀✕✕ Chez Nico
★★★★❀❀ Connaught Hotel
**W1**★★★★★❀ Inter-Continental Hotel (Le Soufflé)
❀❀❀✕✕✕✕ Le Gavroche
★★★★★❀ Le Meridien Hotel (Oak Room)
❀✕✕✕✕✕ Ninety Park Lane
❀✕✕✕ Rue St Jacques
❀✕✕ Stephen Bull
❀✕✕ Sutherlands
**WC2**❀✕✕✕ Boulestin
★★★★★❀ Savoy Hotel (Savoy Restaurant)

## NORFOLK

**Grimston**★★★❀ Congham Hall Hotel
**Norwich**❀✕✕ Adlard's

## NORTHAMPTONSHIRE

**Horton**❀✕✕ French Partridge

## OXFORDSHIRE

**Great Milton**★★★❀❀❀ Le Manoir aux Quat' Saisons
**Horton-cum-Studley**★★★❀ Studley Priory
**Stonor**❀✕✕ Stonor Arms

## SOMERSET

**Williton**★★❀ White House Hotel
**Wiveliscombe**★❀ Langley House Hotel

## STAFFORDSHIRE

**Waterhouses**❀✕✕ Old Beams

## SUFFOLK

Hintlesham★★★⊛ Hintlesham Hall Hotel
Long Melford⊛ ✗✗ Chimneys

## SURREY

Bagshot★★★★⊛ Pennyhill Park
Claygate⊛ ✗✗ Les Alouettes
Haslemere⊛ ✗✗ Morel's

## TYNE & WEAR

Gateshead★★⊛ Eslington Villa

## WARWICKSHIRE

Billesley★★★⊛ Billesley Manor Hotel
Leamington Spa★★★⊛ Mallory Court Hotel

## WEST MIDLANDS

Birmingham⊛ ✗✗✗ Sloan's
Hockley Heath★★★⊛ Nuthurst Grange Hotel
Solihull⊛ ✗✗ Liaison

## WEST SUSSEX

Amberley★★★⊛ Amberley Castle
East Grinstead★★★⊛ Gravetye Manor Hotel
Pulborough⊛ ✗ Stane Street Hollow
Storrington⊛ ✗✗✗ Manleys
Thakeham★★★⊛ Abingworth Hall Hotel

## WEST YORKSHIRE

Pool⊛ ✗✗✗ Pool Court
Ilkley⊛ ✗✗✗ The Box Tree

# WALES

## GWENT

Llanddewi Skyrrid⊛ ✗ Walnut Tree

## GWYNEDD

Llandudno★★⊛ St Tudno Hotel
Pwllheli★★⊛ Plas Bodegroes

## POWYS

Llangammarch Wells★★★⊛ Lake Hotel
Three Cocks★★⊛ Three Cocks Hotel

# SCOTLAND

## CENTRAL

Dunblane★★★⊛ Cromlix House Hotel

## DUMFRIES & GALLOWAY

Portpatrick★★⊛ Knockinaam Lodge Hotel

## FIFE

Anstruther⊛ ✗✗ The Cellar
Cupar⊛ ✗ Ostler's Close
Peat Inn⊛ ✗✗ Peat Inn

## HIGHLAND

Ardelve★⊛ Loch Duich Hotel
Kentallen★★⊛ Ardsheal House
Kingussie⊛ ✗ The Cross
Skye, Isle of; Culnacnoc★⊛ Glenview Inn
　　　　　Isle Ornsay★★⊛ Kinloch Lodge
Ullapool⊛ ✗✗ Altnaharrie Inn

## LOTHIAN

Gullane⊛ ✗ La Potinière

## STRATHCLYDE

Barrhill★★★⊛ Kildonan Hotel
Port Appin★★⊛ Airds Hotel

## TAYSIDE

Dunkeld⊛ ✗✗✗ Kinnaird
Perth★★★⊛ Murrayshall Country House
Hotel

# B.I.T.O.A.

## The British Incoming Tour Operators Association

Founded in 1977, BITOA is now recognised as the professional collective voice of those involved in providing hospitality for foreign tourists visiting Britain - the incoming tourism industry. In addition to tour operators, the association includes, as associate members, those supplying the industry - hotels, hotel chains, restaurants and transportation companies.

BITOA is active in promoting the interests of incoming tour operators both at EEC and national government level; the issues under discussion range from practical problems of baggage handling at airports to the preparation of submissions to the European Commission. Our training programme plays an important role in developing the product knowledge of our members and provides a regular series of educational visits, seminars and training courses. Particular attention is paid to the development of junior staff.

The hotels sub-committee has been influential in the development of customer care programmes, in discussions on price-moderation and a vociferous contributor to the debate on further hotel building, particularly in the budget sector. We are concerned not only to look after the interests of our members, but to try to fight on behalf of the consumer, as we firmly believe that it is only by maintaining client satisfaction that the British Travel Trade can continue to attract foreign visitors to these shores. Efficient operating procedures, high standards of cleanliness and service are therefore our top priority.

The selection of hotels is a vital part of any tour operators role. Many of our members are experts in this field and have built successful businesses using this valuable knowledge. They assess the facilities offered at an hotel, the quality of rooms, safety and security arrangements, service and food quality. They also take into account the location of the property and make a careful assessment of the prices offered to ensure value for money for their clients.

Yet hotels change rapidly, some through renovation work, some through neglect and others as a result of changes of ownership. Each year an exciting array of new properties come onto the market often setting new standards in service and in value-for-money. To keep abreast of these developments is a mammoth task for the professional hotel contractor; it is sadly an almost impossible one for the business or leisure traveller.

BITOA is particularly impressed by the AA Hotel and Restaurant Guide as a source of reliable and annually updated information on hotels. The AA system of star classification for hotels is the most widely used in this country and is based on annual inspections following objective criteria. This is now augmented by their recently introduced subjective assessment of quality, carried out by their team of experienced professional Inspectors, and the resulting percentage award provides a valuable standard of comparison among hotels at any star rating. May I therefore urge you to read this new edition carefully, in order to make a well-considered choice...and then try it. The real joy of travelling is finding you got it right!

*Neil Haythorne.*

Neil Haythorne
**BITOA Hotels Committee**

# HOW WE CLASSIFY HOTELS AND RESTAURANTS

This guide aims to provide, in an easily understood form, as much up-to-date information as possible about AA-inspected hotels and restaurants in Britain. Classifications are decided on a purely objective basis, as distinct from accolades such as red stars and rosettes which reflect personal opinions. In this edition of the Guide, the AA has extended its system of quality assessment, awarding a percentage rating to all hotels. The AA system of appointing hotels began in 1909. Over the years, standards have been adapted to take into account current trends in hotel construction and operation, and changing requirements.

## THE HOTEL AND RESTAURANT INSPECTORS

Much of the inspectors' work consists of regular and detailed examination of premises, furniture, equipment and facilities. Inspectors either have a background in the hotel and catering industries or have gained wide experience within the Association. This creates a balance between qualified men and women with specialised knowledge of the industry on the one hand, and those with an expert appreciation of AA members' needs on the other. Regular courses serve to keep their knowledge abreast of the times, and consultants are available in each region to assist the inspectors in providing informed and unbiased reports upon which the Committees can base their decisions to grant and withhold recognition. Additional information from AA members is also greatly valued.

## HOTELS

When an hotel applies to the AA for recognition and appointment, the following procedure is adopted. An inspector visits the hotel unannounced, stays overnight and takes every opportunity of testing as many services as possible. Having settled the bill in the morning, the inspector introduces himself or herself and makes a thorough inspection of the entire premises. At subsequent discussions with the management the inspector will draw attention to any points which may affect the classification. Once granted recognition and given a rating, the

hotel is subject to annual inspection to ensure that standards are maintained. If the hotel changes hands, it is automatically deleted until the new proprietor applies for recognition and the hotel has been reassessed. Current applications and possible reclassifications or deletions are considered regularly by the Hotel Appointment Committee. This Committee also keeps the Association's general policy of classification under review. A fee is levied for both registration and appointment.

Basic requirements for appointed hotels are: bedrooms with hot and cold water; adequate bath and lavatory arrangements; service of all meals (with a choice of main dishes) to residents. Full details of the principal requirements for each classification are printed in the leaflet HH5 'AA-Appointed Hotels,' available from the Hotel Services, Fanum House, Basingstoke, Hants RG21 2EA. All classifications shown in this edition of the Hotel and Restaurant Guide reflect an establishment's AA status as at June 1990.

## WHAT CLASSIFICATIONS INDICATE

The star classification of hotels by the AA, in addition to providing an indication of the type of hotel, may be regarded as a universally accepted standard, ranging from the simplest to the most luxurious hotel.

The majority of hotels are classified with black stars, the method introduced and used by the AA since 1912. A new classification, the AA Lodge, denotes a motel-style establishment. Lodges cater for overnight stops and offer good, functional, reasonably priced rooms in a block adjacent to a restaurant.

⇧      Lodge with bedroom accommodation only. At least two-star standard, all rooms with private facilities with adjacent motorway or roadside restaurant.

★      Hotels generally of small scale with good facilities and furnishings. Adequate bath and lavatory arrangements. Meals provided for residents but availability to non-residents may be limited. The AA now accepts private hotels at one and two star level, where the requirements for ready public access and full lunch service may be relaxed.

★★ Hotels offering a higher standard of accommodation and some bedrooms with private facilities. The AA now accepts private hotels at one and two star level, where the requirements for ready public access and full lunch service may be relaxed.

★★★ Well-appointed hotels with more spacious accommodation, the majority of bedrooms having a private bath/shower room with lavatory. Fuller meal facilities are provided.

★★★★ Exceptionally well-appointed hotels offering a high standard of comfort and service, and all bedrooms providing a private bath/shower room with lavatory.

★★★★★ Luxury hotels offering the highest international standard.

🏨 This denotes an AA Country House hotel where a relaxed, informal atmosphere and personal welcome prevail. Some of the facilities may differ, however, from those found in urban hotels of the same classification. Country House hotels are often secluded and, though not always rurally situated, are quiet. Hotels attracting frequent conferences or functions are not normally granted this symbol. See list on page 761.

O Hotels due to open during the currency of this guide which have not been inspected at the time of going to press.

NOTE: Hotels often satisfy some of the requirements for a higher classification than that awarded.

## PERCENTAGE ASSESSMENTS

The percentage assessment score applied to each hotel is a subjective view of relative quality given by the AA to highlight our view of the differences between establishments within the same star classification. It is intended to reflect the inspectors' experiences at the time of the inspection. Inspecting establishments is, of course, a continuous process, and this means that the percentage assessment score is subject to change during the currency of this publication.

## RED STAR HOTELS

Red stars are the AA's highest accolade and were introduced in 1975. They are awarded only to hotels that AA inspectors consider to offer the very best quality of accommodation, services and food within their classification, where you will find a warm welcome and a high standard of hospitality. Red stars are awarded only after a great deal of consideration, and a change of management or ownership is likely to result in the award being carefully reviewed. In the whole of Great Britain there are only 72 Red-Star hotels (see list on page 41). They are highlighted in the gazetteer by a special panel containing a detailed description and a photograph, as well as the standard information. Look out for red stars in the guide and on those familiar, yellow AA hotel signs.

## RESTAURANTS

Restaurants are assessed differently from hotels. For the most part, the approach is made by the Association rather than the proprietor and AA inspectors visit them anonymously. Subsequently they report to the Restaurant Committee who, if they consider the cuisine to be of a high enough standard, award 'crossed knives and forks' to denote the amenities. The basic requirements for recommendation are a high standard of cuisine, prompt and courteous service, pleasant atmosphere and value for money.

✗ Modest but good restaurant.

✗✗ Restaurant offering a higher standard of comfort than above.

✗✗✗ Well-appointed restaurant.

✗✗✗✗ Exceptionally well-appointed restaurant.

✗✗✗✗✗ Luxury restaurant.

N.B. Any accommodation available at classified restaurants must not be assumed to be of a standard suitable for hotel appointment.

## ROSETTES

Very few restaurants are considered worthy of rosettes. This is the AA's highest award for quality of food and service in a restaurant. First introduced in 1955, rosettes are still awarded to only 131 establishments. See page 47.

❀ Food is of a higher standard than expected for its classification.

❀❀ Excellent food and service.

❀❀❀ Outstanding food, and service, equal to the highest international standards.

# SOME POINTS TO REMEMBER

## BOOKING

Book as early as possible, particularly if accommodation is required during a holiday period (beginning of June to end of September, public holidays and, in some parts of Scotland, during the skiing season). Some hotels ask for a deposit, and some also ask for full payment in advance, especially for one-night bookings taken from chance callers. Not all hotels take advance bookings for bed and breakfast for overnight or short stays, and some will not accept reservations from mid-week.

## CANCELLATION

Once the booking has been confirmed, notify the hotel straight away if you are in any doubt about whether you can keep to your arrangements. If the hotel cannot re-let your accommodation, you may be liable to pay about two-thirds of the price you would have paid had you stayed there (your deposit will count towards this payment).

In Britain it is accepted that a legally binding contract has been made as soon as an intending guest accepts an offer of accommodation, either in writing or on the telephone. Illness is not accepted as a release from this contract. For these reasons you are advised to effect insurance cover, e.g. AA Travelsure, against a possible cancellation.

## COMPLAINTS

Guests who wish to complain about food, services or facilities are urged to do so promptly and on the spot. This should provide an opportunity for the hotelier or restaurateur to correct matters. If a personal approach fails, members should inform AA Hotel Services, Fanum House, Basingstoke, Hampshire RG21 2EA.

## FIRE PRECAUTIONS

As far as we can discover, every hotel in Great Britain listed in this book has applied for, and not been refused, a fire certificate. The Fire Precautions Act does not apply to the Channel Islands, or the Isle of Man, which exercise their own rules regarding fire precautions for hotels.

## LICENSE TO SELL ALCOHOL

*Hotels and Restaurants.* All establishments in this guide are licensed unless otherwise stated. Basically, hotel residents can obtain alcoholic drinks at all times, if the owner is prepared to serve them. Restaurant customers can obtain drinks with their meals.

The sale of alcoholic drinks is controlled by separate licensing laws in England, Wales, Scotland, Isle of Man, the Isles of Scilly and each of the islands forming the Channel Islands.

*Licensing hours in public houses* are generally from mid morning to early afternoon and from mid evening to an hour or two before midnight. Some will remain open throughout the afternoon.

*Club Licence.* Drinks can be served only to club members, but an interval of 48 hours must elapse after joining.

*Children under 14* (18 in Scotland) may be excluded from bars, except areas intended for the service of food. Those under 18 may not be allowed to purchase or consume alcoholic drinks.

## MEALS

Unless otherwise stated, the terms quoted in the gazetteer section of this book include full cooked breakfast.

In some parts of Britain, particularly in Scotland, *high teas* (i.e. a savoury dish followed by bread and butter, scones, cakes, etc) is sometimes served instead of dinner, which may, however, be available on request. The last time at which high tea or dinner may be ordered on weekdays is shown, but this may be varied at weekends.

On Sundays, some hotels serve the main meal at midday, and provide only a cold supper in the evening.

## PAYMENT

Most hotels will only accept cheques in payment of accounts if notice is given and some form of identification (usually a cheque card) is produced. Travellers' cheques issued by the leading banks and agencies are accepted by many hotels but not all. If a hotel accepts leading credit or cheque cards, this is shown in the gazetteer entry (see page 58 for details).

## PRICES

The Hotel Industry Voluntary Code of Booking Practice was revised in 1986, and the AA encourages its use in appropriate establishments. Its prime object is to ensure that the customer is clear about the precise services and facilities he is buying, and what price he will have to pay, before he commits himself to a contractually binding agreement. If the price has not been previously confirmed in writing, the guest should be handed a card at the time of registration, stipulating the total obligatory charge.

The Tourism (Sleeping Accommodation Price Display) Order 1977 compels hotels, motels, guesthouses, farmhouses, inns and self-catering accommodation with four or more letting bedrooms to display in entrance halls the minimum and maximum prices charged for each category of room. This order complements the voluntary Code of Booking Practice.

The tariffs quoted in the gazetteer of this book may be affected by inflation, variations in the rate of VAT and many other factors. You should always ascertain the current prices before making a booking. Those given in this book have been provided by hoteliers and restaurateurs in good faith and must be accepted as indications rather than firm quotations. Where information about 1991 prices is not given, you are requested to make enquiries direct.

Prices quoted show minimum and maximum for one or two persons and include a full breakfast unless otherwise stated. Where a Continental breakfast is included in the price, this is stated in the gazetteer. However, some prices may vary for the following reasons:

a) weekday/weekend terms offered

b) season of the year

c) if double room is used for single occupancy

d) dinner is normally charged for separately, but in some areas an inclusive dinner, bed and breakfast option may be offered at a cheaper rate.

Some hotels charge for bed, breakfast and dinner, whether dinner is taken or not. Many hotels, particularly in short-season holiday areas, accept booking only at full-board rate.

For main meals served in hotels and restaurants, minimum and maximum *table d'hôte* (set menu) prices are given. Where an *à la carte* menu is available, the price of a three-course dinner and lunch is shown. Where establishments offer both types of menu, *table d'hôte* prices are the only ones shown but the abbreviation (& alc) is used to indicate that an *à la carte* menu is also available.

VAT is payable, in the United Kingdom and in the Isle of Man, on both basic prices and any service. VAT does not apply in the Channel Islands. With this exception, prices quoted in this guide are inclusive of VAT (and service where this is included on the bill).

# A Signature Of Confidence

Queens Moat Houses offer a choice of over 100 hotels conveniently located throughout the UK and a further 55 across Continental Europe. In every one of our hotels, you will find a warm and friendly team on hand, to ensure that your stay is as comfortable and relaxing as you would want it to be. The flavour and style of each Queens Moat Houses Hotel is as individual as a signature. But they all have one thing in common . . . the hallmark of over twenty years experience that will make your stay with us both enjoyable and memorable.

So the next time you are travelling away on business, or if you simply want to get away from it all, tell us where you are thinking of going. Chances are there's a Queens Moat Houses Hotel nearby.

**Queens Moat Houses**

MOAT 15 12 HOUSE

INTERNATIONAL HOTELIERS

*CONFIDENCE WITH QUEENS MOAT HOUSES HOTELS*

**QUEENS MOAT HOUSES RESERVATIONS 0800 289330 (24 hrs) WORLDWIDE RESERVATIONS 0708 766677 (24 hrs)**

# HOW TO USE THIS GUIDE

**SAMPLE ENTRY** The entry is fictitious

| | |
|---|---|
| <u>BEESTON</u>  Derbyshire Map **15** NJ90 | **1. Town name** |
| ★★★ 65% **Red Lion** The Square AB00 XY1 (GB Hotels)<br>☎(0685) 8276 Telex no 739619 Fax (0685) 6728 | **2. Hotel name** |
| RS Nov–Mar | **3. Restricted service** |
| *Attractive old coaching inn with comfortable, pretty bedrooms.* | |
| 19rm(14⇌5♠) Annexe5rm(8fb)3⊞╳in 5 bedrooms CTV in all bedrooms®╳T sB&B⇌♠£16.50-£24.50 dB&B⇌♠£31-£49 ➡ | **4. Accommodation details** |
| Lift ⟮ CTV 100P 3🏊⇊ CFA ▣ ♫ nc 3yrs | |
| ♦English & French V ♦⚌╳ Lunch £3-£4.50 Tea 85p-£1.40 High Tea £2.75-£6 Dinner £8.25-£11 &alc Last dinner 9pm | **5. Hotel facilities** |
| | **6. Meals** |
| Credit Cards ①②③④⑤ ⓔ | **7. Payment details** |

**1. Town name** listed in gazetteer in strict alphabetical order. This is followed by the county or region, which is the administrative county or region, and not necessarily part of the correct postal address. Towns on islands (not connected to the mainland by a bridge) are listed under the island name. Scottish regions or islands are followed by the old county name in italics. The **map reference** which follows denotes the map-page number and grid reference. Read 1st figure across, 2nd figure vertically, within the appropriate square.

**2. Hotel name,** address (including postcode) and telephone number with classification and percentage (see p 52 for details). When establishments' names are shown in *italics* the particulars have not been confirmed by the management. Within towns hotels are listed in descending order of star rating, with Red Stars first then descending order of percentage ratings. Hotels precede restaurants. London hotels are listed under London postal districts. *Company owned hotels* and marketing consortia are shown using abbreviations (key on page 767). Before its name is shown in the guide a company must own at least five AA-appointed hotels, or a hotel must be affiliated to one of the following marketing consortia: Best Western, Consort, Exec Hotels, Guestaccom, Inter-Hotels, Minotel, Prestige, Relais et Châteaux, Pride of Britain and Welsh

Rarebits. The *telephone exchange* is that of the town heading, unless the name of the exchange is given after the ☎ symbol and before the dialling code and number. In some areas, numbers are likely to be changed during the currency of this book. In case of difficulty check with the operator. When making a reservation by *telex* it is advisable to specify which hotel you wish to book with as some hotels (particularly those in groups) use a central telex service. The same applies to *fax* messages.

**3. Restricted service.** Some hotels, while remaining open, operate a restricted service during the less busy months. This may take the form of a reduction in meals served, accommodation or facilities available, or in some cases both.

**4. Accommodation details.** The first figure shows the number of letting bedrooms. Where rooms have *en suite* bath or shower and WC, the number precedes the appropriate symbol.

Annexe    bedrooms available in an annexe are noted only if they are at least of the same standard as those in the rest of the hotel. Facilities may not be the same as in the main building however, and it is advisable to check the nature of the accommodation and the tariff

56

before making a reservation. In some hotels, accommodation is available only in an annexe.

✂ number of bedrooms and/or area of the restaurant set aside for non-smokers.

fb family bedrooms.

CTV/TV can mean colour or black and white television in lounge or available in bedrooms. Check when making reservations.

✗ no dogs allowed into bedrooms. Some hotels may restrict the type of dogs permitted and the rooms into which they may be taken. Hotels which do not normally accept dogs may accept guide dogs. Generally dogs are not allowed in the dining room. Check when booking, the conditions under which pets are accepted.

T automatic direct-dial telephone facilities available from bedrooms. Many hotels impose a surcharge for calls made from bedrooms, so check before making the call. A public telephone is usually available in the hotel hallway or foyer.

Prices prices given have been provided by hoteliers and restaurateurs in good faith and are indications rather than firm quotations. Unless otherwise stated, they include full cooked breakfast. Some hotels offer free accommodation to children provided they share the parents' room. Check current prices before booking. See also page 54.

**5. Hotel facilities.** For key to symbols see inside front cover.

《 All hotels employing a night porter are shown thus except 4 and 5 star hotels, all of which have night porters on duty.

🚌 No coaches. This information is published in good faith from information supplied by the establishments concerned. Inns, however, have well-defined legal obligations towards travellers, and it is for the customer to take up any queries with the proprietor or the local licensing authority.

♫ Live entertainment should be available at least once a week throughout the year. Some hotels without this symbol will provide entertainment during high season or at certain other specified times only. You are advised to check this information before booking.

nc No children. Where this abbreviation does not appear, the hotels listed will accommodate children, but may not provide any special facilities. A minimum age (e.g. nc4yrs — no children under four years old) may be specified. For very young children, check before booking about such provisions as cots and high chairs and any reductions made.

⚘ establishments with special facilities for children, which will include baby-sitting service or baby intercom system, playroom or playground, laundry facilities, drying and ironing facilities, cots, high chairs and special meals.

CFA hotels which offer conference facilities. Many other hotels offer facilities of this nature but may not be indicated as such. It is therefore advisable to check with the hotel's management.

Suitable Full details for disabled people will be
for the found in AA *Guide for the Disabled*
disabled *Traveller* on sale at AA shops, free to members. Intending guests with any form of disability should notify proprietors so that arrangements can be made to minimise difficulties, particularly in the event of an emergency.

**6. Meals.** Details of the style of food served, last dinner orders and likely price ranges are given. Where the *table d'hôte* prices are given, the abbreviation "& alc" indicates that there is also an *à la carte* menu, which may be considerably dearer than the set menu.

V a choice of vegetarian dishes available (but check before booking).

☕🍵 morning coffee or afternoon tea are served to chance callers. All 4 and 5 star hotels serve morning coffee and, normally, afternoon tea to residents.

Prices See page 46.

**7. Payment details** (but check current position when booking)
1 — Access/Eurocard/Mastercard
2 — American Express
3 — Barclaycard/Visa
4 — Carte Blanche
5 — Diners
£ — Hotel may offer a discount. See p. 2 for details.

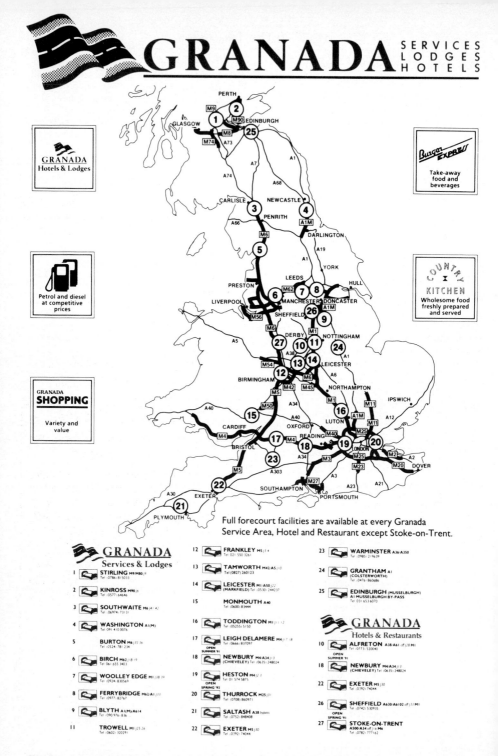

# GRANADA
SERVICES
LODGES
HOTELS

GRANADA
Hotels & Lodges

Take-away
food and
beverages

Petrol and diesel
at competitive
prices

COUNTRY
KITCHEN
Wholesome food
freshly prepared
and served

GRANADA
SHOPPING

Variety and
value

Full forecourt facilities are available at every Granada
Service Area, Hotel and Restaurant except Stoke-on-Trent.

## GRANADA
### Services & Lodges

1  STIRLING M9/M80 J9
   Tel :0786: 815033

2  KINROSS M90 J6
   Tel :0577: 64646

3  SOUTHWAITE M6 (4/ 42
   Tel :06974: 7313)

4  WASHINGTON A1(M)
   Tel: 091: 410 0076

5  BURTON M6 J35 36
   Tel :0524: 781 234

6  BIRCH M62 J18 19
   Tel :061: 655 3403

7  WOOLLEY EDGE M1 J38 39
   Tel :0924: 830569

8  FERRYBRIDGE M62/A1 J11
   Tel :0977: 82767

9  BLYTH A1(M)/A614
   Tel :090 976: 836

11 TROWELL M1 J25 26
   Tel :0602: 320291

12 FRANKLEY M5 J3 4
   Tel 021 550 3261

13 TAMWORTH M42/A5 J10
   Tel :0827: 260123

14 LEICESTER M1/A50 J22
   (MARKFIELD) Tel :0530: 244237

15 MONMOUTH A40
   Tel :0600: 83444

16 TODDINGTON M1 J11 12
   Tel :05255: 5150

17 LEIGH DELAMERE M4 J17 18
   Tel :0666: 837097
   OPEN
   SUMMER '91

18 NEWBURY M4/A34 J13
   (CHIEVELEY) Tel :0635: 248024

19 HESTON M4 J2 3
   Tel 01 574 5875
   OPEN
   SPRING '92

20 THURROCK M25 J31
   Tel :0708: 860971

21 SALTASH A38 (ypos)
   Tel :0752: 848408

22 EXETER M5 J30
   Tel :0392: 74044

23 WARMINSTER A36/A350
   Tel :0985: 219639

24 GRANTHAM A1
   (COLSTERWORTH)
   Tel :0476: 860686

25 EDINBURGH (MUSSELBURGH)
   A1 MUSSELBURGH BY-PASS
   Tel :031: 653 6070

## GRANADA
### Hotels & Restaurants

10 ALFRETON A38/A61 off J28 M1
   Tel :0773: 520040
   OPEN
   SUMMER '91

18 NEWBURY M4/A34 J13
   (CHIEVELEY) Tel :0635: 248024

22 EXETER M5 J30
   Tel :0392: 74044

26 SHEFFIELD A630/A6102 off J31 M1
   Tel :0742: 530935
   OPEN
   SPRING '91

27 STOKE-ON-TRENT
   A500/A34 off J16 M6
   Tel :0782: 777162

For bookings and further information call Central Reservations on 052 55 55 55

ABBERLEY Hereford & Worcester Map **07** SO76

★★★**12**77%, **Elms** WR6 6AT (on A443) (Queens Moat)(Prestige) ☎Great Witley(0299)896666 Telex no 337105 FAX (0299) 896804
*An attractive avenue of limes leads to this lovely Queen Anne house. Early last year the hotel was completely restored and refurbished to a very high standard; all the bedrooms have lovely views over the Teme Valley or over the hotel's formal gardens. A very British menu is prepared in the modern style using top-quality, well-chosen produce, and generous portions are attactively presented.*
16⇨📞Annexe9⇨📞1🛏 CTV in all bedrooms T
✘ (ex guide dogs) ✱ sB&B⇨📞frf80 dB&B⇨📞£95-£135 🏳
《 60P 1🚗 ❀ ℛ (hard) croquet putting *xmas*
⏱ English & French V ❖ ⟁ S% Lunch £10.95-£13.95 Dinner £20 Last dinner 9.30pm
Credit Cards ①②③④⑤⑥

★★63%, *Manor Arms at Abberley* WR6 6BN
☎Great Witley(0299)896507 Telex no 335672
FAX (0562) 747488
*A pleasant village inn, some 300 years old, with well-equipped bedrooms.*
7⇨📞Annexe3⇨ CTV in all bedrooms ⑱ T
40P ❀
V ❖ ⟁ Last dinner 9.30pm
Credit Cards ①③

ABBOTSBURY Dorset Map **03** SY58

★★66%, **Ilchester Arms** 9 Market St DT3 4JR ☎(0305)871243
*The characterful bars and conservatory restaurant of this village inn serve dishes ranging from the usual bar snacks to more imaginative and tasty daily 'specials'; recently renovated bedrooms tend to be small but have been made attractive with individual wallpapers and fabrics.*
8⇨📞Annexe2⇨(2fb)3🛏 CTV in all bedrooms ⑱ T
sB&B⇨📞£40-£45 dB&B⇨📞£55-£65 🏳
40P *xmas*
⏱ English & Continental V ❖ ⟁ ✔ Lunch fr£7.50&alc Dinner £3.50-£8alc Last dinner 9pm
Credit Cards ①③

ABBOT'S SALFORD Warwickshire Map **04** SP05

★★★73%, **Salford Hall** WR11 5UT (Best Western)
☎Evesham(0386)871300 Telex no 336682 FAX (0386) 871301
Closed 23 Dec-4 Jan
*An imposing Tudor manor house, set beside the A439 eight miles from Stratford-on-Avon and close to Evesham, has recently been refurbished to provide comfortable, well-appointed accommodation, bedrooms both in the main hotel and Tudor Court having been provided with modern facilities without sacrificing the character of the original; the restaurant serves very enjoyable meals complemented by a good wine list. Its friendly, relaxing atmosphere, and the attention of cheerful staff who are always eager to please, contribute to its popularity with both tourists and business travellers.*
34⇨📞8🛏 CTV in all bedrooms ⑱ T ✘ (ex guide dogs) ✱
sB&B⇨📞£70-£100 dB&B⇨📞£95-£140 🏳
51P 🚗 ❀ ℛ (hard) snooker sauna solarium croquet
V ❖ ⟁ ✔ Lunch £12.50-£15&alc Dinner fr£18.95&alc Last dinner 10pm
Credit Cards ①②③⑤⑥
**See advertisement under STRATFORD-UPON-AVON**

A rosette is an indication of exceptional standards of cuisine.

ABERDARON Gwynedd Map **06** SH12

★★62%, *Ty Newydd* LL53 8BE ☎(075886)207
RS Dec-Jan
*Friendly and family-run, the hotel gives direct access to the sea shore, all but two of its bedrooms enjoying panoramic views of the bay.*
17rm(8⇨1📞)(3fb) CTV in 12 bedrooms TV in 5 bedrooms ✘ (ex guide dogs)
CTV
⏱ Mainly grills V ❖ Last dinner 9.30pm
Credit Cards ①③

ABERDEEN Grampian *Aberdeenshire* Map **15** NJ90

See **Town Plan Section**
See also **Aberdeen Airport & Westhill**
★★★★51%, **Skean Dhu Altens** Souter Head Rd, Altens AB1 4LF (3m S off A956) (Mount Charlotte (TS))
☎(0224)877000 Telex no 739631 FAX (0224) 896964
RS Xmas wk
*A spacious hotel standing on the main route to Aberdeen Harbour. Some bedrooms have views across the city towards the coast.*
221⇨📞(70fb)⤢in 6 bedrooms CTV in all bedrooms ⑱ T ✱
S10% sB⇨📞£70-£75 dB⇨📞£80-£85 (room only)
Lift 《 ▦ 300P ❀ CFA ⌁(heated) *xmas*
⏱ International V ❖ ⟁ S10% Lunch fr£11.50 Dinner fr£14 Last dinner 10.45pm
Credit Cards ①②③④⑤⑥

# The Manor Arms at Abberley ★ ★

## Abberley Village, Worcestershire WR6 6BN
## Telephone: (0299) 896507

Discover our delightful old beamed village inn with superior accommodation, all en suite, restaurant and bars. Nestling in the Abberley Hills within the glorious Worcestershire countryside, yet conveniently situated for Worcester, Stourport, Kidderminster, the Cotswolds, Malvern Hills, Birmingham and the NEC. For business or leisure always a warm welcome and personal service for everyone. Family owned and run.

**A**

★★★ 72% **Ardoe House** Blairs, South Deeside Rd AB1 5YP (Consort) ☎(0224)867355 Telex no 739413 FAX (0224) 861283
*Just 4 miles west of the city on the South Deeside road, this recently refurbished hotel is an ideal base for the visiting businessman, and a popular venue for local conferences and functions. It is set in 17 acres of parklands and offers every modern comfort, while retaining much of the original character. The comfortable bedrooms are tastefully appointed with stylish fabrics and have been well equipped. Dinner in the wood-panelled restaurant is an enjoyable experience.*
19⇨🛏(2fb)1💷 CTV in all bedrooms ® T 🏋 (ex guide dogs) ✱ S% sB&B⇨🛏£55-£100 dB&B⇨🛏£70-£100
( 100P ♨ putting petanque *xmas*
♀ International V ♦ ♨ S% Lunch £7.50-£8.50alc Dinner £17.50&alc Last dinner 9.30pm
Credit Cards [1][2][3][5]

★★★ 70% **Caledonian Thistle** 10 Union Ter AB9 1HE (Mount Charlotte (TS)) ☎(0224)640233 Telex no 73758 FAX (0224) 641627
*This particularly well-managed hotel is ideally set in the heart of Aberdeen. There is a choice of either well-equipped, generally compact 'club' bedrooms, or larger 'executive club' rooms and suites. Public areas include a café-bar, attractive restaurant, cocktail lounge and a smart function room.*
80⇨🛏(4fb)2💷✂in 2 bedrooms CTV in all bedrooms ® T ✱ sB⇨🛏fr£80 dB⇨🛏fr£85 (room only) 🅿
Lift ( 25P sauna solarium
♀ International ♦ ♨ ✂ Lunch fr£9&alc Dinner fr£14.95&alc Last dinner 10pm
Credit Cards [1][2][3][4][5]

★★★ 67% **Copthorne** 122 Huntly St AB1 1SU ☎(0224)630404 Telex no 739707 FAX (0224) 640573
89⇨🛏✂in 12 bedrooms CTV in all bedrooms ® T ✱ sB⇨🛏£80-£95 dB⇨🛏£90-£105 (room only) 🅿
Lift ( 20♨ ♫ *xmas*
♀ Scottish & French V ♦ ♨ Lunch fr£8.95&alc Dinner fr£12.95&alc Last dinner 10pm
Credit Cards [1][2][3][4][5] £

★★★ 65% **Bucksburn Moat House** Oldmeldrum Rd, Bucksburn AB9 2LN (3m N A947) (Queens Moat) ☎(0224)713911 Telex no 73108 FAX (0224) 714020
Closed 25-26 Dec
*Located at the junction of A96/A947 and close to the airport, this hotel has spacious rooms, some of which have been refurbished, and a pleasantly upgraded restaurant.*
98⇨🛏(20fb)✂in 11 bedrooms CTV in all bedrooms ® T S% sB⇨🛏£47-£80.50 dB⇨🛏£66-£89.70 (room only) 🅿
Lift ( 180P CFA ⊠(heated) *xmas*
♀ Scottish & French V ♦ ♨ Lunch £9-£17&alc Dinner £13-£16&alc Last dinner 10.30pm
Credit Cards [1][2][3][4][5] £

★★★ 63% **Stakis Treetops** 161 Springfield Rd AB9 2QH (Stakis) ☎(0224)313377 Telex no 73794 FAX (0224) 312028
*Popular with both business guests and holiday-makers, this large hotel offers well-equipped bedrooms and a choice of two restaurants.*
113⇨🛏(28fb)1💷✂in 50 bedrooms CTV in all bedrooms ® T ✱ sB⇨🛏£79-£89 dB⇨🛏£92.50-£103 (room only) 🅿
Lift ( CTV 300P ♣ CFA ⊠(heated) ♪ (hard) sauna solarium gymnasium ♫ *xmas*
♀ Scottish & Continental V ♦ ♨ ✂ Lunch £7.50-£9.50&alc Dinner £12.50-£15&alc Last dinner 10pm
Credit Cards [1][2][3][5] £

★★★ 62% **New Marcliffe** 51-53 Queen's Rd AB9 2PE ☎(0224)321371 Telex no 73225 FAX (0224) 311162
*Tasteful conversion of two granite buildings has created a small, elegant hotel with an almost club-like atmosphere. The bedrooms are attractive and well-equipped*

27⇨🛏(3fb) CTV in all bedrooms ® T 🏋 (ex guide dogs) sB&B⇨🛏£67.50-£85 dB&B⇨🛏£76-£105
( 74P ♨
♀ Scottish & French V ♦ ♨ Lunch £8.50-£12.50alc Dinner £17.50-£23.50&alc Last dinner 9.45pm
Credit Cards [1][2][3][5]

★★★ 57% **Swallow Imperial** Stirling St AB9 2JY ☎(0224)589101 Telex no 73365 FAX (0224) 574288
*Conveniently situated close to the station and city centre shops, this Victorian hotel offers neatly-appointed accommodation, the public rooms and half of the bedrooms having been refurbished to a high standard.*
108rm(104⇨🛏)(3fb) CTV in all bedrooms ® T ✱ S% sB&B£45 sB&B⇨🛏£68 dB&B£58 dB&B⇨🛏£78 🅿
Lift ( CTV ✗
V ♦ ♨ S% Lunch £5.45&alc Dinner £12.95&alc Last dinner 9.30pm
Credit Cards [1][2][3][5]

### ABERDEEN AIRPORT Grampian *Aberdeenshire* Map 15 NJ81

★★★★ 67% **Holiday Inn** Riverview Dr, Farburn AB2 0AZ (Holiday Inns) ☎Aberdeen(0224)770011 Telex no 739651 FAX (0224) 722347
*Accommodation at this hotel includes very spacious and well-equipped bedrooms, and some king-size 'Leisure' and 'Club Europe' rooms. The combined coffee shop/restaurant features well-cooked dishes which are inventive and visually appealing.*
154⇨🛏(71fb)✂in 16 bedrooms CTV in all bedrooms ® T ✱ S% sB⇨🛏£82-£104 dB⇨🛏£89-£115 (room only) 🅿
( ⊞ 300P CFA ⊠(heated) sauna solarium gymnasium jacuzzi *xmas*
♀ International V ♦ ♨ S% Lunch £13.50&alc Dinner £15-£30alc Last dinner 10.30pm
Credit Cards [1][2][3][4][5] £

★★★★ 58% **Skean Dhu** Argyll Rd AB2 0DU (adjacent to main entrance 1m N of A96) (Mount Charlotte (TS)) ☎Aberdeen(0224)725252 Telex no 739239 FAX (0224) 723745
*Many spacious bedrooms are available at this modern two-storey hotel which is built around an enclosed central courtyard with outdoor swimming pool; set north west of the city, off the A96, it offers easy access to the airport terminal building.*
148⇨🛏(6fb)✂in 6 bedrooms CTV in all bedrooms ® T sB&B⇨🛏£65-£75 dB&B⇨🛏£75-£85 🅿
( ⊞ 450P ♣ CFA ⊠(heated) *xmas*
♀ Scottish & French V ♦ ♨ Lunch £9-£10&alc High tea £6.90 Dinner £14.50-£16&alc Last dinner 9.45pm
Credit Cards [1][2][3][5] £

★★★ 63% **Skean Dhu Dyce** Farburn Ter AB2 0DW (off A947) (Mount Charlotte (TS)) ☎Aberdeen(0224)723101 Telex no 73473 FAX (0224) 722965
*A friendly and well-managed hotel with modern bedrooms, a coffee shop, restaurant, and very good conference facilities.*
Annexe220⇨🛏(80fb)✂in 12 bedrooms CTV in all bedrooms ® T ✱ sB&B⇨🛏£57.50-£65 dB&B⇨🛏£67.50-£75 🅿
( 250P CFA squash sauna solarium gymnasium pool table tennis *xmas*
♀ Scottish & French V ♦ ♨ Lunch £12.30-£19.95alc Dinner fr£13.45&alc Last dinner 11pm
Credit Cards [1][2][3][5]

### ABERDOUR Fife Map 11 NT18

★★ 66% **Woodside** High St KY3 0SW ☎(0383)860328 Telex no 72165 FAX (0383) 860920
*The public areas of this beautifully renovated hotel feature woodwork from the Mauretania and the ornately decorated captain's cabin from RMS Orontes. Bedrooms are all attractive*

and well-equipped, though some are on the small side. Attentive
service is provided by the hotel staff.
21⇨♦3🖭 CTV in all bedrooms ® sB&B⇨♦fr£48.50
dB&B⇨♦fr£63.50 ⧫
⟮50P ✿ sauna
♦ ☑

Credit Cards ①②③④⑤

★64%, **Fairways** 17 Manse St KY3 0TT ☎(0383)860478
*Friendly resident proprietors have created a cosy hotel with a
homely atmosphere where guests can enjoy home-cooked meals, its
lunch and dinner menus featuring a delightful selection of pies,
both sweet and savoury.*
10rm(2⇨)(2fb) CTV in all bedrooms ® sB&B£22-£26
sB&B⇨£30-£35 dB&B£32-£36 dB&B⇨£40-£45 ⧫
CTV 12P 📶
♦ ☑ ✂ Bar Lunch £1.50-£3.95 Dinner £4.50-£7.50 Last dinner
8.45pm
Credit Cards ① ③ ⓔ

---

ABERDOVEY Gwynedd Map **06** SN69
During the currency of this publication Aberdovey telephone
numbers are liable to change.
★★★🏢 65%, **Plas Penhelig Country House** LL35 0NA (Inter-
Hotels/Welsh Rarebits) ☎(065472)676 FAX (065472) 7783
Closed Jan & Feb
*This large Edwardian country house is situated in an elevated
position on the outskirts of town, and enjoys superb views of the
Dovey Estuary. It is set in 14 acres of grounds, which include 7
acres of delightful gardens, a putting green, a croquet lawn and a
tennis court. The public rooms retain their original charm and
there is a wealth of oak panelling and stained glass windows.
Welcoming log fires burn in the main lounge. The hotel is privately
owned, and run in an informal and friendly manner.*
12⇨♦(3fb) CTV in all bedrooms T ✖ ✱
dB&B⇨♦£101-£107 (incl dinner) ⧫
CTV 48P 📶 ✿ ♪ (hard) croquet putting
🍴 English & French ♦ ☑ Sunday Lunch fr£9.25 Dinner
fr£15 Last dinner 8.45pm
Credit Cards ①②③⑤ⓔ

See advertisement on page 63

★★★ 65%, **Trefeddian** LL35 0SB ☎(065472)213
Closed 3 Jan-14 Mar
*A well furnished hotel in traditional style offers good all-round
comforts and commands outstanding sea views from dining room,
lounge and several bedrooms.*
46rm(37⇨5♦)(4fb) CTV in all bedrooms T ✱
sB&B⇨♦£34-£49 dB&B⇨♦£68-£98 (incl dinner) ⧫
Lift CTV 50P 18🏌 (80p per night) 📶 ✿ 🖾(heated) ♪ (hard)
solarium pool table tennis badminton pitch & putt ஃ xmas
🍴 English & French ♦ ☑ ✂ Lunch £6.75-£8 Dinner £12-£14
Last dinner 8.45pm
Credit Cards ① ③

★★ 68%, **Penhelig Arms Hotel & Restaurant** LL35 0LT
☎(065472)215 due to change to (0654) 767215
Closed 4 days Xmas
*This delightfully furnished hotel overlooking the harbour provides
comfortable bedrooms and a cosy lounge and bars. Good food is
served in the restaurant.*
11⇨♦ CTV in all bedrooms ® sB&B⇨♦£28
dB&B⇨♦£56-£65 ⧫
12P 📶
V ♦ ☑ Lunch £1.30-£5.50 Dinner £14.50 Last dinner 9.30pm
Credit Cards ① ③ ⓔ

For key to symbols see the inside front cover.

**A**

★★66% **Harbour** LL35 0EB ☎(065472)250 & 7792
Telex no 35746 FAX (065472) 459
RS Nov-Mar
*In a central position on the seafront, this is a well-furnished hotel*
*with a homely atmosphere, pleasant bedrooms and good food.*
16rm(3⇨5♠)(4fb)2⊞ CTV in 14 bedrooms ®
sB&B⇨♠£40-£55 dB&B⇨♠£50-£80 **启**
CTV ⨉
♀ English & French V ⍟ ⍩ ⊁ Lunch £3.50-£10.50alc High
tea £2.30-£10.50alc Dinner £15-£17&alc Last dinner 9pm
Credit Cards ①②③⑤ ⓔ

★66% **Maybank Hotel & Restaurant** 4 Penhelig Rd, Penhelig
LL35 0PT ☎(065472)500 due to change to (0654) 767500
Closed 9 Jan-10 Feb & 26 Nov-2 Dec
*The charming little restaurant of this small, well-run hotel*
*overlooking the sea offers a very high standard of home-cooked*
*dishes, and accommodation is of a comparable quality.*
6rm(4♠)(1fb) CTV in all bedrooms ® ✱ sB&B♠£20-£33.95
dB&B♠£36-£51.90 **启**
CTV ⨉ ⊞ ✿ *xmas*
♀ English & Continental V ⍟ Sunday Lunch £7.95-£8.95 High
tea £3.50-£5.95 Dinner £16.50-£19alc Last dinner 10pm
Credit Cards ①③ ⓔ

---

**ABERFELDY** Tayside *Perthshire* Map **14** NN84

★★58% **Weem** Weem PH15 2LD (1m NW B846)
☎(0887)20381
*A friendly roadside inn, full of character and with an interesting*
*history. A popular base for touring holidaymakers, the hotel offers*
*traditional comforts in practical, well-equipped bedrooms.*
14⇨♠(4fb)⊁in 4 bedrooms CTV in all bedrooms ® T ✱
sB&B⇨♠£24-£28 dB&B⇨♠£40-£46 **启**
20P ✿ ✔ shooting loch fishing *xmas*
♀ European V ⍟ ⊁
Credit Cards ②③⑤ ⓔ

---

**ABERFOYLE** Central *Perthshire* Map **11** NN50

✕✕**Braeval Mill** Braeval FK8 3UY ☎(08772)711
*Situated just east of the village on the A821, this original mill has*
*been attractively converted into a cosy little country restaurant,*
*complete with a woodburning stove and paving stone floor. The*
*chef/proprietor, Nick Nairn cooks in the modern style with the*
*emphasis on Scottish meats and seafoods. His wife, Fiona, is a*
*charming hostess, assisted by attentive young staff. The wine list is*
*also noteworthy, and contains a good range of half bottles.*
Closed Mon, 2 wks Feb, 1 wk May/Jun & 2 wks Nov
Lunch not served Tue-Sat
♀ Scottish & French 32 seats Sunday Lunch £12.95-£14.50
Dinner £18-£25alc Last lunch 1.30pm Last dinner 9.30pm 18P
ncl0yrs ⊁
Credit Cards ①②③

---

**ABERGAVENNY** Gwent Map **03** SO21

★★★57% **The Angel** Cross St NP7 5EW (Trusthouse Forte)
☎(0873)7121 FAX (0873) 78059
*A popular town-centre hotel dating back to the 17th century offers*
*extensive conference facilities, well-equipped bedrooms which are*
*due to be upgraded, and friendly, helpful service.*
29⇨(1fb)1⊞⊁in 2 bedrooms CTV in all bedrooms ® T ✱
sB⇨£60-£65 dB⇨£71.50-£77 (room only) **启**
27P *xmas*
V ⍟ ⊒ ⊁ S% Lunch £8.95-£11.95 Dinner £12.95 Last dinner
9.30pm
Credit Cards ①②③④⑤

*1991 marks the 25th anniversary of this guide.*

---

★★70% **Llanwenarth Arms** Brecon Rd NP8 1EP
☎Crickhowell(0873)810550 FAX (0873) 811880
*An hotel perched on the bank of the River Usk, beside the A40 2.5*
*miles west of the town centre, commands spectacular views across*
*the valley from all but three of its eighteen well-equipped*
*bedrooms. The restaurant features an imaginative menu of*
*enjoyable dishes.*
18⇨♠ CTV in all bedrooms ® T ✖ sB&B⇨♠£48
dB&B⇨♠£58 **启**
60P ⊞ ✔
♀ International V ⍟ Lunch £8.20-£18.95alc Dinner
£8.20-£18.95alc Last dinner 10pm
Credit Cards ①②③⑤

✕**Bagan Tandoori** 35 Frogmore St NP7 5AN ☎(0873)4790
*An attractive restaurant just off the town centre offers pleasant*
*surroundings in which to enjoy good Indian cooking – including a*
*good range of curried dishes – all prepared with authentic spices*
*and served by polite, attentive, friendly staff.*
Closed 25-26 Dec
♀ Indian V 36 seats ✱ Dinner £15-£18alc Last lunch 2.30pm
Last dinner 11.30pm nc5yrs
Credit Cards ①②③⑤

---

**ABERGELE** Clwyd Map **06** SH97

★★63% **Kinmel Manor** St Georges Rd LL22 9AS
☎(0745)832014
*Set in open countryside one mile east of the town centre, this much*
*extended country house provides accommodation in simple but well*
*equipped bedrooms which are equally suitable for tourist or*
*business traveller. Conference/function facilities are available, and*
*leisure amenities include an indoor heated swimming pool, steam*
*room, spa bath and solarium.*
25⇨♠(3fb) CTV in all bedrooms ® T sB&B⇨♠£45
dB&B⇨♠£65 **启**
CTV 120P ✿ ▱(heated) sauna solarium gymnasium spa bath
steam room *xmas*
♀ English & French V ⍟ ⊒ ⊁ Lunch £8&alc High tea £4.50
Dinner £13.50&alc Last dinner 9.30pm
Credit Cards ①②③④⑤ ⓔ

---

**ABERLADY** Lothian *East Lothian* Map **12** NT47

★★64% **Kilspindie House** Main St EH32 0RE ☎(08757)682
*A friendly family owned hotel, popular with both business guests*
*and golfers. Improvements continue to be made, and include a wing*
*of comfortable bedrooms, but the characterful Golf Addict's Bar*
*remains unchanged.*
26⇨♠1⊞ CTV in all bedrooms ® T sB&B⇨♠£29-£37
dB&B⇨♠£50-£56 **启**
30P ⊞
V ⍟ ⊒ Sunday Lunch fr£7 High tea fr£5.90 Dinner fr£11&alc
Last dinner 8.30pm
Credit Cards ①③⑤ ⓔ

---

**ABERPORTH** Dyfed Map **02** SN25

★★★62% **Hotel Penrallt** SA43 2BS ☎(0239)810227
FAX (0239) 811375
Closed 23-31 Dec
*Set among a complex of good quality self-catering units and*
*enjoying leisure facilities which now include a small golf course,*
*this large country house provides accommodation in well-equipped*
*bedrooms which are for the most part spacious ; the restaurant*
*features interesting ceiling timbers and wall panelling.*
16⇨♠(2fb) CTV in all bedrooms ® T sB&B⇨♠£44
dB&B⇨♠£68 **启**
CTV 100P ⊞ ✿ ◿(heated) ♪ (hard) sauna solarium
gymnasium pitch & putt ⚬
⍟ ⊒ Sunday Lunch fr£7.95 High tea fr£4 Dinner fr£12.50&alc
Last dinner 9pm
Credit Cards ①②③⑤ ⓔ

---

62

★★65% **Penbontbren Farm** Glynarthen SA44 6PE (3.5m SE off A487) (Welsh Rarebits) ☎(0239)810248
Annexe10⇄♠♙(6fb) CTV in all bedrooms ® T ✱
sB&B⇄♠♙fr£24 dB&B⇄♠♙fr£40 🏳
35P ☆ ❊ ♪
V ↻ ⏃ ⍭ Dinner £8-£13alc Last dinner 8.30pm
Credit Cards ① ③

★★55% **Highcliffe** SA43 2DA (Minotels) ☎(0239)810534
*Conveniently situated above the town and a short walk from two sandy beaches, is this friendly, family run hotel. Bedrooms, although modestly furnished, are well-equipped with modern facilities and are gradually being upgraded.*
9rm(5⇄)Annexe6⇄♙(4fb) CTV in all bedrooms ® T
sB&B£22.50-£30.50 sB&B⇄♠£26.50-£34.50 dB&B£45
dB&B⇄♠£45 🏳
CTV 18P *xmas*
♀ International V ↻ ⏃ Sunday Lunch £5.95-£11 Dinner £11&alc Last dinner 8.30pm
Credit Cards ① ② ③ ⑤ ⓔ

★73% **Glandwr Manor** Tresaith SA43 2JH ☎(0239)810197
Closed Nov-Feb
*This small secluded hotel, reputedly designed by John Nash, is set in pleasant lawns and gardens above the small cove at Tresaith. It provides sparkling accommodation, good food and a warm welcome.*
7rm(2⇄3♠)(2fb) ® ✖ ✱ sB&Bfr£17.50 sB&B⇄♠fr£18.50
dB&Bfr£35 dB&B⇄♠fr£37
CTV 14P ⊞ ❊
↻ ⏃

---

**ABERSOCH** Gwynedd Map **06** SH32

★★★🏱65% **Porth Tocyn** Bwlch Tocyn LL53 7BU
☎(075881)3303 FAX (075881) 3538
Closed end Nov-21 Mar
*This delightfully situated hotel stands in 25 acres of farmland with superb views over Cardigan Bay. Owned by the same family since the 1940's it offers a relaxing informal atmosphere in the excellent lounges and dining room. The cuisine has a good reputation and bedrooms are attractively furnished.*
17⇄♠(1fb) CTV in all bedrooms T S% sB&B⇄♠£36-£47
dB&B⇄♠£57-£87 🏳
CTV 50P ⊞ ❊ ⌇(heated) ℛ (hard) windsurfing
↻ ⏃ Sunday Lunch £12.50 High tea £6 Dinner £15-£21 Last dinner 9.30pm
Credit Cards ① ⓔ

★★★65% **Riverside** LL53 7HW (Exec Hotel) ☎(075881)2419 & 2818
Closed Dec-Feb
*A comfortable hotel on the banks of the river, as its name suggests, and close to both harbour and town centre. It is very popular with holidaymakers, but equally suitable for business people, and the owners ensure that both will feel welcome.*
12⇄♠(4fb) CTV in all bedrooms ® T ✖ 🏳
25P ⊞ ❊ ▱(heated) sailing windsurfing
↻ ⏃
Credit Cards ① ② ③ ⑤

★★★62% **Abersoch Harbour** LL53 7HR ☎(075881)2406 & 3632
RS Jan & Feb
*A well-furnished, comfortable, family owned and run hotel close to the harbour and the river provides good, all-round comforts.*
9rm(7⇄1♠)Annexe5⇄♠(2fb)1ⓔ CTV in all bedrooms ® T
sB&B⇄♠£31-£54 dB&B⇄♠£62-£108 🏳
50P *xmas*
♀ English & French V ↻ ⏃ Lunch fr£12&alc High tea £1.50-£8.80 Dinner fr£12&alc Last dinner 10pm
Credit Cards ① ② ③ ⓔ

---

**A**

★★76%, **Neigwl** Lon Sarn Bach LL53 7DY ☎(075881)2363
*A combination of good friendly hospitality, attentive service, well-equipped bedrooms and enjoyable, imaginative food make this impeccably maintained family run hotel special. It is situated close to a good sandy beach and enjoys excellent views across Cardigan Bay to the Cambrian Mountains.*
7rm(1⇨4↑)Annexe2⇨(2fb) CTV in all bedrooms ®
✖ (ex guide dogs) sB&B£30-£33 sB&B⇨↑£30-£33
dB&B£50-£55 dB&B⇨↑£50-£55 ₽
CTV 30P ✿ ✿ *xmas*
✧ ⚓ Lunch £9 Dinner £15-£16.50 Last dinner 8.30pm
Credit Cards ①③⑤ €

★★61%, *Deucoch* LL53 7LD ☎(075881)2680
*A friendly, family-run hotel in an elevated position on the outskirts of the town commands panoramic views across Cardigan Bay from Snowdonia to mid-Wales. Its accommodation is equally suitable for holiday makers or business travellers, rooms being quite well furnished and having en suite facilities in the majority of cases.*
10rm(3⇨6↑)(2fb) CTV in all bedrooms ® ✖ sB&B£20-£22
sB&B⇨↑£20-£22 dB&B£40-£42 dB&B⇨↑£40-£42 ₽
CTV 50P ✿ ✿ *xmas*
V ✧ ⚓ Bar Lunch £3.50-£5.75alc Dinner fr£11 Last dinner 8pm
Credit Cards ①②③⑤

**ABERYSTWYTH** Dyfed Map **06** SN58

★★★♨66%, **Conrah** Ffosrhydygaled, Chancery SY23 4DF (Welsh Rarebits) ☎(0970)617941 Telex no 35892
FAX (0970) 624546
Closed 24-31 Dec
*A country mansion in Georgian style, set in pleasant lawns and gardens just south of the town. Public areas are elegant and comfortable and the restaurant has earned a good local reputation for the quality of its food.*
13rm(11⇨)Annexe9⇨↑ CTV in all bedrooms ® T ✖
sB&B£42-£46.50 sB&B⇨↑£43-£46.50 dB&B⇨↑£60-£85 ₽
Lift 60P ✿ ✿ ⊠(heated) sauna table tennis croquet nc5yrs
✧ International V ✧ ⚓ ✾ Lunch £7.25-£17alc Dinner £17-£18.50&alc Last dinner 9.30pm
Credit Cards ①②③⑤

★★64%, *Court Royale* Eastgate SY23 2AR ☎(0970)611722
*Small, family-run and friendly, the hotel is convenient for both sea front and town centre. Bedrooms are comfortable, and the busy bar provides a good deal of local atmosphere.*
10⇨↑(3fb) CTV in all bedrooms ® T
▦CTV ✿
V ✧ ⚓ Last dinner 10pm
Credit Cards ①②③

★★63%, **Four Seasons** 50-54 Portland St SY23 2DX
☎(0970)612120
Closed 25 Dec-2 Jan
*Located in a residential area just off the town centre this small family run hotel has pretty and well-equipped bedrooms and a spacious lounge. Enjoyable meals are served in the restaurant.*
14rm(11⇨↑)(1fb) CTV in all bedrooms ® T sB&B£28-£30
sB&B⇨↑£35-£40 dB&B£45-£50 dB&B⇨↑£53-£55 ₽
CTV 10P
✧ English & Continental V ✧ ⚓ ✾ Sunday Lunch £7.75-£8.50 Dinner £10.50-£14 Last dinner 8.30pm
Credit Cards ①③ €

★★61%, **Belle Vue Royal** Marine Ter SY23 2BA ☎(0970)617558
FAX (0970) 612190
Closed 24-26 Dec
*This Victorian hotel, set right on the Promenade and family run with the aid of friendly, attentive staff, provides accommodation in slightly dated bedrooms which are in process of refurbishment; bars are spaciously comfortable, and a new grill room augments the range of dishes served in the main restaurant.*

42rm(16⇨8↑)(6fb) CTV in all bedrooms ® T
✖ (ex guide dogs) sB&B£25-£28 sB&B⇨↑£31-£34
dB&B£44-£48.50 dB&B⇨↑fr£49 ₽
《 CTV 6P 9✿
✧ Continental V ✧ ⚓ Lunch fr£7.95 Dinner fr£11.50&alc
Last dinner 9pm
Credit Cards ①②③⑤ €

★★61%, **Groves** 42-46 North Pde SY23 2NF (Minotels)
☎(0970)617623
Closed Xmas
*A family-run hotel at the centre of the busy university town provides accommodation in compact but well-equipped bedrooms; the pleasant surroundings of the lounge invite relaxation, while both à la carte restaurant and cosy lounge bar offer a choice of meals.*
11⇨↑✖in 1 bedroom CTV in all bedrooms ® T
✖ (ex guide dogs) sB&B⇨↑fr£28.50 dB&B⇨↑fr£48.50 ₽
8P ✿ nc3yrs
✧ International V ✧ Sunday Lunch fr£6.95 Dinner fr£8.50alc
Last dinner 8.30pm
Credit Cards ①②③⑤ €

★★59%, **Bay** 35-37 Marine Ter SY23 2BX ☎(0970)617356
FAX (0970) 612198
Closed 24 Dec-1 Jan
*This modernised hotel is situated on the sea front, with some rooms having good sea views. There is an innovative menu each night as well as the roast of the day.*
32rm(7⇨13↑)(3fb) CTV in all bedrooms ® sB&B£18-£20
sB&B⇨↑£30 dB&B£49-£55 dB&B⇨↑£49-£55
20P pool table
V ✧ ⚓ ✾ Sunday Lunch £7-£9 Dinner £11-£13&alc Last dinner 8.30pm
Credit Cards ①②③ €

★★57%, **Queensbridge** Promenade, Victoria Ter SY23 2BX
☎(0970)612343 & 615025 FAX (0970) 617452
Closed 1wk Xmas
*Standing near the foot of Constitution Hill, within easy walking distance of the town centre, this small, family-run hotel provides tidy en suite bedrooms, an attractive basement restaurant and a cosy bar and lounge.*
15⇨↑(6fb) CTV in all bedrooms ® T ✳ sB&B⇨↑£30
dB&B⇨↑£42 ₽
Lift CTV ✗
✧
Credit Cards ①②③⑤

★★55%, **Cambrian** Alexandra Rd SY23 1LG ☎(0970)612446
Closed 25 Dec
*Friendly, helpful staff and bedrooms which are well equipped, though compact, characterise a small, mock-Tudor hotel which stands in the centre of town, opposite the station.*
12rm(2⇨5↑)(3fb) CTV in all bedrooms ® sB&B£26
sB&B⇨↑£28 dB&B£48 dB&B⇨↑£52 ₽
✗
✧ Welsh, English & Continental V ✧ ⚓ Lunch £7.25-£9.25
High tea fr£1.99 Dinner £9.25-£11.25&alc Last dinner 9.30pm
Credit Cards ①③ €

**ABINGDON** Oxfordshire Map **04** SU49

★★★61%, **Abingdon Lodge** Marcham Rd OX14 1TZ (Consort)
☎(0235)553456 Telex no 837750 FAX (0235) 554117
Closed 25-26 Dec
*Conveniently situated at the junction of the A34/A415 and designed for the popular business market, this new, purpose-built hotel offers comfortable bedrooms with a good range of facilities and equipment, though public rooms are a little restrictive.*
63⇨ CTV in all bedrooms ® T ✖ (ex guide dogs) S10%
sB&B⇨£55-£90 dB&B⇨£60-£95 Continental breakfast ₽
《 85P

♀ English & French V ✿ ⏛ S10% Lunch £7.95-£10.50 Dinner £7.95-£10.50&alc Last dinner 10pm
Credit Cards ① ② ③ ⑤ ⑥

★★★59% **Upper Reaches** Thames St OX14 3JA (Trusthouse Forte) ☎(0235)522311 FAX (0235) 555182
*The hotel overlooks the River Thames on one side and an old mill stream on the other, enjoying one of the most attractive locations in the historic town of Abingdon. The original building was an abbey cornmill, now converted to provide cosy public rooms, including the Mill Wheel Restaurant, and comfortable bedrooms. There is a private mooring beside the hotel and attractive garden terraces prove popular in the summer.*
26⇨🍴in 4 bedrooms CTV in all bedrooms ® ✳ sB⇨ᵈfr£70 dB⇨ᵈfr£85 (room only) ₽
90P ❈ *xmas*
V ✿ ⏛ ⊁
Credit Cards ① ② ③ ④ ⑤

★★61% **Crown & Thistle** Bridge St OX14 3HS (Berni/Chef & Brewer) ☎(0235)522556
*A small, friendly hotel with a popular Berni grill restaurant operation and well-equipped bedrooms. Popular with both commercial and private guests.*
21⇨🍴(3fb)1🖼 CTV in all bedrooms ® T 🐾 (ex guide dogs) sB&B⇨🍴£43-£54 dB&B⇨🍴£70-£75 ₽
《 36P
V ✿ ⊁ Lunch £8-£15alc Dinner £8-£15alc Last dinner 10.30pm
Credit Cards ① ② ③ ⑤

---

**ABOYNE** Grampian *Aberdeenshire* Map **15** NO59

★★61% **Birse Lodge** Charleston Rd AB3 5EL
☎(03398)86253 & 86254
*A former dower house, set in its own garden close to the River Dee and popular with both holidaymakers and sporting enthusiasts, provides good food and a friendly atmosphere; major bedroom refurbishment is planned.*
11⇨🍴Annexe4⇨🍴(2fb) CTV in all bedrooms ® T ✳ sB&B⇨🍴£35 dB&B⇨🍴£70
CTV 80P 🚲 ❈ putting green
♀ International V ✿ ⏛ Lunch £3.50-£8.50alc High tea £3.50-£8.50alc Dinner fr£16 Last dinner 8.30pm
Credit Cards ① ② ③

**See advertisement on page 67**

---

**ABRIDGE** Essex Map **05** TQ49

✗✗ *Roding* Market Pl RM4 1UA ☎Theydon Bois(037881)3030
*Within a beamed building of the 15th century, this restaurant is tastefully appointed and now enhanced by a new lounge area. Caring service and a good selection of reasonably priced wines, though the Chinatown-style menu is perhaps too extensive.*
Closed Mon & 26 Dec-early Jan
Lunch not served Sat
Dinner not served Sun
♀ Chinese 55 seats Last dinner 10pm 20P
Credit Cards ① ② ③ ⑤

---

**ACCRINGTON** Lancashire Map **07** SD72

★★★61% **Dunkenhalgh** Blackburn Rd, Clayton le Moors BB5 5JP (adj to M65, junct 7) (Character)
☎Blackburn(0254)398021 Telex no 63282 FAX (0254) 872230
*An impressive country house with modern bedrooms, attractive public rooms and extensive leisure facilities.*
35⇨🍴Annexe28⇨🍴(3fb)1🖼 CTV in all bedrooms ® T sB&B⇨🍴fr£70 dB&B⇨🍴fr£82 ₽
《 CTV 400P ❈ ▨(heated) snooker sauna solarium gymnasium
🎵 *xmas*
▶

**A**

⌖ International V ❀ ⚖ Lunch fr£9.50 Dinner £12.65-£26alc
Last dinner 9.45pm
Credit Cards [1] [2] [3] [5]

---

**ACHNASHEEN** Highland *Ross & Cromarty* Map **14** NH15

★★⚑70% **Ledgowan Lodge** IV22 2EJ (Best Western)
☎(044588)252 Telex no 75431 FAX (044588) 240
Closed 29 Oct-Mar
*A traditional Highland tourist hotel, formerly a shooting lodge,
offering friendly, attentive service and good wholesome country
cooking.*
13⇨(4fb) CTV in all bedrooms ® T sB&B⇨£35.50-£42.50
dB&B⇨£57-£70
25P ✿
V ❀ ⚖ Lunch £7.50-£15.50 Dinner £17.50-£19.75&alc Last
dinner 9pm
Credit Cards [1] [2] [3] [5] [£]

★★69% **Loch Maree** IV22 2HL ☎Kinlochewe(044584)288
FAX (044584) 241
Closed Nov-11 Apr
18⇨↾(1fb) CTV in all bedrooms ® T
50P ✿ ✦
V ❀ ⚖ Last dinner 9pm
Credit Cards [1] [3]

---

**ACLE** Norfolk Map **09** TG41

○**Travelodge** A47 Acle by pass(Trusthouse Forte)
☎Central reservations (0800) 850950
40⇨

---

**ADLINGTON Cheshire** Map **07** SJ98

○**Travelodge** A523 Adlington(Trusthouse Forte)
☎Central reservations (0800) 850950
Due to have opened summer 1990
32⇨

---

**ADLINGTON Lancashire** Map **07** SD61

★★63% **Gladmar** Railway Rd PR6 9RG ☎(0257)480398
FAX (0257) 482681
Closed 25 Dec & 1 Jan
*This friendly, personally-run commercial hotel in pleasant gardens
now has a small wing of six attractive, well equipped bedrooms,
while its older rooms, though in some cases very compact, are all
carefully maintained and provided with smart en suite facilities.*
20⇨↾(1fb)✂in 2 bedrooms CTV in all bedrooms ® T
➤ (ex guide dogs) ✲ sB&B⇨↾£35-£46 dB&B⇨↾£46-£54 ⑂
CTV 30P ✿
V ❀ ⚖ ✂ Lunch fr£5.50 High tea fr£5.50 Dinner fr£7.80 Last
dinner 8.30pm
Credit Cards [1] [3] [5] [£]

---

**ALCESTER** Warwickshire Map **04** SP05

★★57% **Arrow Mill** Arrow B49 5NL (On A435 S of town)
☎(0789)762419 Telex no 312522 FAX (0789) 765170
Closed 23 Dec-5 Jan
*An historic building set in a tranquil location amidst 55 acres of
rural Warwickshire. Now a family managed hotel, it still retains
its charm and character – an attractive example being the original
water wheel, driven by the stream, in the Miller's Bar.*
18⇨↾(5fb) CTV in all bedrooms ® T ✲ sB&B⇨↾£46-£56
dB&B⇨↾£56-£84 ⑂
250P 6➤ (£10) ✿ ✦ croquet archery clay pigeon shooting
⌖ English & French V ❀ ⚖ Lunch £8.25-£20 High tea
£1.75-£3.50 Dinner fr£14.50 Last dinner 9.30pm
Credit Cards [1] [2] [3] [5] [£]

---

★★55% **Cherrytrees** Stratford Rd B49 6LN ☎(0789)762505
Closed 25 & 26 Dec
*Sound, modest accommodation in chalets, facilities for small
conferences and a restaurant which is well used by residents and
locals alike are provided by a popular, modern hotel set beside the
A422 to the east of the town.*
Annexe22⇨↾ CTV in all bedrooms ®
CTV 80P ✿
⌖ International V ❀
Credit Cards [1] [2] [3]

---

**ALCONBURY** Cambridgeshire Map **04** TL17

★★64% **Alconbury House** Alconbury Weston PE17 5JG (1.5m
N on A1) ☎Huntingdon(0480)890807 FAX (0480) 891259
*An attractive Georgian house set in its own grounds adjacent to the
A1 (northbound). Attentive staff ensure an hospitable welcome
and a good range of dishes is served in both the bar and restaurant.*
24↾(2fb) CTV in all bedrooms ® T S% sB&B↾£25-£49
dB&B↾£38-£59 ⑂
80P ✿ squash snooker sauna solarium
⌖ European ❀ ⚖ Lunch fr£10.50&alc Dinner fr£10.50&alc
Last dinner 9.30pm
Credit Cards [1] [2] [3] [5] [£]
See advertisement under HUNTINGDON

---

**ALDBOURNE** Wiltshire Map **04** SU27

✕✕**Raffles** The Green SN8 2BW ☎Marlborough(0672)40700
*Attractive cottage-style restaurant offering interesting food and
attentive, friendly service.*
Closed Sun, last 2 wks Aug & 25-30 Dec
Lunch not served Mon & Sat
⌖ French 36 seats Lunch £13.50-£17.95alc Dinner
£13.50-£17.95alc Last lunch 2.15pm Last dinner 10.30pm
nc3yrs
Credit Cards [1] [2] [3] [5]

---

**ALDEBURGH** Suffolk Map **05** TM45

★★★67% **White Lion** Market Cross Place IP15 5BJ (Best
Western) ☎(0728)452720 Telex no 94017152
FAX (0728) 452986
*The White Lion is in an attractive position on the sea front. It
dates from 1563 and is Aldeburgh's oldest hotel. All bedrooms
have been recently refurbished and there are some very attractive
four-poster bedrooms. There are two elegant lounges, one of which
is non-smoking, a popular restaurant which serves fresh, well-
prepared food in a relaxed, candle-lit atmosphere, and the Buttery
Bar for snacks and light meals.*
38⇨↾(1fb)⊞ CTV in all bedrooms ® T sB&B⇨↾£50-£60
dB&B⇨↾£65-£90 ⑂
15P ⊞ xmas
⌖ English & French V ❀ ⚖ Sunday Lunch £10.25-£11.25
Dinner £14.95-£15.95&alc Last dinner 8.45pm
Credit Cards [1] [2] [3] [5]

★★★64% **Wentworth** Wentworth Rd IP15 5BD (Consort)
☎(0728)452312
Closed 28 Dec-11 Jan
*Behind the rather drab exterior of this Victorian building facing
the sea lies a comfortable, well-furnished hotel. Bedrooms are
attractive with co-ordinating fabrics whilst framed prints, antiques
and open fires provide warmth and elegance in the comfortable
lounges, small bar and smart dining room.*
31rm(24⇨4↾) CTV in all bedrooms T sB&B£35-£40
sB&B⇨↾£40-£48 dB&B⇨↾£72.50-£95 ⑂
16P ⊞ xmas

---

66

♥ English & French **V** ♦ ♨ Lunch £11.50-£13.50&alc Dinner
£14.50&alc Last dinner 9pm
Credit Cards ① ② ③ ⑤

★★★58% **Brudenell** The Parade IP15 5BU (Trusthouse Forte)
☎(0728)452071
*Comfortable, inviting public areas and good service from a
particularly friendly team of staff are among the attractive
features of a sea-front hotel which offers excellent views from
many of its rooms; accommodation is, for the most part, quite
spacious and well equipped.*
47⇔(3fb)⊁in 8 bedrooms CTV in all bedrooms ® **T** S%
sB&B⇔£40-£50 dB&B⇔£45-£60 ⊟
Lift ℂ 14P 8🏓 games room *xmas*
♥ English & French **V** ♦ ♨ ⊁ S% Lunch £7.50-£9.50&alc
Dinner £11.95-£13.50&alc Last dinner 9pm
Credit Cards ① ② ③ ④ ⑤

★★62% **Uplands** Victoria Rd IP15 5DX ☎(0728)452420
Closed 23-30 Dec
*Set in its own beautifully maintained walled garden on the
approach road to the town, and boasting a 300-year-old mulberry
tree, this house, dating from 1800, retains an Italian moulded
ceiling in the dining room and an impressive stone fireplace in a
hall, overlooked by a balustraded gallery; extensive additions
made in 1904 provide neat, tidy accommodation, cuisine is simple
but mainly fresh and attentive owners take every care to ensure
guests' well-being.*
12rm(9⇔)Annexe8⇔ℝ(2fb) CTV in 17 bedrooms TV in 3
bedrooms ® **T** ✗ (ex guide dogs) sB&Bfr£25 sB&B⇔ℝfr£37
dB&Bfr£55 ⊟
CTV 22P ⇑ nc12yrs
**V** Dinner fr£13&alc Last dinner 8.30pm
Credit Cards ① ② ③ ⑤

# Ledgowan Lodge Hotel ★★ 🏌🚶70% A

## Achnasheen, Wester Ross IV22 2EJ
## Telephone: Achnasheen (044 588) 252

Built as a shooting lodge in 1904 and now
discreetly converted into a Country House
Hotel with most of its original charm and
character. Situated in the peace and quiet of
the beautiful Western Highlands, an ideal
position from which to tour. 13 bedrooms,
all have private bathroom en suite, TV,
telephone, tea/coffee making facilities and
central heating throughout. Privately owned
and fully licensed.

# WENTWORTH
## HOTEL ★★★
## Aldeburgh, Suffolk
## Tel: (0728) 452312

*Enjoy the atmosphere of a traditional
country house hotel, situated overlooking
the beach of the most delightful of East
Anglia's seaside towns. Privately owned
by the Pritt family since 1920, the hotel
has 31 bedrooms, all centrally heated,
28 with private bathroom and many
with superb sea views. Open fires in the
lounges provide a warm welcome in the
Winter. The hotel has a long standing
reputation for good food, fine wines and
personal service.*

**THE BIRSE LODGE HOTEL ★★**

## Aboyne, Royal Deeside AB3 5EL
## Telephone: (03398) 86253

This privately owned Country
House Hotel is set in its own
grounds. Popular with fishers and
shooters also golfing enthusiasts
who have a choice of 5 Golf
Courses all within a few miles of
the hotel.

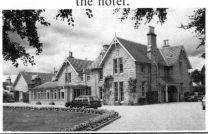

# Alderley Edge - Alloway

**A**

## ALDERLEY EDGE Cheshire Map 07 SJ87

★★★72%, **Alderley Edge Hotel** Macclesfield Rd SK9 7BJ
☎(0625)583033 FAX (0625) 586343
*Situated in an elevated position in a peaceful residential area this hotel has been completely refurbished to provide well-equipped and tastefully appointed bedrooms and comfortable public areas which include a pleasant conservatory where traditional afternoon tea can be enjoyed. Fresh produce, particularly seafood is a feature on the various menus and the extensive wine list includes over one hundred different champagnes. Service throughout is provided by friendly, attentive staff.*
32⇴ CTV in all bedrooms ® T S% sB⇴fr£79 dB⇴fr£97 (room only) ₽
( 90P *xmas*
V ✿ ⚏ Lunch fr£11.95&alc Dinner fr£17.95&alc Last dinner 10pm
Credit Cards ① ② ③ ④ ⑤

## ALDERMINSTER Warwickshire Map 04 SP24

★★★★64%, **Ettington Park** CV37 8BS (Select)
☎Stratford-upon-Avon(0789)740740 Telex no 311825
FAX (0789) 87472
*A Victorian mansion in Gothic style, glimpsed through the mature trees of forty acres of parkland, now offers standards of comfort unprecedented in the many years that it has operated as an hotel. The new wing's modern accommodation, though plainer and more uniform than the spacious, ornate and individually styled bedrooms of the main house, is equally comfortable; the restaurant enjoys a well-earned reputation for good food, a small but attractive leisure centre is available for guests' use.*
48⇴1🛏 CTV in all bedrooms T ✖ (ex guide dogs)
sB&B⇴£105-£195 dB&B⇴£145-£250 ₽
Lift ( 85P ✿ ☐(heated) ♪ (hard) ⌁ ∪ sauna solarium croquet clay pigeon shooting archery nc7yrs *xmas*
♀ English & French V ✿ ⚏ Lunch fr£17.50&alc High tea £10-£15&alc Dinner fr£30&alc Last dinner 9.30pm
Credit Cards ① ② ③ ⑤ ⓔ
**See advertisement under STRATFORD-UPON-AVON**

## ALDERNEY

See **Channel Islands**

## ALDWARK North Yorkshire Map 08 SE46

★★★⚫78%, **Aldwark Manor** YO6 2NF ☎(03473)8146
FAX (03473) 8867
*Set in 180 acres of parkland, which include a nine hole golf course and a clay pigeon shooting ground, this handsome 19th century mansion house has been tastefully converted to provide luxurious bedrooms and elegant public areas. Dinner can be especially recommended, and the service is particularly friendly.*
15⇴(2fb)2🛏✚in 2 bedrooms CTV in all bedrooms ® T ✖ (ex guide dogs) ✳ sB&B⇴£65-£80 dB&B⇴£90-£120 ₽
( 52P ✿ ♪ 9 ⌁ *xmas*
♀ European V ✿ ⚏ Lunch £10.50&alc Dinner £15.50&alc Last dinner 9pm
Credit Cards ① ② ③ ⑤

## ALFORD Lincolnshire Map 09 TF47

★69%, **White Horse** 29 West St LN13 9DG ☎(0507)462218
*Though the accommodation provided by this hotel in the main street is modest, rooms are attractively decorated with co-ordinated soft furnishings; the proprietor and his wife maintain good standards throughout, and a genuine warmth and care for guests' wellbeing is evident.*
9rm(7⇴)(2fb) CTV in all bedrooms ® sB&B£20-£22 sB&B⇴£26-£27 dB&B£30-£33 dB&B⇴£34-£38
10P 3🛏

♀ English & Continental ✿ Lunch £8-£10alc Dinner £8-£17alc
Last dinner 10pm
Credit Cards ① ③

## ALFRETON Derbyshire Map 08 SK45

○**Granada Lodge** A38/A61 DE55 1JH (junc A38/A61)
(Granada) ☎(0773)520040 FAX (0773) 521087
61⇴(10fb)✚in 13 bedrooms CTV in all bedrooms ® T ✖ (ex guide dogs) ✳ sB⇴fr£32 dB⇴fr£36 (room only)
( 130P
V ✿ ⚏ ✚ Lunch £7.15-£12.15alc High tea £2.10-£2.50alc Dinner £8.70-£13.70alc Last dinner 9.30pm
Credit Cards ① ② ③ ⑤
**See advertisement under SWANWICK**

## ALFRISTON East Sussex Map 05 TQ50

★★★57%, **The Star** BN26 5TA (Trusthouse Forte)
☎(0323)870495 FAX (0323) 870922
*An ancient inn endowed with massive oak beams and inglenook fireplaces offers open lounges, a cosy bar, a candlelit restaurant and a choice of bedrooms which includes some in a modern new wing. The Heritage Room is available for meetings.*
34⇴✚in 10 bedrooms CTV in all bedrooms ® T S% sB⇴£65-£75 dB⇴£85-£95 (room only) ₽
36P *xmas*
V ✿ ⚏ ✚ Lunch £9.50-£11.50&alc Dinner £13.50&alc Last dinner 9pm
Credit Cards ① ② ③ ④ ⑤

✖**Moonraker's** High St BN26 5TD ☎(0323)870472
*Delightful small 14th-century cottage restaurant featuring inglenook log fire and a homely lounge. Chef Elaine Wilkinson's cooking is very reliable, wholesome and interesting. A good wine selection is available, particularly Estate and Domaine bottled wines. All is complimented by friendly supervision and service.*
Closed Sun, Mon & 13 Jan-13 Feb
Lunch not served
♀ French V 32 seats Dinner £18.90 Last dinner 9.15pm
♪ nc5yrs

## ALLENDALE Northumberland Map 12 NY85

★★⚫63%, **Bishopfield Country House** NE47 9EJ
☎(0434)683248 FAX (0434) 683830
Closed 24-26 Dec
*Until recently a working farm, buildings in the courtyard at Bishopfield have been converted to a small country-house hotel. The bedrooms are modern and well-equipped, and there are two comfortable lounges. The dinner menu offers honest country cooking.*
12⇴(3fb) CTV in all bedrooms ® T sB&B⇴fr£32 dB&B⇴fr£54
20P ✿ ✳ ⌁
♀ English & French V ✿ ⚏ ✚ Lunch fr£5 Dinner fr£13 Last dinner 8.30pm
Credit Cards ① ③ ⓔ
**See advertisement under HEXHAM**

## ALLOWAY Strathclyde *Ayrshire* Map 10 NS31

★★67%, **Burns Monument** KA7 4PQ (2m S on B7024) (Best Western) ☎Ayr(0292)42466 FAX (0292) 43174
*This comfortable hotel takes its name from the nearby Burns Monument and the Auld Brig O' Doon. Its own setting, in the midst of landscaped gardens overlooking the River Doon, is spectacular, and the recent refurbishment of its rooms makes a bright and welcoming impression. Snacks and light meals are provided in the Alloway Lounge, which has lovely views of the river and the Poet's Restaurant serves an imaginative range of dishes. The Brig O' Doon public bar is busy and full of character.*

9⇄♪(2fb)1⌘ CTV in all bedrooms ® T sB&B⇄♪£35-£40 dB&B⇄♪£60-£70 ⊟
《 CTV 20P ✽ ♪ ⋄ xmas
♀ British & French V ❂ ⬙ Lunch £7.50-£8.50&alc High tea £4.75-£6.50&alc Dinner £12.95-£14.95&alc Last dinner 9.45pm
Credit Cards ①②③⑤
___
✗**Burns Byre** Mount Oliphant Farm KA6 6BU ☎(0292)43644
Closed Mon
Dinner not served Sun
40 seats ✱ Lunch £5.50-£10.80alc Dinner £10-£18.50alc Last lunch 2pm Last dinner 9pm 20P
Credit Cards ①②③⑤

---

**ALMONDSBURY** Avon Map **03** ST68

○**Aztec** Aztec West Business Park BS12 4TS (Shire)
☎Bristol(0454)201090
Due to have opened Sep 1990
88⇄♪

---

**ALNWICK** Northumberland Map **12** NU11

★★★59% **White Swan** Bondgate Within NE66 1TD
☎(0665)602109 FAX (0665) 510400
Located at the centre of the town, with views of the castle to the rear, this business and tourist hotel offers a selection of bedrooms which are all well equipped although they vary in style.
43⇄♪(2fb)⊬in 4 bedrooms CTV in all bedrooms ® T sB&B⇄♪fr£56 dB&B⇄♪fr£75 ⊟
《 30P ✽ xmas
♀ English & French V ❂ ⬙ Lunch fr£6.95&alc High tea £6-£9.50 Dinner £13.95-£15&alc Last dinner 9pm
Credit Cards ①②③⑤ ⓔ

★★73% **The Oaks** South Rd NE66 2PN ☎(0665)510014
Two stone-built private houses, dating from the 18th century have been converted by Avril and Middleton Dand into a very good quality hotel. Bedrooms are thoughtfully equipped, including mini-fridge bars and hairdryers. There is an attractive oak-panelled bar and in the Restaurant the à la carte dinner offers a good range of dishes using fresh local ingredients.
4⇄♪Annexe4⇄ CTV in all bedrooms ®
⊞ 32P
V ❂ Last dinner 9pm
Credit Cards ①③

★★51% **Hotspur** Bondgate Without NE66 1PR ☎(0665)602924
Closed 24-26 Dec & 1 Jan
Historic coaching inn with good comfortable restaurant.
28rm(17⇄1♪)(2fb) CTV in all bedrooms ®
CTV 25P
V ❂ ⬙ Last dinner 9pm
Credit Cards ①③

---

**ALRESFORD** Hampshire Map **04** SU53

✗**Old School House** 60 West St SO24 9AU ☎(096273)2134
This restaurant could justifiably claim to serve the best school dinners in Hampshire Meals of excellent quality, selected from two fixed-price menus, are based on good-quality ingredients, well seasoned and individually cooked ; there is a separate pudding menu and a popular wine list. Service is efficient, attentive and friendly.
Closed Mon & Tue
♀ English & French V 36 seats ✱ Lunch £5-£15 Dinner £20-£30 Last lunch 2pm Last dinner 10pm ♪ ⊬
Credit Cards ①③

---

**ALREWAS** Staffordshire Map **07** SK11

⌂**Travelodge** A38 Rykneld St(Trusthouse Forte)
☎Central res (0800) 850950

---

A modern, well-equipped bedroom unit on the A38 Southbound, adjacent to a Happy Eater restaurant which is open for meals from 7am to 10pm.
40⇄♪(40fb) CTV in all bedrooms ® sB⇄♪£24 dB⇄♪£29.50 (room only)
《 40P ⌘
Credit Cards ①②③

---

**ALSAGER** Cheshire Map **07** SJ75

★★★64% **Manor House** Audley Rd ST7 2QQ
☎Crewe(0270)884000 FAX (0270) 882483
A hotel which stands three miles from junction 16 of the M6 has largely incorporated into its restaurant and bar areas the original farmhouse whose site it occupies.
27⇄♪(1fb)1⌘ CTV in all bedrooms ® T
《 CTV 178P
♀ French & English V ❂ ⬙ Last dinner 9.30pm
Credit Cards ①②③⑤
See advertisement under CREWE

---

**ALSTON** Cumbria Map **12** NY74

★★⬛75% **Lovelady Shield Country House** CA9 3LF
☎(0434)381203 FAX (0434) 381515
Closed 3 Jan-21 Feb
Margaret and Kenneth Lyons are now in their 2nd year at this lovely 19th-century house, and they are certainly making their mark. Improvements have encompassed all areas providing higher levels of comfort and better facilities throughout. Bedrooms vary in size and style but all are well furnished and pretty, and guests can relax in an attractive lounge with a log fire, magazines and fine ornaments.
12⇄♪(1fb)1⌘ CTV in all bedrooms T ✳ sB&B⇄♪£50 dB&B⇄♪£105-£120 (incl dinner) ⊟
20P ⌘ ✽ ♪ (hard) croquet xmas
♀ English & French ❂ ⬙ ⊬ Sunday Lunch £10-£15 High tea £4-£10 Dinner £19 Last dinner 8.30pm
Credit Cards ①②③⑤ ⓔ
See advertisement on page 71

★★67% **Lowbyer Manor Country House** CA9 3JX
☎(0434)381230
This interesting period house on the A686, 1 mile north of the town centre, has a cosy bar, attractive dining room and comfortable lounge.
7⇄♪Annexe4⇄ CTV in all bedrooms ® sB&B⇄♪£29 dB&B⇄♪£50.50 ⊟
CTV 14P ✽ xmas
V ❂ ⬙ Sunday Lunch £8.25 Dinner £13.15-£18.85alc Last dinner 8.30pm
Credit Cards ①②③⑤ ⓔ

★63% **Hillcrest** Townfoot CA9 3RN ☎Hexham(0434)381251 & 381444
A friendly and relaxing hotel, with a comfortable lounge and hospitable bar, situated to the west of town on the A686. The hotel also provides a good standard of cuisine both in the bar and the small restaurant.
11rm(2fb) ✖ (ex guide dogs) ✳ sB&B£19-£29 dB&B£35-£55 CTV 16P 3⬤ ✽ ⋄ xmas
V ❂ ⬙ ⊬ Lunch £6.95&alc High tea £3.25-£6.95alc Dinner £10.25-£16.75alc Last dinner 9pm
Credit Cards ①③ ⓔ

---

**ALTHORPE** Humberside Map **08** SE81

See **Scunthorpe** for details of other hotels.
★★66% **Lansdowne House** Main St DN17 3HJ
☎Scunthorpe(0724)783369
Friendly and attentive service is provided by the proprietors and young staff of this hotel – a Victorian country house which has

▶

*been tastefully converted to provide bedrooms with modern facilities and comfortable public areas.*
7⇔↱Annexe3⇔↱(5fb) CTV in all bedrooms ® **T**
✗ (ex guide dogs) ✱ sB&B⇔↱fr£45.50 dB&B⇔↱fr£55.50
CTV 40P ❊
English & French **V** ♧ ☕ Lunch £13-£25alc Dinner £13-£25alc Last dinner 10pm
Credit Cards [1] [2] [3] [5]

**ALTON Hampshire** Map **04** SU73

**★★★59%** ***Alton House*** Normandy St GU34 1DW
☎(0420)80033 FAX (0420) 89222
*Spacious gardens and a car park surround this comfortable Regency hotel to which a new wing of attractive bedrooms has now been linked by the Fountain Lounge. O'Connors Restaurant serves generous portions of both traditional and more imaginative dishes, while cheerful, friendly staff are keen to please.*
38⇔↱(2fb)1⊞ CTV in all bedrooms ® **T**
( 80P 6🚗 ❊ ⌒(heated) ℘ (hard) snooker
English & Continental **V** ♧ ☕ ⊁ Last dinner 9.45pm
Credit Cards [1] [2] [3]

**★★63%** **Grange** 17 London Rd, Holybourne GU34 4EG
☎(0420)86565 FAX (0420) 541346
Closed Xmas-30 Dec
*Twenty new, well co-ordinated bedrooms have been added to a personally-run hotel with attractive rear gardens and good car parking which stands on the eastern outskirts of the town. The no-smoking restaurant serves soundly cooked meals from both table d'hôte and à la carte menus, and a friendly atmosphere encourages relaxation.*
27rm(23⇔↱)Annexe6⇔↱(2fb)1⊞⊁in 2 bedrooms CTV in all bedrooms ® **T** sB&B£45-£49.50 sB&B⇔↱£45-£49.50 dB&B£49.50-£79.50 dB&B⇔↱£49.50-£79.50
CTV 48P ⊞ ❊ ⌒(heated) croquet putting nc3yrs
English & French **V** ♧ ☕ ⊁ Lunch £7.95-£8.95&alc Dinner fr£9.95&alc Last dinner 9pm
Credit Cards [1] [2] [3] [5]

**ALTON Staffordshire** Map **07** SK04

**★★61%** **Bull's Head Inn** High St ST10 4AQ
☎Oakamoor(0538)702307
RS 4 Nov-Feb
*Conveniently situated for visitors to Alton Towers this small inn lies in the centre of the village. Bedrooms, though on the small side, are prettily decorated and well equipped. The character bar has much local flavour and good food is available in the attractive restaurant.*
6rm(3↱)(2fb) CTV in all bedrooms ® ✗ sB&B£25-£35 sB&B↱£25-£35 dB&B£30-£50 dB&B↱£30-£50
CTV 15P ⊞
**V** ♧ Sunday Lunch £6.50 Dinner £10-£16 Last dinner 9.30pm
Credit Cards [1] [3]

**ALTRINCHAM** Greater Manchester Map **07** SJ78

**★★★64%** ***Woodland Park*** Wellington Rd, Timperley WA15 7RG (Inter-Hotels) ☎061-928 8631 Telex no 635091 FAX 061-941 2821
*A family-owned hotel situated in a quiet residential area. A high standard of accommodation is provided and extensive facilities for functions and conferences are available. The lounge and bar contain antique furniture and gas lamps to create an aura of Victorian elegance.*
44⇔↱(6fb)5⊞ CTV in all bedrooms ® **T** ✗ (ex guide dogs)
( 150P 1🚗 (charged)
International **V** ♧ ☕ Last dinner 9.45pm
Credit Cards [1] [2] [3] [5]

**See advertisement under MANCHESTER AIRPORT**

**★★★63%** **Bowdon** Langham Rd, Bowdon WA14 2HT
☎061-928 7121 Telex no 668208 FAX 061-927 7560
RS 25 & 26 Dec
*An hotel well placed for access to Manchester, the airport and the M56 motorway offers the ideal centre for business meetings and conferences. Modernisation has provided bedrooms of a high standard, well appointed and having en suite facilities, whilst retaining many traditional features.*
82⇔(1fb) CTV in all bedrooms ® **T** sB&B⇔£32-£59 dB&B⇔£46-£72 ⊟
( 168P ♫
English & French **V** ♧ ☕ Lunch £11.50&alc Dinner £11.50&alc Last dinner 10pm
Credit Cards [1] [2] [3] [5]

**★★★63%** **Cresta Court** Church St WA14 4DP (Best Western)
☎061-927 7272 Telex no 667242 FAX 061-926 9194
*A modern building with good car parking facilities stands at the A56/A560 junction, within easy reach of Manchester airport and the city itself. Public areas include two restaurants and three bars, while bedrooms – though compact in some cases – are very well equipped.*
139⇔↱(5fb) CTV in all bedrooms ® **T** ✱ sB&B⇔↱£30-£55 dB&B⇔↱£40-£66 ⊟
Lift ( 200P CFA
English & French **V** ♧ ☕ S% Sunday Lunch fr£7.45&alc Dinner £7-£12.50alc Last dinner 11pm
Credit Cards [1] [2] [3] [5]

**★★★61%** **The Swan** WA16 6RD (De Vere)
☎Bucklow Hill(0565)830295 Telex no 666911
FAX (0565) 830614
(For full entry see Bucklow Hill)

**★★★55%** ***Ashley*** Ashley Rd, Hale WA15 9SF (De Vere)
☎061-928 3794 Telex no 669406 FAX 061-926 9046
Closed 26 Dec RS 27-31 Dec
*Situated in Hale village and part of a shopping complex, this purpose built commercial hotel has friendly and helpful staff and limited public areas.*
49⇔↱ CTV in all bedrooms ® **T**
Lift ( CTV 100P CFA bowling green
English & French **V** ♧ ☕ ⊁ Last dinner 9.45pm
Credit Cards [1] [2] [3] [5]

**★★63%** ***Pelican Inn & Motel*** Manchester Rd WA14 5NH (County Inns) ☎061-962 7414 Telex no 668014
*This attractive mock-Tudor hotel, its compact bedrooms in a courtyard of matching style at the rear of the main building, stands on the A56 about two miles east of the town centre within easy reach of Manchester's centre and airport.*
50↱ CTV in all bedrooms ®
( 150P
English & French **V** ♧ ☕ ⊁ Last dinner 10pm
Credit Cards [1] [2] [3] [5]

**★★60%** ***George & Dragon*** Manchester Rd WA14 4PH (County Inns) ☎061-928 9933 Telex no 665051
*Conveniently situated on the A56 close to the town centre and within easy reach of Manchester Airport and major motorway links, this popular hotel features bedrooms with practical facilities; bars are comfortable and the restaurant has a good reputation.*
47⇔↱(2fb) CTV in all bedrooms ®
Lift ( 80P
English & Continental **V** ♧ ☕ Last dinner 9.45pm
Credit Cards [1] [2] [3] [5]

**★★56%** ***Grove Park*** Park Rd, Bowdon WA14 3JE
☎061-928 6191
*Standing in a suburban area within easy reach of the M56 motorway and Manchester Airport, the hotel features popular restaurants which are open for both lunch and dinner. Bedrooms are modest but service is obliging. Suit business people.*
13⇔↱ CTV in all bedrooms ® **T** ✗

▶

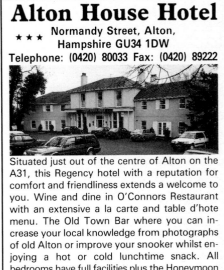

《 CTV 28P
🍴 International **V** ❡ Last dinner 11.30pm
Credit Cards ①③

★**64% Greystone** 305 Manchester Rd, West Timperley
WA14 5PH ☎061-905 2233
*A former detached residence recently modernised and extended
with well-appointed bedrooms. Situated on the A56 between
junction 7 of the M53 and Altrincham.*
12♠ CTV in all bedrooms ⓡ **T**
《 CTV 12P 🚗 sauna
**V** ❡ ⚿ Last dinner 10.30pm
Credit Cards ①②③

**ALVECHURCH** Hereford & Worcester Map **07** SP07

✗✗**Osbornes** The Mill, Radford Rd B48 7LD ☎021-445 4628
Closed Sun, Mon & 18-29 Aug
Lunch not served Sat
🍴 English & French **V** 60 seats ✻ Lunch £10.25-£12.95 Dinner
£18.80&alc Last dinner 9.30pm 20P nc10yrs ♬
Credit Cards ①②③

**ALVESTON** Avon Map **03** ST68

★★★**69% Alveston House** BS12 2LJ ☎Thornbury(0454)415050
Telex no 449212 FAX (0454) 415425
*A tastefully modernised hotel standing beside the A58 between
junctions 14 and 16 of the M5 offers comfortable, well equipped
bedrooms, attractive open-plan public areas and attentive service
from friendly staff.*
30⇄♠(1fb) CTV in all bedrooms ⓡ **T**
sB&B⇄♠£67.50-£72.50 dB&B⇄♠£77.50-£85.50 ▤
CTV 75P ✤ CFA
🍴 English & French **V** ❡ ⚿ Lunch £12.75-£15&alc Dinner
£12.75-£15.75&alc Last dinner 9.30pm
Credit Cards ①②③⑤Ⓔ
                    **See advertisement under BRISTOL**

★★★**58% Post House** Thornbury Rd BS12 2LL (Trusthouse
Forte) ☎Thornbury(0454)412521 Telex no 444753
FAX (0454) 413920
*An extension to the original Ship Inn, the hotel combines character
with modern facilities for the businessman. Bedrooms vary in style
but are all well equipped and comparable in quality, while a wide
range of efficient services includes a range of eating options which
ensures that guests can obtain a meal at any time of day.*
75⇄(13fb)✂in 22 bedrooms CTV in all bedrooms ⓡ **T** S%
sB&B⇄fr£67 dB&B⇄fr£78 (room only) ▤
《 100P ✤ CFA ⌂(heated) mini golf pitch & putt *xmas*
🍴 English & French **V** ❡ ⚿ ✂ Lunch £11&alc Dinner
£15.40&alc Last dinner 10pm
Credit Cards ①②③④⑤

**ALWALTON** Cambridgeshire Map **04** TL19

★★★★**58% Swallow** Lynchwood PE2 0GB (Swallow)
☎Peterborough(0733)371111 Telex no 32422
FAX (0733) 236725
*Opened in summer 1988, this hotel exemplifies both the ever-
improving quality of Swallow hotels, and the modern, expansive
spirit of Peterborough. The hotel faces the East of England
Showground and is designed for business use, but offers useful
leisure facilities too.*
163⇄(10fb)✂in 56 bedrooms CTV in all bedrooms ⓡ **T** ✻
sB&B⇄fr£74 dB&B⇄fr£92 ▤
《 CTV 200P ✤ ⌂(heated) sauna solarium gymnasium steam
room spa bath beauty therapist ♬ *xmas*
🍴 English & French **V** ❡ ⚿ ✂ Lunch £10.25-£12.75&alc
Dinner £13.75-£16.95&alc Last dinner 10.30pm
Credit Cards ①②③④⑤

🏠**Travelodge** A1, Great North Rd PE7 3UR (A1 southbound)
(Trusthouse Forte)
☎Peterborough(0733)231109 Central res (0800) 850950
*Situated on the A1 Southbound the lodge offers well equipped
accommodation and value for money. The adjacent Little Chef is
open 7am – 10pm.*
32⇄♠(32fb) CTV in all bedrooms ⓡ sB⇄♠£24
dB⇄♠£29.50 (room only)
32P 🚗
🍴 Mainly grills
Credit Cards ①②③

**ALYTH** Tayside *Perthshire* Map **15** NO24

★★**⚑58% Lands of Loyal** Loyal Rd PH11 8JQ ☎(08283)3151
*A Victorian mansion house overlooking the valley of Strathmore
and the Sidlaw Hills. Public rooms have a comfortable lived-in
feel, though bedrooms are more modest and offer a variety of
styles.*
11⇄(2fb)1🛏 CTV in 3 bedrooms ⓡ **T**
CTV 20P 6🐎 🚗 ✤ snooker shooting
🍴 Scottish & Continental **V** ❡ ⚿ Last dinner 10pm
Credit Cards ①②③

**AMBERLEY** Gloucestershire Map **03** SO80

★★**68% Amberley Inn** GL5 5AF (Best Western) ☎(0453)872565
Telex no 94012242 FAX (0453) 812738
*A stone-built inn at the heart of the village offers individual and
well equipped bedrooms, including four in an attractive cottage
annexe; characterful public rooms are warmed by log fires during
the winter months.*
10rm(9⇄)Annexe4⇄(1fb) CTV in all bedrooms ⓡ **T**
sB&B⇄£52-£60 dB&B⇄£64-£72 ▤
30P 🚗 ✤ *xmas*
❡ Lunch £7.50-£10.50&alc Dinner £13.50-£15&alc Last dinner
9.30pm
Credit Cards ①②③

**AMBERLEY** West Sussex Map **04** TQ01

🏵★★★**⚑75% Amberley Castle** BN18 9ND
☎Bury(0798)831992 FAX (0798) 831998
*This delightful hotel – rated Regional Best Newcomer in last
year's guide – was created by the clever transformation of a 900-
year-old castle, The beautifully designed and thoughtfully
equipped bedrooms within its ancient walls and battlements, many
of them overlooking lawns and gardens, are complemented by the
three comfortable lounges off the old hall and a first-floor
restaurant which features some fine restoration work. An
enthusiastic chef produces some imaginative menus, and the young
team of staff offers willing service.*
12⇄♠2🛏 CTV in all bedrooms ⓡ ✈ (ex guide dogs)
50P 🚗 ✤ ♪ (grass)
🍴 French **V** ❡ ⚿ Last dinner 10.30pm
Credit Cards ①②③⑤

✗**Quins** Houghton Bridge BN18 9LR (Close to Amberley Station
1m S of village) ☎Bury(0798)831790
*Attractively situated beside the River Arun on the medieval
Houghton Bridge (B2139), and named after the Harlequins rugby
football team, this friendly restaurant is personally run by George
and Marion Walker.*
Closed Mon, Tue & 1 wk end Apr & 1st 2 wks Oct
Dinner not served Sun
🍴 English, French & Swiss **V** 40 seats ✻ Last lunch 2.15pm Last
dinner 9.30pm 20P nc5yrs
Credit Cards ①③⑤

For key to symbols see the inside front cover.

**AMBLESIDE** Cumbria Map **07** NY30

See also **Elterwater**

★★★73% **Rothay Manor** Rothay Bridge LA22 0EH
☎(05394)33605 FAX (05394) 33607
Closed 2 Jan-8 Feb

*An elegant, Regency-style house set in its own well tended lawns and gardens, just outside Ambleside, on the Coniston road. Family run, comfortable and relaxing, service is unobtrusive, and there are many nice touches in bedrooms, such as iced water, fruit and small floral arrangements. Fresh flowers are also displayed throughout the hotel. Dinner is a much acclaimed and imaginative five-course meal. Although set, the menu offers an adequate choice of dishes for each course. Afternoon tea is also highly recommended, taken in the lounge, or on the lawns in summer. A charming hotel in every respect.*

15⇨Annexe3⇨(6fb) CTV in all bedrooms ® **T**
✈ (ex guide dogs) sB&B⇨£58-£63 dB&B⇨£82-£98 ⊟
30P ⊞ ✲ *xmas*
☋ English & Continental **V** ✧ ☕ ⊁ Sunday Lunch fr£12 High tea £4-£6 Dinner £17-£22.50 Last dinner 9pm
Credit Cards [1] [2] [3] [5]

★★★61% **Regent** Waterhead Bay LA22 0ES (1m S A591)
☎(05394)32254

*This comfortable hotel adjacent to Lake Windermere provides modern bedrooms, some in a purpose built block situated across a paved courtyard. The short table d'hôte menu served at dinner in the George IV restaurant is accompanied by an extensive wine list. Happy, young staff are supervised by the Hewitt family.*

21⇨↱(2fb)3⊞ CTV in all bedrooms ® **T** ✱
sB&B⇨↱£38-£43 dB&B⇨↱£64-£84 ⊟
30P ⊞ ⊡(heated) *xmas*
☋ English & French **V** ✧ ☕ ⊁ Bar Lunch £3-£8alc High tea £2-£5alc Dinner fr£16.50&alc Last dinner 9pm
Credit Cards [1] [3]

**See advertisement on page 75**

★★★54% **Waterhead** Lake Rd LA22 0ER (Best Western)
☎(05394)32566 Telex no 65273 FAX (05394) 34072

*A resort hotel at the southern end of town with views over the lake. Bedrooms are mainly compact and functional though some are more spacious and comfortable.*

27⇨↱(6fb) CTV in all bedrooms ® **T** S% sB&B⇨↱£32-£53 dB&B⇨↱£64-£102 ⊟
50P ✲ *xmas*
☋ English & French **V** ✧ ☕ ⊁ S% Sunday Lunch £7.95-£8.50 High tea £4.75-£5.25 Dinner £15.50&alc Last dinner 8.30pm
Credit Cards [1] [2] [3] [5]

★★76% **Wateredge** Borrans Rd, Waterhead LA22 0EP
☎(05394)32332
Closed mid Dec-early Feb

*Two 17th-century fisherman's cottages form the heart of this skilfully extended and remarkably comfortable hotel on the edge of Windermere. From the lounges there are lovely views of the lake, and the hotel's garden extends to the water's edge. Dinner in the oak-beamed dining room is very much a special occasion, with six courses of predominantly home-cooked English fare and a good selection of wines. The young staff provide a friendly and helpful service.*

18⇨↱Annexe5⇨↱(1fb) CTV in all bedrooms ® **T**
sB&B⇨↱£48.50-£59.50 dB&B⇨↱£84-£135 (incl dinner) ⊟
CTV 25P ⊞ ✲ rowing boat nc7yrs
✧ ☕ ⊁ Bar Lunch £2-£10.50alc Dinner £18.90 Last dinner 8.30pm
Credit Cards [1] [2] [3]

**See advertisement on page 75**

1991 marks the 25th anniversary of this guide.


Rothay Manor
HOTEL & RESTAURANT
★★★

*Set in its own grounds near Lake Windermere, this elegant Regency house has been run by the Nixon family for 22 years, and is one of the country's leading Country House Hotels. It is well-known for the excellence of its cuisine and service whilst retaining a relaxed atmosphere.*

**Ambleside, Cumbria LA22 0EH.**
**Tel: (05394) 33605**

*The*
GREY STONE HOTEL
★
***305 Manchester Road, West Timperley, Altrincham***
***Tel: 061-905 2233 Fax: 061-962 1458***

A detached residence recently modernised and extended. All bedrooms have en suite facilities, colour television, tea & coffee making facilities and direct dial telephone. An added luxury of a sauna is available at a nominal fee. Honeymoon Suite with Champagne breakfast. Conference facilities and Function Room are also available. The hotel is situated on the A56 near for junc 7 of the M53. Personal service at all times.

## Ambleside

★★⚑72% **Nanny Brow Country House** Clappersgate
LA22 9NF ☎(05394)32036 Telex no 265871
*This attractive Edwardian country house sits in its own grounds high above the A593, 2 miles from the town. A stylish and comfortable lounge, together with other more traditional rooms of the original house, are complemented by a garden wing of suites and studio bedrooms. The 6-course dinner is predominantly a set menu.*
19rm(16⇊1♠)(3fb)4⌷ CTV in all bedrooms ® T ✱
sB&B⇊♠£53-£88 dB&B⇊♠£86-£156 ₽
20P ⇎ ✿ ♪ solarium croquet spa bath *xmas*
♀ English & French V ♥ ⚏ ⅋ Lunch £8.50 High tea £3.75-£5.75alc Dinner £18.50 Last dinner 9pm
Credit Cards ①②③ⓔ

★★70% **Kirkstone Foot Country House** Kirkstone Pass Rd
LA22 9EH ☎(05394)32232
Closed 8-22 Dec & 3 Jan-early Feb
*A converted 17th-century manor house located in an attractive elevated position above the town with well-kept grounds in which the popular self catering cottages and apartments are situated. Lounges are comfortable and spacious, and provide guests with lots of books relating to local information. Emphasis is on traditional English food. A 5-course dinner, with no choice until pudding, is served at 8pm. Bedrooms are very pretty with all necessary facilities.*
15⇊♠(2fb) CTV in all bedrooms ® T ℋ S%
sB&B⇊♠£35-£47.50 dB&B⇊♠£70-£107 (incl dinner) ₽
35P ⇎ ✿ *xmas*
V ♥ ⚏ ⅋ High tea £5 Dinner £16 Last dinner 8.30pm
Credit Cards ①②③⑤ⓔ

★★70% **Skelwith Bridge** Skelwith Bridge LA22 9NJ (2.5m W A593) ☎(05394)32115 FAX (05394) 34254
*Set in very picturesque surroundings on the A593 2.5 miles from the town, this 17th-century lakeland inn retains a wealth of charm and character. Comfortable and well-equipped modern accommodation includes en suite bath and shower facilities, six bedrooms being located in a quaint stone-built annexe some 75 yards from the main hotel.*
23⇊♠Annexe6⇊♠(3fb)2⌷ℋin 6 bedrooms CTV in all bedrooms ® T sB&B⇊♠£22-£37 dB&B⇊♠£38-£68 ₽
60P ⇎ ♪
♀ English & French V ♥ ⚏ ⅋ Sunday Lunch £7.50-£8.25 Dinner £14.95-£15.95 Last dinner 9pm
Credit Cards ①③ⓔ

★★69% **Riverside** Under Loughrigg, Rothay Bridge LA22 9LJ
☎(05394)32395
Closed Dec-Jan
*Standing amid its own well-tended gardens in a country lane, and looking across the River Rothay to Loughrigg Fell, the hotel offers attractive, comfortable public rooms – its peaceful setting and relaxing ambience belying the fact that the town is only ten minutes' walk away.*
10⇊♠(2fb)1⌷ CTV in all bedrooms ® T ℋ (ex guide dogs) dB&B⇊♠£68-£76 (incl dinner) ₽
CTV 20P ⇎ ✿ ♪ nc8yrs
♀ Continental V ♥ ⚏ ⅋ Bar Lunch £3-£6 Dinner £15-£16alc Last dinner 8pm
Credit Cards ①③

★★68% **Fisherbeck** Lake Rd LA22 0DH ☎(05394)33215
Closed 25 Dec-13 Jan
*A comfortable and efficiently maintained hotel, beside the A591 on its southern approach to the town, provides well-equipped bedrooms and a good standard of cuisine.*
20rm(17⇊♠)(3fb) CTV in all bedrooms ® T ℋ
sB&B£26.50-£49 sB&B⇊♠frf49 dB&B£45-£50
dB&B⇊♠£53-£59 ₽
CTV 24P ⇎

▶

**A**

V ✿ ⍟ Bar Lunch £3.50-£10.50alc Dinner £13.75-£15 Last
dinner 8pm
Credit Cards 1 3

**★★⚑66%, Crow How** Rydal Rd LA22 9PN ☎(05394)32193
RS 10 Nov-8 Apr
*Beautifully located in attractive gardens three-quarters of a mile
north of Ambleside, the hotel provides comfortable, well decorated
bedrooms, a relaxing lounge and a cosy bar.*
9rm(7⇨1�ંⰙ)(2fb) CTV in all bedrooms ® sB&B£20-£23
dB&B£40-£46 dB&B⇨🌘£48-£55 ⅊
9P ⊞ ✿
♔ English & French V ✿ ⍟ Dinner £10 Last dinner 7.30pm
£

**★★64%, Borrans Park** Borrans Rd LA22 0EN ☎(05394)33454
Closed 3 days Xmas
*This fine Georgian house is set in its own landscaped gardens on
the southern outskirts of the town. It has been extended to provide
comfortable public rooms and some very attractive bedrooms. A 4
course dinner is served at about 7pm and breakfasts, too, are
enjoyable. The hotel offers good value for money and pleasantly
relaxed service.*
14rm(9⇨4🌘)(2fb)7⊞ CTV in all bedrooms ® T ✕ S%
sB&B£26-£64 dB&B⇨🌘£52-£64 ⅊
20P ⊞ ✿ nc7yrs
V ⍥ S% Dinner £13 Last dinner 8pm
Credit Cards 1 3

**★★63%, Elder Grove** Lake Rd LA22 0DB (on A591 .5m S)
☎(05394)32504
Closed mid Nov-mid Feb
*Several of this homely, family-run hotel's pleasantly decorated
bedrooms are quite spacious, while public areas include two
lounges, a cosy bar and a restaurant where dinner is served at 7.30
prompt*
12⇨🌘(1fb)1⊞ CTV in all bedrooms ® sB&B⇨🌘fr£23
dB&B⇨🌘fr£46 ⅊
CTV 12P ⊞
V ✿ ⍟ ⍥ Bar Lunch 60p-£3.50 Dinner £11.50-£13 Last dinner
7.30pm
Credit Cards 1 3

**★★60%, Glen Rothay** Rydal LA22 9LR ☎(05394)32524
*A quaint, historical hotel, close to the road yet set back in the
rockside and surrounded by its own gardens. Bedrooms vary
considerably in size.*
11⇨🌘(2fb)3⊞ CTV in all bedrooms ® sB&B⇨🌘fr£25
dB&B⇨🌘fr£50 ⅊
35P ⊞ ✿ ♪ xmas
V ✿ ⍥ Dinner £15.95-£25 Last dinner 8pm
Credit Cards 1 3 £

**★★56%, Horseshoe** Rothay Rd LA22 0EE ☎(05394)32000
*This family-run tourist hotel offers bedrooms in various styles and
compact but tastefully decorated public rooms, the cosy bar serving
drinks to residents and diners only. In the dining room a wholefood
breakfast is available as an alternative to the more traditional
range of dishes.*
20rm(1⇨10🌘)(5fb)1⊞ CTV in all bedrooms ®
19P ⊞
V ⍥ Last dinner 7.30pm
Credit Cards 1 3

**AMERSHAM** Buckinghamshire Map **04** SU99

**★★62%, The Crown** High St HP7 0DH (Trusthouse Forte)
☎(0494)721541 FAX (0494) 431283
*This Elizabethan inn with a handsome Georgian façade retains
many of its original features and embodies the charm of history.
The comfortable accommodation has been tastefully arranged to
suit the building. A varied menu of good, imaginative cooking is
offered.*

23rm(13⇨1🌘) CTV in all bedrooms ® ✳ sBfr£60
sB⇨🌘£70-£75 dBfr£70 dB⇨🌘£85-£90 (room only) ⅊
51P *xmas*
V ✿ ⍟ ⍥ Lunch fr£8.50&alc Dinner £14-£16.95&alc Last
dinner 9.30pm
Credit Cards 1 2 3 4 5

**AMESBURY** Wiltshire Map **04** SU14

⌂**Travelodge** SP4 7AS (on A303) (Trusthouse Forte)
☎(0980)624966 Central res (0800) 850950
*This lodge on the A303, is designed for the motorist, with ample
parking and an adjacent Little Chef restaurant. Bedrooms are
spacious, well equipped and have en suite facilities.*
32⇨🌘(32fb) CTV in all bedrooms ® sB⇨🌘£24
dB⇨🌘£29.50 (room only)
⦅ 32P ⊞
Credit Cards 1 2 3

**AMLWCH** Gwynedd Map **06** SH49

**★★60%, Trecastell** Bull Bay LL68 9SA (Frederic Robinson)
☎(0407)830651
*A detached hotel overlooking the bay offers good all-round
facilities and comforts.*
12rm(8⇨3🌘)(3fb) CTV in 10 bedrooms ® sB&B£20-£22
sB&B⇨🌘£20-£22 dB&B£33-£35 dB&B⇨🌘£33-£35 ⅊
CTV 60P ⊞ ✿
⍥ Bar Lunch £2-£6 Dinner £8.95-£10.95&alc Last dinner
8.30pm
Credit Cards 1 2 3

**AMMANFORD** Dyfed Map **02** SN61

**★★67%, Mill at Glynhir** Glyn-Hir, Llandybie SA18 2TE (3m
NE off A483) (Exec Hotel) ☎(0269)850672
RS 24-28 Dec
*Probably originating as an old flour mill, and reputed to have
connections with the French Revolution, this comfortable hotel
provides well-equipped bedrooms with all modern facilities and
well cooked, enjoyable meals served in the attractive restaurant.
Free golf is available at the adjacent golf course.*
9⇨🌘Annexe2⇨🌘 CTV in all bedrooms ® T S%
sB&B⇨🌘£29 dB&B⇨🌘£58 ⅊
20P ⊞ ✿ ▭(heated) ▶ 18 ♪ nc11yrs
♔ Welsh & French V ✿ S% Dinner £12&alc Last dinner
8.30pm
Credit Cards 1 3

**AMPFIELD** Hampshire Map **04** SU32

**★★★62%, Potters Heron** SO51 9ZF (Lansbury)
☎Southampton(0703)266611 Telex no 47459
FAX (0703) 251359
*A picturesque, thatched hotel of charm with a modern bedroom
block at the rear. Most rooms have been totally refurbished, work
on the remainder is planned for 1991. The very busy Potters Pub
provides a popular pantry food operation, whilst the restaurant
features a choice of menus.*
60⇨🌘(3fb)1⊞🌘in 12 bedrooms CTV in all bedrooms ® ✕
sB&B⇨🌘fr£77 dB&B⇨🌘fr£90 ⅊
Lift ⦅ 200P CFA sauna gymnasium *xmas*
♔ English & French V ✿ ⍟ Lunch fr£11&alc Dinner
fr£11&alc Last dinner 10pm
Credit Cards 1 2 3 5

Entries for red-star hotels are highlighted by a
tint panel. For a full list of these establishments
consult the Contents page.

**A**

**ANDOVER** Hampshire Map **04** SU34

★★★63% **Ashley Court** Micheldever Rd SP11 6LA
☎(0264)57344 FAX (0264) 56755
*This quietly situated business/conference hotel, now offering new bedrooms, has various sizes of conference room (with syndicate rooms) available and supplies conference equipment. The Rendezvous Restaurant presents an à la carte menu at both lunch and dinner, friendly service being provided by smartly uniformed staff.*
35⇨⁴↑✗in 8 bedrooms CTV in all bedrooms ® T
sB&B⇨↑£60-£65
dB&B⇨↑£78-£80 Continental breakfast ⊟
*xmas*
♀ English & Continental V ⍟ ⊒ Bar Lunch £1.50-£6.50alc
Dinner £9.50-£14.50 Last dinner 9.30pm
Credit Cards ①②③④

★★61% **Danebury** High St SP10 1NX ☎(0264)23332
Telex no 47587 FAX (0264) 334021
*Parts of this commercial hotel in the centre of town date back to the sixteenth century, but its comfortable bedrooms provide all the modern facilities expected by today's business user. A varied à la carte menu is available in the informal dining room, and public bars are popular with local trade.*
24⇨1🖼 CTV in all bedrooms ® T 🐾 (ex guide dogs) ✳
sB&B⇨fr£59 dB&B⇨fr£71 ⊟
⊄ CTV 40P 🚲 *xmas*
♀ European V ⍟ ⊒ ✗ Lunch £11-£17alc Dinner £12&alc Last dinner 10.30pm
Credit Cards ①②③⑤④

For key to symbols see the inside front cover.

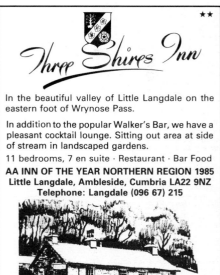

**A**

## ANNAN Dumfries & Galloway *Dumfriesshire* Map **11** NY16

★★65% **Warmanbie Hotel & Restaurant** DG12 5LL
☎(04612)4015
*A modernised country house on the outskirts of town which is
informally run. Bedrooms are well-appointed and reflect some
thoughtful touches; some of the bedrooms are spacious and
traditionally furnished, while others are more compact and modern
in style. With its own stretch of water, this compact Georgian
house is very popular with fishermen.*
7⇁♪(1fb) CTV in all bedrooms ® T sB&B⇁♪fr£39.75
dB&B⇁♪fr£55 ₽
25P 1🐾 ❄ ♪ clay pigeon shooting *xmas*
V ♥ ♨ Sunday Lunch fr£6.95 Dinner fr£12.95 Last dinner
9.30pm
Credit Cards 1 2 3 £

★★64% *Queensberry Arms* ☎(04612)2024
*New owners are refurbishing this town-centre commercial hotel
which offers comfortable and well equipped bedrooms.*
27rm(8⇁16♪)(4fb) CTV in all bedrooms ®
25P 6🐾 ❄
V ♥ ♨ Last dinner 9.30pm
Credit Cards 1 2 3 5

★53%, *Corner House* High St DG12 6DL (Mount Charlotte (TS))
☎(04612)2754
*A friendly, town centre commercial hotel which also caters for
coach tours and local functions. It offers wholesome food and plain,
practical budget accommodation.*
31rm(1⇁)(3fb) ®
CTV 40P
🍴 Mainly grills ♥ ♨
Credit Cards 1 2 3 5

## ANSTRUTHER Fife Map **12** NO50

★★★60% **Craws Nest** Bankwell Rd KY10 3DA ☎(0333)310691
Telex no 727049 FAX (0333) 312216
*Popular with tourists, golfers and business people, this hotel has a
superior annexe wing of spacious and comfortable bedrooms.*
31⇁♪Annexe19⇁♪(4fb)2☷ CTV in all bedrooms ® T
✖ (ex guide dogs) sB&B⇁♪£32-£46 dB&B⇁♪£54-£80 ₽
CTV 150P ❄ solarium games room ♫ *xmas*
V ♥ ♨ Lunch £8.50-£10 High tea £5.50-£8 Dinner
£14.80-£16&alc Last dinner 9pm
Credit Cards 1 2 3 4 5

★★62% **Smugglers Inn** High St KY10 3DQ ☎(0333)310506
*A former inn, set in the main street but having views of the Firth of
Forth to the rear, offers accommodation in bedrooms that are for
the most part compact.*
8⇁♪ CTV in all bedrooms T sB&B⇁♪£23.50-£25
dB&B⇁♪£47-£50
CTV 12P
🍴 Scottish, French & Italian V ♥ Lunch £7-£10 Dinner
£11.50-£14&alc Last dinner 9.30pm
Credit Cards 1 2 3 5

❋✕✕*Cellar* 24 East Green KY10 3AA ☎(0333)310378
*A delightful restaurant specialising in fish, and appropriately
located in a narrow street behind the harbour. Live fires, beams
and warm friendly service combine to create a congenial
atmosphere in which to sample the mouthwatering meat and fish
dishes prepared by chef/proprietor Peter Jukes.*
Closed Sun, 24 Dec-4 Jan & 1 wk May
Lunch not served Mon
🍴 French 32 seats Last lunch 1.30pm Last dinner 9.30pm
nc5yrs ✂
Credit Cards 1 2 3

## ANSTY Warwickshire Map **04** SP38

★★★70%, **Ansty Hall** CV7 9HZ ☎Coventry(0203)612222
FAX (0203) 602155
*Set in 8 acres of garden and parkland, this mellow red-brick
Caroline house has been carefully and sympathetically furnished.
The hotel is spacious and comfortable, and the bedrooms are
particularly well-equipped.*
24⇁♪Annexe6⇁♪✂in 8 bedrooms CTV in all bedrooms T
✖ (ex guide dogs) ✳ sB⇁♪£70 dB⇁♪£90 (room only) ₽
50P 💷 ❄ *xmas*
V ♥ ♨ ✂ Lunch £15-£17.50&alc High tea £6 Dinner
£15-£18.50&alc Last dinner 9.45pm
Credit Cards 1 2 3 5 £
**See advertisement under COVENTRY**

## APPIN Strathclyde *Argyllshire* Map **14** NN04

★★★73%, **Invercreran Country House** Glen Creran PA38 4BJ
☎(063173)414 & 456 FAX (063173) 532
Closed Dec-Feb
*Built originally as a private residence only 20 years ago, this
unique and imposing building is surrounded by its own grounds and
offers magnificent views across the glen from its hillside position. It
is now run as a small, select country house hotel by the Kersley
family, who ensure that hospitality is second to none. The spacious
lounge has french windows leading onto a balcony and takes full
advantage of the hotel's delightful position; drinks are served here,
as there is no bar. In the lovely dining room guests can enjoy a
four-course dinner, cooked in modern style with excellent use made
of the best Scottish seafood, meat and game.*
7⇁♪(3fb)✂in 1 bedroom CTV in all bedrooms T
✖ (ex guide dogs) sB&B⇁♪£71-£86
dB&B⇁♪£120-£170 (incl dinner) ₽
18P ❄ sauna nc5yrs *xmas*
V ♥ ♨ ✂ Lunch £10-£22alc Dinner £25 Last dinner 8pm
Credit Cards 1 3 £

## APPLEBY-IN-WESTMORLAND Cumbria Map **12** NY62

★★★⚑68%, **Appleby Manor Country House** Roman Rd
CA16 6JD (Best Western) ☎Appleby(07683)51571
Telex no 94012971 FAX (07683) 52888
Closed 24-26 Dec

*This red sandstone building, standing amid its own gardens in an
elevated position overlooking the town, was built as a private
residence in Victorian times. Now much extended , it offers
accommodation in thoughtfully equipped bedrooms which are
clean and well maintained – though those in the converted coach
house are rather more compact, and light sleepers may be
disturbed by traffic noise from the adjacent A66. Public areas are
comfortable, a relaxed and informal style of service being provided
throughout.*
23⇁♪Annexe7⇁♪(8fb)2☷ CTV in all bedrooms ® T
sB&B⇁♪£42.50-£53 dB&B⇁♪£65-£84 ₽
40P 3🐾 (£1) ❄ ▣(heated) sauna solarium gymnasium croquet
jacuzzi pool table steam room
V ♥ ♨ ✂ Lunch £13-£14.50&alc Dinner £13-£14.50&alc Last
dinner 9pm
Credit Cards 1 2 3 5

★★★67%, **Tufton Arms** Market Square CA16 6XA (Consort)
☎Appleby(07683)51593 FAX (07683) 52761
*This elegantly restored hotel is situated in the town centre. The
comfortable drawing room with its open fire, the half panelled bar
with interesting photographs, and the luxurious conservatory
restaurant are all in a tasteful Victorian style, and a high standard
of cuisine is offered from the extensive à la carte menu. Bedrooms
have been individually furnished and decorated, two have their own
sitting rooms, and there are also six simpler rooms, designed more
for the business client.*
19⇁♪(2fb) CTV in all bedrooms ® T ✳ sB&B⇁♪£30-£40
dB&B⇁♪£45-£95 ₽
CTV 15P 2🐾 💷 ♪ shooting *xmas*

A

V ✿ ♨ Lunch £7.25-£11.90alc Dinner £11.50&alc Last dinner 9.30pm
Credit Cards 1 3

★★61% **Royal Oak Inn** Bongate CA16 6UN
☎Appleby(07683)51463
*This traditional coaching inn, dating back to the 15th century, has attractive bedrooms and serves very good food.*
6rm(1⇨2♠) CTV in all bedrooms ® ⅻ
ⅲ ♪ ∪
⛬ International ✿
Credit Cards 1 2 3

★★59% **White Hart** Boroughgate CA16 6XG
☎Appleby(07683)51598
*This 18th-century, small, modernised hotel is situated in the town centre.*
15rm(7⇨3♠)(4fb)✂in all bedrooms CTV in all bedrooms ® T
✳ sB&B£14-£25 sB&B⇨♠£17-£30 dB&B£34-£40
dB&B⇨♠£40-£45 ⋤
CTV 6P hairdresser beauty consultant
⛬ International V ✿ ♨ Lunch £9&alc Dinner £9&alc Last dinner 9.30pm
Credit Cards 1 2 3 5 ⓔ

★58% **Courtfield** Bongate CA16 6UP ☎Appleby(07683)51394
*Standing in three acres of gardens on the approach road into the town from the direction of Brough, this one-time vicarage offers wholesome meals, generously served, and the opportunity to relax in comfortable public rooms where log fires blaze during the colder months.*
6rm(2⇨2♠)Annexe5rm(1⇨)(1fb) CTV in 6 bedrooms TV in 2 bedrooms ®
CTV 20P 2🎾 🚗 ✿ ⚸
V ✿ ♨ Last dinner 8pm

**A**

**APPLETON-LE-MOORS** North Yorkshire Map **08** SE78

★★⚔73%, **Dweldapilton Hall** YO6 6TF
☎Lastingham(07515)227 & 452 FAX (07515) 540
Closed Jan
*The early Regency/Victorian house stands in attractively
landscaped grounds at the centre of a moorland village. The public
rooms are furnished in the style of the period and the comfortable
bedrooms have been upgraded and restored. The atmosphere is
relaxing.*
12➩↑1🗗 CTV in all bedrooms ℝ ✹ sB&B➩↑£40
dB&B➩↑£80-£100 🍴
Lift CTV 30P ⇄ ✤ croquet nc12yrs *xmas*
♀ English & Continental V ✿ ⚉ Bar Lunch £5.50-£10.50
Dinner £18.50-£21.50 Last dinner 8.15pm
Credit Cards ①②③①

**ARBROATH** Tayside *Angus* Map **12** NO64

★★★66%, **Letham Grange** Colliston DD11 4RL (Best Western)
☎Gowanbank(024189)373 FAX (024189) 414
*This handsome Victorian mansion, in its two hundred acres of
wooded grounds, provides an ideal centre for either business guest
or leisure-seeker; comfortable, individually designed bedrooms
have been thoughtfully equipped, public areas are elegantly
appointed and outdoor facilities include both and 18-hole
championship golf course and a 4-sheet curling rink.*
19➩↑(4fb)1🗗 CTV in all bedrooms ℝ ✖ (ex guide dogs) ✹
sB&B➩↑£52-£62 dB&B➩↑£80-£90 🍴
《100P ⇄ ↑ 18 ♪ (hard & grass) ∪ croquet putting pool tables
*xmas*
♀ International V ✿ ⚉ Lunch fr£9 High tea fr£6.50 Dinner
fr£16 Last dinner 9.30pm
Credit Cards ①②③⑤①

★★58%, **Hotel Seaforth** Dundee Rd DD11 1QF ☎(0241)72232
*On the southern edge of the town, this hotel is family owned and
managed and offers modest, but serviceable bedrooms which vary
in size. There is a leisure centre and in the small, comfortable
restaurant à la carte and table d'hôte meals are available.*
18➩(2fb) CTV in all bedrooms ℝ T ✹ sB&B➩£29.50-£32.50
dB&B➩£39.50-£42.50 (incl dinner) 🍴
100P ✤ 🗗(heated) snooker sauna solarium gymnasium
jacuzzi *xmas*
V ✿ ⚉ Lunch £5.95-£6.95 Dinner £15&alc Last dinner 9.30pm
Credit Cards ①②③⑤

✖✖*Carriage Room* Meadow Bank Inn, Montrose Rd DD11 5RA
☎(0241)75755
*This small, friendly and well-appointed restaurant stands beside
the A92, forming part of a complex on the northern fringe of the
town. The à la carte menu offers a range of imaginative French
and Scottish dishes with game in season and a selection of fresh,
local sea food which is particularly recommended. Also worthy of
mention is the delicious bread and butter pudding with a yoghurt
sauce.*
Closed Sun, Mon & 1st wk Jan
Lunch not served Sat
♀ Scottish & French V 54 seats Last lunch 2pm Last dinner
9.30pm 200P ⅍
Credit Cards ①②③⑤

**ARCHIRONDEL**

See **Jersey under Channel Islands**

---

All AA-appointed establishments are
inspected regularly to ensure that required
standards are maintained.

---

**ARDELVE** Highland *Ross & Cromarty* Map **14** NG82

✤★76%, **Loch Duich** IV40 8DY ☎Dornie(059985)213
Closed Nov-Etr
(Rosette awarded for dinner only)
*Conveniently placed for travellers to and from the Isle of Skye, this
hospitable small hotel affords its guests a lovely view of that much
photographed Scottish castle, Eilean Donan. It is of course rather
more than the outlook that draws visitors here – Rod, Bryan and
Francis Stenson are good hosts and the cooking of Carol Macrae
is definitely a prospect that pleases. Fresh produce, particularly
seafood, is beautifully cooked, resulting in dishes with genuine
flavour – and all at very reasonable prices. Good bar meals are
also available in the popular public bar where many an impromptu
Ceilidh may enliven the evening. Bedrooms are comfortable but
there are only two with en-suite bathrooms.*
18rm(2➩↑)(1fb)⅍in 2 bedrooms ✹ sB&B£22-£25
dB&B£44-£50 dB&B➩↑£54-£60 🍴
CTV 40P 1➾ ⇄ ✤ fishing shooting
V ✿ ⚉ ⅍ Bar Lunch £1.25-£6alc Dinner fr£16 Last dinner
9pm
Credit Cards ①③①

**ARDENTINNY** Strathclyde *Argyllshire* Map **10** NS18

★★64%, **Ardentinny** PA23 8TR ☎(036981)209 & 275
FAX (036981) 345
Closed Nov-15 Mar
*Friendly roadside inn full of character and delightfully situated
with gardens leading down to the sea. Popular with yachtsmen and
those who enjoy good food.*
11rm(5➩↑)(1fb) CTV in all bedrooms ℝ sB&B➩↑£25-£37
dB&B➩↑£40-£70 🍴
CTV 30P ✤ boating
♀ Scottish, French & German V ✿ ⚉ ⅍ Sunday Lunch
£5-£12alc Dinner £17.50&alc Last dinner 9.30pm
Credit Cards ①②③⑤

**ARDEONAIG** Central *Perthshire* Map **11** NN63

★★57%, **Ardeonaig** South Loch Tayside FK21 8SU
☎Killin(05672)400
Closed 5 Nov-12 Jan
*A relaxed atmosphere prevails in the cosy public areas of this
family run hotel peacefully situated on the south shore of Loch
Tay, much of its original character as a coaching inn having been
retained, and modestly appointed bedrooms are gradually being
upgraded.*
12➩↑(2fb) ℝ sB&B➩↑£25-£27 dB&B➩↑£50-£54 🍴
CTV 40P ⇄ ✤ ♪ clay pigeon shooting canoeing
♀ Scottish, English & Continental ✿ ⚉ Bar Lunch
£6.50-£12.50 Dinner £15-£18 Last dinner 9pm
Credit Cards ①②③⑤

**ARDUAINE** Strathclyde *Argyllshire* Map **10** NM80

★★★68%, **Loch Melfort** PA34 4XG ☎Kilmelford(08522)233
FAX (08522) 214
Closed mid Oct-Etr
*Boldly claiming to be 'The finest location on the west coast', this
family-owned hotel lives up to expectations, with superb views
southwards of the sea and islands, which, on fine days, has few
equals. Many improvements have been made by Philip and
Rosalind Lewis, particularly to the 20 bedroomed Cedar Wing,
where rooms either have balconies or patios from which to enjoy
the view. The table d'hôte menu, with supplements, makes good use
of local seafood and meats, as well as quality imported items. The
Chart Room Bar serves food for most of the day, and is popular
with families and the yachting fraternity.*
6rm(3➩)Annexe20➩ CTV in 3 bedrooms ℝ
CTV 40P ✤

V ✿ ☡ Last dinner 8.30pm
Credit Cards ①

See advertisement under OBAN

**ARDVASAR**
See Skye, Isle of

**ARISAIG** Highland *Inverness-shire* Map **13** NM68

**★★★**

**★★★ ♨ ARISAIG HOUSE**

Beasdale PH39 4NR (3m E
A830) (Relais et Châteaux)
☎(06875)622
Telex no 777279
FAX (06875) 626
Closed 11 Nov-8 Mar
*Externally this house may
strike a sombre note amid its well tended gardens, but inside
all is aglow with natural light. Colourful flower displays
enliven the inner hall with its warm oak staircase and the
drawing room with its unusual Italian vaulted ceiling and deep
armchairs where guests may sink into quiet oblivion. A
number of features from the 1930s, when the present house
was rebuilt on the site of the original Victorian mansion, have
been retained, notably the panelled dining room and the
splendid 2nd-floor billiards room. A new chef was appointed
last year and is already making a good impression – breakfast
is certainly worth getting up for. Day to day running of the
hotel is capably managed by the staff but guests are sure to
make the acquaintance of one or other of the Smithers family
who own Arisaig and to receive a warm welcome.*

15rm(13⇨) CTV in all bedrooms T ✖ (ex guide dogs)
sB&B⇨£77-£82.85 dB&B⇨£198-£242 (incl dinner) 🅱

16P ⇔ ✿ snooker croquet nc10yrs

🎋 British & French ✿ ☡ ✔ Bar Lunch £12-£18alc Dinner
£33 Last dinner 8.30pm
Credit Cards ① ③

---

**★★64%, Arisaig** PH39 4NH ☎(06875)210
*A roadside hotel with commanding views of the island of Eigg.
Highland hospitality is provided by the Stewart family and
includes good, honest food using local produce, particularly
seafood.*
15rm(6⇨)(4fb) Ⓡ T sB&B£22-£30 dB&B£44-£60
dB&B⇨£53-£72.50
CTV 60P ⇔
V ✿ ☡ ✔ Bar Lunch £2-£15alc High tea £2-£15alc Dinner
£15-£21 Last dinner 8.30pm
Credit Cards ① ③

See advertisement on page 83

---

**ARNCLIFFE** North Yorkshire Map **07** SD97

**★★♨76%, Amerdale House** BD23 5QE ☎(075677)250
Closed mid Nov-mid Mar
*This former manor house is set on the edge of a peaceful and
attractive village, within easy access of all the tourist attractions,
and set amid beautiful dales countryside. Bedrooms are
comfortable and well furnished, and there is an elegant drawing
room in which guests can relax. Food is all freshly prepared by the
proprietor, who takes great pride in producing an imaginative and
skilfully prepared menu. The atmosphere is relaxed and the staff
are attentive and welcoming.*
11⇨↿(3fb)1⊠ CTV in all bedrooms Ⓡ ✖ (ex guide dogs) ✱
sB&B⇨↿£46-£49 dB&B⇨↿£82-£88 (incl dinner)
30P ⇔ ✿

---

# Loch Duich Hotel ★ ❀

## Ardelve, Ross & Cromarty
## Telephone: (0599) 85213

*A friendly and comfortable hotel
overlooking the famous Eilean Donan
Castle and the mountains of Skye and
Kintail. The food is imaginative and
makes use of local produce, rosette
awarded for dinner, complemented by
an interesting wine list.*

---

# Carriage Room Restaurant
## ✖✖
## Meadow Bank Inn, Montrose Road, Arbroath, Angus DD11 5RA
## Telephone: 0241 75755

Small, friendly restaurant situated
near the A92. The menu offers a
range of imaginative French and
Scottish dishes with game in season
and a selection of fresh, local
seafood. Children welcome.
Large car park.

*Closed — Sunday & Monday and
lunch Saturday*

Amex    Access    Visa    Diners cards accepted

V ⊬ Dinner £15 Last dinner 8.30pm
Credit Cards [1] [3]

---

**ARRAN, ISLE OF** Strathclyde *Bute* Map **10**

---

**BRODICK** Map **10** NS03

★★★**72%**, *Auchrannie Country House* KA27 8BZ
☎(0770)2234 & 2235
*A modernised and extended Victorian sandstone mansion – former home of the Dowager Duchess of Hamilton – that stands in 10 acres of tree-studded grounds. A good array of facilities in the bedrooms ensures comfort, and the public rooms retain much of their original charm. The Garden Restaurant boasts varied menus, with an emphasis on local produce, and seafood features strongly.*
12⇌(1fb) CTV in all bedrooms ® T ✠
30P ⇱ ✿
♡ Scottish & French V ⊹ 🕮 Last dinner 10pm
Credit Cards [1] [3]

---

**LAGG** Map **10** NR92

★★**65%**, **Lagg** Kilmory KA27 8PQ ☎Sliddery(077087)255
*This picturesque, 18th-century coaching inn stands amid 10 acres of woodland, its well-kept gardens extending to the Lagg Burn. Welcoming log fires burn in the relaxing lounge and bar areas, while bedrooms, though they vary in size and are fairly modestly equipped, are comfortable. Enjoyable home-cooked meals are based on fresh local produce and helpful service is provided by friendly young staff.*
15⇌🔥(3fb) ® S% sB&B⇌🔥£27-£46
dB&B⇌🔥£54-£92 (incl dinner)
CTV 40P ⇱ ✿ ♩ xmas
♡ Scottish & French V ⊹ 🕮 S% Lunch £5.50-£15alc High tea £5-£10alc Dinner £10-£16&alc Last dinner 9pm

---

**LAMLASH** Map **10** NS03

★★**66%**, **Glenisle** KA27 8LS ☎(07706)559 & 258
*Set on the sea front, overlooking Holy Isle, a small, personally-run hotel has been completely refurbished to offer comfortable, well appointed and equipped bedrooms complemented by attractive public areas which include a compact lounge and cocktail bar, enjoyable meals featuring fresh local produce are served in a popular restaurant whose pleasant view takes in both the carefully-tended garden and the sea.*
13⇌🔥 CTV in all bedrooms ® T sB&B⇌🔥£20.50-£25.50
dB&B⇌🔥£41-£51 ◨
10P ⇱ ✿ xmas
V ⊹ Lunch £3.50-£4.50alc Dinner £8-£11.50alc Last dinner 9pm
Credit Cards [1] [3] ④

---

**WHITING BAY** Map **10** NS02

★**57%**, *Cameronia* KA27 8PZ ☎(07707)254
RS Nov-Mar
*A small, homely, family-run hotel looking out across the sea to the mainland.*
5🔥(1fb) CTV in all bedrooms ® ✠
6P ⇱ nc5yrs
⊹ Last dinner 9pm

---

**ARUNDEL** West Sussex Map **04** TQ00

★★★**67%**, **Norfolk Arms** High St BN18 9AD (Forestdale)
☎(0903)882101 Telex no 878436 FAX (0903) 884275
*An original Georgian coaching inn, tastefully and skilfully modernised to retain all its historical features and an atmosphere of traditional permanence, provides well equipped bedrooms with public rooms which include two bars, the Arun Restaurant and breakfast room and a comfortable lounge. Good levels of service are provided by a professional management.*

---

21⇌Annexe13⇌(1fb)6✿⊬in 3 bedrooms CTV in all
bedrooms ® T ✱ sB&B⇌£44.50-£49.50 dB&B⇌£65-£80 ◨
⟪ 15P 15⚘ xmas
♡ International V ⊹ 🕮 ⊬ Lunch £8.95-£9.95 Dinner
£15-£20alc Last dinner 10pm
Credit Cards [1] [2] [3] [4] [5]

★⚑**63%**, **Burpham Country** Old Down, Burpham BN18 9RJ (3m
NE off A27) ☎(0903)882160
*Enjoying a peaceful location, this small, privately-run hotel has attractive bedrooms, furnished in traditional style. Service is friendly and very helpful.*
10rm(8⇌1🔥) CTV in all bedrooms ® ✠ sB&B⇌🔥£36-£40
dB&B⇌🔥£54-£64 ◨
12P ⇱ ✿ nc12yrs xmas
V ⊹ 🕮 ⊬ Lunch £9-£11 Dinner £11.50-£13.50 Last dinner
8pm
Credit Cards [1] [3]

---

**ASCOT** Berkshire Map **04** SU96

During the currency of this publication Ascot telephone numbers are liable to change.

★★★★**56%**, **The Royal Berkshire** London Rd, Sunninghill
SL5 0PP (Hilton) ☎(0990)23322 Telex no 847280
FAX (0990) 27100
*A large, conference-orientated hotel set in several acres of quiet grounds offers leisure facilities, a formal dining room and a choice of accommodation ranging from the larger rooms in the original to modern, purpose-built ones and those in the courtyard.*
64⇌🔥Annexe18⇌(2fb)2✿ CTV in all bedrooms ® T ✱
sB&B⇌🔥£100-£150 dB&B⇌🔥£120-£170 (room only) ◨
⟪ 150P ✿ ◫(heated) ♪ (hard) squash sauna croquet xmas
V ⊹ 🕮 Lunch fr17.50&alc Dinner fr23.50&alc Last dinner
10pm
Credit Cards [1] [2] [3]

★★★★**50%**, **Berystede** Bagshot Rd, Sunninghill SL5 9JH
(Trusthouse Forte) ☎(0990)23311 due to change to
(0344) 23311 Telex no 847707 FAX (0990) 872301
*Set in attractive grounds, this smart, well-appointed hotel continues to upgrade its bedrooms. It is popular with both conferences and private guests.*
91⇌(6fb)2✿⊬in 30 bedrooms CTV in all bedrooms ® T ✱
sB&B⇌🔥fr£86 dB&B⇌🔥fr£103 (room only) ◨
Lift ⟪ 240P 1⚘ ✿ ◲(heated) games room xmas
♡ English & French V ⊹ 🕮 Lunch fr£15 Dinner fr£19 Last
dinner 9.45pm
Credit Cards [1] [2] [3] [4] [5]

---

**ASHBOURNE** Derbyshire Map **07** SK14

★★★**69%**, **Ashbourne Lodge** Derby Rd DE6 1XH (Best
Western) ☎(0335)46666 Telex no 378560 FAX (0335) 46549
*A modern hotel on the main Derby road caters for tourists, business people and functions, combining high standards with an awareness of local traditions and culture.*
51⇌(5fb)⊬in 11 bedrooms CTV in all bedrooms ® T
✠ (ex guide dogs) ✱ sB&B⇌£65-£90 dB&B⇌£80-£95 ◨
Lift ⟪ 180P ✿ CFA xmas
♡ International V ⊹ 🕮 Lunch £4.80-£10&alc Dinner £15&alc
Last dinner 10.45pm
Credit Cards [1] [2] [3] [5] ④

★★★**59%**, **Beresford Arms** Station Rd DE6 1AA
☎(0335)300035 FAX (0335) 300065
*Personally run by Peter and Karen Wells this is a fully renovated town centre hotel with well-equipped, tastefully furnished bedrooms and a quality restaurant.*
12⇌🔥(1fb) CTV in all bedrooms ® T ✠ (ex guide dogs) ✱
sB&B⇌🔥£45-£50 dB&B⇌🔥£50-£55 ◨
30P ⇱ xmas

♀ English & French V ✿ ⌂ Lunch £8-£11&alc High tea fr£5
Dinner £12.50-£15&alc Last dinner 9.30pm
Credit Cards ① ② ③ ⓔ

★★⚑74% **Callow Hall** Mappleton Rd DE6 2AA
☎(0335)43403 & 43164 FAX (0335) 43624
Closed 25-26 Dec & 2 wks Feb
*"Small is beautiful" might well be the motto of this hotel, which
stands half a mile from the town centre in an elevated position
overlooking 14 acres of grounds. The home of the Spencer family,
who personally supervise the day-to-day running, it offers
accommodation in well designed, extremely comfortable and warm
bedrooms; the proprietor is an experienced chef who is well known
in the area for his baking and for his utilisation of fresh ingredients
to create tasty, inviting meals.*
12⇆🛏(2fb)1🚿 CTV in all bedrooms ® T ✖ (ex guide dogs)
sB&B⇆🛏£60-£70 dB&B⇆🛏£80-£110 🅿
20P 1🍴 🛁 ✿ ♪
♀ English & French Sunday Lunch fr£11 Dinner fr£21.50&alc
Last dinner 9.15pm
Credit Cards ① ② ③ ⑤ ⓔ

---

**ASHBURTON** Devon Map 03 SX77

★★⚑69% **Holne Chase** TQ13 7NS (Inter-Hotels)
☎Poundsgate(03643)471 FAX (03643) 453
*An attractive period house in a magnificent setting with most
impressive views.*
12rm(9⇆2🛏)1🚿 CTV in all bedrooms ® T ✱
sB&B⇆🛏£52.50-£62.50 dB&B⇆🛏£72-£120 🅿
30P 🛁 ✿ ♪ croquet putting *xmas*
♀ English & French V ✿ ⌂ ✄ Lunch £12.50 Dinner £19.50
Last dinner 9pm
Credit Cards ① ② ③ ⑤ ⓔ

# Holne Chase Hotel ⚑⚑
# and Restaurant

Open all year. Holne Chase is an
exceptionally peaceful Country House
with very comfortable
accommodation, a good kitchen and
a 200 bin cellar.

Small conference & meeting rooms.
Putting, croquet and salmon fishing
within the grounds.

**Holne Chase Hotel and Restaurant
Nr Ashburton, Devon TQ13 7NS
Tel: (03643) 471.**

# THE ROYAL BERKSHIRE   A

The Royal Berkshire is in the beautiful
Berkshire countryside, with good road
and rail links. It is within 5 miles of
Windsor Castle, Smiths Polo Lawn,
Sunningdale and Wentworth golf
courses, and Ascot racecourse. The hotel
has a well equipped leisure complex.

**The Royal Berkshire, London Road,
Sunninghill, Ascot, Berkshire SL5 0PP.
Tel: 0990 23322, Telex: 847280,
Fax: 0990 27100.**

★★★★

# The ARISAIG HOTEL

**Arisaig, Inverness-shire PH39 4NH
Telephone: (06875) 210**

★★

*Resident Proprietors
George, Janice and son Gordon Stewart*

The hotel stands on the shores of Loch Nan
Ceal, at the edge of Arisaig village. Across
the bay are the islands of Rhum, Eigg and
Muck where boats sail regularly all summer,
some virtually from the front doorstep. The
ideal hotel to get away from it all, relax and
enjoy the comforts of the hotel or spend your
stay taking in the spectacular countryside
steeped in history with many places of
interest to visit. Good wholesome Scottish
food and a family atmosphere with fine
wines and a large range of selected malt
whiskies. A warm welcome awaits you.

## Ashburton - Ashford-in-the-Water

★★ 67% **Tugela House** 68-70 East St TQ13 7AX ☎(0364)52206
*Comfortable family-run hotel in this moorland town, offering*
*attractive bedrooms and public areas, good home cooking and*
*friendly services.*
7rm(6⇨↑) CTV in all bedrooms ✱ sB&B⇨↑fr£25
dB&B⇨↑fr£40
6P 2🚗 ⇔ ✿
♀ English & French **V** ⌾ ✁ Lunch £10-£12alc Dinner
£12-£14alc Last dinner 9pm
ⓔ

★★ 63% **Dartmoor Lodge** Peartree Cross TQ13 7JW (Exec
Hotel) ☎(0364)52232
*Standing near the A38, and providing an ideal base from which to*
*tour Dartmoor, the English Riviera and South Hams, the hotel*
*offers accommodation in naturally and, centrally-heated bedrooms*
*with en suite facilities. Public areas include a busy lounge bar, a*
*split-level function room and a restaurant whose interesting à la*
*carte menu features a good range of home-cooked dishes.*
30⇨↑(6fb)2🛏 CTV in all bedrooms Ⓡ **T** ✱ sB&B⇨↑fr£26.50
dB⇨↑fr£28.50 (room only) 🅿
Lift ⓒ CTV 50P 2🚗 (£1.50) ✿ *xmas*
♀ English & French **V** ⌾ ✁ ✁ Lunch fr£4.15 High tea fr£1.90
Dinner £7.50-£8.95 Last dinner 9.30 pm
Credit Cards ① ② ③

**ASHBY-DE-LA-ZOUCH** Leicestershire Map **08** SK 31

★★★ 60% **Royal Osprey** Station Rd LE6 5GP (Toby)
☎(0530)412833 Telex no 341629
RS 24 Dec-1 Jan
*Situated on the A453 close to the town centre this Georgian*
*building provides quite well equipped accommodation and caters*
*mainly for commercial guests. Recently refurbished bedrooms are*
*spacious and well equipped, providing quality and comfort*
*throughout.*
31⇨↑(3fb)✁in 3 bedrooms CTV in all bedrooms Ⓡ **T**
ⓒ 100P ✿ ♫
♀ English & French **V** ⌾ ✁ ✁ Last dinner 9.45pm
Credit Cards ① ② ③ ④ ⑤

**ASHFORD Kent** Map **05** TR04

**EASTWELL MANOR**

Eastwell Park, Boughton
Lees TN25 4HR (Queens
Moat)(Prestige)
☎(0233)635751
Telex no 966281
FAX (0233) 635530

*For those wishing to*
*experience country living in the grand manner, Eastwell*
*Manor will more than live up to their expectations.*
*Surrounded by extensive grounds, the exterior is imposing,*
*and the carved panelling, stone-mantled fireplaces, leather*
*Chesterfields and antique furniture of lounge, billiards room*
*and bar are scarcely less so. Service, by extremely well trained*
*staff, is professional and at the same time pleasant and*
*attentive. For the active guest, there is tennis or croquet, and*
*golf, squash, shooting and trout fishing can all be arranged.*
*The elegant dining room offers a choice of French and English*
*cuisine.*
23⇨↑ CTV in all bedrooms **T** S12% sB&B⇨↑£95-£116
dB&B⇨↑£110-£215
Lift ⓒ 50P 10🚗 ⇔ ✿ ♫ ♬ (hard) ✍ ∪ snooker croquet
*xmas*

♀ English & French **V** ⌾ ✁ Lunch fr£15.50 Dinner
fr£22.50 Last dinner 10pm
Credit Cards ① ② ③ ⑤

★★★ 65% **Post House** Canterbury Rd TN24 8QQ (Trusthouse
Forte) ☎(0233)625790 Telex no 966685 FAX (0233) 43176
*A 15th-century manor house has been carefully renovated*
*and extended to provide a high standard of modern*
*accommodation whilst still retaining its original charm and*
*character. The Swiss Restaurant is set in a restored barn dating*
*from the 17th century and featuring exposed oak beams and a*
*minstrels' gallery, the adjoining bar and lounge offering*
*comfortable surroundings in which to relax.*
60⇨↑in 10 bedrooms CTV in all bedrooms Ⓡ **T**
ⓒ 95P ✿ ♫
**V** ⌾ ✁ ✁ Last dinner 10pm
Credit Cards ① ② ③ ④ ⑤

★★★ 54% **Master Spearpoint** Canterbury Rd, Kennington
TN24 9QR (Best Western) ☎(0233)636863 Telex no 965978
FAX (0233) 610119
*A pleasant hotel set in five acres of delightful grounds offers*
*functional bedrooms (some in a new wing) and a restaurant that*
*operates as a carvery at lunchtime. The ground level bar/lounge is*
*supplemented by a small lounge on the first floor.*
36⇨↑(1fb) CTV in all bedrooms Ⓡ **T** sB&B⇨↑£57-£70
dB&B⇨↑£75-£91
60P ✿
♀ International **V** ⌾ ✁ Lunch £3.50-£7.50alc Dinner
£10-£20alc Last dinner 9.45pm
Credit Cards ① ② ③ ⑤

**ASHFORD Surrey** London plan **1** *A2* (Page 000)

✕✕**Terrazza** 45 Church Rd TW15 2TY ☎(0784)244887 &
241732
Closed Sun & BH's
Lunch not served Sat
♀ Continental **V** 70 seats Lunch £18.50&alc Dinner
£18.50&alc Last lunch 2.15pm Last dinner 10.30pm ✍
Credit Cards ① ② ③ ⑤

**ASHFORD-IN-THE-WATER** Derbyshire Map **07** SK 17

★★ 73% **Ashford** Church St DE4 1QB ☎Bakewell(0629)812725
*The friendly and informal atmosphere of this comfortable little*
*hotel proves popular with residents and locals alike. Bedrooms are*
*decorated in a delightful rustic style, oak-beamed ceilings are*
*complemented by attractively co-ordinated soft furnishings*
*throughout, and a good range of modern facilities is provided. The*
*restaurant's table d'hôte and à la carte menus offer a wide and*
*interesting selection of dishes, all based on quality produce.*
7⇨↑ CTV in all bedrooms Ⓡ **T** sB&B⇨↑£45-£55
dB&B⇨↑£65-£75 🅿
CTV 50P ⇔ ✿ *xmas*
♀ French **V** ⌾ ✁ ✁ Sunday Lunch £10 Dinner £17&alc Last
dinner 10pm
Credit Cards ① ③ ⓔ

★★ 73% **Riverside Country House** Fennel St DE4 1QF
☎Bakewell(0629)814275 FAX (0629) 812873
*This charming ivy-clad Georgian country house stands in lovely*
*gardens in the centre of this delightful Peak District village. The*
*public rooms are cosy and peaceful, and, like the well equipped*
*bedrooms, are decorated and furnished in a style sympathetic with*
*the character of the house. A five-course fixed-price menu provides*
*an imaginative selection of dishes and takes full advantage of*
*seasonally available fresh produce. It is complimented by a*
*comprehensive wine list and good, attentive service.*
7⇨↑2🛏✁in all bedrooms CTV in all bedrooms Ⓡ **T**
sB&B⇨↑£70-£75 dB&B⇨↑£80-£90 🅿

CTV 30P ⊞ ❖ ♪ ∪ *xmas*
☺ English & French V ♉ ⏛ ⤺ Lunch £13-£15 Dinner £27.50
Last dinner 9.30pm
Credit Cards ① ② ③ ⓔ

---

**ASHINGTON** West Sussex Map **04** TQ11

★★ 69% **Mill House** Mill Ln RH20 3BZ ☎(0903)892426
FAX (0903) 892855
*A cosy 18th-century mill house which has been extended to offer modern accommodation whilst still retaining its charm and character. Personally-run by hospitable proprietors it also has a small conference room.*
10rm(7⇋2♠)2⊞ CTV in all bedrooms ® T sB&Bfr£38.50
sB&B⇋♠fr£42.50 dB&B⇋♠£70-£80 ⊟
CTV 12P ⊞ ❖ ⌀ *xmas*
☺ English & French V ♉ ⏛ Lunch fr£8.75&alc Dinner
fr£12.50&alc Last dinner 9.30pm
Credit Cards ① ② ③ ④ ⑤ ⓔ

✕✕The Willows London Rd RH20 3JR ☎(0903)892575
*This elegant, beamed farmhouse-style restaurant has a bar lounge and log fires, and is personally run by Mr Andrew James. A good value à la carte menu features fresh fish, local produce, and a daily special; all deserts are home made. The service is particularly efficient and helpful.*
Lunch not served Mon & Tue
Dinner not served Sun
☺ International 30 seats ✻ Last lunch 2pm Last dinner 10pm
25P
Credit Cards ① ② ③

1991 marks the 25th anniversary of this guide.

# Eastwell Manor

**A**

★★★★ ⚬⚬

**Eastwell Park, Boughton Aluph**
**Nr Ashford, Kent TN25 4HR**
**Tel: (0233) 35751    Fax: (0233) 35530**
**Telex: 966281 EMANOR**

Eastwell Manor, a luxury 23 bedroom country house, standing in 3,000 acres of private parkland. A beautifully panelled Rose Garden Room is available for executive level meetings up to 24 delegates.

Special mid-week, Easter and Christmas packages are available.

Leisure facilities include tennis court, snooker table and croquet lawn. Horse-riding, golf, squash and fishing nearby.

**ASHLEY HEATH** Dorset Map **04** SU10

★★69% *Struan Hotel & Restaurant* Horton Rd BH24 2EG (2m
W in Dorset) ☎Ringwood(0425)473553 & 473029
FAX (0425) 480529
*Set in a wooded residential area on the edge of the New Forest this
warm, friendly hotel is run by resident proprietors John and
Wendy Haywood. Bedrooms here are quite stunning with quality
co-ordinating fabrics and furnishings.*
10rm(2♠)(2fb) ®
CTV 75P ✿ solarium ♫
♀ English & French V ✝ ⬛ Last dinner 9.30pm
Credit Cards ① ② ③ ⑤

**ASHTON-UNDER-LYNE** Greater Manchester Map **07** SJ99

★★72%, **York House** York Place, Richmond St OL6 7TT
☎061-330 5899 FAX 061-343 1613
Closed Bank Hols
*Warmth and hospitality are regarded as paramount at this family-
run, professional hotel which is situated on the Manchester side of
town, in a quiet side road just off the A635. Accommodation is very
well appointed – the cottage rooms being particularly well
equipped – and the chef combines classical cuisine with a range of
his own seasonal creations.*
24rm(18⇨5♠)Annexe10⇨(2fb)1⊞ CTV in all bedrooms ®
S10% sB&B⇨♠£45-£55 dB&B⇨♠£60 ⊟
《 34P ✿
♀ English & French V ✝ ⬛ S10% Lunch £4.95-£8.50 Dinner
£9-£21alc Last dinner 9.30pm
Credit Cards ① ② ③ ④ ⑤

**ASKRIGG** North Yorkshire Map **07** SD99

★★75% **King's Arms** Market Place DL8 3HQ (Minotels)
☎Wensleydale(0969)50258 FAX (0969) 50635
*18th-century coaching inn of great character and warmth. The
comfortable, modernised bedrooms are furnished in period style
with some beautiful antiques. Ray Hopwood gives guests a warm
welcome, and the 5 log fires set the scene for a relaxing and
enjoyable stay. Liz Hopwood competently prepares the tasty meals
from fresh local produce.*
10rm(3⇨6♠)(1fb)6⊞ CTV in all bedrooms ®
sB&B⇨♠£35-£38 dB&B⇨♠£55-£60 ⊟
14P nc6yrs *xmas*
♀ English & French V ✝ ⬛ ✗ Lunch fr£7.50 Dinner
fr£15&alc Last dinner 9pm
Credit Cards ① ③ ⓔ

**ASPLEY GUISE** Bedfordshire Map **04** SP93

★★★71%, **Moore Place** The Square MK17 8DW
☎Milton Keynes(0908)282000 FAX (0908) 281888
RS 26-28 Dec
*Accommodation of a very high standard is available at this popular
commercial hotel, bedrooms all being tastefully appointed and well
equipped though they vary in size. A bright, conservatory-style
restaurant offers a selection of expertly prepared English and
French dishes, while attentive, willing staff successfully combine
helpfulness with professionalism.*
39⇨Annexe15⇨ CTV in all bedrooms ® T ✱
sB&B⇨£75-£85 dB&B⇨£90-£95 ⊟
《 60P ✿ ♪
V ✝ ⬛
Credit Cards ① ② ③ ⑤

Hotels with a high percentage rating for quality
are highlighted by a % across their
gazetteer entry.

**ASTON CLINTON** Buckinghamshire Map **04** SP81

★★★

✿★★★ **BELL INN**
HP22 5HP (Relais et
Châteaux)
☎Aylesbury(0296)630252
Telex no 83252
FAX (0296) 631250
RS Sun eve & Mon

*The fresh flowers that fill this
beautiful old coaching house raise expectation of friendly
hospitality which are handsomely fulfilled by the owners,
Michael and Patsy Harris. Here one can relax and enjoy the
charm of the old courtyard, also full of flowers, and the stone-
flagged bar. Most of the comfortable, spacious bedrooms are
set apart from the main building, in the inn's former malt
houses and stables, and some are furnished with fine antiques.
A scheme of small sections within the spacious restaurant
makes for intimacy, and young chef Kevin Cape uses the best
fresh produce with innovative skill, producing such dishes as a
light Ravioli filled with wild mushrooms, and superb fillets of
Dover Sole stuffed with spring vegetables with a fluffy herb
mousse. A particularly well-chosen wine list continues to
excite the most fastidious of wine lovers. The greatest
compliment that one can pay this famous long-established inn
is its unerring consistency. The faces may change, but it is
to the eternal credit of the Harris family that standards
remain so uniformly high.*
21⇨♠2⊞ CTV in all bedrooms ® T S%
sB&B⇨♠£86-£95
dB&B⇨♠£100-£125 Continental breakfast
《 150P ⊞ ✿ croquet *xmas*
♀ English & French V ✝ ⬛ ✗ Lunch £10-£17&alc
Dinner £16.50-£19.50&alc Last dinner 9.45pm
Credit Cards ① ③

**ATHERSTONE** Warwickshire Map **04** SP39

★★70%, **Old Red Lion** Lone St CV9 1BB ☎(0827)713156
FAX (0827) 711404
*This 17th-century coaching inn has recently been totally
refurbished to offer particularly well equipped en suite bedrooms
and comfortable, modern public areas which include a restaurant
whose à la carte and table d'hôte menus – including both flambé
and vegetarian selections – are popular with resident and local
alike.*
22⇨♠(1fb)2⊞ CTV in all bedrooms ® T ✖ (ex guide dogs)
sB&B⇨♠£45 dB&B⇨♠£55-£65 ⊟
《 22P
♀ English & French V ✝ ⬛ ✗ Lunch £8&alc Dinner £10&alc
Last dinner 9.45pm
Credit Cards ① ② ③ ⑤ ⓔ

**ATTLEBOROUGH** Norfolk Map **05** TM09

★★60% *Sherbourne Country House* Norwich Rd NR17 2JX
☎(0953)454363
*Standing five minutes' walk from the town, in an acre of mature
grounds next to the old turnpike, this well-maintained 17th-century
house offers comfortable rooms (most having en suite facilities), an
attractive bar and lounge, and good standards of hospitality.*
8rm(4⇨1♠)3⊞ CTV in all bedrooms ®
50P 1⊞ ✿
♀ International ✝ ⬛ ✗ Last dinner 9pm
Credit Cards ① ② ③

See advertisement under **NORWICH**

86

AUCHENCAIRN Dumfries & Galloway *Kirkcudbright*
Map 11 NX75

★★★♨69% **Balcary Bay** DG7 1QZ ☎(055664)217 & 311
Closed Nov-Feb
*A delightful hotel, in a charming coastal situation, whose grounds run down to the waters edge. Bedrooms are bright and airy and public areas comfortable and tastefully appointed.*
13rm(11⇨1♠)(1fb) CTV in all bedrooms ® T sB&B⇨♠£40
dB&B£52 dB&B⇨♠£66-£80 ⊟
50P ∰ ✿ snooker
♀ English & French V ✿ ♨ Lunch £16-£20alc Dinner £16&alc
Last dinner 9pm
Credit Cards ①③

★★61% **Solwayside House** 25 Main St DG7 1QU ☎(055664)280
*This tourist hotel in the village centre, family run on traditional lines, has no bar but serves drinks in its lounges and dining room.*
9rm(3⇨3♠)(4fb) CTV in 3 bedrooms ®
CTV 10P games room ♨
V ✿ ♨ ⊬ Last dinner 7.45pm

AUCHTERARDER Tayside *Perthshire* Map 11 NN91

★★★★★
**THE GLENEAGLES HOTEL**

PH3 1NF ☎(0764)62231
Telex no 76105
FAX (0764) 62134
*All good Americans, as the old saying runs, may go to Paris when they die, but to enjoy themselves on holiday they come to Gleneagles, where the recreational and leisure facilities are unrivalled. Apart from the 2 fine golf courses (and a 3rd under construction) on the 600-acre estate, there is a shooting school, the Mark Phillips equestrian centre, a leisure and health spa embracing a swimming pool, gymnasium, sauna, jacuzzi, squash and tennis courts, plus a snooker room, putting green, pitch and putt course and lovely grounds and gardens. These dazzling facilities must not be allowed to obscure the fact that the heart of the complex is a very fine hotel, largely due to the impressive management skills of Vivien Sirotkin who ensures that the friendly personal service which first established the reputation of Gleneagles is admirably maintained. Executive Chef Alan Hill has an equally formidable task when it comes to feeding the large numbers of guests attracted here. Under his wing come the restaurants in the shooting school, golf club and health spa as well as the two in the hotel itself, the Strathearn and the Glendevon. The Strathearn is the more elegant, but is unfortunately often reserved for conferences and private functions. Massive investment over the past few years has resulted in a marked improvement to the bedrooms, now all beautifully appointed, and though some rooms are still on the compact side rather than the spacious, the very small rooms that used to exist have been abolished. Gleneagles can best be described as a Great Scottish Institution and long may it remain a landmark.*
236⇨♠10⊟ CTV in all bedrooms T sB⇨♠£85-£95
dB⇨♠£140-£170 (room only) ⊟
Lift ℂ 200P ∰ ✿ CFA ⬚(heated) ⊳ 18 ♀ (hard & grass)
♪ squash ∪ snooker sauna solarium gymnasium croquet
bowls putting shooting school ♫ ♨ xmas
♀ International V ⊬ Lunch fr£20 Dinner fr£27.50 Last
dinner 10pm
Credit Cards ①②③④⑤

★★★♨73%, *Auchterarder House* PH3 1DZ (Prestige)
☎(0764)63646 & 63647 FAX (0764)62939
*The owners of this impressive baronial home set in seventeen acres of secluded grounds and surrounded by beautiful countryside extend a warm welcome to guests. Day rooms of charm and character reflect the grandeur of the Victorian age, while individually styled bedrooms are comfortable, tastefully appointed and thoughtfully equipped. The restaurant serves a range of interesting dishes prepared from fresh ingredients.*
12⇨ CTV in all bedrooms T
ℂ 40P ∰ ✿ ♪ croquet lawn pitch & putting green
♀ Scottish & French V ✿ ♨ Last dinner 10pm
Credit Cards ①②③④⑤

★★★♨65%, **Duchally House** PH3 1PN ☎(0764)63071
FAX (0764) 62464
*Standing in 27 acres of grounds, this extended Victorian mansion house has lovely views over the Perthshire countryside. It is decorated and furnished in traditional style and offers comfortable, spacious accommodation. Service is friendly and helpful.*
15⇨♠(3fb)1⊟ CTV in all bedrooms ® T ✱ sB&B£40
sB&B⇨♠£40-£55 dB&B£60-£65 dB&B⇨♠£65-£75 ⊟
30P ✿ ♀ (hard) snooker ♨ xmas
V ✿ ♨ ⊬ Lunch £10-£15&alc Dinner £17.50-£20&alc Last
dinner 9.30pm
Credit Cards ①②③⑤

AUCHTERHOUSE Tayside *Forfarshire* Map 11 NO33
★★★♨70% **Old Mansion House** DD3 0QN ☎(082626)366
FAX (082626) 400
Closed 25 Dec-3 Jan

▶

# Duchally House Hotel
★ ★ ★     ♨

Duchally House is set amidst 27 acres of gardens in the Ochil Hills overlooking Auchterader. This fine country hotel offers the discerning guest, good food, fine wines and a relaxed and friendly atmosphere. An ideal base for touring, fishing, golfing or just simply relaxing.

From £30 – £50 per person.

Conference and meeting facilities are available throughout the year.

*For further information and brochure contact: Duchally House Hotel, Auchterader, Perthshire PH3 1PN. Tel: (0764) 63071. Fax: (0764) 62464.*

**A**

*This 16th-century baronial home, beautifully set in ten acres of garden and wooded grounds amid gentle, rolling countryside, has been sympathetically converted to create a small hotel of some distinction. Comfortably appointed day rooms which retain much of their original charm and character invite relaxation, while bedrooms, are individual in style and thoughtfully equipped with useful extras. Good food is considered a priority and service is both willing and helpful.*
6⇨↑(2fb)1▥ CTV in all bedrooms ® T ✱ sB&B⇨↑£60-£65 dB&B⇨↑£75-£95 ₽
50P 1🏌 ⌗ ✿ ⌐(heated) ♪ (grass) squash croquet
♀ Scottish & French V ↻ ⚗ Lunch fr£14&alc Dinner £20-£25alc Last dinner 9.30pm
Credit Cards ① ② ③ ⑤

---

**AULTBEA** Highland *Ross & Cromarty* Map **14** NG88

★★66% **Aultbea** IV22 2HX ☎(044582)201 FAX (044582) 214
*Delightfully situated on the shore of Loch Ewe, this small friendly family run hotel is an ideal base for touring holidaymakers. The attractive bedrooms, though compact, are comfortable and well equipped and, in addition to the Restaurant, there is the Waterside Bistro which offers an all day meal service.*
8rm(7⇨↑)(1fb) CTV in all bedrooms ® T ✱ sB&B⇨↑£18-£32 dB&B⇨↑£36-£62 ₽
CTV 40P ✿ pool table ♪ ♨ xmas
♀ International V ↻ ⚗ Lunch £2-£11 Dinner £16.50&alc Last dinner 9.30pm
Credit Cards ① ③

---

**AUST MOTORWAY SERVICE AREA (M4)** Avon Map **03** ST58

⇧**Rank Motor Lodge** M4 Motorway (junc 21) BS12 3BJ (Rank)
☎Pilning(04545)3313
51⇨↑(21fb)⅌in 8 bedrooms CTV in all bedrooms ® ✱ sB&B⇨↑£27.50 dB&B⇨↑£34.50 Continental breakfast
《70P ✿
V ↻ ⚗ ⅌
Credit Cards ① ② ③ ⑤

---

**AUSTWICK** North Yorkshire Map **07** SD76

✸69% **The Traddock** LA2 8BY ☎Clapham(04685)224
Closed Oct-Etr
*A Georgian country house of stone construction in its own grounds.*
12rm(11⇨↑)(3fb) CTV in 10 bedrooms ® sB&B⇨↑£23-£26 dB&B⇨↑£38-£44 ₽
12P ✿ nc5yrs
Dinner fr£12 Last dinner 5.30pm

---

**AVIEMORE** Highland *Inverness-shire* Map **14** NH81

★★★61% **Stakis Four Seasons** Aviemore Centre PH22 1PF (Stakis) ☎(0479)810681 Telex no 75213 FAX (0479) 810862
*This hotel with a distinctive modern style occupies a prominent position, commanding particularly fine views of the Spey Valley and surrounding mountains from many of its bedrooms. Boasting a pleasantly situated swimming pool and associated leisure activities, it enjoys a good reputation for package holidays.*
88⇨↑(6fb)⅌in 54 bedrooms CTV in all bedrooms ® T ✱ sB&B⇨↑£50-£64 dB&B⇨↑£88-£104 (incl dinner) ₽
Lift 《 100P ✿ ⌐(heated) sauna solarium gymnasium turkish bath whirlpool ♪ xmas
♀ Scottish, English & French ↻ ⚗ S% Lunch £7 Dinner £15&alc Last dinner 9.30pm
Credit Cards ① ② ③ ⑤ ⓔ

For key to symbols see the inside front cover.

★★★65% **Red McGregor** Main Rd PH22 1RH ☎(0479)810256 FAX (0479) 810685
*A popular tourist hotel in the main street. In addition to the usual facilities it offers a leisure complex, coffee shop, food bar and video hire for showing in bedrooms.*
30⇨↑(8fb) CTV in all bedrooms ® T ✖ (ex guide dogs) sB&B⇨↑£52 dB&B⇨↑£89 (incl dinner) ₽
《 65P ⌐(heated) sauna solarium gymnasium beauty salon steam room xmas
♀ Mainly grills V ↻ ⚗ High tea £3-£4alc Dinner £12-£14alc Last dinner 10pm
Credit Cards ① ② ③ ⑤ ⓔ

★★★55% **Aviemore Highlands** Aviemore Centre PH22 1PJ ☎(0479)810771 Telex no 75597 FAX (0479) 811473
*This modern, purpose-built hotel is situated in the Aviemore Centre and is popular with tour and conference groups. It offers a choice of bars and lounges, and provides practical accommodation.*
103⇨↑(34fb)⅌in 27 bedrooms CTV in all bedrooms ® T ✱ sB&B⇨↑£27.50-£47 dB&B⇨↑£55-£62
Lift 《 140P ✿ solarium games room ♪ ♨ xmas
♀ English & French V ↻ ⚗ S% Bar Lunch £1.75-£7.50 Dinner £10.50&alc Last dinner 9pm
Credit Cards ① ② ③ ④ ⑤ ⓔ

---

**AVON** Hampshire Map **04** SZ19

★★★66% **Tyrrells Ford Country House** BH23 7BH (4m S of Ringwood on B3347) ☎Bransgore(0425)72646 FAX (0425) 72262
*A Georgian hotel on the edge of the New Forest has been extended and refurbished in a style compatible with the period features that have been retained. All rooms are comfortable, public areas including an unusual galleried lounge and a dining room offering both table d'hôte and à la carte menus. There is also an extensive selection of bar food, popular locally, and service is friendly throughout.*
16⇨↑ CTV in all bedrooms ® T ✖ (ex guide dogs) sB&B⇨↑£45-£65 dB&B⇨↑£60-£90 ₽
100P ✿ xmas
♀ English & French V Lunch £9.95-£11.95&alc Dinner £14.95-£17.95&alc Last dinner 10pm
Credit Cards ① ③
**See advertisement under CHRISTCHURCH**

---

**AXBRIDGE** Somerset Map **03** ST45

★★64% **Oak House** The Square BS26 2AP ☎(0934)732444 FAX (0934) 733112
*This hotel of character has cosy lounges and bedrooms which have been upgraded to a good standard. Varied and interesting dishes are served in the restaurant.*
11rm(7⇨3↑)(2fb)2▥ CTV in all bedrooms ® T ✱ sB&B£23.50 sB&B⇨↑£32.50 dB&B⇨↑£51 ₽
P
♀ English & French V ↻ ⚗ Lunch £16.50-£25.50alc High tea £2.50 Dinner £16.50-£25.50alc Last dinner 10pm
Credit Cards ① ② ③ ④ ⑤
**See advertisement under CHEDDAR**

---

**AXMINSTER** Devon Map **03** SY29

★★56% *George* Trinity Square EX13 5DW (Minotels) ☎(0297)32209 FAX (0297) 34234
*A Georgian coaching inn in the centre of the town, featuring one of the country's few remaining 'Adam' fireplaces. It is personally run by Mr and Mrs Andrews who offer a warm welcome. All bedrooms have good facilities. There are two busy bars and a small restaurant with an à la carte menu.*
11⇨↑(5fb)1▥ CTV in all bedrooms ®

CTV 20P
♀ English & French **V** ♥ ⎵ Last dinner 9pm
Credit Cards [1] [2] [3] [5]

---

**AYLESBURY** Buckinghamshire Map **04** SP81

★★★★73% **Forte** Aston Clinton Rd HP22 5AA (Trusthouse Forte) ☎(0296)393388 Telex no 838820 FAX (0296) 392211
*A modern, well-appointed commercial hotel with spacious comfortable public areas and well-equipped bedrooms of a good size. The restaurant offers a choice of menus and the good standard of cooking is complemented by a generally well-balanced wine list, though our Inspector thought it would benefit from a few better quality wines. Service is efficient and helpful.*
94⇌♠(8fb)⚹in 22 bedrooms CTV in all bedrooms ® **T** ✳
sB⇌♠£85-£100 dB⇌♠£95-£120 (room only) ☲
《 150P ✿ ▤(heated) sauna solarium gymnasium *xmas*
**V** ♥ ⎵ ⚹
Credit Cards [1] [2] [3] [4] [5]

★★★ ♨ **HARTWELL HOUSE**

Oxford Rd HP17 8NL
(Prestige) ☎(0296)747444
Telex no 837108
FAX (0296) 747450

*An elegant Grade I listed country house, with a history dating back to the 16th century, Hartwell opened as an hotel in 1989 and is already making its mark. Décor and furnishings throughout are in keeping with the distinguished history of the house, which has in its time been host to several crowned heads; space and grace abounds in the beautifully proportioned reception rooms, and many of the bedrooms can only be described as vast. They are reached by a remarkably ornate Jacobean staircase, almost grotesquely adorned with a profusion of carved figures. Chef Aidan McCormack is in charge of the kitchens and his modern British style of cooking results in some very enjoyable and unusual dishes, for example, a tender fillet of lamb cooked in anchovy oil and served with a robust saffron-flavoured jus – though on occasions some may find his style over-complicated. Hartwell House is the winner for southern England of our Best Newcomer Award for 1990-91 and we are delighted to welcome them to the 25th anniversary edition of the guide.*
32⇌♠5☰ CTV in all bedrooms **T** ✖ (ex guide dogs) S%
sB⇌♠£83-£115 dB⇌♠£127-£185 (room only) ☲
Lift 《 60P ⇱ ✿ ♪ croquet nc8yrs *xmas*
**V** ♥ ⎵ S% Lunch £17-£21.50&alc Dinner £29.50&alc Last dinner 9.45pm
Credit Cards [1] [2] [3] [5]

---

★★58% **Bell** Market Square HP20 1TX ☎(0296)89835
*Comfortable and friendly old coaching house with sound cooking and excellent breakfasts.*
17⇌♠ CTV in all bedrooms ®
♪ ⇱
**V** ♥ ⎵ ⚹ Last dinner 9.30pm
Credit Cards [1] [2] [3] [5]

✖**Pebbles** 1 Pebbles Ln HP20 2JH ☎(0296)86622
*In the friendly atmosphere of this small, intimate restaurant you can enjoy a choice of dishes from both fixed price and à la carte menus, both featuring a range of interesting dishes that illustrate the chef's skill and imagination; an impressive wine list includes some reasonably priced offers, and friendly staff provide efficient service.*
Closed Mon, 26 Dec & 1-3 Jan

Dinner not served Sun
♀ English & French **V** 32 seats ✳ Lunch £16.50-£28 Dinner £28 Last lunch 2.15pm Last dinner 10pm ♪
Credit Cards [1] [3]

---

**AYR** Strathclyde *Ayrshire* Map **10** NS32

★★★61% **Pickwick** 19 Racecourse Rd KA7 2TD
☎(0292)260111 FAX (0292) 43174
*Friendly, personally-run hotel in a Victorian mansion with good parking facilities. Bedrooms are comfortably furnished and equipped whilst public areas are wood panelled with lots of Victorian prints.*
15⇌♠ CTV in all bedrooms ® **T** S%
sB&B⇌♠£40-£47.50 dB&B⇌♠£70-£80 ☲
《 100P ⇱ ✿ ♪ putting green ⚬♨ *xmas*
♀ Scottish & French **V** ♥ ⎵ S% Lunch £5.50-£10.50&alc High tea £5.50-£6.50&alc Dinner £12.95-£14.95&alc Last dinner 9.45pm
Credit Cards [1] [2] [3] [5] [£]

★★★56% **Caledonian** Dalblair Rd KA7 1UG (Embassy)
☎(0292)269331 Telex no 776611 FAX (0292) 610722
*The bright, spacious public areas of this centrally-located, modern hotel include a terrace café which is open from 7am to 11pm. Many of the comfortable bedrooms have sea views and all are attractively presented, with pastel décor and light wood furniture.*
114⇌♠(12fb)⚹in 22 bedrooms CTV in all bedrooms ® **T** S%
sB⇌♠£69-£53 dB⇌♠£89-£98 (room only) ☲
Lift 《 70P CFA ▤(heated) snooker sauna solarium gymnasium jacuzzi *xmas*
♀ Scottish & French **V** ♥ ⎵ ⚹ S% Lunch fr£7.95 High tea fr£4.75 Dinner fr£14.50 Last dinner 10pm
Credit Cards [1] [2] [3] [5]

**★★★★**

Situated in the magnificent Spey Valley, this hotel offers luxurious accommodation, matched only by the breath-taking views. Ideal touring base. All bedrooms ensuite with colour TV/in-house movies/ radio/telephone and tea/coffee facilities. Excellent leisure club with turkish steam room/pool/whirl pool spa/sauna/sunbeds and exercise equipment. "New for 1991 Adventure Holiday Base."
Telephone: (0479) 810681.
Fax: (0479) 810862
━━━ ᛙ STAKIS ━━━
**Four Seasons**
━ A V I E M O R E ━

**A**

★★★53%, **Savoy Park** 16 Racecourse Rd KA7 2UT
☎(0292)266112 FAX (0292) 611488
*Old-established and family-run, this hotel remains a bastion of*
*traditionalism; once a substantial mansion, it has country house*
*style rooms and some smaller, more functional ones.*
16⇨♠(4fb) CTV in all bedrooms ® T sB&B⇨♠£35-£45
dB&B⇨♠£50-£70 ⊟
《 CTV 80P ❀ ⋑ xmas
♀ Scottish & French V ♦ ⚄ Lunch fr£7.50&alc High tea
fr£7.50&alc Dinner fr£17&alc Last dinner 9pm
Credit Cards ① ② ③

★★69%, **Carrick Lodge** 46 Carrick Rd KA7 2RE
☎(0292)262846
*Bright, well-equipped bedrooms, popular bar meals and a nicely-*
*appointed restaurant are features of this well maintained hotel*
*situated on the south side of town.*
8⇨♠(2fb) CTV in all bedrooms ® T ✕
《 25P
V ♦ ⚄ Last dinner 9.45pm
Credit Cards ① ② ③

★★66%, **Elms Court** 21 Miller Rd KA7 2AX ☎(0292)264191 &
282332 FAX (0292) 610254
*Centrally situated between the town and seafront this is a family*
*run hotel with modest accommodation and friendly, professional*
*service. Enjoyable bar meals are served in the recently refurbished*
*lounge bar which is popular with locals at lunchtime.*
20⇨♠(4fb) CTV in all bedrooms ® T sB&B⇨♠fr£28.50
dB&B⇨♠fr£57
《 40P xmas
♀ Scottish & French V ♦ ⚄
Credit Cards ① ② ③

★★50%, **Ayrshire & Galloway** 1 Killoch Place KA7 2EA
☎(0292)262626
RS Xmas & New Year
*Modest commercial hotel in the town centre. Bedrooms with en*
*suite facilities have been upgraded but others remain fairly simple.*
25rm(8⇨)(3fb) CTV in 8 bedrooms ✕ sB&B£15-£18
sB&B⇨£18-£20 dB&B£30-£36 dB&B⇨£36-£40
《 CTV 20P ♫
♦ Bar Lunch fr£3.50alc High tea £5-7.50alc Dinner £7.50-£10
Last dinner 8.30pm
Credit Cards ① ③

★62%, **Aftongrange** 37 Carrick Rd KA7 2RD ☎(0292)265679
*Though this small, family-run, commercial hotel on the south side*
*of the town can offer no lounge facilities other than its large bar, it*
*is popular for the generous portions served in the dining room.*
8rm(1⇨4♠)(2fb) CTV in all bedrooms ® T sB&B£20-£25
sB&B⇨♠£25 dB&B£36 dB&B⇨♠£42 ⊟
30P pool table
V ♦ ⚄ Lunch fr£5 High tea fr£4.50 Dinner fr£8.50 Last
dinner 9pm
£

---

**AYTON, GREAT** North Yorkshire Map **08** NZ51

★★★⚑70%, **Ayton Hall** Low Green TS9 6BW
☎Middlesbrough(0642)723595 FAX (0642) 722149
*A manor house, set in six acres of landscaped gardens and*
*claiming associations with Captain James Cook, has been*
*tastefully furnished in the style of a private residence; bedrooms*
*have been particularly well equipped, with many thoughtful extras.*
*Cuisine is of a high standard, the chef's individual style being*
*complemented by an outstanding wine list.*
9⇨♠(2fb)3⊞ CTV in all bedrooms T ✕ sB&B⇨♠£77-£89
dB&B⇨♠£95-£115 ⊟
《 35P ❀ ♟ (hard) croquet archery nc11yrs xmas
♀ International V ♦ ⚄ ⤬ Lunch fr£10.95&alc Dinner
fr£20.50&alc Last dinner 9.45pm
Credit Cards ① ② ③ ⑤ £

---

**BABBACOMBE**
See **Torquay**

---

**BAGINTON** Warwickshire Map **04** SP37

★★62%, **Old Mill** Mill Hill CV8 2BS (Berni/Chef & Brewer)
☎Coventry(0203)303588
*Once a working mill, as its name suggests, and incorporating such*
*relics of its history as an 18th-century iron mill wheel and the*
*original mill pool in the grounds, the hotel has been restyled and*
*refurbished to offer good, modern accommodation which is proving*
*very popular.*
20⇨♠(4fb)1⊞ CTV in all bedrooms ® T ✕ (ex guide dogs)
sB&B⇨♠£58 dB&B⇨♠£71 ⊟
《 200P ❀ ∪ ⋑
V ♦ ⚄ ⤬ Lunch £8-£15alc Dinner £8-£15alc Last dinner
9.30pm
Credit Cards ① ② ③ ⑤

---

**BAGSHOT** Surrey Map **04** SU96

❀★★★★⚑70%, **Pennyhill Park** London Rd GU19 5ET
(Prestige) ☎(0276)71774 Telex no 858841 FAX (0276) 73217
*Surrounded by acres of garden and parkland – including its own*
*golf course – this impressive, characterful manor house offers a*
*range of individually decorated bedrooms, those in the tastefully*
*designed annexe linked to the main building by a new connecting*
*section which has also extended the lounge and reception facilities.*
22⇨♠Annexe41⇨♠✕ in 15 bedrooms CTV in all bedrooms
T ✕ (ex guide dogs) ❀ sB⇨♠£105-£250
dB⇨♠£130-£250 (room only) ⊟
《 250P ❀ ⌇(heated) ♥ 9 ♟ (hard) ✔ ∪ sauna solarium clay
pigeon shooting xmas
♀ English & French V ♦ ⚄ Lunch fr£19.50&alc Dinner
fr£30alc Last dinner 10.30pm
Credit Cards ① ② ③ ④ ⑤

---

**BAINBRIDGE** North Yorkshire Map **07** SD99

★★68%, **Rose & Crown** Village Green DL8 3EE
☎Wensleydale(0969)50225
*Set in the heart of 'Herriot' country this 15th-century hotel has*
*attractive, well-cared-for bedrooms, three bars and a comfortable*
*lounge. The intimate restaurant provides enjoyable meals, using*
*fresh local produce, the trout from the local fish farm can be*
*especially recommended. Enthusiastic staff provide old-fashioned*
*hospitality.*
12⇨♠(1fb)1⊞ CTV in all bedrooms ® sB&B⇨♠fr£33
dB&B⇨♠fr£58 ⊟
65P ❀ ✔
V ♦ ⚄ Sunday Lunch £7-£9.50alc Dinner £12.50-£15.50alc
Last dinner 9.30pm
Credit Cards ① ③

---

**BAKEWELL** Derbyshire Map **08** SK26

★★★70%, **Hassop Hall** Hassop DE4 1NS
☎Great Longstone(062987)488 Telex no 378485
FAX (062987) 577
Closed 23-26 Dec
*Tranquilly set at the centre of the Peak District National Park,*
*surrounded by parkland and the steep wooded slopes of the*
*Arboretum, an hotel which was once the ancestral home of the*
*Eyre family offers friendly, hospitable service and accommodation*
*in comfortably appointed bedrooms – some of which are positively*
*huge.*
12⇨♠(2fb)2⊞ CTV in all bedrooms T
Lift 60P ❀ ♟ (hard) croquet ♫
V Last dinner 9pm
Credit Cards ① ② ③ ⑤

★★★52% **Rutland Arms** The Square DE4 1BT (Best Western)
☎(0629)812812 Telex no 377077 FAX (0629) 814600
*Situated in the centre of town, this large stone-built former coaching inn dates from 1804 and is reputed to be where the famous Bakewell pudding was accidentally created. It provides modern, well-equipped accommodation to suit both tourists and commercial customers. A young team of staff are genuine and helpful. The Four Seasons Restaurant offers well chosen dishes freshly prepared.*
19⇄Annexe17⇄(2fb) CTV in all bedrooms ® T
sB&B⇄£42-£51 dB&B⇄£59-£69 🅿
《 30P 2🚗 *xmas*
🍴 English & French V ♥ ☞ Lunch £7.95-£9.95 Dinner £15.95&alc Last dinner 9.30pm
Credit Cards ① ② ③ ⑤ ⑤

★★🏅77% **Croft Country House** Great Longstone DE4 1TF
☎Great Longstone(062987)278
Closed 22 Dec-Feb
*This gem of a country house has warm, stylish rooms, very comfortable lounges, charming gardens and extremely hospitable hosts, who really make their guests feel welcome and relaxed.*
9rm(4⇄3🏮) CTV in all bedrooms ® 🏮 (ex guide dogs)
sB&B⇄🏮£44-£49 dB&B£55-£62 dB&B⇄🏮£64-£72 🅿
Lift CTV 30P 🚗 ❀
🍴 English & French V ✂ Dinner £16 Last dinner 7.30pm
Credit Cards ① ③

**See advertisement on page 93**

★★66% **Milford House** Mill St DE4 1DA ☎(0629)812130
Closed Jan & Feb RS Nov, Dec & Mar
*This old Georgian residence is peacefully set in its own attractive gardens, some 300 yards from the town centre. The Hunt family have owned and run the hotel for many years, and offer a high level of old-fashioned hospitality, making it a favourite with regular guests.*
▶

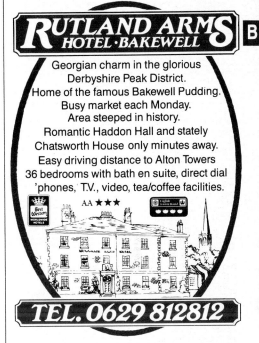

B

## RUTLAND ARMS
### HOTEL·BAKEWELL

Georgian charm in the glorious
Derbyshire Peak District.
Home of the famous Bakewell Pudding.
Busy market each Monday.
Area steeped in history.
Romantic Haddon Hall and stately
Chatsworth House only minutes away.
Easy driving distance to Alton Towers
36 bedrooms with bath en suite, direct dial
'phones, T.V., video, tea/coffee facilities.

AA ★★★

## TEL. 0629 812812

*The Elegant Hayward Suite*

# PENNYHILL PARK PLAYS HOST TO THOSE WHO TREASURE PRIVACY AND QUIET

SURROUNDED by peace and tranquillity Pennyhill Park Hotel stands in 112 acres of legendary parkland and landscaped gardens to be enjoyed whatever the season.

Forty-eight bedrooms and suites, all beautifully furnished and retaining the original charm and character of a country manor.

The Latymer Restaurant provides the elegance and quiet dignity expected from its surroundings. The food and service – known to many, is complemented by an oustanding selection of fine wines.

The Pennyhill Park Country Club's tempting pastimes are a nine-hole golf course, tennis courts, outdoor heated, Roman style swimming pool, horse-riding and clay pigeon shooting.

Whatever the occasion, Pennyhill Park offers a unique setting be it business or pleasure – *slip away now and enjoy us.*

AA ★★★★

### Pennyhill Park
HOTEL & COUNTRY CLUB

Pennyhill Park Hotel, College Ride, Bagshot, Surrey GU19 5ET Telephone: 0276 71774 Telex: 858841 PH PARK G Fax: 0276 73217

12⇨↑ CTV in all bedrooms ® ✈ ✳ sB&B⇨↑£28.75-£32 dB&B⇨↑£50.60-£60
10P 7🚗 ᴴ ✿ nc10yrs
V Sunday Lunch £10.90 Dinner £11.50-£13 Last dinner 7.30pm

---

**BALA** Gwynedd Map **06** SH93

★★ 65% *White Lion Royal* 61 High St LL23 7AE (Consort)
☎(0678)520314
Closed 25 Dec RS 26 Dec
*This High Street inn, one of the oldest in Wales and set at the centre of the Welsh Lakes, offers guests the comfort of well-equipped bedrooms enhanced by hospitable service from friendly staff.*
22⇨↑(3fb) CTV in all bedrooms ® T
CTV 30P
V ✿ ᴸ Last dinner 8.30pm
Credit Cards ①②③⑤

★★ 64% *Bala Lake* LL23 7YF (1m S on B4403) ☎(0678)520344
FAX (0678) 521193
*This Grade II listed building dating from 1790 is set in a 29 acre estate with a terraced swimming pool and a 9-hole golf course leading to the south shore of Bala Lake. Most bedrooms are situated in motel-type blocks with well-equipped en-suite facilities and spectacular views near the lake. The cuisine is wholesome and the atmosphere warm and friendly.*
1⇨Annexe12↑ CTV in all bedrooms ® T ✳
sB&B⇨↑£36-£40 dB&B⇨↑£50-£55 ⊟
40P 10🚗 ≋(heated) ▶9
✿ ᴸ Lunch £9 High tea £2 Dinner £12 Last dinner 8.30pm
Credit Cards ①③⑤

★★ 57% *Plas Coch* High St LL23 7AB ☎(0678)520309
Closed 25 Dec
*An 18th century coaching inn situated on the main street is now a privately owned and run hotel with friendly staff. Rooms are spacious with modest, traditional furnishings and there are two bars and a restaurant.*
10⇨↑(4fb) CTV in all bedrooms ® T S%
sB&B⇨↑£29.50-£40 dB&B⇨↑£47 ⊟
20P 🚗 windsurfing canoeing sailing
V ✿ ᴸ ✗ S% Lunch £5.50-£6.50 Dinner £10.50-£12.25 Last dinner 8.30pm
Credit Cards ①②③⑤ⓔ

---

**BALDOCK** Hertfordshire Map **04** TL23

⌂**Travelodge** Great North Rd (A1), Hinxworth SG7 5EX (A1) (Trusthouse Forte)
☎Hinxworth(0462)835329 Central res (0800) 850950
*This lodge on the A1, offers well-maintained and modern accommodation at good value. Well-equipped bedrooms have ensuite facilities and additional sofabeds. Meals and refreshments are available in the adjacent Happy Eater restaurant.*
40⇨↑(40fb) CTV in all bedrooms ® sB⇨↑£24
dB⇨↑£29.50 (room only)
⦅ 40P 🚗
Credit Cards ①②③

---

**BALLACHULISH** Highland *Argyllshire* Map **14** NN05

See also **North Ballachulish**
★★★ 60% *Ballachulish* PA39 4JY (Inter-Hotels) ☎(08552)606
Telex no 94013696 FAX (08552) 629
*A Scottish baronial-style hotel with good views of Loch Linnhe and the surrounding mountain scenery. It has attractive, well-equipped bedrooms and comfortable public areas with service provided by a team of friendly, young staff.*
30⇨↑(3fb)1 ⒇ CTV in all bedrooms ® T S10%
sB&B⇨↑£39.50-£45 dB&B⇨↑£49.50-£92 ⊟
⦅ 50P 4🚗 ✿ ♫ xmas

---

🏵 International V ✿ ᴸ ✗ S10% Lunch £2.50-£8.50alc High tea £2.50-£7.50alc Dinner £17&alc Last dinner 10pm
Credit Cards ①③ⓔ

---

**BALLASALLA**
See **Man, Isle of**

---

**BALLATER** Grampian *Aberdeenshire* Map **15** NO39

★★★★ 66% *Craigendarroch Hotel & Country Club* Braemar Rd AB3 5XA ☎(03397)55858 Telex no 739952
FAX (0338) 55447
*Set in the heart of Royal Deeside amidst spectacular scenery, this former country house has been sympathetically extended and now forms the centre of an extensive time share complex. There are numerous leisure facilities, and eating options range from the formal Oaks restaurant to the informal Café Jardin.*
29⇨↑(2fb)1 ⒇ CTV in all bedrooms ®
Lift ⦅ 100P ✿ ☒(heated) ᵈ squash snooker sauna solarium gymnasium games room beauty salon ⚕
V ✿ ᴸ Last dinner 10pm
Credit Cards ①②③⑤

★★ 73% *Glen Lui* Invercauld Rd AB3 5RP ☎(03397)55402
FAX (03397) 55545
Closed Nov
*The hotel is quietly situated in 2 acres of grounds next to Ballater Golf Club. There is a choice of well-equipped bedrooms, including 2 suites, most of which have lovely views of Loch Nager. Public rooms have been tastefully furnished and the restaurant makes good use of fresh local produce. Service is well-managed, informal and helpful.*
10⇨↑(1fb) CTV in all bedrooms ® T sB&B⇨↑£25
dB&B⇨↑£45-£65 ⊟
CTV 12P ✿ ⚕ xmas
V ✿ ᴸ Bar Lunch £1.25-£9.50alc Dinner £13.50-£15alc Last dinner 9.30pm
Credit Cards ①②③ⓔ

★★ 67% *Darroch Learg* AB3 5UX ☎(03397)55443
Closed Nov-Jan
*Set in landscaped gardens with magnificent views over the River Dee, this hotel has a relaxed, friendly atmosphere and individually decorated bedrooms. Good, wholesome food is served in the dining room.*
15⇨↑Annexe8rm(3⇨2↑)(2fb) CTV in all bedrooms ® T
25P 🚗 ✿
V ✿ ᴸ Last dinner 8.30pm
Credit Cards ①③

★★ 60% *Monaltrie* 5 Bridge Square AB3 5QJ (Inter-Hotels)
☎(03397)55417 FAX (03397) 55180
*This 19th-century hotel has been extensively modernised and facilities include a good lounge, a spacious bar and a popular restaurant. The bedrooms are well equipped and several overlook the River Dee. Local fishing and golf can be arranged. Staff are friendly and helpful.*
23rm(18⇨3↑)(3fb)1 ⒇ CTV in all bedrooms ® T
sB&B⇨↑£29-£35 dB&B⇨↑£50-£58 ⊟
45P ✿ xmas
V ✿ ᴸ ✗ Bar Lunch £3-£8alc Dinner £15.25&alc Last dinner 8.30pm
Credit Cards ①②③⑤ⓔ

---

**BALLOCH** Strathclyde *Dunbartonshire* Map **10** NS38

○**Cameron House** G83 8QZ ☎(0389)55625
Due to have opened Aug 1990
68rm

93

**BALSALL COMMON** West Midlands Map **04** SP27

★★68%, **Haigs** Kenilworth Rd CV7 7EL
☎Berkswell(0676)33004 FAX (0676) 34572
Closed 26 Dec-3 Jan
*A small, privately owned and run hotel on the A452, conveniently situated for the motorway network and only fifteen minutes' drive from NEC and airport, is popular with the business traveller, for whom it provides comfortable accommodation with good facilities and a well-appointed restaurant offering a good choice of well-prepared dishes.*
13rm(12⇔3🅫) CTV in all bedrooms 🅫 T sB&B£24.50-£32
sB&B⇔3🅫£29.50-£44.50 dB&B⇔3🅫£39-£56
CTV 22P 🚗 ✿ nc4yrs
🍴 French V ✿ Sunday Lunch £8.95-£9.50 Dinner
£13.25-£14.50&alc Last dinner 9pm
Credit Cards 1 2 3 5 £
**See advertisement under BIRMINGHAM (NATIONAL EXHIBITION CENTRE)**

**BAMBURGH** Northumberland Map **12** NU13

★★69%, **Lord Crewe Arms** Front St NE69 7BL ☎(06684)243
Closed Dec-Mar
*This attractive hotel, situated at the centre of the quaint village and managed by friendly resident proprietors, features pretty bedrooms, comfortable lounges and a good-value five-course dinner.*
25rm(14⇔6🅫)(1fb) CTV in all bedrooms 🅫 sB&B£30-£32
dB&B£40-£44 dB&B⇔3🅫£52-£57 🏢
34P 🚗 nc5yrs
🍴 English & French ✿ ✂ Bar Lunch £2.75-£7.50alc Dinner
£15.50-£17 Last dinner 9pm
Credit Cards 1 3

★★55%, **Victoria** Front St NE69 7BP ☎(06684)431
*Family-run hotel, recently refurbished to offer modern bedrooms and character public rooms.*
23rm(15⇔1🅫)(3fb)1🖼 CTV in all bedrooms 🅫 T
sB&B£23-£29 sB&B⇔3🅫£27.50-£34 dB&B£40-£55
dB&B⇔3🅫£46-£66 🏢
7P games room *xmas*
V ✿ Sunday Lunch £7-£7.50 Dinner £14-£15.50&alc Last dinner 8.30pm
Credit Cards 1 2 3 5 £

★57%, **Sunningdale** 21-23 Lucker Rd NE69 7BS ☎(06684)334
*This family-managed hotel offers comfortable accommodation, and friendly service is assured. Bedroom accommodation is basic with some compact rooms.*
19rm(6⇔3)(3fb)✂ in 2 bedrooms sB&B£15-£25 sB&B⇔3£17-£27
dB&B£30-£48 dB&B⇔3£34-£50 🏢
CTV 16P games room *xmas*
V ✿ Bar Lunch 75p-£3 Dinner £9 Last dinner 7.30pm
Credit Cards 1 3 £

**BAMFORD** Derbyshire Map **08** SK28

★★68%, **Rising Sun** Castleton Rd S30 2AL (on main A625 rd)
☎Hope Valley(0433)51323
*Set beside the main A625 road, with well-maintained gardens where children can play in safety, this popular inn has a busy carvery restaurant and well-furnished bedrooms with many extras. A warm welcome and comfortable accommodation are assured.*
11⇔3🅫(1fb) CTV in all bedrooms 🅫 T ✖ (ex guide dogs)
sB&B⇔3🅫£38 dB&B⇔3🅫£55 🏢
70P ✿
V ✿ ✂
Credit Cards 1 3 £

★★56% **Marquis of Granby** Hathersage Rd S30 2BH
☎Hope Valley(0433)51206
*Standing in the beautiful Peak District, this friendly hotel is situated alongside the A625, and looks out on to pleasant lawns and gardens. Panelling from the SS Olympic is much in evidence, and the bedrooms, many of which are beamed, are spacious and well equipped. There is a choice of bars and a good range of restaurant and bar meals. Please note that the restaurant is closed on Mondays.*
7⇔3🅫(2fb)1🖼 CTV in all bedrooms 🅫
CTV 100P ✿ ✔
V ✿ ✂
Credit Cards 1 2 3 5

**BAMPTON** Devon Map **03** SS92

★★68%, **Bark House** Oakford Bridge EX16 9HZ (2.5m W A396) ☎Oakford(03985)236
Closed 21 Dec-1 Mar
*Situated beside the A396 in the hamlet of Oakfordbridge near the River Exe. The hotel is a stone building, formerly a tannery. The well-kept garden is terraced on the hillside of this Devonshire valley to picturesque effect. The bedrooms are comfortable and well-decorated, and the public rooms promote a cottage atmosphere. A warm welcome and good home cooking are offered.*
6rm(2⇔2🅫)(1fb) CTV in 5 bedrooms T ✳ sB&B£16
sB&B⇔3🅫£27-£33 dB&B£36
dB&B⇔3🅫£44-£54 Continental breakfast
12P ✿ (£1) 🚗 ✿ nc5yrs
🍴 English, French & American ✿ ✂ Bar Lunch £2-£7 Dinner £13 Last dinner 8.30pm
Credit Cards 1 3

**BANBURY** Oxfordshire Map **04** SP44

★★★66%, **Whately Hall** Banbury Cross OX16 0AN (Trusthouse Forte) ☎(0295)263451 Telex no 837149 FAX (0295) 271736
*Dating in part from the seventeenth century, the hotel has been upgraded to provide modern comforts and facilities. Comfortable, tastefully-appointed public areas include an interesting restaurant where table d'hôte and à la carte meals display the flair and imagination of the chef, adequately furnished bedrooms are well equipped, and a pleasant helpful staff provides efficient service.*
74⇔3🅫 in 30 bedrooms CTV in all bedrooms 🅫 T S%
sB⇔3🅫£76-£79 dB⇔3🅫£97.50-£130 (room only) 🏢
Lift ( 60P 20🚗 (£5-£8 per night) ✿ CFA croquet *xmas*
V ✿ ✂ ✂ Lunch fr£10.95&alc High tea fr£5.90 Dinner fr£14.50&alc Last dinner 9.15pm
Credit Cards 1 2 3 4 5

★★★60%, **Banbury Moat House** 27-29 Oxford Rd OX16 9AH (Queens Moat) ☎(0295)259361 Telex no 838967
FAX (0295) 270954
*This hotel features modern well-equipped bedrooms, with spacious bathrooms and more traditonal public rooms.*
50⇔3🅫(2fb)1🖼 CTV in all bedrooms 🅫 T S% sB&B£69
dB&B⇔3🅫£79 🏢
《 48P CFA
🍴 International V ✿ ✂ ✂ S% Lunch fr£10.50 Dinner fr£11.50&alc Last dinner 9.45pm
Credit Cards 1 2 3 5

★★61%, **Cromwell Lodge** North Bar OX16 0TB ☎(0295)259781
Telex no 83343
Closed 1 wk Xmas & New Year
*Pleasant, professionally run hotel with pleasant staff. Modern, well-equipped bedrooms and attractive restaurant.*
32⇔3🅫(1fb) CTV in all bedrooms 🅫
《 CTV 25P
🍴 International V ✿ ✂ Last dinner 9.30pm
Credit Cards 1 2 3 4 5

**B**

★★60%, **Lismore Hotel & Restaurant** 61 Oxford Rd OX16 9AJ
(Minotels) ☎(0295)267661
Closed 24 Dec-3 Jan
*A homely hotel, conveniently positioned, offering well-equipped
bedrooms and good food standards. Popular with both business
people and tourists alike.*
14rm(10⇨♪♠)Annexe7⇨♠(4fb)1⊞ CTV in all bedrooms ® T
✳ sB&B£25-£30 sB&B⇨♠£40-£45 dB&B⇨♠£55-£60 ♬
CTV 19P
♡ English & French V ✿ ⍽ Lunch £4.50-£13.50 Dinner
£11.50-£13.50 Last dinner 9.30pm
Credit Cards ①②③④

---

**BANCHORY** Grampian *Kincardineshire* Map **15** NO69

★★★★♨71% **Invery House** Bridge of Feugh AB3 3NJ
(Prestige) ☎(03302)4782 Telex no 73737 FAX (03302) 4712
Closed 5-25 Jan
*A lovely half-mile drive, through silver birches and beech trees and
by the side of the River Feugh, leads to this elegant and luxurious
Deeside mansion. With fishing rights on the river and shooting
parties organised, it is popular with sportsmen and those simply
seeking peace and quiet. A stone-flagged hall leads to a large
foyer-lounge with a lovely drawing room beyond. Quality
furnishings abound, and bedrooms are spacious and well-
appointed. Food is ably cooked by chef Clive Lamb and the
friendly staff ensure that one's stay is enjoyable.*
14⇨♠1⊞ CTV in all bedrooms T ✖ (ex guide dogs)
sB&B⇨♠£85-£115 dB&B⇨♠£95-£165 ♬
《 20P 3🅿 ⇔ ✿ ♪ (grass) ✐ snooker croquet lawn putting
green nc8yrs xmas
♡ Scottish & French V ✿ ⍽ ✗ Lunch £17.50 Dinner £29.50
Last dinner 9.45pm
Credit Cards ①②③⑤
**See advertisement on page 97**

---

# The Banbury Moat House
★★★

This elegant Georgian hotel now has 48 bedrooms all
with private bathroom, colour television, direct-dial
telephone, hair dryer and coffee and tea making facilities.
There is also the Blenheim Suite with its four-poster bed
and jacuzzi bath.

The Restaurant serves both à la Carte and Table d'Hôte
menus and is locally renowned for its superb cuisine.

The Moat House is situated near the town centre with car
parking at the rear.

**Queens Moat Houses PLC**

INTERNATIONAL HOTELIERS

Oxford Road, Banbury, Oxfordshire, OX16 9AH
Telephone: Banbury (0295) 259361

---

★★     RELAIS
ROUTIERS

# CROMWELL LODGE
### ⌒*HOTEL*⌒

*North Bar, Banbury, Oxfordshire OX16 0TB
Tel: 0295-259781*

This 17th century privately run hotel has a large
peaceful garden and patio where summer barbecues are held. All 32 bedrooms are en-suite. Within
25 minutes of Stratford, it is well situated for
visiting the Cotswolds, Warwick and Oxford. Free
car parking. Excellent reputation for food and
hospitality.
All major credit cards.
Weekend breaks available all year.

---

AA ★ ★       ETB

## VICTORIA HOTEL

## Bamburgh,
## Northumberland NE69 7BP
### Tel: Bamburgh (066 84) 431

Stay on Northumbria's enchanted shore, amid
castles, magnificent beaches and tiny fishing
villages — absolutely unspoilt and a paradise
for walkers, golfers and lovers of wildlife.

The famous old Victoria Hotel, in the centre
of Bamburgh, Northumbria's ancient capital,
offers great comfort, good food, a wonderful atmosphere and excellent value. 23 rooms, most
with private bath, all with colour television,
direct-dial telephone and tea/coffee facilities.

★★★

★★★ 🏵 BANCHORY LODGE

AB3 3HS ☎(03302)2625
Closed 13 Dec-Jan

*A charming Georgian country
house on the banks of the
River Dee makes an ideal
retreat for fishermen because
the hotel owns both banks of this stretch of the river and can
arrange fishing. Dugald and Maggie Jaffray have run
Banchory Lodge for many years, imprinting their personality
on the hotel which is beautifully furnished with many fine
antique pieces and decorated with prints, paintings and masses
of fresh flowers. The dining room is gracious, and creates a
lovely atmosphere for the delicious 4-course dinners, and the
comfortable lounges are just right for the indulgence of a
traditional afternoon tea. Service is attentive and courteous.*

23⇄ᐧ(11fb)2🛏 CTV in all bedrooms ®
CTV 50P 🚗 ✿ ♪ sauna pool table
🍴 English & French V 🕯 ⚗ Last dinner 9.30pm
Credit Cards ①②③④⑤

---

★★★🏵75%, **Raemoir** AB3 4ED ☎(03302)4884 Telex no 73315
FAX (03302) 2171
*Magnificently set in 3,500 acres, this elegant 18th-century
mansion is furnished throughout with antiques, many of them
unusual. The panelled morning room dates from 1817 and all the
bedrooms have been individually furnished to preserve the
character of the house. The young chef makes good use of fresh
local ingredients to produce an interesting menu. The friendly
service is complemented by the personal involvement of owner, Kit
Sabin, and her daughter Judy Ollis.*
17⇄ᐧAnnexe6⇄ᐧ(1fb)1🛏 CTV in all bedrooms ® T
sB&B⇄ᐧ£50-£70 dB&B⇄ᐧ£80-£120 🏢
CTV 200P 1🏠 (£1) 🚗 ✿ ▶9 ♫ (hard) ♪ sauna solarium
gymnasium croquet mini golf shooting stalking ♨ *xmas*
🍴 International V 🕯 ⚗ ✂ Sunday Lunch £11.50 Dinner
£19.50&alc Last dinner 9pm
Credit Cards ①②③⑤ ⑥

★★★62%, **Tor-na-Coille** AB3 4AB ☎(03302)2242
FAX (03302) 4012
*Under the ownership of Roxanne Sloan, this hotel is being
dramatically upgraded and its now-restored bedrooms are both
elegant and spacious, with many thoughtful touches. The lounge
bar continues to be a popular venue for bar meals, and the dining
room has been attractively redecorated. Here guests can enjoy
table d'hôte and à la carte meals with a Scottish flavour, served by
friendly local staff.*
24⇄ᐧ(4fb)1🛏 CTV in all bedrooms ® T
sB&B⇄ᐧ£44.50-£72 dB&B⇄ᐧ£72-£85 🏢
Lift 130P ✿ squash croquet lawn *xmas*
🍴 Scottish & French V 🕯 ⚗ ✂
Credit Cards ①②③⑤ ⑥

★★61%, **Burnett Arms** 25 High St AB3 3TD (Consort)
☎(03302)4944 Telex no 739925 FAX (0224) 744354
*This old coaching inn has been completely modernised and
provides a lounge, 2 popular bars, a dining room and bedrooms
which are well equipped and functional. Service is well managed
and friendly and there is a self-contained function suite offering
good facilities for both private and business purposes.*
18rm(4⇄12ᐧ)(5fb) CTV in all bedrooms ® T sB&B£22-£24
sB&B⇄ᐧ£24-£28 dB&B⇄ᐧ£36-£44 🏢
40P ♫ *xmas*

V 🕯 ⚗ Lunch £4.60-£8.50alc High tea £5.60-£9.90alc Dinner
£11-£13 Last dinner 9pm
Credit Cards ①②③⑤

---

**BANFF** Grampian *Banffshire* Map **15** NJ66

★★★56%, **Banff Springs** Golden Knowes Rd AB4 2JE
(Consort) ☎(02612)2881 FAX (02612) 5546
*A popular venue for local functions, this modern, purpose-built
hotel stands on the edge of the town overlooking the Moray Firth.
Bedrooms, though practical in style, are comfortable and well
equipped.*
30⇄ᐧ(4fb) CTV in all bedrooms ® ✳ sB&B⇄ᐧ£35
dB&B⇄ᐧ£50 🏢
⦅ 120P *xmas*
🍴 French V 🕯 ⚗ Dinner £12.50&alc Last dinner 9pm
Credit Cards ①②③④⑤ ⑥

★★58%, **County** 32 High St AB4 1AE (Guestaccom)
☎(02612)5353
*A charming Georgian house in the town centre with bedrooms and
public rooms in period style. Throughout the hotel the ambience of
a country house in former days is retained, enhanced by the
personal involvement of the owners. Good views of Banff Bay.*
7rm(5⇄)(2fb)2🛏 CTV in all bedrooms ® T 🐕 (ex guide dogs)
sB&B⇄ᐧ£30-£32 dB&B⇄ᐧ£45-£48 🏢
7P ✿ ♪ ♨ *xmas*
V 🕯 ⚗ ✂ Sunday Lunch £5-£7alc High tea £3-£5alc Dinner
£10-£20alc Last dinner 9pm
Credit Cards ①②③⑤ ⑥

---

**BANGOR** Gwynedd Map **06** SH57

★★68%, **Menai Court** Craig y Don Rd LL57 2BG
☎(0248)354200
Closed 26 Dec-7 Jan
*This delightful, well-furnished hotel offers well-equipped,
comfortable bedrooms, good food and friendly service.*
12⇄ᐧ(2fb) CTV in all bedrooms ® T sB&B⇄ᐧ£43
dB&B⇄ᐧ£72 🏢
22P 🚗 *xmas*
🍴 British & French V 🕯 Lunch £11.50 Dinner £16&alc Last
dinner 9.30pm
Credit Cards ①③ ⑥

★★65%, **Ty Uchaf** Tal-y-Bont LL57 3UR ☎(0248)352219
Closed 24 Dec-2 Jan
*Good, all-round facilities are provided by this well-furnished and
comfortable hotel which stands in rural surroundings just outside
the town. Bedrooms provide all home comforts, the cosy lounge
and typical Welsh bar are open to diners as well as residents, and
meals of a good standard are served in both restaurant and bar.*
9⇄ᐧ CTV in all bedrooms ® 🐕 (ex guide dogs) ✳
sB&B⇄ᐧ£22.50-£27.50 dB&B⇄ᐧ£37.50-£42.50 🏢
40P ✿ nc10yrs
V 🕯 ⚗ Lunch £7.95 Dinner fr£8.50&alc Last dinner 8.30pm
Credit Cards ①③ ⑥

★★63%, **Telford** Holyhead Rd LL57 2HX ☎(0248)352543
*Friendly, resident owners create a home-like atmosphere at an
hotel which enjoys fine views of Telford's suspension bridge from its
position on the Menai Straits.*
10rm(4ᐧ)(2fb)✂in 2 bedrooms CTV in 9 bedrooms TV in 1
bedroom 🐕 (ex guide dogs) S% sB&B£33-£40.25
sB&Bᐧ£40.25 dB&B£46-£50 dB&Bᐧ£80.50 🏢
⦅⊞CTV 15P ✿ ♪
V 🕯 ⚗ ✂
Credit Cards ①③

---

1991 marks the 25th anniversary of this guide.

B

BARDON MILL Northumberland Map **12** NY76

★**65%, Vallum Lodge** Military Rd, Twice Brewed NE47 7AN
☎Haltwhistle(0434)344248
Closed Dec-Feb
*Standing on earthworks which were once part of Hadrian's Wall and next to the military road ( B6318) that runs alongside it, this small hotel offers bright, comfortable accommodation in a friendly informal atmosphere.*
7rm(2fb) ⑬ sB&B£16-£19 dB&B£31-£39 ▤
CTV 30P 🚗 ✿
🎘 Mainly grills V 🕭 ⬛ ⨆ Lunch £5.50-£6.75alc Dinner £10-£12 Last dinner 8pm

BARFORD Warwickshire Map **04** SP26

★★**62%, The Glebe at Barford** Church St CV35 8BS
☎Warwick(0926)624218 FAX (0926) 624625
*This Georgian house, in a peaceful village setting adjacent to the church, continues to provide inviting, well-cooked meals; bedrooms and parts of the public areas are due for major refurbishment and alteration.*
36⇌⅗♠(3fb)2🖼⨆in 3 bedrooms CTV in all bedrooms ⑬ T
sB&B⇌⅗♠£74.50 dB&B⇌⅗♠£88.50 ▤
Lift ⊄ 56P 🚗 ✿ ▤(heated) sauna solarium gymnasium jacuzzi
xmas
🎘 English & Continental V 🕭 ⬛ Lunch £3.95-£13.50 Dinner £18.50 Last dinner 9.45pm
Credit Cards ① ② ③ ⑤

All AA-appointed establishments are inspected regularly to ensure that required standards are maintained.

**★★★**

## Golden Knowes Road, Banff AB4 2JE Scotland
## Telephone: 02612-2881

Privately owned hotel open all year round, only an hour drive from Aberdeen and the airport.
30 rooms all with private bathrooms, TV etc.
The Restaurant is locally renowned for good food and service.
Facilities available for conferences, dinner dances, weddings – two golf courses a short drive away.

**B**

---

**BAR HILL** Cambridgeshire Map **05** TL36

★★★**61% Cambridgeshire Moat House** CB3 8EU (Queens Moat) ☎Crafts Hill(0954)780555 Telex no 817141
FAX (0954) 780010
Closed 25 Dec
*An hotel conveniently set beside the A604 five-and-a-half miles north of the city centre combines well-equipped accommodation with a good range of conference and banquetting facilities. Its very comprehensive leisure centre, which includes squash courts and a swimming pool, is complemented by an 18-hole championship golf course, and guests have a choice of bars in which to relax. Service is efficient throughout.*
100⇨♠(8fb) CTV in all bedrooms ® T sB&B⇨♠£70-£77 dB&B⇨♠£87-£95 ⋤
《 200P ❈ CFA⬚(heated) ▶ 18 ♪ (hard) squash sauna solarium gymnasium putting green
♀ English & French V ❖ ⬚ Lunch fr£15&alc High tea £2.75-£3.75 Dinner £15-£16.50&alc Last dinner 10pm
Credit Cards ①②③⑤

---

**BARKSTON** Lincolnshire Map **08** SK94

✗✗**Barkston House** NG32 2NH ☎Loveden(0400)50555
*Sound British dishes with fresh produce treated in a light, modern style, from the basis of the short but imaginative menu here, where the quality of food is matched by charming attentive service. The dining room – originally the kitchen of the pleasant eighteenth-century house – has stripped beams, complete with servants' bells, and open fireplace. The warm, country atmosphere carries through to an attractive sitting room and a large, comfortable bar. Two fine bedrooms are available for overnight guests.*
Closed Sun, 25-30 Dec & 2 wks Jun
Lunch not served Sat & Mon
28 seats Lunch £10 Dinner £12-£16alc Last lunch 1.30pm Last dinner 9.15pm 16P
Credit Cards ①②③⑤

---

**BARMOUTH** Gwynedd Map **06** SH61

★★**65% Ty'r Graig** Llanaber Rd LL42 1YN ☎(0341)280470
Closed Nov-Feb
*This large detached late Victorian house, of unusual architecture, is located approximately half a mile from the town centre. It stands in its own attractive gardens and wooded grounds in an elevated position overlooking the beach and Cardigan Bay. The public areas are elegant, and tastefully furnished and decorated, and have a wealth of carved pitch pine woodwork and stained glass leaded windows. The bedrooms are well equipped, all with en suite facilities.*
12⇨♠2⁂ CTV in all bedrooms ® T ✗ (ex guide dogs) sB&B⇨♠fr£30 dB&B⇨♠fr£52 ⋤
15P ⚗ ❈ windsurfing yachting sea fishing
♀ Welsh, English & French V ❖ ⬚ ✄ Sunday Lunch £7.50 Dinner fr£11.50&alc Last dinner 8.30pm
Credit Cards ①③

★★**62% Panorama** Panorama Rd LL42 1DQ ☎(0341)280550
*This large stone built Victorian hotel is aptly named as it does, indeed, enjoy panoramic views from its elevated position. Family run, in an informal manner the hotel provides comfortable accommodation suitable for both holidaymakers and business people alike.*
20rm(15⇨♠)(3fb) CTV in all bedrooms ® ✳ sB&B£15.50 sB&B⇨♠£20-£21 dB&B£31 dB&B⇨♠£40-£42 ⋤
CTV 40P ❈ putting green nc2yrs
V ❖ ⬚ Sunday Lunch £6.95 Dinner £8.95&alc Last dinner 9.30pm
Credit Cards ①③

★**63% Bryn Melyn** Panorama Rd LL42 1DQ ☎(0341)280556
FAX (0341) 280990
Closed Dec-Feb
*A small family run hotel in an elevated position east of the town, commanding splendid views across the Mawddach Estuary to the Cader Mountains. The bedrooms are quite well equipped, the majority have en suite showers and toilets.*
10rm(8♠)(2fb) CTV in 8 bedrooms ® sB&Bfr£18.50 sB&B♠fr£27.50 dB&Bfr£33 dB&B♠fr£45 ⋤
10P ⚗ ❈
V ❖ Dinner fr£10.75 Last dinner 8.30pm
Credit Cards ①③£

★**60% Marwyn** 21 Marine Pde LL42 1NA ☎(0341)280185
*A small, seafront hotel enjoying views of the beach, Cardigan Bay and the Mawddach Estuary. The majority of the well-equipped bedrooms have en suite facilities.*
7⇨♠(1fb)1⁂ CTV in all bedrooms ®
CTV ⚗ nc7yrs
V ❖ ⬚ Last dinner 11pm
Credit Cards ①③

---

**BARNBY MOOR** Nottinghamshire Map **08** SK68

★★★**66% Ye Olde Bell** DN22 8QS ☎Retford(0777)705121
FAX (0777) 860424
*An original 17th-century posting house whose guests have included Queen Victoria and Queen Maud of Norway.*
55⇨♠2⁂✄in 8 bedrooms CTV in all bedrooms ® T ✳ sB&B⇨♠£60-£70 dB&B⇨♠£80-£90 ⋤
《 250P ❈ xmas
♀ English & French V ❖ ⬚ ✄ Lunch £6.95-£7.95&alc Dinner £12.95&alc Last dinner 9.45pm
Credit Cards ①②③④⑤

See advertisement under **RETFORD (EAST)**

---

**BARNHAM BROOM** Norfolk Map **05** TG00

★★★**65% Barnham Broom Hotel Conference & Leisure Centre** NR9 4DD (Best Western) ☎(060545)393 Telex no 975711
FAX (060545) 8224
*Surrounded by two hundred and fifty acres of countryside, yet offering easy access to the A471 Norwich Road, this purpose-built hotel with extensive leisure centre combines well-equipped accommodation and conference/banqueting facilities, competent service being provided throughout. Flints Restaurant serves a carvery lunch, its varied menu making imaginative use of fresh produce. The two golf courses are 18-hole with a par 72.*
52⇨♠(12fb) CTV in all bedrooms ® T ✳ sB&B⇨♠£55-£60 dB&B⇨♠£70-£75 ⋤
《 200P CFA⬚(heated) ▶ 36 ♪ (hard) squash sauna solarium gymnasium hairdressing salon beautician xmas
♀ English & Continental V ❖ ⬚ ✄ Lunch £7.50-£8 Dinner £12-£12.50 Last dinner 9.30pm
Credit Cards ①②③⑤£

See advertisement under **NORWICH**

---

**BARNSDALE BAR** South Yorkshire Map **08** SE51

⌂**Travelodge** Wentbridge (A1), Barnsdale Bar WF8 3JB (Trusthouse Forte)
☎Pontefract(0977)620711 Central res (0800) 850950 Telex no 557457
*Located on the south-bound carriageway of the A1 just eight miles north of Doncaster, the lodge stands adjacent to a Little Chef restaurant and shop in a busy service area.*
56⇨♠(56fb) CTV in all bedrooms ® sB⇨♠£24 dB⇨♠£29.50 (room only)
《 56P ⚗
Credit Cards ①②③

---

**BARNSLEY** South Yorkshire Map **08** SE30

★★★65% **Ardsley Moat House** Doncaster Rd, Ardsley
S71 5EH (Queens Moat) ☎(0226)289401 Telex no 547762
FAX (0226) 205374
Closed 25 Dec
*Comfortable and well-appointed, the hotel offers friendly service
and some very interesting restaurant menus.*
73⇌♠(3fb)3♨ CTV in all bedrooms ® ✱ sB⇌♠£59-£62
dB⇌♠£72-£75 (room only) ♬
《 300P ✿ snooker ♫
♀ English & French V ❖ ⚑ Lunch £10.50 Dinner £14&alc
Last dinner 10.30pm
Credit Cards ①②③⑤

★50% *Royal* Church St S70 2AD ☎(0226)203658
Closed 25 Dec RS Bank Hols
*Comfortable, well-appointed hotel with spacious lounge bars and
restaurant featuring local dishes.*
17rm(1⇌)(1fb) CTV in all bedrooms ®
CTV 2♨
V ❖ ⚑ ✂ Last dinner 9.30pm
Credit Cards ①②③④⑤

○**Travelodge** A633/635, Stairfoot Roundabout(Trusthouse
Forte) ☎Central reservations (0800) 850950
Due to open winter 1990
32⇌

---

**BARNSTAPLE** Devon Map **02** SS53

★★★64% **Imperial** Taw Vale Pde EX32 8NB (Trusthouse
Forte) ☎(0271)45861 FAX (0271) 24448
*Good facilities are provided for both commercial guests and
holiday makers at this busy, town centre hotel. Comfortable
bedrooms are complemented by welcoming public area, both table
d'hôte and à la carte menus are available in the spacious
restaurant, and staff are pleasant and friendly.*
56⇌♠(3fb)✂in 22 bedrooms CTV in all bedrooms ® T
sB⇌♠£60-£65 dB⇌♠£71-£76 (room only) ♬
Lift 《 80P *xmas*
V ❖ ⚑ ✂ Sunday Lunch fr£8.95 High tea £2.50-£3.50 Dinner
fr£14.50&alc Last dinner 9pm
Credit Cards ①②③④⑤

★★★62% **Park** Taw Vale EX32 8NJ (Brend) ☎(0271)72166
Telex no 42551 FAX (0271) 78558
*A small hotel with modern amenities, and a restaurant on the first
floor.*
25⇌♠Annexe17⇌♠(7fb) CTV in all bedrooms ® T
sB&B⇌♠£39-£49 dB&B⇌♠£60-£75 ♬
《 80P *xmas*
♀ English & French V ❖ ⚑ Lunch £6.50-£7.50&alc Dinner
£10-£14&alc Last dinner 9pm
Credit Cards ①②③⑤ ⓔ

★★‡68% **Downrew House** Bishops Tawton EX32 0DY
☎(0271)42497 & 46673 FAX (0271) 23947
*The new and enthusiastic owners of this small, cosy retreat have
created a homely and relaxing atmosphere by their emphasis on
good standards of hospitality. The house, built in 1640 and
enlarged during the reign of Queen Anne, stands amid twelve acres
of meadowland in very attractive countryside just outside the town
and now easily accessible from the new link road. Compact but
attractively appointed and comfortable public areas are
complemented by bedrooms which are for the most part charming
and individually furnished, though those in the adjoining lodge
tend to be a little more functional, while mealtimes offer a good
range of dishes soundly based on quality produce. Leisure
amenities include a full-size billiard table, solarium, croquet lawns,
outdoor swimming pool and private 15-hole golf approach and putt
course.*
6⇌♠Annexe6⇌♠(2fb) CTV in all bedrooms ® T
sB&B⇌♠£63.17-£84 dB&B⇌♠£108.84-£133 (incl dinner) ♬
▶

**B**

12P ⚙ ✤ ◿(heated) ♪ (hard) snooker solarium golf (15 hole approach) croquet lawn nc7yrs *xmas*
♀ English & Continental **V** ✗ Dinner £11.50-£26alc Last dinner 9.15pm
Credit Cards ①③

★★66%, **Royal & Fortescue** Boutport St EX31 1HG (Brend)
☎(0271)42289 Telex no 42551 FAX (0271) 78558
*A choice of dining room and all-day coffee shop is available at this bustling town-centre commercial hotel. Management is efficient and service friendly, whilst the bedrooms are all well equipped, though they vary in style.*
62rm(33◿2♠)(4fb) CTV in all bedrooms ® **T** sB&B£30 sB&B◿♠£38 dB&B£48 dB&B◿♠£55 ₱
Lift ⓒ CTV 20P 6🚗 *xmas*
♀ English & French **V** ♥ ⏤ Lunch £5.50-£6.50&alc Dinner £10-£12&alc Last dinner 9pm
Credit Cards ①②③⑤ⓔ

★

★♨ HALMPSTONE MANOR

Bishop's Tawton EX32 0EA
☎Swimbridge(0271)830321
FAX (0271) 830826

*Guests arriving at Charles and Jane Stanbury's welcoming hotel will readily understand why it won the AA 'Best Newcomer' Award in 1989. The owners and their staff are naturally hospitable, with a manner that makes guests feel immediately at home. They have furnished the house with antiques and ornaments that are mainly family pieces and so sit well in the spacious and attractive rooms, maintaining the informal and home-like atmosphere. Fresh flowers are everywhere, and among the many extras waiting for guests in the bedrooms are a decanter of sherry and bowl of fruit. Meals in the panelled dining room are especially good and the kitchens are supervised by Jane Stanbury who insists on the best quality local produce, with which she and her staff create a range of imaginative and succulent dishes. Tucked away amid quiet lanes just south of Barnstaple, Halmpstone Manor is ideally placed for visiting both North Devon and Somerset.*
5◿♠2⌷ CTV in all bedrooms ® ✗ sB&B◿♠£60 dB&B◿♠£80-£100
12P ⚙ ✤ nc10yrs
♀ English & French Dinner £20&alc Last dinner 9.30pm
Credit Cards ①②③ⓔ

✗✗✗**Lynwood House** Bishops Tawton Rd EX32 9DZ
☎(0271)43695 FAX (0271) 79340
*A detached Victorian residence on the edge of town where the Roberts family have been maintaining their service and facilities for two decades. There is now only one dining room, which is open for both lunch and dinner, the same menu being used for both meals. Only fresh foods are used, especially seafood, and are carefully cooked. Three comfortable bedrooms are also now available.*
♀ British & Continental **V** 50 seats ✳ Lunch £15-£30alc Dinner £15-£30alc Last lunch 2pm Last dinner 9.30pm 30P ✗
Credit Cards ①③

The AA's star-rating scheme is the market leader in hotel classification.

---

# The Lower Pitt Restaurant
# ✗ ✗

EAST BUCKLAND, BARNSTAPLE,
N. DEVON EX32 0TD
Telephone Filleigh 243
Mr. & Mrs. J.T. LYONS

**Reservations essential**

Licensed restaurant noted for its fine cuisine using top quality ingredients. Set in a XVIth century Devon longhouse. Welcoming atmosphere and away from it all. Three cosy double rooms (one with bath, 2 with shower) for overnight dinner guests. Situated in quiet hamlet yet only 2 miles from new North Devon Link Road.

---

**BARRA, ISLE OF** Western Isles *Inverness-shire* Map 13

**TANGUSDALE** Map 13 NF60

★★61%, **Isle of Barra** Tangusdale Beach PA80 5XW (Consort)
☎Castlebay(08714)383 FAX (08714) 385
Closed Nov-Mar RS Apr
*Situated beside one of the island's most attractive sandy beaches, to which there is easy access, this purpose-built, modern hotel offers pleasant, comfortable public areas, and functional bedrooms, some of which enjoy fine views of the sea. Service is friendly and helpful.*
30⇌(2fb) CTV in all bedrooms ® sB&B⇌£30-£45
dB&B⇌£50-£65 ⊟
CTV ✗ ❄ ♪
V ♥ ⚗ S% Dinner £13.50-£15 Last dinner 8.30pm
Credit Cards [1] [3] ⓔ

**BARR, GREAT** West Midlands Map 07 SP09

★★★59%, **Great Barr Hotel & Conference Centre** Pear Tree Dr, off Newton Rd B43 6HS (1m W of junc A34/A4041)
☎021-357 1141 Telex no 336406 FAX 021-357 7557
*This hotel is pleasantly situated in a residential area which is both close to Walsall and convenient for the M6 motorway. Most of its rooms have now been refurbished to offer a wide range of facilities, and the establishment is particularly popular for conferences.*
114⇌ᐟ(1fb) CTV in all bedrooms ® T ✖ (ex guide dogs) ✳
S% sB&B⇌ᐟ£59-£65 dB&B⇌ᐟ£69-£75 ⊟
⟨ 175P ❄
♥ English & Continental V ♥ ⚗ Lunch £7.95-£9&alc Dinner fr£11.75&alc Last dinner 9.45pm
Credit Cards [1] [2] [3] [4] [5] ⓔ
**See advertisement under BIRMINGHAM**

★★★58%, *Post House* Chapel Ln B43 7BG (at junction M6/A34) (Trusthouse Forte) ☎021-357 7444 Telex no 338497 FAX 021-357 7503
*Current refurbishment should provide up-to-date bedrooms in line with the hotel's excellent leisure complex and extensive conference facilities, while the planned improvement of public areas includes the addition of a Traders Restaurant.*
204⇌(42fb) CTV in all bedrooms ®
⟨ 300P CFA ⊠(heated) ⊇ sauna solarium gymnasium ♫
V ♥ ⚗ ✂ Last dinner 10pm
Credit Cards [1] [2] [3] [4] [5]

**BARRHEAD** Strathclyde *Renfrewshire* Map 11 NS45

★★55%, *Dalmeny Park* Lochlibo Rd G78 1LG ☎041-881 9211
*19th-century house with gardens, on the edge of town, with open fires and Georgian-style function suite.*
18rm(3⇌10ᐟ)(2fb) CTV in all bedrooms ®
⟨ 150P ❄
V ♥ ⚗ Last dinner 9.30pm
Credit Cards [1] [2] [3] [4] [5]

**BARRHILL** Strathclyde *Lanarkshire* Map 10 NX28

❀★★★⚜77%, **Kildonan** KA26 0PU ☎(046582)360
FAX (046582) 292
*Located somewhat off the beaten track, this fine Sir Edwin Lutyens designed country house offers a haven for those seeking solitude in beautiful surroundings, yet it is within striking distance of Glasgow and Prestwick Airports. Most bedrooms are spacious and furnished in good traditional style, whilst the food has a Continental flavour due to the influence of Swiss chef Rolf Mueller.*
31⇌ᐟ(7fb)1⊠ CTV in all bedrooms ® T sB&B⇌ᐟ£75-£140
dB&B⇌ᐟ£110-£140 ⊟
⟨ 60P ⇛ ❄ ⊠(heated) ▶ 9 ♞ (hard) ♪ squash snooker sauna solarium gymnasium badminton ♧ xmas

♥ English, French & Swiss V ♥ ⚗ ✂ Lunch £13.50&alc
Dinner £21.95-£25&alc Last dinner 9.30pm
Credit Cards [1] [2] [3] [5] ⓔ

**BARROW-IN-FURNESS** Cumbria Map 07 SD16

★★66%, **Lisdoonie** 307/309 Abbey Rd LA14 5LF ☎(0229)27312
Closed Xmas & New Year
*A compact and homely hotel on the main road.*
12⇌ᐟ(2fb) CTV in all bedrooms ® T ✳
CTV 30P
♥ English & French ♥ ⚗ Dinner £12&alc Last dinner 7.30pm
Credit Cards [1] [2] [3] ⓔ

**BARRY** South Glamorgan Map 03 ST16

See also **Porthkerry**

★★★53%, **Mount Sorrell** Porthkerry Rd CF6 8AY (Consort)
☎(0446)740069 Telex no 497819 FAX (0446) 746600
*This commercial and family hotel, which stands in an elevated position above the Bristol Channel and Barry Island, has recently acquired a new swimming pool and sauna. Fifteen of its bedrooms are fairly modern, though the remainder need upgrading, and conference facilities are available. Friendly service is provided throughout.*
45⇌ᐟAnnexe4⇌(3fb) CTV in all bedrooms ®
sB&B⇌ᐟ£46-£57.50 dB&B⇌ᐟ£55-£72.50 ⊟
⟨ 17P ⊠(heated) sauna gymnasium xmas
♥ Continental V ♥ Lunch £7.50-£10 Dinner £11.50-£12.50
Last dinner 10pm
Credit Cards [1] [2] [3] [4] [5] ⓔ

**BARTON** Lancashire Map 07 SD53

★★★65%, **Barton Grange** Garstang Rd PR3 5AA (Best Western) ☎Broughton(0772)862551 Telex no 67392
FAX (0722) 861267
*A modern hotel adjoining its own garden centre on the A6 offers well-appointed bedrooms, friendly service and a comfortable atmosphere.*
56⇌ᐟAnnexe10⇌(10fb)1⊠ CTV in all bedrooms ® T
✖ (ex guide dogs) sB&B⇌ᐟ£45-£75 dB&B⇌ᐟ£53-£87 ⊟
Lift ⟨ CTV 250P ❄ CFA ⊠(heated)
♥ English & French V ♥ ⚗ Lunch £7.50-£8.50 High tea £5-£8.50 Dinner £13.50-£17 Last dinner 10pm
Credit Cards [1] [2] [3] [5]

**BARTON MILLS** Suffolk Map 05 TL77

⌂**Travelodge** A11 IP28 6AE (Trusthouse Forte)
☎(0638)717675 Central res (0800) 850950
*Situated on the roundabout junction of the A1065, A11 and A1101 at Barton Mills, accessible off the A1101. There is a Little Chef restaurant adjacent to the lodge.*
32⇌ᐟ(32fb) CTV in all bedrooms ® sB⇌ᐟ£24
dB⇌ᐟ£29.50 (room only)
⟨ 32P ⇛
Credit Cards [1] [2] [3]

**BARTON-ON-SEA** Hampshire Map 04 SZ29

★★65%, **The Cliff House** Marine Dr West BH25 7QL
☎New Milton(0425)619333 & 610014 FAX (0425) 612462
*Smoking is not allowed in the cosy, well-appointed bedrooms or popular dining room of this fresh, clean little hotel with uninterrupted sea views.*
9rm(4⇌4ᐟ)(1fb)✂in all bedrooms CTV in all bedrooms ® T
✖ (ex guide dogs) ✳ sB&Bfr£30 sB&B⇌ᐟ£42-£45
dB&B⇌ᐟ£66-£80 ⊟
50P ❄ xmas

**B**

V ♥ � Lunch £8.50-£10.50&alc Dinner fr£12.95&alc Last
dinner 9pm
Credit Cards 1 2 3 5 £

---

**BARTON STACEY** Hampshire Map **04** SU44

⭐Travelodge SO21 3NP (on A303) (Trusthouse Forte)
☎Andover(0264)72260 Central res (0800) 850950
*Single storey purpose-built bedroom block set back from the west
bound A303, behind a Little Chef, offering excellent budget
accommodation.*
20⇨♪(20fb) CTV in all bedrooms ® sB⇨♪£24
dB⇨♪£29.50 (room only)
( 20P ♨
Credit Cards 1 2 3

---

**BARTON UNDER NEEDWOOD** Staffordshire
Map **07** SK11

⭐Travelodge DE13 0ED (on A38) (Trusthouse Forte)
☎(028371)6343 Central res (0800) 850950
*A brick-faced, single-storey lodge on the northbound side of the
very busy A38 Birmingham/Derby road stands adjacent to a Little
Chef restaurant and offers a pleasant canal walk at its rear.*
20⇨♪(20fb) CTV in all bedrooms ® ✳ sB⇨♪£24
dB⇨♪£29.50 (room only)
( 20P ♨
Credit Cards 1 2 3

---

**BASILDON** Essex Map **05** TQ78

★★★**63%** Crest Cranes Farm Rd SS14 3DG (Trusthouse Forte)
☎(0268)533955 Telex no 995141 FAX (0268) 530119
*This refurbished hotel, set in its own grounds, provides easy access
to both the town and the M25 motorway. All the well equipped
bedrooms have an en suite facilities, while the Executive and Lady
Crest rooms offer extra touches. The Water's Edge Restaurant
and Conservatory Bar offer relaxed surroundings in which to enjoy
a meal or a drink.*
110⇨♪� in 25 bedrooms CTV in all bedrooms ® (room only)
♬
Lift ( 200P ♣ CFA snooker snooker room putting green
♀ International V ♥ ⚖ ✳
Credit Cards 1 2 3 5

★★★**61%**, Chichester Old London Rd, Rawreth, Wickford
SS11 8UE ☎(0268)560555 FAX (0268) 560580
2⇨Annexe32⇨ CTV in all bedrooms ® T ✗ (ex guide dogs)
✳ sB&B⇨£52-£55 dB&B⇨£62-£65
( 150P nc5yrs
♀ English & French V Lunch fr£9.50&alc Dinner
£12.50-£15.50alc Last dinner 9.30pm
Credit Cards 1 2 3 5

⭐*Campanile* Miles Grey Rd, Pipps Hill Industrial Estate,
Southend Arterial Rd SS14 3AE (A127) (Campanile)
☎(0268)530810 Telex no 995068
Annexe98⇨♪ CTV in 47 bedrooms ® T
63P
♀ English & French Last dinner 10pm
Credit Cards 1 3

⭐**Watermill Travel Inn** Felmores, East Mayne SS13 1BW
☎(0268)522227 FAX (0268) 530092
Closed 25 & 26 Dec
*Situated next to the popular Watermill Steak House, this
establishment offers a new style of comfortable, modern, well-
equipped accommodation and convenient parking.*
Annexe32⇨♪✉ in 5 bedrooms CTV in all bedrooms ®
✗ (ex guide dogs) ✳ sB⇨♪£27.50 dB⇨♪£27.50 (room only)
160P

♀ Mainly grills V ✘ Lunch £3.50-£10.50alc Dinner
£3.50-£10.50alc Last dinner 10.30pm
Credit Cards 1 2 3 5

---

**BASINGSTOKE** Hampshire Map **04** SU65

See also **Odiham & Sherfield on Loddon**

★★★★⚜**79%, Tylney Hall** RG27 9AJ (Prestige)
☎Hook(0256)764881 Telex no 859864 FAX (0256) 768141
(For full entry see Rotherwick)

★★★★**70%** Audleys Wood Thistle Alton Rd RG25 2JT (Mount
Charlotte (TS)) ☎(0256)817555 Telex no 858273
FAX (0256) 817500
*This attractive Victorian house, which has been thoughtfully
extended, is situated just south of the town. The main house retains
many original features, particularly in the public areas, whilst
bedrooms are spacious and furnished to a high standard. Service is
formal and efficient to meet the needs of the predominantly
commercial clientele.*
71⇨♪(6fb)2♨✘ in 12 bedrooms CTV in all bedrooms ® T ✳
sB⇨♪£75-£95 dB⇨♪£95-£125 (room only) ♬
( 100P ♣ croquet putting bicycles ♫ *xmas*
♀ British & French V ♥ ⚖ Lunch £12.50-£15&alc Dinner
£18.50-£22&alc Last dinner 10pm
Credit Cards 1 2 3 4 5
See advertisement on page 105

★★★**69%** Centre Court Centre Dr, Chineham RG24 0FY
☎(0256)816664 FAX (0256) 816727
*As the name implies, this modern hotel and leisure complex,
conveniently located close to the M3 link and Basingstoke
Business Area, yet peacefully tucked away, offers perhaps some of
the finest tennis facilities in the country. Extensive, floodlit, all-
weather outdoor courts and superb indoor courts offer the standard
and services acknowledged by the tennis professionals. In addition,
the hotel also boasts a comprehensive leisure and recreational* ▶

B

*complex, complete with a bright, indoor pool, sauna/solarium,*
*supervised gym and even a daytime crèche. The hotel offers*
*executive and standard rooms, both promoting excellent comfort,*
*style and an extensive range of facilities, now sought after by*
*today's more discerning traveller. They are richly decorated and*
*furnished with some having the additional benefit of balconies*
*overlooking the tournament courts. Public rooms are bright, with*
*modern furnishings, offering a choice of bars and dining facilities,*
*with a good range of traditional services from well dressed,*
*pleasing staff.*

50⇨↑(6fb)⊁in 25 bedrooms CTV in all bedrooms ⓇT❋S%
sB&B⇨↑£89-£120 dB&B⇨↑£102-£115 日
Lift ⑩CTV 120P ⊠(heated) ♬ (hard) sauna solarium
gymnasium *xmas*
V ⑦ ⚎ ⊁ Lunch £12.50&alc High tea £2.80-£5.70alc Dinner
£15&alc Last dinner 10pm
Credit Cards ①②③⑤

★★★67% **Basingstoke Country** Nately Scures, Hook RG27 9JS
☎(0256)764161 Telex no 859981 FAX (0256) 768341
*This smart, modern hotel on the eastern outskirts of the town, once*
*a pub building, has recently been developed to provide bright and*
*well equipped accommodation for a mainly business clientele;*
*public areas have been extended by the provision of a huge*
*conservatory which houses the swimming pool and coffee shop.*
*Cuisine is ambitious, and a friendly young staff offers willing*
*service.*
70⇨↑1团⊁in 14 bedrooms CTV in all bedrooms ⓇT❋
S10% sB&B⇨↑fr£80 dB&B⇨↑£92-£120 日
Lift ⑩ 200P 棚⊠(heated) gymnasium
V ⑦ ⚎ S10% Lunch fr£16.50&alc Dinner fr£19.50&alc Last
dinner 9.45pm
Credit Cards ①②③④⑤

★★★61% **Crest** Grove Rd RG21 3EE (Trusthouse Forte)
☎(0256)468181 Telex no 858501 FAX (0256) 840081
*Bright modern hotel, conveniently situated on the southern*
*outskirts of the town. Bedrooms have been equipped to suit the*
*needs of the business person. A limited lounge area is provided,*
*together with a choice of two bars and a popular restaurant.*
85⇨↑⊁in 21 bedrooms CTV in all bedrooms Ⓡ 日
⑩ 150P CFA snooker pool table *xmas*
☺ English & French V ⑦ ⚎ ⊁
Credit Cards ①②③④⑤

★★★60% **Hilton National** Popley Way, Aldermaston
Roundabout, Ringway North (A339) RG24 9NV (Hilton)
☎(0256)20212 Telex no 858223 FAX (0256) 842835
*Palms piano bar and eating house create a lively atmosphere.*
*Bedrooms are well equipped and there are good leisure facilities.*
138⇨↑(10fb)⊁in 26 bedrooms CTV in all bedrooms ⓇT
Lift ⑩ 160P CFA ⊠(heated) sauna gymnasium ♬
☺ English & American V ⑦ ⚎
Credit Cards ①②③⑤£

★★★57% **Hilton Lodge** Old Common Rd, Black Dam
RG21 3PR (Hilton) ☎(0256)460460 Telex no 859038
FAX (0256) 840441
*All the well-equipped standard bedrooms of this modern, purpose-*
*built hotel have recently been upgraded, and twenty-four plaza*
*rooms provide such extra touches as chocolates and the provision*
*of bathrobes. The Hillside Restaurant, which extends into a*
*conservatory, offers a fixed-price carvery operation plus a short à*
*la carte menu, and service is friendly and helpful.*
144⇨↑(17fb)⊁in 54 bedrooms CTV in all bedrooms ⓇT❋
S15% sB⇨↑£82-£102 dB⇨↑£92-£112 (room only) 日
⑩ 田100P ❀ ⊠(heated) sauna gymnasium fitness trail *xmas*
☺ International V ⑦ ⚎ ⊁ Lunch fr£12.50 Dinner
fr£15.50&alc Last dinner 10pm
Credit Cards ①②③④⑤

★★62% **Wheatsheaf** RG25 2BB (Lansbury)
☎Dummer(0256)398282 Telex no 859775 FAX (0256) 398253
(For full entry see North Waltham)

★★55% **Red Lion** 24 London St RG21 1NY (Trusthouse Forte)
☎(0256)28525 FAX (0256) 844056
*In a central position with good car parking. Bedrooms are of*
*various standards. The Pavillion Restaurant serves à la carte and*
*Best of British table d'hôte menus. There is no lounge as such.*
62⇨↑(2fb)⊁in 18 bedrooms CTV in all bedrooms Ⓡ ❋ 日
Lift ⑩ 50P *xmas*
V ⑦ ⚎ ⊁ Lunch £6.95-£15&alc Dinner £11.95&alc Last
dinner 9.30pm
Credit Cards ①②③④⑤

⏚**Travelodge** Stag and Hounds, Winchester Rd RG22 6HN
(Trusthouse Forte) ☎(0256)843566 Central res (0800) 850950
*Providing excellent value for money this lodge is situated on the*
*western edge of town at the rear of a Harvester Restaurant which*
*is open 11am – 11pm. Breakfast is not served on site but there are*
*several hotels within a 5 mile radius. One room is specifically*
*designed for the disabled.*
32⇨↑(32fb) CTV in all bedrooms Ⓡ sB⇨↑£24
dB⇨↑£29.50 (room only)
⑩ 32P 棚
Credit Cards ①②③

**BASLOW** Derbyshire Map **08** SK27

★★★ CAVENDISH

DE4 1SP ☎(0246)582311
Telex no 547150
FAX (0246) 582312

*The setting of this hotel is*
*quite superb, affording as it*
*does such fine views of the*
*majestic Chatsworth estate.*
*Eric Marsh and his friendly staff aim to provide unobtrusive*
*service and one feels that no reasonable request from their*
*guests would ever go unanswered. Rooms are supremely*
*comfortable and tastefully furnished, and the alterations to*
*the public rooms have proved very popular with guests, in*
*particular the Garden Room, which offers both informal and*
*flexible eating, serving food and drink throughout the day and*
*well into the evening.*
24⇨↑1团 CTV in all bedrooms ⓇT❌ (ex guide dogs) ❋
sB⇨↑£60-£70 dB⇨↑£75-£85 (room only) 日
⑩ 50P 棚 ❀ ♪ putting green *xmas*
V ⑦ ⚎ ⊁
Credit Cards ①②③⑤

**BASSENTHWAITE** Cumbria Map **11** NY23

★★★★⚑58% **Armathwaite Hall** CA12 4RE
☎Bassenthwaite Lake(059681)551 Telex no 64319
FAX (059681) 220
*Pleasant lounges with many objets d'art and fine pieces of*
*porcelain and pewter give a large hotel with much historical*
*interest and fine views across the lake a pleasant country house*
*atmosphere which is enhanced by helpful service from willing staff.*
42⇨↑(4fb)团 CTV in all bedrooms ⓇT❋
sB&B⇨↑£45-£90 dB&B⇨↑£100-£170 日
Lift ⑩ 100P ❀ ⊠(heated) ♬ (hard) ♪ ⋃ snooker sauna
solarium gymnasium croquet games room pitch & putt *xmas*
☺ English & French V ⑦ ⚎ Lunch fr£10.95 Dinner fr£23.95
Last dinner 9.30pm
Credit Cards ①②③⑤£

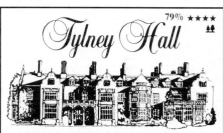

★★★ **59% Castle Inn** CA12 4RG (Best Western)
🕾Bassenthwaite Lake(059681)401 FAX (059681) 604
*This one-time coaching inn, enhanced by recent refurbishment,*
*stands beside the A591 at the head of Bassenthwaite Lake ; ease of*
*access makes it popular with business and leisure users alike and*
*extensive leisure and conference facilities are available.*
36⇨ℕ(7fb)1⚏ CTV in all bedrooms Ⓡ T ✱ S%
sB&B⇨ℕ£44-£54 dB&B⇨ℕ£69-£79 🏳
100P ✿ ⊠(heated) ♪ (grass) snooker sauna solarium
gymnasium badminton table tennis ♫ 🎱 *xmas*
♀ English & French V ✿ ♨ S% Lunch £7.50&alc Dinner
£12.95&alc Last dinner 9.30pm
Credit Cards ①②③⑤ ⓔ

See advertisement under **KESWICK**

★★ **72% Pheasant Inn** CA13 9YE 🕾Keswick(07687)76234
Closed 25 Dec
*Peacefully set between Bassenthwaite Lake and Thornthwaite*
*Forest, this delightful traditional country inn provides comfortable,*
*well furnished bedrooms and attractive public areas which are full*
*of character and atmosphere. The original bar has unique nicotine-*
*coated walls and ceiling. Well prepared fresh produce features on*
*the table d'hôte dinner menu, and the wide choice of freshly-*
*prepared dishes makes this a popular lunchtime venue.*
17⇨ℕAnnexe3⇨ℕ Ⓡ ✖ S10% sB&B⇨ℕ£42
dB&B⇨ℕ£70 🏳
80P 🚗 ✿
V ✿ ♨ ✖ Lunch £8.50&alc Dinner £18 Last dinner 8.30pm

★★⚑ **67% Overwater Hall** Ireby CA5 1HH
🕾Bassenthwaite Lake(059681)566
Closed 24 Dec-23 Feb
*Set in splendid seclusion near Overwater, north of Bassenthwaite,*
*this family-run hotel is popular locally for its dinners. Bedrooms*
*are furnished comfortably and most have unspoilt views over local*
*countryside. There are good lounges – with some fine pieces of*
*china and porcelain on display. In the cocktail bar a grand piano is*
*used as the bar counter.*
13⇨ℕ(4fb)3⚏ CTV in all bedrooms Ⓡ sB&B⇨ℕfr£31
dB&B⇨ℕfr£52 🏳
25P 🚗 ✿
♀ English & French ✿ ♨ Dinner fr£15 Last dinner 8.30pm
Credit Cards ①③

**BATH** Avon Map **03** ST76
See **Town Plan Section.**
See also **Colerne & Limpley Stoke**
★★★★★ **70% Bath Spa** Sydney Rd BA2 6JF (Trusthouse
Forte) 🕾(0225)444424 Telex no 449729 FAX (0225) 444006
*This splendid mansion of Bath stone, built in 1830 by Colonel*
*Augustus Andrews has been magnificently restored by Trusthouse*
*Forte at a cost of some £20 million and is one of the very few hotels*
*in this country to receive a five-star classification. Standing in 7*
*acres of gardens above the city centre, the hotel has been carefully*
*planned to ensure that most rooms have views of gardens or city*
*rather than of the extensive car parking needed for an hotel of this*
*size. Every care has been taken over the restoration and furnishing*
*of the interior to create surroundings that offer luxury and comfort*
*of a very high order while preserving the elegance of a country-*
*house atmosphere. Drawing room, colonnade lounge and*
*restaurant (originally the ballroom) are strikingly lovely and the*
*bedrooms, furnished with a dazzling array of different fabrics and*
*colours, are entirely in keeping with the period of the building.*
*Chef Richard Tonks produces menus that make dining here a*
*special occasion, and the excellent General Manager, Alan*
*McAinsh, ensures that guests receive friendly treatment from his*
*staff, who try very hard to please.*
103⇨ℕ7⚏✖in 31 bedrooms CTV in all bedrooms T ✱ S%
sB⇨ℕfr£100 dB⇨ℕ£125-£350 (room only) 🏳
Lift 〖 156P 🚗 ✿ ⊠(heated) ♪ (hard) sauna solarium
gymnasium croquet ♫ *xmas*

♀ French V ✿ ♨ ✖ S% Lunch fr£18.50&alc Dinner fr£25&alc
Last dinner 10pm
Credit Cards ①②③④⑤

★★★★ **71% Royal Crescent** 16 Royal Crescent BA1 2LS
(Queens Moat)(Prestige) 🕾(0225)319090 Telex no 444251
FAX (0225) 339401
*A change of management has brought Simon Coombe from*
*Eastwell Manor to this hotel which is formed from two of the*
*largest houses in Bath's magnificent Royal Crescent built by John*
*Wood in the 18th century. A noticeable improvement in standards*
*is the immediate result and a programme of refurbishment being*
*carried out, already evident in the comfortable lounges and*
*(mostly) spacious bedrooms. Michael Croft's cooking continues to*
*be praiseworthy, although our Inspectors have noted some*
*inconsistency on occasions.*
27⇨ℕAnnexe17⇨ℕ(8fb)4⚏ CTV in all bedrooms T
✖ (ex guide dogs) ✱ sB⇨ℕfr£89
dB⇨ℕ£110-£165 (room only)
Lift 〖 12🗲 (£4 per night) ✿ croquet boules *xmas*
♀ English & French V ✿ ♨ Lunch £17-£21 Dinner £33&alc
Last dinner 9.30pm
Credit Cards ①②③⑤ ⓔ

★★★ **78% The Priory** Weston Rd BA1 2XT (Select)
🕾(0225)331922 Telex no 44612 FAX (0225) 448276
*An early 19th-century house, standing in a peaceful postion in a*
*residential area not far from the city centre, that has been*
*converted into a particularly comfortable hotel. Bedrooms vary*
*widely in size but all have furniture and soft furnishings of high*
*quality and good large beds. Food is very good indeed, and an*
*interesting menu with occasional 'special' dishes. There is a*
*general atmosphere of friendliness with staff eager to see that you*
*are always fully satisfied. All in all, it is not surprising that many*
*guests return again and again.*
21⇨ℕ1⚏ CTV in all bedrooms T ✖ (ex guide dogs) ✱
sB&B⇨ℕfr£85 dB&B⇨ℕ£120-£170 🏳
24P 1🗲 ✿ ⊠(heated) croquet *xmas*
♀ French V ✿ ♨ ✖ Lunch fr£18 Dinner fr£27.50 Last dinner
9.15pm
Credit Cards ①②③⑤ ⓔ

★★★ **67% *Lansdown Grove*** Lansdown Rd BA1 5EH (Best
Western) 🕾(0225)315891 Telex no 444850 FAX (0225)448092
*Comfortable amenities and attentive, friendly service provided by a*
*traditionally-run hotel which commands magnificent views of the*
*city beyond its small, well-kept garden area.*
45⇨ℕ(3fb)✖in 9 bedrooms CTV in all bedrooms Ⓡ
Lift 〖 38P 🚗 ✿ CFA
♀ English & French V ✿ ♨ Last dinner 9.30pm
Credit Cards ①②③④⑤

See advertisement on page 109

★★★ **66% Compass** North Pde BA1 1LG 🕾(0225)461603
Telex no 44812 FAX (0225) 447758
*Situated in the centre of Bath, close to the Abbey, this hotel was*
*once three Georgian town houses. It has been totally refurbished to*
*provide modern, well-equipped bedrooms and attractive public*
*areas which include a choice of restaurant or coffee shop.*
54⇨ℕ(4fb) CTV in all bedrooms Ⓡ T ✱ sB&B⇨ℕ£55-£65
dB&B⇨ℕ£75-£90 🏳
Lift 〖 ♪ *xmas*
♀ British & French V ✿ ♨ ✖ Lunch £5.50-£9.50 Dinner
£11.50&alc Last dinner 9.30pm
Credit Cards ①②③⑤

See advertisement on page 109

★★★ **63% Bath** Widcombe Basin BA2 4JP (Best Western)
🕾(0225)338855 Telex no 445876 FAX (0225) 428941
*Enjoying picturesque, waterside views from an attractive position*
*where the Kennet and Avon Canal joins the River Avon – yet only*
*a few moments' walk from the city centre – this large, purpose-built*
*hotel offers ninety-six comfortable bedrooms with en suite*

▶

*facilities, equipped to cater for business and leisure guests alike, and a restaurant and bar overlooking the terrace.*
96⇄♠(4fb) CTV in all bedrooms ® T S% sB⇄♠fr£68 dB⇄♠fr£82 (room only) ➡
Lift ℂ 102P *xmas*
V ✿ ⚏ S% Lunch £8.95&alc Dinner £13.50&alc Last dinner 9.30pm
Credit Cards ① ② ③ ④ ⑤

★★★61% **Francis** Queen Square BA1 2HH (Trusthouse Forte)
☎(0225)424257 Telex no 449162 FAX (0225) 319715
*A building of considerable charm and elegance, forming one side of Queen Square, the hotel is only a short walk from some of the city's delightful shops and also has its own car park at the rear. First opened as an hotel over a hundred years ago, it has since seen many improvements in its level of comfort, and a major refurbishment has recently been carried out. Service throughout is unfailingly helpful and friendly.*
94⇄⅍in 30 bedrooms CTV in all bedrooms ® T ✳
sB⇄£75-£81 dB⇄£100-£108 (room only) ➡
Lift ℂ 30P CFA ♫ *xmas*
♈ English & French V ✿ ⚏ ⅍ Lunch £12.50 Dinner £15.50&alc Last dinner 10pm
Credit Cards ① ② ③ ④ ⑤

★★★61% **Pratts** South Pde BA2 4AB (Forestdale)
☎(0225)460441 Telex no 444827 FAX (0225) 448807
*Once the home of Sir Walter Scott, this classically designed and beautifully preserved Georgian building offers well-equipped and comfortable accommodation; its convenient situation, close to both city centre and railway station, make it popular with tourists and business people alike.*
48rm(46⇄)(5fb)1🛏⅍in 2 bedrooms CTV in 46 bedrooms ®
➡
Lift ℂ ♪ *xmas*
♈ English & French V ✿ ⚏ Sunday Lunch £8.95 Dinner £13.75&alc Last dinner 9.30pm
Credit Cards ① ② ③ ⑤ ⓔ

★★69% **Duke's** Great Pulteney St BA2 4DN ☎(0225)463512 Telex no 449227
*A charming, historic hotel (built in 1780) offering well-furnished bedrooms with good facilities. Comfortable public areas include a small, relaxing bar and guests are assured of warm service and hospitality from the resident owners.*
21⇄♠(4fb) CTV in all bedrooms ® T sB&B⇄♠£55-£65 dB&B⇄♠£65-£95 ➡
1🏠 (charged) 🎱
V ✿ ⚏ ⅍ Lunch £10-£15 Dinner £10-£15 Last dinner 8.30pm
Credit Cards ① ② ③

★★65% **Haringtons** 9/10 Queen St BA1 1HE ☎(0225)461728
*Situated in a quiet, attractive, cobbled street in the city centre, this comfortable little hotel and restaurant provides well-furnished bedrooms and friendly family service.*
12rm(5⇄♠)(3fb) CTV in all bedrooms ® ✖ (ex guide dogs)
S% sB&B£24-£40 sB&B⇄♠£28-£40 dB&B£34-£40 dB&B⇄♠£40-£50 ➡
♪
♈ English & French ⚏ Lunch fr£3.95alc Dinner fr£6.95alc Last dinner 10pm
Credit Cards ① ② ③

★★64% **Bailbrook Lodge** 35/37 London Rd West BA1 7HZ
☎(0225)859090
*Situated 200 yards east of junction A46 on the A4, this imposing double-fronted Georgian house has been carefully modernised to provide elegant and comfortable public areas and various sized bedrooms, all with good en suite facilities.*
13⇄♠(2fb)4🛏 CTV in all bedrooms ® ✖ (ex guide dogs) ✱
sB&B⇄♠£40-£55 dB&B⇄♠£45-£60
CTV 14P 🎱 ❀

V ⅍ Bar Lunch £1.95-£5 Dinner £10.50-£12.50 Last dinner 8.30pm
Credit Cards ① ③

★69% **Berni Royal** Manvers St BA1 1JP (Berni/Chef & Brewer)
☎(0225)463134
*An hotel standing opposite the railway station provides a useful base from which to explore the city. Staff are extremely friendly, and guests appreciate particularly the high standard of housekeeping which prevails throughout the warm, well-equipped bedrooms.*
30⇄♠(4fb) CTV in all bedrooms ® T ✖ (ex guide dogs)
sB&B⇄♠£54-£63.50 dB&B⇄♠£70 ➡
ℂ ♪
V ✿ ⅍ Lunch £8-£15alc Dinner £8-£15alc Last dinner 10.30pm
Credit Cards ① ② ③ ⑤
*See advertisement on page 111*

★64% **Gainsborough** Weston Ln BA1 4AB ☎(0225)311380
Closed Xmas & 1st wk Jan
*Spacious rooms and good modern facilities are the attractions of this small, personally-run hotel on the outskirts of the city, close to the village of Weston.*
16⇄♠(2fb)1🛏 CTV in all bedrooms ® T ✖
sB&B⇄♠£28-£35 dB&B⇄♠£52-£66 ➡
17P 🎱 ❀
V Lunch £10 Dinner £10.50 Last dinner 8.30pm
Credit Cards ① ② ③
*See advertisement on page 111*

1991 marks the 25th anniversary of this guide.

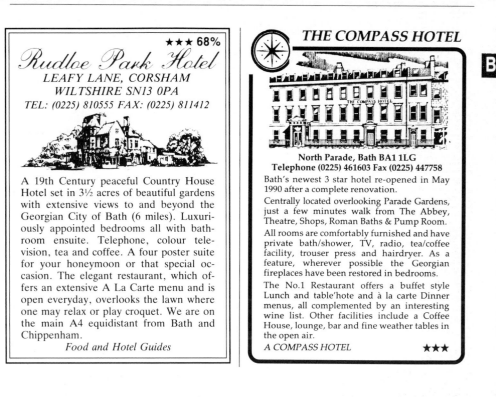
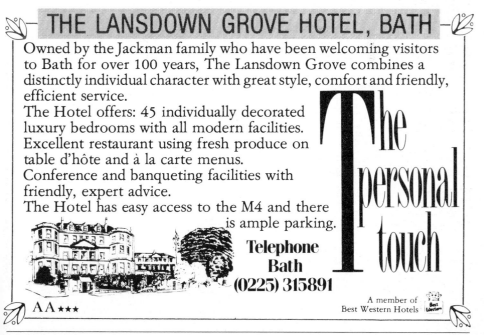

**B**

✗✗✗**Popjoys** Beau Nash House, Sawclose BA1 1EU
☎(0225)460494 FAX (0225) 446319
*Situated adjacent to the Theatre Royal, this fine Regency house, once the home of Beau Nash and Juliana Popjoy, retains many original features. The spacious first floor Drawing Room is luxuriously furnished and is an ideal room in which to relax after enjoying Chef John Headley's imaginative and well cooked dishes. Worthy of particular note is the light chicken liver parfait and the selection of mouth watering sweets.*
Closed Sun & Mon
Lunch not served Sat
♀ English & French **V** 32 seats ✴ Lunch £5-£10 Dinner £25
Last lunch 2pm Last dinner 10.30pm ✗ nc6yrs ✓
Credit Cards ①②③④

✗✗**Rajpoot Tandoori** Rajpoot House, 4 Argyle St BA2 4BA
☎(0225)466833 & 464758 FAX (0225) 442462
*A popular well-appointed Indian-style restaurant near the city centre offering Tandoori and Biriani specialities and some vegetarian dishes. The food is well-cooked and service prompt and polite.*
Closed 25 & 26 Dec
♀ North Indian **V** 110 seats Lunch £13-£20&alc Dinner £13-£20&alc Last lunch 2.30pm Last dinner 11pm ✗
Credit Cards ①②③⑤

✗**Garlands** 7 Edgar Buildings, George St BA1 2EE
☎(0225)442283
*A new partnership has taken over these premises in central Bath. The small restaurant offers an intimate and relaxing atmosphere together with enthusiastic service. Dishes are well presented in the modern French style and include Duck Terrine layered with its own livers, Oyster Mushrooms and hazlenuts and some appetizing desserts.*
Closed Mon & 24-27 Dec
♀ English & French **V** 30 seats Lunch £7.25-£11.95&alc Dinner £16.25&alc Last lunch 2.15pm Last dinner 10.30pm ✗
Credit Cards ①②③

✗**Pino's Hole In The Wall** 16 George St BA1 2EN ☎(0225)25242
*Now under the management of a new owner, this well decorated and furnished restaurant in the city centre offers a varied menu with a strong classical Italian bias, though desserts are decidedly English; a friendly and welcoming young staff provides informal service in keeping with the intimate atmosphere.*
Lunch not served Sun
♀ French **V** 45 seats Last dinner 10pm ✗
Credit Cards ①②③⑤

---

**BATLEY** West Yorkshire Map **08** SE22

★★65%, **Alder House** Towngate Rd, off Healey Ln WF17 7HR
☎(0924)444777 Telex no 51363
*This handsome Gerogian house dates back to 1730 and has been pleasingly converted to meet all today's modern comforts. Bedrooms are attractive and guests are assured of a warm and friendly welcome.*
22rm(20⇩👍♠)(1fb) CTV in all bedrooms ® **T** ✴ sB&B£32 sB&B⇩♠£40-£47 dB&B⇩♠£58-£60 ♬
CTV 50P 2🐾 ✿
♀ English & Continental **V** ✌ ⚲ Lunch £6.25-£8.75 Dinner £10.95-£12.50&alc Last dinner 9.30pm
Credit Cards ①②③

---

All AA-appointed establishments are inspected regularly to ensure that required standards are maintained.

---

**BATTLE** East Sussex Map **05** TQ71

★★★ **▲▲**
**NETHERFIELD PLACE**

Netherfield TN33 9PP (3m NW B2096) (Pride of Britain) ☎(04246)4455
Telex no 95284
FAX (04246) 4024
Closed 2 wks Xmas & New Year

*Built in 1924 this hotel is a fine example of a Georgian country house, with magnificent views over 30 acres of gardens and parkland. Accommodation is comfortable and bedrooms are individually decorated. Michael Collier's kitchens produce good food, served in the panelled and candle-lit dining room, whilst Helen Collier supervises the front-of-house operation with a mixture of considerable charm and dedication.*
14⇩(1fb)1♬ CTV in all bedrooms ✖ (ex guide dogs) ✴ sB&B⇩frf45 dB&B⇩£75-£100 ♬
30P 2🐾 ♨ ✿ ⚲ (hard) croquet
♀ French **V** ✌ ⚲ Lunch £13.50-£14.95&alc Dinner frf17.50&alc Last dinner 9.30pm
Credit Cards ①②③⑤ⓔ
**See advertisement under HASTINGS & ST LEONARDS**

★★74% **Burntwood Hotel & Country Club** Powdermill Ln
TN33 0SU ☎(04246)5151 FAX (04246) 2459
*This delightful small Edwardian country house is set in 18 acres of rolling Sussex countryside. Significant upgrading and refurbishment has been carried out recently; bedrooms in particular are very comfortable and decorated in pleasing colours with coordinating fabrics. Sumptuous Victorian style bathrooms add a degree of luxury, including good quality towels and fine toiletries. Public rooms are equally elegant with a classically furnished quiet lounge, a cosy cocktail bar and the Crystal Room Restaurant in which commendable dishes are nicely presented. One of the main strengths of this hotel, however, is the high level of service and hospitality which would normally be associated with a hotel of much higher classification.*
10⇩♠ CTV in all bedrooms ® **T** sB&B⇩♠£45-£50 dB&B⇩♠£54-£75 ♬
30P ✿ ◿(heated) ⚲ (hard) ✈ ∪ shooting croquet *xmas*
♀ French **V** ✌ ⚲ Lunch frf10.50 High tea £1.50-£4.95 Dinner frf15.50 Last dinner 9.30pm
Credit Cards ①②③⑤

★★72% **La Vieille Auberge** 27 High St TN33 0EA (Minotels)
☎(04246)5171 FAX (04246) 4015
*This small auberge with the ambience of a French provincial hotel offers individually furnished, well equipped bedrooms, a choice of quality menus based on good, fresh, local produce, a fine wine list, and warm personal service.*
7rm(5⇩♠)(1fb)1♬ CTV in all bedrooms ® **T**
✖ (ex guide dogs) sB&B£29.50-£45 dB&B⇩♠£45-£55 ♬
✗ ♨ *xmas*
♀ French **V** ✌ ⚲ Lunch £12.50-£14.50&alc Dinner £16-£21.95&alc Last dinner 10pm
Credit Cards ①②③ⓔ

★★57% **The George** 23 High St TN33 0EA ☎(04246)4466
FAX (04246) 4853
*An old coaching inn set in the centre of this busy historic town. Bedrooms are well-equipped, if functional, and public areas are cosy. There is a range of menus at both lunch and dinner, while service is provided by pleasant young staff supervised by the owner.*

21⇨🛏(3fb)1🛏 CTV in all bedrooms ® ✳ S%
sB&B⇨🛏fr£36.50 dB&B⇨🛏fr£49.50 🅿
30P *xmas*
🍴 English & French V 🕏 ⚓ Lunch £6.25-£8.50 Dinner
fr£10.95
Credit Cards ① ② ③ ④ ⑤

---

**BAWTRY** South Yorkshire Map **08** SK 69

★★★ 66% **Crown Hotel & Posting House** High St DN10 6JW
(Trusthouse Forte) ☎Doncaster(0302)710341 Telex no 547089
FAX (0302) 711798
*A coaching inn dating back to the early seventeenth century has
been sympathetically and tastefully decorated and furnished to
provide modern comforts amd amentities. A restaurant on three
levels, run by a friendly staff, offers a good selection of dishes
which are based on fresh produce wherever possible, while the
Crown Bar serves snacks and bar meals.*
57⇨🛏1🛏✂in 12 bedrooms CTV in all bedrooms ® ✳
sB⇨🛏£65-£70 dB⇨🛏£81-£100 (room only) 🅿
( 40P CFA *xmas*
V 🕏 ⚓ ✂ Lunch fr£8.50&alc Dinner fr£14.50&alc Last dinner
9.30pm
Credit Cards ① ② ③ ④ ⑤

---

**BEACONSFIELD** Buckinghamshire Map **04** SU99

★★★ 56% **Bellhouse** Oxford Rd HP9 2XE (2m E A40) (De
Vere) ☎Gerrards Cross(0753)887211 Telex no 848719
FAX (0753) 888231
*Extensive refurbishment of this busy commercial hotel has
provided not only good business and conference facilities but also
comfortable accommodation in thoughtfully furnished bedrooms
which have been equipped to offer all modern facilities. Varied
menus are available in the bright modern bistro and main
restaurant.*
136⇨🛏(5fb)✂in 18 bedrooms CTV in all bedrooms ® T ✳
S10% sB&B⇨🛏£35-£85 dB&B⇨🛏£85-£110 🅿
Lift ( 405P ❄ CFA ▣(heated) squash snooker sauna solarium
gymnasium pool table tennis beauty therapy room ♫ *xmas*
🍴 English & Continental V 🕏 ⚓ S10% Lunch £12.50-£14.50
Dinner £17.50 Last dinner 10pm
Credit Cards ① ② ③ ④ ⑤

★★ 55% **White Hart Toby** Aylesbury End HP9 1LW (Toby)
☎(0494)671211 Telex no 837882
*A spacious bar and Toby Restaurant form the public areas of this
lively inn, which dates back to the sixteenth century;
accommodation is for the most part in a modern annexe, though
there are a few characterful bedrooms in the main building.*
6🛏Annexe28🛏1🛏 CTV in all bedrooms ®
( 80P
V 🕏 ✂
Credit Cards ① ② ③ ⑤

---

**BEAMINSTER** Dorset Map **03** ST40

★★ 70% **Bridge House** 3 Prout Bridge DT8 3AY (Minotels)
☎(0308)862200
RS 24-29 Dec
*This delightful, 13th-century stone house with a walled garden is
set in the middle of town. It offers well-equipped comfortable
accommodation, excellent food and warm, friendly service.*
9rm(4⇨🛏🛏) CTV in all bedrooms ® T ✳
sB&B⇨🛏£35.50-£42.50 dB&B⇨🛏🛏£55-£65 🅿
22P 🚗 ❄ *xmas*
🍴 International 🕏 Lunch £10-£12 Dinner £16.75 Last dinner
9pm
Credit Cards ① ③

---

👑 👑 👑 ★

# Gainsborough Hotel

**B**

### Weston Lane, Bath, Avon
### Tel: (0225) 311380

Set in its own grounds of half an acre the
Gainsborough provides the comfort & friendly
atmosphere you would expect from a small
country house hotel.

All our bedrooms have private bathroom or
shower and toilet en-suite, plus direct dial
telephone, colour TV, radio and tea & coffee
making facilities. Small dining room and bar
both overlook the garden. The hotel has full
central heating, and our own large car park.
Warm welcome — friendly staff.

---

# The
# Berni Royal Hotel ★
## Manvers Street
## Bath, Avon BA1 1JP
## Telephone: (0225) 63134

A Georgian style hotel built for the
arrival of the railways in Victorian
times. Conveniently situated for the
railway and bus stations. Enter the
hotel and you'll find its warm and
comfortable atmosphere makes it not
only an ideal place to relax after a
long journey but a perfect spot to
plan an excursion into the elegant
city of Bath. All bedrooms
are en-suite and have full
facilities with furnishing
chosen to compliment the
historic character.

**BEARSDEN** Strathclyde *Dunbartonshire* Map **11** NS57

✗✗**La Bavarde** 19 New Kirk Rd G61 3SJ ☎041-942 2202
*Small restaurant run by friendly proprietors.*
Closed Sun, Mon, 2 wks Xmas/New Year & last 3 wks Jul
V 50 seats Lunch £6.50 Dinner £12.20-£16.65alc Last lunch
2pm Last dinner 9.30pm ⅊
Credit Cards ①②③④⑤

✗✗**October Restaurant** 128 Drymen Rd G61 3RB
☎041-942 7272 FAX 041-942 9650
*A complete transformation of the interior of this originally simple
restaurant has created an elegant, sophisticated environment in
which guests can sample such delights as onion and tarragon soup,
cheese soufflé or mussels with garlic from the interesting range of
dishes on a well-balanced menu. Service is friendly and
unpretentious, the small selection of wines represents most of the
growing areas and a short, value-for-money menu is available at
lunchtime.*
Closed BH's, 1 wk Etr & 1st 2 wks Aug
Dinner not served Sun
� International V 48 seats ✳ Lunch £8.25-£9.75 Dinner
fr£21alc Last lunch 2pm Last dinner 10pm ⅊
Credit Cards ①③

**BEATTOCK** Dumfries & Galloway *Dumfriesshire*
Map **11** NT00

See also**Moffat**
★★★63% *Auchen Castle* DG10 9SH (Inter-Hotels) ☎(06833)407
Closed 20 Dec-8 Jan
*Set in 50 acres of grounds and gardens a mile north of the village,
and offering direct access to the A74, this splendid, Victorian
country house provides comfortable, individually styled bedrooms,
relaxing public rooms, and helpful and friendly service from
enthusiastic staff.*
15⇨♪Annexe10♪(1fb) CTV in all bedrooms ®
35P ✿ ♪
V ♥ ⚏ Last dinner 9pm
Credit Cards ①②③④⑤

★★59% *Beattock House* DG10 9QB ☎(06833)403 & 402
*A converted Victorian house – still retaining some of its original
features – is family run to provide guests with traditional comforts
and service. Part of its six-acre grounds form a small caravan
park, and its setting offers convenient access to the A74.*
7rm(3♪)(2fb) CTV in 4 bedrooms TV in 1 bedroom ®
sB&Bfr£23.50 sB&B♪fr£27.50 dB&Bfr£45
dB&B♪fr£47.50 ☐
CTV 30P ✿ ♪ putting
V ♥ ⚏ Lunch £6.95-£7.50 High tea fr£5.25 Dinner fr£14.50
Last dinner 9.30pm
Credit Cards ①②③⑤

**BEAULIEU** Hampshire Map **04** SU30

★★★73% **Montagu Arms** SO42 7ZL ☎(0590)612324
*This creeper-clad listed building at the centre of the picturesque
village features individually furnished and decorated bedrooms
which include three rooms with four-poster beds and three suites. A
dedicated team of chefs prepares the gourmet dishes included in
the set table d'hôte and short à la carte menus, and a good selection
of fine wines is available. A wide choice of meals is also served in
the Wine Press Bar. A friendly but professionally managed and
smartly uniformed staff gives good service throughout.*
24⇨♪(3fb)3🛏 CTV in all bedrooms T ✖ (ex guide dogs) ✳
sB&B⇨♪£60
dB&B⇨♪£87.50-£150 Continental breakfast ☐
《80P 6🏌 ✿ xmas
V ♥ ⚏ ⅙ Lunch £14.50&alc Dinner £22.50&alc Last dinner
9.30pm
Credit Cards ①②③⑤

★★★64% **Beaulieu** Beaulieu Rd SO42 7YQ
☎Southampton(0703)293344 FAX (0703) 283719
*This former 19th-century coaching inn, with well-equipped
refurbished bedrooms, lies adjacent to the Beaulieu Road Railway
Station. The Beaulieu Road Pub is housed in a splendid conversion
and has a carvery-style food operation, whilst the restaurant offers
choice of menus.*
10rm(9♪)(2fb) CTV in all bedrooms ® T S% sB&B♪£59-£69
dB&B♪£85-£95 ☐
Lift CTV 100P ✿ xmas
♁ English & French V ♥ ⚏ ⅙ Dinner £13 Last dinner 8.45pm
Credit Cards ①②③⑤

**BEAULY** Highland *Inverness-shire* Map **14** NH54

★★63% **Priory** The Square IV4 7BX (Inter-Hotels)
☎(0463)782309 FAX (0463) 782531
*This modern hotel stands in the town square and serves meals and
refreshments throughout the day. Bedrooms are well equipped and
there are plans to refurbish the ground floor and to add more
bedrooms.*
11⇨♪(1fb) CTV in all bedrooms ® T
sB&B⇨♪£26.95-£29.95 dB&B⇨♪£39.50-£47.50 ☐
⅊
V ♥ ⚏ Lunch £3.95-£9.95alc High tea £4.95-£7.95alc Dinner
£8.50-£16.50alc Last dinner 9pm
Credit Cards ①②③Ⓔ

**BEAUMARIS** Gwynedd Map **06** SH67

★★67% **Bishopsgate House** 54 Castle St LL58 8AB
☎(0248)810302
Closed 21 Dec-13 Feb
*Family owned and run, this delightful, friendly little hotel offers
good all-round facilities and well-prepared food.*
10⇨♪1🛏 CTV in all bedrooms ® T sB&B⇨♪£24-£27
dB&B⇨♪£42-£48 ☐
10P ⍩ nc5yrs
♁ English & French V ♥ ⅙ Sunday Lunch £7.50 Dinner
£11&alc Last dinner 9pm
Credit Cards ①③Ⓔ

**BEAUMONT**

See**Jersey** under**Channel Islands**

**BEBINGTON** Merseyside Map **07** SJ38

★★61% **Bridge Inn** Bolton Rd, Port Sunlight L62 4UQ
☎051-645 8441
*This popular inn, standing close to the church in the unique setting
of Port Sunlight Village, provides comfortable accommodation in
well-equipped bedrooms.*
16⇨♪(2fb)1🛏 CTV in all bedrooms ® ✖
50P
♁ English & Continental V ♥ ⚏
Credit Cards ①②③⑤Ⓔ

⌂**Travelodge** New Chester Rd L62 9AQ (A41/M53 junc 5)
(Trusthouse Forte) ☎051-327 2489 Central res (0800) 850950
*Situated on the A41 to Liverpool Road at Eastham off junction 5
of the M53. The lodge is set with car park frontage and flower
beds around the building. It maintains a good degree of comfort
and cleanliness, safety and security and provides excellent value
for money.*
31⇨♪(31fb) CTV in all bedrooms ® ✳ sB⇨♪£24
dB⇨♪£29.50 (room only)
《31P ⍩
Credit Cards ①②③

**B**

**BECCLES** Suffolk Map **05** TM49

★★63% *Kings Head* New Market NR34 9HA ☎(0502)712147
*Once a coaching inn, this town-centre hotel with its own car park at
the rear now offers a good base for the leisure user because of its
setting in the Waveney Valley and for the businessman because of
having easy access to the A143 and A146. Bedrooms are homely
and well equipped, bars and lounge/foyer enjoy a convival
atmosphere, and the restaurant features a popular steak menu
augmented by daily blackboard specials.*
12rm(8⇔3♠) CTV in all bedrooms ® T ✖ (ex guide dogs)
18P
V ♥ ⚞ ⌖ Last dinner 9.30pm
Credit Cards ①②③⑤

★★61% *Waveney House* Puddingmoor NR34 9PL
☎(0502)712270
*Standing on the banks of the River Waveney, this old hotel dates
back to the 16th century yet offers modern facilities in its
comfortable rooms. The bar, made busy in summer by the custom
of passing river traffic, serves food both at lunchtimes and in the
evenings.*
13⇔♠(2fb)1⚞ CTV in all bedrooms ®
CTV 100P ❖ ✦
⚐ English & French V ♥ ⚞ Last dinner 9.30pm
Credit Cards ①②③④⑤

**BECKINGHAM** Lincolnshire Map **08** SK85

✖✖**Black Swan** Hillside LN5 0RF ☎Newark(0636)626474
*This family run restaurant nestles on the banks of the River
Witham. A lounge with open fire provides an inviting setting in
which to study the six course menu. The fine style of cuisine,
concentrating on quality not quantity, uses subtle blends of herbs
and natural flavours to delicately enhance dishes such as Duck
Soup with fine herb quenelles or a Seafood Casserole with Saffron.
Service is courteous and attentive.*
Closed Sun, Mon, 2 wks Jan/Feb & 2 wks Sep
⚐ English & French 35 seats ✳ Lunch £11.50-£15.50 Dinner
£17.50-£21.50 Last lunch 2pm Last dinner 10pm 9P
Credit Cards ①③

**BEDALE** North Yorkshire Map **08** SE28

★★63% *Motel Leeming* DL8 1DT (1m NE junc A1/A684)
☎(0677)23611
*Situated within the service area on the northbound carriageway of
the A1 near the town, this hotel offers functional but well-equipped
accommodation which represents good value for money; cafeteria
and à la carte restaurant provide a choice of eating styles, and
there is a comfortable bar lounge.*
40⇔ CTV in all bedrooms ®
⚋ 100P 14🍽 (charged) ❖ ஃ
⚐ English & Continental V ♥ ⚞ ⌖
Credit Cards ①②③⑤

★★61% *White Rose* DL7 9AY ☎(0677)22707 & 24941
FAX (0677) 25123
(For full entry see Leeming Bar)

**BEDDGELERT** Gwynedd Map **06** SH54

★★★63% *Royal Goat* LL55 4YE ☎(076686)224 & 343
FAX (076686) 422
*A well-furnished, family-run hotel in the village centre, lying
amidst spectacular scenery.*
31⇔♠(4fb)1⚞✠in 5 bedrooms CTV in all bedrooms ® T
sB&B⇔♠£36-£75 dB&B⇔♠£66-£80 ⚐
Lift ⚋ 150P ✦ games room *xmas*
⚐ Welsh & French V ♥ ⚞ ⌖ Lunch £9&alc High tea
£5-£10&alc Dinner £16&alc Last dinner 10pm
Credit Cards ①②③⑤ Ⓛ
**See advertisement on page 115**

# ℭhe ℱamous
# ℰlde ℬridge ℑnn
# ℌotel ★★

Bolton Road,
Port Sunlight Village,
Bebington, Wirral,
Merseyside L62 4UQ
Telephone: 051-645 8441

# CHEQUERS INN ★★

**Kiln Lane, Wooburn Common,
Beaconsfield, Bucks HP10 0JQ
Telephone:
Bourne End (06285) 29575
Fax: (0628) 850124**

17 bedrooms all en suite and with
colour TV, telephone, tea & coffee making facilities. Only 2
miles from M40 (junc 2 or 3) and
6 miles from M4 junc 7.

*Restaurant – Wedding Receptions
Conference Facilities
Large Car Park*

**B**

★⚑69%, *Bryn Eglwys Country House* LL55 4NB ☎(076686)210
*A former Georgian country house in its own grounds, standing in
mountainous splendour on the edge of the village, now provides
well-furnished accomodation comprising bedrooms with good
facilities, comfortable lounges and a delightful restaurant which
offers a wide choice of well-prepared dishes.*
16rm(12⇆)(3fb) CTV in 12 bedrooms ®
30P 🚗 ✿
♈ English & French **V** ✿ ⚗ ⌣ Last dinner 9pm
Credit Cards ⑴ ⑶ ⑸

★⚑69%, **Sygun Fawr Country House** LL55 4NE ☎(076686)258
7rm(3⇆3🖤)(1fb) ® ✳ sB&B⇆🖤 fr£17.50 dB&B⇆🖤 fr£35 ☐
CTV 30P 🚗 ✿ sauna *xmas*
**V** ✿ ⚗ Dinner fr£9 Last dinner 8.30pm

★59%, **Tanronen** LL55 4YB (Frederic Robinson) ☎(076686)347
*This small, friendly, village-centre hotel and public house stands
beside the river bridge, surrounded by beautiful mountain scenery.
Bedrooms are warm and comfortable, the cosy lounge is warmed
by log fires in winter and both restaurant and bar offer a good
range of fare.*
8rm CTV in all bedrooms ® ✖ ✳ sB&B£16 dB&B£32 ☐
CTV 12P 3🚗 *xmas*
**V** ✿ ⚗ Lunch £6.50 Dinner £11 Last dinner 9pm
Credit Cards ⑴ ⑶ ⑸

**BEDFORD** Bedfordshire Map **04** TL04

★★★78%, **Woodlands Manor** Green Ln, Clapham MK41 6EP
(2m N A6) ☎(0234)363281 Telex no 825007
FAX (0234) 272390
*A privately-run Victorian manor house, set in wooded grounds and
garden, offers a choice of well-appointed bedrooms, an elegant
restaurant and a drawing room. Chef Rae Johnson shows skill and
flair in the production of the well-seasoned, attractively presented
dishes that make up an attractive à la carte menu.*
26⇆🖤Annexe3⇆🖤 CTV in all bedrooms **T** ✖ ✳
sB&B⇆🖤£55-£85 dB&B⇆🖤£68-£90 ☐
⟪ 100P ✿ nc7yrs
♈ English & French **V** ✿ ⚗ Lunch £14.95-£21&alc Dinner
£21&alc Last dinner 9.45pm
Credit Cards ⑴ ⑵ ⑶

★★★68%, **Bedford Moat House** 2 Saint Mary's St MK42 0AR
(Queens Moat) ☎(0234)55131 Telex no 825243
FAX (0234) 40447
Closed Xmas RS Bank hols
*This commercial hotel, modernised to high standards and ideally
situated by the river, offers well appointed, fully equipped
bedrooms and good conference facilities.*
100⇆🖤(20fb) CTV in all bedrooms ® **T** ✖ (ex guide dogs)
sB&B⇆🖤 fr£68 dB&B⇆🖤 fr£82.50 ☐
Lift ⟪ CTV 72P sauna jacuzzi mini-gym
♈ English & Continental ✿ ⚗ Lunch fr£12.50 Dinner fr£14
Last dinner 9.45pm
Credit Cards ⑴ ⑵ ⑶ ⑸

★★★64%, **The Barns** Cardington Rd, Fenlake MK44 3SA
(Lansbury) ☎(0234)270044 Telex no 827748
FAX (0234) 273102
49⇆🖤(1fb)1 🛏⌣in 11 bedrooms CTV in all bedrooms ® **T**
✖ (ex guide dogs) sB&B⇆🖤 fr£70 dB&B⇆🖤 fr£82 ☐
⟪ 120P ✿ ♪ sauna solarium gymnasium *xmas*
♈ English & Continental **V** ✿ ⌣ Lunch fr£11&alc Dinner
fr£15&alc Last dinner 10pm
Credit Cards ⑴ ⑵ ⑶ ⑸

Book as early as possible for busy holiday
periods.

**BEER** Devon Map **03** SY28

★★60%, **Anchor Inn** EX12 3ET ☎Seaton(0297)20386
Closed 1 wk Xmas
*A traditional-looking business hotel, which faces the slipway to the
beach is popular for its successful combination of original character
and completely refurbished interior . Bedrooms – though not over-
large – are warm, cosy and attractively decorated, while the
character bars and adjacent restaurant offer a good choice of
wholesome fare with the emphasis on seafood. Service is informally
friendly, and in summer the cliff-top beer garden serving real ale is
an attraction.*
9rm(2⇆2🖤)(1fb) CTV in all bedrooms ® ✖ ✳ sB&B£18-£27
sB&B⇆🖤£22-£33 dB&B£36-£40 dB&B⇆🖤£44 ☐
CTV ⚗ 🚗 nc10yrs
✿
Credit Cards ⑴ ⑶

**BEETHAM** Cumbria Map **07** SD47

★62%, **Wheatsheaf** LA7 7AL ☎Milnthorpe(05395)62123
*An attractive, oak-beamed village inn close to lakeland, noted for
its bar food. Bedrooms are compact but cosy.*
6⇆🖤 CTV in all bedrooms ® ✳ sB&B⇆🖤£27
dB&B⇆🖤£38 ☐
CTV 50P
✿ Lunch £1.90-£7alc Dinner £7.50&alc Last dinner 8.30pm
Credit Cards ⑴ ⑶

**BELFORD** Northumberland Map **12** NU13

★★⚑74%, **Waren House** Waren Mill NE70 7EE
☎Bamburgh(06684)581 FAX (06684) 484
*A delightful country house set in 6 acres of wooded grounds on the
west corner of Budle Bay and only 2 miles from the A1. Service is
courteous and friendly, bedrooms comfortable and the restaurant
offers freshly prepared dishes at good value.*
7⇆🖤Annexe2⇆🖤⌣in 6 bedrooms CTV in all bedrooms ® **T**
✖ (ex guide dogs) sB&B⇆🖤£50-£65 dB&B⇆🖤£70-£95 ☐
20P 🚗 ✿ Croquet nc15yrs
♈ European **V** ⌣ Dinner £15-£20alc Last dinner 8.30pm
Credit Cards ⑴ ⑵ ⑶ ⑸

★★70%, **Blue Bell** Market Place NE70 7NE (Consort)
☎(0668)213543 FAX (0668) 213787
RS 13 Jan-21 Feb
*This 18th-century coaching inn has been carefully modernised to
retain much of its original character. Bedrooms are individually
decorated and well equipped; those to the rear overlooking
attractive gardens are more spacious and comfortable. Good
standards of housekeeping throughout.*
17⇆🖤(1fb)1🛏⌣in 4 bedrooms CTV in 15 bedrooms ®
10P 2🚗 (£3 per night) ✿ putting green nc6yrs
**V** ✿ ⌣ Last dinner 8.45pm
Credit Cards ⑴ ⑵ ⑶ ⑸

**BELLINGHAM** Northumberland Map **12** NY88

★★64%, **Riverdale Hall** NE48 2JT (Exec Hotel) ☎(0434)220254
*Just outside the village, the hotel overlooks its own cricket pitch
and the River Tyne. Additional bedrooms and a new lounge have
recently been added, signs of the constant imporovement here.
Friendly and attentive service is assured from the resident
proprietors and their experienced staff.*
20⇆🖤(6fb)3🛏 CTV in all bedrooms ® **T**
sB&B⇆🖤£28-£34.50 dB&B⇆🖤£49-£58 ☐
CTV 60P ✿ ⊡(heated) ♪ sauna *xmas*
♈ English & Danish **V** ✿ ⚗ Lunch £5.95-£7.50&alc High tea
£8-£11 Dinner £13-£15&alc Last dinner 9.30pm
Credit Cards ⑴ ⑵ ⑶ ⑸ ⑥

**BELPER** Derbyshire Map **08** SK34

✗✗*Rémy's Restaurant Français* 84 Bridge St DE5 1AZ
☎(0773)822246
*This small first-floor restaurant, situated on the A6, offers mainly
French cuisine, prepared from good fresh ingredients. Orders are
taken in the small aperitif bar before proceeding to the modestly
furnished restaurant, which encourages a non-smoking clientele.
There is a good wine list, with items to suit all tastes. Chef/
proprietor, Martin Smee, will usually leave the kitchen at some
point to converse with his customers.*
Closed Sun, 1st wk Jan & 2 wks Jul
Lunch not served Sat
♀ French 28 seats Last lunch 1.30pm Last dinner 9.30pm
♪ nc10yrs ✄
Credit Cards ① ② ③ ⑤

**BELTON** Lincolnshire Map **04** SK80

○**Belton Woods Hotel & Country Club** NG32 2LN (Scottish
Highland) ☎Grantham(0476)590924
Due to open Mar 1991
96⇆🐾

**BEMBRIDGE**

See **Wight, Isle of**

**BENLLECH BAY** Gwynedd Map **06** SH58

★★59% **Bay Court** Beach Rd LL74 8SW
☎Tynygongl(0248)852573
*A modern hotel only 200 yards from the beach.*
18rm(2⇆1🐾)Annexe4⇆(5fb) CTV in 14 bedrooms ® ✳
sB&Bfr£16.50 dB&Bfr£33 dB&B⇆🐾fr£43 ⊟
CTV 65P ⇚ *xmas*
♀ English & French **V** ♡ �🗲
Credit Cards ① ② ③ ⑤

**BERKELEY** Gloucestershire Map **03** ST69

★★63% **Old Schoolhouse** Canonbury St GL13 9BG
☎Dursley(0453)811711
Closed 22 Dec-7 Jan
*A small hotel offers friendly, personal service, complementing
distinctive public areas with comfortable bedrooms which include
all modern facilities.*
7⇆🐾(1fb) CTV in all bedrooms ® **T** ✗ ✳ sB&B⇆🐾£38
dB&B⇆🐾£52 ⊟
15P ⇚
♀ International **V** Lunch £8.50-£10.50alc Dinner £9-£15alc
Last dinner 8.45pm
Credit Cards ① ③ ⓕ

★★56%, **Berkeley Arms** Canonbury St GL13 9BG
☎Dursley(0453)810291
*This small hotel, set in the centre of the historic little town, retains
the relaxed, informal atmosphere of the coaching inn that it once
was. Its good choice of bar meals is supplemented by the buffet
lunch and evening set price menus.*
10⇆(1fb) CTV in all bedrooms ® **T** sB&B⇆fr£35
dB&B⇆fr£46 ⊟
50P ✿
♀ English & French **V** ♡ ⚓ Lunch fr£6.50&alc Dinner
fr£11.95alc Last dinner 9.30pm
Credit Cards ① ② ③ ⑤ ⓕ

Entries for red-star hotels are highlighted by a
tint panel. For a full list of these establishments
consult the Contents page.

**B**

Woodlands Manor ★★★

*A Victorian Manor ideally situated in three acres two miles from
Bedford. Frequent direct rail links to the north, London, and
Gatwick Airport provide easy travel to this central location. For
drivers, the town is close to Motorways for rapid access
throughout the country. The Hotel is a popular venue and, during fifteen years of continuous management and ownership, has
gained considerable experience in staging meetings and conferences of all types. Efficient meeting rooms can be fitted with
a wide range of presentational aids. A comfortable stay is assured
with fully equipped bedrooms, tranquil lounges where drinks
are served, and dining rooms commended in the principal
restaurant guides.*

**Green Lane, Clapham, Bedford
Tel: 0234 363281 Telex: 825007 Fax: 0234 272390**

*The Royal Goat Hotel*

**BEDDGELERT, GWYNEDD,
N. WALES LL55 4YE
Telephone 076-686-224/343
WTB AA ★★★**

Situated in the small mythical village
of Beddgelert in the heart of the
Snowdonia National Park stands this
18th century impressive hotel. Resident family owners. Salmon and trout
fishing, golf, horse riding and other
sporting activities. All rooms with
private facilities. Magnificent views.
Centrally heated. Two bars. Two restaurants table d'hôte and à la carte.
Live entertainment on Saturday
nights. Lift. Coral Chandelier Suite
available for functions & conferences.
CTV all rooms.

**B**

---

**BERKELEY ROAD** Gloucestershire Map **03** ST79

★★61% **Prince of Wales** GL13 9HD ☎Dursley(0453)810474
Telex no 437464

*Recent improvements by the new owners of this hotel have resulted in bright, comfortable, modern accommodation and good facilities which are complemented by attentive, friendly service. Its pleasant location near the historic village of Berkeley, yet only a few miles from the business centres of Bristol, Cheltenham and Gloucester, makes it attractive to both tourist and businessman.*

8⇥🏠(1fb) CTV in all bedrooms ® **T**
150P ✿
♀ English & French **V** ✿ 🗷 Last dinner 9pm
Credit Cards 1 2 3

---

**BERRIEW** Powys Map **06** SJ10

★★65% **Lion** SY21 8PQ ☎(0686)640452 & 640844

*A charming 17th-century inn, with beamed ceilings and a stone fireplace, offering comfortable bedrooms and cosy bars. The food is good with a choice of bar meals or an à la carte menu.*

7⇥🏠(1fb)1🍴 CTV in all bedrooms ® **T** ✱ ✻
sB&B⇥🏠£35-£38 dB&B⇥🏠£55-£60 🍴
6P ✔
♀ Welsh, English & Continental **V** ✿ Sunday Lunch £8-£8.95
Dinner fr£15&alc Last dinner 9.30pm
Credit Cards 1 3 £

---

**BERWICK-UPON-TWEED** Northumberland Map **12** NT95

★★★53% **Turret House** Etal Rd, Tweedmouth TD15 2EG
(Inter-Hotels) ☎(0289)330808 FAX (0289) 330467

*Elegant hotel in its own grounds with tastefully decorated open-plan bar, dining room and lounge.*

13⇥🏠(1fb) CTV in all bedrooms ® **T** ✱
sB&B⇥🏠£42.50-£47.50 dB&B⇥🏠£57-£65 🍴
100P ✿
**V** ✿ 🗷 Lunch £4.25-£10.75 Dinner £8.50-£14.50 Last dinner 8.45pm
Credit Cards 1 2 3 5

★59% **Queens Head** Sandgate TD15 1EP ☎(0289)307852

*A characterful little hotel with cosy bar and lounge, very popular both for bar snacks and for its good-value table d'hôte menu, stands in the town centre close to the harbour. Bedrooms are modestly furnished but very well equipped.*

6rm(5fb) CTV in all bedrooms ® **T** sB&B£19.50-£20
dB&B£39-£40
CTV 🅿
♀ Mainly grills **V** ✿ Lunch £6.50-£7.50 High tea fr£5.50
Dinner £9.50-£11 Last dinner 8.30pm
Credit Cards 1 3 £

---

**BETWS-Y-COED** Gwynedd Map **06** SH75

★★★69% **Waterloo** LL24 0AR (Consort) ☎(06902)411
Closed Xmas

*Recent extensive alterations and improvements have resulted in a further sixteen spacious and modern bedrooms, a pleasant coffee shop and a leisure/fitness complex with an indoor pool and a fully supervised gymnasium.*

9⇥Annexe30⇥(2fb) CTV in all bedrooms ® **T** ✱
sB&B⇥£38.50-£45 dB&B⇥£62-£67 🍴
200P ✿ 🏊(heated) ✔ sauna solarium gymnasium *xmas*
♀ International **V** ✿ 🗷 Sunday Lunch £7.50-£8.75 Dinner
£14.25-£14.50 Last dinner 9.30pm
Credit Cards 1 2 3 5 £

---

*The AA's star-rating scheme is the market leader in hotel classification.*

---

★★★⚑64% **Plas Hall** Pont-y-Pant, Dolwyddelan LL25 0PJ
(3m SW A470) (Minotels) ☎Dolwyddelan(06906)206
Telex no 61155

*A delightful Welsh stone building standing in its own grounds on the banks of the River Lleds features an attractive restaurant where local produce forms the basis of a high standard of cuisine; public rooms are well-furnished and bedrooms offer all-round comfort.*

19rm(15⇥1🏠)(3fb)2🍴 CTV in all bedrooms ® **T** ✱
sB&B⇥🏠£38.35-£51.35 dB&B⇥🏠£59-£79 🍴
36P ✿ ✔ ♫ *xmas*
♀ Welsh & French **V** ✿ 🗷 ✂
Credit Cards 1 3 £

---

★★★⚑63% **Craig-y-Dderwyn Country House** LL24 0AS
(Minotels) ☎(06902)293 FAX (06902) 362

*Standing down a narrow lane beside the River Conwy, on the edge of the town, this half-timbered country house complements a relaxing atmosphere with personal service and freshly prepared meals.*

17⇥🏠Annexe1🏠(3fb)🍴 CTV in all bedrooms ® **T**
sB&B⇥🏠fr£45 dB&B⇥🏠fr£60 🍴
60P ✿ 🎱 *xmas*
♀ International **V** ✿ 🗷 Lunch fr£7.25&alc High tea fr£4.50
Dinner fr£15&alc Last dinner 8.45pm
Credit Cards 1 2 3

---

★★★63% **Royal Oak** Holyhead Rd LL24 0AY ☎(06902)219
due to change to (0690) 710219 FAX (06902) 433
Closed 25-26 Dec

*A choice of eating styles and a range of well-equipped bedrooms are available at this nicely appointed hotel in the centre of the village.*

27⇥🏠(5fb) CTV in all bedrooms **T** ✱ sB&B⇥🏠£37-£44
dB&B⇥🏠£50-£68 🍴
⟨ 60P

▶

---

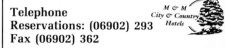

# Craig-y-Dderwen
# Country House Hotel
### Betws-y-coed,
### North Wales LL24 0AS

AA★★★, WTB 4 Crown

Recommended by leading guides. Recently restored to its former grandeur, the hotel offers 18 luxuriously appointed rooms, including 3 four poster suites and a jacuzzi, with most modern facilities as expected by a discerning clientele, complemented by our exciting 5 course menu of freshly prepared local produce by our chef/proprietor and served in our terrace restaurant.

*Special Breaks include: Gourmet weekends, Honeymoon Hushaways and activity holidays arranged.*

**Telephone**
**Reservations: (06902) 293**
**Fax (06902) 362**

*M & M
City & Country
Hotels*

---

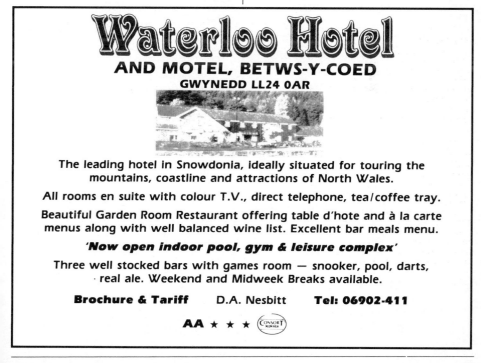

## Betws-y-Coed - Bibury

♀ English, French & Italian V ✿ ⬚ Lunch £7.95-£8.50 High tea £5.50-£7.50alc Dinner £9-£18&alc Last dinner 9.30pm
Credit Cards ①②③⑤

★★69% **Ty Gwyn** LL24 0SG (Best Western) ☎(06902)383 & 787
*A stone built coaching inn that dates back four hundred years stands beside the A5 on the edge of the town, close to Waterloo Bridge ; most of its original features having been preserved, it exhibits a wealth of charm and character.*
13rm(2⇨7↑)(1fb)4⊞ CTV in 8 bedrooms Ⓡ ✱ sB&B⇨↑£17 dB&B£34 dB&B⇨↑£50 ♬
CTV 12P *xmas*
♀ English & French V ✿ Lunch £9-£12.95&alc Dinner £12.95&alc Last dinner 9.30pm
Credit Cards ①③ⓔ

★★68% *Park Hill* Llanrwst Rd LL24 0HD ☎(06902)540
*A small, friendly, privately owned hotel on the A470 just south of Betws-y-Coed, providing well equipped bedrooms.*
11rm(6⇨3↑)(1fb) CTV in all bedrooms Ⓡ
14P ⚙ ✿ ▭(heated) sauna nc6yrs
♀ Welsh, English & French V ✿ ⬚ ✂
Credit Cards ①②③⑤

★62% **Fairy Glen** LL24 0SH ☎(06902)269
Closed Dec & Jan
*A small and friendly hotel, personally run by its resident owners, stands beside the river in a wooded area close to the village.*
10rm(5⇨2↑)(3fb) CTV in all bedrooms Ⓡ sB&B£15-£19 dB&B£30-£34 dB&B⇨↑£34-£38 ♬
⦅ CTV 10P ⚙ ✿
V ✿ ⬚ ✂ Bar Lunch £1-£5 Dinner £10 Last dinner 7.30pm
Credit Cards ①③⑤

### BEVERLEY Humberside Map **08** TA03

★★★68% **Tickton Grange** Tickton HU17 9SH (3m NE on A1035) ☎Hornsea(0964)543666 Telex no 527254
FAX (0964) 542556
RS 25-29 Dec
*A peaceful country house just off the A1079 provides comfortable accomodation, interesting menus and friendly service.*
16⇨↑(1fb)⊞ CTV in all bedrooms Ⓡ T ✱ sB&B⇨↑£63 dB&B⇨↑£78 ♬
65P ✿
V ✿ ⬚ Lunch fr£11.95alc Dinner £13.95-£19.95alc Last dinner 9.30pm
Credit Cards ①②③⑤ⓔ

★★★59% **Beverley Arms** North Bar Within HU17 8DD (Trusthouse Forte) ☎Hull(0482)869241 Telex no 597568
FAX (0482) 870907
*A modernised coaching inn offers sound accommodation in functional, up-to-date bedrooms complemented by public areas whose traditional features have been highlighted to good effect.*
57⇨↑(4fb)✂in 3 bedrooms CTV in all bedrooms Ⓡ T S%
sB⇨↑fr£65 dB⇨↑fr£85 (room only) ♬
Lift ⦅ 70P ♫ *xmas*
V ✿ ⬚ ✂ S% Lunch fr£8.95 Dinner fr£14.95&alc Last dinner 9.45pm
Credit Cards ①②③④⑤

★★71% *Lairgate* 30-34 Lairgate HU17 8EP
☎Hull(0482)882141
*This privately owned, town centre hotel provides a friendly and relaxed environment, created by polite and conscientious staff. Continual upgrading of facilities means modern accommodation with a good range of facilities, and the restaurant offers interesting menus that are popular with both residents and locals alike.*
25rm(9⇨8↑)(2fb)⊞ CTV in all bedrooms Ⓡ
⦅ CTV 18P
♀ English & Continental V ✿ ⬚ Last dinner 9.30pm
Credit Cards ①③

### BEWDLEY Hereford & Worcester Map **07** SO77

★★53% **Black Boy** Kidderminster Rd DY12 1AG
☎(0299)402119
Closed 25 Dec
*An eighteenth-century inn, standing on the A456 close to both the River Severn and the centre of this lovely old town, offers accommodation that is equally suitable for business people and tourists, with simple but comfortable bedrooms, pleasant bar facilities and a small, cosy restaurant.*
17rm(5⇨)Annexe8rm(2⇨)(2fb) CTV in 15 bedrooms Ⓡ T sB&B£27.50-£29.70 sB&B⇨↑£31.90-£41.80 dB&B£41.80-£42.90 dB&B⇨↑£47.30-£59.40 ♬
CTV 28P ⚙ ✿
♀ English and French V ✿ Lunch £8.25&alc Dinner £10.75 Last dinner 8.45pm
Credit Cards ①②③

### BEXHILL-ON-SEA East Sussex Map **05** TV70

See also **Cooden Beach**
★★★64% **Granville** Sea Rd TN40 1EE ☎Bexhill(0424)215437
FAX (0424) 225028
*A friendly hotel, with a pervading sense of charm and peace. The hotel has been refurbished and modernised to provide comfortable bedrooms that have been decorated attractively, a pleasant lounge and popular bar. Staff are helpful and are led by the personal involvement of the proprietors.*
50⇨(1fb) CTV in all bedrooms Ⓡ T sB&B⇨↑fr£43.50 dB&B⇨↑fr£65.50 ♬
Lift ⦅ ♪ ⚙ *xmas*
V ✿ ⬚ Lunch £8.25-£11 Dinner fr£12.50 Last dinner 9pm
Credit Cards ①②③⑤ⓔ

### BEXLEY Greater London Map **05** TQ47

★★★69% **Crest** Black Prince Interchange, Southwold Rd DA5 1ND (Trusthouse Forte) ☎(0322)526900 Telex no 8956539
FAX (0322) 526113
*This efficiently-managed commercial hotel offers a good standard of well-equipped accomodation – and the new bedroom wing will add executive studios, rooms for lady executives and spa rooms. Attractive public areas include a separate lounge bar for residents and a business centre.*
106⇨↑in 20 bedrooms CTV in all bedrooms Ⓡ T ✱ S%
sB⇨↑£82-£95 dB⇨↑£95-£108 (room only) ♬
Lift ⦅ 180P ✿ games room *xmas*
♀ English & French V ✿ ⬚ ✂ Lunch £9-£15.50&alc Dinner £9-£15.50&alc Last dinner 9.45pm
Credit Cards ①②③④⑤

### BIBURY Gloucestershire Map **04** SP10

★★⬚67% **Bibury Court** GL7 5NT ☎(028574)337
FAX (028574) 660
Closed 24-30 Dec
*Set within landscaped walled grounds this fine period building is now a hotel of charm and character. Spacious public areas retain many original features and the well-equipped bedrooms are comfortable. The new Coach House restaurant, 50 yards from the main building, serves imaginative food in intimate surroundings.*
18⇨(1fb)10⊞ CTV in all bedrooms T sB&B⇨↑£40-£50 dB&B⇨↑£60-£66 Continental breakfast ♬
CTV 100P ⚙ ✿ ♩
♀ English & French ✿ ⬚ Lunch £15-£20alc Dinner £15-£20alc Last dinner 9pm
Credit Cards ①③

For key to symbols see the inside front cover.

BIDEFORD Devon Map **02** SS42

See also **Fairy Cross, Landcross & Westward Ho**

★★★ 66% **Royal** Barnstaple St EX39 4AE (Brend)
☎(0237)472005 Telex no 42551 FAX (0271) 78558

*This traditional, older-style hotel has recently been significantly
upgraded and refurbished. Comfortable, spotlessly clean bedrooms
offer an extensive range of modern amenities whilst public rooms
are equally stylish.*

30↰ ᐟ(3fb) CTV in all bedrooms ® T sB&B↰ᐟ£44-£49
dB&B↰ᐟ£66-£77 ₧
₵ 70P *xmas*
♥ English & French **V** ◊ ▱ Lunch £7.50&alc Dinner
£10-£12&alc Last dinner 9pm
Credit Cards ①②③⑤Ⓔ

★★★ 59% **Durrant House** Heywood Rd, Northam EX39 3QB
(Consort) ☎(0237)472361 Telex no 46740

*Attractive building with 30 new comfortable bedrooms in a top
floor extension. The public areas are attractively decorated and
offer a friendly atmosphere to both commercial and holiday trade.
The restaurant offers adequate menus, and steaks and bar meals
are available in the Bridge steak bar.*

79↰ᐟ(6fb)3₩ CTV in all bedrooms ®
Lift 150P ✿ CFA ᐼ sauna solarium
♥ English & French Last dinner 9.30pm
Credit Cards ①②③⑤

See advertisement on page 121

★★ 69% **Sonnenheim** Heywood Rd EX39 2QA ☎(0237)474989
Closed Nov-Feb

*The personally-run country-house-style hotel provides pleasant
bedrooms, comfortable public areas, and a friendly atmosphere
throughout. A table d'hôte menu of honest cooking, using fresh
garden produce whenever possible, offers an interesting choice of
dishes.*

▶

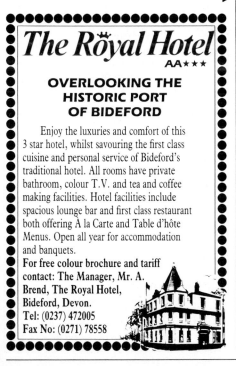

9rm(6⇨2♠)(1fb) CTV in all bedrooms ® ✳ sB&B£19-£22 sB&B⇨♠£24-£26 dB&B⇨♠£38-£40 ⊟
10P 1🛏 (£2 per night) ⊞ ✣
♀ English & Continental V Dinner £12.50-£15&alc Last dinner 8pm
Credit Cards ❶❸ ⓔ

★★67% *Orchard Hill Hotel & Restaurant* Orchard Hill, Northam EX39 2QY ☎(0237)472872
*An hotel looking down on town and river from its elevated position provides comfortable accommodation to suit both businessman and holidaymaker; a relaxed atmosphere prevails in the public lounges and bar, while the refurbished restaurant serves an à la carte menu and resident proprietors give personal service throughout.*
9⇨♠ CTV in all bedrooms ® 🐕 (ex guide dogs)
15P ⊞ ✣ nc6 yrs
V ❖ ⊒ Last dinner 9.30pm
Credit Cards ❶❸

★★60% *Riversford* Limers Ln EX39 2RG (Inter-Hotels) ☎(0237)474239 FAX (0237) 421661
*A family-managed hotel standing about a mile from the centre of the town, provides comfortable bedrooms (most with en suite facilities) and informal public rooms which include a restaurant offering a table d'hôte menu.*
16⇨♠(2fb)2⊞ CTV in all bedrooms ® T sB&B⇨♠£24-£47 dB&B⇨♠£64-£74 ⊟
《 CTV 20P 2🛏 ✣ solarium badminton putting 🏌 *xmas*
♀ English & Continental V ❖ ⊒ ✂ Lunch £7.70 High tea £4-£10 Dinner £16.80 Last dinner 9pm
Credit Cards ❶❷❸❺ ⓔ

★★▟58% *Yeoldon House* Durrant Ln, Northam EX39 2RL ☎(0237)4744OO Telex no 46410 FAX (0237) 476618
RS early Jan
*An hotel in country house style commands an expansive view over the River Torridge – to which its lawns slope down – and across woodland to the village beyond. Bedrooms are well-equipped, and public areas include a comfortable lounge, pleasant dining room and cosy residents' bar.*
10⇨♠(2fb)1⊞ ✂in 1 bedroom CTV in all bedrooms ® T S% sB&B⇨♠£40.75-£45.50 dB&B⇨♠£66-£75.50 ⊟
20P ✣ sauna solarium gymnasium shooting *xmas*
♀ English & Continental V ❖ ⊒ ✂ S% Lunch £9.95-£14.95&alc High tea fr£3.50 Dinner £19.50&alc Last dinner 8.30pm
Credit Cards ❶❷❸❹❺ ⓔ

**BIDFORD-ON-AVON** Warwickshire Map **04** SP05

★★65% *White Lion* High St B50 4BQ ☎(0789)773309 & 773218 FAX (0789)490663
*An intimate dining room and cosy, traditional lounge are attractive features of this small riverside hotel; well-furnished and spacious bedrooms are equipped with a good range of facilities, and a friendly staff provides efficient service.*
10⇨♠1⊞ CTV in all bedrooms ® T
18P ♪
♀ English & French ❖ ⊒ ✂ Last dinner 9.30pm
Credit Cards ❶❷❸❺
**See advertisement under STRATFORD-UPON-AVON**

**BIGBURY-ON-SEA** Devon Map **03** SX64

★69% *Henley* TQ7 4AR (Minotels) ☎(0548)810240
*Commanding beautiful views of both coast and countryside from its elevated position, and having a private cliff path to beach and gardens, the hotel promotes a cottage atmosphere in its thoughfully decorated lounge and well equipped bedrooms. An attractive dining room offers home-cooked food prepared from fresh produce, varying the table d'hôte menu daily; service is friendly, and a 'no smoking' policy is applied.*

8rm(6⇨3♠)(2fb)✂in all bedrooms CTV in all bedrooms ® T sB&B£18.50-£19.50 dB&B⇨♠£39-£45 ⊟
9P ⊞ ✣ *xmas*
♀ English & French ❖ ⊒ ✂ Dinner £11.25&alc Last dinner 8pm
Credit Cards ❶❸

**BIGGAR** Strathclyde *Lanarkshire* Map **11** NT03

★★★▟75%, *Shieldhill* Quothquan ML12 6NA ☎(0899)20035 Telex no 777308 FAX (0899) 21092
*Completely restored to its former elegance, this charming hotel is comfortably furnished and enhanced by lovely antiques and fresh flowers.*
11⇨♠4⊞✂in all bedrooms CTV in all bedrooms T
🐕 (ex guide dogs) sB&B⇨♠£81-£126 dB&B⇨♠£91-£137 ⊟
25P ⊞ ✣ croquet bowls nc15yrs
V ❖ ⊒ ✂ Lunch £15-£25alc Dinner fr£19.95&alc Last dinner 10pm
Credit Cards ❶❷❸❹❺ ⓔ

★★★64%, *Tinto* Symington ML12 6PQ ☎Tinto(08993)454 FAX (08993) 520
*Situated within attractive grounds and close to Tinto Hill, the hotel has been considerably upgraded and is a popular venue for weddings. Keenly-priced light meals are available throughout the day and evening.*
38⇨♠(2fb)1⊞ CTV in all bedrooms ® T ✳ sB&B⇨fr£35 dB&B⇨fr£50 ⊟
《 100P ⊞ ✣ solarium pool table *xmas*
♀ European V ❖ ⊒ Lunch £6.50-£12 High tea £4.75-£10 Dinner £10-£20alc Last dinner 10pm
Credit Cards ❶❷❸❺ ⓔ
**See advertisement under LANARK**

**★★♨ 68% Wyndales House** Symington ML12 6JU (3m W off A72) ☎Tinto(08993)207

*In the hands of its new owners this former mansion is undergoing a phased programme of improvements designed to restore the original charm and character of the Edwardian building. The panelled public rooms, especially the lounge, are comfortable and the bedrooms, individually decorated, are well equipped. The hotel stands in 19 acres of wooded grounds at the foot of Tinto Hill, just off the A73.*

14⇨➚(3fb)1🛏 CTV in 10 bedrooms ® T ✼
sB&B⇨➚£29.50-£35 dB&B⇨➚£39.50-£45 🅿

《 60P ✼ ♫ (grass) *xmas*

♍ International V ↻ ♨ Lunch £7.50-£8.50 Dinner £12.50-£13.50&alc Last dinner 9.30pm

Credit Cards ①②③

---

**BILBROOK** Somerset Map **03** ST04

**★★ 72% Dragon House** TA24 6HQ ☎Washford(0984)40215

*Set in 2.5 acres of beautiful gardens beside the A39, this 17th-century character property stands only six miles from Minehead, providing an excellent centre from which to tour the Exmoor National Park. Beauty and technology combine in attractive, comprehensively equipped bedrooms with extensive en suite facilities, whilst pleasant public areas feature open fires, beams and exposed stonework. Table d'hôte and à la carte menus offer an interesting range of dishes, based exclusively on top-quality fresh produce and complemented by personal service from resident proprietors.*

8⇨➚Annexe2⇨(1fb)1🛏 CTV in all bedrooms ® T
sB&B⇨➚£39-£43 dB&B⇨➚£60-£72.50 🅿

25P 🐾 *xmas*

♍ English & French V ↻ ♨ ✂ Dinner £13.95&alc Last dinner 9pm

Credit Cards ①②③⑤

**See advertisement under DUNSTER**

**★ 68% Bilbrook Lawns** TA24 6HE ☎Washford(0984)40331
Closed Nov-Feb (ex Xmas)

*A small Georgian house with elegant, well proportioned rooms stands back from the road in its own gardens. Bedrooms in country style contain some antique furnishings, while the restaurant serves enjoyable meals in which fresh ingredients have been used to create some interesting and well-flavoured – but not over-elaborate – European dishes ; resident proprietors provide good-natured hospitality.*

7rm(1⇨3➚)(1fb) CTV in all bedrooms ® sB&Bfr£21.50
sB&B⇨➚fr£25 dB&Bfr£33 dB&B⇨➚£38-£44 🅿

8P 🐾 ✼

♍ English & French V ↻ ♨ ✂ Lunch fr£6.50 Dinner fr£10.50 Last dinner 7.30pm

---

**BILBROUGH** North Yorkshire Map **08** SE54

★★★

**★★★♨**
**BILBROUGH MANOR COUNTRY HOUSE**

YO2 3PH
☎Tadcaster(0937)834002
FAX (0937) 834724
Closed 25-29 Dec

*This lovely country house stands in extensive grounds just off the A64 and only 5 miles from York. The high quality of the restoration is the work of Colin and Susan Bell, who bought the hotel in 1986, and is evident throughout, notably in the elegant panelled drawing room and the spacious reception hall. There are 12 beautifully*

*appointed and decorated bedrooms, with views of the gardens and the surrounding countryside, and the service is impeccable. Head Chef Daniel Martelat presents a menu of the new classical French cuisine of a very high standard and the dining room service is ably supervised by Restaurant Manager Antonio Esteve, is beyond reproach.*

12⇨➚1🛏 CTV in all bedrooms ✼ sB&B⇨➚£75-£100 dB&B⇨➚£85-£135 🅿

《 CTV 50P 🐾 ✼ croquet nc12yrs *xmas*

♍ French V ↻ ♨ Lunch £12.50&alc Dinner £19.50-£29.50alc Last dinner 9.30pm

Credit Cards ①②③⑤ⓔ

**See advertisement under YORK**

---

**BILLESLEY** Warwickshire Map **04** SP15

**※★★★♨ 74% Billesley Manor** B49 6NF (3m W off A422) (Queens Moat)(Prestige) ☎Stratford-upon-Avon(0789)400888 Telex no 312599 FAX (0789) 764145

*This old country mansion 3 miles west of Stratford, is imbued with the spirit of Shakespeare country – oak-panelled rooms, real log fires and 11 acres of grounds including a topiary garden set the tone for a comfortable and relaxing stay. The lovely restaurant is a perfect setting for Head Chef Mark Naylor's skills. The table d'hôte menu changes daily and the à la carte menu offers a sensible choice of good, imaginative dishes. A heated indoor swimming pool, croquet lawn, pitch and putt course and two tennis courts take care of the need for exercise.*

41⇨➚(6fb)3🛏 CTV in all bedrooms T ✼ sB&B⇨➚fr£95 dB&B⇨➚fr£117 🅿

《 200P ✼ ⊠(heated) ♫ (hard) croquet shooting pitch & putt *xmas*

♍ English & French V ↻ ♨ Lunch fr£17&alc Dinner fr£23&alc Last dinner 9.30pm

Credit Cards ①②③⑤

---

**BILLINGHAM**

See Stockton-on-Tees

---

**BILLINGTON** Lancashire Map **07** SD73

**✕✕✕Foxfields** Whalley Rd BB6 9HY ☎Whalley(0254)822556 FAX (0254) 824613

*Well furnished and comfortable, a restaurant which stands close to the Pendle Hills and is within easy reach of Blackburn. It offers very high standards of cuisine and service – only the freshest produce is used, daily market specials being highly recommended, and there is a well-balanced wine list. A recently constructed block of bedrooms offers accommodation.*

Lunch not served Sat

V 90 seats ✼ Lunch £8.25-£11.50&alc Dinner £18.50&alc Last lunch 1.30pm Last dinner 9.30pm 75P

Credit Cards ①②③⑤

---

**BINGLEY** West Yorkshire Map **07** SE13

**★★★ 66% Oakwood Hall** Lady Ln BD16 4AW
☎Bradford(0274)564123 & 563569 FAX (0274) 561477
Closed 25-28 Dec

*Situated in a quiet woodland setting, this well furnished family-run hotel provides a good standard of accommodation, with well designed, spacious bedrooms. A high standard of cooking is provided in the charming restaurant.*

18⇨➚(1fb)1🛏 CTV in all bedrooms ® T ✼
sB&B⇨➚£40-£60 dB&B⇨➚£60-£80

《 100P ✼ ᴓ

♍ English & French V ↻ Lunch fr£8.95 Dinner fr£11.25&alc Last dinner 9.30pm

Credit Cards ①②③④⑤ⓔ

**B**

★★★64% **Bankfield** Bradford Rd BD16 1TU (Embassy)
☎Bradford(0274)567123 FAX (0274) 551331
*This modernised country house offers comfortable, well-appointed bedrooms and friendly service.*
103⇄╅(5fb)✂in 6 bedrooms CTV in all bedrooms ® T S%
sB⇄╅£67-£80 dB⇄╅£72-£85 (room only) ⊟
Lift ⟨ 250P 20☎ ✿ CFA pool table tennis ♫ *xmas*
V ♥ ⚓ ✂ Lunch fr£11.50&alc Dinner fr£11.50&alc Last dinner 9.15pm
Credit Cards ①②③⑤

---

**BIRCHGROVE** West Glamorgan Map 03 SS79

★★64% **Oak Tree Parc** Birchgrove Rd SA7 9JR (300yds from M4 junc 44) ☎Skewen(0792)817781
Closed 25-31 Dec
*A small commercial hotel run by the friendly Tilbrook family providing comfortable, well equipped accommodation and well-cooked food. The small lounge/bar area is due to be extended during 1990.*
10⇄╅(2fb) CTV in all bedrooms ® ⊟
⟨ 40P ✿
♀ Welsh, English, French & Italian V ♥ ⚓ ✂
Credit Cards ①②③⑤

---

**BIRCH MOTORWAY SERVICE AREA (M62)** Greater Manchester Map 07 SD80

⌂**Granada Lodge** M62 Service Area OL10 2HQ (Granada)
☎061-655 3403 FAX 061-655 3358
*Situated on the eastbound side of the M62 between junctions 18 and 19 this lodge is well maintained and clean. The adjacent Country Kitchen offers a selection of dishes throughout the day.*
37⇄╅(5fb)✂in 5 bedrooms CTV in all bedrooms ®
✕ (ex guide dogs) ✳ S% sB⇄fr£28 dB⇄fr£31 (room only)
⟨ 60P
V ♥ ⚓ ✂
Credit Cards ①②③⑤

See advertisement under MANCHESTER

---

**BIRDLIP** Gloucestershire Map 03 SO91

★★★59% **Royal George** GL4 8JH (Lansbury)
☎Gloucester(0452)862506 Telex no 437238
FAX (0452) 862277
*The hotel stands in rural surroundings on the edge of the village, and guests can expect to enjoy a much more peaceful stay now that the completed bypass has diverted the majority of the traffic. For a drink in surroundings full of atmosphere, visit the Applecart Pub, converted from a 17th-century chapel.*
34rm(24⇄)Annexe2⇄(4fb)1⊞✂in 6 bedrooms CTV in all bedrooms ® T ✕ (ex guide dogs) sB&B⇄£67 dB&B⇄£80 ⊟
⟨ 120P ✿ sauna solarium 9 hole putting green *xmas*
V ♥ ⚓ ✂ Lunch fr£8.95 Dinner fr£14&alc Last dinner 10pm
Credit Cards ①②③⑤

✕**Kingshead House** GL4 8JH ☎Gloucester(0452)862299
*An 18th-century house that was originally a coaching inn is now a popular restaurant. Poultry and game are prominent in the selection of dishes on the menu, with at least one vegetarian dish on offer. Desserts have strong flavours and the chocolate mousse is especially good. The wine list is well chosen and includes a good variety of half bottles.*
Closed Mon
Lunch not served Sat
Dinner not served Sun
♀ English & French V 30 seats ✳ Lunch £13.50 Dinner £23.50
Last lunch 2pm Last dinner 9.45pm 12P
Credit Cards ①②③⑤

---

**BIRKENHEAD** Merseyside Map 07 SJ38

★★★61% **Bowler Hat** 2 Talbot Rd, Oxton L43 2HH
☎051-652 4931 Telex no 628761
*Peacefully situated in a residential area, this period house with neat, well-tended lawns and gardens offers sound accommodation in both its original building and the modern wing to the rear.*
29⇄╅ CTV in all bedrooms ® T ✳ sB&B⇄╅£33-£51.50
dB&B⇄╅£48-£64 Continental breakfast
⟨ 40P ✿
♀ English, French & Italian V ♥ ⚓ Lunch fr£9.50 Dinner fr£13.50&alc Last dinner 10pm
Credit Cards ①②③⑤⑥

★★68% **Riverhill** Talbot Rd, Oxton L43 2HJ ☎051-653 3773
FAX 051-653 7162
*The restaurant is an attractive feature of this hotel, being recently refurbished in elegant, Victorian style and providing a choice of dishes spanning Bistecchina Casanova on the Anglo-Italian menu to Lamb Noisettes Soubise or Duckling aux Grand Marnier from the more classical range. Resident proprietors create a convivial atmosphere throughout the hotel, and accommodation is in well-appointed bedrooms.*
16⇄╅(1fb)2⊞ CTV in all bedrooms ® ✕ ✳
sB&B⇄╅£33-£43 dB&B⇄╅£47-£64
CTV 30P ⌘ ✿
♀ English, French & Italian V Lunch £7.95&alc Dinner £9.90&alc Last dinner 9.30pm
Credit Cards ①②③⑤

See advertisement on page 125

A rosette is an indication of exceptional standards of cuisine.

## Birmingham

**BIRMINGHAM** West Midlands Map **07** SP08

See **Town Plan Section**

See also **Birmingham Airport, Birmingham (National Exhibition Centre) and Bromsgrove**

★★★★72% **Swallow** 12 Hagley Rd, Five Ways B16 8SJ (Swallow) ☎021-452 1144 Telex no 333806 FAX 021-456 3442

*Recent major conversion of one of Birmingham's landmarks has resulted in an Edwardian-style hotel that is a credit to that lavish period, but with today's luxuries. Fine marble and paintings adorn the interior, and the formally uniformed staff are plentiful and friendly. Chef Idris Caldora offers his strong, flavoursome cooking – classical French in the Elgar Restaurant, and British with regional specialities in the Langtry Restaurant.*

98⇌2🛁¥in 54 bedrooms CTV in all bedrooms ® T ✳ S15% sB&B⇌fr£97.50 dB&B⇌fr£120 ⊟
Lift ( ⊞ 70P 🚗 ⊠(heated) sauna solarium gymnasium ♫ *xmas*
♡ English & French V ✧ ◻ ¥ S% Lunch £15-£50alc Dinner £15-£50alc Last dinner 10.30pm
Credit Cards ①②③⑤

★★★★67% **Plough & Harrow** Hagley Rd, Edgbaston B16 8LS (Trusthouse Forte) ☎021-454 4111 Telex no 338074 FAX 021-454 1868

*This city hotel has a great deal of character and is popular with Birmingham's businessmen. The old sandstone building conceals modern extensions with quiet, comfortable bedrooms whilst the restaurant has a notable reputation for well prepared food and formal, professional service.*

44⇌🛋¥in 9 bedrooms CTV in all bedrooms (room only) ⊟
Lift ( 80P 🚗 sauna
V ✧ ◻
Credit Cards ①②③④⑤

★★★★51% *Albany* Smallbrook Queensway B5 4EW (Trusthouse Forte) ☎021-643 8171 Telex no 337031 FAX 021-631 2528

*An impressive, modern, thirteen-storey building with extensive views over the city.*

254⇌¥in 25 bedrooms CTV in all bedrooms ®
Lift ( ⊞ ✗ CFA ⊠(heated) squash sauna solarium gymnasium health & fitness club
♡ European V ✧ ◻ ¥ Last dinner 11pm
Credit Cards ①②③④⑤

★★★★50% *Holiday Inn* Holliday St B1 1HH (Holiday Inns Inc) ☎021-631 2000 Telex no 337272 FAX 021-643 9018

*International standard hotel reached from Suffolk Street Queensway before junction with Paradise Circus.*

290⇌(210fb)¥in 64 bedrooms CTV in all bedrooms ®
Lift ( ⊞ 300🚗 ⊠(heated) sauna solarium gymnasium
♡ International V ✧ ◻
Credit Cards ①②③④⑤

★★★77% **Norton Place** 180 Lifford Ln, Kings Norton B30 3NT ☎021-433 5656 FAX 021-433 3048

*This former Victorian paper mill has been imaginatively converted into a museum, restaurant, hotel and conference centre, while retaining lovely gardens and an attractive lake. The unique hotel is small with an exclusive atmosphere, and the new residents' block, matching perfectly the earlier buildings, contains ten lavishly equipped bedrooms, reception and a delightful sitting room. In the Lombard Room Restaurant, chef Paul Bingham produces deft interpretations of French classics.*

10⇌🛋2🛁¥in 5 bedrooms CTV in all bedrooms T
✱ (ex guide dogs) sB&B⇌🛋£150-£250
dB&B⇌🛋£170.50-£280.50 Continental breakfast
( 300P 20🚗 🚗 ✿ gymnasium clay pigeon shooting ♫ nc *xmas*
V ✧ ◻ ¥ Lunch £16.50&alc High tea £11&alc Dinner £20.50&alc Last dinner 10pm
Credit Cards ①②③⑤

★★★65%, **Strathallan Thistle** 225 Hagley Rd, Edgbaston B16 9RY (Mount Charlotte (TS)) ☎021-455 9777 Telex no 336680 FAX 021-454 9432

*A striking circular building on the main thoroughfare into the city.*

167⇌🛋(5fb)¥in 18 bedrooms CTV in all bedrooms ® T ✳ sB⇌🛋fr£72 dB⇌🛋fr£82 (room only) ⊟
Lift ( ⊞ 250P 150🚗 CFA
♡ International ✧ ◻ ¥ Lunch fr£15alc Dinner fr£15alc Last dinner 10pm
Credit Cards ①②③④⑤

★★★64% **Royal Angus Thistle** St Chads, Queensway B4 6HY (Mount Charlotte (TS)) ☎021-236 4211 Telex no 336889 FAX 021-233 2195

*A modern city centre hotel with adjacent NCP offers comfortable public areas, extensive conference amenities and rooms equipped with all the facilities a business person would expect.*

135⇌🛋(4fb)¥in 8 bedrooms CTV in all bedrooms ® T ✳ sB⇌🛋fr£72 dB⇌🛋fr£82 (room only) ⊟
Lift ( 600🚗 (charged) CFA
♡ International ✧ ◻ ¥ Lunch fr£10.25&alc Dinner fr£13.50&alc Last dinner 10pm
Credit Cards ①②③④⑤

★★★63% **Novotel Birmingham** 70 Broad St B1 2HT (Novotel) ☎021-643 2000 Telex no 335556 FAX 021-643 9796

148⇌🛋(148fb) CTV in all bedrooms ® T ✳ sB⇌🛋fr£59 dB⇌🛋fr£69 (room only) ⊟
Lift ⊞ 65🚗 🚗 sauna gymnasium jacuzzi
V ✧ ◻ Lunch £12.75-£19.05alc Dinner £12.75-£19.05alc Last dinner mdnt
Credit Cards ①②③⑤

# No workspace?

# No problems.

**novotel**

★ ★ ★

Hotels with desks in all rooms
Novotel Birmingham
70 Broad Street · Birmingham B1 2HT
Tel 021 6432000 · Telex 335556
Fax 021 6439796

124

# Birmingham

**★★★61% Westmead Hotel & Restaurant** Redditch Rd,
Hopwood B48 7AL (Lansbury) ☎021-445 1202 Telex no 335956
FAX 021-445 6163
*The hotel stands near to junction 2 of the M42 in a peaceful rural
location, but convenient for access to Birmingham.
Accommodation is spacious and well equipped, ideally suited for
the business traveller. Conference facilities are extensive.*
60⇩(4fb)2⌷⅔✦in 4 bedrooms CTV in all bedrooms ® T
sB&B⇩£74 dB&B⇩£87 ₽
《250P ✿ *xmas*
♡ English & French V ◊ ⚏ ✦ Lunch fr£8.95 Dinner
fr£14&alc Last dinner 10pm
Credit Cards [1][2][3][5]

**★★★59% Great Barr Hotel & Conference Centre** Pear Tree
Dr, off Newton Rd B43 6HS ☎021-357 1141 Telex no 336406
FAX 021-357 7557
(For full entry see Barr, Great)

**★★★58% Apollo** 243-247 Hagley Rd, Edgbaston B16 9RA
(Mount Charlotte (TS)) ☎021-455 0271 Telex no 336759
FAX 021-456 2394
*A modern motor lodge style hotel with all rooms in annexe blocks
around the main amenity building. The hotel offers a choice of
restaurants – the Rib Room Carvery and the Burgundy French
Restaurant.*
128⇩Ւ(9fb)✦in 22 bedrooms CTV in all bedrooms ® T ✳
S% sB⇩Ւ£64.50-£69.50 dB⇩£69.50-£79.50 (room only) ₽
Lift 《CTV 130P CFA ♫ *xmas*
♡ English & French V ◊ ⚏ S% Lunch £10.75&alc High tea
£6.50 Dinner £11.50-£12.75&alc Last dinner 10.30pm
Credit Cards [1][2][3][5]

**★★★58%, Post House** Chapel Ln B43 7BG (Trusthouse Forte)
☎021-357 7444 Telex no 338497 FAX 021-357 7503
(For full entry see Barr, Great)

**★★★56% Grand** Colmore Row B3 2DA (Queens Moat)
☎021-236 7951 Telex no 338174 FAX 021-233 1465
Closed 4 days Xmas
*Extensive refurbishment has recently been undertaken at what was
a rather dated city centre hotel; accommodation offers excellent
modern facilities, whilst two bars, a carvery and the Penny Black
Restaurant provide a range of eating options. The nearest NCP car
park is a few minutes' walk away.*
173⇩Ւ(7fb) CTV in all bedrooms ® T S% sB&B⇩Ւ£40-£75
dB&B⇩Ւ£55-£90 ₽
Lift 《 ♪ CFA
♡ English & French V ◊ ⚏ Lunch £10.50 Dinner £12.50 Last
dinner 9.45pm
Credit Cards [1][2][3][5] £

**★★67% Wheatsheaf** Coventry Rd, Sheldon B26 3EH
(Porterhouse) ☎021-742 6201 & 021-743 2021
FAX 021-722 2703
Closed 25 & 26 Dec
*A popular hotel on the A45 and convenient for the NEC, with
generally spacious and comfortable rooms. The pleasant
restaurant is manned by friendly, helpful staff.*
86⇩Ւ✦in 10 bedrooms CTV in all bedrooms ® T
✖ (ex guide dogs)
《100P
♡ English, French & Italian V ✦
Credit Cards [1][2][3][5]

**★★66%, Portland** 313 Hagley Rd, Edgbaston B16 9LQ
☎021-455 0535 Telex no 334200 FAX 021-456 1841
*An hotel standing beside the A456 near the city centre attracts
predominantly business users to its well-equipped accommodation
and is busy with conference trade. Staff are friendly and helpful.*
64⇩Ւ(2fb) CTV in all bedrooms ® ✖ (ex guide dogs)
Lift 《 CTV 80P
♡ English & French V ⚏ Last dinner 10pm
Credit Cards [1][2][3][5]

**★★65%, Norwood** 87-89 Bunbury Rd, Northfield B31 2ET
☎021-411 2202
*Personally-run, friendly hotel within easy reach of the M5, M6,
and M42. Bedrooms are modest in size but comfortable and well
equipped. "Beryl's" restaurant overlooks the attractive garden.*
17rm(5⇩6Ւ) CTV in all bedrooms ® T ✳ sB&B£24.75-£25
sB&B⇩Ւ£45 dB&B⇩Ւ£55-£65 ₽
11P ✿
♡ English & French V ⚏ Bar Lunch £4.50-£7.50 Dinner
£13.75 Last dinner 9 30pm
Credit Cards [1][3]

**★★64%, Hagley Court** 229 Hagley Rd, Edgbaston B16 9RP
☎021-454 6514 FAX 021-456 2722
Closed Xmas
*On the western route out of the city centre on the A456, this
privately owned hotel has well-equipped rooms and a hospitable
atmosphere.*
27⇩Ւ(1fb) CTV in all bedrooms ® T ✖ (ex guide dogs) ✳
S% sB&B⇩Ւ£38-£40 dB&B⇩Ւ£46-£60 ₽
《8P ⌷
♡ English & Continental ◊ ⚏ Bar Lunch £2.90-£7.50alc
Dinner fr£11.50&alc Last dinner 9.30pm
Credit Cards [1][2][3][5]

**★★64%, Westbourne Lodge** 27/29 Fountain Rd, Edgbaston
B17 8NJ ☎021-429 1003 FAX 021-429 7436
*A family-run private hotel located just off the A456 at Edgbaston
provides a friendly, informal atmosphere and value-for-money
accommodation in well equipped, efficiently maintained rooms.*
20⇩Ւ(4fb) CTV in all bedrooms ® T sB&B⇩Ւfr£36
dB&B⇩Ւfr£52
CTV 12P
♡ English, French & Italian V ◊ ⚏ Lunch £6.90-£13 High tea
£3.45-£6.90 Dinner £13-£15 Last dinner 7.45pm
Credit Cards [1][3]

**★★62%, Copperfield House** 60 Upland Rd, Selly Park B29 7JS
☎021-472 8344
Closed 24 Dec-2 Jan RS 30 Jul & 14 Aug
*Comfortable, well-equipped accommodation, a friendly
atmosphere and a setting in a pleasant residential area are the
attractions of this small, personally owned and run hotel.*
14⇩(1fb) CTV in all bedrooms ® T ✳ sB&B⇩£32.50
dB&B⇩£42.50
12P ⌷
V ✦ Dinner £9.95 Last dinner 7.30pm
Credit Cards [1][3]

**★★60%, Beechwood** 201 Bristol Rd, Edgbaston B5 7UB
☎021-440-2133 FAX 021-446 4549
*A small, efficiently-managed hotel on the A38, a mile from the city
centre, provides accommodation in simply furnished, well-kept
rooms and features extensive rear gardens with a trout lake.*
18rm(6⇩10Ւ)(4fb) CTV in all bedrooms ®
⊞ CTV 30P ✿ trout lake ♨
V ◊ ⚏ Last dinner 10pm
Credit Cards [1][3][5]

**★★60%, New Cobden** 166 Hagley Rd, Edgbaston B16 9NZ
(Consort) ☎021-454 6621 Telex no 333851 FAX 021-454 1910
*Conveniently located on the A456 close to the centre of
Birmingham, the original hotel has been extended considerably.
Some rooms have been refurbished to a high standard, while the
others tend to be more compact and basic. The hotel has its own
leisure centre that includes solarium, sauna, swimming pool and
gymnasium. The restaurant choice is somewhat limited but the
daily carvery joints are popular.*
230⇩Ւ(8fb)2⌷✦in 40 bedrooms CTV in all bedrooms ® T
S% sB&B⇩Ւ£49-£58.50
dB&B⇩Ւ£58.50-£66 Continental breakfast ₽
Lift 《 200P ✿ ⬓(heated) sauna solarium gymnasium jacuzzi
*xmas*

♡ English & French **V** ✿ ⬚ ✓ S% Lunch fr£7.50 Dinner
£11.75-£14.75&alc Last dinner 9.45pm
Credit Cards ① ② ③ ⑤ ⓔ

★★ 54%, **Norfolk** 257/267 Hagley Rd, Edgbaston B16 9NA
(Consort) ☎021-454 8071 Telex no 339715 FAX 021-454 1910
Closed 24 Dec-2 Jan
*A large hotel on the A456 close to the city centre, offering modestly
decorated and furnished rooms, is particularly popular with
commercial travellers.*
175rm(32⇦56↑)✓in 15 bedrooms CTV in all bedrooms ® T
S% sB&B⇦↑£49-£58.50
dB&B⇦↑£58.50-£66 Continental breakfast ⦆
Lift ⦅ CTV 130P ❖ putting green
**V** ✿ ⬚ ✓ S% Lunch fr£7.50 Dinner £11.75-£14.75&alc Last
dinner 9.45pm
Credit Cards ① ② ③ ⑤ ⓔ

★★ 52%, **Sheriden House** 82 Handsworth Wood Rd,
Handsworth Wood B20 2PL ☎021-554 2185 & 021-523 5960
FAX 021-551 4761
*A small, popular hotel situated in the suburbs of Birmingham and
quite close to junction 7 of the M6. The hotel offers a variety of
bedrooms, a cosy bar and a small lounge. The restaurant offers
limited table d'hôte and à la carte menus.*
12rm(11⇦↑)1⊞ CTV in all bedrooms ® T sB&B£30-£33
sB&B⇦↑£44-£46 dB&B⇦↑£63-£65 ⦆
⦅ CTV 30P
♡ English & French **V** ✿ ⬚ S% Lunch £10.50-£11 High tea
£3.50-£4.50 Dinner £10.50-£11&alc Last dinner 9.30pm
Credit Cards ① ② ③ ⓔ

✿*Campanile* 55 Irving St, Lee Bank B1 1DH (Campanile)
☎021-622 4925 Telex no 333701
*Popular for its proximity to the city centre and for the value-for-
money accommodation it provides in standard rooms with good
modern facilities, this busy hotel is run by a friendly management
couple.*
Annexe48⇦↑ CTV in all bedrooms ®
50P
♡ English & French Last dinner 10pm
Credit Cards ① ③

See advertisement on page 129

❀✕✕✕**Sloan's** 27-29 Chad Square, Hawthorne Rd,
Edgbaston B15 3TQ ☎021-455 6697
*A busy little restaurant specialising in modern French cuisine,
Sloan's has received much favourable publicity over the past year
for Roger Narbert's cooking. Interesting sauces and combinations
of ingredients are its hallmark, but our Inspector commented that
preparation of the dishes was not quite as refined and careful as on
previous visits.*
Closed Sun, 25 Dec-1 Jan & BH's
Lunch not served Sat
♡ French **V** 60 seats Lunch fr£14.50&alc Dinner £22-£25alc
Last lunch 2pm Last dinner 9.45pm 40P nc10yrs ✓
Credit Cards ① ② ③

✕✕**Henry's** 27 St Pauls Square B3 1RB ☎021-200 1136
*This very popular Chinese restaurant stands close to the city's
jewellery quarter and is much used at lunchtimes by businessmen
who appreciate the good, fresh flavours of its dishes; service is
well-supervised, attentive and pleasant.*
Closed Sun, BH's & 1 wk Aug
♡ Cantonese **V** 90 seats Lunch £12-£15&alc Dinner
£12-£15&alc Last lunch 2pm Last dinner 11pm ✗
Credit Cards ① ② ③ ⑤

✕✕**Rajdoot** 12-22 Albert St B4 7UD ☎021-643 8805 &
021-643 8749
*Birmingham's premier Indian restaurant , it has maintained its
elegance, along with its standard of service and its authentic
cuisine, for many years. Recent additions to the menu include
tandoori and massalla quail and pheasant.*

▶

**B**

Closed 25-26 Dec
Lunch not served Sun & BH's
♥ North Indian **V** 74 seats S12.5% Lunch fr£7&alc Dinner
£11.50-£14.50&alc Last lunch 2.15pm Last dinner 11.30pm
♪ ⊬
Credit Cards ① ② ③ ④ ⑤

✗ **Franzl's** 151 Milcote Rd B67 5BN ☎021-429 7920
FAX 021-429 1615
*Set in a quiet, residential area, this popular small restaurant
features a menu offering well-prepared and attractively presented
Austrian specialities served by ladies in national dress; the wine
list features mainly Austrian types and the decor of both the dining
room and its little basement bar echo the theme, making this an
interesting and unique place in which to dine.*
Closed Sun, Mon, 1-22 Aug & 25-29 Dec
Lunch not served
♥ Austrian **V** 40 seats ✳ Dinner £9.55-£15.95 Last dinner
10.30pm ♪ nc5yrs
Credit Cards ① ③

✗ **Henry Wong** 283 High St, Harborne B17 9QH ☎021-427 9799
*Housed in a converted bank in the High Street, this authentic
Cantonese restaurant offers a good range of dishes, the set meals
providing particularly excellent value. Bright, fresh décor combines
with friendly, attentive service to create a pleasant atmosphere.*
Closed Sun, BH's & last wk Aug
♥ Cantonese 140 seats Last lunch 2pm Last dinner 11pm ♪
Credit Cards ① ② ③ ⑤

✗ **J Jays Restaurant** 1347 Stratford Rd, Hall Green B28 9HW
☎021-777 3185
*An attractive and well appointed Indian restaurant situated within
easy reach of the city centre. The best ingredients and careful
spicing combine to produce enjoyable interesting dishes which
diners can see being prepared through a glass partition. Staff are
attentive and happy to explain dishes to guests.*
Closed Sun & 25 Dec
♥ Northern Indian **V** 78 seats Lunch £5.95-£8&alc Dinner
£10.95-£15.50alc Last lunch 2.30pm Last dinner 11.45pm 30P
⊬ ♪
Credit Cards ① ② ③ ⑤

**BIRMINGHAM AIRPORT** West Midlands Map **07 SP18**

★★★54% **Excelsior** Coventry Rd, Elmdon B26 3QW
(Trusthouse Forte) ☎021-782 8141 Telex no 338005
FAX 021-782 2476
*Situated on the A45 close to the NEC, the hotel remains busy
though many rooms are poorly decorated and furnished.
Refurbishment should commence in 1990.*
141⇌🛏(3fb)⊬in 30 bedrooms CTV in all bedrooms ®
sB⇌🛏£67 dB⇌🛏£78 (room only) 🍽
《 150P CFA *xmas*
♥ European **V** ☼ ⚲ ⊬ Lunch £10&alc Dinner £16&alc Last
dinner 10.15pm
Credit Cards ① ② ③ ④ ⑤

**BIRMINGHAM (NATIONAL EXHIBITION CENTRE)**
West Midlands Map **07 SP18**

★★★57% **Arden Hotel & Leisure Club** Coventry Rd,
Bickenhill B92 0EH (A45) ☎Hampton-in-Arden(06755)3221
Telex no 334913 FAX (06755) 3225 ext 317
*Located by the A45, in front of the NEC complex, and convenient
for rail and air travel, this busy hotel features a leisure complex
comprising swimming pool, jacuzzi, solarium and gymnasium.*
76⇌🛏(4fb) CTV in all bedrooms ® T sB⇌🛏£65
dB⇌🛏£72.50 (room only)
Lift 《 150P ✳ CFA ▤(heated) snooker sauna solarium
gymnasium jacuzzi

♥ French **V** ☼ ⚲ Lunch £8.95-£11.45&alc High tea £4.50
Dinner £11.45&alc Last dinner 10pm
Credit Cards ① ② ③ ⑤

**BISHOP AUCKLAND** Co Durham Map **08 NZ22**

★★68% *Park Head* New Coundon DL14 8QT (1m N on A688)
☎(0388)661727
*A popular, well-appointed hotel on the A688 just north east of the
town offers spaciously comfortable bedrooms, traditional menus
based on local produce in its restaurant and an equally high
standard of cuisine in the congenial surroundings of its carvery and
function room.*
8⇌🛏Annexe7⇌🛏(3fb)1🛁 CTV in all bedrooms ®
《 96P ✳ ♫ ♨
♥ English, French & Italian **V** ☼ ⚲ ⊬ Last dinner 9.45pm
Credit Cards ① ② ③ ④ ⑤

★★61% **The Postchaise** 36 Market Pl DL14 7NX
☎(0388)661296
*A commercial hotel, which was once a coaching inn, overlooks the
market square.*
12⇌🛏(1fb)2🛁 CTV in all bedrooms ® 🛏 ✳
sB&B⇌🛏£20-£24 dB&B⇌🛏£30-£33 🍽
♪ 🛁 ♫
⊬ S10%
Credit Cards ① ③ ⑤

**BISHOP'S STORTFORD** Hertfordshire Map **05 TL42**

✗✗ *The Mill* Hallingbury Mill, Old Mill Lane, Gaston Green,
Little Hallingbury CM22 7QS ☎(0279)726554
*Hallingbury Mill, dating back to 1874, was converted by the
present owners to house 2 restaurants. Keen to preserve the
atmosphere of the Mill, the proprietors have retained much of the
machinery, which diners can watch turning as they sip their*  ▶

★★
# Park Head Hotel

**New Coundon, Bishop Auckland, Co Durham**
**Telephone: (0388) 661727**

Built in the 1890's and transformed in 1978 from a
derelict Public House to a stylish 15 bedroomed
hotel. Situated in open countryside and approximately 1½ miles north east of Bishop Auckland,
on the A688. All bedrooms are en suite and
furnished to a high standard. Traditional food
using fresh local produce is served in the Restaurant or Carvery or choose from the Bar menu.
Sporting facilities are well catered for or just relax
in a rowing boat for a leisurely trip on the river.
Ample free parking.

**B**

*aperitifs. Those that come for the peaceful surroundings will not be disappointed, and for those in search of gastronomic satisfaction the Mill's well-served choice of food should prove rewarding.*
Closed Mon
Lunch not served Sat
Dinner not served Sun
♀ English & Continental **V** 45 seats Last lunch 2pm Last dinner 10pm 50P ⚓
Credit Cards [1] [2] [3]

---

BISHOPSTEIGNTON Devon Map **03** SX87
★★ **58% Cockhaven Manor** Cockhaven Rd TQ14 9RF
☎Teignmouth(0626)775252
*Situated in a small village, a short drive from Teignmouth, Torquay and Paignton, this hotel dates back to the 16th century. The bars are lively and the à la carte restaurant offers steak and fish dishes. Bedrooms and public areas are at present undergoing complete refurbishment.*
12rm(4⇨7↑)4⊞⚓in 2 bedrooms CTV in all bedrooms ® **T** sB&B£25 sB&B⇨↑£31 dB&B£40 dB&B⇨↑£52 ⊟
50P games room *xmas*
**V** ✿ 🖵 Lunch £9-£15alc High tea fr£2.50 Dinner £6&alc Last dinner 9.30pm
Credit Cards [1] [3] ⓔ

---

BLACKBURN Lancashire Map **07** SD62
See also **Langho**
★★★ **57% Blackburn Moat House** Preston New Rd BB2 7BE (Queens Moat) ☎(0254)64441 Telex no 63271
FAX (0254) 682435
*A modern functional hotel, with a distinctive gabled roof, set beside the A677 on the western approach to town. Bedrooms are all well equipped and there are spacious conference facilities*
98⇨↑(2fb)⚓in 12 bedrooms CTV in all bedrooms ® **T** ✳ sB&B⇨↑£60 dB&B⇨↑£72 ⊟
Lift ℂ CTV 350P ✿ CFA pool table ♫
♀ English & French **V** ✿ 🖵 Lunch £6.45-£8.45 Dinner £11.95-£12.95 Last dinner 10pm
Credit Cards [1] [2] [3] [4] [5] ⓔ
★★ **76% Millstone** Church Ln, Mellor BB2 7JR (3m NW) (Shire) ☎Mellor(0254)813333 Telex no 635309
FAX (0254) 812628
*Good, interesting food is available in the attractive, wood-panelled dining room of this charming country village inn with its pleasant atmosphere. The attractive bedrooms are well furnished, there is an open-plan bar/lounge area, management is attentive and service willing.*
20⇨↑(1fb)⚓in 4 bedrooms CTV in all bedrooms ® **T** ✳ S%
sB&B⇨↑£47-£56 dB&B⇨↑£70 ⊟
40P *xmas*
♀ English & French **V** ✿ 🖵
Credit Cards [1] [2] [3] [5]

---

BLACKPOOL Lancashire Map **07** SD33
★★★★ **67% Pembroke** North Promenade FY1 2JQ
☎(0253)23434 Telex no 677469 FAX (0253) 27864
*A large, impressive seafront hotel provides comfortable lounges, well appointed bedrooms, extensive leisure facilities and attentive, friendly service.*
278⇨↑(18fb)⚓in 12 bedrooms CTV in all bedrooms ® **T** sB&B⇨↑£85-£95 dB&B⇨↑£107-£117 ⊟
Lift (⊞ 320P ☐(heated) sauna solarium games room *xmas*
♀ English & French **V** ✿ 🖵 ⚓ Lunch £10.95 High tea £1.85 Dinner £12.50&alc Last dinner 10.30pm
Credit Cards [1] [2] [3] [4] [5]

★★★★ **50% Imperial** North Promenade FY1 2HB (Trusthouse Forte) ☎(0253)23971 Telex no 677376 FAX (0253) 751784
*Imposing Victorian building overlooking sea with spacious public areas and elegant modern Palm Court restaurant.*
183⇨↑(9fb)⚓in 50 bedrooms CTV in all bedrooms ® ✳
sB⇨↑£35-£80 dB⇨↑£50-£110 (room only) ⊟
Lift ℂ 200P ☐(heated) sauna solarium gymnasium *xmas*
**V** ✿ ⚓ Lunch £10&alc Dinner £13.50&alc Last dinner 10.30pm
Credit Cards [1] [2] [3] [4] [5]

★★★ **63% Clifton** Talbot Square FY1 1ND ☎(0253)21481
FAX (0253) 27345
*Centrally sited and overlooking the sea, the hotel has well-furnished bedrooms and public areas.*
80⇨↑(2fb) CTV in all bedrooms ® **T** ✳ sB&B⇨↑fr£55 dB&B⇨↑fr£85 ⊟
Lift ℂ ♪ *xmas*
♀ English, French & Italian **V** ✿ 🖵 Lunch fr£7.50 Dinner fr£12.50 Last dinner 9.30pm
Credit Cards [1] [2] [3] [5]

★★ **67% Brabyns** Shaftesbury Av, North Shore FY2 9QQ (Exec Hotel) ☎(0253)54263
*Personally run by friendly and caring proprietors who ensure guests' comfort, this pleasant small hotel just off Queen's Promenade offers rooms which are all well equipped and maintained in good order though they vary in size.*
22⇨↑Annexe3⇨↑(10fb) CTV in all bedrooms ® **T** sB&B⇨↑£28-£31.50 dB&B⇨↑£50-£57 ⊟
CTV 12P *xmas*
**V** ✿ 🖵 Lunch £5-£5.50 Dinner fr£8.50 Last dinner 7.30pm
Credit Cards [1] [3] [5]

★★ **67% Headlands** 611-613 South Prom FY4 1NJ
☎(0253)41179
Closed 2-13 Jan
*A pleasant family hotel, situated on south shore sea front.*
43⇨↑(11fb) CTV in all bedrooms ® sB&B⇨↑£27.50-£38.50 dB&B⇨↑£55-£66 ⊟
Lift CTV 40P 8⚓ snooker solarium ♫ *xmas*
**V** ✿ ⚓ Lunch £8 High tea £4.50 Dinner £11.75 Last dinner 7.30pm
Credit Cards [1] [3]

★★ **65% Hotel Sheraton** 54-62 Queens Promenade FY2 9RP ☎(0253)52723
*The friendly, well-run hotel, overlooking the sea on the north shore, offers good all-round value and is ideal for family holidays.*
119⇨↑(37fb) CTV in all bedrooms ® ✳ sB&B⇨↑£29-£32 dB&B⇨↑£58-£64 ⊟
Lift ℂ ☐(heated) sauna solarium *xmas*
**V** ✿ 🖵 Sunday Lunch £6.50 Dinner £9.50 Last dinner 7.45pm
Credit Cards [1] [3]

See advertisement on page 133

★★ **64% Ruskin** 55-61 Albert Rd FY1 4PW ☎(0253)24063
FAX (0253) 23571
80⇨↑(14fb)⊞ CTV in all bedrooms ® **T** S%
sB&B⇨↑fr£30 dB&B⇨↑fr£50 ⊟
Lift ℂ CTV 16⚓ (£5 for 24hrs) pool table *xmas*
**V** ✿ 🖵 ⚓ Lunch £6.50 High tea £6 Dinner £10 Last dinner 8.30pm
Credit Cards [1] [3] ⓔ

★★ **62% Warwick** 603-609 New South Promenade FY4 1NG (Best Western) ☎(0253)42192 Telex no 677334
FAX (0253) 405776
*Overlooking the seafront at the southern approach to the town, this privately-owned hotel offers bedrooms that are all well equipped and freshly decorated though they vary in size ; pleasant public areas include a comfortable, popular bar and an attractive restaurant.*

▶

B

52⇌↱(10fb) CTV in all bedrooms ® T
sB&B⇌↱£30.50-£38.50 dB&B⇌↱£51.50-£65.50 Ħ
☾ 30P ▭(heated) solarium ♫ *xmas*
V ✿ ⊻ Bar Lunch £2.50-£6alc Dinner £10.95-£12.50 Last dinner 8.30pm
Credit Cards [1] [2] [3] [5] £

**★★60% Revill's** 190-4 North Promenade FY1 1RJ
☎(0253)25768 & 24736
*Improvements continue at this family-owned hotel, situated on the sea front near the North Pier. All bedrooms now have en suite facilities, and the attractive, comfortable public areas feature the colourul new Bobbins bar and bistro.*
47⇌↱(10fb) CTV in all bedrooms ® T ✗ S%
sB&B⇌↱£22-£24 dB&B⇌↱£32-£41.80
Lift ☾ CTV 23P snooker *xmas*
V ✿ ⊻
Credit Cards [1] [3]

**★★59% Cliffs** Queens Promenade FY2 9SG ☎(0253)52388
Telex no 67191 FAX (0253) 500394
*This large sea-front hotel to the north of the town provides well-equipped bedrooms with en suite facilities and a range of amenities which includes an all-day coffee shop, a leisure complex and entertainment.*
162⇌↱(28fb)1⊞ CTV in all bedrooms ® T
sB&B⇌↱£26.50-£58 dB&B⇌↱£53-£86 Ħ
Lift ☾ 70P ▭(heated) squash snooker sauna gymnasium jacuzzi ♫ *xmas*
☋ English & French V ✿ ⊻ ⊬ Bar Lunch £4.50-£8 High tea £4-£8 Dinner £10-£11 Last dinner 8.30pm
Credit Cards [1] [2] [3]

**★★52% Claremont** 270 North Prom FY1 1SA ☎(0253)293122
FAX (0253) 752409
*A large, busy hotel in seafront location close to the centre of town caters well for tourists and conference delegates; bedrooms in a variety of styles and sizes are gradually being refurbished to a good standard.*
143⇌↱Annexe25⇌(51fb) CTV in all bedrooms ® T
✗ (ex guide dogs) S% sB&B⇌↱£25-£35
dB&B⇌↱£50-£70 Ħ
Lift ☾ 60P CFA *xmas*
✿ ⊻ ⊬ S% Lunch £4.50-£5.50 High tea £4-£8 Dinner £9-£10.50 Last dinner 8.30pm
Credit Cards [1] [2] [3] £

**See advertisement on page 135**

**★65% Kimberley** New South Promenade FY4 1NQ
☎(0253)41184
Closed 3-13 Jan
*A friendly, informal hotel, standing in a crescent off the sea front and managed by its resident proprietors, offers a choice of eating styles, the light snacks offered throughout the day by the Coffee Shop complementing restaurant menus.*
54rm(37⇌↱)(8fb) CTV in all bedrooms ® sB&B£22-£24
sB&B⇌↱£24-£27 dB&B⇌↱£42-£48 Ħ
Lift ☾ CTV 26P ⇼ table tennis *xmas*
☋ English & Continental ✿ ⊻ Lunch fr£5.95 Dinner fr£9.50 Last dinner 7.30pm
Credit Cards [1] [3] £

**BLACKWATER** Cornwall & Isles of Scilly Map **02** SW74

**✕Pennypots** TR4 8EY ☎St Day(0209)820347
*It is easy to forget the traffic rumbling past as you enjoy your meal in this period cottage on the A30. Surroundings are simple, the atmosphere relaxing and the cuisine from the short à la carte menu and fish menu is light in style. Of particular delight are Mr Peter's own bresoala and the boned quail stuffed with mushrooms and cashew nuts. The small carefully-chosen wine list represents excellent value for money.*
Closed 2 wks winter
Lunch not served
Dinner not served Sun & Mon
30 seats Dinner £18-£22alc Last dinner 10pm 10P
Credit Cards [1] [2] [3] [5]

**BLACKWOOD** Gwent Map **03** ST19

**★★★50% Maes Manor** NP2 0AG ☎(0495)224551 & 220011
*This carefully restored 19th-century manor is set in 9 acres of secluded woodland and provides good facilities for visiting business people.*
8⇌Annexe14⇌(2fb)2⊞ CTV in all bedrooms ® T ✱
sB&B⇌£41 dB&B⇌£55
☾ 100P ✲
☋ Welsh, English & French V ✿ ⊻ Lunch £9-£19alc Dinner £9-£18alc Last dinner 9.30pm
Credit Cards [1] [2] [3] [5]

**BLAIR ATHOLL** Tayside *Perthshire* Map **14** NN86

**★★60% Atholl Arms** PH18 5SG ☎Blairatholl(079681)205
FAX (0796) 81550
*Situated opposite Blair Castle this long established village hotel is popular with tour groups, holidaymakers and sporting enthusiasts. It offers traditional comforts and has a splendid dining room with a minstrel gallery.*
30⇌↱1⊞ CTV in all bedrooms ® Ħ
100P 3⌂ ✲ ⅃ rough shooting
V ✿ ⊻
Credit Cards [1] [3]

**BLAIR DRUMMOND** Central *Stirlingshire* Map **11** NS79

**✕Broughton's Restaurant** Burnbank Cottages FK9 4XE (1m W on A873) ☎Doune(0786)841897
*This delightful country cottage restaurant offers a warm welcome and cosy atmosphere, while a dedicated chef ensures that a consistently high standard of cuisine is maintained so that its reputation continues to grow. Such seasonal game specialities as venison, rabbit, pigeon and pheasant are particularly enjoyable, but all meals are of excellent quality and based on fresh ingredients, the good-value light lunches being increasingly popular.*
Closed Mon & 2-3 wks Feb
Dinner not served Sun
☋ International V 42 seats Lunch £4-£9.50alc Dinner fr£18 Last lunch 2.30pm Last dinner 10pm 22P nc10yrs ⊬
Credit Cards [1] [3]

**BLAIRGOWRIE** Tayside *Perthshire* Map **15** NO14

**★★★♣75% Kinloch House** PH10 6SG (3m W on A923)
☎Essendy(025084)237 FAX (025084) 333
Closed 20-29 Dec
*Highland cattle graze freely in the 20 acres of grounds surrounding a delightful country hotel at the heart of beautiful Perthshire. Here you can relax peacefully in oak-panelled public rooms hung with fine paintings, furnished with antiques and brought to life by fresh flowers and log fires. Bedrooms vary in size and style, but all are comfortable, with thoughtful personal touches. Menus in the elegant dining room feature typically Scottish dishes, imaginatively prepared with fresh local produce from sea, loch and hillside.*
21⇌↱(1fb)8⊞ CTV in all bedrooms ® T S%
sB&B⇌↱£40.50 dB&B⇌↱£78-£108
CTV 40P ⇼ ✲ ⅃
V ⊬ S% Sunday Lunch £12.50 Dinner £19.50 Last dinner 9.15pm
Credit Cards [1] [2] [3] [5]

For key to symbols see the inside front cover.

★★♨65%, **Altamount House** Coupar Angus Rd PH10 6JN
☎(0250)3512 & 3814
Closed 4 Jan-14 Feb
*An elegant Georgian house set in six acres of lawned and wooded grounds is personally run to provide a comfortable base for touring holidaymakers.*
7⇨♠(2fb) CTV in all bedrooms ® T ✻ sB&B⇨♠fr£28.50 dB&B⇨♠fr£55
40P 3🏮 ✿
♦ ☑ Lunch £3-£9 High tea fr£6.50 Dinner fr£14.50 Last dinner 9pm
Credit Cards ①③

★★60%, **Rosemount Golf** Golf Course Rd, Rosemount
PH10 6LJ ☎(0250)2604
*Popular with golfers, this family-run hotel stands in its own spacious, well-maintained grounds not far from the town's Rosemount Course. A relaxed atmosphere prevails in the comfortable public rooms. Bedrooms are compact but furnished with practical fitted units.*
8⇨♠ Annexe4♠(2fb) CTV in all bedrooms ® T
✕ (ex guide dogs) sB&B⇨♠£27.50-£30 dB&B⇨♠£45 🄿
70P 🎏 ✿
V ♦ Bar Lunch £4-£10alc High tea £4-£10alc Dinner £11.50-£13.50 Last dinner 9pm
Credit Cards ①③ⓔ

★★58%, **Angus** 46 Wellmeadow PH10 6NQ (Consort)
☎(0250)2838 Telex no 76526 FAX (0250) 5289
*The popularity of this town centre holiday hotel, especially with tour parties, is due to its bright modern public areas and good range of leisure facilities.*
85⇨♠(4fb) CTV in all bedrooms ® sB&B⇨♠£24-£30.50 dB&B⇨♠£44-£61 🄿
Lift 60P CFA ▣(heated) squash snooker sauna solarium ♫ xmas
♡ British & French V ♦ ☑ High tea £3.50-£6alc Dinner £12.50-£17alc Last dinner 8.30pm
Credit Cards ①②③

---

**BLAKENEY** Norfolk Map **09** TG04

★★★65%, **Blakeney** The Quay NR25 7NE ☎Cley(0263)740797 FAX (0263) 740795
*Enjoying a perfect location on the quayside of this popular North Norfolk resort, the hotel offers a comfortable and hospitable stay. Both restaurant and bar overlook Blakeney Point.*
41⇨♠Annexe10⇨⅛(4fb)1🛗 CTV in all bedrooms ® T
sB&B⇨♠£39-£59 dB&B⇨♠£78-£118 🄿
《 CTV 100P 🎏 ✿ CFA ▣(heated) sauna solarium gymnasium xmas
♡ English & Continental V ♦ ☑ Lunch £6-£15alc Dinner fr£14.50&alc Last dinner 9.30pm
Credit Cards ①②③⑤

★★61%, **Manor** NR25 7ND ☎Cley(0263)740376
FAX (0263) 741116
Closed 4-27 Dec
*Dating back to the 16th century the Manor Hotel overlooks Blakeney Quay and Point. The main flintstone building houses comfortable public areas and well equipped warm bedrooms, courtyard rooms provide similar comfort on ground level. Good, fresh food features on the menu.*
8⇨♠Annexe27⇨♠(2fb)1🛗 CTV in all bedrooms ® T ✻
sB&B⇨♠£22-£28 dB&B⇨♠£48-£66 🄿
60P ✿ bowling green nc10yrs
♡ English & Continental V ♦ ⊬ Bar Lunch £1.25-£4.50alc Dinner £12&alc Last dinner 8.30pm

1991 marks the 25th anniversary of this guide.

---

**B**

## BLANCHLAND Northumberland Map **12** NY95

**★★67% Lord Crewe Arms** DH8 9SP ☎Hexham(0434675)251
FAX (0434675) 337
*An interesting hotel at the heart of the village near the abbey,
which retains the charm of bygone days in its flagstone floors,
original stonework and the vaulted ceilings that survive in some
public areas. Bedrooms continue the period theme but are
thoughtfully equipped to meet the needs of the modern traveller,
some annexe rooms being contained in an original building across
the square.*
8⇨♠Annexe10⇨♠(3fb)1🛏 CTV in all bedrooms ⑧ T
sB&B⇨♠£60-£72 dB&B⇨♠£84-£96 ₽
𝓕 🐾 ✿ *xmas*
V ✆ ⚲ Sunday Lunch fr£11.50 Dinner £17.50-£21alc Last
dinner 9.15pm
Credit Cards ①②③⑤ ⑥

## BLANDFORD FORUM Dorset Map **03** ST80

**★★★64% Crown** 1 West St DT11 7AJ (Consort)
☎(0258)456626 Telex no 418292 FAX (0258) 451084
Closed 25-28 Dec
*Close to the town centre yet overlooking open countryside the
Crown has majestic panelled public rooms and spacious bedrooms.
The main features of the hotel are the friendly staff and the
skilfully cooked reasonably priced food.*
29⇨♠(1fb)1🛏 CTV in all bedrooms ⑧ T ✳ sB&B⇨♠£52
dB&B⇨♠£62-£70 ₽
80P 4🏊 (£2.50) ✿ ♪ croquet lawn ⚬
V English & French V ✆ ⚲ Lunch £6-£10&alc Dinner
£6-£10&alc Last dinner 9.15pm
Credit Cards ①②③⑤ ⑥

**✕✕La Belle Alliance** Whitecliff Mill St DT11 7BP
☎(0258)452842 FAX (0258) 480054
*This charming 'restaurant with rooms' stands on the edge of town.
The short fixed price menu offers interesting dishes which are
freshly-cooked with skill and flair and presented in the modern
style with well-made sauces. Our inspectors have reported a good
fish mousseline with tomato flavoured butter sauce, breast of
French duck with pineapple sauce and some good flavoursome
desserts. A well-chosen wine list is available and the service and
hospitality is good.*
Closed Mon (ex BH's) & 1st 3 wks Jan
Lunch not served Tue-Sat (ex by arrangement only)
Dinner not served Sun
V British & French 32 seats Lunch £10.50-£11.50 Dinner
£19.50-£21.50 Last dinner 9.30pm 13P ⚲
Credit Cards ①②③

## BLOCKLEY Gloucestershire Map **04** SP13

**★★★64% Crown Inn** High St GL56 9EX ☎(0386)700245
FAX (0386) 700247
*This 16th-century village inn, now tastefully modernised, offers
well equipped, comfortable bedrooms and character public areas
including à la carte and grill restaurants. Friendly, attentive
services are provided by the Champion family.*
13⇨♠Annexe8⇨♠(2fb)4🛏 CTV in all bedrooms ⑧ T ✳
sB&B⇨♠fr£49.50 dB&B⇨♠fr£66.50 ₽
50P *xmas*
V English & Continental V ✆ ⚲ Sunday Lunch fr£12.95
Dinner fr£16.95&alc Last dinner 9.30pm
Credit Cards ①②③

## BLOXHAM Oxfordshire Map **04** SP43

**★★64% Olde School** Church St OX15 4ET (Inter-Hotels)
☎Banbury(0295)720369 FAX (0295) 721748
RS 1 Jan
*One-time village school with small, well-equipped bedrooms and
professional restaurant.*

11⇨♠Annexe27⇨♠3🛏 CTV in all bedrooms ⑧ T
✖ (ex guide dogs) ✳ sB&B⇨♠£50-£58 dB&B⇨♠£68-£75 ₽
《 100P squash games room
V English & French V ✆ ⚲ Lunch £11-£17&alc Dinner
£16-£17&alc Last dinner 10pm
Credit Cards ①②③⑤ ⑥

## BLUE ANCHOR Somerset Map **03** ST04

**★62% Langbury** TA24 6LB ☎Dunster(0643)821375
Closed Nov-Feb
*This small proprietor-run hotel stands in neat gardens close to both
the steam railway and the sea. Many bedrooms have sea views,
there is a comfortable lounge, and simple but fresh English fare is
served in the good-sized dining room.*
9rm(1⇨4♠)(3fb) CTV in all bedrooms ⑧ sB&B£16-£18
sB&B⇨♠£24-£26 dB&B£32-£36 dB&B⇨♠£35-£39 ₽
10P 🐾 ✿ 🅐
✆ ⚲ Bar Lunch £3-£5 Dinner £9 Last dinner 7pm

## BLUNDELLSANDS Merseyside Map **07** SJ39

**★★★59% Blundellsands** Serpentine L23 6TN (Lansbury)
☎051-924 6515 Telex no 626270 FAX 051-931 5364
*Situated in a residential area of Crosby beside the railway station,
this much extended Edwardian building has undergone recent
refurbishment to provide extensive and attractive function facilities
and well appointed bedrooms. Service in the restaurant is friendly
and traditional.*
41⇨♠(6fb)⚲in 7 bedrooms CTV in all bedrooms ⑧ T
sB&B⇨♠£63 dB&B⇨♠£76 ₽
Lift 《 CTV 350P
V English & French V ✆ ⚲ Lunch fr£8.95 Dinner fr£14&alc
Last dinner 9.30pm
Credit Cards ①②③⑤

## BLYTH Nottinghamshire Map **08** SK68

**★★★61% Charnwood** Sheffield Rd S81 8HF ☎(0909)591610
FAX (0909) 591429
*This stone-faced hotel, with charming gardens that include a pond,
has comfortable, well equipped bedrooms, as well as a popular
restaurant offering choices from set or à la carte menus.*
20⇨♠(1fb) CTV in all bedrooms ⑧ T ✖ (ex guide dogs)
sB&B⇨♠£44-£60 dB&B⇨♠£55-£75 ₽
70P 🐾 ✿
V English & French V ⚲ S10% Lunch £8.50-£9.30&alc
Dinner £13.50-£14.25&alc Last dinner 9.45pm
Credit Cards ①②③⑤ ⑥
See advertisement on page 137

**⌂Granada Lodge** Hilltop Roundabout S81 8HG (junct. A1M/
A614) (Granada) ☎(0909)591836 FAX (0909) 591831
*A busy stop over point on the A1(M)/A614 road junction reached
by following the 'Services' signs for both north and southbound
traffic.*
37⇨♠(6fb)⚲in 8 bedrooms CTV in all bedrooms ⑧
✖ (ex guide dogs) ✳ S% sB⇨♠fr£25
dB⇨♠fr£28 (room only)
《 100P
V International V ✆ ⚲ ⚲
Credit Cards ①②③⑤
See advertisement on page 137

**○Travelodge** (Trusthouse Forte)
☎Central reservations (0800) 850950
Due to open winter 1990
32⇨

For key to symbols see the inside front cover.

**B**

---

BOAT OF GARTEN Highland *Inverness-shire* Map **14** NH91

★★★63% **Boat** PH24 3BH (Best Western) ☎(047983)258 FAX (047983) 414

*A friendly, family-run tourist hotel just two minutes' drive from the golf course features a comfortable tasteful lounge and a privileged position overlooking the station which is the home of the preserved Strathspey Steam Railway.*

32⇨🛏(1fb) CTV in all bedrooms ® T ✱ sB&B⇨🛏£41-£46 dB&B⇨🛏£70-£77 🅿

36P 🚗 ✿ CFA 🛴 *xmas*

♡ Scottish, English & French V ✿ ⚗ ✖ Lunch £12.50-£15.50 High tea £6.95 Dinner £16.50-£18.50&alc Last dinner 9.30pm

Credit Cards ①②③⑤

★★★63% **Craigard Country House** Kinchurdy Rd PH24 3BP ☎(047983)206

Closed Nov

*Once a hunting lodge, and still retaining its Victorian style, a comfortable and warmly welcoming hotel which is well furnished throughout looks across the Strathspey Railway and the golf course to the Cairngorms beyond from the setting of its own grounds.*

20⇨🛏(1fb) CTV in all bedrooms ® ✱

sB&B⇨🛏£26.50-£29.50 dB&B⇨🛏£53-£59 🅿

20P 4🚗 (£1) 🚗 ✿ *xmas*

♡ International ✿ ⚗ ✖ Lunch £8-£12 High tea £4-£7 Dinner £15 Last dinner 8.45pm

Credit Cards ①②③

---

BODINNICK Cornwall & Isles of Scilly Map **02** SX15

★71% **Old Ferry Inn** PL23 1LX ☎Polruan(0726)870237 RS Nov-Feb

*A delightful, 400-year-old inn, overlooking the centuries-old Bodinnick/Fowey Ferry, offers comfortable accommodation, a relaxed atmosphere and good food.*

12rm(6⇨3🛏)(1fb) CTV in 10 bedrooms

sB&B£27.50-£31.50 sB&B⇨🛏£30.25-£35.25 dB&B£55-£63 dB&B⇨🛏£60.50-£70.50

8P 2🚗 🛴

♡ English & French ✿ Bar Lunch 90p-£3 Dinner £18&alc Last dinner 8.15pm

Credit Cards ①③

---

BODMIN Cornwall & Isles of Scilly Map **02** SX06

★★55% **Westberry** Rhind St PL31 2EL ☎(0208)72772 Closed 5 days Xmas/New Year

*Most bedrooms are modern and well equipped in this popular commercial hotel within easy reach of the town centre; public areas include a cosy bar, smart restaurant and some leisure and function facilities.*

15rm(5⇨3🛏)Annexe8⇨3🛏(3fb) CTV in 20 bedrooms ® CTV 30P 🚗 snooker sauna gymnasium

V ✿ ⚗ Last dinner 8.45pm

Credit Cards ①③⑤

---

BOGNOR REGIS West Sussex Map **04** SZ99

★62% **Black Mill House** Princess Av, Aldwick PO21 2QU (Minotels) ☎(0243)821945 & 865596 FAX (0243) 821316

*This is a traditional and long established family run hotel offering a friendly atmosphere and conventional style service. Bedrooms vary in size but all are neat and well equipped.*

22rm(18⇨3🛏)Annexe4rm(6fb) CTV in all bedrooms ® T sB&B⇨🛏£25-£31 sB&B⇨🛏£30-£38.50 dB&B£42-£56 dB&B⇨🛏£50-£68 🅿

CTV 13P 🚗 table tennis putting 🛴 *xmas*

♡ English & French V ✿ ⚗ ✖ Lunch fr£7.50 Dinner fr£9 Last dinner 8pm

Credit Cards ①②③⑤ ⑥

---

BOLLINGTON Cheshire Map **07** SJ97

★★★57% **Lukic-Belgrade** Jackson Ln, Kerridge SK10 5BG ☎(0625)573246 Telex no 667554 FAX (0625) 574791

*This Gothic-style Victorian house, which overlooks the village, is reached via a winding shrub-lined drive. There is a modern rear bedroom wing, and two comfortable lounges, one of which is a conservatory.*

54⇨🛏 CTV in all bedrooms ® T ✱ (ex guide dogs) ✻ sB&B⇨🛏£55-£62 dB&B⇨🛏£62-£70 🅿

《 200P ✿ CFA 🎵 *xmas*

♡ English & French V ✿ ⚗ S% Lunch fr£9&alc Dinner fr£11.75&alc Last dinner 10pm

Credit Cards ①②③⑤ ⑥

✗✗**Mauro's** 88 Palmerston St SK10 5PW ☎(0625)573898

*In this attractive little Italian restaurant you can watch the chef/ proprietor at work through a glazed arch, while he and his wife may well wait on you, too, both being very actively involved in the running of the establishment. Pasta is home-made, menus feature a fresh fish each day and you can enjoy all the traditional Italian specialities – accompanied by a reasonably-priced bottle of Italian wine – in a warm, convivial atmosphere.*

Closed Sun, Mon, 25-26 Dec & 2-3 wks Jul/Aug

♡ Italian V 50 seats Last lunch 2pm Last dinner 10pm ✔

Credit Cards ①②③

---

BOLTON Greater Manchester Map **07** SD70

★★★64% **Last Drop** Hospital Rd, Bromley Cross BL7 9PZ (3m N off B6472) (Character) ☎(0204)591131 Telex no 635322 FAX (0204) 54122

*This unique hotel, together with tea room, craft shop and public house, forms part of a village created in 1964 from derelict farm buildings and now one of the north-west's popular tourist attractions. The accommodation on offer has been considerably developed in recent years to comprise very well appointed bedrooms, comprehensive conference and banquetting facilities and an outstanding leisure complex comprising indoor heated swimming pool, solarium, large gymnasium, snooker room and squash court. The old shippon has been converted into a charming restaurant which preserves some of the cattle stalls and associated antique items.*

73⇨🛏Annexe10⇨🛏(35fb)4🚗 CTV in all bedrooms ® T sB&B⇨🛏fr£69 dB&B⇨🛏fr£85 🅿

《 400P ✿ CFA ▨(heated) squash snooker sauna solarium gymnasium *xmas*

♡ International V ✿ ⚗ Lunch fr£10.50 Dinner £16-£30alc Last dinner 10.30pm

Credit Cards ①②③⑤

★★★63% **Egerton House** Blackburn Rd, Egerton BL7 9PL (3m N A666) (Character) ☎(0204)57171 FAX (0204) 593030

*Secluded, in 4·5 acres of grounds and gardens, this comfortable hotel provides accommodation in attractive, well-appointed bedrooms, friendly service, and facilities for banquetting and conferences in a recently converted barn.*

33⇨🛏(8fb) CTV in all bedrooms ® T ✗ (ex guide dogs) sB&B⇨🛏£50-£67 dB&B⇨🛏£65-£80 🅿

《 100P ✿

♡ English & French V ✿ ⚗

Credit Cards ①②③⑤

★★★62% **Crest** Beaumont Rd BL3 4TA (Trusthouse Forte) ☎(0204)651511 Telex no 635527 FAX (0204) 61064

*The hotel – conveniently situated on the A58, close to junction 5 of the M61 motorway – features attractive, well-appointed bedrooms and a pleasant restaurant where à la carte and fixed price menus offer a wide choice of dishes.*

100⇨🛏(10fb)✖in 26 bedrooms CTV in all bedrooms ® T ✱ sB⇨🛏£72-£84 dB⇨🛏£84-£96 (room only) 🅿

《 CTV 150P ✿ CFA games room

---

♥ English & French **V** ❦ ⚏ ⚓ Lunch £10.50 High tea £5.75
Dinner £14.50-£16.50&alc Last dinner 9.45pm
Credit Cards ① ② ③ ④ ⑤

★★★61% **Pack Horse** Bradshawgate, Nelson Square BL1 1DP
(De Vere) ☎(0204)27261 Telex no 635168 FAX (0204) 364352
*In a town centre position, yet within easy reach of the national
motorway network, stands a traditional hotel with an attractive
Georgian façade.*
74rm(68⇨3♠)(4fb)⚓in 14 bedrooms CTV in all bedrooms ⓡ
**T** S% sB&B£63-£66 dB&B⇨♠£80-£85 ♬
Lift ⦅ ⚡ CFA *xmas*
♥ English & French **V** ❦ ⚏ S% Lunch £8.85-£9.50&alc
Dinner £12.50-£14&alc Last dinner 9.45pm
Credit Cards ① ② ③ ⑤ ⓔ

★57% **Broomfield** 33-35 Wigan Rd, Deane BL3 5PX
☎(0204)61570
RS Jul-Aug
*This small, friendly, family-run hotel stands on the A58 just over a
mile from the town centre. Constantly being improved, it now offers
bedrooms with en suite facilities, a comfortable lounge bar, an
attractive restaurant and a cosy lounge.*
15⇨3♠(1fb) CTV in all bedrooms ⓡ ✕ (ex guide dogs) ✱
sB⇨♠£28 dB⇨♠£38 (room only) ♬
CTV 20P ⚙
❦
Credit Cards ① ③ ⓔ

---

**BOLTON ABBEY** North Yorkshire Map **07** SE05

★★★75% **Devonshire Arms Country House** BD23 6AJ (Best
Western) ☎(075671)441 Telex no 51218 FAX (075671)564
*Beautifully located by the River Wharfe, the hotel is set in the
rolling landscape of the Yorkshire Dales near Bolton Abbey. The
restaurant has a good menu, notable for its delicately prepared
dishes and sauces, and all the bread, cakes and pastries are baked
daily on the premises. Up-to-date conference facilities are
available, but the function suites are separate from the other public
rooms and are not too obtrusive.*
40⇨38⚙⚓in 6 bedrooms CTV in all bedrooms ⓡ **T** S10%
sB&B⇨£75-£80 dB&B⇨£95-£110 ♬
⦅ CTV 150P ❄ ♪ clay pigeon shooting *xmas*
♥ French **V** ❦ ⚏ ⚓ S10% Lunch £13.95&alc High tea
£5-£7.50 Dinner £23.50&alc Last dinner 10pm
Credit Cards ① ② ③ ⑤ ⓔ

See advertisement on page 139

---

**BONAR BRIDGE** Highland *Sutherland* Map **14** NH69

★★57% *Bridge* IV24 3EB (Exec Hotel) ☎Ardgay(08632)204 &
685 FAX (08632) 686
Closed 1 & 2 Jan
*Travellers on the A9 or holidaymakers wishing to explore the area
around the Dornoch Firth will find ample accommodation at this
old-fashioned hotel; a good range of bar and restaurant meals is
available, and children are catered for.*
15rm(5⇨5♠)(3fb) CTV in all bedrooms ⓡ **T**
20P
♥ Scottish & French **V** ❦ ⚏ Last dinner 10pm
Credit Cards ① ② ③ ⑤

---

**BONCHURCH**

See **Wight, Isle of**

---

**BONTDDU** Gwynedd Map **06** SH61

★★★65% **Bontddu Hall** LL40 2SU ☎(034149)661
FAX (034149) 284
Closed Jan-Etr RS Nov-Dec
*Standing in two acres of lovely grounds with superb views over the
Mawddach estuary to the mountains beyond, this charming,
delightfully furnished hotel in the style of a Victorian country*

▶

*house offers well-equipped bedrooms and excellent public areas ; service is friendly and professional.*

16⇨🐾Annexe4⇨(6fb)1🖭 CTV in all bedrooms ® T sB&B⇨🐾fr£42.50 dB&B⇨🐾fr£70 🍴
50P 🚷 ✿ putting nc3yrs
🍲 British & French **V** ✆ 🖵 🍽 Lunch £7.50 Dinner £17.50&alc Last dinner 9.30pm
Credit Cards ①②③⑤

---

**BOOTLE** Merseyside Map **07** SJ39

★★★**54%**, **Park** Dunnington Rd, Netherton L30 3SU (De Vere)
🕾051-525 7555 Telex no 629772 FAX 051-525 2481
*Situated beside the busy A5036 not far from Aintree and convenient for the M57 and M58, this commercial and conference hotel is gradually being improved. Those bedrooms which have been refurbished are attractively appointed and well equipped.*
58⇨🐾 CTV in all bedrooms ® T ✳ sB&B⇨🐾£49.50 dB&B⇨🐾£62 🍴
Lift ⟨ 250P 2🏧 CFA *xmas*
🍲 English & French **V** ✆ 🖵 Lunch £6.50-£6.95&alc Dinner fr£9.95&alc Last dinner 9.15pm
Credit Cards ①②③④⑤ ⓔ

---

**BOREHAM STREET** East Sussex Map **05** TQ61

★★★**60%** **White Friars** BN27 4SE (Best Western)
🕾Herstmonceux(0323)832355 Telex no 877440
FAX (0323) 833882
*Family owned and well managed, this 18th-century manor house features chintzy beamed lounges with log fires and quaint bedrooms. Further accommodation is available in the cottage annexe. Guests can eat either in the Ashburham Dining Room or the Cellar Grill and service is cheerful and friendly throughout.*
12⇨🐾Annexe8⇨🐾(2fb)1🖭 CTV in all bedrooms ® T sB&B⇨🐾£44-£55 dB&B⇨🐾£78-£100 🍴
50P ✿ *xmas*
🍲 English & French **V** ✆ 🖵 Lunch £9.50-£12 Dinner £14.25-£16.50&alc Last dinner 10pm
Credit Cards ①②③⑤ ⓔ

---

**BOROUGHBRIDGE** North Yorkshire Map **08** SE36

★★★**64%**, **Crown** Horsefair YO5 9LB (Best Western)
🕾Harrogate(0423)322328 Telex no 57906
*Once a very busy coaching inn, this town-centre hotel is still popular with modern-day coach parties touring the area. The well-equipped bedrooms are equally suitable for both tourists and business travellers.*
42⇨🐾(6fb) CTV in all bedrooms ® T ✳ sB&B⇨🐾£36-£42 dB&B⇨🐾£60-£82.50 🍴
Lift ⟨ ⊞ 60P
**V** ✆ 🖵 Lunch £5.75-£9 Dinner £14.50&alc Last dinner 9.15pm
Credit Cards ①②③⑤ ⓔ

★★★**58%** **Three Arrows** Horsefair YO5 9LL (Embassy)
🕾Harrogate(0423)322245
Closed 27-30 Dec
*An attractive country house with a quiet relaxing atmosphere, set in extensive grounds close to the A1. Bedrooms are generally spacious and the restaurant and bar are decorated in delicate pastel shades.*
17⇨🐾(4fb) CTV in all bedrooms ®
50P ✿
**V** ✆ 🖵 Last dinner 9pm
Credit Cards ①②③⑤

---

✗✗*Fountain House* St James Square YO5 9AR
🕾Harrogate(0423)322241
Closed Mon
Dinner not served Sun

---

🍲 International **V** 40 seats Last lunch 2pm Last dinner 9.30pm
6P
Credit Cards ①②③

---

**BORROWDALE** Cumbria Map **11** NY21

See also **Keswick & Rosthwaite**
★★★★**72%**, **Lodore Swiss** CA12 5UX (Stakis) 🕾(059684)285
Telex no 64305 FAX (059684) 343
Closed 4 Jan-14 Feb
*A delightfully located hotel at the head of the Borrowdale valley, the Lodore Swiss offers an excellent range of leisure facilities, efficient and friendly service and comfortable accommodation.*
70⇨🐾(13fb) CTV in all bedrooms ® T ✖ sB&B⇨🐾£50-£75 dB&B⇨🐾£100-£150 (incl dinner)
Lift ⟨ 55P 24🏧 (£3.50) 🚷 ✿ ▤(heated) ⌇(heated) ♬ (hard) squash sauna solarium gymnasium ♪ ♨ *xmas*
🍲 British, French & Swiss **V** ✆ 🖵 🍽 Lunch fr£10&alc Dinner fr£19.50&alc Last dinner 9.30pm
Credit Cards ①②③⑤

★★★**69%**, **Borrowdale** CA12 5UY 🕾(059684)224
FAX (059684) 338
*A welcoming and relaxing hotel, originally built as a coaching inn, has been carefully modernised to provide guests with comfortable, well-equipped bedrooms, two lounges where log fires blaze in cooler weather and an attractive restaurant. Well-supervised young staff give friendly, efficient service.*
34⇨🐾(8fb)6🖭 CTV in all bedrooms ® T sB&B⇨🐾fr£45 dB&B⇨🐾£74-£90 (incl dinner) 🍴
100P 🚷 ✿ ♨ *xmas*
🍲 English & Continental **V** ✆ 🖵 Lunch £4-£12.65alc Dinner fr£15.50 Last dinner 9.15pm
Credit Cards ① ③

★★★**66%**, **Borrowdale Gates Country House** CA12 5UQ
🕾(059684)204 & 606 Due to change to (07687) 77204
*Set amid beautiful Lakeland scenery and surrounded by almost two acres of wooded gardens, this delightful hotel offers comfortable, well-equipped bedrooms with lovely views. Relaxing lounges are warmed by log fires, an attractive dining room provides meals of a good standard, and personal service is given by friendly owners.*
23⇨🐾(2fb) CTV in all bedrooms ® T ✖ (ex guide dogs)
sB&B⇨🐾£27.50-£42.50 dB&B⇨🐾£51-£85 🍴
35P 🚷 ✿ ♨ *xmas*
🍲 English & French **V** ✆ 🖵 Sunday Lunch £8.25-£8.75 Dinner £15.50-£16.50 Last dinner 8.45pm
Credit Cards ① ③

**See advertisement under KESWICK**

---

**BOSCASTLE** Cornwall & Isles of Scilly Map **02** SX09

★★**63%**, **Bottreaux House** PL35 0BG 🕾(08405)231
Closed Dec-Feb (ex Xmas)
*Standing on a hill overlooking the picturesque harbour village, the personally-run hotel offers a friendly atmosphere and accommodation in bright, clean bedrooms equipped to modern standards. There is a pleasant lounge (with separate bar) and also an attractive dining room providing a good choice of imaginative dishes.*
7⇨🐾 CTV in all bedrooms ® ✳ sB&B⇨🐾£28.50
dB&B⇨🐾£48-£52 🍴
10P 🚷 nc10yrs *xmas*
🍲 English, French & Italian **V** ✆ 🍽 Lunch £8.50-£12.35alc Dinner £8.50-£12.35alc Last dinner 9.30pm
Credit Cards ① ③ ⓔ

---

Book as early as possible for busy holiday periods.

★★62% **The Wellington Hotel** The Harbour PL35 0AQ
☎(08405)202 FAX (08405) 621
Closed 25 Nov-7 Feb
*This turreted Cornish stone coaching inn, dating back to the sixteenth century, stands adjacent to an Elizabethan harbour in National Trust countryside. Personally run by the owners, it provides a relaxed, cheerful atmosphere in which to enjoy the imaginative menus of La Belle Alliance Georgian Restaurant, with its emphasis on fresh local fish, meats and vegetables, or the good range of bar meals available in the locally popular Long Bar.*
21rm(10⇨6♠)1⏀ CTV in all bedrooms ® T sB&B£17-£19 sB&B⇨♠£26-£29 dB&B⇨♠£48-£54 ▤
20P ✿ nc10yrs
♀ French V ✿ ✗ Bar Lunch £1.20-£11.55alc Dinner £12-£15.50 Last dinner 9.30pm
Credit Cards ①②③⑤ £

---

**BOSHAM** West Sussex Map **04** SU80

★★67% **The Millstream** Bosham Ln PO18 8HL (Best Western)
☎(0243)573234 FAX (0243) 573459
*This delightful, peaceful hotel, picturesquely set beside a stream in this pretty village, offers individually decorated and furnished bedrooms which have been provided with modern facilities without sacrificing their charm. The lounge and restaurant have also been refurbished to offer a good standard of amenities.*
29⇨♠(2fb)1⏀ CTV in all bedrooms ® T sB&B⇨♠£55-£65 dB&B⇨♠£85-£105 ▤
《 CTV 40P ✿ xmas
♀ English & French ✿ ⏀ Lunch fr£14.50 Dinner fr£15.50 Last dinner 9.30pm
Credit Cards ①②③⑤

# Bosham - Bournemouth

**✗✗Wishing Well Tandoori** Main Rd PO18 8PG
☎Chichester(0243)572234 & 575016
*Helpful and courteous waiters offer a menu of mainly north Indian cuisine at this modern cottage-style restaurant.*
Closed 25 & 26 Dec
♡ Indian **V** 80 seats ✱ Lunch £10-£20 Dinner £10-£20 Last lunch 2.30pm Last dinner 11.30pm 45P ✔
Credit Cards ①②③⑤

---

**BOSTON** Lincolnshire Map **08** TF34

**★★63%** *White Hart* 1-5 High St, Bridge Foot PE21 8SH
☎(0205)364877
*An impressive, Regency-style building, the White Hart stands on the bank of the River Witham near the town centre, opposite the famous St Botolph's Church (the Stump). It has been tastefully modernised to provide comfortable bedrooms and pleasant public areas which include a choice of restaurants, each with its own bar.*
23rm(8⇨10ᐩ)(2fb) CTV in all bedrooms Ⓡ ✖ (ex guide dogs) ℂ35P
♡ Mainly grills **V** ♥ ⓛ ✔ Last dinner 10.30pm
Credit Cards ①②③⑤

**★★61%** *New England* 49 Wide Bargate PE21 6SH (Trusthouse Forte) ☎(0205)365255 FAX (0205) 310597
*Providing comfortable accommodation and friendly service this market place hotel is also a popular meeting point for visitors and locals. Chaucers restaurant serves traditional roasts and grills, and conference/banqueting facilities are available.*
25⇨✔in 5 bedrooms CTV in all bedrooms Ⓡ S%
sB&B⇨£60-£63 dB&B⇨£65 ᐱ
ℂ✗ *xmas*
♡ Mainly grills **V** ♥ ⓛ ✔ S% Lunch £6.95-£9&alc Dinner £13.25-£13.75&alc Last dinner 10pm
Credit Cards ①②③④⑤

---

**BOTALLACK** Cornwall & Isles of Scilly Map **02** SW33

**✗✗Count House** TR19 7QQ ☎Penzance(0736)788588
*Set in the heart of Penmarric country among ruined mine workings, this is a lofty restaurant with a homely atmosphere. Graham and Helen Ashton offer a short à la carte dinner menu where dishes such as terrine of smoked salmon, pigeon breast with grape and madiera sauce and toffee pudding with hot fudge sauce are complimented by a well-balanced wine list. Light lunches by prior arrangement.*
Closed Mon (& Tue in winter)
Dinner not served Sun
♡ English & French **V** 45 seats Sunday Lunch £9.50-£9.95 Dinner £19.25-£19.95 Last lunch 2pm Last dinner 10pm 50P ✔
Credit Cards ①②③

---

**BOTHWELL** Strathclyde *Lanarkshire* Map **11** NS75

**★★★60%** *Bothwell Bridge* 89 Main St G71 8LN
☎(0698)852246 Telex no 776838
*A modernised Victorian mansion with a new extension, standing in its own grounds. It offers pleasant bedrooms and an attractive restaurant featuring menus and a wine list with a strong Italian influence.*
41⇨ᐩ(5fb)1⚐ CTV in all bedrooms Ⓡ T ✖ (ex guide dogs)
✱ sB&B⇨ᐩ£40-£55 dB&B⇨ᐩ£50-£65 ᐱ
ℂ90P ✿ ♫ *xmas*
♡ Continental **V** ♥ Lunch £5.50 Dinner £11-£15.50 Last dinner 10.45pm
Credit Cards ①②③⑤ Ⓔ

**★★58%** *Silvertrees* Silverwells Crescent G71 8DP
☎(0698)852311
*This large sandstone house stands in spacious grounds in a quiet residential area. Many of the bedrooms are located in well-furnished annexes within the grounds. The hotel caters for all types of functions with an attractive, totally self-contained suite to accommodate large groups.*

7⇨Annexe19⇨ᐩ(1fb)1⚐ CTV in all bedrooms Ⓡ T
sB&B⇨ᐩ£52.50 dB&B⇨ᐩ£70-£80
100P 4🎯 🌳 ✿ ♨
**V** ♥ Lunch £7.50-£9&alc High tea £7 Dinner £11.50&alc Last dinner 8.45pm
Credit Cards ①②③⑤

---

**BOTLEY** Hampshire Map **04** SU51

**✗✗Cobbett's** 15 The Square SO3 2EA ☎(0489)782068
*A delightful 16th-century cottage restaurant, Cobbett's serves French regional food, cooked with all the skill of her native land by Madame Lucie Sipwith. The menu features dishes such as quenelles de truite and terrine de légumes, and to finish the meal there is a choice of lovely desserts. Separate from the restaurant, La Causerie Wine Rooms makes an ideal place to meet.*
Closed Sun, 2 wks summer & BH's
Lunch not served Sat & Mon
♡ French **V** 45 seats Lunch £8.50-£14.50&alc Dinner £16.50&alc Last lunch 1.45pm Last dinner 9.45pm 20P ncl1yrs
Credit Cards ①②③

---

**BOURNE** Lincolnshire Map **08** TF02

**★★54%** *Angel* Market Place PE10 9AE ☎(0778)422346
*Though restored and refurbished over recent years, this former coaching inn effectively retains its old world character; accommodation is provided in compact, modern bedrooms.*
13rm(4⇨6ᐩ)(1fb)2⚐ CTV in all bedrooms Ⓡ
✖ (ex guide dogs)
✗ ⓛ
♡ French **V** ♥ ⓛ
Credit Cards ①③

---

**BOURNEMOUTH** Dorset Map **04** SZ09

See **Town Plan Section** During the currency of this guide some Bournemouth telephone numbers are liable to change.
See also **Christchurch, Longham & Poole**

**★★★★62%** *Royal Bath* Bath Rd BH1 2EW (De Vere)
☎(0202)555555 Telex no 41375 FAX (0202) 554158
*Now 150 years old, this spaciously elegant hotel, attractively set in a commanding position overlooking the sea, has undergone major refurbishment to bring standards to an even higher level of excellence with a new leisure complex and exceptionally good conference facilities which make it particularly popular with the business fraternity. Lively dinner dances take place in the main restaurant on Saturday evenings, 'Oscar's' offering a more serious cuisine in a separate, well-appointed room and a smart and helpful staff providing competent service in all areas.*
131⇨2⚐ CTV in all bedrooms ✖ (ex guide dogs) S%
sB&B⇨£85-£95 dB&B⇨£125-£210 ᐱ
Lift ℂ120🎯 (£3.50 per day) 🌳 ✿ CFA 🏊(heated) sauna solarium gymnasium beauty salon putting green croquet lawn *xmas*
♡ English & French **V** ♥ ⓛ S% Lunch fr£15.10&alc Dinner fr£21.10&alc Last dinner 10.30pm
Credit Cards ①②③④⑤ Ⓔ

**★★★★70%** *Norfolk Royale* Richmond Hill BH2 6EN
☎(0202)551521 Telex no 418474 FAX (0202) 299729
*This splendid 1920s building, recently refurbished to a high standard, now offers very well decorated comfortable bedrooms providing luxuries such as bath robes and toiletries. In the Peacock Restaurant the chef produces good quality, innovative dishes or, alternatively, try the light conservatory-style coffee shop. Staff throughout are smart and amiable.*
95⇨(9fb)✔in 14 bedrooms CTV in all bedrooms Ⓡ T
✖ (ex guide dogs) sB&B⇨£75-£82.50 dB&B⇨£100-£300 ᐱ
Lift ℂ85🎯 ✿ 🏊(heated) sauna steamroom whirlpool ♫ *xmas*
♡ English & French **V** ♥ ⓛ
Credit Cards ①②③④⑤ Ⓔ

**★★★★61% Bournemouth Highcliff** St Michaels Rd, West Cliff BH2 5DU (Best Western) ☎(0202)557702 Telex no 417153 FAX (0202) 292734

*In a cliff top position with sea views this hotel has refurbished bedrooms, including fifty new rooms, and a new conference room with adjoining syndicate rooms. The totally refurbished Hop Inn offers a second food operation with a popular menu and friendly service.*

146⇌ṁ Annexe14⇌(30fb) CTV in all bedrooms ® T ✻ (ex guide dogs) S% sB&B⇌ṁ£70-£80 dB&B⇌ṁ£110-£140 🖪

Lift ₵150P ✿ CFA ⇲(heated) ♬ (hard) snooker sauna solarium croquet putting ⚙ xmas

V ♥ ⊡ ✗ S% Lunch £10-£13&alc High tea £5-£8 Dinner £13-£15.50&alc Last dinner 9.30pm

Credit Cards ①②③⑤①

**★★★68% Durlston Court** Gervis Rd, East Cliff BH1 3DD ☎(0202)291488 FAX (0202) 299615

*Now completely refurbished this small well-managed hotel has well-equipped bedrooms, a series of small lounges and bars and an attractive dining room.*

54⇌ṁ Annexe4⇌ṁ(16fb) CTV in all bedrooms ® T ✱ sB&B⇌ṁ£38-£48 dB&B⇌ṁ£76-£96 (incl dinner) 🖪

Lift ₵50P CFA ⇲(heated) sauna solarium gymnasium ♫ xmas

🍴 English & French V ♥ ⊡ ✗ S% Lunch £7.50&alc High tea £3.50&alc Dinner £9.50 Last dinner 8.30pm

Credit Cards ①②③⑤①

For key to symbols see the inside front cover.

THE
NORFOLK
ROYALE
HOTEL
BOURNEMOUTH

*Your Edwardian Country Home by the Sea*

TELEPHONE: (0202) 551521  FAX: (0202) 299729

Set in 10 acres of scenic grounds, adjacent to the Ferndown Golf Course and located near Bournemouth and the New Forest. All guests have free use of the fully fitted exclusive Leisure Club, featuring indoor pool and squash courts. A la Carte and Table D'Hôte restaurant plus snack bar in addition to the 3 bars. Friday night Barbecue/Dance (Summer Months) and Dinner Dance every Saturday. 134 De Luxe en suite bedrooms. Special Leisure Breaks all year and summer specials (July/August).

Please telephone for brochure and tariff.

# THE DORMY

NEW ROAD, FERNDOWN
DORSET, BH22 8ES
TEL: BOURNEMOUTH (0202) 872121
DE VERE          FAX: (0202) 895388
HOTELS
★★★★

# *Bothwell Bridge Hotel* ★★★

**Main Street, Bothwell G71 8LN**
**TEL. 0698 852246/TELEX: 776838**

At the Bothwell Bridge Hotel we bid you a welcome to a world of friendly hospitality in the peaceful surroundings of an elegant country house

ITALIAN RESTAURANT
SUITABLE FOR ALL OCCASIONS
DINNER DANCE MOST EVENINGS

Fully Licensed
Weddings – Functions – Meetings –
Conferences – Large Car Park – Country
View
Conveniently situated 1½ miles from M74

## Bournemouth

★★★67% **Chine** Boscombe Spa Rd BH5 1AX ☎(0202)396234 Telex no 41338 FAX (0202) 391737

*A large well-maintained conference hotel where bedrooms have recently been upgraded to a high modern standard, and public areas are both spacious and comfortable. The hotel has both indoor and outdoor swimming pools.*

97✑🏠(15fb) CTV in all bedrooms ® T ✖ (ex guide dogs) sB&B✑🏠£35-£45 dB&B✑🏠£70-£90 🅿
Lift ( 40P 3🎯 (£2) ❀ ▨(heated) ▨(heated) sauna solarium gymnasium ♒ *xmas*
♥ English & French V ✆ ⬆ Lunch £10-£12 High tea £6 Dinner £15-£18 Last dinner 8.30pm
Credit Cards 1 2 3 5 £

★★★67% **East Anglia** 6 Poole Rd BH2 5OX ☎(0202)765163 FAX (0202) 752949

*Friendly and well run, the hotel provides a series of smart, well furnished lounges and some leisure facilities. Though bedrooms vary, most are of a good size with modern fitted furnishings, a competent staff serves meals based on fresh ingredients, and a homely atmosphere prevails throughout.*

49✑🏠Annexe24✑🏠(12fb) CTV in all bedrooms ® T ✖ (ex guide dogs) sB&B✑🏠£39-£46 dB&B✑🏠£72-£92 (incl dinner) 🅿
Lift ( 73P CFA ▨(heated) sauna solarium gymnasium jacuzzi games room *xmas*
♥ English & French ✆ ⬆ ✖ Sunday Lunch fr£6.75 Dinner fr£12.50 Last dinner 8.30pm
Credit Cards 1 2 3 5

★★★67% **Piccadilly** Bath Rd BH1 2NN ☎(0202)552559 FAX (0202) 298235

*Centrally situated hotel with friendly staff. Bedrooms have all been upgraded recently. A table d'hôte dinner menu is on offer in The Fountain Restaurant. Conference facilities are also available.*

45✑🏠(2fb)🛏 CTV in all bedrooms ® T ✖ (ex guide dogs) sB&B✑🏠£35-£45 dB&B✑🏠£50-£70 🅿
Lift ( 30P 🎵 *xmas*
♥ English & French V ✆ ✖ Lunch fr£7.50&alc Dinner fr£10.95&alc Last dinner 9pm
Credit Cards 1 2 3 5 £

★★★67% **Wessex** West Cliff Rd BH2 5EU (Forestdale) ☎(0202)551911 FAX (0202) 297354

*Situated on the West Cliffs, this large, well maintained Victorian hotel offers well equipped, recently upgraded, modern bedrooms and a good range of public rooms including a spacious, tastefully appointed lounge and two restaurants, all areas enjoying prompt attentive service. A small leisure and recreational complex has recently been added.*

84✑🏠(15fb)✖in 3 bedrooms CTV in all bedrooms ® T
Lift ( 250P CFA ▨(heated) ▨(heated) snooker sauna solarium gymnasium table tennis 🎵
♥ International V ✆ ⬆ ✖ Last dinner 9.15pm
Credit Cards 1 2 3 5

★★★66% **Hotel Courtlands** 16 Boscombe Spa Rd, East Cliff BH5 1BB (Best Western) ☎(0202)302442 Telex no 41344 FAX (0202) 309880

*Popular with business people and holidaymakers alike, this hotel has newly decorated and furnished bedrooms which are well equipped and comfortable. Sound English food is served in the dining room and staff are pleasant and friendly.*

60✑🏠(15fb) CTV in all bedrooms ® T S% sB&B✑🏠£37-£43 dB&B✑🏠£68-£76 🅿
Lift ( 50P 🚗 ❀ CFA ▨(heated) sauna solarium spa bath 🎵 *xmas*
♥ English & French V ✆ ⬆ S% Sunday Lunch £6.95-£7.95 Dinner £13.50-£15 Last dinner 8.30pm
Credit Cards 1 2 3 5

★★★66% **Langtry Manor** 26 Derby Rd, East Cliff BH1 3QB (Consort) ☎(0202)553887 FAX (0202) 290115

*Built in 1877 by King Edward VII for his mistress Lillie Langtry, it is now an appealing hotel with a romantic atmosphere. Well-equipped bedrooms vary in size and style and there are some suites complete with four poster beds. Edwardian dinner parties are held in the elegant Dining Hall on Saturdays.*

14✑🏠Annexe13✑🏠(6fb)8🛏 CTV in all bedrooms ® T sB&B✑🏠£49.50-£64.50 dB&B✑🏠£76-£142
30P 🚗 ❀ *xmas*
♥ International V ✆ ⬆ ✖ Bar Lunch £5-£12 Dinner £17.75-£18.75&alc Last dinner 9pm
Credit Cards 1 2 3 5 £

★★★64% **Elstead** 12-14 Knyveton Rd BH1 3QP ☎(0202)293071 FAX (0202) 293827 Closed Oct-Mar

*This hotel, in a quiet situation, has undergone complete renovation. Facilities include two bedrooms designed specifically for disabled guests, extensive conference rooms and full-size snooker table and pool table.*

51rm(39✑🏠7🏠)(4fb)✖in 5 bedrooms CTV in all bedrooms ® T ✱ sB&B£22.50-£24 sB&B✑🏠£27.50-£29 dB&B£45-£48 dB&B✑🏠£55-£58
Lift ( 32P snooker 🎵
✆ ⬆ Lunch fr£5.50 Dinner fr£10&alc Last dinner 8.30pm
Credit Cards 1 3

See advertisement on page 145

★★★64% **Moat House** Knyveton Rd BH1 3QQ (Queens Moat) ☎(0202)293311 Telex no 417226 FAX (0202) 292221

*Major refurbishment of this hotel which stands in a quiet area of the town has provided two standards of bedroom, a new indoor pool with its own changing rooms and lounge, the themed Kings Bar and Castles Restaurant, and an extensive range of conference facilities. A full-size snooker table is available for guests' use.*

▶

## Bournemouth

146⇔♠(20fb) CTV in all bedrooms ⓡ T S%
sB&B⇔♠£52.50-£60 dB&B⇔♠£70-£80 ⊟
Lift ⓒ 100P ▨(heated) ⌒ snooker sauna gymnasium table
tennis *xmas*
ⓥ English & French V ♦ ⬚ Lunch £9.50 Dinner £13.50 Last
dinner 9.30pm
Credit Cards [1] [2] [3] [5] ⓔ

★★★64%, **New Durley Dean** Westcliff Rd BH2 5HE
☎(0202)557711 FAX (0202) 292815
*An elegant Victorian red-brick hotel that has been recently*
*refurbished and reopened. Leisure facilities include an indoor pool*
*with whirlpool spa, a Turkish steam room and a well-equipped*
*"trymasium". The Green Room Restaurant offers a buffet style*
*breakfast, a carvery at lunchtime and full service at dinner.*
*Bedrooms are comfortable and well-designed.*
112⇔♠(27fb)5⊞ CTV in all bedrooms ⓡ T ✕ (ex guide dogs)
sB&B⇔♠£37-£52 dB&B⇔♠£74-£104 (incl dinner) ⊟
Lift ⓒ 40P ▨(heated) snooker sauna solarium gymnasium ♫
*xmas*
ⓥ English & Continental V ♦ ⬚ ✗ Lunch £9.50 High tea
£4.50 Dinner £14.50&alc Last dinner 8.30pm
Credit Cards [1] [2] [3] ⓔ

★★★63%, **Chesterwood** East Overcliff Dr BH1 3AR (Inter-
Hotels) ☎(0202)558057 FAX (0202) 293457
*The comfortable public areas of this seafront hotel include a*
*ballroom where guests can dance to live music some evenings,*
*together with a sheltered terrace and outdoor pool which are*
*popular during the summer months. Bedrooms vary in style but are*
*generally light and modern in style.*
49⇔♠Annexe3⇔(13fb)2⊞ CTV in all bedrooms ⓡ T
✕ (ex guide dogs) sB&B⇔♠£36-£50
dB&B⇔♠£64-£96 (incl dinner) ⊟
Lift ⓒ CTV 39P 8🏌 ❋ ⌒(heated) ♫ ⚷ *xmas*
V ♦ ⬚ ✗ Lunch £6-£10.50&alc High tea £2.50-£5.50 Dinner
£9-£12.50 Last dinner 8.30pm
Credit Cards [1] [2] [3] [5] ⓔ

★★★63%, **The Connaught** West Hill Rd, West Cliff BH2 5PH
☎(0202)298020
*Here tastefully furnished and very well equipped modern bedrooms*
*are complemented by public areas including a small television*
*lounge, restaurant, bar and patio. Service is friendly and helpful,*
*and the hotel is set amid sheltered lawns and gardens.*
60⇔♠(15fb)1⊞✗in 12 bedrooms CTV in all bedrooms ⓡ T
S% sB&B⇔♠£48 dB&B⇔♠£78 ⊟
Lift ⓒ 45P ❋ ▨(heated) ⌒(heated) snooker sauna solarium
gymnasium table tennis pool table steam room ♫ ⚷ *xmas*
ⓥ English & French V ♦ ⬚ ✗ S% Lunch £3-£8.50 Dinner
£16.50&alc Last dinner 10pm
Credit Cards [1] [2] [3] [5] ⓔ

★★★63%, **Suncliff** 29 East Overcliff Dr BH1 3AG
☎(0202)291711 Telex no 41363 FAX (0202) 299182
*A large seafront hotel with extensive leisure facilities. Bedrooms*
*vary in size and furnishings (also in price) but all are well*
*decorated and have modern facilities. Staff are cheerful and*
*courteous and entertainment is often provided.*
95⇔♠(30fb)6⊞ CTV in all bedrooms ⓡ T ✱
sB&B⇔♠£26-£44 dB&B⇔♠£52-£104 (incl dinner) ⊟
Lift ⓒ 55P ▨(heated) squash solarium spa bath ♫ *xmas*
ⓥ English & French V ♦ ⬚ ✗ Bar Lunch £1.15-£10.30 High
tea £2-£5 Dinner £13.95 Last dinner 8.30pm
Credit Cards [1] [2] [3] [5]

★★★63%, **Trouville** Priory Rd BH2 5DH ☎(0202)552262
FAX (0202) 294810
*In a central position, convenient for Bournemouth International*
*Centre and the Winter Gardens, this hotel has been owned by*
*more than 40 years by the same family.*
80⇔♠(22fb) CTV in all bedrooms ⓡ T ✱
sB&B⇔♠£35-£43.50 dB&B⇔♠£70-£87 (incl dinner) ⊟

Lift ⓒ 55P 5🏌 (£3.50 per night) sauna solarium gymnasium
jacuzzi *xmas*
ⓥ English & French V ♦ ⬚ Lunch £6.50-£7.50 Dinner
£13.95-£15.95 Last dinner 8.30pm
Credit Cards [1] [3] ⓔ

★★★62%, **Belvedere** Bath Rd BH1 2EU ☎(0202)551080
FAX (0202) 294699
*Comfortable public rooms are matched by neat modern bedrooms,*
*some with sea views. The young, informal staff provide cheerful*
*service. Cuisine is modest.*
63⇔♠(9fb)⊞ CTV in all bedrooms ⓡ T sB&B⇔♠£37-£44
dB&B⇔♠£52-£59 ⊟
Lift ⓒ 50P ♫ *xmas*
ⓥ English & Continental V ♦ Lunch £7.95 Dinner
£11.50-£13.50 Last dinner 9pm
Credit Cards [1] [2] [3] [5] ⓔ

★★★62%, **Cumberland** East Overcliff Dr BH1 3AF
☎(0202)290722 Telex no BH 418297 FAX (0202) 294810
*Conference and holiday guests are equally well catered for by a*
*spacious sea front hotel with sheltered pool and terrace,*
*comfortable, well decorated public rooms, helpful service and a*
*pleasingly informal atmposphere.*
102⇔♠(12fb)3⊞ CTV in all bedrooms ⓡ T ✕ (ex guide dogs)
S% sB&B⇔♠£32.50-£39.50 dB&B⇔♠£65-£79 ⊟
Lift ⓒ CTV 65P ⌒(heated) games room table tennis pool *xmas*
ⓥ British & Continental V ♦ ⬚ S% Lunch £6.95-£8.25 High
tea £2.25-£4.50 Dinner £13.95-£14.95 Last dinner 8.30pm
Credit Cards [1] [3] ⓔ

★★★62%, **Marsham Court** Russell Cotes Rd BH1 3AB
☎(0202)552111 Telex no 41420 FAX (0202) 294744
*A large, conference-orientated hotel with good sea views provides*
*accommodation in comfortable, freshly decorated bedrooms which*
*are for the most part spacious; public areas have also been*
*redecorated and are furnished to a high standard. À la carte*
*menus of mainly British fare are available in the dining room.*
86⇔♠(16fb) CTV in all bedrooms ⓡ T ✕ (ex guide dogs)
sB&B⇔♠£47-£52 dB&B⇔♠£84-£94 ⊟
Lift ⓒ 100P ⌒(heated) snooker *xmas*
ⓥ English & French V ♦ ⬚ Lunch £9.50 High tea £5 Dinner
£13.50&alc Last dinner 9pm
Credit Cards [1] [2] [3] [5] ⓔ

★★★62%, **Pavilion** 22 Bath Rd BH1 2NS ☎(0202)291266
Telex no 418253 FAX (0202) 559264
*This small, smartly decorated hotel has an attractive lounge and*
*dining room. Bedrooms tend to be rather compact, but are well*
*equipped and modern.*
44⇔♠(4fb)2⊞ CTV in all bedrooms ⓡ T sB&B⇔♠£38
dB&B⇔♠£54 ⊟
Lift ⓒ 40P ♫ ⚷ *xmas*
ⓥ English & French ♦ ⬚ ✗ S% Lunch £4.25-£6.25 High tea
£1.50-£3.50 Dinner £12-£14 Last dinner 8.30pm
Credit Cards [1] [2] [3] [5] ⓔ

★★★61%, *Bournemouth Heathlands* 12 Grove Rd, East Cliff
BH1 3AY ☎(0202)23336 Telex no 8954665 FAX (0202) 25937
*Quietly situated near East Cliff, a large, modern hotel provides*
*well co-ordinated public areas which include good leisure,*
*conference and banqueting facilities. Coffee shop type lunches are*
*available, as well as the well-balanced table d'hôte menus available*
*in the evening, and service is provided by smartly-uniformed,*
*professional staff.*
116⇔♠(17fb) CTV in all bedrooms ⓡ
Lift ⓒ 80P ❋ CFA ⌒(heated) sauna solarium gymnasium
croquet boules games room health club ⚷
ⓥ English & French V ♦ ⬚ Last dinner 8.30pm
Credit Cards [1] [2] [3] [5]

**B**

★★★**60%, Grosvenor** Bath Rd, East Cliff BH1 2EX
☎(0202)28858 Telex no 417200
*Centrally situated, and professionally run by the owners and their friendly team of staff, the hotel offers attractive leisure facilities which include mini gym equipment, heated pool and whirlpool bath; more bedrooms have recently been refurbished, and the dining room's varied and well balanced menus include a value-for-money lunchtime selection.*
40rm(33⇔5ſ)(10fb)2⊞ CTV in 38 bedrooms ® T
Lift ℂ CTV 40P ☒(heated) sauna solarium gymnasium spa exercise area ♫
⚑ English & French **V** ✿ ⚏ ✂ Last dinner 8.45pm
Credit Cards ①③

★★★**60%, Savoy** West Hill Rd BH2 5EJ ☎(0202)294241
FAX (0202) 298367
*This large clifftop hotel is set in a splendid garden, where open plan public areas include a sun lounge and a comfortable dining room. Bedrooms were being redecorated and refurbished at the time of inspection, and were to become of a high standard once furnished.*
89⇔ſ(10fb) CTV in all bedrooms ® T sB&B⇔ſ£39-£55 dB&B⇔ſ£66.50-£90 ⊟
Lift ℂ 81P ✿ ☒(heated) sauna games room croquet ♫ *xmas*
⚑ English & French ✿ ⚏ Lunch £6.95-£8 Dinner £9.95-£18 Last dinner 8.45pm
Credit Cards ①②③⑤ⓔ

★★★**59%, Cliffeside** East Overcliff Dr BH1 3AQ
☎(0202)555724 Telex no 418297 FAX (0202) 294810
*In a good seafront location, this is a family run hotel with an informal atmosphere and friendly staff. Bedrooms are continually being upgraded and public rooms are newly refurbished.*
61⇔ſ(10fb) CTV in all bedrooms ® T ✳
sB&B⇔ſ£37.50-£49 dB&B⇔ſ£75-£98 ⊟
Lift ℂ CTV 45P ⊞ CFA ☒(heated) snooker table tennis *xmas*
⚑ French & Italian **V** ✿ ⚏
Credit Cards ①③ ⓔ

★★★**59%, Queens** Meyrick Rd, East Cliff BH1 3DL
☎(0202)554415 Telex no 418297 FAX (0202) 294810
*A large conference and holiday hotel with some modern, purpose built bedrooms while others are more individually styled. The five course dinner menu offers a good choice of fresh dishes.*
114⇔ſ(15fb)1⊞ CTV in all bedrooms ® T ✳
sB&B⇔ſ£39.50-£42.50 dB&B⇔ſ£79-£85 ⊟
Lift ℂ 80P 12🂠 (£1.50) ✿ snooker beauty salon games room *xmas*
⚑ English & French **V** ✿ ⚏ Lunch £8.25-£10 High tea £3.95-£4.95 Dinner £14.95-£15.95 Last dinner 9pm
Credit Cards ①③ ⓔ

★★★**58%, Hermitage** Exeter Rd BH2 5AH ☎(0202)557363
FAX (0202) 559173
*This hotel is in an excellent position with easy access to the sea, shops and BIC. Public rooms are comfortable and bedrooms vary from spacious and well furnished to smaller, modest rooms.*
71⇔ſ(17fb) CTV in all bedrooms ® T ✳ S10%
sB&B⇔ſ£40.50-£44 dB&B⇔ſ£72-£84 ⊟
Lift ℂ CTV 58P CFA sauna solarium *xmas*
⚑ English & French **V** ✿ ⚏ ✂ S10% Lunch £5.35-£9.50alc Dinner £10.50 Last dinner 8.30pm
Credit Cards ①②③⑤ⓔ

★★★**57%, Crest** Lansdowne BH1 2PR (Trusthouse Forte)
☎(0202)553262 Telex no 41232 FAX (0202) 27698
*A modern, circular building, centrally placed for the town and sea, offers well equipped bedrooms of a uniform standard, an up-to-date video bar and some leisure facilities, whilst a good range of dishes is available in the Picnics Restaurant.*
102⇔ſ(78fb)✂in 34 bedrooms CTV in all bedrooms ® T
(room only) ⊟

Lift ℂ CTV 50🂠 snooker table tennis darts games room skittles *xmas*
⚑ English & French **V** ✿ ⚏ ✂
Credit Cards ①②③④⑤

★★★**57%, Embassy** Meyrick Rd, Boscombe BH1 3DW
☎(0202)290751 FAX (0202) 557459
*Quietly located in a tree-lined avenue convenient for the town and the East Cliff, this friendly hotel offers garden annexe bedrooms of a good standard and comfortable lounge areas.*
39⇔ſ Annexe33⇔ſ(12fb)1⊞ CTV in all bedrooms ® T ✳
S% sB&B⇔ſ£29.50-£41 dB&B⇔ſ£55-£79 ⊟
Lift ℂ CTV 75P CFA ☒(heated) *xmas*
⚑ British & Italian ✿ ⚏
Credit Cards ①②③⑤ ⓔ

★★★**57%, Melford Hall** St Peters Rd BH1 2LS ☎(0202)551516
FAX (0202) 292533
*Quietly yet centrally situated, the large, traditional holiday hotel offers excellent value for money, with good parking facilities and substantial meals. The unusual fibre-optic displays in the public areas are worthy of note.*
60rm(59⇔)(17fb) CTV in all bedrooms ® T sB&B£20-£30 sB&B⇔£22-£34 dB&B⇔£44-£68 ⊟
Lift ℂ 65P ✿ ☒(heated) sauna solarium gymnasium *xmas*
⚑ English & French **V** ✿ ⚏ Lunch £6-£7.25 Dinner £9-£9.25 Last dinner 8.30pm
Credit Cards ①②③⑤ⓔ

★★★**56%, Durley Hall** Durley Chine Rd, West Cliff BH2 5JS (Consort) ☎(0202)766886 FAX (0202) 762236
*This recently extended hotel offers bedrooms both in executive style and more modest. A formal dining room is augmented by a coffee shop, and there are new indoor sports facilities and a sun lounge.*

▶

71rm(70⇄♠)Annexe10⇄♠(22fb)1⌷ CTV in all bedrooms
® T sB&B⇄♠£53-£58 dB&B⇄♠£79-£84 ⊟
Lift ℂ 150P ✿ CFA ⬚(heated) ⇲(heated) snooker sauna
solarium gymnasium jacuzzi steam cabinet hairdresser ♫ xmas
♥ English & Continental V ✿ ⚌ Sunday Lunch £6.75 Dinner
£14.50&alc Last dinner 8.45pm
Credit Cards ①②③⑤

★★★55% **Burley Court** Bath Rd BH1 2NP ☎(0202)552824
FAX (0202) 298514
Closed 23 Dec-6 Jan
*The public areas of this holiday hotel include a large lounge and
games room, together with a newly-decorated dining room, and
guests enjoy individual attention from the friendly, helpful staff.*
39rm(29⇄5♠)(8fb)1⌷ CTV in 34 bedrooms TV in 5
bedrooms ® T sB&B⇄♠£25-£38 dB&B⇄♠£49-£76 ⊟
Lift ℂ CTV 35P ✿ ⇲(heated) solarium games room
♥ English & French ✿ ⚌ S5% Dinner £9.50-£10 Last dinner
8.30pm
Credit Cards ①③

★★★50% **Hotel Miramar** East Overcliff Dr, East Cliff
BH1 3AL ☎(0202)556581 FAX (0202) 299573
*Warm, comfortable hotel where many rooms have fine sea views.*
39⇄♠(4fb) CTV in all bedrooms ® T ✖ (ex guide dogs)
sB&B⇄♠£39-£50 dB&B⇄♠£70-£90 ⊟
Lift ℂ CTV 50P 6🚗 (£4 per night) ✿ croquet putting ♫ xmas
V ✿ ⚌ ✕ Lunch £5-£7 High tea £8.50-£10.50 Dinner
£13.50-£15 Last dinner 8.30pm
Credit Cards ①②③⑥

★★71% **Hinton Firs** Manor Rd, East Cliff BH1 3HB (Exec
Hotel) ☎(0202)555409 FAX (0202) 299607
*Beautifully kept and professionally managed this appealing hotel
is set in neat gardens and boasts both indoor and outdoor
swimming pools. Bedrooms are very well equipped and most are
furnished to a high standard.*
46⇄♠(19fb) CTV in 52 bedrooms ® T ✖ ✱
sB&B⇄♠£28-£48.40 dB&B⇄♠£56-£85.20 (incl dinner) ⊟
Lift ℂ CTV 40P ✿ ⬚(heated) ⇲(heated) sauna ♫ xmas
♥ English & French V ✿ ⚌ ✕ Sunday Lunch £6.25 Dinner
£8.25&alc Last dinner 8.30pm
Credit Cards ①③

★★68% **Boltons** 9 Durley Chine Rd South, West Cliff BH2 5JT
☎(0202)760907 & 751517 FAX (0202) 751629
12⇄♠(2fb) CTV in all bedrooms ® T ✱
sB&B⇄♠£23-£28.75 dB&B⇄♠£46-£57.50 ⊟
10P ✿ ⇲(heated) nc5yrs xmas
♥ English & French ✿ ⚌ Lunch £5.50 Dinner £10.50&alc
Last dinner 8.30pm
Credit Cards ①②③

★★66% **Chinehurst** 18-20 Studland Rd, Westbourne BH4 8JA
☎(0202)764583
*A well managed family-run hotel popular with families, but also
well-equipped for business people.*
31⇄♠(4fb)1⌷ CTV in all bedrooms ® T
sB&B⇄♠£18.50-£35 dB&B⇄♠£57-£70 ⊟
14P 2🚗 (£2.50 per night) games room xmas
♥ Continental V ✿ ⚌ ✕ Lunch £1.50-£6.50 Dinner £9.50 Last
dinner 8.30pm
Credit Cards ①②③⑤

See advertisement under POOLE

★★66% **Riviera** Burnaby Rd, Alum Chine BH4 8JF
☎(0202)763653 Telex no 41363 FAX (0202) 299182
Closed 2-31 Jan
*White painted hotel with good facilities. Quietly situated a short
walk from the Promenade, this popular, value-for-money hotel
offers friendly holiday accommodation; many of its well-equipped
bedrooms have verandahs, varied table d'hôte menus are featured*

*in the dining room, entertainment is provided four nights weekly,
and good leisure facilities include two full-sized billiard tables.*
70⇄♠Annexe9⇄♠(24fb) CTV in all bedrooms ® T ✱
sB&B⇄♠£25-£50 dB&B⇄♠£50-£100 (incl dinner)
Lift 79P ⬚(heated) ⇲(heated) snooker sauna solarium 2
games rooms ♫ xmas
♥ French & English V ✿ ⚌ Lunch £7-£8.50 Dinner
£13.50-£15 Last dinner 8.30pm
Credit Cards ①③

★★65% **Arlington** Exeter Park Rd BH2 5BD ☎(0202)552879 &
553012
RS Jan-Mar
*Set in an excellent position – overlooking the Central Gardens and
within walking distance of sea, pier, shops and the BIC – this
friendly, family-run hotel provides bedrooms which, though small,
are neat and well equipped, whilst a loyal team of staff creates a
genial, informal atmosphere.*
28⇄♠Annexe1♠(6fb) CTV in 28 bedrooms ® T ✖ ✱
sB&B⇄♠£26.50-£33.50 dB&B⇄♠£53-£67 (incl dinner) ⊟
Lift CTV 21P ✿ nc2yrs xmas
♥ English & French V ✿ ⚌ ✕ Sunday Lunch £5.95 Dinner
£9.50 Last dinner 8pm
Credit Cards ①③ ⓔ

★★65% **Hartford Court** 48 Christchurch Rd BH1 3PE
☎(0202)551712 & 293682
34rm(6⇄18♠)Annexe6rm(5⇄♠)(6fb) CTV in all bedrooms
® T S% sB&B£19-£21 sB&B⇄♠£21-£23 dB&B£38-£42
dB&B⇄♠£42-£46 ⊟
Lift CTV 36P ✿ nc10yrs xmas
✿ ⚌ S% Dinner £7.50 Last dinner 7.30pm
Credit Cards ①③ ⓔ

★★64% **Overcliff** Overcliff Dr, Southbourne BH6 3JA
☎(0202)428300
Closed 3-30 Jan
*There are views out to the bay from the restaurant and some of the
bedrooms – those with balconies also have colour TV. There is
well-balanced table d'hôte menu for dinner and an extensive range
of bar meals are available at lunchtime. The friendly owners
commit themselves totally to the running of their hotel.*
26rm(17⇄4♠)(10fb) CTV in 4 bedrooms ® ✖ (ex guide dogs)
CTV 22P ♫
V ✿ ⚌ Last dinner 8pm
Credit Cards ①③

★★63% **Durley Chine** Chine Crescent, West Cliff BH2 5LB
☎(0202)551926
*A family owned and run hotel in its own grounds offers many
facilities in its modern bedrooms – fourteen of which are recent
additions – together with a freshly decorated dining room, cosy bar
and lounge areas, friendly service and a relaxing atmosphere.*
22rm(8⇄9♠)Annexe14rm(8⇄2♠)(5fb) CTV in all bedrooms
® T sB&B⇄♠£28.50-£35 dB&B⇄♠£57-£70 (incl dinner) ⊟
40P ✿ ⇲(heated) nc5yrs xmas
♥ English & Continental V ✿ ⚌ ✕ Bar Lunch £4.50-£6.50alc
Credit Cards ①③ ⓔ

★★63% **Gresham Court** 4 Grove Rd, East Cliff BH1 3AX
☎(0202)21732
*A warm, friendly, proprietor-run hotel provides modern bedroom
facilities and spacious public areas which include a ball room with
live entertainment some evenings. Despite specialising in coach
parties, the hotel maintains high standards both in cuisine and
service.*
34⇄♠(12fb) CTV in all bedrooms ® ✱ sB&B⇄♠£23-£32
dB&B⇄♠£46-£64 ⊟
Lift CTV 35P ✿ xmas
✿ ⚌ Dinner £9 Last dinner 7.30pm
Credit Cards ①②③⑤

★★63% *Pinehurst* West Cliff Gardens BH2 5HR ☎(0202)26218
*A substantial red-brick hotel catering for the holiday and coach trade offers some superior bedrooms on its third floor, a choice between the traditional menu of the restaurant and a range of Carvery meals, a themed Tudor bar, and efficient service from a friendly team of staff.*
77rm(46⇋26♠)(11fb) CTV in 75 bedrooms ®
Lift ℂ 48P solarium ♫
Last dinner 8pm
Credit Cards ① ② ③
*See advertisement on page 151*

★★63% *Royal Exeter* Exeter Rd BH2 5AG (Berni/Chef & Brewer) ☎(0202)290566 & 290567
*Very well positioned opposite the BIC and near the sea this hotel has attractive bedrooms which are furnished and equipped to a uniform standard. The ground floor offers a choice of popular restaurants during the summer.*
36♠(10fb) CTV in all bedrooms ® T ✗ (ex guide dogs)
sB&B♠£46-£52.50 dB&B♠£61.50 ☐
Lift ℂ 50P
V ♦ ⚖ ✗ Lunch £8-£15alc Dinner £8-£15alc Last dinner 10pm
Credit Cards ① ② ③ ⑤
*See advertisement on page 151*

★★63% *Ullswater* West Cliff Gardens BH2 5HW ☎(0202)555181
*This friendly hotel, at present being upgraded, has a very comfortable lounge and bar, and some well-furnished bedrooms. It is suitable for both holiday and commercial guests.*
42⇋♠(7fb) CTV in all bedrooms ® T ✗ (ex guide dogs)
sB&B⇋♠£24.50-£33 dB&B⇋♠£49-£66 (incl dinner) ☐
Lift 10P table tennis ♫ xmas
♀ English & French ♦ ⚖ Bar Lunch £1.25-£5alc
Credit Cards ① ③

## BOURNEMOUTH

*Modern family owned hotel with extensive leisure facilities*

Overlooking wooded Alum Chine and Bournemouth Bay, The Riviera Hotel offers the ideal location for family holidays and short breaks.
Indoor and outdoor pools, spa bath, solarium and large snooker room are just some of the leisure facilities on offer.

The
**Riviera**
Hotel
★ ★
BURNABY ROAD, ALUM CHINE,
BOURNEMOUTH
TEL: (0202) 763653

≡**Calotels**≡

---

★★

# The Boltons Hotel    B

## Durley Chine Road Sth., West Cliff, Bournemouth BH2 5JT

The ideal place for that relaxing holiday or business stay. This 12 bedroomed (all en suite) Victorian building, gives you all the luxuries of a large hotel but with the style and comfort of a bygone era.
Placed in a quiet location on the West cliff away from traffic noise, but within 7 minutes walk of the town centre and beach.
Outdoor Heated Swimming Pool (Seasonal)
Very Large Garden   Car Park

**Bargain Breaks from October-May
Any two consecutive nights on a
Half Board Basis £50 inc VAT
Tel: (0202) 760907/751517
Fax: (0202) 751629**

---

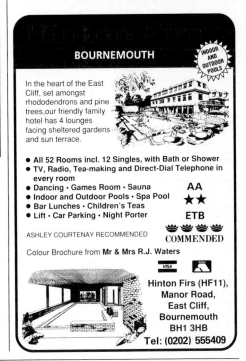

### BOURNEMOUTH

INDOOR AND OUTDOOR POOLS

In the heart of the East Cliff, set amongst rhododendrons and pine trees,our friendly family hotel has 4 lounges facing sheltered gardens and sun terrace.

● All 52 Rooms incl. 12 Singles, with Bath or Shower
● TV, Radio, Tea-making and Direct-Dial Telephone in every room
● Dancing · Games Room · Sauna
● Indoor and Outdoor Pools · Spa Pool
● Bar Lunches · Children's Teas
● Lift · Car Parking · Night Porter

AA
★★
ETB

ASHLEY COURTENAY RECOMMENDED

👑👑👑
COMMENDED

Colour Brochure from **Mr & Mrs R.J. Waters**

VISA

Hinton Firs (HF11),
Manor Road,
East Cliff,
Bournemouth
BH1 3HB
**Tel: (0202) 555409**

# Bournemouth

**★★62%, Chinehead** 31 Alumhurst Rd, Westbourne BH4 8EN
☎(0202)752777
*A small proprietor run hotel popular with both business people and holidaymakers alike. There are well equipped bedrooms, a comfortable lounge bar and a good choice of dishes at dinner.*
21⇌🛏(2fb) CTV in all bedrooms ⓡ T 🛏 (ex guide dogs)
sB&B⇌🛏£24-£28 dB&B⇌🛏£48-£56 🅟
20P 🚗 *xmas*
V ⍋ 🖵 ⚡ Lunch £6.25-£10.50&alc Dinner £8.25-£9.25&alc
Last dinner 8.30pm
Credit Cards ① ③ ⓔ

**★★62%, Winterbourne** Priory Rd BH2 5DJ ☎(0202)296366
Telex no 417153
Closed Jan
*With excellent views of the town and sea this friendly hotel with an informal atmosphere has modern bedrooms, a bar and games room. It is suitable for business people and holidaymakers alike.*
41⇌🛏(12fb) CTV in all bedrooms ⓡ T sB&B⇌🛏£29-£37
dB&B⇌🛏£51-£60 🅟
Lift 32P 1🐾 ❄ △(heated) ⚘ *xmas*
V ⍋ 🖵 Bar Lunch £1.50-£7 High tea fr£3 Dinner fr£10 Last dinner 8pm
Credit Cards ① ③ ⓔ

**★★62%, Woodcroft Tower** Gervis Rd, East Cliff BH1 3DE
☎(0202)558202 & 551807
*Standing in its own grounds, a convenient walking distance from shops, pier and the seafront.*
42rm(22⇌17🛏)(4fb) CTV in all bedrooms ⓡ T
🛏 (ex guide dogs) sB&B⇌🛏£30-£40 dB&B⇌🛏£50-£70 🅟
Lift (60P (charged) ❄ *xmas*
♈ English & French ⍋ Bar Lunch £3-£5 Dinner £10-£12
Last dinner 8.30pm
Credit Cards ① ③

**★★61%, Cottonwood** Grove Rd, East Cliff BH1 3AP (Minotels)
☎(0202)23183
*A traditionally managed seafront hotel on the cliff overlooks neat gardens and provides a cheerful, family atmosphere. Bedrooms have modern facilities, including neat bathrooms whilst public areas include a billiard room and a lounge with a dance floor.*
32⇌🛏(8fb) CTV in all bedrooms ⓡ T
sB&B⇌🛏£38.50-£47.50 dB&B⇌🛏£62-£80 (incl dinner) 🅟
Lift 50P ❄ snooker ♫ *xmas*
♈ English & French V ⍋ 🖵 ⚡ Bar Lunch 85p-£3.50 Dinner £8 Last dinner 8pm
Credit Cards ① ② ③ ⑤ ⓔ

**★★61%, Durley Grange** 6 Durley Rd, West Cliff BH2 5JL
☎(0202)554473 & 290743 FAX (0202) 293774
*A privately owned and run hotel with a friendly atmosphere. The refurbishment of the bedrooms is nearly complete, and rooms are well equipped and have modern, fitted furniture.*
50⇌🛏(6fb) CTV in all bedrooms ⓡ T sB&B⇌🛏£25-£29
dB&B⇌🛏£50-£58 🅟
Lift ( CTV 25P ☐(heated) sauna solarium ♫ nc5yrs *xmas*
♈ English, French & German ⍋ ⚡ Sunday Lunch £6-£7
Dinner £11.50-£12.50 Last dinner 8pm
Credit Cards ① ③ ⓔ

**★★61%, Mansfield** West Cliff Gardens BH2 5HL
☎(0202)552659
Closed 28 Dec-17 Jan
*The hotel stands in a quiet road at West Cliff, an easy walk from cliff top and beach. Friendly, attentive resident owners provide personal service, and the bedrooms are very comfortable.*
30⇌🛏(7fb)1🖭 CTV in all bedrooms ⓡ T 🛏
sB&B⇌🛏£25-£30 dB&B⇌🛏£50-£60 (incl dinner) 🅟
12P 🚗 *xmas*
♈ English & French ⍋ 🖵 ⚡ Sunday Lunch £6 Dinner £7.25
Last dinner 8pm
Credit Cards ① ③

**★★61%, St George** West Cliff Gardens BH2 5HL
☎(0202)26075 due to change to 556075
Closed 3 Jan-2nd week Mar
*Peacefully situated on the West Cliff, overlooking the bay and only ten minutes walk from the town centre and pier.*
22rm(20⇌🛏)(5fb) CTV in all bedrooms ⓡ T
Lift 4P pool table
♈ English, French, Italian & Indian ⍋ 🖵 Last dinner 7.15pm

**★★61%, West Cliff Hall** 14 Priory Rd BH2 5DN (Best Western)
☎(0202)299715
*A busy hotel, centrally situated and only a short walk from both West Cliff and the Conference Centre, caters mainly for the holiday trade; bedrooms vary in style but are all co-ordinated and well-equipped, an attentive, friendly staff creates a relaxed atmosphere, and a stay here represents good value for money.*
49⇌🛏(9fb) CTV in all bedrooms ⓡ T ⚹ sB&B⇌🛏£24-£35
dB&B⇌🛏£48-£70 (incl dinner) 🅟
Lift CTV 36P ♫ *xmas*
V ⍋ 🖵 Lunch £4-£6 High tea £4-£6 Dinner £6-£8 Last dinner 8pm
Credit Cards ① ② ③ ⑤ ⓔ

**★★61%, Whitehall** Exeter Park Rd BH2 5AX ☎(0202)554682
Closed 6 Nov-Feb
*A quiet holiday hotel in an elevated position overlooking the central gardens to the rear and close to the town centre.*
49rm(44⇌🛏)(5fb) CTV in all bedrooms ⓡ T
sB&B⇌🛏£22-£28 dB&B⇌🛏£44-£56 🅟
Lift ( 25P ❄
⍋ 🖵 S%, Bar Lunch £1.25-£4 Dinner fr£8.50 Last dinner 8pm
Credit Cards ① ② ③ ⑤

**★★60%, Hotel Riviera** West Cliff Gardens BH2 5HL
☎(0202)552845
Closed Dec-Mar
*A friendly hotel which has been under the same ownership for 30 years and has acquired a loyal clientele who appreciate its generally pretty fitted bedrooms and the cosy, comfortable public rooms.*
34⇌🛏(5fb) CTV in all bedrooms ⓡ sB&B⇌🛏£22-£27
dB&B⇌🛏£44-£54 🅟
Lift ( CTV 24P 🚗 *xmas*
⍋ 🖵 Dinner £8.50 Last dinner 7.30pm
Credit Cards ① ② ③

**★★59%, Sun Court** West Hill Rd BH2 5PH ☎(0202)551343
*Holiday and commercial trade are catered for equally well by a modern hotel offering a range of accommodation from small budget-priced rooms to spacious ones with balconies – all being very well equipped and carefully looked after. Public areas include a smart, cane-furnished cocktail bar and separate lounge, whilst the dining room, where guests enjoy their choice of a short menu of English dishes, features a dance floor.*
36⇌🛏(4fb) CTV in all bedrooms ⓡ sB&B⇌🛏£31.50-£38.50
dB&B⇌🛏£63-£77 (incl dinner) 🅟
Lift ( CTV 50P 1🐾 △(heated) solarium gymnasium *xmas*
♈ English & Italian ⍋ 🖵 Sunday Lunch £5.75 Dinner £13&alc
Last dinner 8pm
Credit Cards ① ② ③ ⑤

**★★57%, Russell Court** Bath Rd BH1 2EP (Inter-Hotels)
☎(0202)295819 FAX (0202) 293457
*This hotel, in its central location, is suitable as a base for holidays or business. It provides personal friendly service, attractive public areas and well-equipped bedrooms, some with a view to sea.*
62rm(44⇌10🛏)(6fb) CTV in all bedrooms ⓡ T
🛏 (ex guide dogs) S%, sB&B⇌🛏£46
dB&B⇌🛏£86 (incl dinner) 🅟
Lift ( 60P ♫ *xmas*
V ⍋ 🖵 Sunday Lunch fr£6.50 Dinner fr£7.50 Last dinner 8pm
Credit Cards ① ② ③ ⑤ ⓔ

**See advertisement on page 153**

150

**B**

★★**55%**, **Fircroft** 4 Owls Rd, Boscombe BH5 1AE
☎(0202)309771
*Slightly compact but very well equipped bedrooms with mainly modern furnishings, ample lounge space, a ballroom and facilities for squash are available at this hotel.*
49⇨♠(18fb) CTV in all bedrooms ® T sB&B⇨♠£22-£26 dB&B⇨♠£44-£52 ♖
Lift ( CTV 50P squash ♬ *xmas*
V ♥ ⚏ Bar Lunch £1.50-£5 Dinner fr£11 Last dinner 8pm
Credit Cards ⅠⅢ ⓔ

★★**50%**, **County** Westover Rd BH1 2BT ☎(0202)552385
*Well placed close to the pier, gardens and shops, this hotel offers the usual modern bedroom facilities and a lively disco.*
51rm(37⇨9♠)(11fb) CTV in all bedrooms ® T sB&B£20-£25 sB&B⇨♠£30-£35 dB&B£40-£50 dB&B⇨♠£50-£60 ♖
Lift ( ♪ *xmas*
♥ ⚏
Credit Cards ⅠⅡⅢ

★**65%**, **Lynden Court** 8 Durley Rd, West Cliff BH2 5JL
☎(0202)23894
Closed Nov-Mar (ex Xmas & New Year)
*Well-equipped, comfortable bedrooms, attractive public areas and twice-weekly entertainment during the season are provided by a pleasant holiday hotel, quietly located with a garden at the rear.*
32⇨♠(7fb) CTV in 31 bedrooms ®
Lift 20P ♬
Last dinner 7.15pm
Credit Cards ⅠⅡⅢⅤ

★**64%**, **New Dorchester** 64 Lansdowne Rd BH1 1RS
☎(0202)551271
Closed 24 Dec-3 Jan
*A comfortable small hotel, personally run in a relaxed manner by its friendly owners, offers well equipped, simply furnished bedrooms, attractive public areas and a selection of wholesome meals.*
10rm(5⇨) CTV in all bedrooms ® ✱ sB&B£16-£18 sB&B⇨£24-£30 dB&B£30-£34 dB&B⇨£32-£40
10P ⚗ ncl2yrs
♥ Bar Lunch £3-£5 Dinner £7-£9 Last dinner 7pm
Credit Cards ⅠⅡⅢⅤ

★**64%**, **Taurus Park** 16 Knyveton Rd BH1 3QN ☎(0202)557374
*The hotel stands in a quiet, tree-lined avenue, close to the town centre. It is run by a friendly Spanish family, who involve themselves totally with the welfare of their guests. Most bedrooms have been refurbished, the food is simple but wholesome and there is evening entertainment on several nights each week during the holiday season. All in all, good value for money.*
47rm(8⇨17♠)(4fb) CTV in all bedrooms ® ✱ sB&B£16-£22 sB&B⇨♠£18-£28 dB&B£32-£44 dB&B⇨♠£36-£56 (incl dinner)
Lift CTV 30P games room nc3yrs *xmas*
Bar Lunch £1.50-£3.50 Dinner £4.50-£6 Last dinner 7.30pm
ⓔ

★**59%**, **Silver How** West Cliff Gardens, West Cliff BH2 5HN
☎(0202)21537
Closed Jan
*This small, family-managed hotel is quietly situated, yet convenient for the town centre. It offers pleasant public rooms, well-equipped bedrooms, simple home cooking, friendly staff and a relaxed atmosphere.*
22rm(9⇨9♠)(11fb) CTV in all bedrooms ®
12P solarium
Last dinner 7pm
Credit Cards ⅠⅢ

★**55%**, **Commodore** Overcliff Dr, Southbourne BH6 3TD
☎(0202)423150 & 427127
14rm(3⇨7♠)(1fb) CTV in all bedrooms ®
Lift 14P ⚗
♥
Credit Cards ⅠⅡⅢⅤ

✕ ✕**Sophisticats** 43 Charminster Rd BH8 8UE ☎(0202)291019
*In a street of shops about 1.5 miles from the centre of Bournemouth. Booth seating and friendly service create an intimate atmosphere. The à la carte menu has sensibly been extended and is supplemented by daily additions. Local fish and game are delicious, as are some imaginative dishes from the Far East. The menu includes pheasant in red wine with bacon and chipolata, grilled halibut with tarragon and chevril hollandaise and Javanese fillet steak. The vegetables are cooked al dente to retain their colour and flavour.*
Closed Sun, Mon, 2 wks Feb & 2 wks Nov
Lunch not served
♡ International V 34 seats Dinner £18-£25alc Last dinner 10pm ♪

**BOURTON-ON-THE-WATER** Gloucestershire Map 04 SP12

★★**66%**, **Finden Lodge** Whiteshoots Hill, Cirencester Rd
GL54 2LE (Inter-Hotels) ☎Cotswold(0451)20387
*Close to Bourton-on-the-Water on the A429, this hotel is an ideal base for touring the Cotswolds. Accommodation is comfortable and attractive and all rooms are equipped with good modern facilities. It is family-owned and run, hence the friendly and relaxed atmosphere.*
12⇨♠(2fb)1♨❤in 3 bedrooms CTV in all bedrooms ® T ✱ sB&B⇨♠£35-£40 dB&B⇨♠£56-£60 ♖
38P ❀ *xmas*
♡ Continental V ♥ ⚏ ✂ Lunch £8.50 Dinner £12.50&alc Last dinner 9.30pm
Credit Cards ⅠⅢ

★★**66%**, **Old Manse** Victoria St GL54 2BX
☎Cotswold(0451)20082 & 20642
*The Old Manse was built in the 18th century and was the home of the village pastor. It has recently been refurbished to a good standard, tourists will enjoy the relaxing atmosphere whilst business guests will appreciate the modern facilities. Management and staff offer genuine hospitality.*
12⇨♠(2fb)1♨ CTV in all bedrooms ® T ✱ (ex guide dogs) ✱ sB&B⇨♠£35 dB&B⇨♠£55-£105 ♖
12P *xmas*
♡ English & French V ♥ ⚏ Lunch £5.95-£7.95 High tea £3.50 Dinner fr£14.75&alc Last dinner 9.30pm
Credit Cards ⅠⅢ

★★**64%**, **Chester House Hotel & Motel** Victoria St GL54 2BS
(Minotels) ☎Cotswold(0451)20286 FAX (0451) 20471
Closed mid Dec-mid Feb
*Mr and Mrs Davies have taken every care to retain the character and charm of the building whilst renovating and providing modern facilities. A newly discovered well under the dining room is now a feature of the room. There is a choice of traditional and motel-style bedrooms.*
13⇨♠Annexe10⇨♠(5fb)1♨ CTV in all bedrooms ® T sB&B⇨♠£35-£40
dB&B⇨♠£54-£66 Continental breakfast ♖
23P
V ♥ Lunch £10.50 Dinner £14.95 Last dinner 9.30pm
Credit Cards ⅠⅡⅢⅣⅤ ⓔ

★★**63%**, **Old New Inn** High St GL54 2AF
☎Cotswold(0451)20467
Closed 25 Dec
*This part eighteenth-century building has tremendous character and an intriguing model village in the garden. Led by the Morris family, the staff are extremely helpful and pleasant.*

17rm(6⇨1♠)Annexe5rm1⌨ CTV in 9 bedrooms S10%
sB&Bf£24-£30 sB&B⇨♠fr£30 dB&Bfr£48 dB&B⇨♠fr£60 ⊟
CTV 25P 6🐾 (£1) 🎐 ✿
V ⚙ Lunch £8-£9 Dinner fr£14 Last dinner 8.30pm
Credit Cards ⒈ ⒊

---

**BOVEY TRACEY** Devon Map 03 SX87

★★★63% *Edgemoor* Haytor Rd TQ13 9LE ☎(0626)832466
*New owners, Robert and Mary Stephens have significantly
upgraded this hotel, without detriment to its charm and appealing
character. Bedrooms have pleasing co-ordinated décor, some with
4-poster or half-tester beds, and all offer modern comforts. Robert
Stephens, a Master Sommelier has put together a well-balanced
wine list to complement the enjoyable food and, under the daily
management of the Stephens's daughter, Nicola, the hotel offers a
caring and hospitable atmosphere.*
12rm(10⇨)(3fb) CTV in all bedrooms
CTV 45P (charged) 🎐 ✿
🍴 French V ⚙ ⏱ Last dinner 8pm
Credit Cards ⒈ ⒉ ⒊ ⒌

★★63% **Riverside Inn** Fore St TQ13 9AF ☎(0626)832293
FAX (0626) 833880
10⇨♠ CTV in all bedrooms ® T ✱ sB&B⇨♠fr£30
dB&B⇨♠fr£50 ⊟
💰100P ♪ *xmas*
V ⚙ Lunch £6-£8.50 Dinner £6-£8&alc Last dinner 9pm
Credit Cards ⒈ ⒊

★★53% **Coombe Cross** Coombe Cross TQ13 9EY (Inter-Hotels)
☎(0626)832476
*Comfortable and well appointed traditional country hotel,
personally run.*
26rm(23⇨1♠)(2fb) CTV in all bedrooms ® T S%
sB&B£26.95 sB&B⇨♠£34 dB&B⇨♠£53.90 ⊟
▶

**B**

《 CTV 26P ✿
V ✿ 🖵 ✔ S% Bar Lunch fr£4.95 High tea fr£2.75 Dinner
fr£15.95 Last dinner 8pm
Credit Cards ①②③⑤

**BOWMORE**

See Islay, Isle of

**BOWNESS ON WINDERMERE**

See **Windermere**

**BOX** Wiltshire Map **03** ST86

✗✗✗*Clos du Roy* Box House SN14 9NR ☎Bath(0225)744447
Telex no 831476 FAX (0225) 743971
*Philippe and Emma Roy have transplanted their very popular
restaurant from its tiny premises in Bath to a spacious and elegant
Georgian mansion on the outskirts of the village of Box which lies
between Bath and Chippenham. The interior of the house has been
refurbished and now offers three beautifully decorated dining
rooms. The 'menu surprise' offers very good value for money, with
unusual and imaginative combinations of ingredients and flavours;
the delicate sauces which accompany most of the dishes are a
particular strength of Philippe Roy, and the seasonal à la carte
menu may offer such dishes as feuilleté d'asperges, ragoût du
marin or noisettes d'agneau au St Jacques. The raw ingredients
are all of the highest quality, many of the vegetables and herbs
coming from their own kitchen garden.*
♀ French **V** 55 seats Last lunch 2.30pm Last dinner 10pm 35P
Credit Cards ①②③④⑤

**BRACKLESHAM** West Sussex Map **04** SZ89

✗**Cliffords Cottage** Bracklesham Ln PO20 8JA ☎(0243)670250
*Small 17th-century cottage restaurant with a cosy atmosphere,
serving good, honest cooking of a very good standard.*
Closed Tue (winter only)
Lunch not served Mon-Sat
Dinner not served Sun
♀ French **V** 28 seats ✱ Sunday Lunch £9-£9.50 Dinner
fr£15.50&alc Last dinner 9pm 16P nc3yrs
Credit Cards ①②③⑤

**BRACKLEY** Northamptonshire Map **04** SP53

★68% *Crown* Market Square NN13 5DP ☎(0280)702210
*Friendly staff offer a warm welcome at this charming coaching inn.
Bedrooms are comfortable and provide modern facilities whilst
retaining the inn's character.*
14🛏 CTV in all bedrooms ® ✖ (ex guide dogs)
《 CTV 20P
♀ Mainly grills **V** ✿ 🖵 ✔ Last dinner 10pm
Credit Cards ①②③⑤

**BRACKNELL** Berkshire Map **04** SU86

★★★60% *Stirrups Country House* Maidens Green RG12 6LD
(Best Western) ☎Winkfield(0344)882284 FAX (0344) 882300
*Set in ten acres of gardens in a rural location just outside
Bracknell, this popular commercial-style hotel is run on traditional
lines in a pleasing manner. The well-appointed bedrooms are bright
and comfortable and the racing theme of its name is reflected
throughout the public rooms, which include congenial bars and a
restaurant.*
24🛏(6fb) CTV in all bedrooms ® T ✱ sB&B🛏£75-£84
dB&B🛏£87.50-£97.50 🈺
Lift 《 150P ✿ *xmas*
♀ English & Continental **V** ✿
Credit Cards ①②③⑤

**BRADFORD** West Yorkshire Map **07** SE31

★★★★52% **Stakis Norfolk Gardens** Hall Ings BD1 5SH
(Stakis) ☎(0274)734734 Telex no 517573 FAX (0274) 306146
*Though bedrooms tend to be compact and dated in style,
attractively refurbished public areas make this modern city centre
hotel a popular local business venue; an added attraction is
Juliana's Table, where good-value buffet meals are offered
alongside a short à la carte selection.*
126🛏🍴(5fb)✔in 73 bedrooms CTV in all bedrooms ® T ✱
sB🛏🍴£75-£85 dB🛏🍴£95-£105 (room only) 🈺
Lift 《 *xmas*
♀ French **V** ✿ 🖵 Lunch £8.50 Dinner £16.50&alc Last dinner
10pm
Credit Cards ①②③④⑤ ⑥

★★★59% **The Victoria** Bridge St BD1 1JX (Trusthouse Forte)
☎(0274)728706 Telex no 517456 FAX (0274) 736358
*A typically English hotel adjacent to St George's Hall in the heart
of the city. There are spacious public rooms, a fixed price carvery
restaurant and friendly staff to serve you.*
59🛏🍴in 10 bedrooms CTV in all bedrooms ® ✱
(room only) 🈺
Lift 《 40P
♀ Mainly grills **V** ✿ 🖵 ✔
Credit Cards ①②③④⑤

★★★57% *Novotel Bradford* Merrydale Rd BD4 6SA (3m S
adjacent to M606) (Novotel) ☎(0274)683683 Telex no 517312
FAX (0274) 651342
*Conveniently situated just off the A606 and only minutes from the
M62, this functional modern hotel offers basic but clean
accommodation.*
132🛏(132fb) CTV in all bedrooms ® T
Lift 《 ⊞ 180P ✿ ⌬(heated) ♨
♀ English & French **V** ✿ 🖵 Last dinner mdnt
Credit Cards ①②③④⑤

★★63% **Dubrovnik** 3 Oak Av, Manningham BD8 7AQ
☎(0274)543511 FAX (0274) 480407
*A friendly hotel managed by the resident proprietor providing
comfortable bedrooms and pleasant service.*
20🛏🍴(6fb) CTV in all bedrooms ® ✖
《 60P *xmas*
♀ English & Yugoslavian **V** ✿ 🖵
Credit Cards ①③

✗✗**Restaurant Nineteen** 19 North Park Rd, Heaton BD9 4NT
☎(0274)492559
*An elegant restaurant offering comfort, genteel service and an
interesting 4-course menu. Imagination and skill are very evident
in the dishes produced – starters include chicken breast stuffed
with asparagus, smoked trout mousse with yogurt sauce and home
made soup. Main courses may include spring lamb with asparagus
mousse, breast of duck, sea bass and veal, while a tempting array
of desserts, such as cherry and almond pudding, home-made ice
cream and rich chocolate cake, make for a difficult choice.*
Closed Sun, Mon, 1 wk after Xmas, 1 wk Jun & 2 wks Aug/Sep
Lunch not served (ex by arrangement only)
♀ English & French 40 seats ✱ Dinner £24.50-£26.50 Last
dinner 9.30pm 15P nc8yrs ✔
Credit Cards ①②③⑤

Entries for red-star hotels are highlighted by a
tint panel. For a full list of these establishments
consult the Contents page.

**BRADFORD ON AVON** Wiltshire Map **03** ST86

★★★⚑73% **Woolley Grange** Woolley Green BA15 1TX
☎(02216)4705 FAX (02216) 4059
*This delightful, 17th-century Cotswold stone house was recently
opened as a hotel run by the Chapman family with their friendly
staff. The house stands in well-kept grounds with open country
views that encompass a one-acre kitchen garden that provides
vegetables and fruit for the restaurant. Ian Manfield leads the
small team in the kitchen producing modern British cuisine ; the
food is accompanied by a good selection of wines at reasonable
prices. Public areas are comfortable and are furnished in a
Victorian style whilst bedrooms vary in size and facilities. There is
a play area for older children that includes a juke box and table
tennis that adjoins a small nursery with a nanny available from
10am-6pm.*
14⇨🛏Annexe6⇨🛏 CTV in all bedrooms T S%
sB&B⇨🛏£80-£135 dB&B⇨🛏£88-£150 ➡
40P 🚲 ✿ ⊇(heated) ♪ (grass) badminton croquet games
room ₰ xmas
V ✿ ⬡ S% Lunch £14.50-£24.50 High tea fr£5 Dinner
fr£24.50&alc Last dinner 9.45pm
Credit Cards 1 2 3 5

**BRADLEY STOKE** Avon Map **03** ST68

★★★70% **Stakis Leisure Lodge** Woodlands Ln, Patchway
BS12 4JF (Stakis) ☎Almondsbury(0454)201144
Telex no 445774 FAX (0454) 612022
*Located 200 yards south of M5 junction 16 on the A38, this
modern hotel offers very good facilities for business and leisure
guests. Bedrooms are spacious with good en suite bathrooms, firm
beds and comfortable seating. There is an open plan foyer lounge
and indoor heated pool.*
112⇨(35fb)✄in 28 bedrooms CTV in all bedrooms ® T
▶

**B**

( ⊞ 132P ⊠(heated) sauna solarium gymnasium ♫
V ⊹ ⚏ ⅄ Last dinner 10pm
Credit Cards 1 2 3 5

## BRAE
See Shetland

## BRAEMAR Grampian *Aberdeenshire* Map **15** NO19
★★67%, **Braemar Lodge** Glenshee Rd AB3 5YQ
☎(03397)41627
Closed Dec & Apr
*A granite-built lodge, enjoying splendid Highland views from its two-acre grounds, has been tastefully converted to provide well-appointed bedrooms and delightful public rooms warmed by log fires. The food is worthy of note, and service throughout the hotel is willing and friendly.*
8rm(6♠) CTV in all bedrooms ® S% sB&B£15.50-£24
sB&B♠£25-£35 dB&B£31-£48 dB&B♠£50-£60 ₽
20P 1🐾 🐓 ✿
V ⊹ ⚏ ⅄ S% Dinner £15-£19.50 Last dinner 8.30pm
Credit Cards 1 3

## BRAINTREE Essex Map **05** TL72
★★66%, **White Hart** Bocking End CM7 6AB (Lansbury)
☎(0376)21401 Telex no 988835 FAX (0376) 552628
*This popular inn, a focal point of the town since the 15th century, has recently been refurbished without loss of character or charm. Well-appointed bedrooms are tastefully decorated in Laura Ashley designs, the Beefeater Steakhouse restaurant offers a range of popular dishes, and guests are assured of a warm welcome and friendly atmosphere.*
35⇥♠(4fb)1🖨⅄in 5 bedrooms CTV in all bedrooms ® T
✖ (ex guide dogs) sB&B⇥♠fr£60 dB&B⇥♠fr£72 ₽
( 40P
♈ Mainly grills V ⊹ ⅄ Lunch fr£8.50alc Dinner fr£9alc Last dinner 10.30pm
Credit Cards 1 2 3 5

## BRAITHWAITE Cumbria Map **11** NY22
★★64%, **Middle Ruddings** CA12 5RY ☎(059682)436
Telex no 934999
RS mid Nov-Mar (ex New Year)
*After extensive refurbishment, this is now a very comfortable and well-appointed hotel, quality being the keynote throughout.*
13rm(8⇥2♠)1🖨 CTV in all bedrooms ® T ✖ ✳
sB&B⇥♠fr£36 dB&B⇥♠fr£63.80 ₽
20P 2🐾 (£1) 🐓 ✿ bowls
♈ English & French ⊹ ⚏ ⅄ Bar Lunch £1.95-£6.50 Dinner fr£15.50 Last dinner 8.45pm
Credit Cards 1 3 ②

## BRAMHALL Greater Manchester Map **07** SJ88
★★★62%, **Bramhall Moat House** Bramhall Ln South SK7 2EB
(Queens Moat) ☎061-439 8116 Telex no 668464
FAX 061-440 8071
*A recently extended and refurbished hotel with well-appointed bedrooms, catering mainly for a business clientele. Very convenient for the city of Manchester and only a short distance from Manchester International Airport.*
65⇥♠ CTV in all bedrooms ® T ✖ (ex guide dogs)
Lift ( 132P sauna gymnasium
♈ English & French V ⊹ ⚏ Last dinner 9.45pm
Credit Cards 1 2 3 5

1991 marks the 25th anniversary of this guide.

## BRAMHOPE West Yorkshire Map **08** SE24
★★★69%, **Post House** Otley Rd LS16 9JJ (Trusthouse Forte)
☎Leeds(0532)842911 Telex no 556367 FAX (0532) 843451
*Comfortable accommodation is complemented by interesting menus in an hotel which enjoys an attractive rural setting whilst still being within easy reach of Leeds and the airport.*
129⇥½⅄in 30 bedrooms CTV in 130 bedrooms ® T
sB⇥½£86-£92 dB⇥½£97-£103 (room only) ₽
Lift ( 220P ✿ CFA ⊠(heated) sauna solarium gymnasium health and fitness club *xmas*
♈ French V ⊹ ⚏ ⅄ Lunch fr£12.95&alc Dinner fr£15.75&alc Last dinner 10.15pm
Credit Cards 1 2 3 4 5

## BRAMPTON Cambridgeshire Map **04** TL27
★★59%, **Grange** 115 High St PE18 8TG
☎Huntingdon(0480)459516
*Built in about 1773, and once a girls school, this friendly and comfortable family-owned hotel offers good food and facilities.*
9rm(1⇥7♠)(1fb) CTV in all bedrooms ® ✖ sB&B£25
sB&B⇥♠£25-£41.50 dB&B⇥♠£49.50-£52.50
CTV 40P ✿
♈ English & Continental V ⊹ Sunday Lunch £6.95-£8.80 Dinner £9.05-£19.50alc Last dinner 10pm
Credit Cards 1 3

## BRAMPTON Cumbria Map **12** NY56

✸★★🏅 FARLAM HALL
Hallbankgate CA8 2NG
(2.75m SE A689) (Relais et Châteaux)
☎Hallbankgate(06976)234
& 357 FAX (06976) 683
Closed Feb
(Rosette awarded for dinner only)
*Delightful wooded grounds and a gently flowing river contribute to the air of peace and quiet that enfolds this part 17th, part 19th-century house run by the Quinion and Stevenson families for more than 15 years. Throughout your stay the Quinions and their staff will treat you with an old-fashioned courtesy seldom encountered but which prevails everywhere at Farlam Hall. In the evenings around 7.30, the inn is full of expectation as guests gather to sample the excellent 4-course dinners. The cooking, mainly traditional British dishes, is refreshingly uncomplicated and free of gimmickry and only the very strong-minded will be able to resist the display of tempting home-made desserts which round off the meal.*
13⇥♠ CTV in all bedrooms T sB&B⇥♠£80-£90
dB&B⇥♠£130-£180 (incl dinner) ₽
35P 🐓 ✿ croquet nc5yrs
V ⊹ ⚏ Dinner £24-£25 Last dinner 8pm
Credit Cards 1 3

★★69%, **Tarn End** Talkin Tarn CA8 1LS (2m S off B6413)
☎(06977)2340
Closed Feb RS Oct-Jan
*This friendly, peaceful, family-run hotel on the banks of Talkin Tarn is justifiably proud of the standard of its French haute cuisine, offering à la carte and table d'hôte menus at lunch and dinner. Breakfasts also deserve commendation, and lunchtime bar snacks are available.*

6⇘♠(1fb) CTV in all bedrooms ® ✖ (ex guide dogs)
sB&B⇘♠£40 dB&B⇘♠£59.50 🅿
70P 🚗 ✿ ♪ rowing *xmas*
♀ French V ✿ ⬛ Sunday Lunch £7.50 Dinner
£15.50-£25.50alc Last dinner 9pm
Credit Cards ① ② ③ ⑤ ⓔ

---

**BRANDON** Suffolk Map **05** TL78

★★★**70%** **Brandon House** High St 1P27 0AX (Minotels)
☎Thetford(0842)810171 FAX (0842) 814859
*A detached Georgian building set back from the main road in its*
*own grounds. Consistently good standards are maintained*
*throughout and the menu offers fresh imaginative dishes.*
15⇘♠ CTV in all bedrooms ® T ✱ sB&B⇘♠£33-£44.50
dB&B⇘♠£44-£59 🅿
40P 🚗 ✿
♀ English & French V ✿ ⬛ Lunch £11.95&alc Dinner
£11.95&alc Last dinner 9.15pm
Credit Cards ① ② ③ ⓔ

**See advertisement under THETFORD**

---

**BRANDON** Warwickshire Map **04** SP47

★★★**61%** **Brandon Hall** Main St CV8 3FW (Trusthouse Forte)
☎Coventry(0203)542571 Telex no 31472 FAX (0203) 544909
*Standing in its own wooded grounds in a quaint village, this*
*company hotel has recently been refurbished to offer comfortable*
*accommodation and a range of well-equipped facilities, the most*
*popular among them being squash, snooker and pitch and putt.*
60⇘♠(4fb)⚡in 20 bedrooms CTV in all bedrooms ® T ✱
sB⇘♠£76-£86 dB⇘♠£97-£107 (room only) 🅿
《 250P ✿ squash pitch & putt ♫ *xmas*
V ✿ ⬛ ⚡ Lunch fr£9.25&alc Dinner fr£13.50&alc Last dinner
9.30pm
Credit Cards ① ② ③ ④ ⑤

---

**BRANDS HATCH** Kent Map **05** TQ56

★★★★**63%** **Brands Hatch Thistle** DA3 8PE (Mount Charlotte
(TS)) ☎West Kingsdown(0474)854900 Telex no 966449
FAX (0474) 853220
138⇘♠(7fb)1🚗⚡in 12 bedrooms CTV in all bedrooms ® T
✱ sB⇘♠£75-£88 dB⇘♠£87-£100 (room only) 🅿
《 180P ✿ ♫ *xmas*
♀ English & French V ✿ ⬛ Lunch £12.95&alc Dinner
£15.95-£17.95&alc Last dinner 10.30pm
Credit Cards ① ② ③ ④ ⑤

---

**BRANKSOME**

See **Poole**

---

**BRANSTON** Lincolnshire Map **08** TF06

★★★**54%** **Moor Lodge** LN4 1HU (Consort)
☎Lincoln(0522)791366 FAX (0522) 794389
*An interesting hotel offers a variety of accommodation, its newly*
*refurbished bedrooms providing modern facilities and the older*
*ones being more functional. The Parisien theme of the unusually*
*appointed Arnheim Restaurant helps to create a warm and*
*pleasant atmosphere in which to enjoy some fine cooking.*
25⇘♠(3fb)1🚗 CTV in all bedrooms ® T
sB&B⇘♠£57.20-£64.90 dB&B⇘♠£74.80-£85.80 🅿
CTV 150P ♪ *xmas*
♀ English & French V ✿ ⬛ Sunday Lunch fr£12.60&alc
Dinner fr£15.30&alc Last dinner 9.30pm
Credit Cards ① ② ③ ⑤ ⓔ

---

For key to symbols see the inside front cover.

---

**BRAUNTON** Devon Map **02** SS43

★★**64%** *Poyers Hotel & Restaurant* Wrafton EX33 2DV
☎(0271)812149
Closed 23 Dec-4 Jan
*An attractive thatched house standing in its own grounds near the*
*A361 features annexed bedrooms set round a cobbled courtyard ;*
*public rooms in the main building include a cosy restaurant offering*
*an à la carte menu of interesting dishes which make good use of*
*fresh produce, and the whole hotel runs smoothly under the*
*personal supervision of a resident proprietor.*
Annexe10⇘♠ CTV in all bedrooms ® T
20P 🚗 ✿
♀ English, French, German & Italian Last dinner 9.30pm
Credit Cards ① ② ③

---

**BRAY** Berkshire Map **04** SU97

❀❀✖✖✖✖ WATERSIDE, BRAY River Cottage, Ferry Rd
SL6 2AT (Relais et Châteaux) ☎Maidenhead(0628)20691 &
22941 FAX (0628) 784710
*Michel Roux has made this delightful riverside restaurant*
*synonymous with the highest levels of French cuisine in this*
*country. Books by the Roux brothers and literature about their*
*enterprises, generously distributed around the lounge and entrance*
*hall, provide a pleasant distraction for guests waiting for their*
*tables, and an appetiser for the à la carte menu which reflects a*
*balance between classical dishes, modern interpretations and*
*signature dishes such as the delightful starter of a Petit Flan*
*d'Escargots frais en habit vert. High praise also from our Inspector*
*for a perfectly cooked Tournedos with a delicate little Feuilleté of*
*creamed wild mushrooms and an intensely flavoured sauce*
*Périgourdine. A glorious caramelised Tarte Tatin with a globe of*
*apple sorbet and a very good Crème Anglaise completed the meal.*
*Service is highly professional and a knowledgeable sommelier*
*presides over a distinguished wine list that includes such rarities as*
*Château Grillet.*
Closed Mon & 7 wks fr 26 Dec
Lunch not served Tue
Dinner not served Sun (3rd wknd Oct-2nd wknd Apr)
♀ French V 70 seats S% Lunch £25.50-£50&alc Dinner
£50&alc Last lunch 2pm Last dinner 10pm 25P nc6yrs
Credit Cards ① ③ ④ ⑤

---

**BRECHFA** Dyfed Map **02** SN53

★★**67%** **Ty Mawr** SA32 7RA ☎(0267)202332
FAX (0267) 202437
*The relaxed, peaceful atmosphere is one of the virtues of this*
*attractive country hotel, and another is the good food served in its*
*restaurant. An unusual feature is the Bakery, which prepares a*
*selection of wholefood treats using only organic flour.*
5⇘(1fb) ® sB&B⇘fr£38 dB&B⇘fr£58 🅿
45P 🚗 ♪ *xmas*
V ✿ ⬛ Lunch £8.50-£12.50alc Dinner fr£17 Last dinner
9.30pm
Credit Cards ① ② ③

---

**BRECHIN** Tayside *Angus* Map **15** NO56

★★**56%** **Northern** Clerk St DD9 6AE ☎(03562)2156 & 5505
FAX (03562) 2714
RS 1 & 2 Jan
*Though modestly appointed, this family-run commercial hotel in*
*the town centre offers a homely atmosphere and traditional*
*comforts.*
17rm(4⇘11♠) CTV in all bedrooms ® T sB&B£15-£28
sB&B⇘♠£28 dB&B£30-£40 dB&B⇘♠£36-£40 🅿
20P pool table
V ✿ ⬛ Lunch £2.75-£3 High tea £4-£7 Dinner £5-£11.50alc
Last dinner 9pm
Credit Cards ① ② ③

---

**BRECON** Powys Map **03** SO02

★★67% **Wellington** The Bulwark LD3 7AD (Inter-Hotels)
☎(0874)5225
*Conveniently located right in the town centre, this Georgian hotel offers good, modern, well-equipped bedrooms and a comfortable Residents Lounge. Food of an excellent quality is served in the Dukes Bistro and Coffee Shop (open all day), whilst a cobbled arcade includes several shops, a wine bar and popular bars busy with local trade.*
21➪(1fb) CTV in all bedrooms ® T ✖ (ex guide dogs)
sB&B➪£33-£38 dB&B➪£56-£62 🅿
🅟 xmas
♥ Welsh, English & French V ⊘ ⊊ ✂ Lunch £2.10-£10alc
High tea £2.25-£3.75alc Dinner £7-£15alc Last dinner 10pm
Credit Cards ① ② ③ ⑤ ⑥

★★61% **Nant Ddu Lodge Country House** Cwm Taf CF48 2HY
(Minotels) ☎Merthyr Tydfil(0685)79111 FAX (0685) 77088
(For full entry see Nant-Ddu)

★★58% **Castle of Brecon** Castle Square LD3 9DB (Consort)
☎(0874)4611 Telex no 57515 Attn 137 FAX (0874) 3737
*Near the town centre with views across the Usk Valley towards the Brecon Beacons. A traditional coaching inn with modern, comfortable bedrooms and comfortable public areas. As far as food is concerned, there is an à la carte menu and a good range of meals from the bar.*
34➪♠Annexe12♠(3fb)1🛏 CTV in all bedrooms ® T S%
sB&B➪♠£35-£50 dB&B➪♠£50-£65 🅿
30P ✿ xmas
♥ Welsh, English & French V ⊘ S10% Lunch £12-£18alc
Dinner fr£12.50&alc Last dinner 9pm
Credit Cards ① ② ③ ④ ⑤ ⑥

★65% **Lansdowne** 39 The Watton LD3 7EG ☎(0874)3321
*This small, personally-run hotel combines character with charm and friendly service. Recent upgrading has provided comfortable bedrooms with modern private facilities.*
11rm(2➪4♠)(2fb) CTV in all bedrooms ® sB&B£19.50-£21
sB&B➪♠£22-£23.75 dB&B£33-£35.75 dB&B➪♠£38-£41 🅿
CTV 10P 🚲 ✿ pony trekking nc5yrs
♥ English & French V ⊘ ⊊ ✂ Lunch £6-£14.50alc Dinner
£6-£14.50&alc Last dinner 9.30pm
Credit Cards ① ② ③ ⑤ ⑥

**BRENT KNOLL** Somerset Map **03** ST35

★★62% **Battleborough Grange Country** Bristol Rd TA9 4HJ
(Exec Hotel) ☎(0278)760208
*This attractive, detached hotel is set in its own grounds overlooking the Somerset countryside. Décor is pleasant throughout and the hotel provides modern bedrooms and attentive service.*
18rm(8➪6♠)4🛏 CTV in all bedrooms ® T ✖ ✲
sB&B£28-£30 sB&B➪♠£42-£48 dB&B£40-£46
dB&B➪♠£52-£62 🅿
CTV 60P ✿ nc8yrs xmas
♥ English & French V ⊘ ⊊
Credit Cards ① ② ③ ⑤ ⑥

**BRENTWOOD** Essex Map **05** TQ59

★★★66% **Post House** Brook St CM14 5NF (Trusthouse Forte)
☎(0277)260260 Telex no 995379 FAX (0277) 264264
*This hotel is conveniently situated close to the M25/A12 interchange and guests will find ample parking space. The modern bedrooms include some family rooms and all have en suite bath/ shower rooms and are equipped with all the usual facilities, including a mini-bar. For meals, guests can choose between the coffee shop, open throughout the day for light meals, the Oak Bar for lunches, or the Woodland Restaurant which offers both an à la carte and a 'selection of the day' menu. For relaxation there is a health and fitness club with a heated indoor swimming pool.*
120➪✂in 30 bedrooms CTV in all bedrooms ®

Lift ⊄ 148P ✿ CFA ⊟(heated) sauna solarium gymnasium
health & fitness club
♥ International V ⊘ ⊊ ✂ Last dinner 10pm
Credit Cards ① ② ③ ④ ⑤

**BRETBY** Derbyshire Map **08** SK22

★★★64% **Stanhope** Ashby Rd East DE15 0PU (Lansbury)
☎Burton upon Trent(0283)217954 Telex no 347185
FAX (0283) 226199
*The hotel stands by the busy A50 road, but peace can be found at the back of the hotel where there are well-maintained, terraced gardens for guests to relax in. The bedrooms are warm and comfortable, the bar is friendly and the restaurant has been elegantly furnished.*
28➪♠(1fb)1🛏✂in 5 bedrooms CTV in all bedrooms ® T
✖ (ex guide dogs) sB&B➪♠fr£64 dB&B➪♠fr£76 🅿
⊄ 150P ✿ sauna solarium gymnasium 🎯 xmas
♥ Continental V ⊘ ✂ Lunch fr£8&alc Dinner fr£14&alc Last
dinner 10pm
Credit Cards ① ② ③ ⑤

**BRIDGEND**

See Islay, Isle of

**BRIDGEND** Mid Glamorgan Map **03** SS97

★★★71% **Coed-y-Mwstwr** Coychurch CF35 6AF (WR)
☎(0656)860621 FAX (0656) 863122
*A Victorian mansion set in acres of woodland just three miles from juction 35 of the M4 provides bedrooms of excellent quality in a comfortable lounge and bar warmed by a welcoming log fire in cooler weather. Dishes served from the restaurant's four-course menu are all of a very high standard, and service is friendly and attentive throughout the hotel.*
28➪♠ CTV in all bedrooms T ✖ (ex guide dogs)
sB&B➪♠£79.50-£90
dB&B➪♠£90-£140 Continental breakfast 🅿
Lift ⊄ 60P ✿ ⊟(heated) ♪ (hard) snooker 🎵 nc7yrs
♥ French V ⊘ ⊊ Lunch £14.95-£19.95 Dinner £23.95-£25.95
Last dinner 10pm
Credit Cards ① ② ③ ⑤

★★★64% **Heronston** Ewenny CF35 5AW (2m S B4265)
☎(0656)668811 Telex no 498232 FAX (0656) 767391
Closed 25-26 Dec & 1 Jan
*This modern commercial hotel provides excellent leisure and conference facilities. It is situated just south of the A48, the staff are friendly and helpful. Bedrooms are well furnished and equipped, and public areas are spacious and comfortable.*
76➪♠(4fb) CTV in all bedrooms ® T ✖ sB&B➪♠£50-£65
dB&B➪♠£66-£82 🅿
Lift ⊄ CTV 175P 🚲 CFA ⊟(heated) ⊇(heated) snooker
sauna solarium turkish bath jacuzzi
♥ Welsh & French V ⊘ ⊊ Lunch fr£12.50&alc Dinner
fr£12.50&alc Last dinner 10pm
Credit Cards ① ② ③ ④ ⑤

★★58% *Court Colman* Pen-y-Fai CF31 4NG
☎Aberkenfig(0656)720212
*This imposing house, originally a gentleman's country residence, is set amidst woodland and lawns. Inside, there are panelled walls and several beautiful fireplaces. Bedrooms are spacious, public rooms are comfortable and elegant.*
26➪♠(7fb)2🛏 CTV in all bedrooms ®
150P ✿ solarium
⊘ ⊊ Last dinner 9.45pm
Credit Cards ① ② ③ ⑤

1991 marks the 25th anniversary of this guide.

★★54% **Wyndham** Dunraven Place CF31 1JE
☎(0656)652080 & 57431 FAX (0656) 766438
*A busy town centre hotel with popular bars and an attractive restaurant offers friendly service and reasonably well equipped bedrooms; parking is difficult, however, though there are public car parks not too far away.*
28rm(25⇨)1 🛏 CTV in all bedrooms ®
《CTV ♪
♀ English & French V ♥ ⊱ Last dinner 10pm
Credit Cards ①②③⑤

⇧**TraveLodge** Sarn Park Motorway Services CF32 9RW
(Trusthouse Forte) ☎(0656)659218
(For full entry see Sarn Park Motorway Service Area (M4))

**BRIDGE OF ALLAN** Central *Stirlingshire* Map **11** NS79
★★★62% **Royal** Henderson St FK9 4HG ☎(0786)832284
FAX (0786) 834377
*A commercial and tourist hotel right at the centre of town. The general improvement programme is making good progress: the bedrooms and smart restaurant, where work is completed, are evidence of the high standards the proprietors aim to achieve throughout the hotel.*
32⇨ℕ(2fb) CTV in all bedrooms ® T sB&B⇨ℕ£46-£56
dB&B⇨ℕ£69-£80 🅿
Lift 《 60P *xmas*
♀ Scottish & French V ♥ ⊿ Lunch £9.60-£10.95&alc High tea
£5.95-£8.50 Dinner £15.25-£17.25&alc Last dinner 9.30pm
Credit Cards ①②③⑤
**See advertisement under STIRLING**

✗✗**Kipling's Restaurant** Mine Rd FK9 4DT
☎Stirling(0786)833617
*The agreeable restaurant, set in a quiet residential area high above the town, enjoys a sound local reputation for honest unpretentious cooking. An enthusiastic chef/patron will advise on à la carte menus which regularly feature an interesting range of game and seafood dishes, while a keen young team offers courteous service.*
Closed Sun, Mon, 24 Dec-3 Jan & 1st 2 wks Aug
V 68 seats Last lunch 2pm Last dinner 9.30pm 20P
Credit Cards ①②③

**BRIDGE OF CALLY** Tayside *Perthshire* Map **15** NO15
★65% **Bridge of Cally** PH10 7JJ ☎(025086)231
Closed Nov & 1st 2 wks Dec
*Set in its own well tended garden beside the River Ardle, this small, family-run holiday hotel is also a popular base for the sporting and ski enthusiasts. It has a friendly atmosphere, and enjoyable food is served on candlelit tables in the neatly appointed dining room. Bedrooms, though compact, are cheery and comfortable.*
9rm(3⇨3ℕ) ✗ (ex guide dogs) sB&B£23-£24
dB&B£39.70-£40.70 dB&B⇨ℕ£41.90-£42.90 🅿
CTV 40P 👶 ❀ ♪
V ♥ ⊿ Lunch £5.45-£8.50alc Dinner £12.50-£16 Last dinner
9pm
Credit Cards ①③⑤
**See advertisement on page 161**

**BRIDGNORTH** Shropshire Map **07** SO79
★★65% **Parlors Hall** Mill St WV15 5AL ☎(0746)761931
FAX (0746) 767058
*Parts of this fine, mainly Georgian building date from the 15th century, when it was owned by Richard Parlour, whose name it still bears. Set on the one-way system in Lower Town, a short walk from the riverside park and bridge, it offers well equipped bedrooms and public areas, the latter having some fine fireplaces and excellent carved panelling; the restaurant enjoys a particularly pleasant outlook over an enclosed garden, dominated* ▶

**B**

# *the* HERONSTON HOTEL
★ ★ ★
## Ewenny, Bridgend, Mid Glamorgan CF35 5AW
Telephone: (0656) 668811
Fax: (0656) 767391
Telex: 498232
Modern popular hotel with comfortable bedrooms, friendly service and good leisure facilities.

# Battleborough Grange Country Hotel ★★
*BRISTOL ROAD – BRENT KNOLL – SOMERSET*
*Telephone: (0278) 760208*
**GUEST ACCOM Good Room Award**

Surrounded by Somerset countryside nestles in its own grounds at the foot of the historic iron age fort known as Brent Knoll. Excellent accommodation includes spa baths, four posters and luxury suites. All bedrooms have direct dial telephones, colour TV, and tea & coffee making facilities. Our restaurant with a renowned reputation offers both à la carte and table d'hôte menus. Ideal centre for touring Bristol, Bath, Wells, Cheddar, Glastonbury, Longleat and Exmoor. 6 miles Weston Super Mare 3 miles Burnham on Sea (golf course). Ample parking. 1 mile from junc 22 of M5.

*by a large willow tree, and the food served here is sound, although not particularly adventurous.*
16rm(10⇄2🌑)(1fb)2🎏 CTV in all bedrooms Ⓡ T ✹ (ex guide dogs) ✱ sB&B⇄🌑£42 dB&B⇄🌑£50
24P *xmas*
🍴 European V ✿ 🍷
Credit Cards ①③

★★**61%**, **Falcon** St John St, Lowtown WV15 6AG
☎(0746)763134 FAX (0746) 765401
*Old coaching inn in Lowtown, close to River Severn.*
15rm(5⇄7🌑)(3fb) CTV in all bedrooms Ⓡ T sB&Bfr£27.50 sB&B⇄🌑fr£38 dB&B⇄🌑fr£45-£48 🍴
CTV 200P
🍴 English & French V ✿ 🍷 Lunch £10.50-£22alc Dinner £10.50-£25alc Last dinner 9.30pm
Credit Cards ①②③④

★**68%**, **Croft** St Mary's St WV16 6DW (Guestaccom)
☎(0746)762416
*Guests are assured of warm hospitality at this small, town-centre hotel with its well-equipped bedrooms and satisfying, nourishing meals.*
12rm(4⇄6🌑)(3fb) CTV in all bedrooms T ✱ sB&B£22-£24 sB&B⇄🌑fr£40 dB&B⇄🌑fr£48 🍴
CTV 🅿 🎏
V ✿ 🍷 S% Lunch £4.95-£6.95 Dinner £9.95-£13.95 Last dinner 9pm
Credit Cards ①②③

★**65%**, *Whitburn Grange* 35 Salop St WV16 5BH ☎(0746)766786
*A busy well-equipped hotel situated on the old Low Town road close to the Severn Valley Railway Station. Friendly, helpful staff ensure guests have a comfortable stay.*
9rm(2⇄2🌑)Annexe6rm(1⇄)(3fb)1🎏 CTV in all bedrooms Ⓡ
CTV 9P
✿ 🍷
Credit Cards ①②③

---

**BRIDGWATER** Somerset Map 03 ST33

★★★**68%**, **Walnut Tree Inn** North Petherton TA6 6QA (3m S A38) (Best Western) ☎North Petherton(0278)662255
Telex no 46529 FAX (0278) 663946
*A warm welcome and cosy atmosphere are the hallmarks of this busy, commercial High Street hotel. Once a coaching inn, it has now been extended to offer a range of bedrooms that includes those in the luxury class as well as less elaborate chalet accommodation. Similarly, guests can choose between the formal à la carte menus of the dining room, simpler meals served in the Cottage Restaurant, and bar snacks.*
28⇄(2fb)1🎏 CTV in all bedrooms Ⓡ T ✹ (ex guide dogs) sB&B⇄🌑£46-£52 dB&B⇄🌑£62-£74 🍴
ⓒ 70P solarium
🍴 Mainly grills V ✿ 🍷 Lunch £7.50-£13alc Dinner £7.50-£13alc Last dinner 10pm
Credit Cards ①②③⑤ⓔ

★★**64%**, **Friarn Court** 37 St Mary St TA6 3LX ☎(0278)452859
FAX (0278) 452988
*Close to the town centre and recently converted to provide quality bedrooms with modern facilities – all is new and in good order, though the public rooms are small. The proprietor runs the hotel personally with warm hospitality. An all day menu is served in the restaurant.*
12⇄🌑(2fb)1🎏 CTV in all bedrooms Ⓡ T ✹ (ex guide dogs) ✱ sB&B⇄🌑£39.50-£54.50
dB&B⇄🌑£44.50-£69.50 Continental breakfast 🍴
ⓒ 12P *xmas*
🍴 English & French V ✿ 🍷 Lunch £8-£10&alc High tea £4-£6 Dinner £8-£10&alc Last dinner 9.30pm
Credit Cards ①②③⑤ⓔ

---

**BRIDLINGTON** Humberside Map 08 TA16

★★★**66%** **Expanse** North Marine Dr YO15 2LS
☎(0262)675347 FAX (0262) 604928
*Comfortable, well-appointed bedrooms, a wealth of cosy lounges and particularly friendly service are the attractions of this large sea-front hotel.*
48⇄🌑(4fb) CTV in all bedrooms Ⓡ T ✹ (ex guide dogs) sB&B⇄🌑£37.50-£42 dB&B⇄🌑£61-£67 🍴
Lift ⓒ 15P 15⛵ (£1.50) 🎏 *xmas*
🍴 English & French V ✿ 🍷 Lunch £6.50-£7 Dinner £11&alc Last dinner 9pm
Credit Cards ①②③⑤

★★**67%** **Monarch** South Marine Dr YO15 3JJ (Consort)
☎(0262)674447 Telex no 57515 FAX (0262) 604928
Closed 18 Dec-7 Jan
*A comfortable friendly sea-front hotel offering very good value menus.*
40rm(36⇄🌑)(5fb) CTV in all bedrooms Ⓡ T ✹ (ex guide dogs) ✱ sB&B⇄🌑£38-£45 dB&B£50 dB&B⇄🌑£60 🍴
Lift ⓒ CTV 10P 🎏
🍴 English & French V ✿ 🍽 Lunch £6-£12 Dinner £12-£14&alc Last dinner 8.30pm
Credit Cards ①②③⑤ⓕ

★★**66%** **New Revelstoke** 1-3 Flamborough Rd YO15 2HY
☎(0262)672362
*A hotel of pleasing proportions close to the town's facilities and North Sands. It is managed by the resident proprietors who are assisted by their family and the keen, young staff. Bedrooms are well-appointed and generally spacious.*
25rm(17⇄3🌑)(5fb) CTV in all bedrooms Ⓡ T ✹ ✱ sB&B£35.50-£45.50 sB&B⇄🌑£35.50-£45.50 dB&B£55-£70 dB&B⇄🌑£55-£70 🍴

▶

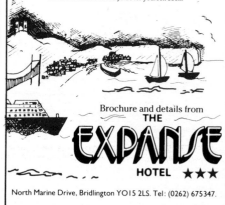

# ★★ Royal Clarence Hotel

THE ESPLANADE, BURNHAM-ON-SEA,
SOMERSET TA8 1BQ
Telephone: 0278 783138

● Good Food ● Pleasant Surroundings ● A Great Range of Beers ● Comfortable Accommodation What more could anybody want?
The Royal Clarence Hotel is the place for you if you're looking for the good life. All our rooms are equipped with drinks facilities, colour televisions and radios. Bathrooms en suite are also available. Situated on the seafront, the Hotel offers something for everybody. The Hotel has three bars to choose from, a first class restaurant and also a function room with dance floor and bar.

● Wedding Receptions ● Discos ● Formal Functions ● Etc.

So if you want to get away from it all for a few days or even a few hours, why not visit the Royal Clarence Hotel at Burnham-on-Sea.

---

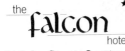 the **falcon** ★★ hotel  B

St John Street, Lowtown,
Bridgnorth, Shropshire WV15 6AG
Telephone: Bridgnorth (0746) 763134
Fax: (0746) 765401

A grade 2 listed 16th Century Coaching Inn, near the banks of the River Severn. The Falcon Hotel offers the kind of hospitality typical of the best English Rural Inn.

The recently refurbished bedrooms, tastefully furnished and equipped with every modern convenience, assure guests of a comfortable and relaxing stay.

A wide variety of food is offered, complemented by a well stocked bar serving several real ales.

The Falcon makes the ideal base to visit the many attractions of Shropshire, the Severn Valley Railway and Ironbridge Gorge to name but a few.

Our Falcon suite is available for private parties, conferences, exhibitions and wedding receptions.

**EGON RONAY RECOMMENDED**

---

# THE WALNUT TREE INN

AA ★ ★ ★

**North Petherton · Bridgwater · Somerset
On A38 (Exit 24 M5 One Mile) Nr. Bridgwater**
You will get a warm welcome at The Walnut Tree Inn. Your comfortable bedroom will have its own bathroom and you can watch TV while you make a cup of tea, or call home on your direct-dial telephone. There is ample parking space for your car. After a relaxing drink in the friendly bar, you can enjoy a pleasant dinner in the charming à la carte restaurant, or a more casual meal if you wish in the Cottage Grill Room.
**PLEASE CALL NORTH PETHERTON (0278) 662255 FOR YOUR RESERVATION.**

---

# Bridge of Cally Hotel

Perthshire PH10 7JJ          ★
Tel: Bridge of Cally 231

Situated on the A93 Braemar Road overlooking the River Ardle surrounded by woodland and the Perthshire hills. Fishing, golf, pony trekking, skiing all available nearby. Nine bedrooms six with private bath. Fully licensed. Restaurant. Noted for good food. Residents' lounge with colour TV. Brochure and tariff on application. Closed end Oct-mid Dec.

**B**

14P

♀ English & French V ✿ ⚗ Lunch £4.10-£10&alc Dinner
£10.50&alc Last dinner 8.30pm
Credit Cards ①②③⑤ ⓔ

---

### BRIDPORT Dorset Map 03 SY49

★★★62% **Haddon House** West Bay DT6 4EL (2m S off B3157
Weymouth rd) ☎(0308)23626 & 25323
*The atmosphere is relaxed and informal at this Regency-style hotel
with its comfortable lounge and spacious, simply furnished but well
equipped bedrooms. An attractive dining room with panelled walls
and a large fireplace offers a varied menu of dishes which make
skilfull use of good produce, local fish being a speciality.*
13↪ℝ(2fb) CTV in all bedrooms ⓡ T
sB&B↪ℝ£39.50-£42.50 dB&B↪ℝ£45-£55 🄿
CTV 70P 4🎱 ✿ *xmas*
♀ English & French V ✿ Lunch £9.95 Dinner £14.50 Last
dinner 9pm
Credit Cards ①②③⑤

★★68% **Roundham House** Roundham Gardens, West Bay Rd
DT6 4BD (Exec Hotel) ☎(0308)22753 & 25779 Telex no 417182
FAX (0308) 421145
Closed mid Nov-Jan
*A solidly built turn-of-the-century house in an elevated position is
personally run by resident proprietors to provide friendly service
and a well priced dinner menu based on fresh local produce ;
recently upgraded bedrooms are comprehensively equipped and
very comfortable.*
8rm(4↪3ℝ)(2fb) CTV in all bedrooms ⓡ T 🏵 ✳
sB&B↪ℝ£27.50-£34 dB&B↪ℝ£39.50-£51.50 🄿
12P ✿
♀ English & French V ✿ ⚗ ✝ Bar Lunch £1.50-£5alc Dinner
£12-£13.50 Last dinner 8.15pm
Credit Cards ①②③⑤ ⓔ

★★67% **Eype's Mouth Country** Eype DT6 6AL (2m SW)
☎(0308)23300
*Set in rural surroundings just five minutes from the sea and coastal
footpath this is a friendly hotel with very clean, well-equipped
bedrooms. Dinner dances are held in the large dining room.*
18↪ℝ1🍴 CTV in all bedrooms ⓡ T sB&B↪ℝfr£37.50
dB&B↪ℝfr£48 🄿
55P ♫ *xmas*
♀ English & French V ✿ ⚗ Lunch fr£6.95&alc Dinner
fr£10.50&alc Last dinner 9pm
Credit Cards ①③

★★57% *Bull* 34 East St DT6 3LF ☎(0308)22878
Closed 24-26 Dec
*A greatly improved town centre hotel, personally supervised by
proprietors who create an intimate, friendly atmosphere, offers
pleasantly appointed, well equipped bedrooms and an attractive
dining room where guests can enjoy an interesting range of
competently prepared dishes.*
22rm(5↪3ℝ)(1fb) CTV in 16 bedrooms ⓡ 🏵
40P 2🎱 🚗 snooker
♀ French ✿
Credit Cards ①③

★56% **Bridport Arms** West Bay DT6 4EN (2m S off B3157
Weymouth rd) ☎(0308)22994
*A thatched inn situated right on the beach. Simple accommodation
is enhanced by warm, friendly service.*
8rm(1↪5ℝ)(2fb) CTV in all bedrooms ⓡ sB&B£19.50-£23.50
sB&B↪ℝ£24-£27.50 dB&B£37-£42 dB&B↪ℝ£45-£55 🄿
CTV 4🎱
V ✿ ✝ Sunday Lunch £6.95-£7.95 Dinner £8.50-£12.95alc Last
dinner 8.45pm
Credit Cards ①③ ⓔ

---

### BRIGHOUSE West Yorkshire Map 07 SE12

★★★★62% **Forte Hotel** Clifton Village HD6 4HW (Trusthouse
Forte) ☎(0484)400400 Telex no 518204 FAX (0484) 400068
*A new hotel built of York stone to blend in with the environment. It
lies in an elevated position just off the A644 close to Junction 25 of
the M62. Bedrooms are comfortable and well-appointed. There
are extensive conference facilities as well as a health and fitness
club.*
94↪ℝ(20fb)✝in 23 bedrooms CTV in all bedrooms ⓡ T S%
sB↪ℝfr£92 dB↪ℝfr£103 (room only) 🄿
⚄155P ✿ ▣(heated) sauna solarium gymnasium croquet *xmas*
♀ British & French V ✿ ⚗ ✝ S% Lunch fr£12 Dinner fr£17
Last dinner 10pm
Credit Cards ①②③④⑤

---

### BRIGHTON & HOVE East Sussex Map 04 TQ30

See **Town Plan Section**
See also **Rottingdean**

★★★58% **Courtlands** 19-27 The Drive BN3 3JE
☎Brighton(0273)731055 Telex no 87574 FAX (0273) 28295
*Situated in a wide tree-lined avenue close to the seafront and town,
this hotel has a nicely appointed restaurant with a choice of menus,
a cosy bar and a variety of bedrooms. Leisure facilities include a
swimming pool, spa and solarium.*
53↪ℝAnnexe5↪ℝ(3fb) CTV in all bedrooms ⓡ T ✳
sB&B↪ℝfr£60 dB&B↪ℝfr£80 🄿
Lift ⚄ CTV 26P ✿ CFA ▣(heated) solarium *xmas*
♀ International V ✿ ⚗ ✝ Lunch fr£9.75&alc Dinner
fr£12.75&alc Last dinner 9.30pm
Credit Cards ①②③⑤

★★70% **Whitehaven** 34 Wilbury Rd BN3 3JP
☎Brighton(0273)778355 Telex no 877159 FAX (0273) 731177
*This pleasantly welcoming hotel offers well equipped modern
accommodation. The Rolling Clock Restaurant is elegant and
offers a good selection of well prepared dishes made from quality
ingredients. There is a charming cosy bar and delightfully
appointed lounge. Service is attentive and caring.*
17↪ℝ(2fb)1🍴 CTV in all bedrooms ⓡ T 🏵 S%
sB&B↪ℝ£42-£51 dB&B↪ℝ£56-£69 🄿
🄿 🚗 solarium nc8yrs
♀ French V ✿ ⚗ Lunch £13.50-£16.50 Dinner £13.50-£16.50
Last dinner 9.30pm
Credit Cards ①②③⑤ ⓔ

★★62% **St Catherines Lodge** Seafront, Kingsway BN3 2RZ
(Inter-Hotels) ☎Brighton(0273)778181 Telex no 877073
FAX (0273) 774949
*This Regency-style hotel, conveniently situated opposite the
seafront Hove Leisure Centre, offers a choice of bedrooms, and
attractive restaurant and a small, wood-panelled bar, service being
well-supervised but friendly throughout.*
50rm(40↪ℝ)(4fb)🍴 CTV in all bedrooms T S10%
sB&Bfr£36 sB&B↪ℝfr£45 dB&Bfr£54 dB&B↪ℝfr£65 🄿
Lift ⚄ CTV 5P 4🎱 (£4) CFA games room *xmas*
♀ European V ✿ ⚗ S10% Lunch £4.50-£6.95&alc Dinner
£9.50-£13.50&alc Last dinner 9pm
Credit Cards ①②③⑤ ⓔ

✕✕✕**Eaton Garden** Eaton Gardens BN3 3TN
☎Brighton(0273)738921 Telex no 877247 FAX (0273) 779201
*A well appointed restaurant, conveniently situated in the
commercial centre of Hove, maintains sound traditional values,
offering skilled, attentive service ; John Stevens – chef here for the
past 22 years – prepares an enjoyable range of English and
Continental dishes, their flavours enhanced with robust sauces.*
♀ International V 100 seats ✳ Lunch fr£13&alc Dinner
£16-£17.50&alc Last lunch 2.15pm Last dinner 9.45pm 40P ✝
Credit Cards ①②③⑤

✕**Chai Talay** 67 Church Rd BN3 2BD ☎Brighton(0273)771170
*This small family-run Thai restaurant (it's name literally means
'by the seaside') features an extensive and informative menu of
authentic dishes which are skilfully prepared using the best
ingredients.*
Closed Mon
♀ Thai **V** 46 seats ✱ S10% Lunch £12-£16alc Last lunch 2pm
Last dinner 10.30pm ♪ nc5yrs
Credit Cards [1] [2] [3] [5]

✕**Hayward's** 51/52 North St BN1 1RH ☎Brighton(0273)24261
*An attractive, modern, first-floor brasserie in the town centre offers
an all-day menu ranging from simple salads to good soufflés and
steaks, additional dishes such as Breast of Guinea Fowl with
Sherry Vinegar Sauce demonstrating the chef's capabilities in a
more refined style of cooking. A short, sensible wine list is
available, and service is efficiently carried out by smart, charming
staff.*
Closed Sun & 25 Dec
♀ English & Continental **V** 70 seats ✱ Lunch fr£12&alc
Dinner £12-£22alc Last lunch 3pm Last dinner 11pm ♪ ♫
Credit Cards [1] [2] [3]

✕**Le Grandgousier** 15 Western St BN1 2PG
☎Brighton(0273)772005
*A small but well-established French restaurant , run by Lewis
Harris. The 6 course fixed price menu, which includes a half bottle
of French table wine, is especially good value, and you can eat as
little or as much as you like.*
Closed Sun & 23 Dec-3 Jan
Lunch not served Sat
♀ French 36 seats S15% Lunch £13.50-£25 Last lunch 1.30pm
Last dinner 9.30pm ♪ nc5yrs
Credit Cards [1] [2] [3]

✕**Whyte's** 33 Western St BN1 2PG ☎Brighton(0273)776618
*Chef patron Ian, and Jane Whyte co-ordinate their skills in
personally running this small, cosy and attractively furnished
restaurant. It features a chef's Fish of the Day as well as a choice
of prix fix courses which might include scallops in white wine au
gratin, coarse duck liver paté, roast rack of lamb with cassis,
supreme of wild salmon and a good selection of desserts and
cheeses. Service is particularly attentive and helpful, under the
supervision of Jane Whyte. Some interesting wines are available to
accompany a meal which represents good value for money.*
Closed Sun
Lunch not served (ex by prior arrangement)
♀ English & French 36 seats ✱ Dinner £15.75 Last dinner
10pm ♪
Credit Cards [1] [2] [3]

**BRIMFIELD** Hereford & Worcester Map **07** SO56

○**Travelodge** A49/B4362 Woofferton(Trusthouse Forte)
☎Central reservations (0800) 850950
Due to have opened summer 1990
32⇆

❀✕**Poppies** Roebuck Inn SY8 4LN ☎(058472)230
*The Roebuck Inn stands in the centre of the village – at the rear,
John and Carole Evans have built up Poppies Restaurant, where
Carole, a self-taught cook, continues to improve the interest and
quality of her menu. The menu is a tempting range of dishes,
making good use of the best local produce. Choices include starters
such as spinach soufflé with anchovy hollandaise and fresh pear
with stilton and walnut sauce. For the main course, diners enjoy
brill with scallops on a bed of sorrel and salmon with ginger in a
cream, vermouth and chive sauce. Desserts are a treat not to be
missed – poppyseed parfait with a ragout of dates, or old favourites
such as bread and butter pudding.*
Closed Sun, Mon, 1 wk Oct & 2 wks Feb
**V** 40 seats ✱ Lunch £15-£24alc Dinner £15-£24alc Last lunch
2pm Last dinner 10pm 30P ✂
Credit Cards [1] [3]

**BRISTOL** Avon Map **03** ST57
See **Town Plan Section**
★★★★57% *Holiday Inn* Lower Castle St BS1 3AD (Holiday
Inns) ☎(0272)294281 Telex no 449720 FAX (0272) 225838
*A large, busy hotel close to the city centre complements spacious,
well-equipped accommodation by extensive conference and
function facilities. Guests can relax in a heated swimming pool,
solarium or gymnasium.*
284⇆🛏(138fb)⤪in 78 bedrooms CTV in all bedrooms
Lift ( ▦ 20✿ CFA ⊡(heated) sauna solarium gymnasium
♀ International **V** ✆ ⚿ ✂ Last dinner 10.45pm
Credit Cards [1] [2] [3] [4] [5]

★★★69% **Redwood Lodge & Country Club** Beggar Bush Ln,
Failand BS8 3TG (2m W of Clifton Bridge on B3129)
☎(0272)393901 Telex no 444348 FAX (0272) 392104
*Signposted off the A369 west of the city centre this hotel, now
extensively refurbished, offers attractive open plan public areas,
very well equipped bedrooms, an excellent range of leisure facilities
and good conference rooms.*
112⇆🛏 CTV in all bedrooms ⓡ **T** ✖ (ex guide dogs) S%
sB&B⇆£88-£99 dB&B⇆£99-£115 ℝ
( CTV 1000P ✿ CFA ⊡(heated) ⌿ ♙ (hard) squash snooker
sauna solarium gymnasium badminton cinema (wknds only)
xmas
♀ English & French **V** ✆ ⚿ ✂ S% Lunch fr£11 Dinner fr£16
Last dinner 10pm
Credit Cards [1] [2] [3] [5] [£]

★★★68% **Crest** Filton Rd, Hambrook BS16 1QX (6m NE off
A4174) (Trusthouse Forte) ☎(0272)564242 Telex no 449376
FAX (0272) 569735
*Set in sixteen acres, with easy access to the M4, M5 and M32
motorways, the modern hotel offers comfortable, well-equipped
accommodation which includes a new wing of upgraded executive
rooms. Among its facilities are the Crest Business Centre, an all-* ▶

# Thornbury Castle ★★★

This beautiful 16th century Castle, built by
Edward Stafford, 3rd Duke of Buckingham,
was once owned by Henry VIII who stayed here
in 1535 with Anne Boleyn. It is the only Tudor
Castle in England operated as an hotel, offering award-winning cuisine and luxurious
accommodation. Some rooms with four-
posters and views of the Tudor gardens.
*Described as one of the '300 Best Hotels in
the World' (Lecler/Harpers and Queen).*

**Thornbury, Avon, BS12 1HH**
**Telephone: (0454) 418511**
**Telex: 449986 Castle G. Fax: (0454) 416188**
*A Pride of Britain Hotel*

*day coffee shop, a leisure club and a well-appointed restaurant serving a wide choice of skilfully-prepared dishes – all complemented by genuine, caring hospitality on the part of the staff.*
197⇌∩(14fb)⊬in 43 bedrooms CTV in all bedrooms ® T (room only) ⊟
Lift ☾ 400P ❁ CFA ▭(heated) sauna solarium gymnasium *xmas*
V ♧ ⊻ ⊬
Credit Cards 1 2 3 5

**★★★65% Avon Gorge** Sion Hill, Clifton BS8 4LD (Mount Charlotte (TS)) ☎(0272)738955 Telex no 444237 FAX (0272) 238125
*Enjoying fine views of the Clifton suspension bridge, this hotel has undergone considerable refurbishment to provide comfortable, well-equipped bedrooms and a choice of eating options. There are plans to extend the public areas and provide a much-needed car park.*
76⇌(6fb)2⊞⊬in 2 bedrooms CTV in all bedrooms ® T sB⇌£67.50-£72.50 dB⇌£79.50-£95 (room only) ⊟
Lift ☾ 20P ❁ CFA ♫ *xmas*
♁ English & French V ♧ ⊻ Lunch fr£10.75&alc High tea fr£3.50 Dinner fr£13&alc Last dinner 10.30pm
Credit Cards 1 2 3 5 £

**★★★63% Henbury Lodge** Station Rd, Henbury BS10 7QQ (4.5m NW of City centre off B4055) ☎(0272)502615 FAX (0272) 509532
*A Georgian country-style hotel situated north of the city close to the M5, and run by the Pearce family. Bedrooms are spacious and well equipped and the food is imaginative and well prepared.*
10⇌∩Annexe6⇌∩(4fb)⊬in 6 bedrooms CTV in all bedrooms ® T sB&B⇌∩£64.50-£74.50 dB&B⇌∩£74.50-£84.50 ⊟
24P ⊞ ❁ sauna solarium gymnasium *xmas*
♁ English & Continental V ♧ ⊻ ⊬ Lunch £12.80 Dinner £14.80 Last dinner 9pm
Credit Cards 1 2 3 5 £

**★★★52% Unicorn** Prince St BS1 4QF (Rank) ☎(0272)230333 Telex no 44315 FAX (0272) 230300
*This modern hotel on the waterfront offers bright, attractive public areas and a good range of facilities which includes a wide choice of eating options. A bedroom refurbishment programme is currently improving both facilities and standards, the new Reserve rooms being spacious and well equipped though many of the Study bedrooms are very compact.*
247⇌∩(29fb) CTV in all bedrooms ® T ✱ sB⇌∩£49-£65 dB⇌∩£75-£85 (room only) ⊟
Lift ☾ 400⊞ CFA *xmas*
♁ International V ♧ ⊻ Lunch fr£10.50&alc Dinner fr£14&alc Last dinner 10pm
Credit Cards 1 2 3 4 5

**★★★50% St Vincent Rocks** Sion Hill, Clifton BS8 4BB (Trusthouse Forte) ☎(0272)739251 Telex no 444932 FAX (0272) 238139
*Some of the rooms of this hotel afford good views of the Avon Gorge and the Clifton Suspension Bridge, near which it stands. Much of the accommodation has been refurbished to a good standard, though there is still work to be done, and the friendly, helpful service provided throughout contributes to its popularity.*
46⇌∩⊬in 7 bedrooms CTV in all bedrooms ® T ✱ S10% sB⇌∩£62-£80 dB⇌∩£77-£100 (room only) ⊟
☾ CTV 18P CFA *xmas*
V ♧ ⊻ ⊬ S10% Lunch £8.50-£10.50&alc Dinner £14-£16.95&alc Last dinner 9.30pm
Credit Cards 1 2 3 4 5

**★★67% Rodney Hotel** Rodney Place, Clifton BS8 4HY ☎(0272)735422 Telex no 449075 FAX (0272) 741082
*Dating back to the eighteenth century and refurbished recently to provide attractive, comfortable accommodation, the hotel complements well-equipped modern bedrooms with public areas which, though limited, are of a good quality – the restaurant featuring a concise, selective à la carte menu that is understandably popular with businessman and tourist alike.*
31⇌∩⊬in 2 bedrooms CTV in all bedrooms ® T sB&B⇌∩£54-£58 dB&B⇌∩£81-£86 ⊟
☾ P̸
♁ English & French V ♧ ⊻ Bar Lunch £1.95-£9.85alc Dinner £12&alc Last dinner 10pm
Credit Cards 1 2 3 5

**★★65% *Parkside*** 470 Bath Rd, Brislington BS4 3HQ ☎(0272)711461 FAX (0272) 715507
*Set on the A4, only a mile from the city centre, the complex of this attractive, character hotel includes its own nightclub, a snooker room and two bars.*
30rm(9⇌1∩)1⊞ CTV in all bedrooms ® T
☾ ⊞ 250P ❁ snooker
V ♧ ⊻ Last dinner 10.30pm
Credit Cards 1 3

**★★62% Clifton** St Pauls Rd, Clifton BS8 1LX ☎(0272)736882 Telex no 449075 FAX (0272) 741082
*This successful hotel, close to University and city centre, offers accommodation with good facilities (though some single rooms are compact) which is particularly popular with business travellers. The vaulted 1930's – style wine bar and Races Restaurant have a lively, informal atmosphere.*
64rm(4⇌41∩)(4fb)⊬in 8 bedrooms CTV in all bedrooms ® T sB&Bfr£28 sB&B⇌∩fr£46 dB&Bfr£46 dB&B⇌∩fr£66 ⊟
Lift ☾ 12P
▶

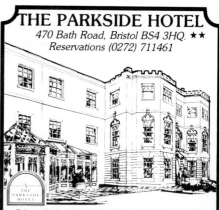

B

🍴 English & French **V** ⬧ 🖵 Lunch £9.90-£15.90alc Dinner £9.50-£12.50&alc Last dinner 10.30pm
Credit Cards 1 2 3 5

○**Berkeley Square** 15 Berkeley Square, Clifton BS8 1HB
☎(0272)254000
Due to have opened Jul 90
43◰⬧🛏

○**Bristol Moat House** Victoria St BS1 6HY (Queens Moat)
☎(0272)255010
Due to have opened Sep 90
132◰⬧🛏

✗✗**Restaurant Danton** 2 Upper Byron Place, The Triangle, Clifton BS8 1JY ☎(0272)268314
*A restaurant in the intimate tradition, the Danton provides attentive yet unobtrusive service and a French cuisine based on fresh ingredients of the best quality.*
Closed Sun, Etr wk & 25-31 Dec
Lunch not served Sat
🍴 French **V** 32 seats ✴ Dinner £14.50-£18.30alc Last lunch 2pm Last dinner 11pm 🅟
Credit Cards 1 2 3 5

✗✗**Restaurant Lettonie** 9 Druid Hill, Stoke Bishop BS9 1EW (2m NW) ☎(0272)686456
*Martin and Sian Blunos are the owners of this small predominantly French restaurant set in a residential area of northwest Bristol. The menu offers dishes that range from a robust braised oxtail with tomatoes, served off the bone, to the delicated pan-fried loin of pork served with braised lettuce, and ravioli filled with smoked haddock and scallops. Ice creams and parfaits are a perfect light ending to the main courses.*
Closed Sun, Mon, Xmas, BH's & last 2 wks Aug
🍴 French 24 seats Lunch £12.50-£18.50 Dinner £18.50 Last lunch 2pm Last dinner 10pm P
Credit Cards 1 2 3

❀✗✗**Markwicks** 43 Corn St BS1 1HT ☎(0272)262658
*One of our 'Best New Restaurants' this year – see the colour feature on page 36. There is a French bias to the cooking here, but culinary skill and flair contribute a degree of innovation and imagination. There is a small à la carte menu which changes to allow for seasonal specialities and is always supplemented by fresh fish. Worthy of special note is the scallop ravioli with a delicate beurre blanc, an outstanding leek tart, bacon-wrapped lamb tournedos placed on à courgette gratin and an iced nougat with honey sauce. Décor is in soft shades of yellow and service is charming and attentive.*
Closed Sat, Sun & BH Mons 10 days Xmas & Etr; 2 wks Aug
**V** 40 seats ✴ S% Lunch £14.50&alc Dinner £20-£25.50alc Last lunch 2pm Last dinner 10.30pm 🅟
Credit Cards 1 3

✗✗**Orient Rendezvous** 95 Queens Rd, Clifton BS8 1LW
☎(0272)745202 & 745231
*A family-owned restaurant on the outskirts of Clifton uses good, fresh ingredients to prepare a selection of Szchewan, Canton and Mandarin dishes, paying fine attention to detail. The Scallop and Black Bean dish is particularly worthy of note. The 73-bin wine list has good coverage and balance, and friendly, attentive service will complete your enjoyment of the meal.*
Closed 25-26 Dec
🍴 Chinese **V** 150 seats ✴ Dinner fr£15alc Last lunch 2.25pm Last dinner 11.30pm 25P ⥾
Credit Cards 1 2 3 5

✗*Bistro Twenty One* 21 Cotham Rd South, Kingsdown BS6 5TZ
☎(0272)421744
*A charmingly simple and informal bistro-style restaurant with a relaxed atmosphere specialises in the French style of cooking, making imaginative use of fresh ingredients, and accompanies its extensive menu with a selective wine list.*
Closed Sun & Xmas-New Year

Lunch not served Sat
🍴 French **V** 40 seats Last lunch 2.30pm Last dinner 11.30pm 🅟

Credit Cards 1 3

✗**Bouboulina's Restaurant** 9 Portland St, Clifton BS8 4JA
☎(0272)731192 & 742833
Closed Sun
🍴 Greek **V** 60 seats Lunch £10.90-£13.95alc Dinner £10.90-£13.95alc Last lunch 2.30pm Last dinner 11.30pm 🅟 ⥾
Credit Cards 1 3

✗**Howard's** 1A-2A Avon Crescent, Hotwells BS1 6XQ
☎(0272)262921
*Run by the Howard family for many years, this restaurant is situated close to the swing bridge in the original city dock area. Food is both imaginative and the scallops grantinee and the Jihn Dory in a chive and vermouth sauce are particularly noteworthy.*
Closed Sun, 1 wk Xmas & 2 wks summer
Lunch not served
🍴 English & French **V** 65 seats Dinner £15-£20alc Last dinner 11pm 🅟 ⥾
Credit Cards 1 3

✗*Raj Tandoori* 35 King St BS1 4DZ ☎(0272)291132
*Cosily tucked away under Bristol's famous King Street and adjacent to the Old Vic Theatre, this cellar restaurant promotes interesting Indian cuisine and in particular caters for the ethnic vegetarian.*
Closed 25 Dec
🍴 English & Indian **V** 85 seats Last dinner mdnt 🅟
Credit Cards 1 2 3 5

**BRIXHAM** Devon Map **03** SX95

★★★61% **Quayside** King St TQ5 9TJ (Inter-Hotels)
☎(08045)55751 Telex no 336682 FAX (0803) 882733
Closed Xmas & New Year
*A beautifully-situated hotel, overlooking the harbour and commanding views across the bay to Torquay, offers compact bedrooms with good facilities and charming public areas; interesting menus make good use of the local fish supply. Car parking is available five hundred yards from the hotel.*
30◰🛏🎂 CTV in all bedrooms Ⓡ sB&B◰🛏fr£35.50 dB&B◰🛏fr£68 🚪
37P
🍴 English & French **V** ⬧ 🖵 Lunch fr£7.95 High tea fr£2.95 Dinner fr£13.95&alc Last dinner 9.45pm
Credit Cards 1 2 3 5

★55% **Smugglers Haunt** Church St TQ5 8HH ☎(08045)3050 & 59416
*A stone-built inn that has stood near the old world harbour for four centuries is a popular venue for tourists and locals alike. Age and architectural features place obvious restrictions on accommodation, so that bedrooms, though soundly equipped are very compact and thus more suited to the needs of transient rather than long-stay guests, but friendly family ownership ensures a relaxing informal atmosphere, and local car parking facilities are conveniently close at hand. The small character public bar and adjacent cottage restaurant serves an extensive range of dishes and bar food featuring the best local fish available, last dinner orders being as late as 10pm.*
14rm(4◰) Annexe2rm(2fb) Ⓡ sB&B£26 sB&B◰🛏£32 dB&B£39 dB&B◰🛏£44
《 CTV 🅟 🚗 xmas
🍴 English & French **V** ⬧ 🖵 Lunch £4.25-£9 Dinner £4.25-£9&alc Last dinner 10pm
Credit Cards 1 2 3 5 ⓔ

For key to symbols see the inside front cover.

**BROADFORD**
See **Skye, Isle of**

---

**BROADSTAIRS** Kent Map **05** TR36

★★★62% **Castle Keep** Joss Gap Rd, Kingsgate CT10 3PQ (Best Western) ☎Thanet(0843)65222 FAX (0843) 65225
*This pleasant hotel overlooks the sea from a superb cliff top setting ; its older section has been refurbished to a high standard, the modern, well-equipped accommodation including some mini suites and the restaurant having been extended to create a conservatory where breakfast is served. A pleasant staff provides helpful service.*
29⇉↑(3fb) CTV in all bedrooms ®
《 ⊞ CTV 100P ✿ ⊐(heated) ♫
♀ English, French & Italian ✪ ⏛ Last dinner 10pm
Credit Cards ① ② ③ ④ ⑤

★★67% **Royal Albion** Albion St CT10 1LO (Consort)
☎Thanet(0843)68071 Telex no 965761 FAX (0843) 61509
*A cosy family-run hotel with well equipped accomodation and friendly service. Many rooms overlook the harbour and bay.*
19⇉↑(3fb)1⊞ CTV in all bedrooms ® T ✟ (ex guide dogs)
S% sB&B⇉↑£55-£60 dB&B⇉↑£65-£75 ➡
《 CTV 20P 2🐎 *xmas*
♀ French V ✪ ⏛
Credit Cards ① ② ③ ⑤ ⓔ

★★65% **Castlemere** Western Esplanade CT10 1TD
☎Thanet(0843)61566
*This long-established, family-run hotel facing the sea has been completely refurbished in recent years. Accommodation now comprises a choice of traditionally furnished modern bedrooms, an attractive, well-appointed restaurant and good bar and lounge facilities.*
37rm(24⇉6↑)(5fb)2⊞ CTV in all bedrooms ® T S10%
sB&B£28-£31.50 sB&B⇉↑£32-£35.50 dB&B£52-£59
dB&B⇉↑£60-£70.50 ➡
《 CTV 30P ✿ *xmas*
♀ English & French ✪ ⏛ Bar Lunch fr£1.50alc Dinner £12
Last dinner 7.45pm
Credit Cards ① ③

---

**BROADWAY** Hereford & Worcester Map **04** SP03

See also **Buckland**

★★★★

★★★★ LYGON ARMS
WR12 7DU (Prestige)
☎(0386)852255
Telex no 338260
FAX (0386) 858611

*This characterful and famous inn prides itself on the warm welcome and personal attention provided by the friendly staff. Service is willingly provided in the comfortable public rooms and the Great Hall restaurant which offers both modern and traditional English dishes. Bedrooms are well equipped and have quality fabrics and soft furnishings, with a choice of delightful period rooms or modern style rooms in the garden wings.*
61⇉↑5⊞ CTV in all bedrooms T sB&B⇉↑£105-£115
dB&B⇉↑£135-£190 Continental breakfast ➡
《 CTV 100P 4🐎 (£7.50 per night) 🚗 ✿ CFA ♪ (hard)
*xmas*

♀ International ✪ ⏛ Lunch fr£17.50 Dinner fr£27.50
Last dinner 9.45pm
Credit Cards ① ② ③ ⑤

★★★68% **Dormy House** Willersey Hill WR12 7LF (2m E off A44 in Gloucestershire) ☎(0386)852711 Telex no 338275 FAX (0386) 858636
Closed 25 & 26 Dec
*Such original features as Cotswold stone and exposed beams enhance the individual charm of this privately-owned hotel, which enjoys fine views of the Vale of Evesham from its superb elevated location. Individually decorated and furnished bedrooms are provided with good modern facilities, though some are quite compact, while public areas include several intimate seating areas and a restaurant where the extensive and interesting menu is complemented by a good wine list and professional service.*
26⇉↑Annexe23⇉(3fb)2⊞ CTV in all bedrooms ® T
sB&B⇉↑£54-£70 dB&B⇉↑£108-£130 ➡
《 80P 🚗 ✿ CFA
♀ English & French V ✪ ⏛ ✂ Lunch £14.25-£16.50&alc
Dinner £24.95&alc Last dinner 10pm
Credit Cards ① ② ③ ⑤
**See advertisement on page 171**

---

All hotels are now given a percentage grading for the quality of their facilities. A full explanation can be found within 'How we Classify Hotels and Restaurants' at the front of the book.

---

★★★62% **Broadway** The Green WR12 7AB (Inter-Hotels)
☎(0386)852401
*This hotel, at the heart of the Cotswold village, was converted from a sixteenth-century house once used by the Abbots of Pershore. Many bedrooms have now been refurbished, and the lounge, with its log fires, original timbers and gallery, is elegantly comfortable.*
12rm(11⇨↱)Annexe10rm(9⇨↱)(2fb)1⊞⚡in 4 bedrooms CTV in all bedrooms ® T ✗ ✱ sB&B⇨↱£48.50-£56 dB&B⇨↱£74-£91 ℞
30P ⛟ ✽ putting green *xmas*
♉ English & French V ♡ ⅅ Lunch £12.50-£14.50 Dinner £17-£18.50&alc Last dinner 9.30pm
Credit Cards 1 2 3 5 £

---

★★♛70% **Collin House** Collin Ln WR12 7PB
☎(0386)858354 & 852544
Closed 24-27 Dec
*Quietly located just off the A44 to the west of the town, and surrounded by eight acres of grounds and gardens, this lovely, 16th-century Cotswold stone house has décor and furnishings which are in keeping with its charm and character, and an ambience which is pleasantly relaxing.*
7rm(5⇨1↱)2⊞ ® ✗ ✱ S% sB&Bfr£37.50 dB&B⇨↱£69-£79 ℞
CTV 35P ⛟ ✽ ⛱ croquet *xmas*
V S% Lunch £12.50-£17alc Dinner £15-£17alc Last dinner 9pm
Credit Cards 1 3

---

✗✗✗**Hunter's Lodge** High St WR12 7DT ☎(0386)853247
*A fine Cotswold house where friendly and attentive services are provided by Dotty Friedli and her staff whilst husband Kurt presides over a kitchen which produces imaginative food. His Swiss origin is very much in evidence with mouth-watering pastry work and delicate sauces.*
Closed Mon, 1st 2 wks Feb & 1st 2 wks Aug
Dinner not served Sun
♉ English & French V 50 seats ✱ Lunch fr£12&alc Dinner fr£18.50&alc Last lunch 2pm Last dinner 9.45pm 20P nc8yrs
Credit Cards 1 2 3 5

---

**BROCKENHURST** Hampshire Map **04** SU20

---

★★★ 69% **Careys Manor** Lyndhurst Rd SO4 7RH
☎Lymington(0590)23551 FAX (0590) 22799
*Features of this hotel include modern bedroom wings with a choice of accommodation, a French staffed cafe/bar restaurant and a professionally-run health and leisure centre. The main restaurant serves imaginative food with a good choice of sweets, and staff are friendly and efficient.*
80⇨↱6⊞⚡in 30 bedrooms CTV in all bedrooms ® T sB&B⇨↱£75.90-£89.90 dB&B⇨↱£99.90-£119.90 ℞
☾180P ⛟ ✽ ⛆(heated) sauna solarium gymnasium jacuzzi steam room beauty therapist *xmas*
♉ English & French V ♡ ⚡ Lunch £12.95&alc Dinner £19.95-£24.95&alc Last dinner 10pm
Credit Cards 1 2 3
**See advertisement in colour supplement**

---

★★★ 68% **New Park Manor** Lyndhurst Rd SO42 7QH
☎Lymington(0590)23467 FAX (0590) 22268
26⇨↱(2fb)2⊞⚡in 10 bedrooms CTV in all bedrooms ® T ✱ sB&B⇨↱fr£62 dB&B⇨↱fr£104 ℞
60P 1⌂ ✽ ⛱(heated) ℘ (hard) ∪ solarium ♫ ♘ *xmas*
♉ French ♡ ⅅ Lunch £7.50-£17.50&alc High tea £3.50&alc Dinner £17.50-£25&alc Last dinner 9.30pm
Credit Cards 1 2 3

---

★★★ 62% **Balmer Lawn** Lyndhurst Rd SO42 7ZB (Hilton)
☎Lymington(0590)23116 Telex no 477649 FAX (0590) 23864
*This former hunting lodge enjoys views over the New Forest. The majority of bedrooms have been refurbished in dramatic style and all are well equipped. Good conference and leisure facilities.*
58⇨↱(8fb)⚡in 26 bedrooms CTV in all bedrooms ® T sB&B⇨↱£50-£75 dB&B⇨↱£80-£95 ℞
Lift ☾ 90P ✽ CFA ⛆(heated) ⛱(heated) ℘ (hard) squash sauna gymnasium *xmas*
V ♡ ⅅ ⚡ Lunch fr£8.50 Dinner £14-£15 Last dinner 9.30pm
Credit Cards 1 2 3 4 5

---

★★★62% **Rhinefield House** Rhinefield Rd SO42 7QB
☎Lymington(0590)22922 Telex no 477617 FAX (0590) 22500
34⇨↱1⊞⚡in 6 bedrooms CTV in all bedrooms ® T ✗ (ex guide dogs)
☾ 80P ✽ ⛆(heated) ⛱(heated) ℘ (hard) sauna solarium gymnasium jacuzzi table tennis pool table croquet
V ♡ ⅅ Last dinner 10pm
Credit Cards 1 2 3 5

---

★★★60% **Forest Park** Rhinefield Rd SO4 7ZG (Forestdale)
☎Lymington(0590)22844 Telex no 47572 FAX (0590) 23948
*A pretty roadside hotel on the outskirts of Brockenhurst. Most bedrooms have recently been refurbished and are ideally equipped to suit both leisure and business guests. Cuisine is straightforward and the service is relaxed.*
38⇨↱(5fb)3⊞⚡in 3 bedrooms CTV in all bedrooms ® T ℞
☾ 80P ✽ ⛱(heated) ℘ (hard) ∪ sauna solarium pool table *xmas*
♉ English & French V ♡ ⅅ ⚡
Credit Cards 1 2 3 4 5 £

---

★★♛69% **Whitley Ridge Restaurant Country House** Beaulieu Rd SO4 7QL ☎Lymington(0590)22354 FAX (0590) 22856
*You can quite often see a small herd of fallow deer in the area of the New Forest surrounding an eighteenth century Royal hunting lodge which today offers individually styled, well-equipped bedrooms and a restaurant whose cuisine exhibits a skill and flair that makes it popular with residents and locals alike.*
11⇨↱1⊞ CTV in all bedrooms ® T sB&B⇨↱£68-£72 dB&B⇨↱£76-£88 (incl dinner) ℞
CTV 30P ✽ ℘ (hard)
♉ English & French V ♡ ⅅ Lunch £9-£9.50 High tea £3-£5 Dinner £16-£17&alc Last dinner 9pm
Credit Cards 1 2 3 5 £

---

★★ 67% **The Cottage Hotel & Restaurant** Sway Rd SO42 7SH
☎Lymington(0590)22296
*A cosy cottage hotel run personally by the resident proprietors. There is a small restaurant, a beamed open-plan lounge and a choice of modern bedrooms, some of which have excellent bathrooms. Service is friendly and helpful and there is good car parking.*
6⇨↱ CTV in all bedrooms ® ✗ ✱ sB&B⇨↱£38-£40 dB&B⇨↱£58-£64 ℞
11P ✽ nc16yrs *xmas*
♉ English & French V ♡ ⅅ ⚡ Sunday Lunch fr£7.50 Dinner £12.50&alc Last dinner 9.30pm
Credit Cards 1 3

---

★★ 60% ***Watersplash*** The Rise SO42 7ZP
☎Lymington(0590)22344
*Standing in its own well-tended gardens, a Victorian house has been extended to create a happy and relaxed family-run hotel with upgraded bar and bedrooms, most popular with holidaymakers.*
23⇨↱(6fb)1⊞ CTV in all bedrooms ®
CTV 25P 4⌂ (£1.50 per night) ✽ ⛱(heated)
♉ English & Continental V ♡ ⅅ ⚡ Last dinner 8pm
Credit Cards 1 3

---

★ 65% ***Cloud*** Meerut Rd SO4 7DJ ☎Lymington(0590)22165 & 22254
Closed 29 Dec-14 Jan
*The Owton family have created a relaxed and friendly atmosphere at this hotel for over twenty years. It offers comfortable bedrooms, well-cooked fresh food and four cosy lounge areas all overlooking open forest heathland.*
▶

★ ★ ★

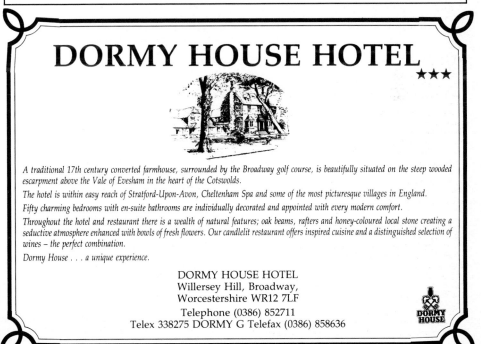

**B**

19rm(5fb)
CTV 20P 2✿ (£1.25 per night) ⌘
V ♦ ◻ Last dinner 8pm

❀ ✕ ✕ *Le Poussin* 57-59 Brookley Rd SO42 7RB
☎Lymington(0590)23063(Rosette awarded for dinner only)
*Hidden behind double-fronted shop windows at the heart of a New Forest village, this pretty restaurant offers a haven of peace in which you can relax to enjoy delicious food efficiently served by professional French waiters. Simple table d'hôte lunches represent good value for money, while a short à la carte dinner menu includes a set 'gastronomique' and features such delicacies as Timbale of Smoked Salmon, Roast Monkfish with Tomatoes and Herbs, Crepinette of Veal and Le Grand Dessert du Poisson (a collection of five small portions to experience).*
Closed Mon (ex private parties), 3 wks Jan & 1 wk Jun
Dinner not served Sun (ex BH's)
♀ British & French **V** 35 seats Last lunch 1.45pm Last dinner 9.45pm 2P ✂
Credit Cards ①③④

**BRODICK**
See **Arran, Isle of**

**BROMBOROUGH** Merseyside Map **07** SJ38

★★★64% **Cromwell** High St L62 7HZ (Lansbury)
☎051-334 2917 Telex no 628225 FAX 051-346 1175
*Situated in the town centre, this hotel offers particularly well-appointed bedrooms and good food in its Cromwell restaurant. Service is friendly.*
31⇨(3fb)1 ⌗ ✂in 5 bedrooms CTV in all bedrooms ® T
sB&B⇨£64 dB&B⇨£77 ☐
《 110P sauna solarium gymnasium
♀ English, French & Italian **V** ♦ ◻ ✂ Lunch fr£8.95 Dinner fr£14&alc Last dinner 10pm
Credit Cards ①②③⑤

★★64% *Dibbinsdale* Dibbinsdale Rd L63 0HJ ☎051-334 5171
19⇨1⌗ CTV in all bedrooms ® T ✖ (ex guide dogs)
《 60P ⌘
♀ International **V** ♦ ✂
Credit Cards ①②③⑤

**BROME** Suffolk Map **05** TM17

★★♨67%, **Oaksmere** IP23 8AJ ☎Eye(0379)870326
FAX (0379) 870051
*Set amid the ancient gardens and topiary of its own grounds, this faithfully restored Victorian house features a most beautiful restaurant with adjoining vine-clad conservatory. Accommodation is particularly well furnished and comfortable, fresh flower arrangements adorn the public areas, and the friendly, informal bar is built over a well, still visible through a glass plate.*
11⇨♠(3fb)4⌗ CTV in all bedrooms ® T ✽
sB&B⇨♠fr£48.50 dB&B⇨♠fr£72 ☐
90P ✿ *xmas*
♀ English & French **V** ♦ ◻ S10% Lunch £16-£18alc High tea fr£4.50alc Dinner £16-£18alc Last dinner 9.30pm
Credit Cards ①②③⑤ ⑥

★★63% **Brome Grange** IP23 8AP (on A140 )
☎Eye(0379)870456 FAX (0379) 870921
*Situated on the A140 south of Diss, Brome Grange provides well-equipped, spacious rooms in a courtyard complex to the rear of the main building. The bar has a cosy, convivial atmosphere and service and cuisine are of a good standard.*
Annexe22⇨♠ CTV in all bedrooms ® T ✽ S%
sB&B⇨♠£37.50-£47.50 dB&B⇨♠£50.50-£60.50 ☐
CTV 100P ✿ *xmas*
♀ English & French **V** ♦ ◻
Credit Cards ①②③⑤

**BROMLEY** Greater London

See **LONDON** plan 1*F2*(pages 426-7)
★★★54% **Bromley Court** Bromley Hill BR1 4JD (Consort)
☎081-464 5011 Telex no 896310 FAX 081-460 0899
*Modernised commercial hotel with informal atmosphere and good lounges.*
122⇨♠(5fb) CTV in all bedrooms ® T ✖ (ex guide dogs)
sB&B⇨♠£70 dB&B⇨♠£95 ☐
Lift 《 100P ✿ CFA ♬ *xmas*
♀ English & French **V** ♦ ◻ ✂ Lunch £11.25&alc Dinner £12.75&alc Last dinner 9.45pm
Credit Cards ①②③⑤

**BROMPTON-BY-SAWDON** North Yorkshire Map **08** SE98

✕ **Brompton Forge** YO13 9DP ☎Scarborough(0723)85409
*On the A170, a few miles west of Scarborough, stands a pleasant small restaurant where the table d'hôte menu offers memorable value for money, particularly since the portions are so generous – though varying from it can increase the cost significantly. Good use is made of east coast seafoods in the tantalising choice of starters and main courses, whilst the sticky toffee pudding is particularly worthy of note among the desserts.*
Closed Mon & 2 wks Feb
Lunch not served Tue-Sat
Dinner not served Sun
♀ English & French **V** 70 seats ✽ Lunch fr£11 Dinner £16-£17 Last lunch 1.15pm Last dinner 9pm 20P

**BROMSGROVE** Hereford & Worcester Map **07** SO97

★★★66% **Country Court** Birmingham Rd B61 0JB (Stakis)
☎Staverton(0327)705911 FAX (0327) 300821
*Friendly service, spacious and comfortable accommodation, good leisure and conference facilities and a convenient location on a pleasantly landscaped site close to the M5 (junction 49 and the M42 (junction 1) have made this hotel popular for both business and pleasure.*
70⇨♠✂in all bedrooms CTV in 141 bedrooms ® T
sB⇨♠fr£35 dB⇨♠£82 (room only) ☐
《 160P ▣(heated) sauna solarium gymnasium *xmas*
**V** ♦ ◻ ✂ Lunch £11.50&alc Dinner £12.50&alc Last dinner 10pm
Credit Cards ①②③④⑤

★★★58% **Perry Hall** Kidderminster Rd B61 7JN (Embassy)
☎(0527)579976 Telex no 8813387 FAX (0527)575998
*A former home of poet A E Houseman, the hotel has added modern extensions. It is popular with businessmen.*
55⇨♠ CTV in all bedrooms ® T sB⇨♠£60.50-£71.50 dB⇨♠£70.50-£81.50 (room only) ☐
《 120P ✿ CFA *xmas*
♀ English & French **V** ♦ ◻ ✂ Lunch fr£10.95&alc Dinner fr£10.95 Last dinner 9.45pm
Credit Cards ①②③④⑤

✕ ✕ ✕**Grafton Manor** Grafton Ln B61 7HA ☎(0527)579007
FAX (0527) 575221
*A grand manor house, once owned by the Earls of Shrewsbury, where you can really dine in style. Dinner is a set price 5-course meal with French country style cooking. Many unusual ingredients have their flavour enhanced by herbs from the extensive gardens. Some lovely bedrooms are available.*
Lunch not served Sat
**V** 45 seats ✽ Lunch £15.75-£19.75 Dinner £26.50 Last lunch 1.45pm Last dinner 9pm 50P nc7yrs
Credit Cards ①②③⑤

1991 marks the 25th anniversary of this guide.

**BROOK (near Cadnam)** Hampshire Map **04** SU21

★★★69% ***Bell Inn*** SO43 7HE ☎Southampton(0703)812214 FAX (0703) 813958

*A pleasant inn on the edge of the New Forest. It is run in conjunction with one of the two adjacent golf courses, and free use of this course is offered to residents. À la carte and table d'hôte menus are served in the restaurant, but the bar features a central servery where you can choose from a good variety of bar meals.*

22⇌🚿(3fb) CTV in all bedrooms ® **T**

150P ⛟ ❉ ⚑36

♁ English & French ♔ ☕ Last dinner 9.30pm

Credit Cards 1 2 3 5

**BRORA** Highland *Sutherland* Map **14** NC90

★★★58% **Links** Golf Rd KW9 6QS (Best Western) ☎(0408)21225 Telex no 75242

Closed 25 Dec-Jan

*This holiday hotel situated next to an 18 hole golf course enjoys fine uninterrupted sea views. The traditionally furnished bedrooms vary in size but all are well equipped, and there are spacious public areas in which to relax.*

22⇌(2fb) CTV in all bedrooms ® **T** S% sB&B⇌£39-£43 dB&B⇌£72-£80 ⛁

55P ❉ ⚑18 ⌂

♁ International **V** ♔ ☕ ⚡ S% Bar Lunch £6.50-£10 Dinner £15-£17.50 Last dinner 9pm

Credit Cards 1 2 3 5 £

★★62% **Royal Marine** Golf Rd KW9 6QS ☎(0408)21252 Telex no 76165

*The good range of leisure facilities featured by this popular holiday hotel includes special golfing, fishing and curling packages; bedrooms are comfortable and well-equipped, while welcoming log fires burn in the traditionally furnished public areas.*

11rm(9⇌1🚿)(1fb)1⛿ CTV in all bedrooms ® **T** sB&B⇌🚿£45-£65 dB&B⇌🚿£70-£95 ⛁

CTV 40P 6🚘 ⛟ ❉ ⛆(heated) ⚑18 🎾(hard) ⚓ snooker sauna ice curling rink in season *xmas*

♁ Scottish & French ♔ ☕ Lunch £7.95-£8.50 High tea £6-£10alc Dinner £15-£16 Last dinner 9pm

Credit Cards 1 2 3 5

**BROUGH** Cumbria Map **12** NY71

★★57% **Castle** Main St CA7 4AX ☎(09304)252

*An hotel with attractive dining room, lounge and cosy lounge bar offers bedrooms ranging from the spacious and traditional to the more modern and compact.*

14⇌🚿(2fb) CTV in all bedrooms ® **T** ✗ (ex guide dogs) ✱ S% sB&B⇌🚿£25 dB&B⇌🚿£35 ⛁

CTV 60P *xmas*

♁ Mainly grills **V** ♔ ☕ Sunday Lunch £3.95-£9.50alc Dinner £5.50-£11&alc Last dinner 9.30pm

Credit Cards 1 3 £

**BROUGHTON IN FURNESS** Cumbria Map **07** SD28

★★61% **Eccle Riggs** Foxfield Rd LA20 6BN ☎(0229)716398 & 716780

*This Victorian mansion sits in parkland 1 mile south of the village. Popular with commercial and business travellers it has very well-equipped bedrooms of varying size and standard.*

12⇌🚿(6fb) CTV in all bedrooms ® **T** ✗ (ex guide dogs) ✱ sB&B⇌🚿fr£39.50 dB&B⇌🚿fr£64.50 ⛁

120P ❉ ⛆(heated) ⚑9 sauna solarium clay pigeon shooting *xmas*

♁ English & French **V** ♔ ☕ Sunday Lunch fr£4.75 Dinner £10.50&alc Last dinner 9pm

Credit Cards 1 2 3 5 £

Eccle Riggs Manor Hotel ★★

Foxfield Road, Broughton in Furness, Cumbria LA20 6BN

Telephone: (0229) 716398 & 716780

Set in 35 acres of gardens and woodlands this splendid hotel, built in 1865, has been tastefully refurbished and offers every modern amenity. Ten of the 13 bedrooms have private facilities and all have colour TV with remote control plus in house video system, radio, coffee/tea making facilities, hair dryer, trouser press and direct dial telephone. The Restaurant overlooks the lawns and Duddon Estuary. A heated indoor swimming pool with adjoining patio is open all year. The hotel is an ideal base for the golfing enthusiast with a 9 hole golf course or those who enjoy the outdoor life.

The Cloud Hotel

★

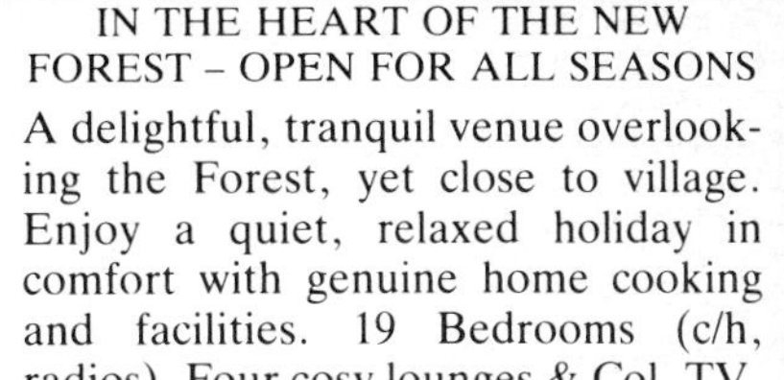

IN THE HEART OF THE NEW FOREST – OPEN FOR ALL SEASONS

A delightful, tranquil venue overlooking the Forest, yet close to village. Enjoy a quiet, relaxed holiday in comfort with genuine home cooking and facilities. 19 Bedrooms (c/h, radios). Four cosy lounges & Col. TV. Licensed. Mini-breaks. 4 nights for price of 3. Send for Colour Brochure.

**MEERUT ROAD, BROCKENHURST, HANTS, SO42 7TA.**

**Tel: (0590) 22165/22254.**

## Broughton in Furness - Buckingham

**★59%** *Old King's Head* Station Rd LA20 6HJ ☎(0229)716293
*Old white-washed village inn.*
5rm(1🏠)(1fb) CTV in all bedrooms Ⓡ
50P ✿
♧ Last dinner 9pm

---

**BROXTED** Essex Map **05** TL52

✿ **★★★78%** **Whitehall** Church End CM6 2BZ (Pride of Britain)
☎Bishops Stortford(0279)850603 FAX (0279) 850385
Closed 26-30 Dec
(Rosette awarded for dinner only)
*A delightful country manor house with some unrivalled rural views captures an atmosphere of peace and tranquility. Individually decorated and furnished bedrooms have been equipped with the best of modern facilities whilst retaining their original character, and guests enjoy modern-style cuisine – including a six-course gourmet menu – in an historic restaurant with a wealth of exposed beams. Public areas also include a comfortable lounge and pleasant bar.*
11⇨🏠 CTV in all bedrooms 🐾 (ex guide dogs)
sB&B⇨🏠£70-£85 dB&B⇨🏠£95-£120 🏢
35P 2🚗 ✿ ☖ ♪ (hard) nc5yrs
♥ French **V** Lunch fr£17.50 Dinner fr£29 Last dinner 9.30pm
Credit Cards 1️⃣ 2️⃣ 3️⃣ 5️⃣

---

**BROXTON** Cheshire Map **07** SJ45

**★★★62%** **Broxton Hall Country House** Whitchurch Rd
CH3 9JS ☎(082925)321
*A seventeenth-century black and white mansion is now a well-furnished and comfortable hotel run by the resident owners, standing in three acres of landscaped gardens and lawns, within easy reach of Chester. Rooms are well equipped and attractively appointed.*
12⇨(1fb)1🏢✂in 1 bedroom CTV in all bedrooms Ⓡ T 🏢
30P ✿ ✿ nc12yrs
♥ English & French **V** ♧ ☖ ✂ Lunch £6-£14 High tea £8
Dinner £17 Last dinner 9.30pm
Credit Cards 1️⃣ 3️⃣ Ⓔ

**See advertisement under CHESTER**

---

**BRUTON** Somerset Map **03** ST63

✕✕**Claire de Lune** 2-4 High St BA10 0EQ ☎(0749)813395
*A high standard of cooking is maintained in this attractive country restaurant whose short set-price menu of French provincial and English cuisine is thoughtfully prepared and accompanied by a range of popular wines at reasonable prices, a keen young staff providing attentive service.*
Closed Mon (ex dinner by prior arrangement) & 2 wks Aug
Lunch not served Tue-Sat
Dinner not served Sun
40 seats Sunday Lunch £7.95-£11.50 Dinner £14.75-£16.95 Last dinner 9.45pm ✗

Credit Cards 1️⃣ 3️⃣

✕**Truffles** 95 High St BA10 0AR ☎(0749)812255
*A small, quality restaurant run by a husband and wife team features a stone-walled dining-room with a fine fireplace, warm-coloured soft furnishings and contrasting stained tables. The fixed price menu offers five choices, dishes being skilfully prepared from a variety of top-quality ingredients, and polite – though unhurried – service is provided by cheerful staff. You are advised to make a reservation, as the establishment has a strong local following.*
Closed Mon & 3 wks Sep
Lunch not served Tue
Dinner not served Sun
♥ French **V** 20 seats Lunch £17.95 Dinner £17.95 Last lunch 2pm Last dinner 10.30pm ✗ nc5yrs

---

**BUCKDEN** Cambridgeshire Map **04** TL16

**★★★62%** *George* High St PE18 9XA
☎Huntingdon(0480)810307
*Legend has it that Dick Turpin frequently stayed at this sixteenth-century former coaching inn beside the old Great North Road; today's traveller, however, is offered accommodation in well equipped bedrooms which provide a standard of comfort unknown in that era.*
16⇨🏠(1fb)1🏢 CTV in all bedrooms Ⓡ T 🐾 (ex guide dogs)
20P ♫
**V** ♧ ☖ Last dinner 9.30pm
Credit Cards 1️⃣ 2️⃣ 3️⃣ 4️⃣ 5️⃣

---

**BUCKDEN** North Yorkshire Map **07** SD97

**★★67%** **Buck Inn** BD23 5JA ☎Kettlewell(075676)227
*Charming Dales inn set amid beautiful scenery offering a warm, friendly welcome.*
15⇨🏠(2fb)1🏢 CTV in all bedrooms Ⓡ T ✳
sB&B⇨🏠£25-£35 dB&B⇨🏠£50-£70 🏢
36P xmas
**V** ♧ ☖ Bar Lunch £2.50-£10 High tea fr£2.50 Dinner
£12.50-£15 Last dinner 9pm
Credit Cards 1️⃣ 3️⃣ Ⓔ

---

**BUCKHURST HILL** Essex London plan 1 F5 (pages 426–7)

**★★57%** **The Roebuck** North End IG9 5QY (Trusthouse Forte)
☎081-505 4636 FAX 081-504 7826
*Standing beside Epping Forest, the hotel contains small, elegant public rooms and well-equipped bedrooms.*
29⇨🏠✂in 5 bedrooms CTV in all bedrooms Ⓡ T sB⇨£70-£83
dB⇨£91-£97 (room only) 🏢
45P xmas
**V** ♧ ☖ ✂ Lunch fr£10.75&alc Dinner fr£15.50&alc Last dinner 9.30pm
Credit Cards 1️⃣ 2️⃣ 3️⃣ 4️⃣ 5️⃣

---

**BUCKIE** Grampian *Banffshire* Map **15** NJ46

**★★57%** **Cluny** 2 High St AB5 1AL ☎(0542)32922
Closed 1-2 Jan
*A long-established commercial hotel, conveniently situated in the town centre, offers good value practical accommodation in simple, well-equipped bedrooms.*
10⇨🏠Annexe4rm(1fb) CTV in all bedrooms Ⓡ T
sB&B⇨🏠£19-£23 dB&B⇨🏠£34-£39 🏢
16P
♥ Scottish & French ♧ ☖ Lunch £5-£6 High tea £5-£8 Dinner £8-£14alc Last dinner 8pm
Credit Cards 1️⃣ 2️⃣ 3️⃣ 5️⃣ Ⓔ

---

**BUCKINGHAM** Buckinghamshire Map **04** SP63

**★★50%** **White Hart** Market Square MK18 1NL (Trusthouse Forte) ☎(0280)815151 FAX (0280) 822215
*18th century traditional hotel with comfortable modernised bedrooms.*
19⇨🏠(1fb)✂in 2 bedrooms CTV in all bedrooms Ⓡ (room only) 🏢
30P
**V** ♧ ☖ ✂
Credit Cards 1️⃣ 2️⃣ 3️⃣ 4️⃣ 5️⃣

---

All hotels are now given a percentage grading
for the quality of their facilities. A full explanation
can be found within 'How we Classify Hotels
and Restaurants' at the front of the book.

**B**

---

BUCKLAND (near Broadway) Gloucestershire Map **04** SP03

★★★

❀★★★⚹
BUCKLAND MANOR

WR12 7LY
☎Broadway(0386)852626

Closed mid Jan-early Feb

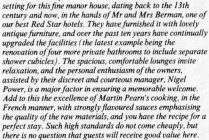

*A peaceful, charming Cotswold village, two miles outside Broadway, is the setting for this fine manor house, dating back to the 13th century in the hands of Mr and Mrs Berman, one of our best Red Star hotels. They have furnished it with lovely antique furniture, and over the past ten years have continually upgraded the facilities (the latest example being the renovation of four more private bathrooms to include separate shower cubicles). The spacious, comfortable lounges invite relaxation, and the personal enthusiasm of the owners, assisted by their discreet and courteous manager, Nigel Power, is a major factor in ensuring a memorable welcome. Add to this the excellence of Martin Pearn's cooking, in the French manner, with strongly flavoured sauces emphasising the quality of the raw materials, and you have the recipe for a perfect stay. Such high standards do not come cheaply, but there is no question that guests will receive good value here.*

11⇄♪(2fb)2⊞ CTV in all bedrooms T 🎵 ✳
sB&B⇄♪£125-£200 dB&B⇄♪£135-£210
30P 🚗 ❀ ⚫ ⌒(heated) ♪ (hard) ∪ croquet lawn putting green nc12yrs *xmas*
♀ International V ❖ ⚑ Lunch £18.75-£28.15alc Dinner £18.75-£28.15alc Last dinner 8.45pm
Credit Cards [1] [3]

---

BUCKLERS HARD Hampshire Map **04** SU40

★★★ 66% *Master Builders House* SO4 7XB ☎(0590)616253
FAX (0590) 612624
*The public rooms of this hotel – once the home of eighteenth-century shipbuilder Henry Adams – command wonderful views over the estuary, and the bedrooms in the original building retain considerable character and charm, although those in the annexe are more stereotyped. Guests can choose between the modern-style cuisine of the main restaurant and the self-service buffet of the beamed Yachtsman's Bar. Management is professional, with service by a smartly uniformed staff.*
6⇄♪Annexe17⇄(1fb)3⊞ CTV in all bedrooms ®
80P 🚗 ❀ ⚫ clay pigeon shooting boating
♀ English & French V ❖ ⚑ ✂ Last dinner 9.45pm
Credit Cards [1] [2] [3] [5]

---

BUCKLOW HILL Cheshire Map **07** SJ78

★★★ 61% **The Swan** WA16 6RD (De Vere) ☎(0565)830295
Telex no 666911 FAX (0565) 830614
*Cavaliers and Roundheads once sought sanctuary in this historic hotel where darkened oak beams still add character to both the recently refurbished public areas in the main building and the bedrooms in an adjoining stable block.*
70⇄♪(11fb)3⊞ ✂in 14 bedrooms CTV in all bedrooms ® T
S% sB&B⇄♪£30-£70 dB&B⇄♪£60-£82 ⊟
⟪ 200P ❀
♀ French & English V ❖ ⚑ S% Lunch £9-£13.75&alc Dinner £13.75&alc Last dinner 10pm
Credit Cards [1] [2] [3] [5] ⓔ

---

BUDE Cornwall & Isles of Scilly Map **02** SS20

★★★ 64% **Hartland** Hartland Ter EX23 8JY (Exec Hotel)
☎(0288)355661
Closed Dec-Feb (ex Xmas)
*Friendly, attentive service will enhance your stay at this family-run hotel with its fine views over town and sea. Modestly furnished bedrooms are comfortable and well equipped, entertainment is provided nightly, and an outdoor swimming pool with good sunbathing facilities is an additional attraction during the summer months.*
29⇄♪(2fb)3⊞ CTV in all bedrooms T
sB&B⇄♪£32.20-£36.80 dB&B⇄♪£55.20-£62.10 ⊟
Lift 30P ❀ ⌒(heated) ♪ *xmas*
♀ International ❖ ⚑ Lunch £12.50 Dinner £15-£16.50 Last dinner 8.30pm

★★ 65% **Bude Haven** Flexbury Av EX23 8NS ☎(0288)352305
*Resident proprietors extend a warm welcome to this clean and very well maintained hotel with its freshly decorated, well equipped bedrooms, new dining room, comfortable lounge and small bar.*
13⇄♪(1fb) CTV in all bedrooms ® S% sB&B⇄♪£17-£18
dB&B⇄♪£34-£36 ⊟
CTV 8P
V ❖ ⚑ S% Bar Lunch £1-£5 Dinner £6-£7 Last dinner 7.30pm
Credit Cards [1] [3] ⓔ

★★ 64% **Camelot** Downs View EX23 8RE ☎(0288)352361
FAX (0288) 355470
*Well-kept and proprietor run, a hotel with strong ties to the golf course across the road offers well-equipped bedrooms and a genial atmosphere.*
21⇄♪(3fb) CTV in all bedrooms ® T 🎵 (ex guide dogs) ✳
sB&B⇄♪£22-£25 dB&B⇄♪£44-£50 ⊟

▶

# The
# Old Kings Head*

## Broughton in Furness, Cumbria LA20 6HJ
## Telephone: (0229) 716293

Claimed to be one of the oldest inns within the district, with recorded history spanning at least 300 years. Inside is full of character, the upstairs was once the town theatre and downstairs interesting reminders of the famous Broughton family of clockmakers. A traditional country town pub with an eye for modern day comforts. All the bedrooms are well equipped with central heating throughout. The restaurant has an enviable reputation and offers a full bar menu equally highly praised. Situated in the centre just a couple of hundred yards in any direction to the edge of town and the open countryside.

21P 🍴 solarium *xmas*
V ✔ Dinner £10-£12&alc Last dinner 8.30pm
Credit Cards 1 3 £

★★62%, **St Margaret's** Killerton Rd EX23 8EN
☎(0288)352252 & 352401 FAX (0409) 254351
*Small, comfortable hotel near town centre.*
10⇄🏾(3fb) CTV in all bedrooms ® T sB&B⇄🏾£30-£34
dB&B⇄🏾£46-£50
CTV 6P 🍴 ✿ games room *xmas*
♀ English & Continental V ✿ ⚲
Credit Cards 1 3 £

★★61%, **Penarvor** Crooklets Beach EX23 8NE ☎(0288)352036
Closed Nov-Feb
*A family-run hotel, standing in a quiet situation, offers friendly, attentive service and good food. Attractively furnished, well-equipped bedrooms are complemented by comfortable public rooms.*
16⇄🏾(3fb) CTV in all bedrooms ® T
sB&B⇄🏾£21.50-£22.50 dB&B⇄🏾£43-£45 🍴
25P ✿ solarium gymnasium pool table games room
♀ English & French ✔ Bar Lunch £1.50-£4.95 Dinner fr£12&alc Last dinner 8pm
Credit Cards 1 3 £

★★60%, *Florida* 17-18 Summerleaze Crescent EX23 8HJ
☎(0288)352451
Closed Nov-Feb
*A personally-run small hotel with a friendly atmosphere, which offers well-organised activity holidays which are especially suitable for adventurous children. Brightly decorated bedrooms, though not very large, are well equipped and there is also a small selection of student/teenager rooms. Public areas include a choice of comfortable lounges and a pleasant dining room where the short table d'hôte menu includes some interesting dishes. Set in a row of terraced properties near to both the town centre and Summerleaze Beach, the hotel commands good views over the river estuary and out to sea.*
21rm(11🏾)(4fb) CTV in all bedrooms ® ✖
10P games room
V ✿ Last dinner 7.30pm

★63%, **Meva Gwin** Upton EX23 0LY ☎(0288)352347
Closed 6 Oct-28 Mar
*A popular family holiday hotel set on the cliff top midway between Bude and Widemouth Bay. Bedrooms, though simply furnished, are light, airy and well equipped and traditional English cooking is served in the dining rooms. This hotel offers superb value for money.*
11rm(4⇄6🏾)(4fb) CTV in all bedrooms ® ✖ ✳ sB&B£13-£16
sB&B⇄🏾£15-£18 dB&B£26-£32 dB&B⇄🏾£30-£36
CTV 44P ✿ ◊
✿ ⚲ ✔ Bar Lunch £3.50-£7.50 Dinner £7.50 Last dinner 7.30pm

★59%, **Edgcumbe** Summerleaze Crescent EX23 8HJ
☎(0288)353846
*Personally run hotel specialising in family holidays.*
15rm(8🏾)(5fb) CTV in all bedrooms ® sB&Bfr£13.50
sB&Bfr£16 dB&Bfr£27 dB&B🏾fr£32 🍴
CTV 7P pool table *xmas*
V ✿ ⚲ Bar Lunch £3-£6 Dinner fr£7 Last dinner 7.30pm
Credit Cards 1 3

★56%, **Maer Lodge** Crooklets Beach EX23 8NG ☎(0288)353306
Closed 12 Oct-1 Dec
*Detached, family holiday hotel close to Crooklets Beach with fine views.*
19rm(7⇄8🏾)(3fb) CTV in all bedrooms ® S%
sB&B£17.50-£22.50 sB&B⇄🏾£21-£26 dB&B£33-£43
dB&B⇄🏾£38-£48 🍴

CTV 20P ✿ pool table mini-golf *xmas*
♀ English & French ✿ ✱ ⚲ ✔
Credit Cards 1 3 £

**BUILTH WELLS** Powys Map 03 SO05

★★★🏩64%, *Caer Beris Manor* LD2 3NP ☎(0982)552601
FAX (0982) 552586
*A tastefully restored country manor house a mile from the town centre features attractive, well-equipped bedrooms, comfortable public areas and extensive gardens.*
21⇄(1fb)4🛏 CTV in all bedrooms
30P 2🐴 ✿ ✱ ✓ ◑ clay pigeon shooting ♫
♀ International V ✿ ⚲ Last dinner 10pm
Credit Cards 1 2 3 5

★★64%, **Pencerrig Country House** LD2 3TF (Consort)
☎(0982)553226 FAX (0982) 552347
*This former gentleman's residence situated off the A483 offers good food and comfortable modern bedrooms. It is also a popular meeting place for locals.*
20⇄🏾(1fb)1🛏 CTV in all bedrooms ® T
sB&B⇄🏾£32-£39.50 dB&B⇄🏾£50-£64 🍴
《 40P ✿ *xmas*
♀ English & French V ✿ ⚲ Lunch £7.50 Dinner £16.50 Last dinner 9pm
Credit Cards 1 2 3 5 £

★★56%, **Lion** 2 Broad St LD2 3DT ☎(0982)553670
*Situated near the River Wye at the centre of the busy market town, and attracting much local trade to its busy bar, this traditional hotel offers bedrooms which retain their old world character despite the provision of modern comforts.*
20rm(12⇄2🏾)(4fb)1🛏 CTV in all bedrooms ® T ✱
sB&B£24-£30 sB&B⇄🏾£26-£30 dB&B£34-£38
dB&B⇄🏾£42-£48 🍴
12P *xmas*
♀ English & French V ✿ ⚲ Lunch fr£6.25&alc Dinner fr£9&alc Last dinner 9.30pm
Credit Cards 1 3 £

**BUNGAY** Suffolk Map 05 TM38

★59%, **King's Head** Market Place NR35 1AF ☎(0986)893583
12rm(4⇄5🏾)1🛏 CTV in all bedrooms ® ✱ sB&Bfr£23
sB&B⇄🏾fr£32.50 dB&Bfr£40 dB&B⇄🏾fr£46 🍴
CTV 28P 🍴 *xmas*
V ✿ ⚲ Lunch £3-£9alc Dinner £12-£17alc Last dinner 9pm
Credit Cards 1 2 3 £

**BUNWELL** Norfolk Map 05 TM19

★★🏩62%, **Bunwell Manor** Bunwell St NR16 1QU
☎(095389)8304
*A warm welcome, friendly service and tasty, wholesome food in the British style are among the attractions of an hotel set at the heart of this tiny village ; the building dates back to the sixteenth century, but amenities are of a standard to meet the expectations of modern travellers.*
10⇄🏾(2fb) CTV in all bedrooms ® T sB&B⇄🏾£42-£46
dB&B⇄🏾£55-£65 🍴
30P ✿ ◊ *xmas*
V ✿ Lunch £10&alc Dinner £10&alc Last dinner 9.30pm
Credit Cards 1 3 £

**BURBAGE** Wiltshire Map 04 SU26

★★55%, **Savernake Forest** Savernake SN8 3AY (1m NE off A346) ☎Marlborough(0672)810206
*A hotel in rural setting on the edge of the forest, beside the Kennet and Avon Canal, offers well-equipped bedrooms (about half of which have been refurbished), a Buttery lunch and dinner menu in the bar which is augmented by the restaurant's evening table d'hôte*

and à la carte choice, and informal service from a friendly local staff.

10⇨🏠Annexe6⇨🏠(2fb)1⊞ CTV in all bedrooms ® T ✳
sB&B⇨🏠fr£50 dB&B⇨🏠fr£70 ⊟
CTV 80P ✿ ♪ xmas
🍴 English & French V ۞ Sunday Lunch fr£8.50 Dinner
fr£12.50&alc Last dinner 9.15pm
Credit Cards 1 2 3 5

**See advertisement under MARLBOROUGH**

---

### BURFORD Oxfordshire Map 04 SP21

★★★62% **Inn For All Seasons** Little Barrington OX8 4TN (3m
W on A40) ☎Windrush(04514)324 FAX (04514) 508
Retaining much of the original character and charm, with old stone
walls and exposed beams, the former coaching inn provides well-
furnished bedrooms and good standards of food.
9⇨🏠(1fb) CTV in all bedrooms ® T ✠ S% sB&B⇨🏠£39.50-£45
dB&B⇨🏠£65-£70 ⊟
30P ✿ Shooting nc10yrs xmas
V ۞ ᴸᴸ S% Sunday Lunch £8.50-£9.50 Dinner £14.50-£15.75
Last dinner 9.30pm
Credit Cards 1 3 £

★★63% **Cotswold Gateway** Cheltenham Rd OX8 4HX
☎(0993)822695 FAX (0993) 823600
Recently completely refurbished during a twelve month closure the
hotel now has very well-equipped, modern bedrooms together with
a formal, panelled dining room, a smart bar and an all day coffee
shop.
13⇨🏠Annexe4⇨(4fb) CTV in all bedrooms ® T ✳
sB&B⇨£47.50 dB&B⇨£65 ⊟
60P ⏹ xmas
🍴 English & French V ۞ ᴸᴸ Lunch £12.50 Dinner
£12.50-£18.50 Last dinner 9.45pm
Credit Cards 1 2 3 5

★★63% **Golden Pheasant** High St OX8 4RJ ☎(099382)3223
Telex no 849041 FAX (099382) 2621
In the heart of this attractive Cotswolds town, the Golden
Pheasant is a small, family-owned hotel which has recently been
renovated. Many of the original beams and stonework have been
exposed and large fireplaces provide a cosy atmosphere. Cottage-
style bedrooms combine character with a good range of modern
facilities and a particularly charming room in the roof space has a
17th-century 4-poster bed. Worthy standards of food place the
emphasis on the imaginative use of fresh produce.
12⇨🏠(2fb)2⊞ CTV in all bedrooms ® T ✳
sB&B⇨🏠£50-£69 dB&B⇨🏠£69-£88 ⊟
CTV 18P ⏹ xmas
🍴 French V ۞ ᴸᴸ Lunch £6.95-£12.95 High tea £2-£5
Dinner £12.95-£20.95 Last dinner 9.30pm
Credit Cards 1 3

---

### BURGH HEATH Surrey Map 04 TQ25

★★58% **Heathside** Brighton Rd KT20 6BW ☎(0737)353355
Telex no 929908 FAX (0737) 370857
This hotel offers modern accommodation. The staff are cheerful,
and a cosy atmosphere pervades the compact Milly's bar and
restaurant. Additionally, there is a Happy Eater restaurant where
breakfast is available.
47⇨🏠(19fb) CTV in all bedrooms ® sB⇨🏠£55-£65
dB⇨🏠£65-£75 (room only) ⊟
⟮ 100P ✿ CFA ⬛(heated) sauna gymnasium xmas
🍴 English & French ۞ ᴸᴸ ✂ Lunch fr£7 Dinner fr£10 Last
dinner 10pm
Credit Cards 1 2 3 5

For key to symbols see the inside front cover.

---

### BURLEY Hampshire Map 04 SU20

★★★64% **Moorhill House** BH24 4AG ☎(04253)3285
Situated on the edge of the forest in three acres of gardens and
lawns, refurbishment has recently been completed : bedrooms are
relaxing with good colour coordination, there is an elegant
restaurant, a bar that has been extended with views of the indoor
pool and plush lounges with leather upholstery.
24⇨🏠(7fb) CTV in all bedrooms ® T sB&B⇨🏠£59-£69
dB&B⇨🏠£85-£95 ⊟
CTV 40P ⏹ ✿ ⬛(heated) sauna jacuzzi spa bath xmas
V ۞ ᴸᴸ ✂ Sunday Lunch £9.95 Dinner £13 Last dinner 9pm
Credit Cards 1 2 3 5

★★★58% **Burley Manor** Ringwood Rd BH24 4BS (Forestdale)
☎(04253)3522 Telex no 41565 FAX (04253) 3227
This 19th century manor house is set in 54 acres of parkland,
within the New Forest, with skilfully extended ground floor
accommodation. There is a large meeting room and open style
country house bar, lounge and restaurant. Riding stables are
nearby, and a seperate conference and banqueting suite adjoins the
main house. Service is relaxed and friendly and particularly well
managed by Miss Sally Whittle, the general manager. An
interesting and reliable standard of cooking is available, along with
a good wine list.
21⇨🏠Annexe9⇨🏠(3fb)4⊞ ✂in 4 bedrooms CTV in all
bedrooms ® T ✳ sB&B⇨🏠fr£60 dB&B⇨🏠£75-£85 ⊟
60P ✿ ⬛(heated) ♪ ∪ croquet xmas
V ۞ ᴸᴸ Sunday Lunch fr£8.95 Dinner £13.25-£20alc Last
dinner 10pm
Credit Cards 1 2 3 5

1991 marks the 25th anniversary of this guide.

The ★★
# Golden Pheasant Hotel

**The High Street, Burford, Oxfordshire OX8 4RJ**
**Tel: Burford (0993 82) 3223 or 3417**

"The Golden Pheasant is a beautiful historic hotel holding the oldest set of property deeds in Burford.

Parts of the builing can be identified as being from the 14th century. As well as being particularly well placed for visiting many famous Cotswold beauty spots. The Golden Pheasant is quite an attraction in its own right.

Whether you are visiting for an over-night stay, a holiday, a dinner party, a casual meal or just using the hotel as a rendezvous for meeting friends, you will appreciate the attention to detail and the friendly personal service."

**B**

## BURNHAM Buckinghamshire Map **04** SU98

★★★67%, **Burnham Beeches Moat House** Grove Rd SL1 8DP (Queens Moat) ☎(0628)603333 FAX (0628) 603994

*Once a hunting lodge, and still surrounded by 600 acres of forest and parkland, this commercial hotel has been tastefully refurbished in the style and luxury of a bygone era. Its elegant lounges are comfortably furnished, whilst a well-appointed restaurant offers both à la carte and table d'hôte menus of carefully prepared dishes based on fresh, quality produce. Some spacious and thoughtfully appointed bedrooms have been well equipped, and there are excellent leisure facilities.*

75⇌2🛏✠in 8 bedrooms CTV in all bedrooms ⓇT ✳ sB&B⇋🛏£80-£85 dB&B⇋🛏£91-£95 🄵

Lift ⦅150P ✿ ▣(heated) ℘ (hard) sauna solarium gymnasium putting croquet *xmas*

🍴 French V ♥ ⚱

Credit Cards 1 2 3 4 5

★★65%, *Grovefield* Taplow Common Rd SL1 8LP (Best Western) ☎(0628)603131 Telex no 846873
Closed 1 wk Xmas

*Once a Victorian country house, this tastefully modernised hotel sits in 7.5 acres of gardens and parkland overlooking unspoilt countryside. Accommodation is in comfortable, well-equipped bedrooms, and a restaurant decorated in pastel shades offers interesting international cuisine.*

42⇌🛏 CTV in all bedrooms Ⓡ

Lift ⦅100P 🅿 ✿ ♨

🍴 International V ♥ Last dinner 10.30pm

Credit Cards 1 2 3 4 5

## BURNHAM-ON-CROUCH Essex Map **05** TQ99

★64%, **Ye Olde White Harte** The Quay CM0 8AS
☎Maldon(0621)782106
RS 25-26 Dec

*Pleasantly set beside the quay, with its own mooring jetty, this historic free-house comprises a choice of individual and well-equipped bedrooms – some overlooking the estuary – with four additional very basic rooms in an annexe. Public areas include the restaurant, two particularly convivial beamed bars with log fires and a separate cosy lounge, service throughout being friendly and informal under the personal supervision of members of the proprietor's family.*

11⇌🛏(2fb) CTV in all bedrooms S10% sB&B⇋🛏£28.60-£33 dB&B⇋🛏£46-£52

CTV 15P

V ♥ Lunch fr£8.50 Dinner £9-£10 Last dinner 9pm

£

## BURNHAM-ON-SEA Somerset Map **03** ST34

★★61%, **Royal Clarence** 31 The Esplanade TA8 1BQ (Minotels)
☎(0278)783138

*Situated on the seafront, this family-run hotel has recently been upgraded throughout. The accommodation is comfortable and bedrooms are well equipped. Comprehensive table d'hôte and à la carte menus are offered in the dining room, and dishes are well prepared. Guests can also sample the real ale made on the premises.*

15rm(5⇌8🛏)(2fb) CTV in all bedrooms Ⓡ T sB&B⇋🛏fr£25 dB&B⇋🛏frf£40 🄵

CTV 20P ♨

V ♥ ⚱ Lunch fr£5.50 Dinner fr£9&alc Last dinner 8.30pm

Credit Cards 1 2 3 5 £

See advertisement under **BRIDGWATER**

A rosette is an indication of exceptional standards of cuisine.

## BURNLEY Lancashire Map **07** SD83

★★★71%, **Oaks** Colne Rd, Reedley BB10 2LF (Shire)
☎(0282)414141 Telex no 635309 FAX (0282) 33401

*A country house has been sympathetically converted to offer comfortable, tastefully modernised bedrooms and fine public rooms which retain its original character.*

58⇌🛏(10fb)2🛏✠in 28 bedrooms CTV in all bedrooms Ⓡ T ✳ sB&B⇋🛏£65-£75 dB&B⇋🛏£80-£90 🄵

⦅CTV 110P ✿ ▣(heated) ℘ (hard) squash snooker sauna solarium gymnasium spa pool *xmas*

🍴 English & French V ♥ ⚱

Credit Cards 1 2 3 4 5

★★★63%, **Keirby** Keirby Walk BB11 2DH ☎(0282)27611 Telex no 63119 FAX (0282) 36370
Closed 24-26 Dec

*Staff are friendly and helpful at this purpose-built commercial hotel in the town centre; all the well-equipped bedrooms are maintained to a good standard, though some are fairly compact.*

49⇌🛏✠in 12 bedrooms CTV in all bedrooms Ⓡ T S% sB&B⇋🛏£49-£58.50 dB&B⇋🛏£58.50-£66 Continental breakfast 🄵

Lift ⦅CTV 100P 20🅰

🍴 English & French V ♥ ⚱ ✠ S% Lunch fr£7.50 Dinner £11.75-£14.25&alc Last dinner 10pm

Credit Cards 1 2 3 5 £

★★65%, **Rosehill House** Rosehill Av B11 2PW ☎(0282)53931
RS 25 Dec-1 Jan

*A tastefully converted country house offers comfortable accommodation and interesting menus.*

20⇌🛏(1fb)1🛏 CTV in all bedrooms Ⓡ T ✳ sB&B⇋🛏£20-£34.50 dB&B⇋🛏£30-£50 🄵

60P 2🅰 ♨ ✿

V ♥ Lunch £8.50-£10.25 Dinner £8.50-£10.25 Last dinner 9.30pm

Credit Cards 1 3 5 £

⬆**Travelodge** Cavalry Barracks, Barracks Rd BB11 4AS (Trusthouse Forte) ☎(0282)416039 reservations (0800) 850 950

*This small unit, conveniently situated just off the M65 at junction 10, offers comfortable accommodation which represents particularly good value for money; meals are taken at a Happy Eater restaurant located in the car parking area.*

32⇌🛏(32fb) CTV in all bedrooms Ⓡ sB⇋🛏£24 dB⇋🛏£29.50 (room only)

⦅32P ♨

Credit Cards 1 2 3

## BURNSALL North Yorkshire Map **07** SE06

★★69%, *Fell* BD23 6BT ☎(075672)209

*Beautifully situated with spectacular views of the surrounding fells and River Wharfe, this is a family run hotel providing warm Yorkshire hospitality. Many of the cosy bedrooms have recently been refurbished and guests can relax in two lounges.*

14rm(10⇌1🛏)(4fb) Ⓡ

CTV 60P ✿ ♨

V ♥ ⚱

Credit Cards 1 2 3

★★66%, **Red Lion** BD23 6BU ☎(075672)204

*Situated in the heart of the picturesque Dales village of Burnsall, overlooking the River Wharfe, this charming hotel offers comfortable accommodation. Bedrooms are located in the main hotel and in an adjacent annexe. A good selection of food is available either from the attractive restaurant or from the cosy public bar, and all food is cooked to a high standard. Guests can relax in the comfortable lounge.*

8rm(1⇨)Annexe4⇨🏠(2fb) CTV in 2 bedrooms ® ✖ S10%
sB&B⇨🏠fr£27 dB&Bfr£38 dB&B⇨🏠fr£49.50
CTV 40P ♪
S10% Sunday Lunch fr£7 Dinner fr£10 Last dinner 9pm

---

**BURNTISLAND** Fife Map **11** NT28

★★67%, **Inchview Hotel** 69 Kinghorn Rd KY39EB
☎Kirkcaldy(0592)872239
*Overlooking the links, this small family-run hotel features a
deservedly popular restaurant.*
12⇨🏠(3fb)1🎗 CTV in all bedrooms ® T sB&B⇨🏠£33.50
dB&B⇨🏠£48-£56 🈂
15P *xmas*
♀ International V ✿ ⚘ Lunch £8.50&alc High tea £4.50
Dinner £12.95&alc Last dinner 9.45pm
Credit Cards 1 2 3 £

---

**BURNT YATES** North Yorkshire Map **08** SE26

★★68%, **Bay Horse Inn & Motel** HG3 3EJ
☎Harrogate(0423)770230
*Originally an eighteenth-century coaching inn, the Bay Horse
retains its original atmosphere with low beams, log fires and a
traditionally friendly welcome. Meals are of a particularly good
standard – the bar food's local popularity making for brisk trade –
while bedrooms are prettily decorated and well equipped, some
being situated in an adjacent house of later date.*
5🏠Annexe10🏠 CTV in all bedrooms ® T sB&B🏠£32-£35
dB&B🏠£43-£50 🈂
100P *xmas*
♀ English & French V ✿ ⚘ Lunch £8.95 High tea £6.50-£8.50
Dinner £11.95-£13.95&alc Last dinner 9.30pm
Credit Cards 1 2 3 £

---

**BURRINGTON** Devon Map **02** SS61

★★★♨67%, *Northcote Manor* EX37 9LZ (2m NW of village
towards Station & A377) (Best Western)
☎High Bickington(0769)60501
Closed Nov-Feb
*Set peacefully in its own grounds, surrounded by open countryside,
a charming hotel offers comfortable bedrooms, an attractive lounge
bar and drawing room, and an elegant split level dining room
serving a simple table d'hôte menu.*
12⇨ CTV in all bedrooms ®
20P 🎗 ✿ croquet nc7yrs
♀ English & French ✿ ⚘ ✗ Last dinner 8.15pm
Credit Cards 1 2 3 5

---

**BURTON UPON TRENT** Staffordshire Map **08** SK22

See also **Rangemore**
★★★63%, **Riverside Inn** Riverside Dr, Branston DE14 3EP
☎(0283)511234 FAX (0283) 511441
Closed 30 Dec RS 24-26 & 31 Dec
*Situated in a residential area, yet enjoying the rural setting of
lovely gardens that stretch down to the banks of the River Trent,
this popular hotel features a new function suite much in demand for
conferences and social occasions.*
21⇨ CTV in all bedrooms ® T sB&B⇨£53 dB&B⇨£64 🈂
℄130P ✿ ♪
♀ English & French V ✿ ⚘ Lunch fr£9.95 Dinner
fr£12.95&alc Last dinner 10pm
Credit Cards 1 2 3

---

Hotels with a high percentage rating for quality
are highlighted by a % across their
gazetteer entry.

---

**BURY** Greater Manchester Map **07** SD81

❀★★★71%, **Normandie** Elbut Ln, Birtle BL9 6UT
☎061-764 3869 & 061-764 1170 Telex no 635091
FAX 061-764 4866
Closed 26 Dec-8 Jan RS Sun
*Situated on a hillside a mile off the B6222 and enjoying panoramic
views over the Manchester plain, this one-time small country inn
has, over the years, been enlarged and extended in a variety of
architectural styles. All bedrooms are well equipped, but the
superior ones are particularly well appointed and comfortable, with
smart, modern and well-lit bathrooms. The highlight of this hotel,
however, is the restaurant, where a dedicated team under the
direction of Pascal Pommier, working with only the best
ingredients, produces memorable meals of consistent quality. Our
inspector was particularly impressed with the quality of fish in a
perfectly executed Ragoût de fruits de mer, crème au noilly. If one
can resist the delicious puddings there is an impressive selection of
French and English cheese. Service in the restaurant and
throughout the hotel is professional, attentive and caring.*
21⇨🏠Annexe3⇨🏠 CTV in all bedrooms ® T
✖ (ex guide dogs) ✱ sB&B⇨🏠£55-£65
dB&B⇨🏠£69-£79 Continental breakfast
Lift ℄ 60P 🎗 ✿
♀ French V ✗ Lunch £21.70-£28.65alc Dinner £18.50&alc
Last dinner 9.30pm
Credit Cards 1 2 3 5

★★60%, **Bolholt** Walshaw Rd BL8 1PU ☎061-764 5239 &
061-764 3888 FAX 061-763 1789
*Formerly a mill owners residence with a modern bedroom wing,
other extensions and its own helicopter pad. Situated in an open
grassy area with lakes and gardens reclaimed from industrial land.*
38rm(28⇨8🏠)(2fb)2🎗 CTV in all bedrooms ® ✖ ✱
sB&B⇨🏠£43-£47 dB&B⇨🏠£54-£60 🈂

▶

179

CTV 200P ❄ ♬ (hard) ♪ sauna gymnasium bowling
♀ International **V** ⊕ ♨ Lunch £8&alc Dinner £10-£14&alc
Last dinner 9pm
Credit Cards ①②③⑤

★**60% Woolfield House** Wash Ln BL9 6BJ ☎061-797 9775
*Conveniently situated between the M66 and the town centre, this
privately owned and managed commercial hotel offers compact but
well equipped bedrooms, the newer ones with smart modern shower
rooms. Guests staying at weekends should check meal
arrangements.*
16rm(3⇔7↑)1⊞ CTV in 10 bedrooms TV in 6 bedrooms ® T
✹ (ex guide dogs)
40P nc
⊕ ♨ Bar Lunch £2.95-£5.50alc Dinner £7.95-£15alc Last
dinner 8.30pm
Credit Cards ①③

---

**BURY ST EDMUNDS** Suffolk Map **05** TL86

See also **Lawshall**
★★★**76%, Angel** Angel Hill IP33 1LT ☎(0284)753926
Telex no 81630 FAX (0284) 750092
*Situated opposite the Abbey, this 18th-century, ivy-clad building is
of long standing repute. It is a hotel where hospitality and good
personal services are readily provided, and all rooms are
individually fashioned and furnished, and share the same range of
facilities, levelled at quality and comfort. The large lounge is
comfortably furnished with plump cushioned sofas and armchairs.
The elegant Regency Restaurant offers classical English dishes,
presented with care, and prepared only with the finest fresh
produce. The 'Vaults' complements by adding a variety of simpler
dishes, with an informal service. It is with great pride and genuine
pleasure that the Gough family run this fine establishment.*
41⇔↑4⊞ CTV in all bedrooms T ✱ sB⇔↑£63-£73
dB⇔↑£90-£115 (room only) ⏚
⒞50P 12🚗 CFA ♫
♀ English & French **V** ⊕ ♨ Lunch £14.50&alc Dinner
£14.50&alc Last dinner 9.45pm
Credit Cards ①②③⑤ ⓔ

★★★✤**76% Ravenwood Hall** Rougham IP30 9JA (3m E off
A45) ☎Beyton(0359)70345 FAX (0359) 70788
*This Tudor country house, steeped in local history, stands in seven
acres of woodland beside the A45 Ipswich road just outside the
town. Accommodation is furnished to a high standard, many
extras ensuring guests' comfort, while the above-average cuisine –
based largely on old English recipes – uses only fresh ingredients.
A small team of staff works under the personal supervision of the
proprietor to provide friendly, informal service throughout.*
7⇔1⊞ CTV in all bedrooms ® sB&B⇔£64.50-£75
dB&B⇔↑£85.50-£96.50 ⏚
100P 3🚗 ⊞ ❄ ⊇(heated) ♬ (hard) ∪ croquet shooting
parties arranged *xmas*
**V** ⊕ ♨ Lunch £16
Credit Cards ①②③⑤

★★★**64%, Butterfly** Symonds Rd, Moreton Hall IP32 7BW
(Consort) ☎(0284)760884 Telex no 818360 FAX (0284) 755476
*Overall value for money and friendly, efficient service based on a
genuine desire to help are provided by a hotel standing beside the
A45 on the outskirts of the town. Single bedrooms are particularly
well designed for the comfort of the user, and the open-plan public
areas are in country style. Meals are all freshly prepared on the
premises, imaginative dishes of the day complementing the buffet
and roast ranges.*
50⇔↑(2fb) CTV in all bedrooms ® T ✹ (ex guide dogs)
⒞70P
♀ European **V** ⊕ ♨ ✔ Last dinner 10pm
Credit Cards ①②③⑤

★★**77%, Kingshotts Hotel & Restaurant** 12 Angel Hill IP33 1UZ
☎(0284)704088 FAX (0284) 763133
*This delightful hotel is a new addition to the guide this year and
can, perhaps, best be described as a country house in the town.
Resident proprietors, Gary and Dianne Kingshott have
sympathetically converted a small 18th-century town house to
provide generally spacious bedrooms, each with its own character
and style. Public areas are compact but of good quality and the
well-appointed restaurant has gained a good local reputation.*
6⇔↑1⊞ CTV in all bedrooms T ✹ (ex guide dogs) ✱
sB&B⇔↑£55-£60 dB&B⇔↑£75-£85 ⏚
3P ⊞
**V** ⊕ Lunch £13-£25.90alc Dinner £13-£25.90alc Last dinner
9pm
Credit Cards ①③

★★**66%, The Suffolk** 38 The Buttermarket IP33 1DC
(Trusthouse Forte) ☎(0284)753995 FAX (0284) 750973
*In the heart of Bury St Edmunds, surrounded by shops, this
friendly hotel offers attentive service. Bedrooms are comfortable
and well-equipped and there are plans to improve the remainder of
the ground floor following recent works in the restaurant. Enquire
on booking for directions to their small garage.*
33⇔↑✹in 15 bedrooms CTV in all bedrooms ® T S10%
sB⇔↑£70-£80 dB⇔↑£80-£95 (room only) ⏚
⒞20P 16🚗 *xmas*
**V** ⊕ ♨ ✔ S10% Lunch £8.25-£11.50&alc Dinner £13.50-£15
Last dinner 9.30pm
Credit Cards ①②③④⑤

✕**Mortimer's Seafood** 31 Churchgate St IP33 1RG
☎(0284)760623
*At this busy seafood restaurant close to the Abbey Gates, guests
are served simply prepared dishes of good quality fish, their
enjoyment enhanced by the establishment's lively atmosphere and
no-fuss service. A counter "dish of the day" such as Fish Lasagne
will always represent very good value for money, but more
expensive items – Grilled Seabass accompanied by a Fennel Butter
Sauce, for example – are also available, and the accompanying
wine list is well chosen.*
Closed Sun, BH's & following Tue, 2 wks Aug & 23 Dec-3 Jan
Lunch not served Sat
♀ British & French 60 seats ✱ Lunch £7.50-£15alc Dinner
£10-£15alc Last lunch 2pm Last dinner 9pm ♪P ✔
Credit Cards ①②③⑤

---

**BUSBY** Strathclyde *Lanarkshire* Map **11** NS55

★★**Busby** 1 Field Rd G76 8RX ☎041-644 2661
Closed 25 Dec-1 Jan
*Attractively situated hotel in conservation area with popular bar
and function trade.*
14⇔↑(1fb)1⊞ CTV in all bedrooms ®
Lift ⒞60P ⊞
**V** ⊕ Last dinner 9pm
Credit Cards ①②③⑤

---

**BUSHEY** Hertfordshire Map **04** TQ19

★★★**58% Hilton National** Elton Way, Watford Bypass
WD2 8HA (Hilton) ☎Watford(0923)35881 Telex no 923422
FAX (0923) 220836
*A conference centre and leisure complex are features of this large
modern hotel. Bedrooms are being refurbished to a high
standard of well-equipped and comfortable accommodation. The
restaurant and bar are due to be extended and refurbished.*
196⇔↑✹in 5 bedrooms CTV in all bedrooms ® T ✱
S% sB⇔↑£80-£96 dB⇔↑£95-£112 (room only) ⏚
Lift ⒞350P CFA ⊡(heated) sauna solarium gymnasium ♫
♀ International **V** ⊕ ♨ S% Lunch fr£15 Dinner £15.75-£17.50
Last dinner 9.45pm
Credit Cards ①②③⑤

**BUTE, ISLE OF** Strathclyde *Buteshire* Map **10**

**ROTHESAY** Map **10** NS06

★**60%**, *St Ebba* 37 Mountstuart Rd, Craigmore PA20 9EB
☎(0700)2683
*A substantial Victorian end-of-terrace stone house situated on the seafront facing Loch Striven and the Kyles of Bute. Homely meals are made from fresh local produce. Simply furnished bedrooms and friendly, relaxed atmosphere. No smoking in the dining room or TV lounge.*
12rm(1⇗10♠)(3fb) CTV in 11 bedrooms ®
CTV 5P ♨
V ✿ ⱸ

**BUTTERMERE** Cumbria Map **11** NY11

★★**66%**, *Bridge* CA13 9UZ ☎(059685)252 & 266
*Between Buttermere and Crummock Water, surrounded by high fells, this warm and friendly hotel provides accommodation in comfortably furnished bedrooms with modern facilities. The lower floor is made up of an elegant residents' lounge, an attractive dining room, and spacious bars in which real ale is served.*
22⇗2♨ ® T ✱ sB&B⇗£49.50-£53.50
dB&B⇗£84-£92 (incl dinner) ☐
36P ♨ *xmas*
♀ English & French V ✿ ⱸ ✔ Bar Lunch £3-£8.50 High tea £1.50-£4 Dinner fr£15 Last dinner 8.30pm

**BUXTON** Derbyshire Map **07** SK07

★★★**66%**, **Lee Wood** 13 Manchester Rd SK17 6TQ (Best Western) ☎(0298)23002 & 70421 Telex no 669848
FAX (0298) 23228
Closed 24-29 Dec
*This large stone-built house, now a privately owned hotel, is situated close to the town centre and is set amongst delightful gardens. The bedrooms are comfortable and well equipped and are suitable for both tourists and business people alike, and also delegates using the conference facilities. A large attractive conservatory is used as the restaurant, and diners can enjoy the views of the garden whilst eating.*
38⇗♠(2fb) CTV in all bedrooms ® T sB&B⇗♠£56-£74
dB&B⇗♠£64-£82 ☐
Lift ⟨ CTV 50P ✿ CFA ♨
♀ English & French V ✿ ⱸ Lunch £10-£18alc Dinner £15-£17.50&alc Last dinner 9.30pm
Credit Cards ⟦1⟧⟦2⟧⟦3⟧⟦5⟧⟦£⟧

★★★**60%**, **Palace** Palace Rd SK17 6AG (Trusthouse Forte)
☎(0298)22001 Telex no 668169 FAX (0298) 72131
*This impressive Victorian building overlooking the spa town provides recently upgraded bedrooms and elegant public areas. Guests can also enjoy the gymnasium, swimming pool and well laid out gardens.*
122⇗(12fb)✔in 33 bedrooms CTV in all bedrooms ® T ✱ S%
sB⇗fr£70 dB⇗fr£92 (room only) ☐
Lift ⟨ 200P ✿ CFA ⊟(heated) snooker sauna solarium gymnasium *xmas*
♀ English & French V ✿ ⱸ S% Lunch fr£8&alc Dinner fr£14&alc Last dinner 9.30pm
Credit Cards ⟦1⟧⟦2⟧⟦3⟧⟦5⟧

★★**66%**, **Portland** 32 St John's Rd SK17 6XQ ☎(0298)71493
FAX (0298) 27464
*Situated just minutes' away from the town centre, yet providing an ideal base from which to explore the surrounding Peak District, this welcoming family-run hotel has ever-improving standards. Freshly prepared meals are served in a conservatory restaurant, a comfortable lounge invites relaxation, and there is a small conference room.*
25⇗♠(4fb)2♨✔in 1 bedroom CTV in all bedrooms ® T
sB&B⇗♠fr£42 dB&B⇗♠fr£55 ☐

▶

★ ★ ★

## HOTEL – RESTAURANT – BAR

Bury St. Edmund's new hotel – informal, comfortable and relaxing – full of style

At the BUTTERFLY you will find all the modern facilities today's travellers require, in a rustic traditional setting, that's welcoming and friendly. Bedrooms fully equipped, all with private bathroom or shower rooms

Walt's Place – Restaurant and Bar – Where you can enjoy good food, wines and service at affordable prices

**A45, BURY EAST EXIT**
**BURY ST. EDMUNDS, SUFFOLK**
For reservations please 'phone **(0284) 760884**

★★★

# The
# Angel Hotel

**Bury St Edmunds, Suffolk**
**Telephone: (0284) 753926**
**Telex: 81630 (Angel G)**
**Fax: (0284) 750092**

In the centre of East Anglia's loveliest town, Bury St Edmunds, and convenient for Newmarket and Cambridge. All rooms individually decorated to a high standard of comfort and luxury and with private bathroom, direct dial telephone and colour television. The hotel offers two restaurants, one in the 12th century Undercroft and one overlooking Angel Hill and the Abbey Gateway.

18P
♀ English & French V ✿ ⚗ Lunch fr£8 High tea fr£4 Dinner fr£14.50&alc Last dinner 9pm
Credit Cards ①②③⑤ ⑥

★63% **Hartington** 18 Broad Walk SK17 6JR ☎(0298)22638
Closed 23 Dec-Jan & 3rd wk Jul RS Nov-Mar
*Set in a quiet residential area, with attractive views over the lake at the Pavilion Gardens, this family-run hotel is reached via Hartington Road, as Broad Walk is closed to traffic.*
17rm(3⇆4♠)(3fb) CTV in 7 bedrooms ® ✖ (ex guide dogs)
sB&B£20-£25 sB&B⇆♠£33 dB&B£38 dB&B⇆♠fr£48 ▱
CTV 15P
✔ Dinner fr£9 Last dinner 8pm
Credit Cards ①③ ⑥

---

**CADNAM** Hampshire Map **04** SU21

★★★63% **Bartley Lodge** Lyndhurst Rd SO4 2NR
☎Southampton(0703)812248 FAX (0703) 812075
*This listed, red-brick, Georgian manor house in tranquil New Forest setting enjoys its reputation as flagship of the Care Leisure group of hotels. Accommodation is of a high standard, with attractively co-ordinated bedrooms which vary in size but not in quality, a galleried, oak-panelled foyer lounge, and conference/function facilities.*
19⇆♠(3fb)1🛏 CTV in all bedrooms ® T sB&B⇆♠£59-£69
dB&B⇆♠£85-£95 ▱
CTV 50P ❀ ⊒(heated) ♟ (hard) *xmas*
V ✿ ⚗ ✔ S% Lunch £13 Dinner £13&alc Last dinner 8.45pm
Credit Cards ①②③⑤

---

**CAERLEON** Gwent Map **03** ST39

✖✖**Bagan Tandoori** 2 Cross St NP7 5AN ☎(0633)422489 & 430086
Closed 25 & 26 Dec
♀ Indian V 36 seats ✱ Lunch fr£5.50 Dinner fr£16alc Last dinner 11.30pm ⅌ ✔
Credit Cards ①②③

---

**CAERNARFON** Gwynedd Map **06** SH46

★★★⚐79% **Seiont Manor** Llanrug LL55 2AQ
☎(0286)76887 & 77349 FAX (0286) 2840
*Midway between Caernarfon and Llanberis, Seiont Manor Hotel has been created from a group of farm buildings close to the Georgian manor house. The appearance of the farmstead has been carefully preserved and it still has its mill pond and surrounding pastures. All the bedrooms are spacious and airy and have been given individual character with interesting and unusual pieces of furniture from around the world. A small, intimate cocktail bar leads to the drawing room, where a 'secret' door in the bookshelves gives access to the charming residents' lounge. The dining room consists of 4 separate but interconnected rooms, and it is here that chef Richard Treble, formerly at Le Manoir aux Quat' Saisons, is gaining a good reputation for his French cooking and also for the skill with which he prepares the Welsh dishes on the menu. There is a fine leisure centre, and outdoor activities include a jogging course around the extensive grounds, or the more leisurely passtime of angling.*
28⇆♠(7fb)1🛏 CTV in all bedrooms ® T ✖ (ex guide dogs)
✱ sB&B⇆♠fr£60 dB&B⇆♠fr£80 ▱
⦗ 30P ❀ ◱(heated) ♨ sauna solarium gymnasium *xmas*
♀ French V ✿ ⚗ ✔ Lunch fr£10 High tea fr£7.50 Dinner fr£12.95&alc Last dinner 10pm
Credit Cards ①②③⑤

★★★61% **Stables** LL54 5SD (Minotels)
☎Llanwnda(0286)830711 & 830935 FAX (0286) 830413
(For full entry see Llanwnda)

---

★64% **Menai Bank** North Rd LL55 1BD ☎(0286)673297
*As suggested by its name, the family-run hotel stands just north of the town centre overlooking the Menai Straits; the comfortable and well-maintained accommodation it provides is equally suitable for tourist or business user.*
15rm(4⇆5♠)(3fb) CTV in all bedrooms ® sB&B£17-£19
dB&B£28-£32 dB&B⇆♠£34-£38 ▱
CTV 10P pool table
✿ Dinner £9-£10 Last dinner 7.30pm
Credit Cards ①③

★62% **Chocolate House** Plas Treflan, Caeathro LL55 2SE
☎(0286)672542
Closed Nov-Mar
2♠Annexe7♠✔in 1 bedroom CTV in all bedrooms ®
sB&B♠£22-£24.50 dB&B♠£32-£37 ▱
15P ⚘ ❀ solarium nc10yrs
V ✔ Dinner fr£11.50alc Last dinner 8pm
Credit Cards ①③

---

**CAERPHILLY** Mid Glamorgan Map **03** ST18

★★62% **Griffin Inn Motel** Rudry CF8 3EA ☎(0222)869735
Closed Xmas
*A character inn adjacent to Rudry church has now been extended to provide a further block of well equipped bedrooms, and a new leisure complex is planned for late 1990; the restaurant is popular locally.*
Annexe20⇆ CTV in all bedrooms ® ✖ (ex guide dogs)
⦗ 100P ⚘ ❀ ◱(heated)
♀ English & French V Last dinner 10pm
Credit Cards ①②③⑤

---

**CALDBECK** Cumbria Map **11** NY34

★★67% **Monoleys Hotel & Restaurant** CA7 8DX
☎(06998)234 & 367 Telex no 64494 FAX (06998) 478
*This attractive converted store barn is situated in the centre of this very pretty village. Bedrooms are well furnished and a very good standard of cooking is provided in the cosy restaurant. The service is provided by the resident owners, and is always friendly.*
9rm(6♠)(1fb)✔in all bedrooms CTV in 8 bedrooms ® T ✱
sB&Bfr£23.50 sB&B♠fr£27 dB&Bfr£47 dB&B♠fr£54 ▱
5P *xmas*
✿ ⚗ ✔ Lunch £6.50-£10.50alc Dinner £14.50-£23.50alc Last dinner 9.30pm
Credit Cards ①②③⑤

---

**CALLANDER** Central *Perthshire* Map **11** NN60

★★★⚐68% **Roman Camp** FK17 8BG ☎(0877)30003
Telex no 9312132123 FAX (0877) 31533
*Reminiscent of a small French château, this delightful hotel is set in 20 acres of grounds and is now under the personal direction of the Brown family, who also own Auchterarder House. Public areas are elegant and comfortable, with a choice of period-style lounges, and of particular interest is the tiny turret chapel. Bedrooms are individual in shape, size and style, but all are comfortable and well equipped.*
14⇆♠(3fb)1🛏 CTV in all bedrooms ® T sB&B⇆♠£65-£80
dB&B⇆♠£75-£110 ▱
30P ❀ ♣ croquet *xmas*
♀ Scottish & French ✿ ⚗ ✔ Lunch £15-£18&alc Dinner £25-£30&alc Last dinner 9pm
Credit Cards ①②③⑤

★★67% **Glenorchy** Leny Rd FK17 8AL ☎(0877)30329
Closed 8-31 Jan
*Run by friendly enthusiastic owners this small holiday hotel offers various sized bedrooms, a cosy bar, lounge and the Poppies restaurant.*
11rm(3⇆4♠) CTV in all bedrooms ® T ✖ sB&B£18-£38
dB&Bfr£36 dB&B⇆♠£46-£52 ▱

16P ⌨
V ✆ ⊆ Lunch £8-£12alc Dinner £8-£12alc Last dinner 9pm
Credit Cards ① ③ ⓒ

★68%, **Lubnaig** Leny Feus FK17 8AS (off A84) ☎(0877)30376
Closed Nov-Etr
*A delightful, small, family-run hotel, quietly set in its own grounds
on the edge of the village, offers pleasant, comfortable bedrooms
with individual décor and pretty, soft furnishings; its tastefully
appointed, warmly welcoming day rooms invite peaceful
relaxation.*
6🐾Annexe4🐾 ⓇsB&B🐾£42-£46
dB&B🐾£64-£72 (incl dinner) 🍴
CTV 14P 2🅿 (£2 per night) ⌨ ✣ croquet nc7yrs
🥄

★59%, **Pinewood** Leny Rd FK17 8AP ☎(0877)30111
FAX (0877) 31337
*This family-run holiday hotel is set in its own grounds beside the
main road on the edge of town. It offers a friendly atmosphere,
comfortable public rooms and functional bedrooms.*
16rm(2⇄7🐾)(3fb) CTV in all bedrooms Ⓡ T
sB&B£16.65-£18.50 sB&B⇄🐾£19.35-£21.50 dB&B£31.50-£35
dB&B⇄🐾£36-£40 🍴
CTV 30P ✣ putting ⌾ *xmas*
V ✆ ⊆ 🥄 Lunch £6-£12alc High tea £6-£12alc Dinner
£12.50-£13.50alc Last dinner 8.30pm
Credit Cards ① ② ③ ⓒ

**CALNE** Wiltshire Map 03 ST97

★★66%, **Lansdowne Strand Hotel & Restaurant** The Strand
SN11 0JR ☎(0249)812488
*Dating back to the sixteenth century, when it was a coaching inn,
the hotel retains many original features, the medieval brewhouse
being of particular interest. En suite bedrooms are well equipped
and supplied with thoughtful extras, each of the bars has its
individual ambience, and an interesting range of dishes is served in
the restaurant.*
21⇄🐾Annexe5⇄(2fb)1🍴 CTV in all bedrooms Ⓡ T
sB&B⇄🐾£48-£52 dB&B⇄🐾£56-£60 🍴
21P
♿ English & French V ✆ ⊆ Lunch £8.50-£9.50&alc High tea
fr£5alc Dinner £9.50-£10.50&alc Last dinner 10pm
Credit Cards ① ② ③ ⑤

**CAMBERLEY** Surrey Map 04 SU86

★★★62%, **Frimley Hall** Portsmouth Rd GU15 2BG (Trusthouse
Forte) ☎(0276)28321 Telex no 858446 FAX (0276) 691253
*Set amidst four acres of beautiful, carefully-maintained gardens,
this elegant Victorian manor retains much of the charm and classic
splendour of its era. Bedrooms are comprehensively equipped, the
more characterful among them being situated in the main hotel
building, and public areas include the cosy Sandhurst Bar as well
as a well appointed restaurant and lounge.*
66⇄🥄in 10 bedrooms CTV in all bedrooms Ⓡ T ✱
sB⇄£70-£79 dB⇄£96-£110 (room only) 🍴
⓿ 200P ✣ CFA *xmas*
V ✆ ⊆ 🥄 Lunch £11.50-£17.75&alc Dinner
£13.75-£18.75&alc Last dinner 10pm
Credit Cards ① ② ③ ④ ⑤

★★★60%, **Lakeside International** Wharf Rd, Frimley Green
GU16 6JR ☎Deepcut(0252)838000 Telex no 858095
FAX (0252) 837857
*The unique lakeside setting gives bedrooms with balconies an
excellent and relaxing panorama, which extends to the very
informal carvery-style restaurant. Function rooms are on offer at
this hotel, and the accommodation has been particularly well
equipped with every modern facility. Live entertainment is usually
provided in the restaurant during the evening.*
97⇄ CTV in all bedrooms Ⓡ T 🐾 (ex guide dogs)

▶

**C**

Lift ℂ 250P ✿ squash snooker *xmas*
♀ French **V** ✿ ℒ Lunch £12.50&alc High tea fr£3.50 Dinner
£12.50&alc Last dinner 10.30pm
Credit Cards ①②③⑤

---

**CAMBRIDGE** Cambridgeshire Map **05** TL45

★★★★55% **Garden House** Granta Place, Mill Ln CB2 1RT
(Queens Moat) ☎6ambridge(0223)63421 Telex no 81463
FAX (0223) 316605
*Approached via Trumpington Street, this modern-style hotel,*
*situated in 3 acres of attractive gardens on the banks of the River*
*Cam, is undergoing a lengthy programme of refurbishment.*
*Bedrooms are spacious and comfortable.*
118➪🟊(4fb)⊁in 15 bedrooms CTV in all bedrooms Ⓡ **T**
✖ (ex guide dogs) sB&B➪🟊£73-£125
dB&B➪🟊£99-£150 Continental breakfast 🍴
Lift ℂ 180P ✿ CFA ✎ punting *xmas*
♀ English & French **V** ✿ ℒ Lunch £15.75&alc Dinner
£18.50-£29.50&alc Last dinner 9.30pm
Credit Cards ①②③⑤ ⓔ

★★★★55% **Post House** Lakeview, Bridge Rd, Impington
CB4 4PH (2.5m N, on N side of rdbt jct A45/B1049) (Trusthouse
Forte) ☎(0223)237000 Telex no 817123 FAX (0223) 233426
*Situated north of Cambridge, adjacent to the A45 with access from*
*the B1049, this hotel offers comfortable accommodation with a*
*good standard of cleanliness. The hotel also has a Business Centre*
*and a Health and Leisure Club.*
120➪🟊(14fb)⊁in 16 bedrooms CTV in all bedrooms Ⓡ **T** ✳
S10% sB➪🟊£84-£92 dB➪🟊fr£103 (room only) 🍴
ℂ 250P ✿ ⊠(heated) sauna solarium gymnasium *xmas*
♀ International **V** ✿ ℒ ⊁ S10% Lunch £15.50-£17.50&alc
High tea £4.50-£10 Dinner fr£16.50&alc Last dinner 10.30pm
Credit Cards ①②③④⑤

★★★★55% **University Arms** Regent St CB2 1AD (De Vere)
☎(0223)351241 Telex no 817311 FAX (0223) 315256
*Though the bedrooms of this famous city centre hotel have been*
*refurbished and its entrance and public rooms restyled to present a*
*more welcoming aspect, the De Vere group have taken care to*
*preserve all the unique features of the establishment.*
117➪(7fb) CTV in all bedrooms Ⓡ **T** sB&B➪£75-£85
dB&B➪fr£90 🍴
Lift ℂ 80P CFA ♫ *xmas*
♀ English & French **V** ✿ ℒ Lunch fr£12&alc Dinner
fr£15&alc Last dinner 9.45pm
Credit Cards ①②③⑤ ⓔ

★★★61% **Cambridgeshire Moat House** CB3 8EU (Queens
Moat) ☎Crafts Hill(0954)780555 Telex no 817141
FAX (0954) 780010
(For full entry see Bar Hill)

★★★61% **Gonville** Gonville Place CB1 1LY ☎(0223)66611
Closed 4 days at Xmas
*Located in the city centre, overlooking Parkers Piece, the hotel is*
*ideal for both tourists and commercial users, offering spotless, well-*
*equipped rooms and consistently high standards throughout.*
62➪(6fb) CTV in all bedrooms Ⓡ
Lift ℂ CTV 100P CFA
**V** ✿ ℒ
Credit Cards ①②③④ ⓔ

★★70% **Cambridge Lodge** Huntingdon Rd CB3 0DQ
☎(0223)352833 FAX (0223) 355166
RS Sat
*A detached Edwardian house, located one mile north of the town*
*centre on the A1207. The accommodation is well furnished and*
*comfortable and the good table d'hôte and à la carte menus in the*
*restaurant offer an interesting range of dishes, prepared from fresh*
*ingredients.*
11➪🟊 CTV in all bedrooms Ⓡ **T** S% sB&B➪🟊£42-£58
dB&B➪🟊£60-£80 🍴

---

20P 🚗 ✿
♀ English & Continental **V** Lunch £13.95-£15.95&alc Dinner
£18.50-£19.95&alc Last dinner 9.30pm
Credit Cards ①②③⑤

★★67% **Arundel House** 53 Chesterton Rd CB4 3AN
☎(0223)67701
Closed 25-26 Dec
*Situated on the edge of Jesus Green and close to the city centre,*
*this hotel has grown in both size and quality. Some rooms are*
*above average for this classification whilst others, although more*
*dated and modestly furnished, are comfortable and well equipped.*
*A good range of well prepared dishes are served in both the bar and*
*restaurant.*
66rm(20➪33🟊)Annexe22➪🟊(7fb) CTV in all bedrooms Ⓡ **T**
✖ sB&B£26.50-£34 sB&B➪🟊£36-£47 dB&B£39.50
dB&B➪🟊£50-£65 Continental breakfast 🍴
ℂ 70P
♀ English, French & Italian **V** ✿ ℒ ⊁ Lunch £7.50&alc
Dinner £11.75&alc Last dinner 9.30pm
Credit Cards ①②③⑤

★54% **Quy Mill** Newmarket Rd CB5 9AG ☎(0223)853383
FAX (0223) 853770
(For full entry see Stow Cum Quy)

✖✖**Midsummer House** Midsummer Common CB4 1HA
☎(0223)69299
*Situated on the edge of Midsummer Common this restaurant*
*comprises a series of small dining areas, elegantly furnished and*
*distinctively decorated. Chef/Patron Hans Schweitzer continues to*
*produce skilful, imaginative dishes using good quality fresh*
*ingredients. A warm winter salad could be followed by roast*
*pheasant garnished with truffle, red cabbage and dauphinois*
*potatoes. An extensive and fine wine list accompanies the*
*frequently changing menu.*
Closed Sun
Lunch not served Sat
♀ International **V** 55 seats Lunch £14.50-£29.50 Dinner
£22.50-£29.50 Last lunch 2pm Last dinner 9.30pm ✐
Credit Cards ①③⑤

---

**CAMPBELTOWN** Strathclyde *Argyllshire* Map **10** NR72

★★63% **Royal** Main St PA28 6AG ☎(0586)52017
*A corner-site commercial hotel overlooking the harbour offers*
*extensive dinner menus in its first floor restaurant.*
16rm(8➪4🟊)(2fb) CTV in all bedrooms Ⓡ **T** ✳ sB&B£19.75
sB&B➪🟊£23.75 dB&B£32.95 dB&B➪🟊£39 🍴
Lift CTV 4P ♫
♀ English & French **V** ✿ ℒ ⊁ Lunch £3.50&alc High tea
£3.95-£7.95 Dinner £11.25&alc Last dinner 9pm
Credit Cards ①③

★65% **Seafield** Kilkerran Rd PA28 6JL ☎(0586)54385
*A small, homely family-run hotel with a cosy little lounge bar.*
*Most of the well-equipped bedrooms are contained in a modern*
*bungalow at the rear.*
3🟊Annexe6🟊 CTV in all bedrooms Ⓡ **T** ✳
sB&B🟊£27.50-£30 dB&B🟊£44-£48 🍴
11P
**V** ✿ Lunch £3.50-£8.95&alc High tea £6.50-£7.50&alc Dinner
£10.50-£13.50&alc Last dinner 9pm
Credit Cards ①③ ⓔ

★61% **The Ardshiel Hotel** Kilkerran Rd PA28 6JL
☎(0586)52133
*This friendly, family-run, commercial/tourist hotel provides*
*accommodation in modestly furnished but well equipped*
*bedrooms ; a programme of upgrading is planned for early 1991.*
10➪🟊(2fb) CTV in all bedrooms Ⓡ **T** ✳ S%
sB&B➪🟊£25-£30 dB&B➪🟊£40-£50 🍴

20P ❀
V ✿ ⚗
Credit Cards 1 3 £

---

**CANNICH** Highland *Inverness-shire* Map **14** NH33

★★1♣67% **Cozac Lodge** Glen Cannich IV4 7LX (8m W on unclass Glen Cannich rd) ☎(04565)263
*This charming and hospitable country house hotel is situated beside Loch Sealbanach at the top of a rugged and remote Highland glen, amid spectacular scenery where wildlife is abundant. Bedrooms are comfortably appointed and well equipped with useful extras, and the elegant public rooms have a tranquil atmosphere.*
7⇱🛏(1fb) CTV in all bedrooms ® sB&B⇱🛏£33-£41
dB&B⇱🛏£54-£64 ♺
CTV 12P 🚲 ❀ ✔
❤ International ✿ ⚗
Credit Cards 1 2 3

---

**CANNOCK** Staffordshire Map **07** SJ91

★★★60% **Roman Way** Watling St, Hatherton WS11 1SH (on A5) (Crown & Raven) ☎(0543)572121 FAX (0543) 502749
*A modern hotel with good standards that meets the needs of business and tourist guests. It lies on the A5 close to junctions 11 and 12 of the M6. Bedrooms have good facilities and there is a choice of bars.*
56⇱🛏 CTV in all bedrooms ® T sB&B⇱🛏fr£53.35
dB&B⇱🛏fr£68.75 ♺
⟨ 200P 🎵
❤ English & French V ✿ ⚗ Lunch fr£6.95&alc High tea fr£3.95 Dinner fr£11.50&alc Last dinner 10pm
Credit Cards 1 2 3 5

🏠**Longford House Travel Inn** Watling St, Longford WS11 1SJ
☎(0543)572721 FAX (0543) 466130
*A modern bedroom complex situated at the rear of a Georgian house on the A5, close to junction 12 of the M6.*
38⇱🛏(2fb)⚹in 14 bedrooms CTV in all bedrooms ®
✗ (ex guide dogs) ✳ sB⇱🛏£27.50 dB⇱🛏£27.50 (room only)
115P ❀
V ✿ ⚹ Lunch £3.65-£10.95alc Dinner £5.45-£10.95alc Last dinner 10.30pm
Credit Cards 1 2 3 5

---

**CANTERBURY** Kent Map **05** TR15

★★★60% **Falstaff** St Dunstans St CT2 8AF (Lansbury)
☎(0227)462138 Telex no 96394 FAX (0227) 463525
*A skilfully modernised sixteenth-century coaching inn near the Westgate Tower offers a choice of particularly well-equipped accommodation where the charm of turret room and four-poster bed is successfully combined with the convenience of modern facilities. After enjoying a traditional meal in the Two Seasons Restaurant, guests can relax in a small beamed lounge, and there is a first-floor conference room; a friendly staff offers helpful service, and the hotel has made good provision for car parking.*
24⇱🛏(2fb)2🛁⚹in 6 bedrooms CTV in all bedrooms ®
✗ (ex guide dogs) sB&B⇱🛏fr£69 dB&B⇱🛏fr£85 ♺
⟨ 50P xmas
❤ English & Continental V ✿ ⚗ Lunch fr£11&alc Dinner fr£11&alc Last dinner 10pm
Credit Cards 1 2 3 5

★★★54% **The Chaucer** Ivy Ln CT1 1TU (Trusthouse Forte)
☎(0227)464427 Telex no 965096 FAX (0227) 450397
*This large hotel, mostly rebuilt since the war, offers compact bedrooms in the main, though there are some larger double rooms at the front; its restaurant is spacious and there is a pleasant lounge bar.*
45⇱🛏⚹in 10 bedrooms CTV in all bedrooms ® T ✳
sB⇱🛏£64-£69 dB⇱🛏£79-£85 (room only) ♺

▶

---

《 45P CFA xmas

♡ English & French V ♦ ⌨ ✕ S% Lunch £6.50-£10.75&alc Dinner £13-£14&alc Last dinner 9.45pm

Credit Cards [1] [2] [3] [4] [5]

★★ 60% Canterbury 71 New Dover Rd CT1 3DZ
☎(0227)450551 Telex no 965809 FAX (0227) 450873
*A pleasant hotel in Georgian-style provides bedrooms which are all well equipped, though some are compact ; a small lounge bar complements the nicely appointed restaurant, and the atmosphere is friendly throughout.*
27➩♠(4fb) CTV in all bedrooms ® ✱ sB&B➩♠fr£45 dB&B➩♠fr£58 ⊟

Lift CTV 40P

♡ English & French ♦ ⌨ Lunch fr£6 Dinner fr£11.50&alc Last dinner 10pm

Credit Cards [1] [2] [3] [5] ④

✕✕Michael's Restaurant 74 Wincheap CT1 3RS
☎(0227)767411
*New owners have improved the amenities of this hotel, a grade II listed sixteenth-century building where open log fires create a cosy atmosphere in winter. The interesting and imaginative dishes featured on both à la carte and additional lunchtime set-price menus are skilfully prepared by the chef/proprietor and accompanied by a wine list which is comprehensive overall though it lacks good half bottles.*
Closed Sun, 26-30 Dec, 1 wk Etr & BH'S

Lunch not served Sat

♡ British & French V 34 seats ✱ Lunch fr£13&alc Dinner fr£18&alc Last lunch 2.30pm Last dinner 9.30pm 10P ✕

Credit Cards [1] [3]

✕Ristorante Tuo e Mio 16 The Borough CT1 2DR
☎(0227)761471
*An appealing restaurant with a comprehensive Italian menu which includes seafood specialities and dishes of the day. Décor is clean and bright with a certain charm and elegance and the staff are pleasant and helpful.*
Closed Mon & last 2 wks Aug

Lunch not served Tue

♡ Italian V 40 seats ✱ S10% Lunch £15-£25alc Last dinner 10.45pm ♪

Credit Cards [1] [2] [3] [5]

## CAPEL CURIG Gwynedd Map 06 SH75

★★ 63% Cobdens LL24 0EE (on A5) ☎(06904)243 & 308
19rm(10➩6♠)(2fb) CTV in all bedrooms ® T ✱
60P ✿ ♨ ♪ ♫

♡ British V ♦ ⌨

Credit Cards [1] [3]

## CARBIS BAY

See St Ives

## CARCROFT South Yorkshire Map 08 SE50

○Travelodge A1 Great North Rd(Trusthouse Forte)
☎Central reservations (0800) 850950
40➩

## CARDIFF South Glamorgan Map 03 ST17

See Town Plan Section

★★★★ 66% Holiday Inn Mill Ln CF1 1EZ (Holiday Inns)
☎(0222)399944 Telex no 497365 FAX (0222) 395578
*An impressive, modern hotel near the city centre and railway station with well appointed bedrooms and open plan public areas. Good conference and leisure facilities.*
182➩♠(78fb)✕in 36 bedrooms CTV in all bedrooms ® T
S10% sB➩♠£80-£236 dB➩♠£94-£236 (room only) ⊟

Lift (⊞ 90P ⊠(heated) squash sauna solarium gymnasium turkish bath beauty therapist ♫ xmas

♡ English & French V ♦ ⌨ ✕ S10% Lunch £10.75-£12.45 Dinner £12-£14.50 Last dinner 10.30pm

Credit Cards [1] [2] [3] [4] [5] ④

★★★★ 54% Park Park Place CF1 3UD (Mount Charlotte (TS))
☎(0222)383471 Telex no 497195 FAX (0222) 399309
*A busy, city-centre hotel, well equipped to handle both conferences and private functions. Renovation and refurbishment of all rooms is well under way, and the management hopes to completely redesign the public areas in the near future.*
119➩♠(7fb)✕in 30 bedrooms CTV in all bedrooms ® T ✱
sB➩♠£62.50-£75 dB➩♠£72.50-£82.50 (room only) ⊟

Lift ( 80P CFA xmas

♡ English & French V ♦ ⌨ Lunch £7.75-£8.75&alc Dinner fr£12.95&alc Last dinner 9.30pm

Credit Cards [1] [2] [3] [4] [5]

★★★ 64% Crest Castle St C71 2XB (Trusthouse Forte)
☎(0222)388681 Telex no 497258 FAX (0222) 371495
*The modern, company-owned hotel stands adjacent to the National Stadium and overlooks Cardiff Castle. Its popular bars and well equipped bedrooms attract a firm business following.*
159➩♠(24fb)✕in 20 bedrooms CTV in all bedrooms ® ⊟

Lift ( 120P CFA xmas

♡ English & French V ♦ ⌨ ✕

Credit Cards [1] [2] [3] [5]

★★★ 59% Post House Pentwyn Rd, Pentwyn CF2 7XA (Trusthouse Forte) ☎(0222)731212 Telex no 497633 FAX (0222) 549147
*Situated alongside the city's Eastern Avenue bypass, this busy comercial hotel has good function facilities, as well as leisure facilities, well equipped bedrooms, an à la carte restaurant and a coffee shop.*
150➩♠(50fb)✕in 30 bedrooms CTV in all bedrooms ®

Lift ( 210P ✿ CFA ⊠(heated) sauna solarium gymnasium

♡ International V ♦ ⌨ ✕ Last dinner 10pm

Credit Cards [1] [2] [3] [4] [5] ④

★★★ 56% Royal Saint Mary's St CF1 1LL (Embassy)
☎(0222)383321 Telex no 498062 FAX (0222) 222238
*This city centre hotel has a range of popular bars and provides good function facilities. The public rooms have recently been upgraded, and are smart and comfortable.*
63rm(39➩8♠)(3fb)✕in 6 bedrooms CTV in all bedrooms ®
sB£35-£37.50 sB➩♠£60-£75 dB£45-£50
dB➩♠£70-£100 (room only) ⊟

Lift ( CTV ♪ CFA snooker ♫ xmas

♡ British & French V ♦ ⌨ Lunch £4.95-£8.95&alc Dinner £12.50-£14.50&alc Last dinner 10pm

Credit Cards [1] [2] [3] [4] [5] ④

★★ 64% Riverside Hotel 53-59 Despenser St, Riverside CF1 8RG ☎(0222)378866 FAX (0222) 388306
*Situated directly across the River Taff from Cardiff Arms Park and the Empire Pool, this extended Victorian house has been modernised to provide well equipped en suite bedrooms and a good range of facilities, including a night spot and a carvery restaurant. Friendly and attentive services are provided by Mrs Stephens and her staff.*
36➩♠(3fb) CTV in all bedrooms ® T ✱ S% sB&B➩♠£38.50 dB&B➩♠£52-£75 ⊟

《 22P ♪ xmas

V ♦ ⌨ Bar Lunch £3-£6alc Dinner £4.50-£12alc Last dinner 9.30pm

Credit Cards [1] [2] [3] [5]

For key to symbols see the inside front cover.

★★59% **The Phoenix** 199 Fidlas Rd, Llanishen CF4 5NA
☎(0222)764615 FAX (0222) 747812
24rm(5⇌16♠)(2fb) CTV in all bedrooms ⓇＴ sB&B⇌♠£39
dB&B£46 dB&B⇌♠£51.50
Lift ₵ CTV 30P ♫
♀ English & French V ♧ ⓛ Lunch £7.95&alc Dinner
£7.95&alc Last dinner 10pm
Credit Cards ①③④ⓔ

★★57% *Lincoln* 118 Cathedral Rd CF1 9LQ ☎(0222)395558
Telex no 497492
*Comfortable modern accommodation is complemented by a cosy*
*bar, friendly service and an informal, relaxing atmosphere in this*
*converted Victorian hotel which stands very close to the Sophia*
*Gardens and only a few minutes' walk from castle and city centre.*
18⇌♠(1fb) CTV in all bedrooms Ⓡ ✘ (ex guide dogs)
₵ 18P
V ♧ ⓛ Last dinner 9.30pm
Credit Cards ①②③⑤

See advertisement on page 189

♫*Campanile* Caxton Place, Pentwyn CF2 7HA (Campanile)
☎(0222)549044 Telex no 497553
Annexe47⇌♠ CTV in all bedrooms Ⓡ Ｔ
50P
♀ English & French Last dinner 10pm
Credit Cards ①③

See advertisement on page 189

♫**Rank Motor Lodge** Cardiff West CF7 8SB (M4, junct 33)
(Rank) ☎(0222)892255
*This brand new complex is situated within the Cardiff West*
*Service Area at junction 33 of the M4. All bedrooms are very well*
*equipped and food is available 24 hours a day at the adjoining*
*service area.*
▶

50⇨♦(25fb)⊬in 7 bedrooms CTV in all bedrooms ® ✱
sB&B⇨♦£27.50 dB&B⇨♦£34.50 Continental breakfast
₵50P
Credit Cards [1][2][3][5]

○**Travelodge** Circle Way East, Off A48 (M), Llanederyn
CF3 7ND (Trusthouse Forte)
☎Central reservations (0800) 850950
32⇨

✕**La Chaumière** 44 Cardiff Rd, Llandaff CF5 2DS
☎(0222)555319
*Situated behind the Maltsters public house, close to the the
cathedral, this intimate restaurant is enthusiastically run by Karen
Duncan and Rory Garvey. Rory is a charming and attentive host,
whilst chef Karen produces imaginative food which includes
mouth-watering pastry work.*
Closed Mon
Lunch not served Sat
Dinner not served Sun
ᛘ French 34 seats Lunch £12.50-£15.75 Dinner £21-£24alc
Last lunch 2pm Last dinner 10pm 20P
Credit Cards [1][2][3]

✕*Gibsons* Romilly Crescent CF1 9NR ☎(0222)341264
*This simple, split-level, ground-floor restaurant in the north-west
suburb of the city features short but imaginative à la carte and
table d'hôte menus offering a selection of imaginative dishes with a
French influence and is particularly popular at lunch time with
local business people ; service is informally friendly and there is a
delicatessen shop on the premises.*
Closed Tue, BH's & 26 Dec
Dinner not served Sun & Mon
ᛘ French V 38 seats Last lunch 2.15pm Last dinner 10pm 5P
Credit Cards [1][2][3][5]

✕*Le Cassoulet* 5 Romilly Crescent, Canton CF1 9NP
☎(0222)221905
*Claire and Gilbert Viader originate from Toulouse and have
named their restaurant after one of the city's most famous dishes.
The region's strong flavours feature prominently on the menu,
which is changed daily, and there is a small but well chosen wine
list.*
Closed Sun, Mon & 4 weeks in summer.(Ring for details)
Lunch not served Sat
ᛘ French 36 seats Lunch £15-£24alc Dinner £15-£24alc Last
lunch 2pm Last dinner 10pm ℱ
Credit Cards [1][3]

✕*Polydores Fish* 89 City Rd, Roath CF2 4BN ☎(0222)481319
*Situated alongside the car show room of the busy City Road, this
very pleasant restaurant specialises in fish, especially the unusual
variety. Tuna, red mullet, barracuda and skate feature, and meat
and poultry are available for those who prefer it. As well as the
usual à la carte menu, an inexpensive lunchtime special has been
introduced.*
Lunch not served Sat
Dinner not served Sun & Mon
V 40 seats Last lunch 2.30pm Last dinner 10.30pm ℱ
Credit Cards [1][2][3][5]

✕*Riverside* 44 Tudor St CF1 8RH ☎(0222)372163
*This restaurant can be reached by taking the side entrance, and
not the most obvious corner entrance, and stairs take you into the
world of Hong Kong. The first floor dining room is large, split into
several areas, and ornate with elaborate moulded walls, full of
entwining dragons and flowers. Very well patronised by the
Chinese population of Cardiff and the food is certainly
authentically Chinese. It has all the expected dishes, but also many
unusual Cantonese ones.*
Closed 24-25 Dec
ᛘ Cantonese V 140 seats Last dinner 11.45pm ℱ
Credit Cards [1][2][3][5]

**CARFRAEMILL** Borders *Berwickshire* Map 12 NT55

★★66% **Carfraemill** Oxton TD2 6RA ☎Oxton(05785)200
Telex no 336587 FAX (05785) 640
*A warm welcome is extended to both residents and diners by this
comfortable hotel at the A697/A68 juction. Interesting menus
represent good value for money, and a friendly atmosphere prevails
throughout.*
8rm(2⇨)(2fb) CTV in all bedrooms ® ✱ sB&Bfr£21.50
sB&B⇨♦fr£26.50 dB&Bfr£40 dB&B⇨♦fr£45 ▯
100P 3⚐
ᛘ International V ❂ ⚑
Credit Cards [1][2][3][5]

**CARLISLE** Cumbria Map 11 NY45
See also **Hayton**
★★★68% **Cumbrian** Court Square CA1 1QY ☎(0228)31951
Telex no 64287 FAX (0228) 47799
*This totally renovated hotel stands next to the railway station and
offers first class accommodation for both business and leisure users
alike. The complete rebuilding of the ground floor has provided
tastefully modern and more spacious lounges and bars, without
losing the character of the building. The magnificent ballroom has
been most elegantly restored.*
70⇨♦(3fb)1⚏⊬in 4 bedrooms CTV in all bedrooms ® T ✱
sB⇨♦fr£72.50 dB⇨♦£87.50-£99.50 (room only) ▯
Lift ₵ 15P 30⚐ CFA ♫ xmas
ᛘ Continental V ❂ ⚑ ⊬ Lunch £10.75&alc Dinner
£16.50&alc Last dinner 10pm
Credit Cards [1][2][3][5]Ⓔ

★★★63% **The Central Plaza** Victoria Viaduct CA3 8AL (Inter-
Hotels) ☎(0228)20256 FAX (0228) 514657
*Recently refurbished city centre hotel with a comfortable lounge
bar.*
84⇨♦(2fb) CTV in all bedrooms ® T ✱ sB&B⇨♦£55-£66
dB&B⇨♦£66-£76 ▯
Lift ₵ CTV 20⚐ pool xmas
ᛘ English & French V ❂ ⚑ Lunch fr£6&alc High tea fr£5.50
Dinner fr£14.50&alc Last dinner 9pm
Credit Cards [1][2][3][5]

★★★62% **Swallow Hilltop** London Rd CA1 2PQ (Swallow)
☎(0228)29255 Telex no 64292 FAX (0228) 25238
*Large modern hotel with very good facilities and new leisure
complex.*
92⇨♦(10fb)⊬in 13 bedrooms CTV in all bedrooms ® T S%
sB&B⇨♦fr£67 dB&B⇨♦fr£80 ▯
Lift ₵ CTV 350P ❈ CFA ◲(heated) sauna solarium
gymnasium table tennis massage putting green ♫ ⚭ xmas
ᛘ English & French V ❂ ⚑ S% Lunch £8 Dinner £14.75 Last
dinner 10pm
Credit Cards [1][2][3][5]

All hotels are now given a percentage grading
for the quality of their facilities. A full explanation
can be found within 'How we Classify Hotels
and Restaurants' at the front of the book.

★★★61% **Crest** Parkhouse Rd, Kingstown CA4 0HR (junc 44/
M6) (Trusthouse Forte) ☎(0228)31201 Telex no 64201
FAX (0228) 43178
*Purpose-built hotel, just south of junction 44 of the M6/A74/A7 on
the northern outskirts of the town, popular with business clientele.*
94⇆✿(12fb)⅄in 23 bedrooms CTV in all bedrooms ®️ T
(room only) 🏲
《 CTV 200P CFA ⊠(heated) snooker sauna solarium
gymnasium ♫ *xmas*
♉ International V ✿ ⛾ ⅄
Credit Cards ①②③④⑤

★★59% **Pinegrove** 262 London Rd CA1 2QS ☎(0228)24828
Closed 25 & 31 Dec
*Conveniently situated on a main road on the south side of the city,
a commercial hotel offers a range of bedroom styles.*
32rm(9⇆13✿)(8fb) CTV in all bedrooms ®️ T S%
sB&B£24-£34 sB&B⇆✿£34 dB&B£36-£46 dB&B⇆✿£46
CTV 30P ✾
V ✿ ⛾ ⅄ S% Lunch £9.50-£14.50 Dinner £9.50-£14.50 Last
dinner 9pm
Credit Cards ①③

★★57% **Woodlands** 264/266 London Rd CA1 2QS (Minotels)
☎(0228)45643
Closed 24 Dec-8 Jan
*A family run hotel providing traditional bedrooms, a spacious
lounge bar and a nicely appointed restaurant. Situated on the A6,
two miles from junction 42 of the M6.*
15rm(6⇆1✿)(1fb) CTV in all bedrooms ®️ T sB&Bfr£25
sB&B⇆✿fr£33 dB&Bfr£42 dB&B⇆✿fr£50 🏲
20P ⚫
V ✿ Bar Lunch £3-£7.85 High tea £4.95 Dinner £11.50-£14.50
Last dinner 9pm
Credit Cards ①②③⑤ ⓔ

See advertisement on page 191

---

# Carlisle - Cartmel

★58% **Vallum House** Burgh Rd CA2 7NB ☎(0228)21860
Closed 25 & 26 Dec
*This family run, mainly commercial hotel, is situated on the western edge of town on the road to Burgh by Sands. Bedrooms vary in size, some singles are very compact, staff are helpful and the bar meals popular.*
9rm(1⇨4🟊)(1fb) CTV in 6 bedrooms TV in 3 bedrooms Ⓡ
CTV 30P ✿
🍴 English & French V ٥ ⏍ Last dinner 9pm
Credit Cards 1

---

### CARMARTHEN Dyfed Map 02 SN42

★★★64% **Ivy Bush Royal** Spilman St SA31 1LG (Trusthouse Forte) ☎(0267)235111 Telex no 48520 FAX (0267) 234914
*Large and popular, the hotel is ideally situated for touring West Wales and also offers good conference facilities. Many bedrooms are now a little dated – though upgrading is planned – but public areas are pleasant and relaxing.*
79⇨🟊(3fb)⊁in 8 bedrooms CTV in all bedrooms Ⓡ T S%
sB⇨🟊fr£58 dB⇨🟊fr£68 (room only) 🏳
Lift ⊄ 75P 3🚗 ✿ CFA sauna *xmas*
V ٥ ⏍ ⊁ Lunch fr£8.50&alc Dinner fr£12.50&alc Last dinner 9.30pm
Credit Cards 1 2 3 4 5

---

### CARNFORTH Lancashire Map 07 SD47

★★66% **Royal Station** Market St LA5 9BT ☎(0524)732033 & 733636
*Spaciously comfortable bedrooms, good-value menus and friendly services are attractive features of this town-centre hotel, conveniently situated opposite the railway station.*
12⇨🟊(1fb) CTV in all bedrooms Ⓡ T sB&B⇨🟊£24.50 dB&B⇨🟊£42 🏳
8P 10🚗
🍴 English, French & Italian V ٥ ⏍
Credit Cards 1 2 3 5

---

### CARNOUSTIE Tayside *Angus* Map 12 NO53

★★59% **Glencoe** Links Pde DD7 7JF ☎(0241)53273
Closed 1 Jan
*Homely, family hotel overlooking golf course, offering very good value meals.*
11rm(3⇨5🟊)(2fb) CTV in all bedrooms T S10%
sB&Bfr£19.50 dB&B⇨🟊fr£46
CTV 10P 🚗
🍴 Scottish & French V ٥ ⏍ S10% Bar Lunch £1-£7.50alc Dinner £10.50-£16.50 Last dinner 9pm
Credit Cards 1 2 3 5

★★57% **Carlogie House** Carlogie Rd DD7 6LD ☎(0241)53185
Closed 1-3 Jan
*A small family-run commercial and holiday hotel set in its own grounds on the northern fringe of the village. It has a friendly atmosphere and offers bedrooms which are somewhat practical in style, though well equipped.*
11⇨🟊(1fb) CTV in all bedrooms Ⓡ T 🐾 (ex guide dogs) ✳
sB&B⇨🟊£30 dB&B⇨🟊£45
CTV 150P 4🚗 ✿
🍴 Scottish & French V ٥ ⏍ Lunch fr£12&alc High tea fr£4.80 Dinner fr£12 Last dinner 9.30pm
Credit Cards 1 2 3 5

★58% **Station** DD7 6AR ☎(0241)52447
*Small, friendly, town centre hotel next to the station and near the beach, with modest, practical accommodation.*
9rm(3🟊)(1fb) CTV in 3 bedrooms Ⓡ
CTV 10P pool ♫
V ٥ ⏍ Last dinner 9pm
Credit Cards 1 3

---

### CARPERBY North Yorkshire Map 07 SE08

★★64% **Wheatsheaf** DL8 4DF ☎Wensleydale(0969)663216
*Run in an informal, friendly manner by the Mackay family the hotel has prettily decorated bedrooms, a character bar and cosy lounge. It was here that James Herriot and his wife Helen spent their honeymoon in 1941.*
8⇨🟊(1fb)2🛏 CTV in all bedrooms Ⓡ
50P 🚗 ✿ nc12yrs
V ٥ ⏍
Credit Cards 1 2 3 5

---

### CARRADALE Strathclyde *Argyllshire* Map 10 NR83

★★65% **Carradale** PA28 6QQ ☎(05833)223
*Standing in its own grounds overlooking Kilbrannan Sound and the Isle of Arran, this pleasant holiday hotel offers modest bedrooms and public rooms and a small leisure centre. The golf course is conveniently situated next to the hotel.*
14rm(4⇨3🟊)Annexe6rm(1⇨3🟊)(2fb) Ⓡ
CTV 20P 🚗 ✿ squash sauna solarium
V ٥ ⏍ Last dinner 8.45pm
Credit Cards 1 3

---

### CARRBRIDGE Highland *Inverness-shire* Map 14 NH92

★★70% **Dalrachney Lodge** PH23 3AT ☎(047984)252 FAX (047984) 382
*This former shooting lodge is now a fine country house hotel, with spacious, lofty bedrooms, a delightful lounge and an elegant dining room. Service is extremely attentive and the artistically presented food features the best of Scottish beef, game and fish. The lodge lies just east of the village, close to the River Dulnain.*
11rm(8⇨1🟊)(3fb) CTV in all bedrooms Ⓡ T sB&B£26-£29.50 sB&B⇨🟊£26-£29.50 dB&B£52-£59 dB&B⇨🟊£52-£59 🏳
40P 🚗 ♪
🍴 Scottish & French V ٥ ⏍ ⊁ Sunday Lunch £5.95 Dinner £13.95&alc Last dinner 9pm
Credit Cards 1 2 3 £

---

### CARRUTHERSTOWN Dumfries & Galloway *Dumfriesshire* Map 11 NY17

★★★64% **Hetland Hall** DG1 4JX (Best Western) ☎Dumfries(0387)84201 Telex no 776819 FAX (0387) 84211
*Standing within the tranquil setting of its own extensive gardens, yet having direct access from the A75, this spacious country house is managed by its resident proprietors to provide friendly, informal service.*
27⇨🟊(3fb)⊁in 3 bedrooms CTV in all bedrooms Ⓡ T S%
sB&B⇨🟊£44-£49 dB&B⇨🟊£66-£74 🏳
⊄ CTV 60P ✿ ♪ snooker sauna solarium gymnasium Indoor badminton *xmas*
🍴 International V ٥ ⏍ Lunch £8-£12.50alc Dinner £15-£16&alc Last dinner 9.30pm
Credit Cards 1 2 3 5 £

**See advertisement under DUMFRIES**

---

### CARTMEL Cumbria Map 07 SD37

★★67% **Priory** The Square LA11 6QB ☎(05395)36267
Closed Jan
*A small, creeper-clad, family-run hotel offering traditional style bedrooms, a comfortable lounge, cosy bar, tea room and an attractive first-floor dining room. Alcoholic drinks are served to residents and diners only.*
9rm(5⇨)(2fb)1🛏 Ⓡ
CTV 8P
🍴 French V ٥ ⏍ ⊁ Last dinner 8.45pm
Credit Cards 1 3

★★58% **Aynsome Manor** LA11 6HH (1m N on unclass rd)
☎(05395)36653
Closed 2-28 Jan
*This lovely old manor house is surrounded by farmland and features open fires in its comfortable lounge. Bedrooms are thoughtfully equipped and have their own style and character. The restaurant provides a freshly-prepared five-course dinner of a very high standard.*
11rm(9⇄1♠)Annexe2⇄(2fb)1⌗ CTV in all bedrooms ® T ✱
sB&B⇄♠£33-£44 dB&B£62-£83
dB&B⇄♠£67-£88 (incl dinner) ◫
20P 🅿 ✿ *xmas*
♀ English & French V ✧ ✗ Sunday Lunch £9 Dinner £16 Last dinner 8.15pm
Credit Cards ①②③

⊛✗✗**Uplands** Haggs Ln LA11 6HD
☎(05395)36248(Rosette awarded for dinner only)
*In the 5 years since Diana and Tom Peter left Miller Howe to open their own restaurant, Uplands has grown in stature and is now held in high esteem throughout the country. The restaurant, housed in a charming country house between Cartmel village and Grange-over-Sands, has a lovely atmosphere and the 4-course set menu (changed every day) features many interesting dishes. Our Inspector found the hot salmon mousse delectable and the choice of main dishes included a baked fillet of sea bass with tarragon and Chambéry sauce, roast duckling with a spiced kumquat and green peppercorn sauce, or loin of lamb marinaded in red wine, all served with beautifully cooked vegetables. Wines are reasonably priced. Four pleasant bedrooms are also available.*
Closed Mon & 2 Jan-25 Feb
30 seats ✱ Lunch £12.50 Dinner £20 Last lunch 1pm Last dinner 8pm 14P nc8yrs ✗
Credit Cards ①②③

---

**CASTERTON** Cumbria Map **07** SD67

★★66% **Pheasant Inn** LA6 2RX
☎Kirkby Lonsdale(05242)71230
*Comfortable village inn, popular for its restaurant dinners and bar lunches. Annexe bedrooms are contained in a modernised coach house.*
10⇄♠(1fb)1⌗ CTV in all bedrooms ® T sB&B⇄♠£30-£35
dB&B⇄♠£50-£55 ◫
CTV 60P ✿ ⋈ *xmas*
V ✧ ⌾ ✗ Lunch £8.50-£12.50 Dinner £11-£13.50&alc Last dinner 9pm
Credit Cards ①③

---

**CASTLE ASHBY** Northamptonshire Map **04** SP85

★★65% **Falcon** ☎Yardley Hastings(060129)200
FAX (060129) 673
*This pleasant hotel is set in a picturesque rural village. Bedrooms in the main hotel are beautifully decorated and furnished, while those in the cottage annexe are simpler. Attractive public areas include a well appointed restaurant and a cosy bar.*
6rm(5⇄)Annexe8⇄♠2⌗ CTV in all bedrooms ®
✖ (ex guide dogs)
CTV 75P ✿
✧ ⌾ Last dinner 9.30pm
Credit Cards ①②③

**See advertisement on page 193**

See 'How we Classify Hotels and Restaurants'
at the front of the book for an explanation
of the AA's appointment and
award scheme.

## Castle Combe - Chaddesley Corbett

**C**

**CASTLE COMBE** Wiltshire Map **03** ST87

★★★★♣**70%, Manor House** SN14 7HR ☎(0249)782206
Telex no 449931 FAX (0249) 782159

*The hotel stands in a park-like combe just beyond the busy tourist village. Bedrooms in the main house have been completely refurbished to a high standard achieving a more distinctive character than those in the annexe. The spacious dining room features interesting and carefully prepared local dishes and staff are friendly yet very professional, offering full service in the comfortable lounges.*

12➪ℾAnnexe24➪ℾ6⊞ CTV in all bedrooms T
dB➪ℾ£85-£200 (room only) ⊟

⟪100P ✿ ⊒(heated) ♪ (hard) ✈ croquet lawn jogging track xmas

♀ English & French V ✿ � Lunch £14.50-£16.50alc Dinner £22.50&alc Last dinner 10pm
Credit Cards ①②③⑤

---

**CASTLE DONINGTON** Leicestershire Map **08** SK42

★★★**66%, Donington Thistle** East Midlands Airport DE7 2SH (Mount Charlotte (TS)) ☎Derby(0332)850700 Telex no 377632 FAX (0332) 850823

*This modern purpose-built hotel sits on the perimeter of the East Midlands Airport and has proved a popular venue for meetings. The up-to-date leisure club and the Sherwood restaurant are further attractions.*

110➪ℾ(4fb)✕in 15 bedrooms CTV in all bedrooms ® T ✱
sB➪ℾfr£68 dB➪ℾfr£85 (room only) ⊟

⟪180P ✿ ⊒(heated) sauna solarium gymnasium ⚿
♀ International V ✿ ⊒ Lunch fr£10&alc Dinner fr£13&alc Last dinner 10pm
Credit Cards ①②③⑤

★★★**60%, Donington Manor** High St DE7 2PP
☎Derby(0332)810253 Telex no 934999 FAX (0332) 850330
Closed 27-30 Dec

*A family owned and run hotel at the edge of the village, conveniently situated for access to the East Midlands Airport, offers good value for money in its well furnished, comfortable accommodation and interesting menus.*

35rm(33➪)Annexe3rm(1➪)(3fb)⊞ CTV in all bedrooms ®
T ✖ (ex guide dogs) ✱ S% sB&B➪£52-£60
dB&B➪£60-£70 ⊟

⟪60P
♀ English & French ✿ ⊒ S10% Lunch £6.50&alc Dinner £8.50&alc Last dinner 9.30pm
Credit Cards ①②③⑤

---

**CASTLE DOUGLAS** Dumfries & Galloway
*Kirkcudbrightshire* Map **11** NX76

★★**70%, Douglas Arms** King St DG7 1DB ☎(0556)2231

*Managed by the friendly resident proprietors, this comfortable high street hotel offers attentive service, cosy bedrooms and inviting lounges and bars. The menus at both lunch and dinner are good value.*

22rm(15➪)(2fb) CTV in all bedrooms ® T ✱ sB&B£14-£20
sB&B➪£17.50-£25 dB&B£26.50-£38 dB&B➪£31.50-£45 ⊟

⟪6P 8✿ xmas
V ✿ ⊒ Bar Lunch £4.40-£10.80alc Dinner fr£8.50&alc Last dinner 9pm
Credit Cards ①③

★★**62%, Imperial** King St DG7 1AA ☎(0556)2086 & 3009
RS 25-26 Dec & 1-2 Jan

*Situated in the main street and easily distinguished by its striking black-painted exterior, this former coaching inn is a favourite meeting place with locals, which means that its lounge bar is often very busy. Quiet relaxation is possible, however, in a comfortable first-floor lounge, and the whole hotel is well equipped and very*

---

*clean; those bedrooms having private bathrooms are the most comfortable, but all are gradually being improved.*

13rm(9➪ℾ)✕in 2 bedrooms CTV in all bedrooms ® T ✱
S10% sB&Bfr£18.50 sB&B➪ℾfr£23.50 dB&Bfr£34
dB&B➪ℾfr£42 ⊟

20P 9✿ sailing water-skiing
V ✿ ⊒ Bar Lunch £3.25-£6.50&alc High tea £4.75-£5.75
Dinner £7.50-£8.50&alc Last dinner 8pm
Credit Cards ①③£

★★**62%, King's Arms** St Andrew's St DG7 1EL ☎(0556)2626
Closed 1 Jan

*Occupying a corner site just off the main street this traditional, small hotel provides modest but comfortable and well-decorated accommodation. Local staff offer cheerful service.*

15rm(5➪3ℾ)(2fb) CTV in 8 bedrooms
CTV 17P ✐
♀ French V ✿ Last dinner 8.30pm
Credit Cards ①②③⑤

---

**CASTLETOWN**
See **Man, Isle of**

---

**CATEL (CASTEL)**
See **Guernsey** under Channel Islands

---

**CATTERICK BRIDGE** North Yorkshire Map **08** SE29

★★**58%, Bridge House** DL10 7PE ☎Richmond(0748)818331

*Overlooking Catterick Race Course this coaching inn, dating from 1442, was mentioned in The Holly Tree by Charles Dickens. Accommodation is functional with an old fashioned ambience. The restaurant, which overlooks the River Swale, provides an intimate setting for an enjoyable meal.*

15rm(4➪9ℾ)(2fb)1⊞ CTV in all bedrooms ® T sB&B£22-£25
sB&B➪ℾ£35-£40 dB&B£36-£40 dB&B➪ℾ£45-£52 ⊟
CTV 70P ✈
♀ English & French V ✿ Lunch £7.50-£12.50alc Dinner £9.50-£15alc Last dinner 10pm
Credit Cards ①②③⑤£

---

**CHADDESLEY CORBETT** Hereford & Worcester
Map **07** SO87

★★★♣**75%, Brockencote Hall Country House** DY10 4PY (0.50 m W, off A448) ☎(0562)777876 Telex no 333431
Closed 26 Dec-3rd wk Jan

*This elegant country house is set in 70 acres of grounds, and is located on the A448 between Kidderminster and Bromsgrove. The well equipped rooms are each individually decorated, comfortable and spacious, with some thoughtful extras provided. The well appointed restaurant provides a delightful setting in which to enjoy the well prepared meals. Friendly staff are attentive, and the owners, Alison and Joseph Petitjean, play an active role in providing personal service to guests.*

8➪ℾ(2fb)1⊞ CTV in all bedrooms ® T ✖ S%
sB&B➪ℾ£57-£108 dB&B➪ℾ£85-£108 ⊟
45P ✐ ✿
♀ French V ✿ ⊒ Lunch £16 Dinner £21.50-£28.90 Last dinner 9.30pm
Credit Cards ①②③⑤

---

Hotels with a high percentage rating for quality
are highlighted by a % across their
gazetteer entry.

**CHADLINGTON** Oxfordshire Map **04** SP32

★★🏮79%, **The Manor** OX7 3LX ☎(060876)711
*David Grant has created a comfortable country house of
international standard in this small Cotswold stone building behind
the village church. Bedrooms are attractively decorated and
furnished with antiques, while the public areas are elegant and
welcoming. Chris Grant produces a 4-course dinner of fresh
English fare.*
7⇸ CTV in all bedrooms T ✗ (ex guide dogs) ✳ S%
sB&B⇸£70-£90 dB&B⇸£100-£130
20P 🚗 ✿ xmas
S% Dinner £24.50-£25.50 Last dinner 9pm
Credit Cards ① ③

★★62%, **Chadlington House** OX7 3LZ ☎(060876)437
Telex no 83138
Closed Jan & Feb
*In a rural location, this delightful hotel, with attractive secluded
gardens and grounds, offers a welcoming atmosphere, homely
accommodation and good cooking standards.*
11rm(5⇸5♠)(2fb)1🚾 CTV in all bedrooms Ⓡ
✗ (ex guide dogs) ✳ sB&B⇸♠£25-£37.50 dB&B£40-£80
dB&B⇸♠£40-£80 🅿
CTV 20P 2🚗 ✿
♀ English & French V ♥ ☒ ✁ Sunday Lunch £10.50-£15
High tea fr£5 Dinner £15-£20 Last dinner 8.30pm
Credit Cards ① ③ Ⓔ

All hotels are now given a percentage grading
for the quality of their facilities. A full explanation
can be found within 'How we Classify Hotels
and Restaurants' at the front of the book.

# THE
# FALCON ★★

**C**

### Castle Ashby, Northampton
**Telephone: Yardley Hastings 060 129 200**
**Fax: 060 129 673**

The Falcon is a 16th century country inn situated
at the heart of a 10,000 acre estate which has
been owned by the Marquess of Northampton's
family for over four centuries.

All 16 bedrooms have direct dial telephone, tea
& coffee making facilities and colour TV. The
16 bedrooms are en suite, including one executive
suite with lounge/office/kitchen/2 double
bedrooms/bathroom.

The restaurant is open for luncheon Sunday-
Friday inclusive and for dinner Monday-Sunday.
Private parties for up to 100 guests can be catered
for. Before dining you can enjoy an aperitif in
the lounge area with its cocktail bar and log fire
or in the cellar bar with its exposed beams.
Barbecues and special events take place on a
number of weekends.

# The Manor House

## at
## Castle Combe

## NEWLY AWARDED 4th STAR

The Manor House at Castle Combe has a setting of idyllic tranquillity; 26 acres of gardens and
parkland, a gently flowing trout stream and the romance of a terraced Italian garden. Only two
hours drive from central London and close to the M4/M5 network.
Rooms have been individually restored in sympathy with their historical significance creating the
ultimate degree of luxury.
A friendly relaxed atmosphere, excellence of service, food and customer care are combined in a
Country House of exceptional charm.
Elegant lounges, Executive Boardrooms, own helipad, trout fishing, outdoor pool, tennis court
and croquet lawn.

AA ★ ★ ★ ★

*Winter Breaks Available.*
For Reservations and details
Tel: Castle Combe (0249) 782206   Castle Combe, Nr Chippenham, Wilts SN14 7HR

CHAGFORD Devon Map 03 SX78

### ★★★

**★★★★♨ GIDLEIGH PARK**

TQ13 8HH (Relais et
Châteaux)
☎(0647)432367 & 432225
Telex no 42643
FAX (0647) 432574

*A major, but not by any
means the only, attraction of
this superb country-house
hotel is its 40 acres of grounds, through which the River Teign
flows, and its lovely location. To reach this idyllic spot,
however, you must negotiate 2 miles of narrow winding lane ;
guests paying a return visit will know that perseverance will be
amply repaid ; first-time visitors have a treat in store. Paul
and Kay Henderson continue to make improvements to the
hotel – the latest being a charming pavilion in the grounds
which provides two extra bedrooms. The cooking of Shaun
Hill remains a major attraction of a stay here. There is a
choice of two dining rooms in which to enjoy his skills, and the
two fixed-price menus reflect the influence of Asian, European
and American cuisine which he has combined in an eclectic
style all his own ; flavours are not confused, however, on the
contrary they remain robust and clear. It is much to his credit
that he recruits and trains a new brigade for his kitchens every
year, and imbues them with the enthusiasm to maintain the
high reputation this hotel has built up over the years. Service is
courteous and correct, always a mark of the Relais et
Châteaux style of hotel operation.*

12↵Annexe2↵ CTV in all bedrooms T ✱
sB&B↵£165-£315
dB&B↵£200-£350 Continental breakfast (incl dinner) ⊟
25P ⇛ ✿ ♬ (hard) ♪ croquet
✿ ☑ Lunch £33-£44alc Dinner £44-£50alc Last dinner
9pm
Credit Cards [1] [3]

---

**★★★♨ 75% Mill End** Sandy Park TQ13 8JN (2m N on A382)
☎(0647)432282 FAX (0647) 433106
Closed 13-23 Dec & 12-22 Jan RS Nov-12 Dec & 23 Jan-Mar
*A former flour mill, dating back to the seventeenth century and
converted into an hotel in 1929, stands beside the River Teign in its
own well-kept gardens just one-and-a-half miles from the stannary
town of Chagford. Interesting features include the waterwheel,
retained to enhance the public rooms. Comfortable bedrooms offer
every facility for both business client and holiday-maker. Varied
and interesting menus are complemented by personal service, and
the excellence of the food – all freshly prepared on the day that it is
to be eaten – ensures that guests return again and again.*
17rm(15↵♠)(2fb) CTV in all bedrooms ® T sB£30-£40
sB↵♠£50-£60 dB↵♠£60-£70 (room only) ⊟
CTV 17P 4⊞ (£2.50) ⇛ ✿ ♪ shooting *xmas*
♀ English & French V ♥ ☑ Lunch £20-£25 Dinner £20-£25
Last dinner 9pm
Credit Cards [1] [2] [3] [5]

*All hotels are now given a percentage grading
for the quality of their facilities. A full explanation
can be found within 'How we Classify Hotels
and Restaurants' at the front of the book.*

---

**❀★★★♨ RTeignworthy** Frenchbeer TG13 8EX (2m S on
unclass rd to Thornworthy) ☎(0647)433355
(Rosette awarded for dinner only)
*A granite and slate country hotel, tucked away in an elevated
position and commanding views across Dartmoor, provides
personal service and a tranquil atmosphere. Cosy public rooms and
attractively furnished bedrooms alike – both in the main building
and the adjacent cottage – are generously supplied with books,
magazines, flowers and chocolates. The restaurant's table d'hôte
menu changes daily and makes use of seasonal produce and
locally grown ingredients in imaginative dishes, so that you
might enjoy pheasant pâté, filo pastry followed by noisettes of
Devon lamb cooked in their own juices, with a blackcurrant soufflé
to conclude the meal – all complemnted by wines chosen from a
well balanced list.*
6↵Annexe3↵1⊞ CTV in all bedrooms ✕
sB&B↵£65-£71.50 dB&B↵£110-£121 ⊟
20P 2⊞ ⇛ ✿ ♬ (grass) ♪ sauna solarium nc10yrs *xmas*
V ♥ ☑ ✕ Lunch £25-£35
Credit Cards [1] [3]

---

**★★ 63% Easton Court** Easton Cross TQ13 8JL (1.5m E A382)
☎(0647)433469
Closed Jan
*This part thatched hotel is run in a friendly and informal manner
by owners Graham and Sally Kidson. Public areas are cosy, with
open fires during the cooler months, and bedrooms offer a variety
of styles. Evelyn Waugh's 'Brideshead Revisited' was written here.*
8↵♠2⊞ CTV in all bedrooms ® ✱
dB&B↵♠£96-£104 (incl dinner) ⊟
CTV 20P ⇛ nc14yrs *xmas*
♀ English & Continental V ♥ ☑ Dinner £18.50-£22.50 Last
dinner 8.30pm
Credit Cards [1] [2] [3] [5] (£)

---

CHALE

See Wight, Isle of

---

CHALFORD Gloucestershire Map 03 SO80

**★★ 72% Springfield House Hotel & Restaurant** London Rd
GL6 8NW (on A419) ☎Brimscombe(0453)883555
*New family proprietors have brought great enthusiasm and a
caring attitude to their guests and this is reflected in genuinely
friendly and hospitable service. The food is good and bedrooms
have modern facilities.*
7↵♠2⊞ CTV in all bedrooms ® T
20P ✿ croquet
♀ English & French V ♥ ☑ ✕ Last dinner 9.30pm
Credit Cards [1] [2] [3] [5]

---

CHANNEL ISLANDS Map 16

---

ALDERNEY

**★★ 63% Inchalla** St Anne ☎(048182)3220
*A comfortable, modern hotel commanding delightful sea views
from its position on the outskirts of St Anne. The only AA-
recommended establishment on this charming little island offers
pleasant, particularly well equipped bedrooms, limited public
areas, good home cooking and friendly, informal service.*
11rm(8↵♠)(2fb) CTV in all bedrooms ® ✕
8P ⇛ ✿ sauna solarium jacuzzi
♀ English & French V ♥ ☑ Last dinner 8.30pm
Credit Cards [2] [3]

## GUERNSEY

### CATEL (CASTEL)

★★65% **Hotel Hougue du Pommier** Hougue Du Pommier Rd
☎Guernsey(0481)56531 Telex no 4191664 FAX (0481) 56260
*This attractive and well-managed hotel is set in 10 acres of grounds which includes a 6-acre pitch and putt course. Chef Fergus Mackay has won many local awards for his cooking, which can be enjoyed in the candle-lit restaurant.*
39➪🝔(12fb) CTV in all bedrooms ® T 🕇 (ex guide dogs) (incl dinner)
《 CTV 87P ✿ ⇗(heated) ▶ 18 solarium gymnasium games room ♬
♀ English & Continental V ⌾ ⨏ Sunday Lunch fr£7.50 Dinner fr£7.25&alc Last dinner 9.45pm
Credit Cards [1][2][3][4]

### FERMAIN BAY

★★★64% **Le Chalet** (Consort) ☎Guernsey(0481)35716
Telex no 4191342 FAX (0481) 35718
Closed mid Oct-May
*In one of the finest positions on the island, Le Chalet is on a quiet road leading to the bay and has its own extensive woodland. Most of the bedrooms have been refurbished and the bright, attractive restaurant, lounge and bar have commanding sea and woodland views. Friendly and attentive service is provided by British and Austrian staff, many of whom wear national costume.*
47➪🝔 CTV in all bedrooms ® T sB&B➪🝔£31.50-£36 dB&B➪🝔£52-£68
35P 🚗 ✿
♀ English, Austrian & French V ⌾ ⨏ Sunday Lunch £10-£12alc Dinner £12-£25alc Last dinner 9.30pm
Credit Cards [1][2][3][4][5]

★★★63% **La Favorita** ☎Guernsey(0481)35666
Telex no 94016631 FAX (0481) 35413
Closed 21 Dec-7 Feb RS 1-20 Dec & 8-28 Feb
*This privately owned hotel overlooking the bay has been upgraded to a good standard, with some particularly fine public rooms and comfortable bedrooms. The restaurant offers a reasonably priced table d'hôte menu and the coffee shop is open throughout the day.*
29➪🝔 CTV in all bedrooms ® T 🕇 sB&B➪🝔£29-£40 dB&B➪🝔£54-£76 (incl dinner) 🅿
40P 🚗
V ⌾ ⨏ 🍴 Lunch fr£8.50&alc Dinner £9.50-£14 Last dinner 9pm
Credit Cards [1][3]

### PERELLE

★★★66% **L'Atlantique** Perelle Bay ☎Guernsey(0481)64056
FAX (0481) 63800
*Situated on the coast road and overlooking the bay, this modern hotel stands in well-tended gardens and offers bright, well-equipped bedrooms and tastefully decorated public areas. A wide choice of eating options includes good table d'hôte and à la carte menus and a carvery.*
21➪🝔(3fb) CTV in all bedrooms ® T 🕇 (ex guide dogs) ✳ S%
sB&B➪🝔£18-£30 dB&B➪🝔£36-£60 🅿
80P ✿ ⇗(heated) *xmas*
♀ International V ⌾ Lunch £7.50 High tea £2-£3 Dinner £8-£8.75&alc Last dinner 9.30pm
Credit Cards [1][2][3][5]

# Hotel Hougue du Pommier ★★

**CÂTEL, GUERNSEY. Tel: 5631/2 53904 (0481)**

This 1712 Farmhouse now transformed into an elegant 2 star Hotel, which stands in its own 10 acres of ground, with a solar heated swimming pool, 18 hole putting green, 9 hole pitch and putt golf course offers you pleasure and relaxation. Enjoy our famous Carvery luncheons in our Tudor Bar or superb Dining Room. An à la carte candlelit dinner in this renowned Farm House Restaurant with its extensive wine menu is a must. We are looking forward to welcoming you here to the Hougue du Pommier.

*Mill End* HOTEL ★★★ ♨

**Sandy Park, Chagford, Devon TQ13 8JN Tel: (0647) 432282 Fax: (0647) 433106**

This old flour mill, with its wheel still turning in the peaceful courtyard, nestles in the Teign Valley on the edge of Dartmoor about one and a half hours drive from Bristol and three and a half hours from London.

The whole atmosphere is one of a rather comfortable private house, with lots of nooks and corners. Tea by the fire in Winter, drinks on the lawn in Summer – it is a most relaxing place.

The restaurant is open every day for all meals; prior booking strongly recommended.

**C**

## ST MARTIN

★★★66%, **Hotel Bella Luce** La Fosse ☎Guernsey(0481)38764
*Situated in the quiet rural and residential area of La Fosse, this hotel is set in large mature landscaped gardens. The building dates back to Norman times and the public areas offer both character and comfort. Bedrooms vary in style but all are comfortable and well equipped. The restaurant provides a good table d'hôte and an extensive à la carte menu and service is attentive and friendly.*
31⇨♠(9fb) CTV in all bedrooms T sB&B⇨♠£24-£42
dB&B⇨♠£38-£84
( 50P ⊞ ✿ ⊇(heated) sauna solarium croquet putting *xmas*
♀ English & Continental V ☼ ⅏ Lunch £7-£9.95&alc High tea
£2.95-£5.95&alc Dinner £7-£9.95&alc Last dinner 10pm

★★★62%, **Green Acres** Les Hubits ☎Guernsey(0481)35711
FAX (0481) 35978
*Peacefully set on the outskirts of the town in beautiful gardens that feature a south-facing patio and a heated swimming pool, the hotel offers well-equipped bedrooms with private facilities, a professionally supervised restaurant where both menu and wine list represent good value for money, and the services of a smart friendly staff.*
48⇨♠(3fb) CTV in all bedrooms ⓡ T ✖ (ex guide dogs)
sB&B⇨♠£40-£70 dB&B⇨♠£60-£90 (incl dinner)
75P ⊞ ✿ ⊇(heated) solarium *xmas*
♀ English & French V ☼ ⅏ ⅍ Bar Lunch £5.80-£11.90
Dinner £9.50-£10.50&alc Last dinner 8.30pm
Credit Cards ①③

★★★58% **St Margaret's Lodge** Forest Rd
☎Guernsey(0481)35757 Telex no 4191664 FAX (0481) 37594
*Conveniently located for the airport, and set in beautifully laid out gardens in the rural parish of St. Martin, the hotel offers well-equipped bedrooms with private facilities and, in some cases, with balconies overlooking the grounds. A good table d'hôte menu is available in the air conditioned "Anniversary" restaurant with its well-appointed bar lounge, whilst the tastefully furnished à la carte dinning room and cocktail bar are open to non-residents.*
47⇨ CTV in all bedrooms ⓡ T ✖
Lift ( 100P ⊞ ✿ CFA ⊇(heated) sauna solarium ♫ ⍟
♀ English & French V ☼ ⅏
Credit Cards ①②③€

★★★50%, **St Martin's Country** Les Merriennes
☎Guernsey(0481)35644
Closed Nov-Feb
*Quietly set in 15 acres of grounds, this hotel offers bedrooms of many shapes and sizes, but all are furnished in the modern style with varying degrees of comfort.*
60⇨(24fb) CTV in all bedrooms T ✽ sB&B⇨£16-£29.50
dB&B⇨£32-£59 ⅋
Lift ( CTV 250P 1⊞ ✿ CFA ⊇(heated) ♪ (hard) putting
green croquet table tennis ⍟
♀ English & French V ☼ ⅏ ⅍ Bar Lunch £3-£7.50alc Dinner
fr£7.75&alc Last dinner 9pm
Credit Cards ①②③④⑤

★★68%, **Windmill** La Rue Poudreuse ☎Guernsey(0481)35383
Telex no 4191501
Closed Nov-Mar
18⇨♠(6fb) CTV in all bedrooms ⓡ T
sB&B⇨♠£30.50-£37.50 dB&B⇨♠£55-£69 (incl dinner) ⅋
CTV 18P ⊞ ✿ ⊇(heated) pool table nc3yrs
♀ International ☼ ⅏ ⅍ Lunch £9 Dinner £9 Last dinner
7.30pm
Credit Cards ①②③⑤

★★63%, **Idlerocks** Jerbourg Point ☎Guernsey(0481)37711
FAX (0481) 35592
*This bright and friendly cliff-top holiday hotel has commanding extensive views out to sea. Bedrooms tend to vary in size, from spacious to those which are a little more compact. However, all of the rooms are brightly decorated and well equipped, although the*

*en suites are compact. The pleasant, modern bar and restaurant have picture windows, giving glorious views. Services are conducted in a friendly, informal style from resident management and local staff. A very picturesque location and relaxing retreat.*
23⇨♠(4fb)2⊞ CTV in all bedrooms ⓡ T ✽
dB&B⇨♠£18-£35 (incl dinner)
( CTV 100P ✿ ⊇(heated) ⍟ *xmas*
♀ English & French V ☼ ⅏ Lunch £6-£12 Dinner £9.50&alc
Last dinner 10pm
Credit Cards ①②③④⑤

## ST PETER PORT

★★★★72%, **St Pierre Park** Rohais ☎Guernsey(0481)28282
Telex no 4191662 FAX (0481) 712041
*Set in 40 acres of parkland with an ornamental lake and fountain, this modern and elegantly furnished hotel combines excellent facilities with professional service and good management. There are two quality restaurants and a brasserie, complemented by 24-hour room service. Indoor facilities include hairdressing and beauty salons, shopping arcade and snooker, while the grounds include a 9-hole golf course.*
135⇨♠(1fb) CTV in all bedrooms ⓡ T ✖ (ex guide dogs) ✽
sB&B⇨♠£85 dB&B⇨♠£115 ⅋
Lift ( 350P ✿ ⊟(heated) ♪ 9 ♪ (hard) snooker sauna
solarium gymnasium croquet childrens playground ♫ ⍟ *xmas*
♀ English & French V ☼ ⅏ ⅍ Sunday Lunch £8.50-£12.50
High tea £5-£10alc Dinner £12-£25alc Last dinner 10pm
Credit Cards ①②③⑤

★★★★58% **Old Government House** Ann's Place
☎Guernsey(0481)24921 Telex no 4191144 FAX (0481) 24429
*Long established, modernised hotel with swimming pool, basement disco and comfortable lounge. There are good views over the harbour.*
74⇨♠(8fb) CTV in all bedrooms T ✽ sB&B⇨♠£31-£51
dB&B⇨♠£62-£102
Lift ( 20P CFA ⊇(heated) solarium ♫ ⍟ *xmas*
♀ English, French & Italian V ☼ ⅏ Lunch £7&alc Dinner
£10&alc Last dinner 9.15pm
Credit Cards ①②③⑤

★★★70%, **La Fregate** Les Cotils ☎Guernsey(0481)24624
FAX (0481) 20443
*This delightful 18th-century manor house is tucked away on a garden hillside overlooking the harbour. Bedrooms are in the modern style and are well equipped – 6 have balconies and all but 2 have stunning views. The restaurant has acquired a reputation for fresh seafood and home-grown vegetables and Head Chef and Manager Oswald Steinsdorfer continues to produce reliable and professional standards of cooking. Service is very attentive.*
13⇨♠ CTV in all bedrooms ⓡ T ✖ S% sB&B⇨♠£50
dB⇨♠£90 (room only)
25P ⊞ ✿ nc14yrs
♀ Continental V S% Lunch fr£12 Dinner fr£16 Last dinner
9.30pm
Credit Cards ①②③④⑤

★★★68%, **Hotel de Havelet** Havelet(Consort)
☎Guernsey(0481)22199 Telex no 4191342 FAX (0481) 714057
*Originally built in the 16th century, this hotel is set on a hillside in 1.5 acres of gardens and enjoys lovely views over Castle Cornet. A choice of restaurants, converted from the stables and coach house, adjoins the main building and chef Hans Herrmann produces reliable standards of cooking. Service is well managed, attentive and very friendly.*
34⇨(4fb) CTV in all bedrooms ⓡ T ✖ sB&B⇨£32.50-£45
dB&B⇨£53.50-£84 ⅋
40P ⊞ ✿ ⊟(heated) sauna gymnasium *xmas*

🍴 English, Austrian & French **V** ♻ 🍽 Lunch £10-£20alc
Dinner £12&alc Last dinner 9.30pm
Credit Cards ①②③④⑤

★★★64%, **Moore's** Pollet(Consort) ☎Guernsey(0481)24452
Telex no 4191342 FAX (0481) 714037
*Situated on the attractive shopping street of Le Pollet, this
Georgian building has undergone extensive refurbishment. It offers
bright, well-equipped bedrooms and an attractive verandah
restaurant and coffee shop.*
42⇄ᐟ🛏Annexe6⇄ᐟ🛏(8fb) CTV in all bedrooms ® **T**
sB&B⇄ᐟ🛏£22-£56 dB&B⇄ᐟ🛏£36-£66 🅿
Lift ( ℙ 🚲 *xmas*
🍴 English & French **V** ♻ 🍽 Lunch £9-£20alc Dinner
£10-£12&alc Last dinner 9pm
Credit Cards ①②③④⑤

**See advertisement on page 199**

★★★60%, **La Collinette** St Jacques ☎Guernsey(0481)710331
FAX (0481) 713516
*A friendly, informal hotel under the personal supervision of the
owner provides modestly furnished, well-equipped bedrooms and
attentive service.*
27⇄ᐟ🛏 CTV in all bedrooms ® ✗ (ex guide dogs) 🅿
CTV 25P 🚲 ❀ ⇔(heated) sauna solarium spa bath ♫
🍴 English & Continental **V** ♻ 🍽 Sunday Lunch fr£7.50 High
tea fr£3 Dinner £8.50 Last dinner 8.30pm
Credit Cards ①②③⑤

**See advertisement on page 199**

★★65% **Sunnycroft** 5 Constitution Steps
☎Guernsey(0481)723008
Closed Nov-Mar
*Hospitality is a strong feature of this small privately owned
holiday hotel. Bedrooms are well equipped and a reasonably priced
set menu of well prepared dishes is available in the dining room.* ▶

# Saint Margaret's Lodge Hotel ★★★ C

**Forest Road, St Martin, Guernsey, CI**
**Tel: Guernsey 35757 Telex: 4191664**

This elegant 47 bedroomed, 3 Star 4 Crowned
Hotel set within beautiful garden surroundings
and only 10 minutes drive from St Peter Port,
the Harbour and Airport. All bedrooms
completely refurbished to the highest possible
standards. Two restaurants and bar luncheon
featuring fresh local seafood and produce.
Conferences catered for.

# La Frégate Hotel & Restaurant

3 STARS

## St Peter Port, Guernsey, Channel Islands
## Telephone: (0481) 24624   Fax: (0481) 20443

La Frégate is a Country House
Hotel tucked away in scented
gardens in a quiet corner of St
Peter Port with views over the
harbour and islands of Herm
and Sark. The French Res-
taurant is superb. Open all year
round, 13 bedrooms, en suite,
central heating, trouser press,
hair dryer, TV.

14⇘🏲 CTV in all bedrooms ⓡ T ✹ ✱ sB&B⇗🏲£17-£26 dB&B⇗🏲£34-£52 (incl dinner)
CTV ✿ nc14yrs
♦ ⚸ Dinner £8 Last dinner 7.30pm
Credit Cards ⬜1 ⬜3

✗✗✗**Le Nautique** Quay Steps ☎Guernsey(0481)21714
*This first-floor restaurant with a côte d'Azur ambience is very popular with an international clientele for its friendly atmosphere, imaginative daily menus which make a particular feature of fresh fish, and carefully chosen wine list.*
Closed Sun & 1st 2 wks Jan
♱ French V 68 seats S10% Lunch £15-£20alc Dinner £15-£20alc Last lunch 2pm Last dinner 10pm ✗ nc5yrs
Credit Cards ⬜1 ⬜2 ⬜3 ⬜5

✗✗**La Piazza Ristorante** Under the Arch, Trinity Square ☎Guernsey(0481)25085
*Situated opposite Holy Trinity Church, this comfortable, intimate restaurant, in shades of pink and grey, spills onto its attractive walled courtyard in warmer months. The cooking style is very Italian, but great use is made of local fish – nine varieties at the time of our visit – and other fresh produce. Of particular note are the Scallops Brettona and the Veal Marsala, accompanied by an imaginative selection of vegetables. It is also a pleasure to find an Italian restaurant which will prepare a Zabaione for one. The small wine list is carefully balanced and offers good value.*
Closed Sun & 24 Dec-23 Jan
♱ French & Italian 55 seats ✱ Lunch £12-£20alc Last lunch 2pm Last dinner 10pm ✗ nc6yrs
Credit Cards ⬜1 ⬜2 ⬜3

### VALE

★★★65%, *Novotel Guernsey* Les Dicqs(Novotel)
☎Guernsey(0481)48400 Telex no 4191306 FAX (0481) 48706
*Purpose-built, and overlooking the bay from its own grounds, the hotel is run with the needs of families in mind. Spacious bedrooms are well-equipped, and the dinning room offers meals from noon until midnight (with set menus at lunch and dinner), while leisure facilities include a sun terrace, open-air swimming pool with adjacent children's pool and a gymnasium.*
99⇘(99fb) CTV in all bedrooms
Lift 120P ✿ ⚊(heated) gymnasium ⚬
♱ English & Continental V ♦ ⚸ Last dinner mdnt
Credit Cards ⬜1 ⬜2 ⬜3 ⬜4 ⬜5

### HERM

★★71%, **White House** ☎Guernsey(0481)22159
FAX (0481) 710066
Closed Oct-Mar
*The only hotel on the island, the White House is reached via a 5-minute walk along the cliff path from the boat, while guests' luggage is transported by tractor. Colonial in style, the hotel has nearby cottages which are used as an annexe in the summer. The lounges are attractive and comfortable, with open log fires, and there is a separate bar lounge. In the split-level restaurant guests can choose from interesting set menus or à la carte, and there is an adjacent carvery. Bedrooms are simply appointed, but all have en suite facilities and some have balconies with delightful views.*
10⇘ ⓡ ✹ ✱ sB&B⇗£36-£60 dB&B⇗£72-£98 (incl dinner)
✗ ⚽ ✿ ⚊ ♪ (hard)
♱ English & French V ♦ ⚸ ✖ Lunch fr£8.50 Dinner fr£13.50
Last dinner 9pm
Credit Cards ⬜1 ⬜3

Entries for red-star hotels are highlighted by a tint panel. For a full list of these establishments consult the Contents page.

### JERSEY

### ARCHIRONDEL

★★67%, **Les Arches** Archirondel Bay ☎Jersey(0534)53839
Telex no 4192085 FAX (0534) 56660
*A popular and lively hotel with nightclub offers a choice of modern bedrooms with views of sea, pool or rear garden. Public areas include a well-run dining room and a residents' bar and lounge, there are extensive leisure facilities, and the Bar Papillon and Les Arches Nightclub feature nightly musical entertainment.*
54⇘🏲 CTV in all bedrooms ⓡ T S% sB&B⇗🏲£27.50-£39 dB&B⇗🏲£55-£78 ❚
《 CTV 120P ⚽ ✿ ⚊(heated) ♪ (hard) sauna gymnasium ⚬ xmas
♱ English & Continental V ♦ ⚸ Lunch £9.50-£16 Dinner £11.50-£25 Last dinner 8.45pm
Credit Cards ⬜1 ⬜3 ⬜4 ⓔ

### BEAUMONT

★★58%, **Hotel L'Hermitage** ☎Jersey(0534)33314
Telex no 4192170
Closed Nov-mid Mar
*An attractive hotel with pleasant, well-kept gardens. The hotel offers good leisure facilities including an indoor and outdoor pool. Accommodation is modest with most rooms located away from the main building arrayed 'chalet style' around the pool. The hotel is popular with holidaymakers and is within easy reach of the airport.*
109⇘🏲 CTV in all bedrooms ⓡ ✹ S%
sB&B⇗🏲£20.35-£26.85 dB&B⇗🏲£38.70-£65.25
《 100P ⚽ ✿ ⚊(heated) ⚊(heated) sauna solarium spa bath ♪ nc14yrs
♱ French & English ♦ ⚸ Lunch £5.25 Dinner £7 Last dinner 8pm

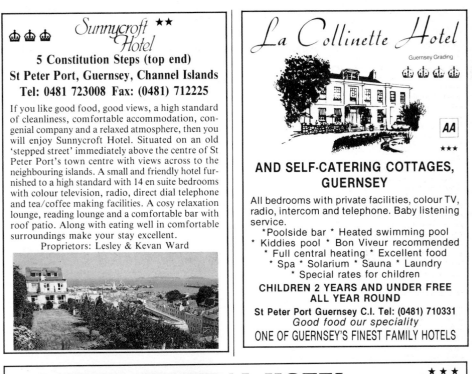

# Channel Islands, Jersey

## CORBIERE

**✗✗✗Sea Crest Hotel Restaurant** Petit Port JE3 8HH
☎Jersey(0534)46353
*Commanding a fine cliff-side position, this popular hotel restaurant has a well-established reputation on the island. Fresh fish is a speciality here and the à la carte menu also offers a good selection of other well-prepared European dishes. Service is pleasant and courteous.*
Closed Mon & Feb
Dinner not served Sun (Nov-Mar)
♡ English, French & Italian V 60 seats Lunch £9&alc Dinner £14-£20alc Last lunch 2pm Last dinner 10pm 30P
Credit Cards ① ③ ④

## GOREY

**★★★62%. Old Court House** JE3 9EX ☎Jersey(0534)54444
Telex no 4192032 FAX (0534) 53587
Closed Nov-Feb
*Situated in its own grounds on the edge of Gorey and opposite the beach, the Old Court House has modern, well-equipped bedrooms, many with balconies overlooking the garden and pool. Recent refurbishment has upgraded the cocktail bar and lounge, and the restaurant has been extended, while preserving the original 15th-century section.*
58➩🏲(4fb) CTV in all bedrooms T 🗙 ✱
sB&B➩🏲£29.80-£41.50 dB&B➩🏲£58.80-£90 (incl dinner)
Lift ℂ 40P ⌘ ⌔(heated) sauna solarium
♡ English, French & Italian ✧ ♫ Lunch £4.50-£6alc Dinner £10&alc Last dinner 9pm
Credit Cards ① ② ③ ⑤

**★★64% The Moorings** Gorey Pier ☎Jersey(0534)53633
Telex no 4192085 FAX (0534) 56660
*This small, well-appointed hotel offers thoughtfully equipped bedrooms – some overlooking the harbour – a comfortable lounge, two bars and a long-established, popular restaurant specialising in seafood.*
16➩🏲 CTV in all bedrooms ® T S% sB&B➩🏲£30-£39 dB&B➩🏲£60-£78 🍴
ℂ CTV ♪ ⌘ xmas
♡ English & Continental V ✧ S% Lunch £9.25-£22 Dinner £13-£30 Last dinner 10.15pm
Credit Cards ① ② ③ ④ ⑥

## L'ETACQ

**★★★66%. Lobster Pot Hotel & Restaurant**
☎Jersey(0534)82888 Telex no 4192605 FAX (0534) 81574
*A popular and long-established restaurant is the focal point of this skilfully converted 18th century granite farmhouse with its coach house bar and patio; comfortable bedrooms are particularly well furnished and equipped, service is generally efficient and the standard of cooking is reliable.*
13➩🏲(1fb) CTV in all bedrooms ® T 🗙 (ex guide dogs)
sB&B➩🏲£45-£63.50 dB&B➩🏲£70-£107
ℂ ▦ 56P ✻ ♫ nc14yrs xmas
♡ English, Continental & North American V ✧ Lunch fr£9.50 Dinner fr£14 Last dinner 10.15pm
Credit Cards ① ② ③ ④ ⑤

## ROZEL BAY

**★★★≜74%. Chteau la Chaire** Rozel Valley
☎Jersey(0534)63354 Telex no 437334 FAX (0534) 65137
*Tasteful refurbishment of an attractive country house in peaceful rural surroundings has provided comfortable and well-equipped accommodation with a friendly, relaxed atmosphere. Helpful service is rendered by charming staff, and meals of a high standard are available in the attractive restaurant with its simple conservatory extension.*
13➩🏲(1fb)1🛏 CTV in all bedrooms T 🗙 (ex guide dogs)
sB&B➩🏲£48-£90 dB&B➩🏲£70-£105 🍴

ℂ 30P ✻ nc7yrs xmas
♡ French V ✧ ⫰ ⊱ Lunch £9.95-£10.95&alc Dinner £15-£22.50alc Last dinner 10pm
Credit Cards ① ② ③ ⑤

**✗Granite Corner** Rozel Harbour ☎Jersey(0534)63590
*The French chef and proprietor Jean Luc Robin with his wife Louise offer regional French dishes at their delightful little restaurant perched right at the water's edge in Rozel. Some ingredients are specially imported to prepare dishes that include home made terrine of goose foie gras, and ballotine of duck. Sweets are deliciously fresh and brightly presented, there is cinnamon parfait on fresh strawberry coulis or walnut gateau, amongst others. The restaurant has a keen following, so booking is essential.*
Closed 15 Dec-10 Jan
Lunch not served
Dinner not served Sun
♡ French 24 seats ✱ Dinner £20-£35alc Last dinner 9pm
♪ nc12yrs
Credit Cards ① ② ③ ⑤

## ST AUBIN

**★★★62%. Somerville** Mont du Boulevard
☎Jersey(0534)41226 Telex no 4192505 FAX (0534) 46621
Closed 2nd wk Nov-mid Mar
*A popular resort hotel situated on a hill overlooking St Aubin Bay, the Somerville has well appointed rooms, a spacious restaurant, good leisure facilities and entertainment in the evenings.*
51rm(48➩2🏲)(7fb) CTV in all bedrooms ® T 🗙 ✱
sB&B➩🏲fr£24 dB&B➩🏲fr£43
Lift ℂ CTV 40P ⌘ ⌔(heated) games room nc4yrs
♡ English & French V ✧ ♫
Credit Cards ① ② ③ ④

## ST BRELADE

**★★★★71%. Hotel L'Horizon St** Brelade's Bay
☎Jersey(0534)43101 Telex no 4192281 FAX (0534) 46269
*A well-appointed holiday hotel with good leisure facilities and a pleasant setting on the seafront offers comfortable, well-equipped bedrooms and public areas; comprehensive menus and a good wine list make its two restaurants popular.*
104➩🏲(7fb)1🛏 CTV in all bedrooms T 🗙 (ex guide dogs)
sB&B➩🏲fr£65 dB&B➩🏲fr£150 🍴
Lift ℂ 125P ⌘ CFA ⌔(heated) sauna gymnasium windsurfing/water skiing spa steam baths ⌀ xmas
♡ English, French & Italian V ✧ ♫ Lunch fr£10.50 Dinner fr£19.50 Last dinner 10.45pm
Credit Cards ① ③

**★★★66%. Atlantic** La Moye ☎Jersey(0534)44101
Telex no 4192405 FAX (0534) 44102
Closed Jan-Feb
*A modern purpose built hotel overlooking St Ouens Bay and adjoining La Moye Golf Course. Although bedrooms (and public rooms) are not large they are all well furnished and equipped to high standards with further accommodation available in two sumptuous suites and two garden studio rooms. Service is professional, well-managed and attentive.*
50➩🏲 CTV in all bedrooms T 🗙 (ex guide dogs)
sB&B➩🏲£70-£100 dB&B➩🏲£100-£170 🍴
Lift ℂ 60P ⌘ ✻ CFA ⌔(heated) ⌔(heated) ℛ (hard) sauna solarium gymnasium spa pool xmas
♡ International V ✧ ♫ Lunch fr£10.75&alc Dinner fr£18.25&alc Last dinner 9.15pm
Credit Cards ① ② ③ ⑤

1991 marks the 25th anniversary of this guide.

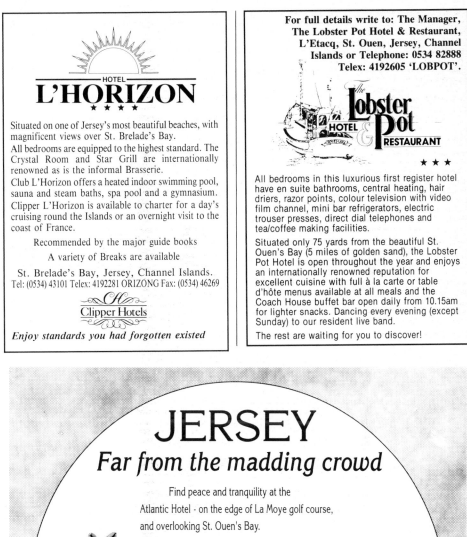

## Channel Islands, Jersey

**★★★66% Château Valeuse** Rue de Valeuse, St Brelade's Bay
JE3 8EE ☎Jersey(0534)46281 FAX (0534) 47110
Closed Jan-Feb
*This friendly hotel has modern, nicely appointed bedrooms, many of which have balconies with lovely views. An outdoor swimming pool is set amongst well-kept gardens and the beach is only a few minutes' walk away. There is a pleasant lounge and bar as well as a small sun terrace.*
33⇸♠(1fb) CTV in all bedrooms T ✖ sB&B⇸♠£32-£38
dB&B⇸♠£64-£76 ◨
《 50P ⇶ ✿ ➘(heated) nc5yrs *xmas*
♀ French V ♥ ⬭ Lunch fr£8.50&alc Dinner fr£12&alc Last dinner 9.15pm
Credit Cards ①③

**★★★63% St Brelade's Bay** ☎Jersey(0534)46141
Telex no 4192519
Closed 17 Oct-21 Apr RS 22-30 Apr & 7-16 Oct
*Set in an ideal position overlooking St Brelades Bay this friendly, personally-run holiday hotel provides good lounge facilities and bedrooms which are all very well equipped though they vary in size and degree of comfort. Helpful staff offer attentive, willing service, the garden is attractive and there are excellent leisure amentities.*
72⇸(2fb) CTV in all bedrooms T ✖ (ex guide dogs)
Lift 《 ⊞ CTV 60P ⇶ ✿ ➘(heated) ♪ (hard) snooker sauna solarium croquet putting green petanque ♫
V ♥ ⬭ ✕ Lunch £9 Dinner £15 Last dinner 9pm
Credit Cards ①②③⑤

**★★65% Beau Rivage** St Brelades Bay ☎Jersey(0534)45983
Telex no 4192341 FAX (0534) 68330
Closed Dec-Feb
27⇸♠(9fb) CTV in all bedrooms ✖ (ex guide dogs)
Lift 《 14P
♀ English, French & Italian V ♥ ⬭ Last dinner 7.30pm
Credit Cards ①②③

### ST HELIER

**★★★★59% The Grand** The Esplanade(De Vere)
☎Jersey(0534)22301 Telex no 4192104 FAX (0534) 37815
*The hotel stands facing the sea, offering comfortable public areas and bedrooms in a variety of styles which continue to be upgraded. As well as the main dining room, Victoria's Restaurant provides a pleasant atmosphere and a good selection of interesting dishes which makes it popular with local residents.*
115⇸♠ CTV in all bedrooms ® CTV ✱ sB&B⇸♠£50-£77
dB&B⇸♠£95-£150 ◨
Lift 《 15P 25🏌 ⇶ CFA ⬛(heated) snooker sauna solarium gymnasium spa bath hairdresser massage parlour ♫ *xmas*
♀ English, French & Italian V ♥ ⬭ ✕ Lunch £13.50-£15.50&alc Dinner £14.50-£17.50&alc Last dinner 10pm
Credit Cards ①②③⑤

**★★★63% Beaufort** Green St ☎Jersey(0534)32471
Telex no 4192160 FAX (0534) 20371
*The provision of a good range of de luxe bedrooms is just part of the upgrading which is in evidence throughout this centrally-situated hotel. An indoor swimming pool and whirlpool spa is another new addition and there are plans to further increase leisure facilities. Nicely decorated throughout, the hotel has comfortable public rooms and staff are efficient and friendly.*
54⇸♠(2fb)1 ⊞ CTV in all bedrooms ® T ✖ ✱
sB&B⇸♠£41-£62 dB&B⇸♠£65-£72 ◨
Lift 《 40P ⬛(heated) jacuzzi spa bath ♫ *xmas*
♀ English & French V ♥ ⬭ ✕ Bar Lunch fr£5.50 Dinner fr£9.50 Last dinner 8.45pm
Credit Cards ①②③⑤

**★★★63% Pomme D'Or** The Esplanade ☎Jersey(0534)78644
Telex no 4192309 FAX (0534) 37781
*Central, modernised hotel facing harbour, and having extensive public rooms, coffee shop and carvery. Popular with businessmen.*
150⇸♠(3fb) CTV in all bedrooms ® T ✖ (ex guide dogs)
Lift 《 ♪ ♫
♀ International V ♥ ⬭ ✕ Last dinner 9pm
Credit Cards ①②③⑤

**★★★62% Apollo** St Saviours Rd ☎Jersey(0534)25441
Telex no 4192086 FAX (0534) 22120
*Situated right in the heart of St Helier, but built around its own quiet courtyard, the Apollo has recently been significantly renovated. Bedrooms are bright and comfortable and their modern facilities include satellite TV and teletext. Public rooms have been tastefully decorated, with lounges and a cocktail bar in modern style. The attractive indoor leisure centre includes a stylish coffee shop terrace which in the evening takes on a bistro atmosphere amid the soft-lit waters of the adjacent pool.*
85⇸(5fb)1 ⊞ CTV in all bedrooms ® T ✖ ✱ S%
sB&B⇸£37.50-£56 dB&B⇸£60-£81 ◨
Lift 《 50P ⬛(heated) sauna solarium gymnasium jacuzzi spa bath ♪ *xmas*
♀ English & French V ♥ ⬭ Sunday Lunch fr£7.50 High tea fr£1.50 Dinner fr£8.50 Last dinner 8.45pm
Credit Cards ①②③⑤

**★★★60% Hotel Savoy** Rouge Bouillon ☎Jersey(0534)27521 FAX (0534) 37162
Closed Jan-14 Apr & 22 Oct-Dec
*This family-run holiday hotel offers a friendly informal atmosphere and comfortable accommodation with some well-equipped bedrooms. Traditional cooking is served in the spacious restaurant.*
61⇸♠(1fb) CTV in all bedrooms ✖
Lift 《 55P ⇶ ➘(heated) pool table ♫
♀ English, French, Italian & Spanish V ♥ ⬭ ✕ Last dinner 8.30pm
Credit Cards ①

**★★68% Sarum Hotel** 19-21 New St John's Rd
☎Jersey(0534)58163
Closed Nov-mid Mar
56rm(23⇸12♠)(1fb) CTV in all bedrooms
Lift 《 CTV ♪
Last dinner 7.30pm
Credit Cards ③

**★★63% Royal Yacht** The Weighbridge ☎Jersey(0534)20511
Telex no 4192642 FAX (0534) 67272
*Retaining much of its original Victorian style and atmosphere, the hotel nevertheless provides accommodation in consistently well equipped bedrooms, all furnished to the same high standard; guests can eat in either the London Grill or Victoria's Carvery, there is a choice of popular bars, and a fifth-floor sun lounge offers an excellent view of the harbour.*
45⇸♠ CTV in all bedrooms ® T S% sB&B⇸♠£30-£34
dB&B⇸♠£60-£72
Lift 《 CTV ♪ *xmas*
♀ English, French & Italian V ♥ ⬭ S% Lunch £5.50-£12 Dinner £10.50-£21.50 Last dinner 8.45pm
Credit Cards ①②③④ⓔ

### ST LAWRENCE

**★★★74% Little Grove** Rue De Haut ☎Jersey(0534)25321
FAX (0534) 25325
*Built of pink granite, this delightful hotel is run very much in the country house style, with attractive cosy lounges and bar and an elegant restaurant. Bedroom upgrading continues and some are now splendid. Interesting and enjoyable food is served in the restaurant and throughout the hotel staff are polite and attentive.*

▶

# *Apollo Hotel*

St. Saviour's Rd, St. Helier, Jersey, JE2 4LA, Channel Islands.
Telephone 0534 25441  Telex 4192086  Fax 0534 22120

Modern 3 Star Hotel with an Indoor Leisure Centre, built around a quiet courtyard in the middle of St. Helier.

86 rooms with bathroom en suite, colour television with satellite link, direct dial telephone, tea and coffee making facilities, and trouser press.

Indoor swimming pool, jacuzzi, saunas, sun beds, gymnasium and games room.
'The Coffee Grove' overlooking the pool, 'Le Petit Jardin' for aperitifs and fine cuisine. 'Haughty Pigeon' bar for local atmosphere.

Centrally heated throughout.
Ample car parking.
Open all year.

AA ★★★ *A Huggler Hotel*

# Beaufort Hotel

BH

St. Helier, Jersey, JE2 4UH, Channel Islands.
Telephone: 0534 - 76500
Telex: 4192160
Fax: 0534 - 20371

**Modern 3 Star Hotel well situated for shopping, business or beach in St. Helier's commercial centre. The Beaufort has been designed to offer every amenity for today's traveller. Brummels Bar for aperitifs. The Rib Room for fine cuisine. Ample car parking.**

INDOOR SWIMMING POOL AND SPA

**All Bedrooms are equipped with:-**
- Full Bathroom and Shower.
- Hairdryer and Trouser Press.
- Tea and Coffee making facilities.
- 2 Direct Dial Telephones.
- Colour T.V. with Satellite Channels.
- Full Lounge armchairs.
- Writing Desk.
- Mini Bars.

AA ★★★ *A Huggler Hotel*

## Channel Islands, Jersey - Charlbury

13↩🛏 CTV in all bedrooms T ✗ ✻ sB&B↩🛏£74.50-£96
dB&B↩🛏£99-£132 🏠
《 30P 🚌 ✻ ⊒(heated) croquet nc12yrs xmas
♀ English & French V ✿ 🍷 S10% Lunch £11.50&alc Dinner
£22.50&alc Last dinner 9.30pm
Credit Cards 1 2 3 5

### ST PETER

★★★60% Mermaid ☎Jersey(0543)41255 Telex no 4192249
FAX (0534) 45826
*Eighteen acres of grounds and gardens surround this hotel, and
many of its bedrooms have balconies overlooking a natural lake.
Leisure facilities comprise an 18-hole putting green, all-weather
tennis courts, a gym and a 45-foot-long indoor swimming pool. A
small grill room augments the more formal restaurant and there is
an historic public bar. Standards of service are formal and
reasonably efficient in all areas.*
68↩1🛏 CTV in all bedrooms ® T ✗ ✻ sB&B↩🛏£35.25-£58
dB&B↩🛏£48.50-£87 🏠
《 250P 🚌 ✻ ⊒(heated) ▶ 18 ♪ (hard) sauna solarium
gymnasium jacuzzi putting green ♫ xmas
♀ English & French V ✿ 🍷 Sunday Lunch fr£9 High tea fr£3
Dinner fr£10.50 Last dinner 9.30pm
Credit Cards 1 2 3 5

### ST SAVIOUR

❀★★★★🔔
**LONGUEVILLE MANOR**

JE2 7SA (off St Helier/
Grouville Rd A3) (Relais et
Châteaux)
☎Jersey(0534)25501
Telex no 4192306
FAX (0534) 31613
(Rosette awarded for dinner
only)

*This historic manor house, parts of which date back to the
13th century, deserves its reputation as Jersey's finest hotel.
Family owned for more than 40 years, it is run by the
partnership of Simon and Sue Dufty and Malcolm and
Ragnhild Lewis, who assure guests of a warm personal
welcome with every attention to their comfort. Bedrooms are
sumptuous, furnished and decorated individually in keeping
with the manorial atmosphere, and the sense of wellbeing is
heightened by the deep sofas, easy chairs and antique
furniture of bar and drawing room. Fresh garden flowers and
log-burning fires add to the country-house atmosphere, which
extends to the fine, panelled restaurant overlooking the
garden. Andrew Baird returns to the hotel as chef de cuisine to
continue the high standard of cooking with its emphasis on
'big flavours'. Creative patisserie and excellent bread making
now complement the range of dishes on offer, and service is
particularly well managed to high professional standards.*
33↩1🛏 CTV in all rooms T S10% sB&B↩🛏£68-£82
dB&B↩🛏£104-£167 🏠
Lift 《 40P 🚌 ✻ ⊒(heated) nc7yrs xmas
V ✿ 🍷 S10% Lunch £17 Dinner £24.50&alc Last dinner
9.30pm
Credit Cards 1 2 3 5 ⓔ

---

### CHAPELTOWN South Yorkshire Map 08 SK39

★★★64% **Staindrop Lodge** Lane End S30 4UH
☎Sheffield(0742)846727 FAX (0742) 846783
Closed 25 & 26 Dec
*A nineteenth-century building of some architectural interest,
standing in its own grounds in a quiet area of Sheffield, has been
suitably converted into an up-to-date hotel where the interesting
international menu and good value wine list are complemented by
friendly family service.*
13↩🛏(1fb) CTV in all bedrooms ® T ✗ sB&B↩🛏£55-£60
dB&B↩🛏£68-£80 🏠
《 60P ✻
♀ English & French V ✿ Lunch £8.50-£10.50&alc Dinner
£17.50-£20&alc Last dinner 9.30pm
Credit Cards 1 2 3 5 ⓔ

### CHARDSTOCK Devon Map 03 ST30

★★★71% **Tytherleigh Cot** EX13 7BN
☎South Chard(0460)21170 FAX (0460) 21291
*Set in this small village on the Devon/Somerset/Dorset borders, a
charming listed building dating from the 14th century offers
bedrooms in carefully converted stables and barns, all providing
high standards of comfort and excellent facilities. The elegant, air-
conditioned restaurant is housed in a Victorian-style conservatory
that overlooks an ornamental pond. Guests can enjoy a wide range
of imaginative dishes – timbale des champignons forestière, for
example, perhaps being followed by escalope de saumon braisée
dorée, and the meal ending with an apple mousse swan on an
apricot base.*
3↩Annexe16↩6🛏 CTV in all bedrooms ® T S%
sB&B↩🛏£45-£48.50 dB&B↩🛏£77-£82 🏠
25P ✻ ⊒(heated) sauna solarium nc12yrs xmas
V ✿ 🍷 🍴 Lunch £7.45-£11.95&alc High tea £2.50-£7.95
Dinner £17.95-£19.95&alc Last dinner 9.30pm
Credit Cards 1 3 ⓔ

### CHARINGWORTH Gloucestershire Map 04 SP13

❀★★★🔔77% **Charingworth Manor** GL55 6NS (on B4035 3m E
of Chipping Campden) ☎Paxford(0386)78555
Telex no 333444 FAX (0386) 78353
*This former 14th-century manor has been intelligently restored
and extended to create a hotel of real charm, which incorporates
all the modern comfort one would expect. The attractive lounges
mix different styles of furniture to pleasing effect and it is worth
mentioning that the corridors, so often a neglected area in hotels,
have also been beautifully decorated and provided with
comfortable seating, with clever use of display cabinets to lend
style and atmosphere. Tony Robson-Burrell presides over the
kitchens and his mouth-watering soufflés and the robust sauces
accompanying the locally produced meat and poultry dishes are
particularly successful. The extensive wine list has a strong French
bias, but includes some worthwhile Australian and American
bottles. Staff are attentive and hardworking.*
25↩2🛏 CTV in all bedrooms T ✗ (ex guide dogs) ✻
sB&B↩🛏£80-£180 dB&B↩🛏£95-£195 🏠
《 50P 🚌 ✻ croquet xmas
♀ English & French V ✿ 🍷 Lunch £15.50&alc Dinner
£24.50&alc Last dinner 10.30pm
Credit Cards 1 2 3 5

### CHARLBURY Oxfordshire Map 04 SP31

★★62% **The Bell** Church St OX7 3AP (Best Western)
☎(0608)810278 Telex no 837883 FAX (0608) 811447
*This privately owned 17th-century hotel of character offers a
warm, cosy atmosphere and some attractive bedrooms. Well-
prepared dishes are served in the intimate dining room.*
10↩🛏Annexe4↩🛏(1fb) CTV in all bedrooms ® T
sB&B↩🛏£45-£50 dB&B↩🛏£65-£75 🏠

---

For key to symbols see the inside front cover.

CTV 50P ✿ clay pigeon shooting fishing riding *xmas*
V ✿ ⊡ Lunch £8-£15alc Dinner £12-£25alc Last dinner 9pm
Credit Cards ① ② ③ ④ ⑤ ⓔ

---

**CHARLECOTE** Warwickshire Map **04** SP25

---

**★★★61% Charlecote Pheasant Country** CV35 9EW (Queens
Moat) ☎Stratford-upon-Avon(0789)470333 Telex no 31688
FAX (0789) 470222
*This hotel complex has a variety of annexe bedrooms converted
from former farm buildings. They offer many modern facilites,
though some are compact and simply decorated.*
Annexe60⇨ ♠(1fb)8 ⊞ ✗in 6 bedrooms CTV in all bedrooms
® T sB&B⇨ ♠£65 dB&B⇨ ♠£80 ⮔
( 120P ✿ ⊴(heated) ℘ (hard) sauna solarium gymnasium
croquet lawn pool table
♡ English & French V ✿ ⊡ Lunch fr£9.95 Dinner fr£12.95
Last dinner 10pm
Credit Cards ① ② ③ ⑤ ⓔ
**See advertisement under STRATFORD-UPON-AVON**

---

**CHARLTON KINGS** Gloucestershire Map **03** SO92

○**Afortie** London Rd GL52 6UU ☎Cheltenham(0242)231061
Due to have opened Sep 1990
14rm

---

**CHARMOUTH** Dorset Map **03** SY39

**★★69% White House** 2 Hillside, The Street DT6 6PJ
☎(0297)60411
Closed Dec-Feb RS Mar
*A charming little Regency house which has been thoughtfully and
tastefully decorated and furnished throughout. Accommodation is
in compact but well furnished and comfortable bedrooms. An*

*especially noteworthy standard of cuisine can be enjoyed in the
elegant dining room and the hotel's proprietors do their utmost to
ensure that a stay here is both relaxed and enjoyable.*
7rm(6⇨3 ♠) CTV in all bedrooms ® T sB&B£46-£48.50
sB&B⇨ ♠£46-£48.50 dB&B£72-£77 dB&B⇨3 ♠£72-£77 ⮔
15P ⇔ nc14yrs
✿ ⊡ Lunch £11.50-£14.50alc High tea £8-£10alc Dinner
£16.50-£18.50&alc Last dinner 9pm
Credit Cards ① ③

**★★57% Queen's Armes** The Street DT6 6QF ☎(0297)60339
Closed 2nd wk Nov-2nd wk Feb
*Nicely-appointed hotel with low, beamed ceilings and comfortable
rooms. Table d'hôte and à la carte menus are available at
reasonable prices.*
11rm(5⇨55 ♠)(1fb)1 ⊞ ✗in all bedrooms CTV in all bedrooms
® ✳ sB&B⇨3 ♠£21-£24 dB&B⇨3 ♠£42-£48 ⮔
CTV 20P ⇔ ✿ nc5yrs
♡ English & French V ✿ ✗ Bar Lunch £2.50-£5alc Dinner
£6-£11alc Last dinner 8.30pm
Credit Cards ① ③

**★★52% Charmouth House** The Street DT6 6PH ☎(0297)60319
*An attractive 16th-century thatched building with neat gardens
and an outdoor pool. Modest bedrooms are complemented by a
large lounge bar, and simple English food is served in the
restaurant.*
12rm(7⇨31 ♠)(2fb) CTV in all bedrooms ® sB&B£20-£24
sB&B⇨3 ♠£20-£24 dB&B£38-£44 dB&B⇨3 ♠£38-£44 ⮔
23P ✿ ⊴(heated) sauna *xmas*
V ✿ Bar Lunch £1.50-£5alc Dinner £7.50-£18alc Last dinner
9pm
Credit Cards ① ③

**CHARNOCK RICHARD** Lancashire Map **07** SD51

★★★63% *Park Hall Hotel, Leisure & Conference Centre*
PR7 5LP (off A49 W of village) ☎Eccleston(0257)452090
Telex no 677604 FAX (0257) 451838
*This modern hotel, adjacent to the Camelot Theme Park, forms part of a complex of new clubs, shops and exhibition halls not far from the Lake and Spanish Village.*
55⇋♠(2fb)1☷⊬in 13 bedrooms CTV in all bedrooms ® ✻
Lift ( ⊞CTV 2500P ☒(heated) squash snooker sauna solarium gymnasium ♫
♔ English & French V ✿ ⚏ Last dinner 10pm
Credit Cards ①②③⑤
**See advertisement under PRESTON**

**CHARNOCK RICHARD MOTORWAY SERVICE AREA
(M6)** Lancashire Map **07** SD51

★★★54% **Welcome Lodge** Mill Ln PR7 5LR (Trusthouse Forte)
☎Coppull(0257)791746 Telex no 67315
*Functional but comfortable accommodation, with meals and drinks available to Lodge residents, forms part of the service area complex and is accessible from both carriageways of the M6.*
103⇋⊬in 10 bedrooms CTV in all bedrooms ® ♬
( CTV 120P ☷
♔ Mainly grills V ✿ ⚏ ⊬
Credit Cards ①②③④⑤

**CHEDDAR** Somerset Map **03** ST45

★56% **Gordons** Cliff St BS27 3PT ☎(0934)742497
Closed 23 Dec-Jan
*A former farmhouse at the foot of the famous Cheddar Gorge now offers comfortable, simply furnished bedrooms, a cosy lounge and bar and a steak house restaurant; service is very informal and the atmosphere friendly.*
11rm(2⇋1♠)Annexe2⇋♠(2fb) CTV in 5 bedrooms TV in 8 bedrooms ® sB&B£16-£17.50 sB&B⇋♠£25-£27.50 dB&B£32-£35 dB&B⇋♠£35-£42
CTV 10P ✿ ☒(heated) ⊿(heated)
V ✿ ⚏ Lunch £6.50-£8.50alc Dinner £6.50-£10.50alc Last dinner 9pm
Credit Cards ①③⑤⑤Ⓔ

**CHELFORD** Cheshire Map **07** SJ87

★★61% **Dixon Arms** Knutsford Rd SK11 9AS
☎Macclesfield(0625)861313 FAX (0625) 861443
Closed 24 Dec-1 Jan
*Standing beside the A537 in a small Cheshire village famous for its livestock markets, and conveniently close to the main line railway station, this hotel offers well-equipped bedrooms, a comfortable lounge and character public bars.*
11♠(2fb) CTV in all bedrooms ® T sB♠£38-£40 dB♠£40-£50 (room only)
100P ✿ CFA bowling
♔ English & French ✿ Lunch fr£7.50 High tea £3-£5alc Dinner £6-£18alc Last dinner 10pm
Credit Cards ①②③④⑤Ⓔ

**CHELMSFORD** Essex Map **05** TL70

★★★74% **Pontlands Park Country** West Hanningfield Rd,
Great Baddow CM2 8HR ☎(0245)76444 Telex no 995256
FAX (0245) 478393
Closed 28 Dec-4 Jan
*Although it dates back to the mid 16th century, Pontlands Park was rebuilt as a Victorian mansion and subsequently converted into a country house hotel. It has a tastefully appointed lounge and an elegant restaurant offering interesting menus and a good wine list. Individually furnished bedrooms and suites are spacious and well equipped. Within the beautiful grounds is 'Trimmers' health and leisure centre.*

17⇋(1fb)3☷⊬in 6 bedrooms CTV in all bedrooms T ✻ (ex guide dogs) ✳ S10% sB⇋£66-£78 dB⇋£76-£96 (room only) ♬
( 60P ☷ ✿ ☒(heated) ⊿(heated) sauna solarium gymnasium jacuzzi
♔ English & French V ✿ ⚏
Credit Cards ①②③⑤

★★★59% **Saracens Head** 3-5 High St CM1 1BE
☎(0245)262368 FAX (0245) 262418
*The recently refurbished bedrooms of this hotel provide en suite facilities and a wide range of amenities, including satellite TV. The Chambers Bar, set across an arch opposite the tastefully appointed Restaurant Grill, offers a wide choice of traditional ales, draught and Continental lagers.*
18⇋♠1☷ CTV in all bedrooms ® T sB⇋♠£62 dB⇋♠£83 (room only)
( ♪
♔ International V ✿ ⚏ ⊬ Lunch £3.75-£16 Dinner £4.25-£16 Last dinner 10.30pm
Credit Cards ①②③⑤Ⓔ

★★★59% **South Lodge** 196 New London Rd CM2 0AR
☎(0245)264564 Telex no 99452 FAX (0245) 492827
*Situated in pleasant grounds just outside the town centre, this hotel has compact bedrooms with facilities to suit visiting business people. The sun lounge room is ideal for small functions and the restaurant offers both table d'hôte and à la carte menus.*
24⇋♠Annexe17⇋(3fb)⊬in 8 bedrooms CTV in all bedrooms ® T S10% sB&B⇋♠£40-£70 dB&B⇋♠£50-£80 Continental breakfast ♬
( 50P ☷
♔ International V ✿ ⚏ ⊬ S10% Lunch £12-£18alc Dinner £14-£25alc Last dinner 9.30pm
Credit Cards ①②③⑤

★★★60% *County* Rainsford Rd CM1 2QA ☎(0245)491911 FAX (0245) 492762
Closed 27-30 Dec
*Busy commercial hotel with modern bedrooms.*
30rm(24⇋4♠)Annexe23rm(7⇋)(1fb) CTV in all bedrooms ® ( 80P
♔ English & French V ✿ ⚏
Credit Cards ①②③⑤

**CHELTENHAM** Gloucestershire Map **03** SO92

See also **Cleeve Hill**
★★★★56% **Golden Valley Thistle** Gloucester Rd GL51 0TS (Mount Charlotte (TS)) ☎(0242)232691 Telex no 43410 FAX (0242) 221846
*Popular with businessmen and offering good conference facilities, the hotel is easily accessible from junction 11 of the M5; modern bedrooms reflect the needs of a business clientele and the new Leisure Club will make a good range of activities available.*
97⇋♠(24fb)⊬in 9 bedrooms CTV in all bedrooms ® T ✻ sB⇋♠fr£69 dB⇋♠fr£78 (room only) ♬
Lift ( 275P ✿ CFA ☒(heated) sauna solarium gymnasium hairdresser ⚘
♔ International ✿ ⚏ ⊬ Lunch fr£11.50&alc Dinner fr£14.50&alc Last dinner 10pm
Credit Cards ①②③④⑤

★★★★54% **The Queen's** Promenade GL50 1NN (Trusthouse Forte) ☎(0242)514724 Telex no 43381 FAX (0242) 224145
*A large, traditional-style hotel with spacious public areas stands in a central position overlooking the town gardens. A programme of refurbishment is at present in progress.*
77⇋(8fb)1☷⊬in 7 bedrooms CTV in all bedrooms ® T sB⇋£80-£85 dB⇋£100-£120 (room only) ♬
Lift ( 50P CFA *xmas*

V ✿ ⬚ ✔ Lunch £11.95-£14.75&alc Dinner
£17.95-£18.95&alc Last dinner 9.45pm
Credit Cards 1 2 3 4 5

★★★

❀★★★⚑ GREENWAY

Shurdington GL51 5UG
(Pride of Britain)
☎(0242)862352
FAX (0242) 862780
Closed 28 Dec-13 Jan RS
Sat & BH Mon

*Tree-lined hills provide a pleasing backdrop to Tony Elliott's delightful Cotswold hotel which stands well back from the Stroud road out of Cheltenham. There is a comfortable informality about the staff, concealing their professional expertise, which makes guests feel immediately at their ease. Comfort is the keynote of the remodelled bedrooms, both in the main house and the more recently converted coach house, and there is ample space for the superb beds, deep armchairs or settees and all the attendant luxuries expected by today's guests. Meals, in the attractive conservatory dining room, are the concern of Edward Stephens, who took over as chef in 1990. The menu features many exciting specialities, such as freshly made noodles, half coloured with squid ink and half with deep, rich egg yolk and accompanied by strips of tender squid or Cornish crab served with fresh yoghourt infused with basil. For the main course, try tiny mignons of veal coated with a lime and ginger farce, wrapped in the thinnest of crêpes. A good example of the vegetarian dishes are sweetcorn pancakes* ▶

★★★★AA

♨
## GOLDEN VALLEY
### THISTLE HOTEL

*Gloucester Road*
*Cheltenham GL51 0TS*
*Telephone: 0242 232691 Telex: 43410*
*Facsimile: 0242 221846*

Set in its own grounds just outside this spa town, the hotel is the perfect centre for touring the Cotswolds and the Welsh Border Country. All bedrooms have private bathroom, TV, radio, telephone and tea and coffee making facilities. The hotel also has an excellent restaurant, cocktail bar, lounge, a spacious conservatory and an extensive leisure centre including outside tennis courts. It is also an ideal conference venue.

*For Reservations at over 90 Mount Charlotte Thistle Hotels telephone London: 071 937 8033 or Leeds: 0532 444866.*

A MOUNT CHARLOTTE THISTLE HOTEL

C

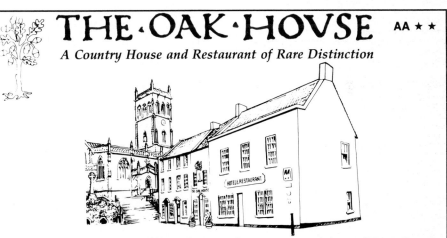

# THE·OAK·HOVSE AA ★ ★
## A Country House and Restaurant of Rare Distinction

People have been enjoying The Oak House for centuries and the tradition of good food and warm hospitality lives on with Joan & John Crew who own and run this charming, comfortable country hotel and restaurant in Axbridge, a medieval town in the heart of Somerset. Only 5 minutes from the M5 motorway. 11 Bedrooms all ensuite with comfortable modern facilities, colour TV and direct dial telephone in all rooms. Special Hideaway Weekend Rates Available.

**The Oak House Hotel and Restaurant, Axbridge, Somerset, BS26 2AP**
**Tel: Axbridge (0934) 732444**

**C**

*served with numerous vegetables enclosed in filo pastry and a herb sauce.*

10⇔𝄞Annexe8⇔𝄞 CTV in all bedrooms **T ⋈ ✳**
sB&B⇔𝄞£85 dB&B⇔𝄞£105-£185 ⊟

50P ⊞ ✿ croquet ♫ nc7yrs *xmas*

V Lunch fr£15 Dinner fr£25 Last dinner 9.30pm

Credit Cards ⟦1⟧⟦2⟧⟦3⟧⟦4⟧⟦5⟧

---

**★★★69%, Wyastone** Parabola Rd GL50 3BG ☎(0242)516654 & 245549 FAX (0242) 522659
Closed 24 Dec-2 Jan
*Enthusiastic, caring proprietors and a small, friendly team of staff will ensure that your stay here is a pleasant one. The Victorian Restaurant offers a short, quality menu with its emphasis on fresh local ingredients presented in a traditionally British style.*
13⇔𝄞(2fb)1⊞ CTV in all bedrooms ⓇT ⋈ ✳ sB⇔𝄞£48 dB⇔𝄞£65-£80 (room only) ⊟
17P ⊞
♀ English & Continental V ✿ ⚖ ⅄ Lunch £7.50-£12.50alc Dinner £13.25-£16.95 Last dinner 9pm
Credit Cards ⟦1⟧⟦3⟧ ⓔ

---

**★★★65%, Carlton** Parabola Rd GL50 3AQ ☎(0242)514453 Telex no 43310 FAX (0242) 226487
*A large double fronted late Georgian house close to the Promenade, with good conference facilities and public rooms which retain many original features. Bedrooms are constantly being upgraded and new rooms are spacious and very comfortable.*
68⇔𝄞(2fb)3⊞ CTV in all bedrooms ⓇT sB&B⇔𝄞fr£55 dB&B⇔𝄞£72-£85 ⊟
Lift ⓒ 35P CFA *xmas*
✿ Lunch fr£9.50&alc Dinner fr£11.50&alc Last dinner 9pm
Credit Cards ⟦1⟧⟦2⟧⟦3⟧⟦5⟧ ⓔ

---

**★★★65%, Hotel De La Bere** Southam GL52 3NH (3m NE A46) (Trusthouse Forte) ☎(0242)237771 Telex no 43232 FAX (0242)236016
*Situated on the Broadway road two miles from the town centre, this former Tudor mansion retains many original features, including fine oak panelling and beams in both public areas and the well equipped bedrooms. Extensive well tended grounds and good leisure facilities make this an ideal venue for the businessman and tourist.*
32⇔𝄞Annexe25⇔(2fb)6⊞⅄in 14 bedrooms CTV in all bedrooms Ⓡ T sB⇔𝄞fr£70 dB⇔𝄞fr£91 (room only) ⊟
ⓒ 150P ✿ CFA ⌂(heated) ♟ (hard) squash snooker sauna solarium badminton *xmas*
♀ English & French V ✿ ⚖ ⅄ Lunch fr£9 Dinner fr£17 Last dinner 10pm
Credit Cards ⟦1⟧⟦2⟧⟦3⟧⟦4⟧⟦5⟧

---

**★★★63%, White House** Gloucester Rd, Staverton GL51 0FT (3m W off B4063) ☎Gloucester(0452)713226 FAX (0452) 857590
*New owners have completely restyled and refurbished this hotel to provide sound modern accommodation, most of its well equipped bedrooms being of reasonable size and all having en suite facilities; public areas are both comfortable and attractively decorated, with co-ordinated colour schemes throughout.*
50⇔(3fb)2⊞ CTV in all bedrooms Ⓡ T ⋈ (ex guide dogs) ✳ sB⇔fr£59 dB⇔fr£69 (room only) ⊟
ⓒ 100P ✿ *xmas*
♀ English & French V ✿ ⚖ Lunch £5-£10 Dinner £13.50&alc Last dinner 9.30pm
Credit Cards ⟦1⟧⟦2⟧⟦3⟧⟦5⟧ ⓔ

---

**★★68%, Prestbury House** The Burgage, Prestbury GL52 3DN (2m NE A46) ☎(0242)529533 & 30106 FAX (0242) 227076
*This hotel is popular for its peaceful situation and friendly owners and staff. Bedrooms in the attractive new annexe have similar modern facilities to those in the main house, but are more compact in size.*
9⇔𝄞Annexe9⇔𝄞(3fb)1⊞⅄in 8 bedrooms CTV in all bedrooms Ⓡ T S10% sB&B⇔𝄞£55 dB&B⇔𝄞£65 ⊟
CTV 30P ✿ ∪ ⚭ *xmas*
♀ English, French & Italian V ✿ ⚖ S10% Lunch £16.50-£18.50&alc High tea £2.50-£5 Dinner £16.50-£18.50&alc Last dinner 9.30pm
Credit Cards ⟦1⟧⟦3⟧ ⓔ

---

**★★59%, Cotswold Grange** Pitville Circus Rd GL52 2QH ☎(0242)515119 FAX (0242) 241537
Closed 24 Dec-1 Jan
*A family run hotel of mellow Cotswold stone situated in the Pittville area of town, close to the centre. Service is informal and relaxed and guests are made to feel very welcome.*
25⇔𝄞(4fb) CTV in all bedrooms Ⓡ T ✳ sB&B⇔𝄞£34 dB&B⇔𝄞£45
CTV 20P ✿ ⚭
V ✿ ⚖ ⅄ Lunch £4.50-£9.50alc Dinner £6.50-£16.50alc Last dinner 7.30pm
Credit Cards ⟦1⟧⟦3⟧

---

**✱ ✕✕Le Champignon Sauvage** 24 Suffolk Rd GL50 2AQ ☎(0242)573449
*This French restaurant is operated by David and Helen Everitt-Matthias who have justifiably won the respect of their regular clientele. David's skill as a pattisier and saucier are very much in evidence and the combinations of original flavours he uses enhance rather than mask the main ingredients. Of particular note are the distinctly flavoured Jerusalem artichoke mousse with light tomato sauce and the noisettes of lamb with ratatouille mousse accompanied by a robust rosemary scented sauce. The wine list has a strong French bias and the sensible pricing policy ensures an overall experience that won't break the bank.*
Closed Sun, 2 wks in Jun, BH's & Xmas-New Year
Lunch not served Sat
♀ French V 32 seats Lunch £13.95-£21&alc Dinner £21-£22.95&alc Last lunch 1.30pm Last dinner 9.30pm ⅃
Credit Cards ⟦1⟧⟦2⟧⟦3⟧

---

**✕✕Cleeveway House** Bishops Cleeve GL52 4SA (3m N A435) ☎Bishop's Cleeve(0242)672585
*This well appointed country house restaurant makes commendable use of game, fish and raw materials in season.*
Closed 1 wk Xmas & 2 wks annual hols
Lunch not served Sun (ex by reservation) & Mon
Dinner not served Sun
♀ English & French V 38 seats ✳ Lunch £12-£18alc Dinner £12-£18alc Last lunch 1.45pm Last dinner 9.45pm 30P
Credit Cards ⟦1⟧⟦3⟧

---

**✕Mayflower Chinese** 32-34 Clarence St GL50 3NX ☎(0242)522426 & 511580 FAX (0242) 251667
*This small, personally-run, Chinese restaurant is served by a helpful and friendly staff. The menu offers a good choice of authentic Cantonese-style dishes, cooked with care and well presented.*
Closed 25-28 Dec
Lunch not served Sun
♀ Cantonese V 80 seats ✳ Lunch £7.50-£25&alc Dinner £7.50-£25&alc Last lunch 1.30pm Last dinner 10.30pm ⅃
Credit Cards ⟦2⟧⟦5⟧

**See advertisement on page 211**

---

1991 marks the 25th anniversary of this guide.

For key to symbols see the inside front cover.

**CHELWOOD** Avon Map **03** ST66

★★**72%, Chelwood House** BS18 4NH
☎Compton Dando(0761)490730 Telex no 44830
RS 24 Dec-15 Jan
*A charming, 300-year-old building, tastefully transformed to provide country house style accommodation, retains a tranquil ambience despite its setting on the A37; individually decorated rooms incorporate an excellent range of modern facilities and carefully prepared food is based on quality ingredients – the breakfast menu featuring some particularly appetising and unusual dishes.*
11⇔👤(1fb)3🛏 CTV in all bedrooms ® T 🔾 (ex guide dogs)
sB&B⇔👤£59-£65 dB&B⇔👤£69-£95 🍴
15P 🚗 ❋ croquet nc10yrs
🍷 English, French & German ♦ 🍴 Lunch fr£14.50 Dinner £16.50-£24alc Last dinner 9pm
Credit Cards ①②③⑤ⓔ

**See advertisement under BRISTOL**

**CHENIES** Buckinghamshire Map **04** TQ09

★★★**62%, Bedford Arms Thistle** WD3 6EQ (Mount Charlotte (TS)) ☎Chorleywood(09278)3301 Telex no 893939
FAX (09278) 4825
*Set in a small, peaceful village, this attractive country hotel offers comfortable well-equipped bedrooms and good hospitality. The intimate oak-panelled restaurant has a comprehensive menu of well-prepared dishes.*
10⇔👤(4fb)🔾in 1 bedroom CTV in all bedrooms T ✱
sB⇔👤fr£68 dB⇔👤fr£80 (room only) 🍴
《 120P
🍷 International ♦ 🍷 🍴 Lunch fr£15alc Dinner fr£15alc Last dinner 10pm
Credit Cards ①②③④⑤

**CHEPSTOW** Gwent Map **03** ST59

★★★**69%, St Pierre Hotel, Golf & Country Club** St Pierre Park NP6 6YA (2.5m W off A48) ☎(0291)625261 Telex no 497562
FAX (02912) 79975
*This elegant and historic mansion, with its own Norman church, is set in 400 acres of attractive parkland. Lounge and bar areas are spacious and comfortable and the bedrooms, most of which are in a modern annexe or converted outbuildings, are very well equipped. There are two golf courses and extensive leisure and conference facilities.*
107⇔👤Annexe43⇔👤(2fb)1🛏 CTV in all bedrooms ® T 🔾 (ex guide dogs) ✱ S% sB&B⇔👤£86-£96
dB&B⇔👤£105-£120 🍴
《 ⊞ CTV 300P ❋ ▣(heated) ▶ 18 ♪ (hard) squash snooker sauna solarium gymnasium beauty salon badminton steam room xmas
🍷 International V 🍴 S% Lunch fr£15 Dinner fr£15 Last dinner 9.30pm
Credit Cards ①②③⑤ⓔ

★★**66%, Castle View** 16 Bridge St NP6 5EZ ☎(02912)70349
FAX (0291) 627397
*This very friendly ivy-clad hotel, some 300 years old, stands opposite the castle. It has an abundance of timbers, and other features include an oak staircase. Homemade food using local produce is available in the restaurant and bar.*
9⇔👤Annexe2⇔👤(5fb) CTV in all bedrooms ® T
sB&B⇔👤£39.50-£46.50 dB&B⇔👤£57.50-£60.50 🍴
🍷 🚗 ❋
V ♦ 🍴 Lunch £9-£9.50&alc Dinner £12.50-£13.50&alc Last dinner 9pm
Credit Cards ①②③⑤ⓔ

★★**62%, Beaufort** Beaufort Square, Saint Mary St NP6 5EP (Inter-Hotels) ☎(0291)625074 & 622497 Telex no 498280
*Originally a 16th-century coaching inn, this busy hotel with its attractive panelled restaurant is near the town centre. Bedrooms are modern and well equipped and a good choice of food is available, including bar meals.*
18rm(10⇔3👤)(2fb) CTV in all bedrooms ® T
12P 🚗
🍷 International V ♦ 🍴 Last dinner 9.30pm
Credit Cards ①②③

★★**61%, First Hurdle** 9/10 Upper Church St NP6 5EX
☎(0291)622189
*A quaint little hotel with friendly proprietors stands on the northern edge of the town centre, close to a large, free, public car park. It offers simple but comfortable accommodation furnished with antique pieces and a pleasant Edwardian-style restaurant, easy access to the M4 motorway making it convenient for both tourists and travelling business clients.*
11rm(3⇔3👤)(1fb) CTV in all bedrooms ®
CTV 🚗
🍷 English & French V ♦ 🍷 Last dinner 10pm
Credit Cards ①②③

★★**55%, The George** Moor St NP6 5DB (Trusthouse Forte)
☎(0291)625363
*Small friendly hotel with comfortable bedrooms.*
15⇔👤🔾in 5 bedrooms CTV in all bedrooms ® S%
sB&B⇔👤fr£60 dB&B⇔👤fr£65 🍴
25P xmas
🍷 English & French V ♦ 🍷 🍴 S% Lunch fr£9.50 Dinner fr£13.50&alc Last dinner 9.30pm
Credit Cards ①②③④⑤

**CHESTER** Cheshire Map **07** SJ46

❀★★★★
**THE CHESTER GROSVENOR**

Eastgate St CH1 1LT
(Prestige) ☎(0244)324024
Telex no 61240
FAX (0244) 313246
Closed 25-26 Dec
*This is a hotel worthy of the beautiful and historic city at whose centre it lies. Recently refurbished, its public rooms, with their wealth of polished wood, clever lighting, brass and sparkling mirrors give a feeling of comfort and the illusion of space. The bedrooms, large (as most are) or small, lack for nothing and the soft furnishings are superb. The restaurant, named after the famous Aintree steeplechaser, Arkle, more than lives up to the expectations aroused by the rest of the hotel. Chef Paul Reed has raised the standard of cooking to award-winning status, and his Gourmet Menu is particularly to be recommended (we have received many letters in praise of it). The Brasserie, open for long hours throughout the day, serves less elaborate meals and snacks and is an excellent alternative for those wishing to eat more informally. The management team of Jonathan Slater and Jonathan Ritchie have brought together a first-class team of professional staff who, we are confident, will maintain our Red Star standards.*
86⇔👤🛏 CTV in all bedrooms T 🔾 (ex guide dogs)
sB⇔👤fr£110 dB⇔👤fr£165 (room only) 🍴
Lift 《 ⊞ ♪ CFA sauna solarium gymnasium ♫

▶

**C**

♡ British & French **V** ♙ ⚑ ⚒ ✗ Lunch £12.50-£14.50
Dinner fr£17 Last dinner 11pm
Credit Cards ⟦1⟧ ⟦2⟧ ⟦3⟧ ⟦4⟧ ⟦5⟧

★★★★71%, **Chester International** Trinity St CH1 2BD (Queens
Moat) ☎(0244)322330 Telex no 61251 FAX (0244) 316118
*Overlooking the renowned Roodee racecourse and commanding
fine views of the distant Welsh hills, this large and elegant modern
hotel – designed to reflect the county's heritage – was only opened
in 1989. Guests' comfort is ensured and their every need met by a
wealth of facilities and standards of hospitality and service which
have been described as exemplary.*
150↙♙✗in 22 bedrooms CTV in all bedrooms ®
sB&B↙£45-£94 dB&B↙£80-£135 ⚑
Lift ⟨ 70P sauna solarium gymnasium jacuzzi steam bath ♫
*xmas*
♡ Continental **V** ♙ ⚑ ⚒ S% Lunch £17&alc Dinner £17-£21&alc
Last dinner 10.45pm
Credit Cards ⟦1⟧ ⟦2⟧ ⟦3⟧ ⟦4⟧ ⟦5⟧ ⓕ

★★★★65%, **Mollington Banastre** Parkgate Rd CH1 6NN
(A540) (Best Western) ☎(0244)851471 Telex no 61686
FAX (0244) 851165
*Modern extensions have been added to the orignal house, not only
incorporating pleasant, uiniformly equipped bedrooms, but also
improving the public areas to include a large, comfortable lounge.
Outside, a real pub called the Good Intent offers another
atmosphere to sample, while the addition of a leisure complex with
its own restaurant and bar, widens the scope of this hotel still
further.*
64↙(6fb)1⚑✗in 5 bedrooms CTV in all bedrooms ® ✳
sB&B↙£73-£85 dB&B↙£89-£100 ⚑
Lift ⟨ 300P ❄ CFA ☐(heated) ⚘ (hard & grass) squash ♲
sauna solarium gymnasium hairdressing health & beauty salon
♫ *xmas*
♡ English & French **V** ♙ ⚑ ⚒ ✗ S% Lunch fr£9.50&alc Dinner
fr£17&alc Last dinner 10.30pm
Credit Cards ⟦1⟧ ⟦2⟧ ⟦3⟧ ⟦5⟧

★★★⚑71%, *Crabwall Manor* Parkgate Rd, Mollington
CH1 6NE (Prestige) ☎(0244)851666 Telex no 61220
FAX (0244) 851400
*Just outside Chester, but within view of the historic city, Crabwall
Manor is set in spacious leafy grounds. The beautifully furnished
and comfortable bedrooms and bathrooms are a major attraction,
and there are several pretty lounges for drinks before dinner. Word
about Crabwall is spreading, and during the week it is increasingly
used by business people, who find that the hotel's discreet meeting
and seminar facilities more than fulfil their needs.*
48↙⚑1⚑✗in 2 bedrooms CTV in all bedrooms
⚑ (ex guide dogs)
⟨ 100P ❄ snooker croquet lawn nc5yrs
♡ English & French **V** ♙ ⚑ ⚒ ✗ Last dinner 9.45pm
Credit Cards ⟦1⟧ ⟦2⟧ ⟦3⟧ ⟦5⟧

★★★64%, **Hoole Hall** Warrington Rd, Hoole Village CH2 3PD
(Crown & Raven) ☎(0244)350011 Telex no 61292
FAX (0244) 320251
*This impressive Georgian and Victorian mansion is set in 5 acres of
parkland, just 2 miles from the city centre. It offers attractive
public areas, comfortable modern bedrooms and good conference
and function facilities.*
99↙(3fb)✗in 16 bedrooms CTV in all bedrooms ® **T** ✳
sB&B↙£76.25-£88.25 dB&B↙£96.50-£108.50 ⚑
Lift ⟨ ⊞ 200P ❄ *xmas*
♡ European **V** ♙ ⚑ ⚒ ✗ Lunch fr£9.75&alc Dinner
fr£14.50&alc Last dinner 9.45pm
Credit Cards ⟦1⟧ ⟦2⟧ ⟦3⟧

★★★64%, **Post House** Wrexham Rd CH4 9DL (Trusthouse
Forte) ☎(0244)680111 Telex no 61450 FAX (0244) 674100
*A modern hotel on the outskirts of town on the A55 ring road close
to its junction with the A483. The hotel now boasts a popular
leisure centre and conference suite.*
106↙✗in 31 bedrooms CTV in all bedrooms ® **T** ✳
sB↙£70-£77 dB↙£90-£97 (room only) ⚑
⟨ 250P CFA ☐(heated) sauna solarium gymnasium spa pool ♨
*xmas*
**V** ♙ ⚑ ⚒ ✗ S15% Sunday Lunch fr£8.95 Dinner fr£14.10&alc
Last dinner 10pm
Credit Cards ⟦1⟧ ⟦2⟧ ⟦3⟧ ⟦4⟧ ⟦5⟧

★★★61%, **Abbots Well** Whitchurch Rd, Christleton CH3 5QL
(Embassy) ☎(0244)332121 Telex no 61561 FAX (0244) 335287
*In spacious grounds beside the southern bypass stands a modern
hotel catering for both business clients and tourists; conference and
banqueting facilities are available, and a well-equipped leisure
centre has recently been opened.*
127↙✗in 6 bedrooms CTV in all bedrooms ® **T** S15%
sB↙⚑£75-£87 dB↙⚑£93-£103 (room only) ⚑
⟨ 200P ❄ CFA ☐(heated) sauna solarium gymnasium jacuzzi
pool *xmas*
♡ English & French **V** ♙ ⚒ S15% Lunch £8.95&alc Dinner
£13.75&alc Last dinner 10pm
Credit Cards ⟦1⟧ ⟦2⟧ ⟦3⟧ ⟦5⟧

★★★61%, **Blossoms** St John St CH1 1HL (Trusthouse Forte)
☎(0244)323186 Telex no 61113 FAX (0244) 346433
*An original coaching house made of timber and brick that dates
back to the 17th-century. It stands in the city centre in a good
position for the tourist, while its facilities and attractiveness would
also appeal to business people. There are elegant public rooms
where you can rest to the accompaniment of soft piano music. The
bedrooms have been furnished and decorated to a high standard.*
64↙⚑(1fb)✗in 13 bedrooms CTV in all bedrooms ® **T**
sB↙⚑fr£75 dB↙⚑fr£97 (room only) ⚑
Lift ⟨ ⚘ CFA ♫ *xmas*
♡ English & French **V** ♙ ⚑ ⚒ ✗ Lunch fr£9.95&alc Dinner
fr£13.95&alc Last dinner 9.45pm
Credit Cards ⟦1⟧ ⟦2⟧ ⟦3⟧ ⟦5⟧

★★★60%, **Rowton Hall** Whitchurch Road, Rowton CH3 6AD
(2m SE A41) (Consort) ☎(0244)335262 Telex no 61172
FAX (0244) 335464
Closed 25-26 Dec
*Improvements are continually being made at this one-time
Georgian country house, now a popular conference and function
venue. Several of the bedrooms have been refurbished to a high
standard and the spacious public areas include a comfortable
lounge and smart new leisure complex.*
42↙↙(4fb)3⚑ CTV in all bedrooms ® **T** ✳
sB&B↙⚑£70-£80 dB&B↙⚑£86-£96 ⚑
⟨ CTV 120P ❄ ☐(heated) sauna solarium gymnasium
♡ French **V** ♙ ⚒ Lunch fr£10&alc Dinner fr£12.50&alc Last
dinner 9.30pm
Credit Cards ⟦1⟧ ⟦2⟧ ⟦3⟧ ⟦5⟧

★★★58%, **Plantation Inn** Liverpool Rd CH2 1AG
☎(0244)374100 Telex no 61263 FAX (0244) 379240
*Conveniently situated just off the A41, within walking distance of
the city centre, this hotel offers accommodation which is for the
most part compact and functional; a number of rooms, however,
have now been upgraded to an executive standard and are of a very
high quality. The colourful Coral Reef Restaurant features
intrenational cuisine on both table d'hôte and à la carte menus,
and there is dancing on several evenings a week. Good conference
facilities and a spacious car park are also provided.*
75↙↙(4fb) CTV in all bedrooms ® **T** S% sB↙⚑£46-£70
dB↙⚑£57-£90 (room only) ⚑
Lift ⟨ ⊞ 150P solarium ♫ *xmas*

▶

# ROWTON HALL HOTEL

AA ★ ★ ★      Member of BHRCA

Delightfully situated in the rural outskirts of Chester, Rowton Hall is renowned for the warm informal country house welcome it extends to guests. Fresh home grown produce, log fires and relaxed atmosphere make the ideal setting for both business and pleasure.

- 42 en-suite bedrooms with many extras.
- Hamiltons Leisure Club includes indoor swimming pool, multi-gym, sauna and solarium. Children under 6 not admitted.
- A choice of 4 conference rooms for up to 200 delegates.
- Bar, lounge and restaurant open to non residents for light refreshments, lunch and dinner.
- Easy access from motorway network with ample parking.
- Set in 8 acres of gardens and pastureland.

\*
\* **SPECIAL WEEKEND RATES** \*
\*

**Whitchurch Road, Rowton, Chester CH3 6AD**
**Telephone: Chester (0244) 335262**
Telex: 61172 Rowtel      Fax: (0244) 335464

---

# LLYNDIR HALL
# Country House Hotel★ ★ ★

**Llyndir Lane, Rossett, Near Chester,**
**Clwyd LL12 0AY**
**Tel: (0244) 571648 Fax: (0244) 571648**

C

Set in quiet, country surroundings the hotel offers all the time and space you need to unwind in a true Country House atmosphere. Built in the 19th century the hotel has undergone recent modernisation but you will still find comfort and tradition. The Restaurant opens out into a conservatory overlooking the lawns. There are 38 luxuriously fitted bedrooms. A newly completed Leisure Complex and Function Room seating up to 150 guests. For further details and colour brochure please contact the hotel.

---

AA ★ ★ ★

# BROXTON HALL
# Country House Hotel

**Whitchurch Road, Broxton,**
**Chester CH3 9JS**
**Tel: (0829) 782 321    Fax: (0244) 314 798**

Beautiful 17th Century Country House Hotel, situated in 5 acres of delightful English gardens, set amidst Cheshire's finest countryside. On cool evenings log fires are lit in 17th Century fireplaces, giving a warm cosy atmosphere. Privately owned. 12 Bedrooms en suite bath, telephone, TV, tea/coffee making facilities. Business lunches and conferences handled with person attention.

---

CHESTER INTERNATIONAL HOTEL

TRINITY STREET, CHESTER,
CHESHIRE CH1 2BD
Tel: 0244-322330. Fax: 0244-316118. Telex: 61251

The very latest in 4 star luxury is waiting for you in the heart of the historic city of Chester. Chester International Hotel can offer you: 150 luxury bedrooms, air conditioned bars and restaurant with spectacular views over the hills of Wales, air conditioned conference & banqueting facilities up to 400. Mini leisure facilities & car parking for 80 vehicles.

INTERNATIONAL HOTELIERS

**C**

♅ Continental **V** ♯ ⚒ S% Lunch fr£6.50 Dinner
£11.50-£13.50&alc Last dinner 10.30pm
Credit Cards ①②③④⑤

**★★66% Green Bough** 60 Hoole Rd CH2 3NL ☎(0244)326241
FAX (0244) 326265·
Closed 21-28 Dec RS 29 Dec-6 Jan
*A warm and friendly hotel, in main road position about a mile from
the city centre, is personally run by its resident owners to provide
delightfully furnished accommodation with a good range of
facilities; public areas include a comfortable, cosy lounge with
separate bar and an attractive, intimate restaurant where guests
can enjoy a well-cooked meal.*
14⇨♠️Annexe2⇨♠️(5fb)1🛏 CTV in all bedrooms ® T
sB&B⇨♠️£34.50-£38 dB&B⇨♠️£43-£47 🄿
CTV 21P
**V** S% Lunch £5.50-£6.60 Dinner £9-£10 Last dinner 8pm
Credit Cards ①③ⓔ

**★★62% Dene** Hoole Rd CH2 3ND ☎(0244)321165
FAX (0244) 350277
*Standing in its own grounds on the A56 one mile from the city
centre, the hotel offers neat functional accommodation in both the
main house and the motel block. The well equipped rooms all have
en suite facilities, and there are good parking arrangements for
resident guests.*
41rm(39⇨♠️)Annexe8⇨♠️(4fb) CTV in all bedrooms ® T
sB&B£26-£28 sB&B⇨♠️£35-£37 dB&B⇨♠️£46-£48 🄿
CTV 55P ✿
**V** ♯ ⊬ Dinner £7-£8&alc Last dinner 8.30pm
Credit Cards ①③

**★★58% Royal Oak** Warrington Rd, Mickle Trafford CH2 4EX
(3m NE A56) (Toby) ☎(0244)301391 Telex no 61536
*This hotel is situated on the outskirts of Chester, and has recently
had the restaurant and the lounge bar refitted, to complement the
well equipped bedrooms and the small conference room.*
36⇨♠️(10fb) CTV in all bedrooms ®
( 150P ✿
**V** ♯ ⚒
Credit Cards ①②③⑤

**CHESTERFIELD** Derbyshire Map **08** SK37

**★★★63% Chesterfield** Malkin St S41 7UA (Best Western)
☎(0246)271141 Telex no 547492 FAX (0246) 220719
*A fully modernised hotel situated adjacent to the station. The
interior is decorated in the 1920's style and facilities include a
stylish function room.*
72⇨♠️(10fb)⊬in 18 bedrooms CTV in all bedrooms ® T
sB&B⇨♠️£36-£68 dB&B⇨♠️£56-£72 🄿
Lift ( 100P ▣(heated) snooker sauna solarium gymnasium ♫
*xmas*
♅ International **V** ♯ ⚒ Lunch £5.25-£7.25 Dinner £10.95 Last
dinner 10pm
Credit Cards ①②③ⓔ

**★★65% Ringwood Hall** Brimington S43 1DQ (Consort)
☎(0246)280077 FAX (0246) 472241
*This large hotel, lying north east of the town on the A619, has a
very busy function and conference trade; both function facilities
and residential accommodation have recently been upgraded.*
24⇨♠️(2fb)2🛏⊬in 3 bedrooms CTV in all bedrooms ® T ✱
sB&B⇨♠️£55-£75 dB&B⇨♠️£65-£75 🄿
( CTV 170P ✿ bowling green ♫ *xmas*
♅ English & Continental **V** ♯ ⚒ Lunch £5.95-£12.50 Dinner
£14 Last dinner 10pm
Credit Cards ①②③⑤ⓔ

**1991 marks the 25th anniversary of this guide.**

**★★61% Portland** West Bars S40 1AY ☎(0246)234502 &
234211 FAX (0246) 550915
*A comfortable, friendly, city centre hotel offers guests a lunchtime
choice between the Fountain Restaurant's à la carte or carvery
meals and the bistro-style bar meals of the Pantry.*
27rm(15⇨1♠️)(4fb) CTV in all bedrooms ® T
✖ (ex guide dogs) sB&B£27.50-£32 sB&B⇨♠️£32-£43.50
dB&B⇨♠️£43.50-£57 🄿
( CTV 30P
♅ Mainly grills **V** ♯ Lunch £5-£7.50 Dinner £5-£10 Last dinner
10pm
Credit Cards ①③

○**Travelodge** A61 Brimmington Rd, Inner Ring
Rd(Trusthouse Forte) ☎Central reservations (0800) 850950
Due to open winter 1990
20⇨

**CHESTERFORD, GREAT** Essex Map **05** TL54

**★★59% The Crown House** CB10 1NY
☎Saffron Walden(0799)30515 FAX (0799) 30683
*Friendly and personally owned, a commercial hotel with a
relaxing, informal atmosphere provides accommodation in
bedrooms which are generally spacious and thoughtfully
appointed; two dining rooms offer a choice of table d'hôte and à la
carte menus, dishes being carefully prepared and well cooked.*
8⇨Annexe14⇨🛏4🛏 CTV in all bedrooms ® T
✖ (ex guide dogs) ✳ sB&B⇨♠️£50-£60 dB&B⇨♠️£70-£85 🄿
CTV 30P 🚗 ♫ *xmas*
♅ English & French **V** ♯ ⚒ ⊬ Lunch £5.75-£17alc Dinner
fr£17&alc Last dinner 9.45pm
Credit Cards ①③ⓔ

**CHICHESTER** West Sussex Map **04** SU80

**★★★72% Goodwood Park** PO18 0QB ☎(0243)775537
Telex no 869173 FAX (0243) 533802
(For full entry see Goodwood)

**★★★61% The Dolphin & Anchor** West St PO19 1QE
(Trusthouse Forte) ☎(0243)785121 FAX (0243) 533408
*A charming town centre hotel, originally two ancient inns,
conveniently situated opposite the cathedral. Parking and access
can be difficult, however, so guests would be well advised to ask for
directions in advance. Bedrooms vary, though there is a continuing
refurbishment programme, while public areas include a popular
coffee shop, bar, attractively appointed restaurant and comfortable
lounge.*
51⇨♠️(5fb)⊬in 22 bedrooms CTV in all bedrooms ® S15%
sB⇨♠️£65 dB⇨♠️£81 (room only) 🄿
( 6P 20🚗 CFA *xmas*
♅ English & French **V** ♯ ⚒ ⊬ S15% Lunch fr£7.25&alc High
tea fr£2.25 Dinner fr£13 Last dinner 9.30pm
Credit Cards ①②③④⑤

**★★55% Ship** North St PO19 1NH ☎(0243)782028
FAX (0243) 774254
*Situated in the centre of the town, this traditional-style hotel is
undergoing gradual refurbishment. Work on the public areas is
almost complete and has been carried out to a good standard, but a
number of the bedrooms remain rather functional. Cheerful staff
and straightforward cuisine ensure its popularity, particularly with
business guests.*
37rm(32⇨5♠️)(4fb) CTV in all bedrooms ® T sB&B£32-£44
sB&B⇨♠️£65 dB&B£48-£71 dB&B⇨♠️£67-£107 🄿
Lift ( 35P 3🚗 (£3 per night) *xmas*
**V** ♯ ⚒ Lunch £4.50-£7&alc High tea £3-£7alc Dinner
£12.50&alc Last dinner 9.30pm
Credit Cards ①③⑤

★66%, **Bedford** Southgate PO19 1DP ☎(0243)785766
FAX (0243) 533175
*A popular and friendly hotel in a good central position with easy*
*access to the town centre and railway station. Accommodation is*
*neat and modern and a good standard of home cooking is served in*
*the pleasant restaurant.*
24rm(4⇌8♠)(2fb) CTV in all bedrooms ® T ✳ S% sB£30-£35
sB⇌♠£39-£45 dBfr£46 dB⇌♠£55-£58 (room only) ⊨
CTV 6P ♨
♚ English V ✿ ☑
Credit Cards ① ② ③ ⑤

✗✗**Comme Ça** 149 St Pancras PO19 1SH ☎(0243)788724
*This small, cottage-style restaurant specialises in traditional*
*French cuisine, a comprehensive range of popular regional dishes*
*being prepared from totally fresh ingredients. Basic sauces are*
*particularly good, and guests' enjoyment of the meal is further*
*enhanced by an excellent selection of good-value Burgundy wines*
*and efficient service.*
Closed Mon, 25 Dec, 1 Jan & BH's
Lunch not served Sat
Dinner not served Sun
♚ French V 39 seats Lunch £15-£20alc Last lunch 1.45pm Last
dinner 10.45pm ℙ
Credit Cards ① ③

**CHIEVELEY SERVICE AREA (off M4)** Berkshire
Map **04** SU46

○**Granada** Oxford Rd RG16 8XX (Granada)
☎Central reservations (05255)5555
Due to have opened Aug 1990
60⇌♠

# Ⓣhe Ⓓene Ⓗotel ★★

**HOOLE ROAD (A56) CHESTER CH2 3ND**
**Tel: (0244) 321165 Fax: (0244) 350277**

Ⓒ

Set in its own grounds and adjacent to
Alexandra Park yet only 1 mile from the
City Centre, this pleasant family run hotel
has Residents' Bar, lounge and Elizabethan restaurant. All bedrooms have private
bathrooms, colour TV, tea and coffee
making facilities and direct dial telephones.

*Ample Parking. Motel Accommodation.*
*Bargain Breaks Available.*

AA ★★★

## ⓉHE CHESTERFIELD HOTEL

*FINE ENGLISH HOTELS*

# COMFORT & CARE ON THE EDGE OF THE PEAK DISTRICT

The market town of Chesterfield is an ideal centre from
which to tour the Peak District and the Chesterfield Hotel
in the town centre is renowned for its high standards and
friendly atmosphere, whether you visit for business or
pleasure.

74 comfortable en suite bedrooms are augmented by an
excellent Restaurant and the superb new Peak Leisure
Centre which must rank among the best available in the
North Midlands, offering a 20m. indoor pool, snooker,
gymnasium, sauna and solarium.
The Chesterfield is also an ideal choice for conferences
and seminars.

*Ask for our full colour brochure*

Malkin Street · CHESTERFIELD · S41 7UA
Telephone: (0246) 71141

AA ★★★

*The* Ⓟlantation Ⓘnn

*FINE ENGLISH HOTELS*

# COMFORT AND STYLE IN ANCIENT CHESTER

Situated just 500 metres from the city's Medieval
Centre, and a few minutes walk from the Roman
Walls, The Plantation Inn is ideally placed for a
stay in Chester and the perfect base for exploring
North Wales and the Welsh Borderlands.

78 comfortable en suite bedrooms offering every
facility for the business and leisure traveller are
complemented by an elegant restaurant with
excellent cuisine and friendly service, and five
fully air-conditioned conference suites offer the
perfect venue for conferences or seminars.

*Ask for our full colour brochure*

Liverpool Road · CHESTER · CH2 1AG
Telephone: (0244) 374100

**C**

## CHILGROVE West Sussex Map 04 SU81

**✗✗White Horse Inn** PO18 9HX ☎East Marden(024359)219 & 251 FAX (024359) 301
*This small, wisteria-clad free house at the foot of the South Downs has a softly-lit dining room where friendly staff, led by a very able manager, create a warm atmosphere. A fixed price menu is prepared from local produce, including fresh fish, and though dishes tend to be simple, flavours are good and clear. The wine list is possibly the longest and richest in rare vintages in the country.*
Closed Mon, 3 wks Feb & 1 wk Oct
Dinner not served Sun
♀ English & French **V** 60 seats Lunch £16.50 Dinner £22-£24.50 Last lunch 1.45pm Last dinner 9.30pm 200P
Credit Cards ①③④⑤

## CHILLINGTON Devon Map 03 SX74

**★★64% Oddicombe House** TQ7 2JD ☎Frogmore(0548)531234
Closed Nov-Etr
*Family-run hotel featuring comfortable bedrooms, good home cooking and an extensive garden with a swimming pool. The atmosphere is relaxed and informal and the hotel is well situated for touring the South Hams.*
8rm(6⇨¾)Annexe2rm(1⇨¾)(3fb)⑧ S% sB&B£22-£25 sB&B⇨¾£28-£31 dB&B£44-£50 dB&B⇨¾£50-£54
CTV 15P ⋙ ✿ ⌂
♀ European ✿ ♨ ✂ Dinner fr£13 Last dinner 8.15pm

**★69% White House** TQ7 2JX ☎Kingsbridge(0548)580580
Closed Nov-Etr (ex Xmas)
*Ideally situated for touring the South Hams coastline, this Georgian house in its own carefully tended gardens offers eight individually furnished, well equipped bedrooms (most with en suite facilities), the comfortably decorated Normandy Bar and a drawing room in elegant peaceful style where coffee can be enjoyed after a pleasant home-cooked meal home which will have made use of local produce wherever possible.*
8rm(3⇨¾3♠)(1fb) CTV in all bedrooms ⑧ dB&B£40.40-£46.30 dB&B⇨¾♠£45.90-£59 ⋤
CTV 8P ⋙ ✿ croquet badminton nc5yrs *xmas*
♀ English, French & Italian ✿ ♨ ✂ Dinner £10.75 Last dinner 8.05pm

## CHIPPENHAM Wiltshire Map 03 ST97

See also **Sutton Benger**
**★59% The Bear** 12 Market Place SN15 3HJ ☎(0249)653272
Closed 25 Dec
*This small, friendly hotel, under the personal supervision of the proprietors, features two lively bars and a first-floor restaurant ; considerable improvements have been made, and sound, simple standards of service prevail.*
9rm(2⇨¾)(1fb) CTV in all bedrooms ⑧ ✱ sB&B£18-£24.50 sB&B⇨¾£35 dB&B£36 dB&B⇨¾£45
6P
♀ Mainly grills **V** ✿
Credit Cards ①③

## CHIPPERFIELD Hertfordshire Map 04 TL00

**★★66% The Two Brewers Inn** The Common WD4 9BS
(Trusthouse Forte) ☎King's Langley(0923)265266
FAX (0923)261884
*You will find a welcoming atmosphere and a popular beamed bar at this charming and cosy 17th-century inn which overlooks the village green. Bedrooms offer well-equipped, modern accommodation and there is a spacious and comfortable lounge.*
20⇨¾♠in 4 bedrooms CTV in all bedrooms ⑧ T ✱ sB⇨¾♠£45-£78 dB⇨¾♠£75-£84 (room only) ⋤
25P ⋙ *xmas*

♀ French **V** ✿ ♨ ✂ Lunch £14.50&alc Dinner £15.50&alc
Last dinner 10pm
Credit Cards ①②③④⑤

## CHIPPING Lancashire Map 07 SD64

**★68% The Brickhouse** PR3 2QH ☎(0995)61316
RS Mon & Sun eve
5⇨¾♠(2fb) CTV in all bedrooms ⑧ ✈ (ex guide dogs) sB&B⇨¾♠fr£33 dB&B⇨¾♠fr£45.50 ⋤
100P ✿
♀ English & Continental **V** ✿ ♨ Lunch fr£8.50&alc Dinner fr£14.95&alc Last dinner 9.30pm
Credit Cards ①③

## CHIPPING CAMPDEN Gloucestershire Map 04 SP13

**★★★70% Cotswold House** The Square GL55 6AN
☎Evesham(0386)840330 FAX (0386) 840310
Closed 25-27 Dec
*This Regency town house has recently been restored to its former elegance and splendour. The bedrooms are individually designed and fitted and the spacious lounges are comfortable. Well presented imaginative cuisine is served in the charming dining room.*
15⇨¾♠1♨ CTV in all bedrooms T ✈ sB&B⇨¾♠£50-£60 dB&B⇨¾♠£80-£142 ⋤
12P ⋙ ✿ croquet ♫ nc8yrs
**V** ✿ ♨ ✂ Sunday Lunch £15.95 Dinner £19.50&alc Last dinner 9.30pm
Credit Cards ①②③⑤ⓔ

**★★64% Noel Arms** High St GL55 6AT (Exec Hotel)
☎Evesham(0386)840317 FAX (0386) 841136
*Public areas of this hotel still reflect the simplicity and character of the original 14th-century coaching inn, while bedrooms offer a range of facilities and are clean and well maintained.*
26⇨¾♠2♨ CTV in all bedrooms ⑧ T ✈ (ex guide dogs) sB&B⇨¾♠£45-£55 dB&B⇨¾♠£70-£90 ⋤
40P *xmas*
**V** ✿ ♨ Sunday Lunch £9.50-£12 Dinner £8-£15 Last dinner 10pm
Credit Cards ①②③

○**Seymour House** High St GL55 6AH ☎(0386)840429
Due to have opened Aug 90
15rm

## CHIPPING NORTON Oxfordshire Map 04 SP23

**✗Vittles** 7 Horsefair OX7 5AL ☎(0608)644490
*The new owners of this cosy cottage restaurant, Ian and Eve Chapman, have instigated significant refurbishment to give the place a simple yet quality, classical appearance. Ian's cuisine bears evidence of some originality, whilst Eve leads the hospitable and conscientious service in the restaurant.*
Closed Sun , last wk Nov & 1st 2 wks Feb
♀ English & Continental **V** 35 seats ✱ Lunch £10.75&alc Dinner £10.75&alc Last lunch 2pm Last dinner 11pm ⚘ nc7yrs
Credit Cards ①②③

## CHIPPING SODBURY Avon Map 03 ST78

**✗Sultan** Melbourne House, 29 Horse St BS17 6DA
☎(0454)323510
*An Indian restaurant with a difference, the Sultan serves well cooked and authentic regional dishes in the comfortable and relaxed atmosphere of a traditionally-furnished Georgian house typical of this charming Cotswold market town.*
♀ Indian **V** 44 seats Last lunch 1.45pm Last dinner 11pm ⚘
Credit Cards ①②③

See advertisement on page 219

**CHITTLEHAMHOLT** Devon Map **02** SS62

★★★♨**74%, Highbullen** EX37 9HD ☎(07694)561
FAX (07694) 492

*Standing on high ground between the Mole and Taw valleys, this hotel is in 60 acres of wooded parkland, which includes a 9-hole golf course and a large herd of Manchurian sika deer. Bedrooms are located in the main building and various annexes and all are centrally heated, with private facilities. A varied menu makes good use of local fish, meat, game and vegetables and the standard of cuisine is high. Sports and leisure facilities are excellent.*
12⇆Annexe23⇆ CTV in all bedrooms ⓇT ⋈ S%
sB&B⇆£50-£65
dB&B⇆£90-£120 Continental breakfast (incl dinner)
60P ⇞ ✿ ☐(heated) ⌒(heated) ▶9 ♗ (hard) ♪ squash snooker sauna solarium gymnasium croquet putting table tennis nc10yrs
♉ International V ✿ ♨ ⚹ Bar Lunch £2-£6alc Dinner £16.50 Last dinner 9pm

**CHOLLERFORD** Northumberland Map **12** NY97

★★★**65%, George** NE46 4EW (Swallow)
☎Humshaugh(043481)611 FAX (0434) 681727
*Set on the banks of the River North Tyne, this tourist and business hotel offers a mixture of modern and traditional bedrooms.*
50⇆(5fb)1⊞ CTV in all bedrooms Ⓡ T
《70P ✿ ☐(heated) ♪ sauna solarium putting
♉ International V ✿ ♨
Credit Cards ①②③⑤

**CHORLEY** Lancashire Map **07** SD51

★★★**65%, Shaw Hill Hotel Golf & Country Club** Preston Rd,
Whittle-le-Woods PR6 7PP (2m N A6) ☎(02572)69221
FAX (02572) 61223
*This comfortably-converted country house is situated on a golf course and has a very good restaurant.*
22⇆♣(1fb)⊞ CTV in all bedrooms Ⓡ T ✳ S%
sB&B⇆♣£40-£57.50 dB&B⇆♣£49.50-£79.50 ⧰
《CTV 200P ✿ ▶18 ♪ snooker sauna solarium *xmas*
♉ International V ✿ ♨
Credit Cards ①②③⑤ ⓔ

★★★**63%, Park Hall Hotel, Leisure & Conference Centre**
PR7 5LP ☎Eccleston(0257)452090 Telex no 677604
FAX (0257) 451838
(For full entry see Charnock Richard)

★★**66%, Hartwood Hall** Preston Rd PR6 7AX ☎(02572)69966
FAX (02572) 41678
Closed 25-30 Dec
*Situated to the north of town on the A6 close to its junction with the M61 this privately owned hotel offers well appointed if fairly compact bedrooms. Housekeeping standards are good and service throughout is friendly and helpful.*
12rm(8⇆♣)Annexe10⇆♣(2fb)1⊞ CTV in all bedrooms Ⓡ
✳ sB&B£35-£45 sB&B⇆♣£35-£45 dB&B£45-£50
dB&B⇆♣£50-£55 ⧰
CTV 150P ⇞
♉ English & Continental V ✿ ♨ Lunch £7.50&alc Dinner £11&alc Last dinner 9pm
Credit Cards ①②③⑤ ⓔ

*All AA-appointed establishments are inspected regularly to ensure that required standards are maintained.*

**CHRISTCHURCH** Dorset Map **04** SZ19

See also **Avon**

★★★**72%, Waterford Lodge** 87 Bure Ln, Friars Cliff,
Mudeford BH23 4DN (2m E off B3059) (Best Western)
☎Highcliffe(0425)272948 & 278801 Telex no 41588
FAX (0425) 279130
*Family-run to provide a warm, friendly atmosphere, and standing in attractive gardens amid peaceful surroundings, the hotel offers comfortable accommodation with spacious, well equipped bedrooms.*
20⇆(3fb)1⊞ CTV in all bedrooms Ⓡ T sB&B⇆£47-£55
dB&B⇆£68-£76 ⧰
38P ⇞ ✿ *xmas*
♉ English & French V ✿ ♨ Lunch £5.95-£9.95 High tea fr£4.50 Dinner £14.50&alc Last dinner 8.30pm
Credit Cards ①②③⑤
**See advertisement also under BOURNEMOUTH**

★★★**60%, The Avonmouth** Mudeford BH23 3NT (2m E off B3059) (Trusthouse Forte) ☎(0202)483434
*A popular resort hotel with fine views of the sea offers modest but well equipped bedrooms, comfortable public areas, good leisure facilities and a friendly, informal atmosphere throughout.*
27⇆Annexe14⇆(3fb)⚹in 4 bedrooms CTV in all bedrooms Ⓡ
《66P ✿ ⌒(heated) ♫ ♤
♉ English & French V ✿ ♨ ⚹ Last dinner 9pm
Credit Cards ①②③④⑤

★★**65%, Fisherman's Haunt** Salisbury Rd, Winkton BH23 7AS
(2.5m N on B3347) ☎(0202)477283 & 484071
Closed 25 Dec
*This busy hotel, attractively creeper-clad and set in its own grounds near the River Avon, provides an ideal base for fishermen, offering comfortable bedrooms and public bars.*
4rm(1⇆2♣)Annexe15rm(13⇆)(4fb)2⊞ CTV in all bedrooms
Ⓡ T ✳ sB&Bfr£25 sB&B⇆♣£32-£34 dB&Bfr£49
dB&B⇆♣£52-£56 ⧰
100P ✿
V ✿ ♨ Lunch £7-£7.50alc Dinner £15-£20alc Last dinner 10pm
Credit Cards ①②③⑤
**See advertisement on page 223**

**CHURCH STRETTON** Shropshire Map **07** SO49

★★★**58%, Stretton Hall** All Stretton SY6 6HE ☎(0694)723224
*A small hotel in country manor style, its well-kept gardens featuring a pond and fountain, offers a friendly, relaxed atmosphere which makes it ideal for the guest seeking a few days "away from it all".*
13⇆♣(1fb) CTV in all bedrooms Ⓡ
CTV 60P ⇞ ✿
♉ English & French ✿ ♨ ⚹ Last dinner 9pm
Credit Cards ①②③⑤

★★**69%, Mynd House** Little Stretton SY6 6RB (2m S B4370)
(Exec Hotel) ☎(0694)722212 FAX (0694) 724180
Closed Jan
*Set high in pleasant gardens, a large Edwardian house in the peaceful and picturesque village of Little Stretton enjoys good views of the valley and hills opposite ; it offers modern, well-equipped accommodation and a warm welcome from the proprietors.*
8⇆♣1⊞ CTV in all bedrooms Ⓡ T sB&B⇆♣£30-£32
dB&B⇆♣£48-£75 ⧰
16P ⇞ ✿ *xmas*
♉ English, French & Italian V ✿ ♨ ⚹ Bar Lunch £3.50-£6 Dinner £12.50-£14.50&alc Last dinner 9.15pm
Credit Cards ①③ ⓔ

**CHURT** Surrey Map **04** SU83

★★★50% *Frensham Pond* GU10 2QB ☎Frensham(025125)3175
Telex no 858610

*Spacious bedrooms combined with garden chalet bedrooms provide a varied choice of accommodation here. There is a small cocktail bar and the well-managed Fountain restaurant provides good standards of service and an above average wine list. A new addition is 'Fathoms' leisure centre.*

7⊸♪◖Annexe12⊸◖ CTV in all bedrooms ℞ ⋈
《 100P ♨ ✻ ▣(heated) squash sauna solarium gymnasium jacuzzi ♫
♀ English & French **V** ☼
Credit Cards ①②③④⑤

**CIRENCESTER** Gloucestershire Map **04** SP00

★★★69% *Fleece* Market Place GL7 2NZ ☎(0285)658507
Telex no 437287 FAX (0285) 651017
*This Tudor inn in the town centre offers a high standard of bedroom accommodation and a comfortable lounge. The dining room serves new English dishes and a new wine bar will offer char-grilled food. Staff are friendly and courteous.*

25⊸(4fb)2▤ CTV in all bedrooms ℞ **T** ✶ S% sB⊸£60-£70
dB⊸£70-£80 (room only) ▤
12P ♨ ♫ *xmas*
♀ English & French **V** ☼ ⌧ Lunch fr£11.95 Dinner fr£13.95
Last dinner 9.30pm
Credit Cards ①②③⑤ ⓔ

★★★65% **The Crown of Crucis** Ampney Crucis GL7 5RS
☎(0285)851806 FAX (0285) 851735
Closed 25 Dec
*This completely refurbished sixteenth-century inn, situated on the A417 three miles east of the town, retains the character and charm of its origins in bar and split-level restaurant, which between them* ▶

**C**

offer a wide range of food. Comfortable, well equipped bedrooms with good en suite facilities surround a garden courtyard, many also overlooking Ampney Brook and the cricket club.
26⇨🎠 CTV in all bedrooms ® T sB&B⇨🎠£46-£50 dB&B⇨🎠£58-£65 ☒
82P *xmas*
V ✿ 🍽 Lunch £3-£7alc Dinner £9.50-£12.50&alc Last dinner 10pm
Credit Cards ①②③⓵

★★★ **65%, King's Head** Market Place GL7 2NR (Best Western)
☎(0285)653322 Telex no 43470 FAX (0285) 655103
Closed 27-30 Dec
Situated in the market square, this hotel provides spacious, comfortable public areas of character and well-equipped bedrooms of varying standards. Very friendly and attentive service is provided by Mr Haigh-Gannon and his staff.
70⇨🎠(4fb)2🛏 CTV in all bedrooms ® T S%
sB&B⇨🎠£45-£60 dB&B⇨🎠£67-£79 ☒
Lift ( 25P pool skittle alley darts table tennis *xmas*
V ✿ 🍽 ⌀ S% Lunch fr£10.50&alc Dinner fr£14&alc Last dinner 9pm
Credit Cards ①②③④⑤ ⓵

★★★ **52%, Stratton House** Gloucester Rd GL7 2LE (Forestdale)
☎(0285)651761 FAX (0285) 640024
Set in an attractive walled garden on the outskirts of town, Stratton House dates from Jacobean times with later additions of mellow Cotswold stone. Run on country house lines, it has welcoming log fires in the cooler months in the flagstoned entrance hall, the elegant lounge and the timbered bar.
25⇨🎠 CTV in all bedrooms ® T ✱ sB&B⇨🎠£49.50-£55 dB&B⇨🎠fr£65 ☒
( 100P ✿ *xmas*
♨ English & French V ✿ 🍽 Lunch £8.80-£13.50 Dinner £8.80-£13.50 Last dinner 9.45pm
Credit Cards ①②③⑤ ⓵

★★ **58%, Corinium Court** Gloucester St GL7 2DG
☎(0285)659711 FAX (0285) 885807
Situated in the oldest part of town, this former 16th-century wool merchant's house is now a hotel with good modern facilities. Public areas have charm and character and the dining room offers imaginative food.
16⇨🎠(1fb) CTV in all bedrooms T
40P 🚗
V ✿ 🍽
Credit Cards ①②③⑤

**CLACHAN-SEIL** Strathclyde *Argyllshire* Map **10** NM71

★★ **65%, Willowburn** PA34 4TJ (Guestaccom)
☎Balvicar(08523)276
Closed Nov-mid Mar
6⇨🎠 CTV in all bedrooms ® sB&B⇨🎠£31-£35 dB&B⇨🎠£62-£70 (incl dinner) ☒
36P 🚗 ✿ *xmas*
✿ 🍽 Bar Lunch £3-£10&alc Dinner £12-£14&alc Last dinner 8.30pm
Credit Cards ①③

**CLACTON-ON-SEA** Essex Map **05** TM11

★★ **61%, King's Cliff** King's Pde, Holland on Sea CO15 5JB
☎(0255)812343 Telex no 817589 FAX (0284) 706502
This imposing sea-front hotel has comfortable bedrooms and the public areas have, for the most part, been refurbished to a good standard. The popular lounge bar includes a food counter which offers good hot and cold snacks at lunchtime, whilst for the more discerning guest there is a new cocktail bar adjacent to the formal restaurant.
15⇨🎠(5fb)1🛏 CTV in all bedrooms ® ✖
( CTV 80P 5🚗 (£1 per night) ✿

▶

♨ European V ✿ 🍽 ✖
Credit Cards ①②③

**CLANFIELD** Oxfordshire Map **04** SP20

✖✖✖ **Plough at Clanfield** Bourton Rd OX8 2RB
☎(036781)222 & 494 Telex no 449848 FAX (036781) 596
Nestling in the heart of the Cotswolds the Plough is a fine example of an Elizabethan manor house. Chef Stephen Parker is responsible for the fine cooking at both lunch and dinner. An excellent wine list complements the food. Some well appointed bedrooms are available.
♨ English & French V 45 seats Lunch £14 Dinner £24.95-£29.95 Last lunch 2pm Last dinner 10pm 30P nc7yrs ✖
Credit Cards ①②③⑤

**CLARE** Suffolk Map **05** TL74

★★ **70%, Bell** Market Hill CO10 8NN (Minotels)
☎(0787)277741 FAX (0787) 278474
This hotel is a former inn with additional accommodation centred around a courtyard. Public areas are a mixture of old and new, perfectly harmonised to create a warm atmosphere, and bedrooms are well equipped.
10rm(3⇨4🎠)Annexe11⇨(1fb) CTV in all bedrooms ® T 15P
♨ English, French & Italian ✿ 🍽 Last dinner 9.30pm
Credit Cards ①②③⑤

★ **71%, The Seafarer** Nethergate St CO10 8NP ☎(0787)277449
Mr and Mrs Ross have preserved the original character of this 17th-century village inn while providing all modern comforts in the carefully furnished and decorated rooms. The atmosphere is friendly and informal.
5rm(3🎠) CTV in all bedrooms ® ✱ sB&B£28.95 sB&B🎠£38.95 dB&B£39.95 dB&B🎠£49.95 ☒
10P ✿ *xmas*

# The Bell Hotel★★

### Clare, West Suffolk, England CO10 8NN
### Telephone Clare 277741
### Code 0787

20 bedrooms – private bathrooms – wine bar – conference rooms. Beamed Restaurant. 16th-century posting house within easy reach of LONDON (62 miles) and ferry ports of HARWICH (40 miles) and FELIXSTOWE (47 miles). Ideal centre for touring East Anglia all year round.

*Resident Proprietors:*
*Brian and Gloria Miles*
MINOTELS

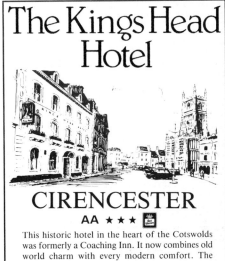

♔ English & French **V** ✿ 🍷 Lunch £6.45-£25alc Dinner £10-£12&alc Last dinner 10pm
Credit Cards ① ② ③ ⑤

---

## CLAWTON Devon Map **02** SX39

★★▚68% **Court Barn Country House** EX22 6PS (Exec Hotel)
🕾North Tamerton(040927)219
Closed 1-14 Jan
*Dating back to around the 14th century and re-built in 1853, this hotel stands in 5 acres of grounds and gardens. Personally run, it offers cosy public rooms with a choice of lounges and comfortable, spotlessly clean bedrooms, each individually furnished and decorated with William Morris wallpapers and fabrics. Many also have good views over the countryside. Plentiful home cooking is based on quality produce and complemented by an extensive wine list and a comprehensive selection of teas.*
8rm(4⇩3🏠)(3fb)1🖩🗲in all bedrooms CTV in all bedrooms Ⓡ sB&B⇩🏠£30-£35 dB&B⇩🏠£60-£68 🅿
CTV 16P 2🏌 ✿ Ú solarium gymnasium croquet putting outdoor badminton 🏌 *xmas*
♔ English & French **V** ✿ 🍷 ✂ Lunch £7.95-£9.95 High tea £1.95-£3alc Dinner fr£16.95 Last dinner 9.15pm
Credit Cards ① ② ③ ⑤ ⓔ

---

## CLAYGATE Surrey

**See LONDON plan** *1B1*(pages 426-7)
❋✕✕**Les Alouettes** High St KT10 0JW 🕾Esher(0372)64882
FAX (0372) 65337
*A popular French restaurant not only noted for its food, but for the warm friendly atmosphere created by the charming French owner. The decor is attractive and tasteful, creating a relaxing and pleasant environment. There is an interesting menu of French cuisine, with thoughtfully prepared dishes from good fresh basic ingredients. There is a well chosen wine list with good vintages and selection from a number of countries. The young staff provide good formal service.*
Closed Sun, 1-12 Jan, 12-29 Aug & BH's
Lunch not served Sat
♔ French 70 seats ✳ Lunch £18-£23 Dinner £23-£29 Last lunch 2.15pm Last dinner 9.30pm 🅿

✕**Le Petit Pierrot** 4 The Parade KT10 0NU 🕾Esher(0372)65105
*A charming little family-run restaurant with a relaxed, welcoming atmosphere and heirloom-adorned walls offers a short – but thoughtfully composed and seasonally appropriate – menu of wholesome dishes based on good-quality ingredients which represent excellent value for money. As food is prepared to order there may be some delay, but the proprietor makes it his business to ensure that every guest's visit is enjoyable.*
Closed Sun
Lunch not served Sat
♔ French 28 seats ✳ Lunch £16.50 Dinner £18.50 Last lunch 2.15pm Last dinner 10pm 🅿 nc10yrs
Credit Cards ① ② ③ ⑤

---

## CLAYWORTH Nottinghamshire Map **08** SK78

★★★65% **Royston Manor** St Peters Ln DN22 9AA
🕾Retford(0777)817484 FAX (0777) 817155
*A delightful Elizabethan manor dating from 1588 and overlooking open countryside houses the bar, lounge and restaurant of this hotel, its well-furnished and comfortable bedrooms being peacefully set in the attractive gardens.*
Annexe22⇩🏠(2fb)3🖩 CTV in all bedrooms Ⓡ **T** ✱
sB&B⇩🏠£32-£42 dB&B⇩🏠£45-£54 🅿
▦ 150P 🚗 ✿ *xmas*
♔ English & French **V** ✿ 🍷 ✂ Lunch £8.75 Dinner £10.60-£16&alc Last dinner 9.30pm
Credit Cards ① ② ③ ⑤

---

## CLEARWELL Gloucestershire Map **03** SO50

★★★65% **Clearwell Castle** Church Rd GL16 8LG
🕾Dean(0594)32320 FAX (0594) 35523
*An eighteenth-century Neo-Gothic castle, standing in glorious farmland amid the wooded surroundings of the Forest of Dean, features an imposing reception hall and drawing room; some of the bedrooms are built to the same scale, dwarfing the four-poster or half-tester beds they house, but the comforts of the twentieth century are present in the form of well-equipped modern bathrooms, one having a whirlpool bath and others with additional shower cubicles. Sherry and fruit greet guests on their arrival, and throughout their stay they are assured of a wide range of spontaneous service from friendly, helpful staff.*
14⇩ CTV in all bedrooms Ⓡ **T** ✘ (ex guide dogs)
⟮ 100P 3🏌 (£5) ✿ 🏌
♔ English & French **V** ✿ 🍷 Last dinner 9.30pm
Credit Cards ① ② ③

★★★63% **Wyndham Arms** GL16 8JT 🕾Dean(0594)33666
FAX (0594) 36450
*A family-owned village inn dating back to the 14th century with modern facilities installed. The staff are helpful and friendly and the good food is popular with the local community as well as hotel guests.*
5⇩Annexe12⇩(3fb) CTV in all bedrooms Ⓡ **T** S10% sB&B⇩🏠£30-£48 dB&B⇩🏠£60 🅿
52P 2🏌 🚗
♔ International **V** ✿ Lunch £8&alc Dinner £14.25&alc Last dinner 9.30pm
Credit Cards ① ② ③ ④ ⑤ ⓔ

---

## CLEETHORPES Humberside Map **08** TA30

★★★69% **Kingsway** Kingsway DN35 0AE 🕾(0472)601122
Telex no 527920
Closed 25-26 Dec
*This traditional hotel is managed by the owning family who, along with their staff, provide warm courteous service. Bedrooms are comfortable and well appointed and public rooms are tasteful.*
53⇩🏠 CTV in all bedrooms Ⓡ **T** ✘ (ex guide dogs)
sB&B⇩🏠£54-£59 dB&B⇩🏠£75-£79 🅿
Lift ⟮ 30P 20🏌 (£1.50) 🚗 nc5yrs
♔ English & French **V** ✿ Lunch £10&alc Dinner £14.50&alc Last dinner 9pm
Credit Cards ① ② ③ ⑤

★★66% **Wellow** Kings Rd DN35 0AQ 🕾(0472)695589
*This modern hotel stands facing the sea in its own grounds with ample parking and a children's play area. The smart, modern bars and the restaurant prove popular with tourists and regulars, and the bedrooms similarly prove popular, and are modern and well equipped, although some are compact.*
10⇩🏠(4fb) CTV in all bedrooms Ⓡ **T** ✘ (ex guide dogs) ✳
sB&B⇩🏠£27.50-£32.50 dB&B⇩🏠£38.50-£47
60P *xmas*
♔ English & Continental **V** ✿ 🍷 Lunch 95p-£11.95 Dinner 95p-£11.95 Last dinner 10pm
Credit Cards ① ③

---

## CLEEVE HILL Gloucestershire Map **03** SO92

★★★57% **Rising Sun** GL52 3PX (Lansbury)
🕾Bishops Cleeve(0242)676281 Telex no 437410
FAX (0242) 673069
*In a commanding position overlooking the Malvern Hills, four miles south of Cheltenham on the Broadway road, this hotel offers well-equipped bedrooms of varying standards, and a popular restaurant operation.*
24⇩(3fb)1🖩✂in 6 bedrooms CTV in all bedrooms Ⓡ **T**
sB&B⇩🏠£63 dB&B⇩🏠£76 🅿
⟮ 56P ✿ sauna *xmas*

**V** ✿ ⚏ ✂ Lunch fr£8.95 Dinner fr£14&alc Last dinner 10.30pm
Credit Cards ① ② ③ ⑤

**❀✕✕Redmond's at Malvern View** GL52 3PR
☎Cheltenham(0242)672017(Rosette awarded for dinner only)
*This very popular restaurant occupies a lovely hillside location with fine views of the surrounding countryside. Redmond Heywood is an innovative and talented cook, and his touch with pastry and light, delicious soufflés is particularly fine. He also has a good instinct for unusual combinations of flavours. His wife, Pippa, is knowledgeable about the wine list, which offers some 50 bins – with a separate list of half-bottles, and ensures that service is attentive and friendly.*
Closed Mon & 1st wk Jan
Lunch not served Sat (by prior arrangement midweek)
Dinner not served Sun
36 seats Lunch £16.50 Dinner £28 Last lunch 1.45pm Last dinner 10pm 16P nc5yrs ✂
Credit Cards ① ③

---

**CLEOBURY MORTIMER** Shropshire Map 07 SO67

**★★69% Redfern** DY14 8AA (Minotels) ☎(0299)270395
Telex no 335176 FAX (0299) 271011
*This busy village hotel has good quality bedrooms, and a friendly atmosphere prevails. Generous portions of well prepared food are served in the country-kitchen style restaurant.*
5⇔𝅒Annexe6⇔𝅒(4fb)1⊞ CTV in all bedrooms ® T S10% sB&B⇔𝅒£38-£49 dB&B⇔𝅒£55-£68 ⊟
20P ⚗ clay pigeon shooting pheasant shooting *xmas*
♌ English & French **V** ✿ ⚏ S10% Lunch £2-£4&alc Dinner £14.50&alc Last dinner 9.30pm
Credit Cards ① ② ③ ⑤ ⓔ

**Clayworth, Near Retford, Notts DN22 9AA**
**Telephone: (0777) 817484 Fax: (0777) 817155**

Situated in four acres of well kept gardens and enjoying superb views of the Idle Valley without a house in sight for five miles. Royston Manor Hotel offers modern facilities whilst retaining the character of a traditional English Manor House, original building dates from 1588. All 22 bedrooms are en suite with some having four poster and half tester beds. A superb menu is provided in the restaurant which overlooks the gardens. Wedding receptions, conferences or a quiet relaxing break in the country Royston Manor Hotel is the ideal venue.

---

## Fisherman's Haunt Hotel

WINKTON CHRISTCHURCH DORSET
Telephone: Christchurch 477283/484071

Dating back to 1673 this lovely olde worlde Wisteria covered Country House offers, Lounge and Buffet Bars with Log Fires in Winter, River View Restaurant. Comfortable Bedrooms all with private facilities, also some bedrooms adapted for disabled guests. Four Poster Beds, Free House, Real Ale, Large Car Park, Children's Corner, Credit Cards taken. Fishing on the River Avon (tickets available locally).

★ ★ AA   Egon Ronay Rec.                    Resident Proprietor: James Bochan.

**C**

★★**61%**, *Talbot* High St DY14 8DQ ☎(0299)270036 270205
*A 15th-century coaching inn of charming appearance. Service is
friendly and informal. All the bedrooms have been well-equipped
and are maintained efficiently, most of them are 'en suite'.*
8rm(2⇨4ƒ⋔)(1fb)3🛏 CTV in all bedrooms ®
✖ (ex guide dogs)
CTV
V ♥ 🍷 ⚡ Last dinner 10pm
Credit Cards 1 3

---

**CLEVEDON** Avon Map **03** ST47

★★★**58%**, **Walton Park** Wellington Ter BS21 7BL
☎(0272)874253 FAX (0272) 343577
*On higher ground above the town, the hotel has splendid views
across the Bristol Channel to the South Wales coast. Considerable
refurbishment have taken place during 1990 to provide quite
spacious rooms with modern facilities. Staff are friendly and it is a
popular venue for small conferences.*
36⇨ƒ⋔(3fb) CTV in all bedrooms ® T ✳
sB&B⇨ƒ⋔£25-£49.50 dB&B⇨ƒ⋔£47-£65 🍴
Lift ⚡ 37P ✿ *xmas*
♡ English & French V ♥ 🍷 Lunch £7.95-£8.45 Dinner
£11-£12.50&alc Last dinner 9pm
Credit Cards 1 2 3 5

---

**CLIMPING** West Sussex Map **04** TQ00

★★★⚑**72%**, *Bailiffscourt* BN17 5RW
☎Littlehampton(0903)723511 Telex no 877870
FAX (0903) 723107
*Situated in rural tranquility and built only 50 years ago, this
replica of a 13th-century courthouse has been furnished with
sturdy antiques. Several bedrooms have open fireplaces and the
thatched house can be reached by an underground passage. Chef
Jonas Tester continues to impress with a menu which changes
weekly and the levels of service can be extensive particularly
during the summer months.*
18⇨Annexe2⇨ƒ⋔(1fb)9🛏 CTV in all bedrooms T
50P ✿ ⌗ ♪ (hard) ♻ croquet nc 8yrs
♡ French V ♥ 🍷 Last dinner 10pm
Credit Cards 1 2 3 5

---

**CLOVELLY**

See **Horn's Cross**

---

**CLUN** Shropshire Map **07** SO38

✖**Old Post Office** 9 The Square SY7 8JA ☎(05884)687
*Chef-proprietor Richard Arbuthnot uses quality ingredients to
produce a small à la carte menu which features light, flavoursome
sauces. His wife, Anne, runs the front of the house in a relaxed, yet
professional manner. The restaurant is housed in a converted shop
with rear extensions giving views onto the village rooftops.*
Closed Mon (ex BH), Tue, 20 Jan-8 Mar & 23 Dec-3 Jan
Lunch not served Wed
V 30 seats ✳ Lunch £3.50-£13.50alc Dinner £19.50-£28.50alc
Last lunch 1.30pm Last dinner 9.30pm nc10yrs
Credit Cards 1 3

---

**CLYDEBANK** Strathclyde *Dunbartonshire* Map **11** NS56

○**Patio** Clydebank Business Park G81 2RW ☎041-951 1133
Now open
80⇨ƒ⋔

---

Hotels with a high percentage rating for quality
are highlighted by a % across their
gazetteer entry.

---

**COALVILLE** Leicestershire Map **08** SK41

★★**66%**, **Bardon Hall** Beveridge Ln, Bardon Hill LE6 5BY
☎(0530)813644
*A recently-built hotel stands two-and-a-half miles east of the town,
nine-and-a-half miles west of Leicester and conveniently close to
junction 22 of the M1. Public areas include a large, split-level
lounge bar, an attractive restaurant with a conservatory for family
groups and a self-contained function room which holds up to two
hundred people. All the well-equipped bedrooms are contained in
cottage-style annexes standing between 70 and 200 yards from the
main building.*
35⇨ƒ⋔ CTV in all bedrooms ® T ✖ (ex guide dogs) ✳
sB&B⇨ƒ⋔£38 dB&B⇨ƒ⋔£46 🍴
150P
V ♥ 🍷 ⚡ S% Lunch fr£7.50alc Dinner fr£7.50alc Last dinner
10pm
Credit Cards 1 2 3 5

---

**COCKERMOUTH** Cumbria Map **11** NY13

★★★**63%**, **Grecian Villas** Crown St CA13 0EH ☎(0900)827575
FAX (0900) 827772
*This attractive sandstone building, with Greek-style frontage, is
situated in the centre of the town. The hotel is well furnished in all
areas, and offers good comforts, service and food.*
13⇨ƒ⋔(1fb)1🛏 CTV in all bedrooms ® T ✳ sB&B⇨ƒ⋔£35
dB&B⇨ƒ⋔£46.50
⚡ 25P *xmas*
♡ International ♥ 🍷 Lunch £6.50 Dinner £13.95&alc Last
dinner 9.30pm
Credit Cards 1 3

★★★**61%**, **Broughton Craggs** Great Broughton CA13 0XP
☎(0900)824400
*A small country hotel and restaurant that is favoured by business
clientele. It sits in its own gardens beside a vicarage 2 miles west of
Cockermouth. To reach it you should turn off the A66 at the
signpost for Great Broughton, cross a bridge and then bear right
uphill towards Keith.*
14⇨ƒ⋔(1fb)1🛏 CTV in all bedrooms ® T ✖ (ex guide dogs)
sB&B⇨ƒ⋔£38-£40 dB&B⇨ƒ⋔£50 🍴
60P 🚗 ✿ ♪
♡ English & Continental V ♥ 🍷 ⚡ Lunch fr£14 Dinner
fr£14&alc Last dinner 9.30pm
Credit Cards 1 2 3 5 £

★★★**61%**, **The Trout** Crown St CA13 0EJ ☎(0900)823591
FAX (0900) 827514
*An attractive hotel which prides itself on its floral displays and has
immaculate side gardens running down to the river bank offers
bedrooms enhanced by recent improvements.*
22⇨ƒ⋔(1fb) CTV in all bedrooms ® T sB&B⇨ƒ⋔£45-£55
dB&B⇨ƒ⋔£55-£59.50 🍴
⚡ 80P ✿ ♪ *xmas*
♡ English, French & Italian V ♥ Lunch £7.50-£9&alc Dinner
£13.95-£16.95&alc Last dinner 9.30pm
Credit Cards 1 3

★★**56%**, **Globe** Main St CA13 9LE (Consort) ☎(0900)822126
Telex no 57515 FAX (0900) 823705
*Originally a coaching inn, this hotel is popular with the coach tour
and commercial trade. Its practical bedrooms vary in size.*
30rm(20⇨5ƒ⋔)(3fb) CTV in all bedrooms ® T ✳ sB&Bfr£30
sB&B⇨ƒ⋔fr£30 dB&B⇨ƒ⋔fr£45 🍴
CTV 12🚗 *xmas*
V ♥ 🍷 ⚡ Lunch £5.50 Dinner fr£13 Last dinner 9.30pm
Credit Cards 1 2 3 5 £

For key to symbols see the inside front cover.

**COGGESHALL** Essex Map 05 TL82

★★★61% **White Hart** Market End CO6 1NH (Select)
☎(0376)561654 FAX (0376) 561789
*An old hostelry of great character with magnificent roof timbers and a beamed bar lounge with copper tables and log fires in winter. The hotel has been tastefully restored and incorporates many original features. Bar snacks and room service supplement the well-appointed restaurant, which also has a dance floor. The young staff are friendly.*
18⇨🏲 CTV in all bedrooms T 🏋 (ex guide dogs) ✳
sB&B⇨🏲£60-£80 dB&B⇨🏲£80-£95 🗗
30P 3🏰 ✿
V ✿ ⚖ Lunch fr£12.50&alc Dinner fr£17.50&alc Last dinner 9pm
Credit Cards [1][2][3][5][£]

**COLBOST**

See **Skye, Isle of**

**COLCHESTER** Essex Map 05 TL92

★★★63%, **George** 116 High St CO1 1TD (Queens Moat)
☎(0206)578494 FAX (0206) 761732
*A town centre coaching inn featuring a choice of bars, a carvery restaurant, cosy public areas and well equipped bedrooms. There is also a fitness room. Good car parking can be found at the rear of the hotel.*
47⇨🏲(3fb) CTV in all bedrooms ® T ✳ sB&B⇨🏲fr£57
dB&B⇨🏲fr£72 🗗
⚓ 50P sauna solarium gymnasium
✿ ⚖ Lunch £7.25-£10.25 Dinner fr£10.25 Last dinner 10pm
Credit Cards [1][2][3][5]

★★★63%, **Red Lion** High St CO1 1DJ (Best Western)
☎(0206)577986 Telex no 987185 FAX (0206) 578207
*Among the many historic attractions of this Grade 1 listed building are the carefully preserved walls of wattle and daub. Bedrooms are cosy, with antique or Victorian pine furnishings, and there is a small lounge. In the beamed dining room, head chef Tim Morris provides innovative menus using good, fresh ingredients.*
24⇨🏲1🎬 CTV in all bedrooms ® T ✳ S% sB&B⇨🏲£59
dB&B⇨🏲£72 🗗
⚓🎬
♀ English & French V ✿ ⚖
Credit Cards [1][2][3][5]

★★65%, **Kings Ford Park** Layer Rd, Layer De La Haye
CO2 0HS (2.5m S B1026) ☎(0206)34301 Telex no 987562
FAX (0206) 34512
RS Sun
*Comfortable Regency house in woodland park with some modernised bedrooms.*
13⇨🏲(2fb)1🎬 CTV in all bedrooms ® T ✳ sB&B⇨🏲fr£55
dB&B⇨🏲fr£70 🗗
CTV 200P ✿ pitch & putt *xmas*
♀ International V ✿ ⚖ Lunch £15-£25alc Dinner
£11.95-£13.45&alc Last dinner 9.30pm
Credit Cards [1][2][3][5]

**COLEFORD** Gloucestershire Map 03 SO51

★★69%, **Lambsquay House** GL16 8QB ☎Dean(0594)33127
RS Jan
*A small, attractive Georgian house set in peaceful surroundings on the outskirts of the town provides well equipped en suite bedrooms with a good range of facilities, home cooking of good quality and friendly, attentive service.*
9⇨🏲(1fb) CTV in all bedrooms ® T sB&B⇨🏲£30-£48
dB&B⇨🏲£42-£65 🗗
30P 🎬 ✿ *xmas*

▶

♀ English & Continental ♥ ⬚ Bar Lunch £3-£8alc Dinner
£8-£19.50alc Last dinner 8.30pm
Credit Cards [1] [3] [5]

**★★63% The Speech House** Forest of Dean GL16 7EL
(Trusthouse Forte) ☎Dean(0594)822607 FAX (0594) 823658
*In the heart of the Forest of Dean, well outside the town, this 17th-century house is signposted from all directions. Its historic Verderers Court Room – now a dining room – is still occasionally used for passing judgement on affairs unique to the forest. Some bedrooms contain massive four-poster beds and friendly caring staff have earned the hotel a reputation for good service.*
14rm(3⇨)(2fb)3⊞⊬in 3 bedrooms CTV in all bedrooms ® T
sB£35-£45 sB⇨£45-£55 dB£55-£66
dB⇨£65-£76 (room only) ⊟
40P ✿ *xmas*
V ♥ ⬚ ⊬ S10% Lunch £8.50-£11&alc High tea £1.50-£5
Dinner £11.50-£12.95&alc Last dinner 9pm
Credit Cards [1] [2] [3] [4] [5]

---

**COLERNE** Wiltshire Map **03** ST87

**★★★★75% Lucknam Park** SN14 8AZ (Prestige)
☎(0225)742777 Telex no 445648 FAX (0225) 743536
*This magnificent country-house hotel offers a very high standard of comfort, service and cuisine. The main house, set in extensive parkland of 280 acres and approached down a mile-long, tree-lined drive, will have 39 bedrooms (including nine suites). The Georgian house has been sympathetically restored to offer gracious and beautifully furnished public rooms, including a spacious drawing room and panelled library with a fine selection of books. The bedrooms are all of comfortable size and well-appointed and some of the larger suites are furnished with a delicate sense of historical context. Near to the house, the former mews have been converted into a bedroom wing. Other facilities at Lucknam Park include a boardroom with adjacent dining room overlooking the quiet courtyard, plus an excellent leisure spa with large indoor swimming pool, steam room, jacuzzi, solarium, beauty parlour and hairdressing salon. There are also a snooker room with an antique snooker table and two outdoor tennis courts.*
39⇨5⊞ CTV in all bedrooms T ✠ (ex guide dogs) ⊟
( 90P ⊞ ✿ ⊠(heated) ♪ (hard) snooker sauna solarium gymnasium jacuzzi croquet beauty salon *xmas*
V ♥ ⬚ ⊬
Credit Cards [1] [3] ⓔ

---

**COLESHILL** Warwickshire Map **04** SP28

**★★★62% Grimstock Country House** Gilson Rd, Gilson
B46 1AJ (off A446 W of Coleshill) ☎(0675)462369 & 462121
Telex no 334256 FAX (0675) 467646
*This attractive house with a modern extension stands in well-kept gardens, conveniently situated for the NEC and the M42 and M6 motorways. Its comfortable, well furnished bedrooms are complemented by a pleasant restaurant offering an à la carte menu, friendly service being provided by the resident owner and his young staff.*
44⇨♠(1fb) CTV in all bedrooms ® T sB&B⇨♠£50-£55
dB&B⇨♠£60-£65 ⊟
( 80P ⊞ ✿
♀ English & French V ♥ ⬚ Lunch £5.50-£10alc High tea
£5-£6 Dinner £12-£15alc Last dinner 9.15pm
Credit Cards [1] [2] [3] [5]

**★★63% Coleshill** 152 High St B46 3BG (Lansbury)
☎(0675)465527 Telex no 333868 FAX (0675) 464013
*Situated close to Junction 4 of the M6. The comfortable modern hotel looks much older than it is, for materials from old buildings were cleverly used in its construction in 1982.*
15⇨♠Annexe8⇨♠2⊞⊬in 8 bedrooms CTV in all bedrooms
® T ✠ (ex guide dogs) sB&B⇨♠fr£62 dB&B⇨♠fr£74 ⊟
( 48P

---

♀ English & French V ♥ ⊬ Lunch frf9.75&alc Dinner
frf14.75&alc Last dinner 10pm
Credit Cards [1] [2] [3] [5]

**★★63% Swan** High St B46 3BL (Porterhouse) ☎(0675)464107
FAX (0675) 467493
*Fully modernised hotel popular with business people.*
32⇨♠ CTV in all bedrooms ® T
( CTV 80P 8☂
V ♥ ⬚
Credit Cards [1] [2] [3] [5]

---

**COLONSAY, ISLE OF** Strathclyde *Argyllshire* Map **10**

---

**SCALASAIG** Map **10** NR30

**★71% Colonsay** PA61 7YP ☎Colonsay(09512)316
FAX (09512) 353
Closed 6 Nov-28 Feb ex 28 Dec-11 Jan
*Kevin Byrne, the owner of this delightful island hotel has a warm welcome for guests, and meets them personally from the ferry. For those who find walking or using the hotel bicycles too strenuous, transport is willingly provided. Accommodation is comfortable, rooms are prettily furnished and the good home cooking, based on local produce, is very enjoyable. Mr Byrne is also extremely knowledgeable about island flora and fauna.*
10rm(1⇨7♠)Annexe1rm(1fb) TV in 6 bedrooms ®
sB&B£43-£60 dB&B⇨♠£86-£120 (incl dinner) ⊟
32P ⊞ ✿ bicycles sailing equipment
♀ European ♥ ⬚ ⊬ Bar Lunch £1.25-£4alc High tea £10
Dinner £15 Last dinner 7.30pm
Credit Cards [1] [2] [3] [5]

---

**COLSTERWORTH** Lincolnshire Map **08** SK92

⌂**Granada Lodge** A1 NG33 5JR (Granada)
☎Grantham(0476)860686 FAX (0476) 861078
*Comfortable, well equipped and good value accommodation is offered here, and a high standard of cleanliness is maintained. The Country Kitchen, open 24 hours a day serves a range of hot and cold food and beverages.*
38⇨♠(9fb)⊬in 4 bedrooms CTV in all bedrooms ®
✠ (ex guide dogs) ✳ sB⇨♠£25 dB⇨♠£28 (room only)
P
V ♥ ⬚ ⊬
Credit Cards [1] [2] [3] [5] ⓔ
**See advertisement under GRANTHAM**

⌂**Travelodge** A1 New Fox, South Witham LE15 8AU
(Trusthouse Forte) ☎Thistleton(057283)586 Central
Res 0800 850950
*Situated about nine miles south of Grantham on the northbound side of the A1. For southbound traffic, take the turning signed South Witham and then re-join the dual-carriageway northbound. There is a Little Chef restaurant adjacent.*
32⇨♠(32fb) CTV in all bedrooms ® sB⇨♠£24
dB⇨♠£29.50 (room only)
( 32P ⊞
Credit Cards [1] [2] [3]

---

**COLVEND** Dumfries & Galloway *Kirkcudbrightshire*
Map **11** NX85

**★★63% Clonyard House** DG5 4QW ☎Rockcliffe(055663)372
*Peacefully situated in seven acres of woodland this pleasant, family-run small hotel is an ideal base from which to explore the Solway coast, with several spacious modern ground floor bedrooms and a comfortable bar, popular for light meals both at lunchtime and during the evening.*
9⇨♠(2fb) CTV in all bedrooms ® T sB&B⇨♠£30
dB&B⇨♠£50 ⊟
CTV 40P ⊞ ✿ ♁

---

♀ British & French **V** ♨ Sunday Lunch £6-£12alc Dinner
£10-£15alc Last dinner 9pm
Credit Cards ①③

---

**COLWYN BAY** Clwyd Map **06** SH87

★★★68%, **Norfolk House** Princes Dr LL29 8PF ☎(0492)531757
Telex no 61155 FAX (0492) 70009
*This friendly privately owned hotel provides well equipped,*
*comfortable accommodation and is equally popular with both*
*holidaymakers and business people. It is conveniently situated for*
*the town centre and the beach.*
25⇨↑(3fb) CTV in all bedrooms ® sB&B⇨↑£39.50-£43
dB&B⇨↑£58-£62 ⊟
Lift ( 30P ✿
♀ English & French **V** ♨ ⊡ ⊬ S%
Credit Cards ①②③⑤

★★★58%, **Hotel 70 Degrees** Penmaenhead LL29 9LD (2m E
A547) (Best Western) ☎(0492)516555 Telex no 61362
FAX (0492) 515565
*Enjoying panoramic views of town and sea from its cliff-top*
*position east of Colwyn Bay, this large, purpose-built hotel*
*provides well equipped accommodation which is equally suitable*
*for holidaymakers or business people, including delegates making*
*use of the establishment's conference facilities.*
43⇨↑(7fb)1⊞ CTV in all bedrooms ® T S%
sB&B⇨↑£52-£62 dB&B⇨↑£75-£85 ⊟
( 200P ♬ *xmas*
♀ English & French **V** ♨ ⊡ Lunch £9.50-£10.95 High tea
£3-£5 Dinner £15.75-£18.75 Last dinner 9.30pm
Credit Cards ①②③④⑤ ⑤
**See advertisement on page 229**

★★70%, **Hopeside** Princes Dr, West End LL29 8PW
☎(0492)533244
*Set in a mainly residential area just off the A55, a few minutes'*
*walk from both town centre or beach, this detached, white-painted*
*hotel with a car park in front provides very clean and well-equipped*
*accommodation, all bedrooms having en suite facilities. Guests*
*receive a genuinely warm welcome from hosts who personally*
*supervise their wellbeing, and they can select an enjoyable meal*
*from the varied selection of dishes featured on the dining room's*
*table d'hôte and à la carte menus.*
19⇨↑(2fb) CTV in all bedrooms ® T sB&B⇨↑£20-£35
dB&B⇨↑£40-£55 ⊟
CTV 25P solarium nc5yrs
♀ French **V** ♨ ⊡ Lunch £5-£12&alc High tea £3.50-£6 Dinner
£10.50&alc Last dinner 9pm
Credit Cards ①②③⑤

★★65% **Lyndale** 410 Abergele Rd, Old Colwyn LL29 9AB
(Guestaccom) ☎(0492)515429
*A happy atmosphere pervades this small, friendly hotel; bedrooms*
*are well equipped, and the dining room offers both an extensive*
*menu and generous portions which make it popular with*
*commercial and holiday clients alike.*
14⇨↑(3fb)1⊞ CTV in all bedrooms ®
CTV 20P
♀ European **V** ♨ ⊡ ⊬ Last dinner 8.30pm
Credit Cards ①②③
**See advertisement on page 229**

★★64%, **Ashmount** 18 College Av, Rhos-on-Sea LL28 4NT
(Minotels) ☎(0492)45479 & 44582
*This large detached late Victorian house, now a family-run hotel, is*
*situated in a quiet residential road close to the seafront at Rhos-on-*
*Sea. It provides well-equipped bedrooms and a car park.*
18⇨↑(4fb) CTV in all bedrooms ® T sB&B⇨↑£22.70-£32
dB&B⇨↑£37.50-£54 ⊟
10P *xmas* ▶

## Clonyard House Hotel ★★
### COLVEND, DALBEATTIE
### DUMFRIES & GALLOWAY, SCOTLAND
Telephone: Rockcliffe (055-663) 372

*BEAUTIFUL GALLOWAY*

Set in this lovely, peaceful corner of South West
Scotland, with its mild climate, CLONYARD is a
Country House Hotel in wooded grounds, 4 miles from
Dalbeattie on A710 — Solway Coast Road. All rooms
en suite, with colour TV, direct dial telephone and tea
making facilities also available. 6 ground floor
bedrooms.
Bar and 'Taste of Scotland' Restaurant open to
non-residents.
Open all year. Winter breaks.

Visa and Access

★ ★

# Lambsquay House Hotel

**Royal Forest of Dean, Nr. Coleford, Glos.**
The Lambsquay Hotel offers a high standard of accommodation and cuisine. All
rooms are en-suite and have colour T.V.,
telephone, radio and beverage tray. The
restaurant and lounge bar are open to non-
residents in the evening. Come and enjoy
our hospitality and discover this beautiful
part of the country. Ideal base to explore
many places of interest. Excellent walking
area. Children and pets are welcome, there
is a family suite and mini-breaks are
available all year (except Bank holidays).
**Telephone (0594) 33127 for a brochure &**
*Les Routiers* **details.** *Ashley Courtenay*

V ✿ ♀ ⚔ Lunch £2-£6 Dinner £9.50-£10.25&alc Last dinner 8pm
Credit Cards [1] [2] [3] [5] £

---

★★64% **Edelweiss** Lawson Rd LL29 8HD (Consort) ☎(0492)532314

*Conveniently close to the town centre and seafront this large Victorian detached house stands in a large garden with its own car park. Accommodation is well equipped and the hospitality friendly.*

25⇌↱(3fb) CTV in all bedrooms ® T sB&B⇌↱fr£25 dB&B⇌↱fr£42 ⊟
CTV 25P ✻ sauna solarium children's play area games room *xmas*
♉ Welsh, English, French & Italian V ✿ ♀ ⚔ Bar Lunch fr£2.75 Dinner fr£11.50 Last dinner 8.30pm
Credit Cards [1] [2] [3] [5] £

---

★67% **West Point** 102 Conway Rd LL29 7LE ☎(0492)530331
Closed last 2 wks Dec & 1st 2 wks Jan

*A comfortable, well maintained and family-run hotel, set on the western side of the town but within walking distance of both centre and sea front, provides good, friendly hospitality.*

10rm(2⇌3↱)(3fb) CTV in all bedrooms ® sB&B£14.75 sB&B⇌↱£17 dB&B£29.50 dB&B⇌↱£34 ⊟
CTV 8P
♉ English & French V ✿ ⚔ Bar Lunch £2.50-£4.50 Dinner £8 Last dinner 7pm
Credit Cards [1] [3]

---

★65% **Whitehall** Cayley Promenade, Rhos on Sea LL28 4EP ☎(0492)47296
Closed Nov-Etr

*A small, pleasant, family-run hotel on the promenade at Rhos-on-Sea. Bedrooms are well-equipped and the hotel has its own car park.*

13rm(1⇌6↱)(2fb) CTV in all bedrooms ®
CTV 5P ⛟
V ✿ ⚔
Credit Cards [1] [3]

---

★64% **Marine** West Promenade LL28 4BP ☎(0492)530295
Closed Nov-Feb

*This well-maintained, family-run hotel stands on the Promenade, offering good sea views from several rooms, and has the advantage of its own car park. The town centre and leisure centre are both within easy reach.*

14rm(9↱)(4fb) CTV in 11 bedrooms TV in 3 bedrooms ® ✱ sB&Bfr£19.15 sB&B↱£22-£23 dB&B£37.20-£38.30 dB&B↱£40-£42 (incl dinner) ⊟
CTV 11P ⛟
V ✿ ♀ Bar Lunch £2-£5 Dinner fr£6 Last dinner 7.30pm
Credit Cards [2] [5] £

---

★55% **Stanton House** Whitehall Rd, Rhos-on-Sea LL28 4ET ☎(0492)44363

*This small, simple and homely hotel, though situated in a quiet residential road, is within easy reach of both sea shore and shopping centre.*

11rm(3⇌)(3fb)⚔in 2 bedrooms CTV in 4 bedrooms TV in 1 bedroom ® S% sB&B£17.50-£18 sB&B⇌£19.50-£21 dB&B£33-£36 dB&B⇌£37.50-£43.50 ⊟
CTV 8P
✿ ♀ ⚔ S% Lunch £4.50-£7.95 Dinner £7.50-£7.95 Last dinner 7.30pm
Credit Cards [1] [3] £

---

Entries for red-star hotels are highlighted by a tint panel. For a full list of these establishments consult the Contents page.

---

## COLYTON Devon Map 03 SY29

★★65% **White Cottage** Dolphin St EX13 6NA ☎(0297)52401
Closed 2wks Xmas

*The White Cottage is a Grade II listed building on the edge of a historic East Devon village. The bedrooms, while retaining some original features, provide comfort and good facilities. There is a friendly atmosphere in the lounge and bar and an interesting choice of dishes is available in the charming dining room.*

6⇌↱(1fb)1⊞ CTV in all bedrooms ® ✱ sB&B⇌↱£26-£27.50 dB&B⇌↱£52-£55 ⊟
15P ⛟ ✻
♉ International ✿ Lunch £3.50-£9alc Dinner £12.50-£19.50alc Last dinner 9.15pm
Credit Cards [1] [3] £

## COMBE MARTIN Devon Map 02 SS54

★★59% **Rone House** King St EX34 0AD ☎(0271)883428
Closed Nov-Feb (ex 23-27 Dec)

*Small, family-run hotel in the centre of Combe Martin, providing comfortable accommodation, simple menus and a friendly atmosphere.*

11rm(4⇌4↱)(4fb) TV in all bedrooms ® ✱ sB&B£13.75-£15.95 dB&B£27.50-£31.90 dB&B⇌↱£29.70-£34 ⊟
CTV 15P ⛟ ✻ ⛱(heated) *xmas*
Dinner £9.50&alc Last dinner 9.30pm
Credit Cards [1] [3]

## COMRIE Tayside *Perthshire* Map 11 NN72

★★63% **Royal** Melville Square PH6 2DN ☎(0764)70200
Telex no 76277
RS Oct-Mar

*Originally a famed hostelry with royal and historic connections. Traditional hospitality, courteous service and comfortable accommodation can now be found here, in the village centre and close to the River Earn. Bedrooms are well furnished and bathrooms are particularly well appointed.*

9rm(8⇌)1⊞ CTV in all bedrooms ® T sB&B⇌£25.50-£27 dB&B⇌£45-£48 ⊟
30P 2⛍ ♩ snooker *xmas*
♉ Scottish & French V ✿ Lunch £3.50-£10alc Dinner £14&alc Last dinner 9.30pm
Credit Cards [1] [2] [3] £

---

★★60% ***Comrie*** Drummond St PH6 2DY ☎(0764)70239
RS Nov-Etr

*Traditional hospitality and good-value accommodation are provided by a small, family-run hotel at the west end of the village. Undergoing a programme of improvements, it provides a popular base for visiting golfers and holidaymakers.*

9rm(1⇌5↱)Annexe2⇌ CTV in all bedrooms ®
24P ⛟ nc5yrs
✿ ♀ Last dinner 9pm
Credit Cards [1]

## CONISTON Cumbria Map 07 SD39

★★65% **Coniston Sun** LA21 8HQ ☎(05394)41248

*Enjoyable Cordon Bleu meals are a feature of this spaciously comfortable family-run hotel which stands high above the village amid fine Lakeland scenery.*

11rm(7⇌3↱)2⊞ CTV in all bedrooms ® T ✱ sB&B⇌↱£30-£35 dB&B⇌↱£60-£70 ⊟
20P ✻
♉ English & French V ✿ ♀ ⚔ Bar Lunch £1.10-£6.50alc Dinner £15.50-£18 Last dinner 8.30pm
Credit Cards [1] [3]

**★★63% Yewdale** Yewdale Rd LA21 8LU ☎(05394)41280
*A charming little village-centre hotel dating back to 1896 has
recently been redecorated to provide extremely attractive, well-
equipped bedrooms, a small but comfortable lounge and an
attractive bar; guests are assured of a warm welcome from the
resident proprietors.*
12rm(2⇨8♠)(4fb) CTV in all bedrooms ® S%
sB&B£18.95-£26.95 dB&B£37.90 dB&B⇨♠£46.50-£53.90 ⊟
6P
V ✿ ♨ ⊁ S% Lunch £2.95-£6.95alc High tea £1.20-£1.63alc
Dinner £12.50-£13.50 Last dinner 8.45pm
Credit Cards ①③

**★⚑72% Old Rectory** Torver LA21 8AX ☎(05394)41353
Closed 2-3 wks Jan
*Standing in three acres of wooded grounds, this charming
Victorian country house has been refurbished throughout to a very
high standard. The atmosphere is warm and friendly and there are
fine views over the surrounding meadowland and fells from most of
the rooms. It is about 2.5 miles south of Coniston off the A593.*
7⇨♠(1fb) CTV in all bedrooms ® ✗ (ex guide dogs)
10P 🚗 ❁
⍾ English & Continental ⊁

**★66% Black Bull** Yewdale Rd LA21 8DU ☎(05394)41335
*A charming country inn at the centre of the village takes pride in
its standards of cooking, and extensive menus are still available in
the cosy bar on those winter nights when the restaurant may not be
open. Bedrooms, though compact, are very well equipped.*
11⇨♠(3fb)⊁in 1 bedroom CTV in all bedrooms ® T
sB&B⇨♠fr£25 dB&B⇨♠fr£50 ⊟
CTV 12P 3🐴 ❁ pony trekking sailing *xmas*
⍾ English & French V ✿ ♨ Lunch £5.50-£6.75alc High tea
fr£4.50alc Dinner fr£9.50alc Last dinner 9pm
Credit Cards ①③

**CONNEL** Strathclyde *Argyllshire* Map **10** NM93

**★★64% Falls of Lora** PA37 1PB (Inter-Hotels) ☎(063171)483
FAX (063171) 694
Closed Xmas & New Year
*This spacious tourist hotel has lovely views of Loch Etive and a
pleasant, relaxing atmosphere. Bedrooms in the main house are
individual in style, those in the modern wing are more uniform, but
all are well equipped. For meals there is a choice of the formal
restaurant or the bistro bar.*
30⇨♠(4fb)1⊞ CTV in all bedrooms T sB&B⇨£24.50-£47.50
dB&B⇨£35-£91 ⊟
CTV 40P 9🐴 🚗 ❁
⍾ Scottish & French V ✿ ♨ ⊁ Bar Lunch £4.75-£9.50alc
High tea £5-£6.50alc Dinner fr£14.50 Last dinner 8pm
Credit Cards ①②③⑤ⓕ

**CONSTANTINE BAY** Cornwall & Isles of Scilly
Map **02** SW87

**★★★76% Treglos** PL28 8JH (Consort) ☎Padstow(0841)520727
FAX (0841) 521163
Closed 4 Nov-7 Mar
*A country house-style hotel with views over rocky coastline. The
restaurant serves imaginative food, well-cooked and presented.
Golfing facilities adjacent.*
44⇨(12fb) CTV in all bedrooms T sB&B⇨♠£46-£66
dB&B⇨♠£87-£126 (incl dinner)
Lift ℂ 50P 8🐴 (90p) 🚗 ❁ CFA ⊠(heated) snooker croquet
jacuzzi
⍾ English & French V ✿ ♨ ⊁ Lunch £9.95&alc Dinner
£16.95&alc Last dinner 9.30pm
Credit Cards ①

**See advertisement under PADSTOW**

**CONTIN** Highland *Ross & Cromarty* Map **14** NH45

**★★57% Craigdarroch Lodge** Craigdarroch Dr IV14 9EH
☎Strathpeffer(0997)21265
Closed 25 Dec & 2 Jan-Feb
*Situated in twelve acres of woodland, this former shooting lodge
and clan dower house has been extended to offer pleasantly
appointed bedroom accommodation which blends the modern with
the traditional, and simply furnished but comfortable public rooms.
Fishing and shooting can be arranged. New owners are gradually
improving the hotel and ensure a relaxed and friendly atmosphere
prevails.*
13rm(8⇨2♠)(1fb) CTV in 11 bedrooms ® sB&B£16-£25
sB&B⇨♠£21-£38 dB&B£32-£40 dB&B⇨♠£42-£56
CTV 30P 🚗 ❁ ⊠(heated) ♪ (hard) ♪ snooker sauna
solarium sailing windsurfing
⊁ Bar Lunch £1.50-£14alc Dinner £14.50&alc Last dinner
9.30pm

**CONWY** Gwynedd Map **06** SH77

See also **Rowen**

**★★★65% Sychnant Pass** Sychnant Pass Rd LL32 8BJ
☎Aberconwy(0492)596868 & 596869 Telex no 61155
FAX (0492) 70009
*This delightful house is situated at the foot of the Sychnant Pass
amidst superb scenery. Tastefully extended and converted a few
years ago it is now a pleasant, comfortable, personally run hotel
with well-equipped modern accommodation.*
13⇨♠(2fb) CTV in all bedrooms ® T ✱
sB&B⇨♠£24.50-£37 dB&B⇨♠£39-£54 ⊟
CTV 30P ❁ sauna solarium sailing squash *xmas*
⍾ British & French ✿ ♨ Lunch £7.95-£10.95alc High tea
£4.50-£6.50alc Dinner £13.95-£18.95alc Last dinner 9.30pm
Credit Cards ①②③⑤ⓕ

**★★72% Castle Bank** Mount Pleasant LL32 8NY
☎Aberconwy(0492)593838
Closed Jan RS Dec & Feb
*Imposing early Victorian house situated just outside the ancient
town walls and overlooking the estuary of the River Conwy with
comfortable, well-equipped bedrooms and friendly proprietors the
hotel is popular with both commercial guests and holidaymakers.*
9rm(8♠)(3fb) CTV in all bedrooms ® ✗ sB&B£23-£27.50
sB&B♠fr£27.50 dB&B♠fr£46 ⊟
CTV 12P 🚗
⍾ International V Sunday Lunch fr£8.25 Dinner fr£13 Last
dinner 8pm
Credit Cards ①③ⓕ

**★★64% Berthlwyd Hall** Llechwedd LL32 8DQ
☎Aberconwy(0492)592409
*A stone-built Victorian manor house set in unspoilt countryside in
the Conwy Valley, Berthlwyd Hall offers well furnished and
comfortable accommodation, and the French-style restaurant
serves good French country dishes.*
6rm(4⇨)(2fb) CTV in all bedrooms ® ✗ (ex guide dogs)
40P 🚗 ❁ ⊐(heated)
⍾ French V ✿ ♨ Last dinner 9.30pm
Credit Cards ①②③

**★★61% The Park Hall** Bangor Rd LL32 8DP
☎Aberconwy(0492)592279
*Standing on the outskirts of the town, in over two acres of wooded
and lawned gardens, this imposing Victorian house caters well for
the commercial user, providing modest accommodation and mainly
British food.*
9⇨♠(2fb) CTV in all bedrooms ® T sB&B⇨♠£22.50-£25
dB&B⇨♠£42-£48
40P 🚗 ❁ *xmas*
⍾ English, French & Italian V ✿ Sunday Lunch fr£5.50alc
Dinner £10-£12&alc Last dinner 9.30pm
Credit Cards ①②③⑤ⓕ

★★59% **The Castle** High St LL32 8DB (Trusthouse Forte)
☎Aberconwy(0492)592324 FAX (0492) 583351
*An early coaching house hotel, parts of which date back to the*
*fifteenth century, stands beside the castle walls, close to the quay.*
*Warm and comfortable throughout, it offers well-equipped*
*bedrooms and pleasant public areas which include the Shakespeare*
*Restaurant, where the speciality is fresh fish.*
29➪⇥ℿ(1fb)1 ♯ ⅄in 2 bedrooms CTV in all bedrooms ® T
S12.5% sB➪⇥ℿ£60-£65 dB➪⇥ℿ£75-£86 (room only) ➡
30P *xmas*
V ๖ ⅄ S12.5% Sunday Lunch fr£7.95 Dinner fr£12.50&alc
Last dinner 9pm
Credit Cards [1][2][3][4][5]

---

**COODEN BEACH** East Sussex Map **05** TQ70

★★★65% **Cooden Resort** TN39 4TT ☎Cooden(04243)2281
FAX (04243) 6142
*Situated close to the beach, the accommodation at this hotel has*
*been extensively upgraded and bedrooms are particularly well*
*equipped. The formal restaurant and cocktail bar are*
*complemented by extensive services and good leisure amenities.*
34➪⇥ℿ(6fb)⅄in 3 bedrooms CTV in all bedrooms ® T ✱
sB➪⇥ℿfr£50 dB➪⇥ℿfr£65 (room only) ➡
《 60P ❋ ▣(heated) ⌂(heated) sauna solarium jacuzzi hair
salon *xmas*
۞ English & French V ๖ ⌐ Lunch fr£11.50 Dinner fr£16.50
Last dinner 9.30pm
Credit Cards [1][2][3][5] £
        **See advertisement under BEXHILL-ON-SEA**

---

**COOKHAM** Berkshire Map **04** SU88

✗✗**Cookham Tandoori** High St SL6 9SL
☎Bourne End(06285)22584 FAX (0628) 770520
*The furnishings and décor of this smart Indian restaurant are*
*more subdued than many. Division into three sections gives an*
*intimate atmosphere, and a selection of well-cooked dishes from*
*the north regions of India are reasonably priced, though more*
*expensive specialities are obtainable by giving 24 hours' notice.*
Closed 25 & 26 Dec
۞ Indian V 85 seats Lunch £15-£25alc Dinner £15-£25.30alc
Last lunch 2pm Last dinner 10.30pm ₤ nc7yrs ⅄
Credit Cards [1][2][3][5]

---

**COPTHORNE**

See Gatwick Airport

---

**CORBIERE**

See Jersey **under Channel Islands**

---

**CORBRIDGE** Northumberland Map **12** NY96

★★63% **The Lion of Corbridge** Bridge End NE45 5AX
☎Hexham(0434)632504 FAX (0434) 632571
*Located in the attractive village of Corbridge, this hotel is situated*
*on the banks of the River Tyne. A wing of new bedrooms has just*
*recently been added, providing comfortable, well equipped rooms.*
*There are also 4 rooms in the original building, and all of these are*
*en suite. A comfortable lounge has recently been provided, where*
*diners can relax, away from the busy public bar. Meals are served*
*in the attractive restaurant or in the bar/diner, which is very*
*popular for light meals and snacks. It is a family-run hotel, which*
*offers friendly and informal service.*
14rm(13➪ℿ)1 ♯ CTV in all bedrooms ® T ✖ (ex guide dogs)
sB&B➪ℿ£45 dB&B➪ℿ£58 ➡
30P ❋ *xmas*
V ๖ ⅄ Sunday Lunch £8.50 Dinner £3.30-£7.50 Last dinner
9.30pm
Credit Cards [1][2][3][5] £

*Sychnant Pass Hotel* ★★★
and FOUR SEASONS RESTAURANT

Sychnant Pass Road, Conwy, Gwynedd LL32 8BJ
Tel: (0492) 596868/9 Telex: 61155 Ref SI Fax: (0492) 870009

Renowned for its comfort, its friendly atmosphere
and particularly its splendid FOUR SEASONS
RESTAURANT. This lovely country home, built in
Swiss chalet style, nestles in three acres of grounds
which include a stream, duck pond and beautiful wooded area. Adjacent is the majestic Snowdonia National
Park, medieval Conwy and Bodnant Gardens. The
hotel is charmingly decorated, with four bedrooms on
the ground floor, one carefully designed for disabled
guests. The renowned restaurant provides a balanced
amalgam of tradition and flair in well presented cuisine,
which is complemented by an imaginative wine list. Our
reputation and unique brochure should persuade you.

---

# THE FALLS OF LORA HOTEL

**AA★★**

Oban 5 miles, only 2½-3 hours drive north-west of
Edinburgh or Glasgow, overlooking Loch Etive this
fine 2-star owner-run Hotel offers a warm welcome,
good food, service and comfort. Most rooms have
central heating, private bathroom, radio/intercom,
colour television and telephone. From luxury rooms
(one with four-poster bed and king size round bath,
another with a 7ft round bed and 'Jacuzzi'
bathroom en suite) to inexpensive family rooms with
bunk beds. FREE accommodation for children sharing parents' room. Relax in super cocktail bar with
open log fire, there are over 100 brands of Whisky
to tempt you and an extensive Bar Bistro Menu.
Fishing, Gliding, Water-sports and Pony Trekking
can be arranged. Out of season mini-breaks.

**OPEN ALL YEAR. A FINE OWNER-RUN SCOTTISH HOTEL**

**Connel Ferry, By Oban, Argyll PA37 1PB**
**Tel: (063171) 483   Fax: (063171) 694**

**★★59%** **Angel Inn** Main St NE45 5LA ☎(0434)632119
*This small, creeper-clad hotel features an attractive split-level restaurant, a wood-panelled foyer lounge where popular bar meals are served, and modern bedroom accommodation.*
5⇄🛏 CTV in all bedrooms ® T ✗ ✱ sB&B⇄🛏fr£30 dB&B⇄🛏£46
5P
♡ English, French & Italian V ♦ Lunch £7.25&alc Dinner £2.15-£4.95&alc Last dinner 10pm
Credit Cards ①②③⑤

**★66%** *Riverside* Main St NE45 5LE (Guestaccom)
☎(0434)632942
Closed Xmas & Jan
*This small, friendly hotel is managed by the courteous resident proprietors. Comfy bedrooms are offered, some with antique furnishings, and an inviting lounge overlooks the Tyne Valley. The imaginative dishes offered on the dinner menu are especially recommended.*
11rm(3⇄4🛏)(1fb) CTV in all bedrooms ®
10P 🚗
♡ English & French Last dinner 8pm

**✗✗Ramblers Country House** Farnley NE45 5RN (1m SE on A695) ☎Hexham(0434)632424
*The elegant, country-house restaurant has charming dining rooms, a very comfortable coffee lounge with log fire and a cheerful cocktail bar. An interesting selection of German dishes is offered, and the staff are very happy to give advice on both the menu and the wine list.*
Lunch not served (by arrangement only)
♡ Continental V 80 seats ✱ Lunch fr£7.50 Dinner £16-£21alc Last dinner 10pm 25P
Credit Cards ①②③⑤

---

**CORBY** Northamptonshire Map **04** SP88

See also **Cottingham**

**★★★61%** **Crest** Rockingham Rd NN17 1AE (Trusthouse Forte) ☎(0536)401348 Telex no 341752 FAX (0536) 66383
*A modern, purpose-built hotel close to the picturesque village of Rockingham and Rockingham Castle. Spacious, well-equipped rooms, function and banqueting facilities, and a large carpark make this peaceful hotel an excellent base for both the businessman and the tourist alike.*
70⇄🛏⊬in 12 bedrooms CTV in all bedrooms ® T (room only)
🅿
《 120P
♡ International V ♦ ⎇ ⊬
Credit Cards ①②③④⑤

---

**CORFE CASTLE** Dorset Map **03** SY98

**★★70%** **Mortons House** East St BH20 5EE ☎(0929)480988 FAX (0929) 480820
*A charming listed Elizabethan manor house in the midst of this much visited, picturesque village. It has been extended in keeping with the original building and provides delightful well-equipped bedrooms. Head Chef Graham Burton-Pye creates food in the modern British style, carefully cooked to retain natural flavours and with original ideas. The wine list is well chosen and comprehensive.*
14⇄🛏Annexe3⇄🛏(1fb)1🏴 CTV in all bedrooms ® T sB&B⇄🛏£45-£55 dB&B⇄🛏£70-£80 🅿
40P 🚗 ✱
V ♦ ⎇ ⊬ Lunch £9-£15alc Dinner fr£18.50alc Last dinner 9.30pm
Credit Cards ①③

---

**CORNHILL-ON-TWEED** Northumberland Map **12** NT83

**★★★⚑58%** **Tillmouth Park** TD12 4UU
☎Coldstream(0890)2255
*Set in extensive grounds, 3 miles north-east of the village, this Victorian mansion, which retains its traditional character, has long been popular with the fishing fraternity. The bedrooms, some of which are massive, have all modern amenities.*
12⇄🛏Annexe1⇄🛏(1fb)1🏴 CTV in all bedrooms ® T ✱ sB&B⇄🛏£40-£45 dB&B⇄🛏£60-£70 🅿
50P ✱ ✔
♡ International V ♦ ⎇ Lunch £5-£6alc Dinner £14.75&alc Last dinner 9.30pm
Credit Cards ①②③④⑤ ⓔ

---

**CORSE LAWN** Hereford & Worcester Map **03** SO83

**★★★68%** **Corse Lawn House** GL19 4LZ ☎Tirley(045278)479 & 771 Telex no 437348 FAX (045278) 840
*This elegant Queen Anne house, with a friendly peaceful atmosphere, is set in a quiet village close to Tewkesbury. Rooms are individually decorated, furnished with antiques and include thoughtful extras. Food is enjoyable with some unusual dishes, all created using the best fresh produce.*
19⇄🛏2🏴 CTV in all bedrooms ® T S% sB&B⇄🛏£60-£75 dB&B⇄🛏£75-£95
50P 🚗 ✱ ⊇(heated) ♪ (hard) croquet lawn *xmas*
♡ English & French V ♦ ⎇ S% Lunch fr£15.50&alc Dinner fr£22.50&alc Last dinner 10pm
Credit Cards ①②③⑤

---

**CORSHAM** Wiltshire Map **03** ST86

**★★★68%** **Rudloe Park** Leafy Ln SN13 0PA
☎Bath(0225)810555 FAX (0225) 811412
*The continued refurbishment of this Victorian hotel has resulted in very well-appointed bedrooms, though lounge facilities, which are still rather limited, can prove inadequate when conferences are in progress. Sound standards of service are matched by the quality of the meals, and a superb wine list details over 500 different bottles.*
11⇄🛏(1fb)1🏴 CTV in all bedrooms ® T S10%
sB&B⇄🛏£60-£65 dB&B⇄🛏£90-£100 🅿
70P 🚗 ✱ croquet lawn nc10yrs *xmas*
♡ International V ♦ ⎇ ⊬ Lunch fr£14&alc Dinner fr£16.50&alc Last dinner 9.30pm
Credit Cards ①②③④⑤ ⓔ
See advertisement under BATH

**★★66%** **Methuen Arms** High St SN13 0HB (Exec Hotel)
☎(0249)714867 FAX (0249) 712004
RS Sun
*Large oak beams, ancient stonework and mullioned windows survive in this hotel – relics of a nunnery built in the early 15th century. Today it offers modern bedrooms, comfortably furnished and well equipped. Guests who do not wish to eat formally in the candle-lit dining room can enjoy a lighter meal in one of the licensed bars – perhaps the interesting Long Bar, so called because it extends for 100ft, which has housed a skittle alley for more than a century.*
19rm(17⇄🛏)Annexe6⇄🛏(2fb) CTV in all bedrooms ® T ✗ sB&B⇄🛏£37-£42 dB&B⇄🛏£53-£58 🅿
60P ✱ skittle-alley ⚑
♡ English & French V ♦ S10% Lunch £10.95-£14.75&alc Dinner £14.75&alc Last dinner 9.30pm
Credit Cards ①③ ⓔ

**✗✗Copperfields** 1 High St SN13 0ES ☎(0249)713982
*This attractive, first-floor restaurant in the town centre offers friendly, attentive service and a good menu selection of well prepared, imaginative dishes.*
Lunch not served Tue-Sat
Dinner not served Sun

**V** 34 seats ✳ Sunday Lunch £11.50 Dinner £15.75&alc Last dinner 9.30pm ✗ nc5yrs ✍
Credit Cards ① ③

---

**COTTINGHAM** Northamptonshire Map **04** SP89

★★58% **Hunting Lodge** High St LE16 8XN
☎Rockingham(0536)771370
RS 25-26 Dec & 1 Jan
*Located in a pleasant village, this hotel provides modern, well-equipped bedrooms, all situated in two purpose-built annexes. A 16th-century building with stone walls and exposed beams houses the restaurant and bar facilities.*
Annexe23⇔ CTV in all bedrooms ® ✳ sB&B⇔£25-£45 dB&B⇔£35-£55 ♬
CTV 120P ✿
♀ English & French **V** ⚹ ⚑ Lunch £6.50 Dinner £12.50-£18.50alc Last dinner 10.30pm
Credit Cards ① ③ ⑤

---

**COVENTRY** West Midlands Map **04** SP37

★★★★52% **De Vere** Cathedral Square CV1 5RP (De Vere)
☎(0203)633733 Telex no 31380 FAX (0203) 225299
*Modern hotel with choice of bars and restaurants and large conference/banqueting facilities.*
190⇔(9fb) CTV in all bedrooms ® **T** sB&B⇔£81.50 dB&B⇔£98 ♬
Lift ( 130 CFA *xmas*
♀ International **V** ⚹ ⚑ ✍ Lunch £10.50 High tea £5-£7.50alc Dinner £15&alc Last dinner 10.15pm
Credit Cards ① ② ③ ④ ⑤

★★★67% **Brooklands Grange Hotel & Restaurant** Holyhead Rd CV5 8HX ☎(0203)601601 FAX (0203) 601277
*Situated 1 1/2 miles from the city centre on the A4114, this former Jacobean house has been extended and converted into a hotel, ideally suited to the tourist and modern businessman. Bedrooms are comfortable and very well equipped and the public areas retain many original features. Imaginative food and friendly services are provided by the resident owners and their staff.*
30⇔(1fb) CTV in all bedrooms ® **T** ✖ (ex guide dogs)
sB&B⇔£75-£80 dB&B⇔£90-£95
( 52P ✿ *xmas*
**V** ⚹ ⚑ ✍ Lunch £4.50-£10.50 Dinner £15&alc Last dinner 9.30pm
Credit Cards ① ② ③

**See advertisement on page 235**

★★★63% **Crest** Hinckley Rd, Walsgrave CV2 2HP (Trusthouse Forte) ☎(0203)613261 Telex no 311292 FAX (0203) 621736
RS Xmas
*A large modern hotel located close to junction 2 of the M6 with extensive conference facilities and a popular new leisure club. Rooms, due to be refurbished during 1990, are well equipped.*
147⇔(6fb)✍in 30 bedrooms CTV in all bedrooms ® (room only) ♬
Lift ( 450P ✿ CFA ▨(heated) sauna solarium gymnasium pool tables *xmas*
♀ English & French **V** ⚹ ⚑ ✍
Credit Cards ① ② ③ ④ ⑤

**See advertisement on page 235**

★★★60% **Chace Crest** London Rd, Willenhall CV3 4EQ (Trusthouse Forte) ☎(0203)303398 Telex no 311993
FAX (0203) 301816
*Situated beside the A423, the hotel is convenient for the city centre and the NEC. Public areas and some good standard bedrooms are located in the main Victorian house, whilst rooms of a lesser quality are situated in a modern extension. The hotel is popular with the conference trade.*

▶

68⇨ᴺ(2fb)1 ⌗⊁in 10 bedrooms CTV in all bedrooms Ⓡ (room only) 🍴
《80P ✿ pool table *xmas*
♀ English & French V ✧ ⚏ ⊬
Credit Cards ⓵ ⓶ ⓷ ⓸ ⓹

★★★**60%**, *Novotel Coventry* Wilsons Ln CV6 6HL (Novotel)
☎(0203)365000 Telex no 31545
*Well situated for access to the M6 this modern hotel provides accommodation with good facilities. The continental-style restaurant is open throughout the day.*
100⇨ᴺ(100fb) CTV in all bedrooms Ⓡ
Lift 《 ⊞ 160P ✿ CFA ⩫(heated) squash sauna solarium gymnasium pool table petanque putting table tennis ♨
♀ British & French V ✧ ⚏
Credit Cards ⓵ ⓶ ⓷ ⓸ ⓹

★★★**59%**, **Hylands** Warwick Rd CV3 6AU (Best Western)
☎(0203)501600 Telex no 312388 FAX (0203) 501027
Closed 24-26 Dec
*This hotel is in a pleasant location overlooking a park and close to the city centre. Many bedrooms have been redecorated over the past year, and all have good facilities. The Carver restaurant is popular with businessmen.*
55rm(54⇨)(4fb) CTV in all bedrooms Ⓡ ✳
sB&B⇨£59-£64.50 dB&B⇨£68-£77 🍴
《 CTV 60P pool table
♀ English & Continental V ✧ ⚏ ⊬
Credit Cards ⓵ ⓶ ⓷ ⓹

★★★**57%**, *Allesley* Birmingham Rd, Allesley Village CV5 9GP
☎(0203)403272 Telex no 311446
*Situated in the village of Allesley, just off the A45 with convenient access to Coventry, this hotel is a popular venue for conferences. Some rooms have been refurbished while others remain rather dated.*
73rm(40⇨26ᴺ)Annexe15⇨ᴺ⊬in 17 bedrooms CTV in all bedrooms Ⓡ
Lift 《 500P
♀ English & French V ✧ ⚏
Credit Cards ⓵ ⓶ ⓷ ⓹

★★★**57%**, **Post House** Rye Hill, Allesley CV5 9PH (Trusthouse Forte) ☎(0203)402151 Telex no 31427 FAX (0203) 402235
*Situated on the A45 close to Coventry and convenient for Birmingham this hotel is due to be refurbished this year as some areas are looking rather tired. There are good conference facilities.*
184⇨ᴺ⊬in 19 bedrooms CTV in all bedrooms Ⓡ T S%
sB⇨ᴺ£67-£77 dB⇨ᴺ£77-£87 (room only) 🍴
Lift 《 250P CFA *xmas*
V ✧ ⚏ ⊬ S% Lunch fr£9&alc Dinner £14.50&alc Last dinner 10pm
Credit Cards ⓵ ⓶ ⓷ ⓸ ⓹

★★**62%**, **Old Mill** Mill Hill CV8 2BS (Berni/Chef & Brewer)
☎(0203)303588
(For full entry see Baginton)

★★**60%**, **Beechwood** Sandpits Ln, Keresley CV6 2FR (3m NW on B4098) ☎(0203)338662 FAX (0203) 337080
*In semi-rural surroundings just two miles from the city centre, this hotel was formerly a farmhouse. Rooms are well kept and have modern facilities, although simple in terms of decor and furnishings.*
24⇨(1fb) CTV in all bedrooms Ⓡ T ✳ sB&B⇨£40 dB&B⇨£53
《 62P ✿
V ✧ ⚏ Lunch £7.50-£10 Dinner £10-£20 Last dinner 9.30pm
Credit Cards ⓵ ⓶ ⓷ ⓹

⛫*Campanile* 4 Wigston Road/Hinkley Rd, Walsgrave CV2 2NE (Campanile) ☎(0203)622311 Telex no 317454

*This lodge stands beside the A46 close to the M6. Bedrooms are housed in an adjacent annexe, and the value for money accommodation is understandably popular.*
Annexe47⇨ᴺ CTV in all bedrooms Ⓡ T
50P ✿
♀ English & French Last dinner 10pm
Credit Cards ⓵ ⓷

⛫**Travelodge** Bedworth CV12 0BN (A444) (Trusthouse Forte)
☎Nuneaton(0203)382541 Central Res (0800) 850950
*This lodge is situated on the A444, on the Nuneaton to Coventry side of the dual carriageway.*
40⇨ᴺ(40fb) CTV in all bedrooms Ⓡ sB⇨ᴺ£24 dB⇨ᴺ£29.50 (room only)
《 40P ⌸
Credit Cards ⓵ ⓶ ⓷

**COWES**
See **Wight, Isle of**

**CRAIGELLACHIE** Grampian *Banffshire* Map **15** NJ24
★★★**72%**, **Craigellachie** AB3 9SS ☎(03404)204 & 205
FAX (03404) 253
*This Victorian fishing hotel, situated 12 miles south of Elgin at the junction of the A95 and A941, has been completely refurbished to provide attractive accommodation. Staff are friendly and standards of housekeeping commendable, which endears the hotel to business clients as well as to fishermen.*
30⇨ᴺ(4fb)1⌗ CTV in all bedrooms Ⓡ T ✳
sB&B⇨ᴺ£43-£63 dB&B⇨ᴺ£70-£90 🍴
《 70P ⌸ ✿ ♪ snooker sauna solarium gymnasium *xmas*
V ✧ ⚏ ⊬ Lunch fr£18.50&alc High tea fr£7.50&alc Dinner fr£18.50&alc Last dinner 9.30pm
Credit Cards ⓵ ⓶ ⓷ ⓸ ⓹

# Beechwood Hotel

★★

**Sandpits Lane, Keresley, Coventry CV6 2FR**
**Telephone: 0203 338662 (3 lines)**

All rooms have private bathrooms, colour TV, tea & coffee making facilities and direct dial telephone.

*Coventry's Country Hotel set in over 2 acres of grounds. Personally managed by the Proprietor. Open all the year. Ideal for the National Exhibition Centre, Coventry City centre only 2½ miles, Birmingham 18 miles.*

*Ideal for Conferences, Weddings & private parties. Restaurant open to Non Residents.*

# The Crest Hotel Coventry

C

Ideally located fifteen minutes from the city centre and close to the N.E.C. 147 bedrooms including Executive and Lady Crest rooms, plus a bedroom with spa bath. Sensations Leisure Club offering swimming pool, sauna, solarium and fitness room. Ample free parking.

Inclusive short break packages available. Please request our Welcome Breaks brochure.

## CREST HOTEL
### COVENTRY

**Hinckley Road** ★★★
**Coventry CV2 2HP**
**Tel: (0203) 613261**
**Telex: 311292. Fax: (0203) 621736**

# No parking?

# No problems.

## novotel

★★★
Novotel Coventry
Wilsons Lane Longford
Tel 0203 365000 Telex 31545
Free Parking

# Brooklands Grange

★★★

*Hotel & Restaurant*

## Brooklands Grange Hotel & Restaurant
## Holyhead Road Coventry CV5 8HX
**Telephone: (0203) 601601 Fax: (0203) 601277**

Surround yourself in the comfort and charm of this beautifully restored and refurbished 16th Century Jacobean farmhouse. Offering you executive accommodation and an excellent restaurant serving you the very best in contemporary English cooking. Ideally located for easy and direct access to Birmingham International Airport, the N.E.C. and the City of Coventry.

**CRAIGHOUSE**

See **Jura, Isle of**

**CRAIGNURE**

See **Mull, Isle of**

**CRAIL** Fife Map **12** NO60

★**62% Croma** Nethergate KY10 3TU ☎(0333)50239
Closed Nov-Mar
*Located in an attractive, quiet area, yet very close to amenities, this small, friendly hotel is managed by resident proprietors who create a comfortable, homely atmosphere.*
8rm(4⇌1♠)(2fb) CTV in 2 bedrooms
CTV 10P ∰ ✿
V ♦ ⌂ Last dinner 10pm
£

**CRAMLINGTON** Northumberland Map **12** NZ27

○**Travelodge** A1 East(Trusthouse Forte)
☎Central reservations (0800) 850950
32⇌

**CRANBORNE** Dorset Map **04** SU01

★★**64% Fleur de Lys** 5 Wimborne St BH21 5PP ☎(07254)282
RS 24-27 Dec
*Situated in the centre of the village, this hotel has attractively decorated bedrooms and a busy bar which is very popular with the locals. Table d'hôte, à la carte and extensive bar menus are available.*
8rm(2⇌4♠)(1fb) CTV in 7 bedrooms ® sB&B£22-£24
sB&B⇌♠£25-£30 dB&B£33-£36 dB&B⇌♠£38-£42
35P
V ♦ Sunday Lunch £7.95-£11.95 Dinner £10.95-£11.95&alc
Last dinner 9.30pm
Credit Cards ①②③ £

**CRANBROOK** Kent Map **05** TQ73

★★⚑**70% Kennel Holt Country House** Goudhurst Rd
TN17 2PT ☎(0580)712032 FAX (0580) 712931
*Set in six acres of gardens with its own duck pond and paddock this Elizabethan manor house offers individually furnished bedrooms, comfortable lounges and an enterprising standard of cooking. Further improvements are planned later this year. Formal business meetings can be arranged.*
9⇌♠Annexe1♠2♨ CTV in all bedrooms ® T ✱
sB⇌♠£60-£80 dB⇌♠£70-£95 (room only) ⊟
CTV 35P ✿ croquet 9 hole mini golf putting green nc6yrs
xmas
♥ English & French V ♦ ⌂ ⊁ Lunch £11.50-£16.75&alc
Dinner £19.75&alc Last dinner 9pm
Credit Cards ①③ £

**CRANTOCK** Cornwall & Isles of Scilly Map **02** SW76

★★**65% Crantock Bay** West Pentire TR8 5SE (Minotels)
☎(0637)830229
Closed late Nov-mid Mar
*Beautifully situated to overlook Crantock Bay, this owner-run hotel offers good facilities.*
36⇌♠(4fb) CTV in all bedrooms ® sB&B⇌♠fr£30.75
dB&B⇌♠£84 (incl dinner) ⊟
35P ∰ ✿ ▢(heated) ♪ (hard) sauna gymnasium putting
croquet ♫ ☗
♦ ⌂ ⊁ Bar Lunch fr£2.50 Dinner £9.75-£11.75 Last dinner
8pm
Credit Cards ①②③⑤ £

**CRATHORNE** North Yorkshire Map **08** NZ40

★★★★⚑**57% Crathorne Hall** TS15 0AR
☎Stokesley(0642)700398
*The large Edwardian country house retains many of its original features and, although our recent inspection found its elegance slightly fading, by the time this guide is published a major refurbishment programme will have been completed and its former style restored.*
90⇌2♨ CTV in 39 bedrooms ® ✖ (ex guide dogs)
( CTV 100P ✿ snooker pool table ☗
♥ French V ♦ ⌂ Last dinner 10pm
Credit Cards ①②③⑤

**CRAWLEY**

See **Gatwick Airport**

**CREWE** Cheshire Map **07** SJ75

★★★**58% Crewe Arms** Nantwich Rd CW1 1DW (Embassy)
☎(0270)213204 FAX (0270) 588615
*This Victorian hotel, which stands very near to the busy railway station, reflects its origins in the interior design of public areas which include a small games room and function suite.*
53⇌♠(3fb)⊁in 7 bedrooms CTV in all bedrooms ® S%
sB⇌♠£50-£65 dB⇌♠£70-£85 (room only) ⊟
( 250P CFA games room xmas
♥ English & French V ♦ ⌂ ⊁ S% Lunch fr£9.50&alc Dinner
£11.75-£13.25&alc Last dinner 9.30pm
Credit Cards ①②③④⑤

★★**64% White Lion** Weston CW2 5NA (2m S A5020)
☎(0270)587011 & 500303
Closed Xmas & New Year
*A building that was originally a Tudor farmhouse now provides the "inn" element of this fully modernised hotel in village setting, its comfortable bedrooms being housed in a new wing to the rear. Meals are taken in an elegant restaurant with a good local reputation.*
16⇌♠(2fb)⊁in 2 bedrooms CTV in all bedrooms ® T ✱
sB&B⇌♠£32.50-£42.50 dB&B⇌♠£42.50-£52.50 ⊟
( 100P ✿ crown green bowling
♥ English & French V ♦ ⌂ Lunch £9.75
Credit Cards ①②③④⑤

**CREWKERNE** Somerset Map **03** ST40

★★**60% Old Parsonage Hotel & Restaurant** Barn St TA18 8BP
(Exec Hotel) ☎(0460)73516
*An old stone house on the edge of the town. There is a cosy lounge bar and a dining room with candlelight. Bedrooms vary from large rooms in the main building to the more compact ones in the annexe. The hotel is managed by the friendly proprietors and is popular with business people and holiday makers.*
4⇌♠Annexe6⇌♠ CTV in all bedrooms ®
12P
♥ British & French V ♦ ⌂ Last dinner 9pm
Credit Cards ①②③⑤

**CRICCIETH** Gwynedd Map **06** SH43

★★★⚑**66% Bron Eifion Country House** LL52 0SA (Inter-
Hotels) ☎(0766)522385 FAX (0766) 522003
*This large, stone-built country house was built in the 1870s and stands in spacious grounds and gardens on the edge of town. The interior has a wealth of Pitch and Oregon pine, which is featured in the panelled walls, doors, magnificent staircase and the delighful minstrels' gallery. The well equipped bedrooms are suitable for both holidaymakers and business people. A keen and enthusiastic proprietor is constantly improving and upgrading the hotel.*
19⇌♠(4fb)5♨ CTV in all bedrooms ® T ✱
sB&B⇌♠£42-£45 dB&B⇌♠£56-£70 ⊟
CTV 80P ✿ clock golf table tennis xmas

♀ French **V** ✿ ⚊ Lunch fr£7.50 Dinner fr£14.50&alc Last
dinner 9.30pm
Credit Cards 1 3

★★66% **Gwyndy** Llanystumdwy LL52 0SP ☎(0766)522720
Closed Dec & Jan
*Situated in the village of Llanystumdwy (famous for its Lloyd
George connections), the main house dates back to the 17th
century and contains the dining room and public areas. Bedrooms
are spacious and well furnished.*
Annexe10⇨(5fb) CTV in all bedrooms ® ✳ sB&B⇨fr£25
dB&B⇨fr£40
CTV 20P ⚑ ✔
♀ British & French ✿ ⚊ Lunch fr£7.50 Dinner fr£8.50 Last
dinner 9pm

★★66% **Parciau Mawr** High St LL52 0RP ☎(0766)522368
Closed Nov-Feb
*A pleasant, family-run hotel in its own grounds at the edge of the
village offers warm, well-furnished bedrooms, a delightful lounge
overlooking the gardens and a good standard of home cooking.*
6⇨Annexe6↑(1fb) CTV in all bedrooms ® ✳
sB&B⇨↑£23.50-£25.50 dB&B⇨↑£37-£43 ⊟
30P ⚑ ❆ nc5yrs
♀ English & French ✿ ⚊ ✂ Dinner £8 Last dinner 8pm
Credit Cards 1 3 £

★★♨64% **Mynydd Ednyfed Country House** Caernarfon Rd
LL52 0PH ☎(0766)523269
Closed 25-26 Dec
*This stone-built manor house, a quarter of a mile off the road, is set
in 7 acres of grounds comprising woods, pastureland and cultivated
gardens. There are warm, well equipped bedrooms, and a
restaurant that gives a choice of home- prepared meals using local
fresh produce.*
8rm(4⇨2↑)(1fb)2⊟ CTV in all bedrooms ® **T** ✳
sB&B£23-£27.50 sB&B⇨↑£25-£27.50 dB&B£46
dB&B⇨↑£46-£50 ⊟
30P ❆
♀ English & Continental **V** Sunday Lunch fr£7.95
Credit Cards 1 3 5

★★63% **Plas Isa** Porthmadog Rd LL52 0HP ☎(0766)522443
*Overlooking the sea and providing fine views of the castle, this
well-furnished, family owned and run hotel offers bedrooms
equipped to modern standards and good meals with an extensive
choice of dishes.*
14⇨↑(3fb) CTV in all bedrooms ® **T** sB&B⇨↑£25-£27.50
dB&B⇨↑£40-£45 ⊟
CTV 14P water sports
♀ Chinese, French, Indian & Italian **V** ✿ Dinner
£7.95-£11&alc Last dinner 8.45pm
Credit Cards 1 3 5 £

★★62% **Plas Gwyn** Pentrefelin LL52 0PT (1m NE A497)
☎(0766)522559 FAX (0766) 523200
*This family run hotel provides well-equipped accommodation and
is popular with commercial visitors, although it is equally suitable
for tourists. It stands on the A497 one mile east of the town.*
14⇨↑(6fb) CTV in all bedrooms ® **T**
sB&B⇨↑£19.50-£21.50 dB&B⇨↑£37-£42 ⊟
CTV 50P
♀ English, French & Italian **V** ✿ ⚊ Lunch £6.50-£8.50 High
tea £6.50-£8.50 Dinner £10.95-£15 Last dinner 9pm
Credit Cards 1 2 3 5

★★58% **Lion** Y Maes LL52 0AA ☎(0766)522460
RS Nov-Mar
*The resident owner of this old coaching inn offers a warm welcome
to guests, and a stay in its adequately furnished accommodation
represents good value for money.*
36rm(27⇨↑)(4fb) CTV in all bedrooms ® ✳ sB&Bfr£18
sB&B⇨↑fr£20.50 dB&Bfr£35 dB&B⇨↑fr£39 ⊟
▶

C

C

Lift 20P 12🚗 *xmas*
🍷 Welsh & French **V** ♥ ☕ Lunch £5.50-£8 High tea fr£6 Dinner £11-£13.50 Last dinner 8.15pm
Credit Cards [1] [2] [3] [5] £

**★★57% *George IV*** LL52 0BS (Consort) ☎(0766)522168
*A high street hotel dating from 1800 and considerably enlarged in 1900, offering quite simple but fairly well-equipped accommodation suitable for holidaymakers, commercial visitors and golfing and fishing parties. The new owners are planning extensive refurbishment in 1991.*
37rm(28⇌6♒)(8fb) CTV in 34 bedrooms ®
Lift CTV 60P ❊
**V** ♥ ☕ Last dinner 9pm
Credit Cards [1] [3]

**★65% Abereistedd** West Pde LL52 0EN ☎(0766)522710
Closed 30 Oct-Feb
*Situated on the seafront, with views across Cardigan Bay, this is a small, well-maintained family-run hotel offering well-equpped bedrooms suitable for holidaymakers and commercial visitors alike.*
12rm(8♒)(2fb) CTV in all bedrooms ® ✱ sB&B£14-£15.50 sB&B♒£14-£15.50 dB&B£28-£31 dB&B♒£28-£31 ⊟
12P
🍷 English & French **V** ♥ ☕ ⚟ Lunch £5.50-£6.50 Dinner £7.50 Last dinner 7.30pm
Credit Cards [1] £

**★62% Caerwylan** LL52 0HW ☎(0766)522547
Closed Nov-Etr
*A well-furnished and comfortable family-run hotel overlooking the sea.*
25rm(17⇌2♒) CTV in all bedrooms ® ✱ sB&Bfr£14.50 sB&B⇌♒fr£16 dB&Bfr£29 dB&B⇌♒fr£32 ⊟
Lift CTV 8P 8🚗 (75p) ❊
♥ ☕ Lunch fr£5.30 Dinner fr£6.50 Last dinner 7.30pm

## CRICK Northamptonshire Map 04 SP57

**★★★65% Post House** NN6 7XR (Trusthouse Forte)
☎(0788)822101 Telex no 311107 FAX (0788) 823955
*Enjoying an enviable position, close to junction 18 of the M1 and convenient for many business centres, this hotel has particularly good conference facilities. There are two bars and the leisure centre is under professional supervision.*
96⇌♒⚟in 28 bedrooms CTV in all bedrooms ® **T** sB⇌♒£72-£82 dB⇌♒£83-£93 (room only) ⊟
( 150P ❊ CFA ▢(heated) sauna solarium gymnasium *xmas*
**V** ♥ ☕ ⚟ Lunch fr£11.50&alc Dinner fr£15&alc Last dinner 10pm
Credit Cards [1] [2] [3] [4] [5]

## CRICKHOWELL Powys Map 03 SO21

**★★♛72% Gliffaes Country House** NP8 1RH
☎Bwlch(0874)730371 FAX (0874) 730463
Closed Jan-9 Mar
*Set amid rare trees and shrubs in 30 acres of magnificent grounds, the distinctive hotel commands fine views of the River Usk and its wooded valley. An informal, friendly atmosphere prevails and the standard of the good home cooking is consistent. Elegant lounges and character bedrooms are well-equipped with modern facilities.*
19rm(15⇌3♒)Annexe3⇌♒(3fb) CTV in 3 bedrooms ® **T** ✗ (ex guide dogs) S8% sB&B⇌♒£27.50-£31.90 dB&B⇌♒£55-£74.50 ⊟
CTV 34P ❊ 🎾 (hard) 🎣 snooker painting croquet putting 🏠
🍷 European **V** ♥ ☕ ⚟ S10% Lunch £9.80-£14.20 Dinner £15.30&alc Last dinner 9.15pm
Credit Cards [1] [2] [3] [5]

**★★65% *Bear*** NP8 1BW (WR) ☎(0873)810408
FAX (0873) 811696
*This 15th century coaching inn is the focal point of the bustling market town. Most bedrooms have now been upgraded to excellent standards, public areas are spacious and comfortable and the food imaginative and enjoyable.*
14rm(7⇌6♒)Annexe13⇌(6fb)1 ▣ CTV in all bedrooms ®
CTV 38P ⛟
🍷 English & French **V** ♥ Last dinner 9.30pm
Credit Cards [1] [2] [3]

**✕Glan-y-Dwr** Brecon Rd NP8 1BT ☎(0873)810756
*A well-maintained and attractive restaurant on the main road in the centre of town commended for the cooking and hospitality of the Belgian owner. He displays his skill and versatility through his international menu and by holding regular gourmet evenings that offer food from China, Italy, France and, of course, Belgium. There are also four good bedrooms, two of which have 'en suite' facilities.*
Closed Mon & 2nd & 3rd wks Jan
Dinner not served Sun
🍷 French **V** 30 seats ✱ Lunch £17-£40alc Dinner £17-£40alc Last lunch 1pm Last dinner 9pm 12P
Credit Cards [1] [3]

## CRICKLADE Wiltshire Map 04 SU09

**✕✕ *Whites*** 93 High St SN6 6DF ☎Swindon(0793)751110
*The ambience of this cottage-style restaurant is enhanced by a warm welcome and simple, friendly service. The chef/patron brings skill and dedication to bear in the preparation of appetisers, fish dishes and such meat specialities as pot-cooked beef, his sauces being particularly tasty. A limited choice of sweets includes some delicious home-made options.*
Closed Sun, 2 wks Aug & 1wk Jan/Feb
Lunch not served Mon
🍷 English, French & Italian **V** 32 seats Last lunch 2pm Last dinner 9.30pm 🅿̸
Credit Cards [1] [3]

## CRIEFF Tayside *Perthshire* Map 11 NN82

**★★67% Murray Park** Connaught Ter PH7 3DJ (Inter-Hotels)
☎(0764)3731 FAX (0764) 5311
*Genuine hospitality, together with consistently good and imaginative food, add to the appeal of this welcoming family-run hotel. Comfortable public rooms invite easy relaxation and the smart bedrooms are well equipped.*
13⇌(1fb) CTV in all bedrooms ® ✱ sB&B⇌£35-£38 dB&B⇌£53-£56
50P ⛟ ❊ shooting stalking
🍷 Scottish & French **V** ♥ Lunch £10-£12 Dinner £16.50-£18&alc Last dinner 9.30pm
Credit Cards [1] [2] [3] [5] £

**★★♛64% Cultoquhey House** PH7 3NE ☎(0764)3253 & 4535
Closed Feb & Mar
*A popular and efficiently run country hotel two miles east of the town offers warmly welcoming public areas with a "lived-in" feel to them and well-equipped bedrooms with traditional comforts. Sound country cooking remains consistantly appetising and hospitality is outstanding.*
11rm(10⇌♒)(3fb)3 ▣ CTV in all bedrooms ® **T** sB&Bfr£30 sB&B⇌♒£35-£40 dB&B£48 dB&B⇌♒£52-£70 ⊟
50P ⛟ ❊ 🎾 (hard) 🎣 Ü snooker game & clay pigeon shooting croquet 🏠 *xmas*
🍷 Scottish & French ♥ ☕ ⚟ Bar Lunch £6.50-£12 Dinner £15.50 Last dinner 8.30pm
Credit Cards [1] [2] [3] [5] £

★★58%, **Crieff** 47-49 East High St PH7 3JA ☎(0764)2632
*Now under new ownership, this small, family-run hotel, situated close to the town centre, is a convenient base for business guests and the touring holidaymaker. It offers a smartly refurbished lounge bar, a range of beauty and fitness facilities and well-prepared meals. Bedrooms are modest in appointment, but improvements are planned.*
8⇨↑(2fb) CTV in all bedrooms ® T ✳ sB&B⇨↑£24.75 dB&B⇨↑£46.50
CTV 9P sauna solarium gymnasium hair & beauty salon
✧ Bar Lunch £6.35 High tea £4.50
Credit Cards 1 2 3 £

★66%, *Lockes Acre* Comrie Rd PH7 4BP ☎(0764)2526
RS Nov-Mar
*This attractive little tourist hotel on the edge of the village overlooks the Ochil Hills. It offers a friendly atmosphere and comfortable, modern bedrooms, though some are limited in size.*
7rm(4↑)(2fb) CTV in all bedrooms ® ✖ (ex guide dogs) 20P 🛗
✧ ⚊ ✖ Last dinner 9pm
Credit Cards 1 3

★60%, *Gwydyr House* Comrie Rd PH7 4BP ☎(0764)3277
Closed Nov-Etr
*A small family-run hotel standing in its own grounds at the west end of town and enjoying fine views of the surrounding hills. It provides a friendly atmosphere and simple, good value accommodation.*
10rm(4fb) CTV in all bedrooms ® sB&B£12.25-£14.50 dB&B£24.50-£29 ⊟
CTV 15P ❀
☺ British & Continental V ✧ Bar Lunch £4.30-£7.95alc Dinner £8.50-£8.50&alc Last dinner 8pm
£

**CROCKETFORD** Dumfries & Galloway *Kirkcudbrightshire* Map 11 NX87

★60%, *Lochview Motel* Crocketford Rd DG2 8RF
☎(055669)281
Closed 26 Dec & 1 Jan
*This simple roadside motel offers compact, but clean and freshly decorated bedrooms. Public areas are rather limited, but there is a popular lounge bar/restaurant with stunning views of Loch Auchenreoch. Food can be obtained throughout the day and the atmosphere is relaxed and friendly.*
7↑ CTV in all bedrooms ® ✖
80P ♪ ♫
✧ ⚊
Credit Cards 1 3

**CROMARTY** Highland *Ross & Cromarty* Map 14 NH76
★★62%, **Royal** Marine Ter IV11 8YN ☎(03817)217
*An hospitable hotel overlooking the harbour and Cromarty Firth has a very good reputation for its cooking, offering huge breakfasts, extensive bar meals, afternoon tea and a "Taste of Scotland" menu at dinner ; walking, fishing and shooting holiday packages can be arranged, or guests may choose simply to relax in the sheltered gardens.*
10rm(5⇨2↑)(2fb) CTV in all bedrooms ® sB&B⇨↑fr£22 dB&B⇨↑fr£44 ⊟
CTV 20P 3❀ ❀ games room 🎱
V ✧ ⚊ Lunch fr£7.75 High tea fr£6 Dinner fr£13.95 Last dinner 8pm
Credit Cards 1 2 3

*The AA's star-rating scheme is the market leader in hotel classification.*

✕ **Le Chardon** Church St IV11 8XA ☎(03817)471
*A pretty little restaurant is sited in a quiet street of this former seaport on the Black Isle. Food is innovative and well cooked.*
Closed Mon
Lunch not served (ex by arrangement only)
☺ French V 30 seats Last lunch 2pm Last dinner 9.30pm 3P nc8yrs ✖
Credit Cards 1 2 3

**C**

**CROOKLANDS** Cumbria Map 07 SD58
★★★65%, **Crooklands** LA7 7NW (Best Western) ☎(04487)432
Telex no 94017303 FAX (04487) 525
*This hotel was at one time a 16th century Croft and Ale house, and this is reflected by the low beamed ceilings and stone walls in the public areas, but now, with a recently opened modern bedroom wing, the accommodation is very much 20th century, although the hotel's old-world charm is still retained. The attractive hayloft restaurant is renowned for its international cuisine.*
31rm(15⇨) CTV in all bedrooms ® T ✖ S% sB&B⇨£60-£75 dB&B⇨£75-£100 ⊟
150P xmas
☺ French V ✧ Bar Lunch £3.95-£6.50 Dinner £8.50-£18.50&alc Last dinner 9.30pm
Credit Cards 1 2 3 5 £

**CROSBY-ON-EDEN** Cumbria Map 12 NY45
★★★⚑69%, **Crosby Lodge Country House** High Crosby CA6 4QZ ☎(022873)618 due to change to (0228) 573618
FAX (0228) 573428 (1991)
Closed 24 Dec-mid Jan RS Sun
*Elegantly furnished, spacious, comfortable bedrooms are a feature of this relaxing family owned hotel. The restaurant, also especially recommended, provides a high standard of British and Continental cuisine.*

▶

9⇨♠Annexe2⇨(3fb)2⊞ CTV in all bedrooms T
sB&B⇨♠£60-£65 dB&B⇨♠£80-£90 ℞
40P ⇔ ❖
♀ English & French V ♦ Lunch £14.25-£17.75&alc Dinner
£20.50-£24.50&alc Last dinner 9pm
Credit Cards ① ② ③

**★★★56%** Newby Grange CA6 4RA ☎(022873)645 due to
change to (0228) 573645 FAX (0228) 573420 (1991)
*An attractive five acres of grounds is the setting for this hotel. A
very popular venue for functions and weddings, Newby Grange
offers efficient and friendly service. Bedrooms vary in size and
style, but are all well equipped.*
20⇨♠(4fb)1⊞ CTV in all bedrooms ® T ✱ sB&B⇨♠£45
dB&B⇨♠£60 ℞
《 CTV 200P ❖ ♪ xmas
V ♦ ⍯ Lunch £6.50&alc Dinner £10.95&alc Last dinner
10.30pm
Credit Cards ① ③ £

---

**CROSS HANDS** Dyfed Map **02** SN51

⬒**Travelodge** SA14 6NW (A48) (Trusthouse Forte)
☎(0269)845700 Central Res (0800) 850950
*A modern bedroom complex standing alongside the Little Chef
restaurant, just off the A40 three miles west of the end of the M4.*
32⇨♠(32fb) CTV in all bedrooms ® sB⇨♠£24
dB⇨♠£29.50 (room only)
《 32P ⇔
Credit Cards ① ② ③

---

**CROSSMICHAEL** Dumfries & Galloway *Kirkcudbrightshire*
Map **11** NX76

**★★≠59%** Culgruff House DG7 3BB ☎(055667)230
RS Oct-Etr
*Genuine warmth and hospitality are foremost in this baronial
mansion, furnished with many antiques. Overlooking the village
and the Ken Valley, it is set in 35 acres of grounds in which
peacocks roam. The lounges with log fires are particularly
comfortable and electric blankets are provided on the beds.*
16rm(4⇨)(8fb) CTV in 14 bedrooms TV in 1 bedroom
sB&B£13-£15 sB&B⇨£19.50 dB&B£23-£34 dB&B⇨£39 ℞
CTV 50P 8➾ (70p) ❖
V ♦ ⍯ ⊱ Lunch £7.50&alc High tea £5-£5.60&alc Dinner
£11&alc Last dinner 7.30pm
Credit Cards ① ② ③ ⑤ £

---

**CROWTHORNE** Berkshire Map **04** SU86

**★★★55%** Waterloo Duke's Ride RG11 7NW (Trusthouse
Forte) ☎(0344)777711 Telex no 848139 FAX (0344) 778913
*Modern facilities and friendly service are found in this basically
Victorian building.*
58⇨♠1⊞⊱in 10 bedrooms CTV in all bedrooms ® T ✱
sB⇨♠fr£70 dB⇨♠£85-£95 (room only) ℞
《 120P xmas
V ♦ ⍯ ⊱ Lunch £9.95-£10.95&alc High tea £1.25-£5.50
Dinner £13.95&alc Last dinner 10pm
Credit Cards ① ② ③ ④ ⑤

---

**CROYDE** Devon Map **02** SS43

**★★66%** Kittiwell House St Mary's Rd EX33 1PG
☎(0271)890247
Closed mid Jan-mid Feb
*This thatched longhouse stands on the edge of the village, within
walking distance of the excellent surfing beaches. All its bedrooms
now offer en suite facilities, whilst characterful public areas have
enormous charm and the heavily beamed restaurant offers a choice
of table d'hôte or à la carte menus.*
12⇨♠(2fb)3⊞⊱in 4 bedrooms CTV in all bedrooms ® ✱
sB&B⇨♠£47-£52 dB&B⇨♠£80-£90 (incl dinner) ℞

CTV 21P ⇔ ❖ xmas
♀ English & French V ♦ ⍯ Sunday Lunch £8-£9 Dinner
£13-£14&alc Last dinner 9.30pm
Credit Cards ① ② ③ ⑤

**★★65%** Croyde Bay House Moor Ln, Croyde Bay EX33 1PA
☎(0271)890270
Closed mid Nov-Feb
*Family-run establishment in an elevated position overlooking
Croyde Bay. The hotel has a cottagey atmosphere and personal
service is provided by the friendly proprietors.*
7⇨♠(2fb) CTV in all bedrooms ® sB&B⇨♠£27-£43
dB&B⇨♠£54-£70 ℞
8P ⇔
♦ ⍯ ⊱ Dinner fr£15 Last dinner 8pm
Credit Cards ① ③

---

**CROYDON** Greater London

See **LONDON plan** 1*D1* (page 427)
**★★★★62%** Selsdon Park Sanderstead CR2 8YA (3m SE off
A2022) (Best Western) ☎081-657 8811 Telex no 945003
FAX 081-651 6171
*A mansion set in beautiful gardens amid 200-acre grounds has
been sympathetically upgraded to retain most of its original
character. An impressive entrance lobby features fine carved
woodwork and some good pieces of furniture, while the spacious
restaurant's light, airy surroundings provide an ideal setting in
which to enjoy your choice of dishes from table d'hôte or à la carte
menus. Most of the bedrooms have been refurbished to a high
standard and are well equipped. New conference facilities are
available, and good leisure amenities are provided both indoors
and out.*
170⇨♠(7fb)1⊞ CTV in all bedrooms ® T S10%
sB&B⇨♠£115-£129 dB&B⇨♠£156-£170 ℞
Lift 《 250P 15➾ (£1.50) ❖ CFA ▨(heated) ⊿(heated) ▸ 18
♬ (hard & grass) squash snooker sauna solarium gymnasium
croquet jacuzzi putting boules ♬ xmas
♀ International ⊱ S10% Lunch fr£18.50&alc Dinner
fr£21&alc Last dinner 9.30pm
Credit Cards ① ② ③ ⑤

**See advertisement on page 243**

**★★★63%** Post House Purley Way CR9 4LT (Trusthouse Forte)
☎081-688 5185 Telex no 893814 FAX 081-681 6438
*Northbound access off the A23 is recommended although
southbound access is possible via the deliveries entrance. A new
wing offers modern accommodation whilst other bedrooms are
slowly being refurbished. Chef Victor Firth provides creative
international cuisine and service is particularly friendly.*
86⇨♠in 28 bedrooms CTV in all bedrooms ® T S%
sB⇨♠£80-£90 dB⇨♠£92-£102 (room only) ℞
《 70P CFA xmas
♀ English & French V ♦ ⍯ ⊱ S% Lunch £8.95-£13&alc High
tea £5.50-£8.50 Dinner £13.95-£15.95&alc Last dinner 10pm
Credit Cards ① ② ③ ⑤

**★★★59%** Holiday Inn 7 Altyre Rd CR9 5AA (Holiday Inns Inc)
☎081-680 9200 Telex no 8956268 FAX 081-760 0426
*A modern, functional hotel in the town centre and close to the East
Croydon railway station. There is a choice of very well-equipped
spacious bedrooms (some for non-smokers), a popular bar, 24-
hour room service and good recreational and conference facilities.*
214⇨♠(40fb)⊱in 26 bedrooms CTV in all bedrooms
Lift 《 ⊞ 118P ▨(heated) squash sauna solarium gymnasium
whirlpool bath
♀ International V ♦ ⍯ ⊱ Last dinner 10pm
Credit Cards ① ② ③ ④ ⑤

---

1991 marks the 25th anniversary of this guide.

★★57% **Briarley** 8 Outram Rd CR0 6XE ☎081-654 1000
FAX 081-656 6084
*This privately-run commercial hotel stands in a residential area off the A215 West Wickham road. Most of its well-equipped bedrooms are located in a rear annexe some distance from the main building.*
18⇄♪♠Annexe20⇄♪(3fb)1♬ CTV in all bedrooms ® T S%
sB&B⇄♪♠fr£55 dB&B⇄♪♠fr£65 🅿
CTV 20P
♡ Mainly grills V ⚔ S% Sunday Lunch fr£10.50 Dinner
fr£10.50&alc Last dinner 10pm
Credit Cards ① ② ③ ⑤ ⓔ

★62% **Central** 3-5 South Park Hill Rd, South Croydon
CR2 7DY ☎081-688 0840 & 081-688 5644 FAX 081-760 0861
*Set in a quiet residential area half a mile south of the town centre, a commercial hotel which is constantly being improved offers modestly furnished but well equipped bedrooms and an attractive garden-themed dining room.*
23rm(7⇄13♠)(1fb)1♬ CTV in all bedrooms ® T
✘ (ex guide dogs) sB&B⇄♪♠£48-£55 dB&B⇄♪♠£60-£65 🅿
《CTV 15P
V ♡ ⚟
Credit Cards ① ③ ⓔ

✘ **Le Saint Jacques** 1123 Whitgift Centre CR0 1UZ
☎081-760 0881
*This cosy little French restaurant, situated in a modern shopping centre, is well frequented and particularly popular at lunchtime. The concise menu offers a good selection of well-prepared dishes such as an enjoyable Magret de Caneton au Coulis de Pêche, and a competent Crême Brulée. Service is charming and attentive.*
Closed Sun & 24 Dec-4 Jan & BH's
Lunch not served Sat
Dinner not served Mon-Wed
▶

Comfortable 7 bedroom hotel, situated at the edge of the beach near the village of Croyde on the beautiful north Devon coast and in an area of outstanding natural beauty. Many sporting facilities nearby including championship golf course and miles of National Trust walks on the doorstep. All rooms have bath or shower en suite, colour television, tea making facilities and with lovely views of the beach and sea. Good food in relaxing surroundings.

*Croyde Bay House Hotel*
★ ★
**Croyde Bay, Braunton,
N. Devon EX33 1PA**
ETB 👑👑👑                Ashley Courtenay
Commended                    recommended
*Please telephone Croyde
(0271) 890270 for brochure*

♔ French 36 seats ✳ Lunch £12-£18alc Dinner fr£13.50alc
Last lunch 2.45pm Last dinner 10pm ✗ nc8yrs
Credit Cards ① ② ③ ④ ⑤

---

**CRUDWELL** Wiltshire Map **03** ST99

★★68%, **Crudwell Court** SN16 9EP ☎(06667)7194 & 7195
FAX (06667) 7853
*A former vicarage of Cotswold stone, set in attractive gardens
which include a well-screened pool, has been lovingly refurbished in
pastel shades and co-ordinating Sanderson fabrics to create a
relaxed, airy atmosphere ; friendly staff offer obliging service, while
carefully prepared food shows imaginative touches.*
15⇔♪(3fb) CTV in all bedrooms ® T sB&B⇔♪fr£40
dB&B⇔♪£77-£100 ₿
20P ⌕ ✿ ⌂(heated) croquet lawn *xmas*
◊ ⚘ Lunch fr£17 Dinner fr£17 Last dinner 9.30pm
Credit Cards ① ② ③ ⑤ ⓔ

★★66%, **Mayfield House** SN16 9EW ☎(06667)409 & 7198
FAX (06667) 7977
*Owned by the Dodson family this hotel serves a good selection of
bar food and an imaginative à la carte restaurant menu. Bedrooms
are neat and warm and the staff friendly and attentive.*
20⇔♪(1fb) CTV in all bedrooms ® T sB&B⇔♪£40-£42
dB&B⇔♪£55-£58 ₿
CTV 50P ✿
♔ English & French ◊ ⚘ Lunch £8.50 Dinner £9.50-£16alc
Last dinner 9pm
Credit Cards ① ② ③ ⓔ

---

**CRUGYBAR** Dyfed Map **03** SN63

★★⚑69%, **Glanrannell Park** SA19 8SA (WR)
☎Talley(0558)685230
Closed Nov-Mar
*Mr and Mrs Davies extend a warm welcome to guests at this hotel,
run by the same family for over twenty years. Bedrooms are
sparkling and bright and the food, chosen from a small but sensible
menu, is consistently enjoyable.*
8rm(5⇔)(2fb) ® sB&B£27 sB&B⇔£31.50 dB&B£46
dB&B⇔£55 ₿
CTV 30P 3🏌 (£3) ⌕ ✿ ⚓
♔ International ◊ ⚘ ✂ Bar Lunch fr£1.50 High tea fr£3
Dinner fr£12.50 Last dinner 8pm

---

**CUCKFIELD** West Sussex Map **04** TQ32

★★★72%, **Ockenden Manor** Ockenden Ln RH17 5LD
☎Haywards Heath(0444)416111 FAX (0444)415549
*An attractive manor house dating from 1520, providing wood-
panelled public rooms and individually furnished and named
bedrooms which, in addition to every modern amenity, retain much
of their original character and charm. The restaurant offers a prix
fixe menu, cooking in the modern English style being
complemented by an outstanding wine list and attentive service.*
22⇔♪4🏌 CTV in all bedrooms ® T ✹ sB&B⇔♪£70-£110
dB&B⇔♪£90-£155 Continental breakfast ₿
⟨40P ⌕ ✿ *xmas*
V ◊ ⚘ Lunch £15.95 Dinner £21.95-£28 Last dinner 9.15pm
Credit Cards ① ② ③ ⑤

★★⚑55%, **Hilton Park** RH17 5EG
☎Haywards Heath(0444)454555
*Attractively and peacefully set in three acres of grounds this hotel
provides old fashioned bedrooms and a fixed price menu of
predominantly English home-style cooking. Services are limited.*
14rm(10⇔)(5fb) CTV in all bedrooms ® T sB&Bfr£45
sB&B⇔fr£48 dB&Bfr£61 dB&B⇔fr£66 ₿
50P 2🏌 ⌕ ✿
♔ English & French ◊ ⚘ Lunch fr£12 High tea fr£5 Dinner
fr£15 Last dinner 8pm
Credit Cards ① ② ③ ⑤

---

✗ **Jeremy's at the Kings Head** South St RH17 5JY
☎Haywards Heath(0444)440386
*Jeremy's – named after its talented chef/patron – retains the
character of an English inn with its simple appointments, log-
burning fires and friendly service. Daily menus offer a good range
of dishes, professionally and skilfully cooked, including fresh fish
as available ; popular choices include fish soup with coriander,
Stilton soufflé, wild salmon with samphire and Gressingham duck
with Madeira, while a tasty pudding provides a fitting end to an
enjoyable meal.*
Dinner not served Mon
V 38 seats 10P
Credit Cards ① ② ③ ⑤

---

**CULLERCOATS** Tyne & Wear Map **12** NZ37

★★57%, **Bay** Front St NE30 4QB ☎091-252 3150
*Improvements are gradually being made to this seafront hotel
which now has a smart first-floor dining room, cocktail bar and
residents' lounge, all of which overlook Cullercoats Bay. There are
extensive and popular bars and a separate carvery. Bedroom
accommodation remains rather modest.*
19rm(4⇔4♪)(2fb)1🏌 CTV in all bedrooms ® T
✹ (ex guide dogs) ✳ sB&B£16-£22 sB&B⇔♪£22
dB&B£30-£38 dB&B⇔♪£38-£42
CTV 9P sailing sea fishing *xmas*
♔ English & French ◊ ⚘ Lunch £2.95-£6.25 Dinner
£5.50-£6.25&alc Last dinner 9pm
Credit Cards ① ② ③ ④ ⑤ ⓔ
**See advertisement under WHITLEY BAY**

---

**CULNACNOC**

See Skye, Isle of

---

**CUMNOCK** Strathclyde *Ayrshire* Map **11** NS51

★★61%, **Royal** 1 Glaisnock St KA18 1BP ☎(0290)20822
*This commercial hotel at the town centre, though somewhat
traditional in style, is homely, comfortable and very clean ; meals
are simple and home-cooked, good afternoon/high teas being
available.*
11rm(2⇔1♪)(1fb) CTV in 4 bedrooms TV in 1 bedroom ®
sB&B£20-£22 dB&B£40-£44 dB&B⇔♪£44-£48
CTV 10P
V ◊ ⚘ Lunch £5-£6.50 High tea £5-£6.50 Dinner £10-£12 Last
dinner 9pm
Credit Cards ① ③

---

**CUPAR** Fife Map **11** NO31

⌗✗**Ostlers Close** Bonnygate KY15 4BU ☎(0334)55574
*The enthusiasm and skill of the proprietors are reflected in the
interesting and daily-changing menus at this attractive 'cottagey'
restaurant. Jimmy Graham produces mouthwatering dishes, using
local produce wherever possible, while Amanda Graham takes care
of guests in the dining room. Our Inspector chose fresh asparagus,
served in a pastry case, followed by a seafood ragoût with an
almond and pear tart to finish, enjoyed every dish and found the
meal very good value for money.*
Closed Sun, Mon & 2 wks Jun
♔ French & Swiss 28 seats Lunch £9-£14alc Dinner £15-£25alc
Last lunch 2pm Last dinner 9.30pm ✗ nc6yrs
Credit Cards ① ③

---

**DALKEITH** Lothian *Midlothian* Map **11** NT36

★★64%, **Eskbank Motor** 29 Dalhousie Rd EH22 3AT
☎031-663 3234 FAX 031-660 4347
*Situated beside the A7 on the outskirts of Edinburgh, this motel
has been substantially refurbished. The main building offers a TV
lounge, a small panelled restaurant and a smart lounge bar with an
all-day licence. The modern, compact well-equipped bedrooms are
located in the chalet block.*

▶

★★★★

16⇨🌂(3fb)1🛏 CTV in all bedrooms ⓡ T ✳
sB&B⇨🌂£36-£45 dB&B⇨🌂£50-£70 🍴
《 CTV 40P 6🍴 ✿
🍴 International V ✿ ᴸ Lunch £5-£7&alc High tea £5-£7
Dinner £5-£7&alc Last dinner 9pm
Credit Cards ①②③⑤⑥
                        **See advertisement under EDINBURGH**

---

DALWHINNIE Highland *Inverness-shire* Map **14** NN68

★★56% **Loch Ericht** PH19 1AF (Inter-Hotels) ☎(05282)257
FAX (05282) 270
*Amidst splendid scenery in the Highlands' highest village, this*
*former lodge is conveniently placed for the A9. It has been*
*extended to provide modern, functional accommodation. Meals are*
*available all day in the split-level bar and restaurant.*
27⇨🌂(4fb) ⓡ ✳ sB&B⇨🌂£27.25 dB&B⇨🌂£45 🍴
CTV 50P ✿ ♩ shooting ski-ing ♫ *xmas*
V ✿ ᴸ Lunch £2.50-£6.50 High tea £5-£7.50 Dinner £5-£10
Last dinner 9pm
Credit Cards ①②③⑥

---

DARESBURY Cheshire Map **07** SJ58

★★★67% **Lord Daresbury** Chester Rd WA4 4BB (De Vere)
☎Warrington(0925)67331 Telex no 629330 FAX (0925) 65615
*This large and popular modern hotel is set in open countryside*
*close to junction 11 of the M56. It has a very good leisure centre*
*and comprehensive conference facilities and, of the two*
*restaurants, The Terrace sets the more formal style.*
141⇨🌂(7fb)✂in 27 bedrooms CTV in all bedrooms ⓡ T ✳
sB&B⇨🌂£60-£90 dB&B⇨🌂£90-£110 🍴
Lift 《 400P CFA ▣(heated) squash snooker sauna solarium
gymnasium jacuzzi
🍴 English & French V ✿ ᴸ ✂ Lunch £11-£16&alc High tea
£5-£11 Dinner £16&alc Last dinner 9.45pm
Credit Cards ①②③⑤⑥

---

DARLINGTON Co Durham Map **08** NZ21

See also **Neasham & Teeside Airport**

★★★★61% **Blackwell Grange Moat House** Blackwell Grange
DL3 8QH (Queens Moat) ☎(0325)380888 Telex no 587272
FAX (0325) 380899
*An impressive, spacious country house on the outskirts of the city.*
*Bedrooms are attractive and comfortable.*
99⇨🌂(11fb)3🛏✂in 14 bedrooms CTV in all bedrooms ⓡ T
S% sB&B⇨🌂£75-£120 dB&B⇨🌂£100-£148 🍴
Lift 《 250P 3🍴 ✿ CFA ▣(heated) ▶ 18 ♬ (hard) sauna
solarium gymnasium boule croquet ♫ *xmas*
🍴 International V ✿ ᴸ ✂ Lunch £8.50-£13.75&alc High tea
£5.50 Dinner £13.75-£17.50&alc Last dinner 9.45pm
Credit Cards ①②③⑤

★★★62% *White Horse* DL1 3AD ☎(0325)382121
Telex no 778704 FAX (0325) 355953
*A Tudor-style building, on the A167 on the outskirts of town, with*
*a modern bedroom extension of very well appointed and*
*comfortable rooms. Public areas are limited to bars and a*
*restaurant serving mainly grills and additional daily dishes.*
40⇨🌂(6fb)✂in 20 bedrooms CTV in all bedrooms ⓡ
Lift 《 120P
🍴 Mainly grills V ✿ ᴸ ✂ Last dinner 10pm
Credit Cards ①②③⑤

★★★61% **Swallow King's Head** Priestgate DL1 1NW (Swallow)
☎(0325)380222 Telex no 587112 FAX (0325) 382006
*Victorian four-storey town centre hotel.*
60⇨🌂(1fb)✂in 25 bedrooms CTV in all bedrooms ⓡ T ✳ S%
sB&B⇨🌂fr£58 dB&B⇨🌂fr£75 🍴
Lift 《 P CFA *xmas*

---

🍴 English, French & Italian V ✿ ᴸ S% Lunch fr£9.75 Dinner
fr£11.50 Last dinner 9.30pm
Credit Cards ①②③⑤

✗✗**Bishop's House** 38 Coniscliffe Rd DL3 7RG ☎(0325)382200
FAX (0325) 489746
*A smart, intimate restaurant reached through an arch and across*
*an attractive courtyard, close to the centre of the town. Fixed price*
*lunch and dinner menus, featuring modern English and French*
*cooking, represent good value for money. Puddings are*
*particularly notable.*
Closed Sun
Lunch not served Sat
🍴 English & French V 35 seats ✳ Lunch £10.50-£12.50&alc
Dinner £19.50-£23&alc Last lunch 2pm Last dinner 9.30pm 🌂
Credit Cards ①②③⑤

✗**Victor's** 84 Victoria Rd DL1 5JW ☎(0325)480818
*Housed in shop-fronted premises between railway station and*
*football ground, with a public car park close by, a tiny,*
*unpretentious restaurant features lunch and dinner menus that*
*represent exceedingly good value for money, cuisine being British*
*in style and offering a varied choice of meat, poultry and fish dishes*
*which are normally preceded by a home-made soup in the four-*
*course evening meal.*
Closed Sun & Mon
V 30 seats ✳ Lunch £6.50 Dinner £16 Last lunch 2.30pm Last
dinner 10.30pm 🌂 ✂
Credit Cards ①②③⑤

---

DARTMOUTH Devon Map **03** SX85

★★★69% **Royal Castle** 11 The Quay TQ6 9PS ☎(0803)833033
FAX (0803) 835445
*Set alongside the inner harbour, with glorious views across to*
*Kingswear, this former 17th-century hostelry has been*
*sympathetically restored to retain its charm and character whilst*
*providing modern day comforts. The elegant Adam Restaurant*
*overlooks the river and is noted for its worthy food standards which*
*feature local seafood and other produce. Parking is limited, but*
*there are public car parks nearby.*
25⇨🌂6🛏 CTV in all bedrooms ⓡ T sB&B⇨🌂£34-£44
dB&B⇨🌂£58-£90 🍴
《 7🍴 (£1.50) ♫ *xmas*
🍴 English & French V ✿ ᴸ Lunch £9.45 Dinner
£14.50-£21.50 Last dinner 9.45pm
Credit Cards ①③⑤

★★★62% **Dart Marina** Sandquay TQ6 9PH (Trusthouse Forte)
☎(0803)832580
*From its beautiful situation beside the River Dart, the hotel enjoys*
*views up and down the river and across to Kingswear, the best*
*being from the first floor public lounge and the more compact bar*
*and dining room on the ground floor, where an interesting table*
*d'hôte menu is changed nightly. The recently refurbished bedrooms*
*all provide a high standard of decor and furnishings, with excellent*
*facilities for both commercial travellers and holidaymakers; there*
*is ample car parking.*
31⇨🌂(4fb)✂in 10 bedrooms CTV in 35 bedrooms ⓡ T S%
sB⇨🌂£65-£75 dB⇨🌂£86-£116 (room only) 🍴
75P 🚗 *xmas*
V ✿ ᴸ ✂ S% Lunch £7.50-£9&alc Dinner £15-£20 Last dinner
9.15pm
Credit Cards ①②③④⑤

★★★55% *Stoke Lodge* Cinders Ln, Stoke Fleming TQ6 0RA
(2m S A379) ☎Stoke Fleming(0803)770523
*Personal service and a friendly atmosphere are provided by a*
*family hotel in the village of Stoke Fleming, about three miles from*
*Dartmouth. Well-equipped bedrooms have en suite facilities, public*
*areas are extensive, and the leisure complex includes both indoor*
*and outdoor pools, spa bath, sauna, games room and hard tennis*
*court. An interesting table d'hôte menu is served in the Garden*
*Restaurant.*

24⇨🏃(5fb)1🛏 CTV in all bedrooms ®
50P 4🏊 (£2.50) 🎱 ✻ ☒(heated) ⌕(heated) ♪ (hard) sauna solarium gymnasium jacuzzi putting
🍽 English & Continental V ♦ ☑ Last dinner 9.00pm

★★65% **Royle House** Mount Boone TQ6 9HZ ☎(0803)833649
RS Dec-Feb
*Family-run hotel in its own gardens, approximately 5 minutes walk from the town centre and the river.*
10⇨🌿in 2 bedrooms CTV in all bedrooms ® T ✱
sB&B⇨fr£43 dB&B⇨🏃£58-£78 🍴
CTV 15P 🎱 ✻ ☒(heated) sauna solarium hairdressing salon nc9yrs
V ♦ 🌿 Dinner fr£12.95 Last dinner 8pm
Credit Cards ①③

🏵✕✕**Carved Angel** 2 South Embankment TQ6 9BB
☎(0803)832465
*This is a restaurant to which patrons return time and again. Its setting, on Dartmouth's historic quayside, could not be more appropriate for a menu with so many appetising fish dishes, and its relaxed and friendly but efficient atmosphere is equally delightful. Joyce Molyneux's repertoire derives inspiration from the freshly caught local seafood (buckets of crab and prawns are delivered several times a day by Devon fishermen). Twice-baked lobster soufflé, terrine of brill and vegetables with delicious herb mayonnaise, pickled samphire or asparagus, accompanied by home-made bread and brioches, give a taste of the range of first courses, to be followed perhaps by Gressingham duck served with apple and sweet potato, or poached skate with caper. To finish, an iced ginger meringue with butterscotch sauce may well tempt the diner. There is a very sound wine list, with the House Bordeaux and Loire wines giving excellent value for money. Vegetarians can be catered for.*
Closed Mon, Xmas, Jan & beginning of Feb
Dinner not served Sun
🍽 International 34 seats ✱ S% Lunch fr£22.50&alc Dinner £30-£35 Last lunch 1.45pm Last dinner 9.30pm 🥢

🏵✕✕**The Mansion House** TQ6 9AG ☎(0803)835474
*Formerly the chef/patron of Bistro 33, Richard Cranfield has now opened this attractive new restaurant in an elegant mansion near the quay, once the home of an 18th-century mayor of Dartmouth. These new, larger premises have enabled him to provide both a bistro-style wine bar on the ground floor and a formal restaurant on the first floor. As befits a leading Dartmouth restaurant, his menu features many excellent fish dishes – sea bass hot-smoked over fennel, with garlic and rosemary butter, charcoal-grilled turbot steak with a parsley-scented veal stock, or cervelas of salmon, halibut and prawns on a bed of creamed leeks. Mansion-House desserts are particularly good too.*
Closed Mon, 1st 2 wks Feb & 1st 2 wks Nov
Lunch not served Sat
Dinner not served Sun
🍽 English & French 32 seats ✱ Lunch fr£18.50 Dinner £22-£26 Last lunch 1.30pm Last dinner 10pm 🥢

**DARWEN** Lancashire Map 07 SD62

★★★56% **Whitehall** Springbank, Whitehall BB3 2JU
☎(0254)701595 FAX (0254) 773426
Closed 25 & 26 Dec
*Set in its own grounds in a residential area close to the main road this traditional hotel with modern extensions is a popular venue for conferences and functions. Family owned and managed, the service is friendly and informal.*
18rm(14⇨🏃) CTV in all bedrooms ® T sB&B£30
sB&B⇨🏃£50 dB&B⇨🏃£60 🍴
60P ✻ ☒(heated) snooker sauna solarium
🍽 English & French V ♦ 🌿 Lunch £8.50 Dinner £10.50 Last dinner 10pm
Credit Cards ①②③④⑤ⓔ

**DATCHET** Berkshire Map 04 SU97

★★52% **The Manor** The Village Green SL3 9EA (Consort)
☎Slough(0753)43442 Telex no 41363 FAX (0202) 299182
*This commercial hotel overlooks the village green and is next to the railway station. The functional bedroom accommodation is equipped with modern facilities and there are two bars and a restaurant.*
30⇨🏃(2fb)1🛏 CTV in all bedrooms ® T ✱ sB&B⇨🏃£69
dB&B⇨🏃£89 🍴
⦅ 30P *xmas*
🍽 English, French, Italian & Spanish V ♦ 🌿 Lunch £15 Dinner £16&alc Last dinner 10pm
Credit Cards ①②③⑤
See advertisement under **WINDSOR**

**DAVENTRY** Northamptonshire Map 04 SP56
○**Holiday Inn** Ashby Rd (A361)(Holiday Inns)
☎Central reservations(0295)252555
Due to have opened autumn 1990
140rm

**DAWLISH** Devon Map 03 SX97

★★★59% **Langstone Cliff** Dawlish Warren EX7 0NA (1.5m NE off A379 Exeter rd) (Consort) ☎(0626)865155
Telex no 57515 FAX (0626) 867166
*This well-established family-run hotel has been improved and upgraded in recent times. The well-equipped bedrooms have modern furnishings and are softly decorated in pastel colours. Situated in its own grounds with sea views the hotel is popular with families during the summer whilst mini conferences are a feature during the autumn and winter.*
64⇨🏃(52fb) CTV in all bedrooms ® T sB&B⇨🏃£40-£45
dB&B⇨🏃£70-£80 🍴
Lift ⦅ CTV 200P ✻ CFA ☒(heated) ⌕(heated) ♪ (hard) snooker solarium table tennis 🎵 ♨ *xmas*
V ♦ 🌿 Lunch fr£9 High tea fr£3 Dinner fr£10.50 Last dinner 9pm
Credit Cards ①②③⑤
See advertisement on page 247

**DEAL** Kent Map 05 TR35

✕**Captain's Table** Cliffe Rd, Kingsdown CT14 8AJ
☎(0304)373755
*There is a distinctly naval flavour at this restaurant, with dishes such as Lemon Sole Nelson, Duck Dreadnought, Captain's Special and Veal Viceroy on the à la carte menu. However, chef Mark Giblin was trained in a college rather than a galley and, assisted by his father Michael, produces honest and wholesome standards of cooking. Service is very warm and friendly, personally supervised by Mrs Gillian Giblin, and as well as the candle-lit dining room, there is a comfortable bar lounge and four bedrooms.*
🍽 English & French 45 seats ✱ Lunch £6.50-£8.50 Dinner £9.95&alc Last lunch 1.45pm Last dinner 10pm 20P
Credit Cards ①③

**DEDDINGTON** Oxfordshire Map 04 SP43

★★66% **Holcombe Hotel & Restaurant** High St OX5 4SL (Best Western) ☎(0869)38274 Telex no 83147 FAX (0869) 37167
*In a picturesque village setting this small 17th century family-run hotel has undergone complete refurbishment. Some good sized bedrooms are comfortable and well equipped, and the restaurant offers thoughtfully prepared dishes.*
17⇨🏃(3fb) CTV in all bedrooms ® T sB&B⇨🏃£58-£69
dB&B⇨🏃£69.50-£85 🍴
CTV 60P ♨ *xmas*

▶

D

♀ English & French **V** ✿ ♨ ⚲ Lunch £12.50-£15.50&alc High tea £2.20-£3.95alc Dinner £16.95-£18.95&alc Last dinner 9.30pm
Credit Cards ① ② ③ ⑤ ⑥

---

### DEDHAM Essex Map **05** TM03

# ★★★

**★★★ ♨ MAISON TALBOOTH**

Stratford Rd CO7 6HN
(Pride of Britain)
☎Colchester(0206)322367
Telex no 987083
FAX (0206) 322752
*Gerald Milsom's long-established hotel enjoys a secluded position overlooking the village and will most easily be found by following signs from the A12 to Stratford St Mary. Meals, apart from breakfast, are not served in the hotel itself, but transport is available to take diners to the Maison Talbooth, well-known for its fine cuisine, or there is a Rotisserie in nearby Dedham Vale or yet another Milson venture, the Pier Restaurant in Harwich. Guests who decide to stay put in the hotel can have a range of snacks and drinks comfortably served in their room. There is also an elegant lounge and one of the chief virtues of staying here is the experience of peace and privacy.*
10⇨♠(1fb) CTV in all bedrooms **T** ✹ ✳
sB&B⇨♠£80-£105
dB&B⇨♠£100-£135 Continental breakfast
12P ⇗ ✿ croquet
**V** S10% Lunch £16&alc Dinner £26-£33alc Last dinner 9.30pm
Credit Cards ① ③

---

✿×××Le **Talbooth** CO7 6HP ☎Colchester(0206)323150
Telex no 987083 FAX (0206) 322752
*Since joining the Talbooth team in January 1988 from Le Meridien in Piccadilly, chef Steven Blake has put this famous restaurant back on the rails with his fine cuisine. The timber-framed house has undergone change too, and a sympathetic extension now runs along the bank of the River Stour. The menu features both tried and tested dishes and some innovative ideas, with a leaning towards flavours from the Far East. Vegetables have been disappointing, but sauces are generally good. A sherry vinegar sauce with a pithivier of sweetbreads was excellent, and canon of lamb with truffle-juice sauce also impressed.*
♀ English & French **V** 70 seats ✳ Lunch fr£16&alc Dinner £26-£33alc Last lunch 2pm Last dinner 9pm 40P
Credit Cards ① ③

---

### DEGANWY Gwynedd Map **06** SH77

**★★66% Bryn Cregin Garden** Ty Mawr Rd LL31 9UR (Exec Hotel) ☎(0492)585266
Closed Jan
*Standing in its own grounds overlooking the Conwy Estuary this warm comfortable and well furnished hotel was once the home of a successful sea captain.*
16⇨♠ CTV in all bedrooms ⑧ **T** ✹ ✳ sB&B⇨♠£44-£58
dB&B⇨♠£54-£76 ₱
30P ⇗ ✿
♀ International **V** ✿ ♨ ⚲ Dinner fr£14.50&alc Last dinner 9pm
Credit Cards ① ③

---

### DERBY Derbyshire Map **08** SK33

**★★★68% Crest** Pasture Hill, Littleover DE3 7BA (Trusthouse Forte) ☎(0332)514933 Telex no 377081 FAX (0332) 518668
*Located adjacent to the junction of the A5250 and B5019 at Littleover on the southern edge of the city. Management and staff provide polite and friendly service to complement the consistently good accommodation.*
66⇨Annexe2⇨♠⚲in 21 bedrooms CTV in 66 bedrooms ⑧ **T**
⟨ 250P
♀ International **V** ✿ ♨ ⚲
Credit Cards ① ② ③ ④ ⑤

**★★★61% International** Burton Rd (A5250) DE3 6AD (Consort) ☎(0332)369321 Telex no 377759 FAX (0332) 294430
*Situated on the A5250 the hotel has extremely well-equipped bedrooms and a restaurant that offers extensive menus. Speciality evenings are a feature.*
41⇨♠Annexe10⇨♠(2fb) CTV in all bedrooms ⑧ **T** S%
sB⇨♠£25-£70 dB⇨♠£35-£80 (room only) ₱
Lift ⟨ 70P gymnasium ♫ *xmas*
♀ English & Continental **V** ✿ ♨ S% Lunch £6.95-£7.50 High tea £5-£7 Dinner £11.50-£12.80 Last dinner 10.30pm
Credit Cards ① ② ③ ⑤ ⑥

**★★★61% Midland** Midland Rd DE1 2SQ ☎(0332)45894
Telex no 378373 FAX (0332) 293522
Closed 25-26 Dec & 1 Jan
*This busy commercial hotel is located next to the railway station and has conference rooms of various sizes. To the rear is a garden with mature trees and a patio area.*
60⇨♠1 ▦ CTV in all bedrooms ⑧ **T** sB&B⇨♠£57.50-£74
dB&B⇨♠£69.50-£86 ₱
⟨ 95P 15✿ CFA ♫
♀ English & French **V** ✿ ♨ Lunch £9.50-£22.50alc Dinner £11.50-£17.50 Last dinner 10pm
Credit Cards ① ② ③ ⑤

**★★70% Kedleston** Kedleston Rd, Quarndon DE6 4JD (3m NW) ☎(0332)559202 & 556507 FAX (0332) 558822
*Dating from the mid 18th century, Kedleston Country House Hotel stands in open countryside 3 miles north-west of Derby. The hotel is being upgraded, but retains its Georgian character. Staff are friendly and attentive.*
14⇨♠1 ▦ CTV in all bedrooms ⑧ **T** ✹ sB&B⇨♠£39-£43
dB&B⇨♠£51-£64
120P ⇗ ♫
♀ English & French **V** ✿ ♨ Sunday Lunch £9.50 Dinner £9.50-£11&alc Last dinner 9.15pm
Credit Cards ① ② ③ ④ ⑤ ⑥

---

### DESBOROUGH Northamptonshire Map **04** SP88

○**Travelodge** A6 Southbound, Harborough Rd(Trusthouse Forte) ☎Central reservations (0800) 850950
Due to have opened summer 1990
32⇨

---

### DEVIZES Wiltshire Map **04** SU06

**★★★61% Bear** Market Place SN10 1HS ☎(0380)722444
Closed 25-26 Dec
*Dating from the 16th century, this popular former coaching inn has recently been upgraded and provides comfortable, well-equipped bedrooms. An attractive restaurant offers table d'hôte and à la carte menus and there is also a grill room restaurant and comfortable lounge. Service is friendly and attentive.*
24⇨♠(5fb)3 ▦ CTV in all bedrooms ⑧ **T** S% sB&B⇨♠£35-£45
dB&B⇨♠£60-£75 ₱
CTV 25P (50p) ✿ (£1)
**V** ✿ ♨ ⚲ Lunch fr£10.95&alc Dinner £14-£15&alc Last dinner 10pm
Credit Cards ① ③ ⑥

★★66% **Castle** New Park St SN10 1DS ☎(0380)729300
FAX (0380) 729155
Closed 26 Dec
*This former coaching inn, dating back to the 1760s, is at the centre
of this bustling Wiltshire market town. Bedrooms are comfortable
and well equipped and the bar is popular with locals. An extensive
selection of bar food is available and Squires Restaurant (closed
on Sunday evenings) serves both table d'hôte and grill menus.
There is a small first-floor no-smoking lounge.*
18⇋♠ CTV in all bedrooms ® T ✳ sB&B⇋♠fr£38
dB&B⇋♠fr£51
4🚗
V ❦ ⚗ Lunch fr£10 Dinner fr£10 Last dinner 9.45pm
Credit Cards ①②③⑤

---

**DINAS MAWDDWY** Gwynedd Map **06** SH81

★★61% *Buckley Pines* SY20 9LP ☎(06504)261
Closed Nov-Jan
*The family-run hotel provides comfortable accommodation and
specialises in vegetarian dishes. Its setting in the Dovey Valley is
particularly picturesque.*
12rm(3⇋2♠)(1fb) CTV in all bedrooms ®
40P 🚗 ✿ ✔
Last dinner 9pm
Credit Cards ①③

---

**DINNINGTON** South Yorkshire Map **08** SK58

★★★67% *Dinnington Hall* Falcon Way S31 3NY
☎Worksop(0909)569661 FAX (0909)563411
*A 17th-century building of architectural and historical interest,
Dinnington Hall is located in a quiet residential area. Run in
country house style, it is distinguished by its interesting restaurant
menu.*
10⇋♠(2fb)1🛏 CTV in all bedrooms ®
《 60P 🚗 ✿
🍽 French ❦ ⚗ ✄
Credit Cards ①②③

---

**DISLEY** Cheshire Map **07** SJ98

★★★62% **Moorside** Mudhurst Ln, Higher Disley SK12 2AP
(Best Western) ☎(0663)64151 Telex no 665170
FAX (0663) 62794
*An extensive leisure complex has now opened to complement the
other amenities at this extended hotel, which is set amidst open
moorland.*
96rm(95⇋♠)(2fb)1🛏 CTV in all bedrooms ® T
sB⇋♠£75-£78 dB⇋♠£95-£98 (room only) 🍴
《 250P ✿ CFA ▨(heated) ▶ 9 squash snooker sauna solarium
gymnasium
🍽 English & French V ❦ ⚗ Lunch £10-£15&alc Dinner
£16-£20&alc Last dinner 10pm
Credit Cards ①②③⑤ⓔ

---

**DISS** Norfolk Map **05** TM18

✗✗**Salisbury House** 84 Victoria Rd IP22 3JG ☎(0379)644738
*In an attractively refurbished Victorian home, Barry and Sue
Davies offer well-cooked food in the light, modern style with the
imaginative use of fresh ingredients. In addition to the elegant
dining room there are two comfortable lounges. Two attractive
bedrooms with en suite facilities are also available.*
Closed Sun & Mon, 1wk Xmas & 2wks Summer
Lunch not served Sat
🍽 British & French 34 seats Lunch fr£11&alc Dinner
£18-£25alc Last lunch 1.45pm Last dinner 9.15pm 10P ✄
Credit Cards ①③

---

**DOLGELLAU** Gwynedd Map **06** SH71

★★67% **George III Hotel** Penmaenpool LL40 1QD
☎(0341)422525 FAX (0341) 423565
Closed 24 Dec-7 Jan RS May Day
*A friendly, informal hotel set on the banks of the Mawddach
estuary complements the accommodation in the main building with
quality bedrooms in a lodge that was once part of a railway
station.*
6rm(5⇋3♠)Annexe6⇋3♠ CTV in all bedrooms ® T ✳ S10%
dB&B£44-£46 dB&B⇋♠£77-£88 🍴
100P 🚗 ✿ ✔
🍽 Welsh, English & French V ❦ S10% Sunday Lunch fr£7.50
Dinner £12-£28alc Last dinner 8.45pm
Credit Cards ①②③

---

★★64% **Royal Ship** Queens Square LL40 1AR (Frederic
Robinson) ☎(0341)422209
*A coaching inn built at the beginning of the nineteenth century and
set at the very centre of the town has been improved to create some
beautifully furnished bedrooms and attractive public areas.*
24rm(13⇋3♠) CTV in all bedrooms ® ✖ (ex guide dogs) ✳
sB&B£15.75 sB&B⇋♠£26 dB&B£31.50 dB&B⇋♠£52 🍴
Lift CTV 8P *xmas*
V ❦ ⚗ Lunch £6 Dinner £10.50 Last dinner 9pm
Credit Cards ①③⑤

*See advertisement on page 249*

---

★★63% **Dolserau Hall** LL40 2AG (Minotels) ☎(0341)422522
*Standing in its own delightful grounds, this recently refurbished
Victorian building is surrounded by beautiful Welsh countryside.*
14rm(13⇋♠)(4fb) CTV in all bedrooms ® T sB&B£32.50
sB&B⇋♠£35 dB&B⇋♠£65 🍴
Lift 70P ✿ *xmas*

▶

# A friendly hotel with a host of facilities

Set in 19 acres of wooded grounds, overlooking
the sea and Exe estuary, this luxurious hotel has
64 centrally heated en suite bedrooms with
colour TV, radio, intercom, baby listening and
telephone. There are 3 bars, heated indoor and
outdoor pools, excellent food, air conditioned
restaurant, dancing and entertainment.

Cabaret weekends

It's terrific for kids and the beach is just 500
yards away. So too is an 18 hole golf course.

Free colour brochure from
Langstone Cliff Hotel, Dept AA.,
Dawlish, S. Devon, EX7 0NA
Tel: (0626) 865155
AA★★★          ETB 4 Crowns

V ♧ ⊈ Sunday Lunch fr£8.50 High tea fr£2.50 Dinner fr£15&alc Last dinner 8.30pm
Credit Cards [1] [3]

★63% **Clifton House** Smithfield Square LL40 1ES ☎(0341)422554
*At this attractive stone building in the centre of the town you can enjoy a meal in a basement restaurant which was once the local gaol – although the warm and friendly service offered by the resident owners creates a very different atmosphere today*
7rm(3⇌↱)(1fb) CTV in all bedrooms ® ✗ ✱ sB&B£16-£20 sB&B⇌↱£20-£24 dB&B£28-£32 dB&B⇌↱£36-£40 ⊟
3P ⇎
V ♧ ⊈ Lunch £5-£7.50alc Dinner £7-£12.50alc Last dinner 9.30pm
Credit Cards [1] [3] Ⓛ

## DOLPHINTON Strathclyde *Lanarkshire* Map **11** NT14

★★★♛64% **Dolphinton House** EH46 7AB ☎(0968)82286 FAX (0899) 20456
*Standing in 186 acres of parkland and woods, this 19th-century sandstone house has been carefully converted to provide up to date facilities while retaining many of its original Victorian features. Bedrooms and bathrooms are generally spacious and well equipped and the lounge is relaxing. The small bar boasts an extensive range of malt whiskies. A small team of staff provide informal but attentive service.*
12⇌↱(2fb)2⊞ CTV in all bedrooms ® T ✱ sB&B⇌↱fr£50 dB&B⇌↱£85-£115 ⊟
40P ⇎ ✲ croquet *xmas*
V ♧ ⊈ ⅟ Lunch £9.50-£13.50alc Dinner £24.95 Last dinner 9.30pm
Credit Cards [1] [2] [3] [4] [5] Ⓛ

## DOLWYDDELAN Gwynedd Map **06** SH75

★★64% **Elen's Castle** LL25 0EJ (Guestaccom) ☎(06906)207
Closed Oct-Mar
*Personal attention and friendly service are provided by a pleasant hotel in an attractive setting on the edge of the village.*
10rm(3⇌4↱)(1fb)1⊞⅟in 1 bedroom ® sB&B£16-£19 sB&B⇌↱£19-£32 dB&B£32-£38 dB&B⇌↱£40-£44
CTV 40P 3⌂(£1) ⇎ ✲ ♩ sauna ⛰
V ♧ ⊈ ⅟ Bar Lunch £2-£3.50 Dinner £7.90-£9.90 Last dinner 7pm

## DONCASTER South Yorkshire Map **08** SE50

★★★69% **Doncaster Moat House** Warmsworth DN4 9UX (2.5m SW on A630 at junc with A1) (Queens Moat) ☎(0302)310331 Telex no 547963 FAX (0302) 310197
*Situated at Warmsworth on the A630 with easy access to the A1 (M) and the M18. The hotel is attractively decorated and management provide food, service and hospitality of a high standard. There is ample car parking space and comfortable accommodation. The hotel also has extensive banquet facilities, both in the main building and in the adjoining Warmsworth Hall.*
70⇌↱⅟in 10 bedrooms CTV in all bedrooms ® T ⊟
☾ 200P ✲
☋ French V ♧ ⊈ ⅟
Credit Cards [1] [2] [3] [4] [5]

★★★64% **Mount Pleasant** Great North Rd DN11 0HP ☎(0302)868696 & 868219 FAX (0302) 865130
(For full entry see Rossington)

★★★55% **Danum Swallow** High St DN1 1DN (Swallow) ☎(0302)342261 Telex no 547533 FAX (0302) 329034
*This town centre hotel has new meeting rooms which are popular with the business community, and the comfortable Danum Lounge is frequented by guests and non-residents alike. The first floor bar and restaurant were refurbished during 1990.*
66⇌↱(2fb)1⊞⅟in 20 bedrooms CTV in all bedrooms ® T ✱ sB&B⇌↱£59 dB&B⇌↱£74 ⊟
Lift ☾ 60P 25⌂ CFA *xmas*
V ♧ ⊈ Lunch £6.95-£7.95 Dinner fr£12.50 Last dinner 9.45pm
Credit Cards [1] [2] [3] [4] [5]

★★68% **Regent** Regent Square DN1 2DS ☎(0302)364180 & 364336 Telex no 54480 FAX (0302) 322331
Closed 25 Dec & 1 Jan RS Bank Hols
*Refurbishment and alterations of two of the three bars took place during 1990 as part of a continual upgrading process. Returning guests list highly the 'comfortable and relaxed atmosphere' as an important asset.*
35⇌↱(2fb)2⊞ CTV in all bedrooms ® T ✱ sB&B⇌↱£35.50-£47.50 dB&B⇌↱£42.50-£57.50 ⊟
Lift ☾ 20P sauna
☋ English & French V ♧ ⊈ Lunch £3.95-£9.50 Dinner £9.50&alc Last dinner 10pm
Credit Cards [1] [2] [3] [4] [5] Ⓛ

⌂ ***Campanile*** Doncaster Leisure Park, Bawtry Rd DN4 7PD (Campanile) ☎(0302)370770 Telex no 547942
*A hotel standing close to the racecourse in an extensive leisure park.*
48⇌↱ CTV in all bedrooms ® T
56P
☋ English & French Last dinner 10pm
Credit Cards [1] [3]

## DONNINGTON

See **Telford**

## DORCHESTER Dorset Map **03** SY69

★★★71% ***King's Arms*** DT1 1HF (Exec Hotel) ☎(0305)65353 FAX (0305) 60269
*This sympathetically modernised 18th-century coaching inn provides a focal point for local residents and offers comfortable, well appointed and equipped accommodation in tastefully furnished bedrooms. Public areas are good, with a choice of two restaurants.*
31⇌(1fb) CTV in all bedrooms ®
Lift 36P ⇎
♧ ⊈ ⅟ Last dinner 8.30pm
Credit Cards [1] [2] [3]

**See advertisement on page 251**

## DORCHESTER-ON-THAMES Oxfordshire Map **04** SU59

★★★70% **White Hart** High St OX9 8HN ☎Oxford(0865)340074 FAX (0865) 341082
*This well-established and personally-run 17th-century coaching inn has particularly well furnished and individually styled bedrooms offering a high standard of comfort. The cosy, intimate public rooms are also comfortable, and tempting, well prepared food is available in the two restaurants.*
20⇌↱(2fb)2⊞ CTV in all bedrooms ® T ✗ (ex guide dogs) ✱ S10% sB&B⇌↱£60-£65 dB&B⇌↱£85-£90 ⊟
CTV 25P ⇎
☋ English & French V ♧ ⅟ Lunch £11&alc Dinner £15-£25alc Last dinner 9pm
Credit Cards [1] [2] [3] [5]

**See advertisement on page 251**

★★65% ***George*** High St OX9 8HH ☎Oxford(0865)340404 Telex no 83147
Closed 1 wk Xmas
*Reputedly one of the oldest coaching inns in England, the hotel offers a warm, friendly atmosphere and comfortable, well-appointed bedrooms which retain much of the building's original charm. The slightly more modern style of the dining room complements the delightful architectural character of the other* ▶

# The Campanile Hotel Doncaster

Part of the international budget hotel chain 'Campanile' the hotel offers 50 bedrooms. Comfortable double or twin rooms with en suite bathrooms, tea and coffee making facilities, radio alarm, remote control colour TV and direct dial telephone at competitive rates.

Our informal restaurant provides a variety of home cooked English & Continental cuisine and personal service at affordable prices.

Our seminar room is available for business meeting or small functions.

**Doncaster Leisure Park,
Bawtry Road, Doncaster, S Yorks
Telephone: (0302) 370770
Telex: 547942**

**Restaurant
Hotel**

Campanile

---

# Dolserau Hall HOTEL ★★

A warm welcome awaits you where your comfort and enjoyment are our main concern. The hotel stands in 5 acres of Snowdonia National Park amidst mountains and meadows outside Dolgellau providing an ideal centre for walking, riding or touring. With its full central heating, comfortable lounges, spacious bedrooms and excellent food, it offers an ideal escape throughout the year. Fishing is available at no extra charge on the Wnion, Mawddach and Lyn Cynwch. Marion and Peter Kaye look forward to meeting you!

Dolgellau, Gwynedd, Wales LL40 2AG.
Telephone: Dolgellau (0341) 422522

**D**

---

# Mount Pleasant Hotel
## and Restaurant ★★★
**Old Great North Road (A638)
Nr Rossington, Doncaster, S. Yorks
Tel: (0302) 868696 Fax: (0302) 865130**

Charming Country House in delightful rural setting. Only 5m from Doncaster Racecourse – Exhibition Centre. Bloodstock Sales. Excellent base for touring the Dukeries (Robin Hood) Lincoln – York – Pilgrim Father and John Wesley country. Accommodation for business executives and travellers. Licensed Restaurant – Buffet Lounge – Private Rooms –Conference/Party suite. Weddings. Stables. Kennels. Free Parking.
*Owned and managed by this family since 1939.*
**BROCHURE UPON REQUEST**

---

# ROYAL SHIP HOTEL ★★
Queens Square, Dolgellau, Gwynedd.
Telephone Dolgellau 0341 422209

Family Rooms
Colour TV in Bedrooms
Ideally situated for touring North & Mid Wales
Great Little Trains of Wales
Slate Mines at Blaenau
Pony Trekking
Golf
Robinson's Traditional Draught Beer
Access and Barclaycard accepted
Colour Brochure on request

public areas, and the dishes served there – ranging from a
Mousseline of Cornish Seafood on a Langoustine Sauce to a Peach
Cheese-cake with White Chocolate and Orange – are of a high
quality.
9⇨♠Annexe8⇨♠2⊞ CTV in all bedrooms ®
CTV 60P ⏍ ✲
♵ English & French V ♦ ⅄ Last dinner 9.45pm
Credit Cards ①②③⑤

---

**DORKING** Surrey Map **04** TQ14

★★★★65% **The Burford Bridge** Burford Bridge, Box Hill
RH5 6BX (2m NE A24) (Trusthouse Forte) ☎(0306)884561
Telex no 859507 FAX (0306) 880386
Set amidst beautiful gardens on the banks of the River Mole, this
hotel was a fashionable rendezvous for country weekends as far
back as the 18th century. It continues to offer a warm welcome and
comfortable accommodation in well-equipped bedrooms, many of
which have been refurbished. Service is well executed by pleasant,
courteous and friendly staff.
48⇨⅄in 16 bedrooms CTV in all bedrooms ® T ✱ sB⇨fr£87
dB⇨fr£105 (room only) ♬
《 100P ✲ CFA ➘(heated) xmas
♵ English & French V ♦ ⅃ ⅄ Lunch fr£15 High tea fr£3.95
Dinner fr£18.50 Last dinner 10pm
Credit Cards ①②③④⑤

★★★56% **The White Horse** High St RH4 1BE (Trusthouse
Forte) ☎(0306)881138 FAX (0306) 887241
Centrally situated, this 16th-century coaching inn retains some of
the old world atmosphere alongside the modern facilities expected
in a well equipped hotel with annexe bedrooms. Space is somewhat
restricted in the bar lounges and restaurant, and service can be
slow at times. An extensive range of air-conditioned conference
and meeting facilities are available.
36⇨♠Annexe32⇨(1fb)1⊞⅄in 20 bedrooms CTV in all
bedrooms ® T ✱ sB⇨♠£70-£86
dB⇨♠£86-£95 (room only) ♬
《 73P ➘(heated) xmas
V ♦ ⅃ ⅄ Lunch £10-£13&alc Dinner £15&alc Last dinner
9.30pm
Credit Cards ①②③④⑤

⏚**Travelodge** A25, Reigate Rd RH4 1QB (on A25) (Trusthouse
Forte) ☎(0306)740251 Reservations 0800 850 950
The consistently good, carefully maintained, modest
accommodation provided by this purpose-built lodge represents
value for money – all its well equipped bedrooms offering en suite
facilities and meals being available in an adjacent restaurant.
29⇨♠(29fb) CTV in all bedrooms ® sB⇨♠£24
dB⇨♠£29.50 (room only)
《 29P ⏍
Credit Cards ①②③

**Partners West Street** 2–4 West St RH4 1BL ☎(0306)882826
The new premises of Partners 23 of Sutton, and run along the same
lines by Tim McEntire and Andrew Thomason.
Lunch not served Sat
Dinner not served Sun
♵ English/French 45 seats

---

**DORNIE** Highland Ross & Cromarty Map **14** NG82

★★56% **Castle Inn** IV40 8DT ☎(059985)205
RS Jan (ex New Year) & Feb
This small family-run village inn is conveniently situated on the
main tourist route to the Isle of Skye, close to Eilean Donan
Castle. It has a friendly atmosphere and recent refurbishment has
provided comfortable, modern standards of accommodation.
12rm(1⇨6♠)(1fb) CTV in all bedrooms ® ✱ sB&B£22-£27
sB&B⇨♠£27 dB&B£44 dB&B⇨♠£54 ♬
20P ⏍ ✲ xmas
♦ ⅃ Lunch fr£8
Credit Cards ①③

---

**DORNOCH** Highland Sutherland Map **14** NH78

★★★53% **Royal Golf** Grange Rd IV25 3LG ☎(0862)810283
Telex no 75300
Closed 27 Oct-22 Mar
Set in its own grounds overlooking the famous links course this
popular golfing hotel is enjoying widespread upgrading with
bedrooms already substantially improved and refurbishment of the
public areas planned.
24⇨♠Annexe8⇨(2fb) CTV in 31 bedrooms ® T
✕ (ex guide dogs)
《 30P ✲
♵ Scottish & Continental ♦ ⅃
Credit Cards ①②③⑤ⓔ

★★60% **Dornoch Castle** Castle St IV25 3SD (Inter-Hotels)
☎(0862)810216
Closed Nov-mid Apr
This hotel is located in the town centre and is popular as a base for
golfers and tourists. It has lounges with comfortable furnishings
and an appealing cocktail bar. The best bedrooms are in the older
part of the castle, those in the wing being modern and practical in
style.
17⇨♠(4fb) CTV in 4 bedrooms ® T sB&B⇨♠£30-£32
dB&B⇨♠£52-£68 ♬
Lift CTV 16P ⏍ ✲
♵ Scottish & Continental V ♦ ⅃ ⅄ Sunday Lunch fr£5alc
Dinner fr£14.50 Last dinner 8.30pm
Credit Cards ①②③

All AA-appointed establishments are
inspected regularly to ensure that required
standards are maintained.

**ROYAL GOLF HOTEL DORNOCH**

Standing on the famous Royal Dornoch Golf
Course ranked among the leading ten courses
in the world. Well-appointed rooms with
Colour TV and Direct-Dial telephone, etc.
An excellent restuarant and a cordial welcome
in superb highland scenery await you. *Inclusive
Midweek & Weekend Golf Holidays available.
Parties welcome.*
*For reservations and further details
please phone:*                           *AA*★★★
**Tel: (0862) 810283**
**Telex: 75300**

### DORRINGTON Shropshire Map **07** SJ40

**✗✗Country Friends Restaurants** SY5 7JD ☎(074373)707
*The restaurant forms part of a most attractive black and white timbered house which is set above the A49 at the centre of the village. Produce from local farms and game are very prominent in its menus, but fish and home-made pasta are equally well presented in light modern style. Vegetables are particularly interesting, the method of preparation really exploiting their flavours. A modestly priced wine list offers a wide choice which includes a good selection of half bottles.*
Closed Sun & Mon, 5 days Xmas, 1 wk Feb, 2 wks end Jul & 2 wks Oct
40 seats ✻ Lunch £15&alc Dinner £15&alc Last lunch 2pm Last dinner 9pm 30P
Credit Cards ⒈ ⒉ ⒊

### DOUGLAS

See **Man, Isle of**

### DOVER Kent Map **05** TR34

**★★★64%, Crest** Singledge Ln, Whitfield CT16 3LF (3m NW junc A2/A256) (Trusthouse Forte) ☎(0304)821222
Telex no 965866 FAX (0304) 825576
RS 23-27 Dec
*A hotel in modern style combines warm hospitality with a friendly atmosphere. Bedrooms are well appointed and equipped, Le Jardin restaurant offers a selection of well chosen dishes, and guests can take their ease in either the comfortable foyer lounge or an attractive conservatory-style bar.*
67⇪🉐(15fb)⊁in 13 bedrooms CTV in all bedrooms ⓡ T ✖ (ex guide dogs)
⑆75P ✻
♈ International V ✿ ⚼ ⊁
Credit Cards ⒈ ⒉ ⒊ ⒋ ⒌

**★★★54%, White Cliffs** Marine Pde, (Waterloo Crescent) CT17 9BW ☎(0304)203633 Telex no 965422 FAX (0304) 216320
Closed 24-26 Dec
*This long established hotel, old fashioned and traditionally furnished, offers a choice of bedrooms, those at the front having uninterrupted sea views. Public areas include a small lounge, bar, restaurant with verandah and a room which can be made available for conferences.*
54⇪🉐(6fb) CTV in all bedrooms ⓡ T sB&B⇪🉐£50-£56 dB&B⇪🉐£70-£80 ☲
Lift ⑆ CTV 25🛆 (£1 per night)
✿ ⚼ Sunday Lunch fr£7.50 Dinner £8-£11&alc Last dinner 9.30pm
Credit Cards ⒈ ⒉ ⒊ ⒋ ⒌ ⓔ

### DOWNHAM MARKET Norfolk Map **05** TF60

**★★56%, Castle** High St PE38 9HF ☎(0366)384311
Telex no 817787 FAX (0366) 384770
*A 300-year-old coaching inn, standing in the centre of this market town, which is described as the gateway to Norfolk, offers rooms which are well equipped though modestly decorated and furnished. Meals are freshly prepared and enjoyable.*
11rm(4⇪5🉐)2☷ CTV in all bedrooms ⓡ T ✱ S10% sB&B£30 sB&B⇪🉐£33 dB&B£39 dB&B⇪🉐£42 ☲
⑆30P 1🛆 xmas
♈ English & Continental V ✿ ⚼ ⊁ S10% Lunch fr£8.50&alc Dinner fr£9.90&alc Last dinner 9pm
Credit Cards ⒈ ⒉ ⒊ ⒌ ⓔ

**★57%, Crown** Bridge St PE38 9DH ☎(0366)382322
*This hotel, located in the town centre, dates back to the 17th century. There are good facilities in the bedrooms and well-prepared food and real ales can be enjoyed here.*
10rm(5⇪2🉐) CTV in 7 bedrooms ⓡ T ✱ sB&Bfr£24 sB&B⇪🉐fr£32 dB&Bfr£34 dB&B⇪🉐fr£42 ☲

CTV 30P
V ✿ ⚼ Lunch £6-£13&alc High tea £1.90&alc Dinner £6-£13&alc Last dinner 9.45pm
Credit Cards ⒈ ⒉ ⒊ ⒌ ⓔ

### DOWN THOMAS Devon Map **02** SX55

**★★58%, Langdon Court** PL9 0DY ☎(0752)862358
FAX (0752) 863428
*Modernised Elizabethan mansion on an unclassified road between Wembury and Down Thomas.*
15⇪🉐(3fb) CTV in all bedrooms ⓡ T sB&B⇪🉐£31-£42 dB&B⇪🉐£42-£57 ☲
100P ✻ pool room nc5yrs
♈ French V ✿ ⚼ S% Sunday Lunch fr£8alc Dinner fr£13.50&alc Last dinner 9.30pm
Credit Cards ⒈ ⒉ ⒊ ⒌

### DRAYCOTT Derbyshire Map **08** SK43

**★★★56%, Tudor Court** Gypsy Ln DE7 3PB (Best Western) ☎(03317)4581 Telex no 377313 FAX (03317) 3133
*Standing in 8 acres of grounds, this modern hotel, built in traditional style, offers good conference facilities. There is also a popular night club within the complex.*
30⇪🉐(8fb) CTV in all bedrooms ⓡ
⑆300P ✻
♈ English & French V ✿ ⚼ Last dinner 10pm
Credit Cards ⒈ ⒉ ⒊ ⒌

### DRIFFIELD, GREAT Humberside Map **08** TA05

**★★★67%, Bell** 46 Market Place YO25 7AP (Best Western) ☎Driffield(0377)46661 Telex no 52341 FAX (0377) 87698 (due to change to 43228)
*The Bell Hotel is a coaching inn that has been carefully modernised to preserve the historic character and atmosphere. Accommodation is comfortable with appealing décor.*
14⇪2🉐 CTV in all bedrooms ⓡ T ✖ (ex guide dogs) sB&B⇪🉐£54-£59.50 dB&B⇪🉐£75-£82.50 ☲
⑆50P ✻ ▣(heated) squash snooker sauna solarium gymnasium steam room whirlpool masseur nc12yrs xmas
V ✿ ⚼ ⊁ Sunday Lunch fr£6.95 High tea £4-£6 Dinner £12-£15alc Last dinner 9.30pm
Credit Cards ⒈ ⒉ ⒊ ⒌

**★★⚑60%, Wold House Country** Nafferton YO25 0LD (3m E A166) ☎Driffield(0377)44242
Closed 24-27 Dec
*Georgian-style country house with rural views.*
11rm(7⇪3🉐)Annexe1🉐(4fb) CTV in all bedrooms ⓡ sB&B£30 sB&B⇪🉐£36 dB&B£42 dB&B⇪🉐£52 CTV 40P ✻ ▵(heated) snooker putting table tennis V ✿ Lunch £6.75-£7.25 Dinner £12.50-£15 Last dinner 8.30pm
Credit Cards ⒈ ⒊ ⓔ

### DROITWICH Hereford & Worcester Map **03** SO86

**★★★★70%, Château Impney** WR9 0BN ☎(0905)774411
Telex no 336673 FAX (0905) 772371
Closed Xmas
*In the style of a French château, this beautiful and elegant hotel was built as a private house in the mid-19th century and stands in extensive landscaped parkland. Popular with a wide variety of guests, it offers good attentive service, well-equipped bedrooms and many other attributes. It also offers arguably the best conference, function and exhibition facilities in the country, certainly in the Midlands.*
67⇪🉐(1fb)1☷ CTV in all bedrooms T ✱
sB⇪🉐£39.95-£89.95 dB⇪🉐£49.95-£99.95 (room only)
Lift ⑆ CTV 600P ✻ CFA ♟ (hard)

♥ English & French **V** ✿ ⚓ Lunch £9.99-£10.99&alc Dinner £10.99-£15.99&alc Last dinner 9.30pm
Credit Cards ① ② ③ ⑤

★★★★66% **Raven** Saint Andrews St WR9 8DU
☎(0905)772224 Telex no 336673 FAX (0905) 772371
Closed Xmas
*Situated close to the centre of town, and within a few minutes drive of junction 5 of the M5, this hotel offers friendly and attentive service by a professional team of staff. Extensive conference and function facilities make this one of the most popular conference venues in the Midlands. Bedrooms continued to be upgraded throughout 1990.*
50⇆📞(2fb) CTV in all bedrooms **T** ✳ sB⇆📞£39.95-£89.95 dB⇆📞£49.95-£99.95 (room only)
Lift ℂ CTV 250P ✿ CFA
♥ English & French ✿ ⚓ Lunch £9.99-£10.99&alc Dinner £10.99-£15.99&alc Last dinner 9.30pm
Credit Cards ① ② ③ ⑤

🏠**Travelodge** A38, Rashwood Hill WR9 8DA (on A38)
(Trusthouse Forte)
☎Wychbold(052786)545 Reservations 0800 850 950
*Standing beside the A58, one mile north of the town centre and a hundred yards north of junction 5 of the M5, this lodge offers the usual good-value bedroom accommodation with meals available at the on-site Little Chef.*
32⇆📞(32fb) CTV in all bedrooms ℝ sB⇆📞£24 dB⇆📞£29.50 (room only)
ℂ 32P 🏕
Credit Cards ① ② ③

For key to symbols see the inside front cover.

# White Cliffs Hotel

Sea Front, Dover 🏆🏆🏆🏆    AA ★ ★ ★
Telephone Dover (0304) 203633
Telex 965422 Fax (0304) 216320

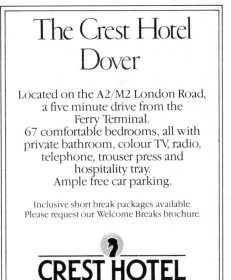

This renowned hotel, situated on the Sea Front in quiet location, close to Eastern and Western Docks, Hoverport and Jetfoil, offers first-class service and true comfort. Fully Licensed with Bar and Restaurant overlooking Harbour. Well-appointed bedrooms, all with private bathrooms, are fitted with colour television, radios, direct dial telephone and tea and coffee-making facilities. Charges are reasonable and the hotel is admirably suited to the needs of cross Channel travellers and for those wishing to explore the many tourist attractions in this part of south east England. A warm welcome awaits you at the White Cliffs Hotel.

# ℂudor Court Hotel ★★★

GYPSY LANE, DRACOTT, DERBYS DE7 3PB
Tel: Draycott (03317) 4581 (10 lines)
Telex: 377313 TUDOR Fax: 03317-3133

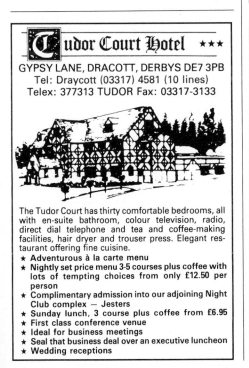

The Tudor Court has thirty comfortable bedrooms, all with en-suite bathroom, colour television, radio, direct dial telephone and tea and coffee-making facilities, hair dryer and trouser press. Elegant restaurant offering fine cuisine.
★ Adventurous à la carte menu
★ Nightly set price menu 3-5 courses plus coffee with lots of tempting choices from only £12.50 per person
★ Complimentary admission into our adjoining Night Club complex — Jesters
★ Sunday lunch, 3 course plus coffee from £6.95
★ First class conference venue
★ Ideal for business meetings
★ Seal that business deal over an executive luncheon
★ Wedding receptions

# The Crest Hotel Dover

Located on the A2/M2 London Road, a five minute drive from the Ferry Terminal.
67 comfortable bedrooms, all with private bathroom, colour TV, radio, telephone, trouser press and hospitality tray.
Ample free car parking.

Inclusive short break packages available.
Please request our Welcome Breaks brochure.

# CREST HOTEL
===DOVER===

Whitfield, Dover
Kent CT16 3LF    ★★★
Tel: (0304) 821222
Telex: 965866. Fax: (0304) 825576

**DRONFIELD** Derbyshire Map **08** SK37

★★60%, *Chantry* Church St S18 6QB ☎(0246)413014
*A small residential hotel, set in reasonably peaceful surroundings and having a well-tended garden that is the owner's pride and joy during the summer months, offers a friendly, caring atmosphere and very clean accommodation with quality soft furnishisngs and modern bathrooms, though a few bedrooms are compact.*
7⇨ CTV in all bedrooms
CTV 28P
Last dinner 8pm

★★53%, **Manor** 10 High St S18 6PY ☎(0246)413971
RS Sun evenings
*A small, proprietor-run hotel, situated in Old Dronfield, and dating from the 16th and 18th centuries. The hotel reflects a period atmosphere with a beamed lounge bar and stylish restaurant, the latter offering good à la carte and daily menus.*
10⇨(1fb) CTV in all bedrooms ® ✱
sB&B⇨£31.50-£42.50 dB&B⇨£38.75-£55.50 🗗
17P
♡ English & French V ♦ ⌂ Lunch £6.95&alc Dinner £12.50&alc Last dinner 10pm
Credit Cards ①②③⑤

**DRUMNADROCHIT** Highland *Inverness-shire* Map **14** NH52

★★♨67%, **Polmaily House** IV3 6XT ☎(04562)343
Closed Nov-Mar
*This small hotel, on the slopes of Glen Urquhart, is notable for its peaceful surroundings and comfortable accommodation. The nine bedrooms are individually decorated and furnished. Cooking is excellent, but choice on the set-price menu is limited.*
9rm(7⇨)(1fb)1🛏 ✖ (ex guide dogs) sB&B£40 dB&B⇨£90
CTV 25P ✿ ✱ ≙ ♪ (hard) croquet
✖ High tea £5-£7.50 Dinner fr£17.50 Last dinner 9.30pm
Credit Cards ①③

**DRYBRIDGE** Grampian *Banffshire* Map **15** NJ46

✖✖**The Old Monastery** AB5 2JB (1m E off Deskford Rd)
☎Buckie(0542)32660
*This popular country restaurant – once, as the name suggests, a monastery – enjoys lovely views to Spey Bay and the Murray coast from its setting on a hill. Game and seafood are prominent on an interesting menu which offers a tempting range of dishes competently prepared by chef/patron Douglas Grey who makes excellent use of the best fresh produce available locally, and a friendly staff provides attentive service.*
Closed Sun, Mon, 2 wks Nov, 3 days Xmas & 3 wks Jan
♡ Scottish & French 40 seats ✱ Lunch £7.55-£12.60alc Dinner £13.45-£17.95alc Last lunch 1.45pm Last dinner 9.30pm 20P nc8yrs ✖
Credit Cards ①②③

**DRYMEN** Central *Stirlingshire* Map **11** NS48

★★★65%, **Buchanan Highland** G63 0BQ (Scottish Highland)(Consort) ☎(0360)60588 Telex no 778215 FAX (0360)60943
*Originally a coaching inn, this village hotel has tastefully refurbished modern bedrooms, while the public rooms have a more traditional style of comfort and character.*
51⇨(3fb)1🛏 CTV in all bedrooms ® T sB&B⇨£60-£65 dB&B⇨£85-£95 🗗
⊄ 100P ✿ ▣(heated) squash sauna solarium gymnasium bowling green *xmas*
♡ Scottish & French V ♦ ⌂ Lunch fr£10 Dinner fr£16&alc Last dinner 9.30pm
Credit Cards ①②③④⑤

**DUDLEY** West Midlands Map **07** SO99
See also Himley

★★★61%, **Ward Arms** Birmingham Rd DY1 4RN (Crown & Raven) ☎(0384)458070 Telex no 335464
*A group hotel standing just across the road from Dudley Zoo offers convenient access to Birmingham because of its proximity to the M5. Major extension and refurbishment has provided modern accommodation, and Mrs Simpson's Carvery – popular with residents and non-residents alike – offers daily roasts in addition to an à la carte menu.*
48⇨ CTV in all bedrooms ® T ✱ sB&B⇨fr£56.65 dB&B⇨fr£71.50 🗗
⊄ 150P
♡ English & French V ♦ ≙ ⌂ ✖ Lunch £9-£15&alc Dinner fr£10 Last dinner 9.30pm
Credit Cards ①②③

★★60%, **Station** Birmingham Rd DY1 4RA (Crown & Raven) ☎(0384)253418 Telex no 335464 FAX (0384) 457503
*The hotel stands close to the town centre, opposite Dudley Zoo, and has ample car parking. Major refurbishment, now complete, has resulted in modern public rooms and well-appointed bedrooms.*
38⇨(7fb) CTV in all bedrooms ® T ✱ sB&B⇨fr£51.70 dB&B⇨fr£65.45 🗗
Lift ⊄ 75P *xmas*
♡ English & French V ♦ ⌂
Credit Cards ①②③

○**Travelodge** A461 Dudley Rd(Trusthouse Forte)
☎Central reservations (0800) 850950
32⇨

**DULNAIN BRIDGE** Highland *Morayshire* Map **14** NH92

★★♨67%, **Muckrach Lodge** PH26 3LY ☎(047985)257
*This privately owned and run small hotel, situated in an elevated position and surrounded by two well maintained grounds close to the Dulnain River, was once a hunting lodge. Today it offers comfortable, thoughtfully appointed rooms with smart modern bathrooms, a quiet, relaxing lounge and a cosy bar where interesting sandwiches are a lunchtime speciality. Its position makes it a good base for exploring the many activities available in the Spey Valley.*
10⇨(3fb) CTV in all bedrooms ® T ✖ (ex guide dogs) sB&B⇨fr£29.50 🗗
50P ✿ ✱ ♪
♡ British & French Lunch £5.50-£8.50alc Dinner £18.50 Last dinner 8.45pm
Credit Cards ①②③⑤

**DULVERTON** Somerset Map **03** SS92

★★★♨72%, **Carnarvon Arms** TA22 9AE (2m S on B3222)
☎(0398)23302 FAX (0398) 24022
Closed 8-29 Feb
*Set in 50 acres on the edge of Exmoor, this long-established hotel offers extensive outdoor sporting activities including shooting and fishing. Lovely lounges have log fires, the bedrooms are traditional in style, and service is warm and friendly.*
25rm(21⇨1♩)(2fb) CTV in all bedrooms T ✱ sB&B£43-£46 dB&B£80-£107 dB&B⇨£86-£114 (incl dinner) 🗗
120P ✿ ✱ ▢(heated) ♪ (hard) ♪ snooker clay pigeon shooting *xmas*
V ♦ ✱ ✖ Lunch fr£8.95&alc Dinner fr£15.75 Last dinner 8.30pm
Credit Cards ①③ ⓔ

1991 marks the 25th anniversary of this guide.

★★

 **ASHWICK HOUSE**

TA22 9QD (3m N W off
B3223) ☎(0398)23868

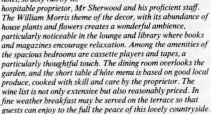

*The beauty of its location,
high on Exmoor, adds to the
charm of this Edwardian
hotel, so ably run by its
hospitable proprietor, Mr Sherwood and his proficient staff.
The William Morris theme of the decor, with its abundance of
house plants and flowers creates a wonderful ambience,
particularly noticeable in the lounge and library where books
and magazines encourage relaxation. Among the amenities of
the spacious bedrooms are cassette players and tapes, a
particularly thoughtful touch. The dining room overlooks the
garden, and the short table d'hôte menu is based on good local
produce, cooked with skill and care by the proprietor. The
wine list is not only extensive but also reasonably priced. In
fine weather breakfast may be served on the terrace so that
guests can enjoy to the full the peace of this lovely countryside.*

6⇄ CTV in all bedrooms ✖ sB&B⇄£58.50-£74.80
dB&B⇄£97-£129.60 (incl dinner) 🅱

25P 2🚗 (£2) ⊞ ❀ solarium nc8yrs *xmas*

♖ International ⊹ ⏢ ✔ Sunday Lunch fr£12.50 Dinner
fr£19.75 Last dinner 8.30pm

ⓔ

---

★★ **64%** **Lion** Bank Square TA22 9BW ☎(0398)23444
*Set on the edge of Exmoor, the Lion Hotel is believed to be at least
500 years old. It provides a good base for touring this lovely area,
and major renovations have resulted in 12 well-equipped en suite
bedrooms. Guests can choose to relax in the cosy residents' lounge,
the lounge bar or the popular tap bar.*
12⇄🌣(1fb)1⊞ CTV in all bedrooms Ⓡ T ✱
sB&B⇄🌣£25-£30 dB&B⇄🌣£50-£60 🅱
CTV 6P ⚊(heated) ♟ (hard) ♪ ∪ snooker clay pigeon
shooting ♫ *xmas*
V ⊹ ⏢ Lunch £7 Dinner £10.50 Last dinner 9pm
Credit Cards ① ③

---

**DUMBARTON** Strathclyde *Dunbartonshire* Map **10** NS37

★★ **69%** **Dumbuck** Glasgow Rd G82 1EG ☎(0389)34336
Telex no 778303
*Popular and friendly privately owned hotel in a converted 18th-
century house. Bedrooms have recently been refurbished to a good
standard and public areas offer character and style.*
22⇄🌣CTV in all bedrooms Ⓡ T ✱ sB&B⇄£38
dB&B⇄£50
⦅ 200P ❀ pool table
V ⊹ ⏢ Lunch £8&alc High tea £7 Dinner £10.25&alc Last
dinner 9.30pm
Credit Cards ① ② ③ ④ ⑤

⧨**Travelodge** A82, Milton G82 2TY (1m E) (Trusthouse Forte)
☎(0389)65202 Reservations 0800 850 950
*Positioned behind the Little Chef, this lodge is situated the north
side of the River Clyde 6 miles from Loch Lomond and 12 miles
from Glasgow.*
32⇄🌣(32fb) CTV in all bedrooms Ⓡ sB⇄🌣£24
dB⇄🌣£29.50 (room only)
⦅ 32P ⊞
Credit Cards ① ② ③

---

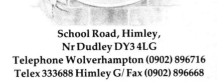

**DUMFRIES** Dumfries & Galloway *Dumfriesshire*
Map **11** NX97

See also Carrutherstown
★★★66% **Cairndale** English St DG1 2DF (Inter-Hotels)
☎(0387)54111 Telex no 777530 FAX (0387) 50555
*A traditional hotel with comfortable bedrooms, interesting good value menus and friendly service. Conveniently located very close to the town centre.*
60⇌♠(4fb) CTV in all bedrooms ® T S% sB&B⇌♠£30-£64 dB&B⇌♠£66-£94 ⊟
Lift ℂ CTV 70P *xmas*
♡ British & French V ✿ ⊒ S% Lunch £7 High tea fr£5 Dinner fr£12.95&alc Last dinner 9.30pm
Credit Cards ①②③④⑤ ⓔ

★★★64% **Station** 49 Lovers Walk DG1 1LT (Consort)
☎(0387)54316 Telex no 778654 FAX (0387) 50388
*Convenient for the station and the town centre, this hotel, dating from 1896, provides well equipped and attractively appointed bedrooms. There is a spacious lounge bar, and a small team of friendly staff provide good service in the comfortable restaurant.*
32⇌♠(1fb) CTV in all bedrooms ® T sB&B⇌♠£55-£65 dB&B⇌♠£70-£80 ⊟
Lift ℂ 40P
♡ British, Italian & Spanish V ✿ ⊒ Bar Lunch £2-£15alc High tea £6.50 Dinner £17.50 Last dinner 10pm
Credit Cards ①②③⑤ⓔ

★64% **Skyline** 123 Irish St DG1 2NS ☎(0387)62416
Closed 25 Dec & 1-2 Jan
*Right in the centre of town, but set in a quiet side street and conveniently provided with its own spacious car park, a friendly little hotel under the personal supervision of its proprietors offers modest but well decorated and efficiently maintained accommodation.*
6rm(2♠)(2fb) CTV in all bedrooms ® ✖
CTV 20P
V

**DUNBAR** Lothian *East Lothian* Map **12** NT67

★★66% **Redheugh** Bayswell Park EH42 1AE ☎(0368)62793
*Comfortable, well-appointed bedrooms, home-cooked meals and particularly friendly service are provided by an hotel quietly located in a residential area.*
10⇌♠(2fb) CTV in all bedrooms ® T ✱ sB&B⇌♠£35-£45 dB&B⇌♠£44-£55 ⊟
♪ ⊞
V ✿ Lunch £7.50-£10&alc Dinner £10&alc Last dinner 9pm
Credit Cards ①②③ⓔ

★★65% **Bayswell** Bayswell Park EH42 1AE (Exec Hotel)
☎(0368)62225
*A friendly atmosphere prevails at this comfortable sea-front hotel. It has cheery, well-equipped bedrooms, a cosy bar and a smart restaurant where good, wholesome food is served.*
13⇌♠(2fb) CTV in all bedrooms ® T sB&B⇌♠fr£36.30 dB&B⇌♠fr£54 ⊟
CTV 20P ✿ putting green *xmas*
V ✿ ⊒ Lunch fr£8.50 High tea fr£4.50 Dinner fr£12.50&alc Last dinner 9pm
Credit Cards ①②③ⓔ

**DUNBLANE** Central *Perthshire* Map **11** NN70

❀★★★ ⚐ **CROMLIX HOUSE**
Kinbuck FK15 9JT (3 m NE B8033) (Pride of Britain)
☎(0786)822125
Telex no 779959
FAX (0786) 825450
Closed 1-14 Feb
(Rosette awarded for dinner only)
*The stresses of the late 20th century seem very far away from this charming Victorian and Edwardian country house. The Edwardian conservatory has recently been restored, and makes a further attractive public area in addition to the fascinating library, comfortable morning room and spacious halls. There is also a chapel where weddings are held to this day. Fine prints and paintings, porcelain, silver and other antiques abound, and welcoming touches include good toiletries, books and magazines in the bedrooms. Eight of these have sitting rooms. The setting is a beautiful, 5,000-acre family estate, and both estate game and locally caught salmon often feature in the memorable fixed-price menu of 6 courses. Chef Simon Burns who has replaced Mark Salter shows much imagination and skill in his cooking which results in many satisfying dishes. A good range of Scottish cheese is also provided, and the fine food is complemented by an outstanding wine list. The young staff are all trained in the Cromlix manner, being courteous, pleasant and helpful at all times.*
14⇌♠ CTV in all bedrooms
50P 1🎜 ⊞ ✿ ♫ (hard) ⏏ ∪ clay pigeon shooting croquet
♡ British, French, German & Swiss V ✿ ⊒ Last dinner 10.30pm
Credit Cards ①②③⑤

**DUNDEE** Tayside *Angus* Map **11** NO43

★★★66% **Stakis Earl Grey** Earl Grey Place DD1 4DE (Stakis)
☎(0382)29271 Telex no 76569 FAX (0382) 200072
*A modern hotel, its position on the banks of the River Tay commanding panoramic views, offers well-appointed bedrooms and public areas, together with a small leisure complex.*
104⇌(4fb)⊬in 45 bedrooms CTV in all bedrooms ® T
✖ (ex guide dogs) (room only) ⊟
Lift ℂ 120P ◻(heated) sauna solarium gymnasium ♫ *xmas*
♡ Scottish & French V ✿ ⊒ ⊬ Lunch £8.50 High tea £1.55-£4.75 Dinner £14.75&alc Last dinner 10pm
Credit Cards ①②③④⑤ ⓔ

★★★65% **Swallow** Kingsway West, Invergowrie DD2 5JT (3.5m W off A972 Dundee Ring Road) (Swallow)
☎(0382)641122 Telex no 76694 FAX (0382) 568340
*This former mansion house has been considerably extended and refurbished to a high standard. Public rooms are warm and inviting, and meals are served in the attractive Garden Restaurant. Bedrooms are comfortably appointed and well equipped.*
110⇌♠2⊞⊬in 21 bedrooms CTV in all bedrooms ® T sB&B⇌♠fr£75 dB&B⇌♠fr£95 ⊟
ℂ 80P ✿ ◻(heated) sauna solarium gymnasium ♉ *xmas*
♡ Scottish & French V ✿ ⊒ ⊬ Lunch fr£11.50 Dinner fr£17.50 Last dinner 9.45pm
Credit Cards ①②③⑤

★★★61%, **Angus Thistle** 10 Marketgait DD1 1QU (Mount Charlotte (TS)) ☎(0382)26874 Telex no 76456 FAX (0382) 22564
*This busy tourist, business and conference hotel is conveniently located in the city centre. Modern public areas are tastefully appointed, and the bedrooms are comfortable and well equipped.*
58⇨🅱🟥(4fb)2🟥½in 11 bedrooms CTV in all bedrooms ® T ✱ sB⇨🅱🟥fr£60 dB⇨🅱🟥fr£70 (room only) 🅱
Lift ( 20P CFA games room whirlpool
♫ International ✧ ☑ ½ Lunch fr£7.75&alc Dinner fr£12.95&alc Last dinner 10pm
Credit Cards ①②③④⑤

★★★59%, **Queens** 160 Nethergate DD1 4DU (Inter-Hotels) ☎(0382)22515 FAX (0382) 202668
*At the time of inspection, a major transformation was taking place at this popular business, conference and function hotel, which is conveniently situated in the city centre. A new leisure complex is planned for 1991.*
47⇨🅱🟥(2fb) CTV in all bedrooms ® T ✖ (ex guide dogs) sB⇨🅱🟥£40-£60 dB⇨🅱🟥£60-£80 (room only)
Lift ( 50P *xmas*
♫ Scottish & French V ✧ ☑ Lunch £5.25-£15 High tea £5.25 Dinner £8-£18alc Last dinner 9.30pm
Credit Cards ①②③④⑤

**DUNDONNELL** Highland *Ross & Cromarty* Map **14** NH08

★★★70%, **Dundonnell** IV23 2QS (Inter-Hotels) ☎(085483)234 FAX (085483) 366
*Enjoying the fine views down Little Loch Broom from its position beneath the An Teallach mountain range, this roadside hotel has been systematically improved by its resident owners so that it now provides comfortable and attractive accommodation, both in public areas and well-appointed bedrooms. The standard of housekeeping is very good throughout and staff are friendly and helpful.* ►

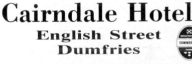

24⇌↱(2fb) CTV in all bedrooms ® T sB&B⇌↱£29.50-£37 dB&B⇌↱£53-£68 ⊟
60P *xmas*
V ♔ ⊻ Bar Lunch £5-£12alc Dinner £14.95-£15.50&alc Last dinner 8.30pm
Credit Cards [1] [3]

## DUNFERMLINE Fife Map 11 NT08

**★★★67% King Malcolm Thistle** Queensferry Rd, Wester Pitcorthie KY11 5DS (Mount Charlotte (TS)) ☎(0383)722611 Telex no 727721 FAX (0383) 730865
*Located on the southern outskirts of town and convenient for the Forth Road Bridge, this purpose-built hotel offers friendly service and well-equipped bedrooms.*
48⇌↱⊬in 12 bedrooms CTV in all bedrooms ® T ✱ sB⇌↱fr£49 dB⇌↱fr£58 (room only) ⊟
☾ 60P
☋ International ♔ ⊻ ⊬ Lunch fr£7.25&alc Dinner fr£11.95&alc Last dinner 9.30pm
Credit Cards [1] [2] [3] [4] [5]

**★★★65% Pitbauchlie House** Aberdour Rd KY11 4PB (Consort) ☎(0383)722282 Telex no 727756 FAX (0383) 620738
*Friendly service features highly at this well managed hotel. Accommodation is comfortable, the bedrooms offering many extras. The dinner menu boasts a range of interesting dishes, and is very good value.*
32⇌↱(2fb) CTV in all bedrooms ® T ✱ sB&B⇌↱£39-£42 dB&B⇌↱£49-£52
☾ 70P ❖ solarium
V ♔ ⊻ Lunch fr£7.50&alc Dinner fr£12.50&alc Last dinner 9pm
Credit Cards [1] [2] [3] [5] ⓔ

**★★★64% Keavil House** Crossford KY12 8QW (2m W A994) (Best Western) ☎(0383)736258 Telex no 728227 FAX (0383) 621600
*The converted fortified mansion has an elegant new bedroom wing and two attractive restaurants, the main dining room and a cocktail bar being complemented by a characterful lounge bar and adjoining supper restaurant. The hotel attracts both tourists and business trade.*
32⇌↱(1fb)1⊞ CTV in all bedrooms ® T sB&B⇌↱£50-£60 dB&B⇌↱£65-£80 ⊟
☾ 100P ⊞ ❖ *xmas*
☋ International V ♔ Lunch £9-£15alc High tea £5-£10alc Dinner £14.50-£16.50 Last dinner 9.30pm
Credit Cards [1] [2] [3] [5] ⓔ

**★★★62% Pitfirrane Arms** Main St, Crossford KY12 8NJ (0.5 W A994) ☎(0383)736132 Telex no 728255 FAX (0383) 621760
*Situated in the village of Crossford, 1.5 miles west of Dunfermline, this modern hotel has evolved from an old coaching inn. The bedrooms are mostly compact, with those in the modern wing more suited to business clientele. The menus offer a good choice of food, including some Italian dishes, and generous portions.*
38⇌↱(1fb) CTV in all bedrooms ® T ⋈ (ex guide dogs) ✱ sB&B⇌↱£35-£42 dB&B⇌↱£47-£54 ⊟
☾ 72P sauna solarium ♫ *xmas*
☋ Scottish & Italian V ♔ Lunch £8.20-£20alc Dinner £8.50-£18alc Last dinner 10.15pm
Credit Cards [1] [2] [3] ⓔ

**★★76% Elgin** Charlestown KY11 3EE ☎Limekilns(0383)872257
*Conveniently situated just off the A985 and close to junction 1 of the M90, this delightful family-managed hotel offers friendly service, very comfortable bedrooms and good value freshly cooked meals.*
13⇌↱(3fb) CTV in all bedrooms ® T ⋈ (ex guide dogs) ✱ sB&B⇌↱£39-£41 dB&B⇌↱£50-£54 ⊟
70P ❖
V ♔ Bar Lunch £6.50-£12 Dinner £6.50-£12&alc Last dinner 9pm
Credit Cards [1] [3]

**★★61% City** 18 Bridge St KY12 8DA ☎(0383)722538
RS 1 & 2 Jan
*Town centre commercial hotel with neat well-equipped bedrooms.*
17⇌↱(1fb)1⊞ CTV in all bedrooms ® T S10% sB&B⇌↱£36-£39 dB&B⇌↱£52-£56 ⊟
☾ 20P
☋ French V ♔ ⊻ S10% Sunday Lunch £8.75-£9.75 High tea £5.20-£9.80 Dinner £10.50-£11.50&alc Last dinner 9pm
Credit Cards [1] [3] ⓔ

## DUNHOLME Lincolnshire Map 08 TF07

**★★★50% Four Seasons** Scothern Ln LN2 3QP ☎Welton(0673)60108 FAX (0673) 62784
*Located on the A46 Lincoln/Grimsby road this is a purpose built motel block with the adjacent main building providing the hotel services. Clean and well-decorated accommodation is complemented by cheerful, willing staff.*
24⇌↱(1fb) CTV in all bedrooms ® T ✱ sB&B⇌↱£35-£45 dB&B⇌↱£35-£60 ⊟
CTV 130P ❖ *xmas*
☋ English & French V ♔ ⊻ Lunch £7.95-£9.95&alc Dinner £8.95-£9.95&alc Last dinner 10pm
Credit Cards [1] [2] [3]

## DUNKELD Tayside *Perthshire* Map 11 NO04

**★★★★62% Stakis Dunkeld House** PH8 0HX (Stakis) ☎(03502)771 Telex no 76657 FAX (03502) 8924
*Set in its own extensive grounds on the banks of the River Tay, the house, built by the seventh Duke of Atholl, has been sympathetically extended, and is a busy conference centre, as well as a popular base for the touring holidaymaker. It offers an extensive range of leisure and sporting activities, and the bedrooms, though varied in size, are comfortably appointed and well equipped.*
92⇌(13fb)⊬in 24 bedrooms CTV in all bedrooms ® T ⋈ (ex guide dogs) sB&B⇌fr£90 dB&B⇌fr£100 (incl dinner)
Lift ☾ CTV 70P ❖ ⊡(heated) ℘ (hard) ⌡ sauna solarium gymnasium table tennis archery croquet putting ♫ *xmas*
☋ International V ♔ ⊻ Lunch fr£15 Dinner fr£22.50 Last dinner 9.45pm
Credit Cards [1] [2] [3] [5]

**★★★63% Birnam** Birnam PH8 0BQ (Consort) ☎(03502)462 Telex no 57515 FAX (03502) 8979
*This comfortable, friendly hotel, family run on traditional lines and situated just off the A9 on its southern approach to the town, features a spacious lounge, first-floor dining rooms and bedrooms with en suite facilities; all floors are served by a lift.*
28⇌↱(1fb)1⊞ CTV in all bedrooms ® T sB&B⇌↱£39-£70 dB&B⇌↱£60-£85 ⊟
Lift 50P ❖
☋ English & French V ♔ Lunch fr£7.50 Dinner £14.95-£16.95 Last dinner 8.30pm
Credit Cards [1] [2] [3] [5] ⓔ

**❀✕✕✕Kinnaird House** Kinnaird Estate PH8 0LB ☎Ballinluig(079682)440 FAX (079682) 289
*One of our 'Best New Restaurants' this year – see the colour feature on page 36. Situated in a fine country mansion at the heart of the Kinnaird estate, this excellent restaurant is the setting for John Webber's excellent cooking. Based on traditional French cuisine, he brings originality and flair to dishes such as hot mousse of sweetbreads on a carrot and Sauternes sauce and a delicious quail set on creamed leek tartlets with an intense red wine sauce. Puddings are equally rich, although a perfectly formed hot mango soufflé was found to be surprisingly lacking in flavour. However, the cooking has impressed our inspectors and, coupled with the*

*caring and attentive service, the whole dining experience is a real treat.*
Closed Feb
50 seats ✱ Lunch £14.50-£18 Dinner £29.50 Last lunch 2pm
Last dinner 9pm 18P nc12yrs
Credit Cards [1] [3]

---

**DUNMOW, GREAT** Essex Map **05** TL62

★★52% **The Saracen's Head** High St CM6 1AG (Trusthouse
Forte) ☎(0371)873901 FAX (0371) 875743
*17th century inn, now a well run hotel with cosy lounges and
spacious, comfortable well-equipped bedrooms.*
24↩⁴⁄in 5 bedrooms CTV in all bedrooms ® ✱ sB↩£70
dB↩£76 (room only) ⬛
⬛ 60P xmas
V ♥ ☑ ⁴⁄ Lunch £8.95-£10&alc High tea £3.50-£5.50 Dinner
£12.95&alc Last dinner 9.30pm
Credit Cards [1] [2] [3] [4] [5]

✗✗**Starr** Market Place CM6 1AX ☎Great Dunmow(0371)4321
FAX (0371) 876337
*A comfortable and attractive 14th century restaurant, which
produces fine food from many local ingredients. It also offers an
outstanding wine list.*
Closed 1st wk Jan
Lunch not served Sat
Dinner not served Sun
♥ English & French **V** 60 seats ✱ Lunch £18 Dinner
£27.50-£30alc Last lunch 1.30pm Last dinner 9.30pm 16P ⁴⁄
Credit Cards [1] [2] [3]

---

**DUNNET** Highland *Caithness* Map **15** ND27

★★59% *Northern Sands* KW14 8DX ☎Barrock(084785)270
*A small tourist hotel close to a delightful sandy beach. All
bedrooms now have en-suite facilities and there are three
comfortable bars. French and Italian cuisine is served in the neat
dining room.*
9↩⬛(3fb) CTV in all bedrooms ® ⊁
CTV 50P
♥ French & Italian **V** ♥ ☑ Last dinner 8.30pm
Credit Cards [3]

---

**DUNOON** Strathclyde *Argyllshire* Map **10** NS17

★★78% **Enmore** Marine Pde, Kirn PA23 8HH ☎(0369)2230 &
2148
Closed Xmas & New Year RS Nov-Feb
*With fine views across the Firth of Clyde, David and Angela
Wilson's attractive hotel is run in the style of a country house. A
complimentary glass of sherry is brought to your room prior to
dinner and you will be introduced to fellow guests in the lounge.
Bedrooms are individually styled and thoughtfully equipped; two
have waterbeds.*
12↩⬛(2fb)3⬛ CTV in all bedrooms ® **T** sB&B↩⬛£35-£38
dB&B↩⬛£74-£106 ⬛
20P ⬛ ✿ squash games room ⬛
♥ Scottish & French **V** ♥ ☑ ⁴⁄ Lunch £10-£18alc High tea
£5-£10alc Dinner £18 Last dinner 8.30pm
Credit Cards [1] [3] [5] ①

★★62% *Firpark* Ardnadam PA23 8QG (3m N A815)
☎(0369)6506
*A small, well-appointed hotel situated at Lazaretto Point, is on the
south shore of the Holy Loch. Built in the 1850's, it features a
unique Minstrel's Gallery in the first floor drawing room.
Bedrooms are individually decorated and very comfortable. Bar
meals and a buttery menu are available. Friendly staff.*
6↩ CTV in all bedrooms ®
▶

---

**The Starr**     ✗✗

## RESTAURANT WITH ROOMS
### MARKET PLACE, GREAT DUNMOW
### ESSEX CM6 1AX
**Tel: 0371 4321   Fax: 0371 6337**
Family run restaurant with eight letting
bedrooms all with private bathrooms,
TV, telephone. As all dishes are cooked
to order vegetarian or special diets are
no problem, an English restaurant with
a definite French accent.

Two elegant rooms on the first floor
available for private dining or meetings.

We are situated between London and
Cambridge close to Thaxted, Saffron
Walden and London's Stansted Airport.

---

CTV 30P ⇔ ✿

⟡

Credit Cards ③

★★56% **Abbeyhill** Dhailing Rd PA23 8EA ☎(0369)2204

*A family-run hotel set in its own garden on a hillside overlooking the Firth of Clyde. It has a friendly informal atmosphere and offers practical well-equipped accommodation.*

14⊸➤(3fb) CTV in all bedrooms ⓡ sB&B⊸➤£25 dB&B⊸➤£38 🅿

40P ⇔ ✿

⟡ Dinner £6.50-£8.50&alc Last dinner 8.30pm

Credit Cards ① ② ③ ⓔ

★★**Hunter's Quay** Marine Pde, Hunter's Quay PA23 8JH ☎(0369)4190

*This friendly, family-run hotel stands opposite the ferry terminal, overlooking the Firth of Clyde. In its comfortable dining room the menu reflects good, imaginative cooking with an emphasis on Scottish game dishes.*

18rm(5⊸2➤)(5fb) CTV in all bedrooms ⓡ

《 CTV 20P ✿ solarium sailing ♫

♀ Scottish & French V ✿ ⚖ Last dinner 10pm

Credit Cards ① ③ ⑤

✗✗**Beverley's** Ardfillayne Hotel, West Bay PA23 7QJ ☎(0369)2267 FAX (0369) 2501

*Bill and Beverley McCaffrey's charming small restaurant forms part of the Ardfillayne Hotel, which overlooks the West Bay of Dunoon and the Firth of Clyde. The hand-written à la carte menu features local seafood and beef dishes and the good use of fresh ingredients, coupled with the relaxed, friendly atmosphere, makes dining here an enjoyable experience.*

Lunch not served (ex by arrangement)

♀ French V 40 seats ✷ Dinner £20-£25alc Last lunch 2pm Last dinner 9.30pm 20P ✂

Credit Cards ① ② ③ ⑤

---

DUNSTABLE Bedfordshire Map **04** TL02

★★★69% **Old Palace Lodge** Church St LU5 4RT ☎(0582)662201 FAX (0582) 696422

*This is a charming old ivy-clad building with plenty of character. The spacious bedrooms have been thoughtfully furnished and equipped, and although lounge facilities are limited, the bar lounge is very comfortable. The well-appointed restaurant offers a varied menu of English-style dishes, well prepared from good ingredients. A very friendly and well-managed hotel.*

49⊸(6fb)2✿✂in 6 bedrooms CTV in all bedrooms ⓡ T ✷ S10% sB⊸£50-£85 dB⊸£55-£100 (room only)

Lift 《 70P ⇔

♀ Continental V ✿ ⚖ Lunch £20-£34alc Dinner £20-£34alc Last dinner 10pm

Credit Cards ① ② ③ ④ ⑤

★★59% **Highwayman** London Rd LU6 3DX ☎Luton(0582)601122 Telex no 825353 FAX (0582) 471131

*This popular, friendly comercial hotel offers attentive service with willing and helpful staff. The public areas are limited, but comfortable.*

38⊸➤ CTV in all bedrooms ⓡ T ✷ sB&B⊸➤£45 dB&B⊸➤£56 🅿

《 60P

V ✿ ⚖ Bar Lunch fr£2

Credit Cards ① ② ③ ⑤

---

Entries for red-star hotels are highlighted by a tint panel. For a full list of these establishments consult the Contents page.

---

DUNSTER Somerset Map **03** SS94

★★★62% **The Luttrell Arms** High St TA24 6SG (Trusthouse Forte) ☎(0643)821555 FAX (0643) 821567

*In the centre of this attractive Exmoor town, the Luttrell Arms dates back to the 15th century. Refurbishment has been carefully carried out to retain many original features and preserve the wealth of character and interest. Some of the bedrooms are in adjacent cottages but all have access frosm the main building. The split-level restaurant offers à la carte as well as the simple table d'hôte menu. The hotel has been under the same management for 23 years and has a welcoming, family-run atmosphere.*

27⊸➤4⊞✂in 2 bedrooms CTV in all bedrooms ⓡ S% sB⊸➤£65 dB⊸➤£81-£92 (room only) 🅿

3⇔ ⇔ ✿ xmas

V ✿ ⚖ ✂ Lunch £7.95&alc Dinner £15&alc Last dinner 9.30pm

Credit Cards ① ② ③ ④ ⑤

★★67% **Exmoor House** West St TA24 6SN ☎(0643)821268 Closed Dec & Jan

*A small, village hotel, personally run by the proprietors, achieves a country house style of operation, providing an excellent standard of hospitality and a menu of good, fresh, local dishes. Bedrooms are well kept and very clean, there are two comfortable lounges and the dining room is well spaced.*

7⊸➤✂in all bedrooms CTV in all bedrooms ⓡ sB&B⊸➤£29.50-£31.50 dB&B⊸➤£44-£48 🅿

CTV ✗ ⇔ nc12yrs

✿ ⚖ ✂ Bar Lunch £5-£8 Dinner £14 Last dinner 7.30pm

Credit Cards ① ② ③ ⑤ ⓔ

---

DUNVEGAN

See **Skye, Isle of**

---

DURHAM Co Durham Map **12** NZ24

See also **Thornley**

★★★★68% **Royal County** Old Elvet DH1 3JN (Swallow) ☎091-386 6821 Telex no 538238 FAX 091-386 0704

*Recently extended and refurbished to a very high standard, this old-established hotel comprises well-appointed bedrooms, comfortable lounge areas, a variety of restaurants and excellent leisure facilities; its river bank setting commands views of the nearby castle and cathedral.*

152⊸➤(4fb)1⊞✂in 49 bedrooms CTV in all bedrooms ⓡ T ✷ S15% sB&B⊸➤£70-£85 dB&B⊸➤£85-£95 🅿

Lift 《 120P CFA ▣(heated) sauna solarium gymnasium Steam room plunge pool impulse showers xmas

♀ International V ✿ ⚖ S%, Lunch fr£10.50 Dinner fr£16.50 Last dinner 10.15pm

Credit Cards ① ② ③ ④ ⑤

★★★69% **Ramside Hall** Belmont DH1 1TD (3m NE A690) (Consort) ☎091-386 5282 Telex no 537681 FAX 091-386 0399

*Lying in extensive grounds off the A690 and close to the A1(M), this hotel caters for business people, and offers a choice of restaurants and some luxury bedrooms.*

82⊸➤(10fb)6⊞✂in 36 bedrooms CTV in all bedrooms ⓡ T ✗ (ex guide dogs) sB&B⊸➤£68-£86 dB&B⊸➤£88-£105 🅿

Lift 《 ⊞ 700P ✿ ♫ ♨

V ✿ ⚖ Lunch £7.50-£9.50 High tea £5.75-£7.50 Dinner £9.50-£12.50&alc Last dinner 10pm

Credit Cards ① ② ③ ⑤ ⓔ

★★★67% **Hallgarth Manor** Pittington DH6 1AB (3m E between A690 & B2183) (Best Western) ☎091-372 1188 Telex no 537023 FAX 091-372 1249

*This attractive hotel is situated in a country location, 3·5 miles from Durham city centre. Bedrooms feature genuine antique furniture, and a beautiful chandelier hangs above the main staircase. Lunch and dinner are served in the Elemore Restaurant,* or alternatively, lunch bar snacks are available in the popular *Village Tavern*, which adjoins the main hotel. A relaxing atmosphere prevails.

23⊸⋔ CTV in all bedrooms ® T sB&B⊸⋔£60-£66 dB&B⊸⋔£71-£77 ⊟

ℂ 101P ✿

⊐ International V ⊕ ⊡ Lunch fr£8.95 Dinner fr£14&alc Last dinner 9.15pm

Credit Cards ①②③⑤

★★★66% **Three Tuns** New Elvet DH1 3AQ (Swallow)
☎091-386 4326 Telex no 583238 FAX 091-386 1406

*A short walk from the city centre, this old coaching inn retains some of its original features, whilst providing modern facilities for the business traveller.*

48⊸⋔(2fb)1⊞⅍in 16 bedrooms CTV in all bedrooms ® T S% sB&B⊸⋔£65-£72 dB&B⊸⋔fr£80 ⊟

ℂ 60P CFA *xmas*

⊐ English & French V ⊕ ⊡ Lunch £9.50&alc Dinner £12.50&alc Last dinner 9.45pm

Credit Cards ①②③⑤

★★★59% *Bowburn Hall* Bowburn DH6 5NT (3m SE junc A177/A1(M)) ☎091-377 0311 Telex no 537681

*This business hotel, formerly a country house, stands three miles south of the city, between the A1(M) and the A177.*

19⊸ CTV in all bedrooms ® ✖

CTV 100P ✿ ♨

V ⊕ ⊡ Last dinner 10pm

Credit Cards ①②③⑤

Book as early as possible for busy holiday periods.

---

---

**Durham - Eastbourne**

**D**

★★★57% *Bridge Toby* Croxdale DH1 3SP (2.25m S off A167)
(Toby) ☎091-378 0524 Telex no 538156 FAX 091-378 9981
*The restaurant and bar here have been converted from a roadside
inn; the bedrooms are in a separate single-storey purpose-built
building at the back.*
46⇢🔌(2fb)⊬in 16 bedrooms CTV in all bedrooms ®
( 150P ❀
♀ Mainly grills V ❖ ⚏ ⊬ Last dinner 9.45pm
Credit Cards ①②③⑤

★67% *Redhills* Redhills Ln, Crossgate Moor DH1 4AN
☎091-386 4331 Telex no 537681
*A popular and friendly hotel, attractively decorated and with
nicely appointed bedrooms. Substantial meals are served in the
restaurant and lounge bar. Very good car parking facilities.*
6rm CTV in all bedrooms ✻
100P
V ❖ ⚏ Last dinner 10pm
Credit Cards ①②③⑤

**DUROR** Highland *Argyllshire* Map **14** NM95
★★77% *Stewart* PA38 4BW (Best Western) ☎(063174)268
Telex no 94014994 FAX (063174) 328
Closed Nov-Etr
*A comfortable and nicely appointed Highland hotel successfully
blending modern facilities with original features.*
20⇢🔌(2fb) CTV in all bedrooms ® T sB&B⇢£35-£40
dB&B⇢£70 🅿
30P 🚗 ❀ sauna solarium clay pigeon shooting sailing
V ❖ ⚏ ⊬ Lunch £12.50 Dinner £22 Last dinner 9.30pm
Credit Cards ①②③⑤

**DUXFORD** Cambridgeshire Map **05** TL44
★★★64% *Duxford Lodge* Ickleton Rd CB2 4RU
☎Cambridge(0223)836444 FAX (0223) 832271
RS Sat
*Set in its own beautifully maintained grounds and centrally located
in the village, offering easy access to A11, A505 and the nearby
Duxford War Museum, this hotel is run in the style of a country
house. Well furnished, individually decorated rooms are
complemented by comfortable, cosy public areas, the restaurant
offering an above average menu of imaginative and skilfully
prepared dishes.*
11⇢🔌Annexe5⇢ CTV in all bedrooms ® T
sB&B⇢🔌£45-£60 dB&B⇢🔌£65-£80 🅿
34P 🚗 ❀
♀ English & French V S% Lunch £13.50-£14.50 Dinner
£16.25-£20 Last dinner 9.30pm
Credit Cards ①②③⑤

**EARL SHILTON** Leicestershire Map **04** SP49
★★63% *Fernleigh* 32 Wood St LE9 7ND ☎(0455)847011
*Completion of a new extension of thirteen good quality bedrooms,
and a new lounge bar, together with improvements to public
public areas have made this a pleasant, sound hotel popular with
business people.*
28⇢🔌(4fb)2🛏 CTV in all bedrooms ® ✳ sB&B⇢🔌£25-£45
dB&B⇢🔌£45-£55 🅿
CTV 100P 10🚗 solarium
♀ English, French & Italian V ❖ ⚏ Lunch £3.50-£8.25 Dinner
fr£8.25&alc Last dinner 9.30pm
Credit Cards ①③

*Hotels with a high percentage rating for quality
are highlighted by a % across their
gazetteer entry.*

**EARL STONHAM** Suffolk Map **05** TM15
✕✕*Mr Underhills* Norwich Rd IP14 5DW
☎Stowmarket(0449)711206
*This is a small restaurant but it is homely and comfortable with
attractive furnishings. There is a set menu and the cooking is of a
very high standard. The wine list presents the customer with a good
selection and service is friendly.*
Closed Sun, Mon & BH's
Lunch not served Tue-Sat (ex by arrangement)
♀ English & French 24 seats Lunch £20-£25 Dinner
£23.45-£29.50 Last dinner 8.30pm 10P ⊬
Credit Cards ①③

**EASINGTON** Cleveland Map **08** NZ71
★★★♨72% *Grinkle Park* TS13 4UB (2m S off unclass rd
linking A174/A171) ☎Guisborough(0287)40515
FAX (0287) 41278
*Located between coast and moorland, and surrounded by 35-acre
grounds with a lake and attractive gardens, a house lovingly
converted into an hotel in 1947 retains many original features and
much of its former character. Individually designed bedrooms are
particularly attractive and well appointed, lounges are elegantly
cosy, and guests can try their skills on billiard table or croquet
lawn; the establishment's most noteworthy feature, however, must
be the level of service provided by friendly, caring staff.*
20⇢🔌2🛏 CTV in all bedrooms ® T sB&B⇢🔌£55.50
dB&B⇢🔌£72-£81 🅿
130P 2🚗 (£2 per night) ❀ ♟ (hard) ♪ snooker croquet *xmas*
♀ English & French V ❖ ⚏ Lunch £7.50-£21 High tea £3.55
Dinner £14.50&alc Last dinner 9.30pm
Credit Cards ①②③⑤ⓔ

**EASINGWOLD** North Yorkshire Map **08** SE56
★★★60% *The Garth* York Rd, Easingwold YO6 3PG
☎(0347)22988
*This is an extended country cottage which stands on the A19 to the
south of Easingwold. Bedrooms are well furnished and friendly,
and attentive service is provided by the resident proprietors, Mr
and Mrs Clayton.*
10⇢🔌(2fb)⊬in 4 bedrooms CTV in all bedrooms ® T ✻ ✳
sB&B⇢🔌£45 dB&B⇢🔌£70 🅿
40P 🚗 ❀
V ❖ ⚏ ⊬ Lunch £5-£9.50 Dinner £12.95-£15.95 Last dinner
8.30pm
Credit Cards ①③

**EASTBOURNE** East Sussex Map **05** TV69
See **Town Plan Section**
★★★★60% *Grand* King Edwards Pde BN21 4EQ (De Vere)
☎(0323)412345 Telex no 87332 FAX (0323) 412233
*The sheer grandeur of this white, palatial hotel at one end of
Eastbourne's promenade, is a visual delight. Public areas are
spacious, with high ceilings and nearly all the bedrooms have been
refurbished. Recent additions include a leisure club and the small,
select Mirabelle restaurant. Manager, Peter Hawley, is a
dedicated professional and his team of young staff provide a
friendly, welcoming atmosphere.*
161⇢(10fb)1🛏 CTV in all bedrooms T S% sB&B⇢£85-£100
dB&B⇢£110-£160 🅿
Lift ( 60P 🚗 ❀ CFA ▤(heated) ⌒(heated) snooker sauna
solarium gymnasium spa bath hairdressing beauty & massage
♪ ♨ *xmas*
♀ English & French V ❖ ⚏ Lunch £12-£17&alc Dinner
fr£22.50&alc Last dinner 10.30pm
Credit Cards ①②③④⑤ⓔ

262

★★★★61% **Cavendish** Grand Pde BN21 4DH (De Vere)
☎(0323)410222 Telex no 87579 FAX (0323) 410941
*An elegant hotel in a fine sea front position retains its charm and*
*traditional feeling. The large and rather elaborate restaurant is*
*complemented by a cocktail bar and popular sun lounge, whilst*
*bedrooms are variable – those at the front offering some*
*magnificent views.*
114⇌♪♠ CTV in all bedrooms ® T S10% sB&B⇌♠£70-£80
dB&B⇌♠£115-£150 ▤
Lift ( 50P CFA snooker games room ♬ *xmas*
♥ English & French V ♥ ⚏ S10% Lunch fr£10alc Dinner
fr£16alc Last dinner 9.30pm
Credit Cards ① ② ③ ④ ⑤

★★★69% **Lansdowne** King Edward's Pde BN21 4EE (Best
Western) ☎(0323)25174 Telex no 878624 LANS G
FAX (0323) 39721
Closed 28 Dec-12 Jan
*In a prime sea-front position, this fine, well-managed hotel has*
*been owned by the same family since 1912. They provide*
*traditional hospitality and service, along with well-furnished*
*bedrooms, excellent lounges and good standards of cooking.*
130⇌♠(7fb) CTV in all bedrooms ® T S10%
sB&B⇌♠£43-£57 dB&B⇌♠£68-£88 ▤
Lift ( CTV 22🛏 (£2.80 per night) CFA snooker games room
*xmas*
V ♥ ⚏ ✂ S10% Lunch £3-£8alc High tea fr£6.25 Dinner
fr£13.50 Last dinner 8.30pm
Credit Cards ① ② ③ ⑤ ⓔ

★★★64% **The Wish Tower** King Edward's Pde BN21 4EB
☎(0323)22676 FAX (0323) 21474
*Bedrooms ranging from sumptuous to modest are available in a*
*hotel whose prime sea-front position opposite the Wish Tower and* ▶

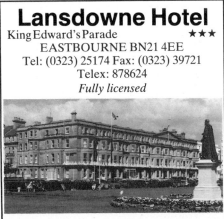

# Eastbourne

*Gardens makes it the ideal location for a pleasant break ; its comfortable, well-appointed restaurant, bar and lounge are managed particularly efficiently, while service is friendly and helpful.*
67rm(59⇆)✔in 6 bedrooms CTV in all bedrooms ® T ✱
sB&B⇆£55-£59 dB&B⇆£75-£82 ⊟
Lift ( 🛆 (£3 per day)'🛺 CFA xmas
♌ English & French V ✿ ◻ ✁ Sunday Lunch £8.95-£9.95
Dinner £13.50-£14.50 Last dinner 8.45pm
Credit Cards ①②③④⑤

★★★57% **Chatsworth** Grand Pde BN21 3YR ☎(0323)411016
FAX (0323) 643270
Closed Jan-mid Mar
*This traditional hotel benefits from a superb seafront location and the accommodation, though old fashioned, is comfortable and well equipped. The personal involvement of the proprietor ensures friendly and helpful service.*
45⇆(2fb) CTV in all bedrooms ✱ sB&B⇆♖£32-£42
dB&B⇆♖£64-£84 ⊟
Lift ( CTV ⚲ CFA xmas
✿ ◻ Sunday Lunch fr£10 Dinner fr£11.50 Last dinner 8.30pm
Credit Cards ①③ 🛺

★★★56% **Queens** Marine Pde BN21 3DY (De Vere)
☎(0323)22822 Telex no 877736 FAX (0323) 31056
*Situated opposite the pier, this busy hotel has long been popular with small conference groups and weekend visitors. It offers well-equipped bedrooms of good size, some facing the sea. There is also a large restaurant, feature bars and service which is both extensive and helpful.*
108⇆♖(5fb) CTV in all bedrooms ® T S15%
sB&B⇆♖£65-£70 dB&B⇆♖£115-£120 ⊟
Lift ( 90P CFA snooker xmas
♌ English & French V ✿ ◻ Lunch fr£10.50 Dinner fr£14 Last dinner 9pm
Credit Cards ①②③⑤ ⓔ

★★★53% **Cumberland** Grand Pde BN21 3YT ☎(0323)30342
*Occupying a wonderful position facing the sea and opposite the band stand, accommodation here is currently being refurbished and upgraded. Service is generally acceptable with a reasonable standard of cooking. A large function room is available.*
70⇆♖(5fb) CTV in all bedrooms ®
Lift ( CTV ⚲ CFA ♫ 🎱
♌ English & French V ✿ ◻ Last dinner 8.30pm
Credit Cards ①②③

★★★51% **Princes** Lascelles Ter BN21 4BL ☎(0323)22056
FAX (0323) 27469
*This long-established, family-run hotel offers traditional services and management. There is a comfortable lounge, friendly restaurant, a bar and conference rooms.*
48rm(37⇆7♖)(3fb) CTV in all bedrooms ® ✖
Lift ( ⚲ CFA table tennis pool table ♫
♌ English & French ✿ ◻ Last dinner 8.15pm
Credit Cards ①②③⑤

★★★73% **Langham** Royal Pde BN22 7AH ☎(0323)31451
Closed 13 Nov-21 Mar
*Set in a fine position overlooking the sea, this privately-run and professionally-managed hotel maintains a consistently high level of service and reliable standards of cooking. Recent improvements have added ten new bedrooms and further upgrading is planned. In-house entertainment and activity weekends are always featured.*
87⇆♖(5fb) CTV in all bedrooms ® T sB&B⇆♖£29-£32
dB&B⇆♖£58-£64 (incl dinner)
Lift ( CTV 3🏊 (£3.50 per night) ♫
♌ European ✿ ◻ Lunch fr£5.95 Dinner fr£8.95 Last dinner 7.30pm
Credit Cards ①③

For key to symbols see the inside front cover.

★★69% **Farrar's** 3-5 Wilmington Gardens BN21 4JN
☎(0323)23737
*This well managed and long established family-run hotel close to the town's theatres and Conference Centre is an ideal choice for either holidaymaker or businessman, providing comfortable lounges, a variety of bedrooms, private car parking and friendly, helpful service.*
42⇆♖(2fb) CTV in all bedrooms ®
Lift ( CTV 26P
♌ English & French V ✿ ◻ Last dinner 8pm
Credit Cards ①②③

★★69% **West Rocks** Grand Pde BN21 4DL ☎(0323)25217
Closed mid Nov-20 Mar
*Conveniently set midway along the seafront, between the bandstand and the Wishtower, this long established, family owned and well managed hotel features three comfortable lounges, a spacious dining room and a choice of bedrooms ; service is extensive and particularly helpful.*
54rm(8⇆32♖)(4fb) CTV in all bedrooms ® T ✖ ✱ S10%
sB&B£20-£26 sB&B⇆♖£30-£38 dB&B£36-£44
dB&B⇆♖£44-£80 ⊟
Lift ( CTV ⚲ 🛺 nc3yrs
♌ English & French V ✿ ◻ Lunch £3-£8alc
Credit Cards ①②③⑤ ⓔ

★★68% **Croft** 18 Prideaux Rd BN21 2NB ☎(0323)642291
*Attractively set in terraced gardens, a quiet, mock Tudor hotel and restaurant under the personal supervision of the chef/patron offers a choice of modern bedrooms which are consistent in standard though they vary in size. Well-cooked meals are based on quality ingredients and home-grown vegetables, one of the two dining rooms being reserved for the use of residents.*
11rm(10⇆) CTV in all bedrooms ® ✖
CTV 20P 🛺 ✿ ≏(heated) ⚲ (hard)
♌ English & French V ✿ ◻ Last dinner 9.30pm
Credit Cards ①②③⑤

★★65% **New Wilmington** 25 Compton St BN21 4DU
☎(0323)21219
Closed Jan & Feb
*Friendly, family-run hotel with comfortable, well-equipped bedrooms.*
41⇆♖(4fb) CTV in all bedrooms ® T sB&B⇆♖£35-£39.50
dB&B⇆♖£58-£67 (incl dinner) ⊟
Lift ( CTV 3🏊 (£2 per day) ♫ xmas
♌ English, French & Italian ✿ ◻ ✁ Bar Lunch £4-£6 Dinner fr£10 Last dinner 8pm
Credit Cards ①②③ ⓔ

★65% **Downland** 37 Lewes Rd BN21 2BU (Minotels)
☎(0323)32689
Closed Jan
*Conveniently located just off the A22. The accommodation has been recently upgraded and more improvements are planned. There is an attractive restaurant and bar, a separate lounge and compact modern bedrooms. Cooking is very creditable, reflecting the flair and individualistic style of the chef/proprietor.*
15⇆♖(4fb)1⊞ CTV in all bedrooms ® T ✖ (ex guide dogs)
sB&B⇆♖£27.50-£37.50 dB&B⇆♖£55-£75 ⊟
CTV 10P 🛺 xmas
V ✿ ◻ Lunch fr£14.50&alc Dinner fr£14.50&alc Last dinner 9pm
Credit Cards ①②③⑤

★61% **Oban** King Edward's Pde BN21 4DS ☎(0323)31581
Closed Dec-Etr RS Nov
*A friendly family-run hotel standing next to the Wish Tower features very well maintained bedrooms equipped in modern style, a generously furnished lounge and bar area and a compact, efficiently run basement restaurant.*
31⇆♖(3fb) CTV in all bedrooms ® T sB&B⇆♖£22-£27
dB&B⇆♖£44-£54 ⊟

▶

E

# The Croft Hotel

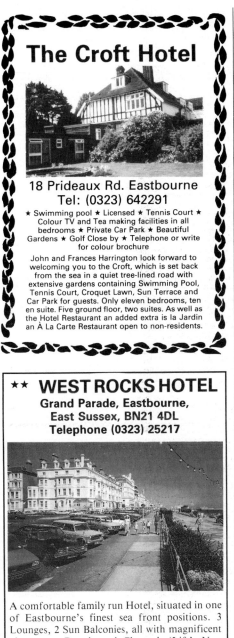

## 18 Prideaux Rd. Eastbourne
## Tel: (0323) 642291

★ Swimming pool ★ Licensed ★ Tennis Court ★ Colour TV and Tea making facilities in all bedrooms ★ Private Car Park ★ Beautiful Gardens ★ Golf Close by ★ Telephone or write for colour brochure

John and Frances Harrington look forward to welcoming you to the Croft, which is set back from the sea in a quiet tree-lined road with extensive gardens containing Swimming Pool, Tennis Court, Croquet Lawn, Sun Terrace and Car Park for guests. Only eleven bedrooms, ten en suite. Five ground floor, two suites. As well as the Hotel Restaurant an added extra is la Jardin an À La Carte Restaurant open to non-residents.

---

# FARRAR'S HOTEL ★★
## WILMINGTON GARDENS, EASTBOURNE, SUSSEX BN21 4JN
## Telephone: 0323 23737
### OPEN ALL YEAR

**E**

A well-established family-run hotel where hospitality means so much. Excellent cuisine. 200 yards from sea-front. Close to theatres & conference centre. Full central heating. All 42 bedrooms have private bath/shower, remote control T.V., Radio, Direct dial telephone, Tea & Coffee making facilities. Large private car park.

---

## ★★ WEST ROCKS HOTEL
### Grand Parade, Eastbourne, East Sussex, BN21 4DL
### Telephone (0323) 25217

A comfortable family run Hotel, situated in one of Eastbourne's finest sea front positions. 3 Lounges, 2 Sun Balconies, all with magnificent views over Parade and Channel. 'Lift', New cocktail bar. All rooms have en-suite facilities, colour TV/radio, direct dial telephone and complimentary tea/coffee tray.

*Please write or 'phone for Brochure.*

---

# THE CUMBERLAND HOTEL EASTBOURNE ★★★
### TELEPHONE (0323) 30342

### Grand Parade, EASTBOURNE BN21 3YT

Premiere, privately owned seafront hotel enjoying magnificent views of the promenade and English Channel.

Excellent sea-facing restaurant serving superb cuisine.

The hotel is spacious with luxury lounges and a large sun lounge. There are 70 comfortable en-suite bedrooms, all with colour TV, direct dial telephone, radio, hair dryer, trouser press and tea/coffee makers.

Entertainment throughout high season.

Lift (( CTV 𝒫 ♫

V ✧ ☑

(£)

**★56%, Lathom** 4-6 Howard Square, Grand Pde BN21 4BG
☎(0323)641986

Closed Nov-Feb (ex Xmas & New Year)

*The comfortable, privately-owned hotel provides nicely-appointed bedrooms, some of which are on the ground floor and an attractive lounge. The proprietors and their team of young staff are particularly helpful.*

45rm(2⇔41↑)(5fb) CTV in all bedrooms ® ⋈ sB&B£24-£26 sB&B⇔↑£26-£28 dB&B⇔↑£52-£56

Lift (( 6P (£2 per day) *xmas*

V ✧ Lunch fr£4 Dinner fr£6.50 Last dinner 8.30pm

Credit Cards [1] [2] [3]

**✗Byrons** 6 Crown St, Old Town BN21 1NX ☎(0323)20171

*An enchanting little cottage-style restaurant, lit by candles and complementing a consistently good standard of cooking with particularly efficient and helpful service, offers a short choice of original dishes which use only free range and organically reared produce. Fresh fish is generally available, and other popular dishes include Hot Spinach Mousse, Homemade Ravioli, Duck Liver Truffle Pâté, Gressingham Duck, Noisettes of Lamb and Sussex Beef.*

Closed Sun, 1 wk Xmas & BH

Lunch not served Sat (bookings only Mon-Fri)

♈ French **V** 22 seats S% Lunch £15-£20alc Dinner £15-£20alc Last lunch 1.30pm Last dinner 10.30pm 𝒫 nc8yrs

Credit Cards [2] [3] [5]

---

**EAST BUCKLAND** Devon Map 03 SS63

**✗✗Lower Pitt** EX32 0TD ☎Filleigh(05986)243

*Situated near the church, this charming 16th-century cottage is now a 'restaurant with rooms'. A low doorway (mind your head) leads to a pleasant lounge/bar, where a log fire burns in winter, and the restaurant. The menu features British dishes, ably prepared with fresh ingredients by the proprietress, Suzanne Lyons. There are three letting bedrooms.*

Closed Sun, 25 Dec & 1 Jan

Lunch not served

Dinner not served Mon

♈ International 30 seats Dinner £15-£20alc Last dinner 9pm 12P nc10yrs

Credit Cards [1] [2] [3]

See advertisement under **BARNSTAPLE**

---

**EAST DEREHAM** Norfolk Map 09 TF91

**★★64%, King's Head** Norwich St NR19 1AD
☎Dereham(0362)693842 & 693283 FAX (0362) 693776

*A 16th-century inn situated only a few minutes away from the town centre, with ample car parking space and a walled garden which is home to the Bowls Club. Accommodation is well equipped and carefully maintained, both in the main part of the hotel – which retains the style and atmosphere of the original building – and in the annexe, while courteous staff provide proficient service throughout.*

10rm(4⇔2↑)Annexe5⇔↑(1fb) CTV in all bedrooms ® **T** ✱ sB&Bfr£30.50 sB&B⇔↑fr£33 dB&Bfr£42 dB&B⇔↑fr£45 ➡

CTV 30P 3⛳ ♪ (grass) bowling

♈ English, French & Italian **V** ✧ Lunch £6.95-£10.50&alc Dinner £7.25-£10.95&alc Last dinner 9pm

Credit Cards [1] [2] [3] [5] (£)

**★★55%, The Phoenix** Church St NR19 1DL (Trusthouse Forte)
☎Dereham(0362)692276

*Set close to the church, in a quiet road just off the main street of the bustling market town, the hotel offers well equipped accommodation which is equally suited to the needs of businessmen and tourists.*

---

23⇔↑⅓in 6 bedrooms CTV in all bedrooms ® **T** ✱ sB&B⇔↑fr£43 dB&B⇔↑fr£49 ➡

40P 2⛳ *xmas*

♈ French & English **V** ✧ ☑ Sunday Lunch fr£6.95 Dinner fr£10.95&alc Last dinner 9.30pm

Credit Cards [1] [2] [3] [4] [5]

**★70%** *George* Swaffham Rd NR19 2AZ (Berni/Chef & Brewer)
☎Dereham(0362)696801

*This small coaching inn, dating from the seventeenth century, has been tastefully refurbished to provide spacious guest rooms, excellently appointed and offering a good range of facilities; the staff are friendly and the managers anxious to ensure that guests enjoy their stay.*

8⇔↑(1fb) CTV in all bedrooms ® ⋈ (ex guide dogs)

40P

V ✧ ☑ Last dinner 9.30pm

Credit Cards [1] [2] [3] [5]

---

**EAST GRINSTEAD** West Sussex Map 05 TQ33

❀★★★★⬧

**GRAVETYE MANOR**

RH19 4LJ (3m SW off unclass rd joining B2110 & B2028) (Relais et Châteaux)
☎Sharpthorne
(0342)810567

Telex no 957239

FAX (0342) 810080

RS 25 Dec

*Peter Herbert first converted this Elizabethan manor into a country-house hotel over 30 years ago and, minor niggles apart (a few inefficient showers and the non-acceptance of credit cards), it remains a shining example of consistently high standards of hotel keeping. The hotel's setting, in 30 acres of grounds within 1,000 acres of Forestry Commission land, gives it an aura of peace and privacy, reinforced by the discreet and courteous service. The wood-panelled public rooms, lovely antique furniture and the high standards of maintenance and cleanliness are other notable attributes. The head chef, Mark Raffan, specialises in British cooking, experimenting successfully with combinations of different flavours. Fish features predominantly on his menus, and the wine list is outstanding. It is a pleasure also to record the promotion of Andrew Russell to General Manager and to applaud his enthusiasm and eye for detail in the running of the hotel.*

14⇔↑🛏 CTV in all bedrooms ⋈ (ex guide dogs) ✱ sB⇔↑£86.25-£98.90 dB⇔↑£103.50-£204.70 (room only)

25P ⇔ ♪ croquet nc7yrs

⅓ Lunch £21.85-£25.30&alc Dinner £25.30&alc Last dinner 9.30pm

---

**★★★65%** *Woodbury House* Lewes Rd RH19 8UD
☎(0342)313657

Closed 25-26 Dec

*A unique style of hospitality is provided at this popular hotel, which has recently been upgraded to provide well-equipped and thoughtfully appointed bedrooms. There is a choice of restaurants – a Bistro with a relaxing, informal atmosphere and the attractive garden restaurant offering a more formal style of service. Here, the table d'hôte and à la carte menus offer a variety of dishes and the standard of cooking is high.*

6⇔↑Annexe1↑1🛏 CTV in all bedrooms ®

30P ⇔ ❀

✧ ☑

Credit Cards [1] [2] [3] [4] [5]

**EAST HORNDON** Essex Map **05** TQ68

⭐**Travelodge** CM13 3LL (3m E of M25 junc 29) (Trusthouse Forte) ☎Brentwood(0277)810819 Central Res (0800) 850950
22⇨👁(22fb) CTV in all bedrooms ® sB⇨👁£24 dB⇨👁£29.50 (room only)
⊄ 22P
♡ Mainly grills
Credit Cards ① ② ③

---

**EAST HORSLEY** Surrey Map **04** TQ05

★★★63% **Thatchers Resort** Epsom Rd KT24 6TB
☎(04865)4291 FAX (04865) 4222
*Accommodation at this hotel consists of a choice of modern and very well equipped bedrooms, a summer poolside annexe and an attractive beamed cottage. Chef Paul O'Dowd provides a good standard of cooking in the restaurant.*
36⇨👁Annexe23⇨👁(4fb)2⊟⊬in 6 bedrooms CTV in all bedrooms ® T ⊁ (ex guide dogs) sB⇨👁£65-£75 dB⇨👁£75-£85 (room only) ⊟
⊄ 60P ✿ ≏(heated) ♫
♡ English & French V ♥ ⊒ Lunch fr£13.75 Dinner fr£16.50 Last dinner 9.30pm
Credit Cards ① ② ③ ⑤ ⓔ

---

**EAST KILBRIDE** Strathclyde *Lanarkshire* Map **11** NS65

★★★62% **Bruce** Cornwall St G74 1AF (Swallow)
☎(03552)29771 Telex no 778428 FAX (03552) 42216
*This purpose-built hotel, located conveniently close to the town centre complex, provides bedrooms which are all well equipped though they vary in style and size. There is no lounge bar as such, drinks being served in the spacious general-purpose central lounge.*
80⇨👁⊬in 6 bedrooms CTV in all bedrooms ® T ✸
sB&B⇨👁£55-£75 dB&B⇨👁£80-£85
Lift ⊄ 15P 25🚗 CFA ♫
♡ International ♥ ⊒ Lunch £4.95&alc High tea £4.50 Dinner £12.95&alc Last dinner 9.45pm
Credit Cards ① ② ③ ⑤ ⓔ

★★★60% **Stuart** 2 Cornwall Way G74 1JR ☎(03552)21161 Telex no 778504 FAX (03552) 64410
Closed 25 Dec & 1 Jan
*Bedrooms in two styles, both varying in size, are available at this town centre business hotel.*
39⇨👁(1fb)1⊟ CTV in all bedrooms ® T ✸
sB&B⇨👁£43-£49 dB&B⇨👁£55-£59 ⊟
Lift ⊄ ⊞ CTV 🎿 ♫ *xmas*
♡ European V ♥ ⊒ Lunch £6.50&alc
Credit Cards ① ② ③ ⑤

---

**EASTLEIGH** Hampshire Map **04** SU41

★★★63% **Crest** Leigh Rd, Passfield Av SO5 5PG (Trusthouse Forte) ☎(0703)619700 Telex no 47606 FAX (0703) 643945
RS 25 Dec & 1 Jan
*An attractive and well-designed, modern hotel with generous bedrooms and extensive, friendly service. There are particularly good standards of cooking in the Beatrix Restaurant.*
120⇨👁(10fb)⊬in 18 bedrooms CTV in all bedrooms ®
Lift ⊄ 200P
♡ English & French V ♥ ⊒ ⊬
Credit Cards ① ② ③ ④ ⑤

○**Travelodge** Twyford Rd(Trusthouse Forte)
☎Central reservations (0800) 850950
32⇨

**1** ▷ Want to be seen with the leaders? . . . Then drive straight to

★★★

**BRUCE HOTEL**
**E A S T   K I L B R I D E**

**NUMBER 1** For eating out.

**NUMBER 1** For accommodation and function facilities including weddings.

**NUMBER 1** For conferences and meetings.

*For further information and reservations please call us on (03552) 29771. Town Centre, Cornwall St., East Kilbride*

**E**

267

**E**

---

**EAST LINTON** Lothian Map **12** NT57

★★62% **The Harvesters** Station Rd EH40 3DP ☎(0620)860395
*Conveniently located south of Edinburgh, only yards from the A1, the hotel offers cosy bedrooms, good-value menus and friendly service.*
5⇨🛏Annexe7rm(4⇨🛁) CTV in all bedrooms ® T sB&B£28
sB&B⇨🛁🌂£42 dB&B£50 dB&B⇨🛁🌂£64-£74 🏢
30P ✿ ✔
ⓖ International **V** ✿ 🎿 Lunch £4.50-£8&alc High tea £6
Dinner £6-£10&alc Last dinner 9pm
Credit Cards ①②③⑤ ⓔ

---

**EAST MOLESEY** Surrey

See **LONDON** plan **1** *B1* (pages 426–7)
✗✗**Lantern** 20 Bridge Rd KT8 9HA ☎081-979 1531
*Tastefully decorated restaurant with conservatory, run by the chef-patron and his wife.*
Closed Sun, Aug & BH's
Lunch not served Mon & Sat
ⓖ French **V** 50 seats Last lunch 2.15pm Last dinner 10.30pm
✗ nc8yrs
Credit Cards ①②③⑤

---

**EAST PORTLEMOUTH** Devon Map **03** SX73

★★63% **Gara Rock** TQ8 8PH (Minotels)
☎Salcombe(054884)2342 FAX (054884) 3033
Closed Nov-Etr
*A converted coastguard station on the cliff edge has been converted to provide comfortable hotel accommodation with panoramic views. There are good facilities for children and service is friendly.*
21rm(14⇨🛁5🌂)(15fb) CTV in all bedrooms ® T sB&B£23-£39
dB&B⇨🛁🌂£50-£86 🏢
60P ♿ ✿ ≈(heated) ♪ (hard) ✔ games room 🎱
ⓖ English & French **V** ✿ 🎿 ⵊ Bar Lunch £2.50-£8 High tea
fr£4.75 Dinner fr£13 Last dinner 8.30pm
Credit Cards ①③⑤
See advertisement under SALCOMBE

---

**EATHORPE** Warwickshire Map **04** SP36

★★56% **Eathorpe Park** Fosse Way CV33 9DQ (Exec Hotel)
☎Marton(0926)632245 FAX (0926) 632481
Closed 25 Dec evening & 26 Dec
*This imposing Victorian hotel is situated on the Fosse Way, close to the village centre. Improvements to the spacious public areas are now complete, with many original features retained. Bedrooms are, at the time of going to press, receiving the same attention.*
14⇨🛁🌂(3fb) CTV in all bedrooms **T** ✖ (ex guide dogs)
sB&B⇨🛁🌂£45-£65 dB&B⇨🛁🌂£55-£75 🏢
CTV 200P ✿ solarium
ⓖ English & French **V** ✿ 🎿 Lunch £12-£14&alc
Credit Cards ①②③⑤ ⓔ

---

**ECCLESHALL** Staffordshire Map **07** SJ82

★★65% **St George** Castle St ST21 6DF ☎(0785)850300
FAX (0785) 851452
*Popular with business people, this fully-renovated inn at the centre of the village offers good quality accommodation, a friendly local bar atmosphere and a restaurant in traditional style which serves good wholesome meals.*
10⇨🛁🌂1🏢 CTV in all bedrooms ® ✖ (ex guide dogs) ✳
sB&B⇨🛁🌂fr£45 dB&B⇨🛁🌂£65-£80 Continental breakfast 🏢
17P ♿
ⓖ English & French **V** ✿ 🎿 ⵊ
Credit Cards ①②③⑤ ⓔ

---

**EDENBRIDGE** Kent Map **05** TQ44

✗✗✗**Honours Mill** 87 High St TN8 5AU ☎(0732)866757
*The fixed price menus for lunch and dinner offer an appealing choice of French dishes at this tastefully restored mill.*
Closed Mon, 2 wks Jan & 2 wks Jun
Lunch not served Sat
Dinner not served Sun
ⓖ French 38 seats Last lunch 2pm Last dinner 10pm
✗ nc10yrs
Credit Cards ①③

---

**EDENHALL** Cumbria Map **12** NY53

★★63% **Edenhall** CA11 8SX ☎Langwathby(076881)454
*The hotel dining room, with its large expanse of windows, offers fine views of the garden.*
29⇨🛁Annexe8⇨🛁(3fb) CTV in 29 bedrooms ✖
🎛 CTV 80P 2🏍 ✿
ⓖ English, French & Italian **V** ✿ 🎿 Last dinner 9pm
Credit Cards ①③

---

**EDINBURGH** Lothian *Midlothian* Map **11** NT27

See **Town Plan Section**

★★★★★65% **Caledonian** Princes St EH1 2AB (Queens
Moat)(Pride of Britain) ☎031-225 2433 Telex no 72179
FAX 031-225 6632
*'The Caley', as this famous hotel is affectionately called, stands at one end of Princes Street and is overlooked by Edinburgh Castle. Deservedly praised for the friendliness of its staff, it is greatly to the credit of new General Manager, David Clarke, that the combination of warmth and efficiency continues to set standards that some other five star hotels might care to emulate. Both restaurants – the popular Gazebo and the classical Pompadour – are under the direction of Chef Jeff Bland and some of his dishes in the Pompadour earn special praise. On the debit side, the recent battles over, and resulting changes of ownership, have meant that the urgently needed upgrading and refurbishment of the bedrooms has not proceeded as quickly as anticipated. Though some are spacious, there are many that are small and lacking in the quality and comfort expected. There are, however, clear signs that the new owning company intends to address the situation, which is no more than a hotel of this standing deserves.*
237⇨🛁✖in 36 bedrooms CTV in all bedrooms **T**
✖ (ex guide dogs) sB⇨🛁fr£110 dB⇨🛁fr£155 (room only) 🏢
Lift ⓒ 60P CFA *xmas*
ⓖ Scottish & French **V** ✿ 🎿 ⵊ S10% Lunch £15.75&alc
Dinner fr£18.75&alc Last dinner 10.30pm
Credit Cards ①②③④⑤

★★★★63% **George** George St EH2 2PB ☎031-225 1251
Telex no 72570 FAX 031-226 5644
*This popular business and tourist hotel is located in the city centre just a short walk from Princes Street. It has elegant and tastefully-appointed public rooms and offers a choice of restaurants. Bedrooms, some of which are compact, have been thoughtfully equipped.*
195⇨🛁🌂(10fb)✖in 4 bedrooms CTV in all bedrooms ® T ✳
sB⇨🛁🌂£93.50-£115.50 dB⇨🛁🌂£132-£143 (room only) 🏢
Lift ⓒ 24P CFA *xmas*
ⓖ Scottish, English & French **V** ✿ 🎿 ⵊ Lunch £13-£20&alc
Dinner £13-£20&alc Last dinner 10pm
Credit Cards ①②③⑤

★★★★62% **Carlton Highland** North Bridge EH1 1SD (Scottish
Highland) ☎031-556 7277 Telex no 727001 FAX 031-556 2691
*Situated within easy reach of the main shopping areas, the Royal Mile and the railway station, this modern hotel offers accommodation in rooms which are, for the most part, spacious; a good range of eating options is available and the sizeable leisure centre is extremely well equipped.*

---

207⇌(20fb) CTV in all bedrooms ® **T** ✻ sB&B⇌£82-£90 dB&B⇌£116-£125 ⊟
Lift ( ⊞ ⚐ CFA ⊡(heated) squash snooker sauna solarium gymnasium jacuzzi table tennis dance studio creche ♫ ⌂ *xmas*
☋ Scottish & French **V** ✿ ⊻ Lunch fr£15&alc High tea fr£8 Dinner fr£15 Last dinner 10.30pm
Credit Cards 1 2 3 4 5

---

★★★69% **Roxburghe** Charlotte Square EH2 4HG (Best Western) ☎031-225 3921 Telex no 727054 FAX 031-220 2518
*A handsome Georgian building, featuring some fine examples of Adam architecture, situated in the heart of the city close to Princes Street. Public rooms are elegant and offer a club atmosphere with traditional comforts, whilst bedrooms are thoughtfully equipped, though they do vary in size and style.*
75⇌1⊟ CTV in all bedrooms ® **T** S10% sB&B⇌£55-£85 dB&B⇌£70-£130 Continental breakfast ⊟
Lift ( ⚐ ⊞ CFA *xmas*
☋ French **V** ✿ ⊻ Lunch £8.50-£10&alc Dinner £14.50-£16&alc Last dinner 10pm
Credit Cards 1 2 3 5

---

★★★68% **King James Thistle** 107 St James Centre EH1 3SW (Mount Charlotte (TS)) ☎031-556 0111 Telex no 727200 FAX 031-557 5333
*This well-appointed city-centre hotel has attractive public areas and comfortable bedrooms which have been furnished and decorated to a high standard. Service is extensive and efficient.*
147⇌⌐(20fb)⊬in 14 bedrooms CTV in all bedrooms ® **T** ✻ sB⇌⌐fr£65 dB⇌⌐fr£85 (room only) ⊟
Lift ( 21P 8⌂ CFA
☋ International ✿ ⊻ ⊬ Lunch fr£13alc Dinner fr£16alc Last dinner 10.20pm
Credit Cards 1 2 3 4 5

---

★★★67% **Barnton Thistle** Queensferry Rd, Barnton EH4 6AS (Mount Charlotte (TS)) ☎031-339 1144 Telex no 727928 FAX 031-339 5521
*On the western outskirts of the city, this extended and refurbished hotel offers elegant public areas and modern, well-equipped bedrooms. Two restaurants provide contrasting styles of cuisine, 'Crichtons' being particularly recommended.*
50⇌⌐(9fb)1⊟⊬in 10 bedrooms CTV in all bedrooms ® **T** ✻ sB⇌⌐fr£65 dB⇌⌐fr£75 (room only) ⊟
Lift ( 100P sauna hairdresser
☋ International ✿ ⊻ ⊬ Lunch fr£8.95&alc Dinner fr£12alc Last dinner 10pm
Credit Cards 1 2 3 4 5

---

★★★67% **Capital Moat House** Clermiston Rd EH12 6UG (Queens Moat) ☎031-334 3391 Telex no 728284 FAX 031-334 9712
*A comfortable, modern hotel in the west end of the city, equally suitable for business people and tourists, offers smart, well-equipped bedrooms, a choice of restaurants and good conference and leisure facilities.*
98⇌⌐(10fb)1⊟ CTV in all bedrooms ® **T** sB&B⇌⌐£72-£88 dB&B⇌⌐£82-£110 ⊟
Lift ( 150P ⊡(heated) sauna solarium gymnasium hairdressing *xmas*
☋ Scottish & French **V** ✿ ⊻ Sunday Lunch £7.50-£8.50 Dinner £14.95-£16.95&alc Last dinner 9.45pm
Credit Cards 1 2 3 4 5

---

★★★65% **Post House** Corstorphine Rd EH12 6UA (Trusthouse Forte) ☎031-334 0390 Telex no 727103 FAX 031-334 9237
*On the western city approach and backed by Edinburgh Zoo this comfortable and spacious hotel offers fine views over the city.*
207⇌(98fb)⊬in 12 bedrooms CTV in all bedrooms ® sB⇌fr£67 dB⇌fr£78 (room only) ⊟
Lift ( 158P CFA

▶

V ♦ ⬛ ⤫ Lunch £7.95-£9.50&alc High tea £6.75-£7.95&alc
Dinner £13.95-£14.50 Last dinner 10pm
Credit Cards ①②③④⑤

★★★64% **Holiday Inn** Queensferry Rd EH4 3HL (Holiday Inns
Inc) ☎031-332 2442 Telex no 72541 FAX 031-332 3408
*This comfortable, modern high-rise hotel enjoys a fine outlook over
the capital. It offers a range of comfortable modern bedrooms, each
well equipped and of ample proportions. The attractive foyer
lounge leads to the popular lounge bar and smart restaurant.
Conference and business facilities are available.*
118⇨🛏(8fb)⤫in 26 bedrooms CTV in all bedrooms ® T S%
sB⇨🛏fr£85 dB⇨🛏fr£110 (room only) 🍴
Lift ( 80P *xmas*
🎇 International V ♦ ⬛ ⤫ S% Lunch fr£10 Dinner fr£15.50
Last dinner 10pm
Credit Cards ①②③④⑤

★★★63% **Bruntsfield** 69/74 Bruntsfield Place EH10 4HH (Best
Western) ☎031-229 1393 Telex no 727897 FAX 031-229 5634
*Located just south of the city centre, this popular business and
holiday hotel has undergone major refurbishment. Some of the
bedrooms are compact, but all are comfortable and well equipped,
and there is a choice of bars and restaurants. A new leisure
complex is under development.*
51⇨🛏(1fb)1🎀 CTV in all bedrooms ® T sB&B⇨🛏£50-£65
dB&B⇨🛏£75-£115 Continental breakfast 🍴
Lift ( 25P CFA *xmas*
🎇 International V ♦ Lunch £6-£8&alc Dinner £14.50-£16&alc
Last dinner 10.30pm
Credit Cards ①②③⑤ⓔ

★★★61% **Donmaree** 21 Mayfield Gardens EH9 2BX
☎031-667 3641
*An attractive hotel south of the city centre with richly appointed
Victorian-style public areas and consistently good cuisine.*
9⇨🛏Annexe8rm(3⇨2🛏) CTV in all bedrooms ®
( CTV 6P
🎇 French ♦ Last dinner 10pm
Credit Cards ①②③⑤

★★★61% **The Howard** Great King St EH3 6QH (Select)
☎031-557 3500 Telex no 727887 FAX 031-557 6515
*Splendidly appointed hotel in the city's Georgian New Town area
with club-style lounges and cocktail bars and individually-styled
bedrooms.*
16⇨🛏3🎀 CTV in all bedrooms T ✕ (ex guide dogs) ✱
sB&B⇨🛏£100-£105 dB&B⇨🛏£150-£190
Lift ( 12P 🚗 CFA
V ♦ ⬛ Lunch fr£15&alc Dinner fr£28.50&alc Last dinner
10pm
Credit Cards ①②③⑤

★★★61% *Norton House* Ingliston EH28 8LX ☎031-333 1275
Telex no 727232 FAX 031-333 5303
*A comfortable hotel, set in its own gardens and conveniently
located beside Edinburgh airport, offers accommodation in
bedrooms equipped to meet the needs of the modern traveller. Its
cuisine enjoys a good local reputation, and service (in particular,
porterage) is commendable, whilst those desiring less formal
surroundings should visit the adjacent Norton Tavern for a pub
snack.*
19⇨🛏(3fb) CTV in all bedrooms ®
( 100P ✿ putting green pool table
🎇 French V ♦ ⬛ Last dinner 9.30pm
Credit Cards ①②③⑤

★★★58% *Albany* 39-43 Albany St EH1 3QY ☎031-556 0397
Telex no 727079
Closed 24-26 Dec & 1-2 Jan
*An attractive Georgian building with a smartly refurbished
basement restaurant and bar. Bedrooms are more practical, with
modest appointments, though improvements are planned.*

20⇨🛏(2fb) CTV in all bedrooms ®
( ✗
🎇 Scottish & French V ♦ Last dinner 9.30pm
Credit Cards ①②③④⑤

★★★58% **Stakis Grosvenor** Grosvenor St EH12 5EF (Stakis)
☎031-226 6001 Telex no 72445 FAX 031-220 2387
*The recently refurbished hotel caters for business and coach
markets with a choice of two attractive restaurants.*
136⇨🛏(18fb)1⤫in 18 bedrooms CTV in all bedrooms ® T
✱ sB⇨🛏£79-£82 dB⇨🛏£102-£105 (room only) 🍴
Lift ( CTV ✗ *xmas*
🎇 Scottish, French & Italian V ♦ ⬛ ⤫ Lunch £8.50-£18alc
High tea £3.40-£3.80 Dinner £12.50-£13.50 Last dinner 9.30pm
Credit Cards ①②③⑤ⓔ

★★★57% **Old Waverley** Princes St EH2 2BY (Scottish
Highland) ☎031-556 4648 Telex no 727050 FAX 031-557 6316
*A modernised city centre hotel. The carvery dining room is
particularly popular at lunchtime when it serves keenly-priced,
straightforward dishes.*
66⇨🛏(6fb) CTV in all bedrooms ® T sB&B⇨🛏£60-£65
dB&B⇨🛏£90-£98 🍴
Lift ( ✗ CFA *xmas*
V ♦ ⬛ Lunch £4.25-£5.75 High tea £6-£7 Dinner £11.25&alc
Last dinner 9.30pm
Credit Cards ①②③⑤

★★★57% *Royal Scot* 111 Glasgow Rd EH12 5NF (Swallow)
☎031-334 9191 Telex no 727197 FAX 031-316 4507
*This large, purpose-built hotel is convenient for the airport.
Facilities include a choice of restaurants and a leisure centre. The
best bedrooms are in the north wing, though major refurbishment
to the remaining rooms is in progress.*
252⇨🛏(18fb) CTV in all bedrooms ®
Lift ( 200P ✿ CFA ⬛(heated) sauna solarium gymnasium
pitch & putt ♫
🎇 French ♦ ⬛
Credit Cards ①②③⑤

★★★56% **Braid Hills** 134 Braid Rd, Braid Hills EH10 6JD
(2.5m S A702) ☎031-447 8888 Telex no 72311
FAX 031-452 8477
*This popular tourist/commercial hotel offers an interesting blend of
the old and the new. Comfortable public rooms have a traditional
air, while the well-equipped bedrooms are furnished in the modern
style.*
68⇨🛏2🎀⤫in 8 bedrooms CTV in all bedrooms ® T ✱
sB&B⇨🛏£50-£65 dB&B⇨🛏£70-£78 🍴
( 38P ✿ *xmas*
🎇 Scottish & French V ♦ Lunch fr£7.95 Dinner fr£14.95 Last
dinner 9pm
Credit Cards ①②③⑤ⓔ

★★★55% **Mount Royal** 53 Princes St EH2 2DG (Embassy)
☎031-225 7161 Telex no 727641 FAX 031-220 4671
*Occupying a central position looking out over Princes Street
Gardens and the Castle, the hotel has recently been effectively
refurbished.*
159⇨🛏(14fb)⤫in 6 bedrooms CTV in all bedrooms ® T ✱
sB⇨🛏£75-£89.50 dB⇨🛏£95-£105 (room only) 🍴
Lift ( ✗ CFA *xmas*
🎇 Scottish & French V ♦ ⬛ ⤫ Lunch £7.50-£8.50 Dinner
£12.50&alc Last dinner 9.30pm
Credit Cards ①②③④⑤

★★★54% *Ellersly House* 4 Ellersly Rd EH12 6HZ (Embassy)
☎031-337 6888 Telex no 727860 FAX 031-313 2543
*This West End hotel is set in two acres of grounds and is a popular
base for businessmen and tourists alike. Public areas offer modern
comforts and the bedrooms, though well equipped, are somewhat
plain and practical.*
55⇨🛏(3fb)1🎀⤫in 10 bedrooms CTV in all bedrooms ®

Lift ⟨ 50P ⤢ ❖ croquet pool table
V ✤ ⛾ Last dinner 9.30pm
Credit Cards ① ② ③ ④ ⑤

★★67% **Westbury** 92-98 St Johns Rd, Corstophine EH12 8AT
☎031-316 4466 FAX 031-316 4333
*Though the well-appointed bedrooms of this new hotel are*
*comfortable in traditional style, its open-plan theme bar features*
*unusual bric à brac, modern music and friendly, informal service,*
*whilst the menu offers a truly international cuisine.*
30⇨✦in 6 bedrooms CTV in all bedrooms ® T
sB&B⇨♦£60-£72 dB&B⇨♦£65-£78 ⊟
⟨ 30P *xmas*
❡ Continental V ✤ ⛾ ✁ Lunch £7.50-£12.50alc
Credit Cards ① ② ③ ⓔ

★★63% **Murrayfield** 18 Corstorphine Rd EH12 6HN
☎031-337 1844 FAX 031-346 8159
*A pleasant old house, conveniently located on the outskirts of the*
*city, and offering good access to the bypass, airport and road*
*bridge. It has been modernised to provide comfortable, well-*
*appointed accommodation.*
23⇨♦Annexe13rm CTV in 23 bedrooms ® T sB&B⇨♦£51
dB&B⇨♦£70 ⊟
⟨ CTV 30P
✤ ⛾ Lunch £6.50-£15alc Dinner £10-£15alc Last dinner
9.30pm
Credit Cards ① ② ③ ⑤ ⓔ

★★61% **Lady Nairne** 228 Willowbrae Rd EH8 7NG (Berni/
Chef & Brewer) ☎031-661 3396 FAX 031-652 2789
*A welcoming village inn has been converted to provide comfortable*
*accommodation comprising well-appointed bedrooms and a cosily*
*inviting lounge and bars. Service is warm and friendly throughout,*
*and menus offer a good-value range of interesting dishes.*
33⇨♦(1fb) CTV in all bedrooms ® T ✖ (ex guide dogs)
sB&B⇨♦£48-£57 dB&B⇨♦£74.50 ⊟
Lift ⟨ 100P
V ✤ ⛾ ✁ Lunch £8-£15alc Dinner £8-£15alc Last dinner
10pm
Credit Cards ① ② ③ ⑤

★★59% **Harp Toby** St John's Rd, Corstorphine EH12 (3.5m W
on A8) (Toby) ☎031-334 4750
*The recently refurbished public areas of this hotel provide superior*
*bars and a split-level carvery restaurant ; bedrooms, though*
*compact, are tastefully appointed and well equipped.*
27⇨♦(2fb)✁in 9 bedrooms CTV in all bedrooms ®
⟨ 50P
✤ ⛾ ✁
Credit Cards ① ② ③ ⑤

★★57% **Iona** Strathearn Place EH9 2AL ☎031-447 6264 &
031-447 5050 FAX 031-452 8574
*A small commercial hotel, situated in a quiet residential area south*
*of the city centre, offers good-value, practical accommodation. It*
*has well-maintained bedrooms, a busy lounge bar and a quiet,*
*comfortable first-floor lounge.*
21rm(2⇨2♦)(2fb) CTV in all bedrooms ® T sB&Bfr£28.85
sB&B⇨♦fr£42.50 dB&Bfr£51.50 dB&B⇨♦fr£58.80
CTV 20P ⤢
V ✤ Lunch fr£5.90 Dinner £9-£13.50alc Last dinner 9pm
Credit Cards ① ③

★★56% **Suffolk Hall** 10 Craigmillar Park EH16 5NE
☎031-668 4333 FAX 031-668 4506
*Located in a residential area between the by-pass and the city*
*centre, this small hotel offers comfortable bedrooms and friendly,*
*informal service.*
12rm(11⇨♦)(4fb) CTV in all bedrooms ® T
✖ (ex guide dogs) ✳ sB&B£35-£40 sB&B⇨♦£40-£45
dB&B⇨♦£50-£60 ⊟

▶

《CTV 12P ⇔ ✿
V ✿ ⚏ Bar Lunch £3-£5 Dinner £10-£12&alc Last dinner 9pm
Credit Cards ①②③⑥

★★55% **Clarendon** Grosvenor St EH12 5EG (Scottish
Highland) ☎031-337 7033 Telex no 72450 FAX 031-346 7606
*Recently refurbished, the quiet, friendly hotel is situated in the
attractive West End of the city.*
51⇨ñ(5fb) CTV in all bedrooms ⑧ T S% sB&B⇨ñ£50-£56
dB&B⇨ñ£75-£85 ⊟
Lift 《CTV ℙ *xmas*
V ✿ ⚏ Lunch £5.50-£12alc High tea £5.50-£6.25 Dinner
£10.75-£13.20&alc Last dinner 9.30pm
Credit Cards ①②③⑤

★★55% **Rothesay** 8 Rothesay Place EH3 7SL ☎031-225 4125
Telex no 727025 FAX 031-220 4350
*A popular, family-run tourist and commercial hotel in the West
End of the city provides good-value, practical accommodation.*
35rm(26⇨3ñ)(1fb) CTV in all bedrooms ⑧ T sB&B£20-£29
sB&B⇨ñ£25-£42 dB&B£30-£45 dB&B⇨ñ£35-£65
Lift 《CTV ℙ
ǒ Mainly grills ✿ ⚏ Dinner £8.50-£15.50alc Last dinner 9pm
Credit Cards ①②③④⑤

★★51% **Cairn** 10-18 Windsor St EH7 5JR ☎031-557 0175
FAX 031-556 8221
*This informal hotel, conveniently situated to the east of the city
centre, has been completely refurbished to provide well-equipped
bedrooms and bright public areas.*
52⇨ñ(12fb) CTV in all bedrooms ⑧ T ✱ sB&B⇨ñ£25-£55
dB&B⇨ñ£45-£75 ⊟
《CTV ℙ
ǒ Mainly grills V ✿ ⚏ Lunch £3.50-£7.50 High tea
£4.50-£6.50 Dinner £10.50&alc Last dinner 9pm
Credit Cards ①②③⑤⑥

○**North British** Princes St EH2 2EQ (Queens Moat)
☎031-566 2414
Due to open spring 1991
189rm

○**Travelodge** A720 Ring Rd South(6m S) (Trusthouse Forte)
☎Central reservations (0800) 850950
Due to open Oct 1990
40⇨
P

✗✗**Alp-Horn** 167 Rose St EH2 4LS ☎031-225 4787
*New owners Sami and Pat Denzler have maintained the
popularity of this intimate Swiss restaurant. An interesting range
of Swiss artefacts are on display, including an impressive wall-
mounted alp-horn in the non-smoking area. The à la
carte menu includes such delights as Bouche aux Fruits de Mer,
Trois Filets Monsieur, and a fine Apfelstrudel. Booking is
advisable for dinner.*
Closed Sun, 1st wk Jan & 2 wks Jul
ǒ Swiss 66 seats S10% Lunch £11-£12.50&alc Dinner
fr£17&alc Last lunch 2pm Last dinner 10pm ℙ ✂
Credit Cards ①③

✗✗**L'Auberge** 56 St Mary's St EH1 1SX ☎031-556 5888
*You will find L'Auberge, one of the city's most popular
restaurants, just off the Royal Mile. Dishes are prepared from the
best available Scottish ingredients, but the innovative cooking, like
the atmosphere, is decidedly French. It offers a choice of menus
and the extensive wine list is worthy of note.*
Closed 26 Dec-2 Jan
ǒ French V 55 seats Lunch £8-£11.75&alc Dinner
£17.50-£32&alc Last lunch 2pm Last dinner 9.30pm ℙ
Credit Cards ①②③⑤

✗✗**Martins** 70 Rose St, North Ln EH2 3DX ☎031-225 3106
*Tucked away in a small lane off the city's famous Rose Street, this
popular and now well-established little restaurant continues to
offer reliable and imaginatively prepared food. The menu is
constantly changing, but may include dishes such as Mousseline of
Salmon with a delicate red pepper sauce, or pigeon breast in a
sauce of strawberry and port. Service is friendly and attentive.*
Closed Sun, Mon & 2 Dec-21 Jan
Lunch not served Sat
28 seats Lunch £12.95-£14&alc Dinner £24-£30alc Last lunch
2pm Last dinner 10pm ℙ nc8yrs ✂
Credit Cards ①②③⑤

✗✗**The Vintners Rooms** The Vaults, 87 Giles St, Leith EH6 6BZ
☎031-554 8423 & 031-554 6767
*Situated in the fashionable, historic port of Leith and revitalised
by Tim and Sue Cumming who previously owned the Hole in the
Wall at Bath, this restaurant and its wine bar occupy the ground
floor of a large stone building whose vaults date back to the twelfth
century and which is reputedly the oldest continuously-used
commercial premises in Scotland. Since it was initially used for the
storage of claret and then became the home of a wine and spirits
merchants, it is appropriate that its style of cuisine should
perpetuate the "auld alliance" – Scottish seafood, meat and game
being prepared in the French provincial manner; a small but
carefully compiled main course selection varies according to
availability, while starters and puddings offer a wide choice, but all
dishes are notable for their honest, uncomplicated flavours. Food is
also served in the bar.*
Closed Sun ex during Edinburgh Festival Xmas
ǒ Scottish, French & Italian V 48 seats ✱ Lunch £17-£22&alc
Dinner £17-£22&alc Last lunch 2.30pm Last dinner 10.30pm
3P ✂
Credit Cards ①②③

✗**Philippine Islands** 1 Barony St, (off Broughton St) EH1 3SB
☎031-556 8240
*Robust, distinctive flavours are a feature at Scotland's first
Filipino restaurant. Orders are taken in the simple basement bar
and most of the main dishes are served in palayoks (clay pots with
charcoal burners to keep the food hot). They are generously
portioned, encouraging sharing, and all are accompanied by rice –
try the garlic or coconut variety.*
Lunch not served Sat & Sun
ǒ Filipino V 60 seats ✱ Lunch fr£5.50 Dinner fr£10.90&alc
Last dinner mdnt ℙ ♫
Credit Cards ①②③

✗**Shamiana** 14 Brougham St EH3 9JH ☎031-228 2265
*Just off the city centre, this restaurant specialises in north Indian
and Kashmiri cuisine, its menu offering a most interesting range of
chicken and lamb dishes which are described in some detail. A
wine recommendation is also given for each item.*
Closed 25 Dec & 1 Jan
Lunch not served Sat & Sun
ǒ Kashmiri & North Indian V 42 seats ✱ Lunch £7-£12alc
Dinner £12-£25alc Last lunch 1.30pm Last dinner 11.30pm ℙ
Credit Cards ①②③④⑤

**EDZELL** Tayside *Angus* Map **15** NO56

★★★58% **Glenesk** High St DD9 7TF ☎(03564)319
*Situated beside the golf course at the edge of the village, this
family-run hotel, with its range of leisure facilities, is popular with
golfers and holidaymakers. It has a cosy bar, traditional lounges,
and modestly appointed bedrooms which are comfortable and well
equipped.*
25rm(22⇨ñ)(3fb) CTV in all bedrooms ⑧ T ✱ sB&Bfr£32
sB&B⇨ñ fr£34 dB&Bfr£58 dB&B⇨ñ fr£60 ⊟
150P 8∞ ⇔ ✿ ▣(heated) ♪ snooker sauna solarium
gymnasium *xmas*
V ✿ ⚏
Credit Cards ②③⑤

**E**

★★61% *Panmure Arms* 52 High St DD9 7TA (Inter-Hotels)
☎(03564)420 & 427
*A relaxed atmosphere, good leisure facilities and well-equipped bedrooms are provided by this extensively refurbished, family-run hotel at the edge of the village.*
16⇒♠(2fb) CTV in all bedrooms ®
30P ▣(heated) ♪ squash snooker sauna solarium
V ♥ ⅙ Last dinner 9pm
Credit Cards ① ② ③ ⑤

EGHAM Surrey Map **04** TQ07

★★★★64% **Runnymede** Windsor Rd TW20 0AG
☎(0784)436171 Telex no 934900 FAX (0784) 436340
125⇒♠(34fb) CTV in all bedrooms ® T ✱ sB⇒♠£80-£95
dB⇒♠£95-£110 (room only) ☒
Lift ℂ 250P ♣ putting green croquet ♫ xmas
♡ International V ♥ ⌂ Lunch £14.75-£16.25&alc Dinner £16.95-£18.45&alc Last dinner 9.45pm
Credit Cards ① ② ③ ⑤
See advertisement on page 275

✕✕La Bonne Franquette 5 High St TW20 9EA ☎(0784)439494
*Cosy Anglo-French restaurant and bar featuring seasonal dishes with a good wine list and efficient service.*
Closed 25 & 26 Dec
Lunch not served Sat
♡ French 46 seats ✱ Lunch fr£16.50&alc Dinner fr£21&alc
Last lunch 2pm Last dinner 9.30pm 16P
Credit Cards ① ② ③ ⑤

EGLWYSFACH Dyfed Map **06** SN69

★★★♨70% **Ynyshir Hall** SY20 8TA ☎Glandyfi(065474)209
*This Georgian house, which stands in ten acres of woodland and gardens off the A487 a few miles west of Machynlleth, is surrounded by a wild bird reserve. Owners and staff are friendly and hospitable, public rooms are warmed by log fires, bedrooms are both comfortable and attractive, and painting courses are available for the budding artist.*
9rm(6⇒2♠)(1fb)1 ⊞ CTV in all bedrooms T
20P ♨ ♣ painting & drawing courses
♡ Welsh, English & French ♥ ⌂ ⅙ Last dinner 8.30pm
Credit Cards ① ② ③ ⓔ

EGREMONT Cumbria Map **11** NY01

★★★56% **Blackbeck Bridge Inn** CA22 2NY (Blackbeck 2.75m A595) ☎Beckermet(094684)661
*This is mainly a commercial hotel, with an attractive little restaurant and a spacious lounge bar, situated on the A595, 3 miles south of Egremont. The bedrooms are well equipped, but those in the older part of the hotel are more compact.*
22⇒♠(1fb)1 ⊞ CTV in all bedrooms ® sB&B⇒♠£23-£43.50
dB&B⇒♠£35-£55 ☒
60P ♣ ♫
♡ Mainly grills V ♥ ⌂ Lunch £5-£10alc Dinner £9.95&alc
Last dinner 10pm
Credit Cards ① ② ③ ⑤

ELCOT Berkshire Map **04** SU36

★★★65% **Elcot Park Resort** RG16 8NJ (1m N off A4) (Best Western) ☎Kintbury(0488)58100 Telex no 846448
FAX (0488) 58288
*Dating back to 1678, this smart hotel sits within 16 acres of grounds and affords fine views of the surrounding countryside. Some of the bedrooms are housed in the annexe, 100 yards from the main building, and all are well equipped and have extra facilities. Meeting and conference facilities are available, and all public areas are elegant and comfortable. A variety of interesting dishes are included on the menu, all carefully prepared from fresh produce and complemented by a selection of fine wines.*

▶

# GRANADA
## Lodge, Edinburgh

A1, Old Craighill, Musselburgh,
Edinburgh EH21 8RE
Tel: 031 653 6070 Fax: 031 653 6106

**AA** ⌂  Located on the A1
Musselburgh By-pass

A high standard of bedroom accommodation at budget prices

All bedrooms have private bathroom, colour television, radio, wake-up alarm and tea & coffee making facilities.

Meals available in Country Kitchen Restaurant in adjacent service area

Ample free parking

For further information or central reservations call 052 555 555

THE
# CAIRN
HOTEL
—— ★★ ——
**10/18 Windsor Street,
Edinburgh EH7 5JR
Telephone: 031 557 0175**

Situated within the Georgian area of the city and minutes from Princes Street. A warm and friendly welcome awaits. 52 comfortable bedrooms fully equipped. Relax in the cosy Windsor Lounge and enjoy a delicious bar meal in the Shaftesbury Lounge. The restaurant offers a varied à la carte menu and a wide selection of good wines.

**Why not visit a sister hotel with similar facilities.**

16⇱Annexe18⇱(2fb)4🛏⅄in 4 bedrooms CTV in all bedrooms ® T ✳ sB⇱£70-£85 dB⇱£85-£95 (room only) 🅿
《100P ✿ ♬ (hard) hot air ballooning at wknds *xmas*
♽ English & Continental V ♦ ⚖ Lunch fr£12.95 Dinner fr£19.50 Last dinner 9.30pm
Credit Cards ①②③⑤ⓔ

---

**ELGIN** Grampian *Morayshire* Map **15** NJ26

★★★71% **Mansion House** The Haugh IV30 1AW
🕾(0343)548811 FAX (0343) 547916
*The creation of a smart new leisure centre and additional high quality bedrooms are welcome developments at this comfortably appointed business and tourist hotel. Imaginative food is served in the attractive restaurant and willing staff provide efficient service throughout.*
18⇱®(3fb)8🛏 CTV in all bedrooms ® T ✹
sB&B⇱®£49-£60 dB&B⇱®£75-£95 🅿
《30P ✿ ▣(heated) sauna solarium gymnasium *xmas*
V ♦ ⚖ Lunch £8-£10alc High tea £5-£10alc Dinner £15-£20alc Last dinner 9pm
Credit Cards ①③

★★★57% **Eight Acres** Sheriffmill IV30 3UN (Consort)
🕾(0343)543077 FAX (0343) 540001
*This purpose-built hotel stands on the A96, on the western outskirts of the town . The bedrooms vary in size and are mainly functional, but those built in 1985 in conjunction with the sports and leisure complex are very tastefully appointed .*
57⇱®(5fb) CTV in all bedrooms ® T ✳ sB&B⇱®fr£45.95 dB&B⇱®fr£65 🅿
《CTV 200P ✿ CFA ▣(heated) squash snooker sauna solarium gymnasium *xmas*
♽ Scottish, French & Italian V ♦ ⚖ Lunch fr£5.50 High tea fr£6 Dinner fr£13 Last dinner 9pm
Credit Cards ①②③⑤ⓔ

★★66% **Park House** South St IV30 1JB 🕾(0343)547695 & 543112 FAX (0343) 541594
*The basement restaurant of this impressive Georgian house on the western perimeter road enjoys a fine reputation, and the bedrooms are thoughtfully furnished and equipped ( though rather compact in some cases ).*
6⇱® CTV in all bedrooms ® T ✳ sB&B⇱®fr£35 dB&B⇱®fr£54 🅿
《30P
♽ Scottish & French V ♦ ⚖ Lunch fr£5.80 High tea fr£4.80 Dinner fr£16alc Last dinner 9.30pm
Credit Cards ①③⑤

★★58% *Laichmoray* Station Rd IV30 1QR 🕾(0343)540045 FAX (0343) 540055
*Georgian-style, family run hotel with a friendly atmosphere. Modern, well-equipped bedrooms are found in the new section of the hotel, while the others are more traditional. Choice of bars in this popular commercial hotel.*
32rm(11⇱11®)(3fb) CTV in all bedrooms
CTV 60P ✿ pool table
V ♦ ⚖
Credit Cards ①②③⑤

★55% **St Leonards** Duff Av IV30 1QS 🕾(0343)547350
*Set in a quiet residential area this small family-run commercial hotel is a popular venue for local functions. Public areas have been substantially refurbished but bedrooms remain plain and practical.*
16rm(13⇱®)(2fb) CTV in all bedrooms ® sB&B£20-£25 sB&B⇱®£30-£35 dB&B£35-£40 dB&B⇱®£50-£55 🅿
60P ✿
♽ Scottish & French V ♦ ⚖ ⅄ S% Lunch £6.90-£7.50 High tea £5-£8.75 Dinner £13.80-£15 Last dinner 9pm
Credit Cards ①③

✗**Qismat Tandoori** 202/204 High St IV30 1BA 🕾(0343)541461
*This elegant Indian restaurant features some interesting specialities and authentic dishes, skilfully prepared and full of flavour. The service, under the supervision of the two partners, is efficient and friendly.*
Closed 25 Dec & 1 Jan
♽ European & Indian V 76 seats Lunch £2.40-£4.75&alc Dinner £5.50-£15.80alc Last lunch 2pm Last dinner 11.45pm ℘
Credit Cards ①②③

---

**ELLESMERE PORT** Cheshire Map **07** SJ47

★★65% *Berni Royal* Childer Thornton L66 1QW (Berni/Chef & Brewer) 🕾051-339 8101
*Situated on the A41, near junction 5 of the M53, a comfortable hotel which was formerly a Georgian house offers well appointed bedrooms – a number with oak beams – and thoughtfully designed public areas which include fully equipped meeting/conference rooms.*
47⇱®(2fb)2🛏 CTV in all bedrooms ® T ✹ (ex guide dogs)
《CTV 180P
♽ Mainly grills V ♦ ⚖ ⅄
Credit Cards ①②③⑤

---

**ELTERWATER** Cumbria Map **07** NY30

★★★69% **Langdale Hotel & Country Club** LA22 9JD
🕾Langdale(09667)302 FAX (09667) 694
*This hotel combines stylish interiors and extensive leisure facilities within the 23 acres of landscaped woodlands and streams in which it stands. A commendable range of slate lodge and cottage bedrooms, which blend perfectly with the environment, have been tastefully decorated and furnished, some with spa baths. The pine-canopied Purdeys Restaurant offers interesting, imaginative cuisine, and service throughout is prompt and friendly.*
65⇱®(6fb)2🛏 CTV in all bedrooms ® T ✹ (ex guide dogs)
✳ dB&B⇱®£110-£120 🅿
《100P ✿ ▣(heated) ♬ (hard) ♪ squash snooker sauna solarium gymnasium croquet mountain bicycle hire ♧ *xmas*
♽ International V ♦ ⚖ S% Lunch £3.50-£11.50alc Dinner £12-£30alc Last dinner 10pm
Credit Cards ①②③⑤ⓔ

★★👥68% **Eltermere Country House** LA22 9HY (On unclass rd between A593 & B5343) 🕾Langdale(09667)207
Closed 25-26 Dec RS mid Nov-mid Feb
*A charming country house, overlooking Elterwater and the surrounding fells from its two acres of grounds and gardens, offers attractive bedrooms and two cosy lounges.*
18rm(8⇱7®)(4fb) CTV in all bedrooms ® ✳ sB&B£27 dB&B⇱®£54 🅿
25P 🚅 ✿ putting
♽ English & Continental ♦ ⅄ Dinner £13.95 Last dinner 7.30pm

---

**ELY** Cambridgeshire Map **05** TL58

★★★62% *Fenlands Lodge* Soham Rd, Stuntney CB7 5TR (2m SE A142) 🕾(0353)667047
*Originally a farmhouse stood on this spot, two miles south of the town on the A142 Newmarket road, and this building houses the restaurant of today's hotel, having been sympathetically extended to provide an elegantly relaxing bar and lounge. The former stable block – once used to breed the local shire horses which can still be seen a short distance away – has similarly been converted to more comfortable accommodation set around an open courtyard. Meals are an enjoyable feature of a stay here, the table d'hôte menu offering a good range of flavoursome and freshly prepared dishes.*
Annexe9⇱® CTV in all bedrooms ® T
《25P
♽ English & French V ♦ ⚖ Last dinner 9.30pm
Credit Cards ①②③⑤

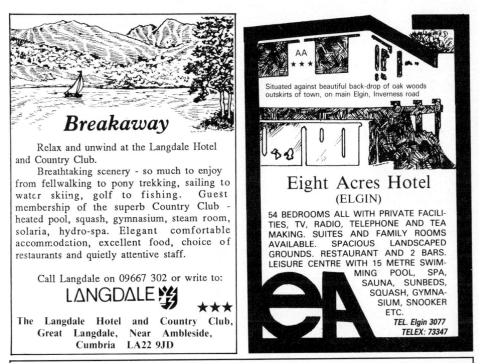

**★★66% Lamb** 2 Lynn Rd CB7 4EJ (Queens Moat)
☎(0353)663574
*The bulk of the cathedral dominates Ely and close by is The Lamb Hotel, on a busy central road junction. The décor is light and fresh, bedrooms are comfortable and well-equipped and there is a choice of bars as well as restaurant and buttery. The staff are friendly and predominantly young.*
32⇨🎢(6fb)2🛏 CTV in all bedrooms ® T sB&B⇨🎢fr£55 dB&B⇨🎢fr£72 🅿
《1🐾 *xmas*
♀ English & French V ✿ ♨ Lunch fr£8.95&alc High tea fr£3&alc Dinner fr£12 Last dinner 9.45pm
Credit Cards ①②③⑤£

**★58% Nyton** 7 Barton Rd CB7 4HZ ☎(0353)662459
*Situated south of the town centre, just off the A10, this pleasant old house is set in 2·5 acres of attractive grounds and gardens. It is family run and offers simple but fairly well equipped accommodation and friendly informal service.*
9⇨🎢Annexe5⇨🎢(2fb) CTV in all bedrooms ® 🕷
sB&B⇨🎢£30-£35 dB&B⇨🎢£40-£45
25P ❄
V S% Lunch £12-£15&alc Dinner £12-£15&alc Last dinner 8.30pm
Credit Cards ①②③⑤

**❀✕Old Fire Engine House** 25 Saint Mary's St CB7 4ER
☎(0353)662582
*As its name suggests, this delightful restaurant of character is sited in a former fire station, also home to an art gallery. A well-compiled menu of good wholesome dishes includes tomato and onion soup, pigeon with bacon, rabbit and pork pie and a roast. Seconds are offered and are difficult to refuse, but for the selection of puddings, home made ice creams and pies.*
Closed 2 wks fr 24 Dec & BH's
Dinner not served Sun
36 seats Lunch £15-£19alc Dinner £15-£19alc Last lunch 2pm Last dinner 9pm 8P ✂

---

**EMBLETON** Northumberland Map **12** NU22

**★★Dunstanburgh Castle** NE66 3UN ☎(066576)203
*The family hotel stands in rural surroundings within easy reach of the sea.*
17rm(9⇨)(3fb) ®
CTV 20P 1🐾 🚲
♀ English & French ✿ ♨
Credit Cards ①③

---

**EMBOROUGH** Somerset Map **03** ST65

**★★60% Court** BA3 4SA ☎Stratton-on-the-Foss(0761)232237
*Privately owned and run, an hotel dating back to the seventeenth century stands in three acres of grounds overlooking the Mendip countryside. Its functional, well-equipped accommodation is popular with businessmen and tourists alike.*
10⇨🎢(2fb)2🛏 CTV in all bedrooms ®
40P ❄
♀ English & French V ✿ ♨ ✂ Last dinner 9.00pm
Credit Cards ①②③

---

**EMPINGHAM** Leicestershire Map **04** SK90

**★★70% The White Horse Inn** Main St LE15 8PR
☎(078086)221 FAX (078086) 521
*A stone-built, 17th century courthouse on the edge of Rutland Water has been converted into a delightful hotel, with attractive bedrooms, particularly those in the stable-block annexe. Bar meals are good, and the owner lays great emphasis on fresh produce in the preparation of the imaginative restaurant menu.*

3rmAnnexe8⇨🎢(4fb)1🛏✂in 1 bedroom CTV in all bedrooms ® T ✳ sB&Bfr£21.50 sB&B⇨🎢fr£32.50 dB&Bfr£29.50 dB&B⇨🎢£42.50-£55 🅿
60P 🐾 *xmas*
V ✿ ♨ ✂ Lunch £9.95-£10.65 Dinner £8-£20alc Last dinner 9.45pm
Credit Cards ①②③⑤£
**See advertisement under OAKHAM**

---

**EMSWORTH** Hampshire Map **04** SU70

**★★★64% Brookfield** Havant Rd PO10 7LF ☎(0243)373363 FAX (0243) 376342
Closed 25 Dec-1 Jan
*This friendly family-run hotel with good bedrooms has now been by-passed by the new road. The Hermitage Restaurant, completely refurbished, overlooks a colourful garden and offers table d'hôte and à la carte menus which represent good value for money.*
41⇨🎢1🛏 CTV in all bedrooms ® T 🕷 (ex guide dogs)
sB&B⇨🎢£53 dB&B⇨🎢£63 🅿
《80P 🚲 ❄
♀ English & French V ✿ ♨ Lunch £11.50&alc Dinner £11.50&alc Last dinner 9.30pm
Credit Cards ①②③⑤

**✕✕36 On The Quay** 47 South St PO10 7EG
☎Chichester(0243)375592 & 372257
*Don't be confused by the name – this charming little restaurant is actually at 47 South Street, but it is on the quay. In the 3 small, but stylish interconnecting dining rooms, Raymond Shoutland offers some unusual combinations of flavours, the more simple dishes being the most successful. Daily specials include lobsters from the tank, oysters, turbot with a herb crust and breast of pheasant with cranberry sauce. The cooking, in the modern British style, tends to be rich, and at times cloying, but the combination of originality, location and service (diners press the bell beside each table for attention) make a visit here well worthwhile.*
Closed Sun
Lunch not served Sat
♀ French V 40 seats ✳ Lunch £12.50-£17.50 Dinner £25.95-£32.95alc Last lunch 2pm Last dinner 10pm 6P nc9yrs ✂
Credit Cards ①②③④

---

**ENFIELD** Greater London Map **04** TQ39

**★★54% Holtwhites** 92 Chase Side EN2 0QN ☎081-363 0124 FAX 081-366 9089
*A busy, commercial hotel offering a choice of modern, well-equipped bedrooms and a generally acceptable standard of cooking.*
30rm(28⇨🎢)(1fb) CTV in all bedrooms ® T 🕷 (ex guide dogs) sB&B⇨🎢£65-£70 dB&B⇨🎢£97 🅿
《CTV 30P 4🐾 🚲 nc5yrs
♀ International V ✿ ♨ ✂ Bar Lunch £2.50-£11.50alc Dinner £10-£20alc Last dinner 8.30pm
Credit Cards ①②③⑤£

**✕✕Norfolk** 80 London Rd EN2 6HU ☎081-363 0979 & 081-363 1153
*This is an old fashioned, but friendly, restaurant with roasts and flambé dishes featured on the menu. The wines are reasonably priced.*
Closed Sun, 1st 3 wks Aug & BH's
Lunch not served Sat
Dinner not served Mon
♀ English & French V 90 seats ✳ Lunch £15-£25alc Dinner £15-£25alc Last lunch 2pm Last dinner 10pm ✂
Credit Cards ①②③④⑤

**EPPING** Essex Map **05** TL40

**★★★57% Post House** High Rd, Bell Common CM16 4DG (Trusthouse Forte) ☎(0378)73137 Telex no 81617 FAX (0378) 560402

*Annexe accommodation provides a varied range of well-equipped bedrooms at this carefully modernised old coaching inn. The choice of set price or à la carte menus in its tastefully refurbished "Turpins" restaurant is complemented by a simple wine list and attentively friendly service.*

Annexe82⇌(22fb)⚡in 25 bedrooms CTV in all bedrooms ® T S% sB⇌£72-£83 dB⇌£83-£94 (room only) 
( 95P CFA ♫ *xmas*
English & French V S% Lunch fr£10.50 High tea fr£2.75 Dinner fr£16 Last dinner 10.30pm
Credit Cards 1 2 3 4 5

**EPSOM** Surrey Map **04** TQ26

**★★58% Heathside** Brighton Rd KT20 6BW ☎Burgh Heath(0737)353355 Telex no 929908 FAX (0737) 370857
(For full entry see Burgh Heath)

**ERBISTOCK** Clwyd Map **07** SJ34

**✕Boat Inn** LL13 0DL ☎Bangor-on-Dee(0978)780143 FAX (0978) 780312

*This lovely 16th-century, stone-built inn stands near the church on the banks of the River Dee. A small flagstoned bar leads to the basement restaurant, where the table d'hôte and à la carte menus are varied. Chef, Martin Rae, creates interesting sauces, such as peach and brandy or orange and mango. There is also a vegetarian menu and a recent introduction is an organic wine list.*

English & French V 70 seats ✱ Lunch fr£8.95&alc Dinner fr£11.95 Last lunch 2.15pm Last dinner 9pm 50P
Credit Cards 1 2 3 5

**ERISKA** Strathclyde *Argyllshire* Map **10** NM94

★★★

**★★★ ISLE OF ERISKA**

PA37 1SD
☎Ledaig(063172)371
Telex no 777040
Closed Dec-mid Mar

*Situated on an island belonging to its owner, the Reverend Robin Buchanan-Smith, Eriska is a truly baronial house, offering seclusion, a tranquil setting rich in wildlife, and space. The large bedrooms retain a somewhat old-fashioned atmosphere, but have all the comforts of a luxury hotel. From the attractive drawing room there are fine views of Loch Linnhe and the surrounding hills to delight the eye whilst waiting to enjoy the sound cooking of chef Vilas Roberts as exemplified in the 6-course dinners which are such a feature of the evenings. Staff are friendly, many of them taken on for the season from Australasia and what they may lack in conventional training is more than compensated for by their unaffected charm and willingness to please.*

16⇌(1fb) CTV in all bedrooms ®
( 36P (hard) croquet watersports
Last dinner 8.30pm
Credit Cards 1 2 3

**ERMINGTON** Devon Map **02** SX65

**★★62% Ermewood House** Totnes Rd PL21 9NS (Exec Hotel) ☎Modbury(0548)830741
Closed 23 Dec-9 Jan

*Friendly, country-house-style hotel catering for the tourist and commercial trade.*

12⇌(1fb)1 CTV in all bedrooms ® T sB&B⇌£45 dB&B⇌£60
15P
English & Continental ⚡ Dinner £16.50 Last dinner 8.30pm
Credit Cards 1 3 £

**See advertisement under PLYMOUTH**

E

**ERSKINE** Strathclyde *Renfrewshire* Map **11** NS47

**★★★64% Crest Hotel-Erskine Bridge** North Barr PA8 6AN (Trusthouse Forte) ☎041-812 0123 Telex no 777713 FAX 041-812 7642

*Standing on the banks of the Clyde with views over Erskine Bridge, this modern hotel is designed for the residental conference trade and business clientele. There is an extensive leisure complex.*

168⇌(4fb)⚡in 35 bedrooms CTV in all bedrooms ® T Lift ( 300P CFA (heated) snooker sauna solarium gymnasium
V ⚡
Credit Cards 1 2 3 4 5

All hotels are now given a percentage grading for the quality of their facilities. A full explanation can be found within 'How we Classify Hotels and Restaurants' at the front of the book.

# The Erskine Bridge Crest Hotel

Situated twelve miles from the centre of Glasgow, the hotel offers panoramic views over the River Clyde and is easily accessible from the M8.
166 bedrooms including Lady Crest, Executive and Executive Study Rooms, plus 2 bedrooms with spa bath.
Sensations Leisure Club with swimming pool, sauna, solarium and fitness room.
Ample free car parking.

Inclusive short break packages available.
Please request our Welcome Breaks brochure.

**ERSKINE BRIDGE CREST HOTEL**
GLASGOW
**Erskine ★★★**
**Renfrewshire PA8 6AN**
**Tel: (041) 812 0123**
**Telex: 777713. Fax: (041) 812 7642**

**ESHER** Surrey

**See LONDON plan 1***B1*(pages 426–7)

★★**64%** **Haven** Portsmouth Rd KT109AR (1 m NE on A307) (Inter-Hotels) ☎081-398 0023 FAX 081-398 9463

*This pleasant family-run commercial hotel is near Sandown Park. It provides a homely atmosphere, with refurbished bedrooms providing modern facilities. Good, home-cooked meals are served in the nicely appointed dining room.*

16⇨ᶠ▜Annexe4⇨ᶠ▜(4fb) CTV in all bedrooms ® T sB&B⇨ᶠ▜£55-£62 dB&B⇨ᶠ▜£65-£72 ▤ CTV 20P 1🅰 🚲

♀ International **V** ✿ ⟂ Bar Lunch £3.50-£5 High tea £3.50-£5 Dinner £8-£10.50 Last dinner 8.30pm

Credit Cards ⒈ ⒉ ⒊ ⒋ ⒌

✕✕**Good Earth** 14-18 High St KT109RT ☎(0372)62489 & 66681

*This popular, well managed, modern restaurant specialises in regional Chinese dishes, making skilful use of fresh ingredients and spices. Pleasant staff provide attentive service.*

Closed 24-27 Dec

♀ Cantonese, Pekinese & Szechuan **V** 100 seats ✶ Lunch £15.50-£22.50 Dinner £15.50-£22.50 Last lunch 2.30pm Last dinner 11pm ✔

Credit Cards ⒈ ⒉ ⒊ ⒌

---

**ESKDALE GREEN** Cumbria Map **06** NY10

★★**61%** **Bower House Inn** CA19 1TD (Best Western) ☎Eskdale(09403)244

*This country inn is popular with tourists and hillwalkers. Most of the bedrooms are contained in 2 annexe buildings.*

5⇨ᶠ▜Annexe17⇨ᶠ(3fb) CTV in all bedrooms ® T ✕ ✶ sB&B⇨ᶠ▜fr£35 dB&B⇨ᶠ▜fr£50 ▤ 60P ✿ *xmas*

♀ English & French **V** ✿

Credit Cards ⒈ ⒊

---

**ESKDALEMUIR** Dumfries & Galloway *Dumfriesshire* Map **11** NY29

★★**67%** **Hart Manor** DG13 0QQ ☎(03873)73217

Closed 25 Dec

*Set in beautiful countryside, this small hotel offers traditional accommodation and courteous, attentive service. Dinners are freshly prepared and are very good value.*

7rm(2⇨3ᶠ▜)(2fb) CTV in all bedrooms ® ✶ sB&B£19-£21.50 dB&B£38-£43 dB&B⇨ᶠ▜£41-£48 ▤ CTV 30P ✿ ✿ ✔

**V** ✿ ✔ Sunday Lunch fr£4alc Dinner £12.50-£15 Last dinner 8pm

---

**EVERCREECH** Somerset Map **03** ST63

★★**57%** *Pecking Mill Inn & Hotel* BA6 6PG (On A371 1m W of village) (Best Western) ☎(0749)830336

*A charming 16th-century inn on the A371 enjoying pleasant rural views. Bedrooms are compact, but well equipped, and the intimate dining room serves a comprehensive menu of mainly grills. Staff are friendly and helpful.*

6ᶠ▜ CTV in all bedrooms ®

23P 🚲

♀ Mainly grills ✿ Last dinner 10pm

Credit Cards ⒈ ⒉ ⒊ ⒌

---

Entries for red-star hotels are highlighted by a tint panel. For a full list of these establishments consult the Contents page.

---

**EVERSHOT** Dorset Map **03** ST50

★★ **SUMMER LODGE**

DT2 0JR ☎(0935)83424 FAX (0935) 83029

Closed 2-18 Jan

*We are delighted to make an award of red stars this year to a charming hotel, owned by the Corbett family and run by Manager Michael Ash. Guests cannot fail to be enchanted both by the delightful grounds and gardens surrounding the Georgian house, and by the friendly young staff who are always willing to put themselves out to be helpful. Public rooms, with their colourful flower arrangements, have a pleasant and comfortable atmosphere, just right for a traditional afternoon tea or quiet browse through books or magazines. Bedrooms vary in size and style but are all tastefully furnished and well equipped. A new chef, Roger Jones, from the Rising Sun at St Mawes, has recently joined the staff and will no doubt be keen to make his own contribution to the high reputation the hotel has always enjoyed for its cuisine.*

11⇨Annexe6⇨(1fb) CTV in 6 bedrooms ® T sB&B⇨£75-£90 dB&B⇨£113-£170 (incl dinner) ▤ CTV 40P 🚲 ✿ ⌣(heated) ♪ (hard & grass) croquet nc8yrs *xmas*

**V** ✿ ⟂ Lunch fr£14.50 Dinner fr£23 Last dinner 8.30pm

Credit Cards ⒈ ⒉ ⒊

---

**EVESHAM** Hereford & Worcester Map **04** SP04

★★★**66%** **The Evesham** Coopers Ln, off Waterside WR11 6DA ☎(0386)765566 Telex no 339342 FAX (0386) 765443

Closed 25 & 26 Dec

*Situated close to the river and convenient for the town centre, this is a pleasant family-run hotel with attractive gardens. Built as a mansion house in 1540, it now offers comfortable, modern accommodation, complemented by an imaginative menu and an extensive selection of wines.*

40⇨ᶠ▜(1fb) CTV in all bedrooms ® T S% sB&B⇨ᶠ▜£48-£55 dB&B⇨ᶠ▜£66-£76 ▤ 50P 🚲 ✿ ▣(heated) croquet putting

♀ International **V** ✿ ⟂ S% Lunch £10-£21alc Dinner £14-£21alc Last dinner 9.30pm

Credit Cards ⒈ ⒉ ⒊ ⒌

★★★**65%** **Northwick Arms** Waterside WR11 6BT ☎(0386)40322 Telex no 333686 FAX (0386) 41070

*This small hotel is set next to the River Avon, south-east of the town centre. The bedrooms are modern, comfortable and well equipped, and the public areas are pleasant and attractive. The hotel caters for tourists and business people, and offers a small conference facility.*

25⇨ᶠ▜(1fb) 🚻 CTV in all bedrooms ® T sB&B⇨ᶠ▜fr£46 dB&B⇨ᶠ▜fr£56 ▤ ₵ 90P

♀ English & French **V** ✿ ⟂ S% Lunch £8-£10&alc Dinner £12-£15&alc Last dinner 10pm

Credit Cards ⒈ ⒉ ⒊ ⒌ ⓔ

---

Book as early as possible for busy holiday periods.

★★77% **The Mill At Harvington** Anchor Ln, Harvington
WR11 5NR (4.5m NE, off A439) ☎(0386)870688
Closed 24-27 Dec
*Included for the first time in our guide, this delightful new hotel is highly recommended by our Inspector. Simon and Jane Greenhalgh have lovingly and painstakingly converted the 16th-century malting mill to provide very comfortable, well-equipped accommodation. The food is imaginative and well prepared and the hospitality is outstanding. It is situated just off the A439, four miles from Evesham.*
15⇨↑ CTV in all bedrooms ® T ⋈ (ex guide dogs) ✻
sB&B⇨↑£45-£48 dB&B⇨↑£65-£70 ▤
50P ♨ ✿ ⌂(heated) ♪ nc10yrs
♀ English & French Lunch £10.95-£13.50 Dinner £17.50-£20.50 Last dinner 9.30pm
Credit Cards ①③

★★77% **Riverside** The Parks, Offenham Rd WR11 5JP
☎(0386)446200 FAX (0386) 40021
RS Nov-Feb
*The cottage-style hotel and its riverside moorings can be found by following the signs for Offenham; there is no access to the hotel from the By-Pass. Public rooms and bedrooms are pretty and comfortable enjoying fine views of the River Avon, but the outstanding feature of the hotel is the highly imaginative cooking which makes good use of top quality produce.*
7⇨↑ CTV in all bedrooms ® T ⋈ (ex guide dogs) S10%
sB&B⇨↑£45-£50 dB&B⇨↑£60-£70 ▤
40P ✿ ♪ xmas
♀ English & French V ♢ Lunch £11.95-£13.95 Dinner £15.95-£17.95 Last dinner 9pm
Credit Cards ①③£

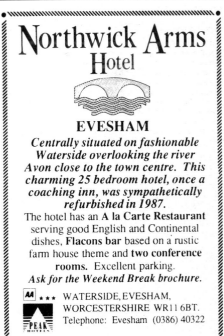

# The Mill at Harvington

Peaceful, owner-run hotel, tastefully converted from a beautiful Georgian house and former baking mill. Set in acres of gardens on the bank of the Avon, it sits ¼ mile from the A439 between Stratford and Evesham. All bedrooms overlook the river, and each has private bath and shower, colour TV, telephone and tea facilities. Excellent restaurant, beams and open fires. Fishing, heated pool, tennis court.

*Special Short Break Rates*

Anchor Lane, Harvington, Evesham, Worcs WR11 5NR
Tel: Evesham (0386) 870688

Ashley Courtenay. AA ★ ★ 77%

---

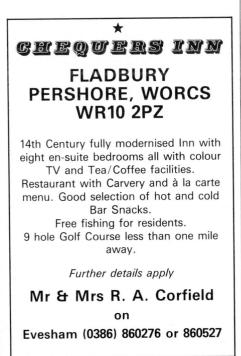

E

**E**

★★73% **Waterside** 56 Waterside WR11 6JZ ☎(0386)442420
*Proprietors Linda and David Young offer a warm welcome and*
*comfortable accommodation which is well equipped with an array*
*of modern facilities. The Waterside is ideal for both business*
*guests and tourists.*
8rm(2⇌4♠)Annexe4⇌♠(3fb) CTV in all bedrooms ® T
sB&B£23.60 sB&B⇌♠£43.80 dB&B£39.40
dB&B⇌♠£54.70 月
30P ⊞ ✔
V ♦ 및 ⊁
Credit Cards ①②③

★56% **Park View** Waterside WR11 6BS ☎(0386)442639
Closed 24 Dec-3 Jan
*A family owned hotel just across the road from the river and with*
*easy access to the town centre. It offers a homely atmosphere and*
*good value for money, though accommodation is modest and rather*
*old fashioned.*
29rm(2fb) sB&B£17.60-£20 dB&B£30.50-£33.50
CTV 40P
♦ 및 Sunday Lunch £7.75-£8.50 Dinner £7.75-£8.50 Last
dinner 7pm
Credit Cards ① ③ ⓔ

---

**EXEBRIDGE** Somerset Map **03** SS92

★★65% **Anchor Inn** TA22 9AZ ☎Dulverton(0398)23433
*Set on the banks of the River Exe this delightful 16th-century inn*
*offers comfortable well appointed accommodation and a warm and*
*friendly atmosphere. Thoughtfully prepared dishes are served in*
*the restaurant.*
6⇌♠(2fb)1月 CTV in all bedrooms ® T sB&B⇌♠fr£35
dB&B⇌♠£54-£60
CTV 100P ✿ ✔
V ♦ 및 Lunch fr£8.25 Dinner fr£12.95 Last dinner 9pm
Credit Cards ①③

**See advertisement on page 281**

---

**EXETER** Devon Map **03** SX99

See **Town Plan Section**
See also Stoke Canon &Topsham

★★★71% **The Forte** Southernhay East EX1 1QF (Trusthouse
Forte) ☎(0392)412812 Telex no 42717 FAX (0392) 413549
*A large, modern city centre hotel with tastefully decorated,*
*comfortable bedrooms which are well equipped for the commercial*
*traveller. The table d'hôte and à la carte menus offer some*
*interesting dishes. The hotel also has leisure facilities, conference*
*rooms and its own car park.*
110⇌♠(6fb)⊁in 31 bedrooms CTV in all bedrooms ® T
sB⇌♠£89-£97 dB⇌♠£99-£108 (room only) 月
Lift ( 115P ⊞ ⬚(heated) sauna solarium gymnasium *xmas*
♀ English & International V ♦ 및 ⊁ Lunch £12.50-£21&alc
High tea fr£5.50 Dinner £17-£21&alc Last dinner 10.15pm
Credit Cards ①②③④⑤

★★★68% **Buckerell Lodge Crest** Topsham Rd EX2 4SQ
(Trusthouse Forte) ☎(0392)52451 Telex no 42410
FAX (0392) 412114
*A modern hotel of some character, situated on the Topsham to city*
*centre road, appeals to businessman and tourist alike with its wide*
*range of facilities and friendly, attentive service. Both standard*
*and executive bedrooms are well-equipped and comfortable, bright*
*public areas are up-to-date in design, and restaurant menus are*
*complemented by the range of meals available in the popular bar.*
54⇌♠(2fb)⊁in 8 bedrooms CTV in all bedrooms ® T
sB⇌♠£70-£85 dB⇌♠£82-£97 (room only) 月
( 200P ⊞ ✿ *xmas*
♀ English & French V ♦ 및 ⊁ Lunch £8.25-£9&alc Dinner
£14.30-£15.25&alc Last dinner 9.45pm
Credit Cards ①②③④⑤

---

★★★67% **Rougemont** Queen St EX4 3SP (Mount Charlotte
(TS)) ☎(0392)54982 Telex no 42455 FAX (0392) 420928
*Located in the heart of the city opposite Exeter Central Station,*
*this character hotel has, over recent times, received significant*
*refurbishment. The bedrooms have been transformed into bright*
*modern rooms and public rooms have had similar good work. The*
*hotel has five function rooms and a range of conference facilities.*
90⇌♠(5fb)1⊞⊁in 13 bedrooms CTV in all bedrooms ® T ✳
sB⇌♠fr£60 dB⇌♠fr£69.50 (room only) 月
Lift ( 40P CFA *xmas*
♀ English & French V ♦ 및 ⊁ Lunch fr£7.50&alc Dinner
fr£12.50&alc Last dinner 10pm
Credit Cards ①②③⑤

★★★66% **St Olaves Court** Mary Arches St EX4 3AZ
☎(0392)217737 FAX (0392) 413054
Closed 25 Dec-4 Jan
*Cosily tucked away in secluded grounds at the heart of the city,*
*this Georgian hotel is an attractive place to stay. Due to the age of*
*the building, some rooms are limited as to space, but all are well*
*equipped and there are now a number of new executive rooms in*
*the adjacent annexe which are spacious and offer the luxury of en*
*suite jacuzzis. The hotel is justly proud of its restaurant, named*
*after the original owner of the house, James Goldsworthy. A*
*typical selection from the menu might be Mousseline of salmon*
*infused with fennel, followed by Rosettes de boeuf à l'estragon or*
*Suprême de canard au vinaigre de vin rouge.*
13rm(11⇌♠)Annexe4⇌♠(4fb) CTV in all bedrooms ® T
✖ (ex guide dogs) sB&B£33 sB&B⇌♠£53-£59
dB&B⇌♠£46-£70 月
( CTV 15P 2⬤ ⊞ ✿
♀ French V ♦ 및 Lunch fr£10.95&alc Dinner fr£14.95&alc
Last dinner 9.30pm
Credit Cards ①②③⑤ⓔ

★★★63% **Granada** Moor Ln, Sandygate EX2 4AR (M5 jnct 30)
(Granada) ☎(0392)74044 FAX (0392) 410406
*A purpose-built modern hotel attached to Granada Services,*
*recently extended to provide more well-equipped bedrooms. Open-*
*plan public areas are limited, the bar extending into a simply-*
*appointed dining room where an à la carte menu is comlemented by*
*a short wine list.*
76⇌♠(22fb)⊁in 18 bedrooms CTV in all bedrooms ® T
✖ (ex guide dogs) ✳ S% sB⇌♠fr£32
dB⇌♠fr£36 (room only) 月
( CTV 80P ✿
♀ English & French V ♦ 및 ⊁ S% Lunch fr£5 Dinner
fr£7&alc Last dinner 9.30pm
Credit Cards ①②③⑤

**See advertisement on page 283**

★★★63% **White Hart** 65 South St EX1 1EE ☎(0392)79897
Telex no 42521 FAX (0392) 50159
Closed 25-26 Dec
*This former coaching inn, steeped in history, offers character*
*charm and cosiness. Bedrooms in the main building vary in shape*
*and size but are, like those in the new wing, well-equipped with*
*modern furnishings and facilities. Guests can choose to eat in the*
*Wine Bar, Coffee Shop or extensive à la carte restaurant.*
61rm(42⇌16♠) CTV in all bedrooms T ✖ (ex guide dogs)
sB&B£33-£49 sB&B⇌♠£49-£53 dB&B⇌♠£71-£75 月
Lift ( CTV 80P ⊞
V ♦ 및 Lunch £7-£8&alc Dinner £11.40-£23alc Last dinner
9.45pm
Credit Cards ①②③⑤ⓔ

---

A rosette is an indication of exceptional
standards of cuisine.

## ★★★AA

# ROUGEMONT HOTEL

Queen Street
Exeter EX4 3SP
Telephone: 0392 54982 Telex: 42455
Facsimile: 0392 420928

This centrally located hotel is ideally situated for either the leisure or business traveller.

Each of the 90 tasteful bedrooms offer private bathroom, colour television and tea and coffee making facilities.

There is a first class restaurant and several bars to chose from.

Meeting facilities are also available.

*For Reservations at over 90 Mount Charlotte Thistle Hotels telephone London: 071 937 8033 or Leeds: 0532 444866.*

**E**

# ANCHOR INN HOTEL

A charming, fully licensed, residential country inn, on the banks of the River Exe. Salmon and Trout Fishing — an ideal place for exploring Exmoor. Comfortable accommodation, with good food and the personal service of the resident proprietors John and Judy Phripp. Dine in style at the Stable Block Restaurant overlooking the romantic River Exe.

AA★★ ETB ♚ ♚ ♚ ♚

## EXEBRIDGE, NR DULVERTON.
## TEL. (0398) 23433

*A. Courtenay Recomm. Derek Johansen's Inns with Restaurant Guide*

# The Barton Cross Hotel

## xvii century

The only six bedroom hotel in Great Britain with a ★ ★ ★ AA rating 73% British Tourist Authority Commended Hotel.

International Standard Accommodation with Superb Cuisine. Set in glorious Devon Countryside yet only four miles Exeter. Easy access Dartmoor, Exmoor and Coast. Relaxing Weekend and Midweek Breaks. Christmas House Party.

**BARTON CROSS HOTEL & RESTAURANT**
at Huxham, Exeter, EX5 4EJ
Telephone: (0392) 841245 Telex: 42603
Fax: (0392) 50402
*See gazetteer under Stoke Canon*

# St Olaves Court Hotel AA★★★

The Country House Hotel
In The Heart Of The City

A small, exclusive, Georgian Hotel set in its own delightful walled garden.

The candlelit Golsworthy's Restaurant has fast earned a reputation as the leading place to eat in the city. Nouvelle and classical French cuisine are served in a warm intimate atmosphere. The restaurant and cocktail bar overlook the pond and gardens.

Helpful friendly staff and the many facilities available will make your stay a delightful experience.

**MARY ARCHES STREET**
**Exeter EX4 3AZ Tel: 217736**
**GOLSWORTHY'S RESTAURANT**

**E**

**★★★61% Countess Wear Lodge** Topsham Rd, Exeter Bypass EX2 6HE (Queens Moat) ☎Topsham(0392)875441
Telex no 42551 FAX (0392) 876174
*Conveniently positioned off the M5 and just outside the city, this hotel features motel-style ground-floor bedrooms, the majority being set round an open car park. Though compact, they have recently been refurbished to a high standard and are well equipped. Public areas have been similarly upgraded to offer a comfortable reception lounge and a choice of bright conference and function suites. As well as the traditional restaurant, home-made fare and lighter snacks are available in Reilly's Food and Wine Bar.*
44⇌↑(1fb)⊁in 4 bedrooms CTV in all bedrooms ® T ✳ sB&B⇌↑£30-£49 dB&B⇌↑£48-£60 ⊟
《 120P ✿ CFA ♬ (hard) *xmas*
♀ English & French V ♦ ⚖ Lunch £13.50-£20alc High tea £5 Dinner £7-£10&alc Last dinner 9.45pm
Credit Cards ①②③⑤ⓔ

**★★★59% Imperial** St David's Hill EX4 4JX ☎(0392)211811
Telex no 42551 FAX (0392) 420906
*Built as a mansion during the Queen Anne period, this hotel is situated in five acres of spacious sheltered grounds.*
27rm(21⇌2↑)(1fb) CTV in all bedrooms ® T ✳ sB&B£29.50-£47.50 sB&B⇌↑£47.50 dB&B£42.50-£60 dB&B⇌↑£60 ⊟
《 70P ✿ CFA riding water ski-ing windsurfing *xmas*
♀ European V ♦ ⚖ Lunch £9.50&alc Dinner £11.95&alc Last dinner 9pm
Credit Cards ①②③⑤ⓔ

**★★★57% Gipsy Hill** Gipsy Hill Ln, Pinhoe EX1 3RN (3m E on B3181) (Consort) ☎(0392)65252 Telex no 57515
FAX (0392) 64302
Closed 25-30 Dec
*Set in attractive gardens, with easy access to the M5 from its position on the eastern edge of the city, the hotel caters for conferences and banquets, and has twenty bedrooms with en suite facilities, together with comfortable public rooms.*
20⇌↑Annexe3⇌↑(3fb)2🏮 CTV in 20 bedrooms ® T ✳ sB&B⇌↑£50-£55 dB&B⇌↑£62-£70 ⊟
《 60P ✿ ♫
♀ English & French V ♦ ⚖
Credit Cards ①②③⑤

**★★★54% Devon Motel** Exeter Bypass, Matford EX2 8XU (Brend) ☎(0392)59268 Telex no 42551 FAX (0392) 413142
*Situated on the Exeter Bypass, this modern hotel offers a choice of standard and well-equipped executive rooms. Meals are taken in the adjacent former Manor House where the eating options includes a lunchtime carvery.*
Annexe41⇌↑(3fb) CTV in all bedrooms ® T
sB&B⇌↑£44-£50 dB&B⇌↑£57-£70 ⊟
《 250P
♀ English & French V ♦ ⚖ Lunch £9&alc Dinner £11-£13&alc Last dinner 9pm
Credit Cards ①②③⑤ⓔ

**★★★50% Exeter Arms Toby** Rydon Ln, Middlemoor PH7 4BP (Toby) ☎(0392)435353 FAX (0392) 420826
*Modern purpose-built complex alongside primary road on outskirts of city.*
37⇌↑(6fb)⊁in 10 bedrooms CTV in all bedrooms ®
✖ (ex guide dogs)
《 380P
V ♦ ⚖ ⊁ Last dinner 10pm
Credit Cards ①②③⑤

**★★67% St Andrews** 28 Alphington Rd EX2 8HN (Exec Hotel)
☎(0392)76784 FAX (0392) 50249
Closed 24 Dec-1 Jan
*The distinctive character of this long-established family-owned hotel appeals equally to business travellers and tourists. It offers light comfortably furnished and particularly well-equipped*

*bedrooms and equally comfortable public areas including a choice of lounges and a cheerful dining room where good home-cooked meals are served. Service is prompt and unfailingly pleasant throughout.*
17⇌↑(2fb) CTV in all bedrooms ® T sB&B⇌↑£35-£48.40 dB&B⇌↑£54-£68.90 ⊟
20P 🚲
♦ ⚖ Bar Lunch £2-£8 Dinner fr£11&alc Last dinner 8.15pm
Credit Cards ①②③

**★★61% Fairwinds Hotel** EX6 7UD ☎(0392)832911
(For full entry see Kennford)

**★★58% Red House** 2 Whipton Village Rd EX4 8AR
☎(0392)56104
*Guests can choose between à la carte, carvery and bar snack menus at this small, family-run commercial hotel on the outskirts of the city. Compact bedrooms, though simply decorated and furnished, are fully equipped with modern facilities.*
12⇌↑(2fb) CTV in all bedrooms ® T S% sB&B⇌↑£25-£34 dB&B⇌↑£38-£46 ⊟
28P
♀ English & French V ♦ ⚖ S% Lunch £5.50-£8.50&alc Dinner fr£9.50&alc Last dinner 9.30pm
Credit Cards ①③ⓔ

**EXMOUTH** Devon Map **03** SY08

**★★★59% Royal Beacon** The Beacon EX8 2AF (Best Western)
☎(0395)264886 FAX (0395) 268890
*Modernised Georgian posting house, overlooking the sea.*
35⇌↑(3fb)2🏮⊁in 1 bedroom CTV in all bedrooms ® T sB&B⇌↑£39-£42.35 dB&B⇌↑£67.30-£72.60 ⊟
Lift CTV 20P 10🚗 CFA snooker *xmas*
♀ English & French V ♦ ⚖ ⊁
Credit Cards ①②③④⑤ⓔ

★★

# Ebford House Hotel

Exmouth Road, Ebford, Devon EX3 0QH

TEL. Exeter (0392) 877658

A beautifully restored Georgian country house set in lovely gardens in rural Devon. Our elegant restaurant is renowned for its imaginative cuisine. In Frisco's Bistro dine in a more informal atmosphere. Gym with sauna, solarium and jacuzzi. Central for Exeter, Dartmoor and beaches.

BTA Highly Commended.
Ashley Courtenay Recommended.
*See gazetteer under Topsham*

**F**

★★★58%, **The Imperial** The Esplanade EX8 2SW (Trusthouse Forte) ☎(0395)274761
*Set in grounds which include an outdoor pool and command extensive views across Lyme Bay, this popular family hotel offers good amenities and friendly service.*
57⇨ᛗ(9fb) CTV in all bedrooms ® sB⇨ᛗ£65
dB⇨ᛗ£87 (room only) ᛨ
Lift ( 61P ⇎ ✿ ⊃(heated) ♪ (hard) ♫ ⚬ xmas
V ✿ ⚚ ⊁ S15% Sunday Lunch £7.50 Dinner £13.25&alc Last dinner 9pm
Credit Cards ①②③④⑤

★★65%, **Barn** Foxholes Hill, off Marine Dr EX8 2DF
☎(0395)274411
*Set in its own well-kept gardens, this hotel occupies an elevated site and commands excellent sea views. Bedrooms are clean and bright and there is a comfortable lounge and informal reception bar. Good plain home cooking and a warm welcome are offered to guests.*
11⇨ᛗ(4fb) CTV in all bedrooms ® ℋ
sB&B⇨ᛗ£24.50-£33.50 dB&B⇨ᛗ£49-£57 ᛨ
30P 3⛐ (£1 per night) ⇎ ✿ ⊃ croquet putting green
V ✿ ⚚ ⊁ Lunch £7.25-£12 Dinner fr£12 Last dinner 8pm
Credit Cards ①③ ⓔ

★58%, **Aliston House** 58 Salterton Rd EX8 3EW ☎(0395)274119
*The Aperitif Bar of this friendly, welcoming hotel features an old, black-leaded range. Throughout, rooms are attractively decorated and the standard of service is good.*
12rm(2⇨5ᛗ)Annexe2ᛗ(2fb) CTV in all bedrooms ®
sB&B£18-£20 sB&B⇨ᛗ£20-£23 dB&B£36-£40
dB&B⇨ᛗ£40-£44 ᛨ
CTV 16P xmas
V ✿ ⚚ Lunch fr£6 High tea fr£4 Dinner £7-£8.50 Last dinner 8.30pm

---

**FAIRBOURNE** Gwynedd Map **06** SH61

★★58%, *Brackenhurst* LL38 2HX ☎(0341)250226
*A pleasant family-owned hotel in an elevated position with excellent views over the Mawddach Estuary.*
10rm(3⇨1ᛗ)(2fb) CTV in all bedrooms ®
CTV 11P ⇎ ✿
V ✿ ⚚ ⊁ Last dinner 8pm
Credit Cards ⑤

---

**FAIRFORD** Gloucestershire Map **04** SP10

★★★60%, **Hyperion House** London St GL7 4AH (Consort)
☎Cirencester(0285)712349 FAX (0285) 713126
RS 1-7 Jan
*Situated in the heart of the village, this Cotswold stone house has been carefully refurbished and enlarged to provide well-equipped bedrooms and bright, attractive open-plan public areas.*
26⇨ᛗ(4fb) CTV in all bedrooms ® T sB&B⇨ᛗ£62.50-£70
dB&B⇨ᛗ£72.50-£80 ᛨ
( 40P ✿ xmas
V ✿ ⚚ Lunch £11.50 Dinner £20 Last dinner 9.30pm
Credit Cards ①②③⑤ ⓔ

---

**FAIRY CROSS** Devon Map **02** SS42

★★★⚐69%, **Portledge** EX39 5BX (off A39) (Best Western)
☎Horns Cross(02375)262 & 367 Telex no 9312132625
FAX (02375) 717
*Steeped in history and surrounded by beautiful Devonshire countryside, this thirteenth-century manor house was converted to hotel use in 1947. Its pride is the Armada wing – built from the proceeds of a Spanish galleon's wreck on the nearby coast – but all bedrooms have ensuite facilities and are spacious and tastefully decorated. The public areas are elegantly comfortable, their blend of modern comfort and old world charm complemented by a tranquil atmosphere and friendly service. À la carte and table d'hôte menus offer a range of interesting dishes based on local*
*produce. A heated swimming pool, tennis court, crazy golf course and private beach, are available for guests' use.*
26⇨ᛗAnnexe9⇨ᛗ(5fb)1⇎ CTV in all bedrooms ® T
sB&B⇨ᛗ£32-£62.50 dB&B⇨ᛗ£64-£105 ᛨ
CTV 100P ✿ CFA ⊃(heated) ♪ (hard) ♪ table tennis pool table xmas
♀ English & French V✿ ⚚ Lunch fr£5 Dinner £18 Last dinner 9.15pm
Credit Cards ①②③⑤

See advertisement under BIDEFORD

---

**FAKENHAM** Norfolk Map **09** TF92

★★59%, *Crown* Market Place NR21 9BP ☎(0328)851418
*Set in the centre of the town, its good-sized car park accessible via an archway from the main road, this charmingly old world hotel complements heavily beamed ceilings and fireplaces with a Victorian/cottage decor ; well-equipped bedrooms have every modern comfort, however, and a popular restaurant caters for healthy appetites.*
11⇨ᛗ CTV in all bedrooms ® ℋ (ex guide dogs)
25P
V ✿ ⚚ ⊁ Last dinner 9.30pm
Credit Cards ①②③⑤

---

**FALFIELD** Avon Map **03** ST69

★★64%, **Park Hotel & Restaurant** GL12 8DR ☎(0454)260550
*Situated south of the village on the A38 and one mile from junction 14 of the M5, this small hotel occupies four acres of grounds, and parts of the original building are 400 years old. Bedrooms are comfortable, well furnished and equipped, and friendly and attentive services are provided by hosts Ken and Rouha Manley and their staff.*
10rm(4⇨3ᛗ)(2fb) CTV in all bedrooms ® T
ℋ (ex guide dogs) ✳ sB&B£40 sB&B⇨ᛗ£45 dB&B£50
dB&B⇨ᛗ£55 ᛨ
CTV 120P ✿ xmas
♀ French V ✿ ⚚ ⊁ S% Sunday Lunch £5.95 Dinner £10-£16alc Last dinner 10pm
Credit Cards ①②③

---

**FALKIRK** Central *Stirlingshire* Map **11** NS88

★★★59%, *Stakis Park* Arnot Hill, Camelon Rd FK1 5RY
(Stakis) ☎(0324)28331 Telex no 776502 FAX (0324) 611593
*Modern purpose-built business and tourist hotel on the edge of the town. It offers a choice of bars, good-function facilities and well-equipped bedrooms which have been upgraded to a comfortable standard.*
55⇨ᛗ(3fb)⊁in 12 bedrooms CTV in all bedrooms ®
Lift ( 151P CFA ♫
♀ English, French & Italian V ✿ ⚚ ⊁ Last dinner 9.45pm
Credit Cards ①②③⑤

✗**Pierre's** 140 Graham's Rd FK2 7BQ ☎(0324)35843
Closed Sun, Mon, 25-26 Dec & 1-5 Jan
Lunch not served Sat
♀ French 38 seats ✳ Lunch £6.90&alc Dinner £8.65-£10.35&alc Last lunch 2.15pm Last dinner 9.30pm 12P
Credit Cards ①②③⑤

All hotels are now given a percentage grading for the quality of their facilities. A full explanation can be found within 'How we Classify Hotels and Restaurants' at the front of the book.

FALMOUTH Cornwall & Isles of Scilly Map **02** SW83

See **Town Plan Section**
See also **Mawnan Smith**
★★★♨ 76% **Penmere Manor** Mongleath Rd TR11 4PN (Best
Western) ☎(0326)211411 Telex no 45608 FAX (0326) 317588
Closed 24-26 Dec
*Under the control of dedicated, experienced owners and set in five
acres of garden and woodland, the hotel features a fitness trail, a
children's adventure playground and the Fountain Leisure Club
with its indoor pool, jacuzzi, sauna and trimnasium; twelve new
garden rooms will shortly complement existing accommodation.*
39⇌♪↑(15fb) CTV in all bedrooms ® T sB&B⇌♪↑£45-£63
dB&B⇌♪↑£68-£99 ⊟
《50P ⚗ ❀ ▭(heated) ⌿(heated) sauna solarium gymnasium
jacuzzi croquet table tennis ♪ *xmas*
V ♡ ⊡ ⌿ Bar Lunch fr£1.75 High tea £4.50-£5.50 Dinner
£17-£18&alc Last dinner 9pm
Credit Cards ①②③⑤

★★★ 69% **Greenbank** Harbourside TR11 2SR ☎(0326)312440
Telex no 45240 FAX (0326) 211362
Closed 1-15 Jan
*Beautifully situated on the river's edge, with views across to
Flushing, the harbour and the docks, this hotel offers spacious
accommodation with good facilities, suitable for both business
client or holidaymaker, the skilful combining of antiques with
modern décor and furnishings in the public rooms creating a
comfortable atmosphere. Both à la carte and table d'hôte menus
are available in the river-fronting restaurant.*
43rm(36⇌6↑)(1fb) CTV in all bedrooms ® T
sB&B⇌♪↑£30-£65 dB&B⇌♪↑£80-£115 ⊟
Lift 《50P 24🚗 ✦ solarium hairdressing beauty salons ♪
☺ English & French V ♡ ⊡ Lunch £9&alc High tea £3.50-£7
Dinner £15.50&alc Last dinner 9.45pm
Credit Cards ①②③⑤

An ideal base from which to
explore the nearby cities of
Edinburgh and Stirling.
Travel east to the Firth of Forth
coastline and explore the
charming seaside villages.
Well appointed modern
bedrooms, some family rooms,
all ensuite with Col TV,
telephone, tea/coffee maker and
complimentary bowl of fruit.
Telephone: 0324 — 28331.

——— ᵮ STAKIS ———

# Park Hotel ★★★
——— F A L K I R K ———

**F**

# PENMERE MANOR HOTEL

## THE HOTEL

Situated in 5 acres of garden woodland overlooking
Falmouth Bay, the Penmere Manor Hotel is owned
and managed by the Pope family. The elegant
ambience of a country house is retained throughout,
and the lounges and Fountain Bar are peaceful and
relaxing. The attractive bedrooms are individually
decorated and all have private facilities en-suite,
colour TV, hair dryer, clock radio, telephone and
tea/coffee making facilities.

## FOUNTAIN LEISURE CLUB

The Fountain Leisure Club offers indoor and outdoor
swimming pools, jacuzzi spa, sauna, trimnasium,
solarium, 3/4 size snooker table, games cellar,
croquet, outdoor giant chess, playground and
woodland fitness trail.

## THE GARDEN ROOMS

The individually designed Garden Rooms are not
only superior in size, but also in luxury and
facilities.

## BOLITHO'S RESTAURANT

Excellent food and wine can
be enjoyed in Bolitho's
Restaurant. Choices from
either A la Carte or
Table d'hote menus.

Mongleath Road, Falmouth,
Cornwall TR11 4PN
Tel: (0326) 211411
Fax: (0326) 317588
Telex: 45608

Best Western
HOTELS WORLDWIDE

AA ★★★ ♨

# Falmouth

★★★**66% Royal Duchy** Cliff Rd TR11 4NX (Brend)
☎(0326)313042 Telex no 42551 FAX (0326) 319420
*In a good position with fine views of the bay, this hotel offers varied accommodation from small singles and compact family rooms to de luxe suites, all well furnished. Fairly spacious public areas include a semi-formal restaurant.*
50⇨(9fb) CTV in all bedrooms ® T sB&B⇨£44-£50 dB&B⇨£77-£125 ♬
Lift ℂ CTV 50P ✿ ◳(heated) sauna solarium spa bath table tennis ♨ *xmas*
♡ English & French V ✧ ⚑ Lunch £8&alc Dinner £13.50-£15&alc Last dinner 9pm
Credit Cards ①②③⑤

★★★**62% Green Lawns** Western Ter TR11 4QJ ☎(0326)312734
Telex no 45169 FAX (0326) 211427
Closed 24-30 Dec
*Built in 1910 in the style of a French château, and set amid terraced lawns, the hotel offers purpose-built, well-equipped bedrooms; the extensive menus of the Garras Restaurant should satisfy most tastes, and there is a modern leisure complex for guests' use.*
40⇨ʰ(8fb)2♬ CTV in all bedrooms ® T sB&B⇨ʰ£42.55-£60.20 dB&B⇨ʰ£58.64-£89.70 ♬
ℂ 60P 9⇔ ✿ CFA ◳(heated) ⅋ (hard & grass) squash sauna solarium gymnasium jacuzzi ♫
♡ English & French V ✧ ⚑ ⅍ Lunch £2.50-£7.50&alc High tea £1.50-£10 Dinner £15-£16&alc Last dinner 10pm
Credit Cards ①②③④⑤ ⓔ

★★★**61% Falmouth** TR11 4NZ ☎(0326)312671 Telex no 45262 FAX (0326) 319533
*An elegant hotel with an outdoor swimming pool in its grounds overlooks the beaches and harbour of Falmouth. Bedrooms with good facilities and warm, comfortable public areas attract commercial traveller and holidaymaker alike. The spacious dining room offers a table d'hôte menu of well-prepared dishes, and both conference facilities and a ballroom are available.*
73⇨(8fb)1♬ CTV in all bedrooms ® ✳ sB&B⇨£44-£51 dB&B⇨£77-£92 ♬
Lift ℂ 150P ✿ CFA ⌒(heated) snooker sailing croquet putting pool table *xmas*
♡ French & Italian V ✧ ⚑ ⅍ Lunch fr£7.50 Dinner fr£14.50&alc Last dinner 9.30pm
Credit Cards ①②③⑤ ⓔ

★★★**61% St Michaels** Stracey Rd TR11 4NB (Consort)
☎(0326)312707 & 318084 Telex no 45540 FAX (0326) 319147
*Recently upgraded to a high standard, the hotel offers picturesque views of the bay from its situation close to the beach; bedrooms are well-equipped and public areas spacious, a wide range of indoor and outdoor leisure facilities also being available.*
60⇨ʰAnnexe15⇨ʰ(22fb) CTV in all bedrooms ® T sB&B⇨ʰ£63-£71 dB&B⇨ʰ£118-£130 (incl dinner) ♬
ℂ 100P ✿ ◳(heated) ⅋ (hard & grass) squash snooker sauna solarium gymnasium jacuzzi windsurfing ♨ *xmas*
♡ English & French V ✧ ⚑ ⅍ Sunday Lunch £7.50&alc High tea £8 Dinner £13-£16&alc Last dinner 9.30pm
Credit Cards ①②③⑤ ⓔ

★★**76% Crill Manor Hotel & Restaurant** Budock Water
TR11 5BL (2.5m W on unclass rd) ☎(0326)211880
FAX (0326) 211229
*This small, comfortable, friendly hotel in a peaceful rural location has been totally refurbished to provide a high standard of accommodation.*
11⇨ʰ CTV in all bedrooms ® T ✳ sB&B⇨ʰ£42.50-£57.50 dB&B⇨ʰ£85-£125 (incl dinner) ♬
25P ✿ ⌒(heated) *xmas*
♡ English & Continental V ✧ ⚑ Lunch £9-£12.50&alc Dinner £13.50-£16.50&alc Last dinner 9.30pm
Credit Cards ①③ ⓔ

See advertisement on page 289

★★**61% Park Grove** Kimberley Park Rd TR11 2DD
☎(0326)313276
Closed Jan
*Occupying a good position overlooking Kimberley Park, this long-established family-run hotel attracts a regular clientele and also specialises in golfing holidays. It offers an informal, relaxed atmosphere, wholesome food and friendly service.*
17rm(15ʰ)(4fb) CTV in all bedrooms ® T S% sB&B£22-£25 sB&Bʰ£22-£25 dB&B£44-£50 dB&Bʰ£44-£50
25P 3⇔
✧ ⚑ Bar Lunch £2-£5 Dinner £7.50-£12 Last dinner 7.30pm
Credit Cards ①③ ⓔ

See advertisement on page 289

★★**60% Carthion** Cliff Rd TR11 4AP ☎(0326)313669
Closed Nov-Feb
*In a prime, elevated position on the sea front, with an attractive garden terrace, this hotel has a homely relaxing atmosphere. The helpful service is supervised by the proprietors and their family.*
18⇨ʰ CTV in all bedrooms
18P ⇔ nc10yrs
♡ English & French V ✧ ⚑ ⅍ Last dinner 8pm
Credit Cards ①②③⑤

★★**60% Gyllyngdune Manor** Melvill Rd TR11 4AR
☎(0326)312978
Closed Jan
*A family-run Georgian Manor where service is informal and friendly. Bedrooms are generally compact and are furnished in either traditional or modern styles. The hotel has a games room and an indoor swimming pool which is situated next to the bar.*
35rm(29⇨)(3fb)3♬ CTV in all bedrooms ®
►

# Go on...
# spoil yourself!

## ST MICHAELS
OF FALMOUTH

⟪ 35P 4🍴 (charged) ❀ ▣(heated) sauna solarium gymnasium table tennis pool table ♫
♀ Continental ✧ ⬭
Credit Cards ①②③⑤

★★54% *Melville* Sea View Rd TR11 4NL ☎(0326)312134 RS Nov-Jan
*Set in 2 acres of sub-tropical gardens, this Victorian hotel has distant sea views and a friendly atmosphere.*
22➪🏠(3fb) ℝ 🗙 (ex guide dogs)
CTV 20P 10🍴 (charged) ❀ croquet lawn putting green
♀ English & Continental Last dinner 8pm

★★*Lerryn Hotel* De Pass Rd TR11 4BJ ☎(0326)312489
Closed 7 Oct-Apr
*Small hotel in a quiet position near seafront.*
20➪🏠(2fb) CTV in all bedrooms ℝ 🗙
13P 2🍴 (£12) 🚭 nc6yrs
✧ ⬭ Last dinner 8pm

---

**FAREHAM** Hampshire Map **04** SU50

★★66% **Red Lion** East St PO16 0BP (Lansbury)
☎(0329)822640 Telex no 86204 FAX (0329) 823579
*This centrally located former coaching inn retains much of its original character in the beams and exposed brickwork of its public areas. Bedrooms are nicely coordinated and well equipped. Bar meals are served as well as the à la carte selections in the restaurant and the wine list includes popular items. Service is friendly and relaxed.*
44➪(3fb)1🛏✂in 6 bedrooms CTV in all bedrooms ℝ
🗙 (ex guide dogs) sB&B➪fr£69 dB&B➪fr£82 🅿
⟪ CTV 136P 3🍴 🚭
♀ English & Continental V ✧ Lunch fr£11&alc Dinner fr£11&alc Last dinner 10pm
Credit Cards ①②③⑤

★★63% **Maylings Manor** 11A Highlands Rd PO16 7XJ
☎(0329)286451 FAX (0329) 822584
*This extended Edwardian manor house is set in 2·5 acres on the western edge of Fareham. Bedrooms, recently upgraded, are well equipped, and the Cams Rose Restaurants offers a choice of menus with light meals also served in the Raffles Bar. There are two popular conference/function rooms.*
26rm(24➪)(2fb)2🛏 CTV in all bedrooms ℝ T ✱ S10%
sB&B➪£48-£52 dB&B➪£58-£62 🅿
87P ❀
♀ English & French V ✧ ⬭ Lunch £8.75-£10&alc Dinner £8.75-£10&alc Last dinner 9.30pm
Credit Cards ①②③⑤ⓔ

○**Solent** Solent Business Park, Whiteley PO15 7AJ (Shire)
☎(0489)880000
Due to open Nov 1990
88➪🏠

---

**FARNBOROUGH** Hampshire Map **04** SU85

★★★63% *Queens* Lynchford Rd GU14 6AZ (Trusthouse Forte)
☎(0252)545051 Telex no 859637 FAX (0252) 377210
*The imposing character façade of this hotel conceals a redesigned interior with generous public areas; Berties Coffee Shop offers two or three course buffet lunches at fixed prices and a grill menu in the evening, whilst the à la carte and fixed price menus of the Club Room emphasise fresh ingredients presented in modern style. Some particularly spacious and comfortable bedrooms are available, as are the facilities of the Glades Leisure Club should guests wish to keep in trim, the atmosphere throughout being welcoming and friendly.*
110➪(2fb)2🛏✂in 20 bedrooms CTV in all bedrooms ℝ

⟪ 170P CFA ▣(heated) sauna solarium gymnasium health & fitness centre ♨
V ✧ ⬭ ✂ Last dinner 10pm
Credit Cards ①②③④⑤

★★58% *Falcon* Farnborough Rd GU14 6TH ☎(0252)545378
FAX (0252) 522539
Closed 24 Dec-2 Jan
*Accommodation is well equipped and maintained at this popular hotel with its modern bedroom extension, open-plan bar/lounge and restaurant with conservatory.*
30➪🏠(2fb)🛏✂in 8 bedrooms CTV in all bedrooms ℝ T 🗙
sB&B➪🏠£57 dB&B➪🏠£67
30P 🚭
♀ International V ✧ ⬭ ✂ Lunch fr£12.50alc Dinner fr£15.50alc Last dinner 9.30pm
Credit Cards ①③

**See advertisement on page 291**

✗ **Wings Cottage Chinese** 32 Alexandra Rd, North Camp GU14 6DA ☎(0252)544141
Closed Sun
Lunch not served Sat
♀ Chinese 70 seats S10% Lunch £17-£24&alc Dinner £17-£24&alc Last lunch 2pm Last dinner 10.30pm 20P nc10yrs ♫
Credit Cards ①②③⑤

---

**FARNHAM** Surrey Map **04** SU84

★★★64% *Hog's Back* Hog's Back GU10 1EX (Embassy)
☎Runfold(02518)2345 Telex no 859352 FAX (02518) 3113
(For full entry see Seale)

## The Gyllyngdune Manor Hotel

AA ★ ★

**Melvill Road, Falmouth,
Cornwall TR11 4AR
Telephone: (0326) 312978**

Old Georgian manor house, romantically situated in one acre of beautiful gardens, overlooking the Bay and Estuary. Guaranteed away from traffic, but within ten minutes' walk of the town centre and two minutes from the beach. Very large car park, covered space if required. Luxury indoor heated swimming pool, games room, Sauna and Solarium. Golf at Falmouth Golf club. 95% rooms en-suite all with colour TV, direct dial telephone and tea/coffee making facilities. Every comfort with personal attention the primary consideration.

## The Park Grove Hotel

**Kimberley Park Road, Falmouth.
Tel: (0326) 313276    ★ ★**

A small but distinguished hotel. Centrally situated, occupying a lovely position overlooking beautiful Kimberley Park. The proprietors take a special pride in the excellent cuisine. The harbour, beaches and town are all within easy walking distance. Licensed. 17 bedrooms (15 with shower/toilet en suite). Colour TV, radio, intercom, child listening system, tea/coffee making facilities in all bedrooms.

F

289

★★★**56%, Bush** The Borough GU9 7NN (Trusthouse Forte)
☎(0252)715237 Telex no 858764 FAX (0252) 733530
*A 17th-century Coaching House with well equipped bedrooms,*
*friendly, helpful staff, coffee shop and restaurant.*
68⇨♠(2fb)1⚋⊁in 20 bedrooms CTV in all bedrooms ® T ✱
S15% sB⇨♠£65-£76 dB⇨♠£80-£91 (room only) ☐
《 60P ✿ CFA *xmas*
V ✧ ⚗ ⊁ Lunch £9.50-£12.50&alc High tea £1.50-£5 Dinner
£14.95&alc Last dinner 9.30pm
Credit Cards ①②③④⑤

★★**56%, Trevena House** Alton Rd GU10 5ER ☎(0252)716908
FAX (0252) 722583
Closed 24 Dec-4 Jan
*Standing in 5 acres of grounds one mile west of Farnham off the*
*eastbound carriageway of the A31. This country house style of*
*hotel retains many of the original Gothic-Victorian features. With*
*an informal atmosphere it is popular for business conferences and*
*all social occasions.*
20⇨♠ CTV in all bedrooms ® T ✱ sB&B⇨♠£25-£48
dB&B⇨♠£40-£60 ☐
30P ⚗ ✿ ⌓ ♪ (hard)
✧ ⚗ Dinner £10-£15alc Last dinner 9.15pm
Credit Cards ①②③⑤ ⓔ

**FARRINGTON GURNEY** Avon Map **03** ST65

★★**67%, Country Ways** Marsh Ln BS18 5TT
☎Temple Cloud(0761)52449 FAX (0761) 53360
Closed 24-31 Dec
*A warm welcome is offered to guests at this small country hotel off*
*the A37 south of the village. The 6 en suite bedrooms are full of*
*character, the attractive restaurant serves imaginative food and the*
*staff are friendly.*
6⇨♠ CTV in all bedrooms ® T ✱ ✱ sB&B⇨♠£45-£49.50
dB&B⇨♠£55-£60 ☐
12P ⚗ ✿
✧ ⚗ ⊁ Lunch £17-£20alc Dinner £17-£20alc Last dinner 9pm
Credit Cards ①③⑤

**See advertisement under WELLS**

**FARTHING CORNER MOTORWAY SERVICE AREA**
**(M2)** Kent Map **05** TQ86

⌂**Rank Motor Lodge** Hartlip ME8 8PW (between juncts 4 & 5
M2) (Rank) ☎Medway(0634)377337
58⇨♠(12fb)⊁in 6 bedrooms CTV in all bedrooms ® ✱
sB&B⇨♠£27.50 dB&B⇨♠£34.50 Continental breakfast
《 60P
Credit Cards ①②③⑤

**FAUGH** Cumbria Map **12** NY55

★★★**54%, String of Horses Inn** CA4 9EG ☎Hayton(0228)70297
FAX (0228) 70675
Closed 24-25 Dec
*A village inn of charm and character features oak beams and*
*roaring log fires; bedrooms are very elaborate, most having*
*canopied or four-poster beds and double sunken baths.*
14⇨♠3⚋ CTV in all bedrooms ® T S% sB&B⇨♠£55-£68
dB&B⇨♠£62-£88 ☐
《 50P ⌁(heated) sauna solarium whirlpool spa
⚘ English & French V ✧ Lunch fr£9.95 Dinner fr£14.95&alc
Last dinner 10pm
Credit Cards ①②③⑤ ⓔ

Hotels with a high percentage rating for quality
are highlighted by a % across their
gazetteer entry.

**FAVERSHAM** Kent Map **05** TR06

★★★**72%, Throwley House** Ashford Rd, Sheldwich ME13 0LT
(2m S of M2 jnct 6 on A251 ) ☎(0795)539168
*An 18th-century country house in 16 acres of gardens and*
*parkland has been sympathetically furnished to preserve its charm.*
*Spacious bedrooms combine luxury with comfort, being well*
*equipped with modern facilities as well as those extra touches*
*which are so welcoming. Public areas are both attractive and*
*comfortable, including two elegant restaurants where skilfully*
*prepared dishes of a high quality are featured on a short but*
*imaginative menu which changes fortnightly. The wine list is well*
*balanced. The owners' personal supervision of this hotel ensures a*
*warm and friendly atmosphere.*
12⇨♠(1fb) CTV in all bedrooms ✱ (ex guide dogs)
《 65P ⚗ ✿ ☉ putting green ncl 1yrs
⚘ French V ✧ ⚗ ⊁ Last dinner 10pm
Credit Cards ①②③⑤

❋✕✕**Read's** Painters Forstal ME13 0EE (2m S A251)
☎(0795)535344
*The hallmark of David Pitchford's cooking is his generous and*
*properly constructed sauces. His flair for classical recipes is being*
*advanced by his gift for combining wild and farm-reared produce*
*to create exciting and original flavours. Our Inspector simply could*
*not decide on his favourite dish from among such temptations as:*
*Terrine de foie gras et poireaux (fresh foie gras with baby leeks) in*
*a Sauternes jelly, Barquettes de moules safranées (delicate pastry*
*boats with mussels and white Burgundy sauce), Caneton*
*Gressingham poêlé suédoise (pot-roasted duck breasts, wild and*
*domestic, in cider sauce with apples, dates, Calvados and*
*marinated sultanas), Mélange de poissons grillés beurre de cerfeuil*
*(mixed grill of sole, red mullet, monkfish, langoustine and mussels*
*on a rich chervil butter sauce), so recommended all. To finish with,*
*the patisseries and petits fours are delightful. The wine list features*
*over 200 bins, including Louis Latour Burgundies, unusual wines*
*and around 30 bottles at £12 or under for good value. Service is*
*considerate and attentive.*
Closed Sun, Mon, 26 Dec & 2 wks Aug
⚘ English & French 44 seats Lunch £12.50 Dinner
£24-£28&alc Last lunch 2pm Last dinner 10pm 40P
Credit Cards ①②③⑤

**FEARNAN** Tayside *Perthshire* Map **11** NN74

★**60%, Tigh-an-Loan** PH15 2PF (Guestaccom)
☎Kenmore(08873)249
Closed Oct-Etr
*This small family-run hotel set on the picturesque shore of Loch*
*Tay provides an ideal base for touring holidaymakers, offering*
*peaceful relaxation, traditional comforts and good home cooking.*
8rm(3⇨)(1fb) ® sB&Bfr£21 dB&Bfr£42 dB&B⇨fr£47
CTV 25P ⚗ ✿ ♪
V ✧ ⚗ S% Bar Lunch fr£3.50 Dinner fr£10 Last dinner 8pm
Credit Cards ①③

**FELIXSTOWE** Suffolk Map **05** TM33

★★★**69%, Orwell Moat House** Hamilton Rd IP11 7DX (Queens
Moat) ☎(0394)285511 Telex no 987676 FAX (0394) 670687
*Maintaining many traditional characteristics, in spite of a modern*
*extension, this hotel is located close to the railway station and*
*convenient for the docks and the A45. Staff are friendly and*
*willing to please. The bedrooms are pleasantly furnished and*
*decorated; there are choices of bars, restaurants and lounges.*
58⇨♠(10fb) CTV in all bedrooms ® T ✱ sB⇨♠fr£55
dB⇨♠fr£70 (room only) ☐
Lift 《 150P 20☎ ✿ CFA ♫
⚘ English & French V ✧ ⚗ Lunch £12.50&alc Dinner
£15&alc Last dinner 9.45pm
Credit Cards ①②③⑤ ⓔ

F

★★★62%, **Brook** Orwell Rd IP11 7PF ☎(0394)278441
Telex no 987674
*A modern, well-furnished hotel situated in a residential area close
to the town centre and the sea.*
25⇨(1fb) CTV in all bedrooms ® ✻
《 20P
✿ ⬚
Credit Cards 1 2 3 5

★★66%, **Marlborough** Sea Front IP11 8BJ ☎(0394)285621
Telex no 987047 FAX (0394) 670724
*Situated on the seafront, the hotel offers comfortable well-equipped
accommodation, a choice of menus and a popular 'joint of the day'
carvery. Conference and banqueting facilities are available.*
45⇨⋔(2fb)1⊞ CTV in all bedrooms ® T
sB⇨⋔£36.95-£46.50 dB⇨⋔£52.50-£54.50 (room only) ♬
Lift 《 CTV 19P windsurfing *xmas*
♀ English & French V ✿ ⅍ Lunch £8.95&alc Dinner
£11.95&alc Last dinner 9.45pm
Credit Cards 1 2 3 5 ⓔ

**FELLING** Tyne & Wear Map **12** NZ26

⌂**Travelodge** Lean Ln NE10 8YB (Trusthouse Forte)
☎091-438 3333 Central res (0800) 850950
41⇨⋔(41fb) CTV in all bedrooms ® sB⇨£24
dB⇨⋔£29.50 (room only)
《 41P ⊞
Credit Cards 1 2 3

**FELMINGHAM** Norfolk Map **09** TG22

★★⚑74% **Felmingham Hall Country House** NR28 0LP
☎Swanton Abbott(069269)631 FAX (069269) 320
*Situated on the B1145 between Aylesham and North Walsham,
this Elizabethan Tudor residence is signposted from the village. It
stands in 15 acres of countryside, the immediate areas around the
house level to lawn and well tended borders. Inside, the hotel is
furnished throughout with style and comfort, whilst retaining many
of the original fire places and covings. The restaurant is well
appointed and has a small, but daily-changed menu. The chef uses
good quality produce and with his small, professional team, serves
imaginative dishes. The accommodation is of similar quality, with
some very spacious rooms, including lovely genuine four-poster and
half-tester beds. A charming drawing room with log burner
complete the picture of a quality country house.*
12⇨⋔Annexe6⇨⋔2⊞ CTV in all bedrooms ® T
✻ (ex guide dogs) ✳ sB&B⇨⋔£50-£70
dB&B⇨⋔£110-£130 (incl dinner) ♬
P ⊞ ✿ ☞ croquet nc12yrs *xmas*
♀ English & French V ✿ ⅍ Lunch £12-£15 Dinner
£18.95-£22.95 Last dinner 9.30pm
Credit Cards 1 2 3

**FENNY BRIDGES** Devon Map **03** SY19

★64% **Fenny Bridges** EX14 0BQ ☎Honiton(0404)850218
FAX (0404) 850920
*This roadside inn maintains its busy bar trade and, having been
completely renovated following a serious fire a couple of years ago,
offers extremely attractive en suite bedrooms whose excellent
facilities attract both holidaymaker and businessman. A compact
residents' lounge provides a quiet area on the first floor, while
meals from an à la carte blackboard menu are available in the
dining area of the lounge bar.*
6⇨⋔(1fb)⋔in 2 bedrooms CTV in all bedrooms ® T
sB&B⇨⋔£26.50-£32.50 dB&B⇨⋔£39.50-£43.50 ♬
CTV 75P ✿ ⌁
♀ English & French V ✿ ⬚ ⅍ Lunch fr£3.95&alc Dinner
fr£4.45&alc Last dinner 10pm
Credit Cards 1 2 3 5 ⓔ

★61% **Greyhound Inn** EX14 0BJ (Berni/Chef & Brewer)
☎Honiton(0404)850380
10⇨⋔1⊞ CTV in all bedrooms ® T ✻ (ex guide dogs)
sB&B⇨⋔£36.50 dB&B⇨⋔£49.50 ♬
80P
V ✿ ⅍ Lunch £8-£15alc Dinner £8-£15alc Last dinner 10pm
Credit Cards 1 2 3 5

**FENSTANTON** Cambridgeshire Map **04** TL36

○**Travelodge** A604, Huntingdon Rd(Trusthouse Forte)
☎Central reservations (0800) 850950
Due to open winter 1990
40⇨
P

**FENWICK** Strathclyde *Ayrshire* Map **11** NS44

★★61% **Fenwick** Kilmaurs Rd KA3 6AX ☎(05606)478
FAX (05606) 334
*Access to the Fenwick Hotel is more easily obtained from the A77
than from the centre of the village. The Fenwick now has new
owners, who have embarked on a programme of renovation, and
the hotel's cuisine is already attracting considerable interest. Bar
food is also good.*
10rm(7⋔) CTV in all bedrooms ® T ✳ sB&B£28 sB&B⋔£35
dB&B£40 dB&B⋔£50
150P
♀ French V ✿ ⬚ Lunch £9&alc High tea £5.50-£11.50 Dinner
£14&alc Last dinner 10pm
Credit Cards 1 3

1991 marks the 25th anniversary of this guide.

★★

**Falcon Hotel**

**FARNBOROUGH ROAD
FARNBOROUGH, HAMPSHIRE GU14 6TH
TEL: (0252) 545378**

Situated on the A325 overlooking Farnborough's
aerospace centre, home of the world-famous air
show. Close to M3 and Aldershot military town.

★ 30 bedrooms each with private bathroom,
  direct dial telephone, colour TV and tea &
  coffee making facilities
★ Restaurant & Bar
★ Car Park

ETB ♻♻♻♻ **Ashley Courtenay recommended**

**RESERVATIONS: (0252) 545378**

**FERMAIN BAY**

See **Guernsey under Channel Islands**

---

**FERNDOWN** Dorset Map **04** SU00

★★★★**61%, Dormy** New Rd BH22 8ES (De Vere)
☎Bournemouth(0202)872121 Telex no 418301
FAX (0202) 895388
*Attractive hotel with well-appointed bedrooms, some in individual bungalows in hotel's extensive grounds.*
130⇍🏠(8fb)2🛏 CTV in all bedrooms ® T
sB&B⇍🏠£90-£240 dB&B⇍🏠£120-£270 🍴
Lift ( CTV 220P ✿ CFA 🖾(heated) *P* (hard) squash snooker sauna solarium gymnasium 🎜 *xmas*
V ✆ 𝒟 Lunch fr£10&alc Dinner £15-£16&alc Last dinner 9.30pm
Credit Cards ①②③④⑤
**See advertisement under BOURNEMOUTH**

★★**60%, Coach House Inn** Tricketts Cross BH22 9NW (junc A31/A348) (Consort) ☎(0202)861222 FAX (0202) 894130
*This modern hotel, with its friendly, informal atmosphere and keen, attentive staff, provides accommodation in good-sized bedrooms furnished with all modern amenities and contained in four blocks outside the main building.*
Annexe44⇍🏠 CTV in all bedrooms ® T ✱ S%
sB&B⇍🏠£37-£45 dB&B⇍🏠£53-£60 🍴
100P 25🚗 CFA
⍾ English & Italian V ✆ 𝒟
Credit Cards ①②③⑤ ⓔ

---

**FERRYBRIDGE SERVICE AREA** West Yorkshire Map **08** SE42

☖**Granada Lodge** (A1/M62 jnct 33) (Granada)
☎Knottingley(0977)670488
*Located within the service area at the intersection of the A1 and M62, this modern, purpose-built hotel offers comfortable and well equipped accommodation, and is very good value. All meals can be obtained from the two restaurants in the adjacent main service area, which are self-service all day and with waitress service in the evening.*
35⇍🏠(6fb)⚥in 5 bedrooms CTV in all bedrooms ®
🕇 (ex guide dogs) ✱ S% sB⇍🏠fr£25
dB⇍🏠fr£28 (room only)
60P
⚥
Credit Cards ①②③⑤

---

**FETTERCAIRN** Grampian *Kincardineshire* Map **15** NO67

★★**64%, Ramsay Arms** AB3 1XX ☎(05614)334
FAX (05614) 500
12⇍🏠(1fb)1🛏 CTV in all bedrooms ® T ✱ sB&B⇍🏠£28
dB&B⇍🏠£40 🍴
CTV 12P ✿ sauna solarium gymnasium 🎜
V ✆ 𝒟 Lunch £4.95-£12.55alc Dinner £5.65-£14.30alc Last dinner 9pm
Credit Cards ①③

---

**FILEY** North Yorkshire Map **08** TA18

★★**69%, Wrangham House** 10 Stonegate, Hunmanby YO14 0NS (3m SW off A165) ☎Scarborough(0723)891333
*This one-time vicarage has lost nothing of its former charm. The friendly atmosphere, the excellent home-cooking and the log fires lit in the two very comfortable lounges on chillier days provide a warm welcome. Bedrooms are all attractively decorated and individually styled.*
9⇍🏠Annexe4⇍🏠⚥in all bedrooms CTV in all bedrooms ®
🕇 (ex guide dogs) sB&B⇍🏠£30 dB&B⇍🏠£60 🍴

20P 🚗 ✿ nc12yrs *xmas*
V ✆ 𝒟 ⚥ Lunch fr£3.50&alc
Credit Cards ①②③⑤ ⓔ

---

**FINDON** West Sussex Map **04** TQ10

★★**62%, Findon Manor** High St BN14 0TA ☎(090671)2733
*An old rectory dating from the sixteenth century has retained many original features in its beamed foyer lounge, pleasant dining room and Snooty Fox Bar. All bedrooms are individually furnished, standards of cooking are good, and informal service is casually relaxed.*
11⇍🏠2🛏 CTV in all bedrooms ® T
30P
✆ 𝒟
Credit Cards ①②③⑤

---

**FIR TREE** Co Durham Map **12** NZ13

★★★**70%, Helme Park Hall Country House** DL13 4NW
☎Bishop Auckland(0388)730970
*This much extended farmhouse, converted to hotel use in 1987, stands in its own grounds just off the A68/A689 two miles north of Fir Tree; tastefully appointed and offering the services of friendly, attentive staff, it commands superb views west over Weardale and the North Pennines from its elevated position.*
10⇍🏠(3fb)1🛏 CTV in all bedrooms ® 🕇 (ex guide dogs)
40P ✿ solarium ⛳
⍾ English & French V ✆ 𝒟 Last dinner 9.45pm
Credit Cards ①②③

---

**FISHGUARD** Dyfed Map **02** SM93

★★**58%, Cartref** 15-19 High St SA65 9AW ☎(0348)872430
*This very friendly little hotel, situated at the middle of the market town, is convenient both as a stop-over for the Rosslare Ferry and as a base from which to tour the area. Bedrooms are bright and clean, and guests can relax in a small bar or in one of the two comfortable lounges.*
12rm(4🏠) CTV in 8 bedrooms 🕇 ✱ sB&Bfr£22 sB&B🏠£29
dB&Bfr£37 dB&B🏠£45 🍴
( CTV 20P 2🚗 🚗 nc7yrs *xmas*
V ✆ 𝒟 ⚥ Lunch fr£4&alc High tea fr£3&alc Dinner fr£8&alc
Last dinner 10pm
Credit Cards ①③ ⓔ

★**60%, Abergwaun** The Market Square SA65 9HA
☎(0348)872077
*Situated right on the square of this small town, the Abergwaun has recently had its ground floor areas completely modernised. Bedrooms remain modestly appointed and a wide range of food is available at the Bumbles Bistro, which is popular with locals.*
12rm(1fb) CTV in all bedrooms ®
CTV *P*
⍾ English & French V ✆ 𝒟 Last dinner 9pm
Credit Cards ①②③

---

**FITTLEWORTH** West Sussex Map **04** TQ01

★★**65%, Swan** Lower St RH20 1EW ☎(079882)429
*A haven for both fishermen and artists, this delightful, low-beamed, fourteenth-century village inn set amid the rolling Sussex Downs features a beamed bar and a candlelit restaurant where guests can choose from a well balanced menu of skilfully prepared dishes; its attractive modern bedrooms are fully equipped, whilst bathrooms are of good quality and contain showers.*
10rm(6⇍2🏠)2🛏 CTV in all bedrooms ® 🕇 (ex guide dogs)
25P ✿ ∪
✆ 𝒟 ⚥ Last dinner 9.30pm
Credit Cards ①②③⑤

**FIVE OAKS** West Sussex Map **04** TQ02

⚓**Travelodge** RH14 9AE (on A29) (Trusthouse Forte)
☎Billingshurst(0403)812711 Central Res (0800) 850950
*On the A29 north of Billingshurst, the lodge provides well-appointed ground floor accommodation, meals being taken at the nearby Little Chef restaurant.*
26⇌🉂🉂(26fb) CTV in all bedrooms ® sB⇌🉂🉂£24
dB⇌🉂🉂£29.50 (room only)
《 26P 🖨
Credit Cards ① ② ③

**FLADBURY** Hereford & Worcester Map **03** SO94

★66% **The Chequers Inn** Chequers Ln WR10 2PZ
☎Evesham(0386)860276 & 860527
*Standing at the end of a quiet lane in the village of Fladbury, this hotel offers a good standard of accommodation, equipped with modern facilities and equally suitable for either businessmen or leisure users; its traditional lounge bar is popular with guests and local residents alike.*
8⇌🉂(1fb) CTV in all bedrooms ® T ✳ sB&B⇌🉂fr£35
dB&B⇌🉂fr£50 🍴
25P 🖨 ♩
V ♥ Lunch £9.60-£20alc Dinner £9.60-£20alc Last dinner
9.30pm
Credit Cards ① ③ ④
                    **See advertisement under EVESHAM**

**FLAMBOROUGH** Humberside Map **08** TA26

★66% *Flaneburg* North Marine Rd YO15 1LF
☎Bridlington(0262)850284
Closed Jan & Feb
*A three-storey building on the edge of the village near the famous cliffs, this friendly hotel provides accommodation in nicely appointed bedrooms, which are complemented by comfortable public rooms.*
13rm(8🉂)(2fb) CTV in all bedrooms ® ✖
CTV 20P 🖨
V ♥

**FLEET** Hampshire Map **04** SU85

★★★56% **Lismoyne** Church Rd GU13 8NA ☎(0252)628555
FAX (0252) 811761
*Set in a quiet residential area and surrounded by over two acres of pleasant gardens, a Victorian hotel offers a variety of bedrooms, public rooms with old world charm, and the services of pleasant, friendly staff.*
44⇌🉂(1fb) 🗐 CTV in all bedrooms ® T ✳ S%
sB&B⇌🉂£62-£72 dB&B⇌🉂£80 🍴
《 80P ✿
♡ English & French V ♥ ⧫ S% Lunch £11.75&alc Dinner
£12.95&alc Last dinner 9.30pm
Credit Cards ① ② ③ ④ ⑤ ④

**FLEETWOOD** Lancashire Map **07** SD34

★★★60% **North Euston** The Esplanade FY7 6BN
☎(03917)6525 FAX (03917) 77842
*In a prominent position overlooking the Wyre Estuary this hotel, which dates back to 1841, has attractive bedrooms equipped with modern facilities. The restaurant has recently undergone refurbishment and the Chatterbox Bistro is being extended.*
59rm(55⇌🉂)(2fb) CTV in all bedrooms ® T
✖ (ex guide dogs) ✳ sB&B⇌🉂£37-£48 dB&B⇌🉂£53-£58 🍴
Lift 《 60P table tennis pool table *xmas*
♥ ⧫ Lunch £8 Dinner £11.50 Last dinner 9.30pm
Credit Cards ① ② ③ ⑤ ④

## Helme Park Country House Hotel

Near Fir Tree, Bishop Auckland, Co. Durham DL13 4NW. Tel: 0388 730970

Northumbria's newest hotel. Five acres of gardens. Highest standards of service, cuisine and appointments. A la carte and bar meals. Highly convenient location, tranquil setting and magnificent views for 25 miles over the hills and dales. A perfect centre to explore Northumbria. Ten en suite bedrooms.

★ ★ ★

---

**FLIMWELL** East Sussex Map **05** TQ73

✗ *Woods'* High St TN5 7PB ☎(058087)342
*The restaurant stands just off the A21 at the traffic lights – and any trouble involved in finding it is amply repaid by the professionalism which makes its meals so enjoyable. An international style is reflected in such dishes as Shellfish Mornay, Roast Crispy Duck with Plum Sauce, Wood's Fillet with Oysters, Veal Escalopes and Pork Calvados. There is a separate pudding menu and a good wine list, guests' pleasure in the meal being completed by particularly friendly service.*
Closed Mon
Lunch not served (ex Sun by.reservation only)
Dinner not served Sun
♀ International **V** 26 seats Last dinner 9.30pm 6P
Credit Cards ①③

---

**FLITWICK** Bedfordshire Map **04** TL03

★★★⚑71% *Flitwick Manor* Church Rd MK45 1AE
☎(0525)712242 Telex no 825562
Closed 24-28 Dec
*Attractively converted to hotel use and tastefully appointed, this 17th-century house offers accommodation in comfortable, well-equipped bedrooms. A Regency-style restaurant provides interesting la carte dinner menus and a good set lunch, both comprised of skilfully-prepared, imaginative dishes and complemented by a carefully chosen wine list.*
15⇌🏠(2fb)5🛏 CTV in all bedrooms ✗ (ex guide dogs)
50P 🚗 ✿ ♪ (hard) 🛥 croquet table tennis bicycles putting
**V** Last dinner 9.30pm
Credit Cards ①②③

---

**FLORE** Northamptonshire Map **04** SP66

★★★64% Heyford Manor The High St NN7 4LP (Lansbury)
☎Weedon(0327)349022 Telex no 312437 FAX (0327) 349017
*Offering easy access to junction 16 of the M1 from its position on the A45 Weedon to Northampton road, the hotel provides well-equipped accommodation on two floors, an attractive lounge and bar area, and a restaurant serving an imaginative menu of dishes based on good quality fresh produce.*
56⇌🏠(7fb)✂in 11 bedrooms CTV in all bedrooms ® **T**
✗ (ex guide dogs) sB&B⇌🏠fr£76 dB&B⇌🏠fr£88 🏴
《 CTV 100P sauna gymnasium *xmas*
♀ English & Continental **V** ♿ ♫ ✂ Lunch fr£12&alc Dinner fr£16.25&alc Last dinner 10pm
Credit Cards ①②③⑤

---

**FOCHABERS** Grampian *Morayshire* Map **15** NJ35

★★60% Gordon Arms High St IV32 7DH ☎(0343)820508
FAX (0343) 820300
*The former coaching inn, lying close to the River Spey on the main Aberdeen-Inverness road, offers comfortable and well-equipped bedrooms, a spacious residents' lounge and a choice of two bars, both of which are popular with the fishing fraternity who frequent this conveniently-sited hotel.*
13⇌🏠(2fb) CTV in all bedrooms ® **T** ✱ sB&B⇌🏠£40 dB&B⇌🏠£55 🏴
CTV 50P 2🚗 (£10 per day) ✿ *xmas*
♀ Scottish, French & Italian **V** ♿ ♫ Lunch £6.50 High tea £4.50-£7.50 Dinner £7.90-£17&alc Last dinner 9.45pm
Credit Cards ①②③

---

**FOLKESTONE** Kent Map **05** TR23

★★★63% Clifton The Leas CT20 2EB (Consort)
☎(0303)851231 Telex no 57515
*Situated in a commanding cliff-top location, this hotel offers a pleasing combination of well equipped accommodation and traditional services. Bedrooms vary in size, and are all gradually*
*being upgraded to the same standard. Meeting and conference failities are available.*
80⇌🏠(4fb) CTV in all bedrooms ® **T**
sB&B⇌🏠£42.50-£54.50 dB&B⇌🏠£59-£69 🏴
Lift 《 ♪ ✿ solarium games room *xmas*
♀ English & French **V** ♿ ♫ Lunch £9.25-£10.25&alc Dinner £14.50-£15.95&alc Last dinner 9pm
Credit Cards ①②③⑤

✗✗La Tavernetta Leeside Court, Clifton Gardens CT20 2EP
☎(0303)54955 & 55044
*Good Italian food is served by this friendly restaurant, which combines a welcoming atmosphere with courteously professional service and accompanies both its à la carte selection and the value-for-money fixed-rate lunch menu with a well-balanced and reasonably priced wine list.*
Closed Sun, 25-26 Dec & BH's
♀ Italian **V** 65 seats ✽ Lunch £8.35&alc Dinner £20-£30alc
Last lunch 2.30pm Last dinner 10.30pm ♪
Credit Cards ①②③⑤

---

**FONTWELL** West Sussex Map **04** SU90

⇧Travelodge BN18 0SB (on A27) (Trusthouse Forte)
☎Eastergate(0243)543973 Central Res (0800) 850950
*A block of modern, well-appointed family rooms stands to the rear of the Little Chef restaurant at the A27/A29 roundabout, west of the village.*
40⇌🏠(40fb) CTV in all bedrooms ® sB⇌🏠£24 dB⇌🏠£29.50 (room only)
《 40P 🚗
Credit Cards ①②③

---

**FORD** Wiltshire Map **03** ST87

★★59% *White Hart Inn* SN14 8RP
☎Castle Combe(0249)782213
*A quietly located inn with beams, fires and a busy bar trade contributing to a nicely informal atmosphere. An à la carte menu is available in the restaurant or try the bar food.*
3🏠Annexe8⇌🏠(1fb) CTV in all bedrooms ®
CTV 100P ✿ ⚊(heated)
♀ English & French **V** ♿ Last dinner 9.30pm
Credit Cards ①③

---

**FORDEN** Powys Map **07** SJ20

★★⚑67% *Edderton Hall* SY21 8RZ ☎(093876)339 & 410
FAX (093876) 452
*Set on the outskirts of Welshpool with panoramic views of the Severn Valley, this personally-run Georgian house features warm hospitality and an imaginative menu with the emphasis on the combination of flavours, although main meals are also available.*
8⇌🏠2🛏 CTV in all bedrooms ®
《 40P ✿
**V** ♿ ♫ Last dinner 9.30pm
Credit Cards ①②③⑤

---

**FORDINGBRIDGE** Hampshire Map **04** SU11

★★66% Ashburn Hotel & Restaurant Station Rd SP6 1JP
(Minotels) ☎(0425)652060
*Situated on a quiet hillside on the edge of town this hotel offers a choice of original and modern new wing bedrooms most with good views over the lawn and swimming pool. Service is friendly and personally supervised and the standard of cooking is very reliable. Fully equipped conference room.*
23⇌🏠(3fb)1🛏 CTV in all bedrooms ® **T** ✱
sB&B⇌🏠£32-£37 dB&B⇌🏠£56-£64 🏴
CTV 60P ✿ ⚊(heated)

♀ English & French V ☺ ⚌ ✔ Sunday Lunch £6.50 High tea £1.50-£4 Dinner £10.50&alc Last dinner 9pm
Credit Cards 1 3 £

✗ ✗ **Hour Glass** Burgate SP6 1LX ☎(0425)652348
Closed Mon
Dinner not served Sun
♀ English & French V 45 seats ✷ Dinner £15.95&alc Last lunch 1.45pm Last dinner 9.45pm 40P nc5yrs ✔
Credit Cards 1 2 3 5

●✗**The Three Lions** Stuckton SP6 2HF ☎(0425)652489
*Karl and June Wadsack have steadily built up the reputation of this friendly restaurant with its cottagey atmosphere. The excellent quality of the ingredients is apparent in Karl's skilful cooking of dishes such as the duck liver pâté au poivre vert, and the wings of pheasant and pigeon Baden-Baden. June presides over the pleasant dining-room service, and is a knowledgeable guide through the extensive wine list which includes over 200 bins.*
Closed Mon, Sun, 22 Dec-8 Jan & 2 wks Jul/Aug
♀ International 56 seats ✷ Lunch £11.50-£28alc Dinner £20-£30alc Last lunch 1.30pm Last dinner 9pm 40P nc14yrs
Credit Cards 1 3

**FOREST ROW** East Sussex Map 05 TQ43

★★★**58% Roebuck** Wych Cross RH18 5JL (2m S junc A22/A275) (Embassy) ☎(034282)3811 FAX (034282) 4790
*Conveniently situated on the A22 south of the village, and currently being refurbished, the hotel provides a good level of comfort in its beamed and wood-panelled public areas, while some bedrooms enjoy a pleasant outlook over well-groomed gardens.*
28⇨🌶 CTV in all bedrooms ® T ✷ S15% sB⇨🌶£55-£65 dB⇨🌶£65-£75 (room only) 🏳
《 150P ❖ *xmas*
♀ English & French V ☺ S15% Lunch £12.95-£16.95 Dinner £12.95-£16.95 Last dinner 9.15pm
Credit Cards 1 2 3 4 5 £

★★**63% Brambletye** The Square RH18 5EZ (Inter-Hotels)
☎(0342)824144 FAX (0342) 824833
*Parts of this family-run establishment date back to the seventeenth century, and the building has been used as an hotel since about 1866 ; skilful extension has now added a modern annexe at the rear. The overall Sherlock Holmes theme is reflected in the Deerstalker restaurant, which features English food and friendly service which is personally supervised by the resident proprietor.*
9⇨🌶Annexe13⇨(3fb) CTV in all bedrooms ® T sB&B⇨🌶£48-£52.50 dB&B⇨🌶£55-£70 🏳
⊞40P
V ☺ ⚌ Sunday Lunch £7.50-£10alc Dinner £10.50-£17alc Last dinner 9.30pm
Credit Cards 1 2 3 5 £

**FORRES** Grampian *Morayshire* Map 14 NJ05

★★**63% Ramnee** Victoria Rd IV36 0BN (Inter-Hotels)
☎(0309)72410
*Fine two-storey stone villa standing back from the main road in well-kept grounds.*
20⇨🌶(3fb)1🖽 CTV in all bedrooms ® T sB&B⇨🌶£34.50-£45 dB&B⇨🌶£49.40-£65 🏳
CTV 50P 🚲 ❖ shooting fishing golf ⛳
♀ Scottish & French V ☺ ⚌ Lunch £7.25-£7.50 Dinner fr£12.50&alc Last dinner 9pm
Credit Cards 1 2 3 5

★★**56% Royal** Tytler St IV36 0EL ☎(0309)72617
*A substantial Victorian building situated in the west end and convenient for the railway station. Public areas offer traditional comforts while the bedrooms provide practical commercial standards.*

19rm(1⇨5🌶)(4fb) CTV in all bedrooms ® sB&B£23.50 sB&B⇨🌶£29 dB&B£36 dB&B⇨🌶£46 🏳
CTV 40P ❖ pool room
♀ European V ☺ ⚌ Lunch £3.75-£6alc High tea £4.75-£12.50alc Dinner £3.75-£14alc Last dinner 8.30pm
Credit Cards 1 2 3 £

**FORT AUGUSTUS** Highland *Inverness-shire* Map 14 NH30

★★**66% Lovat Arms** PH32 4BH ☎(0320)6206
*This traditional hotel, with spacious and comfortable lounges, is situated in an elevated position overlooking the Benedictine monastery and Loch Ness. It is ideal for those wishing to tour the Highlands.*
26rm(22⇨2🌶)(3fb) CTV in all bedrooms ® T S% sB&B£20.50-£23.50 sB&B⇨🌶£23.50-£29.50 dB&B⇨🌶£47-£59 🏳
CTV 50P ❖ putting *xmas*
V ☺ ⚌ S% Sunday Lunch fr£6.50 Dinner £12.50-£16.50 Last dinner 8.45pm
Credit Cards 1 3 4 5 £

★★**63% Caledonian** PH32 4BQ ☎(0320)6256
Closed Oct-Mar
*Many guests return year after year to this small, family-run, Highland holiday hotel, which is especially noted for its warm and friendly hospitality. It offers enjoyable home cooking and good value accommodation.*
12rm(2⇨2🌶)(2fb) ® ✖ (ex guide dogs) ✷ sB&B£16-£22 dB&B£32-£45 dB&B⇨🌶£37-£50 🏳
CTV 20P ❖
♀ Scottish & French V ☺ ⚌ ✔ Bar Lunch £5-£10 Dinner £12-£14 Last dinner 9.30pm

**F**

★★63% **Inchnacardoch Lodge** Loch Ness PH32 4BL (Consort)
☎(0320)6258
Closed Dec-1 Apr
*A converted hunting lodge overlooking Loch Ness. Recently upgraded, it offers good-sized bedrooms and modern, well-furnished public areas. Food is imaginative and good.*
16rm(15⇌3♠)(5fb) CTV in 8 bedrooms ® T sB&B£30-£55 sB&B⇌♠£30-£55 dB&B£40-£60 dB&B⇌♠£40-£60 ♬
CTV 40P 2☎ ❀
♥ International V ♦ ♫ ⊁ Bar Lunch £3-£10alc Dinner £16-£20 Last dinner 9pm
Credit Cards ① ② ③ ⑤ ⓔ

★★62% **The Brae** PH32 4DG ☎(0320)6289
Closed Nov-mid Jan
*A former church manse, converted and extended to create a small, personally-run holiday hotel, provides comfortable accommodation with a friendly atmosphere and is an ideal touring base.*
8rm(2⇌3♠)(1fb) CTV in all bedrooms ®
CTV 12P ⊞ ❀ nc7yrs
⊁ Last dinner 8.15pm
Credit Cards ① ③

**FORTINGALL** Tayside *Perthshire* Map **14** NN74

★★61% **Fortingall** PH15 2NQ ☎Kenmore(08873)367
RS Nov-Feb
*This friendly family-run village hotel is a popular base for the visiting fisherman and touring holidaymaker alike. It has a relaxed atmosphere and provides traditional services and comforts. Good progress is being made with bedroom improvements.*
9rm(3♠)(2fb) ® S% sB&B£21-£25 sB&B⇌♠£23-£25 dB&B£42-£50 dB&B⇌♠£50 ♬
CTV 15P 5☎ ❀ ♪ sailing pony trekking
♥ French V ♦ ♫ Lunch £4.50-£7 Dinner £15-£17 Last dinner 8.30pm
Credit Cards ① ② ③ ⓔ

**FORTON MOTORWAY SERVICE AREA (M6)** Lancashire Map **07** SD45

⌂**Rank Motor Lodge** LA2 9DU (between juncts 32 & 33)
(Rank) ☎Lancaster(0524)792227
*Situated south of Lancaster between junctions 32 and 33 of the M6, and accessible from either carriageway, this new lodge provides well-equipped and comfortable accommodation at reasonable prices. Included within the complex is a restaurant open 24 hours a day.*
41⇌♠(21fb)⊁in 7 bedrooms CTV in all bedrooms ® ✳
sB&B⇌♠27.50 dB&B⇌♠£34.50 Continental breakfast ⊄50P
Credit Cards ① ② ③ ⑤

**FORTROSE** Highland *Ross & Cromarty* Map **14** NH75

★52% **Royal** Union St IV10 8SU ☎(0381)20236
*Set in the main street of this charming little town on the banks of the Moray Firth, near the historic cathedral square, this distinctive hotel offers functional accommodation, substantial meals (in either the dining room or the popular cocktail bar) and friendly service.*
11rm(3⇌1♠)(2fb) ® ✖
CTV 8P ⊞
♥ Scottish & French V ♦ ♫ Last dinner 9pm
Credit Cards ① ③

See 'How we Classify Hotels and Restaurants'
at the front of the book for an explanation
of the AA's appointment and
award scheme.

---

**FORT WILLIAM** Highland *Inverness-shire* Map **14** NN17
Telephone numbers are due to change during the currency of this guide.

★★★★
★★★★ ⊞
INVERLOCHY CASTLE

PH33 6SN (3m NE A82)
(Relais et Châteaux)
☎(0397)2177
Telex no 776229
FAX (0397) 2953
Closed mid Nov-mid Mar
*There are several British hotels which have a delightful natural setting; some that have created round themselves lovely grounds and gardens; some that combine space, comfort, pleasing decor and fine antique furniture; a few that have luxuriously appointed bedrooms and bathrooms; a handful that offer food of exceptional quality and maintain high professional standards of service and housekeeping. One must, however, seriously doubt if there is any other hotel in the British Isles that combines all these virtues to the same extent as Inverlochy Castle. All credit due to the distinguished owner, Grete Hobbs, and her very able Managing Director, Michael Leonard. They will, alas, feel the lack of Head Chef Graham Newbold who, as we go to print, has just left the hotel, and therefore it is not appropriate to consider awarding any rosettes this year, but we are confident that the award will be restored once his successor has settled in and built up his own team.*
16⇌♠ CTV in all bedrooms T ✖ ✳ sB&B⇌♠£121
dB&B⇌♠£180
⊄ 16P 1☎ ⊞ ❀ ₽ (hard) ♪ snooker
♥ International V ♫ ⊁
Credit Cards ① ② ③

★★★65% **Moorings** Banavie PH33 7LY (3m N of Fort William off A830) (Exec Hotel) ☎Corpach(03977)797 due to change to (0397772) 797 FAX (03977) 441 due to change to (0397772) 441
*Located 3 miles from Fort William, off the A380, this professionally managed, family run hotel has recently been extended to provide a spacious new lounge, bar and wine bar. Bedrooms are modern in style and service throughout is particularly helpful.*
21⇌♠Annexe3♠1⊞ CTV in all bedrooms ® T
✖ (ex guide dogs) sB&B⇌♠£48-£65 dB&B⇌♠£56-£76 ♬
60P ❀ nc10yrs xmas
V ♦ ♫ ⊁ Lunch £7.90-£12&alc Dinner £17&alc Last dinner 9.30pm
Credit Cards ① ② ③ ⑤ ⓔ

★★★58% **Alexandra** The Parade PH33 6AZ ☎(0397)2241
Telex no 777210 FAX (0397) 5554
*Traditional in style and situated close to the main shopping area, the hotel offers compact bedrooms which have recently been upgraded. The popular Great Food Shop provides meals and snacks from 9.30am until 11.00pm, supplementing the main restaurant which serves only dinner.*
98⇌♠(7fb) CTV in all bedrooms ® T sB⇌♠£39-£52
dB⇌♠£50-£74 (room only) ♬
Lift ⊄ 50P ♫ xmas
♥ Scottish & French V ♦ ♫ ⊁ Lunch £5-£10 High tea £5-£7 Dinner £6.50-£16 Last dinner 11pm
Credit Cards ① ② ③ ⑤ ⓔ

F

## Onich Hotel — Onich ★★
### NEAR FORT WILLIAM
### INVERNESS-SHIRE PH33 6RY
Tel: Onich (08553) 214, Visitors 266
Fax: (08553) 484

Occupying one of the finest situations in the Scottish Highlands this hotel is the only one in the area with gardens extending to the lochside. The views over Loch Linnhe to Glencoe & Morvern are absolutely breathtaking. This family run hotel has a very real reputation for excellent food and a warm welcoming atmosphere. The new Deerstalker Lounge is open all day for meals and drinks and offers a large selection of malt whisky & real ale on draught. This is an ideal base for climbing, hillwalking, windsurfing, skiing, touring or just relaxing. All 27 rooms have Bath/ Shower, TV/Radio, Phone and Tea/Coffee maker. In-house facilities includes Solarium, Jacuzzi, Exercise Equipment, Games Room.

## THE MOORINGS
### HOTEL & RESTAURANT
### BANAVIE, FORT WILLIAM
Tel: (0397) 772 797. Fax: (0397) 772 441
AA ★ ★ ★                              STB 👑👑👑👑

Access Visa Diners Amex Accepted

**F**

Resident Proprietors:
**James and Mary Sinclair**

This family run hotel stands in its own grounds beside the Caledonian Canal, at Neptune's Staircase 3 miles from Fort William. Magnificent views of Ben Nevis and the surrounding mountain range can be enjoyed from the hotel. The hotel offers first class facilities in all 24 bedrooms.

The hotel's Jacobean styled Restaurant is one of the most popular in the area, renowned for its Taste of Scotland menu with the emphasis on using fresh local produce. Table d'hôte and à la carte available. New Cellar bar — Mariners — serving Bistro Meals Lunch and Dinner. Both with their own extensive wine selections.

The hotel is located in a perfect situation for day tours to Skye, Mallaig, Inverness, Oban, Pitlochry, Glencoe and Aviemore. Private car park. Brochure & terms on request. Ashley Courtenay Recommended Exechotels Taste of Scotland.

## ALEXANDRA HOTEL FORT WILLIAM
**AA**  The Parade. PH33 6AZ
★★★  Telephone: 0397 2241
       Telex: 777210

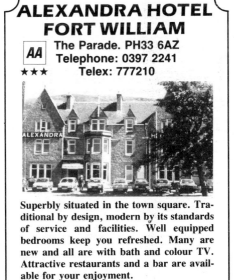

**Superbly situated in the town square. Traditional by design, modern by its standards of service and facilities. Well equipped bedrooms keep you refreshed. Many are new and all are with bath and colour TV. Attractive restaurants and a bar are available for your enjoyment.**

*Whether you're at work or at play, the Alexandra is the place to stay. Send for our colour brochure or simply phone to secure.*

*"Astounding Situation. Most Remarkable Hotel"*

## THE LODGE ON THE LOCH
In the heart of the Highlands, where mountains and Gulf Stream meet in tranquility.
Panoramic views from designer bedrooms, each with private facilities.
Renowned restaurant serving local seafood, salmon, trout and venison with home baking as well as health foods.

**ONICH nr Fort William, Inverness-shire.**
Tel: (08553) 238. Tlx: 94013696. Fax: (08553) 463
Norman, Jessie and Laurence McP Young
*See gazetteer entry under ONICH*  | Scottish Tourist Board COMMENDED 👑👑👑👑
★★★

**★★61% Imperial** Fraser's Square PH33 6DW ☎(0397)2040 &
3921 FAX (0397) 6277
Closed 3-31 Jan
*Enjoying views of Loch Linnhe from its convenient town centre
position, this long established commercial hotel has been
refurbished to offer well equipped, modern bedrooms and
comfortable, attractive public areas.*
34⇦⬗♠(3fb) CTV in all bedrooms ® sB&B⇦⬗♠£25-£44
dB&B⇦⬗♠£40-£66 ⊟
CTV 20P *xmas*
♀ Scottish & French ⅄ Lunch £4-£6.50alc Dinner
£12.50-£14.50&alc Last dinner 9pm
Credit Cards ①③£

**★★60% Nevis Bank** Belford Rd PH33 6BY (Best Western)
☎(0397)5721 due to change to 705721 Telex no 94016892
FAX (0397) 6275 due to change to 706275
*Situated beside the A82 on the northern outskirts of the town, this
friendly, privately owned hotel caters for both tourist and
commercial guest. Bedrooms are well equipped if rather compact,
and the choice of two bars is enjoyed by visitors and locals alike.*
35⇦♠Annexe7⇦♠(2fb) CTV in all bedrooms ® T
sB&B⇦⬗♠£38-£41 dB&B⇦⬗♠£56-£65 ⊟
25P sauna solarium gymnasium *xmas*
V ✿ ⚏ Bar Lunch fr£5.95alc Dinner £14.95-£19.95 Last
dinner 9pm
Credit Cards ①②③⑤£

**★★59% Grand** Gordon Square PH33 6DX ☎(0397)2928
FAX (0397) 5060
*Three-storey hotel on a corner site at west end of shopping centre
and adjacent to Pier.*
33⇦⬗(4fb) CTV in all bedrooms ® sB&B⇦fr£25
dB&B⇦fr£45 ⊟
⟮ 150P
V ✿ ⚏ Lunch fr£7.50 Dinner fr£13.95 Last dinner 8.30 pm
Credit Cards ①②③⑤£

**★★55% Milton** North Rd PH33 6TG ☎(0397)2331
Telex no 777210 FAX (0397) 3695
*Situated on the northern fringe of the town, overlooking Ben Nevis,
this busy holiday hotel has benefited from extensive refurbishment
in recent years and offers good-value, practical accommodation.
Popular with tour groups.*
56⇦♠Annexe67⇦♠(6fb) CTV in all bedrooms ®
sB⇦♠£30-£48 dB⇦♠£36-£64 (room only) ⊟
⟮ 150P
♀ Scottish & French ✿ ⚏ Lunch £5-£10 High tea £6-£7
Dinner £6.50-£14 Last dinner 8.30 pm
Credit Cards ①②③④⑤£

**★★50% *Cruachan*** Achintore Rd PH33 6RQ (Consort)
☎(0397)2022
Closed Nov-Etr
*Large hotel overlooking Loch Linnhe with modern bedroom
extension at rear. Caters for tour parties.*
54⇦♠(2fb) CTV in all bedrooms ®
⟮ 30P snooker ♫
Last dinner 9pm

★ **FACTOR'S HOUSE**
Torlundy PH33 6SN
☎(0397)5767
Telex no 776229
FAX (0397) 2953
Closed 16 Dec-15 Jan RS 16
Jan-14 Mar

*Described by our Inspector as
a little gem of an hotel, the Factor's House, owned by Peter
Hobbs, sits under the shadow of Ben Nevis, just 3 miles north
of the town. Manager Ranald Duff and his staff make guests
feel very much at home in the attractive surroundings, and the
restaurant serves excellent dinners, the menu being displayed
on a blackboard and reflecting the best of Scottish seafood.,
meat and game. Portions are ample, particularly where the
vegetables are concerned. Keen walkers will be pleased to
know that Peter's dog, Pancho, will take them out for a hike
as long as he has his owner's permission first.*
7⇦♠ CTV in all bedrooms T ✖ (ex guide dogs) ✳
sB&B⇦♠£40.25-£63.25 dB&B⇦♠£57.50-£80
CTV 30P ⇔ ✿ ♪ (hard) ♩ sailing nc6yrs
♀ Scottish & Continental Dinner £17.50-£23 Last dinner
9.30pm
Credit Cards ①②③⑤

---

**FOSSEBRIDGE** Gloucestershire Map **04** SP01

**★★65% Fossebridge Inn** GL54 3JS ☎(0285)720721
*The centrepiece of this hotel is the popular and characterful Bridge
Bar, which dates back to the original fifteenth-century inn. It
remains much as it was then, with fine Yorkshire floors, oak beams
and inglenook fireplaces, and offers a comprehensive range of bar
snacks.*
9⇦♠Annexe4⇦⬗(3fb) CTV in all bedrooms ® T
sB&B⇦⬗£35-£45 dB&B⇦♠£50-£65 ⊟
40P ✿ ♩
♀ English & French V ✿ ⚏
Credit Cards ①②③⑤

---

**FOUR MARKS** Hampshire Map **04** SU63

⬆**Travelodge** 156 Winchester Rd GU34 5HZ (on A31)
(Trusthouse Forte)
☎Alton(0420)62659 Central Res (0800) 850950
31⇦⬗(31fb) CTV in all bedrooms ® ✳ sB⇦⬗£24
dB⇦♠£29.50 (room only)
⟮ 31P ⇔
Credit Cards ①②③

---

**FOWEY** Cornwall & Isles of Scilly Map **02** SX15

**★★75% Marina** Esplanade PL23 1HY ☎(0726)833315
Closed Nov-Feb
*Commanding a unique waterfront location an elegant Georgian
hotel offers tastefully furnished, modernised accommodation at a
very high standard throughout, complemented by the Waterside
Restaurant and Terrace, with attentive service personally
supervised by the proprietors. The absence of a car park is
overcome by the provision of courtesy transport when checking out
of the hotel.*
11⇦♠ CTV in all bedrooms ® T sB&B⇦⬗£29-£36
dB&B⇦♠£46-£68 ⊟
⟮ ♪ ⇔ ♩ windsurfing sailing
♀ English & French V ✿ ⅄ Bar Lunch £2-£7 High tea fr£3.50
Dinner £14&alc Last dinner 8.30pm
Credit Cards ①②③⑤

All AA-appointed establishments are
inspected regularly to ensure that required
standards are maintained.

✕✕**Food for Thought** The Quay PL23 1AT ☎(0726)832221
*Fresh fish, transformed by the innovative skill of the chef/
proprietor, is the speciality of this intimate restaurant set on the
quayside of the picturesque Cornish village. Well-flavoured dishes
are attractively presented and complemented by a wine list of
medium length. Quenelles of Fowey River salmon, and the
Rendezvous of freshly caught fish and shellfish with a lobster sauce
are two popular choices.*
Closed early Jan-early Feb
Lunch not served
♀ French 40 seats ✱ Dinner £16.50&alc Last dinner 9.30pm
✗ nc10yrs
Credit Cards ① ③

---

**FOWLMERE** Cambridgeshire Map **05** TL44

✕✕**Chequers Inn** SG8 7SR ☎(076382)369
*A fine little inn dating back to the 16th century displays among its
ancient timbers such relics of the past as mid 17th-century
talismans, some business cards from around 1850 and photographs
of airmen from fighter squadrons who, in two world wars, made
this their second home. Food of a high standard is served in a tiny
restaurant where some tables are set up in the gallery, the skilfully
prepared dishes on the menu including such delicacies as flowering
courgettes stuffed with a light salmon mousse, or chicken breasts
stuffed with smoked trout, wrapped in lettuce, steamed and served
with a nettle, fromage blanc and yogurt sauce – though a
traditional roast is usually also featured. A small but carefully
selected list of wines accompanies the meal, some of them being
available by the glass.*
Closed 25 Dec ▶

# NEVIS BANK HOTEL ★★
**BELFORD ROAD,
FORT WILLIAM PH33 6BY
Tel: (0397) 705721
Fax: (0397) 706275**

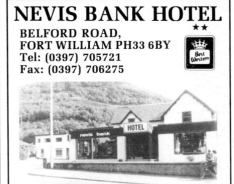

Nevis Bank Hotel is a privately owned hotel situated on the eastern side of the town 10 minutes walk from the Main Street & Travel Centre and at the foot of the access road to Ben Nevis, Britain's highest mountain. The Hotel is famous for its Home Cooking and comfortable surroundings. Cabaret in Ceilidh Bar some weekends throughout the year.

# *Marina Hotel*
## ESPLANADE, FOWEY, CORNWALL PL23 1HY
Telephone: 072683 3315
AA ★★ Ashley Courtenay

The Marina has a unique waterfront position overlooking the harbour. It is a charming Georgian residence with some bedrooms having balconies and the majority of bedrooms overlooking the water and harbour activities.

The restaurant also has panoramic views across the harbour and the menu provides a delicious range of local fish, meat & game.

The Hotel has its own quayside access to the water and moorings are available to guests.

# *IMPERIAL HOTEL* ★★
(Fraser's Square, Fort William)
Inverness-shire PH33 6DW
**Telephone: Fort William 0397 2040**

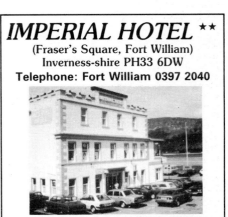

Situated in the heart of Fort William, close to the shopping centre and with panoramic views of Loch Linnhe and the surrounding countryside. The Hotel offers the ideal base to explore and discover the beauty of the West Highlands by car or coach. It is one of the oldest established hotels in Fort William and has developed over the years a reputation for Highland hospitality and good food. The hotel has been substantially refurbished to provide quality accommodation at reasonable prices. All rooms with private bathroom, TV and tea and coffee facilities.

♡ English & French **V** 30 seats ✳ Lunch £14.50 Dinner
£16.10-£24.20alc Last lunch 2pm Last dinner 10pm 50P
Credit Cards ① ② ③ ⑤

---

**FOWNHOPE** Hereford & Worcester Map **03** SO53

★★**65% Green Man Inn** HR1 4PE ☎(043277)243
FAX (043277) 207
*This village inn, originally dating from 1485, has been considerably
extended by the present owners. Bedrooms, both those in the main
building and the pretty cottage annexe, have excellent modern
amenities, and the beamed bars are cosy with open fires.*
10➪🛏Annexe5➪🛏(3fb)1🗗 CTV in all bedrooms ®
CTV 75P ❀ ♪
♡ ⌨ Last dinner 9pm
Credit Cards ① ③

---

**FRAMLINGHAM** Suffolk Map **05** TM26

★★**68% The Crown** Market Hill IP13 9AN (Trusthouse Forte)
☎(0728)723521 FAX (0728) 724274
*Dating from the 16th century this extremely comfortable small
hotel is situated in the centre of town. Bedrooms are particularly
good, mostly spacious and equipped with antique or good
reproduction furniture, and with warm modern bathrooms. The
staff are friendly and helpful.*
14➪🛏🗗✂in 1 bedroom CTV in all bedrooms ® sB➪£65
dB➪£81-£91 (room only) 🍴
15P *xmas*
**V** ♡ ⌨ ✂ S% Lunch £8.95-£14&alc Dinner £14&alc Last
dinner 9.30pm
Credit Cards ① ② ③ ④ ⑤

---

**FRANKLEY MOTORWAY SERVICE AREA (M5)** West
Midlands Map **07** SO98

⌂**Granada Lodge** Illey Ln B32 4AR (3m SE at M5 Service
Area) (Granada) ☎021-550 3261 FAX 021-501 2880
*A modern lodge, situated on the M5 with easy access to the
Midlands business centres. It provides value-for-money
accommodation, with meals available in the nearby Country
Kitchen.*
41➪🛏(13fb)✂in 9 bedrooms CTV in all bedrooms ®
🛏 (ex guide dogs) ✳ S% sB➪🛏fr£28
dB➪🛏fr£31 (room only)
**See advertisement under BIRMINGHAM**

---

**FRASERBURGH** Grampian *Aberdeenshire* Map **15** NJ96

★★**60%, Station** Seaforth St AB4 5BB ☎(0346)23343
FAX (0346) 23171
*Attractive public areas have been refurbished to a good modern
standard and bedrooms, though modestly furnished, are well
equipped at this popular commercial hotel which stands convenient
to the harbour in the town centre.*
20rm(3➪2🛏)(3fb) CTV in all bedrooms ®
⊄ CTV 30P snooker solarium
**V** ♡ ⌨
Credit Cards ① ② ③ ⑤

★★**52% Royal** Broad St AB4 5AV ☎(0346)28524
*Situated in the town centre, convenient to the harbour, this small
family-run commercial hotel provides practical value-for-money
accommodation and caters for local functions.*
15rm(12➪)(1fb) CTV in all bedrooms ®
CTV ♪
**V** ♡ ⌨ Last dinner 9pm
Credit Cards ③

1991 marks the 25th anniversary of this guide.

---

**FRESHFORD** Avon Map **03** ST75

❀★★★⚑**78% Homewood Park** Hinton Charterhouse
BA3 6BB (Between A36 & village)
☎Limpley Stoke(0225)723731 Telex no 444937
FAX (0225) 723820
*Red Stars have been withdrawn from Homewood Park this year
only because the hotel was due to change hands just after we went
to press. We hope the loss will only be temporary – it still remains a
fine house with comfortable, well-planned and nicely furnished
bedrooms and relaxing public rooms, all set amidst lovely gardens
yet only a short distance from Bath.*
15➪🛏(2fb) CTV in all bedrooms **T** 🛏 (ex guide dogs)
sB&B➪🛏£85 dB&B➪🛏£98-£165 Continental breakfast 🍴
30P ❀ ♀ (hard) *xmas*
**V** ♡ ⌨ ✂ Lunch £16.50 Dinner £27-£29.50 Last dinner
9.30pm
Credit Cards ① ② ③ ④ ⑤

---

**FRESHWATER**
See **Wight, Isle of**

---

**FRESSINGFIELD** Suffolk Map **05** TM27

✗**Fox & Goose** IP21 5PB ☎(037986)247
*A well established restaurant, south of Harleston, housed in a
timbered inn dating back to 1509. Chef/patron Adrian Clarke
prepares imaginative but uncomplicated dishes enhanced by
sauces, salmon with a subtle saffron sauce is served with vermicelli
and spinach. Ices and sorbets are home made and there is a
particularly good wine list.*
Closed Tue, 24-27 Dec, 2 wk late Jan/Feb & 2 wks Sep
Dinner not served Sun (ex BH's)
♡ English & French 26 seats Last lunch 1.30pm Last dinner
9pm 29P nc10yrs
Credit Cards ① ② ③ ⑤

---

**FREUCHIE** Fife Map **11** NO20

★★**62% Lomond Hills** Parliament Square KY7 7EY (Exec
Hotel) ☎Falkland(0337)57329 & 57498 FAX (0337) 58180
*Set in the centre of this small village, a former coaching inn offers
well equipped bedrooms which vary in size and style.*
25➪🛏(3fb)1🗗 CTV in all bedrooms ® **T** sB&B➪🛏£33-£40
dB&B➪🛏£47-£55 🍴
30P sauna
♡ Scottish & French **V** ♡ ⌨
Credit Cards ① ② ③ ⑤

---

**FRINTON-ON-SEA** Essex Map **05** TM21

★★**64% Maplin** Esplanade CO13 9EL ☎(0255)673832
Closed Jan
*Some spacious, comfortably appointed bedrooms with modern
facilities are available at this friendly family-run hotel overlooking
the sea; public areas are comfortable, and the dining room offers
both table d'hôte and à la carte menus of unpretentious dishes, with
the accent on English cuisine.*
12rm(9➪1🛏)(2fb) CTV in all bedrooms ® ✳ sB&B£35
dB&B➪🛏£72-£82
CTV 12P ⚄ ⌂(heated) nc10yrs *xmas*
**V** ♡ ⌨ S10% Lunch fr£14.75&alc Dinner fr£16.50&alc Last
dinner 9.30pm
Credit Cards ① ② ③ ⑤

★**69% Rock** The Esplanade, 1 Third Av CO13 9EQ
☎(0255)677194
Closed Jan
*Mr. and Mrs Benmore provide warm, friendly and informal
hospitality at this hotel facing the sea and close to the golf club.
Bedrooms have recently been upgraded and enlarged. There is no
car park, but street parking is virtually unrestricted.*

---

6rm(5♠)(3fb)1⊞ CTV in all bedrooms ® S%
sB&Bf'£40.50-£43 dB&Bf'£53.50-£56.50
CTV 12P ⇔ solarium
V Lunch £7.50-£10&alc Dinner £11.50&alc Last dinner 9pm
Credit Cards [1][2][3][5] £

---

**FROME** Somerset Map **03** ST74

★★★62% **Mendip Lodge** Bath Rd BA11 2HP (Best Western)
☎(0373)63223 Telex no 44832 FAX (0373) 63990
*A motel block of bedrooms, built in the 1960s and 1970s, has now
been updated to today's standards, whilst extensions to the original
Edwardian building beside it have made good use of the potential
for country views. Staff are friendly and helpful throughout the
hotel, and the standard of food served is better than that in many
similar establishments.*
40⇌(12fb)⅛in 10 bedrooms CTV in all bedrooms ® T ✱
sB&B⇌£55 dB&B⇌£70-£80 Continental breakfast ᗺ
《 60P 12🏔 ✿ CFA ⚏
V ✿ ⚘ Lunch fr£18&alc Dinner fr£18&alc Last dinner
9.30pm
Credit Cards [1][2][3][5]

★★66% **George** 4 Market Place BA11 1AF ☎(0373)62584
FAX (0373) 51945
*A former coaching inn in the town centre with a friendly, informal
atmosphere. Bedrooms have been upgraded to a high standard and
the chef produces well-prepared dishes on both menus.*
20⇌♠(3fb)1⊞ CTV in all bedrooms ® T sB&B⇌♠fr£42.50
dB&B⇌♠fr£54.50 ᗺ
17🏔 solarium
♀ English & Continental V ✿ ⚘ Lunch £5.50-£9alc Dinner
fr£10.45&alc Last dinner 9.30pm
Credit Cards [1][2][3][5] £

---

**GAINSBOROUGH** Lincolnshire Map **08** SK88

★★64% *Hickman-Hill* Cox's Hill DN21 1HH ☎(0427)3639
*This large, white Georgian detached house stands in its own
grounds and maintains a country house atmosphere throughout its
public areas. Accommodation is attractive and well equipped and
the restaurant offers well prepared popular dishes.*
8rm(3⇌3♠)(1fb) CTV in all bedrooms ®
CTV 25P ⇔ ✿ solarium
V ✿ ⚘ Last dinner 9pm
Credit Cards [1][3]

---

**GAIRLOCH** Highland *Ross & Cromarty* Map **14** NG87

★★62% **The Old Inn** Flowerdale IV21 2BD ☎(0445)2006
*Set back from the road, this charming 18th century former
coaching inn stands in its own grounds overlooking the fishing
harbour, in a picturesque setting of loch and mountains. The
atmosphere is welcoming and the bedrooms are practical and well
equipped. Fresh highland produce and real ale are served and the
public areas are cosy.*
14⇌♠(4fb) CTV in all bedrooms ® T
sB&B⇌♠£22.50-£29.50 dB&B⇌♠£45-£59 ᗺ
50P ⇔ ⚏ xmas
✿ ⚘ Lunch fr£6.50 High tea fr£5.50 Dinner fr£14.50 Last
dinner 9pm
Credit Cards [1][2][3]

---

**GALASHIELS** Borders *Selkirkshire* Map **12** NT43

★★★65% *Kingsknowes* Selkirk Rd TD1 3HY ☎(0896)58375
*This impressive Victorian sandstone mansion is situated just south
of the town on the A7. The public areas are comfortably elegant,
and the bedrooms, although modernised, have retained the original
character and comfort.*
11rm(8⇌2♠)(2fb) CTV in all bedrooms ®
50P ⇔ ✿ ♪ (hard)

---

V ✿ Last dinner 8.45pm
Credit Cards [1][2][3][4][5]

★★★65% **Woodlands Country House Hotel & Restaurant**
Windyknowe Rd TD1 1RG ☎(0896)4722
*Set in its own gardens above the town and dating from the mid-
19th century, this impressive country house complements
comfortable, tastefully furnished bedrooms in a variety of shapes
and sizes with elegant public areas containing many interesting
features. Very courteous resident proprietors obviously enjoy
caring for their guests – whether resident or diners – and both
restaurant and bar meals are particularly worthy of
recommendation.*
9⇌♠(3fb) CTV in all bedrooms ® T sB&B⇌♠£40
dB&B⇌♠£60 ᗺ
30P ✿ xmas
♀ English & French V ✿ ⚘ Lunch £7.95&alc Dinner
£12-£19alc Last dinner 9.30pm
Credit Cards [1][3]

★★61% **Abbotsford Arms** 63 Stirling St TD1 1BY ☎(0896)2517
Closed 24-25, 31 Dec & 1 Jan
*Bedrooms with modern facilities and substantial meals – served in
either the attractive restaurant or a comfortable lounge bar – are
available at this family-run hotel which stands in the city centre,
beside the re-aligned A7.*
13rm(3⇌6♠)(2fb) CTV in all bedrooms ® 🗙 (ex guide dogs)
sB&B£18-£20 sB&B⇌♠£22-£25 dB&B£30-£36
dB&B⇌♠£40-£44
《 CTV 15P ⇔
V ✿ ⚘
Credit Cards [1][3] £

---

**GANLLWYD** Gwynedd Map **06** SH72

★★★🏅66% **Dolmelynllyn Hall** LL40 2HP ☎(034140)273
RS Dec-Feb
*Parts of this stone-built country house date back to the 16th
century, and it has a wealth of charm and character. It stands in
extensive grounds and delightful formal gardens, off the A410, 3
miles north of Dolgellau. Jon Barkwith and his daughter Jo, who is
also the chef, acquired the house in 1988, and have painstakingly
restored and converted it into a very pleasant country house hotel,
with well equipped accommodation, and elegant, comfortable
public rooms.*
11⇌♠1⊞⅛in 2 bedrooms CTV in all bedrooms ® T ✱
sB&B⇌♠£42.50-£47.50 dB&B⇌♠£85-£105 (incl dinner) ᗺ
25P ⇔ ✿ ⚏ nc10yrs
✿ ⚘ ⅛ Lunch £10.75 Dinner £16 Last dinner 9pm
Credit Cards [1][2][3] £

★62% *Tyn-Y-Groes* LL40 2NH ☎(034140)275
*This former coaching inn, now a privately-owned small hotel, is
situated on the A470 4 miles north of Dolgellau in a popular
holiday area. Rooms are modern and well maintained.*
8rm(4⇌3♠)(1fb) CTV in 3 bedrooms ®
CTV 24P ⇔
♀ French V ✿ ⅛ Last dinner 9pm

---

**GARFORTH** West Yorkshire Map **08** SE43

★★★66% **Hilton National** Wakefield Rd, Garforth Rdbt
LS25 1LH (junc A63/A642 6m E of Leeds) (Hilton)
☎Leeds(0532)866556 Telex no 556324 FAX (0532) 868326
*Modern and functional, this purpose-built hotel offers comfortable,
well appointed bedrooms.*
144⇌♠(21fb)⅛in 4 bedrooms CTV in all bedrooms ® T ✱
sB⇌♠£72-£92 dB⇌♠£89-£109 (room only)
《 250P ✿ CFA ⬚(heated) sauna gymnasium pool xmas
V ✿ ⚘ ⅛ Lunch £8.50-£12.50 Dinner £9.50-£17.50&alc Last
dinner 10pm
Credit Cards [1][2][3][5]

**F**

**GARSTANG** Lancashire Map **07** SD44

★★♨**72%**, **The Pickerings** Garstang Rd, Catterall PR3 0HA (2m S B6430) ☎(0995)602133 FAX (0995) 602100
RS 26 & 27 Dec
*A small, personally-run hotel surrounded by attractive and well-maintained gardens. Bedrooms are particularly spacious and equipped to a high standard. The restaurant offers interesting menus which feature fresh local produce and the helpful young staff provide cheerful service.*
14⇨♠(1fb)3♨ CTV in all bedrooms ® T ✗ (ex guide dogs) sB&B⇨♠£37-£50 dB&B⇨♠£58-£90 ☗
50P ✿ *xmas*
♡ English & Continental V ♦ Lunch £9-£10 Dinner £16-£25
Last dinner 10pm
Credit Cards ① ③ ⑤ ④

★★**68%** **Crofters** Cabus PR3 1PH (A6) (Consort)
☎(0995)604128
*A modern hotel offering well-appointed bedrooms, attractive public areas and interesting menus. Service is courteous and friendly.*
19⇨♠(4fb) CTV in all bedrooms ® T sB&B⇨♠£44-£57 dB&B⇨♠£49.50-£62 ☗
《 200P ♫ *xmas*
♡ English & French V ♦ Lunch £11.50-£15alc Dinner £13&alc Last dinner 10pm
Credit Cards ① ② ③ ⑤ ④

**GARVE** Highland *Ross & Cromarty* Map **14** NH36

★★**64%** **Inchbae Lodge** Inchbae IV23 2PH
☎Aultguish(09975)269
*This former hunting lodge is now a comfortable, family-run hotel providing modestly-appointed bedrooms, spacious public areas including a cosy bar, and imaginative, well-cooked food.*
6rm(3⇨)Annexe6♠(2fb) ® ✱ sB&B£27.50 sB&B⇨♠£29.50 dB&B£47 dB&B⇨♠£49 ☗
30P ♨ ✿ ♪ clay pigeon shooting *xmas*
♡ Scottish & French ♦ ♨ Bar Lunch £1.50-£10alc High tea £1.50-£10alc Dinner £15.95 Last dinner 8.30pm
④

**GATEHOUSE OF FLEET** Dumfries & Galloway *Kirkcudbrightshire* Map **11** NX55

★★★★**64%** **Cally Palace** DG7 2DL ☎Gatehouse(05574)341 Telex no 777088 FAX (05574) 522
Closed 3 Jan-Feb
*This impressive country house is set in its own grounds, which feature some interesting walks. Both the public areas, with their wealth of lounges, and the bedrooms have been refurbished to provide a high degree of comfort, the latter being pleasantly spacious and furnished with many thoughtful extras. Staff are particularly courteous throughout, and the hotel is very popular with family parties.*
55⇨(7fb)1♨ CTV in all bedrooms ® T ✱ sB&B⇨£30-£45 dB&B⇨£60-£90 ☗
Lift 《 100P ♨ ✿ ♪ (hard) ♪ croquet putting green ♫ *xmas*
♡ Scottish & French V ♦ ♨ ✂ Lunch fr£7.50 Dinner fr£16.50 Last dinner 9.30pm
Credit Cards ③

★★★**63%** **Murray Arms** DG7 2HY (Best Western)
☎Gatehouse(05574)207 FAX (05574) 370
*A traditional, long-established hotel extends a warm welcome to guests, providing relaxing lounges and comfortable bedrooms with bathrooms, many of them having been modernised to a high standard.*
12⇨Annexe1⇨(3fb) CTV in all bedrooms ® T S10% sB&B⇨£32-£35 dB&B⇨£64-£70 ☗
《 CTV 50P ✿ croquet *xmas*

V ♦ ♨ Bar Lunch £3-£10alc High tea £3-£10alc Dinner £14-£15 Last dinner 8.45pm
Credit Cards ① ② ③ ⑤ ④

**GATESHEAD** Tyne & Wear Map **12** NZ26

★★★**69%** **Springfield** Durham Rd NE9 5BT (Embassy)
☎091-477 4121 Telex no 538197 SPRING G FAX 091-477 7213
*Recently modernised to a most comfortable standard. The elegant restaurant offers a carvery as well as the standard menu.*
60⇨♠(4fb)✂in 7 bedrooms CTV in all bedrooms ® T ✱ S15% sB&B⇨♠£48.50-£69 dB&B⇨♠£68-£79 (room only) ☗
Lift 《 100P ♫ *xmas*
V ♦ ♨ Lunch fr£8.95 Dinner fr£11.95 Last dinner 9.30pm
Credit Cards ① ② ③ ④ ⑤

★★★**66%** **Swallow** High West St NE8 1PE (Swallow)
☎091-477 1105 Telex no 53534 FAX 091-478 7214
*Situated just off the southern approach to Newcastle, this modern hotel offers spacious accommodation.*
103⇨♠(6fb)✂in 19 bedrooms CTV in all bedrooms ® T S% sB&B⇨♠£68-£110 dB&B⇨♠£78-£125 ☗
Lift 《 CTV 90P 50☎ CFA ☒(heated) sauna solarium gymnasium spa bath steam room ♫ *xmas*
♡ International V ♦ ♨ S% Lunch £9.95&alc Dinner £10.95-£14.75&alc Last dinner 10pm
Credit Cards ① ② ③ ④ ⑤

❀★★**73%**, **Eslington Villa** 8 Station Rd, Low Fell NE9 6DR
☎091-487 6017
Closed 25 Dec-2 Jan
*This charming Edwardian country house is situated in its own gardens overlooking Team Valley, but despite its urban setting, nothing distracts from the comfort, warmth and hospitality provided by the proprietors, Melanie and Nick Tulip, and their enthusiastic staff. Bedrooms are well equipped and the public rooms are comfortable and very tastefully appointed, but pride of place goes to the restaurant, an elegant room with polished tables, in which dishes prepared by chef Allan O'Neil, surpass all expectations. Mouth-watering steamed salmon wrapped in cabbage, with a chive cream sauce was one dish sampled by an inspector, followed by medallions of beef coated with sesame seeds served with a delicate mustard sauce. The vegetables are excellent, and the wine list is well balanced. Service is faultless.*
14⇨♠(2fb)1♨ CTV in all bedrooms ® T ✱ sB&B⇨♠£29.50-£49.50 dB&B⇨♠£39.50-£59.50
《 15P ♨ ✿
♡ English & French ✂ Lunch fr£10.95 Dinner fr£16.95&alc Last dinner 10pm
Credit Cards ① ② ③ ⑤

**GATTONSIDE** Borders *Roxburghshire* Map **12** NT53

✗✗**Hoebridge Inn** TD6 9LZ ☎Melrose(089682)3082
Closed Mon, 2 wks Apr, 1 wk Oct, Xmas & New Year
Lunch not served
♡ French & Italian V 46 seats Dinner £10-£18alc Last dinner 10pm 15P
Credit Cards ① ③

All hotels are now given a percentage grading for the quality of their facilities. A full explanation can be found within 'How we Classify Hotels and Restaurants' at the front of the book.

G

**GATWICK AIRPORT (LONDON)** West Sussex
Map **04** TQ24

See **Town Plan Section** under **London Airports**
See also **Burgh Heath, Dorking, East Grinstead, Reigate and South Godstone**

★★★★71% **London Gatwick Airport Hilton** RH6 0LL (Hilton)
☎Gatwick(0293)518080 Telex no 877021 FAX (0293) 28980
*This hotel provides excellent access to the airport, being directly linked to the terminals. Bedrooms are equipped to a high standard, featuring air-conditioning, mini-bars and television displays of flight information. The reception lobby holds a replica of the Gypsy Moth aeroplane flown by Amy Johnson, after whom the lounge is named. Garden restaurant and bar, with their efficient, well-managed service, will please the discerning diner, while the amenities include a hairdressing salon, bank, shop, business centre, satellite television and indoor swimming pool.*
552⇌✝(4fb)⊱in 34 bedrooms CTV in all bedrooms T ✱
sB⇌✝£105-£115 dB⇌✝£115-£130 (room only) ⃞
Lift ⟨ ⊞ 100P (80p per hour) ✷ CFA ⊠(heated) sauna solarium gymnasium
♲ Continental V ♦ ♨ ⊱ Lunch £12.50-£15&alc High tea £3.50-£3.75 Dinner £18.50-£22.50&alc Last dinner 11pm
Credit Cards ①②③④⑤

★★★★66% **Copthorne** Copthorne Road, Copthorne RH10 3PG
(on A264 2m E of A264/B2036 rbt) (Best Western)
☎Copthorne(0342)714971 Telex no 95500 FAX (0342) 717375
*Only minutes from the airport, but centered round a sixteenth-century farmhouse in a hundred acres of farm and woodland, this hotel offers a choice of modern bedrooms, the new executive wing also housing the Lion D'Or Restaurant and self-service Garden Carvery. Public areas also include bar lounge, pub, conference/ banqueting rooms and extensive health and leisure facilities.*
225⇌*(10fb)4⊞⊱in 34 bedrooms ® T ✱
S% sB⇌£95-£125 dB⇌£105-£195 (room only) ⃞
▶

**Gatehouse-of-Fleet**
**Dumfries & Galloway**
*AA* ★ ★ ★ ★
*Scottish Tourist Board* ♥ ♥ ♥ ♥ *Highly Commended*
Set in 100 acres of its own beautiful grounds, the Cally Palace is a haven of peace and tranquillity.
Combined with the 55 superbly appointed suites and bedrooms, and fine traditionally cooked Scottish Produce, a visit to this hotel is a must.
It is an ideal base to explore the unspoiled South West corner of Scotland.
Work has begun, and is due to be finished at the end of 1990, on an indoor leisure complex comprising swimming pool, jacuzzi, sauna and solaria. Outdoor facilities include tennis, putting, and croquet. Free golf and fishing are also offered.
**Write or telephone (05574) 341 for full details**

**H|LTON**
INTERNATIONAL
★★★★

The London Gatwick Airport Hilton is in a central position within the Gatwick Airport complex with excellent conference and leisure facilities. There are fast and frequent travel connections to London, and in-room TV with flight information.

London Gatwick Airport Hilton,
Gatwick Airport, West Sussex RH6 0LL.
Tel: 0293 518080, Telex: 877021,
Fax: 0293 28980.

**THE**
**PICKERINGS**
★★
**COUNTRY HOUSE RESTAURANT**
**AND HOTEL**

*"Tastefully Different"*
Garstang Road · Catterall
Nr. Garstang · Lancashire
Telephone: (0995) 602133
Facsimile (0995) 602100

## Gatwick Airport (London) - Gerrards Cross

◖ CTV 300P ✿ CFA squash sauna solarium gymnasium croquet putting 🏌 *xmas*
♡ English & Continental V ♨ ☲ ✠ Lunch £12.50-£30&alc Dinner £12.50-£30&alc Last dinner 10.30pm
Credit Cards ① ② ③ ⑤ £

**★★★★60% Copthorne Effingham Park** West Park Road, Copthorne RH10 3EU ☎Copthorne(0342)714994 Telex no 95649 FAX (0342) 716039
*Set in 40 acres of parkland and gardens, this purpose-built hotel offers a range of well equipped and tastefully appointed bedrooms. There is a choice of restaurants, in addition to the popular leisure club bar lounge, and there are extensive facilities, including a 9-hole golf course, indoor swimming pool and beauty salon. Staff are efficient, helpful and friendly.*
122 ⇨³ ↑(6fb)✠in 27 bedrooms CTV in all bedrooms ® T ✳
sB ⇨³ ↑£95-£115 dB ⇨³ ↑£105-£125 (room only) ☒
Lift ◖ 500P ✿ ◳(heated) ▶9 ♪ sauna solarium gymnasium dance studio jacuzzi plunge pool
♡ English & French V ♨ ☲ ✠ Lunch fr£12.50&alc Dinner fr£12.50&alc Last dinner 10.30pm
Credit Cards ① ② ③ ⑤

**★★★70% Holiday Inn** Langley Dr RH11 7SX (Holiday Inns Inc) ☎Crawley(0293)29991 due to change to 529991 Telex no 877311 FAX (0293) 515913
*Recently refurbished throughout, with major new features including the Crest Sensations Leisure Club and indoor pool, the prestigious Colonnade restaurant, La Brasserie, a cocktail lounge and a business centre. Function rooms are nearly complete, and the choice of compact bedrooms includes Lady Crest and Executive. Service is well-managed and helpful.*
225 ⇨³ ↑(9fb)✠in 45 bedrooms CTV in all bedrooms ® T S%
sB ⇨³ ↑fr£90 dB ⇨³ ↑fr£105 (room only) ☒
Lift ◖ 300P ◳(heated) snooker sauna solarium gymnasium jacuzzi steam rooms *xmas*
♡ English & French V ♨ ☲ ✠ S% Lunch fr£15.50 Dinner fr£15.50 Last dinner 9.30pm
Credit Cards ① ② ③ ④ ⑤

**★★★65% The George** High Street, Crawley RH10 1BS (Trusthouse Forte) ☎Crawley(0293)24215 Telex no 87385 FAX (0293) 548565
*This historic inn stands in the centre of Crawley, easily recognised by its rare gallows sign which spans the High Street. Its interior combines the old world charm of exposed beams and timbers with modern standards of comfort, particularly in the bedrooms of both the main building and its new rear extensions. The Shire Restaurant features cuisine in English style, whilst other amenities include coffee shops, a historic public bar and good car parking.*
86 ⇨³ ↑(3fb)✠in 20 bedrooms CTV in all bedrooms ® T ✳
S15% sB ⇨³ ↑fr£70 dB ⇨³ ↑fr£90 (room only) ☒
◖ 89P CFA *xmas*
V ♨ ☲ ✠ S15% Lunch £9.50-£11.95&alc Dinner £13.95-£16&alc Last dinner 9.30pm
Credit Cards ① ② ③ ④ ⑤

**★★★62% Chequers Thistle** Brighton Road, Horley RH6 8PH (Mount Charlotte (TS)) ☎Horley(0293)786992 Telex no 877550 FAX (0293) 820625
*Once a Tudor coaching inn, this pleasant, friendly hotel offers well appointed bedrooms, equipped with the most modern facilities. The Halfway Halt lounge bar has a low oak-beamed ceiling, while restaurant and cocktail bar favour a more formal style.*
78 ⇨³ ↑(54fb)✠in 5 bedrooms CTV in all bedrooms ® T ✕ ✳
sB ⇨³ ↑fr£72 dB ⇨³ ↑fr£85 (room only) ☒
◖ 190P CFA ◳(heated) ♫
♡ International ♨ ☲ ✠ Lunch fr£7.95&alc Dinner fr£14.50&alc Last dinner 10pm
Credit Cards ① ② ③ ④ ⑤

**★★★62% Goffs Park** 45 Goffs Park Road, Crawley RH11 8AX ☎Crawley(0293)35447 Telex no 87415 FAX (0293) 542050
*Situated in a residential area south of Crawley, this busy commercial hotel offers a choice of well equipped, modern bedrooms and service of a good standard. Other amenities include a popular bar and restaurant, and fine conference facilities.*
37 ⇨³ ↑Annexe28 ⇨³ ↑ CTV in all bedrooms ® T
sB&B ⇨³ ↑fr£69.50 dB&B ⇨³ ↑fr£89.50
◖ 92P CFA
♡ English & French V ♨ ☲ Lunch fr£9&alc Dinner fr£12&alc Last dinner 9.30pm
Credit Cards ① ② ③ ⑤

**★★★60% Post House** Povey Cross Road, Horley RH6 0BA (Trusthouse Forte) ☎Horley(0293)771621 Telex no 877351 FAX (0293) 771054
*A modern, purpose-built hotel – much used by airport passengers, for whom it operates a courtesy bus service – offers accommodation in well equipped bedrooms with up-to-date facilities, executive rooms providing additional comforts. Both table d'hôte and à la carte menus are available in the restaurant, while a lighter meal can be obtained in the coffee shop.*
216 ⇨³ ↑(126fb)✠in 65 bedrooms CTV in all bedrooms ® T ✳
sB ⇨³ ↑£80-£90 dB ⇨³ ↑£90-£100 (room only) ☒
Lift ◖ 300P CFA ◳(heated) *xmas*
♡ International V ♨ ☲ ✠ Lunch fr£11 High tea fr£8 Dinner fr£15 Last dinner 10.30pm
Credit Cards ① ② ③ ④ ⑤

**★★★59% Gatwick Concorde** Church Rd, Lowfield Heath, Crawley RH11 0PQ (Queens Moat) ☎Crawley(0293)33441 Telex no 87287 FAX (0293) 35369
*Recently completely refurbished, this hotel now offers well furnished bedrooms equipped to a high standard, some overlooking the runway and others situated in the new wing. Facilities include the Aviators Brasserie, Rounds Pub – a popular meeting place and lunchtime diner – and several function rooms.*
121 ⇨³ ↑(7fb) CTV in all bedrooms ®
Lift ◖ 137P (charged) CFA
♡ English, French & Italian V ♨ ☲ Last dinner 10.45pm
Credit Cards ① ② ③ ⑤

**★★63% Gatwick Manor** London Rd, Lowfield Heath, Crawley RH10 2ST (Berni/Chef & Brewer) ☎Crawley(0293)26301 & 35251 Telex no 87529
*Original beamed Tudor buildings in the grounds of this spacious hotel, have been skilfully extended to offer well-equipped modern bedrooms with friendly and efficiently managed service. Guests have a choice of two bars and two Berni restaurants; grill cooking is of a high standard and supplemented by a self-service salad bar. Conference facilities are available, and the hotel runs a courtesy minibus service to the airport.*
30 ⇨³ ↑(3fb) CTV in all bedrooms ® T ✕ (ex guide dogs)
sB&B ⇨³ ↑£70 dB&B ⇨³ ↑£77.50 ☒
◖ CTV 250P ✿
V ♨ ✠ Lunch £8-£15alc Dinner £8-£15alc Last dinner 10.30pm
Credit Cards ① ② ③ ⑤

◯**Gatwick Sterling** RH6 0PH ☎(0293)567070 FAX (0293) 567739
Due to have opened Sep 1990
474rm

---

**GERRARDS CROSS** Buckinghamshire Map 04 TQ08

**★★64% Ethorpe** Packhorse Rd SL9 8HY (Berni/Chef & Brewer) ☎(0753)882039
*The bedrooms at this friendly commercial-style hotel are comfortable and spacious with co-ordinating soft furnishings and fabrics.*
29 ⇨³ ↑(4fb)1 ☒ CTV in all bedrooms ® T ✕ (ex guide dogs)
sB&B ⇨³ ↑£69-£77.50 dB&B ⇨³ ↑£84 ☒

《 80P ❀
V ✿ ✂ Lunch £8-£15alc Dinner £8-£15alc Last dinner
10.30pm
Credit Cards ① ② ③ ⑤

---

**GIFFNOCK** Strathclyde *Renfrewshire* Map **11** NS55

★★★67% **Macdonald Thistle** Eastwood Toll G46 6RA (Mount
Charlotte (TS)) ☎041-638 2225 Telex no 779138
FAX 041-638 6231
*Modern hotel at the Eastwood Toll roundabout (A77), on the*
*southern outskirts of Glasgow.*
56⇋♠(1fb) CTV in all bedrooms ® T ✲ sB⇋♠fr£65
dB⇋♠fr£75 (room only) ₽
《 200P CFA sauna solarium gymnasium games room ♫
♀ International ✿ ₤ ✂ Lunch fr£7.50&alc Dinner
fr£12.95&alc Last dinner 10pm
Credit Cards ① ② ③ ④ ⑤
See advertisement under GLASGOW

✗**Turban Tandoori** 2 Station Rd G46 6JF ☎041-638 0069
*Standing conveniently close to the railway station, on the southern*
*access road to the city, this well-established restaurant boasts a*
*reputation achieved largely by attentive service and an innovative*
*range of curries, Karami, Jaipuri, Nentara and Masaledar*
*specialities being featured as well as the more popular 'sizzling'*
*Tandoori dishes. Dim lighting adds to the intimate atmosphere*
*created by clever partitioning.*
Closed 25 Dec & 1 Jan
Lunch not served
♀ Indian V 70 seats ✳ Last dinner mdnt 150P
Credit Cards ① ② ③
See advertisement under GLASGOW

---

**GIFFORD** Lothian *East Lothian* Map **12** NT56

★★71% *Tweeddale Arms* EH41 4QU (Consort) ☎(062081)240
*This character village hotel offers good modern comforts combined*
*with old world charm and traditional hospitality. The smart*
*restaurant serves British and continental cuisine. Bedrooms are*
*comfortable and well equipped and the relaxing lounge has an*
*inviting log fire when the weather demands it.*
15⇋♠(2fb) CTV in all bedrooms ®
♪ snooker
V ✿ ₤ Last dinner 9pm
Credit Cards ① ② ③

---

**GIGHA ISLAND** Strathclyde *Argyllshire* Map **10** NR64
(Car ferry from Tayinloan (mainland))

★★64% **Gigha** PA41 7AD ☎Gigha(05835)254 FAX (05835) 282
*This old inn, enjoying views across the Sound of Gigha to the*
*mainland, has been tastefully renovated and extended to provide a*
*comfortable hotel and a haven for visiting yachtsmen. Service is*
*informal and very friendly.*
13rm(11⇋♠) ® ✖ (ex guide dogs) ✳ sB&B⇋♠£47
dB&B⇋♠£94 (incl dinner) ₽
CTV 20P ⊞ ⊩ 9 ♪ xmas
♀ International V ✿ ₤ Lunch £1-£15 Dinner £16.50 Last
dinner 9.30pm
Credit Cards ① ③

---

**GILLAN** Cornwall & Isles of Scilly Map **02** SW72

★★62% *Tregildry* TR12 6HG ☎Manaccan(032623)378
Closed 15 Oct-Etr
*Imaginative menus of well-cooked dishes are offered at this family-*
*run hotel with elevated views over Falmouth Bay.*
10⇋♠(2fb) CTV in 6 bedrooms ®
CTV 20P ⊞ ❀
♀ International ✿ ₤ ✂ Last dinner 8.30pm
Credit Cards ① ③

★★

**Nearest and Fairest of the Hebrides.**

# Isle of Gigha

The Isle of Gigha (pronounced Ghee-a), is 3 miles
from Kintyre and just 2½ hours' drive from
Glasgow with a regular daily ferry service from
Tayinloan. Splendid views, sandy beaches, birds &
wild flowers plus a 9-hole golf course. The great
shrub & woodland gardens of Achamore, known
to experts throughout the world, are open daily to
the public.
The Gigha Hotel is situated overlooking Ardminish
Bay with thirteen comfortable bedrooms all en
suite. There is a cheerful bar and comfortable
lounge. The restaurant features local speciality
products combined with worldwide dishes to
produce excellent cuisine. The hotel has two self
catering crofts and a self catering house. Coffee,
snacks and crafts are available at the Boat House.
For Ferry times phone **088073 253/4.**
For Hotel and Self Catering bookings
contact: Alison or Steve Hyatt
on Gigha **(05835) 254**

**G**

---

# Ghyll Manor
# Hotel
★★★
## Rusper, Nr. Horsham,
## West Sussex RH12 4PX.
## Telephone: (0293) 871571

Beautiful country house hotel
set in 40 acres of landscaped
gardens. 28 bedrooms including five suites and five 4-poster
rooms.

Renowned restaurant featuring
English cuisine.

Heated swimming pool, tennis
court, sauna and solarium.

### GILLINGHAM Dorset Map 03 ST82

★★

★★ STOCK HILL HOUSE

Stock SP8 5NR
☎(0747)823626
RS Sun dinner, Mon

*A splendid Victorian manor, set in 10 acres of wooded parkland, the hotel is superbly run by Nita and Peter Hauser. Furnishings are ornate and lavish, yet the atmosphere is both pleasing and undemanding. The bedrooms are stunning, each one different, and among the notable pieces of furniture is a wrought-iron bed that once belonged to a Spanish princess. Peter Hauser's unfussy cooking has strong Austrian overtones and his pastries are unforgettable. The 5-course dinner is excellent and our Inspector particularly enjoyed monkfish with tomato butter and tarragon, and the braised ox tongue served with Madeira sauce.*

8⇔♠1⌬ CTV in all bedrooms T ✖ ✱ sB&B⇔♠£70-£75 dB&B⇔♠£140-£150 (incl dinner)
25P ⇔ ✿ ⬛(heated) croquet nc7yrs *xmas*
♀ English, Austrian & French V ✗ Lunch £18 Dinner £25 Last dinner 8.45pm
Credit Cards ①③

### GILLINGHAM Kent Map 05 TQ76

⬧**Rank Motor Lodge** Hartlip, ME8 8PW (Rank)
☎Medway(0634)377337
(For full entry see Farthing Corner Motorway Service Area (M2))

### GIRVAN Strathclyde *Ayrshire* Map 10 NX19

★★63% **King's Arms** Dalrymple St KA26 9AE ☎(0465)3322
*This family-run hotel places the emphasis on good food and friendly service, whilst golfing cocktails such as 'The Perfect Slice' are a feature of the Bunker bar. Recently upgraded, the bedrooms have ensuite facilities.*
25⇔♠(4fb) CTV in all bedrooms ® T ✖ (ex guide dogs)
sB&B⇔♠£33 dB&B⇔♠£96 🏳
⚄ 100P 1🛏 (£2) snooker ♫ *xmas*
♀ Scottish & French V ✿ ⚏ Last dinner 9.30pm
Credit Cards ①③ⓔ

### GISBURN Lancashire Map 07 SD84

★★★61% **Stirk House** BB7 4LJ (Consort) ☎(0200)445581
Telex no 635238 FAX (0200) 445744
*Once an impressive country house, this hotel offers accommodation in a modern wing to complement the comfortable, interesting lounges and bars in the old building.*
36⇔♠Annexe12⇔♠(2fb) CTV in all bedrooms ® T
✖ (ex guide dogs) ✱ sB&B⇔♠£55-£60 dB&B⇔♠£66-£76 🏳
⚄ 100P ✿ CFA ⬛(heated) squash sauna solarium gymnasium
♀ English & French V ✿ ⚏ ✗ Lunch £8.50-£10.50&alc Dinner £15.50-£17&alc Last dinner 9.30pm
Credit Cards ①②③④⑤ⓔ

All AA-appointed establishments are
inspected regularly to ensure that required
standards are maintained.

### GITTISHAM Devon Map 03 SY19

★★★⚖67% **Combe House** EX14 0AD (Pride of Britain)
☎Honiton(0404)42756 & 43560 FAX (0404) 46004
Closed 7 Jan-1 Mar
*This large, impressive Elizabethan manor house stands in an extensive parkland estate, and promotes a relaxed and genteel style in the country house manner, combining casual informality with competence. The interior is notable for its wood-panelled Great Hall. Bedrooms and bathrooms vary in size, but all are well equipped. The dining room offers a good choice of well presented dishes.*
15⇔2⌬ CTV in all bedrooms T S12.5% sB&B⇔£55.50-£88 dB&B⇔£85.50-£119.50 🏳
50P 1🛏 (£2.50 per night) ⇔ ✿ ◢ croquet *xmas*
♀ English & French V ✿ ⚏
Credit Cards ①②③⑤

### GLAMIS Tayside *Angus* Map 15 NO34

★★★⚖69% **Castleton House** DD8 1SJ ☎(030784)340
FAX (030784) 506
Closed 1 Jan
*This welcome addition to Scotland's country house hotels is set in eleven acres of grounds three miles south of the town. Built on the site of a fort and surrounded by a dry moat, it has been sympathetically refurbished to retain much of its character. The day rooms, with their welcoming log fires, are tastefully appointed to invite easy relaxation, while bedrooms with individual décor and luxury bathrooms have an air of elegance.*
6⇔♠ CTV in all bedrooms ® T ✖ (ex guide dogs)
sB&B⇔♠£50-£60 dB&B⇔♠£80-£90
15P ⇔ ✿ putting green *xmas*
♀ European V ✿ ⚏ ✗ Lunch fr£10.50 Dinner fr£21 Last dinner 9.30pm
Credit Cards ①②③ⓔ

### GLASGOW Strathclyde *Lanarkshire* Map 11 NS56

See **Town Plan Section**

★★★★63% **Stakis Grosvenor** 1/10 Grosvenor Ter, Great Western Rd G12 0TA (Stakis) ☎041-339 8811 Telex no 776247 FAX 041-334 0710
*Situated in the popular west of the city, overlooking the Botanic Gardens, an hotel with a fine façade offers well-equipped bedrooms and spacious public areas. Guests can choose between the Steakhouse and the attractive Lafayette restaurant, attentive and friendly staff providing the same high standard of service in both.*
95⇔♠(12fb)⌬in 50 bedrooms CTV in all bedrooms ® ✱
sB⇔♠£84.50-£100 dB⇔♠£99-£120 (room only) 🏳
Lift ⚄ 12P 70🛏
♀ French V ✿ ⚏ ✗ Lunch fr£7.25&alc Dinner fr£16.95 Last dinner 10.30pm
Credit Cards ①②③④⑤ⓔ

★★★★61% **Holiday Inn Glasgow** Argyle St, Anderston G3 8RR (Holiday Inns) ☎041-226 5577 Telex no 776355 FAX 041-221 9202
*This typical, large, city-centre hotel has some efficient staff, but the general atmosphere can be rather impersonal. Although the restaurant layout is interesting, our inspector found the dishes on its à la carte menu to be expensive and unmemorable. The cocktail bar, where a pianist plays in the evenings, is comfortable, with a pleasant outlook over the pool, and the hotel is well equipped to cater for meetings and functions.*
298⇔♠(80fb)⌬in 38 bedrooms CTV in all bedrooms ® T ✱
S% sB⇔♠£98-£106 dB⇔♠£118-£133 (room only) 🏳
Lift ⚄ 180P ⬛(heated) squash sauna solarium gymnasium heated whirlpool ♫ *xmas*
♀ European V ✿ ⚏ ✗ S% Lunch £16.26 High tea £2.50-£6 Dinner £16.25&alc Last dinner 10.30pm
Credit Cards ①②③④⑤

★★★★60% *The Albany* Bothwell St G2 7EN (Trusthouse Forte) ☎041-248 2656 Telex no 77440 FAX 041-221 8986
*A large city centre business hotel offers a mixture of compact and spacious bedrooms complemented by two substantial and extensive banqueting and conference facilities. Recently completely renovated, it plans to open a health and fitness club incorporating a swimming pool.*
251⇨⅄in 27 bedrooms CTV in all bedrooms ®
Lift ( ⊞ 25P CFA snooker
♔ Scottish & French V ✿ ⚏ ⅄ Last dinner 10pm
Credit Cards ①②③④⑤

★★★★59% *Hospitality Inn* 36 Cambridge St G3 3HN (Mount Charlotte (TS)) ☎041-332 3311 Telex no 777334 FAX 041-332 4050
*This large city centre hotel, offering spacious, well-appointed bedrooms and having its own car park underneath, is ideal for business traveller and holidaymaker alike.*
316⇨(3fb) CTV in all bedrooms ®
Lift ( 250🅰 CFA ♫
♔ Scottish, Danish & American V ✿ ⚏
Credit Cards ①②③④⑤

★★★75% *One Devonshire Gardens* 1 Devonshire Gardens G12 0UX ☎041-339 2001 & 041-334 9494 FAX 041-337 1663
*This elegant hotel is housed in a fine, end-terrace Victorian mansion house and provides spacious and comfortable accommodation. The restaurant attracts an extensive local clientele, and service is unobtrusive but efficient.*
18⇨♗(2fb)6⊞ CTV in all bedrooms
( 8P 🚳
♔ French ✿ ⚏ Last dinner 10pm
Credit Cards ①②③④⑤

★★★71% *Copthorne Hotel* George Square G2 1DS (Best Western) ☎041-332 6711 Telex no 778147 FAX 041-332 4264
*Situated on historic George Square, in the busy commercial area of the city, this well-modernised hotel offers a range of facilities to suit business and leisure guests. Staff are friendly and hospitable. The main shopping areas and theatres are within easy walking distance and the hotel is close to Queen Street and Central stations.*
141⇨ CTV in all bedrooms ® ✗ (ex guide dogs)
Lift ( ♪
♔ International V ✿ ⚏ ⅄ Last dinner 9.45pm
Credit Cards ①②③⑤

★★★69% *Crest Hotel Glasgow-City* Argyle St G2 8LL (Trusthouse Forte) ☎041-248 2355 Telex no 779652 FAX 041-221 1014
*A comfortable foyer lounge and attractive first floor restaurant – which caters for vegetarian and diabetic diets – are features of this bright, modern business hotel.*
121⇨♗(6fb)⅄in 35 bedrooms CTV in all bedrooms ® T
✗ (ex guide dogs) sB⇨♗£74 dB⇨♗£86 (room only) 🅿
Lift ( ♪ CFA *xmas*
♔ Continental V ✿ ⚏ ⅄ Lunch £9.25&alc Dinner £13.75-£14.95&alc Last dinner 10pm
Credit Cards ①②③⑤
See advertisement on page 309

★★★66% *Tinto Firs Thistle* 470 Kilmarnock Rd G43 2BB (Mount Charlotte (TS)) ☎041-637 2353 Telex no 778329 FAX 041-633 1340
*A modern purpose built hotel set in a residential area on the south side of the city combines style and comfort in its bedrooms and attractive public rooms.*
28⇨♗(4fb)⅄in 2 bedrooms CTV in all bedrooms ® T ✳
sB⇨♗fr£65 dB⇨♗fr£75 (room only) 🅿
( 46P ✿ ♫
♔ International ✿ ⚏ ⅄ Lunch fr£7.75&alc Dinner fr£12.50&alc Last dinner 9.45pm
Credit Cards ①②③④⑤

**G**

# Glasgow

★★★62% **Kelvin Park Lorne** 923 Sauchiehall St G3 7TE
(Queens Moat) ☎041-334 4891 Telex no 778935
FAX 041-337 1659
*With total refurbishment completed early in 1990, this hotel now
offers new, comfortable public areas, including an elegant
restaurant, and two styles of well equipped bedrooms.*
98⇨♪(7fb)2🚭🖐in 20 bedrooms CTV in all bedrooms ® T ✱
sB⇨♪fr£65 dB⇨♪fr£75 (room only) ☐
Lift ( 40🍴 ♫ *xmas*
♡ French V ✿ ஐ Lunch £8.95&alc High tea £3.25-£7.50
Dinner £11.95&alc Last dinner 10.30pm
Credit Cards ①②③④⑤ⓔ

★★★60% **The Buchanan** 185 Buchanan St G1 2JY (Best
Western) ☎041-332 7284 Telex no 776320 FAX 041-332 2534
*An hotel set in a city-centre cul-de-sac offers well-appointed
bedrooms and lounge facilities: meals are taken in the Italian
restaurant which forms part of the hotel.*
54⇨♪ CTV in all bedrooms ® T ✱ sB&B⇨♪£45-£60.50
dB&B⇨♪£55-£75
Lift ( CTV *xmas*
♡ Italian V ✿ ஐ Lunch £4.50 Dinner £8.50 Last dinner 11pm
Credit Cards ①②③⑤

★★★60% **Jurys Pond** Great Western Rd G12 0XP
☎041-334 8161 Telex no 776573 FAX 041-334 3846
*A purpose-built hotel and leisure centre, offering convenient access
to the north west from its position just off the A82, provides
comfortable, well equipped bedrooms and seating throughout the
day in the two main bars though actual lounge facilities are
limited.*
132⇨♪(6fb)🖐in 55 bedrooms CTV in all bedrooms ®
Lift ( CTV 200P ❄ ☐(heated) sauna solarium gymnasium
V ✿ ஐ 🖐 Last dinner 10pm
Credit Cards ①②③⑤

★★★59% **Stakis Ingram** Ingram St G1 1DQ (Stakis)
☎041-248 4401 Telex no 776470 FAX 041-226 5149
*A city centre hotel close to George Square provides
accommodation in bedrooms which, though functional, are
comfortable and well equipped ; lounge facilities are limited.*
90⇨♪(1fb)🖐in 62 bedrooms CTV in all bedrooms ® T ✱
sB⇨♪£69-£72 dB⇨♪£81-£83 (room only) ☐
Lift ( 30P CFA *xmas*
♡ Scottish, English & French V ✿ ஐ 🖐 Lunch fr£8.50 Dinner
£11.95-£12.95 Last dinner 9.45pm
Credit Cards ①②③⑤

★★★58% **Central** 99 Gordon St G1 3SF (Consort)
☎041-221 9680 Telex no 777771 FAX 041-226 3948
*This long established businessman's hotel is located in the heart of
the city, and is also a popular conference venue. It has been
substantially refurbished and offers a choice of lounges, a Carvery
restaurant and well equipped, modern bedrooms. A leisure centre is
planned.*
221rm(190⇨21♪)(10fb)🖐in 40 bedrooms CTV in all
bedrooms ® T ✱ sB&B⇨♪£49.50-£59.50
dB&B⇨♪£65-£69.50 Continental breakfast ☐
Lift ( *xmas*
♡ European V ✿ ஐ 🖐 Lunch £9.65&alc Dinner £11.65&alc
Last dinner 9.30pm
Credit Cards ①②③④⑤

★★★58% **Swallow** 517 Paisley Rd West G51 1RW (Swallow)
☎041-427 3146 Telex no 778795 FAX 041-427 4059
*Situated near to the M8, a purpose-built hotel currently
undergoing a programme of improvements now boasts attractive,
new public areas and a smart, modern leisure complex. All
bedrooms are well equipped and comfortable, though some have
still to be refurbished.*
119⇨♪(1fb)🖐in 34 bedrooms CTV in all bedrooms ® T
S10% sB&B⇨♪£75 dB&B⇨♪£85 ☐
Lift ( 150P CFA ☐(heated) sauna solarium gymnasium *xmas*

♡ English & French V ✿ ஐ S10% Lunch £10&alc Dinner
£14&alc Last dinner 9.30pm
Credit Cards ①②③⑤ⓔ

★★64% **Ewington** 132 Queens Dr, Queens Park G42 8QW
☎041-423 1152 FAX 041-422 2030
*Friendly, traditional hotel in a terrace overlooking the park.*
45rm(19⇨17♪)(1fb) CTV in all bedrooms ® T sB&Bfr£35
sB&B⇨♪£45-£55 dB&B⇨♪£55-£75 ☐
Lift ( 18P snooker
V ✿ ஐ Lunch £5.50-£7.50 High tea £5.50-£6.50 Dinner
£10.50-£12.50&alc Last dinner 9pm
Credit Cards ①②③⑤

★★58% *Newlands* 290 Kilmarnock Rd G43 2XS
☎041-632 9171
Closed 1 Jan
*Set on the south side of the city, this small hotel offers comfortable,
compact bedrooms with a lively lounge bar providing non-stop
music.*
17⇨♪ CTV in all bedrooms ® T
( 🖐 ♫
♡ French & Italian V ✿ Last dinner 9.30pm
Credit Cards ①②③⑤

See advertisement on page 311

★★58% **Sherbrooke** 11 Sherbrooke Av, Pollokshields G41 4PG
☎041-427 4227 FAX 041-427 5685
*An attractive red sandstone building located in a residential area
close to the M77 and enjoying good views across the city. The
annexe wing offers a more modern style of accommodation.*
10⇨♪ Annexe11⇨♪(3fb)🖐in 2 bedrooms CTV in all
bedrooms ® T sB&B⇨♪fr£55 dB&B⇨♪fr£65 ☐
( CTV 50P ❄
♡ English & French V ✿ ஐ 🖐
Credit Cards ①②③⑤ⓔ

○**Town House** West George St G2 1NG ☎041-332 3320
due to have opened Jul 1990
34⇨♠

---

✕✕✕**Fountain** 2 Woodside Crescent G3 7UL ☎041-332 6396
*This long-established restaurant continues to exude an air of relaxed sophistication, despite the changes that have taken place over the years. In its split-level well-appointed dining room guests can enjoy a range of international dishes – though the tone is predominantly French – and there is a comfortable cocktail lounge; very civilised service is provided under the direction of proprietor Luigi Giusti.*
Closed Sun
Lunch not served Sat
♀ French V 70 seats ✱ Lunch £9&alc Dinner £13.95&alc Last lunch 2.30pm Last dinner 11pm ⁄P nc3yrs
Credit Cards 1 2 3 5

G

---

✕✕**Buttery** 652 Argyle St G3 8UF ☎041-221 8188
FAX 041-204 4639
*In contrast to the urban development surrounding it, this restaurant is reminiscent of yesteryear, with its plush bar area and well appointed wood-panelled dining room. Carefully prepared dishes are based on sound ingredients and acccompanied by a well-balanced and reasonably priced wine list.*
Closed Sun & BH's
Lunch not served Sat
♀ Scottish & French V 50 seats ✱ Lunch fr£12.50&alc Dinner £19.30-£35.53alc Last lunch 2.30pm Last dinner 10pm 30P
Credit Cards 1 2 3 5

---

✕✕**Kensingtons** 164 Darnley St, Pollokshields G41 2LL
☎041-424 3662 FAX 041-221 2762
Closed Sun & 4 days New Year
Lunch not served Sat
♀ International V 30 seats ✱ Lunch £8.95&alc Dinner £18.95&alc Last lunch 2pm Last dinner 9.30pm ⁄P
Credit Cards 1 2 3 5

---

✕✕**Rogano** 11 Exchange Place G1 3AN ☎041-248 4055 & 041-248 4913 FAX 041-248 2608
Closed Sun & BH's
V 50 seats ✱ Lunch £17.50-£25alc Dinner £17.50-£25alc Last lunch 2.30pm Last dinner 10.30pm ⁄P
Credit Cards 1 2 3 5

---

✕✕**The Triangle** 37 Queen St G1 3EF ☎041-221 8758
FAX 041-204 3189
*This stylish newcomer to the Glasgow scene offers the choice of a popular brasserie or a more formal dining room. It is the latter which has pleased our inspectors with its spacious and elegant style. The food is innovative, following the modern trend, with the addition of some classical dishes such as Beef Wellington and Tornedos Rossini and a variety of fish dishes. Staff are enthusiastic and friendly.*
Closed Sun
♀ International V 70 seats ✱ Lunch £17.50-£26 Dinner fr£10alc Last lunch 3pm Last dinner 11pm ⁄P nc14yrs
Credit Cards 1 2 3 5

---

✕***Killermont House Restaurant*** 2022 Maryhill Rd, Maryhill Park G20 0AB ☎041-946 5412
*Located in the northern suburbs, this converted manse provides comfortable and elegant surroundings in which to enjoy reliable and straightforward cuisine based on good quality Scottish ingredients. The fixed-price lunch and dinner menus are varied monthly to take advantage of seasonal produce, and on warm summer days one can eat al fresco in the sheltered walled garden.*
Closed Mon
Lunch not served Sat
Dinner not served Sun
♀ French 60 seats Last lunch 2.15pm Last dinner 10pm 22P
Credit Cards 1 2 3

---

✕***Loon Fung*** 417 Sauchiehall St G2 3LG ☎041-332 1240
*The popularity and success of this restaurant is evidenced by the large number of Chinese families who patronise it. The new owners have much improved the service, but some of the dishes, while strong in flavour, seem to lack the quality of fresh produce. Presumably one of the attractions for the discerning palate are speciality dishes that do not appear on the regular menu.*
♀ Cantonese V 140 seats Last lunch 2pm Last dinner 11.30pm ⁄P
Credit Cards 1 2 3 5

---

✕**Peking Inn** 191 Hope St G2 2 ☎041-332 8971
Closed Sun & Chinese New Year
♀ Cantonese & Pekinese V 60 seats Lunch fr£5 Dinner £15.50-£20&alc Last lunch 2pm Last dinner 11.30pm ⁄P
Credit Cards 1 2 3 5

---

**GLASGOW AIRPORT** Strathclyde *Renfrewshire*
Map **11** NS46

---

★★★★**55% The Excelsior** Abbotsinch, Paisley PA3 2TR (Trusthouse Forte) ☎041-887 1212 Telex no 777733
FAX 041-887 3738
*Standing alongside the city's airport terminal, this modern tower block hotel offers bedrooms of varying standards and styles.*
300⇨(8fb)⁄in 35 bedrooms CTV in all bedrooms ® ⊟
Lift ( ⊞ 35P CFA solarium
V ♡ ⊥ ⁄
Credit Cards 1 2 3 4 5

---

★★★**64% Crest Hotel-Erskine Bridge** North Barr PA8 6AN (Trusthouse Forte) ☎041-812 0123 Telex no 777713
FAX 041-812 7642
(For full entry see Erskine)

---

★★★**64% *Stakis Normandy*** Inchinnan Rd, Renfrew PA4 5EJ (2m NE A8) (Stakis) ☎041-886 4100 Telex no 778897
FAX 041-885 2366
*A well run modern hotel offers compact, well-equipped bedrooms with 24 hour room service from friendly, helpful staff. A choice of eating options is available, the buffet breakfast in the Juliana's restaurant being particularly impressive. The hotel also provides a courtesy bus service to the airport.*
141⇨♠(3fb)⁄in 16 bedrooms CTV in all bedrooms ®
Lift ( 350P ♫
♀ International ♡ ⊥ Last dinner 10pm
Credit Cards 1 2 3 5

---

★★★**60% Dean Park** 91 Glasgow Road, Renfrew PA4 8YB (3m NE A8) (Queens Moat) ☎041-886 3771 Telex no 779032
FAX 041-885 0681
120⇨♠(4fb) CTV in all bedrooms ® **T** S15%
sB&B⇨♠£65-£75 dB&B⇨♠£78-£88 ⊟
( 200P ✲ CFA solarium
♀ French V ♡ ⊥ ⁄
Credit Cards 1 2 3 5 £

---

★★★**58% Glynhill Hotel & Leisure Club** Paisley Road, Renfrew PA4 8XB (2m E A741) ☎041-886 5555
Telex no 779536 FAX 041-885 2838
*Well placed for motorway and airport, this much-extended commercial hotel now has two restaurants, one of which is a carvery, three lounge bars and a leisure complex.*
125⇨♠(34fb)2⊟ CTV in all bedrooms ® **T**
sB&B⇨♠£50-£80 dB&B⇨♠£60-£90 ⊟
( 200P 30🚗 CFA ⊡(heated) snooker sauna solarium gymnasium spa bath steam room ♫ *xmas*
♀ International V ♡ ⊥ ⁄ S10% Lunch £8.50-£9.50&alc Dinner £11.50-£16&alc Last dinner 10.30pm
Credit Cards 1 2 3 5 £

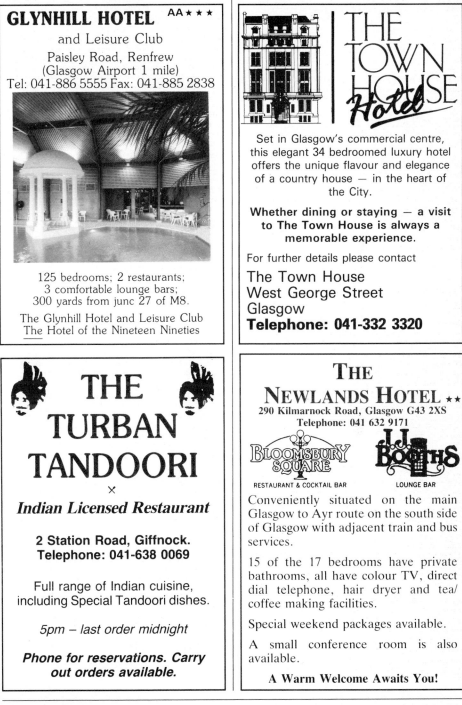

# Glasgow Airport - Glenshee (Spittal of)

★★58%, **Rockfield** 125 Renfrew Road, Paisley PA3 4EA (2m SE off A741) ☎041-889 6182 FAX 041-889 9526
*Modest bedroom accommodation, good value meals and very friendly service can be found at this hotel situated just off M8 junction 27.*
20⇩➤(1fb)1⌘ CTV in all bedrooms ® T sB&B⇩➤fr£41 dB&B⇩➤fr£62
50P
♀ European ◊ ✂ Bar Lunch fr£3 Dinner fr£10.50&alc Last dinner 9.30pm
Credit Cards ①②③⑤ ④

---

## GLASTONBURY Somerset Map 03 ST53

✗✗**Number Three Dining Rooms** 3 Magdalene St BA6 9EW ☎(0458)32129
Closed Sun, Mon & 3 wks Jan
Lunch not served Tue & Sat
♀ English & French V 28 seats S% Dinner £24-£30 Last lunch 1.30pm Last dinner 9pm 8P ✂
Credit Cards ②③

---

## GLEMSFORD Suffolk Map 05 TL84

✗✗**Barrett's** 31 Egremont St CO10 7SA ☎(0787)281573
Closed Mon & 10 days Jan
Lunch not served Tue-Sat
Dinner not served Sun
18 seats ✱ Sunday Lunch £12.95 Dinner fr£25alc Last lunch 2pm Last dinner 9.30pm 10P
Credit Cards ①③

---

## GLENCOE Highland *Argyllshire* Map 14 NN15

★★50%, *Glencoe* PA39 4HW ☎Ballachulish(08552)245 & 673
*Modernised stone building at the western end of Glencoe overlooking Loch Leven. Comfortable, well-appointed public areas and a separate bars complex. Choice of food varies according to the time of year.*
13rm(4⇩1➤)(3fb) CTV in all bedrooms ®
CTV 30P ✿ games room ♫
V ◊ ⚏ ✂ Last dinner 10pm
Credit Cards ①②③⑤

---

## GLENEAGLES

See **Auchterarder**

---

## GLENFARG Tayside *Perthshire* Map 11 NO11

★★60%, **Bein Inn** PH2 9PY ☎(05773)216
*Set in picturesque Glen Farg, this former drovers inn is a popular base for the businessman, tourist and sporting enthusiast. It offers an interesting blend of the old and new, and has a relaxed atmosphere. The best bedrooms are located in the annexe.*
9rm(7⇩)Annexe4⇩➤ CTV in all bedrooms ®
✱ (ex guide dogs) ✱ sB&B£28 sB&B⇩➤£33 dB&B£42 dB&B⇩➤£46-£58 ⊟
60P ⌗ ✿ *xmas*
♀ Scottish, English & French V ◊ ⚏ Lunch £10-£20 High tea £5-£8 Dinner £15-£25alc Last dinner 9.30pm
Credit Cards ①③ ④
See advertisement under PERTH

★★57%, **Glenfarg** Main St PH2 9NU ☎(05773)241
*A small, personally-managed hotel in the centre of the village has undergone major refurbishment and offers comfortable accommodation with a friendly atmosphere.*
14⇩➤(2fb) CTV in all bedrooms ® ⊟
39P ✿ *xmas*
V ◊ ⚏ ✂
Credit Cards ①②③⑤
See advertisement under PERTH

---

## GLENRIDDING Cumbria Map 11 NY31

★★63%, **Glenridding** CA11 0PB (Best Western) ☎(07684)82228 FAX (07684) 82555
Closed 4-23 Jan
*This friendly tourist hotel, situated in the centre of the village, has fine views of both the harbour and the mountains. Bedrooms vary in shape and size, but are well equipped. There is a traditional dining room, a popular bar and an attractive budget restaurant, together with a gift shop and a tea room next door, all under the direction of the hotel.*
43⇩➤(6fb)2⌘ CTV in all bedrooms ® T sB&B⇩➤fr£41 dB&B⇩➤fr£65 ⊟
Lift 40P *xmas*
V ◊ ⚏ ✂ Bar Lunch fr£6.50 Dinner fr£17.50 Last dinner 9.30pm
Credit Cards ①②③⑤ ④

---

## GLENROTHES Fife Map 11 NO20

★★★72%, **Balgeddie House** Balgeddie Way KY6 3ET ☎(0592)742511 FAX (0592) 621702
Closed 1 & 2 Jan
*Large privately owned mansion dating from 1936 standing on a hillside in six acres of land.*
18⇩➤ CTV in all bedrooms ® T ✱ (ex guide dogs) ✱ S10% sB⇩➤fr£53 dB⇩➤fr£68 (room only) ⊟
CTV 100P ✿ ∪ pool
♀ English & French V ◊ ⚏ S10% Lunch £12&alc Dinner £12&alc Last dinner 9.30pm
Credit Cards ①②③⑤

★★75%, **Rescobie** Valley Dr, Leslie KY6 3BQ ☎(0592)742143
*Delightful service, comfortable bedrooms and good value menus of freshly prepared dishes are features of this hotel.*
8⇩➤ CTV in all bedrooms ® T sB&B⇩➤£43 dB&B⇩➤£60-£65 ⊟
20P ⌗ ✿ ♨
♀ International V ◊ ⚏ Lunch £8.50 Dinner £13.50&alc Last dinner 9pm
Credit Cards ①②③⑤

★★53%, **Greenside** High St, Leslie KY6 3DA (2m W A911) ☎(0592)743453 FAX (0592) 756341
Closed 1 Jan
*Managed by the resident proprietors, this small hotel caters mainly for comercial visitors.*
12⇩➤ CTV in all bedrooms ®
⊄ 50P
♀ English & French V ◊
Credit Cards ①②③

---

## GLENSHEE (Spittal of) Tayside *Perthshire* Map 15 NO16

★★♦64%, **Dalmunzie House** PH10 7QG ☎Glenshee(025085)224
Closed Nov-27 Dec
*This impressive and warmly welcoming Scottish mansion, set in a secluded position amid the lovely hills of north Perthshire, promotes a relaxed, informal atmosphere throughout. Public areas retain a comfortably lived-in feeling and facilities include golf, tennis, fishing, shooting and stalking. Major improvements to bedrooms are planned.*
17rm(15⇩➤) sB&B£25-£28 sB&B⇩➤£34-£41.50 dB&B£50-£56 dB&B⇩➤£54-£69
Lift CTV 30P 2⊛ ⌗ ✿ ▶ 9 ♔ (hard) ◀ shooting clay pigeon shooting *xmas*
♀ Scottish & French V ◊ ⚏ Bar Lunch £2-£6.50alc Dinner £15.50 Last dinner 8.30pm
Credit Cards ①③

★55%, *Dalrulzion Highland* PH10 7LJ
☎Blacklunans(025082)222
*The family-run hotel has been created from a historically interesting building that was originally a hunting lodge.*
12rm(5⊸3)(4fb) CTV in 7 bedrooms ® ✹ (ex guide dogs) CTV 60P ✿ ✦ hang gliding pony trekking shooting ♫
♀ Scottish & Continental V ♦ ⬚ Last dinner 9pm
Credit Cards ③

---

**GLENSHIEL (SHIEL BRIDGE)** Highland *Ross & Cromarty*
Map **14** NG91

★★63%, **Kintail Lodge** IV40 8HL ☎Glenshiel(059981)275
Closed 24 Dec-2 Jan RS Nov-Mar
*Situated on the shore of Loch Duich, and surrounded by magnificent scenery, this former shooting lodge, with its 4 acres of walled garden, continues to be improved. Bedrooms, most of which enjoy loch views, vary in shape and size, are modestly furnished, but generally comfortable, while public areas include two inviting lounges, one with a small bar, and a neat dining room where enjoyable home-cooked meals are served.*
12rm(7⊸3♪)(2fb) CTV in all bedrooms ® S% sB&B£37-£44 sB&B⊸3♪£39-£48 dB&B£74-£88
dB&B⊸3♪£78-£96 (incl dinner) 🄱
20P ♿ ✿ ♫
♀ Scottish & French V ♦ ⬚ ⊁ Bar Lunch £1.25-£7alc Dinner £15-£20 Last dinner 8.30pm
Credit Cards ① ③

---

**GLOSSOP** Derbyshire Map **07** SK09

★★73%, **Wind in the Willows** Derbyshire Level, off Sheffield Rd SK13 9PT (A57) ☎(0457)868001 FAX (0457) 853354
*Comfort, quality and a relaxed atmosphere are the hallmarks of this Victorian country house, pleasantly set in 5 acres of grounds adjacent to the local golf course. Traditional furnishings and open fires enhance the atmosphere of relaxed comfort.*
8⊸3♪(1fb) CTV in all bedrooms ® T ✹ (ex guide dogs) sB&B⊸3♪£53-£72 dB&B⊸3♪£64-£94
CTV 12P ♿ ✿ nc10yrs
♦ Dinner fr£19.25 Last dinner 7.30pm
Credit Cards ① ② ③

---

**GLOUCESTER** Gloucestershire Map **03** SO81

★★★75%, **Hatton Court** Upton Hill, Upton St Leonards GL4 8DE (3m SE B4073) ☎(0452)617412 Telex no 437334
FAX (0452) 612945
*Surrounded by 37 acres of carefully maintained gardens and pasture land, with attractive views of the Severn Valley, this popular hotel provides comfortable, well-appointed bedrooms and good levels of friendly service.*
18⊸3♪Annexe28⊸3♪ 2🎌 CTV in all bedrooms T
✹ (ex guide dogs) sB&B⊸3♪£72-£84 dB&B⊸3♪£92-£110 🄱
《 75P ✿ ≈(heated) croquet *xmas*
♀ English & French V ♦ ⬚ Lunch fr£14&alc High tea fr£5.25 Dinner fr£19.50&alc Last dinner 10pm
Credit Cards ① ② ③ ⑤

★★★68%, **Gloucester Hotel & Country Club** Robinswood Hill GL4 9EA (2.5m SE off B4073) (Embassy) ☎(0452)25653
Telex no 43571 FAX (0452) 307212
*Squash courts, golf courses, a dry ski slope and a swimming pool are among the facilities provided by this large, well managed complex 3 miles from the city. The main block's comfortable, well-equipped accommodation has recently been upgraded, and guests have a choice of 4 bars. The original barn houses a restaurant, extensive conference and banqueting facilities are available, and service throughout the hotel is considerate and attentive.*
97⊸3♪Annexe10⊸3♪(11fb)⊁in 5 bedrooms CTV in all bedrooms ® T ✱ S% sB⊸3♪£75-£85
dB⊸3♪£85-£95 (room only) 🄱
▶

---

★★

*Dalmunzie House*

Situated 1½ miles off the main A93 Perth to Braemar Road, this family run country house hotel offers an ideal base for touring Royal Deeside and The Highlands.
A relaxing informal atmosphere where roaring log fires, traditional Scottish cooking, elegant spacious bedrooms nearly all with private bathroom and personal service are our hallmarks.
Golf, tennis, fishing and shooting are available on our 6000-acre estate.

**Spittal o'Glenshee, Blairgowrie
Perthshire PH10 7QG
Telephone: Glenshee (025 085) 224**

---

# Greenside Hotel
AA ★ ★
High Street, Leslie, Glenrothes,
Fife, Scotland
**Tel: Glenrothes (0592) 743453**
Proprietors: Mr & Mrs T. E. Smith

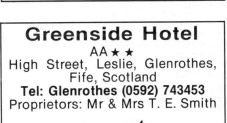

The Greenside Hotel is a family run Hotel situated in the Royal Burgh of Leslie, midway between Edinburgh and Dundee.
Visitors will be delighted to know that Fife offers golfers the choice of 33 golf courses, all within a 20 mile radius, with The Old Course, St Andrews, only 35 minutes away and Gleneagles 40 minutes away. Glenrothes has one of the most modern sports complexes in Scotland, offering a choice of swimming, squash, badminton, gymnasium and saunas.
Our 12 bedroomed hotel prides itself on the friendly and efficient service offered, ensuring for our guests a comfortable and happy stay. Nine bedrooms have private bathrooms, television, telephone and radio alarms, each enjoying the picturesque view of the Lomond Hills to the North.

**G**

⟪ CTV 300P ✿ ⌷(heated) ▐ 18 ♫ (hard) squash snooker sauna solarium gymnasium jacuzzi dry skiing skittle alley ♫ *xmas*
♀ French V ✿ ⚐ S% Lunch £7.95-£10.75 Dinner £14-£14.50 Last dinner 10pm
Credit Cards ①②③⑤⑥

★★★66% **Crest** Crest Way, Barnwood GL4 7RX (Trusthouse Forte) ☎(0452)613311 Telex no 437273 FAX (0452) 371036
*Situated on the Barnwood bypass, two miles from the City centre, this modern hotel has recently been completely refurbished and now offers attractive open-plan public areas and comfortable well-equipped bedrooms. There is a good indoor leisure centre and facilities for business meetings.*
123⇌(30fb)⅟in 24 bedrooms CTV in all bedrooms ®
⟪ 200P ✿ ⌷(heated) sauna solarium gymnasium spa pool steam room games room
♀ English & French V ✿ ⚐ ⅟
Credit Cards ①②③④⑤

★★66% **New County** Southgate St GL1 2DU ☎(0452)307000 FAX (0452) 500487
*At the time of our inspection, this city-centre hotel was in the final stages of a complete refurbishment. Accommodation is well equipped with modern facilities designed with the business traveller in mind. Although there is no car park, there are public car parks within two minutes' walk.*
31⇌(3fb) CTV in all bedrooms ® T ✹ (ex guide dogs) ✳
sB&B⇌⋔£46.75-£51.75 dB&B⇌⋔£56.50-£61.50 ⏢
⟪
V ✿ ⚐ Lunch £10-£16alc Dinner £10-£16alc Last dinner 9.30pm
Credit Cards ①②③⑤

★★63% **Twigworth Lodge** Tewkesbury Rd, Twigworth GL2 9PG ☎(0452)730266 FAX (0452) 730099
*Set in three acres of farmland alongside the A38, just two miles north of the city centre, this good value commercial hotel provides well equipped bedrooms, an indoor heated pool and snooker facilities.*
31⇌⋔(2fb) sB&B⇌⋔£45-£48 dB&B⇌⋔£56-£64 ⏢
50P ✿ ⌷(heated)
♀ European V ✿ ⚐ Lunch fr£8.50&alc Dinner £10-£18alc Last dinner 10pm
Credit Cards ①②③⑤⑥

★64% **Rotherfield House** 5 Horton Rd GL1 3PX ☎(0452)410500
*Small, friendly and informally relaxed in atmosphere, this hotel provides simple but clean bedrooms and a comfortable lounge on the ground floor.*
13rm(8⋔)(2fb) CTV in all bedrooms ® sB&B£16.95-£18.95 sB&B⋔£26.95 dB&B⋔£36.95 ⏢
CTV 9P ⇹
♀ English & Continental V ✿ ⚐ ⅟ Dinner £7.75&alc Last dinner 7.15pm
Credit Cards ①②③⑤⑥

★★★58% **Golden Pheasant** LL20 7BB ☎(069172)281 Telex no 35664
*Enjoying beautiful country views this unpretentious, tranquil hotel, with the character of an inn, is ideal for a relaxing break. Popular with the locals.*
18⇌⋔(7fb)3⊞ CTV in all bedrooms ® T S%
sB&B⇌⋔£34-£52 dB&B⇌⋔£63-£103 ⏢
45P ✿ ☉ game shooting during season ♋ *xmas*
♀ English, French & Italian V ✿ ⚐ Lunch £9.50 High tea £1.75-£4.95 Dinner £16.95 Last dinner 9pm
Credit Cards ①②③⑤⑥

★★70% **Inn On The Moor** YO22 5LZ ☎Whitby(0947)86296
*This hotel provides an ideal retreat for those seeking a quiet relaxing stay in comfortable surroundings. Rooms are well equipped and maintained and the lounge, with its welcoming log fire, is particularly inviting.*
28rm(20⇌2⋔)(2fb)4⊞ CTV in all bedrooms ® T S%
sB&B⇌⋔£35-£45 dB&B⇌⋔£70-£90 (incl dinner) ⏢
CTV 30P ✿ croquet lawn hairdressing salon ♋
V ✿ ⚐ ⅟ Lunch £7.50 High tea £3.50-£7.50 Dinner £13.50-£14.50&alc Last dinner 8.30pm
Credit Cards ①③

★★69% **Mallyan Spout** YO22 5AN ☎Whitby(0947)86206 & 86341
*An attractive stone building, standing in its own grounds in the centre of the village, offers attractive Laura Ashley style bedrooms (some of which are on the small side), good service by friendly staff under the supervision of professional proprietors, and enjoyable meals featuring delicious fresh fish from Whitby.*
24rm(22⇌)(4fb)2⊞ CTV in all bedrooms T ✳
sB&B⇌⋔£35-£50 dB&B⇌⋔£55-£100 ⏢
50P ✿ *xmas*
♀ English & French V ✿ ⚐ ⅟ Lunch £10.50-£12.50&alc Dinner £17.50-£20&alc Last dinner 8.30pm
Credit Cards ①②③⑤⑥

★63% **Whitfield House** Darnholm YO22 5LA (Guestaccom) ☎Whitby(0947)86215
Closed 10 Nov-10 Jan
*A converted stone-built 'period' style cottage on the North Yorkshire moors.*
9rm(2⇌6⋔) ® sB&B⇌⋔£19.50 dB&B⇌⋔£39
CTV 10P ⇹ nc3yrs
✿ ⚐ ⅟ Dinner £9-£12.50 Last dinner 6.30pm

✕✕ **Lakeview Restaurant** Inn On The Lake, Ockford Rd GU7 1RH ☎(04868)5575 FAX (0483) 860445
*An elegant and attractively decorated restaurant, centred round an indoor ornamental pool, supplements its à la carte range of dishes with two reasonable fixed-price menus. Enterprising cuisine shows a definite French influence and is complemented by a fairly extensive wine list. Good bar facilities are available and pleasant service is provided by cheerful young staff.*
♀ International V 80 seats Lunch fr£14&alc Dinner fr£14&alc Last lunch 3pm Last dinner 10pm 100P
Credit Cards ①②③⑤

★★63% **Cormorant** PL23 1LL ☎Fowey(072683)3426
*In a picturesque setting overlooking the Fowey Estuary, this peaceful hotel offers tranquility with caring hospitality. The thoughtfully furnished bedrooms and comfortable lounge have superb views of the river and wooded slopes beyond. Good food, using fresh local produce, is served in the intimate restaurant.*
11⇌⋔in 1 bedroom CTV in all bedrooms ® T ✳
sB&B⇌£43-£48 dB&B⇌⋔£66-£76 ⏢
24P ⇹ ⌷(heated) *xmas*
♀ French V ✿ ⚐ Lunch £12-£20&alc High tea fr£5.50 Dinner fr£17 Last dinner 8.45pm
Credit Cards ①③⑥

★★63% **Sutherland Arms** Old Bank Rd KW10 6RS ☎(04083)3234 & 3216
*Established as the first coaching inn in Sutherland, this friendly, small hotel is enthusiastically run by the resident proprietors and offers comfortable, well-maintained accommodation. First floor*

*bedrooms are attractively decorated, some containing fine traditional pieces of furniture.*
16rm(9⇨2♠)(4fb)1♨ CTV in all bedrooms ® T ✱
sB&B£25-£30 sB&B⇨♠£25-£30 dB&B£50-£60
dB&B⇨♠£50-£60 ➡
CTV 25P ✿
V ♥ ⚑ Lunch £5-£10alc High tea £7-£9alc Last high tea 6pm
Credit Cards ③

★★55% **Golf Links** KW10 6TT ☎(04083)3408
*Overlooking the sea this small family-run hotel provides traditional comforts and is particularly popular with golfers.*
9⇨♠ CTV in all bedrooms ® sB&B⇨♠£20-£25
dB&B⇨♠£40-£44 ➡
20P ▥ ✿
ℚ Scottish & French V ♥ ⚑
Credit Cards ① ③

---

**GOODRICH** Hereford & Worcester Map **03** SO51

★★57% **Ye Hostelrie** HR9 6HX ☎Symonds Yat(0600)890241
*This privately owned inn in a quiet rural village close to the River Wye is popular with shooting and fishing parties. Accommodation is modest with old fashioned furnishings and few modern day facilities.*
8rm(2⇨5♠) CTV in all bedrooms ® sB&B£30 sB&B⇨♠£34
dB&B⇨♠£56 (incl dinner)
CTV 25P ▥ ✿
V ♥ Bar Lunch £2-£7.50alc Dinner £10-£12 Last dinner 9pm
**See advertisement under ROSS-ON-WYE**

---

**GOODRINGTON**

See **Paignton**

---

**GOODWOOD** West Sussex Map **04** SU80

★★★72% **Goodwood Park** PO18 0QB
☎Chichester(0243)775537 Telex no 869173
FAX (0243) 533802
*Recent extensions have transformed what was originally a coaching inn into this modern, purpose-built leisure development. A choice of bedrooms with every up-to-date facility is complemented by the classic cuisine and professionally efficient service of Dukes Restaurant.*
89⇨♠(3fb)1♨ CTV in all bedrooms ® T sB&B⇨♠£95-£105
dB&B⇨♠£105-£120 ➡
⚓100P ✿ ▱(heated) ↑18 ℛ (hard) squash snooker sauna
solarium gymnasium beauty salon *xmas*
V ♥ ⚑ ✂ Lunch fr£10.95 Dinner fr£17.25 Last dinner 9.30pm
Credit Cards ① ② ③ ⑤ ⓔ

---

**GOOLE** Humberside Map **08** SE72

★★59% **Clifton** 1 Clifton Gardens, Boothferry Rd DN14 6AL
☎(0405)761336 FAX (0405) 762350
*The resident proprietor and his hard-working young team of staff create a friendly, informal atmosphere throughout this small, cosy hotel with its clean and modestly equipped bedrooms.*
10rm(5⇨3♠)1♨ CTV in all bedrooms ® T sB&B£22-£28
sB&B⇨♠£32-£35 dB&B⇨♠£36-£42 ➡
CTV 8P
ℚ English & Continental V ♥ Lunch fr£7.95 Dinner fr£7.95
Last dinner 9pm
Credit Cards ① ② ③ ⑤ ⓔ

★★
**Goathland, Whitby
N Yorkshire
YO22 5AN
Telephone:
(0947) 86206**

**G**

A stone-built, ivy clad building situated on the green of a beautiful Yorkshire village overlooking the wide expanses of the famous moors. The hotel takes its name from a small picturesque waterfall flowing into a wooded valley, a short walk below the hotel. Three spacious lounges command a view of the garden, moors and the beautiful Esk Valley, and in the winter you are warmed by roaring fires. Mallyan Spout is an ideal location for outdoor pursuits on the peaceful pleasures of fine food, good wine and friendly hospitality. 24 cottage style bedrooms with private bath including 2 new rooms with balconies and superb views.

*Twigworth Lodge Hotel
&
Coach House Restaurant*

A delightful 2 star hotel set in the heart of Gloucestershire close to the Cotswolds.

- **30 Bedrooms**
- **Conference Facilities**
- **Indoor Swimming Pool**
- **Games Room**
- **Parking for over 60 cars**

Our lively and bustling **Coach House Restaurant** and Lounge Bar offer the best in traditional English food

**AA** ★★ TWIGWORTH LODGE HOTEL
TEWKESBURY ROAD, TWIGWORTH
GLOUCESTER GL2 9PG
Tel. 0452 730266 *Fax. 0452 730099*

# Gordano Motorway Service Area (M5) - Grantham

**GORDANO MOTORWAY SERVICE AREA (M5)** Avon
Map **03** ST57

⬆**Travelodge** BS20 9XG (Trusthouse Forte)
☏Pill(027581)3709 Central Res (0800) 850950
*Situated within the Gordano service centre on the A5 and thus very well placed for both Bristol city centre and Avonmouth, the lodge provides a good choice of eating options on site as well as the usual well equipped, good value bedroom accommodation.*
40⇨ᐟᐟ(40fb) CTV in all bedrooms ℝ sB⇨ᐟᐟ£24
dB⇨ᐟᐟ£29.50 (room only)
《 40P ⬚

Credit Cards ①②③

---

**GOREY**

See **Jersey under Channel Islands**

---

**GORLESTON-ON-SEA**

See **Yarmouth, Great**

---

**GOSPORT** Hampshire Map **04** SZ69

★★53%, *Anglesey* Crescent Rd, Alverstoke PO12 2DH
☏(0705)582157 & 523932
*An hotel set in a Regency terrace complements the à la carte menu of the elegant restaurant, featuring fish specialities, with an extensive value-for-money selection of bar meals. Well equipped bedrooms are undergoing refurbishment and the atmosphere is relaxed and friendly throughout.*
18⇨ᐟᐟ(1fb)1⬚ CTV in all bedrooms ℝ T
CTV 2⬚ (£1.50) ♫
♀ Continental V ✿ Last dinner 9.45pm
Credit Cards ①②③

---

**GOUDHURST** Kent Map **05** TQ73

★★71%, *Star & Eagle* High St TN17 1AL ☏(0580)211512
*Parts of this attractive and well-managed hotel date back to the early fourteenth century, and it has been tastfully modernised to retain such original features as low ceilings and oak beams. Bedrooms are particularly well furnished and equipped to a high standard, while both bar and restaurant offer attentive service.*
11rm(9⇨ᐟᐟ)2⬚ CTV in all bedrooms ℝ sB&Bfr£40
sB&B⇨ᐟᐟfr£50 dB&Bfr£50 dB&B⇨ᐟᐟ£66-£80 ⽖
24P xmas
♀ European V ✿ ♫ Lunch £15-£20alc Dinner £15-£20alc Last dinner 9.30pm
Credit Cards ①②③ⓔ

---

**GRANGE-OVER-SANDS** Cumbria Map **07** SD47

★★★65%, *Grange* Lindale Rd, Station Square LA11 6EJ
(Consort) ☏(05395)33666 FAX (05395) 35064
*Accommodation which will appeal equally to tourist and commercial guest is housed in a substantial Victorian building which overlooks town and bay from its setting in well-tended gardens.*
41⇨ᐟᐟ(6fb) CTV in all bedrooms ℝ T ✱
sB&B⇨ᐟᐟ£33.50-£37.50 dB&B⇨ᐟᐟ£51-£59 ⽖
《 CTV 100P ✿ CFA ♫ ⬚ xmas
♀ English & French V ✿ ♫ Lunch £7.50 Dinner £13.50&alc Last dinner 9.30pm
Credit Cards ①②③⑤ⓔ

★★69%, *Netherwood* Lindale Rd LA11 6ET ☏(05395)32552
*The hotel, an imposing building dating from the 19th century and retaining some fine interior wood panelling and carving, occupies a prime position in 11 acres of attractive gardens and woodland which overlook the River Kent Estuary on Morecambe Bay.*
33rm(27⇨ᐟᐟ)(4fb)ƴin 10 bedrooms CTV in all bedrooms ℝ T
sB&B£32.75-£33.75 sB&B⇨ᐟᐟ£32.75-£33.75
dB&B£65.50-£67.50 dB&B⇨ᐟᐟ£65.50-£67.50 ⽖

---

Lift 《 CTV 100P ✿ ▭(heated) gymnasium ⛵
♀ English & French ✿ ♫ Lunch £7.50-£9&alc High tea £6.95-£8.25 Dinner £10-£13.50&alc Last dinner 8.30pm

★★❋66%, **Graythwaite Manor** Fernhill Rd LA11 7JE
☏(05395)32001 & 33755
*Large country house in beautiful grounds, with home grown produce used in restaurant. Situated high above the town, with superb views of the bay, the hotel offers tastefully refurbished, comfortable rooms where an old-fashioned charm prevails.*
22rm(20⇨ᐟᐟ)(1fb) CTV in all bedrooms ℝ T
ℋ (ex guide dogs) sB&B⇨ᐟᐟ£37.50-£55
dB&B⇨ᐟᐟ£74-£104 (incl dinner) ⽖
18P 14⬚ (£1) ⬚ ✿ ♪ (hard) helicopter landing area putting
♀ English & French V ✿ ♫ ƴ Lunch fr£8.50 Dinner fr£16.50 Last dinner 8.30pm
Credit Cards ①③

★68%, **Clare House** Park Rd LA11 7HQ ☏(05395)33026 & 34253
Closed Nov-Mar
*Situated beside the main road west of the town, overlooking Morecambe Bay from its gardens, this family-run establishment offers warm, comfortable accommodation, some rooms having balconies and sea views. Particularly enjoyable meals are prepared by the proprietor's son, who makes good use of fresh local produce.*
17rm(16⇨ᐟᐟ)(1fb) CTV in all bedrooms ℝ T
ℋ (ex guide dogs) ✱ sB&B£31-£33 sB&B⇨ᐟᐟ£33-£36
dB&B⇨ᐟᐟ£66-£72 (incl dinner) ⽖
CTV 18P ⬚ ✿ croquet putting nc5yrs
✿ ♫ ƴ Dinner £14 Last dinner 7.15pm
ⓔ

---

**GRANTHAM** Lincolnshire Map **08** SK93

★★★65%, **Angel & Royal** High St NG31 6PN (Trusthouse Forte) ☏(0476)65816 FAX (0476) 67149
*Built some time prior to the 13th century and steeped in history, the hotel is approached through a 15th-century stone archway which bears a carving of an angel carrying a crown. Accommodation is comfortable and furnished to a high standard, whilst the King's Room Restaurant serves international cuisine.*
24⇨ᐟƴin 6 bedrooms CTV in all bedrooms ℝ ⽖
《 60P xmas
♀ English & French V ✿ ♫ ƴ Lunch fr£8.95&alc Dinner fr£13.95&alc Last dinner 9pm
Credit Cards ①②③④⑤

★★56%, **Kings** North Pde NG31 8AU ☏(0476)590800
*Situated on the outskirts of the town centre on the B1174 (A1 north), this Georgian house set in its own grounds provides a comfortable lounge, a choice of restaurants and well equipped accommodation.*
23rm(16⇨5ᐟᐟ) CTV in all bedrooms ℝ T sB&B⇨ᐟᐟ£40
dB&B⇨ᐟᐟ£55 ⽖
《 36P ✿ ♪ (hard) ♫
♀ French V ✿ ♫ Lunch £9.25-£13.95&alc Dinner £9.25-£13.95&alc Last dinner 9.30pm
Credit Cards ①②③⑤ⓔ

⬆**Travelodge** Grantham Service Area NG32 2AB (4m S of Gratham) (Trusthouse Forte)
☏(0476)77500 Central Res (0800) 850950
*Situated about four miles north of Grantham at the Welcome Break Service area on the A1, of the roundabout junction on the southbound side for services.*
40⇨ᐟᐟ(40fb) CTV in all bedrooms ℝ sB⇨ᐟᐟ£24
dB⇨ᐟᐟ£29.50 (room only)
《 40P ⬚
Credit Cards ①②③

**GRANTOWN-ON-SPEY** Highland *Morayshire* Map **14** NJ02

★★★64%, **Garth** Castle Rd PH26 3HN (Inter-Hotels)
☎(0479)2836 & 2162 FAX (0479) 2116
*Set in its own grounds close to the town centre, this hotel, converted from a 17th-century building, has a country house atmosphere, combined with friendly informal service. Bedrooms are equipped to modern standards.*
17⇦🁢 CTV in all bedrooms ® T 🍴 ✱ sB&B⇦🁢£28-£34
dB&B⇦🁢£56
22P 🚗 ❀
♀ French V ❂ ⚲ ✄ Bar Lunch £3-£6alc Dinner £16&alc Last dinner 8.30pm
Credit Cards [1][3][4][5] ⓔ

★★65%, **Coppice** Grant Rd PH26 3LD (Exec Hotel)
☎(0479)2688
*Standing in a quiet residential area of the town, this family-run hotel offers comfortable and well-maintained accommodation. An extensive range of malt whiskies is available in the refurbished bar, and service throughout is friendly and attentive.*
26🁢(3fb) CTV in all bedrooms ® sB&B🁢£22.50-£24.50
dB&B🁢£40-£44
CTV 50P ❀ shooting *xmas*
.V ❂ ⚲
Credit Cards [1][3]

★★65%, **Seafield Lodge** Woodside Av PH26 3JN (Minotels)
☎(0479)2152 FAX (0479) 2340
Closed 4 Nov-9 Dec
*Family-owned and run, this well-furnished and comfortable hotel is in a quiet side street and offers good bedroom accommodation and a friendly welcome.*
14⇦🁢(2fb) CTV in all bedrooms ® sB&B⇦🁢£26.50-£34
dB&B⇦🁢🁢£38-£52 🍴 `
15P *xmas*
Bar Lunch £3-£6alc Dinner £15&alc Last dinner 9pm
Credit Cards [1][3] ⓔ
**See advertisement on page 319**

★73%, **Tyree House** 8 The Square PH26 3HF ☎(0479)2615
*This delightful hotel, set at the head of the attractive town square, is personally managed by friendly resident proprietors who maintain very high standards throughout. Both accommodation and meals represent excellent value for money.*
9🁢(1fb) CTV in all bedrooms ® ✱ sB&B🁢£22 dB&B🁢£34
CTV 20P 🚗 ❀ *xmas*
V ❂ Bar Lunch £3-£5 Dinner £10-£15&alc Last dinner 9pm
Credit Cards [1][3] ⓔ
**See advertisement on page 319**

★60%, **Dunvegan** Heathfield Rd PH26 3HX ☎(0479)2301
Closed 16-31 Oct & 23-27 Dec
*Quietly situated in a residential area close to the golf course, this small hotel is run in a friendly and informal manner by the resident proprietors. Neat bedrooms are modestly furnished and public areas are comfortable.*
8rm(2🁢)(5fb) sB&B£12-£14 dB&B🁢£31-£35 🍴
CTV 9P 🍴 (£1) 🚗 *xmas*
❂ ⚲ Bar Lunch £2-£4 Dinner £10 Last dinner 7.30pm
ⓔ

**GRASMERE** Cumbria Map **11** NY30

★★★★64%, **Wordsworth** LA22 9SW ☎(09665)592
Telex no 65329 FAX (09665) 765
*The hotel has been steadily improving since it reopened under private ownership in 1987; the most recent phase of development has added some splendid bedrooms – including two suites – on the second floor and a sun lounge overlooking the attractive swimming pool, overlooking the well-tended gardens. Service is of a good standard throughout, friendly management and staff creating a relaxed atmosphere.*
▶

**G**

37⇨🛏2🖺 CTV in all bedrooms T ✳ (ex guide dogs)
sB&B⇨🛏£46-£48 dB&B⇨🛏£96-£118 🅿

Lift ℂ 60P 🚗 ✿ CFA ☒(heated) sauna solarium gymnasium
table tennis pool jacuzzi *xmas*

♉ English & French V ✿ .☲ Lunch £10.50-£12.50&alc Dinner
fr£25 Last dinner 9pm

Credit Cards ①②③⑤ⓔ

★★★

❋★★★🔟 **MICHAEL'S NOOK**
**COUNTRY HOUSE**

LA22 9RP (Pride of Britain)
☎(09665)496
Telex no 65329
FAX (09665) 765

(Rosette awarded for dinner
only)

*A charming hotel just outside
Grasmere, Michael's Nook reflects owner Reg Gifford's love of
antique furniture. Bedrooms, individually decorated, are most
comfortable and one features a magnificent antique bathroom
suite. The highlight of this, as of many other Lakeland hotels,
are the excellent 5-course dinners (it is to be hoped that guests
are keen walkers who have worked up an appetite) devised by
Heinz Nagler. Dishes enjoyed on the inspection visit included
a Galette of Ratatouille with grilled Angler fish and turbot,
Barbary duck with piquant potatoes, and escalope of salmon
filled with chicken mousse. Service is both courteous and
attentive, and ensures that guests depart with the pleasantest
of memories of their stay.*

11⇨🛏1🖺 CTV in all bedrooms T ✳ sB&B⇨🛏£98
dB&B⇨🛏£155-£225 (incl dinner) 🅿

20P 🚗 ✿ nc12yrs *xmas*

♉ English & French ✔ Sunday Lunch £22.50 Dinner
fr£34alc Last dinner 8.30pm

Credit Cards ①②③⑤

★★★66% **The Swan** LA22 9RF (Trusthouse Forte)
☎(09665)551 FAX (09665) 741

*This very popular hotel provides traditional hospitality in beautiful
surroundings. The en suite bedrooms are very well appointed and
comfortable lounges feature open fires. The restaurant specialises
in local dishes including the renowned tea cup trifle.*

36⇨🛏✔in 10 bedrooms CTV in all bedrooms ⓡ T
sB⇨🛏£70-£80 dB⇨🛏£86-£106 (room only) 🅿

40P 🚗 ✿ *xmas*

V ✿ .☲ ✔ S10% Lunch fr£9.50&alc Dinner fr£18&alc Last
dinner 9pm

Credit Cards ①②③④⑤

★★★65% **Gold Rill Country House** Red Bank Rd LA22 9PU
☎(09665)486
Closed Jan

*This comfortable hotel, peacefully situated just to the west of the
village and enthusiastically run by resident proprietors, commands
fine views on every side. Bedrooms vary in size, but public areas
offer ample space in which to relax, with an attractive restaurant
overlooking the well-kept gardens.*

17⇨🛏(2fb)🖺 CTV in all bedrooms ⓡ sB&B⇨🛏£35-£45
dB&B⇨🛏£70-£90 (incl dinner) 🅿

35P ✿ ⌇(heated) putting green croquet lawn *xmas*

✿ ✔ Bar Lunch £1.50-£4.50 Dinner £16-£17 Last dinner
8.30pm

Credit Cards ①③ⓔ

★★★64% **Prince of Wales** LA22 9PR (Mount Charlotte (TS))
☎(09665)666 Telex no 65364

*Comfortable accommodation and friendly service are provided by
a traditional hotel on the shore of the lake.*

77⇨🛏(7fb)🖺 CTV in all bedrooms ⓡ
ℂ 100P ✿ CFA ✔

♉ English & French ✔ ✿ .☲ Last dinner 9pm

Credit Cards ①②③④⑤

★★★61% **Red Lion** Red Lion Square LA22 9SS (Consort)
☎(09665)456

*A tourist hotel set at the heart of this popular village commands
fine views over surrounding countryside.*

36⇨🛏(4fb) CTV in all bedrooms ⓡ T S% sB&B⇨🛏£25-£33
dB&B⇨🛏£50-£66 🅿

Lift 26P ✿ CFA *xmas*

V ✿ .☲ ✔ Lunch £14&alc Last dinner 8.50pm

Credit Cards ①②③⑤ⓔ

★★68% **Rothay Garden** Broadgate LA22 9RJ ☎(09665)334
FAX (09665) 723

*This charming hotel, set in attractive gardens, offers pretty
bedrooms and an elegant restaurant where very good food is
served.*

21⇨🛏(2fb)5🖺 CTV in all bedrooms ⓡ T sB&B⇨🛏£45-£55
dB&B⇨🛏£72-£125 (incl dinner) 🅿

30P 🖺 ✿ ✔ *xmas*

♉ English & Continental V ✿ .☲ ✔ Lunch £9.50 Dinner
£16.50 Last dinner 9pm

Credit Cards ①③

The AA's star-rating scheme is the market
leader in hotel classification.

---

# GOLD RILL
## Country House Hotel
### ★★★

Argueably the most perfectly positioned hotel in Grasmere.
Situated alongside the lake yet only two minutes walk from the village centre, this beautiful spacious hotel set in two acres of lawned gardens has views of the lake and fells from the lounge, dining rooms and most bedrooms.
The hotel is privately owned and managed and we offer warm hospitality and imaginative cooking at its very best.

Paul and Cathy Jewsbury
Gold Rill Hotel, Grasmere,
English lakes, Cumbria LA22 9PU.
Tel: Grasmere 09665 486

**The Square, Grantown on Spey, Morayshire**
**Telephone: (0479) 2615**

Situated in the Square and sheltered by trees, ideal for family holidays. Only 10 minutes walk through the town for golf course, fishing, bowling green and tennis courts. Facilities for the sportsman with secure gun room and rod room. All nine bedrooms are tastefully decorated and have private facilities, TV and complimentary tea/coffee and biscuits. Comfortable residents lounge enjoys views across the square and is open at all times. Dinner can be provided in the à la carte restaurant open every evening. Ample parking. Full licence.

**G**

---

*A four-star luxury Hotel in the very heart of English Lakeland . . .*

## The ★★★★
# WORDSWORTH HOTEL
### AND "PRELUDE RESTAURANT"
#### GRASMERE, CUMBRIA
**Telephone: GRASMERE (09665) 592 Telex: 65329**

All bedrooms have bathrooms, colour TV, radio and telephone. There are spacious lounges and cocktail bar, indoor heated pool, jacuzzi, sauna, solarium, minigym, hairdressing, terrace and garden.
In the delectable "Prelude Restaurant" the finest fresh produce is skilfully presented on à la carte and table d'hôte menus. Non-residents most welcome. Exceptional Conference and Banqueting Facilities.

Proprietors
Nancy &
Peter Austen

SLH

Tel: (0479) 2152
Fax: (0479) 2340

# Seafield Lodge Hotel
★★
## Grantown-on-Spey, Moray
### PH26 3JN

# & Woodside Restaurant
VENUE FOR THE ARTHUR OGLESBY FLY FISHING COURSES.

Too small to take coaches, but large enough to provide a good restaurant, & comfortable bar, where you can enjoy a relaxing drink. All rooms have private facilities, telephone, & hair driers. TWO LUXURY SUITES WITH SPA BATHS. You will find us close to the famous river Spey, & convenient for Grantown's golf course.

## Grasmere - Gretna (with Gretna Green)

★★67%, **Grasmere** Broadgate LA22 9TA ☎(09665)277
Closed Jan
*A friendly atmosphere prevails at this small, personally-run hotel
set in its own gardens with lawns leading down to the river. Dinner,
served in the attractive dining room at 7.30pm, offers a good blend
of quality and quantity. Bedrooms are thoughtfully equipped.*
12➪↑1⌗ CTV in all bedrooms ® T sB&B➪↑£30-£40
dB&B➪↑£56-£80 ₽
14P ⌗ ✿ croquet nc7yrs ♨
♀ English & French ✿ ✂ Dinner fr£14 Last dinner 8pm
Credit Cards ⃞1 ⃞3

★★67%, **Oak Bank** Broadgate LA22 9TA (Guestaccom)
☎(09665)217
Closed Xmas-Jan
*This personally-run hotel offers comfortable bedrooms and public
areas which include an attractive conservatory dining room where
guests can enjoy a four-course dinner prepared from good raw
ingredients and fresh local produce.*
14➪↑(1fb)2⌗ CTV in all bedrooms ® T S%
sB&B➪↑£30-£36 dB&B➪↑£52-£64 ₽
CTV 14P ⌗ ✿
♀ English & Continental V ✿ ✑ ✂ S%
Credit Cards ⃞1 ⃞3

★

⊛★ WHITE MOSS HOUSE

Rydal Water LA22 9SE
☎(09665)295
Closed Dec-Feb
(Rosette awarded for dinner
only)
*Overlooking Rydal Water,
this hotel, with its ivy-clad
stone walls and small, pleasantly scented garden, epitomises
everyone's dream of the Lake District and indeed the house
once belonged to the poet Wordsworth. The present owners,
Susan and Peter Dixon have long since firmly established
White Moss House as one of the best small hotels in the
country, and Peter has rightly earned much praise for his fine
interpretations of British cooking. The set 5-course dinner is
served around 8pm and this arrangement enables him to
present innovative and perfectly cooked meals. The extensive
wine list offers some very reasonably priced bottles. The hotel
also owns a charming cottage, Brockstone, set on the hillside
behind the hotel, only a short walk or drive away, and offering
pleasant accommodation and breathtaking views.*
5➪Annexe2➪↑ CTV in all bedrooms T ✖ S%
dB&B➪↑£70-£95
10P ⌗ ✿
✂ Dinner fr£22alc Last dinner 8pm

**GRASSINGTON** North Yorkshire Map **07** SE06

★60%, **Black Horse** Garrs Ln BD23 5AT ☎(0756)752770
*Quaint, prettily decorated bedrooms are an attractive feature of
this family-run hotel, centrally located in a charming Dales village.
Meals are wholesome and filling and the bar menu is especially
popular.*
11➪↑(1fb)2⌗ CTV in all bedrooms ® ✳ sB&B➪↑£29-£37
dB&B➪↑£44-£54 ₽
CTV 2P
V ✿ Lunch £1.50-£10alc Dinner £10.50-£12.50&alc Last dinner
9.30pm
Credit Cards ⃞1 ⃞3

**GRAVESEND** Kent Map **05** TQ67

★★★62%, **Inn on the Lake** Watling St DA12 3HB
☎Shorne(047482)3333 Telex no 966356 FAX (047482) 3175
(For full entry see Shorne)

**GRAYSHOTT** Hampshire Map **04** SU83

⊛ ✖ **Woods** Headley Rd GU26 6LB (1m SW B3002 off A3)
☎Hindhead(0428)605555
*This former butcher's shop retains its original tiling and meat
racks, complementing them with simple pine furniture and fresh
flowers. Its short à la carte menu offers a range of dishes carefully
prepared from the finest ingredients, enhancing natural flavours
with delicate sauces. Fillet of Brill with Saffron Sauce might be
followed by Saddle of Hare, with Crumbed Brie as a savoury or
Nutty Meringue as a sweet to end the meal. All this can be enjoyed
in a pleasant, relaxed atmosphere and a setting suitable for any
occasion.*
Closed Sun, Mon & 1 wk Xmas
Lunch not served
♀ Continental 35 seats ✳ Dinner £24-£29.80alc Last dinner
11pm ✗
Credit Cards ⃞1 ⃞2 ⃞3 ⃞5

**GREAT** Places incorporating the word 'Great' will be found
under the actual place name – eg Great Yarmouth is listed
under Yarmouth, Great.

**GREENLAW** Borders *Berwickshire* Map **12** NT74

★★⚑63%, **Purves Hall** TD10 6UJ (4m SE off A697)
☎Leitholm(089084)558
*Enjoying an attractive rural setting, this charming, comfortable
Edwardian country house hotel stands in ten acres of secluded
gardens and grounds off the A697, four miles south east of
Greenlaw. Facilities include an outdoor heated swimming pool, a
croquet lawn and a putting green; stables are also available.*
7➪↑(1fb) CTV in all bedrooms ® T sB&B➪↑£30-£33
dB&B➪↑£55-£60 ₽
20P ⌗ ✿ ⌁(heated) ♪ (hard) croquet putting
♀ International ✿ ✑ Lunch £8 Dinner £15 Last dinner
8.45pm
Credit Cards ⃞1 ⃞2 ⃞3 ⃞5 ⃞£

**GRETA BRIDGE** Co Durham Map **12** NZ01

★★63%, **Morritt Arms** DL12 9SE ☎Teesdale(0833)27232 &
27392 FAX (0833) 27570
*Old coaching inn retaining Dickensian character.*
17➪(3fb)1⌗ CTV in all bedrooms ® T sB&B➪£42
dB&B➪£65 ₽
100P 3🐎 ⌗ ✿ ♪ xmas
♀ English & French ✿ ✑ Sunday Lunch £10.50 Dinner £18
Last dinner 8.45pm
Credit Cards ⃞1 ⃞2 ⃞3 ⃞5

**GRETNA (with Gretna Green)** Dumfries & Galloway
*Dumfriesshire* Map **11** NY36

★★68%, **Solway Lodge** Annan Rd CA6 5DN (Minotels)
☎Gretna(0461)38266 FAX (0461) 37791
Closed 25 & 26 Dec RS 10 Oct-Mar
*A comfortable hotel managed by friendly resident proprietors with
a choice of cosy well-appointed motel rooms or the very attractive
main house rooms. Good value menus are offered.*
3➪↑Annexe7➪↑1⌗ CTV in all bedrooms ® T
sB&B➪↑£29.50-£42 dB&B➪↑£40-£65
25P ⌗
V ✿ ✑ Bar Lunch £2.50-£11.50 Dinner £8-£14alc Last dinner
9pm
Credit Cards ⃞1 ⃞2 ⃞3 ⃞5

G

★★65% **Gretna Chase** CA6 5JB (0.25m S on B721 in England)
☎Gretna(0461)37517
Closed Jan
*Situated on the English side of the River Sack, in award winning*
*gardens, this comfortable hotel offers warm, friendly service and*
*good value menus. A feature of the hotel is the interesting antique*
*bric-a-brac which abounds throughout.*
9rm(3⇨3♠)1🛏 CTV in all bedrooms ® ✠ (ex guide dogs)
sB&B£33-£35 sB&B⇨♠£35-£50 dB&B£42 dB&B⇨♠£53-£80
40P ✿
♀ English & French V ♥ Lunch £10.50-£14.50&alc Dinner
£10.50-£16.50alc Last dinner 8.30pm
Credit Cards ①②③⑤ⓔ

⛪**Travelodge** CA6 5HQ (on A74) (Trusthouse Forte)
☎Gretna(0461)37566 Central Res (0800) 850950
*This lodge offers modern accommodation, and is situated in a*
*service area, adjoining the A74 just north of Gretna Green, with*
*access from both north and southbound carriageways.*
41⇨♠(41fb) CTV in all bedrooms ® sB⇨♠£24
dB⇨♠£29.50 (room only)
⟨41P 🚗
♀ Mainly grills ✀
Credit Cards ①②③

---

**GRIMSBY** Humberside Map **08** TA20

★★★66% **Humber Royal Crest** Littlecoates Rd DN34 4LX
(Trusthouse Forte) ☎(0472)350295 Telex no 527776
FAX (0472) 241354
*Comfortable accommodation and a good restaurant are the*
*attractions of this modern hotel.*
52⇨♠(2fb)✀in 8 bedrooms CTV in all bedrooms ®
Lift ⟨250P ✿ CFA
♀ English & French V ♥ ⠒ ✀
Credit Cards ①②③④⑤

★★★61% **Crest** St James' Square DN31 1EP (Trusthouse Forte)
☎(0472)359771 Telex no 527741 FAX (0472) 241427
Closed Xmas
*This purpose-built hotel is situated in the town centre adjacent to*
*the main shopping area. Bedrooms are well equipped with modern*
*facilities and meals and snacks are served throughout the day.*
128⇨♠(6fb)✀in 20 bedrooms CTV in all bedrooms ® T
Lift ⟨100P CFA sauna
♀ English & French V ♥ ⠒ ✀
Credit Cards ①②③④⑤

★★★59% **Yarborough** Bethlehem St DN31 1LY (Consort)
☎(0472)242266
*Carefully restored to its original style, with attractive and elegant*
*public areas, a Victorian hotel conveniently located beside the*
*railway station offers well-equipped and pleasantly decorated*
*bedrooms, a comfortable lounge area and a choice of two bars.*
51⇨♠(2fb)✀in 2 bedrooms CTV in all bedrooms ® T ✱
sB&B⇨♠fr£47.50 dB&B⇨♠fr£57.50
Lift ⟨10P
♀ English & French V ♥ ⠒
Credit Cards ①②③⑤

Entries for red-star hotels are highlighted by a
tint panel. For a full list of these establishments
consult the Contents page.

G

## GRIMSTON Norfolk Map 09 TF72

®★★★⚑ CONGHAM HALL
COUNTRY HOUSE

Lynn Rd PE32 1AH (Pride of
Britain)
☎Hillington(0485)600250
Telex no 81508
FAX (0485) 601191

*Forty acres of parkland with
orchards, a paddock and
colourful gardens are the setting for this elegant Georgian
house. Fresh flowers, magazines and open fires provide a most
welcoming atmosphere, and the comfortable sitting room is
filled with fine porcelain, pictures and antiques. A resident
pianist performs on the grand piano at weekends. The dining
room has been enlarged, but remains an attractive setting for
menus such as the gourmet, 8-course, fixed-price example.
The wine list is comprehensive and reasonably priced.
Bedrooms are individually decorated and well equipped.
Some are small, but all are provided with thoughtful touches.*

14⇔🛏2⚑ CTV in all bedrooms T ✱ sB&B⇔🛏£70-£110
dB&B⇔🛏£95-£165 🅡

50P 🚗 ✻ ⇨(heated) ♪ (hard) croquet jacuzzi cricket
nc12yrs *xmas*

V ♥ ✔ Lunch £12.50-£14.50alc

Credit Cards 1️⃣2️⃣3️⃣5️⃣
**See advertisement under KING'S LYNN**

## GRINDLEFORD Derbyshire Map 08 SK27

★★★67%, **Maynard Arms** Main Rd S30 1HN
☎Hope Valley(0433)30321 FAX (0433) 30445
*Though busy, this traditional-style hotel manages to retain a
relaxed atmosphere – perhaps most evident in the elegantly
comfortable lounge, with its views across the gardens to the
Derwent Valley.*

13rm(9⇔2🛏)(1fb)2⚑ CTV in all bedrooms ® T
sB&B⇔🛏fr£57 dB&B⇔🛏£80-£85 🅡

90P 3🚗 🚗 ✻ *xmas*

♀ English & French V ♥ Lunch fr£8.95alc Dinner fr£14.95alc
Last dinner 9.30pm
Credit Cards 1️⃣2️⃣3️⃣5️⃣

## GRIZEDALE Cumbria Map 07 SD39

★★70%, **Grizedale Lodge** LA22 0QL ☎Hawkshead(09666)532
Closed Jan-mid Feb
*A peaceful, relaxing hotel in the idyllic surroundings of Grizedale
Forest, enthusiastically run by its friendly owners to provide
comfortable accommodation and skilfully prepared meals.*

6⇔🛏(1fb)1⚑✔in all bedrooms CTV in all bedrooms ® ✱
sB&B⇔🛏£40-£46 dB&B⇔🛏£68-£80 (incl dinner) 🅡

20P *xmas*

♀ English & French ♥ ♫ ✔ Bar Lunch fr£1.50alc Dinner
£15.50 Last dinner 8.30pm
Credit Cards 1️⃣3️⃣

## GROBY Leicestershire Map 04 SK50

★61%, **Brant Inn** Leicester Rd LE6 0DU
☎Leicester(0533)872703 FAX (0533) 875292
*Set beside the A50 on the NW outskirts of the city, a large, busy
public house provides simple accommodation; a marquee is
available for functions of up to two hundred people.*

10rm(8🛏) CTV in all bedrooms ® T ✱ sB&Bfr£25
sB&B🛏£29.50 dB&B🛏£42.50-£49.50

---

200P ✻
♀ English & French V Lunch £4.95-£8.95&alc Dinner
£7.75&alc Last dinner 10pm
Credit Cards 1️⃣3️⃣5️⃣

## GUERNSEY
See **Channel Islands**

## GUILDFORD Surrey Map 04 SU94

★★★★64%, **Post House** Egerton Rd GU2 5XZ (Trusthouse
Forte) ☎(0483)574444 Telex no 858572 FAX (0483) 302960
121⇔🛏✔in 34 bedrooms CTV in all bedrooms ® T S10%
sB⇔🛏£97 dB⇔🛏£108 (room only) 🅡
( 190P ✻ ⊠(heated) sauna solarium gymnasium ♫ *xmas*
♀ French V ♥ ♫ ✔ S10% Lunch £14.50-£15.95&alc High tea
£3.50-£6.50 Dinner £16.50&alc Last dinner 9.45pm
Credit Cards 1️⃣2️⃣3️⃣4️⃣5️⃣

★★★70%, **The Manor** Newlands Newlands Corner GU4 8SE
(3m E A25) ☎(0483)222624 FAX (0483) 211389
Closed 25(after lunch)-31 Dec
*Set in the peace and tranquility of nine acres of well-kept gardens
and grounds, this charming hotel offers tastefully decorated
bedrooms of individual character, comfortably furnished and well-
equipped. Public areas include a wood-panelled bar, a pleasant
restaurant and a relaxing bar off the foyer. Courteous, hospitable
staff provide pleasant and efficient service throughout.*
20⇔🛏(1fb) CTV in all bedrooms T ✱ (ex guide dogs) ✱
sB&B⇔🛏£80-£85 dB&B⇔🛏£90 🅡
100P 5🚗 ✻
♀ English & French V ♥ ♫ S% Lunch £11.50-£12.50&alc
Dinner fr£16.50&alc Last dinner 9.30pm
Credit Cards 1️⃣2️⃣3️⃣4️⃣5️⃣

✕**Rum-Wong** 16-18 London Rd GU1 2AF ☎(0483)36092
*A smart modern restaurant offering carefully prepared authentic
food is split into two sections. The first, the 'Khan Tok' room,
features Thai dancers and low tables from which to eat your meal
while reclining on cushions in the traditional way; the other allows
the less brave to dine in a more conventional manner, with standard
furnishings and service.*
Closed Mon, 25-29 Dec & 2 wks Aug
♀ Thai V 100 seats ✱ Lunch fr£14&alc Dinner £14&alc Last
lunch 2.30pm Last dinner 10.30pm ♪
Credit Cards 1️⃣3️⃣

## GUIST Norfolk Map 09 TF92

✕✕**Tollbridge** Dereham Rd NR20 5NU
☎Foulsham(036284)359
*Guests can enjoy a meal with a view at this lovely restaurant on
the banks of the River Wensum, with a terrace which is floodlit at
night. There is a timbered ceiling and an elegant lounge in the
building, which dates back to 1773, and the menu is simple but well
chosen. A light mousseline of local fish and saddle of Venison with
a port and wild mushroom sauce were recommended by our
Inspector for their natural and subtle flavours. There is a good
cheese board, usually with one or two Irish cheeses chosen by chef
patron Patrick Murphy, and the wine list is well chosen and
moderately priced. Booking is essential in high season.*
Closed Mon & 1st 3 wks Jan
Lunch not served Tue-Sat
Dinner not served Sun
♀ English & French 50 seats ✱ Sunday Lunch £8.50 Dinner
£19.50-£21.50 Last dinner 9pm 20P
Credit Cards 1️⃣3️⃣

---

A rosette is an indication of exceptional
standards of cuisine.

**GULLANE** Lothian *East Lothian* Map **12** NT48

★★★♨81% **Greywalls** Duncar Rd EH31 2EG (Pride of Britain) ☎(0620)842144 FAX (0620) 842241
Closed Nov-mid Mar
*The combined talents of architect Sir Edwin Lutyens and horticulturist Gertrude Jekyll have contributed to the charm of this attractive country house, now converted into an hotel of great character by the Weaver family. Greywalls has the added benefit of overlooking the 9th and 18th greens of Muirfield golf course, which often plays host to the Open Championship. The hotel is exceptionally comfortable and retains its atmosphere of family home, while for those looking for the ultimate in peace and quiet, a room in the nearby lodge offers an ideal retreat.*
17⇨↟Annexe5⇨↟1🚪 CTV in all bedrooms T ✱
sB&B⇨↟£65-£67.50 dB&B⇨↟£105-£115 🅱
⟮ 40P ⊞ ✿ ♬ (hard) croquet shooting
♡ 🕮 Lunch £12.50 Dinner £27 Last dinner 9pm
Credit Cards ⟨1⟩⟨2⟩⟨3⟩⟨4⟩⟨5⟩

✿✕**La Potinière** Main St EH31 2AA ☎(0620)843214
*Hilary and David Brown continue to earn praise for the good food and wine they have served for many years at this unpretentious little haven. The set lunch menu offers no choice, concentrating on four courses of carefully prepared food. A typical meal may begin with a well-constructed tomato soup, with a tangy after-taste of fresh mint, followed by a creamy Arbroath Smokie mousse, pigeon breasts with lentils in a morel-flavoured cream sauce accompanied by exquisite pommes dauphinoises and crisp salad, to be finished with a rich orange soufflé glacé. The magnificent catalogue of French wines has been carefully chosen and is most reasonably priced. Guests should note that lunch, although relaxed and informal, is a serious affair and not to be rushed. Allow plenty of time to enjoy this charming restaurant where booking is preferred and usually necessary.*
Closed Wed, 1 wk Jun & Oct
Lunch not served Sat & Fri
Dinner not served Sun-Thu (dinner served Fri & Sat only)
♡ French 32 seats Lunch fr£14.50 Dinner £22.50 Last lunch 1pm 10P ✴

**GULWORTHY** Devon Map **02** SX47

✕✕✕*Horn of Plenty* PL19 8JD ☎Tavistock(0822)832528
*This peaceful country restaurant with rooms has marvellous views which extend as far as Bodmin Moor. As we go to press, we learn of a change of hands at this restaurant.*
Closed 25 & 26 Dec
Lunch not served Thu & Fri
♡ Continental V 60 seats Last lunch 2pm Last dinner 9.30pm
30P nc10yrs
Credit Cards ⟨1⟩⟨2⟩⟨3⟩

**GWBERT-ON-SEA** Dyfed Map **02** SN15

★★★54% *Cliff* SA43 1PP ☎Cardigan(0239)613241
Telex no 48440 FAX (0239) 615361
*A family, holiday hotel with a friendly atmosphere, the Cliff stands perched on its own 30 acres of headland with fine sea views and offers a good range of facilities.*
75⇨↟(4fb)2🚪 CTV in all bedrooms T
⟮ CTV 200P ✿ CFA ⇴(heated) ▶9 ♪ squash snooker sauna solarium gymnasium sea fishing
♡ Welsh, English & French ♡ 🕮 Last dinner 9pm
Credit Cards ⟨1⟩⟨2⟩⟨3⟩⟨5⟩

**GWITHIAN** Cornwall & Isles of Scilly Map **02** SW54

★63% **Sandsifter** Godrevy Towans TR27 5ED
☎Hayle(0736)753314
*This busy, fully licensed, small hotel on the edge of the sand dunes offers an extensive selection of bar meals in addition to the table d'hôte and à la carte menus of the Fountain Restaurant ; though a few bedrooms are compact, all are well equipped, and friendly service is provided by the proprietor's family and local employees.*
7⇨↟ CTV in all bedrooms ® ✖ (ex guide dogs) ✱
sB&B⇨↟£15-£20 dB&B⇨↟£30-£40 🅱
80P ✿ nc12yrs *xmas*
♡ English & French ♡ ✴ Lunch £6.50-£7.50&alc High tea £2.50 Dinner £7.50-£8.50&alc Last dinner 9pm
Credit Cards ⟨1⟩⟨3⟩£

**HACKNESS** North Yorkshire Map **08** SE99

★★★♨66% **Hackness Grange Country** North Yorkshire National Park Y013 0JW (Best Western)
☎Scarborough(0723)82345 FAX (0723) 82391
*Beautifully located in the North Yorkshire Moors National Park, the hotel stands in attractive gardens which include a lake and a tennis court ; an indoor swimming pool is also available for guests' use. Bedrooms – whether in the main house or the courtyard – are simply furnished but well equipped, substantial meals are competently prepared from fresh produce, and a courteous team of staff provides friendly service.*
11⇨↟Annexe15⇨↟(2fb)1🚪 CTV in all bedrooms ® T ✖
sB&B⇨↟£44-£55 dB&B⇨↟£88-£110
⟮ CTV 60P ⊞ ✿ ▤(heated) ▶9 ♬ (hard) ♪ croquet *xmas*
V ♡ ✴ Lunch £7.50-£9&alc Dinner £16.50 Last dinner 9pm
Credit Cards ⟨1⟩⟨2⟩⟨3⟩⟨5⟩£
**See advertisement under SCARBOROUGH**

G-

## The Manor
### at Newlands

Owner managed
Country House Hotel, 3
miles east of Guildford
on A25 to Dorking (30
minutes from Heathrow
and Gatwick)

AA ★ ★ ★

Set in 9 acres and surrounded by beautiful countryside, The Manor offers comfort and tranquility with 20 en suite luxury bedrooms. The excellent restaurant is open for lunch and dinner seven days a week. Receptions and small conferences a speciality.

**NEWLANDS CORNER
GUILDFORD
SURREY GU4 8SE
Telephone (0483) 222624**

## HADLEY WOOD Greater London Map **04** TQ29

**★★★★62%, West Lodge Park** Cockfosters Rd EN4 0PY
☎081-440 8311 Telex no 24734 FAX 081-449 3698
*Built in 1838, this hotel is attractively situated in 35 acres of parkland with its own arboretum. The owner, Mr T Beale, has gradually upgraded and improved standards and the hotel is starting to develop its own elegant and individual style. Chef Jonathan Binns' creative cooking has influenced the standard of cuisine and service is attentive and professional.*
48⇌🏠Annexe2⇌🏠3🛏 CTV in all bedrooms ® T
🎯 (ex guide dogs) ✳ sB&B⇌🏠£75-£82.50
dB&B⇌🏠£99.50-£115 🏮
Lift ( 200P 🚲 ✿ CFA putting croquet
♡ International V ✿
Credit Cards ①②③

## HADLOW Kent Map **05** TQ65

**★★62%, Leavers Manor** Goose Green TN11 0JH
☎Tonbridge(0732)851442
*A charming Georgian house provides a variety of comfortable accommodation, including a new bedroom wing and relaxing public areas, with willing, attentive service from helpful staff; well-cooked meals are based on good raw materials, both table d'hôte and à la carte menus being available.*
30⇌🏠(2fb) CTV in all bedrooms ® T 🎯 (ex guide dogs)
S10% sB&B⇌🏠£50-£55 dB&B⇌🏠£60-£70 🏮
100P 🚲 ✿
♡ English & French ⬙ Lunch fr£10 Dinner fr£10 Last dinner 9.30pm
Credit Cards ①②③⑤

## HAILSHAM East Sussex Map **05** TQ50

**★★75%, The Olde Forge** Magham Down BN27 1PN
☎(0323)842893
Closed 25 Dec-2 Jan
*Conveniently located on the A271 a mile and a half east of the town, this small but good quality cottage hotel complements a beautifully furnished interior with personal service from the resident proprietors. The cosy, low-beamed lounge bar and restaurant are made welcoming by fresh flower displays and a log-burning fire.*
8rm(1⇌5🏠)1🛏 CTV in all bedrooms ® sB&B£25
sB&B⇌🏠£27.50-£30 dB&B£40 dB&B⇌🏠£42-£48 🏮
12P 🚲
♡ English & French V Lunch £9.50 Dinner £10.50&alc Last dinner 9.15pm
Credit Cards ①②③⑤Ⓔ

○**Travelodge** A22 Hellingly(Trusthouse Forte)
☎Central reservations (0800) 850950
Due to open winter 1990
40⇌

## HALESOWEN West Midlands

⌂**Granada Lodge** Illey Ln B32 4AR (Granada) ☎021-550 3261
FAX 021-501 2880
(For full entry see Frankley Motorway Service Area (M5))

## HALIFAX West Yorkshire Map **07** SE02

**★★★73%, Holdsworth House** Holmfield HX2 9TG (3m NW off
A629 Keighley Road) ☎(0422)240024 Telex no 51574
FAX (0422) 245174
Closed 25 & 26 Dec
*This charming seventeenth-century house with extensions stands in its own grounds and gardens just off the A629 Keighley road three miles from Halifax. Bedrooms are very well equipped and comfortably furnished, while the delightfully appointed public areas include an intimate restaurant which serves meals of a very high standard.*

40⇌🏠(1fb)5🛏🎯✝in 9 bedrooms CTV in all bedrooms T ✳
sB&B⇌🏠£65-£80 dB&B⇌🏠£80-£95 🏮
( 40P ✿ CFA
♡ English & French V ✿ ⬙ Lunch £18-£25alc Dinner
£18-£25alc Last dinner 9.30pm
Credit Cards ①②③⑤

**★★★67%, The Imperial Crown** 42/46 Horton St HX1 1BR
☎(0422)342342 FAX (0422) 349866
*A well furnished and comfortable hotel situated in the centre of town close to the railway station. Bedrooms are very attractive and have good facilities, and the Wallis Simpson restaurant offers an interesting choice of home produced dishes.*
42⇌🏠(3fb) CTV in all bedrooms ® T 🎯 sB&B⇌🏠£37-£52
dB&B⇌🏠£47-£62 🏮
( CTV 16P 🚲 xmas
♡ French V ✿ Sunday Lunch £7.50-£9.75 Dinner £9.75&alc
Last dinner 10pm
Credit Cards ①②③⑤Ⓔ

**★★★59%, Wool Merchants** Mulcture Hall Rd HX1 1SP
☎(0422)368783
*Converted from a woollen warehouse, this well-furnished hotel retains much of its original charm and character. Bedrooms have good facilities and an extensive Italian-style menu is available in both restaurants. It is situated near the town centre and railway station.*
25⇌🏠(2fb) CTV in all bedrooms ® T ✳
sB&B⇌🏠£28.50-£45 dB&B⇌🏠£43-£55
Lift CTV 200P
♡ International V ✿ ⬙
Credit Cards ①②③

## HALKIRK Highland *Caithness* Map **15** ND15

See **John O'Groats**

**★★60%, Ulbster Arms** Bridge St KY12 6XY ☎(084783)206 &
641
*Particularly popular with sporting guests for its high standards of Highland accommodation, food and friendliness, this well-established hotel stands by the banks of the longest privately owned "fly only" river in Britain.*
12rm(7⇌🏠) CTV in all bedrooms ® T sB&B£28-£30.25
dB&B⇌🏠£60.50-£65 🏮
CTV 30P 6🚗 (£2 per day) 🚲 ✔ shooting stalking
V ✿ ⬙ Lunch £5-£6.75 High tea £6-£9 Dinner £12.50-£15
Last dinner 8.30pm
Credit Cards ①③Ⓔ
**See advertisement under JOHN O'GROATS**

## HALKYN Clwyd Map **07** SJ27

⌂**Travelodge** CH8 8RF (on A55) (Trusthouse Forte)
☎(0352)780952 Central Res (0800) 850950
*A single-storey, purpose-built lodge stands adjacent to the Little Chef restaurant where guests take their meals; all its modern bedrooms are comfortable and well equipped, one being specifically designed to meet the needs of a disabled person. The hotel's elevated position on the A55 commands views over the River Dee and Wirral Peninsular.*
31⇌🏠(31fb) CTV in all bedrooms ® sB⇌🏠£24
dB⇌🏠£29.50 (room only)
( 32P 🚲
Credit Cards ①②③

## HALLAND East Sussex Map **05** TQ41

**★★66%, Halland Forge** BN8 6PW (Inter-Hotels) ☎(082584)456
FAX (082584) 773
*Conveniently situated on the A22, with easy access and parking, this family-run motel offers a choice of well-equipped, self-contained bedrooms complemented by a lounge bar, a restaurant*

**H**

and a separate coffee shop that serves light meals throughout the day.
Annexe20⇉♠2🛏 CTV in all bedrooms ® ✱
sB⇉♠£38.50-£42.50 dB⇉♠£48.50-£53.50 (room only) 🍴
70P ✿ nc5yrs
♥ English & French V ♦ ⚘ Lunch £8.95-£9.95&alc High tea fr£5 Dinner £14.50-£15.50&alc Last dinner 9.30pm
Credit Cards 1 2 3 5 £

---

**HAMBLETON** North Yorkshire Map 08 SE53

★★63%, **Owl** Main Rd YO8 9JH (4m W A63)
☎Selby(0757)82374
An 18th century gentleman's residence has been converted and extended to provide a popular venue for functions and bar meals. Accommodation is neat and modestly furnished and the atmosphere is friendly. Located on the A65, 5 miles from the A1 and 3 miles west of Selby.
9⇉♠(1fb)1🛏 CTV in all bedrooms ® T 🐾 (ex guide dogs) ✱
sB&B⇉♠£28.50-£32.50 dB&B⇉♠£38.50-£42.50
50P 🚲
♦ ⚘ Lunch £6&alc Dinner £6-£14alc Last dinner 10pm
Credit Cards 1 3 £

---

**HAMILTON MOTORWAY SERVICE AREA (M74)**
Strathclyde Map 11 NS75

⌂*Roadchef Lodge* M74 Northbound ML3 6JW
☎Hamilton(0698)891904 FAX (0698) 891682
Closed 25 & 26 Dec
36⇉(23fb)⚥in 10 bedrooms CTV in all bedrooms ® T
🐾 (ex guide dogs)
( 120P ✿
Credit Cards 1 2 3 5

---

**HAMPSON GREEN** Lancashire Map 07 SD45

★★58%, **Hampson House** Hampson Ln LA2 0JB (off A6 at M6 junct 33) ☎Galgate(0524)751158
An hotel conveniently situated on the A6, close to junction 33 of the M6, offers modern accommodation and a choice of menus.
13rm(6⇉5♠)(3fb) CTV in all bedrooms ®
45P ✿ ♪ (grass)
♦ ⚘
Credit Cards 1 3

---

**HANCHURCH** Staffordshire Map 07 SJ84

★★★79% **Hanchurch Manor** ST4 8SD
☎Stoke-on-Trent(0782)643030 FAX (0782) 643035
A distinguished country house in charming rural surroundings, yet within easy reach of the motorway. The chef, Peter Puddo, has created two menus – a fixed price gourmet menu and a seasonal à la carte, with the emphasis on fresh, healthy produce.
7⇉Annexe5⇉♠2🛏 CTV in all bedrooms T 🐾
sB&B⇉♠£75-£85 dB&B⇉♠£95-£105 🍴
( 25P 🚲 ✿ ♪ nc12yrs xmas
V ♦ ⚥ ⚘ Lunch £11-£13 Dinner £19-£25&alc Last dinner 9.30pm
Credit Cards 1 2 3 5 £

---

**HANDFORTH** Cheshire Map 07 SJ88

★★★★61% **Belfry** Stanley Rd SK9 3LD ☎061-437 0511
Telex no 666358 FAX 061-499 0597
A family-run hotel, conveniently situated for Manchester Airport or the city centre, offers every facility for business traveller and tourist alike. Recent refurbishment has improved its compact bedrooms, but the restaurant takes pride of place, serving such mouthwatering delicacies as wholemeal pancake filled with seafood and served with tomato flavoured Hollandaise sauce, a

whole roast crispy duck served with port and orange essence, all meals being accompanied by an outstanding wine list.
82⇉ CTV in all bedrooms T ✱ sB⇉£68.50-£82.50
dB⇉£79.20-£92 (room only) 🍴
Lift ( 150P ✿ CFA ♫
♥ International V ♦ ⚘ Lunch £10.25-£11.25&alc Dinner fr£13.50&alc Last dinner 10pm
Credit Cards 1 2 3 5

---

**HANSLOPE** Buckinghamshire Map 04 SP84

★★★⚐68% **Hatton Court** Bullington End, Hanslope
MK19 7BQ ☎Milton Keynes(0908)510044 FAX (0908) 510945
Closed 26 Dec & 1 Jan
The conversion of this building, dating from 1850, into a hotel has skilfully retained its fine architectural features. It is furnished with antiques and all bedrooms have been lavishly decorated and provided with good quality, generous sized bathrooms. The restaurant features a conservatory extension and the cooking is inventive. The hotel is set in seven acres of private grounds, surrounded by open countryside. Conference facilities are available in an adjacent converted barn.
12⇉♠Annexe8⇉♠ CTV in all bedrooms ® T
🐾 (ex guide dogs) ✱ sB&B⇉♠£40-£80
dB&B⇉♠£80-£110 🍴
( 60P 🚲 snooker
♦ ⚘ Lunch £13.50 Dinner £25 Last dinner 9.30pm
Credit Cards 1 2 3 5

Hotels with a high percentage rating for quality are highlighted by a % across their gazetteer entry.

# West Lodge Park

The nearest country hotel to London — only 12 miles from the West End, and one mile from exit 24 on the M25, but set in 35 acres of parkland and fields. Country house atmosphere with antiques and log fires.
Individually decorated bedrooms with carefully chosen fabrics and furnishings. Some four poster bedrooms and whirlpool baths. Ask for colour brochure and details of weekend breaks.

**West Lodge Park**
Hadley Wood, Barnet, Herts
Tel: 081-440 8311.   Telex: 24734
Fax: 081-449 3698
AA ★ ★ ★ ★

**H**

**HARBERTONFORD** Devon Map **03** SX75

★★★67%, **Old Mill Country House** TQ9 7SW ☎(080423)349
*This former mill, peacefully located in riverbank setting, has been tastefully converted to provide comfortable bedrooms, and an intimate lounge and bar ; the restaurant is popular locally, offering an interesting table d'hôte menu of carefully prepared dishes, whilst the proprietors, who live in the grounds, do everything in their power to ensure guests' enjoyment.*
5⇄Annexe1⇄1🖛⅍in 1 bedroom CTV in all bedrooms ® T
Ӿ ✳ sB&B⇄£30-£40 dB&B⇄£38-£58 ﬡ
《 60P ✿ ✔ croquet nc12yrs
♡ English & French V ✿ ⊉ Sunday Lunch £11.95 Dinner £14.95 Last dinner 9.30pm
Credit Cards ① ③

**HAREWOOD** West Yorkshire Map **08** SE34

★★★66%, **Harewood Arms** Harrogate Rd LS17 9LH ☎(0532)886566 FAX (0532) 886064
*Once a coaching inn, and dating back to 1815, the hotel has been carefully restored and renovated to provide comfortable accommodation with modern amenities, whilst at the same time retaining its original character.*
24⇄ℿ(1fb) CTV in all bedrooms ® T ✳ sB&B⇄ℿ£54-£56 dB&B⇄ℿ£66-£70.50 ﬡ
100P ✿ *xmas*
♡ English & French V ✿ ⊉ Lunch £6.50-£8.50 Dinner £11.95-£14.95&alc Last dinner 10pm
Credit Cards ① ② ③ ④ ⑤

**HARLECH** Gwynedd Map **06** SH53

See also **Talsarnau**
★★63%, **The Castle** Castle Square LL36 2YH ☎(0766)780529
*Personally run by the owners, and commanding fine sea views from its position next to the famous castle, the hotel has been refurbished throughout to provide warmth and comfort.*
10⇄ℿ(2fb)1🖛 CTV in all bedrooms ®
CTV 30P ⊞ ▶ 18 ♪ (hard) ∪
♡ English & French V ✿ ⊉ ⅍ Last dinner 9.30pm
Credit Cards ① ③

★57%, **Noddfa** Lower Rd LL46 2UB ☎(0766)780043
*Overlooking St Davids golf course this family-run hotel offers good value for money and home cooked dishes.*
6rm(3⇄ℿ)(1fb) CTV in 5 bedrooms ® Ӿ (ex guide dogs) S%
sB&B£20 sB&B⇄ℿ£23-£30 dB&B£30 dB&B⇄ℿ£36-£50 ﬡ
CTV 40P ⊞ ✿ solarium archery nc3 yrs *xmas*
♡ International V S% Lunch £13-£15&alc Dinner £13-£16 Last dinner 8.30pm
Credit Cards ① ③ ⓔ

✗**Cemlyn** High St LL46 2YA ☎(0766)780425
*Dinner guests at this small, village centre restaurant enjoy fine views of superb sunsets from its west-facing windows. Local lamb, fish and shellfish are ably cooked by the owner/chef, and you are advised to book a table in advance.*
Closed mid Oct-Etr
Lunch not served (ex by arrangement)
♡ International V 42 seats Dinner £13.95-£17.95 Last dinner 9.30pm ♪ nc8yrs ⅍
Credit Cards ① ③

**HARLESTON** Norfolk Map **05** TM28

★★61%, *Swan* The Thoroughfare IP20 9AG ☎(0379)852221
14⇄ℿ(1fb) CTV in all bedrooms ® T
CTV 45P
♡ English & French V ✿ ⊉ ⅍ Last dinner 9.30pm
Credit Cards ① ③

**HARLOSH**

See **Skye, Isle of**

**HARLOW** Essex Map **05** TL41

★★★70%, **Churchgate Manor** Churchgate St, Old Harlow CM17 0JT (Best Western) ☎(0279)420246 Telex no 818289
FAX (0279) 437720
*Set in its own landscaped gardens, this charming hotel has retained some of the original features of the old Jacobean house and has been extended to include conference facilities, an indoor swimming pool and leisure centre, and the Manor Restaurant. Bedrooms are well-equipped with lots of extra facilities. The bar overlooking the floodlit garden fountains, is an ideal setting for an aperitif.*
85⇄(8fb) CTV in all bedrooms ® T ✳ sB&B⇄£52-£85 dB&B⇄£65-£97 ﬡ
《 120P ✿ 🖾(heated) sauna solarium gymnasium *xmas*
♡ English & French V ✿ ⊉ Lunch £10.95-£15&alc Dinner fr£14.95&alc Last dinner 9.45pm
Credit Cards ① ② ③ ⑤

★★★65%, **Harlow Moat House** Southern Way CM18 7BA (Queens Moat) ☎(0279)22441 due to change to 422441
Telex no 81658 FAX (0279) 635094
Closed 24 Dec-3 Jan
*Large hotel with modern and well-equipped bedrooms and recently refurbished public rooms. The hotel offers conference and banqueting facilities.*
120⇄ℿ⅍in 20 bedrooms CTV in all bedrooms ® T
Ӿ (ex guide dogs) ✳ sB&B⇄ℿ£40-£75 dB&B⇄ℿ£55-£85 ﬡ
《 180P CFA
♡ English & French V ✿ ⊉ Lunch fr£13.50 Dinner fr£13.50&alc Last dinner 10pm
Credit Cards ① ② ③ ⑤ ⓔ

★★★51%, **Green Man** Mulberry Green, Old Harlow CM17 0ET
(Trusthouse Forte) ☎(0279)442521 Telex no 817972
FAX (0279) 626113
*Now under new management, providing superior-type bedrooms in the annexe – though others are in need of refurbishment – and willing, helpful service, this characterful coaching inn features an interesting beamed restaurant.*
Annexe55⇄ℿ⅍in 8 bedrooms CTV in all bedrooms ® T
sB⇄£67-£78 dB⇄£78-£89 (room only) ﬡ
《 75P *xmas*
V ✿ ⊉ ⅍ S10% Lunch fr£11.80 Dinner fr£14.50&alc Last dinner 10pm
Credit Cards ① ② ③ ④ ⑤

**HARLYN BAY** Cornwall & Isles of Scilly Map **02** SW87

★66%, **Polmark** PL28 8SB (off B3276) ☎Padstow(0841)520206
*Set only a few minutes' walk from a sandy beach, this attractive stone house offers particularly comfortable public rooms, some well-equipped, newly-built bedrooms and some older-style simpler accommodation.*
13rm(8⇄ℿ)(2fb) ® ✳ sB&Bfr£30 sB&B⇄ℿfr£38 dB&Bfr£70 dB&B⇄ℿfr£70 (incl dinner)
CTV 40P ✿ ⊴(heated) *xmas*
V ✿ ⊉ Lunch fr£1.50 Dinner fr£10&alc Last dinner 7pm
Credit Cards ③

**HAROME**

See **Helmsley**

**HARPENDEN** Hertfordshire Map **04** TL11

★★★66%, **Harpenden Moat House** 18 Southdown Rd AL5 1PE
(Queens Moat) ☎(0582)764111 Telex no 826938
FAX (0582) 769858
Closed 26-31 Dec

*The hotel retains many of its elegant Georgian features, the restaurant being of particular interest. Rooms have been refurbished to offer a good standard of modern accommodation and are generally spacious.*
18⇾♠Annexe37⇾(3fb)2⚌⽊in 5 bedrooms CTV in all bedrooms ⓇT
⟨ 80P ✿ boules croquet lawn
♀ French V ✿ ⚏
Credit Cards ①②③⑤

★★★64% **Glen Eagle** 1 Luton Rd AL5 2PX ☎(0582)760271 FAX (0582) 460819
*Pleasant and friendly, the hotel offers a comfortable country-house style and atmosphere; most bedrooms have recently been refurbished to provide modern accommodation, there is a well appointed lounge bar, and the elegant restaurant features both table d'hôte and à la carte menus.*
51⇾♠(12fb)2⚌ CTV in all bedrooms ⓇT✳S%
sB&B⇾♠£70-£86 dB&B⇾♠£86-£104 ➡
Lift ⟨ 100P CFA *xmas*
♀ English & French V ✿ ⚏ Lunch fr£14&alc Dinner fr£16.25&alc Last dinner 10pm
Credit Cards ①②③④⑤

---

**HARRIS, ISLE OF** Western Isles *Inverness-shire* Map **13**

---

**TARBERT** Map **13** NB10

★★60% **Harris** PA85 3DL ☎Harris(0859)2154 FAX (0859) 2281
*Conveniently situated for the ferry terminal, this long-established family-run hotel offers traditional standards of hospitality and service with good home cooking. Bedrooms vary in size and are generally well maintained.*
25rm(13⇾4♠)(2fb) S% sB&Bfr£25.90 sB&B⇾♠fr£29.90 dB&Bfr£48.90 dB&B⇾♠fr£55.50 ➡
CTV 30P ✿ ⚹ *xmas*
V ✿ ⚏ ⽊ Bar Lunch £2-£5 Dinner £12.50-£13.75 Last dinner 8.30pm
Credit Cards ①③ⓔ

---

**HARROGATE** North Yorkshire Map **08** SE35

See also **Burnt Yates**
★★★★⚑72% **Nidd Hall** Nidd HG3 3BN ☎(0423)771598 FAX (0423) 770931
*This fine country manor, within 23 acres of attractive grounds, complete with punt on the private lake, has only recently been converted to a spacious and elegant hotel. Bedrooms are mostly spacious, with their own individual styles. The public rooms are peaceful and relaxing. The chef, Frank Eckerman, gives a touch of finesse to the cooking, in his own modern style, and for those seeking less formal arrangements, the hotel's leisure club in the basement has an Italian-themed 'Cellar' restaurant, which proves very popular. The hotel is best reached by taking the B6165, off the A61 at Ripvey, and travelling 1/4 mile towards Knaresborough. Nidd Hall is just 4 miles North of Harrogate.*
38⇾♠Annexe4⇾♠(1fb)4⚌⽊in 12 bedrooms CTV in all bedrooms ⓇT⽊ (ex guide dogs) S15% sB&B⇾♠£90 dB&B⇾♠£100-£135 ➡
Lift ⟨ 90P ✿ ⊠(heated) ♪ (hard) ⚑ squash snooker sauna solarium gymnasium beauty salon punting rowing ⚹ *xmas*
♀ French & Italian V ✿ ⚏ S15% Lunch £14&alc Dinner £22&alc Last dinner 9.30pm
Credit Cards ①②③⑤

★★★★62% **The Majestic** Ripon Rd HG1 2HU (Trusthouse Forte) ☎(0423)568972 Telex no 57918 FAX (0423) 502283
*Situated near Harrogate's new conference centre, this hotel is very imposing, with spacious and lofty public rooms, well-tended gardens and good leisure facilities. A bedroom-refurbishment*

*programme is nearly complete, providing every bedroom with modern facilities.*
156⇾♠(10fb)⽊in 42 bedrooms CTV in all bedrooms ⓇT S%
sB⇾♠£81-£99 dB⇾♠£103-£115 (room only) ➡
Lift ⟨ 180P ✿ CFA ⊠(heated) ♪ (hard) squash snooker sauna solarium gymnasium health & fitness centre *xmas*
♀ International V ✿ ⚏ ⽊ S% Lunch £11.50-£14&alc High tea fr£5 Dinner fr£15.50&alc Last dinner 9.45pm
Credit Cards ①②③④⑤

★★★★60% **Moat House International** Kings Rd HG1 1XX (Queens Moat) ☎(0423)500000 Telex no 57575 FAX (0423) 524435
*The modern, purpose-built, multi-storey hotel stands adjacent to the Conference Centre, providing accommodation in smart, modern bedrooms, a spacious reception lounge and conference facilities. The restaurant, with its popular lounge bar, offers high quality cuisine, or guests may eat at the Orangery Coffee Shop.*
214⇾♠⽊in 38 bedrooms CTV in all bedrooms ⓇT✳
sB&B⇾♠£90 dB&B⇾♠£108 ➡
Lift ⟨ ▤ 130P *xmas*
♀ English & French V ✿ ⚏ ⽊ Lunch fr£9.50 Dinner fr£14.50 Last dinner 10pm
Credit Cards ①②③④⑤ⓔ

★★★★57% **The Crown** Crown Place HG1 2RZ (Trusthouse Forte) ☎(0423)567755 Telex no 57652 FAX (0423) 502284
*18th-century building near Valley Gardens and the Royal Baths.*
121⇾♠(3fb)⽊in 5 bedrooms CTV in all bedrooms ⓇT✳S%
sB⇾♠£78-£83 dB⇾♠£91-£98 (room only) ➡
Lift ⟨ 50P CFA *xmas*
♀ French V ✿ ⚏ ⽊ S10% Lunch fr£9.50&alc High tea £5.50-£7.50 Dinner fr£16&alc Last dinner 9.30pm
Credit Cards ①②③④⑤

# Harrogate

**★★★69%** **Balmoral Hotel & Restaurant** Franklin Mount
HG1 5EJ ☎(0423)508208 FAX (0423) 530652
*This stylish and elegantly furnished hotel is situated close to all the
town's amenities including the conference centre. Keith and Alison
Hartwell have refurbished the hotel to provide elegant and
attractively furnished bedrooms, equipped to a high standard. The
bar and restaurant are full of character, furnished to a high
standard and ideal settings in which to enjoy the freshly prepared
food from the imaginative menus.*
20⇨♠(2fb)7♬ CTV in all bedrooms ® T ✳ S% sB⇨♠fr£48
dB⇨♠fr£70 (room only) ₱
12P ⇔ ❖ solarium
V ✿ ♫ Bar Lunch £1.50-£10 Dinner fr£13.50&alc Last dinner
9pm
Credit Cards ① ② ③ ⓔ

**★★★68%** **Grants** 3-11 Swan Rd HG1 2SS ☎(0423)560666
FAX (0423) 502550
*A smart, privately-owned and well-run hotel near the town centre,
extensively refurbished over the years, offers attractive,
individually furnished and very well equipped bedrooms, some of
which are rather compact. Public areas include a comfortable
lounge, a cosy cocktail bar and the pleasant, efficiently-run
Chimney Pots restaurant which serves a range of interesting dishes
to suit all tastes. Friendly yet professional staff create a welcoming
atmosphere.*
37⇨♠(2fb)3♬ CTV in all bedrooms ® T
sB&B⇨♠£32.50-£75 dB&B⇨♠£37.50-£95 ₱
Lift ⓒ 21P ♫ xmas
♀ English & French V ✿ ♫ ⅋ Lunch £9.50 Dinner
£13.95&alc Last dinner 9.30pm
Credit Cards ① ② ③ ⑤ ⓔ

**★★★64%** **Hospitality Inn** Prospect Place, West Park HG1 1LB
(Mount Charlotte (TS)) ☎(0423)564601 Telex no 57530
FAX (0423) 507508
*Standing in the city centre but overlooking urban greenery, the
hotel offers a tranquility rarely found in a town setting ;
accommodation is comfortable and well-appointed.*
71⇨♠(5fb) CTV in all bedrooms ® T ✳
sB&B⇨♠£60-£69.50 dB&B⇨♠£69.50-£79.50 ₱
Lift ⓒ 40P CFA xmas
♀ English & French V ✿ ♫ Sunday Lunch £8.75-£9.50 Dinner
£13.75&alc Last dinner 9.30pm
Credit Cards ① ② ③ ⑤

**★★★64%** **Hotel St George** 1 Ripon Rd HG1 2SY (Swallow)
☎(0423)561431 Telex no 57995 FAX (0423) 530037
*A busy hotel with well-appointed bedrooms, a good leisure suite
and a delightful new bar lounge and brasserie.*
93⇨♠(14fb) CTV in all bedrooms ® T S% sB&B⇨♠£80
dB&B⇨♠£105 ₱
Lift ⓒ 60P CFA ⊠(heated) sauna solarium gymnasium
boutique beautician masseuse xmas
♀ English & French V ✿ ♫ S% Lunch £10.95 Dinner
£15.25&alc Last dinner 9.30pm
Credit Cards ① ② ③ ⑤

**★★★63%** *Studley* Swan Rd HG1 2SE ☎(0423)560425
Telex no 57506
*This busy, popular hotel features a very attractive and comfortable
new lounge, together with well-appointed bedrooms. The French
restaurant maintains its reputation for a high standard of cuisine,
whilst service is efficient and friendly throughout.*
36⇨ CTV in all bedrooms ®
Lift ⓒ CTV 14P nc8 yrs
♀ French ✿ Last dinner 10pm
Credit Cards ① ② ③ ⑤

For key to symbols see the inside front cover.

**★★72%** *Albany* 22-23 Harlow Moor Dr HG2 0JY
☎(0423)565890
*Standing opposite the attractive Valley Gardens, conveniently
situated for the town centre and its conference facilities, the hotel
offers well equipped bedrooms, a comfortable lounge and home-
cooked meals of a good standard; the proprietors are most
welcoming, and guests are assured of a comfortable stay.*
14♠(3fb) CTV in all bedrooms ® ✗ (ex guide dogs)
♀ English & Continental V ⅋ Last dinner 7.30pm
Credit Cards ① ③

**★★72%** **Russell** Valley Dr HG2 0JN ☎(0423)509866
FAX (0423) 506185
Closed 27-30 Dec
*Quietly located overlooking the Valley Gardens, this welcoming
hotel offers a good level of service, well-equipped bedrooms and
cosy lounges. An elegant wood-panelled dining room provides the
ideal setting in which to enjoy cuisine of a high standard, the dishes
on its interesting menu being based on fresh ingredients and
professionally served.*
34⇨♠(4fb) CTV in all bedrooms ® T ✗ (ex guide dogs) ✳
sB&B⇨♠£45.95 dB&B⇨♠£59.95-£69.50 ₱
Lift ⓒ ♪ xmas
♀ French V ✿ ♫ ⅋ Dinner £14.95&alc Last dinner 10pm
Credit Cards ① ② ③ ④ ⑤ ⓔ

**★★68%** **Ascot House** 53 Kings Rd HG1 5HJ (Minotels)
☎(0423)531005 FAX (0423) 503523
*Centrally situated close to the town centre and conference centre,
this hotel provides good old-fashioned service. The lounges are
comfortable and the menus offer good value for money.*
25rm(13⇨♠)(1fb) CTV in all bedrooms ® T sB&B£35-£43.95
sB&B⇨♠£37.50-£49.50 dB&B£47.50-£66
dB&B⇨♠£54-£76.50 ₱
14P xmas
♀ English & Continental V ✿ ♫ Bar Lunch £1.50-£7.50alc
Dinner £10.95-£12.45&alc Last dinner 9pm
Credit Cards ① ② ③ ⑤ ⓔ

**★★68%** *White House* 10 Park Pde HG1 5AH (Exec Hotel)
☎(0423)501388
*This elegant hotel, overlooking 'The Stray', has many interesting
features including a lovely Italian tiled floor in the hall. An
interesting à la carte menu is offered in the restaurant and the food
is of a very good standard. There is a comfortable lounge and
lounge bar.*
13⇨♠(1fb)1♬ CTV in all bedrooms ®
CTV 10P ⇔ ❖
V ✿ ♫ Last dinner 9pm
Credit Cards ① ② ③ ⑤

**★★67%** **Green Park** Valley Dr HG2 0JT (Consort)
☎(0423)504681 Telex no 57515 FAX (0423) 530811
*In a pleasant situation opposite the famous Valley Gardens, and
convenient for the town's shopping centre and conference venues,
this hotel offers a choice of two comfortable lounges and well-
equipped en suite bedrooms. Staff provide a warm welcome and
particularly helpful service.*
43⇨♠(2fb) CTV in all bedrooms ® T ✳ sB&B⇨♠£45
dB&B⇨♠£63 ₱
Lift ⓒ 10P xmas
♀ International V ✿ ♫ ⅋ Sunday Lunch £6.25 Dinner
£10.75&alc Last dinner 8.30pm
Credit Cards ① ② ③ ⑤

**★★62%** *Fern* Swan Rd HG1 2SS (Inter-Hotels) ☎(0423)523866
Telex no 57583 FAX (0423) 501825
*Centrally located close to all of the town's amenities, the Fern
Hotel is a privately-owned establishment, which has been
converted from a listed Victorian building. The Portico Restaurant
provides an elegant setting for the extensive menu of freshly
prepared food. There is a comfy lounge and bar in a open plan
configuration. Bedrooms vary in size and standard, from the newly* ▶

**H**

*refurbished to the traditional and more modest rooms. All,*
*however, are equipped with en suite facilities.*
27rm(26⇊)Annexe7⇊(4fb) CTV in all bedrooms ®
✻ (ex guide dogs)
( ♪
♥ French V Last dinner 9.30pm
Credit Cards 1 2 3 5

**★★61% West Park** West Park HG1 1BL (Porterhouse)
☎(0423)524471
*Good bedrooms and comfortable lounge bars are offered by this*
*centrally situated hotel. The Porterhouse restaurant serves a good*
*range of dishes, and service throughout is friendly and attentive.*
17⇊ CTV in all bedrooms ® T
▦ 20P
V ♥
Credit Cards 1 2 3 5

**★73% Gables** 2 West Grove Rd HG1 2AD ☎(0423)505625
*A small family-run hotel providing a warm welcome, comfortable*
*surroundings and home cooked food. It is conveniently located for*
*Harrogate's conference venues and the town centre, and has its*
*own car park.*
9rm(8⇊⋔)(2fb) CTV in all bedrooms ® T sB&B⇊⋔£22-£25
dB&B⇊⋔£44-£50 ➡
9P
♥ Continental Lunch £4.50-£9.50alc Dinner fr£9.50alc Last
dinner 8.30pm
Credit Cards 1 3 £

**★71% Britannia Lodge** 16 Swan Rd HG1 2SA ☎(0423)508482
*Pleasant and friendly family-run hotel with a cosy lounge and*
*comfortable bedrooms. Good, home cooked-dinners are served.*
12⇊(4fb) CTV in all bedrooms ® T ✻ ✻ sB&B⇊⋔fr£42
dB&B⇊⋔fr£58 ➡
▦ CTV 6P 1🎱 ⊞
♥ French V ♥ ⌁ ✻ Dinner £12 Last dinner 7pm
Credit Cards 1 3 £

**★70% Caesars** 51 Valley Dr HG2 0JH ☎(0423)565818
Closed Xmas & New Year
*Competently prepared and attractively served meals are a feature*
*of this comfortable, family-run hotel which stands close to the town*
*centre, overlooking the Valley Gardens. Comfortably furnished*
*bedrooms are well equipped and there is a pleasant lounge bar.*
12⇊⋔(4fb) CTV in all bedrooms ® T ✻ ✻ (ex guide dogs)
sB&B⇊⋔£42.50 dB&B⇊⋔£60 ➡
CTV ♪ ⊞
♥ English & French ✻ Dinner £13.50 Last dinner 8.30pm
Credit Cards 1 3

**★66% Young's** 15 York Rd HG1 2QL ☎(0423)567336 & 521231
*Friendly little hotel with a spacious, comfortable lounge and*
*attractive, well-equipped bedrooms.*
16⇊⋔(2fb) CTV in all bedrooms ® T ✻ sB&B⇊⋔£28-£38
dB&B⇊⋔£44-£60 ➡
18P ✿
♥ English & French Dinner fr£9.95 Last dinner 7pm
Credit Cards 1 3 £

**★65% Alvera Court** 76 Kings Rd HG1 5JX ☎(0423)505735
*This comfortable and friendly hotel has well-equipped bedrooms*
*and is situated near the conference centre.*
12⇊⋔(4fb) CTV in all bedrooms ® T ✻ (ex guide dogs)
sB&B⇊⋔£26-£30 dB&B⇊⋔£52-£60 ➡
CTV 4P ⊞ xmas
V Dinner fr£10&alc Last dinner 7pm
Credit Cards 1 3

**★62% The Croft** 42-46 Franklin Rd HG1 5EE ☎(0423)563326
*This small family-run hotel provides modest but well-equipped*
*accomodation and friendly, informal service. Close to the*
*Conference Centre and the town, it offers good value for money.*
14rm(12⇊⋔)1⊞ CTV in all bedrooms ® T S% sB&Bfr£18.50
sB&B⇊⋔£25-£27.50 dB&Bfr£35 dB&B⇊⋔£40-£48 ➡
10P
♥ English & French V ♥ ⌁ S% Dinner £7-£15alc Last dinner
9.30pm
Credit Cards 1 3 £

**✕✕Emilio's** 3 Ripon Rd HG1 2SX ☎(0423)565267
FAX (0423) 568701
Closed Sun, 25-26 Dec, 1 Jan & BH's
♥ French & Spanish V 70 seats ✻ Lunch £8.90-£10&alc
Dinner £14.50-£16&alc Last lunch 2pm Last dinner 11pm 22P
Credit Cards 1 2 3

**✕Grundy's** 21 Cheltenham Crescent HG1 1DH ☎(0423)502610
*A smart, attractive little restaurant situated near the Conference*
*Centre offers an interesting and varied menu; Crab Terrine, for*
*example, might be followed by roast duckling in a cream, white*
*wine and green peppercorn sauce, the meal being concluded by a*
*deliciously sticky Toffee Sponge.*
Closed Sun & 2 wks winter, 1 wk summer
Lunch not served
Dinner not served BH's
♥ English & French V 40 seats ✻ Dinner £10.75&alc Last
dinner 9.30pm ♪ nc10yrs
Credit Cards 1 2 3

---

**HARROW** Greater London

See **LONDON plan 1**B5(page 426)
**★★63% Harrow** Roxborough Bridge, 12-22 Pinner Rd
HA1 4HZ ☎081-427 3435 Telex no 917898 FAX 081-861 1370
RS Xmas
*Close to public transport systems which give good access to the*
*City and West End. Much of the modern, well-equipped*
*accommodation is annexed – the Park House has its own bar/*
*lounge and breakfast room.*
76⇊⋔(4fb)1⊞ CTV in all bedrooms ® T ✻
sB&B⇊⋔£55-£75 dB&B⇊⋔£75-£95 ➡
( 67P
♥ International V ♥ ⌁ Lunch fr£10.95&alc Dinner
fr£16.95&alc Last dinner 9.45pm
Credit Cards 1 2 3 5

**★★59% Cumberland** 1 St Johns Rd HA1 2EF ☎081-863 4111
Telex no 917201 FAX 081-861 5668
*Privately owned commercial hotel with informal, friendly*
*atmosphere.*
30⇊ Annexe51⇊⋔(3fb) CTV in all bedrooms ® T
✻ (ex guide dogs) ✻ sB&B⇊⋔fr£60 dB&B⇊⋔fr£73 ➡
( 55P
♥ English & French V ♥ ✻ S% Lunch fr£6.50&alc Dinner
fr£10.95&alc Last dinner 9.30pm
Credit Cards 1 2 3 5

**★★59% Monksdene Hotel** 2-12 Northwick Park Rd HA1 2NT
☎081-427 2899 Telex no 919171 FAX 081-863 2314
Closed 25-31 Dec
*This busy comercial hotel has been recently refurbished, and*
*provides compact, but well equipped bedrooms. Attentive staff offer*
*friendly, efficient service, and the hotel is well managed. The*
*restaurant has a table d'hôte and an à la carte menu, and the*
*dishes are nicely prepared.*
66⇊⋔ Annexe24⇊(3fb) CTV in all bedrooms ® T
✻ (ex guide dogs) ✻ sB&B⇊⋔£58-£63 dB&B⇊⋔£75-£78 ➡
( CTV 65P
♥ English & French V ♥ ⌁ Lunch £14.95&alc Dinner
£14.95&alc Last dinner 9.45pm
Credit Cards 1 2 3 5

## HARTINGTON Derbyshire Map 07 SK16

★55% **Charles Cotton** SK17 0AL ☎(029884)229
*Situated in the centre of this popular Peak District village, the old, stone-built inn provides simple but adequate accommodation. It is named after the famous 17th-century angler and author, who lived locally.*
11rm(3fb) CTV in all bedrooms ®
CTV 50P ❄ ✔
♀ English & French **V** ⊕ Ⲗ Last high tea 6pm
Credit Cards ① ③

## HARTLAND Devon Map 02 SS22

★50% **Hartland Quay** EX39 6DU ☎(02374)41218
Closed Nov-mid Mar RS mid Mar-29 Mar
*Standing beside the old harbour, the hotel was converted from the harbour master's cottage and stores.*
16rm(7⇦1🌂)(2fb) ® S% sB&B£14.50-£16.50
sB&B⇦🌂£16-£18 dB&B£29-£33 dB&B⇦🌂£32-£36
CTV 100P ⟿
⊕ Ⲗ S% Bar Lunch £1.50-£9alc Dinner £7-£9&alc Last dinner 8pm
Credit Cards ① ③

## HARTLEBURY Hereford & Worcester Map 07 SO87

〇**Travelodge** A449 Shorthill Nurseries(Trusthouse Forte)
☎Central reservations (0800) 850950
32⇦

## HARTLEPOOL Cleveland Map 08 NZ53

★★★55% **Marine** 5/7 The Front, Seaton Carew TS25 1BS
☎(0429)266244
*Recently modernised and extended to a good standard, this hotel stands in the Seaton Carew area of the town, overlooking the sands. Bedrooms have all been thoughtfully equipped and decorated. The large lounge bar is popular with all age groups, and a pretty carvery restaurant offers good value.*
25⇦🌂(3fb)3🛏🗲in 3 bedrooms CTV in all bedrooms ® T
🐾 (ex guide dogs) ✳ sB&B⇦🌂£40-£50 dB&B⇦🌂£50-£60 🏱
《 ⊞ 60P
**V** ⊕ Ⲗ 🗲 Lunch £6.50 Dinner £6.50-£9.50 Last dinner 9.30pm
Credit Cards ① ② ③ ⑤

★★69% **Ryedale Moor** 3 Beaconsfield St, Headland TS24 0NX
☎(0429)231436 & 264224 FAX (0429) 863787
11⇦🌂(2fb)🗲in 5 bedrooms CTV in all bedrooms ® T 🐾
《 ⊞ CTV 7P 🚗 nc12yrs
♀ French & Indian **V** ⊕ Ⲗ 🗲
Credit Cards ① ② ③ ⑤
See advertisement on page 333

✗**Krimo's** 8 The Front, Seaton Carew TS25 1BS (2m S A178)
☎(0429)266120
*A modest yet delightful little restaurant on the seafront providing extremely good value for money, particularly business lunches. The emphasis is on good produce, with classic-style dishes prepared in the light modern style. Service is friendly and informal.*
Closed Sun, Mon, & 1st 2 wks Aug
Lunch not served Sat
♀ Algerian, French & Italian **V** 26 seats Lunch £4.50-£7
Dinner £14-£18alc Last lunch 1.30pm Last dinner 9.30pm
🍷 nc8yrs
Credit Cards ① ③

# Harrow Hotel

**12-22 Pinner Road, Harrow, Middlesex HA1 4HZ**
**Tel: 01-427 3435**
**Telex: 917898 HARTEL G    Fax: 01-861 1370**

Our professionally run Harrow Hotel, where every person is treated as a welcome guest, is the natural choice for the discerning business executive and the well-travelled tourist who require very high standards of accommodation and food at a reasonable cost.

All our bedrooms have private facilities and full amenities.

For dining and entertaining we offer exclusive menus and excellent service.

## 🦢 THE FERN HOTEL ⚡⚡

**SWAN ROAD, HARROGATE, HG1 2SS**

Situated on a beautiful tree lined road this grade II listed building epitomises the charm and elegance of the regency period, owned and operated by the Fern family.

29 bedrooms all en-suite ● Direct dial telephone Colour television ● Coffee and tea making facilities Spacious friendly bar ● 2 mins. walk from Conference Centre. 5 mins. from town Centre.

Set in the elegant style that benefits this lovely regency building. The Portico Restaurant offers full à la carte and haute cuisine menus carefully prepared for you by Chef and presented for your enjoyment by maître d'Hôtel.

FOR RESERVATIONS:
TEL: (0423) 523866 TELEX: 57583

**HARVINGTON (near Evesham)** Hereford & Worcester
Map **04** SP04

See also **Evesham**

★★77%, **The Mill At Harvington** Anchor Ln, Harvington
WR11 5NR ☎Evesham(0386)870688
(For full entry see Evesham)

---

**HARWICH** Essex Map **05** TM23

★★64%, *The Pier at Harwich* The Quay CO12 3HH
☎(0255)241212 Telex no 987083 FAX (0206) 322752
*Standing on the quay, with splendid views over the estuary, an
establishment which has long been renowned for its fish restaurant
now offers six quality bedrooms.*
6⇲🛏CTV in all bedrooms ® ✲ (ex guide dogs)
⟮ 10P ♫
♀ English & French **V** Last dinner 9.30pm
Credit Cards [1] [2] [3] [5]

★★59%, **Tower** Mai Rd, Dovercourt CO12 3PJ ☎(0255)504952
RS 25 & 26 Dec
*In this recently converted Victorian building modern bedrooms are
complemented by friendly service.*
15⇲🛏(2fb) CTV in all bedrooms ® **T** ✲ sB&B⇲🛏£37-£45
dB&B⇲🛏£49-£55 🍴
⟮ 50P 1🚗 ⛟
**V** ♦ ♨ Lunch fr£8.50 Dinner £10-£20alc Last dinner 10pm
Credit Cards [1] [2] [3] [5] [£]

★★53%, **Cliff** Marine Pde, Dovercourt CO12 3RD
☎(0255)503345 Telex no 98372
*This informal sea-front hotel improves each year and bedrooms are
now equipped with modern facilities. The restaurant offers a choice
of menu and the main bar is popular with the locals. Staff are
friendly and helpful.*
28⇲🛏 CTV in all bedrooms ® **T** sB&B⇲🛏£43
dB&B⇲🛏£53 🍴
⟮ 60P
**V** ♦ ♨ Lunch £8-£16&alc Dinner fr£9.50 Last dinner 9pm
Credit Cards [1] [2] [3] [4] [5]

---

**HASLEMERE** Surrey Map **04** SU93

Telephone numbers are due to change during the currency of
this guide.

★★★67%, **Lythe Hill** Petworth Rd GU27 3BQ (1.25m E B2131)
☎(0428)51251 due to change to 651251 Telex no 858402
FAX (0428) 4131 due to change to 644131
*Nestled among the Surrey hills and once an ancient hamlet, this
charming hotel preserves some marvellous Tudor architecture;
modern wings have been added, but they are sympathetically
blended in with the original farmhouse. Most of the main building's
spacious, modern and comfortable rooms offer attractive views over
surrounding countryside, whilst the separate Auberge de France
provides six delightful period rooms as well as an additional
restaurant. Good service is rendered by pleasant, helpful staff
throughout the hotel.*
40⇲🛏(8fb) 🛁 CTV in all bedrooms ® **T** ✲ sB⇲🛏£74-£150
dB⇲🛏£85-£150 (room only) 🍴
⟮ 200P ❖ CFA ♪ (hard) ♪ boules croquet pitch & putt *xmas*
♀ English & French **V** ♦ ♨ Lunch £16&alc Dinner £16&alc
Last dinner 9.15pm
Credit Cards [1] [2] [3]

❋✕✕**Morels** 23/27 Lower St GU27 2NY ☎(0428)51462
*Chef/patron, Jean-Yves Morel and his wife Mary Anne have built
up an enviable reputation for consistently high standards at this
delightful restaurant. The table d'hôte and à la carte menus
feature many long-standing favourites, such as Cassoulette de pied
de porc et lentilles aux St-Jacques (diced pigs trotters and lentils
surrounded by fresh scallops), Coussin froid d'oeufs brouillés aux
langoustines (cold scrambled eggs filled with fresh langoustines),
Blini pancakes with smoked salmon, yoghourt and Danish caviar,*

*Poitrine de canard de Gressingham, confit de chataignes (crisp
breast of Gressingham duck with a confit of chestnuts and a red
wine fumet). For variety, if this were not enough, a daily fish
special is offered. One of our Inspectors particularly enjoyed a
méli-mélo of Dover sole with lobster sauce accompanied by a
strudel of wild mushrooms aux pétales d'aux. There is a fine wine
list, featuring a selection of dessert wines to accompany the
separate pudding menu.*
Closed Sun, Mon, 2 wks Feb, 2 wks Sep & BH's (ex Good Fri)
Lunch not served Sat
♀ French **V** 48 seats ✲ Lunch fr£16&alc Dinner fr£19&alc
Last lunch 1.45pm Last dinner 10pm ⚲
Credit Cards [1] [2] [3] [5]

✕**Shrimpton's of Kingsley Green** 2 Grove Cottages, Midhurst
Rd, Kingsley Green GU27 3LF ☎Haslemere(0428)3539
*Located on the A286 Haslemere-Midhurst road, this delightful
17th-century beamed cottage offers fresh food and quality wines in
a romantic setting. Chef John Holman's style of cooking has an
oriental influence, with generous use of spices, soy and good
marination.*
Closed Sun, 26 Dec, 1 Jan & BHs
Lunch not served Sat
♀ English & French **V** 42 seats Lunch £13.75&alc Dinner
£18.50&alc Last lunch 1.45pm Last dinner 9.45pm 4P nc3yrs
Credit Cards [1] [2] [3] [5]

---

**HASTINGS & ST LEONARDS** East Sussex Map **05** TQ80

★★★73%, **Beauport Park** Battle Rd TN38 8EA (3m N off
A2100) (Best Western) ☎Hastings(0424)851222
Telex no 957126 FAX (0424) 852465
*A charming Georgian country house situated in thirty-three acres
of picturesque grounds and woodlands overlooks the formal Italian
sunken gardens from both restaurant and cocktail bar; the elegant
lounge with its log fire offers a relaxed and friendly ambience,
while all the tastefully furnished and decorated bedrooms are
equipped with modern facilities.*
23⇲🛏(2fb)1🛁 CTV in all bedrooms ® ✲ sB&B⇲🛏fr£50
dB&B⇲🛏fr£68 🍴
60P 4🚗 (£1.50) ❖ ☆(heated) ⚑ 18 ♪ (hard) squash ∪
snooker putting croquet *xmas*
♀ French **V** ♦ ♨ Lunch fr£12&alc High tea fr£8 Dinner fr£14
Last dinner 9.30pm
Credit Cards [1] [2] [3] [5]

See advertisement on page 335

❋✕**Roser's** 64 Eversfield Place TN37 6DB
☎Hastings(0424)712218
*Look carefully for this delightful, unobtrusive seafront restaurant
where the food is reliable and the service cheerful and friendly. Its
chef-patron offers a creative selection of dishes, particularly
notable for their use of fresh seafood. Start your meal with mussels
in a saffron sauce served with a julienne of vegetables, and follow
this with lamb in a red wine and tarragon sauce, leaving room for a
delectable pudding which will be well worth every ounce you gain.*
Closed Sun, Mon & 1st 2 wks Jan
Lunch not served Sat
♀ French 40 seats Lunch fr£14.95&alc Last lunch 2pm Last
dinner 10.30pm ⚲
Credit Cards [1] [2] [3] [5]

---

**HATFIELD** Hertfordshire Map **04** TL20

★★★65%, **Hazel Grove** Roehyde Way AL10 9AF
☎(0707)275701 Telex no 916580 FAX (0707) 266033
*This hotel is purpose built, and is conveniently situated just off the
A1. The building has been skilfully extended to include a number
of executive bedrooms and open plan suites. The two teir Gallery
Restaurant features a la carte and table d'hôte menus, with
friendly and well managed service. Extensive conference facilities
are available, with good syndicate rooms. There is also excellent
car parking.*

▶

# netherfield place
★ ★ ★

This Georgian style country house hotel lies at the heart of one of the most beautiful and unspoilt areas of England.

Each of the 14 bedrooms has a private bathroom, colour TV, radio and direct dialling telephone.

Standing in 30 acres Netherfield Place is a haven for those who enjoy peace and tranquility in a grand setting; with two hard tennis courts, putting green and croquet lawn within the grounds.

Conference and Banqueting information on request.

*Helen and Michael Collier*
*Netherfield Place, Battle, East Sussex.*
*Tel: Battle (04246) 4455 Telex: 95284*

# THE RYEDALE MOOR HOTEL
★ ★

Provides charm and elegance with luxurious surroundings. The business is family run and has glorious views over Hartlepool's beautiful esplanade and yet is within easy reach of the town centre, harbour and beach

The Hotel provides
CONFERENCE FACILITIES
for business and boasts
ONE OF THE BEST
RESTAURANTS in the area

This can be enjoyed by non residents but advance booking is essential

**TEL: 0429 231436**

3 Beaconsfield Street,
Headlands, HARTLEPOOL

H

# Lythe Hill Hotel & Restaurants
★ ★ ★

*A hamlet in the foothills of Surrey.*

*Luxury and character in a country hotel. Clustered on its own slope in the beautiful and peaceful Surrey hills is the ancient hamlet of Lythe Hill. The original 14th-century farmhouse has period bedrooms, one with a four-poster and L'Auberge de France renowned as one of the finest restaurants in the South — superb classic French cuisine in luxurious surroundings, cocktail bar and terrace overlooking parkland gardens and lake.*

*Across the courtyard in sympathetically converted farm buildings is the main hotel with 32 luxurious rooms and family suites, an English restaurant, bar and Italian Garden, tennis, croquet, sauna within the grounds.*

*Ideal touring centre for unspoilt local villages, antique hunting, stately houses, golf courses, traditional country pubs, scenic walks — the perfect country retreat.*

**Lythe Hill** Hotel & Restaurants
PETWORTH ROAD, HASLEMERE, SURREY GU27 3BQ
Tel: Haslemere (0428) 651251

333

76⇨(14fb)⚥in 38 bedrooms CTV in all bedrooms ⓇTﾟ*
sB&B⇨£60-£80 dB&B⇨£70-£80
℄ 120P gymnasium
V ✿ ⚓ Sunday Lunch fr£9 Dinner fr£15&alc Last dinner
9.30pm
Credit Cards ①②③⑤

★★★57% **Comet** 301 St Albans Rd West AL10 9RH (junc A1/
A414) (Embassy) ☎(0707)265411 FAX (0707) 264019
RS Xmas
*Named after the De Haviland Comet, a model of which stands in
the forecourt, the hotel provides accommodation in bedrooms
which are, for the most part, spacious ; its popular carvery
restaurant also features some more adventurous dishes.*
57rm(52⇨2♠)(3fb)⚥in 12 bedrooms CTV in all bedrooms Ⓡ
Tﾟ* sB£26-£39 sB⇨♠£29-£62.50
dB⇨♠£40-£82.50 (room only) 🅟
℄ 150P ✿
♀ English & French V ✿ ⚓ ⚥ Lunch fr£10.95&alc Dinner
fr£10.95&alc Last dinner 9.55pm
Credit Cards ①②③⑤

✗✗✗**Salisbury** 15 The Broadway, Old Hatfield AL9 5JB
☎(0707)262220 & 267957
*An elegant and spacious restaurant with a large lounge bar where
aperitifs may be enjoyed whilst selecting from the imaginative à la
carte and good-value table d'hôte menus. Staff are courteous and
efficient.*
Closed Mon & 26 Dec for 2 wks
Lunch not served Sat
Dinner not served Sun
V 60 seats Lunch £15 Dinner £25 Last lunch 2pm Last dinner
9.30pm 16P
Credit Cards ①②③⑤

---

**HATHERSAGE** Derbyshire Map **08** SK28

★★★64% **George** Main Rd S30 1BB (Lansbury)
☎Hope Valley(0433)50436 Telex no 547196
FAX (0433) 50099
*A 16th-century coaching inn has been restored and modernised to
provide a well e quipped hotel with spacious bedrooms, attractive
restaurant, lounge bar and separate private bar.*
18⇨♠(3fb)1🏠⚥in 5 bedrooms CTV in all bedrooms ⓇT
✗ (ex guide dogs) sB&B⇨♠fr£64 dB&B⇨♠fr£78 🅟
40P ✿ xmas
♀ International V ✿ ⚥ Lunch fr£8.25&alc Dinner
fr£14.25&alc Last dinner 10pm
Credit Cards ①②③⑤

★★64% **Hathersage Inn** Main St S30 1BB (Best Western)
☎Hope Valley(0433)50259 FAX (0433) 51199
*Situated in the centre of the village, this charming old inn offers
attractive accommodation, the new bedrooms in the adjacent
Morley House being particularly comfortable.*
11⇨♠Annexe4rm1🏠 CTV in all bedrooms ⓇTﾟ*
sB&B⇨♠£45-£50 dB&B⇨♠£60-£70 🅟
20P xmas
V ✿ ⚓ ⚥ Sunday Lunch £7.95 Dinner £12.50 Last dinner
9.30pm
Credit Cards ①②③⑤ⓔ

---

**HAVANT** Hampshire Map **04** SU70

★★★60% **The Bear** East St PO9 1AA (Lansbury)
☎(0705)486501 Telex no 869136 FAX (0705) 470551
*This sixteenth-century coaching inn, used for Divisional Petty
Sessions before the Court House was built, offers upgraded
bedroom accommodation which is provided with trouser presses
and hairdriers, a character beamed bar, a Henekey's Restaurant
which serves grills plus a range of more imaginative dishes at both
lunch and dinner time, and good parking at the rear of the hotel.*

42⇨(3fb)1🏠⚥in 5 bedrooms CTV in all bedrooms Ⓡ
✗ (ex guide dogs) sB&B⇨fr£72 dB&B⇨fr£85 🅟
Lift ℄ 90P xmas
♀ European V ✿ ⚓ Lunch fr£11&alc Dinner fr£11&alc Last
dinner 10.30pm
Credit Cards ①②③⑤

---

**HAVERFORDWEST** Dyfed Map **02** SM91

★★59% **Hotel Mariners** Mariners Square SA61 2DU
☎(0437)763353 FAX (0437) 764258
Closed 26-27 Dec & 1 Jan
*This historic hotel, parts of which date back to 1625, now provides
accommodation which is popular with both commercial clients and
with tourists, for whom it provides an ideal base from which to
explore the old county of Pembrokeshire. Public areas are cosy
and welcoming, food is good, and friendly staff offer helpful
service.*
32rm(26⇨♠)(5fb) CTV in all bedrooms ⓇT
sB&B⇨♠£39-£45 dB&B⇨♠£60-£74 🅟
℄ 40P
♀ French V ✿ ⚓ Sunday Lunch fr£7 Dinner £10-£12&alc Last
dinner 9.30pm
Credit Cards ①②③⑤

★★57% **Pembroke House** Spring Gardens SA61 2EJ
☎(0437)763652
*A Georgian, house, attractively covered in Virginia Creeper and
situated only a short walk from the town centre, provides a popular
gathering place for the business fraternity in its comfortably
furnished bar ; cosy bedrooms are well equipped and good food is
available.*
21rm(13⇨6♠)(4fb)1🏠 CTV in all bedrooms ⓇT sB&B£30
sB&B⇨♠£35 dB&B£50 dB&B⇨♠£55 🅟
CTV 18P
✿ ⚓ Dinner £10.50&alc Last dinner 9.30pm
Credit Cards ①②③⑤

---

**HAWES** North Yorkshire Map **07** SD88

★★76% **Simonstone Hall** Simonstone DL8 3LY ☎(0969)667255
FAX (0969) 667741
*The former home of the Earls of Wharncliffe, built in 1733, is now
a comfortable and elegant hotel run by John and Sheila Jeffryes. A
fine, relaxed atmosphere prevails and service is provided by
friendly young staff.*
10⇨♠1🏠 CTV in all bedrooms Ⓡ dB&B⇨♠£90-£115 🅟
24P ♿ ✿ potholing hang gliding xmas
♀ English & French V ✿ ⚓ Lunch fr£9.75 Dinner
fr£18.50&alc Last dinner 8.30pm
Credit Cards ①③ⓔ

★★74% *Rookhurst Georgian Country House* Gayle DL8 3RT
☎Wensleydale(0969)667454
Closed 16 Dec-Jan
*Ins and Joe Van der Steen provide a wonderful welcome for their
guests at this small intimate hotel. Bedrooms are full of character,
with four poster and half tester beds ; some rooms have beautifully
preserved Victorian baths. Home cooking is of the highest
standard and the best use is made of fresh local produce.*
6rm(3⇨1♠)2🏠⚥in all bedrooms CTV in all bedrooms Ⓡ
✗ (ex guide dogs)
10P ♿ nc
✿ ⚓ ⚥ Last dinner 7.30pm

★★‡69% **Stone House** Sedbusk DL8 3PT
☎Wensleydale(0969)667571 FAX (0969) 667720
Closed Jan RS mid Nov-Dec & Feb-mid Mar
*Dating back to the turn of the century, this country house has been
carefully modernised to preserve the good features and
atmosphere. Managed by the resident proprietors, the service is
very courteous. Dinner is especially recommended.*

15rm(14⇄↑↑)(1fb)2🛏 CTV in all bedrooms Ⓡ T sB&B£25
sB&B⇄↑↑£25 dB&B£40 dB&B⇄↑↑£50-£60 🍴
15P ❀ ♬ (grass) *xmas*
V ✿ ⚓ Dinner £12.95 Last dinner 8pm
Credit Cards 1 3
★★62% **Fountain** Market Place DL8 3RD ☎(0969)667206
*Modernised town centre hotel, family owned and run.*
13⇄↑↑(2fb) CTV in all bedrooms Ⓡ T sB&B⇄↑↑fr£28
dB&B⇄↑↑fr£46
10P *xmas*
✿
Credit Cards 1 3 ₤
**See advertisement on page 337**
★70% **Herriots** Main St DL8 3QU ☎(0969)667536
Closed Nov-Jan RS Feb-mid Mar
*Courteous resident proprietors manage this small, friendly hotel,*
*ensuring that its restaurant offers excellent value for money.*
6↑↑(1fb) CTV in all bedrooms Ⓡ ✖ sB&B↑↑£28
dB&B↑↑£38-£42 🍴
♬ *xmas*
♘ International V ✿ Lunch £6.95-£7.45alc Dinner
£10.35-£12.85alc Last dinner 9.30pm
Credit Cards 1 3

**HAWICK** Borders *Roxburghshire* Map **12** NT51
★★69% **Kirklands** West Stewart Place TD9 8BH (Exec Hotel)
☎(0450)72263
*Small well-appointed hotel with attractive dining room and*
*thoughtfully equipped bedrooms.*
6rm(2⇄1↑↑)Annexe7⇄↑↑ CTV in all bedrooms Ⓡ T ✳
sB&B£32-£36 sB&B⇄↑↑£33-£36 dB&B£50 dB&B⇄↑↑£55 🍴 ▶

Architecturally unique, the Comet Hotel was
built to honour the local aircraft industry.
Today with a friendly atmosphere and
comfortable surroundings, the Comet is well
patronised by holiday makers and business
people who appreciate the good value and
high standards of service in which the Comet
staff take pride.
The 54 bedrooms each have private
bathrooms and there is parking for 150 cars.
**Comet Hotel,**
**301 St, Albans Road West, Hatfield,**
**Herts AL10 9RH. Tel: 070 7265411**

**Embassy⊡Hotels** ★★★

**H**

## PEMBROKE HOUSE HOTEL ★★ & RESTAURANT

### Spring Gardens
### Haverfordwest, Pembrokeshire
### Tel: (0437) 763652

21 bedrooms, 19 en suite, all rooms with
TV, tea and coffee and direct dialling. Car
park. Night porter. Intimate restaurant
serving à la carte and table d'hôte. Bed &
breakfast from £30.00.
Bed & breakfast
double from
£50.00.
Visa
Access
Amex
Diners
Club

## The Beauport Park Hotel
### Hastings, Sussex TN38 8EA ★★★
### Telephone: 0424 851222

A Georgian country house hotel set in 33 acres
of parkland with its own swimming pool,
tennis courts, putting green, croquet lawn and
country walks. Candle-lit restaurant and open
log fires. Adjacent to an 18 hole golf course,
riding stables and squash courts.

**Resident proprietors:**
**Kenneth and Helena Melsom**

**Special country house bargain breaks available**
**all year. Please send for our colour brochure**
**and tariff.**

**Telex: 957126.**          **Fax: 0424 851465**

20P ✿ snooker games room
♀ International **V** ✿
Credit Cards ①②③⑤ⓔ

**✕The Old Forge** Newmill-on-Teviot TD9 0JU (3m SW A7)
☎Teviotdale(04585)298
*This delightful restaurant, run by Mr and Mrs Irving, is housed in what used to be the village smithy, hence the name. Cooking is of Cordon Bleu standard and offers good value for money.*
Closed Sun, Mon, first 2 wks May & first 2 wks Nov
Lunch not served
♀ International **V** 28 seats S% Dinner £11.50-£13.50 Last dinner 9.30pm 10P
Credit Cards ①③

---

**HAWKCHURCH** Devon Map **03** ST30

**★★★⚏71% Fairwater Head** EX13 5TX ☎(02977)349
Closed Jan RS Dec
*Commanding panoramic views of the countryside from its setting in beautiful gardens above the Axe Valley, an elegant hotel dating from the turn of the century offers warm, comfortable bedrooms complemented by public areas with a peaceful, relaxed atmosphere. The restaurant provides both table d'hôte and à la carte dinner menus, and special diets can be catered for. Resident proprietors offer a warm welcome to guests and take a personal interest in their well-being.*
14➪♠Annexe7➪♠ CTV in all bedrooms ® T
sB&B➪♠£61-£64.50 dB&B➪♠£108-£113 (incl dinner) ⊟
30P ⚗ ✿ croquet ♫ ♨
✿ ⚖ ✄ Sunday Lunch £9.50 High tea £3-£7 Dinner £16.50-£18 Last dinner 8.30pm
Credit Cards ①②③⑤
**See advertisement under LYME REGIS**

---

**HAWKHURST** Kent Map **05** TQ73

**★★68% Tudor Court** Rye Rd TN18 5DA (Best Western)
☎(0580)752312 Telex no 957565 FAX (0580) 753966
*A pleasant, welcoming atmosphere pervades this charming hotel with its large, cheerful Garden Restaurant and extended bar.*
18➪♠(1fb)2⚗ CTV in all bedrooms ® T S10%
sB&B➪♠fr£52 dB&B➪♠£82-£87 ⊟
CTV 50P 2🚗 (£1.50) ✿ ♪ (hard) croquet clock golf *xmas*
♀ International ✿ ⚖ ✄ S10% Lunch fr£11&alc Dinner fr£12.50&alc Last dinner 9.15pm
Credit Cards ①②③⑤

---

**HAWKSHEAD (near Ambleside)** Cumbria Map **07** SD39

**★★★⚏56% Tarn Hows** Hawkshead Hill LA22 0PR
☎Hawkshead(09666)330 FAX (09666) 294
*Situated at Tarn Hows on an unclassified road between Ambleside and Hawkshead, this comfortable hotel offers the ultimate in peace and tranquility. Guests will find service friendly and attentive.*
15➪♠(2fb)2⚗ CTV in all bedrooms ® S% sB&B➪♠£35-£40 dB&B➪♠£70-£80 ⊟
CTV 40P ✿ ⚖(heated) ♪ sauna solarium *xmas*
V ✿ ⚖ ✄ S% Lunch fr£8.50 High tea fr£5 Dinner fr£16.50&alc Last dinner 8.45pm
Credit Cards ①②③⑤

**★★⚏75% Field Head House** Outgate LA22 0PY
☎Hawkshead(09666)240
Closed 14 Jan-8 Feb RS Tue
*Bob and Eeke Van Gulik run this small hotel single handed, with love, dedication and enthusiasm. Bob is responsible for the excellent 5-course dinners and although there is no choice until pudding, the emphasis is on quality and presentation. Eeke's cheery personality ensures a convivial atmosphere in this former shooting lodge, peacefully set in mature grounds.*

---

7➪♠(2fb)✄in all bedrooms CTV in all bedrooms ® S%
dB&B➪♠£95-£115 (incl dinner) ⊟
15P ⚗ ✿ Croquet *xmas*
✄ S% Dinner fr£18

**★★63% Queen's Head** Main St LA22 0NS
☎Hawkshead(09666)271
*An historic inn right at the centre of the village, popular for both its bar meals and its à la carte dinners, offers accommodation in bedrooms with some attractive touches.*
10rm(1➪5♠)Annexe2➪(3fb)✄in 1 bedroom CTV in 10 bedrooms ® T ⛧ sB&B£23.50 sB&B➪♠£23.50-£30 dB&B£36-£39 dB&B➪♠£43-£46 ⊟
CTV 10P nc8 yrs *xmas*
♀ English & Continental **V** ✿ Lunch £8.50 Dinner £12-£17alc Last dinner 9.30pm
Credit Cards ①②③

**★⚏73% Highfield House** Hawkshead Hill LA22 0PN
☎Hawkshead(09666)344
Closed 24-26 Dec
*Sitting in its own grounds, three quarters of a mile from the village, this country house enjoys magnificent panoramic Lakeland views. Some of the comfortable bedrooms are extremely spacious, there is a relaxing lounge and the inventive country cooking offers excellent value for money.*
11rm(8➪♠)(2fb) CTV in all bedrooms ® sB&B£19-£21 sB&B➪♠£25-£27 dB&B£36-£40 dB&B➪♠£43-£56 ⊟
12P ⚗ ✿
♀ English & Continental **V** ✿ ⚖ ✄ Bar Lunch £3-£5alc Dinner £12 Last dinner 8pm
Credit Cards ③

---

**HAWNBY** North Yorkshire Map **08** SE58

**★★70% Hawnby** YO6 5QS ☎Bilsdale(04396)202
*This extremely comfortable little hotel is situated in the unspoilt and picturesque village of Hawnby, in the North Yorkshire Moors National Park. Bought by the family of the Earl of Mexborough, the hotel is personally supervised by Lady Mexborough, who has recently totally refurbished the hotel, using pretty Laura Ashley fabrics and furniture. The 6 attractive bedrooms are all very well equipped, individually decorated and all are fully en suite. The high standards are carried right through the hotel, and there is a cosy lounge, adjoining the dining room where traditional English food is freshly prepared and served. There is also a full range of bar snacks available in the character public bar. A warm welcome for guests is assured at this relaxing, comfortable and quality hotel.*
6➪♠ CTV in all bedrooms ® T ⛧ ✳ sB&B➪♠£40 dB&B➪♠£60 ⊟
25P ✿ ♪ (hard) ♪ nc8yrs
V ✿ ⚖ Lunch fr£4.95 Dinner £10.50 Last dinner 8.30pm
Credit Cards ①③

---

**HAWORTH** West Yorkshire Map **07** SE03

**★★★58% Five Flags** Manywells Heights BD13 5EA (near junc A629/B6429) (Consort) ☎Bradford(0274)834188 & 834594 FAX (0274) 833340
*A stone building set in a moorland location yet close enough to Halifax, Keighley and Bradford. Two styles of dining are provided and bedrooms are spacious and well furnished.*
26➪♠(4fb) CTV in all bedrooms ® T ⛧
⚓ CTV 100P ✿
♀ French, Greek & Italian **V** ✿ ✄ Last dinner 11pm
Credit Cards ①②③⑤ⓔ

A rosette is an indication of exceptional standards of cuisine.

★★71% **The Rydings Country** Bridgehouse Ln BD22 8QE
☎(0535)45206 & 46933 FAX (0535) 46997
*Bill and Lesley Jackson have carefully furnished the hotel in a*
*light modern style, incorporating the traditional warmth of pine.*
*Bedrooms are exceptionally well equipped and prettily decorated*
*and the food is imaginative, wholesome and home cooked. Located*
*near the centre of town, the hotel has good parking facilities.*
10⇨ゐ♠(2fb) CTV in all bedrooms ® T ✘ (ex guide dogs) ✳
sB&B⇨ゐ♠£22-£32 dB&B⇨ゐ♠£36-£42 ⊟
《 CTV 20P *xmas*
♡ English, French & Italian V ✿ ⵎ Lunch £5.95-£6.95alc
Dinner £6.95-£9.95&alc Last dinner 10pm
Credit Cards ①②③⑤

★★64% **Old White Lion** 6 West Ln BD22 8DU ☎(0535)42313
*Stone-built coaching inn standing at the top of the main road.*
14⇨ゐ♠(2fb) CTV in all bedrooms ® T ✘ (ex guide dogs)
sB&B⇨ゐ♠£29.50 dB&B⇨ゐ♠£42.50 ⊟
CTV 10P 2🐾 *xmas*
♡ English & French V ✿ Lunch £5.05-£7.50 Dinner
£8-£8.50&alc Last dinner 9.30pm
Credit Cards ①②③⑤
See advertisement under KEIGHLEY, page 367

✕ **Weavers** 15 West Ln BD22 8DU ☎(0535)43822
*An attractive and comfortable little restaurant set in a row of*
*former weavers' cottages. The menu features a good range of*
*interesting home cooked meals such as sea food bake, beef pie and*
*sticky pudding. Service is friendly.*
Closed Mon, 2 wks Xmas & 2 wks Jun/July
Lunch not served Tue-Sat & Sun (Etr-Oct)
Dinner not served Sun
V 45 seats Sunday Lunch £9.50-£10.50 Dinner
£9.50-£10.50&alc Last dinner 9pm ⌿ ⼬
Credit Cards ①②③

**H**

## HAYDOCK Merseyside Map 07 SJ59

★★★★65% **Haydock Thistle** Penny Ln WA11 9SG (Mount Charlotte (TS)) ☎Ashton-in-Makerfield(0942)272000 Telex no 67034 FAX (0942) 711092
*This elegant hotel, with an attractive Georgian-style façade and formal courtyard gardens, is situated just off junction 23 of the M6 motorway, close to Haydock Park Racecourse. Bedrooms are spacious and particularly well equipped, and the elegant appearance of the hotel extends to the lounges, bar and restaurant.*
139⇋(13fb)⊁in 30 bedrooms CTV in all bedrooms ® T ✳ S%
sB⇋£65-£80 dB⇋£80-£95 (room only) ⊟
《 180P ✿ ⊠(heated) sauna solarium gymnasium pool table steam room whirlpool *xmas*
♀ English & Continental V ⊹ ⚏ S% Lunch £7-£12.50&alc Dinner £14&alc Last dinner 10pm
Credit Cards ① ② ③ ④ ⑤

★★★66% **Post House** Lodge Ln, Newton-Le-Willows WA12 0JG (adj to M6 junct 23) (Trusthouse Forte)
☎Wigan(0942)717878 Telex no 677672 FAX (0942) 718419
*Conveniently situated close to junction 23 of the M6, this purpose built hotel has recently been enlarged to provide more spacious and comfortable public areas and a wing of superior bedrooms. The hotel also possesses a modern keep-fit complex, including a pleasant swimming pool.*
142⇋in 21 bedrooms CTV in all bedrooms ® ✳
sB⇋£67-£77 dB⇋£77-£87 (room only) ⊟
《 197P ✿ CFA ⊠(heated) sauna solarium gymnasium *xmas*
♀ International V ⊹ ⚏ ⊁ Sunday Lunch £8.95 Dinner fr£10.50&alc Last dinner 10.30pm
Credit Cards ① ② ③ ④ ⑤

○**Travelodge** A580 Piele Rd WA11 9TL (Trusthouse Forte)
☎Central reservations (0800) 850950
40⇋

## HAYDON BRIDGE Northumberland Map 12 NY86

★★60% **Anchor** John Martin St NE47 6AB (Exec Hotel)
☎(0434)684227
*Bedrooms vary in size at this former inn, which sits on the south side of the River Tyne, close to the old bridge.*
12rm(10⋔)(1fb) CTV in all bedrooms ® T sB&Bfr£26
sB&B⋔fr£33 dB&Bfr£42 dB&B⋔fr£48 ⊟
25P ♪
♀ English & French V ⊹ Bar Lunch £4-£6alc Dinner £13-£15alc Last dinner 8.30pm
Credit Cards ① ② ③ ⑤ ⓔ

✕**General Havelock Inn** Ratcliffe Rd NE47 6ER ☎(0434)684376
Closed Mon, Tue, 2 wks Jan & last wk Aug-1st wk Sep
Dinner not served Sun
♀ English & French V 28 seats Lunch £6-£9alc Dinner £15-£18 Last lunch 1.30pm Last dinner 9pm 12P

## HAYLE Cornwall & Isles of Scilly Map 02 SW53

★★57% **Hillside** Angarrack TR27 5HZ (1m E of Hayle on unclass rd off A30) ☎(0736)752180
Closed 23-31 Dec & wknds Nov-31 Mar
*Set in a small village a short distance from Hayle and surrounded by a walled garden, an hotel of which parts date back to the sixteenth century is personally run to provide a homely atmosphere and a limited choice of home cooking.*
10rm(1⇋4⋔)(3fb) ✖ (ex guide dogs) sB&B£22.50-£24
sB&B⇋⋔£28-£30 dB&B£39-£42 dB&B⇋⋔£47-£52 ⊟
CTV 8P ⇛ ✿
V ⊹ ⚏ ⊁ Lunch £5.50-£6.95 High tea £4.50-£6.75 Dinner £9.75-£12 Last dinner 7.30pm
Credit Cards ① ③ ⓔ

## HAYLING ISLAND Hampshire Map 04 SU70

★★★61% **Post House** Northney Rd PO11 0NQ (Trusthouse Forte) ☎(0705)465011 Telex no 86620 FAX (0705) 466468
*The hotel is situated off the A3023, overlooking the estuary from the north shore of the island. Facilities include a well-run coffee shop and bar, the dignified Club House Restaurant with cocktail lounge, and a modern health and fitness club. Accommodation is in a choice of comfortable and well-equipped bedrooms.*
96⇋(6fb)⊁in 16 bedrooms CTV in all bedrooms ® ✳
sB⇋£72-£82 dB⇋£83-£93 (room only) ⊟
《 CTV 150P ✿ CFA ⊠(heated) sauna solarium gymnasium *xmas*
♀ French V ⊹ ⚏ ⊁ S% Lunch £8.95&alc Dinner £11.95&alc Last dinner 10pm
Credit Cards ① ② ③ ④ ⑤

## HAY-ON-WYE Powys Map 03 SO24

★★★66% **The Swan** Church St HR3 5DQ (Best Western)
☎(0497)821177 & 821188 FAX (0497) 821424
*This Georgian hotel has been completely modernised and refurbished with all modern facilities. The lounge is particularly elegant, and the two bars offer a choice of atmosphere. Service is professional.*
15⇋⋔Annexe4⇋⋔(1fb)⚏ CTV in all bedrooms ®
sB&B⇋⋔£35-£40 dB&B⇋⋔£50-£75 ⊟
18P ♪ *xmas*
V ⊹ ⚏ Lunch £8.50-£15&alc Dinner £10-£25alc Last dinner 9.30pm
Credit Cards ① ② ③ ⑤

★★66% **Olde Black Lion** 26 Lion St HR3 5AD ☎(0497)820841
*A village inn of charm and character, personally owned and with friendly service , the hotel has cosy, comfortable bedrooms and a nice cottage restaurant offering imaginative menus and good home cooking.*
6⋔Annexe4rm(2⇋)(2fb) CTV in all bedrooms ® T
sB&Bfr£17.50 dB&Bfr£35.50 dB&B⇋⋔fr£39.50 ⊟
CTV 20P ⇛ ♪ *xmas*
V ⊹ ⚏ Lunch £6.45 Dinner £3-£8&alc Last dinner 9pm
Credit Cards ① ③

★★64% **Kilvert Country** The Bull Ring HR3 5AG
☎(0497)821042 Telex no 35315 FAX (0497) 821004
*This town centre hotel with Jacobean origins now offers comfortable, well-equipped bedrooms and good food. The local atmosphere can be enjoyed in the cosy bar.*
11⇋⋔(1fb)⊁in 3 bedrooms CTV in all bedrooms ®
《 CTV 10P ✿ ♪
♀ International V ⊹ ⚏ ⊁ Last dinner 10pm
Credit Cards ① ② ③

## HAYTON Cumbria Map 12 NY55

★★★69% **Hayton Castle** Kennedy CA4 8QD ☎(0228)70651 FAX (0228) 70010
*Set in extensive grounds off the A69, 2.5 miles west of Brampton this listed building is in the throes of an ambitious upgrading and expansion programme, which has already improved the restaurant and added new bedrooms.*
13⇋⋔ CTV in all bedrooms ® T ✖ ✳ S10%
sB&B⇋⋔£49-£68 dB&B⇋⋔£65-£90 ⊟
《 150P ✿ ♪ snooker ⚬
V ⊹ ⚏ ⊁ Lunch £9.95 Dinner £14.95&alc Last dinner 9.30pm
Credit Cards ① ② ③ ④

Book as early as possible for busy holiday periods.

H

HAYTOR Devon Map **03** SX77

Telephone numbers are due to change during the currency of this guide.

★★★❦❦ 70% **Bel Alp House** TQ13 9XX
☎(03646)217 Due to change to (0364) 661217
Closed Dec & Jan RS Nov & Feb

*Set in an elevated position on the south-eastern edge of Dartmoor, this elegant Edwardian country mansion commands breathtaking views across the moors to Torbay and the sea beyond. Nine spacious and individually decorated bedrooms offer every comfort for holidaymaker and business traveller alike, whilst the lounges provide for complete relaxation. Dcor is simple throughout the hotel, a carefully chosen blend of soft furnishings and antiques creating an atmosphere of warmth and quality. The set 5-course evening meal, prepared from first-class local produce, offers such alternatives as Persian chicken with a tomato, almond and sultana sauce, or roast rack of Devonshire lamb with a redcurrant and green pepper sauce, perhaps followed by hot brandied peach crunch. The food is complemented by a well balanced wine list.*

9⇩🐾 CTV in all bedrooms ® T sB&B⇩🐾£66-£78
dB&B⇩🐾£108-£132
Lift 20P 🚗 ✿ snooker
♀ English & French Lunch fr£20 Dinner fr£30 Last dinner 8.30pm
Credit Cards ⃞1⃞ ⃞3⃞

★★ 68% **Rock Inn** TQ13 9XP ☎(03646)305 & 465
FAX (03646) 242

*Busy, family-run, convivial inn, with inglenook fireplaces and exposed beams. Bedrooms are well equipped, and the extensive bar and table d'hôte menus use fresh seasonal produce.*

9⇩🐾(2fb)1 ⌘✂in 2 bedrooms CTV in all bedrooms ® T
✻ (ex guide dogs) ✻ sB&B⇩🐾£38.50 dB&B£45
dB&B⇩🐾£58.50-£65 ⏸
CTV 20P 🚗 ✿ xmas

▶

**Lion Street, Hay-on-Wye, Hereford HR3 5AD
Tel. (0497) 820841**

Nestling in the heart of Hay on Wye, characterful 13th Century Coaching Inn. Atmospheric beamed bar, beautiful beamed dining room, 10 comfortable letting rooms, 8 en suite, ample private car-park, pleasant patio, garden for spring and summer. Al Fresco eating, Private Fishing on Wye, Golf and Pony Trekking by arrangement.

**Superb à la carte dinner menu. 38 choice bar menu of infinite variety. Steak menu of unmatched quality. Exciting sweet menu. Traditional Sunday lunch.**

*Contact the attentive and caring Resident owners John and Joan Collins and staff and visit this fine Inn in this quaint International Bibliography Town.*

**H**

---

## Kilvert Court Hotel
### ★ ★

**BULL RING, HAY-ON-WYE,
via HEREFORD HR3 5AG**

Enjoy a relaxing break with gourmet food in the world renowned Town of Books set in the picturesque Brecon Beacons National Park. Well appointed rooms with every amenity. Fishing, Golfing, Walking, Pony Trekking, Water Sports, etc. all conveniently nearby. Our mini breaks offer superb value. Telephone for further information. Brochures sent on request.

**Tel: 0497 821042    Fax: 0497 821004**

---

# Haytor - Heathrow Airport (London)

♀ English & French V ♥ ⚲ Bar Lunch £2-£12&alc Dinner
£16.95 Last dinner 9.30pm
Credit Cards ①②③ⓔ

**HAYWARDS HEATH** West Sussex Map **04** TQ32

★★★60%, **Birch** Lewes Rd RH17 7SF ☎(0444)451565
FAX (0444) 440109

*Originally built in 1887 as a private residence, this property combines Victorian character with modern facilities. Bedrooms are bright and well furnished and equipped for today's traveller. There is a choice of dining, in either the Pavillion restaurant, or more informal, lighter meals in the Lewes bar. Comercially styled and operated, the hotel is conveniently positioned for Gatwick Airport or the South coast.*

52➪ᴺ CTV in all bedrooms Ⓡ T ✱ S% sB&B➪ᴺ£39.50-£63
dB&B➪ᴺ£49.50-£73 ◪
⟨ 90P
♀ English & French V ♥ ⚲ S% Lunch £8.75-£10.95&alc
Dinner £13.75&alc Last dinner 10pm
Credit Cards ①②③④⑤

**HEATHROW AIRPORT (LONDON)** Greater London
Map **04** TQ07

See **Town Plan Section** under **London Airports**
See also **Ashford (Surrey), Hounslow and Staines**

★★★★64%, **The Excelsior** Bath Rd, West Drayton UB7 0DU
(adj M4 spur at junc with A4) (Trusthouse Forte)
☎081-759 6611 Telex no 24525 FAX 081-759 3421

*Stylish and extensive refurbishment has transformed this very popular hotel located close to the airport terminals. Amenities include a keep fit club, indoor swimming pool and airport courtesy transport. Function facilities are available.*

840➪ᴺ⚲in 130 bedrooms CTV in all bedrooms Ⓡ T S12%
sB➪ᴺ£100-£125 dB➪ᴺ£115-£145 (room only) ◪
Lift ⟨ ⊞ 500P (charged) CFA ◪(heated) sauna solarium
gymnasium health & fitness centre jacuzzi *xmas*
♀ English, French & Italian V ♥ ⚲ ⚲ S12% Lunch
£13.95&alc Dinner £13.95&alc Last dinner 10.45pm
Credit Cards ①②③④⑤

★★★★64%, **Heathrow Penta** Bath Rd, Hounslow TW6 2AQ
☎081-897 6363 Telex no 934660 FAX 081-897 1113

*Bedrooms are functional rather than luxurious at this airport hotel, but they are air-conditioned and double-glazed. Public areas include an impressive marbled entrance hall, two theme bars – one providing evening entertainment – and the London Chop House Restaurant featuring good set meal and à la carte menus ; the popular leisure complex and swimming pool have recently reopened after refurbishment. Room service and the coffee shop offer 24-hour service and the hotel runs a courtesy coach to and from the airport.*

635➪ᴺ⚲in 15 bedrooms CTV in all bedrooms Ⓡ T
✗ (ex guide dogs) S% sB➪ᴺ£95-£103
dB➪ᴺ£107-£116 (room only) ◪
Lift ⟨ ⊞ 600P (£2.75) CFA ◪(heated) sauna solarium
gymnasium *xmas*
♀ International V ♥ ⚲ ⚲ S% Lunch £13.20&alc Dinner
£14.25&alc Last dinner 10.30pm
Credit Cards ①②③⑤ⓔ

★★★★61%, *Holiday Inn* Stockley Rd, West Drayton UB7 9NA
(2m N junc M4/A408) (Holiday Inns Inc)
☎West Drayton(0895)445555 Telex no 934518
FAX (0895) 445122

*A modern transit/conference hotel with spacious, well-equipped bedrooms is in process of improvement which will provide more rooms for ladies and non-smokers. The Farmhouse Kitchen serves refreshments throughout the day, or you can choose a more formal meal from the comprehensive menu of the Tudor Restaurant. Good leisure facilities are available.*

396➪ᴺ(220fb)⚲in 21 bedrooms CTV in all bedrooms Ⓡ

Lift ⟨ ⊞ 400P ✿ ❀ CFA ◪(heated) ▶ 9 ♪ (hard) sauna
solarium gymnasium ⚲
♀ International V ♥ ⚲ ⚲
Credit Cards ①②③④⑤

★★★64%, *Berkeley Arms* Bath Road, Hounslow TW5 9QE
(2.5m E on A4) (Embassy) ☎081-897 2121 Telex no 935728
FAX 081-897 7014

*An additional sixteen well-equipped bedrooms have recently been added to the comfortable accommodation of this modern, purpose-built hotel. Meals are taken in a carvery-style restaurant which also features a short à la carte menu, and staff are pleasant and friendly throughout.*

56➪ᴺ CTV in all bedrooms Ⓡ
Lift ⟨ 85P ❀ ♫
♀ International V ♥ ⚲ Last dinner 9.45pm
Credit Cards ①②③⑤

★★★62%, **Post House** Sipson Road, West Drayton UB7 0JU
(2m N A408) (Trusthouse Forte) ☎081-759 2323
Telex no 934280 FAX 081-897 8659

*Conveniently situated for terminals 1, 2, and 3, this large, purpose-built hotel offers good, well-equipped accommodation ; carvery and popular restaurants are open at times to suit both transit and business clients.*

569➪ᴺ(176fb)⚲in 60 bedrooms CTV in all bedrooms Ⓡ T ✱
sB➪ᴺ£85-£100 dB➪ᴺ£95-£110 (room only) ◪
Lift ⟨ ⊞ 400P CFA
♀ English, Chinese & Italian V ♥ ⚲ ⚲
Credit Cards ①②③④⑤

★★★60%, **The Ariel** Bath Rd, Hayes UB3 5AJ (1.5m E junc A4/
A437) (Trusthouse Forte) ☎081-759 2552 Telex no 21777
FAX 081-564 9265

*A popular hotel on the A4 with quick access to the airport. The ground floor has been completely upgraded to include a new foyer, lounge, bar, carvery and fish restaurant. Service is well managed and friendly and the porterage very helpful.*

177➪ᴺ(6fb)⚲in 12 bedrooms CTV in all bedrooms Ⓡ T ✱
S% sB➪ᴺfr£90 dB➪ᴺfr£100 (room only) ◪
Lift ⟨ ⊞ 100P CFA *xmas*
V ♥ ⚲ ⚲ S% Lunch fr£13.50 Dinner fr£14.50 Last dinner
11pm
Credit Cards ①②③④⑤

★★★60%, *Master Robert* Great West Rd TW5 0BD
☎081-570 6261 Telex no 9413782 FAX 081-569 4016
(For full entry see Hounslow)

★★54%, **Hotel Ibis Heathrow** 112/114 Bath Road, Hayes
UB3 5AL ☎081-759 4888 Telex no 929014 FAX 081-564 7894

*The modern-style accommodation available at this hotel comprises inexpensive rooms which, though functional, are reasonably comfortable ; service is limited, and open-plan public areas include provision for guests to partake of light snacks as an alternative to the more normal table d'hôte and à la carte menus.*

244➪ᴺ(4fb) CTV in all bedrooms T ✱ sB➪ᴺ£49
dB➪ᴺ£54 (room only) ◪
Lift ⊞ 120P *xmas*
♀ International V ♥ ⚲ Lunch £1.50-£10alc Dinner fr£8.75
Last dinner 10.30pm
Credit Cards ①②③⑤

⌂**Granada Lodge** M4 Service Area, North Hyde Ln TW5 9NA
(Granada) ☎081-574 5875 FAX 081-574 1891
(For full entry see Heston)

All hotels are now given a percentage grading
for the quality of their facilities. A full explanation
can be found within 'How we Classify Hotels
and Restaurants' at the front of the book.

**HEBDEN BRIDGE** West Yorkshire Map **07** SD92

**★★★68%**, **Carlton** Albert St HX7 8ES (Consort)
☎(0422)844400 Telex no 518176
RS 25-31 Dec
*An elegant, traditional hotel in the town centre provides*
*comfortable, well appointed accommodation and courteous service.*
18⇾🛁ᒥ CTV in all bedrooms ® T 🎄 (ex guide dogs) ✳
sB&B⇾🛁ᒥ£37-£47 dB&B⇾🛁ᒥ£57-£67 ➡
Lift ⦅ ⅌ ⇆
V ⇖ 🍷 Sunday Lunch fr£9.25 Dinner fr£14.50 Last dinner
9.30pm
Credit Cards ①②③

**★★67%**, **Hebden Lodge** New Rd HX7 8AD (Exec Hotel)
☎(0422)845272
Closed 23-29 Dec
*Standing in the town centre, close to the Rochdale Canal, this*
*imposing Victorian sandstone building is family owned and run.*
*Well furnished in all areas and offering a friendly welcome to every*
*guest, it has a comfortable lounge and cosy bar as well as the*
*attractive restaurant in which a good standard of home cooking*
*can be enjoyed.*
13⇾🛁ᒥ(1fb) CTV in all bedrooms ® T sB&B⇾🛁ᒥfr£28
dB&B⇾🛁ᒥfr£55 ➡
⅌
🍷 English & Continental V ⇖ 🍷 Lunch £6.45-£10.35alc
Dinner £13-£16alc Last dinner ᵒpm
Credit Cards ①②③⑤

**HEDGE END** Hampshire Map **04** SU41

**★★★64%**, **Botleigh Grange** SO3 2GA (Best Western)
☎Botley(0489)787700 FAX (0489) 788535
*This 17th-century building with ornamental lakes forms the focal*
*point of a small new business park. It offers value for money food,*
*and a modern wing of bedrooms with two four-poster rooms.*
*Remaining accommodation is due to be refurbished during 1990/*
*91, when a spacious new foyer and restaurant is also planned.*
42⇾🛁ᒥ(4fb)4🎄 CTV in all bedrooms ® T sB&B⇾🛁ᒥ£60-£80
dB&B⇾🛁ᒥ£73-£100 ➡
⦅ 120P ✿ ♪ putting *xmas*
🍷 English & French V ⇖ 🍷 Lunch £9-£12&alc High tea
£5.50-£7.50alc Dinner £9-£12&alc Last dinner 10pm
Credit Cards ①②③⑤ⓔ
**See advertisement under SOUTHAMPTON**

**HELENSBURGH** Strathclyde *Dunbartonshire* Map **10** NS28

**★★★61%**, *Commodore Toby* 112 West Clyde St G84 8ER
(Toby) ☎(0436)76924 Telex no 778740
*Set on the seafront on the north side of town this purpose built hotel*
*offers well-equipped bedrooms and bright cheerful public rooms*
*including a popular carvery restaurant.*
45⇾🛁 CTV in all bedrooms ®
Lift ⦅ 120P
V ⇖ 🍷 🍴 Last dinner 9.30pm
Credit Cards ①②③⑤

**HELFORD** Cornwall & Isles of Scilly Map **02** SW72

**✕✕** **Riverside** TR12 6JU ☎Manaccan(032623)443
*Situated in the village centre, this intimate restaurant is run by*
*Edward and Susan Darrell, who provide good food in a friendly*
*and relaxed atmosphere. The extensive menu changes daily, with*
*an emphasis on fresh fish: an unusual fish terrine and light,*
*mouthwatering soufflés feature among the starters. Duck, lamb*
*and game can also be found on the main course selection, and there*
*is an extensive wine list.*
Closed Nov-Mar

Lunch not served Mon-Thu, May-Jul
🍷 English & French 30 seats ✳ Lunch £10-£20alc Dinner
£24-£26 Last dinner 9.30pm 10P nc12yrs

**HELMSLEY** North Yorkshire Map **08** SE68

**★★★76%**, **Black Swan** Market Place YO6 5BJ (Trusthouse
Forte) ☎(0439)70466 Telex no 57538 FAX (0439) 70174
*Overlooking the market square, the Black Swan has preserved all*
*of its original character, both inside and out. Bedrooms are*
*furnished and equipped to a very high standard and have many*
*thoughtful little extras. Service by young staff is pleasant and*
*helpful.*
44⇾🛁(4fb)🍴in 7 bedrooms CTV in all bedrooms ® T
sB⇾🛁£75-£85 dB⇾🛁£108-£138 (room only) ➡
⦅ CTV 60P ✿ croquet *xmas*
🍷 English & French V ⇖ 🍷 🍴 Lunch fr£9.60 Dinner
£29.50-£45 Last dinner 9.30pm
Credit Cards ①②③④⑤

**★★★64%**, **Feversham Arms** 1 High St YO6 5AG (Best Western)
☎(0439)70766 Telex no 57966 FAX (0439) 70346
*This characterful hotel, centrally situated in the attractive market*
*town, features a superb outdoor tennis court and poolside terrace*
*area, while many of the comfortable and well equipped bedrooms*
*boast four poster beds and delightful hand-painted bathroom*
*suites.*
18⇾🛁(4fb)5🎄 CTV in all bedrooms ® T sB&B⇾🛁£45-£55
dB&B⇾🛁£70-£80 ➡
30P ✿ ≋(heated) ♪ (hard)
🍷 English, French & Spanish V ⇖ Lunch £12-£18 Dinner
£18-£25 Last dinner 9.30pm
Credit Cards ①②③⑤ⓔ
**See advertisement on page 343**

341

★★71% **Pheasant** Harome YO6 5JG (2.5m SE on unclass rd)
☎(0439)71241
Closed Jan-Feb
*A very comfortable hotel has been established in premises that once housed the village blacksmith and shop. Bedrooms are furnished to a very high standard, several of them looking out onto the duck pond, and the resident proprietors create an atmosphere in which it is easy to relax and unwind.*
12⇌Annexe2⇌ CTV in all bedrooms ® T sB&B⇌£38.50-£50 dB&B⇌£77-£100 (incl dinner) ⊟
20P ⊞ ✲ nc12 yrs
♧ ✗ Bar Lunch £1-£7alc Dinner £16-£17.50 Last dinner 8pm

---

★★67% **Crown** Market Square YO6 5BJ ☎(0439)70297
*A 16th-century coaching inn with low beams, log fires and stone floors has been carefully restored and renovated to preserve its original charm whilst providing comfortable and well equipped accommodation. Afternoon tea, served in the quaint, cosy dining room, is popular, and all the wholesome meals on offer are carefully prepared from fresh ingredients.*
14rm(3⇌9↱)(1fb) CTV in all bedrooms ® T sB&B£24 sB&B⇌↱£26 dB&B£48 dB&B⇌↱£52 ⊟
CTV 17P 3⌂ ⊞ ✲
V ♧ ☐ ✗ Lunch £5-£7.50&alc High tea £3-£6 Dinner £10-£13&alc Last dinner 8pm
Credit Cards [1] [3]

---

★★62% **Feathers** Market Place YO6 5BH ☎(0439)70275
Closed 23 Dec-31 Jan
*Local stone house, partly 14th century and partly 17th century, with Georgian modifications.*
17rm(6⇌7↱)(4fb) CTV in all bedrooms ® ✱ S% sB&Bfr£22 sB&B⇌↱£26.50-£31.50 dB&Bfr£44 dB&B⇌↱fr£53 ⊟
CTV 12P 1⌂ ✲
♀ English & Continental V ♧ Lunch £7.50-£12.50 Dinner £12.50-£19.50 Last dinner 9.00pm
Credit Cards [1] [2] [3] [5] (£)

## HELSTON Cornwall & Isles of Scilly Map 02 SW62

★★♣70% **Nansloe Manor** Meneage Rd TR13 0SB
☎(0326)574691
Closed 25-30 Dec
*Set within four-and-a-half acres of wooded grounds and enjoying rural views from all its windows, a Georgian/Victorian hotel features charming, individually furnished and decorated bedrooms and a Georgian restaurant serving an imaginative à la carte menu; patrons Angela and Harry Davy Thomas were formerly owners of the establishment voted Inn of the Year 1985.*
7⇌↱1⊟ CTV in all bedrooms ® T sB&B⇌↱£28-£46 dB&B⇌↱£50-£84
40P ⊞ ✲ croquet nc10 yrs
♀ English & Continental V Lunch £9.10-£12.35alc Dinner £13.70-£20.05alc Last dinner 9.30pm
Credit Cards [1] [3]

---

★★63% **The Gwealdues** Falmouth Rd TR13 8JX
☎(0326)572808
*This commercial/holiday hotel, standing beside the Falmouth road on the outskirts of the town and popular for functions, provides soundly furnished and well appointed accommodation in a friendly, informal atmosphere.*
12rm(4⇌5↱)(2fb) CTV in all bedrooms ® T ✱ sB&B£25 sB&B⇌↱£30 dB&B£30 dB&B⇌↱£40 ⊟
60P ⊞ ≏
V ♧ ☐ Sunday Lunch £4.50 Dinner £8.50&alc Last dinner 9.30pm
Credit Cards [1] [3]

For key to symbols see the inside front cover.

## HEMEL HEMPSTEAD Hertfordshire Map 04 TL00

★★★57% **Aubrey Park Hotel** Hemel Hempstead Rd AL3 7AF
☎Redbourn(058285)2105 Telex no 82195 FAX (058285) 2001
(For full entry see Redbourn)

---

★★★55% **Post House** Breakspear Way HP2 4UA (Trusthouse Forte) ☎(0442)51122 Telex no 826902 FAX (0442) 211812
*Attractively decorated and furnished hotel about 2 miles from the town centre.*
Annexe107⇌(8fb)✗in 21 bedrooms CTV in all bedrooms ® ✱ S% sB⇌£43-£73 dB⇌£54-£94 (room only) ⊟
Lift ☾ 140P ✲ CFA *xmas*
V ♧ ☐ ✗ S% Lunch £11-£12&alc Dinner £16&alc Last dinner 10pm
Credit Cards [1] [2] [3] [4] [5]

## HEMSWELL Lincolnshire Map 08 SK99

★★64% **Hemswell Cliff** Lancaster Green, Hemswell Cliff DN21 5TU ☎(042773)8181 & 8182 FAX (042773) 483
*Set on the A631 not far from its junction with the A15, this former RAF Officers' Mess has been modernised and refurbished to offer up-to-date accommodation and spacious public rooms, its traditional association with the air force making it popular for reunions.*
22⇌↱ CTV in all bedrooms ® T ✗ (ex guide dogs) ✱ S% sB&B⇌↱£38.50-£45 dB&B⇌↱£60-£70 ⊟
50P 22⌂ ✲ squash *xmas*
♀ English & Continental V ♧ ☐ S10% Lunch £8.50-£10.50&alc Dinner £10.50-£16&alc Last dinner 9.30pm
Credit Cards [1] [2] [3] (£)

1991 marks the 25th anniversary of this guide.

H

---

**HENLEY-IN-ARDEN** Warwickshire Map **07** SP16

**✗✗ Le Filbert Cottage** 64 High St B95 5BX ☎(05642)2700
*Maurice Ricaud and his charming English-born wife have brought
a touch of rural France to this half-timbered and oak-beamed
16th-century restaurant in the centre of the village. Dishes such as
moules mariniere and sherry-laced oxtail jardiniere are
complimented by a good wine list and attentive, friendly service.*
Closed Sun, Mon, 26 Dec & BHs
♀ French 30 seats Lunch £18.50-£22.50&alc Dinner
£18.50-£25alc Last lunch 1.45pm Last dinner 9.45pm ✗ nc6yrs
Credit Cards ①②③④⑤

---

**HENLEY-ON-THAMES** Oxfordshire Map **04** SU78

**★★★62%, Red Lion** Hart St RG9 2AR ☎(0491)572161
Telex no 83343 FAX (0491) 410039
*A recent change of ownership has prompted significant
improvement and upgrading throughout this character hotel, which
stands next to the river at the heart of the town. Public rooms are
particularly comfortable, comprising cosy lounges, public and
cocktail bars and an elegant restaurant, all attractively decorated,
richly furnished, and softened by the skilful use of colourful quality
fabrics. Bedrooms have been refurbished to some extent and are
scheduled for improvement work to bring them up to the standard
of the public areas. Imaginative food is commendably well
prepared, whilst traditional standards of service result in prompt,
friendly attention.*
26rm(22⇨)(1fb)1 CTV in all bedrooms T ✗ S% sB£35
sB⇨£65 dB£68 dB⇨£78-£90 (room only) ⊟
⦅ 25P ⇔
V ♀ ⠓ Lunch £18-£28.50alc Dinner £18-£28.50alc Last dinner
10pm
Credit Cards ①②③

---

**HEREFORD** Hereford & Worcester Map **03** SO54

See also **Much Birch**
**★★★68%, Hereford Moat House** Belmont Rd HR2 7BP (Queens
Moat) ☎(0432)354301 FAX (0432) 275114
Closed Xmas
*Recently completed extensions and improvements have provided
this hotel with an elegant new restaurant and spacious, comfortable
foyer lounge, as well as an additional 28 bedrooms to supplement
the existing motel-type accommodation; it is a popular venue for
functions, and conference facilities are also available, its position
on the A465 south-west of the city centre making for easy access.*
28⇨♠Annexe32⇨♠ CTV in all bedrooms ® T
⦅ 150P ❖
♀ English & French V ♦ ⠓ ✗ Last dinner 9.45pm
Credit Cards ①②③⑤

**★★★61%, The Green Dragon** Broad St HR4 9BG (Trusthouse
Forte) ☎(0432)272506 Telex no 35491 FAX (0432) 352139
*A refurbishment programme is underway at this traditional city
centre hotel to improve rooms which although well equipped are, in
some cases, rather dated. Attractive public areas include an oak-
panelled restaurant. Staff are friendly and obliging.*
88⇨2 ✂ ✗in 9 bedrooms CTV in all bedrooms ® ✳
sB⇨£65-£76 dB⇨£81-£94 (room only) ⊟
Lift ⦅ 90 CFA *xmas*
V ♦ ⠓ ✗ Lunch £8-£15&alc Dinner £15.50&alc Last dinner
10.15pm
Credit Cards ①②③④⑤

**★★75%, Merton Hotel & Governors Restaurant** Commercial
Rd HR1 2BD (Minotels) ☎(0432)265925 FAX (0432) 354983
RS Sun
*A very pleasant privately owned hotel well situated for the city
centre. It offers attractive and very well equipped accommodation
and the popular Governors restaurant.*
15⇨♠Annexe4⇨♠(1fb) CTV in all bedrooms T
sB&B⇨♠frf41.50 dB&B⇨♠frf64 ⊟

CTV 6P sauna solarium gymnasium *xmas*
♀ International V ♦ ⠓ ✗ Lunch £10-£12.50&alc High tea
£3.50-£9 Dinner frf15&alc Last dinner 9.30pm
Credit Cards ①②③⑤ⓔ

**★★65%, Dormington Court Country House** Dormington
HR1 4DA (3.5m E off A438) ☎(0432)850370
*This charming, small hotel on the A438 about 5 miles from
Hereford offers rooms which are bright, fresh and most
comfortable, as are the public areas. Its peaceful location and
attentive service make it a good choice for either business or
pleasure. Enjoyable and imaginative dishes are served in the
intimate dining room.*
7rm(6⇨)(1fb)1 CTV in all bedrooms ® ✳ sB&B⇨£25-£39
dB&B⇨£50-£60 ⊟
16P ⇔ ❖
♀ English & French V ♦ ⠓ Lunch £8.50-£15alc Dinner
£12-£18alc Last dinner 8.45pm
Credit Cards ①③

**★★ 64%, Netherwood Country House** Tupsley HR1 1UT
☎(0432)272388
*A charming early Victorian country house in two acres of grounds
and gardens, standing just off the A438 to the east of the city, once
belonged to the Baskerville family and is reputed to be the setting
for Conan Doyle's famous novel. Today it offers accommodation in
well-equipped bedrooms and friendly personal service by the
proprietors.*
7rm(6⇨♠)(2fb) CTV in all bedrooms ® T ✗ (ex guide dogs)
✳ S% sB&B⇨♠frf42 dB&B⇨♠frf60 ⊟
CTV 36P ❖ ♪
V ♦ ⠓ S% Lunch frf12 High tea frf5 Dinner frf15 Last
dinner 9.30pm
Credit Cards ①②③

**★★61%, Castle Pool** Castle St HR1 2NR (Exec Hotel)
☎(0432)356321
*Described by its proprietors as "the country hotel in the city", this
mid-eighteenth-century house stands in attractive gardens which
extend to what was once the moat of Hereford Castle, its tranquil
setting a complete contrast to the bustling city centre only a few
moments' walk away.*
26⇨♠(3fb)2 CTV in all bedrooms ® T sB&B⇨♠frf44
dB&B⇨♠frf60 ⊟
CTV 14P ❖ *xmas*
♀ International V ♦ ⠓ Lunch frf7.50 High tea frf5.50 Dinner
frf15 Last dinner 9.30pm
Credit Cards ①②③⑤

**✗ Fat Tulip Wine Bar & Bistro** The Old Wye Bridge, 2 St
Martin's St HR2 7RE ☎(0432)275808
*This pleasant, informal restaurant overlooking the River Wye is
just a short walk from the city centre. The short, well-chosen menu
features home made soups and main courses such as beef with
anchovy sauce and salmon and leek puree in a pastry case.*
Closed Sun, 24-30 Dec & BHs
♀ English, French & Italian 35 seats Last lunch 2pm Last
dinner 10pm ✗
Credit Cards ①②③

---

**HERM**

See **Channel Islands**

---

**HERSTMONCEUX** East Sussex Map **05** TQ61

**✗✗ Sundial** BN27 4LA ☎(0323)832217
*Set in rural, village surroundings, the elegant, country restaurant
has a warm, friendly atmosphere and is personally supervised by
the chef/patron and his charming French wife. The French cuisine,
which specialises in fish cookery, is prepared to a very high
standard.*
Closed Mon, 10 Aug-10 Sep & 23 Dec-20 Jan
Dinner not served Sun

♀ French **V** 60 seats Lunch fr£14.50&alc Dinner fr£22.50&alc
Last lunch 2pm Last dinner 9.30pm 25P ✂
Credit Cards 1 2 3 5

---

**HERTFORD** Hertfordshire Map **04** TL31

★★★61% **White Horse** Hertingfordbury SG14 2LB (1m W on
A414) (Trusthouse Forte) ☎(0992)586791 FAX (0992) 550809
*A pleasant, characterful hotel with a warm atmosphere invites
relaxation in its newly extended bar and lounge and offers a well
balanced menu in an attractive restaurant with a conservatory
style area. Most bedrooms have now been refurbished to provide a
good standard of modern accommodation.*
42⇩(20fb)✂in 6 bedrooms CTV in all bedrooms ® S%
sB⇩£70-£75 dB⇩£86-£92 (room only) 🅿
《 60P ✿ ♫ *xmas*
**V** ✿ ♨ S% Lunch £10.95-£14.95 High tea £1.20-£6 Dinner
£13.95-£15.95&alc Last dinner 9.30pm
Credit Cards 1 2 3 4 5

---

**HESLEDEN** Durham Map **08** NZ43

★★67% **Hardwicke Hall Manor** TS27 4PA (2.5m N of town on
A1086) ☎Hartlepool(0429)836326
*An old manor house, boasting a wealth of historical features and
interesting stories, offers comfortable accommodation and meals
that can be recommended both for quality and value.*
11⇩ℝ(2fb)2🛏 CTV in all bedrooms ® T sB&B⇩ℝ£40-£55
dB&B⇩ℝ£50-£65 🅿
50P ✿
♀ French **V** ✿ ♨
Credit Cards 1 2 3 5 £

---

**HESTON MOTORWAY SERVICE AREA (M4)** Greater
London

See **LONDON plan 1***A***3**(page 426)

⇧**Granada Lodge** M4 Service Area, North Hyde Ln TW5 9NA
(Granada) ☎081-574 5875 FAX 081-574 1891
*Conveniently situated between London and Heathrow, on the
westbound carriageway, the Lodge provides accommodation in
well equipped, modern bedrooms with fully tiled bathroom
facilities. Meals can be taken at the Country Kitchen Restaurant
in the adjoining service area.*
46⇩ℝ(15fb)✂in 6 bedrooms CTV in all bedrooms ®
✖ (ex guide dogs) ✳ S% sB⇩ℝfr£32
dB⇩ℝfr£36 (room only)
**See advertisement under HEATHROW AIRPORT
(LONDON)**

---

**HESWALL** Merseyside Map **07** SJ28

★★60% *Hill House* Mount Av L60 4RH ☎051-342 5535
*A friendly hotel with a popular bar and well-appointed bedrooms
stands amid sweeping lawns in its own grounds, close to the centre
of the village.*
8⇩ CTV in all bedrooms ® T ✖ (ex guide dogs)
《 34P ✿
♀ Mainly grills **V** ✿ Last dinner 10pm
Credit Cards 1 2 3 5

---

**HETHERSETT** Norfolk Map **05** TG10

★★★70% **Park Farm** NR9 3DL ☎Norwich(0603)810264
FAX (0603) 812104
Closed 25-29 Dec

---

*Set amid arable and pasture land, approached by a long tree-lined
avenue, the hotel, a former farm and outbuildings, enjoys a quiet
and secluded position only 6 miles south of Norwich, and just off
the A11. The outbuildings have been tastefully converted in brick
and pantile, in an informal courtyard arrangement, each providing
well equipped and individually designed accommodation. An
elegant restaurant offers a good selection of menus. All dishes use
fresh ingredients, while the Chef's monthly specialities have more
skilfully prepared dishes with a light delicate and imaginative
style.*
6⇩ℝAnnexe29⇩ℝ12🛏 CTV in all bedrooms ®
✖ (ex guide dogs) sB&B⇩ℝ£52-£88 dB&B⇩ℝ£65-£105 🅿
100P 1🏊 🚲 ✿ ☐(heated) ♪ (hard) sauna solarium putting
croquet
♀ English & French **V** ✿ ♨ ✂ Lunch £8-£9&alc High tea
£3-£5 Dinner £10.50-£11.50&alc Last dinner 9.30pm
Credit Cards 1 2 3 4 5 £
**See advertisement under NORWICH**

---

**HEXHAM** Northumberland Map **12** NY96

★★★70% **Beaumont** Beaumont St NE46 3LT ☎(0434)602331
Closed 25-26 Dec & 1 Jan
*This very comfortable, traditional hotel overlooks parkland, and is
situated close to the Abbey. It has recently been totally
refurbished, and now offers attractive, individually designed
bedrooms and inviting lounges. Serivce from local staff, supervised
by the resident proprietors, is courteous and friendly.*
23⇩ℝ(1fb)1🛏✂in 15 bedrooms CTV in all bedrooms ® T ✖
sB&B⇩ℝ£42 dB&B⇩ℝ£66
Lift 《 6P gymnasium small fitness room
♀ International **V** ✿ ♨ ✂ Lunch £5-£12alc Dinner
£7.50-£16alc Last dinner 9.45pm
Credit Cards 1 2 3 5

★★62% **Royal** Priestpopple NE46 1PQ (Consort)
☎(0434)602270
*A family-run, town centre, commercial hotel with an attractive first floor restaurant, a separate Bistro and a cosy residents and diners bar. Bedrooms are well equipped.*
24⇌♠(3fb) CTV in all bedrooms ® T ✱ sB&B⇌♠£37-£40 dB&B⇌♠£57-£60 ☒
CTV 24P
♀ English, Scottish & French V ♦ ⊻ Bar Lunch £2.50-£6 Dinner £12&alc Last dinner 9.30pm
Credit Cards ① ② ③ ⑤ ⓔ

★★61% **County** Priestpopple NE46 1PS ☎(0434)602030
*Warm, comfortable, small hotel with good wholesome food.*
9⇌♠(3fb) CTV in all bedrooms ® T sB&B⇌♠£38 dB&B⇌♠£53 ☒
《2P
♀ International V ♦ ⊻ Bar Lunch £6-£8alc High tea £2.75-£8.50alc Dinner £10&alc Last dinner 9.30pm
Credit Cards ① ② ③

○**Slaley Hall Sheraton** Slaley NE47 0BY ☎(0434)673671
FAX (0434) 673616
Due to open spring 1991
140rm

**HIGHBRIDGE** Somerset Map 03 ST34

★★59% **Sundowner** 74 Main Road, West Huntspill TA9 3QU (1m S on A38) ☎Burnham on Sea(0278)784766
*Comfortable accommodation, meals of a reasonable standard and a friendly, informal atmosphere are provided at this small, family-run commercial hotel.*
8⇌♠(1fb) CTV in all bedrooms ®
CTV 24P ✿ solarium
♀ Mainly grills V ♦ ⊻ Last dinner 10pm
Credit Cards ① ② ③ ⑤

**HIGH WYCOMBE** Buckinghamshire Map 04 SU89

★★★65% **Crest** Crest Rd, Handy Cross HP11 1TL (Trusthouse Forte) ☎(0494)442100 Telex no 83626 FAX (0494) 439071
*This modern hotel provides excellent facilities for conference clientele. Bedrooms are well equipped and public rooms have recently been refurbished. The restaurant serves both English and French cuisine.*
110⇌♠(12fb)⊱in 21 bedrooms CTV in all bedrooms ® T ✱ (ex guide dogs) ✱ S% sB&B⇌♠fr£82 dB⇌♠£94-£130 (room only) ☒
《173P CFA *xmas*
♀ English & French V ♦ ⊻ ⊱ Lunch £8.95-£12.15&alc Dinner fr£14.95&alc Last dinner 10.30pm
Credit Cards ① ② ③ ④ ⑤

**HILLINGDON** Greater London

See LONDON plan 1*A4*(page 426)
★★★61% **Master Brewer Motel** Western Av UB10 9NX ☎Uxbridge(0895)51199 Telex no 946589 FAX (0895) 810330
*Conveniently situated for Heathrow and the M25, the motel offers a range of popular eating options, well-equipped bedrooms being provided in separate modern blocks.*
106⇌(22fb) CTV in all bedrooms ®
《200P ✿ CFA ⚬
♀ Continental V ♦ ⊻ Last dinner 11pm
Credit Cards ① ② ③ ⑤

**HILLINGTON** Norfolk Map 09 TF72

★★61% **Ffolkes Arms** Lynn Rd, Hillington PE31 6BJ ☎Hillington(0485)600210 FAX (0485) 601196
*This character coaching inn, which was built over 300 years ago, has recently been completely modernised without losing its original character. A new accommodation annexe has been added which*

---

*gives a good range of facilities, including ground floor bedrooms and a special disabled room. The hotel proves popular for its eating options, with a choice of bar snacks, carvery or à la carte.*
Annexe20⇌♠(1fb)1⌸ CTV in all bedrooms ® T ✱(ex guide dogs) ✱ sB⇌♠£33 dB⇌♠£43-£50 (room only)
200P ✿ pool table *xmas*
♀ English & French V ♦ ⊻ ⊱ Lunch £4.50-£7.95&alc High tea £2.50-£3.95 Dinner £7.95&alc Last dinner 9.45pm
Credit Cards ① ② ③

**HILTON PARK MOTORWAY SERVICE AREA (M6)** West Midlands Map 07 SJ90

⚜**Rank Motor Lodge** Hilton Park Services (M6), Essington WV11 2DR (on M6 between juncts 10a & 11) (Rank)
☎Cheslyn Hay(0922)414100 FAX (0922) 418762
*On the southern carriageway of the M6, 7 miles from Wolverhampton and about 45 minutes drive from the NEC. Value-for-money accommodation is provided, the rooms at the rear having rural views. Meals are available in the adjacent Oasis service area, but Continental breakfasts can be delivered to rooms.*
64⇌♠(22fb)⊱in 6 bedrooms CTV in all bedrooms ® ✱ S% sB&B⇌♠£27.50 dB&B⇌♠£34.50 Continental breakfast
《60P
V ♦ ⊻ ⊱
Credit Cards ① ② ③ ⑤

**HIMLEY** Staffordshire Map 07 SO89

★★★66% **Himley Country Club & Hotel** School Rd DY3 4LG ☎Wombourne(0902)896716 Telex no 333688
FAX (0902) 896668
*A modern business style of hotel, in a rural location, with two restaurants, bars and well-equipped bedrooms.*
76⇌♠ CTV in all bedrooms ® T ✱ (ex guide dogs)
sB⇌♠£48-£53 dB⇌♠£57 (room only)
《⌸ 126P ⚬
♀ Continental V ⊻ Lunch fr£13
Credit Cards ① ② ③ ⑤
**See advertisements under WOLVERHAMPTON & DUDLEY**

★★68% **Himley House** DY3 4LD (On A449 N of Stourbridge) (Berni/Chef & Brewer) ☎Wombourne(0902)892468
*Originally dating from the 17th century this hotel has an elegant interior, well furnished bedrooms and friendly helpful staff.*
17⇌♠Annexe7⇌♠(2fb) CTV in all bedrooms ® T ✱ (ex guide dogs) sB&B⇌♠£50 dB&B⇌♠£69 ☒
《120P ✿
V ♦ ⊱ Lunch £8-£15alc Dinner £8-£15alc Last dinner 10.30pm
Credit Cards ① ② ③ ⑤

**HINCKLEY** Leicestershire Map 04 SP49

★★★72% **Sketchley Grange** Sketchley Ln, Burbage LE10 3HU (Best Western) ☎(0455)251133 Telex no 34694
FAX (0455) 631384
*This friendly, privately-owned hotel is pleasantly situated in four acres of grounds with views of unspoilt countryside, yet is conveniently placed for the M69 and A5.*
34⇌♠2⌸⊱in 10 bedrooms CTV in all bedrooms ® T ✱ (ex guide dogs)
《200P
♀ English & French V ♦ ⊻ ⊱ Last dinner 10.45pm
Credit Cards ① ② ③ ⑤

★★74% **Kings Hotel & Restaurant** 13/19 Mount Rd LE10 1AD ☎(0455)637193 FAX (0455) 636201
*This large Victorian house is set in a quiet road close to the town centre. It provides comfortable, well-equipped accommodation. There is an interesting choice of food and the wine list is extensive.*
7⇌♠⊱in 3 bedrooms CTV in all bedrooms ® ✱ ✱
sB&B⇌♠£49.50-£59.50 dB&B⇌♠£64.50-£69.50

12P 1🏨 (£5) 🎵
♀ English, French & Hungarian V ♥ Lunch £7-£12 Dinner
£15.50-£20.50 Last dinner 9.30pm
Credit Cards ① ② ③ ⑤ ⓔ

---

**HINDHEAD** Surrey Map **04** SU83

★★★58% **Devils Punch Bowl** London Rd GU26 6AG
☎(042873)6565 Telex no 858918 FAX (042873) 5713
*A friendly hotel provides pleasant, modern accommodation, both in
the main building and its annexe ; Squire's Restaurant offers a
popular menu and the lively bar is much used.*
40➪🏔(1fb) CTV in all bedrooms ® T ✱ sB&B➪🏔fr£55.50
dB&B➪🏔fr£65.50 🅱
《 70P CFA 🎵 xmas
♀ English & French V ♥ ♫ ✱ Sunday Lunch £9.75&alc
Dinner £8-£15alc Last dinner 9.30pm
Credit Cards ① ② ③ ⑤

---

**HINDON** Wiltshire Map **03** ST93

★★70% **Lamb at Hindon** SP3 6DP ☎(074789)573
FAX (074789) 605
*This attractive inn provides modern accommodation, healthy home
cooking and a refreshing style of friendly service.*
15rm(10➪1🏔)(2fb)1🛏 CTV in all bedrooms ®
🏃 (ex guide dogs)
CTV 26P 2🏨 ⊞ ✱ 🟊 shooting fishing
♥ ♫ Last dinner 9.30pm
Credit Cards ① ② ③

---

**HINTLESHAM** Suffolk Map **05** TM04

★★★

❀★★★♨
HINTLESHAM HALL

IP8 3NS (Relais et Châteaux)
☎(047387)334 & 268
Telex no 98340
FAX (047387) 463
RS Sat
*This beautiful country house,
with its charming façade and
reputation for excellent cuisine retains its Red Stars despite
having changed hands. All the key staff have been retained,
including the dedicated General Manager, Tim Sunderland,
and this has ensured that the consistently high standards of
service and hospitality have been maintained. The
refurbishment and additional wing of bedrooms have been
completed and it is hoped that the newly constructed golf
course will be open next year.*
33➪🏔(1fb)2🛏🏃in 12 bedrooms CTV in all bedrooms T
✱ S15% sB&B➪🏔£60-£95
dB&B➪🏔£90-£140 Continental breakfast 🅱
《 100P ⊞ ✱ 🏃 18 ♪ (hard) 🟊 ∪ snooker croquet clay &
game shooting xmas
♀ English & French V ✂ S15% Lunch £17.50-£25alc
Dinner £25-£35alc Last dinner 10pm
Credit Cards ① ② ③ ⑤ ⓔ

---

**HITCHIN** Hertfordshire Map **04** TL12

★★★55% **Blakemore Thistle** Little Wymondley SG4 7JJ (3m
SE A602) (Mount Charlotte (TS)) ☎Stevenage(0438)355821
Telex no 825479 FAX (0438) 742114
*Originally a Georgian house, and still enjoying a peaceful location
in its own grounds, this popular commercial hotel has been
extended to provide modern bedroom accommodation, whilst the
style of the public areas is more in keeping with that of the original
building.*

---

82➪🏔(6fb) CTV in all bedrooms ® T ✱ sB➪🏔fr£64
dB➪🏔fr£75 (room only) 🅱
Lift 《 200P ✱ ⌇(heated) sauna games room
♀ International ♥ ♫ Lunch fr£11.25&alc Dinner
fr£13.50&alc Last dinner 9.30pm
Credit Cards ① ② ③ ④ ⑤

---

**HOAR CROSS** Staffordshire Map **07** SK12

○**Hoar Cross Hall Health Hydro** DE13 8QS ☎(028375)671
Due to open Nov 1990
100rm

---

**HOCKLEY HEATH** West Midlands Map **07** SP17

❀★★★♨79% **Nuthurst Grange Country House** Nuthurst
Grange Ln B94 5NL (off A34, 2m S junction 4 M42)
☎Lapworth(05643)3972 Telex no 333485 FAX (05643) 3919
*This luxuriously appointed hotel stands secluded in extensive
landscaped wooded grounds, seemingly a world away from the
A34, M42 and M40, from which it is in fact easily accessible.
Tastefully decorated and furnished, its comfortable rooms are
made welcoming by the provision of such extra touches as a bowl of
fruit and chocolates. Food in the restaurant is lovingly prepared by
Chef Patron David Randolph. Dishes sampled and enjoyed by our
Inspector were a terrine of baby leeks and foie gras, Gressingham
duck with a Marsala and gherkin sauce, rounded off by a delicious
steamed date pudding with toffee sauce.*
8➪🏔1🛏 CTV in all bedrooms T 🏃 (ex guide dogs)
sB&B➪🏔fr£85 dB&B➪🏔£99-£125 Continental breakfast 🅱
50P 6🏨 ⊞ ✱ croquet
♀ English & French V ♥ Lunch fr£17.50 Dinner £27.50-£32.50
Last dinner 9.30pm
Credit Cards ① ② ③ ⑤ ⓔ

*Bishop Field Country* ★★
*House Hotel & Restaurant*

**Allendale, Hexham, Northumberland**
**Tel: (0434) 683248 Fax: (0434) 683830**

Personally owned and run by Kathy & Keith
Fairless and daughter Bridget. Bishop Field
is one of the leading hotels in the area
where you can relax in an informal atmosphere, enjoy freshly prepared food and
leave the rest to us. All bedrooms are individually designed and guests have the
choice of two lounges, one non smoking.
A reputation for good food and wine is well
deserved and the standards never falter,
with the menu changed daily. 10 miles
south west of Hexham on B6305.

---

**HOCKLIFFE** Bedfordshire Map **04** SP92

○**Travelodge** A5(Trusthouse Forte)
☎Central reservations (0800) 850950
Due to open winter 1990
28⇨

---

**HODNET** Shropshire Map **07** SJ62

★★6⅝% **Bear** TF9 3NH ☎(063084)214 & 787
FAX (063084) 351
*The character and quality of this quaint village inn have been
retained and enhanced to create compact but well-equipped
bedrooms which appeal to tourist and businessman alike ; both
restaurant meals and bar snacks are popular, while the Mediaeval
Feasts held in the Banqueting Hall provide a memorable
experience.*
6⇨♪♠ CTV in all bedrooms ® T ✹ (ex guide dogs) ✳
sB&B⇨♠£35-£37.50 dB&B⇨♠£52.50-£57.50 ⊟
100P ✿ ♫
♡ International V ♦ ♨ ✦ Bar Lunch £1.75-£4.50alc Dinner
£7-£12alc Last dinner 10pm
Credit Cards ①③

---

**HOLDENBY** Northamptonshire Map **04** SP66

✕✕**Lynton House Country Restaurant & Hotel** The Croft
NN6 8DJ ☎Northampton(0604)770777
*This restaurant with rooms, once a rectory, stands in its own
grounds offering views across the terrace to lawns with trees and
shrubs. Its fine cuisine is Italian-based though with a difference,
and each dish is uncomplicated and freshly prepared from top-
quality produce. Service is quietly efficient under the supervision of
the proprietor, and a reasonable wine list is available. The
establishment's popularity makes it advisable to book for an
evening meal, while the lunchtime table d'hôte menu represents
extremely good value for money.*
Closed Xmas 3 days, 1 wk in spring, 2 wks Aug
Lunch not served Sat & Mon
Dinner not served Sun
♡ Italian V 55 seats Lunch fr£12.95 Dinner fr£18.75 Last
lunch 1.45pm Last dinner 9.45pm 25P nc6yrs ✦
Credit Cards ①③

---

**HOLFORD** Somerset Map **03** ST14

★★⚑69% **Combe House** TA5 1RZ ☎(027874)382
Closed Jan RS mid Nov-Dec & Feb-mid Mar
*A country house lying in a secluded valley of the Quantock Hills
offers bedrooms with good facilities and cosy, comfortable public
areas. Other attractions include beautiful gardens, a hard tennis
court and a heated indoor swimming pool. Table d'hôte menus
provide an extensive choice of good, home-cooked dishes, while
staff are relaxed and friendly.*
20rm(13⇨2♠)(2fb)1⚑ CTV in all bedrooms ® T S%
sB&B⇨♠£27-£30 sB&B⇨♠£36-£39 dB&B£51-£60
dB&B⇨♠£61-£80 ⊟
15P ⇏ ✿ ☒(heated) ♪ (hard) sauna solarium
♦ ♨ S% Bar Lunch £2-£8alc Dinner £11.50-£12.75alc Last
dinner 8.30pm
Credit Cards ①②③

---

**HOLLINGBOURNE** Kent Map **05** TQ85

★★★66% **Great Danes** Ashford Rd ME17 1RE (Embassy)
☎Maidstone(0622)30022 Telex no 96198 FAX (0622) 35290
*A house dating back to the 1840's has been greatly enlarged and
modernised to provide well-equipped, modern accommodation. As
well as pleasant service and a choice of bars and eating places, this
popular hotel offers extensive leisure facilities.*
126⇨♠(4fb)✦in 13 bedrooms CTV in all bedrooms ® T ✳
sB⇨♠£75 dB⇨♠£85 (room only) ⊟

---

Lift ℂ 400P ✿ CFA ☒(heated) ♪ (hard) ✦ snooker sauna
solarium gymnasium pool table pitch & putt croquet ♫ *xmas*
♡ English & French V ♦ ♨
Credit Cards ①②③⑤
**See advertisement under MAIDSTONE**

---

**HOLMES CHAPEL** Cheshire Map **07** SJ76

★★★67% **Old Vicarage** Knutsford Rd CW4 8EF
☎(0477)32041 FAX (0477) 35728
*Located on the A50 north of Holmes Chapel, this old house with a
modern bedroom extension has a choice of restaurants, which
provide imaginative cuisine, carefully prepared by the chef,
Richard Birchall and his brigade.*
22⇨♠ CTV in all bedrooms ® T ✹ (ex guide dogs)
sB&B⇨♠£54-£56 dB&B⇨♠£68-£70 ⊟
ℂ 70P
♡ English & French V ♦ ♨ S% Lunch £9.50-£10.50&alc
Dinner £13.50-£14.50&alc Last dinner 10pm
Credit Cards ①②③

---

**HOLT** Norfolk Map **09** TG03

★★★63% *Feathers* 6 Market Place NR25 6BW ☎(0263)712318
*Situated on a busy main street with rear car parking, the Feathers
has a warm inviting bar with a cosy, convivial atmosphere. Rooms
are attractively furnished in a cottage style and very well equipped.*
13rm(10⇨) CTV in all bedrooms ® ✹ (ex guide dogs)
50P
V ♦ ♨ ✦ Last dinner 9.30pm
Credit Cards ①②③⑤

---

**HOLYHEAD**
See **Trearddur Bay**

---

**HOLYWELL** Clwyd Map **07** SJ17

★★66% **Stamford Gate** Halkyn Rd CH8 7SJ (Best Western)
☎(0352)712942 & 712968 FAX (0352) 713309
*Close to the A55 just south of the town, this hotel provides
comfortable and well-equipped accommodation and a large
restaurant.*
12⇨♠ CTV in all bedrooms ® ✹ ✳ sB&B⇨♠£32
dB&B⇨♠£46
100P
♡ English & Italian V ♦ Lunch £6.50-£7.50&alc Dinner
£10.75&alc Last dinner 10pm
Credit Cards ①③④

---

**HOLYWELL GREEN** West Yorkshire Map **07** SE01

★★68%, **Rock Inn** HX4 9BS (Best Western)
☎Halifax(0422)379721 FAX (0422) 379110
*Peacefully situated, though only a mile and a half from junction 24
of the M62, the comfortable village hotel offers well-appointed
bedrooms featuring many extras, and spacious, inviting public
areas. The restaurant menu is interesting, the extensive bar menu is
good value, and service throughout is spontaneous and friendly.*
18♠ CTV in all bedrooms ® T
100P 2⇏ ✿ solarium
♡ English & French V ♦ ♨ Last dinner 9.45pm
Credit Cards ①②③⑤

---

**HONILEY** Warwickshire Map **04** SP27

★★★68% **Honiley Court** Honiley CV8 1NP (3m W of
Kenilworth on A4117) (Lansbury) ☎Kenilworth(0926)484234
FAX (0926) 484474
*Situated on the A4117 close to the village, this modern hotel is an
extension of the character Honiley Boot Inn and combines up-to-
date facilities with some character. A night club, good conference*

rooms and well-equipped bedrooms make it an ideal venue for both business and leisure guests.

64⇌ CTV in all bedrooms ℝ T

Lift ℂ 150P

♀ English & French V ✿ ⚹ Last dinner 10pm

Credit Cards ① ② ③ ⑤

---

## HONITON Devon Map 03 ST10

★★★⚑65%, *Deer Park* Weston EX14 0PG (2.5m W off A30)

☎(0404)41266

Set in 30 acres of parkland this former Georgian mansion, dating from 1721, is now a character hotel. Recently upgraded it now presents elegant, comfortable lounges and a good range of refurbished bedrooms. The restaurant offers commendable country cooking complemented by an extensive classical wine list. The leisure facilities include five miles of fishing rights.

15⇌Annexe14⇌(2fb) CTV in all bedrooms ✗

CTV 100P 4🚗 🚸 ✿ CFA ⊒(heated) ♪ (hard) ✦ squash snooker sauna solarium croquet putting shooting ♘

♀ English & French V ✿ ⚥ Last dinner 10pm

Credit Cards ① ② ③ ⑤

★★66%, *Home Farm* Wilmington EX14 9JR (2m E)

☎Wilmington(040483)278

Closed Dec-Jan

A cottage-style family-run hotel standing about 3 miles from the town features individually decorated bedrooms, some of them located in an annexe ; characterful public rooms include a small, informal restaurant offering an à la carte menu.

7rm(3⇌)Annexe6⇌ʂ(3fb) CTV in all bedrooms ℝ T

sB&B£24-£28 sB&B⇌ʂ£24-£28 dB&B£48-£52

dB&B⇌ʂ£48-£52 ℝ

CTV 25P ✿ golf practice nets

▶

**H**

V ♆ ♋ Lunch £3.50-£7.50alc Dinner £10.50&alc Last dinner 9pm
Credit Cards [1] [2] [3] (£)

**★★55% New Dolphin** High St EX14 8HE ☎(0404)42377
Telex no 42479
*Set in the centre of the town, this hotel offers good facilities for both businessman and holidaymaker. Steaks and grills predominate on the restaurant's menu, and the lounge bar attracts a busy local trade.*
10rm(5⇨3⌐)Annexe5⇨⌐(3fb) CTV in all bedrooms ® **T** ✱
sB&B⇨⌐fr£30 dB&B⇨⌐fr£45
12P
V ♆ Lunch £4-£15alc Dinner £6-£15alc Last dinner 9.30pm
Credit Cards [1] [3]

## HOOK Hampshire Map 04 SU75

**★★60% Raven** Station Rd RG27 9HS (0.75m N of M3 junc 5 on B3349) (Lansbury) ☎(0256)762541 Telex no 858901
FAX (0256) 768677
*Ideal for either business or leisure, and conveniently located near the station, this popular commercial hotel has been completely refurbished. Bedrooms are particularly well-equipped. The spacious, lively bar lounge and the busy restaurant present a welcoming atmosphere.*
38⇨(3fb)1 ⊟ ⊁in 5 bedrooms CTV in all bedrooms ®
✗ (ex guide dogs) sB&B⇨fr£71 dB&B⇨fr£85 ⊨
☾ 100P CFA sauna *xmas*
♉ European **V** ♆ ♋ ⊁ Lunch fr£11&alc Dinner fr£11&alc
Last dinner 10.30pm
Credit Cards [1] [2] [3] [4] [5]

## HOOK Wiltshire Map 04 SU08

**★★70% School House Hotel & Restaurant** Hook St SN4 8EF
☎Swindon(0793)851198 Telex no 449703 FAX (0793) 851025
*This listed former school features new spacious bedrooms opened in July 1989, incorporating every modern amenity and furnished with a Victorian theme. In the lofty beamed schoolroom guests can enjoy cuisine in the modern style, dishes being prepared with imagination and flair.*
10⇨⌐ CTV in all bedrooms ® **T** ✗ (ex guide dogs) ✱ S%
sB&B⇨⌐£65 dB&B⇨⌐£72 ⊨
30P ⇼ ✲ ⌂ *xmas*
♉ English & French **V** ♆ ♋ ⊁ S% Lunch fr£13.75alc High tea fr£10.75alc Dinner £16.50-£21.75alc Last dinner 10pm
Credit Cards [1] [2] [3] [5] (£)

## HOOTON ROBERTS South Yorkshire Map 08 SK49

**★★70% Earl of Strafford** Doncaster Rd S65 4PF
☎Rotherham(0709)852737 FAX (0709) 851903
*Standing on the A630, ideally situated for access to the motorways, to Doncaster and to Rotherham itself, this friendly, family-run hotel provides comfortable, well appointed bedrooms, luxury bathrooms with whirlpool baths, and extensive leisure facilities.*
27⇨(3fb)2 ⊟ CTV in 26 bedrooms ® **T** ✗ (ex guide dogs)
sB&B⇨£50-£60 dB&B⇨£60-£70 ⊨
☾ 100P ✲ ⊡(heated) snooker sauna solarium gymnasium *xmas*
♉ English & French **V** ♆ ♋
Credit Cards [1] [2] [3] [5] (£)

## HOPE COVE Devon Map 03 SX64

**★★68% Cottage** Inner Hope Cove TQ7 3HJ
☎Kingsbridge(0548)561555
Closed 2-30 Jan
*This family-managed establishment, beautifully set in its own grounds overlooking Hope Cove, offers a warm welcome and friendly but professionally managed service. Public areas in traditional style include a restaurant offering both an extensive à la carte and a six-course table d'hôte menu.*
35rm(17⇨2⌐)(5fb) CTV in 19 bedrooms **T** S10%
sB&B£29-£40 dB&B£58-£80
dB&B⇨⌐£79-£102 (incl dinner) ⊨
CTV 50P ⇼ ✲ *xmas*
♉ English & French ♆ ♋ S10% Lunch £7.70 Dinner £15.20&alc Last dinner 8.45pm

**★★68% Lantern Lodge** TQ7 3HE ☎Kingsbridge(0548)561280
Closed Dec-Feb
*Enjoying extensive views of the sea and fishing village, this personally run hotel offers nicely furnished bedrooms and very comfortable public rooms, including a new restaurant bar complex. The indoor heated swimming pool with a sauna and solarium is an added attraction.*
14⇨⌐(1fb)3 ⊟ CTV in all bedrooms ® **T** ✗ (ex guide dogs)
✱ sB&B⇨⌐£31.35-£44.55 dB&B⇨⌐£55-£81 (incl dinner)
15P 1⌂ ⇼ ⊡(heated) sauna solarium putting green nc9yrs
♉ English & French **V** ♆ ⊁ Dinner £14 Last dinner 8.30pm
Credit Cards [1] [3]

**★★59% *Sun Bay*** Inner Hope Cove TQ7 3HH
☎Kingsbridge(0548)561371
Closed 19 Oct-27 Mar
*Overlooking the unspoilt harbour of Inner Hope Bay, on the edge of the village, this family-run hotel has a relaxed, informal atmosphere. Bedroom, whilst compact, are brightly decorated and have modern furnishings. Refreshments are served on the sun terrace in the summer.*
14rm(10⇨2⌐)(7fb) CTV in all bedrooms ®
CTV 12P ⇼ ✲
**V** ♆ ♋ Last dinner 8.30pm

**★61% Greystone** TQ7 3HH ☎Kingsbridge(0548)561233
*The comfortable public rooms of the hotel have large windows giving magnificent views of Hope Cove. The substantial home-prepared meals and friendly informal service make for an enjoyable stay.*
7rm(4⇨2⌐)Annexe2⇨ ® ✱ sB&B⇨⌐£27
dB&B⇨⌐£54 (incl dinner) ⊨
CTV 15P 3⌂ (£1 per night) ⇼ ✲ nc7yrs *xmas*
♆ ♋ Lunch fr£5.75 Dinner £9.50-£12 Last dinner 9.30pm
Credit Cards [1] [3]

## HORLEY Hotels are listed under **Gatwick Airport**

## HORNBY Lancashire Map 07 SD56

**★★54% *Castle*** Main St LA28 8JT ☎(0468)21204
*This famous 17th-century coaching inn, set by the roadside at the centre of the village, offers modest accommodation, a good range of bar meals and friendly, informal service.*
13rm(4⇨4⌐)(2fb) CTV in all bedrooms
50P ⇼
♉ English & Continental **V** ♆ ♋
Credit Cards [1] [2] [3]

## HORNCHURCH Greater London Map 05 TQ58

**★★★59% Hilton National** Southend Arterial Rd RM11 3UJ
(Hilton) ☎Ingrebourne(04023)46789 Telex no 897315
FAX (04023) 41719
*Modern hotel with comfortable bedrooms. The popular 'Palms' cocktail bar and eating house has been enlarged and there is a new leisure centre.*
137⇨⌐(10fb)⊁in 25 bedrooms CTV in all bedrooms ® **T** ✱
sB⇨⌐£75-£90 dB⇨⌐£85-£100 (room only) ⊨
☾ 180P ✲ CFA ♫ ⌂

H

♀ International **V** ♥ ⚿ Lunch £10.50-£32.20alc Dinner £10.50-£32.20alc Last dinner 10.30pm
Credit Cards ①②③⑤ⓔ

## HORNING Norfolk Map 09 TG31

★★★62%, **Petersfield House** Lower St NR12 8PF
☎(0692)630741 FAX (0692) 630745
*A family-run hotel in a superb position, tucked away in its own landscaped gardens close to the River Bure, providing friendly service and extending a warm welcome to guests. Comfortable, well-equipped rooms make it equally suitable for tourists and business people.*
18⇱ᠺ(1fb) CTV in all bedrooms ® **T** sB&B⇱ᠺ£52-£58 dB&B⇱ᠺ£65-£75 ₽
70P 🚗 ✿ ♪ ♫ xmas
♀ English & Continental **V** ♥ ⚿ Lunch fr£12&alc High tea £3.50-£5 Dinner fr£14&alc Last dinner 9.30pm
Credit Cards ①②③⑤

★61% **Swan** Lower St NR12 8AA ☎(0692)630316
*Delightfully situated beside the River Bure in a charming Broadland village, this small hotel offers well furnished, attractively decorated bedrooms with good facilities and a bar that is very busy with passing boat trade.*
11⇱ᠺ(2fb) CTV in all bedrooms ® ✖ (ex guide dogs)
150P ✿ ♪ billiards
**V** ♥ ⚿ Last dinner 9.30pm
Credit Cards ①②③⑤

## HORN'S CROSS Devon Map 02 SS32

★★★⚑68%, **Foxdown Manor** EX39 5PJ (Signed from A39 W of village) ☎Horns Cross(02375)325 & 642
Closed Jan & Feb
*Halfway between Bideford and Clovelly, just off the A39, this elegant manor is delightfully situated in twenty acres of gardens and woodland, its style being reflected in the tasteful decoration and furnishing of its public areas; ensuite, well equipped bedrooms are particularly spacious. A table d'hôte menu offers interesting dishes which make use of local produce whenever possible. Family proprietors and their staff offer a warm welcome to guests, assuring them of personal service.*
7⇱ᠺ(1fb)🛏 CTV in all bedrooms ® **T** ✳ sB&B⇱ᠺ£34-£42 dB&B⇱ᠺ£53-£68 ₽
30P 🚗 ✿ ⌒(heated) ♪ (hard) sauna solarium croquet putting ☍ xmas
♀ English & French **V** ♥ ⚿ Sunday Lunch £9 High tea £6 Dinner £16&alc Last dinner 8.45pm
Credit Cards ①②③

## HORRABRIDGE Devon Map 02 SX57

★★66% **Overcombe** PL20 7RN ☎Yelverton(0822)853501
*In village centre position close to the main road, the hotel complements comfortable, well-modernised bedrooms with ample public areas where open fires burn in the colder months. Relaxed, friendly service and the provision of thoughtful extras combine to give a real 'home from home' feeling.*
11rm(10⇱ᠺ)(2fb) CTV in all bedrooms ® ✳ sB&B£18-£23 sB&B⇱ᠺ£23 dB&Bfr£36 dB&B⇱ᠺ£36-£41 (incl dinner) ₽
CTV 10P 🚗 croquet
**V** ✂
Credit Cards ①③ⓔ
See advertisement under YELVERTON

All AA-appointed establishments are inspected regularly to ensure that required standards are maintained.

## HORSFORTH West Yorkshire Map 08 SE23

✖✖✖**Low Hall** Calverley Ln LS18 4EF ☎Leeds(0532)588221
*An elegant Tudor house has been converted into a comfortable hotel where the relaxing atmosphere is largely due to the attentive but unobtrusive service provided by its courteous staff. The restaurant features an interesting range of menus – particularly for the evening meal – starters such as smoked salmon, terrines, home-made soups and Yorkshire puddings with onion and red wine gravy being followed by a choice of main courses including lobster, lamb and beef; puddings, also home made, are a delight, while the wine list has been carefully chosen to complement the menu as a whole.*
Closed Sun, Mon, Xmas, 26-27 May & BH's
Lunch not served Sat
♀ English & French **V** 80 seats Last lunch 2pm Last dinner 9.30pm 70P
Credit Cards ①③
**See advertisement under LEEDS**

## HORSHAM West Sussex Map 04 TQ13

★★★★⚑63%, **South Lodge** Brighton Rd RH13 6PS (Prestige)
☎Lower Beeding(0403)891711 Telex no 877765
FAX (0403) 891253
(For full entry see Lower Beeding)

★★69% **Ye Olde King's Head** RH12 1EG ☎(0403)53126
*Good standards of cooking are matched by particularly well-managed and efficient service at an historic coaching inn which offers a choice of comfortable modern bedrooms; public areas include restaurant, coffee shop, bar lounge and Ye Olde Wine Cellar.*
43rm(6⇱35ᠺ)(2fb)1🛏 CTV in all bedrooms ® **T** ✳ sB&Bfr£49.50 sB&B⇱ᠺ£59.50 dB&B⇱ᠺ£72 ₽
40P CFA

▶

**HOME FARM**
COUNTRY HOUSE HOTEL & RESTAURANT
Wilmington, Nr Honiton,
Devon EX14 9JR ★★

*Small but beautiful thatched farm house.
*14 lovely rooms all with TV, coffee & tea, hair drier, clock radio alarm, telephone, baby listening.
*Far reaching views, from our 4 acres of glorious grounds.
* Draught beer, super food, log fires.
* 5 miles inland from sea.
**Brochure: (040 483) 278**

# Horsham - Howtown (near Pooley Bridge)

V ♿ ⌂ Lunch £9.15-£10.15 Dinner £13.50&alc Last dinner 9.45pm
Credit Cards ⬚1⬚ ⬚2⬚ ⬚3⬚ ⬚5⬚

---

## HORTON Northamptonshire Map 04 SP85

❀✕✕**French Partridge** NN7 2AP ☎Northampton(0604)870033 (Rosette awarded for dinner only)

*Set 4-course meals are served at this well known, family-run restaurant near to Northampton and accessible from junction 15 of the M1. The light, delicately flavoured dishes cooked by Mr Partridge have earned much praise, and particularly from our Inspector for a scallop mousse with an excellent red pepper sauce. There are three separate sittings for dinner, so booking is advisable and service can be a little slow.*

Closed Sun, Mon, 2 wks Xmas, 2 wks Etr & 3 wks Jul-Aug Lunch not served
♀ French V 40 seats ✳ S10% Dinner £18-£19 Last dinner 9pm 50P ⅄

---

## HORTON-CUM-STUDLEY Oxfordshire Map 04 SP51

❀★★★⚑67%, **Studley Priory** OX9 1AZ (Consort)
☎Stanton St John(086735)203 & 254 Telex no 23152 FAX (086735) 613

*Woods and parkland surround this former Benedictine nunnery which has been transformed into a most comfortable hotel with a notable restaurant, now being refurbished to provide a suitable setting for the excellent cooking. At dinner, among several table d'hôte menus, the gourmet menu is the one that our Inspectors recommend, singling out the Quail filled with chestnut soufflé, the chicken and filo pastry canelloni and the Petit Tournedos of beef with a shallot, snail and wild mushroom sauce, for their special praise.*

19⇨1¶2⚏ CTV in all bedrooms ® ✖ sB&B⇨¶£75-£100 dB&B⇨¶£88-£135 ☐
100P 1☎ ✿ ✍ (grass) croquet clay pigeon shooting *xmas*
♀ English & French V Lunch £20-£28 Dinner £28-£38 Last dinner 9.30pm
Credit Cards ⬚1⬚ ⬚2⬚ ⬚3⬚ ⬚4⬚ ⬚5⬚

---

## HORWICH Greater Manchester Map 07 SD61

★★64%, **Swallowfield** Chorley New Rd BL6 6HN
☎(0204)697914 FAX (0204) 68900

*Managed by resident proprietors this comfortable and friendly hotel stands in its own gardens close to junction 6 of the M61.*

31⇨¶(6fb) CTV in all bedrooms ® T sB&B⇨¶£37-£40 dB&B⇨¶£51-£55 ☐
35P ⚏ ✿
♿ ⌂ Lunch £9-£12&alc High tea £2-£5&alc Dinner £9-£12&alc Last dinner 8.30pm
Credit Cards ⬚1⬚ ⬚3⬚

---

## HOUNSLOW Greater London

See **LONDON plan 1**B3(page 426)
★★★60%, **Master Robert** Great West Rd TW5 0BD (A4)
☎081-570 6261 Telex no 9413782 FAX 081-569 4016

*Popular motel-style accommodation, close to Heathrow Airport, on the busy A4. The bedrooms are housed in separate buildings, together with 19 chalets ; each has its own parking space. The Steak House Carvery Restaurant and bars offer good value and service throughout is friendly and well managed. Conference and banqueting facilities are available.*

100⇨(8fb) CTV in all bedrooms ® T ✖ (ex guide dogs)
( 100P 35☎ ✿
♀ Mainly grills V ♿ ⌂
Credit Cards ⬚1⬚ ⬚2⬚ ⬚3⬚ ⬚5⬚

---

## HOVE East Sussex

See **Brighton & Hove**

---

## HOVINGHAM North Yorkshire Map 08 SE67

★★★65%, **Worsley Hotel Arms** YO6 4LA ☎(0653)628234 FAX (0653) 628130

*Situated within the peaceful and picturesque village of Hovingham, this hotel has recently undergone extensive refurbishment. There is a range of comfortable lounges for guests use, and the freshly prepared dishes can be enjoyed in the elegant restaurant. The bedrooms are individually decorated to a high standard, and all have en suite bathrooms. Some are situated in a cottage close by. The young staff provide a friendly service.*

14⇨1⚏ CTV in all bedrooms T sB&B⇨£47-£52 dB&B⇨£66-£74 ☐
CTV 50P 3☎ ✿ ♨ *xmas*
V ♿ ⌂ Lunch £8-£9.50 High tea £5.25-£7.25 Dinner £16.50-£18.50 Last dinner 9pm
Credit Cards ⬚1⬚ ⬚3⬚ ⬚£⬚

---

## HOW CAPLE Hereford & Worcester Map 03 SO63

★★62%, *How Caple Grange* HR1 4TF ☎(098986)208

*This impressive stone-built house, dating back to 1730 but considerably enlarged in Victorian times, stands in five acres of grounds and gardens on the B4224 between Hereford and Ross-on-Wye. Its spacious bedrooms are well equipped to suit tourist or business traveller, and leisure amenities include a solarium, sauna and jacuzzi, as well as an unheated swimming pool in the grounds.*

26rm(18⇨) CTV in 18 bedrooms ®
CTV 100P ✿ ⟿ sauna solarium gymnasium putting
♿ Last dinner 9pm

---

## HOWTOWN (near Pooley Bridge) Cumbria Map 12 NY41

❀❀★★★⚑ SHARROW BAY COUNTRY HOUSE

Sharrow Bay CA10 2LZ (at Pooley Bridge take unclass road S for 4m) (Relais et Châteaux) ☎Pooley Bridge(07684)86301 & 86483 FAX (07684) 86349
Closed end Nov-early Mar

*Brian Sack and Francis Coulson, joint owners of this splendid Lakeland hotel have lost none of their enthusiasm for hotel keeping in the 42 years they have reigned here. Bedrooms, whether in the main house, in one of the cottages in the grounds, or at Bank House, just over a mile away and overlooking the lakeside, are charming and echo the style of the public rooms with their wealth of porcelain and objets d'art. Bank House has its own quiet lounges and a magnificent dining room where breakfast is served. At the main house, lunch, afternoon tea and dinner remain as popular as ever, which at times can place considerable pressure on available seating. Meals continue to achieve high standards, with interesting choices available for each of three principal courses. Many of the management and staff will be familiar faces to those lucky enough to make frequent return visits, and we once again congratulate everybody responsible for maintaining the high reputation of Sharrow Bay, a reputation that we are delighted to honour by nominating this hotel as one of the winners of the AA's new 'Courtesy and Care' Award.*

12rm(8⇄)Annexe18⇄♠ CTV in all bedrooms ® T ✗ S%
sB&B£73 sB&B⇄♠£82-£110 dB&B£146
dB&B⇄♠£185-£242 (incl dinner)
25P 2🅰 ⇔ ❁ nc13yrs
♀ English & French V ❁ ⬚ ✄ S% Lunch £23-£25 Dinner
£35-£37 Last dinner 8.45pm

---

## HUDDERSFIELD West Yorkshire Map **07** SE11

See also **Marsden**

★★★67% **Pennine Hilton National** HD3 3RH (Hilton)
☎Elland(0422)375431 Telex no 517346 FAX (0422) 310067
*Situated just off the M62 at junction 24 this well furnished modern
hotel provides a high standard of comfort and service.*
118⇄♠ ✄in 60 bedrooms CTV in all bedrooms ® T
✗ (ex guide dogs) 🅱
Lift ℂ 250P CFA ▨(heated) sauna gymnasium children's pool
xmas
♀ English, French & Italian V ❁ ⬚
Credit Cards ①②③⑤

★★★65% **The George** St George's Square HD1 1JA
☎(0484)515444 FAX (0484) 435056
*At this traditional hotel, convenient for the station and the town
centre, there are good facilities for both business travellers and
holiday-makers. The Shines Restaurant offers à la carte and table
d'hôte menus, and many items are Yorkshire specialities – some
with interesting sauces. The staff are friendly and the atmosphere
relaxed and comfortable.*
60⇄♠(2fb)✄in 15 bedrooms CTV in all bedrooms ® T
sB⇄♠fr£60 dB⇄♠fr£75 (room only) 🅱
Lift ℂ 12P CFA ♫ xmas
V ❁ ⬚ ✄ S10% Lunch £6.50 Dinner £12.95 Last dinner 10pm
Credit Cards ①②③④⑤ⓔ

★★★61% **Briar Court** Halifax Road, Birchencliffe HD3 3NT
☎(0484)519902 Telex no 518260 FAX (0484) 431812
*This is a busy, modern hotel, near junction 24 of the M62 leading
into the town. A feature of the hotel is the Da Sandro Italian
restaurant, renowned for its pizza, baked in the traditional
Neopolitan way.*
48⇄♠(3fb) CTV in all bedrooms ® T ✗ (ex guide dogs) S%
sB&B⇄♠fr£60 dB&B⇄♠fr£76 🅱
ℂ 140P ❁
♀ English & Italian V ❁ ⬚ S% Lunch fr£7.50&alc Dinner
fr£11.50&alc Last dinner 11.00pm
Credit Cards ①②③⑤

★★68% **Huddersfield** 33-47 Kirkgate HD1 1QT ☎(0484)512111
Telex no 51575 FAX (0484) 435262
*A busy, family run hotel in the town centre, close to the ring road,
providing comfortable, well-equipped bedrooms, a bistro-style
restaurant, nightclub, wine bar and the popular Boy and Barrel
Inn.*
40⇄♠(4fb)2⊞ CTV in all bedrooms ® T sB&B⇄♠£20-£40
dB&B⇄♠£30-£50
Lift ℂ CTV 30P sauna solarium jacuzzi pool-table darts ♫
xmas
V ❁ ⬚ Lunch £4.50-£7.50&alc Dinner £6-£9.50&alc Last
dinner mdnt
Credit Cards ①②③④⑤

---

All hotels are now given a percentage grading
for the quality of their facilities. A full explanation
can be found within 'How we Classify Hotels
and Restaurants' at the front of the book.

---

✗ **Weavers Shed** Acre Mills, Knowl Rd, Golcar HD7 4AN (3m
W off A62) ☎(0484)654284
*The restaurant is housed in a quaint old weavers shed, which has
been delightfully converted to retain the original character and
atmosphere. The menu of traditional British dishes features
unusual home-made soups. Main course dishes change regularly to
make the best use of seasonal produce : fish, meat and game are all
used. Sweets range from light trifles to crumbles and sticky toffee
pudding.*
Closed Sun, Mon, 1st 2 wks Jan & last 2 wks Jul
Lunch not served Sat
40 seats Lunch £8.95&alc Dinner £15.15-£18.95alc Last lunch
1.45pm Last dinner 9pm 30P
Credit Cards ①②③

---

## HULL Humberside Map **08** TA02

★★★★67% **Post House** Castle St HU1 2BX (Trusthouse Forte)
☎(0482)225221 Telex no 592777 FAX (0482) 213299
*Attractively set by the marina, within the redeveloped docks area
and near the city centre, this hotel has spacious public areas,
pleasant bedrooms and a health and fitness club.*
99⇄(12fb)✄in 11 bedrooms CTV in all bedrooms ®
Lift ℂ 130P ❁ ▨(heated) ♪ (grass) sauna solarium
gymnasium
♀ English & French V ❁ ⬚ ✄ Last dinner 10.30pm
Credit Cards ①②③④⑤

★★★75% **Grange Park** Main St HU10 6EA (Best Western)
☎(0482)656488 Telex no 592773 FAX (0482) 655848
(For full entry see Willerby)

★★★69% **Willerby Manor** Well Ln HU10 6ER ☎(0482)652616
Telex no 592629 FAX (0482) 653901
(For full entry see Willerby)

# The Willerby Manor Hotel
### ★★★

*Renowned for its cuisine, high
standards, warm welcome to travellers
and diners alike. Situated within easy
access of Hull & Beverley offers you
the ideal rendezvous for your
Conference, Banquet, Wedding or
Party. Savour and enjoy the
specialities in the Restaurant Lafite.*

**The Willerby Manor Hotel, Well Lane,
Willerby. Tel: Hull 652616 Fax: 0482 653901**

**H**

## Hull

★★★67%, **Crest Hotel-Hull** Ferriby High Rd HU14 3LG
(Trusthouse Forte) ☎(0482)645212 Telex no 592558
FAX (0482) 643332
(For full entry see North Ferriby)

★★★58%, **Valiant House** 11 Anlaby Rd HU1 2PJ
☎(0482)23299 FAX (0482) 214730
*A commercial hotel in the centre of Hull, adjacent to the railway
station and with easy access to the shops. Modern accommodation
includes particularly well equipped bedrooms.*
58⇨ⁿ CTV in all bedrooms ® T
Lift ( 10P
♡ English & French V ✿ ⊡ Last dinner 10pm
Credit Cards ① ② ③ ⑤

★★★57%, **Royal Hotel** Ferensway HU1 3UF (Consort)
☎(0482)25087 Telex no 592450 FAX (0482) 23172
*Spacious public areas complement well appointed bedrooms at this
traditional city centre hotel.*
123⇨ⁿ(4fb)2⚿⊬in 19 bedrooms CTV in all bedrooms ® T
S% sB&B⇨ⁿ£46-£56
dB&B⇨ⁿ£56-£66 Continental breakfast ➡
Lift ( CTV 60P gymnasium *xmas*
♡ English & French V ✿ ⊡ ⊬ Lunch fr£7.50 Dinner
£11.75-£14.75&alc Last dinner 9.30pm
Credit Cards ① ② ③ ④ ⑤ ⓔ

★★71%, **Waterfront** Dagger Ln HU1 2LS ☎(0482)227222
*This interesting hotel occupies an historic warehouse which has
been carefully converted to retain its original character. It provides
guests with modern comforts and facilities of a very good standard.*
30⇨ⁿ2⚿ CTV in all bedrooms ® T sB⇨ⁿ£27-£61
dB⇨ⁿ£43-£73 (room only)
( 32P ⏣
♡ English & French V ✿ ⊡ Sunday Lunch £3.95-£6.95alc
Dinner £10-£16alc Last dinner 10.30pm
Credit Cards ① ③ ⓔ

★★63%, **Pearson Park** Pearson Park HU5 2TQ ☎(0482)43043
FAX (0482) 447679
Closed 24 Dec-1 Jan
*This hotel enjoys a surprisingly different and delightful situation
within a well established and well kept public park, and yet is only
one mile from the city centre. Because of its location, it is both
handy for the city, yet offers a more peaceful environment,
enhanced by the personal attention of the proprietors and their
small team of staff.*
35rm(29⇨ⁿ)(4fb)1⚿ CTV in all bedrooms ® T sB&B£26-£32
sB&B⇨ⁿ£29-£42 dB&B⇨ⁿ£39-£54 ➡
( 30P
♡ English & French V ✿ ⊡ S% Lunch £5 Dinner £9&alc Last
dinner 9pm
Credit Cards ① ② ③ ⑤

**See advertisement on page 357**

⏏**Campanile** Beverley Rd HU2 9AN (Campanile)
☎(0482)25530 Telex no 592840
*A modern, purpose-built unit provides simple bedrooms as an
annexe to the restaurant.*
Annexe48⇨ⁿ CTV in all bedrooms ® T
60P
♡English & French Last dinner 10pm
Credit Cards ① ③

**See advertisement on page 357**

✕✕**Cerutti's** 10 Nelson St HU1 1XE ☎(0482)28501
FAX (0482) 587597
Closed Sun, 24 Dec-3 Jan & BHs
Lunch not served Sat
♡ International 36 seats ✳ Lunch £12-£25alc Dinner
£12-£25alc Last lunch 2.00pm Last dinner 9.30pm 10P
Credit Cards ① ③

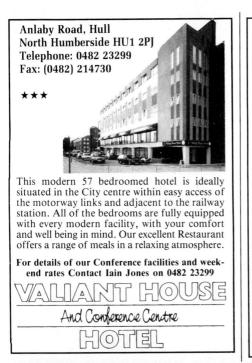

H

---

**HUMBIE** Lothian *East Lothian* Map **12** NT46

★★★≛**66%** *Johnstounburn House* EH36 5PL (1m S on A6137) (Mount Charlotte (TS)) ☎(087533)696 Telex no 557934

*Set in forty acres of secluded grounds and gardens, this charming seventeenth-century house offers well-equipped, individually styled bedrooms and comfortable public rooms which make it easy to relax.*

11➬♠Annexe9➬♠(9fb) CTV in all bedrooms ®
20P ⇔ ✿ clay pigeon shooting ⚐
V ✿
Credit Cards ① ② ③ ⑤

---

**HUNGERFORD** Berkshire Map **04** SU36

★★★**64%** **Bear** Charnham St RG17 OEL ☎(0488)682512 FAX (0488) 684357

*This charming hotel offers the atmosphere of a traditional English inn, with open fires, antiques and exposed beams. Bedrooms are well equipped with modern facilities and the popular restaurant provides a good choice of menus.*

14➬Annexe27➬♠(2fb)1⊞ CTV in all bedrooms ® T ✱
sB➬♠£65-£75 dB➬♠£75-£85 (room only) ♬
《 80P ⇔ *xmas*
V ✿ ⚖ Lunch fr£13.95 Dinner fr£17.95 Last dinner 9.30pm
Credit Cards ① ② ③ ⑤ ⓔ

---

**HUNSTANTON** Norfolk Map **09** TF64

★★**67%** **Caley Hall** PE36 6HH ☎(04853)33486
Closed Jan-Feb RS Sun evening

*Situated in a quiet location, just off the coastal road (the A149), right on the edge of Old Hunstanton, The Caley Hall Hotel offers good accommodation. The King family aim to provide a friendly, informal stay, in a relaxed atmosphere, and with so many guests making return visits, we think they have succeeded. Bedrooms are in chalet-style annexes, which have been sympathetically added to complement the 17th century manor house and the converted old stables, the latter housing the lounge, restaurant and bar.*

Annexe29rm(27➬)(5fb) CTV in all bedrooms ® ✱
sB&B£23-£26 sB&B➬£23-£26 dB&B£46-£52
dB&B➬£46-£52 ♬
50P ✿ nc *xmas*
⚑ International V ✿ Sunday Lunch fr£10.50 Dinner fr£10.50&alc Last dinner 9pm
Credit Cards ① ③

★★**62%** **Lodge** Hunstanton Rd, Old Hunstanton PE36 6HX
☎(04853)2896

*A character hotel offers friendly service and comfortable bedrooms with modern amenities; children are welcomed and have their own safe play area, whilst the restaurant makes full use of local produce, particularly fish and game in season.*

15➬♠(2fb) CTV in all bedrooms ® T ♬
70P ✿ snooker
⚑ English, French & Italian V ✿ ⚖
Credit Cards ① ② ③

★**74%** **Sunningdale** 3-5 Av Rd PE36 5BW ☎(04853)2562

*Just a few minutes walk from the beach and town centre, this hotel provides attractive, well equipped accommodation and imaginatively prepared food. Mr and Mrs Wright maintain high standards throughout.*

11➬♠(1fb)⚹in 2 bedrooms CTV in all bedrooms ®
sB&B➬♠£25-£26.50 dB&B➬♠£40-£47
𝄞 nc7yrs *xmas*
⚑ English & Continental ✿ ⚖ ⚹ Bar Lunch £3-£5&alc Dinner £8-£10&alc Last dinner 8pm
ⓔ

---

★**57%** **Wash & Tope** Le Strange Ter PE36 5AJ ☎(04853)2250

*Situated close to the seafront, with many rooms enjoying sea views, this inn provides comfortable accommodation and friendly service. Dishes are mainly grills.*

10rm(4➬2♠)(1fb)1⊞ CTV in all bedrooms ®
12P 2⚘ pool
V ✿
Credit Cards ① ② ③

---

**HUNSTRETE** Avon Map **03** ST66

★★★≛ HUNSTRETE HOUSE

BS18 4NS ☎Compton
Dando (0761)490490
Telex no 449540
FAX (0761) 490732

*We are delighted to reinstate the red star award for this gracious hotel which changed hands in 1989, and to report that the atmosphere and the surroundings have remained as pleasing as ever, indeed in some respects could be said to have improved. Paintings and antiques abound, and both lounges and dining rooms are exceptionally attractive. The larger of the dining rooms, some may be pleased to note, is exclusively for non-smokers, while those who enjoy the luxury of a cigarette will feel at ease in the other. Bedrooms are comfortable, and are equipped with every conceivable extra. Head chef Robert Elsmore remains in charge of the kitchens, specialising in British food of an extremely high standard, the regularly changing set-price menu featuring dishes of considerable flair and imagination. Staff attitudes are worthy of mention, and the Deputy Manager, Gill Meade, combines efficiency with genuine warmth of manner and interest in her guests.*

13➬♠Annexe11➬♠2⊞ CTV in all bedrooms T
✕ (ex guide dogs) sB&B➬♠fr£95 dB&B➬♠fr£170 ♬
《 40P ⇔ ✿ ≏(heated) ⨏ (hard) croquet lawn nc9yrs *xmas*
⚑ English & French V ✿ ⚖ ⚹ Lunch fr£15&alc Dinner fr£32 Last dinner 10pm
Credit Cards ① ③

See advertisement under BATH

---

**HUNTINGDON** Cambridgeshire Map **04** TL27

★★★**69%** **The Old Bridge** PE18 6TQ ☎(0480)52681
Telex no 32706 FAX (0480) 411017

*An ivy-clad Georgian property, set only a short walk from the town centre in gardens which run down to the River Ouse, offers individually decorated bedrooms with modern facilities. Guests can choose between the restaurant good range of well prepared dishes and the lighter, more informal meals served in the Terrace Lounge.*

26➬♠(3fb)1⊞ CTV in all bedrooms T ✱
sB&B➬♠£71.50-£80 dB&B➬♠£96.80-£110 ♬
《 50P ✈ private mooring for boats *xmas*
V ✿ ⚖ Lunch £14.25-£21.95&alc Dinner fr£21.95&alc Last dinner 10.15pm
Credit Cards ① ② ③ ⑤

★★★**61%** **The George** George St PE18 6AB (Trusthouse Forte)
☎(0480)432444 FAX (0480) 453130

*A hotel set just off the High Street was once the home of Oliver Cromwell's grandfather, and parts of it date back to early Stuart times. Most bedrooms are spacious, and all of them offer modern*

▶

*facilities, while Chaucer's Restaurant features some tradtional English dishes.*
24⇨🏮(2fb)⊬in 4 bedrooms CTV in all bedrooms ® T S%
sB⇨🏮£65-£75 dB⇨🏮£87-£92 (room only) ➡
71P *xmas*
V ❦ ⚲ ⊬ S% Lunch £9-£11&alc Dinner fr£15&alc Last dinner 9.30pm
Credit Cards 1 2 3 4 5

---

## HUNTLY Grampian *Aberdeenshire* Map **15** NJ53

★★⚑53% **Castle** AB5 4SH ☎(0466)2696
*Once the family home of the Gordons, this personally managed, traditional hotel in an elevated position on the outskirts of the town is popular with anglers. There are few modern conveniences, but welcoming open fires and comfortable, spacious rooms, give the hotel a charm of its own.*
24rm(7⇨2🏮)(2fb)1⊞ CTV in 12 bedrooms ®
sB&B£21-£28.50 sB&B⇨🏮£25-£32.50 dB&B£31-£38.50
dB&B⇨🏮£35-£42.50
CTV 50P 3🚗❀ ⚘ *xmas*
V ❦ ⚲ Lunch £5-£15 High tea £2-£10 Dinner £7.50-£15 Last dinner 10pm
Credit Cards 1 2 3 £

---

## HURLEY Berkshire Map **04** SU88

★★★63% **Ye Olde Bell** SL6 5LX
☎Littlewick Green(0628)825881 FAX (0628) 825939
*This ancient inn traces its history back to 1136 and retains much original character plus comfortable bedrooms and friendly, willing service.*
10⇨🏮Annexe15⇨🏮(1fb)3⊞ CTV in all bedrooms ® T ✲
sB⇨🏮£70-£85 dB⇨🏮£85-£90 (room only) ➡
☾90P 🚗 ❀ *xmas*
♀ English & French V ❦ ⚲ ⊬ Lunch fr£14.50 Dinner fr£17.50 Last dinner 9.30pm
Credit Cards 1 2 3 5 £

---

## HURSTBOURNE TARRANT Hampshire Map **04** SU35

★★⚑71% *Esseborne Manor* SP11 0ER (Pride of Britain)
☎(0264)76444 FAX (0264) 76473
*Nestled among well-kept gardens and parkland in a peaceful rural atmosphere, the Georgian/Victorian farmhouse features individually decorated bedrooms which combine charm and comfort, luxury extras and modern facilities, some being located in an annexe to the rear of the main house. Public areas are tastefully furnished and decorated with antiques, while the restaurant offers a carefully balanced selection of dishes prepared from good quality fresh ingredients. little hotel.*
6⇨🏮Annexe6⇨🏮CTV in all bedrooms ✖ (ex guide dogs)
30P 🚗 ❀ ⚘ (hard) croquet putting net nc12yrs
♀ English & French ❦ ⚲ Last dinner 9.30pm
Credit Cards 1 2 3 5

---

## HURST GREEN Lancashire Map **07** SD63

★★77% **Shireburn Arms** BB6 9QJ ☎Stonyhurst(025486)518
*A delightful country inn offering friendly, genteel service throughout. Bedrooms are comfortable and feature many thoughtful extras, whilst bars and lounges are full of character. The restaurant provides interesting menus and good value.*
16⇨🏮(1fb)1⊞ CTV in all bedrooms ® T
sB&B⇨🏮£39.50-£52 dB&B⇨🏮£58-£69.50 ➡
CTV 71P ❀ putting green *xmas*
♀ English & French V ❦ ⚲ Lunch £6.25-£10.50 Dinner £11.50 Last dinner 9.30pm
Credit Cards 1 3 £

---

## HYTHE Kent Map **05** TR13

★★★★66% **The Hythe Imperial** Princes Pde CT21 6AE (Best Western) ☎(0303)267441 Telex no 965082 FAX (0303) 264610
*A good choice of comfortable and tastefully furnished bedrooms, well equipped and appointed, is provided by this large sea-front hotel; public areas are pleasant, staff are friendly, and an extensive range of sports and leisure facilities is available.*
100⇨🏮(5fb)⊞ CTV in all bedrooms ® T ✖ (ex guide dogs)
sB&B⇨🏮£70-£90 dB&B⇨🏮£100-£140 ➡
Lift ☾150P ❀ ▣(heated) ⟟9 ⚘ (hard & grass) squash snooker sauna solarium gymnasium croquet bowls putting karts beauty salon ♫ ◉ *xmas*
♀ English & French V ❦ ⚲ ⊬ Lunch £13.50-£16&alc High tea £3.75-£7 Dinner £17-£20&alc Last dinner 9pm
Credit Cards 1 2 3 5

★★★60% **Stade Court** West Pde CT21 6DT (Best Western) ☎(0303)268263 Telex no 965082 FAX (0303) 264610
*An hotel in pleasant sea-front location features a range of accommodation stretching from family suites to singles – some rooms even having their own small sun lounges – together with a pleasant lounge and cosy bar.*
39⇨🏮(5fb)⊬in 4 bedrooms CTV in all bedrooms ® T
sB&B⇨🏮£43-£49 dB&B⇨🏮£68 ➡
Lift 12P 2🚗 (£3 per night) CFA ▣(heated) ⟟9 ⚘ (hard & grass) squash snooker sauna solarium gymnasium *xmas*
♀ English & Continental V ❦ ⚲ ⊬ Lunch fr£7.50&alc Dinner fr£14.50&alc Last dinner 9pm
Credit Cards 1 2 3 5

---

## ILFRACOMBE Devon Map **02** SS54

★★65% **Elmfield** Torrs Park EX34 8AZ ☎(0271)863377
Closed Nov-Mar (ex Xmas)
*From an elevated position overlooking Ilfracombe and the surrounding countryside, this friendly hotel offers well-equipped bedrooms, comfortable public rooms and the use of a heated swimming pool.*
12rm(11🏮) CTV in all bedrooms ® T ✖ sB&B🏮£32
dB&B🏮£64 (incl dinner) ➡
14P 🚗 ❀ ▣(heated) sauna solarium gymnasium pool table darts jacuzzi spa bath nc8yrs *xmas*
♀ English & Continental V ⊬ Bar Lunch £5-£10 Dinner £9.50&alc Last dinner 7.30pm
Credit Cards 1 3

★★61% **Tracy House** Belmont Rd EX34 8DR
☎(0271)863933 & 868979
Closed Nov-Feb RS Mar & Oct
*This informally-run hotel stands near the town centre yet within walking distance of beaches. All bedrooms offer good facilities and public areas are comfortably furnished, the bar promoting a pleasantly relaxed atmosphere and the dining room serving a simple table d'hôte menu.*
11rm(4⇨5🏮)(2fb) CTV in all bedrooms ® T ✲ sB&B£20-£22
sB&B⇨🏮£24-£26 dB&B£35.50-£40 dB&B⇨🏮£44-£53 ➡
11P 1🚗 (£2) 🚗 ❀ putting
♀ English & Continental ❦ ⚲ Bar Lunch £4.50 Dinner £8.50 Last dinner 8pm
Credit Cards 1 2 3

★★57% **Ilfracombe Carlton** Runnacleave Rd EX34 8AR
(Consort) ☎(0271)862446 FAX (0271) 865379
*A popular holiday hotel offering easy access to both town centre and beaches, and featuring daily entertainment during the season, provides accommodation in simply-appointed bedrooms; spacious public areas include a dining room where the table d'hôte menu is changed nightly.*
50rm(20⇨20🏮)(6fb) CTV in all bedrooms ®
✖ (ex guide dogs) sB&B£17.50-£21 sB&B⇨🏮£20-£23.50
dB&B£35-£42 dB&B⇨🏮£40-£47 ➡

Lift 《 25P ♫ *xmas*
♥ ⫴ ⤔ Bar Lunch 95p-£2.95 Dinner £10.50 Last dinner
8.30pm
Credit Cards ①②③ⓔ

★★56% **Arlington** Sommers Crescent EX34 9DP
☎(0271)862252 FAX (0271) 862015
Closed Dec-27 Jan
*Set in an elevated position with some sea views, this resort hotel caters in particular for the needs of family groups; the restaurant offers a four-course table d'hôte menu, entertainment is laid on during the season, and there is an outdoor swimming pool.*
29⇾ᐟↄ(6fb) CTV in all bedrooms Ⓡ T sB&B⇾ↄ£28-£37
dB&B⇾ↄ£56-£75 (incl dinner) ⊟
Lift CTV 30P ◿(heated) sauna solarium *xmas*
♥ ⫴ Bar Lunch £2-£3 High tea £2-£3 Dinner £12.50 Last
dinner 8pm
Credit Cards ①②③ⓔ

★★55% **St Helier** Hillsborough Rd EX34 9QQ
☎Barnstaple(0271)864906
Closed Oct-Apr
*The family-run hotel occupies a commanding position with sea views, yet is within comfortable walking distance of shops, amusements, sports facilities and beaches.*
23rm(16⇾ↄ1ↄ)(8fb) CTV in all bedrooms Ⓡ sB&B£18-£20
dB&B£34-£38 dB&B⇾ↄ£38-£42 ⊟
CTV 20P 9⇰ ⇷ ✿ pool table
♀ Austrian, French & Italian ♥ ⫴ Dinner £6.50-£7 Last
dinner 7.30pm
Credit Cards ①③

★57% **Torrs** Torrs Park EX34 8AY ☎(0271)862334
Closed Nov-8 Mar
*A friendly, family-run resort hotel in an elevated position enjoying views over the sea, town and countryside. Bedrooms, whilst compact, are simply furnished and well equipped.*
14⇾ↄ(5fb) CTV in all bedrooms Ⓡ ✱ sB&B⇾ↄ£18-£19.50
dB&B⇾ↄ£36-£39 ⊟
16P ⇷ solarium nc5yrs
V ♥ ⫴ ⤔ S10% Lunch £6.50-£9alc High tea £2.50 Dinner
£8.50&alc Last dinner 7.30pm
Credit Cards ①②③④⑤ⓔ

---

**ILKLEY** West Yorkshire Map **07** SE14

★★★58% **Cow & Calf** Moor Top LS29 8BT ☎(0943)607335
Closed Xmas
*A family-owned and run hotel, situated on the moor and overlooking the town. It offers efficient service, comfortable accommodation and a good standard of well-cooked food, served in the pleasant restaurant.*
17⇾ↄ(1fb)1⇷ CTV in all bedrooms Ⓡ T sB&B⇾ↄ£55-£65
dB&B⇾ↄ£65-£75 ⊟
100P ⇷ ✿
♀ English & French V ♥ Lunch £7.50-£10 Dinner £13.50&alc
Last dinner 9pm
Credit Cards ①②③④⑤

★★76% **Rombalds** 11 West View, Wells Rd LS29 9JG
☎(0943)603201 Telex no 51593 FAX (0943) 816586
Closed 28-30 Dec
*The proprietors' personal supervision of this comfortable, tastefully furnished hotel ensures courteous, friendly service, and its restaurant features an imaginative range of freshly-prepared dishes complemented by a well-balanced wine list; on Sundays visitors can enjoy the "Edwardian Breakfast" – a brunch which is served from breakfast time and through the lunch period.*
16⇾ↄↄ(5fb) CTV in all bedrooms Ⓡ sB&B⇾ↄ£55-£75
dB&B⇾ↄ£85-£95 ⊟

《 28P ⇷ *xmas*
V ♥ ⫴ Lunch £8.50-£11.25&alc Dinner £17-£25alc Last
dinner 10pm
Credit Cards ①②③⑤ⓔ

★★60% *Greystones* 1 Ben Rhydding Rd LS29 8RJ
☎(0943)607408
Closed 25 Dec & 1 Jan
*This stone-built suburban mansion, personally owned and run, is comfortable throughout and offers good value for money.*
10⇾ↄↄ(1fb) Ⓡ
CTV 17P ✿
♥
Credit Cards ①②③⑤

★65% **Grove** 66 The Grove LS29 9PA ☎(0943)600298
Closed 24-31 Dec
*A warm and comfortable little hotel near the town centre provides particularly well furnished accommodation and friendly, efficient service from resident owners.*
6⇾ↄↄ(2fb) CTV in all bedrooms Ⓡ sB&B⇾ↄↄ£33-£36
dB&B⇾ↄↄ£46-£48 ⊟
CTV 5P ⇷ nc3yrs
Lunch £7.50-£10alc Dinner £10-£12alc Last dinner 7.30pm
Credit Cards ①③

❀✕✕✕**Box Tree** Church St LS29 9DR ☎(0943)608484
FAX (0943) 816793(Rosette awarded for dinner only)
*Rich colour schemes, objets d'art and a profusion of oil paintings, prints and china give this long-established restaurant an atmosphere all of its own. In the evenings, a classical guitarist helps to set a relaxed tone, making this an ideal place for an intimate dinner. Guests have the option of eating from the Carte du Jour, with several items at each course, or the cheaper 3-course prix-fixe menu. Whatever is chosen, diners can be sure of a*

▶

*memorable evening. Chef Edward Denny combines sound technique with a flair for flavour that results in some well-constructed sauces – for example a wonderfully pungent smoked cheese sauce accompanying the Swiss Cheese Soufflé or the subtle Sauce Caramel compounding the richness of a liqueur-soaked chocolate marquise. Other highlights of the inspection meal were the perfectly cooked vegetables, and the ravioli filled with mushroom and tarragon that exploded with flavour in a fine sauce of consommé and wine, redolent of garlic and basil, and surrounding a noisette of lamb perched on a bed of spinach.*

Closed Mon, 25-26 Dec & 1 Jan
Lunch not served Tue-Sat
Dinner not served Sun
♀ French 50 seats ✻ Sunday Lunch fr£14.95 Dinner fr£18.50&alc Last dinner 10pm ♪ ♫
Credit Cards ①②③⑤

---

### ILMINSTER Somerset Map 03 ST31

★★60% **Shrubbery** TA19 9AR (Consort) ☎(0460)52108
Telex no 46379 FAX (0460) 53660
*Standing on the outskirts of the town, with its own large car park and heated outdoor pool, this ancient Ham-stone building complements public areas and extensive conference facilities which have recently been refurbished with bedrooms in process of upgrading in the main house and more compact but equally well equipped accommodation in a modern annexe. Bar snack, table d'hôte and à la carte menus offer a good range of eating options.*
12➡♠(3fb) CTV in all bedrooms ® ♬
CTV 100P ✻ ➡(heated) ♪ (grass) deep-sea fishing
♀ English & French V ♥ ⚖
Credit Cards ①②③④⑤

○**Travelodge** A303(Trusthouse Forte)
☎Central reservations (0800) 850950
32➡

---

### INCHNADAMPH Highland *Sutherland* Map 14 NC22

★★58% **Inchnadamph** IV27 4HL ☎Assynt(05712)202
Closed Nov-14 Mar
*A haven for anglers and an ideal base from which to explore the beautiful north west Highlands, this friendly family hotel is run on traditional lines, many a fishing yarn being swapped over a glass of malt in its comfortable lounges.*
27rm(10➡)(5fb) sB£20-£21.50 dB£40-£43
dB➡£45-£48 (room only)
CTV 30P 4➡ (£1.50) ♻ ♪
V ♥ ⚖ Lunch fr£7.85 Dinner fr£11.25 Last dinner 7.30pm
Credit Cards ①③⑤

---

### INGATESTONE Essex Map 05 TQ69

★★★65% **Heybridge Moat House** Roman Rd CM4 9AB
(Queens Moat) ☎(0277)355355 Telex no 995186
FAX (0277) 353288
*The original 15th-century building has been carefully renovated and now houses the restaurant and banqueting suites. The modern bedroom wing offers well equipped accommodation.*
22➡♠(3fb) CTV in all bedrooms ® T ✖ sB➡♠fr£72
dB➡♠fr£81 (room only)
《 CTV 200P ✻ ♫
♀ International V ♥ ⚖ Lunch fr£12&alc Dinner fr£12&alc
Last dinner 10.30pm
Credit Cards ①②③④⑤ ⑥

Hotels with a high percentage rating for quality
are highlighted by a % across their
gazetteer entry.

---

### INGLESHAM Wiltshire Map 04 SU29

✖✖**Inglesham Forge** SN6 7QY ☎Faringdon(0367)52298
*This old forge and cottage has been converted into a smart restaurant whilst still retaining its character with exposed beams, stone walls and a log fire. The comprehensive menus contain interesting dishes prepared from fresh ingredients.*
Closed Sun, last 2 wks Aug & 24-31 Dec
Lunch not served Sat & Mon
V 30 seats ✻ Lunch £18.50-£25.50 Dinner £18.50-£25.50 Last lunch 2pm Last dinner 9.30pm 15P
Credit Cards ①②③⑤

---

### INSTOW Devon Map 02 SS43

★★★61% **Commodore** Marine Pde EX39 4JN ☎(0271)860347
FAX (0271) 861233
*This modern hotel has a commanding position with views across the river to Appledore. The bedrooms are comfortable and well equipped, the public areas relaxing and the views from the recently refurbished restaurant (which offers both table d'hôte and à la carte menus) are simply glorious.*
20➡♠(3fb) CTV in all bedrooms ® T ✖ sB&B➡♠£47-£49
dB&B➡♠£70-£80 ♬
150P ♻ ✻ *xmas*
♀ English & Continental V ♥ ⚖ Lunch £9.50-£10.90 Dinner £16&alc Last dinner 9.15pm
Credit Cards ①②③
**See advertisements under BARNSTAPLE & BIDEFORD**

---

### INVERARAY Strathclyde *Argyllshire* Map 10 NN00

★68% **Fernpoint** PA32 8UX ☎(0499)2170
Closed Nov-Feb
*A period house with recent extensions, featuring friendly service and hospitality. Comprehensive bar meals are served throughout the day and evening. The hotel is situated near the pier with views of Loch Fyne.*
6➡♠(4fb) CTV in all bedrooms ® ✻ dB&B➡♠£48-£60 ♬
CTV 12P ✻ boating ♻ *xmas*
V ♥ ⚖ Bar Lunch £3-£6 Dinner £10-£15 Last dinner 9pm
Credit Cards ①③

---

### INVERGARRY Highland *Inverness-shire* Map 14 NH30

★★⚑61% **Glengarry Castle** PH35 4HW ☎(08093)254
FAX (08093) 207
Closed 23 Oct-27 Mar
*Ruins of Invergarry Castle are to be found in the grounds of this Victorian mansion.*
27rm(24➡♠)(4fb)2➡ CTV in 17 bedrooms ® sB&B£24-£29
sB&B➡♠£30-£35 dB&B£40-£44 dB&B➡♠£52-£76
CTV 30P 2➡ ♻ ♪ (hard)
♀ Scottish, English & Continental V ♥ ⚖ Lunch £8 Dinner £13.50 Last dinner 8.15pm
Credit Cards ①③

---

### INVERKEILOR Tayside *Angus* Map 15 NO64

✖**Gordon's** Homewood House, Main St DD11 5RN
☎(02413)364
*In the relaxed, friendly atmosphere of this unpretentious little village restaurant guests can select dishes in the French style from an à la carte menu which, though short, is imaginative without being over-adventurous; much care and skill goes into the preparation of meals here, and excellent use is made of fresh produce.*
Closed Mon & Last 2 wks Jan
Lunch not served Sat
Dinner not served Sun

♀ French 25 seats ✱ Dinner £16.80-£22alc Last dinner 9.30pm
6P nc8yrs ✂
Credit Cards ①③

---

**INVERMORISTON** Highland *Inverness-shire* Map **14** NH41

**★★68%** **Glenmoriston Arms** IV3 6YA
☎Glenmoriston(0320)51206
*This traditional Highland hotel offers friendly service with the
proprietors fully involved. The bar also boasts a fine collection of
malt whiskies.*
8⇄♠1⊞ CTV in all bedrooms ® T sB&B⇄♠£32-£35
dB&B⇄♠£45-£52 ⒫
28P ♨ ✿ ✱ stalking shooting
V ۞ ⚓ Sunday Lunch £6-£10alc Dinner £15-£16.50&alc Last
dinner 8.30pm
Credit Cards ①③ ⓔ

---

**INVERNESS** Highland *Inverness-shire* Map **14** NH64

**See Town Plan Section**
**★★★★58%** *Culloden House* Culloden IV1 2NZ (2m E off A96)
(Prestige) ☎(0463)790461 Telex no 75402 FAX (0463) 792181
*This fine country house was Bonnie Prince Charlie's base during
the Battle of Culloden, and is furnished in keeping with the period.
Proprietors Mr and Mrs McKenzie offer real hospitality, and
cuisine of a good standard is accompanied by an excellent wine
list.*
20⇄(1fb)5⊞ CTV in all bedrooms ✖
⚓ 50P 2☎ ♨ ✿ ♫ (hard) snooker sauna solarium nc10yrs
♀ Scottish & French V ۞ ⚓ ✂ Last dinner 9pm
Credit Cards ①②③⑤

**★★★♨73%** **Bunchrew House** Bunchrew IV3 6TA (3m W off
A862) ☎(0463)234917
*Steeped in history and standing in 15 acres of gardens and
woodland on the shores of the Beauly Firth, this beautifully
furnished 17th-century Scottish castle features a very comfortable
lounge with open log fire and good bedrooms of individual design.
Meals served in the delightful restaurant exhibit a high standard
of cuisine, whilst owners and staff offer a warm welcome and caring
service throughout.*
6⇄♠(2fb)1⊞✂in 1 bedroom CTV in all bedrooms T
sB&B⇄♠£50-£65 dB&B⇄♠£70-£105 ⒫
40P 2☎ ♨ ✿ ♫ clay pigeon shooting ⚘ xmas
♀ International V ۞ ⚓ ✂ Lunch £7.50-£10.50 Dinner £21
Last dinner 9pm
Credit Cards ①②③ⓔ

**★★★73%** **Craigmonie** 9 Annfield Rd IV2 3HX (Best Western)
☎(0463)231649 Telex no 94013304 FAX (0463) 233720
*A splendid indoor leisure complex and pool have recently been
added to this very comfortable, personally owned and managed
hotel with its well equipped bedrooms and the elegant restaurant
where good food is complemented by first-rate service.*
35⇄♠(3fb)3⊞✂in 10 bedrooms CTV in all bedrooms ® T
✖ (ex guide dogs) sB&B⇄♠£51-£65 dB&B⇄♠£85-£104 ⒫
Lift ⚓ 60P ✿ ☒(heated) sauna solarium gymnasium beauty
therapy treatments xmas
♀ Scottish & French V ۞ ⚓ ✂ Lunch £6.95-£8.95 Dinner
£15-£16.50&alc Last dinner 9pm
Credit Cards ①②③⑤

**★★★65%** **Caledonian** Church St IV1 1DX (Embassy)
☎(0463)235181 Telex no 75232 FAX (0463) 711206
*This smart town-centre hotel has been tastefully refurbished to
provide attractive accommodation with an extended range of
services and facilities. Comfortable, well-equipped bedrooms are
furnished and decorated in modern style, and guests are offered a
choice of bars, meals in a pleasant restaurant with views over the
river, and the use of a new leisure club.*
100⇄♠(12fb) CTV in all bedrooms ® T sB⇄♠£63-£79
dB⇄♠£84-£99 (room only) ⒫

---

Lift ⚓ ⊞ 80P CFA ☒(heated) snooker sauna solarium
gymnasium whirlpool spa-bath xmas
♀ International V ۞ ⚓ Lunch fr£8&alc High tea fr£9 Dinner
fr£15.75&alc Last dinner 9pm
Credit Cards ①②③⑤

**★★★64%** **Kingsmills** Culcabock Rd IV2 3LP (Swallow)
☎(0463)237166 Telex no 75566 FAX (0463) 225208
*A major upgrading and refurbishment programme has been carried
out at this popular business and tourist hotel. It offers a range of
bedroom styles and standards – though all are comfortable and
well equipped. The smart new leisure complex is a welcome
development.*
78⇄♠Annexe6⇄♠(22fb)✂in 33 bedrooms CTV in all
bedrooms ® T S% sB&B⇄♠£64-£81 dB&B⇄♠£86-£104 ⒫
Lift ⚓ 100P ✿ ☒(heated) sauna solarium gymnasium putting
green xmas
V ۞ ⚓ S% Lunch £8-£13 Dinner £15.75&alc Last dinner
9.45pm
Credit Cards ①②③⑤

**★★★58%** **Mercury** Nairn Rd IV2 3TR (junc A9/A96) (Mount
Charlotte (TS)) ☎(0463)239666 Telex no 75377
FAX (0463) 711145
*This purpose-built modern hotel is situated on the outskirts of town
with convenient access to the A9 and a major refurbishment
programme started in 1989 provides a high standard of comfort.*
118⇄♠(11fb)✂in 6 bedrooms CTV in all bedrooms ® T ✱ '
sB⇄♠£52.50-£67.50 dB⇄♠£70-£79.50 (room only) ⒫
Lift ⚓ 150P ✿ xmas
V ۞ ⚓ Lunch £6.70-£7.25 Dinner fr£12.50&alc Last dinner
9.30pm
Credit Cards ①②③⑤ⓔ

**★★★57%** **Station** 18 Academy St IV1 1LG ☎(0463)231926
Telex no 75275
Closed 10 days at Xmas/New Year
*Situated next to the railway station, this well-established hotel
offers traditional comforts combined with modern day facilities.
The public rooms are large, the bedrooms well equipped and the
foyer/lounge is a popular rendezvous.*
66rm(43⇄10♠)(6fb) CTV in all bedrooms ®
Lift ⚓ 10P
♀ French V ۞ ⚓ Last dinner 9.15pm
Credit Cards ①②③④⑤

**★★★56%** **Palace** Ness Walk IV3 5NE ☎(0463)223243
Telex no 777210 FAX (0463) 236865
*Situated near the river, this hotel caters for business and tourist
trade. Bedrooms are well equipped and the atmosphere friendly
and informal.*
43⇄♠Annexe41⇄(12fb) CTV in all bedrooms ® T
sB⇄♠£39-£54 dB⇄♠£56-£78 (room only) ⒫
Lift ⚓ 40P ♨ xmas
♀ Scottish & French V ۞ ⚓ Lunch £5.50-£10 High tea £5-£7
Dinner £6.50-£16 Last dinner 9pm
Credit Cards ①②③⑤ⓔ

See advertisement on page 363

**★★♨74%** **Dunain Park** IV3 6JN ☎(0463)230512
RS 2wks Nov & Feb
*Delightful country house in 6 acres of grounds near Loch Ness, it is
run in a friendly and congenial manner by Ann and Edward Nicoll.
Good country cooking is provided in the well appointed dining
room, and the charming bedrooms are thoughtfully equipped with
many extras.*
12rm(10⇄♠)(2fb)1⊞✂in 2 bedrooms CTV in all bedrooms T
dB&B⇄♠£110-£130 ⒫
20P ♨ ☒(heated) sauna croquet badminton xmas
♀ Scottish & French V ۞ ⚓ ✂ Dinner £22.50 Last dinner
9pm
Credit Cards ①②③⑤

★★ **71% Glen Mhor** 10 Ness Bank IV2 4SG ☎(0463)234308
Telex no 75114 FAX (0463) 713170
Closed 31 Dec-2 Jan
*Occupying a prime position facing the River Ness, the hotel offers bedrooms equipped to a very high standard, particularly those in the cottage annexe. Service is well managed and the cuisine in the dining room is reliable, matched by an excellent wine list.*
21rm(8⇨10♠)Annexe10⇨♠(1fb)1☷ CTV in all bedrooms
Ⓡ T ✱ sB&B£20-£25 sB&B⇨♠£45-£55 dB&B⇨♠£50-£80 �🅿
30P pool table *xmas*
♚ International V ✿ ⚗ Lunch fr£7.50&alc High tea £5.30-£9.50alc Dinner fr£16.50&alc Last dinner 9.30pm
Credit Cards ① ② ③ ⑤ Ⓔ

★★ **65% Lochardil House** Stratherrick Rd IV2 4LF
☎(0463)235995
*This handsome, castellated, Victorian house set in 3 acres of grounds still retains much of its original charm. Bedrooms are modern with modern-day facilities.*
11⇨♠(2fb) CTV in all bedrooms Ⓡ T ✖ (ex guide dogs) ✳
sB&B⇨♠£42.50-£45 dB&B⇨♠£65-£75 ⼂
120P 3🅖 ✿
♚ Scottish & French V ✿ ⚗
Credit Cards ① ② ③ ⑤

★★ **57% Beaufort** 11 Culduthel Rd IV2 4AG ☎(0463)222897
*A family-owned hotel in a residential area caters mainly for the commercial trade, providing satisfactory standards of accommodation and service.*
36⇨♠(6fb) CTV in all bedrooms Ⓡ T ✱ sB&B⇨♠£30-£40
dB&B⇨♠£50-£60 ⼂
⊞ 50P ♪ ♨
V ✿ ⚗ S% Lunch £3.75-£7.50 High tea £5-£9 Dinner £7.50-£15&alc Last dinner 10pm
Credit Cards ① ② ③ ⑤ Ⓔ

★★ **57% Cummings** Church St IV1 1EN ☎(0463)232531
FAX (0463) 236541
*Conveniently located in the town centre with its rear private car park this is an old fashioned commercial hotel with modern bedrooms. Good function and banqueting facilities are available and bar meals are served at lunchtime.*
34rm(14⇨5♠)(2fb) CTV in all bedrooms Ⓡ T
✖ (ex guide dogs) ✳ sB&B£30-£33 sB&B⇨♠£35-£38
dB&B£42-£48 dB&B⇨♠£48-£54
Lift ⓒ CTV 25P
V ✿ Lunch £4.50-£6&alc Dinner £8-£10&alc Last dinner 8pm
Ⓔ

★★ **57% Loch Ness House** Glenurquhart Rd IV3 6JL (Consort)
☎(0463)231248
*A family-run hotel situated on the edge of town beside the Caledonian Canal and popular with both businessmen and tourists alike. Public areas offer traditional comforts while the compact well equipped bedrooms are more practical in style.*
23rm(4⇨13♠)(1fb)☷ CTV in all bedrooms Ⓡ T S10%
sB&B£25-£35 sB&B⇨♠£35-£52.50 dB&Bfr£45
dB&B⇨♠£50-£80 ⼂
60P 🅖 ✿ ♪ ♨ *xmas*
♚ Scottish & French V ✿ ⚗ Bar Lunch £4.50-£5.50&alc High tea fr£5.50 Dinner £12.50-£13.50&alc Last dinner 9pm
Credit Cards ① ② ③ Ⓔ

★ **62% Redcliffe** 1 Gorden Ter IV2 3HD ☎(0463)232767
*A good standard of food is served in the pleasant restaurant of this small, well-furnished, family-run hotel which stands in a quiet area close to the town centre. Resident owners ensure that guests' needs are met efficiently.*
9rm(6♠)(1fb) CTV in all bedrooms Ⓡ T sB&Bfr£12
sB&B♠£18-£25 dB&B£31-£33 dB&B♠£37-£40 ⼂
12P ✿

V ✿ ⚗ Lunch £4-£7alc High tea £3.50-£12&alc Dinner £8-£15&alc Last dinner 9pm
Credit Cards ① ② ③ Ⓔ

**INVERURIE** Grampian *Aberdeenshire* Map **15** NJ72

★★★ **64% Strathburn** Burghmuir Dr AB5 9GY ☎(0467)24422
FAX (0467) 25133
*This small, purpose built and family-owned hotel is off the A96 on the fringe of the town. Efficiently run, it has a friendly atmosphere and complements comfortable well-equipped bedrooms with neatly appointed public areas in modern style.*
15⇨♠(1fb) CTV in all bedrooms Ⓡ T ✖ (ex guide dogs)
sB&B⇨♠£34-£43 dB&B⇨♠£47-£58 ⼂
40P 🅖
V ✿ ⚗ Lunch £5.75-£15.50&alc Dinner £14.75&alc Last dinner 9.30pm
Credit Cards ① ② ③ Ⓔ

★★ **56% Gordon Arms** Market Place AB5 9SA ☎(0467)20314
FAX (0467) 21792
*A long-established commercial hotel, conveniently situated in the town centre, offers traditional hospitality and clean, practical accommodation.*
11rm(6♠) CTV in all bedrooms Ⓡ sB&Bfr£22.95
sB&B♠fr£24.95 dB&Bfr£33.50 dB&B♠fr£36.50 ⼂
CTV 🅟
♚ European V ✿ Lunch £4.95-£5.95 High tea £3.50-£7.50 Dinner £6.50-£8.50 Last dinner 8pm
Credit Cards ① ② ③ ⑤ Ⓔ

**IPSWICH** Suffolk Map **05** TM14

❀★★★🏨 HINTLESHAM HALL
IP8 3NS (Relais et Châteaux) ☎Hintlesham(047387)334 & 268
Telex no 98340 FAX (047387) 463
(For full entry see Hintlesham)

★★★ **71% Marlborough** Henley Rd IP1 3SP ☎(0473)257677
FAX (0473) 226927
RS 25 Dec
*Situated in a leafy suburb overlooking Christchurch Park, the two outstanding features of this hotel are the standard of hospitality and the 'good table' it provides. Accommodation is comfortable, with a high standard of cleanliness.*
22⇨♠(3fb) CTV in all bedrooms Ⓡ T ✱ sB⇨♠£63-£77
dB⇨♠£85-£95 (room only) ⼂
ⓒ CTV 60P 🅖 ✿ mini croquet *xmas*
♚ French V ✿ ⚗ ✂ S% Lunch £10.50-£13.50&alc Dinner £16-£19&alc Last dinner 9.30pm
Credit Cards ① ② ③ ⑤ Ⓔ

★★★ **62% Novotel Ipswich** Greyfriars Rd IP1 1UP (Novotel)
☎(0473)232400 Telex no 987684 FAX (0473) 232414
*Located on the periphery of the city centre this hotel has open plan style public areas and spacious, well-equipped rooms well suited for both the business traveller and families alike. The restaurant/grill is open from 6am-midnight.*
101⇨♠(6fb)✂in 38 bedrooms CTV in all bedrooms Ⓡ T
Lift 50P
♚ International V ✿ ⚗ ✂ Last dinner 11.30pm
Credit Cards ① ② ③ ⑤

See advertisement on page 365

★★★ **61% Ipswich Moat House** London Rd, Copdock IP8 3JD
(just off A12 near Copdock village) (Queens Moat)
☎Copdock(047386)444 Telex no 987207 FAX (047386) 801
*Three miles south of Ipswich, off the A12, this modern hotel is set in landscaped gardens and attracts those in search of leisure as well as a flourishing conference trade. Accommodation is attractively furnished and staff are pleasant and helpful.*
45⇨♠Annexe29⇨♠(2fb)1☷ CTV in all bedrooms Ⓡ T ✱
sB&B⇨♠£38-£63 dB&B⇨♠£62-£73 ⼂

►

Lift ⟨ 400P ❖ ⊠(heated) sauna solarium gymnasium *xmas*
♤ English & Continental **V** ⊕ ⊿ Lunch £6.95-£13alc Dinner
£12.75-£13&alc Last dinner 9.50pm
Credit Cards ①②③④⑤ⓔ

★★★53% **Post House** London Rd IP2 0UA (Trusthouse Forte)
☎(0473)690313 Telex no 987150 FAX (0473) 680412
*Located about two miles north of the town and giving easy access
to the A45 at its junction with the A1071, a hotel much used by
business travellers provides well-equipped accommodation, a
restaurant offering a choice of menus, and the popular Millers Bar.*
118⇔�ંⁿ(35fb)⅊in 35 bedrooms CTV in all bedrooms Ⓡ **T** ✱
S% sB⇔�ⁿ£39.50-£67 dB⇔�ⁿ£39.50-£82 (room only) 🄱
⟨ 175P CFA ⌁(heated) ♧ *xmas*
♤ English & French **V** ⊕ ⊿ ⅊ S% Lunch £7.95-8.95 Dinner
£13.50&alc Last dinner 10pm
Credit Cards ①②③④⑤

✕✕**The A La Carte** Orwell House, 4A Orwell Place IP4 1BB
☎(0473)230254
*Situated in the heart of the city centre, this building is believed to
have been a Malthouse at some time and more recently a copper
studio. The two in one Restaurant House is an interesting and
attractive venue. The à la carte restaurant is on the galleried
mezzanine floor, and is more formally furnished than the
downstairs bistro. Service is quite formal but friendly and
informative. The menu offers a good variety of dishes with
particular emphasis on sea food, Lobster Valcany with a light
sauce, delicately flavoured with red and green peppers. There is
also a very good, small range of imaginative vegetarian dishes.
Chef, John Gear, continues to maintain the standard.*
Closed Sun, 26 Dec, 1 Jan & BH Mons
Dinner not served Mon & Tue
♤ French **V** 28 seats ✱ Lunch £15-£26alc Dinner fr£15alc Last
lunch 2pm Last dinner 9.30pm 10P ⅊
Credit Cards ①②③⑤

**IRONBRIDGE** Shropshire Map **07** SJ60

★★★60% **Valley** TF8 7DW ☎(0952)452247 & 453280
FAX (0952) 452308
*A Georgian house with lawns at the rear which merge with a park
before reaching the banks of the River Severn. Beautiful decorative
tiles adorn the hall which leads to Chez Maw restaurant. There is
a choice of menus, including an interesting vegetarian selection.*
17⇔�ⁿ2🄱 CTV in all bedrooms Ⓡ **T** ✖ (ex guide dogs) ✱
sB&B⇔�ⁿ£35.75-£42 dB&B⇔�ⁿ£44.50-£55 🄱
50P ❖
♤ International **V** ⊕ ⊿ Lunch £11&alc Dinner £11.25&alc
Last dinner 9.30pm
Credit Cards ①③

**See advertisement under TELFORD**

**IRVINE** Strathclyde *Ayrshire* Map **10** NS33

★★★★63% **Hospitality Inn** Annick Rd, Annickwater
KA11 4LD (Mount Charlotte (TS)) ☎(0294)74272
Telex no 777097 FAX (0294) 77287
*This popular business, tourist and conference hotel is conveniently
situated close to the A78. There is a choice of restaurants including
one which is beside the spectacular tropical lagoon. Bedrooms are
comfortable and well equipped.*
128⇔�ⁿ(44fb)⅊in 16 bedrooms CTV in all bedrooms Ⓡ **T**
sB⇔�ⁿ£65-£75 dB⇔�ⁿ£80-£90 (room only) 🄱
⟨ 250P ❖ ⊠(heated) ♪ jacuzzi football pitch ♫ *xmas*
♤ French **V** ⊕ ⊿ Lunch £9.20-£11.45&alc Dinner
fr£12.50&alc Last dinner 11pm
Credit Cards ①②③④⑤

**ISLAY, ISLE OF** Strathclyde *Argyllshire* Map **10**

**BOWMORE** Map **10** NR35

★★57%, **Lochside** 19 Shore St PA43 7LB ☎(049681)244 & 266
*This small hotel is situated on the main street, but backs onto the
shore of the loch and there are lovely views from the bar, the dining
room and some of the bedrooms. The hotel boasts an extensive
range of malt whiskies.*
7rm(2⇔) CTV in all bedrooms Ⓡ
⅊
**V** ⊕ ⊿ Last dinner 8.30pm
Credit Cards ①③

**BRIDGEND** Map **10** NR36

★★65% **Bridgend** PA44 7PQ ☎Bowmore(04961)212
*This long established fishing and tourist hotel is located close to the
island's main road junction. Public rooms retain the hotel's
Victorian character, whilst the bedrooms, which vary in size, are
more modern and well equipped.*
10rm(5⇔4�ⁿ)(3fb) CTV in all bedrooms Ⓡ ✱ sB&B£28-£33
sB&B⇔�ⁿ£28-£35 dB&Bfr£56 dB&B⇔�ⁿ£56-£70
30P ♪ ⚭
Lunch fr£12.50 Dinner £12.75-£13.50 Last dinner 8pm

**PORT ASKAIG** Map **10** NR46

★★59% **Port Askaig** PA46 7RD ☎(049684)245 & 295
9rm(2⇔2�ⁿ)(1fb) CTV in all bedrooms Ⓡ S% sB&B£23-£24.50
sB&B⇔�ⁿ£25-£28 dB&B£38-£42 dB&B⇔�ⁿ£40-£50 🄱
CTV 15P 6🄱 🄯 ❖ nc5yrs
**V** ⊕ ⊿ Sunday Lunch £6.25 Dinner £12 Last dinner 9pm

**ISLE OF** Places incorporating the words 'Isle of' or 'Isle' will
be found under the actual name, eg Isle of Wight is listed under
Wight, Isle of.

**ISLE ORNSAY**
See Skye, Isle of

**IXWORTH** Suffolk Map **05** TL97

✕✕**Theobalds** 68 High St IP31 2HJ ☎Pakenham(0359)31707
*Dating back over 300 years, with exposed beams and an inglenook
fireplace, the restaurant offers a relaxing atmosphere in which to
enjoy perfectly cooked dishes accompanied by imaginative sauces
and simple vegetables. The menu changes regularly to
accommodate fresh seasonal produce.*
Closed 25-26 Dec & BH's
Lunch not served Mon & Sat
Dinner not served Sun
♤ English & French **V** 36 seats S% Lunch fr£13.50&alc Dinner
£19.50-£25.50alc Last lunch 2pm Last dinner 10pm ⅊ nc8yrs
⅊
Credit Cards ①③

**JERSEY**
See Channel Islands

**JEVINGTON** East Sussex Map **05** TQ50

✕✕**Hungry Monk** BN26 5QF
☎Polegate(03212)2178 Due to change to (0323) 482178
*Situated in the heart of the charming village of Jevington, this is a
restaurant of character with a cosy and comfortable lounge area
and an intimate and well appointed dining room. The blackboard
menu changes according to the season and good use is made of
local produce – especially game. The wine list is extensive and
good value. Good service is provided by the long-skirted
waitresses. A relaxed and enjoyable experience at this restaurant
is ensured.*

Closed 24-26 Dec & BH Mons
Lunch not served Mon-Sat (ex by reservation)
♀ English & French V 38 seats ✳ Sunday Lunch £16.95-£18.45
Dinner £16.95-£18.45 Last dinner 10.15pm 14P nc3yrs ⚓

---

**JOHN O'GROATS**

See Halkirk and Lybster

---

**JURA, ISLE OF** Strathclyde *Argyllshire* Map **10**

---

**CRAIGHOUSE** Map **10** NR56

★★55% *Jura* PA60 7XU ☎Jura(049682)243
Closed 20 Dec-6 Jan
*This modestly appointed traditional island hotel looks out across the old pier and bay to the mainland. Jura Distillery lies right across the road.*
17rm(4➪1♠)(1fb) CTV in 1 bedroom ®
CTV 10P 6🏌 ✿ ♪
♦ ⌲ Last dinner 9pm
Credit Cards ①②③⑤

---

**KEGWORTH** Leicestershire Map **08** SK42

★★★61% **Yew Lodge** 33 Packington Hill DE7 2DF
☎(0509)672518 Telex no 341995 Ref 211 FAX (0509) 674730
*Well-equipped bedroom accommodation and conference facilities are available at this busy hotel just off the A6, popular with businessmen because it is conveniently close to junction 24 of the M1 and also within easy reach of the East Midlands Airport.*
54➪♠(3fb) CTV in all bedrooms ® T sB&B➪♠£53-£64
dB&B➪♠£71-£84 🏢
Lift ( 120P
♀ English & French V ♦ ⌲ Lunch fr£7.30 Dinner fr£12.50
Last dinner 10pm
Credit Cards ①②③⑤ ⑤

---

**KEIGHLEY** West Yorkshire Map **07** SE04

★★66% **Dalesgate** 406 Skipton Rd, Utley BD20 6HP (2m NW
A629) ☎(0535)664930 FAX (0535) 611253
*Personal management ensures courteous, friendly service at this converted Victorian house with its comfortable, compact accommodation.*
21➪♠(1fb) CTV in all bedrooms ® T
( 30P
Dinner £8.50-£13.75alc Last dinner 9pm
Credit Cards ①②③⑤ ⑤

---

**KELSO** Borders *Roxburghshire* Map **12** NT73

★★★⚐76% **Sunlaws House** Heiton TD5 8JZ (2m SW A698)
☎Roxburgh(05735)331 Telex no 728147 FAX (05735) 611
*An impressive country house situated three miles west of the town amidst woodland and well tended gardens. Elegant, inviting sitting rooms, a comfortable bar, lounge and an intimate restaurant have all been sympathically decorated and furnished. The menus feature skillfully prepared and attractively presented dishes. Owned by the Duke of Roxburghe, the hotel also has facilities for the sporting fraternity. Management and staff exhibit a friendly, relaxed manner in keeping with the style of the establishment.*
22➪♠(2fb)1⛶ CTV in all bedrooms ® T ✖ (ex guide dogs)
✳ sB&B➪♠£50-£72 dB&B➪♠£77-£130 🏢
( 30P ✿ ♪ (hard) ♪ shooting croquet *xmas*
V ♦ ⌲ Lunch £13.75 Dinner £22.50&alc Last dinner 9.30 pm
Credit Cards ①②③⑤ ⑤
**See advertisement on page 367**

---

**K**

**★★★64%, Ednam House** Bridge St TD5 7HT ☎(0573)24168
FAX (0573) 26319
Closed 25 Dec-10 Jan
*A fine Georgian mansion situated in 3 acres of gardens overlooking the River Tweed. The hotel is renowned for its warm and friendly atmosphere and tastefully combines modern facilities with traditional values. Popular with fishing and shooting enthusiasts.*
32⇔⁴♠(2fb) CTV in all bedrooms T ✱ sB&B⇔⁴♠fr£36
dB&B⇔⁴♠£53-£73 ⊟
CTV 100P ⊞ ❅
V ♦ ⍰ Sunday Lunch fr£9 Dinner fr£15.50 Last dinner 9pm
Credit Cards ① ③

**★★★60%, Cross Keys** 36-37 The Square TD5 7UL (Exec Hotel)
☎(0573)23303 FAX (0573) 25792
*One of Scotland's oldest coaching inns, now bedecked with window boxes and offering spotless accommodation. Overlooks Kelso's cobbled square.*
24⇔⁴♠(4fb) CTV in all bedrooms ® T S%
sB&B⇔⁴♠£34.50-£39 dB&B⇔⁴♠£44-£52 ⊟
Lift (( ⊞ CTV snooker sauna solarium gymnasium *xmas*
V Scottish & Continental V S% Lunch £6.90 Dinner
£12.50&alc Last dinner 9.15pm
Credit Cards ① ② ③ ⑤ ⓔ

**★61%, Bellevue House** Bowmont St TD5 7DZ ☎(0573)24588
*A friendly and homely atmosphere prevails at this comfortable hotel which overlooks the bowling green and tennis courts, just north of the town centre. Just a short distance away is Floors Castle.*
9rm(1⇔⁴4♠) CTV in 6 bedrooms ® ✗ sB&B£19.50-£21.50
sB&B⇔⁴♠£19.50-£21.50 dB&B£35-£40 dB&B⇔⁴♠£39-£43 ⊟
CTV 10P ❅
V ♦ ⍰ Lunch fr£5 High tea fr£5 Dinner £10-£12&alc Last dinner 9pm
Credit Cards ① ③ ⓔ

**KENDAL** Cumbria Map **07** SD59

**★★★69%, Riverside** Stramongate Bridge LA9 4BZ
☎(0539)724707 FAX (0539) 740274
*This newly-built hotel, formerly a tannery, situated on the banks of the River Kent, features spacious and very well appointed bedrooms, all with en suite facilities. The Riverside Restaurant provides a high standard of cuisine with lighter dishes served in Tannerman's Buttery.*
47⇔⁴♠(4fb)✗in 4 bedrooms CTV in all bedrooms ® T
✗ (ex guide dogs) sB&B⇔⁴♠£40-£56 dB&B⇔⁴♠£51-£74 ⊟
Lift (( 36P *xmas*
V International V ♦ ⍰ Lunch £8.50&alc Dinner £13.50&alc
Last dinner 10pm
Credit Cards ① ② ③ ⑤ ⓔ

**★★★60%, Woolpack** Stricklandgate LA9 4ND ☎(0539)723852
Telex no 728256 FAX (0539) 728608
*Modernised coaching inn with character bars including the Crown Carvery and popular Laurels coffee House. The Crown Bar, with its beams and open fires, was Kendal's wool auction room.*
53⇔⁴♠(5fb)✗in 6 bedrooms CTV in all bedrooms ®
sB&B⇔⁴♠fr£62 dB&B⇔⁴♠fr£75 ⊟
(( 60P CFA *xmas*
V English & French V ♦ ⍰ Lunch fr£7.50 Dinner
£13.50-£15&alc Last dinner 9.30pm
Credit Cards ① ② ③ ⓔ

**★★69%, Garden House** Fowl-ing Ln LA9 6PH ☎(0539)731131
FAX (0539) 740064
Closed 4 days Xmas
*Peacefully situated off the A685 to the north east of the town centre, a pleasant Regency-style house surrounded by mature trees and formal gardens features individually decorated and particularly well equipped bedrooms whose numbers are written in old Westmorland dialect; comfortable public areas have a relaxed,*

*homely feel, and a new conservatory provides an attractive additional eating area. Resident proprietors and local staff provide efficient professional service throughout.*
10⇔⁴♠(2fb)1⊞✗in 8 bedrooms CTV in all bedrooms ® T
✗ (ex guide dogs) sB&B⇔⁴♠£47-£51 dB&B⇔⁴♠£59-£63 ⊟
40P ⊞ ❅
V English & French V ♦ ✗ Dinner £14.75-£16.50 Last dinner 9pm
Credit Cards ① ② ③ ⑤ ⓔ

**KENILWORTH** Warwickshire Map **04** SP27

**★★★60%, De Montfort** The Square CV8 1ED (De Vere)
☎(0926)55944 Telex no 311012 FAX (0926) 57830
*Situated close to the town centre, this hotel offers well equipped bedrooms, conference facilities, and attractive public areas, including a choice of Restaurant and Coffee Shop.*
96⇔⁴♠ CTV in all bedrooms ® T ✱ sB&B⇔⁴♠fr£69
dB&B⇔⁴♠fr£97 ⊟
Lift (( 85P CFA games room *xmas*
V ♦ ⍰ ✗ Lunch fr£11.50 Dinner fr£13.75 Last dinner 9.45pm
Credit Cards ① ② ③ ⑤ ⓔ

**★★68%, Clarendon House** Old High St CV8 1LZ ☎(0926)57668
Telex no 311240 FAX (0926)50669
*The public areas and some bedrooms of this hotel have recently been refurbished to provide comfort and greater convenience; all accommodation is well equipped with modern facilities, though some rooms are rather compact.*
31⇔⁴♠(1fb)4⊞ CTV in all bedrooms ® T ✱
sB&B⇔⁴♠£45-£50 dB&B⇔⁴♠£68-£75 ⊟
30P ⊞
V European V ♦ Sunday Lunch £8.25 Dinner £11.50-£16.50
Last dinner 9.30pm
Credit Cards ① ③

**✗Restaurant Bosquet** 97A Warwick Rd CV8 1HP ☎(0926)52463
Closed Sun, Mon, BH's, 10 days Xmas & 3 wks Jul
Lunch not served (ex by reservation)
V French 26 seats Last dinner 9.30pm ✗
Credit Cards ① ② ③

**KENNFORD** Devon Map **03** SX98

**★★61%, Fairwinds** EX6 7UD ☎Exeter(0392)832911
Closed 7-30 Dec
*This friendly hotel, just south of Exeter and close to the A38/M5, is run in an informal manner by the resident owners, Mr and Mrs Price. The cosy and well-equipped bedrooms are suitable for business guests and holidaymakers alike.*
8rm(6⇔⁴♠)✗in 2 bedrooms CTV in all bedrooms ® T ✗
sB&B£20-£22 sB&B⇔⁴♠£32-£38 dB&B⇔⁴♠£42-£46 ⊟
8P ✗
V ✗ Lunch £2-£6 Dinner £7.95-£10.95 Last dinner 8pm
Credit Cards ① ③ ⓔ

All hotels are now given a percentage grading
for the quality of their facilities. A full explanation
can be found within 'How we Classify Hotels
and Restaurants' at the front of the book.

**K**

**KENTALLEN** Highland *Argyllshire* Map **14** NN05

**⊛★★♔ 74% Ardsheal House** PA38 4BX ☎Duror(063174)227 FAX (063174) 342
Closed Nov-Mar
(Rosette awarded for dinner only)
*Lying at the end of a mile long single track road, this fine period house is in an elevated position, with superb panoramic views across Loch Linnhe to the peaks of Morven. A congenial houseparty atmosphere prevails, although this does not include a communal dining table, and owners Jane and Robert Taylor are fully involved hosts. Chef George Kelso ensures that Ardsheal's reputation for fine food deservedly continues and although his five-course dinners offer a minimum of choice, the best use is made of first class raw materials to provide superb flavours. It is worth noting that dinner is normally served at the set time of either 8.15 or 8.30 and no earlier. Bedrooms are done out in traditional country house manner and there are many different lounge areas. The tiny bar, styled from the original butler's pantry, has great character.*
13rm(11⇨↱)(1fb) sB&B⇨↱£75
dB&B⇨↱£110-£148 (incl dinner)
CTV 20P ⛟ ✲ ℘ (hard) snooker
☋ International ♉ ☋ ⚘ Lunch £6.50-£14.50 High tea fr£10
Dinner £28 Last dinner 8.30pm
Credit Cards [1] [2] [3]

**★★68% Holly Tree** Kentallen Pier PA38 4BY
☎Duror(063174)292 FAX (063174) 345
Closed Nov-mid Feb
*Beautifully set on the shore of Loch Linnhe and overlooking the Movern Hills, this delightful holiday hotel has been created by careful conversion of the former railway station. Cosy public areas where much of the original character has been preserved invite easy relaxation, the smart restaurant serves interesting and imaginative* ▶

Sunlaws House Hotel
Sunlaws is a lovely country house hotel situated in the heart of the Scottish Borders. The hotel is owned by the Duke of Roxburghe and has all the quality and charm of an 18th century gentleman's retreat. Relax in over 200 acres of secluded woodlands. Enjoy croquet, shooting, tennis or fishing on our private stretches of the Teviot and Tweed. Sunlaws House is situated three miles from Kelso, off the A698. Stop for coffee, lunch or a long weekend.
You will find excellent cuisine and a warm Scottish welcome.
Visit Sunlaws and enjoy the Borders at its best.
Sunlaws House Hotel★★★
Kelso
Roxburghshire TD5 8JZ
Telephone: (05735) 331

Shap Wells Hotel ★★
SHAP, Nr. PENRITH, CUMBRIA, CA10 3QU
Telephone: SHAP (09316) 628/744
Large country hotel midway between Kendal and Penrith, set in 30 acres of secluded wooded grounds, only five minutes from M6 motorway (junction 39). Ideally situated location from which to explore the Lake District, Yorkshire Dales and Border Country. All rooms have radio, most have private facilities. Other amenities include games room, hard tennis court and local fishing. Special rates for two or more days.
*See gazetteer entry under Shap.*

★★
OLD WHITE LION HOTEL
HAWORTH, KEIGHLEY, WEST YORKSHIRE
Tel. HAWORTH (0535) 42313

This family run hotel is situated at the centre of this famous village close to the Bronte museum, church and parsonage. Catering for the discriminating businessman as well as tourists from all over the world. Fourteen comfortable bedrooms, all with en-suite facilities, colour TV, tea making facilities and magnificent views. Central Heating throughout, Residents' Lounge, Cocktail and Lounge Bars. Beamed candlelit restaurant open 7 days a week –Table D'Hôte and A la Carte. Sunday lunch a speciality. Open to non-residents. Hot and cold bar snacks prepared by our chefs at all meal times. Special weekend rates available.

*meals which are produced by the chef/patron, and most of the attractive modern bedrooms enjoy spectacular loch views.*
12⇌⬣♠(3fb) CTV in all bedrooms ® T sB&B⇌♠£44-£63
dB&B⇌♠£92-£118 (incl dinner) ⊟
30P ❖ ♪
♀ International ⊙ ⬛ ✔ Lunch fr£7alc Dinner fr£25 Last dinner 9.30pm
Credit Cards ① ② ③

---

**KESWICK** Cumbria Map 11 NY22
See **Town Plan Section**
See map 11 for details of other hotels in the vicinity
★★★73% **Brundholme Country House** Brundholme Rd
CA12 4NL ☎(07687)74495
Closed 20 Dec-Jan
*Converted to a country house hotel of style in 1988, this fine Georgian mansion commands superb views across the town to the surrounding hills. The emphasis is on quality throughout from the cosy cocktail lounge and large comfortable drawing room, to the well-equipped, and often spacious bedrooms. Chef/proprietor Ian Charlton's cooking is excellent, and his wife Lynn and their staff offer friendly and personal attention to guests at all times.*
11⇌⬣♠2⊞ CTV in all bedrooms ® T ✳ sB&B⇌♠£35-£45
dB&B⇌♠£70-£90 ⊟
20P ⬚ ❖ croquet bowls nc11yrs
♀ English & French V ⊙ ✔ Lunch £8-£10 Dinner £17.50 Last dinner 8.45pm
Credit Cards ① ③ ⓔ

★★★57% **Derwentwater** Portinscale CA12 5RE (Consort)
☎(07687)72538 FAX (07687) 71002
*An hotel which looks towards Derwentwater from its setting of neat lawns and gardens and has recently been enhanced by the upgrading of public areas and a partial refurbishment of bedrooms.*
52⇌⬣♠(2fb)2⊞ CTV in all bedrooms ® T sB&B⇌♠£45-£52
dB&B⇌♠£77-£85 ⊟
Lift ℂ 120P ❖ ♪ putting ♫ *xmas*
♀ English & French V ⊙ ⬛ ✔ Bar Lunch £2.25-£7.95alc Dinner £12.95-£14.50&alc Last dinner 9.30pm
Credit Cards ① ② ③ ⑤ ⓔ

★★70% **Grange Country House** Manor Brow, Ambleside Rd
CA12 4BA ☎(07687)72500
Closed 3 Nov-21 Mar
*Standing just off the A591 Grasmere road on the outskirts of town, this charming hotel has been comfortably furnished and thoughtfully equipped by welcoming proprietors who successfully create a relaxed, informal atmosphere. High standards of housekeeping are evident throughout the hotel, and individually decorated bedrooms continue to be upgraded, while the pleasant dining room overlooking the garden serves enjoyable, carefully prepared, home-cooked meals that make good use of fresh produce.*
11⇌⬣♠2⊞ CTV in all bedrooms ® T sB&B⇌♠£34.50-£39.50
dB&B⇌♠£54-£64 ⊟
12P 1⬛ ⬚ ❖ nc5yrs
V ⊙ ⬛ ✔ Dinner £11.75-£14.75 Last dinner 8pm
Credit Cards ① ③ ⓔ

★★66% **Chaucer House** Ambleside Rd CA12 4DR
☎(07687)72318 & 73223
Closed 29 Oct-21 Mar
*In the public areas of this friendly, comfortable hotel, several spacious lounges (including one warmed by a real fire) are complemented by a very attractively appointed dining room and lounge bar.*
35rm(21⇌⬣♠)(6fb)✂in 6 bedrooms CTV in all bedrooms ®
25P
♀ English & French ⊙ ✔ Bar Lunch £5 Dinner £9.30 Last dinner 7.30pm
Credit Cards ① ② ③ ④ ⓔ

The Grange ★★
COUNTRY HOUSE HOTEL

**Manor Brow, Keswick, Cumbria. CA12 4BA**
**Telephone (07687) 72500**

*The Grange, 19th Century built, is a graceful Hotel with individually decorated bedrooms and lovely lounges with log fires which create an atmosphere of a cosy Country House Hotel. Quietly situated on the hillside overlooking Keswick and commanding magnificent views of the mountains from bedrooms, restaurant and garden terrace. The highest standards are maintained at the Grange with our excellent cuisine, attentive service and first-class wines complementing the splendour of a Lakeland holiday. Duncan and Jane Miller look forward to welcoming you to the Grange.*

*Ashley Courtenay recommended*

The Borrowdale Gates
Country House Hotel ★★★

**Grange-in-Borrowdale, Keswick, Cumbria**
**CA12 5UQ**
**Borrowdale (0596 84) 204**
**Due to change to (07687) 77204**

*Located amidst the breathtaking scenery of the Borrowdale Valley, the hotel nestles peacefully in two acres of wooded gardens on the edge of the ancient hamlet of Grange.*
*All 23 bedrooms are en suite with colour television, direct dial telephone, radio and morning tea and coffee making facilities.*
*A varied table d'hôte menu is offered each evening with a good choice of cuisine, complemented by a thoughtfully chosen wine list.*

# THE DERWENTWATER HOTEL ★★★

Portinscale, Keswick, Cumbria CA12 5RE
Telephone: (07687) 72538 Telex: 57515 Extension 11

Set in 16 acres of prime lakeside grounds on shores of Lake Derwentwater. All 85 bedrooms have en-suite facilities, colour television, tea making equipment, radio and direct dial telephone. Many bedrooms and the hotel lounges have spectacular views of both lake and fells.

FOUR POSTER BEDS AVAILABLE
PRIVATE FISHING IN HOTEL GROUNDS
NINE HOLE PUTTING GREEN
SPECIALITY WEEKEND BREAKS
CHIRISTMAS & NEW YEAR PROGRAMME

CONSORT HOTELS

MEMBER

*"More than a Hotel"*

# UNBEATABLE VALUE!

We would love to tell you more about our extensive leisure facilities, idyllic setting, superb food and relaxed atmosphere so please contact us for a brochure.

ETB ❀❀❀❀ AA ★★★

## CASTLE INN HOTEL
**Bassenthwaite, Nr Keswick**
**Cumbria CA12 4RG**
**TELEPHONE Bass Lake (07687) 76401**

# Keswick

★★66% **Crow Park** The Heads CA12 5ER ☎(07687)72208
*The attractive public areas of a very well maintained hotel set in a terraced row overlooking the head of Borrowdale feature historic photographs of Lakeland.*
26⇋♠(1fb) CTV in all bedrooms ® T sB&B⇋♠£19-£24 dB&B⇋♠£38-£48 ⊟
CTV 26P 🚗 *xmas*
♀ English & Continental V ♦ ✔ Bar Lunch £4-£5.50 Dinner £9-£12 Last dinner 8pm
Credit Cards ① ③

★★♨66% **Red House** Underskiddaw CA12 4QA (on A591) ☎(07687)72211
Closed mid Jan-mid Feb
*Set amidst 8 acres of woodland just north of Keswick, this Victorian country house commands superb views of northern Lakeland. Always a popular hotel with families – its games and recreation cellar proves a boon in wet weather.*
22⇋(7fb)1⚘ CTV in all bedrooms ® sB&B⇋£42-£48 dB&B⇋♠£78-£88 (incl dinner) ⊟
CTV 25P 🚗 ❋ ⇲ putting green games room Ꮽ *xmas*
♀ European ♦ ✔ Dinner £15 Last dinner 8.30pm
Credit Cards ① ③

★★♨64% **Lyzzick Hall Country House** Under Skiddaw CA12 4PY ☎(07687)72277
Closed Feb
*Set on the lowest slopes of Skiddaw, on the A591 2.5 miles from the town centre, this stone-built country house enjoys extensive views of the valley and surrounding hills. Comfortable bedrooms are well equipped and all have en suite shower or bath facilities.*
19⇋♠Annexe1⇋♠(4fb) CTV in all bedrooms ® T ✖ ✱ sB&B⇋♠£23.50-£25 dB&B⇋♠£47-£50 ⊟
40P 🚗 ❋ ⇲(heated) Ꮽ *xmas*
♀ International V ♦ Lunch £2.50-£9 Dinner £10-£12&alc Last dinner 9.30pm
Credit Cards ① ② ③ ⑤

★★63% **Walpole** Station Rd CA12 4NA ☎(07687)72072
*Featuring a cosy bar which serves drinks to residents and diners only, this traditional tourist hotel offers good food and friendly service.*
17rm(10⇋♠)(4fb) CTV in all bedrooms ® sB&B£22 sB&B⇋♠£23.50 dB&B£44 dB&B⇋♠£47 ⊟
9P 🚗 *xmas*
♀ English & French V High tea fr£3&alc Dinner fr£11&alc Last dinner 8pm
Credit Cards ① ③ £

★★62% **Queen's** Main St CA12 5JF (Exec Hotel) ☎(07687)73333 FAX (07687) 71144
Closed 24-26 Dec
*Built of local stone and standing in the centre of town, this early Victorian former posting house is well equipped and is one of the oldest buildings in Keswick.*
35⇋♠(16fb) CTV in all bedrooms ® T ✖ S% sB&B⇋♠£26-£32.40 dB&B⇋♠£42-£54 ⊟
Lift 12🅿 (charged)
♀ English & French V ♦ ㏋ S% Bar Lunch £3-£6.50 Dinner £10.50-£12 Last dinner 9pm
Credit Cards ① ② ③ ⑤ £

★★61% **Skiddaw** Main St CA12 5BN ☎(07687)72071 FAX (07687) 74850
Closed Xmas
*A stay at this well-run hotel in the town centre represents good value for money, offering bedrooms with en suite facilities, a comfortable first floor lounge, a good range of bar meals and an extensive à la carte menu in the evening.*
40⇋♠(7fb)1⚘ CTV in all bedrooms ® T sB⇋♠£21.50-£24.50 dB⇋♠£37-£42 (room only) ⊟
Lift 12P sauna solarium

♀ English & French V ♦ ㏋ Lunch fr£5alc Dinner £11-£15alc Last dinner 9pm
Credit Cards ① ② ③

★★59% **Lairbeck** Vicarage Hill CA12 5QB ☎(07687)73373
*Family hotel with clean accommodation and good home cooking.*
15rm(6⇋4♠)(5fb) CTV in all bedrooms ® T ✖ (ex guide dogs) sB&B£16-£20 dB&B£32-£40 dB&B⇋♠£38-£46 ⊟
25P 🚗 ❋ *xmas*
♀ English & French ✔ Dinner £10-£11 Last dinner 8pm
Credit Cards ① ③

★73% **Priorholm** Borrowdale Rd CA12 5DD ☎(07687)72745
Closed Dec
*Near the town centre, this charming house, built in 1836, and a converted 200-year-old cottage provide well maintained, good quality accommodation and pleasant, cosy public areas.*
8rm(6⇋♠)(1fb) CTV in 7 bedrooms ® ✖ (ex guide dogs) ✱ sB&Bfr£18 sB&B⇋♠fr£32 dB&Bfr£35 dB&B⇋♠fr£46
CTV 7P 🚗
✔ Dinner £14 Last dinner 7.30pm
Credit Cards ① ③ £

★72% **Highfield** The Heads CA12 5ER ☎(07687)72508
Closed Nov-Mar
*An immaculate hotel under the personal supervision of its resident proprietors enjoys splendid views towards Borrowdale from its elevated position. The atmosphere is particularly warm and friendly, the owners, who have lived in the area for many years, willingly giving advice and information on places of interest around the English Lakes.*
19rm(15⇋♠)(3fb) ® sB&B£15.50 sB&B⇋♠£23 dB&B£38-£46
CTV 19P 🚗 nc5yrs
V ♦ ㏋ ✔ Dinner £10.50 Last dinner 6.30pm

★72% **Swinside Lodge** Newlands CA12 5UE ☎(07687)72948
Closed Dec-mid Feb
*This is a charming Victorian lakeland house, situated in an unspoilt area of the Lake District. It is only a short stroll through leafy lanes and woods to the shores of Derwentwater. The hotel is three miles from Keswick, midway on the Portinscale to Grange road, and can also be reached by leaving the A66 at the signpost for Newlands Valley. It has nine superbly appointed bedrooms, all with private facilities and many other extras, along with two lounges and an attractive dining room in which a five course meal is served each evening. The atmosphere is warm and friendly, and the service is personal and attentive. It is in an ideal location in which to relax after an energetic day walking the fells. The hotel is not licensed, but guests may bring their own wine, for which there is no corkage charge.*
9rm(6⇋2♠) CTV in all bedrooms ® ✖ (ex guide dogs) sB&Bfr£40 sB&B⇋♠£44-£52 dB&Bfr£65 dB&B⇋♠£74-£86 (incl dinner) ⊟
10P 🚗 ❋ nc12yrs
✔

★67% **Latrigg Lodge** Lake Rd CA12 5DQ ☎(07687)73545
*There is a continental feel to what is essentially a restaurant with bedrooms, situated in a cul de sac at the centre of town. Bedrooms, though fairly compact, are well furnished and equipped, and there is a quiet, comfortable first-floor lounge. Most enjoyable, reasonably priced evening meals are provided by the popular restaurant – and late sleepers will appreciate the fact that breakfast is served until 10am.*
7⇋♠1⚘ CTV in all bedrooms ® T ✱ sB&B⇋♠fr£27 dB&B⇋♠fr£44 ⊟
7P 🚗 *xmas*
㏋
Credit Cards ① ③

K

★67% **Linnett Hill** 4 Penrith Rd CA12 4HF ☎(07687)73109
*This small, friendly hotel, situated on the A591, overlooks a park,
and is close to the town centre. All bedrooms have en suite facilities
and colour televisions. There is a small bar, a cosy lounge and a
private car park which is situated at the rear of the hotel.*
9⇌♪⊁in all bedrooms CTV in all bedrooms ®
sB⇌♪£20-£25 dB⇌♪£36-£38 (room only) ♬
12P nc5yrs
♡ International V ♡ ⚏ ⊬ Lunch £5-£8.50 Dinner £8.50&alc
Last dinner 7pm
Credit Cards ① ③ ⓔ

---

**KETTLETHORPE** West Yorkshire Map **08** SK 87

★★69% **Hunting Lodge** Standbridge Ln WF2 7NT
☎Wakefield(0924)254339 FAX (0924) 240163
30rm(28⇌)(2fb)2▦ CTV in all bedrooms ® T
✠ (ex guide dogs) ✱ sB&B£52-£90 sB&B⇌£52-£90
dB&B£63-£90 dB&B⇌£63-£90 Continental breakfast ♬
《 ▦ 30P sauna solarium gymnasium
♡ ⚏ Lunch fr£8.50&alc High tea fr£3 Dinner fr£8.50&alc
Last dinner 10pm
Credit Cards ① ② ③ ⑤

---

**KETTLEWELL** North Yorkshire Map **07** SD97

★★66% *Racehorses* BD23 5QZ ☎(075676)233
*An 18th-century former coaching inn, situated on the riverside in
village centre .*
16⇌♪(2fb) CTV in all bedrooms ®
CTV 20P ♪
V ♡ ⚏
Credit Cards ① ③

---

★★ **The Racehorses Hotel**

Kettlewell,
Skipton,
Yorkshire
BD23 5QZ
Telephone:
Kettlewell
(075676) 233

Standing on the bank of the River Wharfe this
former coaching inn with part of the building
dating from 17th century and surrounded by the
Yorkshire Dales National Park. The hotel has 15
bedrooms all with private toilet and bath or
shower, TV and tea/coffee making facilities. Open
throughout the year. The ideal centre from which
to walk or tour the Dales by car. Fishing and riding
are available locally and a leisure centre some four
miles away.

---

# Latrigg ★ Lodge Hotel and Restaurant

Conveniently situated
a few minutes walk
from market square
and lakeside.

**Hotel** Proprietor-run, offering friendly and personal service and an exceptionally high standard
of comfort and service at realistic prices.

**Restaurant** A wide choice of dishes from the
table d'hôte and à la carte menus prepared by our
head chef. Complimenting the superb cuisine is
an interesting and sensibly priced wine list.

Any time bargain breaks. 2 days B/B/EM £60.00

### Tel: (07687) 73545
### Lake Road, Keswick,
### Cumbria, CA12 5DQ.

**K**

---

## *The* Skiddaw Hotel
### Market Square
### Keswick-on-Derwentwater
### Cumbria CA12 5BN
### Tel: (07687) 72071

English Tourist Board

AA ★★

Overlooking the Market Square and
famous Moot Hall, the Skiddaw
Hotel is centrally situated in the Old
Market Town of Keswick. The Hotel
offers a high standard of comfort
and cuisine to help make your stay
in the Lake District a memorable
one. All 40 bedrooms have private
facilities, television, tea and coffee
making, telephone and hairdryer.
The Hotel has its own Saunas &
Solarium with Golf and Squash
available through the Hotel.

*A full brochure is available.*

### KEW Greater London

See LONDON plan 1*B3*(page 426)

**✗Chez Max** 291 Sandycombe Rd ☎081-940 3590
*Although space and comfort are somewhat confined in this tiny family-run bistro, the exciting and hectic atmosphere of cooking 'a la minute' more than compensates, with twin brothers Marc and Max Renzland specialising in classic French cuisine Bourgoise. Marc's skill in the kitchen is mirrored by the personal service and attention provided by Max. The daily-changing fixed price menu offers such dishes as Escalope de Foie Gras de Canard Poëch, Pigeonneau de Bresse en Cocotte, Coq au Vin, Cotes du Boeuf Angus and delightful Patisserie Assiettes. The fixed price menu, with supplementary charges, can be expensive, but the popularity of the restaurant makes early reservations strongly advisable.*
Closed Mon
♀ French 34 seats
Credit Cards [1] [2] [5]

### KEYSTON Cambridgeshire Map 04 TL07

**✗✗Pheasant Inn** PE18 0RE ☎Bythorn(08014)241
*This unspoilt thatched inn is situated on the village green just a short distance from the A604. The timbered bar offers an excellent choice of bar meals, whilst the small, characterful restaurant features dishes such as Pigeon Terrine with rich Cumberland Sauce and Seafood Casserole with a hint of garlic.*
Dinner not served 25 & 26 Dec
♀ English & French **V** 55 seats ✶ Lunch £16-£24alc Dinner £6-£12alc Last lunch 2pm Last dinner 10pm 50P
Credit Cards [1] [2] [3] [5]

### KIDDERMINSTER Hereford & Worcester Map 07 SO87

**★★★★55% Stone Manor** Stone DY10 4PJ (2m SE on A448)
☎Chaddesley Corbett(0562)777555 Telex no 335661
FAX (0562) 777834
RS 25 Dec
*An attractive, mock Tudor hotel, standing in 25 acres of woodland and gardens, Stone Manor has extensive conference and function facilities. Most of its bedrooms are modern and bright, but a few of the older rooms were, at the time of our inspection visit, beginning to show their age.*
53⇆🎇4🛏 CTV in all bedrooms ® **T** ✶ sB⇆🎇£62.75-£70.50 dB⇆🎇£78-£85.50 (room only) 🍴
(( CTV 400P ✿ CFA ➢ ♪ (hard)
♀ International **V** ♥ ⚗ Lunch £9.75-£11.25&alc Dinner £16.25-£30alc Last dinner 10pm
Credit Cards [1] [2] [3] [5] ⓔ

**★★★64% Granary Hotel & Restaurant** Heath Ln, Shenstone DY10 4BS ☎Chaddesley Corbett(0562)777535 & 777251
FAX (0562) 777722
Closed 25 Dec
Annexe19⇆🎇 CTV in all bedrooms ® **T**
(( 60P ✿
**V** ♥ ⚗ Last dinner 9.30pm
Credit Cards [1] [2] [3] [5]

**★★68% Gainsborough House** Bewdley Hill DY11 6BS (Consort)
☎(0562)820041 Telex no 333058 FAX (0562) 66179
*A popular hotel located between Kidderminster and Bewdley, offering comfortable, well-equipped accommodation, relaxing public areas and a good range of conference facilities. This hotel has many attributes indicative of a higher classification.*
42⇆🎇(4fb)1🛏🎇in all bedrooms ® **T** sB&B⇆🎇£54.50-£66 dB&B⇆🎇£72-£88 🍴
(( 130P CFA xmas
♀ English & Continental **V** ♥ ⚗ Lunch £4.95-£7.95&alc Dinner £11.95-£12.95&alc Last dinner 10pm
Credit Cards [1] [2] [3] [5] ⓔ

### KILCHRENAN Strathclyde *Argyllshire* Map 10 NN02

**★★★♨ ARDANAISEIG**
PA35 1HE (Pride of Britain)
☎(08663)333
FAX (08663) 222
Closed end Oct-mid Apr
*This fine example of a Scottish baronial country house belongs to Jane and Jonathan Brown, who head a team of first-class staff whose charm and professionalism have made the hotel so outstanding. A new chef, Martin Vincent, has recently joined them and clearly the dining room's reputation will continue to be high. Redecoration is in hand which will give the rooms a lighter, brighter appearance without detracting from their character. Ardanaiseig stands well away from major roads (10 miles from the A85) in lovely countryside dominated by Ben Cruachan. The hotel's own gardens leading down to Loch Awe are world-famous and open to the public.*
14⇆ CTV in all bedrooms ✶ sB&B⇆£80-£88 dB&B⇆£136-£192 (incl dinner)
20P 🚘 ✿ ♪ (hard) ♪ snooker croquet clay pigeon shooting boating nc8yrs
♥ ⚗ Lunch £5-£15 Dinner £28.50 Last dinner 9pm
Credit Cards [1] [2] [3] [5]

**★★★♨66% Taychreggan** PA35 1HQ ☎(08663)211
FAX (08663) 244
Closed Jan-Feb RS Oct-Dec
*Beautifully set on the tranquil western shore of Loch Awe, and built around a courtyard, a country house hotel offers accommodation in a range of individually decorated bedrooms which vary both in style and size. Guests have a choice of lounges in which to relax, and the attractive, candle-lit restaurant serves good meals in the country house tradition.*
16rm(15⇆)1🛏 **T** ✶ sB&B£50-£55 sB&B⇆£50-£55 dB&B⇆£110-£118 (incl dinner)
CTV 30P 🚘 ✿ ♪ clay pigeon shooting xmas
♀ International ♥ ⚗ Lunch £15-£17 High tea £5-£6 Dinner £25 Last dinner 9pm
Credit Cards [1] [2] [3] ⓔ

### KILDRUMMY Grampian *Aberdeenshire* Map 15 NJ41

**★★★♨75% Kildrummy Castle** AB3 8RA (Best Western)
☎(09755)71288 Telex no 9401252 FAX (09755) 71345
*Situated in peaceful Donside and overlooking the ruins and beautiful gardens of the 13th-century Kildrummy Castle, this most comfortable hotel manages to blend old and new to great effect. The public areas have all the features expected in a grand house, such as elaborate impressive fireplaces and tapestry-covered walls, and the bedrooms are spacious and well equipped.*
16⇆🎇(4fb)1🛏 CTV in all bedrooms ® **T** sB&B⇆🎇£49 dB&B⇆🎇£84-£90 🍴
30P 🚘 ✿ ♪ snooker shooting ෯ xmas
♀ Scottish & French **V** ♥ ⚗ ✗ Lunch £12-£13.50&alc Dinner £20&alc Last dinner 9pm
Credit Cards [1] [2] [3] [4]

**K**

**KILDWICK** West Yorkshire Map **07** SE04

★★★60%, **Kildwick Hall** BD20 9AE ☎Cross Hills(0535)632244
Telex no 517495 FAX (0535) 606343
*A splendid Jacobean manor house set in an elevated position above the village and enjoying fine views over the Aire valley features an attractive beamed foyer lounge with inglenook fireplace and wood panelling. Improvements continue to be made to the individually decorated bedrooms, which come in a variety of shapes and sizes, and service is friendly and helpful throughout.*
13⇌♪Annexe4⇌♪2⌸ CTV in all bedrooms ® T ⊟
《 CTV 60P ✿ *xmas*
🍴 French V ᕉ ⬛
Credit Cards ①②③⑤
**See advertisement under SKIPTON**

**KILFINAN** Strathclyde *Argyll* Map **10** NR97

★★77%, **Kilfinan** PA21 2EP ☎(070082)201 FAX (070082) 205
*Total refurbishment has given this inn an air of cosy elegance, whilst retaining much of its Victorian character. Bedrooms are comfortable and well equipped, but the main attraction here is the food. Chef David Kinnear cooks in the modern style, using the best Scottish produce, and his dishes are generously portioned.*

11⇌♪(1fb) CTV in all bedrooms sB⇌♪fr£35
dB⇌♪fr£48 (room only)
50P ⇎ ✿ ✦ clay pigeon shooting deer stalking *xmas*
🍴 Scottish & French V ᕉ ⬛ Bar Lunch fr£3.50 Dinner
fr£20&alc Last dinner 9pm
Credit Cards ①②③

**KILLIECRANKIE** Tayside *Perthshire* Map **14** NN96

★★67%, **Killiecrankie** PH16 5LG ☎Pitlochry(0796)3220
FAX (0796) 2451
Closed Dec-mid Feb
*A warm welcome awaits guests at this charming holiday hotel which stands in four acres of wooded grounds close to the famous Pass of Killiecrankie. Brightly decorated bedrooms are comfortably appointed, public areas, with their friendly informal atmosphere, invite easy relaxation, and imaginative meals are skilfully prepared from the best fresh produce available.*
11⇌♪(2fb) CTV in all bedrooms ® T sB&B⇌♪£39.75
dB&B⇌♪£75.50 ⊟
30P ⇎ ✿ croquet putting ⛳
V ᕉ ⬛ ✗ Dinner £20.25-£20.75 Last dinner 8.30pm
Credit Cards ①③ⓔ
**See advertisement on page 375**

**KILLIN** Central *Perthshire* Map **11** NN53

★★65%, **Morenish Lodge** Loch Tayside FK21 8TX
☎(05672)258
Closed mid Oct-Etr
*Magnificent panoramic views across Loch Tay can be enjoyed from this country hotel which stands alone 2.5 miles north east of the town – that from the dining room being one of the most striking. Another attractive feature is the warm hospitality offered by friendly owners who are fully involved in the running of the hotel.*
13rm(4⇌8♪)(1fb)2⌸ ® ✗ sB&B£31-£35 sB&B⇌♪£40-£45
dB&B⇌♪£62-£70 (incl dinner) ⊟
CTV 20P ⇎ ✿ nc4yrs
Dinner £12-£15 Last dinner 8.15pm
Credit Cards ①③

★58%, **Falls of Dochart** Main St FK21 8UW ☎(05672)237
*Modest, reasonably-priced accommodation in an informal atmosphere is provided by this small, family-run hotel in the village centre.*
9rm(1⇌4♪)(2fb) ® ✗ (ex guide dogs)

# TAYCHREGGAN

## Stay at Taychreggan, and you will always come back

25 Acres of Highland countryside around you, full of birdlife, Loch Awe in front of you; that's Taychreggan, Scotland's most beautifully situated country hotel. Fish or sail in the 23 miles of Loch Awe; walk, ride or stalk deer in Inverliever forest. Taychreggan is ideally placed for Touring the Western Highlands. We now have 15 double bedrooms each with private bath. Cuisine is superb, with a full wine cellar and an extensive range of malt whiskies. A British Tourist Authority Commended Country House Hotel.

For full information contact:
**\*\*\*A A   TAYCHREGGAN HOTEL
KILCHRENAN, BY TAYNUILT,
ARGYLL PA35 1HQ
Telephone: Kilchrenan (086 63) 211**

**K**

★ ★ ★

# The Granary

## HOTEL AND RESTAURANT

### Shenstone, Nr Kidderminster, Worcestershire

### Tel: (0562) 777535

The Granary is situated in lovely peaceful surroundings and lies amid some of Worcestershire's most beautiful countryside. Small and family run, with 18 fully appointed bedrooms, The Granary is ideally located for a weekend break in the HEART OF ENGLAND. (Special rates apply.) Our long-established Carvery Restaurant has the reputation of being one of the finest English Carveries in the region and will ensure your stay is a memorable one.

**Killin - Kingsbridge**

CTV 20P
V ⍟ ⬛ Last dinner 9pm
Credit Cards ①③

**KILMARNOCK** Strathclyde *Ayrshire* Map **10** NS43

★★★55% *Howard Park* Glasgow Rd KA3 1UT ☎(0563)31211
Telex no 53168 FAX (0563) 27795
*A modern purpose-built hotel situated just to the north of town.*
*The ground floor of this hotel has recently been refurbished to*
*provide an attractive restaurant, cocktail bar and foyer lounge*
*area. Bedrooms are compact and functional.*
46⇋(6fb)⊬in 14 bedrooms CTV in all bedrooms ® T
Lift ℭ 200P
♀ Scottish & French V ⍟ ⬛ Last dinner 9.30pm
Credit Cards ①②③⑤

**KILMARTIN** Strathclyde *Argyllshire* Map **10** NR89

✕**Cairn** PA31 8RQ ☎(05465)254
Closed Nov-Mar
Lunch not served Mon
♀ Scottish & Continental V 50 seats Bar Lunch £3-£8alc
Dinner £5-£12alc Wine £4.95 Last lunch 3pm Last dinner
10pm 25P
Credit Cards ①②③⑤

**KILMELFORD** Strathclyde *Argyllshire* Map **10** NM81

★★67% *Cuilfail* PA34 4XA ☎(08522)274
Closed Jan-Feb
*Friendly, informal and family-run, the hotel has retained much of*
*its original coaching inn character.*
12rm(4⇋3♠)(2fb) ® sB&B£18-£25 sB&B⇋♠£18-£29
dB&B£36-£42 dB&B⇋♠£36-£50
CTV 20P ⊕ ✿
V ⍟ ⬛ ⊬ Bar Lunch £5.25-£9.50alc Dinner £5.25-£16alc Last
dinner 9pm
Credit Cards ①③

**KILNSEY** North Yorkshire Map **07** SD96

★★63% **Tennant Arms** BD23 5PS ☎Grassington(0756)752301
*Situated right by the impressive Kilnsey Crags, this busy, popular*
*inn offers good bedrooms and an oak-panelled restaurant.*
10⇋♠(2fb) CTV in all bedrooms ® ✳
dB&B⇋♠£66.50-£86.50 (incl dinner) 🄱
40P ♪ *xmas*
V ⍟ Dinner £10.95 Last dinner 8.30pm
Credit Cards ①③

**KILWINNING** Strathclyde *Ayrshire* Map **10** NS34

★★★⚑67% *Montgreenan Mansion House* Montgreenan
Estate KA13 7QZ (4m N of Irvine off A736, 3m E B785) (Best
Western) ☎(0294)57733 Telex no 778525 FAX (0294) 85397
*A fine country mansion set in 45 acres of wooded grounds features*
*elegant and comfortably-appointed public rooms. Bedrooms are*
*thoughtfully equipped, the larger among them being provided with*
*en suite spa baths.*
16⇋1🄵 CTV in all bedrooms ® ✘ (ex guide dogs)
Lift ℭ 50P ⊕ ✿ ♪ 5 ♪ (hard) snooker clay-pigeon shooting
croquet
♀ Scottish & French V ⍟ ⬛ Last dinner 9.30pm
Credit Cards ①②③⑤

All AA-appointed establishments are
inspected regularly to ensure that required
standards are maintained.

**KIMBOLTON** Cambridgeshire Map **04** TL06

✕**La Côte d'Or** 19 High St PE18 0HB
☎Huntingdon(0480)861587
Closed Tue & 25-26 Dec
Dinner not served Sun
♀ French 30 seats S10% Lunch £8.20&alc Dinner £21.95&alc
Last lunch 1.45pm Last dinner 9pm ♪ nc6yrs
Credit Cards ①③

**KINCLAVEN** Tayside *Perthshire* Map **11** NO13

★★★⚑76% **Ballathie House** PH1 4QN (Best Western)
☎Meiklour(025083)268 Telex no 76216 FAX (025083) 396
Closed 17 Feb-2 Mar RS Dec-Feb
*In an idyllic setting on the banks of the River Tay, this handsome,*
*baronial mansion has been sympathetically converted and*
*refurbished to provide modern-day facilities, whilst retaining much*
*of the original character. A warm welcome is assured and dinner*
*here is a pleasurable experience.*
28⇋♠(2fb)1🄵 CTV in all bedrooms ® T sB&B⇋♠£42-£65
dB&B⇋♠£75-£120 🄱
50P ⊕ ✿ CFA ♪ (hard) ♪ putting croquet clay pigeon
shooting *xmas*
♀ Scottish & Continental ⍟ ⬛ Lunch £1.50-£16alc Dinner
£18.75-£22&alc Last dinner 8.30pm
Credit Cards ①②③⑤

**KINGHAM** Oxfordshire Map **04** SP22

★★★69% **Mill House Hotel & Restaurant** OX7 6UH
☎(060871)8188 Telex no 849041 FAX (060871) 492
*The recent appointment of Stephen Taylor (one-time 2nd chef to*
*Chris Oakes at the Royal Crescent in Bath and at the Castle in*
*Taunton) as head chef has introduced commendable standards of*
*cuisine to the restaurant of this delightful Cotswold-stone hotel.*
*Dishes worthy of mention are his mousseline of Lemon Sole with*
*flevrons of puff pastry and wild mushrooms in a delicate fish stock*
*with dill sauce ; his breast of grouse with cranberries and Calvados,*
*and the delicious sweets such as a chocolate and hazelnut soufflé.*
*The hotel has recently upgraded its bedrooms, and the standards*
*of decoration and furnishings are exceptionally pleasing, as is the*
*hospitality offered by the owners Mr and Mrs Barnett and their*
*staff. The Mill House enjoys delightful rural surroundings and a*
*mill stream running through its attractive grounds has given the*
*hotel its name.*
21rm(20⇋)(1fb)1🄵 CTV in all bedrooms ® T ✘ ✳
sB&B£45-£56 sB&B⇋♠£45-£56 dB&B⇋♠£70-£92 🄱
60P ✿ ♪ croquet nc5yrs *xmas*
♀ English & French V ⍟ ⬛ Lunch £12.95-£20&alc Dinner
fr£16.95&alc Last dinner 9.30pm
Credit Cards ①②③④⑤

**KINGSBRIDGE** Devon Map **03** SX74

★★★⚑76% **Buckland-Tout-Saints** Goveton TQ7 2DS (2.5m
NE on unclass rd) (Prestige) ☎(0548)853055 Telex no 42513
FAX (0548) 856261
Closed 3 Jan-2 Feb
*From its garden setting, this charming Queen Anne house*
*commands views of the South Devon countryside. The hotel forms*
*part of an estate whose written history goes back for nine centuries*
*and, with its panelled lounges and dining room, offers true country-*
*house hospitality. Standards of comfort are high and the*
*restaurant menu, in the French and modern English style, offers*
*such dishes as salad of wood pigeon (smoked on the premises),*
*noisettes of lamb served with celeriac and a madeira sauce, with*
*pear frangipan for dessert.*
12⇋♠1🄵 CTV in all bedrooms T ✘ S10% sB&B⇋♠£75-£85
dB&B⇋♠£95-£145 🄱
14P ⊕ ✿ croquet putting nc8yrs *xmas*

374

✿ ☑ ✟ S10% Lunch £17.50-£22.50 Dinner £25-£30 Last
dinner 9pm
Credit Cards ① ② ③ ④ ⑤

See advertisement on page 377

★★62% **Kings Arms** Fore St TQ7 1AB (Exec Hotel)
☎(0548)852071 FAX (0548) 852977
*This cosy coaching inn is personally run by an enthusiastic and
conscientious manager to provide a relaxed, welcoming atmosphere
and friendly service. Popular bars and a cottage-style restaurant
offer flexible meal times and a good range of home-cooked dishes,
while bedrooms – which have received some upgrading – reflect the
style and architecture of the building, The majority having four
poster or half tester beds and traditional furnishings ; a small
indoor swimming pool will please the more energetic guest.
Positioned as it is at the heart of a historic town, the hotel makes
an excellent base from which to tour South Devon generally and
the rolling South Hams in particular.*
11rm(8⇄1Ⴖ✿)10⊠ ® sB&B⇄ႶႶ£27.50-£30
dB&B⇄Ⴖ£50-£55 ▤
CTV 40P ⚏ ▣(heated) nc8yrs
♀ English & French V ✿ ✟ Lunch £5.50-£8alc Dinner
£12-£18alc Last dinner 9.00pm
Credit Cards ① ③ ⓔ

★★57% **Rockwood** Embankment Rd TQ7 1JZ ☎(0548)852480
Closed 24-27 Dec
*Small villa with new extension overlooking estuary.*
6⇄Ⴖ CTV in all bedrooms ® ✱ sB&B⇄Ⴖ£23-£27
dB&B⇄Ⴖ£44-£50 ▤
CTV 9P 3☻ ⚏
♀ English & Continental V ✿ ☑ ✟ Sunday Lunch £6.50-£7.50
High tea £2.50-£6.50alc Dinner £9.75-£10.75&alc Last dinner
9pm
Credit Cards ① ③ ⓔ

---

**KING'S LYNN** Norfolk Map 09 TF62

★★★69% **Knights Hill** Knights Hill Village, South Wootton
PE30 3HQ (junct A148/A149) (Best Western) ☎(0553)675566
Telex no 818118 KNIGHT G FAX (0553) 675568
*Accommodation is provided both in the main building – a former
hunting lodge – and in the converted courtyard buildings, which
also include the Farmers Arms Inn and Restaurant. The Garden
Restaurant is most attractive and offers a variety of freshly cooked
dishes. Situated on the outskirts of the town at the junction of the
A148 and A149, this hotel offers a good range of facilities for both
business and leisure guests.*
40⇄Ⴌ Annexe18⇄Ⴌ1⊠✟in 13 bedrooms CTV in all
bedrooms ® T S% sB⇄Ⴌ£55-£68
dB⇄Ⴌ£65-£80 (room only) ▤
ℂ 350P ✿ ▣(heated) ♪ (hard) snooker sauna solarium
gymnasium jogging circuit croquet spa bath ♫ xmas
♀ International V ✿ ☑ S% Lunch fr£7.50alc Dinner
fr£15.50&alc Last dinner 9.30pm
Credit Cards ① ② ③ ⑤ ⓔ

★★★64% **Butterfly** Beveridge Way, Hardwick Narrows
PE30 4NB (junct A10/A47) (Consort) ☎(0553)771707
Telex no 818313 FAX (0553) 768027
*The Butterfly offers well designed modern accommodation which is
well equipped. The semi self-service buffet style of dining uses well-
prepared fresh produce and staff are friendly and efficient.*
50⇄Ⴌ(2fb) CTV in all bedrooms ® T ✖ (ex guide dogs)
ℂ 70P
♀ European V ✿ ☑ ✟ Last dinner 10pm
Credit Cards ① ② ③ ⑤

See advertisement on page 377

---

For key to symbols see the inside front cover.

★★★60% **The Duke's Head** Tuesday Market Pl PE30 1JS (Trusthouse Forte) ☎(0553)774996 Telex no 817349 FAX (0553) 763556
*Situated in the town centre facing Tuesday Market Place this hotel has particularly comfortable and attractive lounge, two bars, a restaurant and coffee shop, and banqueting and conference facilities. Service is generally friendly and efficient.*
72⇌(1fb)⊬in 10 bedrooms CTV in all bedrooms ® T S% sB⇌£65-£78 dB⇌£81-£87 (room only) ⊟
Lift 《 41P CFA *xmas*
♀ English & French V ♥ ♨ ⊬ S% Lunch fr£8&alc Dinner fr£14&alc Last dinner 9.30pm
Credit Cards ①②③④⑤

★★69% *Stuart House* 35 Goodwins Rd PE30 5QX ☎(0553)772169 Telex no 817209
Closed Xmas & New Year
*An hotel located in a quiet residential area of the town offers well equipped and spotlessly clean rooms, plain but interesting cuisine based on fresh produce which includes home-grown vegetables and herbs, a warm, friendly welcome from the proprietors and enthusiastic service.*
19rm(12⇌3ᐱ)(6fb) CTV in all bedrooms ® T ⋈ CTV 25P
♀ European V Last dinner 8.30pm
Credit Cards ①②③

★★64% *Globe* Tuesday Market Pl PE30 1EZ (Berni/Chef & Brewer) ☎(0553)772617
*Occupying a corner site in the Market Place the Globe is a popular meeting place. The bars and restaurants offer reasonably-priced Berni dishes and comfortable surroundings. Bedrooms are modestly furnished and well equipped.*
40⇌ᐱ(2fb) CTV in all bedrooms ® T ⋈ (ex guide dogs) sB&B⇌ᐱ£42-£50.50 dB&B⇌ᐱ£59.50 ⊟
《 15P 8🍴
V ♥ ♨ ⊬ Lunch £8-£15alc Dinner £8-£15alc Last dinner 10.30pm
Credit Cards ①②③⑤

★★64% **The Tudor Rose** St Nicholas St, off Tuesday Market Pl PE30 1LR ☎(0553)762824 Telex no 818752 FAX (0553) 764894
*Comfortable, modestly furnished rooms and good service from a small team of staff are provided by this fifteenth-century inn just off Tuesday Market Place in the town centre. Bars feature beamed ceilings, as does a restaurant serving French/English cuisine which specialises in freshly caught local sea food and uses only the best of ingredients.*
14rm(4⇌7ᐱ)(1fb) CTV in all bedrooms ® T ✱ sB&B£19.95 sB&B⇌ᐱ£30 dB&B⇌ᐱ£45 ⊟
🍴
♀ English & French V ♥ ♨ ⊬ High tea fr70palc
Credit Cards ①②③⑤

★★62% *Grange* Willow Park, South Wootton Ln PE30 3BP ☎(0553)673777 & 671222
*This detached Edwardian hotel, set in well-tended gardens on the outskirts of Kings Lynn, combines modern facilities with friendly personal service.*
6rm(3⇌2ᐱ)Annexe4⇌ CTV in all bedrooms ®
15P 1🍴
♥ ♨ Last dinner 8.30pm
Credit Cards ①②③

**KINGSTEIGNTON** Devon Map 03 SX87

★★★71% **Passage House** Hackney Ln TQ12 3QH ☎Newton Abbot(0626)55515 FAX (0626) 63336
*Modern hotel with conference facilities and leisure complex including indoor pool, jet stream, jacuzzi, sauna and solarium. Overlooks the Teign Estuary and its wild-life.*
39⇌ᐱ CTV in all bedrooms ® T ✱ sB&B⇌ᐱ£55-£65 dB&B⇌ᐱ£85-£95 ⊟
Lift 《 300P ❀ ☐(heated) ♪ sauna solarium gymnasium *xmas*
V ♥ ♨ Lunch £8.50&alc Dinner £13.75&alc Last dinner 9.30pm
Credit Cards ①②③⑤ ⓔ

**KINGSTON UPON THAMES** Greater London

**See LONDON plan 1**B2(page 426)
★★★63% **Kingston Lodge** Kingston Hill KT2 7NP (Trusthouse Forte) ☎081-541 4481 Telex no 936034 FAX 081-547 1013
*Modern hotel with cocktail bar and popular courtyard restaurant. Some bedrooms have courtyard balconies.*
61⇌ᐱ1𝄢⊬in 20 bedrooms CTV in all bedrooms ® T ✱ sB⇌ᐱ£87-£98 dB⇌ᐱ£103-£114 (room only) ⊟
《 74P *xmas*
♀ English & French V ♥ ♨ ⊬ Lunch £11.95-£19.75&alc Dinner £15.50-£19.75&alc Last dinner 9.45pm
Credit Cards ①②③⑤

Entries for red-star hotels are highlighted by a tint panel. For a full list of these establishments consult the Contents page.

# The Grange Hotel AA★★

**Willow Park, Off South Wootton Lane King's Lynn, Norfolk PE30 3BP Telephone: (0553) 673777/671222**

Our impressive Edwardian Hotel offers you a warm welcome. Set in its own grounds. Spacious centrally heated, en-suite, bedrooms, with C.T.Vs, direct dial telephones, coffee & tea making facilities. Ideal base to explore North West Norfolk. Resident & Restaurant licence.

All AA-appointed establishments are inspected regularly to ensure that required standards are maintained.

---

### KINGSWINFORD West Midlands Map 07 SO88

★★★63% **The Kingfisher** Kidderminster Rd, Wall Heath
DY6 0EN ☎(0384)273763 & 401145 FAX (0384) 277094
*This renowned Midlands cabaret club has extended its facilities to
include well-equipped, comfortable bedrooms. It is situated on the
A449 Kidderminster to Wolverhampton road, six miles from
Dudley.*
23⇔♠(2fb) CTV in all bedrooms ⓡ T ✖ (ex guide dogs) ✱
sB&B⇔♠£25-£45 dB&B⇔♠£35-£63
《 200P ✿ ⍨(heated) *xmas*
V ♦ ♨ Lunch £7.95-£8.95 Dinner £7.95-£8.95&alc Last dinner
10.30pm
Credit Cards [1] [2] [3]
**See advertisement under WOLVERHAMPTON**

---

### KINGTON Hereford & Worcester Map 03 SO25

★★66% **Burton** Mill St HR5 3BQ (Exec Hotel) ☎(0544)230323
*A combination of friendly service, bright public areas and well-
equipped bedrooms make this old town centre inn popular with
both tourists and business people alike. Situated close to the Welsh
Border and Offa's Dyke.*
15⇔♠(3fb)1🛏 CTV in all bedrooms ⓡ T sB&B⇔♠fr£36.50
dB&B⇔♠fr£48 🅟
50P ✿
♀ International V ♦ ♨ Lunch fr£12.50 High tea fr£5.50
Dinner fr£12.50 Last dinner 9.30pm
Credit Cards [1] [2] [3] [5]

○**Penrhos Court Hotel & Restaurant** Penrhos Court HR5 3LH
☎(0544)230720
Due to have opened Jan 1990
19rm

---

### KINGUSSIE Highland *Inverness-shire* Map 14 NH70

★★67% **Columba House** Manse Rd PH21 1JF ☎(0540)661402
*A warm, friendly and hospitable hotel which stands in a slightly
elevated position at the north end of the town offers spacious,
particularly well appointed bedrooms and a large garden in which
guests can relax on summer days.*
7⇔♠(2fb) CTV in all bedrooms ⓡ T sB&B⇔♠£18-£24
dB&B⇔♠£36-£48 🅟
12P 🚗 ✿ ♪ (grass) croquet 9-hole putting *xmas*
V ♦ ♨ Lunch £5-£10 Dinner £12-£14 Last dinner 8.30pm
£

★65% **Osprey** Ruthven Rd PH21 1EN ☎(0540)661510
Closed Nov-27 Dec
*Peacefully situated in the heart of the Spey Valley is this friendly
little hotel informally run by Duncan and Pauline Reeves. The
food is imaginatively and competently prepared by Mrs Reeves
whilst Mr Reeves is keen to explain to guests the details of his
excellent wine list.*
8rm(1⇔3♠) sB&B£34-£44 sB&B⇔♠£42-£52 dB&B£68-£78
dB&B⇔♠£74-£104 (incl dinner)
CTV 10P 🚗 nc3yrs
♀ Scottish, English & French ♦ ♨ ✘ Dinner £17-£20 Last
dinner 8pm
Credit Cards [1] [2] [3] [4] [5] £

❀✖**The Cross** High St PH21 1HX ☎(0540)661762
Rosette awarded for dinner only
*Tony and Ruth Hadley's delightful little restaurant can be found
in the centre of the High Street, and has a truly friendly
atmosphere that envelops you from the moment you set foot in the
cosy lounge. The menu is a fixed price one with, usually, a choice of
three dishes at each course, plus a soup. Mountain hare, salmon
and venison are often featured, according to the season, and the
excellent wine list includes many interesting clarets. As the
restaurant seats only 20, it is advisable to make a reservation, and
there are bedrooms for diners wishing to stay overnight.*

Closed Mon, Sun, 1-25 Dec & 3 wks May/Jun
Lunch not served
20 seats ✱ Dinner £23-£30 Last dinner 9.30pm ₽ nc12yrs ✘

---

### KINLOCHBERVIE Highland *Sutherland* Map 14 NC25

★★★60% **Kinlochbervie** IV27 4RP ☎(097182)275
FAX (097182) 438
RS mid Nov-Feb
*Set high in this rugged but beautiful corner of Scotland and
commanding fine views over the harbour and out to sea, this
purpose-built hotel offers comfortable, well equipped bedrooms
with smart modern bathrooms. Guests can eat either in an informal
bistro or in the attractively appointed candle-lit restaurant where a
daily-changing menu features fresh local produce.*
14⇔♠(3fb) CTV in all bedrooms ⓡ T S% sB&B⇔♠£50-£80
dB&B⇔♠£70-£90 🅟
《 CTV 30P 🚗 ♪ snooker
♀ French ♦ ♨ Bar Lunch £5-£12alc High tea £5-£12alc Last
high tea 6pm
Credit Cards [1] [2] [3] [5] £

---

### KINLOCHEWE Highland *Ross & Cromarty* Map 14 NH06

★★60% *Kinlochewe* IV22 2PA (Minotels) ☎(044584)253
*Small, relaxing, family-run hotel offering well-appointed
accommodation and honest cooking based on good ingredients.*
10rm(3⇔2♠) ⓡ
CTV 20P 🚗 salmon & sea trout fishing deer stalking nc
♀ Scottish, English & French V ♦ ♨ ✘
Credit Cards [1] [3]

---

### KINROSS Tayside *Kinross-shire* Map 11 NO10

★★★66% *Windlestrae* The Muirs KY13 7AS (Consort)
☎(0577)63217 FAX (0577) 64733
*Efficiently run by owners, this comfortable business and tourist
hotel features an attractive split-level bar, a smart restaurant and
bedrooms which have been refurbished to a good modern standard.*
18⇔♠(2fb)1🛏 CTV in all bedrooms ⓡ
《 🎠 60P 1🚗 (charged) ✿ sauna ♨
♀ International V ♦ ♨ Last dinner 9.30pm
Credit Cards [1] [2] [3] [5]

★★★62% **Green** 2 The Muirs KY13 7AS (Best Western)
☎(0577)63467 Telex no 76684 FAX (0577) 63180
RS 23-28 Dec
*A friendly atmosphere prevails at this popular business and holiday
hotel, which offers a wide range of sporting and leisure facilities.
Traditional lounges invite easy relaxation, and bedrooms, though
compact and practical, are well equipped.*
40⇔♠(6fb) CTV in all bedrooms ⓡ T sB&B⇔♠£48-£60
dB&B⇔♠£66-£80 🅟
《 60P ✿ CFA ⍨(heated) ▶ 18 ♪ squash sauna solarium
gymnasium curling croquet putting ♨ *xmas*
♀ French V ♦ ♨ Bar Lunch £5-£10.50alc High tea
£5.25-£6.75 Dinner £14.50-£16&alc Last dinner 9.30pm
Credit Cards [1] [2] [3] [5]

★★65% **Bridgend** High St KY13 7EN (Consort) ☎(0577)63413
FAX (0577) 64769
*Conveniently located just off the M90, between junctions 5 and 6,
the hotel has recently been refurbished to offer well appointed
modern accommodation and comfortable public areas.*
15⇔♠(1fb)1🛏 CTV in all bedrooms ⓡ T
sB&B⇔♠£32-£38.50 dB&B⇔♠£42.50-£72.50 🅟
《 CTV 40P *xmas*
V ♦ ♨ Lunch £5.95-£12&alc High tea £6.50 Dinner
£7.95-£15&alc Last dinner 10pm
Credit Cards [1] [2] [3] [5] £

**K**

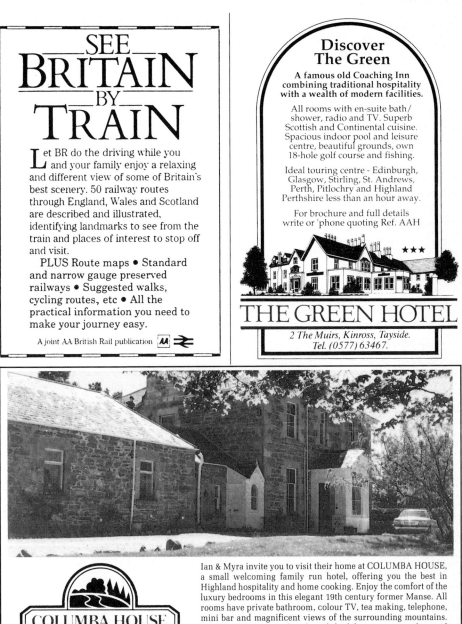
K

★★★62% **Kirklands** 20 High St KY13 7AN ☎(0577)63313
*Conveniently situated in the High Street, this former coaching inn has been substantially refurbished to provide comfortable modern accommodation.*
9⇄🎄 CTV in all bedrooms ® T ✠ (ex guide dogs)
sB&B⇄🎄£30 dB&B⇄🎄£46
30P ✿
V ⍟ ⚏ Bar Lunch £4-£6.50 Dinner fr£6.50&alc Last dinner 9pm
Credit Cards ①③£

⬠**Granada Lodge** Kincardine Rd KY13 7HQ (on A977, off junct 6 of M90) (Granada) ☎(0577)64646 FAX (0577) 64108
*Situated at junction 6 of the M90 with easy access from both sides of the motorway, this lodge offers good value and practical accommodation. The adjacent Country Kitchen provides 24-hour catering facilities.*
34⇄(15fb)⊀in 6 bedrooms CTV in all bedrooms ®
✠ (ex guide dogs) ✳ S% sB⇄fr£25 dB⇄fr£28 (room only)

---

### KINTBURY Berkshire Map 04 SU36

✕✕**Dundas Arms** RG15 0UT ☎(0488)58263 & 58559
*A smart country pub restaurant, on the Kennet and Avon canal, with a friendly and informal atmosphere. The chef offers a short dinner menu of simple English and French dishes complimented by a well-chosen wine list.*
Closed Sun, Mon & Xmas-New Year
⚐ English & French 36 seats Lunch £16 Dinner £24-£28 Last lunch 1.30pm Last dinner 9.15pm 50P ⊀
Credit Cards ①②③

---

### KIRBY MISPERTON North Yorkshire Map 08 SE77

★★61% *Beansheaf Restaurant Motel* Malton Rd YO18 0UE
☎(065230)614 & 488
RS Monday
*The friendly owners of this establishment have worked hard to create an informal atmosphere, modern value-for-money accommodation and a noteworthy restaurant which is popular with guests and local residents alike.*
20⇄🎄(2fb)1⊞ CTV in all bedrooms ®
60P ✿ sauna solarium
⚐ English & Continental V ⍟ ⚏ ⊀ Last dinner 10pm
Credit Cards ①③

---

### KIRKBY FLEETHAM North Yorkshire Map 08 SE29

★★★✢72% **Kirkby Fleetham Hall** DL7 0SU (Pride of Britain)
☎Northallerton(0609)748711 FAX (0609) 748747
*An impressive Georgian house in 30 acres of parkland, the hotel boasts its own lake and offers the advantages of a really peaceful atmosphere, spacious, comfortable lounges and bedrooms, charming staff and good, interesting cooking.*
22⇄🎄(2fb)3⊞ CTV in all bedrooms T S% sB&B⇄🎄fr£75 dB&B⇄🎄£102-£175 ₧
40P ⚗ ✿ ⌂(heated) ✔ croquet xmas
⚐ British & French V ⍟ ⚏ S% Sunday Lunch fr£15 Dinner fr£28 Last dinner 9pm
Credit Cards ①②③④⑤

---

### KIRKBY LONSDALE Cumbria Map 07 SD67

★★★55% *Royal* Main St LA6 2AE (Minotels) ☎(05242)71217 FAX (05242) 72228
*A former private residence, converted into a coaching inn, set in the centre of this market town. Bar meals are popular, with more formal meals served in the restaurant.*
20rm(15⇄1🎄)1⊞ CTV in all bedrooms ®
CTV 25P 8🏤 snooker ♫
V ⍟ ⚏ Last dinner 10pm
Credit Cards ①②③⑤

---

✕**Cobwebs Country House & Restaurant** Leck, Cowan Bridge LA6 2HZ ☎(05242)72141
Closed Jan-mid Mar
Lunch not served
Dinner not served Sun
18 seats ✳ Dinner fr£17.50 Last dinner 7.30pm 20P nc12yrs ⊀
Credit Cards ①③

---

### KIRKBYMOORSIDE North Yorkshire Map 08 SE68

★★68% **George & Dragon** 17 Market Place YO6 6AA
☎(0751)31637
*Welcoming 13th-century inn with modern bedrooms in converted stables.*
14⇄🎄Annexe8⇄🎄(3fb) CTV in all bedrooms ® T
sB&B⇄🎄£30 dB&B⇄🎄£55 ₧
22P ✿ xmas
V ⍟ Sunday Lunch fr£9 Dinner fr£17 Last dinner 9.30pm
Credit Cards ①③

---

### KIRKBY STEPHEN Cumbria Map 12 NY70

★★62% **King's Arms** Market St CA17 4QN ☎(07683)71378
Closed 25 Dec
*Resident proprietors create a warm, friendly atmosphere at this comfortable hotel which was originally a coaching inn. Set at the centre of the historic market town, it lies between the Yorkshire Dales and Lake District – a good base for exploring both areas. Enjoyable, home-cooked dishes, including local specialities, are served in the attractive, antique-furnished dining room.*
9rm(1⇄2🎄)(1fb) ® T ✳ sB&Bfr£24.50 sB&B⇄🎄fr£29 dB&Bfr£40 dB&B⇄🎄fr£47.50 ₧
CTV 4P 5🏤
V ⍟
Credit Cards ①③

---

### KIRKCALDY Fife Map 11 NT29

★★★65% **Dean Park** Chapel Level KY2 6QW ☎(0592)261635 Telex no 727071
*Situated two miles north of the town off the A910 this is a comfortable hotel with modern well-appointed bedrooms and inviting bar lounges. Interesting, good value menus are offered at both lunch and dinner.*
20⇄🎄Annexe12🎄(3fb)1⊞ CTV in all bedrooms ®
✠ (ex guide dogs)
⟮100P ⚗ ✿ snooker
⚐ Scottish & French V ⍟
Credit Cards ①②③⑤

★★67% **The Belvedere** Coxstool, West Wemyss KY1 4SN
☎(0592)54167
*Situated on the Firth of Forth, this comfortable hotel enjoys superb views across to Edinburgh. Bedroom accommodation is inviting and well appointed, service very friendly and the restaurant offers good value, interesting menus.*
5⇄🎄Annexe16⇄🎄(1fb) CTV in all bedrooms ® T
✠ (ex guide dogs) ✳ sB&B⇄🎄fr£39 dB&B⇄🎄fr£50
40P
⚐ Scottish & French V ⍟ ⚏ Lunch £10 Dinner £13 Last dinner 9pm
Credit Cards ①③

---

### KIRKCUDBRIGHT Dumfries & Galloway *Kirkcudbrightshire* Map 11 NX65

★★65% **Selkirk Arms** Old High St DG6 4JG ☎(0557)30402 FAX (0557) 31639
*An hotel situated in the old part of this attractive fishing town, dating back to 1770 and reputedly the place where Burns wrote The Selkirk Grace, has been completely refurbished to provide attractive and comfortable public areas and bedrooms of a comparable standard, being well appointed and thoughtfully*

K

*equipped though fairly compact. Efficient housekeeping ensures
good levels of service throughout.*
14⇨**î**Annexe1⇨(2fb) CTV in all bedrooms ® T ✱
sB&B⇨**î**fr£36.50 dB&B⇨**î**fr£65 ➡
4P 16🛋 ✿ *xmas*
🖳 Scottish & Continental V ✿ ⬚ Sunday Lunch fr£6.45
Dinner fr£12.50&alc Last dinner 9.30pm
Credit Cards ⓵ ⓶ ⓷ ⓹

See advertisement on page 383

---

**KIRKHILL** Highland *Inverness-shire* Map **14** NH54

★66% **Inchmore** IV5 7PX (at junct A862/B9164 )
☎Inverness(0463)83296
*The small, friendly, family-run hotel set at the roadside offers a
relaxed and informal atmosphere. The compact bedrooms are
pleasant and well-equipped. Public areas include an attractive
dining room and two popular and lively bars.*
6⇨(1fb) CTV in all bedrooms ® T ✱ sB&B⇨£20-£25
dB&B⇨£35-£40 ➡
80P
✿ ⬚ Lunch £6.50-£8 Dinner £8.50-£10&alc Last dinner
8.30pm
Credit Cards ⓵ ⓷ Ⓔ

---

**KIRK LANGLEY** Derbyshire Map **08** SK23

★★63% **Meynell Arms** Ashbourne Rd DE6 4NF (Minotels)
☎(033124)515
*This Georgian manor house on the A52 close to Derby, now a busy
hotel, is well-known in the area for its value-for-money bar snacks.*
10rm(5⇨2**î**)(2fb)2⌗ CTV in all bedrooms ® T sB&B£24-£28
sB&B⇨**î**£28-£34 dB&B£38-£45 dB&B⇨**î**£45-£52 ➡
▶

**K**

# DEAN PARK
### —— H O T E L ——
## CHAPEL LEVEL,
## KIRKCALDY KY2 6QW
## Telephone: 0592 261635
### ★ ★ ★ AA
Enjoy the comfort of a professionally run and
beautifully equipped hotel where every guest's
requirements receive our individual attention.
Offering comprehensive facilities and competitive packages for business executives and
conference delegates and set in own peaceful
grounds, Dean Park is a popular venue, with its
superb cuisine and friendly service.
**TO AVOID DISAPPOINTMENT BOOK EARLY**

# The Kirklands
# Hotel
# Kinross
## Telephone (0577) 63313

STB ✿✿✿✿ COMMENDED

AA ★ ★

100P ✿
V ✿ Lunch £8-£10alc Dinner £10-£15alc Last dinner 9.30pm
Credit Cards ①③ⓔ

**KIRKMICHAEL** Tayside *Perthshire* Map **15** NO06

★★58%, **Aldchlappie** PH10 7NS ☎Strathardle(025081)224
*A comfortable, attractively modernised, personally managed hotel*
*beside the River Ardle, which caters for summer tourists and*
*winter ski enthusiasts. The cosy Malt Room bar is noted for its*
*extensive range of malt whiskies.*
7rm(5⇨3)(1fb)⅟in 5 bedrooms ® ✖ (ex guide dogs)
sB&B£17-£20.50 dB&B⇨3£34-£41 ₽
CTV 20P 2🐾 ✿ ⌀
✿ ⌂ ⅟ Sunday Lunch fr£8 Dinner fr£12 Last dinner 9.30pm
Credit Cards ①②③ⓔ

★★58%, **Log Cabin** PH10 7NB (Exec Hotel)
☎Strathardle(025081)288
*Built from Norwegian pine logs and roofed with turf, this*
*attractive, modern and popular hotel stands nine hundred feet up*
*amid rugged moorland, offering glorious views of the surrounding*
*countryside. Compact, practical bedrooms, enjoyable food and*
*attractive public areas.*
13⇨3♠(5fb) TV available ® sB&B⇨3♠£25.95-£30.95
dB&B⇨3♠£41.90-£45.90 ₽
CTV 50P ✿ ⌀ shooting ski-ing *xmas*
V ✿ ⌂ ⅟ Sunday Lunch £7.95 Dinner £14.95 Last dinner
8.45pm
Credit Cards ①②③⑤

★55%, **Strathlene** Main Rd PH10 7NT
☎Strathardle(025081)347
*This family-run holiday hotel at the centre of a picturesque village*
*combines an informal atmosphere and good-value accommodation.*
7rm(5⇨3♠)(1fb) ® sB&B£15-£18 sB&B⇨3♠£15-£20
dB&B£28-£30 dB&B⇨3♠£32-£34 ₽
CTV 3P 🚲
V ✿ Lunch £4.50-£11 Dinner £9.50 Last dinner 8.30pm
Credit Cards ①③ⓔ

**KIRKNEWTON** Lothian *Midlothian* Map **11** NT16

○**Dalmahoy Hotel, Golf & Country Club** EH27 8EB
☎031-333 1845
Due to have opened Sep 1990
116rm

**KIRKWALL**
See **Orkney**

**KIRKWHELPINGTON** Northumberland Map **12** NY98

★★61%, *The* **Knowesgate** NE19 2SH (Inter-Hotels)
☎Otterburn(0830)40261
*Modern hotel complex.*
16⇨3♠ CTV in all bedrooms ® T
100P games room
V ✿ ⌂ ⅟
Credit Cards ①②③⑤

**KNARESBOROUGH** North Yorkshire Map **08** SE35

★★★69%, **Dower House** Bond End HG5 9AL (Best Western)
☎Harrogate(0423)863302 Telex no 57202 FAX (0423) 867665
Closed 25 Dec RS 24 & 26 Dec
*An attractive Grade II listed building retains an old world charm*
*in bedrooms and public areas which still have the original timbers;*
*sympathetic extension has added a pleasant conservatory to the*
*dining room and has provided an excellent, well-equipped leisure*
*centre with a poolside bar. Helpful staff provide friendly service.*

28⇨3♠Annexe4⇨3♠(2fb) CTV in all bedrooms ® T ✖
sB&B⇨3♠£42.50-£60 dB&B⇨3♠£60-£88 ₽
《 80P 🚲 ✿ ▣(heated) sauna solarium gymnasium
♥ English & French V ✿ ⅟ Lunch £7.95-£16alc Dinner
£14.75-£16.50&alc Last dinner 9.30pm
Credit Cards ①②③⑤

✖✖*Four Park Place* 4 Park Place HG5 0ER
☎Harrogate(0423)868002
*A delightful and intimate restaurant to be found just off the High*
*Street. The menu features interesting dishes skillfully prepared.*
*Salmon, scallops, scampi, pigeon and veal are all to be found*
*cooked and served in many different ways. There is also a good*
*selection of starters and desserts. Service is attentive and*
*unobtrusive.*
Closed Sun, 1 wk Jan, 1 wk Aug & 25-26 Dec
Lunch not served Sat
28 seats Last lunch 2.30pm Last dinner 9.30pm 5P nc5yrs ⅟
Credit Cards ①③

**KNIGHTON** Powys Map **07** SO27

★★★66%, **The Knighton** Broad St LD7 1BL ☎(0547)520530
FAX (0547) 520529
*This hotel, built in 1860, adjoins the town's old assembly rooms*
*which have now been converted to a very attractive function suite.*
*The hotel has been completely modernised and features a*
*magnificent galleried central staircase. A good choice of food is*
*available, with vegetarians well catered for.*
15⇨3♠ CTV in all bedrooms ® T sB&B⇨3♠£46-£59
dB&B⇨3♠£66-£76 ₽
Lift 10P snooker *xmas*
♥ International V ✿ ⌂ Lunch fr£8.50 High tea fr£7 Dinner
£12.50-£19.50alc Last dinner 9.30pm
Credit Cards ①②③⑤ⓔ

★★71%, **Milebrook House** Milebrook LD7 1LT (WR)
☎(0547)528632
*This 18th century house is situated 2 miles east of the town,*
*alongside the A4113. A mile stretch of fly fishing is available to*
*guests and the lawns and gardens are very attractive. Most food is*
*local, with vegetables and herbs grown in the hotel's own kitchen*
*garden. Bedrooms are attractive and comfortable and public rooms*
*are cosy and relaxing.*
6⇨3♠ CTV in all bedrooms ® ✖ sB⇨3♠£39.50
dB⇨3♠£53 (room only) ₽
20P ✿ ⌀ Croquet nc8yrs
♥ English & French V ✿ Lunch fr£13.50 Dinner £12.50-£16.95
Last dinner 8.30pm
Credit Cards ①③ⓔ

**KNIGHTWICK** Hereford & Worcester Map **03** SO75

★60%, **Talbot** WR6 5PH ☎(0886)21235
Closed 25 Dec evening
*This inn is situated on the banks of the River Teme, close to the*
*A44 between Worcester and Leominster. Bedrooms are well*
*equipped, with simple furnishings and décor. The service is*
*informal and casual, and staff are friendly. Hearty meals are*
*served in the bar or in the small dining room.*
10rm(5⇨2♠)(2fb) CTV in all bedrooms ® T ✳ sB&B£20
sB&B£25 dB&B£35 dB&B⇨3♠£47.50
CTV 50P ✿ ⌀ squash sauna
V ✿ ⌂ Lunch £7.50-£15alc Dinner £10-£20alc Last dinner
9.30pm
Credit Cards ①③ⓔ

Book as early as possible for busy holiday
periods.

**KNUTSFORD** Cheshire Map **07** SJ77

★★★65% **Cottons** Manchester Rd WA16 0SU (Shire)
☎(0565)50333 Telex no 669931 FAX (0565) 55351
*Situated in rural surroundings just north-west of Knutsford, this hotel is only minutes away from Junction 19 of the M6 and Manchester Airport. The hotel has comprehensive conference facilities and a leisure club with swimming pool, gym and a floodlit tennis court.*
86⇌♪(6fb)3⊞⊁in 18 bedrooms CTV in all bedrooms ® T ✱
sB&B⇌♪£84-£94 dB&B⇌♪£100-£108 ⊟
Lift ☾ CTV 180P ✲ ⊡(heated) ℘ (hard) sauna solarium gymnasium spa bath *xmas*
☋ English & French V ♥ ☕
Credit Cards [1] [2] [3] [5]

★★72% **The Longview** Manchester Rd WA16 0LX (Exec Hotel)
☎(0565)2119 FAX (0565) 52402
Closed Xmas & New Year
*This delightful, privately owned hotel is situated on the A50 close to the town centre. Its pleasant public areas have been tastefully decorated and furnished to suit the Victorian character of the building and the attractive bedrooms are very well equipped.*
13⇌Annexe10⇌(4fb) CTV in all bedrooms ® T ✱
sB&B⇌£29-£42 dB&B⇌£45-£50 ⊟
16P ⊞
☋ English & Continental V ♥ ☕ Bar Lunch £5-£8 Dinner fr£11.75 Last dinner 9pm

★★57% **Royal George** King St WA16 6EE (Berni/Chef & Brewer) ☎(0565)4151
*Standing at the centre of the well-known Cheshire town – which owes its fame to authoress Mrs Gaskell – this elegant Georgian hotel offers bedrooms which have been modernised to a high standard and provided with en suite facilities, three also having four-poster beds.*
25⇌♪Annexe6⇌(4fb)3⊞ CTV in all bedrooms ® T
✗ (ex guide dogs) sB&B⇌♪£59-£65 dB&B⇌♪£73 ⊟
Lift ☾ 40P 7⊞ ♫
V ♥ ☕ ⊁ Lunch £8-£15alc Dinner £8-£15alc Last dinner 10.30pm
Credit Cards [1] [2] [3] [5]

⌂ **Travelodge** Chester Rd, Tabley WA16 0PP (A556)
(Trusthouse Forte) ☎(0565)52187 Central Res (0800) 850950
*This lodge stands in well-tended gardens only a short distance from junction 9 of the M6, in the service area on the Manchester and airport side of the A556. Its modern, sensibly planned, en suite rooms are ideal for families, and a Little Chef restaurant and petrol filling station are conveniently close.*
32⇌♪(32fb) CTV in all bedrooms ® sB⇌♪£24
dB⇌♪£29.50 (room only)
☾ 32P ⊞
Credit Cards [1] [2] [3]

✗✗ **La Belle Epoque** 60 King St WA16 6DT ☎(0565)3060 & 2661 FAX (0565) 4150
*A charming restaurant steeped in history fittingly decked out with objets d'art and curios. Chef David Williams conjures up delicious fare in the modern French style. Diners are strongly advised not to miss out on the excellent cheese board. Service in this restaurant is friendly and attentive assuring diners of a relaxed and enjoyable (as well as delicious) meal.*
Closed Sun, 1st wk Jan & BHs
Lunch not served
☋ French 85 seats ✱ Dinner £30-£45alc Last dinner 10.30pm
⊁ nc14yrs
Credit Cards [1] [2] [3] [4] [5]

The AA's star-rating scheme is the market leader in hotel classification.

K

## Knutsford - Lamphey

**✗✗David's Place** 44 King St WA16 6DT ☎(0565)3356
*David has moved his "place" to the centre of the village, the new
premises providing a spacious restaurant on three levels which is
attractively and comfortably furnished. A good range of dishes is
featured in the ever-changing menu and blackboard list of
"specials", well cooked fresh meats and fish being served with some
interesting sauces and accompanied by a well-balanced wine list.*
Closed Sun & BH's
♟ International V 60 seats ✱ Lunch £8.50-£15&alc Dinner
£14&alc Wine £6 Last lunch 2pm Last dinner 10pm ✔
Credit Cards ①②③⑤

**KYLE OF LOCHALSH** Highland *Ross & Cromarty*
Map **13** NG72

★★★52% *Lochalsh* Ferry Rd IV40 8AF ☎Kyle(0599)4202
Telex no 75318
*A busy tourist hotel beautifully situated on a rocky promontory
overlooking the Isle of Skye beside the ferry terminal. Bedrooms
and restaurant have been vastly improved by a recent programme
of refurbishment.*
40rm(38⇨)(8fb) CTV in all bedrooms ®
Lift ( 20P 6⛟
V ♥ ⚏ Last dinner 9pm
Credit Cards ①②③④⑤

★★65% **Kyle** Main St IV40 8AB ☎Kyle(0599)4204
*A reasonably-priced hotel, with a modern extension, offering
compact, comfortable accommodation.*
32⇨♠ CTV in all bedrooms ® T sB&B⇨♠£25-£32
dB&B⇨♠£50-£60 🅱
CTV 80P ✔ 9 ♫ *xmas*
V ♥ ⚏ Sunday Lunch £4.95 High tea £3.25-£4.75 Dinner
£17&alc Last dinner 9.30pm
Credit Cards ③ ⓔ

**LACEBY** Humberside Map **08** TA20

★★★66% *Oaklands* Barton St DN37 7LE
☎Grimsby(0472)72248
*A Victorian country house set in attractive grounds with bedroom
wings built on to provide spacious and modern accommodation. A
recent addition to this hotel is the leisure facilities for residents'
sole use.*
46⇨♠(3fb)1🛏 CTV in all bedrooms ® T
( 100P ⇺ ✱ ⊟(heated) sauna solarium gymnasium golf
driving range ♫ ⚙
♟ International V ♥ ⚏ Last dinner 10pm
Credit Cards ①②③⑤

**See advertisement under GRIMSBY**

**LAGG**
See Arran, Isle of

**LAGGAN BRIDGE** Highland *Inverness-shire* Map **14** NN69

★★★62% **Gaskmore House** PH20 1BS ☎Laggan(05284)250
FAX (05284) 207
*Just east of Laggan Bridge, this tastefully modernised family-run
hotel has well-equipped bedrooms and comfortable public rooms
where log fires burn in season.*
9⇨♠Annexe2♠(3fb) CTV in all bedrooms ® T
sB&B⇨♠£27.50 dB&B⇨♠£55 🅱
40P ✱ *xmas*
V ♥ ⚏ ✂ Lunch £17.50 Dinner £17.50 Last dinner 9pm
Credit Cards ①③ ⓔ

*A rosette is an indication of exceptional
standards of cuisine.*

**LAIRG** Highland *Sutherland* Map **14** NC50

★★★60% **Sutherland Arms** IV27 4AT (Scottish Highland)
☎(0549)2291 Telex no 778215 FAX (0549) 2261
Closed Nov-Mar
*This long established, traditional fishing and tourist hotel
overlooks Loch Shin from its position at the centre of the village.*
27rm(20⇨2♠)(3fb) CTV in all bedrooms ® T sB&B£45
sB&B⇨♠£48 dB&B£72 dB&B⇨♠£78 🅱
30P ✱ ♪
♥ ⚏ Bar Lunch £1.75-£5.75 Dinner £14.75-£15.75 Last dinner
8.30pm
Credit Cards ①②③⑤

**LAMLASH**
See Arran, Isle of

**LAMORNA COVE** Cornwall & Isles of Scilly Map **02** SW42

★★★59% *Lamorna Cove* TR19 6XH (Inter-Hotels)
☎Penzance(0736)731411
*This former church for Cornish miners has been tastefully
converted to provide comfortable accommodation. Cosy lounges,
good home cooking using local produce and beautiful views of
Lamorna Cove all make for an enjoyable stay.*
18⇨♠(3fb)1🛏 CTV in all bedrooms
Lift 30P ⇺ ✱ ≋(heated) sauna diving ⚙
♥ ⚏ ✂
Credit Cards ①②③

**LAMPETER** Dyfed Map **02** SN54

★★★63% **Falcondale Country House** SA48 7RX ☎(0570)422910
*An eighteenth-century mansion set in fourteen acres of park and
woodland, with its own kitchen gardens, offers comfortably
furnished, well equipped bedrooms, enjoyable food and helpful
service from friendly staff.*
21⇨♠(8fb)2🛏 CTV in all bedrooms ® T
sB&B⇨♠£38-£48 dB&B⇨♠£55-£65 🅱
Lift 80P ✱ ♪ (hard) ⚘ putting green *xmas*
♟ English & French V ♥ ⚏ Sunday Lunch £10 Dinner £15
Last dinner 9.30pm
Credit Cards ①③

**LAMPHEY** Dyfed Map **02** SN00

★★★64% **Court** SA71 5NT (Best Western) ☎(0646)672273
Telex no 48587 FAX (0646) 672480
*Several acres of pleasant lawns, gardens and woodlands surround
a family-run hotel where guests enjoy friendly, attentive service,
the comfort of well-equipped accommodation and the use of an
excellent leisure complex.*
22⇨♠Annexe8⇨♠(15fb) CTV in all bedrooms ® T
sB&B⇨♠£48-£58 dB&B⇨♠£84-£95 🅱
🎬 CTV 50P ✱ ⊟(heated) sauna solarium gymnasium *xmas*
♟ English & French V ♥ ⚏ Lunch £14-£20alc High tea £3-£6
Dinner £14.50&alc Last dinner 9pm
Credit Cards ①②③⑤

**See advertisement under PEMBROKE**

★★69% *Bethwaite's Lamphey Hall* SA71 5NR ☎(0646)672394
*Originally a vicarage, this small hotel has comfortable modern
bedrooms, an attrative open plan lounge/restaurant and a separate
Bistro. Staff are friendly and attentive.*
10⇨♠(2fb)1🛏 CTV in all bedrooms ® T
30P
♟ English & French V ♥ ⚏ Last dinner 8.30pm
Credit Cards ①③

**K**

384

## LANARK

See **Biggar**

---

**LANCASTER** Lancashire Map **07** SD46

★★★ 59% **Post House** Waterside Park, Caton Rd LA1 3RA (close to junc 34 M6) (Trusthouse Forte) ☎(0524)65999 Telex no 65363 FAX (0524) 841265

*Modern, well furnished riverside hotel with very comfortable bedrooms.*

117⇋♠(23fb)1♿⎚in 39 bedrooms CTV in all bedrooms ® S% sB⇋♠£72-£83 dB⇋♠£83-£94 (room only) ♨
Lift ( 180P ✿ ⎙(heated) sauna solarium gymnasium health & fitness centre *xmas*
V ♦ ⍩ ⅙ S% Lunch £10.75-£11&alc Dinner £13.95&alc Last dinner 10.30pm
Credit Cards ①②③④⑤

---

★★★ 67% **Royal Kings Arms** Market St LA1 1HP ☎(0524)32451 Telex no 65481 FAX (0524) 841698

*A comfortable city centre hotel with spacious public rooms and modern well-appointed bedrooms. Service is cheerful and courteous.*

55⇋♠(2fb) CTV in all bedrooms ® T sB&B⇋♠fr£55 dB&B⇋♠fr£70 ♨
Lift ( 20P *xmas*
♀ English & French V ♦ ⍩ Lunch fr£7 Dinner fr£12&alc Last dinner 9.30pm
Credit Cards ①②③⑤⑥

---

★★ 56% *Slyne Lodge* Slyne LA2 6AZ (2m N on A6) ☎Hest Bank(0524)823389

*Situated on the A6 north of the city this hotel has a bedroom annexe at the rear in a quiet location, and a popular steakhouse-style restaurant*

10⇋(3fb) CTV in all bedrooms ®
100P ✿ ♘
♀ Mainly grills V ♦ ⍩ ⅙ Last dinner 10.30pm
Credit Cards ①②③④⑤

---

**LANDCROSS** Devon Map **02** SS42

★★ 50% *Beaconside* EX39 5JL (1m SW on A388) ☎Bideford(02372)77205

*Comfortable small, secluded hotel with good food and atmosphere.*

9rm(4⇋2♠)(2fb) CTV in all bedrooms ✻
CTV 16P ✿ ⍨(heated) ♪ (hard)
♦ ⍩ ⅙
Credit Cards ①⑤

---

**LANGBANK** Strathclyde *Renfrewshire* Map **10** NS37

★★★⚜ 70% **Gleddoch House** PA14 6YE ☎(047554)711 Telex no 779801
Closed 26-27 Dec & 1-2 Jan

*The one-time family home of the Lithgows, with its magnificent views across the Clyde, has been sympathetically extended to create a fine hotel which, despite its popularity as a business venue, retains many of the features of a private country house. All the comfortable bedrooms are well-equipped, public areas are attractive – though they can become a little congested at particularly busy times – and standards of service are high throughout. Menus based on top-quality Scottish produce provide guests with interesting and imaginative combinations of flavours, and an exceptional wine list includes many fine Clarets and Burgundies.*

33⇋♠(6fb)1♿ CTV in all bedrooms ® T sB&B⇋♠£85-£99 dB&B⇋♠£125 ♨
( 100P ✿ ♟ 18 squash ∪ snooker sauna plunge pool *xmas*
V ♦ ⍩
Credit Cards ①②③⑤

---

## LANGDALE, GREAT

See **Elterwater**

---

**LANGHO** Lancashire Map **07** SD73

★★★ 64% **Mytton Fold Farm** Whalley Rd BB6 8AB ☎Blackburn(0254)240662 FAX (0254) 248119
RS Xmas week

*Comfortable bedrooms, friendly service and a very good restaurant are provided at this family-run hotel.*

27⇋♠2♿ CTV in all bedrooms ® T ✻ (ex guide dogs)
sB&B⇋♠£31-£51 dB&B⇋♠£50-£73 ♨
150P ✿ nc6yrs
V ♦ ⅙ Sunday Lunch £5.95-£6.60 High tea £5.95-£6.60 Dinner £6.95-£18.50alc Last dinner 9.30pm
Credit Cards ①③⑥

---

✗✗✗**Northcote Manor** Northcote Rd BB6 8BE ☎Blackburn(0254)240555 FAX (0254) 246568

*A comfortable, peaceful atmosphere pervades this country house restaurant which stands on the fringe of the Ribble Valley yet just off the A59 and within easy reach of motorways. Both the traditionally English fixed price lunch menu and the à la carte dinner menu with its definite Swiss influence feature the innovative modern style of cuisine.*

Closed 25-26 Dec & 1 Jan
V 55 seats ✳ Lunch £11-£14&alc Dinner £21-£35alc Last lunch 1.30pm Last dinner 9.30pm 40P
Credit Cards ①③

---

Entries for red-star hotels are highlighted by a tint panel. For a full list of these establishments consult the Contents page.

---

# TINTO HOTEL
★★★

## SYMINGTON, Nr BIGGAR, CLYDE VALLEY ML12 6PQ
## TELEPHONE TINTO (089 93) 454

Set in beautiful Clyde Valley countryside at the foot of Tinto Hill the Hotel has twenty eight modern bedrooms all with private facilities, two suites and a quiet residents lounge overlooking the garden. A high standard of food is served in the Pennyfarthing A La Carte Restaurant and also in the less formal Tapestry Room Restaurant.
The Hotel is within easy commuting distance of both Edinburgh and Glasgow (32 Miles) and there are facilities locally for fishing and golf. The rolling hills of TINTO AND COULTER are ideal for country walks and there are many places of historical interest worthy of a visit.

*See gazetteer under Tinto*

# MITCHELL'S
# STAR PERFORMERS

## THE ELMS HOTEL ★★★

*Situated a short way from the sea front at the North end of Morecambe which is famous for its magnificent sunsets over the lakeland hills and Morecambe Bay. The Hotel has 40 en-suite rooms, tastefully furnished, and excellent facilities for conferences. Four separate rooms can take from 20 to 150 people, complete with video players, screens, over head projectors etc.*

*The superb restaurant and banqueting facilities can cater for up to 200 people, there are well stocked cocktail and lounge bars, and a small public house called The Owl's Nest in the grounds of the Hotel. There is a quiet peaceful garden to sit in and contemplate the world, together with a large car park for the guests.*

The Elms Hotel, The Crescent, Morecambe LA4 6DD   Tel: (0524) 411501   Fax: (0524) 831979

## THE CLARENDON HOTEL ★★

*Situated on the sea front of Morecambe built circa 1910, 30 en-suite rooms with direct dial telephones, TV, hot drink facilities, lift to all floors, lounge, bar and restaurant. The major feature of this Hotel is its cellar bar called Davey Jones' Locker due to the fact that he visited this bar on several occasions over the years.*

The Clarendon Hotel, West End, Marine Road, Morecambe LA4 4EP   Tel: (0524) 410180

## THE ROYAL STATION HOTEL ★★

*A 2 star Hotel one and a half miles south of the M6 Junction 35. A 16 en-suite roomed country town Hotel with intimate restaurant, lounge bar and sportsman's bar. There are conference facilities in the Hotel at first floor level, which comprises of a small conference room to seat up to 25 people, its own separate bar, adjoining a further conference room / ballroom which will seat another 100 people.*

*This Hotel is an ideal spot for visiting the Lake District and the Dales.*

The Royal Station Hotel, Market Street, Carnforth, Lancashire   Tel: (0524) 732033

## MITCHELL'S OF LANCASTER
### BREWERS OF FINE ALES AND WINE MERCHANTS SINCE 1880
Head Office: 11 Moor Lane, Lancaster LA1 1QB   Tel: (0524) 63773 / 60000 / 66580

**LANGHOLM** Dumfries & Galloway *Dumfriesshire*
Map **11** NY38

★★55% **Eskdale** Market Place DG13 0JH (Minotels)
☎(03873)80357
*An historic coaching hostelry providing modernised accommodation. Popular with businessmen.*
16rm(3⇌7♠)(2fb)⊬in 3 bedrooms CTV in all bedrooms ⓇT
sB&B£20.50 sB&B⇌♠£23 dB&B£35 dB&B⇌♠£40
⦅10P ♪
V ✿ ⚏ Sunday Lunch £5.95 Dinner £10&alc Last dinner 8.30pm
Credit Cards ①③④Ⓣ

**LANGLAND BAY** West Glamorgan Map **02** SS68

See also **Mumbles** and **Swansea**
★★★59% **Osborne** Rotherslade Rd SA3 4QL (Embassy)
☎Swansea(0792)366274 FAX (0792) 363100
*Popular hotel on cliff top, offering warm and friendly service.*
36rm(32⇌♠)(4fb) CTV in all bedrooms ⓇT
sB&B⇌♠£60-£75 dB&B⇌♠£75-£95 ⋿
Lift ⦅40P ♪ *xmas*
♀ Welsh, English & French V ✿ ⚏ Lunch fr£11.50&alc
Dinner fr£14&alc Last dinner 9pm
Credit Cards ①②③④⑤

★★66% **Langland Court** Langland Court Rd SA3 4TD (Best Western) ☎Swansea(0792)361545 Telex no 498627
FAX (0792) 362302
*Set in small but attractive gardens in a quiet residential area convenient for the Bay, an oak-panelled, Tudor-style country house with galleried staircase provides comfortable, well-equipped bedrooms and good function facilities.*
16⇌♠Annexe5⇌♠(5fb)1⌗⊬in 2 bedrooms CTV in all bedrooms ⓇT sB&B⇌♠£46-£50 dB&B⇌♠£64-£68 ⋿
45P 4🍴 (charged) ✣
♀ English & Continental V ✿ Lunch £6.50-£9.85 Dinner £13.50-£14.45&alc Last dinner 9.30pm
Credit Cards ①②③⑤
See advertisement under SWANSEA

**LANGSTONE** Gwent Map **03** ST38

★★65% **New Inn** NP6 2JN (Porterhouse)
☎Newport(0633)412426 FAX (0633) 413679
*Standing beside the A48 just east of Newport and within easy reach of the M4, a busy hotel with grill room restaurant provides modern, well-equipped accommodation which would suit tourist or businessman; a useful function suite is also available.*
34⇌♠(1fb) CTV in all bedrooms ⓇT ✖ (ex guide dogs) ⋿
CTV 150P
V ✿
Credit Cards ①②③⑤

**LANREATH** Cornwall & Isles of Scilly Map **02** SX15

★★58% **Punch Bowl Inn** PL13 2NX ☎(0503)20218
*The popular restaurant of this early 17th-century coaching inn offers both table d'hôte and à la carte menus, whilst an extensive selection of dishes is also available in the cosy bars, which have log fires and polished brasses. Bedrooms, named after Punch characters, range from antique-furnished to modern in style.*
14rm(10⇌2♠)(2fb)3⌗ CTV in all bedrooms Ⓡ ✳
sB&B£15-£17.50 sB&B⇌♠£21-£24 dB&B£30-£35
dB&B⇌♠£42-£48 ⋿
CTV 50P
V ✿ ⊬ Sunday Lunch £5.95 High tea fr£5alc Dinner £8.50&alc Last dinner 9.30pm
Credit Cards ①③
See advertisement under LOOE

**LARGS** Strathclyde *Ayrshire* Map **10** NS25

★★59% **Charleston** 34 Charles St KA30 8HL ☎(0475)672543
*Although this is predominantly a function hotel, the personal involvement of the friendly owners lends a much more homely atmosphere than one might expect. Bedrooms are spacious and the dinner menu is complemented by an extensive range of bar meals. The hotel is situated in a side street, just off the main road, but with the seafront just a few minutes' walk away.*
7rm(6⇌3)(6fb) CTV in all bedrooms Ⓡ ✳ sB&Bfr£20
sB&B⇌fr£26 dB&Bfr£30 dB&B⇌fr£38
30P ✣ ♫
V ✿ ⚏ Bar Lunch £4.50-£10alc Dinner £10-£15alc Last dinner 8.30pm
Credit Cards ①③

★★59% **Springfield** Greenock Rd KA30 8QL ☎(0475)673119
*Set on the seafront of this popular resort, the hotel caters for both tourist and coach trade, offering pleasant comfortable bedrooms – with en suite facilities in many cases – and spacious, neatly appointed public rooms.*
47rm(41⇌♠)(3fb) CTV in all bedrooms ⓇT sB&B£23
sB&B⇌♠£35 dB&B£40 dB&B⇌♠£48 ⋿
Lift CTV 80P ✣ putting ♫ *xmas*
♀ Scottish, French & Italian V ✿ ⚏ ⊬ Lunch £3.75-£8.50&alc High tea £3.75-£9&alc Dinner £12.50&alc Last dinner 8.30pm
Credit Cards ①②③⑤

★★55% **Elderslie** John St, Broomfields KA30 8DR
☎(0475)686460
Closed 25-26 Dec
*A 19th-century building on Largs seafront commanding magnificent views.*
25rm(9⇌4♠) CTV in all bedrooms ⓇT sB&B£25
sB&B⇌♠£30 dB&B£50 dB&B⇌♠£60
CTV 30P ✣ *xmas*
✿ Lunch £8.50-£11 Dinner £12.50-£15&alc Last dinner 8.30pm
Credit Cards ①②③⑤Ⓓ

**LARKFIELD** Kent Map **05** TQ65

★★★60% **Larkfield** London Rd ME20 6HJ (Trusthouse Forte)
☎West Malling(0732)846858 Telex no 957420
FAX (0732) 846786
*A skilfully extended modern hotel with a choice of bedrooms, all traditionally furnished and well-equipped. The Club House restaurant provides good food served by friendly staff and a full range of conference and meeting rooms are available.*
52⇌♠1⌗⊬in 17 bedrooms CTV in all bedrooms ⓇT ✳
sB⇌♠£70-£80 dB⇌♠£86-£92 (room only) ⋿
⦅80P ✣ CFA *xmas*
♀ International V ✿ ⚏ ⊬ Lunch £8.95-£12.50&alc Dinner £14.50&alc Last dinner 10pm
Credit Cards ①②③④⑤
See advertisement under MAIDSTONE

**LASTINGHAM** North Yorkshire Map **08** SE79

★★⚑75% *Lastingham Grange* YO6 6TH ☎(07515)345
Closed mid Dec-Feb
*A 17th-century house of local stone set in attractive gardens and providing a comfortable lounge, with a real fire, well appointed bedrooms and excellent service.*
12⇌ CTV in all bedrooms Ⓡ
30P 2🍴 ⌗ ✣ ♠
V ✿ ⚏ ⊬
Credit Cards ②⑤

**LAUNCESTON**
See Lifton

# THE ARUNDELL ARMS HOTEL
## Lifton, Devon. PL16 0AA
★ ★ ★

A 250-year-old former coaching inn near Dartmoor, now a famous sporting hotel with 20 miles of our own salmon and trout rivers, pheasant and snipe shoots, riding and golf. Log-fire comfort with superb food and wines; winter gourmet evenings by our French-trained chef. Splendid centre for exploring Devon and Cornwall. Excellent conference facilities.
Details: Anne Voss-Bark.
Tel. Lifton (0566) 84666
Fax. (0566) 84494
On A30, 38 miles from M5 motorway at Exeter.

Best Western

---

★ ★

The Eskdale Hotel

**Langholm, Dumfriesshire DG13 0JH**
**Telephone: Langholm (03873) 80357**
The Eskdale Hotel is a former coaching inn in the centre of Langholm on the Scottish border. The hotel offers a high degree of comfort, facilities and good quality home cooking. There are tea/coffee making facilities, colour TV, radio and full central heating in all rooms, $2/3$ of rooms have en suite facilities. Lively atmosphere with two bars, games room and à la carte restaurant. Ample parking is available in the hotel which is a good base for touring the Border region. Fishing, shooting and golf are all available in the area. Fishing permits available from Hotel.

---

# ⌂ ELDERSLIE HOTEL LARGS
★ ★ AA

Situated on the sea front at Largs 'Elderslie' commands breathtaking views over the Firth of Clyde.
Fully licensed with central heating throughout.
Extensive Lounges ★ Private car park
Wide choice of menus ★ A warm welcome guaranteed
All bedrooms are equipped with television, wash basin, radio, telephone and tea making facilities
Many have private bathroom or shower.

**Send now for our colour brochure and tariff**

**ELDERSLIE HOTEL,
BROOMFIELDS, LARGS, AYRSHIRE KA30 8DR.
Tel: Largs 686460**

### LAVENHAM Suffolk Map 05 TL94

★★★70%, **The Swan** High St CO10 9QA (Trusthouse Forte)
☎(0787)247477 Telex no 987198 FAX (0787) 248286
*This beautiful, timbered hotel, based on a building dating from the
fourteenth century, offers bedrooms in a variety of shapes and
sizes and spacious, delightful lounges where open fires and
harpsichord music create an ideal setting for the enjoyment of
afternoon tea; meals are served in a heavily beamed restaurant
with minstrels gallery.*
47⇨↑(1fb)2⊞¥in 4 bedrooms CTV in all bedrooms ⓡ T
《 60P ✿ ♫
V ⓥ ⚗ ¥ Last dinner 9.30pm
Credit Cards ① ② ③ ④ ⑤

✗✗**The Great House** Market Place CO10 9QZ ☎(0787)247431
*This beautifully renovated building, providing a wealth of charm
and character, is an ideal setting for the restaurant. The food is
competently cooked and ranges from the classic to the
imaginatively new and light dishes. Fresh fish features strongly on
the menu and is particularly good. Light snacks or full meals are
served at lunchtime.*
Closed Mon (in winter) & last 3 wks Jan
Dinner not served Sun (in winter)
♀ Continental V 40 seats Lunch £7.90-£15 Dinner
fr£13.95&alc Last lunch 2.30pm Last dinner 9.30pm 6P
Credit Cards ① ③

### LAWSHALL Suffolk Map 05 TL85

★★65% **Corders** Bury Rd IP29 4PJ ☎(0284)830314
*A family-owned hotel situated on the outskirts of the village some
6 miles south of Bury St Edmunds offers guests a warm welcome
and genuine hospitality. Well-equipped and comfortable en suite
accommodation is complemented by pleasant public areas, many
rooms enjoying views over open countryside.*
8⇨(2fb)1⊞ CTV in all bedrooms ⓡ T ✗ (ex guide dogs)
CTV 30P ✿ sauna jacuzzi nc5yrs
♀ English & French V ¥ Last dinner 9pm
Credit Cards ① ② ③ ⑤ ⓔ

### LEAMINGTON SPA (ROYAL) Warwickshire Map 04 SP36

# ★★★

❀★★★ ⚓ MALLORY COURT

Harbury Ln, Bishop's
Tachbrook CV33 9QB (2m S
off A452) (Relais et
Châteaux)
☎Leamington Spa
(0926)330214
Telex no 317294
FAX (0926) 451714

Closed 25 Dec evening-29 Dec

*Ten acres of landscaped gardens, with resplendent herbaceous
borders, a walled rose garden and a herb garden surround the
mellow stone manor owned by Jeremy Mort and Allan
Holland. Guests are certain of receiving a friendly welcome
and luxurious accommodation both in the public rooms and in
the attractive bedrooms where the floral theme of the fabrics
seems to reflect the lovely views of the gardens and
countryside. Allan Holland is once more in charge of the
kitchens, following changes in personnel, and produces
consistently good modern French cuisine. Specialities we can
recommend are the lobster terrine and the fillet of beef foie
gras. Whatever your choice, the natural flavours of high-
quality fresh produce are evident in every dish.*

10⇨↑(1fb) CTV in all bedrooms T ✗ sB&B⇨↑fr£102
dB&B⇨↑£92-£180 Continental breakfast ⋒
50P 2⚓ (£6) ⇶ ✿ ⚗ ⚐ ♪ (hard) squash croquet nc12yrs
♀ French ⓥ ⚗ Lunch fr£21 Dinner fr£38.50 Last dinner
9.45pm
Credit Cards ① ③

★★★62% **Regent** 77 The Parade CV32 4AX (Best Western)
☎(0926)427231 Telex no 311715 FAX (0926) 450728
*Situated in the centre of this fine Georgian spa town, the hotel has
come to the end of a major refurbishment programme, which has
upgraded facilities to modern expectations, whilst retaining the
original charm and character of the building. Staff are friendly and
attentive.*
80⇨↑(7fb)1⊞ CTV in all bedrooms ⓡ T sB&B⇨↑£55-£80
dB&B⇨↑£75-£92.50 ⋒
Lift 《 CTV 70P 30⚓ CFA table tennis pool table ♫ xmas
♀ English, French & Italian V ⓥ ⚗ Lunch fr£9.50 Dinner
fr£15&alc Last dinner 10.45pm
Credit Cards ① ② ③ ⑤

★★★61% **Falstaff** 20 Warwick New Rd CV32 5JQ
☎(0926)312044 Telex no 333388 FAX (0926) 450574
*Situated on the outskirts of town this hotel is undergoing complete
refurbishment to provide comfortable, well-equipped modern
bedrooms and public areas of quality.*
65⇨↑(3fb)2⊞ CTV in all bedrooms ⓡ T ⋒
Lift 《 80P ✿ CFA xmas
♀ English & French V ⓥ ⚗
Credit Cards ① ② ③ ④ ⑤

★★★54% **Manor House** Avenue Rd CV31 3NJ (Trusthouse
Forte) ☎(0926)423251 FAX (0926) 425933
*This large, company hotel, set in lovely gardens and conveniently
situated for the railway station and for access to the town centre,
offers bedrooms in a variety of styles and sizes, but all have modern
en suite facilities.*
53⇨↑(2fb)¥in 12 bedrooms CTV in all bedrooms ⓡ T S15%
sB⇨↑£60-£66 dB⇨↑£75-£80 (room only) ⋒
Lift 《 100P CFA xmas
V ⓥ ⚗ ¥ S% Lunch £9.50-£12.50 Dinner £14.50-£16.50&alc
Last dinner 10pm
Credit Cards ① ② ③ ④ ⑤

★★67% **Adams** 22 Av Rd CV31 3PQ
☎Leamington Spa(0926)450742 & 422758 FAX (0926) 313110
*An impressive Georgian residence on the outskirts of the town,
lovingly restored by the owners to create a comfortable hotel offers
good standards of housekeeping and maintenance throughout. A
good, if limited, choice of home-cooked meals is enhanced by
friendly personal service.*
14⇨↑ CTV in all bedrooms ✗ sB&B⇨↑£33-£45
dB&B⇨↑£48-£52
14P ⇶ ✿
V ⓥ ⚗ Lunch £14-£18 Dinner £15-£20alc Last dinner 8pm
Credit Cards ① ② ③ ⑤ ⓔ

★★62% **Angel** 143 Regent St CV32 4NZ
☎Royal Leamington Spa(0926)881296
*A pleasing hotel near the town centre features a small, intimate
restaurant serving a wide range of dishes. Recent extension has
provided a wing of new bedrooms with good furnishings and
excellent facilities.*
37rm(29⇨7↑)(7fb)2⊞ CTV in all bedrooms ⓡ ✳
sB&B£30-£35 sB&B⇨↑£35-£49.50 dB&B⇨↑£39-£59.50
Lift 《 40P
♀ English & French V ⓥ ⚗ Lunch £7.95 Dinner £11.50 Last
dinner 9.30pm
Credit Cards ① ② ③

★★ **61% Beech Lodge** Warwick New Rd CV32 5JJ
☎Leamington Spa(0926)422227
RS 24 Dec-3 Jan
*Personal service from the proprietors ensures a comfortable stay at this privately owned and run hotel midway between Leamington Spa and Warwick. Simply furnished bedrooms, though compact, offer a good range of modern facilities, the cosy public areas are welcoming and an attractive restaurant serves generous portions of home-cooked food.*
12rm(1⇨8🖐) CTV in all bedrooms ® T sB&B£29.50
sB&B⇨🖐£39.50 dB&B⇨🖐£50-£55 🗦
CTV 16P 🕮
🖓 English & French V Sunday Lunch £7.25 Dinner £8.50-£14.50alc Last dinner 9pm
Credit Cards ① ② ③ ⓔ

★★ **60% Abbacourt** 40 Kenilworth Rd CV32 6JF
☎Leamington Spa(0926)451755 FAX (0926) 450330
*Resident proprietors, aided by a small, helpful team, provide friendly and attentive service at this hotel, a large converted house beside the A452 in the residential outskirts of the town.*
27rm(8⇨13🖐)(4fb) CTV in 20 bedrooms TV in 7 bedrooms ®
T sB&Bfr£25 sB&B⇨🖐fr£50 dB&Bfr£60 dB&B⇨🖐fr£70 🗦
30P
🖓 Continental V ✤ 🖵 Lunch £11&alc High tea fr£2.50&alc Dinner £11 Last dinner 10pm
Credit Cards ① ② ③ ④ ⑤ ⓔ

★ LANSDOWNE

87 Clarendon St CV32 4PF
☎Leamington Spa
(0926)450505
RS 24 Dec-7 Jan
*This attractive Regency hotel fits beautifully into its central location in this pleasant Warwickshire town. Owners David and Gillian Allen have been steadily carrying out improvements over the years, and with the acquisition of an adjoining house have been able to make more bedrooms with en suite bathrooms – their ultimate aim is to convert them all to this standard. The Allens are delightful hosts, and the meals, cooked by Gillian, are something to look forward to in the evenings.*
15rm(12⇨🖐)(1fb) ® T 🏋 sB&Bfr£27.95
sB&B⇨🖐£44.95 dB&Bfr£39.30 dB&B⇨🖐£53.90 🗦
CTV 11P 🕮 nc5yrs
🖓 English, French & Italian ✤ Dinner £14.95 Last dinner 8.30pm
Credit Cards ① ③ ⓔ

**LEDBURY** Hereford & Worcester Map **03** SO73
★★★ **52% Feathers** High St HR8 1DS ☎(0531)5266
FAX (0531) 2001
*This high-street hotel retains much of the character of its Elizabethan origins, with sloping floors and exposed beams. Room sizes vary, some being quite compact, and are individually decorated and have good modern facilities. As well as the restaurant there is the more informal 'Fuggles', and the busy bar is popular with locals.*
11⇨🖐(2fb)1🛏 CTV in all bedrooms ®
(( 10P 🖘 squash
🖓 English & French V ✤ 🖵
Credit Cards ① ② ③ ⑤

⊕★★🔔 **72% Hope End Country House** Hope End HR8 1JQ
(2.5m NE unclass rd) ☎(0531)3613
Closed Mon-Tue & Dec-Feb
(Rosette awarded for dinner only)
*A charming hotel, set in 40 acres of parkland tucked away on the south-west flank of the Malvern Hills. Craftsmen-made furniture and hand-woven curtains lend atmosphere to the house, and Mrs Hegarty's flock of free-range bantams completes the rural scene. At mealtimes, fresh vegetables and herbs from the walled garden, supplemented by other local produce, feature prominently on the menu. Dinner offers a small choice of first and last courses, with a set main course, backed up by an excellent wine list. The food is very enjoyable. with dishes such as scallops and bacon in a ginger and coriander sauce, followed by a traditional steamed pudding being particularly noted by our Inspector.*
7⇨Annexe2⇨ CTV in 1 bedroom ® 🏋 sB&B⇨£78-£122
dB&B⇨£88-£132 🗦
10P 🕮 ❀ nc14yrs
⚰ Dinner £27 Last dinner 8.30pm
Credit Cards ① ③

**LEEDS** West Yorkshire Map **08** SE33

★★★★ **67% Holiday Inn** Wellington St LS1 4DL (Holiday Inns)
☎(0532)442200 Telex no 557879 FAX (0532) 440460
*This is a large, modern hotel, situated in the city centre. Bedrooms are very comfortable and have useful facilities. The elegant restaurant provides a good standard of cooking and there are good leisure facilities as well as adequate parking.*
125⇨🖐⚰in 25 bedrooms CTV in all bedrooms ® T S%
sB⇨🖐fr£120 dB⇨🖐fr£135 (room only) 🗦
Lift (( 🛗 25P 100🖘 ⬜(heated) snooker sauna solarium gymnasium whirlpool spa beauty studio steam room *xmas*
🖓 English & French V ✤ 🖵 ⚰ S% Lunch fr£16 Dinner fr£16 Last dinner 10.30pm
Credit Cards ① ② ③ ④ ⑤

★★★★ **64% Hilton International** Neville St LS1 4BX (Hilton)
☎(0532)442000 Telex no 557143 FAX (0532) 433577
*A comfortable city-centre hotel close to the railway station and with good access to the M1. Choice of menus in the restaurant – interesting à la carte and very good value buffet.*
210⇨(6fb)⚰in 52 bedrooms CTV in all bedrooms ® T ✳ S%
sB⇨£98-£175 dB⇨£110-£175 (room only) 🗦
Lift (( 2P 70🖘 CFA 🎵
🖓 International V ✤ 🖵 ⚰ S% Lunch £12&alc Dinner £16&alc Last dinner 10pm
Credit Cards ① ② ③ ⑤

★★★★ **61% The Queen's** City Square LS1 1PL (Trusthouse Forte) ☎(0532)431323 Telex no 55161 FAX (0532) 425154
*This large, traditional hotel stands in the city centre, next to the station. Much restored in recent years, it offers very well equipped bedrooms featuring items of furniture which were there before the house became a hotel in the late 1930's. Recent improvements to the public areas include the provision of a new restaurant.*
188⇨🖐⚰in 62 bedrooms CTV in all bedrooms ® T
sB⇨🖐£54-£108 dB⇨🖐£65-£108 (room only) 🗦
Lift (( 🅿 CFA *xmas*
🖓 French V ✤ 🖵 ⚰ Lunch £10-£14&alc Dinner £13-£14&alc Last dinner 10pm
Credit Cards ① ② ③ ④ ⑤

★★★ **66% Hilton National** Wakefield Rd, Garforth Rdbt LS25 1LH (Hilton) ☎(0532)866556 Telex no 556324
FAX (0532) 868326
(For full entry see Garforth)

★★★ **66% The Post House, Leeds/Selby** LS25 5LF (Trusthouse Forte) ☎South Milford(0977)682711 Telex no 557074
FAX (0977) 685462
(For full entry see Lumby)

★★★65% **Parkway** Otley Rd LS16 8AG (Embassy)
☎(0532)672551 Telex no 556614 FAX (0532) 674410
*Situated on the A660 just one mile north of the ring road, this hotel offers a choice of restaurants, well-appointed bedrooms and new leisure facilities.*
103⇌♪(8fb)⊬in 11 bedrooms CTV in all bedrooms ® T
✕ (ex guide dogs) ✱ S% sB⇌♪£79-£89
dB⇌♪£95-£105 (room only) ✍
Lift ℭ 250P ⬚ ❀ ▣(heated) ♪ (hard) snooker sauna solarium gymnasium steam room beauty salon *xmas*
♡ English & French V ✧ ⌂ ⊬
Credit Cards ①②③④⑤ⓔ

★★★64% **Stakis Windmill** Mill Green View, Seacroft
LS14 5QP (Stakis) ☎(0532)732323 Telex no 55452
FAX (0532) 323018
*A well furnished and comfortable business hotel with modern bedrooms, built around an old windmill. It is conveniently situated on the Leeds ringroad, at the junction with the A64.*
100⇌♪⊬in 22 bedrooms CTV in all bedrooms ® T ✱
sB⇌♪£70-£80 dB⇌♪£82-£92 (room only) ✍
Lift ℭ 200P *xmas*
♡ English, French & Italian ✧ ⌂ Lunch fr£7.95 Dinner fr£13.95 Last dinner 10pm
Credit Cards ①②③④⑤ ⓔ

★★★62% *Grove Crest* The Grove LS26 8EJ (Toby)
☎(0532)826201 Telex no 557646 FAX (0532) 829243
(For full entry see Oulton)

★★★50% **Merrion** Merrion Centre LS2 8NH (Mount Charlotte (TS)) ☎(0532)439191 Telex no 55459 FAX (0532) 423527
*A functional city centre hotel.*
120⇌♪⊬in 42 bedrooms CTV in all bedrooms ® T ✱
sB⇌♪£64.50 dB⇌♪£69.50 (room only) ✍
Lift ℭ P CFA ♪ *xmas*
♡ English & French V ✧ ⌂ Lunch £12.25&alc Dinner £12.25&alc Last dinner 10.30pm
Credit Cards ①②③⑤

◯**Haleys Hotel & Restaurant** 8 Shire Oak Rd, Headingley
LS6 2DE ☎(0532)784446
Due to have opened summer 1990
22rm

**LEEK** Staffordshire Map **07** SJ95

★★58% *Jester At Leek* 81 Mill St ST13 8EU ☎(0538)383997
Closed 26-28 Dec
*A popular restaurant serving generous portions of freshly prepared food and accommodation in compact but warm and well-equipped bedrooms are the attractions of a family-run hostelry which stands beside the busy Macclesfield road in the town centre.*
14rm(9⇌2♪)(4fb) CTV in all bedrooms ® T
sB&B£25.50-£27.50 dB&B⇌♪£37.50-£40.50 ✍
70P snooker
♡ English & Continental V ✧ ⌂ ⊬ Lunch £5.10-£9.25alc Dinner £6.25-£12.55alc Last dinner 10pm
Credit Cards ①③ⓔ

**LEEMING BAR** North Yorkshire Map **08** SE28

★★63% *Motel Leeming* DL8 1DT ☎Bedale(0677)23611
(For full entry see Bedale)

★★61% **White Rose** DL7 9AY ☎Bedale(0677)22707 & 24941
FAX (0677) 25123
*A roadside hotel near the A1 and Leeming Air Base providing comfortable accommodation in well-equipped en suite bedrooms. Public areas include a lounge and a range of bars.*
18⇌♪(1fb) CTV in all bedrooms ® T sB&B⇌♪fr£25
dB&B⇌♪fr£40 ✍
CTV 50P

V ✧ ⌂ Lunch £4.50-£5.10&alc High tea fr£5.75 Dinner fr£9.50&alc Last dinner 9pm
Credit Cards ①②③⑤ ⓔ

**LEE-ON-THE-SOLENT** Hampshire Map **04** SU50

★★★64%, **Belle Vue** 39 Marine Pde East PO13 9BW
☎Portsmouth(0705)550258 FAX (0705) 552624
Closed 25 & 26 Dec
*This busy commercial hotel on the sea front has been completely refurbished to a high standard. Bedrooms are particularly comfortable and well equipped and though public areas are limtied there is a spacious bar. The bright restaurant offers a short à la carte menu.*
24⇌♪Annexe3⇌♪(4fb) CTV in all bedrooms ® T ✱
sB&B⇌♪£54 dB&B⇌♪£65 ✍
ℭ 80P ♪
♡ English V ✧ Lunch £7.95-£19.05alc Dinner £7.50&alc Last dinner 9.45pm
Credit Cards ①③

**LEICESTER** Leicestershire Map **04** SK50

★★★66%, **Country Court** Braunstone LE3 2WQ (Stakis)
☎(0533)630066 Telex no 34429 FAX (0533) 630627
*This modern hotel is close to junction 21 of the M1, and has easy access to Leicester and the M69. Accommodation is spacious, comfortable and very well equipped, with facilities that the business traveller will appreciate. Comfortable public areas compliment the hotel, particularly the striking foyer. Leisure facilities include a swimming pool and fitness centre, and excellent conference facilities are available.*
141⇌♪(39fb)⊬in 73 bedrooms CTV in all bedrooms ® T
✕ (ex guide dogs)
(ℭ ▤ ⬚▣(heated) sauna solarium gymnasium jacuzzi
♡ English & Continental V ✧ ⌂ ⊬ Last dinner 10pm
Credit Cards ①②③⑤

★★★60%, **Holiday Inn** St Nicholas Circle LE1 5LX (Holiday Inns Inc) ☎(0533)531161 Telex no 341281 HI LEIC
FAX (0533) 513169
*Large, modern purpose-built hotel close to the city centre, adjacent to multi-st orey car park.*
188⇌♪(106fb)⊬in 78 bedrooms CTV in all bedrooms ® T
S% sB⇌♪£72-£80 dB⇌♪£77-£89 (room only) ✍
Lift ℭ ▤ ♪ CFA ▣(heated) sauna solarium gymnasium whirlpool health bar steam room ♪
♡ International V ✧ ⌂ ⊬ S% Lunch fr£9.50 Dinner fr£14.75&alc Last dinner 10.15pm
Credit Cards ①②③④⑤

★★★58% **Grand** Granby St LE1 6ES (Embassy)
☎(0533)555599 Telex no 342244 FAX (0533) 544736
*Impressive Victorian city-centre building standing on the main A6.*
92⇌♪(2fb)2⬚⊬in 19 bedrooms CTV in all bedrooms ® T
S% sB⇌♪£70-£80 dB⇌♪£82.50-£92.50 (room only) ✍
Lift ℭ 120P ⬚
♡ English & French V ✧ ⌂ S% Lunch £7.95-£10.95 Dinner £7.95-£10.95 Last dinner 10pm
Credit Cards ①②③④⑤

★★★65% **Belmont** De Montfort St LE1 7GR (Best Western)
☎(0533)544773 Telex no 34619 FAX (0533) 470804
Closed 25-28 Dec
*The busy, popular, privately-owned hotel, located conveniently close to both city centre and railway station, continues to improve and extend its facilities, many of the well-equipped bedrooms having recently been refurbished to a good standard and work being in progress on a new conference wing.*
46⇌♪Annexe22⇌♪(7fb)⊬in 9 bedrooms CTV in all bedrooms ® T sB&B⇌♪£65-£82 dB&B⇌♪£75-£92 ✍
Lift ℭ 50P CFA ♪

☋ English & French V ♰ ⅅ Lunch £8.95-£9.95&alc Dinner £12.95&alc Last dinner 10pm
Credit Cards 1 2 3 5

---

★★★65% **Leicestershire Moat House** Wigston Rd, Oadby LE2 5QE (3m SE A6) (Queens Moat) ☎(0533)719441
Telex no 34474 FAX (0533) 720559
*The hotel is located adjacent to the A6 at Oadby, about three miles from the city centre. New bedrooms have proved popular and existing rooms have been refurbished to a similar standard. The popular Czars restaurant has a carvery and à la carte menu.*
57⇌♪(4fb)⊁in 14 bedrooms CTV in all bedrooms ® T ✱
sB⇌♪£60-£67.50 dB⇌♪£70-£85 (room only) ⊟
Lift ☾ CTV 190P ✲ ♫
☋ English & French V ♰ ⅅ ⊁ Lunch £6.25-£9.20&alc High tea £2.95 Dinner £11.50&alc Last dinner 9.45pm
Credit Cards 1 2 3 5 £

---

★★★62% **Hotel Saint James** Abbey St LE1 3TE
☎(0533)510666 Telex no 342434 FAX (0533) 515183
*Located on top of a multi-storey car park in the city centre, this recently refurbished hotel has comfortable and well appointed bedrooms and public areas.*
72⇌♪(3fb) CTV in all bedrooms ® T S% sB⇌♪£57-£60
dB⇌♪£67-£70 (room only) ⊟
Lift ☾ ℱ sauna solarium gymnasium steam room jacuzzi
☋ English & French V ♰ ⅅ Lunch fr£8 Dinner fr£10.50 Last dinner 10pm
Credit Cards 1 2 3 5

---

★★★62% **Stage** 299 Leicester Rd, Wigston Fields LE8 1JW (on A50) (Consort) ☎(0533)886161 FAX (0533) 811874
*Situated on the A50, three miles south of the city centre, this pleasant hotel has recently reopened following extensive improvements which include a new block of thirty-eight well-* ▶

L

*equipped modern bedrooms. An attractive, split-level, open-plan area contains the restaurant and lounge bar, and additional facilities include a large self-contained function suite and a bedroom designed for disabled guests.*
Annexe38⤳🟌(8fb) CTV in all bedrooms ⓇT
🅧 (ex guide dogs) S% sB&B⤳🟌£42-£52
dB&B⤳🟌£52-£62 🍴
Lift 200P 🎵 *xmas*
🍴 International V ✧ ⚲ 🍴 Lunch £5.95-£9.95 High tea £1-£8
Dinner £9.95&alc Last dinner 10pm
Credit Cards ①②③④⑤ⓔ

★★★61% **Park International** Humberstone Rd LE5 3AT
☎(0533)620471 Telex no 341460 FAX (0533) 514211
Closed 25-31 Dec
*A large, busy, city-centre hotel providing well equipped accommodation, catering mainly for business people and conference delegates.*
209⤳(7fb)🍴in 22 bedrooms CTV in all bedrooms Ⓡ T
sB⤳£28-£60 dB⤳£38-£70 (room only) 🍴
Lift ⓒ P 25🚗 *xmas*
V ✧ ⚲ Lunch £7.05 Dinner £8.55 Last dinner 10.30pm
Credit Cards ①②③④⑤ⓔ

★★★61% **Post House** Braunstone Ln East LE3 2FW
(Trusthouse Forte) ☎(0533)630500 Telex no 341009
FAX (0533) 823623
*A large and busy hotel on the A46, conveniently placed for access to the M1, M69 and city centre. Popular with business people and a conference centre this hotel has three grades of well-equipped bedrooms and a choice of restaurants.*
172⤳🟌(38fb)🍴in 51 bedrooms CTV in all bedrooms Ⓡ T ✳
S10% sB⤳🟌£67-£78 dB⤳🟌£78-£89 (room only) 🍴
Lift ⓒ 240P CFA 🚗 *xmas*
🍴 International V ✧ ⚲ 🍴 S10% Lunch £8.50-£11&alc Dinner
fr£14&alc Last dinner 10pm
Credit Cards ①②③④⑤

★★★60% **Leicester Forest Moat House** Hinckley Rd,
Leicester Forest East LE3 3GH (Queens Moat) ☎(0533)394661
FAX (0533) 394952
RS 25-26 Dec
*Situated on the A47 Leicester to Hinckley road, four miles from the city centre, this busy commercial hotel offers modern accommodation with a further twenty two. Executive-style bedrooms planned during 1990. The refurbished bar provides flexible eating options.*
34⤳🟌 CTV in all bedrooms Ⓡ T ✳ sB⤳🟌fr£56
dB⤳🟌fr£66 (room only) 🍴
ⓒ 200P ✿ putting
🍴 English & French V ✧ ⚲ Lunch £8&alc Dinner £10.50&alc
Last dinner 9.45pm
Credit Cards ①②③⑤

★★69% **Red Cow** Hinckley Rd, Leicester Forest East LE3 3PG
☎(0533)387878
31⤳🟌(27fb) CTV in all bedrooms Ⓡ T 🅧 ✳ sB&B⤳🟌fr£38
dB&B⤳🟌fr£46
CTV 120P
V ✧ ⚲ 🍴 Lunch £7.50-£10alc Dinner £7.50-£10alc Last
dinner 10.30pm
Credit Cards ①②③⑤

★★64% **Old Tudor Rectory** Main St, Glenfield LE3 8DG
☎(0533)320220 FAX (0533) 876002
Closed Xmas wk
*Set at the centre of Glenfield on the outskirts of the city, this former rectory has sections which date back to the sixteenth century. Hospitality is warm and friendly, accommodation simple but well-equipped, and ample opportunity for relaxation is provided in Halfpenny's, the restaurant and bar facilities contained in a converted schoolhouse in the grounds.*

16rm(6⤳7🟌)Annexe1rm(3fb)2🛏 CTV in all bedrooms Ⓡ T
✳ sB&B⤳🟌£28.75-£33.35 dB&B⤳🟌£46-£51.75 🍴
37P ✿
✧ ⚲ Lunch fr£8.75 Dinner fr£8.95 Last dinner 10pm
Credit Cards ①③ⓔ

★★63% **Regency** 360 London Rd LE2 2PL ☎(0533)709634
*Conveniently situated on the A6 just 1·5 miles south of the city centre, this hotel is well equipped and provides good value for money. It is popular with business people, but equally suitable for tourists and others visiting the area.*
37⤳🟌(2fb) CTV in all bedrooms Ⓡ 🅧 (ex guide dogs)
ⓒ 40P
🍴 English & Continental V ✧ Last dinner 11.30pm
Credit Cards ①②③⑤

★★60% **Alexandra** 342 London Rd, Stoneygate LE2 2PJ
☎(0533)703056 FAX (0533) 705464
Closed Xmas
13rm(3⤳9🟌)(3fb) CTV in all bedrooms Ⓡ T 🅧 ✳
sB&B⤳🟌£32-£35 dB&B⤳🟌£46-£48
CTV 16P 🚗
V ✧ ⚲ 🍴 Dinner £9 Last dinner 8.30pm
Credit Cards ①③ⓔ

✕✕✕**The Manor** Glen Parva Manor, The Ford, Little Glen
Rd, Glen Parva LE2 9TL (3m SW on A426) ☎(0533)774604
*A 16th-century house just south of the city in Glen Parva village. June and John Robson have worked wonders since coming here in 1987, most notably with the appointment of chef Martin Zalesny to lead the kitchen brigade. An extensive à la carte menu is offered, but most popular are the speciality lunch and dinner menus, featuring the best of the day's market. Thin slices of calf's liver on a potato pancake, strips of salmon and plaice in a watercress sauce, steamed chocolate and rum pudding, coffee and petit fours is an example of the choices, which are excellent value for money.* ▶

## The Old Tudor Rectory ★★

Fifteenth Century House in Garden Setting.
Original Staircases and Wealth of Old Timbers.

Four Poster Beds. All Rooms Ensuite.

A la Carte Restaurant.

Ten minutes from M1 and City Centre.

**Glenfield, Leicester. Tel. (0533) 320220**

## THE STAGE HOTEL

299 LEICESTER ROAD (A50)
Wigston Fields, Leicester LE8 1JW
Phone: (0533) 886161
Fax:     (0533) 811874

**AA** ★★★

All 38 newly built bedrooms have en-suite bathroom with bath and shower, heated towel rail, direct dial phone. Remote Control Colour TV with Teletext, Radio with wake-up alarm clock. Complimentary tea and coffee making facilities. Trouser press, Hair Drier.

Bedroom adapted for disabled use.

The Restaurant offers extensive cuisine including à la Carte, table d'hote and a Carvery.

Conference facilities for up to 200 people.

Easy access from Motorways and major trunk roads.

NEC Birmingham only 30 minutes drive.

L

**EVERARDS ORIGINAL INNS**

### The Red Cow ★★
Hinckley Road, Leicester Forest East,
Leicester LE3 3PG. Telephone: 0533 387878
* 31 Ensuite Bedrooms, TV, Tea & Coffee
making facilities, Hair Dryer, Trouser Press,
Direct Dial Telephone * A la Carte
* Conservatory * Childrens Play Area
* Fine Traditional Ales.

### Bardon Hall ★★
Beveridge Lane, Bardon Hill, Nr Coalville,
Leicestershire. Telephone: 0530 813644.
* 35 Ensuite Bedrooms, TV, Tea & Coffee
making facilities, Hair Dryer, Trouser Press,
Direct Dial Telephone * A la Carte
Restaurant * Lounge Bar & Bar Meals
* Fine Traditional Ales * Childrens
Play Area.

FOR FURTHER DETAILS OF EVERARDS ORIGINAL INNS.
PLEASE WRITE TO EVERARDS BREWERY LTD. CASTLE ACRES, NARBOROUGH, LEICESTER LE9 5BY.
Tel: 0533 630900

*The extensive wine list features some classic chateaux and
outstanding years.*
Closed 25-26 Dec
Lunch not served Sat
Dinner not served Sun
♀ French **V** 70 seats ✻ Lunch £11.50&alc Dinner £19.50&alc
Last lunch 2pm Last dinner 10pm 90P
Credit Cards ⬜1 ⬜2 ⬜3 ⬜5

---

**LEIGH DELAMERE MOTORWAY SERVICE AREA (M4)**
Wiltshire Map **03** ST87

⌂**Granada Lodge** M4 Service Area SN14 6LB (Granada)
☎Chippenham(0666)837097 FAX (0666) 837112
*Bedroom accommodation of a high standard, tastefully furnished
and equipped with en suite facilities, is provided at a budget price
in this modern, two-storey block (which can also cater for the
needs of disabled clients). The Country Kitchen Restaurant serves
a range of refreshments, snacks and full meals 24 hours a day,
whilst a shop in an adjacent building sells confectionery, gifts,
newspapers and magazines.*
35⇔🛏(6fb)⊁in 8 bedrooms CTV in all bedrooms ®
✖ (ex guide dogs) ✳ S% sB⇔🛏fr£25
dB⇔🛏fr£28 (room only)
        **See advertisement under CHIPPENHAM**

---

**LEIGHTON BUZZARD** Bedfordshire Map **04** SP92

★★★71% **Swan** High St LU7 7EA ☎(0525)372148
FAX (0525) 370444
RS 25 Dec & 1 Jan
*High standards of service from helpful, willing staff and a relaxing,
friendly atmosphere are attractive features of this comfortably
appointed Georgian coaching inn; bedrooms are tastefully
furnished and well equipped, while a pleasant dining room offers an
interesting menu of competently prepared dishes.*
38⇔🛏(1fb)1🏠 CTV in all bedrooms ® T ✖ (ex guide dogs)
✳ sB&B⇔🛏£72.50-£85 dB&B⇔🛏£85-£100 🅿
《10P ♨
**V** ♥ ⚺ ⊁ Lunch £12-£15 Dinner £17.50-£18.75&alc Last
dinner 9.30pm
Credit Cards ⬜1 ⬜2 ⬜3 ⬜5 ⬜£

---

**LEISTON** Suffolk Map **05** TM46

★67% **White Horse** Station Rd IP16 4HD ☎(0728)830694
FAX (0728) 833105
*This comfortable hotel in the centre of the town now includes a
children's play area in its large garden. It offers warm hospitality,
a popular bar and accommodation in bedrooms which, though quite
modest, are well equipped, clean and tidy.*
10rm(1⇔5🛏)Annexe3🛏(1fb) CTV in all bedrooms ® T
sB&Bfr£29.50 sB&B⇔🛏fr£33.50 dB&Bfr£45
dB&B⇔🛏fr£52 🅿
CTV 14P 3🚗 ♨ ✿ ♫ *xmas*
♀ English & French **V** ♥ ⚺ ⊁ Lunch £8-£13alc Dinner
£8-£13alc Last dinner 9.30pm
Credit Cards ⬜1 ⬜3 ⬜£

---

**LENHAM** Kent Map **05** TQ85

★★65% **Dog & Bear** The Square ME17 2PG
☎Maidstone(0622)858219
*This friendly village hotel offers a great deal of character in its
accommodation, having nicely appointed, well equipped bedrooms
and featuring a wood beamed restaurant which provides grills and
chef's specials. Efficient service is rendered by helpful staff.*
21⇔🛏(1fb) CTV in all bedrooms ® T sB&B⇔🛏fr£40.50
dB&B⇔🛏fr£52 🅿
40P *xmas*

♀ English & Continental **V** ♥ ⚺ Lunch £5-£20alc Dinner
£5-£20alc Last dinner 10pm
Credit Cards ⬜1 ⬜2 ⬜3 ⬜5
        **See advertisement under MAIDSTONE**

---

**LEOMINSTER** Hereford & Worcester Map **03** SO45

★★★53% **Talbot** West St HR6 8EP (Best Western)
☎(0568)6347 Telex no 35332
*Parts of this town-centre hotel date back to the fifteenth century,
and much of its original charm and character has been retained in
the large-scale improvements recently undertaken by the new
owners to provide comfortable, well-equipped accommodation
which will appeal equally to tourists and business users.*
23⇔🛏(3fb) CTV in all bedrooms ® T ✖ sB&B⇔🛏£43-£50
dB&B⇔🛏£70-£84 🅿
20P *xmas*
♀ English & French **V** ♥ ⚺ Lunch £9-£10&alc Dinner
£14-£16&alc Last dinner 9.30pm
Credit Cards ⬜1 ⬜2 ⬜3 ⬜5

★★60% **Royal Oak** South St HR6 8JA (Minotels) ☎(0568)2610
*Close to the town centre, this former Georgian coaching inn
provides simple but comfortable accommodation and informal
service. Equally suitable for tourists and business people, its
ground floor annexe bedroom with access from the car park makes
it accessible for disabled guests.*
17⇔🛏Annexe1⇔🛏(2fb)1🏠 CTV in all bedrooms ® ✳
sB&B⇔🛏£25.50-£28.50 dB&B⇔🛏£38-£42 🅿
CTV 24P 1🚗
**V** ♥ ⚺ Lunch £13-£14alc Dinner £13-£14alc Last dinner 9pm
Credit Cards ⬜1 ⬜2 ⬜3 ⬜5

★🏆77% **Marsh Country** Eyton HR6 0AG ☎(0568)3952
*Martin and Jacqueline Gilleland have created a delightful small
hotel in this timber and red brick house dating from the 14th
century. The oldest part, with massive vaulted beams, is now the
lounge, while later additions contain the pretty dining room and
cosy bar. This is one of our Top Twenty One-Star Hotels – see
colour feature at the front of the guide.*
6⇔🛏 CTV in all bedrooms T ✖ (ex guide dogs) ✳
sB&B⇔🛏fr£69 dB&B⇔🛏fr£93 🅿
15P ♨ ✿ *xmas*
♀ French ♥ ⚺ S% Lunch fr£13.50 Dinner fr£21 Last dinner
9.30pm
Credit Cards ⬜1 ⬜2 ⬜3

---

**LERWICK**

See Shetland

---

**L'ETACQ**

See Jersey **under** Channel Islands

---

**LETHAM** Fife Map **11** NO31

★★★🏆64% *Fernie Castle* KY7 7RU ☎(033781)381
Telex no 295141 FAX (033781) 422
*The needs of both tourist and business user are met in this imposing
castle which lies in its own grounds off the A914. Bedrooms vary in
size, while public areas include an interesting vaulted cocktail bar,
a comfortable drawing room and a restaurant serving high quality
dishes cooked in modern style.*
16⇔🛏(2fb)1🏠 CTV in all bedrooms ®
CTV 50P ✿ putting clay pigeon shooting
♀ French **V** ♥ ⚺
Credit Cards ⬜1 ⬜2 ⬜3 ⬜5

For key to symbols see the inside front cover.

**LETHAM** Tayside *Angus* Map **15** NO54

★★★♨66% **Idvies House** DD8 2QJ ☎(030781)787
Telex no 76252 FAX (030781) 8933
Closed 26 & 27 Dec RS 24 & 25 Dec
*Set in 12 acres of peaceful grounds, this delightful country mansion is a welcome retreat for visiting businessmen and holidaymakers alike. It offers individually furnished and well equipped bedrooms, relaxing public rooms and competent country house cooking. A warm welcome is assured, and service by the young staff is efficient and attentive.*
9⌐⇥ᕀ(1fb)2⌗ CTV in all bedrooms Ⓡ T ✳ sB&B⌐⇥ᕀ£30-£40 dB&B⌐⇥ᕀ£40-£70 🍴
60P ✿ squash croquet clay pigeon shooting
V ⓥ ⌶ Lunch £10-£13.50 High tea £5-£7.50 Dinner £12.50-£20&alc Last dinner 9.30pm
Credit Cards ⓵ ⓶ ⓷ ⓹

**LETTERFINLAY** Highland *Inverness-shire* Map **14** NN29

★★64% **Letterfinlay Lodge** PH34 4DZ (off A82)
☎Spean Bridge(039781)622
Closed Nov-Feb
*A long established, family-run hotel in its own grounds beside the main north road, overlooking Loch Lochy. Touring holidaymakers will find a warm welcome and traditional hospitality.*
13rm(11⌐⇥ᕀ)(5fb) S10% sB&B⌐⇥ᕀ£18-£25 dB&B£32-£46 dB&B⌐⇥ᕀ£36-£50
▦CTV 100P 🚗 ✿ ✔
V ⓥ ⌶ S10% Lunch £1-£15alc Dinner fr£13.50alc Last dinner 8.30pm
Credit Cards ⓵ ⓶ ⓷ ⓸ ⓹ ⓔ

**LEVEN** Fife Map **11** NO30

★★★59% **New Caledonian** 81 High St KY8 4NG
☎(0333)24101 FAX (0333) 21241
*Modern business hotel replacing one which was damaged by fire some years ago.*
17⌐⇥ᕀ(1fb) CTV in all bedrooms Ⓡ T ✳ sB&B⌐⇥ᕀ£35-£45 dB&B⌐⇥ᕀ£47-£55 🍴
⟨▦CTV 50P
♈ English & French V ⓥ ⌶ ⅄ Lunch £6.95&alc High tea £6.95-£8.50 Dinner £10.95-£12.95&alc Last dinner 9.30pm
Credit Cards ⓵ ⓶ ⓷ ⓹ ⓔ

**LEWDOWN** Devon Map **02** SX48

★★

⊛★★♨
**LEWTRENCHARD MANOR**

EX20 4PN (Pride of Britain)
☎(056683)256 & 222
FAX (056683) 332
Closed 2-3 wks Jan
(Rosette awarded for dinner only)

*This magnificent early 17th-century house owned by Susan and James Murray stands in extensive gardens on the edge of Dartmoor and is awarded red stars for the first time this year. Among the many original features of the house which its owners have been careful to retain are the ornate ceilings, wood panelling and a splendid gallery displaying antique furniture and objets d'art, thus creating a home-like atmosphere which, with the very hospitable service, puts guests in a relaxed mood in preparation for the fine cooking. Chef David Shepherd prepares an excellent Menu Gourmand for the evenings as well as the à la carte selection. A salad of squab pigeon accompanied by fresh raspberry dressing,*

*followed by Sea Bass, grilled with lemon and herbs and rounded off by glazed apricot pancakes, are typical of the dishes you may enjoy here.*
8rm(7⌐⇥ᕀ)2⌗ CTV in all bedrooms T sB&B⌐⇥ᕀfr£75 dB&B⌐⇥ᕀ£90-£130 🍴
50P 🚗 ✿ ✔ croquet clay pigeon shooting nc8yrs *xmas*
♈ English & French V ⓥ ⌶ ⅄ Lunch fr£15&alc Dinner £25&alc Last dinner 9.30pm
Credit Cards ⓵ ⓶ ⓷ ⓹

**LEWES** East Sussex Map **05** TQ41

★★★54% **Shelleys** High St BN7 1XS (Mount Charlotte (TS))
☎(0273)472361 Telex no 86719 FAX (0273) 483152
*This former inn, dating from 1526, was converted into a manor house and became the home of the Shelley family in 1663. Now providing comfortable accommodation and modern facilities, the hotel also has a pretty restaurant offering a choice of menus.*
21⌐⇥ᕀ2⌗ CTV in all bedrooms T sB⌐⇥ᕀ£60-£75 dB⌐⇥ᕀ£85-£120 (room only) 🍴
⟨25P 3🅿 ✿ CFA *xmas*
V ⓥ ⌶ Lunch £11.75-£12.50&alc Dinner £14.50-£15.50&alc Last dinner 9.15pm
Credit Cards ⓵ ⓶ ⓷ ⓹

★★60% **White Hart** 55 High St BN7 1XE (Best Western)
☎(0273)474676 & 476694 Telex no 878468 FAX (0273) 476695
*Much of the original character and olde worlde charm of this 15th-century town centre hotel has been retained. Facilities include a carvery, conservatory restaurant and coffee shop.*

▶ **L**

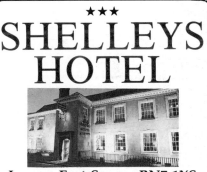

★★★
# SHELLEYS HOTEL

## Lewes, East Sussex BN7 1XS
## Telephone: (0273) 472361

The country house atmosphere and antique furniture reflect the graceful life of the 17th and 18th centuries. With parts of the hotel dating back to 1526 when originally an Inn called The Vine and then converted to a fine Manor House in 1663, has now been tastefully modernized. A choice of continental and English dishes are offered on both the table d'hôte and à la carte menus with an excellent wine cellar. Ideally situated for all sporting activities and venues.

19rm(14⇌ॉ⁀)Annexe21⇌ॉ⁀(4fb)2⊞ CTV in all bedrooms Ⓡ
**T ✱** sB&B£36 sB&B⇌ॉ⁀£36-£51 dB&B£48
dB&B⇌ॉ⁀£68-£78 ▤
《 50P *xmas*
♀ English & French **V** ✿ ⚌ 𝄌 Lunch £6.90-£11.50&alc
Dinner £6.90-£11.50&alc Last dinner 10pm
Credit Cards ①②③⑤

---

**LEWIS, ISLE OF** Western Isles *Ross & Cromarty* Map **13**

---

**STORNOWAY** Map **13** NB43
★★★**64%** **Caberfeidh** PA87 2EU (Best Western) ☎(0851)2604
FAX (0851) 5572
*This purpose built hotel, situated on the southern approach to the
town, offers comfortable and well appointed accommodation.
Bedrooms with smart, modern bathrooms are equipped to a good
standard, and the recently refurbished public areas are attractive
and inviting. Service throughout is attentive and friendly.*
40⇌ॉ⁀ CTV in all bedrooms Ⓡ **T ✳** sB&B⇌ॉ⁀£52-£57
dB&B⇌ॉ⁀£69-£74 ▤
Lift 《 CTV 100P ✿
♀ French **V** ✿ ⚌ Lunch fr£6.50 High tea £4-£6 Dinner
fr£12.50&alc Last dinner 9.30pm
Credit Cards ①②③④⑤ £

---

**LEYBURN** North Yorkshire Map **07** SE19
★**57%** **Golden Lion** Market Place DL8 5AS
☎Wensleydale(0969)22161
Closed 25 & 26 Dec
*A good range of both bar meals and à la carte dinners is served at
this busy, popular village inn.*
14rm(10⇌ॉ1ॉ⁀)(5fb) CTV in all bedrooms Ⓡ **T** sB&B£18-£23
sB&B⇌ॉ⁀£21-£26 dB&B£36-£46 dB&B⇌ॉ⁀£44-£52 ▤
Lift ⫝ ⌗
♀ English & Continental **V** ✿ S% Sunday Lunch £4-£7 Dinner
£6.50-£11.50alc Last dinner 9pm
Credit Cards ①③

---

**LEYLAND** Lancashire Map **07** SD52
★★★**67%** **Pines** Clayton-le-Woods PR6 7ED (1m S of M6 junc
29 on A6) ☎Preston(0772)38551 Telex no 67308
Closed 25 & 26 Dec
*Set beside the A6 at Clayton-le-Woods three miles north of the
town is this extended Victorian house. Bedrooms vary in size and
comfort, the best have comfortable armchairs and impressive
bathrooms.*
25⇌ॉ⁀ CTV in all bedrooms Ⓡ **T ✖** sB&B⇌ॉ⁀£40-£60
dB&B⇌ॉ⁀£65-£80 ▤
《 100P ⌗ ✿
**V** ✿ ⚌ Lunch £10&alc Dinner £9.85-£18.70alc Last dinner
9.30pm
Credit Cards ①②③⑤

★★★**56%** **Penguin Hotel** Leyland Way PR5 2JX
☎Preston(0772)422922 Telex no 677651 FAX (0772) 622282
*Functional modern hotel just off junction 28 of the M6.*
93⇌ॉ⁀(9fb)𝄌in 13 bedrooms CTV in all bedrooms Ⓡ **T ✳**
sB⇌ॉ⁀£52-£57 dB⇌ॉ⁀£64-£70 (room only) ▤
《 CTV 150P CFA *xmas*
♀ English & French **V** ✿ ⚌ Lunch fr£7.95&alc Dinner
fr£11.25&alc Last dinner 10pm
Credit Cards ①②③⑤ £

---

All AA-appointed establishments are
inspected regularly to ensure that required
standards are maintained.

---

**LICHFIELD** Staffordshire Map **07** SK10

---

★★★**60%** **Little Barrow** Beacon St WS13 7AR ☎(0543)414500
FAX (0543) 415734
*Just a short distance from the centre of town and close to the
Cathedral is this popular hotel. Bedrooms are well designed,
particularly for the businessman, and Carters Restc. irant enjoys a
good reputation.*
24⇌ॉ⁀ CTV in all bedrooms Ⓡ **T ✖** (ex guide dogs) sB&B⇌£55
dB&B⇌£65 ▤
《 ⊞ CTV 70P
♀ French **V** ✿ Lunch £7.50&alc Dinner fr£11.50&alc Last
dinner 9.30pm
Credit Cards ①②③⑤

★★★**59%** **George** Bird St WS13 6PR (Embassy)
☎(0543)414822 FAX (0543) 415817
RS Xmas
*Situated close to the town centre and the cathedral, this 18th
century hotel caters for both tourists and business clientele alike.
The open plan lounge and bar areas are cosy and comfortable, and
a good range of food is available, including a popular carvery.*
38⇌ॉ⁀(3fb)𝄌in 5 bedrooms CTV in all bedrooms Ⓡ **T**
sB⇌ॉ⁀fr£59 dB⇌ॉ⁀fr£66 (room only) ▤
《 40P 3⬤ CFA ♫ *xmas*
♀ International **V** ✿ ⚌ Lunch fr£9.75 Dinner fr£13.50 Last
dinner 9.30pm
Credit Cards ①②③④⑤

★★**72%** **Angel Croft** Beacon St WS13 7AA ☎(0543)258737
FAX (0543) 415605
Closed 25 & 26 Dec RS Sun evenings
*This Georgian house with well-tended gardens at its rear, standing
on the edge of the town centre, offers friendly, helpful service,
accommodation in warm, spacious bedrooms and freshly prepared
cuisine which includes a tempting sweet trolley.*
11rm(3⇌6ॉ⁀)Annexe8⇌ॉ⁀(2fb)1⊞ CTV in all bedrooms Ⓡ **T
✖** (ex guide dogs) **✱** sB&B£27.50-£34 sB&B⇌ॉ⁀£38-£55
dB&B£39.50-£49.50 dB&B⇌ॉ⁀£48-£65 ▤
60P ✿
✿ ⚌ Lunch £8.25-£15 Dinner £9.25-£16 Last dinner 9pm
Credit Cards ①③⑤

★★**60%** **Fradley Arms** Rykneld St, Fradley WS13 8RD (on A38,
3m NE) ☎Burton-on-Trent(0283)790186 & 790977
FAX (0283) 791464
*A family-run hotel, standing beside the A38 Birmingham to Derby
road in extensive lawns which include a children's play area. It
features a popular restaurant serving freshly prepared meals and a
large new function room which can cater for 200 people.*
6⇌ॉ⁀(1fb) CTV in all bedrooms Ⓡ **T ✳** sB&B⇌ॉ⁀£36-£40
dB&B⇌ॉ⁀£48-£56 ▤
CTV 200P ✿ ♫
♀ English & French **V** ✿ ⚌ Lunch £6-£7 Dinner fr£11&alc
Last dinner 9.30pm
Credit Cards ①②③⑤ £

---

**LIFTON** Devon Map **02** SX38
★★★**71%** **Arundell Arms** PL16 0AA (Best Western)
☎(0566)84666 FAX (0566) 84494
Closed 4 days Xmas
*Significant and sympathetic refurbishment to this charming former
coaching inn provides stylish public rooms and individually styled
bedrooms equipped with modern day comforts. The cuisine is
equally noteworthy, flair and imagination are used in traditional
French and English dishes. This premier fishing hotel has twenty
miles of its own water on the River Tamar.*
24⇌ॉ⁀ CTV in all bedrooms Ⓡ **T** sB&B⇌ॉ⁀£46-£50
dB&B⇌ॉ⁀£75-£82 ▤
80P ⌗ ✿ CFA ⚓ skittle alley games room *xmas*

♀ English & French V ✿ ⬛ ✂ Lunch £13&alc Dinner
£22&alc Last dinner 9pm
Credit Cards ① ② ③ ⑤
**See advertisement under LAUNCESTON**

★★ 60% **Lifton Cottage** PL16 0DR ☎(0566)84439
*A cosy atmosphere permeates the intimate, character public rooms
and bright, compact, well-equipped bedrooms of this small family-
run hotel. Its position beside the A30 makes an ideal base for
touring the area.*
12rm(10⇨ℿ)(3fb) CTV in all bedrooms ® T sB&Bfr£19.50
sB&B⇨ℿfr£24 dB&B⇨ℿfr£45 ☐
CTV 25P ✿
V ✿ ⬛ ✂ Lunch fr£6.50 Dinner fr£9.50 Last dinner 9pm
Credit Cards ① ② ③ ⑤

---

**LIMPLEY STOKE (near Bath)** Wiltshire Map **03** ST76

★★★⬛ 63% **Cliffe** Crowe Hill BA3 6HY (Best Western)
☎(0225)723226 Telex no 445731 FAX (0225) 723871
Closed 3-31 Jan
*The new Canadian proprietor and his wife have, after only a few
months, refurbished this converted country house. Set in three
acres of gardens and grounds it has a beautifully landscaped
swimming pool which is a great attraction in the summer months.
Cuisine in the tastefully appointed restaurant has a Canadian
influence and service is pleasant.*
11⇨ℿ(3fb)1⬛ CTV in all bedrooms ® T ✱
sB&B⇨ℿ£65-£85 dB&B⇨ℿ£75-£95 ☐
40P ⬛ ✿ ⬛(heated) *xmas*
♀ English & French V ✿ ⬛ ✂ Sunday Lunch fr£9.95 High tea
£5-£10alc Dinner £12-£18&alc Last dinner 9.30pm
Credit Cards ① ② ③ ⑤

## Beacon Street, Lichfield, Staffordshire
## Telephone: (0543) 414500

A modern and popular hotel offering old world
charm combined with every comfort you would
expect of a first class hotel. Situated in Beacon
Street, the hotel is in the perfect position for the
business man or the tourist. There is a large car
park to the rear and most of the city's business,
tourist and shopping areas are within walking
distance.

The ★★★
Little Barrow
Hotel

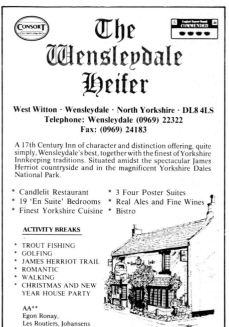

**LINCOLN** Lincolnshire Map **08** SK 97

★★★★63% *The White Hart* Bailgate LN1 3AR (Trusthouse Forte) ☎(0522)26222 Telex no 56304 FAX (0522) 531798
*Early Georgian house with a slate Victorian façade, standing in the shadow of Lincoln cathedral.*
50⇨(4fb)≯in 12 bedrooms CTV in all bedrooms ®
Lift ( CTV 25P 35⬟ CFA ♫
V ✿ ⚐ ≯ Last dinner 9.45pm
Credit Cards ①②③⑤

★★★⚡67% **Washingborough Hall Country House** Church Hill, Washingborough LN4 1BE (3m E B1190) (Minotels) ☎(0522)790340
*Situated three miles from Lincoln and within sight of the the Cathedral, this hotel is set in three acres of gardens and woodland. Décor and furnishings, though modest, are well cared for and Mr and Mrs Shillaker provide warm hospitality.*
12⇨♪♠1 ⌘♪≯in 2 bedrooms CTV in all bedrooms ® T
sB&B⇨♪£42-£55 dB&B⇨♪£59-£75 ⊟
50P ⊞ ❈ ⌣
⚐ International V ✿ ⚐ ≯ Sunday Lunch £7.50 Dinner £12.50&alc Last dinner 9pm
Credit Cards ①②③⑤ ⑥

★★★58% **Eastgate Post House** Eastgate LN2 1PN (Trusthouse Forte) ☎(0522)520341 Telex no 56316 FAX (0522) 510780
*Ideal for both holiday and commercial guests, this hotel has ample parking space, well-equipped bedrooms and conference/banqueting facilities. The Palatinate Restaurant overlooks the Cathedral and offers an interesting menu.*
71⇨(1fb)≯in 21 bedrooms CTV in all bedrooms ® T S15%
sB⇨£67-£78 dB⇨£78-£90 (room only) ⊟
Lift ( 110P CFA xmas
⚐ English & French V ✿ ⚐ ≯ S15% Lunch £9.75-£12 Dinner fr£14&alc Last dinner 10pm
Credit Cards ①②③④⑤

★★★54% **Moor Lodge** LN4 1HU (Consort) ☎(0522)791366 FAX (0522) 794389
(For full entry see Branston)

★★★50% **Four Seasons** Scothern Ln LN2 3QP ☎Welton(0673)60108 FAX (0673) 62784
(For full entry see Dunholme)

★★71% **Hillcrest** 15 Lindum Ter LN2 5RT (Guestaccom) ☎(0522)510182
Closed 20 Dec-3 Jan
*The hotel stands in an elevated position in a quiet residential area to the north-east of Lincoln, and guests can enjoy views of part of the city from the conservatory, lounge bar and dining room. Thoughtfully planned bedrooms are well equipped, and friendly, attentive staff create a relaxed atmosphere throughout.*
17⇨♪♠(4fb) CTV in all bedrooms ® T sB&B⇨♪£36.50 dB&B⇨♪£49.50 ⊟
8P
⚐ International V ✿ ⚐ ≯ Bar Lunch £1.50-£5alc Dinner £7.50-£12alc Last dinner 8.45pm
Credit Cards ①③ ⑥

★★70% **The Lodge** 38 & 40 Nettleham Rd LN2 1RE ☎(0522)513001 FAX (0522) 513002
*Large detached house on a tree-lined main road, tastefully converted to offer spacious, attractive and well-equipped rooms. The hallway retains some original features and the house is furnished in keeping with its era. The hotel is run in an informal and caring manner and a good selection of fresh, excellently prepared dishes is featured on the table d'hôte menu.*
16⇨♪♠(2fb)1 ⊞ CTV in all bedrooms ® T
sB&B⇨♠£42.50-£52 dB&B⇨♠£52-£65 ⊟
Lift CTV 16P ⚹ xmas

⚐ English, French & Italian V ✿ ⚐ ≯ Sunday Lunch £10.50-£11.50&alc High tea £3.50-£4.50 Dinner £11.50-£12.50&alc Last dinner 9.30pm
Credit Cards ①③④ ⑥

★★66% **Loudor** 37 Newark Rd, North Hykeham LN6 8RB (3m SW A1434) ☎(0522)680333 & 500474 FAX (0522) 680403
*Despite its location on the busy A46, three miles south-west of the city, this is a quiet, informal and friendly hotel where guests receive personal service from the proprietors; small and comfortable, the house has been completely remodelled to provide accommodation which is clean and very well maintained, though compact in some instances.*
9⇨♪♠Annexe1♠(1fb) CTV in all bedrooms ® T ✖ ✳
sB&B⇨♪£28-£32 dB&B⇨♪£40-£42
12P ⊞
⚐ English & French ✿ ≯
Credit Cards ①②③⑤

★★59% **Duke William** 44 Bailgate LN1 3AP ☎(0522)533351
Closed 25 Dec
*Situated close to the castle and within easy walking distance of the cathedral, the hotel has a large carpark at the rear of the building, off Chapel Lane. Staff are friendly, there is a popular public bar and a restaurant with a small table d'hôte menu.*
11♠(3fb) CTV in all bedrooms ® T ✖ (ex guide dogs) S10%
sB&B♠£35-£48 dB&B♠£50-£58 ⊟
( 12P ⊞
V ✿ S10% Lunch £2.50-£5.95 Dinner £7.95-£9.95 Last dinner 9.30pm
Credit Cards ①②③⑤ ⑥

★★56% **Castle** Westgate LN1 3AS ☎(0522)38801
*Once a Victorian school, and conveniently situated between cathedral and castle, the hotel has been re-styled to offer more up-to-date accommodation in simply furnished bedrooms with a range of modern facilities; a friendly young team of staff creates a relaxed, informal atmosphere.*
15⇨Annexe6♠(2fb) CTV in all bedrooms ®
21P nc8yrs
⚐ Continental V
Credit Cards ①②③⑤

★★55% **Barbican** Saint Marys St LN5 7EQ ☎(0522)528374 & 543811
*An unusual feature of this hotel is the Barnum's Lager Bar. Decorated and furnished on the Barnum's Circus theme, it certainly provides a lively atmosphere. Good standards of décor prevail throughout the public areas and the modern bedrooms which are individually furnished and well equipped, though some are rather compact.*
20rm(13♠)(2fb) CTV in all bedrooms ® T
CTV ⚐
⚐ Mainly grills V ✿ ⚐ ≯ Last dinner 9.30pm
Credit Cards ①②③⑤

**LINLITHGOW** Lothian *West Lothian* Map **11** NS97

✕✕✕**Champany** EH49 7LU (2m NE off A904) ☎Philipstoun(050683)4532 & 4388 FAX (050683) 4302
Closed Sun & 24 Dec-9 Jan
Lunch not served Sat
⚐ International 48 seats ✳ Lunch £12.50-£30alc Dinner £12.50-£30alc Last lunch 2pm Last dinner 10pm 100P nc8yrs
Credit Cards ①②③⑤

**LIPHOOK** Hampshire Map **04** SU83

✕✕**Lai Quilla** 15 The Square GU30 7AB ☎(0428)722095
⚐ Indian Last dinner 11.30pm ⚐
Credit Cards ①②③⑤

LISKEARD Cornwall & Isles of Scilly Map **02** SX26

## ★★

❀★★♨ WELL HOUSE

St Keyne PL14 4RN
☎(0579)42001

*It may be the scent of jasmine
round the door or the sunlight
which constantly changes the
colour of the secluded valley
below the house that gives Nick Wainford's Victorian manor
its uniquely welcoming air, but whatever the season or
occasion, Well House is an ideal and exclusive retreat. Nick
and his dedicated small brigade of staff meet every guest with
a combination of genuine hospitality and attentive service that
makes each one feel more like a house guest than a hotel
resident. The bedrooms, furnished in styles ranging from Art
Deco to traditional country-house, are decorated with water-
colours and abundant fresh flowers; the cosy sitting room with
its open fires offers a pleasant outlook over the garden, and the
dining room provides memorable meals, created by Chef
David Pope, whose career embraces several of Britain's best
country-house hotels. His innovative dishes express superb
combinations of flavours: his Panache of scallops, salmon and
turbot with an excellent chive sauce, or Terrine of foie gras
show his meticulous attention to detail, and main courses like
Medallions of veal with glazed shallots and leeks in a Dijon
sauce, or Noisettes of English lamb in a robust Port sauce are
equally worthy of mention. The well-researched wine list is
realistically priced.*

7⇦(1fb) CTV in all bedrooms **T** ✳ sB&B⇦£60
dB&B⇦£65-£95 Continental breakfast
30P ⇑ ❖ ⌇(heated) ♪ (hard) croquet
✿ ⌂ Lunch £21-£27.50 Dinner £27.50 Last dinner 9pm
Credit Cards ①②③

★★♨61% **Country Castle** Station Rd PL14 4EB ☎(0579)42694
Closed Nov RS Jan & Feb
*Quietly set in 2.5 acres of grounds, with magnificent views over the
Looe Valley, this hotel provides individually decorated and
attractively furnished bedrooms and an elegant lounge. The
personal involvement of the proprietors maintains old-fashioned
standards of hospitality, serving wholesome food and offering
individual service.*
11rm(5⇦5♠)(1fb) CTV in all bedrooms ℝ ✳ S%
sB&B⇦♠frf36 dB&B⇦♠£50-£60 �📢
50P ❖ ⌇ croquet boule *xmas*
⚲ English & French **V** ✿ ⌂
Credit Cards ①③£

★★58% **Lord Eliot** Castle St PL14 3AQ ☎(0579)42717
*Small hotel built around the character house of a one-time country
landlord.*
15rm(4⇦10♠)(3fb) CTV in all bedrooms ℝ
⟨ CTV 60P ♫
⚲ English & French **V** ✿ ⌂ Last dinner 9.30pm
Credit Cards ①③

---

LITTLEBOURNE Kent Map **05** TR25

★★69% **The Bow Window Inn** High St CT3 1ST
☎Canterbury(0227)721264
8⇦♠(2fb)2⊞ CTV in all bedrooms ℝ ✕ (ex guide dogs)
20P

---

⚲ English & French **V** ✿ ⌂ Last dinner 9.30pm
Credit Cards ①②③⑤
See advertisement under CANTERBURY

---

### LITTLE HALLINGBURY
See Bishop's Stortford

---

### LITTLE LANGDALE Cumbria Map **07** NY30

★★64% **Three Shires Inn** LA22 9NZ ☎Langdale(09667)215
Closed Xmas-Jan RS mid Nov-mid Feb
*A few miles west of Ambleside and north of Coniston, this former
AA Northern Region "Inn of the Year" offers spotless
accommodation for walkers, climbers and other holidaymakers.
The slate-floored Cavalier bar and landscaped gardens are popular
for substantial bar meals.*
11rm(7⇦♠)(1fb) ℝ ✕ ✳ sB&B£23 dB&B£46
dB&B⇦♠£54 �📢
CTV 20P 2⊛ ⇑ ❖
⚲ British & Continental ✿ ⌂ ✕ Bar Lunch £1.30-£10alc
Dinner £13.95 Last dinner 8pm
See advertisement under AMBLESIDE

---

### LITTLE WEIGHTON Humberside Map **08** SE93

★★★♨66% **Rowley Manor** Rowley Rd HU20 3XR
☎Hull(0482)848248 FAX (0482) 849900
*Tranquilly set amid attractive gardens which include a croquet
lawn, its courteous staff supervised by resident proprietors, the
hotel offers friendly service and a range of interesting menus.*
16⇦♠2⊞ CTV in all bedrooms **T** sB&B⇦♠£48-£60
dB&B⇦♠£66-£88 �📢
⟨ 80P ❖ solarium croquet *xmas*

▶

**L**

## ★★

# the
# LODGE
# HOTEL

## 38/40 Nettleham Road, Lincoln LN2 1RE
## Tel: (0522) 513001   Fax: (0522) 513002

The unique charm of the hotel is reflected
both outside and in — firstly by its
elegant Edwardian architecture and
secondly by its intimate and personalised
inner decor, based on the flavour of a
country house. This results in a warm and
relaxing home away from home, while
handily situated only two minutes walk
from the Cathedral. This is complemented
by a menu which prides itself on its
exciting and excellent home cooked
cuisine. Large car park. Conferences &
weddings accommodated.

**Resident proprietors: Carol & Gregory James**

♀ International **V** ✿ ⌨ Lunch £8.50-£16.50&alc Dinner
£14.95-£16.50&alc Last dinner 9.30pm
Credit Cards [1][2][3][5] ⓔ

**See advertisement under HULL**

---

**LIVERPOOL** Merseyside Map **07** SJ39

See **Town Plan Section**
See also Blundellsands **and** Bootle
★★★★57% **Liverpool Moat House** Paradise St L1 8JD
(Queens Moat) ☎051-709 0181 Telex no 627270
FAX 051-709 2706
*Modern purpose-built hotel close to city centre.*
251⇨♪🛏(202fb)⊬in 40 bedrooms CTV in all bedrooms ⓇT
sB&B⇨♪£77.50-£87.50 dB&B⇨♪£99-£109 🄿
Lift ( ⊞ ⨍ CFA ▤(heated) sauna solarium gymnasium
whirlpool *xmas*
♀ English & French **V** ✿ ⌨ S12.5% Lunch £11-£13.50&alc
High tea £6.60-£11 Dinner £17.60-£19.80&alc Last dinner
10.30pm
Credit Cards [1][2][3][4][5] ⓔ

★★★★56% **Atlantic Tower** Chapel St L3 9RE (Mount
Charlotte (TS)) ☎051-227 4444 Telex no 627070
FAX 051-236 3973
*A distinctive building on Liverpool's famous waterfront, with fine
views over the Mersey from many of the compact, but well-
appointed bedrooms. The Stateroom restaurant offers a high
standard of cuisine and the Clubcar Carver, designed like a
Pulman carriage, is noted for its tasty roasts.*
226⇨♪🛏(6fb)⊬in 24 bedrooms CTV in all bedrooms ⓇT ✱
sB⇨♪£67.50 dB⇨♪£75 (room only) 🄿
Lift ( ⊞ 60P 45🛏 CFA ♫ *xmas*
♀ European **V** ✿ ⌨ Lunch £14.50&alc Dinner £14.95&alc
Last dinner 10.15pm
Credit Cards [1][2][3][4][5]

★★★66% *Trials* 56-62 Castle St L2 7LQ ☎051-227 1021
Telex no 626125
*A building that once housed a bank has been converted into a
luxury hotel where the delightfully furnished bedrooms all have
corner spa baths. Attentive service successfully combines
friendliness with professionalism.*
20⇨♪(2fb)4🛏⊬in 3 bedrooms CTV in all bedrooms ⓇT ✂
Lift ( 24🛏 🛏 🄿 (grass) ⚬
✿ ⌨ Last dinner 10.30pm
Credit Cards [1][2][3][4][5]

★★★63% **Crest Hotel Liverpool-City** Lord Nelson St L3 5QB
(Trusthouse Forte) ☎051-709 7050 Telex no 627954
FAX 051-709 2193
*Large, city-centre hotel with comfortable public areas and its own
adjacent car park. Bedrooms are spacious but rather dated,
although progressive upgrading is underway. Staff are friendly and
helpful.*
150⇨♪(2fb)⊬in 53 bedrooms CTV in all bedrooms Ⓡ
Lift ( 300P (charged) CFA snooker
♀ French **V** ✿ ⌨ ⊬
Credit Cards [1][2][3][4][5]

★★★60% *St George's* St John's Precinct, Lime St L1 1NQ
(Trusthouse Forte) ☎051-709 7090 Telex no 627630
FAX 051-709 0137
*Built in 1972 as part of an extensive city centre development, this
large hotel provides well-equipped accommodation and is popular
with a wide range of customers from tourists to business people
using the extensive conference facilities.*
155⇨♪⊬in 15 bedrooms CTV in all bedrooms Ⓡ
Lift ( 1🛏 CFA
**V** ✿ ⌨ ⊬ Last dinner 10pm
Credit Cards [1][2][3][4][5]

---

★★59% **Grange** Holmfield Rd, Aigburth L19 3PQ
☎051-427 2950 FAX 051-427 9055
*A detached Victorian house with neat lawns and gardens at its rear
stands in a residential area off the A561, 1.5 miles from the airport
and 3.5 miles from the city centre. Standards of cuisine are above
average, a varied choice of dishes being offered on table d'hôte and
à la carte menus, whilst service is friendly, willing and competent
throughout.*
25⇨♪🛏(1fb)4🛏 CTV in all bedrooms Ⓡ T ✂ (ex guide dogs)
sB&B⇨♪£31.60-£48.80 dB&B⇨♪£50.20-£65.25 🄿
CTV 50P ✿
♀ French **V** ✿ ⌨ ⊬ Sunday Lunch £7.75-£8.75 Dinner
£11.95-£16.95&alc Last dinner 9pm
Credit Cards [1][2][3][5]

★★59% **Green Park** 4/6 Greenbank Dr L17 1AN
☎051-733 3382
*A Victorian building, situated close to Sefton Park and within easy
reach of the city centre, offering comfortable accommodation with
up-to-date facilities and friendly staff.*
23rm(8⇨8♪)(6fb) CTV in all bedrooms sB&B£26
sB&B⇨♪£30 dB&B£35 dB&B⇨♪£40 🄿
( ⊞ CTV 25P ✿
**V** ✿ ⌨ Lunch £5.50-£7.50 High tea £2-£6 Dinner
£5.50-£7.50&alc Last dinner 9pm
Credit Cards [1][2][3][5] ⓔ

---

**LIVINGSTON** Lothian *West Lothian* Map **11** NT06

★★★60% **Hilton National** Almondvale East EH54 6QB
(Hilton) ☎(0506)31222 Telex no 727680 FAX (0506) 34666
*Popular business hotel with conference and leisure facilities.*
120♪(18fb)⊬in 15 bedrooms CTV in all bedrooms ⓇT ✱
sB♪£75-£95 dB♪£95-£120 (room only) 🄿
( ⊞ 200P ✿ ▤(heated) sauna gymnasium trim track *xmas*
♀ British & French **V** ✿ ⌨ ⊬ Lunch fr£11.50 Dinner
fr£11.50&alc Last dinner 10pm
Credit Cards [1][2][3][5]

---

**LIZARD, THE** Cornwall & Isles of Scilly Map **02** SW71

★★66% **Housel Bay** Housel Cove TR12 7PG
☎The Lizard(0326)290417 FAX (0326) 290359
Closed Jan-Feb 10
*House of Victorian origin superbly situated in cliffside grounds.
Breathtaking views from all the public rooms & gardens.*
23⇨♪🛏⊬in 2 bedrooms CTV in all bedrooms ⓇT
sB&B⇨♪£20-£27 dB&B⇨♪£40-£74 🄿
Lift CTV 25P 4🛏 (£2 per night) ✿ *xmas*
♀ International **V** ✿ ⌨ ⊬ Sunday Lunch fr£7.50 Dinner
fr£13&alc Last dinner 9pm
Credit Cards [1][2][3] ⓔ

★68% **Kynance Bay House** Penmenner Rd TR12 7NR
☎The Lizard(0326)290498
Closed 3 Jan-mid Feb
*Commanding fine coastal views from its position at the edge of the
village, a well-run hotel with a happy family atmosphere offers
comfortable bedrooms, a good choice of meals from its short à la
carte menu and the charm of a sheltered hidden garden.*
9rm(7♪)⊬in all bedrooms TV available Ⓡ ✱ sB&B£15-£22
sB&B♪£15-£22 dB&B£30-£44 dB&B♪£30-£44 🄿
CTV 9P ✿ photographic courses *xmas*
♀ Continental **V** ✿ ⌨ ⊬ Lunch £6.50-£10&alc Dinner
£10&alc Last dinner 9pm
Credit Cards [1][2][3][5] ⓔ

---

Book as early as possible for busy holiday
periods.

LLANARMON DYFFRYN CEIRIOG Clwyd Map **07** SJ13

★★71% **West Arms** LL20 7LD (WR) ☎(069176)665
FAX (069176) 262
*This former 16th-century village inn boasts a wealth of charm and character and provides good, friendly personal service. Recent extensive refurbishment has enhanced the accommodation considerably and all the bedrooms are pleasant and comfortable.*
14⇥(1fb)✂in 5 bedrooms CTV in 2 bedrooms
sB&B⇔£45-£50 dB&B⇔£70-£80 🅿
CTV 30P 2🏮 ⌘ ✿ ♪ *xmas*
🍴 English & Continental V ✿ ⌐ Sunday Lunch £9.75 Dinner £17.50 Last dinner 9pm
Credit Cards ①②③⑤

---

LLANBEDR Gwynedd Map **06** SH52

★★🏩60% **Cae Nest Hall** LL45 2NL ☎(034123)349
Closed Nov-Feb (ex Xmas & New Year)
*This 15th-century manor house enjoys a peaceful location on the outskirts of the village, sheltered by 3 acres of grounds. Owners Anita and Robert Mann offer friendly and informal service, while striving hard to upgrade all the accommodation. In the evenings, Robert, a talented pianist and organist, regularly entertains guests in the lounge.*
10⇥🛏(2fb) CTV in all bedrooms ® 🐾 (ex guide dogs) S10%
sB&B⇔🛏fr£22 dB&B⇔🛏fr£46 🅿
12P ⌘ ✿ ♪ *xmas*
🍴 Continental V ⤫ S10% Dinner fr£11.50 Last dinner 7.30pm

---

★★60% **Ty Mawr** LL45 2NH ☎(034123)440
*A pleasant stone building set in its own grounds on the outskirts of the village offers well-furnished bedrooms and public areas; warm, friendly service ensures guests' comfort.*
10⇥🛏(2fb) CTV in all bedrooms ® ✳ sB&B⇔🛏£22-£24
dB&B⇔🛏£44-£48 🅿
CTV 30P ⌘ ✿ ♪ *xmas*
🍴 Continental V ✿ ⌐ S% Lunch fr£5alc High tea fr£2alc Dinner fr£10alc Last dinner 8.45pm

See advertisement on page 405

---

LLANBERIS Gwynedd Map **06** SH56

★61% **Gallt-y-Glyn** Caernarfon Rd LL55 4EL ☎(0286)870370
Closed 25 Dec RS 26 Dec
*Although extended over the years, part of this hotel dates back to the 17th-century. Now a comfortable small hotel, personally owned and run.*
8rm(2🛏)(1fb)✂in 1 bedroom 🐾 ✳ sB&Bfr£16.50
sB&B🛏£18.50-£25 dB&Bfr£31 dB&B🛏fr£37
CTV 12P ⌘ ✿
V ⤫
Credit Cards ①
See advertisement on page 405

---

✗✗Y **Bistro** Glandwr, 43-45 Stryd Fawr LL55 4EU
☎(0286)871278
*At the centre of this village in the heart of Snowdonia a warm Welsh welcome is offered by a delightful restaurant, which also provides comfortable lounges where guests can relax before and after dining. The menu, typically Welsh in flavour, uses only the very best of local produce, including lamb and the fresh fish of the day, which are always good.*
Closed 3 wks Jan
Lunch not served
🍴 Welsh & French V 50 seats S% Dinner £17.50-£20 Last dinner 9.30pm ₽ ⤫
Credit Cards ①③

*1991 marks the 25th anniversary of this guide.*

### LLANDDEWI SKYRRID Gwent Map 03 SO31

❀✗**Walnut Tree Inn** NP7 8AW (3m NE of Abergavenny)
☎Abergavenny(0873)2797
*This charming little inn can be reached by taking the B4521 road north east of Abergavenny. The food, mainly Italian-style, is consistently enjoyable. Lunch is not served in the restaurant, but the same menu is available in the cosy bar, with its highly polished Britannia tables. The owners, Franco and Ann Taruschio, have been producing excellent food here for over a quarter of a century, and only fresh produce is ever used. Herbs and spices, distinctively Italian in flavour, enhance the dishes and the restaurant is especially noted for the quality of its fish and meat. There is a fine wine list, with a wide range on offer including interesting regional varieties.*
Closed Sun, 4 days Xmas & 2 wks Feb
Lunch not served Mon
♀ French & Italian **V** 45 seats Last lunch 2.30pm Last dinner 10.15pm 30P

### LLANDEGAI Gwynedd Map 06 SH57

◯**Rank Motor Lodge** Bangor Services LL57 4BG (Rank)
☎Central reservations 081-569 7120
Due to open Feb 1991
35⇨♪↑(20fb)⊁in 6 bedrooms CTV in all bedrooms ® ✳ S%
sB&B⇨♪↑£27.50 dB&B⇨♪↑£34.50 Continental breakfast
₵ 35P
Credit Cards ①②③⑤

### LLANDEGLA Clwyd Map 07 SJ15

★★♣74%, **Bod Idris Hall** LL11 3AL (WR) ☎(097888)434
FAX (097888) 335
*In a secluded situation surrounded by hills and moorland, this beautifully preserved old house is steeped in history. Bedrooms are spacious, comfortable and well equipped and public areas are full of charm and character. The hotel is reached by way of a long lane off the A5104, 1.5 miles NE of Llandegla.*
9⇨♪↑(2fb)6⊞ CTV in all bedrooms ® **T** 乂 (ex guide dogs)
sB&B⇨♪↑£45.50-£59.50 dB&B⇨♪↑£65-£85 🖻
CTV 40P ✿ ♪ clay & game shooting *xmas*
♀ Welsh & Continental **V** ♦ ⚏ Lunch £9-£13.50&alc Dinner £10-£15.50&alc Last dinner 9pm
Credit Cards ①②③⓸

### LLANDEILO Dyfed Map 02 SN62

★★★52%, **Cawdor Arms** SA19 6EN ☎(0558)823500
*Elegant, very comfortable Georgian house offering good quality food.*
17⇨♪↑2⊞ CTV in all bedrooms
7P
♀ English & French ♦ ⚏
Credit Cards ①②③⑤

### LLANDOVERY Dyfed Map 03 SN73

See also **Crugybar**
★★65%, **Castle** Kings Rd SA20 0AW (Minotels) ☎(0550)20343
*A family-run coaching inn in the centre of the old market town offers character bars and good food. Bedrooms are well equipped with modern facilities – and a half-tester bed used by Lord Nelson during a visit in 1802 is still in good condition.*
27rm(21⇨♪↑)(4fb)2⊞ CTV in all bedrooms ® **T**
CTV 40P ♪ (hard) ♪
**V** ♦ ⚏ Last dinner 9pm
Credit Cards ①③

For key to symbols see the inside front cover.

### LLANDRILLO Clwyd Map 06 SJ03

★★♣76%, **Tyddyn Llan Country House Hotel & Restaurant**
LL21 0ST (WR) ☎(049084)264
*Peter and Bridget Kindred have carefully and tastefully restored this delightful Georgian country house and its lovely gardens. The good quality well equipped bedrooms are individually styled and public areas are comfortable and welcoming. It has a deservedly high reputation for food and the short but imaginative set menu takes advantage of local produce.*
10⇨♪↑(2fb) ® **T** ✳ sB&B⇨♪↑£37-£41.50
dB&B⇨♪↑£60-£67 🖻
CTV 30P ⊞ ✿ ♪ croquet lawn *xmas*
**V** ♦ ⚏ Sunday Lunch £10.50 Dinner £17 Last dinner 9.30pm
Credit Cards ①③

### LLANDRINDOD WELLS Powys Map 03 SO06

See also **Newbridge-on-Wye and Penybont**
★★★63%, **Hotel Metropole** Temple St LDI 5DY
☎(0597)822881 Telex no 35237 FAX (0597) 824828
*This large and well run hotel, which has been in the same family for over 100 years, now has an excellent leisure centre. Conference facilities are also extensive, and public rooms spacious and well equipped. Most bedrooms are modern and well appointed.*
121⇨♪↑(2fb) ® **T** in 10 bedrooms CTV in all bedrooms ® **T**
sB&B⇨♪↑frf45 dB&B⇨♪↑frf62 🖻
Lift ₵ 150P ✿ ☒(heated) sauna solarium steamroom whirlpool beauty salon *xmas*
**V** ♦ ⚏ Lunch £9.50 Dinner £15 Last dinner 9pm
Credit Cards ①②③④⑤⓸

### LLANDUDNO Gwynedd Map 06 SH78

See **Town Plan Section**
During the currency of this publication Llandudno telephone numbers are liable to change.

★★★♣
**BODYSGALLEN HALL**
LL30 1RS (on A470
Llandudno link road)
(Prestige/Welsh Rarebits)
☎Aberconwy(0492)584466
Telex no 617163
FAX (0492) 582519

*On high ground midway between the resort and the A55 coast road, this 17th-century house was restored and converted to hotel use by Historic House Hotels Ltd and recently celebrated its 10th anniversary. Fine old panelling and many pieces of period furniture give great character to the public rooms, whilst deep armchairs and settees and the overall peace of sitting rooms can cause more than the occasional snoozing guest. Bedrooms still have the air of a bygone age, but now with the 20th century comforts expected. Nine cottages add further character to the accommodation and are especially liked by those guests seeking even more peace. Even small conferences or functions can be accommodated without detracting from this gentle peacefulness – they are housed in a former stable block. Certainly the memory most visitors take away is of beautifully maintained gardens set in 200 acres of parkland and which provide many lovely cut flowers for the house and, more particularly, herbs for the kitchen from the rare knot garden where box hedges have protected delicate plants since the 17th century.*
19⇨♪↑Annexe9⇨♪↑(3fb)1⊞ CTV in all bedrooms ® **T**
S10% sB⇨♪↑frf85 dB⇨♪↑frf135 (room only) 🖻

( 70P 1🏌️ 🚗 ✿ ♪ (hard) croquet nc8yrs *xmas*
V ఈ ☑ S10%
Credit Cards ① ② ③ ⑤

★★★73%, **Empire** Church Walks LL30 2HE ☎(0492)860555
Telex no 617161 FAX (0492) 860791
Closed 23 Dec-2 Jan
*A warm, comfortable hotel, personally managed to a high standard by the resident owners and their families, offers an extensive range of facilities which includes indoor and outdoor pools, sauna and solarium; bedrooms contain antiques complemented by every modern amenity (including satellite TV), lounges are designed for comfort, and good food is served in the delightful restaurant.*
56⇲Annexe8⇲(7fb) CTV in all bedrooms ® T S%
sB&B⇲£40-£55 dB&B⇲£65-£90 ⊟
Lift 35P 5🏌️ (£5 per night) 🚗 CFA ▣(heated) ⏃(heated) sauna solarium ♫
♿ French V ఈ ☑ S% Lunch £5.25-£12.50 Dinner £14.95 Last dinner 9.30pm
Credit Cards ① ② ③ ④ ⑤

★★★64%, **Gogarth Abbey** West Shore LL30 2QY ☎(0492)76211
*This large, attractive house was built in 1862 as the summer residence of the Reverend Henry George Liddel, whose daughter, Alice, was the inspiration of Charles L Dodgeson (Lewis Carroll) when he wrote 'Alice in Wonderland' and 'Alice Through the Looking Glass'. The hotel is quietly situated on the town's west shore, and enjoys splendid views across the Conwy Estuary of Snowdonia and Anglesey. The public areas are quiet and relaxing, and the bedrooms are well equipped. Additional facilities include an indoor heated swimming pool, a solarium and a sauna. The hotel also benefits from having ample car parking space.*
40⇲♟️(4fb) CTV in all bedrooms ® T ✖ (ex guide dogs)
sB&B⇲♟️£30-£38 dB&B⇲♟️£60-£76 ⊟
( 40P ✿ ▣(heated) sauna solarium table tennis *xmas*
♿ English & French V ఈ ☑ ✂ Lunch frf8.50 High tea frf4.50
Dinner frf17 Last dinner 8.45pm
Credit Cards ① ② ③ ⑤ ⓔ

★★★64%, **Imperial** The Promenade LL30 1AP (Best Western)
☎(0492)77466 Telex no 61606 FAX (0492) 78043
*This large hotel on Llandudno's promenade offers many attractions for visitors, being convenient for access to the pier, the shopping centre and other amenities of this popular resort. Bedrooms are all well equipped, and the spacious public areas give guests a choice of bars and a large, attractive restaurant. There are good leisure facilities, including a beauty therapist and hairdressing salon.*
100⇲♟️(10fb) CTV in all bedrooms ® T sB&B⇲♟️£45-£65
dB&B⇲♟️£75-£85 ⊟
Lift ( 40P CFA ▣(heated) snooker sauna solarium gymnasium steam room beauty therapist hairdressing *xmas*
V ఈ ☑ Lunch £9.50-£12.50 Dinner £15.50-£19.50&alc Last dinner 9pm
Credit Cards ① ② ③ ⑤

See advertisement on page 407

★★★61%, **Chatsworth House** Central Promenade LL30 2XS
☎(0492)860788
Closed 28 Dec-12 Jan
*A large hotel conveniently situated on the central promenade provides well-equipped accommodation, spacious public areas, a pleasant Victorian-style coffee shop, conference facilities and a leisure centre with heated indoor swimming pool, sauna and games room.*
58⇲♟️(13fb)1🛏 CTV in all bedrooms ® T
Lift ( 9P ▣(heated) sauna solarium jacuzzi ♫
V ఈ ☑ ✂ Last dinner 8.30pm
Credit Cards ① ③ ⓔ

See advertisement on page 407

---

---

L

## Llandudno

★★★61% **Risboro** Clement Av LL30 2ED (Inter-Hotels)
☎(0492)76343 Telex no 617117 FAX (0492) 879881
*Family-owned and run hotel, in a residential area, with a pleasant atmosphere an d friendly staff.*
65⇌♠(7fb)1🛏 CTV in all bedrooms ® T sB&B⇌♠£30-£40 dB&B⇌♠£60-£85 🅿
Lift ( 40P CFA 🖵(heated) U snooker sauna solarium gymnasium ♫ *xmas*
♡ English & French V ♦ ⚆ Lunch £7.50 Dinner £15 Last dinner 8.45pm
Credit Cards [1][2][3][5] (£)

See advertisement on page 409

❋★★ ST TUDNO

Promenade LL30 2LP
☎(0492)874411
Telex no 61400
FAX (0492) 860407

Closed 28 Dec-10 Jan

*This is an hotel that fully deserves to be described as a colourful and a delightful place to stay. Not only are all the rooms decorated and furnished with a view to combining comfort with elegance and style, but the welcome from owners and staff is memorable. Janette Bland has an outgoing personality that few would fail to respond to, and takes great pains to ensure that guests are happy. Martin Bland and Head Chef, David Harding, presides over the cooking, which is of a very high standard, selecting the best local produce for the à la carte and daily set menus, and the wine list is equally well chosen. The hotel has the added advantage of occupying a prime position overlooking the promenade, beach and the bay.*
21⇌♠(4fb)1🛏 CTV in all bedrooms ® T ✻ (ex guide dogs) ✳ sB&B⇌♠£45-£65 dB&B⇌♠£64-£108 🅿
Lift 4P 2🚗 (£4) ⏦ 🖵(heated) *xmas*
V ♦ ⚆ ⅙ Lunch £9.95-£11.50&alc High tea £5-£12.50alc Dinner £20.95&alc Last dinner 9.30pm
Credit Cards [1][2][3] (£)

★★72% **Dunoon** Gloddaeth St LL30 2DW ☎(0492)860787
FAX (0492) 860031
Closed Nov-mid Mar
*A combination of friendly, attentive service, well equipped bedrooms and attractive public areas account for the well deserved popularity of this privately owned hotel. Close to the town centre, with access to the seafront and other amenities.*
56⇌♠Annexe14⇌(22fb) CTV in all bedrooms ® T ✻ (ex guide dogs) S% sB&B⇌♠£23-£29 dB&B⇌♠£42-£58
Lift CTV 24P solarium
V ♦ ⚆ S% Lunch £6.50-£7.50 Dinner £9-£12 Last dinner 8pm
Credit Cards [1][3]

★★69% **Rose Tor** 124 Mostyn St LL30 2SW ☎(0492)870433
*This very pleasant and well-maintained hotel is well situated for both the town centre and seafront. Family-run, it provides well-equipped bedrooms which are equally suitable for holidaymakers and business guests.*
17⇌♠(2fb) CTV in all bedrooms ® T dB&B⇌♠£31-£35 🅿 ♪ *xmas*
V ♦ ⅙ Lunch fr£6.75 Dinner fr£6.75&alc Last dinner 9.30pm
Credit Cards [1][2][3]

★★69% **Tan-Lan** Great Orme's Rd, West Shore LL30 2AR
☎(0492)860221
Closed Nov-17 Mar
*This elegant family-run hotel provides comfortable bedrooms and warm hospitality .*
18⇌♠(4fb) CTV in all bedrooms ®
15P ⏦
♡ English, French & Italian ♦ ⚆ Lunch £6.50&alc Dinner £10&alc Last dinner 8pm
Credit Cards [1][3]

See advertisement on page 408

★★68% **Belle Vue** 26 North Pde LL30 2LP ☎(0492)879547
Closed Dec-Feb RS Nov & Mar
*A friendly, family-run holiday hotel in an elevated position with lovely sea and promenade views. Accommodation is comfortable and well equipped and the food enjoyable.*
17⇌♠(2fb) CTV in all bedrooms ® T sB&B⇌♠£22-£24 dB&B⇌♠£44-£52
Lift 12P ⏦ table tennis
♡ French & Italian ♦ Bar Lunch £3.50-£5 Dinner £8&alc Last dinner 8pm
Credit Cards [1][3][5] (£)

See advertisement on page 408

★★67% **Merrion** South Pde LL30 2LN ☎(0492)860022
FAX (0492) 860378
Closed Feb
*A well furnished and comfortable hotel occupying a prime position on the Promenade. Family owned and run, it offers good bedrooms, relaxing lounges and well prepared food from an imaginative menu.*
67⇌♠(7fb) CTV in all bedrooms ® T

▶

L

Lift ℂ CTV 16P 25🚗 ♫
♀ English & French **V** ♿ ⅏ Last dinner 8.30pm
Credit Cards ①②③

See advertisement on page 411

★★67% **Sandringham** West Pde LL30 2BD ☎(0492)76513 & 76447
Closed Nov-Feb
*Excellent views of the Conwy Estuary can be enjoyed from this well maintained hotel on its west shore. All the bedrooms are well furnished and all have en suite facilities.*
18⇋✿(4fb) CTV in all bedrooms ® **T** ✖ sB&B⇋✿£20-£23 dB&B⇋✿£40-£46 ◲
6P games room
**V** ♿ ✗ Lunch £6.50-£7.50 Dinner £9 Last dinner 7.30pm
Credit Cards ①③

★★66% **Plas Fron Deg** 48 Church Walks LL30 2HL
☎(0492)77267 & 860226
Closed Nov-Jan
*Set in a quiet side road within easy reach of both seafront and shopping area, and fronted by a large terraced garden, this beautifully preserved and maintained Victorian house retains such original features as exquisitely carved fireplaces and some magnificent stained glass windows. Bedrooms are comfortable and well equipped, and friendly proprietors provide informal but attentive service.*
9⇋✿(1fb) CTV in all bedrooms ® **T** ✖ (ex guide dogs)
sB&B⇋✿£33.35-£37.50
dB&B⇋✿£66.70-£75 (incl dinner) ◲
7P 🚗 nc11yrs
**V** ✗
Credit Cards ①③⑤ⓔ

★★65% **Bryn-y-Bia Lodge** Craigside LL30 3AS
☎(0492)49644 & 40459
*A delightful detached house set in its own grounds on the Coastal Road, near the Little Orme, features well-equipped modern bedrooms and elegantly furnished public areas. Good food, ably prepared by the resident owner and served in an attractive dining room, high standards of hospitality and quality accommodation combine to make this hotel something a little special.*
13⇋✿(2fb)1⌷ CTV in all bedrooms ® **T** ✱
sB&B⇋✿£23.50-£32.50 dB&B⇋✿£45-£52 ◲
20P 🚗 ❀
♀ English & Continental **V** ♿ ✗ Bar Lunch £3-£7alc Dinner £16&alc Last dinner 8.30pm
Credit Cards ①②③ⓔ

★★64% **Bromwell Court** Promenade LL30 1BG
☎(0492)78416 & 874142
*This small and friendly family-run hotel is situated on the Promenade to the east of the town centre. It is very well maintained throughout and the bedrooms are well equipped.*
11rm(3⇋6✿)(2fb) CTV in all bedrooms ® **T**
✖ (ex guide dogs) sB&B⇋✿fr£23 dB&B⇋✿fr£42 ◲
✗ 🚗
**V** ♿ ⅏ Dinner fr£9 Last dinner 7.30pm
Credit Cards ①③ⓔ

★★64% **Sefton Court** Church Walks LL30 2HL ☎(0492)75262
*This delightful hotel stands between the main part of the town and the West Shore, set in its own well-kept gardens under the lea of the Great Orme.*
14rm(10⇋1✿)(6fb)✗in 1 bedroom CTV in all bedrooms ®
CTV 13P
♀ Welsh, English & French **V** ♿ ⅏ ✗ Last dinner 8pm
Credit Cards ①③

See advertisement on page 411

## Llandudno

★★63% **Bedford** Promenade LL30 1BN ☎(0492)76647
*Gigolos' Italian Restaurant and Pizzeria is a feature of this very*
*well furnished and comfortable hotel on the Promenade.*
27⇨(2fb) CTV in all bedrooms ® T
Lift ℂ CTV 20P
♥ English, French & Italian V ♥ ⏛
Credit Cards 1 3

★★62% *Headlands* Hill Ter LL30 2LS (Exec Hotel)
☎(0492)77485
Closed Jan-Feb
*Overlooking the bay from a commanding position, this well*
*furnished and comfortable family-run hotel offers bedrooms with*
*good facilities, two comfortable lounges and a pleasant restaurant*
*with panoramic sea views.*
17rm(12⇨3♠)(4fb)3♛ CTV in all bedrooms ® T
CTV 7P ⏃
♥ ⌿ Last dinner 8.30pm
Credit Cards 1 3 5

★★61% **Castle** Vaughan St LL30 1AG ☎(0492)77694 & 76868
Closed Jan
*An hotel formerly known as the North Western stands at the heart*
*of the town, with busy roads running all round it. Friendly staff are*
*directed by caring proprietors who are eager to ensure that your*
*stay here is an enjoyable one.*
56rm(51⇨3♠)(19fb) CTV in all bedrooms ® ✱ sB&B£18-£20
sB&B⇨♠£20-£22 dB&B⇨♠£36-£40
Lift ℂ (30P 7🚗 (£10 per wk) games room ♫ *xmas*
V ♥ ⏛ ⌿ Lunch £6.50 Dinner £8.50&alc Last dinner 7.30pm
Credit Cards 3 ⓔ

★★60% **Ormescliffe** Promenade LL30 1BE ☎(0492)77191
FAX (0492) 860311
*A family-style hotel on the seafront with views of the bay and the*
*Little and Great Ormes. There is a comfortable lounge and*
*entertainment is provided during the summer season.*
60⇨♠(11fb) CTV in all bedrooms ® ✈ (ex guide dogs) ✱
sB&B⇨♠£20-£23 dB&B⇨♠£40-£46
Lift ℂ CTV 12P pool table tennis ⚽ *xmas*
♥ International ♥ ⏛ Bar Lunch £2-£6 Dinner £9.50 Last
dinner 8pm
Credit Cards 1 3

★★60% **Somerset** St Georges Crescent, Promenade LL30 2LF
☎(0492)76540
Closed Nov-Feb
*Family-run, Victorian seafront hotel with good views of the bay.*
37⇨♠(4fb) CTV in all bedrooms ®
Lift 20P
V ♥ ⌿ Last dinner 8pm
Credit Cards 1 3

★★59% **Esplanade** Glan-y-Mor Pde, Promenade LL30 2LL
☎(0492)860300 Telex no 61155 FAX (0492) 860418
*A large hotel on the promenade and overlooking the pier. The*
*simple but well-equipped bedrooms are popular with*
*holidaymakers and commercial visitors alike. Coach parties are*
*catered for.*
57⇨♠(16fb) CTV in all bedrooms ® T sB&B⇨♠£30-£35
dB&B⇨♠£60-£70 🅱
Lift ℂ CTV 30P games room *xmas*
♥ English & French ♥ ⏛ Sunday Lunch £6.95 High tea
£2.50-£10alc Dinner £10.50-£17.50 Last dinner 8.30pm
Credit Cards 1 2 3 5 ⓔ

★★59% **Royal** Church Walks LL30 2HW ☎(0492)76476
*Close to the sea, yet standing in a quiet side road, this large, well*
*furnished and family run hotel offers value-for-money*
*accommodation in recently upgraded bedrooms.*
38rm(15⇨13♠)(11fb) CTV in all bedrooms ® T
✈ (ex guide dogs) sB&B£19.50 sB&B⇨♠£22 dB&B£56
dB&B⇨♠£61-£70 🅱

▶

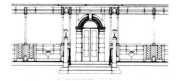

L

# Llandudno

Lift 30P ✿ dry ski slope putting green ♫ *xmas*
V ✿ ⚅ Bar Lunch fr£1alc Dinner fr£11.50 Last dinner 8pm
Credit Cards ⊞ ③

**★★58% *Four Oaks*** Promenade LL30 1AY ☎(0492)76506
RS Nov-Feb
*This large, privately owned hotel is situated on the promenade, within easy reach of the town centre. Many of its bedrooms enjoy sea views, and it is particularly popular with coach tour parties.*
57rm(19⇆8🅵)(25fb) CTV in all bedrooms Ⓡ
Lift 《 CTV 🎾 ♫ ♨
V ✿ ⚅ Last dinner 7.30pm

**★★55% Lynwood** Clonmel St LL30 2LE ☎(0492)76613
*Just a stone's throw away from the main promenade and the town centre, this cosy and friendly family-run hotel has recently been improved, and now provides well equipped bedrooms. There is a small bar and a large basement restaurant.*
26rm(16⇆4🅵)(3fb)1🛏 CTV in all bedrooms Ⓡ T
🅼 (ex guide dogs) ✱ sB&B£19-£22 sB&B⇆🅵£22-£25
dB&B£32-£38 dB&B⇆🅵£38-£44
games room *xmas*
✿ ⚅ ✂ Lunch £1.95-£3.50 Dinner fr£6 Last dinner 7.30pm
Credit Cards ⊞ ③

**★68% *Banham House*** 2 St Davids Rd LL30 2UL ☎(0492)75680
*This small, bright hotel is run by the very friendly Sharpe family, and is situated in a quiet residential area, yet not too far away from the sea and shopping centre. There is a small, comfortable lounge, and modern bedrooms.*
8rm(2⇆4🅵)(2fb) CTV in all bedrooms Ⓡ 🅼 ✱ sB&Bfr£14
sB&B⇆🅵fr£16 dB&Bfr£28 dB&B⇆🅵fr£32
CTV 🎾 ♨ *xmas*
✿ ✂ Lunch fr£3.50 Dinner fr£4.75 Last dinner 7.30pm

**★68% *Clontarf*** 1 Great Ormes Rd, West Shore LL30 2AR
☎(0492)77621
Closed 30 Dec-Feb
*A small, select hotel, situated in the quieter part of the town and only a short distance from the West Shore, is managed by friendly proprietors who offer warm, clean and well-maintained accommodation.*
10rm(1⇆3🅵)(2fb) Ⓡ 🅼
CTV 10P ♨ ✿ nc3yrs
V ✿ ⚅ ✂ Last dinner 7.30pm

**★66% Gwesty Leamore** 40 Lloyd St LL30 2YG ☎(0492)75552
Closed Xmas
*A pleasant well-maintained family-run hotel, conveniently situated for the town centre, beaches and theatres. Accommodation is modest but well equipped, and the proprietors are friendly and hospitable.*
12rm(1⇆6🅵)(4fb) CTV in all bedrooms Ⓡ 🅼 S%
sB&B£14-£16.50 sB&B⇆🅵£16.50-£18.50 dB&B£26-£30
dB&B⇆🅵£30-£34 🍴
CTV 4P ♨
V ✂ Bar Lunch £2-£4 Dinner £7-£8 Last dinner 7.30pm

**★66% Ravenhurst** West Pde LL30 2BB ☎(0492)75525
Closed Dec-Jan
*A pleasant, privately owned and run hotel on the town's West Shore with well-kept accommodation with good facilities. The hotel has two traditional lounges and a games room.*
23⇆🅵Annexe1⇆(4fb) CTV in all bedrooms Ⓡ
sB&B⇆🅵£30-£31 dB&B⇆🅵£60-£62 (incl dinner) 🍴
15P table tennis pool table ♫
V ✿ ⚅ Lunch £6 Dinner £8 Last dinner 7pm
Credit Cards ⊞ ③ ⑤ ④

---

1991 marks the 25th anniversary of this guide.

---

**★65% Sunnymede** West Pde LL30 2BD ☎(0492)77130
Closed mid Nov-Feb
*This pleasant, well furnished and personally run hotel is situated on the West Shore, and enjoys good views of the Conwy Estuary and beyond. The bedrooms are comfortable and well equipped, and many have en suite facilities.*
18rm(14⇆3🅵)(3fb)2🛏 CTV in all bedrooms Ⓡ
dB&B⇆🅵£50-£64 (incl dinner) 🍴
18P
✿ ⚅
Credit Cards ⊞ ③ ④

**★64% Crickleigh** Lloyd St LL30 2YG ☎(0492)75926
*Centrally located for both beach and shopping, this friendly, family-run hotel has a small rose garden at the front and a car park at the rear.*
15rm(7🅵)(4fb) Ⓡ 🅼 (ex guide dogs) ✱ sB&B£15.40-£22.80
dB&B£30.80-£45.60 dB&B⇆🅵£35.80-£50.60 (incl dinner) 🍴
CTV 12P *xmas*
♔ International V ✿ ⚅ Lunch £7.40 Dinner £7.40 Last dinner 7pm
Credit Cards ⊞ ③ ④

**★63% Quinton** 36 Church Walks LL30 2HN ☎(0492)76879 & 75086
Closed Nov-Jan (ex Xmas)
*Homely, personally-run hotel situated NW of the town centre between the two beaches. Popular with golfing parties.*
15rm(4⇆5🅵)(8fb) CTV in all bedrooms Ⓡ S% sB&Bfr£15
sB&B⇆🅵fr£17 dB&Bfr£30 dB&B⇆🅵fr£34 🍴
12P *xmas*
✿ ⚅
Credit Cards ⊞ ④

**★62% *Bransome*** Lloyd St LL30 2YP ☎(0492)75989
Closed Jan-Mar
*A friendly atmosphere, caring owners who are continually improving facilities and a good position, just a few minutes level walk from both shops and Promenade ensure that many guests return to this hotel.*
48rm(7⇆10🅵)Annexe5rm(10fb)
CTV 12P sauna solarium gymnasium ♫
♔ English, French & Italian V ✿ ⚅

**★62% Oak Alyn** Deganwy Av LL30 2YB ☎(0492)860320
Closed Dec-Jan RS early-mid Feb
*This very friendly small hotel, well furnished in all areas, represents particularly good value for money.*
14⇆🅵(2fb) CTV in all bedrooms Ⓡ ✱ S%
sB&B⇆🅵£13.50-£15.50
dB&B⇆🅵£27-£31 Continental breakfast 🍴
CTV 16P
♔ British & Continental ✿ ✂ Bar Lunch £1.50-£3 Dinner £7-£8.50 Last dinner 7.30pm
Credit Cards ⊞ ③

**★61% Bron Orme** 54 Church Walks LL30 2HL ☎(0492)76735
Closed Nov-Feb
*A pleasant small family-run hotel offering excellent value and good home cooking. Set in its own grounds and sheltered by the Great Orme, it is located close to all the town's attractions.*
9rm(4🅵)(2fb) Ⓡ 🅼 (ex guide dogs) ✱ sB&B£11.50-£14
sB&B🅵£14 dB&B£21 dB&B🅵£26
CTV 🎾 ♨ nc5yrs
♔ English & French ✿ ⚅ ✂ Lunch £3-£6 High tea £2.50-£5 Dinner £7-£10.50 Last dinner 7pm

**★61% Hilbre Court** Great Ormes Rd, West Shore LL30 2AR
☎(0492)76632
Closed Nov-Feb (ex Xmas)
*Situated in a quiet side road on the West Shore, this family-run hotel offers friendly service and good home comforts.*
10rm(3⇆3🅵)(1fb)✂in 2 bedrooms CTV in all bedrooms Ⓡ 🍴

CTV 6P ⊕ xmas
V ✤ ☭ ⚥ Lunch £5-£6alc High tea £3.50-£4 Dinner
£6.50-£7.50 Last dinner 8pm
Credit Cards 1 2 3 £

★59% **Min-y-Don** North Pde LL30 2LP ☎(0492)76511
Closed Nov-Jan
*A traditional resort hotel situated on the Promenade with simply furnished, warm rooms and friendly proprietors.*
28rm(2⇋17↟)(12fb) CTV in all bedrooms ® ✖
sB&B£15.80-£18.70 sB&B⇋↟£18.70 dB&B£31.60-£37.40
dB&B⇋↟£37.40 ☐
⊞ CTV 5P xmas
V ✤ ☭ ⚥ Lunch fr£4 Dinner fr£6 Last dinner 7.30pm
Credit Cards 1 3 £

✖✖✖**La Mouette** Merrion Hotel, Promenade LL30 2LN
☎(0492)860022 FAX (0492) 860378
*One of our 'Best New Restaurants' this year – see the colour feature on page 36. Situated at the pier end of the Promenade, this French restaurant provides a high standard of cooking, prepared by chef Gareth Bream, who pays fine attention to detail. The atmosphere is intimate, with soft lighting and décor and good quality furnishings. Service is provided by skilled and attentive French waiters.*
Closed Mon 1-14 Feb & 10-24 Aug
Lunch not served ex by prior arrangement
♈ French V 32 seats ✱ Lunch £18.50&alc Dinner £18.50&alc
Last dinner 10pm 8P nc10yrs ♫
Credit Cards 1 2 3

✖✖**Floral** Victoria St, Craig-y-Don LL30 1LJ ☎(0492)75735
*A friendly, well-furnished restaurant standing in a side street just off the Promenade offers a wide choice of dishes, all well prepared from fresh ingredients, including such specialities as Chicken Buckingham (breast of chicken in a cream and prune sauce). An extensive wine list carries a full description of each item, staff are particularly helpful and attractive décor enhances the pleasant atmosphere.*
Closed Mon
Lunch not served Sat
Dinner not served Sun
♈ Welsh & French V 60 seats Lunch £6.95 Dinner £10.95&alc
Last lunch 1.30pm Last dinner 9.30pm ✗ nc10yrs ⚥
Credit Cards 1 3

✖✖**Lanterns** 7 Church Walks LL30 2HD ☎(0492)77924
*A well-furnished, comfortable restaurant just off the Promenade, in the heart of the town, specialises in fresh, locally caught fish, though meat dishes are also available. In addition to the richly appointed restaurant there is a basement bistro offering a blackboard menu; service is professional but friendly and a good wine list is available.*
Closed Sun, 25-30 Dec & mid Feb-mid Mar
Lunch not served
♈ English & French V 24 seats Dinner £17.50 Last dinner
9.30pm ✗ nc10yrs
Credit Cards 1 2 3 5

---

**LLANELLI** Dyfed Map **02** SN50

★★★59% **Diplomat** Felinfoel SA15 3PJ (Best Western)
☎(0554)756156 FAX (0554) 751649
*This popular and busy hotel in a quiet, residential part of town has modern bedrooms, a leisure centre, coffee shop and conference/function facilities.*
31⇋Annexe8rm(2fb) CTV in 23 bedrooms ®
Lift 300P ✿ ▣(heated) sauna solarium gymnasium turkish
bath ♫
♈ English & French V ✤ ☭ Last dinner 9.45pm
Credit Cards 1 2 3 5 £
**See advertisement on page 415**

---

★

# Crickleigh Hotel

37/39 Lloyd Street, Llandudno, Gwynedd LL30 2YG
Telephone: (0492) 75926

Open all year and Christmas. Mid week book-
ings accepted. Several single rooms on first floor.
Packed lunches on request. Tea & coffee mak-
ing facilities. School & ski parties welcome.
Vegetarians & weightwatchers catered for.
Separate tables in dining room. Central heating.
Ample car parking. En suite.

For colour brochure write or phone
George & Carol Clark.

WTB ♨ ♨ ♨          VISA

L

# Royal Hotel ★★
# Church Walk,
# Llandudno LL30 2HW
# Telephone: 0492 76476

The Royal is Llandudno's oldest hotel
which has been tastefully extended
and modernised. Situated in its own
secluded gardens, close to both beach
and town centre.

The five course table d'hôte dinner
menu is changed daily with a comprehensive choice of dishes. Varied
entertainment is provided most of the
year.

*Special terms for short breaks
and Golf Holidays*

**★★★56% Stradey Park** Furnace SA15 4HA (Trusthouse Forte)
☎(0554)758171 Telex no 48521
*This is a large, well run hotel in an elevated position with fine views over the bay. Public areas have recently been upgraded, and similar work is due to start on the bedrooms.*
80⇗(3fb)⊬in 8 bedrooms CTV in all bedrooms ® ✳ S8%
sB&B⇗£50-£55 dB&B⇗£55-£60 ☒
Lift ⟨ 120P CFA *xmas*
♀ International V ♡ ⏠ ⊬ S% Lunch £8.50-£10.75&alc Dinner £10.75-£11.95&alc Last dinner 9.30pm
Credit Cards ①②③④⑤

### LLANFAIR PWLLGWYNGYLL Gwynedd Map 06 SH57

**★★★63% Carreg Bran Country** Church Ln LL61 5YH
☎Llanfairpwll(0248)714224 Telex no 61464
FAX (0248) 715983
*This former country house, considerably extended in recent times, provides modern well-equipped accommodation and pleasant public areas. It is situated close to the Anglesey end of the Britannia Bridge and is convenient for the A5.*
29⇗🏠Annexe4⇗🏠(4fb) CTV in all bedrooms ® T ✳
sB&B⇗🏠£42 dB&B⇗🏠£62.50 ☒
⟨ 150P ✿
♀ Welsh & French V ♡ ⏠ Lunch £7.95 Dinner £13.75 Last dinner 10pm
Credit Cards ①②③⑤ ⓔ

### LLANFYLLIN Powys Map 06 SJ11

**★★★⚑72% Bodfach Hall** SY22 5HS ☎(069184)272
Closed 17 Nov-24 Dec & Jan-1 Mar
*Set back from the main road just north of the town, an elegant 17th-century country house with ornate ceilings and wood-panelled walls nestles amid trees and lawns. Bedrooms and public areas are comfortable and well-equipped, food is good, and the hotel is personally run by its friendly owners.*
9⇗🏠(2fb) CTV in all bedrooms ® sB&B⇗🏠fr£27.50
dB&B⇗🏠fr£55 ☒
20P ✿ ✧ ♪ *xmas*
V ♡ Sunday Lunch fr£8.75 Dinner fr£13.50&alc Last dinner 8.45pm
Credit Cards ①②③⑤

### LLANGAMMARCH WELLS Powys Map 03 SN94

**❀★★★⚑76% Lake** LD4 4BS (WR) ☎(05912)202 & 474
FAX (05912) 457
*Popular with fishermen and birdwatchers, this elegant and hospitable Victorian house stands in 50 acres of beautiful grounds. Tennis, pitch-and-putt, horseriding, billiards and clay pigeon shooting are available as well as fishing. Individually styled bedrooms combine character with comfort, and the innovative cooking uses local produce. Smoked duck and chicken in filo pastry with a wild bramble sauce, and a selection of seafoods in a lemon butter sauce, have been recommended by our inspectors.*
19⇗(1fb)3☷⊬in 6 bedrooms CTV in all bedrooms T ✳
sB&B⇗£65 dB&B⇗£80-£95 ☒
⟨ 70P 2🚗 🚲 ✿ ♬ (hard) ♪ snooker clay pigeon shooting
*xmas*
♀ English & French ♡ ⏠ ⊬ Sunday Lunch £10.50 Dinner £19.50 Last dinner 8.45pm
Credit Cards ①②③ⓔ

All hotels are now given a percentage grading
for the quality of their facilities. A full explanation
can be found within 'How we Classify Hotels
and Restaurants' at the front of the book.

### LLANGEFNI Gwynedd Map 06 SH47

**★★★⚑77% Tre-Ysgawen Hall** Capel Coch LL77 7UR
☎(0248)750750 FAX (0248) 750035
*This large stone-built late Victorian mansion in spacious grounds some four miles north of Llangefni, opened last year after extensive restoration work. The result is a fine, elegant country house hotel with spacious relaxing public areas including a delightful restaurant which makes the perfect setting in which to enjoy the excellent and imaginative cuisine of chef Raymond Duthie. The bedrooms are all beautifully arranged, many with four-poster beds, and all have cleverly chosen colour schemes to set off the fine pieces of furniture. Bathrooms are luxurious, especially those with jacuzzi baths. The owners Mr and Mrs Craighead have put heart and soul into making this a really distinguished hotel in the grand manner, but because their own style is so friendly, and they have gathered around them such an enthusiastic and well managed team of staff, Tre-Ysgawen has a lovely atmosphere and is a wonderful place to relax in. We are delighted to welcome them to the guide, and to make them the National Winners of the AA Best Newcomer Award for 1990 to 1991.*
19⇗🏠(5fb)3☷ CTV in all bedrooms T ✖ (ex guide dogs)
sB⇗🏠£71.50 dB⇗🏠£93.50-£140 (room only) ☒
⟨ 110P ✿ ▱ clay pigeon shooting ♧ *xmas*
♀ French V ♡ ⏠ Lunch £8.50-£12.50 Dinner £15.95-£21&alc Last dinner 9.30pm
Credit Cards ①②③

**★★62% Nant-yr-Odyn** Llanfawr LL77 7YE (S of junction A5/A5114) ☎(0248)723354
*Formerly a block of old stonebuilt farm buildings cleverly converted into a small hotel, with well equipped bedrooms. Family run, in an informal manner, it is quietly situated 1·5 miles south of Llangefni and within easy reach of the A5.*
14⇗🏠 CTV in all bedrooms ® T ✖
30P 🚲
♡ ⏠
Credit Cards ①③

### LLANGOLLEN Clwyd Map 07 SJ24

**★★★⚑65% Bryn Howel** LL20 7UW (2.75m E on A539)
☎(0978)860331 FAX (0978) 860119
Closed 25 Dec
*This Tudor-style hotel with modern extensions is situated down a quiet country lane on the outskirts of Llangollen. The large restaurant which has panoramic views of the Dee Valley is renowned for its quality meals created from the freshest of ingredients, often locally produced. Visitors to Bryn Howel can also explore the 6-acre grounds and take advantage of the game fishing facilities. This hotel is also popular for all types of conferences and functions.*
38⇗🏠 CTV in all bedrooms ® T
Lift CTV 200P ✿ CFA ♪ sauna solarium
V ♡ ⏠ Last dinner 9.30pm
Credit Cards ①②③

**★★★56% The Royal** Bridge St LL20 8PG (Trusthouse Forte)
☎(0978)860202 FAX (0978) 861824
*Three-storey stone hotel, situated in the centre of town on the bank of the River Dee.*
33⇗(3fb)⊬in 6 bedrooms CTV in all bedrooms ®
20P ♪
V ♡ ⏠ ⊬ Last dinner 9.30pm
Credit Cards ①②③④⑤

**★★64% Ty'n-y-Wern** Shrewsbury Rd LL20 7PH (1m E on A5)
(Exec Hotel) ☎(0978)860252
*A small, friendly hotel which stands beside the A5 on the outskirts of the town features a restaurant with interesting views over the Vale of Llangollen; guests can choose from an extensive range of dishes supplemented by the chef's daily "specials".*
12⇗🏠⊬in 2 bedrooms CTV in all bedrooms ® T

CTV 80P ❊ ♪ ♫
♀ English & French **V** ✿ ⚲ Last dinner 9.30pm
Credit Cards ①③

See advertisement on page 417

---

**LLANGURIG** Powys Map **06** SN98

★★69% **Glansevern Arms** Pant Mawr SY18 6SY (4m W on Aberystwyth Rd) ☎(05515)240
Closed 10 Days at Xmas
*Comfortable modern facilities, good food, and a welcome as warm as its log fires are the hallmarks of this cosy inn, set just above the River Wye on the main A44 road.*
8⇨♪ CTV in all bedrooms ⒽsB&B⇨♪£35-£40
dB&B⇨♪£50-£55 ✠
40P ⇤
✿ Sunday Lunch fr£11 Dinner fr£16 Last dinner 8pm

---

**LLANGYBI** Gwent Map **03** ST39

★★★★67% **Cwrt Bleddyn Hotel & Country Club** NP5 1PG (WR) ☎Tredunnock(0633)49521 FAX (0633) 49220
*Originally a small country manor house set in fine gardens, Cwrt Bleddyn has been extensively but sympathetically extended over the years. A leisure complex is a recent addition.*
29⇨♪Annexe7⇨♪(5fb)3⊞ CTV in all bedrooms Ⓡ T
✗ (ex guide dogs) sB&B⇨♪£62.50-£115
dB&B⇨♪£79.50-£115 ✠
《 CTV 200P ❊ ◪(heated) ♪ (hard) squash snooker sauna
solarium gymnasium croquet boules clay pigeon shooting ♪ ๑
xmas
♀ Welsh & French **V** ✿ ⚲ Lunch £17.95&alc Dinner
£17.95&alc Last dinner 10pm
Credit Cards ①②③⑤

See advertisement under USK

---

## LLANIDLOES Powys Map **06** SN98

★**60%** *Red Lion* Longbridge St SY18 6EE ☎(05512)2270
Closed 25 Dec
*A friendly family-run inn situated in the centre of this small town. Bedrooms are modestly furnished, bright and clean, and very good value food is served in the bars and restaurant. Popular with the locals.*
6rm(1fb) CTV in all bedrooms ®
CTV 10P
V ⚗
Credit Cards ① ② ③

## LLANRWST Gwynedd Map **06** SH76

★★★**63%** *Plas Maenan Country House* Maenan LL26 OYR (3m N) ☎Dolgarrog(049269)232
*Overlooking the beautiful Conwy Valley, this elegant country mansion, located just off the A470, is set in 20 acres of grounds. Bedrooms, although a little dated, are spacious and comfortable, and a good choice of food includes vegetarian specialities.*
15⇌(2fb)1🛏⚔in 3 bedrooms CTV in all bedrooms ® T 🗡
sB&B⇌£30-£38 dB&B⇌£50-£60 🍴
80P ❊ *xmas*
♡ Welsh, English & French V ⚗ ⚗ Lunch £6.95 Dinner £13.50 Last dinner 9pm
Credit Cards ① ③ ⑤ ④

★★★**62%** *Maenan Abbey* Maenan LL26 0UL (Exec Hotel) ☎Dolgarrog(049269)247 & 230
*This impressive Victorian building on the A470, 1.5miles north of the town, stands within pleasant gardens which include a children's play area. The spacious well-equipped bedrooms are equally suitable for holidaymakers and business guests.*
12⇌⋔(2fb) CTV in all bedrooms ®
60P ❊ ⚓ clay pigeon shooting ♫
♡ Welsh, English & French V ⚗ ⚗
Credit Cards ① ② ③ ⑤

★★★**67%** *Meadowsweet* Station Rd LL26 0DS (WR) ☎(0492)640732
*Situated on the A470 just north of the town centre, this small family-run hotel offers imaginative cuisine, complemented by an extensive selection of wines.*
10⋔(3fb) CTV in all bedrooms T sB&B⋔£38-£50 dB&B⋔£56-£80 🍴
10P 🚗
♡ French ⚗ ⚔ Dinner £16.50-£27.50&alc Last dinner 9.30pm
Credit Cards ① ③ ④

★★**61%** *Eagles* LL26 0LG ☎(0492)640454
*Situated close to the town centre, this large, imposing hotel offers modest, but quite well-equipped accommodation. Suitable for business guests and tourists alike.*
12⇌⋔(5fb) CTV in all bedrooms ®
CTV 50P ⚓ sauna solarium gymnasium pool ⚽
♡ Welsh, English & French V ⚗ ⚔ Last dinner 9pm
Credit Cards ① ③ ⑤

## LLANTWIT MAJOR South Glamorgan Map **03** SS96

★★**67%** *West House Country Hotel & Restaurant* West St CF6 9SP ☎(0446)792406 & 793726
*Comfortable and relaxing hotel facilities are now provided by this converted 250-year-old farm house. Bedrooms are well equipped, the bar is warm and cosy and a recently completed Victorian conservatory provides a delightful setting in which to enjoy morning coffee or afternoon tea; meals are consistently good and staff friendly.*
21rm(14⇌3⋔)(1fb)1🛏 CTV in all bedrooms ® T ✱
sB&Bfr£29.50 sB&B⇌⋔fr£37 dB&Bfr£39.50
dB&B⇌⋔fr£47 🍴
《 CTV 60P ⚽ *xmas*

♡ English & French V ⚗ ⚗ ⚔ Lunch £3.15-£6.50 High tea £2.95 Dinner £9.50&alc Last dinner 9.30pm
Credit Cards ① ② ③ ④

✗✗✗*Colhugh Villa* Flanders Rd CF6 9RL ☎(0446)792022
Closed Mon
Lunch not served Tue-Sat
V 75 seats ✱ Sunday Lunch £8.75-£10.75alc Dinner £14-£25alc Last dinner 9.30pm 40P
Credit Cards ① ② ③ ⑤

## LLANWDDYN Powys Map **06** SJ01

★★★🏵**71%** *Lake Vyrnwy* SY10 0LY (WR) ®☎(069173)692 FAX (069173) 259
*Set in 24,000 acres at the foot of the Berwyn Mountains this country house, with its country sports facilities, provides elegant public rooms and well-equipped bedrooms. Food from the carefully selected menu is most enjoyable and the separate Tavern Bar is popular with the locals.*
30⇌⋔(12fb)2🛏 CTV in all bedrooms T ✱ sB&B⇌⋔fr£37.75 dB&B⇌⋔fr£45.50-£95.50 🍴
70P ❊ ⚔ (hard) ⚓ clay & game shooting sailing *xmas*
♡ British & French V ⚗ ⚗ Bar Lunch £1-£5
Credit Cards ① ② ③ ④ ⑤

## LLANWNDA Gwynedd Map **06** SH45

★★★**61%** *Stables* LL54 5SD (Minotels) ☎(0286)830711 & 830935 FAX (0286) 830413
*With the exception of a pleasant suite situated in the original Victorian building, all the other modern well-equipped bedrooms are contained within a purpose-built, single storey, motel-style block.*
Annexe14⇌⋔(2fb)1🛏 CTV in all bedrooms ® T ✱
sB&B⇌⋔£36-£41 dB&B⇌⋔£54-£64 🍴
40P ❊ ⚗
♡ International V ⚗ ⚗ Lunch £6.50 Dinner £8.95-£12.95 Last dinner 9.30pm
Credit Cards ① ② ③

## LLECHRYD Dyfed Map **02** SN24

★★★🏵*Castell Malgwyn* SA43 2QA (0.5m S unclass rd towards Boncath) ☎(023987)382
*An elegant 18th-century mansion set in 40 acres of gardens and woodland. Inside, the hotel's public areas are spacious and comfortable while outside guests can use the heated swimming pool. Salmon and trout fishing in the Teifi is also available.*
22⇌⋔(3fb) CTV in all bedrooms ®
50P ❊ ⚗(heated) ⚓ putting croquet
V ⚗ ⚗ Last dinner 9.30pm
Credit Cards ① ② ③ ⑤

All hotels are now given a percentage grading for the quality of their facilities. A full explanation can be found within 'How we Classify Hotels and Restaurants' at the front of the book.

**LLYSWEN** Powys Map **03** SO13

★★★★♨72% **Llangoed Hall** LD3 0YP ☎Brecon(0874)754525

*This quite splendid house was the first important commission
undertaken by architect Sir Clough Williams Ellis in 1912 and its
original splendours are once again being restored due to a latter-
day Knight's ambition to recreate the atmosphere of an Edwardian
country house in his dream of the perfect hotel. Sir Bernard
Ashley, the present owner, is that Knight, and he has lavished
considerable time and money on his dream, even providing his
superb personal collection of paintings and drawings to hang in the
gallery and public rooms. The house stands just north of the
village, off the A470, and most rooms look out over the lovely
Upper Wye Valley. Bedrooms are mostly spacious and very
comfortable with splendid beds and ample armchairs or settees.
Sitting rooms are also comfortable, whether the Studio, Great Hall
or Library, the latter having a billiard table and which can be
converted for private function use. Chef Mark Salter was a good
choice ; he uses fresh local produce to good effect in the small fixed
price menus and certainly achieves very flavoursome cooking. The
extensive gardens are already providing many herbs and
vegetables and more variety is expected as they become
established.*

23⇨🌂(5fb)9🛏 CTV in all bedrooms **T 🏋** (ex guide dogs) ✳
sB&B⇨🌂£85 dB&B⇨🌂£105-£195 🍴
( 50P 5🍽 ✿ ♪ (hard) croquet *xmas*
**V** ✿ ⏣ ✂ Lunch fr£17.50alc Dinner fr£32.50alc Last dinner
9.30pm
Credit Cards [1] [2] [3] [5]

★★ 62% **Griffin Inn** LD3 0UR ☎(0874)754241
Closed Feb

*Standing alongside the A470 between Builth Wells and Brecon,
this charming inn is well known for its good range of food and
warm welcome. Log fires feature in the character bar and the two
new residents' lounges.*

8rm(5⇨2🌂) ® **T** S% sB&B£25.50-£27 sB&B⇨🌂£25.50-£27
dB&B⇨🌂£48.50-£50 🍴
CTV 14P 📶 ♪
**V** ✿ Lunch £2.50-£10alc Dinner £9-£20alc Last dinner 9pm
Credit Cards [1] [2] [3] [5]

**LOCHBOISDALE**
See **South Uist, Isle of**

**LOCHCARRON** Highland Map **14** NG83

★★ 61% **Lochcarron** IV54 8YS ☎(05202)226
*An hotel beautifully situated on the shores of the loch provides an
ideal base from which to tour the Highlands and coastal area.
Bedrooms, though simply furnished, are clean, comfortable and
well-equipped, while the enjoyable meals served in an attractive
dining room overlooking the loch make a speciality of fresh local
fish.*

11rm(8⇨3🌂)(1fb) CTV in all bedrooms ® sB&Bfr£22.50
sB&B⇨🌂fr£22.50 dB&Bfr£39 dB&B⇨🌂fr£48
30P 📶 boat
**V** ✿ ⏣ Lunch £1.50-£10alc Dinner fr£13.50&alc Last dinner
8.30pm
Credit Cards [1] [3]

**LOCHEARNHEAD** Central *Perthshire* Map **11** NN52

★ 68% **Mansewood Country House** FK19 8NS ☎(05673)213
Closed Dec-Feb

*Set amidst beautiful scenery, this charming little family-run hotel
offers a cosy atmosphere, peaceful relaxation and good home
cooking. Bedrooms are compact, but cheery and comfortable.*

7rm(4⇨1🌂) ® ✳ sB&Bfr£17.75 sB&B⇨🌂fr£21.75
dB&B£35.50 dB&B⇨🌂£41.50

16P 📶 ✿ surfing sailing canoeing water-skiing
✿ ✂ Bar Lunch £2.50 Dinner £10&alc Last dinner 8.30pm
Credit Cards [1] [3] (£)

★ 58% **Lochearnhead** Lochside FK19 8PU ☎(05673)229
Closed mid Nov-Feb

*Homely comforts and a friendly atmosphere are among the
attractions of this small, family-run hotel, pleasantly situated on
the picturesque shore of Loch Earn.*

14rm(1⇨3🌂) CTV in all bedrooms ® sB&B£19.05-£25.50
sB&B⇨🌂£19.05-£25.50 dB&B£30.40-£42.50
dB&B⇨🌂£30.40-£42.50
CTV 80P 📶 ✿ ♪ squash water skiing windsurfing sailing
♡ Scottish & French **V** ✿ ⏣ Bar Lunch £1-£9.20alc Dinner
£14 Last dinner 9pm
Credit Cards [1] [2] [3] [5]

**LOCHGILPHEAD** Strathclyde Map **10** NR88

★★ 67% **The Stag** Argyll St PA31 8NE ☎(0546)2496
*This well-maintained commercial/tourist hotel in the town centre
features an attractive restaurant which maintains a nice balance of
quantity and quality in its enjoyable meals. Bedrooms are fully
equipped and there is a comfortable lounge area.*

17⇨🌂 CTV in all bedrooms ® **T** sB&B⇨🌂fr£27.50
dB&B⇨🌂fr£49.50 🍴
♫ *xmas*
**V** ✿ ⏣ Lunch £5-£10&alc High tea fr£5 Dinner £12.50-£17.50
Last dinner 8.30pm
Credit Cards [1] [3]

**LOCHINVER** Highland *Sutherland* Map **14** NC02

★★★ 76% **Inver Lodge** IV27 4LU (Best Western) ☎(05714)496
Telex no 75206 FAX (05714) 395
Closed 19 Nov-Apr

*This carefully built modern hotel occupies a commanding position
above the village, every room enjoying fine views over Inver Bay
and out to sea. Spacious bedrooms with up-to-date bathrooms are
particularly well appointed, while the delightful first-floor
residents' lounge provides a very comfortable area in which to
relax. The whole hotel is well maintained with a friendly, smart
young staff providing efficient service.*

20⇨🌂(2fb) CTV in all bedrooms ® **T** sB&B⇨🌂£62.30-£88
dB&B⇨🌂£94-£176 🍴
30P 📶 ✿ ♪ snooker sauna solarium
♡ Scottish & French ✿ ⏣ Bar Lunch £8.45-£16.45alc Dinner
£24.50 Last dinner 9pm
Credit Cards [1] [2] [3] [5]

**LOCKERBIE** Dumfries & Galloway *Dumfriesshire*
Map **11** NY18

★★★ 62% *Lockerbie Manor* Boreland Rd DG11 2RG (1m N off
B273) (Consort) ☎(05762)2610 Telex no 57515 ext 17
FAX (05762) 3046

*A range of oriental and traditional English food is available in the
'East Meets West' restaurant of this attractive country house,
which stands in extensive grounds on the northern outskirts of the
town. There is also another restaurant and several comfortable,
attractive lounges. Bedrooms are all well equipped, though they
vary in size and quality. Staff are friendly and the hospitable
proprietors extend a particularly warm welcome to visitors.*

26⇨🌂(2fb)3🛏 CTV in all bedrooms ® **T**
CTV 100P 1🍽 ✿
♡ English & French **V** ✿ ⏣ ✂ Last dinner 9.30pm
Credit Cards [1] [2] [3] [5]

For key to symbols see the inside front cover.

★★74% **Somerton House** Carlisle Rd DG11 2DR
☎(05762)2583 & 2384
*Individually appointed bedrooms, comfortably and tastefully
fitted, are offered by a charming Victorian house which boasts
unusual, ornate wood and plasterwork. Service is relaxed but
courteous, and the restaurant's freshly prepared dishes represent
good value.*
7⊣♪♠(2fb) CTV in all bedrooms ® T ✱ sB&B⊣♠£28-£32
dB&B⊣♠£45-£50
150P ✿
♀ International V ♦ ⅓ Lunch £8.50-£12.25alc Dinner
£9.50-£16alc Last dinner 9.30pm
Credit Cards ① ② ③

★★67% **Queens** Annan Rd DG11 2RB ☎(05762)2415 & 3005
FAX (05762) 3901
*An impressive Victorian house adjacent to the A74 has been
comfortably converted and extended to offer modern bedrooms and
leisure facilities; public areas have, on the whole, retained much of
their original character.*
21⊣♠(2fb) CTV in all bedrooms ® T sB&B⊣♠£35
dB&B⊣♠£55 ᕬ
200P ✿ ▭(heated) snooker sauna solarium gymnasium
putting green
♀ English, French & Italian V ♦ ⊿ ⅓ Lunch fr£6.50 Dinner
fr£11.75&alc Last dinner 9.30pm
Credit Cards ① ③ ⓔ

**See advertisement on page 421**

★★64% **Dryfesdale** DG11 2SF ☎(05762)2427 & 2121
FAX (05762) 4187
*Peacefully situated in its own grounds and yet conveniently close to
the A74, this former manse offers comfortable accommodation and
is personally managed by the resident proprietors. In the attractive
restaurant guests can enjoy not only well-prepared meals but also
fine views of the surrounding countryside.*

▶

# *Mansewood*
COUNTRY HOUSE

**Lochearnhead, Perthshire, Scotland FK19 8NS
Telephone: 05673 213**
*Farm Holiday Guide Award Winner 1986
Recommended Scottish Good Hotels Book*
**GUESTACCOM          AA★          RELAIS ROUTIERS**
Mansewood Country House is a small informal,
friendly hotel, ideally situated for touring some of the
loveliest areas of Scotland. As there is no television,
guests can enjoy an evening of friendly conversation
with each other in the lounge, sun lounge or small
residents' bar. We offer a good standard of food.
Dinner is served between 19.30 and 20.30 hrs and
breakfast from 8.30 until 9.30am. All bedrooms are
double glazed and beds have electric blankets. There
is a log fire in the diningroom and a wood burning
stove in the lounge. The hotel has full central
heating. Rooms with en-suite available. For brochure
please telephone or send a stamp.
**Sue and Jeff Jeffrey look forward to welcoming old
and new friends to their lovely home.**

L

### *Lockerbie Manor* ★★★
COUNTRY HOTEL

**LOCKERBIE, DUMFRIES & GALLOWAY DG11 2RG
TELEPHONE: (05762) 2610        FAX: (05762) 3046**
A delightful country mansion set amidst 78 acres of
woodland with 26 en suite rooms and offering the best
in comfort, hospitality and good food.

An ideal staging post for the traveller, situated ½ mile
from the main A74 London — Glasgow road, 1 mile
north of Lockerbie, 25 miles north of Carlisle.

Non residents welcome in the Restaurant and Bar.

# *Lochcarron Hotel* ★★
*Lochcarron, Ross-shire IV54 8YS      Tel. 05202 226*

Our long established Highland Hotel has
been tastefully modernised and occupies a
spectacular, south facing, lochside
position, in Wester Ross close to the
dramatic "Pass of the Cattle" road to
Applecross — the steepest road in Britain.
We are in a perfect location for touring
the rugged grandeur of the West Coast.
The Hotel has a boat for hire to residents
and Golf is available locally.
You will enjoy your stay with us — that's
a promise.

15🛏🝔(1fb) CTV in all bedrooms ® T sB&B🛏🝔fr£40
dB&B🛏🝔fr£60 🖥
50P 🚗 ✿ ఠ్
♀ English & French V ♔ ◫ Lunch £9&alc Dinner £12.50&alc
Last dinner 9.30pm
Credit Cards [1] [2] [3]

---

★**64% Ravenshill House** 12 Dumfries Rd DG11 2EF
☎(05762)2882
*Set within its own walled garden and managed by resident
proprietors, this small country house provides comfortable
accommodation, good-value menus and friendly, informal service.*
5rm(1🛏3🝔)(1fb)1🏠 CTV in all bedrooms ® ✱ sB&Bfr£20
sB&B🛏🝔fr£22.50 dB&Bfr£32 dB&B🛏🝔fr£38
35P ✿
♀ Scottish, French & Italian V Lunch £4-£7.10alc Dinner
£4.90-£13.75alc Last dinner 9pm
Credit Cards [1] [2] [3]

---

**LOLWORTH** Cambridgeshire Map **05** TL36

⌂**Travelodge** Huntingdon Rd CB3 8DR (5m N Cambridge on
A604) (Trusthouse Forte)
☎Crafts Hill(0954)781335 Central Res (0800)850950
*Standing beside a Little Chef restaurant on the north-bound
carriageway of the A604 5m north of Cambridge, this lodge offers
clean, well-equipped accommodatio which represents good value
for money.*
20🛏🝔(20fb) CTV in all bedrooms ® sB🛏🝔£24
dB🛏🝔£29.50 (room only)
《 50P 🚗
Credit Cards [1] [2] [3]

**ANNAN ROAD, LOCKERBIE, DUMFRIESSHIRE**
Telephone: Management (05762) 2415
*Proprietor:* R. G. Matthews

21 en-suite bedrooms, all with direct dial telephone, tea/
coffee making facilities, colour television with free video
channel, radio alarm and hair dryer.

Leisure complex which includes swimming pool, sauna,
jacuzzi, sunbed, fully equipped gym and full sized snooker
table.

Cocktail and lounge bars, restaurant and coffee lounge.

Bar, à la carte and table d'hôte menus.

Conference and banqueting facilities.

**Lockerbie** ★★
**Telephone 05762 2427**

Quietly situated very close to the A74
overlooking Lockerbie with panoramic
views of the surrounding countryside.

A beautifully appointed family run hotel
where comfort and relaxation are the key-
words. 16 bedrooms all but 2 en suite and 6
on the ground floor with full facilities for
disabled persons.

The restaurant has a renowned reputation
and a wide selection of bar meals is also
available.

Open all the year round.

# Alphabetical Index of
# LONDON HOTELS & RESTAURANTS

London

## London Hotels and Restaurants

| | | | |
|---|---|---|---|
| Fuji Japanese (W1) ✘ | 451 | 22 | Plan 2 B3 |
| Le Gavroche (W1) ✿✿✿✘✘✘✘ | 448 | 36 | Plan 3 E5 |
| Gavvers (SW1) ✘✘ | 439 | 37 | Plan 3 E2 |
| Gay Hussar (W1) ✘✘ | 449 | 24 | Plan 2 B4 |
| Ginnan (EC4) ✘ | 435 | 2 | Plan 5 A4 |
| Gloucester (SW7) ★★★ | 442 | 38 | Plan 3 A2 |
| Good Earth (NW7) ✘✘ | 437 | | Plan 1 C5 |
| Good Earth, Brompton Rd (SW3) ✘✘ | 441 | 40 | Plan 3 C3 |
| Goring (SW1) ★★★ | 438 | 8 | Plan 4 A2 |
| Great Nepalese (NW1) ✘ | 436 | | (not on plan) |
| The Greenhouse (W1) ✘✘✘ | 448 | 41 | Plan 3 E5 |
| Grosvenor House (W1) ★★★★★ | 445 | 43 | Plan 3 E5 |
| Halkin (SW1) ○ | 439 | | (not on plan) |
| Happy Wok (WC2) ✘ | 457 | 25 | Plan 2 D4 |
| Harvey's (SW17) ✿✿✘✘ | 443 | | Plan 1 C2 |
| Hilaire (SW7) ✿✘✘ | 442 | 44 | Plan 3 B2 |
| L'Hippocampe (W1) ✘ | 451 | 3 | Plan 2 B4 |
| Holiday Inn-Marble Arch (W1) ★★★★ | 447 | 46 | Plan 3 C6 |
| Holiday Inn-Swiss Cottage (NW3) ★★★★ | 436 | | Plan 1 D4 |
| Hospitality Inn (W2) ★★★ | 452 | 47 | Plan 3 A5 |
| Hyatt Carlton Tower (SW1) ★★★★★ | 438 | 48 | Plan 3 D3 |
| The Hyde Park (SW1) ★★★★★ | 438 | 49 | Plan 3 D4 |
| Inn on the Park (W1) ★★★★★ | 444 | 50 | Plan 3 E4 |
| Inter-Continental (Le Soufflé) (W1) ✿★★★★★ | 445 | 51 | Plan 3 E4 |
| Kalamara's (W2) ✘ | 452 | 53 | Plan 3 A5 |
| Keats (NW3) ✿✘✘ | 436 | | (not on plan) |
| Ken Lo's Memories of China (SW1) ✿✘✘ | 439 | 10 | Plan 4 A1 |
| Ken Lo's Memories of China (SW10) ✘✘ | 443 | | (not on plan) |
| Kensington Close (W8) ★★★ | 453 | | Plan 1 C3 |
| Kensington Palace Thistle (W8) ★★★★ | 453 | 54 | Plan 3 A3 |
| Kensington Place (W8) ✘ | 454 | | Plan 1 C3 |
| Kerzenstuberl (W1) ✘ | 451 | 55 | Plan 3 E6 |
| Koto Japanese (NW1) ✘ | 436 | | Plan 1 D4 |
| Lal Qila (W1) ✘✘ | 450 | 11 | Plan 4 A6 |
| Langan's Brasserie (W1) ✘✘ | 450 | 12 | Plan 4 A3 |
| Lee Ho Fook (W1) ✘ | 451 | 31 | Plan 2 B3 |
| Leith's (W11) ✘✘✘ | 454 | | Plan 1 C3 |
| Hotel Lexham (W8) ★★ | 453 | 56 | Plan 3 A2 |
| Lindsay House (W1) ✘✘ | 450 | 32 | Plan 2 C4 |
| Little Akropolis (W1) ✘ | 451 | | (not on plan) |
| London Embassy (W2) ★★★ | 451 | 58 | Plan 3 A5 |
| London Hilton (W1) ★★★★★ | 445 | 45 | Plan 3 E4 |
| London Hilton Hotel (Trader Vic's) (W1) ✘✘✘ | 448 | 45 | Plan 3 E4 |
| London Kensington Hilton (W11) ★★★ | 454 | | Plan 1 C3 |
| London Marriot (W1) ★★★★ | 446 | 60 | Plan 3 E6 |
| London Ryan (WC1) ★★★ | 455 | | (not on plan) |
| London Tara (W8) ★★★★ | 453 | | Plan 1 C3 |
| Ma Cuisine (SW3) ✘ | 441 | 62 | Plan 3 C2 |
| Magic Dragon (SW3) ✘ | 442 | | (not on plan) |
| Mandeville (W1) ★★★ | 448 | 63 | Plan 3 E6 |
| Mario (SW3) ✘✘ | 441 | 64 | Plan 3 C2 |
| The Marlborough (WC1) ★★★★ | 454 | 33 | Plan 2 C5 |
| Martin's (NW1) ✘✘ | 436 | 65 | Plan 3 D6 |
| Maxim Chinese (W13) ✘ | 454 | | Plan 1 B4 |
| May Fair Inter-Continental (W1) ★★★★★ | 446 | 13 | Plan 4 A4 |
| Le Mazarin (SW1) ✿✘✘ | 439 | | Plan 1 D3 |
| Ménage à Trois (SW3) ✘✘ | 441 | 68 | Plan 3 D3 |
| Le Meridien London (Oak Room) (W1) ✿★★★★★ | 445 | 35 | Plan 2 A2 |
| Le Mesurier (EC1) ✘ | 435 | | (not on plan) |
| Michel (W8) ✘ | 454 | | Plan 1 C3 |
| Mijanou (SW1) ✘✘ | 439 | 70 | Plan 3 E2 |
| Ming (W1) ✘ | 451 | 23 | Plan 2 C4 |
| Mr Kai of Mayfair (W1) ✘✘ | 450 | 71 | Plan 3 E5 |
| Mr Ke (NW3) ✘ | 436 | | Plan 1 D4 |
| Montcalm (W1) ★★★★ | 446 | 72 | Plan 3 D6 |
| Mostyn (W1) ★★★ | 448 | 69 | Plan 3 D4 |
| Mount Royal (W1) ★★★ | 448 | 73 | Plan 3 D6 |
| M'sieur Frog (N1) ✘ | 435 | | Plan 1 D4 |
| Nayab Indian (SW6) ✘✘ | 442 | | Plan 1 C3 |

| Name | | | |
|---|---|---|---|
| New World (W1) ✗ | 451 | 37 | Plan 2 C3 |
| Ninety Park Lane (W1) ⊛✗✗✗✗✗ | 448 | 43 | Plan 3 E5 |
| Novotel London (W6) ★★★ | 452 | | Plan 1 C3 |
| Number 10 (W1) ✗✗ | 450 | 14 | Plan 4 A4 |
| Odin's (W1) ⊛✗✗ | 450 | | (not on plan) |
| Oh! Poivrier! (WC2)✗✗ | 456 | 29 | Plan 2 D4 |
| 190 Queen's Gate (SW7)✗✗✗ | 442 | | (not on plan) |
| Park Court (W2) ★★★ | 452 | 74 | Plan 3 A5 |
| Park Lane (W1) ★★★★ | 447 | 75 | Plan 3 E4 |
| Peter's Bistro (NW6) ✗ | 437 | | Plan 1 C4 |
| Le Plat du Jour (NW1) ✗ | 436 | | Plan 1 D4 |
| Pollyanna's (SW11) ✗ | 443 | | Plan 1 D3 |
| La Pomme d'Amour (W11) ✗✗ | 454 | | Plan 1 C3 |
| Poon's of Russell Square (WC1) ✗✗ | 455 | 15 | Plan 4 C6 |
| Portman Inter-Continental (W1) ★★★★ | 446 | 77 | Plan 3 D6 |
| Post House (NW3) ★★★ | 436 | | Plan 1 D4 |
| Le Poulbot (EC2) ⊛✗✗✗ | 435 | 3 | Plan 5 B4 |
| Princess Garden of Mayfair (W1) ✗✗✗ | 449 | 79 | Plan 3 E6 |
| Quincy's 84 (NW2) ✗ | 436 | | Plan 1 C4 |
| Ramada (W1) ★★★★ | 447 | 42 | Plan 2 A5 |
| Red Fort (W1) ✗✗ | 450 | 43 | Plan 2 B3 |
| Regent Palace (W1) ★★ | 448 | 44 | Plan 2 B3 |
| Rembrandt (SW7) ★★★ | 442 | 81 | Plan 3 C3 |
| Restaurant 192 (W11) ✗ | 454 | | Plan 1 C3 |
| Ristorante L'Incontro (SW1)✗✗ | 439 | | (not on plan) |
| Ritz (W1) ★★★★★ | 445 | 16 | Plan 4 A3 |
| River Cafe (W6)✗ | 452 | | (not on plan) |
| Royal Garden (W8) ★★★★★ | 452 | 82 | Plan 3 A4 |
| Royal Horseguards Thistle (SW1) ★★★ | 439 | 46 | Plan 2 D1 |
| Royal Lancaster (W2) ★★★★ | 451 | 83 | Plan 3 B5 |
| Royal Trafalgar Thistle (WC2) ★★★ | 456 | 47 | Plan 2 C2 |
| Royal Westminster Thistle (SW1) ★★★★ | 438 | 17 | Plan 4 A1 |
| RSJ The Restaurant on the South Bank (SE1) ✗ | 437 | 18 | Plan 4 E3 |
| Rubens (SW1) ★★★ | 439 | 19 | Plan 4 A2 |
| Rue St Jacques (W1) ⊛✗✗✗ | 449 | 48 | Plan 2 B5 |
| Hotel Russell (WC1) ★★★★ | 454 | 20 | Plan 4 C6 |
| St George's (W1) ★★★★ | 447 | 21 | Plan 4 A5 |
| St Quentin (SW3) ✗✗ | 441 | 84 | Plan 3 C3 |
| Salloos (SW1) ⊛✗✗ | 440 | 85 | Plan 3 D3 |
| Santini (SW1) ✗✗ | 440 | 22 | Plan 4 A1 |
| Savoy (WC2) ⊛★★★★★ | 455 | 50 | Plan 2 E3 |
| Savoy Grill (WC2) ✗✗✗✗✗ | 456 | 50 | Plan 2 E3 |
| Selfridge (W1) ★★★★ | 447 | 87 | Plan 3 E6 |
| Seven Dials (WC2) ✗✗ | 456 | 51 | Plan 2 C4 |
| Sheraton Park Tower (SW1) ★★★★★ | 438 | 88 | Plan 3 D4 |
| Stafford (SW1) ★★★★ | 438 | 52 | Plan 2 A1 |
| Stephen Bull (W1)✗✗ | 450 | | (not on plan) |
| Strand Palace (WC2) ★★★ | 456 | 53 | Plan 2 E3 |
| Le Suquet (SW3) ✗ | 442 | 90 | Plan 3 C2 |
| Sutherlands (W1) ⊛✗✗ | 450 | 54 | Plan 2 A4 |
| Swallow International (SW5) ★★★ | 442 | 91 | Plan 3 A2 |
| Tante Claire (SW3) ⊛⊛⊛✗✗ | 441 | 92 | Plan 3 D1 |
| Taste of India (WC2) ✗ | 457 | 55 | Plan 2 E4 |
| Thomas de Quincey's (WC2) ✗✗ | 456 | 56 | Plan 2 E3 |
| Tiger Lee (SW5) ✗✗ | 442 | 93 | Plan 3 A1 |
| Tower Thistle (E1) ★★★★ | 435 | 4 | Plan 5 C3 |
| Tui (SW7)✗ | 443 | | (not on plan) |
| Turners (SW3) ⊛✗✗ | 441 | 95 | Plan 3 C2 |
| Very Simply Nico (SW1)✗ | 440 | | (not on plan) |
| Wakaba (NW3) ✗ | 436 | | Plan 1 D4 |
| Waldorf (WC2) ★★★★ | 455 | 57 | Plan 2 E4 |
| Waltons (SW3) ✗✗✗✗ | 440 | 96 | Plan 3 C2 |
| Welcome Lodge (NW7)★★ | 437 | | (not on plan) |
| Westbury (W1) ★★★★ | 447 | 26 | Plan 4 A4 |
| White's (W2) ★★★★ | 451 | 97 | Plan 3 B5 |
| Yumi (W1) ✗✗ | 450 | 98 | Plan 3 D6 |
| Zen Central (W1)✗✗ | 450 | | (not on plan) |
| Zen Chinese (SW3) ✗✗✗ | 440 | 99 | Plan 3 D1 |
| Zenw 3 Chinese (NW3) ✗ | 437 | | Plan 1 D4 |

London

# London Postal Districts and ways in and out of London

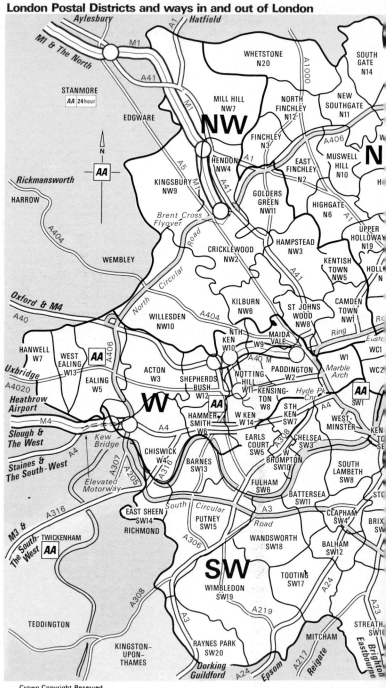

London Postal Area Boundary
London Postal District Boundaries
Main Roads into and out of London
Signposted North and South Circular
Roads & Ring Road
Other Main Roads

Service Centre **AA**

Scale of Miles

0    1    2    3    4

**London**

(5/90) © The Automobile Association

# London Plan 1

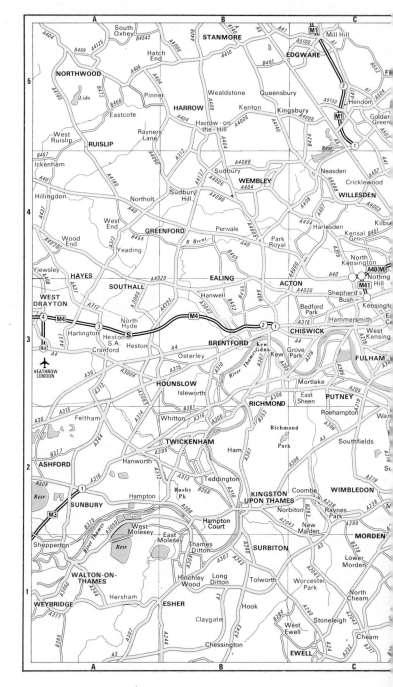

# London Plan 1

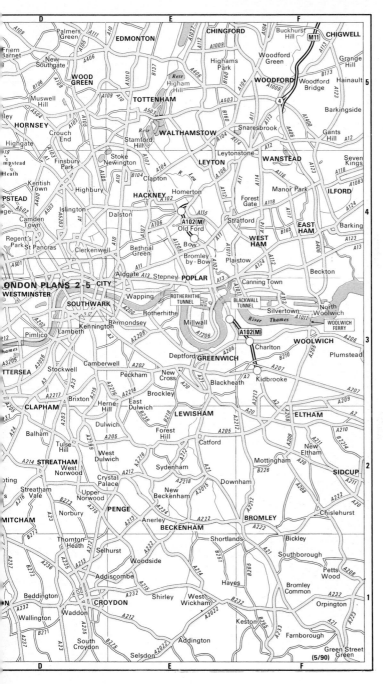

# London Plan 2

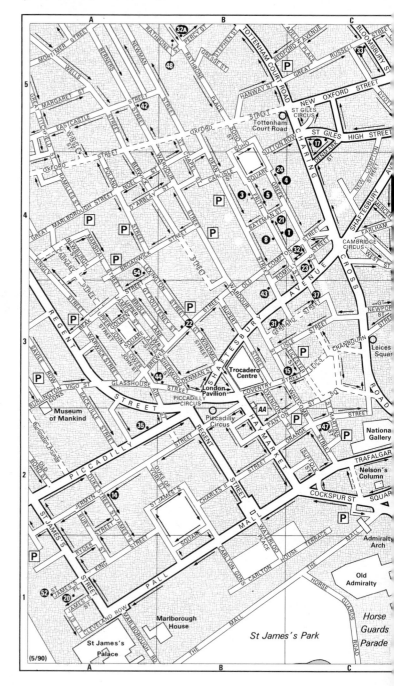

(5/90)

# London Plan 2

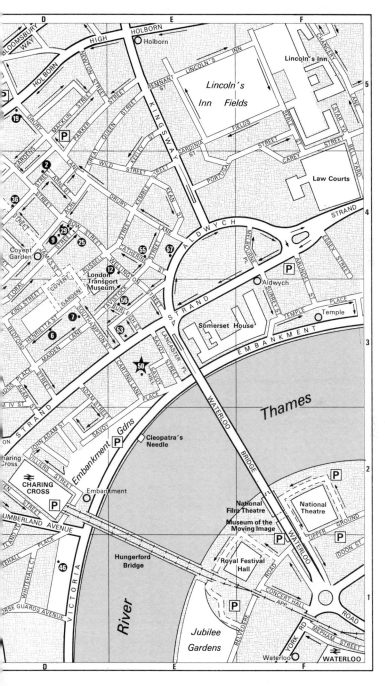

# London Plan 3

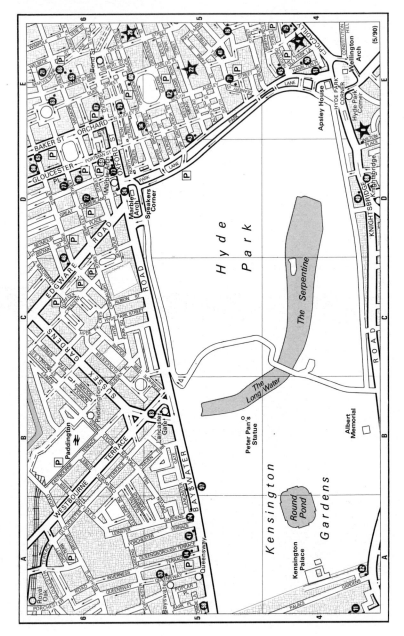

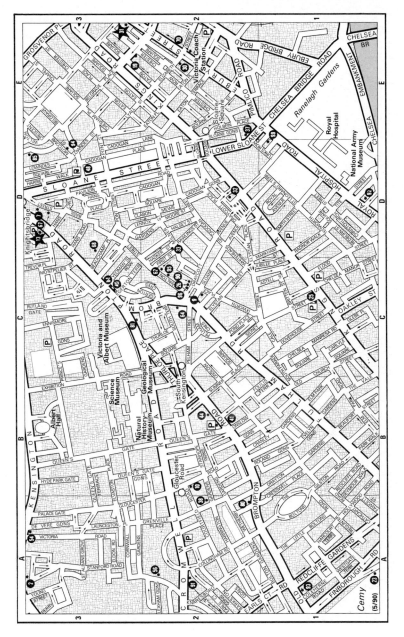

# London Plan 4

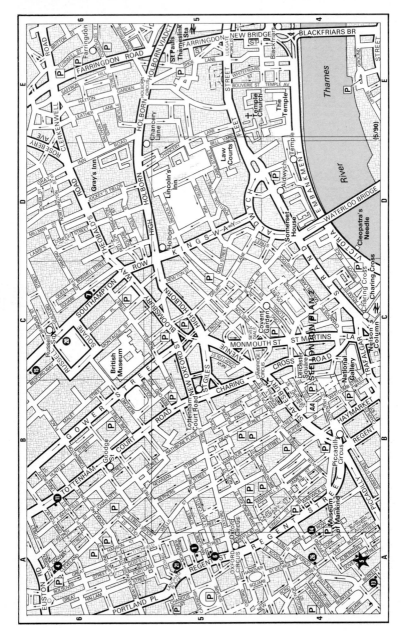

# London Plan 4

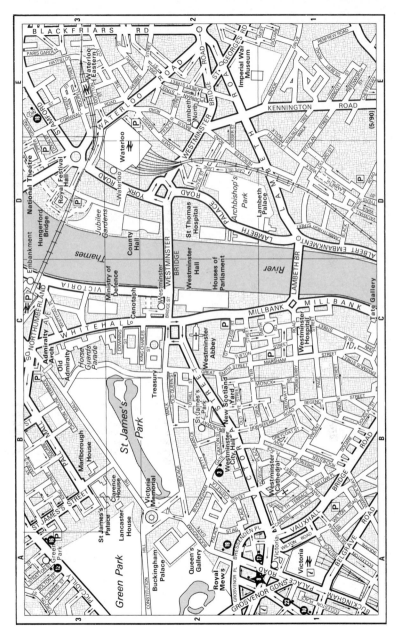

# London Plan 5

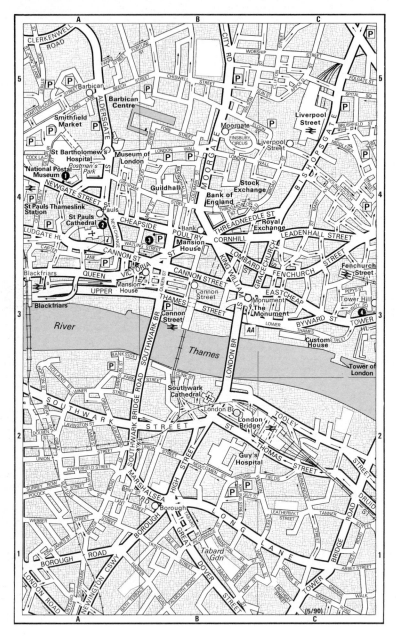

**LONDON** Greater London Plans 1-5, pages 426-434 (Small scale maps 4 & 5 at back of book) A map of the London postal area appears on pages 424-425, listed below in postal district order, commencing East, then North, South and West, with a brief indication of the area covered. Detailed plans 2-5 show the locations of AA-appointed hotels and restaurants within the Central London postal districts which are indicated by a number , followed by a grid reference e.g. A5 to help you find the location.plan 1 shows the districts covered within the outer area keyed by a grid reference e.g. A1. Other places within the county of London are listed under their respective place names and are also keyed to this plan or the main map section. If more detailed information is required the AA Motorists map of London, on sale at AA offices, is in two parts : the 'West End and the City' shows one-way systems, banned turns, car parks stations, hotels , places of interest etc. 'Outer London' gives primary routes, car parks at suburban stations etc. A theatre map of the West End is included. For London Airports see town plan section at the back of this book.

---

**E1 Stepney and east of the Tower of London**

★★★★60% **Tower Thistle** St Katharine's Way E1 9LD (Mount Charlotte (TS)) ☎071-488 4134 Telex no 885934
FAX 071-488 4106
*Overlooking Tower Bridge from its spectacular location on the banks of the Thames, this large modern hotel normally teems with activity. Smart public areas offer a range of eating options which includes both the comfortable Princes Room and an informal café which doubles as a night club after dark. The rather functional bedrooms are shortly to be upgraded, and some of them offer splendid views, whilst service in most areas reflects a genuine desire to please.*
808⇄**ก**(24fb) CTV in all bedrooms ® T **✕** ✳ sB⇄**ก**fr£99 dB⇄**ก**fr£112 (room only) **ㅏ**
Lift (▥ 136P (charged) 116🍴 (charged) CFA ♫
♈ International ✧ ♨ ✂ Lunch fr£18.75&alc Dinner fr£24.50&alc Last dinner 10.30pm
Credit Cards ①②③④⑤

---

**EC1 City of London**

✕**La Bastille** 116 Newgate St EC1A 7AE ☎071-600 1134
*The small, intimate, city restaurant has some good wood carvings, and the portraits of Victorian judges on the walls set an atmosphere. A sound standard of French provincial cuisine is provided, the menu changing daily.*
Closed Sat, Sun, 1 wk Aug, 2 wks Dec & BH's
Dinner not served
♈ French 55 seats Last lunch 2.30pm
Credit Cards ①②③④⑤

✕**Le Mesurier** 113 Old St EC1V 9JR ☎071-251 8117
*In this tiny, bright restaurant, chef patron Gillian Fenthoven offers a short fixed price à la carte menu which usually comprises a choice of four main dishes, all properly constructed with skill and care. Specially recommended are the chicken mousse with madeira sauce, red sea-bream with crab and herb crust, fillet of beef with wild mushrooms, and floating islands. There is a limited list of popular French wines and service is prompt and attentive. Dinners are available by private arrangement.*
Closed Sat, Sun & 24 Dec-2 Jan & 3 wks Aug
Dinner not served ex by appointment
♈ French 24 seats ✳ S12.5% Lunch £15-£26.50alc Dinner £20-£26.50alc Last lunch 3pm Last dinner 8.30pm ✗ nc5yrs
Credit Cards ①②③

All AA-appointed establishments are inspected regularly to ensure that required standards are maintained.

---

**EC2 City of London**

✖✕✕✕**Le Poulbot** 45 Cheapside EC2V 6AR ☎071-236 4379
FAX 071-622 5657
(Rosette awarded for lunch only)
*Chef Nicholas Reade has taken charge of this well-established City restaurant, one of the Roux Brothers' highly successful enterprises. Standards remain high, but the emphasis has shifted a little, to a more straightforward style of modern French cuisine and a number of classical dishes such as Gratin Lyonnaise and Oeufs Florentines. The Filet d'agneau roti, jus de romarin, followed by a Tarte Tatin were our Inspector's favourites. The set-price menu and short wine list continue to offer very good value for money.*
Closed Sat, Sun, Xmas & BH's
Dinner not served
♈ French **V** 50 seats ✳ S% Lunch fr£28.50 Last lunch 3pm
✗ nc10yrs
Credit Cards ①②③⑤

---

**EC4 City of London**

✕**Ginnan** 5 Cathedral Place EC4M 7EA ☎071-236 4120
*Simple, modern Japanese restaurant with small party room.*
Closed Sun & BH's
Dinner not served Sat
♈ Japanese 60 seats Last dinner 10pm ✗
Credit Cards ①②③⑤

---

**N1 Islington**
**See LONDON plan 1D4**
✕✕**Frederick's** Camden Passage N1 8EG ☎071-359 2888
FAX 071-359 5173
*Dating back from the 18th-century, and originally called 'The Gun', this very popular and well-appointed restaurant was renamed in honour of Prince Augustus Frederick who died in 1813. The enterprising menu is changed fortnightly but always includes some delectable puddings, and the formal service is very efficient.*
Closed Sun, 25-26 Dec, 1 Jan, Good Fri & BH Mons
♈ International **V** 150 seats ✳ S15% Lunch £18-£24alc Wine £5.85 Last lunch 2.30pm Last dinner 11.30pm ✗
Credit Cards ①②③④⑤

✕**Annas Place** 90 Mildmay Park N1 4PR ☎071-249 9379
*A small very friendly Swedish café where simplicity and honesty combine to produce outstanding and authentic Swedish cooking. Anna's warm and sincere involvement is complemented by her loyal team of friendly staff. There is a good selection of wines on offer. This restaurant is marvellous value for money.*
Closed Sun, Mon, 2 wks Xmas, 2 wks Etr & 4 wks Aug
♈ Swedish **V** 50 seats ✳ Lunch £16-£22alc Dinner £16-£22alc Last lunch 2.15pm Last dinner 10.30pm ✗

✕**M'Sieur Frog** 31A Essex Rd N1 2SE ☎071-226 3495
*A good choice of dishes is available at this lively and very popular bistro.*
Closed Sun, 1 wk Xmas & 1 wk Aug
Lunch not served Sat
♈ French 63 seats Last lunch 2.30pm Last dinner 11.15pm ✗
Credit Cards ①③

---

**N6 Highgate**
**See LONDON plan 1D5**
✕✕**Bayleaf Tandoori** 2 North Hill N6 4PU ☎081-340 1719 & 081-340 0245
*Well-appointed contemporary restaurant and take-away featuring specialities and seafoods. All dishes are grilled on charcoal. Service is dignified and attentive.*
♈ Indian **V** 100 seats Last lunch 2.45pm Last dinner 11.15pm 20P
Credit Cards ①②③⑤

### NW1 Regent's Park

See LONDON plan 1*D4*

✗✗**Martin's** 239 Baker St NW1 6XE ☎071-935 3130 &
071-935 0997
*A contemporary and very smart restaurant bar where the menu
offers particularly good value, skilfully-prepared dishes.*
Closed Sun & BH's
Lunch not served Sat
♨ English & French 60 seats Lunch £17.50-£21 Dinner
£17.50-£21 Last lunch 3pm Last dinner 10.30pm ✗ nc10yrs
Credit Cards ①②③⑤

✗**Great Nepalese** 48 Eversholt St NW1 ☎071-388 6737
*The unassuming exterior and simple appointments of this
restaurant belie the quality of the cooking here. This as a warm
and welcoming restaurant serving well-flavoured, freshly prepared
food including Tandoori dishes and Nepalese specialities, and
represents excellent value for money.*
Closed 25 & 26 Dec
♨ Nepalese **V** 48 seats ✱ S% Lunch fr£5 Dinner fr£6 Last
lunch 2.45pm Last dinner 11.30pm ✗
Credit Cards ①②③⑤

✗**Koto Japanese** 75 Parkway NW1 7AL ☎071-482 2036
*A small and very friendly traditional restaurant is personally run
by the proprietor, Yoko Arai. Specialities include Sashimi and
Tempora, and there are others which can be cooked at your table.
Service is very attentive, and there is a traditional dining room
upstairs.*
Closed Sun
♨ Japanese 22 seats Last dinner 10.30pm ✗
Credit Cards ①②③④⑤

✗**Le Plat du Jour** 19 Hampstead Rd NW1 3JA
☎071-387 9644 & 071-387 7291
*Popular lunchtime restaurant/wine bar offering excellent value for
money with French regional dishes and daily specialities.*
Closed Sat, Sun, 24 Dec-1 Jan & BH's
♨ French & Italian **V** 70 seats S12.5% Lunch £12-£23 Dinner
£12-£23 Last lunch 3pm Last dinner 10.30pm ✗
Credit Cards ①②③⑤

### NW2 Cricklewood, Willesden

See LONDON plan 1*C4*

✗**Quincy's 84** 675 Finchley Rd NW2 2JP ☎071-794 8499
*Flair and imagination are evident in the cooking at this restaurant,
where dishes from a short but interesting menu are served in a
friendly, informal atmosphere under the personal supervision of the
owner.*
Closed Sun, Mon & 24 Dec-14 Jan
Lunch not served
♨ English & French **V** 30 seats ✱ S% Dinner £19.50 Last
dinner 11.30pm ✗
Credit Cards ①③

### NW3 Hampstead and Swiss Cottage

See LONDON plan 1*D4*

★★★★**65% Holiday Inn Swiss Cottage** 128 King Henry's Rd,
Swiss Cottage NW3 3ST (Holiday Inns) ☎071-722 7711
Telex no 267396 FAX 071-586 5822
*A modern, multi-storey hotel ideally placed for access to Central
London. Bedrooms, recently refurbished, are spacious and well
equipped, the split-level lounge and cocktail bar extremely
comfortable and the restaurant pleasant and airy. This hotel also
has a leisure club with an indoor heated pool.*
303 ⇔↑(166fb) ⊁in 52 bedrooms CTV in all bedrooms ® T ✱
sB ⇔↑£119-£139 dB ⇔↑£140-£162 (room only) ⊟
Lift ℂ ⊞ 50P 100🚗 🏊(heated) sauna solarium gymnasium
*xmas*

♨ International **V** ✧ � ⊁ Lunch fr£17.50 High tea fr£7.50
Dinner fr£18 Last dinner 10.30pm
Credit Cards ①②③④⑤ⓔ

★★★**59% Charles Bernard** 5-7 Frognal, Hampstead NW3 6AL
☎071-794 0101 Telex no 23560 FAX 071-794 0100
*Close to central London, this commercial hotel offers nicely
appointed, well-equipped bedrooms.*
57 ⇔↑ CTV in all bedrooms ® T 🏋 ✱ S% sB&B ⇔↑£52-£72
dB&B ⇔↑£64-£87 ⊟
Lift ℂ CTV 15P
✧ ⊿welcome Lunch £9-£15.75alc High tea £3.50-£5.50alc Dinner
£9-£15.75alc Last dinner 9.15pm
Credit Cards ①②③⑤ⓔ

★★★**58% Post House** Haverstock Hill NW3 4RB (Trusthouse
Forte) ☎071-794 8121 Telex no 262494 FAX 071-435 5586
*Known for its comfortable surroundings this hotel has fine south-
west views across the city. In the restaurant the daily roast is worth
recommending, but our Inspector found that dishes from the à la
carte menu lacked the flavour expected from fresh produce.*
140 ⇔↑in 28 bedrooms CTV in all bedrooms ® T ✱
sB ⇔↑fr£79 dB ⇔↑£90-£95 (room only) ⊟
Lift ℂ 70P *xmas*
♨ English & French **V** ✧ ⊿welcome ⊁ Lunch fr£11.95 Dinner
fr£11.95&alc Last dinner 10.30pm
Credit Cards ①②③④⑤

⊛✗✗**Keats** 3 Downshire Hill NW3 1NR ☎071-435 3544 &
071-435 1599
*This attractively revamped restaurant has, like the Phoenix, risen
from the ashes under the new ownership of chefs Berger and
Sawyer. Their interesting à la carte menu is both sensible and
innovative, whilst set menus provide good value for money. Cuisine
is stylish and refined, perhaps a little too dainty for some, but
highly competent nevertheless, and presented in stunning fashion.
Starters might include a delicious ravioli of truffles with celeriac
and parsley, followed, perhaps, by a perfectly cooked fillet and
kidney of lamb with a light coriander-flavoured sauce. The
attention to detail extends to the trimmings – vegetables are
thoughtfully prepared and breads and coffee are first rate. The
range of desserts is limited but nicely balanced. Service is polite,
professional and agreeable, and the menus are complimented by a
youthful but comprehensive wine list with heavy French emphasis.*
Closed Sun, Mon, Xmas, Etr & 3 wks Aug
♨ French 40 seats ✱ S12.5% Lunch fr£15.50&alc Dinner
£21-£32&alc Last lunch 2.30pm Last dinner 10pm
Credit Cards ①②③

✗**Café Flo** 205 Haverstock Hill NW3 2AG ☎071-435 6744
FAX 071-433 3896
Closed 1 week at Xmas
♨ French **V** 38 seats ✱ Lunch £5.95&alc Last lunch 3.00pm
Last dinner 11.30pm ✗
Credit Cards ①③

✗**Mr Ke** 7 New College Pde, Finchley Rd NW3 5EP
☎071-722 8474
*Small, family-run contemporary restaurant specialising in Peking
and Szechwan cuisine. All dishes are cooked to order and offer
excellent value for money.*
♨ Jiangnan, Pekinese & Szechwan **V** 55 seats ✱ Dinner
£13.50-£22&alc Last lunch 2.30pm Last dinner 11.30pm ✗
Credit Cards ①②③⑤

✗**Wakaba** 122a Finchley Rd NW3 5JD ☎071-586 7960
*The functional bland interior design of this restaurant, by architect
John Paulson, is both modern and unusual. A range of set dinners
based on traditional Japanese recipes is available, together with
old favourites like Tempura and Sashimi; many specialities are
cooked at the table, and there is a separate Sushi Bar.*
Closed Mon, 4 days Xmas, 4 days Etr & 1 wk Aug
Lunch not served

♥ Japanese **V** 38 seats Last dinner 11pm ✔
Credit Cards ①②③⑤

**✗ Zenw 3 Chinese** 83 Hampstead High St NW3 1RE
☎071-794 7863 FAX 071-437 0641
*Interior and furnishings are in the 'Art Deco' style at this
restaurant which provides the 'New Wave' style of cooking with
salads, charcoal grills and iron plate food.*
Closed Xmas
♥ Chinese **V** 140 seats Last dinner 11.30pm ✔
Credit Cards ①②③④⑤

---

### NW6 Kilburn

See LONDON plan 1*C4*
**✗ Peter's Bistro** 63 Fairfax Rd NW6 4EE ☎071-624 5804
*Green awning and fresh plants make the frontage of this
restaurant very impressive. Inside the relaxed intimate atmosphere
provides the ideal setting for a well-cooked bistro-type meals.*
Lunch not served Sat
Dinner not served Sun
♥ French 60 seats ✔ ⚋
Credit Cards ①②③⑤

---

### NW7 Mill Hill

See LONDON plan 1*C5*
**★★62% Welcome Lodge** M1 Scratchwood Service Area, Mill
Hill NW7 3HB (Access from Motorway only) (Trusthouse Forte)
☎081-906 0611 FAX 081-906 3654
*This motorway lodge provides comfortable, well-equipped
bedrooms and a small restaurant offering short à la carte and
carvery menus; friendly staff give efficient and helpful service.*
100⇱(12fb) CTV in all bedrooms Ⓡ T
《 100P CFA
V ✿ ⚋ ⚋
Credit Cards ①②③⑤

**✗✗ Good Earth** 143-145 Broadway, Mill Hill NW7 4RN
☎081-959 7011 FAX 071-823 8769
*Smart, cheerful and popular restaurant with appealing menu of
authentic Cantonese cooking.*
Closed 24-27 Dec
♥ Cantonese, Pekinese & Szechwan **V** 100 seats ✳ Lunch
£15.50-£22.50 Dinner £15.50-£22.50 Last lunch 2.30pm Last
dinner 11.15pm 12P
Credit Cards ①②③⑤

---

### SE1 Waterloo

**✗ RSJ The Restaurant on the South Bank** 13A Coin St SE1 8YQ
☎071-928 4554 & 071-928 9768
*Stylish and elegant restaurant where chef Ian McKenzie
demonstrates his flair for 'New Wave' cooking. There are some
excellent wines from the Loire region.*
Closed Sun & 25-28 Dec
Lunch not served Sat
♥ French 60 seats Last lunch 2pm Last dinner 11pm ✔
Credit Cards ①②③

---

### SE3 Blackheath

**★★64% Bardon Lodge** Stratheden Rd SE3 7TH ☎081-853 4051
FAX 081-858 7387
*One of our first 'Courtesy and Care' award winners, Bardon Lodge
is an elegant house just off the heath offering good quality public
rooms, well equipped bedrooms and a popular restaurant.*
37rm(5⇱23🌰)(3fb)2⚌ CTV in all bedrooms Ⓡ T
🐕 (ex guide dogs) ✳ sB&B£46 sB&B⇱🌰£54 dB&B£65
dB&B⇱🌰£75-£110 🍴
《 CTV 16P ✿
V ✿ ⚋ ⚋ Dinner £12.85 Last dinner 9.15pm
Credit Cards ①②③

---

### SW1 Westminster

★★★★★ THE BERKELEY
Wilton Place,
Knightsbridge SW1X 7RL
☎071-235 6000
Telex no 919252
FAX 071-235 4330
*Over the past 2 or 3 years
considerable refurbishment
has been carried out here,
which includes the provision of a more attractive restaurant,
the 'softening' of the corridors, re-decoration of the drawing
room and bedrooms and further improvement of some of the
already fine suites. There is a heated swimming pool on the
top floor, together with a sauna and mini-gym. The standard
of French cuisine in the restaurant is sound, and the popular
'Le Perroquet' bar and adjoining Buttery offer a wide range of
good-value dishes. Service thoughout is formal, extensive and
traditional – staff tend to smile more when greeting customers
they know. At other times it has to be said that an air of
aloofness prevails, until one comes to appreciate the distinctive
style of The Berkeley. Discretion is considered to be as
important as meeting the high standards of a discerning
clientele, which in turn helps to explain why it attracts such a
loyal following.*
160⇱🌰 CTV in all bedrooms 🐕 S15% sB⇱🌰£150-£215
dB⇱🌰£215-£265 (room only) 🍴
Lift 《 ⊞ 50🐕 (£19 per night) 🚗 ⌱(heated) sauna
solarium gymnasium cinema ♫ *xmas*
▶

**London**

♀ International V ♥ ⚲ S15% Lunch fr£17.50&alc Dinner £30-£45alc Last dinner 11pm
Credit Cards ⓵ ⓶ ⓷ ⓹

---

★★★★★77% **The Hyde Park** Knightsbridge SW1Y 7LA (Trusthouse Forte) ☎071-235 2000 Telex no 262057 FAX 071-235 4552
*This elegant and dignified hotel is situated in the centre of fashionable Knightsbridge overlooking Hyde Park. A stately entrance leads to the reception area – ornate with marble, high, gilded ceilings and huge, fresh flower displays. The lounge and bar is a popular rendezvous which leads into the Park Room Restaurant where the piano is played. Downstairs, the oak-panelled Grill Room offers English roasts and French specialities. Bedrooms and suites, individually decorated by leading designers, are superbly equipped.*
186 ⇌ ⅙ in 6 bedrooms CTV in all bedrooms T S%
sB ⇌ £199-£225 dB ⇌ £250-£265 (room only) 뮤
Lift ( ⊞ ℐ 뀸 CFA ♫ xmas
♀ English & French V ♥ ⚲ ⅙ S% Lunch £20-£24&alc Dinner £25&alc Last dinner 11pm
Credit Cards ⓵ ⓶ ⓷ ⓸ ⓹

★★★★★72% **Hyatt Carlton Tower** Cadogan Place SW1X 9PY ☎071-235 5411 Telex no 21944 FAX 071-235 9129
*A somewhat regimented, modern hotel with some good facilities. These include the refurbished Rib Room Restaurant, attractive Chelsea Room Restaurant and a new health centre that also has a relaxing lounge. Bedrooms are modestly furnished and prices comparatively expensive.*
224 ⇌ ⋔ ⅙ in 23 bedrooms CTV in all bedrooms T ✈ (ex guide dogs) 뮤
Lift ( ⊞ 40 뀸 (£2 per hour) 뀸 CFA ♪ (hard) sauna solarium gymnasium beauty treatment hair salon ♫
♀ French and International V ♥ ⚲ Lunch £23.50&alc High tea £15-£20alc Dinner £22-£35alc Last dinner 11.15pm
Credit Cards ⓵ ⓶ ⓷ ⓸ ⓹ £

★★★★★63% **Sheraton Park Tower** 101 Knightsbridge SW1X 7RN ☎071-235 8050 Telex no 917222 FAX 071-235 8231
*Modern facilities, elegant furnishings and exceptional views are the distinguishing features of the Sheraton Park's bedrooms, and the upper-floor executive rooms, with their TV/videos, individual air-conditioning, mini-bars, etc, are ideally suited for business travellers. The Edwardian-style restaurant and conservatory make an inviting setting for the tempting menus, while light meals and snacks are served throughout the day in the Champagne Bar.*
295 ⇌ ⋔ ⅙ in 20 bedrooms CTV in all bedrooms T ✈ ✳
sB ⇌ ⋔£180-£230 dB ⇌ ⋔£200-£230 (room only) 뮤
Lift ( ⊞ 70 뀸 (£9 per day) 뀸 ♫ xmas
♀ International V ♥ ⚲ Lunch £16.75-£17.50&alc High tea £5-£8.25alc Dinner £23-£33alc Last dinner 11.30pm
Credit Cards ⓵ ⓶ ⓷ ⓸ ⓹

---

## ★★★★

★★★★ **GORING**

Beeston Place, Grosvenor Gardens SW1W 0JW
☎071-834 8211
Telex no 919166
FAX 071-834 4393

*Praise from all quarters continues to be showered on this well established, family-run hotel, particularly for its outstanding hospitality and service. Having a number of long-serving staff contributes much to the consistency and continuity of its reputation, which*

---

*is admirably upheld by the expertise of the General Manager William Cowpe. Great care has been given to the décor and furnishing of the reception area and public rooms, thus creating a cheerful and welcoming atmosphere, carried through in the planning of the well equipped bedrooms which means that even in the smaller rooms the best use of available space is achieved. The elegant and attractive restaurant offers interesting set-price and à la carte menus, particularly notable for their fish dishes, and the well-balanced wine list is reasonably priced.*
90 ⇌ ⋔ CTV in all bedrooms T ✈ S10% sB ⇌ ⋔£105-£115
dB ⇌ ⋔£155-£165 (room only)
Lift ( 10P (£7.50) 4 (£7.50) 뀸 ♫
♀ English & French V ♥ ⚲ Lunch fr£20&alc Dinner fr£24&alc Last dinner 10pm
Credit Cards ⓵ ⓶ ⓷ ⓹

---

★★★★73% *Duke's* 35 St James's Place SW1A 1NY (Prestige) ☎071-491 4840 Telex no 28283 FAX 071-493 1264
*A charming, Edwardian hotel in a peaceful, secluded setting where the highly professional staff manage to create a relaxed and friendly atmosphere. In addition to the superbly furnished and equipped bedrooms, this hotel now has well-appointed suites as well. Public areas are comfortable and the small intimate restaurant offers a short but interesting menu of English and French cuisine skilfully prepared by chef Tony Marshall.*
58 ⇌ (22fb)1 CTV in all bedrooms ✈ (ex guide dogs)
Lift ( ℐ 뀸 nc5yrs
♥ ⚲ Last dinner 10pm
Credit Cards ⓵ ⓶ ⓷ ⓸ ⓹

★★★★72% *Stafford* 16-18 St James's Place SW1A 1NJ (Prestige) ☎071-493 0111 Telex no 28602 FAX 071-493 7121
*In an unobtrusive setting in St James Place the hotel is an oasis of calm in the heart of the West End. Bedrooms, some rather compact, are individually furnished in soft elegant fabrics. Good food and fine wines are a feature of the hotel and traditional afternoon tea is a must.*
62 ⇌ 1 CTV in all bedrooms ✈
Lift ( 5 (£12 per night) 뀸
♀ French ♥ ⚲ Last dinner 10pm
Credit Cards ⓵ ⓶ ⓷ ⓸ ⓹

★★★★67% **Royal Westminster Thistle** 40 Buckingham Palace Rd SW1W 0QT (Mount Charlotte (TS)) ☎071-834 1821 Telex no 916821 FAX 071-931 7542
*Bedrooms here are spacious and well appointed, there is a comfortable lounge and impressive entrance lobby. The two options when it comes to eating are the formal restaurant – the St Germain Brasserie – or the more casual Café St Germain and the service in both is helpful and friendly.*
134 ⇌ ⋔ (69fb) ⅙ in 67 bedrooms CTV in all bedrooms T ✈ ✳
sB ⇌ ⋔fr£105 dB ⇌ ⋔fr£130 (room only) 뮤
Lift ( ⊞ ℐ
♀ English & French ♥ ⚲ ⅙ Lunch fr£15.95&alc Dinner fr£15.95&alc Last dinner 11.30pm
Credit Cards ⓵ ⓶ ⓷ ⓸ ⓹

★★★★63% **The Cavendish** Jermyn St SW1Y 6JF (Trusthouse Forte) ☎071-930 2111 Telex no 263187 FAX 071-839 2125
*The Cavendish is carrying out a programme of refurbishment, designed to improve the comfort of the bedrooms, some of the best of which have balconies affording superb views over London. The restaurant is well supervised and meals are served by friendly and attentive staff. There is also a gallery lounge where drinks and snacks, including traditional afternoon tea, can be ordered throughout the day.*
253 ⇌ ⅙ in 63 bedrooms CTV in all bedrooms T ✳
sB ⇌ £120-£135 dB ⇌ £150-£170 (room only) 뮤
Lift ( 80 (fr £16) 뀸 CFA xmas

♀ French V ✧ ℒ ⊱ Lunch £18.50-£23.50 Dinner £20&alc
Last dinner 11pm
Credit Cards 1 2 3 4 5

★★★68% **Rubens** Buckingham Palace Rd SW1W 0PS
☎071-834 6600 Telex no 916577 FAX 071-828 5401
*Delightfully located facing the mews to Buckingham Palace and
the Royal Parks this hotel has been tastefully refurbished and now
has air conditioning in the Masters restaurant. Bedrooms are well
equipped and staff are pleasantly polite.*
191⇌ᶚ♖(3fb)⊱in 44 bedrooms CTV in all bedrooms Ⓡ T
✖ (ex guide dogs) ✱ sB⇌ᶚ♖£85-£95
dB⇌ᶚ♖fr£105 (room only) ♬
Lift ( ℱ *xmas*
♀ International V ✧ ℒ ⊱ S10% Lunch fr£14.95 Dinner
fr£15.50 Last dinner 10pm
Credit Cards 1 2 3 5 ©

★★★63% **Royal Horseguards Thistle** Whitehall Court
SW1A 2EJ (Mount Charlotte (TS)) ☎071-839 3400
Telex no 917096 FAX 071-925 2263
*Guests of many nationalities frequent this large, imposing and
conveniently located hotel. All bedrooms have modern facilities,
though accommodation in the new wing is superior to the more
compact rooms of the original building, whilst public areas include
a majestically appointed lounge next to the elegant reception area,
a choice of restaurants and a cosy bar.*
376⇌ᶚ♖(98fb)⊱in 95 bedrooms CTV in all bedrooms Ⓡ T ✖
✱ sB⇌ᶚ♖fr£93 dB⇌ᶚ♖fr£99 (room only) ♬
Lift ( ℱ CFA ♫
♀ International ✧ ℒ ⊱ Lunch fr£15.75&alc Dinner
fr£15.75&alc Last dinner 10.30pm
Credit Cards 1 2 3 4 5

★

★**EBURY COURT**

26 Ebury St SW1 0LU
☎071-730 8147
FAX 071-823 5966

Closed 21 Dec-4 Jan

*The Ebury Court hotel has
become a London legend
under the long ownership of
Mrs Topham, and although she has now handed over the
running of it to her daughter and son-in-law, it is to be hoped
that this very English institution will continue in the same vein,
with the emphasis on traditional service and a gentle, old-
fashioned charm and atmosphere. Among the improvements
being undertaken by Mr and Mrs Kingsford are the
refurbishing of some of the bedrooms which, though small, are
very prettily furnished. In the dining room menus are now
shorter, and there is a move towards more ambitious cooking
than hitherto.*
43rm(19⇌ᶚ♖)(3fb)4⌗ CTV in all bedrooms Ⓡ T ✱
sB&Bfr£50 dB&B£75 dB&B⇌ᶚ♖£95
Lift ( ℱ ⌗
♀ English & Continental V ✧ ℒ
Credit Cards 1 3

○**Halkin** Halkin St, Belgravia SW1X 7DJ ☎071-333 1000
Due to have opened Oct 1990
41rm

✖ ✖ ✖**Auberge de Provence** (St James Court Hotel),
Buckingham Gate SW1E 6AF ☎071-821 1899 Telex no 938075
FAX 071-630 7587
*Chef Yves Gravelier shows his flair for the cooking of Provence
with well-constructed dishes, authentic sauces and home-made
pâtisserie. Service, under the direction of Monsieur Perrodin,*

*remains traditionally French and thoroughly professional, with
knowledgeable advice about the wine list.*
Closed Sun, BH's, 26 Dec-15 Jan
Lunch not served Sat
♀ French V 88 seats S% Lunch £19.50-£25&alc Dinner
£30-£45alc Last lunch 2.30pm Last dinner 11pm ℱ ⊱
Credit Cards 1 2 3 4 5

✖ ✖**Gavvers** 61-63 Lower Sloane St SW1W 8HP
☎071-730 5983 & 071-823 4772 FAX 071-622 5657
*A Roux Brothers enterprise, the restaurant offers a very popular,
value for money, fixed price menu, the charge covering not only
half a bottle of wine but also service and VAT.*
Closed Sun, Xmas-1 Jan & BH's
Lunch not served Sat
♀ French V 58 seats ✱ S% Lunch £11.50-£13.50 Dinner fr£22
Last lunch 2.30pm Last dinner 11pm ℱ
Credit Cards 1 2 3 5

❋✖✖**Ken Lo's Memories of China** 67 Ebury St SW1W 0NZ
☎071-730 7734
*The only Chinese restaurant in London currently qualifying for a
rosette award, Ken Lo's restaurant continues to attract a
cosmopolitan clientele. The à la carte menu offers several splendid
dishes, the seafood (lobster, crab, sea bass) dishes being
particularly memorable. The set menus are interesting, with freshly
prepared dishes providing all the contrasts of flavour expected of
Chinese cuisine.*
Closed Sun & BH's
♀ Chinese V 80 seats Last dinner 10.45pm ℱ
Credit Cards 1 2 3 5

❋✖✖**Le Mazarin** 30 Winchester St, Pimlico SW1V 4NE
☎071-828 3366 & 071-630 7604
(Rosette awarded for dinner only)
*Always popular, this intimate basement restaurant offers an
imaginative menu, with dishes skilfully prepared by René Bajard.
Our inspector found it difficult to pick out just one item from
among so many tempting choices, but finally decided on the
Médaillons de lotte à l'Armoricaine et son riz sauvage. At
lunchtime from Tuesday to Saturday there is a set-price menu
which offers very good value.*
Closed Sun, Mon, 1 wk Xmas, BH's & last 2 wks in Aug
♀ French 55 seats Last lunch 2pm Last dinner 11pm ℱ
Credit Cards 1 2 3 5

✖✖**Mijanou** 143 Ebury St SW1W 9QN ☎071-730 4099
FAX 071-823 6402
*Sonia Blech, continues to maintain a high standard in her
imaginative cooking. The menu is not large, but will suit most
tastes, and good fresh produce is well used. A good, comprehensive
wine list accompanies the food and some interesting wines are
available. There is a friendly, informal atmosphere, with Nevelle
Blech keeping a watchful eye on the service. The décor is tasteful
and the atmosphere pleasant, enhanced for some by the provision of
a no-smoking area.*
Closed Sat, Sun, 2 wks Xmas, 1 wk Etr, 3 wks Aug & BH's
♀ French V 30 seats ✱ Lunch £16.50-£29.50 Dinner £25-£36
Last lunch 2pm Last dinner 11pm ℱ ⊱
Credit Cards 1 2 3 5

✖✖**Ristorante L'Incontro** 87 Pimlico Rd SW1W 8PH
☎071-730 3663
*Incorporating the best recipes from the Veneziana region, a well
balanced and interesting menu is offered here. Chef Danilo
Minvezo uses the best quality ingredients and market-fresh
produce with which to perform his traditional skills. Such dishes as
Funghi con Polenta, Pasta e Fagioli, Venetian Brown Soup,
Seppioline alla Briglia (grilled small cuttlefish) and Piccata al
Mango (veal escalopes with fresh mango sauce) are featured.
Pasta is all home-made and there is always a choice of delicious
desserts. The wine list includes a fine selection of Italian wines and
a classic Bordeaux section. Parking can be difficult and
reservations are strongly advised.*

▶

Dinner not served Sun
♡ Italian 80 seats ✻ S% Last dinner 11.30pm
Credit Cards ① ② ③ ④ ⑤

✗ ✗ *Salloos* 62-64 Kinnerton St SW1X 8ER ☎071-235 4444
*An unassuming first floor Pakistani restaurant tucked away in a quiet area of Knightsbridge. The menu boasts that no artificial colours are used in cooking and certainly the cuisine is of a style and standard not usually found in this type of restaurant. Spicy marinated meats from the Tandoori oven, the chicken in cheese (a souffle dish) and the naan bread which almost melts in the mouth are all recommended. Salloo himself is a genial host. Beware the hefty cover and service charges.*
Closed Sun & BH's
♡ Pakistani V 70 seats Last lunch 2.30pm Last dinner 11.15pm ₽
Credit Cards ① ② ③ ⑤

✗ ✗ *Santini* 29 Ebury St SW1W 0NZ ☎071-730 4094 & 071-730 8275 FAX 071-730 0544
*A bright and stylish very Italian restaurant where tables are close together and the atmosphere is noisy and convivial. The menu is à la carte supplemented by daily specials, and the fresh pasta, fresh fish and the Italian dishes that are served are of a quality not often found in this country. Good, value-for-money Italian and fine French wines complement the menu and the puddings should not be missed.*
Closed Xmas, Etr & BH's
Lunch not served Sat & Sun
♡ Italian V 60 seats S12% Lunch £29.50-£48.50alc Dinner £33.50-£48.50alc Last lunch 2.30pm Last dinner 11.30pm ₽
Credit Cards ① ② ③ ④ ⑤

✹ ✗ *Ciboure* 21 Eccleston St SW1W 9LX ☎071-730 2505
*A bright, friendly little French restaurant where the personality of Jean Louis Journade inspires the attentive service and welcoming atmosphere. Chef Melanie Dixon shows a flair for using good quality ingredients to best effect with light but tasty sauces. A hot timbale of leeks and mushrooms, followed by fillet of beef with wild mushrooms and bone marrow or a well executed salad of delicious red mullet followed by a gutsy casserole of guinea fowl display her skills admirably. Good French cheeses or an outstanding Tarte des Demoiselles Tatin will complete a refreshingly simple meal, notable for its honest flavours. Staff are agreeable and help to make the experience of eating here so pleasant.*
Closed Sun, Sat & 14 Aug-04 Sep
♡ French 36 seats ✻ Lunch £13-£14.50 Dinner £17-£20alc Last lunch 2.30pm Last dinner 11pm ₽ nc5yrs
Credit Cards ① ② ③ ⑤

✗ *Eatons* 49 Elizabeth St SW1W 9PP ☎071-730 0074
*Artichoke and cucumber soup and boneless, stuffed quail with a cream and brandy sauce are just two examples from the menu of this cosy and friendly restaurant. The normal menu has seasonal additions. Service is pleasant and courteous.*
Closed Sat, Sun & BH's
♡ Continental 40 seats ✻ S12.5% Lunch £14.70-£17.70&alc Last dinner 11.15pm ₽
Credit Cards ① ② ③ ⑤

✗ *Very Simply Nico* 48a Rochester Row SW1P 1JU ☎071-630 8061
*This popular restaurant has taken on the lively, buzzing atmosphere of a French-style bistro, characterised by aproned waiters rushing around with baskets of French bread. The food is wholesome, well prepared and substantial and, although the menu is not extensive, there is a well balanced choice of good seasonal dishes. Our Inspector recommended a duck paté or Mediterranean fish soup to start and a confit of pork or poached trout to follow.*
Closed Sun, last 10 days Jul-1st 10 days Aug
Lunch not served Sat
♡ French 48 seats ✻ S10% Lunch fr£21 Dinner fr£21 Last lunch 2pm Last dinner 11pm ₽ nc4yrs
Credit Cards ① ③

## SW3 Chelsea, Brompton

★ ★ ★ ★

✱★★★★ CAPITAL
Basil St, Knightsbridge
SW3 1AT (Relais et
Châteaux) ☎071-589 5171
Telex no 919042
FAX 071-225 0011
*This modern hotel has a reputation as a place of character, and the news this year is of a refurbishment in 'fin de sicle' style. The particularly pleasant atmosphere remains unchanged, however, as do the high standards which amply compensate for the hotel's lack of space. Bedrooms vary in size, but all are furnished to a high standard of comfort, with extras such as bathrobes and seasonal fresh fruit, as well as air-conditioning and other good modern facilities. Valet room service is pleasant and polite, and efficiency prevails in all departments. The prettily decorated restaurant, in pastel pink, green and beige, is now under the supervision of a recently promoted and charming manager, who, with Maitre Chef Elliot, deserves a special mention for the combination of skilful cooking and welcoming atmosphere. Together they create a sense that this is somewhere very special, and the wine list is naturally very good too. The proprietor, David Levin, is continually improving the hotel, and is once again to be congratulated on making it such a delightful place. It enjoys a quiet setting for London, and nearby is another of its assets, the very good Le Metro wine bar.*
48⇌ CTV in all bedrooms T
Lift ( ▦ 12🐾 (£8) ⇱
♡ French V ✆ ⚏
Credit Cards ① ② ③ ④ ⑤

★★★62% **Basil Street** Basil St, Knightsbridge SW3 1AH
☎071-581 3311 Telex no 28379 FAX 071-581 3693
*A well-established hotel stylishly and comfortably furnished. The lounge area, wine bar, Punch Restaurant and the Ladies Club are especially attractive and popular.*
92rm(72⇌) CTV in all bedrooms
Lift ( ₽ ⇱ xmas
♡ International V ✆ ⚏ Lunch £13.75-£15.75 Dinner £20-£24alc Last dinner 9.45pm
Credit Cards ① ② ③ ④ ⑤

✗ ✗ ✗ *Waltons* 121 Walton St SW3 2JJ ☎071-584 0204
*Chef Tony Cameron has brought his own adventurous style of cooking to this long-established and famous restaurant. Surroundings are opulent, the wine list excellent, and diners may choose between the prix fixe and the more expensive à la carte menus. Service is very professional, but impersonal.*
Closed 25-26 Dec
V 65 seats Lunch £14.50&alc Dinner £30-£45alc Last lunch 2.30pm Last dinner 11.30pm ₽ nc2yrs
Credit Cards ① ② ③ ④ ⑤

✗ ✗ ✗ *Zen Chinese* Chelsea Cloisters, Sloane Av SW3 3DZ
☎071-589 1781 FAX 071-437 0641
*A popular restaurant serving an appealing selection of well-prepared dishes. The staff are attentive and courteous and offer good Chinese hospitality.*
Closed Xmas
♡ Chinese V 120 seats Last lunch 2.30pm Last dinner 11.30pm ₽
Credit Cards ① ② ③ ④ ⑤

❀ ✕✕**Bibendum** Michelin House, 81 Fulham Rd SW3 6RD ☎071-581 5817 FAX 071-823 7925
*This cool and sophisticated Conran-designed restaurant on the first floor of the distinctive Michelin building, is home to the cooking of the now firmly established Simon Hopkinson, with its emphasis on rusticity, prime ingredients and honest, striking flavours. Starters might include Soupe au Poisson with croutons and rouille, or a warm tomato tart richly flavoured with basil and parmesan. Main dishes are equally accomplished – for example, tender French rabbit with mustard sauce or roast best end of lamb with a garlicked mushroom persillade are dishes that our Inspector has enjoyed this year. The outstanding wine list features a range of sweet wines to accompany the skilfully made desserts. The service is competent and now seems less stand-offish than we have experienced in the past.*
Closed 24-28 Dec
♡ Continental **V** 74 seats ✻ S15% Lunch £24.75 Dinner £35-£45alc Last lunch 2.30pm Last dinner 11.30pm ₰ nc5yrs
Credit Cards ①③

✕✕**Daphne's** 110-112 Draycott Av, Chelsea SW3 3AE ☎071-584 6883 & 071-589 4257
*Warm cosy restaurant with fine French and English cuisine.*
Closed Sun & BHs
Lunch not served Sat
♡ English & French 95 seats ✻ Lunch £5-£30alc Dinner £20-£30alc Last lunch 2.30pm Last dinner mdnt ₰
Credit Cards ①②③⑤

✕✕**English Garden** 10 Lincoln St SW3 2TS ☎071-584 7272
*Well-researched old English recipies, cooked with considerable skill, are featured in a fashionable conservatory, English-garden setting.*
Closed 25-26 Dec
**V** 65 seats Lunch £14.50&alc Dinner £25-£35alc Last lunch 2.30pm Last dinner 11.30pm ₰
Credit Cards ①②③⑤

✕✕**The English House** 3 Milner St SW3 2QA ☎071-584 3002
*This elegant, well-appointed restaurant serves thoroughly researched traditional English dishes; supervision and service are excellent.*
Closed 25-26 Dec
**V** 40 seats Lunch £14.75&alc Dinner £25-£35alc Last lunch 2.30pm Last dinner 11.30pm ₰
Credit Cards ①②③⑤

✕✕**Good Earth** 233 Brompton Rd SW3 2EP ☎071-584 3658 FAX 071-823 8769
*A loyal and appreciative clientèle ensure that this good, serious Chinese restaurant is always busy. Cantonese, Pekinese and Szechwan specialities offer a choice of styles ranging from fiery chilli dishes to the milder, delicate flavour of crispy lamb wrapped in lettuce and served with yellow plum sauce. Whole fish and fresh lobster are generally available at a market price.*
Closed 24-27 Dec
♡ Cantonese, Pekinese & Szechwan **V** 155 seats ✻ Lunch £15.50-£22.50 Dinner £15.50-£22.50 Last lunch 11.15pm ₰
Credit Cards ①②③⑤

✕✕*Mario* 260-262A Brompton Rd SW3 2AS ☎071-584 1724
*An interesting selection of Italian wines complements the reliable and authentic regional dishes produced by Chef Cannas. Pasta is fresh and made on the premises, sauces well flavoured, the vegetables fresh and cooked with care.*
Closed Mon & BH's
♡ Italian **V** 80 seats Last lunch 3pm Last dinner 11.30pm ₰
Credit Cards ①②③⑤

✕✕**Ménage à Trois** 15 Beauchamp Place SW3 1NQ ☎071-589 4252 & 071-589 0984 FAX 071-589 8860
*This lively, basement restaurant has an intimate atmosphere, open fires in season and live piano music. The menu consists of starters and sweets only and the cheerful young staff are happy to help diners make their selections. Especially recommended by our*

*inspector was the "menage a trois" cheese-filled parcels and the splendid array of chocolate puds.*
Closed 25-26 Dec, Good Fri & Etr Sun
Lunch not served Sat & Sun
♡ French **V** 70 seats ✻ Lunch £15-£17.50&alc Dinner £18.50-£35alc Last lunch 3.15pm Last dinner 11.45pm ₰ ♫
Credit Cards ①②③⑤

✕✕**St Quentin** 243 Brompton Rd SW3 2EP ☎071-589 8005 & 071-581 5131 FAX 071-584 6064
*This small, intimate brasserie offers a well chosen menu where the fish dishes are to be highly recommended. The wine list is comprehensive and offers a choice of reasonably priced bottles, the staff are friendly and efficient.*
♡ French 80 seats ✻ Lunch fr£11.90&alc Dinner fr£14.90&alc Last lunch 3pm Last dinner mdnt ₰ nc
Credit Cards ①②③⑤

❀❀❀ ✕✕ **TANTE CLAIRE, LONDON** 68 Royal Hospital Rd SW3 4HP (Relais et Châteaux) ☎071-352 6045 & 071-351 0227 FAX 071-352 3257
*Without doubt this is one of the finest restaurants in the country. Chef patron Pierre Koffmann's apron strings are still firmly attached to his own kitchens, reflecting his dedication and earning the respect of his peers. We are delighted to recognise his pre-eminence by the award of 3 rosettes this year, making this one of the very few restaurants to gain the AA's highest award for food. Signature dishes such as the stuffed Pied de Cochon braisé or the marvellous Selle de chevreuil au vinaigre de framboises et chocolat amer, are consistently memorable, but some experimental dishes, such as the Eventail d'agneau roti, hachis partmentier et jus aux épices doux, where our Inspector found the strength of the eastern spices at odds with the flavour of the lamb, are less successful.*
Closed Sat, Sun, BH's, 10 days Xmas, 10 days Etr & 3 wks Aug/Sep
♡ French 38 seats ✻ Lunch fr£19.50&alc Dinner £40-£60alc Last lunch 2pm Last dinner 11.15pm ₰
Credit Cards ①②③⑤

❀ ✕✕*Turners* 87-89 Walton St SW3 2HP ☎071-584 6711
*Brian Turner spends much time with his customers, and with his infectious enthusiasm has created a warm and friendly restaurant. The cuisine is modern French in style with good use made of fresh ingredients. Diners make their selection from the set menu du jour or a longer menu.*
Lunch not served Sat
♡ French 52 seats Last dinner 11pm ₰
Credit Cards ①②③⑤

✕*Dans* 119 Sydney St SW3 6NR ☎071-352 2718
*The warm, cheerful atmosphere and attractive décor have helped to make this a popular restaurant. The cooking is of good quality and dishes are unpretentious and well prepared. Terrine of game, followed by a succulent loin of lamb en croûte with a dessert of poached pear attractively presented on a raspberry sauce are typical of the lunch dishes.*
Closed BH's & Xmas-New Year
Dinner not served Sun
♡ English & French 50 seats ✻ Dinner £19 Last lunch 2.30pm Last dinner 10.45pm ₰
Credit Cards ①②③⑤

✕*Ma Cuisine* 113 Walton St SW3 2HP ☎071-584 7585
*A cosy little Chelsea restaurant specialising in robust French provincial cuisine. The cooking seems to have lost some edge since a change of ownership, but hearty dishes such as daube de canard continue to be enjoyable, and are served by good-humoured staff.*
Closed Sun
♡ French 32 seats ✻ Lunch £25-£30alc Dinner £25-£30alc Last lunch 2pm Last dinner 11pm ₰
Credit Cards ①②③④⑤

**441**

✕**Magic Dragon** 99 Fulham Rd SW3 6RH ☎071-225 2244
FAX 071-929 5690
*High-tech oriental contemporary design combines with an exciting
and varied picture-styled menu which features the best provincial
dishes from Peking, Szechwan and Canton, creating a whole new
approach to Chinese cooking. Recommended dishes include spring
rolls, slices of pork in garlic sauce, beef in oyster sauce and sautéed
shrimps with cashew nuts. Service is very efficient and friendly and
offers excellent value for money.*
Closed Good Fri, Aug BH & 25-26 Dec
♉ Chinese **V** ✳ S% Lunch fr£9.50&alc Dinner £15-£34&alc
Last lunch 2.30pm Last dinner 10.50pm ♪
Credit Cards ①②③

---

✕**Le Suquet** 104 Draycott Av SW3 3AE ☎071-581 1785
*With French Riviera connections it comes as no surprise to find
seafood a speciality at this corner-sited restaurant. Commendable
dishes include Loup de Mer au beurre blanc and lobster fresh from
the tank. Booking is essential, particularly if a single diner.*
♉ French 50 seats Last dinner 11.30pm ♪
Credit Cards ①②③⑤

---

### SW5 Earl's Court

★★★67% **Swallow International** Cromwell Rd SW5 0TH
(Swallow) ☎071-973 1000 Telex no 27260 FAX 071-244 8194
*A large city-centre hotel with comfortable, well-equipped
accommodation. The tastefully appointed Fountain Brasserie is
open throughout the day and in the evening the newly refurbished
Blayne's Restaurant and piano bar features a traditional menu.
The hotel now has an exclusive leisure club.*
417❤️🎄(36fb)✂in 39 bedrooms CTV in all bedrooms ® T S%
sB&B❤️🎄£95-£103
dB&B❤️🎄£115-£123 Continental breakfast 🅱
Lift ⦅ 45P (£12.50 per day) 30🚗 ⌂(heated) sauna solarium
gymnasium whirlpool spa turkish steamroom ♫ *xmas*
♉ International **V** ♥ ♫ Lunch £11.50&alc Dinner £15&alc
Last dinner mdnt
Credit Cards ①②③⑤

---

✕✕**Tiger Lee** 251 Old Brompton Rd SW5 9HP
☎071-370 2323 & 071-370 5970 Telex no 919660
FAX 071-244 6032
*The elegantly modern Chinese restaurant specialises in seafood
and offers dishes with such evocative names as "Shadow of a
Butterfly". The attentive and professional service is excellent and
there are some fine French wines on the wine list.*
Lunch not served
♉ Cantonese **V** 56 seats ✳ Dinner £18-£40&alc Wine £9.20
Last dinner 11.15pm ♪✂
Credit Cards ①②③⑤

---

### SW6 Fulham

See LONDON plan 1C3
✕✕**The Blue Elephant** 4 Fulham Broadway SW6 1AA
☎071-385 6595 FAX 071-386 7665
Lunch not served Sat
♉ Thai **V** 250 seats ✳ S15% Lunch £25-£35alc Dinner
£30-£40alc Last lunch 2.30pm Last dinner mdnt ♪
Credit Cards ①②③⑤

---

✕**Nayab Indian** 309 New King's Rd SW6 4RF ☎071-731 6993 &
071-736 9596
*Owners Praveen and 'Naz' Rai have enjoyed a regular following
for many years since their 'Park Walk' days, with a fine reputation
for authentic Indian cooking. Chef Molik Mian uses good quality
fresh ingredients and specialises in the authentic flavour of India.
Our inspector particularly recommends Chicken Tikka Masala,
Lamb Pasanda and Footpath Hotel Curry from Delhi. Service,
supervised by 'Naz' Rai is particularly attentive and adds another
dimension to this well run restaurant. A take-away service is
available on request.*
Closed 24-26 Dec & 1 Jan

♉ Indian **V** 50 seats Lunch £7.90-£20.30alc Dinner
£8.50-£21.05alc Last lunch 2.45pm Last dinner 11.45pm
♪ nc5yrs
Credit Cards ①②③⑤

---

### SW7 South Kensington

★★★★65% **Gloucester** 4-18 Harrington Gardens SW7 4LH
(Rank) ☎071-373 6030 Telex no 917505 FAX 071-373 0409
*A pleasant modern hotel with an open-plan foyer/lounge and two
restaurants, one of which offers a traditional à la carte menu,
whilst the other provides an all day light meal and snack service.
Bedrooms are spacious and well equipped, and pleasant, cheerful
staff provide 24-hour room service. In addition to the cocktail
lounge there is also a wine cellar and real ale pub.*
550❤️🎄(2fb)✂in 51 bedrooms CTV in all bedrooms ® T ✳
sB❤️🎄£122-£142 dB❤️🎄£142-£172 (room only) 🅱
Lift ⦅ ▦ 100🚗 (fr £6.50) CFA *xmas*
♉ English & Continental **V** ♥ ♫ ✂
Credit Cards ①②③④⑤

---

★★★56% **Rembrandt** Thurloe Place SW7 2RS ☎071-589 8100
Telex no 295828 FAX 071-225 3363
*Well located for the West End the hotel dates back to the
beginning of the century. Bedrooms vary in size and comfort but all
are well equipped. Fully air conditioned conference facilities can
cater for up to 250 and guests can make use of the Aquilla Health
Club for a nominal fee.*
200❤️🎄(25fb)✂in 28 bedrooms CTV in all bedrooms ®
🐕 (ex guide dogs) ✳ sB❤️🎄£85 dB❤️🎄£105 (room only)
Lift ⦅ ♪ ⌂(heated) sauna solarium gymnasium beauty parlour
massage spa bath
**V** ♥ ♫ S10% Lunch £14.95 Dinner £14.95 Last dinner 9.30pm
Credit Cards ①②③④⑤

---

✕✕✕**Bombay Brasserie** Courtfield Close, 140 Gloucester Rd
SW7 4TH ☎071-370 4040 & 071-373 0971 FAX 071-835 1669
*This restaurant serves authentic regional dishes in an elegant
colonial atmosphere.*
♉ Indian **V** 175 seats ✳ Lunch fr£12.95 Dinner fr£30alc Last
lunch 2.45pm Last dinner mdnt ♪ ♫
Credit Cards ①③

---

✕✕✕**190 Queen's Gate** 190 Queen's Gate SW7 5EU
☎071-581 5666 FAX 071-581 8261
*This basement restaurant offers a good standard of cooking, with
skill and care taken in the preparation of dishes for the à la carte,
set price menu and chef's recommendations. The fish dishes are of
particular note and there is an excellent wine list covering many
countries, including some fine clarets and Burgundies. Professional
and attentive service is of a high standard.*
Closed 25-26 Dec, Good Fri & Etr Sun
Lunch not served Sat
Dinner not served Sun
**V** 70 seats ✳ Lunch fr£11.50&alc Dinner fr£32.50alc Last
lunch 3.30pm Last dinner 11.30pm ♪
Credit Cards ①②③⑤

---

❀✕✕**Hilaire** 68 Old Brompton Rd SW7 3JX ☎071-584 8993 &
071-584 7601
(Rosette awarded for dinner only)
*This two-storey Kensington restaurant maintains a high standard
of cooking. Here Bryan Webb uses his skill and flair to produce
flavoursome dishes accompanied by well-prepared fresh
vegetables. The puddings will not disappoint and the wine list is
well balanced and reasonably priced. A plainer menu is available
at lunchtime.*
Closed 1 wk Xmas, Etr, last 2 wks Aug & BH's
Lunch not served Sat
Dinner not served Sun
♉ European **V** 48 seats ✳ Lunch fr£14.50 Dinner
£23.50-£32.50 Last lunch 2.30pm Last dinner 11pm ♪
Credit Cards ①②③④⑤

**London**

✗**Tui** 19 Exhibition Rd SW7 2HE ☎071-584 8359
*This simple but attractive Thai restaurant on two floors provides a high standard of authentic cuisine, combining good fresh ingredients with subtly blended native flavours. Along with the well-known 'Sateh' and the wonderful creamy curries, are dishes such as Gai Yarng, grilled marinated baby chicken with chilli sauce, Mee Grob, a cold dish of crispy noodles, finely chopped pork and shrimps and a delicious tamarind sauce, and very good traditional Thai soups. There is a short list of well chosen wines and refreshing ginger tea as an alternative. Staff are friendly and helpful.*
Closed Public Hols
♡ Thai 19 seats ✱ S% Lunch £10 Dinner £15 Last lunch 2.30pm Last dinner 11.30pm ♪
Credit Cards ⊡ ② ③ ⑤

---

**SW8 Battersea**
See LONDON plan 1D3
See also SW11
⑧✗✗**L'Arlequin** 123 Queenstown Rd SW8 3RM
☎071-622 0555
*Christian Delteil continues to delight with his refreshingly understated menu concealing dishes of great finesse. The virtues of modern French cuisine are exemplified by stunning presentation, gentle cooking and shiny sauces, resulting in highly satisfying food. An honest fish mousseline with butter sauce, chosen from the excellent prix fixe luncheon menu, was outstanding, and a tender breast of Mallard, served with an intense, red-wine glaze was accompanied by the crispy legs. The wine list complements the cuisine and service in this smart little restaurant under the supervision of Madame Delteil, is relaxed and 'sympathique'.*
Closed Sat, Sun, 1 wk winter & 3 wks Aug
♡ French 45 seats Last dinner 10.30pm ♪ nc5yrs
Credit Cards ⊡ ② ③ ⑤

⑧✗✗**Cavaliers'** 129 Queenstown Rd SW8 3RH ☎071-720 6960
*Well constructed and beautifully presented dishes mark David Cavalier's un-fussy, unpretentious menu which shows off his individual style to perfection. Lobster and salmon terrine with tomato and fennel, a soup of lamb, pearl barley and vegetables, his famous chicken and mushroom ravioli (with brown lentils) are a few of the dishes that carry his unmistakeable signature. Susan Cavalier is responsible for the desserts, which are extraordinarily tempting, in particular the Grand Marnier soufflé with caramel sauce which our Inspector found irresistible. Service is well supervised and the excellent wine list includes many half bottles.*
Closed Sun, Mon, 2 wks Aug & 2 wks Xmas
♡ English & French 50 seats ✱ Lunch £16.50-£33 Dinner £33
Last lunch 2pm Last dinner 10.30pm ♪ nc8yrs
Credit Cards ⊡ ② ③ ⑤

---

**SW10 West Brompton**
See LONDON plan 1C3
✗✗**Brinkley's** 47 Hollywood Rd SW10 9HX ☎071-351 1683
FAX 071-376 5083
*Located off the Fulham Road, Brinkley's is allied to a wine bar and wine shop. Whether you choose from the 'Dishes of the Day' or the à la carte menu, you are sure to enjoy the skilful cooking of Chef Graham Day. This is a deservedly popular restaurant, offering good value for money, and friendly, attentive service. The candlelight and soft lighting create an intimate atmosphere in the evenings.*
Closed Sun, Xmas & Etr
Lunch not served
♡ English & French V 60 seats ✱ Dinner £18-£20&alc Last dinner 11.30pm ♪
Credit Cards ⊡ ③

✗✗**Ken Lo's Memories of China** Chelsea Harbour Yard, Chelsea Harbour SW10 ☎071-352 4953 FAX 071-351 2096
*Set in the heart of the latest and most fashionable of waterside developments, Ken Lo's second 'Memories of China' restaurant has a particularly popular and appealing contemporary atmosphere and offers an interesting à la carte, regional and principal dishes, traditional set meals and a Dim Sum bar. Our Inspectors particularly recommend Peking Duck (one hour's notice required), Cantonese onion and ginger lobster, black bean sauced dishes and iron plate sizzled dishes, choosing the main ingredients. Service is particularly well supervised and an international wine list is augmented by a very good wine by the glass list. A take-away service is available.*
Closed 25-26 Dec & 1 Jan
Dinner not served Sun
♡ Chinese V 160 seats ✱ Lunch £13.50 Dinner £25 Last lunch 2.30pm Last dinner 10.45pm
Credit Cards ⊡ ② ③ ⑤

✗**La Croisette** 168 Ifield Rd SW10 9AF ☎071-373 3694
*Popular small French restaurant specialising in shell fish. Good main basement ambience.*
Closed Mon & 2 wks Xmas
Lunch not served Tue
♡ French 55 seats Last dinner 11.30pm ♪
Credit Cards ⊡ ② ③ ⑤

---

**SW11 Battersea**
See LONDON plan 1D3
See also SW8
✗**Pollyanna's** 2 Battersea Rise SW11 1ED ☎071-228 0316
*Fashionable bistro-style décor is complemented by skilful and reliable cooking supervised by the proprietor.*
Closed 4 days Xmas & 1 Jan
Lunch not served Mon-Sat
Dinner not served Sun
♡ French V 40 seats ✱ Sunday Lunch £14.95 Dinner £14-£22alc Last dinner mdnt ♪
Credit Cards ⊡ ③

---

**SW14 East Sheen**
See LONDON plan 1C3
✗**Crowthers** 481 Upper Richmond Rd West, East Sheen SW14 7PU ☎081-876 6372
*Small family-run, tastefully decorated restaurant offering a fixed price menu.*
Closed Sun (ex Mothers Day), 1 wk Xmas & 2 wks summer
Lunch not served Sat & Mon
♡ French V 28 seats ✱ Lunch £15 Dinner £21 Last lunch 1.45pm Last dinner 10.45pm ♪
Credit Cards ⊡ ② ③

---

**SW17 Wandsworth Common**
See LONDON plan 1C2
⑧⑧✗✗ **HARVEY'S, LONDON** 2 Bellevue Rd, Wandsworth Rd SW17 7EQ ☎081-672 0114
*Marco Pierre White's chic little restaurant may be a little cramped, and service may from time to time be rather less than assured, but on the plate, where it counts, the customer can hardly fail to be impressed. The carte features many tried and tested dishes, some showing the influence of his mentors, and some that truly reflect his innovative genius. The set-price luncheon menu is often used as the breeding ground for new ideas which, if he is pleased with them, are later refined and added to the repertoire on a permanent basis. Some work better than others, but his consistency of touch is remarkable and a meal at Harvey's is invariably laced with memorable dishes. One such dish, a blanquette of scallops and langoustines, with delicately prepared cucumber and strips of ginger, was so good that it broke one's heart*

▶

London

*to come to the last mouthful. Other favourites, such as the delicious ravioli of sweetbreads, served with an intense truffle fumet, have been equally acclaimed. There is an excellent wine list of around 400 bins, but the seeker after bargains will have his work cut out to find any.*

Closed Sun, last 2 wks Aug & last wk Dec-1st wk Jan
Lunch not served Sat
45 seats Last dinner 11pm ✗ nc5yrs
Credit Cards ①②③

---

### SW19 Wimbledon

**See LONDON plan 1***C2*

★★★★63% **Cannizaro House** West Side, Wimbledon
Common SW19 4UF (Mount Charlotte (TS)) ☎081-879 1464
Telex no 9413837 FAX 081-879 7338

*Set in its own beautiful parkland, this historic Georgian mansion provides guests with all the peace and tranquillity of the countryside. Bedrooms are beautifully furnished and have marble-tiled bathrooms. Recent visits have indicated that service levels can be disappointing.*

48➪ॱ🛏4🛏 CTV in all bedrooms T ✱ sB➪ॱ🛏fr£85
dB➪ॱ🛏fr£99 (room only) 🅿
《 60P ✿ ♫
♡ International ⚘ ⏺ Lunch fr£16.50&alc Dinner
fr£16.50&alc Last dinner 10.30pm
Credit Cards ①②③④⑤

---

### W1 West End

★★★★★

★★★★★ **CLARIDGE'S**

Brook St W1A 2JQ
☎071-629 8860
Telex no 21872
FAX 071-499 2210

*This Grande Dame of hotels, favourite of royalty and celebrities, is not resting on its laurels. The majority of the bedrooms and nearly all the superb suites have been refurbished, and work continues on upgrading the rest, with air-conditioning among other welcome new features. The kitchens have also undergone a major transformation costing several million pounds. None of these improvements have been carried out at the expense of the supremely high standards which make Claridge's the epitome of fine English hotel-keeping. Standing in the heart of Mayfair, it adheres rigidly to its traditional values of exclusiveness, discretion and professional service of the highest order. Much of the credit for preserving the ambience and individual style must go to Michael Bentley, manager now for 20 years. To witness his greeting of loyal guests and to hear him talk with pride and affection for this distinguished hotel is to understand why Claridge's attracts such a devoted following. The General Manager and Director, Ron Jones, has brought such life, enthusiasm and personality that it has lifted the spirits of all the staff, and these two gentlemen will undoubtedly ensure that Claridge's remains a very special and uniquely British hotel.*

190➪ॱ🛏 CTV in all bedrooms T 🛏 (ex guide dogs) S15%
sB➪ॱ🛏£190-£220 dB➪ॱ🛏£245-£285 (room only) 🅿
Lift 《 ✗ ♨ ♫ *xmas*
♡ International V ⚘ ⏺ S15% Lunch £29-£48alc High tea
£8-£8alc Dinner £31-£54alc Last dinner 11.15pm
Credit Cards ①②③⑤

---

★★★★★

❀❀★★★★★ **CONNAUGHT**

Carlos Place W1Y 6AL
☎071-499 7070

*Discretion is the Connaught's watchword; behind its unobtrusive portals you will not find such modern fads as gymnasia, beauty salons or saunas, but you will find an impeccably trained staff who are famed for remembering every idiosyncracy of their regular clientele. Managing Director Paolo Zago's adherence to these high traditional standards of hotel-keeping has made the Connaught a favourite retreat of those who value their privacy. Chef Michel Bourdin and his team excel at preparing classical French cuisine. Dishes that have excited our Inspectors include an intriguing 'Black Swan Nellie Melba', choux pastry filled with a smooth parfait of foie gras with grated truffles, followed by a Blanc de Turbot soufflé à l'oseille, sauce Champagne – perfectly cooked fish complemented by the sharpness of the sauce. Don't avoid ordering the Pommes soufflées either – they can hardly be bettered. At lunchtime guests will also find some classic British dishes on the menu – steak, kidney and mushroom pie or pudding, for example. This is also one of the few restaurants to serve that lovely finale to a meal, the savoury, so why not try a special treat to round off an excellent dinner, say, a Scotch woodcock or a superbly prepared Welsh Rarebit. When there is so much to say in praise of the Connaught, it is sad that reports about the food continue to be mixed and this year therefore we make the award of two rosettes with just a few reservations.*

90➪ॱ🛏 CTV in all bedrooms 🛏
Lift 《 ✗ ♨
♡ English & French ⏺
Credit Cards ①

---

★★★★★78% **Inn on the Park** Hamilton Place, Park Ln
W1A 1AZ (Prestige) ☎071-499 0888 Telex no 22771
FAX 071-493 1895 & 6629

*The Inn on the Park is possibly the best modern hotel in London. It is certainly elegant and attractive, with every attention paid to the comfort and convenience of its guests. The entrance lobby, with marbled floors and dark wood panelling, is enhanced by lots of fresh flowers and greenery. There are places to sit and a variety of quality shops. The foyer lounge provides snacks and drinks throughout the day and traditional afternoon teas to the sound of the harp or piano. A double staircase leads to the first floor where there is a further sitting area, the Four Seasons Restaurant with cocktail lounge and the Lanes Restaurant where a pianist plays each evening. Executive Chef, Eric Deblonde, and Chef de Cuisine, Bruno Loubet, are in charge of the catering and have created menus with some imaginative dishes. The bedrooms are spacious, well appointed and individually decorated with tasteful soft furnishings and the added benefit of air conditioning. The valet room service is pleasantly polite and an efficient service prevails throughout the hotel. Overseeing the whole operation, with the same commitment, attention to detail, professionalism and care, is the most charming and courteous Ramon Pajares.*

228➪ॱ🛏✗in 48 bedrooms CTV in all bedrooms T 🛏 ✱ S%
sB➪ॱ🛏£201.25-£224.25 dB➪ॱ🛏fr£247.25 (room only) 🅿
Lift 《 ⊞ 65🐾 (£9) ♨ ♫ *xmas*
♡ International V ⚘ ⏺ ✗ Lunch £20.50-£27 High tea
fr£10&alc Dinner £24.50-£38.50&alc Last dinner mdnt
Credit Cards ①②③④⑤

**✿★★★★★73% Inter-Continental** 1 Hamilton Pl, Hyde Park Corner W1V 0QY ☎071-409 3131 Telex no 25853 FAX 071-493 3476

*One of London's largest modern hotels, the Intercontinental maintains high standards of service in all departments, and rooms that are smartly furnished and equipped with all modern comforts expected at this level. Of the three restarants, Le Soufflé is the most elegant and renowned for Peter Kromberg's cooking – specialities, as one might expect from the name are indeed soufflés, of which there a great variety on the menu. Hamilton's Restaurant also embraces a nightclub, and there is a Coffee House, the only part of the hotel operation with which our Inspectors find fault. Breakfasts are served here, and both the lack of space and self-service buffet of pre-cooked dishes seem scarcely in keeping with the style of a five-star hotel.*

467⇨⁵𝄞✝in 58 bedrooms CTV in all bedrooms T ✖ (ex guide dogs) ✳ S% sB⇨⁵𝄞£195.50-£212.75 dB⇨⁵𝄞£207-£253 (room only) ꊉ

Lift ℂ ⊞ 100🍽 (£21.50 24 hrs) 🚗 CFA sauna gymnasium health centre ♬ xmas

♌ English, French, Italian & Oriental V ✆ ⚏ ✝ Lunch £24&alc Dinner £40&alc Last dinner 11.30pm

Credit Cards ①②③④⑤

**★★★★★72% Grosvenor House** Park Ln W1A 3AA (Trusthouse Forte) ☎071-499 6363 Telex no 24871 FAX 071-493 3341

*After several years of refurbishment, this hotel has been restored to its rightful position as one of the leading 5-star hotels in the country. Besides the renowned banqueting suites, there are a number of shops, and a large lounge where afternoon tea is especially popular. There is a choice of three restaurants – 90 Park Lane, the Pavilion Restaurant (particularly good value at lunchtime) and the attractive Pasta Vino e Fantasia where Italian cuisine is served.*

454⇨⁵𝄞✝in 47 bedrooms CTV in all bedrooms ⑧ T ✖ ✳ S% sB⇨⁵𝄞£185-£215 dB⇨⁵𝄞£205-£235 (room only) ꊉ

Lift ℂ 20P 100🍽 (charged) CFA ▦(heated) sauna solarium gymnasium health & fitness centre ♬ xmas

♌ English, French & Italian V ✆ ⚏ ✝ S% Lunch fr£19 Dinner fr£22.50 Last dinner 10.45pm

Credit Cards ①②③④⑤

**★★★★★71% Ritz** Piccadilly W1V 9DG (Prestige) ☎071-493 8181 Telex no 267200 FAX 071-493 2687

*A bastion of fine hotel keeping, the Ritz occupies a pleasant location by Green Park, over which many of the fine suites and the magnificent restaurant enjoy views. It is the attitude of management and staff which make staying at the Ritz such an enjoyable experience. Chef Keith Stanley has significantly improved the quality of food; the classical dishes have a hint of modern influence.*

130⇨⁵𝄞 CTV in all bedrooms T ✖ S15% sB⇨⁵𝄞fr£185 dB⇨⁵𝄞fr£215 (room only) ꊉ

Lift ℂ 🅿 🚗 ♬ xmas

♌ International V ✆ ⚏ S15% Lunch fr£25&alc Dinner fr£39.50&alc Last dinner 10.45pm

Credit Cards ①②③④⑤

**✿★★★★★67% Le Meridien London** 21 Piccadilly W1V 0BH ☎071-734 8000 Telex no 25795 FAX 071-437 3574

*This French-owned hotel offers all the services that one would expect in a five star hotel but the bedrooms are not, at the time of our Inspector's visit, as elegant and comfortable as at some other hotels of this class. We understand that a programme of refurbishment is in hand. The Oak Room Restaurant, however, with its Chef David Chambers, is highly recommended. Our Inspector particularly praised the intensity of flavour achieved both in his own creations and in the preparation of classical dishes. The hotel's leisure facilities are second to none in the city.*

284⇨⁵𝄞1🔲 CTV in all bedrooms T ✖ (ex guide dogs) ✳ S% sB⇨⁵𝄞£184-£201.25 dB⇨⁵𝄞£201.25-£224.25 (room only) ꊉ

Lift ℂ ⊞ 🅿 🚗 ▦(heated) squash snooker sauna solarium gymnasium health & leisure club ♬

♌ International V ✆ ⚏ ✝ Lunch fr£14.50&alc Dinner £16.95-£37.50alc Last dinner 11.30pm

Credit Cards ①②③④⑤

**★★★★★66% The Churchill** 30 Portman Square W1A 4ZX ☎071-486 5800 Telex no 264831 FAX 071-486 1255

*This hotel has a lovely location overlooking Portman Square Gardens. The flower-filled lobby, attractive arcade of shops, the sunken lounge where afternoon tea is served to the accompaniment of a harp, and the choice of bar, coffee shop and sophisticated restaurant are just some of the facilities made available to guests staying here.*

452⇨⁵𝄞✝in 66 bedrooms CTV in all bedrooms T S% sB⇨⁵𝄞£212.75-£258.75 dB⇨⁵𝄞£235.75-£281.75 (room only) ꊉ

Lift ℂ ⊞ 60🍽 (£2.50 per 2hrs) 🚗 ✿ CFA ♪ (hard) ♬ ♌ International V ✆ ⚏ ✝ S% Lunch fr£25&alc Dinner fr£30&alc Last dinner 11pm

Credit Cards ①②③④⑤ⓔ

**★★★★★59% London Hilton** 22 Park Ln W1A 2HH (Hilton) ☎071-493 8000 Telex no 24873 FAX 071-493 4957

*From its prime position at the heart of Mayfair the Hilton's rooms command superb views over Hyde Park, Green Park and St James's Park. Bedrooms are well equipped and offer free cable and satellite TV as well as the usual facilities. The lively Polynesian restaurant beneath the hotel is very popular and there is also a roof restaurant and a discotheque. Staff are cosmopolitan, well trained and very helpful, contributing much to the character of the hotel.*

448⇨⁵𝄞✝in all bedrooms CTV in all bedrooms T ✳ sB⇨⁵𝄞£178.25-£253 dB⇨⁵𝄞£247.25-£287.50 (room only) ꊉ

Lift ℂ 🅿 sauna solarium ♬ xmas ▶

London

♀ International V ✿ ☑ ✠ S15% Lunch £23.50-£29 Dinner
£45&alc Last dinner 1am
Credit Cards ① ② ③ ④ ⑤

★★★★★58%, *May Fair Inter-Continental* Stratton St W1A 2AN
☎071-629 7777 Telex no 262526 FAX 071-629 1459
*This long-established hotel is now under new management.*
*Facilities include an elegant restaurant, a popular coffee house and*
*the new Starlight leisure club. A multi-million pound programme*
*to redevelop most public areas is under review.*
322⇅♠(14fb) CTV in all bedrooms ✖ (ex guide dogs)
Lift ⟨ ⊞ ⱽ ⇔
♀ English & French V ✿ ☑ Last dinner 10.30pm
Credit Cards ① ② ③ ④ ⑤

★★★★ ATHENAEUM

Piccadilly W1V 0BJ
(Rank)(Pride of Britain)
☎071-499 3464
Telex no 261589
FAX 071-493 1860

*One of the more modern West*
*End Hotels, the Athenaeum*
*has been completely*
*refurbished to a very high standard, with extremely*
*comfortable suites and bay-windowed rooms overlooking the*
*Park furnished to meet the expectations of a sophisticated and*
*international clientele. Drawing room and restaurant are*
*equally attractive and the chef, Derek Fuller, has added a*
*further dimension to his skilful cooking with regular*
*'promotions' of French regional dishes, game, and 'menus*
*dégustations'. His mousselines and light traditional sauces are*
*particularly well constructed. General Manager Nicholas*
*Rettie sets standards of customer care that could be a model*
*for other hotels and contribute much to the attractions of this*
*friendly hotel. A number of serviced apartments are also*
*available and should prove popular.*
112⇅♠✠in 27 bedrooms CTV in all bedrooms T
✖ (ex guide dogs) ✱ sB⇅♠fr£160
dB⇅♠£173-£188 (room only) ⋿
Lift ⟨ ⊞ 300☗ (£20.50) ⇔ CFA *xmas*
♀ International V ✿ ☑
Credit Cards ① ② ③ ④ ⑤

★★★★ BROWN'S

Albemarle St, Dover St
W1A 4SW (Trusthouse Forte)
☎071-493 6020
Telex no 28686
FAX 071-493 9381

*Where else, in the heart of*
*Mayfair, would the newly*
*arrived guest be greeted as an*
*old and valued customer? The strength of Brown's Hotel lies*
*in the ability of the staff to make you feel at home, and the*
*standard of service throughout is highly commendable. The*
*response to requests for room service is both prompt and*
*courteous and our Inspector, clearly suffering from*
*unfortunate experiences elsewhere, specially praised both the*
*quality and the temperature of the hot meal served to him in*
*his room. L'Apéritif Restaurant, with its wood panelling, has a*
*club-like atmosphere in keeping with the rest of the hotel, but*

*praise for the menu is not unanimous among our Inspectors,*
*who report that the blend of sound classical cuisine with*
*modern methods is not always successful. One report remarks*
*that 'the charming and attentive Restaurant Manager will*
*take care to explain some of the more obscurely named*
*dishes.' This apart, however, Brown's remains a hotel that*
*really cares for its guests and is highly recommended.*
133⇅♠(14fb)✠in 12 bedrooms CTV in all bedrooms T
✖ (ex guide dogs) S% sB⇅♠£145-£155
dB⇅♠£185-£225 (room only) ⋿
Lift ⟨ ⱽ ⇔ CFA gents hairdresser *xmas*
♀ English & French V ✿ ☑ ✠ Lunch £25.75-£26.75&alc
Dinner £29.95-£30.95&alc Last dinner 9.30pm
Credit Cards ① ② ③ ④ ⑤

★★★★75%, *Britannia Inter-Continental* Grosvenor Square
W1X 3AN ☎071-629 9400 Telex no 23941 FAX 071-629 7736
*High standards continue to be maintained in this friendly and*
*popular hotel. Service is professional and the staff helpful.*
*Bedrooms range from small singles to spacious de luxe, but all are*
*tastefully decorated and well equipped. The Adams Restaurant*
*offers a number of imaginative dishes, well and freshly prepared by*
*an enthusiastic staff. Puddings are also a delight.*
353⇅✠in 5 bedrooms CTV in all bedrooms T
✖ (ex guide dogs)
Lift ⟨ ⊞ 15P CFA Satellite TV ♫
♀ English, American & Japanese V ✿ ☑ ✠ Last dinner
10.30pm
Credit Cards ① ② ③ ④ ⑤

★★★★75%, *London Marriott* Grosvenor Square W1A 4AW
☎071-493 1232 Telex no 268101 FAX 071-491 3201
*Overlooking Grosvenor Square, this tastefully-furnished hotel*
*offers a choice of eateries, particularly well-equipped bedrooms*
*and good business and function facilities.*
223⇅♠ CTV in all bedrooms T ✖ (ex guide dogs) ✱
sB⇅♠£184-£207 dB⇅♠£207-£224.25 (room only) ⋿
Lift ⟨ ⊞ ⱽ ⇔ CFA ♫ *xmas*
♀ International V ✿ ☑ ✠ Lunch £16.50-£25alc Dinner
£16.50-£25alc Last dinner 12.30am
Credit Cards ① ② ③ ④ ⑤

★★★★74%, *Portman Inter-Continental* 22 Portman Square
W1H 9FL ☎071-486 5844 Telex no 261526 FAX 071-935 0537
*An inviting lobby with clusters of comfortable armchairs, the*
*popular bakery and pub, Truffles Restaurant, a choice of modern*
*bedrooms or penthouse suites and superb function facilities – just*
*some of the services to be enjoyed in this hotel.*
272⇅♠✠in 14 bedrooms CTV in all bedrooms T
✖ (ex guide dogs) sB&B⇅♠£145-£149
dB&B⇅♠£174-£194 ⋿
Lift ⟨ ⊞ ⱽ CFA ♫ *xmas*
♀ French V ✿ ☑ ✠ S% Lunch £19.50-£20.50&alc Dinner
£29.50&alc Last dinner 11.30pm
Credit Cards ① ② ③ ④ ⑤ ⓔ

★★★73%, *Montcalm* Great Cumberland Place W1A 2LF
☎071-402 4288 Telex no 28710 FAX 071-724 9180
*This terraced Georgian building has been tastefully modernised to*
*provide comfortable accommodation and well-equipped bedrooms.*
*The Celebrités restaurant offers an interesting menu of skilfully*
*prepared dishes and service is professional and friendly.*
115⇅♠(9fb) CTV in all bedrooms T ✖ (ex guide dogs) ✱
S15% sB⇅♠£152-£162 dB⇅♠£169-£195 (room only) ⋿
Lift ⟨ ⊞ ⱽ ⇔ ♫
♀ French V ✿ ☑ ✠ Lunch £14-£15.95 Dinner £21.95&alc
Last dinner 10pm
Credit Cards ① ② ③ ④ ⑤ ⓔ

★★★★ 73% *Park Lane* Piccadilly W1Y 8BX ☎071-499 6321
Telex no 21533 FAX 071-499 1965
*The old-fashioned atmosphere based on traditional levels of service
and hospitality coupled with good management are the secrets of
this hotel's success. In addition, residents can enjoy the Palm
Court lounge, Bracewells Restaurant and the Brasserie. Leisure
facilities are also available.*
321⇨↑(32fb)⊁in 44 bedrooms CTV in all bedrooms
Lift ( 180🚗 (charged) CFA gymnasium
♀ International V ✿ ♨ Last dinner 10.30pm
Credit Cards ①②③⑤

★★★★ 68% **Selfridge** Orchard St W1H 0JS (Mount Charlotte
(TS)) ☎071-408 2080 Telex no 22361 FAX 071-629 8849
*A modern hotel with fine public rooms including a panelled lounge
and country pub-style cocktail bar. There are two restaurants –
one formal and very comfortable and the other very informal.
Bedrooms tend to be small but very well equipped.*
296⇨↑(25fb)⊁in 110 bedrooms CTV in all bedrooms T ✈ ✳
sB⇨↑fr£125 dB⇨↑fr£145 (room only) ▤
Lift ( ▥ ♪
♀ International ✿ ♨ ⊁ Lunch fr£16.95&alc Dinner
fr£16.95&alc Last dinner 10.30pm
Credit Cards ①②③④⑤

★★★★ 63% **The Westbury** Bond St, Conduit St W1A 4UH
(Trusthouse Forte) ☎071-629 7755 Telex no 24378
FAX 071-495 1163
*An attractive hotel, ideally set in Mayfair, greets winter guests
with a glowing fire in its marbled foyer. The compact Polo Bar,
with its murals, leads into the gracious, pine-panelled Polo Lounge
which serves refreshments 24 hours a day, while a cosy and
tastefully appointed restaurant offers a range of interesting menus.
Individually decorated bedrooms – some of which are designated
"non smoking" – are attractive and comfortable, though en suite
facilities can be on the small side, whilst the valet room service is
polite and efficient.*
243⇨↑↑⊁in 40 bedrooms CTV in all bedrooms T ✳ S15%
sB⇨↑£160-£175 dB⇨↑£190-£210 (room only) ▤
Lift ( ▥ 15P 🚗 CFA ♪ xmas
♀ French V ✿ ♨ S15% Lunch £18.50-£20.50&alc Dinner
£20.50-£22.50&alc Last dinner 10.30pm
Credit Cards ①②③④⑤

★★★★ 58% **The Cumberland** Marble Arch W1A 4RF
(Trusthouse Forte) ☎071-262 1234 Telex no 22215
FAX 071-724 4621
*This popular commercial and tourist hotel is continuing to upgrade
its accommodation and most rooms are now both well equipped
and comfortable, as are the lounges and reception area. The choice
of restaurants includes a carvery and a coffee-shop as well as the
main restaurant and, for those who like the exotic, one in Japanese
style.*
894⇨↑(25fb)⊁in 117 bedrooms CTV in all bedrooms ® T
✈ (ex guide dogs) S15% sB⇨↑£118
dB⇨↑£419 (room only) ▤
Lift ( ♪ CFA ♪ xmas
V ✿ ♨ ⊁ Lunch £15-£18 High tea £3.50-£12 Dinner £19-£35
Last dinner 10.45pm
Credit Cards ①②③④⑤

★★★★ 58% **Holiday Inn – Marble Arch** 134 George St
W1H 6DN (Holiday Inns) ☎071-723 1277 Telex no 27983
FAX 071-402 0666
*Well-managed, modern high-rise hotel with varied international
clientele. As we went to print a new European restaurant was being
introduced to complement the existing coffee shop. Staff are willing
and helpful, and the well-equipped bedrooms are particularly
spacious. Free parking for residents is a bonus.*
241⇨↑(135fb)⊁in 32 bedrooms CTV in all bedrooms
Lift ( ▥ 5P 60🚗 CFA ⌷(heated) sauna solarium gymnasium
♀ European V ✿ ♨ ⊁ Last dinner 11pm
Credit Cards ①②③④⑤

★★★★ 55% **Ramada** 10 Berners St W1A 3BA ☎071-636 1629
Telex no 25759 FAX 071-580 3972
*A magnificent lounge and dining room are the key features of this
hotel conveniently located just off Oxford Street. The successful
carvery lunch operation is supplemented by an à la carte menu, and
afternoon teas are also extremely popular. Bedrooms satisfy
modern commercial needs and the refurbishment program should
now be complete.*
235⇨↑(10fb)⊁in 105 bedrooms CTV in all bedrooms T ✈ ✳
S10% sB⇨↑£92-£130 dB⇨↑£150-£230 (room only) ▤
Lift ( ♪ ♪ xmas
♀ English & French V ✿ ♨ ⊁ S10%
Credit Cards ①②③④⑤

★★★★ 50% **St George's** Langham Place W1N 8QS (Trusthouse
Forte) ☎071-580 0111 Telex no 27274 FAX 071-436 7997
*The hotel shares its building just north of Oxford Circus with the
BBC, and bedrooms, recently refurbished and upgraded, are all
above the ninth floor. The Summit Restaurant, bar and lounge
afford panoramic views over London.*
86⇨↑(8fb)⊁in 10 bedrooms CTV in all bedrooms ® T
✈ (ex guide dogs) S% sB⇨↑fr£105
dB⇨↑fr£130 (room only) ▤
Lift ( ▥ 2P 🚗 ♪ xmas
V ✿ ♨ ⊁ S% Lunch £18.50&alc High tea £6.75 Dinner
£18.50&alc Last dinner 10pm
Credit Cards ①②③④⑤

See 'How we Classify Hotels and Restaurants'
at the front of the book for an explanation
of the AA's appointment and
award scheme.

**London**

★★★73%, **Clifton-Ford** 47 Welbeck St W1M 8DN
☎071-486 6600 Telex no 22569 FAX 071-486 7492
*All bedrooms will have been upgraded to executive standard by the spring of 1991 at this mainly business hotel in the heart of the West End. There are also six penthouse suites with an oriental theme. Spacious lounge areas include the split-level Howard de Walden Bar, while the restaurant serves a good buffet breakfast. The efficient staff combine professionalism with friendliness to provide excellent service.*
211➪ⓝ(4fb) CTV in all bedrooms ® T ✸ S%
sB➪ⓝ£115-£138 dB➪ⓝ£138-£201.25 (room only)
Lift ( 10🛗 (£12) ♫
♥ International V ✿ ⚏ Lunch £11-£21 Dinner £19-£39alc Last dinner 11pm
Credit Cards ①②③⑤

★★★70%, **Chesterfield** 35 Charles St W1X 8LX ☎071-491 2622
Telex no 269394 FAX 071-491 4793
*This traditional hotel in the centre of Mayfair now has the new Butlers restaurant, which offers an outstanding buffet lunch in addition to its à la carte menu. The colourful bedrooms are furnished to a high standard, and a warm atmosphere is created by flowers and antiques in the ground floor public rooms, which include a wood-panelled library.*
113➪ⓝ1ⓕ CTV in all bedrooms ✠ (ex guide dogs)
Lift ( ✗ 🚭
✿ ⚏ Last dinner 10.30pm
Credit Cards ①②③⑤

★★★66%, **Mandeville** Mandeville Place W1M 6BE
☎071-935 5599 Telex no 269487 FAX 071-935 9588
*With easy access to the West End, Knightsbridge and theatreland, this hotel has well designed bedrooms equipped with remote control TVs and in-house films. The extended room service is pleasantly polite and efficient service prevails throughout.*
165➪ⓝ CTV in all bedrooms
Lift ( ✗ 🚭
V ✿
Credit Cards ①②③⑤

★★★66%, **Mostyn** Bryanston St W1H 0DE ☎071-935 2361
Telex no 27656 FAX 071-487 2759
*Dating from the mid-18th century, and retaining many original features, this hotel has bedrooms which range from compact to spacious de-luxe, all tastefully decorated and well equipped. The Tea Planter Restaurant has a British Empire theme and offers char grills and oriental specialities.*
122➪ⓝ(24fb) CTV in all bedrooms ® T ✠ (ex guide dogs) ✸
S10% sB➪ⓝ£86-£94 dB➪ⓝ£103-£113 (room only)
Lift (
V ✿ ⚏ ⚕ S10% Lunch £12.95&alc High tea fr£6alc Dinner £12.95&alc Last dinner 11.45pm
Credit Cards ①②③⑤

★★★59%, **Mount Royal** Bryanston St, Marble Arch W1A 4UR
(Mount Charlotte (TS)) ☎071-629 8040 Telex no 23355
FAX 071-499 7792
*This large commercial and tourist hotel near Marble Arch incorporates a conference/banqueting suite and a number of boutiques and kiosks. The Terrace Grill serves not only grills but also a choice of table d'hôte menus, while the Coffee House (open until 10pm) offers a variety of meals and snacks. Harry's Bar is ideal for a relaxing drink.*
701➪ⓝ(31fb)⚕in 40 bedrooms CTV in all bedrooms ® ✠
Lift ( ✗ CFA
♥ Mainly grills ✿ ⚏ ⚕ Last dinner 11pm
Credit Cards ①②③④⑤

★★52%, **Regent Palace** Glasshouse St, Piccadilly W1A 4BZ
(Trusthouse Forte) ☎071-734 7000 Telex no 23740
FAX 071-734 6435
*Good accommodation in this outstanding value-for-money hotel, adjacent to Piccadilly Circus.*

882rm(34fb)⚕in 210 bedrooms CTV in all bedrooms ® S15%
sB&Bfr£56 dB&Bfr£73 🏠
Lift ( ✗ CFA
V ✿ ⚏ ⚕ Lunch fr£13.95 High tea fr£3 Dinner fr£13.95 Last dinner 9pm
Credit Cards ①②③④⑤

❀ ✗✗✗✗✗**Ninety Park Lane** 90 Park Ln W1 ☎071-409 1290
Telex no 24871 FAX 071-493 3341
*This elegantly appointed restaurant continues to be noteworthy both for its high standards of attentive but unobtrusive service and the finesse of the dishes on the small but well-chosen menu. An hors d'oeuvre of crab with avocado pear makes a delicately flavoured light introduction to the main courses, of which the Filet de Boeuf, Sauce Chambertin particularly caught our Inspector's eye. Desserts, attractively presented and well prepared bring an excellent meal to a satisfactory conclusion.*
Closed Sun
Lunch not served Sat
♥ French V 78 seats Wine £10.50 Last lunch 2.45pm Last dinner 10.45pm 10P nc3yrs ⚕ ♫
Credit Cards ①②③④⑤

❀❀❀ ✗✗✗✗ LE GAVROCHE, LONDON 43 Upper Brook St
W1Y 1PF ☎071-408 0881 & 071-499 1826 FAX 071-409 0939
*Under the guidance of the ebullient Albert Roux, son Michel has now firmly established himself in the kitchens of London's premier restaurant. His cooking becomes increasingly assured, and some dishes tasted by one Inspector recently have been quite brilliant. For example, a tender, corn-fed pigeon poached in the lining of a pig's bladder was carved at the table and served with the cooking juices enriched with cream and subtly flavoured with star aniseed and truffles. The result was as near perfection as we believe can be achieved ; likewise a Mignonette of beef accompanied by a silky red-wine sauce. Among other dishes that can be highly recommended are a light Soufflé Suissesse to start with and a fine Tartelette de Prunes à l'Armagnac to end the meal. Attention to detail is outstanding throughout this attractively appointed restaurant and the highly skilled and agreeable staff are well directed by a knowledgeable Maître d'. The wine list is of library proportions, abounding in quality and featuring excellent selections of champagne, burgundies and fine clarets.*
Closed Sat, Sun & 22 Dec-2 Jan
♥ French V 65 seats ✸ S% Lunch £24-£53&alc Dinner £53&alc Last lunch 2pm Last dinner 11pm ✗ nc6yrs
Credit Cards ①②③④⑤

✗✗✗**The Greenhouse** 27A Hay's Mews W1X 7RJ
☎071-499 3331 Telex no 919042 FAX 071-225 0011
*Modern elegant dining room with formal but friendly service accompanying English and French cuisine.*
Closed Sun, 1wk after Xmas & BH's
Lunch not served Sat
♥ English & French 85 seats ✸ Lunch £20-£22alc Dinner £20-£22alc Last lunch 2.30pm Last dinner 11pm ✗ nc5yrs
Credit Cards ①②③④⑤

✗ ✗✗**London Hilton Hotel (Trader Vic's)** 22 Park Ln W1A 2HH
☎071-493 7586 Telex no 24873 FAX 071-493 4957
*With décor and furnishings based on those of a Polynesian long house, this basement restaurant at the Hilton Hotel offers a mainly Chinese menu which includes some French and English dishes. The experience is unique, a "fun" thing to do and relaxed service is in keeping with the atmosphere ; cuisine, however, is taken seriously, all dishes being carefully prepared.*
Closed 25 Dec
Lunch not served Sat
♥ French & Chinese V 150 seats Last dinner 11.45pm ✗
Credit Cards ①②③④⑤

For key to symbols see the inside front cover.

London

✗✗✗*Princess Garden of Mayfair* 8-10 North Audley St
W1Y 1FA ☎071-493 3223
*Quietly decorated and smart this large Chinese restaurant with a separate bar has an extensive menu of Pekinese and regional dishes such as Squid Superb, Steamed Dumplings and Mongolian Lamb, accompanied by a quality wine list.*
Closed Xmas & Etr
♧ Pekinese **V** 150 seats Last dinner 11.20pm ✗ nc7yrs
Credit Cards 1 2 3 5

❀✗✗✗**Rue St Jacques** 5 Charlotte St W1P 1HD
☎071-637 0222
*After a number of less favourable reports, Chef/patron Günter Schlender and his brigade appear to be back on the right track. In full flow, this smart, elegant ground-floor restaurant can be the match of any of our single-rosetted establishment, and the attractive menus (biased towards game in season) are always thoughtfully constructed. Bordering on heavy-handedness on occasions, sauces are rich and powerful, but by contrast, meats and vegetables are treated with much more restraint. Try a light Brioche stuffed with delicious pink veal kidneys and sweetbreads and a port and cream sauce to start, and amongst main courses tested by our Inspectors, a fillet of lamb was beautifully roasted and arranged on a bed of very fine ratatouille, with a 'sparkling' pimento sauce. The three chocolate mousses must be tried. A fine wine list is not surprisingly inclined towards French selections, and the well supervised service is courteous and polite.*
Closed Sun, Xmas, Etr & BH's
Lunch not served Sat
♧ French **V** 70 seats ✳ Lunch £23 Last lunch 2.30pm Last dinner 11.15pm ✗
Credit Cards 1 2 3 5

❀✗✗**Au Jardin Des Gourmets** 5 Greek St W1V 6NA
☎071-437 1816 FAX 071-437 0043
*The food at this fashionable Soho restaurant is exceptionally good and, in true French style, uncomplicated and honest, being based solely on high quality fresh produce. Both fixed price and à la carte menus are offered, and although the choice of vegetables is limited they are well chosen for dishes on the menu. The extensive wine list is reasonably priced and the service is professional.*
Closed Sun, Xmas & Etr
Lunch not served Sat & BH's
♧ French 85 seats ✳ Lunch £16.50-£20.60 Dinner £16.50-£20.60 Last lunch 2.15pm Last dinner 11.30pm ✗ ⼲
Credit Cards 1 2 3 5

✗✗**La Bastide** 50 Greek St W1V 5LQ ☎071-734 3300
*This elegant Georgian style restaurant creates a pleasant and caring ambience. Regional French dishes are the speciality, executed with a high degree of competance and there are fixed price menus as well as the à la carte. The wine list is comprehensive, with a good general appeal.*
Closed Sun & BH's
Lunch not served Sat
♧ French 45 seats ✳ Lunch £18.50-£21&alc Dinner £18.50-£21&alc Last lunch 2.30pm Last dinner 11.30pm ✗ nc12yrs
Credit Cards 1 2 3 5

✗✗*Chambeli* 12 Great Castle St W1N 7AD ☎071-636 0662
*Predominantly North Indian dishes are well prepared in this modern restaurant whose two floors are air-conditioned. The staff are helpful, efficient and attentive and the atmosphere is friendly.*
Closed Sun & 25-26 Dec
♧ Indian **V** 86 seats Last dinner 11.30pm ✗
Credit Cards 1 2 3 5

✗✗**Chesa** (Swiss Centre), 10 Wardour St W1V 3HG
☎071-734 1291 Telex no 8811646 FAX 071-439 6129
Closed 25-26 Dec
♧ Swiss **V** 54 seats ✳ S% Lunch fr£11.75&alc Dinner £12.50-£14.50&alc Last lunch 2.30pm Last dinner 11pm ✗ ⼲
Credit Cards 1 2 3 5

❀❀❀✗✗ **CHEZ NICO, LONDON** 35 Great Portland St W1N 5DD
☎071-436 8846
*Nico Ladenis's masterful cooking is most evident in his ability to produce consistently outstanding sauces which combine intensity of flavour with fine balance and clarity to create many memorable dishes. The à la carte menu, priced for two courses, changes regularly and is usually supplemented by a wonderful choice of fresh fish. Favourites from his repertoire include Ravioli de langoustines au beurre de truffe or à la mousse de champignons sauvages (freshly made ravioli filled with langoustine and truffles or with wild mushroom mousse); les petits Rossini (fillet of beef with foie gras, truffle and meat glaze sauce; Pintade au vieux Xérès et son safran pistaché (guinea fowl cooked with old sherry and served with pistachio and veal sweetbreads); Jannet de veau braisé jardinière (knuckle of veal with braised spring vegetables). Desserts are memorable, with a selection of rich ice-creams, delightful petit-fours and truffles. Although service is efficient, it can on occasion seem hurried and a bit lacking in romance and loving care. A fine selection of Pomerol, Château Palmer and Château d'Yquem adds a further dimension to the well chosen wine list. For private parties there is a separate dining room which will seat up to 12 persons.*
Closed Sun, Sat, Xmas-New Year, 3 wks Aug-Sep & 4 days Etr
♧ French **V** 48 seats S15% Lunch fr£27&alc Dinner fr£38alc
Last lunch 2pm Last dinner 11pm nc10yrs
Credit Cards 1 3 5

✗✗**Gay Hussar** 2 Greek St W1V 6NB ☎071-437 0973
*This very popular Soho restaurant has a well-earned international reputation and a very loyal clientele. Chef Laslo Holecz combines authentic Hungarian dishes with Transylvanian specialities, using game and fresh fish with strong flavours and wholesome portions. Featured dishes include a veal goulash, saddle of carp, fish dumplings, goose and pork paté and wild mushroom and cherry soups. Some rare Tokajis wines date from 1889. Credit cards are not accepted and parking can be very difficult.* ▶

**London**

Closed Sun, 25 Dec, 1 Jan & BHs

☺ Hungarian 70 seats ✻ S% Lunch £13.50 Dinner £12.50-£20alc Last lunch 2.30pm Last dinner 11pm ⨍

✗✗**Lal-Qila** 117 Tottenham Court Rd W1P 9HL
☎071-387 4570 & 071-387 5332
*Smart, air-conditioned Tandoori restaurant with a short but interesting menu composed mainly of specialities. The pungent and highly spiced sauces compliment the good quality ingredients used. A take-away service is also available.*
Closed 25 & 26 Dec
☺ Indian V 74 seats Lunch £10-£25&alc Dinner £15-£25&alc Last lunch 3pm Last dinner 11.30pm 10P
Credit Cards ① ② ③ ⑤

✗✗*Langan's Brasserie* Stratton St W1X 5FF ☎071-491 8822
*Very fashionable, popular and sometimes noisy brasserie and first-floor Venician Room. The stylish menu changes daily and the standard of cooking is always reliable.*
Closed Sun & Public hols
Lunch not served Sat
☺ English & French V 200 seats Last lunch 3.00pm Last dinner 11.45pm ⨍ ♫
Credit Cards ① ② ③ ⑤

✗✗**Lindsay House** 21 Romilly St W1V 5TG ☎071-439 0450
*The elegant, tastefully-appointed restaurant specialises in traditional English cuisine, offering meals of a high standard and a very high level of service, excellently supervised.*
Closed 25-26 Dec
V 30 seats Lunch £14.50&alc Dinner £30-£40alc Last lunch 2.30pm Last dinner 11.30pm ⨍ ♫
Credit Cards ① ② ③ ⑤

✗✗**Mr Kai of Mayfair** 65 South Audley St W1Y 5FD
☎071-493 8988
*Sophisticated, elegant restaurant serving both classical and regional Chinese dishes.*
Closed Xmas & Bank Hols
☺ Pekinese & Cantonese 120 seats Wine £6.95 Last lunch 2.30pm Last dinner 11.15pm ⨍ nc6yrs
Credit Cards ① ② ③ ⑤

✗✗*Number 10* 10 Old Burlington St W1X 1LA
☎071-439 1099 & 071-734 5010
*A modern restaurant which has, as its name suggests, a political flavour in its décor, with many pictures and caricatures of past Prime Ministers and politicians. Not surprisingly, the menu offers typically English dishes such as sausage and mash, black pudding and fish cakes.*
Closed Sat, Sun, 1 wk Xmas & 1 wk Aug BH
Dinner not served Mon
V 68 seats Last lunch 3.30pm Last dinner 10.30pm
Credit Cards ① ② ③ ⑤

✗✗*Odin's* 27 Devonshire St W1N 1RJ ☎071-935 7296
*Always busiest at lunchtime, this attractive restaurant just off Marylebone High Street is one of those under the joint ownership of Richard Shephard and Michael Caine. It is richly appointed and the walls are adorned with fine paintings, but the cuisine is refreshingly unfussy. The list of starters is indeed quite straightforward, but is lifted above the average by ingredients of the best quality. Commendable main dishes include loin of lamb baked in pastry and served with an intense Madeira sauce, and medallion of venison with beetroot and port. Mrs Langan's chocolate pudding is a classic which should not be missed. The short wine list is well balanced and service is good humoured, but sensible prices are unfortunately boosted by hefty service and cover charges.*
Closed Sun & Public hols
Lunch not served Sat
☺ French 60 seats Last lunch 2.30pm Last dinner 11.30pm ⨍
Credit Cards ① ② ③ ⑤

✗✗**Red Fort** 77 Dean St W1V 5HA ☎071-437 2525 & 071-437 2115 FAX 071-434 0721
*The exterior of this new Indian restaurant has the air of a pink palace. Inside, exquisite girls in red saris serve cocktails and such regional dishes as spiced and marinated quail baked in a charcoal fire.*
Closed 25-27 Dec
☺ Indian V 160 seats ✻ Lunch £14&alc Dinner £15-£30alc Last lunch 2.45pm Last dinner 11.15pm ⨍ nc5yrs
Credit Cards ① ② ③ ⑤

❀✗✗**Stephen Bull** 5-7 Blandford St W1H 3AA ☎071-486 9696
*One of our 'Best New Restaurants' this year – see the colour feature on page 36. The surroundings are smart and modern and the pleasant relaxed service is not pretentious in any way. A menu 'du Marché' is changed twice daily and is sensibly balanced between straightforward starters, such as a sweet confiture of onions baked in vine leaves with a precise tomato coulis, and less earthy main dishes of John Dory and Salmon with a fennel and tomato butter sauce. Plain chicken and pears or huge fresh sardines might be the basis of other choices, but leave space for a flavoursome redcurrant tartlet or an iced damson parfait. Good sense prevails, too, in the contents of the wine list, providing excellent value for money.*
Closed Sun
Lunch not served Sat
V 60 seats ✻ Last lunch 2.15pm Last dinner 11pm ⨍
Credit Cards ① ③

❀✗✗✗**Sutherlands** 45 Lexington St W1R 3LG ☎071-434 3401 FAX 071-287 2997
*A stylish and well-frequented restaurant housed in a listed Georgian terrace in Soho. The service provided by the young staff is warm and friendly and the innovative but delicious dishes prepared by chef Garry Hollihead are prepared from top-quality ingredients.*
Closed Sun & BH's
Lunch not served Sat
☺ English & French V 45 seats ✻ Lunch £33.50&alc Dinner £36&alc Last lunch 2.15pm Last dinner 11.15pm ⨍
Credit Cards ① ③

✗✗**Yumi** 110 George St W1H 6DJ ☎071-935-8320
*The typical Japanese menu offers well prepared and interesting dishes. Guests are welcomed by traditionally dressed waitresses and at lunchtime there is a choice of reasonably priced set menus.*
Closed Sun, 2 wks Xmas, 1 wk Aug & Public Hols
Lunch not served Sat
☺ Japanese 70 seats Last dinner 10.30pm ⨍
Credit Cards ① ② ③ ⑤

✗✗**Zen Central** 20-22 Queen St W1X 7PJ ☎071-629 8103
*Chef patron Michael Leung's exciting and individual style of cooking has placed Zen Central among the best of central London's fashionable restaurants and he combines imagination and traditional skills with the best quality produce to create dishes which achieve new culinary heights. Tempting hot appetisers, traditional soups, lunchtime dumplings and Dim Sum, Zen Specials, seafood dishes and marinated poultry and meats gives a varied and interesting choice and his sauces are particularly well reduced and full of flavour. The well turned out and professionally trained staff are on hand to advise on the combination of dishes, and service is supervised by the helpful Mr Antony Au-Yeung. A good selection of wines, including rice wine, is available.*
Closed 25 Dec
☺ Chinese V 110 seats ✻ ⨍
Credit Cards ① ② ③ ④ ⑤

All AA-appointed establishments are inspected regularly to ensure that required standards are maintained.

**⊛✗Alastair Little** 49 Frith St W1V 5TE ☎071-734 5183
*The high standards of cooking ensure that this small, fashionable restaurant maintains its popularity, so much so that advance booking is always advisable. The menu, changed at every meal, is short but imaginative; the wine list, on the other hand, is comprehensive and reasonably priced.*
Closed Sun, 1 wk Xmas & BHs
Lunch not served Sat
♀ International 36 seats ✳ Lunch £24-£40alc Dinner £24-£40alc Wine £7.50 Last lunch 2.30pm Last dinner 11.30pm ₽

**✗Aunties** 126 Cleveland St W1P 5DN ☎071-387 1548 & 071-387 3226
*English restaurant specialising in home-made pies.*
Closed Sun, 25-26 Dec, 1 Jan, PH's & 2 wks Aug
Lunch not served Sat
30 seats ✳ Lunch £18.50 Last lunch 2pm Last dinner 11pm ₽
Credit Cards ① ② ③ ⑤

**✗Bahn Thai** 21a Frith St W1V 5TS ☎071-437 8504
Closed Xmas, 1 Jan & BH's
♀ Thai V 80 seats Last dinner 11.15pm nc
Credit Cards ① ② ③

**✗Frith's** 14 Frith St W1V 5TS ☎071-439 3370 & 071-734 7535
*An informal atmosphere, attentively efficient service and a varied, interesting menu all contribute to the popularity of this bright, modern hotel. The dishes offered in both the lunch time time table d'hôte and evening à la carte selections are expertly produced from good fresh produce and accompanied by a short but comprehensive wine list.*
Closed Sun, 2 wks Xmas, Etr & BH's
Lunch not served Sat
♀ British & Italian V 60 seats Lunch £22-£35alc Dinner £22-£35alc Wine £8.50 Last lunch 2.30pm Last dinner 11.15pm ₽
Credit Cards ① ③

**✗Fuji Japanese** 36-40 Brewer St W1R 3HP ☎071-734 0957
Closed 2 wks Xmas
Lunch not served Sat & Sun
♀ Japanese 54 seats Last dinner 10.45pm ₽
Credit Cards ① ② ③ ⑤

**✗Kerzenstuberl** 9 St Christopher's Place W1M 5HB ☎071-486 3196 & 071-486 8103
*Here you can relax in a typically Austrian atmosphere to enjoy authentic Austrian food and wine. Personal service is provided by the proprietors, and in the late evenings staff and guests sing along together to the strains of an accordion.*
Closed Sun, Xmas, Etr & 31 Jul-27 Aug
Lunch not served Sat
♀ Austrian V 50 seats Lunch £14.50-£17.50&alc Dinner £20-£25alc Last lunch 2.15pm Last dinner 11pm ₽ ♫
Credit Cards ① ② ③ ⑤

**✗L'Hippocampe** 63 Frith St W1V 5TA ☎071-734 4545 FAX 071-736 3287
*Fish is the speciality of this small brasserie-type restaurant, the young French chef demonstrating flair and skill in producing dishes of a high standard from the best quality ingredients. The menu, though short, is comprehensive and accompanied by a reasonablay priced wine list, helpful staff offer willing service, and the atmosphere is both friendly and informal.*
Closed Sun
Lunch not served Sat
♀ French 60 seats ✳ Lunch £25-£35alc Last lunch 3pm Last dinner mdnt ₽
Credit Cards ① ② ③

**✗Lee Ho Fook** 15 Gerrard St W1V 7LA ☎071-734 9578
*Authentic Chinatown atmosphere in this intimate restaurant.*
Closed 25 & 26 Dec
♀ Chinese V 150 seats Lunch £7-£10&alc Dinner fr£9&alc Last dinner 11.30pm ₽
Credit Cards ① ② ③ ⑤

**✗Little Akropolis** 10 Charlotte St W1P 1HE ☎071-636 8198
*Small, intimate, candlelit, Greek restaurant.*
Closed Sun & BH's
Lunch not served Sat
♀ Greek V 32 seats Last dinner 10.30pm ₽
Credit Cards ① ② ③ ⑤

**✗Ming** 35-36 Greek St W1V 5LN ☎071-734 2721 & 071-437 0292 FAX 081-847 2772
*An attractive friendly little restaurant specialising in dishes which became part of the Chinese culinary tradition during the creative Ming Dynasty, 1368-1644. Recommendations include Yuunam Prawns fermented in Bean Curd, Gansu Duck simmered in herbs and Mr. Edward's Pork. Car parking can be very difficult.*
Closed Sun, 25 & 26 Dec
♀ Chinese V 80 seats Last dinner 11.45pm ₽ ✄
Credit Cards ① ② ③ ④ ⑤

**✗New World** 1 Gerrard Place W1V 7LL ☎071-734 0677 & 071-434 2508
*This large and popular Chinese restaurant offers a wide selection of dishes based on good-quality ingredients. Throughout the day, heated trolleys circulate among the tables, enabling guests to choose from a tempting array of Dim Sum; service is generally courteous and friendly.*
Closed 25 Dec
♀ Chinese V 600 seats Last lunch 5.45pm Last dinner 11.30pm ₽
Credit Cards ① ② ③ ⑤

### W2 Bayswater, Paddington

**★★★★72%, White's** Lancaster Gate W2 3NR (Mount Charlotte (TS)) ☎071-262 2711 Telex no 24771 FAX 071-262 2147
*This small hotel which overlooks Hyde Park offers high standards of service, cuisine and accommodation, and enjoys a club-like atmosphere. Helpful, correct and friendly service is provided by all staff who have earned the AA's new 'Courtesy & Care' award.*
54⇌1♨✂in 10 bedrooms CTV in all bedrooms T ✠ (ex guide dogs) ✳ s⒝⇌£130 d⒝⇌£170-£210 (room only) ⒝
Lift ℭ ⊞ 25P ⌘ ❋ ♫ xmas
♀ English & French V ♨ ⌸ Lunch fr£15.50&alc Dinner fr£15.50&alc Last dinner 10.30pm
Credit Cards ① ② ③ ④ ⑤

**★★★★67%, Royal Lancaster** Lancaster Ter W2 2TY (Rank) ☎071-262 6737 Telex no 24822 FAX 071-724 3191
*Overlooking Hyde Park, many bedrooms and all major suites have unrivalled views of the Italian Gardens, though some executive bedrooms lack the space and comfort expected at this level. The Rosette restaurants provide a choice of menus, but for a less informal meal try the Pavement Café. The banqueting facilities have been extended.*
418⇌❨(40fb) CTV in all bedrooms T ✠ (ex guide dogs) ✳ s⒝⇌❨£140-£215 d⒝⇌❨£160-£215 (room only) ⒝
Lift ℭ ⊞ 50P (£7.50-£10) 50⊛ (£7.50-£10) ⊞ CFA xmas
♀ International V ♨ ⌸ ✂ Lunch £15-£17&alc High tea fr£4.30alc Dinner £20-£23&alc Last dinner 10.45pm
Credit Cards ① ② ③ ④ ⑤

**★★★65%, London Embassy** 150 Bayswater Rd W2 4RT (Embassy) ☎071-229 1212 Telex no 27727 FAX 071-229 2623
*Modern commercial and tourist hotel overlooking Hyde Park. A pre-theatre meal, fixed price carvery and small à la carte menu are available in the restaurant. Helpful staff provide some lounge and room service.*

▶

193⇨**¶**⊁in 10 bedrooms CTV in all bedrooms ® T
✻ (ex guide dogs) S% sB⇨**¶**£95-£108
dB⇨**¶**£108-£130 (room only) **⊟**
Lift ℂ 20P 20🍴 (£2) CFA
♀ International **V** ♱ ⚗ S% Lunch £12&alc Dinner
£7.50-£12&alc Last dinner 10.15pm
Credit Cards ①②③⑤

★★★62% **Park Court** 75 Lancaster Gate, Hyde Park W2 3NN
(Mount Charlotte (TS)) ☎071-402 4272 Telex no 23922
FAX 071-706 4156
*A very popular tour hotel which is rapidly increasing its
involvement in the business and conference markets. It backs onto
the Bayswater Road and Hyde Park, boasting its own garden with
barbeque area. The lower ground floor Park Brasserie offers
informal buffet-style meals, and a complete bedroom refurbishment
designed to upgrade all accommodation to executive standards is
well advanced.*
398⇨**¶**(11fb)⊁in 227 bedrooms CTV in all bedrooms ® T
sB⇨**¶**fr£72.50 dB⇨**¶**fr£91.50 (room only) **⊟**
Lift ℂ ⚡ ✿ CFA *xmas*
**V** ♱ ⚗ ⊁ Lunch fr£12.50 High tea fr£10 Dinner fr£14 Last
dinner 11pm
Credit Cards ①②③④⑤ ⓔ

★★★60% **Central Park** Queensborough Ter W2 3SS
☎071-229 2424 Telex no 27342 FAX 071-229 2904
*A modern, purpose-built hotel providing tastefully furnished well-
equipped rooms of various sizes. The lower ground floor restaurant
can be a bit dull, but 24-hour room service is available for guests
who choose to take meals in their rooms. The Leisure Point
gymnasium has a sauna and solarium.*
251rm(210⇨31**¶**)(10fb) CTV in all bedrooms ® T S%
Lift ℂ 10P (£1.50) 20🍴 (£1.50) sauna solarium gymnasium
*xmas*
♀ International **V** ♱ ⚗
Credit Cards ①②③⑤

★★★59% **Hospitality Inn Bayswater** 104/105 Bayswater Rd
W2 3HL (Mount Charlotte (TS)) ☎071-262 4461
Telex no 22667 FAX 071-706 4560
*Some rooms in this Bayswater Road hotel overlook the park, and
though these would benefit from refurbishment bedrooms are
equipped with every modern convenience. Staff are friendly and
service is willing throughout the hotel.*
175⇨**¶** CTV in all bedrooms ® T S% sB⇨**¶**£78-£86.50
dB⇨**¶**£94.50-£103 (room only) **⊟**
Lift ℂ ⊞ 20P 40🍴 CFA ♫ *xmas*
♀ International **V** ♱ ⚗ Lunch fr£7.90&alc Dinner £12-£17alc
Last dinner 10.30pm
Credit Cards ①②③④⑤

✗**Kalamara's** 76-78 Inverness Mews W2 3JQ ☎071-727 9122 &
071-727 2564
*There are two Kalamara's restaurants in Inverness Mews – a
smaller, unlicenced one and this, which provides an all-Greek wine
list to complement the authentic Greek cuisine.*
Closed Sun & BHs
Lunch not served
♀ Greek **V** 86 seats ✽ Dinner £12.50-£18alc Last dinner mdnt
⚡
Credit Cards ①②③⑤

## W5 Ealing

See LONDON plan 1*B4*
See also **W13 Ealing (Northfields)**
★★★70% **Carnarvon** Ealing Common W5 3HN (Consort)
☎081-992 5399 Telex no 935114 FAX 081-992 7082
*A modern hotel, on the edge of Ealing Common and handy for the
North Circular Road, looks from the outside severely functional,
but inside is spacious, bright and comfortable with well equipped
bedrooms. A first-class management team and good hotelkeeping
personable staff prove that good hotelkeeping standards can still
flourish. A bonus for visitors to London are the extensive car-
parking facilities.*
145⇨**¶** ⊁in 10 bedrooms CTV in all bedrooms ® T
✻ (ex guide dogs) sB⇨**¶**£79.50
dB⇨**¶**£105.50 (room only) **⊟**
Lift ℂ 150P CFA
♀ European ♱ ⚗ ⊁
Credit Cards ①②③⑤

## W6 Hammersmith

See LONDON plan 1*C3*
★★★58% *Novotel London* 1 Shortlands W6 8DR (Novotel)
☎081-741 1555 Telex no 934539 FAX 081-741 2120
*The hotel enjoys a pleasant location close to Hammersmith Centre
and is popular both with businessmen and with tourists exploring
the capital. Accommodation is spacious and staff now offer a warm
welcome and good standards of hospitality, but facilities can be
stretched on occasions by sheer volume of trade. Light snacks are
available throughout the day in La Terrasse, as are more
substantial meals in Le Grill and an à la carte menu in La Peniche.*
640⇨**¶**⊁in 20 bedrooms CTV in all bedrooms
Lift ⊞ CTV 230🍴 (£6.50)
♀ English & French **V** ♱ ⚗ ⊁ Last dinner mdnt
Credit Cards ①②③⑤

✗**River Cafe** Thames Wharf Studio's, Rainville Rd,
Hammersmith W6 9HA ☎071-381 8824
*A popular and fashionable restaurant in a converted Thames-side
warehouse. The service, like the décor, is simple and uncomplicated
and the Italian cuisine provides food which is fresh, simple and not
over-refined.*
Closed 1 wk Xmas
Lunch not served Mon
Dinner not served Sat & Sun
♀ Italian **V** 60 seats ✽ Lunch £20-£30alc Dinner £30-£35alc
Last lunch 2.30pm Last dinner 9.15pm
Credit Cards ①③

## W8 Kensington

See LONDON plan 1*C3*
★★★★★61% **Royal Garden** Kensington High St W8 4PT
(Rank) ☎071-937 8000 Telex no 263151 FAX 071-938 4532
*Suites, studios and bedrooms are all tastefully furnished, equipped
with all five-star facilities and afford views over Kensington
Gardens and Hyde Park or the lively scene of Kensington High
Street. The Garden Café serves meals throughout the day, and
shares beautiful views over the park with the adjacent Garden Bar,
where a resident pianist entertains. If you prefer a club-like
atmosphere, there is the comfortable Gallery Bar, and the Roof
Restaurant is an ideal rendezvous for dining and dancing.*
380⇨**¶**7🛏⊁in 10 bedrooms CTV in all bedrooms
✻ (ex guide dogs) ✽ sB⇨**¶**£135-£165
dB⇨**¶**£168-£185 (room only) **⊟**
Lift ℂ ⊞ 142🍴 (£2.50-£15) CFA *xmas*
♀ International **V** ♱ ⚗ ⊁
Credit Cards ①②③④⑤

★★★★68% **Kensington Palace Thistle** De Vere Gardens
W8 5AF (Mount Charlotte (TS)) ☎071-937 8121
Telex no 262422 FAX 071-937 2816
*The rooms in this busy hotel have been upgraded to provide modern amenities. The restaurant offers interesting and enjoyable dishes and there is also a coffee shop for lighter meals. Service from the friendly and willing staff is attentive and efficient.*
298◻⇨🜚(27fb)⊁in 32 bedrooms CTV in all bedrooms Ⓡ T ✹
✻ sB◻⇨🜚fr£90 dB◻⇨🜚fr£105 (room only) 🛏
Lift ℂ 🍴 CFA ♫
♲ International ✧ ⚗ Lunch fr£17.50&alc Dinner
fr£17.50&alc Last dinner 10.45pm
Credit Cards ①②③④⑤

★★★★57% *London Tara* Scarsdale Place, off Wrights Ln
W8 5SR (Best Western) ☎071-937 7211 Telex no 918834
FAX 071-937 7100
*Well into a major bedroom and public area improvement programme, this hotel also offers a good range of eating options and very good check-in facilities.*
831◻⇨⊁in 96 bedrooms CTV in all bedrooms
✹ (ex guide dogs)
Lift ℂ ⊞ 30P 80🍴 (£8 per 24hours) CFA
♲ French V ✧ ⚗ Last dinner 11pm
Credit Cards ①②③④⑤

★★★62% **Kensington Close** Wright's Ln W8 5SP (Trusthouse Forte) ☎071-937 8170 Telex no 23914 FAX 071-937 8289
*Quietly situated this large hotel offers a range of well-equipped bedrooms and two restaurants, the Grill and the more popular Rendez Vous which is open throughout the day for snacks. The health and fitness club includes a swimming pool, two squash courts and a gymnasium.*
532◻⇨🜚⊁in 11 bedrooms CTV in all bedrooms Ⓡ T ✻
sB◻⇨🜚£80 dB◻⇨🜚£95 (room only) 🛏
Lift ℂ 40P (£3.50 2 hours) 60🍴 (charged) CFA ▨(heated)
squash sauna solarium gymnasium health & fitness centre *xmas*
♲ Mainly grills V ✧ ⚗ ⊁ S% Lunch £3.50-£13.95&alc Dinner
£3.50-£13.95&alc Last dinner 11pm
Credit Cards ①②③④⑤

★★57% **Hotel Lexham** 32-38 Lexham Gardens W8 5JU
☎071-373 6471 Telex no 268141 FAX 071-244 7827
Closed 23 Dec-2 Jan
*Accommodation in this traditional hotel is very good value, especially for central London. What it lacks in modern facilities it makes up for in service. There is no bar, but a choice of two lounges, and the staff are pleasant and cheerful.*
64rm(40◻⇨🜚)(13fb) CTV in all bedrooms T ✹ ✻ S10%
sB&Bfr£32.50 sB&B◻⇨🜚fr£44.50 dB&Bfr£41.50
dB&B◻⇨🜚£58.50-£64.50 🛏
Lift ℂ CTV 🍴 ⇌ ❀
♲ English & Continental ✧ ⚗ S% Lunch fr£5 Dinner fr£8.25
Last dinner 8pm
Credit Cards ①③

✕✕✕**Belevedere** Holland House, Holland Park W8 6LU
☎071-602 1238
*The elegantly-situated, aristocratic house retains its formal English flower garden and its peaceful atmosphere. The chef has a particular flair with white fish, and many daily specialities appear among the reliable and enterprising dishes on the menu. Service is efficient and very attentive.*
Closed Sun, BH's & Xmas-New Year
Lunch not served Sat
♲ International V 60 seats ✻ S12.5% Lunch fr£19.50&alc
Dinner £30-£40alc Last lunch 2.30pm Last dinner 10.30pm 🍴
Credit Cards ①②③⑤

1991 marks the 25th anniversary of this guide.

✕✕**Boyd's** 135 Kensington Church St W8 7LP ☎071-727 5452
Closed Sat, Sun & 1 wk Xmas
♲ French V 36 seats ✻ Lunch £12.50-£15.50 Dinner
£19.50-£25 Last lunch 2.30pm Last dinner 10.30pm 🍴
Credit Cards ①②③

✕✕**Clarke's** 124 Kensington Church St W8 4BN
☎071-221 9225
*This fresh, bright restaurant offers a short lunch menu and no choice at all in the evenings – but its quality is beyond question. Chef/patronne Sally Clarke's light, American and Eastern-influenced style is exemplified in dishes such as a deliciously spicy corn chowder, and char-grilled meat and fish with imaginative sauces and crisp vegetables. Breads and pastries are excellent, and the wine list includes a good North American range. The bakery and coffee shop next door also sells Californian wines and splendid home-made pickles.*
Closed Sat, Sun, Xmas, Etr & 3 weeks Aug-Sep
♲ British & Italian V 90 seats S% Lunch £18-£20 Dinner
fr£30alc Last lunch 2pm Last dinner 11pm 🍴
Credit Cards ①③

✕**The Ark** 35 Kensington High St W8 5BA ☎071-937 4294
*Long established and extremely popular, this restaurant maintains very reliable standards. Freshly prepared dishes include daily specialities, and a limited selection of good value French wines is available.*
Closed 4 days Xmas & 4 days Etr
Lunch not served Sun
♲ French V 95 seats ✻ Lunch £11.20-£18.30alc Dinner
£11.20-£18.30alc Last lunch 3pm Last dinner 11.30pm 🍴
Credit Cards ①②③⑤

For key to symbols see the inside front cover.

✗**Kensington Place** 201/205 Kensington Church St W8 7LX
☎071-727 3184 FAX 071-229 2025
*Rowley Leigh presides over this lively, popular restaurant,
situated at the Notting Hill end of Kensington Church Street, and
open 12 hours a day. Cooking is excellent and dishes range from
the homely (cod with parsley sauce or rabbit stew, for example), to
the more imaginative, such as griddled foie gras with sweetcorn
pancake, or the red and grey mullet with wild rice and ginger
particularly enjoyed by our inspector. Service is relaxed and
friendly but tables are very close together, so not ideal for private
conversation. The set lunch is good value and there is a range of
reasonably priced wines.*
Closed 25 Dec & Aug BH
♡ European 90 seats ✱ Lunch £12.50&alc Dinner £20-£30alc
Last lunch 2.45pm ₽
Credit Cards 1 3

✗**Michel** 343 Kensington High St W8 6NW ☎071-603 3613
*This small, lively restaurant, pretty in pink, has a French/
Mediterranean style menu of sound innovative cooking.*
Closed Sun & BH's
♡ French V 55 seats ✱ S15% Lunch £11.50-£14.50&alc Last
lunch 2.30pm Last dinner 11pm ₽ ✄
Credit Cards 1 2 3 4 5

---

### W11 Holland Park, Notting Hill

**See LONDON plan 1C3**

★★★73% **London Kensington Hilton** Holland Park Av
W11 4UL (Hilton) ☎071-603 3355 Telex no 919763
FAX 071-602 9397
*Large and exceptionally comfortable hotel with a distinctly
international flavour, well placed for access to and from the West
End and A40. A choice of three places to eat – the à la carte/
carvery Market Restaurant, a 24-hour drink and snack bar and
the Hiroko where authentic Japanese cuisine is served. There are
several shops in the foyer and car parking for 100 available
underneath the hotel.*
606⇥✄in 100 bedrooms CTV in all bedrooms ® T
sB⇥£98-£158 dB⇥£118-£188 (room only) ☒
Lift ( ▦ 100🅿 (£8.50) CFA ♫ xmas
♡ International V ♦ ♩ S10% Lunch £18-£22&alc Dinner
£20-£35&alc Last dinner 10.30pm
Credit Cards 1 2 3 4 5

✗✗✗**Leith's** 92 Kensington Park Rd W11 2PN ☎071-229 4481
*Popular, well-established restaurant that continues to offer
reliable and unusual food, particularly the varied starters. Good
fixed price menu.*
Closed 26-27 Aug & 24-27 Dec
Lunch not served
♡ International V 85 seats S15% Dinner £28.50-£37.50 Last
dinner 11.30pm ₽ nc7yrs
Credit Cards 1 2 3 5

✗✗**La Pomme d'Amour** 128 Holland Park Av W11 3GG
☎071-229 8532
*French regional cooking of a reliable standard forms the basis of
the menu here, complemented by a choice of imaginative
specialities devised by the chef and combining good-quality
ingredients with well constructed sauces. Service is attentive and
agreeably supervised.*
Closed Sun & BH's
Lunch not served Sat
♡ French V 64 seats Last lunch 2.15pm Last dinner 10.45pm
₽ nc10yrs
Credit Cards 1 2 3 5

✗**Restaurant 192** 192 Kensington Park Rd W11 2ES
☎071-229 0482
*A simple restaurant-cum-wine-bar on two floors which offers a
short, high-quality menu of mostly English dishes well prepared
from good, basic ingredients. The atmosphere is friendly and
informal and the service attentive.*

Closed BH's
Dinner not served Sun
♡ French V 80 seats Last lunch 2.30pm Last dinner 11.30pm
₽
Credit Cards 1 2 3

---

### W13 Ealing (Northfields)

**See LONDON plan 1B4**
See also **W5**
✗**Maxim Chinese** 153-155 Northfield Av W13 9QT
☎081-567 1719 & 081-840 1086
*Staff are friendly and service is well supervised at a large,
tastefully appointed restaurant which is popular with locals. As
well as a selection of authentic Pekinese dishes, menus also feature
a good choice of fixed price set meals, and the wine list includes a
very acceptable house wine.*
Closed 25-28 Dec
Lunch not served Sun
♡ Pekinese V 120 seats S5% Lunch £10-£21&alc Dinner
£10-£21&alc Last lunch 2.30pm Last dinner mdnt
Credit Cards 1 2 3 5

---

### W14 West Kensington

✗**Chinon** 25 Richmond Way W14 0AS ☎071-602 5968 &
071-602 4082
*This small, candlelit restaurant specialises in its own original
variations on British cuisine, dishes being beautifully presented and
garnished. A choice of two fixed price menus offers excellent value
for money.*
Closed Sun, Etr & Aug BH
V 28 seats Last lunch 2pm Last dinner 11pm ₽ nc10yrs
Credit Cards 1 2 3

---

### WC1 Bloomsbury, Holborn

★★★★69% **The Marlborough** Bloomsbury St WC1B 3QD
☎071-636 5601 Telex no 298274 FAX 071-636 0532
*The hotel provides comfortable accommodation and has an
attractive restaurant offering a wide choice of dishes. Service is
efficient and friendly.*
169⇥✄in 57 bedrooms CTV in all bedrooms ® T S%
sB⇥🎄fr£128 dB⇥🎄fr£148 (room only)
Lift ( ₽ xmas
♡ French V ♦ ♩ ✄ Lunch £16.50&alc Dinner £16.50&alc
Last dinner 11.30pm
Credit Cards 1 2 3 4 5

★★★★61% **Hotel Russell** Russell Square WC1B 5BE
(Trusthouse Forte) ☎071-837 6470 Telex no 24615
FAX 071-837 3612
*The imposing entrance hall, with large chandelier, marble pillars
and staircase, ushers guests into this large, commercial hotel.
Bedrooms are on the whole comfortable, though some can only be
described as 'compact'. Service is good, however, and there are two
restaurants – an informal, colourful brasserie and a well appointed
carvery which also offers an à la carte menu.*
326⇥(1fb)✄in 20 bedrooms CTV in all bedrooms T
sB⇥£107-£115 dB⇥£130-£135 (room only) ☒
Lift ( ₽ CFA ♫ xmas
♡ International V ♦ ♩ ✄ S7.5% Lunch fr£14.50&alc Dinner
fr£14.50&alc Last dinner 10.30pm
Credit Cards 1 2 3 4 5

★★★69% **Bloomsbury Crest** Coram St WC1N 1HT (Trusthouse
Forte) ☎071-837 1200 Telex no 22113 FAX 071-837 5374
*Situated between the West End and the City this hotel provides
ideal facilities for both business and leisure visitors. Extensive
refurbishment has transformed the hotel's exterior, the new stone
façade is enhanced by a glass domed entrance. The first floor
restaurant complex offers an extensive choice of meals, or try the
informal Café Shaw. The hotel has a purpose built business centre.*

**London** (vertical sidebar text)

284⇌(29fb)⊁in 67 bedrooms CTV in all bedrooms ® **T**
✖ (ex guide dogs) ⊟
Lift ☾ 100⛟ (£8.40 per night)
☋ International **V** ✿ ⊻ ⊁
Credit Cards 1 2 3 4 5

★★★**60% Bonnington** 92 Southampton Row WC1B 4BH
☏071-242 2828 Telex no 261591 FAX 071-831 9170
*Occupying a prime position between the City and the West End, the Bonnington is presently enjoying general upgrading and improvements. Accommodation is of a high standard, and although some bedrooms and bathrooms can be compact, all are well equipped. Food is also of good quality, the 'Bonnington Grill' offering à la carte and set priced menus, whilst a less formal meal is served in the lounge bar, all being complemented by polite and helpful staff.*
215⇌(16fb)⊁in 54 bedrooms CTV in all bedrooms ® **T**
sB&B⇌fr£76 dB&B⇌fr£100 ⊟
Lift ☾
☋ English & French **V** ✿ ⊻ Lunch fr£12&alc Dinner fr£12&alc Last dinner 11.30pm
Credit Cards 1 2 3 5 £

★★★**55% London Ryan** Gwynne Place, Kings Cross Rd WC1X 9QN (Mount Charlotte (TS)) ☏071-278 2480
Telex no 27728 FAX 071-837 3776
*Though bedrooms are simply furnished and a little clinical at this Mount Charlotte Thistle hotel, they are nevertheless well equipped and some have double glazing. The compact restaurant becomes very busy in the evening, so it is advisable to make a table reservation. Situated within walking distance of Kings Cross, the hotel is an ideal base from which to reach any part of London.*
210⇌↱(73fb)⊁in 20 bedrooms CTV in all bedrooms ® **T**
✖ (ex guide dogs) ✱ sB&B⇌↱£64.50-£74.50
dB&B⇌↱£74.50-£89 Continental breakfast ⊟
Lift ☾ 28P 8⛟
☋ English & Continental **V** ✿ ⊻ Lunch fr£10.75 Dinner fr£12.50 Last dinner 9.30pm
Credit Cards 1 2 3 5

✕✕***Poons of Russell Square*** 50 Woburn Place, Russell Square WC1 0JU ☏071-580 1188
*Elegant Chinese restaurant offering an extensive choice of authentic dishes.*
Closed 25-26 Dec & Sun prior to BH
☋ Cantonese **V** 120 seats Last lunch 3pm Last dinner 11.30pm
P̸
Credit Cards 1 2 3 5

## WC2 Covent Garden

★★★★★

❀★★★★★ **THE SAVOY**

Strand WC2R 0EU
☏071-836 4343
Telex no 24234
FAX 071-240 6040
(Rosette awarded for Savoy Restaurant)

*Turning off the Strand into the Savoy's entrance must be among any guest's most treasured memories of this world-famous hotel. The experience of being greeted by the team of uniformed staff who so easily take over all one's worries and uncertainties and make the transition from the bustle of the streets to the calm that reigns inside is also a rare pleasure. The Savoy has a very grand history and 100 years of exemplary service to live up to. Its staff, from the youngest school-leaver to the long-serving Assistant Banqueting Manager who has worked there for 40 years, have the one aim of pleasing their guests and keeping alive the Savoy traditions. The most famous of its restaurants, overlooking the Thames, has the same name as the hotel, and is very much the domain of the famous Maitre Chef Anton Edelmann. The Grill, too, is something of a London landmark, and its daily specials, such as Jugged Hare, Irish Stew or Farmhouse Sausage with creamed potato and fried onions, are much appreciated. Bowing to popular request, the Grill has re-introduced some of the flambé dishes that were for many years a spectacular part of its repertoire, served with much panache. A specialist Champagne and Seafood Café – 'Upstairs' – is a more recent venture and now also serves 'healthy' breakfasts during the week. Afternoon tea, served in the Thames Foyer Lounge, to the accompaniment of a pianist, is another cherished tradition now becoming popular again. No description of the Savoy is complete without a mention of the bedrooms and suites, some of which preserve their 1920s and 1930s furniture, and the particularly well appointed and spacious bathrooms.*
200⇌↱⊁in 30 bedrooms CTV in all bedrooms **T**
✖ (ex guide dogs) S15% sB⇌↱fr£170
dB⇌↱£200-£265 (room only) ⊟
Lift ☾ 58⛟ (£7-£19) ⛟ CFA ♫ *xmas*
☋ English & French **V** ✿ ⊻ Lunch £24.50-£26.50&alc Dinner £38.50-£42.50&alc Last dinner 11.30pm
Credit Cards 1 2 3 5

★★★★**69% The Waldorf** Aldwych WC2B 4DD (Trusthouse Forte) ☏071-836 2400 Telex no 24574 FAX 071-836 7244
*Edwardian elegance is the keynote of this hotel, which originally opened in 1908, and this is now combined with modern amenities. Bedrooms vary considerably in size, but in compensation the hotel has many outstanding attractions – notably the Palm Court, the two bars and the Waldorf Restaurant.*
▶



London

310⇄(11fb)⊁in 40 bedrooms CTV in all bedrooms T
✹ (ex guide dogs) S15% sB⇄£130-£162
dB⇄£162-£199 (room only) 🏪
Lift ( ℐ CFA hairdressing salon ♫ xmas
V ✿ ⌾ ⊁ Lunch £17.50-£19.50&alc Dinner
£22.50-£24.50&alc Last dinner 10pm
Credit Cards ① ② ③ ④ ⑤

★★★67% **Drury Lane Moat House** 10 Drury Ln WC2B 5RE
(Queens Moat) ☎071-836 6666 Telex no 8811395
FAX 071-831 1548
*Conveniently situated for the theatre, Covent Garden and the
Opera House, this stylish purpose-built hotel provides comfortable
accommodation and a choice of à la carte or buffet-style meals.
Efficient service prevails throughout.*
153⇄(15fb) CTV in all bedrooms T sB⇄£109-£119
dB⇄£139-£153.50 (room only) 🏪
Lift ( ⊞ 7♠ (£8)
♀ French V ✿ ⌾ Lunch fr£14&alc Dinner fr£17.50alc Last
dinner 10.30pm
Credit Cards ① ② ③ ④ ⑤ ⑤

★★★56% **Royal Trafalgar Thistle** Whitcomb St WC2H 7HG
(Mount Charlotte (TS)) ☎071-930 4477 Telex no 298564
FAX 071-925 2149
*Located in the heart of London this hotel has compact, well-
equipped bedrooms. Hamilton's French-style brasserie features
daily specials, whilst, in total contrast, real ale and lunchtime
snacks are served in the traditional atmospshere of the hotel pub.
Room service is available 24 hrs a day.*
108⇄🌣⊁in 36 bedrooms CTV in all bedrooms ® T ✳
sB⇄🌣fr£87 dB⇄🌣fr£99 (room only) 🏪
Lift ( ℐ
♀ English & French ✿ ⌾ ⊁ Lunch fr£12.50&alc Dinner
fr£12.50&alc Last dinner 11.30pm
Credit Cards ① ② ③ ④ ⑤

★★★55% **Strand Palace** Strand WC2R 0JJ (Trusthouse Forte)
☎071-836 8080 Telex no 24208 FAX 071-836 2077
*Ideally located in the heart of theatreland, midway between the
City and the West End. Bedrooms, many of which are being
refurbished and decorated, offer a variety of styles, but all have en
suite facilities and are well equipped. Facilities include two popular
bars, a Carvery, a variety of shops and a coffee shop.*
777⇄⊁in 80 bedrooms CTV in all bedrooms ® T ✳
sB⇄£85-£95 dB⇄£100-£110 (room only) 🏪
Lift ( ℐ xmas
♀ International V ✿ ⌾ ⊁ Lunch £14.95-£15.95&alc Dinner
£14.95-£15.95&alc Last dinner mdnt
Credit Cards ① ② ③ ④ ⑤

✗✗✗✗✗**Savoy Grill** Strand WC2R 0EU ☎071-836 4343
Telex no 24234 FAX 071-240 6040
*Maître chef Alan Hill combines his talented creativity with the
traditional dishes that are now synonymous with the Grill Room.
Service is highly professional and very discreet in the fine Savoy
tradition.*
Closed Sun & Aug
Lunch not served Sat
♀ English & French V 80 seats ✳ Dinner £27 Last lunch
2.30pm Last dinner 11.15pm ℐ nc12yrs
Credit Cards ① ② ③ ⑤

Entries for red-star hotels are highlighted by a
tint panel. For a full list of these establishments
consult the Contents page.

❋✗✗✗**Boulestin** 1A Covent Garden, Covent Garden
WC2E 8PS ☎071-836 3819 & 071-836 7061
*The Edwardian luxury of the décor makes a fine setting for this
traditional French restaurant, where the house speciality, their
soufflé, is an experience worth savouring time and again. The menu
gives the skilful kitchen staff ample opportunity to demonstrate
their talents, and the wine list, although not cheap, will excite the
interest of most wine lovers. French waiters provide professional
service, efficient without being intrusive.*
Closed Sun, 1 wk Xmas, BH's & last 3 wks Aug
Lunch not served Sat
♀ French V 70 seats Last lunch 2.30pm Last dinner 11.15pm
ℐ nc5yrs
Credit Cards ① ② ③ ④ ⑤

✗✗**Oh! Poivrier!** 7-8 Bow St WC2E 7AH ☎071-836 9864
FAX 071-379 6859
*Informal atmosphere, honest French cooking and good value for
money.*
♀ European V 70 seats ✳ Lunch £8-£12alc Dinner £10-£15alc
Last dinner 11.30pm ℐ
Credit Cards ① ② ③ ⑤

✗✗**Seven Dials** 5 Neal's Yard, Covent Garden WC2E 9DP
☎071-836 0984
*This pleasant, airy restaurant is attractively designed in
conservatory style. Its atmosphere is friendly, service being
cheerful and helpful, and an international menu is supported by a
fairly priced wine list. Set-priced menus are available for two or
three course meals.*
♀ French V 80 seats Last dinner 11.30pm ℐ
Credit Cards ① ② ③ ④ ⑤

✗✗**Thomas de Quincey's** 36 Tavistock St WC2E 7PB
☎071-240 3972 & 071-240 3773
*The menu makes interesting reading, offering a range of unusual
and original dishes. Standards of cooking are fairly consistent, the
restaurant is attractive and friendly, but front-of-house
management could occasionally be thought lacking. The sweet
trolley may present an overwhelming temptation, but do give the
waiter a chance to explain how very good the selection of cheeses
can be.*
Closed Sun, 2 wks Aug & BH's
Lunch not served Sat
♀ French V 50 seats S% Lunch £21&alc Dinner £25-£35alc
Last lunch 3pm Last dinner 11.15pm ℐ
Credit Cards ① ② ③ ④ ⑤

✗**Ajimura Japanese** 51-53 Shelton St WC2H 9HE
☎071-240 0178 & 071-240 9424
*This Japanese restaurant, run bistro-style, has an interesting menu
of authentic dishes.*
Lunch not served Sat
♀ Japanese V 55 seats ✳ Lunch £7.50-£27&alc Last lunch 3pm
Last dinner 11pm ℐ
Credit Cards ① ② ③ ⑤

✗**Le Cafe des Amis du Vin** 11-14 Hanover Place WC2E 9JP
☎071-379 3444
*French provincial cooking of a very high standard has made this
traditional French restaurant and brasserie an extremely popular
eating place. The atmosphere is relaxed, informal and friendly,
and the well balanced wine list offers some interesting bottles.*
Closed Sun
♀ French V 116 seats ✳ Lunch £10-£15&alc Dinner
£10.50-£16&alc Last lunch 5pm Last dinner 11.30pm ℐ ♫
Credit Cards ① ② ③ ⑤

✗**Le Café du Jardin** 28 Wellington St WC2E 7BD
☎071-836 8769 & 071-836 8760
*In the heart of theatreland, this popular brasserie with its delicious
and wholesome food, attentive and friendly French staff and
pianist who plays each evening, has a lively and very French
atmosphere.*
Closed 25-26 Dec

Lunch not served Sat & BHs

♀ French **V** 116 seats ✳ Lunch fr£18 Dinner fr£18 Last lunch 2.30pm Last dinner 11.30pm ₽

Credit Cards ①②③④⑤

✗ **Happy Wok** 52 Floral St WC2E 9DA ☎071-836 3696
*Well-prepared Pekinese and Cantonese dishes are available at this small, simple Chinese restaurant. Specialities such as Peking Duck and steamed fish are served by attentive and efficient waiters.*

Closed Sun, 25 Dec & BHs (ex 26 Dec)

Lunch not served Sat

♀ Chinese **V** 50 seats ✳ Dinner £17.50-£27.65&alc Last dinner 11.30pm ₽

Credit Cards ①②③⑤

✗ **Taste of India** 25 Catherine St WC2B 5JS ☎071-836 6591 & 071-836 2538
*A modern Indian restaurant on two floors offering an interesting menu with some specialities. Dishes are freshly prepared with skilful use of herbs and spices. Service is friendly, helpful and efficient.*

Closed 25 & 26 Dec

♀ Indian **V** 125 seats ✳ Lunch £7.95-£18.95&alc Last lunch 2.30pm Last dinner mdnt ₽ ✂

Credit Cards ①②③⑤

## LONDON AIRPORTS

See under Gatwick & Heathrow

## LONG EATON Derbyshire Map 08 SK43

See also **Sandiacre**

★★★58% *Novotel Nottingham Derby* Bostock Ln NG10 4EP (S of M1 junc 25) (Novotel) ☎(0602)720106 Telex no 377585
*A purpose-built hotel almost adjacent to junction 25 of the M1. Bedrooms are spacious and functional and the Grill Restaurant is open from 6am for light snacks and more substantial meals.*

110⇨ℝ(110fb) CTV in all bedrooms ®

Lift ⊞ 180P ✿ CFA ⌲(heated) mini golf course putting green

♀ English & French **V** ♥ ⬛ Last dinner mdnt

Credit Cards ①②③⑤

See advertisement under NOTTINGHAM

★★57% *Europa* 20 Derby Rd NG10 1LW ☎(0602)728481
Telex no 377494
RS 23 Dec-2 Jan
*This busy town centre hotel, which has recently been refurbished, features a restaurant popular for its wholesome and freshly prepared meals. Ample car parking facilities are available.*

19rm(14⇨ℝ)(1fb) CTV in all bedrooms ® **T**
✶ (ex guide dogs) ✳ S% sB&B£22-£28 sB&B⇨ℝ£28-£35 dB&B⇨ℝ£38-£45 ☵

《 CTV 27P ⊞

**V** ♥ ⬛ Lunch £5-£7.50 Dinner £8.95-£13.45 Last dinner 8.30pm

Credit Cards ①②③⑤ ⓔ

All hotels are now given a percentage grading for the quality of their facilities. A full explanation can be found within 'How we Classify Hotels and Restaurants' at the front of the book.

## LONGHAM Dorset Map 04 SZ09

★★★73% **Bridge House** 2 Ringwood Rd BH22 9AN
☎Bournemouth(0202)578828 Telex no 418484
FAX (0202) 572620
Closed 25 & 26 Dec
*Situated on the banks of the River Stour, this is a modern 'Mediterranean-style' hotel, providing comfortable, well-equipped accommodation. Public rooms are bright and colourful. The attractive restaurant offers good table d'hôte and à la carte menus of well-prepared food, using good basic ingredients. Service is helpful and attentive.*

37⇨3 ♬ CTV in all bedrooms ® **T** ✶ ✳ sB&B⇨ℝ£45-£60 dB&B⇨ℝ£60-£80 Continental breakfast ☵

《 200P ✿ ✒

♀ English, French & Greek **V** ♥ ✂ Sunday Lunch £12.50-£15 Dinner fr£14.50&alc Last dinner 10.30pm

Credit Cards ①②③

## LONGHORSLEY Northumberland Map 12 NZ19

★★★★74% **Linden Hall** NE65 8XF (Prestige)
☎Morpeth(0670)516611 Telex no 538224 FAX (0670) 88544
*Dating from the early 19th century, Linden Hall is a beautiful ivy-clad mansion set in 300 acres of fine park and woodland. Bedrooms vary from the palatial to the compact but all are prettily decorated and feature many personal touches. Staff are welcoming and attentive.*

45⇨ℝ(4fb)4♬ CTV in all bedrooms ® **T** S%
sB&B⇨ℝ fr£92.50 dB&B⇨ℝ£110-£176 ☵

Lift 《 260P ✿ CFA ℘ (hard) snooker sauna solarium croquet putting clay-pigeon shooting ♬ ⬥ xmas

**V** ♥ ⬛ S% Lunch fr£15.95 Dinner fr£19.50&alc Last dinner 10pm

Credit Cards ①②③⑤ ⓔ

See advertisement under MORPETH

## LONG MELFORD Suffolk Map 05 TL84

★★★59% **The Bull** Hall St CO10 9JG (Trusthouse Forte)
☎Sudbury(0787)78494 FAX (0787) 880307
*This former Posting House, close to the village green, offers every modern convenience amidst the comfort and charm of open fireplaces, wooden rafters and carvings. The Cordell Room restaurant serves interesting, freshly-made dishes.*

25⇨3(4fb)✂in 10 bedrooms CTV in all bedrooms ® **T**
sB⇨3£70-£78 dB⇨3£87-£92 (room only) ☵

40P ♬ xmas

♀ English & French **V** ♥ ⬛ ✂ Lunch £10.95-£15.50 Dinner £15.25-£18.80&alc Last dinner 9.30pm

Credit Cards ①②③④⑤

See advertisement on page 459

★★59% **Crown Inn** Hall St CO10 9JL ☎Sudbury(0787)77666
FAX (0787) 881883
*Set among the eighteenth and nineteenth-century buildings of this lovely village's main street, the hotel provides comfortable and well-equipped en suite accommodation, some rooms having four-poster beds. A friendly, convivial atmosphere pervades its lounges and bar – the meals served in the latter being popular with local customers.*

7rm(3⇨3ℝ)Annexe5⇨ℝ(1fb)4♬ CTV in all bedrooms ® **T**
☵

6P gymnasium

♀ English & French **V** ♥ ⬛

Credit Cards ①③ ⓔ

See advertisement on page 459

1991 marks the 25th anniversary of this guide.

❀ ✕✕**Chimneys** Hall St CO10 9JR ☎Sudbury(0787)79806 FAX (0787) 247276

*The 16th-century Tudor exterior of this delightful restaurant provide a focus of interest in the long main street of this aptly named and picturesque village. The owner, Samuel Chalmers, and his chef, Colin Liddy have devised an imaginative menu based wherever possisble on local produce. The essence of their dishes are the skilfully prepared but uncomplicated sauces that enhance the flavour of creations such as a filo pastry tartlet of crab with a chive and orange sauce or guinea fowl with a confit of cabbage and bacon served on a Madeira sauce. There is a good selection of desserts and well kept cheeses. The extensive wine list will not be disappointing.*

Closed Mon

Dinner not served Sun

☋ English & French **V** 50 seats Lunch £12.50&alc Dinner £20-£24alc Last lunch 2pm Last dinner 9.30pm 10P

Credit Cards 1 3

---

**LONGRIDGE** Lancashire Map **07** SD63

★★61% **Blackmoss Country House** Thornley PR3 2TB (2m NE off Chipping rd) ☎(0772)783148

Closed 25 Dec

*The personally-owned sandstone house, set in three and a half acres of grounds, offers bright, well-furnished bedrooms and good home cooking.*

10⇌↱(1fb)⊁in 2 bedrooms CTV in all bedrooms ® ✗ S% sB&B⇌↱£29-£32 dB&B⇌↱£39-£50

65P ❊ ⛀(heated) ♪ sauna solarium pool table

⊁ Lunch £6-£10&alc High tea £7-£10 Dinner £7-£14&alc Last dinner 9pm

Credit Cards 1 2 3 5

---

**LONG SUTTON** Lincolnshire Map **09** TF42

○**Travelodge** A17(Trusthouse Forte)

☎Central reservations (0800) 850950

Due to have opened autumn 1990

40⇌

---

**LOOE** Cornwall & Isles of Scilly Map **02** SX25

★★★60% **Hannafore Point** Marine Dr, Hannafore PL13 2DG (Best Western) ☎(05036)3273 Telex no 45604 FAX (05036) 3272

*In a spectacular position, with views over the bay, this hotel has upgraded over half of its bedrooms, which now offer good facilities. Table d'hôte and à la carte menus are available at dinner, whilst a wide range of hot and cold bar meals are on offer in St Georges bar at lunchtime.*

38⇌↱(10fb) CTV in all bedrooms ® **T** ✱ sB&B⇌↱£45.50-£66 dB&B⇌↱£72-£100 ⊟

Lift ☾ 35P ⛀(heated) squash sauna solarium gymnasium short tennis court *xmas*

☋ English, French & Italian **V** ♈ ☿ Sunday Lunch £6.95-£7.75 High tea £1-£6 Dinner £14-£17&alc Last dinner 9.30pm

Credit Cards 1 2 3 5

★★71% **Commonwood Manor** St Martin's Rd PL13 1LP ☎(05036)2929

Closed Nov-Feb

*The well-appointed, personally-run hotel enjoys rural surroundings, nestled into the hillside overlooking the harbour. Comfortable lounges, well-appointed bedrooms and a warm, friendly atmosphere combine to make your stay a pleasant one.*

10⇌↱(2fb) CTV in all bedrooms **T** sB&B⇌↱£27-£32 dB&B⇌↱£48-£56

CTV 20P ⛟ ❊ ⛀(heated) nc8yrs

☋ English & Continental ♈ ☿ Bar Lunch £1.50-£4 Dinner £12.50-£14 Last dinner 8pm

Credit Cards 1 2 3

★★65% **Fieldhead** Portuan Rd PL13 2DR ☎(05036)2689

Closed Dec-Jan

*An hotel enjoying views across the Bay to Millandreath, Seaton and Downderry from its attractive setting in a terraced garden with heated outdoor pool offers a warm welcome, comfortable accommodation and friendly service; public rooms have recently been redecorated and the restaurant serves a choice of home-cooked fare.*

14rm(9⇌3↱)(2fb)1⛟ CTV in all bedrooms ® ✗ ✱ sB&B⇌↱£26-£36 dB&B⇌↱£44-£59 ⊟

9P 5⛍ ❊ ⛀(heated) nc5yrs

**V** ♈ ☿ Bar Lunch £2-£4 Dinner £10.75&alc Last dinner 8.30pm

Credit Cards 1 2 3

---

**LOSTWITHIEL** Cornwall & Isles of Scilly Map **02** SX15

★★67% **Restormel Lodge** Hillside Gardens PL22 0DD (Consort) ☎Bodmin(0208)872223 FAX (0208) 873568

*A friendly and relaxed hotel, its situation in the ancient town making it the ideal base for either a touring holiday or a business trip, has been upgraded to provide well-equipped bedrooms; the restaurant, which serves both table d'hôte and à la carte menus, is popular with locals and residents alike, and there are good car parking facilities.*

21⇌↱Annexe12⇌(3fb) CTV in all bedrooms ® **T** S% sB⇌↱£30-£33 dB⇌↱£40-£44 (room only) ⊟

40P ❊ ⛀(heated) *xmas*

**V** ♈ ☿ S% Bar Lunch £1.20-£7alc Dinner £10-£14&alc Last dinner 9.30pm

Credit Cards 1 2 3 5 £

---

**LOUGHBOROUGH** Leicestershire Map **08** SK51

★★★63% **King's Head** High St LE11 2QL (Embassy) ☎(0509)233222 FAX (0509) 262911

RS Xmas

*Situated in the town centre and only 3 miles from the M1, this hotel, with its well-equipped accommodation, conference and function facilities, is understandably popular with business people. It is also popular for weekend breaks.*

78⇌↱(2fb)⊁in 24 bedrooms CTV in all bedrooms ® **T** ✱ S10% sB⇌↱£52.50-£62.50 dB⇌↱£65-£75 (room only) ⊟

Lift ☾ 80P CFA games room

☋ English & French **V** ♈ ☿ S10% Lunch fr£10.50&alc Dinner fr£11.50&alc Last dinner 9.15pm

Credit Cards 1 2 3 4 5

★★★62% **Cedars** Cedar Rd LE11 2AB ☎(0509)214459 & 217834 FAX (0509) 233573

Closed 26-28 Dec RS Sun

*Set in a residential area south of the town centre, just off the A6, this well-established hotel provides comfortable accommodation which is equally suitable for tourists or business people.*

37⇌↱(4fb) CTV in all bedrooms ® **T** ✱ sB&B⇌↱£25-£45 dB&B⇌↱£38-£55 ⊟

☾ 50P ❊ ⛀(heated) sauna solarium

**V** ♈ Lunch £6.55-£9.45alc Dinner £10.90-£15.70alc Last dinner 9.30pm

Credit Cards 1 2 3 5

★★54% **Great Central** Great Central Rd LE11 1RW (Minotels) ☎(0509)263405 FAX (0509) 264130

RS 24-31 Dec

*A small commercial hotel standing close to the Old Great Central Railway line. The modest accommodation has a relaxed, informal atmosphere and the public bars are popular with the locals.*

18⇌↱(1fb)1⛟ CTV in all bedrooms ® **T** sB&B⇌↱£25-£40 dB&B⇌↱£35-£50 ⊟

40P ⛫

☋ English & French **V** ♈ Lunch £2.50-£10 Dinner £9.95-£12&alc Last dinner 9pm

Credit Cards 1 2 3 5 £

**✗ ✗ Restaurant Roger Burdell** The Manor House, Sparrow Hill LE11 1BT ☎(0509)231813
*A manor house which stands near the town centre, facing the church, reflects the character of the timbered building by the décor and furnishings of its three separate dining rooms. The imaginative, interesting à la carte menu and chef's recommendations comprise well-prepared dishes based on fresh, usually local, produce and reflect seasonal patterns in such items as braised pheasant cooked in cider with apple and juniper berries.*
Closed BH's (ex Xmas day)
Lunch not served Mon
Dinner not served Sun
♡ English, French & Italian V 65 seats ✻ Lunch £10.50-£21.50alc Dinner £16.20-£21.50alc Last lunch 2pm Last dinner 9.15pm 6P
Credit Cards [1] [3]

---

LOUTH Lincolnshire Map **08** TF38

**★★64%, Priory** Eastgate LN11 9AJ ☎(0507)602930
Closed 24 Dec-2 Jan
*Although close to the town centre, this hotel is set in two acres of well-tended gardens. A relaxing atmosphere pervades the comfortable public areas and bedrooms are all well maintained. The menus offer a good variety of freshly prepared dishes.*
12rm(6⇴3♪)(2fb) CTV in all bedrooms ® ✹ (ex guide dogs) CTV 24P 🚗 ✿
V ♦ Last dinner 8.30pm
Credit Cards [1] [3]

---

LOWER BEEDING West Sussex Map **04** TQ22

**★★★★♨63%, South Lodge** Brighton Rd RH13 6PS (Prestige) ☎(0403)891711 Telex no 877765 FAX (0403) 891253
*Built towards the end of the 19th century, South Lodge is set in 90 acres of woodland, with a glorious display of rhododendrons and azaleas in the season. There is also a trout lake where guests can fish, and other activities include tennis, croquet, riding and clay pigeon shooting. The interior of the house is splendid, with a grand staircase, wood panelling, attractive plasterwork and fine period furniture. Bedrooms range in style from the cottagey to the grandiose, but all are well equipped and comfortable. Fixed price and à la carte menus are provided in the dining room, with service by cheerful and friendly young staff.*
39⇴2🛏 CTV in all bedrooms T ✹ (ex guide dogs)
sB⇴£65-£110 dB⇴£100-£135 (room only) 🅿
( 80P 🚗 ✿ ♪ (hard & grass) golf-driving net croquet shooting ♫ xmas
♡ English & French V ♦ ⚖ ✖ Lunch £15-£17.50 Dinner £23-£30&alc Last dinner 10.30pm
Credit Cards [1] [2] [3] [4] [5] ④

---

LOWER SLAUGHTER Gloucestershire Map **04** SP12

**★★★♨**
**LOWER SLAUGHTER MANOR**

GL54 2HP (Prestige)
☎Cotswold(0451)20456
Telex no 437287
FAX (0451) 22150
*This elegant manor stands beside the Parish Church at the heart of an unspoilt*

*Cotswold village and the whole atmosphere speaks of rest and relaxation. Bedrooms are beautifully furnished, whether in the manor or the adjacent coach house, and thoughtfully provided*

---

*with home-made biscuits, magazines, books and flowers. Service is generally competent and friendly, though some inconsistencies have been noticed, and earlier in the year there were a few problems with the quality of the cooking.*
11⇴Annexe8⇴2🛏 CTV in all bedrooms T
sB&B⇴£79-£125
dB&B⇴£99-£170 Continental breakfast 🅿
( 60P 🚗 ✿ ☐(heated) ♪ (hard) ♪ sauna solarium croquet ♫ nc8yrs xmas
♡ English & French V ♦ ⚖ Lunch fr£15.50 Dinner fr£25.95 Last dinner 9.30pm
Credit Cards [1] [2] [3] [5] ④

---

LOWESTOFT Suffolk Map **05** TM59

**★★★59%, Broadlands** Bridge Rd, Oulton Broad NR32 3LN (Consort) ☎(0502)516031 Telex no 975621
*Part of a small shopping precinct in Oulton Broad this is a modern purpose built hotel with friendly services and a lively convivial atmosphere. It has a popular carvery and the Chequers disco.*
52⇴(2fb) CTV in all bedrooms ® T
( CTV 120P ☐(heated) snooker sauna solarium gymnasium
♡ English & Italian ♦ ⚖
Credit Cards [1] [2] [3] [5]

**★★★57%, Victoria** Kirkley Cliff Rd NR33 0BZ ☎(0502)574433 FAX (0502) 501529
*This family hotel, with comfortable old fashioned style accommodation, is situated on the southern side of Lowestoft in an elevated position on the sea front. The restaurant offers a good selection of mainly English dishes. Popular with both commercial and leisure guests.*
36⇴♪(6fb)1🛏 in 25 bedrooms CTV in all bedrooms ® T
sB&B⇴♪fr£45.50 dB&B⇴♪fr£68.50 🅿
Lift ( CTV 50P ✿ ☐(heated) ♫ xmas
♡ English, French & Italian V ♦ ⚖ ✖ Lunch £10&alc Dinner £9.95&alc Last dinner 10pm
Credit Cards [1] [2] [3] [5] ④

**★66%, Denes** Corton Rd NR32 4PL (Toby) ☎(0502)564616 & 500679
*Situated in a pleasant residential area, north of the town on the Lowestoft/Corton Road, this hotel provides attractive, clean and very well equipped accommodation. The restaurant offers a carvery selection of roasts and fresh vegetables and a small menu of popular dishes.*
12♪ CTV in all bedrooms ® T
15P
♡ Mainly grills V ♦ ⚖ ✖ Last dinner 10pm
Credit Cards [1] [2] [3] [5]

---

LOWESWATER Cumbria Map **11** NY12

**★★♨64%, Scale Hill** CA13 9UX ☎Lorton(090085)232
Closed Dec-Feb (ex Xmas & New Year)
*A haven of peace and tranquility, this one-time coaching inn enjoying fine views of the surrounding countryside provides comfortable accommodation in traditional style, with plenty of cosy areas in which to read or relax.*
15⇴♪Annexe2⇴♪(2fb)1🛏 S% sB&B⇴♪£62 dB&B⇴♪£96-£116 (incl dinner)
25P 🚗 ✿
♦ ⚖ S% Dinner £16 Last dinner 7.45pm

**★65% Grange Country House** CA13 0SU
☎Lamplugh(0946)861211 & 861570
Closed 20-30 Dec RS 1-19 Dec & 5 Jan-Feb
*A friendly hotel surrounded by its own grounds, in a peaceful location at the northern end of the lake, which offers accommodation both in the main building and in a purpose-built annexe.*

---

7rm(6⇨)Annexe5rm(4⇨)(1fb)2⌗ CTV in 6 bedrooms Ⓡ
sB&B£23-£24 sB&B⇨£25-£27 dB&B£46-£48 dB&B⇨£50-£54
CTV 20P 2☎ (charged) ⇮ ✲
V ⍟ ⬙ Lunch £6.50-£9 High tea £6.50-£8.50 Dinner
£10-£12.50 Last dinner 8pm

---

**LUDLOW** Shropshire Map **07** SO57

★★★67% **Dinham Hall** SY8 1EJ (Pride of Britain)
☎(0584)876464 & 873699
12⇨ᒥ(1fb)2⌗ CTV in all bedrooms Ⓡ T ✖ (ex guide dogs)
S% sB&B⇨ᒥ£60 dB&B⇨ᒥ£75-£125
17P ⇮ ✲ sauna gymnasium nc6yrs *xmas*
V S%
Credit Cards ① ② ③

★★★66% **Overton Grange** SY8 4AD ☎(0584)873500
FAX (0584) 873524
*An Edwardian mansion set in two acres of lawned gardens on the*
*outskirts of the town, recently tastefully modernised and*
*refurnished, features popular function/banqueting facilities.*
16rm(10⇨3ᒥ)(2fb) CTV in all bedrooms Ⓡ T
✖ (ex guide dogs) ✻ sB&B£29.50-£35 sB&B⇨ᒥ£45-£50
dB&B£49.50-£52 dB&B⇨ᒥ£65-£88
80P ✲ *xmas*
V ⍟ ⬙ Lunch fr£12.50&alc Dinner fr£13.95&alc Last dinner
9.30pm
Credit Cards ① ② ③ ⑤ ④

★★★65% **The Feathers at Ludlow** Bull Ring SY8 1AA
☎(0584)875261 Telex no 35637 FAX (0584) 876030
*This fine example of timber-framed Jacobean architecture stands*
*at the centre of the historic market town, its charm and character*
*making it understandably popular with both tourists and*
*businessmen. A wide variety of bedrooms is on offer, some quite*
*luxurious but all well equipped.*
40⇨ᒥ(3fb)10⌗ CTV in all bedrooms Ⓡ T ✖
sB&B⇨ᒥ£60-£80 dB&B⇨ᒥ£86-£102 ⮃
Lift ⦅ 37P CFA snooker *xmas*
V ⍟ ⬙ ⅄ Lunch £6-£13.50&alc Dinner £3-£23alc Last dinner
9pm
Credit Cards ① ② ③ ④ ⑤ ④

★★65% **Dinham Weir** Dinham Bridge SY8 1EH (Minotels)
☎(0584)874431
6⇨ᒥ1⌗ CTV in all bedrooms Ⓡ T ✖ sB&B⇨ᒥ£35-£40
dB&B⇨ᒥ£50-£55 ⮃
10P ⇮ nc5yrs
V ⍟ Lunch £10.50-£11.50&alc Dinner £10.50-£11.50&alc Last
dinner 9pm
Credit Cards ① ② ③ ⑤ ④

★★63% *Cliffe* Dinham SY8 2JE ☎(0584)872063
*Set in attractive grounds, this family-run hotel has fine views of*
*Ludlow Castle. With well-furnished rooms and a popular bar,*
*guests are assured of an informal, friendly stay.*
10rm(3⇨4ᒥ)(1fb) CTV in all bedrooms Ⓡ
CTV 50P ⇮ ✲
V ⍟ Last dinner 8.45pm
Credit Cards ① ③

---

**LUDWELL** Wiltshire Map **03** ST92

★★66% **Grove House** SP7 9ND (2m E A30)
☎Donhead(0747)828365
Closed Dec-Jan
*Attractive gardens, in which guests may catch sight of feeding*
*badgers, are an appealing feature of this friendly, personally-run*
*hotel. Bedrooms are tastefully decorated and furnished and public*
*areas include a comfortable lounge with log fire, a spacious lounge*
*bar and a dining room where guests can enjoy a table d'hôte menu*
*of home cooked dishes.*
▶

11rm(4⇋6♠)(1fb) CTV in all bedrooms ®
sB&B⇋♠£24.50-£27 dB&B⇋♠£49-£54 🏢
12P ⇔ ❀ nc5yrs
♀ English & Continental ✿ ✂ Sunday Lunch £7.50-£12.50
Dinner £13.50-£15 Last dinner 7.30pm
Credit Cards [1] [3]

---

**LUGWARDINE** Hereford & Worcester Map **03** SO53

★★★♨ **64%**, **Longworth Hall** HR1 4DF
☎Hereford(0432)850223 FAX (0432) 850817
*Dating from 1788, and set in its own pleasant grounds on the A438*
*four miles south east of Hereford, this friendly, family-run hotel*
*commands panoramic views of the surrounding countryside. Guests*
*can relax in comfortable, well-equipped accommodation, or enjoy*
*such pursuits as golf, pigeon shooting or horse riding, all of which*
*can be arranged locally.*
10⇋♠(1fb)1 ⊠ CTV in all bedrooms ® T sB&B⇋♠frf44.85
dB&B⇋♠£74.75-£86.25 🏢
30P ❀ ♪ *xmas*
♀ English & French V ✿ ✂ Lunch frf9.95 High tea frf4.50
Dinner frf13.95&alc Last dinner 9.45pm
Credit Cards [3] [5] (£)

---

**LUMBY** North Yorkshire Map **08** SE43

★★★ **66%**, **Post House, Leeds/Selby** LS25 5LF (southern junc A1/
A63) (Trusthouse Forte) ☎South Milford(0977)682711
Telex no 557074 FAX (0977) 685462
*A modern, purpose-built hotel situated at the junction of the A1/*
*A63 and close to the M62. Recently refurbished, this hotel offers*
*greatly improved bedrooms, a leisure centre, two bars and the*
*Traders' Restaurant.*
109⇋♠(3fb)✂in 12 bedrooms CTV in all bedrooms ®
《 300P ❀ CFA ⊠(heated) ♪ (hard) sauna 9 hole pitch & putt
♀ European V ✿ ✂ Last dinner 10pm
Credit Cards [1] [2] [3] [4] [5]

---

**LUNDIN LINKS** Fife Map **12** NO40

★★★ **72%**, **Old Manor** Leven Rd KY8 6AJ ☎(0333)320368
Telex no 727606
*Comfortably converted to offer well-appointed bedrooms this hotel*
*is attractively located and backs on to the golf course and the sea.*
*Interesting menus offer very good value and service is friendly and*
*courteous.*
20rm(15⇋)(2fb) CTV in 19 bedrooms ® ✖
《 80P ❀
♀ Continental V ✿ ✂
Credit Cards [1] [2] [3]

*See advertisement in the colour section*

---

**LUSS** Strathclyde *Dunbartonshire* Map **10** NS39

★★ **54%**, **Inverbeg Inn** Inverbeg G83 8PU (3m N on A82)
☎(043686)678 FAX (043686) 645
*An attractive inn with modern, comfortable facilities, the Inverbeg*
*stands close to the banks of Loch Lomond.*
14rm(7⇋)(1fb)✂in 3 bedrooms CTV in all bedrooms ® T
sB&B£20-£30 sB&B⇋£25-£35 dB&B£30-£50
dB&B⇋£35-£55 🏢
《 80P ❀ ♪ water skiing windsurfing ⊶ *xmas*
♀ British & French V ✿ ✂ ✂ Lunch £6-£12 High tea £7
Dinner £15&alc Last dinner 9.30pm
Credit Cards [1] [2] [3] (£)

---

All AA-appointed establishments are
inspected regularly to ensure that required
standards are maintained.

---

**LUTON** Bedfordshire Map **04** TL02

★★★ **69%**, **Strathmore Thistle** Arndale Centre LU1 2TR (Mount
Charlotte (TS)) ☎(0582)34199 Telex no 825763
FAX (0582) 402528
*Good conference facilities are available at this commercial hotel,*
*and there are two eating options – less expensive meal of the*
*coffee shop or the table d'hôte and à la carte menus of an*
*attractive, well appointed restaurant. Bedrooms have been*
*upgraded to provide a good standard of well equipped*
*accommodation, and public areas are comfortable.*
150⇋♠(7fb)✂in 33 bedrooms CTV in all bedrooms ® T ✖ ✱
sB⇋♠frf70 dB⇋♠frf84 (room only) 🏢
Lift 《 44P CFA
♀ International ✿ ✂ ✂ Lunch frf12.50&alc Dinner
frf16&alc Last dinner 10pm
Credit Cards [1] [2] [3] [4] [5]

★★★ **63%**, **Chiltern Crest** Waller Av, Dunstable Rd LU4 9RU
(Trusthouse Forte) ☎(0582)575911 Telex no 825048
FAX (0582) 581589
*Hotel bedrooms are due to be upgraded this year to provide*
*modern well-equipped accommodation. The restaurant offers a*
*varied choice of dishes. This hotel is popular with commercial/*
*conference guests.*
93⇋♠✂in 17 bedrooms CTV in all bedrooms ® T 🏢
Lift 《 150P CFA
♀ English & French V ✿ ✂ ✂
Credit Cards [1] [2] [3] [4] [5]

★★★ **59%**, **Crest Hotel-Luton** Dunstable Rd LU4 8RQ
(Trusthouse Forte) ☎(0582)575955 Telex no 826283
FAX (0582) 490065
*This good, well-equipped conference/commercial hotel offers an*
*attractive restaurant and helpful service from friendly staff.*
*Currently being upgraded.*
117⇋✂in 21 bedrooms CTV in all bedrooms ® 🏢
Lift 《 130P CFA pool table
♀ International V ✿ ✂ ✂
Credit Cards [1] [2] [3] [4] [5]

★★ **62%**, **Red Lion** Castle St LU1 3AA (Lansbury)
☎(0582)413881 Telex no 826856 FAX (0582) 23864
*Recently refurbished, the bedrooms and public areas of this town*
*centre hotel have been decorated in keeping with its character.*
*Friendly service is offered in the busy coffee shop and restaurant.*
39⇋♠(4fb)1 ⊠✂in 6 bedrooms CTV in all bedrooms ® T
✖ (ex guide dogs) sB&B⇋♠frf72 dB&B⇋♠frf84
《 50P
♀ English & Continental V ✿ ✂ ✂ Lunch frf12alc Dinner
frf16alc Last dinner 10.30pm
Credit Cards [1] [2] [3] [5]

---

**LUTTERWORTH** Leicestershire Map **04** SP58

★★★ **72%**, **Denbigh Arms** High St LE17 4AD (Consort)
☎(0455)553537 Telex no 342545 FAX (0455) 556627
Closed 24-26 Dec & 1-2 Jan
*An 18th-century coaching inn in the centre of this small town,*
*thoroughly and sympathetically modernised to provide warm,*
*comfortable bedrooms and bright, modern public rooms. Very*
*popular as a venue for lunch and dinner, this well-equipped hotel*
*provides value for money and attentive service.*
34⇋(1fb) CTV in all bedrooms ® T ✖ (ex guide dogs) ✱
sB&B⇋£35-£76 dB&B⇋£45-£90 🏢
《 30P ⇔
V ✿ ✂ Lunch £7.95-£23 Dinner £7.95-£23 Last dinner 10pm
Credit Cards [1] [2] [3] [5]

**LYBSTER** Highland *Caithness* Map **15** ND23

See **John O'Groats**

★★58% **Portland Arms** K W 3 6BS ☎(05932)208

*Standing at the crossroads on the edge of the village beside the A9, this popular holiday, business and fishing hotel offers comfortable, well equipped bedrooms varying in size and style, an attractive lounge with chintzy seating and a cosy panelled bar.*

19⇨✿(3fb)2⊞ CTV in all bedrooms ® T ✳
sB&B⇨✿fr£27.50 dB&B⇨✿fr£42 ▤
《 CTV 50P ▶ 9 ✔ *xmas*
♡ Scottish & French **V** ✧ ⊡ Lunch £4-£8 High tea £3-£8
Dinner £14-£16 Last dinner 9.30pm
Credit Cards ①③£

---

**LYDDINGTON** Leicestershire Map **04** SP89

★★★54% **Marquess of Exeter** Main Rd LE15 9LT (Best Western) ☎Uppingham(0572)822477 FAX (0572) 821343

*Charming 17th-century rural inn, with modern bedrooms in annexe.*

Annexe17⇨✿ CTV in all bedrooms ® T ✻
sB&B⇨✿£45-£55 dB&B⇨✿£50-£70 ▤
70P ✻♨ ❀
♡ English & French **V** ✧ ⊡ Lunch £12.95&alc Dinner £12.95&alc Last dinner 9.45pm
Credit Cards ①②③⑤

---

**LYDFORD** Devon Map **02** SX58

★★⚑67% **Lydford House** EX20 4AU (Minotels) ☎(082282)347 FAX (082282) 442

*This delightful, granite-built country house was formerly the home of the Victorian artist William Widgery, whose scenes of Dartmoor still hang in the cosy residents' lounge. The Boulter family have gradually been upgrading the accommodation over a number of years. Service is personal and attentive, and the home cooking very enjoyable. Eight acres of gardens and pasture surround the property, and there is a riding school run by the owners' daughter.*

13rm(11⇨✿)(2fb)1⊞½in 1 bedroom CTV in all bedrooms ®
T sB&B⇨✿£26 dB&B⇨✿£52 ▤
30P ✻♨ ❀ ⃝ nc5yrs
✧ ✕ Sunday Lunch fr£6 Dinner fr£11 Last dinner 8pm
Credit Cards ①②③⑤

---

**LYDNEY** Gloucestershire Map **03** SO60

★★59% **Feathers** High St GL15 5DN ☎Dean(0594)842815 & 842826

*There is a friendly atmosphere in this popular town-centre hotel, which offers a choice of à la carte dining room or carvery, and there are also good bar menus available.*

14⇨✿(3fb)1⊞½in 2 bedrooms CTV in all bedrooms ® T
sB&B⇨✿£35.50-£39.50 dB&B⇨✿£47.50-£49.50 ▤
50P
**V** ✧ ⊡ ✕ Lunch £6-£10 High tea £2.95-£4.95 Dinner £6-£10&alc Last dinner 9pm
Credit Cards ①②③£

---

**LYME REGIS** Dorset Map **03** SY39

See also **Rousdon**

★★★65% **Alexandra** Pound St DT7 3HZ ☎(02974)2010 & 3229
Closed 23 Dec-6 Feb

*Built in 1735, this hotel occupies a prime position with beautiful views over Lyme Bay. Tastefully modernised, public rooms retain their charm and character and bedrooms are currently being upgraded to a very attractive standard. The table d'hôte menu of fresh English dishes changes daily.*

24⇨✿(6fb) CTV in all bedrooms ® T sB&B⇨✿£45-£50 dB&B⇨✿£90-£110 (incl dinner) ▤

▶

**L**

**Lyme Regis**

24P ⚗ ♨ ❀
♡ English & French V ✿ ⚖ Lunch fr£7.95&alc Dinner £14.50&alc Last dinner 8.30pm
Credit Cards 1 3

★★★62% **Mariners** Silver St DT7 3HS ☎(02974)2753
FAX (02974) 2431
Closed 8 Jan-13 Feb
*A 17th-century coaching inn with a friendly and relaxing atmosphere, personally supervised by the owners. Considerable improvements are making this hotel very comfortable. It also has an attractive restaurant which specialises in dishes using fresh local fish.*
17⇨🎇(1fb) CTV in 16 bedrooms ⓇT sB&B⇨🎇£37-£45 dB&B⇨🎇£74-£90 (incl dinner) ⊟
26P croquet *xmas*
♡ International V ✿ ⚖ Lunch £7-£12&alc High tea £3&alc Dinner £14&alc Last dinner 9pm
Credit Cards 1 2 3 5 £

★★★56% **Devon** Lyme Rd DT7 3TQ (Best Western)
☎(02974)3231 Telex no 42513 FAX (0392) 431645
(For full entry see Uplyme)

★★66% **St Michael's** Pound St DT7 3HZ ☎(02974)2503
*This warm, friendly, family-run hotel offers views of the sea from its position high above the Cobb. Its fresh, clean accommodation provides some modern facilities, the dining room is spacious, and there is a comfortable lounge and sun lounge.*
13rm(5⇨7🎇)(1fb)CTV in all bedrooms Ⓡ S%
sB&B£25-£30.50 sB&B⇨🎇£25-£30.50 dB&B£50-£61 dB&B⇨🎇£50-£61
12P 1🐎 🚲 solarium hairdressing salon
✿ ⚖ ✄
Credit Cards 1 3

★★65% **Buena Vista** Pound St DT7 3HZ ☎(02974)2494
*This attractive Regency building offers fine views of the bay, homely accommodation with some modern facilities, two comfortable lounges and a sun lounge.*
18⇨🎇(1fb) CTV in all bedrooms Ⓡ T sB&B⇨🎇£30-£34 dB&B⇨🎇£52-£78 ⊟
20P ⚗ 🚲
V ✿ ⚖ ✄ High tea £5 Dinner £12.50 Last dinner 8pm
Credit Cards 1 2 3 5

★★65% **Dorset** Silver St DT7 3HX ☎(02974)2482
Closed Nov-Feb
*Georgian in style but with later additions, this hotel is set high above the town with views over Golden Cap. Its clean and well-kept accommodation is ideal for holidaymakers, offering simply furnished bedrooms, good home cooking and a warm, friendly atmosphere.*
12rm(3⇨7🎇)(2fb) CTV in all bedrooms Ⓡ
sB&B⇨🎇£20.25-£24.75 dB&B⇨🎇£61.50-£69.50 ⊟
13P
V ✿ ⚖ Bar Lunch fr£2.90 Dinner fr£11 Last dinner 8pm
Credit Cards 1 3

★★62% **Bay** Marine Pde DT7 3JQ ☎(02974)2059
Closed Dec-Feb
*This family-owned and run hotel, with an informal atmosphere, has the distinction of being the only hotel on the front. It has an attractive bar and dining room, together with a sun terrace, and whilst bedrooms are not large, they are well kept.*
21rm(9⇨3🎇)(3fb) Ⓡ
CTV 5P 20🐎 🚲
♡ English & French ✿ ⚖ Last dinner 8.30pm
Credit Cards 1

For key to symbols see the inside front cover.

★★62% **Royal Lion** Broad St DT7 3QF ☎(02974)5622
*Situated in the heart of town, yet close to the sea, this is a 16th-century coaching inn with 20th-century additions. Bedrooms are well equipped and cater for business people and holiday makers alike and there is a range of leisure facilities.*
30⇨🎇(4fb)1 🖵 CTV in all bedrooms Ⓡ T sB&B⇨🎇£30-£33 dB&B⇨🎇£60-£66 ⊟
36P ⚗ 🖵(heated) snooker gymnasium games room 🎯
✿ ⚖ ✄ Sunday Lunch £5.50-£6.50 Dinner £11.50-£12.50 Last dinner 10pm
Credit Cards 1 2 3 5

★56% **Tudor House** Church St DT7 3BU ☎(02974)2472
Closed Nov-mid Mar
*Right in the centre of town, this historic hotel has two cosy lounges and a basement bar with its own spring. It offers warm, genuine hospitality.*
17rm(4⇨🎇)(10fb) Ⓡ ✳ S10% sB&B£12.50-£15.50 dB&B£25-£31 dB&B⇨🎇£27.50-£33.50
CTV 12P
✿ ⚖ S10% Bar Lunch fr£3.50 Dinner £5.50-£7.50 Last dinner 7.30pm
Credit Cards 1 3

L

**LYMINGTON** Hampshire Map **04** SZ39

★★★⚑73%, **Passford House** Mount Pleasant Ln SO41 8LS (2m NW on Sway rd) ☎(0590)682398 FAX (0590) 683494

*Quietly standing in 9 acres of gardens and paddocks on the edge of the New Forest, this hotel has three comfortable lounges, an elegant restaurant and well-equipped and co-ordinated bedrooms. There are separate modern leisure facilities.*

54⇄📞(2fb)1⌨ CTV in all bedrooms ® T sB&B⇄📞£65-£80 dB&B⇄📞£95-£120 ⊟
《 CTV 100P 4🛆 (£3) ⌘ ❋ CFA ▣(heated) ⊿(heated) ♪ (hard) sauna solarium gymnasium croquet putting table tennis pool table 🔕 xmas
♈ English & French ✧ ⚏ Lunch fr£9.95 Dinner fr£17.50&alc Last dinner 9pm
Credit Cards ① ② ③

★★★72%, **Stanwell House** High St SO41 9AA ☎(0590)677123 Telex no 477463 FAX (0590) 677756

*Set in the heart of the town, yet within an acre of walled gardens, this is a modernised Georgian house with a recently built business suite. Food, fresh from the market, is well cooked in the traditional English style and the wine list is quite outstanding. Conveniently situated for sailing or exploring the New Forest.*

35⇄1⌨ CTV in all bedrooms ® T ✠ (ex guide dogs) sB&B⇄fr£62.50 dB&B⇄fr£80 ⊟
《 ♪ ⌘ ❋ xmas
♈ English & French V ✧ ⚏ Lunch fr£10.50 Dinner fr£17.50 Last dinner 9.30pm
Credit Cards ① ③

**LYMM** Cheshire Map **07** SJ68

★★★56%, **Lymm** Whitbarrow Rd WA13 9AQ (De Vere) ☎(092575)2233 Telex no 629455 FAX (092575) 6035 RS New Year

*Conveniently situated for easy access to the M6 and Manchester Airport, this hotel offers bedrooms of a good standard and a large lounge with plenty of comfortable seating.*

22⇄📞Annexe47⇄📞(1fb) CTV in all bedrooms ®
《 120P CFA nc
♈ English & French V ✧ ⚏ Last dinner 10pm
Credit Cards ① ② ③ ⑤

**LYMPSHAM** Avon Map **03** ST35

★★⚑60%, **Batch Farm Country** BS24 0EX ☎Weston-super-Mare(0934)750371 Closed Xmas

*This small hotel, part of a working farm, is set in a tranquil rural location only short drive from Weston-super-Mare. Soundly appointed accommodation offers some modern facilities, lounge areas are comfortable and there is a car park.*

8⇄(4fb)✙in 2 bedrooms CTV in all bedrooms ® ✠ sB&B⇄£28-£31 dB&B⇄£46-£48 ⊟
CTV 50P ⌘ ❋ ♩ snooker croquet
V ✧ ⚏ ✂ Bar Lunch £5-£6 Dinner £9-£10&alc Last dinner 8pm
Credit Cards ① ② ③ ⑤ ⑥

See advertisement under WESTON-SUPER-MARE

**LYMPSTONE** Devon Map **03** SX98

✕✕ **River House** The Strand EX8 5EY ☎Exmouth(0395)265147

*The entrance to this detached red brick building is in the main street of the village, but there are fine views of the estuary from the lounge and dining room. The menu offers a good selection of freshly prepared dishes. The atmosphere is relaxing and the service attentive.*

Closed Mon
Dinner not served Sun

♈ English & French V 34 seats ✳ Lunch £29.50 Dinner £29.50 Last lunch 1.30pm Last dinner 9.30pm ♪ nc6yrs
Credit Cards ① ② ③

**LYNDHURST** Hampshire Map **04** SU30

★★★68%, *Crown* High St SO43 7NF (Best Western) ☎(0703)282922 Telex no 9312110733 FAX (0703) 282751

*An attractive hotel of considerable charm situated in the centre of this New Forest town. Comfortable public areas have a traditional appeal, and major bedroom refurbishment is well under way at the time of going to print. Straightforward cuisine is served by pleasant young staff, and bar meals in particular are very reasonably priced.*

41⇄(6fb)1⌨ CTV in all bedrooms ®
Lift 《 CTV 60P CFA board & computer games
♈ European V ✧ ⚏ Last dinner 9.30pm
Credit Cards ① ② ③ ⑤

See advertisement also under SOUTHAMPTON

★★★⚑66%, *Parkhill* Beaulieu Rd SO43 7FZ ☎(0703)282944 FAX (0703) 283268

*Set in open downland, this Georgian hotel has an attractive restaurant serving the best of modern British cuisine. Bedrooms are comfortable and the staff are young and friendly.*

15⇄📞Annexe5⇄📞(1fb) CTV in all bedrooms ® T
75P ⌘ ❋ ⊿(heated) croquet
♈ French V ✧ ⚏ ✂ Last dinner 10pm
Credit Cards ① ② ③ ④ ⑤

★★★63%, **Forest Lodge** Pikes Hill, Romsey Rd SO43 7AS ☎(0703)283677 FAX (0703) 283719

*An attractive small Georgian hotel on the edge of Lyndhurst and the New Forest. Totally refurbished, it now provides bedrooms which are comfortable and well equipped. The spacious*

▶

*restaurant offers table d'hôte and à la carte menus which are good value for money.*
19⊸🛏(1fb)1🛏✕in 5 bedrooms CTV in all bedrooms ® T
sB&B⊸🛏£59-£69 dB&B⊸🛏£85-£95 🏳
CTV 50P ✿ ⌲(heated) pitch & putt *xmas*
♀ English & French V ♦ ◻ ✕ S% Sunday Lunch £9.95
Dinner £13&alc Last dinner 8.45pm
Credit Cards ①②③⑤

★★★60%, **Lyndhurst Park** High St SO43 7NL (Forestdale)
☎(0703)283923 Telex no 477802 FAX (0703) 283019
*A popular hotel set in its own grounds, this Georgian mansion has been sympathetically modernized to offer a choice of bedrooms, restaurant, bar, games rooms and good conference facilities.*
59⊸🛏(3fb)3🛏✕in 3 bedrooms CTV in all bedrooms ® T ✱
sB&B⊸🛏£55-£66.50 dB&B⊸🛏£70 🏳
Lift ⓒ 100P ✿ CFA ⌲(heated) ♪ (hard) snooker sauna table
tennis ⚬ *xmas*
♀ English & Continental V ♦ ◻ ✕ Lunch £11.50-£18.30alc
High tea £3.75 Dinner £13&alc Last dinner 10pm
Credit Cards ①②③④⑤

★★62%, *Evergreens* Romsey Rd SO43 7AR (Minotels)
☎(0703)282175 & 282343
*In its own garden setting on the edge of town this hotel offers an excellent value table d'hôte menu with dishes to suit all tastes. Most rooms have been tastefully refurbished with pretty co-ordinating fabrics.*
20rm(10⊸8🛏)Annexe2⊸(1fb)3🛏 CTV in all bedrooms ® T
34P 3🏕 ✿
♀ English & Continental V ♦ ◻ Last dinner 9pm
Credit Cards ①③⑤

## LYNMOUTH Devon Map 03 SS74

See also **Lynton**
★★★61%, *Tors* EX35 6NA ☎Lynton(0598)53236
Closed 4 Jan-9 Mar
*Comfortable hotel in five acres of grounds, set on a hill above Lynmouth. There are fine views over the bay.*
35⊸🛏(5fb) CTV in all bedrooms ®
Lift CTV 40P ✿ CFA ⌲(heated)
♀ English & French ♦ ◻ Last dinner 8.45pm
Credit Cards ①②③⑤

★★69%, **Rising Sun** Harbourside EX35 6EQ
☎Lynton(0598)53223
*A 14th century, thatched smugglers' inn beside the harbour has been sympathetically restored to meet modern standards yet retain the charm of the original with its thick walls, crooked ceilings, uneven wooden floors and the oak panelling of dining room and bar. Bedrooms in both the main building and its adjacent cottages are cosy and sparkling clean, with compact en suite facilities, attractive pine furnishings and pleasant décor. Commendable food standards are maintained in the restaurant, which regularly features dishes making good use of quality local seafood and Exmoor game. Shelley's Cottage - so called because the poet spent his honeymoon there - now provides a private suite with its own garden adjoining the hotel's beautiful terraced grounds.*
11⊸🛏Annexe5⊸🛏(2fb)2🛏✕in 6 bedrooms CTV in all
bedrooms ® T ✱ sB&B⊸🛏£35-£48 dB&B⊸🛏£75-£90 🏳
CTV ♪ 🚗 ✿ ♪ nc5yrs *xmas*
♀ English & French V ♦ ✕ Lunch £6.50-£8.50&alc Dinner
£16.50&alc Last dinner 9pm
Credit Cards ①②③ⓕ

★★59%, **Bath** Sea Front EX35 6EL (Exec Hotel)
☎Lynton(0598)52238
Closed Nov-Feb RS Mar
*Set beside the harbour at the centre of this attractive village, a traditional, family-managed hotel provides bright, sound bedrooms - many of them having views over the harbour to the sea*

*beyond - and a choice of public rooms, with friendly service throughout.*
24⊸🛏(9fb) CTV in all bedrooms ® T S10%
sB&B⊸🛏fr£27.50 dB&B⊸🛏£48-£63 🏳
11P 4🏕 (£1.50 per night)
♀ English & French ♦ ◻ S10% Lunch £6.25-£8&alc Dinner
fr£13 Last dinner 8.30pm
Credit Cards ①②③⑤ⓔ

★**Rock House** EX35 6EN ☎Lynton(0598)53508
*A busy tea garden is one of the attractions of this delightful little Georgian hotel. Overlooking the harbour, it occupies a unique position beside the River Lyn, the foreshore and the Manor Gardens.*
6rm(1⊸3🛏)(2fb)1🛏 CTV in all bedrooms ® sB&B£21
sB&B⊸🛏£28 dB&B£42 dB&B⊸🛏£56 🏳
CTV 7P 🚗
♀ English & French V ♦ ◻ Sunday Lunch £7 Dinner £11&alc
Last dinner 8.45pm
Credit Cards ①②③⑤

## LYNTON Devon Map 03 SS74

See also **Lynmouth**
★★★69%, **Lynton Cottage** North Walk EX35 6ED
☎(0598)52342 FAX (0598) 52597
Closed Jan
*John and Maisie Jones, together with their daughter Judy, continue to generate praise for their cosy, hospitable, country house style of hotel. The majority of bedrooms have been upgraded to provide a high standard of comfort and facilities, and chef Robert Schyns produces freshly cooked dishes with flair and imagination.*
17⊸🛏1🛏 CTV in all bedrooms ®
dB&B⊸🛏£105-£122 (incl dinner) 🏳
26P 🚗 ✿ nc10yrs *xmas*
♀ French ♦ ◻ Sunday Lunch fr£12.50&alc Dinner
fr£18.50&alc Last dinner 8.45pm
Credit Cards ①②③⑤

★★69%, **Gordon House** Lee Rd EX35 6BS ☎(0598)53203
Closed Nov-Mar
7⊸🛏(1fb)2🛏 CTV in all bedrooms ® sB&B⊸🛏£19-£22
dB&B⊸🛏£38-£44 🏳
CTV 7P 🚗
♀ English & Continental V ✕ Dinner £9 Last dinner 7.30pm
ⓕ

★★67%, *Castle Hill House* Castle Hill EX35 6JA ☎(0598)52291
Closed Nov-Etr
*Situated in the town centre, this tall, Victorian house is personally run by owners Peter and Wendy Harris, who provide friendly and attentive service. Bedrooms are pretty and well equipped and imaginative food is served in the tented restaurant.*
9⊸🛏(2fb)✕in 2 bedrooms CTV in all bedrooms ®
🐕 (ex guide dogs)
♪ 🚗 nc5yrs
♀ English & Continental V ♦ ◻ ✕ Last dinner 9.30pm
Credit Cards ①③

★★🎖65%, *Hewitts* North Walk EX35 6HJ ☎(0598)52293
RS mid Nov-mid Mar
*A friendly, relaxing atmosphere prevails at Robert and Susan Mahon's secluded cliff-top Victorian mansion now a stylish country house in 27 acres of woodland. Public rooms include a galleried lounge and intimate restaurant which features imaginative menus based on English cuisine with some French influence.*
12rm(9⊸🛏)(1fb)1🛏✕in 2 bedrooms CTV in all bedrooms
10P 🚗 ✿ clay pigeon shooting jaccuzi
V ♦ ◻ ✕ Last dinner 9.30pm
Credit Cards ①②③⑤

★★62%, **Neubia House** Lydiate Ln EX35 6AH (Guestaccom)
☎(0598)52309 & 53644
Closed 20 Nov-11 Feb
12⇨3👤(3fb)⊬in 4 bedrooms CTV in all bedrooms Ⓡ T
sB&B⇨3👤£26.75 dB&B⇨3👤£53.50 🅿
14P 🚗 nc4yrs
V ⊬ Dinner £11-£12 Last dinner 7.30pm
Credit Cards 1 3 £

★★59% **Crown** Sinai Hill EX35 6AG (Inter-Hotels)
☎(0598)52253
Closed Jan
*Dating back to 1760 and once a coaching inn, this character hotel maintains its position as the local hostelry, with a reputation for fine beer. Family run, it combines soundly equipped, cosy bedrooms with a popular restaurant and bars, whilst its central yet secluded position makes it an ideal base from which to tour the area.*
16⇨3👤(6fb)5🚿 CTV in all bedrooms Ⓡ T ✳
sB&B⇨3👤£31.50-£34.50 dB&B⇨3👤£53-£59 🅿
20P 🚗 xmas
🍴 English & French V 🍽 Bar Lunch £2-£4 Dinner
fr£13.50&alc Last dinner 8.30pm
Credit Cards 1 2 3 5

★★57%, **Sandrock** Longmead EX35 6DH ☎(0598)53307
Closed Dec-Jan
*Compact, cosy rooms are provided by a friendly little touring and holiday hotel which has been owned by the same family for many years. Located conveniently close to the town centre, it also offers easy access to the expanses of Exmoor National Park and headland.*
9rm(5⇨2👤)(3fb) CTV in all bedrooms Ⓡ T sB&B£17.50-£21
dB&B⇨3👤£37-£45 🅿
9P 🚗

▶

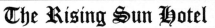

L

✧ ⬰ Bar Lunch £2.50-£4.50 Dinner £10.50-£12.50 Last dinner 7.45pm
Credit Cards 1 2 3 £

★⬩⬩66% **Combe Park** Hillsford Bridge EX35 6LE
☎(0598)52356
Closed mid Nov-mid Mar (ex Xmas)
*Former hunting lodge set in six acres of woodland.*
9rm(6⊱2⋔) ℝ sB&B⊱⋔fr£52
dB&B⊱⋔£64-£75 (incl dinner)
CTV 11P ⬤ ❋ bird watching nc12yrs *xmas*
⬰ ⊬ Dinner fr£14.50 Last dinner 7.30pm

★65% **Rockvale** Lee Rd EX35 6HW ☎(0598)52279 & 53343
Closed 15 Nov-15 Feb
*Former Bristol merchant's holiday home, the hotel has been modernised and offers comfortable accommodation.*
8rm(5⊱1⋔)(2fb)⊞ CTV in 7 bedrooms TV in 1 bedroom ℝ
T S% sB&B£17.50-£20.50 dB&B⊱⋔£35-£43 ⏚
9P ⬤ ❋ nc4yrs
✧ ⬰ Lunch £5-£8 Dinner £9.50-£11 Last dinner 7.30pm
Credit Cards 1 3 £

★65% **Seawood** North Walk EX35 6HT ☎(0598)52272
Closed Dec-Feb
*A friendly, family-run hotel of charm and character commands unrestricted and magnificent views from its elevated setting, looking right across Lynmouth Bay to Countisbury headland where Exmoor meets the sea. Originally built in 1848 as a retreat for wealthy Victorian families, it offers well-equipped, spotlessly clean and comfortable bedrooms with modern en suite facilities, complemented by equally relaxing public rooms which include a choice of lounges and an attractive little dining room where wholesome home cooking is served promptly and efficiently.*
12⊱⋔(1fb)4⊞ CTV in all bedrooms ℝ ❋ sB&B⊱⋔£23-£27
dB&B⊱⋔£42-£52 ⏚
10P ⬤ ❋
⬀ English & Continental **V** Dinner £10-£12 Last dinner 7.30pm
£

★63% **Chough's Nest** North Walk EX35 6HJ ☎(0598)53315
Closed mid Oct-Etr
*Comfortable holiday hotel, situated high above the bay.*
11⊱⋔(2fb)2⊞ CTV in all bedrooms ℝ ❌
sB&B⊱⋔£25-£28.75 dB&B⊱⋔£60-£62.10 (incl dinner)
10P ⬤ ❋ nc2yrs
**V** ✧ ⬰ ⊬

★59% **North Cliff** North Walk EX35 6HJ ☎(0598)52357
Closed 10 Nov-15 Feb
*This small, family-run hotel, commanding unrestricted sea views from its elevated position, provides cosy bedrooms, a relaxed atmosphere and friendly service.*
15rm(11⊱2⋔)(2fb) CTV in 10 bedrooms ℝ
sB&B⊱⋔£26.50-£29 dB&B⊱⋔£53-£58 (incl dinner)
CTV 15P ⬤ table tennis pool table
✧
£

★**Fairholme** North Walk EX35 6ED ☎(0598)52263
Closed Oct-Mar
*The small hotel stands in a breathtaking position overlooking the Bristol Channel.*
12rm(7⊱2fb) ❌ sB&B⊱£16.50-£17.50 dB&B⊱£33-£35
CTV 12P ⬤ ❋ ⬱(heated)
✧ ⬰

Book as early as possible for busy holiday periods.

---

**LYTHAM ST ANNES** Lancashire Map **07** SD32

★★★★61% **Clifton Arms** West Beach, Lytham FY8 5QJ
(Lansbury) ☎(0253)739898 Telex no 677463
FAX (0253) 730657
*Guests will experience delightfully courteous service in every area of this very comfortable hotel.*
41⊱⋔1⬤⊬ in 6 bedrooms CTV in all bedrooms ℝ T ❋
sB&B⊱⋔£79-£87 dB&B⊱⋔£92-£100 ⏚
Lift ℂ 50P CFA sauna solarium jacuzzi *xmas*
⬀ English & French **V** ✧ ⬰ ⊬ Lunch fr£8.95 Dinner
fr£14&alc Last dinner 10pm
Credit Cards 1 2 3 5

★★★68% **Bedford** 307-311 Clifton Dr South FY8 1HN (Exec Hotel) ☎(0253)724636 FAX (0253) 729244
*A very friendly hotel, managed by the resident proprietors, providing comfortable accommodation throughout. There is a choice of eating options – the main restaurant, a coffee shop and a quaint lower-ground-floor bistro.*
36⊱⋔(6fb)1⊞ CTV in all bedrooms ℝ T
sB&B⊱⋔£27.50-£30 dB&B⊱⋔£50-£60 ⏚
Lift ℂ CTV 20P sauna solarium gymnasium jacuzzi steam room *xmas*
⬀ English & Continental **V** ✧ ⬰ Lunch fr£6.95&alc High tea fr£5&alc Dinner fr£12.50&alc Last dinner 8.30pm
Credit Cards 1 3

★★69% **Chadwick** South Promenade FY8 1NP ☎(0253)720061
FAX (0253) 714455
*Good leisure facilities, well-appointed bedrooms and friendly service are provided at this sea-front hotel.*
70⊱⋔(24fb)1⊞ CTV in all bedrooms ℝ T ❌ (ex guide dogs)
S% sB&B⊱⋔£29.50-£34 dB&B⊱⋔£39.50-£42 ⏚
Lift ℂ 40P ⬤ CFA ⬱(heated) sauna solarium turkish bath jacuzzi games room ♫ ⚬ *xmas*
⬀ English & French **V** ✧ ⬰ ⊬ S% Lunch £6.50 Dinner £11.50
Last dinner 8.30pm
Credit Cards 1 2 3 5

★★66% **St Ives** 7-9 South Promenade FY8 1LS ☎(0253)720011
FAX (0253) 724447
Closed 24-26 Dec
*Spacious lounge areas, well-appointed bedrooms and leisure facilities are features of this comfortable, well-managed hotel.*
71rm(61⊱3⋔)(44fb) CTV in all bedrooms ℝ T ❌ ❋
sB&B⊱⋔£35-£41 dB&B£44-£56
dB&B⊱⋔£50-£62 (incl dinner) ⏚
ℂ ⊞ CTV 100P CFA ⬱(heated) snooker sauna solarium ♫ *xmas*
⬀ English & French **V** ✧ ⬰ Bar Lunch £1.10-£2.95 Dinner fr£9.50 Last dinner 8.30pm
Credit Cards 1 2 3 5

★★62% **New Glendower** North Promenade FY8 2 (Consort)
☎(0253)723241
*A large seafront hotel, refurbished to provide pleasant, comfortable public areas, offering accommodation in bedrooms which are all well equipped and maintained to a good standard. Those overlooking the sea are the more spacious and attractive.*
60⊱(17fb) CTV in all bedrooms ℝ T ❋ sB&B⊱£27.50-£33
dB&B⊱£55-£66 ⏚
ℂ CTV 45P ⬱(heated) sauna solarium games room badminton ♫ ⚬ *xmas*
**V** ✧ Bar Lunch £2-£4 High tea £3.50-£4.75 Dinner £11.95-£12.50 Last dinner 8pm
Credit Cards 1 2 3 5

★★58% **Langdales** 320-326 Clifton Dr North FY8 2PB
☎(0253)728657
*Situated close to the town centre and to the sea, this adequately furnished, family-run hotel offers good value for money, and friendly, helpful service from the team of staff.*

20rm(11⇌1🟥)(8fb) CTV in 12 bedrooms ℞
CTV 24P
🏡 ⚲
Credit Cards ① ③

★61% **Lindum** 63-67 South Promenade FY8 1LZ
🕿(0253)721534 & 722516 FAX (0253) 721364
*Dinner represents good value at this seafront hotel which provides friendly, unobtrusive service under the supervision of its resident owners.*
80⇌🟥(25fb) CTV in all bedrooms ℞ T ✱ sB&B⇌🟥£24-£30 dB&B⇌🟥£38-£40 🍴
Lift ℂ CTV 20P CFA sauna solarium jacuzzi *xmas*
V 🏡 ⚲ Sunday Lunch £6.50 High tea £6 Dinner £8.50 Last dinner 7pm
Credit Cards ① ② ③ ⓔ

★60% **Ennes Court** 107 South Prom FY8 1NP 🕿(0253)723731
*A small, friendly, sea-front hotel, personally supervised by the resident proprietors and offering well equipped bedrooms.*
10⇌🟥(2fb) CTV in all bedrooms ℞ 🐾 (ex guide dogs) ✱
sB&B⇌🟥£17-£21.50 dB&B⇌🟥£34-£43 (incl dinner)
CTV 9P 🚗 nc3yrs *xmas*

★57% **Carlton** 61 South Promenade FY8 1LZ 🕿(0253)721036
Closed Jan & Feb
*Pleasant, family-run hotel overlooking the promenade gardens.*
21rm(5⇌5🟥)(6fb) CTV in all bedrooms ℞ ✱ sB&B£16 dB&B£32 dB&B⇌🟥£37.50
CTV 10P *xmas*
V 🏡 ⚲ ⚲
Credit Cards ① ⓔ

---

**MACCLESFIELD** Cheshire Map 07 SJ97

See also **Bollington**
★★65% **Park Villa** Park Ln SK11 8AE 🕿(0625)511428 & 614173 FAX (0625) 614637
*A late Victorian house with a well-tended garden providing well appointed accommodation and particularly comfortable lounges. Bridge weekends are arranged at certain times during the year.*
7⇌🟥(2fb)✂in 2 bedrooms CTV in all bedrooms ℞ T
sB&B⇌🟥£38.50-£54 dB&B⇌🟥£55-£77 🍴
Lift ℂ CTV 14P 🚗 *xmas*
V 🏡 ⚲ ✂ Lunch fr£6.25 Dinner fr£11 Last dinner 8.45pm
Credit Cards ① ② ③ ⑤ ⓔ

★★63% **Crofton** 22 Crompton Rd SK11 8DS 🕿(0625)34113
*A small cosy hotel in a residential area yet just a few minutes from all the amenities. Generous meals and genuine hospitality are features here.*
8rm(2⇌5🟥)(2fb) CTV in 7 bedrooms ℞ 🐾
🍴
🍴 English & Continental V 🏡 ⚲ Last dinner 11pm
Credit Cards ① ③

---

**MACDUFF** Grampian *Banffshire* Map 15 NJ76

★★★51% **The Highland Haven** Shore St AB4 1UB
🕿(0261)32408 FAX (0261) 33652
*Compact, well-equipped bedrooms and a good range of leisure facilities are available at a small family-run commercial and tourist hotel which overlooks the harbour from a waterfront location.*
20⇌🟥(2fb) CTV in all bedrooms ℞ T S%
sB&B⇌🟥£19.95-£29.95 dB&B⇌🟥£38-£49.50 🍴
ℂ CTV 6P snooker sauna solarium gymnasium turkish bath whirlpool spa *xmas*
V 🏡 ⚲ S% Lunch £4-£8alc High tea £3-£7alc Dinner £11.65&alc Last dinner 9pm
Credit Cards ① ③ ④ ⓔ

---

# The Old Rectory ★ ⊲
## A Country House Hotel

This delightful Georgian Rectory, which during the last decade has been lovingly restored to its present high standard, coupled with our personal service, creates an ambience expected by the discerning guest of today. For those looking for a bolt hole on Exmoor, from which to escape the pressures of the nineties, may we offer The Old Rectory as a haven of peace and tranquillity.

*Please write or phone for our colour brochure & tariff.*

**Resident Proprietor: Tony Pring**
**The Old Rectory, Martinhoe, Parracombe, N. Devon. Tel: (05983) 368**
*See gazetteer entry under Martinhoe.*

**L**

---

## SANDROCK HOTEL ★★
## LYNTON, DEVON
### Tel: Lynton (0598) 53307

A family-run hotel offering friendly personal service. Situated in a quiet position in Lynton, it makes a good centre for exploring Exmoor. Full central heating. All bedrooms with colour TV, telephone, radio and intercom, baby listening, tea-making facilities. All double rooms en suite. Fully licensed with two bars. Games room. Mid-week bookings. Free car park. Colour brochure on request.

**Resident Proprietors:**
**John & Maria Harrison**

**MACHYNLLETH** Powys Map **06** SH70

★★63% ***Dolguog Hall*** SY20 8UJ ☎(0654)702244
*An elegant seventeenth-century gentleman's residence is now the centre of a modern holiday complex of log chalets set on the lovely wooded slopes which line the Dulas River. Public rooms are spacious and comfortable, the new Victorian Conservatory Restaurant providing good food and friendly service.*
9⇌🚿(1fb) CTV in all bedrooms ® 🐕
20P ✲ ♩
🍷 Continental **V** ♱ ☕ ⚟ Last dinner 9pm
Credit Cards 1 3 5

★★63% ***Wynnstay Arms*** Maengwyn St SY80 8AE
☎(0654)702941
*Former coaching inn situated in the centre of this market town.*
20⇌⚟in 2 bedrooms CTV in all bedrooms ®
42P
**V** ♱ ☕ ⚟
Credit Cards 1 2 3 4 5

**MADELEY** Staffordshire Map **07** SJ74

★★67% **Crewe Arms** Wharf St, Madeley Heath CW3 9LP
☎Stoke-on-Trent(0782)750392
*This recently modernised and extended country inn now provides good quality and well equipped bedrooms and relaxing bars and lounges. There is a good choice of food, with bar meals and an à la carte restaurant.*
10⇌(2fb) CTV in all bedrooms ® **T** 🐕 (ex guide dogs) ✱
sB&B⇌fr£40 dB&B⇌fr£50
CTV 50P pool table *xmas*
**V** ♱ ☕ Sunday Lunch £5.75
Credit Cards 1 3

**MADINGLEY** Cambridgeshire Map **05** TL36

✕✕**Three Horseshoes** High St CB3 8AB ☎(0954)210221
*Though situated only a few miles from Cambridge, this is a picture-postcard, thatched village inn, its setting park-like and its interior beamed and panelled. Food is mainly British, with a French country influence, and game figures prominently.*
**V** 52 seats Last dinner 10pm 50P
Credit Cards 1 2 3 5

**MAIDENCOMBE**

See **Torquay**

**MAIDENHEAD** Berkshire Map **04** SU88

❀★★★★71% **Fredrick's** Shoppenhangers Rd SL6 2PZ
☎(0628)35934 Telex no 849966 FAX (0628) 771054
Closed 24-30 Dec
*Bedrooms are well appointed, equipped with all the usual modern facilities and nicely co-ordinated, whilst public areas are quite glitzy and elegant. Highly competent staff are pleasant and courteous, none more so than those in the restaurant, where robust enjoyable cuisine is served. Dishes such as breast of partridge with lentil salad to start, followed by noisettes of lamb with lime and thyme have been enjoyed by our inspectors and desserts are always well presented on the trolley.*
37⇌🚿 CTV in all bedrooms **T** 🐕 sB&B⇌🚿£79.50-£110
dB&B⇌🚿£135-£145
☾ 90P ⛟ ✲
🍷 English & French **V** ♱ Lunch £22.50&alc Dinner fr£35.50alc Last dinner 9.45pm
Credit Cards 1 2 3 5

★★★70% ***Boulters Lock*** Boulters Island SL6 8PE
☎(0628)21291 Telex no 848742 FAX (0628) 26048
*Boulters Lock was part of the inspiration for Jerome K Jerome's famous book "Three Men in a Boat". The inn which stands on the site today enjoys a fine reputation for quality cuisine and has now, with the development of its outbuildings taken on a new role in providing very comfortable and well equipped accommodation.*
Annexe19⇌🚿1⊟ CTV in all bedrooms ® **T**
☾ 37P ⛟ ♫
🍷 International **V** ♱ ☕ Last dinner 11pm
Credit Cards 1 2 3 5

★★★57% **Thames Riviera** At the Bridge SL6 8DW
☎(0628)74057 Telex no 846687 FAX (0628) 776586
*This efficiently-run hotel is situated next to the 13th-century bridge which brought wealth to medieval Maidenhead. Jerome's Restaurant and the modern coffee shop offer a good choice of food.*
35⇌🚿Annexe18⇌🚿(3fb)1⊟ CTV in all bedrooms ® **T**
sB⇌🚿fr£82.50 dB⇌🚿fr£93.50 (room only)
☾ 50P 10🚘 ♩ ♫
🍷 English & French **V** ♱ ☕ Lunch fr£15&alc Dinner fr£18&alc Last dinner 9.45pm
Credit Cards 1 2 3 4 5

✕✕✕**Shoppenhangers Manor** Manor Ln SL6 2RA
☎(0628)23444 Telex no 847502 FAX (0628) 770035
*The present Manor House, with its beautiful antique appearance, is actually a replica of the original 16th-century merchant's house, re-built after a disastrous fire in 1937. An ideal venue for private parties and business meetings, the à la carte menu is imaginative and well complimented by the list of wines. Service by the smart young staff is efficient and courteous.*
Closed Sun & BH's
Lunch not served Sat
🍷 International 40 seats S% Lunch fr£18.50 Dinner fr£29.50 Last lunch 2pm Last dinner 10.30pm 80P nc12yrs
Credit Cards 1 2 3 5

**MAIDSTONE** Kent Map **05** TQ75

★★★67% **Tudor Park** Ashford Rd, Bearstead ME14 4NQ
☎(0622)34334 Telex no 966655 FAX (0622) 35360
*Located two miles east of Maidstone, this modern hotel combines extensive and exciting golf and country club facilities with spacious, well equipped bedrooms and 24-hour room service. Public areas include a cocktail lounge, piano bar, the Garden Restaurant and the Waterside Grill. Extensive conference facilities are also available.*
120⇌🚿(6fb)⚟in 29 bedrooms CTV in all bedrooms ® **T** ✱
sB&B⇌🚿£90-£100 dB&B⇌🚿£105-£120 ⊟
☾ ⊞ 320P ⛆(heated) ⚑ 18 ♪ (hard) squash snooker sauna solarium gymnasium table tennis beautician ♫ ♤ *xmas*
🍷 International **V** ♱ ☕ ⚟ Lunch £12.50 Dinner £16.50 Last dinner 9.45pm
Credit Cards 1 2 3 5

★★★60% **Larkfield Hotel** London Rd ME20 6HJ (Trusthouse Forte) ☎West Malling(0732)846858 Telex no 957420
FAX (0732) 846786
(For full entry see Larkfield)

**See advertisement on page 475**

★★61% **Boxley House** Boxley Rd, Boxley ME14 3DZ (3m N between A249 & A229) (Exec Hotel) ☎(0622)692269
FAX (0622) 683536
*A seventeenth-century house set in twenty acres of parkland has been modernised to preserve much of its original character whilst providing a choice of well-equipped bedrooms, a function/dining room with Minstrels Gallery and separate breakfast room, an open-plan lounge/bar and a comfortable annexe.*
11⇌🚿Annexe7⇌🚿(1fb)2⊟ CTV in all bedrooms ® **T** ✱
sB&B⇌🚿£50 dB&B⇌🚿£70
150P ⛟ ✲ ⛆(heated) ♫
▶

M

♀ English & French V ✿ ⌾ Lunch £9.95-£12.50 Dinner
£15-£18 Last dinner 9pm
Credit Cards 1 2 3 5

★★**61%, Grange Moor** St Michael's Rd ME16 8BS (off A26)
☎(0622)677623 FAX (0622) 678246
*A friendly family-run hotel and free house situated off the A26
Tonbridge road, with well-equipped modern bedrooms, a Tudor-
style restaurant and attractive bars serving snacks and bar meals.
The Function Suite is very popular, and there are good car parking
facilities.*
36rm(1⇨31♠)(3fb)1⌗ CTV in all bedrooms ® T
sB&B⇨♠£30-£48 dB&B⇨♠£42-£62 ⊟
60P
♀ English & French V ✿ ⌾ Lunch £10-£15 Dinner
£11.50&alc Last dinner 10pm
Credit Cards 1 3 £

✗✗**Suefflé** The Green, Bearsted ME14 4DW (2m E A20)
☎(0622)37065
Closed Sun, Mon, 1-5 Nov & 25-31 Dec
Lunch not served Sat
♀ French V 40 seats ✹ Lunch £17.50-£28.50 Dinner
£17.50-£28.50 Last lunch 1.45pm Last dinner 9.45pm 14P
Credit Cards 1 2 3 5

**MALDON** Essex Map **05** TL80

★★**55%** *The Blue Boar* Silver St CM9 7QE (Trusthouse Forte)
☎(0621)852681
*The proximity of a 13th-century church enhances the charm and
character of this period hotel with its beamed restaurant, cosy
lounge accommodation and well-equipped bedrooms. Service,
though simple, is efficient and the friendly staff create a pleasant
atmosphere.*
23⇨♠Annexe5⇨✕in 3 bedrooms CTV in all bedrooms ® T
43P
V ✿ ⌾ ✕ Last dinner 9.45pm
Credit Cards 1 2 3 4 5

✗**Francine's** 1A High St CM9 7PB ☎(0621)856605
*The simplicity of this restaurant and the very easy manner of the
chef patron create a most relaxing atmosphere. Here, freshly
prepared dishes are cooked with great care, while a selection of
good value French wines is also available. An unpretentious
restaurant, well worth a visit.*
Closed Sun, Mon, 1st 2 wks Feb & Aug
Lunch not served (ex by arrangement)
♀ French 24 seats ✹ Dinner £17-£20alc Last lunch 2pm Last
dinner 9.15pm 8P nc12yrs
Credit Cards 1 3

**MALLAIG** Highland *Inverness-shire* Map **13** NM69

★★**58%** **Marine** PH41 4PY ☎(0687)2217
Closed Xmas & New Year RS mid Nov-Mar
*Good-value accommodation is provided by this substantially
refurbished family-run commercial and tourist hotel, which stands
beside the railway station, close to the bustling fishing harbour and
ferry terminal.*
23rm(10⇨♠)(1fb) CTV in all bedrooms ® sB&B£18-£24
sB&B⇨♠£25-£30 dB&B£36-£40 dB&B⇨♠£40-£48 ⊟
CTV 6P
✿ ⌾ Bar Lunch fr£4.50alc Dinner £11.50-£13.50 Last dinner
8.30pm
Credit Cards 1 2 3

★★**55% West Highland** PH41 4QZ ☎(0687)2210
FAX (0687) 2130
Closed 10 Oct-21 Apr
*This family-run Highland hotel enjoys a fine outlook over the Inner
Minch towards Skye, Rhum and Eigg from its setting high on a hill*

*above the town. Catering for both coach parties and touring
holidaymakers, it offers good-value traditional comforts.*
26⇨♠(6fb) ® sB&B⇨♠£25-£27 dB&B⇨♠£50-£54 ⊟
CTV 30P ✿ ♫
V ✿ ⌾ Lunch £7 Dinner £12.50 Last dinner 8.30pm
Credit Cards 1 3 £

**MALLWYD** Gwynedd Map **06** SH81

★**59% Brigand's Inn** SY20 9HJ ☎Dinas Mawddwy(06504)208
Closed Feb
*This former 15th-century coaching inn, with later additions, is
situated at the junction of the A458 and A470. It provides modest
accommodation and is popular with fishermen.*
14rm(4⇨1♠)(2fb) ®
CTV 40P ⊞ ♪
V ✿ ⌾
Credit Cards 1 3

**MALMESBURY** Wiltshire Map **03** ST98

★★★⚑**76% Whatley Manor** Easton Grey SN16 0RB
☎(0666)822888 Telex no 449380 FAX (0666) 826120
*An elegant tree-lined drive leads to this delightful Cotswold
Manor House. Bedrooms, both those in the main building and
those in the Court House, are charming, spacious and tastefully
furnished, whilst the panelled public rooms have roaring log fires.
Leisure facilities include all-weather tennis, croquet, swimming
pool, sauna, solarium and spa bath.*
18⇨Annexe11⇨(2fb)1⌗ CTV in all bedrooms ® T
sB&B⇨£70-£80 dB&B⇨£99-£115 ⊟
⟨ 60P ⊞ ✿ ⌖(heated) ♙ (hard) ♪ sauna solarium croquet
putting table tennis jaccuzzi *xmas*
♀ English & Continental V ✿ ⌾ Lunch £14-£15 Dinner fr£26
Last dinner 9pm
Credit Cards 1 2 3 5

★★★**68%, Old Bell** Abbey Row SN16 0BW ☎(0666)822344
FAX (0666) 825145
*Possibly the oldest hotel in the county, standing next to the Abbey,
the Old Bell retains many interesting features including a 700-
year-old fireplace. The spacious dining room serves quality English
food, including sumptuous sweets. There is also an elegant lounge,
a large bar and a separate cocktail bar, cheerful with fresh flowers
and log fires. Some bedrooms are newly built, others are furnished
with antiques, but all have the usual modern facilities. The staff are
good natured and their attitude makes this hotel a special place to
stay.*
37⇨♠Annexe1⇨1⌗ CTV in 37 bedrooms ® T
✖ (ex guide dogs) sB&B⇨♠fr£65 dB&B⇨♠fr£80 ⊟
⟨ 30P ✿ *xmas*
♀ English & French V ✿ ⌾ Lunch fr£10.50 Dinner fr£17.50
Last dinner 9.30pm
Credit Cards 1 3

**MALTON** North Yorkshire Map **08** SE77

★★**67% Talbot** Yorkersgate YO13 0PB ☎(0653)694031
FAX (0653) 693355
*An attractive 18th-century house on the outskirts of town and
overlooking the River Derwent. Traditional Yorkshire fayre is
served in the elegant dining room, and the bedrooms, which vary in
style from modern to traditional, are all well equipped.*
29⇨♠(3fb)1⌗ CTV in all bedrooms ® T ✹ sB&B⇨♠fr£39
dB&B⇨♠fr£66
⟨ 30P 6🚗 (£3 per night) ✿ *xmas*
V ✿ ⌾ Lunch £8.50-£12.50 Dinner £12.50-£16.50 Last dinner
9pm
Credit Cards 1 2 3 5

**See advertisement on page 477**

M

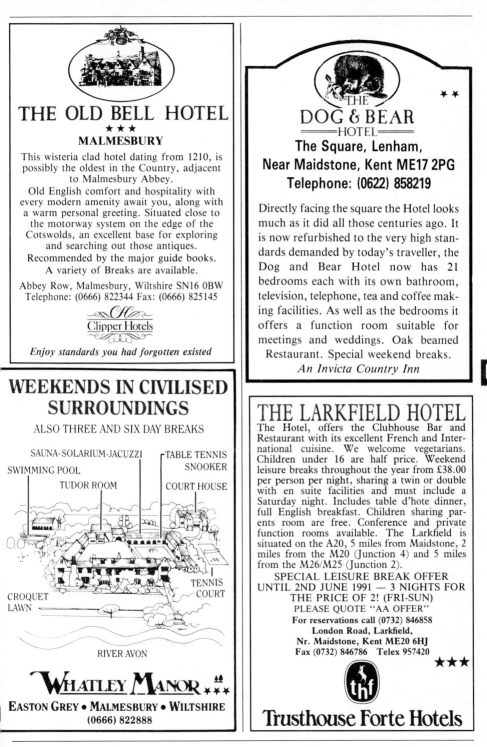

★**60% Wentworth Arms** Town St, Old Malton YO17 0HD
☎(0653)692618
Closed Xmas Day
*Bedrooms are modestly furnished and clean in this sound little
coaching inn which dates back to the early 1700's and preserves
some of its original beams and exposed stone walls in the cosy
dining room.*
6rm(2↑) CTV in all bedrooms ® ⊁ sB&B£17-£18
dB&B£34-£36 dB&B↑£38-£40
30P ₩ nc6yrs
⌂ ⌧ Lunch £6-£7&alc High tea fr£4alc Dinner fr£7alc Last
dinner 8.45pm
Credit Cards ①③

---

**MALVERN** Hereford & Worcester Map **03** SO74

★★★**65% Abbey** Abbey Rd WR14 3ET (De Vere)
☎(0684)892332 Telex no 335008 FAX (0684) 892662
*This large, central hotel standing next to the famous priory, is a
popular conference venue. Rooms continue to be refurbished to a
good modern standard and offer very good facilities.*
105⇨↑(4fb)1⊞ CTV in all bedrooms ® T sB&B⇨↑£62
dB&B⇨↑£88 ₽
Lift ⊄ 120P ❖ CFA
V ⌂ ⌧ Lunch fr£9.50&alc Dinner fr£12.50&alc Last dinner
8.30pm
Credit Cards ①②③⑤

★★★**65% Cottage in the Wood** Holywell Rd, Malvern
Wells WR14 4LG (3m S A449) (Consort) ☎(0684)573487
Telex no 339342 ATTN COTTAGE FAX (0684) 560662
Closed 6-12 Jan
*This privately-owned hotel, a former Georgian dower house, enjoys
a superb location with magnificent views across the Severn Valley.
Sympathetic refurbishment has provided cosy, comfortable rooms,
many of which are situated in the Coach House and Beech
Cottage. The hotel has a relaxing atmosphere and Mr & Mrs
Pattin and their staff offer a warm welcome.*
8⇨Annexe12⇨2⊞ CTV in all bedrooms ® T S% sB⇨£55
dB⇨£72-£105 (room only) ₽
50P ₩ ❖ xmas
V ⌂ ⌧ S% Lunch £5.65-£12.50&alc Dinner £16-£23alc Last
dinner 9pm
Credit Cards ①③

★★★**64% Colwall Park** Colwall WR13 6QG (3m SW B4218)
(Inter-Hotels) ☎(0684)40206 FAX (0684) 40847
*A privately-owned hotel on the A4218 just south of Malvern,
providing comfortable, well-maintained bedrooms and a relaxing
atmosphere that makes it ideal for a weekend break. The
interesting menu makes good use of fresh produce.*
20⇨↑(2fb) CTV in all bedrooms ® S%
sB&B⇨↑£46.50-£52.50 dB&B⇨↑£65-£75 ₽
50P ❖ croquet xmas
V ⌂ ⌧ Lunch fr£9.50 High tea fr£6.50 Last high tea 6pm
Credit Cards ①②③④

★★★**61% Foley Arms** Worcester Rd WR14 4QS (Best Western)
☎(0684)573397 Telex no 437287 FAX (0684) 892275
*Built in 1810 as a coaching inn, The Foley Arms is the oldest hotel
in Malvern and is situated in the centre of the town. It is a
traditional hotel which offers good hospitality and service. The
rooms have been equipped with modern facilities and some have
spectacular views across the Severn Valley.*
26⇨↑Annexe2rm(1fb)2⊞⊁in 1 bedroom CTV in 26
bedrooms ® ✱ sB&B⇨↑£56 dB&B⇨↑£72 ₽
⊄ 45P 4⊜ ❖ CFA xmas
V ⌂ ⌧ ⊁ Sunday Lunch £10.50 Dinner £13.50 Last dinner
9.30pm
Credit Cards ①②③⑤④

★★★**72% Holdfast Cottage** Welland, Malvern Wells
WR13 6NA (4m SE) ☎Hanley Swan(0684)310288
*This delightful small hotel, within in its own grounds, is situated
just outside Malvern. The accommodation is attractive, and the
cottage-style décor and furnishings are enhanced by some
thoughtful extras – even a teddy bear and bath ducks. The public
areas are compact, but cosy and of good quality – the pleasant
dining room overlooks the garden. The menu is short and
interesting, making good use of fresh local produce. Service is
provided by the resident proprietors, Diana and Dennis
Beetlestone.*
8⇨↑ CTV in all bedrooms ® T sB&B⇨↑£36-£39
dB&B⇨↑£72-£78 ₽
16P ₩ ❖ croquet xmas
♡ English & French V ⌂ ⌧ ⊁ Dinner £16&alc Last dinner
9pm
Credit Cards ①③④

★★**66% Royal Malvern** Graham Rd WR14 2HN (Minotels)
☎(0684)563411 FAX (0684) 560514
Closed 25 Dec
*Equally suitable for business people and tourists, this 18th-century
town centre hotel has been tastefully converted to provide
comfortable and well-equipped accommodation.*
14rm(12⇨↑) CTV in all bedrooms ® T sB&B£30-£35
sB&B⇨↑£38-£45 dB&B£40-£46 dB&B⇨↑£48-£58 ₽
Lift 10P
V ⌂ ⌧ ⊁ Bar Lunch £4.45-£15.20alc Dinner £4.45-£19.50alc
Last dinner 9.30pm
Credit Cards ①②③⑤④

★★**64% Broomhill** West Malvern Rd, West Malvern
WR14 4AY (2m W B4232) ☎(0684)564367
*A pleasant, homely, small hotel situated outside the town centre on
the West Malvern road. There are superb views from the public
areas and some of the bedrooms.*
9rm(2⇨↑) CTV in all bedrooms ® sB&B£19.75-£23.50 sB&B⇨↑£19.75-£23.50
dB&B£39.50-£45 dB&B⇨↑£39.50-£45 ₽
CTV 9P ₩ xmas
V ⌂ ⊁ Bar Lunch 90p-£5.50 Dinner £10 Last dinner 8.15pm
④

★★**64% Malvern Hills** Wynds Point WR13 6DW (4m S A449)
☎Colwall(0684)40237 FAX (0684) 40327
*Situated on the A449 between Malvern and Ledbury, close to the
Herefordshire Beacon. Most rooms have now been attractively
decorated and the comfortable accommodation is popular for
holiday and business purposes. There is an 'olde worlde' bar and a
small lounge for residents.*
16rm(11⇨4↑)(1fb)1⊞ CTV in all bedrooms ® T
sB&B⇨↑£35-£38.50 dB&B⇨↑£55-£57.50 ₽
CTV 35P ₩ ❖ solarium xmas
♡ English & French V ⌂ Sunday Lunch £10-£10.50 Dinner
£12-£13.50&alc Last dinner 9.45pm
Credit Cards ①③

★★**63% Cotford** 51 Graham Rd WR14 2JW ☎(0684)572427
Closed 25 Dec-11 Jan
*Built in 1851 for the Bishop of Worcester, this hotel is within
walking distance of the town centre. Rooms are simply furnished,
have good modern facilities and are suitable for business guests
and holidaymakers alike. A friendly, homely atmosphere prevails
throughout.*
16rm(7⇨5↑)(3fb) CTV in all bedrooms ® T sB&B£25-£30
sB&B⇨↑£30-£32 dB&B⇨↑£50-£55
15P ₩ ❖
V ⊁ Dinner fr£14 Last dinner 9pm
Credit Cards ①③

1991 marks the 25th anniversary of this guide.

★★63% *Essington* Holywell Rd, Malvern Wells WR14 4LQ (3m S A449) ☎(0684)561177
*Small, family-run hotel with 2 acres of terraced gardens. Personal service and home cooking are offered.*
9⇄🛏(1fb)1🖩 CTV in all bedrooms ®
30P ⇔ ❀
❦ ⅍ Last dinner 8.15pm
Credit Cards ⊡ ⊡

★★63%, **Mount Pleasant** Belle Vue Ter WR14 4PZ
☎(0684)561837 FAX (0684) 892363
Closed 25 & 26 Dec
*Set in attractive gardens, this large Georgian house, close to the town centre, stands opposite the priory church. It is run in a friendly and informal manner by the proprietors, who provide comfortable and well-equipped accommodation for both tourists and travelling business people alike. There are also facilities for functions and conferences. The small intimate restaurant offers a mainly Spanish theme menu and there is an adjoining coffee shop.*
14⇄🛏 CTV in all bedrooms ® T 🐾 (ex guide dogs)
sB&B⇄🛏 £40-£47 dB&B⇄🛏 £57.50-£63
20P ❀ nc7yrs
♈ English & Spanish V ❦ ⅏ Lunch £8.50-£9.50 Dinner
£9.95-£10.95&alc Last dinner 9.30pm
Credit Cards ⊡ ⊡ ⊡ ⊡ ⊕

★★58% **Montrose** 23 Graham Rd WR14 2HU ☎(06845)2335
Closed 1 wk Xmas
*Reputedly the first purpose-built hotel in this famous spa resort, this large old house is conveniently close to the town centre and provides simple but comfortable accommodation with friendly service.*
14rm(5⇄6🛏)(1fb) CTV in 12 bedrooms ® ✳ sB&B£25-£40
sB&B⇄🛏£27-£45 dB&B£35-£40 dB&B⇄🛏£40-£50 🏋
CTV 18P ❀
V ⅏ Lunch £8-£10 Dinner £10 Last dinner 7pm
Credit Cards ⊡ ⊡ ⊡

### *Mount Pleasant* ★★
### *Hotel*

#### Great Malvern, Worcs.
#### Telephone: (0684) 561837
*Break offers all year*
Situated in the centre of town overlooking Abbey with direct access from 1½ acres of terraced gardens to the hills behind. The hotel has been completely refurbished and offers spacious accommodation in an elegant Georgian house with central heating and log fires. The hotel is run on an informal basis with the emphasis on personal attention, warmth and good food.

**All rooms have Bath/WC, Colour TV, Radio, Alarm, Tea-making facilities and Direct Dial telephone.**
*Conference facilities available*

Holywell Road, Malvern Wells, Worcs.
Tel: (0684) 573487   Fax: (0684) 560662

### THE COTTAGE IN THE WOOD
★★★
A delightful country house hotel and restaurant set high on the Malvern Hills with 30 mile views. Our seven acres open directly onto the Hills. Fabulous walks. Proprietor owned and run.

Short break inclusive rates all year.

20 en-suite bedrooms.

Open for lunch, afternoon tea and dinner.

**M**

*The* T A L B O T
HOTEL *and* RESTAURANT
AA ★ ★   **Yorkersgate, Malton,**
**North Yorkshire YO17 0AA**
**Telephone: 0653 694031 Fax: 0653 693355**

Situated in the heart of this pleasant Market Town, the Talbot is an early Georgian Coaching Inn surrounded by its own grounds with views over the River Derwent and the Yorkshire Wolds, yet close to Castle Howard and the beautiful Minster City of York.
The Restaurant and Bars offer traditional Yorkshire Fare and the elegant Lounge furnished with fine antiques is ideal for pre-dinner drinks and lazy nightcaps.
All 27 bedrooms are en-suite with colour television, radio, hairdryer, trouser press and direct dial telephone.
Luxury Four Poster bedrooms, Suites and Family Rooms are also available.
**For further details and brochures:**
**Telephone: 0653 694031**

MAN, ISLE OF Map **06**

---

BALLASALLA Map **06** SC27

**✗ *La Rosette*** ☎Castletown(0624)822940
*It is advisable to book well in advance at this charming little French restaurant, for it is equally popular with local people and tourists. Cosy and well-furnished, it offers an array of attractive, good-value dishes coupled with friendly service.*
Closed Sun & Mon
♥ French 45 seats Last lunch 4pm Last dinner 10.30pm nc4yrs
✻
Credit Cards 1 3

---

CASTLETOWN Map **06** SC26

**★★★63%, Castletown Golf Links** Fort Island(Best Western)
☎(0624)822201 Telex no 627636 FAX (0624) 824633
*Popular with golfers because it stands beside the Castletown golf links, on the edge of Derryhaven Bay and close to the airport, this hotel has recently been upgraded.*
58rm(44⇨12♠)(1fb)1⊞ CTV in all bedrooms ® T ✻
sB&B⇨♠£52.50-£85 dB&B⇨♠£75-£160 ₽
《 CTV 100P ✿ CFA ⊠(heated) ▶ 18 snooker sauna solarium shooting *xmas*
♥ French V ✆ ⊻ ✻ Lunch £12.50-£14.50&alc Dinner
£14.50-£17.50&alc Last dinner 10pm
Credit Cards 1 2 3 5

---

DOUGLAS Map **06** SC37

**★★★64%, Empress** Central Promenade ☎(0624)27211
Telex no 627772 FAX (0624) 73554
*There are two restaurants at this large, well-furnished, seafront hotel overlooking Douglas Bay.*
102⇨♠ CTV in all bedrooms ® T ✻ (ex guide dogs) ✻
sB⇨♠£45-£70 dB⇨♠£80-£90 (room only)
Lift 《 ⊞ ♪ ♨ ⊠(heated) sauna solarium gymnasium
♥ French V ✆ ⊻ ✻ Lunch fr£15alc High tea fr£5alc Dinner
fr£15alc Last dinner 11pm
Credit Cards 1 2 3 5

**★★★64%, Sefton** Harris Promenade ☎(0624)26011
FAX (0624) 76004
*Overlooking Douglas Bay from its seafront position, this comfortable hotel complements well-appointed bedroom accommodation with a unique coffee shop on the first floor, excellent leisure facilities, a fully self-contained conference/banqueting suite and a modern business centre.*
80⇨♠(5fb) CTV in all bedrooms ® T ✻ (ex guide dogs) ✻
sB&B⇨♠£29-£42 dB&B⇨♠£45-£78 ₽
Lift 《 40P ♨ ⊠(heated) sauna solarium gymnasium steam rooms
V ✆ ⊻ ✻ Lunch £4-£6 High tea £5 Dinner £12.50&alc Last dinner 9.45pm
Credit Cards 1 2 3 5

**★ *Woodbourne*** Alexander Dr ☎(0624)21766
Closed 29 Sep-23 May
*Friendly, comfortable public house in a residential area.*
10rm ✻
CTV ♪ ♨ nc12yrs
✆

**✗✗✗ *Boncompte's*** Admiral House, Loch Promenade
☎(0624)29551
*This friendly restaurant offers a very high standard of international cuisine and is popular with both locals and visitors alike. Dishes are cooked to order using the best fresh produce and although fish is prominently featured, the menu is wide ranging, with prime meat and game in season and flambé specialities. The seafood soufflé can be especially recommended. A wide choice of wines complements the excellent cooking.*

---

Lunch not served Sat
♥ French V 85 seats Last lunch 2pm Last dinner 10pm 20P nc3yrs
Credit Cards 1 3 5

---

RAMSEY Map **06** SC49

**★★★★60%, Grand Island** Bride Rd ☎(0624)812455
Telex no 629849 FAX (0624) 815291
*Terraced lawns lead down to the beach from this Georgian country house which stands in an elevated position overlooking the bay. Now a welcoming hotel which can cater for all tastes and pursuits, it augments its magnificent views and famed croquet lawns with such modern leisure facilities as a swimming pool, sauna, gym and snooker room, while more traditional services have been extended by the provision of beauty and hairdressing salons.*
54⇨♠(4fb)1⊞ ✻in 2 bedrooms CTV in all bedrooms ® T
✻ (ex guide dogs) ✳ sB&B⇨♠£48-£148
dB&B⇨♠£74-£148 ₽
Lift 《 150P ♨ ✿ ⊠(heated) ♪ (hard) ∪ snooker sauna
solarium gymnasium shooting steam room croquet putting
*xmas*
♥ International V ✆ ⊻ Lunch £10.50&alc Dinner £18.75&alc
Last dinner 10pm
Credit Cards 1 2 3 5

---

MANCHESTER Greater Manchester Map **07** SJ89

See **Town Plan Section**
See also **Salford**
**★★★★66%, Holiday Inn Crowne Plaza** Peter St M60 2DS
(Holiday Inns Inc) ☎061-236 3333 Telex no 667550
FAX 061-228 2241
*Neither Mr Rolls nor Mr Royce, who first met at this splendid Edwardian building, would recognise the interior now, although modernisation has not detracted from the luxury and elegance for which the hotel is renowned. In addition to the 3 restaurants, there are excellent conference and banqueting facilities and, in the lower areas, comprehensive leisure facilities. Efficient service is provided by friendly and helpful staff.*
303⇨♠(23fb)✻in 54 bedrooms CTV in all bedrooms T ✻
sB⇨♠fr£97 dB⇨♠fr£121 (room only) ₽
Lift 《 ⊞ 40♨ ⊠(heated) squash sauna solarium gymnasium
jacuzzi *xmas*
♥ English & French V ✆ ⊻
Credit Cards 1 2 3 5

**★★★★66%, Hotel Piccadilly** Piccadilly M60 1QR (Embassy)
☎061-236 8414 Telex no 668765 FAX 061-228 1568
*Situated in the city centre, this hotel has been totally refurbished over recent years to provide comprehensive facilities. Bedrooms, though not large, are well equipped, public rooms are spacious and comfortable and a high standard of cuisine has been achieved in the elegant Pavilion and Verandah Restaurants.*
271⇨♠3⊞✻in 35 bedrooms CTV in all bedrooms ® T
sB⇨♠£95-£120 dB⇨♠£120-£140 (room only) ₽
Lift 《 80P ⊠(heated) sauna solarium gymnasium *xmas*
♥ English & French V ✆ ⊻ ✻ Lunch £12-£14&alc Dinner
£18.50-£22&alc Last dinner 10.30pm
Credit Cards 1 2 3 4 5

**★★★65%, Ramada Renaissance** Blackfriars St M3 2EQ
☎061-835 2555 Telex no 669699 FAX 061-835 3077
*A large, modern, city-centre hotel with spacious and well-appointed bedrooms. The young staff provide service in a cheerful and helpful manner.*
205⇨♠(5fb)✻in 48 bedrooms CTV in all bedrooms T
sB⇨♠£95 dB⇨♠£110 (room only) ₽
Lift 《 80♨ *xmas*
V ✆ ⊻ Bar Lunch £2.75-£12
Credit Cards 1 2 3 4 5 £

**M**

★★★★55% **Portland Thistle** 3/5 Portland St, Piccadilly Gdns M1 6DP (Mount Charlotte (TS)) ☎061-228 3400 Telex no 669157 FAX 061-228 6347

*Conveniently situated in the city centre and undergoing a progressive programme of refurbishment, this hotel offers accommodation in bedrooms which are for the most part compact and in some cases functionally appointed, though all have modern amenities. A range of eating options is complemented by an extensive selection of champagnes and malt whiskies, staff are generally eager to please and the atmosphere is busy and vibrant.*

205⇨↱(6fb)2⊞✂in 51 bedrooms CTV in all bedrooms ® T ✱ sB⇨↱fr£79 dB⇨↱fr£95 (room only) ⊟

Lift ☾ ⊞ P̸ ⊡(heated) sauna solarium gymnasium whirlpool hairdresser

♡ International ♧ ⊻ ✂ Lunch fr£11.95&alc Dinner fr£13.95&alc Last dinner 10pm

Credit Cards 1 2 3 4 5

★★★58% **Willow Bank** 340-342 Wilmslow Rd, Fallowfield M14 6AF ☎061-224 0461 Telex no 668222 FAX 061-257 2561

*Situated 3 miles from the city centre, on the B5117, and popular with business guests, this former Edwardian house with a purpose-built extension is gradually being improved. Public areas are attractive and 24-hour room service is available.*

124rm(110⇨12↱)(2fb) CTV in all bedrooms ® T ✗ (ex guide dogs) S% sB⇨↱£41-£47 dB⇨↱£57-£62 (room only) ⊟

☾ CTV 70P 30🚗 CFA ♫

♡ English & Continental V ♧ ⊻ ✂ S% Lunch £6&alc High tea £3.50 Dinner £10&alc Last dinner 10.15pm

Credit Cards 1 2 3 5 £

**See advertisement on page 481**

# Manchester

**★★★57%** *Novotel Manchester West* Worsley Brow M28 4YA (Novotel) ☎061-799 3535 Telex no 669586 FAX 061-703 8207 (For full entry see Worsley)

---

**★★★56%** **Parkers** 109-111 Corporation St M4 4DX
☎061-953 9550 FAX 061-835 3805
*Close to Victoria Station, in an area of the city undergoing re-development, this Edwardian hotel offers sizeable bedrooms, a spacious foyer and a large restaurant in period style. A variety of conference and banqueting facilities are available and for those in need of exercise, a gym and sauna.*
112⇌🕯(8fb)1🛏 CTV in all bedrooms ® T ✱ S%
sB⇌🕯£25-£57 dB⇌🕯£35-£77 (room only)
Lift (( 35P sauna solarium gymnasium
♀ French V ✿ ⚹ S% Lunch £7.50&alc Dinner £12.50&alc
Last dinner 10.15pm
Credit Cards ⒈⒉⒊⒌

---

**★★★53%** **Post House** Palatine Rd, Northenden M22 4FH (Trusthouse Forte) ☎061-998 7090 Telex no 669248 FAX 061-946 0139
*Conveniently situated on the B5167 close to the M56, M63 and M66 this purpose-built hotel is beginning to show its age, but a major programme of refurbishment should be completed by the time this guide is published.*
200⇌🕯(50fb)✠in 52 bedrooms CTV in all bedrooms ® ✱
sB⇌🕯£67-£77 dB⇌🕯£77-£87 (room only)
Lift (( 123P 120🍴 CFA
V ✿ ⚹ ✠ Lunch £10-£11.50&alc Dinner £14.50&alc Last dinner 10.30pm
Credit Cards ⒈⒉⒊⒋⒌

---

**★★62%** *Mitre* Cathedral Gates M3 1SW ☎061-834 4128 Telex no 669581
*An historic hotel standing near the cathedral and close to Victoria Station offers friendly service and well-equipped bedrooms, many with en suite facilities.*
28rm(3⇌6🕯)(1fb) CTV in all bedrooms ® ✖ (ex guide dogs)
(( CTV ✗
♀ English & French V ✿ ⚹ Last dinner 9.45pm
Credit Cards ⒈⒉⒊⒌

---

**★★60%** *Cornish House* 122 Withington Rd M16 8FB
☎061-226 2235 Telex no 36274
*The recently refurbished hotel, situated about a mile south of the city centre and within easy reach of Trafford Park Industrial Estate, caters mainly for commercial guests. All bedrooms have en suite facilities, and friendly staff provide helpful service.*
25⇌🕯(3fb) CTV in all bedrooms ® T
(( CTV 60P 4🍴
♀ English & French V ✿ ⚹ Last dinner 9.30pm
Credit Cards ⒈⒉⒊⒌

---

**★★60%** *Crescent Gate* Park Crescent, Victoria Park M14 5RE
☎061-224 0672 FAX 061-257 2822
Closed Xmas
*Small, friendly hotel in a quiet crescent off the A6061 Wilmslow Road, south of the city centre.*
15rm(2⇌3🕯)Annexe11⇌🕯(1fb) CTV in all bedrooms ® T
sB&B£25 sB&B⇌🕯£30 dB&B⇌🕯£45
CTV 18P 🚲
✿ ⚹ ✠ Bar Lunch £1.50-£5 Dinner £8 Last dinner 8pm
Credit Cards ⒈⒉⒊⒌ⓕ

---

○**Castlefield** Liverpool Rd, Castlefield M3 4JR ☎061-832 7073
Due to have opened Jul 1990
48rm

---

○**Grand** Aytoun St M1 3DR (Trusthouse Forte) ☎061-236 9559 Telex no 667580
Due to have opened summer 1991
*Previously awarded three stars, this Victorian hotel is currently undergoing a complete refurbishment and is due to reopen in the summer of 1991.*

142⇌🕯(3fb)✠in 10 bedrooms CTV in all bedrooms ®
Lift (( ✗ CFA
V ✿ ⚹ ✠
Credit Cards ⒈⒉⒊⒋⒌

---

✖✖**Gaylord** Amethyst House, Marriot's Court, Spring Garden M2 1EA ☎061-832 6037 & 061-832 4866
*Set in a side street close to the Arndale Centre this comfortable, friendly restaurant is part of an international chain. The menu features well-spiced Mughlai and Karahi specialities based on prawns, chicken and lamb and provides good value at lunchtime and in the evening.*
Closed 25 Dec & 1 Jan
♀ Indian V 102 seats Last lunch 3pm Last dinner 11.30pm
✗✠
Credit Cards ⒈⒉⒊⒌

---

✖✖**Rajdoot** St James House, South Kings St M2 6DW
☎061-834 2176
*Tandoori specialities and other exotic Indian dishes together with friendly and attentive service are features of this long established, colourful restaurant situated near Manchester's main shopping area.*
Lunch not served Sun
♀ Indian 87 seats Last lunch 2.30pm Last dinner 11.30pm ✗
Credit Cards ⒈⒉⒊⒌

---

✖✖**Woodlands** 33 Shepley Rd, Audenshaw M34 5DJ
☎061-336 4241
*Fresh fish features on both the set menu and à la carte at this pleasant and relaxed family-run restaurant, situated just off the A6017. Competent cooking using good raw ingredients makes this a popular restaurant, particularly at lunchtime, and it is advisable to book in advance. On Saturdays, only the à la carte menu is offered.*
Closed Mon, Sun (ex party bookings) 1 wk after Xmas, 1 wk Etr & 2 wks Aug
Lunch not served Sat (ex party bookings)
♀ French V 40 seats ✱ Lunch fr£11.95&alc Dinner fr£13.95
Last lunch 2pm Last dinner 9.30pm 10P
Credit Cards ⒈⒊

---

✖✖**Woo Sang** 19-21 George St M1 4AG ☎061-236 3697
*An old established Cantonese restaurant, with colourful paintings, a fish tank and pot plants, situated above a supermarket in the heart of Manchester's Chinatown. Service is friendly and helpful with advice willingly given on any of the varied dishes on the extensive menu.*
Closed 25-26 Dec
♀ Cantonese V 220 seats Last lunch 2pm Last dinner 11.45pm ✗
Credit Cards ⒈⒉⒊⒌

---

✖✖**Yang Sing** 34 Princess St M1 4JY ☎061-236 2200 FAX 061-236 5934
*This bustling basement restaurant is well patronised by the local Chinese community. The extensive menu contains several dishes which should prove popular with the more adventurous diner, and a good selection of Dim Sum is available during the day. Service is decidedly easy going and informal.*
Closed Xmas Day
♀ Cantonese V 140 seats Last dinner 11pm ✗
Credit Cards ⒈⒉⒊

---

✖**The Koreana** Kings House, 40 King St West M3 2WY
☎061-832 4330
*Service is particularly helpful and friendly at this tastefully decorated restaurant which provides delicate and delicious Korean food. Spicy soups, Gaeram Chim (steamed egg) and Modurn Jurn (oysters coated in egg and shallow fried, with pork coated in breadcrumbs and deep fried) are just some of the dishes offered.*
Closed Sun, 25 Dec, 1 Jan & BH's (ex party bookings)
Lunch not served Sat

▶

481

♬ Korean **V** 60 seats ✷ S% Lunch £4.30-£6.95&alc Dinner £11.50-£17.50&alc Last lunch 2.30pm Last dinner 11pm ✗
Credit Cards ① ② ③ ⑤

✗ *Kosmos Taverna* 248 Wilmslow Rd, Fallowfield M14 6LD
☎061-225 9106
*A jolly, bustling Greek taverna where friendly helpful staff offer many traditional dishes including meze, hummus and taramasalata. Situated two miles south of the city centre on the Wilmslow Road.*
Lunch not served
♬ Greek **V** 70 seats ✗
Credit Cards ① ③

✗ **Market** Edge St, 104 High St M4 1HQ ☎061-834 3743
*This intriguing little restaurant close to the former Smithfield Market in the heart of old Manchester has a simple décor and a 'junk shop' collection of bric-a-brac. A collection of recipes begged and borrowed from around the world form the basis for an unusual range of dishes which include stewed lamb with rhubarb.*
Closed Sun, Mon, Aug, 1 wk Xmas & 1 wk Spring
Lunch not served
**V** 40 seats Dinner £10.80-£17.90alc Last dinner 9.30pm ✗
Credit Cards ① ② ③ ⑤

**MANCHESTER AIRPORT** Greater Manchester
Map **07** SJ88

★★★★66% **Manchester Airport Hilton** Outwood Ln,
Ringway M22 5WP (Hilton) ☎061-436 4404 Telex no 668361 FAX 061-436 1521
*A large, modern hotel which features lots of greenery and an attractive little stream running through its public areas. Enhanced recently by the opening of a stylish new restaurant and additional well-appointed bedrooms, it is busy, with a lively atmosphere. There are extensive conference and banqueting facilities and an appealing leisure complex.*
223⇆☖(10fb)⊁in 20 bedrooms CTV in all bedrooms ® T S% sB&B⇆☖fr£105 dB&B⇆☖£135-£155 ➡
Lift ⓒ ⊞ 260P ⌧(heated) sauna gymnasium
♬ European **V** ⊕ ⊡ Lunch £8.50-£30alc Dinner £8.50-£40alc Last dinner 11pm
Credit Cards ① ② ③ ⑤ ⓔ

★★★★57% **The Excelsior** Ringway Rd, Wythenshawe
M22 5NS (Trusthouse Forte) ☎061-437 5811 Telex no 668721 FAX 061-436 2340
*A good-sized hotel, incorporating a leisure centre with swimming pool, sauna and gym, forms part of the airport complex and is within easy reach of the national motorway network.*
300⇆(3fb)⊁in 80 bedrooms CTV in all bedrooms ® ✷ sB⇆fr£91 dB⇆fr£103 (room only) ➡
Lift ⓒ ⊞ 350P ✿ CFA ⌧(heated) sauna solarium gymnasium health & fitness centre
**V** ⊕ ⊡ ⊁ Lunch fr£11.50&alc Dinner fr£16.95&alc Last dinner 10.15pm
Credit Cards ① ② ③ ④ ⑤

★★★59% **Wilmslow Moat House** Altrincham Rd SK9 4LR
(Queens Moat) ☎Wilmslow(0625)529201 Telex no 666401 FAX (0625) 531876
*Behind its distinctive Swiss Chalet exterior, this hotel offers every modern amenity, including excellent leisure facilities. Some of the bedrooms are compact, but the newer ones are sizeable. The public rooms in the older part of the hotel are due to be refurbished. Food is enjoyable and the staff are helpful.*
125⇆2▥⊁in 4 bedrooms CTV in all bedrooms ® T ✷ sB⇆£70-£75 dB⇆£80-£85 (room only) ➡
Lift ⓒ 400P ✿ CFA ⌧(heated) squash snooker sauna solarium gymnasium jacuzzi steam room beauty therapy
♬ International **V** ⊕ ⊡ Lunch £8.95&alc Dinner £10.50 Last dinner 10.30pm
Credit Cards ① ② ③ ⑤ ⓔ

**M**

✗✗**Moss Nook** Ringway Rd M22 5NA ☎061-437 4778
*The plush, Edwardian-style interior, together with the attentive, friendly and efficient service from smartly dressed staff, make for a comfortable and relaxed dining experience at this charming French restaurant, which is much used for business entertaining. Fruit flavourings feature strongly on the à la carte menu which is supplemented with a number of daily dishes featuring the best produce from that day's market. A recent visit suggested that more care was needed in some areas of the preparation, however, a well judged apple and raspberry sauce was an inventive and effective partner to excellent medallions of venison. A double room with lounge and two bathrooms is available adjacent to the restaurant for those who may wish to stay overnight. Booking is usually essential.*

Closed Sun, Mon & 25 Dec-8 Jan
Lunch not served Sat
♀ French 50 seats ✱ S% Lunch £24&alc Dinner £24&alc Last lunch 1.30pm Last dinner 9.30pm 50P nc12yrs
Credit Cards ① ② ③ ⑤

---

**MANORBIER** Dyfed Map **02** SS09

★★59% **Castle Mead** SA70 7TA ☎(0834)871358
Closed Nov-Etr
*There are beautiful views of the sea, castle and church from the rear windows of this small family-run hotel, which stands at the head of a small wooded valley. Bedrooms are modestly furnished, but comfortable, and the food is consistently good.*
5⇌Annexe3⇌(2fb)✗in 2 bedrooms CTV in all bedrooms ®
sB&B⇌£36 dB&B⇌£72 ▤
20P 🚗 ✿
V ✿ ☑ Dinner fr£9 Last dinner 8pm
Credit Cards ① ② ③

---

**MANSFIELD** Nottinghamshire Map **08** SK56

★★61% *Pine Lodge* 281-283 Nottingham Rd NG18 4SE
☎(0623)22308
*This family owned and run hotel, situated just outside the town centre in a residential area on the Nottingham road, is well furnished in all areas, has good facilities in the bedrooms and serves meals of a high standard in the pleasant restaurant.*
21rm(13⇌3 ♠)(2fb) CTV in all bedrooms ® T ✻
40P 🚗 sauna solarium
✿ ☑
Credit Cards ① ② ③

---

**MARAZION** Cornwall & Isles of Scilly Map **02** SW53

★★66% **Mount Haven** Turnpike Rd TR17 0DQ (Minotels)
☎Penzance(0736)710249
Closed 24-27 Dec
*Set in its own grounds on the edge of the village, with panoramic views over Mount's Bay and St Michael's Mount, this personally-run hotel features some double rooms with small balconies; its split-level restaurant, decorated to a nautical theme, enjoys a good reputation locally.*
17⇌(5fb)1 🛏 CTV in all bedrooms ® T S% sB&B⇌£21-£35
dB&B⇌£42-£58 ▤
40P 🚗
♀ English & French V ✿ ☑ ✗ S% Sunday Lunch fr£6.95alc
Dinner £12&alc Last dinner 9pm
Credit Cards ① ② ③

**See advertisement under PENZANCE**

---

The AA's star-rating scheme is the market
leader in hotel classification.

---

**MARCH** Cambridgeshire Map **05** TL49

★65% **Olde Griffin** High St PE15 9EJ ☎(0354)52517
FAX (0354) 50086
*The proprietors, Mr and Mrs Reeve have created a warm and friendly atmosphere at this former coaching inn located in the town centre. Public areas are undergoing sympathetic refurbishment and are due to re-open early in the summer. Good rear car park.*
21rm(15⇌3 ♠)(2fb) CTV in all bedrooms ® T ✻
sB&B⇌♠£35-£45 dB&B⇌♠£45-£55
50P 🚗
♀ English & Continental V ✿
Credit Cards ① ③

---

**MARCHWIEL** Clwyd Map **07** SJ34

★★65% **Cross Lanes Hotel & Restaurant** Cross Lanes
LL13 0TF ☎Bangor-on-Dee(0978)780555 FAX (0978) 780568
RS 25-26 Dec
*This Victorian country house, set in seven acres of grounds beside the A525 about three miles south east of Wrexham, offers well equipped bedrooms which are popular with business clients, including those making use of the hotel's conference facilities.*
18⇌♠(1fb)1 🛏 CTV in all bedrooms ® T sB&B⇌♠£47
dB&B⇌♠£68 ▤
80P ✿ ▥(heated) sauna
♀ International V ✿ ☑ ✗ Lunch £8.95 Dinner £12.95 Last dinner 9pm
Credit Cards ① ② ③ ⑤ ⓔ

---

**MARFORD** Clwyd Map **07** SJ35

★65% **Trevor Arms** Springfield Ln LL12 8TA
☎Chester(0244)570436
*The inn, and other buildings in the village, were constructed by Flemish builders in the early 1800's and have a unique architectural style. Inside there are old beams and open fires, and bedrooms are well equipped and comfortable. Varied meals are served, with 'specials' displayed on boards.*
10♠(1fb)1 🛏 CTV in all bedrooms ® T ✻ (ex guide dogs) S%
sB&B♠£25-£27.50 dB&B♠£33-£40 Continental breakfast ▤
70P ✿ 🐴
V ✿ ☑ ✗ Lunch £6.75-£11.95alc High tea fr£2.25alc Dinner
£6.75-£11.95alc Last dinner 10pm
Credit Cards ① ③ ⓔ

---

**MARKET DRAYTON** Shropshire Map **07** SJ63

★★★♨68% **Goldstone Hall** Goldstone TF9 2NA
☎Cheswardine(0630)86202 & 86487
*This personally run country home has a relaxing and informal atmosphere. The restaurant has gained a good local reputation and reservations are necessary, especially at weekends. Take the A529 south from Market Drayton towards Hinstock, then follow the signs to the hamlet of Goldstone.*
8⇌♠1 🛏 CTV in all bedrooms ® T ✻ (ex guide dogs) ✱
sB&B⇌♠fr£44.50 dB&B⇌♠£55-£66 ▤
40P ✿ ✿ ✐ snooker croquet lawn
V ✿ ☑ Lunch £8.50-£11.50 Dinner fr£17.50 Last dinner 10pm

★★52% **Corbet Arms** High St TF9 1PY ☎(0630)2037
FAX (0630) 2961
*This historic inn where Thomas Telford once stayed, is believed to have a ghost that appears only to bachelors. Bars are cosy and the bedrooms are well equipped.*
12rm(8⇌2♠)(2fb) CTV in all bedrooms ® T ✻ sB&B⇌♠£38
dB&B⇌♠£55 ▤
60P crown green bowling *xmas*
♀ Mainly grills V ✿ ☑ ✗ Lunch fr£7.25 Dinner £9.50-£12.50
Last dinner 9.30pm
Credit Cards ① ② ③ ⑤

---

MARKET HARBOROUGH Leicestershire Map **04** SP78

★★★61% **Three Swans** 21 High St LE16 7NJ (Best Western)
☎(0858)66644 due to change to 466644 Telex no 342375
FAX (0858) 33101
*Recent major refurbishment has altered and extended both public
rooms and bedrooms to provide the modern, comfortable facilities
demanded by today's discerning guests; bedrooms are particularly
well equipped, all having en suite facilities, most with shower
rooms.*
21⇨🛏Annexe16⇨🛏2🖾⊁in 2 bedrooms CTV in all
bedrooms ⓡ T 🗙 (ex guide dogs) sB&B⇨🛏£67-£71
dB&B⇨🛏£77-£81 🍴
⦅ 40P 8🕸
♀ International V ✧ ⚗ Lunch £10.95-£15 High tea £5.50-£7
Last high tea 6pm
Credit Cards ①②③④⑤ Ⓔ

---

MARKFIELD Leicestershire Map **08** SK41

★★★72% **Field Head** Markfield Ln LE6 0PS (Lansbury)
☎(0530)245454 Telex no 342296 FAX (0530) 243740
28⇨🛏(2fb)1🖾⊁in 6 bedrooms CTV in all bedrooms ⓡ T
🗙 (ex guide dogs) sB&B⇨🛏fr£72 dB&B⇨🛏fr£84 🍴
⦅ 70P *xmas*
♀ English & French V ✧ ⊬ Lunch fr£8.75&alc Dinner
fr£15.50&alc Last dinner 10pm
Credit Cards ①②③⑤

⬆**Granada Lodge** Little Shaw Ln LE6 0PP (Granada)
☎(0530)244237 FAX (0530) 244580
39⇨🛏⊬in 5 bedrooms CTV in all bedrooms ⓡ
🗙 (ex guide dogs) ✳ S% sB⇨🛏fr£25 dB⇨🛏fr£28 (room only)
60P
V ✧ ⚗ ⊬ S% Dinner fr£6 Last dinner 9.30pm
Credit Cards ①②③⑤
**See advertisement under LEICESTER**

---

MARKHAM MOOR Nottinghamshire Map **08** SK77

⬆**Travelodge** DN22 0QU (A1 northbound) (Trusthouse Forte)
☎Retford(0777)838091 Central Res (0800) 850950
*A single-storey lodge, surrounded by lawns and flower beds and
with a car park in front, stands at the A1/A57 intersection
roundabout on the northbound carriageway. Maintaining a good
degree of comfort and cleanliness, with safety and security a
priority, it provides excellent value for money. Meals can be taken
at the adjacent Little Chef (open 7am-10pm) but there is also a
coffee shop which serves beverages, sandwiches and pastries.*
40⇨🛏(40fb) CTV in all bedrooms ⓡ sB⇨🛏£24
dB⇨🛏£29.50 (room only)
⦅ 40P 🚲
Credit Cards ①②③

---

MARKINCH Fife Map **11** NO20

★★★★🏨73%, **Balbirnie House** Balbirnie Park KY7 6NE
☎Glenrothes(0592)610066 FAX (0592) 610529
*Set in 416 acres of parkland, and just a chip from the first tee on
the golf course, stands this magnificent mansion house. After
recent refurbishment, Balbirnie House now offers comfortable
bedrooms and inviting lounges. However, great care has been
taken to preserve the features, and its mid 1700s era.*
30⇨🛏(9fb)1🖾 CTV in all bedrooms ⓡ T ✳ sB⇨🛏£59-£69
dB⇨🛏£69-£130 (room only) 🍴
⦅ 120P ❀ gymnasium *xmas*
♀ International V ✧ ⚗ Lunch £9.50-£15alc Dinner
£22-£27.50alc Last dinner 9.30pm
Credit Cards ①②③⑤
**See advertisement under ST ANDREWS**

# THE SUN INN

Marston Trussell, Market Harborough,
Leicestershire LE16 9TY
Telephone: Market Harborough (0858) 65531
★★

One of the oldest buildings in this delightful little
village, only 2 miles south-east of Market Harborough. The Inn dates back to the late 17th
century and offers modern amenities, subtly
combined with historic charm. All 20 bedrooms
are en suite and have colour TV, tea & coffee
making facilities and direct dial telephone. An
excellent restaurant offers a superb choice to the
discerning diner. Bar meals are available lunch
times & evenings. Conference facilities and a
private function room also available.

M

# The Moss Nook

## RESTAURANT ××

Ringway Road, Moss Nook, Manchester 22
(One mile from Manchester Airport and M56 Junction 5)

Recommended by Egon Ronay and
the Academy of British Gastronomes as one of the
top 25 French restaurants in the UK

Begin your evening with our
special champagne cocktails

Lunch Tuesday to Friday 12 noon to 2 pm
Dinner Tuesday to Saturday from 7 pm

Proprietors Pauline and Derek Harrison

**For reservations please telephone
061-437 4778**

**MARKINGTON** North Yorkshire Map **08** SE26

★★★♨74% **Hob Green** HG3 3PJ (Best Western)
☎Harrogate(0423)770031 Telex no 57780 FAX (0423) 771589
*Beautifully placed hotel in 870 acres of farm and woodland, with splendid views. The drawing room and hall are relaxing with their antique furnishings and open fires, and the traditionally styled bedrooms have very up-to-date facilities. Service by mainly young staff is hospitable and discreet.*
12⇨♠1🛏 CTV in all bedrooms ® T sB&B⇨♠£59-£65 dB&B⇨♠£78-£85 🅿
40P 🚗 ✿ croquet
♡ English & French V ♦ ⚟ Bar Lunch £4.50-£7.50alc Dinner £16.50-£18.50alc Last dinner 9.30pm
Credit Cards 1️⃣2️⃣3️⃣5️⃣
**See advertisement under HARROGATE**

**MARLBOROUGH** Wiltshire Map **04** SU16

★★★72% **Ivy House Hotel & Garden Restaurant** High St SN8 1HJ (Best Western) ☎(0672)515333 Telex no 449703 FAX (0672) 515338
Closed 25-26 Dec
*A listed Georgian hotel overlooking the famous High Street offers individually furnished and decorated bedrooms. The elegant Garden Restaurant offers table d'hôte and à la carte menus and has a comprehensive wine list, while 'Toddy's', a small bistro restaurant, provides a more relaxed and informal style of meal. Service is attentive, friendly and professional.*
12⇨♠Annexe16⇨♠(4fb) CTV in all bedrooms ® T sB⇨♠£55-£75 dB⇨♠£58-£105 (room only) 🅿
30P 🚗 nc12yrs
♡ English & French V S% Lunch fr£13.50&alc Dinner fr£19.50&alc Last dinner 9.30pm
Credit Cards 1️⃣2️⃣3️⃣5️⃣£

★★★64% **The Castle & Ball** High St SN8 1LZ (Trusthouse Forte) ☎(0672)515201 FAX (0672) 515895
*Located in the centre of this lovely market town, this 17th-century inn, with an attractive tile-hung Georgian façade, offers prompt and friendly standards of service. The interior has been completely modernised, yet retains its charm and character. Public rooms are cosy and traditional.*
36⇨♀in 11 bedrooms CTV in all bedrooms ® S% sB⇨♠£76-£81 dB⇨♠£92-£97 (room only) 🅿
50P *xmas*
V ♦ ⚟ ♀
Credit Cards 1️⃣2️⃣3️⃣4️⃣5️⃣

**MARLEY HILL** Tyne & Wear Map **12** NZ25

★★★66% **Beamish Park** Beamish Burn Rd NE16 5EU
☎Stanley(0207)230666 FAX (0207) 281260
47⇨♠(7fb) CTV in all bedrooms ® T sB&B⇨♠£44-£54 dB&B⇨♠£59-£69 🅿
⚟ CTV 100P ✿ *xmas*
♡ English & French V ♦ ⚟ Sunday Lunch fr£7.95alc High tea fr£5 Dinner fr£12.50&alc Last dinner 9.30pm
Credit Cards 1️⃣2️⃣3️⃣5️⃣£

All AA-appointed establishments are inspected regularly to ensure that required standards are maintained.

**MARLOW** Buckinghamshire Map **04** SU88

★★★★73% **The Compleat Angler** Marlow Bridge SL7 1RG (Trusthouse Forte) ☎(06284)4444
Due to change to (0628) 484444 Telex no 848644
FAX (06284) 6388 due to change to (0628) 486388
*Ideally situated on the Thames and set in its own lovely gardens, the hotel complements tastefully appointed accommodation with willing, helpful service and a relaxing atmosphere.*
46⇨♠in all bedrooms CTV in all bedrooms T S% sB⇨♠£108-£130 dB⇨♠£130-£146 (room only) 🅿
⚟ 100P 🚗 ✿ CFA ♪ (hard) ♪ ♫ *xmas*
V ♦ ⚟ ✕ S% Lunch fr£21&alc Dinner £30-£50alc Last dinner 10pm
Credit Cards 1️⃣2️⃣3️⃣4️⃣5️⃣

○**Danesfield House** Medmenham SL7 3ES
☎Maidenhead(0628)891010
Due to open Mar 1991
92⇨♠

**MARPLE** Greater Manchester Map **07** SJ98

★69% **Springfield** Station Rd SK6 6PA ☎061-449 0721
*Fronted by well-tended gardens, this delightful, small hotel offers well-equipped bedrooms and enjoyable meals home cooked by the resident proprietor.*
6⇨♠ CTV in all bedrooms ® T ✱ sB&B⇨♠fr£38 dB&B⇨♠fr£48 🅿
CTV 10P 🚗 ✿
Dinner fr£12.50 Last dinner 8.30pm
Credit Cards 1️⃣2️⃣3️⃣5️⃣

**MARSDEN** West Yorkshire Map **07** SE01

★★★63% **Hey Green** Waters Rd HD7 6NG
☎Huddersfield(0484)844235 FAX 847605
*Situated in a quiet area just off the A62, surrounded by seven acres of woodland with a trout lake, this well-furnished, comfortable hotel serves meals of a good standard.*
10⇨♠1🛏 CTV in all bedrooms ® T ✱ sB&B⇨♠£50 dB&B⇨♠£65 🅿
70P ✿ ♪ orienteering course
V ♦ ⚟ Lunch £12.50-£15.50 Dinner £12.50-£15.50 Last dinner 9pm
Credit Cards 1️⃣2️⃣3️⃣5️⃣

**MARSTON MORETAINE** Bedfordshire Map **04** SP94

⇧**Travelodge** Beancroft Rd Junction MK43 0PZ (on A421) (Trusthouse Forte)
☎Bedford(0234)766755 Central Res (0800) 850950
*A modern building on the A5140 Woburn Sands/Bedford road offers comfortable, well-appointed accommodation with limited services. Guests take their meals at the on-site Little Chef restaurant.*
32⇨♠ CTV in all bedrooms ® sB⇨♠£24 dB⇨♠£29.50 (room only)
⚟ 32P 🚗
Credit Cards 1️⃣2️⃣3️⃣

**MARSTON TRUSSELL** Northamptonshire Map **04** SP68

★★63% **Sun Inn Hotel & Restaurant** LE16 9TY
☎Market Harborough(0858)65531
*Situated in the quiet village of Marston Trussell, this small hotel is still popular with locals as a traditional inn. The hotel has been recently refurbished and extended to provide modern bedrooms and public rooms. The resident managers and their small team of staff, work hard to provide a ready service in a friendly, informal atmosphere.*
10⇨ CTV in all bedrooms ®
CTV 35P 2📢 ✿ ♧

☉ English & Continental **V** ✿ Last dinner 9.30pm
Credit Cards ①②③
See advertisement under MARKET HARBOROUGH

---

**MARTINHOE** Devon Map 03 SS64

★▲70% **Old Rectory** EX31 4QT ☎Parracombe(05983)368
Closed Dec-Feb
*This nineteenth century country house retreat, run by Tony and Elizabeth Pring, is surrounded by National Trust land and the Exmoor National Park. Sympathetically restored to combine modern facilities with character surroundings, the public rooms, including a non-smoking lounge, are comfortable and the sun lounge overlooks the sheltered landscaped garden with its pretty stream and small lake. Quality home cooking makes use of fresh local produce and the menu shows some imagination. With no bar, a glass of sherry is offered before dinner and the hotel promotes a sound and reasonably-priced wine list.*
9⇨🏠 CTV in 5 bedrooms sB&B⇨🏠£43-£45
dB&B⇨🏠£86-£90 (incl dinner) 🅑
14P 🚗 ✿ putting nc12yrs
**V** ✿ ✂ Bar Lunch £2.50-£5.50 Dinner £12.50-£14 Last dinner 7.45pm
£

See advertisement under LYNTON

---

**MARTOCK** Somerset Map 03 ST41

★★72% **The Hollies** Bower Hinton TA12 6LG ☎(0935)822232
Annexe15⇨🏠(2fb)✂in 4 bedrooms CTV in all bedrooms Ⓡ T
✻ (ex guide dogs) sB&B⇨🏠£39.50 dB&B⇨🏠£55 🅑
CTV 50P ✿ 🔥

**V** Lunch £10-£16.95alc Dinner £10-£16.95alc Last dinner 9.30pm
Credit Cards ①③ £

See advertisement under YEOVIL

---

**MARYCULTER** Grampian *Aberdeenshire* Map 15 NO89

★★★68% *Maryculter House* AB1 6BB (Minotels)
☎Aberdeen(0224)732124 FAX (0224) 733510
*Set in five acres of grounds on the south bank of the River Dee, some eight miles from Aberdeen, this popular business hotel has undergone major refurbishment. Individually decorated bedrooms are comfortable and well equipped and there are two restaurants. Service throughout is friendly.*
12⇨🏠(2fb) CTV in all bedrooms Ⓡ T ✻ (ex guide dogs)
℄100P ✿ ▶ 18 ⚙ clay pigeon shooting 🔥
**V** ✿ ⚗ ✂ Last dinner 9.45pm
Credit Cards ①②③⑤

---

**MARYPORT** Cumbria Map 11 NY03

★★64% *Ellenbank* Birkby CA15 6RE (2m NE A596)
☎(0900)815233
*Standing in its own grounds 2 miles north-east of Maryport, this old house is gradually being improved and extended, but still retains it's Victorian character and charm.*
14⇨🏠(3fb) CTV in all bedrooms Ⓡ
CTV 40P ✿
☉ English & Continental **V** ✿ ⚗ Last dinner 9.30pm
Credit Cards ①③
See advertisement on page 489

★58% *Waverley* Curzon St CA15 6LW ☎(0900)812115
*Homely commercial hotel with an extensive bar/dining room menu offering honest home cooking.*
20rm(2⇨2🏠)(2fb) CTV in all bedrooms Ⓡ ✳ sB&Bfr£16
sB&B⇨🏠fr£26 dB&Bfr£30 dB&B⇨🏠fr£39 🅑
CTV 🎱 pool table ▶

---

# the savernake forest hotel

## Savernake, Burbage, ★★
## Nr. Marlborough,
## Wilts SN8 3AY
## Tel: (0672) 810206

Delightful Country Hotel on the edge of Savernake Forest, and alongside the Kennet & Avon Canal. All bedrooms with private facilities & colour TV.
Restaurant, Buttery Bar. One mile of private coarse fishing.

**M**

---

# THE IVY HOUSE HOTEL
## and Garden Restaurant ★★★

High Street, Marlborough, Wiltshire SN8 1HJ
Telephone: (0672) 515333

This Grade II Georgian Residence, overlooking the famous high street, has been completely transformed by resident owners David Ball and Josephine Scott into a 3 star luxury hotel which offers the best in comfort, facilities and service. Their aim is to provide first class hospitality and service in a friendly country house hotel atmosphere. They offer quality accommodation, excellent food and wine and relaxing lounges and bars. A team of dedicated and professional staff ensure that guests to the Ivy House enjoy efficient and courteous service.

⚘ English & Continental **V** ✧ ⏛ Lunch fr£5.50 High tea
fr£4.50 Dinner fr£7.50 Last dinner 9pm
Credit Cards ⊡ ③ ⓔ

---

**MARY TAVY** Devon Map **02** SX57

★★⚏62%, **Moorland Hall** Brentor Rd PL19 9PY
☎(082281)466
*Converted from a farmhouse in 1877 the hotel stands gracefully in
four acres of private gardens, offering attractive and comfortable
accommodation in peaceful surroundings.*
8⇱Ⓕ(1fb)2⊞ CTV in all bedrooms ⓡ sB&B⇱Ⓕ£30
dB&B⇱Ⓕ£46
20P ⇛ ✿ croquet lawn *xmas*
⚘ English & French **V** ⚓ Dinner £14 Last dinner 8pm
Credit Cards ⊡ ③

---

**MASHAM** North Yorkshire Map **08** SE28

★★⚏74%, **Jervaulx Hall** HG4 4PH ☎Bedale(0677)60235
FAX (0969) 23206
Closed Nov-mid Mar
*A quiet and secluded hotel, standing adjacent to the Abbey, run by
John and Margaret Sharp in a lovely welcoming and informal
manner. Log fires and antiques set the scene in the reception
rooms, whilst the comfortable bedrooms are individually furnished.*
10⇱(1fb) ⓡ sB&B⇱£82.50
dB&B⇱£110-£120 (incl dinner) ➟
CTV 15P ⇛ ✿ croquet
ⓔ

---

**MATLOCK** Derbyshire Map **08** SK36

★★★⚏70%, **Riber Hall** DE4 5JU (Pride of Britain)
☎(0629)582795 FAX (0629) 580475
*A quiet country house hotel full of charm and character dating
back to Elizabethan times, that has been tastefully and
thoughtfully restored to maintain its period feel. The bedrooms, all
in the annexe, are extremely well appointed and in keeping with
the rest of the house, with much exposed woodwork and antique
furniture. Chef Jeremy Brezelle has created an interesting menu
which is augmented by the quality, comprehensive wine list.*
Annexe11⇱9⊞ CTV in all bedrooms ⓡ **T** ✻ (ex guide dogs)
sB&B⇱£59-£75 dB&B⇱£78-£120 Continental breakfast ➟
50P ⇛ ✿ ⚑ (hard) nc10yrs
⚘ English & French **V** ✧ ⏛ Lunch fr£12.50 Dinner fr£25alc
Last dinner 9.30pm
Credit Cards ⊡②③④⑤ ⓔ

★★★58%, **The New Bath** New Bath Rd DE4 3PX (2m S A6)
(Trusthouse Forte) ☎(0629)583275 FAX (0629) 580268
*Five acres of grounds overlooking the River Derwent surround this
rambling hotel which is popular for leisure breaks as well as for
conferences. Recent refurbishment has made the public rooms
attractive and many of the bedrooms have beautiful views.*
55⇱✹in 11 bedrooms CTV in all bedrooms ⓡ ➟
⚘ 250P ✿ CFA ⊇ ⚑ (hard) sauna solarium thermal plunge
pool *xmas*
**V** ✧ ⏛ ✹ S10% Lunch £8-£9.50 Dinner £15&alc Last dinner
9.30pm
Credit Cards ⊡②③④⑤

★★67%, *Temple* Temple Walk, Matlock Bath DE4 3PG
☎(0629)583911
*Set high on a steep wooded hillside the hotel enjoys panoramic
views of the 'Little Switzerland' scenery of picturesque Matlock
Bath. Chef/patron Siegfried Essl has a good local reputation for
his buffet-style and à la carte menus featuring seasonal specials,
particularly game, when available.*
14⇱(1fb) CTV in all bedrooms ⓡ **T** ✻

---

⚓ CTV 40P ✿
⚘ English, French & Austrian **V** ✧ ⏛ ⚓ Last dinner 9.45pm
Credit Cards ⊡②③⑤

★★⚏65%, **Red House** Old Rd, Darley Dale DE4 2ER (2.5m N
A6) ☎(0629)734854
*Though situated within easy reach of all Derbyshire's attractions,
the small, family owned and personally run hotel provides a rural
retreat, each room having panoramic views of the countryside and
the large rear garden inviting relaxation.*
7⇱Ⓕ Annexe2⇱Ⓕ 1⊞ CTV in 7 bedrooms ⓡ **T**
sB&B⇱Ⓕ£43-£45 dB&B⇱Ⓕ£60-£72 ➟
16P ⇛ ✿
⚘ English & French **V** Lunch £10.50 Dinner £15.50 Last
dinner 9pm
Credit Cards ⊡②③⑤

★★61%, *Woodland Lodge* Temple Walk, Matlock Bath
DE4 3PG ☎(0629)580540
*An attractive chalet-style stone building set in a wooded valley just
off the A6, providing comfortable and well equipped lodge-style
bedroom accommodation in the grounds. Its unique restaurant
features an animated Tiki bird show, as seen at Disneyland.*
Annexe10⇱ CTV in all bedrooms ⓡ **T** ✻
30P ⇛
✧ ⏛
Credit Cards ⊡ ③

---

**MAWGAN PORTH** Cornwall & Isles of Scilly Map **02** SW86

★★64%, **Tredragon** TR8 4DQ (Inter-Hotels)
☎St Mawgan(0637)860213 FAX (0637) 860269
*This hospitable hotel extends a welcome to guests that merits the
description; commanding splendid sea views from its elevated
position, it offers bedrooms with good facilities, an informal dining
room where the table d'hôte menu is supplemented by a salad
buffet, and the use of an indoor heated swimming pool, sauna and
solarium.*
27⇱Ⓕ(12fb) CTV in all bedrooms ⓡ **T** ✱ S12%
sB&B⇱Ⓕ£29-£41 dB&B⇱Ⓕ£50-£66 ➟
CTV 30P ✿ ▣(heated) sauna solarium *xmas*
⚘ English & French **V** ✧ ⏛ Sunday Lunch £9-£10 Dinner
£9-£10 Last dinner 8pm
Credit Cards ⊡ ③ ⓔ

---

**MAWNAN SMITH** Cornwall & Isles of Scilly Map **02** SW72

★★★⚏73%, **Meudon** TR11 5HT ☎Falmouth(0326)250541
Telex no 45478 MEUDON G FAX (0326) 250543
Closed Dec-Feb
*Friendly, relaxing manor house where comfortable lounges
overlook superb subtropical gardens.*
32⇱Ⓕ(1fb)1⊞ CTV in all bedrooms ⓡ **T** sB&B⇱Ⓕ£65-£93
dB&B⇱Ⓕ£112-£188 ➟
⚓ 50P ⚑ (£5 per night) ⇛ ✿ CFA ⚘ ∪ nc5yrs
⚘ English & French **V** ✧ ⏛ Lunch fr£14 High tea £4-£5.50
Dinner fr£25&alc Last dinner 9pm
Credit Cards ⊡ ③⑤
**See advertisement under FALMOUTH**

★★★69%, **Budock Vean** TR11 5LG ☎Falmouth(0326)250288
Telex no 45795 FAX (0326) 250892
Closed Jan & Feb
*This very professionally run hotel stands in its own golf course,
which runs down to the Helford River.*
59⇱Ⓕ(6fb)1⊞ CTV in all bedrooms **T** sB&B⇱Ⓕ£47-£71
dB&B⇱Ⓕ£94-£142 (incl dinner)
Lift ⚓ 100P ⇛ ✿ ▣(heated) ⚑ 9 ⚑ (hard) ⚓ snooker ♫ *xmas*
⚘ English & French **V** ✧ ⏛ Lunch £11.50 Dinner £16.75&alc
Last dinner 9pm
Credit Cards ⊡②③⑤
**See advertisement under FALMOUTH**

★★★62%, **Trelawne** TR11 5HS ☎Falmouth(0326)250226
FAX (0326) 250909
Closed 30 Dec-Feb
*Set in rural surroundings, with its own 2.5-acre grounds, and within easy reach of the sea, this spotlessly clean, family-run holiday hotel maintains good standards of cooking, menus exhibiting some flair and imagination. Bedroom accommodation is comfortable, public rooms pleasant and the atmosphere is cosy.*
15rm(11⇨2♠)(2fb) CTV in all bedrooms ® T
sB&B⇨♠£39-£43 dB&B⇨♠£69-£76 ☐
20P ⊞ ✿ ⊠(heated) *xmas*
✧ ⊡ ⊬ Bar Lunch £1.40-£6alc Dinner £15.50 Last dinner 8.30pm
Credit Cards [1] [2] [3] [5]
**See advertisement under FALMOUTH**

---

**MAYBOLE** Strathclyde *Ayrshire* Map **10** NS20
★★♨79% **Ladyburn** KA19 7SG ☎Crosshill(06554)585
FAX (06554) 580
Closed Feb
*David and Jane Harburn transformed this old Dower House into a charming country-house hotel in June 1989 and run it in a truly hospitable manner, making their guests feel cossetted. Ladyburn stands in its own grounds in fine countryside south of Maybole.*
8rm(4⇨3♠) CTV in all bedrooms ® T ✖ (ex guide dogs)
sB&B⇨♠£55-£95
dB&B⇨♠£115-£150 Continental breakfast ☐
12P ⊞ ✿ croquet nc12yrs *xmas*
⚇ French V ✧ ⊡ ⊬ S% Lunch £12.50-£17.50&alc
Credit Cards [1] [2] [3]

---

**MAYPOOL (near Churston)** Devon Map **03** SX85
★★★64% **Lost & Found** TQ5 0ET ☎Churston(0803)842442
*A change of ownership should not deter the visitor from seeking out this cosy and friendly hotel. Neatly tucked away down country lanes amid peaceful surroundings, the very comfortable hotel affords commanding views of the Dartmouth Estuary. A homely interior accommodates a well-stocked lounge bar and a restaurant with an informal atmosphere, offering a good range of well-prepared dishes. Bedrooms are bright and well equipped, and service from the family management and local staff, is friendly and helpful.*
16⇨♠(1fb)1⊞ CTV in all bedrooms ® T ✳
dB&B⇨♠£92-£120 (incl dinner) ☐
24P ⊞ ✿ *xmas*
⚇ French V ✧ ⊡ Sunday Lunch £7.95 High tea £4 Dinner fr£14.95&alc Last dinner 9.30pm
Credit Cards [1] [2] [3]

---

**MEALSGATE** Cumbria Map **11** NY24
★★66% **Pink House** CA5 1JP ☎Low Ireby(09657)229
*The small hotel is friendly and cosy, with a comfortable lounge and an attractive bar where enjoyable meals are served.*
6⇨♠(2fb) CTV in all bedrooms ® T ✖ (ex guide dogs)
sB&B⇨♠£30 dB&B⇨♠£42 ☐
CTV 30P ✿
V ✧ ⊡ Lunch £4-£10.50alc Dinner £6.60-£11.75alc Last dinner 9pm
Credit Cards [1] [3] [5]

---

**MELBOURN** Cambridgeshire Map **05** TL34
✖✖**The Pink Geranium** Station Rd SG8 6DX
☎Royston(0763)260215 FAX (0763) 261936
*This 16th-century thatched cottage, set amidst an abundance of geraniums, is where chef Nigel Raffles offers a predominantly English style of cooking, with Eastern and French influences. Dishes such as Breast of Chicken in Ginger and Spring Onion, and Guinea Fowl cooked pink on a wild mushroom Madiera base, are*
▶

**M**

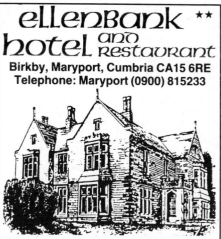

*complimented by a well chosen wine list. The restaurant also provides a Rolls Royce chauffeur service and créche facilites. It is advisable to book in the evenings.*
Closed Mon & 26 Dec
Dinner not served Sun
V 70 seats Lunch £12.95-£13.95&alc Dinner £20.90-£33alc Last lunch 2.30pm Last dinner 10pm 25P ✠
Credit Cards ⊡ ⊡

---

**MELKSHAM** Wiltshire Map **03** ST96

★★★♨74% **Beechfield House** Beanacre SN12 7PU (1m N A350) ☎(0225)703700 FAX (0225) 790118
*An elegant Victorian country house of mellow Bath stone with a sympathetically converted stable annexe is set in eight acres of grounds which include walled gardens with a swimming pool. Well co-ordinated and comfortable bedrooms have many thoughtful touches, while the à la carte and table d'hôte menus available at both lunch and dinner feature dishes prepared with imagination and flair from fresh ingredients – much of the fruit and vegetables being grown in the hotel's own gardens – and are accompanied by a good wine list.*
24⇨1⊞✠in 8 bedrooms CTV in all bedrooms T
✕ (ex guide dogs) ✷ sB⇨£72.50-£83
dB⇨£90-£105 (room only) 🅿
40P ⇿ ✻ ⊒(heated) ♫ (grass) croquet ⚬ xmas
V ♥ ⊒ ✠ Lunch £14.50-£17.50&alc Dinner £18.50&alc Last dinner 9.30pm
Credit Cards ⊡ ⊡ ⊡ ⊡ £

★★64% **Kings Arms** Market Place SN12 6EX ☎(0225)707272 FAX (0225) 702085
*This market place coaching inn is the centre-piece of the town, its cobbled forecourt decorated with colourful flower displays, whilst the antique oak furniture of the dining room and the rustic ambience of the popular bar make the interior equally characterful. Bedrooms vary in style, but old beamed rooms and modern additions alike are well equipped, most having en suite bathroom facilities.*
14rm(9⇨1✿) CTV in all bedrooms ⓡ T sB&B£30
sB&B⇨✿£40 dB&B£50 dB&B⇨✿£50 🅿
40P
V ♥ ⊒ Lunch £8.50&alc Dinner £10&alc Last dinner 9pm
Credit Cards ⊡ ⊡ ⊡ ⊡ £

★★63% **Conigre Farm** Semington Rd SN12 6BX
☎(0225)702229
*An ivy-clad seventeenth-century listed farm house, centrally situated, maintains a comfortable, relaxed atmosphere, providing accommodation in rooms named after Dickens characters, some being contained in a converted stable block. Mr Bumbles Restaurant features old-fashioned English menus, waitresses in appropriate costumes serving the well cooked food, and there is a spacious conservatory lounge to the rear.*
4rm(1⇨)Annexe5⇨✿1⊞ CTV in all bedrooms ⓡ T ✕
sB&B£27-£34 sB&B⇨✿£34-£38 dB&B£44-£48
dB&B⇨✿£48-£60 🅿
⟨12P 2🐾 ⇿ ✻
V ♥ ⊒ Lunch £5.95-£6.95&alc Dinner £8.50-£11.50 Last dinner 10pm
Credit Cards ⊡ ⊡

★★62% *Shaw Country* Bath Rd, Shaw SN12 8EF (2m NW A365) ☎(0225)702836 & 790321 FAX (0225) 790275
*A 400 year-old building, set in its own grounds on the edge of the town centre, has been tastefully restored to provide comfortable accommodation. Staff are friendly and attentive, and meals are chosen from extensive menus of freshly prepared dishes.*
10⇨✿(1fb)⊞ CTV in all bedrooms ⓡ T ✕
25P ✻ ⊒(heated) ⚬
🍴 English & French V ♥ ⊒ Last dinner 9pm
Credit Cards ⊡ ⊡ ⊡

---

**MELLING** Lancashire Map **07** SD57

★★61% **Melling Hall** LA6 2RA (Exec Hotel)
☎Hornby(05242)21298
*Improvements continue to be made at this 17th-century manor house situated at the northern edge of the village. Those bedrooms which have undergone refurbishment are particularly attractive and tastefully furnished. There are two pleasant bars and service is provided by friendly local staff.*
14rm(7⇨3✿)(1fb) CTV in all bedrooms ⓡ T sB&B£25-£28
sB&B⇨✿£35-£40 dB&B£40-£45 dB&B⇨✿£48-£55 🅿
40P ✻ xmas
🍴 English & French ♥
Credit Cards ⊡ ⊡ ⊡ ⊡

---

**MELROSE** Borders *Roxburghshire* Map **12** NT53

★★64% **Burt's** The Square TD6 9PN ☎(089682)2285
FAX (089682) 2870
*Dating from 1722, this converted town house is of architectural interest.*
21⇨✿ CTV in all bedrooms ⓡ T sB&B⇨✿£32-£38
dB&B⇨✿£56-£62 🅿
40P ⇿ ✻ snooker shooting game fishing
🍴 English & French V ♥ Lunch £11.50-£15 Dinner £13-£20alc Last dinner 9.30pm
Credit Cards ⊡ ⊡ ⊡ ⊡

★★55% **George & Abbotsford** TD6 9PD (Consort)
☎(089682)2308 FAX (089682) 3363
*A former coaching inn, situated in the centre of town with comfortable and recently upgraded public areas and friendly helpful staff.*
31⇨✿(3fb) CTV in all bedrooms ⓡ T
⊞CTV 150P 1🐾 ✻
🍴 British & French V ♥ Last dinner 9.30pm
Credit Cards ⊡ ⊡ ⊡ ⊡

---

**MELTON MOWBRAY** Leicestershire Map **08** SK71

★★★★♨76% **Stapleford Park** Stapleford LE14 2EF (Prestige)
☎Wymondham(057284)522 Telex no 342319
FAX (057284) 651
*If Leicestershire is, as Bob Payton staunchly maintains, the most beautiful county in England, then Stapleford Park, former home of the Earls of Harborough, is the jewel in its crown, set in a 500-acre estate and surrounded by gardens. Its rooms are magnificent, and the Paytons have seen to it that the furnishings both match them in elegance and provide a sense of luxurious comfort. Staff are friendly and very natural in manner, concealing a fine professional ability to attend to the needs of the guests. The emphasis at Stapleford is on relaxation and country-house pursuits such as riding (the stables are well worth seeing), clay-pigeon shooting, fishing, croquet, tennis on all-weather courts, miniature golf and, introducing a transatlantic touch, basket ball. The newly arrived chef, Rick Tramonto, was head-hunted in New York by Bob Payton, and provides a wide range of fish, beef and pasta dishes, cooked in American style making the best use of good quality fresh produce, many of the herbs and vegetables coming from the hotel's own gardens. Much praise has rightly been lavished on the highly individual bedrooms, decorated by designer 'names' such as Wedgwood, Nina Campbell, Crabtree and Evelyn and David Hicks. All are spacious and some can only be described as fabulous. Bob Payton has made Stapleford Park a showpiece.*
35⇨✿1⊞ CTV in all bedrooms T sB&B⇨✿£115-£275
dB&B⇨✿£115-£275 Continental breakfast
Lift ⟨ 120P ✻ ♫ (hard) ♪ ∪ mini golf croquet basketball shooting nc10yrs xmas

♀ American **V** ♨ ✗ Lunch fr£20 Dinner fr£27.50&alc Last dinner 11pm
Credit Cards ①②③④⑤ⓔ

★★★57% **Harboro'** Burton St LE13 1AF (Trusthouse Forte)
☎(0664)60121
*Commercial hotel, which was formerly a coaching inn, situated on the A606.*
26↩⇨☝(3fb)✗in 5 bedrooms CTV in all bedrooms ⓡ
✠ (ex guide dogs)
⟨ 40P
**V** ✿ ♨ ✗
Credit Cards ①②③

★★62% **Sysonby Knoll** Asfordby Rd LE13 0HP ☎(0664)63563
FAX (0664) 410364
Closed Xmas
*A much-extended house standing beside the A6006 about a mile from the town centre provides well-equipped accommodation which is popular with tourists and business travellers alike ; six bedrooms on the ground floor are particularly suitable for disabled guests. Pleasant gardens and grounds, which include a pitch and putt course and a swimming pool, stretch down to the River Eye.*
25rm(20↩3☝)Annexe1rm(2fb)2⌷ CTV in all bedrooms ⓡ T
S% sB&B£24 sB&B↩☝£33 dB&B£33 dB&B↩☝£42-£44 ⌷
CTV 30P ✿ ⌣
♀ English & French **V** ✿ Sunday Lunch £7.50 Dinner
£7.50&alc Last dinner 8.30pm
Credit Cards ①③

**See advertisement on page 493**

1991 marks the 25th anniversary of this guide.

## The King's Arms Hotel
### Melksham, Wiltshire
★★ **Tel. (0225) 707272**

The King's Arms is a traditional family-run Inn where hospitality and good food are always to be found.

All your meals are cooked to order using fresh produce and the expertise of the chef/proprietor. Fourteen excellently appointed bedrooms, a cosy lounge and the bar 'Local' all reflect the atmosphere of well-being.

**M**

## Shaw Country Hotel
★★ & Restaurant

SHAW, NR MELKSHAM, WILTS SN12 8EF
Telephone: Melksham (0225) 702836/790321
Fax: 790275

Proprietors Mr & Mrs C Briggs

This 400 year old farmhouse is now an elegant Country Hotel with a glowing reputation for fine food. 13 Bedrooms all with en-suite facilities, colour TV, radio, direct line telephone, beverage facilities and fresh fruit. (3 rooms with four poster bed, one with jacuzzi bath.) Table d'hôte and à la carte menus available in the large licensed restaurant. Ample Car Parking. Ideal centre for touring Bath, Lacock, Longleat etc.

★★★
## BEECHFIELD HOUSE
Set amidst 8 acres of gardens, this elegant 24 bedroom country house hotel offers, quite simply, the finest Wiltshire has to offer.

**Whether dining or staying — a visit to Beechfield House is always a memorable experience.**

For further details please contact:
Beechfield House, Beanacre,
Melksham, Wiltshire SN12 7PU
**Telephone: (0225) 703700**

**MELVICH** Highland *Caithness* Map **14** NC86

★★63%, **Melvich** KW14 7YJ ☎(06413)206
RS 25 Dec & 1-2 Jan

*Improvements continue to make this friendly and comfortable hotel which enjoys spectacular views across the Pentland Firth. A modern wing houses well-maintained bedrooms and a good range of meals is available in the spacious bar.*

14♠ CTV in all bedrooms ® ✳ sB&B♠fr£22.50 dB&B♠fr£42
10P ♣♯ ✳ ◢ snooker deer stalking bird watching
V ♥ ◻ ✂ Lunch £7.50 High tea £3-£9 Dinner £12.50-£16 Last dinner 8pm
Credit Cards ①③ ④

**See advertisement under THURSO**

**MENAI BRIDGE** Gwynedd Map **06** SH57

★★65%, **Anglesey Arms** LL59 5EA ☎(0248)712305
*This well-maintained and friendly hotel stands at the Anglesey end of the famous Telford suspension bridge. It offers comfortable bedrooms, a pleasant restaurant, lounge bar and foyer lounge, and a cocktail bar overlooking the attractive gardens.*

17rm(10⇆6♠) CTV in all bedrooms ® sB&Bfr£29
sB&B⇆♠fr£32 dB&B⇆♠fr£50 ☐
CTV 25P ✳ *xmas*
V ♥ ◻ Lunch £5-£10 Dinner £10-£18.50&alc Last dinner 10pm
Credit Cards ①③ ④

★★64%, **Gazelle** Glyn Garth LL59 5PD (2m NE A545)
(Frederic Robinson) ☎(0248)713364
*Pleasant and well furnished, commanding views of the Snowdonia mountains across the estuary, the hotel serves well-cooked meals of a good standard in its restaurant and bars.*

9rm(4⇆1♠) CTV in all bedrooms ® T ✘ (ex guide dogs)
40P ✳ sailing sea fishing watersports
♥ ◻
Credit Cards ①③

**MERE** Wiltshire Map **03** ST83

★★59%, **Old Ship** Castle St BA12 6JE ☎(0747)860258
FAX (0747) 860501

*A 16th-century building of architectural interest, where comfortable bedrooms include a four poster in the main building and modern annexe accommodation. The restaurant, originally a hayloft, serves an imaginative à la carte menu.*

14rm(6⇆)Annexe10⇆♠(3fb)2♯ CTV in all bedrooms ® ✳
sB&B£29 sB&B⇆♠£33 dB&B£40 dB&B⇆♠£48 ☐
50P
♀ English & French V Lunch £12-£18alc Dinner £2-£8alc Last dinner 9.30pm
Credit Cards ①③④ ④

**MERIDEN** West Midlands Map **04** SP28

★★★72%, **Forest of Arden Hotel, Golf & Country Club**
Maxstoke Ln CV7 7HR ☎(0676)22335 Telex no 312604
FAX (0676) 23711

*This new hotel and leisure development occupies part of Lord Aylesford's 10,000 acre estate and offers excellent facilities for both business and leisure guests. All of the bedrooms are very well equipped and comfortably furnished and indoor facilities include a heated swimming pool, squash courts and health and fitness studios. Outside there is a championship golf course, extensive fishing rights and, of course, the delightful parkland. A separate conference wing offers the latest technological facilities.*

152⇆♠in 20 bedrooms CTV in all bedrooms ® T ✳ S%
sB&B⇆♠fr£95 dB&B⇆♠fr£110 ☐
Lift ( CTV 360P ✳ ▣(heated) ▸ 18 ♪ (hard) ◢ squash snooker sauna solarium gymnasium dance studio steam room *xmas*

♀ English & French V ♥ ◻ ✂ Lunch frf15&alc Dinner frf15&alc Last dinner 9.45pm
Credit Cards ①②③④ ⑤

★★★68%, **Manor** CV7 7NH (De Vere) ☎(0676)22735
Telex no 311011 MANORM FAX (0676) 22186

*An elegant Georgian building conveniently situated for the Midlands motorway network and the NEC. The hotel has been refurbished to a very good standard and rooms offer excellent facilities. Comfortable public areas include the Regency restaurant and two bars. A popular venue for conferences.*

74⇆♠ CTV in all bedrooms ® T sB&B⇆♠fr£75
dB&B⇆♠fr£90 ☐
( 250P ✳ CFA ≘(heated)
♀ English & French V ♥ ◻ Lunch frf15&alc Dinner frf15&alc Last dinner 10pm
Credit Cards ①②③ ⑤

**MERTHYR TYDFIL** Mid Glamorgan Map **03** SO00

See also **Nant-Ddu**

★★★64%, **Baverstock** The Heads Of Valley Rd CF44 0LX
☎(0685)6221 FAX (0685) 723670
*This modern hotel is situated north of the town on the A465. it offers well-equipped bedrooms, spacious and comfortable public rooms and a good choice of food.*

53⇆♠(3fb) CTV in all bedrooms ® T ✘ (ex guide dogs)
sB&B⇆♠£45-£50 dB&B⇆♠£55-£60 ☐
( CTV 300P ✳ pool table half size snooker table *xmas*
♀ European V ♥ ◻ ✂ Lunch £14&alc High tea £3.50-£5.95
Dinner £14&alc Last dinner 10.30pm
Credit Cards ①②③ ⑤

★★64%, **Tregenna** Park Ter CF47 8RF ☎(0685)723627 & 82055
FAX (0685) 721951
*Well furnished bedrooms are offered at this modern hotel which stands only a short walk from the town centre. Public areas are comfortable and an extensive choice of dishes is offered in the dining room. The friendly proprietor and staff extend a particularly warm welcome to guests.*

14⇆♠Annexe7⇆♠(6fb)1♯ CTV in all bedrooms ® T
sB&B⇆♠£34-£38 dB&B⇆♠£45-£49 ☐
( CTV 21P *xmas*
♀ English, Indian & Italian V ♥ ◻ Lunch frf6.50&alc Dinner frf7.50&alc Last dinner 10pm
Credit Cards ①②③ ④

**MEVAGISSEY** Cornwall & Isles of Scilly Map **02** SX04

★★62%, **Spa** Polkirt Hill PL26 6UY ☎(0726)842244
*Family-run hotel in a commanding position on Polkirt Hill, with well-equipped bedrooms and a pleasant garden.*

12rm(11⇆♠)(4fb) CTV in all bedrooms ® sB&B£22-£26.50
dB&B⇆♠£44-£53
CTV 14P ♣♯ ✳ putting green pool table *xmas*
♀ English & French V ♥ ◻ Bar Lunch £1.30-£3.60 Dinner £10-£11 Last dinner 8pm
Credit Cards ①②③

★★50%, **Trevalsa Court** Polstreath PL26 6TH ☎(0726)842468 & 843794
Closed mid Nov-mid Mar
*Occupying a fine position facing the sea and offering access to the beach from its garden, the hotel complements a choice of traditionally-furnished bedrooms ( some of which are conveniently situated on the ground floor) with a comfortable lounge, dining room and bar.*

10⇆♠(2fb) CTV in 8 bedrooms TV in 2 bedrooms ® ☐
40P ♣♯ ✳ sea fishing trips shooting horse riding nc
♀ English, French & Italian V ♥ ◻
Credit Cards ①②③ ⑤

**M**

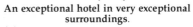
M

★69% **Sharksfin** The Quay PL26 6QU ☎(0726)843241
Closed Dec & Jan
*This former sardine cannery, in a unique quayside position, has been converted to provide a restaurant where cheerful local staff serve a good range of meals. Accommodation is available in second-floor bedrooms.*
11rm(4♠)(2fb) CTV in all bedrooms ® ➤< ✱
sB&B£19.50-£28.50 dB&B£29-£36 dB&B♠£37-£45
CTV ⚡ ⇛
V ◊ ◭ Lunch £6.05-£20.50alc Dinner £6.05-£20.50alc Last
dinner 9pm
Credit Cards ①②③⑤ⓔ

---

MICKLETON Gloucestershire Map **04** SP14

★★★60% **Three Ways** GL55 6SB (Inter-Hotels) ☎(0386)438429
Telex no 337242 FAX (0386) 438118
*A traditional hotel, at the heart of a charming village, Three Ways is run by the Turner family, who are attentive and friendly hosts. Rooms have character as well as comfort, and the intimate dining room offers a good range of dishes. The selection of traditional English puddings is highly acclaimed.*
40⇨♠(5fb) CTV in all bedrooms ® sB&B⇨♠£39-£49
dB&B⇨♠£62-£72 🅿
《 37P ❖ CFA ♫ xmas
♡ English & Continental V ◊ ◭
Credit Cards ①②③⑤

---

MIDDLEHAM North Yorkshire Map **07** SE18

★★71% **Millers House** Market Place DL8 4NR
☎Wensleydale(0969)22630
Closed Jan
*Friendly attentive service and good cooking using fresh produce can be found at this small Georgian 'country house hotel in town'.*
7rm(6⇨)1♯ CTV in all bedrooms ® T ➤< (ex guide dogs)
sB&B£30-£33 dB&B⇨£64-£67 🅿
8P ⇛ nc10yrs xmas
♡ English & French V ◊ ✌ Dinner fr£16 Last dinner 8.30pm
Credit Cards ①③

---

MIDDLESBROUGH Cleveland Map **08** NZ42

★★★50% **Marton Way Toby** Marton Rd TS4 3BS (Toby)
☎(0642)817651 Telex no 587783
Closed 25 Dec
*The purpose-built, motel style bedroom block of this modern hotel, two miles from the town centre, provides good-value, well-equipped accommodation, while its light, airy public areas include a carvery restaurant.*
53⇨(4fb)✌in 18 bedrooms CTV in all bedrooms ®
《 500P CFA
♡ British & Continental V ◊ ◭
Credit Cards ①②③⑤

★★62% **Highfield** 358 Marton Rd TS4 2PA (Berni/Chef & Brewer) ☎(0642)817638
*Set in its own grounds on the A1721, in a quiet residential area south of the town centre, the hotel offers comfortable, well-equipped bedrooms and a large, popular restaurant.*
23⇨♠2♯ CTV in all bedrooms ® T ➤< (ex guide dogs)
sB&B⇨♠£41-£47.50 dB&B⇨♠£54 🅿
《 CTV 100P 4🚗
V ◊ ◭ ✌ Lunch £8-£15alc Dinner £8-£15alc Last dinner
10.30pm
Credit Cards ①②③⑤

★62% **The Grey House** 79 Cambridge Rd, Linthorpe TS5 5NL
☎Middlesborough(0642)817485
*Charming Edwardian house in well-tended gardens, owner-run with friendly informality. All bedrooms have en suite facilities.*

---

8⇨♠(1fb) CTV in all bedrooms ® ✱ sB&B⇨♠£23-£32
dB&B⇨♠£32-£36
10P ⇛ nc

---

MIDDLETON-IN-TEESDALE Co Durham Map **12** NY92

★★65% **Teesdale** Market Place DL12 0QG
☎Teesdale(0833)40264
*This friendly, family-run hotel in the town centre offers attractive, well-appointed bedrooms, a cosy residents' lounge, a spacious bar where a coal fire glows in winter and a popular restaurant.*
14rm(7⇨)(1fb) CTV in 13 bedrooms
CTV 14P ⇛
♡ English, French, German & Italian ◊ ◭ Last dinner
8.30pm
Credit Cards ①③

---

MIDDLETON STONEY Oxfordshire Map **04** SP52

★★65% **Jersey Arms** OX6 8SE ☎(086989)234 & 505
FAX (086989) 565
*This charming Cotswold inn with bare stone walls and large open fires offers a range of accommodation from spacious, comfortable suites in the courtyard, to cosy, well-equipped rooms in the main building. The smart restaurant provides food of a commendable standard.*
6⇨Annexe10⇨1♯ CTV in all bedrooms T ➤< ✱ S%
sB&B⇨£49.50-£70 dB&B⇨£64-£90 🅿
55P ⇛ ❖
♡ English & French V ◊ ◭ Lunch £15-£24alc Dinner
£15-£24alc Last dinner 9.30pm
Credit Cards ①②③⑤

---

MIDDLE WALLOP Hampshire Map **04** SU23

★★72% **Fifehead Manor** SO20 8EG ☎Andover(0264)781565
FAX (0264) 781400
Closed 2wks Xmas
*A small manor house on the fringe of the village has been tastefully restored to provide comfortable accommodation in both the main building and annexe. In the restaurant a sophisticated à la carte menu of French cuisine is served by a willing young staff.*
10⇨ CTV in all bedrooms T ✱ sB&B⇨£45-£50
dB&B⇨£75-£85 🅿
50P ⇛ ❖ croquet
♡ English & French ◊ ◭ Lunch £15&alc High tea £3-£6&alc
Dinner £22&alc Last dinner 9.30pm
Credit Cards ①②③⑤

✗**Old Drapery Stores** SO20 8HN ☎Andover(0264)781301
Lunch not served ex by arrangement only
♡ English & French V 48 seats Lunch £14.50&alc Dinner
£14.50&alc Last lunch 2pm Last dinner 10pm 17P ✌ ♫
Credit Cards ①③

---

MIDHURST West Sussex Map **04** SU82

See also **Trotton**
★★★66% **Spread Eagle** South St GU29 9NH (Best Western)
☎(0730)816911 Telex no 86853 FAX (0730) 815668
*The lounge bar of this hotel is in a part of the building which dates back to 1430, and its individually furnished and decorated bedrooms are co-ordinated with taste and charm – five of them having four-poster beds and the Queen's Suite boasting a wig powder closet. Dinner is served by candlelight, the restaurant's fixed-price menu displaying the innovative style of cuisine for which the establishment is famed, and lighter lunchtime meals can be taken in the Coal Hole Bar.*
37⇨Annexe4♠5♯✌in 4 bedrooms CTV in all bedrooms T
S10% sB&B⇨♠£70-£130 dB&B⇨♠£80-£175 🅿
《 80P ❖ CFA xmas

M

♨ English & French ✧ ◻ S10% Lunch £16.50-£27.50 Dinner £26.50-£30 Last dinner 9.30pm
Credit Cards ①②③⑤ⓔ

✗ **Hindle Wakes** 1 Church Hill GU29 9NX ☎(0730)813371
*Chef Lisa Francis-Lang offers a short, fixed-price menu of imaginative and stylishly cooked starters and main courses. Terrines are particularly good, and light sauces complement main courses such as lamb cutlets with tarragon mousse, and pigeon with honey and fresh fig. Service is very attentive, and a good selection of wines is available too.*
Closed Sun, Mon & 24-26 Dec
Lunch not served Tue
V 20 seats ✱ Lunch £8.95-£16.50 Dinner £8.95-£21.50 Last lunch 1.45pm Last dinner 9.30pm ◢ ⸖
Credit Cards ①③

---

**MIDSOMER NORTON** Somerset Map 03 ST65

★★★62% **Centurion** Charlton Ln BA3 4BD ☎(0761)417711
FAX (0761) 418357
*Situated on the outskirts of the town, the modern hotel offers accommodation in attractive, particularly well equipped rooms and adjoins a Country Club which gives guests access to a nine-hole golf course, squash courts, a swimming pool and facilities for snooker.*
44⇌ CTV in all bedrooms ® T ✗ (ex guide dogs)
sB&B⇌£42-£53 dB&B⇌£53-£73 ⊟
⦅ 100P ✿ ◰(heated) ▶ 9 squash snooker sauna
♨ English & Continental V ✧ ◻ Lunch £8-£9&alc Dinner £8-£9&alc Last dinner 10pm
Credit Cards ①②③⑤

---

**MILDENHALL** Suffolk Map 05 TL77

★★★62% **Riverside** Mill St IP28 7DP (Best Western)
☎(0638)717274 FAX (0638) 715997
*Popular with families from the nearby Air Force Base, the listed red brick house stands at the end of the town's main road, its rear lawns stretching down to the River Lark.*
19rm(10⇌5🝊)(4fb)1⊞ CTV in all bedrooms ® T
sB&B⇌🝊fr£44 dB&B⇌🝊fr£60-£70 ⊟
Lift 45P ✿ ✔ private boats ₰ xmas
♨ International V ✧ ◻ Lunch fr£9.50 High tea fr£5 Dinner £11-£17 Last dinner 9pm
Credit Cards ①②③⑤ⓔ

★★★61% **Smoke House Inn** Beck Row IP28 8DH
☎(0638)713223 Telex no 817430 FAX (0638) 712202
*Situated on the B1101 at Beck Row, three miles from Mildenhall, this single-storey complex of brick and pantiles includes a shopping centre and conference and banqueting facilities, all in extensive grounds. Accommodation is arranged in long corridors and rooms are well equipped. Staff are smartly dressed and friendly and the choice of breakfasts includes traditional English, Continental and American style.*
105⇌Annexe10⇌(20fb) CTV in all bedrooms ® T
✗ (ex guide dogs) S10% sB&B⇌£55-£60 dB&B⇌£70-£80 ⊟
⦅ CTV 200P ✿ ♫ xmas
V ✧ ◻ Lunch £10-£12 High tea £10-£12 Dinner £12-£15&alc Last dinner 10pm
Credit Cards ①②③ⓔ

★★62% **Bell** High St IP28 7EA ☎(0638)717272
*Situated in the town's main street, opposite the church, with car park access via the shopping precinct to the rear. This ivy-clad inn offers comfortable, well-equipped rooms, good levels of hospitality and service and a convivial atmosphere in the bar.*
17rm(14⇌2🝊)(2fb) CTV in all bedrooms ® T
sB&B⇌🝊£40-£48 dB&B⇌🝊£55-£60
24P xmas
V ✧ Lunch £10.25&alc Dinner £10.25&alc Last dinner 9pm
Credit Cards ①②③⑤ⓔ

**M**

## MILFORD HAVEN Dyfed Map 02 SM90

★★63% **Lord Nelson** Hamilton Ter SA73 3AL ☎(0646)695341
Telex no 48622 FAX (0646) 692274
*Comfortable public areas and well-equipped, well-furnished*
*bedrooms are provided by this efficiently run commercial hotel*
*which overlooks the harbour from a town-centre position.*
32⇦⇨♠(1fb)1🛏✎in 2 bedrooms CTV in all bedrooms ® T ✳
sB&B⇦⇨♠fr£39 dB&B⇦⇨♠fr£60 戸
《 CTV 26P ❀
♥ English & French V ♥ Lunch £11.20-£17.55alc Dinner
£11.20-£17.55alc Last dinner 9.30pm
Credit Cards ①②③⑤£

★★59% *Sir Benfro* Herbrandston SA73 3TD (3m W on unclass
rd) ☎(0646)694242
RS 25 Dec
*What was once a busy farm house has been converted into a small,*
*proprietor-run hotel to which a modern wing of bedrooms has been*
*added ; bar meals are available as an alternative to the full à la*
*carte service in the restaurant (or on the sun terrace during the*
*warmer months) and there is a cosy residents' lounge on the first*
*floor.*
12⇦⇨(1fb) CTV in all bedrooms ®
▦ 50P ❀ ➘ ♫
♥ English & French V ♥ ⌷ Last dinner 9.45pm
Credit Cards ①③

## MILFORD ON SEA Hampshire Map 04 SZ29

★★★72% **South Lawn** Lymington Rd SO41 0RF
☎Lymington(0590)643911 FAX (0590) 644820
Closed 20 Dec-12 Jan
*This former Dower House, set in well-kept grounds, provides a*
*warm welcome and personal service. There is a comfortable lounge*
*and spacious dining room, and bedrooms and bathrooms are also of*
*a good size and spotlessly clean. Fresh food, full of flavour, is*
*complemented by a well-chosen wine list, neither being over priced.*
*Many of the guests return regularly.*
24⇦⇨♠(2fb) CTV in all bedrooms T ✠ sB&B⇦⇨♠fr£45
dB&B⇦⇨♠fr£80 戸
50P ❀ nc7yrs
♥ International V ♥ ⌷ Sunday Lunch fr£9.25 Dinner fr£12.50
Last dinner 8.30pm
Credit Cards ①③

**See advertisement under LYMINGTON**

★★★64% **Westover Hall** Park Ln SO41 0PT
☎Lymington(0590)643044 FAX (0590) 644490
*Swiss owned and managed, you are assured of the personal*
*attention of the proprietors at this hotel, where service is warm and*
*informal. It is a late Victorian house with fine, wood-panelled*
*walls, well appointed bedrooms and fine sea views across to the Isle*
*of Wight. The carefully produced table d'hôte menus are*
*imaginative.*
13⇦⇨ CTV in all bedrooms ® T S8% sB&B⇦⇨£32-£50
dB&B⇦⇨£64-£120 戸
50P ⇱❀ xmas
♥ English & French V ♥ ⌷ S10% Lunch fr£12.50&alc High
tea fr£4.95 Dinner fr£12.50&alc
Credit Cards ①②③⑤£

## MILNGAVIE Strathclyde *Dunbartonshire* Map 11 NS57

★★★59% **Black Bull Thistle** Main St G62 6BH (Mount
Charlotte (TS)) ☎041-956 2291 Telex no 778323
FAX 041-956 1896
*A former coaching inn has been tastefully restored to retain the*
*character of its historic past. Quality and tradition are reflected in*
*the beamed ceilings, polished oak and tapestries of the public*
*rooms, whilst bedrooms offer all modern facilities.*
27⇦⇨♠(2fb) CTV in all bedrooms ® T ✳ sB⇦⇨♠fr£55
dB⇦⇨♠fr£60 (room only) 戸

《 120P
♥ International ♥ ⌷ ✂ Lunch fr£6.75&alc Dinner
fr£12.75&alc Last dinner 9.30pm
Credit Cards ①②③④⑤

## MILTON Dyfed Map 02 SN00

★★61% *Milton Manor* SA70 8PG (Exec Hotel)
☎Carew(0646)651398 FAX (0646) 651897
*This Georgian manor house, convenient for Tenby and Pembroke,*
*is set in 7 acres of attractive lawns and woodland. It is run by the*
*friendly Richardson family and their local staff who provide well*
*equipped bedrooms which are being steadily improved.*
19⇦⇨♠(1fb) CTV in all bedrooms ® T sB&B⇦⇨♠£33-£39
dB&B⇦⇨♠£49-£55 戸
40P 3🚗 ❀ putting ⚬ xmas
♥ International V ♥ ⌷ Bar Lunch £1.50-£6.75
Credit Cards ①③

## MILTON ABBAS Dorset Map 03 ST80

★★♨63% *Milton Manor* DT11 0AZ ☎(0258)880254
*Tudor style hotel in its own grounds.*
12rm(6⇦⇨3♠)(2fb)1🛏 CTV in all bedrooms ® T
✠ (ex guide dogs)
CTV 50P ⇱❀ putting green croquet
V ♥ ⌷ Last dinner 9pm
Credit Cards ①③

## MILTON COMMON Oxfordshire Map 04 SP60

★★★64% **Belfry** Brimpton Grange OX9 2JW (Inter-Hotels)
☎Great Milton(0844)279381 Telex no 837968
FAX (0844) 279624
Closed 25-30 Dec
*Large, half-timbered country house in extensive grounds.*
60⇦⇨♠ CTV in all bedrooms ® T ✳ sB&B⇦⇨♠£65-£72.50
dB&B⇦⇨♠£77.50-£85 Continental breakfast 戸
《 200P ❀ CFA 🖾(heated) sauna solarium gymnasium
♥ English & Continental V ♥ ⌷ Lunch £13.50-£14.50&alc
Dinner £16-£18&alc Last dinner 9.30pm
Credit Cards ①②③⑤

## MILTON, GREAT Oxfordshire Map 04 SP60

# ★★★

❀❀❀★★★ ♨ LE MANOIR
AUX QUAT' SAISONS

OX9 7PD (Relais et
Châteaux) ☎Great Milton
(0844)278881
Telex no 837552
FAX (0844) 278847
Closed 22 Dec-20 Jan

*Le Manoir has steadily*
*grown from what Raymond Blanc originally opened as a*
*Restaurant with Rooms into a first-class hotel. Nine superb*
*new bedrooms (including 2 suites) have now been added to the*
*accommodation, and the restaurant has been extended by the*
*building of an elegant conservatory. Happily all these*
*alterations have not, in our view, detracted from the charm of*
*the 15th-century manor house, although some may not agree.*
*The drawing room (where, incidentally, an excellent*
*afternoon tea is served) remains unchanged, as does the quiet*
*lounge. Other pleasant features of the hotel are the water-*
*garden, fine kitchen garden, pool and tennis court. The main*
*reason for a visit to Le Manoir, however, remains the cuisine*
*which is at the highest level here, if at times lacking the*

M

unmistakeable touch of the Master himself. Monsieur Blanc, although involved in other projects these days, is never too far away from his own kitchens. The variety and innovation of the menu is exemplified in such memorable dishes as the Caille farcie au jus de Charentes which successfully incorporates a grapefruit and wine sauce. Even more excitingly different is the Salade aux herbes du jardin pôelée de Coquilles St Jacques et langoustines aux rubans de légumes frits. Professional service, under the guidance of the General Manager Nicholas Dickinson, is enlivened with much natural warmth and zest from the staff and makes its own contribution to the sense of occasion. Although prices (with the Menu Gourmand at £56) are amongst the highest in the land, few would cavil when the experience of eating here is so worthwhile.

19⇨³♠4⊞ CTV in all bedrooms T ✕ ✳ S%
dB⇨³♠£150-£300 (room only) ⊟
《60P ✿ ⌐(heated) ℘ (hard) croquet
♀ French V ♥ ⊡ ⊬ S% Lunch fr£24.50&alc Dinner fr£54&alc Last dinner 10.30pm
Credit Cards ①②③④⑤

---

**MILTON KEYNES** Buckinghamshire Map **04** SP83

See also Newport Pagnell & Woburn
★★★64% **Post House** 500 Saxon Gate West MK9 2HQ (Trusthouse Forte) ☎(0908)667722 Telex no 826842 FAX (0908) 674714
This modern commercial hotel is in process of upgrading to provide a higher standard of accommodation and a new coffee shop to supplement the traditional restaurant's choice of an à la carte and two set price menus. Food is well prepared from high quality fresh products, helpful staff provide friendly, efficient service, and good leisure facilities are available.
163⇨³(4fb)⊬in 50 bedrooms CTV in all bedrooms ® T ✳ sB⇨³£92 dB⇨³£103 (room only) ⊟
Lift 《 ⊞ 80P ☐(heated) sauna solarium gymnasium health & fitness centre xmas
V ♥ ⊡ ⊬ S% Lunch £9.75-£21.50&alc Dinner £15.75-£21.50&alc Last dinner 10.30pm
Credit Cards ①②③⑤

★★★63% **Friendly** Monks Way, Two Mile Ash MK8 8LY (junct A5/A422) (Consort) ☎(0908)561666 Telex no 826152 FAX (0908) 568303
A modern hotel with conference facilities, which has the spacious well-equipped and comfortable bedrooms expected of a busy commercial hotel. The restaurant has a carvery and à la carte menu. Service is friendly and informal.
50⇨³(8fb)2⊞⊬in 8 bedrooms CTV in all bedrooms ® T ✳ sB&B⇨³£52-£62.50
dB&B⇨³£68.50-£73 Continental breakfast ⊟
《CTV 76P (charged) ✿ mini gym
♀ English & French V ♥ ⊡ S% Lunch fr£7.50 Dinner £11.75-£14.75&alc Last dinner 10pm
Credit Cards ①②③⑤⑥
See advertisement on page 499

---

**M**

## MINEHEAD Somerset Map 03 SS94

**★★★70%, Benares** Northfield Rd TA24 5PT (Consort)
☎(0643)704911
Closed 5 Nov-mid Mar (ex Xmas)
*Friendly holiday and business hotel, with good restaurant and fine gardens.*
20rm(19⇨3♠)(2fb) CTV in all bedrooms ® T
sB&B⇨3♠£32.50-£36.50 dB&B⇨3♠£58.50-£68 ⊟
20P 2🚗 (£1.75) ✍ ❁ ѳ& *xmas*
🖵 English, French & Italian V ♥ ⚿ ✗ Bar Lunch £7-£15alc
Dinner £14.85&alc Last dinner 8.30pm
Credit Cards ①②③⑤

**★★★67%, Northfield** Northfield Rd TA24 5PU (Best Western)
☎(0643)705155 Telex no 42513
*Set in 2 acres of interesting gardens, just 100 yards from the sea, this beautifully kept hotel offers good lounges as well as indoor sports facilities. It is very popular with retired British holidaymakers.*
24⇨3♠(7fb) CTV in all bedrooms ® T sB&B⇨3♠£42
dB&B⇨3♠£74-£84 ⊟
Lift 44P ✍ ❁ ⌂(heated) gymnasium putting green steam room spa bath ѳ& *xmas*
V ♥ ⚿ ✗ Lunch fr£2.75&alc Dinner £11.95 Last dinner 8.30pm
Credit Cards ①②③⑤

**★★61%, Beaconwood** Church Rd, North Hill TA24 5SB
☎(0643)702032
Closed Nov-Feb
*Peaceful, family-run hotel outside the town centre.*
16rm(12⇨3♠)(3fb) CTV in all bedrooms ® T sB&B£25-£30
sB&B⇨3♠£30-£35 dB&B£40-£45 dB&B⇨3♠£50-£55 ⊟
《 25P ❁ ⌂(heated) ℘ (grass) ѳ&
V ♥ ⚿ ✗ Bar Lunch £1.25-£3.50 Dinner £11 Last dinner 8pm
Credit Cards ①③⑥

**★70%, Kingsway** Ponsford Rd TA24 5DY ☎(0643)702313
Closed 7 Nov-21 Mar
*Comfortable, privately-owned and run hotel.*
8⇨3♠(2fb) CTV in all bedrooms ® ✳ dB&B⇨3♠£36-£46 ⊟
CTV 8P ✍ nc10yrs *xmas*
♥ ⚿ ✗

**★64%, Mentone** The Parks TA24 8BS ☎(0643)705229
Closed Nov-Mar
*The small, privately owned and personally run hotel offers thoughtfully prepared , imaginative menus and provides an ideal centre for touring.*
9rm(5⇨2♠) CTV in all bedrooms ® ✗
5P 2🚗 ✍ nc8yrs
🖵 English, Asian & Continental ♥ ⚿ ✗ Last dinner 6.45pm

## MINSTEAD Hampshire Map 04 SU21

**✗ *Honeysuckle Cottage*** SO43 7FX ☎Southampton(0703)813122
Lunch not served
🖵 English & French 45 seats Last dinner 9.30pm 20P
Credit Cards ①

All hotels are now given a percentage grading for the quality of their facilities. A full explanation can be found within 'How we Classify Hotels and Restaurants' at the front of the book.

## MISKIN Mid Glamorgan Map 03 ST08

**★★★73%, Miskin Manor** CF7 8ND ☎Pontyclun(0443)224204
FAX (0443) 237606
Closed 24-31 Dec
*A lovely manor house whose history stretches back to the late tenth century stands on the bank of the Ely river in twenty acres of woodland and gardens, yet just off junction 34 of the M4. Bedrooms are spacious and comfortable, extensive conference and leisure facilities are available, and elegant wood-panelled public areas include a dining room serving very enjoyable meals.*
32⇨3♠2🚗✍✗in 12 bedrooms CTV in all bedrooms T
✗ (ex guide dogs) ✳ sB⇨3♠£70-£90
dB⇨3♠£90-£95 (room only) ⊟
《 150P ✍ ❁ 🖂(heated) squash snooker sauna solarium gymnasium steam room, badminton, clay pigeon shoot ѳ&
V ♥ ⚿ ✗ Lunch £15&alc Dinner £15&alc Last dinner 9.45pm
Credit Cards ①②③⑤ⓔ
**See advertisement under CARDIFF**

## MOFFAT Dumfries & Galloway *Dumfriesshire* Map 11 NT00
See also **Beattock**

**★★★62%, Moffat House** High St DG10 9HL (Exec Hotel)
☎(0683)20039 FAX (0683) 21288
*A traditional family-run hotel featuring cosy bedrooms, inviting lounges and interesting menus both in the bar and restaurant.*
16⇨3♠(3fb) CTV in all bedrooms ® T sB&B⇨3♠£32.50-£37
dB&B⇨3♠£54-£60 ⊟
40P 2🚗 ❁ ѳ&
🖵 Scottish & French V ♥ ✗ Bar Lunch £3.50-£10alc Dinner £9-£20alc Last dinner 8.45pm
Credit Cards ①②③⑤ⓔ

**★★70%, Beechwood Country House** Harthope Place DG10 9RS
☎(0683)20210
Closed Jan
*In an elevated position overlooking the town and the Annan valley this gracious Victorian house is now a small, personally run hotel. Bedrooms are generally spacious and well equipped and there are two homely lounges. Local produce features on the five course dinner menu and light lunches are available in the recently built conservatory.*
7⇨3♠(1fb) CTV in all bedrooms ® T sB&B⇨3♠£49.37-£55.25
dB&B⇨3♠£79.60-£91.80 (incl dinner) ⊟
15P ✍ ❁ *xmas*
🖵 English & French V ♥ ⚿ ✗ Sunday Lunch £10.50 High tea £2.50 Dinner £15.50 Last dinner 9pm
Credit Cards ①②③

**★★70%, The Star** 44 High St DG10 9EF ☎(0683)20156
*Managed by the friendly owners, Mr and Mrs Leighfield, this comfortable hotel offers very good value menus throughout the day and evening. Lounge accommodation is somewhat limited, possibly due to its reputation as the narrowest hotel in Great Britain.*
8⇨3♠(1fb) CTV in all bedrooms ® T ✳ S% sB&B⇨3♠£28-£30
dB&B⇨3♠£38-£42 ⊟
℘
V ♥ ⚿ ✗ Lunch fr£3.50 High tea fr£5 Dinner £5-£12 Last dinner 9pm
Credit Cards ①③

**★76%, Well View** Ballplay Rd DG10 9JU ☎(0683)20184
7rm(1⇨34♠)(1fb)1✍✗in 2 bedrooms CTV in all bedrooms ®
sB&B£19-£22 sB&B⇨3♠£34-£38 dB&B£38-£44
dB&B⇨3♠£50-£70 ⊟
8P ✍ ❁ *xmas*
🖵 Scottish & French ♥ ⚿ ✗ Lunch £7-£8 Dinner £13-£16
Last dinner 8.15pm
Credit Cards ①③

## MOLD Clwyd Map **07** SJ26

See also **Northop Hall**
★★63% **Bryn Awel** Denbigh Rd CH7 1BL ☎(0352)58622
FAX (0352) 58625
*A family-run hotel, with well-equipped bedrooms and pleasant public areas, situated on the A541 on the north west outskirts of the town. It is equally popular with tourists and travelling business people.*
7⇌🏠Annexe10⇌🏠1🛏✂in 5 bedrooms CTV in all bedrooms Ⓡ T sB&B⇌🏠fr£30 dB&B⇌🏠£43-£50 ◲
40P 4🛆 ✿ 🐟
♈ English & Continental V ❂ ⚷ Lunch £5-£7.50&alc High tea £3-£8.50 Dinner £8-£12alc Last dinner 9.30pm
Credit Cards ⊞⊡Ⓔ

## MONIAIVE Dumfries & Galloway *Dumfriesshire* Map **11** NX79

★★64% **Woodlea** DG3 4EN ☎(08482)209
Closed Nov-Mar
*This off-beat country hotel caters particularly for family holidays, the exuberantly youthful enthusiasm of its proprietors creating a very lively atmosphere and providing a comprehensive range of pursuits during the high season. Prospective guests can send for the hotel's video.*
12rm(10⇌)(7fb) CTV in all bedrooms Ⓡ
CTV 20P ✿ ▨(heated) ♟ (hard) sauna solarium pony riding croquet putting games room 🐟
V ❂ ⚷ Last dinner 8.30pm

## MONK FRYSTON North Yorkshire Map **08** SE52

★★★🏆 68% **Monk Fryston Hall** LS25 5DU
☎South Milford(0977)682369 Telex no 556634
FAX (0977) 683544
*This historic manor house is situated in attractive and extensive grounds off the A63, close to the A1. There is a great wealth of charm and character in the oak panelled lounge and bar, where open fires burn in the cooler months. Bedrooms are located in a modern wing and in the original house. All are well equipped and comfortable, and although sizes may vary, on the whole most are attractive and comfortable. The young staff are friendly and efficient.*
29⇌🏠(2fb)1🛏 CTV in all bedrooms Ⓡ T sB&B⇌🏠£54-£68 dB&B⇌🏠£76-£90 ◲
℄ 60P 🚗 ✿ *xmas*
❂ ⚷ Lunch £9.60-£10.50&alc Dinner £15-£16&alc Last dinner 9.30pm
Credit Cards ⊞⊡⊟

## MONMOUTH Gwent Map **03** SO51

★★★63% **Kings Head** Agincourt Square NP5 3DY (Welsh Rarebits) ☎(0600)2177 Telex no 497294 FAX (0600) 3545
*Professionally-run by the Gough family for over two decades, this comfortable 17th-century inn provides good food and conference facilities.*
29⇌🏠(2fb)1🛏 CTV in all bedrooms T sB⇌🏠£48-£57.50 dB⇌🏠£70 (room only) ◲
℄ 20P CFA *xmas*
♈ English, French & Italian V ❂ Lunch £10.50-£12.50 Dinner £20-£22 Last dinner 9pm
Credit Cards ⊞⊡⊟⊠Ⓔ

★★68% **Riverside** Cinderhill St NP5 3EY (Minotels)
☎(0600)5577 & 3236
6🏠Annexe6🏠(2fb) CTV in all bedrooms Ⓡ T
🗶 (ex guide dogs) sB&B🏠£39 dB&B🏠£58 ◲
30P *xmas*
♈ European V ❂ ⚷ Lunch fr£9.85 Dinner 95p-£13alc Last dinner 9.30pm
Credit Cards ⊞⊟

## MONTACUTE Somerset Map **03** ST41

★★64% **Kings Arms Inn** TA15 6UU ☎Martock(0935)822513
*A charming well run village inn with a relaxing and informal atmosphere. The bedrooms have been comfortably and thoughtfully upgraded, whilst the restaurant offers food of a good standard.*
11⇌1🛏 CTV in all bedrooms Ⓡ T 🗶 (ex guide dogs) ✳
sB&B⇌£42-£55 dB&B⇌£58-£72 ◲
15P 🚗✿
♈ English & French V ❂ ⚷ ⚷ Lunch £7.20-£7.90 Dinner £12.50-£15alc Last dinner 9pm
Credit Cards ⊞⊡⊟Ⓔ
**See advertisement under YEOVIL**

## MONTROSE Tayside *Angus* Map **15** NO75

★★★58% **Park** 61 John St DD10 8RJ ☎(0674)73415
Telex no 76367 FAX (0674) 77091
*Popular with visiting business people and catering for local functions, this hotel is just a few minutes' walk from both the town centre and the beach. There is a choice of standard or superior bedrooms, all of which are well equipped.*
59rm(48⇌5🏠)(4fb) CTV in all bedrooms Ⓡ T ✳ sB&Bfr£30 sB&B⇌🏠£35-£55 dB&B⇌🏠£46-£76 ◲
℄ CTV 50P ✿ CFA 🐟 *xmas*
V ❂ ⚷ Lunch £5.70-£7.50&alc Dinner £12.50&alc Last dinner 9.30pm
Credit Cards ⊞⊡⊟⊠Ⓔ

## MORAR Highland *Inverness-shire* Map **13** NM69

★★58% **Morar** PH40 4PA ☎Mallaig(0687)2346
FAX (0687) 2130
Closed 21 Oct-Mar
*This family-run hotel overlooks the silver sands and Small Isles and caters for tour groups and holidaymakers alike, with its relaxed, friendly atmosphere and good-value accommodation.*
27⇌🏠(3fb) CTV in 10 bedrooms Ⓡ sB&B⇌🏠£24-£26 dB&B⇌🏠£48-£52
CTV 50P ➴
V ❂ ⚷ Lunch £7-£9 Dinner £13-£15 Last dinner 8.30pm

## MORCOTT Leicestershire Map **04** SK90

○**Travelodge** A47, Uppingham(Trusthouse Forte)
☎Central reservations (0800) 850950
Due to have opened summer 1990
40⇌

## MORDEN Greater London

See **LONDON plan 1**C*1*(page 426)
○**Travelodge** A24 Epsom Rd(Trusthouse Forte)
☎Central reservations (0800) 850950
Due to have opened summer 1990
32⇌

## MORECAMBE Lancashire Map **07** SD46

★★★71% *Headway* Marine Rd East LA4 5AN ☎(0524)412525
Closed 18 Dec-4 Jan RS Nov-Apr
*Modern, comfortable and providing courteously attentive service, the hotel offers views across the bay to the Cumbrian fells.*
53⇌🏠(4fb) CTV in all bedrooms Ⓡ 🗶
Lift ℄ 20P
V ❂ ⚷ Last dinner 8pm
Credit Cards ⊞⊡⊟⊠

★★★65% **Strathmore** East Promenade LA4 5AP (Best
Western) ☎(0524)421234 Telex no 65452 FAX (0524) 414242
*Friendly traditional hotel with resident proprietors.*
51⇨🛏(6fb) CTV in all bedrooms ® T ✖ (ex guide dogs)
sB&B⇨🛏£45-£50 dB&B⇨🛏£57-£62 🖪
Lift ( 30P 12🏌 ♫ *xmas*
♀ French **V** 🕯 ⬚ Lunch £7.25-£8&alc Dinner £12.25-£14&alc
Last dinner 10pm
Credit Cards 1 2 3 5 ⓔ

★★★52% **Elms** Bare LA4 6DD (Consort) ☎(0524)411501
Telex no 57515 FAX (0524) 831979
*Pleasant, comfortable hotel serving home grown English food.*
40⇨🛏(1fb)2🛏 CTV in all bedrooms ® T sB&B⇨🛏£44-£52
dB&B⇨🛏£66-£73 🖪
Lift ( CTV 70P ✿ CFA *xmas*
♀ English & French **V** 🕯 ⬚ Lunch £7.50-£8.50 Dinner
£11.25-£11.75 Last dinner 8.45pm
Credit Cards 1 2 3 5 ⓔ

★★58% **Clarendon** Promenade, West End LA4 4EP
☎(0524)410180
Closed Xmas wk
*Well furnished bedrooms with good facilities, a popular bar and a
cosy dining room serving a good range of food are provided by this
traditional seaside hotel on the Promenade.*
33rm(20⇨7🛏)(4fb) CTV in all bedrooms ® T ✳
sB&B⇨🛏fr£28 dB&B⇨🛏fr£39 🖪
Lift ( CTV ♟ games room
Credit Cards 1 2 3 4 5
**See advertisement under LANCASTER**

MORETONHAMPSTEAD Devon Map 03 SX78

★★68% **The White Hart** The Square TQ13 8NF (Minotels)
☎(0647)40406 FAX (0647) 40565
*Built in 1637 and retaining much of its original character, this
small country hotel is enthusiastically run and provides a relaxing
retreat, with well-equipped bedrooms and comfortable public
rooms. Meals range from a wide variety of bar meals to
imaginative and wholesome cooking from the restaurant.*
20⇨🛏(3fb) CTV in all bedrooms ® T sB&B⇨🛏£33-£36
dB&B⇨🛏£53-£58 🖪
12P snooker nc10yrs *xmas*
♀ English & French **V** 🕯 ⬚ ✂ Sunday Lunch £5.50-£8alc
Dinner £10.95-£11.95&alc Last dinner 8.30pm
Credit Cards 1 2 3 5 ⓔ

★★⚫66% *Glebe House* North Bovey TQ13 (1.5m SW)
☎(0647)40544
Closed 20 Dec-Feb
*Welcoming former Victorian vicarage offering well-prepared food.*
9⇨🛏(1fb) T
CTV 40P 🏕 ✿
♀ International 🕯 ⬚
Credit Cards 1 3

MORETON-IN-MARSH Gloucestershire Map 04 SP23

★★★66% **Manor House** High St GL56 0LJ ☎(0608)50501
Telex no 837151 FAX (0608) 51481
*This 16th-century house set in the heart of town retains many
original features within its public areas including beams and open
log fires. Bedrooms vary in style and all are well equipped, whilst
service is friendly and attentive.*
38rm(34⇨3🛏)4🛏 CTV in all bedrooms T ✖ ✳ sB&Bfr£55
sB&B⇨🛏fr£55 dB&B⇨🛏fr£68 🖪
Lift ( 25P 🏕 ✿ 🏊(heated) ♪ (hard) sauna spa bath nc12yrs
*xmas*
**V** 🕯 ⬚ Lunch £8.95-£10.95 Dinner £17.50-£23 Last dinner
9pm
Credit Cards 1 2 3 5

★★★

## *Headway Hotel*

**East Promenade, Morecambe, Lancashire
Telephone: (0524) 412525**

Ideally located on the East Promenade
with breathtaking views across the magnificent bay to the hills of the Lake
District. Everything for your comfort is
assured with friendly staff always on hand
to make your stay enjoyable. The 53
tastefully decorated and furnished bedrooms are fully equipped with all comforts. Lift and car park available. The
Headway is renown for its high standard
of cuisine, served in the spacious restaurant.

**M**

**AA**

★★★ *The Chequers*

**COUNTRY** **HOUSE HOTEL**

★ SET IN 40 ACRES OF WOODLAND
★ 29 LUXURY BEDROOMS
★ A LA CARTE RESTAURANT
★ WE SPECIALISE IN WEDDING RECEPTIONS
PRIVATE DINNER PARTIES, SILVER WEDDINGS
21st BIRTHDAYS ETC.
★ CONFERENCE FACILITIES FOR 10-120

**DEESIDE (0244) 816181**
FAX: 814661 — TELEX: 617112
**GWESTY CHEQUERS HOTEL, CHESTER ROAD
NORTHOPHALL VILLAGE, MOLD, CLWYD CH7 6HG**

**★★73% Redesdale Arms** High St GL56 0AW (County Inns)(Exec Hotel) ☎(0608)50308 Telex no 837928 FAX (0608) 51843

*This hotel, one of the better preserved Cotswold coaching inns, is full of eighteenth-century charm, retaining such historic features as the Queen Anne panelling in the Archway Bar. It is continually improving its facilities, however, and offers up-to-date accommodation with a good range of amenities, together with modern English cuisine, both complemented by friendly, attentive service throughout.*

9⊶♠ Annexe8⊶♠ (2fb) CTV in all bedrooms ® T ⊁ (ex guide dogs) sB&B⊶♠ fr£44.50 dB&B⊶♠ fr£65 ⊟ 20P *xmas*

♀ English & French V ❖ ♨ Lunch £10.95&alc Dinner £13.95&alc Last dinner 9.30pm
Credit Cards ①③⑤

**★★61% The White Hart Royal** High St GL56 0BA (Trusthouse Forte) ☎(0608)50731 FAX (0608) 50880

*The inn, originally a seventeenth-century manor house, retains such character features as the large open fireplace in the Cavalier Bar and the cobbled hallway leading to its attractive courtyard.*

18rm(9⊶♠)1⊟⊱in 5 bedrooms CTV in all bedrooms ® ✻ S10% sB&Bfr£38 sB&B⊶♠ fr£44 dB&Bfr£44 dB&B⊶♠ fr£49 ⊟
CTV 10P *xmas*

V ❖ ♨ ⊁ S10% Sunday Lunch fr£8.60 Dinner fr£14&alc Last dinner 9.30pm
Credit Cards ①②③④⑤

**MORFA NEFYN** Gwynedd Map **06** SH24

**★★58% Linksway** LL53 6BG ☎Nefyn(0758)720258

*A holiday hotel situated in a residential area of the village just a short walk from the beach and local golf course. Bedrooms are neat and compact and the open-plan public areas are spacious and comfortable. Good food is served by friendly staff.*

26rm(11⊶10♠)(1fb) CTV in all bedrooms ®
60P 2❀✻ ♫
♀ English & Italian ❖ ♨ Last dinner 9pm

**MORLEY** Derbyshire Map **08** SK34

○**Breadsall Priory** Moor Rd DE7 6DL ☎Derby(0332)832235 FAX (0332) 833509
Due to have opened Aug 1990
94⊶♠

**MORPETH** Northumberland Map **12** NZ28

**★★★★74% Linden Hall** NE65 8XF (Prestige) ☎(0670)516611 Telex no 538224 FAX (0670) 88544
(For full entry see Longhorsley)

**MORTEHOE**
See **Woolacombe**

**MOTTRAM ST ANDREW** Cheshire Map **07** SJ87

**★★★67% Mottram Hall** Prestbury SK10 4QT (De Vere) ☎Prestbury(0625)828135 Telex no 668181 FAX (0625) 829284

*Georgian mansion built in 1721, standing in formal gardens surrounded by 120 acres of parkland.*

95⊶♠(10fb)8⊟⊱in 12 bedrooms CTV in all bedrooms ® T S% sB&B⊶♠ frf90 dB&B⊶♠ frf110 ⊟
《250P ❀ ✻ CFA ▣(heated) ♪ (hard & grass) ♪ squash snooker sauna solarium gymnasium croquet putting ♫ *xmas*
♀ English & French V ❖ ♨ S% Lunch fr£12.50&alc Dinner fr£17.50&alc Last dinner 9.45pm
Credit Cards ①②③⑤

**MOULSFORD-ON-THAMES** Oxfordshire Map **04** SU58

**★★68% Beetle & Wedge** Ferry Ln OX10 9JF ☎Cholsey(0491)651381

*A character hotel in a superb setting on the banks of the Thames, which has been upgraded to provide comfortable, well-appointed accommodation. The meals served in the restaurant represent a very high standard of cuisine.*

10⊶Annexe2♠(1fb)1⊟ CTV in all bedrooms ®
54P ❀ ♪
V ❖ Last dinner 9.45pm
Credit Cards ①②③⑤

**MOULTON** North Yorkshire Map **08** NZ20

✗✗**Black Bull Inn** DL10 6QJ ☎Darlington(0325)377289 FAX (0325) 377422
Closed Sun & 23-31 Dec
Lunch not served Sat
100 seats ✻ Lunch £8.75&alc Dinner £15.25-£33.50alc Last lunch 2pm Last dinner 10.15pm 80P nc7yrs
Credit Cards ①②③

**MOUNT HAWKE** Cornwall & Isles of Scilly Map **02** SW74

**★75% Tregarthen Country Cottage** Banns Rd TR4 8BW ☎Porthtowan(0209)890399

*A charming, cottage-style hotel, on the edge of the village and only two miles from beautiful sandy surfing beaches. The six bedrooms are tastefully decorated and the lounges and bar have a homely atmosphere. The menu, with a limited choice, is based on traditional home cooking.*

6⊶♠⊱in all bedrooms ⊁ (ex guide dogs) sB&B⊶♠ £35-£40 dB&B⊶♠ £70-£80 (incl dinner) ⊟
CTV 12P ❀ ✻
Dinner £10-£12 Last dinner 8pm

**MOUSEHOLE** Cornwall & Isles of Scilly Map **02** SW42

**★★59% Lobster Pot** South Cliff TR19 6QX ☎Penzance(0736)731251 FAX (0736) 731140
Closed last 3 wks Jan RS Feb-mid Mar

*This popular restaurant features a verandah section which overhangs the village harbour, commanding panoramic views over Mounts Bay. Bedrooms are compact – with low ceilings in some instances – but well appointed.*

13⊶♠Annexe12rm(7⊶2♠)(5fb) CTV in all bedrooms ® T S10% sB&B£23-£35.50 sB&B⊶♠ £29.50-£42.50 dB&B£46-£70 dB&B⊶♠ £59-£85 ⊟
♪ *xmas*
♀ English & French V ❖ ♨ ⊁ S10% Sunday Lunch £8.25 Dinner £14.50&alc Last dinner 9.45pm
Credit Cards ①②③⑤

**★★58% Carn Du** Raginnis Hill TR19 6SS ☎Penzance(0736)731233
Closed Feb

*The small, personally-run hotel serves home-cooked food with an emphasis on fresh local fish and vegetables. Its windows offer panoramic views across Mount's Bay.*

7rm(1⊶5♠) CTV in 3 bedrooms TV in 1 bedroom ® ⊁ sB&B£20-£25 sB&B⊶♠ £20-£25 dB&B⊶♠ £40-£50 ⊟
CTV 12P ❀ ✻
♀ English & German V ❖ ⊁ Bar Lunch fr£3 Dinner fr£12 Last dinner 8pm
Credit Cards ①②③

Entries for red-star hotels are highlighted by a tint panel. For a full list of these establishments consult the Contents page.

**MUCH BIRCH** Hereford & Worcester Map **03** SO53

★★★61% **Pilgrim** HR2 8HJ ☎Golden Valley(0981)540742
Telex no 35332 FAX (0981) 540620
*A former rectory, with a modern bedroom extension, located on the A49. The young team of staff at this privately-owned hotel are genuinely friendly and welcoming.*
20⇌♠(1fb)2⊟ CTV in all bedrooms ® **T** ✱
sB&B⇌♠£44-£54 dB&B⇌♠£54-£68 ⊟
40P ⊞ ✲ croquet putting pitch & putt badminton *xmas*
☋ English & French **V** ♈ ☋ Lunch £8.75 Dinner £16.75&alc
Last dinner 9.45pm
Credit Cards [1] [2] [3] [5] £

**See advertisement under HEREFORD**

**MUCH WENLOCK** Shropshire Map **07** SO69

★★69% **Wheatland Fox** TF13 6AD ☎(0952)727292
Closed mid Dec-mid Jan
*Set on the edge of the town yet with the atmosphere of a country house, a small personally run hotel offers very comfortable bedrooms and freshly prepared meals.*
4⇌♠Annexe2⇌♠ CTV in all bedrooms ® **T** ✗
sB&B⇌♠£40-£50 dB&B⇌♠£55-£65 ⊟
12P ⊞ nc7yrs
☋ English & French **V** ♈ Dinner £17.50 Last dinner 9.30pm
Credit Cards [1] [2] [3] £

★★54% **Gaskell Arms** Bourton Rd TF13 6AQ ☎(0952)727212
*A red brick Regency hotel beside the A458 Shrewsbury/Kidderminster road offers neat, tidy bedrooms and character bars with local atmosphere.*
11rm(3⇌)(2fb) CTV in all bedrooms ® ✗ sB&B£25-£28
sB&B⇌£30-£35 dB&B£38-£40 dB&B⇌£50-£55
30P 1⊞ ✲
**V** ♈ Lunch £10.95-£12 Dinner £7-£20alc Last dinner 9.30pm
Credit Cards [1] [3] £

**MUDEFORD**

See **Christchurch**

**MUIR OF ORD** Highland *Ross & Cromarty* Map **14** NH55

★★57% **Ord Arms** Great North Rd IV6 7XR
☎Inverness(0463)870286 FAX (0463) 870048
*A holiday and business hotel on the northern fringe of the village accommodates guests in bedrooms which are comfortable, though a little dated; its neatly appointed restaurant serves a range of imaginative dishes, and the atmosphere is friendly throughout.*
11rm(4⇌3♠)(2fb) CTV in all bedrooms ® **T** S% sB&Bfr£25
sB&B⇌♠fr£27 dB&Bfr£38.50 dB&B⇌♠fr£44 ⊟
CTV 120P 6⊞ ✲ ♩ solarium ♫ *xmas*
**V** ♈ ☋ Lunch £7.95 High tea £5.20 Dinner £11 Last dinner 9pm
Credit Cards [1] [2] [3] [5] £

**See advertisement on page 505**

**MULL, ISLE OF** Strathclyde *Argyllshire* Map **10**

**CRAIGNURE** Map **10** NM73

★★★58% **Isle Of Mull** PA65 6BB (Scottish Highland)
☎(06802)351 Telex no 778215 FAX (06802) 462
Closed 2 Nov-24 Mar
*Conveniently placed for the ferry terminal and commanding spectacular sea views, this popular modern hotel provides airy, comfortable public rooms and a range of bedrooms which are more practical in style, though improvements are gradually being made, the best accommodation being in the south wing.*
60⇌(8fb) CTV in all bedrooms ® **T** sB&B⇌£48
dB&B⇌£78 ⊟
☾ 50P ✲ ♫

▶



M

♈ Scottish & French V ✿ ☑ Bar Lunch £2.50-£4.50alc Dinner
£13-£14 Last dinner 8.30pm
Credit Cards ⓵ ⓶ ⓷ ⓹

**TOBERMORY**  Map **13** NM55

★70%  **Tobermory** 53 Main St PA75 6NT ☎(0688)2091
*Delightful, little waterfront hotel with charming lounges, bright,
cheerful bedrooms and a cosy dining room.*
15rm(3⇦2♠)(3fb) ® sB&B£19-£21 dB&B£38-£42
dB&B⇦♠£46-£50
CTV ♪ 🚲
♈ European V ✿ ☑ ½ Dinner £13 Last dinner 7.45pm

★63%  **Ulva House** PA75 6PR ☎(0688)2044
Closed Nov-Feb
*This family-run Victorian house sits high above the town, with
splendid views of the bay. David Woodhouse, a talented artist and
authority on the island's wildlife, organises wildlife expeditions,
with the possibility of spotting otters, badgers and many other
kinds of animals and birds. Joy Woodhouse's hearty cordon bleu
dinners provide the perfect conclusion to the day.*
6rm(1♠)(3fb) ® sB&B£21-£31 sB&B♠£26.50-£36.50
dB&B£42 dB&B♠£53
8P 🚲 ❀
♈ International V ✿ Lunch £13.95&alc Dinner £13.95&alc
Last dinner 8pm

★56%  **Mishnish** Main St PA75 6NU ☎(0688)2009
FAX (0688) 2462
*This busy, harbour-front hotel has an attractive first floor
restaurant, with views of the bay, and modestly decorated and
furnished bedrooms. There are no lounge facilities. Entertainment
is provided most evenings in the popular lounge bar.*
12rm(7⇦3♠)(2fb) CTV in all bedrooms ® ✳
sB&B⇦♠£25-£30 dB&B⇦♠£50-£60
CTV ♪ ♪ squash ◡
V ✿ ☑ Lunch £5-£10alc Dinner £12.50-£15&alc Last dinner
9pm

**MULLION**  Cornwall & Isles of Scilly Map **02** SW61

★★★73%  *Polurrian* TR12 7EN ☎(0326)240421
Telex no 94015906 FAX (0326) 240083
Closed 8 Dec-14 Mar
*Family holiday hotel superbly situated in 12 acres of terraced
grounds overlooking Polurrian Cove with its fine surfing beach.*
39⇦♠(20fb)5🖵 CTV in all bedrooms T
《 CTV 60P 3🎱 (£5) 🚲 ❀ CFA ▣(heated) ⌐(heated) ♪
(hard) squash snooker sauna solarium gymnasium cricket net
whirlpool putting ♪🏌
♈ English & French V ✿ ☑ Last dinner 8.30pm
Credit Cards ⓵ ⓶ ⓷ ⓹

★★56%  **Mullion Cove** TR12 7EP ☎(0326)240328
Closed 6 Nov-2 Mar
*The hotel offers a relaxed, friendly atmosphere and panoramic
views over Mount's Bay.*
36rm(17⇦4♠)(8fb) CTV in all bedrooms ® sB&B£22-£25
dB&B£44-£50 dB&B⇦♠£49-£66 🖵
CTV 50P ❀ ⌐(heated) ♪ (hard) sauna solarium *xmas*
♈ English & Continental V ✿ ☑ Sunday Lunch £4-£7.50 High
tea £3.50 Dinner £16 Last dinner 8.30pm
Credit Cards ⓵ ⓷ ⓹ ⓺

See 'How we Classify Hotels and Restaurants'
at the front of the book for an explanation
of the AA's appointment and
award scheme.

**MUMBLES (near Swansea)**  West Glamorgan Map **02** SS68
See also **Langland Bay** and **Swansea**
★59%  **St Anne's** Western Ln SA3 4EY ☎Swansea(0792)369147
Telex no 498450 FAX (0222) 374671
*This hotel enjoys panoramic views of Swansea Bay and the town
from its elevated position, just a short walk from the sea front.
Public areas are spacious, as are most of the bedrooms, and,
although choice is limited, the food represents good value.*
24rm(15⇦3♠)Annexe4rm(2♠)(1fb) CTV in all bedrooms ®
T ✳ ✱ sB&B£23 sB&B⇦♠£28 dB&B£38 dB&B⇦♠£42 🖵
CTV 50P ❀ snooker ⚬
V ✿ ☑ Lunch £7 High tea £3 Dinner £7-£8 Last dinner
8.30pm
Credit Cards ⓵ ⓷ ⓺

**MUNGRISDALE**  Cumbria Map **11** NY33
★73%  **The Mill** CA11 0XR (Guestaccom)
☎Threlkeld(07687)79659
Closed Dec & Jan
*A former mill cottage dating back to 1651, set amid beautiful
mountain scenery and bounded by a trout stream. It offers
comfortable, delightfully furnished bedrooms, a cosy lounge with a
log fire and a separate TV room. Resident hosts provide personal
attention and home-cooked meals of a very high standard are
served in the attractive dining room.*
8rm(5⇦)(1fb) CTV in 5 bedrooms ® sB&B£25.50-£28.50
sB&B⇦£30.50-£35.50 dB&B£43-£49 dB&B⇦£50-£59
CTV 15P 🚲 ❀ ♪ games room
♈ English & French V ✿ ☑ ½ Dinner £15 Last dinner 8pm

**MUSSELBURGH**  Lothian *Midlothian* Map **11** NT37
⌂**Granada Lodge** A1 Old Craighall EH21 8RE (Granada)
☎031-653 6070 & 031-653 2427 FAX 031-653 6106
*This establishment is conveniently situated on the B6415, only a
few yards from the junction of the A1 and the A720 Edinburgh
bypass.*
44⇦♠(10fb) CTV in all bedrooms ® ✱ (ex guide dogs) ✳
sB⇦♠fr£26.50 dB⇦♠fr£28.50 (room only)
92P
V ✿ ☑ ½
Credit Cards ⓵ ⓶ ⓷ ⓹
**See advertisement under EDINBURGH**

**NAILSWORTH**  Gloucestershire Map **03** ST89

✱✱**Flynn's** 3 Fountain St GL6 0BL ☎(0453)835567
*Australian-born Gary Flynn offers imaginative food at this
intimate, town-centre restaurant. Worthy of particular note is the
goats cheese soufflé and the orange and Grand Marnier soufflé.
The carefully selected wine list represents good value for money
and friendly and attentive service is provided by Deborah Reid.*
Closed Sun
Lunch not served Mon
♈ English, Australian & French V 40 seats ✳ Lunch
fr£13.50&alc Dinner £18.95-£24.50alc Last lunch 2pm Last
dinner 9.30pm P
Credit Cards ⓵ ⓷

**NAIRN**  Highland *Nairnshire* Map **14** NH85
★★★★58%  **Golf View** Seabank Rd IV12 4HG ☎(0667)52301
Telex no 75134 FAX (0667) 55267
*Set on a shore of the Moray Firth, with a beach at the bottom of its
garden, this hotel in traditional style offers modernised
accommodation that is ideal for golfers, business people or
holidaying families. Facilities include an outdoor swimming pool, a
putting green, a games room and a gymnasium.*
55⇦♠(5fb)1🖵 CTV in all bedrooms T 🖵

**M**

Lift ⟨ 40P ❋ CFA ⌒(heated) ♪ (hard) sauna gymnasium putting green *xmas*
☺ Scottish & Continental ⊹ ⌐⊈
Credit Cards ① ② ③ ⑤ ⑥

**★★★59%, Newton** Inverness Rd IV12 4RX (Consort)
☎(0667)53144 FAX (0667) 54026
*A baronial-style hotel with grounds adjoining the championship golf course enjoys fine views over the Moray Firth. Lounges and entrance hall are particularly elegant, the latter being beautifully panelled and exhibiting a variety of paintings, many of which are for sale. Staff are friendly and helpful.*
30⇨🌓Annexe14⇨🌓(6fb)1⌘ CTV in all bedrooms ® T ✸
sB&B⇨🌓£39-£52 dB&B⇨🌓£50-£90 ☐
Lift ⟨ CTV 100P ❋ ♪ (hard) sauna solarium putting *xmas*
☺ Scottish & French V ⊹ ⌐⊈ Lunch fr£6.75&alc High tea fr£5.75 Dinner £12.95-£13.50&alc Last dinner 9.15pm
Credit Cards ① ② ③ ⑤

**★★★58%, Windsor** Albert St IV12 4HP ☎(0667)53108
*This well-decorated and maintained family-run hotel has modern bedrooms of varying sizes.*
60rm(30⇨24🌓)(7fb) CTV in all bedrooms ®
Lift ⟨ CTV 40P ❋ CFA U bowling ♫
☺ Scottish & French V ⊹ ⌐⊈ Last dinner 9.30pm
Credit Cards ① ② ③ ⑤

**★★62%, Carnach House** Delnies IV12 5NT (2m W A96)
☎(0667)52094
*This attractive Edwardian house stands in eight acres of wooded grounds 2 miles west of the town, close to the A96 and within easy reach of Inverness airport. Bedrooms are generally spacious, traditional and well-appointed – several offering views of the Moray Firth – and there are a relaxing lounge and attractive cocktail bar; personal supervision by resident proprietors ensures that a stay here represents good value for money.*
14rm(11⇨🌓)(1fb)⌘ CTV in all bedrooms ® T sB&B£31.50
sB&B⇨🌓£31.50 dB&B£63 dB&B⇨🌓£63 ☐
15P ⊕ ❋ u *xmas*
V ⊹ ⌐⊈ ⊬ Sunday Lunch fr£7.50 Dinner £4.50-£16.50&alc
Last dinner 9pm
Credit Cards ① ② ③ ⑥

**★★58%, Alton Burn** Alton Burn Rd IV12 5ND ☎(0667)52051
RS Oct-Mar
*Peacefully situated on the western outskirts of Nairn overlooking the golf course and Moray Firth, this family owned resort hotel provides comfortable, traditional accommodation and a variety of leisure activities.*
19rm(14⇨3🌓) CTV in 18 bedrooms
CTV 30P ❋ ⌒(heated) ♪ u putting green
☺ International ⊹
Credit Cards ① ③

**NANT-DDU (near Merthyr Tydfil)** Powys Map 03 SO01

**★★61%, Nant Ddu Lodge** Cwm Taf CF48 2HY (5m N of
Merthyr Tydfil on A470 near Brecon) (Minotels)
☎Merthyr Tydfil(0685)79111 FAX (0685) 77088
*Situated 5 miles north of Merthyr on the Brecon road, this hotel was once the shooting lodge of Lord Tredegar, and is set in pleasant grounds within the Brecon Beacons. Bedrooms have been recently modernised and there is a good choice of bar meals available in addition to the à la carte restaurant.*
15⇨🌓(1fb)1⌘ CTV in all bedrooms ® T ✸ sB&B⇨🌓£37.50
dB&B⇨🌓£47
30P ❋
V ⊹ ⌐⊈ Lunch £10.95&alc Dinner £10.95 Last dinner 9.30pm
Credit Cards ① ② ③ ⑤

M

**NANTWICH** Cheshire Map **07** SJ65

★★★♨78%, **Rookery Hall** Worleston CW5 6DQ (2m N B5074) (Select) ☎(0270)626866 Telex no 367169 FAX (0270) 626027
*Situated outside Nantwich, this Georgian hotel continues to set high standards and has exciting prospects for the future. Conversion of an adjacent stable block into 34 modern bedrooms and high quality meeting rooms will be ready for 1991. Staff, under the personal direction of general manager David Tearle, are particularly courteous and attentive, and chef Chris Phillips' cooking has a robust style and wide range of flavours, and the menus contain some interesting vegetarian dishes. The restaurant is a good rendezvous for a special occasion; its dark mahogany, cut glass and candlelight give it a particularly romantic atmosphere.*
30⇥♠Annexe15⇥♠5🛏 CTV in all bedrooms T
✖ (ex guide dogs) sB&B⇥♠£92.50-£235
dB&B⇥♠£140-£260 🛏
Lift ⟮ CTV 150P ⚘ ❋ ♬ (hard) ♪ clay pigeon shooting putting croquet nc10yrs *xmas*
♀ English & French V ✿ ♨ ✄ Lunch £16.50-£20 Dinner £27.50-£32.50&alc Last dinner 9.30pm
Credit Cards ⊡ ② ③ ⑤

★★63%, **Alvaston Hall** Middlewich Rd CW5 6PD (Character) ☎(0270)624341 Telex no 36311 FAX (0270) 623395
*Set in rural surroundings off the A530, about two miles north of the town, this half-timbered Victorian hotel provides accommodation in well-equipped bedrooms situated in the main building and elsewhere in the extensive grounds, and offers comprehensive leisure and conference facilities.*
36⇥♠Annexe52⇥♠(3fb) CTV in all bedrooms ® T
sB&B⇥♠£75-£109 dB&B⇥♠£90-£135 🛏
⟮ 250P ❋ CFA 🏊(heated) ♬ (hard) squash sauna solarium gymnasium whirlpool bath, beauty therapist *xmas*
V ✿ ♨ ✄
Credit Cards ⊡ ② ③ ④ ⑤

★★63%, **Crown** High St CW5 5AS (Best Western) ☎Crewe(0270)625283 FAX (0270) 628047
18⇥(2fb) CTV in all bedrooms ® T ❋ sB⇥£38-£43
dB⇥£44-£55 (room only) 🛏
⟮ 60P
♀ English & Continental V ✿ ♨ Lunch fr£3.25 High tea fr£3 Dinner fr£11.95 Last dinner 11pm
Credit Cards ⊡ ② ③ ⑤

★★57%, **Cedars Hotel & Restaurant** 136 Crewe Rd CW5 6NB ☎(0270)626455
*This family-run hotel, located on the edge of the town, offers friendly service and generous meals. It is popular with business people during the week, and has a large function room which has its own bar.*
24rm(19⇥♠) Annexe 3⇥♠ (4fb)2🛏 CTV in all bedrooms ®
T sB&B£15-£30 sB&B⇥♠£19.50-£35 dB&B£20-£40
dB&B⇥♠£29.50-£48 🛏
⟮ 60P ❋ *xmas*
♀ English & French V ✿ ♨ ✄ S% Lunch £6.95&alc Dinner £12.50&alc Last dinner 9.30pm
Credit Cards ⊡ ② ③ ⑤ ⓔ

○**Travelodge** A51 Nantwich Rd, Calveley(Trusthouse Forte) ☎Central reservations (0800) 850950
Due to open winter 1990
40⇥

**NARBERTH** Dyfed Map **02** SN11

★★61%, **Plas-Hyfryd** Moorfield Rd SA67 7AB (Guestaccom) ☎(0834)860653
*A converted 18th-century mansion which once served as the local rectory is now run as an hotel by friendly owners who are very much involved in every aspect of its management. Bedrooms are neat and compact, the bar and lounge are cosy and relaxing, and food is good.*

12⇥♠(1fb) CTV in all bedrooms ® T ❋ sB&B⇥♠£24-£34
dB&B⇥♠£34 🛏
CTV 30P ❋ ⊐(heated) *xmas*
♀ British, French & Spanish V ✿ ♨ Lunch £9-£13.50alc Dinner £9-£13.50alc Last dinner 9.30pm
Credit Cards ⊡ ③ ⓔ

**NARBOROUGH** Leicestershire Map **04** SP59

★★63%, **Charnwood** 48 Leicester Rd LE9 5DF (off A46 2m S of M1, junc 21) ☎Leicester(0533)862218 FAX (0533) 750119
Closed 1 wk from 25 Dec RS Sun
*Well placed for the M1, M69 and Leicester city centre, this friendly hotel with its large garden is popular with business clients.*
20⇥♠ CTV in all bedrooms ® T sB&B⇥♠£30-£48
dB&B⇥♠£45-£60 🛏
50P ❋
♀ English & French V ✿ ♨ Lunch £7.50&alc High tea £1.50-£6.50 Dinner £11.50&alc Last dinner 9.30pm
Credit Cards ⊡ ② ③ ⓔ

**NEASHAM** Co Durham Map **08** NZ31

★★★63%, **Newbus Arms Hotel & Restaurant** Hurworth Rd DL2 1PE (Best Western) ☎Darlington(0325)721071 FAX (0325) 721770
*Elegant period house in its own gardens, with impressive public and conference areas.*
15⇥♠3🛏 CTV in all bedrooms ® T ❋ sB&B⇥♠£45-£65
dB&B⇥♠£60-£90 🛏
80P 2🚗 (£5 per night) ⚘ ❋ squash
♀ European V ✿ ♨ Lunch £2.25-£20alc Dinner £4.50-£25alc Last dinner 10pm
Credit Cards ⊡ ② ③ ⑤ ⓔ

**NEATH** West Glamorgan Map **03** SS79

★★64%, **Castle Hotel** The Parade SA11 1RB (Lansbury) ☎(0639)641119 & 643581 Telex no 48119 FAX (0639) 641624
28⇥♠(8fb)1🛏✖in 4 bedrooms CTV in all bedrooms ® T ❋
sB&B⇥♠£56 dB&B⇥♠£69 🛏
⟮ ⊞ CTV 20P sauna solarium exercise bike
♀ English & Continental V ✿ ♨ ✄ Lunch fr£8.95 Dinner fr£14&alc Last dinner 10.30pm
Credit Cards ⊡ ② ③ ⑤

**NEEDHAM MARKET** Suffolk Map **05** TM05

★★66%, **Limes** IP6 8DQ (Select) ☎(0449)720305 FAX (0449) 722233
Closed Xmas
*Built some five hundred years ago and centrally sited in the historic market town, this relaxing little hotel offers comfortable accommodation with good facilities; one of its two bars dates back to the sixteenth century and is popular with local residents as well as guests.*
11⇥(4fb) CTV in all bedrooms ® T ❋ sB&B⇥fr£39.50
dB&B⇥fr£55 🛏
60P
♀ English & French V ✿ ♨ Lunch fr£8.95&alc Dinner fr£9.95&alc Last dinner 9.30pm
Credit Cards ⊡ ② ③ ⑤

**NEFYN** Gwynedd Map **06** SH34

★★★68%, **The Nanhoron Arms** Ffordd Dewi Sant LL53 6EA ☎(0758)720203
*This fine example of Edwardian architecture near the town centre is reputed to be the first purpose-built hotel in the area. Since 1989 new owners have undertaken an extensive programme of modernisation and refurbishment to provide comfortable, well-equipped bedrooms and attractive public areas, facilities including*

**N**

*a "family" room where parents can enjoy a drink or bar meal without having to abandon their offspring, and a safe children's play area ; the friendly, obliging service provided throughout this establishment is one of its notable features.*
19⇒♠(2fb) CTV in all bedrooms ® T ✗ (ex guide dogs)
sB&B⇒♠£30-£35 dB&B⇒♠£55-£61 ⊟
60P *xmas*
V ♦ ⊡ ✗ Lunch £7.50-£9.50 High tea £1.50-£10 Dinner
£13.50-£16&alc Last dinner 9.45pm
Credit Cards ① ② ③ ⑤ ⓔ
**See advertisement under PWLLHELI**

★**60%** **Caeau Capel** Rhodfar Mor LL53 6EB ☎(0758)720240
Closed Nov-Etr
*A delightful house, standing in its own grounds close to the sea and an 18-hole golf course, offers good value for money in its pleasantly furnished, comfortable accommodation.*
20rm(6⇒4♠)(6fb) ® ✳ sB&B£17.53-£18.98
sB&B⇒♠£20.70-£23 dB&B£35.06-£39.96
dB&B⇒♠£41.40-£46 ⊟
CTV 20P ✿ ♪ (grass) putting pool
V ♦ ⊡ Bar Lunch £3.50-£6 Dinner fr£10.25 Last dinner
7.30pm
Credit Cards ① ③ ⓔ

---

**NETHER WASDALE** Cumbria Map **11** NY10

★★**59%** **Low Wood Hall** Wasdale CA20 1ET
☎Seascale(09467)26289
Closed Xmas & New Year
*In picturesque village setting, and ideally situated for walkers and those wishing to explore the English Lakes, this Victorian country residence in its own neat gardens enjoys lovely views of the surrounding hills. Some bedrooms are in an adjoining house, but all are well equipped and provided with private facilities.*
13⇒♠ CTV in all bedrooms ® ✗ sB&B⇒♠£26-£30
dB&B⇒♠£40-£44
CTV 24P ⤒ ✿ billiard & pool tables
V ✗ Dinner £10-£15&alc Last dinner 8.45pm

---

**NEVERN** Dyfed Map **02** SN03

★★**65%** *Trewern Arms* SA42 0NB ☎Newport(0239)820395
*Modernised and extended 18th-century inn of some character, in a picturesque and secluded valley.*
8⇒♠(1fb) CTV in all bedrooms ®
CTV 100P ✿ ♪ ∪ solarium gymnasium pool table
V ♦ Last dinner 9.30pm
Credit Cards ①

---

**NEWARK-ON-TRENT** Nottinghamshire Map **08** SK75

★★**66%** *Grange* 73 London Rd NG24 1RZ
☎Newark(0636)703399
Closed 24 Dec-2 Jan
*A warm, friendly and comfortable hotel, personally run by the resident owners, who offer well-cooked food and good bedrooms. Located just south of the town centre in a residential area.*
9⇒♠(2fb) CTV in all bedrooms ® T ✗ sB&B⇒♠£40-£50
dB&B⇒♠£50-£55 ⊟
9P ⤒
V Lunch £7.50-£10alc Dinner £10-£17.50alc Last dinner 9pm
Credit Cards ① ③

★★**55%** *Midland* Muskham Rd NG24 1BL ☎(0636)73788
*This family-run budget style hotel lies adjacent to the cattle market near a railway line on the edge of town.*
10rm(2⇒)(2fb) CTV in all bedrooms ® ✗
CTV 20P
V ♦ Last dinner 8.30pm
Credit Cards ① ② ⑤

---

★**63%** **South Parade** 117-119 Baldertongate NG24 1RY
(Minotels) ☎Newark(0636)703008 FAX (0522) 510182
Closed 21 Dec-2 Jan
*Simple, clean, comfortable accommodation and well-presented, mainly English meals are provided by this privately-owned hotel – a red-brick, detached Georgian house standing on the Balderton road – which caters mainly for commercial users.*
16rm(8⇒♠)(2fb) CTV in all bedrooms ® T sB&B£30
sB&B⇒♠£36 dB&B£44 dB&B⇒♠£49.50 ⊟
《 10P ⤒
⊡ English & French V ♦ ⊡ Sunday Lunch £6.50 Dinner
£12.50-£14alc Last dinner 8.30pm
Credit Cards ① ③ ⓔ

⛺**Travelodge** North Muskham NG23 6HT (3m N A1)
(Trusthouse Forte) ☎Newark(0636)703635 Central
Res (0800) 850950
30⇒♠(30fb) CTV in all bedrooms ® sB⇒♠£24
dB⇒♠£29.50 (room only)
《 30P ⤒
⊡ Mainly grills
Credit Cards ① ② ③

---

**NEWBRIDGE** Cornwall & Isles of Scilly Map **02** SW43

✗✗**Enzo of Newbridge** TR20 8QH ☎Penzance(0736)63777
*Situated in a small hamlet between Penzance and St Just, the restaurant is in two sections – a small, stone-walled area, and the modern plant-adorned conservatory where cooking is carried out under a copper canopy in the corner. An extensive menu features Italian food, with pastas as starters or main courses and a good selection of other dishes, whilst a separate menu concentrates on the use of local fish and fresh well-cooked vegetables. A list of mainly Italian wines is available, and smiling attentive service is offered by uniformed waitresses.*
Closed Thu (Dec-Apr) & 1-21 Nov
Lunch not served
⊡ Italian V 70 seats Dinner fr£12.65&alc Last dinner 9.30pm
25P ✗
Credit Cards ① ② ③ ⑤

---

**NEWBRIDGE-ON-WYE** Powys Map **03** SO05

★★**64%** *New Inn* LD1 6HY ☎Newbridge on Wye(059789)211
Closed Xmas
*A small family-run village inn, recently refurbished to provide good comfortable bedrooms and public areas which include an extensive lounge, offers enjoyable well-cooked meals and four miles of free fishing on the River Wye.*
8rm(2⇒1♠)(3fb) CTV in all bedrooms ®
CTV 30P ⩲(heated)
V ♦ ⊡
Credit Cards ①

---

**NEWBURY** Berkshire Map **04** SU46

See also **Chieveley Elcot and Thatcham**
★★★★**63%** **Regency Park** Bowling Green Rd RG13 3RP
☎Thatcham(0635)71555 Telex no 847844 FAX (0635) 71571
(For full entry see Thatcham)
**See advertisement on page 509**

★★★**56%** *The Chequers* Oxford St RG13 1JB (Trusthouse
Forte) ☎(0635)38000 Telex no 849205 FAX (0635) 37170
*Bedrooms vary in style and standard, but improvements are continuing steadily at this former coaching inn. Public areas are pleasant and comfortable, whilst service throughout is helpful and friendly.*
56⇒♠(3fb)⤵in 12 bedrooms CTV in all bedrooms ®
《 60P CFA
V ♦ ⊡ ✗ Last dinner 9.45pm
Credit Cards ① ② ③ ④ ⑤

○**Millwaters** London Rd RG13 2BY ☎(0635)528838
FAX (0635) 523406
34rm

---

**NEWBY BRIDGE** Cumbria Map **07** SD38

★★★**69% Whitewater** The Lakeland Village LA12 8PX
☎(05395)31133 Telex no 54173 FAX (05395) 31881
*Imaginatively converted from what was originally a mill standing
beside the turbulent River Leven, this is a smart complex, built of
local stone and slate. The hotel has spacious, well-appointed and
comfortable bedrooms and, together with an excellent health and
leisure club, forms part of the Lakeland Village time-share resort.*
35⇌♪♠(10fb)1☷ CTV in all bedrooms ® T ✖ (ex guide dogs)
✳ sB&B⇌♪♠£60 dB&B⇌♪♠£85 ➡
Lift ℂ 50P ♨ ▣(heated) ♪ (hard & grass) squash sauna
solarium gymnasium putting ♫ *xmas*
V ◊ ⚖ Sunday Lunch fr£8.95 Dinner fr£14.95&alc Last
dinner 9pm
Credit Cards ① ② ③ ⑤ ④

**See advertisement on page 511**

★★★**67% Lakeside** LA12 8AT (Consort) ☎(05395)31207
Telex no 65149 FAX (05395) 31699
*A long-established, well-managed hotel set right on the shore at the
southern end of Lake Windermere has been extended and
refurbished to provide attractive, comfortable bedrooms, many
with fine views of the lake; helpful service is given by friendly
young staff.*
79⇌♪♠(3fb)2☷ CTV in all bedrooms ® T ✳ S10%
sB&B⇌♪♠£55-£60 dB&B⇌♪♠£80-£90 ➡
Lift ℂ CTV 100P ✿ launching for boats private jetty ♫ *xmas*
◊ ⚖ S10% Sunday Lunch £8.50 Dinner £16.50 Last dinner
9.30pm
Credit Cards ① ② ③ ⑤ ④

**See advertisement on page 511**

★★★**63% The Swan** LA12 8NB (Exec Hotel) ☎(05395)31681
Telex no 65108 FAX (05395) 31917
Closed 2-11 Jan
*Guests may arrive by car, boat or helicopter at this modernised
coaching inn, attractively set on the River Leven at the southern
end of Lake Windermere. Spacious bedrooms are well furnished
and equipped, and the de luxe rooms are provided with many
thoughtful extras. Dinner is in the first-floor restaurant, full of
character and next to an elegant and comfortable cocktail bar.
Lighter meals and lunches are served in the Mailcoach Wine bar,
open all day.*
36⇌♪(6fb) CTV in all bedrooms ® T ✖ (ex guide dogs)
sB&B⇌♪£46-£66 dB&B⇌♪£74-£105 ➡
CTV 100P 4♣ ♨ ✿ ♪ croquet table tennis ♧ *xmas*
♡ English & French V ◊ ⚖ Sunday Lunch £9-£10.25 Dinner
£15.50-£18&alc Last dinner 9.30pm
Credit Cards ① ② ③ ⑤

**See advertisement on page 511**

★★**61% The Newby Bridge** LA12 8NA ☎(05395)31222
FAX (0900) 823705
*Well-equipped bedrooms, an attractive restaurant serving meals of
a good standard, an extensive range of bar meals and friendly,
helpful service are provided by this well-furnished hotel at the
southern end of Lake Windermere.*
17⇌♪♠(3fb)☷ CTV in all bedrooms ® T ✳ sB&B⇌♪♠£30
dB&B⇌♪♠£40
100P ♨ ✿ ♪ ♫
♡ European V ◊ ⚖ ⤭
Credit Cards ① ② ③ ⑤

Hotels with a high percentage rating for quality
are highlighted by a % across their
gazetteer entry.

---

**NEWCASTLETON** Borders *Roxburghshire* Map **12** NY48

✗*Copshaw Kitchen* TD9 0RB ☎Liddesdale(03873)75250
*This attractive restaurant was once a grocer's shop; today, a
thriving antique business has developed in parallel with the
restaurant trade, and many of the delightful articles that surround
you as you eat are actually for sale. It is for its interesting and
varied menu and the standard of its cuisine, however, that the
Copshaw Kitchen is particularly noteworthy.*
Closed Tue, Jan & most of Feb
Dinner not served Sun & Mon
♡ British V 36 seats Last lunch 6pm Last dinner 9pm 12P ⤭

---

**NEWCASTLE-UNDER-LYME** Staffordshire Map **07** SJ84

★★★**62% Clayton Lodge** Clayton Rd ST5 4AF (A519)
(Embassy) ☎(0782)613093 Telex no 36547 FAX (0782) 711896
*This busy commercial hotel is reached from junction 15 of the M6
along the A519. There is a large banqueting suite, and the hotel
has its own pub in the complex – the Copeland Arms.*
50⇌♪♠(46fb) CTV in all bedrooms ® T S10%
sB⇌♪♠£67-£77 dB⇌♪♠£77-£87 (room only) ➡
ℂ 400P 6♣ ✿ CFA
♡ English & French V ◊ ⚖ S10% Lunch £10.30&alc Dinner
£11.30&alc Last dinner 10pm
Credit Cards ① ② ③ ④ ⑤

★★★**60% Post House** Clayton Rd ST5 4DL (Trusthouse Forte)
☎(0782)717171 Telex no 36531 FAX (0782) 717138
*A hotel which provides a popular meeting point for travellers, being
just off junction 15 of the M6, offers a choice of restaurants and the
amenities of a new leisure complex.*
126⇌♪(46fb)⤭in 55 bedrooms CTV in all bedrooms ® T ✳
sB⇌♪£72-£82 dB⇌♪£83-£93 (room only) ➡
ℂ 128P ✿ ▣(heated) sauna solarium gymnasium *xmas*

▶

**N**

## Regency Park Hotel

# *SOMEWHERE SPECIAL IN ROYAL BERKSHIRE*

*If you are searching for a relaxing venue, look no further
than the Regency Park Hotel. Nestling peacefully in the idyllic Berkshire
countryside, it will soothe away your cares and provide you with
the facilities and service you would expect from a 4-Star Hotel.*

**\*   COMFORT AND RELAXATION**
*In the peace and quiet of our 50 triple-glazed luxury bedrooms with a host of facilities, including direct-line telephones and satellite TV. The hotel is an ideal centre for exploring the many places of interest in Royal Berkshire. Our many services include baby-sitting, limousine service and laundry/dry cleaning.*

**\*   SERVICES AND FACILITIES**
*We cater for individuals and a wide range of organisations. In purpose-designed suites our special business centre provides full conference facilities, fully equipped with audio-visual equipment. Fax/telex, typing and photocopying services are also available, together with a complete range of business services.*

**\*   ELEGANCE AND STYLE**
*Relax in the luxurious Fountains Bar, then enjoy excellent food in the sophisticated surroundings of the Terraces Restaurant. For private functions, dine in our spacious Parkside Room, complete with its own dance floor.*

**\*   LOCATION**
*At the Regency Park Hotel, our staff treat you as SOMEONE SPECIAL. We are just a short distance from the M4 Junction 13, but a world away from the hustle and bustle of everyday life.*

### *THE REGENCY PARK HOTEL*
*because you deserve something special
Call now for reservations or a copy of our brochure.*

**Bowling Green Road, Thatcham, Newbury, Berkshire, RG13 3RP
TELEPHONE (0635) 71555
FAX (0635) 71571    TELEX 847844**

V ✿ ⚲ ✂ Lunch £8.95-£10.95&alc High tea fr£4.95 Dinner
£16.50-£18.75&alc Last dinner 10.30pm
Credit Cards ① ② ③ ④ ⑤

★★61% **Borough Arms** King St ST5 1HX ☎(0782)629421
FAX (0782) 712388
*The Borough Arms stands by the A53 just off the town centre. In
its time it has been both a pottery and a brewery, before being
converted into an hotel that is popular with business travellers and
local people. Bedrooms in the main building have recently been
refurbished to a good standard, and a similar programme of
renovation is under way in the annexe.*
30⇔🁢Annexe15⇔ CTV in all bedrooms ⓇT
✖ (ex guide dogs) ✳ sB&B⇔🁢£33-£43 dB&B⇔🁢£48-£57
⚓40P ♫
♥ International V ✿ Lunch £5.75 Dinner £10.25-£11&alc Last
dinner 9.30pm
Credit Cards ① ② ③ ⑤

★56% **The Deansfield** 98 Lancaster Rd ST5 1DS
☎(0782)619040
*Bedrooms with good facilities are available at this small, family
owned and run hotel situated in a quiet side road near to the town
centre.*
6🁢Annexe5🁢(2fb) CTV in all bedrooms ⓇT sB&B🁢£28
dB&B🁢£34 ₽
⚓CTV 35P 1🏌 🚲 ✿ ♧ *xmas*
♥ English & French V ✿ ✂ S% Lunch fr£6alc High tea
fr£4.50alc Dinner fr£10alc Last dinner 9pm
Credit Cards ① ② ③ ⑤

NEWCASTLE UPON TYNE Tyne & Wear Map **12** NZ26
See**Town Plan Section**
See also **Marley Hill, Seaton Burn & Whickham**
★★★★70% **Swallow Gosforth Park** High Gosforth Park,
Gosforth NE3 5HN (Swallow) ☎091-236 4111 Telex no 53655
FAX 091-236 8192
*Modern hotel with extensive leisure facilities and choice of
restaurants serving interesting, well-prepared food.*
178⇔🁢(14fb)3🛌✂in 24 bedrooms CTV in all bedrooms ⓇT
✳ S% sB&B⇔🁢£98 dB&B⇔🁢£118 ₽
Lift ⚓ CTV 200P ✿ CFA ⬛(heated) ⚑18 ♘ (hard) squash
sauna solarium gymnasium spa pool steam room beauty
therapy ♫ *xmas*
♥ English & French V ✿ ⚲ Lunch £13.50-£17.50alc Dinner
fr£19.50&alc Last dinner mdnt
Credit Cards ① ② ③ ⑤

★★★★54% **Holiday Inn** Great North Rd NE13 6BP (Holiday
Inns) ☎091-236 5432 Telex no 53271 FAX 091-236 8091
(For full entry see Seaton Burn)

★★★69% **Springfield** Durham Rd NE9 5BT (Embassy)
☎091-477 4121 Telex no 538197 SPRING G
FAX 091-477 7213
(For full entry see Gateshead)

★★★68% **Washington Moat House** Stone Cellar Rd, District
12 NE37 1PH (Queens Moat) ☎091-417 2626 Telex no 537143
FAX 091-415 1166
(For full entry see Washington)

★★★67% **New Kent Hotel** Osborne Rd NE2 2TB (Best
Western) ☎091-281 1083 FAX 091-281 3369
*Located just out of the city centre, this family-owned hotel offers
modern, well appointed accommodation, friendly service and good
value dinners.*
32⇔🁢(4fb) CTV in all bedrooms ⓇT ✖ (ex guide dogs) ✳
sB&B⇔🁢£35-£59.50 dB&B⇔🁢£56-£69.50 ₽
⚓16P 🚲
♥ International V Bar Lunch fr£4.95&alc Dinner
£9.90-£11.90&alc Last dinner 10pm
Credit Cards ① ② ③ ④ ⑤

★★★66% **Swallow Hotel-Gateshead** High West St NE8 1PE
(Swallow) ☎091-477 1105 Telex no 53534 FAX 091-478 7214
(For full entry see Gateshead)

★★★63% **County Thistle** Neville St NE99 1AH (Mount
Charlotte (TS)) ☎091-232 2471 Telex no 537873
FAX 091-232 1285
*Comfortable city-centre hotel opposite the main railway station.
The delightful Café Mozart serves good food.*
115⇔🁢(4fb)✂in 10 bedrooms CTV in all bedrooms ⓇT ✳
sB⇔🁢fr£65 dB⇔🁢fr£75 (room only) ₽
Lift ⚓ 25P CFA ♫
♥ International ✿ ⚲ ✂ Lunch fr£8.45&alc Dinner fr£12&alc
Last dinner 9.45pm
Credit Cards ① ② ③ ④ ⑤

★★★63% **Newcastle Crest** New Bridge St NE1 8BS
(Trusthouse Forte) ☎091-232 6191 Telex no 53467
FAX 091-261 8529
*Functional accommodation and a choice of restaurants are offered
by this modern city centre hotel.*
166⇔🁢✂in 58 bedrooms CTV in all bedrooms ⓇT
sB⇔🁢£74 dB⇔🁢£86 (room only) ₽
Lift ⚓ CFA ♫
V ✿ ⚲ ✂ Lunch fr£12 Dinner £14.50 Last dinner 10pm
Credit Cards ① ② ③ ④ ⑤

★★★63% *Swallow* Newgate Arcade NE1 5SX ☎091-232 5025
Telex no 538230 FAX 091- 232 8428
*Purpose-built hotel with sixth-floor cocktail lounge and restaurant
giving good views across the city. A leisure complex is planned.*
93⇔🁢✂in 41 bedrooms CTV in all bedrooms ⓇT
Lift ⚓ 120P CFA ♫
♥ English & French V ✿ ⚲ Last dinner 10pm
Credit Cards ① ② ③ ⑤

★★★61% **Post House** Emerson Distrist 5 NE37 1LB
(Trusthouse Forte) ☎091-416 2264 Telex no 537574
FAX 091-415 3371
(For full entry see Washington)

★★★59% **Imperial** Jesmond Rd NE2 1PR (Swallow)
☎091-281 5511 Telex no 537972 FAX 091-281 8472
*Mainly commercial, modernised city centre hotel with neat
bedrooms, open plan public areas and an attractive leisure
complex. Restaurant and coffee shop facilities.*
129⇔🁢(6fb)✂in 38 bedrooms CTV in all bedrooms ⓇT ✳
sB&B⇔🁢£65-£75 dB&B⇔🁢£75-£85 ₽
Lift ⚓ ⊞150🏌 CFA ⬛(heated) sauna solarium gymnasium
steam room spa bath ♫ *xmas*
V ✿ ⚲ Lunch £7.50-£8.50&alc Dinner £12.50-£13.50&alc Last
dinner 9.45pm
Credit Cards ① ② ③ ⑤

★★★58% **Hospitality Inn** 64 Osborne Rd, Jesmond NE2 2AT
(Mount Charlotte (TS)) ☎091-281 7881 Telex no 53636
FAX 091-281 6241
*The well-equipped bedrooms of this hotel include four delightful
suites, but eating facilities are limited to a coffee shop and small
table d'hôte restaurant unless guests care to make use of the
Garden Restaurant at The Northumberland, a sister hotel which
stands opposite.*
89⇔🁢(6fb)1🛌✂in 10 bedrooms CTV in all bedrooms ⓇT
✖ (ex guide dogs)
Lift ⚓ 90P 10🏌 (£3) sauna
♥ English & French V ✿ ⚲ ✂
Credit Cards ① ② ③ ⑤

★★★57% **Newcastle Moat House** Coast Rd NE28 9HP (Queens
Moat) ☎091-262 8989 & 091-262 7044 Telex no 53583
FAX 091-263 4172
(For full entry see Wallsend)

N

★★ **61% Whites** 38-40 Osborne Road, Jesmond NE2 2AL
☎091-281 5126
*A friendly family-run hotel recently extended into a similar*
*Victorian terraced property. Public rooms are cosy and*
*comfortable and the restaurant is popular. Situated in a residential*
*area not far from the city centre.*
25rm(15⇨7♠)(1fb) CTV in all bedrooms ® ✠
⟨ CTV 30P
V ✿ ⚍ Last dinner 9.30pm
Credit Cards ①②③⑤
See advertisement on page 513

★★ **60% Cairn** 97/103 Osborne Road, Jesmond NE2 2TJ
☎091-281 1358 FAX 091-281 9031
*Recent upgrading has enhanced both the public rooms and the*
*well-equipped bedrooms at this mainly commercial hotel. Situated*
*close to the city centre within easy reach of the major road links.*
51⇨♠(6fb)2⊟ CTV in all bedrooms ® T sB&B⇨♠£42-£46
dB&B⇨♠£59.50-£65 ⅊
⟨ 20P *xmas*
V ✿ ⚍ Lunch £6.50-£7.50 High tea £3.50-£5 Dinner
£9.50-£10.50 Last dinner 9.15pm
Credit Cards ①②③⑤ⓕ
See advertisement on page 513

★★**Morrach** 82-86 Osborne Road, Jesmond NE2 2AP
☎091-281 3361 FAX 091-281 9031
*Modest accommodation is available at this family-run hotel.*
*Dinners represent good value, and there is also a small coffee shop*
*which remains open throughout the day and evening.*
32rm(21⇨♠)(2fb)1⊟ CTV in all bedrooms ® T sB&B£23-£28
sB&B⇨♠£30-£38 dB&B£36-£45 dB&B⇨♠£44-£55 ⅊
20P 3☎ ⇷ pool table
V ✿ ⚍
Credit Cards ①②③

★64% **Osborne** Osborne Road, Jesmond NE2 2AE
☎091-281 3385
*Although generally fairly compact and modestly furnished,*
*bedrooms at this friendly hotel are comfortable and well equipped.*
*Sound home cooking is served in the traditional dining room.*
26rm(1➪9♠)(2fb) CTV in all bedrooms ® T sB&Bfr£30
sB&B➪♠fr£38 dB&Bfr£48 dB&B➪♠£56-£58 ⊟
CTV 6P 1🏊 (£2) 🚿
V ♥ ⌿ Bar Lunch fr£3 Dinner fr£7.50 Last dinner 8.30pm
Credit Cards ① ③

✗✗✗**Fishermans Lodge** Jesmond Dene, Jesmond NE7 7BQ
☎091-281 3281 & 091-281 3724 FAX 091-281 6410
*Situated in the peace and quiet of Jesmond Dene, yet within easy*
*reach of the city centre, is this stylish and very popular restaurant.*
*Fresh seafood is a speciality but the imaginative menu also*
*features game, poultry and delicious sweets.*
Closed Sun, BH's & 25-28 Dec
Lunch not served Sat
♀ French V 65 seats Lunch £12.50-£14&alc Dinner £22-£30alc
Last lunch 2pm Last dinner 11pm 45P nc9yrs
Credit Cards ① ② ③ ⑤

✗✗✗**21 Queen Street** Quayside NE1 3UG ☎091-222 0755
*A smart modern restaurant under the ownership and personal*
*supervision of Terence and Susan Laybourne who provide modern*
*French-style cooking of the highest order. A most delicately*
*textured hot mousseline of sole with mussels has been highly*
*praised as has the delicious honey roast duck with oriental spices.*
Closed Sun
Lunch not served Sat
♀ French 50 seats ✱ Lunch fr£12&alc Dinner
£19.20-£32.90alc Last lunch 2pm Last dinner 10.45pm 𝒫
Credit Cards ① ② ③ ⑤

✗✗**King Neptune** 34-36 Stowell St NE1 4XB ☎091-261 6657 &
091-261 6660
*Situated in Newcastle's small but thriving Chinatown, this*
*attractive restaurant specialises in seafood and Peking cuisine*
*along with a variety of other mouthwatering dishes which should*
*please connoisseurs of Chinese cooking.*
Closed 25 Dec & 1 Jan
♀ Pekinese V 120 seats ✱ Lunch £5-£9&alc Dinner £12-£30alc
Last lunch 1.30pm Last dinner 10.30pm P
Credit Cards ① ② ③ ⑤

**NEWCASTLE UPON TYNE AIRPORT** Tyne & Wear
Map **12** NZ17

★★★64% **Airport Moat House** Woolsington NE13 8DJ
(Queens Moat) ☎Ponteland(0661)24911 Telex no 537121
FAX (0661) 860157
*Situated within the airport complex, this modern hotel has*
*comfortable and well-appointed bedrooms, open-plan lounge areas*
*and an attractive restaurant and cocktail bar.*
100➪♠✄in 59 bedrooms CTV in all bedrooms ® T
sB&B➪♠£45-£75 dB&B➪♠£55-£85 ⊟
Lift ℂ 200P CFA *xmas*
♀ English & French V ♥ ⌿ ✄ Lunch £12.95&alc Dinner
£12.95&alc Last dinner 9.45pm
Credit Cards ① ② ③ ⑤

**NEWMARKET** Suffolk Map **05** TL66

★★★62% **Newmarket Moat House** Moulton Rd CB8 8DY
(Queens Moat) ☎(0638)667171 FAX (0638) 666533
*Situated close to the town centre and Heath this well run hotel has*
*a good atmosphere created by a friendly staff. Accommodation is*
*well cared for and there are good conference facilities.*
49➪♠(2fb) CTV in all bedrooms ® T sB&B➪♠£65-£85
dB&B➪♠£85-£95 ⊟
Lift ℂ CTV 60P 10🏊 CFA

♀ English & French V ♥ ⌿ Lunch £15&alc Dinner £15&alc
Last dinner 9.45pm
Credit Cards ① ② ③ ⑤

★★71% **Bedford Lodge** Bury Rd CB8 7BX (Best Western)
☎(0638)663175 Telex no 97267 FAX (0638) 667391
*Managed by a proprietress who successfully combines*
*professionalism with genuine helpfulness, and standing adjacent to*
*a riding stable in three acres of pleasant and secluded gardens*
*close to the town centre, this former Georgian hunting lodge offers*
*beautifully decorated, comfortably furnished bedrooms with*
*modern amenities; public areas of an equally high standard*
*include conference/banqueting facilities, a relaxed convivial bar,*
*and the Godolphin Restaurant, where a varied and imaginative*
*range of competently prepared dishes is attractively served.*
11➪♠Annexe7rm(1fb)1⊞ CTV in 11 bedrooms ®
ℂ 60P ✿
♀ English & French V ♥ ⌿ Last dinner 9.30pm
Credit Cards ① ② ③ ⑤

★★70% **Rosery Country House** 15 Church St, Exning CB8 7EH
(2m NW B1103) ☎Exning(063877)312
*Situated just off the A45 this hotel offers genuine hospitality,*
*modest accommodation and comfortable, attractive public areas.*
11rm(7➪1♠)1⊞ CTV in all bedrooms ® T ✗ (ex guide dogs)
20P 🚿 ✿ croquet ⚬
♀ English & French V ♥ ⌿ Last dinner 9.30pm
Credit Cards ① ② ③ ⑤

★★58% **White Hart** High St CB8 8JP (Consort)
☎(0638)663051 FAX (0638) 667284
*Set on the town's main street, directly opposite the National Horse*
*Racing Museum, a former coaching inn dating from the sixteenth*
*century provides comfortable, well equipped accommodation which*
*is attractively furnished and decorated. The convivial atmosphere*
*of the public areas makes them popular with locals, while the*
*restaurant offers some interesting dishes based on fresh produce.* ▶

23⇨↑1🛏 CTV in all bedrooms ® T sB&B⇨↑£50-£60
dB&B⇨↑£70-£80 🍴
《 30P *xmas*
♀ English & French **V** ✿ ⚘ Lunch £9.50-£10.50&alc Dinner
£9.50-£10.50&alc Last dinner 9.30pm
Credit Cards ⊡ ② ③ ⑤ ⑤

---

**NEW MILTON** Hampshire Map **04** SZ29

# ★★★★

**CHEWTON GLEN**

Christchurch Rd BH25 6QS
(Relais et Châteaux)
☎Highcliffe(0425)275341
Telex no 41456
FAX (0425) 272310

*It is interesting to note that
this well established and pre-
eminent hotel has not let the grass grow under its feet in the
last year. Building work has been going on to create 12 more
bedrooms and another lounge, a leisure centre and health club
which will provide a hairdressing salon and treatment rooms
as well as the usual array of swimming pool, gymnasium and
saunas. Away from the house there will also be two indoor
tennis courts and there is already a par 3 golf course. Owner
Martin Skan and his fine team of staff have worked
unstintingly to make Chewton Glen a landmark among hotels,
and guests cannot fail to feel cossetted here. Bedrooms all now
have either a terrace or a balcony, which is not only enjoyable
for the guests but has also added character to the already
attractive house. Chef Pierre Chevillard continues to create
superb dishes, making the elegant restaurant, with its 3
distinct dining areas, one of the most popular in the county.
Service, under the supervision of Restaurant Manager Patrick
Gaillard is attentive and professional.*
58⇨↑1🛏 CTV in all bedrooms T ✖ (ex guide dogs)
S10% dB⇨↑£155-£400 (room only) 🍴
《 100P ❋ CFA ⌂(heated) ▶9 ♪ (hard) snooker nc7yrs
*xmas*
♀ French **V** ✿ ⚘ S10% Lunch fr£20 Dinner £37.50-£63alc
Last dinner 9.30pm
Credit Cards ⊡ ② ③ ④ ⑤

---

**NEWPORT Gwent** Map **03** ST38

★★★★65% **Country Court** Chepstow Rd, Langstone NP6 2LX
(Stakis) ☎(0633)413737 Telex no 497147 FAX (0633) 413713
*This newly opened hotel, close to the M4 and with easy access to
the town, offers spacious accommodation which is comfortable and
modern, with a good range of facilities. Comfortable public areas
include the popular Seasons Restaurant, and there is a good range
of leisure facilities for the more energetic.*
141⇨↑(39fb)✗in 73 bedrooms CTV in all bedrooms ® T
✖ (ex guide dogs) ❋ sB⇨↑frf£64 (room only) 🍴
《 ⊞ 160P ⌂(heated) sauna solarium gymnasium jacuzzi
♀ English & Continental **V** ✿ ⚘ ✗ Lunch £2.90-£12.25alc
Dinner £2.40-£14.50alc Last dinner 10pm
Credit Cards ⊡ ② ③ ⑤

★★★★63% **Celtic Manor** Coldra Woods NP6 2YA
☎Llanwern(0633)413000 FAX (0633) 412910
*The 19th-century manor, once used as a maternity home, is
situated close to the motorway. It offers well-appointed bedrooms,
elegant public rooms, two good restaurants and a cellar bar.*
73⇨↑(1fb)2🛏 CTV in all bedrooms T ✖ (ex guide dogs) ❋
sB⇨↑£79 dB⇨↑£99 (room only) 🍴

Lift 《 150P 1🚗 ❋ ▣(heated) ♪ (hard) sauna solarium
gymnasium trim trail, pitch & putt ♫ *xmas*
♀ French **V** ✿ ⚘ ✗ Lunch £20&alc Dinner £20&alc Last
dinner 10.30pm
Credit Cards ⊡ ② ③ ⑤

★★★67% **Kings** High St NP9 1QU ☎(0633)842020
Telex no 497330 FAX (0633) 244667
Closed 25-30 Dec
*This busy city-centre hotel near the railway station and convenient
for junction 26 of the M4, is a fine example of a modern hotel. It
has well-equipped bedrooms, comfortable public areas and offers
the choice of an à la carte menu or a popular carvery. There are
good conference facilities.*
47⇨↑(10fb)✗in 2 bedrooms CTV in all bedrooms ® T
✖ (ex guide dogs) ✳ S% sB&B⇨↑£52-£57
dB&B⇨↑£60-£67 🍴
Lift 《 20P 10🚗
♀ International **V** ✿ ⚘ ✗ S% Lunch £5.95-£8.95&alc Dinner
£7.25-£11.45&alc Last dinner 9.30pm
Credit Cards ⊡ ② ③ ⑤ ⑤

★★★61% **Westgate** Commercial St NP1 1TT ☎(0633)244444
Telex no 498173 FAX (0633) 246616
*A historic hotel, dating back to the 15th century and notorious in
the 19th century as a centre of the famous Chartist Rebellion. It
has now been completely refurbished, to provide comfortable and
well equipped accommodation, and is a popular venue for functions
and conferences. There is a residents' bar and also a locally very
popular Scrum Bar.*
69⇨↑(11fb) CTV in all bedrooms ® T sB&B⇨↑£55
dB&B⇨↑£65 🍴
Lift 《 CTV CFA *xmas*
♀ French & Italian **V** ✿ ⚘ Lunch £6 Dinner £10.95&alc
Last dinner 10pm
Credit Cards ⊡ ② ③ ⑤ ⑤

★★★57% **Hilton National** The Coldra NP6 2YG (Hilton)
☎(0633)412777 Telex no 497205 FAX (0633) 413087
*Conveniently situated close to junction 24 of the M4 this popular
commercial hotel now has a new leisure complex. Most bedrooms
have been modernised and it is hoped to complete the programme
shortly. Guests have a choice of the popular carvery or the à la
carte waitress service.*
119⇨↑(20fb)✗in 22 bedrooms CTV in all bedrooms ® T
sB⇨↑£75-£85 dB⇨↑£93-£105 (room only) 🍴
《 400P ❋ ▣(heated) sauna gymnasium steam room ♪ *xmas*
♀ European **V** ✿ ⚘ ✗ Lunch £5.25-£8.50 Dinner
£2.25-£22.50alc Last dinner 10.30pm
Credit Cards ⊡ ② ③ ⑤ ⑤

★★65% **New Inn Motel** NP6 2JN (Porterhouse) ☎(0633)412426
FAX (0633) 413679
(For full entry see Langstone)

★★61% **Priory** High St, Caerleon NP6 1XD (3m NE B4236)
☎Caerleon(0633)421241
*Character hotel in village. Comfortable bedrooms and popular
restaurant.*
16⇨↑Annexe5⇨↑(1fb) CTV in all bedrooms ® ✖
70P ❋ ▶9
♀ English & French ✿ ⚘ Last dinner 9.45pm
Credit Cards ⊡ ② ③

---

**NEWPORT Shropshire** Map **07** SJ71

★★64% **Royal Victoria** St Mary's St TF10 7AB (Crown &
Raven) ☎(0952)820331 Telex no 335464 FAX (0952) 820209
*Sympathetically modernised to retain the aura of its Victorian
origins, this town-centre hotel features a stylish bar and a large
function suite/ballroom.*
24rm(16⇨↑7↑)(1fb) CTV in all bedrooms ® T
sB&B⇨↑frf£46.75 dB&B⇨↑frf£63.80 🍴
《 100P

ℙ English & French **V** ✿ ᴴ Lunch fr£11.50&alc Dinner
fr£11.50&alc Last dinner 10pm
Credit Cards 1 2 3

---

**NEWPORT PAGNELL** Buckinghamshire Map **04** SP84

★★★66% **Coach House** London Rd, Moulsoe MK16 0JA
(Lansbury) ☎(0908)613688 Telex no 825341
FAX (0908) 617335
*Situated just south of the town close to the M1, this attractive
Georgian building has been sympathetically extended to form a
pleasant quadrangle. Thoughtfully decorated and furnished, it
offers comfortable, well-equipped bedrooms and in the elegant
restaurant, with its central raised platform, both table d'hôte and à
la carte menus are available.*
49⇨ℝ(2fb)1 ☰⚹in 15 bedrooms CTV in all bedrooms ® **T**
✗ (ex guide dogs) sB&B⇨ℝfr£82 dB&B⇨ℝfr£95 ♬
ℂ 162P sauna solarium gymnasium
ℙ English & Continental **V** ✿ ⚹ Lunch fr£11.50&alc Dinner
fr£15.75&alc Last dinner 10pm
Credit Cards 1 2 3 5

★★61% **Swan Revived** High St MK16 8AR ☎(0908)610565
Telex no 826801 FAX (0908) 210995
*This family-run commercial hotel, recently upgraded to provide
comfortable accommodation in adequately furnished, well-
equipped rooms, offers a friendly, informal atmosphere and helpful
service; limited public areas include a well appointed restaurant
featuring an à la carte menu.*
42⇨ℝ(2fb)1 ☰ CTV in 40 bedrooms ® **T** sB&B⇨ℝ£25-£55
dB&B⇨ℝ£38-£65 ♬
Lift ℂ CTV 15P 3🅿
ℙ English & Continental **V** ✿ ᴴ Lunch £8.95-£16alc Dinner
£9.50-£16alc Last dinner 10pm
Credit Cards 1 2 3 5 £

★★★

*The* **Kings Hotel**

👑 Ideal location in town centre, opposite train station and minutes from exit 26 of M4.
👑 47 luxurious en suite bedrooms with colour &
satellite TV, radio & direct dial telephone, tea
& coffee making facilities, hair drier, trouser
press. Special weekend breaks available on
request.
👑 Elegant lounge bar and Egon Ronay recommended restaurant with hot carvery, cold table
& extensive à la carte menu.
👑 A range of five function suites for conference
meetings & banquets to hold 2-600 people.
**A genuine warm & friendly welcome awaits you.**

**High St., Newport, Gwent NP9 1QU**
**Tel: (0633) 842020 Telex: 497330**
**Fax: (0633) 244667**

**N**

★★

**THE
PRIORY
COUNTRY HOTEL**

**High Street, Caerleon, Gwent.
Telephone: 0633 421241**

The Priory Hotel is set in its own beautiful
grounds, backing on to open countryside.
The 24 bedrooms all have en-suite bathrooms and/or showers, colour television,
radio and tea & coffee making facilities.
Video films shown nightly. Room service
is available on request.

We specialise in catering for wedding
receptions, garden parties, banquets and
private parties. Details of suggested menus
are available at reception and we are always
available to discuss your individual requirements.

★★★★

*THE*
*Celtic Manor*
*HOTEL*

**Coldra Woods, Newport, Gwent
(M4 - Junction 24)
Tel: Newport 413000**

★ 75 elegant comfortable rooms, all with bath,
colour TV, radio, 24 hour room service.
★ Special weekend-break rates.
★ Two luxurious restaurants and two intimate bars.
★ Conference and Banqueting up to 300.
★ Impeccable service in this beautifully restored
Manor House.
★ Heated indoor pool, sauna, solarium, multi gym.
★ Welsh Chef of the Year and Restaurant of the Year
(Gwent).

**NEWQUAY Cornwall & Isles of Scilly** Map **02** SW86

See **Town Plan Section**

★★★ 60% **Barrowfield** Hillgrove Rd TR7 2QY ☎(0637)878878 FAX (0637) 879490

*Spacious and modern, this hotel is in a residential area, yet within walking distance of the town centre and beaches. Bedrooms offer good facilities for both holidaymakers and business guests and the table d'hôte menu offers a choice of dishes in the restaurant. There are good leisure facilities.*

81⇌⌒(18fb)11⊞ CTV in all bedrooms ® **T** sB&B⇌⌒£42 dB&B⇌⌒£84 (incl dinner) ⊟

Lift ☾ CTV 34P 16⌂ CFA ⊡(heated) ⌓(heated) snooker sauna solarium gymnasium *xmas*

☋ French **V** ♁ ⌒ Sunday Lunch £7.50 Dinner £11&alc Last dinner 8.30pm

Credit Cards [1] [3]

★★★ 60% **Hotel Bristol** Narrowcliff TR7 2PQ ☎(0637)875181 FAX (0637) 879347

*Spaciously comfortable public rooms and well-equipped bedrooms of various sizes are offered at this hotel, which occupes a fine position on the Promenade. Service combines friendliness and skill throughout.*

86rm(66⇌)(18fb) CTV in all bedrooms **T** S% sB&B£35-£37 sB&B⇌£41-£46 dB&B£59-£66 dB&B⇌£68-£82 ⊟

Lift ☾ CTV 100P 5⌂ (£3.50 daily) CFA ⊡(heated) snooker sauna solarium *xmas*

**V** ♁ ⌒ Lunch fr£8.50 Dinner fr£14 Last dinner 8.30pm

Credit Cards [1] [2] [3] [5]

★★★ 60% **Edgcumbe** Narrowcliff TR7 2RR ☎(0637)872061 FAX (0637) 879490

*Set near the town centre, but offering some good sea views, this modern hotel provides extensive indoor and outdoor leisure facilities for the whole family. Simply appointed bedrooms are well equipped, guests can relax in either the lively bar and ballroom or some quieter lounge areas, and the restaurant features both table d'hôte and à la carte menus.*

85rm(65⇌19⌒)(43fb)2⊞ CTV in all bedrooms ® **T** sB&B⇌⌒£27.60-£35.65 dB&B⇌⌒£55.20-£71.30 (incl dinner) ⊟

Lift ☾ CTV 70P ⊡(heated) ⌓(heated) snooker sauna solarium games room whirlpool ⌂ *xmas*

**V** ♁ ⌒ Dinner £10 Last dinner 8.30pm

Credit Cards [1] [3]

★★★ 60% **Euro** Esplanade Rd, Pentire TR7 1PS ☎(0637)873333 FAX (0637) 878717

*This modern resort hotel is in an elevated position above Fistral Beach. The bedrooms are clean and comfortable, with en suite facilites, direct dial telephones and remote control colour televisions. The public areas have recently been completely refurbished, and an excellent range of leisure facilities, including indoor and outdoor pools, disco and créche, is available. A simple table d'hôte menu is offered in the spacious dining room.*

78rm(66⇌10⌒)(39fb) CTV in all bedrooms ® **T** ✳ sB&B⇌⌒£24-£44 dB&B⇌⌒£44-£84 (incl dinner) ⊟

Lift ☾ 34P ⊡(heated) ⌓(heated) sauna solarium games room ⌂ *xmas*

**V** ♁ ⌒

Credit Cards [1] [3]

**See advertisement in colour section**

★★★ 60% ***Hotel Mordros*** 4 Pentire Av TR7 1PA ☎(0637)876700

*This purpose-built hotel is in an elevated position overlooking Fistral Beach. The bedrooms are spacious and simply furnished, and the staff provide a friendly and relaxed service.*

30⇌⌒(10fb) CTV in all bedrooms ® ✗

Lift CTV P ⌓(heated) sauna solarium gymnasium ♫

☋ English & Continental ♁ ⌒

★★★ 60% **Trebarwith** Island Estate TR7 1BZ ☎(0637)872288 Closed Jan-27 Mar & 3 Nov-Dec

*Overlooking the bay from a particularly fine position, this traditional hotel offers accommodation in a mixture of bedrooms; there are wide open-plan lounge areas and a good indoor swimming pool.*

42⇌⌒(8fb)4⊞ CTV in all bedrooms ® **T** ✗ (ex guide dogs) sB&B⇌⌒£27-£39.50 dB&B⇌⌒£46-£79 (incl dinner)

☾ CTV 40P ✲ ⊡(heated) ♩ snooker sauna solarium spa bath video theatre games room ♫ ⌂

**V** ♁ ⌒ Bar Lunch £1-£5 Dinner £10-£12&alc Last dinner 8.30pm

Credit Cards [1] [3]

★★★ 57% ***Kilbirnie*** Narrowcliff TR7 2RS ☎(0637)875155

*Occupying a commanding position overlooking the bay, this owner-managed hotel offers spacious, comfortable public areas and simply-appointed, but well-equipped bedrooms. Additional facilities include indoor and outdoor swimming pools.*

74⇌⌒(17fb) CTV in all bedrooms ®

Lift ☾ ⊞ CTV 60P 8⌂ ⌓(heated) snooker sauna solarium ♫ ♁ ⌒

Credit Cards [1] [3]

★★★ 54% **Riviera** Lusty Glaze Rd TR7 3AA ☎(0637)874251 Telex no 42513

*Good interesting food is a feature of this comfortable, proprietor-run cliff top hotel.*

50⇌⌒(9fb) CTV in all bedrooms **T** sB&B⇌⌒£34.75-£41.75 dB&B⇌⌒£65-£79.50 ⊟

Lift ☾ CTV 60P CFA ⌓(heated) squash snooker sauna ⌂ *xmas*

☋ English & Continental **V** ♁ ⌒ Lunch fr£7.50 Dinner fr£12.50 Last dinner 8.30pm

Credit Cards [1] [2] [3]

★★ 68% **Water's Edge** Esplanade Rd, Pentire TR7 1QA ☎(0637)872048

Closed Nov-Apr

*Situated overlooking the famous Fistral Beach, this hotel is ideal for surfers. Vera and Les Semke run this mainly holiday hotel on personal lines, in a friendly manner. Bedrooms are comfortable, coordinated and well equipped. The refurbished dining room is long and narrow and well appointed. Care is taken with the table d'hôte dinner menu. Fresh ingredients are used, to prepare the imaginative food prepared by the young chef.*

20rm(12⇌5⌒)(2fb)1⊞ CTV in all bedrooms ® **T** ✗ (ex guide dogs) sB&B£27.50-£42 dB&B⇌⌒£55-£84 (incl dinner) ⊟

18P ⊞

☋ English & French **V** Dinner £11.95 Last dinner 8pm

Credit Cards [1] [3] £

★★ 64% **Philema** 1 Esplanade Rd, Pentire TR7 1PY ☎(0637)872571 FAX (0637) 873188

Closed Nov-Feb

*Located only a short walk from Fistral Beach, and looking across the golf course to the distant coastline, a relaxed, comfortable, family holiday hotel with a convivial atmosphere represents excellent value for money.*

37rm(32⇌⌒)(24fb)1⊞ CTV in all bedrooms ® **T** ✳ sB&Bfr£21 sB&B⇌⌒fr£22 dB&Bfr£42 dB&B⇌⌒fr£44 (incl dinner) ⊟

34P ⊞ ⊡(heated) sauna solarium table tennis pool table jacuzzi *xmas*

☋ English & Continental **V** ♁ ⌒ Bar Lunch £1-£3 High tea £1.50-£4 Dinner £5-£7.50 Last dinner 7.30pm

Credit Cards [1] [3]

★★ 63% **Corisande Manor** Riverside Av, Pentire TR7 1PL (Exec Hotel) ☎(0637)872042

Closed 14 Oct-11 May

*Designed by a ship's surgeon in late Victorian times, and peacefully situated overlooking National Trust land from three acres of garden which lead down to the estuary, this comfortable,*

*relaxing, personally-run hotel offers a varied menu and good value for money.*
19rm(4⇥2⬆11⬥)(3fb) CTV in all bedrooms ⓇⓈ sB&B£15-£21 sB&B⇥⬥£16.50-£22 dB&B£30-£42 dB&B⇥⬥£33-£44 ▯
19P ⚙ ✿ solarium croquet putting green outdoor chess nc3yrs
Ⓖ English, French & Italian ✿ ⬛ Bar Lunch £2.50-£7 Dinner £10 Last dinner 8pm
Credit Cards ①③

★★60% *Cross Mount* 58-60 Church St, St Columb Minor
TR7 3EX ☎(0637)872669
Closed 1 wk New Year
*Dating from the 17th century, this small family-run hotel retains some original features, but offers modern standards of accommodation. The attractive beamed restaurant has a pleasant atmosphere and provides table d'hôte and à la carte menus.*
12rm(4⇥2⬥)(3fb) CTV in all bedrooms Ⓡ ✖
CTV 10P ⚙
Ⓖ English & French V ✿ Last dinner 9.45pm
Credit Cards ①③

★★59% *Minto House* 38 Pentire Crescent, Pentire TR7 1PU
☎(0637)873227
*Situated on a sloping site, overlooking the channel estuary, this hotel provides a relaxed atmosphere. An all weather bowling green has been constructed, and is in a delightful setting. The bar lounge has been enlarged in a nautical theme, and there is entertainment during the season. In the restaurant, there is a simple table d'hôte menu, with an extensive array of sweets.*
40⇥⬥Annexe5⇥⬥(14fb) CTV in all bedrooms Ⓡ T
40P ✿ ⌂(heated) ♪ sauna solarium dinghy, windsurfing ♫
Ⓖ English & Continental V ✿ ⬛ Last dinner 8pm
Credit Cards ①③

# *Philema* ★★
# *Hotel*

PENTIRE·NEWQUAY·CORNWALL
Tel: (0637) 872571   Fax: (0637) 873188
Resident Proprietor: Jim Nettleton

A family Hotel gloriously situated in its own grounds, 150 yards from Fistral beach, 31 bedrooms and 6 apartments enjoying superb views of beach and golf course and all with excellent facilities.
* Indoor heated pool * Sauna * Solarium * Spa Bath * Full Central Heating * Laundry Room * Coffee shop with sun patio open all day * Excellent food and wines * Ideal for short breaks.

# *Kilbirnie Hotel* ★★★

## Narrowcliff,
## Newquay,
## Cornwall TR7 2RS
## Telephone:
## Newquay (0637) 875155

### *A luxury hotel for all the family*

The hotel occupies one of the finest positions in Newquay, where you can enjoy a really relaxing holiday with the accent on comfort and attention to detail. Particular care has been taken in choosing the furnishings, decor and colour schemes, from the bedrooms to public rooms. All the bedrooms have colour television with video and en suite facilities, central heating, radio, shaver point and telephone. Family rooms have baby listening service. Heated indoor & outdoor swimming pool, sauna and solarium plus Games Room with full size snooker table and pool table are all available for your relaxation. Entertainment during the high season provides enjoyment for all the family.

**★★59% Porth Veor Manor House** Porthway TR7 3LW
☎(0637)873274
Closed Nov
*The John family have created a relaxed holiday atmosphere at this quietly situated hotel overlooking Porth Beach. Accommodation is simply furnished and decorated and meals are freshly prepared.*
16⇨♪(3fb) CTV in all bedrooms ® sB&B⇨♪£24-£31 dB&B⇨♪£48-£62 (incl dinner) ♬
48P ♨ ✿ ♪ (grass) putting
♀ International V ♦ ♫ ⚡ S% Sunday Lunch fr£5.95 Dinner £6.95-£10.15&alc Last dinner 9pm
Credit Cards ① ③

**★★58% Tremont** Pentire Av TR7 1PB ☎(0637)872984
Closed end Nov-Feb (ex Xmas-New Years eve)
*Overlooking Fistral Beach from its elevated position, a large, busy coaching hotel with cheerfully obliging staff provides well-equipped basic bedrooms and simple, wholesome meals; leisure facilities are good and there is a children's play room.*
55rm(26⇨24♪)(25fb) CTV in all bedrooms ® T ✱
sB&B⇨♪£25-£35 dB&B⇨♪£50-£70 (incl dinner) ♬
Lift 60P ✿ ▣(heated) ♪ (hard) squash snooker sauna solarium gymnasium putting table tennis ♬ ♨ *xmas*
♦ ♫
Credit Cards ① ③

**★★57% Cedars** Mount Wise TR7 2BA ☎(0637)874225
Closed Dec-Mar (ex Xmas)
*This family-run hotel commands some sea views from its elevated position in the centre of the town. Bedrooms are simple, but well equipped and public areas include a restaurant offering both table d'hôte and à la carte menus.*
36rm(15⇨16♪)(8fb) CTV in all bedrooms ® T
CTV 40P 2♨ ✿ ⌑(heated) sauna solarium gymnasium
♦ ♫ ⚡

**★★Beachcroft** Cliff Rd TR7 1SW ☎(0637)873022
Closed mid Oct-early Apr
*Large family hotel in its own gardens, close to the town centre and beach.*
69rm(29⇨25♪)(12fb) CTV in 59 bedrooms ® T S%
sB&B£21.21-£27.14 sB&B⇨♪£21.50-£27.42
dB&B£42.42-£54.85 dB&B⇨♪£42.85-£54.85 (incl dinner)
Lift ℂ CTV 80P ✿ ▣(heated) ⌑(heated) ♪ (hard) sauna solarium games room putting ♨
V ♦ ♫ Bar Lunch fr50p
Credit Cards ① ③ ⓔ

**★★Bewdley** 10 Pentire Rd TR7 1NX ☎(0637)872883
RS Nov-Mar
*On the outskirts of town overlooking Fistral Beach and the Gannel Estuary.*
29rm(8⇨19♪)(6fb) CTV in all bedrooms ®
CTV 40P ⌑(heated) ♬ ♨
♦
Credit Cards ① ③

**★★Cumberland** 8-10 Henver Rd TR7 3BJ ☎(0637)873025
FAX (0637) 873097
*This comfortable, modern hotel has a convivial atmosphere and is a short walk from the beach and town centre.*
33⇨♪(4fb) CTV in all bedrooms ® T ♬
CTV 38P ⌑(heated) solarium nc *xmas*
♦ ♫
Credit Cards ① ③

**★★Whipsiderry** Trevelgue Road, Porth TR7 3LY
☎(0637)874777
Closed Nov-Etr
*Friendly hotel offering good restaurant, comfort and excellent value.*
24rm(5⇨14♪)(5fb) CTV in all bedrooms ® sB&B£17-£23.50
sB&B⇨♪£19.50-£26 dB&B£34-£47 dB&B⇨♪£39-£52 ♬

CTV 30P ✿ ⌑(heated) sauna putting green pool table ♬ ♨
♀ English & Continental V ♦ ♫ Bar Lunch £2.25-£5.50
Dinner £7.50-£10.50 Last dinner 8pm
ⓔ

**★64% Trevone** Mount Wise TR7 2BP ☎(0637)873039
Closed 20 Oct-19 Apr
*Small family hotel situated close to town centre and beaches.*
32rm(27⇨3♪)(3fb) ® ✈ (ex guide dogs) ✱ sB&B£13-£20
sB&B⇨♪£14-£21 dB&B£26-£40 dB&B⇨♪£28-£42 ♬
CTV 20P ✿ games room
♀ English, French, Indian & Italian ♦ ✕ Bar Lunch £1-£3.50
Dinner £7.50-£8.50 Last dinner 7.30pm

**★58% Lowenva** 103 Mount Wise TR7 2BT ☎(0637)873569
Closed Nov-Feb
*A small, friendly, modern hotel which is centrally situated.*
18rm(12♪)(8fb) CTV in all bedrooms ®
CTV 15P ⌑(heated) pool table
V ♦ ♫ ✕ Last dinner 7pm
Credit Cards ① ③

---

**NEW QUAY Dyfed Map 02 SN35**

**★★60% Black Lion** SA45 9PT ☎(0545)560209
*Dating back to the early 19th century, and enjoying fine views over the harbour, this friendly inn has a character bar offering a choice of food. Bedrooms have been improved and equipped with modern amenities and there is a comfortable lounge.*
7rm(4⇨2♪)(3fb) CTV in all bedrooms ® ✱ sB&B£28-£40
sB&B⇨£28-£45 dB&B£38-£50 dB&B⇨♪£50-£60
CTV 40P ♨ ♬
♀ British & Continental V ♦ Bar Lunch £2.50-£8.50alc Dinner £9.25-£14.25 Last dinner 9.30pm
Credit Cards ① ② ③ ⑤

---

**NEWTON ABBOT Devon Map 03 SX87**

**★★61% Queens** Queen St TQ12 2EZ ☎(0626)63133 & 54106
FAX (0626) 55179
*Further good work by Tony and Fay Jelly in restoring this traditional hotel has resulted in more modern en suite facilities and upgrading of bedrooms. Wholesome Devon cooking is served in the restaurant with informal meals available in the bar.*
24rm(17⇨1♪)(1fb) CTV in all bedrooms ® T sB&B£32
sB&B⇨♪£42 dB&B£46 dB&B⇨♪£56 ♬
8P *xmas*
♀ English & French V ♦ ♫ Lunch £12.25&alc High tea £3.25
Dinner £12.25&alc Last dinner 9pm
Credit Cards ① ③ ⓔ
**See advertisement on page 521**

**★62% Hazlewood** 33A Torquay Rd TQ12 2LW ☎(0626)66130
*This cosy little hotel and restaurant stands only five minutes walk from the town centre and is also within easy reach of the station. Its well-appointed dining room features ecclesiastical panelling and offers imaginative menus, whilst bedrooms have been upgraded with the addition of more en suite facilities.*
7rm(1⇨4♪)(1fb) CTV in all bedrooms ® T ✱ sB&Bfr£25.50
sB&B⇨♪fr£33 dB&Bfr£37.50 dB&B⇨♪fr£44 ♬
6P
♀ English & French V ♦ ♫ Lunch £4.95-£7.95 Dinner £5.95-£8.25&alc Last dinner 8pm
Credit Cards ① ③ ⓔ
**See advertisement on page 521**

---

# BLACK LION HOTEL ★★

## New Quay, Dyfed, Wales
## Tel: 0545 560209

New Quay, Dyfed famous for its boating, fishing and resident dolphin population is ideal for that family holiday or long restful weekend away.

The Black Lion Hotel overlooking Cardigan Bay is 5 mins away from the safe sandy beach and harbour.

Comfortable rooms mostly en-suite, all with colour television and tea or coffee making facilities. Olde-worlde bar, where Dylan Thomas was a regular. Good food and well stocked cellars. Private car park.

# Cumberland Hotel   AA ★★

8 Henver Road, Newquay,
Cornwall TR7 3BJ
Telephone (0637) 873025
Fax: (0637) 873097

A bright, modern family run hotel, 34 bedrooms all with colour TV, tea making facilities, telephone, radio, intercom and en suite. Heated outside pool and sun patio. Large ballroom and cocktail bar. Entertainment nightly during main season. Two large car parks. Open all year, including Christmas. Modern sequence dance tours and bowls tours catered for.

**Please send for full colour brochure to Mrs Marion Faulkner.**

---

### AA ★★
# Whipsiderry Hotel

**TREVELGUE ROAD, PORTH,
NEWQUAY, CORNWALL, TR7 3LY
Telephone: (0637) 874777**

Overlooking Porth beach and standing in its own grounds (approx 2½ acres) this hotel has breathtaking views of both sea and country. A very attractive lounge bar and a heated swimming pool set in the most beautiful surroundings. We serve a 6 course dinner with choice of menu. Bar snacks available.

★ Heated swimming pool ★ Full central heating ★ Detached launderette ★ Licensed for residents ★ Excellent and varied cuisine ★ All rooms en suite with tea making facilities ★ Putting green. Detached American Pool Room ★ Colour TV, radio and intercom all rooms ★ Entertainments.

*Ashley Courtenay recommended*

# Porth Veor Manor

### AA★★ ETB ♚♚♚
**A Family run Country House Hotel**

One of the finest positions on the North Cornish Coast. With Panoramic Views from all rooms. Two acres of garden and private path to beach. All rooms Ensuite, Colour TV and full central heating.
High Class Restaurant offering a choice of superb food with table d'hôte and à la Carte menu.
9 Hole Putting Green. Grass Tennis Court.
**Special Autumn, Spring & Winter Breaks**
**PORTH VEOR MANOR HOTEL**
PORTH WAY, PORTH BEACH
NR. NEWQUAY, CORNWALL TR7 3LW
**TELEPHONE (0637) 873274**

## Newton Ferrers - Newtown

**NEWTON FERRERS** Devon Map **02** SX54

★★✿70% *Court House* Court Rd PL8 1AQ (Exec Hotel)
☎Plymouth(0752)872324
Closed 24 Dec-15 Jan
*Fine, creeper-clad Georgian hotel combining modern facilities with comfort and character. Owned and run by Alan and Mary Ann Gilchrist, with friendly service complemented by the latter's imaginative cooking.*
10⇝1♨ CTV in all bedrooms ® T
20P ⬟ ❀ ⊒(heated) croquet nc8yrs
♀ British & French **V** ✿ ⏒ Last dinner 9pm
Credit Cards 1 3

                    **See advertisement under PLYMOUTH**

**NEWTON-LE-WILLOWS** Merseyside Map **07** SJ59

★★60% *Kirkfield* 2/4 Church St WA12 9SU ☎(09252)28196 & 20489
*Standing on the A49 opposite the church, a friendly hotel offers well equipped bedrooms, most having en suite facilities.*
16⇝♠(1fb)1♨ CTV in all bedrooms ® ✖ (ex guide dogs) CTV 50P
✿ ⏒
Credit Cards 1

★★57% **The Pied Bull** 58 High St WA12 9SH
☎Warrington(0925)224549
*A friendly public house with well equipped bedrooms and a spacious public bar, situated in the centre of the busy High Street of this Merseyside town.*
11rm(2⇝5♠)Annexe7⇝ CTV in all bedrooms ® T ✖
sB&B£27.50 sB&B⇝♠£35 dB&B£42.50 dB&B⇝♠£48 ⊟
CTV 45P 2🏎 ♫
**V** ✿ ⏒ ⊬ Lunch £3.25-£10&alc High tea £4.50 Dinner £6.50-£18alc Last dinner 9.15pm
Credit Cards 1 3

**NEWTON POPPLEFORD** Devon Map **03** SY08

★★66% **Coach House Hotel** Southerton EX11 1SE
☎Colaton Raleigh(0395)68577 FAX (0395) 68946
Closed 2-31 Jan
*In a rural situation and within 2.5 acres of landscaped gardens lies this personally-run small country house hotel and restaurant, tastefully converted from the coach house of a former country estate. Stylish bedrooms are well-equipped and comfortable with some nice personal touches whilst good cooking standards prevail in the restaurant.*
6⇝♠2♨ CTV in all bedrooms ® T ✖ (ex guide dogs) ❀
sB&B⇝♠£29-£39 dB&B⇝♠£48-£68
CTV 16P ⬟ ❀ nc14yrs *xmas*
♀ International **V** ⊬ Lunch £5.50-£6.50 Dinner £12.50&alc
Last dinner 9pm
Credit Cards 1 3 ⓔ

**NEWTON SOLNEY** Derbyshire Map **08** SK22

★★★52% **The Newton Park** DE15 0SS (Embassy)(Consort)
☎Burton-on-Trent(0283)703568 FAX (0283) 703214
*Set on the edge of a quiet village this hotel is a popular venue for business meetings and conferences. Bedrooms which have recently been refurbished offer a good range of modern facilities but some old rooms do not meet these standards and represent poor value.*
46⇝(1fb)⊬in 2 bedrooms CTV in all bedrooms ® T ❀
sB⇝£60-£70 dB⇝£70-£80 (room only) ⊟
Lift ( 150P ❀ *xmas*
♀ English & French **V** ✿ ⏒ Lunch £7.95&alc Dinner £10.95-£11.95 Last dinner 9.30pm
Credit Cards 1 2 3 4 5

**NEWTON STEWART** Dumfries & Galloway *Wigtownshire* Map **10** NX46

★★★★✿55% *Kirroughtree* Minnigaff DG8 8AN ☎(0671)2141
Closed 4 Jan-3 Feb
*This hotel, located in a most tranquil setting well within its own attractive grounds, is conveniently situated just off the A75. The bedrooms vary in size, and the dinner menu, although limited in range, offers dishes which are imaginative and very skilfully cooked and presented.*
20⇝♠Annexe2⇝♠(2fb) CTV in all bedrooms T
( 40P ⬟ ❀ bowls croquet pitch and putt nc10yrs
♀ French ✿ ⏒ ⊬ Last dinner 9.30pm
Credit Cards 1 2 3 5

★★★57% **Bruce** 88 Queen St DG8 6JL ☎(0671)2294
Telex no 934999
Closed Dec & Jan
*An informal, family-run hotel with friendly personal service from the proprietors and their young staff, offering guests enjoyable, freshly prepared meals. There is an attractive and comfortable lounge bar and some bedrooms have recently been redecorated.*
18⇝♠(2fb) CTV in all bedrooms ® T sB&B⇝♠£32-£35 dB&B⇝♠£52-£57 ⊟
20P ⬟ solarium gymnasium 👌
♀ English & French **V** ✿ Lunch £6-£12alc High tea £7-£13alc
Dinner £14.50-£16 Last dinner 8.30pm
Credit Cards 1 2 3 5

★★65% **Creebridge House** DG8 6NP (Consort) ☎(0671)2121
*Peacefully situated across the river from the town centre and surrounded by attractive gardens, this was once a shooting lodge for the Earls of Galloway. Now a pleasant country house hotel, it offers well equipped bedrooms of which those overlooking the gardens are the more spacious and comfortable, relaxing lounges and a lively bar, popular with locals, where enjoyable bar meals are served.*
17⇝♠(2fb) CTV in all bedrooms ® T ❀
sB&B⇝♠£29.50-£39.50 dB&B⇝♠£59-£69 ⊟
CTV 50P ❀ *xmas*
♀ Scottish & French **V** ✿ ⏒ Bar Lunch £3.95-£13.50alc
Dinner £13.50&alc Last dinner 8.30pm
Credit Cards 1 3 ⓔ

★★57% **Crown** 101 Queen St DG8 6JW ☎(0671)2727
*Neat and clean, if fairly modest, accommodation is provided in a listed building which stands beside the market on the eastern approach to the town, its pleasant bars well patronised by locals and visitors alike.*
10rm(4⇝1♠)(1fb) CTV in all bedrooms ® ✖ (ex guide dogs)
sB&B£17-£19 sB&B⇝♠£23-£25 dB&B£34-£38
dB&B⇝♠£38-£40
CTV 20P ♪
**V** ✿ ⏒
Credit Cards 1 3

**NEWTOWN** Powys Map **06** SO19

★★63% **Elephant & Castle** Broad St SY16 2BQ ☎(0686)626271
FAX (0686) 622123
RS 24-26 Dec
*A Severn-side hotel – the birthplace of the famous Welsh pioneer Robert Owen – has been further extended by the creation of eleven cosy, private, pine-furnished rooms in a beamed cottage which stands near the main building. Function facilities are extensive, public bars have been refurbished, and meals are well presented and enjoyable.*
25⇝♠Annexe11⇝♠(3fb) CTV in all bedrooms ® T ❀
sB&B⇝♠£35 dB&B⇝♠£50
( ⊞CTV 60P ♪
**V** ✿ ⏒ S% Lunch £7.70-£10 High tea £5-£7.50 Dinner £9-£16alc Last dinner 9.30pm
Credit Cards 1 2 3 5

NEWTOWN LINFORD  Leicestershire Map **04** SK 50

★★63%  *Johnscliffe Hotel & Restaurant* 73 Main St LE6 OAF
☎Markfield(0530)242228 & 243281
Closed 24 Dec-4 Jan
*Friendly proprietors and staff create a relaxing and informal*
*atmosphere at this village hotel which is convenient for the*
*motorway. Seven new bedrooms all offer modern en suite facilities.*
8rm(2⇌4♠)(1fb)3🖾 CTV in all bedrooms ® T
CTV 30P ✿
♥ English & French V ♥ ⊑ Last dinner 9.45pm
Credit Cards ⬚1 ⬚2 ⬚3 ⬚5

NOLTON HAVEN  Dyfed Map **02** SM81

★★60%  **Mariners Inn** SA62 3NH ☎Camrose(0437)710469
*Nestling in a beautiful cove within the Pembrokeshire National*
*Park this friendly inn provides compact and cosy bedrooms. Public*
*areas have recently been altered, a character bar and an à la carte*
*restaurant are now available. A good range of bar meals are also*
*served.*
14⇌♠1🖾 CTV in all bedrooms ® T ✱
sB&B⇌♠£25.95-£31.95 dB&B⇌♠£39.95-£53.95
70P ⋃ snooker ♣
♥ Welsh, English & French V ♥ ⅙ Sunday Lunch £7.95&alc
Dinner £8.95&alc Last dinner 9.30pm
Credit Cards ⬚1 ⬚3

**See advertisement on page 523**

Entries for red-star hotels are highlighted by a
tint panel. For a full list of these establishments
consult the Contents page.

**N**

## NORMAN CROSS Cambridgeshire Map 04 TL19

★★★ 62% **Crest** Great North Rd PE7 3TB (Trusthouse Forte)
☎Peterborough(0733)240209 Telex no 32576
FAX (0733) 244455

*This hotel offers a range of well-equipped accommodation which includes particularly good executive study rooms and the thoughtfully designed and decorated Lady Crest rooms. Though public areas are limited, a new leisure centre was due to open in the summer of 1990 and willing service throughout the hotel ensures guests' enjoyment of their stay.*

97⇌♠↖in 24 bedrooms CTV in all bedrooms ® 🅿
《 120P ❀ CFA 🖾(heated) sauna solarium gymnasium games room leisure centre *xmas*
V ✿ ⚌ ⊬
Credit Cards ①②③④⑤

## NORMANTON Leicestershire Map 08 SK84

★★★⚌ 72% **Normanton Park** LE15 8RP (1m E unclass road on south shore of Rutland Water) ☎Stamford(0780)720315
FAX (0780) 721086

*The hotel is situated on the south side of Rutland Water, 5 miles from Stanton and 6 miles from Oakham. Using the A606 follow signs for South Shore or Edith Weston then signs for Normanton Park. Converted from a magnificent coach house the hotel has modern accommodation with well-equipped bedrooms and a popular restaurant.*

8rm(6⇌1↖)Annexe8⇌(5fb) CTV in all bedrooms ® T ✱
sB&B£13 sB&B⇌↖£43-£55 dB&B£44 dB&B⇌↖£57-£66 🅿
CTV 60P ❀ sailing canoeing windsurfing
♀ English & French V ✿ ⚌ Lunch £11.75&alc High tea
£3.50-£5.80 Dinner £15-£17.50&alc Last dinner 10pm
Credit Cards ①②③⑤ ④

**See advertisement under OAKHAM**

## NORTHALLERTON North Yorkshire Map 08 SE39

★★★ 70% **Solberge Hall** Newby Wiske DL7 9ER (3.25m S off A167) (Best Western) ☎(0609)779191 FAX (0609) 780472

*A delightful country house hotel standing in ten acres of parkland offers accommodation in particularly well furnished bedrooms and the comfort of peaceful lounges; staff are friendly and helpful throughout, and the standard of cooking is good.*

30⇌(2fb)2📺 CTV in all bedrooms ® T ✱ S% sB&B⇌£62-£85
dB&B⇌£75-£83 🅿
100P ❀ snooker croquet clay pigeon shooting *xmas*
♀ English & French V ✿ ⚌ Lunch £10-£20alc Dinner £17&alc
Last dinner 9.30pm
Credit Cards ①②③⑤

★★★ 67% **Sundial** Darlington Rd DL6 2XF ☎(0609)780525
FAX (0609) 780491

*Modern and purpose-built, the hotel stands in three-and-a-half acres of grounds on the A167 a mile north of the town. Its particularly well-equipped bedroom accommodation, together with an elegant restaurant in which the imaginative range of dishes is competently cooked and efficiently served, makes it popular with a business clientèle. Some rooms have a separate sitting-room and the hotel is noted for its good value weekend packages.*

28⇌↖(8fb)⊬in 22 bedrooms CTV in all bedrooms ® T ✱
sB⇌↖£55 dB⇌↖£66-£110 (room only) 🅿
《 🍽 60P ❀ ♫
♀ English & French V ✿ ⚌ ⊬ Lunch fr£6.50 Dinner
fr£11.50&alc Last dinner 9.30pm
Credit Cards ①②③⑤

★★ 59% *The Golden Lion* Market Place DL7 8PP (Trusthouse Forte) ☎(0609)777411

*On the attractive main street of Northallerton, the Golden Fleece offers comfortable accommodation in bedrooms which are equipped to a good standard. The bar, lounge and restaurant are also comfortable.*

28rm(15⇌)⊬in 12 bedrooms CTV in all bedrooms ® T
CTV 60P
V ✿ ⚌ ⊬ Last high tea 6pm
Credit Cards ①②③④⑤

## NORTHAMPTON Northamptonshire Map 04 SP76

★★★★ 55% **Swallow** Eagle Dr NN4 0HW (off A5, between A428 & A508) (Swallow) ☎(0604)768700 Telex no 31562
FAX (0604) 769011

*Overlooking a lake from its position close to the southern ring road, just outside the town, a modern hotel with two restaurants, a leisure centre and very good business facilities (including excellent audio/visual aids) provides accommodation in bedrooms which are for the most part spacious and modern in style.*

122⇌↖⊬in 38 bedrooms CTV in all bedrooms ® T ✱
sB&B⇌↖fr£75 dB&B⇌↖fr£95 🅿
《 166P 🖾(heated) sauna solarium gymnasium jacuzzi steam room ♫
♀ French V ✿ ⚌ Lunch £11-£13&alc Dinner £13-£18.50&alc
Last dinner 10.30pm
Credit Cards ①②③⑤

★★★ 67% **Northampton Moat House** Silver Street, Town Centre NN1 2TA (Queens Moat) ☎(0604)22441
Telex no 311142 FAX (0604) 230614

*Rooms are attractive, comfortable and well equipped at this large, modern hotel in the centre of the town. Snacks and light meals are available throughout the day in 'Le Jardin' restaurant, with an imaginative à la carte menu in the evening. There is also a leisure centre, and extensive conference facilities are available.*

142⇌↖(4fb)⊬in 2 bedrooms CTV in all bedrooms ® T ✱
sB&B⇌↖£64.50 dB&B⇌↖£79.50 🅿
Lift 《 200P (£2.50) CFA sauna solarium gymnasium jacuzzi hairdresser
♀ English & French V ✿ ⚌ Lunch fr£10.50&alc Dinner
fr£12&alc Last dinner 10.30pm
Credit Cards ①②③④⑤

★★★ 63% **Westone Moat House** Ashley Way, Weston Favell NN3 3EA (3m E off A45) (Queens Moat) ☎(0604)406262
Telex no 312587 FAX (0604) 415023
Closed Xmas-New Years Day

*Built as a country house in 1914, this well-managed hotel on the edge of the town offers comfortable, well-equipped rooms, both in the main house and in the annexe. Staff are friendly and welcoming and the hotel is particularly popular with a business clientele and for conferences.*

30⇌Annexe36⇌(3fb)⊬in 15 bedrooms CTV in all bedrooms ® sB&B⇌↖£64 dB&B⇌↖£74 🅿
Lift 《 CTV 100P 2🚗 (£5) ❀ sauna solarium gymnasium croquet putting *xmas*
♀ International V ✿ ⚌ S10% Lunch £9.50&alc Dinner
£10.50&alc Last dinner 9.45pm
Credit Cards ①②③⑤

**See advertisement on page 525**

★★★ 50% **Grand** Gold St NN1 1RE ☎(0604)250511
Telex no 311198 FAX (0604) 234534
62⇌↖(2fb) CTV in all bedrooms ® T sB&B⇌↖£50
dB&B⇌↖£60 🅿
Lift 《 70P 20🚗 CFA
V ✿ Lunch £4.50-£6 Dinner £10-£12&alc Last dinner 9.30pm
Credit Cards ①②③⑤ ④

★★ 69% *Lime Trees* 8 Langham Place, Barrack Rd NN2 6AA (from city centre follow sign A508 Leicester) (Inter-Hotels)
☎(0604)32188
Closed 25-26 Dec RS 27 Dec-New Year

*A very pleasant and popular hotel, just one mile from the centre of town. Rooms are well equipped and the standard of maintenance exceptional. The hotel continues to improve, to the credit of the*

▶

resident proprietors who, with their team of staff, offer genuine hospitality.
20rm(2⇆13♠)(2fb) CTV in all bedrooms ® ✖
CTV 20P 🚗
V 🛇 ⬚ Last dinner 9pm
Credit Cards ①②③⑤

★★ 64% *Thorplands Toby* Talavera Way, Round Spinney NN3 4RN (Toby) ☎(0604)494241
Closed 25, 26 Dec & 1 Jan
*Conveniently situated for the M1 and the town centre, this hotel offers comfortable well-equipped rooms in a modern accommodation block. The popular Mr Toby's Grill provides a good choice of meals in pleasant surroundings.*
30⇆(2fb)⚲in 8 bedrooms CTV in all bedrooms ® ✖
《 100P ❋ pool table
V 🛇 ⬚ ⚲ Last dinner 10.30pm
Credit Cards ①②③⑤

⏱**Travelodge** Upton Way NN5 6EG (A45, towards M1 junct 16) (Trusthouse Forte)
☎(0604)758395 Central res (0800) 850950
*On the A45 close to Northampton. Good value accommodation is provided in pleasant rooms, and meals are available throughout the day and evening at the adjacent Little Chef restaurant.*
40⇆♠(40fb) CTV in all bedrooms ® sB⇆♠£24
dB⇆♠£29.50 (room only)
《 40P 🚗
Credit Cards ①②③

✖**Vineyard** 7 Derngate NN1 1TU ☎(0604)33978
*This small French restaurant is within easy walking distance of the town centre. Don't be deterred by the ordinary-looking exterior – inside you will find a charmingly informal style, with attentive service and well-presented food of good flavour.*
Closed Sun & Mon
😋 English & French V 30 seats ❋ Lunch £8-£25alc Dinner £15-£25alc Last lunch 1.50pm Last dinner 10.10pm 𝒫
Credit Cards ①②③⑤

## NORTH BALLACHULISH Highland *Inverness-shire* Map **14** NN06

★★ 55% **Loch Leven** Onich PH33 6SA ☎Onich(08553)236 & 459
*Family run hotel on the shores of Loch Leven with magnificent views. Geared to the activity holidaymaker, with simply-appointed bedrooms and a good range of public areas including a childrens' room. Relaxed and friendly atmosphere, meals are good and imaginative, including a wide choice of bar meals available at lunchtimes and evenings.*
12rm(4⇆1♠)(2fb) CTV in 5 bedrooms sB&B£20-£24 dB&B£40-£48 dB&B⇆♠£46-£54
CTV 60P 🚗 ❋
😋 Scottish & Continental V 🛇 ⬚ Bar Lunch £3.50-£10alc Dinner £14-£17alc Last dinner 8.30pm
Credit Cards ①③

## NORTH BERWICK Lothian *East Lothian* Map **12** NT58

★★★ 64% **The Marine** Cromwell Rd EH39 4LZ (Trusthouse Forte) ☎(0620)2406 Telex no 72550 FAX (0620) 4480
*This popular golfing and conference hotel stands beside the championship golf links overlooking the Firth of Forth. Public rooms have been upgraded to a good standard, as have also most of the comfortable and well-equipped bedrooms.*
83⇆♠⚲in 20 bedrooms CTV in all bedrooms ® T S%
sB⇆♠£70-£75 dB⇆♠£80-£85 (room only) 🏳
Lift 《 200P 20🚗 ❋ CFA ⬚(heated) 𝒫 (hard) squash snooker sauna solarium ⚽ *xmas*
😋 International V 🛇 ⬚ ⚲ S% Lunch fr£7.50 Dinner £15.50-£17&alc Last dinner 9.30pm
Credit Cards ①②③④⑤

★★ 61% **Nether Abbey** 20 Dirleton Av EH39 4BQ ☎(0620)2802
*A family-run hotel which is quietly located on the outskirts of the town, with views over the Firth of Forth. At the time of our inspection, a programme of refurbishment was under way, the completed areas being very elegant and inviting.*
16rm(4⇆6♠)(5fb) CTV in all bedrooms ® T 🏳
CTV 40P ❋
V 🛇 Lunch £8.75&alc High tea £5.75 Dinner £14.50&alc Last dinner 8.30pm
Credit Cards ①③ ⓔ

★★ 56% *Point Garry* West Bay Rd EH39 4AW ☎(0620)2380
Closed Nov-Mar
*Popular with golfers, this family-run hotel overlooks the West Course and sea front. Some of the public areas have recently been refurbished and the modest bedrooms are gradually being improved.*
16rm(5⇆6♠)(6fb) CTV in all bedrooms ®
14P 🚗 snooker
😋 International V 🛇 ⬚ Last dinner 9pm

## NORTH FERRIBY Humberside Map **08** SE92

★★★ 67% **Crest Hotel-Hull** Ferriby High Rd HU14 3LG (Trusthouse Forte) ☎Hull(0482)645212 Telex no 592558
FAX (0482) 643332
RS Xmas & New Year
*Situated just off the M62/A63, the hotel is in a rural setting with views over the River Humber to the impressive Humber Bridge. Comfortable accommodation and interesting menus are complemented by warm, courteous service.*
102⇆(6fb)⚲in 20 bedrooms CTV in all bedrooms ® 🏳
《 120P ❋ CFA
😋 International V 🛇 ⬚ ⚲
Credit Cards ①②③④⑤

## NORTH HUISH Devon Map **03** SX75

★★⚐ **BROOKDALE HOUSE**
TQ10 9NR ☎Gara Bridge (054882)402 & 415
Closed 3-24 Jan

*This former rectory and country mansion is aptly named, as a lively little brook runs through its attractive wooded gardens. North Huish is somewhat off the beaten track, but close to Devon's most beautiful countryside and coast. Six of the bedrooms are in the main house, and another two in a cottage in the garden. All have been furnished and equipped with an emphasis on comfort and quality, with fresh flowers adding a welcoming touch. The comfortable lounge leads to a small bar-lounge which was once the gun-room and retains many of its original features. The table d'hôte menu offers some imaginative dishes, for example terrine of rabbit and pigeon breast with spiced apple butter, or medallions of local pork with a tomato and olive-oil fondue sauce garnished with peppers and onions. The cheeseboard, with its selection of local sheep and goat cheeses, is particularly interesting and the wine list carefully chosen. The atmosphere throughout the hotel is welcoming and personal – much to the credit of the proprietor, Charles Trevor-Roper.*
6⇆♠Annexe2⇆(2fb) CTV in all bedrooms ® T ✖
sB&B⇆♠£70-£75 dB&B⇆♠£75-£95 🏳
20P 🚗 ❋ nc10yrs *xmas*

✂ Dinner £24.50 Last dinner 9pm
Credit Cards ① ③

---

**NORTHIAM** East Sussex Map **05** TQ82

★★ **68% Hayes Arms** Village Green TN31 6NN (Best Western)
☎(0797)253142 & 253169
*This 15th-century farmhouse, skilfully extended in Georgian times, lies close to the 12th-century village church. Well-equipped bedrooms are individually furnished, mostly with antiques, and log burning inglenook fires complement the traditional, relaxing atmosphere. The standard of cooking is good and will satisfy most tastes.*
7⇄🅵1🏢 CTV in all bedrooms ® T ✗ (ex guide dogs) ✳
sB&B⇄🅵£35-£37 dB&B⇄🅵£55-£59
40P ✿ nc10yrs
V ✌ ⚓ Lunch £9.30-£15.50alc Dinner £9.30-£15.50alc Last dinner 9.30pm
Credit Cards ① ③

---

**NORTHLEACH** Gloucestershire Map **04** SP11

★ **63% Wheatsheaf** GL54 3EZ ☎Cotswold(0451)60244
*Relaxed and informal, this small hotel offers sound but simple accommodation with a good range of facilities; a comfortable dining room serves home-cooked meals based on local produce and there are cosy bars.*
9rm(2⇄5🅵)(1fb) CTV in 8 bedrooms TV in 1 bedroom ® ✳
sB&B£15 sB&B⇄🅵£25 dB&B£30 dB&B⇄🅵£40 🏳
20P 3🎝 🚗
V ✌ ⚓ Lunch £9.50-£14.75alc Dinner £9.50-£14.75alc Last dinner 9.30pm
Credit Cards ① ② ③ ⑤

---

**NORTHOP** Clwyd Map **07** SJ26

★★★🕍 **76% Soughton Hall** CH7 6AB (Welsh Rarebits)
☎(035286)811 Telex no 61267 FAX (035286) 382
Closed 1st 2 wks Jan
*This lovely old building, winner of an AA Best Newcomer Award in 1989, stands in landscaped grounds just over the Welsh border from Chester. It is run in very personal style by the Rodenhurst family, who have restored the rooms and installed modern comforts in a style true to the period and origins of the house. The two lounges and the state Dining Room are particularly pleasant and create the right atmosphere in which to enjoy Malcolm Wareham's imaginative cooking. Bedrooms and bathrooms are all spacious, well equipped and named after the style of their fittings – Mahogany, Panel, Tudor, Rosebud are self-explanatory – or their original use, hence Schoolroom and, alas, Cane Room – which is not named after the Rattan furniture it now contains.*
12⇄🅵1🏢 CTV in all bedrooms ® ✗ ✳ sB&B⇄🅵£80-£100
dB&B⇄🅵£92-£135 🏳
⊄ CTV 40P ✿ ♬ (hard) croquet nc12yrs *xmas*
V ✌ ⚓ ✂ Lunch £14.50 High tea fr£7.50 Dinner £19.50&alc
Last dinner 9.30pm
Credit Cards ① ② ③ ⓔ

---

**NORTHOP HALL** Clwyd Map **07** SJ26

★★★ **64% The Chequers Country House Hotel** Chester Rd
CH7 6HJ (Inter-Hotels) ☎Deeside(0244)816181
FAX (0244) 814661
*A country manor house in its own extensive grounds, popular for functions and business conferences, has recently undergone major refurbishment.*
27⇄🅵(2fb)1🏢✂in 2 bedrooms CTV in all bedrooms ® T
sB&B⇄🅵£45-£50 dB&B⇄🅵£60-£80 🏳
100P 2🎝 ✿ *xmas*

---

🍴 International V ✌ ⚓ ✂ Lunch fr£10.50&alc Dinner £14.50-£16.50&alc Last dinner 9.30pm
Credit Cards ① ② ③ ⑤ ⓔ
**See advertisement under MOLD**

---

◯**Travelodge** A55(Trusthouse Forte)
☎Central reservations (0800) 850950
Due to have opened autumn 1990
40⇄⅃

---

**NORTH QUEENSFERRY** Fife Map **11** NT18

★★★ **70% Queensferry Lodge** St Margaret's Head KY11 1HP
☎Inverkeithing(0383)410000 Telex no 727553
FAX (0383) 419708
*Modern and purpose-built, the hotel provides a choice of eating styles – formal, informal and coffee shop – which can all be recommended, tastefully decorated public areas and very comfortable, well appointed bedrooms. A friendly staff renders courteous service under the personal supervision of the owners.*
32⇄🅵 CTV in all bedrooms ® T ✳ sB&B⇄🅵£42.50
dB&B⇄🅵£47-£58 🏳
Lift ⊄ 130P ✿ *xmas*
🍴 Scottish & French V ✌ ⚓ ✂ Lunch £13-£18alc Dinner £13-£18alc Last dinner 10pm
Credit Cards ① ② ③

---

Hotels with a high percentage rating for quality are highlighted by a % across their gazetteer entry.

# WESTONE MOAT HOUSE★★★
### ASHLEY WAY, WESTON FAVELL, NORTHAMPTON NN3 3EA
### Telephone: 0604 406262

The Westone is a fine country house set in its own grounds, 10 minutes from the centre of Northampton and Junction 15 of the M1.
There are 66 luxury bedrooms with private bathroom, direct dial telephone, colour television with video channel, tea and coffee making facilities, hair dryer and trouser press.
The hotel has a locally renowned restaurant which offers an extensive à la carte menu. There is a comfortable lounge bar with a log fire overlooking the terrace and croquet lawn.
For extra relaxation there is a sauna, solarium and mini-gymnasium.
Parking is available for 100 cars.

**NORTH STOKE** Oxfordshire Map **04** SU68

★★★74% **Springs** Wallingford Rd OX9 6BE
☎Wallingford(0491)36687 Telex no 849794 FAX (0491) 36877
*In a peaceful, rural setting this country house has been further upgraded to provide comfortable, well-appointed accommodation. Some of the spacious bedrooms enjoy views of the lake, as does the restaurant which offers an interesting and varied menu of English and French cuisine. Service is professional and helpful.*
37⇨(4fb)2⊠ CTV in all bedrooms **T** ✗ S% sB&B⇨£70-£105 dB&B⇨£105-£130 ▤
( 130P ✲ ⛆(heated) ⚲ (hard) sauna croquet putting nc14yrs *xmas*
♡ English & French **V** ✧ ☕ Lunch fr£15&alc Dinner fr£25&alc Last dinner 10.15pm
Credit Cards [1] [2] [3] [4] [5]

**NORTH WALTHAM** Hampshire Map **04** SU54

★★62% **Wheatsheaf** RG25 2BB (on A30) (Lansbury)
☎Dummer(0256)398282 Telex no 859775 FAX (0256) 398253
*A Lansbury hotel complements spacious, comfortable and well-equipped bedrooms (contained mainly in a modern extension) by the old world charm of public areas furnished with country antiques, promoting friendly, relaxed service throughout.*
28⇨♠(1fb)1⊠ CTV in all bedrooms ® **T** sB&B⇨♠fr£71 dB&B⇨♠fr£85 ▤
( 70P ✲
✧ ☕ Lunch fr£11&alc Dinner fr£11&alc Last dinner 10.30pm
Credit Cards [1] [2] [3] [4] [5]

**NORTHWICH** Cheshire Map **07** SJ67

★★★63% ***Hartford Hall*** School Ln, Hartford CW8 1PW (2m SW off bypass A556) (Consort) ☎Hartford(0606)75711
*A 16th-century country mansion standing in its own extensive grounds with a small lake, just off the A556 Northwich by-pass. Bedrooms are well appointed and the public rooms are in character with the historical style of the house.*
21⇨(1fb) CTV in all bedrooms ®
( CTV 50P ✲ ⌂
**V** ✧
Credit Cards [1] [2] [3] [5]

★★68% **Friendly Floatel** London Rd CW9 5HD (Consort)
☎(0606)44443 FAX (0606) 42592
*A first in the UK, this floating hotel has been built over the river and a very successful concept it is. The bedrooms are modern and well equipped and there is a carvery restaurant which, not surprisingly, overlooks the river.*
60⇨⚟in 10 bedrooms CTV in all bedrooms ® **T** S% sB&B⇨£49-£58.50
dB&B⇨£58.50-£66 Continental breakfast ▤
( 40P
♡ English & French **V** ✧ ☕ ⚟ Lunch fr£7.50 Dinner £11.75-£14.25&alc Last dinner 9.30pm
Credit Cards [1] [2] [3] [5] £

★★64% **Woodpecker** London Rd CW9 8EG (County Inns)
☎(0606)45524 Telex no 668025 FAX (0606) 330350
Closed 25 Dec (pm)
*This well-furnished hotel, situated just off the bypass road, has bedrooms in a modern extension block.*
33⇨♠(3fb) CTV in all bedrooms ® **T** ✱ S% sB&B⇨♠£50-£59 dB&B⇨♠£65-£78 ▤
( 100P ✲
♡ English & French **V** ✧ ☕ S% Lunch £7-£8&alc Dinner £11-£14&alc Last dinner 9.45pm
Credit Cards [1] [2] [3] [5]

★62% **Blue Cap** 520 Chester Rd, Sandiway CW8 2DN (Berni/Chef & Brewer) ☎(0606)883006
*Standing on the A556 three miles south west of Northwich, and well placed for visiting Chester and the surrounding countryside, this hotel features well appointed bedrooms and an attractive restaurant.*
12⇨♠1⊠ CTV in all bedrooms ® ✗ (ex guide dogs) sB&B⇨♠£42-£45 dB&B⇨♠£53 ▤
200P ⛟ ♫
**V** ✧ ⚟ Lunch £8-£15alc Dinner £8-£15alc Last dinner 9.30pm
Credit Cards [1] [2] [3] [5]

**NORTON** Shropshire Map **07** SJ70

★★76% **Hundred House** Bridgnorth Rd TF11 9EE (on A442 6m N of Bridgnorth) (Exec Hotel) ☎(095271)353
FAX (095271) 355
*A uniquely styled village inn on the outskirts of Telford features bedrooms which are strikingly decorated and quite luxurious. Its restaurant is very well patronised, and reservation is recommended.*
9⇨(5fb) CTV in all bedrooms ® **T** sB&B⇨£59-£65 dB&B⇨£65-£75 ▤
40P ✲
♡ English & French ✧ ☕
Credit Cards [1] [2] [3] £

**See advertisement under TELFORD**

**NORWICH** Norfolk Map **05** TG20

★★★73% **Norwich Airport Ambassador** Cromer Rd NR6 6JA
☎(0603)410544 FAX (0603) 789935
*This newly built hotel is conveniently situated on the A140 near to Norwich Airport and within easy reach of the city centre. Rooms are spacious, comfortable and equipped with excellent modern facilities. Its attractions include an impressive leisure complex, conference and banqueting facilities and a restaurant which is already popular in the area both for its à la carte menu and the carvery.*
108⇨♠3⊠⚟in 12 bedrooms CTV in all bedrooms ® **T** ✱ S10% sB&B⇨♠£60-£72.50 dB&B⇨♠£60-£72.50
Lift ( 320P ⛆(heated) sauna solarium gymnasium *xmas*
♡ English & French **V** ✧ ☕ ⚟ S10% Lunch £7.95-£12.95&alc Dinner £7.95-£12.95&alc Last dinner 10.30pm
Credit Cards [1] [2] [3] [4] [5]

★★★68% **Post House** Ipswich Rd NR4 6EP (Trusthouse Forte)
☎(0603)56431 Telex no 975106 FAX (0603) 506400
*Consistently high standards are maintained by an hotel set beside the A140 Ipswich road on the outskirts of the city. Its well-furnished family rooms and the Health and Fitness Centre make it attractive to holidaymaker and business traveller alike.*
116⇨⚟in 24 bedrooms CTV in all bedrooms ® **T** sB⇨£72 dB⇨£83 (room only) ▤
( 200P ✲ CFA ⛆(heated) sauna solarium gymnasium health & fitness centre *xmas*
♡ English & French **V** ✧ ☕ ⚟ Lunch £7.50-£9.50&alc High tea fr£6.50 Dinner fr£13.95&alc Last dinner 10pm
Credit Cards [1] [2] [3] [4] [5]

★★★65% **Sprowston Manor** Wroxham Road, Sprowston NR7 8RP (2m NE A1151) (Best Western) ☎(0603)410871
Telex no 975356 FAX (0603) 423911
*On the A1151 Wroxham road just north of Norwich, this fine old manor house has been considerably extended and improved and is popular with both businessmen and tourists alike. Further bedrooms and a leisure centre are under construction.*
25⇨♠Annexe14⇨♠(1fb)2⊠ CTV in all bedrooms ® **T** sB&B⇨♠£60-£75 dB&B⇨♠£75-£100 ▤
( 120P ✲ CFA croquet *xmas*

N

♥ English & French **V** ☼ ⬚ Lunch £9-£11&alc Dinner £11.95-£13.95&alc Last dinner 10pm
Credit Cards ① ② ③ ⑤ ⓔ

★★★63% **Hotel Nelson** Prince of Wales Rd NR1 1DX
☎(0603)760260 Telex no 975203 FAX (0603) 620008
*Well situated alongside the river, across from the railway station and within walking distance of the city centre, this purpose built hotel offers a choice of bar and restaurants, all aptly named in nautical terms. The Trafalgar Restaurant offers a fine view over the river, and has a varied menu – meats and fish a speciality, smoked on the premises. Accommodation is very well equipped and thoughtfully designed, appealing to both business people and holidaymakers alike.*
121⇄♠(24fb)3⬚⅄in 4 bedrooms CTV in all bedrooms ® T
✕ (ex guide dogs) ⊟
Lift ℂ 119P 30⬛ ✿ sauna *xmas*
**V** ☼ S% Lunch £11.95-£12.50&alc
Credit Cards ① ② ③ ④ ⑤

★★★63% **Norwich Sport Village** Drayton High Rd, Hellesdon
NR6 5DU ☎(0603)788898 FAX (0603) 406845
56⇄♠(2fb) CTV in all bedrooms ® T ✳ S%
sB&B⇄♠£35-£55 dB&B⇄♠£50-£64 ⊟
Lift ℂ P ✿ ⊑(heated) ℛ (hard) squash snooker sauna solarium gymnasium jacuzzi ⚬ *xmas*
**V** ☼ ⬚
Credit Cards ① ② ③ ⑤

★★★62% **Maids Head** Tombland NR3 1LB (Queens Moat)
☎(0603)761111 Telex no 975080 FAX (0603) 613688
*Historic hotel with 13th-century features, in the shadow of the cathedral. There are three bars and many lounge areas. Some rooms have recently been refurbished.*
81⇄♠(2fb)1⬚ CTV in all bedrooms ® T sB&B⇄♠£73-£81 dB&B⇄♠£86-£91 ⊟

▶

# Park Farm Hotel & Restaurant

**Hethersett, Norwich, NR9 3DL**
**Tel: Norwich (0603) 810264 FAX: 0603 812104**

Attractive family-run hotel set in beautiful landscaped gardens off the A11. 35 individually furnished bedrooms all with private bath or shower, colour TV, telephone and tea-making facilities. A superb selection of executive rooms, with four poster beds and whirlpool baths – ideal for honeymooners. First class restaurant, sauna, solarium, hard tennis court and all year indoor heated swimming pool. Special weekend rates. Open all year.

Ashley Courtenay, Egon Ronay, AA ★★★

# BARNHAM BROOM HOTEL

**• CONFERENCE AND LEISURE CENTRE •**
★★★
**NORWICH, NORFOLK NR9 4DD**
**Telephone: (060545) 393. Fax: (060545) 8224**
**Telex: 975711**

Situated 8 miles west of Norwich and set in 250 acres the complex incorporates two 18 hole golf courses, Squash/Tennis Courts, Swimming Pool, Fitness Gym, Sauna, Solarium, Hairdressing Salon and Beautician. 52 Bedrooms all with private bath/shower, colour TV, radio, direct dial telephone, tea/coffee making facilities. A venue attracting sports enthusiasts, holidaymakers and business persons requiring after meeting relaxation. Lunches from £7.50, Table d'hôte dinner £12.00.

**N**

## Fri⊙ndly
# NORTHWICH

Friendly Floatel, London Road,
Northwich, Cheshire CW9 5HD.
**AA ★★**
· Staterooms ·
· Free Quayside Parking · Mini-gym ·
The U.K's first floating hotel, situated in the heart of beautiful Cheshire, close to the M6, makes a memorable stop over point for business or pleasure.
***FOR RESERVATIONS* (office hours)**
***TELEPHONE FREEPHONE***

# 0800 591910

***or call direct on 0606 44443***
***FAX: 0606 42596***

## Fri⊙ndly
**HOTELS PLC**

IT'S BEST TO STAY FRIENDLY

Lift ⟨ 80P 20🛏 CFA *xmas*
🍴 English & French V ✵ 🍷 ✂ Lunch £9.25-£11.50alc Dinner
£12.75&alc Last dinner 9.45pm
Credit Cards ①②③⑤

★★★62% **Hotel Norwich** 121-131 Boundary Rd NR3 2BA (Best
Western) ☎(0603)787260 Telex no 975337 FAX (0603) 400466
*Ideally placed beside the A47 ring road north of the city, the hotel
offers well-equipped, purpose-built accommodation with a pleasant,
friendly restaurant and bar. High standards are maintained
throughout, ample car parking is available and there are good
conference/banqueting facilities.*
102⇔🛏(16fb)in 5 bedrooms CTV in all bedrooms ⓇT
🐕 (ex guide dogs) ✳ sB&B⇔🛏£57-£62 dB&B⇔🛏£67-£72 🍴
⟨ 225P CFA *xmas*
🍴 International V ✵ 🍷 Lunch £5.50-£16.95alc Dinner
£11&alc Last dinner 10pm
Credit Cards ①②③⑤

★★★60% **Friendly** 2 Barnard Rd, Bowthorpe NR5 9JB
(Consort) ☎(0603)741161 Telex no 975557 FAX (0603) 741500
*West of the city centre, on the A47, this modern purpose-built hotel
has open-plan public areas leading to a carvery/buffet style
restaurant offering a variety of freshly prepared dishes. The
bedrooms are simply furnished in light woods and pastels, with
'Premier Plus' rooms particularly well equipped with the business
guest in mind.*
80⇔🛏(14fb)2🚭✂in 11 bedrooms CTV in all bedrooms ⓇT
✳ sB&B⇔🛏£52-£62.50
dB&B⇔🛏£68.50-£73 Continental breakfast 🍴
⟨ 100P 🖥(heated) sauna solarium gymnasium jacuzzi *xmas*
🍴 English & French V ✵ 🍷 ✂ Lunch £8.50-£8.95 Dinner
£11.25&alc Last dinner 9.45pm
Credit Cards ①②③⑤ⓔ

★★★56% **Arlington** 10 Arlington Ln Newmarket Rd NR2 2DA
☎(0603)617841 Telex no 975392 FAX (0603) 663708
*Conveniently close to the A11, yet in a quiet area on the outskirts
of the city, this hotel offers well-equipped accommodation and
warm hospitality. There is a European flavour to the fresh dishes in
the restaurant; the bar and grill room are also popular and meals
are available from noon to 11pm.*
44⇔🛏(3fb)1🚭 CTV in all bedrooms Ⓡ ✳ sB&B⇔🛏£55-£65
dB&B⇔🛏£70-£80 🍴
⟨ 60P *xmas*
🍴 English & French V ✵ 🍷 Lunch £7.95-£12.95&alc Dinner
£7.95-£12.95&alc Last dinner 10pm
Credit Cards ①②③⑤

★★★55% **Lansdowne** 116 Thorpe Rd NR1 1RU (Embassy)
☎(0603)620302 FAX (0603) 761706
*Situated just half a mile from the historic city centre, the
Lansdowne provides comfortable accommodation for both leisure
and commercial guests. Bedrooms are well equipped and there is a
cocktail bar and a restaurant decorated in pastel colours.*
39rm(28⇔🛏10🛏)(1fb)✂in 4 bedrooms CTV in all bedrooms Ⓡ
Lift ⟨ CTV 60P CFA
🍴 French ✵ Last dinner 9.15pm
Credit Cards ①②③④⑤

★★65% **Annesley** 6 Newmarket Rd NR2 2LA ☎(0603)624553
Closed Xmas
*A Victorian house, situated on the Norwich/Thetford road close to
the city centre, has been tastefully and sympathetically decorated
to enhance its period features. Accommodation in bright, well-
equipped rooms is complemented by caring personal service from
the proprietors. The lovely garden at the rear of the hotel is
overlooked by a vine-covered sun lounge.*
19rm(1⇔🛏10🛏)(1fb) CTV in all bedrooms ⓇT
🐕 (ex guide dogs) ✳ sB&B£32.50 sB&B⇔🛏£41.50-£44
dB&B£43.50 dB&B⇔🛏£52-£55 🍴
30P ✿

🍴 English & French V ✵ 🍷 Lunch £12.95 Dinner £12.95&alc
Last dinner 9pm
Credit Cards ①②③⑤

★★★65% **Oaklands** 89 Yarmouth Rd, Thorpe St Andrew
NR7 0HH ☎(0603)34471 FAX (0603) 700318
*Set in its own well tended grounds overlooking the River Yare, this
hotel has been recently refurbished to offer good quality
accommodation, a range of dishes which includes fish specialities,
and a choice of bars. Ample car parking. Situated two miles east of
the City on the B1074/A47 Gt Yarmouth road.*
39rm(38⇔🛏)(4fb) CTV in all bedrooms ⓇT ✳
sB&B⇔🛏£46.50-£60 dB&B⇔🛏£65-£80 🍴
⟨ CTV 90P ✿ *xmas*
V ✵ 🍷 Lunch £10.95&alc Dinner £10.95&alc Last dinner
9.30pm
Credit Cards ①②③⑤ⓔ

✿ ✕✕**Adlard's** 79 Upper St Giles St NR2 1AB ☎(0603)633522
*David Adlard and his small team prepare dishes of the finest
quality, delicately enhanced by well constructed sauces. Our
Inspector was especially complimentary about a ragôut of seafood
with a coulis of red peppers, and a loin of venison with oyster
mushrooms on a wild mushroom sauce. Service is friendly and it is
pleasing to note that Adlard's is now serving lunch as well as
dinner.*
Closed Sun & Mon
Lunch not served Sat
🍴 French 35 seats S% Lunch £14-£16 Dinner £24.50-£26 Last
lunch 1.45pm Last dinner 9pm 🥄
Credit Cards ①③

✕✕**Marco's** 17 Pottergate NR2 1DS ☎(0603)624044
*Centrally situated, this busy and popular little restaurant produces
both classic and some more imaginative Italian dishes. Competent
service and a relaxing atmosphere complement the highly
enjoyable food. Not a run-of-the-mill pizzeria by any means.*
Closed Sun, Mon & 20 Aug-20 Sep
🍴 Italian V 20 seats ✳ Lunch fr£16&alc Dinner fr£27alc Last
lunch 2pm Last dinner 9.30pm 🥄 nc12yrs
Credit Cards ①②③④⑤

✕**Greens Seafood** 82 Upper St Giles St NR1 1AQ
☎(0603)623733
*Decorated and furnished in rich greens and reds, this restaurant
offers a wide variety of dishes including salmon and turbot rose –
an elaborate presentation in the form of a rose accompanied by a
delicate watercress sauce. There are a few meat dishes and the
wines are reasonable and varied.*
Closed Sun, Mon, 10 days Xmas, 2 wks mid Aug & BH's
Lunch not served Sat
V 48 seats Wine £5.80 Last lunch 2pm Last dinner 10.30pm 6P
nc8yrs 🎵
Credit Cards ①③

**NOTTINGHAM** Nottinghamshire Map **08** SK54

See **Town Plan Section**
★★★★63% **Royal Moat House International** Wollaton St
NG1 5RH (Queens Moat) ☎(0602)414444 Telex no 37101
FAX 475667
Closed 25-26 Dec
*This is a busy and most popular modern hotel with extensive public
rooms, it offers a choice of four restaurants and a similar number of
bars. A unique and pleasant feature of the hotel is an arcade of
tropical trees and plants giving access to the first floor bars and
restaurants. Car parking is in the multi-storey car park adjacent.*
201⇔🛏(20fb)✂in 44 bedrooms CTV in all bedrooms ⓇT
🐕 (ex guide dogs) ✳ sB&B⇔🛏£28.60-£64.90
dB&B⇔🛏£71.50-£82.50 🍴
Lift ⟨ 🎾 600P squash solarium gymnasium *xmas*

**N**

♀ English, French & American **V** ♧ ℒ ⊬ Lunch
£3.95-£5.25&alc Dinner £5.95-£8.95&alc Last dinner 11pm
Credit Cards ① ② ③ ⑤

★★★★59% *The Albany* Saint James's St NG1 6BN (Trusthouse
Forte) ☎(0602)470131 Telex no 37211 FAX (0602) 484366
*Just off the central ring road, with good views of city and castle
from many rooms.*
139⇨¼⊬in 20 bedrooms CTV in all bedrooms ®
Lift ( ⊞ 🎇 CFA
♀ English & French **V** ♧ ℒ ⊬ Last dinner 10.15pm
Credit Cards ① ② ③ ④ ⑤

★★★56% **Nottingham Moat House** Mansfield Rd NG5 2BT
(Queens Moat) ☎(0602)602621 Telex no 377429
FAX (0602) 691506
*This large, busy, modern hotel stands less than a mile from the city
centre and provides good parking facilities.*
172⇨¼⊬in 66 bedrooms CTV in all bedrooms ®
✵ (ex guide dogs) ✱ sB⇨♪£25-£54.95
dB⇨♪£55-£69.95 (room only) ➡
Lift ( 250P 90🏊
♀ International **V** ♧ ℒ ⊬ Lunch £7.50 Dinner £10.85 Last
dinner 11pm
Credit Cards ① ② ③ ⑤

★★★69% **Swans Hotel & Restaurant** 84-90 Radcliffe Rd,
West Bridgford NG2 5HH ☎(0602)814042 FAX (0602) 455745
*A row of houses now thoughtfully converted into an attractive
hotel, on the A6011, east of West Bridgeford. Chef, Ian Pascoe,
provides inviting menus which make the best of seasonal produce.*
31⇨♪(2fb)¼⊬in 2 bedrooms CTV in all bedrooms ® T
✵ (ex guide dogs) ✱ sB&B⇨♪£25-£70 dB&B⇨♪£46-£80 ➡
Lift ( 33P *xmas*
♀ English & French **V** ♧ ℒ ⊬ Lunch fr£7.95&alc Dinner
£13.95&alc Last dinner 10pm
Credit Cards ① ② ③ ⑤ ⓔ

**N**

★★★ 63% **Waltons** 2 North Road, The Park NG7 1AG
☎(0602)475215 FAX (0602) 475053
Closed 25-26 Dec
*This early nineteenth century hunting lodge now provides well
furnished accommodation within walking distance of the city
centre and serves good food in its elegant dining room.*
13⇨↑1⌂ CTV in all bedrooms ® T ✱ sB&B⇨↑£42-£55
dB&B⇨↑£65-£75
《 CTV 14P 4✿ ✿ ✿ ⌢ sauna solarium ♫ *xmas*
♡ French V ✿ ⬚ Lunch £12-£15alc Dinner £12-£15alc Last
dinner 9.45pm
Credit Cards ①②③ⓔ

★★★ 61% **Stakis Victoria** Milton St NG1 3PZ (Stakis)
☎(0602)419561 Telex no 37401 FAX (0602) 484736
*This traditional town-cente hotel is just yards away from the
Victoria shopping centre. The comfortable ground floor lounge is
an excellent place to relax with a pot of tea after a busy day.*
166⇨↑(15fb)1⌂↙in 23 bedrooms CTV in all bedrooms ® T
S10% sB⇨↑£62-£68 dB⇨↑£75-£81 (room only) ♬
Lift 《 25P *xmas*
V ✿ ⬚ ↙ S% Lunch £7.50 Dinner £12.50&alc Last dinner
9.45pm
Credit Cards ①②③⑤ⓔ

★★★ 61% **Strathdon Thistle** Derby Rd NG1 5FT (Mount
Charlotte (TS)) ☎(0602)418501 Telex no 377185
FAX (0602) 483725
*Modern city-centre hotel with high standard of cuisine.*
69⇨↑(8fb)↙in 8 bedrooms CTV in all bedrooms ® T ✱
sB⇨↑fr£56 dB⇨↑fr£72 (room only) ♬
Lift 《 10P 5✿ CFA ♫
♡ International ✿ ⬚ ↙ Lunch fr£9.40&alc Dinner
fr£10.75&alc Last dinner 10.30pm
Credit Cards ①②③④⑤

★★ 67% **Hotel Windsor Lodge** 116 Radcliffe Rd, West
Bridgford NG2 5HG ☎(0602)813773 FAX (0602) 819405
Closed 25-26 Dec
*This family-run hotel offers good quality accommodation and a
simple, but enjoyable, English menu in the restaurant, freshly
prepared to order. There is a small conference suite, which also
contains a snooker table and trim gym unit.*
49⇨↑(15fb) CTV in all bedrooms ® T ✱ S%
sB&B⇨↑£35-£40 dB&B⇨↑£48-£52
CTV 50P ⊞ sauna gymnasium
S% Bar Lunch £3 Dinner £10 Last dinner 8.30pm
Credit Cards ①②③⑤

★★ 65% **Westminster Hotel** 310-318 Mansfield Rd, Carrington
NG5 2EF (on A60 1.5m N of town centre) ☎(0602)623023
FAX (0602) 691156
*Well-furnished, modern and comfortable, an hotel situated just one
mile from the city centre on the A60 Mansfield Road offers good
all-round facilities.*
57⇨↑ CTV in all bedrooms ® T ✖ S% sB&B⇨↑£22.50-£48
dB&B⇨↑£45-£58 ♬
Lift 《 38P
✿ ⬚ S% Dinner £11.95-£16.95 Last dinner 9.15pm
Credit Cards ①③

★★ 63% *Priory* Derby Rd, Wollaton Vale NG8 2NR (Toby)
☎(0602)221691
*Set in its own grounds on the A52 at Wollaton Vale, three miles
from the city centre, an attractive modern hotel offers
accommodation in well furnished bedrooms linked to the Toby grill
and bars.*
31⇨↑(4fb)↙in 7 bedrooms CTV in all bedrooms ® T
✖ (ex guide dogs)
《 200P
♡ Mainly grills V ✿ ⬚ ↙ Last dinner 10.15pm
Credit Cards ①②③⑤

## ꜧotel ꝡindsor Lodge
★★
**116 Radcliffe Road, West Bridgford,
Nottingham NG2 5HG
Telephone: (0602) 813773 & 811229
Fax: (0602) 819405**

Well appointed family run hotel, 58 en suite
bedrooms with telephone, television, tea making and hair dryer. Games room with full
snooker table. Large conference room. Situated
on the A6011 & A52 Grantham Road, ½ mile
Trent Bridge Cricket Ground, 1½ miles City
centre, 1 mile Holme Pierrepont Water Sports
Centre. Parking for 60 cars. Same owners for
18 years.

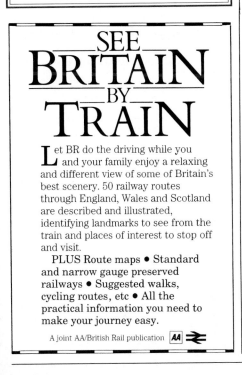

★★ **63% Rufford** 53 Melton Road, West Bridgford NG2 7NE
☎(0602)814202 FAX (0602) 455801
Closed Xmas
*A well-furnished, family owned and run hotel on the Melton road near Trent Bridge offers well cooked meals and bedrooms with good facilities.*
35♠ CTV in all bedrooms ® T ✱ (ex guide dogs) ✱
sB&B♠£29.90-£39.10 dB&B♠£46-£52.90 ♬
《CTV 35P
✿ ⍩ Dinner £10.35-£12.65 Last dinner 8pm
Credit Cards ①②③⑤

✕✕ **Les Artistes Gourmands** 61 Wollaton Rd, Beeston NG9 2NG
☎(0602)228288
Closed Sun & 1 wk Jan
Lunch not served Sat & Mon
♀ French **V** 70 seats ✱ Lunch £15.90&alc Dinner £19.90&alc
Last lunch 1.45pm Last dinner 9.30pm 1P ✂
Credit Cards ①②③⑤

---

**NUNEATON** Warwickshire Map **04** SP39

★★ **61% Chase** Higham Ln CV11 6AG (Porterhouse)
☎(0203)341013 FAX (0203) 383406
*A nineteenth-century manor house, set off the main Hinkley road east of the town centre, has become a busy modern hotel which attracts both businessmen and tourists ; it has a popular bar and restaurant trade, steaks being the strength of the menu.*
28⇨♠ CTV in all bedrooms ® T ♬
300P ✿ childrens play area
♀ English & French **V** ✿ ⍩ ✂
Credit Cards ①②③⑤

⛵ ***Griff House Travel Inn*** Coventry Rd CV10 7PJ
☎(0203)343584
Closed Christmas Day & Boxing Day
*Easily accessible from the M6 on the outskirts of Nuneaton, the Griff House is situated close to the roundabout junction of the A444 and B4113 with access of the latter road.*
38⇨ CTV in all bedrooms ✱
120P
♀ Mainly grills Last dinner 10.30pm
Credit Cards ①②③⑤

⛵ ***Longshoot Toby*** Watling St CV11 6JH (Toby) ☎(0203)329711
Telex no 311100
Closed 24 Dec-4 Jan
*Busy motel at the A5/A47 junction.*
Annexe47⇨♠ CTV in all bedrooms ® ✱
《 120P
**V** ✿ ✂ Last dinner 10pm
Credit Cards ①②③⑤

---

**NUNNINGTON** North Yorkshire Map **08** SE67

✕✕ **Ryedale Lodge** YO6 5XB ☎(04395)246
*Elegant small restaurant, delightfully converted from a Victorian railway station on the edge of the Vale of Pickering. The four-course table d'hôte offers mainly English dishes such as pigeon pie, roast duck, breast of smoked goose and duck, and local Ryedale red deer, with a stimulating wine list and delicious desserts. Seven bedrooms are available at present.*
Closed Jan
Lunch not served
♀ European **V** 30 seats Dinner £25 Last dinner 9.30pm 30P ✂
Credit Cards ①③

---

**NUTFIELD** Surrey Map **04** TQ35

★★★ **74% Nutfield Priory** RH1 4EN ☎Redhill(0737)822066
FAX (0737) 823321
*Set high on the Nutfield Ridge the hotel, dating from 1872, commands extensive views over the Surrey and Sussex countryside. The accommodation has been tastefully furnished throughout and the spacious bedrooms are equipped with every modern facility. Fine food and wines, extensive conference amenities and a leisure centre are other features of this hotel.*
34⇨♠ 2⌷✂in 12 bedrooms CTV in all bedrooms T ✱
sB&B⇨♠£65-£75
dB&B⇨♠£85-£105 Continental breakfast ♬
Lift 《130P ⏚ ✿ ▣(heated) squash snooker sauna solarium gymnasium badminton, steam room, beauty treatment *xmas*
**V** ✿ ✂ Lunch £15.50-£25&alc Dinner £15.50-£20&alc Last dinner 9.45pm
Credit Cards ①②③⑤ ⓔ

See advertisement under **REDHILL**

---

**OAKHAM** Leicestershire Map **04** SK80

❀★★★★♨
**HAMBLETON HALL**

Hambleton LE15 8TH (3m E off A606) (Relais et Châteaux) ☎(0572)756991
Telex no 342888
FAX (0572) 724721

*This splendid house sits at the western end of Rutland Water and offers guests a relaxing stay lapped on every side by luxury and in the care of General Manager Jeffrey Crockett and his friendly young staff. Owners Tim and Stefa Hart have furnished the rooms in a delightful manner, and those bedrooms decorated in Indian style with rich colours and wonderful patterns are especially attractive. Chef Brian Baker offers a varied à la carte menu, and a daily 4-course set menu. Game dishes are a speciality, and we can highly recommend the squab, pot-roasted and served on a bed of braised cabbage with whole roast garlic cloves. The wine list offers a choice of around 270 bottles, all of a character and quality to complement the cooking.*
15⇨♠1▣ CTV in all bedrooms T ✱ sB&B⇨♠£98-£200
dB&B⇨♠£98-£200 Continental breakfast ♬
Lift 40P ⏚ ✿ ♪ (hard) nc9yrs *xmas*
**V** ✿ Lunch £24.50&alc Dinner £35&alc Last dinner 9.30pm
Credit Cards ①③

---

★★★ **76% Barnsdale Country Club** Exton LE15 8AB (2m E on A606) ☎(0572)757901 FAX (0572) 756235
*Originally built in 1890 for the Earl Fitzwilliam family, Barnsdale Hall, is now at the centre of a luxurious time-share development set in 60 acres of grounds which reach to the edge of Rutland Water. As well as the time-share apartments, there are two blocks of good quality, well-equipped hotel rooms and the range of leisure facilities is extensive.*
Annexe57rm(51⇨)(10fb) CTV in all bedrooms ® T
✱ (ex guide dogs) ✱ sB&B£72 sB&B⇨£72 dB&B£105-£127
dB&B⇨£105-£127 Continental breakfast ♬
Lift 《 CTV 100P ⏚ ✿ ▣(heated) ♪ (hard) squash snooker sauna solarium gymnasium croquet bowls pitch & putt pool table ♫ *xmas*
**V** Lunch fr£15alc Dinner fr£15alc Last dinner 9.30pm
Credit Cards ①②③⑤ ⓔ

## NORMANTON PARK HOTEL

Normanton Park, Rutland Water South Shore,
Leics LE15 8RP
Telephone: Stamford (0780) 720315
Fax: (0780) 721086

**16 bedroomed**

Family owned and run being the only hotel situated on the shores of Rutland Water.

The hotel has direct access to the lake and 25 miles of shoreline.

*Award winning conversion of a listed*
★★★ *Coach House.* **Johansen**

## *Barnsdale Country Club*

RUTLAND WATER ★★★

Situated on the north shore of Rutland Water in 60 acres of wooded parkland with beautiful views overlooking the water.

Superb sports and leisure facilities on site:
*Indoor swimming pool, gymnasium, tennis, squash, croquet, bowls, crazy golf, snooker, putting green, beauty shop.* Nearby *golf, fishing, windsurfing, horse-riding, sailing.*

Luxury bedrooms with all facilities, excellent bars and restaurants.

Conference facilities for up to.120 delegates. Easy access to A1.

**Barnsdale Country Club Hotel,
Barnsdale, Exton, Nr. Oakham, Rutland, Leics.
Tel: 0572 757901 Fax: 0572 756235**

# *Rufford Hotel* ★★

**0**

### 53 Melton Road, West Bridgford, Nottingham NG2 7NE
### Telephone: Nottingham (0602) 814202 & 811233
### Fax No. (0602) 455801

*Welcome to Nottingham*

A regular visitor or just passing through, why not enjoy a stay in one of Nottingham's premier locations. Ideally situated just 1½ miles from the City Centre and close to the International Water Sports Centre at Holme Pierrepont, two Football Grounds and the famous Trent Bridge Cricket Ground make this quality hotel the ideal choice.

Family owned and managed for the last 20 years, the Rufford boasts 35 bedrooms all with private facilities, colour television and telephone. A comprehensively stocked bar complete with friendly efficient staff to make your visit that touch more enjoyable.

Top of the list for Nottingham in a leading American Tourist Guide.
Small Wedding Receptions a speciality.

533

**★★★⚑72% Normanton Park** LE15 8RP
☎Stamford(0780)720315 FAX (0780) 721086
(For full entry see Normanton)

**★★★70% Barnsdale Lodge** The Avenue, Exton LE15 8AH (3m
E on A606) ☎(0572)724678 FAX (0572) 724961
*Barnsdale Lodge is a country farmhouse hotel which is situated*
*approximately 3 miles east of Oakham on the A606. This newly*
*created hotel provides interesting, traditional English cuisine in the*
*Edwardian-style restaurant, and a series of 3 individually-styled*
*rooms. The Edwardian theme continues through all public rooms*
*and the modern, comfortable bedrooms.*
17⇨🛉(2fb)1🛏 CTV in all bedrooms ® T ✱
sB&B⇨🛉fr£39.95 dB&B⇨🛉fr£55 🍴
《 P ✿ ὠ xmas
V ᛫ ᛫Ϫ Lunch £9-£22 High tea £4.50 Dinner £9-£22 Last
dinner 9.30pm
Credit Cards 1 2 3 5

**★★★70% Whipper-in Hotel** Market Place LE15 6DT
☎(0572)756971 FAX (0572) 757759
*Furnished with antiques, this 17th-century inn has been*
*transformed into a comfortable hotel. Chef Paul Cherrington*
*promotes modern British cuisine with refreshing skill, and the*
*restaurant is popular. Parking may be restricted on market days –*
*check when booking.*
21⇨🛉Annexe3⇨2🛏 CTV in all bedrooms ® T S%
sB&B⇨🛉fr£68 dB&B⇨🛉fr£80 🍴
《
V ᛫ ᛫Ϫ S% Lunch fr£12.95 Dinner fr£18.95 Last dinner
9.30pm
Credit Cards 1 2 3 5 £

**★★61% Boultons** 4 Catmose St LE15 6HW ☎(0572)722844
FAX (0572) 724473
*Next to the castle of this pleasant old market town stands an hotel*
*with an abundance of original exposed beams, parts of its fabric*
*dating back to the sixteenth century. Accommodation is well*
*equipped, and improvements currently taking place include the*
*provision of twelve additional bedrooms with en suite bathrooms,*
*new conference and function facilities, a new restaurant and a new*
*bar.*
25⇨🛉(2fb)⅍in 7 bedrooms CTV in all bedrooms ® T
15P 1🏮
♀ French ᛫ ᛫Ϫ
Credit Cards 1 2 3 5

**★61% Rutland Angler** Mill St LE15 6EA ☎(0572)55839
*Simple but comfortable bedrooms and modest public areas with a*
*choice of bars are provided by a small stonebuilt inn which stands*
*close to the city centre and is popular with both tourists and*
*commercial guests.*
9rm(1⇨)(1fb) CTV in all bedrooms
20P ♫
♀ Spanish V
Credit Cards 1 2 5

**OAKHILL** Somerset Map 03 ST64

**✕✕Oakhill House** Bath Rd BA3 5AQ ☎(0749)840180
*In the relaxed, informal atmosphere of this delightful 17th-century*
*country house with its elegant bar and spacious dining room, the*
*proprietors present a short, mainly English, menu of imaginative*
*dishes based on local produce and making effective use of fruit*
*sauces; poultry is raised on the premises and herbs are gathered*
*from the garden.*
Closed Mon
Lunch not served Sat
Dinner not served Sun
V 45 seats Lunch £9.75-£16.50&alc Dinner £9.75-£16.50&alc
Last lunch 2pm Last dinner 9.30pm 40P
Credit Cards 1 2 3

**OBAN** Strathclyde *Argyllshire* Map **10** NM83

**★★★55% Caledonian** Station Square PA34 5RT ☎(0631)63133
Telex no 777210 FAX (0631) 62998
*Set in the town centre close to the railway and bus station, this five-*
*storey Victorian building overlooks the bay and harbour.*
70⇨(10fb) CTV in all bedrooms ® T sB⇨£39-£52
dB⇨£50-£74 (room only) 🍴
Lift 《 6P 🚗 xmas
♀ Scottish & French V ᛫ ᛫Ϫ ⅍ Lunch £5-£12&alc High tea
£5-£6 Dinner £6-£14&alc Last dinner 11pm
Credit Cards 1 2 3 5 £

**★★★52% Alexandra** Corran Esplanade PA34 5AA (Scottish
Highland) ☎(0631)62381 Telex no 778215 FAX (0631) 64497
Closed Nov-Mar
*This popular coach-tour hotel on the waterfront enjoys fine views*
*over the bay. A programme of gradual refurbishment is taking*
*place, and standards of accommodation range from modest to*
*good.*
55⇨🛉(1fb) CTV in all bedrooms ® T sB&B⇨🛉£50
dB&B⇨🛉£80 🍴
Lift 《 80P pool table ♫
♀ International V ᛫ ᛫Ϫ Lunch fr£7.50 Dinner fr£12&alc Last
dinner 9pm
Credit Cards 1 2 3 5

**★★76% Manor House** Gallanach Rd PA34 4LS ☎(0631)62087
Closed 25-31 Dec
*A charming little hotel which overlooks the Bay from its attractive*
*situation to the south of the town has been refurbished to reflect its*
*Georgian origins; bedrooms, though fairly compact, are*
*thoughtfully equipped, comfortable and have neat modern*
*bathrooms, while the tastefully appointed dining room offers*
*enjoyable dinners which specialise in fresh local seafood. Service is*
*particularly friendly and attentive throughout.*
11⇨🛉 CTV in all bedrooms ® T sB&B⇨🛉£50-£70
dB&B⇨🛉£70-£140 (incl dinner) 🍴
20P 🚗 ✿ nc10yrs
♀ Scottish, French & German V ᛫ ᛫⅍ Lunch £12-£25alc
Dinner £19.50&alc Last dinner 8.30pm
Credit Cards 1 3

**★★59% Rowan Tree** George St PA34 5NX ☎(0631)62954
*A small, modern hotel which stands near the Esplanade, beside the*
*cinema, provides friendly service and a short à la carte menu of*
*enjoyable food; the combined foyer bar and lounge area offers an*
*interesting outlook onto the main street in which it is situated.*
24⇨🛉 CTV in all bedrooms ® sB&B⇨🛉£24-£35
dB&B⇨🛉£40-£60
《 12P
᛫ ᛫Ϫ
Credit Cards 1 2 3 5

**★★58% Lancaster** Corran Esplanade PA34 5AD ☎(0631)62587
*A number of indoor leisure facilities are available in this extended*
*Mock Tudor house which is pleasantly situated on the sea front*
*with fine views of the bay and offshore islands. Bedrooms are all*
*well equipped, though they tend to be compact and modestly*
*furnished.*
27rm(3⇨21🛉)(3fb) CTV in all bedrooms ® ✱ sB&Bfr£22
sB&B⇨🛉fr£27.50 dB&B⇨🛉fr£48
20P 🚗 🖃(heated) sauna solarium jacuzzi
V ᛫ ᛫Ϫ Lunch fr£5.50&alc Dinner fr£9&alc Last dinner 8pm

**★★50% Argyll** Corran Esplanade PA34 5PZ ☎(0631)62353
FAX (0631) 65472
*At the time of inspection, this modest, family-run hotel was*
*steadily undergoing improvements. It is centrally located, and is*
*popular with local parties. Live entertainment is a popular feature*
*on selected nights during the summer, and the friendly staff provide*
*a good standard of service.*
28rm(2⇨7🛉)(3fb) ® ✱ sB&B£17-£22 sB&B⇨🛉£20-£24
dB&B£40-£44 dB&B⇨🛉£44-£52 🍴

《 CTV 6P ♫
🍴 European V ♥ ⚿ Lunch £3.75-£7.50 High tea £4.25 Dinner
£12 Last dinner 8.30pm
Credit Cards 1 3 £

★⚷67%, **Foxholes** Cologin, Lerags PA34 4SE ☎(0631)64982
Closed Nov-Etr
7⇌𝄐 CTV in all bedrooms ® sB&B⇌𝄐£37.60-£44
dB&B⇌𝄐£57.14-£70 (incl dinner)
8P ⇱ nc7yrs

★55%, **King's Knoll** Dunollie Rd PA34 5JH ☎(0631)62536
*Good value accommodation is provided by this small, family-owned hotel which stands on a hillside overlooking the bay.*
15rm(2𝄐)(8fb) CTV in all bedrooms ®
CTV 7P
V ♥ ⚿ Last dinner 7.30pm
Credit Cards 1

---

**OCKLEY** Surrey Map 04 TQ13

★★67% **Gatton Manor** RH5 5PQ ☎Oakwood Hill(030679)555
FAX (030679) 713
*This small country house provides modern, comfortable bedrooms and has a very busy bar and restaurant. It is set in 200 acres of splendid grounds which includes an 18-hole golf course and, not surprisingly, is popular with golfers.*
10⇌𝄐 CTV in all bedrooms ® T 🐾 (ex guide dogs) ✱
sB&B⇌𝄐fr£45 dB&B⇌𝄐fr£70 🍴
150P ⇱ ✿ ⨾ 18 ♪ (grass) ↗ bowling green *xmas*
🍴 English & French ♥ ⚿ Lunch £6.50-£12.50 Dinner
£7.50-£18alc Last dinner 9.45pm
Credit Cards 1 3

---

## CALEDONIAN
## HOTEL · OBAN

**AA** | Station Square. PH34 5RT
★★★ | Telephone: 0631 63133
| Telex: 777210

**Panoramic bedrooms overlook the bustling fishing harbour towards the Isle of Mull. Experience a taste for the Highlands by staying at this attractive hotel. The modern bedrooms are well equipped to ensure your comfort and the restaurant is well renowned for its standards of cuisine.**

*Whether on holiday or on business, the Caledonian is the place to stay. Send for our colour brochure or phone to secure.*

---

# Loch Melfort
# Hotel***

### The finest location on the West
### Coast of Scotland

19 miles south of Oban (A816)

The perfect place for a relaxing holiday
or short break.

Comfortable accommodation with full
ensuite facilities and spectacular views.

Superb cuisine in our elegant dining room.
Seafood a speciality – especially lobsters.

Non-residents welcome for all meals.

Spring and Autumn Breaks available.

**Arduaine, by Oban, Argyll PA34 4XG**
**Tel 08522 233          Fax 08522 214**

---

★ ★

# The
# White Horse Hotel

**2 Main Street, Empingham, Nr Oakham,**
**Rutland, Leicestershire LE15 8PR**
**Telephone: Empingham (078086) 221/521**
Situated halfway between Stamford and Oakham
on the A606 close to the dam on Rutland Water,
this stone built Inn offers a warm welcome.
Originally a 17th century court house has been
carefully modernised but retaining the character.
All bedrooms are tastefully decorated and en
suite. The restaurant is popular and offers an interesting menu with a good selection of wines.
A separate Conference Room is available for up
to 60 people, ideal for business conferences,
parties and weddings. Large car park for over
50 cars.

O

## ODIHAM Hampshire Map **04** SU75

★★65% **George** High St RG25 1LP ☎(0256)702081
FAX (0256) 704213

*Set at the centre of the small town, a coaching inn dating back to the 16th century retains much of its original character whilst offering modern standards of comfort with the provision of a new bedroom annexe. Bar meals are modest, but you can enjoy a good meal in the restaurant featuring 16th-century panelling and used for ministerial courts in the 1700's.*

9⇨Annexe9⇨(1fb)2⌘⊁in 3 bedrooms CTV in all bedrooms
Ⓡ T ✱ sB&B⇨£37.50-£55 dB&B⇨£55-£75 ℗
20P ⊯

♉ English & French V ♨ ⚓ Lunch £12.50
Credit Cards ①②③⑤

## OKEHAMPTON Devon Map **02** SX59

⏰**Travelodge** Sourton Cross EX20 4LY (4m SW on A30)
(Trusthouse Forte) ☎(0837)52124 Central Res (0800) 850950

*Modern, purpose-built lodge conveniently positioned adjacent to the A30 at Sourton Cross. Comfortable, bright and spacious bedrooms, two of which are fitted for disabled travellers. Convenient stopover; Little Chef restaurant on site.*

32⇨℟(32fb) CTV in all bedrooms Ⓡ sB⇨℟£24
dB⇨℟£29.50 (room only)
《32P ⊯

Credit Cards ①②③

## OLD BURGHCLERE Hampshire Map **04** SU45

✗✗**The Dew Pond** RG15 9LH ☎Burghclere(063527)408
*Surrounded by beautiful downland scenery, this appealing restaurant is in an attractive and welcoming 16th-century house, with a cosy lounge bar and an open fire in the dining room. The chef/patron offers an interesting selection of dishes in French style, making the best use of quality seasonal ingredients, including local game.*
*6.25 miles south of Newbury, off A34 ; follow signs for Beacon Hill, then unclassified road to Old Burghclere*

Closed Sun, Mon, 2 wks from 3rd Jan & 2 wks mid Aug
Lunch not served Sat
♉ English & French V 40 seats ✱ Lunch £14.50-£16.50 Dinner £21-£25 Last lunch 2pm Last dinner 10pm 20P nc3yrs
Credit Cards ①③

## OLDBURY West Midlands Map **07** SO98

★★★74% **Jonathans'** 16-24 Wolverhampton Rd B68 0LH
☎021-429 3757 FAX 021-434 3107

*This very unusual hotel transports its guests back in time to the Victorian era, its rooms unashamedly cluttered with Victoriana— don't be surprised to find in your room a piano, a pool table or a huge four-poster bed! Jonathan's Restaurant offers an interesting old England menu and the traditional puddings should not be missed. Staff are caring and a stay here is sure to be memorable.*

10⇨⌘⊁in 2 bedrooms CTV in all bedrooms Ⓡ T
✹ (ex guide dogs) ✱ sB⇨£65-£85 dB⇨£75-£95 (room only) ℗
《12P ⊯
V ♨ ⚓ Lunch £15-£24alc High tea fr£5.50alc Dinner £15-£24alc Last dinner 10.30pm
Credit Cards ①②③

⏰**Travelodge** Wolverhampton Rd B69 2BH (on A4123)
(Trusthouse Forte) ☎021-552 2967 Central Res (0800) 850950
*This newly-opened lodge, conveniently situated on the A4123 close to junction 2 of the M5, offers value-for-money modern bedroom accommodation, meals being available in the nearby Little Chef restaurant.*

33⇨℟(33fb) CTV in all bedrooms Ⓡ sB⇨℟£24
dB⇨℟£29.50 (room only)
《33P ⊯
Credit Cards ①②③

## OLDHAM Greater Manchester Map **07** SD90

★★★70% **Hotel Smokies Park** Ashton Rd, Bardsley OL8 3HX
(Consort) ☎061-624 3405 Telex no 667490 FAX 061-627 5262

*This modern hotel has tasteful and comfortable public areas and well-equipped bedrooms; second-floor rooms have recently been enlarged to offer extra facilities. Service throughout is friendly and helpful. There is a small 'trimnasium' for guests' use and at weekends there is a nightclub.*

47⇨℟ CTV in all bedrooms Ⓡ T ✹ (ex guide dogs)
sB&B⇨℟£52-£75 dB&B⇨℟£60-£80 ℗
《120P sauna solarium gymnasium steam room
♉ English & French V ♨ ⚓ Lunch £11-£20alc High tea £3.50
Dinner £11.50&alc Last dinner 10.30pm
Credit Cards ①②③⑤

★★★66% **Avant** Windsor Rd, Manchester St OL8 4AS (Best Western) ☎061-627 5500 Telex no 668264 FAX 061-627 5896
*This modern, purpose-built hotel, which stands beside the A62 to the south-west of the town centre, is popular with business people and as a conference and function venue. Well-equipped bedrooms are provided with 24-hour service, and the young staff are very helpful.*

103⇨℟(2fb)⊁in 12 bedrooms CTV in all bedrooms Ⓡ T ✱
sB&B⇨℟£56-£59 dB&B⇨℟£62-£66 ℗
Lift 《120P ♫ xmas
♉ English & French V ♨ ⚓ ⊁ Lunch £7.95-£12.50&alc High tea £3.50-£4 Dinner fr£12.50&alc Last dinner 10pm
Credit Cards ①②③⑤

★★★58% **The Bower** Hollinwood Av, Chadderton OL9 8DE
(2.25 SW A6104) (De Vere) ☎061-682 7254 Telex no 666883
FAX 061-683 4605
RS 25-31 Dec
*Surrounded by pleasant grounds, this former private house has been extended and recently refurbished to provide attractive public areas. Although bedrooms are not over spacious. they are well equipped and the hotel is popular for functions and conferences.*
66⇨℟(1fb)⌘ CTV in all bedrooms Ⓡ T ✱ S10%
sB&B⇨℟£26-£74 dB&B⇨℟£52-£80 ℗
《140P ✤ CFA ♫
♉ Continental V ♨ ⚓
Credit Cards ①②③⑤

★★70% **High Point** Napier St OL8 1TR ☎061-624 4130
FAX 061-627 2767
*A friendly, family-run hotel with exceptionally well-appointed bedrooms. Situated in an elevated position looking towards the town centre. Recent expansion has enhanced the public areas.*

19rm(8⇨7℟)(4fb)1⌘ CTV in all bedrooms Ⓡ T sB&B£32.50
sB&B⇨℟£45 dB&B£45 dB&B⇨℟£55-£68 ℗
《42P 2🅿 ♫
♉ English & French V ♨ ⚓ Lunch fr£7&alc Dinner fr£9.95&alc Last dinner 9.45pm
Credit Cards ①②③⑤

## OLD MELDRUM Grampian *Aberdeenshire* Map **15** NJ82

★66% **Meldrum Arms** The Square AB5 0DS ☎(06512)2238 &
2505

*Family-run village hotel with an attractive lounge bar, well-equipped, compact bedrooms and a wide range of keenly-priced meals. Service is friendly.*

7℟ CTV in all bedrooms Ⓡ T ✹ ✱ sB&B℟£25 dB&B℟£40
25P
V ♨ ⚓ Bar Lunch £3.55-£5.65alc High tea £4-£8alc Dinner £7.35-£12.50alc Last dinner 9.30pm
Credit Cards ①②③

1991 marks the 25th anniversary of this guide.

---

**OLD SODBURY** Avon Map **03** ST78

★★66% **Cross Hands** BS17 6RJ
☎Chipping Sodbury(0454)313000 FAX (0454) 324409
RS Xmas Night
*Set only one-and-a-half miles from the M4 motorway, this hotel
dating back to the fourteenth century has the distinction of having
provided shelter for the Queen during a blizzard in 1981
Bedrooms offer good facilities and there are two restaurants, the
Old Sodbury Grill being particularly popular with a local clientele.*
24rm(3⇨17♠)1🛏 CTV in all bedrooms Ⓡ T sB&B£34-£43
sB&B⇨♠£48-£55 dB&B£55
dB&B⇨♠£72-£80 Continental breakfast 🖪
《 200P ✿
♵ International V ♥ ⅙ Lunch £10-£15&alc Dinner
£10-£15&alc Last dinner 10.30pm
Credit Cards ① ② ③ ⑤
                    **See advertisement under BRISTOL**

---

**OLNEY** Buckinghamshire Map **04** SP85

✗✗**Dhaka Dynasty** 2-3 Stanley Court, Weston Rd MK46 5NH
☎Bedford(0234)713179 & 713188
*A modern, tastefully-appointed Indian restaurant featuring
traditional Moghul and Tandoori dishes. Among those
recommended are Murgh Makhani, Lamb Pasanda, Mawabi,
Gosht Makhani, King Prawn Bhuna and Murgh Jalfrezi. Good
basic ingredients and fresh produce are used, including, where
possible, fresh spices and herbs. The atmosphere is warm and
informal, with friendly, efficient service.*
♵ Indian & Moghul 50 seats Last dinner 11pm 20P
Credit Cards ① ② ③ ④ ⑤

---

For key to symbols see the inside front cover.

---

**ONICH** Highland *Inverness-shire* Map **14** NN06

★★★65% **Lodge on the Loch** Creag Dhu PH33 6RY
☎(08553)237 Telex no 94013696 FAX (08553) 463
Closed Nov-Jan (ex Xmas-New Year)
*Relaxing, family-run hotel with magnificent views of Loch Linnhe
and surrounding mountains from most bedrooms. A ground floor
bedroom has been specially designed for disabled guests.*
18⇨♠(1fb) CTV in all bedrooms Ⓡ T
sB&B⇨♠£29.50-£46.50 dB&B⇨♠£59-£105 🖪
25P 🚗 ✿ 🐟 xmas
♵ International V ♥ ⅏ ⅙ Lunch £5.50-£9alc Dinner
£16.50&alc Last dinner 10pm
Credit Cards ① ③ Ⓔ
                    **See advertisement under FORT WILLIAM**

★★69% **Allt-Nan-Ros** PH33 6RY ☎(08553)210
FAX (08553) 462
Closed Nov-Etr
*A friendly, hospitable hotel which commands splendid views over
Loch Linnhe and the surrounding mountains from its slightly
elevated position beside the A82 is particularly proud of its
cooking, successfully combining modern, French and traditional
Scottish recipes in its varied fixed-price menu. Bedrooms are very
well appointed, and a recent expansion of the ground floor has
provided airy and spaciously comfortable public rooms, all with a
southerly aspect.*
19⇨♠(2fb)1🛏 CTV in all bedrooms Ⓡ T ✳
sB&B⇨♠£32.75-£43 dB&B⇨♠£65.50-£86 🖪
50P 🚗 ✿
♵ Scottish & French ♥ ⅏ ⅙
Credit Cards ① ② ③ ⑤
                    **See advertisement on page 539**

---

## Onich - Oswestry

★★65% **Onich** PH33 6RY (Consort) ☎(08553)214 & 266
RS Nov-Mar
*This spacious lochside hotel has splendid views and gardens which lead down to a shingle beach. Bedrooms are neat and comfortable and a few have balconies.*
27⇄♠(6fb) CTV in all bedrooms ® T sB&B⇄♠£30-£37.50
dB&B⇄♠£50-£65 ₽
50P ⊞ ✿ solarium gymnasium jacuzzi games room ♂♂
♀ International ♦ ♨ Bar Lunch £3.75-£8.50alc Dinner
£15-£16.50 Last dinner 8.30pm
Credit Cards ⓵ ⓶ ⓷ ⓹ ⓔ
**See advertisement under FORT WILLIAM**

---

**ONNELEY** Staffordshire Map **07** SJ74

★★67% **Wheatsheaf Inn at Onneley** Barhill Rd CW3 9QF
☎Stoke-On-Trent(0782)751581 FAX (0782) 751499
*This small country inn, situated on the A525, offers traditional hospitality and is popular with business guests and tourists alike. Recently refurbished rooms provide excellent facilities and the intimate restaurant serves a good range of enjoyable meals.*
5♠ CTV in all bedrooms ® T sB&B♠£37-£42
dB&B♠£42-£52 ₽
150P ▶ 9 ♫ ✿
♀ English & French V ♦ ♨ Sunday Lunch £5.95-£8.45 Dinner
fr£12.95&alc Last dinner 9.30pm
Credit Cards ⓵ ⓶ ⓷ ⓔ

---

**ORFORD (near Woodbridge)** Suffolk Map **05** TM44

★★65% *The Crown & Castle* IP12 2LJ ☎Orford(0394)450205
*An 18th-century posting house once associated with smugglers.*
9rm(1⇄)Annexe10⇄♠¼in 1 bedroom CTV in all bedrooms ®
20P ⊞ ✿
V ♦ ♨ ¼ Last dinner 8.30pm
Credit Cards ⓵ ⓶ ⓷ ⓸ ⓹

---

**ORKNEY** Map **16**

**KIRKWALL** Map **16** HY41

★★65% *Ayre* Ayre Rd KW15 1QX ☎(0856)3001
Closed 1-2 Jan
*Recent refurbishment at this friendly, privately owned hotel has resulted in spacious and comfortable public areas and a new wing of well appointed bedrooms. Original bedrooms remain modest, but are well maintained and clean.*
32rm(4⇄6♠)(2fb) CTV in all bedrooms ®
25P sauna trout & sea fishing
♀ International V ♦ ♨ Last dinner 9pm
Credit Cards ⓵ ⓷

---

**ST MARGARET'S HOPE** Map **16** ND48

✗**Creel** Front Rd KW17 2SL ☎(0856)83311
*An unpretentious little restaurant stands on the waterfront, looking across Scapa Flow. Under the personal supervision of the owners, it provides a most enjoyable range of dishes, making good use of local fish and seafood. Service is simple, as befits the surroundings.*
Closed Mon, Tue & Jan
Lunch not served
40 seats ✱ Dinner £10-£16alc Last dinner 9.45pm 15P
Credit Cards ⓵ ⓷

---

Hotels with a high percentage rating for quality
are highlighted by a % across their
gazetteer entry.

---

**ORMSKIRK** Lancashire Map **07** SD40

★★★67% **Beaufort** High Ln, Burscough L40 7SN
☎Burscough(0704)892655 FAX (0704) 895135
*This newly-built hotel situated at Birscough on the A59 one mile north of Ormskirk, offers comfortable, modern accommodation and enjoyable meals. Service throughout is friendly, attentive and well supervised.*
21⇄♠ CTV in all bedrooms ® T ✱ S% sB&B⇄♠£27-£54
dB&B⇄♠£54-£67
《 126P ⊞
♀ International V ♦ ♨ Lunch £5.50-£7.30 Dinner
£14.95-£16.95 Last dinner 10pm
Credit Cards ⓵ ⓶ ⓷ ⓔ

---

**OSBOURNBY** Lincolnshire Map **08** TF03

★59% **Whichcote Arms** London Rd NG34 0DG
☎Culverthorpe(05295)239 & 500
*This detached stone building on the A15, six miles south of Sleaford is a former farm manager's house of the Whychcote Estate. Accommodation is modest and the restuarant serves good standard, popular dishes. There are good car parking and banqueting facilities.*
7♠(1fb) CTV in all bedrooms ® 🐾 (ex guide dogs) ✱
sB&B♠£25 dB&B♠£34 ₽
40P ✿
V ♦ ♨ ¼ Lunch fr£6.75 Dinner £7-£10alc Last dinner 10pm
Credit Cards ⓵ ⓷ ⓔ

---

**OSTERLEY** Greater London

See **LONDON plan 1**B3(page 426)
★★57% **Osterley** 764 Great West Rd TW7 5NA (Consort)
☎081-568 9981 Telex no 915059 FAX 081-569 7819
*Situated on the Great West Road, the Osterley has an attractive Tudor-style exterior. It offers a steak restaurant with small cocktail bar, and a pub and wine bar which serves real ale. Bedrooms are modern and well equipped.*
57⇄♠Annexe5rm(9fb) CTV in all bedrooms ® T
sB&B£50-£55 sB&B⇄♠£63-£66 dB&B£55-£60
dB&B⇄♠£70-£75 Continental breakfast ₽
《 140P 3🅿
V ♦ ♨ ¼ Lunch £8-£9&alc Dinner £9.50-£11&alc Last dinner
10pm
Credit Cards ⓵ ⓶ ⓷ ⓹

---

**OSWESTRY** Shropshire Map **07** SJ22

★★★67% **Wynnstay** Church St SY11 2SZ ☎(0691)655261
FAX (0691) 670606
*Completely transformed this hotel now offers very comfortable bedrooms and a ground floor area which consists of an elegant library lounge bar, the Camellia restaurant, a conservatory and a function/banqueting suite.*
26⇄♠(4fb)2🏋¼in 12 bedrooms CTV in all bedrooms ® T ✱
sB⇄♠£42-£95 dB⇄♠£53-£110 (room only) ₽
《 70P ✿ crown green bowling *xmas*
V ♦ ♨ ¼ Lunch £10.50-£12.50 High tea £7-£10 Dinner
£12.50-£19 Last dinner 10pm
Credit Cards ⓵ ⓶ ⓷ ⓸ ⓹

★★♨64% **Sweeney Hall** Morda SY10 9EU (1m S on A483)
☎(0691)652450
*Now conveniently accessible from the A483 bypass, an impressive nineteenth-century house surrounded by attractive woodland and meadows provides very comfortable public rooms and bedrooms which are, for the most part, spacious; guests can enjoy a well cooked meal in either the bar or the restaurant.*
9rm(6⇄♠) ® S% sB&B⇄♠£30-£35 dB&B£49-£54
dB&B⇄♠£54-£59
CTV 50P ⊞ ✿ putting green

♡ English, French & Italian **V** ♥ Lunch fr£11&alc Dinner fr£11&alc Last dinner 9.30pm
Credit Cards [1] [3]

⌂**Travelodge** Mile End Service Area SY11 4JA (junct A5/A483) (Trusthouse Forte) ☎(0691)658178
*This busy lodge – part of a complex comprising petrol station, Little Chef restaurant and Tourist Board bureau – is strategically positioned on the Oswestry bypass, close to the Shrewsbury junction.*
40⇔♠(40fb) CTV in all bedrooms ® sB⇔♠£24 dB⇔♠£29.50 (room only)
《 40P ⇘
♡ Mainly grills
Credit Cards [1] [2] [3]

**OTLEY** West Yorkshire Map **08** SE24

★★★66% **Chevin Lodge Country Park** Yorkgate LS21 3NU ☎(0943)467818 Telex no 51538 FAX (0943) 850335
*Constructed of pine in Scandinavian style, the hotel stands in 50 acres of birch wood. Attractively appointed bedrooms and public areas, maintaining the pinewood theme throughout, offer modern comforts and facilities, whilst the restaurant's three menus provide a choice between local and international dishes, supported by a good wine list.*
18⇔♠Annexe34⇔♠(5fb) CTV in all bedrooms ® T
✕ (ex guide dogs) S% sB&B⇔♠£55-£80 dB&B⇔♠£68-£92.50 ℞
《 ⊞ 100P ❀ ♪ (hard) ♪ sauna solarium cycling games room *xmas*
♡ English & French **V** ♥ ⚏ Lunch fr£9.50&alc Dinner fr£14.75&alc Last dinner 9.30pm
Credit Cards [1] [2] [3]

**See advertisement in colour section**

**OTTERBURN** Northumberland Map **12** NY89

★★57% **Otterburn Tower** NE19 1NP ☎(0830)20620
RS 25 Dec
*This historic building, standing in its own grounds, dates back to 1706 and offers bedrooms which are, for the most part, spacious and attractively decorated, though lounge accommodation is, at present, limited. Friendliness is the keynote of the establishment, and the proprietors have created a genuine country house atmosphere.*
11rm(5⇔3♠)(5fb)2⚑ CTV in 8 bedrooms TV in 1 bedroom ® T sB&B£25-£35 sB&B⇔♠£35-£45 dB&B£50-£55 dB&B⇔♠£55-£65 ℞
CTV 50P ❀ CFA ♪ *xmas*
**V** ♥ ⚏ Lunch £7-£10&alc Dinner £11-£13&alc Last dinner 9.30pm
Credit Cards [1] [2] [3] [5] ⓔ

**OTTERY ST MARY** Devon Map **03** SY19

★★★58% **Salston** EX11 1RQ (1m SW off B3174 towards West Hill) (Best Western) ☎(0404)815581
*Set on the edge of this historic town, the 18th-century country house with modern extensions enjoys lovely views over the East Devon countryside. Upgrading of the function rooms and well-equipped bedrooms is continuing. The hotel caters for small conferences and has some recreational amenities.*
26⇔♠(13fb)2⚑⚏in 10 bedrooms CTV in all bedrooms ® T sB&B⇔♠fr£55 dB&B⇔♠fr£70 ℞
《 CTV 100P ❀ CFA ☒(heated) ♪ squash sauna solarium gymnasium croquet & putting lawns ⚘ *xmas*
♡ English & French **V** ♥ ⚏ ⅍ Lunch £10-£20&alc Dinner £15&alc Last dinner 9.30pm
Credit Cards [1] [2] [3] [5] ⓔ

**See advertisement under EXETER**

★★68% **Tumbling Weir Hotel & Restaurant** EX11 1AO (Minotels) ☎(0404)812752
*A short riverside walk from the car park will bring guests to this attractive thatched property with its modern extension; bedrooms are well equipped, while the busy restaurant offers an extensive à la carte menu, and guests are assured of both a warm welcome and personal service.*
13⇔♠ CTV in all bedrooms ® T sB&B⇔♠fr£31.50 dB&B⇔♠fr£49.50 ℞
CTV 3P ❀ ♪ *xmas*
♡ French & Italian **V** ♥ ⚏ ⅍ Sunday Lunch £8.50 Dinner £16 Last dinner 9.45pm
Credit Cards [1] [3] ⓔ

**OULTON** West Yorkshire Map **08** SE32

★★★62% **Grove Crest** The Grove LS26 8EJ (Toby) ☎Leeds(0532)826201 Telex no 557646 FAX (0532) 829243
*Conveniently located at the junction of the A639 and A642, the up-to-date hotel offers motel-style accommodation in a wing separated from the public areas by spacious car parks. Guests can relax in good lounge bars and an attractive, well appointed restaurant.*
40⇔⅍in 5 bedrooms CTV in all bedrooms ®
《 200P pool table
**V** ♥ ⚏ ⅍
Credit Cards [1] [2] [3] [4] [5]

**OUNDLE** Northamptonshire Map **04** TL08

★★★62% **The Talbot** New St PE8 4EA (Trusthouse Forte) ☎(0832)273621 Telex no 32364 FAX (0832) 274545
*There is a relaxed and peaceful atmosphere at this historic hotel, built around a courtyard. Rooms are comfortable and well equipped and the staff are friendly.*
38rm(18⇔17♠)(3fb) CTV in all bedrooms ®

▶

☾ 60P CFA
V ♣ ☕ ⅟ Last dinner 10pm
Credit Cards [1] [2] [3] [4] [5]

**OUTLANE** West Yorkshire Map **07** SE01

**★★ 62% Old Golf House Hotel** New Hey Rd HD3 3YP (Lansbury) ☎Elland(0422)379311 Telex no 51324 FAX (0422) 372694
*Standing beside the M62 at junction 23, an hotel which was formerly the club house of the local golf club provides comfortable, well equipped bedrooms and a pleasant restaurant where both the à la carte and table d'hôte menus offer good value for money.*
50⇌⋒(3fb)2⊟⅟in 4 bedrooms CTV in all bedrooms ® **T** ✗ (ex guide dogs) sB&B⇌⋒fr£65 dB&B⇌⋒fr£77 ⊟
☾ 70P ✲ sauna solarium gymnasium *xmas*
☋ English & Continental **V** ♣ ⅟ Lunch fr£9.50&alc Dinner fr£13.75&alc Last dinner 10pm
Credit Cards [1] [2] [3] [5]

**OXFORD** Oxfordshire Map **04** SP50

See **Town Plan Section**
See also **Milton Common**

**★★★★ 56% The Randolph** Beaumont St OX1 2LN (Trusthouse Forte) ☎(0865)247481 Telex no 83446 FAX (0865) 791678
*Major refurbishment is in progress at this splendid old city-centre hotel. The improvement of the public areas has been completed, and all have been tastefully decorated to provide a high degree of comfort.*
109⇌⋒(5fb)⅟in 30 bedrooms CTV in all bedrooms ® **T** S%
sB⇌⋒£92-£103 dB⇌⋒£105-£216 (room only) ⊟
Lift ☾ 60⌂ CFA ♫ *xmas*
☋ International **V** ♣ ☕ ⅟ S% Lunch £16-£17&alc Dinner £20-£21&alc Last dinner 10pm
Credit Cards [1] [2] [3] [4] [5]

**❀❀❀★★★⚑ LE MANOIR AUX QUAT' SAISON** OX9 7PD (Relais et Châteaux) ☎Great Milton(0844)278881 Telex no 837552 FAX (0844) 278847
(For full entry see Milton, Great)

**❀★★★⚑ 67% Studley Priory** OX9 1AZ (Consort) ☎Stanton St John(086735)203 & 254 Telex no 23152 FAX (086735) 613
(For full entry see Horton-cum-Studley)

**★★★ 64% *Cotswold Lodge*** 66A Banbury Rd OX2 6JP ☎(0865)512121 Telex no 837127
Closed 25-30 Dec
*A friendly, family-run commercial hotel with nicely appointed and well equipped bedrooms, comfortable public rooms and an attractive restaurant which provides a good standard of cooking.*
52⇌(2fb) CTV in all bedrooms **T**
☾ 60P
☋ English & French **V** ♣ ☕ Last dinner 10.30pm
Credit Cards [1] [2] [3] [5]

**★★★ 63% Oxford Moat House** Godstow Rd, Wolvercote Rbt OX2 8AL (Queens Moat) ☎(0865)59933 Telex no 837926 FAX (0865) 310259
*Comfortable, modern hotel on the outskirts of the city, providing well-equipped bedrooms, extensive sport and leisure amenities and prompt service. The comprehensive range of business and conference facilities make the hotel popular with commercial guests.*
155⇌(17fb)⅟in 12 bedrooms CTV in all bedrooms ® **T**
sB&B⇌fr£85 dB&B⇌fr£110 ⊟
☾ 250P ▣(heated) squash snooker sauna solarium gymnasium whirlpool pitch & putt
☋ English & French **V** ♣ ☕ Lunch fr£12.50 Dinner fr£18 Last dinner 9.45pm
Credit Cards [1] [2] [3] [5]

**★★★ 58% Linton Lodge** Linton Rd OX2 6UJ (Hilton) ☎(0865)53461 Telex no 837093 FAX (0865) 310365
*Situated just north of the city, this commercial style of hotel has recently been refurbished and offers a blend of modern and traditional well-equipped accommodation.*
71⇌⋒(1fb)1⊟⅟in 6 bedrooms CTV in all bedrooms ® **T** ✱
sB⇌⋒£81-£91 dB⇌⋒£96-£115 (room only) ⊟
Lift ☾ 40P ✲ CFA pool table *xmas*
**V** ♣ ☕ ⅟ Lunch £9.75-£11 Dinner £13.50-£14.50&alc Last dinner 9.30pm
Credit Cards [1] [2] [3] [5] Ⓔ

**★★★ 55% Eastgate** The High, Merton St OX1 4BE (Trusthouse Forte) ☎(0865)248244 Telex no 83302 FAX (0865) 791681
*Standing at the heart of the city, the hotel has recently been remodelled to include elegantly furnished public rooms with a smart carvery restaurant and busy student bar. Bedrooms range from the sumptuous to the more modest, but cheerful service is provided throughout.*
43⇌1⊟⅟in 6 bedrooms CTV in all bedrooms ® **T** S15%
sB⇌£75-£85 dB⇌£90-£135 (room only) ⊟
Lift ☾ 43P CFA *xmas*
**V** ♣ ☕ ⅟ Lunch £7.25-£12.95&alc Dinner £14.95&alc Last dinner 9.30pm
Credit Cards [1] [2] [3] [4] [5]

**★★ 66% The Tree Hotel** Church Way, Iffley OX4 4EY (3m SE off A4158) ☎(0865)775974 & 778190 FAX (0865) 747554
*Lying three miles south-east of the city centre in Iffley village, this Victorian public house has been transformed into a friendly and comfortable small hotel by Dave and Ann Bowman. Bedrooms in particular are attractively furnished and well-equipped, as are the spotless en suite facilities. The ground floor has a comfortable bar with character, and a homely little dining room. Honest home cooking and hospitable service from staff and owners alike make this an excellent base for the business traveller or tourist.*
7⇌⋒(1fb)1⊟ CTV in all bedrooms ® **T** ✗ (ex guide dogs)
sB&B⇌⋒£55-£60 dB&B⇌⋒£66-£77
20P 3⌂ (£1 per night)
**V** ♣ ☕ ⅟
Credit Cards [1] [2] [3]

**★★ 62% *Royal Oxford*** Park End St OX1 1HR (Embassy) ☎(0865)248432 FAX (0865) 250049
*Conveniently positioned close to the station, a small company-owned city hotel has recently been refurbished to provide bright, modern, well-equipped bedrooms, pleasantly decorated in soft colours and furnished in complementary style; there is also a small modern restaurant and a choice of two bars which are popular locally.*
25rm(12⇌)(2fb) CTV in all bedrooms ®
☾ 12P
**V** ♣ ☕
Credit Cards [1] [2] [3] [5]

**★★ 60% Welcome Lodge** Peartree Roundabout OX2 8JZ (junc A34/A43) (Trusthouse Forte) ☎(0865)54301 Telex no 83202 FAX (0865) 513474
*Comfortable bedrooms are well equipped and styled to suit the touring guest at this modern hotel on the road services site; there is also a popular bar and bright carvery restaurant – with additional facilities available in the nearby Little Chef. The lodge occupies a convenient position just north of the city and adjacent major link roads.*
100⇌(41fb)⅟in 10 bedrooms CTV in all bedrooms ® ⊟
120P ✲ CFA ⛆(heated)
☋ Mainly grills **V** ♣ ☕ ⅟
Credit Cards [1] [2] [3] [4] [5]

★★ **56% Victoria** 180 Abingdon Rd OX1 4RA ☎(0865)724536
Telex no 837031
Closed 20 Dec-20 Jan
*Conveniently positioned adjacent to the Abingdon Road, just south*
*of the city, this friendly family-run hotel offers well-equipped*
*bedrooms although some rooms are a little restrictive.*
23rm(14⇨¾)(2fb) CTV in all bedrooms ® T ✱
sB&B£35.50-£37.50 sB&B⇨£45.50-£48.50
dB&B£48.50-£49.50 dB&B⇨£55.50-£62.50 ⊟
CTV 15P
♀ Italian & Yugoslav V ✿ ⌑ ⅙ Lunch fr£8.50 High tea
fr£4.45 Dinner fr£12.95&alc Last dinner 9pm
Credit Cards ⊡ ⊟ ⓔ

★ **60% River** 17 Botley Rd OX2 0AA ☎(0865)243475
FAX (0865) 724306
Closed 21 Dec-1 Jan
*A small, friendly, family-run hotel in a riverside setting.*
*Moderately priced accommodation includes a good annexe.*
16rm(6⇨5♠)Annexe8rm(3⇨3♠)(3fb) CTV in all bedrooms
® T ✖ (ex guide dogs) sB&Bfr£33 sB&B⇨♠£40-£45
dB&B⇨♠£50-£55
CTV 25P ⇔ ✿ ♪
✿ ⌑ Bar Lunch fr£3 High tea fr£2 Dinner fr£7 Last dinner
7.30pm
Credit Cards ⊡ ⊟

✕✕✕ **Restaurant Elizabeth** 82/84 St Aldates OX1 1RA
☎(0865)242230
*An early 17th century building, full of character, and with a cosy,*
*intimate, first floor restaurant. The short but interesting menu*
*offers French, Spanish and Greek cuisine which is complimented by*
*a well-balanced, reasonably-priced wine list.*
Closed Mon, 25-31 Dec & Good Fri
♀ French, Greek & Spanish V 45 seats Last lunch 2.30pm Last
dinner 11pm ⅌ ⅙
Credit Cards ⊡ ⊡ ⊟ ⊡

✕✕ **Bath Place** 4 & 5 Bath Place, Holywell St OX1 3SU
☎(0865)791812 FAX (0865) 790760
Closed Mon & 2 wks mid Jan-mid Feb
Dinner not served Sun
♀ French V 36 seats ✱ S12% Lunch £12.95 Dinner £24.50 Last
lunch 2pm Last dinner 9.30pm 4P
Credit Cards ⊡ ⊡ ⊟ ⊡

✕✕ **Gees** 61A Banbury Rd OX2 6PE ☎(0865)53540 & 59736
*Pleasant and attractive bistro restaurant within a bright, stylish*
*conservatory providing friendly, informal service and imaginative*
*dishes from a short, well-balanced menu.*
♀ European V 80 seats ✱ Lunch £10.95-£12.95alc Dinner
£17.50-£25alc Last lunch 2.30pm Last dinner 11pm ⅌
Credit Cards ⊡ ⊡ ⊟ ⊡

✕✕ **Paddyfield** 39-40 Hythe Bridge St OX1 2EP ☎(0865)248835
FAX (0235) 555912
*A recent face-lift has provided a bright, stylish, modern interior to*
*this popular Chinese restaurant, but service remains as cheerful*
*and friendly as ever. Well-prepared, authentic Cantonese and*
*Pekinese dishes include such specialities as crispy aromatic duck*
*with plum sauce, sizzling monkfish with black bean sauce and*
*steamed scallops in garlic butter, with plentiful jasmine tea served*
*in pretty china cups to complete the meal.*
Closed 25-27 Dec
♀ Cantonese, Pekinese & Szechwan V 150 seats ✱ Lunch
£4.50-£6.95&alc Last lunch 2.15pm Last dinner 11.45pm 20P
Credit Cards ⊡ ⊡ ⊟ ⊡

✕ **15 North Parade** 15 North Pde Av OX2 6LX ☎(0865)513773
*A stylish, modern, small restaurant offering warm hospitality and*
*a good standard of imaginative cuisine is cosily tucked away in the*
*northern outskirts of the city. Its efficiently short menu features a*
*range of mainly English dishes in which quality ingredients are*
*complemented by a range of tasty and unusual sauces.*

▶

*Surroundings are bright and cheerful, service friendly and unhurried, whilst prices – especially for the set lunch – are sensible.*
Dinner not served Sun
♀ English & French **V** 60 seats ✳ Lunch fr£10.75&alc Dinner fr£15.75&alc Last lunch 2pm Last dinner 10pm ♪ ⅄
Credit Cards [1] [3]

---

**PADSTOW** Cornwall & Isles of Scilly Map **02** SW97
See also **Constantine Bay**
**★★58%**, **The Metropole** Station Rd PL28 8DB (Trusthouse Forte) ☎(0841)532486 FAX (0841) 532867
*Large detached traditional hotel in an elevated position overlooking the river estuary.*
44⇌(11fb)⅄in 5 bedrooms CTV in all bedrooms ℝ S%
sB⇌£60-£65 dB⇌£80-£87 (room only) ⋤
Lift ⟨ 35P ✿ ⌒(heated) pitch & putt trampoline paddling pool xmas
**V** ✿ ⚑ ⅄ S10% Sunday Lunch £6.95-£8.95 Dinner £13.75&alc Last dinner 9.15pm
Credit Cards [1] [2] [3] [4] [5]

**★★59%** **Old Custom House Inn** South Quay PL28 8ED
☎(0841)532359
Closed Jan & Feb RS Nov, Dec & Etr
*Pleasant personally-run inn by harbour's edge and once the old custom house.*
24⇌(2fb) CTV in all bedrooms ℝ
CTV ♪
♀ English & French **V** ✿ Last dinner 9.30pm
Credit Cards [1] [2] [3] [5]

❋✕✕**Seafood** PL28 8BY ☎(0841)532485 FAX (0841) 533344
(Rosette awarded for dinner only)
*This fine restaurant has built up an excellent reputation for its fresh fish and shellfish. The daily changing menu offered by chef patron Rick Stein shows off his creative flair and intelligent use of herbs in flavouring. Highly recommended are his Ravioli of Crayfish with tarragon, a Meurette of Sander (a mixture of pike and perch stewed in red wine) and a braised fillet of brill with basil. Rick Stein's book, 'English Seafood Cookery' is on sale in the restaurant and should inspire guests to try out some of the dishes they have sampled here.*
Closed Sun, 15 Dec-1 Feb
Lunch not served
♀ English & French 75 seats ✳ Dinner £23.95&alc Last dinner 9.30pm 10P
Credit Cards [1] [2] [3]

---

**PAIGNTON** Devon Map **03** SX86
**★★★62%** **The Palace** Esplanade Rd TQ4 6BJ (Trusthouse Forte) ☎(0803)555121 FAX (0803) 527974
*Commanding fine views of sea and beach from its position on the seafront, this traditional hotel provides comfortable, spacious public rooms, well-equipped bedrooms which have recently been refurbished and a small sports/leisure complex. Service is attentive and pleasant throughout.*
52⇌(5fb)⅄in 14 bedrooms CTV in all bedrooms ℝ **T** S%
sB⇌fr£65 dB⇌fr£86 (room only) ⋤
Lift ⟨ 60P ✿ CFA ⌒ ♪ (hard) ☻ xmas
**V** ✿ ⚑ ⅄ S% Sunday Lunch £6.95-£7.50 Dinner fr£11.50&alc Last dinner 9pm
Credit Cards [1] [2] [3] [5]

**★★★60%** **Redcliffe** Marine Dr TQ3 2NL ☎(0803)526397 FAX (0803) 528030
*Dating back to the turn of the century this extended building on the Esplanade offers a choice of bedrooms and public areas which have recently been upgraded. Function rooms are available during the winter.*

60⇌ſ(8fb) CTV in all bedrooms ℝ **T** ✖ (ex guide dogs)
sB&B⇌ſ£34-£42 dB&B⇌ſ£68-£84 ⋤
Lift ⟨ CTV 80P ✿ CFA ⌒(heated) ⚡ putting green table tennis ๑ xmas
♀ English & French **V** ✿ ⚑ Sunday Lunch £6.75-£7.50 Dinner £10.75-£12.50 Last dinner 8.30pm
Credit Cards [1] [3]

---

**★★67%**, **Sunhill** Alta Vista Rd TQ4 6DA (Inter-Hotels)
☎(0803)557532 FAX (0803) 663850
*An hotel overlooking and having direct access to Goodrington Sands has recently been totally upgraded to provide value-for-money accommodation, some bedrooms having verandahs and awnings; meals are freshly cooked and experienced staff offer friendly service.*
31⇌ſ(5fb) CTV in all bedrooms ℝ **T** ✳ sB&B⇌ſ£25-£34 dB&B⇌ſ£50-£68 ⋤
Lift 31P snooker sauna solarium nc4yrs xmas
♀ English & French ✿ ⚑ ⅄ Dinner fr£12 Last dinner 7.30pm
Credit Cards [1] [3] [£]

---

**★★62%**, **Dainton** 95 Dartmouth Rd, Three Beaches, Goodrington TQ4 6NA ☎(0803)550067 & 525901
*Of modern construction, but Tudor in style, the hotel stands on a corner site, with the side road leading to the beach. This small, personally-run hotel has been upgraded under the new ownership to provide spotlessly clean, compact but well-equipped bedrooms, bright public rooms and a cosy intimate restaurant. Service is prompt and conducted in a friendly manner.*
11⇌ſ(3fb) CTV in all bedrooms ℝ **T** ✳ sB&B⇌ſfr£22.50 dB&B⇌ſfr£40 ⋤
⟨ CTV 20P ⊞ solarium ♫ xmas
♀ English & Continental **V** ✿ ⚑ ⅄ Lunch fr£5.50&alc High tea fr£5 Dinner fr£8&alc Last dinner 9.30pm
Credit Cards [1] [3]

**P**

# SUNHILL HOTEL

Alta Vista Road, Goodrington Sands, Paignton,
Devon TQ4 6DA

Tel: (0803) 557532    Fax: (0803) 663850

An English Tourist Board 4-crown rated hotel and a member of the prestigious Inter-Hotel Group, The Sunhill is privately owned and managed and situated in a delightful position overlooking Goodrington Sands.

All 29 bedrooms are fully en-suite including tea/coffee making facilities, radio, television, direct dialling telephones and a choice of balcony, seaview and standard rooms.

Recently refurbished throughout to the very highest standards, there is a lift, central heating for the winter months, a large car park, sauna, snooker room with a full size match play table and comprehensive conference facilities.

A spacious sun terrace overlooks the bay while in the dining room the freshly prepared and varied cuisine can be complimented by a wide choice of selected wines.

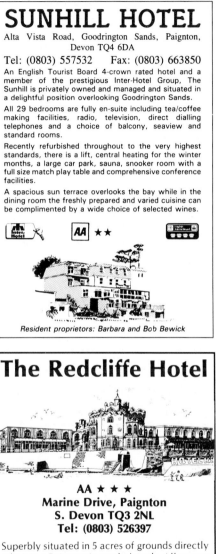

*Resident proprietors: Barbara and Bob Bewick*

★ ★

## THE OLD CUSTOM HOUSE

**South Quay, Padstow**

**Cornwall PL28 8ED**

**Telephone: 0841 532359**

During the early 1800's the Custom House was the focal point of Padstow Quay. Formerly a grain warehouse, the Caledonia Inn, a spit and sawdust bar, and custom house were converted into The Old Custom House Hotel which was opened in 1973. Full of interest and character the hotel offers 27 lovely bedrooms and a superb restaurant where the chef makes sure of getting fresh fish straight from the quay.

# The Redcliffe Hotel

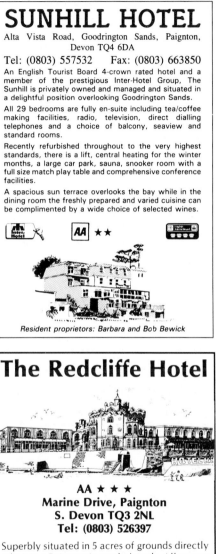

AA ★ ★ ★
**Marine Drive, Paignton**
**S. Devon TQ3 2NL**
**Tel: (0803) 526397**

Superbly situated in 5 acres of grounds directly adjoining Paignton's sandy beach. All rooms have private bathroom, radio, telephone, colour TV and tea making facilities, the majority with fine sea and coastal views.

*Heated Outdoor Pool
*Putting Green
*Hairdressing Salon
*Ample parking
*Ballroom with regular dancing
 during the season
*Excellent cuisine and service.

## Treglos Hotel

★★★

**Constantine Bay, Nr Padstow, Cornwall PL28 8JH**
**Telephone: (0841) 520727 Fax: (0841) 521163**
Guests return year after year to enjoy the personal attention, high standard of service, the superb restaurant and luxurious comfort. Specializing in local seafood, vegetables from the hotel garden and home made desserts with cornish cream. Six course table d'hôte, and extensive à la carte menu.
***Write to owner managers Ted and Barbara Barlow for colour Brochure.***
     See gazetteer under Constantine Bay
*Associate hotel – Budock Vean, Mawnan Smith*

P

**★★61% Torbay Holiday Motel** Totnes Rd TQ4 7PP
☎(0803)558226 FAX (0803) 663375
Closed 24-31 Dec
*Conveniently positioned on the Totnes road just outside Paignton, the friendly family-owned and run motel complex complements spacious, well-equipped bedrooms with pleasant, recently upgraded bars and restaurant. Holiday studio apartments and suites are also available, either self-catering or on a full-board basis, for guests who like to combine greater freedom and space with the convenience of hotel facilities.*
16⇘♠ CTV in all bedrooms ® T sB&B⇘♠£23-£26
dB&B⇘♠£36-£42
150P ⊞ ❀ ⊠(heated) ⌇(heated) sauna solarium gymnasium
crazy golf, adventure playground
♥ English & French V ♦ Bar Lunch £4-£6alc Dinner
£8.50&alc Last dinner 9pm
Credit Cards ① ③

**★★55% *Seaford*** 2-4 Stafford Rd TQ4 6EU (off Sands Road)
☎(0803)557341
*A friendly, informal, family-owned hotel popular with both tourists and commercial guests alike. The bedrooms, though rather compact, are well-equipped for the size of the hotel and the public rooms are bright and cosy. Situated close to the seafront.*
23rm(12⇘9♠) CTV in all bedrooms ® T ✖ (ex guide dogs)
Lift 10P
♥ English & French V ♦ Last dinner 9pm
Credit Cards ① ③

**★70% Oldway Links Hotel** 21 Southfield Rd TQ3 2LZ
☎(0803)559332
*In an elevated position with lovely views across the town to the sea, this elegant, detached hotel, now completely refurbished, provides compact bedrooms with good facilities, and an informal bar. Good, home cooked dishes feature on the table d'hôte menu.*
13rm(4⇘6♠)(2fb) CTV in all bedrooms ®
sB&B£16.50-£19.50 sB&B⇘♠£20-£23 dB&B£33-£39
dB&B⇘♠£40-£46 ⊟
40P ⊞ ❀ ♿
♥ English & French ♦ Bar Lunch £2.45-£4.75 Dinner £11.50
Last dinner 8.00pm
Credit Cards ① ③ ⓔ

**★62% Preston Sands** 10/12 Marine Pde TQ3 2NU
☎(0803)558718
*Bedrooms have fresh, modern décor and furnishings, while public areas include a very attractive and comfortable lounge complemented by a new bar and dining room, at an hotel which is well managed and friendly though both food and service tend to be simple.*
26⇘♠(2fb) CTV in all bedrooms ® sB&B⇘♠£18-£25
dB&B⇘♠£36-£48 ⊟
CTV 24P nc10yrs
V ♦ ⑃
ⓔ

**PAINSWICK** Gloucestershire Map 03 SO80

**★★★64% *Painswick*** Kemps Ln GL6 6YB ☎(0452)812160
Telex no 43605
*Although it is located in the centre of the village, this hotel is in a secluded position within the parish church, and the reception area was once a private chapel. The oak-panelled bar lounge has an open fire and a friendly atmosphere prevails throughout. Attentive service and an interesting menu are offered in the restaurant.*
15⇘♠(2fb) CTV in all bedrooms ® T
25P ⊞ ❀ snooker croquet
♥ French V ♦ ⑃ Last dinner 9.30pm
Credit Cards ① ② ③ ⑤

**PAISLEY** Hotels are listed under Glasgow Airport.

**PANGBOURNE** Berkshire Map 04 SU67

**★★★70% The Copper Inn** Church Rd RG8 7AR
☎Reading(0734)842244 Telex no 849041 FAX (0734) 845542
*Built as the Elephant in the hey day of the coaching era, the Inn has since been sympathetically modernised. Bedrooms are individually decorated and the restaurant offers an imaginative menu.*
22⇘♠(1fb)1⊞ CTV in all bedrooms ® T ✳ sB⇘♠£65-£75
dB⇘♠£75-£90 (room only) ⊟
30P ⊞ ❀
♥ English & French V ♦ ⑃ Lunch fr£13.50&alc Dinner
fr£16.95&alc Last dinner 9.30pm
Credit Cards ① ② ③ ⑤

**PARBOLD** Lancashire Map 07 SD41

**★69% Lindley** Lancaster Ln WN8 7AB ☎(02576)2804
Closed 24, 25, 31 Dec & 1 Jan
*Situated in an elevated position on the B6246 close to the village, this friendly hotel has recently been refurbished to provide most attractive and comfortable accommodation. There are lovely views from the smart restaurant.*
8⇘♠(1fb) CTV in all bedrooms ® T ✳ sB&B⇘♠£35-£45
dB&B⇘♠£40-£50
60P ⊞ ❀
♥ English & French V ♦ ⑃ ✂ Lunch £6.50-£7.50
Credit Cards ① ② ③ ⓔ

**PARKGATE** Cheshire Map 07 SJ27

**★★★57% The Ship** The Parade L64 6SA (Trusthouse Forte)
☎051-336 3931
*Relaxed, traditional small hotel with excellent views of the Dee Estuary and its wild bird life.*
26⇘2⊞✂in 2 bedrooms CTV in all bedrooms ® S8%
sB&B⇘£60-£65 dB&B⇘♠£65-£76 ⊟
⦅ 100P *xmas*
V ♦ ⑃ S% Lunch fr£8.50 Dinner fr£12.50&alc Last dinner
9.30pm
Credit Cards ① ② ③ ④ ⑤

**★★62% Parkgate** Boathouse Ln L64 6RD (Lansbury)
☎051-336 5001 Telex no 629469 FAX 051-336 8504
*This recently extended and refurbished hotel is well appointed for the business traveller.*
27⇘♠(3fb)1⊞✂in 5 bedrooms CTV in all bedrooms ® T
sB&B⇘♠£63 dB&B⇘♠£76 ⊟
⦅ 150P *xmas*
♥ English & French V ♦ ⑃ Lunch fr£8.95 Dinner fr£14&alc
Last dinner 10pm
Credit Cards ① ② ③ ⑤

**PARKHAM** Devon Map 02 SS32

**★★★64% Penhaven Country House** EX39 5PL
☎Horns Cross(02375)388 & 711
*Standing on the edge of the village in 11 acres of wooded grounds, a Victorian rectory has been sensitively restored to create a small hotel with a friendly, relaxed atmosphere. Well-equipped country-style bedrooms are individually decorated, while public rooms are cosy and comfortable. A small restaurant offers imaginative menus, making good use of such local specialities as Devon beef or Bideford Bay seafood, complemented by the hotel's own vegetables, and Parkham Cheddar cheese is featured on the cheese board. Accommodation with full use of the hotel's services and facilities is also available in 5 adjoining cottages.*
12⇘♠(5fb)⊞ CTV in all bedrooms ® T
sB&B⇘♠£42.50-£48.50 dB&B⇘♠£85-£97 (incl dinner) ⊟
50P ⊞ ❀ nc10yrs *xmas*

♀ English & French **V** ♥ ⛱ ✂ Lunch fr£7.50&alc High tea fr£4 Dinner £12.95-£13.95&alc Last dinner 9.30pm
Credit Cards ①②③⑤ⓔ

## PATELEY BRIDGE North Yorkshire Map **07** SE16

✗✗*Sportsman's Arms* Wath-in-Nidderdale HG3 5PP (2m NW unclass rd) ☎Harrogate(0423)711306
*Nestling in the beautiful Nidderdale countryside this restaurant is housed in an attractive building dating from the 17th century. Cuisine is basically British with game (in season), salmon, beef, duck, pork and fish expertly cooked and served. The food is complemented by an extensive wine list.*
Closed 25-26 Dec
Lunch not served Mon-Sat
Dinner not served Sun
♀ English & Continental **V** 45 seats Last dinner 9.30pm 30P
Credit Cards ①②③⑤

## PATHHEAD Lothian *Midlothian* Map **11** NT36

★★★59% **Stair Arms** EH37 5TX ☎Ford(0875)320277
FAX (0875) 320929
*Conveniently situated twelve miles south of Edinburgh on the A68 this attractive hotel offers comfortable, well-appointed bedrooms and good value menus. Managed by the resident proprietors, service is attentive and friendly.*
12rm(10⇔)(1fb)1⊞ CTV in all bedrooms ® **T** ✱
sB&B£29-£35 sB&B⇔↑£35-£48 dB&B⇔↑£45-£55 �ᵽ
《 50P ✿ ⳿⳿ *xmas*
**V** ♥ Lunch fr£1.50
Credit Cards ①②③⑤

## PATTERDALE Cumbria Map **11** NY31

★★57% **Patterdale** CA11 0NN ☎Glenridding(07684)82231
FAX (07684) 82440
Closed Jan-Feb
*Owned by the same family for over sixty years, this hotel has recently upgraded its bedrooms to provide a good standard of accommodation.*
57⇔↑(4fb) CTV in all bedrooms ® **T** ✱ sB&B⇔↑£25-£30 dB&B⇔↑£50-£60
CTV 30P 1❦ ✿ ✔ *xmas*
**V** ♥ Lunch fr£9 Dinner fr£12 Last dinner 8pm
Credit Cards ①③ⓔ

## PATTINGHAM Staffordshire Map **07** SO89

★★★56% **Patshull Park** Patshull WV6 7HR (1.5m W of Pattingham) ☎(0902)700100 Telex no 334849
FAX (0902) 700874
*Popular for functions and residential golfing breaks, with an 18-hole golf course, 65-acre fishing lake and a large leisure/fitness complex within the spacious grounds.*
48⇔↑(4fb) CTV in all bedrooms ® **T** sB&B⇔↑£60-£70 dB&B⇔↑£74-£85 ᵽ
《 ⊞ CTV 200P ✿ ⛱(heated) ▶ 18 ✔ snooker sauna solarium gymnasium beautician *xmas*
♀ English & French **V** ♥ ⛱ Lunch fr£7.75 Dinner fr£11.75&alc Last dinner 9.30pm
Credit Cards ①②③⑤ⓔ

## PEASMARSH East Sussex Map **05** TQ82

★★66% **Flackley Ash** TN31 6YH (Best Western) ☎(079721)651
Telex no 957210 FAX (079721) 510
*A Georgian manor house has been skilfully extended to provide additional bedrooms of a luxurious standard and good indoor leisure facilities. All rooms are well equipped and furnished in modern style, the informal service provided throughout being in keeping with the relaxed atmosphere of the hotel.*

30rm(21⇔3↑)(3fb)3⊞ CTV in all bedrooms ® **T**
sB&B⇔↑£52.50-£66.50 dB&B⇔↑£79.50-£94.50 ᵽ
70P ✿ ⛱(heated) sauna solarium gymnasium spa bath croquet *xmas*
♀ English & French **V** ♥ ⛱ Lunch £10.95-£11.95 High tea £3.75-£5alc Dinner £13.95-£21.50alc Last dinner 9.30pm
Credit Cards ①②③⑤

## PEAT INN Fife Map **12** NO40

✿✗✗**The Peat Inn** KY15 5LH ☎(033484)206
*Master Chef David Wilson continues to earn high praise for this delightful country inn. The daily set menu offers six courses, and there is also a full à la carte menu, both promoting local produce and game dishes. The lunchtime set menu, served at 1pm, is excellent value and deservedly popular. Should diners wish to stay overnight, there are eight suites, attractively and comfortably furnished.*
Closed Sun, Mon, 2 wks Jan & 2 wks Nov
♀ French 48 seats ✱ Lunch £16.50 Dinner fr£26&alc Last lunch 1pm Last dinner 9.30pm 24P ✂
Credit Cards ①②③⑤

## PEEBLES Borders *Peeblesshire* Map **11** NT24

★★★64% **Peebles Hydro** EH45 8LX (Consort) ☎(0721)20602
Telex no 72568 FAX (0721) 22999
*Majestically placed above the town, this elegant Edwardian hotel has a swimming pool, tennis courts and a putting green. The supervised play rooms and other facilities will also appeal to families with young children, and there are excellent conference and function rooms.*
134⇔↑(25fb) CTV in all bedrooms ® **T** ✗ (ex guide dogs)
S% sB&B⇔↑£54.75-£60.50
dB&B⇔↑£75-£120.50 (incl dinner) ᵽ                    ▶

**P**

Lift ⟨ 200P ❀ CFA ▣(heated) ♪ (hard) squash ∪ snooker sauna solarium gymnasium pitch & putt badminton beautician ♫ ⌀ xmas
V ✆ ⚏ ⚡
Credit Cards ① ② ③ ⑤ £

**★★★58% Park** Innerleithen Rd EH45 8BA ☎(0721)20451
Telex no 72568 FAX (0721) 22999
*This traditional town-centre hotel, set in an attractive garden, enjoys pleasant views over the surrounding countryside and offers accommodation in well-equipped, comfortable bedrooms; after eating in the charming oak-panelled restaurant guests can relax in a comfortable lounge or make use (free of charge) of the sports and leisure facilities at the nearby Peebles Hydro, a sister hotel.*
24⇨↑Annexe1⇨1▥ CTV in all bedrooms ® T ✱
sB&B⇨↑£45.50-£51
dB&B⇨↑£67.50-£105.50 (incl dinner) ⊟
⟨ 50P ❀ xmas
V ✆ ⚏ Sunday Lunch £8.75 Dinner £12.75-£19.25 Last dinner 9.30pm
Credit Cards ① ② ③ ⑤

**★★★50% The Tontine** High St EH45 8AJ (Trusthouse Forte)
☎(0721)20892
*Traditional, friendly and well-equipped hotel in the centre of the picturesque town.*
37⇨↑in 5 bedrooms CTV in all bedrooms ® T S%
sB&B⇨↑£45-£50 dB&B⇨↑£50-£60 ⊟
30P 4⊜ CFA xmas
♀ Scottish & French V ✆ ⚏ ⚡ S% Bar Lunch £3.40-£7 High tea £5-£7 Dinner fr£11.50&alc Last dinner 9pm
Credit Cards ① ② ③ ④ ⑤

**★★⚉77% Cringletie House** EH45 8PL ☎Eddleston(07213)233
FAX (07213) 244
Closed 2 Jan-8 Mar
*A romantically splendid country house featuring crow-stepped gables and fairytale turrets. Owned and managed by the Maguire family, supported by a courteous and attentive staff, warm and spontaneous service is assured. Bedroom accommodation is cosy and inviting, as are the two spacious lounges. The home cooked dinners are very good value for money.*
13⇨↑(2fb) CTV in all bedrooms T sB&B⇨↑£39-£50
dB&B⇨↑£72 ⊟
Lift 40P ⊞ ❀ ♪ (hard) putting croquet
♀ International ✆ ⚏ ⚡ Lunch £5-£12.50 Dinner fr£20 Last dinner 8.30pm
Credit Cards ① ③

**★★67% Kingsmuir** Springhill Rd EH45 9EP ☎(0721)20151
FAX (0721) 21795
*Comfortable and friendly under the management of its resident proprietors, the hotel offers home-cooked meals in both bar and restaurant which represent particularly good value for money.*
10⇨↑(2fb) CTV in all bedrooms ® T sB&B⇨↑£28-£35
dB&B⇨↑£50-£58 ⊟
27P ⊞ ❀ ⌀
V ✆ ⚡ Lunch £8&alc Dinner £12.50&alc Last dinner 8.30pm
Credit Cards ① ② ③ £

**★★⚉62% Venlaw Castle** Edinburgh Rd EH45 8QG
☎(0721)20384
Closed Nov-Mar
*Pleasantly secluded by trees, yet commanding beautiful views from its upper windows, this baronial-style house in the hills above the town has been owned by the same family for more than thirty years. Traditional standards of hospitality and service are maintained throughout, a particularly relaxing lounge and unique library bar being attractive features.*
12rm(5⇨4↑)(4fb) CTV in all bedrooms ® ✱ sB&B£22-£26
sB&B⇨↑£26-£28 dB&B£40-£44 dB&B⇨↑£50-£54 ⊟
20P ⊞ ❀

V ✆ Bar Lunch £4.50-£6 Dinner £11.50-£12.50 Last dinner 8pm
Credit Cards ① ② ③ ④ ⑤ £

**PELYNT** Cornwall & Isles of Scilly Map **02** SX25

**★★63% Jubilee Inn** PL13 2JZ ☎Lanreath(0503)20312
*An inn of charm and character has been tastefully modernised to provide comfortable accommodation; the atmosphere is relaxing and friendly, helpful service being rendered by charming staff.*
9⇨↑(2fb)▥ CTV in all bedrooms
CTV 80P 6⊜ ❀ ⌀
♀ English & Continental V ✆ ⚏ Last dinner 10pm
Credit Cards ① ③

**PEMBROKE** Dyfed Map **02** SM90

See also **Lamphey**
**★★59% Coach House Inn** 116 Main St SA71 4HN (Exec Hotel)
☎(0646)684602 FAX (0646) 687456
Closed 24-26 Dec
*The yard of an old coaching inn has been roofed to create an attractive bar with a small but comfortable gallery lounge; bedrooms are pine-fitted, and the good food on offer includes a fine vegetarian selection.*
14⇨↑(3fb)⚡in 4 bedrooms CTV in all bedrooms ® T
✖ (ex guide dogs) sB&B⇨↑£31-£34 dB&B⇨↑£44-£46 ⊟
10P ❀ solarium
♀ English & French V ✆ ⚏ Lunch £11.05-£20.85alc Dinner £12.50&alc Last dinner 9pm
Credit Cards ① ② ③ ⑤ £

**★★59% Old Kings Arms** Main St SA71 4JS ☎(0646)683611
Closed 25-26 Dec & 1 Jan
*Bedrooms are compact but well equipped at this small, historic hotel which stands right in the centre of the town. The slab-floored Kitchen Dining Room offers a good choice of food, and meals are also available in the two popular bars.*
21⇨↑ CTV in all bedrooms ®
21P
V ✆ Last dinner 10pm
Credit Cards ① ② ③

**PENARTH** South Glamorgan Map **03** ST17

**★65% Walton House** 37 Victoria Rd CF6 2HY ☎(0222)707782
FAX (0222) 711012
RS Sun
*This small, friendly, family-run hotel, situated in a quiet part of the town, provides accommodation in bedrooms that are continually being improved. An attractive restaurant offers a wide choice of enjoyable meals.*
12rm(9⇨↑) CTV in all bedrooms ® ✖ (ex guide dogs) ✱ sB&B£21 sB&B⇨↑£25.50-£28.50 dB&B£35 dB&B⇨↑£39
16P ⊞ ❀
♀ English, French, Italian & Spanish V Lunch £9.50&alc Dinner £9.50&alc Last dinner 9pm
Credit Cards ① ③

**✖Il Pescatore** The Esplanade ☎(0222)703428
*Standing beside the yacht club, with lovely views over the Bristol Channel, this little restaurant complements its variety of Italian dishes with a few in English style among both main courses and sweets. Pasta items such as Tagliatelli Napoletana or Alfredo, tempt the palate, and there is a good range of Italian wines available. There is also a more modestly priced Pizzeria, open both at lunchtime and in the evening.*
Closed Mon
Lunch not served Sat
Dinner not served Sun

▶

♀ French & Italian **V** 46 seats Lunch £6.50-£15alc Dinner
£6.50-£15alc Last lunch 2.30pm Last dinner 11pm ≯
Credit Cards [1] [2] [3]

---

**PENCOED** Mid Glamorgan Map **03** SS98

⬘**Travelodge** Old Mill, Felindre Rd CF3 5HU (Trusthouse
Forte) ☎(0656)864404 Central Res (0800) 850950
*From junction 35 on the M4 take the A473 to Pencoed. Take the
first right signposted Cemetery, then first left. The Travelodge is
adjacent to the Harvesters Restaurant.*
40⇌♠(40fb) CTV in all bedrooms ® sB⇌♠£24
dB⇌♠£29.50 (room only)
《 40P ⇗
Credit Cards [1] [2] [3]

---

**PENCRAIG** Hereford & Worcester Map **03** SO52

★★♨62%, **Pencraig Court** HR9 6HR (off A40)
☎Ross-on-Wye(0989)84306
Closed Xmas, New Year & Jan-Feb
*Just off the A40, four miles south of Ross-on-Wye, this hotel is set
in three-and-a-half acres of grounds, with some superb views of the
surrounding countryside. The hotel is privately owned and has a
relaxed, informal atmosphere.*
11⇌(2fb)1⊞ CTV in all bedrooms ® ✖ (ex guide dogs)
sB&B⇌£31-£37 dB&B⇌£40-£52 ฿
25P ✿ ∪
♀ English & French **V** ♡ ⌷ S% Bar Lunch fr£3.25 Dinner
fr£12.50&alc Last dinner 9pm
Credit Cards [1] [2] [3] [5]

---

**PENKRIDGE** Staffordshire Map **07** SJ91

✖**William Harding's House** Mill St ST19 5AY ☎(0785)712955
Closed Mon & 26-29 Dec
Lunch not served ex Sun Autumn & Winter
♀ English & French 24 seats ✱ Dinner fr£16.90 Last dinner
9.30pm ≯ nc15yrs
Credit Cards [1] [3]

---

**PENMAEN** West Glamorgan Map **02** SS58

★★62%, **Nicholaston House** Nicholaston SA3 2HL
☎Swansea(0792)371317
*Now converted to provide good modern accommodation this hotel
offers warm friendly hospitality and well-equipped bedrooms. A
full size snooker table is available.*
11⇌(4fb)1⊞ CTV in all bedrooms ® ✱ sB&B⇌£16-£30
dB&B⇌£32-£65 ฿
CTV 35P ✿ snooker 9 hole putting green
**V** ⌇ Sunday Lunch fr£7.50alc Dinner £4.95-£18.50alc Last
dinner 9pm
Credit Cards [1] [3]

---

**PENNAL** Gwynedd Map **06** SH60

★★60%, **Llugwy Hall Country House** SY20 9JX (1m E on A483)
☎(065475)228 FAX (065475) 231
*The hall stands in a picturesque setting beside the Dovey River,
and part of it has been converted into an Outdoor Pursuits Centre;
in the remainder, however, guests can enjoy modern comforts, good
cooking and friendly service.*
15rm(13⇌♠)(4fb)⌇in 1 bedroom CTV in all bedrooms ® T
sB&B£37.50-£45 sB&B⇌♠£37.50-£45 dB&B£65-£75
dB&B⇌♠£65-£75 ฿
40P ✿ croquet badminton clay pigeon shooting *xmas*
**V** ♡ ⌷ Sunday Lunch £5.95-£8 Dinner £11.50&alc Last dinner
9pm
Credit Cards [1] [2] [3] [5]

---

★**50%, Riverside** SY20 9DW ☎(065475)285
*Located in the centre of the village by the river bridge, this inn
caters for locals and tourists alike.*
7rm(1fb) ® ✱ sB&Bfr£18.50 dB&Bfr£37
CTV 60P 4🍴 ✿
**V** ♡ Lunch £5.95-£9.50 Dinner £10.95-£12.95 Last dinner
9.30pm

---

**PENRHYNDEUDRAETH** Gwynedd Map **06** SH63

★★★76%, **The Hotel Portmeirion** LL48 6ET (2m W,
Portmeirion village is S off A487) ☎Porthmadog(0766)770228
Telex no 61540 FAX (0766) 771331
Closed 14 Jan-8 Feb
*The hotel is an important part of the Italian-style village which was
built by Sir Clough Williams-Ellis between 1925 and 1972.
Destroyed by fire in 1981 the hotel, now painstakingly restored,
offers superbly elegant accommodation, good quality imaginative
cuisine and attentive, professional service. Fourteen main house
bedrooms are supplemented by another twenty individually styled
rooms situated in nine houses and cottages throughout the village.
Free transport to and from the main house is available if required.
The village, which has lovely sandy beaches and walks is a popular
tourist attraction and was the location for the TV series 'The
Prisoner'.*
14⇌Annexe20⇌(2fb)2⊞ CTV in all bedrooms ® T
✖ (ex guide dogs) ✱ dB⇌£45-£115 (room only) ฿
《 40P ⇗ ✿ ≏(heated) ♫ *xmas*
♡ ⌇ ⌷ Lunch £10.50-£12.50 Dinner £20.50 Last dinner
9.30pm
Credit Cards [1] [2] [3] [5]

---

**PENRITH** Cumbria Map **12** NY53

See also **Edenhall and Shap**
★★★73%, **North Lakes** Ullswater Rd CA11 8QT (Shire)
☎(0768)68111 Telex no 64257 FAX (0768) 68291
*A modern, well-appointed hotel, situated close to the M6, with
extensive leisure and conference facilities. It offers every comfort to
its guests, whether on holiday or on business. Bedrooms are
attractively furnished and very well equipped and public areas are
full of character. The Martindale restaurant is particularly
efficient and friendly.*
85⇌(6fb)4⊞⌇in 12 bedrooms CTV in all bedrooms ® T ✱
sB&B⇌£74-£90 dB&B⇌£90-£114 ฿
Lift 《 CTV 150P ≏(heated) squash snooker sauna solarium
gymnasium spa pool *xmas*
♀ English & French **V** ♡ ⌷
Credit Cards [1] [2] [3] [5]

★★64%, **George** Devonshire St CA1 7SU ☎(0768)62696
FAX (0768)68223
Closed 25-26 Dec & 1 Jan
*While providing a good standard of modern amenities, this
traditional town centre hotel retains much of its earlier character
as a coaching inn. Good value lunches are served in its attractive
dining room and enjoyable afternoon teas in the comfortable foyer
lounges.*
31⇌♠(1fb) CTV in all bedrooms ® T sB&B⇌♠fr£37
dB&B⇌♠fr£49.50 ฿
《 30P
♀ English & French ♡ ⌷ Lunch fr£6.50 Dinner fr£10.50 Last
dinner 8.30pm
Credit Cards [1] [3] [£]

★★59%, *Clifton Hill* Clifton CA10 2EJ (2.75m S A6)
☎(0768)62717
*Set back from the A6 in its own grounds, three miles south of the
town, a family owned and run hotel features organised tours of the
Lake District.*

57⇨♠(2fb) CTV in all bedrooms
CTV 200P 25🏰 ✤
V ✿ ⚏ ⚡

★★ 55% **Roundthorn Country** Beacon Edge CA11 8SJ
☎(0768)63952
Closed Nov-Feb RS Mar & Nov
7⇨♠(2fb)1⊞ CTV in all bedrooms Ⓡ ✱ sB&B⇨♠£20-£25
dB&B⇨♠£35-£45 ⌷
40P 2🏰 ✤ nc3yrs
Dinner £9.50-£12&alc
Credit Cards ⊡ ⊡

★ 56% **Glen Cottage** Corney Square CA11 7PX ☎(0768)62221
Closed 25-26 Dec & 1 Jan
*An eighteenth-century house in the centre of the town offers
adequate accommodation, friendly service and good value for
money.*
7rm(4⇨♠)(3fb) CTV in all bedrooms Ⓡ sB&B£19.50-£21
sB&B⇨♠£22.50-£25 dB&B£30-£32 dB&B⇨♠£33-£36
3🏰 (50p per night)
✿ Lunch £3.95-£5.50 Dinner £5.50-£7.50 Last dinner 9pm
Credit Cards ⊡ ⊡ ⊡ ⊡

⬆**Travelodge** Redhills CA11 0DT (A66) (Trusthouse Forte)
☎(0768)66958 Central Res (0800) 850950
*Standing beside the A66, just west of its junction with the M6, the
Lodge offers a good standard of reasonably-priced
accommodation, meals (mainly grill type) being available at the
adjacent Little Chef.*
32⇨♠(32fb) CTV in all bedrooms Ⓡ sB⇨♠£24
dB⇨♠£29.50 (room only)
⊛ 32P ⚑
Credit Cards ⊡ ⊡ ⊡

P

**PENYBONT** Powys Map **03** SO16

★★62%, **Severn Arms** LD1 5UA ☎(059787)224 & 344
Closed Xmas wk
*This historic inn, situated alongside the A44, has bright clean bedrooms. The restaurant provides good food and, like the bars, has a popular local following. Free fishing is available for residents.*
10⇆(6fb) CTV in all bedrooms ® T ✱ sB&B⇆£24 dB&B⇆£42 ♬
CTV 20P 2🏊 ❈ ♪
V 🕸
Credit Cards ①③ ⓔ

---

**PENZANCE** Cornwall & Isles of Scilly Map **02** SW43

★★★♨62%, **Higher Faugan** Newlyn TR18 5NS (off B3315)
☎(0736)62076 FAX (0736) 51648
*Built for Stanhope Forbes in 1904, this Cornish stone house stands in 10 acres of gardens and paddocks and is now a relaxing venue for both business and holiday travellers. Bedrooms are individually furnished and a short table d'hôte menu is offered at dinner.*
12⇆♟(2fb)1 ♨ ⅓ in 3 bedrooms CTV in all bedrooms ® T
✖ (ex guide dogs) ✱ sB&B⇆♟£38 dB&B⇆♟£60-£78 ♬
20P 3🏊 ♨ ❈ ⌣(heated) ♪ (hard) snooker solarium gymnasium putting green *xmas*
♘ English, French & Italian 🕸 ⚆ Dinner fr£10 Last dinner 8.30pm
Credit Cards ①②③⑤ ⓔ

★★★60%, **Mount Prospect** Britons Hill TR18 3AE (Exec Hotel)
☎(0736)63117 FAX (0736) 50970
*Well-appointed hotel in gardens overlooking Mounts Bay and Penzance harbour.*
26⇆♟(2fb)⅓in 6 bedrooms CTV in all bedrooms ® T
sB&B⇆♟£34.50-£35.65 dB&B⇆♟£55.20-£57.50 ♬
《 CTV 14P ❈ ⌣(heated)
♘ English & Continental 🕸 ⚆ Bar Lunch £3.50-£7.20alc Dinner fr£11.50&alc Last dinner 9pm
Credit Cards ①②③⑤

★★★52%, **Queen's** The Promenade TR18 4HG ☎(0736)62371
FAX (0736) 50033
*Large, traditional hotel on the sea front with exceptional views over Mount's Bay.*
71⇆♟(9fb)1♨ CTV in all bedrooms ® T sB&B⇆♟£33-£44 dB&B⇆♟£60-£80 ♬
Lift 《 100P snooker sauna solarium gymnasium *xmas*
♘ English & French V 🕸 ⚆ ⅓ Sunday Lunch fr£7.50 Dinner £14-£17.50&alc Last dinner 8.45pm
Credit Cards ①②③⑤ ⓔ

★★62%, **Kenegie Manor** Gulval TR20 8YN ☎(0736)69174
FAX (0736) 63272
*The hotel forms the focal point of a holiday village consisting of around 100 units. It has good leisure facilities, including an indoor pool and there is live entertainment in the Tudor Bar during the season. Bedrooms are all pleasantly furnished to a similar standard. The dining room offers a carvery-style operation at both breakfast and dinner.*
21⇆♟(9fb) CTV in all bedrooms ® T ✱ sB&B⇆♟£30-£32 dB&B⇆♟£60-£64 ♬
▦ CTV 80P ❈ ▣(heated) ⌣ ♪ (hard) sauna solarium ໑ *xmas*
V 🕸 ⚆ ⅓ Dinner £13.50 Last dinner 9.30pm
Credit Cards ①③

★★60%, **Sea & Horses** 6 Alexandra Ter TR18 4NX
☎(0736)61961
Closed mid Nov-mid Feb
*A homely atmosphere and good value for money are provided by a small, personally-run hotel with views over St Mounts Bay. The single-fronted, Victorian, mid-terrace premises offer simple,*

*comfortable bedrooms, honest, home-cooked meals and a good standard of housekeeping throughout.*
11rm(2⇆6♟)(4fb) CTV in all bedrooms ® T ✖ ✱
sB&B£17.50-£19 sB&B⇆♟£17.50-£19 dB&B£32-£36 dB&B⇆♟£35-£38
8P 1🏊 (£1) 🚭
V 🕸 ⚆ Bar Lunch 85p-£3.50 Dinner £8.50 Last dinner 7.30pm
Credit Cards ①③

★73%, **Estoril** 46 Morrab Rd TR18 4EX ☎(0736)62468 & 67471
Closed Dec-Jan
*This comfortable private hotel, centrally situated a short walk from both promenade and shops, provides accommodation in well-appointed, individually furnished bedrooms, wholesome home-cooked meals and a family atmosphere.*
10⇆♟(2fb) CTV in all bedrooms ® T ✖ sB&B⇆♟£23-£24 dB&B⇆♟£46-£48 ♬
4P 🚭
V Lunch £6 Dinner £10 Last dinner 7.30pm
Credit Cards ①③ ⓔ

# Estoril Hotel

★
**46 Morrab Road, Penzance, Cornwall
Telephone:
(0736) 62468/67471**

You will find this small comfortable hotel ideally situated between the promenade and the town centre.

A warm welcome awaits guests at all times. Highly recommended. All rooms en suite. Special diets catered for.

Access                                         Visa

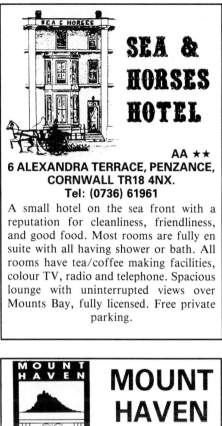

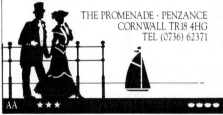
551

★**70%, Tarbert** 11-12 Clarence St TR18 2NU (Minotels)
☎(0736)63758
Closed Dec-15 Jan
*Ideally situated for touring the Penwith Peninsula and West Cornwall, this listed Georgian building within walking distance of the town centre offers freshly decorated bedrooms (most with Laura Ashley prints), well equipped and provided with en suite facilities. Cosy lounges combine quality, character and charm, whilst an informal dining room provides both table d'hôte and à la carte menus, with personal service from the resident proprietors.*
12⇅ᐃ♪ CTV in all bedrooms ® T Ⅺメ sB&B⇅ᐃ♪£22.50-£25.50 dB&B⇅ᐃ♪£39-£51 ➡
CTV 5P ⇛ nc12yrs
♡ English & French V ♥ ⌁ Bar Lunch £1.50-£4.50 Dinner £10.50&alc Last dinner 8pm
Credit Cards [1][2][3][5]

★**61%** *Alexandra* Alexandra Ter, Seafront TR18 4NX
☎(0736)62644 Telex no 934999
*A double-fronted Victorian holiday hotel in end-of-terrace position provides well-equipped bedrooms, simple wholesome food and a homely atmosphere.*
33rm(6⇅24♪)(12fb) CTV in all bedrooms ®
21P ♫
♡ International V ♥ ⌁ Last dinner 7.45pm
Credit Cards [1][2][3]

## PERELLE

See **Guernsey** under **Channel Islands**

## PERRANPORTH Cornwall & Isles of Scilly Map **02** SW75

★**67%, Beach Dunes** Ramoth Way, Reen Sands TR6 0BY
☎Truro(0872)572263 FAX (0872) 573824
Closed Nov & Dec RS Jan & Feb
*Set in the sand dunes above the beach, at the end of its own private road, a small, family-run hotel with a relaxed and friendly atmosphere offers accommodation in well-equipped bedrooms. Spacious lawns and patios provide ideal suntraps, and guests have the use of the hotel's squash court and indoor swimming pool.*
7rm(3⇅♪)Annexe3⇅♪(2fb) CTV in all bedrooms ® T Ⅺメ (ex guide dogs) sB&B£20.50-£25.50
sB&B⇅♪£20.50-£25.50 dB&B£41-£51 dB&B⇅♪£41-£51
15P ⇛ ❄ ☐(heated) squash exercise equipment nc3yrs
V ♥ ⌁ ⅍ Bar Lunch £3-£7alc
Credit Cards [1][3]

## PERRANUTHNOE Cornwall & Isles of Scilly Map **02** SW52

★**60%,** *Ednovean House* Ednovean Ln TR20 9LZ (on A394 5m E of Penzance) ☎Penzance(0736)711071
*A personally-run hotel of character with fine views over the bay and St Michael's Mount from its quiet rural setting. Comfortable public areas and bedrooms which, though compact, are bright, well furnished and fully equipped. Good meals, which cater for vegetarian and other diets, and a friendly, informal atmosphere make this the ideal retreat. Guests can relax in the attractive, mature gardens and the beach is only a short walk away.*
9rm(6♪)(2fb) ®
CTV 16P ⇛ ❄ putting green, croquet ♧
V ♥ ⌁ ⅍
Credit Cards [1][3]

All AA-appointed establishments are inspected regularly to ensure that required standards are maintained.

## PERTH Tayside *Perthshire* Map **11** NO12

See town plan section

❀ ★★★**78%, Murrayshall Country House Hotel** New Scone PH2 7PH ☎(0738)51171 Telex no 76197 FAX (0738) 52595
*A country-house hotel just north of Perth, Murrayshall has its own golf course and separate club house so that golfing parties do not intrude on the quiet atmosphere. The major attraction, however, is the excellent cooking of master chef Bruce Sangster. The 4-course table d'hôte menu provides a choice at each course and displays a subtlety and skill rarely encountered outside London and the Home Counties. A pianist and harpist provide entertainment in the evenings, creating a relaxing atmosphere for diners. Accommodation, especially in the main house, is spacious, though rooms in the new wing are more compact.*
19⇅ᐃ(1fb) CTV in all bedrooms T Ⅺ (ex guide dogs)
sB&B⇅ᐃ♪£70-£75 dB&B⇅ᐃ♪£105-£115 ➡
⟜ 50P ⇛ ❄ ⚑ 18 ♟ (hard) bowling green croquet *xmas*
♡ British & French ♥ ⌁ Lunch fr£17.50 Dinner fr£35 Last dinner 9.30pm
Credit Cards [1][2][3][5]

★★★**62%,** *Huntingtower* Crieff Rd, Almondbank PH1 3JT (3m W off A85) ☎(0738)83771 FAX (0738) 83777
*This popular business and tourist hotel is situated in 3.5 acres of beautiful grounds, just a short drive west of the city bypass. Public areas offer traditional comforts, while the neatly appointed bedrooms, some with en suite jacuzzi baths, have been thoughtfully equipped with useful extras. Dinner in the candlelit panelled restaurant is a pleasurable experience.*
17⇅ᐃ♪Annexe7rm(4⇅ᐃ)(2fb) CTV in 17 bedrooms ®
⟜ CTV 100P ❄ putting
♡ Scottish & Continental V ♥ ⌁ ⅍ Last dinner 9.30pm
Credit Cards [1][2][3][5]

★★★**62%, Queens Hotel** Leonard St PH2 8HB ☎(0738)25471 Telex no 76531 FAX (0738) 38496
*Close to the station and city centre, this extensively refurbished business and tourist hotel offers a range of conference and leisure facilities.*
50rm(40⇅9♪)(7fb)1 ✿ CTV in all bedrooms ® T Ⅺ
sB&B⇅ᐃ♪£52-£56 dB&B⇅ᐃ♪£68-£72 ➡
Lift ⟜ 30P ☐(heated) sauna solarium gymnasium *xmas*
V ♥ ⌁
Credit Cards [1][2][3] £

★★★**59%, Lovat** 90 Glasgow Rd PH2 0LT ☎(0738)36555
Telex no 76531 FAX (0738) 43123
*Popular business, tourist and conference hotel just south of city centre, with one bar reserved for non-smokers.*
26⇅ᐃ♪(3fb) CTV in all bedrooms ® T Ⅺ (ex guide dogs)
sB&B⇅ᐃ♪£44 dB&B⇅ᐃ♪£60 ➡
⟜ 60P *xmas*
V ♥ ⌁ ⅍ Lunch £6.75-£10 High tea £4.75-£9 Dinner £10-£14&alc Last dinner 9.30pm
Credit Cards [1][2][3] £

★★★**58%, Stakis City Mills** West Mill St PH1 5QP (Stakis) ☎(0738)28281 Telex no 778704 FAX (0738) 43423
*A former water mill, imaginatively converted into an interesting hotel with a choice of bars and restaurants.*
78rm(76⇅)(2fb)2✿⅍in 50 bedrooms CTV in all bedrooms ® T ✳ sB⇅ᐃ£59.50-£60 dB⇅ᐃ£71-£81 (room only) ➡
⟜ 75P CFA ♫ *xmas*
♡ International V ♥ ⌁ ⅍ Lunch fr£8&alc Dinner fr£11&alc Last dinner 10pm
Credit Cards [1][2][3][5] £

★★★**57%, Newton House** Glencarse PH2 7LX (Inter-Hotels)
☎Glencarse(073886)250 FAX (073886) 717
*Set back from the busy A85, in its own grounds, this small hotel is personally managed by the resident proprietors. The lunch and dinner menus feature well-prepared Scottish produce which is served in either the dining room or cosy bar.*

10⇨♪♠(2fb) CTV in all bedrooms ® T sB&B⇨♪♠£44-£50
dB&B⇨♪♠£64 ⊟
CTV 50P ✿ ♨ xmas
♋ Scottish & French V ♦ ⌑ Lunch £10-£14&alc High tea
£5-£11alc Dinner £19&alc Last dinner 9pm
Credit Cards ①③⑤ⓔ

*See advertisement on page 555*

★★★57%, **The Royal George** Tay St PH1 5LD (Trusthouse
Forte) ☎(0738)24455 FAX (0738) 30345
RS Jan-Feb
*A popular hotel standing beside the river and close to the town
centre amenities. Refurbishment has considerably enhanced the
public areas, but though bedroom improvements are underway,
some rooms remain rather dated.*
43⇨♪⚥in 16 bedrooms CTV in all bedrooms ® T ✳ sB⇨♪fr£65
dB⇨♪£81-£90 (room only) ⊟
《 20P 12🐾 xmas
♋ International V ♦ ⌑ ⚥ Lunch fr£8.95&alc High tea
£5.75-£6.75 Dinner fr£11.50&alc Last dinner 9.30pm
Credit Cards ①②③④⑤

★★★56%, **Isle of Skye Toby** Queen's Bridge, Dundee Rd
PH2 7AB (Toby) ☎(0738)24471 Telex no 76185
*Comfortable, spacious bedrooms and bright, modern public areas
are provided by this virtually rebuilt hotel. The original building
houses the popular Carving Room and additional bedrooms, some
of which are rather compact.*
56⇨♪♠in 14 bedrooms CTV in all bedrooms ®
✖ (ex guide dogs)
Lift 《 70P CFA
♦ ⌑ ⚥ Last dinner 9pm
Credit Cards ①②③⑤

★★★

This converted mill has 78
bedrooms all with en suite
bathrooms, colour television,
tea and coffee facilities. Our two
restaurants offer excellent
cuisine. Conference facilities
from 2 to 150, Weddings,
Dinner Dances and Seminars.
Easy access by road and rail.
Tel: (0738) 28281

—— 🏛 STAKIS ——

# City Mills Hotel

—— P E R T H ——

P

**✗ ✗ *Number Thirty Three*** 33 St George St PH1 5LA
☎(0738)33771
*Located in the heart of town this small sophisticated restaurant creates the modern concept of a 30's theme. Here the emphasis is on seafood though other tastes are catered for. Choice varies according to the season but a typical dinner might be Oak smoked Queenies with a piquant sauce, followed by baked Monkfish vegetable parcel accompanied by a delicate saffron sauce, and to finish sticky toffee pudding or perhaps a croque monsieur can be recommended.*
Closed Sun, Mon & 10 days Xmas-New Year
♡ Scottish & French **V** 48 seats Last lunch 2.30pm Last dinner 9.30pm ✗ nc5yrs
Credit Cards 1 2 3

---

**PETERBOROUGH** Cambridgeshire Map **04** TL19

**★★★68%, Peterborough Moat House** Thorpe Wood PE3 6SG
(Queens Moat) ☎(0733)260000 Telex no 32708
FAX (0733) 262737
*A modern, purpose-built hotel on the west side of the city just off the ring road. The well-equipped, comfortable accommodation appeals to both commercial and holiday visitors and amenities include a small leisure centre and banqueting/conference facilities.*
125⇨♪↖⊱in 28 bedrooms CTV in all bedrooms ® **T** ✱
sB⇨♪£66 dB⇨♪£76 (room only) ₧
Lift ( 230P ✿ CFA ▣(heated) sauna solarium gymnasium jacuzzi spa pool ♫
♡ International **V** ⊕ ⊿ Lunch £12.95&alc Dinner £13.95&alc Last dinner 9.45pm
Credit Cards 1 2 3 5 £

**★★★66%, *Butterfly*** Thorpe Meadows, Off Longthorpe Parkway PE3 6GA (Consort) ☎(0733)64240 Telex no 818360
FAX (0733) 65538
*A purpose-built hotel standing within Thorpe Country Park and Wildlife Sanctuary, with easy access to the A1, A15 and A47, provides accommodation in light, thoughtfully designed and well equipped rooms and an open-plan Victorian-style restaurant/bar/ lounge area overlooking the River Nene. Efficient service is given by a competent young staff whose members are particularly caring and friendly.*
70⇨♪(2fb) CTV in all bedrooms ® **T** ✖ (ex guide dogs)
( 70P
♡ European **V** ⊕ ⊿ ⊱ Last dinner 10pm
Credit Cards 1 2 3 5

**★★★62%, Crest Hotel** Great North Rd PE7 3TB (Trusthouse Forte) ☎(0733)240209 Telex no 32576 FAX (0733) 244455
(For full entry see Norman Cross)

**★★★60%, Bull** Westgate PE1 1RB ☎(0733)61364
Telex no 329265 FAX (0733) 557304
*This former coaching inn in the town centre dates back to Tudor times and is full of warmth and character. Friendly and helpful staff complement the hotel's range of facilities.*
112⇨(3fb) CTV in all bedrooms ® **T** sB&B⇨£64-£70
dB&B⇨fr£79 ₧
( 100P CFA
♡ English & French **V** ⊕ ⊿ Lunch fr£10.95&alc Dinner fr£10.95&alc Last dinner 10.30pm
Credit Cards 1 2 3 5

---

**PETERHEAD** Grampian *Aberdeenshire* Map **15** NK14

**★★★67%, Waterside Inn** Fraserburgh Rd AB4 7BN (Consort)
☎(0779)71121 Telex no 739413 FAX (0779) 70670
*This modern hotel is well-equipped for the business traveller and has helpful and friendly staff.*
70⇨♪Annexe40⇨♪(40fb) CTV in all bedrooms ® **T**
( 250P ✿ CFA ▣(heated) snooker sauna solarium gymnasium steam room spa bath ♫
♡ Scottish & French **V** ⊕ ⊿
Credit Cards 1 2 3 5 £

---

**PETTY FRANCE** Avon Map **03** ST78

**★★★71%, Petty France** GL9 1AF (on A46 S of junct with A433)
☎Didmarton(045423)361 FAX (045423) 768
*The former dower house of the Beaufort estate, which stands on the A46 not far from Badminton, has been refurbished to provide character accommodation in the main building and compact modern rooms in the former stables. Public areas – all situated within the house – are comfortably furnished and tastefully decorated, their original character enhanced by good pictures and occasional antiques.*
8⇨♪Annexe12⇨♪(1fb)1⊞ CTV in all bedrooms ® **T**
sB&B⇨♪£55-£95
dB&B⇨♪£75-£110 Continental breakfast ₧
50P ⊞ ✿ croquet *xmas*
♡ International **V** ⊕ ⊿ S%, Lunch £11-£16alc Dinner £16-£30alc Last dinner 10pm
Credit Cards 1 2 3 5 £

---

**PEVENSEY** East Sussex Map **05** TQ60

**★★56%, Priory Court** Castle Rd BN24 5LG
☎Eastbourne(0323)763150
*A busy free house which dates back to the 15th century and retains a wealth of beams and original architectural features, standing in two acres of grounds opposite Pevensey Castle. It provides a choice of bedrooms, lounge, restaurant and lounge bar which features a wide range of bar snacks, friendly service being supervised throughout by the resident proprietors.*
9rm(5⇨1♪)(1fb)1⊞ CTV in 6 bedrooms ® ✱ sB&B£25
sB&B⇨♪£30 dB&B£45 dB&B⇨♪£50-£60
CTV 60P ⊞ ✿
♡ Mainly grills **V** ⊕ ⊿ Lunch £10.65-£22alc Dinner £10.65-£22alc Last dinner 9.30pm
Credit Cards 1 3

---

**PICKERING** North Yorkshire Map **08** SE78

**★★68%, Crossways Hotel** Eastgate YO18 7DW ☎(0751)72804
*Wholesome Yorkshire fare is served at this comfortable hotel, centrally situated on town's main through route. Access to the car park is through a pleasant walled garden.*
10rm(7⇨♪)(3fb) CTV in all bedrooms ® ✖ (ex guide dogs)
sB&B£20-£25 dB&B£40-£50 dB&B⇨♪£46-£56 ₧
CTV 15P *xmas*
⊕ ⊿ Lunch £4.50-£7.50 High tea £4-£6.50 Dinner £10-£12.50 Last dinner 9pm
Credit Cards 1 3 £

**★★68%, Forest & Vale** Malton Rd YO18 7DL (Consort)
☎(0751)72722 Telex no 57515
*Comfortable country hotel with well-kept garden. Large restaurant serving mainly English food.*
16⇨♪Annexe5⇨♪(3fb) CTV in all bedrooms ® **T**
sB&B⇨♪£45-£58 dB&B⇨♪£70-£82 ₧
70P ✿
♡ English & French **V** ⊕ ⊿ Bar Lunch fr£3.50 High tea fr£3.50 Dinner £14.50 Last dinner 9.30pm
Credit Cards 1 2 3 5

**★★67%, Burgate House** 17 Burgate YO18 7AU ☎(0751)73463
*Situated in the town centre close to the Castle, this hotel is mainly Victorian with some 16th-century features. Accommodation is comfortable and well equipped and meals are prepared with imagination and skill.*
7rm(2⇨♪)(2fb) CTV in all bedrooms ® **T** ✖ (ex guide dogs)
sB&B£20-£25 sB&B⇨♪£25-£30 dB&B£30-£48
dB&B⇨♪£52-£56 ₧

▶

## Pickering - Pitlochry

▦ CTV 8P *⊞ xmas*
♀ English & French **V** ✿ Sunday Lunch fr£6.95 Dinner
fr£10.95 Last dinner 9pm
Credit Cards ⌷1⌷ ⌷3⌷

★★64% **White Swan** Market Place YO18 7AA ☎(0751)72288
*Situated in the town centre, the stone-faced White Swan offers
well-equipped accommodation and a convivial atmosphere. The
restaurant St Emillion combines an interesting menu with an
extensive, quality wine list.*
13⇨♠(1fb)⊁in 2 bedrooms CTV in all bedrooms ® **T**
sB&B⇨♠£38.50 dB&B⇨♠£60-£80 ⊟
35P *⊞ xmas*
♀ English & French **V** ✿ Lunch £8.50-£10 Dinner £15-£20
Last dinner 9pm
Credit Cards ⌷1⌷ ⌷3⌷

★61% **Cottage Leas Country** Nova Ln, Middleton YO18 8PN
(Consort) ☎(0751)72129
*Formerly a farmhouse, this small, family run hotel stands on the
edge of the North York Moors and is ideally placed for
holidaymakers. Food is all freshly prepared and served in an
attractive dining room overlooking the Vale of Pickering.*
12⇨♠(2fb)2⊞ CTV in all bedrooms ® **T ✱**
sB&B⇨♠£32-£36 dB&B⇨♠£54-£60 ⊟
60P ✿ ℘ (hard) *xmas*
♀ English & French **V** ✿ 辺 Lunch £7.50-£12.50alc Dinner
£10.50-£15.50alc Last dinner 9.30pm
Credit Cards ⌷1⌷ ⌷3⌷

### PIDDLETRENTHIDE Dorset Map 03 SY79

★★58% **Old Bakehouse** DT2 7QR ☎(03004)305
Closed 25-26 Dec & Jan
*Resident proprietors offer a warm welcome to this charming little
hotel. What bedrooms lack in quality is made up for in character,
whilst the lounge and bar, though small, are comfortable.*
3⇨♠Annexe7⇨♠3⊞ CTV in all bedrooms ®
sB&B⇨♠£24.50 dB&B⇨♠£44-£50 ⊟
16P *⊞ ✿ ⊇*(heated) nc12yrs
♀ English & Continental **V**
Credit Cards ⌷1⌷ ⌷3⌷

### PIMPERNE Dorset Map 03 ST90

★★59% **The Anvil Hotel & Restaurant** Salisbury Rd DT11 8UQ
☎Blandford(0258)453431 & 480182
*Charming, thatched 16th-century inn of great character.
Bedrooms vary in size but all are comfortable, and cosy, beamed
restaurant offers a varied menu. Owners Mr and Mrs Palmer
ensure a warm, friendly atmosphere.*
9⇨♠ CTV in all bedrooms ® **T** sB&B⇨♠fr£37.50
dB&B⇨♠fr£55 ⊟
CTV 25P ♫
**V** ✿ 辺 Lunch fr£13.25alc Dinner fr£13.25alc Last dinner
9.45pm
Credit Cards ⌷1⌷ ⌷2⌷ ⌷3⌷ ⌷5⌷

### PITLOCHRY Tayside *Perthshire* Map 14 NN95

★★★⇣68% **Pine Trees** Strathview Ter PH16 5QR
☎(0796)2121 FAX (0796)2460
Closed 4-31 Jan
*Run by the MacLellan family, this delightful Victorian country
house is set in 14 acres of secluded grounds. The public rooms are
elegant, and the well-equipped bedrooms are constantly being
improved.*
19rm(18⇨♠) CTV in all bedrooms ® **T ✱** (ex guide dogs)
sB&B⇨♠£30-£35 dB&B⇨♠£60-£70 ⊟
40P *⊞ ✿ putting xmas*
♀ Scottish & French **V** ✿ 辺 Lunch fr£10 High tea fr£14alc
Credit Cards ⌷1⌷ ⌷3⌷

★★★62% **Green Park** Clunie Bridge Rd PH16 5JY
☎(0796)3248
Closed 2 Nov-26 Mar
*Set in its own grounds on the picturesque shores of Loch Faskally,
this friendly, family-run hotel has a relaxed atmosphere and is an
ideal base for the touring holidaymaker. It offers comfortable
lounges and neatly decorated, well equipped bedrooms.*
37⇨♠(10fb) CTV in all bedrooms ® **T ✱** sB&B⇨♠£30-£37
dB&B⇨♠£60-£74 ⊟
50P 4☎ (£1.50) *⊞* ✿ CFA ✔ putting table tennis bar billiards
♀ Scottish & French **V** ✿ 辺 ⊁ Lunch fr£6 Dinner
£14.50-£16.50 Last dinner 8.30pm
Credit Cards ⌷1⌷ ⌷3⌷

★★★61% **Pitlochry Hydro** Knockard Rd PH16 5JH (Scottish
Highland) ☎(0796)2666 FAX (0796)2238
Closed Jan
*The volume of coach business has been reduced at this upgraded
popular tourist hotel, where refurbished bedroom accommodation
and an exciting new leisure centre now complement spacious and
comfortably-appointed public rooms.*
64⇨♠(4fb) CTV in all bedrooms ® **T ✱** (ex guide dogs)
sB&B⇨♠£48-£52 dB&B⇨♠£78-£85 ⊟
Lift ℂ CTV 100P ✿ ▢(heated) snooker sauna solarium
gymnasium putting green croquet *xmas*
♀ Scottish, English & French **V** ✿ Bar Lunch £2.50-£7 Dinner
£13.50 Last dinner 9pm
Credit Cards ⌷1⌷ ⌷2⌷ ⌷3⌷ ⌷5⌷

★★★58% **Scotland's** 40 Bonnethill Rd PH16 5BT (Best
Western) ☎(0796)2292 Telex no 76392 FAX (0796) 3284
*This busy holiday and conference hotel is well situated for the
town. It has a friendly atmosphere and offers good value, practical
accommodation which is gradually being improved. A new leisure
centre is due to open in the Spring.*
60⇨♠(14fb) CTV in all bedrooms ® **T** sB&B⇨♠£33-£49
dB&B⇨♠£54-£78 ⊟
Lift ℂ CTV 80P ✿ CFA pool table *xmas*
**V** ✿ 辺 Lunch fr£9.50 Dinner fr£12.50 Last dinner 9pm
Credit Cards ⌷1⌷ ⌷2⌷ ⌷3⌷ ⌷5⌷ Ⓔ

★★★56% **The Atholl Palace** Atholl Rd PH16 5LY (Trusthouse
Forte) ☎(0796)2400 Telex no 76406 FAX (0796) 3036
*A popular holiday and conference hotel standing in 48 acres of
grounds, with a wide range of leisure facilities. Spacious public
rooms offer traditional comforts, while bedrooms are modest and
somewhat practical.*
84⇨♠(6fb)1⊞⊁in 12 bedrooms CTV in all bedrooms ® **T**
sB&B⇨♠£67.50-£72.50 dB&B⇨♠£100-£110 ⊟
Lift ℂ 150P ✿ CFA ⊇(heated) ℘ (hard) snooker sauna
solarium pitch & putt ⊿ *xmas*
**V** ✿ 辺 ⊁ Lunch £7.95-£9.95 Dinner £13.95-£14.50&alc Last
dinner 9pm
Credit Cards ⌷1⌷ ⌷2⌷ ⌷3⌷ ⌷4⌷ ⌷5⌷

★★68% **Dundarach** Perth Rd PH16 5DJ (Consort)
☎(0796)2862
Closed Feb
*On the southern edge of Pitlochry, off the A924, this family-run
hotel stands in its own gardens and there are uninterrupted views
of the surrounding hills from the two spacious lounges and the
dining room. Bedrooms vary in size, but all are comfortable and
well equipped. The hotel is run in traditional manner and the young
staff are friendly and helpful.*
23rm(16⇨5♠)Annexe3⇨(2fb) CTV in all bedrooms ® **T ✱**
sB&B⇨♠£36 dB&B⇨♠£55 ⊟
CTV 30P ✿
**V** ✿ 辺
Credit Cards ⌷1⌷ ⌷3⌷

★★65% **Claymore** 162 Atholl Rd PH16 5AR ☎(0796)2888
Closed 4-30 Nov & 3-26 Jan
*Situated just west of the town centre, this small family-run hotel stands in its own well tended grounds and is a popular base for the touring holidaymaker. It is efficiently run by enthusiastic owners, Joyce and Harold Beaton, and offers neatly appointed public rooms, together with comfortable and well equipped bedrooms.*
7⇨♠Annexe4rm(2♠)(1fb) CTV in all bedrooms ℝ T ✱
sB&B£19-£27.50 dB&B⇨♠£38-£55 ⊞
25P ⊞ ✿ *xmas*
V ✿ ⊡ ✕ Bar Lunch £2.10-£4.85 Dinner £13.50&alc Last dinner 9pm
Credit Cards 1 3

★★64% **Acarsaid** 8 Atholl Rd PH16 5BX ☎(0796)2389
Closed 3 Jan-1 Mar
*Friendly, family-run hotel in its own grounds, popular as a base for touring holidaymakers.*
18⇨♠(1fb) CTV in all bedrooms ℝ T ✖ sB&B⇨♠£21-£25
dB&B⇨♠£42-£50
CTV 20P ✿ putting *xmas*
V ✿ ⊡ ✕ Lunch £8.75-£13.50alc Dinner £12.50-£15 Last dinner 8pm
Credit Cards 1 3

★★64% **Birchwood** 2 East Moulin Rd PH16 5DW (Inter-Hotels)
☎(0796)2477
Closed Dec-Feb
*This attractive Victorian house, set in its own grounds and offering well-equipped bedroom, modern standards of comfort and a friendly atmosphere, is a popular base for tourists seeking quiet relaxation.*
12⇨♠Annexe5♠(4fb) CTV in all bedrooms ℝ T ✱
sB&B⇨♠£40.50-£45.25
dB&B⇨♠£73-£82.50 (incl dinner) ⊞
25P ✿
✿ ⊡ ✕ Lunch £5-£8alc Dinner £14.50&alc Last dinner 8pm
Credit Cards 1 3

★★63% **Airdaniar** 160 Atholl Rd PH16 5AR (Guestaccom)
☎(0796)2266
Closed Jan
*Set just north of the town centre in 3 acres of beautiful gardens, this friendly, family-run hotel combines bright, modern and comfortable public areas with practically-styled and well-equipped bedrooms, in a range of sizes.*
9⇨♠(1fb) CTV in all bedrooms ℝ T sB&B⇨♠£36.50
dB&B⇨♠£53-£55 ⊞
18P ⊞ ✿ ♪ *xmas*
V ✿ ✕ Bar Lunch £6.45-£11alc Dinner £14 Last dinner 8.30pm
Credit Cards 1 3

★★60% **Craigvrack** West Moulin Rd PH16 5EQ (Minotels)
☎(0796)2399
*Rob and Janette Wallace's small, comfortable hotel is a popular base for holidaymakers. It has a friendly, informal atmosphere and the public rooms are peaceful and relaxing. The comfortable bedrooms are well equipped, though some are a little compact.*
19rm(8⇨6♠)(2fb) CTV in all bedrooms ℝ
22P ⊞
☺ Scottish & English V ✕ Last dinner 8.30pm
Credit Cards 1 2 3

★★55% **Craigower** 134/136 Atholl Rd PH16 5AB ☎(0796)2590
*Catering mainly for the tourist market, this small family-run hotel in the town centre offers a friendly atmosphere and good-value accommodation in bedrooms which are currently being refurbished.*
23rm(1⇨15♠)(6fb) CTV in 18 bedrooms ℝ
CTV 15P
V ✿ ⊡ Last dinner 8.30pm
Credit Cards 1 3

# Acarsaid Hotel
## PITLOCHRY ★★
## PERTHSHIRE PH16 5BX
Telephone 0796 2389 *(Management)*, 2220 *(Guests)*

- Ideally situated — level walk to Festival Theatre/Village Centre.
- Excellent food. Spacious Dining Room overlooking Tummel Valley.
- 18 warm, comfortable bedrooms (5 ground floor) equipped with bathroom, TV, tea/coffee tray, hair drier and telephone.
- Relaxed informal atmosphere with high standards of service. ALWAYS!

★★
# CLAYMORE HOTEL
**Atholl Road, Pitlochry, Perthshire PH16 5AR**
**Telephone: (0796) 2888**

A small exclusive hotel beautifully situated in 2 acres of gardens yet within walking distance of the town centre and the Festival Theatre.
— Fully licensed. Bar snacks and table d'hôte or à la Carte available. Extensive wine list.
— Most bedrooms ensuite.
— Colour TV and tea/coffee trays as standard.
— No supplement for single rooms.
— Heating throughout.
— Bargain Breaks for low season.
**Resident Proprietors: Joyce and Harold Beaton**

★71% **Knockendarroch House** Higher Oakfield PH16 5HT
☎(0796)3473
Closed 15 Nov-Mar
*An attractive family-run hotel enjoying a pleasant outlook from its own grounds offers bright, airy bedrooms, nicely appointed lounges that invite relaxation and a neat dining room where the short menu is based on local produce.*
12⇨↑(1fb)2⊟ CTV in all bedrooms ® ✱
dB&B⇨↑£42-£56 ₽
( 12P ⇔ ✥
♀ Scottish & French Dinner £12.50 Last dinner 7.30pm
Credit Cards [1] [2] [3] [5] ⓔ

★69% **Balrobin** Higher Oakfield PH16 5HT ☎(0796)2901
Closed Nov-Mar
*A delightful, efficiently run small hotel, standing in its own grounds and commanding fine views over the surrounding hills, combines comfortable, well-equipped accommodation with the opportunity to enjoy good home cooking in its attractive dining room and to relax in an attractive lounge.*
12rm(1⇨10↑)(1fb) CTV in all bedrooms ®
sB&B⇨↑£20-£22 dB&B⇨↑£40-£48 ₽
12P ⇔ ✥ nc10yrs
✕ Dinner £8-£10 Last dinner 7.30pm
ⓔ

★60% **Craig Urrard** 10 Atholl Rd PH16 5BX ☎(0796)2346
*Situated at the east end of town, this small, friendly, family-run tourist hotel is well maintained and offers good value accommodation.*
10rm(6↑)Annexe2↑(3fb) CTV in all bedrooms ® ✖
sB&B£14.50-£17.50 dB&B£29-£35 dB&B↑£32-£38
CTV 12P ⇔ ✥
✕ Bar Lunch £1.25-£5alc Dinner £9&alc Last dinner 8pm
Credit Cards [1] [2] [3]

---

**PLOCKTON** Highland *Ross & Cromarty* Map **14** NG83

★★76% **Haven** IV52 8TW ☎(059984)223 & 334
Closed 21 Dec-9 Feb RS 10 Feb-1 Apr & Nov-20 Dec
*This friendly, privately owned hotel is aptly named, and is sought out by many both for its lovely West Highland setting, and for the high standards of comfort it offers. Bedrooms are particularly well equipped, and there are two comfortable (though non-smoking) lounges.*
13rm(10⇨) CTV in all bedrooms ® T sB&B⇨£25-£28
dB&B⇨£50-£56 ₽
7P ⇔ nc7yrs
V ♥ ♨ ✕ Lunch £1.50-£15alc Dinner £16-£18 Last dinner 8.30pm
Credit Cards [1] [3]

---

**PLYMOUTH** Devon Map **02** SX45

See **Town Plan Section**
See also **Down Thomas**
★★★★65% **Copthorne** Armada Centre, Armada Way
PL1 1AR (Best Western) ☎(0752)224161 Telex no 45756
FAX (0752) 670688
*Popular modern city-centre hotel, with comfortable and well-equipped bedrooms, attractive public areas and a small leisure centre. The Burlington Restaurant offers an interesting choice of dishes cooked in the modern classical style, while Bentley's Brasserie provides an alternative menu in more informal surroundings. Service is prompt and conducted in a pleasant manner.*
135⇨↑(29fb)✕in 18 bedrooms CTV in all bedrooms ® T ₽
Lift ( 40🅰️ ⌫(heated) sauna solarium gymnasium pool table
♀ International V ♥ ♨ ✕ Lunch £10.95&alc High tea £3.95
Dinner £10.95&alc Last dinner 10.30pm
Credit Cards [1] [2] [3] [5] ⓔ

★★★★60% **Plymouth Moat House** Armada Way PL1 2HJ
(Queens Moat) ☎(0752)662866 Telex no 45637
FAX (0752) 673816
*The 12-storey purpose-built modern hotel commands views over the city and across Plymouth Hoe. It offers a good choice of restaurants – the Penthouse boasting a superb outlook and Mongers, on the ground floor, specialising in seafood – and a variety of bars. Bedrooms, currently undergoing some upgrading, are well equipped, attractively decorated and spacious, although some bathrooms are rather small, and the 5th floor is a non-smoking area. A small leisure complex complements the indoor swimming pool.*
213⇨↑(106fb)✕in 14 bedrooms CTV in all bedrooms ® T ✱
sB⇨↑£72-£87 dB⇨↑£82-£97 (room only) ₽
Lift ( ⊞ 30P 100🅰️ CFA ⌫(heated) sauna solarium
gymnasium ♫ *xmas*
♀ Continental V ♥ ♨ ✕ Lunch £15 High tea £6-£8alc Dinner
£13&alc Last dinner 10pm
Credit Cards [1] [2] [3] [5]

★★★66% **Mayflower Post House** Cliff Rd, The Hoe PL1 3DL
(Trusthouse Forte) ☎(0752)662828 Telex no 45442
FAX (0752) 660974
*In an elevated position on the Hoe, the bars, lounge and restaurant enjoy glorious views of Plymouth Sound. Most of the comfortable, well-equipped bedrooms (some with balconies) share the view. The comprehensive menu is complimented by an extensive wine list and there is a special menu for children.*
106⇨↑(74fb)✕in 32 bedrooms CTV in all bedrooms ® T ✱
sB⇨↑£67 dB⇨↑£78-£89 (room only) ₽
Lift ( 149P ✱ CFA ⌫(heated) *xmas*
♀ English & Continental V ♥ ♨ ✕ Lunch £9.50 High tea
fr£3.95 Dinner £14&alc Last dinner 10pm
Credit Cards [1] [2] [3] [4] [5]

★★★64% **Elfordleigh** Colebrook, Plympton PL7 5EB
☎(0752)336428 FAX (0752) 344581
*Within 65 acres of rolling grounds and countryside, the hotel has magnificent views over the Plym Valley, and is surrounded by its own golf course, gardens and woodland. The main house itself has been sympathetically restored, together with the sensitive addition of an attractive conservatory restaurant, and a bright, modern leisure complex, the facilities of which include an indoor and outdoor pool, a gym, beauty salon, squash, all-weather tennis courts and an extensive range of recreational facilities. There is a choice of three bars and, of course, the golf club-house. Bedrooms are richly decorated in pleasing, coordinating colours and fabrics, with quality, fully-tiled en suites, and they are all well equipped for today's modern hotel guest. There is also a choice of dining, with a family country pantry for more informal eating, in conjunction with the conservatory à la carte style restaurant. Services are conducted in a prompt and friendly manner. The hotel is located just outside the city itself, being convenient for the A38 and major link roads.*
18⇨↑(3fb)1⊟ CTV in all bedrooms ® T ✖ ✱ sB&B⇨↑£49
dB&B⇨↑£79-£89 ₽
250P ⇔ ✥ ⌫(heated) ⌫(heated) ▶ 9 ♪ (hard) ♪ squash
snooker sauna solarium gymnasium jacuzzi beauty therapy
croquet *xmas*
♀ European V ♥ ♨ ✕ Lunch £6-£12alc Dinner £14.95&alc
Last dinner 9.30pm
Credit Cards [1] [2] [3]

★★★63% **New Continental** Millbay Rd PL1 3LD
☎(0752)220782 Telex no 45193 FAX (0752) 227013
Closed 24 Dec-2 Jan
*Well-established city centre hotel close to the Hoe and the Barbican. The comfortable bedrooms have good facilities and the spacious restaurant offers a large selection of interesting dishes. A large leisure complex includes an indoor heated pool and beauty treatment room.*
84⇨↑(14fb)2⊟ CTV in all bedrooms ® ✱ sB&B⇨↑£55
dB&B⇨↑£50-£68 ₽
Lift ( 100P ⌫(heated) sauna solarium gymnasium

☝ English, French & Greek **V** ✪ Lunch £7.75-£8.50&alc
Dinner £14.75&alc Last dinner 10pm
Credit Cards ① ② ③ ⑤ Ⓔ

★★★**61%** **Strathmore** Elliot St, The Hoe PL1 2PP (Consort)
☎(0752)662101 Telex no 45193 FAX (0752) 223690
*This busy commercial hotel is part of a terrace, just a stone's throw
away from the celebrated Plymouth Hoe. All rooms have now been
refurbished, and are well appointed. A wide choice of dishes are on
offer in the charming restaurant, and service is provided by the
friendly team of staff.*
53⇨🛏(6fb) CTV in all bedrooms Ⓡ **T** sB&B⇨🛏fr£45
dB&B⇨🛏fr£55 🖪
Lift ( ℙ
☝ English & Continental **V** ✪ Lunch fr£7&alc Dinner
fr£11.50&alc Last dinner 10pm
Credit Cards ① ② ③ ⑤ Ⓔ

★★★**58%** *Novotel Plymouth* Marsh Mills Roundabout, 270
Plymouth Rd PL6 8NH (Novotel) ☎(0752)221422
Telex no 45711
*Modern hotel with pleasant atmosphere and a French theme in the
restaurant.*
101⇨🛏 CTV in all bedrooms Ⓡ
Lift ( 140P ✿ CFA ⌂ ፙ
☝ French **V** ✪ ⏠ ⅄ Last dinner mdnt
Credit Cards ① ② ③ ④ ⑤

Entries for red-star hotels are highlighted by a
tint panel. For a full list of these establishments
consult the Contents page.

# No sleep?

# No problems.

## novotel

★ ★ ★
Hotels with double beds in all rooms
Novotel Plymouth  Marsh Mills
Roundabout  Plymouth Road
Tel 0752 221422  Telex 45711

---

P

★★★57%, *Astor* Elliot Street, The Hoe PL1 2PS (Mount Charlotte (TS)) ☎(0752)225511 Telex no 45652
*Popular, and therefore busy, commercial hotel, conveniently situated for the city and within walking distance of The Hoe. Bedrooms are being upgraded and are soundly equipped. Service is friendly and prompt.*
56rm(49⇔4ſ\)(3fb) CTV in all bedrooms ® ⅛
Lift ( ⅌ CFA
V ◊ Last dinner 9.30pm
Credit Cards ① ② ③ ⑤

★★65%, *Camelot* 5 Elliot St, The Hoe PL1 2PP (Minotels) ☎(0752)221255 & 669667 FAX (0752) 603660
*Near the Hoe and Barbican, and within walking distance of the city centre, an informal terraced hotel offers comfortable well-equipped bedrooms, and compact public areas with a lively atmosphere; the latter include a cosy dining room serving an imaginative menu, and a bar where snacks are available.*
17⇔ſ\(4fb) CTV in all bedrooms ® T ⅛ (ex guide dogs)
sB&B⇔ſ\fr£34 dB&B⇔ſ\fr£47 ₽
CTV ⌘
V ◊ ⬚ Lunch fr£10.50 Dinner fr£10.50&alc Last dinner 9.30pm
Credit Cards ① ② ③ ⑤ ⑥

★★61%, *Invicta* 11-12 Osborne Place, Lockyer Street, The Hoe PL1 2PU ☎(0752)664997
Closed 25 Dec-5 Jan
*A family-owned hotel overlooking Drake's famous Bowling Green. Bedrooms are comfortable and well equipped, there is a choice of menus in the dining room and the public lounge bar offers a lively atmosphere.*
23rm(9⇔11ſ\)(4fb) CTV in all bedrooms ® T
⅛ (ex guide dogs) ✳ sB&B⇔£38 dB&Bfr£38
dB&B⇔ſ\£50 ₽
CTV 10P
⍰ Mainly grills ◊ ⬚ Dinner £8.25-£13.50alc Last dinner 9pm
Credit Cards ① ③

★★55%, *Grosvenor* 9 Elliot Street, The Hoe PL1 2PP ☎(0752)260411
*This busy commercial hotel, converted from a Georgian-style house, features a lower ground restaurant whose wall murals depict various ghouls.*
14rm(8⇔5ſ\) CTV in 13 bedrooms ® T ⅛
CTV ⌘
◊ ⬚
Credit Cards ① ② ③

★61%, *Imperial* Lockyer Street, The Hoe PL1 2QD ☎(0752)227311
Closed 25-31 Dec
*The public rooms of a detached Victorian hotel near the Hoe are pleasantly warmed by real fires in winter, and its bedrooms are well equipped, though compact; proprietors and staff offer friendly, attentive service.*
22rm(4⇔12ſ\)(4fb) CTV in all bedrooms ® T ⅛
sB&B£27-£28 sB&B⇔ſ\£36-£38 dB&B£38-£40
dB&B⇔ſ\£44-£46 ₽
CTV 18P games room
V ◊ ⬚ Bar Lunch £2.50-£5 Dinner £10.95-£11.95 Last dinner 8.15pm
Credit Cards ① ② ③ ⑤ ⑥

★56%, *Drake* 1 & 2 Windsor Villas, Lockyer Street, The Hoe PL1 2QD ☎(0752)229730
Closed Xmas
*This small, functional, family-managed hotel stands on the Hoe, within walking distance of the city centre.*
36rm(25⇔ſ\)(3fb) CTV in all bedrooms ® T ✳ sB&Bfr£22
sB&B⇔ſ\£31-£35 dB&Bfr£38 dB&B⇔ſ\£40-£45 ₽
25P 2⍰ ⌘

⍰ Mainly grills V ◊ Lunch fr£7.80&alc Dinner fr£7.80&alc Last dinner 9pm
Credit Cards ① ② ③ ⑤
See advertisement on page 563

⬧*Campanile* Marsh Mills, Longbridge Rd, Forder Valley PL6 8LD (Campanile) ☎(0752)601087 Telex no 45544
*Set beside the A38 about 1.5 miles from the city centre this Lodge has bedrooms with outside access from the car park. All are simply appointed with good facilities for the short-stay guest. Adjacent is a bistro-style restaurant with a French influence, and a bar.*
48⇔ſ\ CTV in all bedrooms ® T
56P ✿
⍰ English & French Last dinner 10pm
Credit Cards ① ③
See advertisement on page 563

✗*The Chez Nous* 13 Frankfort Gate PL1 1QA ☎(0752)266793
*This haven of good French cooking is a welcome discovery in the centre of Plymouth, and attracts a regular clientele who are greatly appreciative both of the atmosphere and the cuisine. Jacques and Suzanne Marchal present an excellent daily menu.*
Closed Sun, Mon, 3 wks Feb, 3 wks Sep & BH's
⍰ French 28 seats ✳ Lunch fr£23.50&alc Dinner fr£23.50&alc Last lunch 2pm Last dinner 10.30pm ⅌
Credit Cards ① ② ③ ⑤

**POCKLINGTON** Humberside Map **08** SE84

★★65%, *Feathers* Market Square YO4 2AH ☎(0759)303155
*This small market place inn proves a popular venue with local trade and hotel guests alike. The inn has well appointed bedrooms, in both the main house and the purpose-built annexe. A selection of good value menus are offered in the small restaurant.* ▶

# INVICTA HOTEL
## 11/12 OSBORNE PLACE
## LOCKYER STREET, THE HOE
## PLYMOUTH PL1 2PU
### Tel: (0752) 664997  AA★★

This modernised Family Run Hotel, is situated directly opposite the famous Plymouth Hoe, very close to the City Centre & Brittany Ferries.

★ 23 appointed bedrooms mostly en-suite, with C/H, Colour TV, telephone & tea/coffee making facilities.
★ Excellent restaurant food. Bar.
★ Wedding Receptions & Conferences catered for.
★ Private lock-up Car Park.

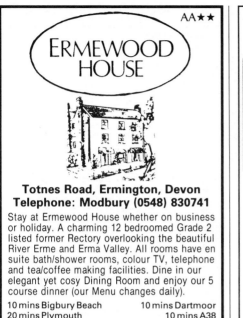
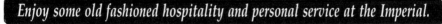

6⇔↖Annexe6⇔(1fb)1⊟ CTV in all bedrooms ® **T**
✗ (ex guide dogs)
CTV 60P 6⌂
**V** ✿ Last dinner 9.30pm
Credit Cards [1] [2] [3] [5]

**PODIMORE** Somerset Map **03** ST52

⌂**Travelodge** BA22 8JG (A303, S of junct with A37) (Trusthouse Forte) ☎Yeovil(0935)840074 Central Res (0800) 850950
*Located at the roundabout junction of the A303 with the A37, this lodge offers excellent value family accommodation in new and well equipped bedrooms. Meals and light refreshments are available from seven in the morning until ten at night in the Little Chef restaurant which stands a short walk across the car park.*
31⇔↖(31fb) CTV in all bedrooms ® sB⇔↖£24 dB⇔↖£29.50 (room only)
☾31P ⊞
Credit Cards [1] [2] [3]

**POLMONT** Central *Stirlingshire* Map **11** NS97

**★★★ 67% Inchyra Grange** Grange Rd FK2 0YB (Best Western) ☎(0324)711911 Telex no 777693 FAX (0324) 716134
*This extended mansion, though peacefully set in eight acres of grounds, offers convenient access to M9 at junction 4. Major refurbishment has provided well-equipped bedrooms in modern style and the new Pelican Leisure Club is a popular development.*
33⇔↖ CTV in all bedrooms ® **T** sB&B⇔↖£66-£78 dB&B⇔↖£85-£110 ⊟
☾150P ✻ ⊡(heated) snooker sauna solarium gymnasium jacuzzi steam room beauty therapy room
♀ Scottish & French **V** ✿ ⊻ Lunch £7.50-£9.50&alc Dinner £13-£14.50&alc Last dinner 9.30pm
Credit Cards [1] [2] [3] [5]

**POLPERRO** Cornwall & Isles of Scilly Map **02** SX25

**★ 66% Claremont** Fore St PL13 2RG ☎(0503)72241
RS 16 Oct-23 Mar
*A small holiday hotel with a warm French influence providing comfortable accommodation and well-cooked food.*
11rm(10⇔↖)(3fb) CTV in all bedrooms ® **T** sB&B⇔↖£18-£23 dB&B£26-£31 dB&B⇔↖£34-£46 ⊟
CTV 16P ⊞ *xmas*
♀ French ✿ ⊻ Lunch £5.25-£8alc Dinner £10.95-£16.50&alc Last dinner 8.30pm
Credit Cards [1] [3] £

**POLZEATH** Cornwall & Isles of Scilly Map **02** SW97

**★★ 70% Pentire Rocks** PL27 6US ☎Trebetherick(0208)862213
Closed 29 Dec-Jan
*One is assured of a warm welcome at this family-run hotel that overlooks Polzeath. As well as its hospitality, is also offers a restaurant with style and flair, headed by the chef, Graham Holder.*
16rm(1⇔14↖)(3fb) CTV in all bedrooms ® **T**
✗ (ex guide dogs) ✱ sB&Bfr£25 sB&B⇔↖fr£25 dB&Bfr£50 dB&B⇔↖fr£50 ⊟
CTV 20P ⊞ ✻ ⌒(heated)
✿ ⊻
Credit Cards [1] [3]

All hotels are now given a percentage grading for the quality of their facilities. A full explanation can be found within 'How we Classify Hotels and Restaurants' at the front of the book.

**POOLE** Dorset Map **04** SZ09

**For hotel locations see Town Plan Section under Bournemouth**
See also **Bournemouth**

**★★★★ 51% Hospitality Inn** The Quay BH15 1HD (Mount Charlotte (TS)) ☎(0202)666800 Telex no 418374 FAX (0202) 684470
*Modern, well-equipped commercial hotel with good harbour views and a spacious restaurant.*
68⇔↖(65fb) CTV in all bedrooms ® **T** sB⇔↖fr£72 dB⇔↖fr£85 (room only) ⊟
Lift ☾150P CFA *xmas*
♀ French **V** ✿ ⊻ Lunch fr£14 Dinner fr£15 Last dinner 10pm
Credit Cards [1] [2] [3] [4] [5]

**★★★ 75% Mansion House** Thames St BH15 1JN ☎(0202)685666 FAX (0202) 665709
Closed 24 Dec-2 Jan
*Situated a short distance from the quay, this elegant Georgian town-house has the twin virtues of friendly service and good, honest cooking in the Dining Club Restaurant. A separate breakfast room, an intimate lounge with antique furnishings, and every conceivable facility in the bedrooms, ensure that guests will have a comfortable stay.*
28⇔↖(2fb) CTV in all bedrooms **T** sB&B⇔↖£69-£75 dB&B⇔↖£91-£104 ⊟
☾40P ⊞ CFA
♀ English & French **V** ✿ ⊻ Lunch £12.95-£14.50 Dinner £17.50-£22.50 Last dinner 10pm
Credit Cards [1] [2] [3] [5] £

**★★★ 72% *Salterns*** 38 Salterns Way, Lilliput BH14 8JR (Best Western) ☎(0202)707321 Telex no 41259 FAX (0202) 707488
*Owned and run by Mr and Mrs Smith, this welcoming and attractive hotel enjoys a unique setting overlooking the marina. A very comfortable first-floor lounge gives good harbour views, and the intimate restaurant serves and an interesting menu of well-prepared dishes.*
16⇔ CTV in all bedrooms ®
☾150P ⊞ ✻ ♩ squash snooker
♀ French & English ✿ ⊻ Last dinner 10pm
Credit Cards [1] [2] [3] [5]

**★★★ 70% Haven** Sandbanks BH13 7QL ☎(0202)707333 Telex no 41338 FAX (0202) 708796
*A hotel ideally situated overlooking the sea is being upgraded to a high standard, providing well equipped bedrooms and comfortable public areas. A new business centre is available for conference, there are excellent leisure facilities, and the restaurant offers a comprehensive menu of sound, well-prepared dishes. Service is efficient throughout, staff being willing and helpful.*
96⇔↖(6fb) CTV in all bedrooms ® **T** ✗ (ex guide dogs) sB&B⇔↖£50-£70 dB&B⇔↖£100-£140
Lift ☾150P ✻ ⊡(heated) ⌒(heated) ♩ squash sauna solarium gymnasium steam room spa pool *xmas*
♀ English & French **V** ✿ ⊻ ⚔ Lunch £11-£15 High tea £6 Dinner £18-£22&alc Last dinner 8.30pm
Credit Cards [1] [2] [3] [5] £

**★★★ 66% Harbour Heights** 73 Haven Rd, Sandbanks BH13 7LW ☎(0202)707272 FAX (0202) 708594
*This friendly, family-run hotel is situated high up, with panoramic views of the bay. Bedrooms vary in size but are decorated and furnished in a modern style and most have comfortable armchairs and balconies. There is a small dining room offering à la carte and table d'hôte menus as well as the popular carvery serving informal meals and snacks.*
49⇔↖ CTV in all bedrooms ® **T** sB&B⇔↖£43 dB&B⇔↖£70 ⊟
Lift ☾84P ⊞ ✻
♀ English & French **V** ✿ ⊻ Sunday Lunch £11.50 Dinner £15&alc Last dinner 9.30pm
Credit Cards [1] [2] [3] [5]

★★★63% **Sandbanks** Banks Rd, Sandbanks BH13 7PS
☎(0202)707377 Telex no 41338 FAX (0202) 708796
*Ideally situated for family holidays and offering very good facilities for children, an hotel in process of upgrading provides an informal atmosphere, willing, helpful service and extensive leisure amenities.*
115⇄🛏❧ CTV in all bedrooms ® T ✱ (ex guide dogs)
sB&B⇄🛏❧£40-£50 dB&B⇄🛏❧£80-£100 🏠
Lift ℂ 200P ❖ CFA ⊠(heated) sauna solarium gymnasium
steam room ஃ *xmas*
♀ International V ♦ ⌂ Lunch £10-£12 High tea £6 Dinner
£15-£18 Last dinner 8.30pm
Credit Cards ①②③⑤£

★★★56% **Dolphin** High St BH15 1DU ☎(0202)673612
Telex no 417205 FAX (0202) 674197
*Centrally located close to the shops and railway station, this modern hotel has busy public areas which include a coffee shop, carvery restaurant serving a good range of meals and snacks and a large bar with live music. Bedrooms tend to be small but are well furnished.*
66⇄🛏❧1🛁 CTV in all bedrooms ® ✳ sB&B⇄🛏❧£32.50-£68
dB&B⇄🛏❧£54-£78 🏠
Lift ℂ 50P
♀ French V ♦ ⌂ Lunch £4.95-£20&alc High tea £3-£10alc
Dinner £9.95&alc Last dinner 10.30pm
Credit Cards ①②③⑤

★★60% **Sea Witch** 47 Haven Rd, Canford Cliffs BH13 7LH
☎(0202)707697
Closed 25 Dec-3 Jan
*A modern, family-run hotel within easy distance of the centres of both Poole and Bournemouth offers simply-appointed bedrooms whose good facilities appeal to the holidaymaker and business traveller alike, together with a popular restaurant featuring both à* ▶

*la carte and table d'hôte menus. Ample car parking space is available.*

9⇨🏠🛏(2fb) CTV in all bedrooms ® T ✹
40P 🅿
♙ International V ✧ ⏛
Credit Cards ①③

★★ 59% **Antelope** High St BH15 1BP (Lansbury)
☏(0202)672029 Telex no 418387 FAX (0202) 678286
*Set in the High Street, not far from the quay, and recently completely renovated, the Antelope offers bedrooms with modern facilities and many extras. A cheerful young staff provides helpful service in the rustic-style Henekey's restaurant.*
21⇨🛏(1fb)✂in 3 bedrooms CTV in all bedrooms ®
✹ (ex guide dogs) sB&B⇨🛏fr£63 dB&B⇨🛏fr£76 🏱
⦅20P *xmas*
♙ European V ✧ ⏛ Lunch fr£11&alc Dinner fr£11&alc Last dinner 10.30pm
Credit Cards ①②③④⑤

★★ 59% **Norfolk Lodge** 1 Flaghead Rd, Canford Cliffs
BH14 7JL ☏Bournemouth(0202)708614 & 708661
*In a pleasant location close to Sandbanks, this attractive Victorian house with modern extensions offers bright comfortable public rooms and well equipped bedrooms. Eight of these are of recent construction and offer particularly good quality accommodation. The hotel is personally owned and run, with friendly informal service, and is well suited to the holiday market.*
19rm(15⇨🛏)(4fb) CTV in all bedrooms ® T sB&B£22-£25
sB&B⇨🛏£32-£35 dB&B£50-£54 dB&B⇨🛏£54-£58 🏱
16P 🅿 ✿ *xmas*
✧ ⏛ ✂ Lunch fr£7 Dinner fr£8.50 Last dinner 8pm
Credit Cards ①②③£

★ 64% **Fairlight** 1 Golf Links Rd, Broadstone BH18 8BE (3m
NW B3074) ☏(0202)694316 & 605349
*You will need directions to find this small hotel, quietly situated in a residential area, but its warm, friendly atmosphere and wide choice of carefully cooked food – with diets catered for and a wholefood breakfast available – make the effort worthwhile.*
10rm(7⇨🛏)(1fb) sB&B£26-£29 sB&B⇨🛏£26-£29
dB&B£36-£42 dB&B⇨🛏£40-£46 🏱
CTV 10P 🅿 ✿
✧ ✂ Dinner £12-£15.50 Last dinner 7.30pm
Credit Cards ①③

✕✕**Le Château** 13 Haven Rd, Canford Cliffs BH13 7LE
☏(0202)707400
*A pleasant and hospitable little restaurant in Canford Cliffs, offering well-prepared, flavoursome dishes and a wine list of about 38 bins.*
Closed Sun & Mon
♙ English & French V 35 seats ✳ Lunch £16-£20alc Dinner
£16-£20alc Last lunch 2pm Last dinner 10pm 4P
Credit Cards ①②③

**POOLEWE** Highland *Ross & Cromarty* Map **14** NG88

★★ 61% **Pool House** IV22 2LE ☏(044586)272
Closed 15 Oct-Etr
*Delightfully situated at the head of Loch Ewe, this small, family-run, holiday hotel is a popular touring base ; now substantially refurbished, it offers compact but comfortable accommodation.*
13rm(10⇨🛏1🛏)(1fb) CTV in all bedrooms ® ✹ sB&B£24-£28
sB&B⇨🛏£26-£30 dB&B⇨🛏£52-£60 🏱
20P 🅿
✧ ⏛ ✂ Dinner £14 Last dinner 8.30pm
Credit Cards ①③

★ 58% **Poolewe** IV22 2JX ☏(044586)241
*This small, family-run hotel has a friendly atmosphere and is popular with touring holidaymakers. Bedrooms have been refurbished to a comfortable modern standard and public areas are gradually being improved.*
9rm(4⇨🛏1🛏)(1fb)✂in 3 bedrooms CTV in all bedrooms ® ✳
sB&B£18-£22 dB&B£35-£46 dB&B⇨🛏£37-£48 🏱
CTV 50P ∪ snooker 🎵 *xmas*
V ✧ ⏛ ✂ Lunch £6.50-£9.50 High tea £6.50-£9.50 Dinner
fr£11.50&alc Last dinner 9pm
Credit Cards ①②③

**POOLEY BRIDGE** Cumbria Map **12** NY42

★★ 63% **Swiss Chalet Inn** CA10 2NN ☏(07684)86215
Closed 3-18 Jan
*Not only the architecture of this hotel, but also the style of the bar and restaurant and many of the dishes featured on its comprehensive menu, reflect a Swiss theme. Pleasantly set in a small village on the northern tip of Lake Ullswater, the inn provides accommodation in well equipped rooms with en suite facilities.*
6⇨🛏(1fb)1🛏 CTV in all bedrooms ® sB&B⇨🛏£25-£30
dB&B⇨🛏£40-£48 Continental breakfast
40P ✿
♙ Continental V ✧ ⏛ Bar Lunch £4.90-£15.20alc Dinner
£4.90-£15.20alc Last dinner 9.30pm
Credit Cards ①③£

See advertisement under ULLSWATER

**POOL-IN-WHARFEDALE** West Yorkshire Map **08** SE24

❀✕✕✕**Pool Court** Pool Bank LS21 1EH ☏Leeds(0532)842288
FAX (0532) 843115
(Rosette awarded for dinner only)
*Much care and attention to detail has been devoted to the creation of this long established and comfortable restaurant which also has six en suite bedrooms available for its guests. The main bill of fare is a four-course dinner priced according to the main dish chosen and features first class ingredients, mainly British, such as Cornish oysters, potted rabbit, Aylesbury duck and sirloin of beef. Chef David Watson has a lightness of touch which is seen at its best in the consistency of his delicate mousses, although one could sometimes wish for greater depth of flavour. The comprehensive wine list includes some notable burgundies and a good selection of half bottles. Service is highly professional and at the same time friendly and personable.*
Closed Sun, Mon, 2wks from 25 Dec & 2 wks mid-summer
Lunch not served (ex parties by arrangement)
♙ British & French V 65 seats Dinner £10&alc Last dinner
9.30pm 65P
Credit Cards ①②③⑤

**PORLOCK** Somerset Map **03** SS84

★★ 71% **The Oaks** Doverhay TA24 8ES ☏(0643)862265
*Resident proprietors have created a delightful hotel with a blazing log fire in the front hall on colder days and welcoming lounges. Well-equipped and beautifully clean bedrooms are for the most part furnished with antiques, the restaurant offers a good choice of fresh local food at dinner, and a friendly atmosphere prevails throughout.*
11⇨🛏(2fb) CTV in all bedrooms ® T S% sB&B⇨🛏fr£36
dB&B⇨🛏fr£57.50 🏱
12P 🅿 ✿ *xmas*
✧ ✂ S% Dinner £15 Last dinner 8.30pm
£

**P**

1991 marks the 25th anniversary of this guide.

For key to symbols see the inside front cover.

★★

❀★★ AIRDS

PA38 4DF (Relais et Châteaux)
☎Appin(063173)236 & 211
Closed mid Nov-mid Mar
(Rosette awarded for dinner only)

*The setting of this charming little hotel never ceases to appeal, as one gazes from the restaurant across the waters of Loch Linnhe to the distant hills beyond. Resplendent in his kilt, the bearded Mr Allen looks totally at home in his West Highland setting, and guests soon discover that he, his wife, their son Graeme and their manager Alison McCorquodale are totally dedicated hosts with a natural warmth of manner and lack of pretence that inspires all the staff. Bedrooms are very attractive, comfortable and well appointed, as are the two inviting lounges and last though not least the dining room, where the small but excellent menu devised by Graeme is served. The 4-course dinners feature the best of Scottish cooking and add the final touch to the pleasures of one's peaceful stay here.*

12⇴❦Annexe2❦ CTV in all bedrooms
✖ (ex guide dogs)
30P ♨ ✿ nc5yrs
♦ ⬚ ✄ Last dinner 8.30pm

**PORT ASKAIG**

See **Islay, Isle of**

**PORT GAVERNE** Cornwall & Isles of Scilly Map **02** SX08

**★★70% Port Gaverne** PL29 3SQ ☎Bodmin(0208)880244
FAX (0208) 880151
Closed 13 Jan-15 Feb
*Situated in a sheltered cove fringed by National Trust land, an early seventeenth-century inn offers accommodation in a convivial atmosphere with well equipped modern bedrooms of various sizes, first floor lounges, popular bars and good services. The restaurant boasts excellent standards of cooking, featuring local sea food, and draws on a fine wine cellar. Reservations are strongly advised.*
16⇌♠Annexe3⇌♠(5fb) CTV in 18 bedrooms ® T
sB&B⇌♠£32-£41 dB&B⇌♠£64-£82 ⊟
CTV 30P ⊞ *xmas*
☋International V ✿ ⊻ S10% Lunch £1.50-£8.75 Dinner £13.50-£25alc Last dinner 9.30pm
Credit Cards 1 2 3 5 £

**★★66% *Headlands*** PL29 3SH ☎Bodmin(0208)880260
*Beautifully situated to command panoramic coastal views across the cove to Port Isaac, the hotel provides comfortable bedrooms and public areas which take advantage of this breathtaking outlook. Table d'hôte and à la carte menus on offer in the attractive restaurant make good use of the best local produce, and welcoming proprietors are on hand to render personal service.*
11⇌♠(1fb) CTV in all bedrooms ®
35P ⊞ ✿ sauna
☋European V ✿ ⊻ Last dinner 9.30pm
Credit Cards 1 2 3 5

**PORTHCAWL** Mid Glamorgan Map **03** SS87

**★★★58% Seabank** The Promenade CF36 3LU (Lansbury)
☎(065671)2261 Telex no 497797 FAX (065671) 5363
*This company-owned, character hotel occupies a commanding position overlooking the Bristol Channel. A recent major refurbishment has created comfortable modern bedrooms, spacious public rooms and a small leisure complex.*
62⇌♠(4fb)⊬in 6 bedrooms CTV in all bedrooms ® T ✱
sB&B⇌♠£63 dB&B⇌♠£76 ⊟
Lift ( 150P ✿ sauna solarium gymnasium jacuzzi *xmas*
☋English & French V ✿ ⊻ ⊬ Lunch fr£8.95 Dinner fr£14&alc Last dinner 10pm
Credit Cards 1 2 3 5

**★★64% *Glenaub*** 50 Mary St CF36 3YA ☎(065671)8242
*At the centre of this seaside town, yet within easy walking distance of the beach, a family-run hotel provides well equipped bedrooms and a cosy restaurant serving good food.*
18⇌ CTV in all bedrooms ® ✗
CTV 12P ⊞
☋International V ✿ ⊻ Last dinner 10pm
Credit Cards 1 2 3 4 5

**★63% Rose & Crown** Heol-y-Capel, Nottage CF36 3ST (2m N B4283) (Berni/Chef & Brewer) ☎(065671)4850
*This small, friendly inn, a short drive from sea and town centre, provides compact but comfortable and well-equipped bedrooms. Though there is no residents' lounge, it offers a choice of 3 popular bars, whilst the Country Carvery restaurant serves a range of good-value meals which always includes a traditional roast.*
8⇌(1fb) CTV in all bedrooms ® T ✗ (ex guide dogs)
sB&B⇌£41 dB&B⇌£54 ⊟
15P
V ✿ ⊬ Lunch £8-£15alc Dinner £8-£15alc Last dinner 9.30pm
Credit Cards 1 2 3 5

**★60% Brentwood** 37-41 Mary St CF36 3YN ☎(065671)2725 & 6815
*A busy hotel located just 100 yards from the sea front and the shopping centre, convenient for both holidaymakers and businessmen. Bedrooms are well-equipped with modern amenities and the à la carte menu offers a good choice of dishes. The two bars are popular with the locals.*
22rm(19⇌2♠)(5fb) CTV in all bedrooms ® T
sB&B⇌♠£24-£30 dB&B⇌♠£36-£42 ⊟
CTV 12P games room *xmas*
V S% Lunch £6-£8&alc Dinner £10-£12&alc Last dinner 10pm
Credit Cards 1 2 3 5

**✕✕Lorelei** Esplanade Av CF36 3YS ☎(065671)2683
FAX (0656) 772712
☋International V 54 seats Lunch £10-£14 Dinner £10-£14&alc Last lunch 2pm Last dinner 10pm ⊁ ⊬
Credit Cards 1 2 3 5

**PORTHKERRY** South Glamorgan Map **03** ST06

**★★★75% Egerton Grey Country House Hotel** CF6 9BZ (WR)
☎Barry(0446)711666 FAX 711690
*This handsome manor house is set in several acres of woodland and lawns, with lovely views down the valley to the sea. Public rooms are elegant and spacious, bedrooms are attractive and comfortable and food is of excellent quality.*
10⇌♠2⊟ CTV in all bedrooms ® T ✗ S% sB&B⇌♠£45-£95 dB&B⇌♠£55-£110 Continental breakfast ⊟
30P ⊞ ✿ ▶18 ♪ (hard) croquet nc10yrs *xmas*
V ✿ ⊻ ⊬ Lunch fr£14.75alc High tea £5-£10alc Dinner £19.50-£24.50alc Last dinner 9.45pm
Credit Cards 1 2 3

**PORTHLEVEN** Cornwall & Isles of Scilly Map **02** SW62

**★★65% Harbour** Commercial Rd TR13 9JD
☎Helston(0326)573876
*A quayside inn that has its own car park and modern, well equipped rooms, some of which overlook the working harbour. There is a choice of bars, including a family room where children of all ages are made welcome.*
10⇌♠(1fb) CTV in all bedrooms ® T ✗ ✱ sB&B£16.50 sB&B⇌♠£25 dB&B£31 dB&B⇌♠£42
CTV 10P ⊞ ♫
V ✿ ⊬ Lunch £4-£10 Dinner £4-£10&alc Last dinner 9.30pm
Credit Cards 1 2 3

**PORT ISAAC** Cornwall & Isles of Scilly Map **02** SW98

See also **Port Gaverne and Trelights**

**★★68% Archer Farm** Trewetha PL29 3RU
☎Bodmin(0208)880522
Closed Nov-Feb
*Standing on the outskirts of the village and extended from a farmhouse, the hotel provides comfortable bedrooms, good home cooking and the friendly services of the owners.*
8rm(1⇌3♠)(1fb) CTV in 1 bedroom T sB&B£23-£25 dB&B£46-£50 dB&B⇌♠£50-£55 ⊟
CTV 8P ⊞ ✿ *xmas*
☋French V Dinner £15 Last dinner 8.30pm

**★★63% Castle Rock** 4 New Rd PL29 3SB (Minotels)
☎Bodmin(0208)880300
Closed 5 Jan-Feb
*Set in an elevated position with spectacular views of the rugged coastline this relaxed, friendly and mainly holiday hotel offers well-equipped comfortable accommodation. Dinners are freshly cooked and wholesome, whilst bar meals are available at lunchtime.*
17rm(12⇌3♠)(3fb) CTV in 16 bedrooms ® T ✱
sB&B⇌♠£24-£28 dB&B£44-£50 dB&B⇌♠£48-£56 ⊟
CTV 20P ✿ *xmas*
V ✿ ⊻ ⊬ Lunch £6.50 Dinner £11&alc Last dinner 8.30pm
Credit Cards 1 3 £

**PORTLAND** Dorset Map **03** SY67

★★★ **59% Portland Heights** Yeates Corner DT5 2EN (Best Western) ☎(0305)821361 FAX (0305) 860081

*Modern style hotel with good amenities overlooking Chesil Beach.*

66⇌↱(4fb)⅟in 5 bedrooms CTV in all bedrooms ® **T** sB&B⇌↱£49-£50 dB&B⇌↱£64-£66 ⊟

( 160P CFA ⌂(heated) squash sauna solarium gymnasium steam room *xmas*

☋ International **V** ♧ ☕ ⅟ Lunch £9 Dinner £13&alc Last dinner 9.30pm

Credit Cards 1 2 3 5 £

★★ **52% Pennsylvania Castle** Pennsylvania Rd DT5 1HZ ☎(0305)820561

*An 18th-century mock castle standing in grounds overlooking the sea.*

12rm(4⇌5↱)(1fb)2⊟ CTV in all bedrooms ® **T** sB&B£27 sB&B⇌↱£36-£48 dB&B£40 dB&B⇌↱£50-£66

( CTV 150P ⊟ ✲ CFA *xmas*

☋ International **V** ♧ ☕ Lunch £12.95&alc Dinner £1.50-£13.95alc Last dinner 10pm

Credit Cards 1 2 3

See 'How we Classify Hotels and Restaurants' at the front of the book for an explanation of the AA's appointment and award scheme.

**The HARBOUR INN** ★★

**Porthleven, Nr Helston, Cornwall**
**Telephone: (0726) 573876**

Situated on the east side of this fishing village within 20 yards of the inner harbour. Still retaining the friendly atmosphere of an old fishermen's pub. The main bar is a focal meeting point for the locals where songs and talk of the sea and ships are commonplace. There is also a comfortable lounge bar and restaurant serving a good selection of food and a wide range of wines. Most of the bedrooms are en suite and have harbour views. Porthleven is ideally situated for touring with many of Cornwall's beauty spots within easy distance.

**★ THE ★**
**CASTLE ROCK HOTEL**

*"The hotel with the view"*

**Port Isaac,**
**North Cornwall PL29 3SB**
**Telephone 0208-880300**

Superbly situated overlooking the Atlantic and Port Isaac Bay. High standard of comfort and cuisine with personal service. Spring, Autumn and Christmas breaks. Brochure with pleasure.

●●●

Full à la carte restaurant. Cocktail bar. Conference facilities October-March.

★★

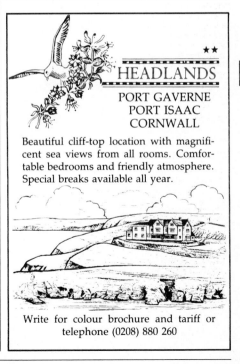

HEADLANDS

PORT GAVERNE
PORT ISAAC
CORNWALL

Beautiful cliff-top location with magnificent sea views from all rooms. Comfortable bedrooms and friendly atmosphere. Special breaks available all year.

Write for colour brochure and tariff or telephone (0208) 880 260

# Portloe - Portscatho

**PORTLOE** Cornwall & Isles of Scilly Map **02** SW93

★★70% *Lugger* TR2 5RD (Inter-Hotels) ☎Truro(0872)501322
FAX (0872) 501691
Closed mid Nov-mid March
*Very hospitable, family-run hotel in delightful harbourside position
in the picturesque village. Comfortable and pretty public areas
include a good-sized terrace for sunny days, and bedrooms are
individually styled. The best are in the annexe. Cooking is
straightforward and enjoyable.*
7⇨🟦Annexe13⇨🟦 CTV in all bedrooms ® ✖ (ex guide dogs)
27P 🏕 sauna solarium nc12yrs
🍴 English & Continental **V** ✆ ⚊ ✗ Last dinner 9pm
Credit Cards 1 2 3 5

**PORT OF MENTEITH** Central *Perthshire* Map **11** NN50

◯**Lake** FK8 3RA ☎(08775)258
Due to have opened Jul 1990
13rm

**PORTPATRICK** Dumfries & Galloway *Wigtownshire*
Map **10** NX05

★★★63% **Fernhill** DG9 8TD ☎(077681)220 FAX (077681) 596
Closed Xmas
*Situated in an elevated position commanding fine panoramic views
over the village and out to sea, this enlarged Victorian house
provides comfortable accommodation. Bedrooms, although
compact and plainly decorated, are clean, fresh and well equipped.
Guests can relax in the elegant lounge and enjoyable meals are
served by friendly young staff in the bright, modern restaurant.*
15rm(14⇨🟦🟦)Annexe4⇨🟦(1fb) CTV in all bedrooms ® **T** ✳
sB&Bfr£30 sB&B⇨🟦£35-£45 dB&B⇨🟦£60-£80 🍴
50P ✢ 🐾 *xmas*
🍴 Scottish & French **V** ✆ ⚊ ✗ Sunday Lunch fr£7 Dinner
fr£14.50&alc Last dinner 10pm
Credit Cards 1 2 3 5

✱★★ ♨
**KNOCKINAAM LODGE**

DG9 9AD (2m S on unclass
rd) (Pride of Britain)
☎(077681)471
FAX (077681) 435

Closed 5 Jan-14 Mar

(Rosette awarded for dinner
only)

*Set at the end of a narrow lane, the Victorian lodge stands in
30 acres of wooded grounds at the foot of a glen, with gardens
running down to a private beach. As a hotel, it is small and
unpretentious but very stylish and, as one would expect from
the French background of owner Marcel Frichot, great
emphasis is laid upon the pleasures of dining. Décor and
furnishings throughout the hotel are attractive and a tribute to
the taste of Corinna Frichot, who is the charming and friendly
hostess.*
10⇨🟦🎴 CTV in all bedrooms **T** sB&B⇨🟦£85
dB&B⇨🟦£140-£170 (incl dinner) 🍴
25P 🏕 ✢ croquet
🍴 French **V** ✆ ⚊ ✗ Lunch £15-£18alc High tea fr£10alc
Last high tea 7pm
Credit Cards 1 2 3 5

★★56% **Portpatrick** DG8 8TQ (Mount Charlotte (TS))
☎(077681)333
Closed last wk Nov-early Mar
*Large cliff-top resort hotel with good amenities for families with
children.*
57⇨🟦(5fb) CTV in all bedrooms ® ✳
sB&B⇨🟦£37.50-£39.50 dB&B⇨🟦£59.50-£63.50 🍴
Lift ℂ 60P ✢ CFA ⚊(heated) ▶9 ♬ (grass) snooker games
room ♬ 🐾 *xmas*
🍴 English & French **V** ✆ ⚊ Bar Lunch £2-£4.50 Dinner
fr£11.50&alc Last dinner 9pm
Credit Cards 1 2 3 5

★53% **Mount Stewart** South Crescent DG9 8LE ☎(077681)291
*A family-run hotel beside the harbour, commanding imposing sea
views. Service is friendly, and local seafoods are a speciality.*
8rm(3🟦)(2fb) CTV in all bedrooms ® sB&B£14-£17
dB&B£30-£34 dB&B🟦£34-£40
15P 🏕
🍴 International **V** Lunch £3.45-£13.50alc High tea
£4.95-£8.95alc Dinner £8-£10.50&alc Last dinner 10pm
Credit Cards 1 3

**PORTREE**

See **Skye, Isle of**

**PORTSCATHO** Cornwall & Isles of Scilly Map **02** SW83

★★★61% **Rosevine** Porthcurnick Beach TR2 5EW
☎(087258)206 & 230
Closed Nov-Etr
*A privately owned Georgian manor house, set in 3.5 acres of
sheltered gardens and run along traditional lines. Bedrooms, some
with balconies, are gradually being upgraded whilst retaining
many original features. The hotel has a good sun lounge and there
is a large restaurant with dance floor.*
14rm(12⇨🟦🟦)(2fb) CTV in all bedrooms ® **T** sB&B£37.50-£44
sB&B⇨🟦£42-£50 dB&B£75-£88
dB&B⇨🟦£88-£120 (incl dinner) 🍴
ℂ CTV 40P 🏕 ✢
🍴 International **V** ✆ ⚊ Bar Lunch £6.50-£8alc Dinner £18.50
Last dinner 8.30pm
Credit Cards 1 3

★★69% **Gerrans Bay** Gerrans TR2 5ED ☎(087258)338
Closed Nov-Mar (ex Xmas)
*Personally supervised by proprietors, Ann and Brian Greaves,
whose total commitment and attention to detail is reflected in this
very well run hotel. Bedrooms are tastefully furnished and daily
menus promote a good standard of cooking.*
14rm(12⇨🟦)(2fb) ® sB&B⇨🟦£29.50-£34.75
dB&B⇨🟦£60-£72.50 (incl dinner)
CTV 16P 🏕 *xmas*
✆ ⚊ Sunday Lunch £8.25 Dinner £13.50-£15.50 Last dinner
8pm
Credit Cards 1 2 3

★★🎴61% **Roseland House** Rosevine TR2 5EW ☎(087258)644
Closed Dec-Feb
*The well-proportioned Edwardian house stands amid well-tended
gardens in a superb cliff-top position with its own private access to
the beach. Bedrooms are comfortable and public rooms intimate.*
19⇨🟦(5fb)2🎴 ✖ (ex guide dogs) S%
dB&B⇨🟦£70-£80 (incl dinner) 🍴
CTV 25P 3🏕 🏕 ✢ ♪ private beach nc5yrs *xmas*
**V** ✆ ⚊ ✗ Sunday Lunch £8-£10 Dinner £13-£15 Last dinner
8pm

**PORTSMOUTH & SOUTHSEA** Hampshire Map **04** SZ69

★★★**71% Crest** Pembroke Rd PO1 2TA (Trusthouse Forte)
☎Portsmouth(0705)827651 Telex no 86397
FAX (0705) 756715
*This recently refurbished purpose-built hotel is ideal for either business or pleasure use, featuring a selection of conference and meeting rooms with a business centre and offering the opportunity for relaxation in its professionally supervised Sensations Leisure Club. Bedrooms vary in size but are all well-equipped and co-ordinated, and guests are provided with a choice of eating styles – the formal restaurant serving table d'hôte and à la carte menus, while the French theme Boulevard Café Bar operates a relaxed all-day service. A young team of staff gives friendly service throughout.*
163♥♪(12fb)✄in 36 bedrooms CTV in all bedrooms ® 🖹
Lift ⸨ 80P CFA ▣(heated) sauna solarium gymnasium *xmas*
♀ English & French **V** ✿ ⚏ ✄
Credit Cards ①②③④⑤

★★★**67% Holiday Inn** North Harbour PO6 4SH (Holiday Inns)
☎Portsmouth(0705)383151 Telex no 86611
FAX (0705) 388701
*This modern, purpose-built hotel on the outskirts of Portsmouth offers public areas which are attractive and bright, making the best of the vast holodrome interior. At the time of inspection, the bedrooms were being refurbished, but were still spacious and well equipped. Cuisine is straightforward, and served by pleasant young staff.*
170♥♪(76fb)✄in 23 bedrooms CTV in all bedrooms ® T
sB♥♪£90-£110 dB♥♪£100-£120 (room only) 🖹
Lift ⸨ ⊞ 200P ✿ CFA ▣(heated) squash sauna solarium gymnasium childrens adventure playground *xmas*
♀ English & French **V** ✿ ⚏ ✄ Lunch £14-£17&alc Dinner £15-£18&alc Last dinner 11pm
Credit Cards ①②③④⑤ⓔ

★★★**55% Hospitality Inn** St Helens Pde PO4 0RN (Mount Charlotte (TS)) ☎Portsmouth(0705)731281 Telex no 86719
FAX (0705) 812572
*This impressive and spacious sea front hotel provides some well appointed and attractively decorated bedrooms. Lounge facilities are limited, but there is a gracious restaurant featuring fine chandeliers, and four function rooms.*
115♥♪(6fb)✄in 13 bedrooms CTV in all bedrooms ® T ✳
sB♥♪fr£60 dB♥♪fr£69.50 (room only) 🖹
Lift ⸨ 50P *xmas*
♀ English & French **V** ✿ Lunch fr£10.50&alc Dinner fr£11.95&alc Last dinner 9.45pm
Credit Cards ①②③⑤

★★**65% Keppels Head** PO1 3DT (Trusthouse Forte)
☎Portsmouth(0705)833231
*Well established modernised hotel with very limited lounge facilities. Some bedrooms enjoy views across the Solent. Close to Royal dockyard, Isle of Wight ferry and Nelson's Victory.*
25♥♪✄in 3 bedrooms CTV in all bedrooms ® S%
sB&B♥♪£58-£64 dB&B♥♪£75-£80 🖹
Lift ⸨ 18P
**V** ✿ ⚏ ✄ S% Lunch £5-£10 Dinner £12-£12.50&alc Last dinner 9.30pm
Credit Cards ①②③④⑤

✕*Bistro Montparnasse* 103 Palmerston Rd PO5 3PS
☎Portsmouth(0705)816754
*A small bistro, brightly decorated with a friendly informal atmosphere. Cooking is of a very good standard with a few specialities.*
Closed Sun, 1st 2 wks Jan & BH's
Lunch not served
♀ French 42 seats Last dinner 10pm nc5yrs
Credit Cards ①②③⑤

**PORT TALBOT** West Glamorgan Map **03** SS79

★★★ **58%** **Aberafan Beach** Princess Margaret Way SA12 6QP (Consort) ☎(0639)884949
*A large, family hotel overlooking Aberafan beach provides reasonably good bedroom accommodation and spacious, open-plan public areas which are currently due for extension and upgrading. Table d'hôte and à la carte menus are supplemented by a range of bar meals, and friendly staff create a homely atmosphere.*
66⇋(6fb) CTV in all bedrooms ® T sB&B⇋£36-£45 dB&B⇋£43-£49 ⊟
Lift ℂ 150P CFA ♫ *xmas*
♥ Welsh, English & French ✿ ⌂ Sunday Lunch fr£7.50 Dinner fr£10&alc Last dinner 10.15pm
Credit Cards ①②③⑤ ⓔ

**PORT WILLIAM** Dumfries & Galloway *Wigtownshire* Map **10** NX34

★★★ 🏌️ **63%** **Corsemalzie House** DG8 9RL (Inter-Hotels) ☎Mochrum(098886)254
Closed 21 Jan-5 Mar
*Very peaceful 19th-century country mansion, surrounded by extensive wooded grounds. Sporting pursuits can be arranged, and the young staff are friendly and efficient.*
15⇋♠(1fb) CTV in all bedrooms ® T sB&B⇋♠£35.50-£43 dB&B⇋♠£57-£67 ⊟
30P ⇷ ✿ ♪ croquet game shooting putting ⚘
♥ Scottish & French V ✿ ⌂ Lunch £8-£11.50 Dinner £14.25-£14.75&alc Last dinner 9.15pm
Credit Cards ①③ ⓔ

★★ **55%** *Monreith Arms* The Square DG8 9SE ☎(09887)232
*A family-run hotel in the village square, close to the harbour, offers modest accommodation and can arrange a number of sporting activities for guests, including sea fishing from its own boat.*
12rm(5⇋6♠)(3fb) CTV in all bedrooms ® T
CTV 10P ♪ snooker
♥ Scottish, English & Italian V ✿ ⌂ Last dinner 9.30pm
Credit Cards ①③

**POTT SHRIGLEY** Cheshire Map **07** SJ97

★★★★ **65%** **Shrigley Hall Golf & Country Club** Shrigley Park SK10 5SB ☎Bollington(0625)575757 FAX (0625) 573323
*A magnificent building set in 260 rolling acres which include an 18-hole championship golf course. Many other sports are offered, as are conference and banqueting facilities. Ten miles from Manchester Airport.*
58⇋5🛏 CTV in all bedrooms ® T S% sB&B⇋£80-£95 dB&B⇋£90-£160 ⊟
Lift ℂ 600P ✿ ⌷(heated) ▶ 18 ℛ (hard) ♪ squash snooker sauna solarium gymnasium ♫ ⚘ *xmas*
♥ English & French V ✿ ⌂ ⊁ Lunch £15-£16.50&alc Dinner £18.50-£21&alc Last dinner 9.45pm
Credit Cards ①②③④⑤

All hotels are now given a percentage grading for the quality of their facilities. A full explanation can be found within 'How we Classify Hotels and Restaurants' at the front of the book.

**POWBURN** Northumberland Map **12** NU01

★★ 🏌️ **75%** **Breamish House** NE66 4LL ☎(066578)266 & 544 FAX (066578) 500
Closed Jan
*Set back from the A697 in its own well-kept and peaceful grounds, this elegant Georgian house offers a very good standard of accommodation throughout. Everything is provided for guests' comfort and a relaxing atmosphere prevails throughout. A five-course dinner, prepared by Cordon Bleu cooks, uses fresh local produce and the equally memorable breakfast might include locally smoked kippers. Breamish House provides a perfect base from which to explore the lovely Northumbrian countryside and coastline.*
10rm(7⇋7♠) CTV in all bedrooms ® T sB&B⇋♠£58-£68 dB&B£90-£100 dB&B⇋♠£95-£130 (incl dinner) ⊟
30P 2🚗 ⇷ ✿ nc12yrs *xmas*
⊁ Sunday Lunch fr£12 Dinner fr£18.50 Last dinner 8pm

**POWFOOT** Dumfries & Galloway *Dumfriesshire* Map **11** NY16

★★ **61%** *Golf* Links Av DG12 5PN ☎Cummertrees(04617)254
*On the Solway coast and next to an 18-hole golf course, this hotel offers spacious public areas and a modern wing of superior bedrooms. Friendly young staff offer polite, helpful service.*
21rm(7⇋7♠)(1fb) CTV in 7 bedrooms ® ✠
▦ CTV 100P 10🚗 ⌷(heated) ▶ 18 ♪
V ✿ ⌂ Last dinner 8.15pm
Credit Cards ①

**PRAA SANDS** Cornwall & Isles of Scilly Map **02** SW52

★★ **57%** **Prah Sands** Chy An Dour Rd TR20 9SY ☎Penzance(0736)762438
*Set beside the beach and commanding an unrestricted view of the coastline, this family-run hotel provides friendly service and good meals. Public rooms achieve a nice balance of comfort and charm, while bedrooms are compact, with simple furnishings and appointments.*
18rm(10⇋)(3fb) CTV in all bedrooms ® ✠ (ex guide dogs) sB&B£28-£31 dB&B£28-£34 dB&B⇋£31-£38 (incl dinner) ⊟
CTV 20P ✿ ⌷(heated) ℛ (hard) croquet
♥ English & French V ✿ ⌂ Bar Lunch £1.50-£4.95 Dinner £10.95-£15.40alc Last dinner 8.30pm
Credit Cards ①③

**PRESTBURY** Cheshire Map **07** SJ97

✗✗✗ **Legh Arms** SK10 4DG ☎(0625)829130 & 827833
*A charming restaurant dating back to the early fifteenth century and retaining its low ceilings and ancient beams is attractively set in this old village. The à la carte menu features a very cosmopolitan selection of skilfully prepared dishes served by a friendly, professional staff and accompanied by an extensive wine list.*
Closed 25 Dec evening & 1 Jan evening
♥ English & French V 90 seats ✳ S12.5% Lunch £8.50&alc Dinner £14.50&alc Last lunch 2pm Last dinner 10pm 60P
Credit Cards ①②③⑤

**PRESTEIGNE** Powys Map **03** SO36

★★ **67%** **Radnorshire Arms** High St LD8 2BE (Trusthouse Forte) ☎(0544)267406 FAX (0544)260418
*A beamed and oak panelled late-sixteenth-century coaching inn set in attractive gardens provides comfortable, character lounges and bars.*
8⇋Annexe8⇋⊁in 5 bedrooms CTV in all bedrooms ® T sB⇋£52-£62 dB⇋£67-£77 (room only) ⊟
20P 6🚗 ✿ *xmas*
V ✿ ⌂ ⊁ Sunday Lunch £9&alc High tea £1-£5alc Dinner £13-£15 Last dinner 9pm
Credit Cards ①②③④⑤

**PRESTON** Lancashire Map **07** SD52

See also **Barton**

★★★72% **Tickled Trout** Preston New Rd, Samlesbury
PR5 0UJ (Character) ☎(0772)877671 Telex no 677625
FAX (0772) 877463
*This comfortable hotel combines modern bedroom accommodation
with a quaint old world restaurant and lounge. Situated just off
junction 31 of the M6.*
72⇨♪♠(54fb)2⊞½in 10 bedrooms CTV in all bedrooms ®
S10% sB&B⇨♠£62-£70 dB&B⇨♠£74-£80 ⊟
《 150P 10 CFA ✔ sauna solarium gymnasium wave pool
steam room ♫ *xmas*
♀ International V ♦ ♫ S10% Lunch fr£8&alc Dinner
fr£12.50&alc Last dinner 9.45pm
Credit Cards 1 2 3 5

★★★71% **Broughton Park Hotel & Country Club** Garstang
Rd, Broughton PR3 5JB (3m N on A6)
☎Broughton(0772)864087 Telex no 67180 FAX (0772) 861728
*Located in extensive grounds just off junction 1 of the M55 north
of Preston, this former late Victorian house has been tastefully
extended in recent years and now provides extensive facilities
including a comprehensive leisure club. The restaurants offer a
choice of fine French cuisine or more traditional dishes.*
98⇨♠(7fb)2⊞½in 11 bedrooms CTV in all bedrooms ® T
✕ (ex guide dogs) ✳ S% sB&B⇨♠£78-£88
dB&B⇨♠£88-£98 ⊟
Lift 《 ⊞ CTV 250P ✿ ⊠(heated) ♪ (hard) squash snooker
sauna solarium gymnasium spa bath steam room beauty salon
*xmas*
♀ English & French V ✕ S% Lunch £9-£20&alc High tea fr£4
Dinner £15-£35&alc Last dinner 10pm
Credit Cards 1 2 3 5 £

★★★63% **Crest** The Ringway PR1 3AU (Trusthouse Forte)
☎(0772)59411 Telex no 677147 FAX (0772) 201923
*The comfortable modern accommodation provided by this brick-
built town centre hotel is particularly popular with a business
clientele. Reception and an open-plan area containing the
restaurant and spacious lounge bar are housed on the first floor.
Car parking is limited, but guests may use an adjacent car park
free of charge.*
126⇨♠(11fb)½in 46 bedrooms CTV in all bedrooms ® T
✕ (ex guide dogs) ⊟
Lift 《 30P CFA
♀ International V ♦ ♫ ✕
Credit Cards 1 2 3 5

★★★63% **Swallow Trafalgar** Preston New Rd, Samlesbury
PR5 0UL (Swallow) ☎(0772)877351 Telex no 677362
FAX (0772) 877424
*Situated at the junction of the A677 and A59 one mile east of the
M6, this roadside hotel offers comfortable and well-appointed
rooms in a modern bedroom wing. Service is friendly and there is a
new leisure club.*
78⇨♠½in 18 bedrooms CTV in all bedrooms ® T ✳ S10%
sB&B⇨♠fr£68 dB&B⇨♠fr£84 ⊟
Lift 《 300P CFA ⊠(heated) squash sauna solarium
gymnasium steam room & spa pool *xmas*
♀ International V ♦ ♫ S10% Lunch fr£9.25 Dinner fr£13.75
Last dinner 9.45pm
Credit Cards 1 2 3 5

★★★56% **Penguin** Leyland Way PR5 2JX ☎(0772)422922
Telex no 677651 FAX (0772) 622282
(For full entry see Leyland)

★★★54% **Novotel Preston** Reedfield Place, Walton Summit
PR5 6AB (Novotel) ☎(0772)313331 Telex no 677164
*A purpose-built hotel conveniently situated just to the east of
junction 29 of the M6 provides functional modern accommodation
and a restaurant which is open from 6am until midnight.*
100⇨♪(100fb) CTV in all bedrooms ®

Lift 《 120P ✿ ⊟(heated) pool table
♀ Continental V ♦ ♫ Last dinner 11.50pm
Credit Cards 1 2 3 5
**See advertisement on page 573**

★★69% **Vineyard** Cinnamon Hill, Chorley Rd, Walton-Le-
Dale PR5 4JN (2m S A49) (Consort) ☎(0772)54646
Closed Xmas Day night & New Years Day night
*Situated in an elevated position to the south of the town, this
attractive and popular hotel has bright and lively public areas.
Bedrooms are comfortable and well equipped.*
14⇨♪(1fb) CTV in all bedrooms ® ✕ (ex guide dogs)
《 200P ♫
♀ French V ♦ ♫ Last dinner 10.15pm
Credit Cards 1 2 3 5

★★68% **Dean Court** Brownedge Ln, Bamber Bridge PR5 6TB
☎(0772)35114
*This comfortable hotel, noteworthy for its particularly friendly
atmosphere, provides a choice of restaurants, both of which offer
interesting menus.*
9⇨♪♠5⊞ CTV in all bedrooms ® T ✕ sB&B⇨♠£25-£45
dB&B⇨♠£37-£59.50
CTV 35P nc10yrs
V ♦ ♫ Lunch fr£5.50&alc Dinner fr£8.75&alc Last dinner
10pm
Credit Cards 1 3 £

**PRESTWICK** Strathclyde *Ayrshire* Map **10** NS32
★★★60% **Carlton Toby** KA9 1TP (Toby) ☎(0292)76811
Telex no 778740
*A bright, modern and conveniently placed hotel. It has a lively
lounge bar and a carvery restaurant, where service is provided by
friendly young staff.*
39⇨♪♠(2fb)½in 9 bedrooms CTV in all bedrooms ® ▶

# Golf Hotel ★★

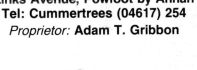

## Links Avenue, Powfoot by Annan
## Tel: Cummertrees (04617) 254
### Proprietor: Adam T. Gribbon

( 100P ✿ ♫
♀ European **V** ✿ ⬚ ⚕ Last dinner 10pm
Credit Cards [1] [2] [3] [5]

**★★60% Parkstone** Esplanade KA9 1QN ☎(0292)77286
*Looking across the Esplanade to the Isle of Arran, the hotel caters*
*for business and function trade as well as tourists. Bedrooms,*
*though compact for the most part, are equipped with modern*
*facilities, and several offer good views.*
15⇨🏳(1fb) CTV in all bedrooms ® ✖ sB&B⇨🏳£35
dB&B⇨🏳£54 🝱
( 30P 4🛏
**V** ✿ Lunch £6.55-£6.95 High tea £5.25-£9.50 Dinner
£10.95-£11.95&alc Last dinner 9pm
Credit Cards [1] [2] [3]

**★★60% St Nicholas** 41 Ayr Rd KA9 1SY ☎(0292)79568
*Cosy, owner-run hotel which is continually being improved.*
*Bedrooms are attractively decorated, and there are two bars. High*
*teas are a speciality in the quieter residents' lounge.*
16rm(10🏳)(4fb) CTV in 10 bedrooms TV in 6 bedrooms ® T
✖ (ex guide dogs) ✳ S10% sB&Bfr£23 sB&B🏳fr£28
dB&Bfr£38 dB&B🏳fr£42
CTV 50P
**V** ✿ S15% Lunch fr£3.50&alc High tea fr£5.50 Dinner
fr£7.50&alc Last dinner 9.30pm
Credit Cards [1] [2] [3] [5]

**PUDDINGTON** Cheshire Map **07** SJ37

**✖✖✖Craxton Wood** Parkgate Rd L66 9PB (on A540 junct
A550) ☎051-339 4717 FAX 051-339 1740
*Set in delightful grounds, a charming country house hotel and*
*restaurant offers an interesting menu which is changed every three*
*months or so to take advantage of seasonal specialities. Cooking is*
*of a consistently high standard, but dishes particularly worthy of*
*praise include a delicious salmon and spinach roulade and rich*
*calves' sweetbreads braised in white wine, filled with duxelle and*
*served in a white onion sauce.*
Closed Sun, 2 wks end Aug & BH's
♀ French **V** 85 seats ✳ Lunch £21.50-£28.85alc Dinner
£21.50-£28.85alc Last lunch 2pm Last dinner 10pm 60P
Credit Cards [1] [2] [3] [5]

**PUDSEY** West Yorkshire Map **08** SE23

**✖Tiberio** 68 Galloway Ln LS28 8LE ☎Bradford(0274)665895
*This small Italian restaurant provides well prepared food which is*
*attractively presented to the table by friendly and helpful staff.*
*Naturally the dishes are mainly Italian, but English and other*
*Continental specialities are available.*
Closed Mon (ex BH's) & 1st 2 wks Jan
Lunch not served Sat
♀ English & Italian **V** 66 seats Lunch £8.50-£12.25&alc Dinner
£7.75-£30alc Last lunch 2pm Last dinner 11pm 30P
Credit Cards [1] [2] [3]

**PULBOROUGH** West Sussex Map **04** TQ01

**★★75% Arun Cosmopolitan** 87 Lower St RH20 2BP
☎(07982)2162 FAX (07982) 2935
*Setting high standards of personal service, this charming hotel*
*offers a warm, friendly and relaxing atmosphere. It is situated in*
*the heart of the village and, although on the road side, it has good*
*views over the River Arun to the rear. Bedrooms are individually*
*decorated and well equipped and public rooms include a*
*comfortable lounge, a well managed restaurant and a lively bar*
*which is popular with the locals.*
6⇨🏳 CTV in all bedrooms ® **T** sB&B⇨🏳£38.50-£45
dB&B⇨🏳£60 🝱
5P 10🛏
**V** ✿ ⬚ Lunch £9.95&alc Dinner £9.95&alc Last dinner 9pm
Credit Cards [1] [2] [3] [5] ⓔ

**★★64% Chequers** Church Place RH20 1AD (Minotels)
☎(07982)2486 Telex no 67596 FAX (07982) 2715
*Welcoming, tile-hung house with beautiful views over the Sussex*
*Downs. Good British food is served, and the well-equipped*
*bedrooms have many useful extras.*
11⇨🏳(2fb)1 🛏 CTV in all bedrooms ® **T**
sB&B⇨🏳£39.50-£44.50 dB&B⇨🏳🏳£53-£63 🝱
11P 🚗 ✿ *xmas*
**V** ✿ ⬚ Lunch fr£5 High tea fr£4.50 Dinner fr£13.50 Last
dinner 8.30pm
Credit Cards [1] [2] [3] [5] ⓔ

**❀✖Stane Street Hollow** Codmore Hill RH20 1BG
☎(07982)2819
*A cosy, charming restaurant housed in what was originally two*
*farm cottages. René Kaiser's appealing menus offer the best of*
*Swiss and French ideas, and the daily fish specialities may include*
*scallops, turbot or pike. The two-course set luncheon is good value,*
*and among the range of desserts, the Tarte aux framboises is*
*delectable. Service is unfailingly attentive.*
Closed Sun, Mon, Tue, 2 wks May, 3 wks Oct & 24-28 Dec
Lunch not served Sat
♀ French & Swiss **V** 35 seats Lunch £8&alc Dinner
£15.50-£20.50alc Last lunch 1.15pm Last dinner 9pm 15P ⚕

**PURTON** Wiltshire Map **04** SU08

**★★★70% The Pear Tree at Purton** Church End SN5 9ED
☎Swindon(0793)772100 FAX (0793) 772369
*This former Victorian vicarage, built of mellow Cotswold stone*
*was opened as a restaurant with rooms at the end of 1987 but has*
*now been extended to provide 18 well-equipped bedrooms. The*
*attractive twin conservatory restaurant is the setting for talented*
*chef, Janet Pichel-Juan's cooking, with a mixture of traditional*
*French recipes and English food. The fixed price menu offers good*
*value for money. Seven and a half acres of grounds surrounding*
*the hotel are currently being laid out as a Victorian garden.*
18⇨🏳(2fb)3🛏 CTV in all bedrooms **T** ✖ (ex guide dogs) ✳
sB&B⇨🏳£75-£85 dB&B⇨🏳£85-£120 🝱
60P 🚗 ✿ croquet ⚓
**V** ✿ ⬚ Lunch £12.50 Dinner £18.50 Last dinner 9.30pm
Credit Cards [1] [2] [3] [5]

**PWLLHELI** Gwynedd Map **06** SH33

**❀★★⬛75% Plas Bodegroes Restaurant** LL53 5TH (1.5m W on
Nefyd rd) (Welsh Rarebits) ☎(0758)612363
FAX (0758) 701247
Closed Jan-Feb
*A charming Georgian country house situated in mature woodlands*
*one mile west of Pwllheli. Bedrooms are well furnished and*
*comfortable and a very high standard of cooking is provided by the*
*chef/proprietor who uses only the freshest ingredients.*
5⇨🏳2🛏 CTV in all bedrooms **T** S% sB&B⇨🏳£35-£45
dB&B⇨🏳£50-£70 🝱
25P 🚗 ✿ croquet *xmas*
⚕ S% Dinner £23&alc Last dinner 9.30pm
Credit Cards [1] [3]

**★64% The Seahaven** West End Pde LL53 5PN ☎(0758)612572
10rm(5🏳)(2fb) CTV in all bedrooms ® ✳ sB&Bfr£17
sB&B🏳fr£21 dB&B£28-£32 dB&B🏳£36-£42 🝱
CTV 🚗
Lunch fr£5 Dinner fr£9.50 Last dinner 7.15pm

---

**QUORN** Leicestershire Map **08** SK 50

★★★★65% **Quorn Country** Charwood House, Leicester Rd
LE12 8BB (on A6 in village centre) ☎(0509)415050
Telex no 347166 FAX (0509) 415557
RS 26 Dec & New Year
*Situated on the A6, within spacious grounds, this attractive hotel*
*provides good quality, modern, well-equipped accommodation.*
*Business executives are especially welcome but the hotel is popular*
*with all guests.*
19⇨♪(1fb)1🛏 CTV in all bedrooms ® ✳ sB⇨♪£68
dB⇨♪£82 (room only) 🅱
《 ▦ CTV 100P ✿ ✔
♀ English & Continental V ✆ ⚌ Lunch fr£11.95 Dinner
fr£15.95 Last dinner 10pm
Credit Cards ①②③⑤
                   **See advertisement under LOUGHBOROUGH**

---

**RAASAY, ISLE OF** Highland *Inverness-shire* Map **13** NG53

★★62% **Isle Of Raasay** IV40 8PB
☎Isle o´ Raasay(047862)222 & 226
Closed Oct-Mar
*Peacefully situated and enjoying glorious views over the Sound of*
*Raasay to the mountains of Skye, a Victorian house with practical*
*modern extensions provides fresh, neat accommodation with a*
*most relaxing atmosphere. Popular with walkers, birdwatchers*
*and nature-lovers in general. Car users should note that no petrol is*
*available on the island.*
12⇨♪ CTV in all bedrooms ® ✳ sB&B⇨♪£25-£27
dB&B⇨♪£50-£54
CTV 12P 🖭 ✿
V ✆ ⚌ ⊬
ⓔ

---

**RAGLAN** Gwent Map **03** SO40

★★67% **Beaufort Arms** High St NP5 2DY ☎(0291)690412
*The public areas of this village-centre inn, parts of which date back*
*to the fifteenth century, have considerable charm and character,*
*while its well-equipped modern bedrooms are equally suitable for*
*tourists or business clients.*
10⇨♪Annexe5⇨♪(2fb) CTV in all bedrooms ® T
⊁ (ex guide dogs) sB&B⇨♪£35 dB&B⇨♪£45 🅱
CTV 80P *xmas*
♀ English, French & Italian V ✆ ⚌ Sunday Lunch £6.95
Dinner £9.95&alc Last dinner 9.30pm
Credit Cards ①②③⑤ⓔ

---

**RAINHILL** Merseyside Map **07** SJ49

★57% **Rockland** View Rd L35 0LG ☎051-426 4603
*This family run hotel, standing in its own grounds in a residential*
*area of the village not far from junction 7 of the M62 motorway,*
*offers conventional, well equipped bedrooms, most of which have en*
*suite facilities.*
10⇨Annexe3⇨♪(5fb) CTV in all bedrooms ® sB&B£23-£29
sB&B⇨♪£29-£35 dB&B£37-£43 dB&B⇨♪£43-£55 🅱
30P ✿
V ✆ ⚌ Lunch £6.50&alc High tea £4 Dinner £9.25&alc Last
dinner 8.15pm
Credit Cards ①③ⓔ

---

**RAMSBOTTOM** Greater Manchester Map **07** SD71

★★★62% **Old Mill** Springwood BL10 9DS ☎(070682)2991
FAX (070682) 2291
*Recently extended, this hotel now has 18 well-equipped new*
*bedrooms as well as an indoor pool, gym and sauna. Facilities will*
*appeal to business and pleasure users alike, public areas offering*
*two restaurants and comfortable bars. The black and white painted*
*exterior is distinctive and there is an attractive water garden.*

36⇨♪(3fb)🛏 CTV in all bedrooms ® T ⊁ ✳
sB&B⇨£29.50-£45 dB&B⇨£46-£59 🅱
《 85P 🖭 ▱(heated) sauna solarium gymnasium *xmas*
♀ French & Italian V ✆ ⚌ Lunch fr£7&alc Dinner
fr£11.50&alc Last dinner 10.30pm
Credit Cards ①②③④⑤

---

**RAMSEY**

See **Man, Isle of**

---

**RAMSGATE** Kent Map **05** TR36

★★53% **Savoy** Grange Rd, 43 West Cliff CT11 9NA
☎Thanet(0843)592637
*Family-run and informal, the hotel offers modern bedrooms (some*
*located in an annexe on the other side of the road) and recently*
*extended public areas which include an attractive restaurant and*
*bar.*
15rm(1⇨7♪)Annexe11⇨♪(3fb) CTV in all bedrooms ®
⊁ (ex guide dogs)
《 15P 2🚗 (£3 per night) 🖭
♀ French V ✆ ⚌ Last dinner 10pm
Credit Cards ①②③⑤

---

**RAMSGILL** North Yorkshire Map **07** SE17

★★72% **Yorke Arms** HG3 5RL ☎Harrogate(0423)75243 due to
change to 755243
*In a picturesque Dales village, the Yorke Arms has prettily*
*decorated bedrooms and although some are rather small, they are*
*all well equipped. Meals are available in the popular bar as well as*
*in the restaurant and there is also a comfortable lounge for*
*residents.*
13⇨♪(2fb) CTV in all bedrooms ® T ⊁ ✳ sB&B⇨£40
dB&B⇨£60-£70 🅱
20P 🖭 ✿ *xmas*
V ✆ ⚌ ⊬ Lunch £8.50-£9 Dinner £10.50-£11.50&alc Last
dinner 9pm
Credit Cards ①③

---

**RANGEMORE** Staffordshire Map **07** SK12

★★🏠70% *Needwood Manor* DE13 9RS
☎Barton-under-Needwood(028371)2932 & 3340
Closed 24-30 Dec
*A tastefully restored manor house, standing in two acres of well-*
*tended gardens, personally run by Mr and Mrs George.*
*Hospitality is the keynote here, along with the cuisine provided by*
*young chef Michael Morris.*
11rm(1⇨1♪)(2fb)1🛏⊬in 1 bedroom CTV in 4 bedrooms ®
⊁
CTV 30P 🖭 ✿
✆
Credit Cards ①③

---

**RANGEWORTHY** Avon Map **03** ST68

★★🏠64% **Rangeworthy Court** Church Ln, Wotton Rd
BS17 5ND (Exec Hotel) ☎(045422)347 & 473
FAX (045422) 8945
*Dating from the 14th century, this former manor house is in a*
*peaceful setting by the church. Some of the bedrooms are rather*
*compact, but all are individually decorated and have good*
*facilities. Personal attention is provided by the proprietors and*
*their friendly staff.*
14⇨♪ CTV in all bedrooms ® T sB&B⇨♪£44-£52
dB&B⇨♪£60-£68 🅱
50P 🖭 ✿ ▱(heated) *xmas*
V ✆ ⚌ Lunch £9.50-£12.50&alc Dinner £15-£17.50&alc Last
dinner 9pm
Credit Cards ①②③⑤ⓔ

## RAVENGLASS Cumbria Map 06 SD09

★59% **Pennington Arms** CA18 1SD ☎(0229)717222 & 717626
*Situated in the village on the estuary of the Rivers Esk, Mite and Irt, this friendly inn offers a good range of food and fairly simple accommodation at a 'value-for-money' price.*
17rm(10⇨3♠)Annexe12rm(2⇨1♠)(6fb) ® sB&B£15.50-£22 sB&B⇨♠£22-£28.50 dB&B£26.50-£37.50
dB&B⇨♠£33-£44 ⊟
CTV 50P 3🅐 pool table
V ⚸ ⎯⌣ Lunch fr£7alc High tea £5-£9alc Dinner £8-£11alc Last dinner 10pm

## RAVENSTONEDALE Cumbria Map 07 NY70

★★73% **Black Swan** CA17 4NG
☎Newbiggin-on-Lune(05873)204
*Accommodation is charming, well furnished and enhanced by some thoughtful finishing touches, at a delightful hotel in quiet, picturesque village setting ; recently-added annexe rooms are of a high standard while public areas retain their original character, appealing to guests and local residents alike.*
14rm(8⇨3♠)Annexe4⇨♠(1fb) CTV in all bedrooms ® T ✻ sB&Bfr£33 sB&B⇨♠fr36.50 dB&B⇨♠fr£49 ⊟
CTV 20P 3🅐 ⇄ ❀ ♪ (hard) **♪** *xmas*
⚸ ⎯⌣ ✂ Lunch £8.50-£15&alc High tea fr£4.50 Dinner fr£16&alc Last dinner 9pm
Credit Cards ①②③ⓔ

★★65% **The Fat Lamb** Cross Bank CA17 4LL (Guestaccom)
☎Newbiggin-on-Lune(05873)242
*A seventeenth-century farmhouse surrounded by open countryside has been made into a friendly, small hotel, enthusiastically run by the proprietors ; bedrooms, though fairly compact, have smart, modern bathrooms, while comfortable public areas invite relaxation.*
12⇨(4fb) ® sB&B⇨£27-£29.50 dB&B⇨£42-£46 ⊟
CTV 60P ❀ *xmas*
♋ International V ⚸ ⎯⌣ Lunch £12.20-£16alc Dinner £13.50&alc Last dinner 9pm
ⓔ

## READING Berkshire Map 04 SU77

★★★★63% **Caversham** Caversham Bridge, Richfield Av RG1 8BD (Queens Moat) ☎(0734)391818 Telex no 846933 FAX (0734) 391665
114⇨♠(6fb) CTV in all bedrooms ® T ✻ sB⇨♠£40-£96 dB⇨♠£50-£96 (room only) ⊟
Lift ⟪ 200P ⊠(heated) sauna solarium gymnasium
V ⚸ ⎯⌣ ⊀ Lunch £14.50 High tea £6.50 Dinner £18 Last dinner 10pm
Credit Cards ①②③⑤ⓔ

★★★★59% **Ramada** Oxford Rd RG1 7RH ☎(0734)586222 Telex no 847785 FAX (0734) 597842
*A modern purpose-built hotel with good sized bedrooms and attractive public areas. Of the two restaurants the Arabesque offers sound French cooking.*
196⇨♠(100fb)⊀in 49 bedrooms CTV in all bedrooms ® T ✖ (ex guide dogs) S% sB⇨♠£82-£92
dB⇨♠£92-£102 (room only) ⊟
Lift ⟪ 75🅐 ⊠(heated) sauna solarium gymnasium turkish bath jacuzzi beauty salon
♋ International V ⚸ ⎯⌣ ⊀ Lunch £8.50&alc Dinner £10-£18&alc Last dinner 11.30pm
Credit Cards ①②③⑤

★★★66% *Kirtons Farm Country Club* Pingewood RG3 3UN ☎(0734)500885 FAX (0734) 391996
30⇨ CTV in all bedrooms ®

▶

★★

## ᴛʜᴇ Black Swan
### AT RAVENSTONEDALE
### Kirkby Stephen, Cumbria CA17 4NG
### Tel: (058 73) 204

Built of Lakeland stone at the turn of the century and situated in the foothills of the Eden Valley. The hotel has fourteen bedrooms all tastefully furnished the majority en suite and three rooms available for disabled guests. The Resident Owner's belief that a hotel should emulate 'home from home' whenever possible, and every effort is made to ensure warm hospitality, great comfort and fine food. Combine all this with the surrounding countryside, and we feel sure you will enjoy your stay and wish to return. Ravenstonedale is less than ten minutes from juction 38 of the M6.

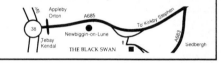

# Rangeworthy 🌲
# Court Hotel ★★

- Cotswold country manor built by Lord Chief Justice Sir Matthew Hale in mid-C17th.
- All bedrooms en-suite, with TV, telephone, movies, hairdryer etc.
- Popular restaurant.
- Excellent base for short holidays: terms available.
- Easy to get to – M4 (M32 junction 1) 15 mins – M5 (junction 14) 10 mins – Central Bristol 20 mins.
- Enjoyable, relaxing place to stay.
- Large garden: ample parking.

**CHURCH LANE, WOTTON ROAD, RANGEWORTHY, NR. BRISTOL BS17 5ND**
**Telephone: 045422-347 or 473**
**Fax: 045422-8945**

**R**

Lift ( ⊞ CTV 200P ▭(heated) ♪ (hard) ♪ squash snooker sauna solarium gymnasium ♫
♡ English & French V ♡ ⌐ Last dinner 10pm
Credit Cards [1] [2] [3] [5]

★★★65% *Post House* Basingstoke Rd RG2 0SL (Trusthouse Forte) ☎(0734)875485 Telex no 849160 FAX (0734) 311958
*Standing beside the A33, between town centre and M4, this modern commercial hotel offers two styles of well equipped bedrooms. Comfortable, functional public areas include a choice of restaurants – one of which serves imaginative cooking of a high standard – and good conference facilities.*
143⇨(43fb)⊬in 14 bedrooms CTV in all bedrooms ®
( 240P ❖ CFA ▭(heated) sauna solarium gymnasium Health & Fitness Centre
♡ English & French V ♡ ⌐ ⊬ Last dinner 10.30pm
Credit Cards [1] [2] [3] [4] [5]

★★60% *George* King St RG1 2HE (Berni/Chef & Brewer)
☎(0734)573445
*This attractive, characterful inn, with its central courtyard, narrow stairs and abundance of heavy timbering, has stood in the town centre for about five hundred years; bedrooms, however, are equipped with all modern comforts, and staff are friendly and helpful.*
68⇨(2fb) CTV in all bedrooms ® T ✖ (ex guide dogs)
sB&B⇨♠£59.50-£65 dB&B⇨♠£70 ◲
(
♡ International V ♡ ⊬ Lunch fr£8&alc Dinner £8-£15alc Last dinner 10.30pm
Credit Cards [1] [2] [3] [5]

🏠*Travelodge* 387 Basingstoke Rd RG2 0JE (Trusthouse Forte)
☎(0734)750618
*This lodge is situated on the A33 southbound, next to the Harvester restaurant, with the Little Chef open for breakfast less than a mile away. Bedrooms are well equipped and tastefully decorated, with en suite facilities. Ample parking space.*
36⇨♠(36fb) CTV in all bedrooms ® sB⇨♠£24 dB⇨♠£29.50 (room only)
( 36P ⚗
Credit Cards [1] [2] [3]

✖✖*Peking Palace* 3 Prospect St. Caversham RG4 8JB
☎(0734)483488 & 483888 FAX (0734) 461650
*This popular, intimate restaurant offers a range of interesting menus featuring authentic regional dishes from Szechwan and Canton as well as honest Peking cuisine, accompanied by service which though informal is attentive and efficient.*
Closed 25 & 26 Dec
♡ Cantonese, Pekinese & Szechwan V 120 seats Lunch £7.50-£16.50&alc Dinner £9.50-£16.50&alc Last lunch 1.45pm Last dinner 11.20pm
Credit Cards [1] [2] [3] [5]

---

**REDBOURN** Hertfordshire Map **04** TL11

★★★57% *Aubrey Park* Hemel Hempstead Rd AL3 7AF
☎(058285)2105 Telex no 82195 FAX (058285) 2001
*Set amongst six acres of gardens and lawns this hotel offers a choice of restaurants, the beamed Ostler's Room serves traditional English food whilst the Beaumont provides a more international selection. Bedrooms vary in standard but all are equipped with modern facilities.*
119⇨♠(2fb) CTV in all bedrooms ® T sB⇨♠£40-£95 dB⇨♠£70-£105 (room only) ◲
( 160P ❖ ⌐(heated) *xmas*
♡ English & French V ♡ ⌐ Lunch £12-£16.50&alc Dinner £12-£19.50&alc Last dinner 9.45pm
Credit Cards [1] [2] [3] [4] [5] ①

---

**REDBROOK** Clwyd Map **07** SJ54

★★64%, *Redbrook Hunting Lodge* Wrexham Rd SY13 3ET (Inter-Hotels) ☎Redbrook Maelor(094873)204 & 533
(For full entry see Whitchurch (Shropshire))

---

**REDCAR** Cleveland Map **08** NZ62

★★★67% *Park* Granville Ter TS10 3AR ☎(0642)490888 FAX (0642) 486147
*An elegant, comfortable, sea-front hotel providing a very good value carvery for both lunch and dinner, as well as a substantial range of bar snacks.*
25⇨♠ CTV in all bedrooms ® T ✖ (ex guide dogs)
sB&B⇨♠£30-£50 dB&B⇨♠£45-£60 ◲
( 20P ⚗
♡ English & French V ♡ ⌐ Lunch £8-£8.75&alc Dinner £8-£8.75&alc Last dinner 9.30pm
Credit Cards [1] [2] [3] [5]

---

**REDDITCH** Hereford & Worcester Map **07** SP06

★★★61% *Southcrest* Pool Bank, Southcrest B97 4JG
☎(0527)541511 Telex no 338455 FAX (0527) 402600
Closed 24 Dec-2 Jan & BH's RS Sun evenings
*A privately owned and run hotel in a secluded position yet accessible to the motorway network, the NEC and the town centre. Accommodation is well equipped, rooms in the main building are of a greater quality than those in the modern extension.*
58⇨♠(2fb)2⌂ CTV in all bedrooms ® T sB&B⇨♠£60-£72 dB&B⇨♠£70-£88 ◲
( 100P ❖
♡ French V ♡ S% Lunch £10-£11&alc Dinner £12-£13&alc Last dinner 9.15pm
Credit Cards [1] [2] [3] [5] ①

🏠*Campanile* Farmoore Ln, Winyates Green B98 0FD (Campanile) ☎(0527)510710 Telex no 339608
*Modern hotel for business travellers and others seeking pleasant, straightforward accommodation. Well placed for the M42.*
Annexe48⇨♠ CTV in all bedrooms ® T
CTV 60P ❖
♡ English & French V ♡ ⌐ Last dinner 10pm
Credit Cards [1] [3]

---

**REDHILL**

See Nutfield **and advertisement on page 579**

---

**REDLYNCH** Wiltshire Map **04** SU22

✖✖*Langley Wood* SP5 2PB ☎Romsey(0794)390348
*An attractive, creeper-clad house, set in its own pleasant grounds among dense woodland at the edge of the village, offers an imaginative menu and a wine list that are both reasonably priced. It is run by a husband and wife team – she cooking with flair and he bringing humour and professionalism to the task of serving.*
Closed Mon, Tue & 2-3 wks Jan/Feb
Lunch not served all week (ex by reservation)
Dinner not served Sun
♡ English & French V 30 seats Sunday Lunch £11.50 Dinner £13-£21alc Last dinner 11pm 30P
Credit Cards [1] [2] [3] [5]

---

**REDRUTH** Cornwall & Isles of Scilly Map **02** SW64

★★★58% *Penventon* TR15 1TE ☎(0209)214141
*This family-owned and run Georgian manor house has elegant dining galleries featuring an extensive à la carte menu and a short table d'hôte menu. Bedrooms are rather compact. The Twilight Zone nightclub in the grounds is well insulated for sound.*
50⇨♠(3fb) ⌘ CTV in all bedrooms ® T ✴ S10%
sB&B⇨♠£20-£38 dB&B⇨♠£38-£70
( 100P ❖ ▭(heated) snooker sauna solarium gymnasium leisure spa jacuzzi masseuse

▶

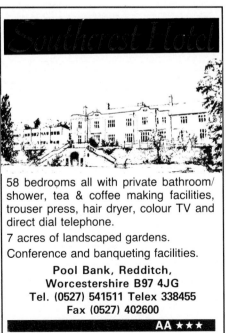
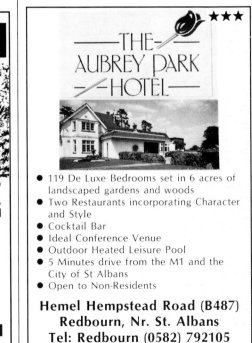
**R**

♿ English French & Italian **V** ✿ ⏰ Lunch £7&alc Dinner
fr£11.95&alc Last dinner 9.30pm
Credit Cards [1][2][3]

★★**68%** *Crossroads Motel* Scorrier TR16 5BP (2m E off A30)
☎(0209)820551 Telex no 45133
*A purpose built hotel, conveniently situated for touring and local
industry, with a choice of restaurants and modern, well-equipped
bedrooms.*
35rm(33⇌♁)(2fb) CTV in all bedrooms ® **T**
Lift 140P
♿ English & French **V** ✿ ⏰ Last dinner 9.30pm
Credit Cards [1][2][3][5]

★★**66%** *Aviary Court* Mary's Well, Illogan TR16 4QZ
☎Portreath(0209)842256
*On the edge of Illogan Woods, between Redruth and Portreath, a
charming 300-year-old Cornish country house stands in two-and-
a-quarter acres of well-tended gardens. Here the Studley family
have created a hospitable, welcoming atmosphere, details like
flowers and fruit in the warm, attractive bedrooms complementing
the high standard of modern facilities. The cosy, comfortably-
furnished lounge is heated by log fires in winter, and its windows
open onto the garden terrace in summer. Cornish produce is put to
good use in the creation of enjoyable meals served in the well-
appointed new restaurant.*
6⇌♟(1fb) CTV in all bedrooms ® **T** ✠
sB&B⇌♟£31.50-£36.50 dB&B⇌♟£46-£51
25P ⌷ ✿ nc3 yrs
♿ English & French Sunday Lunch £7.50 Dinner £9.50&alc
Last dinner 8.45pm
Credit Cards [2][5]

---

**RED WHARF BAY** Gwynedd Map **06** SH58

★**62%** *Min-y-Don* LL75 8RJ ☎Tynygongl(0248)852596
RS Nov-Feb
*Comfortably appointed family run hotel, only a few miles from the
sea.*
15rm(3⇌3♟)(4fb) CTV in 6 bedrooms ® ✲ sB&B£17
sB&B⇌♟£35 dB&B£32 dB&B⇌♟£44
CTV 60P ✿
✿ ⏰
Credit Cards [1][3]

---

**REDWORTH** Co Durham Map **08** NZ22

★★★**69%** *Redworth Hall* DL5 6NL
☎Bishop Auckland(0388)772442 FAX (0388) 775112
*An impressive late 16th-century hall set in twenty five acres of
parkland, with extensive lawns leading down to the A6072, just
south of Bishop Auckland. At the time of the last inspection
additional bedrooms were being built at the rear of the hall,
together with a leisure complex and a new restaurant. These
facilities combined with those provided in the elegant house will
meit the needs of business people and tourists alike.*
17⇌3⏛ CTV in all bedrooms ® **T**
⏛ ⊞ 200P ✿ ◲(heated) squash snooker sauna solarium
gymnasium ◔
♿ British & French **V** ✿ ⏰ Last dinner 9.30pm
Credit Cards [1][2][3][5]

---

**REETH** North Yorkshire Map **07** SE09

★★**64%** *The Buck* DL11 6SW ☎Richmond(0748)84210
*Originally a coaching house, the Buck Inn is situated in the heart
of beautiful Swaledale. Accommodation is provided in prettily
decorated and comfortable bedrooms, with an equally comfortable
lounge and cosy bar. The food is wholesome and home cooked.*
10⇌(1fb) CTV in all bedrooms ® ✠ ✲ sB&B⇌£30
dB&B⇌£44 ⊟

---

🗡 ✿ *xmas*
**V** ✿ Sunday Lunch £6.25 Dinner £10&alc Last dinner 9.30pm
Credit Cards [1][2][3][4] ⓔ

★**75%** *Burgoyne Hotel* DL11 6SN (Guestaccom)
☎Richmond(0748)84292
Closed end Nov-Etr
*Pat and Steve Foster run this small hotel in a most welcoming and
hospitable manner. There are two comfortable lounges, spotlessly
clean bedrooms enjoying spectacular views and meals are freshly
prepared and enjoyable.*
11rm(2⇌2♟)(2fb) CTV in all bedrooms ®
CTV 4P 2⊶ ⌷
Last dinner 8pm
Credit Cards [3]

---

**REIGATE** Surrey Map **04** TQ25

★★★**65%** *Bridge House* Reigate Hill RH2 9RP
☎(0737)246801 & 244821 Telex no 268810 FAX (0737) 233756
*Hillside hotel with wonderful views. Most of the spacious
bedrooms have balconies, and the large, popular restaurant has a
live band playing for dancing on five evenings a week.*
40⇌♟(3fb) CTV in all bedrooms ® **T** ✠ ✲
sB&B⇌♟£40-£58
dB&B⇌♟£58-£85 Continental breakfast ⊟
⏛ 110P ⌷ ♫ *xmas*
♿ English & French **V** ✿ Lunch £14 Dinner £18.50-£21.50
Last dinner 10pm
Credit Cards [1][2][3][5]

★★★**61%** *Reigate Manor Hotel* Reigate Hill RH2 9PF (Best
Western) ☎(0737)240125 Telex no 927845 FAX (0737) 223883
*Popular and welcoming hillside hotel with spacious restaurant. A
new wing has a gym, sauna and solarium.*
51⇌♟(1fb)1⊠ CTV in all bedrooms ® **T** ✠ (ex guide dogs)
sB⇌♟£55-£79.50 dB⇌♟£76-£89 (room only) ⊟
⏛ 130P sauna solarium gymnasium
♿ English & French **V** ✿ ⏰ Lunch £10.25-£11.25&alc Dinner
£14.50-£15.90&alc Last dinner 10pm
Credit Cards [1][2][3][5]

---

**RENFREW** For hotels see **Glasgow Airport**

---

**RENISHAW** Derbyshire Map **08** SK47

★★★**64%** *Sitwell Arms Osprey* S31 9WE (Toby)
☎Eckington(0246)435226 Telex no 547303
Closed Xmas day evening
*Converted 18th-century coaching inn with good quality, spacious,
modern accommodation and imaginative food.*
30⇌♟⊱in 10 bedrooms CTV in all bedrooms ®
⏛ 150P ✿ ◔
♿ English & French **V** ✿ ⏰ ⊱ Last dinner 9.30pm
Credit Cards [1][2][3][5]

---

**RETFORD (EAST)** Nottinghamshire Map **08** SK78

★★★**65%** *West Retford* 24 North Rd DN22 7XG (Situated on
A638) (Character) ☎East Retford(0777)706333
Telex no 56143 FAX (0777) 709951
*The well-furnished and comfortable rooms of an eighteenth-
century manor house are complemented by bedrooms of a high
standard in an adjacent modern annexe.*
Annexe63⇌♟(41fb)⊱in 9 bedrooms CTV in all bedrooms ®
**T** ✲ sB&B⇌♟£35-£62 dB&B⇌♟£50-£76 ⊟
⏛ 130P ✿ CFA ♫ *xmas*
♿ French **V** ✿ ⏰ Lunch fr£9.50&alc Dinner fr£15.50&alc
Last dinner 10pm
Credit Cards [1][2][3][5]

REYNOLDSTON West Glamorgan Map **02** SS48

★★⚑ 70%, **Fairyhill Country House** SA3 1BS (WR)
☎Gower(0792)390139
Closed 25-26 Dec
*This elegant eighteenth-century country mansion, beautifully set in twenty-four acres of park and woodland at the heart of the Gower, is family-run to offer warm hospitality, spaciously comfortable accommodation and first-class meals which make good use of fresh local produce.*
11⇨♪ CTV in all bedrooms ℞ T sB&B⇨♪£65-£75 dB&B⇨♪£75-£88
50P ⚙ ✻ ♪ sauna
♡ English & French V ♥ Dinner £20-£25alc Last dinner 9.15pm
Credit Cards ①③

RHAYADER Powys Map **06** SN96

★★ 66%, **Elan Hotel** West St LD6 5AF ☎(0597)810373
*This small, family-run hotel combines comfortable, well-equipped accommodation with warm hospitality and good-value meals; guests can relax in a compact residents' bar or the cosy lounge with its recently discovered stone inglenook fireplace. Set at the centre of the picturesque mid-Wales town, the establishment provides an ideal base from which to visit the local reservoirs and explore the surrounding countryside.*
11rm(1⇨6♪)(1fb) CTV in all bedrooms ℞ T sB&Bfr£17.50 sB&B⇨♪£30-£35 dB&B£39 dB&B⇨♪£44-£50 ♬
CTV 12P
V ♥ ⬚ Lunch £7.50 High tea £1.10-£5 Dinner £11.50&alc Last dinner 8.30pm
Credit Cards ①③ⓔ

★★ 61%, *Elan Valley Hotel* LD6 5HN (2.5m W of Rhayader)
☎(0597)810448
*Situated in beautiful rural surroundings near the village of Elan, this relaxing hotel provides modern bedrooms, two bars and a spacious lounge with a full size snooker table.*
12rm(2⇨5♪)(1fb) TV available ℞
CTV 50P 2🎱 (£2) ✻ ♪ snooker
V ♥ Last dinner 8pm
Credit Cards ①③

RHU Strathclyde *Dunbartonshire* Map **10** NS28

★★★ 55%, **Rosslea Hall** G84 8NF ☎(0436)820684
Telex no 778695 FAX (0436) 820897
*A mansion situated by the shore of the Gareloch – a popular Clyde anchorage – and dating back to 1849 has been extended to offer a range of eating and function operations.*
31⇨♪(1fb) CTV in all bedrooms ℞ T ✱ sB&B⇨♪£59-£65 dB&B⇨♪£69-£80 ♬
《 ⊞ 80P ✻ *xmas*
♡ Scottish & French V ♥ ⬚ Lunch £8&alc High tea £5-£10 Dinner £12-£15&alc Last dinner 9.30pm
Credit Cards ①②③⑤

RICHMOND North Yorkshire Map **07** NZ10

★★ 67%, **King's Head** Market Square DL10 4HS (Consort)
☎(0748)850220
*A busy inn in the market square with a coffee shop and a pizzeria.*
26⇨♪Annexe4⇨♪(1fb)3⊞✔in 9 bedrooms CTV in 29 bedrooms ℞ T ✱ sB&B⇨♪£42-£45 dB&B⇨♪£62-£65 ♬
《 23P *xmas*
♡ English & Continental V ♥ ⬚ ✔ Sunday Lunch fr£7.95 High tea fr£2.75alc Dinner fr£11.95 Last dinner 9.30pm
Credit Cards ①②③④⑤
**See advertisement on page 581**

R

**★★59%, Frenchgate** 59-61 Frenchgate DL10 7AE
☎(0748)2087 & 3596
Closed Dec-Feb
*Originally a Georgian town house, the hotel is set in a quiet cobbled
street in one of the attractive original gates to the old walled town.
Bedrooms are simply furnished but well equipped, there are several
cosy lounge areas for guests' use and the proprietors offer friendly,
efficient service.*
13rm(3⇨4ſ) CTV in all bedrooms ® sB&Bfr£24
sB&B⇨ſ fr£32 dB&Bfr£44 dB&B⇨ſ fr£50.50 🍴
6P ⇔ nc7yrs
Dinner £9.50&alc Last dinner 8.30pm
Credit Cards ⊞ ② ③ ⑤

## RICHMOND UPON THAMES Greater London

See**LONDON plan 1**B3(page 426)
**★★★60%, Richmond Hill** 146-150 Richmond Hill TW10 6RW
(Best Western) ☎081-940 2247 & 081-940 5466 Telex no 21844
FAX 081-940 5464
*Overlooking the Thames Valley from its location near Richmond
Park, an hotel with a wealth of interesting architectural features
provides accommodation in bedrooms which have been modernised
to a comfortable standard, a cosy bar, and the warmth and
elegance of a wood-panelled dining room. Visitors to this popular,
busy establishment are assured of a warm welcome and pleasant,
helpful service.*
123⇨ſ(9fb)1⊞ CTV in all bedrooms ® ✱ sB&Bſ£65-£80
dB&B⇨ſ£89-£95 🍴
Lift ℭ 150P CFA squash ♫ *xmas*
𝕆 English & French V ♦ ⚌
Credit Cards ⊞ ② ③ ⑤

**✕✕Lichfield's** 13 Lichfield Ter, Sheen Rd ☎081-940 5236
*Chef David Lee-Sang worked for five years at the Churchill Hotel
and, with patron Franco Mattoscio, provides popular French
cookery, influenced by his particular style and Chinese origins. The
mainly classical menu usually includes a short selection of fish and
meat dishes, with some 'Plats du Jour' and delightful creative
puddings. Terrine au Deux Poissons, Ravioli au Crab, Fillet of
Beef Wellington, Rondelles Boeuf aux Girolles and Steak de Veau
Normande have all been recommended by our Inspectors. A short
selection of popular wines is available and service is friendly and
informal.*
Closed Sun & Xmas
𝕆 International 40 seats ✱ Lunch fr£12 Dinner fr£25alc Last
lunch 2.30pm Last dinner 11pm
Credit Cards ⊞ ② ③ ⑤

## RINGWOOD Hampshire Map 04 SU10

**★★69%, Struan Hotel & Restaurant** Horton Rd BH24 2EG
☎(0425)473553 & 473029 FAX (0425) 480529
(For full entry see Ashley Heath)

**★77%, Moortown Lodge Hotel** 244, Christchurch Rd BH24 3AS
☎(0425)471404
Closed 24 Dec-14 Jan
*Jilly and Bob Burrows-Jones have successfully created an
individual hotel with a friendly, relaxed atmosphere, and offering
excellent value for money. A very good table d'hôte menu including
dishes such as steak and kidney or beef in beer pie, and lamb in a
pastry case. Bedrooms are cosy and compact and there is a
comfortable lounge. This hotel is one of our Top Twenty One-star
hotels, and one of the first 'Courtesy and Care' award winners –
see colour features at the front of the book.*
6rm(1⇨4ſ)(1fb) CTV in all bedrooms ® T ✻ sB&B£26-£28
sB&B⇨ſ£33-£37 dB&B£46-£54 dB&B⇨ſ£46-£54 🍴
8P ⇔
𝕆 British & French V ⊁ Dinner £10.50-£14.50&alc Last
dinner 8.30pm
Credit Cards ⊞ ③

## RIPON North Yorkshire Map 08 SE37

**★★★65%, Ripon Spa** Park St HG4 2BU (Best Western)
☎(0765)2172 Telex no 57780 FAX (0765) 690770
*Set in seven acres of attractive gardens only five minutes' walk
from the city, the hotel offers individually decorated bedrooms
which have recently been refurbished to a high standard, spacious
public areas including a comfortable lounge and pleasant public
bar, and friendly service in traditional style.*
40⇨ſ(5fb)2⊞ CTV in all bedrooms ® T ✱
sB&B⇨ſ£48-£60 dB&B⇨ſ£66-£90 🍴
Lift ℭ CTV 80P ✿ CFA *xmas*
V ♦ ⚌ Lunch £9-£14 Dinner £12.95-£18 Last dinner 9pm
Credit Cards ⊞ ② ③ ⑤ ④

**★★77%, Bridge** 16-18 Magdalen Rd HG4 1HX ☎(0765)3687
*Set in attractive gardens beside the River Ure, on the outskirts of
this historic cathedral city, a former Dame School has been
lovingly converted to provide an hotel where individually decorated
en suite bedrooms abounding in ornaments, curios and antique
objects are complemented by two cosy little sitting rooms, a bar
and a delightful restaurant serving interesting, fresh and
competently prepared meals.*
15⇨ſ(7fb)1⊞ ⊁ in 4 bedrooms CTV in all bedrooms ®
✖ (ex guide dogs)
15P ⇔
𝕆 English, French & Italian V ♦ ⚌ ⊁ Last dinner 9.30pm
Credit Cards ⊞ ② ③ ⑤

**★★56%, Unicorn** Market Place HG4 1BP (Consort)
☎(0765)2202 Telex no 57515 FAX (0765) 700321
Closed 24-27 Dec
*This hotel has stood in the medieval market place since its days as
a post house. It provides well-fitted bedrooms, a comfortable first-
floor lounge, and bars and a restaurant retaining some original
features on the ground floor.*
33⇨ſ(4fb) CTV in all bedrooms ® T sB&B⇨ſ£39-£43
dB&B⇨ſ£45-£53 🍴
ℭ 15P 4⇔
𝕆 English & French V ♦ ⚌ ⊁ Lunch £7-£7.95 High tea
£4.50-£5.50 Dinner £11-£12.50 Last dinner 9.30pm
Credit Cards ⊞ ② ③ ⑤

## RIPPONDEN West Yorkshire Map 07 SE01

**✕✕Over The Bridge** Millfold HX6 4DJ ☎Halifax(0422)823722
*The attractively redecorated interior of this pleasant little
restaurant, set beside the old pack horse bridge in a delightful
stone building that was once a row of millworkers' cottages,
provides a relaxing atmosphere in which to enjoy the freshly
produced, well-presented dishes featured on a short but interesting
set price menu and accompanied by an ample wine list.*
Closed Sun & BH's
Lunch not served
𝕆 English & French 48 seats Dinner £19.50 Last dinner
9.30pm 50P nc10yrs
Credit Cards ⊞ ② ③

## ROADE Northamptonshire Map 04 SP75

**✕Roadhouse** 16 High St NN7 2NW ☎(0604)863372
*An attractive, popular restaurant in the High Street where our
Inspector particularly enjoyed the homemade leek soup, chicken
stuffed with spinach and oyster mushrooms, followed by a
wonderful honey parfait with prunes. Just a short drive from
junction 15 of the M1.*
Closed Sun, Mon & 3 wks Summer
Lunch not served Sat
𝕆 French 32 seats S10% Lunch £13-£14&alc Dinner
£17.50-£23alc Last lunch 1.45pm Last dinner 10pm 15P nc5yrs
Credit Cards ⊞ ③

---

**ROBIN HOOD'S BAY** North Yorkshire Map **08** NZ90

★64%, **Grosvenor** Station Rd YO22 4RA ☎Whitby(0947)880320
*A small family-run hotel, modestly furnished with good standards
of cleanliness and good menus. Situated opposite a large car park
and tennis courts in the upper part of the village.*
13rm(3⇨2↑)(2fb) CTV in 6 bedrooms ® T ✕ (ex guide dogs)
✳ sB&B£15 sB&B⇨↑£17.50 dB&B£30 dB&B⇨↑£35 ⊟
CTV
⚘ Lunch £5.25 Dinner £7.25&alc Last dinner 9pm
Credit Cards ①③

---

**ROCHDALE** Greater Manchester Map **07** SD81

★★★68%, **Norton Grange** Manchester Rd, Castleton OL11 2XZ
(Character) ☎(0706)30788 FAX (0706) 49313
*Situated in its own grounds beside the A664 on the southern
outskirts of town at Castleton. This Victorian mansion has been
extended and is now a pleasant hotel with a new wing of
particularly well appointed bedrooms.*
50⇨↑(28fb)1⊞ CTV in all bedrooms ® T ✳ sB&B⇨↑£65
dB&B⇨↑£76 ⊟
Lift ℂ 150P ✿ ♬ *xmas*
♀ International V ⏾ ⚟
Credit Cards ①②③④⑤

★★60%, **Midway** Manchester Rd, Castleton OL11 2XX
☎(0706)32881 Telex no 635220 FAX (0706) 53522
*A commercial hotel standing on the A664 at Castleton, about three
miles south of Rochdale.*
25⇨↑(2fb)1⊞ CTV in all bedrooms ® T ✕ ✳
sB&B⇨↑£35-£50 dB&B⇨↑£50-£60 ⊟
ℂ⊞ 100P ♬ *xmas*
♀ English, French & Italian V ⚟ Lunch £5-£10 Dinner £8-£10
Last dinner 10.30pm
Credit Cards ①②③

---

**ROCHESTER** Kent Map **05** TQ76

★★★75% **Bridgewood Manor Hotel** Bridgewood
Roundabout, Maidstone Rd ME5 9AX (Best Western)
☎Medway(0634)201333 Telex no 965864 FAX (0634) 201330
*A quantity of intricate old woodwork has been incorporated into
the design of this delightful, purpose-built hotel; its comfortable
lounge overlooks a courtyard – as do some of the attractively
decorated, tastefully furnished and well equipped bedrooms – and
public areas also include an elegant restaurant, a welcoming lounge
bar and leisure facilities.*
98⇨(12fb) CTV in all bedrooms ® T sB&B⇨£70-£115
dB&B⇨£90-£135 ⊟
Lift ℂ 178P ✿ ▣(heated) ♪ (hard) snooker sauna solarium
gymnasium spa bath *xmas*
♀ English & French V ⏾ ⚟ Lunch fr£13&alc Dinner
fr£17.50&alc Last dinner 10pm
Credit Cards ①②③⑤

★★★67% **Crest** Maidstone Rd ME5 9SF (on A229 1m N of M2
jnct 3) (Trusthouse Forte) ☎Medway(0634)687111
Telex no 965933 FAX (0634) 684512
*This is a busy, commercial hotel with well-maintained modern
bedrooms, an open plan lounge/bar area, a leisure complex and
business centre. Staff are friendly and pleasant.*
105⇨↑(7fb)⚥in 21 bedrooms CTV in all bedrooms ® ⊟
Lift ℂ 150P ▣(heated) sauna solarium gymnasium
♀ English & French V ⏾ ⚟ ⚥
Credit Cards ①②③④⑤

★★64% **Royal Victoria & Bull Hotel** 16-18 High St ME1 1PX
☎(0634)846266 FAX (0634) 832312
28rm(21⇨↑)(2fb)1⊞ CTV in all bedrooms ® T S10% sB£38
sB⇨↑£45 dB£45 dB⇨↑£55 (room only)
ℂ CTV 25P ♬

▶

---

**AND RESTAURANT**
*Magdalen Road, Ripon,
North Yorkshire HG4 1HA
Tel: (0765) 3687 4 miles from A1*

A period house, situated on the perimeter of this small ancient market city overlooking fields and the River Ure, the BRIDGE hotel provides relaxing and interesting accommodation with many original furnishings and furniture. All rooms have private facilities, hospitality tray, remote control colour television, telephone. Our table d'hôte menu is considered to be excellent, special diets can be catered for.

City of Ripon was granted a charter by Alfred the Great over 1100 years ago. Conveniently situated between the Dales and the Moors, with the Cathedral, Fountains Abbey & Studley Royal, Newby Hall, Norton Conyers (setting for Jane Eyre) just minutes away. James Herriot country, Castle Howard, Riveaux Abbey, York, Harrogate, and so much more, all within easy reach.

**From £28 per person including VAT and à la carte breakfast. 2 day breaks from £70 including 5 course dinner.** Licensed. Car park. Visa, Access, American Express, Diners Club.

★★

**The Market Place, Richmond
North Yorkshire, DL10 4HS
Tel: (0748) 850220**

A fine Georgian Hotel built in 1720 and now restored and refurbished to compliment the period. Situated in the centre of Richmond's ancient, historic cobbled Market Square, it is ideally placed at the head of Swaledale and Wensleydale for touring Herriot country and the Yorkshire Dales. There are 29 bedrooms all equipped to a high standard with En-Suite bathrooms.

♀ International **V** ✿ ✿ ℒ ✗ Lunch £9.95&alc Dinner £9.95&alc
Last dinner 11pm
Credit Cards ❘1❘ ❘2❘ ❘3❘ ❘5❘ Ⓔ

---

**ROCHFORD** Essex Map 05 TQ89

★★★68%, **Hotel Renouf** Bradley Way SS4 1BU
☎Southend-on-Sea(0702)541334 Telex no 995158
FAX (0702) 549563
*A new hotel with some style, privately run, offers well-equipped
bedrooms which are simply but tastefully decorated. In the split-
level restaurant, with its air of grandeur, service is professionally
supervised and the imaginative dishes featured on both the table
d'hôte and à la carte menus are feshly prepared, well-presented
and complemented by a reasonably priced wine list.*
24⇔♠(1fb) CTV in all bedrooms Ⓡ **T** sB&B⇔♠£56-£90
dB&B⇔♠£64-£90
⟨⊞25P ⇔ ✿ *xmas*
♀ French **V** S10% Lunch £19.50&alc Dinner £19.50&alc Last
dinner 8.30pm
Credit Cards ❘1❘ ❘2❘ ❘3❘ ❘5❘

✗✗**Renoufs** 1 South St SS4 1BL
☎Southend-on-Sea(0702)544393 Telex no 995158
FAX (0702) 549563
Closed Sun, Mon, 1-21 Jan & 24 Jun-9 Jul
Lunch not served Sat
♀ English & French **V** 70 seats S10% Lunch £19.50&alc
Dinner £19.50&alc Last lunch 2pm Last dinner 10pm ⋡
Credit Cards ❘1❘ ❘2❘ ❘3❘ ❘4❘ ❘5❘

---

**ROCK (near St Minver)** Cornwall & Isles of Scilly
Map 02 SW97

★★67% *St Enodoc* PL27 6LA ☎Trebetherick(020886)3394
*This sporting hotel offers snooker tables, squash courts and gym
enjoys splendid views over the Camel Estuary. The candlelit dining
room offers a short table d'hôte menu of well prepared English
dishes and bar snacks are also available.*
13⇔♠(2fb) CTV in all bedrooms
33P ⇔ ✿ squash snooker sauna solarium gymnasium water-
skiing, windsurfing, pony-trekking
♀ English & Continental **V** ✿ ℒ Last dinner 9.30pm
Credit Cards ❘1❘ ❘2❘ ❘3❘

★★59%, **Mariners Motel** Slipway PL27 6LD
☎Trebetherick(020886)2312
RS Nov & Feb
*Overlooking the estuary, the motel-type operation is personally
run, offering a friendly atmosphere and a choice of good food from
the well-priced table d'hôte or slightly more expensive à la carte
menus. The main building contains reception, cocktail bar and
dining room on the first floor, with the popular bar at ground level,
whilst comfortable bedrooms are situated across the side road in
Custom House Cottage and a more modern conversion. Some of
these rooms have lounge areas.*
Annexe15⇔♠(2fb) CTV in all bedrooms Ⓡ ✱
sB&B⇔♠£25-£28 dB&B⇔♠£44-£50
30P pool table
**V** ✿ ℒ Bar Lunch £1.90-£7.50 Dinner £1.90-£16&alc Last
dinner 9.30pm
Credit Cards ❘1❘ ❘3❘

---

**ROCKCLIFFE** Dumfries & Galloway *Kirkcudbrightshire*
Map 11 NX85

★★★⛾68%, **Baron's Craig** DG5 4QF ☎(055663)225
Closed mid Oct-Etr
*Handsome mansion, set peacefully in woodland with colourful
gardens and views of the Solway and Rough Firths. Both
traditional and modern bedrooms are offered, and there is a smart
cocktail bar.*

27rm(20⇔♠)(2fb) CTV in all bedrooms **T** sB&B£34-£38.50
sB&B⇔♠£47-£52 dB&B£63-£72 dB&B⇔♠£80-£96 ➡
50P ⇔ ✿ putting
♀ International ✿ ℒ Lunch fr£10 Dinner fr£18.50 Last dinner
9pm
Credit Cards ❘1❘ ❘3❘

---

**ROMALDKIRK** Durham Map 12 NY92

★★70%, **Rose & Crown** DL12 9EB ☎Teesdale(0833)50213
FAX (0833) 50828
*Charming old village inn with wide-ranging inexpensive bar meals.*
6⇔♠Annexe5⇔♠(1fb)1 ➡ CTV in all bedrooms Ⓡ **T**
sB&B⇔♠fr£44 dB&B⇔♠fr£55 ➡
40P *xmas*
♀ English & French ✿ ℒ Sunday Lunch fr£8.50 Dinner
fr£15.50 Last dinner 9.30pm
Credit Cards ❘1❘ ❘3❘ Ⓔ

---

**ROMSEY** Hampshire Map 04 SU32

★★★62%, **Potters Heron Hotel** SO51 9ZF (Lansbury)
☎Southampton(0703)266611 Telex no 47459
FAX (0703) 251359
(For full entry see Ampfield)

★★★61%, **The White Horse** Market Place SO5 8NA
(Trusthouse Forte) ☎(0794)512431 FAX (0794) 517485
*Part-Tudor coaching inn with a Georgian façade, offering elegance
at the Lucella Dixon restaurant and a flower-filled courtyard for
summer bar meals or drinks.*
33⇔♠(7fb)✗in 4 bedrooms CTV in all bedrooms Ⓡ **T** ✱
sB⇔£70-£80 dB⇔£80-£90 (room only) ➡
⟨60P CFA *xmas*
♀ English & French **V** ✿ ℒ ✗ Lunch fr£7 Dinner fr£12.95
Last dinner 9.45pm
Credit Cards ❘1❘ ❘2❘ ❘3❘ ❘4❘ ❘5❘

★★★58%, **New Forest Heathlands** Romsey Rd, Ower SO51 6ZJ
☎Southampton(0703)814333 Telex no 8954665
FAX (0703) 812123
50⇔♠(2fb) CTV in all bedrooms Ⓡ **T** S% sB&B⇔♠£60-£75
dB&B⇔♠£75-£90 ➡
⟨150P ✿ mini-golf jacuzzis ♋ *xmas*
♀ International **V** ✿ ℒ S% Lunch £7.50&alc High tea
£2.60-£5.80 Dinner £14.75&alc Last dinner 9.15pm
Credit Cards ❘1❘ ❘2❘ ❘3❘ ❘5❘ Ⓔ

❀✗✗**Old Manor House** 21 Palmerston St SO51 8GF
☎(0794)517353
*A consistently high standard of French cuisine is maintained at
this pleasant restaurant. Chef patron Bregoli offers a short but
interesting menu with specialities such as Bresaolo, a home-cured
smoked beef, and succulent langoustines served in flaky pastry
with butter sauce. The delicately prepared squab pigeon is highly
recommended, and to accompany the food there is a superb wine
list of more than 600 wines covering many countries. Mrs Bregoli's
charming personality ensures that the hospitality of the welcome
matches her husband's excellent cooking.*
Closed Mon, 24-30 Dec & last 3 wks Aug
Dinner not served Sun
♀ French 46 seats ✱ Lunch £12.50-£19.50 Dinner fr£29.50
Last lunch 2pm Last dinner 9.30pm 12P
Credit Cards ❘1❘ ❘3❘

---

**ROSEBANK** Strathclyde *Lanarkshire* Map 11 NS84

★★★61%, **Popinjay** Lanark Rd ML8 5OB (Consort)
☎Crossford(055586)441 Telex no 776496 FAX (055586) 204
*Mock-Tudor hotel with gardens by the River Clyde. Popular for
functions.*
40⇔♠(1fb)2➡ CTV in all bedrooms Ⓡ **T** sB&B⇔♠fr£50
dB&B⇔♠fr£65 ➡

⟨ 100P ✿ ♪ ൟ

♀ International **V** ♱ ☒ Lunch fr£7&alc Dinner fr£12&alc
Last dinner 10pm
Credit Cards ①②③⑤

---

**ROSEDALE ABBEY** North Yorkshire Map **08** SE79

**★★★68%** **Blacksmiths Arms** Hartoft End YO18 8EN
☎Lastingham(07515)331
*This one-time 16th century farmhouse, has now been carefully*
*restored and extended, and is now a cosy and attractive hotel with*
*period furniture and open fires in winter. The building, however,*
*still retains much of its old world charm and character. Bedrooms*
*have been individually designed, and the dining room, in which*
*delectable dishes are served from a 4 course menu, has been*
*charmingly appointed, and the bars with horse brasses, beams and*
*lots of interesting points, provide an atmosphere in total character*
*with the building.*
14⇥♠ CTV in all bedrooms ⓇT ✕ ✳ sB&B⇥♠fr£33
dB&B⇥♠fr£66 ⊟
80P ⊞ ✿
♀ English & French **V** ♱ ☒ Lunch £11.50 High tea £3.95-£5
Dinner £19.50 Last dinner 8.45pm
Credit Cards ①③⑤ⓔ

**★★73%** **Milburn Arms** YO18 8RA (Guestaccom)
☎Lastingham(07515)312
Closed Xmas day
*A very friendly hotel offering an extensive range of well-prepared*
*bar and restaurant meals, and comfortable accommodation.*
11⇥(2fb)1⊞ CTV in all bedrooms ⓇT ✳ sB&B⇥£31-£47
dB&B⇥£49-£70 ⊟
35P ⊞ ✿ pool table *xmas*
**V** ♱ ⊬ Sunday Lunch £8.90 Dinner £14.50&alc Last dinner
9pm
Credit Cards ①③ⓔ

**R**

## Rosedale Abbey - Ross-on-Wye

★★63% **White Horse Farm** YO18 8SE (Minotels)
☎Lastingham(07515)239
Closed Xmas day
*An hotel commanding superb views from its position at the heart of the North Yorkshire Moors National Park provides accommodation in comfortable, well-equipped bedrooms, whilst quaint public rooms with open log fires and original beams are an effective reminder that the building dates back to 1702.*
11⇦♠Annexe4⇦♠(2fb) CTV in all bedrooms ®
✕ (ex guide dogs) sB&B⇦♠£25-£35 dB&B⇦♠£50-£60 ₽
50P ⇬ ✿ *xmas*
♀ English & Continental **V** Sunday Lunch £6.95-£8.95 High tea £2.50-£5alc Dinner £15.50-£17.50 Last dinner 8.45pm
Credit Cards ①②③⑤ ⓔ

---

**ROSEHALL** Highland *Sutherland* Map **14** NC40

★★57% *Achness* IV27 4BD ☎(054984)239
Closed Oct-Feb
*A popular anglers' retreat, this small highland hotel offers comfort and relaxation in its refurbished public areas and bedrooms which remain simple and practical. Satisfying home cooked dinners are provided at the self service hot buffet.*
5rmAnnexe7⇦ TV in 6 bedrooms ®
CTV 40P ⇬ ✿ ♪ clay pigeon shooting
**V** ♦ ⱹ
Credit Cards ①③

---

**ROSSETT** Clwyd Map **07** SJ35

★★★⚑75% **Llyndir Hall** LL12 0AY ☎Chester(0244)571648
*At the time of inspection extensive alterations were being completed, which would totally transform this former small country house hotel. A large extension was being built which would increase the number of rooms to 38. A large function/conference suite was also being provided, as well as an indoor swimming pool and small gymnasium. New rooms and facilities were finished at the end of Autumn, 1990.*
38⇦♠(4fb)⊬in 3 bedrooms CTV in all bedrooms **T**
✕ (ex guide dogs) sB&B⇦♠£60-£75 dB&B⇦♠£70-£95 ₽
⟮120P ⇬ ✿ ⬛(heated) solarium gymnasium croquet spa bath steam room *xmas*
♀ English & French **V** ♦ ⱹ ⊬ Lunch £9.50-£11.50&alc
Dinner £17.50&alc Last dinner 10pm
Credit Cards ①②③⑤ ⓔ
**See advertisement under CHESTER**

---

**ROSSINGTON** South Yorkshire Map **08** SK69

★★★64% **Mount Pleasant** Great North Rd DN11 0HP (On A638 Great North Rd 1.5m E of village)
☎Doncaster(0302)868696 & 868219 FAX (0302) 865130
Closed Xmas Day
*Situated on the A638 half-way between Bawtry and Doncaster, this much extended building was formerly the estate house to Rossington Hall and dates back to the 1700s. It now offers good accommodation in comfortable surroundings including a range of cosy quiet lounges.*
38rm(23⇦10♠)(2fb)4⇬ CTV in all bedrooms ® **T**
✕ (ex guide dogs) ✳ sB&Bfr£22 sB&B⇦♠fr£39.50
dB&B⇦♠fr£49.50
⟮100P ⟮£1 per night) ✿
**V** ♦ ⱹ Lunch £7.45-£20.15alc High tea fr£4.25 Dinner fr£10 Last dinner 9.30pm
Credit Cards ①②③ ⓔ
**See advertisement under DONCASTER**

---

The AA's star-rating scheme is the market leader in hotel classification.

---

**ROSS-ON-WYE** Hereford & Worcester Map **03** SO62
See also **Goodrich, Pencraig** and **Symonds Yat**

★★★⚑65% **Pengethley Manor** HR9 6LL (4m N on A49 Hereford rd) (Best Western) ☎Harewood End(098987)211
Telex no 35332 FAX (098987) 238
*This country house hotel is set in attractive, extensive grounds with superb views across the beautiful Herefordshire countryside. Rooms in the main house are very well furnished, whilst those in the annexes tend to be more compact. Service is professional and hospitable.*
11⇦Annexe11⇦(3fb)3⇬ CTV in all bedrooms ® **T**
sB&B⇦£60-£110 dB&B⇦£100-£150 ₽
70P ✿ ⬛(heated) ♪ snooker 9 hole mini golf croquet *xmas*
♀ English & French **V** ♦ ⱹ S% Lunch fr£13.75 Dinner fr£18.50&alc Last dinner 9.30pm
Credit Cards ①②③⑤ ⓔ

★★★65% **Royal** Palace Pound HR9 5HZ (Trusthouse Forte)
☎(0989)65105 FAX (0989) 768058
*The Royal was built in 1837, and occupied a prime elevated position, with views across the horseshoe bend of the River Wye. It is a traditional hotel with comfortable, well equipped accommodation – some rooms have small balconies overlooking the gardens. There is a well appointed dining room, a comfortable lounge and conference facilities, which are very popular.*
40⇦♠(4fb)⊬in 10 bedrooms CTV in all bedrooms ® **T** ✳
sB⇦♠fr£70 dB⇦♠fr£90 (room only) ₽
⟮40P ✿ ♪ *xmas*
**V** ♦ ⱹ ⊬ Lunch fr£9&alc High tea fr£4 Dinner fr£14&alc Last dinner 9.30pm
Credit Cards ①②③④⑤

★★★60% **Chase** Gloucester Rd HR9 5LH (Consort)
☎(0989)763161 FAX (0989) 768330
*Set in extensive grounds on the outskirts of town this former country house provides comfortable, well-equipped accommodation, good service and hospitality. It is popular with both conference delegates and tourists.*
40⇦♠(26fb)3⇬ CTV in all bedrooms **T** ✕ (ex guide dogs) S%
sB&B⇦♠£65 dB&B⇦♠£93 ₽
⟮200P ✿ CFA *xmas*
**V** ♦ ⱹ Lunch £15&alc Dinner £15&alc Last dinner 9.30pm
Credit Cards ①②③⑤ ⓔ

---

★★ **WHARTON LODGE COUNTRY HOUSE**
Weston-under-Penyard
HR9 7JX ☎(0989)81795
FAX (0989) 81700
Closed 28 Dec-11 Jan

*We can highly recommend this delightful hotel as a new addition to the guide. It is a Georgian property, standing in 15 acres of parkland on the A40, 3 miles from Ross-on-Wye, which has been home to 4 generations of the Gough family. The elegance and quality of rooms and furnishings makes a lasting impression from the moment you enter, and the traditional service is in keeping with the surroundings. The dinners prepared by chef Hamish Deas are imaginative; try the clear but subtle flavours evident in dishes such as Bass and Mussel mousse with watercress purée, chicken served with a Vermouth, cream and cucumber sauce, followed by a Bavarois of pistachios and coconut with a mango coulis. Manager Jeremy Gough looks after his guests in a friendly, relaxed manner.*

9⇦♠1⇬ CTV in all bedrooms **T** ✕ (ex guide dogs)
sB&B⇦♠£85-£120 dB&B⇦♠£95-£130 ₽

---

584

30P ⊞ ❄ ∪ shooting nc12yrs *xmas*
V ⚘ Lunch £4-£15alc Dinner £20&alc Last dinner 9.30pm
Credit Cards ①②③

---

★★⚑72%, **Peterstow Country House** Peterstow HR9 6LB
☎(0989)62826
*Set in twenty five acres of countryside on the A49, this Georgian*
*rectory has recently been lovingly restored. Rooms are spacious,*
*beautifully decorated and furnished with antiques and the*
*enjoyable meals are made from produce from the local farm where*
*possible.*
9⇨ℂ(3fb) CTV in all bedrooms ⊁ sB&B⇨ℂ£34-£70
dB&B⇨ℂ£41-£85 ⽥
CTV 60P ⊞ ❄ clay pigeon shooting nc7yrs *xmas*
♀ English & French V ⚘ ⌸ Lunch fr£12.50 Dinner fr£16.95
Last dinner 9pm
Credit Cards ①②③⑤ⓔ

---

★★⚑71% **Glewstone Court** Glewstone HR9 6AW
☎Llangarron(098984)367 FAX (098984) 282
Closed 25-27 Dec
*The Reeve-Tucker family run this delightful hotel with warmth*
*and hospitality and with some quirky finishing touches – such as*
*furry cats to put outside the bedroom door instead of a 'do not*
*disturb' sign. Transformed since 1987 from dilapidation to an*
*elegant and comfortable hotel, it is also peacefully situated*
*amongst fruit orchards in its own three acres of grounds. Christine*
*Reeve-Tucker prepares imaginative meals, making the most of*
*local produce.*
9⇨ℂ CTV in all bedrooms ® T sB&B⇨ℂ£43-£51
dB&B⇨ℂ£64-£74 ⽥
20P ⊞ ❄ croquet lawn hot air ballooning ⊘
♀ English & French V ⚘ Lunch fr£12.50 High tea fr£3 Dinner
fr£17 Last dinner 9.30pm
Credit Cards ①②③

---

★★66% **Hunsdon Manor** Gloucester Rd, Weston-Under-
Penyard HR9 7PE (2m E A40) ☎(0989)62748 & 63376
*A 16th-century manor house with later additions, standing in two*
*and a half acres of lawns and gardens.*
14⇨ℂAnnexe10⇨ℂ(3fb)2⊞ CTV in all bedrooms ® T
sB&B£22 sB&B⇨ℂ£32-£34 dB&B⇨ℂ£44-£60 ⽥
55P ⊞ ❄ sauna solarium
♀ English & French V ⚘ ⌸ Sunday Lunch £9.50&alc Dinner
£13-£17alc Last dinner 9.30pm
Credit Cards ①②③⑤ⓔ
See advertisement on page 587

---

★★66% **Orles Barn** Wilton HR9 6AE ☎(0989)62155
Closed Nov
*Standing less than a mile from the town centre, in one-and-a-half*
*acre grounds that include a swimming pool, this former farm offers*
*accommodation in rooms which are all well-maintained and*
*attractive, though some are quite compact; a restaurant*
*overlooking the garden provides guests with a good selection of*
*English and Continental dishes.*
9rm(6⇨2ℂ)(1fb) CTV in all bedrooms ®
sB&B⇨ℂ£27.50-£45 dB&B⇨ℂ£50-£70 ⽥
《 20P ❄ ▭(heated) ⊘
♀ English, French & Spanish V ⚘ ⌸ Lunch fr£8.25 Dinner
fr£9.25&alc Last dinner 9pm
Credit Cards ①②③⑤ⓔ
See advertisement on page 587

---

★★65% **Bridge House** Wilton HR9 6AA (adjacent A40/A49
junc) ☎(0989)62655
*A small, privately-owned hotel in the village of Wilton, just a short*
*drive from the town centre. The well kept garden leads down to the*
*River Wye and guests can enjoy pre-dinner drinks here in the*
*summer. Rooms are comfortable and the proprietors extend a*
*warm welcome.*

▶

R

7⇨🟊1🛏 CTV in all bedrooms ® ✖ sB&B⇨🟊£29-£30 dB&B⇨🟊£48-£50 🖪
CTV 14P 🚭 ✿ nc10yrs *xmas*
♀ English & French Sunday Lunch £8.50-£9.50 Dinner £9.50-£10.50&alc Last dinner 9pm
Credit Cards ① ③

**★★63% King's Head** 8 High St HR9 5HL ☎(0989)763174
Closed 24-26 Dec
*A 14th century town centre inn where the well-equipped bedrooms and public areas retain their olde worlde charm. The lounge bar is popular with hotel guests and residents alike, and meals make the most of fresh local produce.*
14⇨🟊Annexe9⇨(4fb) CTV in all bedrooms ® T 🖪
20P 🚭
V ♦ .🖃
Credit Cards ① ③

**★★58% Chasedale** Walford Rd HR9 5PQ ☎(0989)62423
*Dating back to 1850, the house is surrounded by gardens, including a large kitchen garden. Bedrooms are modestly furnished and the owners are very involved in the running of the hotel.*
11rm(9⇨)(4fb) CTV in all bedrooms ® T sB&B⇨£29-£31 dB&B£35-£37.50 dB&B⇨£46-£50 🖪
14P 🚭 ✿ *xmas*
♀ English & French V ♦ .🖃 ✶ Lunch £7.75-£8.50 Dinner £9.75-£10.50&alc Last dinner 9pm
Credit Cards ① ③ ④ ⑤ ⓔ

---

**ROSTHWAITE** Cumbria Map **11** NY21

See also **Borrowdale**
**★★★60% Scafell** CA12 5XB ☎Keswick(059684)208
FAX (059684) 280
Closed 2 Jan-9 Feb
*Located in the heart of Borrowdale and surrounded by misty fells this very pleasant family-owned hotel offers warm hospitality, comfortable lounges and well-furnished bedrooms. A high standard of food is served in the restaurant.*
20⇨🟊(3fb) CTV in all bedrooms ® T sB&B⇨£40-£45 dB&B⇨🟊£80-£90 (incl dinner) 🖪
50P 🚭 ✿ *xmas*
♀ International V ♦ .🖃 Sunday Lunch £8.50-£9.50 Dinner £15.80&alc Last dinner 9.15pm
Credit Cards ①

**See advertisement on page 589**

---

**ROTHBURY** Northumberland Map **12** NU00

**★★63% Coquet Vale** Station Rd NE65 9QN ☎(0669)20305
*Friendly service, a good-value range of interesting menus and accommodation in spacious, comfortable bedrooms are provided by this privately-owned small hotel.*
14rm(11⇨🟊)(6fb) CTV in all bedrooms ® ✖ (ex guide dogs) ✶ sB&B£23.50 sB&B⇨🟊£40 dB&B⇨🟊£40 🖪
40P ✿ *xmas*
V ♦ Lunch £6.95 High tea £3.75-£7.50 Dinner £9.95&alc Last dinner 9pm
Credit Cards ① ③

---

**ROTHERHAM** South Yorkshire Map **08** SK49

See also **Thurcroft**
**★★★66% Rotherham Moat House** Moorgate Rd S60 2BG (Queens Moat) ☎(0709)364902 Telex no 547810
FAX (0709) 368960
*A modern, well-appointed hotel offering comfortable accommodation. Situated close to the town centre and motorways.*
83⇨🟊(6fb)1🛏✖in 22 bedrooms CTV in all bedrooms ® T ✶ S10% sB⇨🟊fr£58 dB⇨🟊fr£64 (room only) 🖪
Lift ℭ CTV 95P CFA sauna solarium gymnasium jacuzzi ♫

---

♀ English & French V ♦ .🖃 ✶ Lunch fr£6.25 Dinner £11.50-£12.75&alc Last dinner 9.45pm
Credit Cards ① ② ③ ④ ⑤

**★★69% Brentwood** Moorgate Rd S60 2TY ☎(0709)382772
FAX (0709) 820289
Closed 26 & 27 Dec RS Bank Hols
*The restaurant of this impressive country house offers a good-value menu of imaginative dishes, and the accommodation in its original building is supplemented by modern bedroom wings.*
37rm(32⇨🟊)Annexe10⇨🟊(4fb)2🛏 CTV in all bedrooms ® T ✶ sB&B£20-£33 sB&B⇨🟊£20-£48 dB&B£35-£65 dB&B⇨🟊£35-£65 🖪
60P ✿
♀ English & Continental V ♦ Lunch fr£8.50&alc Dinner fr£13.95&alc Last dinner 9.30pm
Credit Cards ① ② ③ ⑤ ⓔ

**★68% Elton** Main St, Bramley S66 0SF (3m E A631)
☎(0709)545681 FAX (0709) 549100
*A popular small hotel in the village of Bramely on the A631, 1/2 mile from junction 1 of the M18. Helpful and friendly staff provide a most hospitable atmosphere, while a good range of dishes is available in the restaurant.*
15rm(2⇨3🟊) CTV in all bedrooms ® T sB&B£22-£29 sB&B⇨🟊£24-£46 dB&B£36-£50 dB&B⇨🟊£40-£54 🖪
ℭ 32P
♀ English & French V ♦ .🖃 Lunch £9.25&alc Dinner £13.75&alc Last dinner 9.30pm
Credit Cards ① ② ③ ⑤ ⓔ

---

**ROTHERWICK** Hampshire Map **04** SU75

**★★★★🛏79% Tylney Hall** RG27 9AJ (Prestige)
☎Hook(0256)764881 Telex no 859864 FAX (0256) 768141
*A magnificent country mansion set within 66 acres of pleasant gardens and woodland, with many of the splendid, spacious bedrooms contained in former coach houses and gardener's cottages. The lounges are grand yet retain a comforting, homely atmosphere it is the attentiveness, efficiency and friendliness of the staff, led by Rita Mooney, which makes staying here such a pleasure. The hotel is popular with the business and seminar market though every effort is made to ensure that other guests are not overwhelmed by these groups. This kind of consideration has helped Tylney Hall become one of our first 'Courtesy and Care' award winners. See the colour feature at the front of the book.*
35⇨🟊Annexe56⇨(1fb)3🛏 CTV in all bedrooms ® T ✖ (ex guide dogs) ✵ S10% sB&B⇨🟊fr£85 dB&B⇨🟊fr£99 🖪
Lift ℭ 120P 🚭 ✿ ▣(heated) ⌇(heated) ♬ (hard) snooker sauna gymnasium croquet lawn archery clay pigeon shooting ♫ *xmas*
♀ English & French V ♦ .🖃 ✶ Lunch fr£17&alc Dinner fr£23.50&alc Last dinner 9.30pm
Credit Cards ① ② ③ ⑤ ⓔ

**See advertisement under BASINGSTOKE**

---

**ROTHES** Grampian *Morayshire* Map **15** NJ24

**★★★🛏64% Rothes Glen** IV33 7AH ☎(03403)254
FAX (03403) 566
Closed Jan
*A baronial-style mansion, set in grounds where Highland cattle roam. The entrance hall is particularly impressive, and the public rooms are elegant and comfortable. The very well-equipped bedrooms include spacious examples furnished with antiques.*
16rm(13⇨)(4fb) CTV in all bedrooms 🖪
CTV 40P 🚭 ✿
♦ S10% Lunch £12.50 Dinner £23 Last dinner 9pm
Credit Cards ① ② ③ ⑤

**ROTHESAY**

See **Bute, Isle of**

---

**ROTHLEY** Leicestershire Map **08** SK51

★★★**70%** *Rothley Court* Westfield Ln LE7 7LG (Trusthouse Forte) ☎Leicester(0533)374141 Telex no 342811 FAX (0533) 374483

*Situated midway between Leicester and Loughborough, and standing in six acres of grounds, this lovely old manor house dates back to the 13th century. Accommodation is comfortable and well equipped, many of the bedrooms are situated in two annexes.*

15⇨♠Annexe21⇨ CTV in all bedrooms ® T
《 100P ✿ CFA croquet
V ✤ ⚓ ⊬ Last dinner 10pm
Credit Cards ①②③④⑤

---

**ROTTINGDEAN** East Sussex Map **05** TQ30

★★**61%** *White Horse* Marine Dr BN2 7HB
☎Brighton(0273)300301

*In a prime seaside location with extensive views, this hotel offers well-equipped modern accommodation decorated in Laura Ashley designs. There is a contemporary restaurant, a smart cocktail bar and a lively lounge bar where lunches are served.*

17⇨(2fb)2⇴ CTV in all bedrooms ® ✖ (ex guide dogs)
Lift 《 45P ⌐
V ✤ ⚓ ⊬ Last dinner 10pm
Credit Cards ①②③⑤

---

**ROUSDON** Devon Map **03** SY29

★★**57%** *Orchard Country* DT7 3XW ☎Lyme Regis(02974)2972
Closed Nov-Mar

*Standing in quiet rural surroundings, its pleasant small grounds set well back for the A3052 between Lyme Regis and Seaton, this personally-run little hotel offers friendly, informal service in a relaxed atmosphere, public rooms which are both cosy and homely, and bright, simply-styled, modern bedrooms.*

12⇨♠ CTV in all bedrooms ® sB&B⇨♠£27-£34
dB&B⇨♠£50-£59 ⊟
CTV 25P ✿ nc8yrs
✤ ⚓ ⊬ Bar Lunch fr£2alc Dinner £12.50 Last dinner 8.15pm
Credit Cards ①③ ⓔ

---

**ROWARDENNAN** Central *Stirlingshire* Map **10** NS39

★★**61%** *Rowardennan (Loch Lomond)* G63 0AR
☎Balmaha(036087)273
Closed Nov RS Oct-Mar

*A modest but homely hotel situated amidst rugged scenery at the end of the road on the east side of Loch Lomond. Popular with walkers travelling the West Highland Way, which passes the hotel. It offers a good range of bar meals and an interesting dinner menu in season.*

11rm(1⇨)(2fb) ® ✱ sB&Bfr£20 sB&B⇨♠fr£25 dB&Bfr£34
dB&B⇨fr£40
CTV 50P ⇴ water-skiing boating
V ✤ Bar Lunch £2.50-£10alc Dinner £10-£12alc Last dinner 8.45pm
ⓔ

---

**ROWEN** Gwynedd Map **06** SH77

★★**64%** *Tir-y-Coed Country House* LL32 8TP
☎Tynygroes(0492)650219
Closed Xmas RS Nov-Feb

*Standing in its own gardens on the edge of the village and surrounded by beautiful scenery, this well-furnished little hotel offers a peaceful, friendly atmosphere.*

7⇨♠Annexe1♠(1fb) CTV in all bedrooms ®
sB&B⇨♠£19.25-£22.75 dB&B⇨♠£36-£41.50 ⊟

---

8P ⇴ ✿ ⚬
✤ ⚓ ⊬ Bar Lunch £2-£5alc Dinner £9.25 Last dinner 7.30pm
ⓔ

---

**ROWNHAMS MOTORWAY SERVICE AREA (M27)** Hampshire

○**Roadchef Lodge** M27 Southbound SO1 8AW ☎(0703)734480
Due to have opened summer 1990
39rm

---

**ROWSLEY** Derbyshire Map **08** SK26

★★★**57%** *Peacock* DE4 2EB (Embassy)
☎Matlock(0629)733518 FAX (0629) 732671

*Popular with visitors and locals, the restaurant here is particularly busy. Accommodation in the main house is of a good standard and there are simpler, lower-priced rooms available in the cottage annexe.*

14⇨♠Annexe6rm(1⇨♠)(4fb)1⇴⊬in 3 bedrooms CTV in all bedrooms ® T sB£36-£48 sB⇨♠£65-£75 dB£48
dB⇨♠£75-£80 (room only) ⊟
《 45P 2⇘ ⇴ ✿ ♪ xmas
V ✤ ⚓ Lunch £9.80-£12.30 Dinner £23.50-£28.50 Last dinner 9pm
Credit Cards ①②③⑤

★★**71%** *East Lodge Country House* DE4 2EF
☎Matlock(0629)734474

*This country house hotel is set in 10 acres of attractive gardens and grounds, and the proprietors, with their small team of staff, provide a personal friendly service. The accommodation has recently been extended, and offers rooms that are well equipped and furnished.*

14⇨♠ CTV in all bedrooms ® T ✖ ✱ sB&B⇨♠£37-£45
dB&B⇨♠£60-£80
30P ⇴ ✿ croquet lawn xmas
♀ International ✤ ⚓ Lunch £9.50-£14.50 Dinner £15.50-£18.50 Last dinner 8.30pm
Credit Cards ① ⓔ

---

**ROY BRIDGE** Highland *Inverness-shire* Map **14** NN28

★★**57%** *Glenspean Lodge* PH31 4AW
☎Spean Bridge(039781)223 FAX (039781) 660

*Attractively situated in an elevated position two miles east of Roy Bridge, this well maintained country house is slowly being refurbished to provide comfortable and well appointed bedrooms. Informal service is rendered by friendly staff and a number of sporting activities can be arranged.*

12rm(8⇨♠)(2fb) CTV in 9 bedrooms ® T ✱ sB&B⇨♠£18-£20
sB&B⇨♠£26-£30 dB&B⇨♠£36-£40 dB&B⇨♠£42-£60 ⊟
CTV 50P ✿ ♪ clay pigeon & rough shooting stalking ⚬ xmas
♀ Scottish & French V ✤ ⚓ ⊬ Bar Lunch £1-£4.75alc
Credit Cards ①③ ⓔ

---

**ROZEL BAY**

See **Jersey under Channel Islands**

---

**RUABON** Clwyd Map **07** SJ34

★★**59%** *Wynnstay Arms* High St LL14 6BL ☎(0978)822187

*In the centre of the village, which is not by-passed, is this mainly 19th-century coaching inn with modest but comfortable accommodation and friendly, hospitable staff. The fine old stable block was the headquarters of Watkin-Wynn's private army, which fought in the Crimean War.*

9rm(3⇨)(1fb) CTV in all bedrooms ® S% sB&B£25
sB&B⇨£30 dB&B£38 dB&B⇨£44
80P 2⇘
♀ English & French V ✤
Credit Cards ①②③④⑤ ⓔ

**RUAN HIGH LANES** Cornwall & Isles of Scilly
Map **02** SW93

★★71% **Hundred House** TR2 5JR ☎Truro(0872)501336
Closed Nov-Feb
*An old Cornish house dating from 1790 which has been extensively refurbished by the owners Mike and Kitty Eccles. Bedrooms are individually furnished and public areas include a small library, a comfortable, spacious bar lounge and separate sitting room. Service is friendly and informal.*
10⇨↑ CTV in all bedrooms ® ✱ S% sB&B⇨↑£24-£27
dB&B⇨↑£48-£54 ⊞
15P ⇔ ✿ croquet nc6yrs
♦ ⊈ ⼇ Dinner fr£15 Last dinner 6pm
Credit Cards ① ③

★★69% **Pendower** Gerrans Bay TR2 5LW
☎Truro(0872)501257 FAX (0452)410440
Closed Nov-Easter
*In a remote position on the peninsula, and surrounded by National Trust land, the hotel has private access to the beach. Bedrooms are furnished in the modern style, there are three lounges and a well-appointed bar. Service is particularly well-managed.*
14⇨(2fb)
CTV 16P 3 (£2 per day) ⇔ ✿
V ♦ ⊈ Last dinner 9pm
Credit Cards ① ② ③

**RUGBY** Warwickshire Map **04** SP57

★★★65% **Post House Hotel** NN6 7XR (Trusthouse Forte)
☎Crick(0788)822101 Telex no 311107 FAX (0788) 823955
(For full entry see Crick)

# GLENSPEAN LODGE HOTEL ★★
## Roy Bridge, Inverness-shire PH31 4AW

You will find a warm friendly atmosphere in this country house hotel, which has been completely refurbished and decorated to a very high standard and your comfort is our keyword. All bedrooms have bathroom en suite and colour TV.

**For a brochure and tariff please telephone the resident proprietors Neal or Isabel Smith on 039 781-224.**

# SCAFELL Hotel ★★★
## ROSTHWAITE, BORROWDALE, CUMBRIA CA12 5XB
## TELEPHONE: BORROWDALE (059684) 208

**R**

Situated in the heart of Borrowdale Valley, just off the main road which goes on to Honister Pass and Buttermere, the Scafell Hotel was formerly a Coaching Inn frequented by travellers making the Journey over Honister Pass From Keswick to Cockermouth.

Tastefully modernised it still retains its old world charm and character.

20 bedrooms – all en suite – our dining room/restaurant (open to non-residents) is renowned for its fine food and wines. 5 course table d'hôte, or late supper menu available. Full licensed with cocktail and public (riverside) bar selling real ale, both well noted for bar lunches.

★★★**60% Grosvenor** Clifton Rd CV21 3QQ ☎(0788)535686
FAX (0788) 541297
*This hotel, formerly three late Victorian houses, has been totally
refurbished during the past four years and now provides modern
well-equipped bedrooms and imaginative food standards. The hotel
also has a new indoor swimming pool and fitness complex.*
21⇨✿ CTV in all bedrooms ® T ✕ (ex guide dogs)
sB&B⇨✿£55-£65 dB&B⇨✿£75-£85
《40P ⊞ ⊠(heated) sauna solarium gymnasium jacuzzi ♫
*xmas*
V ✿ ⊈ Lunch £11.95&alc Dinner £11.95-£20alc Last dinner
10pm
Credit Cards ① ② ③ ⑤

★★**65% Hillmorton Manor** 78 High St, Hillmorton CV21 4EE
(2m SE off A428) ☎(0788)565533 & 572403
*Standing on the outskirts of the town of Hillmorton on the B4429
near its junction with the A428, an hotel under the management of
its resident proprietors takes a particular pride in providing clean
and well-maintained bedroom accommodation with modern en
suite facilities.*
11⇨✿(1fb) CTV in all bedrooms ® T ✕ (ex guide dogs) ✳
sB&B⇨✿fr£45 dB&B⇨✿fr£60
40P
♀ English & French V ✿ Lunch £9 Dinner £13.50 Last dinner
10pm
Credit Cards ① ② ③ ④

---

**RUGELEY** Staffordshire Map **07** SK01

★★**59% Cedar Tree** Main Road, Brereton WS15 1DY
☎(0889)584241
RS Sun evenings
*A commercial-style hotel on the busy A51 in the village of Brereton
has a solarium, squash courts and a popular large function suite.*
14rm(7⇨)Annexe14⇨✿(1fb) CTV in 25 bedrooms ® T ✕ ✳
sB&Bfr£19 sB&B⇨✿£23-£25 dB&Bfr£38 dB&B⇨✿fr£42
CTV 200P squash solarium
♀ English & French V ✿ Lunch £6&alc Dinner £8.50&alc Last
dinner 9.30pm
Credit Cards ① ② ③ ⑤

⭧**Travelodge** Western Springs Rd WS15 2AS (A51) (Trusthouse
Forte) ☎(0889)570096
*Two-storey brick-clad building on the edge of the town centre with
a petrol station and Little Chef on site.*
32⇨✿(32fb) CTV in all bedrooms ® sB⇨✿£24
dB⇨✿£29.50 (room only)
《32P ⊞
Credit Cards ① ② ③

---

**RUNCORN** Cheshire Map **07** SJ58

★★★**64% Crest** Wood Ln, Beechwood WA7 3HA (Trusthouse
Forte) ☎(0928)714000 Telex no 627426 FAX (0928) 714611
*This busy hotel, popular for both business and pleasure, stands in a
residential area which is reached via junction 12 of the M56.*
134⇨✿(12fb)⚥in 30 bedrooms CTV in all bedrooms ® T ⊟
Lift 《250P ✿ CFA ⊠(heated) sauna solarium gymnasium
steam room spa bath pool tables *xmas*
V ✿ ⊈ ⚥
Credit Cards ① ② ③ ④ ⑤

---

**RUSHDEN** Northamptonshire Map **04** SP96

★★**60% The Rilton Hotel** High St NN10 1BT
☎Wellingborough(0933)312189
*This private commercial hotel is on the A6 in the centre of the
town. Rooms are generally spacious and equipped with modern
facilities. The steak house restaurant provides popular dishes and
the bar is busy with locals as well as guests.*
10⇨✿1⊞ CTV in all bedrooms ®

CTV 50P
V ✿ ⊈
Credit Cards ① ③

---

**RUSHYFORD** Co Durham Map **08** NZ22

★★★**59% Eden Arms Swallow Hotel** DL17 0LL (Swallow)
☎Bishop Auckland(0388)720541 FAX (0388) 721871
*A business and conference hotel conveniently situated two miles
from the A1(M).*
46⇨✿(4fb)1⊞⚥in 20 bedrooms CTV in all bedrooms ® T ✳
sB&B⇨✿fr£58 dB&B⇨✿fr£74 ⊟
《200P ✿ ⊠(heated) sauna solarium gymnasium jacuzzi steam
room impulse shower ♫ *xmas*
♀ English & French V ✿ ⊈ Lunch fr£8.25&alc Dinner
fr£11.95&alc Last dinner 9.30pm
Credit Cards ① ② ③ ⑤

---

**RUSPER** West Sussex Map **04** TQ23

★★★**68% Ghyll Manor** RH12 4PX (Trusthouse Forte)
☎(0293)871571 Telex no 877557 FAX (0293) 871419
*Set in forty acres of countryside, with open terraces and
landscaped gardens, this fine, oak-panelled and beamed manor
house has been faithfully restored and well furnished to create a
restaurant, extensive banquetting and conference facilities, a small
lounge and bedrooms which are uniquely and individually
furnished with a wealth of extras – the eight original ones now
augmented by the more modern adjacent stable mews;
accommodation is also provided in historic cottages and very
comfortable suites.*
28⇨✿6⊞⚥in 3 bedrooms CTV in all bedrooms ® ✳
sB⇨✿£86 dB⇨✿£108 (room only) ⊟
《150P ✿ ⊇(heated) ♪ (hard) sauna solarium ♫ ⚭ *xmas*
V ✿ ⊈ Lunch £16.50&alc Dinner £20&alc Last dinner 10pm
Credit Cards ① ② ③ ④ ⑤
See advertisement under GATWICK AIRPORT (LONDON)

---

**RUTHIN** Clwyd Map **06** SJ15

★★★**62% Ruthin Castle** LL15 2NU (Best Western)
☎(08242)2664 Telex no 61169 FAX (08242) 5978
*An authentic castle set in thirty acres of delightful grounds – yet
only a short walk from the town centre – caters equally well for
business people (including delegates using the conference
facilities) and holidaymakers with its well-equipped bedrooms and
extensive public areas.*
58⇨✿(6fb)1⊞ CTV in all bedrooms ® T ✕ (ex guide dogs)
sB&B⇨✿fr£45 dB&B⇨✿fr£69 ⊟
Lift 《CTV 200P ✿ CFA ✍ snooker *xmas*
♀ International V ✿ ⊈ Sunday Lunch fr£7.95 Dinner
fr£14.50&alc Last dinner 9.30pm
Credit Cards ① ② ③ ⑤ ⓕ

---

**RYDE**

See **Wight, Isle of**

---

**RYE** East Sussex Map **05** TQ92

★★★**63% Mermaid Inn** Mermaid St TN31 7EU
☎(0797)223065 Telex no 957141
*With beams and panelling dating from its 1420 rebuilding, the
Mermaid offers good food and warm hospitality. The inn's charm
compensates for the lack of space, and some rooms have four-
posters.*
28rm(21⇨5✿)3⊞ CTV in 14 bedrooms T ✕ (ex guide dogs)
S10% sB&B⇨✿£45-£50 dB&B⇨✿£75-£90 ⊟
《CTV 25P nc8yrs *xmas*
V ✿ S10% Lunch £12-£13&alc Dinner £15-£16&alc Last dinner
9.15pm
Credit Cards ① ② ③ ④ ⑤

★★68% *The George* High St TN31 7JP (Trusthouse Forte)
☎(0797)222114
*An historic coaching inn, whose many original architectural features include an elegant first-floor lounge and banqueting suite, offers bedrooms which are well equipped, though compact in some cases, and a range of enjoyable meals featuring some traditional English recipes in Chaucers restaurant.*
22⇄ CTV in all bedrooms ®
9P 8🐾
V ♧ 🏳 ⊁ Last dinner 9pm
Credit Cards 1 2 3 4 5

★60% **Playden Oasts** Peasmarsh Rd, Playden TN31 7LU
☎(0797)223502
*Standing on the edge of the historic town of Rye, and mentioned in the Doomsday Book, the hotel was used in bygone years for drying hops, grown in nearby fields, which were used to flavour local ales and beers. Dating from 1800, it was still in use until 1965, and the restaurant exhibits the original charm and architecture. The bedrooms in this small, informal and friendly hotel, are simply furnished and soundly equipped with modern facilities such as direct dial telephones, colour televisions and compact en suite bathrooms.*
5⇄🏠Annexe3🏠(2fb) CTV in all bedrooms ® T
✖ (ex guide dogs) ✳ sB&B⇄🏠£20-£30 dB&B⇄🏠£46-£56 🏳
20P ⇔ ❄ xmas
V ♧ 🏳 Lunch £6.95-£7.95 Dinner £9.50-£16alc Last dinner 9pm
Credit Cards 1 2 3 4 5 ⓔ

✖**Landgate Bistro** 5-6 Landgate TN31 7LH ☎(0797)222829
*Nick Parkin and partner Toni Ferguson-Lees consistently produce reliable and good standards of cooking and service. The short menu lists such dishes as wild rabbit with rosemary, breast of duck with port and cognac and a very tasty fish stew.*
Closed Sun, Mon, Xmas, 1 wk Jun & 2 wks Oct
Lunch not served
♀ British & French V 34 seats S% Dinner £13-£19.50alc Last dinner 9.30pm ⊁
Credit Cards 1 2 3 5

---

**SAFFRON WALDEN** Essex Map 05 TL53

★★65% **Saffron** 10-18 High St CB10 1AY ☎(0799)22676
Telex no 81653 FAX (0799) 513979
*A 16th-century hotel combining old-world charm with modern comforts and providing high standards of cuisine.*
21rm(8⇄8🏠)(2fb)1 ⊞ CTV in all bedrooms ® T S% sB&B£28
sB&B⇄🏠£44 dB&B£50
dB&B⇄🏠£60 Continental breakfast 🏳
10P
♀ English & French V ♧ Lunch £7.50-£9.50&alc Dinner £15.95&alc Last dinner 9.30pm
Credit Cards 1 3 ⓔ

---

**ST AGNES** Cornwall & Isles of Scilly Map 02 SW75

★★64% **Rosemundy House** Rosemundy TR5 0UF
☎(087255)2101
Closed 5 Oct-27 Mar & 6 Apr-4 May
*Delightful country-house style hotel, parts of which date back to 1780, set in 4 acres of wooded gardens close to the village centre. This is a busy holiday hotel offering exceptional value for money.*
44⇄🏠(16fb) CTV in all bedrooms ® sB&B⇄🏠£18-£29
dB&B⇄🏠£36-£58
CTV 50P ⇔ ❄ ≋(heated) badminton games room croquet putting
♧ 🏳 ⊁ Bar Lunch £1.20-£5 Dinner £10 Last dinner 8pm

For key to symbols see the inside front cover.

Ruthin, Clwyd, LL15 2NU, Wales

Originally built by Edward I, the present castle stands amidst the 13thC. ruin, including dungeon, whipping pit etc., in 35 acres of gardens. 58 bedrooms, all with private facilities, cocktail bar in the library, table d'hôte and à la carte restaurant and world famous Mediaeval Banquets. Car parking for 200 cars.

Please call 08242 2664, telex 61169 or fax 08242 5978 for reservations.

# THE GROSVENOR HOTEL
## CLIFTON ROAD, RUGBY CV21 3QQ
## WARWICKSHIRE. TEL: 0788 535686 ★★★

A privately run hotel which offers the discerning traveller timelessly elegant surroundings, which take you back to when the emphasis was on comfort and good service.
23 individually styled bedrooms all en suite, and with every convenience for your comfort. Some rooms even feature your own jacuzzi. You can relax in the pleasant atmosphere of our Cocktail Bar whilst making your choice of dishes featured on our monthly changing menu designed by chef "Richard Johnson".
The luxurious indoor Leisure complex includes Swimming pool, Jacuzzi, Gymnasium, Sauna and Sunbed.

**S**

★★**৶**61% **Rose in Vale Country House** Rose in Vale, Mithian
TR5 0QD ☎(087255)2202
Closed Nov-Feb
*This attractive Georgian house with a modern extension is set in pleasant grounds within a secluded valley. The bedrooms, though not particularly spacious, are well equipped and have en-suite facilities and there is a choice of comfortable lounges.*
15⇔♪(3fb)1⌘ CTV in all bedrooms ® T sB&B⇔♪£29.95
dB&B⇔♪£59.90 (incl dinner) ∺
CTV 20P ⇼ ✿ ⊇(heated) solarium croquet badminton table tennis billiards
𝄢 English & Continental ✆ ⚏ ✔ Sunday Lunch £7.50 Dinner £13.95&alc Last dinner 8pm
Credit Cards ①③

★70% **Sunholme** Goonvrea Rd TR5 0NW ☎(087255)2318
Closed Nov-Mar
*Set in well-tended gardens and grounds, commanding magnificent views of coast and countryside, this personally-run hotel promotes a relaxed, convivial atmosphere. Bedrooms are neat and tidy, with en suite showers, there are three compact but well presented interconnecting lounges, the small rear bar houses an unusual collection of milk bottles and home cooked meals represent very good value for money.*
10♪(6fb) CTV in all bedrooms ® T sB&B♪£19.50-£21
dB&B⇔♪£39-£42 ∺
CTV 20P ✿ ๘
V ✆ ⚏ ✔ Dinner £9 Last dinner 7.30pm
Credit Cards ①③ ⓔ

**ST ALBANS** Hertfordshire Map 04 TL10

★★★69% **Noke Thistle** Watford Rd AL2 3DS (2.75m S at junct A405/B4630) (Mount Charlotte (TS)) ☎(0727)54252
Telex no 893834 FAX (0727) 41906
*A comfortable, elegant hotel offering modern, well-equipped bedrooms and pleasant, attentive service. Enterprising French and English cuisine is served in the restaurant.*
111⇔♪(4fb)✔in 5 bedrooms CTV in all bedrooms ® T ✱
sB⇔♪fr£75 dB⇔♪fr£85 (room only) ∺
⚓150P ✿ CFA
𝄢 International ✆ ⚏ ✔ Lunch fr£14.50&alc Dinner fr£17.50&alc Last dinner 10pm
Credit Cards ①②③④⑤

★★★65% **Sopwell House** Cottonmill Ln, Sopwell AL1 2HQ (Best Western) ☎(0727)64477 Telex no 927823
FAX (0727) 44741
*This 18th century mansion is located in its own grounds, and has been recently extended to include outstanding conference facilities, together with comfortable, good quality bedrooms. The conservatory restaurant offers an extensive à la carte menu, with formal service.*
70⇔♪(10fb)22⌘✔in 12 bedrooms CTV in all bedrooms ® T
Lift ⚓150P ✿ CFA
V ✆ ⚏ ✔ Last dinner 10.30pm
Credit Cards ①②③⑤

★★★63% **St Michael's Manor** Fishpool St AL3 4RY
☎(0727)64444 Telex no 917647 FAX (0727) 48909
Closed 27-30 Dec
*Guests experience peace and contentment in the hospitable surroundings of this charming manor house with its five acres of beautiful grounds. Named, individually decorated bedrooms retain their original atmosphere but are equipped with modern facilities, and the restaurant has been extended by the addition of a Victorian-style conservatory overlooking the gardens.*
26rm(13⇔9♪)4⌘ CTV in all bedrooms T S%
sB&B⇔♪£65-£80 dB&B⇔♪£80-£100
⚓CTV 80P ⇼ ✿ nc12yrs

𝄢 English & French V Lunch £15.50-£17&alc Dinner £19-£20&alc Last dinner 9pm
Credit Cards ①②③⑤ ⓔ

**ST ANDREWS** Fife Map 12 NO51

★★★★72% **St Andrews Old Course Hotel** Old Station Rd KY16 9SP ☎(0334)74371 Telex no 76280 FAX (0334) 77668
Closed 26-30 Dec
*Totally transformed following a major refurbishment, this hotel now offers extended public areas, a choice of good restaurants and a very good spa club. It occupies a dominant position overlooking the famous Old Course Links golf course – a view enjoyed by many of the spacious bedrooms and public rooms.*
125⇔♪ CTV in all bedrooms
Lift ⚓⊞150P ✿ ⊡(heated) snooker sauna solarium gymnasium health spa jacuzzi
𝄢 Scottish & French V ✆ ⚏
Credit Cards ①②③④⑤

★★★★60% **Rusack's** Pilmour Links KY16 9JQ (Trusthouse Forte) ☎(0334)74321 FAX (0334) 77896
*Rusacks Hotel occupies a position overlooking the 1st and 18th fairways of the famous Links Golf Course – towards the expanse of beach beyond, and yet is close to the town centre. This makes this well established resort hotel the ideal base for golfers and families. Public areas retain a sense of elegance and the principal lounge offers fine views. Bedrooms provide the expected levels of comfort, with tasteful décor.*
50⇔♪✱in 5 bedrooms CTV in all bedrooms ® T ✱
sB⇔♪£81-£87 dB⇔♪£119-£146 (room only) ∺
Lift ⚓30P sauna solarium *xmas*
V ✆ ⚏ ✔ Lunch £6-£9.25 Dinner £24.50-£32 Last dinner 9.30pm
Credit Cards ①②③④⑤

★★★68% **Rufflets Country House** Strathkinness Low Rd KY16 9TX ☎(0334)72594 FAX (0334) 78703
Closed 7 Jan-19 Feb
*An attractive hotel, situated outside the centre of the town, stands amid splendid, formal gardens. Its ongoing programme of refurbishment has provided comfortable, spacious public areas and well-equipped bedrooms, those in Rose Cottage being particularly charming. Polite staff provide service of a professional standard, especially in the restaurant where meals with a strong Scottish emphasis are served.*
18⇔♪Annexe3⇔♪(2fb)1⌘ CTV in all bedrooms ® T ✖ (ex guide dogs) S10% sB&B⇔♪£46-£60
dB&B⇔♪£92-£120 ∺
⚓50P 2☗ (£1) ✿ putting ๘ *xmas*
V ✆ ⚏ ✔ S10% Lunch fr£9.50 Dinner fr£21 Last dinner 9.30pm
Credit Cards ①②③⑤

★★★67% **St Andrews Golf** 40 The Scores KY16 9AS
☎(0334)72611 Telex no 94013267 FAX (0334) 72188
*This comfortable hotel continues to improve under the personal supervision of the proprietor.*
23⇔♪(10fb) CTV in all bedrooms ® T sB&B⇔♪£47.50-£58
dB&B⇔♪£75-£105 ∺
Lift ⚓6P CFA sauna solarium *xmas*
𝄢 Scottish & French V ✆ ⚏ ✔ Lunch £10.50 High tea £7.50-£10.50alc Dinner £18.50&alc Last dinner 9.30pm
Credit Cards ①②③④⑤

★★★60% **Scores** 76 The Scores KY16 9BB (Best Western)
☎(0334)72451 Telex no 94012061 FAX (0334) 73947
*Situated close to the famous golf course, this is a spacious hotel with two bars, a restaurant and coffee shop. Well-equipped bedrooms vary in size and style. Guests will enjoy the fine views and friendly atmosphere.*
30⇔♪(1fb) CTV in all bedrooms ® T ✱ sB&B⇔♪£54-£62
dB&B⇔♪£65-£105 ∺

▶

S

Lift ( 10P ✤
♋ English & French **V** ✿ ☑ Lunch fr£5.45alc High tea fr£5.50alc Dinner frf£14.50&alc Last dinner 9.30pm
Credit Cards ① ② ③ ④ ⑤

**★★ 67% *Ardgowan*** 2 Playfair Ter KY16 9HX (Consort)
☎(0334)72970
Closed 25 Dec-15 Jan RS Nov-24 Dec & 16 Jan-Apr
*Small, family-run hotel offering reasonably-priced meals both in the attractive restaurant and downstairs bar.*
13rm(7⇨4↑)(2fb) CTV in all bedrooms ®
CTV ℱ
♋ Scottish & French **V** Last dinner 9.30pm
Credit Cards ① ③

**★★ 65% Parklands Hotel & Restaurant** Kinburn Castle, Double Dykes Rd KY16 9DS ☎(0334)73620
*A comfortable, friendly hotel managed by the chef/proprietor who creates interesting and skillfully prepared dishes at both lunch and dinner.*
15rm(8⇨1↑)(2fb)⅍in 3 bedrooms CTV in all bedrooms ® T ✕ (ex guide dogs) ✱ sB&Bfr£22.50 sB&B⇨↑fr£33 dB&Bfr£40 dB&B⇨↑fr£57 ⊟
15P ⇑
♋ French **V** ✿ ⅍ Lunch £8-£10 Dinner fr£12.50&alc Last dinner 8.30pm
Credit Cards ① ③

**★★ 64% *Lathones Manor*** Largoward KY9 1JE
☎Peat Inn(033484)494 & 495 Telex no 76137
*A roadside hotel situated six miles south-west of St Andrews which has been completely renovated in country cottage style to provide well-equipped annexe bedrooms and a cosy, characterful lounge bar in the main building.*
14⇨↑(2fb) CTV in all bedrooms ® T ✕ (ex guide dogs)
50P ⇑ ◢ ◡ ♫
**V** ✿ ☑
Credit Cards ① ② ③

**★★ 64% Russell Hotel** 26 The Scores KY16 9AS ☎(0334)73447
Closed 25 Dec-mid Jan
*Small family-run hotel with views of the sea.*
7⇨↑ CTV in all bedrooms ® T ✕ (ex guide dogs)
sB&B⇨↑£25-£45 dB&B⇨↑£50-£60
CTV ℱ ⇑
♋ Scottish & French **V** ✿ ☑ Dinner £12.50-£15alc Last dinner 9.30pm
Credit Cards ① ② ③ ⓕ

**ST ANNES**

See **Lytham St Annes**

**ST ASAPH** Clwyd Map **06** SJ07

**★★★ 68% Talardy Park** The Roe LL17 0HY ☎(0745)584957
FAX (0745) 584385
*A busy and hospitable hotel situated on the outskirts of the town. Bedrooms are spacious, warm and well equipped. There is a brasserie-style restaurant and a modern, bright lounge bar. To the rear of the hotel, with its own separate entrance, is a premier nightclub.*
11⇨↑(1fb)1⊞ CTV in all bedrooms ® T ✕ (ex guide dogs)
✱ sB&B⇨↑£30-£52.50 dB&B⇨↑£45-£65 ⊟
( CTV 120P ⇑ ✤ *xmas*
**V** ✿ ☑ ⅍ Lunch fr£3.50 High tea fr£2.50 Dinner fr£3.50&alc Last dinner 10pm
Credit Cards ① ② ③ ⑤ ⓕ

1991 marks the 25th anniversary of this guide.

**★★★ 61% Oriel House** Upper Denbigh Rd LL17 0LW
☎(0745)582716 FAX (0745) 582716
*Oriel House, which stands in its own grounds, was a school until 1968. The classrooms and dormitories have long since been replaced by pleasant public areas and well-equipped bedrooms which are equally suitable for holidaymakers and business people, as well as the delegates using the extensive conference/function facilities.*
19⇨↑(1fb)1⊞ CTV in all bedrooms ® T
sB&B⇨↑£38.50-£41.80 dB&B⇨↑£56-£65 ⊟
200P ✤ ◢ snooker ⬯
♋ English, Chinese & French **V** ✿ ☑ Lunch £11&alc High tea £1.50-£8alc Dinner £11&alc Last dinner 9.45pm
Credit Cards ① ② ③ ⑤

**★★ 66% Plas Elwy Hotel & Restaurant** The Roe LL17 0LT (Exec Hotel) ☎(0745)582263 & 582089
Closed 26-31 Dec
*Standing beside the A55 on the edge of the town, a small but busy hotel with cottage-style interior features a popular restaurant where the menu is extensive enough to cater for all tastes.*
7↑Annexe6⇨↑(2fb)1⊞ CTV in all bedrooms ® T ✕ (ex guide dogs) sB&B⇨↑£34.50-£37.50
dB&B⇨↑£47-£53 ⊟
CTV 28P ⇑
**V** ✿ ⅍ Lunch £7.95 Dinner £12&alc Last dinner 10pm
Credit Cards ① ② ③ ⑤ ⓕ

**ST AUBIN**

See **Jersey** under **Channel Islands**

**ST AUSTELL** Cornwall & Isles of Scilly Map **02** SX05

**★★★★ 61% Carlyon Bay** Sea Rd, Carlyon Bay PL25 3RD (Brend) ☎Par(072681)2304 Telex no 42551
FAX (072681) 4938
*Set in 250 acres this hotel has superb indoor and outdoor leisure facilities including its own golf course, and popular conference and banqueting facilities. Most bedrooms enjoy excellent sea views. There are plans to extend and develop the ground floor public rooms.*
70⇨(10fb) CTV in all bedrooms ® T ✕ (ex guide dogs)
sB&B⇨£56-£69 dB&B⇨↑£106-£150 ⊟
Lift ( CTV 100P 1⛟ (£1.75 per night) ⇑ ✤ ⊠(heated)
⊠(heated) ▶ 18 ℙ (hard) snooker sauna solarium spa bath table tennis putting ⬯ *xmas*
♋ English & French **V** ✿ ☑ Lunch £11&alc Dinner £16&alc Last dinner 9pm
Credit Cards ① ② ③ ⑤

**★★★ 63% Cliff Head** Sea Rd, Carlyon Bay PL25 3RB (2m E off A390) ☎Par(072681)2345 FAX (072681) 5571
*Situated close to the beach this modernised hotel provides comfortable public areas and well-equipped bedrooms.*
48rm(30⇨4↑)(10fb) CTV in all bedrooms ® T
sB&B⇨↑£37.03 dB&B⇨↑£64.80 ⊟
( CTV 60P 8⛟ ✤ ⊠(heated) pool table *xmas*
**V** ✿ ☑ ⅍ Lunch £5.95-£7.50 Dinner £10.95 Last dinner 9pm
Credit Cards ① ② ③ ⑤

**See advertisement on page 597**

**★★★ 63% Porth Avallen** Sea Rd, Carlyon Bay PL25 3SG
☎Par(072681)2802 & 2183 FAX (072681) 7097
Closed Xmas & New Year
*Privately-owned resort hotel in an ideal setting, overlooking Carlyon Bay, offering comfortable accommodation. Sound English cooking is nicely prepared and service is friendly and helpful. Good value for money.*
23rm(18⇨1↑)(2fb)2⊞ CTV in all bedrooms ® T
✕ (ex guide dogs) sB&B⇨↑£47.30-£54.25
dB&B⇨↑£66.55-£76.45 ⊟
( CTV 50P 2⛟ ✤

▶

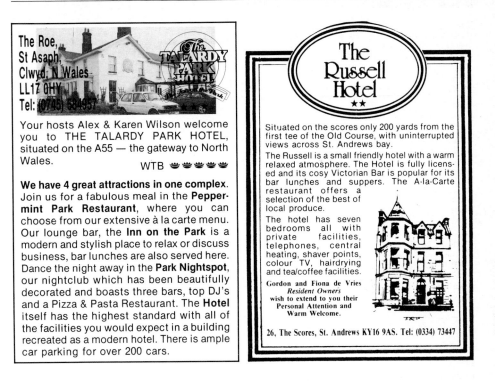

☗ English & French **V** ✿ ⬚ Lunch £7.50 High tea £2.75
Dinner £15-£18 Last dinner 8.30pm
Credit Cards ① ② ③ ⑤

★★⚑75% **Boscundle Manor** Tregrehan PL25 3RL (2m E off
A390) ☎Par(072681)3557 FAX (072681) 4997
Closed mid Oct-mid Apr
*This historic Cornish stone manor is surrounded by nine acres of
natural garden in which there are many wild flowers, an ancient tin
mine, several seating areas and two golf holes. Delightfully
furnished and decorated bedrooms are complemented by
spaciously comfortable public areas with a roaring fire and an
abundance of pictures, prints and antiques. The dinners served in
the dining room are the result of flair and imagination being
brought to bear on good local produce ; breakfast is served in the
conservatory. Staff are obviously hand-picked for their friendliness
and unobtrusive helpfulness.*
9⇨ᐟ🏠Annexe2⇨ᐟ CTV in all bedrooms ® **T** S%
sB&B⇨ᐟ🏠£52.50 dB&B⇨ᐟ🏠£80-£95
15P ⇗ ❀ ⊇(heated) gymnasium croquet practice golf course
☗ International S% Dinner £20 Last dinner 9pm
Credit Cards ① ③

★★60% **White Hart** Church St PL25 4AT ☎(0726)72100
Closed 25 & 26 Dec
*Well appointed, busy inn, centrally located.*
18⇨ᐟ🏠 CTV in all bedrooms ® **T** ✠ (ex guide dogs)
**V** ✿ ⬚ Last dinner 8.20pm
Credit Cards ① ② ③ ⑤

★63% **Selwood House** 60 Alexandra Rd PL25 4QN
☎(0726)65707
11⇨ᐟ🏠Annexe2(2fb) CTV in all bedrooms ® ✳
sB&B⇨ᐟ🏠£21.50-£27.50 dB&B⇨ᐟ🏠£37-£51 🈺
CTV 12P
**V** ✿ ⬚ Dinner £8 Last dinner 7.30pm
Credit Cards ① ② ③ ⑤

**ST BOSWELLS** Borders *Roxburghshire* Map **12** NT53

★★64% **Buccleuch Arms** The Green TD6 0EW ☎(0835)22243
Telex no 336587 FAX (0835) 23965
*A red sandstone hotel on the A68 beside the village cricket ground
features well-appointed bedrooms and a comfortable lounge ; a new
function room enhances previous conference facilities, there is a
secluded garden, and arrangements can be made for guests who
want to hunt, shoot or fish.*
19rm(18⇨ᐟ🏠)(1fb) CTV in all bedrooms ® **T** ✳ S%
sB&B⇨ᐟ🏠£33-£45 dB&B⇨ᐟ🏠£60 🈺
50P 2 ❀ *xmas*
☗ International **V** ✿ ⬚ ✲ S10% Lunch £8-£11.25 High tea
fr£5 Dinner fr£11.25&alc Last dinner 10pm
Credit Cards ① ② ③ ⑤

**ST BRELADE**

See **Jersey under Channel Islands**

**ST CLEARS** Dyfed Map **02** SN21

★★67% **Forge Restaurant & Motel** SA33 4NA ☎(0994)230300
Closed 25 & 26 Dec
*This small, personally-run motel provides comfortable bedrooms
within a small complex well distanced from the A40, together with
bars and a separate grill. New bedrooms and a small leisure
complex have been finished to a high standard.*
Annexe18⇨ᐟ🏠(4fb) CTV in all bedrooms ® ✳ sB&B⇨ᐟ🏠£30
dB&B⇨ᐟ🏠£45
80P ⇗ ❀ ⊆(heated) sauna gymnasium
☗ Mainly grills **V** ✿ ⬚ ✲ Lunch £5-£10alc High tea £5-£10alc
Dinner £5-£10alc Last dinner 9.30pm
Credit Cards ① ③ Ⓔ

**ST COMBS** Grampian *Aberdeenshire* Map **15** NK06

★★61% **Tufted Duck** AB4 5YS ☎Inverallochy(03465)2481
*Converted and extended, the hotel is in a secluded location close to
the beach, commanding impressive sea views. Bedrooms are well
equipped and nicely appointed. The charming wine bar
complements the popular restaurant which offers carvery meals for
Sunday lunch. There is also a public and games room, in addition
to the cosy foyer lounge which has open peat fires in the winter.*
18⇨ᐟ🏠(4fb) CTV in all bedrooms ®
⟨50P ❀ ⚓
☗ Scottish, French & Italian **V** ✿ ⬚ ✲ Last dinner 9.30pm
Credit Cards ① ② ③ ⑤

**ST DAVID'S** Dyfed Map **02** SM72

★★★⚑64% **Warpool Court** SA62 6BN ☎(0437)720300
*Originally built as St David's Cathedral Choir School in the
1860's, and enjoying spectacular scenery, this country-house hotel
looks out over St Bride's from seven acres of Italian gardens. It
offers stylish bedrooms, some containing unique ornamental
Victorian tiles, comfortable public rooms and promising food
standards.*
25⇨ᐟ🏠(3fb) CTV in all bedrooms ® **T** S% sB&B⇨ᐟ🏠£45-£55
dB&B⇨ᐟ🏠£80-£100 🈺
100P ❀ ⊆(heated) ♗ (hard) sauna gymnasium croquet pool
table childrens play area *xmas*
☗ English & French **V** ✿ ⬚ S% Lunch £11.50-£20 High tea
£4.50-£6.50 Dinner £20-£28&alc Last dinner 9.15pm
Credit Cards ① ② ③ ④ ⑤

★★61% **St Non's** SA62 6 (WR) ☎(0437)720239
FAX (0437) 721839
*This comfortable hotel, set only a short drive from local beaches
and convenient for cathedral and shops, provides bedrooms which
are in the process of being upgraded to a good standard and*   ▶

★★★

# 𝔚arpool 𝔠ourt 𝔥otel

*Relax amidst 3,000 individually hand-
painted antique tiles at this famous
Country House Hotel dating back to
1860. Good food, fine wines.*

*Situated on the outskirts of St Davids,
overlooking the coast with beautiful
sea views; Indoor heated swimming
pool (April to September); Sauna and
Gymnasium, games room, in-house
films, direct dial telephones. Tennis
Court, Croquet. Special Winter and
spring time breaks, Christmas and
New Year packages. De luxe rooms
available.*

**St Davids, Pembrokeshire**
**Tel: 0437 720300**
**Fax: 0437 720300**

S

*relaxing, comfortable public rooms; free golf is available at the nine-hole course some two miles away.*
24⇄(5fb) CTV in all bedrooms ® T sB&B⇄£33.50-£43 dB&B⇄£67-£71 ♬
60P ♬ *xmas*
♀ International V ✿ ⌦ Sunday Lunch £9.50-£11.50 Dinner £13.50-£14.85 Last dinner 9pm
Credit Cards ⑴ ⑵ ⑶ ⓔ

★★58% **Old Cross** Cross Square SA62 6SP ☎(0437)720387
Closed Nov-Feb
*A holiday hotel in the centre of the town, just a stone's throw from the Cathedral, features pleasant, comfortable lounges and bars; bedrooms, though on the small side, are all equipped with en suite facilities.*
17⇄♠(5fb) CTV in all bedrooms ® T ✖ (ex guide dogs) ✱
sB&B⇄♠£23-£27 dB&B⇄♠£46-£54 ♬
18P ⇦
♀ English, European & Oriental V ✿ Bar Lunch £2-£4 Dinner fr£12.50&alc Last dinner 8.30pm
Credit Cards ⑴ ⑶

## ST FILLANS Tayside *Perthshire* Map 11 NN62

★★★64% **The Four Seasons Hotel** PH6 2NF ☎(076485)333
Closed Jan-Feb
*This friendly family-run hotel enjoys spectacular views over Loch Earn. It offers a choice of small restaurants, has a snug bar, and the bedrooms, with modern appointments, are comfortable and well equipped. A high standard of food is served in the bright restaurant.*
12⇄♠(2fb) CTV in all bedrooms ® T ✱ sB&B⇄♠£35-£45 dB&B⇄♠£58-£70
25P ⇦ ♬ *xmas*
♀ International V ✿ ⌦ ✂ Lunch £10-£12 Dinner £18-£21&alc Last dinner 9.30pm
Credit Cards ⑴ ⑵ ⑶ ⓔ

## ST HELENS Merseyside Map 07 SJ59

★★★66% **Post House** Lodge Ln, Newton-Le-Willows WA12 OJG (Trusthouse Forte) ☎Wigan(0942)717878
Telex no 677672 FAX (0942) 718419
(For full entry see Haydock)

## ST HELIER

See **Jersey under Channel Islands**

## ST IVES Cambridgeshire Map 04 TL37

★★★62% **Slepe Hall** Ramsey Rd PE17 4RB ☎(0480)63122
FAX (0480) 300706
Closed 25-26 Dec
*Small, comfortable hotel set back from main road.*
16rm(15⇄)(1fb)2☷ CTV in all bedrooms ® T
sB&B⇄fr£57.50 dB&B⇄fr£67.50 ♬
70P 1⇦ ⇦
V ✿ ⌦ ✂ Lunch fr£11.95&alc Dinner fr£11.95&alc Last dinner 9.45pm
Credit Cards ⑴ ⑵ ⑶ ⑸

★★★61% **Dolphin** Bridge Foot, London Rd PE17 4EP ☎(0480)66966 FAX (0480) 495597
*The modern town-centre, purpose-built hotel gives views of the adjacent river and countryside.*
10⇄♠Annexe12⇄♠2☷ CTV in all bedrooms ® T
sB&B⇄♠£48-£52 dB&B⇄♠£58-£62 ♬
⦅ 80P ✿ ♪
♀ English & French V ✿ ⌦ Lunch £11.50&alc Dinner £11.50&alc Last dinner 9.30pm
Credit Cards ⑴ ⑵ ⑶ ⑸

★★64% **St Ives Motel** London Rd PE17 4EX ☎(0480)63857 FAX (0480) 492027
RS 25 & 26 Dec
*An hotel on the perimeter of the town centres round a low main building which houses the recently refurbished, light and airy public areas, adjacent accommodation blocks being reached through a covered walkway. Guests here are assured of a friendly welcome.*
Annexe16⇄(2fb) CTV in all bedrooms ® T
sB&B⇄£28.50-£39.50 dB&B⇄£46-£55 ♬
80P ⇦ ✿
♀ English & French V ✿ ⌦ Lunch £9.50&alc Dinner £10.50&alc Last dinner 9.30pm
Credit Cards ⑴ ⑵ ⑶ ⑸ ⓔ

★56% **Pike & Eel** Overcote Ln, Needingworth PE17 3TW (3m E off A1123) ☎(0480)63336
Closed Xmas Night
*Dating from the 16th century, this popular inn enjoys a very . pleasant location beside the Great Ouse.*
9rm(3⇄)(4fb) CTV in all bedrooms ✖
CTV 100P ✿ ♪
♀ English & French V ✿ ⌦
Credit Cards ⑴ ⑵ ⑶ ⑷

## ST IVES Cornwall & Isles of Scilly Map 02 SW54

★★★67% **Porthminster** The Terrace TR26 2BN (Best Western) ☎Penzance(0736)795221 FAX (0736) 797043
*Traditional hotel in a commanding position overlooking St Ives Bay.*
50⇄♠(9fb) CTV in all bedrooms ® T S% sB&B⇄♠£38-£44 dB&B⇄♠£76-£88 ♬
Lift ⦅ CTV 32P 9⇦ ✿ ⊡(heated) ⊿(heated) sauna solarium gymnasium ⚬ *xmas*
♀ English & French ✿ S% Lunch £9.75-£18alc Dinner £13.75&alc Last dinner 8.30pm
Credit Cards ⑴ ⑵ ⑶ ⑷ ⑸ ⓔ

★★★64% **Garrack** Higher Ayr TR26 3AA ☎Penzance(0736)796199 FAX (0736) 798955
*This secluded family owned and run hotel, which enjoys panoramic views over St. Ives Bay, has a country house atmosphere with cosy public rooms and friendly service. The well-equipped bedrooms range from the modern Terrace rooms to the more intimate accommodation within the main house. The small restaurant promotes well-balanced menus and commendable cooking standards.*
19rm(14⇄2♠)Annexe2rm(3fb) CTV in all bedrooms T ✱
sB&B£26-£31 dB&B£52-£62 dB&B⇄♠£56-£77 ♬
CTV 30P ⇦ ✿ ⊡(heated) sauna solarium *xmas*
♀ English & French ✿ ⌦ Lunch fr£6.50 Dinner fr£13&alc Last dinner 8.30pm
Credit Cards ⑴ ⑵ ⑶ ⑷ ⑸

★★★61% **Chy-an-Drea** The Terrace TR26 2BP (Consort) ☎Penzance(0736)795076
Closed Dec-12 Mar
*A popular, well-established hotel offering a homely atmosphere and prompt, friendly service. Recent upgrading includes a very pleasant foyer lounge and a small leisure complex.*
33⇄♠(fb) CTV in all bedrooms ® T
sB&B⇄♠£26.95-£36.50 dB&B⇄♠£53.90-£73 ♬
5P 20⇦ ⇦ jacuzzi fitness equipment nc5yrs
♀ English & French ✿ Bar Lunch £1.10-£6alc Dinner £13-£14 Last dinner 8.30pm
Credit Cards ⑴ ⑵ ⑶ ⑸

Book as early as possible for busy holiday periods.

**S**

★★★58% **Carbis Bay** Carbis Bay TR26 2NP
☎Penzance(0736)795311
Closed Dec-Etr
*A large detached hotel in a prominent position overlooking its own
private beach and the Bay. Recently upgraded bedrooms offer
modern standards of comfort, with friendly service from local staff.*
32rm(30⇨♠)(9fb)1⚅ CTV in all bedrooms ® T sB&B£25-£30
sB&B⇨♠£30-£35 dB&B£50-£60 dB&B⇨♠£60-£70 ⊟
CTV 200P 6☂ ✿ ⌣(heated) ✔ snooker Hotel has own beach
♫
♥ English & Continental ◊ ⌐ Bar Lunch £1.50-£5 Dinner
fr£16alc Last dinner 8.30pm
Credit Cards ① ② ③ ⑤ ⓔ
**See advertisement on page 601**

★★64% *Pedn-Olva* The Warren TR26 2EA
☎Penzance(0736)796222
*Perched right at the water's edge on a rocky promontory with
unrestricted views over the bay and harbour. This is a small,
personally-managed hotel with a friendly atmosphere, comfortable
public rooms, cosy bedrooms, a sun terrace and outdoor pool. The
small grill room is a dining alternative to the main restaurant.*
20⇨♠Annexe4rm(2fb) CTV in all bedrooms ®
⟨ ♪ ⌣(heated) ♫
♥ English & French V ◊ ⌐
Credit Cards ① ③

★★62% **Cornwallis** Headland Rd, Carbis Bay TR26 2NR
☎Penzance(0736)795294
*This family-run hotel overlooking Carbis Bay specialises in activity
holidays and offers friendly, relaxed service.*
12rm(7⇨3♠)(3fb) CTV in all bedrooms ® ⴜ ✳
sB&B⇨♠£18.40-£23 dB&B⇨♠£36.80-£46 ⊟

▶

**S**

12P ⚘ ❄ ≈(heated)
V ✆ ⚿ ⚼ Dinner £8.05 Last dinner 7.30pm
Credit Cards [1][2][3][5]

---

★★62% **Skidden House** Skidden Hill TR26 2DU
☎Penzance(0736)796899
RS Jan-Feb
7♚ CTV in all bedrooms ® T sB&B♚£29.50-£35
dB&B♚£59-£70 ⊟
CTV 7P ⚘ *xmas*
♼ English & French V ⚼ Bar Lunch £6.95&alc Dinner
£15.50&alc Last dinner 9.30pm
Credit Cards [1][3](£)

---

★★59% **Chy-an-Dour** Trelyon Av TR26 2AD
☎Penzance(0736)796436
*Friendly, personally-run holiday hotel in a peaceful setting with*
*superb views of St Ives and the bay. Public rooms are comfortable*
*and the bedrooms, though compact, are soundly equipped.*
23♚♚(2fb) CTV in all bedrooms ® T ⚼ (ex guide dogs)
sB&B♚♚£22-£33 dB&B♚♚£60-£72 (incl dinner) ⊟
Lift CTV 23P ❄ ♂ *xmas*
♼ English & Continental V ✆ ⚼ Bar Lunch £1-£2.50 Dinner
£9-£11.50 Last dinner 8pm
Credit Cards [1][3](£)

---

★★59% **St Uny** Carbis Bay TR26 2NQ
☎Penzance(0736)795011
Closed early Oct-Etr
*Castle-style, comfortable family hotel, set in its own grounds and*
*gardens close to the beach.*
30rm(14♚5♚)(4fb)1⊞ TV available ⚼ ✳ sB&B£25-£28
sB&B♚♚£27-£35 dB&B£50-£56
dB&B♚♚£54-£70 (incl dinner) ⊟
CTV 28P 4🎱 ❄ snooker table tennis putting nc5yrs
V ✆ ⚿ ⚼ Dinner £11.50 Last dinner 8pm
Credit Cards [1][3]

---

★★58% **Boskerris** Boskerris Rd, Carbis Bay TR26 2NQ
☎Penzance(0736)795295 FAX (0736) 798632
Closed Nov-Etr RS Xmas
*This well-appointed country-house-style hotel enjoys glorious*
*coastal views. Meals are carefully cooked and well balanced.*
18rm(16♚♚)(4fb) CTV in all bedrooms ® T
dB&B♚♚£62-£83.50 (incl dinner) ⊟
CTV 20P ⚘ ❄ ≈(heated) putting, games room *xmas*
♼ English & French V ✆ ⚿
Credit Cards [1][3][5]

---

★★55% **Chy-an-Albany** Albany Ter TR26 2BS
☎Penzance(0736)796759
Closed Nov-Etr RS Xmas
*Family-holiday hotel in elevated position near the beach and the*
*town centre.*
40rm(8♚18♚)(12fb) CTV in all bedrooms ®
⚼ (ex guide dogs) ✳ sB&B£24-£29 sB&B♚♚£27-£32
dB&B£48-£58 dB&B♚♚£54-£64 (incl dinner) ⊟
35P *xmas*
V ✆ ⚿ ⚼ Bar Lunch £1-£5 High tea 50p-£1.50alc Dinner £8
Last dinner 7.30pm
Credit Cards [1][2][3]

---

★59% **Trecarrell** Carthew Ter TR26 1EB
☎Penzance(0736)795707
Closed Nov-Feb RS Mar
*This extended Victorian double-fronted terrace hotel, quietly*
*situated above the town, is personally run to offer good value for*
*money in its simple, bright, clean bedrooms and plain, wholesome*
*meals.*
16rm(2♚7♚)(2fb)⚼in 5 bedrooms CTV in 3 bedrooms TV in
1 bedroom ® ⚼ (ex guide dogs) ✳ sB&B£18.50-£24.50
sB&B♚♚£20.50-£27.50 dB&B£27-£39
dB&B♚♚£39.50-£55 (incl dinner) ⊟

CTV 15P 1🎱 *xmas*
V ✆ ⚿ ⚼ Lunch £3.50-£5 Dinner £5.50-£7 Last dinner 7.15pm
Credit Cards [1][3](£)

---

★**Dunmar** Pednolver Ter TR26 2EL ☎Penzance(0736)796117
*Small, family hotel overlooking the town and the bay.*
17rm(4♚7♚)(7fb) CTV in 15 bedrooms TV in 2 bedrooms ®
✳ sB&B£12.50-£18 sB&B♚≈£14.50-£20 dB&B£25-£36
dB&B♚≈♚£29-£40 ⊟
CTV 20P
✆ ⚿ ⚼
Credit Cards [1][3](£)

---

**ST LAWRENCE**
See **Jersey** under **Channel Islands**

---

**ST LAWRENCE**
See **Wight, Isle of**

---

**ST LEONARDS** Dorset Map **04** SU10

★★★67% **St Leonards Hotel** BH24 2NP (Lansbury)
☎(0425)471220 Telex no 418215 FAX (0425) 480274
*A warm and friendly atmosphere prevails at this hotel. Public*
*areas are limited but the bright, relaxing restaurant serves well-*
*prepared dishes, and there are some exceptionally good bedrooms.*
33♚♚(4fb)1⊞⚼in 5 bedrooms CTV in all bedrooms ® T ⚼
sB&B♚♚fr£65 dB&B♚♚fr£78 ⊟
₵ 250P ❄ sauna gymnasium
♼ European V ✆ ⚿ Lunch fr£11&alc Dinner fr£11&alc Last
dinner 10pm
Credit Cards [1][2][3][5]

---

**ST LEONARDS-ON-SEA**
See **Hastings & St Leonards**

---

**ST MARGARET'S HOPE**
See **Orkney**

---

**ST MARTIN**
See **Guernsey** under **Channel Islands**

---

**ST MARY CHURCH**
See **Torquay**

---

**ST MARY'S**
See **Scilly, Isles of**

---

**ST MAWES** Cornwall & Isles of Scilly Map **02** SW83

★★★61% **Idle Rocks** Tredenhan Rd TR2 5AN ☎(0326)270771
*A hotel in a superb situation on the perimeter of the harbour serves*
*a range of bar lunches on its terrace during the warmer months;*
*public rooms are comfortable.*
14♚♚Annexe6♚♚ CTV in all bedrooms ® T
sB&B♚♚£25-£52 dB&B♚♚£66-£120
🅿 *xmas*
♼ English & Continental V ✆ ⚿ ⚼
Credit Cards [1][2][3][5]

---

All hotels are now given a percentage grading
for the quality of their facilities. A full explanation
can be found within 'How we Classify Hotels
and Restaurants' at the front of the book.

**S**

★★71% *Rising Sun* TR2 5DJ ☎(0326)270233

*This small harbourside hotel, the flagship of the St Austell Brewery, features a new Conservatory Bar overlooking the water. Some bedrooms are compact, but all are comfortable and well-equipped, the excellent dishes on the dining room's interesting menus are skilfully prepared from fresh ingredients, and service, though attentive, is relaxed and friendly.*

12rm(9⇨3)⊁in all bedrooms CTV in all bedrooms ®
6P ⊞ nc10 yrs
♀ English, French & Italian ♥ ⊑ Last dinner 9pm
Credit Cards ①②③

★★60% **St Mawes** The Seafront TR2 5DW ☎(0326)270266
Closed Dec & Jan

*A small, comfortable, quayside hotel dating from the seventeenth century offers well-equipped cottagey bedrooms with such thoughtful provisions as hairdriers, tissues and small jars of sweets; public areas include a character bar with a good deal of atmosphere.*

7rm(5⇨3) CTV in all bedrooms ® S10% sB&B⇨£44
dB&B⇨£80 (incl dinner) ♫
⊁ ⊞ nc5yrs
♀ English & French V ♥ Lunch £9-£16alc Dinner £14-£25alc
Last dinner 8.15pm
Credit Cards ①③

Entries for red-star hotels are highlighted by a tint panel. For a full list of these establishments consult the Contents page.

# The Rising Sun ★★

## St Mawes, Cornwall
### Telephone: (0326) 270233

Set in the heart of St Mawes, looking across the harbour. The Rising Sun is one of Cornwall's most famous waterside inns and reflects all the attractive qualities of its surrounding environment. Elegant dining room, serving the freshest foods. Charming and comfortable bedrooms. Delightful lounge — home from home. The Rising Sun — gorgeous area, beautiful location and the most superb standards, yet retaining all the comfort and charm of a village inn.

★ ★ ★
# THE CARBIS BAY HOTEL

## CARBIS BAY, ST IVES, CORNWALL TR26 2NP
### Telephone 0736-795311

Ideally situated by our own beach. Beautiful views across St Ives Bay. 28 rooms, most with private bathroom, all with Colour Television, radio, intercom and baby listening service. Holiday flats also available.
Excellent English and French cuisine.
Renowned for our superb selection of wines — definitely the hotel for lovers of fine wines. Heated swimming pool, sheltered sunbathing area.
Good centre for walking, riding, surfing and sight seeing.
One mile from West Cornwall Golf Club.

Open Easter to November.
Special terms for early and late season bookings.
Please write or phone for our colour brochure.
Resident Proprietor Mr M W Baker.

S

## ST MAWGAN Cornwall & Isles of Scilly Map 02 SW86

**★★71%** *Dalswinton* TR8 4EZ ☎(0637)860385
*A fine Victorian house, overlooking this charming village from a commanding position, has been carefully converted into an hotel of character, with a variety of small public rooms and comfortable, well equipped bedrooms. The hotel also boasts a spacious, well-tended garden and a heated outdoor swimming pool which is available for guests' use during the warmer months.*
9⇨🏠(4fb) CTV in all bedrooms ®
CTV 15P ⇔ ❄ ◺(heated) ♨
♀ English & Continental ♦ ⚄ ✂ Last dinner 9pm
Credit Cards ① ③

## ST MELLION Cornwall & Isles of Scilly Map 02 SX36

**★★★66%** *St Mellion* PL12 6SD ☎Liskeard(0579)50101
FAX (0579) 50116
Closed Xmas RS 23-27 Dec
*Modern hotel with excellent leisure facilities including a golf course and sports centre. Bedrooms are in a seperate block and there is a smart lounge bar and formal restaurant.*
Annexe24⇨🏠 CTV in all bedrooms ®
❨ CTV 500P ⇔ ❄ ◺(heated) ▶ 18 ♪ (hard) squash snooker sauna solarium gymnasium badminton table tennis keep fit
♀ English & Continental V ♦ ⚄ Last dinner 9.15pm
Credit Cards ① ② ③ ⑤

## ST NEOTS Cambridgeshire Map 04 TL16

**★★64%** *Abbotsley Golf* Eynesbury Hardwicke PE19 4XN
☎Huntingdon(0480)74000
13⇨🏠in 4 bedrooms CTV in all bedrooms ® T
sB&B⇨🏠£21-£25 dB&B⇨🏠fr£42 ▤
CTV 50P ⇔ ❄ ▶ 18 squash snooker sauna solarium *xmas*
♀ English, French & Italian V ✂ Lunch £7.50-£10 Dinner £6.50-£8.50&alc Last dinner 9.30pm
Credit Cards ① ③

## ST PETER

See **Jersey under Channel Islands**

## ST PETER PORT

See **Guernsey under Channel Islands**

## ST SAVIOUR

See **Jersey under Channel Islands**

## ST WENN Cornwall & Isles of Scilly Map 02 SW96

**★⚬61%** *Wenn Manor* ☎St Austell(0726)890240
*A Georgian house which once served as a vicarage stands on the edge of the village in four acres of wooded grounds which include an outdoor swimming pool. Bedrooms are warm, with traditional décor and furnishings, while public areas comprise a cosy bar, separate television lounge, and dining room serving both à la carte and table d'hôte meals.*
8rm(6⇨1🏠)(1fb) CTV in all bedrooms ® ❄ sB&B£17-£19
sB&B⇨🏠£19-£27 dB&B⇨🏠£38-£44
20P 1🛏 ⇔ ◺(heated), putting, croquet *xmas*
♦ ⚄ Bar Lunch £2.80-£6.50 Dinner £6-£8.50 Last dinner 7.30pm
Credit Cards ① ③

A rosette is an indication of exceptional standards of cuisine.

## SALCOMBE Devon Map 03 SX73

**★★★79% Tides Reach** South Sands TQ8 8LJ ☎(054884)3466
FAX (054884) 3954
Closed Dec-Feb
*Perched right on the water's edge, with glorious views of the estuary and coastline, this well-established hotel maintains its high standards. Recent improvements have invested bedrooms with a degree of luxury, as new furnishings and pastel décor bring them up to the standard of the balconied bed-sitting rooms installed a year ago. Richly furnished lounges with fresh-flower arrangements complement a brightly appointed restaurant serving generous portions of fine food with an emphasis on fresh fish. An indoor leisure complex with health and beauty spa completes a good range of facilities, all well served by a dedicated management and staff.*
41⇨🏠(5fb) CTV in all bedrooms T sB&B⇨🏠£52.50-£75
dB&B⇨🏠£96-£180 (incl dinner) ▤
Lift ❨ 100P ⇔ ❄ ◺(heated) squash snooker sauna solarium gymnasium windsurfing nc8yrs
♀ English & Continental V ♦ ⚄ Bar Lunch £2.75-£6.50&alc Dinner fr£22.50&alc Last dinner 10pm
Credit Cards ① ② ③ ⑤

**★★★72% Soar Mill Cove** Soar Mill Cove, Malborough TQ7 3DS (3m W of town off A381 at Malborough)
☎Kingsbridge(0548)561566 FAX (0548) 561223
Closed 29 Dec-11 Feb
*The cove – reached via the village of Malborough, and often described as the most beautiful in England – offers, secluded bathing and accommodation in a family-run hotel which is constantly improving its standards. Relaxing, well-equipped bedrooms in a modern style including a private sun patio, while mainly open-plan public areas are comfortably equipped with quality furniture and warmed by a log fire in cooler weather. Imaginative food is complemented by a well-balanced wine list, while the proprietors and their efficient staff provide friendly, attentive service. Both indoor and outdoor swimming pools are available for guests' use.*
14⇨🏠(2fb) CTV in all bedrooms ® T ✳ sB&B⇨🏠£54-£68
dB&B⇨🏠£98-£119 ▤
30P ⇔ ❄ ◺(heated) ◺ ♪ (grass) ♨ *xmas*
♀ International ♦ ⚄ Lunch £10-£25&alc Dinner £25-£35&alc Last dinner 9pm
Credit Cards ① ③

**★★★69% Bolt Head** TQ8 8LL (Best Western) ☎(054884)3751
FAX (054884) 3060
Closed 10 Nov-23 Mar
*Standing adjacent to National Trust property on the headland 140ft above sea-level, and enjoying outstanding sea views over Salcombe estuary, this personally-owned Swiss-chalet-style hotel has been considerably upgraded over recent years to offer good-quality accommodation. Bright, spotlessly clean, modern bedrooms are furnished in attractive pine and well equipped, whilst comfortable public areas and lounges are richly appointed. Other features available here include private moorings, commendable cuisine based on quality produce, and high standards of service.*
28⇨🏠(6fb) CTV in all bedrooms ® T ✳ sB&B⇨🏠£44-£62
dB&B⇨🏠£88-£124 (incl dinner) ▤
30P ⇔ ❄ ◺(heated)
♀ English & French V ♦ ⚄ Lunch £5.95-£9.15 High tea fr£4&alc Dinner fr£18.50 Last dinner 9pm
Credit Cards ① ② ③ ⑤ ⓔ

**★★68% Grafton Towers** Moult Rd, South Sands TQ8 8LG
☎(054884)2882
Closed Nov-Mar
*Creeper-clad Victorian house, in a fine elevated position overlooking the bay, providing friendly services, comfortable public areas and improving bedrooms.*
14rm(9⇨3🏠) CTV in 12 bedrooms ® sB&Bfr£26
sB&B⇨🏠£31 dB&Bfr£55 dB&B⇨🏠£69 ▤
12P ⇔ ❄
♀ English and French V Dinner fr£12.50 Last dinner 8pm
Credit Cards ① ③

S

★65% **Sunny Cliff** Cliff Rd TQ8 8JU ☎(054884)2207
RS Nov-Mar
*Small friendly holiday hotel in a clifftop location, with grounds
sloping down to the water's edge. There are cosy public rooms and
bright, spotlessly clean bedrooms. Service is informal and prompt.*
15rm(3⇄8♠)Annexe4⇄(3fb) Ⓡ sB&B£23-£27.50
sB&B⇄8♠£26.50-£31 dB&B£46-£55 dB&B⇄8♠£53-£62 ⊟
CTV 14P 1🏨 ✿ ⌓(heated) ✔ moorings and landing stage
♈ English & French ♥ ♨ Bar Lunch £1.20-£4 Dinner £10.50
Last dinner 8pm
Credit Cards [1] [3]

★63% **Knowle** Onslow Rd TQ8 8HY ☎(054884)2846
Closed Nov-Feb
*Small, personally-run hotel in an elevated position with modest
accommodation and public rooms of character.*
9rm(1⇄5♠)Annexe6rm(1⇄1♠)(3fb) CTV in all bedrooms Ⓡ
S%, sB&Bfr£21.85 sB&B⇄8♠£31.05 dB&Bfr£43.70
dB&B⇄8♠£62.10 ⊟
CTV 30P ⌸ ✿ ◍
♈ English & Continental V ♥ ♨ Lunch £5.25 Dinner £11.50
Last dinner 7.45pm
Credit Cards [1] [3]

★**Woodgrange Hotel** Devon Rd TQ8 8HJ (Minotels)
☎(054884)2439 & 2006
Closed Nov-Etr
10⇄8♠(1fb) CTV in all bedrooms Ⓡ T sB&B⇄8♠£21-£24
dB&B⇄8♠£42-£48 ⊟
12P ⌸
♥ ♨ Bar Lunch £1-£5 Dinner £10-£15 Last dinner 7.30pm
Credit Cards [1] [2] [3] [5] ⓔ

---

SALFORD Greater Manchester Map **07** SJ89

See also **Manchester**
★61% **Beaucliffe** 254 Eccles Old Rd, Pendleton M6 8ES
☎061-789 5092 FAX 061-787 7739
Closed 25 Dec
*Well situated for Manchester city centre and the national
motorway network, being sited opposite Hope Hospital just off
junction 2 of the M602, a friendly, well-established hotel features
antiques which give character to its comfortable lounge and other
public areas. Guests are provided with secure car parking.*
21rm(2⇄15♠)(2fb) CTV in all bedrooms Ⓡ ✖ ✳
sB&B£20-£27 sB&B⇄8♠£22-£34 dB&B£25-£40
dB&B⇄8♠£35-£47 ⊟
CTV 25P ⌸
♈ European V ♥ ♨ Bar Lunch £1.75-£8alc Dinner
£8.50-£16alc Last dinner 8.45pm
Credit Cards [1] [2] [3] [5]

★61% **Inn of Good Hope** 226 Eccles Old Rd M6 8AG (Berni/
Chef & Brewer) ☎061-707 6178
*Particularly well appointed bedrooms with en suite facilities are
provided by a popular public house which occupies a corner site on
the A578 almost opposite Hope hospital and within easy reach of
both city centre and motorway network.*
8⇄8♠ CTV in all bedrooms Ⓡ T ✖ (ex guide dogs)
sB&B⇄8♠£41-£46 dB&B⇄8♠£53 ⊟
50P ⌸
♈ International **V** ♥ Lunch £8-£15alc Dinner £8-£15alc Last
dinner 9.30pm
Credit Cards [1] [2] [3] [5]

---

SALISBURY Wiltshire Map **04** SU12

Some Salisbury telephone and fax numbers may change during
the currency of this guide.

★★★69% **Red Lion** Milford St SP1 2AN (Best Western)
☎(0722) 23334 Telex no 477674 FAX (0722) 25756
*Former coaching inn dating from 1320 containing many items of
historic interest.*

57⇄8♠(4fb)3🏨 CTV in all bedrooms Ⓡ T ✖ (ex guide dogs)
sB&B⇄8♠£55-£60 dB&B⇄8♠£80-£90 ⊟
Lift ⓒ 8P 10🏨 CFA *xmas*
♈ English & French V ♥ ♨ Lunch £9.50-£13&alc Dinner
£12.50-£13&alc Last dinner 9pm
Credit Cards [1] [2] [3] [5]

★★★63% **The White Hart** St John St SP1 2SD (Trusthouse
Forte) ☎(0722)27476 FAX (0722) 412761
*The comfortably refurbished foyer lounge of this hotel leads to the
Wavells bar, where open fires enhance traditional décor. The
Chequers Restaurant, offering pleasant views across the courtyard
and garden, serves a varied cuisine from table d'hôte and à la carte
menus.*
68⇄(3fb)✂in 20 bedrooms CTV in all bedrooms Ⓡ T ✳
sB⇄8♠£70-£72 dB⇄8♠£86-£98 (room only) ⊟
ⓒ 85P *xmas*
V ♥ ♨ ✂ Lunch fr£9 Dinner fr£14&alc Last dinner 9.30pm
Credit Cards [1] [2] [3] [4] [5]

★★★60% **Rose & Crown** Harnham Road, Harnham SP2 8JQ
(Queens Moat) ☎(0722)27908 Telex no 47224
FAX (0722) 339816
*Parts of this attractive hotel date back to the 13th century and the
Pavilions Restaurant, with its impressive conservatory extension,
has a fine view across the River Avon to the distant cathedral.
Menus here are varied and extensive. Most of the public areas
have been refurbished and all of the bedrooms, some of which
overlook the river, will have received similar attention during 1990.*
28⇄8♠(6fb)3🏨 CTV in all bedrooms Ⓡ T
sB&B⇄8♠£70.50-£75.50 dB&B⇄8♠£90.50-£95.50 ⊟
ⓒ 40P ✿ CFA *xmas*
♈ English & French V ♥ ♨ ✂ Lunch £8.95-£12.50 High tea
£1.90-£2.50 Dinner £11.50-£12.50 Last dinner 9.30pm
Credit Cards [1] [2] [3] [5] ⓔ

★★64% **County** Bridge St SP1 2ND (Berni/Chef & Brewer)
☎(0722)20229
*A friendly, central hotel, built in 1832 alongside the River Avon.
Bedrooms are comfortable, well equipped and decorated with
Laura Ashley designs. There is a Berni restaurant, a separate
licensed coffee shop and a spacious bar. Lounge area limited.*
31⇄8♠(3fb) CTV in all bedrooms Ⓡ T ✖ (ex guide dogs)
sB&B⇄8♠£53-£62.50 dB&B⇄8♠£70 ⊟
ⓒ 31P
♈ International ♥ ♨ ✂ Lunch £8&alc Dinner £8-£15alc Last
dinner 10pm
Credit Cards [1] [2] [3] [5]

★★63% **Trafalgar** 33 Milford St SP1 2AP ☎(0722)338686
FAX (0722) 414496
*Originally a pick-up point for the Southampton stagecoach, this
renovated hotel dates back to the 15th century, though it was
extended in the 17th. Bedrooms are tastefully decorated, and the
restaurant offers interesting meals and good-quality snacks are
served in the comfortable bar-lounge.*
16⇄8♠1🏨 CTV in all bedrooms Ⓡ T ✖ (ex guide dogs) ✳
sB&B⇄8♠£40-£50 dB&B⇄8♠£58-£70 ⊟
ⓒ ♪ ⌸
♈ International V ♥ ♨ Lunch £6.50-£6.95 Dinner fr£8.95 Last
dinner 9.30pm
Credit Cards [1] [2] [3] [5] ⓔ

★★50% *Cathedral* Milford St SP1 2AJ ☎(0722)20144
*Situated close to the shops and Cathedral Close, this hotel dates
from the 1700s. It has a lively public bar, grill-type restaurant and
1st floor lounge; bedrooms are simply furnished and have some
modern facilities.*
30rm(15⇄4♠)(3fb)1🏨 CTV in all bedrooms Ⓡ
✖ (ex guide dogs)
Lift ⓒ ♪
♈ English & French V ♥ Last dinner 9pm
Credit Cards [1] [3]

★**69%**, **King's Arms** 9-11 St John's St SP1 2SP ☎(0722)27629
*Said to be the city's oldest hostelry, built 90 years before the
foundation stone of the cathedral. It is full of character with
beams, sloping floors and a quaint twisty, slanting staircase leading
to the comfortable and attractive bedrooms. The Cloisters
Restaurant has a realistic à la carte menu and bar meals are also
available.*
12⇄♦Annexe3⇄(1fb)2🛏 CTV in all bedrooms ® T
✻ (ex guide dogs)
V ♰ ♨ ⅓ Last dinner 10pm
Credit Cards ①②③⑤

---

**SALTASH** Cornwall & Isles of Scilly Map **02** SX45

⇧**Granada Lodge** Callington Rd, Carkeel PL12 6LF (Granada)
☎Plymouth(0752)848408 FAX (0752) 848346
*Situated on the A38 close to the Tamar Bridge and Plymouth this
Lodge has pleasing, well-equipped bedrooms. There is a well-
designed and very clean self-service restaurant offering some
cooked-to-order dishes.*
31♦(14fb)⅓in 5 bedrooms CTV in all bedrooms ®
✻ (ex guide dogs) ✳ S% sB♦fr£25 dB♦fr£28 (room only)
Dinner fr£6

---

**SAMPFORD PEVERELL** Devon Map **03** ST01

★**60%**, **Green Headland** EX16 7BJ ☎Tiverton(0884)820255
*Conveniently situated just off the M5 at junction 27, its friendly
atmosphere popular with tourists and businessmen alike. The well-
maintained, family-run hotel is pleasantly set in attractive gardens.*
7rm(3fb) CTV in all bedrooms ®
100P ✿ ♫
V ♰ ♨
Credit Cards ①③

⇧**Travelodge** Sampford Peverell Service Area EX16 7HD (SE
junc 27, M5) (Trusthouse Forte)
☎Tiverton(0884)821087 Central Res (0800) 850950
*Set within easy reach of the Devonshire and Somerset coast, and
offering direct access to the North Devon Link Road from its
location beside junction 27 of the M5, this lodge extends a warm
welcome to travellers at any hour of day or night, providing
accommodation in spotless, well-equipped bedrooms and quick
meals at the Little Chef restaurant across the car park.*
40⇄♦(40fb) CTV in all bedrooms ® sB⇄♦£24
dB⇄♦£29.50 (room only)
40P ⇖
♥ Mainly grills
Credit Cards ①②③

---

**SANDBACH** Cheshire Map **07** SJ76

★★★**65%**, **Chimney House** Congleton Rd CW11 0ST (Lansbury)
☎Crewe(0270)764141 Telex no 367323 FAX (0270) 768916
*Distinguished by its Tudor façade, the hotel is set in spacious
grounds on the A534 not far from junction 17 of the M6.
Comfortable bedrooms are exceptionally well appointed, being
equipped with every modern amenity; and versatile conference
facilities are available.*
50⇄(2fb)⅓in 6 bedrooms CTV in all bedrooms ® T
sB&B⇄£74 dB&B⇄£87 ♬
( 110P ✿ sauna solarium *xmas*
♥ English & French V ♰ ♨ Lunch fr£8.95 Dinner fr£14&alc
Last dinner 10pm
Credit Cards ①②③⑤

★★★**62%**, **Saxon Cross Motor Hotel** Holmes Chapel Rd
CW11 9SE (M6 Junc 17) ☎Crewe(0270)763281 Telex no 367169
FAX (0270) 768723
*This motel-style operation stands beside the A5022, just off
junction 17 of the M6, and is a popular venue for banqueting and
functions. Rooms have a light, cheerful décor and are well
equipped.*

52⇄♦(13fb)⅓in 5 bedrooms CTV in all bedrooms ® T ✻
sB&B⇄♦£56-£60 dB&B⇄♦£70-£72 ♬
( 200P ✿ CFA
♥ English & French V ♰ ♨ Lunch £8-£9.50&alc High tea
£4-£4.20 Dinner £13.80-£14.20 Last dinner 9.30pm
Credit Cards ①②③⑤ £

★★★**61%**, **Old Hall** Newcastle Rd CW11 0AL
☎Crewe(0270)761221 FAX (0270) 762551
*A beautifully preserved timber framed building dating back to
1656. Public rooms have a wealth of oak panelling and some
attractive fireplaces and the bedrooms are quite well equipped.*
12⇄♦Annexe3⇄♦(2fb)4🛏 CTV in all bedrooms ® T ✻
sB&B⇄♦£48 dB&B⇄♦£57-£75 ♬
Lift ( 50P ⇖
♥ English & Continental V ♰ ♨ ⅓ Lunch £8.75&alc Dinner
£13.50&alc Last dinner 9pm
Credit Cards ①②③

---

**SANDBANKS**
See **Poole**

---

**SANDIACRE** Derbyshire Map **08** SK43
See also **Long Eaton**

★★★**52%**, **Post House** Bostocks Ln NG10 5NJ (N of M1 junc
25) (Trusthouse Forte) ☎(0602)397800 Telex no 377378
FAX (0602) 490469
*Modern, purpose built hotel, at junction 25 of the M1, with a
restaurant and a coffee shop which serves snacks and grills
throughout the day.*
107⇄♦(20fb)⅓in 50 bedrooms CTV in all bedrooms ® T ✻
sB⇄♦£67-£78 dB⇄♦£78-£86 (room only) ♬
( 180P ✿ CFA *xmas*
♥ English & French V ♰ ♨ ⅓ Lunch fr£8 Dinner fr£14 Last
dinner 10pm
Credit Cards ①②③④⑤

---

**SANDIWAY** Cheshire Map **07** SJ67

★★★⚑**75%**, **Nunsmere Hall Country House** Tarporley Rd
CW8 2ES ☎Northwich(0606)889100 FAX (0606) 889055
*In an idyllic setting overlooking a lake and surrounded by 10 acres
of gardens and parkland, this hotel is run as an extension of the
owners home, yet with the atmosphere of a quality country house
hotel. Head Chef, Paul Kitching, formerly at Gidleigh Park, is in
charge of the kitchens here, creating dishes with a strong French
influence.*
15⇄♦1🛏 CTV in all bedrooms ® T ✻ (ex guide dogs) ✻
sB&B⇄♦£85-£95 dB&B⇄♦£95-£105 ♬
Lift ( CTV 30P ⇖ ✿ nc12yrs *xmas*
V ♰ ♨ ⅓ Lunch £11.25-£20.50 Dinner £25-£35 Last dinner
9.30pm
Credit Cards ①②③ £

---

**SANDOWN**
See **Wight, Isle of**

---

**SANQUHAR** Dumfries & Galloway *Dumfriesshire*
Map **11** NS70

★★**59%**, **Mennockfoot Lodge** Mennock DG4 6HS
☎(0659)50382 & 50477
*This small cottage hotel enjoys a tranquil position beside the
Mennock Water where it joins the River Nith, just south of the
town. The majority of the bedrooms are contained in a simple
cedarwood annexe behind the main building. There is also a dining
room and bar which have recently been redecorated.*
1⇄Annexe8⇄♦(1fb) CTV in all bedrooms ® T
sB&B⇄♦£25-£28 dB&B⇄♦£38-£42

CTV 25P ✿ ⌀
♀ British & Continental V ⌑ ⚏ Lunch £5.25-£8.90alc High tea fr£5.95alc Dinner £10.75-£18.95alc Last dinner 8.30pm
Credit Cards 1 3 ⓔ

★**58% Nithsdale** 1-7 High St DG4 6DJ ☎(0659)50506
*Improvements continue at a small hotel which now boasts attractively refurbished public areas ; bedrooms, though fairly compact, are clean and freshly decorated.*
6rm(2fb) CTV in all bedrooms ⓡ ✻ sB&Bfr£18 dB&Bfr£36
2P ✿ bowling *xmas*
♀ Mainly grills V ⌑ ⚏ Lunch £6.50-£10.50 High tea £6-£9 Dinner £10.50-£12.50&alc Last dinner 9.30pm
Credit Cards 3

**SARN PARK MOTORWAY SERVICE AREA (M4)** Mid Glamorgan Map 03 SS98

⌂**Travelodge** Sarn Park Motorway Services CF32 9RW (junction 36, M4) (Trusthouse Forte) ☎Bridgend(0656)659218
40➪♠ CTV in all bedrooms ⓡ sB➪♠£24 dB➪♠£29.50 (room only)
⟮ 40P ⇶
♀ Mainly grills
Credit Cards 1 2 3

**SAUNDERSFOOT** Dyfed Map 02 SN10

★★★**65% St Brides** St Brides Hill SA69 9NH (Inter-Hotels)
☎(0834)812304 Telex no 48350 FAX (0834) 813303
Closed 1-14 Jan
*Situated just above the harbour and sandy beach, the restaurant views are exceptional. The public rooms are spacious and comfortable, and the bedrooms, all well equipped, were being upgraded at the time of inspection. The staff are friendly and efficient, and the food is constantly enjoyable.*
45➪♠(4fb)1 ⌸✁in 4 bedrooms CTV in all bedrooms ⓡ T sB&B➪♠£54-£75 dB&B➪♠£85-£115 ⊟
⟮ 70P ✿ CFA ⌇(heated) sauna ♫ *xmas*
♀ English & French V ⌑ ⚏ Lunch £9.50-£12.50&alc Dinner £14.95-£17.50&alc Last dinner 9.15pm
Credit Cards 1 2 3 5
**See advertisement on page 609**

★★ 65% **Rhodewood House** St Brides Hill SA69 9NU
☎(0834)812200 FAX (0834) 811863
*This busy family-run resort hotel offers well-equipped bedrooms, regular entertainment in "Taff's" Bar and facilities for snooker.*
34➪♠(6fb)✁in 6 bedrooms CTV in all bedrooms ⓡ T S%
sB&B➪♠£24-£35 dB&B➪♠£38-£60 ⊟
70P ✿ snooker solarium ♫ ⌀ *xmas*
V ⌑ ⚏ S% Sunday Lunch £5.50-£6.50 Dinner £7-£8.25&alc Last dinner 9.30pm
Credit Cards 1 2 3 5 ⓔ
**See advertisement under TENBY**

★★ 60% **Glen Beach** Swallow Tree Woods SA69 9DE
☎(0834)813430
*Set in lovely woodland just outside the town, with access to the beach, this small, family-run holiday hotel offers neat, cosy bedroom accommodation and attentive service from its friendly owners and staff.*
13➪♠(3fb)1 ⌸ CTV in all bedrooms ⓡ T ✻
sB&B➪♠£27-£30 dB&B➪♠£40-£49 ⊟
35P ✿ *xmas*
♀ English & French V ⌑ Sunday Lunch fr£4.95 Dinner fr£10 Last dinner 9pm
Credit Cards 1 2 3 ⓔ
**See advertisement on page 609**

S

SAUNDERTON Buckinghamshire Map **04** SP70

★★62% **Rose & Crown** Wycombe Rd HP17 9NP (Exec Hotel)
☎Princes Risborough(08444)5299 & 2241
Closed 25-31 Dec
*A privately-owned hotel with a warm, friendly atmosphere has
been tastefully upgraded to provide bedrooms which are
comfortable and well-equipped, though compact, and very
attractive public areas. The dining room's interesting menus
specialise in fresh fish, and good bar meals are available.*
17rm(14➪⋔) CTV in all bedrooms ® T ✙ (ex guide dogs)
sB&Bfr£43.45 sB&B➪⋔£65.50-£72
dB&B➪⋔£65.50-£82.50 ♬

50P ⇛ ✿
♈ English & French ✿ ⏛ Lunch £10.50-£14.95&alc Dinner
£15-£18.50&alc Last dinner 9.30pm
Credit Cards ① ② ③ ⑤

---

SAUNTON Devon Map **02** SS43

★★★★57% **Saunton Sands** EX33 1LQ (Brend)
☎Croyde(0271)890212 Telex no 42551 FAX (0271) 890145
*Beautifully situated hotel enjoying panoramic sea views and direct
access to the beach. The bedrooms vary in size but all offer good
facilities, and a choice of menu is available in the restaurant.
Extensive leisure and recreation facilities include a large indoor
pool, tennis and squash courts, and gift shops.*
90➪(39fb) CTV in all bedrooms ® T ✙ (ex guide dogs)
sB&B➪⋔£56-£69 dB&B➪⋔£104-£138 ♬
Lift ℂ CTV 140P 2☙ ⇛ ✿ CFA ▣(heated) ♪ (hard) squash
snooker sauna solarium putting table tennis spa bath ♫ ঞ
*xmas*
♈ English & French V ✿ ⏛ Lunch £11.50&alc Dinner
£15&alc Last dinner 9pm
Credit Cards ① ② ③ ⑤

See advertisement on page 611

★★64% **Preston House** EX33 1LG ☎Croyde(0271)890472
FAX (0271) 890555
RS Dec-Feb
*Set in its own gardens overlooking the ten mile sweep of Barnstaple
Bay this Victorian hotel has direct access to the beach. Bedrooms
are individually decorated, well equipped and all have en-suite
bathrooms. Breakfast is served in the attractive conservatory
which faces the sea.*
12➪⋔2⋔ CTV in all bedrooms ® T ✙ ✳
sB&B➪⋔£27.50-£37.50 dB&B➪⋔£55-£66
CTV 12P ⇛ ✿ sauna solarium nc12yrs *xmas*
♈ English & Continental V ✿ ⏛ Bar Lunch fr£3 Dinner
fr£12.50&alc Last dinner 8.30pm
Credit Cards ① ③

---

SAVERNAKE

See **Burbage**

---

SCALASAIG

See **Colonsay, Isle of**

---

SCARBOROUGH North Yorkshire Map **08** TA08

See **Town Plan Section**
★★★★53% **Holbeck Hall** Seacliff Rd YO11 2XX (Best
Western) ☎(0723)374374 FAX (0723) 351114
*A mansion built in 1883 and converted to hotel use in 1930
overlooks South Bay and the harbour from its pleasant situation in
three acres of garden. The elegant lounge and restaurant both
enjoy superb sea views, there is an impressive oak panelled
reception hall with minstrels' gallery, and bedrooms are all well
equipped, though they vary in size, shape and décor.*
30➪⋔(3fb) CTV in all bedrooms T ✙ ✳ sB&B➪⋔£42-£47
dB&B➪⋔£84-£94
ℂ CTV 50P ⇛ ✿ ♫ *xmas*

♈ English & French ✿ ⏛ Lunch fr£8.95 Dinner fr£16.50&alc
Last dinner 9.30pm
Credit Cards ① ② ③ ⑤

★★★★64% **Wrea Head Country** Scalby YO13 0PB (3m NW off
A171) (Inter-Hotels) ☎(0723)378211 FAX (0723) 353732
*Converted Victorian residence standing in 14 acres of landscaped
gardens.*
21➪⋔(2fb) CTV in all bedrooms T ✙ sB&B➪⋔£35-£55
dB&B➪⋔£80-£120 ♬
ℂ 50P 4☙ (£3 per night) ⇛ ✿ putting green croquet *xmas*
♈ English & French V ✿ ⏛ Lunch £10.50-£15.50 Dinner
£18.50-£24.50 Last dinner 9pm
Credit Cards ① ② ③ ⑤

★★★63% **Esplanade** Belmont Rd YO11 2AA ☎(0723)360382
FAX (0723) 376137
*An auriole window in the hotel's newly-refurbished restaurant
makes the most of its superb setting on the south cliff, overlooking
the bay. Bedrooms are attractively decorated and well-equipped,
while a good range of bars, lounges and patio areas offer guests
space in which to relax.*
73➪⋔(9fb) CTV in all bedrooms ® T sB&B➪⋔£33-£40
dB&B➪⋔£61-£67.50 ♬
Lift ℂ CTV 24P ✿ CFA darts table tennis *xmas*
♈ English & French V ✿ ⏛ Sunday Lunch £8 Dinner £11&alc
Last dinner 9pm
Credit Cards ① ② ③ ⑤

See advertisement on page 611

★★★62% **Hotel St Nicholas** St Nicholas Cliff YO11 2EU
☎(0723)364101 Telex no 52351 FAX (0723) 500538
*This large, seafront hotel, undergoing a continuous programme of
upgrading, now offers good conference and leisure facilities.*
141➪⋔(18fb)4⋔ CTV in all bedrooms ® T ✳
sB&B➪⋔£55-£65 dB&B➪⋔£80-£90 (incl dinner) ♬    ▶

# Wrea Head ★★★
# Country Hotel

Victorian Country House Hotel set in fourteen
acres of glorious parkland adjacent to the
North Yorkshire Moors. All bedrooms with
private bathroom, colour TV, radio, hairdryer,
direct dial telephone. Honeymoon rooms and
suites available. Ample free car parking. Good
English food with fresh produce from our own
gardens. Putting, Croquet, Stabling all within
the grounds. Fully licensed. Open all year.
*An English Rose Hotel.*

Scalby, Scarborough YO13 0PB Tel: 0723 378211
Fax: 0723 353732

**S**

Lift ₵ 15🛎 (£3) 🖬(heated) sauna solarium children's games room *xmas*
V ✆ ⍾ Sunday Lunch fr£7 Dinner fr£11 Last dinner 9pm
Credit Cards ① ② ③ ⑤ ⓔ

★★★61% **Palm Court** Nicholas Cliff YO11 2ES
☎(0723)368161 Telex no 527579 FAX (0723) 371547
*Beach and local amenities are both within easy reach of a recently modernised hotel near the town centre which offers comfortable public rooms, an indoor swimming pool with sauna, and attentive service from a friendly young staff.*
51⇨☏(11fb) CTV in all bedrooms ® T ✕ (ex guide dogs) ✱
sB&B⇨☏£34-£50 dB&B⇨☏£55-£70 🖪
Lift ₵ CTV 6P (£2 day £3 night) 🚗 🖬(heated) sauna ♫ *xmas*
♀ English & French V ✆ ⍾ Sunday Lunch £8 High tea fr£4
Dinner £10.50-£14&alc Last dinner 9pm
Credit Cards ① ② ③ ⑤

★★★60% **Clifton** Queens Pde YO12 7HX ☎(0723)375691
FAX (0723) 364203
*Victorian in origin, but modern and well-furnished, the hotel overlooks the magnificent North Bay.*
70⇨☏(6fb)2🛏 CTV in all bedrooms ® T ✕ (ex guide dogs)
✱ sB&B⇨☏£28.50-£33 dB&B⇨☏£57-£66
Lift ₵ CTV 30P sauna solarium *xmas*
V ✆ ⍾ Sunday Lunch fr£6.50 Dinner fr£12.50 Last dinner 8.45pm
Credit Cards ① ② ③

★★69% **Gridley's Crescent** The Crescent YO11 2PP
☎(0723)360929 FAX (0723) 354126
*This attractive listed building has been carefully converted into a very comfortable hotel. All bedrooms are well equipped and nicely furnished and guests have a choice of restaurants. The Grindleys own and manage the hotel in a professional manner.*
20⇨☏1🛏✂in 5 bedrooms CTV in all bedrooms ® T
✕ (ex guide dogs) sB&B⇨☏£35-£45 dB&B⇨☏£60-£70 🖪
Lift ₵ ♪ 🚗 nc6yrs
V ✆ ⍾ Sunday Lunch fr£8.25 Dinner fr£12.50&alc Last dinner 10pm
Credit Cards ① ③

★★67% **Red Lea** Prince of Wales Ter YO11 2AJ
☎(0723)362431 FAX (0723) 371230
*Pleasant, family-run hotel, with a smart new leisure centre, offering good value for money.*
67⇨☏(7fb) CTV in all bedrooms ® T ✕ ✱
sB&B⇨☏£22.50-£24.50 dB&B⇨☏£45-£49
Lift ₵ CTV ♪ 🖬(heated) sauna solarium gymnasium *xmas*
♀ International ✆ ⍾ ✂ Lunch fr£6.50 Dinner fr£9 Last dinner 8.30pm
Credit Cards ① ③

★★66% **Bradley Court** 7-9 Filey Rd, South Cliff YO11 2SE
☎(0723)360476 FAX (0723) 376661
*This comfortable, well-appointed hotel, recently extensively refurbished, stands near to South Cliff and only a short distance from the town centre; individually decorated bedrooms are fully equipped, public areas include an attractive lounge bar and the popular Sizzles Restaurant, and a young staff provides friendly service.*
40rm(22⇨17☏)(3fb) CTV in all bedrooms ® T ✕ ✱
sB&B⇨☏£30-£40 dB&B⇨☏£60-£80 🖪
Lift ₵ 40P *xmas*
✆ ⍾ ✂ S% Lunch £8.50-£9.50 Dinner £13.50-£17.50 Last dinner 9pm
Credit Cards ① ② ③ ⓔ

A rosette is an indication of exceptional standards of cuisine.

★★66% **The Pickwick Inn** Huntriss Row YO11 2ED
☎(0723)375787 FAX (0723) 374284
*Centrally situated, next to the town's main shopping area, the hotel provides modern, very comfortable accommodation in attractively decorated, well-equipped bedrooms. A small restaurant serves carefully prepared meals, and the large cosy bars offer an alternative menu.*
11⇨☏ CTV in all bedrooms ® T ✕ (ex guide dogs)
sB&B⇨☏£24-£32 dB&B⇨☏£40-£65 🖪
Lift 🚗 *xmas*
♀ English & French V Lunch £5.95-£9&alc Dinner £9-£10.95&alc Last dinner 10pm
Credit Cards ① ② ③ ⑤

★★61% **Southlands** 15 West St, South Cliff YO11 2QW
(Consort) ☎(0723)361461 Telex no 57515 FAX (0723) 376035
Closed Jan-Feb
*A well furnished and comfortable traditional seaside hotel, personally owned and run, and offering good home comforts. Situated on South Cliff, near the Esplanade.*
58⇨☏(8fb) CTV in all bedrooms ® T sB&B⇨☏£30-£35
dB&B⇨☏£50-£60 🖪
Lift ₵ CTV 45P CFA
V ✆ ⍾ ✂ Bar Lunch £1.25-£10alc Dinner £12&alc Last dinner 8.30pm
Credit Cards ① ② ③ ⑤ ⓔ

Book as early as possible for busy holiday periods.

**S**

S

★★57% **Brooklands** Esplanade Gardens, , South Cliff
YO11 2AW ☎(0723)376576 & 361608
Closed Dec-last 2wks Mar
*A friendly atmosphere prevails in this comfortable, unpretentious hotel, which enjoys the personal supervision of the resident proprietor.*
61rm(48⇔4♠)(5fb) CTV in all bedrooms ® T
✗ (ex guide dogs) ✱ sB&B£20-£21 sB&B⇔♠£21.50-£22.50
dB&B£37-£39 dB&B⇔♠£40-£46
Lift 1♠ (£2) CFA pool table ♫
V ♦ ⚅ Lunch £5 High tea £2.50-£4 Dinner £8 Last dinner 8pm
Credit Cards 1 3

★★50% **Central** 1-3 The Crescent YO11 2PW ☎(0723)365766
*A centrally-located hotel offers basic bedroom accommodation and good, simple meals based on quality ingredients, many dishes being char grilled ; the restaurant – which features an open display kitchen – serves a table d'hôte dinner at 7.00 pm and an à la carte menu after 7.30.*
39rm(13⇔8♠)(3fb) CTV in all bedrooms ® T ✱
sB&B£25-£29 sB&B⇔♠fr£29 dB&Bfr£44 dB&B⇔♠fr£52 ♬
Lift 18P *xmas*
✿ English & Continental V ♦ Dinner £7&alc Last dinner 9.30pm
Credit Cards 1 2 3 5 £

✗✗**Lanterna Ristorante** 33 Queen St YO11 1HQ
☎(0723)363616
*The Lanterna has, for many years, enjoyed a high reputaltion in Scarborough for its Italian cuisine and friendly, attentive service. Situated in a side road close to the centre of town. Booking is advisable.*
Closed Sun & Mon
Lunch not served
✿ Continental V 36 seats Dinner £13.10-£15.50alc Last dinner 9.30pm ✗ nc2yrs
Credit Cards 1 3

**SCILLY, ISLES OF** No map

**ST MARY'S**

★★★67% **Tregarthens** Hugh Town TR21 0PP (Best Western)
☎Scillonia(0720)22540 FAX (0720) 22089
Closed Nov-mid Mar
*Overlooking the harbour from its elevated position, a hotel which has undergone major refurbishment over recent years offers modern, well-equipped bedrooms and spacious, comfortable public areas ; imaginative food is complemented by friendly and attentive service.*
32rm(24⇔)Annexe1rm(5fb) CTV in all bedrooms ® T ✗ ✱
sB&B£42-£49 sB&B⇔£46-£53 dB&B£78-£90
dB&B⇔£92-£120 (incl dinner) ♬
✿ English & French V ♦ ⚅ Bar Lunch £2-£5 High tea £4-£6 Dinner £17.50-£18.50 Last dinner 8pm
Credit Cards 1 2 3 5

★★**Godolphin** Church St, Hugh Town TR21 0JR
☎Scillonia(0720)22316 FAX (0720) 22252
Closed mid Oct-late Mar
*A Georgian house in the town centre offers modern, well-equipped bedrooms and good public areas which include an intimate cocktail bar.*
31rm(25⇔2♠)(3fb) CTV in all bedrooms ® ✗ ✱
dB&B⇔♠£62-£82
✗ ⇘ sauna
✿ British & French ♦ ⚅ ✗ Bar Lunch fr£1.30 Dinner fr£13 Last dinner 8pm
Credit Cards 1 3

**TRESCO**

★★★73% **The Island** TR24 0PU ☎Scillonia(0720)22883
FAX (0720) 23008
Closed Nov-Feb
*Set in a commanding position, with extensive grounds and a private beach, this character hotel is designed to meet the needs of the modern traveller. Bedrooms are comfortable and particularly well-equipped, many of them having sea views, whilst public areas are bright and comfortable – the restaurant, with its panoramic views, menu of well-cooked dishes and balanced wine list being particularly worthy of note. Attentive service is offered throughout by the resident managers and their team of friendly staff.*
40⇔♠ CTV in all bedrooms ® T ✗ (ex guide dogs)
sB&B⇔♠£76-£88 dB&B⇔♠£140-£220 (incl dinner)
CTV ✗ ⛳ ✱ ⇘(heated) ✓ croquet boating table tennis
✿ English & Continental V ♦ ⚅ Sunday Lunch £12 Dinner £21-£25 Last dinner 8.30pm

★★63% **New Inn** TR24 0QQ ☎Scillonia(0720)22844
*This historic inn stands by a small harbour. The atmosphere is friendly and informal. The bedrooms, the lounge and the residents' bar have all been tastefully modernised.*
12rm(10⇔) CTV in all bedrooms ® T ✗ (ex guide dogs)
sB&B£29-£49.50 dB&B⇔£58-£99 (incl dinner) ♬
✗ ⛳ ⇘(heated) sea fishing *xmas*
V ♦ Bar Lunch £1.10-£7.50alc Dinner £9.50-£14.50 Last dinner 8.30pm

**SCOLE** Norfolk Map **05** TM17

★★60% **Scole Inn** IP21 4DR (Best Western)
☎Diss(0379)740481 FAX (0379) 740762
*Dating from 1655, the inn has retained many of its original features, while providing modern facilities. The annexe accommodation is housed in a conversion of the former stable block. Service is informal and friendly and well chosen menus, using fresh ingredients, are available in the restaurant.*
12⇔♠Annexe11⇔♠(2fb)3♬✗in 3 bedrooms CTV in all bedrooms ® T sB&B⇔♠£45-£55 dB&B⇔♠£65-£75 ♬
CTV 60P *xmas*
✿ English & French V ♦ S10% Lunch £10.95-£12&alc Dinner £10.95-£12&alc Last dinner 10pm
Credit Cards 1 2 3 5

**SCOTCH CORNER (near Richmond)** North Yorkshire Map **08** NZ20

★★★65% **Scotch Corner** DL10 6NR ☎Richmond(0748)850900
Telex no 587447 FAX (0748) 5417
*Most conveniently located at the junction of the A1/A66, and recently the subject of extensive refurbishment, this hotel effectively provides for the varied needs of its customers. All its well equipped bedrooms are designed for comfort, there is an attractive open plan lounge/foyer area, and a coffee shop menu widens the choice of meals offered by the two restaurants.*
90⇔♠(4fb)♬ CTV in all bedrooms ® T ✱ sB&B⇔♠fr£65 dB&B⇔♠fr£81.50 ♬
Lift ( CTV 250P ♫ *xmas*
V ♦ ⚅ ✗ Lunch £3.75-£10.50 Dinner fr£12.50&alc Last dinner 10pm
Credit Cards 1 2 3 5 £

⌂**Travelodge** Skeeby DL10 5EQ (Trusthouse Forte)
☎Richmond(0748)3768 Central res (0800) 850950
*This Travelodge/Little Chef operation stands beside the north-bound carriageway of the A1, just three miles south of Scotch Corner.*
40⇔♠(40fb) CTV in all bedrooms ® sB⇔♠£24
dB⇔♠£29.50 (room only)
( 40P ⛳
Credit Cards 1 2 3

○**Rank Motor Lodge** A1/A66, Middleton Tyas Ln DL10 6PQ
(Rank) ☎Darlington(0325)377177
Due to have opened Oct 1990
50⇌⅔♠(12fb)⊁in 7 bedrooms CTV in all bedrooms ® ✱ S%
sB&B⇌⅔♠£27.50 dB&B⇌⅔♠£34.50 Continental breakfast
《50P
V ✿ ⚏ ⊁ High tea £2-£9.25
Credit Cards ①②③⑤

---

SCOURIE Highland *Sutherland* Map **14** NC14

★★68% **Eddrachilles** Badcall Bay IV27 4TH ☎(0971)2080 &
2211
Closed Nov-Feb
*A former manse which enjoys wonderful views of the island-
studded Badcall Bay from the peaceful setting of its own extensive
natural grounds has been refurbished and extended to provide
modern bedrooms that are well equipped though fairly compact;
enlarged public areas now feature an attractive stone-walled,
flagstone-floored dining room and a pleasant conservatory lounge,
while standards of maintenance and house-keeping are sound
throughout.*
11⇌⅔♠(1fb) CTV in all bedrooms ® T ⋊ (ex guide dogs)
sB&B⇌⅔♠£32.20-£41.60 dB&B⇌⅔♠£53.80-£63.30 ⊟
25P ⇎ ❋ ❢ boats for hire nc3yrs
V ✿ Bar Lunch fr£3.50 Dinner fr£9.25&alc Last dinner 8pm

★★65% **Scourie** IV27 4SX (Exec Hotel) ☎(0971)2396
FAX (0971) 2423
Closed Nov-mid Mar RS mid Mar-mid May
*A comfortably appointed and friendly Highland hotel, an
established favourite with the angling fraternity, also provides an
ideal base for the touring holidaymaker.*
18rm(16⇌⅔)Annexe2⇌⅔(2fb) ® T sB&B£25-£30
sB&B⇌⅔£30-£35 dB&B⇌⅔£53-£60 ⊟
30P ⇎ ❢
♀ British & French ✿ ⚏ Dinner £11.50-£12 Last dinner
8.30pm
Credit Cards ①②③⑤

---

SCUNTHORPE Humberside Map **08** SE81

★★★60% **Wortley House** Rowland Rd DN16 1SU
☎(0724)842223 Telex no 527837 FAX (0724) 280646
*The large house, suitably converted and extended, stands near the
town centre; spacious public areas of comfort and style are
complemented by up-to-date bedrooms.*
38⇌⅔♠(2fb)3⇎ CTV in all bedrooms ® S% sB&B⇌⅔♠£60
dB&B⇌⅔♠£70 ⊟
《100P *xmas*
♀ English & French V ✿ ⚏ ⊁ S% Lunch fr£9&alc High tea
fr£5 Dinner fr£9&alc Last dinner 9.30pm
Credit Cards ①②③④⑤ⓔ

★★58% **Royal** Doncaster Rd DN15 7DE (Trusthouse Forte)
☎(0724)282233 Telex no 527479 FAX (0724)281826
RS Public Hols
*Popular, comfortable villa-style hotel with relaxing atmosphere.*
33⇌⅔♠(1fb)⊁in 6 bedrooms CTV in all bedrooms ® ✱
sB&B⇌⅔♠£60-£70 dB&B⇌⅔♠£65-£75 ⊟
《33P CFA *xmas*
V ✿ ⚏ ⊁ Lunch £5.50-£13&alc Dinner £7.45-£13&alc Last
dinner 10pm
Credit Cards ①②③④⑤

**See advertisement on page 615**

---

All AA-appointed establishments are
inspected regularly to ensure that required
standards are maintained.

---

**S**

**SEAHOUSES** Northumberland Map **12** NU23

★★**74%, Beach House** Sea Front NE68 7SR ☎(0665)720337
Closed Nov-Mar
*A warm welcome is extended by the owners of this very pleasant*
*and well-furnished hotel, and bedrooms have good views towards*
*the Farne Islands.*
14⇌ऒ(3fb)1 ⌘ CTV in all bedrooms ⓡ T sB&B⇌ऒ£24-£32
dB&B⇌ऒ£48-£59 ♬
CTV 16P ⅋ ✿ spa bath games table
♉ English & Italian **V** ✿ ✔ Dinner £14.75 Last dinner 8pm
Credit Cards ⊡⊡ Ⓔ

★★**69%, Olde Ship** NE68 7RD ☎(0665)720200
Closed Dec-Jan
*This charming harbour hotel, owned and managed by the same*
*family for more than eighty years, still retains its friendly*
*atmosphere and traditional standards of service whilst also offering*
*the modern facilities expected by today's traveller.*
14⇌ऒ(2fb) CTV in all bedrooms ⓡ T ✹
sB&B⇌ऒ£25.50-£27.50 dB&B⇌ऒ£51-£55
CTV 10P 2⊛ ⅋ putting green
**V** ✿ ℒ Lunch fr£5 Dinner fr£11.50 Last dinner 8.15pm
Credit Cards ⊡⊡

★★**58%, St Aidans** NE68 7SR ☎(0665)720355
Closed 16 Nov-14 Feb
*A compact, homely and friendly tourist hotel with views of the sea*
*and Bamburgh Castle. Bedrooms are simply furnished and vary*
*size, whilst lounge facilities are limited to a small snug with a self-*
*service dispense bar.*
8rm(1⇌3ऒ)(3fb) CTV in all bedrooms ⓡ ✹
10P ⅋ ✿
♉ English & Continental **V** Last dinner 8pm
Credit Cards ⊡⊡

**SEALE** Surrey Map **04** SU84

★★★**64%, Hog's Back** Hog's Back GU10 1EX (on A31)
(Embassy) ☎Runfold(02518)2345 Telex no 859352
FAX (02518) 3113
*This hotel has been extensively redeveloped and upgraded*
*throughout and 26 spacious new bedrooms have been added. John*
*Fielding is an enthusiastic Manager leading a well-co-ordinated*
*team, and Chef David Gregory continues to produce an interesting*
*selection of dishes in the Ambassador Restaurant.*
75⇌ऒ(6fb)✔in 10 bedrooms CTV in all bedrooms ⓡ T ♬
《 130P ✿ ▣(heated) snooker sauna solarium gymnasium *xmas*
♉ English & French **V** ✿ Lunch £8.50-£12.50&alc Dinner
£8.50-£14.50&alc Last dinner 9.30pm
Credit Cards ⊡⊡⊡⊡⊡ Ⓔ

**SEATON BURN** Tyne & Wear Map **12** NZ27

★★★★**54%, Holiday Inn** Great North Rd NE13 6BP (Holiday
Inns) ☎091-236 5432 Telex no 53271 FAX 091-236 8091
*Conveniently situated close to Newcastle Airport, this purpose-*
*built, low-rise hotel provides accommodation which is slowly being*
*upgraded, though some rooms remain functional. Car parking*
*facilities are good, with a courtesy bus service to the airport, there*
*are leisure amenities, and service is generally willing and friendly –*
*especially in the busy carvery-style restaurant.*
150⇌ऒ(77fb)✔in 10 bedrooms CTV in all bedrooms ⓡ T ✹
sB⇌ऒfr£75 dB⇌ऒfr£85 (room only) ♬
《⊞ 200P ✿ CFA ▣(heated) sauna solarium gymnasium
games room ♫ *xmas*
♉ International **V** ✿ ℒ ✔ Lunch fr£14.95 Dinner
fr£15.50&alc Last dinner 10.30pm
Credit Cards ⊡⊡⊡⊡⊡ Ⓔ

**SEAVIEW**

See **Wight, Isle of**

**SEAVINGTON ST MARY** Somerset Map **03** ST41

✗✗**Pheasant** Water St TA19 0QH
☎South Petherton(0460)40502 FAX (0460) 42388
Closed 26 Dec-10 Jan
Dinner not served Sun
♉ English, French & Italian **V** 48 seats ✳ Lunch £3.50-£6.75
Dinner £12.95 Last lunch 2.30pm Last dinner 9.30pm 40P
Credit Cards ⊡⊡⊡⊡

**SEDBERGH** Cumbria Map **07** SD69

★★**64%, Oakdene Country House** Garsdale Rd LA10 5JN
☎(05396)20280
Closed Jan & Feb
*A small, family-run hotel retaining much of the character of its*
*Victorian origin enjoys a rural situation on the A684 a mile east of*
*the town; delightful views of the surrounding countryside are*
*offered by all its refurbished and comfortable bedrooms.*
6⇌ऒ(1fb) CTV in all bedrooms ⓡ ✹ sB&B⇌ऒ£27-£33
dB&B⇌ऒ£54-£60 ♬
15P ⅋ ✿ nc8yrs
♉ English, French & Italian Dinner £10.50&alc Last dinner
8.45pm
Credit Cards ⊡⊡

**SEDGEFIELD** Co Durham Map **08** NZ32

★★★**67%, Hardwick Hall** TS21 2EH ☎(0740)20253
Telex no 537681
*Standing in an attractive country park, yet close to the A1(M),*
*this hotel offers charming accommodation in a peaceful*
*environment. Bedroom refurbishment will be complete in 1990,*
*when all bathrooms will offer spa baths. Meals are of good quality,*
*dinner being especially worthy of recommendation.*
17⇌ऒ(1fb) CTV in all bedrooms ✹
200P ✿ ♨
♉ English & French **V** ✿ ℒ Last dinner 9.30pm
Credit Cards ⊡⊡⊡⊡⊡

★★**66%, Crosshill** 1 The Square TS21 2AB ☎(0740)20153 &
21206
*A friendly, family-run hotel in the centre of the village, overlooking*
*the 13th-century church. The attractive restaurant is renowned for*
*its high standard of cuisine and bar meals are available in the*
*comfortable lounge bar. Bedrooms are nicely decorated and*
*thoughtfully equipped.*
8⇌ऒ(2fb) CTV in all bedrooms ⓡ T S% sB&B⇌ऒ£40-£45
dB&B⇌ऒ£50-£60 ♬
《 CTV 9P *xmas*
♉ English & Continental **V** ✿ ℒ S% Lunch £7.50-£8.50 High
tea £4-£5 Dinner £15-£17&alc Last dinner 9.30pm
Credit Cards ⊡⊡⊡ Ⓔ

**SEDGEMOOR MOTORWAY SERVICE AREA (M5)**
Somerset Map **03** ST35

⌂**Travelodge** M5 Motorway Northbound BS24 0JL (only
accessible from northbound carriageway) (Trusthouse Forte)
☎Weston-Super-Mare(0934)750831
*Modern, purpose-built block of well-equipped rooms offering good*
*value, family accommodation. Food is available in the nearby*
*service area between 7am and 10pm.*
40⇌ऒ(40fb) CTV in all bedrooms ⓡ sB⇌ऒ£24
dB⇌ऒ£29.50 (room only)
《 40P ⅋
Credit Cards ⊡⊡⊡

**SEDLESCOMBE** East Sussex Map **05** TQ71

★★69%, *Brickwall* The Green TN33 0QA ☎(0424)870253
*A welcoming manor house with Tudor origins retains a good deal
of character though it now provides modern bedroom extensions
supplying well equipped accommodation; a popular restaurant
maintains good standards of food and service, and the hotel has a
lively, hospitable atmosphere.*
24rm(10➪8🖑)(2fb)4🛏 CTV in all bedrooms ® T
25P 🚗 ✿ ⩲(heated)
☺ English, French & Italian V ✿ ⚗ Last dinner 8.45pm
Credit Cards 1 2 3 5

**SELBY** North Yorkshire Map **08** SE63

★★65%, **Londesborough Arms** Market Place YO8 0NS (Berni/
Chef & Brewer) ☎(0757)707355
*Standing at the head of the market place, an impressive old
coaching inn has been converted to provide comfortable modern
facilities whilst retaining its original character and atmosphere.*
27rm(14➪9🖑)(1fb)1🛏 CTV in all bedrooms ® T
🎗 (ex guide dogs) sB&B➪🖑£40-£49 dB&B➪🖑£52-£54 🍴
《 CTV 18P 6🍴 ♫
V ✿ ⚗ Lunch £8-£15alc Dinner £8-£15alc Last dinner 9.30pm
Credit Cards 1 2 3 5

★★63%, **Owl** Main Rd YO8 9JH ☎(0757)82374
(For full entry see Hambleton (4m W A63))

**SELKIRK** Borders *Selkirkshire* Map **12** NT42

★62%, **Heatherlie House** Heatherlie Park TD7 5AL
☎(0750)21200
*Quietly situated within its own well-kept gardens this small hotel
offers comfortable accommodation and interesting home-cooked
dishes.*
7rm(6🖑)(2fb) CTV in all bedrooms ® 🎗 sB&B£17
sB&B🖑£23 dB&B🖑£37 🍴
12P 🚗 ✿ CFA
☺ European V ⚡ Bar Lunch £5-£7 High tea £6-£8 Dinner
£8-£9&alc Last dinner 8pm
Credit Cards 1 3 ⓔ

**SENNEN** Cornwall & Isles of Scilly Map **02** SW32

★★★66% **The State House** TR19 7AA
☎Penzance(0736)871844 FAX (0736) 871812
34➪3🛏 CTV in all bedrooms ® T 🎗 (ex guide dogs) 🍴
《 50P *xmas*
☺ English & French V ✿ ⚗
Credit Cards 1 2 3

★★63%, *Old Success Inn* Sennen Cove TR19 7DG
☎(0736)871232
*Set in an enviable beach-side position against the panoramic
backdrop of Sennen Cove, this busy, fully licensed little holiday
hotel, with its character bars, provides a popular venue for both
tourists and the locals. Cosy bedrooms are spotlessly clean, well
decorated and appointed, many of them offering good views across
the cove, while the equally bright and comfortable public rooms
include a restaurant serving skilfully cooked meals which make
effective use of fresh ingredients. Personally managed, the hotel
provides a pleasant retreat or an ideal base from which to explore
the tip of Cornwall.*
11rm(9➪)2🛏 CTV in all bedrooms ® 🎗
CTV 30P
✿ ⚗
Credit Cards 3

1991 marks the 25th anniversary of this guide.

## Yorkshire Dales National Park

### *Oakdene Country House Hotel* ★ ★

1 mile from Sedbergh on A684
Imposing Victorian Country House
retaining all the original features with
magnificent and uninterrupted views
Six en suite bedrooms
Remote control colour TV
Courtesy tea/coffee facilities
Pleasant licensed restaurant with à la
carte and table d'hôte menus
Evening bar snacks
Open to non residents
Special mid week breaks

**Garsdale Road, Sedbergh, Cumbria
Telephone: Sedburgh (05396) 20280
for further information**

**Doncaster Road, Scunthorpe,
South Humberside DN15 7DE
Telephone 0724 282233**
★★

The Royal Hotel has 33 bedrooms,
recently refurbished; all with en suite
facilities, colour television and tea and
coffee making.
We can arrange golf, fishing and
bowling in the nearby indoor bowling
club.
Come and sample the hospitality of
this friendly hotel.
Weekend terms: £26.00 per person
inclusive of VAT, Bed, Breakfast and
Evening Meal. Arrive any night from
Friday to Sunday.

**S**

SETTLE North Yorkshire Map **07** SD86

★★★**62%, Falcon Manor** Skipton Rd BD24 9BD (Consort)
☎(07292)3814 FAX (07292) 2087
*This family-run hotel stands in the busy Dales town that is the
starting point of the famous Settle to Carlisle railway and the
gateway to Ribblesdale and the Yorkshire Dales National Park.
Its two bars and comfortable lounge provide an ideal setting in
which to relax after enjoying the well-prepared food – including
some typical local specialities – served in the elegant restaurant.*
15⇨₳(2fb)3⊞ CTV in all bedrooms ® T ✳
sB&B⇨₳£41-£60 dB&B⇨₳£60-£88 🍴
85P ✿ bowling green *xmas*
♡ English & Continental V ✆ ⚿ Sunday Lunch £7.25 High
tea £5 Dinner £14.75&alc Last dinner 9.30pm
Credit Cards ⌊1⌋⌊3⌋⌊5⌋⍧

★★**73%, *Royal Oak*** Market Place BD24 9ED ☎(07292)2561
Closed Xmas day night
*Dating from 1684 this is a busy, friendly family run hotel. The en
suite bedrooms are pretty and very well equipped and the elegant
oak panelled restaurant provides a good standard of cuisine, or try
the popular bar meals.*
6⇨₳ CTV in all bedrooms ® ✵ (ex guide dogs)
20P 2🚗
♡ English & French V ✆ ⚿ Last dinner 10pm

SEVENOAKS Kent Map **05** TQ55

★★**66%, Royal Oak** Upper High St TN14 5PG ☎(0732)451109
FAX (0732) 740187
*A popular hotel which was originally a coaching inn has been
tastefully refurbished to provide a choice of bedrooms, comfortable
modern lounges, a Victorian bar and an elegant restaurant;
standards of cuisine are high, and service is friendly and attentive.*
21⇨₳ CTV in all bedrooms ® T ✳ sB&B⇨₳fr£65
dB&B⇨₳fr£78 🍴
⌊50P
♡ English & French V ✆ ⚿ ⚿ Lunch fr£13.50 Dinner
fr£16.50 Last dinner 9.30pm
Credit Cards ⌊1⌋⌊2⌋⌊3⌋⌊5⌋⍧

★★**59%, *Sevenoaks Park*** Seal Hollow Rd TN13 3SH
☎(0732)454245 Telex no 95571 FAX (0732) 457468
*The public areas of this friendly, efficient and family-run hotel
include a newly refurbished and extended restaurant and lounge.
There are also some well-appointed annexe rooms peacefully
located in the grounds.*
16rm(3⇨3₳)Annexe10⇨₳(3fb) CTV in all bedrooms ® T
✵
33P 🚗 ✿ ⚿(heated)
♡ English & French Last dinner 9pm
Credit Cards ⌊1⌋⌊2⌋⌊3⌋⌊5⌋

SHAFTESBURY Dorset Map **03** ST82

★★★**64%, Royal Chase** Royal Chase Roundabout SP7 8DB
(Best Western) ☎(0747)53355 Telex no 418414
FAX (0747) 51969
*Formerly a monastery, this privately owned commercial hotel has
been furnished to maintain some of its original character, with
comfortably appointed, well equipped bedrooms and an attractive
restaurant serving an interesting menu of well prepared dishes, all
in a friendly, informal atmosphere.*
35⇨₳(15fb) CTV in all bedrooms ® T S% sB&B⇨₳£43-£65
dB&B⇨₳£64-£99 🍴
CTV 100P ✿ ☐(heated) solarium croquet putting *xmas*
V ✆ ⚿ ⚿ S% Lunch £7-£18alc
Credit Cards ⌊1⌋⌊2⌋⌊3⌋⌊5⌋

★★★**56%, The Grosvenor** The Commons SP7 8JA (Trusthouse
Forte) ☎(0747)52282
*A former coaching inn with a friendly, informal atmosphere and
nicely equipped bedrooms which have been upgraded.*
47rm(41⇨1₳)(2fb)2⊞⚿in 4 bedrooms CTV in all bedrooms
® sB&Bfr£45 dB&Bfr£50 🍴
🎾 *xmas*
V ✆ ⚿ ⚿ Sunday Lunch £8.95 High tea £6.50 Dinner £11&alc
Last dinner 9pm
Credit Cards ⌊1⌋⌊2⌋⌊3⌋⌊4⌋⌊5⌋

SHALDON
See Teignmouth

SHANKLIN
See Wight, Isle of

SHAP Cumbria Map **12** NY51

★★**62%, Shap Wells** CA10 3QU (situated 3m SW of Shap Village
off A6) ☎(09316)628 & 744 FAX (09316) 377
Closed 2 Jan-14 Feb
*Improvements are continually being made to this long-established
family-run hotel. It is peacefully set in its own grounds, but is
conveniently located near the A6 and M6. With its spacious public
areas and new function facilities, social events and conferences are
well catered for, and the newer bedrooms are very comfortable and
well appointed.*
90rm(83⇨₳)(11fb) CTV in all bedrooms ® T ✳
sB&B⇨₳£32-£43 dB&B⇨₳£48-£65 🍴
CTV 200P ✿ ♪ (hard) snooker
♡ English & French V ✆ Lunch £5.50 Dinner £11.50&alc Last
dinner 8.30pm
Credit Cards ⌊1⌋⌊2⌋⌊3⌋⌊5⌋
See advertisement under KENDAL

SHARDLOW Derbyshire Map **08** SK43

★★**63%, The Lady In Grey** Wilne Ln DE7 2HA
☎Derby(0332)792331
*This fully restored old house offers comfortable accommodation in
modern, well-equipped bedrooms. The restaurant, which overlooks
attractive gardens, emphasises Spanish cuisine and offers a good,
reasonably-priced wine list.*
9⇨₳2⊞ CTV in all bedrooms ® T ✵ ✳ sB&B⇨₳£30-£40
dB&B⇨₳£30-£50 🍴
35P 🚗 ✿
♡ English & Continental V ✆ Lunch fr£7.50&alc Dinner
fr£10&alc Last dinner 10pm
Credit Cards ⌊1⌋⌊2⌋⌊3⌋⌊5⌋

SHEFFIELD South Yorkshire Map **08** SK38

★★★★**53%, *Grosvenor House*** Charter Square S1 3EH
(Trusthouse Forte) ☎(0742)720041 Telex no 54312
FAX (0742) 757199
*Modern, fourteen-storey hotel in the town centre.*
103⇨⚿in 14 bedrooms CTV in all bedrooms ®
Lift ⌊ 82🚗 CFA
♡ International V ✆ ⚿ ⚿ Last dinner 10pm
Credit Cards ⌊1⌋⌊2⌋⌊3⌋⌊4⌋⌊5⌋

Hotels with a high percentage rating for quality
are highlighted by a % across their
gazetteer entry.

★★★72% **Charnwood** 10 Sharrow Ln S11 8AA ☎(0742)589411 FAX (0742) 555107
*This charming Georgian mansion offers a relaxed, comfortable atmosphere in quality surroundings. Major alterations and a refurbishment programme are due to be completed in September 1990 and will provide Bridal and disabled suites. The two restaurants both offer a good standard of food.*
26⇨🏠 CTV in all bedrooms ® T 🖾 (ex guide dogs) sB&B⇨🏠£70-£80 dB&B⇨🏠£80-£90
( 22P 🚗 ♫
♀ French V ☺ 🖵 ⁄ Lunch £14.95 Dinner £16.95 Last dinner 10pm
Credit Cards ①②③⑤ⓔ

★★★69% **Sheffield Moat House** Chesterfield Rd South S8 8BW (Queens Moat) ☎(0742)375376 Telex no 547890
FAX (0742) 378140
Closed 25-26 Dec
*Close to the junction of the A61/A6102 ring road, a brand new hotel offers attractive bedrooms, a well-equipped leisure centre and extensive facilities for meetings. Efficient room service is provided by friendly staff.*
95⇨🏠(9fb)⁄in 20 bedrooms CTV in all bedrooms ® T sB⇨🏠£67-£70 dB⇨🏠£78-£83 (room only) 🚪
Lift ( 260P ❊ 🖾(heated) sauna solarium gymnasium Health & beauty treatment room
♀ English & French V ☺ 🖵 ⁄ Lunch £10.25-£11.50&alc High tea £5-£5.50 Dinner £11.95-£13&alc Last dinner 10pm
Credit Cards ①②③⑤

★★★67% **Dinnington Hall Hotel** Falcon Way S31 3NY
☎Worksop(0909)569661 FAX (0909)563411
(For full entry see Dinnington)

★★★65% **Beauchief** 161 Abbeydale Rd S7 2QW (Lansbury) ☎(0742)620500 Telex no 54164 FAX (0742) 350197
*An original coaching inn, pleasantly set amongst trees, has been extended and modernised to provide a good standard of well appointed accommodation; its restaurant is complemented by the popular Michel's Cellar Bar, and pleasant staff create a lively, friendly atmosphere throughout.*
41⇨🏠(2fb)2🛏⁄in 11 bedrooms CTV in all bedrooms ® T 🖾 (ex guide dogs) sB&B⇨🏠fr£76 dB&B⇨🏠fr£88 🚪
( 200P ❊ sauna solarium gymnasium
♀ English & Continental V ☺ ⁄ Lunch fr£9.75&alc Dinner fr£14.75&alc Last dinner 10pm
Credit Cards ①②③⑤

★★★65% **Hallam Tower Post House** Manchester Rd, Broomhill S10 5DX (Trusthouse Forte) ☎(0742)670067
Telex no 547293 FAX (0742) 682620
*Twelve-storey, modern tower block hotel, overlooking the city.*
135⇨🏠⁄in 18 bedrooms CTV in all bedrooms ® T S%
sB⇨🏠£72-£131 dB⇨🏠£83-£131 (room only) 🚪
Lift ( 120P ❊ CFA 🖾(heated) sauna solarium gymnasium Health & Fitness Centre *xmas*
V ☺ 🖵 ⁄ S% Lunch fr£8.95
Credit Cards ①②③④⑤

★★★65% **Mosborough Hall** High St, Mosborough S19 5AE (7m SE A616) ☎(0742)484353 FAX (0742) 477042
*A peaceful country house-style hotel offering friendly service and good restaurant menus.*
24⇨🏠(1fb)4🛏 CTV in all bedrooms ® T sB&B⇨🏠£35-£85 dB&B⇨🏠£55-£100 🚪
( CTV 100P ❊ ♪ (hard)
♀ English & French V ☺ 🖵 ⁄ Lunch £7.50-£10 High tea £5-£12 Dinner £13-£18&alc Last dinner 9.30pm
Credit Cards ①②③

For key to symbols see the inside front cover.

★★★65% **Swallow** Kenwood Rd S7 1NQ (Swallow)
☎(0742)583811 Telex no 547030 FAX (0742) 500138
*Modern hotel situated in own grounds and gardens, close to city centre. Recently updated public rooms offer comfort and relaxation in pleasant surroundings.*
141⇨🏠 CTV in all bedrooms ® T S10% sB&B⇨🏠£60-£75 dB&B⇨🏠£75-£100 🚪
Lift ( 200P ❊ CFA 🖾(heated) ⁄ sauna solarium gymnasium Spa bath ♫ *xmas*
♀ English & French V ☺ 🖵 S10% Lunch fr£12&alc Dinner fr£15&alc Last dinner 10pm
Credit Cards ①②③⑤

★★★64% **Staindrop Lodge** Lane End S30 4UH ☎(0742)846727
FAX (0742) 846783
(For full entry see Chapeltown)

★★69% **Rutland** 452 Glossop Rd, Broomhill S10 2PY
☎(0742)664411 Telex no 547500 FAX (0742) 670348
*Seven detached stone houses, interconnected by walkways, form a modern hotel which is popular with businessmen. Public rooms include a spacious reception lounge with separate public lounge, writing room and small, intimate restaurant with adjoining cocktail bar. An extremely good bedroom annexe stands close by.*
73rm(68⇨🏠1🏠)Annexe17⇨🏠(9fb) CTV in all bedrooms ® T ✳ sB&B£33 sB&B⇨🏠£33-£53 dB&B⇨🏠£52-£58 🚪
Lift ( CTV 80P CFA *xmas*
V ☺ 🖵 Lunch £4.95-£5.50 Dinner £8.95 Last dinner 9.30pm
Credit Cards ①②③⑤ⓔ

★★68% **Andrews Park** 48 Kenwood Rd S7 1NQ
☎(0742)500111 & 500005 FAX (0742) 555423
*Genuine hospitality and service can be found at this small, quiet residential hotel. Exceptionally good standards of maintenance and cleanliness prevail throughout and good home cooking is served in the dining room.*

▶

S

11rm(2⇔5♠)Annexe2⇔♠(2fb) CTV in all bedrooms ® T ✳
sB&B£28-£30 sB&B⇔♠£30-£35 dB&B⇔♠£40-£48
《 CTV 15P
V ✆ ⬚ Lunch £5-£10 Dinner £6.50-£10 Last dinner 9pm
Credit Cards [1][2][3]

★★ **65%, Roslyn Court** 178-180 Psalter Ln, Brincliffe S11 8US
☎(0742)666188 FAX (0742) 684279
*Three-storey building in a residential area.*
31⇔♠(2fb) CTV in all bedrooms ® ✳ sB&B⇔♠£36-£42
dB&B⇔♠£56
《 CTV 25P
♈ English & French V ✆ ⬚ Lunch £5 Dinner fr£7&alc Last
dinner 8.45pm
Credit Cards [1][2][3][5][£]

★ **50%, Montgomery** Montgomery Rd, Netheredge S7 1LN
☎(0742)553454 & 553224 Telex no 54662
*Situated in an attractive residential suburb close to the city centre,*
*the hotel has well-fitted, compact bedrooms and a relaxed*
*atmosphere.*
24rm(1⇔4♠)(2fb) CTV in all bedrooms ®
《 CTV 1P snooker sauna solarium gymnasium
♈ Mainly grills V ✆ ⬚ Last dinner 9.30pm
Credit Cards [1][2][3][5]

⌂**Comfort Inn** George St S1 2PF ☎(0742)739939
FAX (0742) 768332
Closed 24 Dec-3 Jan
*In the very heart of the city, this Lodge provides bedrooms which,*
*though compact, are modern and very well equipped. There is a*
*pleasant bistro-style restaurant open from breakfast through to*
*5.30pm. For dinner you will need to seek out one of the numerous*
*restaurants nearby.*
50⇔♠(2fb)⊁in 7 bedrooms CTV in all bedrooms ® T ✳
sB⇔♠£29.50 dB⇔♠£39.50 (room only) ⊟
Lift 《 ✗
V ✆ ⬚ ⊁
Credit Cards [1][2][3][5]

○**Granada** 340 Prince of Wales Rd S2 1FF (Granada)
☎(0742)530935 FAX (0742) 642731
61⇔♠(10fb)⊁in 10 bedrooms CTV in all bedrooms ® T
✗ (ex guide dogs) ✳ S% sB⇔♠fr£32
dB⇔♠fr£36 (room only) ⊟
《 60P
♈ English & French V ✆ ⬚ ⊁ S% Lunch fr£5 Dinner fr£7
Last dinner 9.30pm
Credit Cards [1][2][3][5]

○**Holiday Inn** Victoria Station Rd S4 7YE (Holiday Inns)
☎(0742)768822
100rm

**SHEPPERTON** Surrey

See LONDON plan 1.A1(page 426)
★★★ **58%, Shepperton Moat House** Felix Ln TW17 8NP
(Queens Moat) ☎Walton-on-Thames(0932)241404
Telex no 928170 FAX (0932) 245231
Closed 26-30 Dec
*Set in eleven acres of parkland close to the River Thames, the hotel*
*is surrounded by marinas and yacht clubs and has its own private*
*moorings. A spacious lobby lounge combines with the piano bar*
*and Roasters Carvery Restaurant, and extensive conference and*
*banqueting facilities are provided. Bedrooms have every modern*
*facility, including daytime room service.*
156⇔♠(4fb) CTV in all bedrooms ® T ✳ sB&B⇔♠£36-£75
dB&B⇔♠£50-£94 ⊟
Lift 《 225P ✿ CFA snooker sauna solarium gymnasium ♫

♈ English & French V ✆ Lunch £13.75 Dinner fr£14&alc Last
dinner 9.30pm
Credit Cards [1][2][3][5]

**SHEPTON MALLET** Somerset Map 03 ST64

✗ ✗ **Bowlish House** Wells Rd, Bowlish BA4 5JD (on the Wells
road A371) ☎(0749)342022
Closed 24-27 Dec
Lunch not served all week (ex by prior arrangement)
♈ International V 26 seats ✳ Dinner fr£18.50&alc Last dinner
10pm 10P ⊬
Credit Cards [1][3]

✗ **Blostin's** 29 Waterloo Rd BA4 5HH ☎(0749)343648
*Small, country town restaurant where blackboard menus offer*
*simple, inexpensive 2 or 3 course meals using good quality fresh*
*produce.*
Closed Sun, Mon, 3-19 Jan, 1-8 Jun & 1 wk Etr
Lunch not served all week (ex prior arrangement Tue-Fri)
♈ French 30 seats Lunch £9.95 Dinner £12.95-£13.95&alc Last
lunch 1.45pm Last dinner 9.30pm ✗
Credit Cards [1][3]

**SHERBORNE** Dorset Map 03 ST61

★★★ **76%, Eastbury** Long St DT9 3BY ☎(0935)813131
Telex no 46644 FAX (0935) 817296
*This characterful, attractive and centrally situated Georgian town*
*house offers a warm, relaxing atmosphere; and well managed*
*service; bedrooms are of good size and comfortably equipped,*
*while tastefully appointed public areas include pleasant lounges*
*and a light, airy restaurant where the well prepared dishes featured*
*in table d'hôte and à la carte menus are accompanied by an*
*excellent wine list.*
15⇔(1fb)1▣ CTV in all bedrooms ® T ✗ (ex guide dogs)
sB&B⇔fr£62.50 dB&B⇔fr£80 ⊟
24P ♨ ✿ croquet *xmas*
♈ English & French V ✆ ⬚ Lunch fr£10.50 Dinner fr£17.50
Last dinner 9.30pm
Credit Cards [1][3]

★★★ **62%, Post House** Horsecastles Ln DT9 6BB (Trusthouse
Forte) ☎(0935)813191 Telex no 46522 FAX (0935) 816493
*Many of the rooms of this hospitable modern hotel have been*
*upgraded to a high standard and all are well-equipped, whilst*
*lounge facilities are comfortable though limited and friendly staff*
*provide helpful service.*
60⇔♠⊁in 10 bedrooms CTV in all bedrooms ®
《 100P ✿ CFA croquet putting
V ✆ ⬚ ⊁ Last dinner 10pm
Credit Cards [1][2][3][4][5]

★★ **60%, Half Moon Toby** Half Moon St DT9 3LN (Toby)
☎(0935)812017
*This former coaching inn, dating back to the seventeenth century,*
*offers well-equipped modern bedrooms, carvery and à la carte*
*menus of competently prepared dishes, and a friendly informal*
*atmosphere.*
15⇔♠(2fb)⊁in 4 bedrooms CTV in all bedrooms ®
44P (charged) ♨ pool table & skittles
V ✆ ⊁ Last dinner 10pm
Credit Cards [1][2][3]

✗ **Pheasants** 24 Greenhill DT9 4EW ☎(0935)815252
*Placed in an old stone cottage this small, intimate restaurant*
*specialises in English and French cuisine. Well-prepared dishes are*
*complimented by an equally well-balanced wine list.*
Closed Mon & Jan
Dinner not served Sun
♈ English & French V 40 seats Lunch £7.95-£9.95&alc Dinner
£13-£16alc Last lunch 2pm Last dinner 10.30pm 10P
Credit Cards [1][3]

**S**

**S**

**SHERFIELD ON LODDON** Hampshire Map **04** SU65

★★63% **Wessex House** Reading Rd RG27 0EX
☎Basingstoke(0256)882243 FAX (0256) 881131
Closed 25 Dec-1 Jan
*In a village setting 5 miles north east of Basingstoke just off the A33. This friendly hotel offers modern bedroom accommodation together with a new bar and restaurant with à la carte and table d'hôte menus.*
17⇨🍫 CTV in all bedrooms ® T ✹ (ex guide dogs) ✱
sB&B⇨🍫£39-£49 dB&B⇨🍫£49-£59
《30P ♫
V
Credit Cards ⌴1⌴⌴2⌴⌴3⌴⌴5⌴

**SHERINGHAM** Norfolk Map **09** TG14

★★64% **Beaumaris** South St NR26 8LL ☎(0263)822370
Closed 19 Dec-Jan
*Situated in a quiet area within walking distance of the town centre and the beach. The proprietors are gradually improving and updating the facilities to meet todays requirements whilst retaining traditional care and attention.*
24rm(22⇨🍫)(5fb) CTV in all bedrooms ® T
sB&B⇨🍫£25.50-£27.50 dB&B£47-£50 dB&B⇨🍫£49-£53 🍴
CTV 25P ♨
V ✿ 𝒟 ✂ Lunch fr£8.95 Dinner fr£11.95&alc Last dinner 8.30pm
Credit Cards ⌴1⌴⌴2⌴⌴3⌴

★★58% **Southlands** South St NR26 8LL ☎(0263)822679
Closed Oct-Etr
*A small, seasonal hotel, conveniently located for access to both town centre and seafront, provides accommodation in modest rooms with some modern facilities and has a comfortable lounge bar.*
18rm(13⇨1🍫)(2fb) CTV in all bedrooms ® ✱ sB&Bfr£23
sB&B⇨🍫fr£26 dB&Bfr£46 dB&B⇨🍫fr£52
22P
✂ Dinner fr£10.50 Last dinner 7.45pm

**SHETLAND** Map **16**

**BRAE** Map **16** HU36

★★★⚑67% **Busta House** ZE2 9QN (Consort) ☎(080622)506
Telex no 9312100 FAX (080622) 588
Closed 23 Dec-2 Jan
*An eighteenth century mansion house is situated on the western shores of Busta Voe with a private quay leading down to its own little harbour. It offers compact but well-equipped bedrooms, two comfortable lounges and a cosy country bar ; the restaurant features a short, carefully chosen dinner menu of good quality which uses only local produce.*
20⇨🍫1🏮 CTV in all bedrooms ® T sB&B⇨🍫£45-£54
dB&B⇨🍫£65-£73 🍴
35P ✿ sea fishing & water sports
♡ International V ✿ 𝒟 ✂ Bar Lunch £6.15-£13 Dinner £18.25-£21.50 Last dinner 9.30pm
Credit Cards ⌴1⌴⌴2⌴⌴3⌴⌴5⌴

**LERWICK** Map **16** HU44

★★★66% **Shetland** Holmsgarth Rd ZE1 0PW ☎(0595)5515
Telex no 75432 FAX (0595) 5828
*Standing opposite the car ferry terminal, this purpose-built, modern hotel provides spacious bedrooms and the services of friendly staff.*
66⇨🍫✂in 5 bedrooms CTV in all bedrooms ® T
sB&B⇨🍫£58 dB&B⇨🍫£66 🍴
Lift 《150P ✿ ⬜(heated) sauna solarium gymnasium ♫

♡ International V ✿ 𝒟 Lunch £4-£7.50 Dinner £13.50&alc
Last dinner 9.30pm
Credit Cards ⌴1⌴⌴2⌴⌴3⌴⌴4⌴⌴5⌴ ⓔ

★★★58% **Lerwick** South Rd ZE1 0RB ☎(0595)2166
Telex no 75128 FAX (0595) 4419
*There are fine views of the bay from this tourist/commercial hotel, purpose-built in the seventies.*
31⇨🍫(1fb) CTV in all bedrooms ® S% sB&B⇨🍫fr£47
dB&B⇨🍫fr£60 🍴
《22P
♡ English & French V ✿ 𝒟 S% Lunch £6.90 Dinner £12.75&alc Last dinner 9pm
Credit Cards ⌴1⌴⌴2⌴⌴3⌴ ⓔ

★★★56% **Kveldsro House** ZE1 0AN ☎(0595)2195
*Standing in a quiet area of the town, this small business hotel offers functional but thoughtfully equipped bedrooms, sound menus which combine quality with quantity, and limited lounge facilities.*
14rm(9⇨) CTV in all bedrooms ® T ✹ (ex guide dogs)
sB&B£33.93 sB&B⇨£46.58 dB&B⇨£57.50
28P ♨
V ✿ 𝒟 Lunch £2.60-£5.10&alc

**SHIELDAIG** Highland *Ross & Cromarty* Map **14** NG85

★★66% **Tigh an Eilean** IV54 8XN ☎(05205)251
Closed Nov-Etr
*A small family-run hotel, beautifully situated on the shores of Loch Torridon.*
13rm(4⇨1🍫)(2fb) ®
CTV 15P ♨ ✈
Credit Cards ⌴1⌴⌴3⌴

**SHIFNAL** Shropshire Map **07** SJ70

★★★★60% **Park House** Silvermere Park, Park St TF11 9BA
(Character) ☎Telford(0952)460128 Telex no 35438
FAX (0952) 461658
*This extensive complex of leisure accommodation is located on the Wolverhampton side of the town. Formed by linking 2 country houses and their grounds the hotel has built a well-deserved reputation for high standards of comfort and friendly caring staff. Recent conversion of a cottage-style annexe adds further accommodation.*
54⇨🍫(2fb)✂in 2 bedrooms CTV in all bedrooms ® T ✱ S%
sB&B⇨🍫£45-£94 dB&B⇨🍫£50-£105 🍴
Lift 《160P ✿ ⬜(heated) sauna solarium jacuzzi *xmas*
♡ French V ✿ 𝒟 Lunch fr£10&alc High tea £1.50-£8alc
Dinner £12.50-£19.45&alc Last dinner 10.30pm
Credit Cards ⌴1⌴⌴2⌴⌴3⌴⌴5⌴

**SHINFIELD** Berkshire Map **04** SU76

❀❀✕✕ **L'ORTOLAN, SHINFIELD** Church Ln RG2 9BY
☎Reading(0734)883783 FAX (0734) 885391
(Rosette awarded for dinner only)
*John Burton-Race has firmly established himself as one of the country's top chefs, and we are delighted to mark his achievement by the award of two rosettes. His distinctive cuisine is innovative and complex and can be breathtakingly successful, though there is a danger of experimentation for experiment's sake, leading occasionally to excess and self-indulgence. However, there is no doubting the genius and dedication that he brings to his cooking, and indeed there is so much to enthuse about that it is difficult to know which individual dishes to highlight. However, the Soufflé de Turbot et Crabe au gingembre was memorable, as was the Filet d'Agneau farci de son ris en enveloppe d'epinards et son jus fleur de thym, and the rich chocolate soufflé which followed was faultless. The wine list fully meets the expectations at this level of haute cuisine and the staff are well directed by the ever-charming Christina Burton-Race.*

Closed Mon, last 2 wks Feb & last 2 wks Aug
Dinner not served Sun
♀ French **V** 55 seats ✳ Lunch £27-£44 Dinner £44-£50 Last
lunch 2.15pm Last dinner 10.15pm 30P
Credit Cards ①②③

---

**SHIPDHAM** Norfolk Map **05** TF90

★★69% **Shipdham Place** Church Close IP25 7LX
☎Dereham(0362)820303
*The peaceful surroundings of what was once Shipdham Rectory,
dating back to the seventeenth century, provide the ideal
opportunity for escape and relaxation. Its charming bedrooms are
individually decorated, comfortable lounge areas are tastefully
furnished, a table d'hôte menu makes good use of quality fresh
ingredients and personal service is rendered by resident owners.*
8rm(7⇥)(1fb)2⊞ **T** sB&B⇦£33-£72 dB&B⇦£44-£85 ➠
CTV 25P ✿
♀ English & French **V** ♥ ⍟ ⚡ Lunch £10.95 Dinner
£18.50-£22.50 Last dinner 9.30pm
Credit Cards ①③

**See advertisement on page 623**

★68% **Pound Green** Pound Green Ln IP25 7LS (4m SW East
Dereham) ☎Dereham(0362)820165
*Clean, comfortable surroundings, friendly service and a choice
between a good à la carte menu and a selection of bar meals
prepared from fresh local produce are offered by a small family-
run hotel in a quiet residential road.*
12rm(7♠)(2fb) CTV in 7 bedrooms ®
CTV 60P 2🐾 ✿ ⌧
**V** ♥ ⚡ Last dinner 9.30pm
Credit Cards ①③

**S**

**SHIPHAM** Somerset Map **03** ST45

**★★★🏵63% Daneswood House** Cuck Hill BS25 1RD ☎Winscombe(093484)3145 & 3945 FAX (093484) 3824
RS 24 Dec-6 Jan

*From its quiet woodland setting in the Mendip Hills, this friendly, personally-run hotel commands rural views across its terraced gardens and the valley beyond. The Edwardian house has recently been upgraded to offer spacious, comfortable bedrooms which retain their original character while providing modern facilities – the three garden suites with their own lounges and patio doors on to the terrace are particularly well designed to offer additional comfort and a degree of independence – and good use has been made of pleasing soft décor and complementary fabrics throughout. Food standards are worthy of note for their imaginative treatment of quality ingredients and local produce. The hotel's site makes it an ideal tourist base and easy access to Bristol and its airport is an attraction for businessmen.*

9⇌↱Annexe3⇌↱(3fb) CTV in all bedrooms ® **T** ✗ (ex guide dogs) sB&B⇌↱£45-£65 dB&B⇌↱£62.50-£89.50 ⊟

( 25P 2🚗 ⊞ ❊

🍷 English & Continental **V** ✿ ☕ ⊁ Lunch £9.95-£11.95alc Dinner £16.95-£19.95alc Last dinner 9.30pm

Credit Cards 1 2 3 5 £

**See advertisement under BRISTOL**

**★50% Penscot Farmhouse** The Square BS25 1TW (Minotels) ☎Winscombe(093484)2659
RS Dec-6 Jan

*Small village hotel popular with ramblers and tourists, with a comfortable lounge bar.*

18rm(12↱)(2fb)1⊞ ® **T** ✱ sB&B£23.75-£27.50 sB&B↱£27.50 dB&B£37.50 dB&B↱£45 ⊟

CTV 40P ❊

**V** ✿ ☕ ⊁

Credit Cards 1 2 3 5 £

**SHIPLEY** West Yorkshire Map **07** SE13

**✕Aagrah** 27 Westgate BD18 3QX ☎Bradford(0274)594660

*This small and extremely popular restaurant is situated in the centre of the town. The menu is extensive and offers a wide range of dishes. The service is quick, and the food is nicely presented. Booking is advisable.*

Closed 23 Aug & 25 Dec

Lunch not served Mon-Sat

🍷 Asian **V** 50 seats ✱ Sunday Lunch £6-£12alc Last dinner 12.45am 20P ⊁

Credit Cards 1 2 3 5

**See advertisement under BRADFORD**

**SHIPTON-UNDER-WYCHWOOD** Oxfordshire Map **04** SP21

**★★63% Shaven Crown** OX7 6BA ☎(0993)830330

*Formerly a 14th-century hospice to Bruern Abbey, and retaining many of its original features, this small family-run hotel and restaurant offers individually styled bedrooms with modern facilities, an intimate candle-lit restaurant and a good range of buffet and bar food.*

9rm(5⇌3↱)(1fb) CTV in all bedrooms ® ✗ (ex guide dogs) sB&B⇌↱fr£29 dB&B⇌↱£59-£62 ⊟

15P ❊ bowling green *xmas*

🍷 Continental **V** ✿ ☕ Sunday Lunch £9.75 Dinner £16.50-£19.50alc Last dinner 9.30pm

Credit Cards 1 3

A rosette is an indication of exceptional standards of cuisine.

***✕Lamb Inn*** High St OX7 6DQ ☎(0993)830465

*This character Cotswold inn features a small restaurant with bright, cosy surroundings where service is friendly and informal. Although the menu is short, its limited range of dishes is prepared with a degree of imagination and flair, making good use of quality produce.*

Closed 25 Dec-1 Jan

Lunch not served Mon-Sat

Dinner not served Sun

30 seats Last dinner 9pm 25P nc14yrs

Credit Cards 1 2 3 5

**SHORNE** Kent Map **05** TQ67

**★★★62% *Inn on the Lake*** Watling St DA12 3HB (A2) ☎(047482)3333 Telex no 966356 FAX (047482) 3175

*Busy hotel in attractive, well-kept gardens with a delightful lake. The accommodation is comfortable and well-maintained and service is pleasant.*

78⇌ CTV in all bedrooms ® ✗ (ex guide dogs)

( 250P ❊ CFA ♪ ♫

🍷 English & French ✿ ☕ Last dinner 9.45pm

Credit Cards 1 2 3 5

**SHRAWLEY** Hereford & Worcester Map **07** SO86

**★★★64% Lenchford** WR6 6TB ☎Worcester(0905)620229
Closed 24, 25 & 26 Dec

*This family-run hotel enjoys an idyllic setting on the banks of the River Severn in a quiet rural location six miles north of Worcester.*

16rm(14⇌1↱)(1fb) CTV in all bedrooms ® ✗ sB&B£32 sB&B⇌↱£47 dB&B⇌↱£57 ⊟

50P ❊ ⛆(heated) ♪

🍷 English & French **V** ✿ Dinner £12-£17.50alc Last dinner 9.30pm

Credit Cards 1 2 3 5

**See advertisement under WORCESTER**

**SHREWSBURY** Shropshire Map **07** SJ41

**★★★★61% Albrighton Hall** Albrighton SY4 3AG (2.5m N on A528) (Character) ☎Bomere Heath(0939)291000
Telex no 35726 FAX (0939) 291123

*Beautifully preserved 17th-century house, set in 14 acres of gardens and grounds , providing high standards of accommodation and facilities for conferences and functions.*

33⇌↱Annexe10⇌↱(2fb)6⊞ CTV in 33 bedrooms ® **T** ✱ sB&B⇌↱£52-£68 dB&B⇌↱£67-£80 ⊟

( 120P ❊ ⛆(heated) squash snooker sauna solarium gymnasium aerobics room beauty room *xmas*

🍷 International **V** ✿ ☕ Lunch £9.75 Dinner fr£15&alc Last dinner 10.30pm

Credit Cards 1 2 3 5

**★★★🏵71% Albright Hussey** Broad Oak SY4 3AF ☎Bomere Heath(0939)290571 FAX (0939) 291143

*Steeped in history, this small family-run hotel is fast growing in popularity, not only for the quality of the bedrooms, but for service and the cuisine prepared by the brothers Guy and Alastair Nickless. A lot of care and attention has been taken to renovate the moated house, which has parts dating back to 1524.*

5⇌Annexe1↱1⊞ CTV in all bedrooms ® **T** ✱ sB⇌↱£50-£75 dB⇌↱£65-£90 (room only) ⊟

( 50P ❊ nc3yrs *xmas*

🍷 International **V** ✿ ☕ Lunch £7.50-£9&alc Dinner £13.50&alc Last dinner 10pm

Credit Cards 1 2 3 4

1991 marks the 25th anniversary of this guide.

★★★ 64% **Prince Rupert** Butcher Row SY1 1UQ (Queens Moat) ☎(0743)236000 Telex no 35100 FAX (0743) 57306
*This traditional style of hotel has been completely remodelled internally to provide comfortable bedrooms and public areas. With its central location, parking could be a problem, but staff will park your car and return it on departure.*
65⇔(4fb)2🖵 CTV in all bedrooms ® ✳ sB&B⇔£58-£60 dB&B⇔£72-£76 🏳
Lift ⟨ 60P CFA games room
♀ English, French & Italian **V** ✿ *⌦* Lunch £9.75&alc Dinner £14.50&alc Last dinner 10.15pm
Credit Cards [1] [2] [3] [5] £

★★★ 61% **Radbrook Hall** Radbrook Rd SY3 9BQ (Berni/Chef & Brewer) ☎(0743)236676
*This extended hotel offers guests well-equipped bedrooms, a grill-style restaurant and a leisure and health centre.*
28⇔🏠(3fb)1🖵 CTV in all bedrooms ® **T** ✗ (ex guide dogs) sB&B⇔🏠£48-£56.50 dB&B⇔🏠£62 🏳
⟨ CTV 250P ✿ squash sauna solarium gymnasium games room **V** ✿ ⅄ Lunch £8-£15alc Dinner £8-£15alc Last dinner 10.30pm
Credit Cards [1] [2] [3] [5]

★★★ 60% **The Lion** Wyle Cop SY1 1UY (Trusthouse Forte) ☎(0743)53107 FAX (0743) 52744
*A 14th-century hotel close to the busy town centre. It has comfortable lounge foyer areas and the Shires Restaurant offers traditional English cuisine and friendly attentive service.*
59⇔(1fb)1🖵⅄in 14 bedrooms CTV in all bedrooms ® **T** sB⇔fr£59 dB⇔£81-£89 (room only) 🏳
Lift ⟨ 72P CFA *xmas*
**V** ✿ *⌦* ⅄ Lunch fr£7.50&alc Dinner £13.50-£17.50&alc Last dinner 10pm
Credit Cards [1] [2] [3] [4] [5]

★★ 68% **Shelton Hall** Shelton SY3 8BH (2m NW A5) ☎(0743)3982 due to change to 343982
Closed Xmas
*This charming little hotel stands in well-manicured grounds just outside the city centre; its busy restaurant features a fixed-price menu offering a varied choice of dishes prepared from fresh ingredients.*
10rm(9⇔🏠)(2fb) CTV in all bedrooms ® **T** ✗ sB&B⇔🏠£50 dB&B⇔🏠£60
CTV 50P 🚗 ✿
♀ English & Continental **V** ✿ Sunday Lunch £11&alc Dinner £15&alc Last dinner 8.30pm
Credit Cards [1] [3]

See advertisement on page 625

★★ 60% **Lion & Pheasant** 49-50 Wyle Cop SY1 1XJ (Consort) ☎(0743)236288
*Once linked with the infamous sport of cock-fighting, this historic and characterful inn with an abundance of exposed timbers and old fireplaces offers well-equipped bedrooms, comfortable public areas and good-value meals.*
20rm(4⇔8🏠)(1fb) CTV in all bedrooms ® **T** sB&B£27.50-£33 sB&B⇔🏠£38.50 dB&B£44 dB&B⇔🏠£55 🏳
CTV 20P
♀ English & French **V** ✿ *⌦* Lunch £7.95-£8.95 High tea £1.25-£2.50 Dinner £10.95-£11.95&alc Last dinner 9.30pm
Credit Cards [1] [2] [3] [5] £

See advertisement on page 625

★★ 59% **The Shrewsbury** Bridge Place, Mardol SY1 1TU ☎(0743)231246 FAX (0743) 247701
*A family-run hotel standing near the Welsh Bridge and the town centre has recently undergone complete refurbishment to provide a choice of bars, a small but comfortable first floor lounge and compact bedrooms which are well furnished and equipped.*
24⇔🏠(5fb) CTV in all bedrooms ® **T** ✳ sB&B⇔🏠£35-£40 dB&B⇔🏠£45-£50 🏳

▶

S

623

( CTV 34P
V ♔ Bar Lunch £2-£5 Dinner £8.95-£10.95 Last dinner 9pm
Credit Cards [1] [2] [3] [5]

**SIBSON** Leicestershire Map **04** SK30

**★★67% Millers Hotel & Restaurant** Main Rd CV13 6LB (6m N of Nuneaton on A444 road to Burton)
☎Tamworth(0827)880223

*Providing easy access to the M6 and M42 from its position on the A444 between Nuneaton and Burton on Trent, and converted to hotel use as recently as 1980, this one-time bakery and water mill reatains such original features as the water wheel and baker's oven, together with font, fountains and courtyards. Bedrooms are all comfortable, well equipped and recently refurnished in a most attractive style, while the aptly-named Millstream Restaurant offers a variety of interesting dishes based on fresh local produce ; guests can also sample the extensive range of popular bar meals served in the friendly atmosphere of the Millwheel Bar.*

40⇌♪(1fb)2⊞ CTV in all bedrooms ® T ✱
sB&B⇌♪fr£49.50 dB&B⇌♪fr£59.50 ⊟
( CTV 100P 2⊜ (£3 per night) games room ⌂ *xmas*
☊ English & Continental V ♔ ⊈ Lunch fr£12.95&alc Dinner fr£14.95&alc Last dinner 9.45pm
Credit Cards [1] [2] [3] [5] (£)

**SIDMOUTH** Devon Map **03** SY18

**★★★★69% Belmont** The Esplanade EX10 8RX (Brend)
☎(0395)512555 Telex no 42551 FAX (0395) 579154

*A totally refurbished hotel with fine sea views stands at the quieter end of the promenade ; bedrooms and public areas alike are comfortable and well-equipped, while friendly, efficient service is provided in all areas.*

54⇌(10fb) CTV in all bedrooms ® T ✗ (ex guide dogs)
sB&B⇌£60-£66 dB&B⇌£90-£145 ⊟
Lift ( 45P ✿ ❊ putting green ♫ ⌂ *xmas*
☊ English & French V ♔ ⊈ Lunch £9.50&alc Dinner £14.50&alc Last dinner 9pm
Credit Cards [1] [2] [3] [5]

**★★★★64% Victoria** Esplanade EX10 8RY (Brend)
☎(0395)512651 Telex no 42551 FAX (0395) 579154

*Set in a prime position overlooking the sea, this fine Victorian hotel complements spaciously comfortable public rooms with a range of leisure activities that includes a hairdressing salon and both indoor and outdoor swimming pools.*

61⇌(18fb) CTV in all bedrooms ® T ✗ (ex guide dogs)
sB&B⇌£60-£68 dB&B⇌£99-£150 ⊟
Lift ( 100P 4⊜ (£4 per day) ✿ ❊ CFA ⊡(heated) ⌓(heated) ⚲ (hard) snooker sauna solarium spa bath putting green ♫ ⌂ *xmas*
☊ English & French V ♔ ⊈ Lunch £10&alc Dinner £16-£18&alc Last dinner 9pm
Credit Cards [1] [2] [3] [5]

**See advertisement on page 627**

**★★★78% Riviera** The Esplanade EX10 8AY ☎(0395)515201
Telex no 42551 FAX (0395) 577775

*Situated in a prime position off the seafront, this fine, bow-fronted Georgian hotel has been totally refurbished to provide tasteful, comfortable public areas and particularly well-equipped quality bedrooms. Staff are friendly and efficient, and a good room service menu is available.*

34rm(29⇌♪)(6fb) CTV in all bedrooms T sB&B⇌♪£47-£63
dB&B⇌♪£94-£126 (incl dinner) ⊟
Lift ( 12P 9⊜ (£2.25 per 24hrs) ❊ *xmas*
☊ English & French V ♔ ⊈ Lunch £10.50&alc Dinner £17.50&alc Last dinner 9pm
Credit Cards [1] [2] [3] [5]

**See advertisement on page 629**

**★★★68% Westcliff** Manor Rd EX10 8RU ☎(0395)513252
FAX (0395) 578203
Closed 21 Dec-13 Feb RS 3 Nov-22 Dec & 14 Feb-25 Mar

*Traditionally hospitable standards of service are offered by this popular, family-owned and personally run hotel, which commands good sea views from a setting amid 2 acres of lawns and gardens – its position directly opposite Connaught Gardens providing a pleasant and picturesque gateway to Jacob's Ladder and the Western Beach. Recent upgrading of the public rooms has brought them to a commendable standard, with the addition of a pleasing new cocktail bar, while many of the spotlessly clean bedrooms boast balconies.*

40⇌♪(15fb) CTV in all bedrooms ® T ✗
sB&B⇌♪£44-£63.25 dB&B⇌♪£80-£132.26 (incl dinner) ⊟
Lift CTV 40P ✿ ❊ ⌓(heated) solarium gymnasium croquet, games room, jacuzzi, pool table ♫ ⌂
☊ English & Continental V ♔ ⊈ ⚟ Sunday Lunch fr£9.50 Dinner fr£16.50&alc Last dinner 8.30pm
Credit Cards [1] [3]

**★★★61% Fortfield** Station Rd EX10 8NU ☎(0395)512403

*A family managed hotel in its own gardens and within easy walking distance of the sea front. It offers simply decorated and furnished bedrooms, a high standard of service and naturally friendly staff.*

52⇌♪(7fb) CTV in all bedrooms ® T sB&B⇌♪£30-£50
dB&B⇌♪£60-£100 ⊟
Lift ( CTV 60P ✿ ❊ CFA ⊡(heated) sauna solarium games room putting green ⌂ *xmas*
♔ ⊈ ⚟ Bar Lunch £2.50-£10 Dinner £12.50&alc Last dinner 8.30pm
Credit Cards [1] [2] [3]

**★★★60% Royal Glen** Glen Rd EX10 8RW ☎(0395)513221 & 578124

*This former residence of the late Duke and Duchess of Kent and their daughter Princess Victoria, later to become Queen, stands in its own grounds and offers a wealth of history and character. Some bedrooms are compact but all are furnished in keeping with the Victorian Style. A table d'hôte menu offers some choice of dishes.*

34rm(32⇌♪)(4fb) CTV in all bedrooms T ✱
sB&B£20.90-£31.02 sB&B⇌♪£24.20-£35.84
dB&B⇌♪£31.36-£47.05 ⊟
⊞ CTV 16P 8⊜ (£1 per night) ✿ ⊡(heated) nc8yrs
♔ ⊈ Lunch fr£5.25 Dinner fr£9.50&alc Last dinner 8pm
Credit Cards [1] [2] [3]

**★★★59% Salcombe Hill House** Beatlands Rd EX10 8JQ
☎(0395)514697
Closed Nov-Feb

*A hotel situated about half a mile from the sea front achieves a country house feeling under the management of proprietors of 35 years' standing ; guests have the use of a well-tended garden and swimming pool.*

32rm(29⇌♪)(5fb) CTV in all bedrooms ® T ✱
sB&B£32.50-£45.45 sB&B⇌♪£32.50-£45.45 dB&B£65-£90.95
dB&B⇌♪£65-£90.95 (incl dinner) ⊟
Lift ( 35P 4⊜ (£2.75 daily) ✿ ❊ ⌓(heated) ⚲ (grass) putting games room nc3yrs
V ♔ ⊈ ⚟ Lunch £7.50&alc Dinner £10.50&alc Last dinner 8.30pm
Credit Cards [1] [3] [5]

**★★68% Abbeydale** Manor Rd EX10 8RP ☎(0395)512060
Closed Dec-Jan (ex Xmas)

*Built at the turn of the last century and opened in 1962 as a private hotel by the present owners, this establishment in its own attractive gardens offers a choice of lounges, a dining room with simple table d'hôte menu, and well-equipped en suite bedrooms, some of which provide sea views.*

18⇌♪(2fb) CTV in all bedrooms ® T ✗ sB&B⇌♪£30-£35
dB&B⇌♪£60-£70

Lift 24P ⇗ ✿ nc4yrs *xmas*
☺ English & French ⟐ ⅏ ✂ Bar Lunch fr£4.25 Dinner fr£13
Last dinner 8pm

★★✦68%, **Brownlands** Sid Rd EX10 9AG ☎(0395)513053
Closed Nov, Jan & Feb RS Dec & Mar
*Set amid trees in 7 acres on the wooded slopes of Salcombe Hill, enjoying panoramic views over Sidmouth and Lyme Bay, this attractive Victorian hotel, family-owned and run in country house style, has been sympathetically restored to provide a delightful retreat. Further upgrading has resulted in a new oak-panelled dining room and bright, restful conservatory overlooking the grounds, while the effect of the comfortable, freshly decorated and well furnished bedrooms is pleasingly softened with attractive fabrics. Public rooms are luxuriously furnished and, like the bedrooms, spotlessly clean.*
15⇨↑(1fb) CTV in all bedrooms ® T
sB&B⇨↑£35.50-£38.50 dB&B⇨↑£71-£96 (incl dinner) ᗡ
CTV 25P ⇗ ✿ ♗ (hard) putting nc8yrs *xmas*
☺ International V ✂ Sunday Lunch £8 Dinner £14.95 Last dinner 8pm

See advertisement on page 626

★★68%, **Mount Pleasant** Salcombe Rd EX12 8JA
☎(0395)514694
Closed Oct-Etr
*Built in the eighteenth century as a home for the vicar of Salcombe Regis, the hotel overlooks the Byes and river from a delightful position within easy reach of the town centre. Careful improvements have produced cosy, individual bedrooms and public areas which include a small, intimate dining room. Well landscaped gardens offer several sunbathing areas for the warmer months.*
16⇨↑(1fb)1⊞ CTV in all bedrooms ® sB&B⇨↑£24-£27 dB&B⇨↑£48-£56 ᗡ
22P 1☂ ⇗ ✿ ♗ 9 nc8yrs
V ⟐ ⅏ ✂

See advertisement on page 626

**S**

## Sidmouth

**★★ 65% Kingswood** Esplanade EX10 8AX ☎(0395)516367
Closed mid Nov-mid Mar
*Centrally situated on the Promenade, this fine terraced house has been owned by the same family for thirty years, and returning guests are very much a part of that family. Upgraded, en suite, bedrooms combine good modern amenities with thoughtful extra touches, while public areas are spacious and comfortably furnished.*
26⇔⬧🖐(7fb)1🎗 CTV in all bedrooms ℝ T
Lift CTV 7P 2🏊
♉ ⬛ Last dinner 7.30pm

See advertisement on page 629

**★★ 65% Littlecourt** Seafield Rd EX10 8HF ☎(0395)515279
*This attractive character property is within walking distance of the sea front and town centre. Public areas, refurbished over the winter, combine comfort and modern quality, and bedrooms are tastefully decorated.*
21rm(12⇔🖐6🖐)(3fb)1🎗 CTV in all bedrooms ℝ sB&B£22-£30
sB&B⇔🖐£25-£41 dB&B⇔🖐£50-£84 (incl dinner) 🅿
CTV 17P ❄ ⌓(heated) *xmas*
♉ English & French V ♉ ⬛ ✗ Lunch £6.80 High tea £4
Dinner £9.50-£10.50 Last dinner 8pm
Credit Cards 1 3

**★★ 63% Royal York & Faulkner** Esplanade EX10 8AZ
☎(0395)513043 & 513184 FAX (0395) 577472
*Regency-style building, personally-run, on the sea front close to shopping facilities.*
68⇔🖐(6fb) CTV in all bedrooms ℝ T sB&B⇔🖐£23-£43.90
dB&B⇔🖐£46-£87 (incl dinner) 🅿
Lift CTV 7P 2🏊 sauna solarium gymnasium jacuzzi spa pool
health complex ♫ *xmas*
♉ English & French V ♉ ⬛ Bar Lunch £5.50-£9.50alc Dinner
£9.50-£10.50 Last dinner 8pm
Credit Cards 1 3

**★★ 62% Applegarth** Church St, Sidford EX10 9QP (2m N
B3175) ☎(0395)513174
*Situated in the village of Sidford, approximately one mile from the sea, this family-run, sixteenth-century character hotel features exposed wooden beams in compact, comfortably furnished public areas which include a restaurant where imaginative home-cooked dishes are offered at lunch and dinner ; cottage-style bedrooms are spotlessly clean, with bright décor and pine furnishings.*
8rm(3⇔1🖐) CTV in all bedrooms ℝ ✂ ✳ sB&B£17.50-£21.50
dB&B£35-£43 dB&B⇔🖐£37-£45 🅿
CTV 12P 🏷 ❄
♉ English & French ♉ ⬛ ✗ Lunch £2-£6 Dinner £9.50&alc
Last dinner 9pm
Credit Cards 1 3

**★★ 54% Woodlands** Station Rd EX10 8HG ☎(0395)513120
*A large, period house on the outskirts of the town offers modestly appointed bedrooms and spacious public areas furnished with good antiques.*
30rm(14⇔4🖐)(1fb) CTV in 4 bedrooms ℝ
CTV 22P 🏷 ❄ putting nc3yrs
♉ ⬛ Last dinner 8pm
Credit Cards 1 3

**★★ 50% Westbourne** Manor Rd EX10 8RR ☎(0395)513774
Closed Nov-Feb
*This family-run hotel, quietly situated within easy reach of beaches and the town centre, offers some bedrooms with en suite facilities and serves a choice of meals from a single table d'hôte menu in the dining room.*

▶

**S**

# The Victoria Hotel
### AA★★★★
## A LUXURY HOTEL SET IN 5 ACRES OVERLOOKING GLORIOUS SIDMOUTH BAY

The unspoilt beauty of East Devon's most exclusive resort can be enjoyed to the full at The Victoria. Enchanting elevated gardens command inspiring views of the sands and superb coastline. Luxurious surroundings reflect a long tradition of excellence in cuisine and personal service. All the amenities that you would expect of one of England's finest hotels are at your disposal - including **indoor & outdoor heated pool, sauna & solarium, private beach, terrace, tennis, hairdressing salon etc.** Private bath & colour T.V. with video films in every room. First class golf, fishing & riding nearby.

**FOR FREE COLOUR BROCHURE AND TARIFF PLEASE CONTACT:**
**J. E. BREND, VICTORIA HOTEL, SIDMOUTH, DEVON EX10 8RY**
**TEL: (0395) 512651     FAX NO: (0395) 579154**

# There's no better choice in East Devon
## The Belmont Hotel
### AA★★★★
### TRADITIONALLY SIDMOUTH'S FINEST SEAFRONT HOTEL

The Belmont hotel enjoys a superb location just a short level walk from the resorts' Regency centre. Relax and savour the delights of a West Country Winter break or Summer holiday with good cuisine, every comfort and personal service. With a lift to all floors each bedroom has private bathroom, colour T.V., radio and telephone, most having superb seaviews. Leisure facilities include putting green with bowling green and tennis courts adjacent.

**FOR FREE COLOUR BROCHURE AND TARIFF PLEASE CONTACT:**
**MR. A. DENNIS, THE BELMONT HOTEL, THE ESPLANADE, SIDMOUTH, DEVON**
**TEL: (0395) 512555     FAX NO: (0395) 579154**

## Brend Hotels
**TRAVEL CENTRE TEL: (0271) 44496**

627

14rm(8⇨1♦)(2fb) CTV in all bedrooms ® S%
sB&B£31.35-£33.35 dB&B£62.70-£67.10
dB&B⇨♦£67.70-£71.50 (incl dinner) ♯
16P ∰
V ⊹ ⊡ ⅙ Bar Lunch £1.50-£5 Dinner £10 Last dinner 7.30pm
Credit Cards [1] [3]

---

**SILLOTH** Cumbria Map **11** NY15

★★★70% *The Skinburness Hotel* CA5 4QY ☎(06973)32332
*An attractive sandstone building situated in a peaceful hamlet.*
*Tastefully furnished throughout it provides good comfort and*
*friendly service. Traditional English fare is served in the delightful*
*restaurant.*
25⇨♦ CTV in all bedrooms ®
70P ✿ snooker sauna solarium gymnasium ♫
♀ English & French V ⊹ ⊡ Last dinner 9pm
Credit Cards [1] [2] [3] [5]

★★66% **Golf** Criffel St CA5 4AB ☎(06973)31438
FAX (06973) 32582
Closed 25 Dec
*Situated close to the southern shore of the Solway Firth, a*
*championship golf course, and the tourist attractions of the Lake*
*District, this hotel has well-equipped bedrooms and is suitable for*
*both commercial visitors and tourists.*
22⇨♦(4fb)1♯ CTV in all bedrooms ® ✱ sB&B⇨♦fr£34
dB&B⇨♦fr£48 ♯
♪
♀ English & Continental ⊹ ⊡ Lunch fr£6.75 Dinner
fr£12.50&alc Last dinner 9.15pm
Credit Cards [1] [2] [3] [5]

---

**SILVERDALE** Lancashire Map **07** SD47

★57% **Silverdale** Shore Rd LA5 0TP ☎(0524)701206
*A conservatory and attractive restaurant have been added to this*
*quaint country inn which is also popular for bar meals. The new*
*owners now plan to improve the modest bedroom accommodation.*
10rm(1⇨1♦)(2fb) CTV in all bedrooms ® T ✱ sB&B£17.50
sB&B⇨♦£22.50 dB&B£28.50 dB&B⇨♦£33.50 ♯
30P
V ⊹ ⊡
Credit Cards [1] [3] £

---

**SIMONSBATH** Somerset Map **03** SS73

★★⚑69% **Simonsbath House** TA24 7SH ☎Exford(064383)259
Closed Dec-Jan
*Set in the natural beauty of Exmoor this fine 17th-century house*
*provides a high degree of comfort and hospitality augmented by*
*freshly prepared food selected from a balanced menu. Bedrooms*
*are well appointed and furnished in keeping with the style of the*
*house, yet have the modern-day facilities; most also have fine*
*countryside views. The owners, Mr & Mrs Burns, extend a very*
*warm welcome – the offer of a tea-tray in front of the log fire in the*
*cooler evenings is most welcome.*
7⇨♦3♯ CTV in all bedrooms ® T ✖ sB&B⇨♦£45-£62
dB&B⇨♦£76-£92 ♯
40P ∰ ✿ nc10yrs
⊹ ⊡ ⅙
Credit Cards [1] [2] [3] [5] £

---

See 'How we Classify Hotels and Restaurants'
at the front of the book for an explanation
of the AA's appointment and
award scheme.

---

**SIX MILE BOTTOM** Cambridgeshire Map **05** TL55

★★★74% **Swynford Paddocks** CB8 0UE ☎(063870)234
FAX (063870) 283
Closed 1 & 2 Jan RS Sat lunch-closed
*Situated on the A1304 six miles south west of Newmarket this*
*former country mansion is set amidst well-maintained gardens and*
*has racehorses grazing in its pastures. The house has been*
*carefully restored and the individually styled bedrooms are*
*furnished to a high standard. The restaurant has a good à la carte*
*menu of imaginative dishes based on fresh produce.*
15⇨♦2♯ CTV in all bedrooms ® T ✱ S%, sB&B⇨♦£60-£65
dB&B⇨♦£90-£130 ♯
60P ∰ ✿ ♪ (hard) croquet putting outdoor chess *xmas*
♀ English & French V ⊹ ⊡ Lunch fr£13.50&alc High tea
£1.50-£6.50alc Dinner fr£18.50&alc Last dinner 9.30pm
Credit Cards [1] [2] [3] [5]

---

**SKEABOST BRIDGE**

See Skye, Isle of

---

**SKEGNESS** Lincolnshire Map **09** TF56

★★55% *County* North Pde PE25 2UB ☎(0754)2461
*A large hotel overlooking the sea stands at the north end of the*
*town, near to such amenities as the bowling green and the sunken*
*garden. Modern bedroom accommodation is complemented by*
*more traditional public areas, and services are also traditional; the*
*restaurant offers both a reasonably priced 5-course table d'hôte*
*menu and a good à la carte selection, a range of vegetarian dishes*
*being included.*
44⇨♦(2fb) CTV in all bedrooms ®
Lift ⊿ 40P 4⊕ sauna
V ⊹ ⊡ Last dinner 9.30pm
Credit Cards [1] [3] [5]

★★53% **Vine** Vine Rd, Seacroft PE25 3DB (Exec Hotel)
☎(0754)3018 & 610611
Closed Xmas
*A few minutes walk from the sea front, the vine is an ivy-clad 17th-*
*century smuggling inn set in its own grounds in a quiet residential*
*area. The accommodation is simply furnished, with old-fashioned*
*comfortable public areas; the restaurant offers a choice of menus.*
20rm(16⇨♦)(4fb) CTV in all bedrooms T ✱ S%
sB&B⇨♦fr£35 dB&B⇨♦fr£50 ♯
100P ✿
V ⊹ ⊡ Lunch £7.50 Dinner £15 Last dinner 9pm
Credit Cards [1] [2] [3] [5] £

---

**SKELMORLIE** Strathclyde *Ayrshire* Map **10** NS16

★★★⚑63% *Manor Park* PA17 5HE
☎Wemyss Bay(0475)520832
Closed 4 Jan-2 Mar
*This delightfully situated small hotel, personally run by resident*
*proprietors, offers fine views over its beautiful, immaculate gardens*
*to the mountains beyond the Clyde. The house features attractive*
*plasterwork, the domed ceiling of the entrance foyer being*
*particularly striking; bedrooms vary in size but are generally*
*spacious and, like the public rooms, traditionally furnished.*
7rm(5⇨1♦) CTV in all bedrooms ® T ✖
150P ✿
♀ Scottish & Continental V ⊹ ⊡ Last dinner 9.30pm

---

**SKIPTON** North Yorkshire Map **07** SD95

⬆**Travelodge** Gargrave Rd BD23 1UD (A65/A59 roundabout)
(Trusthouse Forte) ☎(0756)798091 Central res (0800) 850950
*The lodge stands beside a Little Chef restaurant off the A59*
*ringroad on the north west outskirts of the town.*

▶

---

**S**

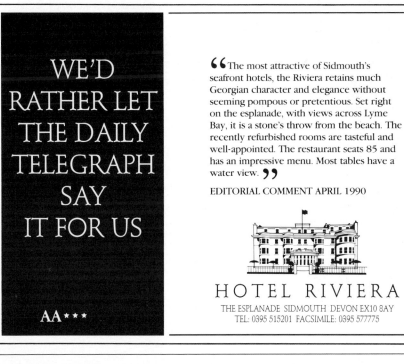
S

32⇨♥(32fb) CTV in all bedrooms ® sB⇨♥£24
dB⇨♥£29.50 (room only)
《 55P ⇨
Credit Cards ①②③

✗✗✗**Oats** Chapel Hill BD23 1NL ☎(0756)798118
FAX (0756) 792369
*Comfortable and elegant, the restaurant offers courteously*
*attentive service and an interesting menu featuring such freshly-*
*cooked dishes as seafood casserole, chicken, oyster and mushroom*
*pie and a mouthwatering range of puddings.*
Closed Mon
Lunch not served Sat
Dinner not served Sun
V 100 seats ✳ Lunch £8.95-£12.95 Dinner £16.95-£19.50 Wine
£6.75 Last lunch 1.45pm Last dinner 9.45pm 20P
Credit Cards ①②③④

---

**SKYE, ISLE OF** Highland *Inverness-shire* Map **13**

---

**ARDVASAR** Map **13** NG62

★★**69% Ardvasar** IV45 8RS ☎(04714)223
Closed 24-25 Dec & 1-3 Jan RS Nov-Mar
*Justifiably popular, the hotel enjoys an attractive setting on the*
*southern tip of the island, conveniently situated for users of the*
*Armadale/Mallaig ferry. The owners provide high standards of*
*housekeeping, hospitality and comfort, the latter making good use*
*of fresh local produce generally and seafood in particular.*
10⇨♥(3fb) CTV in 4 bedrooms ® sB&B⇨♥£25-£30
dB&B⇨♥£50-£60
CTV 30P ⇨
♥ Scottish & French V ♥
Credit Cards ③

---

**BROADFORD** Map **13** NG62

★★**54% Broadford** IV49 9AB ☎(04712)204 & 414
RS Nov-Mar
*Originally an inn, which dates back from 1611, this extended and*
*modernised hotel is situated in the centre of the village, fronted by*
*gardens. At the time of inspection, it was gradually being*
*improved. The accommodation is well equipped, compact and*
*modestly appointed.*
20⇨♥Annexe9⇨♥(3fb) CTV in all bedrooms ® T
sB&B⇨♥£25-£29 dB&B⇨♥£50-£58 ☐
100P ❖ ♪ gymnasium
V ♥ ⚲
Credit Cards ①③

---

**COLBOST** Map **13** NG24

✗**Three Chimneys** IV55 8ZT ☎Glendale(047081)258
*In a remote but beautiful corner of Skye, overlooking Loch*
*Dunvegan, a sympathetically converted crofter's cottage features a*
*beamed ceiling, exposed stone walls and candle-lit tables, these*
*cosy, atmospheric surroundings provide a perfect background to*
*the enjoyment of well-cooked food based on good local ingredients.*
*Menus are à la carte, the simpler lunchtime range offering such*
*dishes as Partan Pie or Stovies, whilst in the evening – when*
*booking is essential – you may enjoy wild Skye salmon, scallops or*
*steak ; delicious home-made bread and puddings may accompany*
*either meal.*
Closed Nov-Mar
Lunch not served Sun
Dinner not served Sun (ex BH wknds)
V 35 seats ✳ Lunch £2-£10alc Dinner £12.50-£28alc Last lunch
2pm Last dinner 9pm 30P ✂
Credit Cards ①③

---

**CULNACNOC** Map **13** NG56

❀★ **74% Glenview Inn** IV51 9JH ☎Staffin(047062)248
Closed mid Oct-Etr
(Rosette awarded for dinner only)
*This charming island inn stands in breathtaking scenery, set*
*between mountains and sea. The Harper family, who run it, offer*
*friendly and informal service, and the cooking of their daughter,*
*Linda Thomson, makes a visit to this lovely part of Skye an*
*additional treat. She uses mostly local produce as the basis for her*
*recipes, giving full scope to here imagination in the creation of a*
*menu that gives diners three choices at every course. At breakfast*
*time, home-made scones and oatcakes accompany the delicious*
*chunky marmalade.*
6rm(3♥) CTV in all bedrooms ® ✳ dB&B♥£25
15P ⇨ ❖
♥ ⚲ Dinner £17.50 Last dinner 9.30pm
Credit Cards ①

---

**DUNVEGAN** Map **13** NG24

★**66% Atholl House** IV55 8WA ☎(047022)219
FAX (047022) 481
Closed Nov
*Enjoying a fine view of Macleod's Table from its village setting,*
*this small, family-run hotel offers relaxed, friendly service, well-*
*equipped bedrooms and home-cooked meals that make use of fresh*
*produce whenever available.*
9rm(7⇨♥)(2fb) CTV in all bedrooms ® T sB&B£21-£23.50
dB&B⇨♥£48-£55 ☐
12P ⇨ xmas
V ♥ ⚲ Bar Lunch £1.50-£4.50alc Dinner £13-£15 Last
dinner 9.30pm
Credit Cards ①③

---

**HARLOSH** Map **13** NG24

★**73% Harlosh House** IV55 8ZG ☎Dunvegan(047022)367
Closed Nov-Mar
*Beautifully situated overlooking Loch Caroy and the majestic*
*Cuillin Hills beyond, this delightful and welcoming small, family-*
*run hotel is an ideal base for the touring holidaymaker seeking*
*quiet relaxation. If offers genuine hospitality, comfortable*
*accommodation, and the food, imaginatively prepared from fresh*
*local produce, ensures that dining in the attractive restaurant is a*
*pleasurable experience.*
7rm(2⇨2♥)(3fb) TV available ® ✠ (ex guide dogs) ✳
dB&B£45 dB&B⇨♥£60
10P ⇨ ❖
✂ Dinner £15-£25alc Last dinner 9pm
Credit Cards ①③

---

**ISLE ORNSAY** Map **13** NG61

★★**66% Duisdale** IV43 8QW ☎(04713)202
Closed 5 Jan-29 Mar
*This former hunting lodge is surrounded by pleasant gardens, and*
*enjoys lovely views over the Sound of Sleat, to the mountains*
*beyond. Although bedrooms are modestly furnished and equipped,*
*public areas are comfortable and relaxing, and a log fire burns in*
*the spacious lounge, on all but the warmest evenings. Enjoyable*
*home-cooked meals using fresh local ingredients are served by*
*pleasant and helpful tartan clad young staff.*
19rm(14⇨♥)(2fb)1⊞ ® sB&Bfr£21 sB&B⇨♥£26-£32.50
dB&Bfr£42 dB&B⇨♥£46.60-£67 ☐
CTV 20P ❖ croquet putting ♬ xmas
V ♥ ⚲ Lunch £7.80 High tea £7.80 Dinner £14-£15.60 Last
dinner 8.30pm
Credit Cards ①③

❋★★♨ 65% **Kinloch Lodge** IV43 8QY ☎(04713)214 & 333
FAX (04713) 277
Closed Dec-14 Mar
(Rosette awarded for dinner only)
*Lord and Lady Macdonald run this charming hotel with the accent on providing comfort, hospitality and a high standard of cooking, many of the dishes coming from Lady Macdonald's own repertoire of interesting recipes. The whole hotel gives on the feeling of a family house, a feeling that the owners and their friendly, helpful staff do their utmost to maintain.*
10rm(8⇨) ® sB&B£65-£80 sB&B⇨£65-£80 dB&B£130-£160 dB&B⇨£130-£160
CTV 18P ⊞ ✿ ♪ stalking
♙ ⚘ ⚓ Dinner £29 Last dinner 8pm
Credit Cards [1] [3]

★ 57% **Hotel Eilean Iarmain** Camuscross IV43 8QR
☎(04713)332 Telex no 75252 FAX (04713) 260
*Peacefully situated close to the water's edge, this traditional Gaelic-speaking, Highland inn enjoys fine views over the Sound of Sleat, and it offers characterful accommodation, with most bedrooms being modestly furnished, but having smart modern bathrooms. There is a cosy and comfortable resident's lounge and an attractive dining room. Service by the local staff is relaxed and informal.*
6rm(2⇨)Annexe6⇨(2fb)1 ⊞ ® T ✳ sB&B£18-£30 sB&B⇨£20-£35 dB&B£40-£60 dB&B⇨£40-£70 ▤
20P ✿ ♪ ♫ *xmas*
V ♙ ⚓ Bar Lunch £2.75-£5.90alc Dinner £13-£15&alc Last dinner 9pm
Credit Cards [1] [3] (£)

For key to symbols see the inside front cover.

---

**PORTREE** Map 13 NG44

★★★ 59% **Cuillin Hills** IV51 9LU ☎(0478)2003
FAX (0478) 3092
*The owners of this long established hotel are undertaking a programme of improvements. One thing that remains unchanged is the magnificent view across the bay to the distant mountains, from which the hotel takes its name.*
17⇨♘Annexe9⇨♘(5fb) CTV in all bedrooms ® T S%
sB&B⇨♘£28-£37 dB&B⇨♘£54-£80 ▤
《 50P ✿ snooker ♫ ⚘ *xmas*
V ♙ ⚓ S%, Lunch £6.50-£12 High tea fr£7.50 Dinner £13.50-£18&alc Last dinner 10pm
Credit Cards [1] [3] (£)

★★ 69% **Rosedale** IV51 9DB ☎(0478)3131
Closed Oct-mid May
*Dating from the early 19th-century and originally three separate buildings, this privately owned waterfront hotel has gradually expanded and developed to provide up-to-date, well-maintained accommodation. All bedrooms are comfortably furnished and freshly decorated, though some are quite compact, while a maze of corridors and stairways links public areas which include two comfortable lounges and a neat first-floor dining room overlooking the harbour of Loch Portree.*
20⇨♘Annexe3⇨♘(1fb) CTV in all bedrooms ®
sB&B⇨♘£30-£35 dB&B⇨♘£55-£66 ▤
18P ⊞
♙ Dinner £15 Last dinner 8.30pm

★★ 64% **Royal** IV51 9BU (Consort) ☎(0478)2525
FAX (0478) 3198
*This traditional tourist and business hotel in the town centre provides some accommodation in a 1970's extension.*
25⇨♘(6fb) CTV in all bedrooms ® ✳ sB&B⇨♘£35-£38 dB&B⇨♘£50-£56 ▤

▶

---

S

4P 🐾
V ✿ ♨ ✗ Lunch £4.95-£8.50 Dinner £13.50-£16&alc Last
dinner 9pm
Credit Cards 1 3

★**59**% **Isles** Somerled Square IV51 9EH ☎(0478)2129
Closed Nov-Mar
*This attractively appointed small hotel, set at the centre of the
harbour town, offers bright, comfortable bedroom accommodation
of a standard higher than its classification would lead one to
expect.*
10rm(5🌂) CTV in all bedrooms ⓇsB&B£20-£21
dB&B🌂£48-£59
CTV ⚟ ✿
Dinner £7.50-£15alc Last dinner 8.30pm

---

**SKEABOST BRIDGE** Map 13 NG44

★★★♨66% **Skeabost House** IV51 9NR ☎(047032)202
Closed 23 Oct-10 Apr
*Peacefully situated in attractive, well-kept gardens which include a
9-hole golf course, and surrounded by twelve acres of woodland,
this whitewashed former hunting lodge enjoys fine views over Loch
Snizort. The well decorated bedrooms, though for the most part
compact, offer modern amenities, service is provided by the resident
proprietors aided by a friendly young staff – and the availability of
eight miles of fishing on the River Snizort makes it a popular
choice with anglers.*
21rm(14🌂6🌂)Annexe5🌂(3fb)1🛏 CTV in all bedrooms Ⓡ T
sB&B🌂£29-£36 dB&B£48 dB&B🌂£82-£102
《 CTV 40P ✿ ⚟ 9 ♪ snooker
✿ ♨ Bar Lunch £3-£5 Dinner £18 Last dinner 8.30pm
Credit Cards 1 3

---

**TEANGUE** Map 13 NG60

★★65% **Toravaig House** IV44 8RJ ☎Isle Ornsay(04713)231
Closed Nov-Etr
*Standing in eight acres of attractive grounds beside the Broadford
to Armadale road, this small, family-owned hotel offers
individually decorated bedrooms and comfortable public areas.*
9🌂🌂 CTV in all bedrooms Ⓡ ✳ sB&B🌂🌂£35-£38
dB&B🌂🌂£50-£54 🎗
CTV 20P 🐾 ✿
✿ ♨ ✗ Dinner £14 Last dinner 8pm
Credit Cards 1 3 £

---

**UIG** Map 13 NG36

★★66% **Uig** IV51 9YE ☎(047042)205 FAX (047042) 308
Closed 8 Oct-mid Apr
*Well appointed family run hotel overlooking Uig Bay.*
11🌂🌂Annexe6🌂🌂(1fb) CTV in all bedrooms Ⓡ T ✳
sB&B🌂🌂£30-£38 dB&B🌂🌂£60-£74 🎗
20P 🐾 ✿ ∪ nc12yrs
V ✿ ♨ ✗ Bar Lunch fr£3.50 High tea fr£6 Dinner fr£15 Last
dinner 8pm
Credit Cards 1 2 3 4 5

★62% **Ferry Inn** IV51 9XP ☎(047042)242
Closed Xmas day & 1-2 Jan RS Nov-Etr
*As its name suggests, this roadside Highland inn is conveniently
situated for those using the ferries to the Outer Hebrides. It offers
accommodation at reasonable prices in bedrooms which, though
modest, are well maintained and those to the front have lovely sea
views. There is a comfortable lounge, two popular small bars and a
smartly decorated dining room.*
6🌂🌂(2fb) Ⓡ ✳ dB&B🌂🌂£32-£40
CTV 12P 🐾
V ✿ ♨ Bar Lunch £1-£4alc Dinner £8-£15.50alc Last dinner
8.30pm
Credit Cards 1 3 £

---

**SLEAFORD** Lincolnshire Map 08 TF04

★★★64% **Mallards** Eastgate NG34 7DJ (Consort)
☎(0529)303062 FAX (0509) 303459
13rm(9🌂🌂) CTV in all bedrooms Ⓡ T ✳ sB&Bfr£24
sB&B🌂🌂fr£30 dB&Bfr£34 dB&B🌂🌂fr£40 🎗
7P 🐾
♀ English & French V ✿ ♨ Lunch fr£9.50 Dinner £10-£12
Last dinner 9pm
Credit Cards 1 2 3 £

○**Travelodge** A17/A15, Holdingham(Trusthouse Forte)
☎Central reservations (0800) 850950
Due to open winter 1990
40🌂

---

**SLINFOLD** West Sussex Map 04 TQ13

★★★66% **Random Hall** Stane St RH13 7QX
☎Horsham(0403)790558 & 790852 FAX (0403) 791046
*This charming road-side hotel, originally a Tudor farmhouse, has
been skilfully modernised to provide attractively furnished, well
equipped bedrooms whilst elsewhere retaining inglenook fireplaces,
dark oak beams and flagstone floors; its atmosphere is warm and
cosy, attentive personal service being particularly well managed.*
16🌂🌂(2fb)2🛏 CTV in all bedrooms Ⓡ T S10%
sB&B🌂🌂fr£55 dB&B🌂🌂fr£75 🎗
CTV 40P 🐾 ☾ xmas
V ✿ ♨ S10% Lunch £13.25&alc High tea £4.95-£13.25 Dinner
£13.25&alc Last dinner 10pm
Credit Cards 1 2 3 £

---

**SLOUGH** Berkshire Map 04 SU97

★★★★64% **Holiday Inn Slough/Windsor** Ditton Road,
Langley SL3 8PT (Holiday Inns) ☎(0753)44244
Telex no 848646 FAX (0753) 40272
*A modern hotel conveniently located for direct access to the M4
and London. Facilities include large conference rooms, a leisure
club and an à la carte restaurant. Lounge service for drinks is
enhanced by live music in the evenings.*
302🌂🌂(102fb)✗in 26 bedrooms CTV in all bedrooms Ⓡ T
sB🌂🌂fr£99-£115 dB🌂🌂£121-£149 (room only) 🎗
Lift 《 ⊞ 385P ✿ CFA ⊠(heated) ♪ (hard) sauna solarium
gymnasium table tennis golf net jogging track ♫ ☾ xmas
♀ International V ✿ ♨ ✗ S10% Lunch £17.50 Dinner
£17&alc Last dinner 11pm
Credit Cards 1 2 3 5

---

**SMALLWAYS** North Yorkshire Map 12 NZ11

★52% **A66 Motel** DL11 7QW ☎Teesdale(0833)27334
*A small hotel on the A66 offers compact modest accommodation
and a comfortable lounge bar where an open fire burns during the
winter months.*
6rm(1🌂) CTV in all bedrooms
30P ✿
V ✿ Last dinner 10.30pm
Credit Cards 1 3 5 £

---

**SNAINTON** North Yorkshire Map 08 SE98

★★62% **Coachman Inn** YO13 9PL ☎Scarborough(0723)85231
*A small village inn with a cosy bar and unpretentious
accommodation. Good home-cooked dinners are served.*
10rm(5🌂3🌂)Annexe2🌂 CTV in 7 bedrooms Ⓡ
CTV 50P ✿
✿ Last dinner 9pm
Credit Cards 1 2 3 5

**S**

---

**SNAKE PASS** Derbyshire Map **07** SK 19

★★**61% Snake Pass Inn** S30 2BJ (on A57 Sheffield to Glossop rd) ☎Hope Valley(0433)51480
*This small inn was built in 1821 for travellers on the then newly constructed turnpike between Manchester and Sheffield, now the A57. It is about halfway between these cities, in the remote and spectacular scenery of the High Peak. The area abounds with footpaths, including the Pennine Way, and the inn is therefore popular with ramblers and walkers.*
7⇌(1fb)1🛏 CTV in all bedrooms ® ✱ S10%
sB&B⇌£19.50-£25 dB&B⇌£35-£55 🍴
40P ✿ *xmas*
V ☼ ⅊ ✸ Lunch £1.20-£10 Dinner £3-£10 Last dinner 9pm
Credit Cards ①③
**See advertisement under SHEFFIELD**

---

**SOLIHULL** West Midlands Map **07** SP17

★★★**69% Regency** Stratford Rd, Shirley B90 4EB (Crown & Raven) ☎021-745 6119 Telex no 334400 FAX 021-733 3801
*A modern hotel close to the town centre with convenient access to the M42. Accommodation is very well appointed and an extension of 54 new rooms was due to be completed by summer 1990. The hotel has two bars and an attractive restaurant and a leisure centre is at present under construction.*
112⇌🌢(10fb)✂in 59 bedrooms CTV in all bedrooms ® T ✱
sB&B⇌🌢fr£76.45 dB&B⇌🌢fr£91.30 🍴
Lift ℂ 300P ☐(heated) sauna solarium gymnasium *xmas*
☺ French V ☼ ⅊ ✸ Lunch £9.50 Dinner £13.25&alc Last dinner 10pm
Credit Cards ①②③

★★★**65% St John's Swallow** 651 Warwick Rd B91 1AT (Swallow) ☎021-711 3000 Telex no 339352 FAX 021-705 6629
*This large, modern hotel on the outskirts of the town, conveniently sited for access to the M42 motorway, offers comfortable accommodation, well appointed public areas, extensive conference facilities and its own leisure centre.*
206⇌(6fb) CTV in all bedrooms ® T ✱ S% sB&B⇌£72 dB&B⇌£86 🍴
Lift ℂ CTV 380P ✿ CFA ☐(heated) sauna solarium gymnasium *xmas*
V ☼ ⅊ S% Lunch £11 Dinner £15 Last dinner 9.45pm
Credit Cards ①②③④⑤

★★★**63% George** High St B91 3RF (Embassy) ☎021-711 2121 Telex no 334134 FAX 021-711 3374
*This modern town centre hotel is built around the original coaching inn. The executive rooms are a particulary impressive alternative to the more compact, standard rooms. The main restaurant overlooks the ancient Crown Bowling Green whilst Georges Rotisserie offers a more informal atmosphere.*
74⇌🌢(5fb)1🛏✂in 20 bedrooms CTV in all bedrooms ® T
sB⇌🌢£68-£93 dB⇌🌢£77-£104 (room only) 🍴
Lift ℂ 120P *xmas*
☺ English & French V ☼ ⅊ ✸ Lunch £11.50-£13.50&alc Dinner £16.50-£18.50 Last dinner 9.45pm
Credit Cards ①②③④⑤ⓔ

★★**67% Saracens Head** Stratford Road, Shirley B90 3AG (Porterhouse) ☎021-733 3888 FAX 021-733 2762
*A popular hotel conveniently positioned for the NEC and M42 and offering a good standard of modern accommodation. The Steak House restaurant is popular with locals and guests alike.*
34⇌🌢 CTV in all bedrooms ® T 🐾 (ex guide dogs)
ℂ 100P
☺ International V ☼
Credit Cards ①②③⑤

---

★★**57% Flemings** 141 Warwick Rd, Olton B92 7HW
☎021-706 0371 FAX 021- 06 4494
Closed 4 days Xmas
*This hotel is particularly popular with business travellers as it offers a home-from-home atmosphere. Rooms are a mixture of standards and sizes, and staff are friendly.*
84⇌🌢 CTV in all bedrooms ® T ✱ S%
sB&B⇌🌢£19-£43 dB&B⇌🌢£36-£54 🍴
ℂ CTV 85P ✿ snooker
☺ Asian & European V ☼ ⅊ S% Bar Lunch fr£2 Dinner fr£10.75 Last dinner 9.30pm
Credit Cards ①②③⑤

○**Brookes** 61 Homer Rd B91 3QD ☎021-711 4700 FAX 021- 711 2696
Due to open Sep 1990
115⇌

✕✕**Liaison French Cuisine** 761 Old Lode Ln B92 8JE ☎021-743 3993
*As we go to press we learn of a change of hands here, but have been unable to re-inspect or verify details.*
Closed Sun, Mon, 1 wk Xmas & Aug
Lunch not served
☺ French V 32 seats Dinner £19.50-£25&alc Wine £7.95 Last dinner 10pm 10P
Credit Cards ①②③⑤

---

**SOMERTON** Somerset Map **03** ST42

★★**72% The Lynch Country House** Behind Berry TA11 7PD ☎(0458)72316 FAX (0458) 74370
*This delightful, small 18th-century country house, a Grade II listed building, is set in well-kept gardens. Tastefully decorated and furnished in keeping with the character of the house it has comfortable public rooms and spacious, well-appointed bedrooms. A set price menu of carefully prepared dishes is available in the elegant dining room.*
6⇌🌢2🛏 CTV in all bedrooms T ✱ sB&B⇌🌢£35-£60 dB&B⇌🌢£55-£90 🍴
15P ⚗ ✿ hot air ballooning croquet
☺ English & Continental V ☼ ⅊ ✸ Dinner fr£17.50 Last dinner 9.30pm
Credit Cards ①②③⑤ⓔ

---

**SOURTON** Devon Map **02** SX59

★★⚘**77% Collaven Manor** EX20 4HH
☎Bridestowe(083786)217 & 522 FAX (083786) 570
*A delightful stone manor, dating back to 1485 and set in five acres of grounds, offers well-equipped bedrooms, charming public rooms and meals cooked with imagination and flair.*
9⇌🌢1🛏 CTV in all bedrooms ® T 🐾 ✱ sB&B⇌🌢fr£55 dB&B⇌🌢£85-£105 🍴
20P ⚗ ✿ croquet, clay pigeon shooting, putting nc12yrs *xmas*
☺ Mainly grills V ☼ Lunch fr£15.50 Dinner £15.50-£22 Last dinner 9.30pm
Credit Cards ①③

---

**SOUTHAMPTON** Hampshire Map **04** SU41

See **Town Plan Section**
★★★**62% Southampton Park** Cumberland Place SO9 4NY (Forestdale) ☎(0703)223467 Telex no 47439
FAX (0703) 332538
Closed 25 & 26 Dec nights
*Formerly the Royal, this hotel offers a choice of restaurants and a new leisure facility. The well-equipped bedrooms are double glazed.*

▶

**S**

72⊂⊐♙2🛏✂in 5 bedrooms CTV in all bedrooms Ⓡ T ✳
sB&B⊂⊐♙£60-£70 dB&B⊂⊐♙£75 🅿
Lift (ℓ ♪ CFA ▣(heated) sauna solarium gymnasium
massage, jet stream, jacuzzi
♟ English & French V ✿ ♨ ✂ Lunch £8.50-£12.50 Dinner
£6.50-£18.50alc Last dinner 11pm
Credit Cards ①②③⑤ Ⓔ

**★★★60% Novotel Southampton** 1 West Quay Rd SO1 0RA
(Novotel) ☎(0703)330550 Telex no 477641
FAX (0703) 222158
*This purpose built, well sound-proofed hotel was opened in April of
1990. There are functional bedrooms, and food is available all day
in the Le Grill Restaurant. The establishment is a French-concept
hotel, with French management, and there is a small leisure facility
for the use of hotel guests only. The first floor bedrooms are all
non-smoking.*
121⊂⊐✂in 21 bedrooms CTV in all bedrooms Ⓡ T
✠ (ex guide dogs) ✳ sB⊂⊐£54-£58 dB⊂⊐£54-£58 (room only) 🅿
Lift (⊞ 300P ▣(heated) sauna gymnasium *xmas*
♟ International V ✿ ♨ Lunch £10.50-£11.50&alc Dinner
£10.25-£12.50&alc Last dinner mdnt
Credit Cards ①②③⑤

**★★★57% Post House** Herbert Walker Av SO1 0HJ
(Trusthouse Forte) ☎(0703)330777 Telex no 477368
FAX (0703) 332510
*Recent refurbishment has brought all bedrooms to a comparable
standard and added the Traders Restaurant, guests now having a
choice between its buffet-style operation and the more formal à la
carte menu. A smartly dressed staff is professionally managed,
while the health and fitness centre is efficiently supervised.*
132⊂⊐♙(3fb)✂in 25 bedrooms CTV in all bedrooms Ⓡ T S%
sB⊂⊐♙£72-£89 dB⊂⊐♙£83-£94 (room only) 🅿
Lift (⊞ 250P ✿ CFA ▣(heated) sauna solarium gymnasium spa
bath *xmas*
♟ English & Continental V ✿ ♨ ✂ Lunch fr£10.80&alc
Dinner fr£15&alc Last dinner 9.45pm
Credit Cards ①②③④⑤

**★★★54% The Dolphin** High St SO9 2DS (Trusthouse Forte)
☎(0703)339955 Telex no 477735 FAX (0703) 333650
*A traditionally-styled town centre hotel with characterful public
areas and a variety of bedrooms currently undergoing much
needed refurbishment.*
73⊂⊐♙✂in 12 bedrooms CTV in all bedrooms Ⓡ ✳
sB⊂⊐♙£65-£72 dB⊂⊐♙£82-£92 (room only) 🅿
Lift (⊞ 70P CFA health & fitness facilities *xmas*
V ✿ ♨ ✂ Lunch £8.50-£9.50&alc Dinner £12.50-£14&alc Last
dinner 9.45pm
Credit Cards ①②③④⑤

**★★★50% The Polygon** Cumberland Place SO9 4DG
(Trusthouse Forte) ☎(0703)330055 Telex no 47175
FAX (0703) 332435
*This city centre commercial hotel is in process of upgrading its
bedrooms to modern standards comparable with those of its fine
conference facilities and the spacious restaurant with its choice of
table d'hôte and à la carte menus.*
119⊂⊐(1fb)✂in 14 bedrooms CTV in all bedrooms Ⓡ T S%
sB⊂⊐£75 dB⊂⊐£92 (room only) 🅿
Lift (⊞ 120P CFA *xmas*
♟ International V ✿ ♨ ✂ S% Lunch £13.95&alc High tea
£5.50 Dinner £18.30&alc Last dinner 10pm
Credit Cards ①②③④⑤

A rosette is an indication of exceptional
standards of cuisine.

**★★63% Elizabeth House** 43-44 The Avenue SO1 2SX
☎(0703)224327
*A small, family owned and run hotel with a friendly atmosphere
offers bedrooms that are furnished in a utilitarian manner but
provided with modern facilities, a smart dining room and a cellar
bar – the whole constituting good commercial accommodation.*
24rm(9⊂⊐11♙) CTV in all bedrooms Ⓡ T ✳ sB&Bfr£30
sB&B⊂⊐♙fr£40 dB&B⊂⊐♙fr£54 🅿
CTV 20P ⊞
♟ English V ✿ Lunch fr£11.75alc Dinner fr£11.75alc Last
dinner 9.15pm
Credit Cards ①②③⑤ Ⓔ

**★★57% Star** High St SO9 4ZA ☎(0703)339939
FAX (0703) 335291
Closed 24-26 Dec
*Centrally situated, with an attractive reception and small lounge
area, this friendly hotel is continually being refurbished and
upgraded. A good choice of meals is available.*
45rm(14⊂⊐21♙)✂in 7 bedrooms CTV in all bedrooms Ⓡ
sB&B£15-£30 sB&B⊂⊐♙£30-£60 dB&B⊂⊐♙£40-£70 🅿
Lift (⊞ 20P 10🚗
V ✿ Lunch £6-£12alc Dinner £10-£15alc Last dinner 9pm
Credit Cards ①②③⑤

**✕✕Browns Brasserie** Frobisher House, Nelson Gate,
Commercial Rd SO1 0GX ☎(0703)332615
*Browns is situated on the ground floor of a modern office block,
and is convenient for the Mayflower Theatre. Richard and Patricia
Brown, along with their head chef Martin Nash, create interesting
menus which are presented in a modern style. A lunchtime
blackboard menu offers dishes such as Highland Chicken, Beef
Olives and Plum and Walnut Mousse. Special theatre suppers are
available.*
Closed Sun
♟ British & French V 44 seats ✳ Lunch £11.45&alc Dinner
£12.45&alc Last lunch 2.30pm Last dinner 11pm P nc12yrs ♫
Credit Cards ①②③⑤

**✕✕Kohinoor Tandoori** 2 The Broadway, Portswood SO2 1WE
☎(0703)582770 & 584339
*The cosiness of this intimate restaurant is emphasised by the high-
backed seats that enclose the tables, and the cheerfully informal
atmosphere is enhanced by the native costumes of the staff.
Outstandingly fresh and well-flavoured food includes some
interesting Tandoori dishes.*
Closed 25 & 26 Dec
♟ Indian & Continental V 40 seats Last lunch 2pm Last dinner
11.30pm 20P ♫
Credit Cards ①②③

See advertisement on page 637

**⊞✕✕Kuti's** 70 London Rd SO1 2AJ ☎(0703)221585
*A very smart, modern North Indian restaurant comfortably
appointed and gaily decorated with Indian murals. In its warm
friendly atmosphere you can enjoy dishes superbly prepared with
spices and herbs, delicately blended to ensure excellent flavour and
served by pleasant, willing staff.*
♟ Indian 80 seats Last lunch 2.30pm Last dinner 11.45pm 20P
Credit Cards ①②③

**⊞✕Golden Palace** 17A Above Bar St SO1 0DQ ☎(0703)226636
*This large, bustling Chinese restaurant has been deservedly
popular for a number of years and maintains its high standard of
cooking. Food is fresh, skilfully prepared and seasoned to achieve
an excellent flavour, delicate and subtle in some dishes such as the
fried or steamed Dim Sum, robust in others, for example the Kung
Po Chilli Chicken. Both the set menu and the à la carte dishes offer
very good value for money, which more than compensates for any
delay in service that might be noticed when the restaurant is busy.*
♟ English & Chinese V 87 seats ✳ Lunch fr£3.60&alc Dinner
fr£9.50alc Last dinner 11.45pm ♪
Credit Cards ①②③⑤

**S**

## SOUTH BRENT Devon Map **03** SX66

★★♨74% *Glazebrook House Hotel & Restaurant* TQ10 9SE
☎(03647)3322
*Owner-managers have sympathetically restored this fine country
house to provide a quality hotel with up-to-date amenities;
restoration of the extensive landscaped gardens is also planned.
Bedrooms are individually furnished to a high standard, and
though they vary in size all are equipped with modern en suite
facilities. Good, interesting food is accompanied by a fine wine list.*
11⇨♠3🛏⊱in 1 bedroom CTV in all bedrooms ® T ✖
CTV 50P 🚗 ❀
♀ English & French ♥ ⚘ ⊱ Last dinner 9pm
Credit Cards [1] [2] [3] [4]

## SOUTHEND-ON-SEA Essex Map **05** TQ88

★★64% **Schulers Hotel & Restaurant** 161 Eastern Esplanade
SS1 2YB ☎Southend(0702)610172
Closed 24 Dec-2 Jan
*This small, well-run hotel has modern, bright and well-equipped
bedrooms, a comfortable lounge and a bar function room, but its
main attraction is the formal restaurant. Swiss chef patron
Manfred Schuler specialises in seafood and professional Haute
Cuisine and the service is well-managed by his wife, Claire.*
9rm(1⇨4♠)(1fb) CTV in all bedrooms ® T ✖ (ex guide dogs)
❋ sB&B£33-£55 sB&B⇨♠£43-£55 dB&B£40-£65
dB&B⇨♠£50-£65
14P
♀ International S10% Lunch £16-£17&alc Dinner £16-£17&alc
Last dinner 9.45pm
Credit Cards [1] [2] [3] [5]

★66% **Balmoral** 34 Valkyrie Rd, Westcliffe-on-Sea SS0 8BU
☎(0702)342947 FAX (0702) 337828
*Enjoying a good reputation, this hotel has steadily improved its
accommodation to provide comfortable, very well-equipped
bedrooms. The relaxing atmosphere is complimented by personal
service.*
22⇨♠(4fb) CTV in all bedrooms ® T sB&B⇨♠£37-£40
dB&B⇨♠£51-£57 🄿
CTV 19P 🚗 ♨
♀ English & French ♥ ⚘ Sunday Lunch £9 High tea £4&alc
Dinner £9&alc Last dinner 7.30pm
Credit Cards [1] [3]

## SOUTH GODSTONE Surrey Map **05** TQ34

✖✖✖**La Bonne Auberge** Tilburstow Hill RH9 8JY
☎(0342)892318 FAX (0342) 893435
Closed Mon & 26-30 Dec
Dinner not served Sun
♀ French **V** 75 seats S% Lunch £16.50-£21 Dinner
£22.50-£32.50&alc Last lunch 2pm Last dinner 10pm 50P ♫
Credit Cards [1] [2] [3] [5]

## SOUTH MIMMS Hertfordshire Map **04** TL20

★★★64% **Crest** Bignells Corner EN6 3NH (junc A1/A6)
(Trusthouse Forte) ☎Potters Bar(0707)43311 Telex no 299162
FAX (0707) 46728
RS Xmas
*This modern purpose-built hotel has recently received a new facia
which compliments the newly refurbished foyer and reception. It
also offers a welcoming split level bar/lounge, a modern style
restaurant, a leisure complex and business and training centres.
Bedrooms are well equipped and comfortable.*
123⇨♠(6fb)⊱in 30 bedrooms CTV in all bedrooms ® T 🄿
《150P ❀ CFA 🏊(heated) sauna solarium gymnasium outdoor
childrens play area pool tables
♀ International **V** ♥ ⚘ ⊱
Credit Cards [1] [2] [3] [4] [5]

## SOUTH MOLTON Devon Map **03** SS72

★★

❋★★♨
**WHITECHAPEL MANOR**

EX36 3EG ☎(07695)3377
FAX (07695) 3797

*One of our 'Best Newcomer'
hotels this year – see the
colour feature on page 25.*
*This delightful Elizabethan
mansion, standing above terraces of formal gardens, has
changed little in character over the centuries and its historic
importance has earned it Grade I listing, due in part to the
excellent restoration work undertaken by owners John and
Patricia Shapland. The bedrooms, some very spacious indeed,
are individually decorated and furnished to a very high
standard, There is also a comfortable sitting room of true
manorial proportions and an elegant dining room in which to
enjoy the superb dishes produced by young French chef
Thierry Lepretre-Granet and his team. Some excellent fish
dishes include a sautéed red mullet with red wine sauce and
purée of artichoke which found particular favour with our
Inspector. Exmoor game and venison, Taw salmon, naturally
reared pork, beef and lamb and a wide variety of local cheeses
all feature on the menu. The well-balanced wine list has some
good vintage clarets and burgundies. Service is efficient and
friendly throughout, and the Shaplands and their staff are
quick to put guests at their ease and ensure a relaxing and
enjoyable stay.*
10⇨♠1🛏 CTV in all bedrooms T ✖ ❋ S%
sB&B⇨♠£55-£140 dB&B⇨♠£80-£150 🄿
40P 🚗 ❀ xmas
♀ French ♥ ⚘ ⊱ S% Sunday Lunch fr£18.50 Dinner
fr£34.50 Last dinner 8.45pm
Credit Cards [1] [3]

★★♨73% **Marsh Hall** EX36 3HQ (1.25m N towards North
Molton) ☎(07695)2666
*Part of this hotel dates back to the 17th century yet the frontage is
Victorian. The bedrooms are spacious, tastefully decorated and
well equipped. Great attention is paid to the quality of dishes which
make up the table d'hôte menu, and service is friendly and warm.*
7⇨♠1🛏 CTV in all bedrooms ® T sB&B⇨♠£28-£35
dB&B⇨♠£56-£70 🄿
15P 🚗 ❀ nc12yrs xmas
♀ English & Continental **V** ♥ Bar Lunch £4-£6alc Dinner
£15.95 Last dinner 8.45pm
Credit Cards [1] [3]

## SOUTH NORMANTON Derbyshire Map **08** SK45

★★★62% **Swallow** Carter Ln East DE55 2EH (junct 28 of M1)
(Swallow) ☎Ripley(0773)812000 Telex no 377264
FAX (0733) 580032
*The hotel was extended and refurbished in January 1990 to give
guests more comfortable lounge and bar areas and new
banqueting/meeting rooms. The coffee shop and Pavilion
restaurant offer a choice of snacks and à la carte menus and the
comprehensive indoor leisure facilities are particularly popular
with families at weekends.*
123⇨♠(6fb)⊱in 61 bedrooms CTV in all bedrooms ® T ❋
sB&B⇨♠fr£72 dB&B⇨♠fr£86 🄿
《200P ❀ CFA 🏊(heated) sauna solarium gymnasium jacuzzi
steam room xmas
♀ International **V** ♥ ⚘ ⊱
Credit Cards [1] [2] [3] [4] [5]

**SOUTHPORT** Merseyside Map **07** SD31

★★★★54% **Prince of Wales** Lord St PR8 1JS (Trusthouse Forte) ☎(0704)536688 Telex no 67415 FAX (0704)543488
*This large hotel in Southport's famous Lord Street, set conveniently close to both seafront and main shopping areas, provides comfortable public rooms and a choice of restaurants.*
104⇨ⓕ(7fb)1⌗ CTV in all bedrooms ⓇT✱ sB⇨ⓕ£70-£80 dB⇨ⓕ£80-£90 (room only) 🅡
Lift ⑄95P ✿ CFA *xmas*
♈ English & French V ✿ ⚏ ⨉ S% Lunch £7.95-£10.75 Dinner £10.50-£13.50&alc Last dinner 10pm
Credit Cards ①②③⑤

★★★62% **Royal Clifton** Promenade PR8 1RB (Best Western) ☎(0704)33771 Telex no 677191 FAX (0704) 500657
*Large seaside hotel overlooking promenade and gardens.*
107⇨ⓕ(2fb)2⌗⨉in 2 bedrooms CTV in all bedrooms ⓇT✱ S% sB&B⇨ⓕ£64-£70 dB&B⇨ⓕ£75-£85 🅡
Lift ⑄40P CFA 🏊(heated) sauna solarium gymnasium sunbed jacuzzi ♫ *xmas*
♈ English & French V ✿ ⚏ S% Lunch fr£7.50 Dinner fr£12.50 Last dinner 9.45pm
Credit Cards ①②③⑤ⓔ

★★★61% **Scarisbrick** Lord St PR8 1NZ ☎(0704)43000 FAX (0704) 33335
*Situated in famous Lord Street this modernised former coaching inn still retains some of its original character with Victorian-style furnishing and décor and some four poster bedrooms.*
66⇨ⓕ(5fb)6⌗ CTV in all bedrooms Ⓡ T S10% sB&B⇨ⓕ£55-£75 dB&B⇨ⓕ£68-£105 🅡
Lift ⑄40P 12🎱 pool tables ♫ *xmas*
♈ English & French V ✿ ⚏ S10% Lunch £5.25-£7.50&alc High tea £4.50-£6.50 Dinner £11.25-£13.50&alc Last dinner 9.30pm
Credit Cards ①②③⑤ⓔ

★★68% **Balmoral Lodge** 41 Queens Rd PR9 9EX ☎(0704)544298 FAX (0704) 501224
*Friendly hotel with well equipped bedrooms. Home cooking.*
15⇨ⓕ(1fb)1⌗ CTV in all bedrooms Ⓡ T ✂
sB&B⇨ⓕ£25-£50 dB&B⇨ⓕ£50-£60 🅡
CTV 10P 🌫 sauna *xmas*
Dinner £11-£13 Last dinner 8.30pm
Credit Cards ①②③⑤ⓔ

*See advertisement on page 639*

★★64% **Bold** Lord St PR9 0BE ☎(0704)32578 FAX (0704) 32528
*A Victorian hotel at the northern end of Lord Street has been completely refurbished to give attractive bedrooms and public areas. The elegant restaurant offers many tantalising dishes from a creative menu and a competitively priced wine list complements the delicious food.*
22rm(15⇨6ⓕ)(4fb) CTV in all bedrooms Ⓡ T
✂ (ex guide dogs) ✱ sB&B⇨ⓕ£45
dB&B⇨ⓕ£50 Continental breakfast 🅡
⑄8P ♫ *xmas*
♈ English, French & Italian V ✿ ⚏ Lunch £5.80-£17.65alc High tea £2.65-£3.65 Dinner £13.40-£21.40alc Last dinner 9.45pm
Credit Cards ①②③④⑤

*See advertisement on page 639*

All AA-appointed establishments are inspected regularly to ensure that required standards are maintained.

**S**

★★61% **Stutelea Hotel & Leisure Club** Alexandra Rd PR9 0NB
☎(0704)544220 FAX (0704) 500232
*Situated within easy reach of the town centre and marine drive, its
well tended gardens creating a relaxing atmosphere, this family-
run hotel offers comfortable accommodaltion; amenities include a
leisure club with well equipped gymnasium and an indoor heated
swimming pool.*
18⇨₨(3fb)2₥ CTV in all bedrooms ® T ✹ (ex guide dogs)
✳ sB&B⇨₨£35 dB&B⇨₨£55-£57 ₧
Lift CTV 18P ⊞ ✿ ▣(heated) sauna solarium gymnasium
games room jacuzzi
V ♦ ⚷ Bar Lunch £1-£4alc Dinner £9.90-£14alc Last dinner
8pm
Credit Cards ①②③⑤ ⓔ

★★60% **Lockerbie House** 11 Trafalgar Rd, Birkdale PR8 2EA
☎(0704)65298
*Situated in a quiet residential area, convenient for Birkdale
Station and not far from the famous golf course, this small hotel is
run in a friendly and informal manner by the enthusiastic
proprietors. Bedrooms continue to be improved, most are spacious
and comfortable.*
14⇨₨(3fb) CTV in all bedrooms ® sB&B⇨₨fr£25
dB&B⇨₨fr£48 ₧
CTV 14P 2☎ ✿ snooker ⚮
V ♦ ⚷ Bar Lunch fr£2.50 Dinner fr£8.50 Last dinner 8pm
Credit Cards ①②③⑤ ⓔ

★★55% **Metropole** Portland St PR8 1LL ☎(0704)36836
*Pleasant, family-run hotel.*
25rm(9⇨9₨)(3fb) CTV in all bedrooms ® T sB&B£20-£22
sB&B⇨₨£27.50-£30 dB&B£33-£40 dB&B⇨₨£47-£53.50 ₧
CTV 12P ⊞ snooker *xmas*
⚑ English & French ♦ Lunch fr£3.75 Dinner fr£8.75 Last
dinner 8.30pm
Credit Cards ①②③

**SOUTH QUEENSFERRY** Lothian *West Lothian*
Map 11 NT17

★★★60% **Forth Bridges Moat House** Forth Bridge EH30 9SF
(Queens Moat) ☎031-331 1199 Telex no 727430
FAX 031-319 1733
*A popular business and tourist hotel, overlooking the Firth from its
convenient situation at the south side of the Forth road bridge, has
been substantially refurbished to provide comfortable modern
accommodation.*
108⇨₨(30fb)⚡in 5 bedrooms CTV in all bedrooms ® T ✳
sB⇨₨£70-£75 dB⇨₨fr£90 (room only) ₧
Lift ⚓ 200P ✿ ▣(heated) squash snooker sauna solarium
gymnasium *xmas*
⚑ English & French V ♦ ⚷ S% Lunch fr£11.95&alc Dinner
fr£13.05&alc Last dinner 9.45pm
Credit Cards ①②③⑤ ⓔ

**SOUTHSEA**
See Portsmouth & Southsea

**SOUTH SHIELDS** Tyne & Wear Map 12 NZ36

★★★58% **Sea** Sea Rd NE33 2LD ☎091-427 0999
Telex no 53533 FAX 091-454 0500
Closed 25-27 Dec
*A mainly commercial hotel on the seafront and overlooking the
harbour mouth, amusement park and other leisure facilities. At the
time of the last inspection bedrooms were still being upgraded to a
good modern standard. Service is friendly and helpful.*
33⇨₨(2fb)1₥ CTV in all bedrooms ® T ✳
sB&B⇨₨£49.80-£54.80 dB&B⇨₨£60.80-£68.80 ₧
⚓40P
⚑ English & French V ♦ ⚷ Lunch £5.60-£7&alc High tea
£2.95 Dinner £7.77&alc Last dinner 9.30pm
Credit Cards ①②③⑤ ⓔ

★★63% **New Crown** Mowbray Rd NE33 3NG ☎091-455 3472
*A large public house, built in the late 1930's, with spacious bars, an
attractive first floor restaurant and functional bedrooms. Situated
overlooking the sea and harbour mouth it is within easy reach of
Newcastle, Sunderland and other commercial centres.*
11rm(6⇨1₨)(1fb) CTV in all bedrooms ® sB&B£28-£32
sB&B⇨₨£31-£36 dB&B£47-£52 dB&B⇨₨£51-£58
50P
⚑ English & Continental V ♦ Sunday Lunch £5.95-£6.45
Dinner £7.45-£9.50&alc Last dinner 9.30pm
Credit Cards ①②③⑤ ⓔ

**SOUTH UIST, ISLE OF** Western Isles *Inverness-shire* Map 13

**LOCHBOISDALE** Map 13 NF71

★★53% **Lochboisdale** PA81 5TH ☎(08784)332
FAX (08784) 367
*This friendly fishing hotel, situated beside the harbour and ferry
terminal, is slowly being improved. The walls of the public areas,
which include a comfortable lounge, lounge bar and a refurbished
dining room, are adorned with fishing prints and local paintings.
Bedrooms are modestly furnished and equipped.*
20rm(11⇨)(1fb) ® sB&B£18.50-£27.50 sB&B⇨₨£18.50-£33
dB&B£37-£47.50 dB&B⇨₨£37-£58 ₧
CTV 50P ✿ ✎ snooker birdwatching trips ♫ ⚮
⚑ French V ♦ ⚷
Credit Cards ①③ ⓔ

**SOUTHWAITE MOTORWAY SERVICE AREA (M6)**
Cumbria Map 12 NY44

⌂**Granada Lodge** Broadfield Site CA4 0NT (on M6) (Granada)
☎Southwaite(06974)73131 FAX (06974) 73669
*Situated between junctions 41 and 42 of the M6, on the south-
bound side, the Lodge provides good-value accommodation which
is well maintained and meticulously clean.*
39⇨₨(10fb)⚡in 6 bedrooms CTV in all bedrooms ®
✹ (ex guide dogs) ✳ S% sB⇨₨fr£25
dB⇨₨fr£28 (room only)
**See advertisement under CARLISLE**

**SOUTHWELL** Nottinghamshire Map 08 SK75

★★★62% **Saracen's Head** Market Place NG25 0HE
(Trusthouse Forte) ☎(0636)812701 Telex no 377201
FAX (0636) 815408
*Timber-framed, and dating back to the reign of Charles I, this
warm, comfortable hotel retains exposed beams and wood
panelling whilst providing modern standards of comfort in its well-
furnished bedrooms, pleasant bars and good restaurant.*
27⇨₨1₥⚡in 6 bedrooms CTV in all bedrooms ® T ₧
⚓80P CFA *xmas*
V ♦ ⚷ ⚡ Lunch fr£9.95 Dinner fr£15 Last dinner 10pm
Credit Cards ①②③④⑤

**SOUTHWOLD** Suffolk Map 05 TM57

★★★65% **Swan** Market Place IP18 6EG ☎(0502)722186
Telex no 97223 FAX (0502) 724800
*Standing in the Market Place this former 17th-century inn, now
restored and totally refurbished, provides good quality,
comfortable accommodation. The restaurant offers a
predominantly English menu using fresh produce.*
27⇨₨ Annexe18⇨₨(2fb) CTV in all bedrooms T ✳
sB&B⇨₨£42-£51 dB&B⇨₨£74-£125 ₧
Lift ⚓ 50P ⊞ *xmas*
V ♦ ⚷ ⚡ Lunch £9.95-£18.75alc Dinner £14.95-£21.95alc
Last dinner 9.30pm
Credit Cards ①②③

★★ 65% **Crown Southwold** 90 High St ɪᴘ18 6ᴅᴘ ☏(0502)722275
Telex no 97223 FAX (0502) 724805
Closed 1st wk Jan
*The hotel is popular with locals and residents alike for its extensive*
*selection of fine wines – Adnams Wine Merchants' main offices*
*being on the premises – which is complemented by an interesting*
*choice of menus in both bar and restaurant.*
12rm(8⇨1ℝ)(1fb) CTV in all bedrooms ✖ (ex guide dogs)
sB&B⇨ℝ£29 dB&B⇨ℝ£46 Continental breakfast
15P 8🚗 🍽 xmas
♀ Italian ✧ ⚖ ⚓ Lunch £11.50-£13.50 Dinner £14.50-£16.50
Last dinner 9.45pm
Credit Cards ① ② ③

---

**SOUTH ZEAL** Devon Map 03 SX69

★★ 64% **Oxenham Arms** EX20 2JT
☏Okehampton(0837)840244 & 840577
*This charming village-centre inn has been a licensed house since*
*1477, the current proprietors providing friendly, relaxed service*
*here for the past eighteen years. Public areas retain such original*
*features as oak beams and open fireplaces – the residents'lounge,*
*with its comfortable sofas and good antiques, being a particularly*
*delightful venue on a winter's evening – whilst bedrooms, though*
*varying in standard, all offer good facilities.*
8rm(7⇨3ℝ) CTV in all bedrooms ® T sB&B£28-£38
sB&B⇨ℝ£38 dB&B£36 dB&B⇨ℝ£55
CTV 8P 🍽 ❉ xmas
♀ International V ✧ ⚖ Lunch £7.50-£11.50alc Dinner
£13.50-£15.50alc Last dinner 9pm
Credit Cards ① ② ③ ⑤ ⑥

---

**SOWERBY BRIDGE** West Yorkshire Map **07** SE02

★★72%, **The Hobbit** Hob Ln, Norlands HX6 3QL
☎Halifax(0422)832202 FAX (0422) 835381
*Set on a hillside overlooking the town is this charming, well-furnished country inn. It offers delightful bedrooms, a good standard of cooking and friendly service.*
17⇄ Annexe5⇄ (2fb)1 ⌨ CTV in all bedrooms ® T ✖
sB&B⇄£25-£48 dB&B⇄£38-£66 ⋿
100P ♫ *xmas*
♡ English, French & Italian V Lunch £7.50 Dinner
£9.95-£12.95 Last dinner 10.30pm
Credit Cards ①②③⑤

**SPALDING** Lincolnshire Map **08** TF22

★★69%, **Woodlands** 80 Pinchbeck Rd PE11 1QF
☎(0775)769933 FAX (0775) 711369
*A tastefully converted Edwardian house standing just north of the town centre has more recently been extended to offer a new wing of bedrooms, a larger restaurant and upgraded public areas. Young, very friendly staff do their best to ensure that your stay here is an enjoyable one.*
18⇄(1fb)✖in 2 bedrooms CTV in all bedrooms ® T ✱
sB&B⇄£25-£45 dB&B⇄£35-£58 ⋿
CTV 60P ✿ ⚬
♡ English & French V ♥ ⚏ ✖ Lunch £17-£23alc Dinner
£17-£23alc Last dinner 10pm
Credit Cards ①②③⑤ⓔ

**SPEAN BRIDGE** Highland *Inverness-shire* Map **14** NN28

See also **Letterfinlay** and **Roy Bridge**
★★57%, **Spean Bridge** PH34 4ES ☎(039781)250
*A family run roadside hotel with a modern, purpose-built annexe, ten modern chalets and a choice of original hotel bedrooms all furnished in the modern style.*
22⇄ Annexe10⇄(4fb) CTV in 22 bedrooms ®
sB&B£21-£31 sB&B⇄£23-£33 dB&B£45-£60
dB&B⇄£49-£64 ⋿
CTV 50P ♪ 9 ♪ snooker games room
V ♥ ⚏ Bar Lunch £1-£9 Dinner £14-£16 Last dinner 9pm
Credit Cards ①③⑤

**STADDLE BRIDGE** North Yorkshire Map **08** SE49

✕✕McCoys (Tontine Inn) DL6 3JB ☎East Harsley(060982)671
*A 1920's atmosphere will greet diners arriving at this unusual restaurant – large plants, enormous, comfortable old-fashioned sofas and armchairs and music from the '20's combine to create a realistic atmosphere. The dining room has large parasols and intimate lighting. The main feature of this restaurant, and rightly so, is the carefully prepared menu which offers individual cooking throughout. The excellent food is complemented by an extensive wine list.*
Closed Sun, 25-26 Dec & 1 Jan
Lunch not served
♡ International V 60 seats ✱ Lunch £7-£15alc Dinner
£10-£40alc Last lunch 2pm Last dinner 11pm 80P
Credit Cards ①②③⑤

All hotels are now given a percentage grading
for the quality of their facilities. A full explanation
can be found within 'How we Classify Hotels
and Restaurants' at the front of the book.

**STAFFORD** Staffordshire Map **07** SJ92

★★★64%, **Tillington Hall** Eccleshall Rd ST16 1JJ (De Vere)
☎(0785)53531 Telex no 36566 FAX (0785) 59223
RS Xmas & New Year
*This smart business-style hotel is reached via junction 14 of the M6. The staff are friendly and helpful, and the restaurant has an à la carte menu or a fixed-price meal which changes daily.*
90⇄(3fb)1 ⌨ CTV in all bedrooms ® T sB&B⇄£50-£77
dB&B⇄£75-£90 ⋿
Lift ℄ 150P CFA ▱(heated) ℘ (hard) snooker gymnasium
table tennis jacuzzi ♫ *xmas*
♡ English & French V ♥ ⚏ ✖ Lunch £9&alc Dinner
fr£10&alc Last dinner 9.45pm
Credit Cards ①②③⑤

★★65%, **Garth** Wolverhampton Rd, Moss Pit ST17 9JR (Crown & Raven) ☎(0785)56124 Telex no 36479 FAX (0785) 55152
RS 25-26 Dec
*Situated just off junction 13 of the M6 and very busy with commercial trade, the hotel provides well equipped accommodation and a restaurant where the set menu is augmented by a more extensive à la carte selection.*
60⇄(2fb)✖in 20 bedrooms CTV in all bedrooms ® T
sB&B⇄fr£52.25 dB&B⇄fr£69.30 ⋿
⟨ 175P ✿
♡ English & French V ♥ ⚏ Lunch £6.95&alc Dinner
£10.55&alc Last dinner 10pm
Credit Cards ①②③

★★63%, **Swan** Greengate St ST16 2JA (Berni/Chef & Brewer)
☎(0785)58142
*This popular hotel in the centre of town is 400 years old and retains many of its original features. The well-equipped bedrooms have 'Laura Ashley' designs with complimentary furnishings.*
32⇄(5fb)2⌨ CTV in all bedrooms ® T ✖ (ex guide dogs)
sB&B⇄£43-£47 dB&B⇄£61 ⋿
⟨ 50P CFA
V ♥ ✖ Lunch £8-£15alc Dinner £8-£15alc Last dinner 10pm
Credit Cards ①②③⑤

★★62%, **Vine** Salter St ST16 2JU (Crown & Raven)
☎(0785)51071 & 44112 Telex no 36479 FAX (0785) 46612
*A busy, town-centre inn which is reputedly the oldest licensed house in Staffordshire serves mainly grill-type meals and boasts a very popular bar.*
27⇄(1fb) CTV in all bedrooms ® T ✱ sB&B⇄fr£43.45
dB&B⇄fr£60.50 ⋿
30P
♡ English & French V ♥ ⚏
Credit Cards ①②③

★★57%, **Abbey** 65-68 Lichfield Rd ST17 4LW ☎(0785)58531
Closed 23 Dec-7 Jan
*This busy commercial hotel on the edge of town has a rear car park. At weekends the restaurant offers a restricted service, bar snacks only are available but these can be served in the dining room.*
21rm(1⇄6♪)(1fb) CTV in all bedrooms ® ✖ ✱
sB&Bfr£18.50 sB&B⇄fr£27.50 dB&Bfr£32
dB&B⇄fr£40 ⋿
CTV 21P 5▱ (£3 per night) ⚐
♡ English & French V ♥ Bar Lunch £2-£4alc Dinner
£5.50-£8&alc Last dinner 8.30pm
Credit Cards ①③

★★55%, **Albridge** 73 Wolverhampton Rd ST17 4AW
☎(0785)54100
Closed Xmas Day RS 26-31Dec
*A games room with pool table is a popular feature of a commercial hotel set beside a busy road leading into the town centre.*

11rm(1⊸8♠)Annexe8rm(2fb) CTV in 12 bedrooms ® T ✳
sB&B£15.50-£21.95 sB&B⊸♠£24.15-£28.55 dB&B£31.95
dB&B⊸♠£38.45 ⊟
CTV 20P
V ⊕ ⬚ ✖ Lunch £6.30-£9.80 Dinner £6.30-£9.80 Last dinner
9.45pm
Credit Cards ①②③⑤

---

**STAINES** Surrey Map **04** TQ07

★★★57% **The Thames Lodge** Thames St TW18 4SF
(Trusthouse Forte) ☎(0784)464433 Telex no 8812552
FAX (0784) 454858
*A riverside setting and good car parking make this a popular venue
for business and social occasions. All bedrooms are well furnished
and equipped, and the ten superior Club Rooms overlook the river.
Facilities include an attractive restaurant, bar, riverside terrace
and good functions rooms.*
44⊸(2fb)✖in 6 bedrooms CTV in all bedrooms ® T S%
sB⊸£80-£88 dB⊸£95-£103 (room only) ⊟
《 32P *xmas*
V ⊕ ⬚ ✖
Credit Cards ①②③④⑤

See 'How we Classify Hotels and Restaurants'
at the front of the book for an explanation
of the AA's appointment and
award scheme.

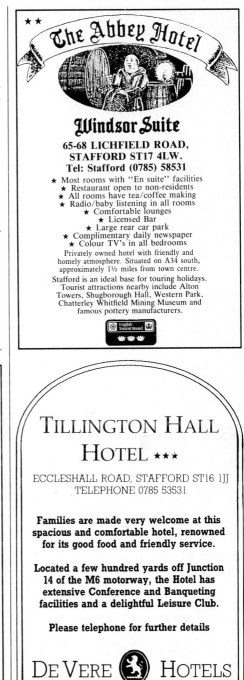

# The Abbey Hotel

## Windsor Suite

### 65-68 LICHFIELD ROAD, STAFFORD ST17 4LW.
### Tel: Stafford (0785) 58531

★ Most rooms with "En suite" facilities
★ Restaurant open to non-residents
★ All rooms have tea/coffee making
★ Radio/baby listening in all rooms
★ Comfortable lounges
★ Licensed Bar
★ Large rear car park
★ Complimentary daily newspaper
★ Colour TV's in all bedrooms
Privately owned hotel with friendly and
homely atmosphere. Situated on A34 south,
approximately 1½ miles from town centre.
Stafford is an ideal base for touring holidays.
Tourist attractions nearby include Alton
Towers, Shugborough Hall, Western Park,
Chatterley Whitfield Mining Museum and
famous pottery manufacturers.

English Tourist Board

# Albridge Hotel

**Wolverhampton Road, Stafford ST17 4AW**
**Telephone Stafford (0785) 54100**

Situated 2¾ miles off the M6, Motorway, Junction 13. (Stafford
South) ½ mile from Town Centre.
A Fine Comfortable Hotel, under owner's supervision ensuring a
good personal service.
★ 19 bedrooms with tea/coffee facilities Radio/Room call H&C.
★ 11 bedrooms en-suite incl. Family rooms.
★ 11 bedrooms with colour TV.
★ Annexe Bedrooms 30yds apart from main hotel. Reduced rates.
★ Classical Bar/Lounge. Sitting Room. Intimate restaurant.

English Tourist Board

# TILLINGTON HALL
# HOTEL ★★★

ECCLESHALL ROAD, STAFFORD ST16 1JJ
TELEPHONE 0785 53531

**Families are made very welcome at this
spacious and comfortable hotel, renowned
for its good food and friendly service.**

**Located a few hundred yards off Junction
14 of the M6 motorway, the Hotel has
extensive Conference and Banqueting
facilities and a delightful Leisure Club.**

**Please telephone for further details**

DE VERE 🦁 HOTELS

**S**

### STAMFORD Lincolnshire Map 04 TF00

★★★ 72% **George of Stamford** St Martins PE9 2LB
☎(0780)55171 Telex no 32578 FAX (0780) 57070
*Originally a 16th-century inn, this beautiful hotel combines historic
charm and atmosphere with the provision of comfort and good
service. Public areas include the lounge with its open log fire, a
garden lounge featuring exotic plants and trees, and an oak-
panelled restaurant where interesting food and good wine are
served; comfortable bedrooms are well furnished, and demand for
them has been increased by the provision of a modern business
centre. The delightful courtyard is particularly popular in summer,
as diners enjoy substantial meals from the Garden Lounge menu.*
47⇨🌂(2fb)4🚻 CTV in all bedrooms T ✱
sB&B⇨🌂£69.50-£85 dB&B⇨🌂£90-£140 🎴
《 120P ✿ CFA croquet *xmas*
♀ English, French & Italian V ♥ ⚄ ✗ Lunch £19-£28alc
Dinner £19-£28alc Last dinner 10.30pm
Credit Cards ①②③⑤

★★★ 69% **Garden House** St Martin's PE9 2LP ☎(0780)63359
Telex no 329230 FAX (0780) 63339
*Set on the town centre's main thoroughfare, south of the river, this
aptly-named hotel has particularly attractive gardens and a
delightful conservatory brimming with plants. Home-produced
dishes of good quality are served in an elegant dining room, the
cosy bar boasts an open log-fire, and bedrooms – though more
modest – are clean. Its outstanding feature is the standard of
hospitality which, together with professional service, creates the
atmosphere more usually associated with a country house.*
20⇨🌂(1fb)1🚻 CTV in all bedrooms ® T sB&B⇨🌂fr£59.75
dB&B⇨🌂fr£75 🎴
25P 5✿ ✿ ⚇
♀ English & French V ♥ ⚄ Lunch fr£15 Dinner fr£15 Last
dinner 9.30pm
Credit Cards ①②③⑤

★★ 62% **Lady Anne's** 37-38 High Street, St Martins PE9 2LJ
☎(0780)53175 Telex no 32376
Closed 27-30 Dec
*Personally supervised by the proprietors, and a popular venue for
weddings and conferences, the hotel is set in its own pleasant
grounds on the B1081 south of the town, easily accessible from the
A1.*
28rm(17⇨9🌂)(6fb)2🚻 CTV in all bedrooms ® T ✱
sB&B⇨🌂£35-£39.50 dB&B⇨🌂£50-£75 🎴
CTV 150P ✿ ♬ (hard) *xmas*
V ♥ ⚄ Lunch £9.50 High tea £1.30-£3.25 Dinner £9.50-£12.50
Last dinner 9.30pm
Credit Cards ①②③④⑤

★★ 51% **Crown** All Saints Place PE9 2AG ☎(0780)63136
Closed 25 Dec
*An old two-storey, stone-built hotel in the town centre.*
18rm(5⇨10🌂)(2fb)1🚻 CTV in all bedrooms ® T ✱ sB&B£35
sB&B⇨🌂£40 dB&B£45 dB&B⇨🌂£50
40P
♀ European V ♥ ⚄ Lunch £7.50-£12 High tea £5.50-£7.50
Dinner £11-£18alc Last dinner 9.30pm
Credit Cards ①②③⑤

### STANDISH Greater Manchester Map 07 SD51

★★★ 69% **Kilhey Court Hotel** Chorley Rd WN1 2XN (on A5106
1.5m N of A49/A5106 junct) (Best Western) ☎(0257)472100
Telex no 67460 FAX (0257) 422401
*Situated in 10 acres of grounds and gardens with a lake, this
extended Victorian mansion provides comfortable accommodation
and excellent cuisine. Conference facilities are available and a new
wing accommodates more bedrooms and a leisure complex.*
54⇨🌂(4fb)1🚻✗in 10 bedrooms CTV in all bedrooms ® T ✱
sB&B⇨🌂£38-£93 dB&B⇨🌂£48-£105 🎴

Lift 《 CTV 180P ✿ 🖃 ⌇ ♪ sauna solarium gymnasium steam
room spa bath ⚇
V ♥ ⚄ Lunch £9-£10&alc Dinner £15-£20&alc Last dinner
10pm
Credit Cards ①②③⑤ £

### STANLEY Tayside Map 11 NO13

★★ 57% **The Tayside** Mill St PH1 4NL (6m N of Perth)
☎(0738)828749 FAX (0738) 33449
*An Edwardian building has been converted and extended to
provide a quiet village hotel which is a popular base for fishing,
shooting and golfing traditions, combining traditional comforts
with practical accommodation.*
17rm(2⇨10🌂)(2fb) CTV in all bedrooms ® sB&B£17-£22.50
sB&B⇨🌂£24.50-£29.50 dB&B£34-£49 dB&B⇨🌂£39-£49 🎴
▦ 50P *xmas*
V ♥ ⚄ Lunch fr£2.90 High tea fr£5.25 Dinner fr£12.50 Last
dinner 8.30pm
Credit Cards ③ £

### STANSTED AIRPORT Essex Map 05 TL52

○ **Harlequin Hotel Stansted** Round Coppice Rd CM24 8SE
☎(0279)680800
Due to have opened Jul 1990
249⇨🌂

### STAVERTON Devon Map 03 SX76

★ 69% **Sea Trout Inn** TQ9 6PA ☎(080426)274
*A comfortable village inn in a peaceful situation offering attentive
service from the resident owners.*
10⇨🌂(2fb)1🚻 CTV in all bedrooms ® T sB&B⇨🌂£35-£45
dB&B⇨🌂£44-£52 🎴
70P 🚐
♀ English & French V ♥ Sunday Lunch £6.95-£7.50 Dinner
£12-£13&alc Last dinner 9.45pm
Credit Cards ①③

### STAVERTON Northamptonshire Map 04 SP56

★★★ 72% **Staverton Park Hotel & Golfing Complex** NN11 6JT
☎Staverton(0327)705911 FAX (0327) 300821
*This modern complex overlooks the well established golf course
and attractive parkland. Bedrooms are spacious and very well
equipped, and the public areas are extensive and comfortable.
There are excellent conference facilites, and a good choice of food
is available.*
50⇨🌂✗in 4 bedrooms CTV in all bedrooms ® T
🐾 (ex guide dogs) sB&B⇨🌂£71.50-£88
dB&B⇨🌂£93.50-£110 🎴
《 250P ▶ 18 snooker sauna solarium Trimnasium ♬ *xmas*
♀ International V ♥ ⚄ Lunch £8 Dinner £12.95 Last dinner
9.30pm
Credit Cards ①②③⑤
**See advertisement under NORTHAMPTON**

### STEEPLE ASTON Oxfordshire Map 04 SP42

★★★ 61% **Hopcrofts Holt** OX5 3QQ ☎(0869)40259
FAX (0869) 40865
*This Cotswold-stone coaching inn has been extended into a popular
commercial and conference style hotel whilst retaining some of the
characteristics of its fifteenth century origins. All bedrooms are
well equipped and furnished, some having small courtyard
balconies, and a recent change of ownership has resulted both in
improvements to facilities and services and in the construction of a
new accommodation complex. Multi-purpose conference rooms,
like the busy restaurant and bars, make the hotel most suitable for
the businessman, though its proximity to major motorway links
also makes it popular with some tourists.*

**S**

88rm(71⇨15♠)(2fb) CTV in all bedrooms ® T S%
sB&B⇨♠£58-£65 dB&B⇨♠£76-£85 ₽
《 CTV 200P ✿ games room *xmas*
♀ English & French V ✿ ⚗ S% Lunch £11&alc Dinner
£14&alc Last dinner 9.30pm
Credit Cards ①②③⑤

STEPPS Strathclyde *Lanarkshire* Map 11 NS66

★★63% **Garfield House** Cumbernauld Rd G33 6HW
☎041-779 2111
*An extended and modernised Victorian house where the majority
of bedrooms have been upgraded to provide modern facilities for
the businessman. The restaurant offers a choice of menus.
Extensive car parking facilities.*
27⇨♠(2fb) CTV in all bedrooms ®
《 80P
V ✿ ⚗ Last dinner 9.30pm
Credit Cards ①②③⑤

STEVENAGE Hertfordshire Map 04 TL22

★★★60% **Hertford Park** Danestrete SG1 1EJ (Queens Moat)
☎(0438)350661 Telex no 825697 FAX (0438) 741880
*Situated in the heart of the town centre, this large, modern hotel
offers functional, well-equipped accommodation. There is a
pleasant restaurant on the first floor, and an open plan-style bar.*
100⇨♠✂in 24 bedrooms CTV in all bedrooms ® T ✳
sB&B⇨♠£30-£62 dB&B⇨♠£42-£72 ₽
Lift 《 ✔
♀ International V ✿ ⚗ Lunch fr£10.75 Dinner fr£10.75 Last
dinner 9.45pm
Credit Cards ①②③④⑤

★★★58% **Novotel Stevenage** Knebworth Park SG1 2AX
(Novotel) ☎(0438)742299 Telex no 826132
FAX (0438) 723872
101⇨(101fb) CTV in all bedrooms ® T
Lift 《 120P ✿ ⚐(heated)
♀ International V ✿ ⚗ ✂ Last dinner mdnt
Credit Cards ①②③⑤

★★★56% **Stevenage Moat House** High St, Old Town SG1 3AZ
(Queens Moat) ☎(0438)359111 FAX (0438) 742169
*A popular hotel of historic interest with a beamed restaurant and
cosy bar lounge. Bedrooms are equipped with most modern
conveniences though rooms do vary in size.*
60⇨♠(4fb)✂in 11 bedrooms CTV in all bedrooms ® T ✳
sB&B⇨♠£57.75-£62.75 dB&B⇨♠£70 ₽
《 100P ✿
♀ English & French V ✿ ⚗ Lunch £9.50-£11.35&alc Dinner
£9.50-£11.35&alc Last dinner 9.45pm
Credit Cards ①②③④⑤

★★★55% **Blakemore Thistle** Little Wymondley SG4 7JJ
(Mount Charlotte (TS)) ☎(0438)355821 Telex no 825479
FAX (0438) 742114
(For full entry see Hitchin)

★★★54% **The Roebuck** Old London Rd, Broadwater SG2 8DS
(Trusthouse Forte) ☎(0438)365444 Telex no 825505
FAX (0438) 741308
*Charming 15th century inn with modern bedrooms.*
54⇨✂in 6 bedrooms CTV in all bedrooms ®
《 80P ✿ CFA
♀ English & French V ✿ ⚗ ✂ Last dinner 9.45pm
Credit Cards ①②③④⑤

*A rosette is an indication of exceptional
standards of cuisine.*

STEWARTON Strathclyde *Ayrshire* Map 10 NS44

★★★⚑75% **Chapeltoun House** KA3 3ED ☎(0560)82696
FAX (0560) 85100
*This charming mansion, set in 20 acres of grounds and gardens in
delightful countryside, offers style and seclusion combined with
character and comfort. Public rooms with their wood panelling,
ornate plasterwork and elaborate stone work are tastefully
decorated and furnished whilst the bedrooms vary in size, are
individually decorated and equipped with many thoughtful extras.
The menus feature traditional dishes using local produce and the
food is complemented by an extensive wine list.*
8⇨♠1🛏 CTV in all bedrooms T sB&B⇨♠£69-£79
dB&B⇨♠£99-£124 ₽
50P 🚗 nc12yrs
♀ French V ✿ ⚗ ✂ Lunch fr£15 Dinner fr£25.50 Last dinner
9pm
Credit Cards ①②③Ⓔ

STILTON Cambridgeshire Map 04 TL18

★★★64% **Bell Inn** Great North Rd PE7 3RA
☎Peterborough(0733)241066 FAX (0733) 245173
*This historic coaching inn has been tastefully extended to provide
modern accommodation round the old courtyard. The elegant
vaulted restaurant is a popular eating place with locals, much
appreciated for its traditional English food. In the 18th century, of
course, the Bell was the inn that was famous for serving the blue-
veined cheese that eventually took its name from the village of
Stilton although it was not made here.*
19⇨♠(1fb)2🛏✂in 4 bedrooms CTV in all bedrooms ® T
✖ (ex guide dogs) ✳ sB&B⇨♠£55-£65 dB&B⇨♠£70-£90 ₽
《 30P 🚗
♀ English & French V ✿ ⚗ ✂ Lunch £12.50&alc Dinner
£15-£30alc Last dinner 9.30pm
Credit Cards ①②③

**S**

**STIRLING** Central *Stirlingshire* Map **11** NS79

See also **Bridge of Allan**

★★**59% Terraces** 4 Melville Ter FK8 2ND (Consort)
☎(0786)72268 Telex no 778025 FAX (0786) 50314
*This small Georgian house, situated in a tree-lined terrace convenient for the town centre, has been converted to provide compact, well-equipped accommodation ; bedrooms are being refurbished, and the atmosphere is friendly.*
15⇌🛏(2fb) CTV in all bedrooms ⑧ T ✳ sB&B⇌🛏fr£45
dB&B⇌🛏fr£57.50 🍴
《 25P *xmas*
🍴 International V ✿ ⊬ Lunch fr£2.95 Dinner fr£10.95&alc
Last dinner 9pm
Credit Cards ①②③⑤ ⑥

★★**58% King Robert** Glasgow Rd, Bannockburn FK7 OLT
☎Bannockburn(0786)811666
*Standing beside the famous Bannockburn battlefield, this modern, privately-owned hotel combines practical commercial standards with modest, yet well-equipped bedrooms.*
24rm(21⇌)(1fb) CTV in 21 bedrooms ⑧ ✖
CTV 100P ✿
V ✿ ⊋
Credit Cards ①②③⑤

⌂**Granada Lodge** Pirnhall Roundabout, Snabhead FK7 8EU
(junct M9/M80) (Granada) ☎(0786)815033
FAX (0786) 815900
*Meals can be obtained from the adjacent Country Kitchen restaurant.*
37⇌(10fb)⊬in 5 bedrooms CTV in all bedrooms ⑧
✖ (ex guide dogs) ✳ S% sB⇌fr£25 dB⇌fr£28 (room only)
Dinner fr£6

**STOCKBRIDGE** Hampshire Map **04** SU33

★★★**61% Grosvenor** High St SO20 6EU (Lansbury)
☎Andover(0264)810606 Telex no 477677
*Set at the heart of an attractive old market village in the Test Valley, the hotel is home to the Houghton Fishing Club. Bedrooms are particularly well equipped, and the standard of cuisine is high, under the close personal supervision of the resident manager.*
25⇌🛏⊬in 5 bedrooms CTV in all bedrooms ⑧ T
✖ (ex guide dogs) sB&B⇌🛏fr£65 dB&B⇌🛏fr£78
《 60P 🚗 ✿ sauna
🍴 Continental V ✿ ⊋ Lunch fr£11&alc Dinner fr£11&alc
Last dinner 10.30pm
Credit Cards ①②③⑤

**STOCKPORT** Greater Manchester Map **07** SJ88

★★★**62% Alma Lodge** 149 Buxton Rd SK2 6EL (Embassy)
☎061-483 4431 Telex no 665026 FAX 061-483 1983
RS Xmas
*Set on the A6 Buxton road, one and a half miles from both the town centre and junction 12 of the M63 motorway, a converted Victorian hotel with modern extensions provides sound accommodation in well-appointed rooms.*
58rm(52⇌)(2fb)⊬in 4 bedrooms CTV in all bedrooms ⑧ T
sBfr£29.50 sB⇌£59.50-£69.50 dB⇌£69.50-£72 (room only) 🍴
《 200P CFA ♫
🍴 English & French V ✿ ⊋ Lunch £11.50&alc Dinner
£11.50&alc Last dinner 9.30pm
Credit Cards ①②③④⑤

★★★**62% Bramhall Moat House** Bramhall Ln South SK7 2EB
(Queens Moat) ☎061-439 8116 Telex no 668464
FAX 061-440 8071
(For full entry see Bramhall)

★★**72% Red Lion Inn** 112 Buxton Rd, High Ln SK6 8ED
☎Disley(0663)65227 FAX (0663) 62170
*This mellow stone hotel, standing beside the busy A6 some six miles south east of Stockport, offers quality bedrooms and a very popular all-day brasserie restaurant which specialises in fresh fish dishes.*
6⇌🛏(1fb) CTV in all bedrooms ⑧ T ✖ (ex guide dogs) ✳
sB&B⇌🛏£20-£39.50 dB&B⇌🛏£40-£55
100P 🚗
V ✿ ⊋ ⊬ Lunch fr£5.50&alc
Credit Cards ①②③⑤ ⑥

★★**64% Rudyard Toby** 271 Wellington Rd North, Heaton
Chapel SK4 5BP (1.5m N off A6) (Toby) ☎061-432 2753
Telex no 668594
*An attractive Victorian building with modern bedrooms and comfortable bars reached by a flower-decked, colonial-style veranda.*
21⇌🛏(2fb)⊬in 8 bedrooms CTV in all bedrooms ⑧
《 82P Golf
V ✿ ⊋ ⊬ Last dinner 10pm
Credit Cards ①②③④⑤

★★**59% Wycliffe Villa** 74 Edgeley Rd, Edgeley SK3 9NQ
☎061-477 5395
RS Sun & BH's
*A friendly atmosphere prevails at this small family-run hotel located three miles from the town centre. Bedrooms are generally compact and modestly furnished but have excellent beds and are kept very clean. Italian food is a speciality.*
12⇌🛏 CTV in all bedrooms ⑧ ✖ ✳ sB&B⇌🛏£35-£40
dB&B⇌🛏£42-£47
CTV 20P 🚗 nc5yrs
🍴 English, French & Italian V Lunch fr£5.50&alc Dinner
fr£12alc Last dinner 9.30pm
Credit Cards ①②③⑤ ⑥

★**58% Acton Court** Buxton Rd SK2 7AB ☎061-483 6172
FAX 061-483 0147
Closed Boxing Day, New Year & Bank Hols
*A gabled and extended building on the A6 about 2 miles south east of the town centre. Recent improvements have considerably enhanced the well-equipped bedrooms and attractive restaurant provides a good standard of cooking.*
37rm(13⇌15🛏) CTV in all bedrooms ⑧ T ✳ sB&B£24-£32
sB&B⇌🛏£31-£42 dB&B£34-£45 dB&B⇌🛏£42-£55 🍴
《 CTV 200P 🚗 ✿ ♫
🍴 French V Lunch £5.95 Dinner £9.50&alc Last dinner 10pm
Credit Cards ①②③⑤

**STOCKTON-ON-TEES** Cleveland Map **08** NZ41

★★★★**55% Swallow** 10 John Walker Square TS18 1QZ
(Swallow) ☎(0642)679721 Telex no 587895
FAX (0642) 601714
*An attractive leisure centre is now available in the basement of this modern town centre hotel which caters well for the business guest. A convenient, undercover free public car park is situated behind the hotel.*
124⇌🛏⊬in 25 bedrooms CTV in all bedrooms ⑧ T S10%
sB&B⇌🛏fr£68 dB&B⇌🛏fr£86 🍴
Lift 《 400P CFA ▨(heated) sauna solarium gymnasium
jacuzzi steam room *xmas*
🍴 English & French V ✿ ⊋ Lunch £10.50-£14.25 Dinner
£14.75-£18.50&alc Last dinner 10pm
Credit Cards ①②③④⑤

★★★**67% Parkmore** 636 Yarm Rd, Eaglescliffe TS16 0DH (3m
S A19) (Best Western) ☎(0642)786815 Telex no 58298
FAX (0642) 790485
*This comfortable, well-run hotel, in an easily accessible position on the A167 and conveniently close to all the North East's commercial centres, provides well-equipped bedrooms, comfortable*

*public areas and an excellent leisure centre. Competently prepared*
*meals are served by a friendly efficient staff.*
55⇨3♠(3fb)4⊟½in 4 bedrooms CTV in all bedrooms ® T
sB&B⇨3♠£46-£54 dB&B⇨3♠£60-£72 ⊟
《 CTV 140P ❖ ⊟(heated) snooker sauna solarium gymnasium
jacuzzi steam room beauty salon
♡ English & French V ✿ ⚌ ½ Lunch fr£9.75 High tea
£5.50-£6.50 Dinner £13.50-£15&alc Last dinner 9.30pm
Credit Cards ①②③⑤④

★★★ 61%**Post House** Low Ln, Thornaby-on-Tees TS17 9LW
(Trusthouse Forte) ☎Middlesbrough(0642)591213
Telex no 58426 FAX (0642) 594989
*Situated one mile east on the A1044 this is a busy hotel with*
*friendly staff, an à la carte restaurant and a coffee shop.*
135⇨3♠(12fb)½in 40 bedrooms CTV in all bedrooms ® T
sB⇨3♠£67 dB⇨3♠£78 (room only) ⊟
《 250P ❖ CFA sauna solarium
V ✿ ⚌ ½ S% Lunch £8.50-£9.75 High tea £9 Dinner £16 Last
dinner 10.15pm
Credit Cards ①②③④⑤

★★★ 52%**Billingham Arms** The Causeway, Billingham
TS23 2HD (3m NE A19) ☎(0642)553661 Telex no 587746
FAX (0642) 552104
*Centrally situated, this hotel caters for a mainly business clientele*
*and has extensive function facilities. Well-equipped bedrooms vary*
*in size and style. A wide range of bars includes a cocktail bar*
*adjoining Bertie's Restaurant. The less formal 'Langtry's' offers*
*light meals.*
69⇨3♠(3fb)2⊟½in 4 bedrooms CTV in all bedrooms ® T ✲
sB⇨3♠£19-£43 dB⇨3♠£38-£54 (room only) ⊟
Lift 《 ⊞ CTV 150P 2🏂 CFA solarium pool table *xmas*
♡ International V ✿ ⚌ Lunch fr£6.95 Dinner fr£9.95 Last
dinner 11pm
Credit Cards ①②③④⑤④

**See advertisement under BILLINGHAM**

★ 66%*Stonyroyd* 187 Oxbridge Ln TS18 4JB ☎(0642)607734
*In a quiet residential area about two miles from the centre of*
*Stockton, this small hotel is owned and run by Mrs Dunne, who not*
*only gives her personal attention to her guests, but also cooks the*
*evening meals. Bedrooms are, on the whole, compact, but well*
*equipped.*
13rm(8♠)(1fb) CTV in all bedrooms ® ✖
CTV 6P 🎮 solarium
♡ International V Last dinner 8pm
Credit Cards ①③

★ 50%**Claireville** 519 Yarm Rd, Eaglescliffe TS16 9BG (3m S
A135) ☎(0642)780378 FAX (0642) 784109
RS Xmas & New Year
*This modestly-furnished, family-run hotel is set in an acre of*
*gardens.*
19rm(16⇨3♠)(2fb) CTV in all bedrooms ® ✱ sB&B£20-£27
sB&B⇨3♠£27-£34 dB&B⇨3♠£38-£45 ⊟
CTV 20P ❖
♡ English & French V ✿ ⚌ Sunday Lunch £6.95 Dinner
£9.75&alc Last dinner 8.30pm
Credit Cards ①③⑤④

All hotels are now given a percentage grading
for the quality of their facilities. A full explanation
can be found within 'How we Classify Hotels
and Restaurants' at the front of the book.

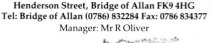

**S**

## STOKE CANON Devon Map 03 SX99

★★★73% **Barton Cross Hotel & Restaurant** Huxham EX5 4EJ
☎Exeter(0392)841245 & 841584 Telex no 42603
FAX (0392) 50402

*Dating back to the 17th century this hotel has attractive inglenook fireplaces, exposed beams and a thatched roof. Bedrooms have been carefully decorated and are exceptionally well equipped for both business clients and holidaymakers. Carefully prepared dishes are served in the interesting galleried restaurant and service throughout is warm and friendly.*

6⇔ↂ CTV in all bedrooms ® T ✱ sB&B⇔ↂ £63-£69 dB&B⇔ↂ£77-£83 ◪
24P ⇔ ✿ windsurfing instruction *xmas*
V ♉ ◿ Lunch £11.50-£23alc Dinner £18.50-£23alc Last dinner 9.30pm
Credit Cards ①②③④⑤

See advertisement under EXETER

## STOKE D'ABERNON Surrey Map 04 TQ15

★★★75% **Woodlands Park** Woodlands Ln KT11 3QB (Select)
☎Oxshott(037284)3933 Telex no 919246

*Extensive restoration and complete refurbishment has resulted in exceptionally well equipped and tastefully furnished bedrooms, whilst public areas retain many original features. Chef Paul Jones prepares imaginative French regional dishes in the restaurant. Service throughout is particularly attentive and keen to please.*

59⇔ↂ2◪ CTV in all bedrooms ® T ✕ (ex guide dogs) ✱ sB&B⇔ↂ£90-£115 dB&B⇔ↂ£100-£120 ◪
Lift ℭ 150P ✿ ℘ (hard) croquet putting 
♉ ◿ Lunch fr£9.75 Dinner fr£20.50 Last dinner 10.30pm
Credit Cards ①②③⑤ ⓔ

## STOKE GABRIEL Devon Map 03 SX85

★★★⚑65% **Gabriel Court** TQ9 6SF ☎(080428)206 & 267
Closed Feb

*Situated on the edge of this character village, a pleasantly proportioned Georgian house offers well-equipped bedrooms and comfortable public areas with some good paintings and antiques. Atmosphere is friendly and service relaxed yet attentive.*

20⇔ↂ CTV in all bedrooms ® T sB&B⇔ↂfr£50
dB&B⇔ↂfr£70
CTV 13P 7⚘ ⇔ ✿ ⊐(heated) croquet  *xmas*
♉ ◿ Sunday Lunch £9-£12 Dinner £19-£27 Last dinner 8.30pm
Credit Cards ①②③⑤

## STOKE-ON-TRENT Staffordshire Map 07 SJ84

See also Newcastle-under-Lyme

★★★69% **Haydon House** 1-13 Haydon St, Basford ST4 6JD
☎(0782)711311 Telex no 36600

*Family-run and progressive, the hotel keeps pace with modern trends, offering warm, well-equipped bedrooms (those in the annexe being of superior quality) and featuring a Victorian-style restaurant which is gaining a fine reputation for its imaginative menus.*

18⇔ↂ CTV in 26 bedrooms ®
52P
♉ English & French V ♉ ◿ Last dinner 10.30pm
Credit Cards ①②③⑤

★★★67% **Stakis Grand** 66 Trinity St, Hanley ST1 5NB (Stakis)
☎(0782)202361 Telex no 367264 FAX (0782) 286464

*A traditional style hotel that has recently been completely and sympathetically refurbished. It is very close to Hanley town centre and has a popular carvery-style restaurant.*

128⇔ↂ(55fb)⅄in 30 bedrooms CTV in all bedrooms ® T ✕ (ex guide dogs) (room only) ◪

Lift ℭ 175P ⊠(heated) sauna solarium gymnasium whirlpool spa *xmas*
V ♉ ◿ ⅄
Credit Cards ①②③⑤

★★★62% **Clayton Lodge** Clayton Rd ST5 4AF (Embassy)
☎Newcastle-under-Lyme(0782)613093 Telex no 36547
FAX (0782) 711896
(For full entry see Newcastle-under-Lyme)

★★55% **George** Swan Square, Burslem ST6 2AE
☎(0782)577544

*A busy commercial hotel where several sizes of function suite are available offers both carvery and à la carte meals supplemented by a popular lunchtime bar-snack menu.*

39rm(21⇔ↂ)(1fb) CTV in all bedrooms ® ✕ (ex guide dogs) ◪
Lift ℭ 14P sauna solarium gymnasium
♉ International V ♉ ◿ Lunch fr£6.75 Dinner fr£8.75 Last dinner 10pm
Credit Cards ①②③⑤ ⓔ

## STONE Staffordshire Map 07 SJ93

★★★62% **Stone House** ST15 0BQ (Lansbury) ☎(0785)815531
FAX (0785) 814764

*An Edwardian house, one mile south of the town, has recently been extended to include extra bedrooms and a leisure and conference complex.*

50⇔ↂ(2fb)⅄in 5 bedrooms CTV in all bedrooms ® T
sB&B⇔ↂ£74 dB&B⇔ↂ£87 ◪
ℭ 100P ✿ ⊠(heated) ℘ (hard) sauna solarium gymnasium croquet putting green *xmas*
♉ International V ♉ ◿ ⅄ Lunch fr£8.95 Dinner fr£14&alc Last dinner 10pm
Credit Cards ①②③⑤

## STON EASTON Somerset Map 03 ST65

★★★ ⚑ STON EASTON PARK

BA3 4DF (Relais et Châteaux)
☎Chewton Mendip (076121)631
FAX (076121) 377

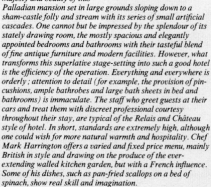

*It is easy to dwell on the majesty and beauty of this Palladian mansion set in large grounds sloping down to a sham-castle folly and stream with its series of small artificial cascades. One cannot but be impressed by the splendour of its stately drawing room, the mostly spacious and elegantly appointed bedrooms and bathrooms with their tasteful blend of fine antique furniture and modern facilities. However, what transforms this superlative stage-setting into such a good hotel is the efficiency of the operation. Everything and everywhere is orderly; attention to detail (for example, the provision of pin-cushions, ample bathrobes and large bath sheets in bed and bathrooms) is immaculate. The staff who greet guests at their cars and treat them with discreet professional courtesy throughout their stay, are typical of the Relais and Château style of hotel. In short, standards are extremely high, although one could wish for more natural warmth and hospitality. Chef Mark Harrington offers a varied and fixed price menu, mainly British in style and drawing on the produce of the ever-extending walled kitchen garden, but with a French influence. Some of his dishes, such as pan-fried scallops on a bed of spinach, show real skill and imagination.*

20rm(19⊸🅜)6🛏 CTV in all bedrooms **T**
✖ (ex guide dogs) ✱ sB&B⊸🅜 fr£65
dB&B⊸🅜£115-£285 Continental breakfast 🛗
《 CTV 40P 🚲 ✿ snooker croquet hot air ballooning
nc12yrs *xmas*
☺ English & French **V** ♿ ☕ Lunch £22 Dinner £32 Last
dinner 9.30pm
Credit Cards ① ② ③ ⑤

---

**STONEHAVEN** Grampian *Kincardineshire* Map **15** NO88
★★ **55%** *County* Arduthie Rd AB3 2EH ☎(0569)64386
Closed 1 Jan
*Plain, practical accommodation, a choice of bars and a range of*
*leisure activities are provided by this busy commercial hotel in a*
*residential area which is also a popular venue for local functions.*
14⊸🅜(4fb) CTV in all bedrooms ®
⊞ CTV 40P ✿ squash sauna solarium gymnasium
☺ Scottish, English & Italian **V** ♿ ☕ Last dinner 8.45pm
Credit Cards ① ② ③

---

**STONEHOUSE** Gloucestershire Map **03** SO80
★★★ **67%** **Stonehouse Court** Bristol Rd GL10 3RA
☎(0453)825155 FAX (0453) 824611
*Situated a mile east of M5 junction 13 on the A419, this imposing*
*Grade 2 listed house has been tastefully refurbished and extended*
*to provide public areas of character and quality. Most of the*
*modern and well equipped bedrooms are in the garden wing, which*
*enjoys uninterrupted views of the surrounding countryside. Five*
*acres of attractive grounds and good modern conference facilities*
*make this an ideal venue for the business and leisure customer.*
37⊸1🛏 CTV in all bedrooms ® **T** ✖ (ex guide dogs)
sB&B⊸fr£67.50 dB&B⊸fr£80 🛗

▶

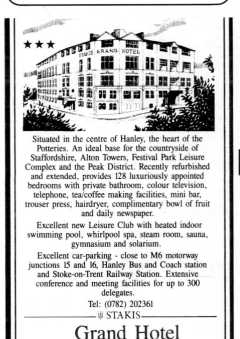
**S**

( 150P ❖ snooker croquet bowls *xmas*
☺ English & French **V** ✿ ⊈ Lunch fr£10.50 Dinner fr£17.50
Last dinner 9.30pm
Credit Cards [1][3]

## STONOR Oxfordshire Map **04** SU78

✹ ✗ ✗**Stonor Arms** RG9 6HE ☏Turville Heath(049163)345
*This 18th-century village inn has been most attractively converted
by Mr and Mrs Frost to make a cosy and intimate restaurant.
Stephen Frost does the cooking, and from a good choice of
imaginative dishes, our Inspector recommended highly the terrine
of scallops and turbot served with a herby tomato sauce, followed
by a superbly prepared braised leg and roast loin of rabbit with a
thyme and mustard sauce. Another terrine, this time of chocolate
ice-cream, with orange and mint sauce, finished the meal. Staff are
young, enthusiastic and very friendly.*
Lunch not served Mon-Sat
Dinner not served Sun
40 seats ✱ Sunday Lunch £18.95-£23.95 Dinner
£26.75-£31&alc Last lunch 1.45pm Last dinner 9.30pm 30P
Credit Cards [1][2][3]

## STORNOWAY

See **Lewis, Isle of**

## STORRINGTON West Sussex Map **04** TQ01

✹ ✗ ✗ ✗**Manleys** Manleys Hill RH20 4BT ☏(0903)742331
*Karl Löderer's appealing restaurant continues to offer a reliably
high standard of cuisine, mainly French in style but with some
Austrian and German influences which add to the richness. The set
menu at lunchtime is extremely good value, with dishes such as the
Millefeuilles de Saumon with langoustine sauce and a superb
interpretation of crème brulée being particularly memorable. A
well chosen wine list and the service by professional but friendly
staff complete one's enjoyment.*
Closed Mon, 1st 2 wks Jan, last wk Aug & 1st wk Sep
Dinner not served Sun
☺ Austrian & French **V** 45 seats ✱ Lunch fr£17.60&alc Last
lunch 2pm Last dinner 9.30pm 25P
Credit Cards [1][2][3][5]

## STOURBRIDGE West Midlands Map **07** SO88

★★**66**% **Talbot** High St DY8 1DW (Crown & Raven)
☏(0384)394350 Telex no 335464 FAX (0384) 371318
*A 16th-century former coaching inn situated in the town centre
offering comfortable, modern, well-equipped rooms. Ask for
directions when booking as the town's one-way system can be
confusing.*
25rm(13⇔7♠)(4fb)1⊠ CTV in all bedrooms ® **T** ✱
sB&B⇔♠fr£53.35 dB&B⇔♠fr£69.30 🅟
( 25P
☺ English & French **V** ✿ ⊈
Credit Cards [1][2][3]

## STOURPORT-ON-SEVERN Hereford & Worcester Map **07** SO87

★★★**63**% **Stourport Moat House** 35 Hartlebury Rd DY13 9LT
(Queens Moat) ☏(0299)827733 Telex no 333676
FAX (02993) 78520
*Set on the eastern outskirts of the town, and once the home of
Stanley Baldwin's family, this nineteenth-century country house
has been considerably altered and extended over recent years to
provide good conference/function facilities, a leisure complex and a
night club, whilst refurbishment of the bedrooms is producing
accommodation which will attract both business guests and
tourists.*
68⇔♠✂in 6 bedrooms CTV in all bedrooms ® **T** ✱
sB&B⇔♠£60-£65 dB&B⇔♠£70-£80 🅟

( 400P ❖ CFA ⚲ ► ♪ (hard) squash snooker sauna
gymnasium clay pigeon shooting
☺ English & French **V** ✿ ⊈ ✂ S% Lunch fr£10.50&alc
Dinner fr£12.50&alc Last dinner 9.55pm
Credit Cards [1][2][3][5]

★★**62**% **Swan** High St DY13 8BX (Porterhouse)
☏(02993)71661 FAX (0299) 827650
*This town-centre hotel has comfortable, refurbished bedrooms and
a popular, value-for-money restaurant.*
33⇔♠(2fb) CTV in all bedrooms ® **T** ✱
sB&B⇔♠£29-£42.50 dB&B⇔♠£42-£65 🅟
CTV 60P
☺ English, French & Spanish **V** ✿
Credit Cards [1][2][3][5]

## STOW CUM QUY Cambridgeshire Map **05** TL56

★**54**% **Quy Mill** Newmarket Rd CB5 9AG
☏Cambridge(0223)853383 FAX (0223) 853770
*Family-run hotel, adjacent to the A45, which is being developed
from several former mill buildings. The newer bedrooms are well
equipped and standards are being raised throughout. Popular for
bar lunches.*
26rm(1⇔19♠)1⊠✂in 10 bedrooms CTV in all bedrooms ®
( CTV 100P ❖ ♪
☺ English, French & Italian **V** ✿ ⊈ Last dinner 9.15pm
Credit Cards [1][3][5]

## STOWMARKET Suffolk Map **05** TM05

★★**60**% **Cedars** Needham Rd IP14 2AJ ☏(0449)612668
FAX (0449) 674704
Closed Xmas-New Year
*Pleasant service and a good standard of cleanliness are the
hallmarks of a hotel which offers easy access to the A45 from its
position beside the B1113 on the outskirts of the town. Bedrooms
are neatly furnished and all have en suite facilities.*
24⇔♠(2fb) CTV in all bedrooms ® **T** sB&B⇔♠£37.50-£40
dB&B⇔♠fr£50 🅟
60P ❖
☺ English & French ✿ ⊈ Lunch £7.50-£15alc Dinner
£7.50-£15alc Last dinner 9pm
Credit Cards [1][2][3]£

⌂**Travelodge** IP14 3PY (A45) (Trusthouse Forte)
☏(0449)615347 Central res (0800) 850950
*Situated about three miles to the north west of Stowmarket on the
A45 westbound carriageway. There is a Little Chef Restaurant
adjacent.*
40⇔♠(40fb) ® sB⇔♠£24 dB⇔♠£29.50 (room only)
( 40P ⇘
Credit Cards [1][2][3]

See 'How we Classify Hotels and Restaurants'
at the front of the book for an explanation
of the AA's appointment and
award scheme.

STOW-ON-THE-WOLD Gloucestershire Map **04** SP12

⬛★★★🏨77%, **Wyck Hill House** Burford Rd GL54 1HY
☎Cotswold(0451)31936 Telex no 43611 FAX (0451) 32243
*Well kept lawns and flower beds brighten the approach to this*
*attractive country-house hotel, on the A424 road out of Stow, run*
*by Peter Robinson. He and his staff ensure a welcoming*
*atmosphere, and Chef Ian Smith creates meals which have earned*
*the hotel an excellent local reputation. Working mostly with good*
*British produce, he devises an imaginative menu featuring dishes*
*such as ballotine of rabbit filled with herb mousse and served on a*
*salad of beans, leeks, tomato and walnuts; fillet of seabass served*
*with ravioli filled with crab on a coriander-flavoured lemon-butter*
*sauce, or from the vegetarian menu, an enticing spinach and cheese*
*strudel with tomato and basil sauce, and an aubergine, tomato and*
*courgette charlotte accompanied by a rosemary-flavoured sauce.*
*Interesting combinations of hot and cold sweets include a lemon*
*trio, with creamy mousse, a sharp sorbet and a piping hot soufflé*
*arranged on a raspberry sauce and decorated with a border of*
*piped chocolate.*
16⇦⤴🏠Annexe17⇦🏠(3fb)3🛏 CTV in all bedrooms ⓇT
sB&B⇦🏠£85-£100 dB&B⇦🏠£100-£175 🛏
Lift ℂ 100P ✿ croquet clay pigeon shooting 🎵 ৶ xmas
♲ British & French V ⏱ 🍴 ✂ Lunch fr£14.25&alc Dinner
fr£27.50&alc Last dinner 9.30pm
Credit Cards ①②③⑤④

★★★59%, **Unicorn Crest** Sheep St GL54 1HQ (Trusthouse
Forte) ☎Cotswold(0451)30257 Telex no 437186
FAX (0451) 31090
*Situated on the main crossroads, this well known hostelry offers*
*public areas of character and charm and a range of en suite*
*bedrooms of varying degrees of style and comfort. Service is*
*friendly and attentive.*
20⇦⤴2🛏✂in 3 bedrooms CTV in all bedrooms ⓇT
sB⇦🏠fr£42 dB⇦🏠fr£72 (room only) 🛏

▶

**S**

CTV 45P *xmas*
☋ English & French V ♈ ☕ ✂ Lunch fr£9.95 Dinner fr£14.21 Last dinner 9.30pm
Credit Cards 1 2 3 4 5

**★★ 76% Grapevine** Sheep St GL54 1AU (Best Western)
☎Cotswold(0451)30344 Telex no 43423 FAX (0451) 32278
Closed 25 Dec-10 Jan
*Situated in the heart of this charming Cotswald village, the team spirit generated by proprietor, Sandra Elliott, and her staff, provides very friendly and willing services, and this, coupled with character public areas and well equipped, individually designed bedrooms, makes a stay at the Grapevine both happy and memorable. The atmosphere here is relaxed and informal and nothing seems too much trouble.*
13⇌↱Annexe4⇌(3fb)1⊞✂in 4 bedrooms CTV in all bedrooms ® T ✗ sB&B⇌↱£57-£74 dB&B⇌↱£78-£106 ⊟
17P ⊞
☋ English, French & Italian V ♈ ☕ ✂ Lunch fr£7.25 Dinner fr£16.95 Last dinner 9.30pm
Credit Cards 1 2 3 5 £

**★★ 72% Stow Lodge** The Square GL54 1AB
☎Cotswold(0451)30485
Closed 20 Dec-mid Jan
*A friendly, privately owned and personally supervised hotel in a relatively peaceful corner of the town provides comfortable, well appointed bedrooms and an attractive lounge with an open exposed stone fireplace where a roaring log fire burns on cooler days.*
12rm(10⇌)Annexe10⇌(2fb)1⊞✂in 1 bedroom CTV in 21 bedrooms ® ✗ ✳ sB&B⇌£34.50-£40 dB&B⇌£44-£62 ⊟
( 30P ⊞ ❀ nc5yrs
♈ ✂ Bar Lunch £8.40-£14alc Dinner £11.50-£12.50&alc Last dinner 9pm
Credit Cards 2 5

**★★ 70% Fosse Manor** GL54 1JX (Consort)
☎Cotswold(0451)30354 FAX (0451) 32486
Closed 24 Dec-5 Jan
*An attractive hotel set in its own grounds provides comfortable accommodation, with willing service from the proprietors and their friendly staff. Dining room and lounge have been carefully refurbished to meet modern standards of comfort whilst retaining the character of the original old manor house.*
14⇌↱Annexe6rm(2⇌)(6fb)1⊞ CTV in all bedrooms ® T ✳ sB&B⇌↱fr£45 dB&B⇌↱fr£76 ⊟
CTV 20P ⊞ ❀ solarium croquet ⌂
☋ English & Continental V ♈ ☕ ✂ Lunch fr£16.95&alc Dinner fr£16.95&alc Last dinner 9.30pm
Credit Cards 1 2 3 5 £

**★★ 66% *Old Farmhouse*** Lower Swell GL54 1LF (1m W B4068)
☎Cotswold(0451)30232
Closed 25-27 Dec RS 25-27 Dec
*This small hotel sits in the peaceful hamlet of Lower Swell just one miles north of Stow-on-the-Wold. Friendly, informal service is complimented by sound accommodation and food.*
5⇌↱Annexe8⇌↱ CTV in all bedrooms ®
25P ⊞ ❀ board games ⌂
☋ International V ♈ ☕ ✂ Last dinner 9pm
Credit Cards 1 3

**★★ 63% Old Stocks** The Square GL54 1AF
☎Cotswold(0451)30666
Closed 17-27 Dec
*Standing next to the green, this hotel comprises three 16th and 17th-century buildings which have been tastefully upgraded and refurbished to retain their original character. Bedrooms are all en suite and equipped with modern facilities, though the nature of the building means that some are rather compact. Under the personal supervision of the resident proprietors, service is friendly and informal.*
17⇌↱(1fb) CTV in all bedrooms ® T sB&B⇌↱£30-£35 dB&B⇌↱£60-£70 ⊟
CTV 14P ❀ ⌂
V ♈ ☕ Sunday Lunch fr£7.95 Dinner £8.95-£14.95 Last dinner 9.30pm
Credit Cards 1 2 3 £

**★★ 63% Royalist** Digbeth St GL54 1BN
☎Cotswold(0451)30670
*Friendly proprietors continue to make improvements throughout the hotel where a small team provides hospitable, polite service.*
14⇌↱1⊞ CTV in all bedrooms ® T sB&B⇌↱£25-£35 dB&B⇌↱£45-£65 ⊟
12P CFA
V ♈ ☕ Bar Lunch £1.50-£10 Dinner £16-£23 Last dinner 9pm
Credit Cards 1 2 3

**❀✗✗ Epicurean** 1 Park St GL54 1AQ ☎Cotswold(0451)31613
*One of our 'Best New Restaurants' this year – see the colour feature on page 36. In a pretty row of Cotswold stone cottages, this outstanding new restaurant is owned and run by chef Patrick McDonald, formerly head chef at Charingworth Manor and Ettington Park, with experience also gained at The Dorchester and Grosvenor House in London. His creations are imaginative, inventive and interesting to look at – Quartet of Lamb has, at the points of the compass, the trimmed loin, wrapped in spinach then steamed, a tiny tartlet filled with sweetbreads, kidney sandwiched between thin filo pastry, and liver, thinly sliced and topping a mould of ratatouille, each an individual masterpiece.*
Closed Mon 2 wks early Feb
Dinner not served Sun
☋ British & French V 30 seats ✳ Lunch £10.50-£16.50&alc Dinner £18.50-£26&alc Last lunch 2.30pm Last dinner 11.30pm nc7yrs ✂
Credit Cards 1 2 3

## STRACHUR Strathclyde *Argyllshire* Map 10 NN00

**★★★ 61% Creggans Inn** PA27 8BX (Minotels) ☎(036986)279 Telex no 777694 FAX (036986) 637
*Extensively and tastefully modernised, this seventeenth-century inn on the shores of Loch Fyne offers compact but cheerful, attractively decorated bedrooms. In the restful split-level restaurant good food is served by friendly, courteous staff.*
21rm(17⇌↱) CTV in all bedrooms T ✳ sB&Bfr£40 sB&B⇌↱fr£48 dB&Bfr£80 dB&B⇌↱fr£90 ⊟
CTV 80P ❀ ♪ *xmas*
☋ French V ♈ ☕ ✂
Credit Cards 1 2 3 5

## STRANRAER Dumfries & Galloway *Wigtownshire* Map 10 NX06

**★★★ 69% North West Castle** DG9 8EH (Exec Hotel)
☎(0776)4413 Telex no 777088 FAX (0776) 2646
*Family owned and managed this spacious, elegant hotel has been sympathetically modernised and extended to provide a wide range of leisure and recreational facilities. Many of the comfortable, well-equipped bedrooms enjoy fine views of Loch Ryan.*
74⇌↱(12fb)1⊞ CTV in all bedrooms ® T ✗ (ex guide dogs) sB&B⇌↱£45-£60 dB&B⇌↱£64-£88 ⊟
Lift ( 100P ⊞ CFA ▭(heated) snooker sauna solarium gymnasium curling (Oct-Apr) games room *xmas*
V ♈ ☕ Dinner fr£18&alc Last dinner 9.30pm

All hotels are now given a percentage grading for the quality of their facilities. A full explanation can be found within 'How we Classify Hotels and Restaurants' at the front of the book.

**STRATFORD-UPON-AVON** Warwickshire Map **04** SP25

See **Town Plan Section**

★★★★73% **Welcombe** Warwick Rd CV37 0NR
☎(0789)295252 Telex no 31347 FAX (0789) 414666
Closed 29 Dec-4 Jan

*Standing on the outskirts of Stratford in a parkland estate which offers an 18-hole golf course and two all-weather floodlit tennis courts, this Jacobean mansion features truly traditional service rendered by a charming and efficient staff. Public rooms are comfortable, and a major refurbishment programme is upgrading most bedrooms to a luxurious standard – including many suites and four poster rooms – though the older, garden wing accommodation remains simple.*

76⇨(2fb)7⊞ CTV in all bedrooms T ✱ sB&B⇨£85-£100 dB&B⇨£120-£135 ⊟

( 100P 6🚗 ❊ CFA ▶18 snooker croquet putting table tennis *xmas*

♁ English & French V ✿ ☐ Lunch fr£16 Dinner fr£25&alc Last dinner 9.30pm

Credit Cards [1] [2] [3] [5]

**See advertisement on page 653**

★★★★57% **The Shakespeare** Chapel St CV37 6ER (Trusthouse Forte) ☎(0789)294771 Telex no 311181 FAX (0789) 415411

*Situated in the heart of town this magnificent timbered building dates back to at least 1637. The hotel offers comfortable public areas, with good levels of service. Bedrooms are continually being sympathetically upgraded to offer modern accommodation, but some of the older rooms are still awaiting attention.*

70⇨↱2⊞⊁in 20 bedrooms CTV in all bedrooms ® T sB⇨↱£75-£85 dB⇨↱£105-£135 (room only) ⊟

Lift ( 45P CFA ♫ *xmas*

♁ English & Continental V ✿ ☐ ⊁ Lunch fr£11&alc High tea £3-£8 Dinner fr£17&alc Last dinner 10pm

Credit Cards [1] [2] [3] [4] [5]


★★

**FOSSE MANOR HOTEL**

**Fosse Way**
**Stow on the Wold**
**Gloucestershire GL54 1JX**
**Tel: (0451) 30354 Fax: (0451) 32486**

Standing in six acres of beautiful gardens 1 mile south of Stow-on-the-Wold on the A429. Ideally situated for Cotswolds, Stratford, Oxford, Cheltenham and Worcester. Tastefully decorated with a warm family welcome. Excellent food and efficient staff.



★★

Old Farmhouse Hotel

***Lower Swell, Stow-on-the-Wold,***
***Glos GL54 1LF***
***Telephone: Cotswold (0451) 30232***

*Well placed for touring, exploring and sound sleeping, a 16th-Century traditional Cotswold farmhouse in a peaceful hamlet 1 mile west of Stow, sympathetically converted to a warm and comfortable small hotel of 15 bedrooms, all different, mostly en suite. The hotel has the relaxed and friendly air of its farmhouse origins and a varied cuisine, including traditional. There are log fires, a walled garden and ample private parking.*



**Stow Lodge Hotel**★★

The Square, Stow-on-the-Wold,
Cheltenham, Glos. GL54 1AB
Tel: (0451) 30485

Set back in its own grounds far enough from the Market Square to allow guests complete peace and relaxation. 20 bedrooms, all with private bath and toilet, television, radio, tea and coffee-making facilities. Full central heating. Open log fires in both the Bar and Lounge. The restaurant which is non smoking seats 30 persons and offers a varied table d'hôte menu and à la carte with traditional English fare at its very best. Fully licensed Bar offering a selection of light lunches daily to the traveller not wishing to linger. Private Car park for approx 30 cars.

*A perfect centre for touring the Cotswolds and Shakespeare country.*


S

★★★★56% **Moat House International** Bridgefoot CV37 6YR (Queens Moat) ☎(0789)414411 Telex no 311127 FAX (0789) 298589

*Situated on the river by Clopton Bridge, and close to the theatre, this large hotel has undergone extensive refurbishment and offers modern, well-equipped bedrooms, a choice of restaurants, shops and a nightclub. There is a good range of conference facilities and an indoor leisure complex.*

249🛁🚿(20fb)⚡in 64 bedrooms CTV in all bedrooms ® T ★ sB🛁🚿£75 dB🛁🚿£99 (room only) ⊟

Lift ☾ ⊞ CTV 350P ✽ 🏊(heated) snooker sauna solarium gymnasium ♫

🍽 British & French V ☘ ☕ Lunch fr£10.75 High tea fr£5.50 Dinner fr£12.95&alc Last dinner 10.30pm

Credit Cards 1 2 3 5

---

❀★★★⚐74% **Billesley Manor Hotel** B49 6NF (Queens Moat)(Prestige) ☎(0789)400888 Telex no 312599 FAX (0789) 764145

(For full entry see Billesley)

---

★★★72% **Windmill Park Hotel & Country Club** Warwick Rd CV37 0PY (Best Western) ☎(0789)731173

*This newly opened hotel and leisure complex on the A439 two miles from Stratford, is convenient for junction 15 of the M40. Accommodation is comfortable and equipped with modern facilities that the business traveller will appreciate. The open plan ground floor areas include 'Traditions' carvery restaurant and a comfortable lounge bar.*

100🛁(4fb)8🛏 CTV in all bedrooms ® T ★ S% sB&B🛁fr£65 dB&B🛁fr£80 ⊟

Lift ☾ 220P ✽ 🏊(heated) 🎾 (hard) sauna solarium gymnasium steam room *xmas*

V ☘ ☕

Credit Cards 1 2 3 5

---

★★★61% **Charlecote Pheasant Country** CV35 9EW (Queens Moat) ☎(0789)470333 Telex no 31688 FAX (0789) 470222

(For full entry see Charlecote)

---

★★★60% **Dukes** Payton St CV37 6UA ☎(0789)69300 Telex no 31430 FAX (0789) 414700

Closed 2 days Xmas

*The hotel offers attractive accommodation in cosy bedrooms which are compact yet well furnished with good facilities. Public rooms are beautifully appointed, the comfortable, spacious lounge and elegant restaurant being of a particularly high standard, as is also the lovingly-tended garden, enjoyed by guests and visitors alike.*

22🛁🚿2🛏 CTV in all bedrooms ® T ✗ sB&B🛁🚿£45-£50 dB&B🛁🚿£70-£90 ⊟

30P 🚗 ✽ nc12yrs

🍽 European V ☘ Lunch £11.50-£18.50alc Dinner £13-£18.50alc Last dinner 9.45pm

Credit Cards 1 2 3 5

---

★★★59% **Alveston Manor** Clopton Bridge CV37 7HP (Trusthouse Forte) ☎(0789)204581 Telex no 31324 FAX (0789) 414095

*An attractive hotel with well-kept gardens just across the river from the theatre and town centre. Afternoon tea can be enjoyed in the cocktail bar which has 16th-century oak panelling.*

108🛁(6fb)1🛏⚡in 30 bedrooms CTV in all bedrooms ® T S10% sB🛁£76-£113 dB🛁£97-£162 (room only) ⊟

☾ 200P ✽ CFA pitch & putt *xmas*

V ☘ ☕ ⚡ S10% Lunch fr£12.50&alc Dinner fr£17.75&alc Last dinner 9.30pm

Credit Cards 1 2 3 4 5

---

★★★55% **Grosvenor House** Warwick Rd CV37 6YT (Best Western) ☎(0789)269213 Telex no 311699 FAX (0789) 266087

Closed 24-27 Dec

*This family-run hotel is particularly hospitable, and a friendly atmosphere prevails; the well-equipped health centre is now an added attraction.*

51🛁🚿(9fb) CTV in all bedrooms ® T ✗ sB&B🛁🚿£50-£60 dB&B🛁🚿£72-£82 ⊟

☾ 40P CFA

V ☘ Lunch £6.50&alc Dinner £9.95&alc Last dinner 8.45pm

Credit Cards 1 2 3 5

---

★★★54% ***Falcon*** Chapel St CV37 6HA (Queens Moat) ☎(0789)205777 Telex no 312522 FAX (0789) 414260

*Located close to the town centre, this busy conference hotel dating back to 1640 offers well-equipped bedrooms in various styles and sizes together with an extensive range of conference/meeting rooms.*

73🛁🚿(13fb)1🛏 CTV in all bedrooms ®

Lift ☾ 100P 24🚗 CFA

🍽 French V ☘ ☕ Last dinner 9pm

Credit Cards 1 2 3 4 5

---

★★★50% **The White Swan** Rother St CV37 6NH (Trusthouse Forte) ☎(0789)297022 FAX (0789) 68773

*Traditional 15th-century inn situated in the town centre.*

42🛁🚿(4fb)1🛏⚡in 5 bedrooms CTV in all bedrooms ® T S% sB🛁🚿£70 dB🛁🚿£98 (room only)

☾ 8P (charged) CFA *xmas*

V ☘ ☕ ⚡ Lunch £10 High tea £2-£4 Dinner £14&alc Last dinner 9pm

Credit Cards 1 2 3 4 5

---

★★★53% **The Swan's Nest** Bridgefoot CV37 7LT (Trusthouse Forte) ☎(0789)66761 FAX (0789) 414547

*Standing beside the River Avon, the hotel is conveniently placed for both town and theatre. It offers guests comfortable bedrooms and a choice of menus.*

60🛁(1fb)⚡in 18 bedrooms CTV in all bedrooms ® T ★ sB🛁£62-£82 dB🛁£72-£82 (room only) ⊟

☾ 100P ✽ CFA *xmas*

▶

S

**S**

V ✿ ⚓ ⍾ Lunch £8.95-£13.70 Dinner £14&alc Last dinner
10pm
Credit Cards 1 2 3 4 5

★★73% **Stratford House** Sheep St CV37 6EF ☎(0789)68288
FAX (0789) 295580
Closed Xmas RS 3 days from Xmas day
*In the heart of Stratford's shopping area and close to the Royal
Shakespeare Theatre this lovely Georgian building is filled with
flowers. Shepherds Restaurant is light and airy and it is here where
chef John George maintains a sound reputation for his excellent
modern British cooking. Bedrooms are a little compact but
comfortably furnished and staff are caring and friendly.*
10rm(6⇄3♠)(1fb) CTV in all bedrooms ® T ✖ sB&B£50-£60
dB&B⇄♠£68-£80 ⊟
✗ ⌺ nc2yrs
♀ English & French ✿ ⚓ Lunch £4.30-£10 High tea £5.45-£7
Dinner £12-£18 Last dinner 9.30pm
Credit Cards 1 2 3 5

★★64% **The Coach House Hotel** 16-17 Warwick Rd CV37 6YW
(Guestaccom) ☎(0789)204109 & 299468
*Two adjoining properties on the A46/A439 Warwick Road, one
Georgian and one Victorian in style, have been merged to create
value-for-money, comfortable accommodation with a good range of
facilities. The Four Seasons Restaurant and Bar offers both a cosy
environment and a good range of choices.*
10⇄♠Annexe13rm(8⇄♠)(3fb)1⍾ ✖in 3 bedrooms CTV in
all bedrooms ® T ✖ (ex guide dogs) sB&B£19-£33.40
sB&B⇄♠£33.40-£39 dB&B£35-£37 dB&B⇄♠£49-£79 ⊟
30P *xmas*
♀ English & French ⍾ Lunch £9.50&alc Dinner
£9.50-£12.50&alc Last dinner 10pm
Credit Cards 1 3 £

★★60% **Swan House** The Green CV37 9XJ ☎(0789)67030 due
to change to 267030 FAX (0789) 204875
(For full entry see Wilmcote)

STRATHAVEN Strathclyde Map **11** NS74

★★56% **Strathaven** Hamilton Rd ML10 6SZ (Consort)
☎(0357)21778 Telex no 776496 FAX (0357) 20789
10⇄♠ CTV in all bedrooms ® T ✳ sB&B⇄♠£45
dB&B⇄♠£55 ⊟
《80P ✿
♀ French V ✿ Lunch fr£5.95&alc Dinner fr£10.25&alc Last
dinner 10pm
Credit Cards 1 2 3 4 5 £

STRATHBLANE Central *Stirlingshire* Map **11** NS57

★★★61% *Country Club* Milngavie Rd G63 9AH
☎Blanefield(0360)70491
*Set in 15 acres of grounds this former country mansion is now a
comfortable hotel with special appeal for the businessman.
Bedrooms are individually decorated and well-equipped and a
good standard of cuisine is served in the restaurant. Lounge
facilities are limited.*
10⇄♠⍾in 2 bedrooms CTV in all bedrooms ®
60P ⍾ ✿
♀ European V ✿ Last dinner 9.30pm
Credit Cards 1 2 3 4 5

★★66% **Kirkhouse Inn** G63 9AA (Minotels)
☎Blanefield(0360)70621 FAX (0360) 70896
*A friendly, hospitable roadside inn stands at the junction of the
A81 and A891 in the village of Strathblane at the foot of the
Campsie Fells. Catering for business and tourists alike and well
equipped throughout, the hotel features a restaurant with a very
good local reputation serving mainly continental cuisine.*
15⇄♠(2fb)1⍾ CTV in all bedrooms ® T S% sB&B⇄♠fr£50
dB&B⇄♠fr£70 ⊟
《350P *xmas*

♀ Scottish & French V ✿ ⚓ S% Lunch fr£10&alc High tea
fr£6 Dinner fr£15&alc Last dinner 10pm
Credit Cards 1 2 3 5

STRATHPEFFER Highland *Ross & Cromarty* Map **14** NH45

★★64% *Holly Lodge* IV14 9AR ☎(0997)21254
*This attractive stone-built hotel stands in its own grounds
overlooking the Victorian spa resort of Strathpeffer. It offers warm
hospitality and good food influenced by a hint of the orient. The
public rooms – in particular the charming residents' lounge area
and the comfortable bedrooms also have an oriental feel about
them.*
7rm(3⇄3♠) CTV in all bedrooms ®
CTV 15P 2☂ ⍾ ✿ shooting ♫
♀ Scottish & Oriental ✿ ⚓ Last dinner 9pm

★68% **Brunstane Lodge** IV14 9AT ☎(0997)21261
Closed 1 & 2 Jan RS mid Oct-Apr
*A small family run hotel offering warm and friendly service and
good facilities. In an elevated position overlooking the village and
hills.*
6rm(2⇄3♠)(1fb) ® ✳ sB&B£16.50-£18.50
sB&B⇄♠£16.50-£20 dB&B⇄♠£33-£37 ⊟
CTV 20P ✿ ⌀
V ✿ ⚓ ⍾ Bar Lunch £3-£5 Dinner £10-£12 Last dinner
8.30pm
Credit Cards 1 3 £

Entries for red-star hotels are highlighted by a
tint panel. For a full list of these establishments
consult the Contents page.

## ★★★

# *The Country Club Hotel*

**MILNGAVIE ROAD STRATHBLANE G63 9AH**
TELEPHONE: BLANEFIELD (0360) 70491

A former country mansion, is set in 15 acres of
wooded Parkland in the very beautiful Blane Valley.
Our 10 extremely well appointed bedrooms are of
spacious proportions and epitomise elegance with a
quiet graciousness.

In the Restaurant the main emphasis is always on
fresh foods with game in season, and our menus
invariably feature a choice of indigenous Scottish
Dishes.

S

**STRATHYRE** Central *Perthshire* Map **11** NN51

★58%, *The Inn* Main St FK18 8NA ☎(08774)224
*Practical, value-for-money accommodation and a homely*
*atmosphere of this small, family-run, roadside inn which dates*
*back to the early eighteenth century.*
6rm(4⇔) ®
CTV 30P
♀ Mainly grills ✆ ⚏ Last dinner 8.30pm

**STREATLEY** Berkshire Map **04** SU58

★★★73%, **Swan Diplomat** High St RG8 9HR
☎Goring-on-Thames(0491)873737 Telex no 848259
FAX (0491) 872554
*Nestling beneath the ancient ridgeway in a fold of hills beside the*
*River Thames, this tastefully renovated hotel offers spacious*
*bedrooms, individually decorated and furnished in traditional*
*mahogany, with river or hill views. Other facilities include the*
*riverside restaurant with its candlelit atmosphere, a cocktail bar*
*and the Magdalen Barge, which is popular for meetings and*
*private functions, weather permitting. More recently a boathouse*
*bar and leisure complex have been added to the hotel's attractions.*
46⇔↑1⚏ CTV in all bedrooms ® T
sB&B⇔↑£89.10-£107.70 dB&B⇔↑£113-£147.40 ₽
℄ CTV 146P ✻ ⊠(heated) sauna solarium gymnasium croquet
row boat *xmas*
♀ French V ✆ ⚏ Bar Lunch fr£6 Dinner £19.50-£21.50 Last
dinner 9.30pm
Credit Cards ①②③⑤ⓔ

**STREET** Somerset Map **03** ST43

★★★66%, **Bear** 53 High St BA16 0EF ☎(0458)42021
*Located opposite the Shoe Museum, an attractive stone hotel with*
*some grounds offers bedrooms of a good size, furnished with a good*
*degree of comfort and quality; public areas are small but cosy, and*
*a pleasant atmosphere prevails throughout.*
10⇔↑Annexe5⇔(3fb) CTV in all bedrooms ® T ✱
sB&B⇔↑£30-£45 dB&B⇔↑£50-£80 ₽
℄36P ✻ *xmas*
♀ English & French V ✆ ⚏ ✂ Lunch £4.95-£6.50 Dinner
£15-£25alc Last dinner 9.30pm
Credit Cards ①②③

**STREETLY** West Midlands Map **07** SP09

★★60%, **Parson & Clerk Motel** Chester Rd B73 6SP (junc
A452/B4138) (Porterhouse) ☎021-353 1747 FAX 021-352 1340
Closed 24-26 Dec
*The motel comprises an accommodation block with its own small*
*bar and breakfast room. Across the car park is a popular*
*Porterhouse Restaurant and bar. Located opposite Sutton Park*
*the motel is conveniently situated for access to Birmingham, Sutton*
*Coldfield and the surrounding districts.*
30⇔↑ CTV in all bedrooms ® T ✗ (ex guide dogs) ₽
CTV 100P
V ✆ ⚏
Credit Cards ①②③⑤

**STRETTON** Cheshire Map **07** SJ68

★★69%, **Old Vicarage** Stretton Rd WA4 4NS
☎Norcott Brook(0925)73706 FAX (0925) 73740
*This old vicarage has now been fully modernised and now operates as a*
*busy commercial hotel. The restaurant overlooks a secluded rear*
*garden, and has a local reputation for good food and service.*
28⇔↑(2fb)1⚏ CTV in all bedrooms ® T ✱
sB&B⇔↑£45-£55 dB&B⇔↑£70 ₽
Lift ℄150P ✻ *xmas*
V ✆ ⚏ Lunch £8.75&alc
Credit Cards ①②③

**STRETTON** Leicestershire Map **08** SK91

★★71%, **Ram Jam Inn** Great North Rd LE15 7QX
☎Castle Bytham(0780)410776 Telex no 342888
FAX (0572) 724721
*On the A1 Great North Road, 9 miles north of Stamford, stands an*
*old, stonebuilt inn; the exterior is the only evidence of its age,*
*however, the interior having been transformed to provide luxurious,*
*extremely well-equipped bedrooms and a modern, split-level public*
*area containing reception, lounge, bar, restaurant and a 'fast food'*
*snack meal operation.*
Annexe8⇔(2fb) CTV in all bedrooms ® sB⇔fr£38.50
dB⇔fr£49.50 (room only)
100P ✻
✆ ⚏
Credit Cards ①②③

**STRONTIAN** Highland *Argyllshire* Map **14** NM86

★★69%, **Kilcamb Lodge** PH36 4HY ☎(0967)2257
Closed 21 Oct-Etr
*The dedicated owners of this charming small hotel by the*
*picturesque shoreline of Loch Sunart, are constantly striving to*
*develop and to improve standards. Guests are assured of a warm*
*welcome, comfortable, tastefully decorated bedrooms and relaxing*
*public areas which include a dining room serving a short but*
*imaginative dinner menu of dishes prepared from fresh local*
*produce.*
9rm(2⇔6↑)(1fb) ® ✗ ✱ sB&B⇔↑fr£50
dB&B⇔↑fr£100 (incl dinner) ₽
CTV 20P ⚗ ✻
♀ Scottish & French V ✆ ✂ Bar Lunch fr£2.50 High tea fr£5
Dinner £19.50 Last dinner 7pm

★★60%, **Loch Sunart** PH36 4HZ ☎(0967)2471
Closed Nov-Etr
*A friendly atmosphere, modest traditional comforts and good*
*home-cooked meals are provided by this extended eighteenth-*
*century country house which overlooks the loch from its position at*
*the edge of the village.*
11rm(4⇔2↑)(1fb) ®
CTV 30P ⚗ ✻
V ✆ ⚏ ✂ Last dinner 7.30pm

**STROUD** Gloucestershire Map **03** SO80

See also **Amberley and Painswick**

★★★♨65% **Burleigh Court** Brimscombe GL5 2PF (2.5m SE
off A419) ☎Brimscombe(0453)883804 FAX (0453) 886870
Closed 25 Dec-10 Jan RS Sun
*Situated three miles from the town centre off the A419 this fine*
*Georgian house is in a commanding position overlooking the*
*surrounding countryside. It has well equipped bedrooms of*
*differing standards, comfortable public areas and an attractive*
*garden with a putting green. Good food and friendly services are*
*provided by the Benson family and their staff.*
11⇔↑Annexe6⇔↑(1fb) CTV in all bedrooms ® T ✗
sB&B⇔↑£54-£59 dB&B⇔↑£70-£80 ₽
40P 1⚗ ⚗ ✆ ⊇(heated) putting green
♀ English & French V ✆ ⚏ ✂ Lunch £10.75-£11.95alc High
tea £3.50-£6.50alc Dinner £17.25-£23.50alc Last dinner 8.45pm
Credit Cards ①②③⑤

★★★56%, **The Bear of Rodborough** Rodborough Common
GL5 5DE (.5m SW) (Trusthouse Forte) ☎(0453)878522
Telex no 437130 FAX (0453) 872523
*Situated on the edge of the common with fine views over the*
*surrounding countryside this historic inn offers character public*
*areas with good food and service standards provided by friendly,*

**S**

*attentive staff. Bedrooms vary in style and standard, some are in need of redecoration and we understand that there is a planned improvement programme.*
47⇨🕯1🛏↳in 5 bedrooms CTV in all bedrooms ® T
sB⇨🕯£65-£70 dB⇨🕯£80-£86 (room only) 🍴
⟮ 200P *xmas*
🍷 European V ❀ ⬚ ↳ Lunch £7.50-£9.50&alc Dinner
£14&alc Last dinner 9.30pm
Credit Cards ①②③④⑤

★★68% **London** 30-31 London Rd GL5 2AJ ☎(0453)759992
*On the A419 east of the town centre, this hotel has undergone major improvements and offers good open plan public areas, and most of the modern well equipped bedrooms have en suite facilities. Friendly and attentive service is provided by hosts Mr and Mrs Portal and their young staff.*
12rm(2⇨6🕯) CTV in all bedrooms ® T ✖ ✳ sB&B£23-£26
sB&B⇨🕯£32-£42 dB&B£36 dB&B⇨🕯£42-£56 🍴
10P 🚭 nc2yrs
🍷 Continental V ❀ ⬚ ↳ Lunch £5.50-£10.25&alc Dinner
£11.95&alc Last dinner 9.30pm
Credit Cards ①②③④⑤Ⓔ

★★64% **Imperial** Station Rd GL5 3AP (Berni/Chef & Brewer)
☎(0453)764077
*Conveniently situated opposite the railway station, a Georgian coaching inn clad in colourful creeping ivy offers well-equipped bedrooms, refurbished and with en suite bathrooms, complemented by a ground floor restaurant featuring the popular 'new look' Berni menu.*
25⇨🕯(2fb)2🛏 CTV in all bedrooms ® T ✖ (ex guide dogs)
sB&B⇨🕯£42-£46 dB&B⇨🕯£58 🍴
15P
🍷 Mainly grills V ❀ ↳ Lunch £8-£15alc Dinner £8-£15alc Last
dinner 10.30pm
Credit Cards ①②③⑤

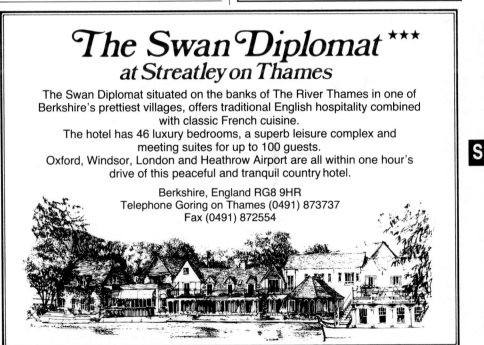
S

657

★★63% **The Bell** Wallbridge GL5 3JA ☎(0453)763556
*This small, privately owned and run hotel is situated in the town centre of Stroud, within a short distance of the railway and bus stations. The hotel is also convenient for the M5, being only 5 miles from junction 13. Rooms have been recently refurbished and offer good, modern facilities, equally suited to the business traveller or the tourist. There is a small bar, which is popular with locals, and an attractive dining room serving a good choice of dishes.*
12rm(4⇄5♠)(1fb)1⊞ CTV in all bedrooms ® T
✕ (ex guide dogs) ✳ sB&B£28-£30 sB&B⇄♠£35-£55 dB&B£40 dB&B⇄♠£48-£70 ➡
CTV 20P *xmas*
♀ Continental V ♥ ℒ Lunch £11.95&alc Dinner £11.95&alc Last dinner 9.30pm
Credit Cards 1 3

★★51% **Alpine Lodge** Stratford Rd GL5 4AJ ☎(0453)764949
RS Sun
*The bars of this small and privately-owned commercial hotel are particularly popular with locals. Its bedrooms, though simple, provide a reasonable range of facilities.*
10rm(8⇄)(4fb) CTV in all bedrooms ® T sB&B£21-£23 sB&B⇄♠£28-£30 dB&B⇄♠£38-£40
CTV 50P 2☙
♀ Mainly grills V ♥ ℒ Lunch £5-£7.50alc Dinner £7.50&alc Last dinner 9pm
Credit Cards 1 3 5 ⓔ

✿✕**Oakes** 169 Slad Rd GL5 1RG ☎(0453)759950
*This immaculately maintained stone house is on the B4070, signposted Slad from the town centre and stands high above the town. You will be met by Caroline Oakes, who is a most friendly and attentive hostess who quickly makes visitors feel at ease. A choice of 3 fixed-price menus is offered and it is quite possible to jump from one to another, but at lunch time, this top quality restaurant offers a superb value-for-money menu where a light meal, still of award winning style, is approximately half the price of the à la carte. However, it is still the place for that special occasion dinner, as the evening atmosphere is delightful. Dishes have such distinctive flavours - ragout of sea food, for example, will have each type of fish easily identifiable, and vegetables, described by one Inspector as 'Good enough to turn a meat-eater into a vegetarian' were perfectly cooked and seasoned. Some dishes may be a little too innovative. 'Bread and butter pudding' needed a designer label - it was more simply a lovely baked custard with a thin lid of fruit bread, with a gorgeous flavour, and so light, but hardly the stuff of schoolboy dreams. However, it is Chris Oakes' immaculate cooking that is the entitlement, and not dish titles, and together with his wife, Caroline, they have continued to maintain exacting standards, and to widen their circle of satisfied and regular customers.*
Closed Mon & end Dec-end Jan
Dinner not served Sun
♀ English & French V 30 seats Lunch £14.50-£32 Dinner £28-£32 Last lunch 1.45pm Last dinner 9.30pm 12P
Credit Cards 1 3

STRUY Highland *Inverness-shire* Map **14** NH33
★★73% **Cnoc** Erchless Castle Estate IV4 7JU ☎(046376)264
*This friendly little hotel, ideal for anglers, offers good, home-made cooking, well-equipped bedrooms with ensuite facilities, and spacious public areas, tastefully furnished. As we go to press, we learn of a change of ownership here, the hotel now being run by Pam and Martin Carr.*
8⇄♠(2fb) ® T ✳ sB&B⇄♠£24-£29 dB&B⇄♠£48-£58 ➡
CTV 40P ✿ ✳ shooting ⚲ *xmas*
♥ ℒ Bar Lunch £3-£5alc
Credit Cards 1 3 ⓔ

STUDLAND Dorset Map **04** SZ08
★★★63% **Knoll House** Ferry Rd BH19 3AH ☎(092944)251 FAX (092944) 423
Closed Nov-Mar
*Overlooking the sea from the delightful setting in well-kept gardens, this family holiday hotel provides excellent facilities for children, including their own dining room; there is also good, comfortable lounges and good leisure amenities.*
57rm(42⇄♠)Annexe22rm(15⇄♠)(30fb) T S% sB&B£45-£58 sB&B⇄♠£55-£68 dB&B£90-£116 dB&B⇄♠£104-£136 (incl dinner)
《 CTV 100P ✿ ✳ ⌒(heated) ▶ 9 ℛ (hard) sauna solarium gymnasium jacuzzi & leisure centre ⚲
♥ ℒ S% Lunch fr£12 Dinner fr£14 Last dinner 8.30pm

★★⚐66% **Manor House** BH19 3AU ☎(092944)288
Closed 19 Dec-Jan
*Gothic-style manor house with secluded gardens and grounds overlooking the sea and cliffs.*
20⇄♠(9fb)4⊞ CTV in all bedrooms ® T S% sB&B⇄♠£50.75-£59 dB&B⇄♠£84.75-£105.50 (incl dinner) ➡
40P ✿ ✳ ℛ (hard) nc5yrs
♀ English & French V ♥ ℒ Bar Lunch £2.50-£7.50 High tea £2.50-£4 Dinner £17 Last dinner 8.30pm
Credit Cards 1 3 ⓔ

STURMINSTER NEWTON Dorset Map **03** ST71
✕✕**Plumber Manor** DT10 2AF (2m SW on Hazlebury Brian road) (Pride of Britain) ☎(0258)72507 FAX (0258) 73370
*This impressive and comfortable restaurant-with-rooms, run by the Prideaux-Brune family, provides good-value English dishes prepared from quality fresh ingredients; the home-made puddings, in particular are not to be missed.*
Closed 1st 2 wks Feb
Lunch not served
♀ English & French V 60 seats ✳ Dinner £18-£25 Last dinner 9.30pm 25P nc12yrs
Credit Cards 1 3

SUDBURY Suffolk Map **05** TL84
★★★61% **Mill** Walnut Tree Ln CO10 6BD (Consort) ☎(0787)75544 Telex no 987623
*Originally a mill dating back nearly 300 years, it is now a more unusual hotel with many features of its past still remaining. The old mill wheel is still working today, and divides the bar and the restaurant. Comfortable accommodation and good service is provided at this hotel.*
50⇄♠(2fb) CTV in all bedrooms ® T ✳ S% sB&B⇄♠£45-£50 dB&B⇄♠£50-£68 ➡
《 60P ♪ *xmas*
♀ English & French V ♥ ℒ Lunch £9.75-£10.50&alc Dinner £14.50-£17.50&alc Last dinner 9.30pm
Credit Cards 1 2 3 5

✕**Mabey's Brasserie** 47 Gainsborough St CO10 7SS ☎(0787)74298
*In this simple brasserie the skill of one of England's most accomplished chefs is brought to the production of interesting country dishes from top quality ingredients. Interested customers can watch Robert Mabey at work - either during the daily routine or in one of his periodic demonstrations - as his cooking area is in full view of diners. An extensive blackboard menu offers such traditional savoury fare as saddle of hare, haunch of wild rabbit, rack of lamb and salmon, all matched with compatible vegetables, and you can complete your meal with an individual bread and butter pudding, a roast apple dessert or rich parfaits.*
Closed Sun, Mon, 1st 2wks Feb & 2nd 2wks Aug

♀ International **V** 38 seats Lunch £9.55-£17.95alc Dinner
£11.55-£17.95alc Last lunch 2pm Last dinner 10pm ♪
Credit Cards ①③

---

**SUNDERLAND** Tyne & Wear Map **12** NZ35

★★★63% **Swallow** Queen's Pde, Seaburn SR6 8DB (Swallow)
☎091-529 2041 Telex no 53168 FAX 091-529 4227
*A well-managed hotel built in the 1930's is pleasantly situated two*
*miles north of the town centre, overlooking the sandy beaches of*
*Whitburn. All bedrooms are well-equipped, though those in the*
*new part of the building are more comfortable and up-to-date; ;*
*there are plans for further extensive modernisation.*
65⇌(4fb)⊬in 30 bedrooms CTV in all bedrooms ® T
sB&B⇌£70-£75 dB&B⇌£80-£100 ₽
Lift ( CTV 110P CFA ◲(heated) sauna solarium gymnasium
xmas
♀ English & French **V** ♥ ⌂ Lunch fr£9.50&alc Dinner
fr£14.50 Last dinner 9.30pm
Credit Cards ①②③⑤

★★63% **Roker** Roker Ter SR6 0PH (Berni/Chef & Brewer)
☎091-567 1786
*Comfortable accommodation and friendly, informal service are*
*offered at this sea-front hotel.*
45⇌ℸ(8fb) CTV in all bedrooms ® T ℋ (ex guide dogs)
sB&B⇌ℸ£42-£48 dB&B⇌ℸ£54 ₽
( 200P
♀ Mainly grills **V** ♥ ⊬ Lunch £8-£15alc Dinner £8-£15alc Last
dinner 10.30pm
Credit Cards ①②③⑤

★★57% *Mowbray Park* Toward Rd SR1 1PR ☎091-567 8221
Telex no 587746
*This town centre, commercial hotel provides a range of bars and*
*good-value menus .*
52rm(33⇌2ℸ)(5fb) CTV in all bedrooms ®
Lift ( CTV 400P (charged) 20⇔ (charged)
♀ French **V** ♥ ⌂ ⊬
Credit Cards ①②③④⑤

★64% **Gelt House** 23 St Bede's Ter SR2 8HS (Exec Hotel)
☎091-567 2990 FAX 091-510 0724
Closed Xmas-New Year
*A small, friendly hotel is situated in a tree-lined private road close*
*to the town centre and offers simple, clean and comfortable*
*accommodation.*
14rm(3⇌6ℸ)Annexe8rm(2fb) CTV in all bedrooms ® T ℋ
sB&B⇌ℸ£34 dB&B⇌ℸ£40
( 14P ⇔
⊬ Dinner fr£8 Last dinner 8.30pm
Credit Cards ①②③⑤

---

**SURBITON** Greater London
See **LONDON plan 1***B1*(page 426)
✗✗**Chez Max** 85 Maple Rd KT6 4AW ☎081-399 2365
*Chef/patron Max Markarian offers a well-balanced fixed-price*
*menu at this cosy restaurant, using seasonal produce to advantage*
*and making good use of sauces. Service is supervised by Mrs*
*Markarian who has a team of charming French waitresses. The*
*wine list remains well-balanced.*
Closed Sun, Mon, 25-26 Dec, 1-2 Jan & Good Fri
Lunch not served Sat
♀ French **V** 40 seats ✳ Lunch £17 Dinner £17.70-£24.55alc
Last lunch 2pm Last dinner 10pm ♪ nc7yrs
Credit Cards ①②③⑤

Book as early as possible for busy holiday
periods.

---

**SUTTON** Greater London
See **LONDON plan 1***B1*(page 426)
○**Holiday Inn** Gibson Rd(Holiday Inns Inc)
☎Central reservations 071-722 7755
Due to open Mar 1991
115⇌ℸin 25 bedrooms CTV in all bedrooms ® T
Lift ( ◲(heated) sauna solarium gymnasium whirlpool spa
steam room
♀ English & French **V** ♥ ⌂ ⊬
Credit Cards ①②③④⑤

✗*Partners 23* 23 Stonecot Hill SM3 9HB ☎081-644 7743
*As we go to press we learn of a change of premises – Tim*
*McEntire and Andrew Thomason are now at 'Partners West*
*Street' in Dorking. See under Dorking for details.*
Closed Sun, Mon & 25 Dec-4 Jan
Lunch not served Sat
♀ English & French 30 seats Last lunch 2pm Last dinner
9.30pm ♪ nc10yrs
Credit Cards ①②③⑤

---

**SUTTON BENGER** Wiltshire Map **03** ST97

★★★58% **Bell House** SN15 4RH ☎Seagry(0249)720401
RS 25 Dec pm
*Set in formal gardens in a pretty village this hotel has ornate*
*bedrooms and a formal well-managed restaurant offering a*
*continental menu.*
12⇌Annexe2⇌(2fb)1 ⊞ CTV in all bedrooms ® T
sB&B⇌£48-£55 dB&B⇌£74-£87 Continental breakfast ₽
40P ✿

★★★

# THE
# KNOLL HOUSE

## A COUNTRY HOUSE HOTEL

- Within a National Trust reserve – overlooking
  three miles of golden beach and native heath.

- An independent country-house hotel under the
  third generation of personal owner management.
  A civilised and relaxing holiday for all ages.

- Six fine lounges and restaurant; tennis courts,
  nine acre golf course and outdoor heated pool.
  Jacuzzi, sauna, Turkish room, plunge-pool and gym.

- Family suites, two games rooms, separate young
  children's restaurant, playroom and
  fabulous SAFE adventure playground.

- The many ground-floor and single rooms are a
  popular all-age asset, rare in most hotels.

- Daily full board terms:
  $45 – $68 incl. VAT and service
  Children's terms
  according to age.

**Open Easter – to end of October 1991**

STUDLAND BAY DORSET
BH19 3AA
092 944 251

♀ International V ♦ ⚓ ✓ Lunch £10-£20alc Dinner £10-£20alc Last dinner 10.30pm
Credit Cards ① ② ③ ⑤

See advertisement under CHIPPENHAM

---

**SUTTON COLDFIELD** West Midlands Map **07** SP19

★★★★70%, **New Hall** Walmley Rd B76 8QX (Mount Charlotte (TS)) ☎021-378 2442 Telex no 333580 FAX 021-378 4637
*Reputedly the oldest fully moated manor house in England, New Hall's history dates back to the 13th century. The hotel, although close to Birmingham, is surrounded by 26 acres of woodland and garden and is very comfortably appointed, a particular feature being the majestic Great Hall, now the dining room, where the menus, devised by the new chef, Glen Purcell, are already proving popular. The range of services offered is extensive and traditional, ably supervised by Caroline Parkes, who manages the running of the hotel superbly.*
64➪♪2⊟ CTV in all bedrooms T ✳ sB➪♪fr£79 dB➪♪fr£95 (room only) 月
《 80P ❀ croquet archery
♀ International V ♦ ⚓ ✓ Lunch £12.50-£15.20 Dinner £19.50-£21.20&alc Last dinner 10pm
Credit Cards ① ② ③ ④ ⑤

★★★★55%, **Penns Hall** Penns Ln, Walmley B76 8LH (Embassy) ☎021-351 3111 Telex no 335789
FAX 021-313 1297
*Just south of the town, the original house dates from the 17th century but is now considerably extended to include a very good leisure centre. The facilities are popular with the locals, and this is also a conference venue.*
114➪♪✓in 13 bedrooms CTV in all bedrooms ® T S% sB➪♪£86-£98 dB➪♪£96-£110 (room only) 月
Lift 《 500P ❀ CFA ☒(heated) ♪ squash snooker solarium gymnasium steam & beauty room childrens play area *xmas*
♀ French & Italian V ♦ ⚓ Lunch fr£18 High tea fr£5 Dinner fr£19 Last dinner 10pm
Credit Cards ① ② ③ ④ ⑤

★★★68%, **Moor Hall** Moor Hall Dr, Four Oaks B75 6LN (Best Western) ☎021-308 3751 Telex no 335127 FAX 021-308 8974
*This privately owned hotel is situated in a residential area and it is advisable to ask for directions when booking. Accommodation is of a good standard with an excellent wing of new executive rooms, and the two restaurants offer a good choice of food. The hotel has its own fitness centre.*
75➪♪(3fb)3⊟✓in 5 bedrooms CTV in all bedrooms ® T sB&B➪♪£70-£95 dB&B➪♪£80-£110 月
Lift 《 180P ❀ CFA sauna solarium gymnasium *xmas*
♀ International V ♦ ⚓ Lunch £5.95-£7.45 Dinner fr£16.95 Last dinner 10.30pm
Credit Cards ① ② ③ ④ ⑤ ⑥

★★★60% **Sutton Court** 60-66 Lichfield Rd B74 2NA (Consort) ☎021-355 6071 Telex no 334175 FAX 021-355 0083
*This popular hotel, much used for conferences, has been extended over many years and now includes some annexe accommodation; rooms throughout are individually decorated and provided with good facilities, while the restaurant offers and interesting range of dishes.*
56➪♪Annexe8➪♪(9fb)1⊟✓in 13 bedrooms CTV in all bedrooms ® T S% sB&B➪♪£35-£75 dB&B➪♪£45-£98 月
《 90P *xmas*
♀ International V ♦ ⚓ ✓ Lunch fr£8&alc Dinner fr£14&alc Last dinner 10pm
Credit Cards ① ② ③ ④ ⑤ ⑥

See advertisement also under BIRMINGHAM (NATIONAL EXHIBITION CENTRE)

---

★★65%, **Berni Royal** High St B72 1UD (Berni/Chef & Brewer) ☎021-355 8222
*Dating from the 19th century this centrally situated hotel was once the home of photographer William Morris Grundy. The accommodation has been modernised with attractive floral décor, pine furnishings and excellent facilities. There are two bars and a popular Berni restaurant.*
22➪(3fb) CTV in all bedrooms ® T ✠ (ex guide dogs) sB&B➪£48-£53 dB&B➪£64 月
《 80P
♀ International V ♦ ⚓ ✓ Lunch £8-£15alc Dinner £8-£15alc Last dinner 11pm
Credit Cards ① ② ③ ⑤

★★63% **The Lady Windsor** 17 Anchorage Rd B74 2PJ ☎021-354 5181 FAX 021-355 0095
*A commercial hotel on a busy residential road on the edge of town. The elegant Garden restaurant at the rear overlooks well-tended gardens and is a popular venue for wedding receptions at weekends.*
26➪♪(2fb)2⊟ CTV in all bedrooms ® T ✠ sB&B➪♪£33-£49 dB&B➪♪£59-£68 月
CTV 46P ⊞ ❀ *xmas*
♀ Continental V ♦ ⚓ Lunch fr£8.95&alc High tea fr£3.95 Dinner fr£10.50&alc Last dinner 9.30pm
Credit Cards ① ② ③ ⑥

---

**SUTTON IN THE ELMS** Leicestershire Map **04** SP53

★★63% **Mill On The Soar** Coventry Rd LE9 6QD ☎Hinckley(0455)282419
*A pleasant country inn with a purpose-built annexe housing well-equipped modern bedrooms. Its facilities include a children's playground and a rare breeds farm. It is within easy reach of the M1 and the M69.*
20➪♪(10fb) CTV in all bedrooms ® T ✳ S% sB&B➪♪fr£38 dB&B➪♪fr£46
200P ❀ ♪
V ♦ ⚓ Lunch £9-£16alc Dinner £9-£16alc Last dinner 10pm
Credit Cards ① ② ③ ⑤

---

**SUTTON ON SEA** Lincolnshire Map **09** TF58

★★60% **Grange & Links** Sea Ln, Sandilands LN12 2RA ☎(0507)441334 FAX (0507) 443033
*An hotel popular with residents and locals alike, providing sound accommodation and good public areas, offers a particularly warm welcome to the golfers who avail themselves of its course (situated a short distance from the hotel); golfing packages are available.*
23➪♪(9fb)1⊟ CTV in all bedrooms ® T ✳ sB&B➪♪fr£46 dB&B➪♪fr£57.50 月
《 CTV 60P ❀ ▶ 18 ♪ (hard) snooker *xmas*
♀ French V ♦ Sunday Lunch fr£10alc Dinner £12.50-£25alc Last dinner 8.30pm
Credit Cards ① ② ③ ⑤

---

**SUTTON SCOTNEY** Hampshire Map **04** SU43

⌂**Travelodge (North)** SO21 3JY (on A34 northside) (Trusthouse Forte) ☎Winchester(0962)761016 Central res (0800) 850950
*Excellent value budget-price accommodation is provided in a single storey block – purpose-built and opened in 1989 – which stands adjacent to the Welcome Break Granary Food operation.*
31➪♪(31fb) CTV in all bedrooms ® sB➪♪£24 dB➪♪£29.50 (room only)
《 31P ⊞
Credit Cards ① ② ③

---

1991 marks the 25th anniversary of this guide.

⭐**Travelodge (South)** A34 Trunk Rd Southside SO21 3JY (on A34 southside) (Trusthouse Forte)
☎Winchester(0962)760779 Central res (0800) 850950
*Excellent value-for-money accommodation, including one room designed specifically for the disabled, is provided in a purpose-built, single-storey, T-shaped building which stands well back from the A34 ; guests can eat in the adjoining Little Chef restaurant and coffee shop.*
40⇆↑(40fb) CTV in all bedrooms ® sB⇆↑£24 dB⇆↑£29.50 (room only)
《 40P ⊞
♘ Mainly grills
Credit Cards ①②③

---

**SUTTON UPON DERWENT** Humberside Map **08** SE74

★★63% **Old Rectory** YO4 5BX ☎Elvington(090485)548
*A former rectory in which guests can enjoy peace and quiet while being looked after by the friendly owners and their staff. Freshly prepared, straightforward cooking is much appreciated by the guests.*
6rm(2↑)(2fb) CTV in all bedrooms ® sB&B£25-£35 dB&B£40-£44 dB&B↑£44-£46 ⋤
50P ⊞ ✿
☼
Credit Cards ① ⓔ

---

**SWAFFHAM** Norfolk Map **05** TF80

★★★61% **George** Station Rd PE37 7LJ (Consort)
☎(0760)721238
*This tastefully restored Georgian house at the centre of the town, next to the market place, offers additional well-equipped accommodation and conference facilities in purpose-built extensions to the rear. Bar and restaurant serve a variety of freshly prepared dishes, while a family team of proprietors provides willing service throughout.*
27rm(24⇆1↑)(1fb)⊞ CTV in all bedrooms ® T sB&B⇆↑£40-£45 dB&B⇆↑£52-£59 ⋤
《 100P CFA *xmas*
♘ English & French V �� ⌂ Lunch fr£11.50&alc Dinner fr£11.50&alc Last dinner 9.30pm
Credit Cards ①②③④⑤

★★69% **Grady's Country House** Norwich Rd PE37 7QS (Best Western) ☎(0760)23355
*Set in its own grounds only a few minutes' walk from the town centre, and providing ample car parking, this Georgian house offers accommodation in attractive, well-equipped bedrooms. The restaurant's menu of freshly cooked dishes is supplemented by a range of popular bar meals, hospitable proprietors are aided by an enthusiastic small staff, and an excellent, self-contained banqueting/conference facility is available.*
12⇆↑(1fb)⊞ CTV in all bedrooms ® T sB&B⇆↑£40-£50 dB&B⇆↑£50-£60 ⋤
《 70P *xmas*
♘ English & French V ♍ ⌂ Lunch £15.50-£23.50alc Dinner £15.50-£23.50alc Last dinner 9.30pm
Credit Cards ①③ ⓔ

---

**SWALLOWFIELD** Berkshire Map **04** SU76

★★57% **The Mill House** RG7 1PY ☎Reading(0734)883124
Telex no 847423
*This attractive Georgian property, tastefully converted and with well-equipped bedrooms, is now under a pleasant husband and wife management team with friendly staff. Our Inspector felt that at the time of his visit, there was room for improvement in the standard of cooking.*
10⇆↑(2fb)⊞ CTV in all bedrooms ®
40P ⊞ ✿ ♩
♘ French V ♍ ⌂ Last dinner 10pm
Credit Cards ①②③⑤

**S**

SWANAGE Dorset Map 04 SZ07

★★★62%, **Grand** Burlington Rd BH19 1LU (Best Western)
☎(0929)423353 Telex no 9401694 FAX (0929) 427068
*Occupying an excellent cliff-top position, this family resort hotel has been upgraded to provide comfortable accommodation in well-equipped bedrooms and relaxing lounges. Other facilities include an unusual and attractively appointed restaurant offering both à la carte and table d'hôte menus, and good leisure amenities which are also open to non residents. Friendly staff offer attentive and efficient services in all areas.*
30⇌🛏(5fb)1🎛 CTV in all bedrooms ⓇT sB&B⇌🛏£35-£45 dB&B⇌🛏£70-£90 🏳
Lift 🛗15P ❋ 🖃(heated) ⚓ sauna solarium gymnasium spa bath table tennis pool table *xmas*
♡ English & French V ♥ ⏣ ⊁ Lunch £9-£16alc Dinner £12.95-£13.95&alc Last dinner 9.30pm
Credit Cards ①②③⑤

★★★55%, **The Pines** Burlington Rd BH19 1LT ☎(0929)425211
Telex no 418297 FAX (0929) 422075
*A family-run resort hotel with an excellent cliff-top location offers spacious, comfortable lounges, well-equipped bedrooms and the services of a friendly, attentive staff.*
51rm(49⇌🛏)(26fb) CTV in all bedrooms T ✻
sB&B£35-£37.50 sB&B⇌🛏£35-£40 dB&B£70-£80 dB&B⇌🛏£70-£80 🏳
Lift 🛗60P 🚘 ❋ CFA 👶 *xmas*
♡ Continental V ♥ ⏣ Lunch fr£8.50 High tea fr£5 Dinner fr£15 Last dinner 9pm
Credit Cards ①③

★59%, **Suncliffe** Burlington Rd BH19 2NZ ☎(0929)423299
*Small, family-run hotel with a warm, friendly atmosphere. Bedrooms, though rather basic, are of a good size and public rooms are comfortable.*
14rm(1⇌🛏)(5fb) ✖
CTV 14P 4🚘 🚘 👶
♡

SWANWICK

See Alfreton

SWANSEA West Glamorgan Map 03 SS69

See also Langland Bay **and** Mumbles
★★★64%, **Hilton National** Phoenix Way, Swansea Enterprise Park SA7 9EG (1m S M4, jct 44 & 45, SW of Llansamlet) (Hilton) ☎(0792)310330 Telex no 48589 FAX (0792) 797535
*This modern commercial hotel is situated within the Swansea Enterprise Zone, convenient for junction 45 of the M4 motorway. Bedrooms are all well equipped, and open-plan public rooms are spacious and comfortable. A popular carvery is available, in addition to an à la carte menu.*
120⇌🛏(18fb)⊁in CTV in all bedrooms ⓇT
sB⇌🛏£74-£100 dB⇌🛏£87-£115 (room only) 🏳
🛗200P ❋ 🖃(heated) sauna gymnasium *xmas*
♡ English & French V ♥ ⏣ ⊁ Lunch £5.50-£8.95&alc Dinner £12.95-£14.25&alc Last dinner 9.45pm
Credit Cards ①②③⑤

★★★63%, **Fforest** Pontardulais Rd, Fforestfach SA5 4BA (on A483 1.5m S of M4 junc 47) (Lansbury) ☎(0792)588711
Telex no 48105 FAX (0792) 586219
*A busy, commercial hotel with good modern bedrooms, a small fitness centre and extensive conference/function facilities. The attractive restaurant serves a good à la carte menu and a range of bar meals is also available. Situated on the Swansea side of the M4, one mile from junction 47.*
34⇌🛏(1fb)1🎛 in 4 bedrooms CTV in all bedrooms ⓇT
sB&B⇌🛏£68 dB&B⇌🛏£82 🏳
🛗CTV 200P sauna solarium

♡ Mainly grills V ♥ ⏣ ⊁ Lunch fr£8.95 Dinner fr£14&alc Last dinner 10.30pm
Credit Cards ①②③⑤

★★★54%, **Dolphin** Whitewalls SA1 3AB (Inter-Hotels)
☎(0792)650011 Telex no 48128 FAX (0792) 642871
*A busy town-centre hotel which is popular with business people provides free parking at a local public car-park. It has an all-day coffee lounge at ground level with a cosy cocktail bar and restaurant on the floor above; bedrooms are all well-equipped, though a little dated.*
65⇌🛏(5fb) CTV in all bedrooms ⓇT
Lift 🛗 🥢
♡ English & Continental V ♥ ⏣ Last dinner 9.30pm
Credit Cards ①②③⑤

★★71%, **Beaumont** 72 Walter Rd SA1 4QA ☎(0792)643956
FAX (0792) 643044
*Situated between the city centre and the uplands area this is a well-run commercial and family hotel. Public areas are comfortable and relaxing, the food is good and the staff very friendly. Bedrooms vary in size, all are well furnished and equipped.*
17⇌🛏🛏2🎛⊁in 1 bedroom CTV in all bedrooms ⓇT
sB&B⇌🛏£45-£56 dB&B⇌🛏£55-£78
10P 🚘
♡ Welsh, French & Italian V ♥ ⏣ Lunch fr£12.50alc High tea fr£6alc Dinner fr£14.50alc Last dinner 9.30pm
Credit Cards ①②③⑤

See advertisement on page 665

★★64%, **Oak Tree Parc** Birchgrove Rd SA7 9JR
☎Skewen(0792)817781
(For full entry see Birchgrove)

★★62%, **Nicholaston House** Nicholaston SA3 2HL
☎(0792)371317
(For full entry see Penmaen)

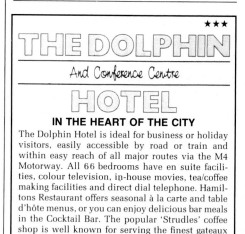

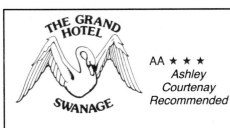

S

★73% **Windsor Lodge** Mount Pleasant SA1 6EG
☎(0792)642158 & 652744 FAX (0792) 648996
Closed 25-26 Dec
*An attractive Georgian house, close to the town centre and very popular with a business clientele, features attractive bedrooms which, though on the small side, are all well equipped with modern facilities. The cosy restaurant provides a good choice of food, there is a comfortable lounge, and friendly staff offer help throughout.*
19rm(11⇨4♠) CTV in all bedrooms ® T ✱
sB&B£21.75-£25.88 sB&B⇨♠£36.80 dB&B£42.55
dB&B⇨♠£51.75 ♬
25P 1🏌 (£2) ⊟ sauna
♡ English & French V ✧ Dinner £12-£16.50 Last dinner 9.30pm
Credit Cards ①②③⑤ ⑥

★65% **Parkway** 253 Gower Rd, Sketty SA2 9JL
☎(0792)201632
Closed 25 Dec-1 Jan
*Situated on Gower Road in a residential suburb, this extended house offers attractive open-plan public areas and modern well-equipped bedrooms. Mr and Mrs Wearing and their staff provide friendly service.*
15♠ CTV in all bedrooms ® T ✱ sB&B♠£31 dB&B♠£39 ♬
CTV 16P ⊟ games room
Lunch £4.50-£7.50&alc Dinner £7.50&alc Last dinner 8pm
Credit Cards ①②③⑤

○**Forte** Kingsway Circle SA1 5LS (Trusthouse Forte)
☎(0792)651074 Telex no 48309 FAX (0792) 456044
Due to re-open spring 1991
*This hotel, previously called The Dragon and awarded four stars, has been closed for extensive refurbishment and is due to re-open in March 1991.*
99⇨♠(12fb)⊬in 30 bedrooms

**SWANWICK** Hampshire Map **04** SU50

✗✗**Yew Tree Farm Restaurant** Botley Rd SO3 7BU
☎Locks Heath(0489)577291
*This restaurant has elegantly furnished dining rooms on two floors and a very comfortable lounge and bar facility. Chef/Manager Michael Ashman specialises in local game and seasonal fish, his individual modern style of cooking is based on classical recipes. Service is quietly efficient. There are no half bottles of wine, but a good connoisseurs list is available.*
Closed Mon & 1st 2wks Jan
Lunch not served Sat
Dinner not served Sun
♡ English & French V 40 seats ✱ Lunch fr£13.50 Dinner fr£21.50&alc Last lunch 2pm Last dinner 10pm 30P ⊬
Credit Cards ①②③

**SWAY** Hampshire Map **04** SZ29

★★60% **White Rose** Station Rd SO41 6BA (Exec Hotel)
☎Lymington(0590)682754
*Substantial red brick house standing in 6 acres of grounds with well-equipped, if plainly-appointed bedrooms, and an attractive bar serving good value imaginative bar meals.*
11rm(9⇨)(2fb) CTV in all bedrooms ® T S10% sB&B£33
sB&B⇨£40 dB&B£52 dB&B⇨£66 ♬
Lift 50P ⊟ ✱ ⊋ *xmas*
V ✧ ⊋ S10% Lunch £11-£17alc Dinner £10&alc Last dinner 9pm
Credit Cards ①③ ⑥

Hotels with a high percentage rating for quality
are highlighted by a % across their
gazetteer entry.

**SWINDON** Wiltshire Map **04** SU18
See also Inglesham

★★★★68% **Blunsdon House Hotel & Leisure Club** Blunsdon
SN2 4AD (3m N off A419) (Best Western) ☎(0793)721701
Telex no 444491 FAX (0793) 721056
*Family owned and run hotel where the proprietors take a personal interest in their guests' well being. Bedrooms are comfortable and well-equipped and there is a formal restaurant and a separate carvery. Supervised crèche for younger guests.*
88⇨♠(13fb)5⊟ CTV in all bedrooms ® T ✈ (ex guide dogs)
✱ sB&B⇨♠£75-£82.50 dB&B⇨♠£85-£92.50 ♬
Lift ℂ 300P ✿ CFA ▣(heated) ♪ (hard) squash snooker sauna
solarium gymnasium spa pool skittles beauty therapy ⊘ *xmas*
♡ English & French V ✧ ⊋ Lunch £8.75-£12&alc Dinner £8.75-£15&alc Last dinner 10pm
Credit Cards ①②③⑤

★★★71% **Holiday Inn** Piper's Way SN3 1SH (Holiday Inns)
☎(0793)512121 Telex no 445789 FAX (0793)513114
*This is a modern, purpose-built hotel, attractively designed, and occupying a convenient site on the edge of town. The public areas are spacious and very well maintained, with an impressive leisure complex, whilst the comfortable bedrooms are equipped to the highest standards. The young staff provide a friendly style of service that will prove popular with the business guest.*
158⇨♠(48fb)⊬in 20 bedrooms CTV in all bedrooms ® T ✱
sB⇨♠£80 dB⇨♠£97 (room only) ♬
Lift ℂ ⊞ 190P ✿ ▣(heated) ♪ (hard) squash sauna solarium
gymnasium Turkish steam bath *xmas*
♡ English & Continental V ✧ ⊋ ⊬ Lunch £10.25-£14.25&alc
Dinner £16.50&alc Last dinner 10.15pm
Credit Cards ①②③④⑤

**S**

**S**

**★★★ 64%, Post House** Marlborough Rd SN3 6AQ (Trusthouse Forte) ☎(0793)524601 Telex no 444464 FAX (0793) 512887
*This sprawling, modern, purpose-built hotel, conveniently located between town centre and motorway, offers accommodation in bedrooms which are in process of upgrading, good health and fitness facilities, and a restaurant serving either table d'hôte or à la carte meals at both lunch and dinner times.*
104⇌(26fb)⊱in 32 bedrooms CTV in all bedrooms ® T ✱ sB⇌fr£75 dB⇌fr£85 (room only) 月
《 200P ✿ CFA ◲(heated) sauna solarium gymnasium jacuzzi xmas
𝒢 English & Continental V ✿ ⚏ ⊱ S% Lunch fr£9.50&alc Dinner fr£12.50&alc Last dinner 10pm
Credit Cards ① ② ③ ④ ⑤

**★★★ 62%, Wiltshire** Fleming Way SN1 1TN (Mount Charlotte (TS)) ☎(0793)528282 Telex no 444250 FAX (0793) 541283
*A purpose-built hotel close to the town centre with parking facilities in a nearby, multi-storey car park. Bedrooms have been completely renovated to provide a high standard of comfort and facilities.*
93⇌ CTV in all bedrooms ® T sB⇌↑£72.50-£85 dB⇌↑£79.50-£92 (room only) 月
Lift 《 ♪ CFA ♫ xmas
𝒢 English & French V ✿ ⚏ Lunch £14.50-£16&alc Dinner £14.50-£16&alc Last dinner 10pm
Credit Cards ① ② ③ ⑤

**★★★ 60%, Crest** Oxford Rd, Stratton St Margaret SN3 4TL (3m NE A420) (Trusthouse Forte) ☎(0793)831333 Telex no 444456 FAX (0793) 831401
*Purpose built hotel on the edge of town with comfortable bedrooms, an attractive restaurant and pleasant staff. Standard bedrooms are plainly furnished but well equipped. Other accommodation includes disabled guest rooms, and 'Lady' guest rooms which have a more feminine décor and extra facilities. There is an open plan bar and carvery restaurant, which also caters for vegetarians and diabetics.*
94⇌↑(13fb)⊱in 23 bedrooms CTV in all bedrooms ® T 月
《 150P ✿ pool table xmas
𝒢 English & French V ✿ ⚏ ⊱
Credit Cards ① ② ③ ④ ⑤

**★★★ 58%, Quality Hotel Swindon** Sandy Ln, South Marston SN3 4SL ☎(0793)827777 Telex no 444634 FAX (0793) 827879
*The hotel offers a choice of Standard or Executive bedrooms, extensive indoor leisure facilities and a selection of conference rooms. The sports bar/coffee lounge is used for discos and other entertainment.*
40⇌(4fb) CTV in all bedrooms ® T ✱ sB&B⇌£27.50-£75 dB&B⇌£55-£85 月
《 CTV 200P 1🏚 ✿ ◲(heated) ⌿(heated) squash snooker sauna solarium gymnasium badminton spa bath table tennis ◷ xmas
𝒢 English & French V ⊱ Lunch fr£9.75 Dinner fr£13.95&alc Last dinner 9.45pm
Credit Cards ① ② ③ ⑤ £

**★★★ 53%, Goddard Arms** High St, Old Town SN1 3EW (Trusthouse Forte) ☎(0793)692313 Telex no 444764 FAX (0793) 512984
*The ivy clad, Cotswold stone building with two modern bedroom annexes is set in three acres of grounds. A warm comfortable atmosphere prevails throughout and staff are pleasant and friendly. Good car parking.*
18⇌↑ Annexe47⇌↑⊱in 12 bedrooms CTV in all bedrooms ® T ✱ sB⇌↑fr£70 dB⇌↑fr£87 (room only) 月
《 120P CFA
V ✿ ⚏ ⊱ Lunch fr£10&alc High tea fr£4 Dinner fr£12.50&alc Last dinner 9.30pm
Credit Cards ① ② ③ ④ ⑤

**★★ 71%, Salthrop House** Salthrop SN4 9QP ☎(0793)812990 FAX (0793) 814380
*Set in 16 acres of grounds and lovingly restored to its former glory, this classical Georgian stone house has only recently been opened as a country hotel. Its ideal situation combines with pleasant accommodation in stylish bedrooms, elegant public areas and a small cellar restaurant to make this hotel perfect for a quiet business seminar or country weekend.*
10⇌↑2🏚 CTV in all bedrooms ® ⋈ ✱ sB&B⇌↑£85 dB&B⇌↑£105 月
CTV 100P ⊕ nc14yrs
𝒢 French Lunch £18.50 Dinner £25 Last dinner 9.15pm
Credit Cards ① ③ ⑤ £

○**De Vere** Shawridge Leisure Park, Shawridge(De Vere) ☎Farnham Common(02814)6505
165rm

**SYMONDS YAT (EAST)** Hereford & Worcester
Map 03 SO51

**★★ 65%, Royal** HR9 6JL ☎Symonds Yat(0600)890238
Closed 3-30 Jan RS Nov-2 Jan & Feb
*This peaceful hotel in a superb location on the banks of the River Wye is ideally placed for touring the Wye Valley. The comfortable accommodation is equally suitable for tourists and business travellers alike.*
20⇌↑4🏚 ® T ⋈ (ex guide dogs) sB&B⇌↑£29.50 dB&B⇌↑£59-£69 月
80P ⊕ ✿ ♪ sauna solarium abseiling canoeing clay pigeon shooting nc12yrs xmas
𝒢 British, French & Italian V ✿ ⚏ Sunday Lunch £8.75 Dinner £15.50-£17.50&alc Last dinner 9.30pm
Credit Cards ① ② ③

**SYMONDS YAT (WEST)** Hereford & Worcester
Map 03 SO51

**★★ 64%, Paddocks** HR9 6BL ☎(0600)890246 FAX (0600) 890964
*This large hotel, set in one of the most popular and picturesque parts of the Wye Valley, but easily reached from the A40, offers well equipped accommodation which is equally suitable for tourists or business guests. Coach parties and users of the extensive function suite also increase its trade. Outdoor facilities include a tennis court and a pitch-and-putt course.*
26rm(24⇌↑)(2fb) CTV in all bedrooms ® T ✱ sB&B£21.50 sB&B⇌↑£26.50 dB&B⇌↑£53 月
150P ✿ 𝒫 (hard) pitch & putt nc12yrs
𝒢 English & French V ✿ ⚏ Lunch £9.20-£17.45alc High tea £3.50-£10alc Dinner £9.20-£17.45alc Last dinner 9.45pm
Credit Cards ① ③ ⑤ £

**TAIN** Highland *Ross & Cromarty* Map 14 NH78

**★★★ 65%, Morangie House** Morangie Rd IV19 1PY ☎(0862)2281 FAX (0862) 2872
*An imposing Victorian mansion standing in three acres of grounds to the north of Tain with uninterrupted views to Dornoch Firth. Bedrooms offer a high standard of comfort whatever their size, and décor is in keeping with the period. Public rooms retain their Victorian stained-glass windows.*
11⇌↑(1fb)1🏚 CTV in all bedrooms ® T sB&B⇌↑£30-£42 dB&B⇌↑£45-£55 月
30P ✿
𝒢 Scottish & Continental V ✿ ⚏ Lunch £6-£13&alc Dinner £5-£15&alc Last dinner 10pm
Credit Cards ① ② ③ ⑤

For key to symbols see the inside front cover.

★★★62% **Royal** High St IV19 1AB (Minotels) ☎(0862)2013
FAX (0862) 3450
*Nicely appointed and comfortable hotel catering for business*
*people and holidaymakers.*
25rm(9⇥13♠) CTV in all bedrooms ® T ♬
10P 6🍴 (£2)
V ♥ ⎶ Dinner £14.50 Last dinner 9pm
Credit Cards ⃞1⃞ ⃞2⃞ ⃞3⃞ ⃞5⃞

TALKE Staffordshire Map 07 SJ85

○**Granada** North Links(Granada)
☎Central reservations (05255) 5555
Due to open Apr 1991
60⇥♠

**See advertisement under STOKE-ON-TRENT**

TALLAND BAY Cornwall & Isles of Scilly Map 02 SX25

★★★♨71% **Talland Bay** PL13 2JB (Inter-Hotels)
☎Polperro(0503)72667 FAX (0503) 72940
Closed 2 Jan-10 Feb
*Lovely gardens surround this charming hotel whose rooms have*
*excellent sea views, are tastefully appointed and well equipped.*
*The food is good, the staff helpful, and the hotel has access to the*
*beach.*
19⇥Annexe2⇥(2fb)1♨ CTV in all bedrooms T
sB&B⇥£40-£70 dB&B⇥£80-£150 (incl dinner) ♬
25P ⊞ ✿ ⌇(heated) sauna solarium croquet games room
putting *xmas*
♉ English & French V ♥ ⎶ Sunday Lunch £7.50 High tea
£5.50-£7&alc Dinner £16.40&alc Last dinner 9pm
Credit Cards ⃞1⃞ ⃞2⃞ ⃞3⃞ ⃞5⃞

TALSARNAU Gwynedd Map 06 SH63

★★

★★ ♨ MAES Y NEUADD
LL47 6YA ( 2m SE on unclass
rd off B4573) (Pride of
Britain)
☎Harlech(0766)780200
FAX (0766) 780211
Closed 9-20 Dec
*Over the past eight years the*
*owners have steadily improved this historic old property, parts*
*of which date back to the 14th century, and we are delighted*
*to award it red stars for the first time this year. Surrounded by*
*several acres of grounds amidst some of the finest scenery*
*Wales can offer, the hotel is the perfect place in which to relax*
*and let yourself be looked after by the particularly friendly*
*staff. Chef Andrew Taylor prepares an imaginative menu,*
*served in the elegant restaurant, which has added to the hotel's*
*popularity. Accommodation has now been extended by the*
*conversion of the former coach house into an annexe with*
*luxurious bedrooms and a second lounge.*
12⇥♠Annexe4⇥♠1♨ CTV in all bedrooms T
sB&B⇥♠£35-£39 dB&B⇥♠£90-£118 ♬
50P ⊞ ✿ nc7yrs *xmas*
V ♥ ⎶ ✂ Lunch £13.95 Dinner £23.50&alc Last dinner
9.15pm
Credit Cards ⃞1⃞ ⃞2⃞ ⃞3⃞ ⃞5⃞

1991 marks the 25th anniversary of this guide.

T

★★**64%** **Tregwylan** LL47 6YG
☎Penrhyndeudraeth(0766)770424
*A farmhouse built in 1906 has been extended to create a*
*comfortable, family-run hotel offering a warm Welsh welcome and*
*commanding superb views over Cardigan Bay from the pleasant*
*setting of its own grounds.*
10rm(8⇨3ℹ)(3fb) CTV in all bedrooms ® ✟ (ex guide dogs)
✱ sB&B⇨3ℹ£21.50 dB&B£31 dB&B⇨3ℹ£37 🅿
CTV 20P 🕭 ✿
V ✧ ⚅ Dinner £9.75 Last dinner 8.30pm
Credit Cards ①③

---

**TAL-Y-BONT (near Conwy)** Gwynedd Map **06** SH76

★★**63%** **Lodge** LL32 8YX ☎Dolgarrog(049269)766
*Resident owners offer a friendly reception to guests at this small,*
*village hotel in the beautiful Conwy Valley. Bedrooms are in a*
*modern, single-storey block at the back of the main building and*
*have good facilities. The standard of food is good.*
Annexe10⇨1🖭 CTV in all bedrooms ® 🅿
50P ✿ *xmas*
� British & French V ✧ ⚅ ✔ Sunday Lunch £5.75-£7.50
Dinner fr£11.50&alc Last dinner 9pm
Credit Cards ①③£

---

**TALYBONT-ON-USK** Powys Map **03** SO12

★★**67%** **Aberclydach House** Aber LD3 7YS (2m SW)
☎(087487)361 FAX (087487) 436
*An elegant eighteenth-century house, set in a wooded valley within*
*the Brecons National Park, has been carefully modernised to*
*provide well-equipped bedrooms and comfortable public areas;*
*meals are of a high standard, and speciality activity holidays are*
*available.*
11⇨3ℹ✔in 4 bedrooms CTV in all bedrooms ® T ✟
sB&B⇨3ℹfr£34 dB&B⇨3ℹfr£58 🅿
CTV 14P ✿
V ✧ ⚅ ✔ Lunch £6.25-£8.50 High tea fr£4.50 Dinner fr£15.50
Last dinner 8.30pm
Credit Cards ①③

---

**TAL-Y-LLYN** Gwynedd Map **06** SH70

★★**62%** **Tyn-y-Cornel** LL36 9AJ ☎Abergynolwyn(065477)282
*A well furnished and comfortable hotel commands superb views*
*from its lakeside setting.*
6⇨3ℹAnnexe9⇨3ℹ(2fb) CTV in all bedrooms ® T ✱
sB&B⇨3ℹ£47-£57 dB&B⇨3ℹ£94 (incl dinner) 🅿
60P 3🖾 🕭 ✿ ⚊(heated) ✈ sauna solarium
♛ English & Continental V ✧ ⚅ Lunch fr£7.50&alc High tea
fr£2.50 Dinner fr£12.50&alc Last dinner 9.30pm
Credit Cards ①②③⑤

★

★ **MINFFORDD**

Minffordd LL36 9AJ
☎Corris(0654) 761665

Closed Jan-Feb RS Nov-
Dec & Mar

*Literally translated,*
*Minffordd means 'edge of the*
*road' and this charming hotel*
*stands at the head of the Dysynni Valley in magnificent*
*scenery, but near to the A487/B4405 junction. Mr and Mrs*
*Pickles have made the old inn such a hospitable place to stay*
*that guests return time and again. Their son, Jonathan, is in*
*charge of the cooking and offers high quality, well prepared*

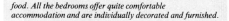

*food. All the bedrooms offer quite comfortable*
*accommodation and are individually decorated and furnished.*

6⇨3ℹ ® T ✟ sB&B⇨3ℹ£51-£56
dB&B⇨3ℹ£82-£92 (incl dinner) 🅿
12P 🕭 ✿ nc3yrs *xmas*
✧ ✔ Dinner £14.75 Last dinner 8.30pm
Credit Cards ①③⑤

---

**TAMWORTH** Staffordshire Map **07** SK20

⌂**Granada Lodge** (A5/M42 jnct 10) (Granada)
☎(0827)260123 FAX (0827) 260145
*This large lodge on junction 10 of the M42 has 24-hour service.*
*Rooms are comfortable and well equipped and offer a limited room*
*service for food throughout the day, and a Continental breakfast in*
*the morning.*
63⇨3ℹ(10fb)✔in 20 bedrooms CTV in all bedrooms ®
✟ (ex guide dogs) ✱ S% sB⇨3ℹfr£28
dB⇨3ℹfr£31 (room only)

---

**TANGUSDALE**

See **Barra, Isle of**

---

**TAPLOW** Buckinghamshire Map **04** SU98

★★★★

★★★★★🏆 CLIVEDEN

SL6 0JF (Prestige)
☎Maidenhead
(0628)668561
Telex no 846562
FAX (0628) 661837

*Owned by the National Trust*
*and leased to Blakeney*
*Hotels, this marvellous*
*stately home, once the home of the Astors, has been awarded*
*Red Stars for the very first time this year. It has been*
*transformed under the guidance of the Hon. John Sinclair into*
*one of the country's finest hotels. Set amidst almost 400 acres*
*of woodland, parkland and formal gardens leading to the*
*banks of the Thames, the house offers a wide range of leisure*
*pursuits that now include a fine indoor swimming pool and*
*health centre. The public areas, steeped in history, abound in*
*opulence and comfort and the simplicity of the main dining*
*room is a refreshing contrast. As we go to press, we learn of*
*the development of a further eating option, in the shape of an*
*intimate basement grill room. The individually styled*
*bedrooms are, for the most part, very generous in size and*
*classical in style, incorporating the highest levels of quality*
*and comfort. Standards of service are exceptionally*
*professional and unobtrusive to reflect the level of formality*
*that the Management feel are appropriate. Ron Maxfield, the*
*talented young chef, is now beginning to show skill and flair in*
*his cooking, producing exceptionally good soups and sauces.*
25⇨3ℹAnnexe6⇨3ℹ2🖾✔in 1 bedroom CTV in all
bedrooms T ✱ S% sB&B⇨3ℹfr£150 dB&B⇨3ℹfr£185
Lift ℭ 30P 3🖾 🕭 ✿ ▣(heated) ⚊(heated) ▶ 4 ♐ (hard)
✈ squash ⚓ snooker sauna solarium gymnasium indoor
tennis turkish bath massage *xmas*

V S% Lunch fr£27&alc Dinner fr£39.80&alc Last dinner
9.30pm
Credit Cards ①③④⑤

## TARBERT

See Harris, Isle of

**TARBERT LOCH FYNE** Strathclyde *Argyllshire*
Map **10** NR86

★★★55% *Stonefield Castle* PA29 6YJ ☎Tarbert(0880)820836
Telex no 776321
*In a quiet, secluded position, surrounded by fifty acres of beautiful grounds, the hotel combines the charm and character of a previous age with modern comforts.*
33rm(30⇌2♠)(4fb) CTV in all bedrooms ®
Lift ( CTV 50P ⇔ ✿ ⌿(heated) ♪ (hard) snooker sauna solarium gymnasium
✿ 🖫 ⌿

Credit Cards ①②③⑤

★59% *West Loch* PA29 6YF ☎Tarbert(0880)820283
*The small, roadside, family-run hotel has a reputation for producing fine, imaginative food. The style of cooking is international and the intentionally limited dinner menu, which is changed daily, features fresh local sea-food and game in season.*
6rm(2fb)
CTV 20P ⇔ ✿
Ⴒ International V ✿ 🖫 ⌿ Last dinner 8.30pm

**TARPORLEY** Cheshire Map **07** SJ56

★★★69% **The Wild Boar** Whitchurch Rd, Beeston CW6 9NW
(2.5m S off A49) ☎Bunbury(0829)260309 Telex no 61222
FAX (0829) 261081
*Located on the A49 about 3 miles south of Tarporley. A new building with good bedroom accommodation has been constructed looking out over the beautiful rolling countryside and blending perfectly with the striking mock-Tudor style of the elegant* ▶

**T**

*restaurant which adjoins. The restaurant itself is quickly earning
favour for its high standard of cuisine.*
37⇌🕯(19fb) CTV in all bedrooms ® T sB&B⇌🕯£45-£68
dB&B⇌🕯£68-£80 🍴
《70P ✿ *xmas*
♀ English & French V ✿ ⬛ Lunch fr£11&alc Dinner
fr£16.50&alc Last dinner 10pm
Credit Cards [1] [2] [3] [5]

★★♨64% **The Willington Hall** Willington CW6 0NB (3m NW
off unclass rd linking A51 & A54) ☎Kelsall(0829)52321
Closed 25 Dec
*A delightful mock-Elizabethan house set in extensive parkland at
the heart of rural Cheshire offers spaciously comfortable bedrooms
with good facilities and cosy dining rooms serving meals of a high
standard.*
10⇌(1fb) CTV in all bedrooms ®
60P 1🏮 🚑 ✿ ✏ (hard) nc5yrs
V
Credit Cards [1] [2] [3] [5]

---

TAUNTON Somerset Map 03 ST22

---

❀ ★★★♨84% **The Mount Somerset Country House** Lower
Henlade TA3 5NB ☎(0823)442500 FAX (0823) 442900
*This gracious Georgian house overlooking Taunton Vale was
opened two years ago after extensive refurbishment. There is both
a fixed-price and an à la carte menu, and although all dishes are in
the modern British style, the food can be more plainly cooked on
request. Philip Vickery, the chef, has imagination, style and flair,
and he uses the freshest produce available – some vegetables and
herbs come from the hotel's kitchen garden. Service is formal and
correct, yet friendly and charming. A fish dish 'from the day's best
catch' is always available. The pastry chef is also very talented and
extremely artistic. Crisp pastry, lined with white chocolate
filled with port-poached damsons, accompanied by a rich lemon ice
cream is a masterpiece. Coffee can be taken in the drawing room,
served with petit fours and an elaborate spun sugar creation. The
wine list is extensive and international, given the correct service by
the experienced staff. The whole Mount Somerset experience is a
treat for a special occasion.*
14⇌🕯2🛏 CTV in all bedrooms T ✖ ✳
sB&B⇌🕯£93.50-£140.25
dB&B⇌🕯£110-£165 Continental breakfast 🍴
Lift 《 54P 🚑 ✿ ✏ (hard) nc12yrs *xmas*
V ✿ ⬛ ✔ Lunch £14.50-£18&alc Dinner £28&alc Last dinner
9.30pm
Credit Cards [1] [2] [3] [5]

★★★65% **Crest Hotel** Deane Gate Av TA1 2UA (Trusthouse
Forte) ☎(0823)332222 Telex no 46703 FAX (0823) 332266
*Spacious, comfortable bedrooms, equipped with good facilities
which will appeal to commercial travellers and holidaymakers
alike, are available at this hotel which stands beside the M5 at
junction 25; conference rooms are available, and open plan public
areas include the Vale restaurant where every care is taken in the
preparation and service of the dishes featured on its table d'hôte
and à la carte menus.*
101⇌🕯(85fb)✔in 8 bedrooms CTV in all bedrooms ® 🍴
Lift 《 250P sauna gymnasium *xmas*
♀ International V ✿ ⬛ ✔
Credit Cards [1] [2] [3] [5]

★★★64% **Rumwell Manor** Rumwell TA4 1EL ☎(0823)461902
10⇌🕯(3fb)3🛏✔in 2 bedrooms CTV in all bedrooms ® T
sB&B⇌🕯£44.50-£49.50 dB&B⇌🕯£59-£75 🍴
CTV 30P 🚑 ✿ ♨
♀ English & French V ✿ ⬛ ✔ Lunch £10.50-£12.50&alc
Dinner fr£13.50&alc Last dinner 8.30pm
Credit Cards [1] [2] [3] [5] £

★★★56% **The County** East St TA1 3LT (Trusthouse Forte)
☎(0823)337651 Telex no 46484 FAX (0823) 334517
*A large, town-centre hotel catering mainly for conferences has
upgraded half its bedrooms to a very high standard and makes
good use of fresh local produce in the dishes featured on its dining
room's English menu.*
67⇌✔in 6 bedrooms CTV in all bedrooms ®
Lift 《 CTV 100P CFA
V ✿ ⬛ ✔ Last dinner 9.30pm
Credit Cards [1] [2] [3] [4] [5]

★★65% **Falcon** Henlade TA3 5DH (3m E A358) (Exec Hotel)
☎(0823)442502 FAX (0823) 442670
Closed 25 Dec
*Guests are assured of a warm welcome at this small, pleasantly
informal hotel, its particularly well-equipped bedrooms and simple,
well-cooked food making it an ideal choice for the business
traveller.*
11⇌🕯(1fb)1🛏✔in 3 bedrooms CTV in all bedrooms ® T ✖
sB&B⇌🕯fr£45 dB&B⇌🕯fr£55 🍴
25P 🚑 ✿ ♨
♀ International V ✿ ⬛ ✔ Lunch fr£8.50&alc Dinner
fr£11&alc Last dinner 9.30pm
Credit Cards [1] [3]

★★58% **Corner House** Park St TA1 4DQ ☎(0823)284683 &
272665 Telex no 46288 FAX (0823) 332276
*Conveniently situated in the town centre, the hotel is privately
owned and run, has some modern, spacious bedrooms, a formal
dining room and is popular with both business people and tourists.*
33rm(23⇌4🕯)(4fb) CTV in all bedrooms ® T
✖ (ex guide dogs) sB&Bfr£36 sB&B⇌🕯£50-£51
dB&B£62.50-£68 dB&B⇌🕯£62.50-£68
CTV 40P 2🏮 🚑
♀ English & French V ✿ ⬛ ✔ Lunch fr£7.50alc Dinner fr£10alc
Last dinner 9.15pm
Credit Cards [1] [3]

---

TAUNTON DEANE MOTORWAY SERVICE AREA (M5)
Somerset Map 03 ST12

---

⛫**Roadchef Lodge** Trull TA1 4BA ☎Taunton(0823)332228
FAX (0823) 338131
*Standing in a service area between junctions 25 and 26 of the M5,
on the southbound carriageway, the lodge offers good quality
accommodation in new and well-equipped bedrooms with modern
comforts. A choice of eating facilities is available, there being a 24-
hour cafeteria only a short walk from the lodge, and the smart new
Hickory's Restaurant with table service across the motorway
bridge.*
39⇌🕯✔in 20 bedrooms CTV in all bedrooms ® T
✖ (ex guide dogs) sB⇌🕯fr£29 dB⇌🕯fr£35 (room only)
《 P
Credit Cards [1] [2] [3] [4] [5]

---

TAVISTOCK Devon Map 02 SX47

---

★★★57% **The Bedford** Plymouth Rd PL19 8BB (Trusthouse
Forte) ☎(0822)613221 FAX (0822)618034
*A stone-built hotel, on the original site of Tavistock Abbey, the
hotel combines traditional character and modern facilities.*
30⇌🕯in 4 bedrooms CTV in all bedrooms ® T ✳ sB⇌🕯fr£65
dB⇌🕯fr£82 (room only) 🍴
24P 5🏮 (£2 per night) ✿ *xmas*
♀ English & French V ✿ ⬛ ✔ Lunch fr£8.95&alc High tea
fr£5.50 Dinner fr£13.95&alc Last dinner 9pm
Credit Cards [1] [2] [3] [4] [5]

The AA's star-rating scheme is the market
leader in hotel classification.

**TAYNUILT** Strathclyde *Argyllshire* Map **10** NN03

★★66%, **Brander Lodge** Bridge of Awe PA35 1HT (Consort)
☎(08662)243 & 225 FAX (08662) 273
*Small, comfortable family run Highland hotel with relaxing, friendly atmosphere.*
20⇨↰(2fb) CTV in all bedrooms ® T
sB&B⇨↰£20.50-£28.50 dB&B⇨↰£41-£57 ⊟
100P ✿ pool table *xmas*
♀ International V ✿ ⊡ Lunch £5-£12alc Dinner
£13.75-£16.50&alc Last dinner 9pm
Credit Cards 1 2 3 5 £

★★57%, **Polfearn** PA35 1JQ (Consort) ☎(08662)251
*Family-run, small granite hotel with gardens and a grazing field at the front.*
16rm(2⇨12↰)(2fb) ®
CTV 20P
V ✿ ⊡ ⅍ Last dinner 9pm
Credit Cards 1 3

---

**TEANGUE**

See **Skye, Isle of**

---

**TEES-SIDE AIRPORT** Co Durham Map **08** NZ31

★★★64%, **St George** Middleton St George DL2 1RH (Mount
Charlotte (TS)) ☎Darlington(0325)332631 Telex no 587623
FAX (0325) 333851
*Modern hotel within airport complex.*
59⇨↰(2fb)1❤⅍in 8 bedrooms CTV in all bedrooms ® T ✱
✕ (ex guide dogs) ✱ sB&B£24.50-£42.50
sB&B⇨↰£55-£65 dB&B⇨↰£65-£70
《 200P 20🚗 (£2.50 per day) ✿ CFA squash sauna solarium
*xmas*
♀ English & French V ✿ ⊡ ⅍ Lunch fr£7.50&alc Dinner
fr£11.75&alc Last dinner 9.45pm
Credit Cards 1 2 3 5

---

**TEIGNMOUTH** Devon Map **03** SX97

★★70%, **Ness House** Marine Dr, Shaldon TQ14 0HP
☎Shaldon(0626)873480 FAX (0626) 873486
*A comfortable Regency hotel with good sea views and modern
accommodation. The attractive restaurant offers a commendable
standard of cooking.*
7⇨↰Annexe5rm(2fb)1❤ CTV in all bedrooms ® T
✕ (ex guide dogs) ✱ sB&B£24.50-£42.50
sB&B⇨↰£24.50-£42.50 dB&B£49-£65 dB&B⇨↰£49-£65 ⊟
20P 🚗 ✿
♀ French V ✿ ⊡ Lunch £12-£20alc Dinner £12-£20alc Last
dinner 10pm
Credit Cards 1 2 3 £

★63%, **Glenside** Ringmoor Rd, Shaldon TQ14 0EP (1m S off
A379) (Guestaccom) ☎Shaldon(0626)872448
Closed Nov & 3-4 weeks during Feb or Mar
*This well-proportioned house on the Shaldon-Newton Abbott road
has been successfully converted to provide an hotel with well-
equipped bedrooms and bright, comfortable public areas. Friendly,
attentive service is rendered by both the owners and their staff.*
10rm(1⇨6↰)(1fb) CTV in all bedrooms ® ✱ sB&B£16-£21.50
sB&B⇨↰£16-£21.50 dB&B£32-£43 dB&B⇨↰£32-£43 ⊟
10P 🚗
V Dinner £9-£10 Last dinner 6.30pm

★61%, **Coombe Bank** Landscore Rd TQ14 9JL ☎(0626)772369
*Central holiday hotel with warm welcome from young owners.*
11rm(1⇨3↰)(2fb) CTV in 9 bedrooms ® ✱ sB&B£15.50-£18
sB&B⇨↰£17.50-£20 dB&B£31-£36 dB&B⇨↰£35-£40 ⊟
CTV 12P

▶

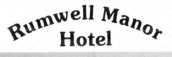

T

♀ English & French **V** ⅟ Bar Lunch £2-£2.50 Dinner £7 Last dinner 7.30pm
Credit Cards 1 3 £

---

**★60%** ***Belvedere*** Barnpark Rd TQ14 8PJ ☎(0626)774561
*Spacious detached Victorian house in a quiet elevated position. Bedrooms are comfortable, many have good en suite facilities, and good home cooking is served in the dining room.*
13rm(3⇌6↱)(4fb) CTV in 4 bedrooms ® ✖
CTV 10P 1🚗 ✲
V ✿ ☕
Credit Cards 1 3

---

**★55% Drakes** 33 Northumberland Place TQ14 8UG
☎(0626)772777
RS 12 Oct-6 Nov
*The running of this small, tastefully appointed and comfortable hotel is personally supervised by the resident owners. An interesting choice of well-cooked food is available throughout the day in the Bistro Coffee Shop, and candlelit suppers are served in the exquisite restaurant.*
6rm(5⇌↱)(1fb) CTV in all bedrooms ® **T** sB&B£16.50-£21 sB&B⇌↱£16.50-£21 dB&B⇌↱£30-£42 ▤
CTV ⅌ ✈ *xmas*
♀ English & Continental **V** ✿ ☕ Lunch £5.50-£10.50&alc High tea £5.50-£6.50 Dinner £5.50-£7.50&alc Last dinner 9.30pm
Credit Cards 1 3 £

---

**★50% Bay** 15 Powerham Terrace, Sea Front TQ14 8BL
☎(0626)774123
Closed mid Nov-Mar (ex Xmas)
*Hotel features comfortable lounge bar overlooking seafront lawns and tennis courts.*
18rm(5⇌9↱)(5fb) CTV in all bedrooms ® ✱ sB&B£17-£20 sB&B⇌↱£19-£22 dB&B£34-£40 dB&B⇌↱£38-£44 ▤
☾ CTV 16P *xmas*
♀ English & Continental **V** ✿ ☕ Lunch £2-£10alc
Credit Cards 1 2 3 5 £

---

## TELFORD Shropshire Map 07 SJ60

See also **Ironbridge**
**★★★73%** ***Madeley Court*** TF7 5DW ☎(0952)680068
FAX (0952) 684275
*Situated close to the town centre with easy access to the M54. Predominantly Elizabethan, the house originally dates from Medieval times, the 13th century hall is now the restaurant with more informal dining available in the Brasserie.*
16⇌↱ CTV in all bedrooms ® **T** ✖ (ex guide dogs)
☾ 110P ♪ ♫
V ✿ ☕ ⅟ Last dinner 10pm
Credit Cards 1 2 3 5

---

**★★★70% Holiday Inn** St Quentin Gate TF3 4EH (Holiday Inns) ☎(0952)292500 Telex no 359126 FAX (0952) 291949
*This modern, purpose built hotel has all the amenities one would expect of a Holiday Inn, including a leisure centre. Situated half a mile south-east of the town centre off the Randlay interchange of the A442.*
100⇌↱⅟in 20 bedrooms CTV in all bedrooms ® **T** S% sB⇌↱fr£80 dB⇌↱fr£92 (room only) ▤
Lift ☾ 100P ▭(heated) sauna solarium gymnasium steam room whirlpool spa *xmas*
♀ English & French **V** ✿ ☕ ⅟ S% Lunch fr£11 Dinner fr£19 Last dinner 10pm
Credit Cards 1 2 3 4 5

---

A rosette is an indication of exceptional standards of cuisine.

---

**★★★68% Telford Moat House** Forgegate, Telford Centre TF3 4NA (Queens Moat) ☎(0952)291291 Telex no 35588
FAX (0952) 292012
Closed 26-30 Dec
*A modern yet relaxing hotel, located close to the main shopping centre, with a leisure complex and extensive conference and banqueting facilities. The restaurant offers carvery, à la carte, vegetarian and diabetic menus.*
148⇌↱(8fb)⅟in 3 bedrooms CTV in all bedrooms ® **T** sB&B⇌↱£66-£89 dB&B⇌↱£70-£108 ▤
Lift ☾ CTV 300P ▭(heated) sauna solarium gymnasium games room mini-gym ♫
♀ English & French **V** ✿ ☕ Lunch fr£14.75&alc Dinner fr£14.75&alc Last dinner 10pm
Credit Cards 1 2 3 4 5

---

**★★★65%** ***Telford Hotel Golf & Country Club*** Great Hay, Sutton Hill TF7 4DT (Queens Moat) ☎(0952)585642
Telex no 35481 FAX (0952) 586602
*A very popular leisure and conference hotel that is found by following the signs to Telford Golf Club. The restaurant enjoys wide views over Ironbridge and offers a choice of set and à la carte menus. A pantry restaurant serves snacks throughout the day.*
59⇌↱(4fb) CTV in all bedrooms ®
☾ 200P ✲ ▭(heated) ▶9 squash snooker sauna ⌂
♀ International **V** ✿ ☕ Last dinner 10pm
Credit Cards 1 2 3 4 5

---

**★★★62% Buckatree Hall** Wellington TF6 5AL (Best Western)
☎(0952)641821 Telex no 35701 FAX (0952) 47540
*Nine acres of woodland surround this modern hotel at the foot of the Wrekin and a mile from junction 7 of the M54. Buckatree has established a flourishing conference trade and has a popular international-style restaurant.*
37⇌↱(1fb)4⊞ CTV in all bedrooms ® **T** sB&B⇌↱£59-£69 dB&B⇌↱£69-£79 ▤
☾ 80P ✲ *xmas*
♀ International **V** ✿ ☕ Sunday Lunch £6.95-£12 Dinner fr£10.50&alc Last dinner 10pm
Credit Cards 1 2 3 5 £

---

**★★65% Charlton Arms** Wellington TF1 1DG (County Inns)
☎(0952)251351 FAX (0952) 222077
*Dating back to the 17th century this busy town centre hotel is reached via Vineyard Road off the A442. The restaurant serves generous meals and orders for these are taken in the library lounge bar.*
26rm(22⇌1↱)(1fb)1⊞ CTV in all bedrooms ® **T** sB&B£36-£39 sB&B⇌↱£47-£50 dB&B£47.50-£50 dB&B⇌↱£59-£62 ▤
☾ 75P *xmas*
♀ European **V** ✿ ☕ Lunch £8.25-£9&alc High tea £5-£6 Dinner £8.25-£9&alc Last dinner 10pm
Credit Cards 1 2 3 5

---

**★★61% White House** Wellington Rd, Muxton TF2 8NG (off A518) ☎(0952)604276
*Once a farmhouse in rural surroundings, the hotel now stands close to the busy new town and offers convenient access to the M54. A modern wing of bedrooms provides all the usual amenities, whilst the comfortable public areas attract an extensive local food and bar trade.*
28rm(20⇌↱)(4fb) CTV in all bedrooms ® **T** sB&B£45-£55 sB&B⇌↱£45-£55 dB&B£60 dB&B⇌↱£65 ▤
100P ✲
♀ English & French **V** ✿ ☕ Lunch £9-£10.50&alc Dinner £9-£10.50&alc Last dinner 9.30pm
Credit Cards 1 2 3 £

---

For key to symbols see the inside front cover.

T

★★53%, **Falcon** Hoylhead Road, Wellington TF1 2DD
☎(0952)255011
Closed Xmas RS Sun
*An ancient and family-owned coaching inn on the old London/Holyhead road features character bars and rooms which, though modestly appointed, are brightly decorated.*
13rm(7⇨♠)(1fb) CTV in all bedrooms ✖ sB&B£27-£33
sB&B⇨♠£30-£37 dB&B£35-£40 dB&B⇨♠£42-£48 ➡
CTV 30P ⊞ nc2yrs
♥ English & Continental **V** ❖ Bar Lunch £1.10-£7alc Dinner £7.50-£15alc Last dinner 9pm
Credit Cards ① ③

★63%, **Arleston Inn** Arleston Ln, Wellington TF1 2LA
☎(0952)501881
*This small, privately owned inn is convenient for Telford and the M54. Accommodation is modern and well equipped, although some rooms are rather compact. Bar areas are cosy and a simply-appointed restaurant serves popular meals.*
6♠ CTV in all bedrooms ® ✖ (ex guide dogs) ✱ sB&B♠£32
dB&B♠£43 ➡
40P ✿
**V** Lunch £4.50-£10alc Dinner £4.50-£10alc Last dinner 10pm
Credit Cards ① ③

○**Travelodge** A5223 New Whitchurch Rd(Trusthouse Forte)
☎Central reservations (0800) 850950
Due to have opened summer 1990
40⇨

Book as early as possible for busy holiday periods.

# THE HUNDRED HOUSE HOTEL ★★

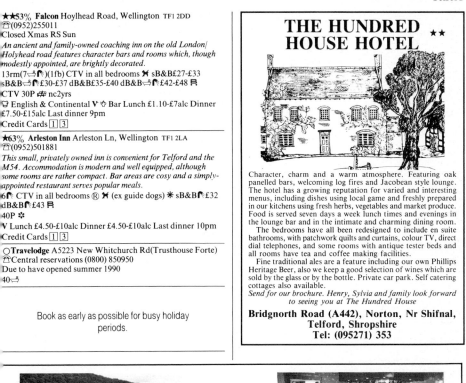

**T**

**TEMPLECOMBE** Somerset Map **03** ST72

★★**59% Horsington House** Horsington BA8 0EG (1m N A357)
☎(0963)70721 FAX (0963) 70554
*A country house of honey-coloured stone stands in eight acres of grounds which include facilities for tennis and croquet. Bridge parties are a speciality, in which the proprietors take an active role.*
23⇨🖰(2fb) CTV in all bedrooms ® T sB&B⇨🖰£46-£55 dB&B⇨🖰£69-£78 ⊟
55P ❊ ♬ (hard) croquet putting ⚗ *xmas*
♉ English & Continental V ☼ � Lunch £9.50-£11 Dinner £15-£20&alc Last dinner 9.30pm
Credit Cards ①②③⑥

---

**TEMPLE SOWERBY** Cumbria Map **12** NY62

★★**74% Temple Sowerby House** CA10 1RZ
☎Kirkby Thore(07683)61578
*This former 17th-century farmhouse is now a well-furnished and comfortable hotel of charm and character. There are two attractive lounges with open fires, and the restaurant serves well-produced cuisine. Staff are thoughtful and friendly.*
8⇨Annexe4⇨(2fb)2☷ CTV in all bedrooms ® T sB&B⇨£40 dB&B⇨£55 ⊟
30P ⚗ ❊ croquet badminton boules ⚗ *xmas*
♉ International V ☼ � ⊁ Lunch £12 Dinner £17 Last dinner 9pm
Credit Cards ①③⑥

---

**TENBY** Dyfed Map **02** SN10

★★⚐**79% Penally Abbey Country House** Penally SA70 7PY (WR) ☎(0834)3033
*Six acres of wooded grounds, which include the ruins of a 14th-century chapel, surround this delightful 200-year-old Flemish-style house which enjoys superb views across the golf links and sand dunes to Carmarthen Bay. The high quality of the bedrooms and public areas reflects the good taste and untiring efforts of the proprietors, who have painstakingly restored and refurbished the housed since acquiring it in 1985. Peace and quiet are assured, and facilities include a small heated indoor swimming pool and a snooker room.*
7⇨Annexe4⇨(3fb)8☷ CTV in all bedrooms ® T ✹ ✲ sB&B⇨£48-£58 dB&B⇨£80-£92 (incl dinner) ⊟
14P ⚗ ⊡(heated) snooker croquet *xmas*
⊁ Bar Lunch £5 Dinner £15&alc Last dinner 9pm
Credit Cards ①③

★★**69% Atlantic** Esplanade SA70 7DU ☎(0834)2881 & 4176
*Overlooking the South Beach from a superb situation which is reached via its Italianate gardens, this family holiday hotel offers good, comfortable accommodation, an elegant lounge and a spacious restaurant which looks out onto the heated indoor swimming pool.*
35⇨🖰(9fb)1☷ CTV in all bedrooms ® T sB&B⇨🖰£35-£38 dB&B⇨🖰£50-£70 ⊟
30P ❊ CFA ⊡(heated) solarium spa bath
♉ French V ☼ � ⊁ Sunday Lunch fr£6.50 Dinner fr£11 Last dinner 8.30pm
Credit Cards ①③

★★**68% Fourcroft** The Croft SA70 8AP ☎(0834)2886
FAX (0834) 2888
Closed Nov-Etr
*The gardens of this family holiday hotel overlook the popular North Beach and harbour, and it also offers its own excellent pool and leisure facilities. The same proprietors have owned it for many years, and they are very much involved in its day-to-day running, providing well-equipped accommodation with friendly, attentive service.*
38⇨🖰(6fb) CTV in all bedrooms ® T ✲ sB&B⇨🖰£35-£40 dB&B⇨🖰£62-£72 ⊟

Lift ☾ 5P (£1.50 per night) ❊ ⊿(heated) sauna gymnasium games room spa pool
♉ International V ☼ ⊁ Bar Lunch £1-£5alc High tea £2-£4 Dinner £13.50-£15 Last dinner 8.30pm
Credit Cards ①③

★★**64% Harbour Heights** 11 The Croft SA70 8AP ☎(0834)2132
*Overlooking the sands of the North Beach, this small, family-run hotel is comfortable and well equipped. Fresh produce is used in the kitchens and the food is good, although the choice of dishes is necessarily fairly small.*
8⇨🖰(4fb) CTV in all bedrooms ® ✲
✗ ⚗ nc8yrs
♉ English & Continental Last dinner 9.30pm
Credit Cards ①②③⑤

★★**63% Albany** The Norton SA70 8AB ☎(0834)2698
23⇨🖰(2fb) CTV in all bedrooms ® S% sB&B⇨🖰£25.50-£31 dB&B⇨🖰£43-£54 ⊟
*xmas*
♉ French V ☼ � ⊁ S% Lunch £7.95 Dinner £7.95&alc Last dinner 9.30pm
Credit Cards ①②③⑥

★★**63% Esplanade** The Esplanade SA70 7DU ☎(0834)3333
*Located on the sea front, over the sandy south beach, this family-run hotel provides modern, comfortable bedrooms and open plan public areas. A small fixed-price menu is available for guests, and the town centre is just a few yards away.*
15⇨🖰Annexe3⇨🖰(5fb) CTV in all bedrooms ® T
✗ ⚗
♉ French ☼ � Last dinner 9.30pm
Credit Cards ①②③⑤

★★**Royal Lion** High St SA70 7ES ☎(0834)2127
Closed Nov-Feb
*This Victorian hotel occupies a fine seafront position with views over the harbour; the comfortable bedrooms are well equipped, and service is friendly.*
36rm(14⇨1🖰)(8fb) CTV in all bedrooms ® T sB&B£22-£30 dB&B£35-£55 dB&B⇨🖰£45-£65 ⊟
Lift CTV 40P
☼ ⊆cue
Credit Cards ①③⑤

★**65% Buckingham** Esplanade SA70 7DU ☎(0834)2622
Closed Dec-Feb
*This small holiday hotel overlooking the South Beach, is run by the friendly Rooke family. A cosy bar/lounge is available for residents, and bedrooms are bright and well equipped.*
8⇨🖰(2fb) CTV in all bedrooms ® sB&B⇨🖰£20-£22 dB&B⇨🖰£37-£40 ⊟
✗ ⚗
V ☼ Lunch £6 Dinner £9.50 Last dinner 7.45pm
Credit Cards ①③

All hotels are now given a percentage grading for the quality of their facilities. A full explanation can be found within 'How we Classify Hotels and Restaurants' at the front of the book.

## TENTERDEN Kent Map **05** TQ83

★★71% **Little Silver Country** Ashford Rd, St Michael's TN30 6SP ☎High Halden(023385)321
*Whilst retaining much of its former 'olde worlde' charm, the house has been lovingly renovated and extended to provide a choice of bedrooms, equipped to the highest standard. The beamed sitting room has an open fire at each end, and also extends into a Victorian-style conservatory, which overlooks the beautifully kept lawned gardens. The octagonal-shaped function suite adds yet another dimension to this charming and relaxing, family-run hotel, where the standards of personal service being provided by the resident proprietors is much appreciated by the regular clientèle.*
10⇌ℕ(3fb)1⊠ CTV in all bedrooms ® **T** ✗ (ex guide dogs)
✱ sB&B⇌ℕ£48-£64 dB&B⇌ℕ£62-£90
CTV 40P *xmas*
**V** ⊁ Lunch £13-£16alc Dinner £13-£16alc Last dinner 9.30pm
Credit Cards 1 3

## TETBURY Gloucestershire Map **03** ST89

★★★

✿★★★♣ **CALCOT MANOR**

Calcot GL8 8YJ (3m W at junc A4135/A46) (Pride of Britain)
☎Leighterton(0666)890391
Telex no 437105
FAX (0666) 890394
Closed 2-10 Jan
*Seen from the road, this attractive group of Cotswold stone buildings does not look like an hotel, but such relaxed and unpretentious style is typical of this charming and comfortable hotel, where guests who appreciate peace, quiet and excellent food will instantly be made to feel at home by the owners Mr and Mrs Ball and their son Richard. The highlight of one's stay at Calcot Manor has to be the cooking of their young chef, Ramon Farthing. It is a delight to experience his successsful combination of flavours in dishes such as the breast of local pigeon with creamed potato, glazed apples, pan-fried chicken livers and a caramelised game sauce, or the starter of red mullet poached in tomato and mushroom vinaigrette served on a crab and potato galette. Breakfasts, too, are excellent, so with the food and hospitality leaving nothing to be desired, it is a pity that some of the bedrooms in the main house are beginning to look tired; on the other hand the newer bedrooms in the annexe are very pleasantly furnished and, arguably, have more character. The lounges are very comfortable indeed, and the two Retrievers who wander amiably around contribute to the relaxing atmosphere that cannot fail to refresh the spirits.*
7⇌ℕAnnexe6⇌ℕ1⊠ CTV in all bedrooms **T**
✗ (ex guide dogs) ✱ sB&B⇌ℕ£80-£100
dB&B⇌ℕ£95-£140 ⊟
40P 3⌂ ⚘ ❉ CFA ⩯(heated) croquet lawn nc12yrs *xmas*
☋ English & French ♆ ⩍ ⊁ Sunday Lunch £16.50-£25
Dinner £30-£38 Last dinner 9.30pm
Credit Cards 1 2 3 5

All AA-appointed establishments are inspected regularly to ensure that required standards are maintained.

★★★77% **Close** 8 Long St GL8 8AQ (Prestige) ☎(0666)502272
FAX (0666) 504401
*A discreet façade which blends beautifully with its High Street neighbours gives no hint of the internal proportions of this most unusual hotel. Lovingly restored and furnished, it offers individually styled bedrooms which combine some striking fabric designs with fine antiques and have superb bathrooms. Two elegant dining rooms are the setting for the interesting and enjoyable dishes produced by Chef Chris Amos, and General Manager, David Broadhead, has put together a first class wine list to accompany the menu.*
15⇌ℕ3⊠ CTV in all bedrooms **T** ✗ (ex guide dogs)
sB&B⇌ℕ£75-£125
dB&B⇌ℕ£95-£155 Continental breakfast ⊟
20P ⚘ nc10yrs *xmas*
**V** ♆ ⩍ ⊁ Lunch £9.50-£14.95 Dinner £17-£27.50 Last dinner 9.45pm
Credit Cards 1 2 3 5

★★★71% **Snooty Fox** Market Place GL8 8DD ☎(0666)502436
FAX (0666) 503479
*Honey coloured Cotswold stone building facing the old Market Hall, this popular hotel has been ambitiously refurbished to a high standard. The bedrooms are individually designed while the oak panelled restaurant provides a delightful setting for the excellent food.*
12⇌ℕ(1fb)1⊠ CTV in all bedrooms **T** ✗ (ex guide dogs) ✱
sB&B⇌ℕ£66-£82 dB&B⇌ℕ£84-£110 ⊟
*P xmas*
☋ English & French **V** ♆ ⩍ Lunch fr£14&alc Dinner fr£18&alc Last dinner 9.45pm
Credit Cards 1 2 3 5 £

★★★62% **Hare & Hounds** Westonbirt GL8 8QL (Best Western)
☎Westonbirt(066688)233 Telex no 94012242
FAX (066688) 241
*This family owned and managed country hotel, run on traditional lines, stands in grounds which extend to almost ten acres, including large, well-tended lawns – on one of which croquet is played – and two hard tennis courts.*
22⇌ℕAnnexe8⇌ℕ(3fb)5⊠ CTV in all bedrooms ® **T**
sB&B⇌ℕ£52-£60 dB&B⇌ℕ£70-£80 ⊟
80P ❉ ♩ (hard) squash croquet table tennis *xmas*
☋ English & French **V** ♆ ⩍ Lunch £10.50&alc Dinner £16.50-£18.50&alc Last dinner 9pm
Credit Cards 1 2 3

★★64% **Hunters Hall Inn** Kingscote GL8 8X2
☎Dursley(0453)860393 FAX (0453) 860707
Annexe12⇌ℕ(1fb) CTV in all bedrooms ® **T**
✗ (ex guide dogs) ✱ S% sB&B⇌ℕ£44 dB&B⇌ℕ£54 ⊟
120P ❉ *xmas*
**V** ♆ ⩍ Lunch £7-£15 Dinner £8-£15alc Last dinner 9.30pm
Credit Cards 1 2 3 5

## TEWKESBURY Gloucestershire Map **03** SO83

★★★68% **Royal Hop Pole Crest** Church St GL20 5RT (Trusthouse Forte) ☎(0684)293236 Telex no 437176
FAX (0684) 296680
*Located on the High Street, this former 14th-century coaching inn was largely rebuilt in the Georgian era and following recent refurbishment is now a hotel of charm and character, meeting the needs of the modern traveller. Previous notable guests include Charles Dickens and the hospitality he enjoyed is still evident in the nineties.*
29⇌ℕ(2fb)1⊠⊁in 6 bedrooms CTV in all bedrooms ® **T** ⊟
☾ 30P ❉ CFA *xmas*
☋ English & French **V** ♆ ⩍ ⊁
Credit Cards 1 2 3 4 5

★★★66% **Tewkesbury Hall** Puckrup GL20 6EL (3m N A38)
☎(0684)296200 FAX (0684) 850788
*Forty acres of grounds surround this country-house-style hotel which is within easy reach of the M5/M50 junction. The interior*

*has been refurbished to a high standard and the bedrooms are well equipped.*
16⇌2⇔ CTV in all bedrooms ® T sB&B⇌£70-£85 dB&B⇌£90-£125 月
80P ⇔ ❖ ✔ croquet putting *xmas*
🍴 English & French V ✿ ⌂ ✂ Lunch £12.50-£14.50 Dinner £19.50-£21.50&alc Last dinner 9.30pm
Credit Cards ①②③⑤

★★★65% **Tewkesbury Park Golf & Country Club** Lincoln Green Ln GL20 7DN ☎(0684)295405 Telex no 43563 FAX (0684) 292386
*This modern hotel and leisure complex is situated south of the town and is surrounded by grounds containing a golf course, tennis courts and parkland. Indoor facilities include a swimming pool, squash courts and health and beauty treatments. Bedrooms are comfortable, public areas are spacious and there is a choice of bars and restaurants.*
78⇌fↄ(10fb) CTV in all bedrooms ® T ✖ (ex guide dogs) sB&B⇌fↄ£92-£104 dB&B⇌fↄ£104-£120 月
《 CTV 180P ❖ CFA 🏊(heated) ⏊ 18 ♟ (hard) squash snooker sauna solarium gymnasium steam room whirlpool *xmas*
🍴 English & French V ✿ ⌂ S% Lunch £10.50 Dinner £15 Last dinner 10pm
Credit Cards ①②③④⑤ⓔ

★★★64% **Bell** Church St GL20 5SA (Best Western)
☎(0684)293293 Telex no 43535
*A distinctive black and white building dating back to Victorian times stands on the western side of the town, easily accessible and with its own generous car parking space. Bedrooms vary in size, but all are modern and equipped with en suite facilities.*
25⇌fↄ(2fb)3⇔✂in 1 bedroom CTV in all bedrooms ® T sB&B⇌fↄ£53-£65 dB&B⇌fↄ£66-£75 月
《 55P CFA *xmas*
🍴 English & French V ✿ ⌂
Credit Cards ①②③⑤ⓔ

★★65% **Tudor House** High St GL20 5BH ☎(0684)297755 FAX (0684) 290306
*The architectural features of this fine old Tudor building include an elegant Queen Anne staircase and the Mayor's Parlour with its hidden Priest's Hole. Bedrooms have been meticulously redecorated to preserve the original character of the building and incorporate a good range of modern facilities, most having en suite facilities.*
16rm(6⇌4fↄ)(2fb)1⇔ CTV in all bedrooms ® ✖ ✱ sB&B⇌fↄ£45-£55 dB&B⇌fↄ£60-£65 月
22P ⇔
🍴 English & French V ✿ ⌂ Dinner fr£10.95 Last dinner 9.30pm
Credit Cards ①②③⑤

**THAKEHAM** (near Storrington) West Sussex Map **04** TQ11

❀★★★↟74%**Abingworth Hall** Storrington Rd RH20 3EF
☎West Chiltington(0798)813636 Telex no 877835 FAX (0798) 813914
Closed 3 wks Jan
*A charming, Edwardian country house, built on the site of a much older manor unfortunately destroyed by fire, Abingworth stands in 10 acres of grounds overlooking the South Downs, and is hospitably run by its owners, Mr and Mrs Bulman. Their Chef, Peter Canon, continues to offer a well balanced selection of good food. Dishes such as a trout mousse served on a watercress and tarragon sauce, or breast of duck with a herb butter sauce show a strong French influence in the modern style.*
21⇌fↄ CTV in all bedrooms T ✖ S% sB&B⇌fↄ£65-£80 dB&B⇌fↄ£88-£150 月
50P ⇔ ❖ 🏊(heated) ⏊ 9 ♟ (hard) croquet lawn nc10yrs *xmas*
🍴 English & French V Lunch fr£15&alc Dinner fr£27&alc Last dinner 9pm
Credit Cards ①②③④⑤

**THAME** Oxfordshire Map **04** SP70

★★★72% **Spread Eagle** Cornmarket OX9 2BW ☎(084421)3661 Telex no 83343 FAX (0844) 261380
Closed 27-30 Dec
*A very special hotel with warm hospitality and modern bedrooms.*
33⇌fↄ(1fb)⇔ CTV in all bedrooms ® T ✖ (ex guide dogs) S% sB&B⇌fↄ£65.95-£72.55
dB&B⇌fↄ£72.55-£82.45 Continental breakfast 月
《 80P CFA *xmas*
🍴 English & French V ✿ Lunch fr£14.80&alc Dinner £15.70-£16.70&alc Last dinner 10pm
Credit Cards ①②③⑤ⓔ
**See advertisement on page 679**

**THATCHAM** Berkshire Map **04** SU56

★★★★63% **Regency Park** Bowling Green Rd RG13 3RP ☎(0635)71555 Telex no 847844 FAX (0635) 71571
*Now extended and refurbished to a high standard, the hotel offers accommodation in spacious bedrooms which are tastefully appointed and well equipped. An attractive modern restaurant features à la carte and table d'hôte menus of dishes which are both imaginatively conceived and properly prepared, lounge facilities are limited but comfortable, and a helpful young staff provides efficiently attentive service.*
50⇌fↄ(12fb) CTV in all bedrooms ® T sB⇌fↄ£75-£87 dB⇌fↄ£90-£100 (room only) 月
Lift 《 114P ⇔ *xmas*
🍴 English & Continental V ✿ ⌂ ✂ Lunch £13.50&alc Dinner £16.95&alc Last dinner 10.30pm
Credit Cards ①②③⑤
**See advertisement under NEWBURY**

**THAXTED** Essex Map **05** TL63

★★65% **The Swan** Bullring, Watling St CM6 2PL ☎(0371)830321 FAX (0371) 831186
13⇌fↄ(1fb) CTV in all bedrooms ® T sB&B⇌fↄ£65 dB&B⇌fↄ£70-£90 月
《 24P *xmas*
🍴 French V ✿ ⌂ Lunch £13.95 Dinner £19.95&alc Last dinner 10pm
Credit Cards ①②③

★★56% **Four Seasons** Walden Rd CM6 2RE ☎(0371)830129
*There has been a inn on this pleasant country site since the 16th century. The hotel has naturally undergone extensive modernization since that time. A good selection of bar food is available in the spacious and comfortable bar lounge, while the tastefully-decorated restaurant offers a choice of freshly-prepared, popular dishes. Bedrooms offer some modern facilities and are comfortable. The proprietors, Mr and Mrs Murfitt, personally supervise the hotel service and a pleasant, hospitable welcome is made at all times.*
9⇌fↄ CTV in all bedrooms ® T ✖ ✱ sB&B⇌fↄfr£50 dB&B⇌fↄfr£65 月
CTV 100P ⇔ ❖ nc12yrs
🍴 English & French V ✿ ✂ Lunch £15-£20alc Dinner £15-£20alc Last dinner 9.30pm
Credit Cards ①②③

**THETFORD** Norfolk Map **05** TL88

See also **Brandon (Suffolk)**
★★★59% **The Bell** King St IP24 2AZ (Trusthouse Forte)
☎(0842)754455 Telex no 818868 FAX (0842) 755552
*This 15th-century coaching house has been carefully converted to an elegant, comfortable hotel.*
47⇌fↄ(4fb)⇔✂in 11 bedrooms CTV in all bedrooms ® T S10% sB⇌fↄ£65-£92 dB⇌fↄ£81-£92 (room only) 月
《 50P ❖ *xmas*

▶

677

V ✿ ✍ ✤ S10% Lunch £8-£10.95&alc High tea £10 Dinner £14.25-£16.50&alc Last dinner 10pm
Credit Cards ① ② ③ ④ ⑤

★★57% **Historical Thomas Paine** White Hart St IP24 1AA (Best Western) ☎(0842)755631 Telex no 58298 FAX (0842) 766505
*Partly Georgian hotel, reputed to be the birthplace of Thomas Paine, a famous son of Thetford.*
14rm(7⇆6♠)(1fb)1⊞ CTV in all bedrooms ® T sB&B£40-£45 sB&B⇆♠£41-£46 dB&B⇆♠£52-£58 ₽
30P ⇝
V ✿ ✍ Lunch £9-£11&alc Dinner £12-£15&alc Last dinner 9.30pm
Credit Cards ① ② ③ ⑤

★★56% **Anchor** Bridge St IP24 3AE ☎(0842)763925
*Set in a good position at the centre of the town, beside the Little Ouse, this well equipped hotel has its own large car park. Most of the attractive, cottage-style bedrooms have en suite facilities, the popular Barnaby's Carvery offers value-for-money meals, and there is a convivial "locals" bar.*
17rm(12⇆3♠) CTV in all bedrooms ® T ✖ (ex guide dogs) 60P
V ✿ ✍ ✤ Last dinner 10pm
Credit Cards ① ② ③ ⑤

**THIRSK** North Yorkshire Map 08 SE48
★★66% **The Golden Fleece** Market Place YO7 1LL ☎(0845)523108 FAX (0845) 523996
*Dating back well over 300 years, this characterful hotel retains an authentically historic atmosphere with open fireplaces and antiques throughout; bedrooms are well equipped, some having en suite facilities.*
22rm(6⇆)2⊞✤in 3 bedrooms CTV in all bedrooms ® T S% sBfr£45 sB⇆fr£55 dBfr£55 dB⇆fr£70 (room only) ₽
50P *xmas*
V ✿ ✍ ✤ S% Lunch fr£6.50&alc Dinner fr£11.50&alc Last dinner 9.15pm
Credit Cards ① ② ③ ④ ⑤ ⓔ

★★65% **Sheppard's** Church Farm, Front St, Sowerby YO7 1JF ☎(0845)523655 FAX (0845) 524720
Closed 1st wk Jan
*Small, family-run and hospitable, the hotel is made up of characterful buildings set around a central cobbled courtyard. A former stable has been converted to provide a restaurant serving imaginative, freshly prepared dishes which include some very enjoyable items, while bedrooms are quaint and comfortable.*
8⇆♠(1fb)1⊞✤in 2 bedrooms CTV in all bedrooms ® T ✖ sB&B⇆♠£45-£50 dB&B⇆♠£55-£65 ₽
35P ⇝ nc10yrs
☺ International ✿ ✍ ✤ Sunday Lunch fr£10alc Dinner fr£16alc Last dinner 9.30pm
Credit Cards ① ③

★63% **Old Red House** Station Rd YO7 4LT ☎(0845)524383
6⇆♠(1fb)1⊞✤in 1 bedroom CTV in all bedrooms ® T ✳
sB&B⇆♠£16-£20 dB&B⇆♠£26-£30 ₽
30P *xmas*
V ✿ ✍ Lunch £6.50-£8.50&alc High tea £4.50-£6.50 Dinner £7-£12&alc Last dinner 10pm
Credit Cards ② ③ ⑤

---

Entries for red-star hotels are highlighted by a tint panel. For a full list of these establishments consult the Contents page.

---

**THORNBURY** Avon Map 03 ST69

★★★ ⊞
**THORNBURY CASTLE**

BS12 1HH (Pride of Britain)
☎(0454)418511
Telex no 449986
FAX (0454) 416188
Closed 2-12 Jan RS 24-29 Dec

*Once owned by Henry VIII, this imposing 16th-century castle conceals behind the grandeur of its walls an exceptionally welcoming and relaxing hotel. The blend of modern comfort and historical interest is very much the creation of its owner Maurice Taylor. The panelled rooms, heraldic shields, tapestries and oil paintings are a wonderful setting, and the spacious bedrooms provide every refinement of luxury and quality. Manager Peter Strong and his staff give a service that successfully blends efficiency and charm to create a lasting impression of genuine hospitality that really makes guests feel welcome (none more so than the engaging Pepe who has been with the hotel for 16 years). In the non-smoking dining room chef Derek Hamlin provides a selection of beautifully presented dishes; some may be a little 'over the top' but on the whole, his cooking, mainly in the British tradition, is very sound, and the wine list is outstanding. Breakfasts are excellent, and of a quality rarely equalled.*
18⇆♠8⊞ CTV in all bedrooms T ✖ ✳
sB&B⇆♠£70-£85
dB&B⇆♠£100-£190 Continental breakfast ₽
《 40P ⇝ ✿ croquet nc12yrs *xmas*
☺ English & French V ✿ ✍ ✤ Lunch £17.50 Dinner £25-£29 Last dinner 9.30pm
Credit Cards ① ② ③ ④ ⑤
**See advertisement under BRISTOL**

---

**THORNE** South Yorkshire Map 08 SE61
★★67% **Belmont** Horsefair Green DN8 5EE ☎(0405)812320 Telex no 54480 FAX (0405) 740508
*A friendly hotel near the town centre offering good value for money.*
23⇆♠(3fb)1⊞ CTV in all bedrooms ® T
sB&B⇆♠£36.50-£38.50 dB&B⇆♠£48.50-£50.50 ₽
30P *xmas*
☺ English & French V ✿ ✍ Lunch £8.95&alc Dinner fr£8.95&alc Last dinner 9.30pm
Credit Cards ① ③ ⓔ

---

**THORNHILL** Dumfries & Galloway *Dumfriesshire* Map 11 NX89
★★72% **Trigony House** Closeburn DG3 5EZ (2m S off A76) ☎(0848)31211
*In an attractive rural location, with direct access from the A76 just south of the town, this tranquil country house offers charming well-appointed bedrooms and inviting public rooms. Resident proprietors and their family provide delightful service and interesting food.*
9rm(2⇆6♠) CTV in all bedrooms ® T ✖ (ex guide dogs)
sB&B⇆♠£29.50 dB&B⇆♠£49-£53 ₽
30P ⇝ ✿ nc8yrs
V ✿ Bar Lunch £5-£9alc Dinner £10-£12alc Last dinner 8.30pm
Credit Cards ① ③

**★★53% Buccleuch & Queensberry Hotel** Drumlanrig St
DG3 5LU ☎(0848)30215
*Very friendly service and good-value menus are attractive features
of this modest High Street inn.*
12rm(9⇨↑)(5fb) CTV in 7 bedrooms ® ✖ (ex guide dogs) ✱
sB&B£23.50 sB&B⇨↑£29 dB&B£44 dB&B⇨↑£50 🅿
CTV 30P *xmas*
♡ Mainly grills **V** ♡ ⏜ Lunch £5-£9 High tea £4.25-£5.50
Dinner £5-£9 Last dinner 9pm
Credit Cards ①③

**★68% George Hotel** Drumlanrig St DG3 5LU ☎(0848)30326
Closed Xmas Day & New Years Day
*The hotel has been carefully modernised to preserve its 'village inn'
atmosphere and the comfortable lounge bar is now proving popular
for its good bar meals.*
8rm(6⇨↑)(1fb) CTV in all bedrooms ® **T** S%
sB&B£22.50-£27.50 sB&B⇨↑£22.50-£27.50 dB&B£35-£45
dB&B⇨↑£35-£45
CTV 10P ♪ Indoor bowling
**V** ♡ Dinner £5-£9.95&alc Last dinner 8.55pm
Credit Cards ①③

---

**THORNLEY** Durham Map **08** NZ33

**★★63% Crossways** Dunelm Rd DH6 3HT (5m SE of Durham
City) ☎Wellfield(0429)821248 FAX (0429) 820034
*Popular with business travellers, this modern, family-run hotel has
compact but well equipped bedrooms. There is a choice of bars and
an attractive, small dining room serving good-value meals.*
23⇨↑(9fb)🛏 CTV in all bedrooms ® **T** ✱
sB&B⇨↑£34-£38.50 dB&B⇨↑£38-£55 🅿
《 CTV 150P ❀ sauna solarium fitness room ♫ ಈ *xmas*
♡ English & French **V** ♡ ⏜ ✂ Lunch £8.50&alc High tea
£3.50-£6.50&alc Dinner £8.50&alc Last dinner 9.45pm
Credit Cards ①②③⑤

**THORNTHWAITE** Cumbria Map **11** NY22

During the currency of this guide Braithwaite telephone numbers are liable to change.

★★**65%** **Thwaite Howe** CA12 5SA ☎Braithwaite(059682)281 Closed Nov-Feb

*A charming Lakeland house set in its own delightful gardens. Well furnished and comfortable bedrooms and a good standard of home cooking is provided by friendly resident owners.*

8⇨ CTV in all bedrooms ® T sB&B⇨£28.50-£43 dB&B⇨£57-£66 (incl dinner) **F**

12P ⇔ ✿ nc12yrs

♀ English & French ✄ Dinner £10.50 Last dinner 7pm

ⓔ

---

★★61% **Ladstock Country House** CA12 5RZ ☎Braithwaite(059682)210 Closed Jan

*Situated 2.5 miles north-west of Keswick, this period house sits in its own attractive gardens with a backdrop of wooded hillside. There are good views across the valley to the peaks of Skiddaw.*

22rm(11⇨7🏠)(2fb)3⇔ CTV in all bedrooms ® T ✖ (ex guide dogs) S% sB&B£24 sB&B⇨🏠£30-£35 dB&B£32 dB&B⇨🏠£45-£64 **F**

CTV 50P ✿ *xmas*

V ✪ 🎦 S% Lunch £7-£8 Dinner £11.95-£12.95 Last dinner 8.30pm

Credit Cards 1 3

---

★★59% **Swan** CA12 5SQ ☎Braithwaite(059682)256 Closed Nov-Etr

*Now peacefully situated, bypassed by the main road, this family-run coaching inn boasts a smart, comfortable bar in addition to its more traditional areas. Bedrooms are furnished with modern fitted units and many of them command fine views of Skiddaw and Lake Bassenthwaite, as does the dining room where guests enjoy meals prepared by the proprietor.*

14rm(3⇨5🏠) CTV in 13 bedrooms S10% sB&B£29.45-£32.40 dB&B£58.90-£64.80 dB&B⇨🏠£66.40-£72.70 (incl dinner) **F**

CTV 60P 3🚗 (£1.75) ⇔ ✿

♀ English & Continental V ✪ 🎦 ✄ Bar Lunch £1.10-£7.25 Dinner £13.50 Last dinner 8.30pm

Credit Cards 1 3

---

**THORNTON CLEVELEYS** Lancashire Map **07** SD34

✗**The River House** Skippool Creek FY5 5LF (2m E A585) ☎Poulton-Le-Fylde(0253)883497 & 883307

*For more years than he cares to remember Bill Scott has run this charming restaurant with enthusiasm and care. The cooking is robust and no-nonsense and the à la carte menu, with its daily variations, offers plenty of choice as does the lengthy wine list. Tuna, scallops and local duck are all likely to feature on the menu. There are also four individually decorated bedrooms.*

Closed Sun & 6-18 Aug

Lunch not served Sat

♀ International 40 seats ✹ Lunch £30-£60alc Dinner £30-£60alc Last lunch 2.30pm Last dinner 9.30pm 20P

Credit Cards 1 3

---

**THORNTON DALE** North Yorkshire Map **08** SE88

★**50%** **New Inn** YO18 7LF ☎Pickering(0751)74226 Closed Nov-Feb

*The New Inn stands at the centre of the village. It is dated at around 1600. Although small it offers good home comfort.*

6rm(1fb) ® ✖ S10% sB&B£19 dB&B£30

CTV 9P 1🚗

V ✪

1991 marks the 25th anniversary of this guide.

---

**THORNTON HOUGH** Merseyside Map **07** SJ38

★★★61% **Thornton Hall** Neston Rd L63 1JF ☎051-336 3938 Telex no 628678

*A large house, set in rural surroundings, with bedrooms in separate wings as well as in the main building. Considerable expansion has taken place recently with extra bedrooms, a function room and upgraded public areas.*

9⇨🏠Annexe28⇨🏠 CTV in all bedrooms ® ✖ (ex guide dogs)

ⓒ 100P ✿

♀ English, French & Italian V ✪ Last dinner 9.30pm

Credit Cards 1 2 3 4 5

---

**THORNTON WATLASS** North Yorkshire Map **08** SE28

★63% **Buck Inn** HG4 4AH ☎Bedale(0677)22461

*An attractive stone inn overlooking the village green where cricket is played in the summer. Bedrooms are pleasantly furnished and there is a separate lounge. The bars are full of local atmosphere.*

6rm(5⇨3🏠)(1fb) ® sB&B⇨🏠fr£20 dB&B⇨🏠fr£40

CTV 10P ✿ ♪ quoits pool table childrens play area 🎵

♀ English & Continental V ✪ 🎦 Lunch £7-£12alc Dinner £7-£14alc Last dinner 9.30pm

Credit Cards 1 3 ⓔ

---

**THORPE (DOVEDALE)** Derbyshire Map **07** SK15

★★★65% **Peveril of the Peak** DE6 2AW (Trusthouse Forte) ☎Thorpe Cloud(033529)333 FAX (033529) 507

*Eccentric and rambling, this comfortable hotel sits in 11 acres of gardens and grounds at the foot of Thorpe Cloud, and it proves a popular retreat for conferences and ramblers. Refurbishment is currently taking place in public areas and the final few remaining bedrooms that are more dated.*

47⇨🏠 4 bedrooms CTV in all bedrooms ® S% sB⇨🏠£65-£85 dB⇨🏠£85-£100 (room only) **F**

ⓒ 60P ✿ CFA ♪ (hard) *xmas*

V ✪ 🎦 ✄ S% Lunch fr£10.50 Dinner fr£15.50&alc Last dinner 9.30pm

Credit Cards 1 2 3 4 5

---

★★★62% **Izaak Walton** DE6 2AY (1m W on Ilam rd) ☎Thorpe Cloud(033529)555 Telex no 378406 FAX (033529) 539

*A much extended 18th-century farmhouse enjoying excellent views of Dovedale.*

34⇨🏠(2fb)3⇔✄ in 6 bedrooms CTV in all bedrooms ® T S10% sB&B⇨🏠fr£63.80 dB&B⇨🏠fr£105.05 (incl dinner) **F**

ⓒ 80P ✿ ♪ 🎵 ✿ *xmas*

♀ English & French V ✪ 🎦 ✄ S10% Lunch fr£9.90&alc High tea fr£4.95 Dinner fr£14.85&alc Last dinner 9pm

Credit Cards 1 2 3 5

---

**THORPE-LE-SOKEN** Essex Map **05** TM12

✗✗ **Thorpe Lodge** Landermere Rd CO16 0NG ☎Clacton-on-Sea(0255)861509

*A converted country vicarage with two dining rooms, where freshly prepared dishes such as crab soufflé and goulash can feature on the menu.*

Lunch by arrangement

♀ English & French V 75 seats Last lunch 2pm Last dinner 9.15pm 25P ✄

Credit Cards 1 3 5

---

**THRAPSTON** Northamptonshire Map **04** SP97

○**Travelodge** A14 Link Rd, Thrapston By-pass(Trusthouse Forte) ☎Central reservations (0800) 850950 Due to open winter 1990

40⇨

---

## THREE COCKS Powys Map 03 SO13

✿★★74% Three Cocks LS3 0SL ☎Glasbury(04974)215
Closed Dec & Jan
(Rosette awarded for dinner only)
*This attractive hotel stands near the small village from which it takes its name, its ivy-clad stone walls suggesting the traditional comforts and friendly service you will find within. Rooms are pleasant and comfortable and the luxury of early morning tea service is an agreeable feature. The owner is justly proud of his restaurant where the food, either on the set menu or the small but well chosen à la carte menu, is excellent, as the rosette award indicates. Cooking is in the modern style and presentation is accomplished and professional.*
7rm(5⇆1♠)(2fb) ✖ dB&B⇆♠£50 🍴
CTV 40P 🚗 ✿
♀ Continental V ♥ Lunch £20&alc
Credit Cards [1][3]£

## THRESHFIELD North Yorkshire Map 07 SD96

★★★66% Wilson Arms Station Rd BD23 5ET
☎Grassington(0756)752666
*A pleasant, friendly hotel with comfortable lounges, where the high standard of cooking is to be particularly recommended.*
14⇆♠(1fb)1🛏 CTV in all bedrooms ® T
sB&B⇆♠£34.50-£48 dB&B⇆♠£69-£96 (incl dinner)
Lift ( CTV 40P ✿ xmas
♀ English & French V ♥ ☑ Lunch £8.50 Dinner £13.95&alc
Last dinner 9.30pm
Credit Cards [1][2][3]
**See advertisement under SKIPTON**

## THRUSSINGTON Leicestershire Map 08 SK61

⬒Travelodge Green Acres Filling Station LE7 8TE (on A46)
(Trusthouse Forte)
☎Rearsby(0664)424525 Central res (0800) 850950
*Situated on the southbound side of the A46, about eight miles north of Leicester and surrounded by open countryside, a value-for-money lodge adjacent to a Little Chef restaurant offers accommodation in well furnished bedrooms.*
32⇆♠(32fb) CTV in all bedrooms ® sB⇆♠£24
dB⇆♠£29.50 (room only)
( 32P 🚗
Credit Cards [1][2][3]

## THURCROFT South Yorkshire Map 08 SK48

★★70% Consort Brampton Rd S66 9JA (Consort)
☎Rotherham(0709)530022 FAX (0709) 531529
*Situated at the M18/M1 intersection, this is a two-storey modern brick and pantile building. Good levels of service are provided by a very friendly team, and the excellent, well equipped accommodation is comfortable and attractive. There is a good selection of bar snacks and restaurant meals, and a very comfortable lounge. A large banqueting suite has facilities for 300.*
18⇆(1fb) CTV in all bedrooms® T ✖ (ex guide dogs) ✳
sB⇆£25-£53 dB⇆£40-£66 (room only)
( 90P 🚗
V ♥ ☑ ⅙ Lunch fr£11.95&alc Dinner fr£11.95&alc Last dinner 9.30pm
Credit Cards [1][2][3]
**See advertisement under ROTHERHAM**

## THURLASTON Warwickshire Map 04 SP47

⬒Travelodge London Rd CV23 9LG (A45) (Trusthouse Forte)
☎Dunchurch(0788)521538 Central res (0800) 850950
*Situated three miles south of Rugby and eight miles from Coventry, this Travelodge offers easy access to the M45.*

40⇆♠(40fb) CTV in all bedrooms ® sB⇆♠£24
dB⇆♠£29.50 (room only)
40P 🚗
Credit Cards [1][2][3]

## THURLESTONE Devon Map 03 SX64

★★★★68% Thurlestone TQ7 3NN ☎Kingsbridge(0548)560382
Telex no 42513 FAX (0548) 561069
*Spacious hotel, built, owned and managed by the Grose family for 90 years, which has fine country and sea views.*
68⇆♠(13fb) CTV in all bedrooms T
Lift ( 100P 19🚗 🚗 ✿ CFA ⬚(heated) ⌿(heated) ▶9 ♀
(hard) squash snooker sauna solarium gymnasium games room badminton spa bath ♨
♀ English & French V ♥ ☑ ⅙ Lunch £5.75-£10&alc Dinner fr£21&alc Last dinner 9pm
Credit Cards [1][3][5]

## THURSO Highland *Caithness* Map 15 ND16

★★61% Pentland Princes St KW14 7AA ☎(0847)63202
*Situated in the centre of town this privately owned commercial and tourist hotel has spacious and comfortable public areas with traditional services provided by local staff.*
53rm(20⇆16♠)(4fb) CTV in all bedrooms T sB&Bfr£16
sB&B⇆♠fr£21 dB&Bfr£32 dB&B⇆♠fr£38
( ⅙ 🚗
V ♥ ☑ Lunch fr£3.30alc High tea fr£5alc Dinner fr£6.50alc
Last dinner 8.30pm
Credit Cards [1][3]

For key to symbols see the inside front cover.

**TIGHNABRUAICH** Strathclyde Map **10** NR97

★★68% **Kames** Kames PA21 2AF (Minotels) ☏(0700)811489
10⇌↱(3fb) CTV in 5 bedrooms ® **T** ✱ sB&B⇌↱fr£22.50 dB&B⇌↱fr£37 ⊟
CTV P ⌘ ✲ childrens play park ♫ *xmas*
☋ Scottish **V** ♧ ☕ ⁄ Bar Lunch £2.50-£7.50 Dinner £13-£16alc Last dinner 9pm
Credit Cards 1 2 3 5

**TINTAGEL** Cornwall & Isles of Scilly Map **02** SX08

★★62% **Bossiney House** PL34 0AX ☏Camelford(0840)770240
Closed Nov-Feb (ex 5 days at Xmas)
*Modern holiday hotel in its own grounds with sea views.*
17rm(15⇌↱)Annexe1⇌(1fb) ® ✱ sB&B£24-£28.50 sB&B⇌↱£25.50-£30 dB&B£38-£42.50 dB&B⇌↱£41-£45.50 ⊟
CTV 30P ✲ ⊡(heated) sauna solarium gymnasium putting green *xmas*
**V** ♧ ☕ Lunch £5-£8 High tea £1.50-£3.50 Dinner £8.25-£10.50 Last dinner 8pm
Credit Cards 1 2 3 5 £

★★56% **Atlantic View** Treknow PL34 0EJ
☏Camelford(0840)770221
*Bedrooms are simply furnished (though some have four-poster beds) and the many lounges are comfortable at this personally-run hotel with lawns and fine sea views.*
9⇌↱(2fb)4⊞ CTV in all bedrooms ® ✱
sB&B⇌↱£16.50-£22.50 dB&B⇌↱£33-£45 ⊟
CTV 20P ⌘ ✲ ⊡(heated) solarium nc2yrs
☋ English & European **V** ♧ ☕ ⁄ Lunch £7 Dinner £11.50&alc Last dinner 9pm
Credit Cards 1 3

**TINTERN** Gwent Map **03** SO50

★★★68% **The Beaufort** NP6 6SF (Embassy) ☏(0291)689777
FAX (0291) 689727
*A busy, popular hotel, situated in the picturesque Wye Valley right opposite Tintern Abbey, offering good quality, well-equipped bedrooms and pleasant public areas which prove equally attractive to tourists and business travellers. Residential conferences are something of a speciality.*
24⇌↱(2fb) CTV in all bedrooms ® **T** S% sB&B⇌↱£60-£75 dB&B⇌↱£80-£100 ⊟
60P ✲ games room *xmas*
☋ English & French **V** ♧ ☕ S% Sunday Lunch £6.50-£11 Dinner £14.95-£16.95 Last dinner 9pm
Credit Cards 1 2 3 4 5

★★63% **Royal George** NP6 6SF ☏(0291)689205
FAX (0291) 689448
*Standing beside the A466 in the picturesque Wye Valley, not far from the famous Abbey, a family-run hotel whose history as an inn dates back to the seventeenth century now offers well-equipped accommodation, the majority of its rooms being contained in annexes overlooking the delightful gardens.*
2rm(1⇌)Annexe14⇌(1fb) CTV in all bedrooms ® **T**
sB&B£30 sB&B⇌£42.35 dB&B⇌£58.85 ⊟
50P ✲ *xmas*
☋ English & French **V** ♧ ☕ S% Sunday Lunch £7.50 Dinner £14.75&alc Last dinner 9.30pm
Credit Cards 1 2 3 5

★★57% **Parva Farmhouse Hotel & Restaurant** NP6 6SQ
☏(0291)689411
*Set almost on the bank of the River Wye, this small, friendly, family-run hotel provides well equipped bedrooms and good meals; there is no actual bar, but an "honesty bar" arrangement operates in the comfortable lounge.*
9rm(7⇌↱)(5fb)3⊞ CTV in all bedrooms ® **T** sB&B£28-£30 sB&B⇌↱£30-£52 dB&B£39 dB&B⇌↱£44-£60 ⊟
10P 2⌂
☋ European **V** Lunch £9.50-£14 Dinner £12.50-£14&alc Last dinner 8.30pm
Credit Cards 1 2 3 5 £

**TISBURY** Wiltshire Map **03** ST92

✕ ***Garden Room*** 2-3 High St SP3 6PS ☏(0747)870907
*This 'little gem' of a restaurant, has a bright garden style décor and an equally bright atmosphere. It is owned and personally run by Jonathan Ford and Paul Firmin. The restaurant is open for both lunch and dinner, with an à la carte menu available at both meals, while a well priced table d'hôte menu is also available at lunch time. The menus are changed frequently, thereby offering seasonal meats, game, fish, and vegetables. Paul Firmin's cuisine is modern in style, creating interesting dishes which are cooked with care, and with appealing presentation but without being fussy. The wine list is well chosen, and you are assured of a warm welcome and attentive service from Jonathan Ford.*
CLOSED
Closed Mon, 2 wks late Feb & 1 wk Sep/Oct
Lunch not served Tue-Sat
Dinner not served Sun
☋ English & Continental **V** 32 seats Last dinner 10pm ⁄
Credit Cards 1 2 3

**TITCHWELL** Norfolk Map **09** TF74

★★70% **Titchwell Manor** PE31 8BB (Best Western)
☏Brancaster(0485)210221 & 210284 Telex no 32376
*A flintstone building, typical of the area, enjoying views of the nature reserve and sea. Accommodation is attractive and comfortable, there is an elegant restaurant and a bar with an open fire.*
11rm(7⇌↱)Annexe4⇌↱(2fb) CTV in all bedrooms ® **T**
sB&B£31-£38 sB&B⇌↱£31-£38 dB&B£62-£76 dB&B⇌↱£62-£76 ⊟
50P ⌘ ✲ *xmas*
☋ European **V** ♧ ☕ ⁄ Lunch £8.95-£15 High tea £1-£5alc Dinner £14.50-£20 Last dinner 9.30pm
Credit Cards 1 2 3 5

**TIVERTON** Devon Map **03** SS91

★★★60% **Tiverton** Blundells Rd EX16 4DB ☏(0884)256120
Telex no 42551 FAX (0884) 258101
*Spacious, well equipped bedrooms, bright, open public areas and a good range of leisure facilities are available at an hotel off the new Link Road, on the outskirts of the town.*
75⇌↱(75fb) CTV in all bedrooms ® **T** sB&B⇌↱£33-£43 dB&B⇌↱£56-£76 (incl dinner) ⊟
☾ 130P CFA ♫ *xmas*
☋ English, French & Italian **V** ♧ ☕ ⁄ Lunch £7.50
Credit Cards 1 2 3 5 £

★★61% **Hartnoll** Bolham EX16 7RA (1.5m N on A396)
☏(0884)252777 FAX (0884) 259195
*A Georgian building in its own well kept gardens just one mile from the town centre and 300 yards from the North Devon link road. Bedrooms are at present being refurbished to a high standard, all offer good facilities including those in the cottage annexe. Snacks are available in the spacious bar whilst the restaurant serves a more imaginative à la carte menu.*
11⇌Annexe5↱(3fb)1⊞ CTV in all bedrooms ® **T**
sB&B⇌↱£20-£40 dB&B⇌↱£27.50-£55 ⊟
100P ✲ *xmas*
☋ English & Continental **V** ♧ ☕ Lunch fr£9.50&alc Dinner £10.50-£17alc Last dinner 10pm
Credit Cards 1 2 3 5 £

T

## TOBERMORY
See Mull, Isle of

## TODDINGTON MOTORWAY SERVICE AREA (M1)
Bedfordshire Map **04** SP92

⛟**Granada Lodge** M1 Motorway LU5 6HR (Granada)
☎(05255)5150 FAX (05255) 5602
*A modern two-storey building on the southbound carriageway of the M1 provides up-to-date and well equipped bedrooms ; continental breakfasts are served in guests' rooms, but other facilities are limited.*
43⇔(10fb)⊬in 5 bedrooms CTV in all bedrooms ®
✠ (ex guide dogs) ✳ S% sB⇔fr£28 dB⇔fr£31 (room only)
《 60P
V ⵁ ⵁ ⊬
Credit Cards ①②③⑤

## TODMORDEN Lancashire Map **07** SD92
★★★✦70%, **Scaitcliffe Hall** Burnley Rd ОL14 7DQ
☎(0706)818888 FAX (0706) 818825
*This attractive country house, which dates back to 1666 is set in its own well-tended grounds on the outskirts of the town. It offers comfortable accommodation and well-prepared food.*
13⇔♜(2fb)1🝙 CTV in all bedrooms ® T ✳
sB⇔♜£29.95-£45.75 dB⇔♜£45.75-£52.25 (room only) 🍴
《 200P ✾ *xmas*
V ⵁ ⵁ
Credit Cards ①②③⑤

## TODWICK South Yorkshire Map **08** SK48
★★★67% **Red Lion** Worksop Rd S31 0DJ (Lansbury)
☎Worksop(0909)771654 Telex no 54120 FAX (0909) 773704
*A roadside inn extended and cleverly converted in the style of a period coaching inn. It offers comfortable accommodation just a short distance from junction 31 of the M1.*
29⇔♜1🝙⊬in 9 bedrooms CTV in all bedrooms ® T
✠ (ex guide dogs) sB⇔♜fr£70 dB⇔♜fr£82 🍴
《 90P *xmas*
🝙 English & French V ⵁ ⊬ Lunch fr£9.25&alc Dinner fr£14.25&alc Last dinner 10pm
Credit Cards ①②③⑤

## TONBRIDGE Kent Map **05** TQ54
★★64% **The Rose & Crown** High St TN9 1DD (Trusthouse Forte) ☎(0732)357966 FAX (0732)357194
*Traditional décor and a wealth of heavy oak beams characterise this busy hotel – a posting and coaching house dating from the sixteenth century – though its well equipped bedrooms, which are mostly contained in the new wing, are all furnished in the modern style. Attentive, friendly and well managed services.*
50⇔♜(2fb)1🝙⊬in 20 bedrooms CTV in all bedrooms ® T ✳
sB⇔♜£60 dB⇔♜£75 (room only) 🍴
《 62P CFA *xmas*
V ⵁ ⵁ ⊬ Lunch £8.50-£10.50&alc Dinner £12.95&alc Last dinner 10pm
Credit Cards ①②③④⑤

## TONGUE Highland *Sutherland* Map **14** NC55
★★58% **Ben Loyal** IV27 4XE ☎(084755)216
*Small, friendly family run tourist hotel.*
13rm(6⇔♜)1🝙 ® sB&B£20-£26.50 sB&B⇔♜£26.50
dB&B£30-£40 dB&B⇔♜£53 🍴
CTV 19P ✾ ♫ *xmas*
V ⵁ ⵁ ⊬ Bar Lunch £3.75 Dinner fr£8.50 Last dinner 8.30pm
Credit Cards ①③

## TOPSHAM Devon Map **03** SX98
★★68%, **Ebford House** Exmouth Rd EX3 0QH (1m E on A376)
☎(0392)877658 FAX (0392) 874424
*Conveniently situated for Exeter and the coastal resorts, this well restored Georgian house offers comfortable bedrooms with excellent en-suite bathrooms. For meals, there is a choice of either a bistro or a formal restaurant.*
18⇔♜↟⊬in 4 bedrooms CTV in all bedrooms ® T
✠ (ex guide dogs) sB&B⇔♜£45-£52 dB&B⇔♜£60-£75 🍴
45P 🝙 ✾ sauna solarium gymnasium
🝙 English & French V ⵁ ⊬ Lunch £12.05-£13.15 Dinner £17-£18.65alc Last dinner 9.30pm
Credit Cards ①②③
**See advertisement under EXETER**

## TORBAY
See under **Brixham, Paignton & Torquay**

## TORCROSS Devon Map **03** SX84
★66% **Grey Homes** TQ7 2TH ☎Kingsbridge(0548)580220
Closed Nov-Mar
*This small, comfortable hotel is in an elevated position, overlooking the unique freshwater lake beside the sea, and the little fishing village of Torcross. Built in the 1920s by the grandfather of the present proprietor, guests are assured of a warm welcome. Bedrooms all share the same beautiful views, and are comfortably decorated and furnished. All offer private facilities, and there is a cosy lounge and a separate bar. A limited menu of home-cooked dishes is available in the relaxed atmosphere of the dining room.*
7⇔(1fb) CTV in all bedrooms ® sB&B⇔fr£25
dB&B⇔£50-£56 🍴
CTV 15P 3🝙 (charged) 🝙 ✾ ♪ (hard) nc2yrs
ⵁ ⵁ Dinner £11 Last dinner 7.30pm
Credit Cards ①③

**T**

**TORMARTON** Avon Map **03** ST77

★★64% **Compass Inn** GL9 1JB (Inter-Hotels)
☎Badminton(045421)242 & 577 FAX (045421) 741
Closed Xmas
*Old, family-run inn offering modern facilities.*
32⇌🟫(7fb)1🛏⊬in 12 bedrooms CTV in all bedrooms Ⓡ T
sB&B⇌🟫£49.95-£59.50 dB&B⇌🟫£64.90-£74.50 **ᄆ**
160P ❀
V ✧ ⊉ Bar Lunch £6-£8 Dinner £13-£18alc Last dinner
9.30pm
Credit Cards ①②③⑤ ⓔ

---

**TORPOINT** Cornwall & Isles of Scilly Map **02** SX45

★67% **Whitsand Bay** Portwrinkle PL11 3BU (5m W, off B3247)
☎St Germans(0503)30276
Closed Jan-mid Mar RS Nov-24 Dec
*A popular family and golfing hotel commanding unrestricted sea*
*views from its position on the headland has been owned and*
*managed by the same family for some considerable time. It*
*provides bedrooms which are bright, though simply furnished and*
*appointed, comfortable lounges, honest home cooking and an*
*attractive new leisure complex adjacent to the golf course ; friendly*
*service throughout contributes to a relaxed atmosphere.*
30rm(28⇌)(10fb) CTV in 1 bedroom Ⓡ ✳ sB&B£15-£17.50
sB&B⇌£17.50-£21 dB&B£30-£34 dB&B⇌£35-£43 **ᄆ**
CTV 60P ❀ ⊡(heated) ▶ 18 sauna solarium gymnasium
beauty salon steam room hairdressers ôồ *xmas*
V ✧ ⊉ ⊬ Sunday Lunch £7-£9 High tea £3.50-£5.50 Dinner
£12.50 Last dinner 8.30pm
ⓔ

---

**TORQUAY** Devon Map **03** SX96

See **Town Plan Section**

★★★★★54% **The Imperial** Park Hill Rd TQ1 2DG (Trusthouse
Forte) ☎(0803)294301 Telex no 42849 FAX (0803) 298293
*This spacious hotel, with its rather functional, unassuming exterior,*
*is situated within easy reach of the town centre, and has marvellous*
*views across the bay. Operated in a traditional resort style, many*
*areas are now quite dated, and a much needed refurbishment*
*programme is planned to take place over the next few years. Many*
*of the Imperial's guests return year after year, and are well looked*
*after, whilst first-time visitors may be attracted by the wide range of*
*leisure facilities. Cuisine is straightforward, and service sometimes*
*lacks polish, but the overall product reflects good value for money.*
167⇌(7fb)⊬in 45 bedrooms CTV in all bedrooms T ✳ S%
sB&B⇌£79-£96 dB&B⇌£138-£172 **ᄆ**
Lift ℂ 200P 60🍽 (£3.50 per day) ❀ CFA ⊡(heated) ⊇(heated)
₽ (hard) squash snooker sauna solarium gymnasium health
fitness centre croquet putting ♫ ôồ *xmas*
V ✧ ⊉ ⊬ S% Lunch £14&alc Dinner £26&alc Last dinner
9.30pm
Credit Cards ①②③④⑤

★★★★53% **Palace** Babbacombe Rd TQ1 3TG ☎(0803)200200
Telex no 42606 FAX (0803) 299899
*Set in 25 acres of attractive grounds this hotel has excellent sports*
*and leisure facilities including tennis, golf, squash, snooker and two*
*swimming pools. Most bedrooms have recently been refurbished to*
*a good modern standard and public areas are popular with the*
*busy conference trade. Our Inspector found the quality of some of*
*the dishes featured on the menu somewhat disappointing.*
141⇌🟫(10fb)6🛏 CTV in all bedrooms Ⓡ T ✴ (ex guide dogs)
✳ S% sB&B⇌🟫£45-£108 dB&B⇌🟫£90-£216 **ᄆ**
Lift ℂ CTV 100P 40🍽 (charged) ❀ CFA ⊡(heated)
⊇(heated) ▶ 9 ₽ (hard) squash snooker sauna croquet putting
table tennis ôồ *xmas*
♡ English & French V ✧ ⊉ Lunch £10&alc High tea £6.50
Dinner £16&alc Last dinner 9.15pm
Credit Cards ①③⑤

★★★★50% **Grand** Sea Front TQ2 6NT ☎(0803)296677
Telex no 42891 FAX (0803) 213462
*This imposing Victorian seafront hotel is undergoing extensive*
*improvements. Public areas are spacious and comfortable and the*
*bedrooms are well-equipped.*
112⇌🟫(30fb) CTV in all bedrooms Ⓡ T sB&B⇌🟫£40-£60
dB&B⇌🟫£80-£140 **ᄆ**
Lift ℂ 35🍽 ❀ CFA ⊡(heated) ⊇(heated) ₽ (hard) sauna
solarium gymnasium jacuzzi hairdressers *xmas*
V ✧ ⊉ Lunch £10-£16&alc High tea £6-£7.50 Dinner
£16.50-£18.50&alc Last dinner 9.30pm
Credit Cards ①③⑤

★★★70% **Corbyn Head** Torquay Rd, Sea Front, Livermead
TQ2 6RH ☎(0803)213611 FAX (0803) 296152
*Situated in a commanding position opposite Livermead Beach this*
*modern hotel has been refurbished with quality and taste to offer*
*comfortable and very well equipped en-suite bedrooms. Public*
*areas are spacious and there is a choice of restaurants. General*
*Manager Mr Quilliam and his staff provide friendly and skilled*
*services.*
51⇌🟫(1fb)3🛏 CTV in all bedrooms Ⓡ T sB&B⇌🟫£30-£48
dB&B⇌🟫£30-£96 **ᄆ**
ℂ 50P CFA ⊇(heated) *xmas*
V ✧ ⊉ Sunday Lunch £9.50-£12.50 Dinner £12.50-£15.50&alc
Last dinner 9pm
Credit Cards ①②③⑤ ⓔ

★★★69% **Abbey Lawn Hotel** Scarborough Rd TQ2 5UQ
☎(0803)299199 FAX (0803) 291460
*Complete refurbishment has restored this fine hotel to its former*
*Georgian elegance and glory. Public rooms are spacious and richly*
*furnished whilst bedrooms are well equipped. Spotlessly clean*
*throughout the hotel is personally managed with prompt,*
*traditional services.*

▶

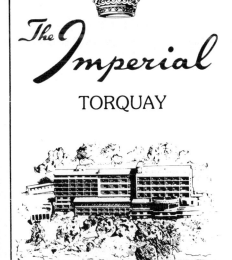
**T**

70⇌↱ CTV in all bedrooms ® T S% sB&B⇌↱£52-£90 dB&B⇌↱£104-£120 ⊟
Lift ℂ 50P ✲ ⌓(heated) ℘ (hard & grass) nc13yrs *xmas*
☋ English & French V ✧ ⅅ ⚟ S% Lunch £9.50-£12.50&alc High tea fr£6.50&alc Dinner fr£15&alc Last dinner 8.30pm
Credit Cards 1 2 3 5 £

---

★★★68% **Homers** Warren Rd TQ2 5TN ☎(0803)213456 FAX (0803) 213458
Closed 2 Jan-7 Feb
*All of the public rooms and most of the well-equipped bedrooms, at this elegant hotel enjoy panoramic views of Tor Bay. Décor throughout is tasteful and the furnishings have been carefully chosen. Interesting dishes are served in the dining room.*
14⇌↱(1fb)1⊞ CTV in all bedrooms T ✱ sB&B⇌↱£28-£40 dB&B⇌↱£54-£108 ⊟
CTV 5P ⊞ ✲ nc7yrs *xmas*
☋ European V ✧ ⅅ ⚟ Dinner £15.85-£25 Last dinner 9pm
Credit Cards 1 2 3 5

---

★★★⚘67% **Orestone Manor House** Rockhouse Ln, Maidencombe TQ1 4SX (Inter-Hotels) ☎(0803)328098 & 328099 FAX (0803) 328336
*This was originally a Georgian country lodge, built in the early 19th century. It is set in its own gardens and grounds that sweep down to the sea, and it has been substantially extended, and now provides twenty bedrooms of varying sizes. All are well equipped, and at the time of inspection were due to be refurbished over the following 18 months. The public lounges and bar are full of character, and comfortably decorated and furnished. Interesting dishes are offered on the table d'hôte menu, with some à la carte choices, and the food is served in the intimate dining room. A games room, an outdoor heated pool and a putting course are also available.*
20⇌↱(4fb) CTV in all bedrooms ® T sB&B⇌↱£27.50-£50 dB&B⇌↱£50-£100 ⊟
CTV 30P ✲ ⌓(heated) putting green games room *xmas*
☋ International V ✧ ⅅ Lunch fr£7.50 Dinner £17.50-£20&alc Last dinner 9pm
Credit Cards 1 2 3 5

---

★★★64% **Overmead** Daddyhole Rd TQ1 2EF (Consort) ☎(0803)297633 & 295666 FAX (0803) 211175
*Stone-built, split level hotel with a modern wing extension set in a quiet position.*
55⇌↱(7fb) CTV in all bedrooms ® T ⊟
Lift ℂ 11P ✲ ⌓(heated) snooker sauna solarium gymnasium ♫ *xmas*
☋ International V ✧ ⅅ Lunch £6-£8.50 High tea £4.50-£8.50 Dinner £14-£16&alc Last dinner 9pm
Credit Cards 1 2 3

---

★★★63% **Livermead Cliff** Torbay Rd TQ2 6RQ (Best Western) ☎(0803)299666 & 292881 Telex no 42424 FAX (0803) 294496
*Beautifully situated on the sea front with easy access to the town, this hotel has comfortable bedrooms with good facilities for commercial or holiday visitors. The lounge, bar and dining room are well positioned to make the best of the sea views.*
64⇌↱(21fb) CTV in all bedrooms ® T S% sB&B⇌↱£27.50-£48 dB&B⇌↱£54-£94 ⊟
Lift ℂ CTV 60P 12⊞ ✲ CFA ⌓(heated) ♪ solarium *xmas*
☋ English & Continental V ✧ ⅅ S% Lunch £7-£8&alc Dinner £12.50-£15&alc Last dinner 8.30pm
Credit Cards 1 2 3 5

---

★★★62% **Sefton** Babbacombe Downs Rd, Babbacombe TQ1 3LH ☎(0803)328728 & 326591
*The Powell family, assisted by a young, friendly staff, have made this Babbacombe hotel popular. All the bedrooms are attractive and there is a large entertainments room, a cocktail bar and a relaxing restaurant.*
47⇌↱(11fb)1⊞ CTV in all bedrooms ® T sB&B⇌↱£31.50-£35.50 dB&B⇌↱£63-£75 ⊟

▶

T

T

Lift 40P snooker ♬ *xmas*
V ♦ ☐ Lunch £6.50-£13.50&alc Dinner £9.50-£13.50&alc Last dinner 9pm
Credit Cards ①②③⑤

★★★61% **Kistor** Belgrave Rd TQ2 5HF ☎(0803)212632 FAX (0803) 293219
*Commercial and tourist hotel close to the beach, affording personal attention.*
59⇨(16fb)1⊞ CTV in all bedrooms ® T sB&B⇨£27.50-£45 dB&B⇨£51-£70 ℞
Lift CTV 45P ❀ CFA ⊠(heated) sauna solarium gymnasium spa pool games room ♬ *xmas*
♡ English & Continental V ♦ ☐ ✂
Credit Cards ①②③⑤⑤

★★★60% **Belgrave** Seafront TQ2 5HE ☎(0803)296666 FAX (0803) 211308
*Situated in a good position overlooking the bay, the hotel offers bright, modern public rooms, attractive bars and well furnished bedrooms.*
68⇨(16fb) CTV in all bedrooms ® T sB&B⇨🝔£32-£45 dB&B⇨🝔£64-£90 ℞
Lift ℂ 80P 6🝔 (£2) ⇱ ❀ CFA ⊒(heated) *xmas*
♡ English & French ♦ ☐ Bar Lunch £3-£8 Dinner £9 Last dinner 8.30pm
Credit Cards ①③⑤

★★★60% **Toorak** Chestnut Av TQ2 5JS ☎(0803)291444 Telex no 42885 FAX (0803) 291666
*This imposing Victorian hotel, close to the centre, is being totally refurbished, but until work is complete, guests can enjoy a wide range of leisure facilities in adjacent hotels under the same management.*
91⇨🝔(25fb) CTV in all bedrooms ® T sB&B⇨🝔£34-£50 dB&B⇨🝔£68-£100 (incl dinner) ℞
Lift ℂ 90P ⇱ ❀ CFA ⊒(heated) ℘ (hard) snooker croquet lawn ♬ *xmas*
♡ English & French V ♦ ☐ Lunch fr£7.50 Dinner fr£12.50&alc Last dinner 8.30pm
Credit Cards ①②③

★★★58% **Lincombe Hall** Meadfoot Rd TQ1 2JX ☎(0803)213361 FAX (0803) 211485
*Built in 1882 as a summer residence, the hotel has retained the elegance and classical simplicity of the period. The bedrooms, some spacious, offer good facilities and public areas are comfortable. A table d'hôte menu is available in the dining room which overlooks the grounds.*
43⇨🝔(6fb)3⊞ CTV in all bedrooms ® T sB&B⇨🝔£37.50-£46.75 dB&B⇨🝔£75-£93.50 ℞
ℂ 60P ❀ CFA ⊒(heated) ℘ (hard) sauna solarium putting spa bath badminton croquet *xmas*
V ♦ ☐ Sunday Lunch fr£7.45 Dinner £12.95&alc Last dinner 8.30pm
Credit Cards ①②③⑤

★★★57% **Livermead House** Torbay Rd TQ2 6QJ (Best Western) ☎(0803)294361 Telex no 42918 FAX (0803) 200758
*Conveniently situated for the town and beaches this hotel has indoor and outdoor leisure facilities, and a range of conference rooms. The compact bedrooms are equipped with good facilities and suitable for holidaymakers and business guests alike.*
62⇨🝔(9fb) CTV in all bedrooms ® T ✗ (ex guide dogs) S% sB&B⇨🝔£29-£41 dB&B⇨🝔£58-£82 ℞
Lift ℂ 90P ❀ ⊒(heated) ℘ (hard) squash snooker sauna solarium gymnasium *xmas*
♡ English & French V ♦ ☐ S% Lunch £6.25-£7&alc Dinner £10.50-£12.50&alc Last dinner 8.30pm
Credit Cards ①②③⑤⑤

## Seafront, Torquay
## Telephone: 0803-294361
## Telex: 42918

Right on the seafront at sea level, the Livermead House Hotel is situated in three acres of gardens and has ample parking. The 62 ensuite rooms all have colour TV, 'phone, hair dryer, radio, tea and coffee trays. Extensive leisure facilities. Restaurant and Bar also open to non-residents for lunch, dinner, bar meals and teas. Conference and function facilities.

**Proprietors: The Rew Family**

*Colour Brochure on Request*

**★★★**

## Lincombe Hall Hotel

## 'By Reputation'

An escape to comfort and hospitality on the English Riviera.
A Georgian Mansion set in 5 acres of gardens, yet just a short walk to Torquay's Harbour, Marina and Beaches.
All 43 rooms have en-suite facilities, radio, colour TV, direct dial telephone, mini-bar, toiletries and hot drinks tray.
Complimentary sauna, spa-bath, jacuzzi and sunbed.

## Meadfoot Road, Torquay, Devon
## Telephone: (0803) 213361
## Fax: (0803) 211485

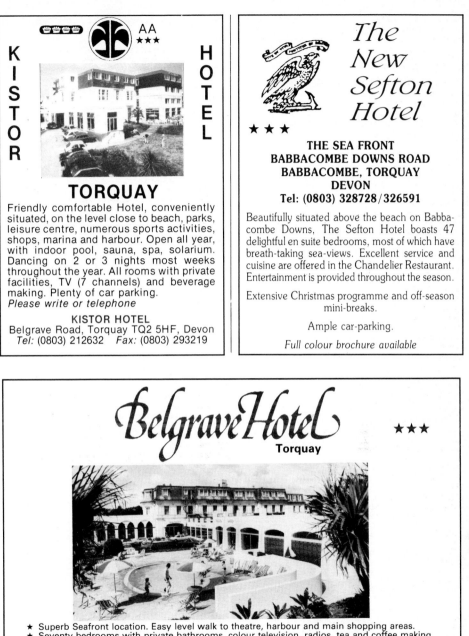
T

# Torquay

★★★51% **_Devonshire_** Parkhill Rd TQ1 2DY ☎(0803)291123
Telex no 42988 FAX (0803) 291710
_Large detached hotel with pleasant garden, set in a quiet position._
47rm(35⇔11♠)Annexe12⇔♠(7fb) CTV in all bedrooms ®
《 ▦ CTV 50P ✿ CFA ⌿(heated) ♪ (hard) snooker horse
riding surfing ♫ ♙
♀ English, French, Italian & German ☼ ⌧ Last dinner
8.30pm
Credit Cards ①②③④⑤

★★69% **_Conway Court_** Warren Rd TQ2 5TS ☎(0803)299699
_Friendly holiday hotel with spectacular views across Tor Bay._
38rm(16⇔19♠)(3fb)4⊞ CTV in all bedrooms ® T
CTV ♙ heated spa pool
☼ ⌧ ⌧ Last dinner 8pm
Credit Cards ①②③⑤

★★68% **_Oscar's Hotel & Restaurant_** 56 Belgrave Rd TQ2 5HY
☎(0803)293563
Closed 12 Nov-17 Dec
_A tall, Victorian, terraced house, tastefully converted, Oscars is in_
_the Belgravia area of Torquay. Bedrooms are comfortable and the_
_intimate bistro is open from March to October._
12rm(1⇔6♠)(2fb) CTV in all bedrooms ® T
✻ (ex guide dogs) ✱ sB&B£14.50-£20.50
sB&B⇔♠£16.50-£22.50 dB&B£28-£40 dB&B⇔♠£30-£45 ₽
CTV 8P ⊞
♀ International V ☼ Dinner £6.50-£8.50&alc Last dinner
8.30pm
Credit Cards ①③④⑤

★★67% **_Coppice_** Barrington Rd TQ1 2QJ ☎(0803)297786
Closed Nov-Apr
_This pleasant, family-run hotel has been further upgraded by the_
_addition of eight comfortable bedrooms, together with a bright new_
_bar lounge and conservatory. It enjoys a quiet position, away from_
_the town centre yet within easy reach of all amenities, and is_
_attractively set amid sub-tropical gardens with an outdoor_
_swimming pool._
38rm(33⇔3♠)(10fb) CTV in all bedrooms ® T
sB&B£16.50-£19.75 sB&B⇔♠£18.50-£21.75 dB&B£33-£39.50
dB&B⇔♠£37-£43.50
《 CTV 30P ✿ ⌧(heated) solarium xmas
☼ Dinner £8 Last dinner 8pm

★★67% **_Frognel Hall_** Higher Woodfield Rd TQ1 2LD
☎(0803)298339
Closed Dec-Feb RS Xmas & New Year
_An owner-managed hotel which commands fine bay views from its_
_elevated position was a private house from 1860 to 1980, and many_
_original features have been retained in the provision of good_
_modern facilities. Spacious public areas include an intimate dining_
_room where guests are served by attentive waitresses clad in_
_Victorian style, and guests receive a warm welcome from_
_proprietors whose main concern is their comfort and happiness._
27rm(12⇔9♠)(4fb) CTV in all bedrooms ®
sB&B£15.50-£23.50 sB&B⇔♠£17.50-£25.50
dB&B⇔♠£35-£50 ₽
Lift CTV 25P ✿ sauna solarium croquet games room xmas
♀ English & French V ☼ ⌧ Bar Lunch £1.50-£4.50 Dinner
£7.95-£10.95 Last dinner 7.30pm
Credit Cards ①③④

★★66% **_Burlington_** 462-466 Babbacombe Rd TQ1 1HN
☎(0803)294374 FAX (0803) 200189
_A tourist hotel situated on a main road about quarter of a mile_
_from beach and town centre._
44⇔♠(7fb)1⊞ CTV in all bedrooms ® T
《 CTV 20P ✿ ⌧(heated) sauna solarium pool table spa bath
♫
♀ English, French & Italian V ☼ ⌧ Last dinner 8pm
Credit Cards ①③

★★66% **Chelston Tower** Rawlyn Rd TQ2 6PQ ☎(0803)607351
Closed Jan
_Built in the 1800's this country house style of hotel stands in its_
_own gardens and enjoys glorious views of the town and sea front._
_Bedrooms are clean and comfortable and the lounge and bar offer_
_a lively atmosphere. A simple table d'hôte menu, which makes_
_good use of fresh produce, is available in the informal restaurant._
24rm(9⇔2♠)(11fb) T sB&B£17.50-£25 sB&B⇔♠£20.50-£28
dB&B£35-£50 dB&B⇔♠£41-£56
CTV 40P ✿ ⌧(heated) games room xmas
V ☼ ⌧ Dinner £12 Last dinner 7.30pm
£

★★66% **Gresham Court** Babbacombe Rd TQ1 1HG
☎(0803)293007 & 293658
Closed Dec-Feb
_Standing on the Babbacombe road close to both harbour and_
_shopping centre, and run by the same family for thirty years, this_
_hotel has now been modernised to provide clean, comfortable_
_bedrooms and a good range of public areas._
30⇔♠(6fb) CTV in all bedrooms ® sB&B⇔♠£19-£25
dB&B⇔♠£38-£50
Lift CTV 4P
V ☼ Bar Lunch £1.20-£4 Dinner £7 Last dinner 8pm
Credit Cards ①③

★★66% **Red House** Rousdown Rd, Chelston TQ2 6PB
☎(0803)607811 FAX (0803) 200592
_As its name suggests this is an attractive red brick hotel within_
_easy reach of the town and beaches. The accommodation is_
_comfortable and the coffee shop, dining room and lounge are all_
_situated near the hotel's excellent leisure facilities._
10⇔♠(3fb) CTV in all bedrooms ® S% sB&B⇔♠£23-£31.50
dB&B⇔♠£37-£55 ₽
10P ⊞ ✿ ⌧(heated) ⌧(heated) sauna solarium gymnasium
games room spa pool xmas
♀ English & French V ☼ ⌧ S% Lunch fr£6alc High tea
£1-£2.80alc Dinner £7.25-£7.95&alc Last dinner 8pm
Credit Cards ①③

★★65% **Ansteys Lea** Babbacombe Rd, Wellswood TQ1 2QJ
☎(0803)294843
_A tastefully restored, large Victorian villa, situated close to_
_Babbacombe beach. Rooms are spacious and comfortable, the staff_
_friendly, and the attractive gardens contain a small, secluded_
_swimming pool._
24rm(15⇔♠)(8fb) CTV in all bedrooms ® S%
sB&B£17-£23.50 sB&B⇔♠£19.50-£26 dB&B£31-£44
dB&B⇔♠£36-£49 ₽
CTV 18P ✿ ⌧(heated) solarium games room table tennis pool
table xmas
♀ English & French ☼ ⌧ S% Bar Lunch £1.10-£4 Dinner £5
Last dinner 7.30pm
£

★★65% **Dunstone** Lower Warberry Rd TQ1 1QS
☎(0803)293185
Closed 31 Oct-Feb
_This fine Victorian house, quietly set in an elevated position_
_overlooking the bay, numbers a magnificent open staircase, ornate_
_cornices and marble fireplaces among its orignal features._
_Tastefully furnished public areas are very comfortable, and guests_
_relaxing in the quiet room after dinner may be lucky enough to_
_hear the proprietor play the boudoir grand piano as he recalls his_
_days as a professional musician._
14rm(13⇔♠)(3fb) CTV in all bedrooms ® T ✻ sB&B£27-£33
sB&B⇔♠£29-£37 dB&B£54-£66
dB&B⇔♠£58-£74 (incl dinner) ₽
CTV 18P ⊞ ✿ ⌧(heated) pool table table tennis badminton
V ☼ ⌧ ⌧ Bar Lunch £2-£4 Dinner £10 Last dinner 8pm
Credit Cards ①③

★★65% *Hunsdon Lea* Hunsdon Rd TQ1 1QB ☎(0803)296538
Closed Nov-Etr
*This friendly, family, holiday hotel enjoys the personal attention of
its proprietors and a quiet setting which is nevertheless
conveniently close to central shopping area, harbour and amenities.*
16rm(8➪3♠)(5fb) CTV in all bedrooms ✕
12P ♨ ➔(heated) solarium pool table & table tennis
V ✿ ☑ ⊬

★★64% **Albaston House** 27 St Marychurch Rd TQ1 3JF
☎(0803)296758
Closed Dec
*Small family-run hotel, occupying a main road position, half a mile
from the town centre.*
13➪3♠(4fb) CTV in all bedrooms ® T ✳ sB&B➪3♠£17-£19
dB&B➪3♠£34-£38 🍴
CTV 12🚘 ♨
♧ English & French V ✿ ☑
Credit Cards ①③ⓔ

★★63% **Mount Nessing** St Lukes Rd North TQ2 5PD
☎(0803)292970
Closed last 2 wks Nov-1st 2 wks Dec
*Sharon and John Davidson have in recent times transformed their
family run hotel into a small, homely and comfortable
establishment. The bright bedrooms are individually decorated and
well furnished in keeping with the Victorian style of the property
whilst public areas include a new conservatory bar lounge and a
stylish restaurant.*
12➪3♠(3fb)1🏧 CTV in all bedrooms ® T ✕ ✳
sB&B➪3♠£16-£20.50 dB&B➪3♠£32-£41 🍴
CTV 10P ♨ *xmas*                    ▶

**T**

# Torquay

☿ English & French **V** ✂ Lunch £8-£12alc Dinner £8-£12alc
Last dinner 8.30pm
Credit Cards [1] [3]

**★★63% Roseland** Warren Rd TQ2 5TT ☎(0803)213829
FAX (0803) 291266
*In an elevated setting enjoying breathtaking views across the Bay
to Paignton and Brixham. Bedrooms have recently been
refurbished and now offer modern facilities and a simple table
d'hôte menu is available in the informal restaurant.*
36➾🏠(3fb)3⚄ CTV in all bedrooms ⓇT sB&B➾🏠£30-£37
dB&B➾🏠£55-£65 (incl dinner) 🍴
Lift 《 36P 2🐾 (£10 per week) ❖ ♫ *xmas*
☿ International **V** ❖ ⚏ ✂ Lunch £8.50 Dinner £14.50&alc
Last dinner 9pm
Credit Cards [1] [2] [3] £

**★★61% Carlton** Falkland Rd TQ2 5JJ ☎(0803)291166
*Following much refurbishment, this family hotel, conveniently
situated for the town centre and beaches, offers clean, brightly
decorated and well equipped bedrooms. The public areas are
spacious, and a full sized snooker table, pool table, outdoor heated
swimming pool, sun patio and lively bars with entertainment are
available for the guests' enjoyment.*
32rm(29➾🏠) CTV in all bedrooms ⓇT ✖ 🍴
Lift 《 26P ➾(heated) snooker ♫ *xmas*
**V** ❖ ⚏ Sunday Lunch £4-£9 Dinner £9.50-£12 Last dinner
7.45pm
Credit Cards [1] [3]

**★★61% Morningside** Babbacombe Downs TQ1 3LF
☎(0803)327025
*Competently managed by owners who have made considerable
improvements since taking over, and set in a good position
overlooking Babbacombe Downs, the hotel provides
accommodation in comfortable, well-equipped bedrooms which all
have en suite facilities, though they vary in size. Spacious, well-
furnished public areas include a dining room offering a table d'hôte
menu all the year round and an additional à la carte selection
during the summer months.*
14➾🏠 CTV in all bedrooms Ⓡ ✖
CTV 16P nc10yrs
**V** ❖ ⚏
Credit Cards [1] [3]

**★★61% Hotel Sydore** Meadfoot Rd TQ1 2JP ☎(0803)294758
*This villa in its own grounds is near town centre and harbour.*
13rm(6➾6🏠)(5fb)1⚄ CTV in all bedrooms Ⓡ S%
sB&B➾🏠£22-£30 dB&B➾🏠£34-£50 🍴
CTV 17P ❖ games room croquet *xmas*
☿ English & Continental **V** ❖ ⚏ S% Sunday Lunch £6.50
Dinner £6.95 Last dinner 8.45pm
Credit Cards [1] [3] £

**★★60% Bancourt** Avenue Rd TQ2 5LG ☎(0803)295077
*Modern, purpose-built and run by the resident owner, this hotel
stands within easy reach of both station and shops; bedrooms,
though compact, are clean, bright and well-equipped, and the
atmosphere is friendly.*
46rm(25➾5🏠)(8fb) CTV in all bedrooms ⓇT ✖
sB&B£23-£29 sB&B➾🏠£25.50-£36.50 dB&B£46-£58
dB&B➾🏠£51-£63 🍴
《 CTV 50P ❖ ⊡(heated) snooker *xmas*
☿ English & French ❖ ⚏ Lunch £4.50-£7.30 Dinner
fr£10.50&alc Last dinner 8pm
Credit Cards [1] [2] [3]

**★★59% Bute Court** Belgrave Rd TQ2 5HQ ☎(0803)293771
*A resort hotel with easy access to the seafront and town centre.
The bedrooms, whilst simply furnished, are equipped with colour
TVs and direct dial telephones. Entertainment is provided during
the season and there is ample car parking.*

46rm(42➾5🏠)(10fb) CTV in all bedrooms Ⓡ T S%
sB&B➾🏠£18.50-£30 dB&B£31-£45 dB&B➾🏠£37-£60 🍴
Lift 《 CTV 37P ❖ ➾(heated) snooker table tennis darts *xmas*
☿ English & Continental ❖ ⚏ S% Bar Lunch £1.40-£3alc
High tea £3-£5alc Dinner £7.50-£9alc Last dinner 8pm
Credit Cards [1] [2] [3] [5] £

**★★58% Hotel Balmoral** Meadfoot Sea Rd TQ1 2LQ
☎(0803)293381 & 299224
*This large, Victorian house is close to Meadfoot beach. Bedrooms,
though small, are well equipped and the public rooms are spacious.*
24➾🏠(7fb) CTV in all bedrooms ⓇT sB&B➾🏠£20-£26
dB&B➾🏠£40-£52 🍴
18P ❖ *xmas*
☿ English & French ❖ ⚏ Lunch £6.50 Dinner £9.50 Last
dinner 8pm
Credit Cards [1] [2] [3]

**★★57% Bowden Close** Teignmouth Rd, Maidencombe
TQ1 4TJ ☎(0803)328029
*A large, extended Victorian house set off the A379 at
Maidencombe provides comfortable public areas and clean, bright,
well-equipped bedrooms.*
20rm(3➾13🏠)(2fb) CTV in all bedrooms Ⓡ sB&B£22-£25
sB&B➾🏠£24-£27 dB&B£44-£50
dB&B➾🏠£48-£54 (incl dinner) 🍴
CTV 25P 2🐾 ❖ pool table clock golf
**V** ❖ ⚏ ✂ Bar Lunch 75p-£3.50alc Dinner £8.50&alc Last
dinner 8pm
Credit Cards [1] [3] £

**★★57% Lansdowne** Babbacombe Rd TQ1 1PW
☎(0803)299599
*A hotel on the Babbacombe road, near the town centre, is very well
geared to the needs of the holidaymaker, offering well equipped
bedrooms of various sizes, bright, attractive public areas and
friendly service from owners and staff.*
27➾🏠(9fb) CTV in all bedrooms ⓇT ✳ S%
sB&B➾🏠£25.50-£31.50 dB&B➾🏠£51-£63 (incl dinner) 🍴
CTV 30P ❖ ➾(heated) pool table table tennis *xmas*
☿ English, French & Italian **V** ❖ ⚏ ✂ Bar Lunch £1.20-£5.75
Dinner fr£8.50 Last dinner 8pm
Credit Cards [1] [2] [3] £

**★★57% Templestowe** Tor Church Rd TQ2 5UU
☎(0803)299499 FAX (0803) 295101
*Situated in an elevated position close to the main shopping areas,
this owner-managed hotel has been extensively improved and offers
modern, well-equipped bedrooms and spacious public areas.
Entertainment is provided nightly.*
87➾🏠(28fb) CTV in all bedrooms ⓇT
sB&B➾🏠£24.50-£37.50 dB&B➾🏠£49-£75
Lift 《 CTV 50P ➾(heated) 𝓅 (hard) solarium crazy golf table
tennis pool table ♫ *xmas*
☿ French **V** ❖ ⚏ Bar Lunch £1.50-£5 Dinner £8&alc Last
dinner 8.30pm
Credit Cards [1] [3] £

**★★55% Norcliffe** 7 Babbacombe Downs Rd, Babbacombe
TQ1 3LF ☎(0803)328456
*This detached Victorian property is located near to the village of
Babbacombe, with some sea views. Bedrooms are simply decorated
and furnished, yet all offer colour television and direct dial
telephones.*
20➾🏠(2fb)1⚄ CTV in all bedrooms ⓇT
Lift 16P
❖ ⚏ Last dinner 7.30pm
Credit Cards [3]

1991 marks the 25th anniversary of this guide.

★★54% *Belvedere House* Braddons Hill Rd West TQ1 1BG
☎(0803)293313
*An elegant building dating from 1892 and situated above the town with some sea views. The attractive lounge and intimate bar are shared with the hotel's four cats and dog. Homecooked dishes make up the simple table d'hôte menu available in the dining room.*
10⇌ᐕ(1fb) CTV in all bedrooms ®
CTV 9P ⌗ nc10yrs
⌾ English & Continental ♥ ⬚ ✂ Last dinner 7.30pm
Credit Cards ① ③

★★52% **Sunray** Aveland Rd, Babbacombe TQ1 3PT
☎(0803)328285
RS Dec-Mar
*Personal service is provided by the owner of a friendly little hotel which offers good-value, basic holiday accommodation.*
22rm(21⇌ᐕ)(3fb) CTV in all bedrooms ® sB&B⇌ᐕ£18-£25 dB&B⇌ᐕ£36-£50 (incl dinner) ▤
CTV 15P 1☂ *xmas*
⌾ English, French & Italian ✂ Bar Lunch 90p-£3.50 Dinner £7.50 Last dinner 8pm
Credit Cards ① ③

★★52% **Vernon Court** Warren Rd TQ2 5TR ☎(0803)292676
Closed Nov-Feb (ex Xmas)
*In superb, commanding position offering panoramic views over Tor Bay and the sea.*
21rm(14⇌5ᐕ)(6fb) CTV in all bedrooms ® ✳
sB&B£17.50-£26.50 dB&B⇌ᐕ£23.50-£26.50
dB&B⇌ᐕ£47-£53 ▤
CTV 9P *xmas*
⌾ English & Continental V ♥ ⬚
Credit Cards ① ② ③ ⑤ Ⓔ

**T**

★★50% **Meadfoot Bay** Meadfoot Sea Rd TQ1 2LQ
☎(0803)294722
Closed Nov-Feb
*Double-fronted villa standing in its own grounds in the Meadfoot Bay area.*
25rm(13⇨7♠)(6fb) CTV in all bedrooms ®
CTV 15P games room
♀ English & French **V** ◊ 〿 Last dinner 7.30pm
Credit Cards [1] [2] [3]

★70% **Fairmount House** Herbert Road, Chelston TQ2 6RW (Guestaccom) ☎(0803)605446
Closed Nov-Feb
*This attractive little hotel is located in a quiet residential area of Torquay. Surrounded by beautifully kept gardens, a warm welcome is assured at this hotel by Maggie and Noel Tolkien, and friendly service is offered. Well equipped bedrooms offer bright décor and coordinating colour schemes. The public rooms include a small bar in a conservatory, off the informal dining room where a table d'hôte menu is offered, made up of well cooked, interesting dishes.*
8⇨♠(3fb) ® sB&B⇨♠£20-£24 dB&B⇨♠£40-£48 **ᖴ**
CTV 9P
♀ English & Continental ◊ 〿 ✗ Sunday Lunch £9.50 Dinner £9.50 Last dinner 7.30pm
Credit Cards [1] [2] [3] [£]

★68% **Westwood** 111 Abbey Rd TQ2 5NP ☎(0803)293818
*Situated near to the centre of the town, and only a short walk away from the harbour and sea front, the Westwood provides clean, comfortable, well equipped bedrooms, and attractive public rooms. A simple table d'hôte menu is offered in the relaxed dining room, and the dishes are home cooked and enjoyable. The warm welcome, friendly service and the party atmosphere, created by the caring proprietors and their team of staff, make a stay at this hotel memorable.*
18rm(14♠)(1fb) CTV in all bedrooms ® ✗ (ex guide dogs) ✳ S% sB&B£13-£16 sB&B♠£15-£19 dB&B£26-£34 dB&B♠£29-£37 **ᖴ**
CTV 9P ✾ xmas
♀ English & French **V** ✗ Sunday Lunch £7&alc Dinner £7-£8&alc Last dinner 7.30pm
Credit Cards [1] [3]

★66% **Shelley Court** Croft Rd TQ2 5UD ☎(0803)295642
*Overlooking the bay from its elevated position, yet close to the town centre, this large, extended Victorian house offers comfortable accommodation in clean, bright bedrooms, many of which have good en suite facilities; spacious public areas are equally comfortable, service being attentive and friendly throughout.*
29rm(3⇨19♠)(3fb) ® ✗
CTV 20P ✾ ♫
◊ Last dinner 7.30pm
Credit Cards [1]

★64% **Sunleigh** Livermead Hill TQ2 6QY ☎(0803)607137
Closed Jan-21 Mar & 3 Nov-23 Dec
*Spaciously comfortable public areas and bedrooms which though compact in some cases are very well equipped – all but one having en suite facilities – are provided by this large, detached Victorian house overlooking Livermead Bay.*
21rm(20♠)(3fb) CTV in all bedrooms ® sB&B♠£21-£26.50 dB&B♠£42-£53 (incl dinner) **ᖴ**
CTV 18P xmas
Dinner £8.75 Last dinner 7pm
[£]

★61% **Hotel Fluela** 15-17 Hatfield Rd TQ1 3BW ☎(0803)297512
*This small, family-run hotel has a friendly atmosphere, and the bedrooms, while compact in places, offer good facilities, and the two lounges are comfortably decorated and furnished. A simple*

*choice of home-cooked dinners makes up the table d'hôte menus and the service is friendly and relaxed.*
13⇨♠(3fb) CTV in all bedrooms ® **T** ✗ (ex guide dogs) S% sB&B⇨♠£12-£18 dB&B⇨♠£24-£36
CTV 20P ▦ xmas
**V** ✗ Bar Lunch 60p-£3.80alc Dinner £7&alc Last dinner 7.30pm
Credit Cards [1] [3]

★60% **Windsurfer** St Agnes Ln TQ2 6QE ☎(0803)606550
Closed 27 Nov-22 Dec & 29 Dec-13 Jan
*Overlooking the sea from its elevated location close to the railway station, a large Victorian semi with spacious rooms and high ceilings offers comfortable, well-equipped accommodation and personal service by the proprietors and their family.*
10⇨♠(5fb) CTV in all bedrooms ® ✗
CTV 14P ✾
Last dinner 8pm
Credit Cards [2]

★**Ashley Rise** 18 Babbacombe Rd, Babbacombe TQ1 3SJ
☎(0803)327282
Closed Dec-Mar ex Xmas
*Detached modern hotel on the main Babbacombe road into Torquay, near the sea front and the shops.*
28rm(4⇨7♠)(5fb) sB&B£16-£18 sB&B⇨♠£18-£20 dB&B£32-£36 dB&B⇨♠£36-£40
CTV 14P xmas
◊ Dinner fr£8.75 Last dinner 7pm
[£]

✱✗✗**The Table** 135 Babbacombe Rd TQ1 3SR ☎(0803)324292
*A cosy, intimate restaurant in the centre of Babbacombe, converted from a shop by Jane and Trevor Brooks. Jane is the charming and attentive hostess, while Trevor is the innovative chef, preparing local produce with fresh herbs and robust sauces. His background as a patissier in some of Britain's finest restaurants reveals itself throughout, from the light home-made rolls to the delicious desserts. The wine list is young but carefully compiled, and offers good value for money.*
Closed Mon, 1-16 Feb & 1-10 Sep
Lunch not served
♀ British & French 20 seats Dinner £22.50-£26 Last dinner 10pm ✗ nc10yrs

✗**Remy's Restaurant Français** 3 Croft Rd TQ2 5UF
☎(0803)292359
*A popular small restaurant with a French atmosphere features interesting and imaginative dishes from the Alsace region. You may enjoy a vegetable terrine or delicate smoked salmon, followed perhaps by Saddle of Venison with Cranberry Sauce or Breast of Pheasant with Madeira and Truffle Sauce, the meal being completed by a delectable range of home-made puddings and accompanied by a wine list containing some Alsation examples which are well worth trying. Booking is advisable.*
Closed Sun, Mon & 2 wks Aug
Lunch not served ex by arrangement
♀ French 33 seats Lunch £16.85 Last dinner 9.30pm ✗ nc7yrs
Credit Cards [1] [2] [3]

---

**TORRINGTON, GREAT** Devon Map **02** SS42

✗**Rebecca's** 8 Potacre St EX38 8BH ☎Torrington(0805)22113
*A fairly recent change of ownership has seen a transformation in this little restaurant, now more stylish and comfortable with the cooking making good use of quality fresh produce. Dishes are well prepared and presented with a recognisable degree of flair and imagination. Dishes might include a mousseline of locally caught fish with a sauce of fresh garden herbs, mayonnaise and Dijon mustard as a starter, Breast of Aylesbury duck with ginger and a lime and plum sauce to follow and a portion of Rebecca's infamous chocolate and hazelnut cheesecake to finish. Raspberry and pear millefeuille on a raspberry sauce is another firm favourite. The*

*wine list is well balanced and reasonably priced and service is informal and friendly.*
Closed Sun & 26-28 Dec
Lunch not served Mon
♌ International 36 seats ✱ Lunch £13.50-£20.50alc Dinner £13.50-£20.50alc Last lunch 2pm Last dinner 10pm ✔ nc2yrs
Credit Cards ①③

---

**TOTLAND BAY**

See Wight, Isle of

---

**TOTNES** Devon Map **03** SX86

See also **Harbertford & Staverton**
★★59% **Royal Seven Stars** TQ9 5DD ☎(0803)862125 & 863241
FAX (0803) 867925
*This town-centre hotel, originally a coaching inn dating back to 1660, offering simply appointed bedrooms, some with en suite facilities. The public bars and restaurants are popular with non-residents, but a quiet residents lounge is available.*
18rm(12⇩🌂)(3fb)2🚻 CTV in all bedrooms ® T sB&Bfr£36 sB&B⇩🌂£46-£58 dB&Bfr£48 dB&B⇩🌂£58-£68 🛗
CTV 20P ♫ *xmas*
♌ English & Continental V ♥ ✱ Lunch £7-£7.50&alc Dinner £12.75-£15&alc Last dinner 9.30pm
Credit Cards ①③⑤

---

**TOWCESTER** Northamptonshire Map **04** SP64

⭐**Travelodge** East Towcester by pass NN12 0DD (A43 East Towcester by-pass) (Trusthouse Forte) ☎(0327)359105
*Offering easy access to Northampton from its position on the A43, the lodge provides value-for-money accommodation of a good standard, meals being available in an adjacent Little Chef restaurant.*
33⇩🌂(33fb) CTV in all bedrooms ® sB⇩🌂£24 dB⇩🌂£29.50 (room only)
《 33P 🚗
Credit Cards ①②③

✖✖**Vine House** 100 High St, Paulerspury NN12 7NA (3m S A5)
☎Paulerspury(032733)267
*This small restaurant, attached to a cottage-style hotel in the picturesque village centre, is fast achieving a high reputation in the country. The young chefs use first-class produce and have a lovely, light lunch with dishes such as Pithiviers of Duck with a Port Wine and pink peppercorn sauce, tartlet of wild mushrooms with a cream and chive sauce, the tomato butter sauce accompanying the pan-fried fillet of salmon showed real depth of flavour, and to conclude the meal there is a small selection of tempting desserts or carefully-chosen selection of cheeses.*
Closed 2 wks before Etr, Xmas-New Year & BHs
Lunch not served Sat & Mon
Dinner not served Sun
♌ French V 45 seats ✱ Lunch £14.95-£32&alc Dinner £14.95-£32&alc Wine £5.65 Last lunch 2pm Last dinner 9.30pm 20P
Credit Cards ①③

---

**TREARDDUR BAY** Gwynedd Map **06** SH27

★★★62% **Beach** LL65 2YT (Best Western) ☎(0407)860332
Telex no 61529 FAX (0407) 861140
*Situated just a few hundred yards from the beach, this privately-owned hotel is ideally suited for the family holidaymaker. The bedrooms are quite well equipped, and the hotel offers a choice of restaurants and bar facilities. There is also a well equipped indoor leisure centre, the facilities of which include a small swimming pool, 2 squash courts and 9 full-sized snooker tables. In short, the hotel offers something for all the family.* ▶

**T**

26⇌🦚(2fb) CTV in all bedrooms ® T ✱ sB&B⇌🦚£33-£40
dB&B⇌🦚£50-£55 Continental breakfast 🍴
《150P squash snooker sauna solarium gymnasium spa ↺ xmas
♀ English & French V ✧ ◡ Sunday Lunch £6.50-£9 Dinner
£10-£20 Last dinner 9.30pm
Credit Cards ①②③⑤ ⓔ

★★★62% *Trearddur Bay* LL68 2UN ☎(0407)860301
Telex no 61609
*This seafront hotel provides well equipped accommodation and
spacious public areas. Equally suitable for both holidaymakers and
business people, facilities include a completely self contained
function suite and an indoor heated swimming pool.*
27rm(20⇌)(7fb) CTV in all bedrooms ®
《CTV 300P ✻ ☒(heated)
V ✧ ◡
Credit Cards ①②③④⑤
See advertisement under HOLYHEAD

★★60% Seacroft Ravenspoint Rd LL65 2YU ☎(0407)860348
*Two-storey hotel near the beach.*
6rm(1⇌2🦚)(3fb) CTV in all bedrooms ® ✈
CTV 30P ✻
♀ French V ✧

TREFRIW Gwynedd Map 06 SH76

★★73% Hafod House LL27 0RQ (Inter-Hotels)
☎Llanrwst(0492)640029 FAX (0492) 641351
*Personally run by the chef/owner and his wife, this delightful small
hotel provides very good standards of both hospitality and cuisine.
Two cosy, comfortable lounges are available for guests' use,
bedrooms are carefully designed to provide good facilities, and a
rural location on the edge of the village commands views over the
Conwy Valley.*
7⇌🦚1🛏 CTV in all bedrooms ® T ✈ (ex guide dogs)
sB&B⇌🦚£29.50 dB&B⇌🦚£59 🍴
20P ✻ nc11yrs xmas
♀ English & French V ✧ ◡ Lunch £10.50-£13.95 Dinner
£14.95 Last dinner 9.30pm
Credit Cards ①②③⑤ ⓔ

TRELIGHTS Cornwall & Isles of Scilly Map 02 SW97

★★58% Long Cross Victorian PL29 3TF
☎Bodmin(0208)880243
Closed Nov-Etr
*Set amongst well tended Victorian gardens, the hotel has a friendly
atmosphere, good bedrooms and bathrooms, and a pleasant, period
atmosphere in its public rooms. Its separate bars open directly onto
the gardens.*
12⇌1🛏 CTV in all bedrooms ® ✻ sB&B⇌fr£26.50
dB&B⇌fr£52 (incl dinner) 🍴
CTV 20P ✻ nc14yrs
V ✧ ◡ Bar Lunch fr£2.25 Dinner fr£14 Last dinner 9pm
Credit Cards ①③ ⓔ

TREMADOG Gwynedd Map 06 SH54

★★57% Madoc LL49 9RB ☎Porthmadog(0766)512021
*Stone-built, and dating back to the early 19th century, the hotel
stands in the market square. Furnishings are comfortable, and the
dining room serves good, honest food.*
21rm(1⇌3🦚)(3fb) ® ✻ sB&B£18.50-£25 sB&B⇌🦚£25-£27
dB&B£40-£45 dB&B⇌🦚fr£45 🍴
CTV 12P 4🚗 ♫
V ✧ ◡ Lunch £6.50 Dinner £7-£15alc Last dinner 9.30pm
Credit Cards ①③

TRESCO
See Scilly, Isles of

TREYARNON BAY Cornwall & Isles of Scilly Map 02 SW87

★★65% Waterbeach PL28 8JW ☎Padstow(0841)520292
Closed Nov-Feb
*A warm welcome awaits guests at this hotel which overlooks bay
and beach from the setting of its own secluded garden. Bedrooms
are well equipped and public areas include a comfortable lounge
and bar as well as the dining room with its imaginative table d'hôte
menu of freshly cooked dishes.*
20rm(7⇌2🦚)(2fb) CTV in all bedrooms ® T ✈ ✱
sB&B£31-£33 dB&B£62-£66 dB&B⇌🦚£68-£72 (incl dinner)
CTV 20P 🚲 ✻ ♪ (hard) putting
V ✧ ◡ Dinner £12.75 Last dinner 8.15pm
Credit Cards ①②③

TRING Hertfordshire Map 04 SP91

★★62% Rose & Crown High St HP23 5AH (Lansbury)
☎(044282)4071 Telex no 826538 FAX (0442) 890735
*The variety of well equipped accommodation available at this
popular coaching inn ranges from rooms which contain four-poster
beds to more compact singles. Public areas include a busy grill-
style restaurant and a bar appointed to retain some of the original
character of the hotel, a lively atmosphere prevailing throughout.*
27⇌🦚(1fb)🚲🛏in 5 bedrooms CTV in all bedrooms ® T
✈ (ex guide dogs) sB&B⇌🦚fr£76 dB&B⇌🦚fr£88 🍴
《50P xmas
♀ Mainly grills V ✧ ✂ Lunch fr£8.25&alc Dinner
fr£13.25&alc Last dinner 10pm
Credit Cards ①②③⑤

⬙*Crows Nest Travel Inn* Tring Hill HP23 4LD ☎(044282)4819
*Ideal for both business and leisure user, offering easy access to
main routes, this neat, well-maintained establishment situated
beside a Beefeater Steak House provides good value
accommodation.*
30⇌🦚 CTV in all bedrooms ® ✈ (ex guide dogs)
140P
V ✧ ✂ Last dinner 10.30pm
Credit Cards ①②③⑤

○*Pendley Manor* Cow Ln HP2 5QY ☎(0442)891891
70rm open

TROON Strathclyde *Ayrshire* Map 10 NS33

★★★★65% Marine Highland KA10 6HE (Scottish Highland)
☎(0292)314444 Telex no 777595 FAX (0292) 316922
*With Troon's championship golf course on its doorstep this hotel is
popular with golfers, tourists and business people alike. The lively
brasserie, main restaurant and comfortable lounges are
complimented by good leisure facilities and a commendable range
of services.*
72⇌(7fb)🛏 CTV in all bedrooms ® T sB&B⇌£70-£80
dB&B⇌£105-£120 🍴
Lift 《200P ✻ CFA ☒(heated) squash snooker sauna solarium
gymnasium shooting fishing golf ♫ xmas
♀ International V ✧ ◡ Lunch £9.95&alc Dinner £17.50&alc
Last dinner 11pm
Credit Cards ①②③⑤

★★★67% Piersland House Craigend Rd KA10 6HD (Consort)
☎(0292)314747 FAX (0292) 315613
15⇌🦚Annexe4⇌(2fb)1🛏 CTV in all bedrooms ® T ✱
sB&B⇌🦚£48-£74 dB&B⇌🦚£74-£95 🍴
《150P ✻ croquet putting xmas
♀ Scottish, English & Contininental V ✧ Lunch £9.95&alc
High tea £5-£9.50alc Dinner £17.50 Last dinner 9.30pm
Credit Cards ①②③⑤

★★62% **Craiglea** South Beach KA10 6EG ☎(0292)311366
*A long-established hotel with views across the South Links and out
to the sea retains its good, old-fashioned values, offering friendly
traditional service and reasonably priced meals.*
20rm(11⇨♠♪)(2fb) CTV in all bedrooms ® T sB&B£28-£35
sB&B⇨♠♪£32-£40 dB&B£40-£50 dB&B⇨♠♪£45-£58 ⊟
CTV 14P *xmas*
V ✧ ⚗ Lunch £7.50-£10.50&alc Dinner £11.50-£13.50&alc
Last dinner 8.45pm
Credit Cards ① ② ③ ⑤

★★60% **Ardneil** 51 St Meddans St KA10 6NU ☎(0292)311611
*A privately-owned, well supervised and friendly hotel close to the
town centre and railway station. Bedrooms are compact but
comfortable and mealtimes are very busy.*
9rm(3⇨4♠♪)(2fb) CTV in all bedrooms ® ✱
sB&B£23.50-£24.50 sB&B⇨♠♪£27.50-£29.50 dB&B£42-£43.50
dB&B⇨♠♪£47.50-£49.50
100P ✿ snooker ♨
V ✧ ⚗ Lunch £5.55-£7.55alc High tea £4.50-£5.50alc Last
high tea 7pm
Credit Cards ① ② ③ ⑥

★★57% **South Beach** South Beach Rd KA10 6EG
☎(0292)312033
*Close to the seafront, the hotel is popular with families and has
recently completed a new leisure centre.*
27⇨♠♪(6fb) CTV in all bedrooms ® T ✱ sB&B⇨♠♪£40-£50
dB&B⇨♠♪£50-£85 ⊟
CTV 50P ♪ sauna solarium gymnasium jacuzzi ♫ *xmas*
♥ English & French ✧ ⚗ Sunday Lunch £6.50 High tea £5
Dinner £14.50-£19.50 Last dinner 8.30pm
Credit Cards ① ② ③

✕*Campbell's Kitchen* 3 South Beach KA10 6EF ☎(0292)314421
*This popular little bistro restaurant enjoys a good local reputation.
The cosy interior is delightfully simple, with subdued lighting and a
friendly relaxed atmosphere. The short, imaginative menu reflects
a French influence, and service is unobtrusively efficient.*
Closed Sun, Mon, 25-26 Dec & 2 wks Jan
♥ Scottish & French 36 seats Last lunch 2.30pm Last dinner
9.30pm ✍
Credit Cards ① ② ③

---

**TROTTON** West Sussex Map **04** SU82

★★★65% **Southdowns** GU31 5JN (Exec Hotel)
☎Rogate(073080)774 & 763 Telex no 86658
FAX (073080) 790
*Tucked away in four acres of grounds at the foot of the South
Downs, an hotel with some magnificent views offers comfortable
and well-equipped accommodation, some of the rooms in the main
section of the house recently having been refurbished. Features
include the popular bar, a restaurant serving a variety of menus,
and an indoor swimming pool.*
22⇨(3fb)1 ♨⚲in 4 bedrooms CTV in all bedrooms ® T ✖
sB&B⇨£45-£60 dB&B⇨£60-£80 ⊟
CTV 70P ✿ ▦(heated) ♪ (hard) ♪ sauna solarium croquet
exercise equipment *xmas*
V ✧ ⚗ ⚲ Lunch £8-£12alc High tea £3.50-£10alc Dinner
£15-£20alc Last dinner 10pm
Credit Cards ① ② ③ ⑥
**See advertisement under MIDHURST**

---

Hotels with a high percentage rating for quality
are highlighted by a % across their
gazetteer entry.

---

**TROUTBECK (near Windermere)** Cumbria Map **07** NY40

★★70% **Mortal Man** LA23 1PL ☎Ambleside(05394)33193
Closed mid Nov-mid Feb
*This delightful historic country inn provides accommodation in
cosy atmospheric public areas and comfortably furnished, well
equipped bedrooms which enjoy beautiful views down the valley to
Lake Windermere; food, service and housekeeping are all of a
high standard.*
12⇨ CTV in all bedrooms ® T S% sB&B⇨£35-£40
dB&B⇨£70 (incl dinner) ⊟
CTV 20P ♨ ✿ nc5yrs
✧ ⚗ S% Sunday Lunch £10 Dinner £16.50 Last dinner 8pm

---

**TROWBRIDGE** Wiltshire Map **03** ST85

★★58% **Polebarn House** Polebarn Gardens, Polebarn Rd
BA14 7EW ☎(0225)777006 FAX (0225) 754164
*A Grade II listed building with an impressive façade offers good,
simply-appointed accommodation; the provision of disco music in
the lower ground floor open-plan lounge area between the bar and
restaurant makes it popular with local young people, and service is
friendly and helpful throughout.*
13rm(2⇨10♠♪)(1fb) CTV in all bedrooms ® T
✖ (ex guide dogs) ✱ sB&B£40-£45 sB&B⇨♠£40-£45
dB&B£53-£60 dB&B⇨♠£53-£60 ⊟
10P 2♨
V ✧ ⚗ Lunch £6-£15 High tea fr£1.50 Dinner £8.50-£12&alc
Last dinner 8.45pm
Credit Cards ① ③ ⑥

★67% **Hilbury Court** Hilperton Rd BA14 7JW ☎(0225)752949
Closed 24-31 Dec
*This attractive, late-Georgian house stands in its own grounds on
the outskirts of Trowbridge. The public rooms are comfortable and
the bedrooms, some with en suite facilities, are tastefully decorated*
▶

**T**

*and very well equipped. The owner's wife is in charge of the dining room, and the food is good, unfussy and freshly prepared.*
13rm(4⇨3♠)(2fb) CTV in all bedrooms ⓡ T
✗ (ex guide dogs) sB&B£32-£39 sB&B⇨♠£39
dB&B£43.50-£50.50 dB&B⇨♠£50.50
CTV 14P ⇨ ✿
V ⊹ ⚏ Sunday Lunch £2-£4 Dinner £8-£12 Last dinner 7.30pm
Credit Cards 1 3

---

**TRURO** Cornwall & Isles of Scilly Map **02** SW84

★★★

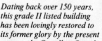

★★★ **ALVERTON MANOR**

Tregolls Rd TR1 1XQ
☎(0872)76633
FAX (0872) 222989

*Dating back over 150 years, this grade II listed building has been lovingly restored to its former glory by the present owners, the Costellos. Once home to the Tweedy family, and latterly to the Sisters of the Epiphany, today's guests at Alverton Manor can once again enjoy many creature comforts. The attractive bar lounge, colourfully decorated with fresh flowers, leads into an elegant dining room where chef Christopher Musgrave cooks in the modern English style. The imaginative à la carte menu features such dishes as duck liver parfait with remoulade of celeriac, or warm seafish mousse studded with vegetables and served with a thyme butter sauce. Main courses may be loin of lamb (cooked as requested) with a timbale of courgettes and roast garlic, or oven-baked pavé of salmon with a potato purée and red wine jus. For those who like really plain food, grilled steaks are always an alternative.*
25⇨♠ CTV in all bedrooms T ✗ (ex guide dogs) ✱
sB&B⇨♠fr£67 dB&B⇨♠fr£90 Continental breakfast ♬
Lift ( 60P ⇨ ✿ snooker ♫ nc12yrs *xmas*
ℱ English & French V ⊹ ⚏ ✗ Lunch £9.95-£16.95 High tea £6.95 Dinner £16.95&alc Last dinner 9.45pm
Credit Cards 1 2 3 5 £

---

★★★63% **Brookdale** Tregolls Rd TR1 1JZ (Inter-Hotels)
☎(0872)73513 & 79305
Closed Xmas wk
*A small and well-managed hotel, pleasantly situated in the centre of Truro. The restaurant offers an imaginative menu and dishes are carefully prepared.*
21⇨♠ CTV in all bedrooms ⓡ T ✱ sB&B⇨♠£46
dB&B⇨♠£62 ♬
50P 10⇨
ℱ English, French & Italian ⊹ ⚏ S% Bar Lunch £1.50-£8.50
Dinner £14.50 Last dinner 8.45pm
Credit Cards 1 2 3 5

---

★★60% **Royal** Lemon St TR1 2QB ☎(0872)70345
FAX (0872)42453
RS Xmas & New Year
*Standing close to the Cathedral this former Georgian coaching inn features well-equipped bedrooms, a grill room and two popular bars.*
34⇨♠(4fb) CTV in all bedrooms ⓡ T ✱
sB&B⇨♠£38.50-£42.50 dB&B⇨♠£50 ♬
( CTV 34P

---

ℱ English & French V ⊹ ⚏ Lunch £6.50&alc Dinner
£6.50&alc Last dinner 9.30pm
Credit Cards 1 2 3 £

★★55% **Carlton** Falmouth Rd TR1 2HL ☎(0872)72450
FAX (0872) 223938
Closed 21 Dec-5 Jan
*Detached Victorian mansion with extension. Family run by Chef proprietor. Quiet situation but close to city centre.*
30rm(5⇨22♠)(4fb) CTV in all bedrooms ⓡ T ✱
sB&B£26-£36.20 sB&B⇨♠£31.25-£36.20 dB&B£39.20-£48.50
dB&B⇨♠£48.50 ♬
32P ⇨ sauna solarium gymnasium spa bath
V ⊹ ⚏ Dinner £7.95&alc Last dinner 8pm
Credit Cards 1 3 £

---

**TUNBRIDGE WELLS (ROYAL)** Kent Map **05** TQ53

★★★73% **Spa** Mount Ephraim TN4 8XJ (Best Western)
☎Tunbridge Wells(0892)20331 Telex no 957188
FAX (0892) 510575
*An elegant Georgian mansion, set in fourteen acres of landscaped gardens with lakes, provides every modern comfort in its individually decorated bedrooms. Meals are served in a charming restaurant, and guests can relax in either the Equestrian Bar or the spaciously comfortable lounge – unless they prefer to take advantage of the hotel's leisure facilities or beauty therapy clinic.*
76⇨♠(9fb) CTV in all bedrooms ⓡ T sB⇨♠£65-£70
dB⇨♠£80-£100 (room only) ♬
Lift ( 120P ✿ CFA ⬛(heated) ℘ (hard) sauna solarium gymnasium *xmas*
ℱ English & French V ⊹ ⚏ ✗ Lunch fr£13&alc Dinner £19&alc Last dinner 9.30pm
Credit Cards 1 2 3 4 5 £

★★62% **Royal Wells Inn** Mount Ephraim TN4 8BE
☎Tunbridge Wells(0892)511188 FAX (0892) 511908
Closed 25-26 Dec RS 1 Jan & BH Mons
*Well equipped bedrooms – some of which have been upgraded – and an attractive first-floor restaurant with interesting menus of skilfully prepared dishes are offered by a family-run commercial hotel with a friendly, informal atmosphere.*
25⇨♠2⇩ CTV in all bedrooms ⓡ S10% sB&B⇨♠£60-£65
dB&B⇨♠£75-£85 ♬
Lift 28P 4⇨ ⇨
ℱ English & French V ⊹ Lunch £12.75-£14.50&alc Dinner £14.50-£16&alc Last dinner 10pm
Credit Cards 1 2 3 5 £

**See advertisement on page 701**

★★61% **Russell** 80 London Rd TN1 1DZ (Inter-Hotels)
☎Tunbridge Wells(0892)544833 Telex no 95177
FAX (0892) 515846
*A friendly, comfortable hotel, personally supervised by the owners, Mr and Mrs Wilkinson, assisted by staff who are enthusiastic and very willing to please. The dinner menu offers plenty of choice of mostly traditional dishes and the bedrooms are spacious and well appointed.*
21⇨♠(3fb)✗in 5 bedrooms CTV in all bedrooms ⓡ T
✗ (ex guide dogs) ✱ sB⇨♠£44-£55
dB⇨♠£44-£55 (room only) ♬
( 20P
ℱ English & French V ⊹ Bar Lunch £1.50-£2.75 Dinner fr£13 Last dinner 9.30pm
Credit Cards 1 2 3 5 £

★★56% **Calverley** Crescent Rd TN1 2LY
☎Tunbridge Wells(0892)26455 Telex no 957565
FAX (0892) 512044
*An old-fashioned hotel offering simple but spacious accommodation, many of the rooms having pleasant views over the rear gardens, is conveniently located for the centre of the town.*

▶

# Russell Hotel ★★
## TUNBRIDGE WELLS

The Russell Hotel is situated in a beautiful position facing the common, yet conveniently only a few minutes walk from the town centre.
21 comfortable ensuite bedrooms with satellite colour TV, radio, telephone, hairdryer, trouser press and hospitality tray.
The restaurant serves a changing variety of high quality fresh food.
A small conference room is available for up to 16 persons.
**Telephone (0892) 544833**
**Telex: 97177 RUSSEL G.   Fax: 0892 515846**
**80 London Road, Tunbridge Wells, Kent TN1 1DZ**

# The Royal Truro

OPEN ALL DAY TO
NON-RESIDENTS
Breakfast, Coffee Bar,
Bar Snacks, Lunches and
Evening Grills

ALL MEALS ARE
REASONABLY
PRICED
Stockroom and
Conference Facilities

34 Bedrooms all En Suite with Colour TV, Telephone, Tea and Coffee making facilities
*Write or telephone for free brochure including details of special week-end-away rates*
**OPEN ALL YEAR**
**The Royal Hotel,** Lemon Street, Truro
*Tel:* (0872) 70345   *Fax:* 42453

# The Carlton Hotel
**Falmouth Road, Truro, Cornwall**
**Tel: 0872 72450**   ★★
**Fax: 0872 223938**

We are a family run hotel with all home cooking, table d'hôte and à la carte menus. 32 bedrooms, most with private bathroom and Colour TV, tea & coffee making facilities. Central heating throughout the Hotel. 3 residents' lounges. Large dining room. Sauna, gym & spa bath.

**Resident proprietors Roy and Sheila Palmer.**

*Your comfort is our concern.*

# Hilbury Court ★ Hotel
**Hilperton Road (A361), Trowbridge**
**Tel: (0225) 752949**

The Hilbury Court is set in its own grounds on the outskirts of Trowbridge. Most rooms have en-suite bathrooms and all rooms have a colour TV, direct dial telephone, radio and tea and coffee making facilities.

The Hotel has a residential licence, and is furnished to a very high standard making it the ideal place for the traveller to stay.

T

44rm(25⇨11↑)(2fb)1⊞ CTV in all bedrooms ® T ✳
sB&B£38 sB&B⇨↑£42 dB&B£56 dB&B⇨↑£65
Lift ℂ CTV 44P ✿ xmas
V 🕭 ⏛ Lunch fr£7 Dinner fr£9 Last dinner 8.30pm
Credit Cards ①③⑤

✕✕Eglantine High St TN1 1XX ☎(0892)24957
Closed Mon & 24-28 Dec
Dinner not served Sun
⊌ French V 35 seats Lunch fr£11 Dinner fr£18 Last lunch
1.45pm Last dinner 9.30pm 🍷 ⌣
Credit Cards ①②③

✿ ✕✕Thackeray's House TN1 1EA
☎Royal Tunbridge Wells(0892)511921
*Chef-patron Bruce Wass has decorated this elegant restaurant,
once the home of the writer William Makepeace Thackeray, with
many paintings, creating an atmosphere reminiscent of Odin's, the
well known London restaurant where he was formerly chef. He
brings style and originality to his interpretation of classical recipes,
and notable dishes from his repertoire include a hot Turbot and
Scallop pâté with sorrel sauce, Breast of wild duck served on
brioche with Madeira and wild mushrooms, and Brill baked in
Chambéry Vermouth and chives. The separate dessert menu
cannot fail to tempt one to indulge oneself. Service, under the eye
of Restaurant Manager Michael Burrows, is particularly caring.
For those wishing to eat less formally, the 'Downstairs' bistro,
offers a set menu produced by the same kitchen: the mousseline of
chicken, the baked fillet of Rye cod cooked in Vermouth and
blackcurrant pavlova can all be recommended.*
Closed Sun, Mon & Xmas
⊌ English & French V 35 seats ✳ S10% Lunch £14.90-£16.85
Dinner £21-£35alc Last lunch 2.30pm Last dinner 10pm 🍷
Credit Cards ①③

✕Cheevers 56 High St TN1 1XF ☎(0892)545524
*The precise and skilfull cooking of chef/patron Timothy J
Cheevers and the warm, friendly supervision of Martin J Miles
results in attractive and individual standards of cuisine. The menu
features dishes such as mousse of crab wrapped in spinach, terrine
of quail and duck, medallions of venison with red wine and raisins,
and hot walnut and ginger pudding.*
Closed Sun, Mon, 1 wk Xmas, 2 wks Etr & 2 wks Summer
34 seats Lunch £15-£20alc Dinner £19 Last lunch 2pm Last
dinner 10.30pm 🍷
Credit Cards ①③

TURNBERRY Strathclyde *Ayrshire* Map **10** NS20

★★★★★63% *Turnberry* KA26 9LT ☎(0655)31000
Telex no 777779 FAX (0655) 31706
*Following a major investment and refurbishment of this fine hotel,
we are delighted to grant Turnberry five stars. Furthermore, an
extra £6 million is currently being spent on creating a new and
impressive leisure centre which will open in September 1991 and
will also include a second restaurant and 16 more bedrooms. These
extra facilities will add to the glowing reputation of a spectacularly
located building that overlooks the championship Ailsa golf course
and the sea beyond. A few bedrooms are limited in space, but the
vast majority are comfortable and very well appointed and with the
creation of a new conference room and extra lounge areas, both the
sports enthusiast and the conference is well catered for.*
115⇨↑(7fb)2⊞ CTV in all bedrooms T
Lift ℂ CTV 200P ⊞ ✿ CFA ▱(heated) ▶18 ♪ (hard) ∪
snooker ₃auna solarium gymnasium pitch & putt putting table
tennis ♫
⊌ Scottish & French V 🕭 ⏛ ⌣ Last dinner 9.30pm
Credit Cards ①②③⑤

★★★66% **Malin Court** KA26 9PB ☎(0655)31457
FAX (0655) 31072
*Set on the coast just north of the famous golf course, a small,
modern hotel which forms an integral part of a residential home for*

---

*the elderly has recently been refurbished to offer attractive public
areas and well appointed bedrooms, the latter all enjoying views of
Ailsa Craig. Friendly, attentive service is provided by a smartly
dressed young staff.*
8↑ CTV in all bedrooms ® T sB&B↑£41.95-£45.95
dB&B↑£71.90-£79.10 🄟
Lift ℂ 50P ♫ xmas
V 🕭 ⏛ Lunch £7.95-£8.50&alc High tea £4.95-£6.50 Dinner
£13.50-£14.95&alc Last dinner 9.30pm
Credit Cards ①②③④⑤ ⓔ

---

TURNERS HILL West Sussex Map **04** TQ33

★★★73% **Alexander House** East St RH10 4QD (Prestige)
☎Copthorne(0342)714914 & 716333 Telex no 95611
FAX (0342) 717328
*The tree-lined driveway leading up to this fine mansion sets the
scene for the English country-house atmosphere of Alexander
House. The décor is stunning, and includes some quite splendid
works of art. Bedrooms are spacious, beautifully designed and
equipped in a luxurious style.*
14⇨2⊞ CTV in all bedrooms ® T 🕱 (ex guide dogs)
sB&B⇨↑fr£90 dB&B⇨↑fr£175 🄟
Lift ℂ CTV 50P ⊞ ✿ ♪ (hard) ✦ croquet ♫ nc7yrs xmas
⊌ English & French V 🕭 ⏛
Credit Cards ①②③⑤

---

TUTBURY Staffordshire Map **08** SK22

★★★66% **Ye Olde Dog & Partridge** High St DE13 9LS
☎Burton-on-Trent(0283)813030 FAX (0283) 813178
Closed 25-26 Dec & 1 Jan
*A charming, friendly 15th-century hotel located in the heart of the
village. Guests can enjoy an informal carvery rotisserie meal or a
more formal, well prepared meal in the Grill Room with some
English specialities such as braised oxtail.*
3⇨Annexe14⇨↑(1fb)3⊞ CTV in all bedrooms ® T ✳
sB&B⇨↑fr£54 dB&B⇨↑fr£66 🄟
ℂ 120P ✿ ♫
⊌ English & French V 🕭 ⌣ Lunch £8.20-£10.50 Dinner
£8.20-£10.50&alc Last dinner 9.45pm
Credit Cards ①②③ ⓔ

---

TUXFORD Nottinghamshire Map **08** SK77

★★70% **Newcastle Arms** Market Place NG22 0LA
☎Retford(0777)870208
*A friendly, well run hotel, in the heart of this small town, offering
warm, cosy rooms and a choice of bars. The restaurant has earned
itself a fine local reputation.*
11⇨↑(1fb)1⊞ CTV in all bedrooms ® T ✳
sB&B⇨↑£42-£52 dB&B⇨↑£52-£67 Continental breakfast
50P 2🛏 snooker
⊌ French V 🕭 ⏛ Lunch £9.25-£14.95 Dinner £13.95-£14.95
Last dinner 9.30pm
Credit Cards ①②③⑤

---

TWICKENHAM Greater London
See **LONDON plan** 1*B2*(page 426)
✕Cezanne 68 Richmond Rd TW1 3BE ☎081-892 3526
*A pretty little restaurant situated close to the town centre, with an
unassuming entrance from the street. The sensible, à la carte
menus offer an interesting choice of freshly prepared food, with
dishes such as sole and smoked trout terrine with a sweet red-
pepper sauce, or roast quail with cassis sauce. The puddings are
good, too, and the wine list is keenly priced. Service is friendly and
informal.*
Closed Sun, 1 wk Xmas & BH's
Lunch not served Sat

# Ye Olde Dog and Partridge ★★★

HIGH STREET, TUTBURY, STAFFS.
Telephone: 0283 813030

This mid 15th-century Inn famed for its association with Bull Running, and Mary Queen of Scots offers luxury accommodation. All rooms have private bath, colour television, radio alarm, tea and coffee-making facilities and a bar fridge.
There is an intimate French restaurant renowned for good food and also a wine Bar Carvery where there is an informal atmosphere with live music.
BTA commended.

# Calverley Hotel ★ ★

Crescent Road, Tunbridge Wells
Kent TN1 2LY
Tel: (0892) 26455
Fax: (0892) 512044    Telex: 957565 CBJ AG

Once the home of Royalty situated in the centre of the town. Extensive gardens. All bedrooms have TV, teamakers and direct telephone. Most have en suite facilities. Residents' TV Lounge, Drawing Room and Lift. Good parking. Royalty Suite is an ideal venue for Conferences, Dinner Dances and Weddings.

**Managers: Mr and Mrs A Phillips MHCIMA MBII**

★ ★

THE ROYAL WELLS INN

Mount Ephraim, Tunbridge Wells, Kent, (0892) 511188
Fax (0892) 511908

Try our magnificent Conservatory Restaurant, with the twin attractions of fine food served in delightful surroundings. The emphasis is on fresh produce superbly prepared by proprietor Robert Sloan and served with friendly efficiency.

For a snack try Alan's food bar— lunchtimes and evenings.

Accommodation—25 rooms, all with full facilities.

Business accounts, conferences and weddings are very welcome.

T

**✗ McClements** 12 The Green TW2 5AA ☎081-755 0176
*Chef John McClements uses his very reliable and skilful*
*standards of cooking to produce a weekly menu of modern French*
*cuisine using the best quality fresh produce. Dishes such as delicate*
*sole mousse with dill and broad beans, bouillabaisse of fresh*
*shellfish and roast pheasant have proved to be long term favourites.*
*Service is attentive and the wine list French.*
Lunch not served Sat
♀ French **V** 30 seats Last lunch 2.15pm Last dinner 10.30pm
✗ ✗
Credit Cards ①②③④

---

## TWO BRIDGES Devon Map **02** SX67

**★★★60%** **Prince Hall** PL20 6SW ☎Princetown(082289)403
FAX (082289) 676
*Set in a south-facing position at the heart of Dartmoor National*
*Park, a hotel commanding views of some breathtaking scenery*
*retains the atmosphere of a family home, offering guests spacious*
*bedroom accommodation with good facilities and public areas with*
*an intimate atmosphere.*
8➪♠(1fb)2⊞ CTV in all bedrooms **T**
sB&B➪♠£52.50-£54.50 dB&B➪♠£85-£89 (incl dinner) ❚
15P ⊞ ✿ ✔ *xmas*
♀ English & French Dinner £16.50 Last dinner 9pm
Credit Cards ①②③⑤ ⓔ

**★★62%** **Two Bridges** PL20 6SW ☎Princetown(082289)581
FAX (082289) 575
*Situated on the Two Bridges crossroads and dating from the*
*eighteenth century, this hotel provides an ideal base for lovers of*
*Dartmoor. Spacious and very traditional public areas comprise a*
*comfortable residents' lounge with log fire, a character bar and a*
*dining room which offers a good range of hot and cold dishes.*
*Recently upgraded bedrooms include additional en suite facilities,*
*while an effective use of pretty soft furnishings ensures that their*
*original charm and character is not lost.*
24rm(18➪♠)(2fb)1⊞⊟in all bedrooms CTV in all bedrooms
® **T ✱** sB&B£19 sB&B➪♠£30-£33 dB&Bfr£33
dB&B➪♠£46-£50 ❚
150P ✿ ✔ ʊ *xmas*
♀ English & French **V** ♥ ⬚ ✗ Sunday Lunch £8.75-£11.75
Dinner £10.50-£12.60&alc Last dinner 9pm
Credit Cards ①②③⑤

---

## TYNEMOUTH Tyne & Wear Map **12** NZ36

**★★★61%** **Park** Grand Pde NE30 4JQ ☎091-257 1406
FAX 091-257 1716
RS Xmas & New Year
*A modern functional hotel situated in a prominent position on sea*
*front.*
49rm(41➪2♠)(4fb)✗in 10 bedrooms CTV in all bedrooms ®
**T** sB&B£36 sB&B➪♠£43-£55.50 dB&B➪♠£65.50 ❚
⟨ 400P sauna solarium gymnasium ♫ *xmas*
♀ English & French **V** ♥ ✗ Lunch £7.50-£10.50&alc Dinner
£9-£11&alc Last dinner 9.30pm
Credit Cards ①②③⑤ ⓔ

---

## TYNET Grampian *Banffshire* Map **15** NJ36

**★★56%** **Mill House** AB5 2HJ ☎Clochan(05427)233
FAX (05427) 331
*This former Meal Mill, now a roadside hotel, offers good value*
*practical accommodation popular with business people.*
15➪♠(2fb) CTV in all bedrooms ® **T ✱** sB&B➪♠£23
dB&B➪♠£40-£45 ❚
CTV 100P ♫
**V** ♥ ⬚ Lunch £6.95-£8alc
Credit Cards ①②③⑤ ⓔ

---

## TYWYN Gwynedd Map **06** SH50

**★58%** **Greenfield** High St LL36 9AD ☎(0654)710354
Closed Nov RS Dec-Feb
*Privately owned and run, a small hotel on the edge of the village*
*offers very good value for money in its warm and comfortable*
*accommodation.*
14rm(2➪)(3fb) ® **✗** (ex guide dogs) sB&B£13.50 dB&B£27
dB&B➪£32
CTV ✗ ⊞
**V** Lunch fr£4.50 Dinner fr£5.75&alc Last dinner 8pm

---

## UCKFIELD East Sussex Map **05** TQ42

### ★★★

**★★★ ⚐ HORSTED PLACE**
Little Horsted TN22 5TS (2m
S A26) (Prestige)
☎Isfield(082575)581
Telex no 95548
FAX (0825) 75459
Closed 1st wk Jan
*This impressive and elegant*
*Victorian country manor has undergone a change of*
*management, though the effective control of the General*
*Manager, Elizabeth Crookston, has not affected the quality of*
*service which continues to be offered by willing and capable*
*staff. The superb Pugin interior centres on a beautifully carved*
*staircase, the grand gallery and the luxurious main lounge,*
*which offers comfort and a warm, relaxed atmosphere.*
*Bedrooms, some of which are quite magnificent, afford some*
*good views, while offering refined comfort with the convenience*
*of modern facilities and luxurious little extras. The chef, Alan*
*Garth, offers a well-balanced and appealing fixed price menu*
*in addition to vegetarian specialities and the à la carte menu.*
*The food is thoughtfully prepared from quality ingredients by*
*skilled hands. The hotel is due to undergo a number of*
*changes this year, including alterations to the restaurant and*
*reception areas. The walled garden will disappear to make*
*way for a new conservatory-style restaurant. It is believed that*
*the changes will allow even more freedom of movement for*
*guests and increase public areas. The hotel now borders a*
*magnificent golf course which is likely to become famous in its*
*own right and, in time, a golf village will be built a few miles*
*away from the hotel. Nevertheless, this should not affect the*
*peaceful country house atmosphere of the hotel.*
17➪♠ CTV in all bedrooms **T ✗** (ex guide dogs)
sB&B➪♠£120-£310 dB&B➪♠£120-£310 ❚
Lift 30P 6🚗 ✿ ⬚(heated) ▶ 18 ♟ (hard) croquet ♫
nc7yrs *xmas*
♀ English & French **V** ♥ ⬚ ✗ Lunch £14.50-£18 Dinner
fr£27.50 Last dinner 9.15pm
Credit Cards ①②③⑤ ⓔ

---

## UDDINGSTON Strathclyde *Lanarkshire* Map **11** NS66

**★★55%** **Redstones** 8-10 Glasgow Rd G71 7AS
☎(0698)813774 & 814843 FAX (0698) 815319
Closed 1-2 Jan
*A well-decorated, privately owned business hotel.*
18rm(16➪♠)2⊞ CTV in all bedrooms ® **T ✗** sB&Bfr£41
sB&B➪♠£50-£58 dB&B£64-£70 dB&B➪♠£64-£70 ❚
⟨ CTV 33P ⊞ ✿
♀ Scottish, French & Italian **V** ♥ Lunch £8.50-£20&alc High
tea £6.50-£7.95 Dinner fr£14.50&alc Last dinner 9.30pm
Credit Cards ①②③⑤

**UIG**

See Skye, Isle of

**UIST (SOUTH), ISLE OF**

See South Uist, Isle of

**ULLAPOOL** Highland *Ross & Cromarty* Map **14** NH19

★★69% *Ceilidh Place* West Argyle St IV26 2TV ☎(0854)2103
*More an experience than simply a hotel, this charming hostelry successfully combines a well stocked bookshop, an all day coffee shop which also acts as a venue for poetry, folk music and jazz, a bright conservatory-style restaurant serving good fresh food and a tastefully furnished and most comfortable first floor lounge which boasts fine views of Loch Broom and where a range of teas and coffee is available at all hours. Cottage-style bedrooms with beamed walls and ceilings are generally compact but comfortable, those with private bathrooms having telephones. The staff provide a friendly service.*
15rm(8⇔)(7fb)
30P ✿
♀ International **V** ♦ ⚑ ⅄ Last dinner 9pm
Credit Cards ① ② ③ ⑤

★57% *Ferry Boat Inn* Shore St IV26 2UJ ☎(0854)2366
*Though bedrooms are compact, standards are gradually improving at this modest waterfront hotel overlooking the bustling harbour, whilst its atmosphere is friendly and informal.*
11rm(2⇔)(1fb) ®
CTV ✔ ⇔
♦ ⚑ ⅄
Credit Cards ① ③ ⑤

❀ ✕ ✕ **Altnaharrie Inn** IV26 2SS ☎Dundonnell(085483)230
(Rosette awarded for dinner only)
*The short boat ride across Loch Broom that transports guests to this unusual and fascinating restaurant is not the least of the charms of an evening out here. Gunn Eriksen's cooking has gained her much celebrity over the years and continues to be both imaginative and artistic in its use of excellent raw ingredients. As would be expected both from its location and from one with her Scandinavian background, fish features predominantly on Gunn's menus, accompanied by some very flavoursome sauces. Service is attentive and pleasantly informal. Bedrooms are available, should guests wish to extend their stay.*
Closed for part of winter
Lunch not served (except to residents)
14 seats Dinner fr£38 Wine £7.50 Last dinner 7.45pm
✔ nc12yrs ⅄

**ULLSWATER**

See Glenridding, Patterdale, Pooley Bridge **&** Watermillock

**ULVERSTON** Cumbria Map **07** SD27

★★65% **Virginia House** Queen St LA12 7AF ☎(0229)54844
*The newly-furnished hotel provides good all-round facilities; set in a delightful Georgian house, family owned and run, it offers good meals in a pleasant restaurant.*
7➧(1fb) CTV in all bedrooms ® **T** ✖ ✻ sB&B➧£30-£35
dB&B➧£40-£50
✔ ⇔ ✿
♀ International **V** ♦ ⚑ Dinner £10.95-£11.50 Last dinner 9pm
Credit Cards ① ③ ⓔ

★★58% **Sefton House** Queen St LA12 7AF ☎(0229)52190
*Just off the A590, close to the town centre, this predominantly commercial hotel offers functional, well equipped rooms, a friendly, informal atmosphere and pleasant service from an enthusiastic young staff.*
14rm(4⇔6➧) CTV in all bedrooms ® **T** ✖ (ex guide dogs)
sB&B£27.50-£32 sB&B⇔➧£32-£40 dB&B£40-£45
dB&B⇔➧£50-£55 ❒

▶

**U**

CTV 15P 3🅿🍴 💶
V ❦ 🖵 Lunch fr£7 Dinner fr£13 Last dinner 8.30pm
Credit Cards ①③

---

**❀ ✖ Bay Horse Inn & Bistro** LA12 9EL ☎(0229)53972
*The conservatory added to this delightful village inn on the Lune
estuary by its chef-Patron Robert Lyons is a charming setting for
the distinctive style of cooking he has developed since leaving
Miller Howe. The à la carte menu changes weekly and there are
daily specials to look forward to for added variety. Pan-fried
calves liver cooked with Dubonnet and oranges was our Inspector's
choice, to be followed by a most delicious chocolate and brandy
roulade. Portions are generous as well as being attractively
presented, and one of the two wine lists features an interesting
selection of New World wines. Service combines friendliness with
professionalism.*
Closed Sun & possible closure in Jan & Feb
Lunch not served Mon
V 30 seats ✳ S10% Lunch fr£11.50 Dinner £7.50-£15alc Last
lunch 1.30pm Last dinner 9pm 🚭 nc12yrs ✍
Credit Cards ①③

---

### UMBERLEIGH Devon Map 02 SS62

★★64% *Rising Sun Inn* EX37 9DU
☎High Bickington(0769)60447
*A small, friendly village inn on the main road provides attractive,
upgraded bedroom accommodation which meets all modern
requirements. Public areas include cosy bars, a lounge and a dining
room offering a short table d'hôte menu of home-cooked dishes.*
6⇌🏾 CTV in all bedrooms ® T ✖ (ex guide dogs)
CTV 20P 2🅿🍴 ♪
V ❦ 🖵 ✍ Last dinner 9pm
Credit Cards ①②③⑤

---

### UPHALL Lothian *West Lothian* Map 11 NT07

★★★🏅65% *Houstoun House* EH52 6JS
☎Broxburn(0506)853831 Telex no 727148 FAX (0506) 854220
Closed 1-3 Jan
*An historic, baronial country hotel with splendid period bedrooms
supplemented by a modern extension. The vaulted cellar bar is a
popular feature and cuisine enterprising and enjoyable.*
28⇌🏾Annexe2⇌10🛁 CTV in all bedrooms ® ✳
sB&B⇌🏾£73-£83 dB&B⇌🏾£98-£125 🅿
(🀫 100P 💶 ✿
V ❦ 🖵 Lunch £14-£16 Dinner £26-£27.50 Last dinner 9.30pm
Credit Cards ①②③④⑤

---

### UPHOLLAND Lancashire Map 07 SD50

★★62% *Holland Hall* 6 Lafford Ln WN8 0QZ ☎(0695)624426
FAX (0695) 622433
RS Xmas Day & 2 Jan
*Situated just off the main road east of the town centre this hotel
has an elegant formal restaurant and a lively pizzeria. Bedrooms
vary, the newer rooms are stylish and comfortable with modern
bathrooms.*
29⇌🏾Annexe5⇌🏾(1fb) CTV in all bedrooms ® ✖
(🀫 200P ✿
♀ English, American & French V ❦ 🖵 Last dinner 10pm
Credit Cards ①②③⑤

---

### UPLYME Devon Map 03 SY39

See also Lyme Regis
★★★56% *Devon* Lyme Rd DT7 3TQ (Best Western)
☎Lyme Regis(02974)3231 Telex no 42513 FAX (0392) 431645
Closed 3 Nov-21 Mar
*Former 16th-century monastery which has been converted into a
relaxing hotel.*
21⇌🏾(4fb) CTV in all bedrooms ® T sB&B⇌🏾£39-£44
dB&B⇌🏾£78-£88 (incl dinner) 🅿

---

30P 💶 ✿ ≏(heated) solarium gymnasium games room
putting green
♀ English & French ❦ 🖵 Lunch £6.50-£9.50 High tea fr£2.50
Dinner £10.95-£16.95 Last dinner 8.30pm
Credit Cards ①②③⑤ ⓔ

---

### UPPER SLAUGHTER Gloucestershire Map 04 SP12

★★★★🏅77% **Lords of the Manor** GL54 2JD
☎Cotswold(0451)20243 Telex no 83147 FAX (0451) 20696
*At the centre of an unspoilt Cotswold village stands this
magnificent 17th-century former rectory, now converted into a
hotel of considerable character, that retains its period charm
despite the introduction of modern amenities. There are several
intimate and comfortable lounge areas, a small bar and several
private dining areas. A meal here is, as our Inspector found, a truly
memorable experience : leek mousse with asparagus and chervil,
delicious seafood in a light sauce, completed by a poached pear in a
butterscotch sauce.*
29⇌🏾3🛁 CTV in all bedrooms T ✖ (ex guide dogs) ✳
sB&B⇌🏾£70-£100 dB&B⇌🏾£90-£135 🅿
(40P ✿ ♪ croquet *xmas*
V ❦ 🖵 ✍ Lunch £10.95-£13.25 Dinner £25&alc Last dinner
9.30pm
Credit Cards ①②③⑤ ⓔ

---

### UPPINGHAM Leicestershire Map 04 SP89

★★★67% *Falcon* High St LE15 9PY (Inter-Hotels)
☎(0572)823535 FAX (0572) 821620
*Former coaching inn situated in the attractive town centre.*
21⇌🏾(2fb)1🛁 CTV in all bedrooms ® T ✳
sB&B⇌🏾£55-£65 dB&B⇌🏾£65-£75 🅿
(25P *xmas*
♀ English & French V ❦ 🖵 Lunch fr£10.50 Dinner
£10.50-£12.50&alc Last dinner 10pm
Credit Cards ①②③⑤ ⓔ

★★74% *Garden* 16 High St West LE15 9QD ☎(0572)822352
FAX (0572) 821156
*Standing opposite the famous Uppingham School, this lovely old
house in its walled garden provides well-equipped, quality
accommodation, home-cooked meals and a warm, friendly
hospitality that makes it popular with business clients and tourists
alike.*
12rm(7⇌3🏾)(1fb) CTV in all bedrooms ® T sB&B£25
sB&B⇌🏾£40 dB&B£35 dB&B⇌🏾£48-£55
CTV 🚭
V ❦ 🖵 Lunch fr£7.50alc Dinner £11.75&alc Last dinner 9pm
Credit Cards ①②③

★★67% *Lake Isle* High St East LE15 9PZ ☎(0572)822951
*Under the personal supervision of David and Clare Whitfield this
high street hotel provides attentive friendly service. David is
justifiably proud of the food and the extensive wine list, both
proving popular with residents and locals alike.*
10⇌🏾(1fb) CTV in all bedrooms ® T sB&B⇌🏾£36-£42
dB&B⇌🏾£54-£62 🅿
4P 1🅿🍴 💶
♀ English & French V Lunch £9.50-£10.75 Dinner £17-£21
Last dinner 10pm
Credit Cards ①②③⑤ ⓔ

---

### UPTON UPON SEVERN Hereford & Worcester Map 03 SO84

★★★56% *White Lion* High St WR8 0HJ (Exec Hotel)
☎Upton on Severn(06846)2551
Closed 25 Dec RS 26 Dec
*This privately owned, former 16th century coaching inn, has
retained many original features, such as beams and sloping floors.
Rooms are individually decorated, some in the original building*

and some in a newer rear wing. *An intimate, character restaurant serves a range of traditional dishes.*
10⇄♪🏠1🛁 CTV in all bedrooms ® T sB&B⇄🅁fr£46 1B&B&🛁🅁fr£64 🍴
18P 1🏨
🞧 English & French **V** ✿ ⌻ Lunch fr£13.50&alc Dinner fr£13.50&alc Last dinner 9.15pm
Credit Cards 1 2 3 5 ⓔ

★★68% *Star* High St WR8 0HQ ☎(06846)2300 & 4601 FAX (06846) 2929
*A seventeenth-century coaching inn near the river has been extensively restored and modernised to provide well-equipped, comfortable accommodation in a friendly, informal atmosphere that makes it suitable for tourist and businessman alike. Public areas retain much of their original character and charm, with attractive oak panelling in the restaurant and an inglenook fireplace in the lounge bar.*
17⇄🅁(2fb)1🛁 CTV in all bedrooms ®
9P ♫
**V** ✿ ⌻ Last dinner 9.30pm
Credit Cards 1 3

## USK Gwent Map 03 SO30

★★74% **Glen-yr-Afon** Pontypool Rd ☎(02913)2302
*Situated on the edge of town in attractive grounds this lovely old house provides good quality, well-equipped accommodation and pleasant, comfortable public areas. It is equally suitable for both tourists and business people. Midweek breaks are available in the winter.*
16rm(10⇄5🅁)(2fb) CTV in all bedrooms T ✱ sB&Bfr£34.50 sB&B⇄🅁£37.95-£40.25 dB&B⇄🅁£51.75 🍴
《 CTV 42P 1🏨 🚼 ❄ croquet *xmas*
**V** ✿ ⌻ 🗡 Lunch fr£3.50&alc High tea fr£1.50&alc Dinner £12.50-£20&alc Last dinner 9.30pm
Credit Cards 1 3

★★61% **Three Salmons** Bridge St NP5 1BQ ☎(02913)2133
Closed 24-26 Dec
*This former coaching inn in the town centre provides modest but fairly well-equipped accommodation both in the main building and two nearby annexes.*
12⇄🅁Annexe18rm(14⇄2🅁)(1fb)2🛁 CTV in 23 bedrooms ® T ✱ sB&B£25 sB&B⇄🅁£30-£35 dB&B⇄🅁£50-£55
40P
✿ Lunch £9.25-£12
Credit Cards 1 2 3 4

## UTTOXETER Staffordshire Map 07 SK03

★★67% *Bank House* Church St ST14 8AG ☎(0889)566922 FAX (0889) 567565
*Pleasant public areas and comfortable, well-equipped bedrooms are provided by this late 18th-century country house on the outskirts of the town centre, once Uttoxeter's first bank. The unsupported spiral staircase is worthy of note, being one of the best examples of its kind in the country.*
16⇄🅁(2fb)1🛁 CTV in all bedrooms ® T
CTV 16P
**V** ✿ ⌻ Last dinner 9.45pm
Credit Cards 1 2 3 5

🏠**Travelodge** Ashbourne Rd ST14 5AA (on A50/A5030)
(Trusthouse Forte) ☎(0889)562043 Central res (0800) 850950
32⇄🅁(32fb) CTV in all bedrooms ® sB⇄🅁£24 dB⇄🅁£29.50 (room only)
《 32P 🚼
Credit Cards 1 2 3

## UXBRIDGE Greater London Map 04 TQ08

★★★61% *Master Brewer Motel* Western Av UB10 9NX ☎(0895)51199 Telex no 946589 FAX (0895) 810330
(For full entry see Hillingdon)

## VALE
See Guernsey **under** Channel Islands

## VENTNOR
See Wight, Isle of

## VERYAN Cornwall & Isles of Scilly Map 02 SW93

★★★73% **Nare** Carne Beach TR2 5PF ☎Truro(0872)501279 FAX (0872) 501856
*Excellent service is only one of the pleasing features of this away-from-it-all hotel which is exceptionally well managed by Mr and Mrs Gray who have completely refurbished its accommodation, providing tasteful and elegant furnishings in keeping with the country-house atmosphere. The restaurant menu features many local seafood specialities. Leisure and fitness facilities are good and the hotel is adjacent to National Trust land, with uninterrupted views of Gerrans Bay and Nare Head.*
39rm(37⇄🅁)(6fb) CTV in all bedrooms ® T sB&B⇄🅁£43-£83 dB&B⇄🅁£72-£136
80P 🚗 ❄ ⌒(heated) ♟ (hard) snooker sauna solarium gymnasium boating windsurfing *xmas*
🞧 English & French **V** ✿ ⌻ Sunday Lunch £11 Dinner £19&alc Last dinner 9.30pm
Credit Cards 1 3

**See advertisement on page 707**

**U**

705

★★**64%**, *Elerkey House* TR2 5QA ☎Truro(0872)501261
Closed Nov-Etr
*Small country hotel in this picturesque old Cornish village.*
*Peaceful atmosphere and pleasant garden.*
7rm(3⇆2♠)⊬in all bedrooms CTV in all bedrooms ® ✗
CTV 12P ⚑ ❖ nc10 yrs
✿ ⊒ ⊬ Last dinner 8.30pm
Credit Cards [1] [3]

✗**Treverbyn House** Pendower Rd TR2 5QL
☎Truro(0872)501201
*This tiny, unsophisticated restaurant with letting rooms provides*
*home cooking at its best. There is a good wine list.*
Closed Mon, Tue & Sun
Lunch not served
✿ International 20 seats ✱ Dinner fr£12.75 Wine £4.90 Last
dinner 8.30pm 9P nc7yrs
Credit Cards [1] [2] [3]

---

**WADEBRIDGE** Cornwall & Isles of Scilly Map **02** SW97

★★**56%**, *Molesworth Arms* Molesworth St PL27 7DP
☎(020681)2055
*A sixteenth-century coaching inn at the centre of the town*
*complements simply furnished bedrooms with a new cocktail bar*
*and restaurant where friendly, informal staff offer a menu*
*featuring mainly grills.*
14rm(8⇆)(2fb) CTV in all bedrooms ® T
CTV 14P
V ✿ ⊒ Last dinner 9.30pm
Credit Cards [1] [3]

---

**WADHURST** East Sussex Map **05** TQ63

★★⚑**66%**, *Spindlewood Country House Hotel & Restaurant*
Wallcrouch TN5 7JG (2.25m SE of Wadhurst on B2099) (Inter-
Hotels) ☎Ticehurst(0580)200430 FAX (0580) 201132
Closed 4 days Xmas RS Bank Hols
*The small, relaxing, family-run hotel is peacefully situated and*
*furnished with antiques. Imaginative country cooking is*
*complemented by good, personal service and attention to detail.*
9⇆♠(1fb) CTV in all bedrooms ® T ✗ (ex guide dogs)
sB&B⇆♠£45.50-£48 dB&B⇆♠£67-£80 ⊟
60P ⚑ ❖
✿ English & French V ✿ S% Lunch £12-£22alc Dinner
£13.50-£15&alc Last dinner 9pm
Credit Cards [1] [2] [3] £

---

**WAKEFIELD** West Yorkshire Map **08** SE32

★★★**65%**, *Cedar Court* Denby Dale Road, Calder Grove
WF4 3QZ ☎(0924)276310 Telex no 557647 FAX (0924) 280221
*This large modern hotel, situated close to the M1 at junction 39,*
*offers a choice of restaurants with English, French and Italian*
*cuisine. The public areas are stylish, and bedrooms are spacious*
*and well appointed.*
151⇆♠(18fb)⊬in 64 bedrooms CTV in all bedrooms ® T ✱
sB&B⇆♠£79.50-£89.50 dB&B⇆♠£95-£105 ⊟
Lift (▥ 240P ❖
✿ English, French & Italian V ✿ ⊒ Lunch fr£2.95alc Dinner
£13.50&alc Last dinner 11pm
Credit Cards [1] [2] [3] [5] £

★★★**63%**, *Waterton Park* Walton Hall, The Balk, Walton
WF2 6PW (3m SE off B6378) (Consort) ☎(0924)257911
FAX (0924) 240082
*Very good leisure facilities are available at this unusual converted*
*country house, set in a nature reserve at the centre of a lake.*
31⇆♠(1fb)3⚑ CTV in all bedrooms ® T ✗ ✱
sB&B⇆♠£62-£68 dB&B⇆♠£80-£88 ⊟
(▥ 100P ❖ ▣(heated) ⚋ squash snooker sauna solarium
gymnasium boating jacuzzi beautician masseur *xmas*

---

✿ English & French V ✿ ⊒ Lunch fr£8.80 High tea fr£5
Dinner fr£14.25&alc Last dinner 9.30pm
Credit Cards [1] [2] [3] [5] £

★★★**61%**, *Post House* Queen's Dr, Ossett WF5 9BE
(Trusthouse Forte) ☎(0924)276388 Telex no 55407
FAX (0924) 280277
*This comfortable modern hotel, situated just off the M1 motorway*
*at junction 40, offers well furnished bedrooms and meals of a good*
*standard.*
99⇆♠⊬in 20 bedrooms CTV in all bedrooms ® T S%
sB⇆♠fr£67 dB⇆♠fr£78 (room only) ⊟
Lift (▥ 140P ❖ CFA *xmas*
V ✿ ⊒ ⊬ S% Lunch £8.50-£10.50&alc High tea £4.50-£6
Dinner £13.50&alc Last dinner 10pm
Credit Cards [1] [2] [3] [4] [5]

★★★**61%**, *Swallow* Queens St WF1 1JV (Swallow)
☎(0924)372111 Telex no 557464 FAX (0924) 383648
*Well-appointed bedrooms and friendly service are features which*
*make this city-centre hotel popular.*
64⇆♠(4fb)⊬in 17 bedrooms CTV in all bedrooms ® T ✱ S%
sB&B⇆♠fr£64 dB&B⇆♠fr£80 ⊟
Lift (▥ 40P CFA *xmas*
✿ English & French V ✿ ⊒ Lunch fr£9 Dinner fr£13.50 Last
dinner 9.15pm
Credit Cards [1] [2] [3] [5]

⭍**Granada Lodge** M1 Service Area, West Bretton WF4 4LQ
(Granada) ☎(0924)830371 & 830569 FAX (0924) 830609
(For full entry see Woolley Edge)

---

**WALKERBURN** Borders *Peeblesshire* Map **11** NT33

★★⚑**66%**, *Tweed Valley Hotel & Restaurant* Galashiels Rd
EH43 6AA (Inter-Hotels) ☎(089687)636 FAX (089687) 639
*The privately owned and managed hotel, which has an attractive*
*wood-panelled dining room, was recently refurbished.*
15⇆♠(2fb)1⚑ CTV in all bedrooms ® T S%
sB&B⇆♠£31.50-£38.50 dB&B⇆♠£63-£66 ⊟
35P ⚑ ❖ ⚋ sauna solarium gymnasium shooting stalking
*xmas*
✿ Scottish English & French V ✿ ⊒ ⊬ S% Lunch
£6-£13.50alc Dinner £14.50&alc Last dinner 9.30pm
Credit Cards [1] [3] £

---

**WALL** Northumberland Map **12** NY96

★★**64%**, *Hadrian* NE46 4EE ☎Humshaugh(043481)232 & 236
*Creeper clad inn, richly furnished with antiques; bedrooms are*
*simple and clean.*
11rm(1⇆2♠)2⚑ CTV in 9 bedrooms ® T
CTV 40P 3❖ ❖ nc14yrs
V ✿ ⊒ ⊬ Last dinner 10pm
Credit Cards [1] [5]

---

**WALLINGFORD** Oxfordshire Map **04** SU68

★★★**66%**, *George* High St OX10 0BS (Mount Charlotte (TS))
☎(0491)36665 Telex no 847468 FAX (0491) 25359
*At the heart of the town, the timbered George Hotel dates from*
*Tudor times and provides a high standard of accommodation in*
*pleasant surroundings. The beamed public bar is a popular*
*rendezvous, and in the restaurant, imaginative dishes are served.*
39⇆♠(1fb)⊬in 9 bedrooms CTV in all bedrooms ® T ✱
sB⇆♠£65 dB⇆♠£80 (room only) ⊟
(▥ 60P *xmas*
✿ English & French V ✿ Lunch £14 Dinner £17.50 Last dinner
10.30pm
Credit Cards [1] [2] [3] [5]

★★★59% **Shillingford Bridge** Shillingford OX10 8LZ (2m N
A329) ☎Warborough(086732)8567 Telex no 837763
FAX (086732) 8636
Closed 24-31 Dec
*The hotel stands on the banks of the River Thames, between
Oxford and Henley-on-Thames, with superb views along the river.
Dinner-dances are frequently held in the pleasant restaurant.*
25⇌2🛏 CTV in all bedrooms ® T ✱ sB&B⇌£55-£65
dB&B⇌£75-£90
100P ❀ ⌂(heated) ♪ squash ♫
V ७ ⌷ Lunch fr£12.50 Dinner fr£12.50 Last dinner 10pm
Credit Cards ①②③⑤

WALLSEND Tyne & Wear Map **12** NZ26

★★★57% **Newcastle Moat House** Coast Rd NE28 9HP (Queens
Moat) ☎091-262 8989 & 091-262 7044 Telex no 53583
FAX 091-263 4172
*Modern and purpose-built, the hotel stands 5 miles from the centre
of Newcastle, at the A1/A1058 junction. Bedrooms, though dated
in style, have every facility, and accommodation should be
enhanced considerably by a planned redevelopment; there is a
small leisure club, and conference/function facilities and sport.*
150⇌📢(8fb)⊬in 10 bedrooms CTV in all bedrooms ® T ✱
sB&B⇌📢£60-£70 dB&B⇌📢£70-£80 🍴
Lift 《 500P sauna solarium gymnasium steam room
🍸 English & Continental V ७ ⌷ ⊬ S% Lunch
£11.95-£12.95&alc Dinner £11.95-£12.95&alc Last dinner
9.45pm
Credit Cards ①②③⑤

WALSALL West Midlands Map **07** SP09

See also **Barr, Great**

★★★66% **Fairlawns** 178 Little Aston Road, Aldridge
WS9 0NU (3m NE off A454) (Consort) ☎Aldridge(0922)55122
Telex no 339873 FAX (0922) 743120
RS 24 Dec-2 Jan
*A privately owned hotel on the A454, close to Walsall and
convenient for Sutton Coldfield and the motorway network. The
rooms have been refurbished and are comfortable and well
equipped whilst the restaurant, which enjoys a good local
reputation, provides well prepared dishes. Service is friendly and
attentive.*
36⇌📢(2fb) CTV in all bedrooms ® T ✱
sB&B⇌📢£39.50-£79.75 dB&B⇌📢£69.50-£79.75 🍴
《 80P ❀
🍸 English & French V ७ ⌷
Credit Cards ①②③④⑤ⓔ

★★★66% **Friendly Hotel** 20 Wolverhampton Rd West,
Bentley WS2 0BS (junction 10, M6) (Consort) ☎(0922)724444
Telex no 334854 FAX (0922) 723148
*At junction 10 of the M6, this modern hotel provides comfortable
and well-equipped accommodation and open-plan public areas.
There is a popular carvery restaurant and a range of leisure
facilities.*
120⇌📢(20fb)2🛏⊬in 30 bedrooms CTV in all bedrooms ® T
S% sB&B⇌📢£52-£62.50
dB&B⇌📢£68.50-£73 Continental breakfast 🍴
《 140P ❀ ◱(heated) sauna solarium gymnasium jacuzzi
🍸 English & French V ७ ⌷ ⊬ Lunch fr£7.50 Dinner
£11.75-£14.75&alc Last dinner 10pm
Credit Cards ①②③⑤ⓔ
**See advertisement on page 709**

★★★62% **Crest Hotel-Birmingham/Walsall** Birmingham Rd
WS5 3AB (Trusthouse Forte) ☎(0922)33555 Telex no 335479
FAX (0922) 612034
*Situated outside the town centre and offering standard
accommodation, this hotel features three bars – one of them a jazz
bar – and an attractive Orangerie Restaurant which contribute to
its popularity with the business and conference trade.*
▶

101⇆♠(3fb)⊁⌂in 21 bedrooms CTV in all bedrooms Ⓡ ⧖
Lift ⦅ 250P CFA 2 pool tables
♉ Continental V ✿ ⚏ ⊁
Credit Cards ①②③④⑤

★★★61% **Barons Court** Walsall Rd, Walsall Wood WS9 9AH
(3m NE A461) (Best Western) ⌂Brownhills(0543)452020
Telex no 333061 FAX (0543) 361276
*This popular hotel stands on the A461 on the outskirts of Walsall.*
*Bedrooms are well equipped, and ornate, many have four poster*
*beds. Guests can choose between the formal restaurant and the new*
*carvery, and there is a popular health hydro.*
100⇆(5fb)23⌘⊁⌂in 6 bedrooms CTV in all bedrooms Ⓡ T
Lift ⦅ 180P CFA ⊠(heated) sauna solarium gymnasium health
hydro whirlpool ♫
♉ English & French V ✿ ⚏ Last dinner 9.45pm
Credit Cards ①②③④⑤

★★69%, **Beverley** 58 Lichfield Rd WS4 2DJ ⌂(0922)614967 &
22999 FAX (0922) 724187
*A privately owned and run hotel stands just outside the town on the*
*A461, offering a good standard of accommodation with an*
*excellent range of modern facilities together with a pool room,*
*sauna, solarium and gymnasium.*
29⇆♠Annexe2⇆♠(1fb)1⌘⊁⌂in 2 bedrooms CTV in all
bedrooms Ⓡ T ✻ (ex guide dogs) sB&B⇆♠£43-£49
dB&B⇆♠£56 ⧖
⦅ CTV 60P sauna solarium gymnasium
♉ English & French V ✿ ⚏ Lunch fr£6.95&alc Dinner
fr£9.95&alc Last dinner 9.30pm
Credit Cards ①③ⓔ

★★63% **Abberley** 29 Bescot Rd WS2 9AD ⌂(0922)27413
FAX (0922) 720933
*The Stone family have continued to expand and improve this*
*predominantly commercial hotel situated close to junction 9 of the*
*M6. Bedrooms have excellent facilities including satellite TV.*
28⇆♠(4fb)1⌘⊁⌂in 4 bedrooms CTV in all bedrooms Ⓡ T ✻
sB&B⇆♠£36.80 dB&B⇆♠£48.30 ⧖
⦅ 29P
♉ English, Asian, Chinese & Vietnamese V ✿ ⚏ Lunch
£7.50&alc High tea £6&alc Dinner £7.95&alc Last dinner
8.30pm
Credit Cards ①③ⓔ

★★60% **Bescot** Bescot Rd WS2 9DG ⌂(0922)22447
FAX (0922) 30256
*A well run, privately owned hotel close to junction 9 of the M6.*
*Rooms are modest with good modern facilities and staff create a*
*'home-from-home' atmosphere for the mainly commercial clientèle.*
13⇆♠(1fb) CTV in all bedrooms Ⓡ T ✻ (ex guide dogs) ✻
sB&B⇆♠fr£25 dB&B⇆♠fr£50 ⧖
⦅ CTV 30P
♉ International V ✿ ⚏ Lunch £8.40-£18.65alc Dinner
fr£8.50&alc Last dinner 9.30pm
Credit Cards ①②③⑤ⓔ

**WALTHAM ABBEY** Essex Map **05** TL30

★★★★60% **Swallow Hotel** Old Shire Ln EN9 3LX (Swallow)
⌂Lea Valley(0992)717170 Telex no 916596
FAX (0992) 711841
*This hotel and leisure club is particularly well situated for the*
*business traveller, close to junction 26 of the M25. Well-appointed*
*bedrooms include honeymoon and executive suites and some have*
*been especially adapted for disabled guests. Public areas are all*
*air-conditioned, and include a brasserie and formal restaurant.*
163⇆(10fb)4⌘⊁⌂in 60 bedrooms CTV in all bedrooms Ⓡ T ✻
sB&B⇆fr£88 dB&B⇆fr£98 ⧖
⦅ ⊞ 240P ⊠(heated) sauna solarium gymnasium steam room
xmas

♉ English & Continental V ✿ ⚏ S% Lunch fr£11 Dinner
£14.50-£20&alc Last dinner 10.30pm
Credit Cards ①②③⑤ⓔ

**WALTON ON THE HILL** Surrey Map **04** TQ25

✕✕**Ebenezer Cottage** 36 Walton St KT20 7RT
⌂Tadworth(0737)813166
*Early 16th-century cottage restaurant offering traditional English*
*food in a number of period styled dining rooms.*
Closed Mon & 18 Jun-2 Jul & 22 Oct-6 Nov
Dinner not served Sun
♉ English & French 65 seats ✱ Lunch fr£13.25&alc Dinner
fr£23.75 Last lunch 1.45pm Last dinner 9.30pm 40P ⊁
Credit Cards ①②③⑤

**WALTON UPON THAMES**
See Shepperton & Weybridge

**WANSFORD** Cambridgeshire Map **04** TL09

★★76% **The Haycock Hotel** PE8 6JA ⌂Stamford(0780)782223
Telex no 32710 FAX (0780) 783031
*A 17th-century riverside coaching inn in the centre of a charming*
*village just off the A1. Both the restaurant and the buttery offer an*
*imaginative range of freshly prepared dishes, and rooms are*
*individually decorated and tastefully furnished to provide*
*maximum comfort. Competent and friendly service compliment the*
*extensive range of facilities.*
51⇆⌂4⌘ CTV in all bedrooms T ✱ S15% sB&B⇆♠£60-£80
dB&B⇆♠£80-£120 ⧖
⦅ 300P ✿ ♪ petanque outdoor chess xmas
V ✿ ⚏ ⊁ Bar Lunch £2.25-£7alc
Credit Cards ①②③⑤

**WANTAGE** Oxfordshire Map **04** SU48

★★56% **Bear** Market Place OX12 8AB (Consort)
⌂(02357)66366 Telex no 41363
*A comfortable hotel in the heart of this bustling market town, the*
*Bear has compact modern bedrooms. The King Alfred Restaurant,*
*on the first floor and overlooking the market place has a good*
*standard of cooking and friendly service.*
33⇆♠(3fb) CTV in all bedrooms Ⓡ
Lift ⫟
♉ French V ✿ ⚏ ⊁
Credit Cards ①②③⑤
**See advertisement under OXFORD**

**WARE** Hertfordshire Map **05** TL31

★★★63% **Ware Moat House** Baldock St SG12 9DR (Queens
Moat) ⌂(0920)465011 Telex no 817417 FAX (0920) 468016
Closed 25-31 Dec
*A good standard of well-equipped accommodation is provided by*
*this purpose-built hotel; a pleasant, conservatory-style restaurant*
*offers both à la carte and table d'hôte menus and there is an*
*attractive, cosy bar.*
50rm(43⇆6♠)(1fb)⊁in 6 bedrooms CTV in all bedrooms Ⓡ T
Lift ⦅ 100P
V ✿ ⚏
Credit Cards ①②③④⑤

○**Hanbury Manor** Thundridge SG1 0SD ⌂(0920)487722
Due to have opened Aug 1990
98⇆♠

A rosette is an indication of exceptional
standards of cuisine.

WAREHAM Dorset Map 03 SY98

★★★77% **Priory** Church Green BH20 4ND ☎(0929)552772 & 51666 Telex no 41143 FAX (0929) 554519

*An attractive 16th-century converted priory, the hotel stands in a tranquil setting with two acres of gardens leading to the river. Tastefully furnished bedrooms combine modern facilities with fine antiques, and some of the bathrooms have whirlpool baths. Public rooms are elegant, with breakfast and lunch taken in the Greenwood Room and dinner served in the intimate Cellar Restaurant.*

5⇨🐾Annexe4⇨2🛏 CTV in all bedrooms T ◀ (ex guide dogs) ✻ sB&B⇨🐾£90-£95 ‖B&B⇨🐾£75-£160 🏳

25P 🚭 ✿ ⚓ croquet sailing ♫ xmas
⚑ ✿ ⚓

Credit Cards ①②③⑤

★★★67% **Springfield Country** Grange Road, Stoborough BH20 5AL (1.5m S off A351) ☎(0929)552177 & 551785 FAX (0929) 551862

*A family-run hotel set in attractive gardens has been upgraded to provide comfortable accommodation in well equipped bedrooms; two restaurants offer skilfully prepared dishes.*

52⇨(7fb) CTV in all bedrooms ® T ✻ S% sB&B⇨fr£59 ‖B&B⇨fr£91 🏳

Lift (100P 🚭 ✿ ⇨(heated) ♪ (hard) snooker solarium table tennis pool table nc2yrs

♫ English & Continental ♦ ⚑ Bar Lunch £1-£8alc High tea £1-£7alc Dinner £12&alc Last dinner 9pm

Credit Cards ①②③

1991 marks the 25th anniversary of this guide.

W

**★★68% Kemps Country House** East Stoke BH20 6AL
☎Bindon Abbey(0929)462563 FAX (0929) 405287
Closed 26-31 Dec
*This Victorian country house, now a professionally run hotel with a pleasantly informal atmosphere and good views across open countryside, is located on the A352 approximately one and a half miles west of Wareham. Bedrooms are all of good size, though they vary from the more traditionally styled in the main building and coach house to spacious, well-furnished newer rooms; comfortable lounges complement the garden-style dining room, half housed in a conservatory, which offers good, interesting dishes prepared from fresh ingredients.*
5rm(1⇨3♠)Annexe10rm(4⇨)(3fb)1⇔ CTV in all bedrooms ℝ T ✱ sB&B£35 dB&B⇨♠£68-£92 🏳
CTV 50P 🚗 ✿
♡ English & French **V** ♥ ⅃ Lunch fr£7.50&alc Dinner fr£14.95&alc Last dinner 9.30pm
Credit Cards ①②③④⑤

**★★61% Worgret Manor** BH20 6AB ☎(0929) 552957
*Quiet Georgian hotel with modern extension.*
9rm(4♠)(3fb) CTV in all bedrooms ℝ
CTV 40P ✿
♡ English & French **V** Last dinner 9.15pm
Credit Cards ①②③⑤

**★★50% Red Lion** Towncross BH20 4AB ☎(0929) 552483
*This typical inn, set in the middle of the town, serves a wide range of meals in its busy, popular bars. Bedrooms vary, some being spacious and well furnished while others are more modest in style.*
20rm(5⇨)(5fb) CTV in all bedrooms ℝ
15P 🚗 snooker skittle alley
**V** ♥ ⅃ Last dinner 9.30pm
Credit Cards ①②③

**WARK** Northumberland Map **12** NY87

**★Battlesteads** NE48 3LS ☎Bellingham(0660)30209
*A pleasant village inn with charm and character conveyed by the proprietors.*
6rm(1fb)
CTV 50P ✿
♡ Mainly grills **V** ♥ ⅃

**WARMINSTER** Wiltshire Map **03** ST84

**★★★★⚑67% Bishopstrow House Hotel** BA12 9HH (Relais et Châteaux) ☎(0985)212312 Telex no 444829
FAX (0985) 216769
*An imposing Georgian house with attractive grounds and excellent leisure facilities. Although a few are compact, most of the bedrooms are spacious, comfortable and tastefully decorated, whilst the public rooms contain fine furniture and prints. Chef Christopher Suter offers varied and interesting menus.*
32⇨♠(3fb)1⇔ CTV in all bedrooms **T** sB&B⇨♠fr£80 dB&B⇨♠fr£110 Continental breakfast 🏳
《 60P ✿ ⊡(heated) ⊇(heated) ℘ (hard) ♪ sauna solarium clay pigeon shooting archery ♫ nc3yrs *xmas*
**V** ♥ ⅃ ⅄ Lunch fr£16&alc Dinner fr£28&alc Last dinner 9pm
Credit Cards ①②③⑤

**⇧Granada Lodge** A36 Bath Rd BA12 7RU (Granada)
☎(0985)219639 FAX (0985) 214380
32⇨♠(10fb)⇨in 7 bedrooms CTV in all bedrooms ℝ
✠ (ex guide dogs) ✱ sB⇨♠fr£25 dB⇨♠fr£28 (room only)

**WARRINGTON** Cheshire Map **07** SJ68

**★★★62% Fir Grove** Knutsford Old Rd WA4 2LD
☎(0925)67471 Telex no 628117 FAX (0925) 67471 ext 246
*Situated just off the A50 on the south-eastern approach to the town, the hotel offers compact bedrooms with every modern facility.*

40⇨♠ CTV in all bedrooms ℝ **T** S10% sB&B⇨♠£50-£55 dB&B⇨♠£60-£65
《 100P *xmas*
♡ French **V** ♥ ⅃ S% Lunch £9.75&alc Dinner £9.75&alc Last dinner 10pm
Credit Cards ①②③⑤

**★★70% Rockfield** 3 Alexandra Rd, Grappenhall WA4 2EL
(1.75m SE off A50) ☎(0925)62898 & 63343
Closed Xmas Day & Boxing Day
*A charming Edwardian building, with immaculate bedrooms, the hotel is in a quiet residential area to the south-east of the town, off the A50 and near to junction 20 of the M6.*
6⇨♠Annexe7rm(5⇨♠) CTV in all bedrooms ℝ **T** ✱
sB&B£40-£45 sB&B⇨♠£45-£50 dB&B£40-£50 dB&B⇨♠£45-£55 🏳
CTV 30P ✿
♡ English, French & Italian **V** ♥ ⅃ Lunch £8-£9.50&alc Dinner £11-£12&alc Last dinner 9pm
Credit Cards ①③⑤

**★★69% Old Vicarage Hotel** Stretton Rd WA4 4NS
☎Norcott Brook(0925)73706 FAX (0925) 73740
(For full entry see Stretton (Cheshire))

**★★58% Patten Arms** Parker St WA1 1LS (County Inns)
☎(0925)36602
Closed Xmas
*A commercial hotel on the A49, opposite Bank Quay station and close to the town centre, offers accommodation in bedrooms with en suite facilities.*
43⇨♠(1fb) CTV in all bedrooms ℝ **T**
《 CTV 18P ♫
**V** ♥ ⅃
Credit Cards ①②③⑤

**★★56% Paddington House** 514 Old Manchester Rd WA1 3TZ (Exec Hotel) ☎(0925)816767
*Conveniently situated off the A57 and a mile from the M6 at junction 21, this hotel has function and conference rooms.*
37⇨♠(1fb)1⇔ CTV in all bedrooms ℝ
Lift 《 ▦ 100P 2🚗 (£5) ✿
♡ French **V** ♥ ⅃ Last dinner 9pm
Credit Cards ①③

**★58% Ribblesdale** Balmoral Rd, Grappenhall WA4 2EB
☎(0925)601197
*Small, quiet, friendly hotel, supervised by resident owners.*
14rm(12⇨) CTV in all bedrooms ℝ **T**
20P 🚗 ✿
♡ French **V** ♥ ⅃ Last dinner 9pm
Credit Cards ①②③

**WARSASH** Hampshire Map **04** SU40

**✕Nook and Cranny** Hook Ln, Hook Village SO3 6HH
☎Locks Heath(0489)584129
*An eighteenth-century cottage in the village of Hook has been converted to an attractive restaurant where chef/proprietor Colin Wood shows his flair for honest, well-constructed French cuisine, with authentic dishes such as rillette, fillet of lamb with Chicken Mousseline and Madeira sauce, fresh salmon poached in the Court Bouillion, and delicious desserts such as Tartes aux Fraises with a fruit coulis. Service is business-like and very industrious.*
Closed Sun, Mon, 1 wk Nov, 25-30 Dec & BH's
Lunch not served Sat
♡ French 50 seats Last lunch 2pm Last dinner 9.45pm 15P
Credit Cards ①③

For key to symbols see the inside front cover.

## WARWICK Warwickshire Map 04 SP26

See also **Barford and Leamington Spa (Royal)**

**★★★ 57% Hilton National** A46, Stratford Rd CV34 6RE (Junc A41/A46/A429) (Hilton) ☎(0926)499555 Telex no 312468 FAX (0926) 410020

*A popular hotel for both leisure and business guests, with modern conference facilities. Bedrooms are well furnished.*

180⇆↑(8fb)✕in 60 bedrooms CTV in all bedrooms ® T ✻ sB⇆↑£75-£85 dB⇆↑£105-£115 (room only) ⊟
Lift ℂ 250P ✿ ⊠(heated) sauna solarium pool table ♬ ஃ *xmas*
♈ International V ✿ ⊘ Lunch £8.50-£10.50&alc High tea fr£5.50 Dinner fr£15.95 Last dinner 10pm
Credit Cards ① ② ③ ⑤

**★★ 66% Warwick Arms** High St CV34 4AJ (Minotels) ☎(0926)492759 FAX (0926) 410587

*Once the property of the Earls of Warwick, this 18th century inn has been refurbished over recent years and now offers bedrooms with good modern facilities and public areas which retain their character.*

35⇆↑(4fb) CTV in all bedrooms ® T 21P
♈ English & French V ✿ ⊘ Last dinner 9.30pm
Credit Cards ① ② ③ ⑤

**See advertisement on page 713**

**★★ 58% Lord Leycester** Jury St CV34 4EJ (Consort) ☎(0926)491481 Telex no 41363 FAX (0202) 299182

*Popular with businessmen for its conference and function facilities – and also because it provides the car parking space which can so often be a problem in the busy town – this centrally positioned hotel offers bedrooms which, though in some cases compact, are continually being upgraded to meet modern standards.*

▶

W

52⇌♪(4fb)1⊟ CTV in all bedrooms ® T ✱ S%
sB&B⇌♪£42 dB&B⇌♪£59 ⊟
Lift ☾ 40P *xmas*
☋ English & French V ✿ ⊡ Lunch £6.75&alc Dinner £12-£15alc Last dinner 8.30pm
Credit Cards [1] [2] [3] [5] £

★66% ***Penderrick*** 36 Coten End CV34 4NP ☎(0926)499399
*Situated on the Leamington Spa Road close to the centre, this large semi-detached Victorian house has been carefully modernised to provide well equipped bedrooms and comfortable public areas. Friendly and attentive services are provided by Alan and Margaret Blackband and their staff.*
7rm(4♪)(2fb) CTV in all bedrooms ®
CTV 9P 2⌂ ⊞ ⌂
✿ ⊡ ⊬ Last dinner 9pm
Credit Cards [1] [2] [3] [5]

✕✕ **Randolph's** Coten End CV34 4NT ☎(0926)491292
*Just out of the town centre, on the Leamington Spa road, this is a charming 17th century black and white timbered cottage in a terrace of mixed building styles. An open wood fire, low beams and attentive service by owners Rudolf and Gillian Prymaka, make it a place for a special occasion. Few kitchens can boast an all female staff such as Randolph's, and imaginative modern dishes are produced, in which herbs and fruit figure strongly to provide unusual, but tasty combinations such as baby vegetables in puff pastry with lemon and herb sauce, lettuce and lovage soup with sorrel pancakes, saddle of venison with juniper berry and port sauce with compôte of rhubarb and pear, clove and honey ice cream served in a dark chocolate box. A well chosen wine list ranges throughout all wine growing countries and has some at modest prices.*
Closed Sun & 25-30 Dec
Lunch not served Sat-Tue
Dinner not served Mon
☋ French V 30 seats ✱ Lunch £18-£22&alc Dinner £25-£29alc Last lunch 1.30pm Last dinner 9.30pm ⁄P nc9yrs
Credit Cards [1] [2] [3]

## WASDALE HEAD Cumbria Map 11 NY10

★★67% **Wasdale Head Inn** CA20 1EX ☎Wasdale(09406)229
Closed mid Nov-mid Mar
*Remotely situated amongst spectacular mountain scenery, this atmospheric small country inn is understandably popular with walkers and climbers but also with the less energetic, as its cosy public areas, thoughtfully equipped bedrooms, traditional hearty home cooking and homely charm make it a delightful place in which to relax 'away from it all'.*
10⇌♪(3fb) ® T ✱ sB&B⇌♪£39-£42
dB&B⇌♪£77-£80 (incl dinner) ⊟
50P ⊞ ❊
V ✿ ⊬ Bar Lunch £3.40-£6.50alc Dinner £14.50 Last dinner 7.30pm
Credit Cards [1] [3]

## WASHINGTON Tyne & Wear Map 12 NZ35

★★★68% **Washington Moat House** Stone Cellar Rd, District 12 NE37 1PH (Queens Moat) ☎091-417 2626 Telex no 537143 FAX 091-415 1166
*Comfortable and well-appointed, the hotel features extensive leisure facilities which include a golf course and driving range.*
106⇌♪(9fb)2⊟⊬in 16 bedrooms CTV in all bedrooms ® T ✱ sB⇌♪£63-£80 dB⇌♪£73-£100 (room only) ⊟
☾ CTV 200P ❊ CFA ⊡(heated) ⚑ 18 squash snooker sauna solarium gymnasium golf driving range hair-dressing salon *xmas*
☋ English & French V ✿ ⊡ ⊬ Lunch fr£7.75 Dinner fr£12.95 Last dinner 10pm
Credit Cards [1] [2] [3] [5]

★★★61% **Post House** Emerson Distrist 5 NE37 1LB (Trusthouse Forte) ☎091-416 2264 Telex no 537574 FAX 091-415 3371
*This large, modern and well furnished hotel stands close to the A1(M) on the south side of Newcastle.*
138⇌♪(52fb)⊬in 30 bedrooms CTV in all bedrooms ® T ✱ sB⇌♪fr£62 dB⇌♪fr£72 (room only) ⊟
Lift ☾ 198P ❊ CFA pitch & putt ⌂ *xmas*
☋ English & Continental V ✿ ⊡ ⊬ Lunch £7.50-£14.20&alc High tea £2.75-£14.20 Dinner £10.50-£14.20 Last dinner 10pm
Credit Cards [1] [2] [3] [4] [5]

## WASHINGTON SERVICE AREA Tyne & Wear Map 12 NZ25

⌂ **Granada Lodge** A1M, Portobello DH3 2SJ (Granada) ☎091-410 0076 FAX 091-410 0057
35⇌♪(10fb)⊬in 6 bedrooms CTV in all bedrooms ®
✗ (ex guide dogs) ✱ S% sB⇌♪fr£25
dB⇌♪fr£28 (room only)
60P
⊬
Credit Cards [1] [2] [3] [5]

## WATCHET Somerset Map 03 ST04

★★53% **Downfield** 16 St Decuman's Rd TA23 0HR ☎(0984)31267 FAX (0984) 34369
*This Victorian house, standing high above the town and commanding splendid views of the harbour and steam railway, is furnished in keeping with its era. Bedrooms are very well equipped, and the restaurant offers various grill menus at a range of prices.*
8⇌♪(2fb) CTV in all bedrooms ® T sB&B⇌♪£25-£30
dB&B⇌♪£28-£40
22P ❊ ⌂ *xmas*
☋ English, French & German V ✿ Lunch £8-£12alc Dinner £9-£14alc Last dinner 9.30pm
Credit Cards [1] [2] [3] [5] £

## WATERGATE BAY Cornwall & Isles of Scilly Map 02 SW86

★★59% **Tregurrian** TR8 4AB ☎St Mawgan(0637)860280
Closed Nov-Feb
*A family-run hotel, close to the beach.*
27rm(1⇌21♪)(8fb) CTV in all bedrooms ® ✱ S%
sB&B£15-£18.50 sB&B⇌♪£16.50-£24 dB&B£30-£37
dB&B⇌♪£36-£45 ⊟
CTV 26P ❊ ⊡(heated) sauna solarium jacuzzi spa pool games room ⌂
✿ ⊡
Credit Cards [1] [3]

## WATERHOUSES Staffordshire Map 07 SK05

❀ ✕✕ **Old Beams Restaurant** Leek Rd ST10 3HW ☎(0538)308254
*This charming restaurant stands beside the main road in the centre of an attractrive moorland village. Chef patron Nigel Wallis cooks excellent dishes with delicate sauces and lots of natural flavour. Ann Wallis supervises the attentive and convivial service so much appreciated by the diners here, many of them regular guests. Six bedrooms have now been added to the restaurant, encouraging guests to linger in this comfortable ambience.*
Closed Mon
Lunch not served Sat
Dinner not served Sun
☋ English & French 50 seats ✱ Lunch £12.50 Dinner £18-£25alc Last lunch 2pm Last dinner 10pm 22P nc4yrs ⊬ ♫
Credit Cards [1] [2] [3] [5]

**WATERINGBURY** Kent Map **05** TQ65

★★★59% **Wateringbury** Tonbridge Rd ME18 5NS (Lansbury)
☎Maidstone(0622)812632 Telex no 96265 FAX (0622) 812720
*This busy hotel provides comfortable and well-equipped
accommodation with a cosy bar and lively restaurant. The menu
offers a variety of popular dishes including some for vegetarians.*
28➪1 ✕ ⅏ in 3 bedrooms CTV in all bedrooms ℞ T ✖
sB&B➪fr£75 dB&B➪fr£88 ঘ
€ 60P sauna *xmas*
♀ European ♿ ⅌ Lunch fr£11&alc Dinner fr£11&alc Last
dinner 10pm
Credit Cards ⊞ ② ③ ⑤

**WATERMILLOCK** Cumbria Map **12** NY42

★★★✦75% **Leeming House** CA11 0JJ (Trusthouse Forte)
☎Pooley Bridge(07684)86622 Telex no 64111
FAX (07684) 86443
*A charming country house set on the western shore of Lake
Ullswater in 20 acres of beautiful grounds. Bedrooms are
tastefully furnished and have good facilities with an additional
bedroom block due to open in late 1990. A six course dinner menu
is served in the elegant restaurant.*
40➪ি✦ in 11 bedrooms CTV in all bedrooms ℞ T S%
sB➪ি£75-£108 dB➪ি£108-£135 (room only) ঘ
CTV 50P ⊞ ❋ ♪ *xmas*
V ♿ ⅌ ✕ S% Lunch £14.50&alc Dinner £29.50 Last dinner
8.45pm
Credit Cards ⊞ ② ③ ④ ⑤

Book as early as possible for busy holiday
periods.

**W**

# Watermillock - Weedon

**★★★★⚑**73% **Rampsbeck Country House** CA11 0LP
🕿 Pooley Bridge(07684)86442 & 86688
Closed 6 Jan-24 Feb
(Rosette awarded for dinner only)
*A warm, friendly hotel, admirably run by Mr and Mrs Gibb. The elegance and comfort of the accommodation is matched by the superb cooking. Local produce is the basis of such skilfully prepared dishes as Fillet of beef with Jerusalem artichoke sauce or roast squab with wild mushrooms. Guests cannot fail to feel well cared for.*
19rm(18⇔♠)(2fb) CTV in all bedrooms ℝ T
sB&B⇔♠£32-£48 dB&B⇔♠£60-£85 ᕮ
30P ♨ ❅ ♪ croquet lawn nc5yrs *xmas*
♡ English & French V ♥ ⚏ Lunch £14-£25alc Dinner £23-£30
Last dinner 9pm
Credit Cards ①③

★★

**★★⚑ OLD CHURCH HOTEL**
CA11 0JN 🕿 Pooley Bridge
(07684)86204
FAX (07684) 86368
Closed Dec-Feb
*Kevin and Maureen Whitemore are dedicated to providing their guests with a restful atmosphere in keeping with the hotel's idyllic setting on the north shore of Ullswater. In pursuit of this policy, the comfortable and attractively furnished bedrooms are free of radio or television sets (though there are telephones), but guests who must view can do so in one of the comfortable lounges, and for other entertainment there is ample provision of books and board games should conversation fail. Hearty 5-course dinners are also very much a feature of the evenings, and at lunchtime lighter but equally tasty dishes are available. Our inspectors are enthusiastic in their praise for this lovely hotel and there is much competition for return visits.*
10⇔T 🗙 (ex guide dogs) ✳ S% sB&B⇔£68-£132 dB&B⇔£136-£176 (incl dinner)
CTV 30P ♨ ❅ ♪ boat hire moorings ⚓
♡ English & French ♥ ⚏ ⅄ S% Lunch £4-£10alc Dinner £23.50 Last dinner 8pm
Credit Cards ①

---

## WATERROW Somerset Map 03 ST02

**★⚑**76% **Hurstone Hotel & Restaurant** TA4 2AT
🕿 Waveliscombe(0894)23441
*One of our Top Twenty One-Star Hotels—see the colour feature on page 37. This is a beautiful Somerset long house, dating in part from the 17th century, which offers a natural friendly atmosphere, thoughtfully equipped bedrooms and a high standard of cooking which uses home grown produce to a large extent.*
6rm(4⇔)(1fb)⅄in 1 bedroom CTV in 5 bedrooms ℝ T ✳
sB&B⇔£43-£48.50 dB&B⇔£60-£69 dB&B⇔£66-£75 ᕮ
CTV 12P ♨ ♪ ⚓ *xmas*
V ♥ ⚏ Lunch £9.25-£10.50 Dinner £12.50-£17.50alc Last dinner 10pm
Credit Cards ①②③

---

## WATFORD Hertfordshire Map 04 TQ19

**★★★**63%, **Dean Park** 30-40 St Albans Rd WD1 1RN (Queens Moat) 🕿 (0923)229212 Telex no 8813610 FAX (0923) 54638
Closed 25-31 Dec
*A modern purpose-built hotel features well equipped, tastefully appointed bedrooms and a pleasant first floor cocktail bar with restaurant offering both à la carte and table d'hôte menus.*

---

90⇔♠(2fb) CTV in all bedrooms ℝ 🗙 (ex guide dogs) ✳ S%
sB&B⇔♠£30-£83 dB&B⇔♠£60-£83 ᕮ
Lift ℂ 12P ♪
♡ French V ♥ ⚏ ⅄ S% Lunch £12&alc Dinner £14&alc Last dinner 10pm
Credit Cards ①②③④⑤

**★★★**58%, **Hilton National** Elton Way, Watford Bypass WD2 8HA (Hilton) 🕿 (0923)35881 Telex no 923422
FAX (0923) 220836
(For full entry see Bushey)

---

## WATTON Norfolk Map 05 TF90

**★★**70%, **Clarence House** 78 High St IP25 6AH (Exec Hotel)
🕿 (0953)884252 & 884487 FAX (0953) 881323
*The small, family-managed hotel provides value-for-money accommodation in comfortable surroundings and a friendly atmosphere.*
6⇔♠(1fb) CTV in all bedrooms ℝ
7P ♨
♡ English & French V ♥ ⚏ Last dinner 9pm
Credit Cards ①②③⑤

---

## WEEDON Northamptonshire Map 04 SP65

**★★★**70%, **Crossroads** NN7 4PX (Best Western) 🕿 (0327)40354
Telex no 312311 FAX (0327) 40849
Closed 24-26 Dec
*Standing at the heart of England, where the A5 and A45 cross, a hotel within easy reach of both Northampton and the M1 offers accommodation in charmingly decorated rooms which are thoughtfully equipped to suit the needs of either business traveller or leisure guest. Brimming with antiques and interesting bric à brac, it provides a friendly, hospitable atmosphere, and the resident proprietors who have developed it with such care plan still further improvements.*
10⇔Annexe40⇔(3fb)3⊞ CTV in all bedrooms ℝ T 🗙 (ex guide dogs) sB&B⇔£60-£80 dB&B⇔£70-£95 ᕮ
100P ❅ ♬ (hard)
V ♥ ⚏ Lunch £15-£25alc Dinner £15-£25alc Last dinner 10.15pm
Credit Cards ①②③⑤
**See advertisement under NORTHAMPTON**

**★★**66%, **Heart Of England** Daventry Rd NN7 4QD
🕿 (0327)40335
*Rooms are attractively furnished and well equipped in an hotel which dates back to the eighteenth century; today it offers convenient access to junction 16 of the M1 from its town centre position beside the A45. Good levels of hospitality and service are maintained by a particularly friendly staff, and a selection of grill meals is available in the Gables Restaurant.*
12rm(1⇔1♠)1⊞ CTV in all bedrooms ℝ 🗙 (ex guide dogs)
70P ♨ ❅
V ♥ ⚏ Last dinner 10pm
Credit Cards ①②③⑤

**★**66%, **Globe** High St NN7 4QD (Inter-Hotels) 🕿 (0327)40336
FAX (0327) 349058
*This eighteenth-century coaching house stands where the A5 crosses the A45, three miles west of junction 16 of the M1. All its attractively furnished and well equipped rooms provide en suite facilities, and in the informal atmosphere of restaurant and bar guests can sample a range of freshly-cooked pies, casseroles, curries, grills, roasts and other popular dishes.*
14⇔♠(1fb) CTV in all bedrooms ℝ T sB&B⇔♠£30-£42 dB&B⇔♠£39.50-£52 ᕮ
CTV 40P ♪
♡ Mainly grills V ♥ ⚏ Lunch £7-£10 Dinner £10-£13alc Last dinner 10pm
Credit Cards ①②③⑤④

**WELLINGBOROUGH** Northamptonshire Map **04** SP86

**★★★50% Hind** Sheep St NN8 1BY (Queens Moat)
☏(0933)222827 FAX (0933) 441921
*Standing in the centre of the town, the Hind dates back to the 17th century and offers modern, well-equipped accommodation in rooms which retain their old character.*
34⇌⋔(1fb)1⊞ CTV in all bedrooms ® **T** sB&B⇌⋔£55-£58 dB&B⇌⋔£70-£74 ⊟
☾ 13P 3⌂ CFA
☋ English & Continental **V** ♁ ☕ ⁄ Lunch fr£8.95&alc Dinner fr£10.95&alc Last dinner 10pm
Credit Cards 1 2 3 4 5 £

**★★58% High View** 156 Midland Rd NN8 1NG ☏(0933)78733 due to change to 278733 FAX (0933) 225948
*This small privately-owned hotel is situated in a quiet area of the town close to the railway station. Accommodation is comfortable and very well equipped. Three rooms are in a separate annexe in a nearby house. Public areas include a simply appointed basement dining room, a small bar and a games room.*
14⇌⋔Annexe3rm(2fb) CTV in all bedrooms ® **T** sB&Bfr£23 sB&B⇌⋔£43 dB&Bfr£33 dB&B⇌⋔£50 ⊟
CTV 8P 1⌂ ❊
**V** ♁ ⁄ Lunch fr£8.10alc Dinner fr£8.10alc Last dinner 8.30pm
Credit Cards 1 2 3 5 £

**★61% Columbia** 19 Northampton Rd NN8 3HG (Consort)
☏(0933)229333 FAX (0933) 440418
Closed 24-27 Dec
*A popular privately-owned hotel close to the town centre, accommodation here is well equipped and ideal for commercial guests. Public areas are open-plan and include a small restaurant where an extensive range of dishes is available. Staff are friendly and helpful and create an amiable atmosphere.*
29⇌⋔(1fb) CTV in all bedrooms ® **T** ✗ (ex guide dogs) ✱ sB&B⇌⋔£28-£43 dB&B⇌⋔£40-£54 ⊟
CTV 18P
☋ English & French **V** ♁ ☕ Lunch £6.95&alc Dinner £9.50-£11.50&alc Last dinner 9.30pm
Credit Cards 1 2 3

**WELLINGTON**

See **Telford**

**WELLS** Somerset Map **03** ST54

**★★★62% Swan** Sadler St BA5 2RX (Best Western)
☏(0749)78877 Telex no 449658 FAX (0749) 77647
*Overlooking the West Front of the cathedral, this 16th-century and Victorian hotel offers spacious and well equipped bedrooms, many with antique furnishings. Other amenities include a bar and lounge with log fires and a cosy dining room whose range of good English food includes traditional roasts.*
32⇌⋔(2fb)9⊞ CTV in all bedrooms ® **T**
sB&B⇌⋔£55-£62.50 dB&B⇌⋔£75-£82.50 ⊟
30P CFA squash *xmas*
**V** ♁ ☕ Lunch fr£11&alc Dinner fr£14.50&alc Last dinner 9.30pm
Credit Cards 1 2 3 5

**See advertisement on page 717**

**★★55% *Crown*** Market Place BA5 2RP ☏(0749)73457
*Standing opposite the Bishop's Palace, this pleasant old coaching-house hotel retains many original features. An attractive restaurant serves well-prepared dishes and the bar serves light meals and afternoon teas.*
15⇌⋔4⊞ CTV in all bedrooms ®
15P squash
**V** ♁ ☕ Last dinner 10pm
Credit Cards 1 2 3 4 5

**See advertisement on page 717**

*The Hind Hotel and Restaurant*

SHEEP STREET · WELLINGBOROUGH
NORTHANTS NN8 1BY

ASHLEY COURTENAY RECOMMENDED

AA★★★

An olde worlde Cromwellian Hotel offering all the modern facilities, good food, comfortable bedrooms all with private bathrooms and an efficient and friendly service. Wellingborough is an ideal location for visiting many stately houses such as Althorp House, a spot of fishing at Grafham Waters, Drag Racing at Santa Pod or a day out for the family at Wicksteed Leisure Park.

**WELLINGBOROUGH (0933) 222827**
**Fax (0933) 441921**

Special Weekend Bargain Breaks available
Please phone or write for full details

**Queens Moat Houses PLC**

MOAT HOUSE
INTERNATIONAL HOTELIERS

★★★ *Rampsbeck Country House Hotel*

**Watermillock, Ullswater, Nr. Penrith, Cumbria CA11 0LP**
**Telephone: 07684 86442**

Rampsbeck is a charming 18th Century Country House. Privately owned and managed the Hotel stands in 18 acres of meadow and garden which includes lake shore and a croquet lawn. The attractive en suite bedrooms have been individually designed and most have views of the lake or garden. Elegant reception rooms have log fires in winter and garden access in summer, and the Dining Room overlooking the lake is noted for its superb cuisine. Cheerful staff provide a competent friendly service. The Hotel is ideally situated for exploring the many Historic and Artistic associations of the Lake District. Golfing, sailing, swimming, riding and shooting facilities are within easy reach.

***Midweek Breaks*** *April, May, June and October. Any two days between Sunday and Thursday £90 to £120 DBB pp.*
***Winter Breaks*** *Any two days November, December and March £80 to £110, DBB pp.*

Listed as one of the most beautifully situated Hotels in Great Britain.

V

★57% **Ancient Gate House** Sadler St BA5 2RR ☎(0749)72029
Closed 24-26 Dec
*A hotel with plenty of character situated close to the Cathedral.*
*Accommodation is basic but is in the process of being upgraded.*
*The Italian cooking is of a good standard and service is friendly*
*and efficient.*
10rm(1⇌2↑)(1fb)6⊞ CTV in all bedrooms ® ✱
sB&B£25-£27 sB&B⇌↑£35-£37 dB&B£40-£42
dB&B⇌↑£45-£47 ▤
4P
♡ English & Italian **V** ♦ Lunch £4.95-£5.95&alc Dinner
£11.75-£12.75&alc Last dinner 10.30pm
Credit Cards ⧈ ② ③ ⑤

WELLS-NEXT-THE-SEA Norfolk Map 09 TF94

★68% **Crown** The Buttlands NR23 1EX (Minotels)
☎Fakenham(0328)710209
*A high standard of French provincial cuisine, the dishes featured in*
*its daily-changing menu using only fresh local produce, can be*
*enjoyed in this restaurant at the heart of Wells. The building,*
*despite its Georgian façade, has its origins in Tudor times, and the*
*comfortable bar areas are still warmed by open log fires, while the*
*town's association with Nelson is reflected in naval prints depicting*
*him. Accommodation, though modest, is both warm and*
*comfortable, informal service being attentive and friendly, so that*
*the hotel offers an ideal base both for commercial clients and for*
*holidaymakers exploring the area.*
16rm(3⇌5↑)(3fb) CTV in all bedrooms ® sB&Bfr£38
sB&B⇌↑fr£45 dB&Bfr£48 dB&B⇌↑fr£55 ▤
10P ⌘ xmas
♡ English & Continental **V** ♦ ⚏ ✂ Lunch fr£13.50&alc
Dinner fr£13.50&alc Last dinner 9.30pm
Credit Cards ⧈ ② ③ ⑤

✗**Moorings** 6 Freeman St NR23 1BA ☎Fakenham(0328)710949
*Locally caught seafood is a speciality of this charming little*
*restaurant that stands close to the harbour of this small Norfolk*
*fishing town. Dishes are predominantly provincial French –*
*mussels, oysters, sea-trout and dogfish are all well-flavoured, with a*
*lavish use of herbs. Vegetarians are particularly well catered for,*
*with dishes such as eggs and broccoli with mustard and cheese*
*sauce or Chinese vegetables with beancurd. The wine list is*
*extensive and modestly priced.*
Closed Wed, 2 wks early Jun & late Nov-mid Dec
Lunch not served Thu
Dinner not served Tue
♡ English & French **V** 40 seats ✱ Lunch fr£14 Dinner fr£15
Last lunch 1.45pm Last dinner 8.45pm ᕽ ✂

WELSH HOOK Dyfed Map 02 SM92

✗✗**Stone Hall** SA62 5NS ☎Letterston(0348)840212
*Stone Hall stand near the hamlet of Welsh Hook between*
*Haverfordwest and Fishguard. The charming restaurant in the*
*600-year-old part of the house serves imaginative food prepared by*
*a talented young chef whose experience was gained in Nice and*
*Brittany.*
Closed Mon (Nov-Mar only) & 6-18 Nov
Lunch not served ex by prior arrangement
♡ French **V** 34 seats ✱ Dinner £12-£13&alc Last dinner
9.30pm 50P
Credit Cards ⧈ ② ③

Entries for red-star hotels are highlighted by a
tint panel. For a full list of these establishments
consult the Contents page.

WELSHPOOL Powys Map 07 SJ20

★★⚑73% **Golfa Hall** Llanfair Rd SY21 9AF ☎(0938)553399
FAX (0938) 554777
*A relaxing, friendly hotel in an elevated position 1.5 miles west of*
*town. Set in 8 acres of grounds it offers warm, bright and*
*comfortable bedrooms and extended lounge areas.*
10⇌↑(3fb) TV available ® T sB&B⇌↑fr£35
dB&B⇌↑fr£60 ▤
50P ⌘ ✿ clay pigeon shooting
**V** ♦ ⚏ ✂ Lunch £15.50 Dinner fr£15.50 Last dinner 8.30pm
Credit Cards ⧈ ③ ⑤

★★64% **Royal Oak** SY21 7DG (Consort) ☎(0938)552217
Telex no 57515
*Dating from the mid 18th century, and right in the heart of this*
*busy mid Wales market-town, this hotel provides a popular*
*function suite and a good choice of bars and lounges. Many*
*bedrooms have recently been modernised, and a good choice of*
*food is available in the timbered restaurant.*
24⇌↑(1fb)1⊞ CTV in all bedrooms ® T ✖ (ex guide dogs)
sB&B⇌↑£32-£34 dB&B⇌↑£57-£60 ▤
CTV 60P 2▥
♡ English, French & Italian **V** ♦ ⚏ Lunch £8-£9&alc Dinner
£10-£11.50&alc Last dinner 9pm
Credit Cards ⧈ ② ③ ⓔ

WELWYN GARDEN CITY Hertfordshire Map 04 TL21

★★★57% **Crest** Homestead Ln AL7 4LX (Trusthouse Forte)
☎(0707)324336 Telex no 261523 FAX (0707) 326447
*A small, lively hotel attracting a busy commercial trade, the hotel*
*is located in a residential area.*
58⇌↑✱in 12 bedrooms CTV in all bedrooms ® T ✱
sB⇌↑fr£71 dB⇌↑fr£84 (room only) ▤
Lift ⓒ 80P ✿ CFA xmas

▶

*AA* ★★⚑                         ᴴᴴᴴᴴ

# GOLFA HALL HOTEL
## WELSHPOOL,
## MONGOMERYSHIRE
### Powys SY21 9AF
### Tel: (0938) 553399 Fax: (0938) 554777

A listed country house set in magnificent
grounds overlooking a wooded vale. A
warm welcome is always assured. Our
rooms are all ensuite & furnished to a
high standard. We are ideally situated
for visiting Powis Castle, Lake Vyrnwy,
local steam railway & golf course. Our
restaurant offers a very high standard of
cuisine and specialises in seasonal local
produce.

**W**

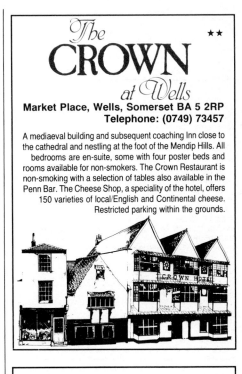

**W**

⚲ International **V** ✆ ⚲ ⚲ Lunch £11-£12.50 Dinner
fr£15&alc Last dinner 10pm
Credit Cards [1] [2] [3] [4] [5]

**WEMBLEY** Greater London

See **LONDON plan 1**B4(page 426)
✗✗**Moghul Brasserie** 525 High Rd HA0 4AG ☎081-903 6967 &
081-902 8665
*Intimate and tastefully appointed, this town-centre restaurant
offers authentic dishes based on good fresh produce, well
marinated prior to cooking. Of particular interest are the succulent
King Prawn Bhuna and a fine selection of breads which includes an
excellent Spinach Paratha.*
Closed 25-26 Dec
⚲ Indian **V** 60 seats Last dinner 11.15pm 20P
Credit Cards [1] [2] [3] [5]

✗**Woodlands** 402A High Rd HA9 7AB ☎081-902 9869
FAX 081-908 0253
*A friendly, intimate atmosphere prevails in this South Indian
vegetarian restaurant.*
Closed 25-26 Dec
⚲ South Indian **V** 55 seats Last lunch 2.30pm Last dinner
10.30pm 2P
Credit Cards [1] [2] [3] [5]

**WENTBRIDGE (near Pontefract)** West Yorkshire
Map **08** SE41
★★★**67%, Wentbridge House** WF8 3JJ (Select)
☎Pontefract(0977)620444 FAX (0977) 620148
Closed Xmas night
*A building dating from 1700, and set in about fifteen acres of
attractive grounds near the A1, has been converted into a
comfortable, family-run hotel; despite its unspoiled village location
it is ideally placed for access to all parts of Yorkshire. The Fleur
de Lys Restaurant, under the close personal supervision of the
proprietors, serves excellent French and International cuisine,
making good use of fresh ingredients and providing consistently
high standards of service. The wine list itemises 333 wines, ranging
from the modest to the more expensive.*
12⇌🏠1🛏 CTV in all bedrooms **T** ✖ (ex guide dogs) S%
sB&B⇌🏠£60-£85 dB&B⇌🏠£73-£100 🍴
100P 🎮 ✿
⚲ French **V** ✆ Lunch £14.50-£18.50&alc Dinner
£22.50-£34.50alc Last dinner 9.30pm
Credit Cards [1] [2] [3] [5]

**WEST BAY**
See **Bridport**

**WEST BEXINGTON** Dorset Map **03** SY58
★★**67%, Manor** Beach Rd DT6 9DF
☎Burton Bradstock(0308)897616
*An attractive stone-built hotel which stands close to the sea and
Chesil Beach offers a pleasantly informal atmosphere and
accommodation in attractive bedrooms provided with such homely
touches as several different types of tea; public areas include a
very comfortable lounge, a formal dining room serving good, fresh
dishes and a cellar bar and conservatory where an extensive range
of bar food is available.*
13⇌🏠(1fb) CTV in all bedrooms ® **T** ✖ ✱
sB&B⇌🏠£33.95-£39.95 dB&B⇌🏠£56-£67 🍴
28P ✿
**V** ✆ Lunch £10-£12.50 Dinner £17.45 Last dinner 10pm
Credit Cards [1] [2] [3] [5] ④

**See advertisement under BRIDPORT**

**WEST BROMWICH** West Midlands Map **07** SP09
See also **Barr, Great**
★★★**63%, West Bromwich Moat House** Birmingham Rd
B70 6RS (Queens Moat) ☎021-553 6111 Telex no 336232
FAX 021-525 7403
*Comfortable, well equipped accommodation and extensive
conference facilities are available at this efficiently managed hotel
which stands beside junction 1 of the M5; its popular Rafferty's
Restaurant serves both carvery and à la carte dishes.*
170⇌🏠✖in 17 bedrooms CTV in all bedrooms ®
Lift ⚲ ⊞ 200P CFA
⚲ English & French **V** ✆ ⚲
Credit Cards [1] [2] [3] [5]

★★★**59%, Great Barr Hotel & Conference Centre** Pear Tree
Dr, off Newton Rd B43 6HS ☎021-357 1141 Telex no 336406
FAX 021-357 7557
(For full entry see **Barr, Great**)

**WEST CHILTINGTON** West Sussex Map **04** TQ01
★★★**61%, Roundabout** Monkmead Ln RH20 2PF (1.75m S)
(Best Western) ☎(0798)813838 Telex no 94013840
FAX (0798) 812962
*The peaceful rural situation of this Tudor-style hotel offers easy
access to many places of interest. Bedrooms are furnished in dark
oak, four rooms have four-poster beds which reflect the
establishment's origins, while the presence of the garden in summer
and the log fires which warm the public in winter both contribute to
the cosy, relaxed atmosphere which is such an attractive feature.*
23⇌🏠(4fb)4🛏 CTV in all bedrooms ® **T** S10% sB&B⇌🏠£60-£64
dB&B⇌🏠£73.75-£77 🍴
46P ✿ nc3yrs *xmas*
⚲ English & French **V** ✆ ⚲
Credit Cards [1] [2] [3] [4] [5]

**WESTCLIFF-ON-SEA**
See **Southend-on-Sea**

**WESTERHAM** Kent Map **05** TQ45
★★★**61%, Kings Arms** Market Square TN16 1AN
☎(0959)62990 FAX (0959) 61240
*This family-owned hotel, a 200-year-old building, has been
attractively decorated and tastefully furnished. It provides
spacious bedrooms, a comfortable bar lounge and a charming
restaurant offering à la carte and, during the week, carvery menus.*
18⇌🏠(2fb)1🛏✖in 3 bedrooms CTV in all bedrooms ® **T** ✱
sB&B⇌🏠£60-£75 dB&B⇌🏠£70-£90
30P 4🚗 🚗
⚲ European **V** ✆ ⚲ Lunch £11.75&alc Dinner
£13.75-£15.75&alc Last dinner 10pm
Credit Cards [1] [2] [3] [5]

**WESTGATE ON SEA** Kent Map **05** TR37
★★★**55%, Ivyside** 25 Sea Rd CT8 8SB ☎Thanet(0843)31082
*A seafront hotel providing functional and varied accommodation
especially designed for families with children features games
rooms, play areas and good indoor leisure facilities; it is also
popular with local residents, friendly service being supervised by
the second generation of the proprietor's family.*
67rm(65⇌🏠)(58fb) CTV in all bedrooms ® **T** ✖ ✱
sB&B⇌🏠£22-£35 dB&B⇌🏠£44-£70
⚲ CTV 30P ✿ CFA ▣(heated) ⚲(heated) squash snooker
sauna solarium gymnasium spa pool steam room table tennis
♫ 🎱 *xmas*
⚲ English & French **V** ✆ ⚲ Lunch £6.50 High tea £2-£4
Dinner £8.50 Last dinner 8.30pm
Credit Cards [1] [3]

**W**

**WESTHILL** Grampian *Aberdeenshire* Map **15** NJ80

★★★61%, **Westhill** AB3 6TT (Consort)
☎Aberdeen(0224)740388 Telex no 739925 FAX (0224) 744354
*This modern, purpose-built hotel stands just off the A944, six miles west of Aberdeen. Popular with businessmen, and catering for local functions, it offers practical accommodation in well equipped bedrooms, a choice of bars and some leisure facilities.*
38⇔Annexe14⇔♪♠(2fb) CTV in all bedrooms ® T ✳
sB&B⇔♠£48 dB&B⇔♠£65
Lift ( ⊞ 350P CFA sauna solarium gymnasium ♫ *xmas*
♀ International V ✿ Bar Lunch £3-£8alc Dinner £12-£25alc
Last dinner 10pm
Credit Cards ① ② ③ ⑤
**See advertisement under ABERDEEN**

**WESTLETON** Suffolk Map **05** TM46

★★72%, **The Crown at Westleton** IP17 3AD ☎(072873)273
Closed 25-26 Dec
*A delightful inn of character and charm, where the hospitality and personal attention of the proprietors are enhanced by an inviting log fire, offers fully en suite accommodation of good quality; its excellent restaurant serves an extensive à la carte menu with fish specialities freshly and skilfully prepared in imaginative style – sea trout poached with champagne and saffron sauce, for example – and a range of schoolboy favourites such as Spotted Dick and Treacle Pudding to complete the meal, whilst the English Breakfast is a feast that challenges the capacity of the heartiest eater*
7rm(3⇔)Annexe7⇔♠(3fb)2⌗ CTV in all bedrooms ®
30P
V ✿ ⊬ Last dinner 9.30pm
Credit Cards ① ② ③ ⑤

**WEST LULWORTH** Dorset Map **03** SY88

★★62%, **Cromwell House** BH20 5RJ ☎(092941)253
FAX (092941) 566
14⇔♠(1fb)1⌗ CTV in all bedrooms ® T sB&B⇔♠£30-£35
dB&B⇔♠£60-£65 (incl dinner) ᕈ
CTV 14P 1🐾 ❀ ≏(heated) solarium *xmas*
V ✿ ♫ Sunday Lunch £7.50-£8.50 High tea £2-£3.50 Dinner £8.50-£9.50&alc Last dinner 8.30pm
Credit Cards ① ③

★★61%, **Gatton House** BH20 5RU ☎(092941)252
Closed 24 Dec-20 Jan
*A small hotel which commands splendid views over surrounding countryside from its position high on a hill is run on friendly lines by its resident proprietors, featuring a comfortable lounge bar with real log fire and a bright, airy dining room which offers a short table d'hôte menu of fresh British dishes.*
8⇔♠(1fb)⊬in 1 bedroom CTV in all bedrooms ® ✳ S%
sB&B⇔♠frf25 dB&B⇔♠£50 ᕈ
CTV 11P 曲
✿ ♫ ⊬
Credit Cards ① ③

★65%, **Shirley** Main Rd BH20 5RL ☎(092941)358
Closed early Nov-Feb
*The hotel has been in the hands of the same proprietors for twenty years, and their good-natured, natural hospitality creates an informal atmosphere which make it ideal for the holidaymaker. Bedrooms, though small in many cases, are fully equipped with modern facilities, books and games are available in the comfortable lounge, and the garden contains a sheltered pool and giant chess set.*
19⇔♠(2fb) CTV in all bedrooms ® T S%
sB&B⇔♠£19.25-£22.25 dB&B⇔♠£38.50-£44.50 ᕈ
20P 曲 ≏(heated) giant chess
V ⊬ S% Dinner £6.55-£6.85&alc Last dinner 8pm
Credit Cards ① ③

**W**

WEST MERSEA Essex Map 05 TM01

✗ **Le Champenois (Blackwater Hotel)** 20-22 Church Rd
CO5 8QH ☎Colchester(0206)383338 & 383038
*Fresh seafood, veal and duck feature in the enjoyable, simple
dishes presented in this attractive French restaurant which forms
part of the Blackwater Hotel on Mersea Island. Charming and
efficient staff provide attentive service and a high standard of
hospitality.*
Closed 6 Jan-6 Feb
Lunch not served Tue
Dinner not served Sun
♀ English & French **V** 42 seats Lunch £9.80-£13&alc Dinner
£17-£23alc Last lunch 2pm Last dinner 9.45pm 15P
Credit Cards ① ② ③

___

WESTON-ON-THE-GREEN Oxfordshire Map 04 SP51

★★★66% **Weston Manor** OX6 8QL (Best Western)
☎Bletchington(0869)50621 Telex no 83409 FAX (0869) 50901
*In the past this 14th-century manor house has been the ancestral
home of earls, then a monastery, and has now been restored to
make a stylish hotel featuring a unique, oak-panelled restaurant
with minstrels' gallery. The bedrooms combine comfort with
character, and there are extensive leisure facilities.*
17⇨↑Annexe20⇨↑(3fb)⚃ CTV in all bedrooms ® T
✖ (ex guide dogs) ✳ sB&B⇨↑£75-£90
dB&B⇨↑£95-£115 ⋒
⋒ 150P ✢ ⩰(heated) squash croquet *xmas*
♀ English & French **V** ⍟ ⍟ Lunch £12.50-£14.50 Dinner
£17.50-£20 Last dinner 9.30pm
Credit Cards ① ② ③ ⑤ ⓔ

___

WESTON-SUPER-MARE Avon Map 03 ST36

★★★65% **The Grand Atlantic** Beach Rd BS23 1BA (Trusthouse
Forte) ☎(0934)626543 FAX (0934) 415048
*A high level of hospitality is the hallmark of this large, traditional,
sea-front hotel where refurbishment continues. Many of the
bedrooms enjoy impressive sea views.*
76⇨↑in 15 bedrooms CTV in all bedrooms ® T S%
sB⇨£60-£70 dB⇨£81-£91 (room only)
Lift ⋒ 150P ✢ CFA ⩰(heated) ♪ (hard) ⚅ *xmas*
♀ English & French **V** ⍟ ⍟ ✄ S10% Lunch £8.60-£9.70&alc
Dinner fr£11.65&alc Last dinner 9.30pm
Credit Cards ① ② ③ ④ ⑤

★★★60% **Commodore** Beach Rd, Sand Bay, Kewstoke
BS22 9UZ (Exec Hotel) ☎(0934)415778 FAX (0934) 636483
*Situated two miles from the town centre, on the sands at Kewstoke,
this modern hotel offers compact but very well equipped bedrooms
and bright, open-plan public areas. A good choice of imaginative
food is available.*
12⇨↑Annexe7rm(4↑)(1fb) CTV in all bedrooms ® T
✖ (ex guide dogs) sB&B£45 sB&B⇨↑£45 dB&B£60
dB&B⇨↑£60 ⋒
85P ✢ ♪ ⚅
♀ English & French **V** ⍟ ⍟ ✄ Lunch fr£7.95&alc Dinner
£11-£15&alc Last dinner 9.30pm
Credit Cards ① ② ③ ⑤ ⓔ

★★★56% **Royal Pier** Birnbeck Rd BS23 2EJ (Best Western)
☎(0934)626644
*Friendly services and spacious public areas are attractive features
of this holiday hotel which commands views of the bay from its
position near Birnbeck Pier ; bedrooms vary in quality but are
currently being upgraded to a higher standard.*
40rm(33⇨3↑)(4fb) CTV in all bedrooms ® T ✖
Lift ⋒ CTV 70P ⚌ pool table & table tennis
♀ European **V** ⍟ ⍟ Last dinner 9.15pm
Credit Cards ① ② ③ ⑤

___

★★69% **Rozel** Madeira Cove BS23 2BU ☎(0934)415268
*A friendly, family-run hotel with some fine sea views offers
bedrooms which have a good selection of modern facilities, most of
them being spacious and some featuring their own small balconies.
Guests enjoy the use of an outdoor heated swimming pool.*
46⇨↑(15fb) CTV in all bedrooms ® T ✳ sB&B⇨↑£35-£40
dB&B⇨↑£58-£70 ⋒
Lift ⋒ 30P 50⬥ ✢ CFA ⩰(heated) ♫ *xmas*
♀ English & French **V** ⍟ ⍟
Credit Cards ① ② ③ ⑤ ⓔ

★★64% **Beachlands** 17 Uphill Rd North BS23 4NG
☎(0934)621401
*A family-run hotel which is situated in a mainly residential area,
overlooking the golf course, offers modern, well-equipped
bedrooms, spacious open-plan public areas and particularly
friendly, attentive services.*
18⇨↑(5fb) CTV in all bedrooms ® T sB&B⇨↑fr£25.75
dB&B⇨↑fr£51.50 ⋒
CTV 15P ⚌ *xmas*
♀ English & French ⍟ ⍟ Bar Lunch £1-£5 High tea £5 Dinner
£9.75 Last dinner 8.30pm
Credit Cards ① ② ③ ⑤

★★62% **Old Manor Inn** Queensway, Worle BS22 9LP
☎(0934)515143 FAX (0934) 521738
*On the site of a former monastery, the hotel offers functional
accommodation. The lively skittle bar is popular with the locals,
and a lounge bar is also available. Leisure facilities include a
sauna, solarium and multi-gym.*
Annexe19⇨↑ CTV in all bedrooms ® T ✳ S%
sB⇨↑fr£32.50 dB⇨↑fr£45 (room only) ⋒
75P sauna solarium gymnasium
**V** ⍟ S% Lunch £4.50-£11alc Dinner £4.50-£11alc
Credit Cards ① ② ③ ⑤

★★60% **Berni Royal** South Pde BS23 1JN (Berni/Chef &
Brewer) ☎(0934)623601
*Situated close to the Promenade, this Victorian hotel has been
modernised to provide well-equipped, en suite bedrooms, popular
bars and a grill restaurant.*
37⇨↑2⚃ CTV in all bedrooms ® T ✖ (ex guide dogs)
sB&B⇨↑£48.50-£59.50 dB&B⇨↑£70 ⋒
Lift ⋒ 150P ✢
**V** ⍟ ⍟ Lunch £8-£15alc Dinner £8-£15alc Last dinner
10.30pm
Credit Cards ① ② ③ ⑤

___

WESTON-UNDER-REDCASTLE Shropshire Map 07 SJ52

★★★53% **Hawkstone Park** SY4 5UY (1m E of A49 between
Shrewsbury & Whitchurch) (Best Western)
☎Lee Brockhurst(093924)611 Telex no 35793
FAX (093924) 311
*A paradise for golfers, with a choice of two 18-hole courses as well
as other sporting activities. Within the hotel there is a choice of
dining places – a traditional restaurant and 'Caspians' bistro.*
43⇨↑Annexe16⇨↑(10fb) CTV in all bedrooms ® T
✖ (ex guide dogs)
⋒ CTV 250P ✢ CFA ⩰ ▶ 18 ♪ (grass) ♩ snooker sauna
solarium gymnasium croquet games room
⍟ ⍟ Last dinner 9pm
Credit Cards ① ② ③ ⑤

___

WEST RUNTON Norfolk Map 09 TG14

★★★65% **Links Country Park Hotel & Golf Club** Sandy Ln
NR27 9QH ☎(026375)691 FAX (026375) 8264
*Standing in 35-acre grounds which include its own popular 9-hole
golf course, and enjoying magnificent views from its position behind
the village, the hotel offers comfortable accommodation which
includes a variety of family rooms all equipped with*

satellite television channels. *More health conscious guests will choose to make use of the tennis court, swimming pool, sauna and solarium (free of charge to residents), and a choice of bars and restaurants is available.*
22⇥🏠Annexe10⇥ CTV in all bedrooms Ⓡ T
sB&B⇥🟰£52-£72 dB&B⇥🟰£104-£154 (incl dinner) ⊟
Lift ℂ 150P ✿ CFA ▣(heated) ▶9 ♬ (hard) sauna solarium
*xmas*
🍴 English & French V ◊ ⌷ Lunch £10.95&alc High tea
£1.50-£4 Dinner £14.95&alc Last dinner 9.30pm
Credit Cards ① ③

---

## WESTWARD HO! Devon Map 02 SS42

★★63% **Culloden House** Fosketh Hill EX39 1JA
☎Bideford(0237)479421
Closed Nov-Feb
*Commanding an excellent view of the bay, a family-run hotel offers comfortable, modern bedrooms, a good lounge with separate bar, an attractive dining room and friendly, personal service ; it is particularly popular for golfing holidays, having a choice of local courses.*
9rm(2⇥5🟰)(2fb) CTV in all bedrooms sB&B£30-£40
sB&B⇥🟰£30-£40 dB&B£55-£65 dB&B⇥🟰£58-£70
CTV 9P 🚗 ✿
V ◊ ⌷
Credit Cards ① ③

---

## WEST WITTON North Yorkshire Map 07 SE08

★★68% **Wensleydale Heifer Inn** DL8 4LS (Consort)
☎Wensleydale(0969)22322 FAX (0969) 24183
*Situated on the main road, the A684, through beautiful Wensleydale, this 17th century inn provides accommodation in the main building and in 2 adjacent houses – 'The Old Reading Room' and 'East View House'. All rooms are attractively decorated, comfortable and are very well equipped. A cosy, chintzy lounge with an open fire, original beams and a similar bar provide the traditional ambiance of the Coaching Inn. Freshly cooked and interesting food is the highlight of a stay here, served in the elegant candlelit dining room. The hotel is family owned, with a young, pleasant staff.*
9⇥🟰Annexe10⇥🟰(1fb)3🖾 CTV in all bedrooms Ⓡ T
sB&B⇥🟰£45 dB&B⇥🟰£60-£80 ⊟
25P *xmas*
V ◊ ⌷ Lunch fr£9.50 Dinner fr£17.50 Last dinner 9.30pm
Credit Cards ① ② ③ ⑤ ⑥
**See advertisement under LEYBURN**

---

## WETHERAL Cumbria Map 12 NY45

★★★66% **Crown** CA4 8ES (Shire) ☎(0228)61888
Telex no 64175 FAX (0228) 61637
*Situated in a charming village, this former 18th-century inn has been extended and carefully modernised to provide comfortable and well-appointed bedrooms with conference facilities and a leisure complex. The young staff are friendly and attentive and the conservatory restaurant is an attractive setting for enjoyable meals.*
49⇥(6fb)1🖾✂in 13 bedrooms CTV in all bedrooms Ⓡ T ⊟
ℂ CTV 80P ✿ CFA ▣(heated) squash snooker sauna solarium
gymnasium spa pool *xmas*
🍴 English & French V ◊ ⌷ ✂
Credit Cards ① ② ③ ⑤
**See advertisement on page 723**

★65% **Killoran** The Green CA4 8ET ☎(0228)60200
*Set at the centre of the pleasant village, overlooking the River Eden from its own grounds, this friendly little hotel is a popular eating place, its attractive bar and restaurant offering a wide range of home-cooked meals at both lunch and dinner. Lounge facilities are limited, but bedrooms are generally spacious and comfortable.* ▶

---

# BATCH FARM
# COUNTRY HOTEL
## AA ★★
### LYMPSHAM, Nr WESTON-SUPER-MARE
### SOMERSET   (0934) 750371
**Proprietors: Mr & Mrs D. J. Brown**

A family run hotel with a long reputation for friendly atmosphere and excellent traditional English food, à la carte menus also available. Delightfully situated in own grounds, panoramic views from all rooms. 5 miles Weston-super-Mare. 5 miles Burnham-on-Sea. Fishing in river. Fully licensed lounge bar. All bedrooms are en suite and have colour TV and tea making facilities. Ample parking, games room. Egon Ronay/Ashley Courtenay recommended.

---

## AA ★★★
### THE *Royal Pier* HOTEL

Birnbeck Road, Weston-Super-Mare
Avon BS23 2EJ Telephone (0934) 626644

### WE LOOK FORWARD TO THE
### PLEASURE OF YOUR COMPANY!

The Royal Pier Hotel is a three star hotel, open all year, managed by resident proprietors. In an unrivalled position on the water's edge, most bedrooms and public rooms have magnificent views of the Bay and Channel. An ongoing programme of refurbishment has produced a high standard of comfort, service and decor, with the majority of bedrooms en suite, and all with colour TV, radio and telephone.

Fully licensed, there are two bars – the renamed luxurious 'Kennedys' or the more informal Prince Consort Bar which also serves a wide selection of bar food. The excellent restaurant offers a choice of food and menus, complemented by a well stocked cellar. Two function rooms are available and ample parking is adjacent. Tariffs including Winter Weekends, Christmas etc., are available.

**W**

10rm(2fb) CTV in 6 bedrooms TV in 4 bedrooms ® S%
sB&B£21.25-£25 dB&B£37-£40
CTV 70P ✿
♥ English & Continental V ✿ ⚖ S% Lunch £2-£8.50 High tea
£3-£6 Dinner £2-£12.50&alc Last dinner 10pm
Credit Cards ① ③ ⓔ

✗**Fantails** The Green CA4 8ET ☎(0228)60239
*A delightful small and friendly restaurant housed in a converted
17th-century hayloft overlooking the village green. There is an
interesting à la carte menu and a vegetarian menu, both of which
are complemented by a well-balanced wine list.*
Closed Sun
♥ English & French V 70 seats Lunch £12.50-£25alc Dinner
£12.50-£25alc Last lunch 2pm Last dinner 9.30pm 15P ✂
Credit Cards ① ③

### WETHERBY West Yorkshire Map 08 SE44

★★★ 🏨 WOOD HALL
Trip Ln, Linton LS22 4JA
(Select) ☎(0937)67271
FAX (0937) 64353

*This palatial Yorkshire
mansion lies just west of the
old market town of
Wetherby, overlooking the
village of Linton from its extensive grounds. Guests are drawn
to it, not only for its setting and elegant, luxurious
accommodation, but also for the warm and hospitable
treatment they receive from staff and management alike.
Drawing room, oak-panelled bar, billiard room and dining
room reinforce the country-house atmosphere, and Chef David
Woolfall presents diners with a selection of delectable dishes
to round off the sense of well-being. Dinner may start with a
confit of leg of duck with a cassis sauce, to be followed by
calves liver with a mustard sauce and braised wild rice, or
escalope of salmon poached in Beaujolais and finished with
cream, parsley and Sevruga caviar. The outstanding wine list
contains many fine vintages.*
16⇨✿Annexe6⇨✿1⚕✂in 4 bedrooms CTV in all
bedrooms T sB&B⇨✿£85-£105 dB&B⇨✿£105-£115 �🅟
《 CTV 70P ✿ ♪ snooker *xmas*
♥ British & French ✿ ⚖ ✂ Lunch fr£14.95 Dinner
fr£29.50&alc Last dinner 9.30pm
Credit Cards ① ② ③ ④ ⑤

★★★76% **Linton Spring Country House** Sickling Hall Rd
LS22 4AF ☎(0937)65353 FAX (0937) 67579
Closed 1-8 Jan
*This delightful country house, situated about two miles west of the
town centre, guarantees a tranquil stay. The new bedrooms are
elegant and comfortable and are provided with many little extras.
The restaurant has been open for some time and has earned a good
reputation for fine cuisine and friendly service.*
12rm(10⇨✿)2⚕ CTV in all bedrooms T ✖ (ex guide dogs) ✱
sB&B£90-£150 sB&B⇨✿£90-£150 dB&B⇨✿£110-£150
《 55P ⚕ ✿ nc5yrs
V ✿ Lunch £12.45 Dinner £22-£28alc Last dinner 9.30pm
Credit Cards ① ② ③ ⑤

★★★57% **Penguin** Leeds Rd LS22 5HE (junc A1/A58)
☎(0937)63881 Telex no 556428 FAX (0937) 580062
*A modern hotel with good facilities, bars and restaurants, the
Penguin is conveniently situated near to the A1.*

72⇨✿(2fb)✂in 8 bedrooms CTV in all bedrooms ® T ✱
S10% sB⇨✿£63-£65 dB⇨✿£78-£80 (room only) �🅟
《 150P ✿ ♪ *xmas*
V ✿ ⚖ ✂ S10% Lunch £8-£8.50 Dinner £10-£30alc Last
dinner 9.45pm
Credit Cards ① ② ③ ⑤ ⓔ

### WETHERSFIELD Essex Map 05 TL73

✗ ✗**Dicken's** The Green CM7 4BS
☎Great Dunmow(0371)850723
*Chef patron John Dickens, a head chef in the Channel Islands for
five years, has brought to this restaurant professional cooking skills
and a flair for distinctive menu composition, with imaginative
French recipes. Foie Gras terrine with home-made brioche, ravioli
or crab with corriander, fillet of beef with wild mushroom sauté,
supreme of salmon with herbs and fricassée of chicken with wild
morel and home-made noodles have all been recommended by our
Inspectors. Maria Dickens provides very attentive and friendly
service.*
Closed Mon & 3 wks in Feb
Lunch not served Sat
Dinner not served Sun
♥ English & French V 45 seats ✱ Lunch fr£11.75 Dinner
£21-£25alc Last lunch 2pm Last dinner 9.30pm 11P
Credit Cards ① ③

### WEYBOURNE Norfolk Map 09 TG14

★★59% **Maltings** NR25 7SY (Consort) ☎(026370)731
Telex no 57515
*Situated in the heart of the village half a mile from the sea this
hotel provides well equipped accommodation and a warm and
friendly atmosphere. A good choice of dishes is available in the
attractive restaurant and the Retreat bar/buttery is popular with
both visitors and residents.*
11⇨✿Annexe11rm(7⇨2✿)(3fb)2⚕ CTV in all bedrooms
sB&B⇨✿£35-£40 dB&B⇨✿£54-£60 �🅟
150P ✿ *xmas*
♥ International V ✿ ⚖ Lunch fr£5 Dinner fr£15&alc Last
dinner 9pm
Credit Cards ① ② ③ ⑤

### WEYBRIDGE Surrey

See **LONDON** plan 1*A1*(page 426)
★★★64% **Ship Thistle** Monument Green KT13 8BQ (Mount
Charlotte (TS)) ☎(0932)848364 Telex no 894271
FAX (0932) 857153
*A friendly hotel offers comfortable, well-appointed bedrooms,
relaxing bar and lounge areas and an elegant restaurant serving
both à la carte and table d'hôte meals.*
39⇨✿ CTV in all bedrooms ® T ✱ sB⇨✿fr£79
dB⇨✿fr£90 (room only) �🅟
《 50P 20🚗 ✿ ♪
♥ International ✿ ⚖ ✂ Lunch fr£9.95&alc Dinner
fr£13.75&alc Last dinner 10pm
Credit Cards ① ② ③ ④ ⑤

### WEYMOUTH Dorset Map 03 SY69

★★66% **Streamside** 29 Preston Rd DT3 6PX
☎Preston(0305)833121
*This privately owned mock Tudor hotel has a friendly, informal
atmosphere and offers small but well-appointed bedrooms and
comfortable public rooms.*
15rm(10⇨1✿)(4fb) CTV in all bedrooms ® T sB&B£34-£38
sB&B⇨✿£38-£45 dB&B£48-£55 dB&B⇨✿£56-£64 �🅟
35P ✿ games room
♥ English & French V ✿ ⚖ Lunch £10-£26alc Dinner
£10.50&alc Last dinner 9.30pm
Credit Cards ① ② ③ ⑤ ⓔ

★★63% **Hotel Rex** 29 The Esplanade DT4 8DN
☎(0305)760400 FAX (0305) 760300
Closed Xmas
*A family holiday hotel overlooking the seafront has been extended
to provide some modern, well-equipped bedrooms. Guests are
assured of efficient service from friendly helpful staff.*
31⇄👗(5fb)1📺 CTV in all bedrooms ® T ✳
sB&B⇄👗£32-£40 dB&B⇄👗£52-£72 🍴
Lift ( CTV 6🎮 (£1 per night)
🖤 International V ♦ ♫ Dinner fr£6.50&alc Last dinner
10.30pm
Credit Cards 1 2 3 ①

★★62% **Glenburn** 42 Preston Rd DT3 6PZ (3m NE A353)
☎Preston(0305)832353
Closed 25 Dec-1 Jan
*Situated away from the noise and bustle of the town centre, this
family-run hotel caters for both holidaymakers and business users ;
its atmosphere is friendly, bedrooms are neat and very clean, and
regular dinner dances are held in the dining room.*
13rm(5⇄7👗)(1fb) CTV in all bedrooms ® ✖ sB&B⇄👗fr£30
dB&B⇄👗fr£57 🍴
30P 🚗 ✿ ♫ nc3 yrs
V ♦ ♫ Lunch fr£4.50 Dinner fr£12 Last dinner 8.30pm
Credit Cards 1 3

★★61% **Crown** 51-52 St Thomas St DT4 8EQ ☎(0305)760800
FAX (0305) 760300
Closed 25-26 Dec
*Centrally situated on the town's complicated one-way system, a
busy coaching hotel of imposing appearance offers good value
accommodation with comfortable bedrooms and simple fare.*
79rm(43⇄10👗)(12fb) ® ✖ (ex guide dogs) sB&B£23-£26
sB&B⇄👗£26-£28.50 dB&B£42-£46 dB&B⇄👗£47-£51 🍴

▶

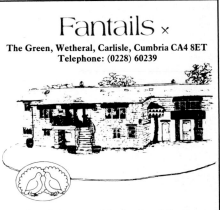

**W**

Lift ( CTV 8🛏 (£1) CFA
V ✿ Sunday Lunch £4.95-£6 Dinner £5.95-£8 Last dinner 8pm
Credit Cards 1 2 3 5 £

★★54% **Hotel Prince Regent** 139 The Esplanade DT4 7NR
(Consort) ☎(0305)771313 Telex no 94011219
Closed 24 Dec-3 Jan
*The attractive dining room of this sea front resort hotel offers both
table d'hôte and à la carte menus of well-prepared dishes, whilst its
popular bar and coffee shop are open throughout the day during the
season. Bedrooms are simply appointed but adequately equipped,
and a friendly staff provides helpful service.*
50rm(37⇨8♠)(25fb) CTV in all bedrooms ® T ✹
sB&Bfr£39.50 sB&B⇨♠fr£49.50 dB&Bfr£56
dB&B⇨♠fr£66 ☐
Lift ( 5P 14🛏 CFA
♀ English & French V ✿ ⚑ ✗ Dinner £11.75-£12.75 Last
dinner 8.30pm
Credit Cards 1 2 3 5

★62% **Alexandra** 27/28 The Esplanade DT4 8DN
☎(0305)785767
*This friendly and relaxing hotel has been attractively upgraded,
with the public areas and first and second floor bedrooms receiving
attention. The bar lounge is spacious and comfortable and
wholesome, simple meals are served in the dining room.*
20rm(5⇨9♠)(4fb) CTV in 14 bedrooms ® ✳ sB&B£15-£20
sB&B⇨♠£17.50-£24.50 dB&B£30-£40 dB&B⇨♠£35-£49 ☐
7P xmas
V ✿ ⚑ Lunch fr£5.50
Credit Cards 1 3

---

**WHATTON** Nottinghamshire Map **08** SK73

★★63% **The Haven** Grantham Rd NG13 9EU ☎(0949)50800
*A privately-owned, family-run hotel on the A52 midway between
Nottingham and Grantham. It offers comfortable modern
bedrooms, a popular function suite and friendly attentive service.*
17⇨♠(3fb)3❋ CTV in all bedrooms ® T ✳
sB&B⇨♠£22-£30 dB&B⇨♠£40-£45
70P ♨ ✿
V ✿ ⚑ Lunch £10-£26alc High tea £4-£6.20 Dinner
£5-£10&alc Last dinner 9.45pm
Credit Cards 1 2 3

---

**WHEATLEY** Oxfordshire Map **04** SP50

◯**Travelodge** London Rd(Trusthouse Forte)
☎Central reservations (0800) 850950
24⇨

---

**WHEDDON CROSS** Somerset Map **03** SS93

★★♨68% **Raleigh Manor** TA4 7BB
☎Timberscombe(0643)841484
Closed Nov-Feb
*Situated on the A396 north of the village crossroads, this small
Victorian country house enjoys splendid views of Snowdrop Valley
and Grabbist Hill. There are two comfortable lounges and an
elegant dining room, where home-cooked food is served. Good-
sized bedrooms, some with antique furnishings, provide modern
facilities. Run by resident proprietors, the hotel has a friendly
atmosphere and offers very good value for money.*
7⇨♠1⚑ CTV in all bedrooms ® sB&B⇨♠£35-£38
dB&B⇨♠£70-£90 (incl dinner)
8P ♨ ✿
✿ ⚑ ✗ Dinner £13-£15 Last dinner 8pm
Credit Cards 3 £

---

**WHICKHAM** Tyne & Wear Map **12** NZ26
See also Newcastle upon Tyne

★★68% **Gibside Arms** Front St NE16 4JG ☎091-488 9292
FAX 091-488 8000
*A hotel offering comfortable modern accommodation, interesting
menus and friendly service.*
13⇨♠(2fb) CTV in all bedrooms ® T ✹ (ex guide dogs)
sB&B⇨♠£44-£54 dB&B⇨♠£59-£69 ☐
Lift ( 20P 10🛏 xmas
♀ English & French V ✿ ⚑ Lunch £9.95&alc High tea fr£1.50
Dinner £12.50&alc Last dinner 10pm
Credit Cards 1 2 3 5

---

**WHIMPLE** Devon Map **03** SY09

★★♨76% **Woodhayes** EX5 2TD ☎(0404)822237
*Conveniently situated between Exeter and Honiton near the cider
apple village of Whimple, this fine Georgian house is managed by
the friendly and enthusiastic Rendle family. The charming public
rooms include two comfortable lounges and a pretty dining room
with polished mahogany tables. Bedrooms are, in general, spacious
and comfortably furnished, offering modern facilities whilst still
retaining much of their original character.*
6rm(5⇨) CTV in all bedrooms ✹ S10% sB&B⇨£55
dB&B⇨£75 ☐
20P 2🛏 ♨ ✿ ⚑ (grass) croquet nc12yrs xmas
♀ English & French V Lunch £14 High tea £5 Dinner £19.50
Last dinner 9.30pm
Credit Cards 1 2 3 5

---

**WHITBY** North Yorkshire Map **08** NZ81

★★68% **Saxonville** Ladysmith Av, (Off Argyle Road)
YO21 3HX ☎(0947)602631
Closed mid Oct-mid May
*A pleasant and friendly family-run hotel, offering good food and
value for money.*
24⇨♠(3fb) CTV in all bedrooms ® T ✹ (ex guide dogs) S%
sB&B⇨♠fr£27.50 dB&B⇨♠fr£55
20P
✿ Bar Lunch fr95palc Dinner fr£11.50&alc Last dinner
8.30pm
Credit Cards 1 2 3 £

★★67% **Sneaton Hall** Beacon Way, Sneaton YO22 5HP (3m S
B1416) ☎(0947)605929
*Situated in a peaceful village, just south of Whitby, this is a
friendly family-run hotel in an elegant Georgian house.*
8⇨♠(2fb) CTV in all bedrooms ® sB&B⇨♠£22.50-£29
dB&B⇨♠£40-£45 ☐
30P ♨
V ✿ ⚑ Lunch fr£6.50 Dinner £10-£13 Last dinner 8.30pm
Credit Cards 1 3

★★65% **Larpool Hall Country House** Larpool Ln YO22 4ND
☎(0947)602737
*This elegant Georgian mansion house is rich in local history. It
stands in 10 acres of beautiful gardens and woodland and offers
lovely views all round. Well furnished in all areas, it offers good
comforts and peaceful surroundings. Very attentive service is
provided by the resident owner, and a good standard of cooking is
served in the pleasant dining room.*
10⇨♠(1fb)♨ CTV in all bedrooms ® T ✹ (ex guide dogs)
✳ sB&B⇨♠£28-£32.50 dB&B⇨♠£50-£70 ☐
CTV 40P ✿ xmas
♀ English & Continental V ✿ ⚑ ✗ Lunch £2.95-£7.50alc
Dinner £11.95-£15.95 Last dinner 9pm
Credit Cards 1 3

---

For key to symbols see the inside front cover.

★★65% **White House** Upgang Lane, West Cliff YO21 3JJ
☎(0947)600469
*Situated just off the A174, next to the Golf Club, and commanding fine views over Sandsend Bay, this family-run hotel provides comfortable accommodation and a friendly ambience.*
12rm(7⇨4♠)(3fb) CTV in all bedrooms ® T
sB&B£16.50-£18.50 sB&B⇨♠£20.50-£22.50
dB&B⇨♠£41-£43 🛋
CTV 50P ✿ ⅋ xmas
♀ English & French V ✿ Sunday Lunch fr£5.95 Dinner
fr£9.50&alc Last dinner 10pm
Credit Cards ①③

★★64% **Stakesby Manor** Manor Close, High Stakesby
YO21 1HL ☎(0947)602773
*A comfortable, converted old manor house where good value dinners are especially recommended.*
8⇨♠ CTV in all bedrooms ® T ✖ (ex guide dogs)
sB&B⇨♠£34.50 dB&B⇨♠£49.50-£52 🛋
40P ⊞ ✿ ⅋
♀ International V ✿ ⅃ Lunch £10.90-£35 Dinner £10.90-£35
Last dinner 9.30pm
Credit Cards ①③ ⓔ

---

**WHITCHURCH** Shropshire Map **07** SJ54

★★★62% **Terrick Hall Country** Hill Valley SY13 4JZ (off A49
NE of town centre) (Minotels) ☎(0948)3031
*A country house style of hotel that has strong links with the adjacent golf course. It is set in four acres of grounds with an ornamental pool and hard tennis court.*
10⇨Annexe7⇨♠(7fb) CTV in all bedrooms ® T ✱ S%
sB&B⇨♠£28.50-£32.50 dB&B⇨♠£45-£49
CTV 50P ✿ ▶9 ℘ (hard) squash snooker sauna
♀ International V ✿ ⅃ Lunch fr£7.45&alc Dinner
fr£9.45&alc Last dinner 9pm
Credit Cards ①②③⑤

★★★56% **Dodington Lodge** Dodington SY13 1EN (Inter-
Hotels) ☎(0948)2539
*This roadside hotel situated at the junction of the A41 and A49 is also popular with the locals who make full use of the small function room for wedding receptions and private meetings.*
10rm(9⇨♠)(2fb)1⊞ CTV in all bedrooms ® T ✱
sB&B⇨♠fr£37.50 dB&Bfr£47.50 dB&B⇨♠fr£47.50 🛋
⟨70P ✿ xmas
V ✿ ⅃ S% Sunday Lunch fr£5.95 Dinner fr£9.75&alc Last
dinner 9.30pm
Credit Cards ①③

★★★64% **Redbrook Hunting Lodge** Wrexham Rd SY13 3ET
(Inter-Hotels) ☎Redbrook Maelor(094873)204 & 533
*An early eighteenth-century hunting lodge, set at the junction of the A495 and A525 about two-and-a-half miles west of Whitchurch, offers well-equipped bedrooms which are equally suitable for tourists or businessmen and a useful function room.*
13⇨♠(3fb)2⊞ CTV in all bedrooms ® sB&B⇨♠fr£40
dB&B⇨♠fr£55 🛋
100P ✿
♀ English & French V ✿ ⅃ Lunch fr£7&alc Dinner
fr£9.25&alc Last dinner 9pm
Credit Cards ①②③ⓔ

Hotels with a high percentage rating for quality
are highlighted by a % across their
gazetteer entry.

**WHITEBRIDGE** Highland *Inverness-shire* Map **14** NH41

★★

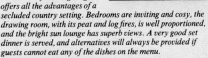

★★ 😊 **KNOCKIE LODGE**
IV1 2UP (Pride of Britain)
☎Gorthleck(04563)276
Closed 30 Oct-29 Apr
*From its eyrie high above Loch Nan Lann, this former 18th-century hunting lodge offers all the advantages of a secluded country setting. Bedrooms are inviting and cosy, the drawing room, with its peat and log fires, is well proportioned, and the bright sun lounge has superb views. A very good set dinner is served, and alternatives will always be provided if guests cannot eat any of the dishes on the menu.*
10⇨♠ T sB&B⇨♠fr£75
dB&B⇨♠£120-£160 (incl dinner)
20P ⊞ ✿ ⅃ snooker sailing nc10yrs
Dinner fr£20 Last dinner 8pm
Credit Cards ①②③⑤

★★62% **Whitebridge** IV1 2UN (Exec Hotel)
☎Gorthleck(04563)226
Closed 21 Dec-Feb
*Situated nine miles from Fort Augustus, this roadside hotel has been much improved over the past few years, and friendly, informal services are provided by the Campbell family.*
12rm(10⇨♠)(3fb) CTV in all bedrooms ® sB&B£22-£27
sB&B⇨♠£25-£30 dB&B£34-£46 dB&B⇨♠£40-£50
▶

**W**

725

30P 2☎ (50p) ⌘ ✿ ♪
✧ ☒ Bar Lunch £5-£10alc Dinner fr£12.50 Last dinner 9pm
Credit Cards ①②③⑤ ⓔ

---

**WHITEBROOK** Gwent Map 03 SO50

★★65% **Crown at Whitebrook** NP5 4TX (Exec Hotel)
☎Monmouth(0600)860254 FAX (0600) 860607
Closed 2wks in Jan
*This pleasant "restaurant with rooms" stands in a quiet wooded valley, yet conveniently near major roads, and offers small comfortable bedrooms and an attractive restaurant and bar.*
12➪♠1⌘ CTV in all bedrooms ® T sB&B➪♠£55-£60
dB&B➪♠£100-£110 (incl dinner) ⊟
40P ⌘ ✿
♀ French V ⊁ Lunch £11.75 Dinner £21.50-£24 Last dinner 9.30pm
Credit Cards ①②③④⑤ ⓔ

---

**WHITING BAY**

See Arran, Isle of

---

**WHITLAND** Dyfed Map 02 SN21

★★★⚑62% **Waungron Country Mansion** SA34 0QX (off B4328)
☎(0994)240232
*Standing in an elevated position over the village this small hotel is run by the friendly Phillips family. Bedrooms, although compact in size, are well equipped and modern, whilst lounges and bars are warm and relaxing. Function facilities are available.*
9➪♠ CTV in all bedrooms T
50P 10☎ ✿ ♪ ♨
V ✧ ☒
Credit Cards ①③

---

**WHITLEY BAY** Tyne & Wear Map 12 NZ37

★★63% **Holmedale** 106 Park Av NE26 1DN ☎091-251 3903 & 091-253 1162 FAX 091-297 0278
*A friendly, family-run hotel on a corner site convenient for both the town and seafront. Most of the well-equipped bedrooms have en suite facilities.*
18rm(7➪9♠)(3fb)1⌘ CTV in all bedrooms ® T
sB&B➪♠£24-£45 dB&B➪♠£34-£55 ⊟
CTV 10P pool table
♀ English & Continental Dinner £6.95-£10&alc Last dinner 8pm
Credit Cards ①②③⑤ ⓔ

★★63% **Windsor** South Pde NE25 8UT ☎091-252 3317 FAX 091-297 0272
Closed 25 Dec
*A recently extended and modernised hotel, offering well-equipped bedrooms designed for the business traveller, and tastefully appointed public rooms.*
55rm(38➪5♠)(14fb) CTV in all bedrooms ® T ⊟
Lift ⓒ CTV 25P 2☎ xmas
♀ European V ✧ ☒ Lunch £9-£10 High tea £6-£9 Dinner £10-£15 Last dinner 9.30pm
Credit Cards ①②③⑤ ⓔ

★57% **Park Lodge Hotel** 160-164 Park Av NE26 1AO
☎091-253 0288 & 091-252 6879 FAX 091-297 1006
*A cheerful, mainly commercial hotel under the personal supervision of the resident proprietress. Situated a short distance from the sea front and within easy reach of the town centre.*
16rm(5➪6♠)(1fb) CTV in all bedrooms ® T � ✳ sB&Bfr£20
sB&B➪♠fr£35 dB&B➪♠fr£55
CTV 8P ⌘ snooker solarium gymnasium nc
✧ ♪ ⊁ Dinner £15 Last dinner 9.30pm
Credit Cards ①③⑤

---

★56% **Cavendish** 51 Esplanade NE26 2AS ☎091-253 3010
*Simple seaside hotel managed by proprietors and his family.*
11rm(5➪1♠)(2fb) CTV in all bedrooms ® ✳
sB&B£17.50-£22.50 sB&B➪♠£22.50 dB&B➪♠£35
CTV 12P
V Sunday Lunch £5.95 Dinner £7.95&alc Last dinner 9.30pm
Credit Cards ①③

---

**WHITTINGTON** Shropshire Map 07 SJ33

★63% **Ye Olde Boot Inn** SY11 4DG (Frederic Robinson)
☎Oswestry(0691)662250
*Standing beside a busy road, yet having views of castle ruins and the village duck pond, a small inn provides comfortable accommodation complemented by a popular bar and restaurant.*
6➪(2fb) CTV in all bedrooms ® ✖ (ex guide dogs) ✳
sB&B➪fr£19 dB&B➪fr£34.50 ⊟
100P
V ✧ ☒ Lunch £4.75 Dinner fr£7.50
Credit Cards ①③

---

**WICK** Highland *Caithness* Map 15 ND35

★★58% **Mackay's** Union St KW1 5ED ☎(0955)2323
Closed 1-2 Jan
*Improvements are gradually being made to this long established family owned commercial hotel. Situated in the town centre beside the River Wick it offers functional, well equipped accommodation and friendly service.*
26rm(23➪1♠)(4fb) CTV in all bedrooms ® T ⊟
Lift ⓒ CTV 12P ⌘
V ✧ ⊁
Credit Cards ①③

---

**WICKHAM** Hampshire Map 04 SU51

✤★★73%**Old House** The Square PO17 5JG ☎(0329)833049 FAX (0329) 833672
Closed 10 days Xmas, 2 wks Etr & 2 wks Jul/Aug RS Mon-Fri
*A charming small hotel standing in the square at the heart of this conservation village. The restaurant is of particular note where chef Nick Harman cooks in the French Regional style using fresh produce, simply presented, with dishes including terrine de volaille et ris de veau à la pistache, Saumon frais d'Ecosse au vinaigre de xérès et terrine au trois chocolats au coulis de cassis.*
9➪♠Annexe3➪♠ (1fb) CTV in all bedrooms ® T ✖ S10%
sB&B➪♠fr£70 dB&B➪♠fr£90
12P ⌘
♀ French V S10% Lunch fr£25alc Dinner fr£25alc Last dinner 9.30pm
Credit Cards ①②③⑤

---

**WICKHAM MARKET** Suffolk Map 05 TM35

✖*Bears* 56 Market Hill ☎(0728)747395
*Standing in the middle of the town's market place, this attractive restaurant emphasises the teddy bear theme in a profusion of paintings and prints. Its simple menu features good hearty food – a starter of meat balls in tomato sauce or rich lentil and bacon soup may be followed by chicken with pecan nut and stilton or pork, apple and cider pie, with good old Spotted Dick to follow.*
Lunch not served
V 50 seats
Credit Cards ①③

---

**WIDNES** Cheshire Map 07 SJ58

★★61% **Hill Crest** 75 Cronton Ln WA8 9AR ☎051-424 1616
Telex no 627098 FAX 051-495 1348
57➪♠(1fb) CTV in all bedrooms ® T ✳
sB&B➪♠£30.50-£40.50 dB&B➪♠£40.50-£62.50
Lift ⓒ 200P ⌘ ♫ xmas

**W**

♀ Continental ♦ ♫ Lunch fr£10.50 Dinner fr£10.50 Last dinner 10pm
Credit Cards 1 2 3 5

---

**WIGAN** Greater Manchester Map **07** SD50

★★★69% **Kilhey Court Hotel** Chorley Rd WN1 2XN (Best Western) ☎Standish(0257)472100 Telex no 67460
FAX (0257) 422401
(For full entry see Standish)

★★66% **Bellingham** 149 Wigan Ln WN1 2NB ☎(0942)43893
FAX (0942) 821027
*Recently extended and almost entirely rebuilt, the hotel is now a modern establishment which retains the traditional hospitality and service. All bedrooms now have ensuite facilities and are very well equipped.*
30⇄♪(4fb)2✠✠in 4 bedrooms CTV in all bedrooms ® T
✠ (ex guide dogs) sB&B⇄♪£35-£50 dB&B⇄♪£47-£60 ☒
Lift ( CTV 45P
♀ English & French V ♦ ♫ ✠ Lunch £5.95&alc Dinner £9.05-£11.95&alc Last dinner 9.45pm
Credit Cards 1 2 3 5 £

★★64% *Bel-Air* 236 Wigan Ln WM1 2NU ☎(0942)41410
FAX (0942) 43967
*Conveniently located a mile north of the town centre and close to the A49, this small, friendly hotel, personally run by the proprietors, offers a pleasant bar and lounge facilities as well as its compact but well appointed bedrooms.*
12⇄♪(3fb)1✠ CTV in all bedrooms ® T
CTV 12P
♀ English & Continental V ♦ ♫
Credit Cards 1 3

★★61% *Brocket Arms* Mesnes Rd WN1 2DD ☎(0942)46283
Telex no 628117
*Situated to the north of the town centre this privately owned commercial hotel offers traditional accommodation with two bars and a small restaurant. The hotel is also popular for weddings and functions.*
27⇄♪ CTV in all bedrooms ® ✠
( 60P
V ♦ Last dinner 9.30pm
Credit Cards 1 2 3 5

---

**WIGHT, ISLE OF** Map **04**

---

**BEMBRIDGE** Map **04** SZ68

★★58% **Birdham** 1 Steyne Rd PO35 5UH
☎Isle of Wight(0983)872875
Closed 24-26 Dec
*Small comfortable inn with good cuisine.*
14rm(12⇄)(5fb)✠in 4 bedrooms CTV in all bedrooms ®
sB&B£18 sB&B⇄£22 dB&B£36 dB&B⇄£44
( CTV 100P ✿ pool table petanque ♤
♀ Continental V ♦ ✠ Lunch £7.50-£12.50&alc Dinner £9-£12
Last dinner 10pm

---

**BONCHURCH** See **Bembridge**

---

**CHALE** Map **04** SZ47

★68% **Clarendon Hotel & Wight Mouse Inn** PO38 2HA
☎Isle of Wight(0983)730431
*Built in or around 1845 to bridge the gap between Casey's Cottage and the historic White Mouse, the hotel now offers a choice of comfortable, family-style bedrooms, extensive bar meals and popular live entertainment, which, coupled with friendly service, ensures a pleasant and lively atmosphere. A link with the past is provided by the panelling in the bar, which was rescued from the wreck of the Varvassi.*

13rm(2⇄7♪)(9fb) CTV in all bedrooms ® sB&B£20-£24.15
sB&B⇄♪£20-£26.45 dB&B£40-£48.30 dB&B⇄♪£40-£52.90
CTV 200P ✿ ♫ ♤
♀ European V ♦ ♫ Lunch £3-£9alc High tea £3-£4alc Dinner £8.50-£16&alc Last dinner 10pm
£

---

**COWES** Map **04** SZ49

★★63% **Cowes** 260 Artic Rd PO31 7PJ
☎Isle of Wight(0983)291541 Telex no 86284
Closed 27 Dec-1 Jan
*A small, well-run hotel facing the River Medina and local wharfs complements modern, well equipped bedrooms with a very popular restaurant and bar; service is extensive, friendly and personally managed by the proprietors.*
15⇄♪(4fb) CTV in all bedrooms ✱ sB&B⇄♪£38-£50
dB&B⇄♪£53-£100 ☒
( 24P ♫ ✿ sauna
♀ English & French V ♦ ♫ Lunch £13.95-£16.95alc High tea fr£1.50 Dinner £13.95-£16.95&alc Last dinner 9.30pm
Credit Cards 1 2 3 5

★★55% *Fountain* High St PO31 7AN
☎Isle of Wight(0983)292397
*Located in West Cowes, alongside the Cowes Ferry and Hydrofoil Terminal and the Quay, this popular coaching inn is ideally placed for business travellers. Accommodation comprises well-equipped, modern bedrooms, the popular Henekey Restaurant and the lively Quayside Bar. Car parking can be difficult.*
20⇄ CTV in all bedrooms ® T ✠ (ex guide dogs)
♪ ♫
♀ European V ♦ ♫ Last dinner 10.30pm
Credit Cards 1 2 3 4 5

**W**

○**New Holmwood** Queens Rd, Egypt Point PO31 8BW
☎(0983)292508
Due to have opened Jul 1990
28rm

✗**Sullivan's** 10 Bath Rd, The Parade PO31 7QN
☎Isle of Wight(0983)297021
*Small cottage-style restaurant run by chef/patron, Michael Sullivan, formerly of the Café des Amis du Vin in Covent Garden, and his wife. The short menu features both new style and classical dishes. Fresh ingredients are prepared with care and flavours and clear and well defined.*
Lunch not served in winter except by prior arrangement
♀ French 42 seats ✻ Lunch £12-£16alc Dinner £12-£16alc Last lunch 3pm Last dinner 11pm ⨍
Credit Cards ⊡ ⊟

---

**FRESHWATER** Map **04** SZ38

★★★50% **Albion** PO40 9RA ☎Isle of Wight(0983)753631
FAX (0983) 755295
*This developing hotel stands in a unique sea-shore position, most of its bedroom having a balcony or terrace facing the sea; a new cocktail lounge has recently been added, and bedroom refurbishment is planned. Good standards of cooking are complemented by acceptable service, though management can be uneven.*
42rm(39⇨🛏)(28fb) CTV in all bedrooms ® T
sB&B⇨🛏£32.50 dB&B⇨🛏£62 🅿
《 CTV 75P ♨ xmas
♀ International V ♥ ⚷ S% Sunday Lunch £8.50 Dinner £15&alc Last dinner 9pm
Credit Cards ⊡⊡⊟⊠

---

**RYDE** Map **04** SZ59

★★★61% **Hotel Ryde Castle** The Esplanade PO33 1JA
☎Isle of Wight(0983)63755 Telex no 869466
FAX (0983) 616436
*An unusual castle-style building offering excellent sea views and an informal, relaxed atmosphere. Many of the comfortable bedrooms have four poster beds and are well-equipped with modern facilities. The restaurant, decorated to resemble the interior of a galleon, offers an interesting menu featuring French and English cuisine of a good standard.*
17⇨🛏7🛏⅌in 1 bedroom CTV in all bedrooms ® T
sB&B⇨🛏£49.50-£64.90 dB&B⇨🛏£65.90-£88 🅿
75P ♨
♀ English & French V ♥ ⚷ Lunch fr£7.95&alc Dinner fr£13.95&alc Last dinner 10pm
Credit Cards ⊡⊡⊟⊠

★★67% **Biskra House Beach** 17 St Thomas's St PO33 2DL
☎Isle of Wight(0983)67913
*An hotel with its own beach frontage on West Sands offers guests a choice of dining rooms including the popular Italian-style Bistro. Bedrooms – one boasting its own private balcony – have been thoughtfully furnished and very well equipped with every possible extra, whilst service is pleasant and the standard of cooking good.*
9⇨🛏 CTV in all bedrooms ® T 🛏 ✳
sB&B⇨🛏£29.50-£33.50 dB&B⇨🛏£47.50-£59.50 🅿
14P ♨
♀ French & Italian ♥ ⚷
Credit Cards ⊡⊟ ⓔ

---

**ST LAWRENCE** Map **04** SZ57

★★66% **Rocklands** PO38 1XH ☎Ventnor(0983)852964
Closed Nov-Apr
*Quietly situated in its own grounds, the hotel maintains impressive levels of hospitality and service and an adequate standard of cooking whilst slowly upgrading its old-fashioned accommodation; good facilities are available for snooker and croquet.*

16⇨🛏🗬Annexe5rm(4⇨🛏🗬)(9fb)1🛌 CTV in all bedrooms
🛏 (ex guide dogs) sB&B⇨🛏£32.20-£34.50
dB&B⇨🛏£64.40-£69
CTV 18P ✿ ≋(heated) snooker sauna solarium croquet ♧
♀ English & Continental V ♥ ⚷ Dinner £10-£11.50 Last dinner 8.15pm

★70% **The Lawyers Rest** Undercliff Dr PO38 1XF
☎Isle of Wight(0983)852610
Closed Nov RS Dec-Feb
*Looking across gardens to the sea from its fine position on a terraced hillside, this impressive and elegantly furnished house, built in 1840, boasts a relaxing drawing room and separate cocktail bar, complemented by a modern restaurant serving fine, freshly produced food and excellent wines. Bedrooms are individually furnished, some enjoying sea views, and friendly service is supervised by the proprietor.*
8⇨🛏 sB&B⇨🛏fr £33.35 dB&B⇨🛏fr £57.50
13P ♨ nc10yrs xmas
♀ International V ♥ ⚷ ⅟ Lunch £6.50-£12alc Dinner £13.50 Last dinner 7pm
Credit Cards ⊡⊡⊟⊠

---

**SANDOWN** Map **04** SZ58

★★★60% **Melville Hall** Melville St PO36 9DH
☎Isle of Wight(0983)406526
*A well-managed, family-run hotel, nestling in a quiet semi-rural setting yet close to all local amemities, is ideal for either short break or holiday. Accommodation comprises bright modern bedrooms, lounge, Coffee Shop, Buttery, Palm Court Restaurant and bar, service being friendly and informal throughout.*
33⇨🛏(11fb) CTV in all bedrooms ® 🛏 (ex guide dogs)
sB&B⇨🛏£33-£44 dB&B⇨🛏£66-£88 (incl dinner) 🅿
《 30P ✿ ≋(heated) 9 hole putting xmas
♀ English & Continental V ♥ ⚷ Sunday Lunch £6.50 Dinner £11.95&alc Last dinner 9.30pm
Credit Cards ⊡⊟ ⓔ

---

**SEAVIEW** Map **04** SZ69

✸★★74%**Seaview** High St PO34 5EX
☎Isle of Wight(0983)612711 FAX (0983) 613729
*The heart of this seaside hotel must be the dining room, where young chef Charles Bartlett produces unpretentious, but innovative cuisine, using mostly local produce and seafood. The rest of the hotel has charm too. Bedrooms are individually styled and thoughtfully provided with many extras, and a drawing room, coffee lounge and ward room are also available. The owners are Nicholas and Nicola Hayward, who personally supervise the extensive services.*
16⇨🛏(2fb) CTV in all bedrooms T sB&B⇨🛏£44-£63
dB&B⇨🛏£66-£73 🅿
12P ♨ xmas
♀ English & French V ♥ ⚷ ⅟ Lunch £14.85-£21.85alc Dinner £14.85-£21.85alc Last dinner 9.30pm
Credit Cards ⊡⊡⊟

---

**SHANKLIN** Map **04** SZ58

★★★58% **Cliff Tops** Park Rd PO37 6BB (Best Western)
☎Isle of Wight(0983)863262 FAX (0983) 867139
*Cliff Tops boasts a superb position with glorious sea views from the front bedrooms and balconies. There is a direct lift access to the beach below, and recent refurbishment has improved the accommodation and leisure facilities. There is a popular carvery restaurant and live bar entertainment most evenings.*
88⇨🛏(8fb) CTV in all bedrooms ® T
Lift 《 40P CFA ⊠(heated) snooker sauna solarium gymnasium steam room beautician hairdresser
V ♥ ⚷ Last dinner 10pm
Credit Cards ⊡⊡⊟⊠ ⓔ

**W**

★★★57% *Holliers* Church Rd, Old Village PO37 6NU
☎Isle of Wight(0983)862764
*Conveniently situated for the town centre and all local amenities, Holliers offers comfortable well-equipped bedrooms, several bars, pleasant restaurant and good indoor leisure facilities.*
37⇔ᶜ(7fb)3⊞ CTV in all bedrooms Ⓡ ✻
40P ⊡(heated) ⩴(heated) sauna solarium ♫
♦ ⚵ Last dinner 8.30pm
Credit Cards ①②③

★★68% *Fernbank* Highfield Rd PO37 6PP
☎Isle of Wight(0983)862790
Closed Xmas
*Set in an acre of well-tended, sheltered gardens enjoying country and woodland views from its peaceful location yet handy for the old village, the hotel offers friendly, relaxed service and good leisure facilities. The restaurant's table d'hôte menu is augmented by an à la carte dinner selection (except after 8pm on Sundays and Tuesdays).*
30⇔ᶜ(7fb)2⊞ CTV in all bedrooms Ⓡ T
sB&B⇔ᶜ£20.30-£28.70 dB&B⇔ᶜ£40.60-£57.40 ⼋
24P ✿ ⊡(heated) sauna solarium pool table whirlpool bath
nc7yrs
♡ English, French & Italian V ♦ ⚵ ⚹ Sunday Lunch £8.50
Dinner £8.50-£9.50&alc Last dinner 10.30pm
Credit Cards ①③ ④

For key to symbols see the inside front cover.

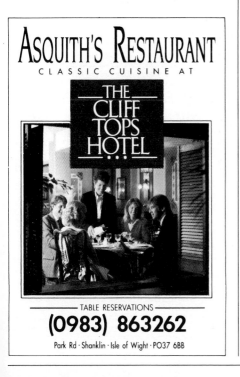
**W**

★★68% **Keats Green** 3 Queens Rd PO37 6AN
📞Isle of Wight(0983)862742
Closed mid Oct-Etr
*Enjoying a prime cliff top position close to the lift, and commanding panoramic views across the bay, this hotel provides accommodation in a choice of bedrooms furnished in the modern style, with generous public rooms. Service is efficient and the five course dinner menu offers good value for money.*
34rm(23⇨10↑)(3fb) CTV in all bedrooms ℝ T
sB&B⇨↑£22-£29 dB&B⇨↑£44-£60 (incl dinner) ⊟
34P ✿ ⌔(heated)
◊ Dinner £9 Last dinner 7.45pm
Credit Cards [1][3][£]

★★61% **Luccombe Hall** Luccombe Rd PO37 6RL (Exec Hotel)
📞Isle of Wight(0983)862719 FAX (0983) 867482
RS 1-25 Jan
*Overlooking the sea and Culver Down, Luccombe Hall is set in a quiet residential area. The comfortable bedrooms are complemented by excellent leisure facilities.*
30⇨↑(14fb)1⊟ CTV in all bedrooms ℝ T sB&B⇨↑£26-£33
dB&B⇨↑£52-£66 ⊟
CTV 30P ✿ ⌔(heated) ⌔(heated) ♪ (grass) squash sauna solarium gymnasium games room *xmas*
Ϙ English & Continental ✧ ⚌ ✔ Lunch £8-£9 Dinner
£13.25-£15 Last dinner 8.30pm
Credit Cards [1][3]

★★61% **Melbourne Ardenlea** Queen's Rd PO37 6AP
📞Isle of Wight(0983)862283
Closed Dec-Feb RS Mar & late Oct
*An ideal family hotel, there is a good choice of family bedrooms, and good leisure facilities. Excellent value for money.*
51⇨↑(9fb) CTV in all bedrooms ℝ sB&B⇨↑£18-£30
dB&B⇨↑£36-£60
Lift CTV 28P ✿ ⌔(heated) sauna solarium games room spa bath ♫ ⌔
Ϙ English & French V Bar Lunch £1.25-£5alc Dinner
£8-£10&alc Last dinner 8pm
Credit Cards [1][3][£]

★★61% **Shanklin Manor House** Manor Rd, Old Village
PO37 6QX 📞Isle of Wight(0983)862777
Closed Nov-mid Jan RS 24-28 Dec
*Set in four-and-a-half acres of grounds, and retaining much of its original Victorian atmosphere, this long-established, family-run holiday hotel features good leisure facilities as well as a choice of bedrooms furnished in modern style and well-appointed public areas which include an attractive dining room.*
38rm(21⇨12↑)(12fb) CTV in all bedrooms ℝ T
✖ (ex guide dogs) ✳ sB&B⇨↑£26-£29 dB&Bfrf£48
dB&B⇨↑£54 ⊟
50P ✿ ⌔(heated) ♪ (hard) sauna solarium gymnasium spa bath putting croquet jacuzzi nc6mths *xmas*
Ϙ English & French ✧ ⚌ Bar Lunch £2.20-£3.10 Dinner
£13.50 Last dinner 8.30pm

✖**La Petite Maison** 34 High St PO37 6JY
📞Isle of Wight(0983)863205
*A small French restaurant combines interesting à la carte French-style cuisine with some fresh fish and Italian dishes. Popular, value for money choices include the smoked trout mousse, fish bisque, Supreme of Chicken and Beef Wellington, all dishes are freshly cooked and well presented.*
Closed 1st 2 wks Nov & Jan
Ϙ Continental V 26 seats Lunch £6.20-£7&alc Dinner
£7.50-£10&alc Last lunch 2.30pm Last dinner 10.30pm ♪
Credit Cards [1][2][3][5]

1991 marks the 25th anniversary of this guide.

**TOTLAND BAY** Map **04** SZ38

★★63% **Sentry Mead** Madeira Rd PO39 0BJ
📞Isle of Wight(0983)753212
*This is a pleasant, cosy, personally-run hotel. The comfortable lounges are a feature here, and the newly-furnished bedrooms have modern facilities.*
12rm(8⇨2↑)(4fb) CTV in all bedrooms ℝ
CTV 10P ⚌ ✿ putting
Ϙ European ✧ ⚌ Last dinner 8pm
Credit Cards [2]

**VENTNOR** Map **04** SZ57

★★★62% **Ventnor Towers** Madeira Rd PO38 1QT (Consort)
📞Isle of Wight(0983)852277 Telex no 8951182
FAX (0983) 855536
*Commanding fine sea views from its cliff-top location, this upgraded, family-run hotel offers comfortable accommodation, a warm, friendly atmosphere and excellent outdoor sporting facilities.*
27rm(17⇨5↑)(4fb) CTV in all bedrooms ℝ
⟮ 40P 1✿ ✿ ⌔(heated) ♪ 9 ♪ (hard) croquet games room
Ϙ English & French V ✧ ⚌ ✔ Last dinner 8.30pm
Credit Cards [1][2][3][5]

★★**Highfield** Leeson Rd, Bonchurch PO38 1PU
📞Isle of Wight(0983)852800 & 854611
Closed Nov-Feb
*This charming Victorian house has a warm, friendly atmosphere and an attractive garden. Tastefully decorated and furnished, it provides good, comfortable accommodation and the resident proprietor/chef offers an interesting menu.*
12⇨↑(1fb)2⊟ CTV in all bedrooms ℝ
12P ⚌ ✿ nc5yrs
Ϙ English & French V ✧ ⚌ ✔ Last dinner 7.30pm
Credit Cards [1][3]

**WOOTTON** Map **04** SZ58

✖**Lugley's** Staplers Rd PO33 4RW 📞Isle of Wight(0983)882202
*Chef/proprietor Angela Hewitt's individual style and attention to detail is very evident – the short menu here includes local game, homemade breads and some of her own specialities, and portions are generous. Reservations are carefully timed to allow for everything being cooked 'à la minute'. The good food is complemented by the quiet country setting of this Edwardian house.*
Closed Sun (in winter), 2 wks Nov & 2 wks Apr
Lunch not served in winter (ex by prior arrangement)
16 seats Lunch £4.95&alc Dinner £17.45-£21.95alc Last lunch
1.30pm Last dinner 9.30pm 10P nc5yrs

**WIGTON** Cumbria Map **11** NY24

★★59% **Greenhill Lodge** Red Dial CA7 8LS (2m S off A595)
📞(06973)43304
*A family-owned and well-run hotel, originally an eighteenth-century mansion, which stands in its own grounds on the A595 at Red Dial offers comfortable standards and a good range of food.*
7⇨↑2⊟ CTV in all bedrooms ℝ T sB&B⇨↑£30-£33
dB&B⇨↑£44-£48 ⊟
100P ✿ nc *xmas*
Ϙ International V ✧ Lunch £5.95-£6.50 Dinner £15-£16.50
Last dinner 9pm
Credit Cards [1][3][£]

★★59% **Wheyrigg Hall** Wheyrigg CA7 0DH (4m NW on
B5302) 📞Abbeytown(06973)61242 FAX (06973) 61020
*This converted farmhouse is situated in rural surroundings on the B5302, 4 miles from Wigton. The hotel restaurant is open for lunch and dinner 7 days a week, and bar meals are available throughout*

*the day. Bedrooms have been well designed, the majority having full en suite facilities.*
6rm(2⇥3♠)(2fb) CTV in all bedrooms ® ➤ ✱ sB&Bfr£22
sB&B⇥♠fr£25 dB&B⇥♠fr£38 ♬
60P ✿ *xmas*
V ✿ ⚿ Lunch fr£5.40 Dinner fr£10.95 Last dinner 9pm
Credit Cards ①②③

---

**WILLERBY** Humberside Map **08** TA03

★★★75% **Grange Park** Main St HU10 6EA (Best Western)
☎Hull(0482)656488 Telex no 592773 FAX (0482) 655848
*Extensive leisure facilities and a creche are popular features of this very comfortable hotel. At mealtimes guests can choose between and intimate atmosphere in the French restaurant and the greater formality of the Italian restaurant, both offering very good value.*
109⇥♠4🖳 CTV in all bedrooms ® T S% sB⇥♠£41-£81
dB⇥♠£56-£92 (room only) ♬
Lift ⓒ ⊞ CTV 600P ✿ ◨(heated) sauna solarium gymnasium
hairdressing beauty clinic ♫ 🚴 *xmas*
♀ English, French & Italian V ✿ ⚿ S% Lunch £11.50&alc
High tea £5-£9.50alc Dinner £15&alc Last dinner 10.30pm
Credit Cards ①②③⑤
**See advertisement under HULL**

★★★69% **Willerby Manor** Well Ln HU10 6ER
☎Hull(0482)652616 Telex no 592629 FAX (0482) 653901
*This attractive old manor house has had two bedroom wings added, providing comfortable well-equipped rooms. Two restaurants offer good value for money.*
36⇥♠4🖳 CTV in all bedrooms ® T ✱ S% sB⇥♠£35-£59
dB⇥♠£45-£75 (room only) ♬
ⓒ 250P ✿ CFA ♫ *xmas*
♀ French V ✿ ⚿ S% Lunch £9&alc High tea £3.95 Dinner
£12.50&alc Last dinner 9.45pm
Credit Cards ①②③£
**See advertisement under HULL**

---

**WILLITON** Somerset Map **03** ST04

❋★★71%**White House** Long St TA4 4QW ☎(0984)32306 &
32777
Closed 6 Nov-16 May
(Rosette awarded for dinner only)
*The personal supervision of Kay and Dick Smith ensures a warm, friendly atmosphere at this attractive Georgian hotel. The bedrooms, some of which are in courtyard rooms, are thoughtfully equipped. The hotel is noted for its cuisine, which is predominantly English with some French dishes. The cooking has a welcome honesty and lack of pretention and the Smiths' interest in wine shows in the exceptionally good list.*
8rm(5⇥3♠)Annexe4⇥(1fb) CTV in all bedrooms T sB&B£29
sB&B⇥♠£33-£42 dB&B£51 dB&B⇥♠£60-£66 ♬
15P 🚗
♀ English & French ✂ Dinner £26 Last dinner 8.30pm
£

---

**WILMCOTE** Warwickshire Map **04** SP15

★★60% **Swan House** The Green CV37 9XJ
☎Stratford-upon-Avon(0789)67030 due to change to 267030
FAX (0789) 204875
Closed 24-28 Dec
*Standing just three miles from Stratford in the little village of Wilmcote, overlooking its green and Mary Arden's House, the hotel provides accommodation in simply furnished bedrooms with en suite facilities. The lounge bar is popular with tourists and locals alike, and there is a separate snooker room with full-size table.*
12⇥♠(1fb)🖳 CTV in all bedrooms ® ➤ (ex guide dogs)
sB&B⇥♠£32-£36 dB&B⇥♠£52-£65 ♬
40P ✿ snooker ♫

---

♀ English & French V ✿ ⚿ Lunch £5.30-£10.65 Dinner
£9-£17.80alc Last dinner 9.30pm
Credit Cards ①②③£
**See advertisement under STRATFORD-UPON-AVON**

---

**WILMSLOW** Cheshire Map **07** SJ88

See also **Manchester Airport**

❋★★★71%*Stanneylands* Stanneylands Rd SK9 4EY
☎(0625)525225 Telex no 8950511 FAX (0625)537282
RS 1 Jan & Good Fri
*Set in its own well-kept grounds and surrounded by farmland, yet not far from Manchester Airport, this attractive, family-managed hotel features a classical interior. The fine, oak-panelled dining room provides an ideal environment in which to enjoy your choice from the innovative short à la carte menu, the 'market special' or a table d'hôte 5-course dinner, dishes such as fillet of seabass cooked with ginger and roast Gressingham duck in a patchwork of puréed vegetables being backed up by an impressive wine list. All bedrooms are comfortable, well equipped and pleasantly decorated, though some are more compact than others.*
33⇥♠2🖳 CTV in all bedrooms ➤
ⓒ 80P 🚗 ✿
V ✿ ⚿ Last dinner 10pm
Credit Cards ①②③⑤
**See advertisement under MANCHESTER AIRPORT**

---

**WIMBORNE MINSTER** Dorset Map **04** SZ09

★★★57% **The King's Head** The Square BH21 1JA (Trusthouse
Forte) ☎(0202)880101 FAX (0202)881667
*This busy, country town hotel offers comfortable well-appointed public areas, an attractive restaurant with table d'hôte and à la carte menus, and well-equipped bedrooms of good size. Service is provided by friendly, willing staff.*
▶

**Leeson Road, Bonchurch, Ventnor, Isle of Wight PO38 1PV**

**★★**

**Telephone: (0983) 852800**

We extend to you a warm invitation to visit our attractive country house hotel which stands amid glorious gardens overlooking the sea in one of the prettiest corners of the Isle of Wight. The hotel is tastefully and attractively furnished and the ideal place to relax, enjoy good food prepared by our chef using only the finest ingredients.
**Resident proprietors: Dennis & Thelma Flaherty**

**W**

27⇨(1fb)⅛in 3 bedrooms CTV in all bedrooms ® ✳ S%
sB⇨£60-£65 dB⇨£75-£81 (room only) 🏥
Lift CTV 25P *xmas*
V ✿ ⅃⊑ ⅛ S% Lunch fr£8.20 Dinner £13.50-£18.35 Last dinner
9pm
Credit Cards 1 2 3 4 5

★★60% **Coach House Inn** Tricketts Cross BH22 9NW (Consort)
☎Ferndown(0202)861222 FAX (0202) 894130
(For full entry see Ferndown)

---

**WINCANTON** Somerset Map 03 ST72

★★♨63% **Holbrook House** Holbrook BA9 8BS ☎(0963)32377
Closed 31 Dec
*Popular for family holidays in the summer and quiet breaks away
in winter, this peaceful country house with extensive outdoor
leisure facilities has been owned by the same family for over 40
years. Some bedrooms are spacious with antique furnishings, but
the smaller top floor rooms are more modest. The foyer lounge and
very comfortable drawing room complement a Victorian-style
dining room. Any lack of modern amenities is fully compensated
for by the charming and courteous staff.*
20rm(8⇨8♠)(2fb) ® V ✗ (ex guide dogs) sB&B£38-£48
sB&B⇨♠£38-£48 dB&B£68-£72 dB&B⇨♠£68-£72 🏥
CTV 30P 4🏌 ≈🏊(heated) ♪ (hard & grass) squash
croquet table tennis *xmas*
V ✿ Lunch £8-£15 Dinner £13.50-£20 Last dinner 8.30pm
Credit Cards 1 2 3

---

**WINCHESTER** Hampshire Map 04 SU42

During the currency of this guide Winchester telephone
numbers are liable to change.
★★★★58% **The Wessex** Paternoster Row SO23 9LQ
(Trusthouse Forte) ☎(0962)61611 Telex no 47419
FAX (0962) 841503
*Conveniently located next to the Cathedral precinct, this modern
hotel offers a varied selection of bedrooms, equipped and furnished
to several different standards. For meals, guests can choose
between the coffee shop and Waltons Restaurant, and there is also
a popular cocktail lounge.*
94⇨⅛in 37 bedrooms CTV in all bedrooms ® T S%
sB⇨♠£86-£97 dB⇨♠£97-£108 (room only) 🏥
Lift ( 25P 40🏌 CFA *xmas*
🍴 French V ✿ ⅃⊑ ⅛ S% Lunch £14.50&alc Dinner £19&alc
Last dinner 10pm
Credit Cards 1 2 3 4 5

❀★★★♨78%,**Lainston House** Sparsholt SO21 2LT (3m NW off
A272) (Prestige) ☎(0962)63588 Telex no 477375
FAX (0962) 72672
(Rosette awarded for dinner only)
*This attractive William and Mary period house is set in 63 acres of
parkland. The individually designed bedrooms are comfortable
and very well equipped with bathrobes and quality bed linen.
Public rooms include a gracious drawing room and a panelled bar.
In the dining room the chef provides a selection of British dishes
such as lobster and crab terrine on a light crab sauce and breast of
guinea fowl filled with a light mousse.*
32rm(30⇨1♠)(1fb) CTV in all bedrooms T sB⇨♠fr£90
dB⇨♠fr£110 (room only) 🏥
( 150P 🏌 ✿ ♪ croquet clay pigeon shooting ♫ ♨ *xmas*
🍴 English & French V ✿ ⅃⊑ Lunch £16.50-£22alc Dinner
£26-£40alc Last dinner 10pm
Credit Cards 1 2 3 4 5

★★★63% *Royal* Saint Peter St SO23 8BS (Best Western)
☎(0962)840840 Telex no 477071 FAX (0962) 841582
*Once a convent, this well-managed hotel is a peaceful haven in the
centre of the city. A modern bedroom extension, overlooking the
colourful gardens, provides particularly comfortable, modern
bedrooms. There is an attractive conservatory style restaurant.*

59⇨♠(4fb)1🛏 CTV in all bedrooms ®
( 60P ✿ fly fishing
🍴 English & French ✿ ⅃⊑ Last dinner 9.30pm
Credit Cards 1 2 3 5

★★★61% **Winchester Moat House** Worthy Ln SO23 7AB
(Queens Moat)(Consort) ☎(0962)68102 due to change to
868102 Telex no 47383 FAX (0962) 840862
*Sited on the former coach station, near to a car park, this purpose-
built hotel offers well-equipped bedrooms and a restaurant
featuring table d'hôte menus.*
72⇨♠(6fb)⅛in 20 bedrooms CTV in all bedrooms ® T S%
sB&B⇨♠£79-£84 dB&B⇨♠£103-£113 🏥
( 72P ≈🏊(heated) sauna solarium gymnasium steam room
jacuzzi *xmas*
🍴 English & French V ✿ ⅃⊑ Lunch £11.50-£13&alc Dinner
£16.50-£18 Last dinner 9.45pm
Credit Cards 1 2 3 5

---

**WINDERMERE** Cumbria Map 07 SD49

See **Town Plan Section**

★★★★59% **The Old England** Church St, Bowness LA23 3DF
(Trusthouse Forte) ☎(09662)2444 Telex no 65194
FAX (09662) 3432
*An elegantly spacious hotel which occupies a prime position beside
the shore of Lake Windermere provides good meals which are
served in an attractive restaurant that looks out onto the water;
several of the well-equipped bedrooms also have lake views, and
there is a delightful lounge.*
82⇨♠(8fb)⅛in 6 bedrooms CTV in all bedrooms ® T 🏥
Lift ( 80P ✿ CFA ≈🏊(heated) snooker sauna solarium croquet
golf driving net *xmas*
V ✿ ⅃⊑ ⅛ Lunch £9.50 Dinner fr£15.95&alc Last dinner
9.15pm
Credit Cards 1 2 3 4 5

*See advertisement on page 735*

★★★69% **Wild Boar** Crook LA23 3NF (2.5m S of Windermere
on B5284 Crook road) (Best Western) ☎(09662)5225
Telex no 65464 FAX (09662) 2498
*This 18th-century country hotel, in a secluded setting of woodland
and fell, has a good atmosphere and personal attention and service.
Low beamed ceilings in the public rooms contribute to the
character, and bedrooms offer traditional country-syle comfort and
appointments with modern facilities.*
36⇨♠(3fb)4🛏⅛in 6 bedrooms CTV in all bedrooms ® T
sB&B⇨♠£40-£50 dB&B⇨♠£80-£100 🏥
60P 🏌 ✿ CFA free boat launching facilities *xmas*
🍴 English & French V ✿ ⅃⊑ ⅛ Lunch £4.45-£9.45&alc Dinner
£18&alc Last dinner 8.45pm
Credit Cards 1 2 3 4 5

★★★♨64% **Langdale Chase** LA23 1LW
☎Ambleside(05394)32201 FAX (05394) 32604
*Despite its proximity to the A591, this old hotel retains the air of a
country house, with an impressive oak-panelled interior and well-
kept gardens running down to Lake Windermere. Bedrooms,
though traditional in style, are equipped with modern amenities,
some commanding the same lake views as are enjoyed by the
terrace and comfortable public areas. For those with a real desire
to be close to the water, a boathouse has been converted into a
particularly restful bedroom, served as efficiently and caringly as
the rest of the hotel.*
26rm(17⇨6♠)Annexe7⇨(2fb)1🛏 CTV in all bedrooms ® T
S% sB&B⇨♠£42-£50 dB&B⇨♠£84-£110 🏥
( 36P 🏌 ✿ ♪ (grass) croquet rowing boats putting *xmas*
🍴 English & French ✿ ⅃⊑ Lunch fr£9.25 Dinner fr£19 Last
dinner 8.45pm
Credit Cards 1 2 3 5

*See advertisement on page 735*

W

# Windermere

★★★63% **Burnside** Kendal Road, Bowness LA23 3EP
☎(09662)2211 Telex no 65430 FAX (09662) 3824
*This large Victorian house in an elevated position, is steadily being
enlarged and improved to provide spacious, comfortable and well-
equipped bedrooms. It boasts new leisure facilities which are also
part of a time-share complex situated within the hotel grounds.*
45⇌(11fb)4🛏 CTV in all bedrooms ® T sB&B⇌£42-£55
dB&B⇌£76-£102 ♬
Lift 80P ❉ ▣(heated) squash snooker sauna solarium
gymnasium watersports steam room badminton ♫ *xmas*
V ❖ ♨ ✗ Sunday Lunch £7-£7.50 High tea £4.50-£6&alc
Dinner £13-£14 Last dinner 9.45pm
Credit Cards 1 2 3 5 £

★★★62% **Burn How Garden House Hotel, Motel &
Restaurant** Back Belsfield Rd, Bowness LA23 3HH
☎(09662)6226
*This hotel is delightfully situated in a slightly elevated position
above Lake Windermere. Accommodation is available in family
chalets, a recently modernised Victorian house, or in a purpose-
built wing offering sun balconies and four-poster beds. The
attractive restaurant specialises in English and French cuisine.*
Annexe26⇌♞(10fb)4🛏 CTV in all bedrooms ® T
✘ (ex guide dogs) ✱ sB&B⇌♞£39-£50 dB&B⇌♞£58-£80 ♬
30P ♨ ❉ sauna solarium gymnasium water sports ⚽ *xmas*
♒ English & French V ❖ ✗ Bar Lunch £2.50-£7alc Dinner
£15&alc Last dinner 9pm
Credit Cards 1 2 3 £

See advertisement on page 737

★★★60% **The Belsfield** Kendal Rd, Bowness LA23 3EL
(Trusthouse Forte) ☎(09662)2448 Telex no 65238
FAX (09662) 6397
*An elegant Victorian residence overlooking Lake Windermere.
Public areas are comfortable and well furnished with fine Lake
views, whilst bedrooms have all modern amenities.*
66⇌♞2🛏✗in 6 bedrooms CTV in all bedrooms ® T
sB⇌♞£65-£70 dB⇌♞£78-£89 (room only) ♬
Lift ⍓ 80P ❉ CFA ▣(heated) ♟ (grass) snooker sauna
solarium mini golf putting green ♫ *xmas*
♒ French V ❖ ♨ ✗ Sunday Lunch £10.50-£12.50 Dinner
£14-£15.50&alc Last dinner 9.30pm
Credit Cards 1 2 3 4 5

★★★58% **Low Wood** LA23 1LP (3m N A591) (Best Western)
☎Ambleside(05394)33338 Telex no 65273 FAX (05394) 34072
*This large and recently refurbished and extended hotel stands on
the shore of Lake Windermere. Extensive leisure amenities include
a water ski and windsurfing school. The hotel also has conference
facilities.*
99⇌♞(10fb)3🛏 CTV in all bedrooms ® T ✱
sB&B⇌♞£54-£85 dB&B⇌♞£108-£150 ♬
Lift ⍓ 200P ❉ CFA ▣ ⚶ ♒ squash snooker sauna solarium
gymnasium water skiing sub aqua diving ⚽ *xmas*
♒ International V ❖ ♨ ✗ Bar Lunch fr£7.70alc Dinner
fr£17&alc Last dinner 10pm
Credit Cards 1 2 3 5

★★★**Hydro** Helm Rd, Bowness LA23 3BA (Mount Charlotte
(TS)) ☎(09662)4455 Telex no 65196 FAX (09662) 88000
*Modernised Victorian hotel overlooking Lake Windermere, with
views of the Langdale Pikes.*
96⇌♞(9fb) CTV in all bedrooms ® ♬
Lift ⍓ 140P *xmas*
V ❖ Lunch £8.50 High tea £4 Dinner £11.50&alc Last dinner
9pm
Credit Cards 1 2 3 5

All AA-appointed establishments are
inspected regularly to ensure that required
standards are maintained.

❀★★ **MILLER HOWE**
Rayrigg Rd LA23 1EY
☎(09662)2536
FAX (09662) 5664
Closed mid Dec-early Mar
(Rosette awarded for dinner
only)
*Despite its international
reputation, this is still an hotel that retains its relaxed,
informal atmosphere, created and maintained over many
years by its famous owner John Tovey. Fine paintings, china
and porcelain adorn the public rooms which are bright with
fresh flowers, and from the depths of the comfortable
armchairs and Chesterfields guests can feast their eyes on
Windermere and the Langdale Fells. Dinner is, as always, a
feast of another order, the five courses cooked by chef Gaulton
Blackiston and his team being carefully chosen to make a well
balanced and original meal, beautifully served. Service is
attentive and friendly throughout, and provided by a most
pleasant team of long-serving staff, whose efforts make this
hotel such an enjoyable place to visit. Incidentally, among the
'extras' provided in the bedrooms are umbrellas, binoculars
and cassette players.*
13⇌♞1🛏 TV available ✱ sB&B⇌♞£85-£90
dB&B⇌♞£130-£220 (incl dinner) ♬
40P ♨ ❉ nc12yrs
V ❖ ♨ ✗ Dinner £27.50 Last dinner 8.30pm
Credit Cards 1 2 3 5

★★⚑84% **Holbeck Ghyll Country House** Holbeck Ln
LA23 1LU ☎Ambleside(05394)32375
Closed Jan
*From its splendid position high on a hillside, this former shooting
lodge offers wonderful views of Lake Windermere and, under the
caring attention of owners David and Patricia Nicholson, has
retained much of its original character. Some of the bedrooms are
truly spacious, some smaller, but all are nicely decorated and well
supplied with comforts. Chef Craig Wright and his team cook
delicious meals, and the spontaneous friendliness from all the staff
makes a lasting impression on the guests.*
14⇌♞(1fb)🛏 CTV in all bedrooms ® T ✱ sB&B⇌£60
dB&B⇌£90-£120 (incl dinner) *xmas*
20P ♨ ❉ putting green *xmas*
♒ English & French V ❖ ♨ ✗ Sunday Lunch £9.50 Dinner
£20 Last dinner 8.45pm
Credit Cards 1 3

See advertisement under AMBLESIDE

★★74% **Cedar Manor Hotel & Restaurant** Ambleside Rd
LA23 1AX (Exec Hotel) ☎(09662)3192
*This charming and peaceful hotel takes its name from the
magnificent 200-year-old cedar tree in the garden. Carefully
decorated and furnished by the friendly proprietors, the bedrooms,
including two delightful rooms in a converted coach house, are
spacious and well-appointed. There is a cosy bar, and well-
prepared food is served in the attractive dining room.*
10⇌♞Annexe2⇌♞(4fb)1🛏 CTV in all bedrooms ® T
sB&B⇌♞£42-£46 dB&B⇌♞£68-£84 (incl dinner) ♬
15P ♨ ❉ *xmas*
♒ English & French V ❖ ♨ ✗ Dinner £14.50-£16.50 Last
dinner 8.30pm
Credit Cards 1 3

**W**

★★♨74% *Linthwaite* Bowness LA23 3JA ☎(09662)3688
Closed Dec-mid Apr
*Set high in fourteen acres which include gardens and woodland,
this immaculate country house enjoys beautiful views across Lake
Windermere and Belle Island. Delightful bedrooms offer good
modern facilities, public areas retain comfort and character, and
there is a well-stocked tarn for guests' use – all these factors
combining to ensure a tranquil and relaxing stay.*
11⇌ CTV in all bedrooms ® ✖
25P 🚗 ✿ ♪ putting green nc8yrs
♀ English & French ♦ ⍅ ⍴
Credit Cards ① ② ③

★★72% *Hillthwaite House* Thornbarrow Rd LA23 2DF
☎(09662)3636 & 6691
*Set on a hill, the hotel has magnificent views of Lake Windermere
and the surrounding fells. Accommodation is comfortable, with a
particularly pleasant lounge and lounge bar.*
25⇌🏲(2fb)8🗗 CTV in all bedrooms ®
26P 🚗 ✿ ⌔(heated) sauna solarium
♀ English & French V ♦ ⍅ Last dinner 9pm
Credit Cards ① ② ③

★★♨72% *Lindeth Fell* Upper Storrs Park Rd, Bowness
LA23 3JP ☎(09662)3286 & 4287
Closed mid Nov-mid Mar
*Beautifully located and standing in fine gardens, this Lakeland
country house hotel enjoys impressive views across the lake to the
Cumbrian mountains. Run very much as an extension of the
owner's private home, the hotel offers high levels of décor, comfort
and catering, the 5-course dinner and its accompanying wine list
representing particularly good value for money.*
14⇌🏲(2fb) CTV in all bedrooms ® T ✖ sB&B⇌🏲£42-£50
dB&B⇌🏲£80-£100 (incl dinner)
20P 🚗 ✿ ⍴ (grass) ♪ croquet putting nc7yrs
♦ ⍅
Credit Cards ① ③

★★68% *Bordriggs Country House* Longtail Hill, Bowness
LA23 3LD ☎(09662)3567 FAX (09662) 6949
Closed Dec & Jan
*Cosy and relaxing, the hotel enjoys a secluded location and has its
own attractive gardens with an outdoor swimming pool.
Accommodation is in comfortable, well cared for rooms with good
facilities, whilst the proprietors and their family both offer a warm
welcome and do their utmost to ensure that guests enjoy their stay.*
9⇌🏲Annexe2⇌🏲(2fb)1🗗⍀in all bedrooms CTV in all
bedrooms T ✖ (ex guide dogs) sB&B⇌🏲fr£30
dB&B⇌🏲fr£55
❲ 20P 🚗 ✿ ⌔(heated) croquet badminton nc10yrs
♀ English & Continental V ⍀ Dinner £15 Last dinner 7.30pm

★★68% *Hideaway* Phoenix Way LA23 1DB ☎(09662)3070
*This traditional Westmorland stone-built Victorian house is
peacefully set on the west side of the village. There are attractive
and comfortable public rooms and the bedrooms are prettily
decorated and well equipped. Good friendly hospitality.*
11rm(4⇌6🏲)Annexe5⇌🏲(3fb)6🗗 CTV in all bedrooms ®
sB&B£31-£45 sB&B⇌🏲£31-£45 dB&B⇌🏲£56-£90 🏳
16P 🚗 ✿ *xmas*
♀ English & Continental V ♦ ⍅ ⍀ Bar Lunch £3.50-£5
Dinner £12.50 Last dinner 7.30pm
£

★★62% *Royal* Queens Square, Bowness LA23 3DB (Best
Western) ☎(09662)3045 Telex no 65273 FAX (09662) 2498
*A hotel reputed to be the oldest establishment in the Lake District,
and one which numbers many famous names among its guests over
the years, stands in the centre of Bowness close to the lake; today's
guests are assured of comfortably furnished accommodation and a
good standard of food.*                                              ▶

---

# 𝕷𝖆𝖓𝖌𝖉𝖆𝖑𝖊 𝕰𝖍𝖆𝖘𝖊 𝕳𝖔𝖙𝖊𝖑
## 𝖂𝖎𝖓𝖉𝖊𝖗𝖒𝖊𝖗𝖊        ★ ★ ★
### LA23 1LW
### ENGLISH LAKES
### Tel: Ambleside (05394) 32201

Magnificently situated on Lake Windermere in beautifully landscaped gardens,
this aristrocrat of Hotels offers you
gracious living from a more leisurely age.

Fully licensed, open to non residents, the
excellent Cuisine and Cellar may be
sampled in our elegant Restaurant.

All the delightfully individual bedrooms
have colour TV, central heating, telephone, tea/coffee making facilities and
the majority with private bathroom.

---

# *The Old England Hotel*

**Bowness-on-Windermere, Cumbria, LA23 3DF.
Tel: Windermere (09662) 2444 Telex 65194**

★★★★

The Old England is an elegant Georgian house situated on the
shores of Lake Windermere. All 80 and 2 suites guest rooms
are comfortably furnished and have private bathroom, colour
television, radio, telephone and tea and coffee making
facilities. Guests can relax in the spacious lounge or on the Sun
Terrace. Within the hotel grounds there is a heated swimming
pool, which is open during the summer months, and golf
driving net. Billiard Room. Hairdressing Salon, Solarium and
Beautician. The hotel is renowned for its lavish English cuisine
and selection of vintage wines. Situated in the heart of
Cumbrian Countryside, yet conveniently located for the M6
Motorway. The Old English also provides the ideal venue for
all types of business functions. Parking facilities for 100 cars.

**W**

29⇆♠(4fb)1⌗ CTV in all bedrooms Ⓡ T S%
sB&B⇆♠£29.50-£39.50 dB&B⇆♠£59-£79 ⊟
16P 5🏊 (£1.50) ✣ sub-aqua diving water skiing pool table ♫
*xmas*
♥ English & French V ✿ ⚅ ✂ Bar Lunch fr£2.95 High tea
£4.75-£5 Dinner £13 Last dinner 9pm
Credit Cards ① ② ③ ④ ⑤

★★60% **The Knoll** Lake Rd, Bowness LA23 2JF
☎(09662)3756 & 88466
Closed Dec-Feb
*There are good views across the Lake from the dining room and
lounge of this late-nineteenth-century house in attractive secluded
location, now a modest privately-owned and run hotel.*
12rm(9⇆♠)(4fb) CTV in all bedrooms Ⓡ T ✕ S10%
sB&Bfr£32 sB&B⇆♠£35-£40
dB&B⇆♠fr£80 (incl dinner) ⊟
CTV 20P ✣ nc3yrs
V ✿ ⚅ ✂ S10% Dinner fr£13.25 Last dinner 7.30pm
Credit Cards ① ③ £

★🏅67% **Quarry Garth Country House** Troutbeck Bridge
LA23 1LF ☎(09662)88282 FAX (09662) 6584
*Set between Windermere and Ambleside, surrounded by 8 acres of
gardens, this small country house is being refurbished by its new
owners. Bedrooms vary in size, but are generally spacious and
comfortable, while pleasant public areas feature fine wood
panelling, polished floors with rugs and log fires on chillier days.
Enjoyable, well-cooked meals are served in an attractive dining
room, and young staff provide attentive service.*
10⇆♠(2fb) CTV in all bedrooms Ⓡ T sB&B⇆♠£40-£55
dB&B⇆♠£80-£100 (incl dinner) ⊟
35P ✣ ♪ *xmas*
♥ English & Continental V ✿ ⚅ Lunch £10-£15alc Dinner
fr£18.50alc Last dinner 9pm
Credit Cards ① ② ③ ⑤ £

★67% **Willowsmere** Ambleside Rd LA23 1ES ☎(09662)3575
Closed Dec-Etr
*The sincere young proprietors of this homely and comfortable little
hotel enjoy meeting their guests' needs and ensure that a friendly
atmosphere prevails.*
13⇆♠(7fb) Ⓡ
CTV 20P ⌗
♥ English & Austrian ✿ ⚅ ✂
Credit Cards ① ② ③ ⑤

✣✕**Porthole Eating House** 3 Ash St, Bowness LA23 3EB
☎(09662)2793
(Rosette awarded for dinner only)
*This friendly little restaurant can be found in a small side street
close to the lake at Bowness. Hugely popular, it is always packed
and though tables may be a bit cramped, the atmosphere is always
cheerful and the food most enjoyable. Pancakes filled with a
mixture of really good fresh fish, or supreme of chicken filled with
pâté, mushrooms and onions are typical of the menu, and the home-
made ice-cream is just one of the many enjoyable puddings.*
Closed Tue & mid Dec-mid Feb
Lunch not served
♥ English, French & Italian V 36 seats ✱ Dinner £15-£21alc
Last dinner 11pm ✗

✕**Rogers** 4 High St LA23 1AF ☎(09662)4954
*The warm atmosphere, attractive décor and quality napery of this
delightful little restaurant on the edge of town help to make it the
ideal setting in which to enjoy a very good meal. The menu offers a
range of French and English dishes, all based on fresh produce,
and features specially set meals in winter. Reservations are
necessary.*
Closed Sun (ex BH's) & 2 wks in Jan, Feb & Mar
Lunch not served (ex by prior arrangement)
♥ English & French 42 seats Dinner £12.50&alc Last lunch
1.30pm Last dinner 9.45pm ✗
Credit Cards ① ② ③ ⑤

**WINDSOR** Berkshire Map **04** SU97
See also **Datchet**

★★★★73% **Oakley Court** Windsor Road, Water Oakley
SL4 5UR (2m W A308) (Queens Moat)(Prestige)
☎Maidenhead(0628)74141 Telex no 849958
FAX (0628) 37011
*A splendid mansion house set in acres of beautifully landscaped
gardens sloping gently to the River Thames. Spacious public rooms
remain as they were in 1859 including the drawing room with
ornate plasterwork. Suites in the mansion house have been restored
to their original splendour with more modern accommodation
available in the Garden and River Wings. The restaurant offers
imaginative cuisine and attentive service.*
65⇆♠Annexe27⇆♠(4fb)5⌗ CTV in all bedrooms T
✕ (ex guide dogs) ✱ sB⇆♠£99-£195
dB⇆♠£115-£325 (room only) ⊟
《 120P ✣ ▶9 ♪ snooker ♫ *xmas*
♥ English & French V ✿ ⚅ Lunch £18.25&alc Dinner
fr£27.50&alc Last dinner 10pm
Credit Cards ① ② ③ ⑤

★★★65% **The Castle** High St SL4 1LJ 6 (Trusthouse Forte)
☎(0753)851011 Telex no 849220 FAX (0753) 830244
*The elegance of this hotel's Georgian frontage and wrought-iron
balconies is reflected inside, the foyer, lounge and reception area
being decorated in traditional English country house style and a
restaurant with candle-lit chandeliers and fresh flowers creating a
delightfully intimate atmosphere – though guests can enjoy a less
formal meal in the Brasserie. Large bedrooms, tastefully and
comfortably furnished, provide all modern amenities.*
103⇆♠(40fb)4⌗✂in 6 bedrooms CTV in all bedrooms Ⓡ ✱
sB⇆♠£80 dB⇆♠£100 (room only) ⊟
Lift 《 90P CFA ♫ *xmas*
♥ French V ✿ ⚅ ✂ S10% Lunch fr£13.50&alc Dinner
fr£18&alc Last dinner 10pm
Credit Cards ① ② ③ ④ ⑤

★★63% **Royal Adelaide** 46 Kings Rd SL4 2AG ☎(0753)863916
FAX (0753) 830682
*Overlooking the Long Walk which runs from the castle, this
Georgian building maintains a warm atmosphere throughout ;
refurbished public areas are tastefully decorated, and all bedrooms
offer good facilities, though some are smaller than others.*
39⇆♠(1fb) CTV in all bedrooms Ⓡ T ✱
sB&B⇆♠£57.50-£67 dB&B⇆♠£68.75-£80 ⊟
《 30P *xmas*
♥ English & French V ✂ Dinner fr£12.75&alc Last dinner
9pm
Credit Cards ① ② ③ ⑤ £

★★59% **Ye Harte & Garter** High St SL4 1PH (Berni/Chef &
Brewer) ☎(0753)863426
*An inn whose name can be traced back to the Knights of the
Garter, though its design is Victorian, overlooks Windsor Castle
from a site used for the same purpose since Tudor times, when two
taverns stood here. Comfortable bedrooms are equipped with
modern facilities and there are two restaurants, the larger offering
a typical Berni/Chef and Brewer menu of steaks and grills.*
50rm(36⇆♠7♠)(8fb) CTV in all bedrooms Ⓡ T
✕ (ex guide dogs) sB&B⇆♠£52-£68.50
dB&B⇆♠£70-£85.50 ⊟
Lift 《 ✗
V ✿ ⚅ ✂ Lunch £8-£15alc Dinner £8-£15alc Last dinner
10.30pm
Credit Cards ① ② ③ ⑤

**W**

★★67% **Aurora Garden** 14 Bolton Av SL4 3JF ☎(0753)868686
FAX (0753) 831394
*Situated in a quiet, tree-lined avenue only a short distance from the town centre, this hotel offers attractive, comfortable and well-equipped bedrooms, a cosy bar/lounge area and conference and banqueting facilities. The terrace at the rear of the hotel overlooks a delightful, well-tended water garden.*
14⇨¶(1fb) CTV in all bedrooms ® T S10%
sB&B⇨¶£58.50-£63.50 dB&B⇨¶£70-£75 ⊟
20P ✿ *xmas*
♥ English & French V ⊕ ⚏ S10% Lunch £12.50-£14 High tea £6.50-£7.50 Dinner £16.50-£18&alc Last dinner 9pm
Credit Cards ①②③⑤ⓕ

**See advertisement on page 739**

★58% **Union Inn** 17 Crump Hill SL4 2QY ☎(0753)861955
FAX (0753) 831378
12⇨¶ CTV in all bedrooms ® T ✗ (ex guide dogs) ✳ S9%
sB&B⇨¶£45.50-£49.50 dB&B⇨¶£57.50-£62.50
32P ♿
♥ English & French V ⊕ ⚏ S% Lunch £9.50&alc Dinner fr£9.50&alc Last dinner 10.15pm
Credit Cards ①②③

All hotels are now given a percentage grading for the quality of their facilities. A full explanation can be found within 'How we Classify Hotels and Restaurants' at the front of the book.

# WILLOWSMERE HOTEL★
## Ambleside Road, Windermere, Cumbria LA23 1ES
### Tel. Windermere 3575

Willowsmere is situated on the main road Windermere – Ambleside (A591) and is an excellent centre from which to tour the whole Lake District.

Near to the Lake (Millerground) for Boating, Fishing, Swimming, Picnics (Public heated swimming pool ¾ mile). Orrest Head and Troutbeck Valley for walking. All bedrooms with private facilities. Tea & Coffee.

Sheltered Private Garden. Central Heating in all rooms. Colour television in one Lounge. Large Free Car Park.

Noted for excellent catering. Residential licence.

Under the Personal Supervision of Resident proprietors.
**Heather & Alan Cook & Family**

# THE
# BURN HOW

❋ *Garden House Hotel · Motel & Restaurant* ❋
*Bowness-on-Windermere, Cumbria*
*Tel. Windermere, (09662)6226*

AA★★★

ETB 👑 👑 👑 👑

Enjoy the unique Burn How experience: elegance, comfort and superb service in a secluded garden setting in the heart of Bowness.

Relax in elegant four poster beds, beautiful en-suite bedrooms or spacious family chalets, and dine in our highly recommended restaurant.

We look forward to welcoming you.

W

## WINSFORD Somerset Map 03 SS93

**★★75% Royal Oak Inn** Exmoor National Park TA24 7JE (Best Western) ☎(064385)455 Telex no 46529 FAX (064385) 388

*Interesting, beamed bedrooms are available in the main building of this thatched and picturesque hotel, but all its pleasantly furnished, well decorated rooms are of a high standard. Public areas include three comfortable lounges, two small bars and a dining room with polished floor and quality furnishings where the table d'hôte menu offers a good range of fresh English dishes and home-made puddings.*

8⇌Annexe6⇌(1fb) CTV in all bedrooms T 🎏
20P 3🐾 ♪ hunting shooting *xmas*
V ♥ 🍺
Credit Cards 1 2 3 5 ⓔ

## WINSLOW Buckinghamshire Map 04 SP72

**★★66% Bell** Market Square MK18 3AB ☎(0296)714091

*This small, privately owned village hotel has been completely refurbished and provides comfortable accommodation. Bedrooms are of a good size and are well equipped. A short à la carte menu is offered and the cooking is of a good standard. Staff are friendly, and provide an efficient and attentive serivce.*

19⇌↑ CTV in all bedrooms ⓡ T
P
♥ 🍺

## WINTERBOURNE ABBAS Dorset Map 03 SY69

**★★61% Whitefriars** Copyhold Ln DT2 9LT ☎Martinstown(0305)889206

*Skilfully prepared meals based on good, fresh produce, spacious, well equipped and tastefully appointed bedrooms and a warm, relaxing atmosphere are the attraction of this charming hotel.*

7⇌↑ CTV in all bedrooms ⓡ T sB&B⇌↑£35
dB&B⇌↑£60-£70 🎏
16P 🚲 ✷ nc12yrs *xmas*
V ♥ 🍺 Lunch £8-£10alc High tea £5-£7alc Dinner £13-£16alc
Last dinner 9.30pm
Credit Cards 1 2 3 5 ⓔ

## WISBECH Cambridgeshire Map 05 TF40

**★★64% Orchard House** 5 North Brink PE13 1JR ☎(0945)474559 FAX (0945) 474497

*The Orchard House Hotel is located on the North Brink, one of the finest rows of Georgian façades in Great Britain. Formerly the Old Whyte Hart, it has now been refurbished to offer character and comfort in the public rooms, with the food in either the wine bar or restaurant proving quite popular. Bedrooms are clean and all en suite, but more modest in appointment.*

18⇌↑(1fb) CTV in all bedrooms ⓡ T ✳ sB&B⇌↑£35
dB&B⇌↑£45 🎏
ℂ CTV 6P 4🐾 *xmas*
🍴 English & French V ♥ 🍺 Lunch £3.75-£14&alc Dinner £7.50-£9.50&alc Last dinner 10pm
Credit Cards 1 3

**★★63% Queens** South Brink PE13 1JJ ☎(0945)583933
Telex no 329197 FAX (0945) 474250

*A well preserved Georgian property, situated alongside the River Nene only a few minutes' walk from the town centre, is family-run to offer comfortable, well-equipped accommodation which is equally suitable for tourist or businessman. Lounge bar and residents' lounge have a pleasant, homely atmosphere, the recently refurbished restaurant is attractive, and addition facilities include a function room for up to 120 guests.*

12⇌↑Annexe6⇌(3fb)2🛏 CTV in all bedrooms ⓡ T ✳
sB&B⇌↑£37.50-£42.50 dB&B⇌↑£47.50-£60 🎏
40P ✷

🍴 English & French V ♥ 🍺 Lunch £9.95&alc Dinner £9.95&alc Last dinner 10pm
Credit Cards 1 2 3 5

**★★55% White Lion** 5 South Brink PE13 1JO ☎(0945)584813

*Situated close to the town centre and the River Nene, this coaching inn offers varying standards of accommodation, some single bedrooms being rather compact. Guests have a choice of 2 bars, and good parking facilities are provided.*

18rm(11⇌5↑)(1fb) CTV in all bedrooms ⓡ T sB&B£35
sB&B⇌↑£40-£45 dB&B£46 dB&B⇌↑£55-£59.95 🎏
25P

🍴 English & French V ♥ 🍺 Lunch £9.50&alc Dinner £9.50-£10.50&alc Last dinner 9.30pm
Credit Cards 1 2 3 5 ⓔ

## WISHAW West Midlands Map 07 SP19

**★★★★66% The Belfry** Lichfield Rd B76 9PR (A446) (De Vere) ☎Curdworth(0675)70301 Telex no 338848 FAX (0675) 70178

*Situated conveniently close to Birmingham and the National Exhibition Centre, this large and luxurious hotel is part of a vast complex which is perhaps best known for its world-famous golfing facilities, having been the venue for the 1989 Ryder Cup tournament. The amenities, all contained within 370 acres of parkland, include a conference centre with extensive facilities, a health and leisure resort and a night club – this combination making it understandably popular with a wide range of visitors.*

219⇌↑(34fb)2🛏 CTV in all bedrooms ⓡ T ✗ (ex guide dogs)
Lift ℂ 1500P ✤ CFA 🏊(heated) ▶ 18 ♟ (hard) squash snooker sauna solarium gymnasium archery clay pigeon shooting 🎣
🍴 French V ♥ 🍺 Last dinner 10pm
Credit Cards 1 2 3 5

**★★★50% Moxhull Hall** Holly Ln B76 9PE (Exec Hotel) ☎021-329 2056 Telex no 333779

*This fine, red-brick house, standing in eight acres of garden and woodland just off the A446, is popular with local families for its leisurely atmosphere and French-style bistro.*

21⇌↑(2fb)1🛏 CTV in all bedrooms ⓡ
60P ✷ croquet 🎵
🍴 English & French V ♥ Last dinner 10pm
Credit Cards 1 2 3 5

## WITHAM Essex Map 05 TL81

**★★58% White Hart** Newland St CM8 2AF (Berni/Chef & Brewer) ☎(0376)512245

18⇌↑(1fb)1🛏 CTV in all bedrooms ⓡ T ✗ (ex guide dogs)
sB&B⇌↑£41.50-£46 dB&B⇌↑£53.50 🎏
43P
🍴 International V ♥ 🍴 Lunch £8-£15alc Dinner £8-£15alc
Last dinner 10pm
Credit Cards 1 2 3 5

## WITHERSLACK Cumbria Map 07 SD48

★

★🏛 OLD VICARAGE
COUNTRY HOUSE

LA11 6RS ☎(044852)381
Telex no 668230
FAX (044852) 373
Closed Xmas wk

*Set well away from the hustle and bustle of the more popular Lakeland towns, this delightful hotel makes an excellent base for holidays. Owners Jill and Roger*

**W**

738

*Burrington-Brown and Irene and Stanley Reeve have steadily improved the accommodation every year, and this year have opened a lovely Orchard House in the grounds, with most of its rooms giving access to a patio. The lavish 5-course meals remain one of the greatest strengths of the Old Vicarage, as do Stanley Reeve's excellent and sustaining breakfasts, where the range of high-quality preserves are a special treat to look forward to, and ensure that you will start your day in style.*

7⇌👤Annexe5⇌👤1 🛏 CTV in all bedrooms ® *
sB&B⇌👤£50-£80 dB&B⇌👤£70-£120 🅿
25P 🚗 ✿ ♪ (hard) nc12yrs
✗ Dinner fr£23.50 Last dinner 6pm
Credit Cards 1 2 3 5

---

**WITHYPOOL** Somerset Map 03 SS83

★★71% **Royal Oak Inn** TA24 7QP ☎Exford(064383)506
Telex no 46529
Closed 25 & 26 Dec
*This small village inn boasts two cosy, beamed bars with log fires and a restaurant which has a strong local reputation for well-prepared fresh food. Friendly and efficiently run, it is popular with visitors to the Moors, providing accommodation in comfortable bedrooms with a good degree of quality, some being furnished with antiques and Sanderson fabrics.*

8rm(3⇌3👤)(1fb)1 🛏 CTV in all bedrooms ® T * sB&Bfr£27
sB&B⇌👤fr£40 dB&Bfr£44 dB&B⇌👤£58-£60
20P 🚗 ♪ shooting nc10yrs xmas
♀ English & French V ✿ ☲ Sunday Lunch fr£8.50 Dinner
£16-£20&alc Last dinner 9pm
Credit Cards 1 2 3 5

★★⚱69% **Westerclose Country House** TA24 7QR
☎Exford(064383)302
Closed Jan-23 Mar & 6 Nov-Dec
*Small, personally owned and set in nine acres of gardens and paddocks, this country house provides freshly decorated and comfortable bedrooms; its two lounges are similarly well furnished, one having a log fire, while the polished dining room offers both table d'hôte and à la carte menus based on fresh local produce.*

11rm(9⇌)Annexe1⇌(3fb)1 🛏 CTV in all bedrooms ®
12P 🚗 ✿ hunting
♀ English & French ✿ ☲ Last dinner 8.30pm
Credit Cards 1 2 3

---

**WITNEY** Oxfordshire Map 04 SP30

★★67% **Witney Lodge** Ducklington Ln OX8 7TS (Consort)
☎(0993)779777 Telex no 83459
*Conveniently located just outside the town, this attractive, recently opened, Cotswold-style hotel is ideally positioned for both business travellers and tourists. Bedrooms are particularly good, their furnishings combining with an extensive range of facilities including tiled, bright bathrooms, and a restaurant in homely style offers good, value-for-money food and friendly service.*

34⇌ CTV in all bedrooms ® T ✗ (ex guide dogs) S%
sB&B⇌£27-£65 dB&B⇌£48-£73 Continental breakfast 🅿
(⚡ 🎱 120P ☲(heated) sauna solarium gymnasium whirlpool spa
♫
V ✿ ☲ S% Lunch £8.50-£9.75&alc High tea £3.50-£4.95
Dinner £9.75-£11&alc Last dinner 10pm
Credit Cards 1 2 3 4 5 £

Entries for red-star hotels are highlighted by a
tint panel. For a full list of these establishments
consult the Contents page.

**W**

WIVELISCOMBE Somerset Map 03 ST02

❀★ **LANGLEY HOUSE**

Langley Marsh TA4 2UF (1m
N on unclass rd)
☎(0984)23318
FAX (0984) 23442
(Rosette awarded for dinner
only)

*Set in quiet rural
surroundings just north of the old market town, Langley
House is a delightful 16th-century hotel, personally run by
Anne and Peter Wilson. Guests will appreciate the comforts of
the attractive sitting room, and the set 5-course dinners
cooked by Peter Wilson will linger pleasantly in the memory.
Dishes are of the highest quality, matched by a comprehensive
and well-chosen wine list. The bedrooms are tastefully and
individually decorated, mineral water, fresh flowers and high
quality toiletries being among the thoughtful extra touches
that contribute to the pleasures of a stay here.*
9rm(6⇌2↑)(1fb)1⌷ CTV in all bedrooms T ✱ S%
sB&B⇌↑£52.50-£62.50 dB&B⇌↑£75-£93 ⊟
16P 4🔥 (£2.50) ⬥ ✿ croquet nc7yrs ⚬ xmas
✿ ⚄ ⅟ S% Dinner £19.75-£23.50 Last dinner 9pm
Credit Cards ①②③

WOBURN Bedfordshire Map 04 SP93

★★62% *The Bell Inn* 34 Bedford St MK17 9OD (Best Western)
☎(0525)290280 FAX (0525) 290017
21⇌↑Annexe6rm(3⇌1↑)(2fb) CTV in all bedrooms ® T
✘ (ex guide dogs)
《 50P 🔥
V ✿ Last dinner 9.30pm
Credit Cards ①②③⑤

✘✘✘Paris House Woburn Park MK17 9QP ☎(0525)290692
FAX (0525) 290471
*A fourteenth-century house enjoyed a superb setting in Woburn
Park has been converted into a most interesting restaurant whose
chef/patron produces an imaginative menu of mainly French
Provincial dishes. Cuisine is of a high standard, only good fresh
produce being used, the wine list is unusually comprehensive, and
staff are young and enthusiastic.*
Closed Mon & Feb
Dinner not served Sun
♉ French V 50 seats ✱ Lunch fr£16.50&alc Dinner fr£32&alc
Wine £8 Last lunch 2pm Last dinner 10pm 30P
Credit Cards ①②③⑤

WOKINGHAM Berkshire Map 04 SU86

★★★★64% Stakis St Anne's Manor London Rd RG11 1ST
(Stakis) ☎Reading(0734)772550 Telex no 847342
FAX (0734) 772526
*Set amidst 25 acres of private gardens and grounds, this 19th-
century hotel has been sympathetically extended and provides
comfortable modern accommodation. There are two restaurants,
one offering a carvery and set price menu, the other a more serious
à la carte choice. Service is professional and efficient. Although
lounge facilities are limited, the bedrooms are spacious. There are
good leisure and conference facilities.*
127⇌↑(30fb)1⌷⅟in 10 bedrooms CTV in all bedrooms ® T
✱ sB⇌↑fr£88 dB⇌↑£105-£115 (room only) ⊟
Lift 《⌷ CTV 170P ✿ ⬠(heated) ♪ (hard) sauna solarium
gymnasium jogging track spa bath steam room ♫ xmas

♉ English & French V ✿ ⚄ ⅟ Lunch £14&alc High tea £7.95
Dinner £17&alc Last dinner 10pm
Credit Cards ①②③④⑤

★★★★52% Reading Moat House Mill Ln, Sindlesham
RG11 5DF (Queens Moat) ☎Reading(0734)351035
Telex no 846360 FAX (0734) 666530
*The River Loddon gently flows through the 19th-century Mill
House, now the backdrop of this new, modern hotel, with well-
equipped bedrooms and à la carte restaurant. Facilities include a
conference and leisure centre, The Poachers pub, coffee shop and
The Mill nightclub.*
96⇌(10fb) CTV in all bedrooms ® T S% sB⇌£97.50-£102
dB⇌£104-£109 (room only) ⊟
Lift 《 350P ✿ sauna gymnasium jacuzzi steam room ♫
♉ International V ✿ ⚄ Lunch fr£16 Dinner fr£20 Last dinner
10.30pm
Credit Cards ①②③⑤ⓕ

★★60% Cantley House Milton Rd RG11 5QG ☎(0734)789912
Telex no 848210 FAX (0734) 774294
*A peaceful, relaxed hotel set amid many acres of picturesque and
open parkland retains much of its Victorian character; bedrooms
are comfortable and well equipped, all having private bathrooms,
and there is a choice of restaurants – Maryline's in the main
building and the Penguin and Vulture pub/brasserie located in the
grounds.*
29⇌(2fb)1⌷ CTV in all bedrooms ® T ✱
sB&B⇌↑£40-£58 dB&B⇌↑£50-£67 ⊟
《 70P ✿ ♪ (hard) croquet ♫
♉ English & French V ✿ Lunch £12.95&alc Dinner £10-£20alc
Last dinner 10pm
Credit Cards ①②③⑤

WOLVERHAMPTON West Midlands Map 07 SO99

See also **Himley**

★★★63% Mount Mount Road, Tettenhall Wood WV6 8HL
(2.5m W off A454) (Embassy) ☎(0902)752055 Telex no 333546
FAX (0902) 745263
*Set in four and a half acres of landscaped gardens and located in a
rural area, the hotel is nevertheless near enough to the centre of
Wolverhampton to be popular with business people.*
49⇌↑(11fb)⅟in 4 bedrooms CTV in all bedrooms ® T
sB⇌↑fr£66 dB⇌↑fr£76.50 (room only) ⊟
《 250P ✿ CFA xmas
♉ English & French V ✿ ⚄ Lunch fr£9.50 Dinner fr£12&alc
Last dinner 9.45pm
Credit Cards ①②③④⑤

★★★61% Park Hall Park Drive, Goldthorn Park WV4 5AJ
(2m S off A459) (Embassy) ☎(0902)331121 Telex no 333546
FAX (0902) 344760
*Located off the A459 just 3 miles from the centre of
Wolverhampton, this much extended 18th-century house provides
modern accommodation with a good range of facilities. Well
managed, with friendly and helpful staff, the hotel also has
extensive conference facilities.*
57⇌↑(20fb)⅟in 4 bedrooms CTV in all bedrooms ® T ✱ S%
sB⇌↑£22-£53 dB⇌↑£32-£63 (room only) ⊟
《 408P ✿ CFA xmas
♉ English & French V ✿ ⚄ S% Lunch £10 Dinner £10 Last
dinner 9.45pm
Credit Cards ①②③④⑤

★★★60% Goldthorn Penn Rd WV3 0ER ☎(0902)29216
Telex no 339516 FAX (0902) 710419
Closed 25-26 Dec
*This large, well-managed hotel, standing beside the A449 on the
outskirts of the town, offers a wide range of accommodation, a
business centre, two bars and a restaurant popular with guests and
non-residents alike, friendly staff provide attentive service
throughout*

**W**

57rm(63⇔3♪)Annexe27⇔♪(1fb)6♯ CTV in all bedrooms
® T ✳ S% sB⇔♪£50-£67 dB⇔♪£60-£75 (room only) ☐
《150P
♬ English & French V ♥ ⌧ Lunch £8.95-£11.95&alc Dinner
£10.95-£12.95&alc Last dinner 9.30pm
Credit Cards ①②③⑤ⓔ

★★62% **York** 138-140 Tettenhall Rd WV6 0BQ (Exec Hotel)
☎(0902)758211 FAX (0902) 758212
Closed 24 Dec-1 Jan
*Small and personally run, a hotel situated on the outskirts of the*
*own provides modest accommodation which is popular with*
*regular business travellers.*
16⇔♪(2fb) CTV in all bedrooms ® T sB&B⇔♪£35-£45
dB&B⇔♪£40-£60 ☐
CTV 20P
♬ English & French V ♥ ⌧ Lunch £6.95-£10.95&alc Dinner
fr£9.95&alc Last dinner 9.30pm
Credit Cards ①②③⑤ⓔ

★★60% **Castlecroft** Castlecroft Rd WV3 8NA ☎(0902)764040
RS Xmas
*The hotel, popular with a business clientele, stands in a residential*
*area of the town, surrounded by well-kept gardens and local sports*
*grounds. The functional accommodation offers good modern*
*facilities; there are three bars and an informal restaurant which is*
*also popular with non-residents.*
20rm(6⇔11♪)(1fb) CTV in all bedrooms ®
100P 6🏌 ❀ solarium
♬ English & French V ♥ ⌧ Last dinner 9pm
Credit Cards ①②③

---

**WOOBURN COMMON** Buckinghamshire Map **04** SU98

★★63% **Chequers Inn** Kiln Ln HP10 0JQ (1m W unclass
towards Bourne End) ☎Bourne End(06285)29575
FAX (0628) 850124
*This busy 17th-century inn has been thoughtfully modernised to*
*provide comfortable and well-equipped accommodation. The*
*service is friendly and helpful, under the personal supervision of the*
*proprietors.*
17⇔♪1♯ CTV in all bedrooms ® T ✗ (ex guide dogs) ✳
sB&B⇔♪fr£70 dB&B⇔♪£75-£90 ☐
60P
♬ English & French V ♥ Lunch fr£13&alc Dinner fr£16 Last
dinner 9pm
Credit Cards ①②③
**See advertisement under BEACONSFIELD**

---

**WOODBRIDGE** Suffolk Map **05** TM24

★★★⚑73% **Seckford Hall** IP13 6NU ☎(0394)385678
Telex no 987446 FAX (0394) 380610
Closed 25 Dec
*This picturesque Elizabethan manor has been tastefully converted*
*to incorporate modern facilities in a historic setting. Among the*
*original features much admired by guests are the linenfold*
*panelling, beamed ceilings, carved doors and massive stone*
*fireplaces of the public rooms. The Tudor tithe barn has recently*
*been converted to house a number of attractive suites and*
*bedrooms where guests have the additional facility of some*
*catering equipment. The indoor swimming pool and adjacent*
*buttery are popular amenities.*
24⇔♪ Annexe10⇔♪(4fb)5♯ CTV in all bedrooms ® T ✳
S10% sB&B⇔♪£64-£95 dB&B⇔♪£75-£120 ☐
《200P ❀ ⊠(heated) ♪ solarium gymnasium spa bath ♫
♬ International V ♥ ⌧ S10% Lunch fr£10.50&alc Dinner
£14-£18.50alc Last dinner 9.30pm
Credit Cards ①②③⑤

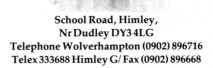 
**W**

## Woodbridge - Woodstock

★★62% **The Crown** Thoro'fare IP12 1AD (Trusthouse Forte) ☎(03943)4242 FAX (03943) 7192
*Ideally situated for the town's centre, quays and waterfront, this former coaching inn retains such traces of its sixteenth-century origins as the oak beamed restaurant with open fireplace which provides a pleasant setting both for morning coffee and for meals; the menu's varied selection of freshly-prepared dishes is served by a delightfully informal but courteous young team of staff.*
10⇄Annexe10⇄(2fb)⊁in 3 bedrooms CTV in all bedrooms ® ⊁
30P *xmas*
♀ English & French V ♥ ⌘ ⊁ Lunch £5.50-£12 Dinner fr£14&alc Last dinner 9pm
Credit Cards ① ② ③ ④ ⑤

○**Travelodge** A12 Eastern by pass, 121 Anson Rd, Martlesham(Trusthouse Forte)
☎Central reservations (0800) 850950
Due to open winter 1990
32⇄

---

**WOODFORD** Greater Manchester Map **07** SJ88

✗**3 Gates** 547 Chester Rd SK7 1PR ☎061-440 8715 & 061 439 7824
*Set next to a rural church on the edge of Manchester's "stockbroker belt" this little restaurant is attractively furnished with mahogany tables and co-ordinating fabrics, fresh flowers and tasteful prints effectively offsetting the simplicity of its red brick walls. Imaginative à la carte menus and daily blackboard specials offer, for example, fresh seawater turbot stuffed with crabmeat and mussels on a bed of spinach with claret essence, or poached fillet of pork with baby leeks in a herb sauce, while puddings include such treats as a deliciously sticky toffee pudding or a white chocolate and raspberry terrine.*
♀ English & French V 46 seats ✳ Lunch £12-£15alc Dinner £22-£25alc Last lunch 2pm Last dinner 10pm 16P
Credit Cards ① ② ③ ⑤

---

**WOODFORD BRIDGE** Devon Map **02** SS31

★★★57% **Woodford Bridge** Milton Damerel EX22 7LL ☎Milton Damerel(040926)481 FAX (040926) 585
*This thatched property, located beside the A388 between Holsworthy and Bideford, dates back to the 15th century. Recent extensions have incuded time share apartments, and a leisure complex in the grounds, and the image is now more of a country club than a roadside inn. The bedrooms offer character, and are well equipped, and there is a choice of lounges and a busier public bar, which along with the popular carvery restaurant, has recently been upgraded.*
12⇄♠(1fb) CTV in all bedrooms ® T ✳ sB&B⇄♠£42 dB&B⇄♠£68 ⊟
《 100P ✿ ☒(heated) ℐ (hard) ⏁ squash snooker sauna solarium gymnasium *xmas*
♀ English & French V ♥ ⌘ ⊁ Lunch £6-£10 Dinner £6-£10&alc Last dinner 10pm
Credit Cards ① ② ③ ⑤ ⓔ

---

**WOODFORD BRIDGE** Greater London

See **LONDON plan 1** *F5* (page 426)
★★★69% **Prince Regent** Manor Rd IG8 8AE ☎081-505 9966 FAX 081-506 0807
*This skillfully converted Georgian manor house is set in 4 acres of landscaped grounds. The accommodation has been elegantly furnished and very well equipped, comprising a choice of luxurious, spacious open style suites, and well furnished bedrooms, all with generous bathroom or shower. Dukes Restaurant combines with the bar and features à la carte and daily fresh fish dishes. An extensive conference centre and banqueting rooms are available, together with 24 hour room service and very good car parking.*
10⇄♠Annexe51⇄♠3⊞ CTV in all bedrooms ® T ✗ (ex guide dogs) ✳ sB&B⇄♠£75 dB&B⇄♠£85

Lift 《 CTV 100P 20🅿 ✿
♀ English & Continental V ♥ ⌘ S12.5% Lunch £15&alc
Credit Cards ① ② ③ ⑤

---

**WOODFORD GREEN** Greater London

See **LONDON plan 1** *F5* (page 427)
★★★68% **Woodford Moat House** Oak Hill IG8 9NY (Queens Moat) ☎081-505 4511 Telex no 264428 FAX 081-506 0941
*In an ideal position on the edge of Epping Forest, there are comprehensive facilities here for both business and pleasure. Bedrooms are comfortable and very well-equipped, and the attractive wood-panelled Churchill Restaurant offers tempting set and à la carte menus. Young staff provide friendly and attentive service.*
99⇄♠ CTV in all bedrooms ® T ✗ (ex guide dogs)
sB&B⇄♠fr£79 dB&B⇄♠fr£92 ⊟
Lift 《 150P CFA
♀ English & French V ♥ ⌘ Lunch £14.25-£28.65alc Dinner £14.25-£28.65alc Last dinner 10.15pm
Credit Cards ① ② ③ ⑤

---

**WOODHALL SPA** Lincolnshire Map **08** TF16

★★★59% **Petwood** Stixwould Rd LN10 6QF (Best Western) ☎(0526)52411 Telex no 56402 FAX (0526) 53473
Closed 24-30 Dec
*This house is set in quiet surroundings of 30 acres of gardens and mature woodland; formerly the house of Sir Archibold Wiesall, and laterly the officers' mess of the famous 'Dambuster' 617 Squadron during World War II. The hotel is currently undergoing a refurbishment programme to enhance and restore public rooms. The bedrooms are modern, with a good range of facilities and are generally spacious.*
46⇄♠(12fb)3⊞⊁in 6 bedrooms CTV in all bedrooms ® T ✗ (ex guide dogs) ✳ sB⇄♠£57-£67
dB⇄♠£67-£87 (room only) ⊟
Lift 《 80P ✿ croquet bowls boules putting green
V ♥ ⌘ ⊁ Lunch fr£7.95 Dinner fr£11.95&alc Last dinner 9.30pm
Credit Cards ① ② ③ ⑤

---

**WOODLANDS** Hampshire Map **04** SU31

★★59% **Busketts Lawn** 174 Woodlands Rd SO4 2GL ☎Ashurst(0703)292272 & 292077 FAX (0703) 292487
*This small, family-run establishment is equally suitable for holidaymaker or business traveller, proving comfortable bedrooms and the services of a particularly helpful and friendly staff; in addition to the hotel's own pool, there are excellent local leisure facilities.*
14⇄♠(3fb)1⊞ CTV in all bedrooms ® T S10%
sB&B⇄♠£32.50-£65 dB&B⇄♠£65-£95 ⊟
CTV 50P ✿ ☒(heated) putting croquet football *xmas*
♀ English & Continental V ♥ ⌘ S10% Lunch £7.50-£10.50 High tea £6.50-£7.50 Dinner £12.50-£14&alc Last dinner 8.30pm
Credit Cards ① ② ③ ⑤
**See advertisement under SOUTHAMPTON**

---

**WOODSTOCK** Oxfordshire Map **04** SP41

★★★67% **Bear** Park St OX7 1SZ (Trusthouse Forte) ☎(0993)811511 Telex no 837921 FAX (0993) 813380
*A busy town centre commecial hotel with some character. The accommodation is comfortable and although some bedrooms are small they are well equipped. Carefully prepared dishes are served in the attractive restaurant.*
33⇄Annexe12⇄(1fb)5⊞⊁in 11 bedrooms CTV in all bedrooms ® T ✳ sB⇄fr£81 dB⇄£108-£165 (room only) ⊟
《 40P CFA *xmas*

---

**W**

V ✿ ⬛ ✠ S% Lunch £10.50-£17.50&alc Dinner
£19.50-£24.50&alc Last dinner 10pm
Credit Cards 1 2 3 4 5

★★70% **Feathers** Market St OX7 1SX ☎(0993)812291
Telex no 83147 FAX (0993) 813158

*Dating from the 17th-century, this delightful hotel has been
beautifully restored. The superb colour schemes, antique furniture
and old prints certainly combine to set off the flag-stoned hall,
wainscoted library, drawing room and smart green bar to the best
advantage. The open fires which burn in the public rooms in season
and lovely flowers perfect the scene. A cobbled courtyard where
guests can sit out in fine weather and take refreshment is another
feature of this hotel not to be missed. As you might imagine,
bedrooms in an old building like this vary in size, but all are
beautifully decorated and well equipped as well as having many
nice little extras. The candle-lit dining room is very elegantly
decorated and appointed with high-backed chairs. Here Nick Gill
prepares the excellent dishes for the fixed price and à la carte
lunch and dinner menus.*

15⇨🅟 CTV in all bedrooms T ✱ sB&B⇨🅟 fr£75
dB&B⇨🅟£90-£145 Continental breakfast 🅿

🅟 🏠 *xmas*

V ✿ ⬛ Lunch £19.50-£34.50 Dinner £29.50-£34.50 Last dinner
9.45pm
Credit Cards 1 2 3 5

★★64% **King's** Market St OX7 1ST (Trusthouse Forte)
☎(0993)811592 & 812073 Telex no 837921 FAX (0993) 813380
*This historic hotel was one of the properties given to the town by
Queen Elizabeth I on her accession. Today the hotel features a
comfortable interior, with compact but very well-equipped
bedrooms, and public rooms with much character. The renowned
Wheelers Fish Restaurant offers an extensive and commendable*

*menu; the alternative is Mario and Franco's, which provides a
variety of fresh pasta dishes accompanied by numerous meat and
vegetable sauces.*
9⇨🅟2🏠 CTV in all bedrooms ® T
🅟
V ✿ ⬛ ✠ Last dinner 10.15pm
Credit Cards 1 2 3 4 5

---

**WOODY BAY** Devon Map 03 SS64

★★77% **Woody Bay** EX31 4QX ☎Parracombe(05983)264
Closed early Jan-mid Feb RS mid Feb-mid Mar & Nov-Dec
*Set in a magnificent spot overlooking the bay on the edge of
Exmoor National Park, this spacious Victorian house offers
comfortable bedrooms – many with sea views, a cosy chintzy
lounge and imaginative cooking. An interesting feature here is a
small sanctuary for injured owls.*
14rm(11⇨2🅟)(1fb)2🏠 ® sB&B£27-£34 dB&B⇨🅟£50-£74 🅿
CTV 15P 🏠 ❀ nc8yrs *xmas*
♀ English & French V ✿ ⬛ Bar Lunch £5-£12alc Dinner
£14.50&alc Last dinner 8.30pm
Credit Cards 1 3

---

**WOOLACOMBE** Devon Map 02 SS44

★★★68% **Watersmeet** Mortehoe EX34 7EB ☎(0271)870333
FAX (0271) 870890
Closed Jan-mid Feb
*Beautifully situated on the headland of Mortehoe, this hotel has
undergone extensive refurbishment to provide individually
designed bedrooms which offer a good combination of quality and
comfort. Relaxing public areas include a restaurant with fine
panoramic views.*
24⇨🅟(4fb)1🏠 CTV in all bedrooms T ⋈ ✱ S%
sB&B⇨🅟£35-£60 dB&B⇨🅟£70-£114 (incl dinner) 🅿
▶

**W**

CTV 20P 10🍴 ⌕ ✿ ⌒(heated) ♪ (grass) clay pigeon
shooting *xmas*
♀ English & French V ✿ ⌑ ✄ S% Bar Lunch fr£2.50 Dinner
fr£19.50 Last dinner 8.30pm
Credit Cards ①②③⑤

★★★63%, **Woolacombe Bay** South St EX34 7BN (Best Western)
☎(0271)870388 Telex no 46761
Closed Jan
*This comfortable family-run hotel overlooks the bay, and has a*
*good range of public rooms, well-equipped bedrooms and an*
*excellent range of indoor and outdoor facilities.*
59⌒🌂(26fb)1🏠 CTV in all bedrooms ® T ✖ (ex guide dogs)
sB&B⌒🌂£43-£95 dB&B⌒🌂£86-£190 (incl dinner) 🍴
Lift ⊄ CTV 100P ✿ ✿ ⌒(heated) ⌒(heated) ♪ 9 ♪ (hard)
squash snooker sauna solarium gymnasium spa bath *xmas*
♀ English & French V ✿ ⌑ Sunday Lunch £7 High tea £5
Dinner £7.50-£15&alc Last dinner 9.45pm
Credit Cards ①②③⑤

★★68%, **Little Beach** The Esplanade EX34 7DJ
☎Barnstaple(0271)870398
Closed Nov-Jan
*Enjoying a prime position overlooking the bay, the hotel provides*
*well equipped, modern bedrooms and spacious public areas*
*enhanced by good antiques; meals are imaginative and service is*
*friendly throughout.*
10rm(4⌒4🌂) CTV in all bedrooms T ✳ sB&B£20-£22.50
dB&B⌒🌂£34.60-£55 🍴
8P 🍴 sauna nc7yrs
♀ English & Continental Dinner £11.50 Last dinner 8pm
Credit Cards ①③

★★64%, **Devon Beach** The Esplanade EX34 7DJ
☎(0271)870449
Closed mid Oct-Etr
*This friendly, personally-run hotel overlooking the sea offers bright*
*bedrooms (some of the sea-facing ones having balconies) and quite*
*spacious public areas which include a lounge for non-smokers.*
36rm(24⌒)(21fb) CTV in all bedrooms ® sB&B£30-£40
sB&B⌒£35-£45 dB&B£60-£80 dB&B⌒£70-£90 (incl dinner)
28P ⌒🍴 (£4 per day) ⌒(heated) solarium ♪ ✿
♀ English, French & Italian ✿ ⌑ ✄ Bar Lunch £1-£4alc
Dinner £8.50-£9.50&alc Last dinner 8.15pm
Credit Cards ①③

★★**Atlantic** Sunnyside Rd EX34 7DG ☎(0271)870469
FAX (0271) 870223
Closed Nov-Feb
*Comfortable, friendly, privately owned holiday hotel, overlooking*
*village and bay.*
16rm(9⌒3🌂)(10fb)✄in 4 bedrooms CTV in all bedrooms ®
✳ sB&B£30-£37.50 sB&B⌒🌂£35-£40
dB&B⌒🌂£65-£80 (incl dinner) 🍴
CTV 16P ✿ table tennis pool table
♀ English & Continental V ✿ ⌑ ✄ S% Bar Lunch
£2.50-£7.90alc Dinner £14&alc Last dinner 7.30pm
£

★70%, **Crossways** The Esplanade EX34 7DJ ☎(0271)870395
Closed Nov-Feb
*This cosy hotel which stands in a fine, elevated position overlooking*
*the bay, has been refurbished to a good standard. Public areas*
*include a comfortable themed bar and a quality lounge with fine*
*sea views, while bedrooms though small are tastefully decorated*
*and well equipped (some having very good en suite facilities).*
*Guests enjoy good home cooking and the services of particularly*
*friendly and attentive hosts.*
9rm(5🌂)(5fb) CTV in all bedrooms ® S% sB&B£14.75-£20.25
dB&B£29.50-£36.30 dB&B🌂£33.50-£40.70 🍴
9P 🍴
✿ ✄ Bar Lunch £1-£2.50 Dinner fr£5 Last dinner 6.30pm

★50%, **Sunnyside** Sunnyside Rd EX34 7DG ☎(0271)870267
Closed Nov-Mar
*Pleasant family holiday hotel in a quiet position.*
16rm(2⌒)(5fb) ®
CTV 12P ✿ ♪ ✿
V ✿ Last dinner 7.15pm

**WOOLER** Northumberland Map **12** NT92

★★53%, **Tankerville Arms** Cottage Rd NE71 6AD (Minotels)
☎(0668)81581
Closed 22-28 Dec
*This large, comfortable inn is managed by resident proprietors who*
*maintain a high level of service.*
14rm(6⌒3🌂)(1fb) CTV in 9 bedrooms ® ✳ sB&B£20-£29.50
sB&B⌒🌂£20-£29.50 dB&B£40
dB&B⌒🌂£47-£53 Continental breakfast 🍴
CTV 100P ✿ ✿
V ✿ ✄ Sunday Lunch £3.95-£6.95 High tea £5.50-£6.50 Dinner
£14.75-£18 Last dinner 9pm
Credit Cards ①③⑤

**WOOLLEY EDGE MOTORWAY SERVICE AREA (M1)**
West Yorkshire Map **08** SE31

⌂**Granada Lodge** M1 Service Area, West Bretton WF4 4LQ
(between junct 38/39, adj to service area) (Granada)
☎Wakefield(0924)830371 & 830569 FAX (0924) 830609
31⌒🌂(4fb)✄in 7 bedrooms CTV in all bedrooms ®
✖ (ex guide dogs) ✳ S% sB⌒🌂fr£25
dB⌒🌂fr£28 (room only)
60P
V ✿ ⌑ ✄
Credit Cards ①②③⑤
See advertisement under WAKEFIELD

**WOOTTON**
See Wight, Isle of

**WORCESTER** Hereford & Worcester Map **03** SO85

★★★71%, **Fownes** City Walls Rd WR1 2AP ☎(0905)613151
Telex no 335021 FAX (0905) 23742
*This former glove factory was transformed into an hotel in 1985.*
*Situated on Worcester's inner ring road it is convenient for the city*
*centre shops and the cathedral. Bedrooms are of a good size and*
*equipped for the needs of commercial guests and holidaymakers*
*alike. The restaurant and 'all day' brasserie allow a choice of*
*eating style.*
61⌒🌂(4fb) CTV in all bedrooms ® T ✖ (ex guide dogs)
sB⌒🌂£76.50-£84.50 dB⌒🌂£91.50-£150 (room only) 🍴
Lift ⊄ 94P sauna gymnasium ♪ *xmas*
♀ English & French V ✿ ⌑ ✄ Lunch £10-£12.50&alc Dinner
£15.95&alc Last dinner 9.45pm
Credit Cards ①②③⑤ £

★★★69%, **Star** Foregate St WR1 1EA (Crown & Raven)
☎(0905)24308 Telex no 335075 FAX (0905) 23440
*This city-centre hotel dates back to the 16th century and was*
*famous as a coaching inn during the 1800s. It has recently*
*benefitted from an extensive programme of improvements.*
*Bedrooms are well equipped, with two specially adapted to meet*
*the needs of disabled guests and there are three luxurious*
*'executive rooms'.*
46⌒🌂(2fb) CTV in all bedrooms ® T ✳ sB&B⌒🌂£56.65
dB&B⌒🌂£69.30 🍴
Lift ⊄ 55P
♀ English & French V ✿ ⌑ Sunday Lunch £7.95 Dinner
fr£11.55&alc Last dinner 10pm
Credit Cards ①②③

★★★56% **The Giffard** High St WR1 2QR (Trusthouse Forte)
☎(0905)726262 Telex no 336689 FAX (0905) 723458
*This busy, modern hotel is located in the city centre, with a nearby NCP car park. The Giffard has extensive conference facilites for up to 200 delegates. The restaurant offers good views of Worcester cathedral, and there is also a coffee shop for light meals and refreshments.*
103⇠✠in 28 bedrooms CTV in all bedrooms ® T ✱
sB&B⇠£58 dB&B⇠£80 ⊟
Lift ( CFA snooker *xmas*
♀ English & International V ✧ ⬛ ✠
Credit Cards [1][2][3][4][5]

★★65% **Loch Ryan Hotel** 119 Sidbury Rd WR5 2DH
☎(0905)351143
*Situated just south of the city centre on the A44, this Grade II listed Georgian building close to the cathedral was once the house of the Bishop of Worcester. The well maintained, comfortable accommodation and friendly, informal service provides good value for money and is equally suitable for tourists and business people.*
12rm(2⇠)Annexe1↑(1fb) CTV in all bedrooms ✖ ✱
sB&B£25 sB&B⇠↑£30 dB&B£42 dB&B⇠↑£50 ⊟
✗ ✿ ⬥
V ✧ ⬛ ✠

★★63% **Ye Olde Talbot** Friar St WR1 2NA (Lansbury)
☎(0905)23573 Telex no 333315 FAX (0905) 612760
*A warm and pleasant atmosphere pervades this old 13th-century coaching inn. The bedrooms and public rooms are sympathetically furnished, comfortable and well-equipped, and the staff are particularly caring and friendly.*
29⇠(6fb)1⧈✠in 3 bedrooms CTV in all bedrooms ® T
✖ (ex guide dogs) sB&B⇠£63 dB&B⇠£76 ⊟
( 8P
♀ Mainly grills V ✧ ⬛ Lunch fr£8.95 Dinner fr£14&alc Last dinner 10pm
Credit Cards [1][2][3][5]

★★61% *Diglis Hotel* Riverside, Severn St WR1 2NF
☎(0905)353518
RS Xmas day night
*Situated on the banks of the River Severn, close to the cathedral and the county cricket ground, a charming old house with terraced gardens has recently been refurbished to provide simple, comfortable accommodation with informal service.*
14rm(3⇠)(1fb) CTV in all bedrooms ®
CTV ✿ ♪
♀ English & French V ✧ ⬛ Last dinner 9.45pm
Credit Cards [1][3]

★61% **Park House** 12 Droitwich Rd WR3 7LJ (Guestaccom)
☎(0905)21816 FAX (0905) 612178
*Located north of the city centre, on the A38 close to its junction with the A449, this small family-run hotel provides simple, but comfortable bedrooms and informal service.*
7rm(3↑)(1fb) CTV in all bedrooms ® ✱ sB&B£20-£22
sB&B↑£26-£32 dB&B£30-£32 dB&B↑£34-£36
CTV 10P ⊞
V ✧ ⬛

✖✖*Brown's* The Old Cornmill, South Quay WR1 2JN
☎(0905)26263
*Situated within a cleverly converted corn mill overlooking the River Severn, close to the cathedral and city centre, this smart restaurant features art nouveau furnishings and a galleried lounge area. The good value fixed price menu offers a good selection of meat dishes which are given a distinctive flavour by charcoal grilling, and fish is always available.*
Closed Xmas wk & BH Mon's
Lunch not served Sat
Dinner not served Sun ▶

W

♀ English & French 70 seats Last lunch 1.45pm Last dinner 9.45pm ✔ nc10yrs
Credit Cards ① ② ③ ⑤

---

### WORFIELD Shropshire Map 07 SJ40

★★★♨68% **Old Vicarage** WV15 5JZ ☎(07464)497
Telex no 35438 FAX (07464) 552
Closed 22 Dec-2 Jan
*The tasteful modernisation and extension of this Edwardian House has resulted in a successful combination of character and the comforts of up-to-date facilities. Peter and Christine Iles look after their guests very well, and the food is most enjoyable, as is the comprehensive wine list. Bedrooms are well equipped, those in the coach-house being particularly spacious, and one has been furnished with a view to providing suitable accommodation for a disabled guest. The public areas retain much of the original character of the house and are furnished in keeping with the period.*
11⇨ℝAnnexe4⇨ℝ(1fb)1🛏⅙in 6 bedrooms CTV in all bedrooms ® T ✱ sB&B⇨ℝ£55-£62.50
dB&B⇨ℝ£69.50-£77.50 🍴
CTV 30P 🚗 ✱
V ♥ 🖵 ✙ Lunch fr£17.50 Dinner £24.50 Last dinner 9pm
Credit Cards ① ② ③

---

### WORKINGTON Cumbria Map 11 NX92

★★★67% **Washington Central** Washington St CA14 3AW
☎(0900)65772 FAX (0900) 68770
Closed 1 Jan
*This modern town-centre hotel is built around a small enclosed courtyard. The bedrooms are pleasant and cosy, there is an attractive cocktail bar, peaceful lounge and a restaurant where well-prepared dishes are served by young and friendly staff. Good home-baking is offered in the all-day coffee shop.*
40⇨ℝ(4fb) CTV in all bedrooms ® T ✘ (ex guide dogs) sB&B⇨ℝ£38.50 dB&B⇨ℝ£59.50 🍴
Lift ℂ 50P 🎵
V ♥ 🖵 ✙ Lunch £8.50&alc Dinner £11.95&alc Last dinner 9.30pm
Credit Cards ① ② ③

★★★55% **Cumberland Arms** Belle Isle St CA14 2XQ
☎(0900)64401 FAX (0900) 68624
Closed 25 Dec
*This large and well furnished hotel, set conveniently close to the railway station and within a short distance of the town centre, offers a good standard of carefully prepared meals.*
29⇨ℝ(1fb) CTV in all bedrooms ®
Lift ℂ CTV 60P pool table
♀ English & French ♥ 🖵
Credit Cards ① ② ③ ⑤ ⑥

★★57% **Crossbarrow Motel** Little Clifton CA14 1XS (3m E on A595) ☎(0900)61443
*A purpose-built complex with modern functional bedrooms.*
Annexe27⇨ℝ CTV in all bedrooms ® T
50P ✱ ♨
V ♥ 🖵 Last dinner 8.30pm
Credit Cards ① ③

---

### WORKSOP Nottinghamshire Map 08 SK57

★★61% **Regancy** Carlton Rd S80 1PS ☎(0909)474108
*A busy family run commercial hotel on the edge of town adjacent to a railway line. The hotel has popular restaurant where friendly local staff serve well-priced meals.*
13rm(7ℝ)(1fb) CTV in all bedrooms ® T sB&B£17 sB&Bℝ£22 dB&B£27 dB&Bℝ£37

---

CTV 25P 5🏠 🚿 sauna solarium gymnasium
Lunch £4&alc Dinner £7-£8&alc Last dinner 8pm
Credit Cards ① ② ③ ⑤

---

### WORMIT Fife Map 11 NO32

★★58% **Sandford Hill** DD6 8RG
☎Newport-on-Tay(0382)541802
Closed 1-2 Jan
*Located 3 miles south of the Tay Road Bridge, this well-established hotel is popular with both businessmen and tourists. The public rooms have a homely atmosphere and the practical modern bedrooms are well-equipped.*
15rm(13⇨ℝ)(3fb) CTV in all bedrooms ® T sB&B⇨ℝ£35.50-£44 dB&B£50-£60 dB&B⇨ℝ£55-£66 🍴
CTV 50P 🚗 ✱ ♬ (hard) ✈ clay pigeon shooting
♀ Scottish & Continental V ♥ 🖵 Lunch £10-£14 High tea £5-£8.50alc Dinner £17.50-£20 Last dinner 9pm
Credit Cards ① ② ③ ⑤ ⑥

---

### WORSLEY Greater Manchester Map 07 SD70

★★★57% **Novotel Manchester West** Worsley Brow M28 4YA (adjacent to M62 junc 13) (Novotel) ☎061-799 3535
Telex no 669586 FAX 061-703 8207
*Just off junction 13 of the M62, this modern hotel provides functional and well-equipped accommodation. Ideal for families and business travellers, this hotel is convenient for Manchester airport.*
119⇨ℝ(119fb)⅙in 20 bedrooms CTV in all bedrooms ®
Lift 133P ✱ ⊇(heated) ♬
♀ English & French V ♥ 🖵 ✙ Last dinner mdnt
Credit Cards ① ② ③ ⑤

See advertisement under MANCHESTER

---

### WORTHING West Sussex Map 04 TQ10

★★★67% **Beach** Marine Pde BN11 3QJ ☎(0903)34001 FAX (0903) 34567
*An hotel which commands extensive sea views from its fine position on the front creates a warmly hospitable atmosphere, retaining some traditional services. Bedrooms are well equipped and there is ample comfortably furnished lounge accommodation.*
78⇨ℝ(8fb) CTV in all bedrooms ® T ✘ sB&B⇨ℝ£45.50-£52 dB&B⇨ℝ£68.50-£77.50 🍴
Lift ℂ 55P 🚗 CFA nc8yrs xmas
V ♥ 🖵 Lunch fr£11.50&alc Dinner fr£16&alc Last dinner 8.45pm
Credit Cards ① ② ③ ④ ⑤

★★★62% **Chatsworth** Steyne BN11 3DU ☎(0903)36103
Telex no 877046 FAX (0903) 823726
*The hotel has an attractive Georgian frontage and overlooks Steyne Gardens and the sea.*
105⇨ℝ(5fb) CTV in all bedrooms ® T sB&B⇨ℝ£52-£64 dB&B⇨ℝ£71.50-£75 🍴
Lift ℂ ✈ CFA snooker sauna solarium gymnasium games room xmas
♀ English & Continental V ✙ Lunch fr£9.85 Dinner fr£13.75 Last dinner 8.30pm
Credit Cards ① ② ③ ⑤

★★★58% **Kingsway** Marine Pde BN11 3QQ ☎(0903)37542 & 37543 FAX (0903) 204173
*A hotel in fine sea front position, personally supervised by proprietors who take pride in their traditional hospitality, features some exceptional rooms, all bedrooms are well equipped, some of them having recently been refurbished, guests can relax in comfortable lounge or cosy bar, and there is a carvery restaurant.*
28⇨ℝ(1fb) CTV in all bedrooms ® T sB&B⇨ℝ£38-£42 dB&B⇨ℝ£52-£64 🍴

---

**W**

Lift ( 12P 🚑 *xmas*
V ✿ ⬧ ₢ Lunch fr£8.95&alc Dinner fr£14 Last dinner 9pm
Credit Cards [1] [2] [3] [5] (£)

★★63% **Ardington** Steyne Gardens BN11 3DZ (Best Western)
☎(0903)30451
Closed Xmas
*This established family-run commercial hotel is conveniently
situated overlooking Steyne Gardens. The bedrooms are well-
equipped, and the resident proprietors' personal service and
supervision complement the friendly and informal atmosphere.*
55rm(22⇨22🅝)(4fb) CTV in all bedrooms ® T ✱
sB&B⇨🅝£38-£48 dB&B⇨🅝£55-£63 🄮
( 16P
♀ International ✿ ⬧ Lunch £6.75-£14.50alc Dinner £10 Last
dinner 8.30pm
Credit Cards [1] [2] [3] [5]

★★61% **Windsor House** 14/20 Windsor Rd BN11 2LX
☎(0903)39655
*Quietly situated off the A259, yet close to the beach and all
holiday facilities, a popular, well-managed and family-run hotel
complements a choice of modern bedrooms with an attractive
carvery-style restaurant, cosy bar, foyer lounge and good function
facilities.*
33rm(17⇨13🅝)(7fb)⩘in 4 bedrooms CTV in all bedrooms ®
T ✖ (ex guide dogs) ✱ sB&B£23.50-£25.50
sB&B⇨🅝£38.50-£45.50 dB&B£47-£51 dB&B⇨🅝£63-£75 🄮
CTV 18P *xmas*
♀ English & French V ✿ ⬧ Lunch fr£7.50 Dinner fr£9&alc
Last dinner 9.30pm
Credit Cards [1] [3] [5] (£)

---

**WREXHAM** Clwyd Map **07** SJ34

See also **Marchwiel and Marford**
★★★🏆73% **Llwyn Onn Hall** Cefn Rd LL13 0NY (WR)
☎(0978)261225
*Though close to the industrial estate, this quietly sedate yet
friendly hotel occupies a secluded position in rolling parkland. It
enjoys a good local reputation for imaginative cuisine – and most
of the produce used in the preparation of meals is grown in its own
garden.*
13⇨🅝1🛏 CTV in all bedrooms T ✱ sB⇨🅝£46-£52
dB⇨🅝£60-£72 (room only) 🄮
70P
V ✿ ⬧ Lunch fr£9.50&alc Dinner fr£13&alc Last dinner 9pm
Credit Cards [1] [2] [3] [5]
**See advertisement on page 749**

★★★63% *Wynnstay Arms* High Street/Yorke St LL13 8LP
(Consort) ☎(0978)291010 Telex no 61674 FAX (0978) 362138
*Modern hotel, situated in the town centre.*
75⇨🅝(8fb)⩘in 4 bedrooms CTV in all bedrooms ® T
Lift ( CTV 50P 20🚗
V ✿ ⬧ ⥅ Last dinner 9.45pm
Credit Cards [1] [2] [3] [5]

⭐Travelodge Wrexham By Pass, Rhostyllen LL14 4EJ (A483/
A5152 Wrexham by-pass) (Trusthouse Forte) ☎(0978)365705
Central res (0800) 850950
*Three miles south of the town, at the junction of the A483 and
A5152, stands a two-storey, purpose-built, modern block which
provides well equipped and spaciously comfortable bedrooms – one
catering specifically for the needs of disabled guests; restaurant
facilities are provided by the adjacent Little Chef.*
32⇨🅝(32fb) CTV in all bedrooms ® sB⇨🅝£24
dB⇨🅝£29.50 (room only)
( 31P 🚑
Credit Cards [1] [2] [3]

**W**

## Wrightington - Wymondham

### WRIGHTINGTON Lancashire Map 07 SD51

★★★64% **Wrightington Hotel & Restaurant** Moss Ln,
WN6 9PB ☎Standish(0257)425803 FAX (0257) 425830
*Set in open green fields close to junction 27 of the M6 this well
furnished hotel offers well-equipped bedrooms, good food and
extensive leisure facilities.*
47⇨³(4fb) CTV in all bedrooms ® T ✱ sB&B⇨³£45-£55
dB&B⇨³£60-£70 ☐
《 80P ⊠(heated) squash sauna solarium gymnasium ♫
♀ International V ⊹ ⚏ Lunch £6.95&alc Dinner
£10.95-£16.50&alc Last dinner 10pm
Credit Cards ①②③

✸✗✗✗**High Moor** Highmoor Ln WN6 9QA junct 27 off M6,
take B5239 ☎Appley Bridge(02575)2364
*The name of this consistently good restaurant aptly desribes its
location overlooking the road between Parbold and Standish. The
old beamed ceilings and open fires give it atmosphere, but is success
is due to James Simes's sound and reliable cooking. The à la carte
menu is frequently changed so the choice is good, and the special
Sunday lunch remains a popular feature.*
Closed Mon
Lunch not served Sat
Dinner not served Sun
♀ English & French V 80 seats ✱ Lunch £17-£25alc Dinner
£17-£25alc Last lunch 1.45pm Last dinner 9.45pm 35P
Credit Cards ①②③⑤

### WROTHAM Kent Map 05 TQ65

★★★★54% **Post House** London Rd, Wrotham Heath
TN15 7RS (Trusthouse Forte) ☎Borough Green(0732)883311
Telex no 957309 FAX (0732) 885850
*A second generation Post House, close to junction 2A of the M26,
with good sized, well-furnished bedrooms, a carvery-style à la
carte restaurant and good leisure facilities. Excellent car parking
makes this an ideal business rendezvous.*
119⇨³♠(22fb)⅓in 24 bedrooms CTV in all bedrooms ® ☐
《 138P ⊠(heated) sauna solarium gymnasium health & fitness
centre ♧ xmas
♀ International V ⊹ ⚏ ⅓ S10% Lunch £12.50-£18.80&alc
Dinner £16.60-£18.80&alc Last dinner 11pm
Credit Cards ①②③④⑤
**See advertisement under MAIDSTONE**

### WROXHAM Norfolk Map 09 TG31

★★★63% *Broads* Station Rd NR12 8UR
☎Norwich(0603)782869
*A centrally situated hotel run by the Bales family who extend a
warm welcome to their guests. Popular with both commercial
visitors and holidaymakers the hotel provides comfortable
accommodation and a variety of well-cooked dishes.*
19rm(12⇨³1♠)Annexe7⇨³♠(2fb) CTV in 19 bedrooms ® T
40P ♫
♀ English & French V ⊹ ⚏
Credit Cards ①②③⑤

★★62% **Hotel Wroxham** Hoveton NR12 8AJ ☎(0603)782061
FAX (0603) 784279
*Many rooms have their own balconies overlooking the water at this
hotel, which enjoys an enviable position at the heart of the Broads.
Extensive public areas include the Riverside Bar, which is
particularly popular for lunchtime snacks, and a restaurant which
offers a wide à la carte selection as well as the d'hôte menu.*
18rm(14⇨³♠)(2fb) CTV in all bedrooms ® T sB&B£28-£39
sB&B⇨³♠£34-£39 dB&B£42 dB&B⇨³♠£52-£57 ☐
CTV 55P ♪ boating facilities ♫ xmas

♀ English & French V ⊹ ⚏ ⅓ Lunch £6.85-£10&alc High tea
£3.50-£4.80 Dinner £9.50&alc Last dinner 9.30pm
Credit Cards ①②③⑤

★62% **Kings Head** Station Rd NR12 8UR (Berni/Chef &
Brewer) ☎(0603)782429
6⇨³♠(2fb) CTV in all bedrooms ® T ✗ (ex guide dogs)
sB&B⇨³♠£36.50-£41 dB&B⇨³♠£48.50 ☐
50P
♀ International V ⊹ ⚏ ⅓ Lunch £8-£15alc Dinner £8-£15alc
Last dinner 9.30pm
Credit Cards ①②③⑤

### WROXTON Oxfordshire Map 04 SP44

★★★67% **Wroxton House** OX15 6QB (Best Western)
☎Banbury(0295)730482 & 730777 Telex no 83409
FAX (0295) 730800
*A small country house hotel, set in this charming village, has been
extended and tastefully upgraded to provide comfortable, well
appointed accommodation with spacious, well-equipped bedrooms
and attractive public rooms boasting some fine period furniture and
paintings. The restaurant, in three sections, creates an intimate
atmosphere in which to enjoy interesting dishes, skilfully prepared
from good fresh produce.*
29⇨³♠ Annexe3⇨³♠2☒ CTV in all bedrooms ® T
sB&B⇨³♠£75-£85 dB&B⇨³♠£95-£120 ☐
《 40P 🚗 ✿ xmas
♀ English & Continental V ⊹ ⚏ ⅓ Lunch £16.50-£18.50&alc
Dinner £24.50-£26.50&alc Last dinner 9.30pm
Credit Cards ①②③④⑤

### WYKEHAM (near Scarborough) North Yorkshire Map 08 SE98

★★62% **Downe Arms** YO13 9QB ☎Scarborough(0723)862471
Telex no 527192 FAX (0723) 864329
*This popular old 18th-century coaching inn offers very good value
for money. The lounge bar and dining room are very attractive,
and there are good facilities for functions and receptions.*
10⇨³♠(2fb) CTV in all bedrooms ® ✱ sB&B⇨³♠£22.50
dB&B⇨³♠£45 ☐
Lift CTV 150P 2🚗 ✿ shooting xmas
♀ English & French V ⊹ ⚏ Sunday Lunch £7.25 Dinner
£10.50&alc Last dinner 9pm
Credit Cards ①②③⑤

### WYMONDHAM Norfolk Map 05 TG10

★★★64% **Sinclair** 28 Market St NR18 0BB ☎(0953)606721
FAX (0953) 601361
*A family owned and run hotel in the town centre which benefits
from constant care and attention. Both table d'hôte and à la carte
menus are available in the restaurant.*
20⇨³(2fb)1☒⅓in 12 bedrooms CTV in all bedrooms ® T ✗
sB&B⇨³♠£39-£45 dB&B⇨³♠£49-£55 ☐
8P ✿ sauna xmas
V ⊹ ⚏ Lunch £9-£12.50 Dinner £9.50-£12.50&alc Last dinner
9.30pm
Credit Cards ①②③
**See advertisement on page 751**

★★62% **Abbey** Church St NR18 0PH (Best Western)
☎(0953)602148 FAX (0953) 606247
*Situated adjacent to Wymondham Abbey the hotel has been
sympathetically updated and retains some of its 16th century and
Victorian features. The accommodation is well equipped and there
are some conference/banqueting facilities. Guests have use of the
excellent leisure/golf centre at Barnham Broom, a sister hotel.*
26⇨³ Annexe1rm(4fb) CTV in 26 bedrooms ® T
sB&B⇨³♠£40-£45 dB&B⇨³♠£60-£65 ☐
Lift 《 25P xmas

▶

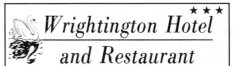

749

V ✿ ⏴ Lunch £6.50-£7.50 Dinner £11.50-£12&alc Last dinner
9.15pm
Credit Cards [1] [2] [3] ⓔ

✗**Jennings** 16 Damgate St NR18 0BQ ☎(0953)603533
*A former 17th-century butcher's shop has been sympathetically
transformed into a friendly and informal restaurant. Sarah and
David Jennings offer a small but well-chosen menu featuring dishes
such as chicken liver and foie gras on a warm salad with raspberry
vinaigrette.*
Closed Sun, Mon & BHs
Lunch not served all week (ex by prior arrangement)
♿ English & French 30 seats Last dinner 10.30pm ♪ ✂
Credit Cards [1] [2] [3]

---

**WYRE PIDDLE** Hereford & Worcester Map **03** SO94

★★**62%, Avonside** Main Rd WR10 2JB (2m NE on B4084)
☎Pershore(0386)552654
*A small, family-run hotel in the village of Wyre Piddle, close to
Pershore. Rooms are very well equipped with modern facilities and
the comfortable lounge overlooks the River Avon. The hotel has an
outdoor swimming pool.*
7⇨🛏(3fb) CTV in all bedrooms ⓡ T ✗ ✳ sB&B⇨🛏fr£40
dB&B⇨🛏fr£52 🍴
10P 🎬 ✿ ≋(heated) ♪ nc7 yrs *xmas*
♿ English & French Dinner fr£14.95 Last dinner 7.30pm
Credit Cards [1] [3]

---

**YARCOMBE** Devon Map **03** ST20

★★**69%, The Belfry Hotel** EX14 9BD (Minotels)
☎Upottery(040486)234 & 588 FAX (040486) 579
6⇨🛏(1fb) CTV in all bedrooms ⓡ T ✗ (ex guide dogs)
sB&B⇨🛏£38.50 dB&B⇨🛏£58 🍴
10P 🎬 nc12yrs *xmas*
♿ English & French V ✿ ⏴ ✂ Lunch £8.25&alc Dinner
£14.90&alc Last dinner 8.45pm
Credit Cards [1] [2] [3] [5] ⓔ

---

**YARM** Cleveland Map **08** NZ41

✗✗*Santoro* 47 High St TS15 9BH ☎Eaglescliffe(0642)781305
*This modern, first-floor restaurant in the High Street features a
spacious, open-plan area which includes an attractive dining room,
small bar and comfortable lounge. The interesting menu shows
both French and Italian influences and offers very good value.*
Closed Sun & BH's
Lunch not served Sat
♿ English, French & Italian V 45 seats Last lunch 2pm Last
dinner 10.15pm 20P
Credit Cards [1] [2] [3] [5]

---

**YARMOUTH, GREAT** Norfolk Map **05** TG50

★★★**70%, Cliff** Gorleston NR31 6DH (2m S A12) (Best
Western) ☎Great Yarmouth(0493)662179 Telex no 975608
FAX (0493) 653617
*This Victorian building of painted brick stands amid terraced
lawns on the cliffside, commanding splendid views of the harbour
and estuary yet within easy reach of town centre and beach. Well-
furnished bedrooms, elegant public rooms and the convivial Cliff
Bar are above average in the style and quality of their décor, the
dining room's à la carte and table d'hôte menus are made up of
dishes which use only the best of fresh local produce, and an
enthusiastic staff ensures a high standard of hospitality and
service.*
30⇨🛏(5fb)1🎬✂in 2 bedrooms CTV in all bedrooms T
⏴ 70P ✿ ➿
V ✿ ⏴ ✂ Last dinner 9.30pm
Credit Cards [1] [2] [3] [5]

★★★**67%, Carlton** Marine Pde NR30 3JE (Consort)
☎Great Yarmouth(0493)855234 Telex no 975642
FAX (0493) 852220
*The Carlton Hotel has just completed a total refurbishment and
now offers comfortable public rooms, and modern accommodation
that is particularly well equipped. A good range of services – a
blend of the formal and informal – are readily provided in a polite
and efficient manner, suitable for both the holidaymaker and
business guest alike.*
95⇨🛏(10fb)4🎬 CTV in all bedrooms ⓡ T ✳
sB&B⇨🛏£45-£60 dB&B⇨🛏£65-£130 🍴
Lift ℂ CTV 30P 30🎬 (£2) hairdressing salon *xmas*
V ✿ ⏴ Sunday Lunch fr£11.95 Dinner fr£13.95 Last dinner
10pm
Credit Cards [1] [2] [3] [4] [5]

★★★**60%, Meridian Dolphin** Albert Square NR30 3JH
☎Great Yarmouth(0493)855070 Telex no 975037
FAX (0493) 853798
*Situated off Marine Parade close to the popular attractions of the
Pleasure Beach this recently refurbished and modernised hotel
provides full en-suite facilities and every modern convenience in the
light and attractively furnished rooms. The same style is continued
in the public areas where service is friendly and informal.*
49⇨🛏(3fb) CTV in all bedrooms ⓡ T S%
sB&B⇨🛏£45-£62 dB&B⇨🛏£56-£75 🍴
ℂ CTV 12P 12🎬 ✿ ≋(heated) sauna gymnasium whirlpool
*xmas*
♿ English & French V ✿ ⏴ S% Bar Lunch £1-£6.50 Dinner
fr£9.50&alc Last dinner 9.30pm
Credit Cards [1] [2] [3] [5] ⓔ

★★**69%, Imperial** North Dr NR30 1EQ
☎Great Yarmouth(0493)851113 FAX (0493) 852229
*This imposing Victorian hotel, set at the quieter end of the sea front
and having its own car park, offers well appointed and equipped
accommodation which is particularly noted for the excellence of
the Rambouillet Restaurant, where guests can enjoy a high
standard of English cuisine prepared under the guidance of the
chef/proprietor. Public areas also include a ballroom and games
room.*
41⇨🛏(7fb) CTV in all bedrooms ⓡ T sB&B⇨🛏£46-£52
dB&B⇨🛏£60 🍴
Lift ℂ CTV 50P CFA *xmas*
♿ English & French V ✿ ⏴ Lunch £10.50&alc Dinner
£13.50&alc Last dinner 10.30pm
Credit Cards [1] [2] [3] [4] [5]

★★**63%, Burlington** 11 North Dr NR30 1EG
☎Great Yarmouth(0493)844568 & 842095
Closed Jan-Feb RS Dec
*This traditional, family-owned, resort hotel stands at the quieter
end of the sea front ; bedrooms are steadily being improved to offer
good modern facilities, and some have fine sea views. Leisure
amenities include a swimming pool, steam room and solarium.*
30rm(28⇨🛏)(9fb) CTV in all bedrooms ⓡ T
✗ (ex guide dogs) sB&B£30-£35 sB&B⇨🛏£40-£45
dB&B£42-£50 dB&B⇨🛏£50-£60 🍴
Lift CTV 40P CFA ≋(heated) sauna solarium gymnasium
jacuzzi turkish steamroom ♪ *xmas*
♿ English & French V ✿ ⏴ Lunch £7.50 High tea £6.50
Dinner £9.50 Last dinner 8pm
Credit Cards [1] [3]

★★**61%, Two Bears** South Town Rd NR31 0HV
☎Great Yarmouth(0493)603198
11⇨🛏 CTV in all bedrooms ⓡ ✗ (ex guide dogs)
120P
V ✿ ⏴ ✂ Last dinner 9.30pm
Credit Cards [1] [2] [3] [5]

**YATTENDON** Berkshire Map **04** SU57

★★65% **Royal Oak** The Square RG16 0UF
☎Hermitage(0635)201325 FAX (0635) 201926
*An appealing 16th-century inn at the heart of the picturesque*
*village now provides accommodation in charming bedrooms,*
*individually decorated and furnished, which have been equipped*
*with many homely extras. Guests relax in a comfortable lounge*
*with open log fire, and good food is served in both the elegant small*
*restaurant and a lively, popular bar.*
5rm(3⇌) CTV in all bedrooms T ✱ sB&Bfr£50 sB&B⇌fr£60
dB&Bfr£60 dB&B⇌fr£70 🏳
30P
🍴 English & French V ❖ ⚏
Credit Cards ①②③

**YELVERTON** Devon Map **02** SX56

★★★70% **Moorland Links** PL20 6DA (Forestdale)
☎(0822)852245 Telex no 45616 FAX (0822) 855004
Closed 24 Dec-2 Jan
*Set in nine acres of grounds with breathtaking views across the*
*Tamar Valley this hotel provides attractive public areas and*
*tastefully decorated bedrooms. Conference facilities are also*
*available.*
30⇌🟊🌶 in 5 bedrooms CTV in all bedrooms ® T
sB&B⇌🌶£57.50-£63.20 dB&B⇌🌶£77-£84.70 🏳
《 120P ❖ CFA ♪ (hard)
🍴 English & French V ❖ ⚏ 🛠 Lunch £13.60-£20alc Dinner
£15-£23alc Last dinner 10pm
Credit Cards ①②③⑤ⓔ

**YEOVIL** Somerset Map **03** ST51

★★★65% **Manor Crest** Hendford BA20 1TG (Trusthouse
Forte) ☎(0935)23116 Telex no 46580 FAX (0935) 706607
*Well-appointed hotel in city centre. Bedrooms are particularly*
*well-equipped. The standard of food and service are especially*
*worthy of mention.*
20⇌🌶Annexe21⇌🌶1🛏🛠in 9 bedrooms CTV in all
bedrooms ® 🏳
《 50P CFA *xmas*
V ❖ ⚏ 🛠
Credit Cards ①②③④⑤

★★★62% *Yeovil Court* West Coker Rd BA20 2NE
☎(093586)3746 FAX (093586) 3990
*A small modern hotel with an informal atmosphere, on the A30*
*towards West Coker. Bedrooms are very well equipped, there are*
*three spacious suites with lounge areas. An ambitious menu of*
*modern British dishes is provided in the dining room.*
15⇌Annexe3⇌(4fb) CTV in all bedrooms ®
75P ❖
🍴 French V ❖ ⚏ Last dinner 10pm
Credit Cards ①②③⑤
See advertisement on page 753

★★★57% **Four Acres** West Coker BA22 9AJ (3m W A30)
☎West Coker(093586)2555 Telex no 46466
*Set back off the A30 Yeovil – Crewkerne Road this stone-built*
*property has a modern wing of bedrooms and an attractive*
*restaurant.*
20rm(16⇌3🌶)Annexe5⇌ CTV in all bedrooms ®
🐕 (ex guide dogs)
40P 5🍲 🚲 ❖ pool table
🍴 French V ❖ ⚏ Last dinner 9.30pm
Credit Cards ①②③⑤
See advertisement on page 753

For key to symbols see the inside front cover.

**Y**

★**60%** *Preston* 64 Preston Rd BA20 2DL ☎(0935)74400
*A small, convivial hotel, family-owned and run, is situated on the*
*Taunton Road at the edge of the town and offers good parking.*
7rm(2⇵3✟)(1fb) CTV in all bedrooms Ⓡ
19P ♨
☺ English & French V ♥ ⚲ ✂
Credit Cards ①③

---

**YORK** North Yorkshire Map **08** SE65

★★★★**63%** *Viking* North St YO1 1JF (Queens Moat)
☎(0904)659822 Telex no 57937 FAX (0904) 641793
*The large, modern hotel is situated beside the River Ouse, in the*
*heart of the city. With a choice of three restaurants, it caters for*
*business people and for tourists.*
188⇵✟(7fb)✂in 6 bedrooms CTV in all bedrooms Ⓡ T
✖ (ex guide dogs) ✳ sB&B⇵✟£68-£78
dB&B⇵✟£90-£100 ☗
Lift ℂ 15P 70🅿 sauna solarium gymnasium spa bath *xmas*
☺ English & French V ♥ ⚲ ✂ Lunch £9-£9.50 High tea £6-£7
Dinner £13.50-£14&alc Last dinner 9.45pm
Credit Cards ①②③⑤Ⓔ

★★★★**62%** *Holiday Inn* Tower St YO1 1SB (Holiday Inns)
☎(0904)648111 Telex no 57566 FAX (0904) 610317
*An elegant hotel with a striking red-brick façade. Additional*
*comforts include spa bathrooms and luxury suites. International*
*cuisine can be sampled in the restaurant and the informal brasserie*
*offers a good choice of popular dishes.*
128⇵✟(10fb)✂in 26 bedrooms CTV in all bedrooms Ⓡ T S%
sB⇵✟fr£80 dB⇵✟fr£95 (room only) ☗
Lift ℂ 40🅿 *xmas*
☺ English & French V ♥ ⚲ ✂ Lunch fr£10.50 Dinner
fr£15.50 Last dinner 10.30pm
Credit Cards ①②③④⑤

★★★ **MIDDLETHORPE HALL**

Bishopthorpe Rd YO2 1QB
(Prestige) ☎(0904)641241
Telex no 57802
FAX (0904) 620176
*This beautifully restored*
*country house set amid*
*delightful gardens dates back*
*to the William and Mary period and has preserved all the*
*elegance and grace of that time, allied to modern comforts.*
*Staff are charming and friendly, and although efficient, not in*
*the least formal. Drawing room, library and sitting room are*
*all comfortable and for meals there is either the panelled*
*dining room or the basement Grill Room with a cosy, club-like*
*atmosphere. Chef Kevin Francksen's cuisine shows much*
*potential and his sauces are particularly commendable. Dishes*
*in the Grill Room are simpler and flambé work is a speciality*
*here. Bedrooms have recently been redecorated and*
*refurbished, greatly improving the comfort for guests, whether*
*in the spacious accommodation in the main house or in the*
*more cottage rooms off the courtyard.*
31⇵✟1✎ CTV in all bedrooms Ⓡ T ✖ S10%
sB⇵✟£80-£93 dB⇵£108-£120 (room only) ☗
Lift ℂ 70P ✿ croquet nc8yrs *xmas*
V ♥ ⚲ S10% Lunch £13.90-£15.90 Dinner fr£26.90&alc
Last dinner 9.45pm
Credit Cards ①②③⑤

---

★★★**78%** *The Grange* Clifton YO3 6AA ☎(0904)644744
Telex no 57210 FAX (0904) 612453
*Our Best Newcomer for the North of England this year—see colour*
*feature on page 33. Situated close to the city centre, this Regency town*
*house has been beautifully restored to provide extremely comfortable,*
*elegant and well appointed accommodation. Lounges with open fires,*
*cosy bars and an elegant hall combine to create a restful atmosphere and*
*the individually designed bedrooms are extremely well equipped. The*
*Ivy Restaurant offers a high standard of cuisine, while the more informal*
*Brasserie provides light meals and snacks throughout the day.*
✳ sB&B⇵✟ fr £74 dB&B⇵✟£88-£110
Lunch £11.50-£12.50 & alc Dinner fr £17.50 & alc
29⇵✟2✎ CTV in all bedrooms T
ℂ 29P
☺ English & French V ♥ ⚲ Last dinner 10pm
Credit Cards ①②③⑤

★★★**71%** *Dean Court* Duncombe Place YO1 2EF (Best
Western) ☎(0904)625082 Telex no 57584 FAX (0904) 620305
*Pleasantly situated beneath the shadow of the Minster, The Dean Court*
*Hotel is located in the heart of this historic city. There are some*
*attractive and comfortable lounges and also a small tea room/snack*
*shop. It is a well managed, privately owned hotel and the young staff*
*provide a friendly service. The bedrooms are very well equipped and*
*decorated, and although sizes vary, most of the bedrooms are*
*comfortable and spacious. A substantial choice is offered in the*
*restaurant, and the food is nicely cooked and presented. The restaurant*
*and many bedrooms have pleasant views of the Minster and its*
*surroundings.*
41⇵✟ CTV in all bedrooms Ⓡ T ✖ sB&B⇵✟£50-£60
dB&B⇵✟£95-£120 ☗
Lift ℂ 25P ♨ *xmas*
☺ English & French V ♥ ⚲ Lunch £10-£12&alc High tea
£5-£10 Dinner £15.50-£17&alc Last dinner 9.30pm
Credit Cards ①②③④⑤

**See advertisement on page 755**

**THE GRANGE**
YORK
★★★

This classical Regency Townhouse,
located just five minutes walk from the
Minster has recently been restored to
create 29 individually decorated bedrooms, all with private bathroom and
satellite TV. The Ivy Restaurant which
serves a combination of French and
English country cooking, using fresh local
produce, and Cafe Brasserie situated in
the brick vaulted cellars of the building.
Car parking is available at the rear of the
hotel.

*The Grange Hotel, Clifton, York YO3 6AA*
*Tel: 0904 644744, Fax: 0904 612453,*
*Telex: 57210*

# York

**★★★70%, Swallow Chase** Tadcaster Rd YP2 2QQ (Swallow)
☎(0904)701000 Telex no 57582 FAX (0904) 702308
*Overlooking the racecourse, just outside the city, this hotel has
been extensively redeveloped and upgraded to offer spacious public
areas and new bedrooms. A popular leisure centre has also been
added. The staff are attentive and cater particularly well for coach
parties.*
112⇌🏠(14fb) CTV in all bedrooms ® T S10%
sB&B⇌🏠 fr£78 dB&B⇌🏠 frf£95 🗮
Lift ℂ CTV 200P 5🏌 ❅ CFA 🗔(heated) sauna solarium
gymnasium putting green golf practise net *xmas*
♀ English & French V ✿ ♨ Lunch £12-£15&alc High tea
£5-£10 Dinner £17-£22&alc Last dinner 10pm
Credit Cards ① ② ③ ⑤

**★★★66%, York Pavilion** 45 Main St, Fulford YO1 4PJ (Best
Western) ☎(0904)622099 Telex no 57305 FAX (0904) 626939
*Situated just 2 miles from the city centre in the old village of
Fulford, The Pavilion is elegant, with a country-house atmosphere,
set in attractive gardens. The bedrooms, which vary in size, are
well equipped and decorated to a good standard, and are located in
the main hotel and a "Stables" annexe. Freshly prepared and
imaginative dishes are served in the elegant restaurant, and there is
a comfortable lounge and a cosy cocktail bar.*
11⇌Annexe10⇌🏠(3fb) CTV in all bedrooms ® T
✻ (ex guide dogs)
46P 🚗
V ✿ ♨ Last dinner 9.30pm
Credit Cards ① ② ③ ⑤

**★★★64%, Post House** Tadcaster Rd YO2 2QF (Trusthouse
Forte) ☎(0904)707921 Telex no 57798 FAX (0904) 702804
*This multi-storey hotel near the race course has spacious,
attractive lounges, a dining room with a garden patio and well-
fitted bedrooms.*
147⇌🏠(28fb)✻in 32 bedrooms CTV in all bedrooms ® T
sB⇌🏠£67 dB⇌🏠£78 (room only) 🗮
Lift ℂ 180P ❅ CFA *xmas*
♀ International V ✿ ♨ ✗ Lunch fr£7.50&alc High tea
£5-£8.50 Dinner £10.50-£12.50&alc Last dinner 10pm
Credit Cards ① ② ③ ④ ⑤

**★★★62%, Novotel** Fishergate YO1 4AD (Novotel)
☎(0904)611660 Telex no 57556 FAX (0904) 610925
124⇌🏠(124fb)✻in 14 bedrooms CTV in all bedrooms ®
Lift ℂ 150P ⌂(heated)
♀ English & French V ✿ ♨ ✗ Last dinner mdnt
Credit Cards ① ② ③ ⑤

**★★★59%, Fairfield Manor** Shipton Rd, Skelton YO3 6XW
(Consort) ☎(0904)625621 Telex no 57476 FAX (0904) 612725
*An attractive Georgian house set on the A19 three miles north of
the city centre has been converted to provide comfortable, well
equipped and generally spacious bedrooms ; pleasant public areas
include wood-panelled lounges.*
22⇌🏠(1fb)2🖉 CTV in all bedrooms ® T sB&B⇌🏠£49-£54
dB&B⇌🏠£71-£77 🗮
50P ❅ *xmas*
♀ English & French V ✿ ♨ Lunch £9.75-£10.50&alc Dinner
£13.50-£15&alc Last dinner 9.15pm
Credit Cards ① ② ③ ⑤ ⓔ

---

---

**★★70%, Heworth Court** 76-78 Heworth Green YO3 7TQ
☎(0904)425156 & 425126 Telex no 57571 FAX (0904) 415290
*Situated on the east side of York, about ten minutes' walk from the
city walls, this hotel provides individually designed and well
equipped bedrooms which range from spacious, traditional style to
compact modern. They are in the main building, in an adjoining
courtyard and in a new block 200 yards away. Public areas include
a cosy lounge, a welcoming bar and a lamplit restaurant where
friendly staff serve imaginative meals, which, like everything else
about this family-run establishment, represent value for money.*
8⇌🏠 Annexe17⇌🏠 CTV in all bedrooms ® T ✻ ✱
sB&B⇌🏠£36-£39.50 dB&B⇌🏠£56-£62 🗮
CTV 25P 1🏌 🚗 *xmas*
V ✿ ♨ Lunch £8.50-£12.50&alc Dinner £12.50&alc Last
dinner 9.30pm
Credit Cards ① ② ③ ⑤ ⓔ

**★★69%, Beechwood Close** 19 Shipton Rd, Clifton YO3 6RE
(Minotels) ☎(0904)658378 FAX (0904) 647124
Closed 25 Dec
*A converted country house with its own gardens stands in a
suburban area to the north of the city. It provides homely public
areas, an attractive restaurant and the attention of friendly
proprietors.*
14⇌🏠(2fb) CTV in all bedrooms ® T ✻
sB&B⇌🏠£31.50-£35 dB&B⇌🏠£54-£60 🗮
CTV 36P 🚗
V ✿ ♨ Lunch £5.95-£6.50 Dinner £10.75-£13 Last dinner 9pm
Credit Cards ① ② ③ ⓔ

**★★69%, Kilima** 129 Holgate Rd YO2 4DE (Inter-Hotels)
☎(0904)658844 & 625787 Telex no 57928 FAX (0904) 612083
*Standing beside the A59 only a short walk from the city centre,
this converted rectory offers fifteen bedrooms which, though
compact, are well equipped with every modern amenity, including
en suite facilities. The original cellars have been developed to* ▶

## ★ ★

# Heworth
# Court
# Hotel RESTAURANT

### 76/78 HEWORTH GREEN
### YORK YO3 7TQ
### Telephone: (0904) 425156/425157

**Comfortable 2 star hotel within easy
walking distance of the city centre.**

**All rooms are en-suite with colour TV
and tea/coffee makers. Cosy bar and
restaurant offering the finest English
cuisine and an extensive wine list
featuring some superb wines.**

**Enquire for Christmas & New Year and
other special breaks.**

**Phone for brochure and
reservations.**

*provide an attractive restaurant in which guests can enjoy freshly prepared meals, and a very comfortable lounge overlooks the rear patio and garden.*
15⇨ñ(1fb)1🛏 CTV in all bedrooms ® T ✱ sB&B⇨ñfr£38 dB&B⇨ñfr£56 ⊟
20P ⚘ xmas
♀ English & French V ᵛ ⬛ ½ Lunch £14.75 Dinner £14.75 Last dinner 9.30pm
Credit Cards ① ② ③ ⑤

★★67% **Town House** 100-104 Holgate Rd YO2 4BB
☎(0904)636171 FAX (0904) 623044
Closed 24-31 Dec
*A row of Victorian town houses dating from 1848 has been converted to create this hotel, which stands close to the city centre on the A59. Bedrooms are comfortable and well equipped, while public areas comprise a comfortably relaxing lounge, the Grapevine restaurant with its good value table d'hôte and à la carte menus of freshly cooked dishes, a conservatory full of plants and an aviary.*
23rm(21⇨ñ)(3fb) CTV in all bedrooms ® T sB&B£25 sB&B⇨ñ£36-£42 dB&B£38-£40 dB&B⇨ñ£48-£60 ⊟
25P
♀ European V ᵛ ⬛ Bar Lunch £2-£5.50alc Dinner £9.50-£11.50&alc Last dinner 9.15pm
Credit Cards ① ③

★★65% *Hudsons* 60 Bootham YO3 7BZ ☎(0904)621267
*Victorian décor preserves the character and atmosphere of a hotel converted from two houses of that era in 1981. Ideally situated, close to the Minster and the ancient city walls, it provides its own excellent parking facilities. Accommodation varies in style, the traditional bedrooms of the main building contrasting with the more modern ones in the new wing; public areas include a cosy downstairs bar and restaurant, and there is a roof garden.*
28⇨ñ(3fb)1🛏 CTV in all bedrooms ® T ✖ (ex guide dogs)
Lift ▦ 34P pool table ♫
♀ English & French V ᵛ ⬛ Last dinner 9.30pm
Credit Cards ① ② ③ ⑤

★★64% **Cottage** 3 Clifton Green YO3 6LH ☎(0904)643711 FAX (0904) 611230
Closed 24-26 Dec
*A pair of town houses overlooking the Green in the village of Clifton has been converted into a cosy, cottage-style hotel, featuring exposed brickwork and beams and furnished in compatibly antique fashion. Traditional English and Yorkshire dishes are served in the dining room by friendly staff.*
16⇨ñAnnexe4⇨ñ(3fb) CTV in all bedrooms ® T ✖ (ex guide dogs) sB&B⇨ñ£35-£45 dB&B⇨ñ£55-£65 ⊟ 12P
V ᵛ Dinner £8-£9.50&alc Last dinner 9pm
Credit Cards ① ② ③ ⑤ ⓔ

★★63% *Abbots' Mews* 6 Marygate Ln, Bootham YO3 7DE
☎(0904)634866 Telex no 5777
*This hotel near the city centre was converted from a coachman's cottage and stables.*
12ñAnnexe34⇨ñ(8fb) CTV in all bedrooms ® T ✖ sB&B⇨ñ£35-£40 dB&B⇨ñ£60-£70 ⊟
30P ✿ xmas
♀ International V ᵛ ⬛ Lunch £6.50 Dinner fr£12&alc Last dinner 9.30pm
Credit Cards ① ② ③ ⑤ ⓔ

★★62% *Alhambra Court* 31 St Mary's, Bootham YO3 7DD
☎(0904)628474
*A pair of tall, impressive town houses has been combined to create this well-equipped hotel within walking distance of the Minster. Public areas include a cosy lounge of character (with satellite TV) and a well-appointed lower-ground floor à la carte restaurant with adjacent matching lounge bar. Well-designed bedrooms combine modern facilities with the charm of the houses' original period.*
25⇨ñ(5fb)1🛏 CTV in all bedrooms ® ✖
►

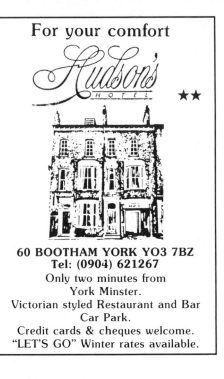

Y

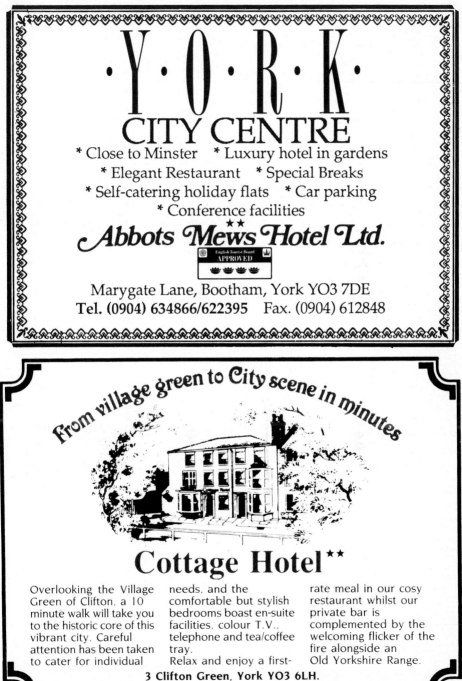
Y

Lift CTV 25P
♀ French & Italian Last dinner 10pm
Credit Cards ① ③

★★62% **Knavesmire Manor** 302 Tadcaster Rd YO2 2HE
☎(0904)702941 FAX (0904) 709274
*A comfortably converted Regency villa enjoys uninterrupted views over the race course.*
13rm(8⇗1♪)Annexe9♪(2fb)1⚑ CTV in all bedrooms ® T
sB&B£35-£45 sB&B⇗♪£39.50-£55 dB&B£43-£49
dB&B⇗♪£45-£69 ◘
Lift 26P 1🎱 ◳(heated) sauna *xmas*
V ❖ ◫ Dinner £13.75-£15&alc Last dinner 9pm
Credit Cards ① ② ③ ⑤ ⓔ

★★60% **Savages** 15 St Peters Grove YO3 6AQ ☎(0904)610818
FAX (0904) 627729
Closed 25 Dec
*Though this pleasant hotel retains traces of Victorian elegance and charm, its bedrooms have been refurbished to offer modern facilities. A welcoming restaurant offers English cuisine, and the comfortable lounge has a small bar.*
18rm(7⇗9♪)(2fb) CTV in all bedrooms ® T
♥ (ex guide dogs) sB&B£28-£30 sB&B⇗♪£32-£36
dB&B£56-£60 dB&B⇗♪£60-£64 ◘
CTV 16P solarium gymnasium
V ❖ ◫ ✄ Lunch fr£6.50 Dinner £10.50-£11.50&alc Last dinner 9pm
Credit Cards ① ② ③ ⑤ ⓔ

★★59% **Disraeli's** 140 Acomb Rd YO2 4HA ☎(0904)781181
Closed 25 Dec-1 Jan
*A detached Victorian house in a quiet residential area on the edge of the city ; public areas comprise a small lounge, a cosy bar and the large restaurant which serves both table d'hôte and à la carte menus, and the hotel is popular with commercial and business clients.*
12⇗♪(4fb) CTV in all bedrooms ® T ♥ (ex guide dogs) ✳
sB&B⇗♪£47-£52 dB&B⇗♪£58-£64 ◘
CTV 40P ⊞ ✿ ⚙
V ❖ ◫ Sunday Lunch £5.90-£6.20 Dinner £11.25-£14.50&alc Last dinner 9.30pm
Credit Cards ① ② ③

★★59% *Lady Anne Middletons Hotel* Skeldergate YO1 1DS
☎(0904)632257 & 630456 Telex no 57577
Closed 24-27 Dec
40rm(38♪)Annexe10♪ CTV in all bedrooms ® T
♥ (ex guide dogs)
℄ CTV 50P ✿ sauna jacuzzi
V ❖ ◫ Last dinner 9pm
Credit Cards ① ② ③

★★58% *The Sheppard* 63 The Mount YO2 2AX ☎(0904)643716
Telex no 57950
*Centrally situated, close to both railway station and city walls, the hotel offers well equipped bedrooms in a variety of shapes, sizes and decorative styles; its converted eighteenth-century cellar contains a cosy restaurant and bar, whilst there are a small residents' lounge and a light new bar on the ground floor.*
19rm(16⇗)(3fb)1⚑✄in 6 bedrooms CTV in all bedrooms ®
♥ (ex guide dogs)
CTV 10P 6🎱 (£1.25) ♪
♀ English & French V ◫ Last dinner 9.30pm
Credit Cards ① ③

★★54% *The Hill* 60 York Rd, Acomb YO2 5LW (Exec Hotel)
☎(0904)790777 Telex no 57567
Closed mid Dec-mid Jan
*The hotel stands in an acre of fine walled gardens on the city's highest point, in the quiet suburb of Acomb. Family-run in a relaxed, informal manner, it offers well-equipped bedrooms, a comfortable lounge and simple, home-cooked meals.*

9⇗(1fb)2⚑ CTV in 10 bedrooms ® ♥
12P ⊞ ✿
V ✄
Credit Cards ① ② ③ ⑤

★★53% **Ashcroft** 294 Bishopthorpe Rd YO2 1LH (Minotels)
☎(0904)659286 FAX (0904) 640107
Closed Xmas & New Year
*Large but quiet house with restful atmosphere and good home cooking.*
11⇗♪ Annexe4⇗♪(3fb) CTV in all bedrooms ® T ❋
sB&B⇗♪fr£33 dB&B⇗♪fr£55 ◘
CTV 40P ✿
V ❖ ◫ Lunch fr£5.50alc High tea fr£5.50alc Dinner fr£9.50&alc Last dinner 8pm
Credit Cards ① ② ③ ⑤

★65% **Clifton Bridge** Water End, Clifton YO3 6LL
☎(0904)610510
Closed 24-31 Dec
*Situated on the northern edge of the city and close to the river this comfortable hotel offers well-equipped, pleasant bedrooms. There is a small car park.*
14⇗♪(1fb) CTV in all bedrooms ® T sB&B⇗♪£30-£35
dB&B⇗♪£52-£60 ◘
12P 2🎱 ⊞
V ❖ ◫ Dinner £6.75-£11.95alc Last dinner 7.45pm
Credit Cards ① ③ ⓔ

Entries for red-star hotels are highlighted by a
tint panel. For a full list of these establishments
consult the Contents page.

★

Clifton Bridge Hotel

Beautifully appointed private hotel, renowned for its friendly service, is ideally situated opposite the pleasant Homestead Park and beside a delightful riverside walk to the city centre and all historical attractions.

All rooms have central heating, colour TV, tea and coffee-making facilities and radio/intercom/baby-listening service and telephones.

There is a large, relaxing lounge, fully licensed bar and charming dining room offering à la carte menu.
Own private car park. Bargain breaks available.
Please contact:
**Elizabeth and Barry Swallow**
Water End, York YO3 6LL
Tel: (0904) 610510   Fax: (0904) 640208

**Y**

## York

★65% **Fairmount** 230 Tadcaster Road, Mount Vale YO2 2ES
☎(0904)638298

*Located on the A1036 close to the racecourse, an attractive
Victorian building has recently been refurbished to provide a good
standard of accommodation in very well equipped bedrooms,
together with a cosy lounge bar, comfortable lounge and pleasant
restaurant serving enjoyable meals.*

10rm(4⇨4♠)(4fb) CTV in all bedrooms ® ✳ sB&B£30-£35
dB&B⇨♠£50-£60 ⊟
7P 3🚗

♗ International V ✿ ⏛ Dinner £12.50-£15 Last dinner 9pm
Credit Cards ① ③ ⓔ

★65% **Newington** 147 Mount Vale YO2 2DJ ☎(0904)625173
Telex no 65430

*Four town houses have been suitably converted to form this hotel
on the A1036 (south) approach road into the city.*

25⇨♠Annexe15⇨♠(3fb)2⍰ CTV in all bedrooms ® T ✖
sB&B⇨♠£35-£40 dB&B⇨♠£48-£58 ⊟
Lift 40P ▣(heated) sauna solarium *xmas*
V ✿ S% Sunday Lunch £5.95-£6.95 Dinner £11-£12.50 Last
dinner 9.30pm
Credit Cards ① ② ③ ⑤ ⓔ

★63% **Holgate Bridge** 106-108 Holgate Rd YO2 4BB
☎(0904)635971
Closed 24-26 Dec

*A friendly little hotel, part of a row of town houses only a short
walk from the city centre, providing modern, well-equipped
bedrooms, a conservatory-style lounge and a basement dining room
serving meals of a good standard.*

14rm(11⇨♠)(4fb)1⍰ CTV in all bedrooms ® T sB&B£18-£22
sB&B⇨♠£30-£36 dB&B£35 dB&B⇨♠£48 ⊟
16P
V Bar Lunch £1.75-£8.50alc Dinner fr£8.50&alc Last dinner
9pm
Credit Cards ① ② ③ ⓔ

✕19 **Grape Lane** 19 Grape Ln YO1 2HU ☎(0904)636366
*Situated in the centre of the city, close to the Minster and main
shopping centre, this restaurant is in a beautiful timbered house,
and it has a wealth of character and original features. Service is
attentive, yet informal, and tables are provided on 2 floors – the top
floor being for smoking guests. Food is refreshingly unpretentious,
and it is competently cooked using the very best fresh ingredients in
traditional dishes with imaginative touches. Delightful home-made
sweets such as treacle tart and sticky toffee pudding are very much
recommended by one of our inspectors. Fish terrines and soups are
full of flavour, and sauces have a good depth of flavour. It is very
good value for money, and there is an honest, relaxed and friendly
atmosphere.*

Closed Sun, Mon, last two wks Jan & 23 Sep-6 Oct
V 34 seats Lunch £8.50&alc Dinner £16.50&alc Last lunch
2pm Last dinner 10.30pm ✗ nc5yrs
Credit Cards ① ③

**Y**

# COUNTRY HOUSE HOTELS

Identified in the gazetteer by the 🏯 symbol, country house hotels are often secluded and though they are not always rurally situated, you will be assured of peaceful surroundings and a restful night. The atmosphere will be relaxed and informal and you will receive a personal welcome. Some of the facilities may differ from those to be found in purpose-built urban hotels of the same star rating. Full details can be found in the gazetteer entries.

## ENGLAND

### AVON

**Freshford**
⊛★★★🏯 78% Homewood Park

**Hunstrete**
★★★🏯 Hunstrete House

**Lympsham**
★★🏯 60% Batch Farm Country Hotel

**Rangeworthy**
★★🏯 64% Rangeworthy Court

**Thornbury**
★★★🏯 Thornbury Castle

### BEDFORDSHIRE

**Flitwick**
★★★🏯 71% Flitwick Manor

### BUCKINGHAMSHIRE

**Aylesbury**
★★★🏯 Hartwell House

**Hanslope**
★★★🏯 68% Hatton Court

**Taplow**
★★★★★🏯 Cliveden

### CHESHIRE

**Chester**
★★★🏯 71% Crabwall Manor

**Nantwich**
★★★🏯 78% Rookery Hall

**Sandiway**
★★★🏯 75% Nunsmere Hall Country House

**Tarporley**
★★🏯 64% The Willington Hall

### CLEVELAND

**Easington**
★★★🏯 78% Grinkle Park

### CORNWALL & ISLES OF SCILLY

**Falmouth**
★★★🏯 76% Penmere Manor

**Helston**
★★🏯 70% Nansloe Manor

**Lamorna Cove**
★★★🏯 59% Lamorna Cove

**Liskeard**
★★🏯 61% Country Castle
⊛★★★🏯 Well House

**Mawnan Smith**
★★★🏯 73% Meudon

**Penzance**
★★★🏯 62% Higher Faugan

**Portscatho**
★★🏯 61% Roseland House

**St Agnes**
★★🏯 61% Rose in Vale

**St Austell**
★★🏯 75% Boscundle Manor

**St Wenn**
★🏯 61% Wenn Manor

**Talland Bay**
★★★🏯 71% Talland Bay

### CUMBRIA

**Alston**
★★🏯 75% Lovelady Shield

**Ambleside**
★★🏯 66% Crow How
★★🏯 72% Nanny Brow

**Appleby in Westmorland**
★★★🏯 69% Appleby Manor

**Bassenthwaite**
★★★★🏯 58% Armathwaite Hall
★★🏯 67% Overwater Hall

**Brampton**
⊛★★★🏯 Farlam Hall

**Coiniston**
★🏯 72% Old Rectory

**Crosby on Eden**
★★★🏯 69% Crosby Lodge

**Elterwater**
★★🏯 68% Eltermere

**Grange over Sands**
★★🏯 66% Graythwaite Manor

**Grasmere**
⊛★★★🏯 Michael's Nook

**Hawkshead**
★★★🏯 75% Field Head House
★🏯 73% Highfield House
★★★🏯 56% Tarn Hows

**Howtown**
⊛⊛★★★🏯 Sharrow Bay

**Keswick**
★★🏯 64% Lyzzick Hall
★★🏯 66% Red House

**Loweswater**
★★🏯 64% Scale Hill

**Thornthwaite**
★★🏯 65% Thwaite Howe

**Watermillock**
★★★🏯 75% Leeming House
★★🏯 Old Church
⊛★★★🏯 73% Rampsbeck

**Windermere**
★★★🏯 84% Holbeck Ghyll
★★★🏯 64% Langdale Chase
★★🏯 72% Lindeth Fell
★★🏯 74% Linthwaite
★🏯 67% Quarry Garth

**Witherslack**
★🏯 Old Vicarage

### DERBYSHIRE

**Ashbourne**
★★🏯 74% Callow Hall

**Ashford in the Water**
★★🏯 73% Riverside

**Bakewell**
★★🏯 77% Croft

**Matlock**
★★🏯 65% Red House
★★★🏯 70% Riber Hall

**Rowsley**
★★🏯 71% East Lodge

### DEVON

**Ashburton**
★★🏯 69% Holne Chase

**Barnstaple**
★★🏯 68% Downrew House
★🏯 Halmpstone Manor

**Bideford**
★★🏯 58% Yeoldon House

**Burrington**
★★★🏯 67% Northcote Manor

**Chagford**
⊛★★★🏯 Gidleigh Park
★★★🏯 75% Mill End

**Chittlehamholt**
★★★🏯 74% Highbullen

**Clawton**
★★🏯 68% Court Barn

**Fairy Cross**
★★★🏯 69% Portledge

**Gittisham**
★★★🏯 67% Combe House

**Hawkchurch**
★★★🏯 71% Fairwater Head

**Haytor**
★★🏯 70% Bel Alp House

**Honiton**
★★★🏯 65% Deer Park

**Horn's Cross**
★★★🏯 68% Foxdown Manor

**Kingsbridge**
★★★🏯 76% Buckland-Tout-Saints

**Lewdown**
⊛★★🏯 Lewtrenchard Manor

**Lydford**
★★🏯 67% Lydford House

**Lynton**
★🏯 66% Combe Park
★★🏯 65% Hewitts

**Martinhoe**
★🏯 70% Old Rectory

**Mary Tavy**
★★★🏯 62% Moorland Hall

**Moretonhampstead**
★★🏯 66% Glebe House

**Newton Ferrers**
★★🏯 70% Court House

**North Hewish**
★★🏯 Brookdale House

**Sidmouth**
★★🏯 66% Brownlands

**Sourton**
★★🏯 77% Collaven Manor

**South Brent**
★★🏯 74% Glazebrook House

**South Molton**
★★🏯 73% Marsh Hall
★★🏯 Whitechapel Manor

**Stoke Gabriel**
★★★🏯 65% Gabriel Court

**Torquay**
★★★🏯 67% Orestone Manor House

**Whimple**
★★76% Woodhayes

### DORSET

**Gillingham**
★★🏯 Stock Hill House

**Milton Abbas**
★★🏯 63% Milton Manor

**Studland**
★★🏯 66% Manor House

### EAST SUSSEX

**Battle**
★★★🏯 Netherfield Place

**Uckfield**
★★★🏯 Horsted Place

**Wadhurst**
★★⬆ 66% Spindlewood

**ESSEX**
**Dedham**
★★★⬆ Maison Talbooth

**GLOUCESTERSHIRE**
**Bibury**
★★⬆ 67% Bibury Court
**Buckland**
★★★⬆ Buckland Manor
**Charingworth**
❀★★★⬆ 77% Charingworth Manor
**Cheltenham**
★★★⬆ Greenway
**Lower Slaughter**
★★★⬆ Lower Slaughter Manor
**Stow-on-the-Wold**
❀★★★⬆ 77% Wyck Hill House
**Stroud**
★★★⬆ 65% Burleigh Court
**Tetbury**
❀★★★ Calcot Manor
**Upper Slaughter**
❀★★★⬆ 77% Lords of the Manor

**HAMPSHIRE**
**Brockenhurst**
★★⬆ 69% Whitley Ridge
**Hurstbourne Tarrant**
★★⬆ 71% Esseborne Manor
**Lymington**
★★★⬆ 73% Passford House
**Lyndhurst**
★★★⬆ 66% Parkhill
**New Milton**
❀★★★★⬆ Chewton Glen
**Rotherwick**
★★★★⬆ 79% Tylney Hall
**Winchester**
❀★★★★⬆ 78% Lainston House

**HEREFORD & WORCESTER**
**Abberley**
★★★⬆ 77% Elms
**Broadway**
★★⬆ 70% Collin House
**Chaddesley Corbett**
★★★⬆ 75% Brockencote Hall
**Hereford**
★★⬆ 64% Netherwood
**Ledbury**
❀★★⬆ 72% Hope End
**Leominster**
★⬆ 77% Marsh
**Lugwardine**
★★★⬆ 64% Longworth Hall
**Malvern**
★★★⬆ 65% Cottage in the Wood
★★⬆ 72% Holdfast Cottage

**Pencraig**
★★⬆ 62% Pencraig Court
**Ross-on-Wye**
★★⬆ 71% Glewstone Court
★★★⬆ 65% Pengethley Manor
★★⬆ 72% Peterstow

**HUMBERSIDE**
**Driffield**
★★⬆ 60% Wold House
**Little Weighton**
★★★⬆ 66% Rowley Manor

**KENT**
**Ashford**
★★★★⬆ Eastwell Manor
**Cranbrook**
★★⬆ 70% Kennel Holt

**LANCASHIRE**
**Garstang**
★★⬆ 72% The Pickerings
**Todmorden**
★★★⬆ 70% Scaitcliffe Hall

**LEICESTERSHIRE**
**Melton Mowbray**
★★★★⬆ 76% Stapleford Park
**Normanton**
★★★★⬆ 72% Normanton Park
**Oakham**
★★★★⬆ Hambleton Hall

**LINCOLNSHIRE**
**Lincoln**
★★★⬆ 67% Washingborough Hall

**NORFOLK**
**Bunwell**
★★⬆ 62% Bunwell Manor
**Felmingham**
★★⬆ 74% Felmingham Hall
**Grimston**
❀★★★⬆ Congham Hall

**NORTH YORKSHIRE**
**Aldwark**
★★★⬆ 78% Aldwark Manor
**Appleton le Moors**
★★⬆ 73% Dweldapilton Hall
**Arncliffe**
★★⬆ 76% Amerdale House
**Ayton, Great**
★★★⬆ 70% Ayton Hall
**Bilbrough**
★★★⬆ Bilbrough Manor
**Crathorne**
★★★★⬆ 57% Crathorne Hall
**Hackness**
★★★⬆ 66% Hackness Grange
**Harrogate**
★★⬆ 72% Nidd Hall

**Hawes**
★★⬆ 69% Stone House
**Kirkby Fleetham**
★★★⬆ 72% Kirkby Fleetham Hall
**Lastingham**
★★⬆ 75% Lastingham Grange
**Markington**
★★★⬆ 74% Hob Green
**Masham**
★★⬆ 74% Jervaulx Hall
**Monk Fryston**
★★⬆ 68% Monk Fryston Hall
**Scarborough**
★★★⬆ 64% Wrea Head

**NORTHUMBERLAND**
**Allendale**
★★⬆ 63% Bishopfield
**Belford**
★★⬆ 74% Waren House
**Cornhill on Tweed**
★★★⬆ 58% Tillmouth Park
**Powburn**
★★⬆ 75% Breamish House

**OXFORDSHIRE**
**Chadlington**
★★⬆ 79% The Manor
**Horton-cum-Studley**
❀★★★⬆ 67% Studley Priory
**Milton, Great**
❀❀❀★★★⬆ Le Manoir aux Quat' Saisons

**SHROPSHIRE**
**Market Drayton**
★★★⬆ 68% Goldstone Hall
**Oswestry**
★★⬆ 64% Sweeney Hall
**Shrewsbury**
★★★⬆ 71% Albright Hussey
**Worfield**
★★★⬆ 68% Old Vicarage

**SOMERSET**
**Dulverton**
★★⬆ Ashwick House
★★★⬆ 72% Carnarvon Arms
**Holford**
★★⬆ 69% Combe House
**Shipham**
★★★⬆ 63% Daneswood House
**Simonsbath**
★★⬆ 69% Simonsbath House
**Ston Easton**
★★★⬆ Ston Easton Park
**Waterrow**
★⬆ 76% Hurstone
**Wheddon Cross**
★★⬆ 68% Raleigh Manor
**Wincanton**
★★⬆ 63% Holbrook House
**Withypool**
★★⬆ 69% Westerclose

**STAFFORDSHIRE**
**Rangemoor**
★★⬆ 70% Needwood Manor

**SUFFOLK**
**Brome**
★★⬆ 67% Oaksmere
**Bury St Edmunds**
★★★⬆ 76% Ravenwood Hall
**Hintlesham**
❀★★★⬆ Hintlesham Hall
**Woodbridge**
★★★⬆ 73% Seckford Hall

**SURREY**
**Bagshot**
❀★★★★⬆ 70% Pennyhill Park

**WARWICKSHIRE**
**Billesley**
❀★★★★⬆ 74% Billesley Manor
**Leamington Spa**
❀★★★★⬆ Mallory Court

**WEST MIDLANDS**
**Hockley Heath**
❀★★★⬆ 79% Nuthurst Grange

**WEST SUSSEX**
**Amberley**
❀★★★⬆ 75% Amberley Castle
**Arundel**
★⬆ 63% Burpham
**Climping**
★★★⬆ 72% Bailiffscourt
**Cuckfield**
★★⬆ 55% Hilton Park
**East Grinstead**
❀★★★⬆ Gravetye Manor
**Lower Beeding**
★★★★⬆ 63% South Lodge
**Thakeham**
❀★★★⬆ 74% Abingworth Hall

**WEST YORKSHIRE**
**Wentbridge**
★★★⬆ 67% Wentbridge House
**Wetherby**
★★★⬆ Wood Hall

**WILTSHIRE**
**Bradford on Avon**
★★★⬆ 73% Woolley Grange
**Castle Combe**
★★★★⬆ 70% Manor House
**Limpley Stoke**
★★★⬆ 63% Cliffe
**Malmesbury**
★★★⬆ 76% Whatley Manor

**Melksham**
★★★⚿ 74% Beechfield House
**Warminster**
★★★★⚿ 67% Bishopstrow House

# CHANNEL ISLANDS

## JERSEY
**Rozel Bay**
★★★⚿ 74% Château la Chaire
**St Saviour**
⊕★★★★⚿ Longueville Manor

# SCOTLAND

## BORDERS
**Greenlaw**
★★⚿ 63% Purves Hall
**Kelso**
★★★⚿ 76% Sunlaws House
**Peebles**
★★⚿ 77% Cringletie House
★★⚿ 62% Venlaw Castle
**Walkerburn**
★★⚿ 66% Tweed Valley

## CENTRAL
**Callander**
★★★⚿ 68% Roman Camp
**Dunblane**
⊕★★★⚿ Cromlix House

## DUMFRIES & GALLOWAY
**Auchencairn**
★★★⚿ 69% Balcary Bay
**Crossmichael**
★★⚿ 59% Culgruff House
**Newton Stewart**
★★★★⚿ 55% Kirroughtree
**Portpatrick**
⊕★★⚿ Knockinaam Lodge
**Port William**
★★★⚿ 63% Corsemalzie House
**Rockcliffe**
★★★⚿ 68% Baron's Craig

## FIFE
**Letham**
★★★⚿ 64% Fernie Castle
**Markinch**
★★★★⚿ 73% Balbirnie House

## GRAMPIAN
**Banchory**
★★★⚿ Banchory Lodge
★★★★⚿ 71% Invery House
★★★⚿ 75% Raemoir
**Huntly**
★★⚿ 53% Castle
**Kildrummy**
★★★⚿ 75% Kildrummy Castle

**Rothes**
★★★⚿ 64% Rothes Glen

## HIGHLAND
**Achnasheen**
★★★⚿ 70% Ledgowan Lodge
**Arisaig**
★★★⚿ Arisaig House
**Cannich**
★★★⚿ 67% Cozac Lodge
**Drumnadrochit**
⊕★★⚿ 67% Polmaily House
**Dulnain Bridge**
★★⚿ 67% Muckrach Lodge
**Fort William**
★★★★⚿ Inverlochy Castle
**Invergarry**
★★⚿ 61% Glengarry Castle
**Inverness**
★★★⚿ 73% Bunchrew House
★★⚿ 74% Dunain Park
**Kentallen**
⊕★★⚿ 72% Ardsheal House
**Whitebridge**
★★⚿ Knockie Lodge

## LOTHIAN
**Gullane**
★★★⚿ 81% Greywalls
**Humbie**
★★★⚿ 66% Johnstounburn House
**Uphall**
★★★⚿ 65% Houstoun House

## STRATHCLYDE
**Appin**
★★★⚿ 73% Invercreran
**Barrhill**
⊕★★★⚿ 77% Kildonan
**Biggar**
★★★⚿ 75% Shieldhill
★★⚿ 68% Wyndales House
**Dolphinton**
★★★⚿ 64% Dolphinton House
**Eriska**
★★★⚿ Isle of Eriska
**Kilchrenan**
★★★⚿ Ardanaiseig
★★★⚿ 66% Taychreggan
**Kilwinning**
★★★⚿ 67% Montgreenan Mansion House
**Langbank**
⊕★★★⚿ 70% Gleddoch House
**Maybole**
★★⚿ 79% Ladyburn
**Oban**
★⚿ 67% Foxholes
**Skelmorlie**
★★★⚿ 63% Manor Park
**Stewarton**
★★★⚿ 75% Chapelton House

# TAYSIDE
**Alyth**
★★⚿ 58% Lands of Loyal
**Auchterarder**
★★★⚿ 73% Auchterarder House
★★★⚿ 65% Duchally House
**Auchterhouse**
★★★⚿ 70% Old Mansion House
**Blairgowrie**
★★⚿ 65% Altamount House
★★★⚿ 75% Kinloch House
**Crieff**
★★⚿ 64% Cultoquhey House
**Glamis**
★★★⚿ 69% Castleton House
**Glenshee**
★★⚿ 64% Dalmunzie House
**Kinclaven**
★★★⚿ 76% Ballathie House
**Letham**
★★★⚿ 66% Idvies House
**Perth**
⊕★★★⚿ 78% Murrayshall
**Pitlochry**
★★★⚿ 68% Pine Trees

# SCOTTISH ISLANDS

## SHETLANDS
**Brae**
★★⚿ 67% Busta House

## SKYE
**Isle Ornsay**
⊕★★⚿ 65% Kinloch Lodge
**Skeabost Bridge**
★★★⚿ 66% Skeabost House

# WALES

## CLWYD
**Llandegla**
★★⚿ 74% Bod Idris Hall
**Llandrillo**
★★★⚿ 76% Tyddyn Llan
**Llangollen**
★★★⚿ 65% Bryn Howel
**Northop**
★★★⚿ 85% Soughton Hall
**Rossett**
★★★⚿ 75% Llyndir Hall
**Wrexham**
★★★⚿ 73% Llwyn Onn Hall

## DYFED
**Aberystwyth**
★★★⚿ 66% Conrah
**Crugybar**
★★⚿ 69% Glanrannel Park
**Eglwysfach**
★★★⚿ 70% Ynishir Hall
**Lamphey**
★★★⚿ 64% Court

**Llechryd**
★★★⚿ Castell Malgwyn
**St Davids**
★★★⚿ 64% Warpool Court
**Tenby**
★★⚿ 79% Penally Abbey
**Whitland**
★★★⚿ 62% Waungron Country Mansion

## GWYNEDD
**Aberdovey**
★★★⚿ 65% Plas Penhelig
**Abersoch**
★★★⚿ 65% Porth Tocyn
**Beddgelert**
★⚿ 69% Bryn Eglwys
★⚿ 69% Sygun Fawr
**Betws-y-Coed**
★★★⚿ 63% Craig-y-Dderwyn
★★★⚿ 64% Plas Hall
**Caernarfon**
★★★⚿ 79% Seiont Manor
**Criccieth**
★★★⚿ 66% Bron Eifion
★★★⚿ 64% Mynydd Ednyfed
**Ganllwyd**
★★★⚿ 66% Dolmelynllyn Hall
**Llanbedr**
★★⚿ 60% Cae Nest Hall
**Llandudno**
★★★⚿ Bodysgallen Hall
**Llangefni**
★★★⚿ 77% Tre-Ysgawen Hall
**Llanrwst**
★★★⚿ 63% Plas Maenan
**Pwllheli**
⊕★★★⚿ 75% Plas Bodegroes
**Rowen**
★⚿ 64% Tir-y-Coed
**Talsarnau**
★★⚿ Maes y Neuadd

## POWYS
**Builth Wells**
★★★⚿ 64% Caer Beris Manor
**Crickhowell**
★★★⚿ 72% Gliffaes
**Forden**
★★⚿ 67% Edderton Hall
**Llanfyllin**
★★★⚿ 72% Bodfach Hall
**Llangammarch Wells**
⊕★★★⚿ 76% Lake
**Llanwddyn**
★★★⚿ 71% Lake Vyrnwy
**Llyswen**
★★★★⚿ 72% Llangoed Hall
**Welshpool**
★★⚿ 73% Golfa Hall

## WEST GLAMORGAN
**Reynoldston**
★★⚿ 70% Fairyhill

# AA LODGES

In 1967, in the first edition of this guide, the AA had a special classification for motels – white stars. Although this kind of accommodation was well established and popular in the USA – and at that time the British still tended to take a lead from things American – motels did not really catch on here and eventually we dropped the special classification.

Then, in 1985, the first Lodge was built at Barton-under-Needwood in Staffordshire – the Little Chef Lodge, now renamed Travelodge by its operating company, Trusthouse Forte. Surely this was the same principal as the motel, in that it provided reasonably priced accommodation in a convenient roadside position, without all the trappings of a full-scale hotel, but this time the concept was right for the travelling British public and before long Lodges were springing up all over the place – usually where there was already a roadside eating place such as Little Chef or a motorway service area.

The AA was quick to recognise this new trend and in the spring of 1987 our new Lodge classification was launched, with 11 establishments appearing in the 1988 edition of the guide. Thirteen more Lodges were appointed during 1988, 32 more in 1989 and a further 36 by the summer of 1990. In this edition of the guide there are no less than 123 – 92 already inspected and appointed and 31 due to open during the currency of the guide.

Recent market research has shown that business travellers, who previously tended to stay in quite expensive hotels, were beginning to shift towards more budget-conscious accommodation and to Lodges in particular. No doubt the economic climate has something to do with that, but no amount of belt-tightening would persuade these customers to change their habits if the standard of accommodation was not up to their expectations. This, we believe, is where the Lodge has scored over the old-style motel. Rooms in Lodges are comfortable, attractive and well designed and offer all you need for an overnight stay, including a colour television, facilities for making tea and coffee, an en suite bathroom and somewhere to work if necessary. They are well-built and well insulated from noise (motels had something of a reputation for paper-thin walls!); booking is efficient with central reservation numbers, and credit-card bookings will reserve the room regardless of your time of arrival. Of course, it is not essential to make a reservation – in most cases you can just pull in and find a room available, even quite late in the evening. This would not always make you a popular guest at an ordinary hotel. Checking out is also efficient, with computerised accounts which can be settled when you arrive to save time next morning.

It is not just the business fraternity that have warmed to the Lodge concept. Holidaymakers, too, are finding that Lodges are an excellent option for a break in their journey, and they are particularly good value for families. Each room has a sofa which converts to two extra beds as well as the double bed, so a family of four can stay, in comfort, for the normal double rate of around £30 a night. Usually there are rooms available which have been specially designed for wheelchair-bound visitors too.

Generally speaking, you will not find anywhere to eat in the Lodge itself, but most, as has already been said, are adjacent to a roadside restaurant where meals are available from breakfast time to late evening, or round the clock at a motorway service area.

At the moment, most of the Lodges we list are fairly standard in the quality and facilities that they offer, but as they become more and more established further developments are likely to appear and we are taking a keen interest in their progress. We are certain that it will not be another 25 years before roadside accommodation takes another step forward – closely followed, of course, by this guide!

| TOWN | COUNTY | NAME | LOCATION |
|---|---|---|---|
| Acle | Norfolk | Travelodge | A47 E of Norwich |
| Adlington | Cheshire | Travelodge | A523 N of Macclesfield |
| Alfreton | Derbys | Granada | A38/A61 |
| Alrewas | Staffs | Travelodge | A38 NE of Lichfield |
| Alwalton | Cambs | Travelodge | A1 SW of Peterborough |
| Amesbury | Wilts | Travelodge | A303 W of Andover |
| Aust Services | Avon | Rank Motor | M4 Junc 21 |
| Baldock | Herts | Travelodge | A1 N of Baldock |
| Barnsdale Bar | S Yorks | Travelodge | A1 N of Doncaster |
| Barnsley | S Yorks | Travelodge | A633/A635 |
| Barton Mills | Suffolk | Travelodge | A11 E of Newmarket |
| Barton Stacey | Hants | Travelodge | A303 E of Andover |
| Barton under Needwood | Staffs | Travelodge | A38 SW of Burton-upon-Trent |
| Basildon | Essex | Campanile | A127 NW of town |
| Basildon | Essex | Watermill Travel Inn | A132 NE of town |
| Basingstoke | Hants | Travelodge | A30 SW of town centre |
| Bebington | Mersey | Travelodge | A41, N of M53 Junc 5 |
| Birch Services | Gt Man | Granada | M62 Junc 18–19 |
| Birmingham | W Mid | Campanile | Off A38 SW city centre |
| Blyth | Notts | Granada | A1 NE of Worksop |
| Blyth | Notts | Travelodge | A1 NE of Worksop |

| TOWN | COUNTY | NAME | LOCATION |
|---|---|---|---|
| Brimfield | Salop | Travelodge | A49/B4362 S of Ludlow |
| Burnley | Lancs | Travelodge | Off M65 Junc 10 |
| Cannock | Staffs | Longford House | A5; off M6 Junc 12 |
| Carcroft | S Yorks | Travelodge | A1 N of Doncaster |
| Cardiff | S Glam | Campanile | Pentwyn M4 Junc 29, off A48 |
| Cardiff | S Glam | Rank Motor | Cardiff West M4 Service area Junc 33 |
| Cardiff | S Glam | Travelodge | Off A48(M) E of city |
| Chesterfield | Derbys | Travelodge | A61 Inner Ring Road |
| Colsterworth | Lincs | Granada | A1 S of Grantham |
| Colsterworth | Lincs | Travelodge | A1 S of Grantham |
| Coventry | W Mid | Campanile | A46 E of city |
| Coventry | W Mid | Travelodge | A444 N of city |
| Cramlington | Northumb | Travelodge | A1 NE of Newcastle |
| Cross Hands | Dyfed | Travelodge | A48 beyond end of M4 |
| Desborough | N'hants | Travelodge | A6 NW of Kettering |
| Doncaster | S Yorks | Campanile | A638 near racecourse |
| Dorking | Surrey | Travelodge | A25 E of town |
| Droitwich | Heref/Worcs | Travelodge | A38 N of town |
| Dudley | W Mid | Travelodge | A461 |
| Dumbarton | Strath | Travelodge | A82 SE edge of town |
| East Horndon | Essex | Travelodge | A127, E of M25 Junc 29 |
| Eastleigh | Hants | Travelodge | A335 N of town |
| Edinburgh | Lothian | Travelodge | A720 Ring Road South |
| Farthing Corner | Kent | Rank Motor | M2 services Junc 4–5 |
| Felling | Tyne & Wear | Travelodge | A194 off A1(M) S of Tyne Tunnel |
| Fenstanton | Cambs | Travelodge | A604 SE of Huntingdon |
| Ferrybridge | W Yorks | Granada | A1/M62 E of Pontefract |
| Five Oaks | W Sussex | Travelodge | A29 SW of Horsham |
| Fontwell | W Sussex | Travelodge | A27 W of Arundel |
| Forton Services | Lancs | Rank Motor | M6 junc 32–33 |
| Four Marks | Hants | Travelodge | A31 SW of Alton |
| Frankley | W Mid | Granada | M5 junc 3–4 |
| Gordano | Avon | Travelodge | M5 Junc 19 W of Bristol |
| Grantham | Lincs | Travelodge | A1 S of town |
| Gretna | Dumf & Gall | Travelodge | A74 |
| Hailsham | E Sussex | Travelodge | A22 NW of town |
| Halkyn | Clwyd | Travelodge | A55 W of Flint |
| Hamilton | Strath | Roadchef | M74 N-bound junc 5–6 |
| Hartlebury | Heref & Worcs | Travelodge | A449 S of Kidderminster |
| Haydock | Mersey | Travelodge | A580 N of St Helens |
| Heston | G Lond | Granada | M4 junc 2–3 |
| Hilton Park | W Mid | Rank Motor | M6 junc 10a–11 |
| Hockliffe | Beds | Travelodge | A5 NW of Dunstable |
| Hull | Humbs | Campanile | A1079 S of town centre |
| Ilminster | Som | Travelodge | A303 |
| Kinross | Tays | Granada | A977, off M90 junc 6 |
| Knutsford | Chesh | Travelodge | A556, off M6 junc 19 |
| Leigh Delamere | Wilts | Granada | M4 junc 17–18 |
| Llandegai | Gwyn | Rank Motor | A55 E of Bangor |
| Lolworth | Cambs | Travelodge | A604 NW of Cambridge |
| Long Sutton | Lincs | Travelodge | A17 midway Spalding & King's Lynn |
| Markfield | Leics | Granada | M1/A50 junc 22 NW of Leicester |
| Markham Moor | Notts | Travelodge | A1 S of Retford |
| Marston Moretaine | Beds | Travelodge | A421 SW of Bedford |
| Morcott | Leics | Travelodge | A47 S of Oakham |
| Morden | G Lond | Travelodge | A24 NE of Epsom |
| Musselburgh | Lothian | Granada | A1 E of Edinburgh |

| TOWN | COUNTY | NAME | LOCATION |
|---|---|---|---|
| Nantwich | Chesh | Travelodge | A51 NW of town |
| Newark-on-Trent | Notts | Travelodge | A1 N of town |
| Northampton | N'hants | Travelodge | A45 W of town, off M1 junc 16 |
| Northop Hall | Clwyd | Travelodge | A55, N of Mold |
| Nuneaton | Warks | Griff House Travel Inn | A444, N of M6 junc 3 |
| Nuneaton | Warks | Longshoot Toby | A5/A47 E of town |
| Okehampton | Devon | Travelodge | A30 |
| Oldbury | W Mid | Travelodge | A4123 SE of Wolverhampton |
| Oswestry | Salop | Travelodge | A5/A483 Oswestry bypass |
| Pencoed | M Glam | Travelodge | Off A473 E of Bridgend, M4 junc 35 |
| Penrith | Cumbria | Travelodge | A66, W of M6 junc 40 |
| Plymouth | Devon | Campanile | A38 N of city centre |
| Podimore | Som | Travelodge | A303, S of junc with A37 W of Wincanton |
| | | | |
| Reading | Berks | Travelodge | A33 S outskirts of town |
| Redditch | Heref & Worcs | Campanile | Off M42 junc 3 |
| Rownhams | Hants | Roadchef | M27 S-bound, junc 3–4 |
| Rugeley | Staffs | Travelodge | A51/B5013 outskirts of town |
| Saltash | C'wall | Granada | A38 W of Plymouth |
| Sampford Peverell | Devon | Travelodge | Off M5, junc 27 |
| Sarn Park | M Glam | Travelodge | M4 junc 36 |
| Scotch Corner | N Yorks | Rank Motor | A1/A66 NE of Richmond |
| Scotch Corner | N Yorks | Travelodge | A1 S of Scotch Corner |
| Sedgemoor | Som | Travelodge | M5 N-bound, junc 25–26 |
| Sheffield | S Yorks | Comfort Inn | Centre of town, near Crucible Theatre |
| | | | |
| Skipton | N Yorks | Travelodge | Off A59, NW outskirts |
| Sleaford | Lincs | Travelodge | A17/A15 N of town |
| Southwaite | Cumbria | Granada | M6 services junc 41–42 |
| Stirling | Central | Granada | Junc M9/M80 S of town |
| Stowmarket | Suffolk | Travelodge | A45 NW of town |
| Sutton Scotney | Hants | Travelodge | A34 N of Winchester |
| Tamworth | Staffs | Granada | M42 junc 10 E of town |
| Taunton Deane | Som | Roadchef | M5 services junc 25–26 |
| Telford | Salop | Travelodge | A5223 off M54 W of town? |
| Thrapston | N'hants | Travelodge | A14 E of Kettering |
| Thrussington | Leics | Travelodge | A46 N of Leicester |
| Thurlaston | Warks | Travelodge | A45/M45 S of Rugby |
| Toddington | Beds | Granada | M1 services junc 11–12 |
| Tring | Herts | Crows Nest Travel Inn | Junc A41(M)/A4011 N of town |
| Uttoxeter | Staffs | Travelodge | A50 |
| Warminster | Wilts | Granada | A36 NW of town |
| Washington | Tyne & Wear | Granada | A1(M) services |
| Wheatley | Oxon | Travelodge | A40 E of Oxford |
| Woodbridge | Suffolk | Travelodge | A12 NE of Ipswich |
| Woolley Edge | N Yorks | Granada | M1 services junc 38–39 |
| Wrexham | Clwyd | Travelodge | A483/A5152 S of town |

# INDEX OF TOWN PLANS

# KEY TO TOWN PLANS

| | | | |
|---|---|---|---|
| - - - | Roads with restricted access | ❸ | Hotel and restaurant |
| ✝ | Churches | ★ | Red Star hotel |
| _i_ | Tourist Information centre | ◀ 2m | Distance to hotels from edge of plan |
| AA | AA Centre | | |
| P | Car parking | | |

**Aberdeen**

1  Bucksburn Moat House ★★★
2  Caledonian Thistle ★★★
3  Copthorne ★★★
4  New Marcliffe ★★★
5  Skean Dhu Altens ★★★★
6  Stakis Treetops ★★★
7  Swallow Imperial ★★★

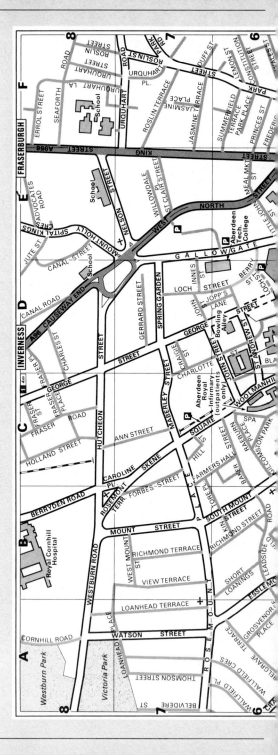

Central Aberdeen
© The Automobile Association 1990

(5/90)

3

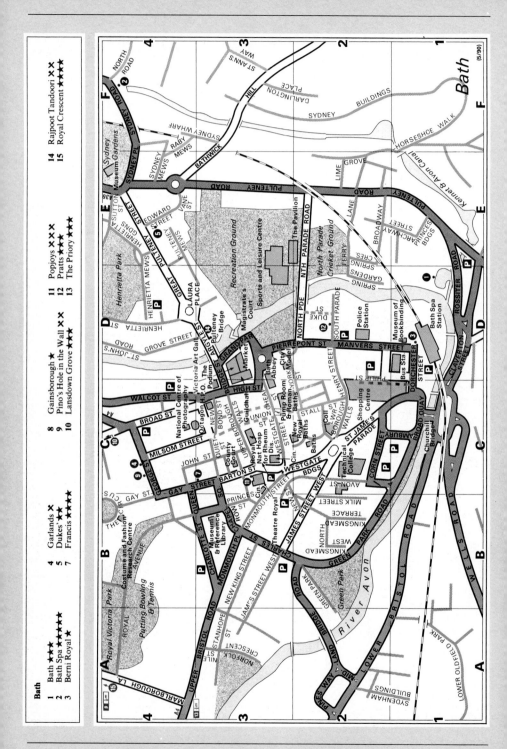

**Bath**

| | | |
|---|---|---|
| 1 | Bath | ★★★ |
| 2 | Bath Spa | ★★★★★ |
| 3 | Berni Royal | ★ |
| 4 | Garlands | ★ |
| 5 | Dukes | ★★ |
| 7 | Francis | ★★★★ |
| 8 | Gainsborough | ★ |
| 9 | Pino's Hole in the Wall | ★★ |
| 10 | Lansdown Grove | ★★★ |
| 11 | Popjoys | ★★★ |
| 12 | Pratts | ★★★ |
| 13 | The Priory | ★★★ |
| 14 | Rajpoot Tandoori | ★★ |
| 15 | Royal Crescent | ★★★★ |

Bath

(5/90)

4

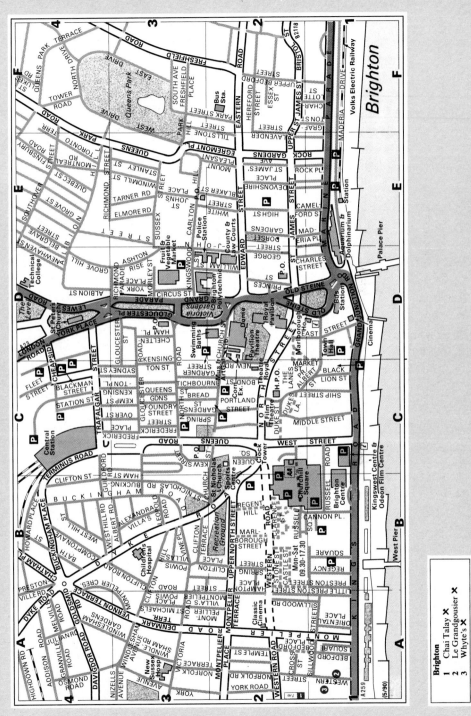

**Brighton**

1 Chai Talay ✗
2 Le Grandgousier ✗
3 Whyte's ✗

A259 (5/90)

Central Birmingham

© The Automobile Association 1990

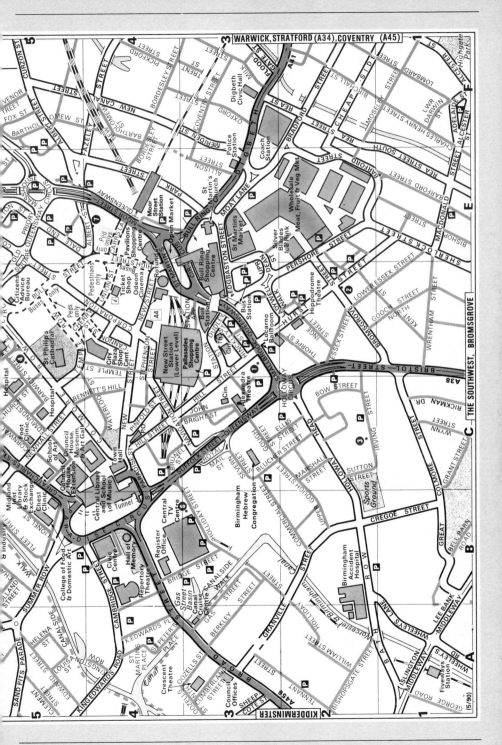

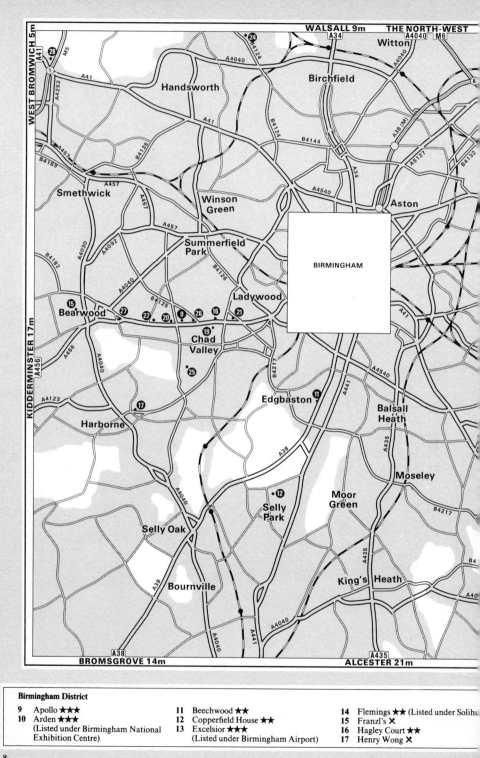

**Birmingham District**

| | | | | | | |
|---|---|---|---|---|---|---|
| **9** | Apollo ★★★ | **11** | Beechwood ★★ | **14** | Flemings ★★ (Listed under Solihu |
| **10** | Arden ★★★ | **12** | Copperfield House ★★ | **15** | Franzl's ✗ |
| | (Listed under Birmingham National | **13** | Excelsior ★★★ | **16** | Hagley Court ★★ |
| | Exhibition Centre) | | (Listed under Birmingham Airport) | **17** | Henry Wong ✗ |

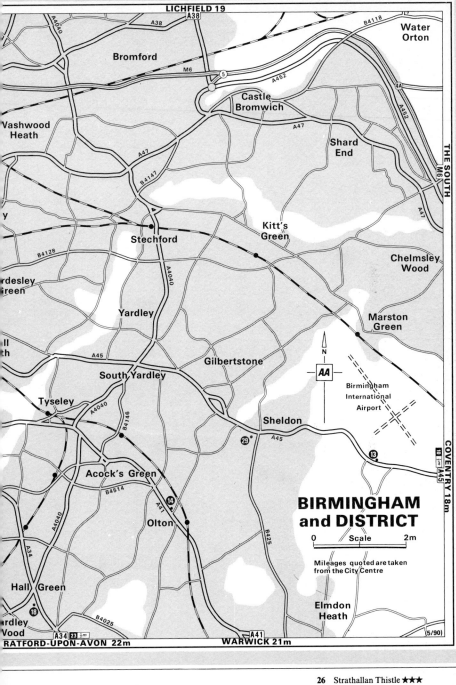

# BIRMINGHAM and DISTRICT

LICHFIELD 19

Water Orton

Bromford

Castle Bromwich

Vashwood Heath

Shard End

Kitt's Green

Stechford

Chelmsley Wood

rdesley Green

Yardley

Marston Green

South Yardley

Gilbertstone

Birmingham International Airport

Tyseley

Sheldon

Acock's Green

Olton

Hall Green

Elmdon Heath

ardley Wood

Scale 0 — 2m

Mileages quoted are taken from the City Centre

STRATFORD-UPON-AVON 22m

WARWICK 21m

THE SOUTH M6

COVENTRY 18m A45

(5/90)

| | 26 | Strathallan Thistle ★★★ |
|---|---|---|
| J Jays ✗ | 22 Portland ★★ | 27 Westbourne Lodge ★★ |
| New Cobden ★★ | 23 Saracens Head ★★ (See under Solihull) | 28 West Bromwich Moat House ★★★ |
| Norfolk ★★ | 24 Sheriden House ★★ | (See under West Bromwich) |
| Plough & Harrow ★★★★ | 25 Sloan's ✗✗✗ | 29 Wheatsheaf ★★ |

9

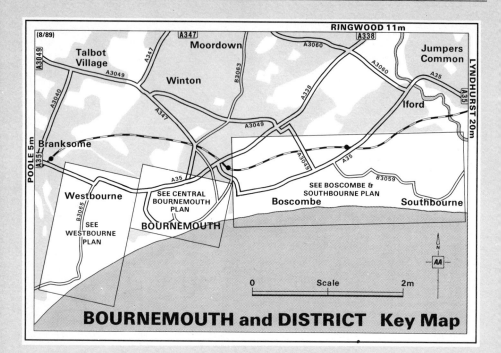

**BOURNEMOUTH and DISTRICT   Key Map**

RINGWOOD 11m

LYNDHURST 20m

POOLE 5m

(8/89)

Talbot Village

Moordown

Jumpers Common

Winton

Iford

Branksome

Westbourne

SEE CENTRAL BOURNEMOUTH PLAN

SEE WESTBOURNE PLAN

BOURNEMOUTH

SEE BOSCOMBE & SOUTHBOURNE PLAN

Boscombe

Southbourne

0   Scale   2m

A3049 | A347 | A338 | A3060 | A35 | A3063 | A347 | A3049 | A3040 | A347 | A3049 | A3049 | A35 | B3059 | A35 | B3065

---

**Bournemouth Central**

| | | | |
|---|---|---|---|
| 1 | Arlington ★★ | 24 | New Dorchester ★ |
| 2 | Belvedere ★★★ | 25 | New Durley Dean ★★★ |
| 3 | Boltons ★★ | 26 | Norfolk Royale ★★★★ |
| 4 | Bournemouth Heathlands ★★★ | 27 | Pavillion ★★★ |
| 5 | Bournemouth Highcliff ★★★★ | 28 | Hotel Piccadilly ★★★ |
| 6 | Burley Court ★★★ | 29 | Pinehurst ★★ |
| 7 | The Connaught ★★ | 30 | Queens ★★★ |
| 8 | County ★★ | 31 | Hotel Riviera (West Cliff Gardens) ★★ |
| 9 | Crest ★★★ | 32 | Royal Bath ★★★★★ |
| 10 | Durley Chine ★★ | 33 | Royal Exeter ★★ |
| 11 | Durley Grange ★★ | 34 | Russell Court ★★ |
| 12 | Durley Hall ★★★ | 35 | St George ★★ |
| 13 | Durlston Court ★★★ | 36 | Savoy ★★★ |
| 14 | East Anglia ★★★ | 37 | Silver How ★ |
| 15 | Embassy ★★★ | 38 | Sophisticats ✕✕ |
| 16 | Gresham Court ★★ | 39 | Sun Court ★★ |
| 17 | Grosvenor ★★★ | 40 | Trouville ★★★ |
| 18 | Hermitage ★★★ | 41 | Ullswater ★★ |
| 19 | Lynden Court ★ | 42 | Wessex ★★★ |
| 20 | Mansfield ★★ | 43 | West Cliff Hall ★★ |
| 21 | Marsham Court ★★★ | 44 | Whitehall ★★ |
| 22 | Melford Hall ★★★ | 45 | Winterbourne ★★ |
| 23 | Hotel Miramar ★★★ | 46 | Woodcroft Tower ★★ |

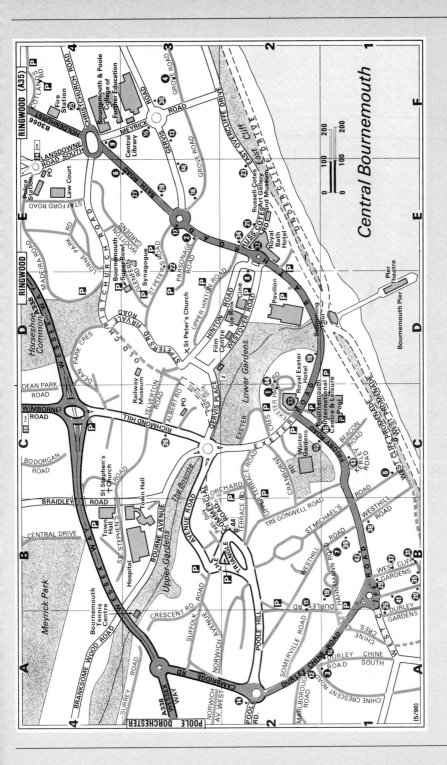

Central Bournemouth

11

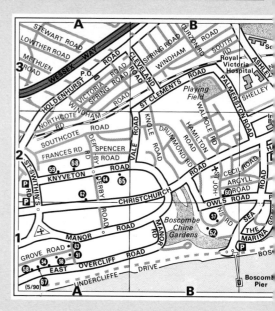

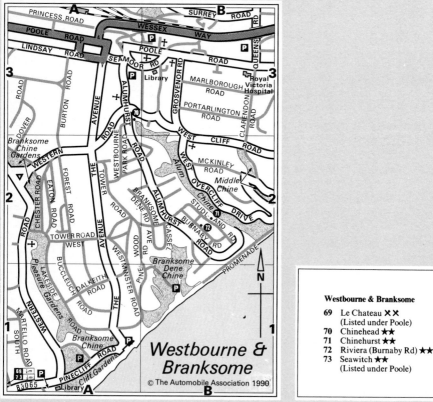

Westbourne & Branksome

© The Automobile Association 1990

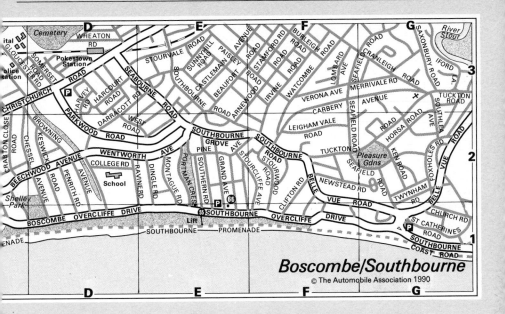

Boscombe/Southbourne
© The Automobile Association 1990

**Boscombe & Southbourne**

51 Chesterwood ★★★
52 Chine ★★★
54 Cliffeside ★★★
55 Commodore ★
56 Cottonwood ★★
57 Hotel Courtlands ★★★
58 Cumberland ★★★
59 Elstead ★★★
60 Fircroft ★★
62 Hartford Court ★★
63 Hinton Firs ★★
64 Langtry Manor ★★★
65 Moat House ★★★
66 Overcliff ★★
67 Suncliff ★★★
68 Taurus Park ★

**Bristol**

1   Avon Gorge ★★★
2   Barbizon ✕✕
3   Bistro Twenty One ✕
4   Bouboulina's ✕
5   Clifton ★★
6   Crest ★★★
8   Henbury Lodge ★★★
10   Holiday Inn ★★★★
11   Howards ✕
17   Orient Rendezvous ✕✕
18   Parkside ★★
19   Raj Tandoori ✕
20   Redwood Lodge & Country Club ★★★
21   Restaurant Danton ✕✕
23   Restaurant Lettonie ✕✕
24   St Vincent's Rocks ★★★
25   Rodney ★★
26   Unicorn ★★★

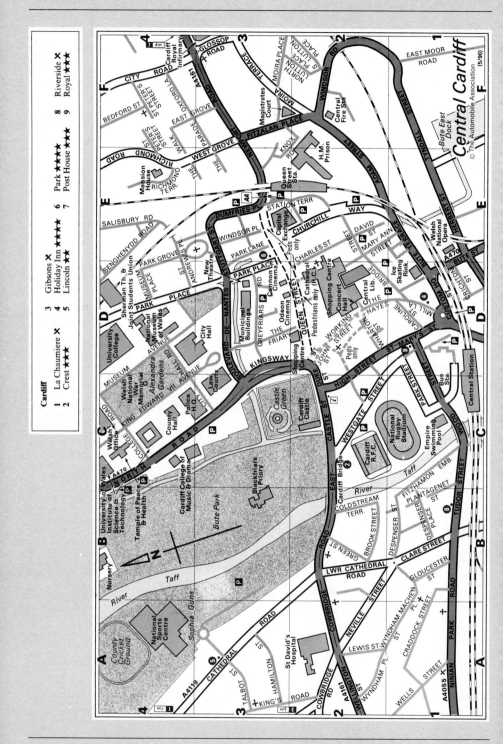

Central Cardiff (5/90)
© The Automobile Association

Cardiff

| | | |
|---|---|---|
| 1 La Chaumiere ✗ | 3 Gibsons ✗ | 8 Riverside ✗ |
| 2 Crest ★★★ | 4 Holiday Inn ★★★★ | 9 Royal ★★★ |
| | 5 Lincoln ★★ | 6 Park ★★★★ |
| | | 7 Post House ★★★ |

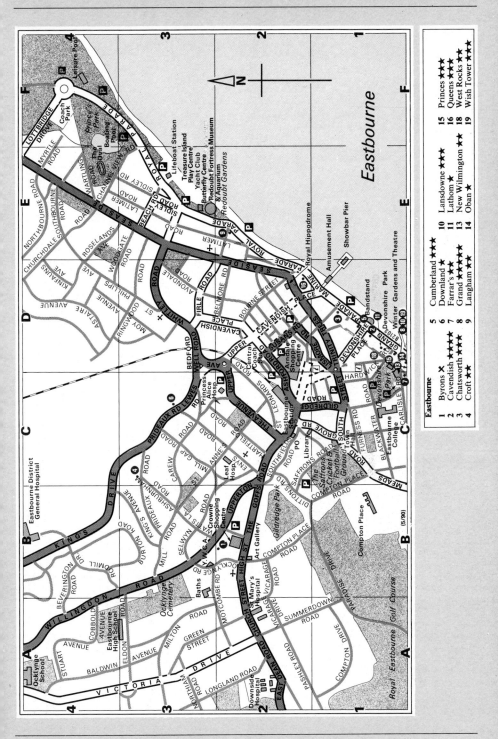

Eastbourne

17

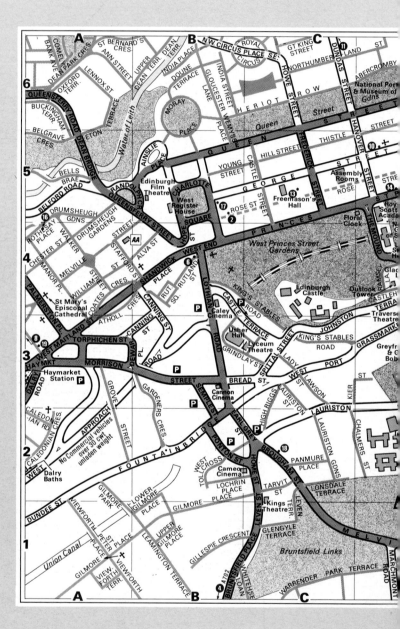

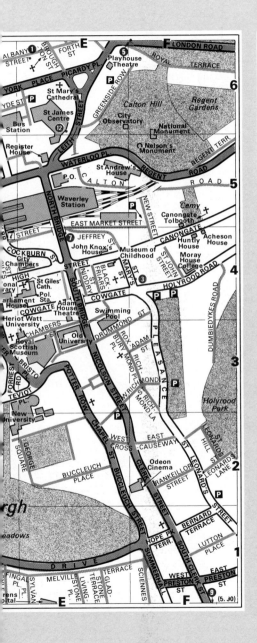

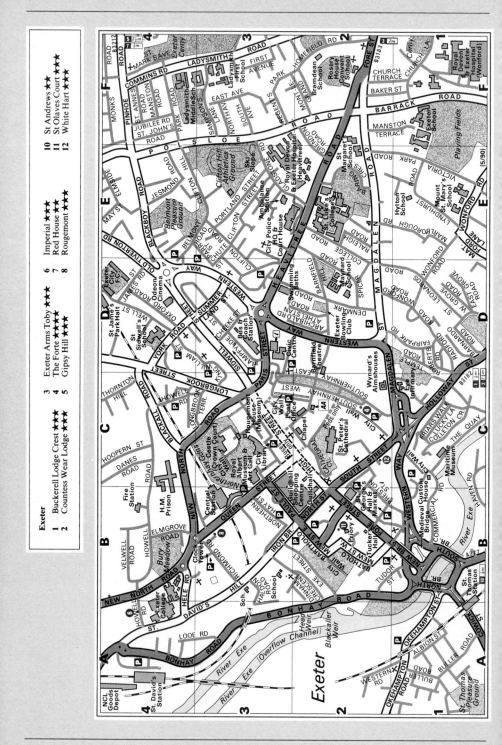

**Exeter**

1 Buckerell Lodge Crest ★★★
2 Countess Wear Lodge ★★★

3 Exeter Arms Toby ★★★
4 The Forte ★★★★
5 Gipsy Hill ★★★

6 Imperial ★★★
7 Red House ★★
8 Rougemont ★★★

10 St Andrews ★★
11 St Olaves Court ★★★
12 White Hart ★★★

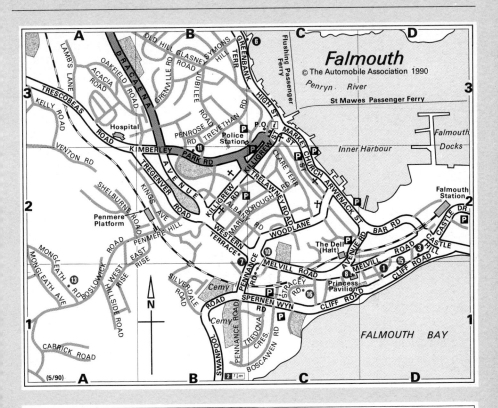

**Falmouth**

1   Carthion ★★
2   Crill Manor Hotel & Restaurant ★★
3   Falmouth ★★★
6   Greenbank ★★★

7   Green Lawns ★★★
8   Gyllyngdune Manor ★★★
10   Melville ★★
11   Park Grove ★★

13   Penmere Manor ★★★★⚑
15   Royal Duchy ★★★
16   St Michaels ★★★

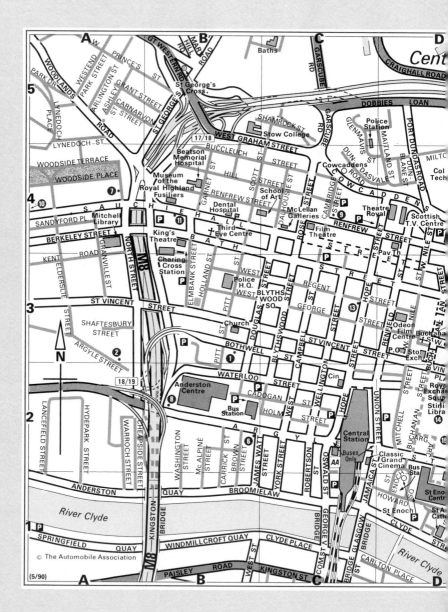

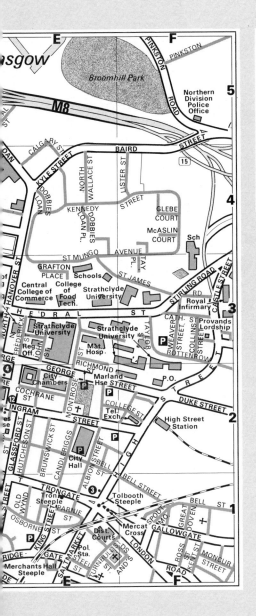

**Glasgow**

1 Albany ★★★★
2 Buttery ✕✕
3 Colonial ✕✕
4 Copthorne ★★★
6 Crest Hotel Glasgow-City ★★★
7 Fountain ✕✕✕
8 Holiday Inn Glasgow ★★★★
9 Hospitality Inn ★★★★
10 Kelvin Park Lorne ★★★
11 Loon-Fung ✕
12 Stakis Ingram ★★★
13 Peking Inn ✕
14 Rogano ✕✕
15 The Triangle ✕✕

Inverness

| | | | | |
|---|---|---|---|---|
| **Inverness** | 4 | Culloden House ★★★★ | 12 | Mercury ★★★ |
| | 5 | Cummings ★★ | 13 | Loch Ness House ★★ |
| 1 | Beaufort ★★ | 8 | Dunain Park ★★★ | 14 | Palace ★★★ |
| 2 | Caledonian ★★★ | 9 | Glen Mhor ★★ | 15 | Redcliffe ★ |
| 3 | Craigmonie ★★★ | 11 | Kingsmills ★★★ | 16 | Station ★★★ |

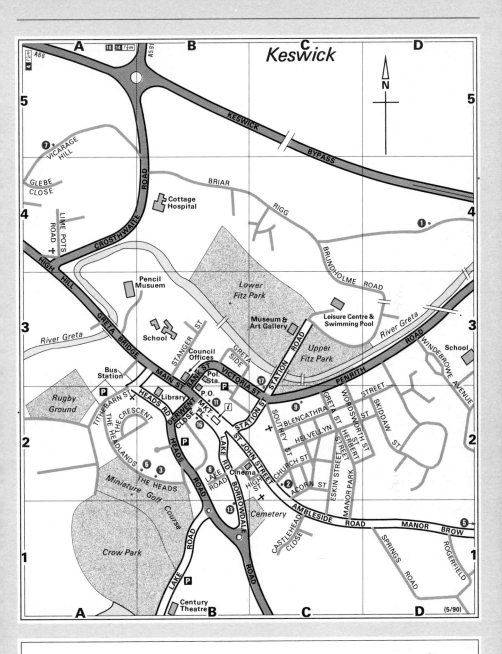

**Keswick**

| | | | | | | |
|---|---|---|---|---|---|---|
| | | | | | **10** | Lyzzick Hill ★★⚑ |
| **1** | Brundholme Country House ★★★ | **5** | Grange Country House ★★ | **11** | Queen's ★★ |
| **2** | Chaucer House ★★ | **6** | Highfield ★ | **13** | Priorholm ★ |
| **3** | Crow Park ★★ | **7** | Lairbeck ★★ | **14** | Red House ★★★⚑ |
| **4** | Derwentwater ★★★ | **8** | Latrigg Lodge ★ | **16** | Skiddaw ★★ |
| | | **9** | Linnett Hill ★ | **17** | Walpole ★★ |

**Liverpool**

1 Atlantic Tower ★★★★
2 Blundellsands ★★★
  (See under Blundellsands)
3 Crest Hotel Liverpool-City ★★★
4 Far East ✕✕
5 Grange ★★
6 Green Park ★★
7 Liverpool Moat House ★★★★
8 Park ★★★ (See under Bootle)
9 St George's ★★★

Central Liverpool

RIVER MERSEY

(5/90)

27

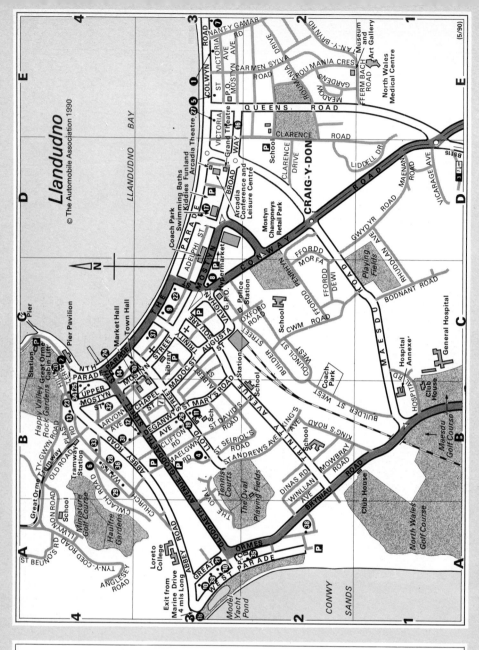

Llandudno
© The Automobile Association 1990

**Llandudno**
1 Bedford ★★
2 Belle Vue ★★
3 Bodysgallen Hall ★★★★⑱
4 Branksome ★
5 Bromwell Court ★★
6 Bryn Orme ★★
7 Bryn-y-Bia Lodge ★★
8 Castle ★★
9 Chatsworth House ★★★
10 Clontarf ★
11 Crickleigh ★★
12 Dunoon ★★★
13 Empire ★★★
14 Esplanade ★★
16 Floral ★★
17 Four Oaks ★★
18 Gogarth Abbey ★★★
19 Gwesty Leamore ★
20 Headlands ★★
21 Hilbre Court ★
22 Imperial ★★★
23 Lanterns ★★
24 Merrion ★★
25 Min-y-Don ★
26 Oak Alyn ★
27 Ormescliffe ★★
28 Plas Fron Deg ★★★
29 Quinton ★
30 Ravenhurst ★
31 Risboro ★★★
32 Rose Tor ★★
33 Royal ★★
34 St Tudno ★★★
35 Sandringham ★★
36 Sefton Court ★★★
37 Somerset ★★
38 Sunnymede ★★
39 Tan-Lan ★★

28

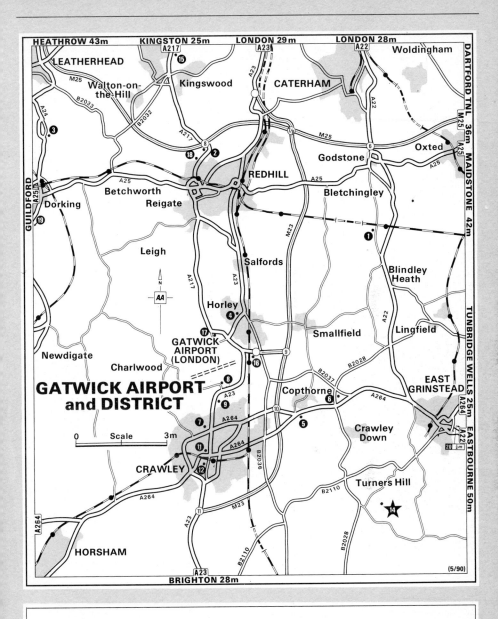

**Gatwick Airport & District**

1   La Bonne Auberge ✗✗✗ (See under South Godstone)
2   Bridge House ★★★ (See under Reigate)
3   Burford Bridge ★★★★ (See under Dorking)
4   Chequers Thistle ★★★
5   Copthorne ★★★★
6   Copthorne Effingham Park ★★★★
7   Holiday Inn Gatwick ★★★
8   Gatwick Concorde ★★★

9   Gatwick Manor ★★
11   George ★★★
12   Goffs Park ★★★
14   Gravetye Manor ★★★⚑ (See under East Grinstead)
15   Heathside ★★ (See under Burgh Heath)
16   London Gatwick Airport Hilton ★★★★
17   Post House ★★★
18   Reigate Manor ★★★ (See under Reigate)
19   The White Horse ★★★ (See under Dorking)
20   Woodbury House ★★ (See under East Grinstead)

**Heathrow Airport**

1  Ariel ★★★
2  Berkeley Arms ★★★
3  Excelsior ★★★★
4  Heathrow Penta ★★★★
5  Holiday Inn ★★★★
6  Hotel Ibis Heathrow ★★
7  Master Robert ★★★ (See under Hounslow)
8  Thames Lodge ★★★ (See under Staines)
9  Post House ★★★
10 Terrazza ✕✕ (See under Ashford)

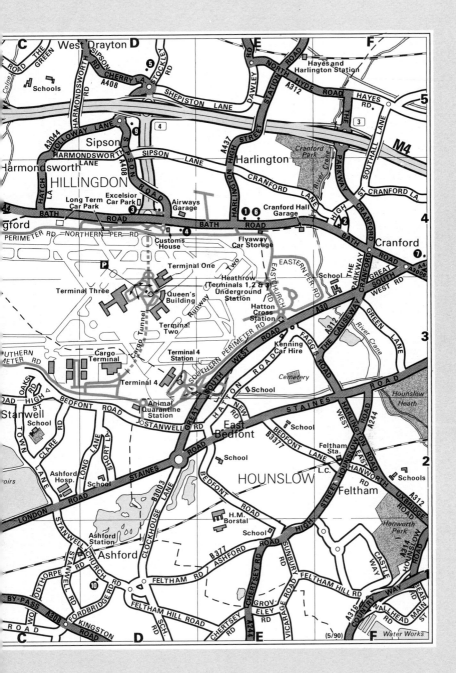

**Manchester**

1    Gaylord ✗✗
1A   Grand ○
2    Holiday Inn Crowne Plaza ★★★★
3    The Koreana ✗
4    Kosmos Taverna ✗
5    Lime Tree ✗
6    Market ✗
7    Hotel Piccadilly ★★★★
8    Portland Thistle ★★★★
9    Post House ★★★
10   Mina-Japan ✗
11   Mitre ★★
12   Rajdoot ✗✗
13   Ramada Renaissance ★★★★
14   Willow Bank ★★★
15   Woodlands ✗✗
16   Woo Sang ✗✗
17   Yang Sing ✗✗

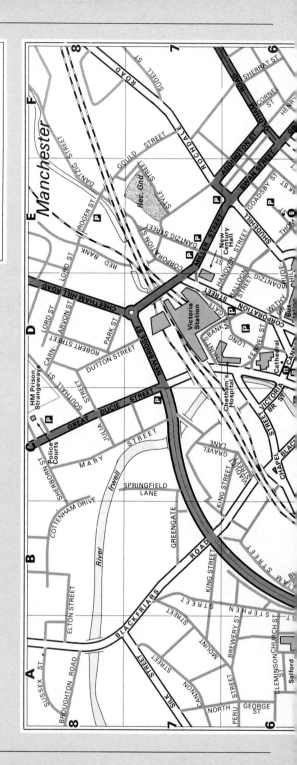

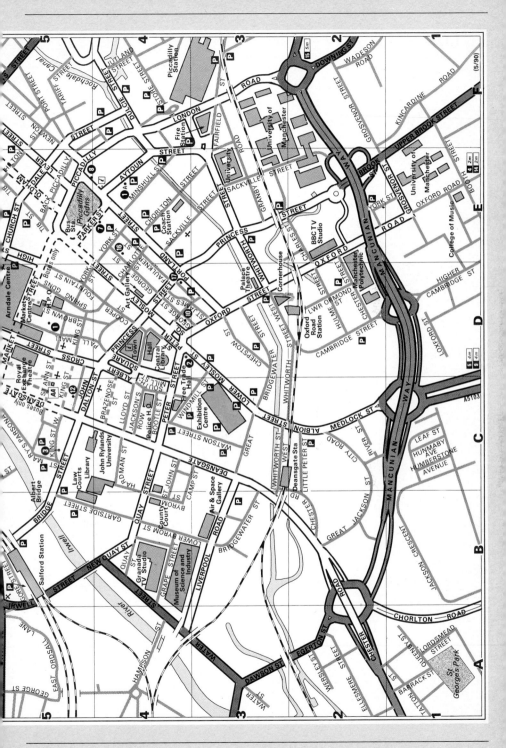

33

**Newcastle Upon Tyne**

1   Hospitality Inn ★★★
2   Cairn ★★
3   County Thistle ★★★
4   Newcastle Crest ★★★
5   Fishermans Lodge ✕✕✕
8   Holiday Inn ★★★★
9   Imperial ★★★
10  King Neptune ✕✕
12  Morrach ★★
13  Osborne ★
14  21 Queen Street ✕✕✕
15  Swallow ★★★
16  Swallow Gosforth Park ★★★★
17  Whites ★★

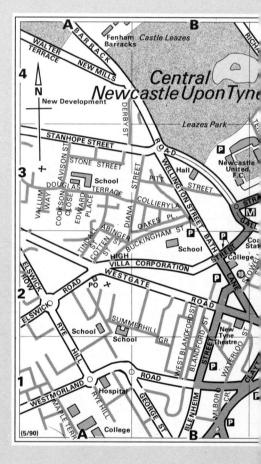

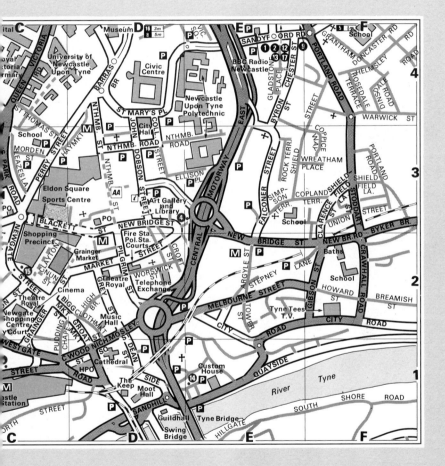

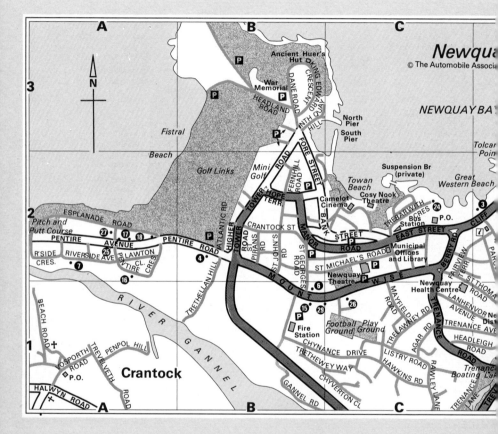

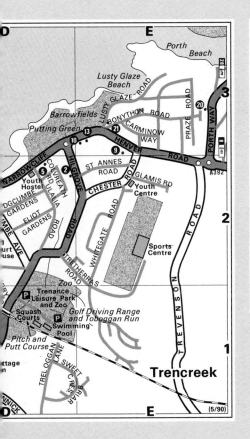

**Newquay**

2  Barrowfield ★★★
3  Beachcroft ★★
4  Bewdley ★★
5  Hotel Bristol ★★★
6  Cedars ★★
7  Corisande Manor ★★
8  Cross Mount ★★
9  Cumberland ★★
10  Edgcumbe ★★★
13  Kilbirnie ★★★
15  Hotel Lowenva ★
16  Minto House ★★
17  Hotel Mordros ★★★
18  Philema ★★
20  Porth Veor Manor House ★★
21  Hotel Riviera ★★★
24  Trebarwith ★★★
25  Tremont ★★
26  Trevone ★
27  Water's Edge ★★
28  Whipsiderry ★★
29  Windsor ★★★

**Nottingham**

1 Albany ★★★★
2 Les Artistes Gourmands ✕✕
3 Nottingham Moat House ★★★★
4 Priory ★★
5 Royal Moat House International ★★★★
6 Rufford ★★
7 Strathdon Thistle ★★★
8 Stakis Victoria ★★★
9 Swans Hotel & Restaurant ★★★
10 Waltons ★★★

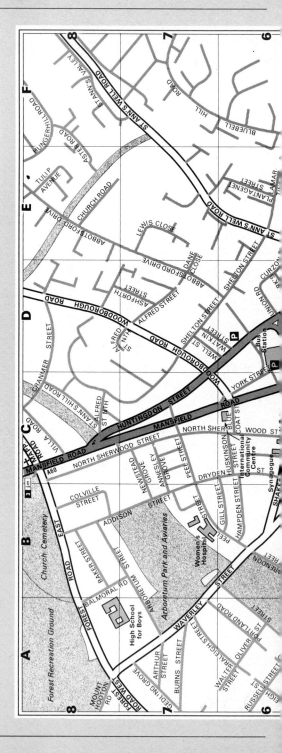

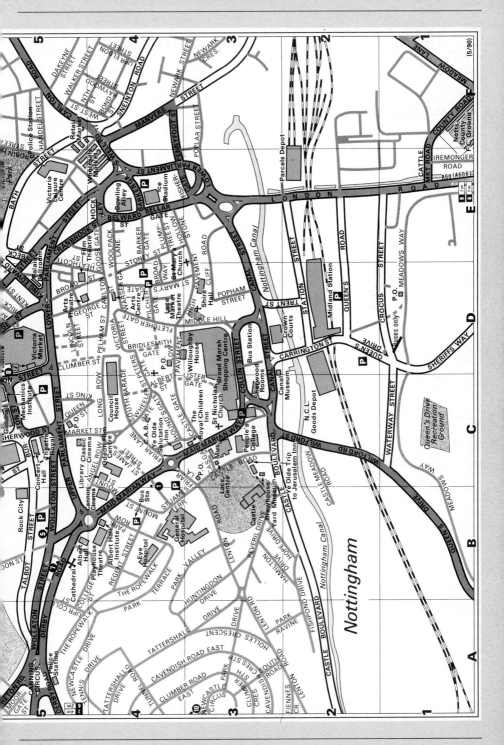

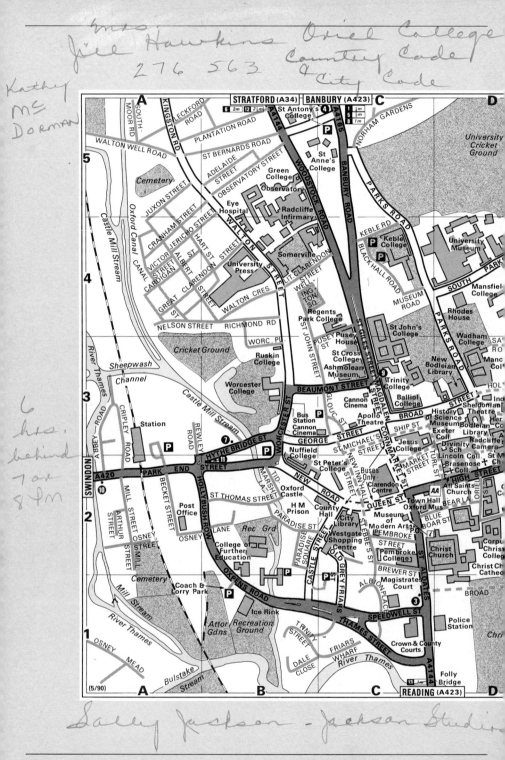

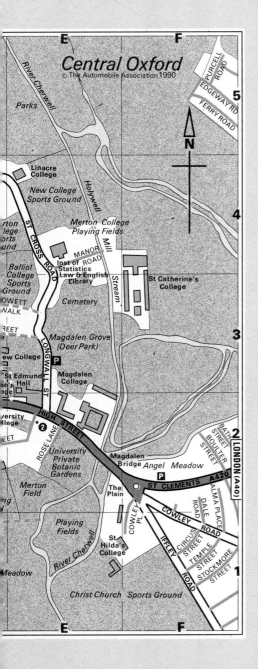

**Central Oxford**
© The Automobile Association 1990

**Oxford**

1  Cotswold Lodge ★★★
2  Eastgate ★★★
3  Restaurant Elizabeth ✗✗✗
4  15 North Parade ✗
5  Linton Lodge ★★★
6  Oxford Moat House ★★★
7  Paddyfield ✗✗
8  Gees ✗✗
9  Randolph ★★★★
10 River ★
11 Royal Oxford ★★
12 Welcome Lodge ★★
13 Victoria ★★

**Plymouth**

1 Astor ★★★
2 Camelot ★★
3 Chez Nous ✕
5 New Continental ★★★
6 Copthorne ★★★★
7 Drake ★
9 Grosvenor ★★
11 Plymouth Moat House ★★★★
12 Imperial ★
13 Invicta ★★
14 Mayflower Post House ★★★
16 Novotel Plymouth ★★★
17 Strathmore ★★

Plymouth

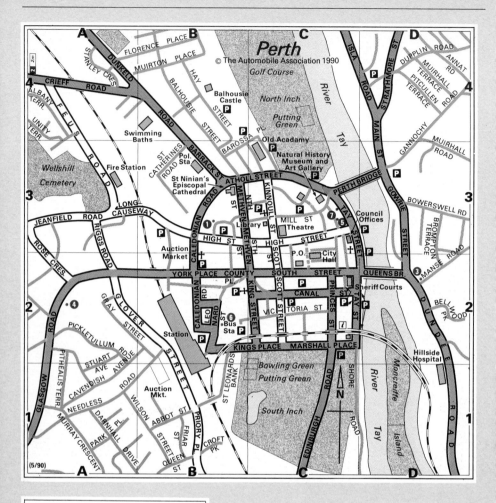

**Perth**

1 Stakis City Mills ★★★
2 Huntingtower ★★★
3 Isle of Skye Toby ★★★
4 Lovat ★★★
5 Number Thirty Three ✕✕
6 Queens ★★★
7 Royal George ★★★

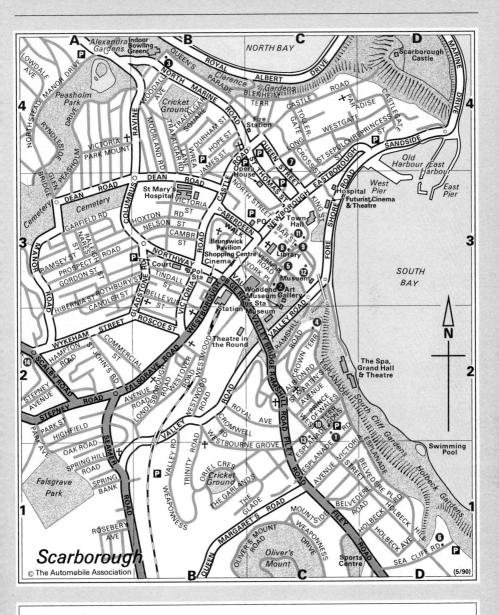

# Scarborough

| | | | | | | |
|---|---|---|---|---|---|---|
| **1** | Brooklands ★★ | **5** | Gridley's Crescent ★★ | **10** | Red Lea ★★ | |
| **2** | Central ★★ | **6** | Holbeck Hall ★★★★ | **11** | Royal ★★★★ | |
| **3** | Clifton ★★★ | **7** | Lanterna Ristorante ✗✗ | **12** | Hotel St Nicholas ★★★ | |
| **4** | Esplanade ★★★ | **8** | Palm Court ★★★ | **13** | Southlands ★★ | |
| | | **9** | Pickwick Inn ★★ | **14** | Wrea Head Country ★★★🏪 | |

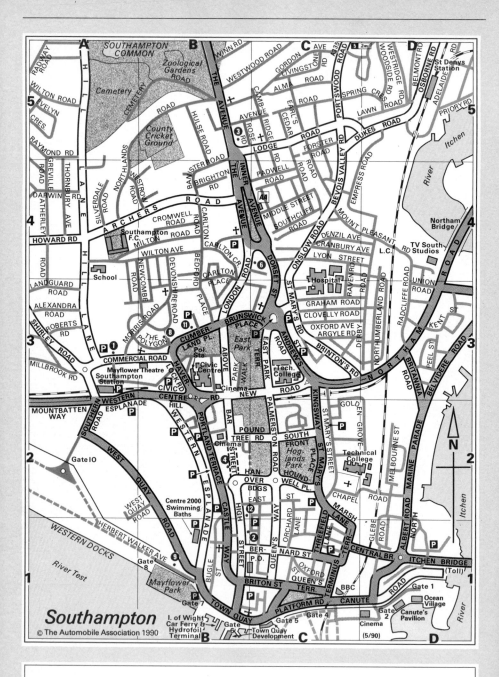

**Southampton**

| | | | | |
|---|---|---|---|---|
| **Southampton** | 3 | Elizabeth House ★★ | 8 | Polygon ★★★ |
| 1 Browns Brasserie ✕✕ | 4 | Golden Palace ✕ | 9 | Post House ★★★ |
| 2 Dolphin ★★★ | 5 | Kohinoor Tandoori ✕✕ | 11 | Southampton Park ★★★ |
| | 6 | Kuti's ✕✕ | 12 | Star ★★ |

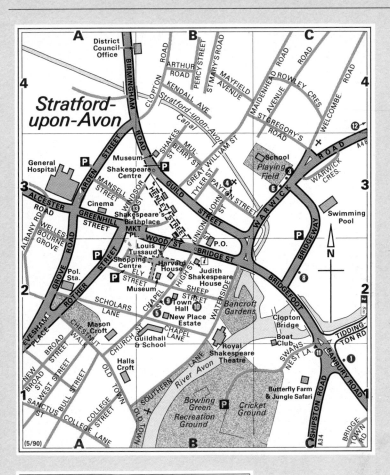

**Stratford-upon-Avon**

1 Alveston Manor ★★★
2 Charlecote Pheasant ★★★ (listed under Charlecote)
3 The Coach House ★★
4 Dukes ★★★
5 Falcon ★★★
6 Grosvenor House ★★★
8 Moat House International ★★★★
9 Shakespeare ★★★★
10 Stratford House ★★
11 Swan's Nest ★★★
12 Welcombe ★★★★
13 White Swan ★★★

**Torquay**

1 Abbey Lawn ★★★
2 Albaston ★★
3 Bancourt ★★
4 Belgrave ★★★
5 Belvedere House ★★
6 Burlington ★★
7 Bute Court ★★
8 Carlton ★★
9 Chelston Towers ★★
10 Conway Court ★★
11 Devonshire ★★★
12 Dunstone ★★
13 Frognel Hall ★★
14 Grand ★★★★
15 Gresham Court ★★
16 Homers ★★★
17 Howden Court ★★
18 Hunsdon Lea ★★
19 Imperial ★★★★★
20 Kistor ★★★
21 Lansdowne ★★
22 Lincombe Hall ★★★
23 Livermead Cliff ★★★
24 Livermead House ★★★
25 Mount Nessing ★★
26 Oscar's ★★
27 Rainbow House ★★★
28 Red House ★★
29 Remy's Restaurant Francais ✕
30 Roseland ★★
32 Shelley Court ★
33 Sydore ★★
34 Templestowe ★★
35 Toorak ★★★
36 Vernon Court ★★
37 Windsurfer ★

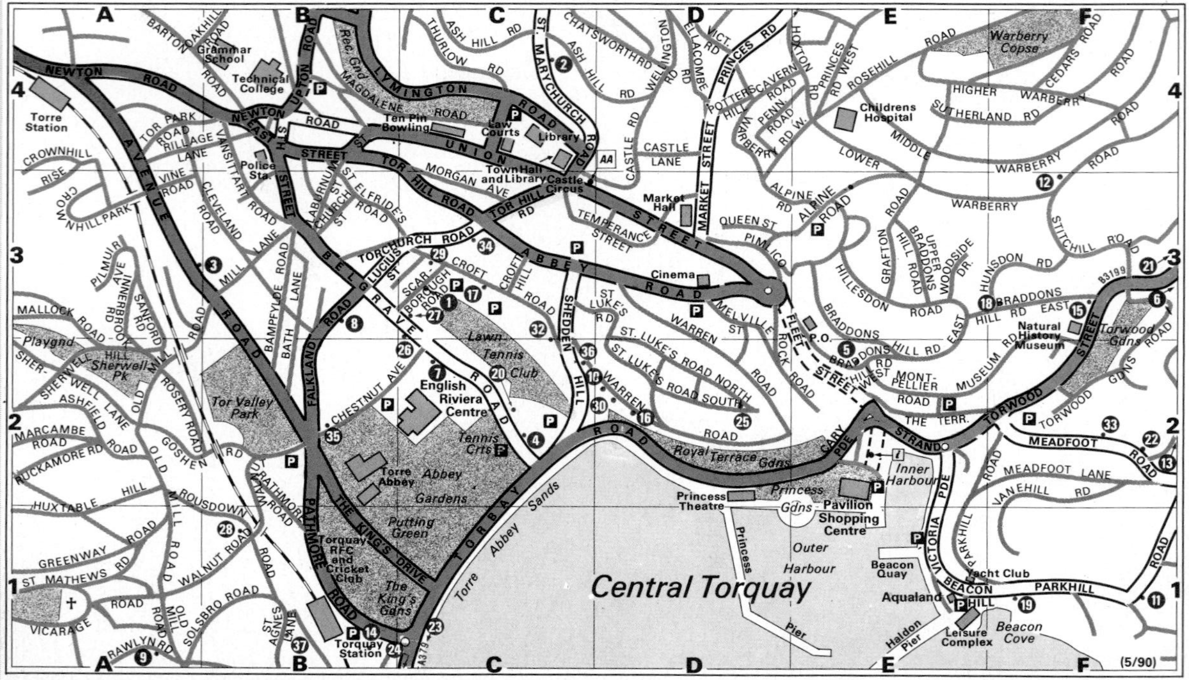

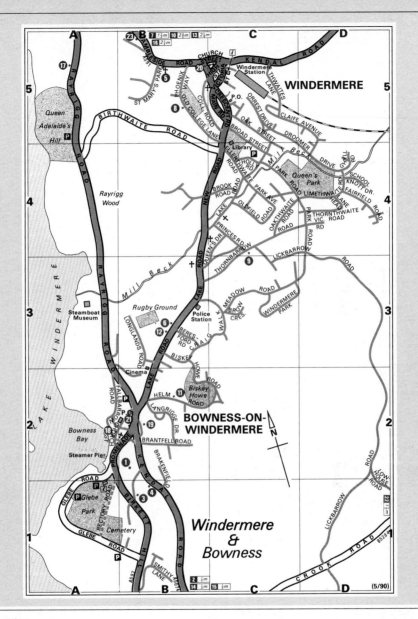

*Windermere & Bowness*

(5/90)

**Windermere**

1 Belsfield ★★★
2 Bordriggs Country House ★★
3 Burn How Garden House Hotel, Motel and Rest ★★★
4 Burnside ★★★
5 Cedar Manor ★★
6 Craig Foot Country House ★★
7 Quarry Garth Country House ★🏠
8 Hideaway ★★

9 Hillthwaite House ★★
10 Holbeck Ghyll ★★★🏠
11 Hydro ★★★
12 Knoll ★★
13 Langdale Chase ★★★★🏠
14 Lindeth Fell ★★★🏠
15 Linithwaite ★★★🏠
16 Low Wood ★★★
17 Miller Howe ★★
18 The Old England ★★★★

19 Porthole Eating House ✗
20 Rogers ✗
21 Royal ★★
22 Wild Boar ★★★
23 Willowsmere ★

49

# HOTEL GROUPS

## Key to abbreviations and central reservation telephone numbers (where applicable)

Special corporate rates are available at hotel companies marked with an *, to those business travellers who have a company account with the AA Business Travel Service.

Bookings may be made via the AA Business Travel Centres listed below

| Company | Abbreviations | Telephone |
|---|---|---|
| Associated Leisure Hotels Ltd | Associated Leisure | 061-941 6848 |
| Berni Chef & Brewer | Berni and Chef & Brewer | |
| *Best Western | Best Western | 081-541 0033 |
| Brend Hotels Ltd | Brend | Barnstaple (0271) 44496 |
| *Consort Hotels Ltd | Consort | York (0904) 643151 |
| *Commonwealth Holiday Inns of Canada Ltd | Holiday Inns | 071-722 7755 |
| Crown & Raven | Crown & Raven | |
| De Vere Hotels Ltd | De Vere | Warrington (0925) 65050 |
| *Embassy Hotels | Embassy | 071-581 3466 |
| Exec Hotels | Exec Hotel | |
| Forestdale Hotels Ltd | Forestdale | |
| Frederic Robinson Ltd | Frederic Robinson | |
| Granada Motorway Services Ltd | Granada | 05255-5555 |
| Greenall Whitley Hotels Ltd | GW Hotels | Warrington (0925) 65050 |
| Guestaccom | Guestaccom | |
| *Hilton National & Associated Hotels Ltd | Hilton | 071-734 6000 |
| Leading Hotels of the World | | Freephone 0800 181123 |
| for Berkeley, Claridges, Connaught, Savoy, Hyde Park, London; Royal Crescent, Bath, Avon; Lygon Arms, Broadway, Worcs; Grosvenor, Chester; Chewton Glen, New Milton, Hants | | |
| Inter-Hotels | Inter-Hotels | 071-373 3241 |
| Minotels | Minotels | Blackpool (0253) 594185 |
| *Mount Charlotte Thistle Hotels Ltd | Mount Charlotte (TS) | Freephone (0800) 700400 |
| *Novotel International | Novotel | 071-724 1000 |
| Porterhouse Restaurants Ltd | Porterhouse | |
| Prestige Hotels | Prestige | 071-439 2365 |
| Pride of Britain Ltd | Pride of Britain | Andover (026476) 444 |
| *Queens Moat House Ltd | Queens Moat | Harrogate (0423) 52644 |
| *Rank Organisation Ltd | Rank | 071-262 2893 |
| Relais et Châteaux Hotels | Relais et Châteaux | |
| Scottish Highland Hotels | Scottish Highland | 041-332 6538 |
| Shire Inns Ltd | Shire | |
| *Stakis Hotels & Inns | Stakis | 041-332 4343 |
| *Swallow Hotels Ltd | Swallow | 091-529 4666 |
| Toby Restaurants Ltd | Toby | |
| *Trusthouse Forte Hotels Ltd | Trusthouse Forte | 081-567 3444 |
| *Whitbread/Lansbury | | |

---

**Automobile Association**
Bookings for hotels belonging to groups marked * can only be made if your company has an account with AA Business Travel Service. Business Travel Centres are located throughout the UK and are listed below with telephone numbers.

| | | | | | |
|---|---|---|---|---|---|
| Aberdeen | (0224) 645138 | Guildford | (0483) 574070 | Twickenham | 081-891 6211 |
| Basingstoke | (0256) 493881 | Halesowen | 021-501 7779 | Manchester | 061-488 7499 |
| Bristol | (0272) 308373 | Haymarket | 071-930 6854 | Northampton | (0604) 231911 |
| Chester | (0244) 350541 | Leeds | (0532) 448981 | Reading | (0734) 580663 |
| Edinburgh | 031-225 7677 | Stanmore | 081-954 6718 | Wolverhampton | (0902) 712345 |
| Glasgow | 041-221 4373 | | | | |

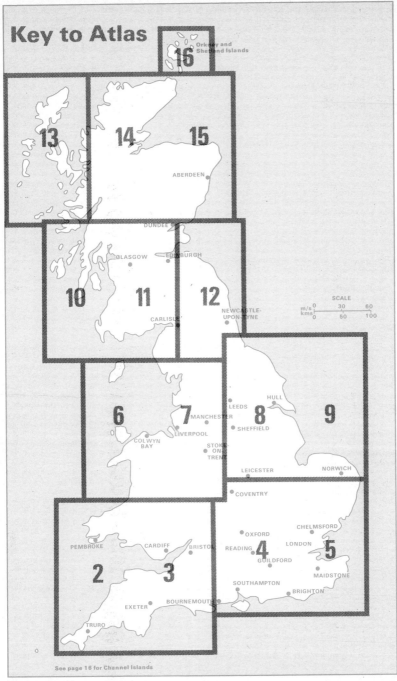

# Key to Atlas

**16** Orkney and Shetland Islands

**13**

**14**

**15**

ABERDEEN

DUNDEE

GLASGOW  EDINBURGH

**10**

**11**

**12**

CARLISLE

NEWCASTLE-UPON-TYNE

SCALE

m/s 0   30   60
kms 0   50   100

HULL

**6**

**7** MANCHESTER   LEEDS

LIVERPOOL   SHEFFIELD

**8**

**9**

COLWYN BAY

STOKE-ON-TRENT

LEICESTER

NORWICH

COVENTRY

CHELMSFORD

OXFORD

**2**

PEMBROKE

CARDIFF   BRISTOL

READING

LONDON

**4**

GUILDFORD

**5**

**3**

SOUTHAMPTON

MAIDSTONE

BRIGHTON

EXETER

BOURNEMOUTH

TRURO

See page 16 for Channel Islands

Maps produced by
The Automobile Association from the Automaps database.
© The Automobile Association 1990.

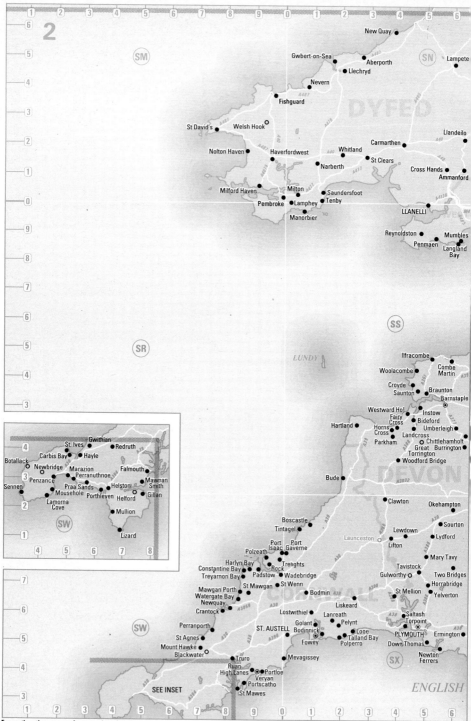

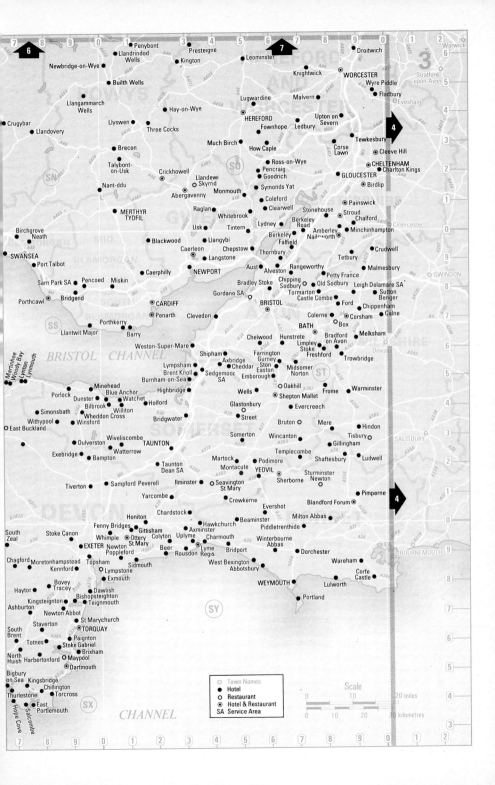

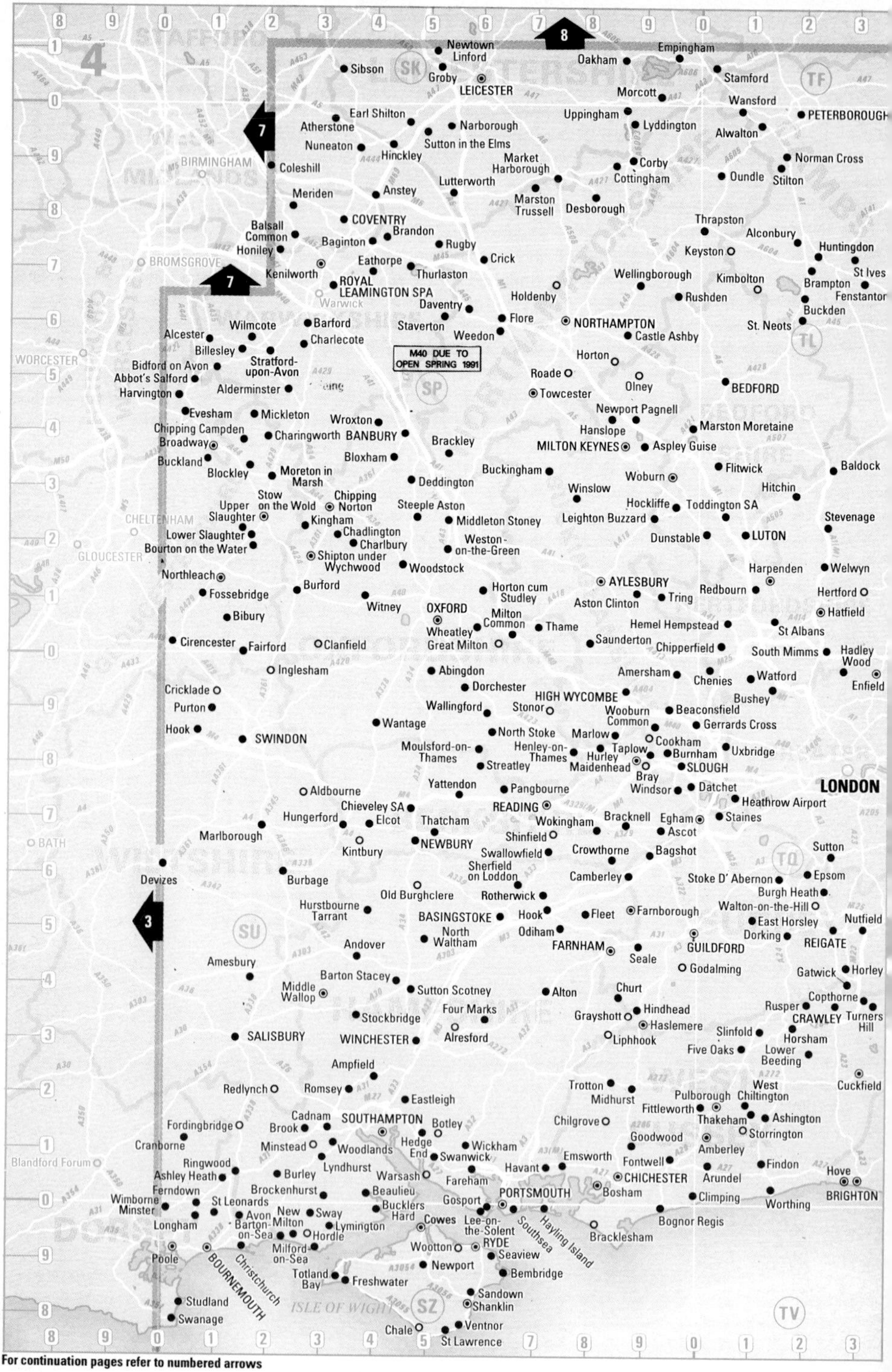

Newtown Linford
Sibson
Groby
LEICESTER
Empingham
Oakham
Stamford
Morcott
Wansford
PETERBOROUGH
Earl Shilton
Atherstone
Narborough
Uppingham
Lyddington
Alwalton
Norman Cross
Nuneaton
Hinckley
Sutton in the Elms
Corby
Oundle
Stilton
Coleshill
Lutterworth
Market Harborough
Cottingham
Anstey
Marston Trussell
Desborough
Meriden
COVENTRY
Brandon
Rugby
Crick
Thrapston
Alconbury
Huntingdon
Balsall Common
Baginton
Eathorpe
Thurlaston
Wellingborough
Kimbolton
Brampton
St Ives
Fenstanton
Honiley
Kenilworth
ROYAL LEAMINGTON SPA
Keyston
Rushden
Buckden
Holdenby
NORTHAMPTON
St. Neots
Wilmcote
Barford
Charlecote
Daventry
Staverton
Weedon
Flore
Castle Ashby
Alcester
Billesley
Bidford on Avon
Abbot's Salford
Stratford-upon-Avon
Alderminster
Harvington
Horton
Roade
Olney
BEDFORD
Towcester
Evesham
Mickleton
Wroxton
Newport Pagnell
Marston Moretaine
Chipping Campden
Charingworth
BANBURY
Brackley
Hanslope
Aspley Guise
Broadway
MILTON KEYNES
Buckland
Blockley
Moreton in Marsh
Bloxham
Buckingham
Woburn
Flitwick
Baldock
Stow on the Wold
Chipping Norton
Deddington
Winslow
Hockliffe
Toddington SA
Hitchin
Upper Slaughter
Kingham
Steeple Aston
Leighton Buzzard
Stevenage
Lower Slaughter
Chadlington
Middleton Stoney
Dunstable
LUTON
Bourton on the Water
Charlbury
Weston-on-the-Green
Northleach
Shipton under Wychwood
Woodstock
Harpenden
Welwyn
Fossebridge
Burford
Witney
OXFORD
Horton cum Studley
AYLESBURY
Redbourn
Hertford
Bibury
Milton Common
Aston Clinton
Tring
Hatfield
Cirencester
Fairford
Clanfield
Wheatley
Thame
Hemel Hempstead
St Albans
Great Milton
Saunderton
Chipperfield
South Mimms
Hadley Wood
Inglesham
Abingdon
Amersham
Chenies
Watford
Enfield
Cricklade
Dorchester
HIGH WYCOMBE
Bushey
Purton
Wallingford
Stonor
Wooburn Common
Beaconsfield
Hook
Wantage
North Stoke
Marlow
Cookham
Gerrards Cross
SWINDON
Moulsford-on-Thames
Henley-on-Thames
Taplow
Burnham
Uxbridge
Streatley
Hurley
Maidenhead
SLOUGH
Yattendon
Pangbourne
Bray
Datchet
LONDON
Aldbourne
Chieveley SA
READING
Windsor
Heathrow Airport
Hungerford
Elcot
Bracknell
Egham
Staines
Marlborough
Kintbury
NEWBURY
Thatcham
Wokingham
Shinfield
Ascot
Sutton
Burbage
Swallowfield
Crowthorne
Bagshot
Epsom
Old Burghclere
Sherfield on Loddon
Camberley
Stoke D'Abernon
Burgh Heath
Hurstbourne Tarrant
Rotherwick
Walton-on-the-Hill
East Horsley
Nutfield
Devizes
BASINGSTOKE
Hook
Fleet
Farnborough
Dorking
REIGATE
Andover
North Waltham
Odiham
FARNHAM
Seale
GUILDFORD
Amesbury
Barton Stacey
Alton
Churt
Godalming
Gatwick
Horley
Middle Wallop
Sutton Scotney
Four Marks
Hindhead
Grayshott
Haslemere
Rusper
Copthorne
Stockbridge
Liphook
Slinfold
CRAWLEY
Turners Hill
SALISBURY
WINCHESTER
Alresford
Five Oaks
Lower Beeding
Horsham
Ampfield
Trotton
Pulborough
West Chiltington
Cuckfield
Redlynch
Romsey
Eastleigh
Midhurst
Fittleworth
Thakeham
Ashington
Cadnam
SOUTHAMPTON
Botley
Chilgrove
Goodwood
Storrington
Amberley
Fordingbridge
Brook
Minstead
Hedge End
Wickham
Emsworth
Fontwell
Findon
Cranborne
Woodlands
Swanwick
Havant
CHICHESTER
Arundel
Hove
Ringwood
Burley
Lyndhurst
Warsash
Fareham
PORTSMOUTH
Bosham
Climping
BRIGHTON
Ashley Heath
Brockenhurst
Beaulieu
Bucklers Hard
Gosport
Worthing
Ferndown
St Leonards
New Milton
Sway
Lymington
Lee-on-the-Solent
Southsea
Bognor Regis
Wimborne Minster
Avon
Hordle
Cowes
RYDE
Bracklesham
Longham
Barton-on-Sea
Milford on Sea
Wootton
Seaview
Poole
Christchurch
Totland Bay
Freshwater
Newport
Bembridge
BOURNEMOUTH
Studland
Sandown
Swanage
ISLE OF WIGHT
Shanklin
Chale
Ventnor
St Lawrence

M40 DUE TO OPEN SPRING 1991

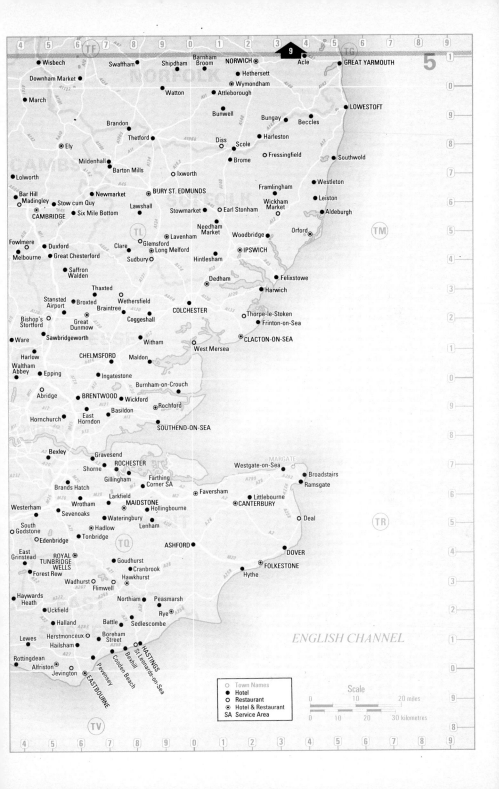

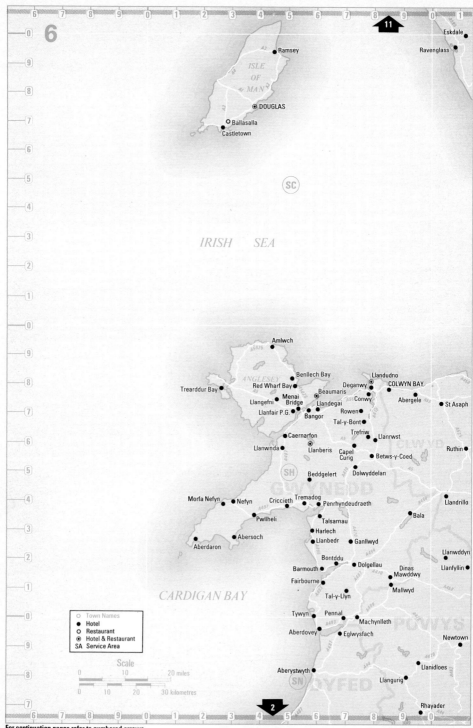

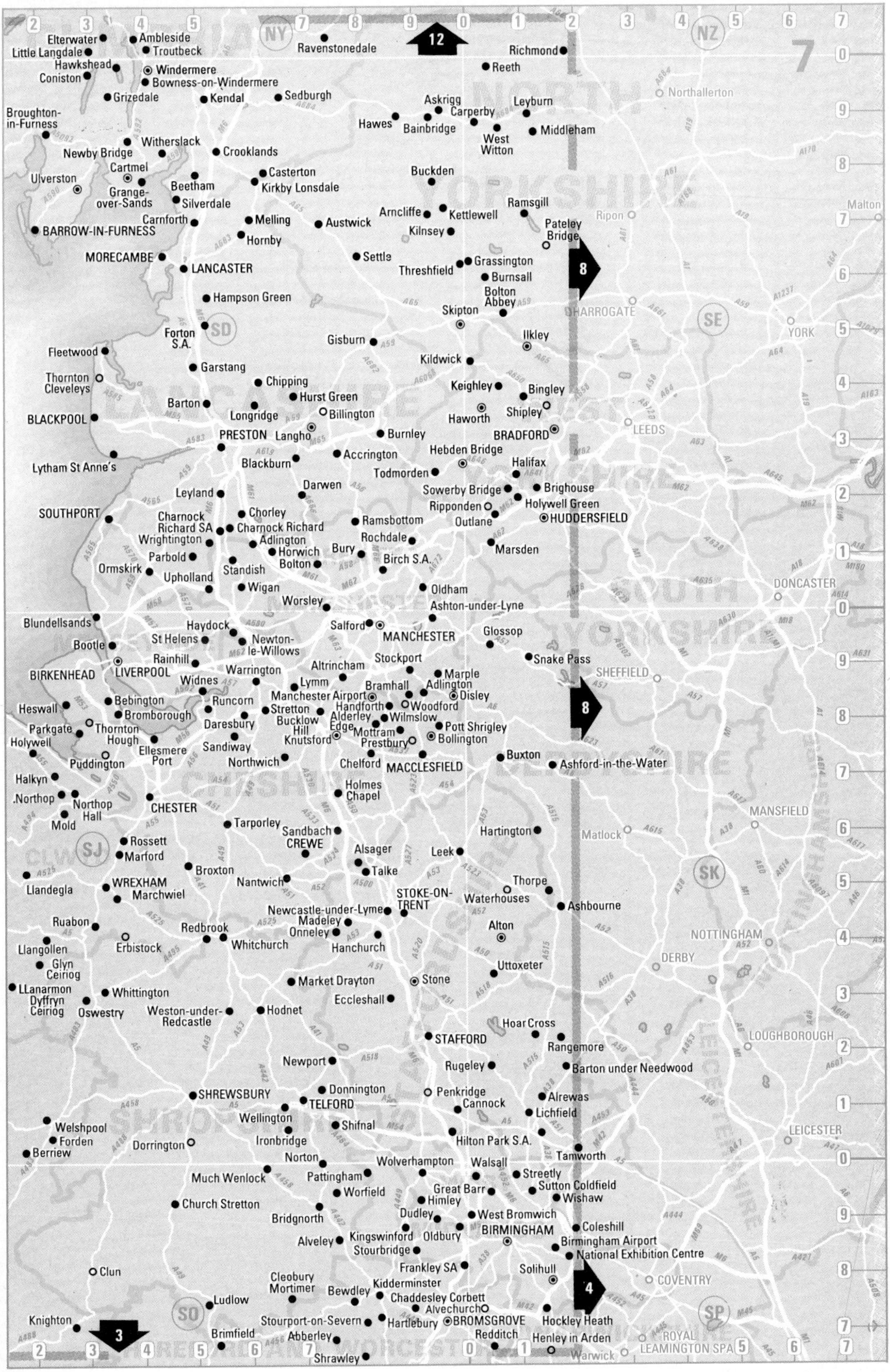

7
12
Elterwater
Ambleside
Little Langdale
Troutbeck
Hawkshead
Windermere
Coniston
Bowness-on-Windermere
Grizedale
Kendal
Sedburgh
Ravenstonedale
Richmond
Reeth
Northallerton
Broughton-in-Furness
Askrigg
Carperby
Leyburn
Hawes
Bainbridge
West Witton
Middleham
Witherslack
Newby Bridge
Crooklands
Cartmel
Ulverston
Grange-over-Sands
Beetham
Silverdale
Casterton
Kirkby Lonsdale
Buckden
Ramsgill
Malton
Carnforth
Melling
Austwick
Arncliffe
Kettlewell
Ripon
Pateley Bridge
BARROW-IN-FURNESS
Hornby
Kilnsey
MORECAMBE
LANCASTER
Settle
Threshfield
Grassington
Burnsall
8
Hampson Green
Bolton Abbey
Skipton
HARROGATE
SE
YORK
Forton S.A.
SD
Gisburn
Ilkley
Fleetwood
Kildwick
Garstang
Thornton Cleveleys
Chipping
Hurst Green
Keighley
Bingley
LANCASHIRE
Barton
Longridge
Billington
Haworth
Shipley
BLACKPOOL
PRESTON
Langho
Burnley
BRADFORD
LEEDS
Hebden Bridge
Accrington
Lytham St Anne's
Blackburn
Halifax
Todmorden
Darwen
Leyland
Sowerby Bridge
Brighouse
Holywell Green
Ripponden
SOUTHPORT
Charnock Richard SA
Chorley
Charnock Richard
Ramsbottom
Outlane
HUDDERSFIELD
Wrightington
Adlington
Rochdale
Horwich
Bury
Marsden
Parbold
Ormskirk
Bolton
Birch S.A.
Standish
Upholland
Wigan
Oldham
DONCASTER
Worsley
Ashton-under-Lyne
Blundellsands
Haydock
Salford
MANCHESTER
Glossop
St Helens
Newton-le-Willows
Bootle
Rainhill
Snake Pass
BIRKENHEAD
LIVERPOOL
Warrington
Altrincham
Stockport
Marple
SHEFFIELD
Widnes
Lymm
Bramhall
Adlington
Disley
Manchester Airport
Bebington
Runcorn
Heswall
Stretton
Handforth
Woodford
Bromborough
Bucklow Hill
Alderley Edge
Wilmslow
Parkgate
Thornton Hough
Daresbury
Pott Shrigley
Holywell
Mottram
Bollington
Knutsford
Ellesmere Port
Sandiway
Prestbury
Puddington
Northwich
Chelford
Buxton
Ashford-in-the-Water
MACCLESFIELD
Halkyn
Holmes Chapel
.Northop
Northop Hall
CHESTER
Mold
MANSFIELD
Tarporley
Sandbach
Hartington
Matlock
SJ
Rossett
CREWE
Marford
Alsager
Leek
Broxton
Talke
SK
Llandegla
WREXHAM
Nantwich
Thorpe
Marchwiel
STOKE-ON-TRENT
Waterhouses
Ashbourne
Newcastle-under-Lyme
Madeley
Ruabon
Redbrook
Onneley
Alton
NOTTINGHAM
Llangollen
Erbistock
Whitchurch
Hanchurch
DERBY
Glyn Ceiriog
Uttoxeter
Market Drayton
Stone
LLanarmon Dyffryn Ceiriog
Whittington
Eccleshall
Oswestry
Weston-under-Redcastle
Hodnet
Hoar Cross
LOUGHBOROUGH
STAFFORD
Rangemore
Newport
Rugeley
Barton under Needwood
SHREWSBURY
Donnington
Penkridge
Alrewas
TELFORD
Cannock
Lichfield
Wellington
Welshpool
Shifnal
LEICESTER
Forden
Ironbridge
Hilton Park S.A.
Dorrington
Berriew
Tamworth
Norton
Wolverhampton
Walsall
Much Wenlock
Pattingham
Streetly
Great Barr
Sutton Coldfield
Worfield
Himley
Wishaw
Church Stretton
Dudley
West Bromwich
Bridgnorth
Coleshill
Kingswinford
Oldbury
BIRMINGHAM
Alveley
Birmingham Airport
Stourbridge
National Exhibition Centre
Frankley SA
Clun
Solihull
Cleobury Mortimer
Kidderminster
COVENTRY
4
Bewdley
Chaddesley Corbett
Ludlow
Alvechurch
SO
SP
Knighton
Stourport-on-Severn
Hartlebury
BROMSGROVE
Hockley Heath
3
Brimfield
Abberley
Redditch
Henley in Arden
ROYAL LEAMINGTON SPA
Shrawley
Warwick

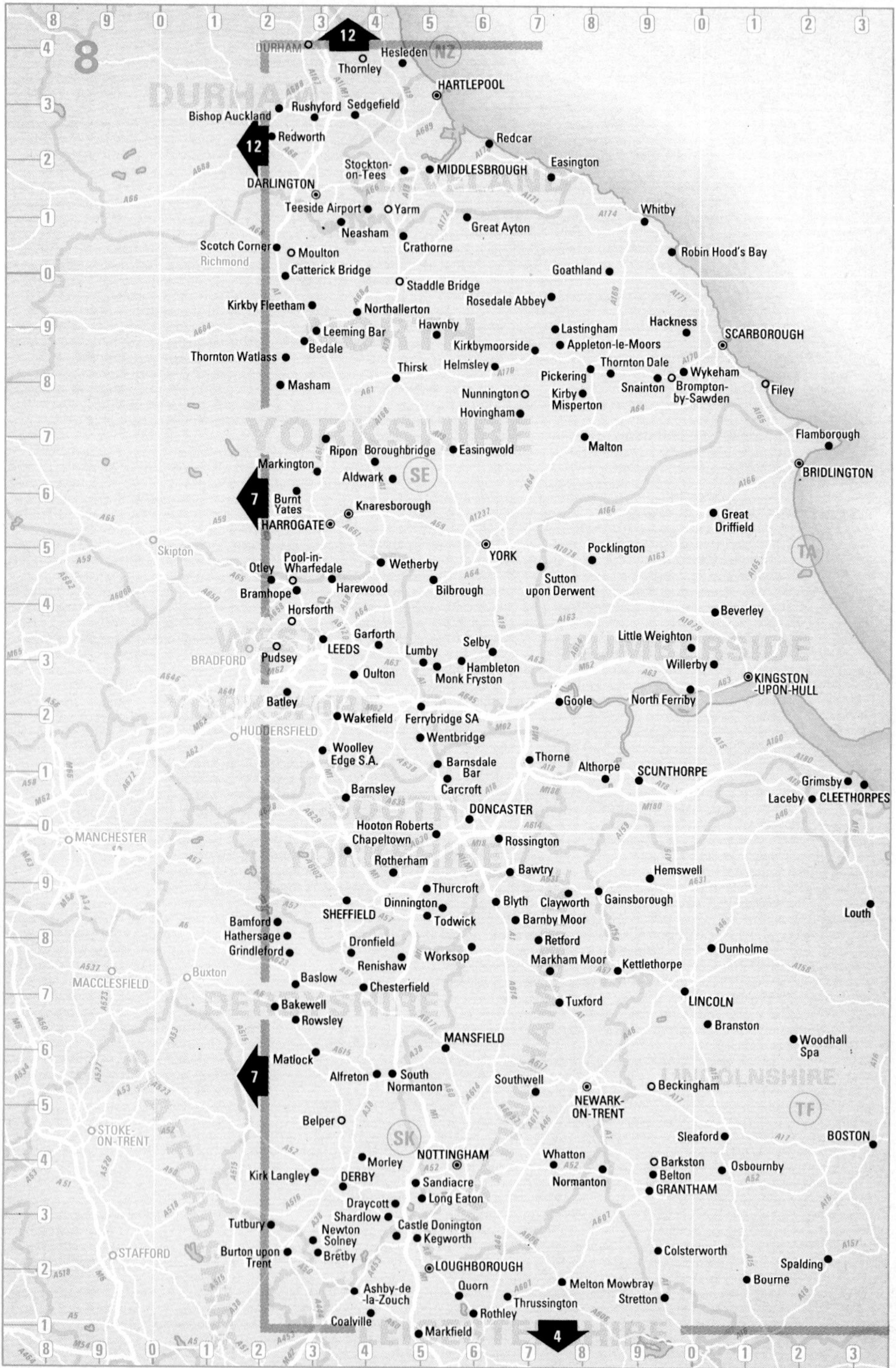

8
12
7
4
NZ
SE
TA
SK
TF
DURHAM
NORTH YORKSHIRE
WEST YORKSHIRE
SOUTH YORKSHIRE
HUMBERSIDE
DERBYSHIRE
STAFFORDSHIRE
NOTTINGHAMSHIRE
LINCOLNSHIRE
LEICESTERSHIRE
CLEVELAND
DURHAM
Thornley
Hesleden
HARTLEPOOL
Bishop Auckland
Rushyford
Sedgefield
Redworth
Redcar
Stockton-on-Tees
MIDDLESBROUGH
Easington
DARLINGTON
Teeside Airport
Yarm
Whitby
Great Ayton
Neasham
Crathorne
Scotch Corner
Moulton
Robin Hood's Bay
Richmond
Catterick Bridge
Goathland
Staddle Bridge
Rosedale Abbey
Kirkby Fleetham
Northallerton
Hackness
Leeming Bar
Hawnby
Lastingham
SCARBOROUGH
Bedale
Kirkbymoorside
Appleton-le-Moors
Thornton Watlass
Thornton Dale
Wykeham
Thirsk
Helmsley
Pickering
Snainton
Brompton-by-Sawden
Filey
Masham
Nunnington
Kirby Misperton
Hovingham
Flamborough
Ripon
Boroughbridge
Easingwold
Malton
Markington
BRIDLINGTON
Aldwark
Burnt Yates
Knaresborough
Great Driffield
HARROGATE
Skipton
YORK
Pocklington
Pool-in-Wharfedale
Wetherby
Otley
Sutton upon Derwent
Bramhope
Harewood
Bilbrough
Horsforth
Beverley
Garforth
Little Weighton
Pudsey
LEEDS
Lumby
Selby
BRADFORD
Hambleton
Willerby
Oulton
Monk Fryston
KINGSTON-UPON-HULL
Batley
Goole
North Ferriby
Wakefield
Ferrybridge SA
HUDDERSFIELD
Wentbridge
Woolley Edge S.A.
Barnsdale Bar
Thorne
Althorpe
SCUNTHORPE
Grimsby
Barnsley
Carcroft
Laceby
CLEETHORPES
DONCASTER
MANCHESTER
Hooton Roberts
Chapeltown
Rossington
Rotherham
Bawtry
Hemswell
Thurcroft
Dinnington
Blyth
Clayworth
Gainsborough
SHEFFIELD
Todwick
Barnby Moor
Louth
Bamford
Hathersage
Dronfield
Retford
Grindleford
Worksop
Dunholme
Renishaw
Markham Moor
Kettlethorpe
Buxton
MACCLESFIELD
Baslow
Chesterfield
LINCOLN
Bakewell
Tuxford
Rowsley
Branston
MANSFIELD
Woodhall Spa
Matlock
Alfreton
South Normanton
Southwell
NEWARK-ON-TRENT
Beckingham
Belper
STOKE-ON-TRENT
Sleaford
BOSTON
NOTTINGHAM
Whatton
Morley
Barkston
Kirk Langley
DERBY
Normanton
Belton
Osbournby
Sandiacre
GRANTHAM
Draycott
Long Eaton
Shardlow
Castle Donington
Tutbury
Newton Solney
Kegworth
Burton upon Trent
Bretby
Colsterworth
STAFFORD
LOUGHBOROUGH
Spalding
Ashby-de-la-Zouch
Quorn
Melton Mowbray
Bourne
Thrussington
Stretton
Rothley
Coalville
Markfield

For continuation pages refer to numbered arrows

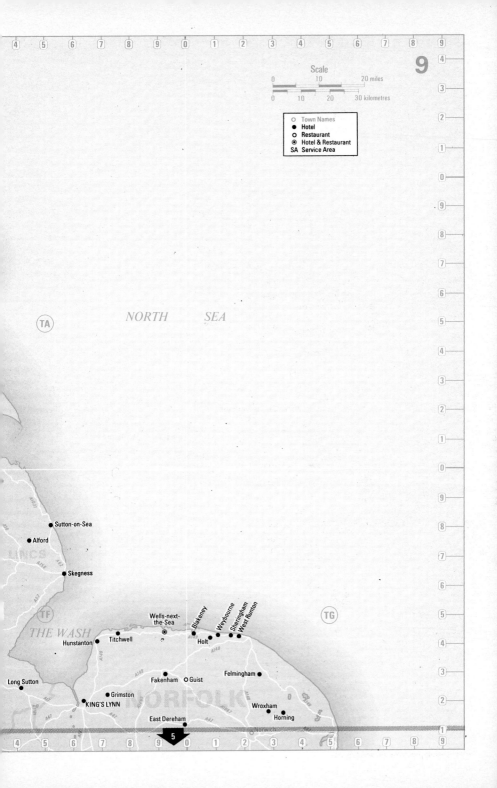

9

4
3
2
1
0
9
8
7
6
5
4
3
2
1
0
9
8
7
6
5
4
3
2
1
9

Scale

0        10        20 miles

0        10        20        30 kilometres

○  Town Names
●  Hotel
○  Restaurant
◉  Hotel & Restaurant
SA  Service Area

NORTH        SEA

TA

TG

Sutton-on-Sea

Alford

Skegness

LINCS

TF

THE WASH

Wells-next-the-Sea

Blakeney

Weybourne

Sheringham

West Runton

Holt

Hunstanton

Titchwell

Felmingham

Fakenham    Guist

Long Sutton

Grimston

KING'S LYNN

NORFOLK

Wroxham

Horning

East Dereham

Norwich

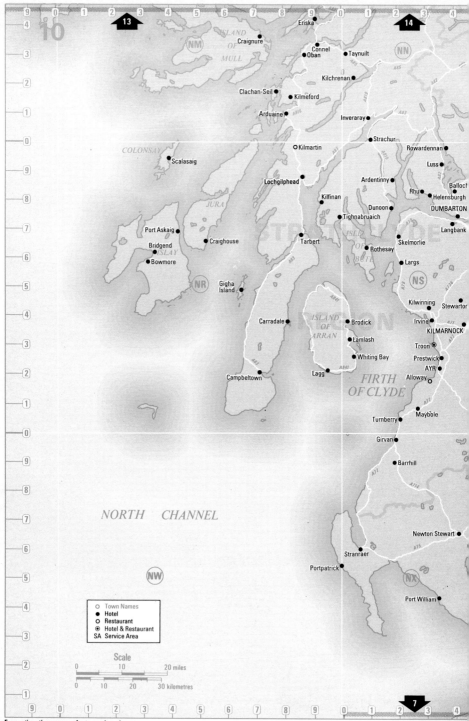

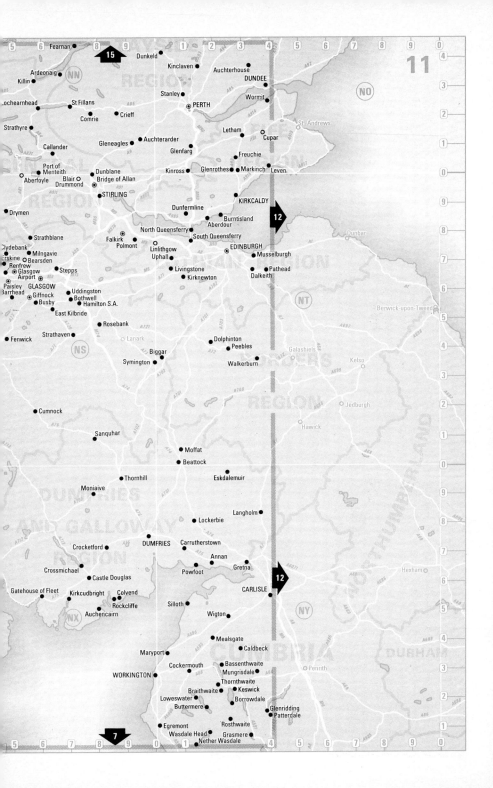

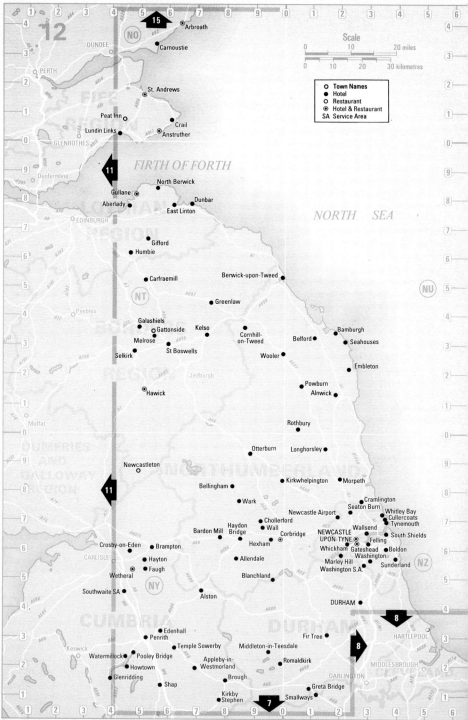

Scale

| 0 | 10 | 20 miles |
| 0 | 10 | 20 | 30 kilometres |

○ Town Names
● Hotel
○ Restaurant
◉ Hotel & Restaurant
SA Service Area

**12**

NO
11
15
11
8
7

Arbroath
Carnoustie
DUNDEE
PERTH
FIFE REGION
St. Andrews
Peat Inn
Crail
Lundin Links
Anstruther
GLENROTHES
Dunfermline

FIRTH OF FORTH

North Berwick
Gullane
Dunbar
Aberlady
East Linton
EDINBURGH
LOTHIAN REGION

NORTH SEA

Gifford
Humbie
Carfraemill
Berwick-upon-Tweed
NT
Peebles
Greenlaw
Galashiels
Gattonside
Kelso
Melrose
Cornhill-on-Tweed
Belford
Bamburgh
Selkirk
St Boswells
Seahouses
Wooler
Embleton
Jedburgh
Hawick
Powburn
Alnwick
Moffat

Rothbury

DUMFRIES AND GALLOWAY REGION
Newcastleton
Otterburn
Longhorsley
NORTHUMBERLAND
Kirkwhelpington
Morpeth
Bellingham
Wark
Cramlington
Seaton Burn
Whitley Bay
Cullercoats
Tynemouth
Newcastle Airport
Chollerford
Haydon Bridge
Wall
Corbridge
Wallsend
Bardon Mill
NEWCASTLE UPON TYNE
Felling
South Shields
Hexham
Whickham
Gateshead
Boldon
Crosby-on-Eden
Brampton
Marley Hill
Washington
Sunderland
NZ
CARLISLE
Hayton
Allendale
Washington S.A.
Faugh
Wetheral
Blanchland
NY
Southwaite SA
Alston
DURHAM

CUMBRIA
DURHAM
Edenhall
Fir Tree
HARTLEPOOL
Penrith
Temple Sowerby
Middleton-in-Teesdale
8
Watermillock
Pooley Bridge
Appleby-in-Westmorland
Romaldkirk
MIDDLESBROUGH
Howtown
Brough
DARLINGTON
CLEVELAND
Glenridding
Keswick
Shap
Greta Bridge
Kirkby Stephen
Smallways
7

For continuation pages refer to numbered arrows

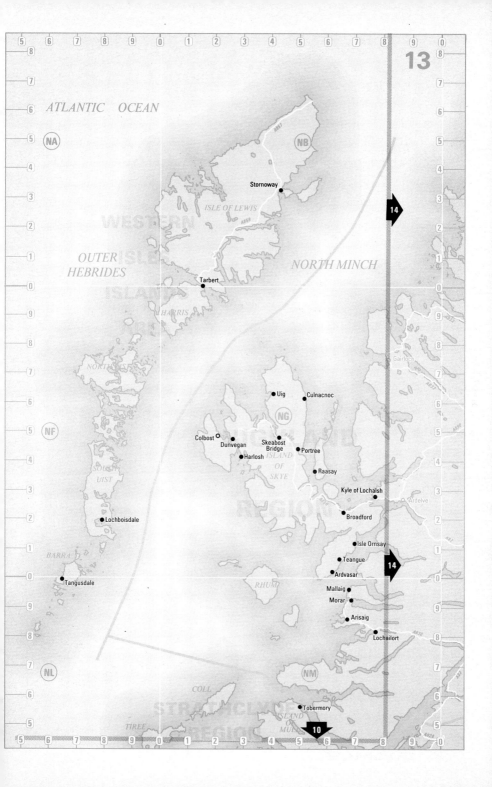

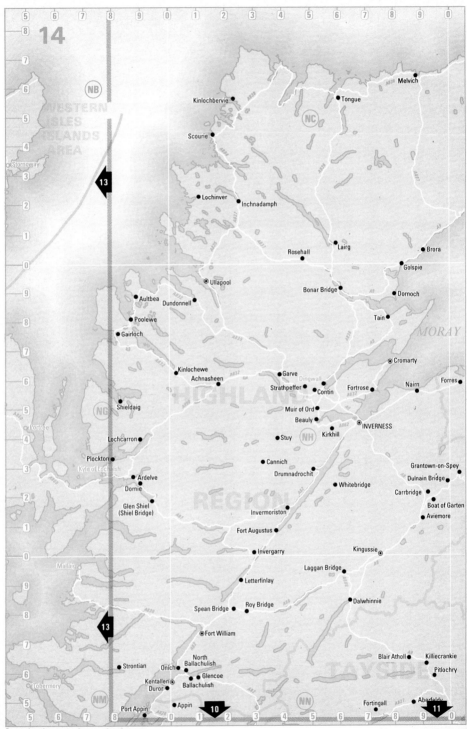

Melvich

Kinlochbervie

Tongue

NB

NC

WESTERN
ISLES
ISLANDS
AREA

Scourie

Stornoway

13

Lochinver

Inchnadamph

Rosehall

Lairg

Brora

Golspie

Ullapool

Bonar Bridge

Dornoch

Aultbea

Dundonnell

Poolewe

Tain

MORAY

Gairloch

Cromarty

Kinlochewe

Achnasheen

Garve

Dingwall

Forres

Strathpeffer

Contin

Fortrose

Nairn

NG

Shieldaig

HIGHLAND

Muir of Ord

Portree

Beauly

INVERNESS

Lochcarron

Stuy

NH

Kirkhill

Plockton

Cannich

Grantown-on-Spey

Kyle of Lochalsh

Drumnadrochit

Dulnain Bridge

Ardelve

Dornie

Whitebridge

Carrbridge

Boat of Garten

Glen Shiel
(Shiel Bridge)

REGION

Invermoriston

Aviemore

Fort Augustus

Mallaig

Invergarry

Kingussie

Laggan Bridge

Letterfinlay

Spean Bridge

Roy Bridge

Dalwhinnie

Fort William

Blair Atholl

Killiecrankie

North
Ballachulish

TAYSIDE

Pitlochry

Strontian

Onich

Glencoe

Kentallen

Ballachulish

Tobermory

Duror

NM

NN

Fortingall

Aberfeldy

Port Appin

Appin

10

11

For continuation pages refer to numbered arrows

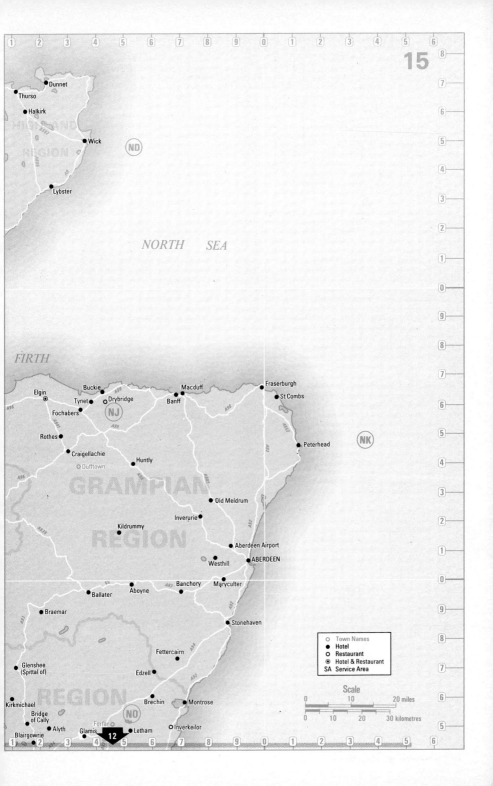

**16**

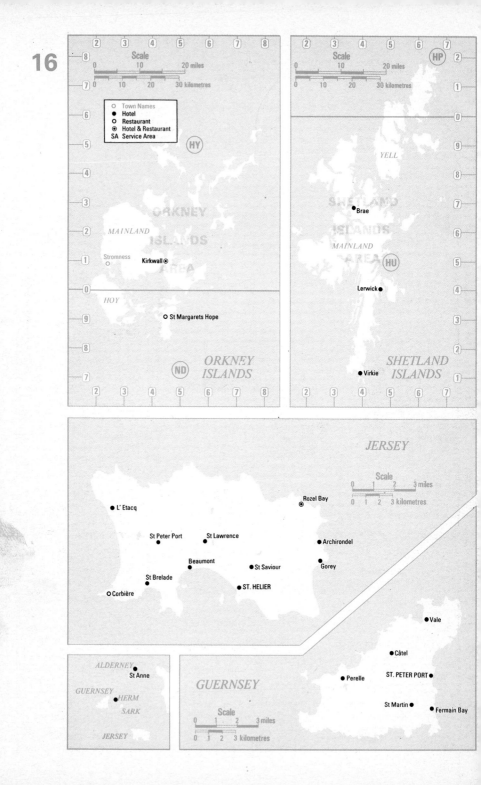

**Scale**

0   10   20 miles

0   10   20   30 kilometres

○ Town Names
● Hotel
○ Restaurant
◉ Hotel & Restaurant
SA Service Area

HY

ORKNEY ISLANDS AREA

MAINLAND

Stromness ○   Kirkwall ◉

○ HOY

○ St Margarets Hope

ND   **ORKNEY ISLANDS**

**Scale**

0   10   20 miles

0   10   20   30 kilometres

HP

YELL

SHETLAND ISLANDS AREA

● Brae

MAINLAND

HU

Lerwick ●

**SHETLAND ISLANDS**

● Virkie

*JERSEY*

● L' Etacq

Rozel Bay ◉

St Peter Port ●   St Lawrence ●

● Archirondel

Beaumont ●

● St Saviour

● Gorey

St Brelade ●

ST. HELIER ●

○ Corbière

**Scale**

0   1   2   3 miles

0   1   2   3 kilometres

*ALDERNEY*

St Anne ●

*GUERNSEY*

● HERM

*SARK*

*JERSEY*

*GUERNSEY*

**Scale**

0   1   2   3 miles

0   1   2   3 kilometres

● Vale

● Câtel

ST. PETER PORT ●

Perelle ●

St Martin ●

● Fermain Bay